THE GREAT AMERICAN
BASEBALL
STAT BOOK 1992

Gary Gillette

A Mountain Lion/Grand Slam Book

HarperPerennial
A Division of HarperCollinsPublishers

Acknowledgments

The Great American Baseball Stat Book is based on eight years of hard work by many people, including the many hundreds of volunteers who gave freely of their time to help Project Scoresheet compile its unique database. It is regrettably impossible to acknowledge all of those people here, other than to dedicate this book to them.

The Project Scoresheet volunteers scored every baseball game play-by-play from 1984 through 1990, producing the database that made this book possible. The 1991 scoring was done under license, with many of the project's members actively participating.

(Project Scoresheet is currently considering reorganizing as a baseball research organization. If you would like information on the project or to order its previously published books or computer disk data, please write to P.O. Box 27614, Philadelphia, PA 19118.)

Special thanks also go to several people whose contributions have been instrumental in compiling the statistics presented here. First and foremost, to David W. Smith, who has been unstintingly generous with his time and his expertise and whose help has been truly indispensable for several years.

To Pete Palmer, who knows more about baseball history, analysis, and statistics than anyone around, and who is the most helpful and selfless person working in the field today.

To John Montague and Bruce Herman of SportSource, Inc., who carried on the work of the project by collecting and compiling the 1991 season data under license.

To David Nichols and Tom Tippett, computer programmers *par excellence*, who are responsible for most of the software that compiles these baseball statistics.

To Craig Christmann, Gord Fitzgerald, and Gary Skoog, for their valuable advice and support over the past few years.

To Eddie Epstein, one of the most astute baseball analysts I've had the pleasure of knowing.

To Jay Virshbo and Jim Keller of Howe Sportsdata International, which provided the minor-league data for the Career Records. HSI is the official statistician for all minor leagues; Jay runs the show there and is always a pleasure to deal with. Jim graciously helped me with my research on 1992 prospects.

To John Monteleone of Mountain Lion, Inc., who made publication of this book a reality, and to Mary Kay Linge of HarperCollins, who was a wonderful editor.

Finally, to Margaret Trejo and Jean Atcheson, who designed the book and prepared the manuscript for publication. They were a delight to work with, both professionally and personally.

A Mountain Lion/Grand Slam Book

ISSN: 1056-5116
ISBN: 0-06-273095-9

92 93   5 4 3 2 1

CONTENTS

INTRODUCTION

The Great American Stat Book 1992 is crammed with as much information as we could possibly fit into 512 pages. It is designed to give you more information on current players and teams than you can obtain from any other source.

Baseball reference books typically deal with only one type of statistics: either official statistics (e.g., AB, R, H, RBI; IP, W, L, ERA) or situational statistics (e.g., vs. left-handers, vs. right-handers; at home, on road). This book contains *both* types of statistics for all players active in 1991 as well as career information for many of the top prospects for 1992 who did not play in the majors in 1991. Other books usually limit their scope to the 500 to 600 players who played most frequently last year, often leaving the reader without useful information on the up-and-coming stars.

The *Stat Book* contains three primary types of information: situational statistics, official career statistics, and special statistics.

○ Situational stats are defined by how a player performs in a specific situation: how he hits against left-handed pitchers, how he pitched on the road, how well he hit with runners on base, or how well he pitched month-by-month during the season. Comprehensive situational stats for 390 players (15 regulars per team) are found in Part 1; the most important situational stats categories (left/right, home/road, bases empty/runners on base) are found in Part 2 for all other 1991 players. Part 3 gives team and league situational stats totals.

○ Official statistics are the traditional baseball statistics listed in newspapers' sports sections, baseball magazines, and reference books. The career records in Part 5 of the book contain complete major-league career statistics for *all* 1991 players. This part includes extensive minor-league career information for all major-leaguers and for top prospects, as well. Unlike other sources which leave out much information, the *Stat Book* includes every official batting and pitching statistics category.

○ The special reports included in Part 4 are a mix of statistics on starting pitching, relief pitching, base-stealing, and defense. These reports break down the official stats into categories useful for analyzing player and team performance.

In addition to giving you more information, the *Stat Book* has been designed to give you really useful information and to skip the trivia. Therefore, you won't find any of those cute little statistics that are churned out in vast quantities by the baseball media —and generally don't mean anything. You know,

details like "Cal Ripkin was the AL leader in multi-hit games last year," or "Pat Tabler hit .333 with the bases loaded in 1991."

The primary problem with the flood of trivia and arcane statistics is that they merely describe coincidences. Take the Cal Ripken example quoted above: Ripken was the leader in multi-hit games because he was among the league leaders in batting average (.323) and was second in total hits (210). Because he played every day and hit for a high average, it's predictable that he would have one of the top multi-hit game totals. Therefore, Cal's high batting average is important, and the fact that he played every day is tremendously important, but his total of multi-hit games is not. It simply describes the result of other important factors; it is not meaningful in itself.

One final note. In order to get the *Stat Book* published as early as possible, all 1991 statistics used in the book are based on the final unofficial totals for the 1991 season. These unofficial totals are released the day after the regular season ends and aren't significantly different from the final official stats that are released two months later. The major leagues don't release final official statistics until baseball's winter meetings in early December—and by then this book was already at the printer's.

You shouldn't notice many differences in the batting and pitching statistics, though. Baseball usually makes very few—and very minor—changes between the final unofficial statistics and the final official statistics. Fielding statistics are another case, because there are normally quite a few changes made between early October and early December. Therefore, there may be small differences between some of the fielding stats in this book and the final official totals. These changes are almost always minor (one game at position here, a couple of putouts or assists there) and don't substantially alter any analysis based on these numbers.

I hope that you enjoy using this book during the 1992 season as much as I enjoyed putting it together. If you have any questions or comments, please drop a note to the publisher. Feedback from fans—especially what readers liked and didn't like—is always welcome. Any suggestions for improvements will be considered for next year's edition of *The Great American Baseball Stat Book*.

By the way, Pat Tabler was 2-for-6 in 1991 with the bases loaded. Does it matter?

— GARY GILLETTE

A USER'S GUIDE

Every baseball reference book you can buy (and there are literally hundreds of them) is chock-full of statistics set in agate type.

What's a baseball fan to do when presented with so many choices? What makes this book more useful than the others? How do you sort out the statistical wheat from the chaff?

Many of the answers to these questions are matters of personal preference. Lots of fans don't want to get bogged down in statistics, feeling that too many stats diminish their appreciation of the game. That's fine: one of the beauties of baseball is that it can be enjoyed in many, very different ways.

However, if you want to use this book to better understand and predict the performance of current players, read this essay first. It will help you to properly interpret the remarkable wealth of statistics the *Stat Book* contains.

AFLOAT IN A SEA OF STATISTICS

Baseball has always had statistics, and its statistics have always given a more complete picture of the game than those of other sports. The familiar traditional stats—batting average, runs, home runs, runs batted in, wins, losses, earned-run average, and strikeouts—obviously have lots of merit, or they wouldn't be universally known and discussed by fans.

In recent years, as the media have been paying more and more attention to baseball statistics, more and more "new" statistics have been published and a statistical backlash has arisen. This takes different forms, but can easily be recognized by such questions as, "What's wrong with the old statistics?" and "Why do we need new stats?" or by complaints about a player's stats "in road games on Tuesdays against a southpaw with a runner on second under a full moon."

Here are some answers to those questions. What's wrong with the old familiar stats is that they haven't changed as the game has changed. They still have value, but newer stats are needed to describe and analyze the way the game is played today. Everything else in life changes over time, so why should baseball—or baseball statistics, for that matter—remain frozen?

Baseball was a radically different game in 1910 when Ty Cobb was terrorizing pitchers. It changed when Babe Ruth became king and instituted the era of the slugger in the 1920s; it changed again with the advent of night baseball and the rise of relief pitching. Maury Wills and the reintroduction of speed changed the game again in the 1960s. Artificial turf, domed stadiums, the adoption of the designated hitter rule, and the increasing special-ization in player roles have altered the face of the game yet again in the past 25 years.

Scholars, doctors, lawyers, politicians, teachers, stock-brokers, mechanics, and many others play largely the same roles in society today as they did 75 years ago. Yet their training isn't the same, their tools are different, the way they approach their jobs has changed, and the amount they get paid has increased manyfold. There is no reason to assume that similar changes haven't affected our national pastime.

Just as our language has altered and our sciences have progressed, so, too, must our understanding of how baseball is played. Baseball statistics are the measure of the game, and the "new" statistics are simply an attempt to assess the modern game more accurately.

APPLY COMMON SENSE TO BASEBALL STATISTICS

Just because the average fan is not a mathematician or a so-called baseball expert doesn't mean that he or she can't use common sense when evaluating baseball stats. The key here is to apply the same rules of good judgment to baseball stats that you apply to real life.

Think critically, be skeptical, ask questions, examine the evidence carefully. If you follow these guidelines when looking at baseball stats, you should be happy with the results.

The first rule for any statistic—baseball or otherwise—is not to read any more significance into it than it was designed for. Two good examples of this are pitchers' won-lost records and ERAs. These stats serve well when evaluating starting pitchers who pitch lots of innings. For relief pitchers, however, their relevance is marginal and when relief pitching became prominent, the Save statistic was invented to better reflect the change in the way the game was played.

A corollary to this rule is never to put more weight on a statistic than it can justifiably support. If a stat doesn't show the complete picture, don't use it to make sweeping judgments. Example: a player can lead the league in homers and runs batted in but not deserve the Most Valuable Player award because of big holes in his game that are not measured by HRs and RBIs. He could be a bad fielder and a terrible baserunner, making him less valuable than a player who does everything well but doesn't quite measure up in the glamour stats categories.

The second rule is to be skeptical of small samples. Even good statistics can be very misleading when measuring small numbers of events. Sometimes a small sample will support a theory or reveal a trend, but the level of chance in small numbers is too great for any reliance to be placed on them. Scott Lusader hit .319 in his rookie year with Detroit in 1987, playing in the heat of a pennant race. Of course, he only had 47 at-bats, so it's not surprising that he has never proven himself as a big-league hitter.

Too obvious an example? Consider Dan Gladden. As a rookie with the Giants, Dan clipped NL pitchers for a .351 average in 342 at-bats in the second half of 1984 after hitting .397 in Triple-A the first half of the year. Lots of people thought he was going to be a bona fide .300 hitter in the big leagues, yet he has never hit more than .295 since then and has a career average of .272. Why should this not have been a surprise to the skeptical? Because one half of a season is too small a sample to base such judgments on, and because Gladden's minor-league history before 1984 showed no such gaudy batting averages to lend additional weight to the evidence.

The third rule is to look for strong trends over time or to look for evidence from multiple sources. The stronger the trend and the longer the period of time over which it occurs, the more reliability you can place on it. The primary value of career statistics when predicting future performance is that they are a much more reliable indicator than single-season stats. The reason for this is that the good luck and bad luck, the fluke performances, and the injuries tend to even out over long periods of time. If a player has averaged 18 home runs a year for six years and then breaks loose for 30 one year, he's much more likely to revert to his average the next season than to hit 30 again.

Be especially wary of expecting too much from players coming off "career" years. For veteran players with established track records, "career" years are just that—the peaks of their careers. Because of skill, good health, favorable circumstances, and a dose of good fortune, a player may exceed his career norms by a wide margin one season. However, because all of these factors will not be present every year, the odds of players returning to normal production after a career year is very high.

PREDICTING PERFORMANCE

Baseball is an exceedingly complex game deceptively cloaked in a mantle of simplicity. If predicting the performance of players and teams were easy, there wouldn't be such delightful surprises as the 1991 Minnesota Twins and Atlanta Braves. No matter how much you know about baseball—and this certainly applies to the experts, too—there is so much more that remains unknown.

In order to have a prayer of a chance of accurately predicting future performance, you must study the evidence carefully, consider past circumstances, try to anticipate future changes in circumstances, and then draw the proper conclusions. This is obviously a lot easier said than done for everyone involved, including managers, coaches, players, writers, and analysts. If it

really were easy to predict performance, scouts wouldn't recommend many more players than succeed, managers wouldn't pencil .180 hitters into the lineup, and pitchers with ERAs over five wouldn't get out of the bullpen except in blowouts.

While predictions are admittedly imperfect, you can certainly increase the accuracy of your hunches by relying on the proper statistics. Some stats are more meaningful than others, some stats are useful only in certain situations, and most stats can mislead if not interpreted properly.

A QUICK TOUR OF THE BOOK

The first two sections of the *Stat Book* present extensive situational statistics for all 1991 major-league players. One of the most important features of this book is that it presents totals for the past eight years in all situations. No other book gives you this information: information that can make it easier to predict next year's performance.

(The reason eight-year totals are used is that Project Scoresheet's database starts with the 1984 season. Since the large majority of major-league players active today made their big-league debuts after 1984, these eight-year totals are also their career totals, which is how they will be referred to here.)

Career situational totals are very important analytical tools for many reasons. If a player was injured or didn't play much in 1991, his totals will be much more meaningful than his 1991 numbers. If you know that a player has changed in some important way (e.g., his batting stance, his pitching motion, or just in the way he's used), you can compare his 1991 stats to his career averages to see how these changes might have made a difference.

Explanations of the situational statistics categories used are listed below, using batters' statistics as examples. A Key to Abbreviations for the statistics used throughout the book follows this User's Guide.

The situational statistics categories shown for pitchers are analogous to those for batters, but are divided into two parts. The first part uses traditional pitching statistics for the home/road, grass/turf, day/night, and monthly breakdowns. The second part shows how opposing batters hit against that pitcher in various situations.

All of the categories listed below are shown for the 390 regular players included in Part 1. The most important categories (vs. left/vs. right, home/road, and bases empty/runners on base) are shown in Part 2 for all other 1991 players.

● "Vs. Left" and "vs. Right" break down batters' statistics into how they batted against left-handed pitchers and how they batted against right-handed pitchers. For pitchers, the breakdowns represent how opposing left-handed and right-handed batters did against them.

o "At Home" and "On Road" break players' statistics into how they performed in games in their home ballpark and how they performed in games in other ballparks.

o "On Grass" and "On Turf" break player's statistics into how they performed in venues with grass fields as opposed to those with artificial turf.

o "Day Games" and "Night Games" separate players' statistics into games starting before 5:00 p.m. local time and those starting after 5:00 p.m.

o The monthly categories are self-explanatory with the exception of the last line. September and October games are totaled and include regular-season games only.

o The "Bases Empty" category breaks down players' statistics into how they batted when there was no runner on base. For regular players, the "Leadoff" line gives statistics when they were the first batter of an inning.

o The "Runners On Base" category breaks down players' statistics into how they batted when there was a runner or runners on base. For regular players, the "Scoring Position" line gives statistics separately with a runner or runners in scoring position (i.e., on second base and/or third base).

o The "Late and Close" line gives players' statistics when the score is close in the late innings of a game. Late and Close situations are defined as at-bats in the 7th inning or later when a player's team is ahead by only one run, the score is tied, or his team is behind but the tying run is at-bat, on-base, or on-deck.

This means that the game is always close if the batter's team is behind by only one run in the 7th inning or later, and that the game can never be close if his team is behind by more than five runs. While the definition of a Late and Close situation does not change, such situations can change from one at-bat to the next if the score or the runners on base change.

Essentially, the game is considered close for an at-bat if it is currently tied, if there is only a one-run difference in the score, or if the team that is currently behind would take the lead, tie the game, or come within one run of tying the game if the batter hit a home run and all runners on base scored. By the way, the Close part of the Late and Close definition is the same as used in the official Save rule for pitchers.

The team and league statistics presented in Part 3 are useful for two reasons. The league statistics give the norms so that you can see how much above or below average a particular player is. The team statistics give you a chance to see where a team was strongest and weakest—information that can help you predict what moves they're likely to make. Better yet, these numbers will help predict what the effects of those moves will be.

The Special Reports found in Part 4 have several functions. The Starting Pitching and Relief Pitching reports give much more detailed information about pitchers than the official stats. There are several key pieces of information in these reports.

For starting pitchers, look closely at their run support. If a pitcher's run support is way above his team's average runs scored per game, it's likely that his record is better than it should be, based solely on his pitching ability. This is frequently a tipoff that he will "slump" next year. The converse is also true. A pitcher who endures a season of miserable support from his mates will generally rebound smartly the following year.

The second set of numbers of value for starters represents their endurance. Looking at how often a pitcher was replaced in certain innings can give you a clue as to how he will be used next year. A starter who can't make it to the 7th inning in many of his starts is a good candidate for bullpen duty in the future.

For ace relief pitchers, look closely at the Blown Save, Save Percentage, and Inherited Runners columns. If an ace reliever blows too many Save opportunities or lets too many inherited runners score, he could be demoted to middle relief fast. For middle relievers, look at their Save opportunities, their Save Conversion Percentages and the innings in which they enter the game. Most middle relievers will have few Save opportunities compared to the number of games they pitch in relief. However, the higher the number of opportunities and the higher the conversion percentage, the greater are their chances of being auditioned for the closer's job if there is a vacancy in the future. But beware of middle relievers who rarely get into games in late innings, since it's a clear sign that they are not trusted to pitch in key situations.

The value of the last part of the book, the Career Records, should be self-evident. The first point to note about this section is that similar batting and pitching statistics are grouped together, allowing for easier analysis than the traditional statistics lines. The second point is that all minor-league stats lines include classifications as well as leagues. Comparing stats across the minor leagues is not easy, and for those who don't know the relevant differences between the Midwest and California leagues, having the classifications listed should help.

USING SITUATIONAL STATS

Because baseball is so complex and unpredictable, experience is in many ways the best teacher. No book of statistics can substitute for years spent following baseball and studying its history and its players. Such experience gives an astute fan a valuable sense of the relative importance of particular statistics and how to apply them.

Many fans feel lost, however, when trying to ascertain the meaning of such new statistics as situationals, so some brief comments on the strengths and weaknesses of the prominent categories may be helpful.

By far the most important situational statistics categories are the left/right and home/road breakdowns. For decades now, managers have regularly been platooning hitters, which serves as an indication of how seriously the people who fill out the lineup cards take the differences between left-handed and right-handed batters. In recent years, the prevalence of what one might call "platoon pitching"—the frequent changing of relief pitchers in late innings to get the platoon advantage over the batter—has increased greatly as well.

There are many theories about why it is true, but no one disagrees with the facts that, overall, right-handed hitters hit left-handed pitchers better than right-handed pitchers, and that left-handed batters are at a distinct disadvantage when facing left-handed pitchers. because this knowledge is applied in every major-league game, the "vs. left" and "vs. right" situational stats lines are most important and enlightening.

The home/road stats breakdowns are also very meaningful, but in a rather different way. Baseball people are well aware of the effects different ballparks have on players, but it is somewhat harder to apply that information every day. For example, it might be clear that a particular starting pitcher performs substantially better in his home park than elsewhere. Even so, most teams cannot afford the luxury of benching key players in road games, so what might be termed "home/road platooning" is much less frequent than left/right platooning.

Frequently, the most valuable information to be gained from studying home/road splits for players is when they have changed teams or when their home ballpark has been radically altered in the off-season. For example, Kevin Mitchell's career road statistics will give you a much better picture of how he will hit in 1992 (away from pitcher-friendly Candlestick Park). If a team performs radical surgery on its park—like moving the fences in much closer in the power alleys—one can use home/road numbers to make an estimate of how much a player's numbers might change (by holding road stats constant and adjusting home stats for the change).

Grass/turf and day/night breakdowns are much less useful than left/right and home/road. Grass/turf numbers are always heavily influenced by a player's home park: because home games will necessarily be all grass or all turf, one of the grass/turf lines will largely reflect a player's home performance. Furthermore, because players on different teams and in different divisions play very different percentages of games on grass and turf, the numbers are even less comparable. The best use of grass/turf numbers, then, is in assessing the performances of players who move from a team with grass to a team with turf, or vice versa.

Monthly stats for one season are a useful means of seeing what happened when—but the real scope of monthly stats is evident in the career totals. Many players show pronounced patterns of playing better or worse in the cold spring and fall months (April, May, September) than in the hot summer months (June, July, August). Some are prone to hot starts and cold finishes; others start slowly and finish strongly. Check for these patterns when evaluating players who are off to especially fast or slow starts in 1992.

The bases empty/runners on base and "late and close" breakdowns are more problematical than the others. Baseball analysts are constantly arguing over the predictive value of so-called clutch statistics; no one has yet been able to do a definitive study of "clutch" performance and show that it remains constant over multiple seasons. While these stats are a lot of fun to look at for past years, their predictive value has not been established.

A last word of advice about the situationals: be sure to make use of the career totals, especially for players who did not play much in 1991. Because of the much larger sampling, these career totals will generally be more accurate than single-season stats in predicting future performance—although you should always consider whether a player's age, injury status, and/or changes in his batting or pitching technique may render the career numbers less useful.

Enough for now. I hope that this has shed just a little more light on the complicated world of baseball statistics and analysis—and that you enjoy perusing the reams of information contained in *The Great American Baseball Stat Book.*

KEY TO ABBREVIATIONS

BATTING AND PITCHING STATISTICS

G	Games
H	Hits
R	Runs
HR	Home Runs
BB	Bases on Balls
IBB	Intentional Bases on Balls
SO	Strikeouts

BATTING STATISTICS

TPA	Total Plate Appearances
AB	At-Bats
2B	Doubles
3B	Triples
TB	Total Bases
RBI	Runs Batted In
HP or HBP	Hit by Pitch
SH	Sacrifice Hits
SF	Sacrifice Flies
SB	Stolen Bases
CS	Caught Stealing
SB%	Stolen Base Percentage [SB/(SB+CS)]
GDP	Grounded into Double Play
BA	Batting Average (H/AB)
OBA	On Base Average [(H+TBB+HBP)/(AB+TBB+HBP+SF)]
SA	Slugging Average (TB/AB)

PITCHING STATISTICS

GS	Games Started
CG	Complete Games
GF	Games Finished
IP	Innings Pitched
TBF	Total Batters Faced
ER	Earned Runs
HB	Hit Batsmen
WP	Wild Pitches
BK	Balks
W	Wins
L	Losses
PCT	Winning Percentage [W/(W+L)]
SHO	Shutouts
S or SV	Saves
ERA	Earned Run Average [(ER/IP) × 9]

FIELDING STATISTICS

G	Games at Position
PO	Putouts
A	Assists
E	Errors
TC	Total Chances (PO+A+E)
DP	Double Plays
TP	Triple Plays
FA	Fielding Average [(PO+A)/(TC)]
PB	Passed Balls

STARTING PITCHING STATISTICS

SP	Starting Pitcher or Starting Pitching
R/GS	Run Support per Game Started
TM/W	Team Wins
TM/L	Team Losses
11,21,...,91,XI	Endurance per Game Started (number of times pitcher left game in 1st inning, 2nd inning, ..., 9th inning, or extra innings)

RELIEF PITCHING STATISTICS

RP	Relief Pitcher or Relief Pitching
GR	Games in Relief
SVS	Games Entered in Save Situation
BSV	Blown Saves
SC%	Save Situation Conversion Percentage (SV/SVS)
SV%	Save Percentage [SV/(SV+BSV)]
<6I	Games Entered before 6th Inning
6I,7I,8I,9I	Games Entered in 6th, 7th, 8th, or 9th Innings
XI	Games Entered in Extra Innings
IR	Inherited Runners
IRS	Inherited Runners Scoring
IRP	Inherited Runners Scoring Percentage

MAJOR LEAGUE TEAMS

AMERICAN LEAGUE (AL)

Eastern Division

BAL	Baltimore Orioles
BOS	Boston Red Sox
CLE	Cleveland Indians
DET	Detroit Tigers
MIL	Milwaukee Brewers
NYA or NY	New York Yankees
TOR	Toronto Blue Jays

Western Division

CAL	California Angels
CHA or CHI	Chicago White Sox
KC	Kansas City Royals
MIN	Minnesota Twins
OAK	Oakland Athletics
SEA	Seattle Mariners
TEX	Texas Rangers

NATIONAL LEAGUE (NL)

Eastern Division

CHN or CHI	Chicago Cubs
MON	Montreal Expos
NYN or NY	New York Mets
PHI	Philadelphia Phillies
PIT	Pittsburgh Pirates
SL or STL	St. Louis Cardinals

Western Division

ATL	Atlanta Braves
CIN	Cincinnati Reds
HOU	Houston Astros
LA	Los Angeles Dodgers
SD	San Diego Padres
SF	San Francisco Giants

CAREER RECORDS

YR	Year
TM/LG	Team/League
CL	Classification (for Minor Leagues)

MINOR LEAGUE TEAMS

MINOR LEAGUE CLASSIFICATIONS

AAA	Triple-A
AA	Double-A
A+	Single-A (Advanced)
A	Single-A
A	Single-A (Short Season)
R+	Rookie (Advanced)
R	Rookie

MINOR LEAGUES

AMA	American Association (Triple-A)
INT	International League (Triple-A)
PCL	Pacific Coast League (Triple-A)
MEX	Mexican League (Triple-A)
EAS	Eastern League (Double-A)
SOU	Southern League (Double-A)
TEX	Texas League (Double-A)
CAL	California League (Single-A, Advanced)
MID	Midwest League (Single-A)
CAR	Carolina League (Single-A, Advanced)
SAL	South Atlantic League, a.k.a. "Sally League" (formerly Western Carolina League-WCL) (Single-A)
FSL	Florida State League (Single-A, Advanced)
NYP	New York-Pennsylvania League (Single-A, Short Season)
NWL	Northwest League (Single-A, Short Season)
PIO	Pioneer League (Rookie, Advanced)
APP	Appalachian League (Rookie, Advanced)
GCL	Gulf Coast League (Rookie)
ARI	Arizona League (Rookie)

CITY/TEAM ABBREVIATIONS

American Association (AMA)

AMA BUF	Buffalo
AMA DEN	Denver
AMA EVA	Evansville
AMA IND	Indianapolis
AMA IOW	Iowa
AMA LOU	Louisville
AMA NAS	Nashville
AMA OC	Oklahoma City
AMA OMA	Omaha
AMA PAW	Pawtucket
AMA VAN	Vancouver
AMA WIC	Wichita

Appalachian League (APP)

APP BLU	Bluefield
APP BRI	Bristol
APP BUR	Burlington
APP ELI	Elizabethton
APP HUN	Huntington
APP JC	Johnson City
APP KIN	Kingsport
APP PAI	Paintsville
APP PIK	Pikeville

APP PUL   Pulaski
APP WYT   Wytheville

Arizona League (ARI)
ARI ANG   Angels
ARI ATH   Athletics

California League (CAL)
CAL BAK   Bakersfield
CAL FRE   Fresno
CAL HD   High Desert
CAL LOD   Lodi
CAL MOD   Modesto
CAL PS   Palm Springs
CAL RED   Redwood
CAL REN   Reno
CAL RIV   Riverside
CAL SAL   Salinas
CAL SB   San Bernardino
CAL SJ   San Jose
CAL SC   Santa Clara
CAL STO   Stockton
CAL VEN   Ventura
CAL VIS   Visalia

Carolina League (CAR)
CAR DUR   Durham
CAR FRE   Frederick
CAR HAG   Hagerstown
CAR KIN   Kingston
CAR LYN   Lynchburg
CAR PEN   Peninsula
CAR PW   Prince William
CAR SAL   Salem
CAR VIR   Virginia
CAR WIN   Winston-Salem

Eastern League (EAS)
EAS ALB   Albany
EAS BRI   Bristol
EAS BUF   Buffalo
EAS CAN   Canton-Akron
EAS GF   Glens Falls
EAS HAG   Hagerstown
EAS HAR   Harrisburg
EAS LON   London
EAS LYN   Lynn
EAS NAS   Nashua
EAS NB   New Britain
EAS PIT   Pittsfield
EAS REA   Reading
EAS VER   Vermont
EAS WAT   Waterbury
EAS WH   West Haven
EAS WIL   Williamsport

Florida State League (FSL)
FSL BC   Baseball City
FSL CHA   Charlotte

FSL CLE   Clearwater
FSL DB   Daytona Beach
FSL DUN   Dunedin
FSL FM   Ft. Myers
FSL FL   Ft. Lauderdale
FSL LAK   Lakeland
FSL MIA   Miami
FSL OSC   Osceola
FSL SAR   Sarasota
FSL SL   St. Lucie
FSL SP   St. Petersburg
FSL TAM   Tampa
FSL VB   Vero Beach
FSL WH   Winter Haven
FSL WPB   West Palm Beach

Gulf Coast League (GCL)
GCL AST   Astros
GCL BJ   Blue Jays
GCL BRA   Braves
GCL CUB   Cubs
GCL DOD   Dodgers
GCL EXP   Expos
GCL IND   Indians
GCL MET   Mets
GCL ORI   Orioles
GCL PHI   Phillies
GCL PIR   Pirates
GCL RAN   Rangers
GCL RS   Red Sox
GCL RED   Reds
GCL ROY   Royals
GCL WS   White Sox
GCL YAN   Yankees

International League (INT)
INT CHA   Charleston, WV
INT COL   Columbus
INT MAI   Maine
INT PAW   Pawtucket
INT RIC   Richmond
INT ROC   Rochester
INT SCR   Scranton-Wilkes-Barre
INT SYR   Syracuse
INT TID   Tidewater
INT TOL   Toledo

Mexican League (MEX)
MEX VER   Veracruz

Midwest League (MID)
MID APP   Appleton
MID BEL   Beloit
MID BUR   Burlington
MID CR   Cedar Rapids
MID CLI   Clinton
MID DAV   Davenport
MID KEN   Kenosha

MID MAD   Madison
MID PEO   Peoria
MID QC   Quad City
MID ROC   Rockford
MID SB   South Bend
MID SPR   Springfield
MID WAT   Waterloo
MID WAU   Wausau

Northwest League (NWL)
NWL BEL   Bellingham
NWL BEN   Bend
NWL CO   Central Oregon
NWL EUG   Eugene
NWL EVE   Everett
NWL MED   Medford
NWL SAL   Salem
NWL SO   Southern Oregon
NWL SPO   Spokane
NWL TRI   Tri-Cities
NWL WW   Walla Walla

New York–Pennsylvania League (NYP)
NYP AUB   Auburn
NYP BAT   Batavia
NYP ELM   Elmira
NYP ERI   Erie
NYP GEN   Geneva
NYP HAM   Hamilton
NYP JAM   Jamestown
NYP LF   Little Falls
NYP NEW   Newark
NYP NF   Niagara Falls
NYP ONE   Oneonta
NYP PIT   Pittsfield
NYP SC   St. Catherines
NYP UTI   Utica
NYP WAT   Watertown
NYP WEL   Welland

Pacific Coast League (PCL)
PCL ALB   Albuquerque
PCL CAL   Calgary
PCL CS   Colorado Springs
PCL DEN   Denver
PCL EDM   Edmonton
PCL HAW   Hawaii
PCL LV   Las Vegas
PCL PHO   Phoenix
PCL POR   Portland
PCL SLC   Salt Lake City
PCL TAC   Tacoma
PCL TUC   Tucson
PCL VAN   Vancouver

Pioneer League (PIO)
PIO BIL   Billings
PIO BUT   Butte

PIO CAL   Calgary
PIO GF   Great Falls
PIO HEL   Helena
PIO IF   Idaho Falls
PIO LET   Lethbridge
PIO MH   Medicine Hat
PIO POC   Pocatello
PIO SLC   Salt Lake City

South Atlantic League (SAL)
SAL AND   Anderson
SAL ASH   Asheville
SAL AUG   Augusta
SAL CHA   Charleston, SC
SAL CHS   Charleston, SC
SAL CHW   Charleston, WV
SAL COL   Columbia
SAL FAY   Fayetteville
SAL FLO   Florence
SAL GAS   Gastonia
SAL GRE   Greensboro
SAL MAC   Macon
SAL MB   Myrtle Beach
SAL SAV   Savannah
SAL SPA   Spartanburg
SAL SUM   Sumter

Southern League (SOU)
SOU BIR   Birmingham
SOU CAR   Carolina
SOU CHA   Charlotte
SOU CHT   Chattanooga
SOU COL   Columbus
SOU GRE   Greenville
SOU HUN   Huntsville
SOU JAC   Jacksonville
SOU KNO   Knoxville
SOU MEM   Memphis
SOU MID   Midland
SOU NAS   Nashville
SOU ORL   Orlando
SOU SAV   Savannah

Texas League (TEX)
TEX AMA   Amarillo
TEX ARK   Arkansas
TEX BEA   Beaumont
TEX EP   El Paso
TEX JAC   Jackson
TEX MID   Midland
TEX SA   San Antonio
TEX SHR   Shreveport
TEX TUL   Tulsa
TEX WIC   Wichita

Western Carolina League (WCL)
WCL GRE   Greenwood

Part 1

Regular Players' Situational Statistics

This part contains situational breakdowns for major-league regulars in 1991. Players are listed alphabetically, separated into batters and pitchers. A team-by-team list of all 390 regulars and an explanation of how they were selected opens the section.

Each player's statistics follow the same format. The first line gives the player's name, how he bats and throws, and his age, effective for the 1992 season. It also lists the team he played for and the positions he played in 1991.

A player's effective age for the season is his age on his birthday that year. So whether a player turns 30 on February 15, June 1, September 30, or December 31, 1992, his Season Effective Age is considered to be 30.

There are two reasons why effective age is used rather than a player's calendar age. First, it really is the age he is closest to for the majority of the season. (For instance, a player who turns 30 on November 1 may be playing at a calendar age of 29 but is actually more than 29½ for the majority of the season, which means that an effective age of 30 is more accurate than his calendar age of 29.) Second, it is a means of standardizing all player ages, allowing for easy and accurate comparisons.

Abbreviations for player's 1992 positions employ the system devised by Pete Palmer for his ground-breaking encyclopedia *Total Baseball*. The player's positions are listed in descending order of most games played; *all* positions played in 1992 are included. Each is represented by a one-letter abbreviation: C for catcher, 1 for 1st base, 2 for 2nd base, 3 for 3rd base, S for shortstop, O for outfield and D for designated hitter. (If a non-pitcher was used as a pitcher, a P will show up in his position abbreviation at the appropriate place.)

An asterisk (*) next to a player's position abbreviation indicates that he played more than 100 games at that position. A slash (/) separates positions at which a player played 10 or more games (to the left of the slash) from those at which he played less than 10 games (to the right of the slash). (If a player played fewer than 10 games at any position, his position abbreviation will start with a slash.)

On the left-hand side of the page are the player's situational statistics for 1991, broken down into the various categories. On the right-hand side of the page are the player's situational statistics totals from 1984–1991. If a player played in the majors every year from 1984 to 1991, it will show "8-Year Totals." If he played in the majors for only part of that period, the header will list the actual number of years he played and the first year he played. For example, a player who played in 1989, 1990, and 1991 would have "3-Year Totals" listed.

1991 REGULAR PLAYERS, BY POSITION

The listings that follow show the 390 regular players included in Part 1. Fifteen regulars, six pitchers, and nine position players were selected for each team, based on their playing time.

The regulars at the eight fielding positions were almost always determined by the most games started at that position. For teams with several players starting many games at multiple positions (e.g., Cleveland 1B-DH and 2B-SS-3B), a judgment call was made as to who to list where. For designated hitters, the number of starts at DH was not always the primary criterion. Many AL teams rotate several players through the DH slot, and the player who started the most at DH frequently starts fewer total games than a player who plays the field as well. The player listed at DH always started a substantial number of games at DH, but he is the player with the most games started overall (who did not qualify as a regular at any fielding position).

Traded players who qualified as regulars are usually listed on the team where they finished the season. The only exceptions are for players like Mike Bielecki, who spent almost all of the season with his first team. When players split the season relatively evenly with two teams, their total playing time was used to determine whether they were a regular. For example, Brook Jacoby played mostly first base in Cleveland and mostly third base in Oakland. Because of his combined playing time, he was selected as Oakland's regular at third base, even though he had fewer starts at third for the Athletics than Ernest Riles did.

For National League teams, which have no designated hitter, the abbreviation UT (Utility) represents the player who had the most playing time (aside from the eight regular position players). This player is somewhat analogous to the AL DH, and is usually a good offensive player who gets as many at-bats as many designated hitters. On most NL teams, this will be a player who played fairly regularly at one or two positions, but it could also be a traditional utility player who put in substantial time at several positions. Frequently, this ninth regular position player is also the primary pinch-hitter for the pitcher.

The regular pitchers selected for most teams were usually their top four starters (determined by games started) and their top two relievers (determined by games finished). Some teams with very stable starting rotations are represented by five starters and one reliever. For a few teams with unstable starting rotations and heavily used bullpens, three starters and three relievers were selected.

S1, S2, S3, S4, S5 indicates a team's regular starting pitchers, ranked by Games Started. R1, R2, R3 indicates a team's regular relievers, ranked by Games Finished. Thus, a team's regular closer will be designated R1 and the second-most-used closer or the top set-up pitcher will be designated R2. Pitchers who started and relieved are listed by their primary role.

C (Catcher), 1B (First Base), 2B (Second Base), SS (Shortstop), LF (Left Field), CF (Center Field), RF (Right Field), and DH (Designated Hitter) are the standard position abbreviations.

AMERICAN LEAGUE

BALTIMORE ORIOLES

S1	Bob Milacki
S2	Jose Mesa
S3	Jeff Ballard
S4	Ben McDonald
R2	Mike Flanagan
R1	Gregg Olson
C	Chris Hoiles
1B	Randy Milligan
2B	Billy Ripken
3B	Leo Gomez
SS	Cal Ripken
LF	Joe Orsulak
CF	Mike Devereaux
RF	Dwight Evans
DH	Sam Horn

BOSTON RED SOX

S1	Roger Clemens
S2	Mike Gardiner
S3	Greg Harris
S4	Joe Hesketh
R2	Jeff Gray
R1	Jeff Reardon
C	Tony Pena
1B	Carlos Quintana
2B	Jody Reed
3B	Wade Boggs
SS	Luis Rivera
LF	Mike Greenwell
CF	Ellis Burks
RF	Tom Brunansky
DH	Jack Clark

CLEVELAND INDIANS

S1	Greg Swindell
S2	Charles Nagy
S3	Eric King
R3	Doug Jones
R2	Shawn Hillegas
R1	Steve Olin
C	Joel Skinner
1B	Carlos Martinez
2B	Mark Lewis
3B	Carlos Baerga
SS	Felix Fermin
LF	Albert Belle
CF	Alex Cole
RF	Mark Whiten
DH	Chris James

DETROIT TIGERS

S1	Bill Gullickson
S2	Frank Tanana
S3	Walt Terrell
S4	Mark Leiter
R2	Paul Gibson
R1	Mike Henneman
C	Mickey Tettleton
1B	Cecil Fielder
2B	Lou Whitaker
3B	Travis Fryman
SS	Alan Trammell
LF	Tony Phillips
CF	Milt Cuyler
RF	Rob Deer
DH	Pete Incaviglia

MILWAUKEE BREWERS

S1	Jaime Navarro
S2	Chris Bosio
S3	Bill Wegman
S4	Don August
R2	Dan Plesac
R1	Chuck Crim
C	B.J. Surhoff
1B	Franklin Stubbs
2B	Willie Randolph
3B	Jim Gantner
SS	Bill Spiers
LF	Greg Vaughn
CF	Robin Yount
RF	Dante Bichette
DH	Paul Molitor

NEW YORK YANKEES

S1	Scott Sanderson
S2	Jeff Johnson
S3	Wade Taylor
R3	Greg Cadaret
R2	Lee Guetterman
R1	Steve Farr
C	Matt Nokes
1B	Don Mattingly
2B	Steve Sax
3B	Pat Kelly
SS	Alvaro Espinoza
LF	Roberto Kelly
CF	Bernie Williams
RF	Mel Hall
DH	Kevin Maas

TORONTO BLUE JAYS

S1	Todd Stottlemyre
S2	Jimmy Key
S3	Dave Wells
S4	Tom Candiotti
R2	Tom Henke
R1	Duane Ward
C	Greg Myers
1B	John Olerud
2B	Roberto Alomar
3B	Kelly Gruber
SS	Manuel Lee
LF	Candy Maldonado
CF	Devon White
RF	Joe Carter
DH	Rance Mulliniks

CALIFORNIA ANGELS

S1	Jim Abbott
S2	Mark Langston
S3	Chuck Finley
S4	Kirk McCaskill
R2	Mark Eichhorn
R1	Bryan Harvey
C	Lance Parrish
1B	Wally Joyner
2B	Luis Sojo
3B	Gary Gaetti
SS	Dick Schofield
LF	Luis Polonia
CF	Dave Gallagher
RF	Dave Winfield
DH	Dave Parker

CHICAGO WHITE SOX

S1	Jack McDowell
S2	Alex Fernandez
S3	Charlie Hough
S4	Greg Hibbard
R2	Scott Radinsky
R1	Bobby Thigpen
C	Carlton Fisk
1B	Dan Pasqua
2B	Scott Fletcher
3B	Robin Ventura
SS	Ozzie Guillen
LF	Tim Raines
CF	Lance Johnson
RF	Sammy Sosa
DH	Frank Thomas

KANSAS CITY ROYALS

S1	Kevin Appier
S2	Mike Boddicker
S3	Bret Saberhagen
S4	Mark Gubicza
S5	Luis Aquino
R1	Jeff Montgomery
C	Mike MacFarlane
1B	Todd Benzinger
2B	Terry Shumpert
3B	Bill Pecota
SS	Kurt Stillwell
LF	Kirk Gibson
CF	Brian McRae
RF	Dan Tartabull
DH	George Brett

MINNESOTA TWINS

S1	Jack Morris
S2	Kevin Tapani
S3	Scott Erickson
S4	Allan Anderson
R2	Steve Bedrosian
R1	Rick Aguilera
C	Brian Harper
1B	Kent Hrbek
2B	Chuck Knoblauch
3B	Mike Pagliarulo
SS	Greg Gagne
LF	Dan Gladden
CF	Kirby Puckett
RF	Shane Mack
DH	Chili Davis

OAKLAND ATHLETICS

S1	Bob Welch
S2	Dave Stewart
S3	Mike Moore
S4	Ron Darling
R2	Steve Chitren
R1	Dennis Eckersley
C	Terry Steinbach
1B	Mark McGwire
2B	Mike Gallego
3B	Brook Jacoby
SS	Mike Bordick
LF	Rickey Henderson
CF	Dave Henderson
RF	Jose Canseco
DH	Harold Baines

SEATTLE MARINERS

S1	Randy Johnson
S2	Rich DeLucia
S3	Brian Holman
S4	Erik Hanson
R2	Bill Swift
R1	Michael Jackson
C	Dave Valle
1B	Pete O'Brien
2B	Harold Reynolds
3B	Edgar Martinez
SS	Omar Vizquel
LF	Greg Briley
CF	Ken Griffey Jr
RF	Jay Buhner
DH	Alvin Davis

TEXAS RANGERS

S1	Kevin Brown
S2	Nolan Ryan
S3	Jose Guzman
S4	OilCan Boyd
R2	Kenny Rogers
R1	Jeff Russell
C	Ivan Rodriguez
1B	Rafael Palmeiro
2B	Julio Franco
3B	Dean Palmer
SS	Jeff Huson
LF	Kevin Reimer
CF	Juan Gonzalez
RF	Ruben Sierra
DH	Brian Downing

CHICAGO CUBS
S1	Greg Maddux
S2	Mike Bielecki
S3	Shawn Boskie
R3	Les Lancaster
R2	Dave Smith
R1	Paul Assenmacher
C	Rich Wilkins
1B	Mark Grace
2B	Ryne Sandberg
3B	Luis Salazar
SS	Shawon Dunston
LF	George Bell
CF	Jerome Walton
RF	Andre Dawson
UT	Chico Walker

PHILADELPHIA PHILLIES
S1	Terry Mulholland
S2	Jose DeJesus
S3	Tommy Greene
S4	Bruce Ruffin
R2	Joe Boever
R1	Mitch Williams
C	Darren Daulton
1B	John Kruk
2B	Mickey Morandini
3B	Charlie Hayes
SS	Dickie Thon
LF	Wes Chamberlain
CF	Lenny Dykstra
RF	Dale Murphy
UT	Ricky Jordan

ATLANTA BRAVES
S1	Charlie Leibrandt
S2	John Smoltz
S3	Steve Avery
S4	Tom Glavine
R2	Alejandro Pena
R1	Juan Berenguer
C	Greg Olson
1B	Sid Bream
2B	Jeff Treadway
3B	Terry Pendleton
SS	Rafael Belliard
LF	Lonnie Smith
CF	Ron Gant
RF	Dave Justice
UT	Otis Nixon

LOS ANGELES DODGERS
S1	Tim Belcher
S2	Mike Morgan
S3	Ramon Martinez
S4	Bob Ojeda
R2	Roger McDowell
R1	Jay Howell
C	Mike Scioscia
1B	Eddie Murray
2B	Juan Samuel
3B	Lenny Harris
SS	Alfredo Griffin
LF	Kal Daniels
CF	Brett Butler
RF	Darryl Strawberry
UT	Gary Carter

MONTREAL EXPOS
S1	Dennis Martinez
S2	Mark Gardner
S3	Brian Barnes
S4	Chris Nabholz
R2	Jeff Fassero
R1	Barry Jones
C	Gilberto Reyes
1B	Andres Galarraga
2B	Delino DeShields
3B	Tim Wallach
SS	Spike Owen
LF	Ivan Calderon
CF	Marquis Grissom
RF	Larry Walker
UT	Dave Martinez

PITTSBURGH PIRATES
S1	Doug Drabek
S2	Zane Smith
S3	John Smiley
S4	Randy Tomlin
R2	Stan Belinda
R1	Bill Landrum
C	Mike LaValliere
1B	Orlando Merced
2B	Jose Lind
3B	Steve Buechele
SS	Jay Bell
LF	Barry Bonds
CF	Andy VanSlyke
RF	Bobby Bonilla
UT	Gary Redus

CINCINNATI REDS
S1	Tom Browning
S2	Jose Rijo
S3	Jack Armstrong
S4	Norm Charlton
R2	Randy Myers
R1	Rob Dibble
C	Joe Oliver
1B	Hal Morris
2B	Bill Doran
3B	Chris Sabo
SS	Barry Larkin
LF	Billy Hatcher
CF	Eric Davis
RF	Paul O'Neill
UT	Mariano Duncan

SAN DIEGO PADRES
S1	Andy Benes
S2	Bruce Hurst
S3	Dennis Rasmussen
S4	Greg Harris
R2	Mike Maddux
R1	Craig Lefferts
C	Benito Santiago
1B	Fred McGriff
2B	Bip Roberts
3B	Tim Teufel
SS	Tony Fernandez
LF	Jerald Clark
CF	Darrin Jackson
RF	Tony Gwynn
UT	Thomas Howard

NEW YORK METS
S1	Frank Viola
S2	David Cone
S3	Dwight Gooden
S4	Wally Whitehurst
R2	Tim Burke
R1	John Franco
C	Rick Cerone
1B	Dave Magadan
2B	Gregg Jefferies
3B	Howard Johnson
SS	Kevin Elster
LF	Kevin McReynolds
CF	Vince Coleman
RF	Hubie Brooks
UT	Keith Miller

ST LOUIS CARDINALS
S1	Bryn Smith
S2	Bob Tewksbury
S3	Ken Hill
S4	Jose DeLeon
S5	Omar Olivares
R1	Lee Smith
C	Tom Pagnozzi
1B	Pedro Guerrero
2B	Jose Oquendo
3B	Todd Zeile
SS	Ozzie Smith
LF	Bernard Gilkey
CF	Ray Lankford
RF	Felix Jose
UT	Milt Thompson

HOUSTON ASTROS
S1	Pete Harnisch
S2	Jim Deshaies
S3	Mark Portugal
S4	Darryl Kile
R2	Al Osuna
R1	Curt Schilling
C	Craig Biggio
1B	Jeff Bagwell
2B	Casey Candaele
3B	Ken Caminiti
SS	Eric Yelding
LF	Luis Gonzalez
CF	Steve Finley
RF	Karl Rhodes
UT	Andujar Cedeno

SAN FRANCISCO GIANTS
S1	Bud Black
S2	John Burkett
S3	Trevor Wilson
S4	Don Robinson
R2	Jeff Brantley
R1	Dave Righetti
C	Steve Decker
1B	Will Clark
2B	Rob Thompson
3B	Matt Williams
SS	Jose Uribe
LF	Kevin Mitchell
CF	Willie McGee
RF	Kevin Bass
UT	Mike Felder

BATTERS

ROBERTO ALOMAR — bats both — throws right — age 24 — TOR — *2

1991	BA	OBA	SA	AB	H	2B	3B	HR	RBI	BB	SO		BA	OBA	SA	AB	H	2B	3B	HR	RBI	BB	SO
												4-YEAR TOTALS (1988–1991)											
Total	.295	.354	.436	637	188	41	11	9	69	57	86		.286	.343	.394	2390	684	119	23	31	226	205	317
vs. Left	.246	.295	.419	191	47	12	3	5	27	11	35		.257	.320	.390	762	196	41	6	16	81	66	128
vs. Right	.316	.379	.444	446	141	29	8	4	42	46	51		.300	.353	.396	1628	488	78	17	15	145	139	189
at Home	.297	.367	.479	313	93	23	8	6	40	35	36		.291	.352	.405	1175	342	50	15	18	131	110	148
on Road	.293	.341	.395	324	95	18	3	3	29	22	50		.281	.334	.384	1215	342	69	8	13	95	95	169
on Grass	.267	.309	.341	255	68	14	1	1	22	15	41		.277	.330	.360	1532	425	64	9	15	145	120	205
on Turf	.314	.383	.500	382	120	27	10	8	47	42	45		.302	.364	.455	858	259	55	14	16	81	85	112
Day Games	.245	.301	.380	208	51	20	1	2	27	18	26		.283	.345	.389	742	210	46	3	9	81	71	91
Night Games	.319	.380	.464	429	137	21	10	7	42	39	60		.288	.342	.396	1648	474	73	20	22	145	134	226
April	.256	.315	.366	82	21	9	0	0	6	7	10		.262	.311	.334	290	76	13	1	2	20	21	37
May	.274	.355	.528	106	29	6	3	5	19	13	18		.288	.342	.410	444	128	19	4	9	48	36	53
June	.290	.356	.411	107	31	9	2	0	9	11	13		.263	.329	.374	422	111	25	5	4	37	41	55
July	.358	.386	.462	106	38	7	2	0	11	5	12		.294	.340	.369	388	114	18	4	1	32	29	49
August	.264	.311	.397	121	32	4	3	2	12	8	17		.282	.345	.402	443	125	23	6	6	40	40	79
Sept—Oct	.322	.395	.443	115	37	6	1	2	12	13	16		.323	.381	.457	403	130	21	3	9	49	38	44
Bases Empty	.295	.351	.449	390	115	21	9	7	7	32	52		.278	.336	.395	1429	397	72	13	23	23	121	197
Leadoff	.295	.372	.484	122	36	8	3	3	3	15	13		.288	.350	.429	538	155	32	4	12	12	50	63
Runners On Base	.296	.358	.417	247	73	20	2	2	62	25	34		.299	.353	.393	961	287	47	10	8	203	84	120
Scoring Position	.280	.341	.420	157	44	15	2	1	58	16	22		.296	.347	.391	530	157	28	5	4	183	49	76
Late and Close	.286	.371	.419	105	30	6	1	2	15	15	20		.274	.350	.359	398	109	16	3	4	39	47	63

CARLOS BAERGA — bats both — throws right — age 24 — CLE — 32/S

1991	BA	OBA	SA	AB	H	2B	3B	HR	RBI	BB	SO		BA	OBA	SA	AB	H	2B	3B	HR	RBI	BB	SO
												2-YEAR TOTALS (1990–1991)											
Total	.288	.346	.398	593	171	28	2	11	69	48	74		.278	.330	.397	905	252	45	4	18	116	64	131
vs. Left	.329	.376	.416	161	53	8	0	2	20	8	14		.295	.330	.386	264	78	12	0	4	36	10	36
vs. Right	.273	.335	.391	432	118	20	2	9	49	40	60		.271	.330	.401	641	174	33	4	14	80	54	95
at Home	.291	.337	.368	299	87	13	2	2	32	20	31		.294	.341	.392	449	132	23	3	5	60	29	53
on Road	.286	.355	.429	294	84	15	0	9	37	28	43		.263	.320	.401	456	120	22	1	13	56	35	78
on Grass	.295	.350	.413	508	150	23	2	11	65	40	53		.287	.336	.419	766	220	39	4	18	107	52	98
on Turf	.247	.323	.306	85	21	5	0	0	4	8	21		.230	.299	.273	139	32	6	0	0	9	12	33
Day Games	.243	.340	.393	173	42	9	1	5	21	25	25		.247	.322	.387	279	69	11	2	8	39	29	46
Night Games	.307	.349	.400	420	129	19	1	6	48	23	49		.292	.334	.401	626	183	34	2	10	77	35	85
April	.255	.317	.382	55	14	1	0	2	3	5	5		.231	.283	.363	91	21	1	1	3	8	7	9
May	.295	.362	.438	105	31	4	1	3	19	10	8		.273	.330	.373	161	44	5	1	5	23	13	15
June	.267	.364	.407	86	23	3	0	3	8	12	10		.246	.331	.418	134	33	8	0	5	18	16	22
July	.320	.372	.417	103	33	7	0	1	9	9	15		.290	.343	.374	131	38	8	0	1	9	11	19
August	.292	.317	.383	120	35	5	0	2	14	4	22		.314	.342	.434	175	55	9	0	4	25	5	30
Sept—Oct	.282	.338	.363	124	35	8	1	0	16	8	14		.286	.333	.399	213	61	14	2	3	33	12	36
Bases Empty	.271	.321	.370	343	93	14	1	6	6	22	43		.267	.316	.370	525	140	22	1	10	10	32	72
Leadoff	.286	.348	.389	126	36	7	0	2	2	11	10		.285	.337	.383	193	55	10	0	3	3	14	18
Runners On Base	.312	.379	.436	250	78	14	1	5	63	26	31		.295	.349	.434	380	112	23	3	8	106	32	59
Scoring Position	.280	.369	.427	150	42	5	1	5	59	20	22		.274	.343	.422	237	65	9	1	8	96	25	40
Late and Close	.224	.284	.327	107	24	5	0	2	10	8	19		.234	.303	.347	167	39	10	0	3	22	15	34

JEFF BAGWELL — bats right — throws right — age 24 — HOU — *1

1991	BA	OBA	SA	AB	H	2B	3B	HR	RBI	BB	SO		BA	OBA	SA	AB	H	2B	3B	HR	RBI	BB	SO
												1-YEAR TOTALS (1991)											
Total	.294	.387	.437	554	163	26	4	15	82	75	116		.294	.387	.437	554	163	26	4	15	82	75	116
vs. Left	.322	.417	.473	205	66	10	0	7	37	32	36		.322	.417	.473	205	66	10	0	7	37	32	36
vs. Right	.278	.369	.415	349	97	16	4	8	45	43	80		.278	.369	.415	349	97	16	4	8	45	43	80
at Home	.296	.392	.431	274	81	15	2	6	35	36	52		.296	.392	.431	274	81	15	2	6	35	36	52
on Road	.293	.382	.443	280	82	11	2	9	47	39	64		.293	.382	.443	280	82	11	2	9	47	39	64
on Grass	.278	.389	.430	158	44	2	2	6	30	28	40		.278	.389	.430	158	44	2	2	6	30	28	40
on Turf	.301	.386	.439	396	119	24	2	9	52	47	76		.301	.386	.439	396	119	24	2	9	52	47	76
Day Games	.269	.342	.418	134	36	6	1	4	18	14	26		.269	.342	.418	134	36	6	1	4	18	14	26
Night Games	.302	.400	.443	420	127	20	3	11	64	61	90		.302	.400	.443	420	127	20	3	11	64	61	90
April	.254	.348	.407	59	15	3	0	2	8	9	17		.254	.348	.407	59	15	3	0	2	8	9	17
May	.270	.356	.416	89	24	2	1	3	11	11	29		.270	.356	.416	89	24	2	1	3	11	11	29
June	.317	.393	.462	104	33	7	1	2	11	13	20		.317	.393	.462	104	33	7	1	2	11	13	20
July	.313	.433	.506	83	26	5	1	3	14	16	15		.313	.433	.506	83	26	5	1	3	14	16	15
August	.267	.378	.381	105	28	4	1	2	20	16	16		.267	.378	.381	105	28	4	1	2	20	16	16
Sept—Oct	.325	.397	.447	114	37	5	0	3	18	9	19		.325	.397	.447	114	37	5	0	3	18	9	19
Bases Empty	.291	.383	.414	302	88	18	2	5	5	41	62		.291	.383	.414	302	88	18	2	5	5	41	62
Leadoff	.275	.360	.342	120	33	8	0	0	0	12	28		.275	.360	.342	120	33	8	0	0	0	12	28
Runners On Base	.298	.391	.464	252	75	8	2	10	77	34	54		.298	.391	.464	252	75	8	2	10	77	34	54
Scoring Position	.301	.397	.458	153	46	5	2	7	65	23	37		.301	.397	.458	153	46	5	2	7	65	23	37
Late and Close	.360	.481	.547	86	31	8	1	2	13	16	19		.360	.481	.547	86	31	8	1	2	13	16	19

HAROLD BAINES — bats left — throws left — age 33 — OAK — *DO

1991

	BA	OBA	SA	AB	H	2B	3B	HR	RBI	BB	SO
Total	.295	.383	.473	488	144	25	1	20	90	72	67
vs. Left	.301	.348	.506	83	25	5	0	4	18	5	14
vs. Right	.294	.390	.467	405	119	20	1	16	72	67	53
at Home	.264	.358	.458	227	60	11	0	11	52	36	38
on Road	.322	.406	.487	261	84	14	1	9	38	36	29
on Grass	.301	.391	.494	405	122	21	0	19	80	62	58
on Turf	.265	.344	.373	83	22	4	1	1	10	10	9
Day Games	.335	.414	.528	161	54	8	1	7	33	23	21
Night Games	.275	.368	.446	327	90	17	0	13	57	49	46
April	.224	.274	.313	67	15	4	1	0	11	4	12
May	.397	.505	.654	78	31	5	0	5	19	17	9
June	.341	.417	.545	88	30	6	0	4	20	13	12
July	.314	.388	.500	86	27	4	0	4	15	11	12
August	.241	.307	.418	79	19	5	0	3	11	8	11
Sept–Oct	.244	.376	.389	90	22	1	0	4	14	19	11
Bases Empty	.279	.357	.431	262	73	13	0	9	9	31	35
Leadoff	.239	.278	.303	109	26	4	0	1	1	6	14
Runners On Base	.314	.412	.522	226	71	12	1	11	81	41	32
Scoring Position	.278	.416	.474	133	37	8	0	6	69	35	20
Late and Close	.205	.333	.370	73	15	3	0	3	10	14	15

8-YEAR TOTALS (1984–1991)

	BA	OBA	SA	AB	H	2B	3B	HR	RBI	BB	SO
Total	.296	.362	.468	4291	1272	220	23	157	696	459	670
vs. Left	.277	.327	.420	1322	366	59	8	38	191	102	248
vs. Right	.305	.376	.490	2969	906	161	15	119	505	357	422
at Home	.298	.364	.480	2073	617	119	11	79	379	229	311
on Road	.295	.360	.457	2218	655	101	12	78	317	230	359
on Grass	.299	.366	.470	3613	1081	188	16	132	603	398	566
on Turf	.282	.337	.460	678	191	32	7	25	93	61	104
Day Games	.309	.376	.480	1180	365	62	8	41	199	137	195
Night Games	.292	.356	.464	3111	907	158	15	116	497	322	475
April	.259	.330	.407	514	133	23	1	17	76	55	83
May	.296	.366	.443	706	209	36	1	22	107	83	97
June	.307	.381	.507	781	240	33	6	37	133	98	125
July	.325	.394	.516	711	231	49	3	27	128	83	118
August	.286	.342	.461	751	215	31	8	28	120	67	110
Sept–Oct	.295	.348	.457	828	244	48	4	26	132	73	137
Bases Empty	.283	.343	.447	2358	667	118	10	83	83	213	374
Leadoff	.269	.324	.407	803	216	37	4	22	22	65	122
Runners On Base	.313	.383	.494	1933	605	102	13	74	613	246	296
Scoring Position	.302	.392	.480	1111	336	57	7	42	521	192	188
Late and Close	.292	.385	.489	638	186	35	2	29	100	96	100

KEVIN BASS — bats both — throws right — age 33 — SF — *O

1991

	BA	OBA	SA	AB	H	2B	3B	HR	RBI	BB	SO
Total	.233	.307	.366	361	84	10	4	10	40	36	56
vs. Left	.243	.281	.450	111	27	5	0	6	15	5	15
vs. Right	.228	.318	.328	250	57	5	4	4	25	31	41
at Home	.210	.298	.335	167	35	2	2	5	17	21	35
on Road	.253	.315	.392	194	49	8	2	5	23	15	21
on Grass	.229	.307	.373	249	57	4	4	8	25	26	47
on Turf	.241	.306	.348	112	27	6	0	2	15	10	9
Day Games	.187	.261	.252	139	26	1	1	2	12	13	30
Night Games	.261	.335	.437	222	58	9	3	8	28	23	26
April	.243	.300	.324	74	18	4	1	0	4	6	14
May	.256	.318	.436	78	20	2	0	4	7	6	9
June	.173	.271	.192	52	9	1	0	0	5	6	6
July	.360	.414	.600	25	9	0	0	2	7	3	4
August	.196	.250	.339	56	11	2	0	2	5	4	10
Sept–Oct	.224	.330	.395	76	17	1	3	2	12	11	13
Bases Empty	.249	.303	.410	205	51	6	3	7	7	14	32
Leadoff	.197	.247	.316	76	15	2	2	1	1	4	10
Runners On Base	.212	.311	.308	156	33	4	1	3	33	22	24
Scoring Position	.198	.316	.333	96	19	2	1	3	33	17	16
Late and Close	.235	.321	.368	68	16	1	1	2	13	9	10

8-YEAR TOTALS (1984–1991)

	BA	OBA	SA	AB	H	2B	3B	HR	RBI	BB	SO
Total	.274	.326	.421	3481	953	173	31	92	444	249	461
vs. Left	.286	.323	.483	1325	379	87	9	52	195	59	183
vs. Right	.266	.328	.382	2156	574	86	22	40	249	190	278
at Home	.274	.332	.404	1722	472	80	12	40	222	140	238
on Road	.273	.321	.437	1759	481	93	19	52	222	109	223
on Grass	.261	.312	.422	1320	345	63	13	41	171	92	189
on Turf	.281	.335	.420	2161	608	110	18	51	273	157	272
Day Games	.248	.296	.385	1028	255	41	8	28	117	69	155
Night Games	.285	.339	.435	2453	698	132	23	64	327	180	306
April	.269	.318	.398	566	152	28	6	11	67	40	80
May	.267	.307	.409	651	174	33	4	17	76	36	74
June	.264	.329	.416	507	134	26	3	15	66	42	60
July	.289	.339	.439	456	132	18	4	14	54	30	65
August	.264	.322	.411	531	140	22	4	16	75	42	83
Sept–Oct	.287	.340	.447	770	221	46	10	19	106	59	99
Bases Empty	.267	.306	.414	2009	537	95	19	54	54	92	252
Leadoff	.253	.287	.409	801	203	41	9	22	22	34	100
Runners On Base	.283	.352	.429	1472	416	78	12	38	390	157	209
Scoring Position	.294	.371	.447	855	251	46	8	23	342	113	128
Late and Close	.283	.347	.420	621	176	23	4	18	101	60	87

JAY BELL — bats right — throws right — age 27 — PIT — *S

1991

	BA	OBA	SA	AB	H	2B	3B	HR	RBI	BB	SO
Total	.270	.330	.428	608	164	32	8	16	67	52	99
vs. Left	.289	.368	.500	194	56	13	5	6	28	25	18
vs. Right	.261	.311	.394	414	108	19	3	10	39	27	81
at Home	.281	.332	.446	303	85	19	5	7	33	23	49
on Road	.259	.327	.410	305	79	13	3	9	34	29	50
on Grass	.237	.301	.363	160	38	8	3	2	13	13	21
on Turf	.281	.340	.451	448	126	24	5	14	54	39	78
Day Games	.280	.332	.446	168	47	14	1	4	20	13	28
Night Games	.266	.329	.420	440	117	18	7	12	47	39	71
April	.183	.234	.254	71	13	3	1	1	5	4	9
May	.276	.333	.540	87	24	5	0	6	19	8	13
June	.321	.374	.481	106	34	5	3	2	10	8	19
July	.311	.359	.462	119	37	6	0	4	15	9	13
August	.246	.295	.360	114	28	8	1	1	5	8	24
Sept–Oct	.252	.349	.432	111	28	5	3	3	13	15	21
Bases Empty	.237	.301	.398	354	84	16	4	11	11	30	61
Leadoff	.343	.420	.636	99	34	5	3	6	6	13	13
Runners On Base	.315	.370	.469	254	80	16	4	5	56	22	38
Scoring Position	.286	.344	.464	140	40	9	2	4	49	14	22
Late and Close	.283	.365	.457	92	26	5	1	3	12	12	14

6-YEAR TOTALS (1986–1991)

	BA	OBA	SA	AB	H	2B	3B	HR	RBI	BB	SO
Total	.254	.318	.375	1812	460	89	20	30	184	167	342
vs. Left	.286	.361	.427	639	183	36	12	10	70	78	95
vs. Right	.236	.294	.346	1173	277	53	8	20	114	89	247
at Home	.256	.319	.375	915	234	51	11	12	80	83	176
on Road	.252	.318	.375	897	226	38	9	18	104	84	166
on Grass	.228	.294	.332	632	144	26	8	8	62	57	130
on Turf	.268	.331	.397	1180	316	63	12	22	122	110	212
Day Games	.266	.332	.402	522	139	36	4	9	60	48	107
Night Games	.249	.313	.364	1290	321	53	16	21	124	119	235
April	.183	.256	.252	230	42	6	2	2	20	21	46
May	.283	.346	.439	244	69	16	2	2	20	21	46
June	.274	.335	.408	223	61	9	6	3	21	20	48
July	.265	.307	.385	317	84	16	2	6	36	20	46
August	.249	.294	.350	366	91	16	3	5	24	23	69
Sept–Oct	.262	.353	.400	432	113	26	5	8	53	58	88
Bases Empty	.227	.301	.338	1055	239	49	6	19	19	106	215
Leadoff	.264	.342	.402	311	82	14	4	7	7	37	68
Runners On Base	.292	.343	.425	757	221	40	14	11	165	61	127
Scoring Position	.283	.330	.435	414	117	19	10	8	147	34	78
Late and Close	.250	.321	.350	260	65	9	4	3	28	28	54

GEORGE BELL — bats right — throws right — age 33 — CHN — *O

1991	BA	OBA	SA	AB	H	2B	3B	HR	RBI	BB	SO		BA	OBA	SA	AB	H	2B	3B	HR	RBI	BB	SO
Total	.285	.323	.468	558	159	27	0	25	86	32	62		.288	.327	.490	4811	1385	257	27	220	797	278	581
vs. Left	.285	.338	.541	207	59	8	0	15	34	17	19		.290	.335	.525	1508	438	75	9	87	268	102	174
vs. Right	.285	.315	.425	351	100	19	0	10	52	15	43		.287	.324	.474	3303	947	182	18	133	529	176	407
at Home	.267	.294	.413	288	77	15	0	9	45	11	30		.290	.334	.480	2329	676	130	17	93	390	151	276
on Road	.304	.354	.526	270	82	12	0	16	41	21	32		.286	.321	.498	2482	709	127	10	127	407	127	305
on Grass	.290	.324	.460	411	119	22	0	16	66	22	39		.283	.317	.477	2136	605	109	5	98	354	109	250
on Turf	.272	.323	.490	147	40	5	0	9	20	10	23		.292	.335	.500	2675	780	148	22	122	443	169	331
Day Games	.271	.311	.440	273	74	13	0	11	46	16	30		.278	.323	.482	1649	459	96	12	72	275	103	210
Night Games	.298	.336	.495	285	85	14	0	14	40	16	32		.293	.330	.494	3162	926	161	15	148	522	175	371
April	.272	.291	.469	81	22	4	0	4	12	2	9		.304	.341	.525	657	200	40	3	33	104	35	80
May	.269	.311	.495	93	25	0	0	7	19	6	8		.285	.323	.485	808	230	34	10	36	139	46	103
June	.324	.374	.495	105	34	6	0	4	15	9	14		.291	.328	.495	859	250	40	3	43	155	51	115
July	.268	.294	.474	97	26	5	0	5	19	3	9		.281	.328	.486	745	209	39	3	36	124	51	90
August	.308	.350	.439	107	33	8	0	2	12	7	12		.307	.350	.532	859	264	61	3	42	155	54	86
Sept–Oct	.253	.300	.427	75	19	4	0	3	9	5	10		.263	.296	.425	883	232	43	5	30	120	41	107
Bases Empty	.290	.343	.502	303	88	13	0	17	17	22	30		.284	.328	.506	2559	728	138	15	133	133	144	331
Leadoff	.324	.365	.647	139	45	9	0	12	12	9	16		.282	.320	.506	1176	332	63	7	62	62	56	149
Runners On Base	.278	.301	.427	255	71	14	0	8	69	10	32		.292	.326	.471	2252	657	119	12	87	664	134	250
Scoring Position	.236	.274	.392	148	35	5	0	6	60	9	23		.293	.334	.485	1323	388	72	7	56	574	107	158
Late and Close	.260	.312	.460	100	26	5	0	5	18	8	16		.286	.331	.501	779	223	39	4	40	143	51	99

8-YEAR TOTALS (1984–1991)

ALBERT BELLE — bats right — throws right — age 26 — CLE — OD

1991	BA	OBA	SA	AB	H	2B	3B	HR	RBI	BB	SO		BA	OBA	SA	AB	H	2B	3B	HR	RBI	BB	SO
Total	.282	.323	.540	461	130	31	2	28	95	25	99		.261	.302	.487	702	183	39	6	36	135	38	160
vs. Left	.288	.312	.568	132	38	11	1	8	34	5	27		.276	.307	.533	199	55	13	1	12	47	10	41
vs. Right	.280	.327	.529	329	92	20	1	20	61	20	72		.254	.301	.469	503	128	26	5	24	88	28	119
at Home	.254	.294	.419	236	60	15	0	8	35	11	49		.250	.288	.412	364	91	21	1	12	62	17	83
on Road	.311	.352	.667	225	70	16	2	20	60	14	50		.272	.318	.568	338	92	18	5	24	73	21	77
on Grass	.278	.321	.540	413	115	26	2	26	85	24	88		.257	.298	.483	606	156	33	4	32	117	33	140
on Turf	.313	.333	.542	48	15	5	0	2	10	1	11		.281	.327	.510	96	27	6	2	4	18	5	20
Day Games	.295	.338	.619	139	41	9	0	12	35	6	25		.271	.321	.552	203	55	12	3	13	49	10	45
Night Games	.276	.316	.506	322	89	22	2	16	60	19	74		.257	.295	.461	499	128	27	3	23	86	28	115
April	.268	.328	.518	56	15	2	0	4	9	3	17		.250	.305	.474	76	19	2	0	5	12	4	20
May	.273	.333	.525	99	27	8	1	5	18	8	18		.265	.324	.510	102	27	8	1	5	18	8	21
June	.194	.194	.355	31	6	2	0	1	5	0	7		.194	.194	.355	31	6	2	0	1	5	0	7
July	.295	.318	.590	78	23	2	0	7	17	4	13		.286	.329	.564	140	40	5	2	10	33	10	28
August	.296	.336	.546	108	32	6	0	7	21	5	23		.249	.280	.466	189	47	9	1	10	32	7	45
Sept–Oct	.303	.337	.584	89	27	11	1	4	25	5	21		.268	.309	.463	164	44	13	2	5	35	9	39
Bases Empty	.242	.280	.480	227	55	13	1	13	13	8	53		.224	.271	.420	357	80	16	3	16	16	18	86
Leadoff	.301	.336	.584	113	34	9	1	7	7	4	19		.277	.335	.528	159	44	9	2	9	9	11	31
Runners On Base	.321	.362	.598	234	75	18	1	15	82	17	46		.299	.334	.557	345	103	23	3	20	119	20	74
Scoring Position	.310	.357	.556	126	39	13	0	6	61	12	31		.321	.355	.579	190	61	18	2	9	94	13	47
Late and Close	.197	.280	.333	66	13	1	1	2	10	7	23		.215	.283	.346	107	23	3	1	3	21	10	34

3-YEAR TOTALS (1989–1991)

RAFAEL BELLIARD — bats right — throws right — age 31 — ATL — *S

1991	BA	OBA	SA	AB	H	2B	3B	HR	RBI	BB	SO		BA	OBA	SA	AB	H	2B	3B	HR	RBI	BB	SO
Total	.249	.296	.286	353	88	9	2	0	27	22	63		.226	.287	.261	1400	316	25	11	1	99	108	230
vs. Left	.250	.296	.272	92	23	2	0	0	4	6	14		.236	.296	.270	441	104	7	4	0	28	35	63
vs. Right	.249	.296	.291	261	65	7	2	0	23	16	49		.221	.282	.258	959	212	18	7	1	71	73	167
at Home	.254	.299	.312	173	44	6	2	0	15	10	26		.215	.278	.256	673	145	11	8	0	52	52	105
on Road	.244	.294	.261	180	44	3	0	0	12	12	37		.235	.295	.267	727	171	14	3	1	47	56	125
on Grass	.248	.297	.295	258	64	8	2	0	19	17	43		.256	.304	.302	577	148	15	4	1	40	36	97
on Turf	.253	.294	.263	95	24	1	0	0	8	5	20		.204	.275	.233	823	168	10	7	0	59	72	133
Day Games	.268	.314	.309	97	26	2	1	0	6	6	7		.236	.299	.280	454	107	8	6	0	32	37	67
Night Games	.242	.289	.277	256	62	7	1	0	21	16	56		.221	.281	.253	946	209	17	5	1	67	71	163
April	.220	.264	.240	50	11	1	0	0	5	3	12		.221	.268	.281	217	48	5	4	0	19	12	41
May	.267	.313	.322	90	24	3	1	0	10	6	17		.248	.308	.296	250	62	7	1	1	23	19	39
June	.207	.224	.220	82	17	1	0	0	3	2	11		.221	.285	.229	340	75	1	1	0	23	28	49
July	.125	.222	.250	16	2	0	1	0	2	2	1		.208	.263	.267	202	42	4	4	0	15	14	28
August	.333	.350	.333	39	13	0	0	0	3	1	9		.217	.279	.237	198	43	2	1	0	11	15	37
Sept–Oct	.276	.360	.329	76	21	4	0	0	4	8	13		.238	.315	.269	193	46	6	0	0	8	20	36
Bases Empty	.234	.286	.268	205	48	5	1	0	0	14	38		.212	.274	.236	798	169	11	4	0	0	63	143
Leadoff	.265	.315	.289	83	22	2	0	0	0	6	12		.215	.275	.237	316	68	3	2	0	0	25	56
Runners On Base	.270	.310	.311	148	40	4	1	0	27	8	25		.244	.304	.296	602	147	14	7	1	99	45	87
Scoring Position	.269	.310	.333	78	21	3	1	0	27	5	13		.251	.326	.316	342	86	9	5	1	94	34	51
Late and Close	.227	.261	.227	44	10	0	0	0	2	2	10		.231	.309	.249	169	39	1	1	0	4	16	33

8-YEAR TOTALS (1984–1991)

TODD BENZINGER — bats both — throws right — age 29 — CIN/KC — 1O/D

5-YEAR TOTALS (1987–1991)

1991	BA	OBA	SA	AB	H	2B	3B	HR	RBI	BB	SO		BA	OBA	SA	AB	H	2B	3B	HR	RBI	BB	SO
Total	.262	.310	.351	416	109	18	5	3	51	27	66		.255	.302	.383	2048	523	99	12	46	286	134	376
vs. Left	.252	.280	.315	143	36	6	0	1	16	6	13		.259	.294	.360	725	188	32	1	13	85	40	82
vs. Right	.267	.324	.370	273	73	12	5	2	35	21	53		.253	.306	.395	1323	335	67	11	33	201	94	294
at Home	.269	.306	.384	216	58	13	3	2	30	10	26		.274	.322	.420	1022	280	64	8	23	143	70	161
on Road	.255	.314	.315	200	51	5	2	1	21	17	40		.237	.282	.346	1026	243	35	4	23	143	64	215
on Grass	.288	.340	.360	139	40	5	1	1	18	11	27		.263	.316	.409	970	255	49	3	29	150	72	186
on Turf	.249	.294	.347	277	69	13	4	2	33	16	39		.249	.289	.359	1078	268	50	9	17	136	62	190
Day Games	.232	.281	.280	125	29	1	1	1	12	9	20		.240	.292	.350	674	162	35	3	11	82	47	131
Night Games	.275	.322	.381	291	80	17	4	2	39	18	46		.263	.307	.399	1374	361	64	9	35	204	87	245
April	.231	.256	.333	39	9	2	1	0	9	2	6		.259	.303	.341	205	53	7	2	2	30	16	28
May	.000	.000	.000	20	0	0	0	0	0	0	2		.245	.277	.349	278	68	15	1	4	41	15	51
June	.217	.309	.317	60	13	1	1	1	2	8	11		.251	.329	.386	319	80	14	1	9	40	34	66
July	.342	.381	.494	79	27	4	1	2	18	4	12		.273	.311	.423	359	98	19	1	11	48	19	68
August	.260	.295	.320	100	26	4	1	0	7	5	15		.232	.265	.370	427	99	21	4	10	60	18	82
Sept–Oct	.288	.341	.364	118	34	7	1	0	15	8	20		.272	.323	.400	460	125	23	3	10	67	32	81
Bases Empty	.279	.319	.365	219	61	9	2	2	2	11	39		.269	.309	.389	1110	299	48	5	25	25	58	197
Leadoff	.289	.317	.320	97	28	3	0	0	0	4	15		.261	.303	.337	463	121	18	1	5	5	26	83
Runners On Base	.244	.300	.335	197	48	9	3	1	49	16	27		.239	.293	.375	938	224	51	7	21	261	76	179
Scoring Position	.267	.322	.344	131	35	5	1	1	46	11	21		.238	.306	.378	609	145	31	3	16	239	64	130
Late and Close	.222	.315	.321	81	18	1	2	1	7	11	13		.220	.291	.338	337	74	8	4	8	48	34	64

DANTE BICHETTE — bats right — throws right — age 29 — MIL — *O/3

4-YEAR TOTALS (1988–1991)

1991	BA	OBA	SA	AB	H	2B	3B	HR	RBI	BB	SO		BA	OBA	SA	AB	H	2B	3B	HR	RBI	BB	SO
Total	.238	.272	.393	445	106	18	3	15	59	22	107		.241	.273	.394	978	236	42	4	33	135	44	217
vs. Left	.253	.299	.429	154	39	5	2	6	18	11	37		.257	.293	.424	413	106	21	3	14	52	22	88
vs. Right	.230	.257	.375	291	67	13	1	9	41	11	70		.230	.259	.372	565	130	21	1	19	83	22	129
at Home	.249	.296	.399	213	53	10	2	6	30	16	46		.245	.280	.403	461	113	21	2	16	68	22	97
on Road	.228	.249	.388	232	53	8	1	9	29	6	61		.238	.267	.385	517	123	21	2	17	67	22	120
on Grass	.245	.277	.406	372	91	15	3	13	57	18	85		.246	.278	.405	820	202	35	4	29	119	36	177
on Turf	.205	.247	.329	73	15	3	0	2	2	4	22		.215	.247	.335	158	34	7	0	4	16	8	40
Day Games	.286	.316	.460	161	46	8	1	6	25	8	31		.247	.291	.417	300	74	13	1	12	44	20	69
Night Games	.211	.248	.356	284	60	10	2	9	34	14	76		.239	.265	.383	678	162	29	3	21	91	24	148
April	.236	.253	.375	72	17	4	0	2	11	2	10		.259	.287	.430	193	50	12	0	7	28	8	29
May	.209	.255	.451	91	19	2	1	6	15	6	27		.229	.261	.403	231	53	11	1	9	34	10	56
June	.235	.308	.397	68	16	2	0	3	9	7	18		.177	.232	.312	141	25	4	0	5	16	10	40
July	.307	.325	.400	75	23	4	0	1	9	3	18		.262	.296	.426	141	37	5	0	6	23	8	36
August	.132	.179	.226	53	7	2	0	0	2	3	16		.227	.284	.341	88	20	2	1	2	8	5	23
Sept–Oct	.279	.287	.442	86	24	4	2	2	13	1	18		.277	.283	.408	184	51	8	2	4	26	3	33
Bases Empty	.234	.271	.385	239	56	10	1	8	8	11	59		.247	.288	.407	526	130	25	1	19	19	27	113
Leadoff	.267	.290	.422	90	24	3	1	3	3	3	22		.242	.276	.398	211	51	10	1	7	7	9	48
Runners On Base	.243	.274	.403	206	50	8	2	7	51	11	48		.235	.256	.378	452	106	17	3	14	116	17	104
Scoring Position	.218	.270	.427	110	24	4	2	5	46	10	28		.233	.263	.408	245	57	9	2	10	104	15	64
Late and Close	.273	.297	.409	88	24	1	1	3	15	2	24		.276	.304	.425	181	50	5	2	6	35	7	47

CRAIG BIGGIO — bats right — throws right — age 27 — HOU — *C/2O

4-YEAR TOTALS (1988–1991)

1991	BA	OBA	SA	AB	H	2B	3B	HR	RBI	BB	SO		BA	OBA	SA	AB	H	2B	3B	HR	RBI	BB	SO
Total	.295	.358	.374	546	161	23	4	4	46	53	71		.272	.339	.371	1667	454	74	9	24	153	162	243
vs. Left	.274	.343	.366	186	51	10	2	1	11	20	19		.253	.330	.333	565	143	21	3	6	41	63	65
vs. Right	.306	.365	.378	360	110	13	2	3	35	33	52		.282	.344	.390	1102	311	53	6	18	112	99	178
at Home	.343	.401	.437	277	95	20	3	0	24	27	39		.279	.346	.380	828	231	43	7	9	77	83	128
on Road	.245	.313	.309	269	66	3	1	4	22	26	32		.266	.332	.361	839	223	31	2	15	76	79	115
on Grass	.243	.296	.289	173	42	2	0	2	15	13	21		.259	.314	.356	517	134	15	1	11	46	40	70
on Turf	.319	.385	.413	373	119	21	4	2	31	40	50		.278	.350	.377	1150	320	59	8	13	107	122	173
Day Games	.363	.409	.471	102	37	6	1	1	8	8	11		.319	.384	.449	408	130	20	3	9	51	40	60
Night Games	.279	.346	.351	444	124	17	3	3	38	45	60		.257	.324	.346	1259	324	54	6	15	102	122	183
April	.359	.400	.469	64	23	1	0	2	5	5	10		.297	.371	.376	165	49	4	0	3	13	19	30
May	.311	.382	.378	90	28	6	0	0	7	11	12		.301	.361	.383	266	80	14	1	2	28	25	41
June	.309	.374	.381	97	30	4	0	1	4	9	8		.268	.337	.366	295	79	11	0	2	24	30	38
July	.273	.326	.307	88	24	1	1	0	10	7	10		.284	.340	.375	331	94	15	3	3	31	24	43
August	.271	.377	.365	96	26	7	1	0	9	16	16		.253	.339	.352	293	74	14	3	3	23	39	44
Sept–Oct	.270	.302	.369	111	30	4	2	1	11	5	15		.246	.304	.375	317	78	16	2	7	34	25	47
Bases Empty	.268	.333	.363	317	85	15	3	3	3	30	36		.266	.329	.380	964	256	45	7	17	17	85	135
Leadoff	.302	.357	.422	116	35	7	2	1	1	10	7		.240	.303	.396	366	88	20	5	9	9	33	39
Runners On Base	.332	.391	.389	229	76	8	1	1	43	23	35		.282	.353	.358	703	198	29	2	7	136	77	108
Scoring Position	.280	.354	.312	125	35	4	0	0	39	16	24		.263	.357	.333	399	105	13	0	5	121	60	78
Late and Close	.258	.351	.289	97	25	3	0	0	12	13	22		.254	.321	.362	315	80	15	2	5	38	29	51

WADE BOGGS — bats left — throws right — age 34 — BOS — *3

1991	BA	OBA	SA	AB	H	2B	3B	HR	RBI	BB	SO		8-YEAR TOTALS (1984–1991) BA	OBA	SA	AB	H	2B	3B	HR	RBI	BB	SO
Total	.332	.421	.460	546	181	42	2	8	51	89	32		.343	.435	.472	4778	1637	342	35	68	520	803	382
vs. Left	.265	.333	.361	166	44	6	2	2	13	17	10		.305	.386	.411	1504	459	78	12	19	182	192	157
vs. Right	.361	.456	.503	380	137	36	0	6	38	72	22		.360	.457	.499	3274	1178	264	23	49	338	611	225
at Home	.389	.482	.587	252	98	28	2	6	32	47	12		.381	.477	.541	2333	888	222	18	39	279	435	201
on Road	.282	.368	.350	294	83	14	0	2	19	42	20		.306	.395	.405	2445	749	120	17	29	241	368	181
on Grass	.330	.420	.470	445	147	34	2	8	47	72	24		.346	.440	.478	4012	1389	297	28	59	441	686	330
on Turf	.337	.429	.416	101	34	8	0	0	4	17	8		.324	.411	.436	766	248	45	7	9	79	117	52
Day Games	.310	.403	.408	184	57	10	1	2	17	30	11		.336	.435	.453	1584	532	108	9	20	158	280	123
Night Games	.343	.431	.486	362	124	32	1	6	34	59	21		.346	.436	.481	3194	1105	234	26	48	362	523	259
April	.304	.429	.507	69	21	5	0	3	5	15	3		.301	.420	.407	599	180	38	1	8	57	127	59
May	.354	.467	.465	99	35	8	0	1	12	21	6		.347	.449	.497	769	267	52	9	15	103	146	67
June	.271	.339	.385	96	26	8	0	1	14	11	8		.347	.436	.481	804	279	62	8	10	89	125	59
July	.415	.495	.598	82	34	10	1	1	8	15	5		.340	.424	.490	823	280	69	9	12	96	126	69
August	.330	.400	.425	106	35	5	1	1	8	13	6		.348	.428	.463	936	326	58	5	13	89	130	72
Sept—Oct	.319	.404	.415	94	30	6	0	1	4	14	4		.360	.454	.477	847	305	63	3	10	86	149	56
Bases Empty	.335	.402	.466	358	120	30	1	5	5	40	19		.340	.421	.473	2893	985	212	21	43	43	395	233
Leadoff	.299	.359	.436	211	63	20	0	3	3	20	7		.346	.422	.470	1468	508	106	5	22	22	193	104
Runners On Base	.324	.453	.447	188	61	12	1	3	46	49	13		.346	.456	.469	1885	652	130	14	25	477	408	149
Scoring Position	.310	.504	.414	87	27	6	0	1	38	40	6		.344	.486	.462	1011	348	70	8	11	425	314	89
Late and Close	.290	.395	.377	69	20	3	0	1	6	12	8		.312	.417	.386	674	210	33	4	3	65	122	74

BARRY BONDS — bats left — throws left — age 28 — PIT — *O

1991	BA	OBA	SA	AB	H	2B	3B	HR	RBI	BB	SO		6-YEAR TOTALS (1986–1991) BA	OBA	SA	AB	H	2B	3B	HR	RBI	BB	SO
Total	.292	.410	.514	510	149	28	5	25	116	107	73		.269	.367	.485	3111	837	184	31	142	453	484	521
vs. Left	.284	.385	.473	201	57	13	2	7	39	32	30		.269	.363	.485	1138	306	74	14	48	179	164	213
vs. Right	.298	.425	.540	309	92	15	3	18	77	75	43		.269	.369	.485	1973	531	110	17	94	274	320	308
at Home	.272	.384	.448	261	71	8	1	12	51	49	42		.257	.358	.463	1515	389	76	16	68	215	235	272
on Road	.313	.436	.582	249	78	20	4	13	65	58	31		.281	.376	.506	1596	448	108	15	74	238	249	249
on Grass	.280	.375	.500	132	37	10	2	5	27	23	18		.272	.357	.472	824	224	52	7	33	110	112	148
on Turf	.296	.422	.519	378	112	18	3	20	89	84	55		.268	.371	.490	2287	613	132	24	109	343	372	373
Day Games	.256	.373	.429	133	34	9	1	4	25	28	23		.251	.353	.455	907	228	53	9	38	110	147	159
Night Games	.305	.424	.544	377	115	19	4	21	91	79	50		.276	.373	.497	2204	609	131	22	104	343	337	362
April	.177	.212	.290	62	11	1	0	2	10	3	15		.251	.311	.484	378	95	28	6	16	47	34	70
May	.280	.400	.451	82	23	3	1	3	16	14	9		.280	.385	.514	471	132	22	8	24	75	76	79
June	.325	.481	.613	80	26	6	1	5	19	25	9		.278	.383	.496	587	163	43	5	25	76	86	89
July	.362	.447	.638	94	34	4	2	6	29	16	11		.294	.393	.520	510	150	28	6	25	90	86	89
August	.287	.417	.553	94	27	7	0	6	22	23	15		.262	.369	.497	583	153	34	2	33	96	100	91
Sept—Oct	.286	.422	.469	98	28	7	1	3	20	26	14		.247	.345	.409	582	144	29	4	19	69	88	96
Bases Empty	.259	.368	.421	259	67	12	3	8	8	43	36		.258	.344	.473	1964	507	116	22	87	87	246	324
Leadoff	.295	.432	.421	95	28	8	2	0	0	21	12		.279	.364	.508	1050	293	70	13	48	48	133	161
Runners On Base	.327	.448	.610	251	82	16	2	17	108	64	37		.288	.404	.507	1147	330	68	9	55	366	238	197
Scoring Position	.345	.471	.588	148	51	10	1	8	87	46	20		.275	.413	.469	684	188	37	6	28	297	180	122
Late and Close	.338	.450	.538	80	27	10	0	2	16	18	14		.258	.363	.422	531	137	32	5	15	60	90	106

BOBBY BONILLA — bats both — throws right — age 29 — PIT — *O3/1

1991	BA	OBA	SA	AB	H	2B	3B	HR	RBI	BB	SO		6-YEAR TOTALS (1986–1991) BA	OBA	SA	AB	H	2B	3B	HR	RBI	BB	SO
Total	.302	.391	.492	577	174	44	6	18	100	90	67		.283	.357	.472	3294	931	201	37	116	527	397	497
vs. Left	.284	.349	.530	232	66	13	1	14	47	25	23		.271	.336	.446	1361	369	75	8	49	215	139	149
vs. Right	.313	.418	.467	345	108	31	5	4	53	65	44		.291	.372	.490	1933	562	126	29	67	312	258	348
at Home	.309	.408	.512	285	88	25	3	9	51	49	29		.273	.352	.451	1600	436	95	16	53	253	199	217
on Road	.295	.374	.473	292	86	19	3	9	49	41	38		.292	.362	.491	1694	495	106	21	63	274	198	280
on Grass	.284	.339	.419	155	44	5	2	5	21	14	23		.301	.368	.488	989	298	51	13	36	156	109	176
on Turf	.308	.409	.519	422	130	39	4	14	79	76	44		.275	.353	.465	2305	633	150	24	80	371	288	321
Day Games	.323	.407	.555	164	53	10	2	8	34	25	20		.299	.362	.514	1036	310	69	8	46	174	103	159
Night Games	.293	.385	.467	413	121	34	4	10	66	65	47		.275	.355	.452	2258	621	132	29	70	353	294	338
April	.315	.407	.521	73	23	6	0	3	17	11	5		.295	.342	.490	447	132	27	3	18	76	33	59
May	.312	.383	.473	93	29	6	0	3	15	12	10		.292	.374	.506	520	152	29	5	24	86	68	75
June	.217	.327	.386	83	18	9	1	1	9	14	11		.266	.344	.442	527	140	38	8	13	75	66	84
July	.330	.379	.563	112	37	4	2	6	23	10	13		.256	.334	.418	543	139	23	4	19	72	66	78
August	.377	.465	.604	106	40	13	1	3	20	19	9		.308	.385	.523	621	191	48	7	24	109	81	94
Sept—Oct	.245	.375	.391	110	27	6	2	2	16	24	19		.278	.358	.451	636	177	36	10	18	109	83	107
Bases Empty	.282	.368	.465	284	80	21	5	7	7	38	29		.277	.342	.469	1750	485	92	21	67	67	166	256
Leadoff	.275	.342	.442	138	38	10	2	3	3	13	11		.290	.344	.474	822	238	46	11	28	28	64	112
Runners On Base	.321	.412	.519	293	94	23	1	11	93	52	38		.289	.373	.475	1544	446	109	16	49	460	231	241
Scoring Position	.310	.415	.513	158	49	12	1	6	75	36	23		.285	.389	.479	898	256	63	9	31	395	179	147
Late and Close	.265	.396	.458	83	22	7	0	2	14	20	15		.256	.360	.402	547	140	25	2	17	82	91	95

MIKE BORDICK — bats right — throws right — age 27 — OAK — S/23

1991	BA	OBA	SA	AB	H	2B	3B	HR	RBI	BB	SO	2-YEAR TOTALS (1990–1991) BA	OBA	SA	AB	H	2B	3B	HR	RBI	BB	SO
Total	.238	.289	.268	235	56	5	1	0	21	14	37	.229	.280	.257	249	57	5	1	0	21	15	41
vs. Left	.224	.274	.241	58	13	1	0	0	6	4	6	.203	.250	.219	64	13	1	0	0	6	4	8
vs. Right	.243	.293	.277	177	43	4	1	0	15	10	31	.238	.290	.270	185	44	4	1	0	15	11	33
at Home	.226	.287	.264	106	24	2	1	0	7	7	14	.216	.275	.252	111	24	2	1	0	7	7	15
on Road	.248	.290	.271	129	32	3	0	0	14	7	23	.239	.284	.261	138	33	3	0	0	14	8	26
on Grass	.222	.271	.259	189	42	5	1	0	11	11	29	.217	.268	.253	198	43	5	1	0	11	12	32
on Turf	.304	.360	.304	46	14	0	0	0	10	3	8	.275	.327	.275	51	14	0	0	0	10	3	9
Day Games	.306	.359	.333	72	22	2	0	0	10	6	9	.286	.345	.312	77	22	2	0	0	10	7	11
Night Games	.209	.257	.239	163	34	3	1	0	11	8	28	.203	.250	.233	172	35	3	1	0	11	8	30
April	.000	.000	.000	0	0	0	0	0	0	0	0	.000	.000	.000	6	0	0	0	0	0	0	2
May	.000	.000	.000	0	0	0	0	0	0	0	0	.000	.000	.000	0	0	0	0	0	0	0	0
June	.200	.200	.300	10	2	1	0	0	0	0	1	.200	.200	.300	10	2	1	0	0	0	0	1
July	.221	.254	.250	68	15	2	0	0	7	3	11	.221	.254	.250	68	15	2	0	0	7	3	11
August	.250	.329	.289	76	19	1	1	0	4	7	11	.250	.329	.289	76	19	1	1	0	4	7	11
Sept–Oct	.247	.287	.259	81	20	1	0	0	10	4	14	.236	.281	.247	89	21	1	0	0	10	5	16
Bases Empty	.207	.265	.233	150	31	4	0	0	0	11	24	.198	.253	.222	162	32	4	0	0	0	11	27
Leadoff	.210	.222	.242	62	13	2	0	0	0	1	13	.200	.212	.231	65	13	2	0	0	0	1	14
Runners On Base	.294	.330	.329	85	25	1	1	0	21	3	13	.287	.330	.322	87	25	1	1	0	21	4	14
Scoring Position	.346	.375	.385	52	18	0	1	0	20	3	6	.333	.373	.370	54	18	0	1	0	20	4	7
Late and Close	.235	.350	.294	17	4	1	0	0	0	3	1	.200	.304	.250	20	4	1	0	0	0	3	3

SID BREAM — bats left — throws left — age 32 — ATL — 1

1991	BA	OBA	SA	AB	H	2B	3B	HR	RBI	BB	SO	8-YEAR TOTALS (1984–1991) BA	OBA	SA	AB	H	2B	3B	HR	RBI	BB	SO
Total	.253	.313	.423	265	67	12	0	11	45	25	31	.263	.333	.422	2387	627	147	10	71	350	265	345
vs. Left	.132	.132	.132	38	5	0	0	0	3	0	8	.230	.274	.369	648	149	36	3	16	83	42	111
vs. Right	.273	.340	.471	227	62	12	0	11	42	25	23	.275	.354	.442	1739	478	111	7	55	267	223	234
at Home	.270	.310	.391	115	31	5	0	3	21	8	15	.265	.332	.437	1132	300	81	6	34	173	117	152
on Road	.240	.315	.447	150	36	7	0	8	24	17	16	.261	.335	.408	1255	327	66	4	37	177	148	193
on Grass	.258	.317	.403	186	48	9	0	6	31	18	21	.249	.317	.379	799	199	37	2	21	108	86	125
on Turf	.241	.302	.468	79	19	3	0	5	14	7	10	.270	.341	.443	1588	428	110	8	50	242	179	220
Day Games	.267	.308	.517	60	16	3	0	4	12	4	10	.259	.335	.414	719	186	47	4	19	92	87	124
Night Games	.249	.314	.395	205	51	9	0	7	33	21	21	.264	.332	.425	1668	441	100	6	52	258	178	221
April	.241	.305	.463	54	13	6	0	2	8	5	7	.251	.337	.460	350	88	26	1	15	39	46	58
May	.287	.330	.512	80	23	3	0	5	20	6	13	.270	.345	.461	423	114	25	4	16	75	51	67
June	.341	.375	.523	44	15	2	0	2	6	3	4	.305	.357	.483	354	108	23	2	12	53	31	46
July	.000	.000	.000	0	0	0	0	0	0	0	0	.249	.322	.369	317	79	15	1	7	51	35	41
August	.200	.333	.300	10	2	1	0	0	0	2	1	.279	.349	.408	380	106	26	1	7	51	42	44
Sept–Oct	.182	.264	.260	77	14	0	0	2	11	9	6	.234	.303	.369	563	132	32	1	14	81	60	89
Bases Empty	.267	.313	.427	150	40	6	0	6	6	10	18	.251	.307	.404	1291	324	73	7	37	37	104	187
Leadoff	.262	.338	.410	61	16	3	0	2	2	7	7	.252	.305	.416	548	138	28	4	18	18	42	70
Runners On Base	.235	.313	.417	115	27	6	0	5	39	15	13	.276	.361	.443	1096	303	74	3	34	313	161	158
Scoring Position	.256	.340	.462	78	20	4	0	4	36	12	10	.262	.364	.400	648	170	37	2	16	258	120	97
Late and Close	.219	.219	.219	32	7	0	0	0	3	0	3	.249	.342	.400	390	97	25	2	10	56	61	57

GEORGE BRETT — bats left — throws right — age 39 — KC — *D1

1991	BA	OBA	SA	AB	H	2B	3B	HR	RBI	BB	SO	8-YEAR TOTALS (1984–1991) BA	OBA	SA	AB	H	2B	3B	HR	RBI	BB	SO
Total	.255	.327	.402	505	129	40	2	10	61	58	75	.298	.382	.488	3890	1160	258	29	141	662	548	414
vs. Left	.234	.309	.353	167	39	12	1	2	18	20	28	.278	.344	.450	1340	373	69	7	49	223	141	162
vs. Right	.266	.337	.426	338	90	28	1	8	43	38	47	.309	.401	.508	2550	787	189	22	92	439	407	252
at Home	.247	.326	.379	243	60	19	2	3	27	30	33	.302	.386	.488	1943	587	121	23	65	347	282	178
on Road	.263	.329	.424	262	69	21	0	7	34	28	42	.294	.377	.488	1947	573	137	6	76	315	266	236
on Grass	.251	.309	.408	211	53	18	0	5	26	19	32	.293	.377	.488	1554	455	107	4	63	255	214	193
on Turf	.259	.340	.398	294	76	22	2	5	35	39	43	.302	.385	.488	2336	705	151	25	78	407	334	221
Day Games	.302	.365	.472	159	48	12	0	5	15	17	18	.315	.387	.531	1026	323	84	6	42	185	125	104
Night Games	.234	.310	.370	346	81	28	2	5	46	41	57	.292	.380	.473	2864	837	174	23	99	477	423	310
April	.170	.220	.170	47	8	0	0	0	0	3	9	.256	.378	.403	422	108	16	2	14	59	86	46
May	.310	.412	.483	29	9	2	0	1	4	5	6	.309	.392	.488	514	159	38	6	14	83	72	56
June	.267	.336	.410	105	28	12	0	1	19	12	13	.290	.374	.451	668	194	49	2	18	102	88	62
July	.284	.345	.500	102	29	10	0	4	17	11	10	.322	.397	.535	777	250	60	5	32	144	102	78
August	.250	.325	.407	108	27	10	2	1	10	13	16	.315	.394	.544	779	245	55	11	34	148	111	93
Sept–Oct	.246	.326	.377	114	28	6	0	4	11	14	21	.279	.355	.462	730	204	40	3	29	126	89	79
Bases Empty	.260	.310	.419	289	75	26	1	6	6	21	46	.284	.354	.481	2081	592	137	17	79	79	217	225
Leadoff	.257	.291	.457	105	27	10	1	3	3	5	20	.283	.349	.506	735	208	48	4	36	36	71	72
Runners On Base	.250	.349	.380	216	54	14	1	4	55	37	29	.314	.411	.497	1809	568	121	12	62	583	331	189
Scoring Position	.239	.381	.349	109	26	7	1	4	45	30	17	.308	.439	.470	1006	310	63	5	30	483	275	125
Late and Close	.197	.326	.316	76	15	3	0	2	15	11	11	.283	.397	.452	584	165	39	3	18	96	112	68

GREG BRILEY — bats left — throws right — age 27 — SEA — *O/D23

1991	BA	OBA	SA	AB	H	2B	3B	HR	RBI	BB	SO
Total	.260	.307	.336	381	99	17	3	2	26	27	51
vs. Left	.231	.250	.333	39	9	2	1	0	9	1	10
vs. Right	.263	.313	.336	342	90	15	2	2	17	26	41
at Home	.249	.310	.314	185	46	4	1	2	12	17	19
on Road	.270	.303	.357	196	53	13	2	0	14	10	32
on Grass	.261	.291	.345	142	37	8	2	0	11	7	25
on Turf	.259	.315	.331	239	62	9	1	2	15	20	26
Day Games	.330	.368	.386	88	29	5	0	0	6	6	14
Night Games	.239	.288	.321	293	70	12	3	2	20	21	37
April	.233	.333	.326	43	10	1	0	1	5	7	6
May	.218	.237	.269	78	17	1	0	1	4	2	9
June	.176	.192	.216	51	9	0	1	0	3	1	16
July	.227	.277	.273	44	10	2	0	0	1	3	3
August	.382	.427	.500	68	26	8	0	0	5	6	5
Sept—Oct	.278	.330	.371	97	27	5	2	0	8	8	12
Bases Empty	.251	.300	.307	231	58	11	1	0	0	16	29
Leadoff	.196	.241	.245	102	20	3	1	0	0	6	13
Runners On Base	.273	.317	.380	150	41	6	2	2	26	11	22
Scoring Position	.243	.282	.357	70	17	1	2	1	22	5	8
Late and Close	.266	.289	.392	79	21	5	1	1	6	3	14

4-YEAR TOTALS (1988–1991)

BA	OBA	SA	AB	H	2B	3B	HR	RBI	BB	SO
.258	.322	.380	1148	296	59	9	21	111	108	187
.256	.319	.357	129	33	6	2	1	19	11	31
.258	.322	.383	1019	263	53	7	20	92	97	156
.230	.300	.338	539	124	19	3	11	53	55	77
.282	.341	.417	609	172	40	6	10	58	53	110
.266	.331	.391	473	126	26	6	7	40	45	86
.252	.315	.372	675	170	33	3	14	71	63	101
.262	.319	.384	294	77	11	2	7	29	24	49
.256	.322	.378	854	219	48	7	14	82	84	138
.225	.309	.342	120	27	11	0	1	11	14	18
.266	.310	.367	188	50	7	0	4	19	12	27
.240	.278	.352	196	47	11	3	3	18	11	41
.299	.368	.490	194	58	10	3	7	28	22	29
.249	.323	.376	237	59	12	3	4	20	25	41
.258	.332	.343	213	55	8	2	2	15	24	31
.257	.322	.370	676	174	32	4	12	12	59	105
.236	.295	.313	259	61	9	1	3	3	20	37
.258	.321	.394	472	122	27	5	9	99	49	82
.247	.303	.381	239	59	7	5	5	83	25	43
.258	.295	.374	198	51	11	3	2	17	11	44

HUBIE BROOKS — bats right — throws right — age 36 — NYN — *O

1991	BA	OBA	SA	AB	H	2B	3B	HR	RBI	BB	SO
Total	.238	.324	.409	357	85	11	1	16	50	44	62
vs. Left	.250	.345	.417	120	30	5	0	5	17	18	13
vs. Right	.232	.313	.405	237	55	6	1	11	33	26	49
at Home	.238	.340	.355	172	41	6	1	4	22	27	28
on Road	.238	.309	.459	185	44	5	0	12	28	17	34
on Grass	.252	.330	.404	270	68	9	1	10	37	32	47
on Turf	.195	.307	.425	87	17	2	0	6	13	12	15
Day Games	.198	.313	.365	96	19	5	1	3	11	14	19
Night Games	.253	.329	.425	261	66	6	0	13	39	30	43
April	.241	.343	.466	58	14	4	0	3	7	8	8
May	.256	.301	.430	86	22	1	1	4	14	6	20
June	.316	.438	.592	76	24	3	0	6	19	17	9
July	.194	.279	.269	93	18	1	0	2	6	10	12
August	.159	.213	.273	44	7	2	0	1	4	3	13
Sept—Oct	.000	.000	.000	0	0	0	0	0	0	0	0
Bases Empty	.262	.301	.477	195	51	6	0	12	12	9	28
Leadoff	.317	.333	.561	82	26	5	0	5	5	1	11
Runners On Base	.210	.348	.327	162	34	5	1	4	38	35	34
Scoring Position	.212	.367	.323	99	21	3	1	2	33	26	23
Late and Close	.211	.328	.351	57	12	2	0	2	6	10	16

8-YEAR TOTALS (1984–1991)

BA	OBA	SA	AB	H	2B	3B	HR	RBI	BB	SO
.274	.323	.433	3956	1085	201	22	127	604	282	676
.292	.353	.487	1227	358	81	7	48	209	114	185
.266	.309	.408	2729	727	120	15	79	395	168	491
.283	.336	.439	1918	543	106	11	57	302	152	330
.266	.311	.426	2038	542	95	11	70	302	130	346
.275	.324	.432	1755	483	74	8	62	256	126	300
.274	.322	.433	2201	602	127	14	65	348	156	376
.266	.317	.436	1212	322	55	11	43	184	89	201
.278	.326	.431	2744	763	146	11	84	420	193	475
.258	.306	.427	539	139	24	2	21	81	37	88
.281	.322	.436	679	191	25	7	22	96	38	129
.307	.370	.495	707	217	42	5	27	119	72	124
.249	.290	.366	763	190	36	1	17	99	46	121
.259	.312	.418	632	164	33	5	19	87	46	103
.289	.334	.459	636	184	41	2	21	122	43	111
.270	.308	.443	2126	573	106	10	81	81	106	340
.285	.314	.449	939	268	54	5	30	30	36	137
.280	.339	.420	1830	512	95	12	46	523	176	336
.283	.353	.447	1099	311	62	8	34	479	137	223
.281	.329	.449	695	195	28	4	27	116	49	142

TOM BRUNANSKY — bats right — throws right — age 32 — BOS — *O/D

1991	BA	OBA	SA	AB	H	2B	3B	HR	RBI	BB	SO
Total	.229	.303	.390	459	105	24	1	16	70	49	72
vs. Left	.254	.321	.423	142	36	7	1	5	22	16	12
vs. Right	.218	.294	.375	317	69	17	0	11	48	33	60
at Home	.256	.335	.453	234	60	16	0	10	39	27	32
on Road	.200	.269	.324	225	45	8	1	6	31	22	40
on Grass	.216	.295	.375	379	82	18	0	14	54	42	56
on Turf	.287	.337	.463	80	23	6	1	2	16	7	16
Day Games	.203	.296	.323	158	32	7	0	4	21	20	31
Night Games	.243	.306	.425	301	73	17	1	12	49	29	41
April	.250	.343	.467	60	15	4	0	3	11	9	8
May	.222	.286	.455	99	22	5	0	6	25	10	12
June	.169	.263	.277	83	14	3	0	2	8	9	16
July	.200	.266	.306	85	17	6	0	1	4	8	14
August	.288	.356	.424	66	19	1	1	2	8	6	10
Sept—Oct	.273	.333	.439	66	18	5	0	2	14	7	12
Bases Empty	.216	.300	.345	232	50	12	0	6	6	26	38
Leadoff	.217	.272	.321	106	23	5	0	2	2	7	19
Runners On Base	.242	.305	.436	227	55	12	1	10	64	23	34
Scoring Position	.232	.299	.423	142	33	4	1	7	56	16	18
Late and Close	.250	.333	.382	68	17	9	0	0	7	9	14

8-YEAR TOTALS (1984–1991)

BA	OBA	SA	AB	H	2B	3B	HR	RBI	BB	SO
.247	.325	.432	4364	1078	202	20	189	647	515	769
.254	.332	.461	1400	356	72	8	67	221	176	180
.244	.322	.419	2964	722	130	12	122	426	339	589
.261	.337	.458	2161	565	113	15	94	354	254	361
.233	.314	.407	2203	513	89	5	95	293	261	408
.237	.320	.431	1937	459	81	4	94	287	237	333
.255	.329	.434	2427	619	121	14	95	360	278	436
.245	.320	.416	1345	329	62	0	56	194	151	247
.248	.328	.440	3019	749	140	20	133	453	364	522
.244	.333	.420	566	138	20	1	26	83	78	97
.281	.358	.490	779	219	35	4	40	151	98	126
.248	.338	.445	742	184	42	4	32	104	101	138
.218	.294	.369	739	161	29	4	25	90	82	136
.260	.325	.457	774	201	38	5	35	110	73	133
.229	.303	.406	764	175	38	2	31	109	83	139
.249	.321	.440	2305	573	104	10	106	106	240	386
.242	.307	.412	1035	250	51	4	39	39	95	166
.245	.329	.424	2059	505	98	10	83	541	275	383
.237	.332	.401	1213	288	55	6	44	445	192	239
.240	.331	.401	691	166	38	2	23	89	98	143

STEVE BUECHELE — bats right — throws right — age 31 — TEX/PIT — *32/S

7-YEAR TOTALS (1985–1991)

1991	BA	OBA	SA	AB	H	2B	3B	HR	RBI	BB	SO		BA	OBA	SA	AB	H	2B	3B	HR	RBI	BB	SO
Total	.262	.331	.440	530	139	22	3	22	85	49	97		.241	.309	.399	2813	679	120	14	98	358	254	548
vs. Left	.298	.404	.573	131	39	7	1	9	26	22	23		.270	.346	.466	903	244	49	4	40	123	103	165
vs. Right	.251	.305	.396	399	100	15	2	13	59	27	74		.228	.291	.366	1910	435	71	10	58	235	151	383
at Home	.275	.343	.446	251	69	14	1	9	32	24	42		.247	.316	.394	1382	341	56	5	46	164	126	256
on Road	.251	.320	.434	279	70	8	2	13	53	25	55		.236	.302	.403	1431	338	64	9	52	194	128	292
on Grass	.267	.331	.438	397	106	18	1	16	60	34	64		.244	.311	.395	2291	559	91	11	78	290	205	433
on Turf	.248	.331	.444	133	33	4	2	6	25	15	33		.230	.297	.412	522	120	29	3	20	68	49	115
Day Games	.211	.286	.358	95	20	2	0	4	16	8	15		.223	.293	.376	537	120	23	1	19	60	48	103
Night Games	.274	.341	.457	435	119	20	3	18	69	41	82		.246	.313	.404	2276	559	97	13	79	298	206	445
April	.255	.333	.431	51	13	3	0	2	3	5	5		.256	.335	.455	336	86	14	1	17	37	36	73
May	.306	.362	.529	85	26	1	0	6	17	8	15		.267	.318	.453	415	111	21	1	18	50	31	79
June	.239	.333	.424	92	22	6	1	3	13	13	21		.220	.297	.349	490	108	25	1	12	56	50	101
July	.264	.337	.440	91	24	2	1	4	15	8	17		.257	.328	.403	474	122	18	3	15	69	46	78
August	.255	.300	.392	102	26	5	0	3	18	5	12		.243	.314	.400	510	124	21	4	17	78	46	92
Sept–Oct	.257	.328	.431	109	28	5	1	4	19	10	27		.218	.276	.364	588	128	21	4	19	68	45	125
Bases Empty	.241	.305	.381	291	70	11	0	10	10	24	62		.236	.299	.406	1588	374	62	7	65	65	132	308
Leadoff	.272	.314	.377	114	31	6	0	2	2	6	18		.253	.299	.445	679	172	27	2	33	33	41	117
Runners On Base	.289	.362	.510	239	69	11	3	12	75	25	35		.249	.321	.389	1225	305	58	7	33	293	122	240
Scoring Position	.300	.390	.547	150	45	7	3	8	66	21	21		.250	.328	.384	701	175	35	4	17	248	80	138
Late and Close	.250	.302	.380	108	27	3	1	3	21	7	24		.255	.317	.382	463	118	18	1	13	53	38	101

JAY BUHNER — bats right — throws right — age 28 — SEA — *O

5-YEAR TOTALS (1987–1991)

1991	BA	OBA	SA	AB	H	2B	3B	HR	RBI	BB	SO		BA	OBA	SA	AB	H	2B	3B	HR	RBI	BB	SO
Total	.244	.337	.498	406	99	14	4	27	77	53	117		.247	.331	.471	1055	261	56	6	56	182	118	320
vs. Left	.240	.371	.486	146	35	5	2	9	26	28	28		.237	.325	.456	371	88	20	2	19	58	44	96
vs. Right	.246	.316	.504	260	64	9	2	18	51	25	89		.253	.335	.480	684	173	36	4	37	124	74	224
at Home	.212	.321	.472	212	45	9	2	14	41	31	71		.231	.323	.468	524	121	27	2	31	87	65	167
on Road	.278	.355	.526	194	54	5	2	13	36	22	46		.264	.339	.475	531	140	29	4	25	95	53	153
on Grass	.301	.377	.582	153	46	3	2	12	32	19	35		.274	.353	.492	445	122	22	3	23	85	48	126
on Turf	.209	.313	.447	253	53	11	2	15	45	34	82		.228	.315	.456	610	139	34	3	33	97	70	194
Day Games	.231	.299	.510	104	24	5	0	8	19	9	42		.275	.345	.557	291	80	20	1	20	55	28	99
Night Games	.248	.349	.493	302	75	9	4	19	58	44	75		.237	.326	.438	764	181	36	5	36	127	90	221
April	.231	.333	.558	52	12	3	1	4	7	8	20		.231	.333	.558	52	12	3	1	4	7	8	20
May	.270	.372	.514	37	10	1	1	2	9	6	12		.239	.333	.435	46	11	1	1	2	11	7	13
June	.182	.318	.364	55	10	1	0	3	12	9	15		.236	.324	.476	246	58	9	1	16	59	26	74
July	.253	.298	.563	87	22	3	0	8	15	5	26		.229	.298	.500	118	27	5	0	9	16	9	35
August	.284	.358	.611	95	27	6	2	7	25	10	27		.288	.365	.554	267	77	23	3	14	49	30	84
Sept–Oct	.225	.351	.338	80	18	0	0	3	9	15	17		.233	.320	.380	326	76	15	0	11	40	38	94
Bases Empty	.256	.353	.507	207	53	5	1	15	15	27	67		.250	.339	.458	557	139	30	1	28	28	66	174
Leadoff	.306	.385	.612	85	26	3	1	7	7	10	21		.285	.359	.532	235	67	14	1	14	14	25	63
Runners On Base	.231	.320	.487	199	46	9	3	12	62	26	50		.245	.323	.486	498	122	26	5	28	154	52	146
Scoring Position	.217	.346	.396	106	23	3	2	4	42	21	29		.257	.347	.463	268	69	14	4	11	115	35	84
Late and Close	.222	.337	.389	72	16	3	0	3	12	13	20		.206	.280	.339	180	37	4	1	6	24	19	57

ELLIS BURKS — bats right — throws right — age 28 — BOS — *O/D

5-YEAR TOTALS (1987–1991)

1991	BA	OBA	SA	AB	H	2B	3B	HR	RBI	BB	SO		BA	OBA	SA	AB	H	2B	3B	HR	RBI	BB	SO
Total	.251	.314	.422	474	119	33	3	14	56	39	81		.283	.344	.461	2558	725	152	24	85	357	226	401
vs. Left	.259	.313	.489	135	35	12	2	5	23	11	21		.299	.366	.467	720	215	48	5	21	101	78	104
vs. Right	.248	.315	.395	339	84	21	1	9	33	28	60		.277	.334	.459	1838	510	104	19	64	256	148	297
at Home	.267	.328	.466	232	62	18	2	8	25	20	36		.301	.366	.492	1234	372	84	11	43	179	123	180
on Road	.236	.301	.380	242	57	15	1	6	31	19	45		.267	.322	.433	1324	353	68	13	42	178	103	221
on Grass	.247	.305	.406	384	95	25	3	10	44	30	65		.285	.346	.462	2159	616	127	18	73	307	195	332
on Turf	.267	.353	.489	90	24	8	0	4	12	9	16		.273	.332	.456	399	109	25	6	12	50	31	69
Day Games	.266	.333	.411	158	42	11	0	4	23	12	33		.287	.357	.457	857	246	47	6	29	132	85	137
Night Games	.244	.304	.427	316	77	22	3	10	33	27	48		.282	.337	.463	1701	479	105	18	56	225	141	264
April	.234	.338	.375	64	15	6	0	1	4	7	15		.269	.367	.430	286	77	19	3	7	35	38	47
May	.295	.356	.411	95	28	5	0	2	7	9	11		.281	.333	.463	462	130	30	4	12	52	36	75
June	.191	.238	.436	94	18	5	0	6	13	6	14		.280	.326	.530	443	124	30	3	25	79	32	62
July	.277	.346	.500	94	26	5	2	4	14	4	18		.312	.374	.521	388	121	27	6	14	57	35	70
August	.250	.303	.402	92	23	9	1	1	10	7	16		.280	.346	.427	558	156	27	5	15	81	57	86
Sept–Oct	.257	.300	.343	35	9	3	0	0	8	2	7		.278	.325	.399	421	117	19	1	10	53	28	61
Bases Empty	.249	.320	.458	249	62	18	2	10	10	22	32		.280	.339	.451	1395	390	73	11	48	48	117	210
Leadoff	.232	.309	.455	99	23	8	1	4	4	10	8		.295	.349	.481	672	198	35	6	26	26	53	84
Runners On Base	.253	.308	.382	225	57	15	1	4	46	17	49		.288	.349	.474	1163	335	79	13	37	309	109	191
Scoring Position	.227	.305	.379	132	30	6	1	4	45	16	29		.283	.353	.483	696	197	32	10	29	287	81	124
Late and Close	.217	.299	.348	69	15	4	1	1	2	6	14		.247	.336	.395	377	93	20	6	8	43	47	76

BRETT BUTLER — bats left — throws left — age 35 — LA — *O

1991	BA	OBA	SA	AB	H	2B	3B	HR	RBI	BB	SO
Total	.296	.401	.343	615	182	13	5	2	38	108	79
vs. Left	.282	.397	.313	252	71	2	3	0	14	48	41
vs. Right	.306	.404	.364	363	111	11	2	2	24	60	38
at Home	.312	.425	.369	295	92	7	2	2	22	59	29
on Road	.281	.377	.319	320	90	6	3	0	16	49	50
on Grass	.304	.406	.348	451	137	10	2	2	34	79	50
on Turf	.274	.387	.329	164	45	3	3	0	4	29	29
Day Games	.280	.362	.324	207	58	4	1	1	15	27	35
Night Games	.304	.420	.353	408	124	9	4	1	23	81	44
April	.316	.369	.382	76	24	2	0	1	6	7	11
May	.243	.381	.282	103	25	2	1	0	5	22	15
June	.312	.409	.339	109	34	1	1	0	4	18	14
July	.337	.444	.367	98	33	1	1	0	11	19	9
August	.351	.451	.441	111	39	3	2	1	10	21	13
Sept–Oct	.229	.345	.263	118	27	4	0	0	2	21	17
Bases Empty	.290	.390	.336	441	128	9	4	1	1	71	57
Leadoff	.304	.398	.368	280	85	7	4	1	1	44	34
Runners On Base	.310	.427	.362	174	54	4	1	1	37	37	22
Scoring Position	.309	.451	.382	110	34	3	1	1	36	30	15
Late and Close	.302	.444	.387	106	32	2	2	1	12	27	15

8-YEAR TOTALS (1984–1991)

BA	OBA	SA	AB	H	2B	3B	HR	RBI	BB	SO
.291	.379	.382	4700	1368	177	72	36	351	663	498
.290	.385	.360	1571	455	47	21	7	128	240	222
.292	.376	.394	3129	913	130	51	29	223	423	276
.307	.396	.394	2287	703	83	36	14	159	337	217
.276	.363	.372	2413	665	94	36	22	192	326	281
.297	.384	.391	3702	1101	146	58	28	287	522	373
.268	.363	.351	998	267	31	14	8	64	141	125
.279	.372	.370	1672	466	57	25	15	130	247	192
.298	.383	.389	3028	902	120	47	21	221	416	306
.302	.384	.402	570	172	28	7	5	39	77	51
.247	.349	.316	805	199	31	9	2	54	124	103
.297	.387	.380	799	237	32	10	5	62	120	75
.290	.369	.368	799	232	22	14	4	62	99	78
.300	.387	.398	819	246	26	12	10	68	113	101
.311	.399	.430	908	282	38	20	10	66	130	90
.288	.371	.384	3260	938	127	53	27	27	418	348
.287	.369	.383	1924	552	74	33	15	15	246	195
.299	.397	.378	1440	430	50	19	9	324	245	150
.298	.408	.389	866	258	33	14	6	307	176	90
.271	.359	.344	723	196	21	4	8	73	101	95

IVAN CALDERON — bats right — throws right — age 30 — MON — *O/1

1991	BA	OBA	SA	AB	H	2B	3B	HR	RBI	BB	SO
Total	.298	.366	.479	470	140	22	3	19	75	53	65
vs. Left	.348	.418	.621	161	56	9	1	11	31	20	23
vs. Right	.272	.339	.405	309	84	13	2	8	44	33	42
at Home	.304	.370	.451	224	68	8	2	7	29	26	36
on Road	.293	.362	.504	246	72	14	1	12	46	27	29
on Grass	.295	.360	.477	132	39	7	1	5	21	13	18
on Turf	.299	.368	.479	338	101	15	2	14	54	40	47
Day Games	.305	.367	.466	131	40	7	1	4	23	14	22
Night Games	.295	.365	.484	339	100	15	2	15	52	39	43
April	.276	.325	.434	76	21	3	0	3	15	5	10
May	.330	.387	.495	91	30	1	1	4	20	11	13
June	.321	.397	.477	109	35	11	0	2	12	14	17
July	.286	.367	.455	77	22	2	1	3	10	11	12
August	.263	.333	.515	99	26	5	1	6	15	10	9
Sept–Oct	.333	.400	.500	18	6	0	0	1	2	2	4
Bases Empty	.281	.377	.474	253	71	13	0	12	12	36	38
Leadoff	.269	.367	.538	78	21	6	0	5	5	11	10
Runners On Base	.318	.352	.484	217	69	9	3	7	63	17	27
Scoring Position	.306	.345	.472	144	44	5	2	5	57	14	15
Late and Close	.344	.435	.567	90	31	5	0	5	12	15	16

8-YEAR TOTALS (1984–1991)

BA	OBA	SA	AB	H	2B	3B	HR	RBI	BB	SO
.277	.338	.456	2903	805	176	21	100	399	271	502
.299	.369	.515	976	292	64	9	43	138	108	153
.266	.322	.426	1927	513	112	12	57	261	163	349
.277	.343	.449	1371	380	80	13	43	190	140	231
.277	.334	.462	1532	425	96	8	57	209	131	271
.284	.344	.463	2010	570	122	16	69	287	189	337
.263	.325	.439	893	235	54	5	31	112	82	165
.273	.340	.443	785	214	61	5	21	123	80	146
.279	.337	.460	2118	591	115	16	79	276	191	356
.244	.319	.399	446	109	24	0	15	61	48	90
.294	.359	.505	545	160	34	3	25	89	56	95
.292	.339	.481	559	163	40	6	18	78	43	94
.272	.339	.405	486	132	23	6	10	61	51	85
.284	.334	.472	475	135	28	2	19	61	36	76
.270	.331	.459	392	106	27	4	13	49	37	62
.282	.345	.466	1583	446	101	10	57	57	145	273
.284	.340	.486	630	179	45	5	24	24	50	98
.272	.329	.443	1320	359	75	11	43	342	126	229
.283	.345	.467	735	208	38	5	29	295	85	129
.291	.366	.442	468	136	32	0	13	55	58	96

KEN CAMINITI — bats both — throws right — age 29 — HOU — *3

1991	BA	OBA	SA	AB	H	2B	3B	HR	RBI	BB	SO
Total	.253	.312	.383	574	145	30	3	13	80	46	85
vs. Left	.306	.343	.493	229	70	14	1	9	43	12	26
vs. Right	.217	.292	.310	345	75	16	2	4	37	34	59
at Home	.253	.307	.422	289	73	18	2	9	48	22	52
on Road	.253	.316	.344	285	72	12	1	4	32	24	33
on Grass	.260	.314	.356	177	46	6	1	3	14	12	22
on Turf	.249	.311	.395	397	99	24	2	10	66	34	63
Day Games	.234	.299	.312	141	33	8	0	1	14	13	26
Night Games	.259	.316	.406	433	112	22	3	12	66	33	59
April	.268	.316	.352	71	19	3	0	1	8	4	7
May	.226	.297	.321	106	24	2	1	2	9	10	11
June	.211	.263	.356	90	19	4	0	3	8	7	18
July	.284	.340	.516	95	27	6	2	4	25	7	11
August	.269	.344	.407	108	29	9	0	2	22	12	21
Sept–Oct	.260	.306	.346	104	27	6	0	1	8	6	17
Bases Empty	.230	.283	.328	296	68	15	1	4	4	17	49
Leadoff	.246	.293	.326	138	34	8	0	1	1	5	23
Runners On Base	.277	.341	.442	278	77	15	2	9	76	29	36
Scoring Position	.290	.370	.452	155	45	11	1	4	63	22	22
Late and Close	.272	.302	.380	92	25	1	0	3	9	4	16

5-YEAR TOTALS (1987–1991)

BA	OBA	SA	AB	H	2B	3B	HR	RBI	BB	SO
.247	.304	.348	1986	490	90	9	31	233	162	337
.283	.323	.416	757	214	41	3	18	103	47	107
.225	.293	.306	1229	276	49	6	13	130	115	230
.263	.318	.376	997	262	55	5	16	125	81	175
.231	.290	.320	989	228	35	4	15	108	81	162
.228	.283	.323	619	141	20	3	11	62	47	106
.255	.314	.359	1367	349	70	6	20	171	115	231
.250	.307	.365	537	134	26	3	10	63	46	105
.246	.303	.342	1449	356	64	6	21	170	116	232
.270	.322	.363	226	61	12	0	3	23	16	38
.257	.314	.357	300	77	8	2	6	35	25	35
.218	.269	.308	289	63	12	1	4	30	22	52
.274	.329	.418	340	93	17	4	8	50	27	44
.233	.306	.325	421	98	25	1	4	57	44	95
.239	.289	.327	410	98	16	1	6	38	28	73
.234	.288	.333	1062	248	51	5	15	15	76	190
.266	.310	.381	443	118	27	3	6	6	24	72
.262	.322	.365	924	242	39	4	16	218	86	147
.279	.355	.390	541	151	29	2	9	197	70	98
.257	.299	.351	373	96	8	3	7	36	23	80

CASEY CANDAELE — bats both — throws right — age 31 — HOU — *203

5-YEAR TOTALS (1986–1991)

1991	BA	OBA	SA	AB	H	2B	3B	HR	RBI	BB	SO		BA	OBA	SA	AB	H	2B	3B	HR	RBI	BB	SO
Total	.262	.319	.362	461	121	20	7	4	50	40	49		.258	.318	.346	1423	367	63	19	8	106	125	151
vs. Left	.282	.345	.353	156	44	6	1	1	13	15	15		.290	.344	.385	496	144	28	5	3	34	41	41
vs. Right	.252	.306	.367	305	77	14	6	3	37	25	34		.241	.304	.325	927	223	35	14	5	72	84	110
at Home	.294	.361	.396	235	69	11	5	1	33	26	27		.270	.333	.364	742	200	31	15	3	65	69	85
on Road	.230	.274	.327	226	52	9	2	3	17	14	22		.245	.301	.326	681	167	32	4	5	41	56	66
on Grass	.237	.273	.319	135	32	5	0	2	11	7	15		.272	.320	.364	371	101	18	2	4	31	28	38
on Turf	.273	.338	.380	326	89	15	7	2	39	33	34		.253	.317	.339	1052	266	45	17	4	75	97	113
Day Games	.250	.296	.333	108	27	4	1	1	10	7	11		.244	.304	.338	397	97	23	4	2	30	33	41
Night Games	.266	.326	.371	353	94	16	6	3	40	33	38		.263	.323	.349	1026	270	40	15	6	76	92	110
April	.267	.346	.467	45	12	3	3	0	8	6	5		.254	.342	.367	169	43	10	3	1	13	23	15
May	.234	.272	.312	77	18	4	1	0	7	4	9		.275	.327	.345	229	63	10	3	0	13	17	26
June	.240	.302	.323	96	23	5	0	1	11	9	12		.218	.284	.315	289	63	13	3	3	23	27	29
July	.329	.404	.532	79	26	3	2	3	8	10	10		.330	.394	.478	209	69	9	5	4	14	22	26
August	.237	.290	.301	93	22	4	1	0	7	7	9		.219	.284	.296	196	43	9	3	0	16	18	22
Sept–Oct	.282	.316	.296	71	20	1	0	0	9	4	4		.260	.300	.308	331	86	12	2	0	27	18	33
Bases Empty	.231	.297	.333	255	59	9	4	3	3	24	25		.249	.311	.344	885	220	42	12	6	6	79	95
Leadoff	.257	.328	.372	113	29	6	2	1	1	12	12		.229	.297	.290	445	102	16	4	1	1	42	58
Runners On Base	.301	.347	.398	206	62	11	3	1	47	16	24		.273	.329	.349	538	147	21	7	2	100	46	56
Scoring Position	.304	.372	.420	112	34	6	2	1	45	14	16		.255	.329	.342	310	79	11	5	2	95	36	40
Late and Close	.265	.336	.324	102	27	4	1	0	16	11	13		.257	.328	.354	280	72	11	5	2	30	30	27

JOSE CANSECO — bats right — throws right — age 28 — OAK — *OD

7-YEAR TOTALS (1985–1991)

1991	BA	OBA	SA	AB	H	2B	3B	HR	RBI	BB	SO		BA	OBA	SA	AB	H	2B	3B	HR	RBI	BB	SO
Total	.266	.359	.556	572	152	32	1	44	122	78	152		.270	.348	.518	3216	867	156	8	209	647	370	870
vs. Left	.250	.370	.493	136	34	9	0	8	21	24	41		.290	.361	.564	876	254	49	4	61	181	93	223
vs. Right	.271	.356	.576	436	118	23	1	36	101	54	111		.262	.343	.501	2340	613	107	4	148	466	277	647
at Home	.270	.371	.506	267	72	15	0	16	46	39	80		.268	.356	.499	1520	407	69	3	92	292	201	405
on Road	.262	.349	.600	305	80	17	1	28	76	39	72		.271	.340	.535	1696	460	87	5	117	355	169	465
on Grass	.257	.356	.531	467	120	27	1	33	91	67	124		.268	.347	.509	2674	716	120	7	170	525	311	714
on Turf	.305	.376	.667	105	32	5	0	11	31	11	28		.279	.351	.565	542	151	36	1	39	122	59	156
Day Games	.306	.390	.597	196	60	16	1	13	49	25	61		.274	.359	.528	1184	324	68	4	75	262	144	327
Night Games	.245	.343	.535	376	92	16	0	31	73	53	91		.267	.341	.512	2032	543	88	4	134	385	226	543
April	.277	.440	.538	65	18	5	0	4	13	18	19		.280	.390	.501	379	106	15	0	23	78	68	111
May	.194	.299	.367	98	19	5	0	4	13	16	32		.275	.356	.525	509	140	19	0	36	105	65	138
June	.272	.362	.685	92	25	8	0	10	23	10	17		.263	.349	.543	438	115	25	1	32	86	53	102
July	.315	.389	.658	111	35	8	0	10	35	13	19		.296	.362	.600	565	167	26	1	48	135	57	142
August	.229	.318	.490	96	22	1	0	8	12	11	35		.243	.305	.453	602	146	34	3	29	102	49	176
Sept–Oct	.300	.366	.582	110	33	5	1	8	26	10	30		.267	.341	.497	723	193	37	3	41	141	78	201
Bases Empty	.264	.357	.560	318	84	20	1	24	24	41	87		.250	.331	.480	1718	429	83	5	101	101	191	504
Leadoff	.330	.438	.739	115	38	5	0	14	14	20	25		.261	.344	.501	617	161	29	1	39	39	70	163
Runners On Base	.268	.362	.551	254	68	12	0	20	98	37	65		.292	.365	.561	1498	438	73	3	108	546	179	366
Scoring Position	.268	.366	.601	153	41	9	0	14	85	25	46		.294	.374	.544	873	257	41	3	57	427	128	227
Late and Close	.237	.292	.588	97	23	7	0	9	28	7	27		.258	.329	.476	508	131	30	0	27	119	52	138

GARY CARTER — bats right — throws right — age 38 — LA — C1

8-YEAR TOTALS (1984–1991)

1991	BA	OBA	SA	AB	H	2B	3B	HR	RBI	BB	SO		BA	OBA	SA	AB	H	2B	3B	HR	RBI	BB	SO
Total	.246	.323	.375	248	61	14	0	6	26	22	26		.257	.328	.422	3265	840	129	8	131	508	330	365
vs. Left	.247	.339	.367	150	37	9	0	3	14	17	16		.273	.359	.448	1222	334	60	2	50	176	165	96
vs. Right	.245	.295	.388	98	24	5	0	3	12	5	10		.248	.309	.406	2043	506	69	6	81	332	165	269
at Home	.216	.298	.304	125	27	2	0	3	11	11	17		.252	.326	.408	1589	401	53	3	63	247	167	187
on Road	.276	.348	.447	123	34	12	0	3	15	11	9		.262	.330	.435	1676	439	76	5	68	261	163	178
on Grass	.238	.314	.362	185	44	8	0	5	19	15	19		.259	.327	.429	2007	520	66	5	88	327	200	244
on Turf	.270	.347	.413	63	17	6	0	1	7	7	7		.254	.330	.412	1258	320	63	3	43	181	130	121
Day Games	.235	.342	.338	68	16	4	0	1	4	10	5		.268	.343	.456	1076	288	49	2	50	185	118	117
Night Games	.250	.315	.389	180	45	10	0	5	22	12	21		.252	.321	.405	2189	552	80	6	81	323	212	248
April	.091	.167	.091	11	1	0	0	0	0	1	1		.248	.330	.430	460	114	22	1	20	80	55	51
May	.211	.326	.421	38	8	2	0	2	7	6	4		.225	.319	.385	524	118	23	2	19	81	67	73
June	.271	.327	.375	48	13	2	0	1	5	3	3		.285	.349	.454	557	159	18	2	24	76	52	57
July	.273	.338	.455	66	18	6	0	2	8	4	9		.264	.321	.428	561	148	24	2	22	95	43	55
August	.292	.320	.417	48	14	3	0	1	4	1	5		.248	.313	.395	565	140	21	0	20	83	52	68
Sept–Oct	.189	.333	.216	37	7	1	0	0	2	7	4		.269	.338	.438	598	161	21	1	26	93	61	61
Bases Empty	.245	.318	.403	139	34	7	0	5	5	12	15		.250	.311	.419	1739	434	66	5	73	73	141	188
Leadoff	.281	.305	.456	57	16	4	0	2	2	1	5		.275	.321	.464	783	215	37	0	37	37	47	79
Runners On Base	.248	.328	.339	109	27	7	0	1	21	10	11		.266	.347	.425	1526	406	63	3	58	435	189	177
Scoring Position	.265	.350	.368	68	18	4	0	1	19	7	9		.276	.366	.425	956	264	34	3	34	377	145	124
Late and Close	.222	.300	.333	54	12	3	0	1	3	6	8		.264	.334	.408	603	159	19	1	22	76	58	85

JOE CARTER — bats right — throws right — age 32 — TOR — *OD

1991	BA	OBA	SA	AB	H	2B	3B	HR	RBI	BB	SO	8-YEAR TOTALS (1984–1991) BA	OBA	SA	AB	H	2B	3B	HR	RBI	BB	SO
Total	.273	.330	.503	638	174	42	3	33	108	49	112	.265	.310	.466	4524	1197	233	26	208	754	266	721
vs. Left	.335	.366	.569	188	63	12	1	10	32	11	28	.271	.314	.469	1282	347	61	8	59	206	83	215
vs. Right	.247	.315	.476	450	111	30	2	23	76	38	84	.262	.308	.464	3242	850	172	18	149	548	183	506
at Home	.290	.348	.583	321	93	23	1	23	64	23	65	.269	.318	.470	2242	604	112	13	104	371	142	368
on Road	.256	.311	.423	317	81	19	2	10	44	26	47	.260	.302	.461	2282	593	121	13	104	383	124	353
on Grass	.263	.322	.441	247	65	12	1	10	37	21	35	.264	.309	.458	3453	910	163	19	157	564	206	543
on Turf	.279	.335	.542	391	109	30	2	23	71	28	77	.268	.313	.489	1071	287	70	7	51	190	60	178
Day Games	.238	.304	.457	210	50	14	1	10	31	17	39	.262	.308	.457	1482	388	73	12	64	229	90	249
Night Games	.290	.343	.526	428	124	28	2	23	77	32	73	.266	.310	.470	3042	809	160	14	144	525	176	472
April	.337	.391	.542	83	28	8	0	3	15	8	13	.266	.313	.461	545	145	28	0	26	94	34	98
May	.240	.310	.394	104	25	5	1	3	10	9	14	.269	.311	.442	710	191	34	7	25	120	42	112
June	.352	.405	.759	108	38	11	0	11	29	8	23	.261	.316	.507	696	182	44	2	41	123	42	113
July	.255	.348	.490	98	25	5	0	6	18	12	20	.256	.304	.448	777	199	37	5	34	126	51	108
August	.248	.262	.448	125	31	7	0	6	20	2	14	.258	.299	.468	818	211	38	4	42	136	42	119
Sept–Oct	.225	.288	.408	120	27	6	2	4	16	10	28	.275	.316	.467	978	269	52	8	40	155	55	171
Bases Empty	.272	.313	.523	346	94	26	2	19	19	16	54	.259	.296	.472	2369	613	117	14	120	120	107	357
Leadoff	.290	.323	.621	124	36	10	2	9	9	5	16	.265	.297	.496	923	245	42	3	55	55	35	128
Runners On Base	.274	.348	.479	292	80	16	1	14	89	33	58	.271	.323	.458	2155	584	116	12	88	634	159	364
Scoring Position	.265	.353	.465	185	49	8	1	9	76	27	40	.271	.337	.445	1294	351	68	4	47	528	131	237
Late and Close	.196	.295	.280	107	21	4	1	1	9	14	25	.246	.303	.409	728	179	23	6	28	121	52	134

ANDUJAR CEDENO — bats right — throws right — age 23 — HOU — S

1991	BA	OBA	SA	AB	H	2B	3B	HR	RBI	BB	SO	2-YEAR TOTALS (1990–1991) BA	OBA	SA	AB	H	2B	3B	HR	RBI	BB	SO
Total	.243	.270	.418	251	61	13	2	9	36	9	74	.236	.262	.405	259	61	13	2	9	36	9	79
vs. Left	.213	.220	.262	80	17	4	0	0	10	1	24	.202	.209	.250	84	17	4	0	0	10	1	26
vs. Right	.257	.293	.491	171	44	9	2	9	26	8	50	.251	.286	.480	175	44	9	2	9	26	8	53
at Home	.224	.250	.396	134	30	7	2	4	21	5	41	.221	.246	.390	136	30	7	2	4	21	5	42
on Road	.265	.293	.444	117	31	6	0	5	15	4	33	.252	.279	.423	123	31	6	0	5	15	4	37
on Grass	.264	.293	.483	87	23	4	0	5	14	3	22	.264	.293	.483	87	23	4	0	5	14	3	22
on Turf	.232	.257	.384	164	38	9	2	4	22	6	52	.221	.246	.366	172	38	9	2	4	22	6	57
Day Games	.261	.271	.478	69	18	4	1	3	10	1	16	.243	.253	.446	74	18	4	1	3	10	1	19
Night Games	.236	.269	.396	182	43	9	1	6	26	8	58	.232	.265	.389	185	43	9	1	6	26	8	60
April	.000	.000	.000	0	0	0	0	0	0	0	0	.000	.000	.000	0	0	0	0	0	0	0	0
May	.000	.000	.000	0	0	0	0	0	0	0	0	.000	.000	.000	0	0	0	0	0	0	0	0
June	.000	.000	.000	0	0	0	0	0	0	0	0	.000	.000	.000	0	0	0	0	0	0	0	0
July	.250	.286	.400	20	5	1	1	0	2	1	6	.250	.286	.400	20	5	1	1	0	2	1	6
August	.239	.256	.385	117	28	5	0	4	18	3	34	.239	.256	.385	117	28	5	0	4	18	3	34
Sept–Oct	.246	.281	.456	114	28	7	1	5	16	5	34	.230	.264	.426	122	28	7	1	5	16	5	39
Bases Empty	.234	.255	.401	137	32	8	0	5	5	3	42	.229	.250	.393	140	32	8	0	5	5	3	44
Leadoff	.169	.183	.322	59	10	3	0	2	2	1	19	.169	.183	.322	59	10	3	0	2	2	1	19
Runners On Base	.254	.287	.439	114	29	5	2	4	31	6	32	.244	.276	.420	119	29	5	2	4	31	6	35
Scoring Position	.254	.297	.463	67	17	1	2	3	28	5	19	.243	.286	.443	70	17	1	2	3	28	5	21
Late and Close	.238	.289	.452	42	10	3	0	2	3	3	16	.233	.283	.442	43	10	3	0	2	3	3	16

RICK CERONE — bats right — throws right — age 38 — NYN — C

1991	BA	OBA	SA	AB	H	2B	3B	HR	RBI	BB	SO	8-YEAR TOTALS (1984–1991) BA	OBA	SA	AB	H	2B	3B	HR	RBI	BB	SO
Total	.273	.360	.357	227	62	13	0	2	16	30	24	.251	.316	.340	1828	458	86	3	24	181	172	223
vs. Left	.324	.387	.398	108	35	8	0	0	8	11	13	.270	.323	.360	745	201	41	1	8	81	59	86
vs. Right	.227	.338	.319	119	27	5	0	2	8	19	11	.237	.312	.327	1083	257	45	2	16	100	113	137
at Home	.293	.365	.390	123	36	9	0	1	12	14	10	.258	.317	.354	978	252	48	2	14	110	87	107
on Road	.250	.355	.317	104	26	4	0	1	4	16	14	.242	.316	.325	850	206	38	1	10	71	85	116
on Grass	.285	.363	.372	172	49	12	0	1	12	21	15	.255	.318	.348	1516	387	71	3	21	161	139	176
on Turf	.236	.354	.309	55	13	1	0	1	4	9	9	.228	.310	.304	312	71	15	0	3	20	33	47
Day Games	.288	.373	.394	66	19	4	0	1	3	8	3	.261	.322	.332	587	153	25	1	5	54	47	74
Night Games	.267	.355	.342	161	43	9	0	1	13	22	21	.246	.314	.344	1241	305	61	2	19	127	125	149
April	.385	.407	.615	26	10	3	0	1	4	0	2	.283	.343	.394	254	72	10	0	6	33	21	33
May	.227	.320	.318	44	10	4	0	0	3	6	3	.266	.335	.369	312	83	14	0	6	29	33	41
June	.204	.361	.224	49	10	1	0	0	3	12	5	.251	.333	.312	263	66	14	1	0	28	31	27
July	.304	.396	.326	46	14	1	0	0	2	7	5	.246	.295	.321	321	79	18	0	2	34	22	33
August	.306	.358	.367	49	15	3	0	0	3	4	6	.251	.309	.336	402	101	16	0	6	34	34	50
Sept–Oct	.231	.286	.538	13	3	1	0	1	1	1	3	.207	.288	.315	276	57	14	2	4	23	31	39
Bases Empty	.302	.353	.410	139	42	9	0	2	2	11	9	.253	.308	.337	1029	260	46	1	13	13	79	125
Leadoff	.333	.403	.450	60	20	4	0	1	1	7	4	.269	.333	.386	420	113	28	0	7	7	39	49
Runners On Base	.227	.370	.273	88	20	4	0	0	14	19	15	.248	.326	.344	799	198	40	2	11	168	93	98
Scoring Position	.204	.418	.224	49	10	1	0	0	12	17	10	.242	.349	.315	422	102	17	1	4	144	74	53
Late and Close	.342	.432	.526	38	13	4	0	1	2	6	4	.235	.316	.304	289	68	14	0	2	25	33	27

WES CHAMBERLAIN — bats right — throws right — age 26 — PHI — O

1991	BA	OBA	SA	AB	H	2B	3B	HR	RBI	BB	SO		BA	OBA	SA	AB	H	2B	3B	HR	RBI	BB	SO
Total	.240	.300	.399	383	92	16	3	13	50	31	73		.245	.300	.408	429	105	19	3	15	54	32	82
vs. Left	.266	.346	.489	139	37	8	1	7	26	16	18		.270	.339	.485	163	44	9	1	8	28	16	25
vs. Right	.225	.273	.348	244	55	8	2	6	24	15	55		.229	.276	.361	266	61	10	2	7	26	16	57
at Home	.265	.317	.445	211	56	9	1	9	32	15	37		.269	.315	.437	238	64	11	1	9	32	15	43
on Road	.209	.280	.343	172	36	7	2	4	18	16	36		.215	.282	.372	191	41	8	2	6	22	17	39
on Grass	.213	.260	.351	94	20	4	0	3	12	6	19		.211	.257	.347	95	20	4	0	3	12	6	19
on Turf	.249	.313	.415	289	72	12	3	10	38	25	54		.254	.312	.425	334	85	15	3	12	42	26	63
Day Games	.188	.261	.366	101	19	6	0	4	15	10	20		.198	.264	.369	111	22	7	0	4	16	10	23
Night Games	.259	.315	.411	282	73	10	3	9	35	21	53		.261	.313	.421	318	83	12	3	11	38	22	59
April	.200	.200	.200	5	1	0	0	0	0	0	0		.200	.200	.200	5	1	0	0	0	0	0	0
May	.000	.000	.000	0	0	0	0	0	0	0	0		.000	.000	.000	0	0	0	0	0	0	0	0
June	.328	.361	.448	58	19	4	0	1	6	2	8		.328	.361	.448	58	19	4	0	1	6	2	8
July	.260	.289	.452	73	19	5	0	3	12	3	12		.260	.289	.452	73	19	5	0	3	12	3	12
August	.267	.356	.483	116	31	3	2	6	18	16	24		.265	.353	.479	117	31	3	2	6	18	16	25
Sept–Oct	.168	.232	.282	131	22	4	1	3	14	10	29		.199	.250	.335	176	35	7	1	5	18	11	37
Bases Empty	.225	.291	.314	204	46	10	1	2	2	18	37		.231	.289	.333	234	54	13	1	3	3	18	45
Leadoff	.232	.293	.319	69	16	1	1	1	1	5	10		.224	.280	.316	76	17	2	1	1	1	5	12
Runners On Base	.257	.311	.497	179	46	6	2	11	48	13	36		.262	.314	.497	195	51	6	2	12	51	14	37
Scoring Position	.250	.333	.500	96	24	4	1	6	36	11	20		.252	.336	.515	103	26	4	1	7	39	12	21
Late and Close	.240	.287	.333	75	18	4	0	1	8	5	13		.229	.273	.313	83	19	4	0	1	8	5	15

2-YEAR TOTALS (1990–1991)

JACK CLARK — bats right — throws right — age 37 — BOS — *D

1991	BA	OBA	SA	AB	H	2B	3B	HR	RBI	BB	SO		BA	OBA	SA	AB	H	2B	3B	HR	RBI	BB	SO
Total	.249	.374	.466	481	120	18	1	28	87	96	133		.262	.406	.491	3061	803	132	10	183	596	752	826
vs. Left	.325	.465	.530	117	38	6	0	6	20	34	22		.297	.471	.546	918	273	48	3	58	177	307	217
vs. Right	.225	.342	.445	364	82	12	1	22	67	62	111		.247	.376	.468	2143	530	84	7	125	419	445	609
at Home	.281	.377	.542	253	71	12	0	18	47	40	68		.257	.396	.487	1512	389	65	5	91	298	357	410
on Road	.215	.372	.382	228	49	6	1	10	40	56	65		.267	.416	.495	1549	414	67	5	92	298	395	416
on Grass	.247	.365	.455	409	101	16	0	23	65	76	116		.257	.403	.480	1890	485	69	4	115	366	467	517
on Turf	.264	.426	.528	72	19	2	1	5	22	20	17		.272	.412	.510	1171	318	63	6	68	230	285	309
Day Games	.290	.387	.574	162	47	10	0	12	34	25	39		.268	.411	.509	1056	283	50	3	66	209	254	283
Night Games	.229	.368	.411	319	73	8	1	16	53	71	94		.259	.404	.482	2005	520	82	7	117	387	498	543
April	.246	.386	.421	57	14	1	0	3	10	12	19		.260	.400	.487	511	133	20	3	30	90	121	150
May	.190	.346	.250	84	16	2	0	1	5	20	29		.279	.415	.493	613	171	30	1	33	123	146	151
June	.216	.352	.473	74	16	1	0	6	14	16	20		.242	.379	.471	637	154	23	3	39	118	141	175
July	.270	.383	.528	89	24	2	0	7	23	17	23		.280	.419	.514	500	140	18	0	33	116	124	135
August	.261	.385	.523	88	23	6	1	5	22	17	19		.242	.403	.480	425	103	23	3	24	83	114	111
Sept–Oct	.303	.394	.573	89	27	6	0	6	13	14	23		.272	.433	.512	375	102	18	0	24	66	106	104
Bases Empty	.236	.339	.421	242	57	6	0	13	13	37	69		.251	.385	.465	1532	384	56	6	87	87	330	440
Leadoff	.230	.319	.385	122	28	4	0	5	5	15	37		.243	.378	.457	733	178	27	5	40	40	156	215
Runners On Base	.264	.407	.510	239	63	12	1	15	74	59	64		.274	.426	.517	1529	419	76	4	96	509	422	386
Scoring Position	.242	.432	.462	132	32	5	0	8	58	47	44		.271	.449	.505	909	246	45	3	54	414	314	253
Late and Close	.205	.278	.386	88	18	1	0	5	8	9	28		.257	.398	.491	538	138	18	3	34	92	128	156

8-YEAR TOTALS (1984–1991)

JERALD CLARK — bats right — throws right — age 29 — SD — O1

1991	BA	OBA	SA	AB	H	2B	3B	HR	RBI	BB	SO		BA	OBA	SA	AB	H	2B	3B	HR	RBI	BB	SO
Total	.230	.298	.355	369	85	16	0	10	47	31	89		.234	.292	.373	526	123	23	1	16	68	39	126
vs. Left	.183	.246	.302	126	23	3	0	4	13	10	30		.188	.240	.307	202	38	4	1	6	16	13	48
vs. Right	.255	.324	.383	243	62	13	0	6	34	21	59		.262	.323	.414	324	85	19	0	10	52	26	78
at Home	.210	.270	.379	195	41	9	0	8	29	14	43		.204	.260	.377	265	54	13	0	11	40	18	60
on Road	.253	.328	.328	174	44	7	0	2	18	17	46		.264	.324	.368	261	69	10	1	5	28	21	66
on Grass	.227	.284	.355	282	64	12	0	8	40	20	74		.228	.279	.384	391	89	17	1	14	57	26	101
on Turf	.241	.340	.356	87	21	4	0	2	7	11	15		.252	.327	.341	135	34	6	0	2	11	13	25
Day Games	.210	.284	.305	105	22	4	0	2	11	10	24		.210	.271	.299	167	35	7	1	2	15	13	40
Night Games	.239	.303	.375	264	63	12	0	8	36	21	65		.245	.301	.407	359	88	16	0	14	53	26	86
April	.288	.366	.452	73	21	3	0	3	13	8	16		.268	.348	.415	82	22	3	0	3	13	9	18
May	.238	.304	.286	21	5	1	0	0	3	1	7		.263	.311	.333	57	15	4	0	0	4	3	17
June	.294	.410	.544	68	20	5	0	4	15	12	11		.283	.374	.511	92	26	6	0	5	17	12	11
July	.209	.242	.308	91	19	3	0	2	8	4	24		.207	.240	.304	92	19	3	0	2	8	4	24
August	.209	.260	.299	67	14	3	0	1	6	4	16		.200	.256	.280	75	15	3	0	1	6	5	17
Sept–Oct	.122	.167	.143	49	6	1	0	0	2	2	22		.203	.239	.367	128	26	4	1	5	20	6	39
Bases Empty	.199	.284	.299	201	40	8	0	4	4	22	55		.213	.283	.329	286	61	10	1	7	7	26	76
Leadoff	.213	.286	.303	89	19	5	0	1	1	8	24		.229	.284	.313	131	30	6	1	1	1	9	31
Runners On Base	.268	.314	.423	168	45	8	0	6	43	9	34		.258	.302	.425	240	62	13	0	9	61	13	50
Scoring Position	.236	.280	.360	89	21	2	0	3	36	3	16		.220	.260	.348	132	29	5	0	4	50	5	27
Late and Close	.239	.276	.352	71	17	2	0	2	12	3	20		.220	.255	.310	100	22	3	0	2	12	4	30

4-YEAR TOTALS (1988–1991)

WILL CLARK — bats left — throws left — age 28 — SF — *1

1991	BA	OBA	SA	AB	H	2B	3B	HR	RBI	BB	SO	6-YEAR TOTALS (1986–1991) BA	OBA	SA	AB	H	2B	3B	HR	RBI	BB	SO
Total	.301	.359	.536	565	170	32	7	29	116	51	91	.302	.372	.512	3265	985	182	34	146	563	370	594
vs. Left	.241	.294	.456	195	47	11	2	9	40	14	34	.294	.344	.478	1175	346	64	13	42	224	86	213
vs. Right	.332	.392	.578	370	123	21	5	20	76	37	57	.306	.387	.532	2090	639	118	21	104	339	284	381
at Home	.283	.344	.558	283	80	19	4	17	47	25	51	.310	.377	.530	1633	507	98	15	77	292	187	286
on Road	.319	.373	.514	282	90	13	3	12	69	26	40	.293	.367	.494	1632	478	84	19	69	271	183	308
on Grass	.295	.353	.532	410	121	22	6	21	74	35	72	.308	.378	.517	2416	744	136	24	107	418	276	446
on Turf	.316	.374	.548	155	49	10	1	8	42	16	19	.284	.358	.499	849	241	46	10	39	145	94	148
Day Games	.338	.397	.653	219	74	17	5	14	46	20	31	.313	.393	.548	1317	412	80	19	64	244	171	233
Night Games	.277	.334	.462	346	96	15	2	15	70	31	60	.294	.358	.488	1948	573	102	15	82	319	199	361
April	.325	.402	.584	77	25	4	2	4	21	10	9	.309	.383	.527	495	153	26	8	22	84	60	93
May	.233	.289	.398	103	24	2	0	5	15	9	19	.259	.328	.497	586	152	29	7	32	98	57	111
June	.333	.361	.513	78	26	1	2	3	20	4	12	.331	.401	.551	477	158	21	6	24	108	60	78
July	.322	.384	.622	90	29	6	0	7	18	8	11	.296	.369	.462	483	143	23	3	17	75	54	95
August	.347	.408	.678	118	41	14	2	7	28	11	16	.316	.377	.544	618	195	44	5	29	104	63	104
Sept–Oct	.253	.312	.414	99	25	5	1	3	14	9	24	.304	.381	.493	606	184	39	5	22	94	76	113
Bases Empty	.276	.327	.452	312	86	18	2	11	11	22	60	.292	.351	.481	1843	539	99	16	72	72	155	339
Leadoff	.262	.303	.369	103	27	3	1	2	2	5	13	.293	.354	.483	644	189	30	7	26	26	54	105
Runners On Base	.332	.395	.640	253	84	14	5	18	105	29	31	.314	.398	.553	1422	446	83	18	74	491	215	255
Scoring Position	.338	.419	.623	151	51	7	3	10	84	24	15	.313	.415	.545	852	267	47	12	42	407	171	163
Late and Close	.303	.382	.528	89	27	7	2	3	23	12	16	.297	.380	.504	548	163	32	6	23	101	73	112

ALEX COLE — bats left — throws left — age 27 — CLE — *O/D

1991	BA	OBA	SA	AB	H	2B	3B	HR	RBI	BB	SO	2-YEAR TOTALS (1990–1991) BA	OBA	SA	AB	H	2B	3B	HR	RBI	BB	SO
Total	.295	.386	.354	387	114	17	3	0	21	58	47	.296	.384	.355	614	182	22	7	0	34	86	85
vs. Left	.387	.500	.500	62	24	5	1	0	8	14	7	.325	.447	.404	114	37	5	2	0	12	24	18
vs. Right	.277	.362	.326	325	90	12	2	0	13	44	40	.290	.368	.344	500	145	17	5	0	22	62	67
at Home	.291	.399	.341	182	53	9	0	0	14	33	27	.297	.399	.353	303	90	11	3	0	23	51	50
on Road	.298	.374	.366	205	61	8	3	0	7	25	20	.296	.367	.357	311	92	11	4	0	11	35	35
on Grass	.282	.373	.333	330	93	13	2	0	19	48	43	.292	.380	.347	524	153	17	6	0	30	74	77
on Turf	.368	.463	.474	57	21	4	1	0	2	10	4	.322	.402	.400	90	29	5	1	0	4	12	8
Day Games	.248	.340	.286	133	33	3	1	0	6	19	21	.272	.377	.318	173	47	4	2	0	8	30	28
Night Games	.319	.410	.390	254	81	14	2	0	15	39	26	.306	.386	.370	441	135	18	5	0	26	56	57
April	.321	.368	.415	53	17	3	1	0	2	4	7	.321	.368	.415	53	17	3	1	0	2	4	7
May	.300	.391	.350	20	6	1	0	0	0	3	0	.300	.391	.350	20	6	1	0	0	0	3	0
June	.278	.384	.292	72	20	1	0	0	4	12	9	.278	.384	.292	72	20	1	0	0	4	12	9
July	.250	.417	.286	56	14	2	0	0	6	16	6	.269	.394	.295	78	21	2	0	0	6	16	9
August	.271	.358	.390	59	16	3	2	0	2	8	12	.303	.388	.394	165	50	7	4	0	11	22	34
Sept–Oct	.323	.392	.378	127	41	7	0	0	7	15	13	.301	.379	.354	226	68	8	2	0	11	29	26
Bases Empty	.311	.410	.377	257	80	13	2	0	0	43	35	.309	.407	.372	401	124	17	4	0	0	65	61
Leadoff	.312	.433	.390	154	48	8	2	0	0	33	23	.300	.422	.365	233	70	9	3	0	0	49	37
Runners On Base	.262	.338	.308	130	34	4	1	0	21	15	12	.272	.338	.324	213	58	5	3	0	34	21	24
Scoring Position	.258	.370	.258	66	17	0	0	0	20	12	7	.284	.380	.293	116	33	1	0	0	31	18	17
Late and Close	.286	.360	.299	77	22	1	0	0	7	8	10	.283	.366	.293	99	28	1	0	0	7	12	13

VINCE COLEMAN — bats both — throws right — age 32 — NYN — O

1991	BA	OBA	SA	AB	H	2B	3B	HR	RBI	BB	SO	7-YEAR TOTALS (1985–1991) BA	OBA	SA	AB	H	2B	3B	HR	RBI	BB	SO
Total	.255	.347	.327	278	71	7	5	1	17	39	47	.264	.327	.339	3812	1008	113	61	16	234	353	675
vs. Left	.250	.310	.308	104	26	3	0	1	4	9	11	.251	.313	.359	1415	355	64	25	13	101	127	260
vs. Right	.259	.368	.339	174	45	4	5	0	13	30	36	.272	.335	.327	2397	653	49	36	3	133	226	415
at Home	.234	.364	.262	107	25	3	0	0	5	22	16	.278	.343	.368	1890	525	62	36	12	134	182	312
on Road	.269	.335	.368	171	46	4	5	1	12	17	31	.251	.312	.310	1922	483	51	25	4	100	171	363
on Grass	.243	.359	.280	189	46	5	1	0	10	34	35	.251	.316	.293	1122	282	23	9	2	59	109	216
on Turf	.281	.319	.427	89	25	2	4	1	7	5	12	.270	.332	.358	2690	726	90	52	14	175	244	459
Day Games	.258	.365	.315	89	23	1	2	0	5	15	16	.267	.328	.353	1311	350	39	25	8	87	121	242
Night Games	.254	.338	.333	189	48	6	3	1	12	24	31	.263	.327	.331	2501	658	74	36	8	147	232	433
April	.219	.345	.301	73	16	2	2	0	5	14	13	.273	.346	.368	538	147	21	12	2	39	59	89
May	.301	.404	.333	93	28	1	1	0	6	16	18	.299	.361	.377	708	212	16	15	3	50	69	128
June	.240	.296	.420	50	12	2	2	1	4	4	6	.253	.317	.333	699	177	22	14	2	36	65	126
July	.318	.348	.318	22	7	0	0	0	0	1	7	.243	.317	.297	572	139	15	5	2	29	61	107
August	.200	.282	.229	35	7	1	0	0	1	4	3	.285	.332	.366	702	200	23	11	4	46	47	109
Sept–Oct	.200	.200	.400	5	1	1	0	0	0	0	0	.224	.285	.280	593	133	16	4	3	34	52	116
Bases Empty	.249	.341	.321	193	48	5	3	1	1	27	33	.268	.335	.343	2606	698	78	40	13	13	255	483
Leadoff	.245	.352	.300	110	27	4	1	0	0	18	19	.270	.339	.347	1653	447	57	26	6	6	164	318
Runners On Base	.271	.361	.341	85	23	2	2	0	16	12	14	.257	.311	.328	1206	310	35	21	3	221	98	192
Scoring Position	.281	.369	.351	57	16	2	1	0	15	8	12	.251	.314	.332	786	197	23	16	3	213	77	143
Late and Close	.308	.400	.385	52	16	2	1	0	6	8	6	.267	.332	.324	621	166	22	5	1	55	60	104

MILT CUYLER — bats both — throws right — age 24 — DET — *O

1991	BA	OBA	SA	AB	H	2B	3B	HR	RBI	BB	SO	2-YEAR TOTALS (1990–1991) BA	OBA	SA	AB	H	2B	3B	HR	RBI	BB	SO
Total	.257	.336	.338	474	122	15	7	3	33	52	92	.257	.334	.339	525	135	18	8	3	41	57	102
vs. Left	.270	.345	.336	122	33	6	1	0	8	13	19	.276	.342	.343	134	37	7	1	0	11	13	19
vs. Right	.253	.332	.338	352	89	9	6	3	25	39	73	.251	.331	.338	391	98	11	7	3	30	44	83
at Home	.244	.355	.303	221	54	6	2	1	15	35	31	.242	.348	.308	240	58	7	3	1	17	36	37
on Road	.269	.318	.368	253	68	9	5	2	18	17	61	.270	.322	.365	285	77	11	5	2	24	21	65
on Grass	.246	.336	.321	386	95	13	5	2	29	49	76	.247	.333	.325	437	108	16	6	2	37	54	86
on Turf	.307	.337	.409	88	27	2	2	1	4	3	16	.307	.337	.409	88	27	2	2	1	4	3	16
Day Games	.275	.354	.397	131	36	6	2	2	20	15	26	.286	.367	.407	140	40	7	2	2	23	17	28
Night Games	.251	.329	.315	343	86	9	5	1	13	37	66	.247	.322	.314	385	95	11	6	1	18	40	74
April	.225	.262	.250	40	9	1	0	0	0	2	6	.225	.262	.250	40	9	1	0	0	0	2	6
May	.265	.386	.353	68	18	1	1	1	11	14	11	.265	.386	.353	68	18	1	1	1	11	14	11
June	.228	.274	.367	79	18	1	2	2	4	3	13	.228	.274	.367	79	18	1	2	2	4	3	13
July	.237	.333	.275	80	19	3	0	0	5	12	17	.237	.333	.275	80	19	3	0	0	5	12	17
August	.224	.325	.318	107	24	6	2	0	7	14	25	.224	.325	.318	107	24	6	2	0	7	14	25
Sept–Oct	.340	.389	.410	100	34	3	2	0	6	7	20	.311	.364	.391	151	47	6	3	0	14	12	30
Bases Empty	.293	.377	.382	283	83	11	4	2	2	36	47	.288	.368	.370	316	91	12	4	2	2	38	55
Leadoff	.275	.354	.374	131	36	4	3	1	1	16	22	.272	.348	.361	147	40	4	3	1	1	17	26
Runners On Base	.204	.274	.272	191	39	4	3	1	31	16	45	.211	.282	.292	209	44	6	4	1	39	19	47
Scoring Position	.186	.266	.274	113	21	3	2	1	30	12	30	.203	.279	.317	123	25	5	3	1	38	13	32
Late and Close	.246	.307	.377	69	17	3	0	2	7	4	15	.244	.306	.359	78	19	3	0	2	7	5	15

KAL DANIELS — bats left — throws right — age 29 — LA — *O

1991	BA	OBA	SA	AB	H	2B	3B	HR	RBI	BB	SO	6-YEAR TOTALS (1986–1991) BA	OBA	SA	AB	H	2B	3B	HR	RBI	BB	SO
Total	.249	.337	.397	461	115	15	1	17	73	63	116	.289	.388	.489	2126	615	114	8	98	335	343	439
vs. Left	.251	.308	.379	203	51	8	0	6	36	19	51	.248	.348	.366	650	161	26	0	17	96	99	151
vs. Right	.248	.359	.411	258	64	7	1	11	37	44	65	.308	.406	.543	1476	454	88	8	81	239	244	288
at Home	.248	.332	.426	242	60	7	0	12	48	31	63	.291	.386	.506	1054	307	56	4	54	175	163	218
on Road	.251	.343	.365	219	55	8	1	5	25	32	53	.287	.391	.472	1072	308	58	4	44	160	180	221
on Grass	.249	.338	.415	357	89	12	1	15	61	49	94	.279	.379	.473	1066	297	51	3	50	183	174	235
on Turf	.250	.333	.337	104	26	3	0	2	12	14	22	.300	.398	.505	1060	318	63	5	48	152	169	204
Day Games	.203	.265	.376	133	27	6	1	5	20	12	35	.274	.371	.506	674	185	41	2	37	115	101	141
Night Games	.268	.365	.405	328	88	9	0	12	53	51	81	.296	.397	.481	1452	430	73	6	61	220	242	298
April	.212	.260	.348	66	14	3	0	2	18	5	13	.276	.378	.495	366	101	25	2	17	64	62	67
May	.278	.303	.389	72	20	2	0	2	9	2	21	.296	.385	.464	358	106	16	1	14	51	49	81
June	.284	.379	.500	88	25	1	0	6	14	14	20	.280	.397	.490	300	84	12	0	17	42	59	62
July	.289	.439	.511	45	13	4	0	2	5	12	13	.291	.392	.467	351	102	27	1	11	47	58	76
August	.209	.327	.253	91	19	1	0	1	10	17	23	.279	.376	.449	405	113	17	2	16	52	64	80
Sept–Oct	.242	.330	.424	99	24	4	1	4	17	13	26	.315	.406	.575	346	109	17	2	23	79	51	73
Bases Empty	.231	.315	.341	255	59	10	0	6	6	30	61	.290	.378	.490	1252	363	68	3	59	59	169	255
Leadoff	.302	.368	.385	96	29	5	0	1	1	9	21	.321	.394	.558	561	180	42	2	29	29	63	107
Runners On Base	.272	.363	.466	206	56	5	1	11	67	33	55	.288	.403	.486	874	252	46	5	39	276	174	184
Scoring Position	.291	.392	.535	127	37	2	1	9	61	25	32	.295	.430	.508	516	152	30	4	24	239	132	121
Late and Close	.237	.318	.329	76	18	4	0	1	14	10	20	.266	.392	.406	323	86	18	0	9	52	69	73

DARREN DAULTON — bats left — throws right — age 30 — PHI — C

1991	BA	OBA	SA	AB	H	2B	3B	HR	RBI	BB	SO	7-YEAR TOTALS (1985–1991) BA	OBA	SA	AB	H	2B	3B	HR	RBI	BB	SO
Total	.196	.297	.365	285	56	12	0	12	42	41	66	.221	.326	.360	1622	359	73	4	48	200	252	337
vs. Left	.147	.226	.253	95	14	4	0	2	9	9	31	.205	.315	.295	312	64	14	1	4	28	49	81
vs. Right	.221	.330	.421	190	42	8	0	10	33	32	35	.225	.329	.376	1310	295	59	3	44	172	203	256
at Home	.211	.320	.428	152	32	9	0	8	23	24	38	.216	.332	.353	779	168	43	2	20	92	136	152
on Road	.180	.271	.293	133	24	3	0	4	19	17	28	.227	.321	.367	843	191	30	2	28	108	116	185
on Grass	.234	.330	.377	77	18	2	0	3	10	11	20	.238	.329	.386	466	111	16	1	17	61	62	122
on Turf	.183	.285	.361	208	38	10	0	9	32	30	46	.215	.325	.349	1156	248	57	3	31	139	190	215
Day Games	.211	.287	.408	76	16	0	0	5	12	9	21	.235	.332	.410	473	111	20	0	21	64	71	116
Night Games	.191	.301	.349	209	40	12	0	7	30	32	45	.216	.324	.339	1149	248	53	4	27	136	181	221
April	.203	.292	.281	64	13	5	0	0	8	7	17	.240	.355	.410	217	52	10	0	9	34	37	51
May	.071	.278	.071	14	1	0	0	0	0	4	7	.161	.292	.254	236	38	8	1	4	21	44	58
June	.167	.250	.367	30	5	0	0	2	5	4	5	.220	.338	.357	255	56	14	0	10	35	48	49
July	.208	.330	.390	77	16	2	0	4	12	14	15	.204	.303	.350	314	64	14	1	10	36	45	50
August	.198	.287	.407	86	17	3	0	5	15	11	18	.239	.332	.398	347	83	16	0	13	40	47	69
Sept–Oct	.286	.333	.643	14	4	2	0	1	2	1	4	.261	.343	.379	253	66	11	2	5	34	31	60
Bases Empty	.173	.272	.393	168	29	7	0	10	10	22	42	.200	.301	.341	916	183	38	2	29	29	128	195
Leadoff	.179	.292	.500	56	10	3	0	5	5	9	14	.207	.284	.342	363	75	19	0	10	10	38	63
Runners On Base	.231	.331	.325	117	27	5	0	2	32	19	24	.249	.358	.385	706	176	35	2	19	171	124	142
Scoring Position	.290	.402	.387	62	18	3	0	1	29	14	7	.240	.365	.363	416	100	18	0	11	148	88	87
Late and Close	.183	.271	.317	60	11	2	0	2	12	8	21	.211	.289	.299	318	67	7	0	7	40	35	88

ALVIN DAVIS — bats left — throws right — age 32 — SEA — *D1

1991	BA	OBA	SA	AB	H	2B	3B	HR	RBI	BB	SO
Total	.221	.299	.335	462	102	15	1	12	69	56	78
vs. Left	.238	.339	.376	101	24	2	0	4	14	16	19
vs. Right	.216	.288	.324	361	78	13	1	8	55	40	59
at Home	.230	.313	.354	226	52	10	0	6	35	29	44
on Road	.212	.286	.318	236	50	5	1	6	34	27	34
on Grass	.209	.287	.291	182	38	3	0	4	21	22	29
on Turf	.229	.307	.364	280	64	12	1	8	48	34	49
Day Games	.240	.297	.372	129	31	2	0	5	19	12	18
Night Games	.213	.300	.321	333	71	13	1	7	50	44	60
April	.203	.325	.290	69	14	0	0	2	9	13	13
May	.222	.261	.358	81	18	3	1	2	14	5	15
June	.253	.351	.434	83	21	3	0	4	13	13	13
July	.254	.309	.324	71	18	2	0	1	13	7	8
August	.104	.205	.194	67	7	0	0	2	8	9	12
Sept–Oct	.264	.327	.374	91	24	7	0	1	12	9	17
Bases Empty	.195	.253	.246	272	53	8	0	2	2	21	51
Leadoff	.184	.215	.216	125	23	4	0	0	0	5	17
Runners On Base	.258	.357	.463	190	49	7	1	10	67	35	27
Scoring Position	.259	.388	.333	108	28	3	1	1	46	29	17
Late and Close	.213	.302	.387	75	16	1	0	4	11	10	15

8-YEAR TOTALS (1984–1991)

	BA	OBA	SA	AB	H	2B	3B	HR	RBI	BB	SO
Total	.281	.381	.453	4136	1163	212	10	160	667	672	549
vs. Left	.268	.367	.406	1272	341	70	3	33	205	195	198
vs. Right	.287	.387	.475	2864	822	142	7	127	462	477	351
at Home	.294	.397	.505	2055	604	117	7	101	376	352	258
on Road	.269	.365	.402	2081	559	95	3	59	291	320	291
on Grass	.266	.361	.406	1590	423	70	1	50	226	243	219
on Turf	.291	.393	.483	2546	740	142	9	110	441	429	330
Day Games	.281	.377	.427	1050	295	51	3	32	156	166	143
Night Games	.281	.382	.462	3086	868	161	7	128	511	506	406
April	.283	.388	.453	552	156	29	1	21	80	97	69
May	.312	.403	.499	680	212	36	2	29	121	108	96
June	.255	.360	.395	693	177	30	2	21	104	113	84
July	.313	.417	.474	597	187	26	2	22	102	109	63
August	.288	.389	.485	784	226	43	0	37	124	130	107
Sept–Oct	.247	.341	.420	830	205	48	3	30	136	115	130
Bases Empty	.273	.365	.436	2274	621	114	4	83	83	315	320
Leadoff	.278	.355	.435	887	247	51	2	28	28	97	107
Runners On Base	.291	.399	.474	1862	542	98	6	77	584	357	229
Scoring Position	.285	.415	.463	1065	304	55	4	42	486	268	135
Late and Close	.251	.372	.417	617	155	28	1	24	87	119	77

CHILI DAVIS — bats both — throws right — age 32 — MIN — *D/O

1991	BA	OBA	SA	AB	H	2B	3B	HR	RBI	BB	SO
Total	.277	.385	.507	534	148	34	1	29	93	95	117
vs. Left	.270	.358	.511	174	47	9	0	11	32	25	36
vs. Right	.281	.397	.506	360	101	25	1	18	61	70	81
at Home	.303	.420	.539	267	81	19	1	14	45	54	51
on Road	.251	.348	.476	267	67	15	0	15	48	41	66
on Grass	.271	.371	.517	203	55	14	0	12	42	33	49
on Turf	.281	.393	.502	331	93	20	1	17	51	62	68
Day Games	.265	.392	.497	147	39	8	1	8	27	32	27
Night Games	.282	.382	.512	387	109	26	0	21	66	63	90
April	.302	.450	.524	63	19	2	0	4	11	16	18
May	.296	.350	.528	108	32	10	0	5	17	9	20
June	.253	.345	.596	99	25	4	0	10	23	15	22
July	.241	.358	.437	87	21	5	0	4	18	17	18
August	.289	.423	.478	90	26	8	0	3	13	21	19
Sept–Oct	.287	.404	.471	87	25	5	1	3	11	17	20
Bases Empty	.255	.339	.462	286	73	12	1	15	15	36	58
Leadoff	.306	.390	.589	124	38	8	0	9	9	17	20
Runners On Base	.302	.433	.560	248	75	22	0	14	78	59	59
Scoring Position	.283	.423	.546	152	43	16	0	3	64	40	37
Late and Close	.343	.478	.571	70	24	7	0	3	14	18	17

8-YEAR TOTALS (1984–1991)

	BA	OBA	SA	AB	H	2B	3B	HR	RBI	BB	SO
Total	.275	.356	.446	4094	1125	199	18	155	617	531	782
vs. Left	.254	.317	.428	1275	324	53	5	53	192	122	257
vs. Right	.284	.373	.454	2819	801	146	13	102	425	409	525
at Home	.277	.360	.438	1974	546	89	8	71	286	267	376
on Road	.273	.351	.453	2120	579	110	10	84	331	264	406
on Grass	.271	.350	.429	2982	809	135	11	104	436	377	579
on Turf	.284	.370	.492	1112	316	64	7	51	181	154	203
Day Games	.272	.353	.437	1482	403	67	8	54	217	195	288
Night Games	.276	.357	.451	2612	722	132	10	101	400	336	494
April	.277	.339	.436	610	169	34	0	21	94	61	124
May	.278	.343	.449	755	210	42	6	25	104	78	128
June	.254	.330	.451	767	195	30	5	37	124	92	133
July	.279	.360	.459	641	179	27	2	28	101	83	124
August	.273	.370	.430	711	194	37	3	23	110	112	150
Sept–Oct	.292	.396	.449	610	178	29	2	21	84	105	123
Bases Empty	.262	.330	.421	2286	600	108	9	79	79	228	416
Leadoff	.267	.332	.446	948	253	47	3	39	39	92	162
Runners On Base	.290	.385	.477	1808	525	91	9	76	538	303	366
Scoring Position	.282	.397	.481	1050	296	55	5	48	462	227	223
Late and Close	.246	.363	.407	676	166	31	3	24	98	127	141

ERIC DAVIS — bats right — throws right — age 30 — CIN — O

1991	BA	OBA	SA	AB	H	2B	3B	HR	RBI	BB	SO
Total	.235	.353	.386	285	67	10	0	11	33	48	92
vs. Left	.229	.359	.362	105	24	5	0	3	11	20	31
vs. Right	.239	.349	.400	180	43	5	0	8	22	28	61
at Home	.243	.376	.393	140	34	6	0	5	18	30	47
on Road	.228	.329	.379	145	33	4	0	6	15	18	45
on Grass	.253	.375	.414	87	22	2	0	4	7	14	27
on Turf	.227	.343	.374	198	45	8	0	7	26	34	65
Day Games	.278	.394	.443	79	22	1	0	4	8	12	29
Night Games	.218	.337	.364	206	45	9	0	7	25	36	63
April	.270	.400	.378	37	10	4	0	0	1	8	9
May	.218	.378	.500	78	17	1	0	7	13	17	23
June	.283	.389	.370	46	13	1	0	1	5	7	17
July	.278	.346	.389	72	20	2	0	2	9	7	21
August	.300	.429	.400	10	3	1	0	0	1	3	3
Sept–Oct	.095	.208	.190	42	4	1	0	1	4	6	19
Bases Empty	.237	.343	.378	156	37	4	0	6	6	21	50
Leadoff	.246	.316	.449	69	17	2	0	4	4	6	16
Runners On Base	.233	.365	.395	129	30	6	0	5	27	27	42
Scoring Position	.217	.378	.348	69	15	3	0	2	21	19	21
Late and Close	.154	.327	.333	39	6	1	0	2	5	9	17

8-YEAR TOTALS (1984–1991)

	BA	OBA	SA	AB	H	2B	3B	HR	RBI	BB	SO
Total	.268	.362	.508	2859	766	119	18	177	533	424	754
vs. Left	.277	.379	.536	953	264	39	5	66	180	157	223
vs. Right	.263	.354	.494	1906	502	80	13	111	353	267	531
at Home	.263	.373	.498	1306	343	52	8	80	251	231	347
on Road	.272	.353	.516	1553	423	67	10	97	282	193	407
on Grass	.275	.362	.511	949	261	35	6	59	164	125	231
on Turf	.264	.363	.506	1910	505	84	12	118	369	299	523
Day Games	.276	.363	.525	918	253	40	9	57	174	125	237
Night Games	.264	.362	.500	1941	513	79	9	120	359	299	517
April	.227	.321	.434	440	100	17	4	22	58	63	121
May	.258	.339	.529	395	102	19	2	28	94	49	108
June	.304	.404	.587	424	129	13	4	30	90	68	105
July	.273	.366	.495	556	152	30	3	29	87	78	149
August	.274	.376	.502	526	144	20	2	32	99	89	134
Sept–Oct	.268	.362	.510	518	139	20	3	33	105	77	137
Bases Empty	.256	.341	.472	1581	405	53	8	91	91	197	410
Leadoff	.274	.348	.534	686	188	29	4	47	47	75	150
Runners On Base	.282	.387	.552	1278	361	66	10	86	442	227	344
Scoring Position	.282	.406	.545	760	214	41	6	49	357	171	213
Late and Close	.269	.373	.512	484	130	19	0	33	114	82	131

ANDRE DAWSON — bats right — throws right — age 38 — CHN — *O

8-YEAR TOTALS (1984–1991)

1991	BA	OBA	SA	AB	H	2B	3B	HR	RBI	BB	SO	BA	OBA	SA	AB	H	2B	3B	HR	RBI	BB	SO
Total	.272	.302	.488	563	153	21	4	31	104	22	80	.278	.322	.490	4279	1188	203	35	212	753	274	635
vs. Left	.292	.316	.543	219	64	8	1	15	43	7	26	.296	.343	.529	1276	378	63	9	72	222	93	168
vs. Right	.259	.293	.453	344	89	13	3	16	61	15	54	.270	.313	.474	3003	810	140	26	140	531	181	467
at Home	.293	.328	.575	280	82	11	1	22	59	11	38	.284	.333	.497	2097	595	88	16	109	368	148	296
on Road	.251	.277	.403	283	71	10	3	9	45	11	42	.272	.312	.484	2182	593	115	19	103	385	126	339
on Grass	.277	.306	.509	405	112	13	3	25	80	15	54	.287	.328	.521	2382	683	109	21	136	452	148	349
on Turf	.259	.292	.437	158	41	8	1	6	24	7	26	.266	.315	.451	1897	505	94	14	76	301	126	286
Day Games	.291	.327	.561	278	81	14	2	19	58	12	34	.300	.347	.547	2080	625	100	19	125	405	144	295
Night Games	.253	.278	.418	285	72	7	2	12	46	10	46	.256	.299	.436	2199	563	103	16	87	348	130	340
April	.329	.376	.595	79	26	4	1	5	17	6	10	.308	.358	.568	600	185	31	10	35	115	47	69
May	.250	.298	.477	88	22	4	2	4	12	3	11	.273	.320	.497	700	191	38	7	35	117	47	101
June	.275	.275	.363	91	25	2	0	2	13	0	16	.261	.300	.428	614	160	27	2	24	91	32	89
July	.286	.312	.583	84	24	4	0	7	26	4	13	.287	.334	.459	687	197	30	2	28	127	49	106
August	.234	.263	.396	111	26	1	1	5	15	4	17	.267	.302	.485	814	217	33	8	43	142	40	130
Sept–Oct	.273	.304	.545	110	30	6	0	8	21	5	13	.275	.324	.503	864	238	44	6	47	161	59	140
Bases Empty	.255	.286	.436	298	76	14	2	12	12	9	49	.268	.300	.478	2226	596	93	21	111	111	87	352
Leadoff	.218	.250	.380	142	31	6	1	5	5	4	23	.251	.279	.460	927	233	43	6	46	46	31	134
Runners On Base	.291	.319	.547	265	77	7	2	19	92	13	31	.288	.345	.503	2053	592	110	14	101	642	187	283
Scoring Position	.297	.339	.576	158	47	4	2	12	76	12	18	.292	.369	.512	1199	350	67	7	61	540	164	169
Late and Close	.220	.250	.424	118	26	3	0	7	19	3	28	.260	.323	.438	753	196	26	3	34	125	69	130

STEVE DECKER — bats right — throws right — age 27 — SF — C

2-YEAR TOTALS (1990–1991)

1991	BA	OBA	SA	AB	H	2B	3B	HR	RBI	BB	SO	BA	OBA	SA	AB	H	2B	3B	HR	RBI	BB	SO
Total	.206	.262	.309	233	48	7	1	5	24	16	44	.223	.270	.345	287	64	9	1	8	32	17	54
vs. Left	.224	.233	.376	85	19	2	1	3	13	2	11	.250	.263	.407	108	27	3	1	4	15	3	13
vs. Right	.196	.277	.270	148	29	5	0	2	11	14	33	.207	.274	.307	179	37	6	0	4	17	14	41
at Home	.241	.304	.411	112	27	5	1	4	19	9	16	.232	.288	.387	142	33	5	1	5	22	10	21
on Road	.174	.221	.215	121	21	2	0	1	5	7	28	.214	.252	.303	145	31	4	0	3	10	7	33
on Grass	.203	.262	.333	177	36	6	1	5	23	13	27	.225	.272	.374	227	51	8	1	8	31	14	36
on Turf	.214	.262	.232	56	12	1	0	0	1	3	17	.217	.262	.233	60	13	1	0	0	1	3	18
Day Games	.218	.302	.337	101	22	4	1	2	16	10	19	.235	.311	.345	119	28	5	1	2	19	11	25
Night Games	.197	.229	.288	132	26	3	0	3	8	6	25	.214	.239	.345	168	36	4	0	6	13	6	29
April	.238	.319	.444	63	15	1	0	4	8	8	16	.238	.319	.444	63	15	1	0	4	8	8	16
May	.145	.158	.236	55	8	2	0	1	5	1	9	.145	.158	.236	55	8	2	0	1	5	1	9
June	.255	.304	.314	51	13	3	0	0	5	2	11	.255	.304	.314	51	13	3	0	0	5	2	11
July	.240	.333	.280	25	6	1	0	0	2	3	3	.240	.333	.280	25	6	1	0	0	2	3	3
August	.000	.000	.000	0	0	0	0	0	0	0	0	.000	.000	.000	0	0	0	0	0	0	0	0
Sept–Oct	.154	.195	.205	39	6	0	1	0	4	2	5	.237	.260	.376	93	22	2	1	3	12	3	15
Bases Empty	.183	.236	.267	131	24	2	0	3	3	8	23	.221	.266	.350	163	36	3	0	6	6	9	29
Leadoff	.173	.232	.269	52	9	2	0	1	1	3	7	.190	.250	.317	63	12	2	0	2	2	4	9
Runners On Base	.235	.293	.363	102	24	5	1	2	21	8	21	.226	.275	.339	124	28	6	1	2	26	8	25
Scoring Position	.138	.194	.224	58	8	0	1	1	16	5	14	.162	.205	.243	74	12	1	1	1	21	5	17
Late and Close	.204	.220	.347	49	10	1	0	2	4	1	10	.185	.200	.315	54	10	1	0	2	4	1	11

ROB DEER — bats right — throws right — age 32 — DET — *O/D

8-YEAR TOTALS (1984–1991)

1991	BA	OBA	SA	AB	H	2B	3B	HR	RBI	BB	SO	BA	OBA	SA	AB	H	2B	3B	HR	RBI	BB	SO
Total	.179	.314	.386	448	80	14	2	25	64	89	175	.218	.325	.437	2971	649	108	11	173	472	452	1079
vs. Left	.196	.327	.449	138	27	6	1	9	18	27	46	.254	.370	.532	897	228	37	4	68	164	167	262
vs. Right	.171	.307	.358	310	53	8	1	16	46	62	129	.203	.304	.396	2074	421	71	7	105	308	285	817
at Home	.193	.332	.399	218	42	5	2	12	31	46	87	.212	.324	.430	1478	314	48	6	87	236	231	534
on Road	.165	.296	.374	230	38	9	0	13	33	43	88	.224	.325	.444	1493	335	60	5	86	236	221	545
on Grass	.183	.316	.390	367	67	12	2	20	51	72	140	.220	.326	.436	2514	552	94	9	144	392	383	909
on Turf	.160	.303	.370	81	13	2	0	5	13	17	35	.212	.316	.442	457	97	14	2	29	80	69	170
Day Games	.170	.293	.369	141	24	4	0	8	21	25	53	.206	.320	.419	887	183	35	2	50	135	142	325
Night Games	.182	.323	.394	307	56	10	2	17	43	64	122	.224	.327	.444	2084	466	73	9	123	337	310	754
April	.197	.338	.500	66	13	3	1	5	17	14	29	.237	.349	.513	359	85	14	2	27	67	58	119
May	.176	.346	.435	85	15	1	0	7	14	22	32	.215	.333	.426	474	102	15	2	27	79	82	170
June	.194	.269	.323	93	18	3	0	3	10	10	35	.206	.291	.419	535	110	16	1	32	87	61	189
July	.181	.277	.434	83	15	3	0	6	10	11	29	.221	.326	.454	412	91	19	1	25	60	62	147
August	.111	.323	.236	72	8	1	1	2	6	23	32	.225	.335	.486	475	107	18	2	34	92	76	172
Sept–Oct	.224	.345	.408	49	11	3	0	2	7	9	18	.215	.324	.377	716	154	26	3	28	87	113	282
Bases Empty	.165	.304	.337	249	41	10	0	11	11	50	98	.208	.312	.415	1588	330	56	6	87	87	230	576
Leadoff	.123	.256	.245	106	13	4	0	3	3	19	39	.222	.320	.436	711	158	30	1	40	40	97	238
Runners On Base	.196	.325	.447	199	39	4	2	14	53	39	77	.231	.339	.462	1383	319	52	5	86	385	222	503
Scoring Position	.168	.328	.366	101	17	2	0	6	35	25	43	.233	.359	.460	776	181	27	1	49	302	158	276
Late and Close	.164	.299	.315	73	12	2	0	3	9	14	32	.200	.312	.388	464	93	17	2	22	64	68	192

DELINO DeSHIELDS — bats left — throws right — age 23 — MON — *2

1991	BA	OBA	SA	AB	H	2B	3B	HR	RBI	BB	SO		2-YEAR TOTALS (1990–1991) BA	OBA	SA	AB	H	2B	3B	HR	RBI	BB	SO
Total	.238	.347	.332	563	134	15	4	10	51	95	151		.262	.360	.361	1062	278	43	10	14	96	161	247
vs. Left	.218	.339	.277	188	41	2	0	3	14	33	58		.239	.346	.321	377	90	10	3	5	29	59	105
vs. Right	.248	.351	.360	375	93	13	4	7	37	62	93		.274	.368	.382	685	188	33	7	9	67	102	142
at Home	.265	.379	.349	238	63	9	1	3	15	44	64		.289	.390	.392	464	134	24	3	6	42	76	105
on Road	.218	.324	.320	325	71	6	3	7	36	51	87		.241	.336	.336	598	144	19	7	8	54	85	142
on Grass	.202	.314	.306	173	35	2	2	4	19	29	49		.220	.310	.316	313	69	7	4	5	25	41	81
on Turf	.254	.362	.344	390	99	13	2	6	32	66	102		.279	.380	.379	749	209	36	6	9	71	120	166
Day Games	.241	.345	.293	174	42	3	0	2	15	29	49		.264	.356	.333	318	84	14	1	2	29	46	82
Night Games	.237	.349	.350	389	92	12	4	4	36	66	102		.261	.362	.372	744	194	29	9	12	67	115	165
April	.288	.388	.438	73	21	1	2	2	6	12	15		.308	.400	.434	143	44	8	2	2	10	22	28
May	.170	.328	.277	94	16	1	0	3	5	21	25		.232	.360	.363	190	44	6	2	5	13	37	44
June	.284	.408	.392	102	29	5	0	2	17	22	31		.287	.401	.387	160	46	6	2	2	19	30	44
July	.256	.350	.289	90	23	3	0	0	3	13	20		.265	.355	.318	151	40	8	0	0	11	21	26
August	.286	.375	.381	105	30	5	1	1	11	14	22		.278	.359	.378	209	58	9	3	2	19	25	39
Sept–Oct	.152	.241	.232	99	15	0	1	2	9	13	38		.220	.306	.301	209	46	6	1	3	24	26	66
Bases Empty	.227	.342	.324	383	87	10	3	7	7	65	108		.261	.356	.361	721	188	25	7	11	11	101	170
Leadoff	.228	.335	.356	219	50	6	2	6	6	33	56		.273	.354	.377	411	112	12	5	7	7	48	83
Runners On Base	.261	.358	.350	180	47	5	1	3	44	30	43		.264	.368	.361	341	90	18	3	3	85	60	77
Scoring Position	.248	.356	.330	109	27	4	1	1	40	21	26		.266	.383	.383	214	57	16	3	1	80	45	48
Late and Close	.245	.355	.330	106	26	4	1	1	10	18	30		.237	.342	.304	207	49	7	2	1	17	32	52

MIKE DEVEREAUX — bats right — throws right — age 29 — BAL — *O

1991	BA	OBA	SA	AB	H	2B	3B	HR	RBI	BB	SO		5-YEAR TOTALS (1987–1991) BA	OBA	SA	AB	H	2B	3B	HR	RBI	BB	SO
Total	.260	.313	.431	608	158	27	10	19	59	47	115		.251	.306	.394	1461	367	63	14	39	160	116	242
vs. Left	.293	.350	.515	167	49	7	6	6	16	14	30		.260	.316	.415	578	150	26	8	16	58	48	81
vs. Right	.247	.299	.399	441	109	20	4	13	43	33	85		.246	.299	.379	883	217	37	6	23	102	68	161
at Home	.252	.302	.420	305	77	13	4	10	35	22	58		.245	.306	.387	695	170	27	6	20	79	62	118
on Road	.267	.324	.442	303	81	14	6	9	24	25	57		.257	.306	.399	766	197	36	8	19	81	54	124
on Grass	.251	.307	.430	505	127	21	9	17	53	41	97		.251	.308	.401	1217	305	49	13	36	136	101	207
on Turf	.301	.345	.437	103	31	6	1	2	6	6	18		.254	.297	.357	244	62	14	1	3	24	15	35
Day Games	.241	.301	.397	141	34	8	1	4	12	11	36		.269	.313	.413	383	103	21	2	10	39	25	62
Night Games	.266	.317	.441	467	124	19	9	15	47	36	79		.245	.303	.387	1078	264	42	12	29	121	91	180
April	.208	.300	.434	53	11	4	1	2	2	6	7		.197	.279	.321	137	27	6	1	3	11	15	16
May	.348	.402	.554	92	32	7	0	4	10	9	22		.303	.340	.474	175	53	13	1	5	19	11	29
June	.203	.261	.358	123	25	4	3	3	11	10	18		.234	.294	.369	244	57	7	4	6	23	22	37
July	.304	.363	.441	102	31	3	1	3	10	10	15		.298	.355	.455	255	76	9	2	9	35	23	42
August	.238	.271	.410	122	29	6	3	3	12	5	26		.226	.289	.355	279	63	10	4	6	30	23	49
Sept–Oct	.259	.301	.422	116	30	3	2	4	14	7	27		.245	.287	.385	371	91	18	2	10	42	22	69
Bases Empty	.266	.318	.437	414	110	18	7	13	13	31	85		.253	.306	.391	897	227	39	8	23	23	66	154
Leadoff	.266	.320	.437	229	61	12	3	7	7	17	46		.250	.308	.385	452	113	22	3	11	11	36	77
Runners On Base	.247	.302	.418	194	48	9	3	6	46	16	30		.248	.306	.397	564	140	24	6	16	137	50	88
Scoring Position	.255	.316	.451	102	26	5	3	3	39	10	18		.243	.296	.418	325	79	15	6	10	120	28	49
Late and Close	.260	.300	.365	104	27	2	0	3	9	6	20		.256	.305	.366	254	65	5	1	7	25	19	43

BILL DORAN — bats both — throws right — age 34 — CIN — 2/01

1991	BA	OBA	SA	AB	H	2B	3B	HR	RBI	BB	SO		8-YEAR TOTALS (1984–1991) BA	OBA	SA	AB	H	2B	3B	HR	RBI	BB	SO
Total	.280	.359	.374	361	101	12	2	6	35	46	39		.269	.355	.380	4052	1090	185	30	68	398	549	479
vs. Left	.262	.362	.412	80	21	4	1	2	8	13	8		.281	.376	.400	1347	379	65	7	27	136	207	139
vs. Right	.285	.358	.363	281	80	8	1	4	27	33	31		.263	.345	.370	2705	711	120	23	41	262	342	340
at Home	.296	.390	.408	169	50	8	1	3	18	26	14		.276	.372	.391	1945	537	97	20	29	199	300	217
on Road	.266	.330	.344	192	51	4	1	3	17	20	25		.262	.339	.369	2107	553	88	10	39	199	249	262
on Grass	.275	.336	.375	120	33	1	1	3	13	12	12		.276	.352	.394	1266	349	58	7	26	140	151	159
on Turf	.282	.370	.373	241	68	11	1	3	22	34	27		.266	.357	.373	2786	741	127	23	42	258	398	320
Day Games	.268	.317	.402	97	26	5	1	2	12	7	12		.267	.343	.389	1115	298	54	5	24	130	129	130
Night Games	.284	.373	.364	264	75	7	1	4	23	39	27		.270	.360	.376	2937	792	131	25	44	268	420	349
April	.333	.441	.396	48	16	3	0	0	2	10	2		.243	.329	.340	573	139	31	2	7	49	74	68
May	.071	.071	.071	14	1	0	0	0	1	0	2		.275	.357	.367	578	159	21	4	8	62	75	60
June	.375	.459	.528	72	27	3	1	2	13	12	6		.292	.379	.428	780	228	28	6	22	97	113	86
July	.253	.317	.379	95	24	3	0	3	8	9	12		.269	.344	.380	758	204	34	4	14	75	87	104
August	.183	.272	.225	71	13	1	1	0	4	9	8		.277	.374	.405	728	202	39	9	12	68	114	94
Sept–Oct	.328	.388	.410	61	20	2	0	1	7	6	9		.249	.339	.339	635	158	32	5	5	47	86	67
Bases Empty	.264	.355	.368	220	58	6	1	5	5	31	32		.259	.346	.373	2579	668	111	24	45	45	340	328
Leadoff	.292	.409	.438	96	28	2	0	4	4	19	15		.279	.356	.408	1204	336	55	11	26	26	142	137
Runners On Base	.305	.365	.383	141	43	6	1	1	30	15	7		.286	.370	.392	1473	422	74	6	23	353	209	151
Scoring Position	.272	.333	.346	81	22	4	1	0	28	9	5		.263	.367	.354	881	232	32	6	12	312	160	114
Late and Close	.244	.322	.346	78	19	3	1	1	11	10	9		.246	.344	.334	674	166	20	3	11	67	102	91

BRIAN DOWNING — bats right — throws right — age 42 — TEX — *D

1991	BA	OBA	SA	AB	H	2B	3B	HR	RBI	BB	SO	8-YEAR TOTALS (1984–1991) BA	OBA	SA	AB	H	2B	3B	HR	RBI	BB	SO
Total	.278	.377	.455	407	113	17	2	17	49	58	70	.269	.374	.450	3904	1050	185	18	162	570	589	561
vs. Left	.281	.401	.511	139	39	5	0	9	17	25	24	.278	.397	.480	1326	368	72	4	63	180	249	199
vs. Right	.276	.364	.425	268	74	12	2	8	32	33	46	.265	.361	.434	2578	682	113	14	99	390	340	362
at Home	.255	.365	.431	204	52	8	2	8	23	32	39	.267	.377	.453	1907	509	85	10	83	275	310	255
on Road	.300	.389	.478	203	61	9	0	9	26	26	31	.271	.371	.448	1997	541	100	8	79	295	279	306
on Grass	.267	.369	.434	348	93	15	2	13	41	50	64	.267	.372	.448	3291	879	150	16	138	475	500	471
on Turf	.339	.426	.576	59	20	2	0	4	8	8	6	.279	.380	.460	613	171	35	2	24	95	89	90
Day Games	.268	.342	.465	71	19	3	1	3	11	7	12	.267	.370	.460	1069	285	55	7	46	170	150	138
Night Games	.280	.384	.452	336	94	14	1	14	38	51	58	.270	.375	.446	2835	765	130	11	116	400	439	423
April	.350	.500	.500	40	14	3	0	1	5	9	6	.274	.397	.480	529	145	24	2	27	97	93	73
May	.354	.430	.585	82	29	2	1	5	11	11	12	.272	.376	.444	637	173	27	4	25	73	95	86
June	.119	.241	.194	67	8	2	0	1	7	9	16	.250	.353	.399	627	157	40	4	15	76	87	89
July	.313	.389	.488	80	25	2	0	4	10	10	14	.270	.374	.448	670	181	24	4	29	96	103	100
August	.294	.362	.529	51	15	3	0	3	8	5	9	.282	.374	.476	660	186	33	1	31	115	89	97
Sept–Oct	.253	.369	.437	87	22	5	1	3	8	14	13	.266	.371	.456	781	208	37	3	35	113	122	116
Bases Empty	.270	.346	.475	259	70	12	1	13	13	25	43	.257	.360	.442	2295	590	111	10	98	98	313	317
Leadoff	.295	.375	.545	156	46	9	0	10	10	16	23	.267	.359	.476	1105	295	59	5	54	54	136	147
Runners On Base	.291	.425	.419	148	43	5	1	4	36	33	27	.286	.393	.461	1609	460	74	8	64	472	276	244
Scoring Position	.256	.410	.400	90	23	2	1	3	33	24	17	.266	.387	.428	952	253	41	7	33	394	194	153
Late and Close	.293	.365	.400	75	22	2	0	2	14	8	11	.280	.380	.459	651	182	27	3	28	113	95	89

MARIANO DUNCAN — bats both — throws right — age 29 — CIN — 2S/O

1991	BA	OBA	SA	AB	H	2B	3B	HR	RBI	BB	SO	6-YEAR TOTALS (1985–1991) BA	OBA	SA	AB	H	2B	3B	HR	RBI	BB	SO
Total	.258	.288	.411	333	86	7	4	12	40	12	57	.252	.297	.370	2256	569	83	24	45	203	129	428
vs. Left	.314	.347	.493	140	44	6	2	5	19	7	22	.309	.345	.465	867	268	48	9	23	99	44	143
vs. Right	.218	.244	.352	193	42	1	2	7	21	5	35	.217	.267	.311	1389	301	35	15	22	104	85	285
at Home	.311	.333	.539	167	52	4	2	10	25	5	25	.259	.300	.376	1117	289	42	10	23	99	60	208
on Road	.205	.243	.283	166	34	3	2	2	15	7	32	.246	.293	.364	1139	280	41	14	22	104	69	220
on Grass	.231	.253	.352	91	21	1	2	2	12	2	16	.235	.284	.332	1266	298	44	12	18	104	76	255
on Turf	.269	.301	.434	242	65	6	2	10	28	10	41	.274	.312	.419	990	271	39	12	27	99	53	173
Day Games	.239	.295	.398	88	21	1	2	3	12	5	8	.258	.302	.386	702	181	26	11	14	65	40	130
Night Games	.265	.285	.416	245	65	6	2	9	28	7	49	.250	.294	.363	1554	388	57	13	31	138	89	298
April	.152	.200	.273	33	5	1	0	1	2	0	9	.262	.325	.402	343	90	16	1	10	28	29	63
May	.240	.267	.323	96	23	2	3	0	10	3	13	.221	.266	.290	421	93	12	4	3	30	23	89
June	.184	.262	.289	38	7	1	0	1	2	4	6	.243	.279	.345	345	84	13	2	6	25	14	55
July	.250	.240	.375	24	6	0	0	1	3	0	6	.247	.288	.377	332	82	15	5	6	28	17	65
August	.439	.452	.756	41	18	2	1	3	11	1	9	.310	.342	.464	390	121	13	7	11	42	18	69
Sept–Oct	.267	.292	.455	101	27	1	0	6	12	4	14	.233	.283	.353	425	99	14	5	9	50	28	87
Bases Empty	.243	.284	.398	206	50	6	1	8	8	11	40	.247	.297	.366	1414	349	54	12	30	30	91	280
Leadoff	.183	.227	.310	71	13	3	0	2	2	3	13	.216	.275	.308	679	147	19	5	11	11	48	137
Runners On Base	.283	.293	.433	127	36	1	3	4	32	1	17	.261	.295	.378	842	220	29	12	15	173	38	148
Scoring Position	.342	.346	.507	73	25	0	3	2	28	0	9	.251	.291	.365	499	125	14	8	9	155	29	94
Late and Close	.231	.245	.269	52	12	0	1	0	6	1	13	.259	.312	.344	355	92	9	3	5	35	24	78

SHAWON DUNSTON — bats right — throws right — age 29 — CHN — *S

1991	BA	OBA	SA	AB	H	2B	3B	HR	RBI	BB	SO	7-YEAR TOTALS (1985–1991) BA	OBA	SA	AB	H	2B	3B	HR	RBI	BB	SO
Total	.260	.292	.407	492	128	22	7	12	50	23	64	.258	.288	.395	3257	840	154	37	73	340	134	569
vs. Left	.230	.269	.366	191	44	7	2	5	18	10	23	.258	.281	.416	954	246	42	14	27	110	33	135
vs. Right	.279	.307	.432	301	84	15	5	7	32	13	41	.258	.290	.386	2303	594	112	23	46	230	101	434
at Home	.295	.329	.451	237	70	10	3	7	26	10	30	.272	.304	.415	1626	443	82	18	38	173	69	279
on Road	.227	.258	.365	255	58	12	4	5	24	13	34	.243	.271	.375	1631	397	72	19	35	167	65	290
on Grass	.280	.312	.440	339	95	14	5	10	39	15	45	.264	.294	.409	2281	603	113	24	56	247	92	403
on Turf	.216	.248	.333	153	33	8	2	2	11	8	19	.243	.274	.364	976	237	41	13	17	93	42	166
Day Games	.285	.312	.438	235	67	11	2	7	25	9	32	.267	.298	.411	1907	510	96	15	49	210	81	332
Night Games	.237	.275	.377	257	61	11	5	5	25	14	32	.244	.273	.373	1350	330	58	22	24	130	53	237
April	.235	.286	.353	68	16	2	0	2	7	5	6	.235	.270	.374	468	110	23	3	12	37	23	69
May	.216	.245	.409	88	19	3	1	4	8	2	15	.269	.303	.427	599	161	34	5	17	66	27	114
June	.255	.282	.398	98	25	4	2	2	12	3	13	.279	.306	.440	527	147	28	6	15	77	18	101
July	.184	.241	.276	76	14	4	0	1	5	6	10	.253	.284	.386	451	114	18	6	10	48	21	79
August	.427	.438	.610	82	35	6	3	1	11	4	13	.270	.291	.392	548	148	23	10	8	58	17	101
Sept–Oct	.237	.262	.375	80	19	3	1	2	7	3	7	.241	.272	.354	664	160	28	7	11	54	28	105
Bases Empty	.268	.309	.421	299	80	15	2	9	9	15	37	.258	.285	.393	1953	504	89	21	44	44	67	364
Leadoff	.292	.338	.446	130	38	8	0	4	4	7	18	.265	.293	.393	859	228	41	9	17	17	30	149
Runners On Base	.249	.268	.383	193	48	7	5	3	41	8	27	.258	.291	.399	1304	336	65	16	29	296	67	205
Scoring Position	.271	.288	.402	107	29	3	4	3	35	7	15	.259	.303	.406	734	190	32	11	18	265	56	126
Late and Close	.357	.395	.527	112	40	6	2	3	13	5	15	.264	.295	.369	580	153	21	5	10	61	24	110

LENNY DYKSTRA — bats left — throws left — age 29 — PHI — O

7-YEAR TOTALS (1985–1991)

1991	BA	OBA	SA	AB	H	2B	3B	HR	RBI	BB	SO		BA	OBA	SA	AB	H	2B	3B	HR	RBI	BB	SO
Total	.297	.391	.427	246	73	13	5	3	12	37	20		.283	.361	.410	2874	812	171	28	46	244	344	310
vs. Left	.315	.422	.511	92	29	6	3	2	6	16	13		.260	.346	.346	743	193	33	8	5	56	93	103
vs. Right	.286	.371	.377	154	44	7	2	1	6	21	7		.290	.367	.432	2131	619	138	20	41	188	251	207
at Home	.322	.424	.492	118	38	7	2	3	6	20	10		.292	.377	.431	1365	399	81	12	28	115	179	138
on Road	.273	.359	.367	128	35	6	3	0	6	17	10		.274	.348	.390	1509	413	90	16	18	129	165	172
on Grass	.272	.366	.346	81	22	4	1	0	4	12	9		.275	.348	.401	1509	415	92	16	22	136	164	176
on Turf	.309	.403	.467	165	51	9	4	3	8	25	11		.291	.376	.419	1365	397	79	12	24	108	180	134
Day Games	.236	.327	.270	89	21	3	0	0	1	12	6		.280	.357	.426	996	279	64	9	21	79	116	111
Night Games	.331	.426	.516	157	52	10	5	3	11	25	14		.284	.364	.401	1878	533	107	19	25	165	228	199
April	.317	.434	.524	82	26	7	2	2	6	17	2		.318	.402	.503	352	112	26	6	9	37	48	34
May	.214	.353	.214	14	3	0	0	0	0	3	0		.307	.380	.432	414	127	25	3	7	33	46	40
June	.000	.000	.000	0	0	0	0	0	0	0	0		.314	.384	.439	433	136	26	5	6	34	49	52
July	.321	.377	.321	56	18	0	0	0	1	4	6		.286	.368	.385	595	170	33	4	6	52	75	61
August	.277	.364	.436	94	26	6	3	1	5	13	12		.247	.321	.377	648	160	38	8	10	47	66	73
Sept–Oct	.000	.000	.000	0	0	0	0	0	0	0	0		.248	.339	.366	432	107	23	2	8	41	60	50
Bases Empty	.307	.386	.425	179	55	9	3	2	2	23	13		.279	.353	.405	2003	558	122	19	31	31	219	216
Leadoff	.303	.397	.440	109	33	5	2	2	2	17	7		.266	.347	.407	1221	325	69	14	25	25	144	136
Runners On Base	.269	.402	.433	67	18	4	2	1	10	14	7		.292	.380	.420	871	254	49	9	15	213	125	94
Scoring Position	.250	.455	.313	32	8	0	1	0	7	12	4		.286	.396	.389	517	148	29	6	4	183	98	62
Late and Close	.314	.435	.451	51	16	4	0	1	3	11	6		.293	.392	.385	447	131	27	1	4	48	73	51

KEVIN ELSTER — bats right — throws right — age 28 — NYN — *S

6-YEAR TOTALS (1986–1991)

1991	BA	OBA	SA	AB	H	2B	3B	HR	RBI	BB	SO		BA	OBA	SA	AB	H	2B	3B	HR	RBI	BB	SO
Total	.241	.318	.351	348	84	16	2	6	36	40	53		.224	.289	.345	1566	351	75	6	34	174	142	240
vs. Left	.297	.360	.373	158	47	9	0	1	14	16	16		.256	.321	.353	589	151	31	1	8	48	57	66
vs. Right	.195	.284	.332	190	37	7	2	5	22	.24	37		.205	.269	.340	977	200	44	5	26	126	85	174
at Home	.265	.335	.376	181	48	11	0	3	14	19	24		.221	.283	.334	797	176	38	2	16	88	67	127
on Road	.216	.300	.323	167	36	5	2	3	22	21	29		.228	.295	.356	769	175	37	4	18	86	75	113
on Grass	.267	.335	.375	232	62	14	1	3	21	24	29		.227	.286	.347	1086	247	55	3	23	127	90	164
on Turf	.190	.286	.302	116	22	2	1	3	15	16	24		.217	.293	.340	480	104	20	3	11	47	52	76
Day Games	.234	.308	.404	94	22	2	1	4	11	10	14		.200	.258	.327	529	106	24	2	13	68	41	72
Night Games	.244	.322	.331	254	62	14	1	2	25	30	39		.236	.304	.354	1037	245	51	4	21	106	101	168
April	.308	.378	.538	39	12	1	1	2	8	5	4		.216	.278	.349	232	50	10	3	5	27	21	36
May	.238	.340	.333	42	10	1	0	1	5	7	6		.220	.302	.325	268	59	7	0	7	29	32	43
June	.194	.250	.284	67	13	6	0	0	9	5	11		.216	.274	.345	296	64	23	0	5	42	23	49
July	.176	.263	.275	51	9	2	0	1	2	5	11		.218	.269	.351	271	59	13	1	7	33	17	43
August	.297	.357	.422	64	19	2	0	2	7	6	10		.259	.319	.364	228	59	9	0	5	21	21	32
Sept–Oct	.247	.333	.318	85	21	4	1	0	5	12	11		.221	.294	.339	271	60	13	2	5	22	28	37
Bases Empty	.230	.313	.346	191	44	8	1	4	4	23	31		.199	.256	.312	898	179	38	3	19	19	64	139
Leadoff	.222	.329	.286	63	14	1	0	1	1	10	8		.215	.265	.339	354	76	10	2	10	10	21	49
Runners On Base	.255	.324	.357	157	40	8	1	2	32	17	22		.257	.330	.389	668	172	37	3	15	155	78	101
Scoring Position	.271	.359	.412	85	23	4	1	2	31	13	10		.249	.341	.377	385	96	19	3	8	136	62	70
Late and Close	.140	.290	.140	57	8	0	0	0	3	12	12		.181	.259	.261	249	45	8	0	4	18	24	42

ALVARO ESPINOZA — bats right — throws right — age 30 — NYA — *S/3P

6-YEAR TOTALS (1985–1991)

1991	BA	OBA	SA	AB	H	2B	3B	HR	RBI	BB	SO		BA	OBA	SA	AB	H	2B	3B	HR	RBI	BB	SO
Total	.256	.282	.344	480	123	23	2	5	33	16	57		.254	.280	.315	1523	387	61	5	7	104	48	190
vs. Left	.261	.294	.342	161	42	10	0	1	15	7	11		.308	.342	.362	494	152	19	1	2	38	25	40
vs. Right	.254	.276	.345	319	81	13	2	4	18	9	46		.228	.249	.292	1029	235	42	4	5	66	23	150
at Home	.248	.273	.327	254	63	12	1	2	14	8	30		.250	.276	.309	776	194	32	4	2	50	25	85
on Road	.265	.292	.363	226	60	11	1	3	19	8	27		.258	.284	.320	747	193	29	1	5	54	23	105
on Grass	.258	.285	.342	403	104	20	1	4	26	15	49		.253	.281	.314	1237	313	52	4	5	82	44	148
on Turf	.247	.266	.351	77	19	3	1	1	7	1	8		.259	.273	.318	286	74	9	1	2	22	4	42
Day Games	.248	.293	.355	141	35	4	1	3	10	8	16		.235	.270	.291	443	104	12	2	3	36	19	50
Night Games	.260	.277	.339	339	88	19	1	2	23	8	41		.262	.284	.324	1080	283	49	3	4	68	29	140
April	.367	.404	.531	49	18	6	1	0	7	3	3		.282	.321	.351	174	49	10	1	0	18	10	23
May	.193	.221	.253	83	16	5	0	0	2	3	10		.211	.238	.242	227	48	7	0	0	11	8	24
June	.268	.302	.366	82	22	2	0	2	6	4	11		.259	.282	.342	243	63	9	1	3	13	8	27
July	.273	.314	.379	66	18	2	1	1	4	4	6		.278	.311	.352	227	63	7	2	2	15	10	28
August	.261	.275	.364	88	23	3	0	2	8	0	9		.257	.269	.306	343	88	9	1	2	28	3	39
Sept–Oct	.232	.243	.277	112	26	5	0	0	6	2	18		.246	.273	.307	309	76	19	0	0	19	9	49
Bases Empty	.245	.270	.340	294	72	12	2	4	4	9	35		.235	.264	.301	926	218	35	4	6	6	32	125
Leadoff	.250	.263	.348	112	28	5	0	2	2	2	9		.227	.249	.291	344	78	14	1	2	2	9	38
Runners On Base	.274	.301	.349	186	51	11	0	1	29	7	22		.283	.304	.335	597	169	26	1	1	98	16	65
Scoring Position	.250	.280	.340	100	25	6	0	1	27	4	12		.269	.294	.327	309	83	13	1	1	93	11	33
Late and Close	.200	.231	.240	75	15	3	0	0	3	3	11		.249	.284	.300	213	53	6	1	1	14	11	22

DWIGHT EVANS — bats right — throws right — age 41 — BAL — OD

1991	BA	OBA	SA	AB	H	2B	3B	HR	RBI	BB	SO		BA	OBA	SA	AB	H	2B	3B	HR	RBI	BB	SO
Total	.270	.393	.378	270	73	9	1	6	38	54	54		.279	.385	.478	4110	1146	221	27	181	714	709	745
vs. Left	.308	.468	.364	107	33	3	0	1	10	32	15		.301	.424	.500	1141	344	57	8	51	189	246	180
vs. Right	.245	.339	.387	163	40	6	1	5	28	22	39		.270	.369	.470	2969	802	164	19	130	525	463	565
at Home	.259	.373	.370	135	35	3	0	4	20	24	25		.288	.390	.491	1982	570	127	17	81	351	336	336
on Road	.281	.413	.385	135	38	6	1	2	18	30	29		.271	.379	.465	2128	576	94	10	100	363	373	409
on Grass	.259	.381	.343	239	62	6	1	4	34	46	48		.278	.385	.471	3483	970	187	24	145	602	607	623
on Turf	.355	.487	.645	31	11	3	0	2	4	8	6		.281	.382	.517	627	176	34	3	36	112	102	122
Day Games	.245	.479	.306	49	12	1	1	0	5	21	11		.281	.389	.500	1347	379	73	9	68	234	236	230
Night Games	.276	.370	.394	221	61	8	0	6	33	33	43		.278	.383	.467	2763	767	148	18	113	480	473	515
April	.300	.390	.400	50	15	2	0	1	8	8	14		.247	.371	.400	563	139	29	3	17	78	113	100
May	.233	.397	.300	60	14	1	0	1	9	17	16		.261	.376	.425	702	183	42	2	23	109	129	135
June	.310	.375	.552	29	9	2	1	1	6	3	0		.298	.395	.497	724	216	37	7	31	142	121	123
July	.267	.450	.400	30	8	1	0	1	5	9	8		.289	.382	.496	629	182	31	3	31	108	92	127
August	.270	.357	.378	37	10	1	0	1	4	5	7		.296	.384	.551	740	219	48	9	41	134	103	136
Sept–Oct	.266	.390	.344	64	17	2	0	1	6	12	9		.275	.395	.480	752	207	34	3	38	143	151	124
Bases Empty	.232	.345	.318	151	35	4	0	3	3	25	31		.268	.375	.464	2134	572	107	13	95	95	354	391
Leadoff	.176	.309	.235	68	12	1	0	1	1	13	12		.259	.352	.458	948	246	50	3	44	44	130	173
Runners On Base	.319	.450	.454	119	38	5	1	3	35	29	23		.290	.394	.493	1976	574	114	14	86	619	355	354
Scoring Position	.359	.511	.547	64	23	3	0	3	32	21	10		.298	.412	.497	1088	324	59	10	46	521	237	200
Late and Close	.221	.341	.324	68	15	1	0	2	8	13	11		.277	.373	.496	678	188	26	1	40	136	102	121

MIKE FELDER — bats both — throws right — age 31 — SF — *O/32

1991	BA	OBA	SA	AB	H	2B	3B	HR	RBI	BB	SO		BA	OBA	SA	AB	H	2B	3B	HR	RBI	BB	SO
Total	.264	.325	.328	348	92	10	6	0	18	30	31		.251	.307	.324	1480	372	37	22	9	117	121	142
vs. Left	.276	.321	.343	105	29	5	1	0	4	7	8		.274	.322	.344	468	128	10	7	3	37	36	37
vs. Right	.259	.326	.321	243	63	5	5	0	14	23	23		.241	.300	.315	1012	244	27	15	6	80	85	105
at Home	.286	.337	.351	168	48	5	3	0	10	13	13		.249	.315	.324	698	174	14	13	4	56	68	62
on Road	.244	.313	.306	180	44	5	3	0	8	17	18		.253	.299	.325	782	198	23	9	5	61	53	80
on Grass	.289	.342	.352	270	78	7	5	0	17	21	26		.250	.303	.324	1230	307	27	19	9	100	98	123
on Turf	.179	.264	.244	78	14	3	1	0	1	9	5		.260	.324	.324	250	65	10	3	0	17	23	19
Day Games	.237	.304	.296	135	32	4	2	0	9	12	13		.229	.287	.300	480	110	11	4	5	34	39	50
Night Games	.282	.338	.347	213	60	6	4	0	9	18	18		.262	.316	.336	1000	262	26	18	4	83	82	92
April	.414	.469	.448	29	12	1	0	0	1	3	4		.277	.346	.330	112	31	2	2	0	9	14	14
May	.307	.333	.446	101	31	4	5	0	8	4	13		.244	.278	.317	205	50	5	5	0	15	9	22
June	.236	.320	.258	89	21	0	1	0	1	10	3		.273	.332	.342	330	90	10	5	1	23	30	25
July	.193	.258	.246	57	11	3	0	0	6	5	4		.222	.261	.290	248	55	6	1	3	19	13	22
August	.188	.235	.188	16	3	0	0	0	0	1	0		.223	.269	.302	179	40	4	2	2	16	12	16
Sept–Oct	.250	.333	.286	56	14	2	0	0	2	7	7		.261	.330	.342	406	106	10	7	3	35	43	43
Bases Empty	.248	.294	.309	246	61	7	4	0	0	16	25		.245	.295	.315	939	230	26	11	6	6	65	92
Leadoff	.242	.288	.281	153	37	4	1	0	0	10	19		.248	.298	.317	499	124	16	3	4	4	44	44
Runners On Base	.304	.393	.373	102	31	3	2	0	18	14	6		.262	.326	.340	541	142	11	11	3	111	56	50
Scoring Position	.279	.371	.361	61	17	3	1	0	17	9	3		.249	.317	.332	325	81	9	6	2	103	38	29
Late and Close	.203	.346	.219	64	13	1	0	0	6	13	7		.236	.313	.309	275	65	6	4	2	30	31	30

FELIX FERMIN — bats right — throws right — age 29 — CLE — *S

1991	BA	OBA	SA	AB	H	2B	3B	HR	RBI	BB	SO		BA	OBA	SA	AB	H	2B	3B	HR	RBI	BB	SO
Total	.262	.307	.302	424	111	13	2	0	31	26	27		.253	.305	.288	1477	373	35	7	1	98	105	95
vs. Left	.281	.341	.314	121	34	4	0	0	8	10	6		.258	.319	.287	450	116	9	2	0	32	41	23
vs. Right	.254	.293	.297	303	77	9	2	0	23	16	21		.250	.299	.288	1027	257	26	5	1	66	64	72
at Home	.290	.339	.348	210	61	8	2	0	20	16	11		.265	.320	.317	735	195	25	5	1	56	56	41
on Road	.234	.274	.257	214	50	5	0	0	11	10	16		.240	.290	.259	742	178	10	2	0	42	49	54
on Grass	.264	.313	.306	363	96	11	2	0	29	24	22		.245	.297	.281	1151	282	30	4	1	82	81	69
on Turf	.246	.270	.279	61	15	2	0	0	2	2	5		.279	.334	.313	326	91	5	3	0	16	24	26
Day Games	.236	.276	.260	127	30	3	0	0	6	7	12		.262	.311	.292	439	115	8	1	1	25	28	35
Night Games	.273	.320	.320	297	81	10	2	0	25	19	15		.249	.303	.286	1038	258	27	6	0	73	77	60
April	.125	.176	.125	32	4	0	0	0	0	2	3		.217	.284	.264	129	28	1	1	1	10	12	7
May	.281	.319	.359	64	18	3	1	0	7	2	2		.252	.297	.296	250	63	7	2	0	15	15	16
June	.260	.297	.292	96	25	3	0	0	4	5	5		.250	.296	.280	268	67	8	0	0	12	18	15
July	.286	.341	.345	84	24	3	1	0	7	7	5		.238	.284	.267	277	66	6	1	0	18	16	19
August	.258	.306	.281	89	23	2	0	0	10	6	8		.280	.330	.324	250	70	9	1	0	27	18	12
Sept–Oct	.288	.333	.322	59	17	2	0	0	3	4	4		.261	.326	.287	303	79	4	2	0	16	26	26
Bases Empty	.251	.287	.285	239	60	8	0	0	0	11	16		.257	.305	.293	861	221	18	5	1	1	57	57
Leadoff	.255	.291	.265	98	25	1	0	0	0	5	5		.264	.316	.298	356	94	5	2	1	1	26	20
Runners On Base	.276	.332	.324	185	51	5	2	0	31	15	11		.247	.305	.281	616	152	17	2	0	97	48	38
Scoring Position	.278	.342	.340	97	27	2	2	0	29	9	6		.228	.290	.265	359	82	9	2	0	93	29	26
Late and Close	.185	.233	.198	81	15	1	0	0	4	5	6		.235	.304	.255	204	48	4	0	0	9	18	14

TONY FERNANDEZ — bats both — throws right — age 30 — SD — *S

1991	BA	OBA	SA	AB	H	2B	3B	HR	RBI	BB	SO	8-YEAR TOTALS (1984–1991) BA	OBA	SA	AB	H	2B	3B	HR	RBI	BB	SO
Total	.271	.336	.358	558	151	27	5	4	38	55	74	.287	.338	.394	4476	1284	218	65	44	439	338	416
vs. Left	.253	.317	.335	182	46	7	1	2	13	17	22	.277	.336	.376	1454	403	66	16	15	135	131	130
vs. Right	.279	.345	.370	376	105	20	4	2	25	38	52	.292	.339	.403	3022	881	152	49	29	304	207	286
at Home	.292	.362	.365	271	79	13	2	1	17	30	38	.291	.345	.401	2180	635	117	39	15	217	174	188
on Road	.251	.310	.352	287	72	14	3	3	21	25	36	.283	.331	.387	2296	649	101	26	29	222	164	228
on Grass	.276	.345	.361	402	111	16	3	4	26	43	59	.283	.333	.383	1961	555	82	20	25	179	142	209
on Turf	.256	.310	.353	156	40	11	2	0	12	12	15	.290	.342	.402	2515	729	136	45	19	260	196	207
Day Games	.255	.333	.393	145	37	5	3	3	16	17	27	.281	.332	.386	1436	404	69	15	17	132	108	129
Night Games	.276	.336	.346	413	114	22	2	1	22	38	47	.289	.341	.398	3040	880	149	50	27	307	230	287
April	.261	.309	.318	88	23	3	1	0	7	6	18	.260	.309	.334	500	130	11	7	4	50	31	61
May	.278	.366	.417	108	30	6	3	1	5	15	14	.269	.333	.373	754	203	40	7	8	67	75	79
June	.327	.394	.408	98	32	5	0	1	3	11	10	.316	.373	.451	788	249	51	14	9	86	70	60
July	.153	.228	.208	72	11	4	0	0	4	7	10	.254	.297	.354	775	197	36	10	7	70	49	77
August	.282	.328	.400	110	31	5	1	2	12	8	13	.309	.356	.434	834	258	41	18	9	91	53	68
Sept–Oct	.293	.356	.341	82	24	4	0	0	7	8	9	.299	.347	.394	825	247	39	9	7	75	60	71
Bases Empty	.249	.319	.335	346	86	17	2	3	3	36	50	.280	.332	.381	2762	774	124	38	26	26	204	273
Leadoff	.298	.365	.395	114	34	6	1	1	1	12	11	.274	.329	.374	1290	354	62	15	12	12	97	122
Runners On Base	.307	.362	.396	212	65	10	3	1	35	19	24	.298	.347	.415	1714	510	94	27	18	413	134	143
Scoring Position	.308	.364	.402	117	36	4	2	1	33	11	17	.311	.368	.430	971	302	63	16	7	371	94	98
Late and Close	.273	.326	.318	88	24	4	0	0	6	7	12	.314	.364	.425	685	215	30	14	6	80	55	54

CECIL FIELDER — bats right — throws right — age 29 — DET — *1D

1991	BA	OBA	SA	AB	H	2B	3B	HR	RBI	BB	SO	6-YEAR TOTALS (1985–1991) BA	OBA	SA	AB	H	2B	3B	HR	RBI	BB	SO
Total	.261	.347	.513	624	163	25	0	44	133	78	151	.261	.346	.527	1703	445	69	3	126	349	214	477
vs. Left	.296	.399	.597	159	47	9	0	13	31	25	29	.289	.376	.602	744	215	37	2	64	155	101	194
vs. Right	.249	.328	.484	465	116	16	0	31	102	53	122	.240	.323	.469	959	230	32	1	62	194	113	283
at Home	.256	.348	.561	305	78	12	0	27	75	41	72	.265	.356	.569	809	214	34	1	70	176	111	222
on Road	.266	.345	.467	319	85	13	0	17	58	37	79	.258	.338	.490	894	231	35	2	56	173	103	255
on Grass	.260	.352	.510	524	136	20	0	37	111	72	127	.256	.351	.513	1204	308	47	1	87	248	170	332
on Turf	.270	.318	.530	100	27	5	0	7	22	6	24	.275	.336	.561	499	137	22	2	39	101	44	145
Day Games	.223	.323	.477	197	44	8	0	14	45	26	41	.209	.305	.454	527	110	16	1	37	103	69	152
Night Games	.279	.358	.529	427	119	17	0	30	88	52	110	.285	.365	.560	1176	335	53	2	89	246	145	325
April	.292	.370	.458	72	21	3	0	3	18	6	18	.226	.297	.452	221	50	8	0	14	50	19	55
May	.238	.350	.485	101	24	4	0	7	18	18	27	.298	.406	.615	262	78	17	0	22	52	46	78
June	.292	.385	.575	106	31	6	0	8	24	15	26	.297	.378	.605	276	82	11	1	24	69	36	76
July	.267	.313	.610	105	28	3	0	11	25	6	21	.271	.351	.564	291	79	11	1	24	54	34	79
August	.223	.299	.463	121	27	8	0	7	26	13	31	.240	.340	.466	313	75	15	1	18	60	46	91
Sept–Oct	.269	.371	.479	119	32	1	0	8	22	20	28	.238	.306	.471	340	81	7	0	24	64	33	98
Bases Empty	.236	.303	.433	326	77	10	0	18	18	30	84	.249	.319	.508	888	221	30	1	66	66	87	252
Leadoff	.213	.280	.419	160	34	3	0	10	10	14	41	.262	.318	.542	413	108	15	1	33	33	31	108
Runners On Base	.289	.392	.601	298	86	15	0	26	115	48	67	.275	.374	.548	815	224	39	2	60	283	127	225
Scoring Position	.286	.400	.560	175	50	9	0	13	88	34	45	.263	.386	.504	460	121	23	2	28	212	93	135
Late and Close	.232	.339	.354	99	23	3	0	3	19	16	26	.212	.329	.323	269	57	6	0	8	36	45	88

STEVE FINLEY — bats left — throws left — age 27 — HOU — *O

1991	BA	OBA	SA	AB	H	2B	3B	HR	RBI	BB	SO	3-YEAR TOTALS (1989–1991) BA	OBA	SA	AB	H	2B	3B	HR	RBI	BB	SO
Total	.285	.331	.406	596	170	28	10	8	54	42	65	.269	.316	.363	1277	343	49	16	13	116	89	148
vs. Left	.246	.286	.306	183	45	6	1	1	16	11	25	.218	.251	.278	335	73	9	1	3	31	15	47
vs. Right	.303	.351	.450	413	125	22	9	7	38	31	40	.287	.339	.393	942	270	40	15	10	85	74	101
at Home	.273	.309	.377	300	82	15	8	0	20	17	36	.248	.291	.328	661	164	28	11	1	44	41	87
on Road	.297	.353	.436	296	88	13	2	8	34	25	29	.291	.342	.399	616	179	21	5	12	72	48	61
on Grass	.328	.367	.475	183	60	10	1	5	19	12	21	.272	.317	.361	771	210	30	7	8	73	51	95
on Turf	.266	.316	.375	413	110	18	9	3	35	30	44	.263	.313	.366	506	133	19	9	5	43	38	53
Day Games	.297	.342	.448	145	43	11	1	3	15	11	17	.244	.294	.328	320	78	16	1	3	23	23	29
Night Games	.282	.328	.392	451	127	17	9	5	39	31	48	.277	.323	.374	957	265	33	15	10	93	66	119
April	.203	.268	.266	64	13	2	1	0	3	6	8	.241	.306	.331	145	35	4	3	1	13	14	16
May	.350	.391	.560	100	35	8	2	3	12	8	9	.262	.310	.398	221	58	13	4	3	22	17	27
June	.270	.342	.360	100	27	3	0	2	10	11	9	.258	.324	.342	225	58	10	0	3	18	20	20
July	.347	.380	.495	95	33	5	3	1	10	4	7	.312	.355	.402	199	62	6	3	2	18	12	25
August	.265	.308	.389	113	30	5	3	1	14	7	17	.283	.322	.372	191	54	8	3	1	20	12	22
Sept–Oct	.258	.290	.339	124	32	5	1	1	7	6	15	.257	.288	.334	296	76	8	3	3	25	14	38
Bases Empty	.296	.339	.417	412	122	19	8	5	5	25	46	.276	.323	.374	815	225	34	11	8	8	53	95
Leadoff	.348	.376	.498	201	70	11	5	3	3	8	24	.289	.330	.397	388	112	19	7	3	3	23	49
Runners On Base	.261	.314	.380	184	48	9	2	3	49	17	19	.255	.304	.342	462	118	15	5	5	108	36	53
Scoring Position	.311	.379	.485	103	32	5	2	2	46	15	12	.279	.340	.401	262	73	9	4	5	104	29	41
Late and Close	.281	.327	.315	89	25	3	0	0	12	7	11	.262	.311	.305	187	49	5	0	1	21	14	28

CARLTON FISK — bats right — throws right — age 45 — CHA — *CD1

8-YEAR TOTALS (1984–1991)

1991	BA	OBA	SA	AB	H	2B	3B	HR	RBI	BB	SO	BA	OBA	SA	AB	H	2B	3B	HR	RBI	BB	SO
Total	.241	.299	.413	460	111	25	0	18	74	32	86	.253	.324	.449	3353	849	155	6	163	541	306	564
vs. Left	.229	.274	.376	157	36	8	0	5	28	9	24	.260	.327	.467	1198	312	62	3	60	201	114	176
vs. Right	.248	.312	.432	303	75	17	0	13	46	23	62	.249	.322	.439	2155	537	93	3	103	340	192	388
at Home	.236	.295	.408	233	55	13	0	9	39	18	41	.250	.322	.427	1661	416	83	3	68	256	164	270
on Road	.247	.304	.419	227	56	12	0	9	35	14	45	.256	.325	.470	1692	433	72	3	95	285	142	294
on Grass	.247	.306	.414	396	98	24	0	14	61	27	71	.254	.323	.447	2832	718	131	6	135	451	259	476
on Turf	.203	.257	.406	64	13	1	0	4	13	5	15	.251	.327	.459	521	131	24	0	28	90	47	88
Day Games	.238	.273	.476	84	20	5	0	5	17	4	16	.231	.305	.423	749	173	30	0	38	115	73	129
Night Games	.242	.305	.399	376	91	20	0	13	57	28	70	.260	.329	.456	2604	676	125	6	125	426	233	435
April	.333	.394	.383	60	20	3	0	0	7	4	7	.271	.339	.445	431	117	22	1	17	59	37	69
May	.237	.319	.350	80	19	6	0	1	8	9	18	.223	.313	.382	497	111	17	1	20	79	57	102
June	.226	.286	.429	84	19	5	0	4	14	6	15	.240	.306	.407	526	126	17	1	23	82	43	98
July	.242	.299	.371	62	15	2	0	2	10	5	15	.248	.312	.475	516	128	25	1	30	83	43	76
August	.287	.326	.563	87	25	6	0	6	19	3	13	.273	.329	.501	704	192	37	2	40	122	54	115
Sept–Oct	.149	.202	.356	87	13	3	0	5	16	5	18	.258	.338	.458	679	175	37	0	33	116	72	104
Bases Empty	.236	.292	.356	225	53	12	0	5	5	14	44	.250	.313	.453	1826	456	81	3	95	95	140	311
Leadoff	.229	.283	.343	105	24	6	0	2	2	4	22	.254	.320	.467	735	187	38	2	38	38	55	126
Runners On Base	.247	.306	.468	235	58	13	0	13	69	18	42	.257	.335	.443	1527	393	74	3	68	446	166	253
Scoring Position	.250	.311	.441	136	34	8	0	6	53	10	25	.261	.353	.425	876	229	41	3	32	355	122	156
Late and Close	.242	.317	.484	91	22	4	0	6	18	8	22	.262	.334	.470	592	155	29	2	30	111	58	126

SCOTT FLETCHER — bats right — throws right — age 34 — CHA — 2/3

8-YEAR TOTALS (1984–1991)

1991	BA	OBA	SA	AB	H	2B	3B	HR	RBI	BB	SO	BA	OBA	SA	AB	H	2B	3B	HR	RBI	BB	SO
Total	.206	.262	.266	248	51	10	1	1	28	17	26	.263	.336	.333	3693	973	155	23	19	353	377	401
vs. Left	.188	.248	.218	101	19	3	0	0	5	6	13	.284	.360	.358	1329	378	57	7	9	108	151	123
vs. Right	.218	.272	.299	147	32	7	1	1	23	11	13	.252	.322	.319	2364	595	98	16	10	245	226	278
at Home	.200	.285	.252	115	23	4	1	0	14	12	10	.276	.348	.348	1811	500	77	13	9	189	185	178
on Road	.211	.241	.278	133	28	6	0	1	14	5	16	.251	.324	.319	1882	473	78	10	10	164	192	223
on Grass	.211	.272	.272	228	48	9	1	1	25	17	23	.267	.339	.337	3074	820	130	17	17	297	313	331
on Turf	.150	.143	.200	20	3	1	0	0	3	0	3	.247	.320	.317	619	153	25	6	2	56	64	70
Day Games	.220	.244	.293	82	18	1	1	1	8	3	11	.266	.339	.340	883	235	39	7	4	79	96	94
Night Games	.199	.270	.253	166	33	9	0	0	20	14	15	.263	.335	.331	2810	738	116	16	15	274	281	307
April	.333	.419	.519	54	18	5	1	1	14	7	3	.257	.353	.328	482	124	15	5	3	56	67	59
May	.152	.209	.165	79	12	1	0	0	3	6	10	.255	.322	.317	703	179	24	7	2	61	69	81
June	.091	.211	.121	33	3	1	0	0	0	4	4	.271	.352	.359	616	167	33	6	3	54	69	66
July	.188	.188	.250	16	3	1	0	0	2	0	2	.290	.342	.363	600	174	32	0	4	56	46	50
August	.258	.258	.290	31	8	1	0	0	5	0	2	.262	.329	.314	641	168	22	1	3	63	59	71
Sept–Oct	.200	.211	.229	35	7	1	0	0	4	0	5	.247	.324	.323	651	161	29	4	4	63	67	74
Bases Empty	.179	.229	.199	156	28	3	0	0	8	8	18	.243	.319	.310	2248	547	88	13	12	12	228	252
Leadoff	.156	.194	.188	64	10	2	0	0	0	3	10	.222	.304	.290	808	179	27	2	8	8	88	86
Runners On Base	.250	.314	.380	92	23	7	1	1	28	9	8	.295	.362	.370	1445	426	67	10	7	341	149	149
Scoring Position	.254	.324	.365	63	16	7	0	0	25	7	7	.294	.367	.366	866	255	43	5	3	319	103	103
Late and Close	.241	.297	.259	58	14	1	0	0	6	3	5	.237	.317	.279	570	135	17	2	1	64	61	81

JULIO FRANCO — bats right — throws right — age 34 — TEX — *2

8-YEAR TOTALS (1984–1991)

1991	BA	OBA	SA	AB	H	2B	3B	HR	RBI	BB	SO	BA	OBA	SA	AB	H	2B	3B	HR	RBI	BB	SO
Total	.341	.408	.474	589	201	27	3	15	78	65	78	.306	.367	.414	4719	1444	217	32	76	588	455	565
vs. Left	.368	.424	.626	155	57	10	3	8	29	16	19	.322	.388	.490	1306	421	83	11	38	176	145	151
vs. Right	.332	.402	.419	434	144	17	0	7	49	49	59	.300	.358	.385	3413	1023	134	21	38	412	310	414
at Home	.344	.409	.480	294	101	13	3	7	40	33	42	.323	.383	.433	2319	749	117	15	36	296	229	251
on Road	.339	.407	.468	295	100	14	0	8	38	32	36	.290	.351	.395	2400	695	100	17	40	292	226	314
on Grass	.342	.413	.488	482	165	22	3	14	68	56	65	.312	.373	.421	3973	1238	191	26	64	500	393	467
on Turf	.336	.388	.411	107	36	5	0	1	10	9	13	.276	.331	.375	746	206	26	6	12	88	62	98
Day Games	.330	.421	.422	109	36	4	0	2	17	16	13	.294	.360	.385	1308	384	55	8	16	155	131	176
Night Games	.344	.405	.485	480	165	23	3	13	61	49	65	.311	.369	.425	3411	1060	162	24	60	433	324	389
April	.239	.271	.313	67	16	2	0	1	6	3	5	.281	.349	.396	623	175	34	1	12	94	64	77
May	.336	.411	.518	110	37	6	1	4	16	13	17	.294	.355	.419	840	247	38	8	17	98	82	128
June	.361	.431	.528	108	39	6	0	4	18	13	18	.306	.365	.419	826	253	34	7	15	100	75	106
July	.330	.408	.407	91	30	4	0	1	10	11	8	.319	.379	.399	749	239	35	2	7	93	73	64
August	.376	.458	.473	93	35	1	1	2	15	14	10	.319	.374	.419	835	266	36	3	14	101	72	98
Sept–Oct	.367	.417	.525	120	44	8	1	3	13	14	20	.312	.375	.424	846	264	40	11	11	102	89	92
Bases Empty	.339	.402	.462	327	111	14	1	8	8	34	40	.303	.359	.404	2679	811	119	17	39	39	226	324
Leadoff	.307	.348	.394	127	39	5	0	2	2	8	14	.303	.350	.396	1037	314	45	5	14	14	72	123
Runners On Base	.344	.416	.489	262	90	13	2	7	70	31	38	.310	.376	.427	2040	633	98	15	37	549	229	241
Scoring Position	.324	.420	.419	148	48	6	1	2	57	24	25	.311	.384	.427	1192	371	57	12	19	492	160	157
Late and Close	.330	.415	.437	103	34	5	0	2	6	15	15	.308	.369	.424	708	218	30	5	14	96	70	79

TRAVIS FRYMAN — bats right — throws right — age 23 — DET — 3S

1991	BA	OBA	SA	AB	H	2B	3B	HR	RBI	BB	SO	BA	OBA	SA	AB	H	2B	3B	HR	RBI	BB	SO
Total	.259	.309	.447	557	144	36	3	21	91	40	149	.270	.320	.454	789	213	47	4	30	118	57	200
vs. Left	.296	.349	.480	152	45	9	2	5	23	11	43	.304	.359	.512	240	73	16	2	10	35	19	59
vs. Right	.244	.293	.435	405	99	27	1	16	68	29	106	.255	.303	.428	549	140	31	2	20	83	38	141
at Home	.249	.303	.421	261	65	15	3	8	42	20	76	.252	.317	.423	369	93	18	3	13	50	34	102
on Road	.267	.313	.470	296	79	21	0	13	49	20	73	.286	.323	.481	420	120	29	1	17	68	23	98
on Grass	.261	.305	.434	472	123	31	3	15	71	31	131	.275	.322	.452	677	186	40	4	24	95	47	173
on Turf	.247	.326	.518	85	21	5	0	6	20	9	18	.241	.309	.464	112	27	7	0	6	23	10	27
Day Games	.238	.291	.387	181	43	10	1	5	27	14	51	.272	.330	.448	239	65	13	1	9	33	21	62
Night Games	.269	.317	.476	376	101	26	2	16	64	26	98	.269	.316	.456	550	148	34	3	21	85	36	138
April	.194	.271	.339	62	12	1	1	2	10	7	11	.194	.271	.339	62	12	1	1	2	10	7	11
May	.247	.290	.412	85	21	5	0	3	19	6	21	.247	.290	.412	85	21	5	0	3	19	6	21
June	.243	.291	.388	103	25	6	0	3	11	7	30	.243	.291	.388	103	25	6	0	3	11	7	30
July	.275	.323	.560	91	25	9	1	5	15	7	28	.271	.321	.542	144	39	10	1	9	22	11	40
August	.269	.310	.454	108	29	6	1	4	17	6	33	.297	.346	.456	195	58	11	1	6	21	13	53
Sept–Oct	.296	.347	.491	108	32	9	0	4	19	7	26	.290	.338	.475	200	58	14	1	7	35	13	45
Bases Empty	.253	.313	.431	297	75	14	3	11	11	25	82	.275	.328	.455	429	118	20	3	17	17	33	108
Leadoff	.296	.355	.541	98	29	8	2	4	4	9	24	.303	.357	.510	145	44	11	2	5	5	12	35
Runners On Base	.265	.304	.465	260	69	22	0	10	80	15	67	.264	.310	.453	360	95	27	1	13	101	24	92
Scoring Position	.292	.324	.455	154	45	16	0	3	64	9	37	.273	.316	.440	209	57	18	1	5	81	15	51
Late and Close	.233	.289	.400	90	21	4	1	3	14	7	25	.259	.303	.411	112	29	6	1	3	16	7	29

GARY GAETTI — bats right — throws right — age 34 — CAL — *3

1991	BA	OBA	SA	AB	H	2B	3B	HR	RBI	BB	SO	BA	OBA	SA	AB	H	2B	3B	HR	RBI	BB	SO
Total	.246	.293	.379	586	144	22	1	18	66	33	104	.259	.309	.432	4456	1155	219	19	171	660	300	746
vs. Left	.239	.303	.396	159	38	7	0	6	26	13	25	.254	.313	.421	1278	324	54	5	50	183	110	195
vs. Right	.248	.289	.372	427	106	15	1	12	40	20	79	.261	.307	.436	3178	831	165	14	121	477	190	551
at Home	.275	.331	.429	280	77	5	1	12	31	20	59	.269	.319	.445	2205	594	112	12	84	334	150	381
on Road	.219	.257	.333	306	67	17	0	6	35	13	45	.249	.299	.419	2251	561	107	7	87	326	150	365
on Grass	.248	.298	.384	487	121	16	1	16	51	29	88	.261	.314	.436	1987	519	91	4	83	291	143	330
on Turf	.232	.264	.354	99	23	6	0	2	15	4	16	.258	.305	.429	2469	636	128	15	88	369	157	416
Day Games	.303	.322	.521	142	43	7	0	8	24	3	22	.265	.314	.424	1322	350	60	0	50	203	85	230
Night Games	.227	.284	.333	444	101	15	1	10	42	30	82	.257	.307	.436	3134	805	159	19	121	457	215	516
April	.273	.296	.429	77	21	4	1	2	9	3	13	.268	.323	.450	622	167	35	3	24	93	51	115
May	.270	.287	.441	111	30	4	0	5	19	1	15	.271	.322	.475	811	220	41	5	38	142	59	138
June	.215	.284	.253	79	17	0	0	1	6	5	15	.255	.310	.426	746	190	37	2	29	104	57	120
July	.255	.297	.351	94	24	3	0	2	11	5	21	.258	.301	.429	779	201	40	3	29	118	45	131
August	.250	.305	.491	108	27	5	0	7	12	8	20	.247	.296	.419	752	186	34	4	29	110	47	128
Sept–Oct	.214	.287	.291	117	25	6	0	1	9	11	20	.256	.301	.393	746	191	32	2	22	93	41	114
Bases Empty	.214	.262	.365	345	74	11	1	13	13	18	59	.250	.296	.423	2444	612	123	12	92	92	137	406
Leadoff	.234	.275	.376	141	33	5	0	5	5	7	17	.251	.292	.446	1044	262	53	5	47	47	51	150
Runners On Base	.290	.336	.398	241	70	11	0	5	53	15	45	.270	.324	.442	2012	543	96	7	79	568	163	340
Scoring Position	.288	.340	.417	132	38	5	0	4	50	11	21	.271	.332	.464	1152	312	60	3	52	499	115	212
Late and Close	.179	.226	.244	78	14	2	0	1	5	5	13	.235	.295	.411	655	154	29	1	28	90	55	106

GREG GAGNE — bats right — throws right — age 31 — MIN — *S

1991	BA	OBA	SA	AB	H	2B	3B	HR	RBI	BB	SO	BA	OBA	SA	AB	H	2B	3B	HR	RBI	BB	SO
Total	.265	.310	.395	408	108	23	3	8	42	26	72	.251	.296	.393	2920	733	159	35	62	292	169	587
vs. Left	.280	.348	.432	118	33	8	2	2	12	12	17	.273	.316	.443	905	247	59	19	19	94	56	183
vs. Right	.259	.294	.379	290	75	15	1	6	30	14	55	.241	.287	.371	2015	486	100	16	43	198	113	404
at Home	.263	.321	.376	194	51	7	3	3	18	15	28	.249	.302	.406	1411	352	80	21	33	156	98	269
on Road	.266	.300	.411	214	57	16	0	5	24	11	44	.252	.290	.381	1509	381	79	14	29	136	71	318
on Grass	.261	.300	.430	165	43	13	0	5	17	11	30	.255	.293	.396	1169	298	65	11	26	98	57	236
on Turf	.267	.317	.370	243	65	10	3	3	25	15	42	.248	.298	.391	1751	435	94	24	36	194	112	351
Day Games	.293	.346	.463	123	36	12	0	3	15	9	28	.237	.287	.377	872	207	44	9	20	83	53	185
Night Games	.253	.294	.365	285	72	11	3	5	27	17	44	.257	.300	.400	2048	526	115	26	42	209	116	402
April	.302	.351	.528	53	16	4	1	2	6	4	11	.267	.325	.418	423	113	26	4	10	40	33	90
May	.316	.386	.506	79	25	6	0	3	10	8	15	.247	.296	.392	482	119	24	8	10	45	33	99
June	.160	.190	.213	75	12	2	1	0	3	3	11	.235	.281	.375	536	126	28	7	11	59	31	114
July	.234	.265	.312	77	18	3	0	1	9	4	12	.241	.281	.352	506	122	29	3	7	43	23	89
August	.288	.333	.442	52	15	3	1	1	5	2	10	.279	.314	.441	456	127	29	9	9	53	23	92
Sept–Oct	.306	.346	.417	72	22	5	0	1	9	5	13	.244	.286	.391	517	126	23	4	15	52	26	103
Bases Empty	.270	.320	.414	215	58	14	1	5	5	15	37	.263	.307	.424	1649	433	99	21	42	42	89	314
Leadoff	.225	.274	.371	89	20	4	0	3	3	6	16	.267	.305	.430	644	172	39	9	16	16	33	108
Runners On Base	.259	.299	.373	193	50	9	2	3	37	11	35	.236	.282	.352	1271	300	60	14	20	250	80	273
Scoring Position	.255	.298	.382	110	28	3	1	3	34	8	19	.235	.291	.364	698	164	35	11	11	219	59	156
Late and Close	.167	.239	.190	42	7	1	0	0	3	2	9	.245	.305	.359	359	88	19	5	4	29	27	82

ANDRES GALARRAGA — bats right — throws right — age 31 — MON — *1

7-YEAR TOTALS (1985–1991)

1991	BA	OBA	SA	AB	H	2B	3B	HR	RBI	BB	SO	BA	OBA	SA	AB	H	2B	3B	HR	RBI	BB	SO
Total	.218	.265	.335	376	82	13	2	9	33	22	86	.269	.326	.436	3082	830	168	14	106	433	223	790
vs. Left	.180	.216	.359	128	23	1	2	6	17	6	34	.284	.337	.489	1014	288	63	2	47	161	81	247
vs. Right	.238	.289	.323	248	59	12	0	3	16	16	52	.262	.320	.410	2068	542	105	12	59	272	142	543
at Home	.222	.252	.333	153	34	6	1	3	14	6	37	.275	.336	.452	1482	407	100	11	47	227	116	378
on Road	.215	.274	.336	223	48	7	1	6	19	16	49	.264	.316	.421	1600	423	68	3	59	206	107	412
on Grass	.216	.256	.342	111	24	5	0	3	10	6	29	.257	.308	.410	825	212	33	0	31	107	56	227
on Turf	.219	.269	.332	265	58	8	2	6	23	16	57	.274	.332	.446	2257	618	135	14	75	326	167	563
Day Games	.238	.301	.418	122	29	3	2	5	13	11	25	.264	.338	.435	938	248	52	3	34	113	93	246
Night Games	.209	.247	.295	254	53	10	0	4	20	11	61	.271	.320	.437	2144	582	116	11	72	320	130	544
April	.234	.319	.328	64	15	3	0	1	2	7	15	.286	.359	.452	409	117	26	0	14	61	37	100
May	.273	.291	.416	77	21	5	0	2	9	2	14	.285	.334	.466	536	153	30	2	21	83	36	127
June	.000	.000	.000	0	0	0	0	0	0	0	0	.289	.351	.485	499	144	37	2	19	77	40	121
July	.191	.247	.235	68	13	1	1	0	4	5	14	.256	.313	.421	461	118	26	4	14	61	33	128
August	.171	.200	.220	82	14	1	0	1	5	2	21	.234	.289	.352	500	117	13	2	14	48	32	132
Sept–Oct	.224	.275	.459	85	19	3	1	5	13	6	22	.267	.315	.439	677	181	36	4	24	103	45	182
Bases Empty	.236	.276	.377	199	47	8	1	6	6	10	40	.265	.311	.434	1674	443	99	8	56	56	96	419
Leadoff	.193	.239	.337	83	16	3	0	3	3	5	19	.274	.325	.438	635	174	40	2	20	20	43	166
Runners On Base	.198	.253	.288	177	35	5	1	3	27	12	46	.275	.342	.439	1408	387	69	6	50	377	127	371
Scoring Position	.173	.257	.245	98	17	2	1	1	21	10	28	.261	.352	.404	827	216	37	6	23	305	106	239
Late and Close	.208	.278	.292	72	15	3	0	1	5	7	16	.248	.318	.418	593	147	31	2	22	78	55	163

DAVE GALLAGHER — bats right — throws right — age 32 — CAL — O/D

5-YEAR TOTALS (1987–1991)

1991	BA	OBA	SA	AB	H	2B	3B	HR	RBI	BB	SO	BA	OBA	SA	AB	H	2B	3B	HR	RBI	BB	SO
Total	.293	.355	.367	270	79	17	0	1	30	24	43	.275	.329	.343	1380	380	59	7	7	115	108	179
vs. Left	.300	.353	.364	110	33	7	0	1	9	8	14	.270	.324	.327	581	157	22	4	1	46	45	66
vs. Right	.287	.356	.369	160	46	10	0	1	21	16	29	.279	.333	.355	799	223	37	3	6	69	63	113
at Home	.270	.343	.333	126	34	8	0	1	10	14	21	.271	.328	.333	669	181	28	4	2	52	56	75
on Road	.313	.365	.396	144	45	9	0	1	20	10	22	.280	.331	.353	711	199	31	3	5	63	52	104
on Grass	.292	.356	.362	243	71	14	0	1	28	23	40	.282	.341	.353	1147	324	51	6	6	101	100	141
on Turf	.296	.345	.407	27	8	3	0	0	2	1	3	.240	.270	.296	233	56	8	1	1	14	8	38
Day Games	.300	.373	.350	60	18	3	0	0	7	7	8	.273	.330	.346	370	101	16	1	3	26	33	37
Night Games	.290	.349	.371	210	61	14	0	1	23	17	35	.276	.329	.343	1010	279	43	6	4	89	75	142
April	.556	.636	.556	9	5	0	0	0	1	2	0	.245	.310	.316	155	38	4	2	1	16	15	15
May	.303	.378	.333	33	10	1	0	0	3	4	5	.301	.373	.350	183	55	4	1	1	12	21	22
June	.271	.340	.333	48	13	3	0	0	5	5	8	.286	.331	.361	255	73	11	1	2	20	17	33
July	.292	.329	.389	72	21	4	0	1	10	3	11	.303	.359	.361	238	72	11	0	1	17	18	40
August	.250	.341	.333	36	9	3	0	0	1	4	6	.235	.265	.293	294	69	13	2	0	25	11	42
Sept–Oct	.292	.346	.375	72	21	6	0	0	10	6	12	.286	.351	.380	255	73	16	1	2	25	26	27
Bases Empty	.305	.360	.402	164	50	13	0	1	1	13	26	.279	.328	.351	858	239	43	2	5	5	60	112
Leadoff	.323	.380	.385	65	21	4	0	0	0	6	8	.287	.334	.360	439	126	24	1	2	2	31	52
Runners On Base	.274	.347	.311	106	29	4	0	0	29	11	17	.270	.332	.331	522	141	16	5	2	110	48	67
Scoring Position	.328	.403	.391	64	21	4	0	0	28	8	12	.267	.339	.320	322	86	12	1	1	102	37	50
Late and Close	.286	.375	.310	42	12	1	0	0	6	6	6	.226	.287	.278	230	52	9	0	1	17	20	23

MIKE GALLEGO — bats right — throws right — age 32 — OAK — *2S

7-YEAR TOTALS (1985–1991)

1991	BA	OBA	SA	AB	H	2B	3B	HR	RBI	BB	SO	BA	OBA	SA	AB	H	2B	3B	HR	RBI	BB	SO
Total	.247	.343	.369	482	119	15	4	12	49	67	84	.232	.315	.318	1743	404	63	9	23	160	197	271
vs. Left	.311	.408	.500	122	38	6	1	5	13	20	16	.257	.333	.359	580	149	30	1	9	55	66	89
vs. Right	.225	.320	.325	360	81	9	3	7	36	47	68	.219	.305	.298	1163	255	33	8	14	105	131	182
at Home	.270	.378	.409	230	62	8	3	6	20	40	34	.244	.334	.329	872	213	29	6	11	74	113	120
on Road	.226	.310	.333	252	57	7	1	6	29	27	50	.219	.294	.307	871	191	34	3	12	86	84	151
on Grass	.251	.348	.365	403	101	13	3	9	36	58	69	.229	.313	.309	1452	332	49	8	17	124	167	222
on Turf	.228	.315	.392	79	18	2	1	3	13	9	15	.247	.322	.364	291	72	14	1	6	36	30	49
Day Games	.253	.349	.413	150	38	5	2	5	13	21	26	.236	.323	.322	673	159	26	4	8	65	79	108
Night Games	.244	.340	.349	332	81	10	2	7	36	46	58	.229	.309	.315	1070	245	37	5	15	95	118	163
April	.222	.382	.259	54	12	0	1	0	2	14	10	.263	.357	.340	194	51	10	1	1	17	28	28
May	.286	.360	.416	77	22	4	0	2	13	8	9	.208	.298	.311	283	59	11	3	4	34	33	45
June	.205	.287	.205	83	17	0	0	0	1	10	13	.233	.298	.274	288	67	4	1	2	21	27	44
July	.298	.377	.500	94	28	5	1	4	16	10	17	.222	.299	.325	329	73	14	1	3	33	33	48
August	.198	.255	.372	86	17	4	1	3	7	6	15	.233	.325	.333	240	56	7	1	5	22	30	29
Sept–Oct	.261	.394	.409	88	23	2	1	3	10	19	20	.240	.323	.328	409	98	17	2	5	33	46	77
Bases Empty	.240	.333	.357	300	72	9	1	8	8	41	56	.219	.313	.307	1013	222	37	2	16	16	135	173
Leadoff	.227	.314	.383	141	32	5	1	5	5	18	23	.206	.300	.316	446	92	14	1	11	11	60	77
Runners On Base	.258	.358	.390	182	47	6	3	4	41	26	28	.249	.317	.333	730	182	26	7	7	144	62	98
Scoring Position	.250	.366	.380	100	25	3	2	2	36	18	15	.234	.321	.304	385	90	15	3	2	127	44	52
Late and Close	.313	.402	.488	80	25	1	2	3	11	11	14	.225	.311	.300	240	54	5	2	3	21	27	45

RON GANT — bats right — throws right — age 27 — ATL — *O

1991	BA	OBA	SA	AB	H	2B	3B	HR	RBI	BB	SO		BA	OBA	SA	AB	H	2B	3B	HR	RBI	BB	SO
Total	.251	.338	.496	561	141	35	3	32	105	71	104		.259	.322	.467	2042	529	109	17	94	283	188	381
vs. Left	.290	.387	.574	162	47	16	0	10	37	25	22		.267	.345	.483	660	176	45	4	30	98	79	102
vs. Right	.236	.317	.464	399	94	19	3	22	68	46	82		.255	.311	.459	1382	353	64	13	64	185	109	279
at Home	.279	.370	.558	258	72	16	1	18	52	36	52		.267	.334	.486	986	263	47	11	49	142	95	176
on Road	.228	.310	.442	303	69	19	2	14	53	35	52		.252	.312	.450	1056	266	62	6	45	141	93	205
on Grass	.260	.338	.521	411	107	23	3	26	80	46	77		.258	.323	.464	1490	384	66	14	71	211	140	282
on Turf	.227	.337	.427	150	34	12	0	6	25	25	27		.263	.320	.476	552	145	43	3	23	72	48	99
Day Games	.273	.371	.467	150	41	5	0	8	29	22	37		.250	.326	.429	560	140	20	4	24	82	59	129
Night Games	.243	.325	.506	411	100	30	3	24	76	49	67		.262	.321	.482	1482	389	89	13	70	201	129	252
April	.162	.250	.294	68	11	6	0	1	7	8	9		.159	.244	.292	195	31	10	2	4	14	22	43
May	.244	.310	.578	90	22	3	0	9	19	8	17		.251	.288	.471	378	95	18	1	21	59	21	78
June	.253	.306	.451	91	23	7	1	3	11	6	16		.273	.327	.513	337	92	18	6	17	48	26	60
July	.348	.423	.674	92	32	7	1	7	22	11	21		.286	.343	.509	332	95	20	3	16	51	29	61
August	.234	.336	.495	107	25	4	0	8	23	16	19		.267	.350	.486	329	88	18	3	16	44	39	57
Sept–Oct	.248	.367	.442	113	28	8	1	4	23	22	22		.272	.343	.461	471	128	25	2	20	67	51	82
Bases Empty	.268	.345	.521	280	75	15	1	18	18	30	51		.271	.331	.498	1205	326	60	11	64	64	101	225
Leadoff	.298	.356	.628	121	36	8	1	10	10	10	15		.294	.344	.566	544	160	29	4	37	37	38	87
Runners On Base	.235	.331	.470	281	66	20	2	14	87	41	53		.243	.310	.423	837	203	49	6	30	219	87	156
Scoring Position	.263	.361	.485	171	45	16	2	6	69	28	29		.247	.320	.396	498	123	32	3	12	175	60	93
Late and Close	.169	.304	.313	83	14	3	0	3	20	15	16		.206	.281	.349	321	66	12	2	10	46	33	69

5-YEAR TOTALS (1987–1991) (right-hand columns above)

JIM GANTNER — bats left — throws right — age 39 — MIL — 32

1991	BA	OBA	SA	AB	H	2B	3B	HR	RBI	BB	SO		BA	OBA	SA	AB	H	2B	3B	HR	RBI	BB	SO
Total	.283	.320	.361	526	149	27	4	2	47	27	34		.273	.317	.345	3695	1009	162	20	21	321	219	301
vs. Left	.266	.304	.288	139	37	3	0	0	13	6	8		.274	.321	.312	1071	293	37	2	0	92	64	79
vs. Right	.289	.325	.388	387	112	24	4	2	34	21	26		.273	.316	.358	2624	716	125	18	21	229	155	222
at Home	.287	.328	.362	254	73	14	1	1	20	15	15		.271	.318	.338	1801	488	81	6	9	160	119	150
on Road	.279	.311	.360	272	76	13	3	1	27	12	19		.275	.316	.352	1894	521	81	14	12	161	100	151
on Grass	.288	.329	.367	458	132	22	4	2	39	26	31		.270	.316	.338	3129	844	130	17	17	259	202	255
on Turf	.250	.254	.324	68	17	5	0	0	8	1	3		.292	.323	.380	566	165	32	3	4	62	17	46
Day Games	.293	.348	.420	150	44	11	4	0	13	13	8		.270	.315	.348	1055	285	53	7	5	101	66	85
Night Games	.279	.308	.338	376	105	16	0	2	34	14	26		.274	.318	.344	2640	724	109	13	16	220	153	216
April	.260	.296	.360	50	13	5	0	0	8	3	9		.246	.293	.320	403	99	16	4	2	38	23	37
May	.299	.327	.355	107	32	6	0	0	5	4	4		.281	.324	.359	605	170	30	1	5	51	33	44
June	.247	.304	.301	73	18	2	1	0	10	5	5		.271	.314	.337	658	178	27	1	5	67	40	48
July	.311	.344	.410	61	19	4	1	0	2	3	3		.276	.325	.337	673	186	29	3	2	59	45	56
August	.283	.291	.336	113	32	4	1	0	12	2	7		.295	.321	.374	641	189	30	6	3	51	52	65
Sept–Oct	.287	.346	.402	122	35	6	1	0	10	10	6		.262	.317	.334	715	187	30	5	4	55	52	65
Bases Empty	.305	.335	.399	311	95	19	2	2	2	12	20		.285	.326	.362	2190	625	107	11	13	13	114	156
Leadoff	.333	.366	.407	135	45	5	1	1	1	6	7		.300	.340	.372	843	253	38	4	5	5	43	50
Runners On Base	.251	.298	.307	215	54	8	2	0	45	15	14		.255	.305	.320	1505	384	55	9	8	308	105	145
Scoring Position	.238	.297	.311	122	29	5	2	0	44	12	10		.248	.314	.312	842	209	28	7	4	285	84	102
Late and Close	.310	.340	.430	100	31	9	0	1	9	4	7		.285	.336	.364	618	176	29	1	6	60	48	55

8-YEAR TOTALS (1984–1991) (right-hand columns above)

KIRK GIBSON — bats left — throws left — age 35 — KC — OD

1991	BA	OBA	SA	AB	H	2B	3B	HR	RBI	BB	SO		BA	OBA	SA	AB	H	2B	3B	HR	RBI	BB	SO
Total	.236	.341	.403	462	109	17	6	16	55	69	103		.269	.360	.470	3612	972	169	29	166	550	489	807
vs. Left	.197	.307	.303	132	26	2	3	2	11	16	31		.245	.332	.415	1211	297	51	7	47	175	138	326
vs. Right	.252	.355	.442	330	83	15	3	14	44	53	72		.281	.374	.497	2401	675	118	22	119	375	351	481
at Home	.222	.327	.343	239	53	5	6	4	26	35	46		.269	.358	.470	1791	482	74	20	82	287	238	390
on Road	.251	.356	.466	223	56	12	0	12	29	34	57		.269	.362	.470	1821	490	95	9	84	263	251	417
on Grass	.261	.372	.521	165	43	7	0	12	26	27	40		.281	.372	.494	2707	760	126	20	137	430	372	603
on Turf	.222	.324	.337	297	66	10	6	4	29	42	63		.234	.323	.398	905	212	43	9	29	120	117	204
Day Games	.178	.281	.301	146	26	4	1	4	13	19	35		.260	.341	.460	1099	286	53	8	50	169	126	233
Night Games	.263	.368	.449	316	83	13	5	12	42	50	68		.273	.368	.474	2513	686	116	21	116	381	363	574
April	.257	.342	.543	70	18	0	1	6	12	9	14		.269	.362	.476	368	99	14	4	18	60	51	87
May	.217	.316	.313	83	18	5	0	1	4	12	16		.285	.364	.510	473	135	28	6	22	65	54	95
June	.235	.321	.459	98	23	5	1	5	19	13	15		.259	.349	.489	767	199	33	7	43	138	103	169
July	.254	.333	.322	59	15	2	1	0	5	5	9		.273	.354	.446	688	188	34	2	27	101	85	140
August	.282	.408	.518	85	24	2	3	4	11	16	20		.281	.383	.473	715	201	31	8	30	99	111	168
Sept–Oct	.164	.321	.209	67	11	3	0	0	4	14	29		.250	.347	.434	601	150	29	2	26	87	85	148
Bases Empty	.226	.326	.357	283	64	7	3	8	8	37	60		.263	.349	.462	2013	529	92	16	92	92	245	466
Leadoff	.221	.319	.404	104	23	3	2	4	4	11	22		.276	.351	.478	678	187	30	6	29	29	69	142
Runners On Base	.251	.364	.475	179	45	10	3	8	47	32	43		.277	.373	.480	1599	443	77	13	74	458	244	341
Scoring Position	.227	.370	.418	110	25	5	2	4	35	25	23		.269	.380	.480	870	234	44	10	40	370	166	197
Late and Close	.177	.309	.342	79	14	1	3	2	11	14	19		.253	.361	.440	554	140	23	6	23	88	87	141

8-YEAR TOTALS (1984–1991) (right-hand columns above)

BERNARD GILKEY — bats right — throws right — age 26 — SL — O

1991	BA	OBA	SA	AB	H	2B	3B	HR	RBI	BB	SO	2-YEAR TOTALS (1990–1991) BA	OBA	SA	AB	H	2B	3B	HR	RBI	BB	SO
Total	.216	.316	.313	268	58	7	2	5	20	39	33	.232	.327	.346	332	77	12	4	6	23	47	38
vs. Left	.185	.295	.267	135	25	5	0	2	9	20	15	.202	.309	.307	163	33	7	2	2	9	24	17
vs. Right	.248	.338	.361	133	33	2	2	3	11	19	18	.260	.345	.385	169	44	5	2	4	14	23	21
at Home	.215	.316	.295	149	32	4	1	2	10	21	14	.203	.303	.286	182	37	5	2	2	11	25	17
on Road	.218	.317	.336	119	26	3	1	3	10	18	19	.267	.356	.420	150	40	7	2	4	12	22	21
on Grass	.277	.364	.489	47	13	1	0	3	7	7	8	.277	.364	.489	47	13	1	0	3	7	7	8
on Turf	.204	.306	.276	221	45	6	2	2	13	32	25	.225	.321	.323	285	64	11	4	3	16	40	30
Day Games	.212	.269	.329	85	18	1	0	3	6	7	12	.231	.283	.346	104	24	3	0	3	8	8	12
Night Games	.219	.336	.306	183	40	6	2	2	14	32	21	.232	.346	.346	228	53	9	4	3	15	39	26
April	.260	.360	.338	77	20	1	1	1	5	12	11	.260	.360	.338	77	20	1	1	1	5	12	11
May	.197	.337	.324	71	14	3	0	2	5	15	7	.197	.337	.324	71	14	3	0	2	5	15	7
June	.243	.282	.297	37	9	0	1	0	2	2	3	.243	.282	.297	37	9	0	1	0	2	2	3
July	.180	.276	.200	50	9	1	0	0	3	6	9	.180	.276	.200	50	9	1	0	0	3	6	9
August	.111	.172	.148	27	3	1	0	0	2	2	3	.111	.172	.148	27	3	1	0	0	2	2	3
Sept–Oct	.500	.556	1.667	6	3	1	0	2	3	2	0	.314	.395	.586	70	22	6	2	3	6	10	5
Bases Empty	.231	.310	.372	156	36	5	1	5	5	17	17	.243	.320	.396	202	49	7	3	6	6	22	19
Leadoff	.266	.341	.468	79	21	4	0	4	4	8	5	.267	.342	.438	105	28	4	1	4	4	11	6
Runners On Base	.196	.324	.232	112	22	2	1	0	15	22	16	.215	.338	.269	130	28	5	1	0	17	25	19
Scoring Position	.213	.390	.279	61	13	2	1	0	15	19	13	.229	.398	.314	70	16	4	1	0	17	21	15
Late and Close	.256	.388	.359	39	10	1	0	1	5	9	5	.267	.404	.400	45	12	3	0	1	5	11	5

DAN GLADDEN — bats right — throws right — age 35 — MIN — *O

1991	BA	OBA	SA	AB	H	2B	3B	HR	RBI	BB	SO	8-YEAR TOTALS (1984–1991) BA	OBA	SA	AB	H	2B	3B	HR	RBI	BB	SO
Total	.247	.306	.356	461	114	14	9	6	52	36	60	.273	.329	.382	3663	1000	165	37	53	338	281	500
vs. Left	.254	.341	.390	118	30	5	4	2	19	16	10	.286	.348	.397	1108	317	54	9	17	99	102	135
vs. Right	.245	.293	.344	343	84	9	5	5	33	20	50	.267	.321	.375	2555	683	111	28	36	239	179	365
at Home	.266	.333	.381	244	65	9	5	3	27	22	33	.288	.350	.402	1817	523	81	20	29	166	159	227
on Road	.226	.275	.327	217	49	5	4	3	25	14	27	.258	.308	.361	1846	477	84	17	24	172	122	273
on Grass	.239	.276	.333	180	43	4	2	3	19	9	20	.262	.323	.359	1807	473	73	8	29	169	146	272
on Turf	.253	.325	.370	281	71	10	7	3	33	27	40	.284	.335	.404	1856	527	92	29	24	169	135	228
Day Games	.192	.257	.250	104	20	3	0	1	7	7	11	.265	.336	.372	1263	335	52	7	23	106	121	189
Night Games	.263	.321	.387	357	94	11	9	5	45	29	49	.277	.325	.387	2400	665	113	30	30	232	160	311
April	.188	.278	.275	69	13	3	0	1	10	7	5	.283	.335	.380	495	140	30	0	6	49	30	60
May	.275	.333	.429	91	25	2	3	2	7	7	11	.265	.315	.389	686	182	35	10	10	60	48	107
June	.304	.368	.405	79	24	3	1	1	6	8	10	.268	.330	.386	567	152	21	5	12	52	48	63
July	.406	.457	.594	32	13	3	0	1	13	3	7	.287	.342	.371	536	154	28	4	3	57	41	66
August	.214	.257	.311	103	22	2	4	0	13	5	8	.261	.319	.346	685	179	22	9	6	61	52	90
Sept–Oct	.195	.247	.264	87	17	1	1	1	3	6	19	.278	.338	.415	694	193	29	9	16	59	62	114
Bases Empty	.248	.310	.328	290	72	7	2	4	4	23	36	.273	.333	.383	2409	658	106	21	39	39	196	342
Leadoff	.250	.310	.342	184	46	3	1	4	4	13	21	.275	.336	.387	1391	383	55	11	26	26	109	191
Runners On Base	.246	.300	.404	171	42	7	7	2	48	13	24	.273	.321	.379	1254	342	59	16	14	299	85	158
Scoring Position	.222	.302	.361	108	24	6	3	1	41	12	18	.263	.320	.365	768	202	37	7	9	270	65	107
Late and Close	.189	.306	.377	53	10	2	1	2	13	8	9	.247	.318	.370	579	143	28	8	9	55	55	102

LEO GOMEZ — bats right — throws right — age 26 — BAL — *3D/1

1991	BA	OBA	SA	AB	H	2B	3B	HR	RBI	BB	SO	2-YEAR TOTALS (1990–1991) BA	OBA	SA	AB	H	2B	3B	HR	RBI	BB	SO
Total	.233	.302	.409	391	91	17	2	16	45	40	82	.233	.308	.393	430	100	17	2	16	46	48	89
vs. Left	.219	.288	.412	114	25	4	0	6	16	13	20	.227	.291	.394	132	30	4	0	6	16	14	21
vs. Right	.238	.308	.408	277	66	13	2	10	29	27	62	.235	.315	.393	298	70	13	2	10	30	34	68
at Home	.232	.303	.414	203	47	12	2	7	23	22	38	.233	.310	.399	223	52	12	2	7	23	26	40
on Road	.234	.302	.404	188	44	5	0	9	22	18	44	.232	.306	.386	207	48	5	0	9	23	22	49
on Grass	.234	.300	.413	334	78	17	2	13	37	34	69	.233	.307	.394	373	87	17	2	13	38	42	76
on Turf	.228	.313	.386	57	13	0	0	3	8	6	13	.228	.313	.386	57	13	0	0	3	8	6	13
Day Games	.231	.307	.374	91	21	4	0	2	9	10	21	.253	.321	.384	99	25	4	0	3	9	10	23
Night Games	.233	.301	.420	300	70	13	2	13	36	30	61	.227	.304	.396	331	75	13	2	13	37	38	66
April	.278	.366	.333	36	10	2	0	0	0	5	7	.278	.366	.333	36	10	2	0	0	0	5	7
May	.000	.000	.000	9	0	0	0	0	0	0	4	.000	.000	.000	9	0	0	0	0	0	0	4
June	.257	.384	.443	70	18	2	1	3	12	13	12	.257	.384	.443	70	18	2	1	3	12	13	12
July	.194	.255	.357	98	19	7	0	3	11	9	17	.194	.255	.357	98	19	7	0	3	11	9	17
August	.212	.269	.471	85	18	2	1	6	13	7	18	.212	.269	.471	85	18	2	1	6	13	7	18
Sept–Oct	.280	.317	.452	93	26	4	0	4	9	6	24	.265	.331	.386	132	35	4	0	4	10	14	31
Bases Empty	.242	.311	.443	219	53	13	2	9	9	20	47	.237	.313	.419	241	57	13	2	9	9	25	51
Leadoff	.207	.309	.390	82	17	3	0	4	4	11	21	.183	.276	.344	93	17	3	0	4	4	11	24
Runners On Base	.221	.291	.366	172	38	4	0	7	36	20	35	.228	.301	.360	189	43	4	0	7	37	23	38
Scoring Position	.188	.265	.287	80	15	2	0	2	25	11	19	.191	.275	.281	89	17	2	0	2	26	13	21
Late and Close	.194	.253	.347	72	14	2	0	3	7	6	18	.195	.267	.338	77	15	2	0	3	7	8	20

JUAN GONZALEZ — bats right — throws right — age 23 — TEX — *O/D

1991	BA	OBA	SA	AB	H	2B	3B	HR	RBI	BB	SO		3-YEAR TOTALS (1989–1991) BA	OBA	SA	AB	H	2B	3B	HR	RBI	BB	SO
Total	.264	.321	.479	545	144	34	1	27	102	42	118		.258	.312	.465	695	179	44	2	32	121	50	153
vs. Left	.299	.366	.531	147	44	7	0	9	27	16	28		.277	.338	.482	195	54	10	0	10	32	19	41
vs. Right	.251	.304	.460	398	100	27	1	18	75	26	90		.250	.302	.458	500	125	34	2	22	89	31	112
at Home	.267	.328	.408	262	70	16	0	7	40	19	62		.263	.318	.422	346	91	20	1	11	53	23	81
on Road	.261	.315	.544	283	74	18	1	20	62	23	56		.252	.306	.507	349	88	24	1	21	68	27	72
on Grass	.282	.337	.493	444	125	28	0	22	83	34	94		.267	.321	.473	562	150	33	1	27	99	41	123
on Turf	.188	.248	.416	101	19	6	1	5	19	8	24		.218	.273	.429	133	29	11	1	5	22	9	30
Day Games	.281	.333	.573	89	25	6	1	6	23	5	18		.256	.310	.513	117	30	7	1	7	24	6	26
Night Games	.261	.319	.461	456	119	28	0	21	79	37	100		.258	.313	.455	578	149	37	1	25	97	44	127
April	.429	.467	.786	14	6	2	0	1	5	1	4		.429	.467	.786	14	6	2	0	1	5	1	4
May	.327	.403	.577	104	34	11	0	5	28	13	20		.327	.403	.577	104	34	11	0	5	28	13	20
June	.255	.336	.402	102	26	3	0	4	17	13	20		.255	.336	.402	102	26	3	0	4	17	13	20
July	.256	.316	.556	90	23	6	0	7	20	7	27		.256	.316	.556	90	23	6	0	7	20	7	27
August	.304	.323	.592	125	38	7	1	9	24	3	24		.203	.252	.340	256	52	15	1	6	27	13	56
Sept–Oct	.155	.205	.227	110	17	5	0	1	8	5	23												
Bases Empty	.234	.276	.399	278	65	22	0	8	8	15	60		.235	.283	.408	358	84	29	0	11	11	21	73
Leadoff	.214	.248	.402	112	24	9	0	4	4	5	21		.210	.253	.399	138	29	11	0	5	5	8	26
Runners On Base	.296	.365	.562	267	79	12	1	19	94	27	58		.282	.342	.525	337	95	15	2	21	110	29	80
Scoring Position	.265	.360	.435	170	45	6	1	7	68	24	37		.260	.344	.409	208	54	8	1	7	78	26	50
Late and Close	.215	.306	.473	93	20	3	0	7	21	9	21		.218	.291	.471	119	26	6	0	8	22	9	26

LUIS GONZALEZ — bats left — throws right — age 25 — HOU — *O

1991	BA	OBA	SA	AB	H	2B	3B	HR	RBI	BB	SO		2-YEAR TOTALS (1990–1991) BA	OBA	SA	AB	H	2B	3B	HR	RBI	BB	SO
Total	.254	.320	.433	473	120	28	9	13	69	40	101		.251	.318	.427	494	124	30	9	13	69	42	106
vs. Left	.168	.256	.261	119	20	6	1	1	13	12	30		.167	.254	.258	120	20	6	1	1	13	12	30
vs. Right	.282	.342	.492	354	100	22	8	12	56	28	71		.278	.338	.481	374	104	24	8	12	56	30	76
at Home	.273	.339	.445	227	62	15	6	4	32	20	41		.274	.342	.444	234	64	16	6	4	32	22	43
on Road	.236	.303	.423	246	58	13	3	9	37	20	60		.231	.295	.412	260	60	14	3	9	37	20	63
on Grass	.250	.309	.426	148	37	6	1	6	25	14	35		.242	.299	.408	157	38	6	1	6	25	12	36
on Turf	.255	.325	.437	325	83	22	8	7	44	28	66		.255	.326	.436	337	86	24	8	7	44	30	70
Day Games	.263	.344	.447	114	30	6	0	5	14	12	21		.254	.336	.426	122	31	6	0	5	14	13	21
Night Games	.251	.312	.429	359	90	22	9	8	55	28	80		.250	.311	.427	372	93	24	9	8	55	29	85
April	.148	.212	.230	61	9	3	1	0	3	4	19		.148	.212	.230	61	9	3	1	0	3	4	19
May	.287	.317	.628	94	27	8	3	6	23	5	18		.287	.317	.628	94	27	8	3	6	23	5	18
June	.224	.327	.365	85	19	7	1	1	5	11	15		.224	.327	.365	85	19	7	1	1	5	11	15
July	.274	.347	.440	84	23	3	1	3	16	8	16		.274	.347	.440	84	23	3	1	3	16	8	16
August	.250	.318	.421	76	19	3	2	2	11	5	21		.250	.318	.421	76	19	3	2	2	11	5	21
Sept–Oct	.315	.375	.438	73	23	4	1	1	11	7	12		.287	.350	.404	94	27	6	1	1	11	9	17
Bases Empty	.247	.308	.427	227	56	13	2	8	8	14	44		.245	.305	.420	245	60	15	2	8	8	15	48
Leadoff	.211	.268	.400	90	19	3	1	4	4	6	15		.219	.279	.406	96	21	4	1	4	4	7	15
Runners On Base	.260	.331	.439	246	64	15	7	5	61	26	57		.257	.330	.434	249	64	15	7	5	61	27	58
Scoring Position	.272	.356	.434	136	37	9	2	3	50	19	40		.268	.356	.428	138	37	9	2	3	50	19	41
Late and Close	.284	.357	.365	74	21	4	1	0	9	6	12		.280	.362	.366	82	23	5	1	0	9	8	16

MARK GRACE — bats left — throws left — age 28 — CHN — *1

1991	BA	OBA	SA	AB	H	2B	3B	HR	RBI	BB	SO		4-YEAR TOTALS (1988–1991) BA	OBA	SA	AB	H	2B	3B	HR	RBI	BB	SO
Total	.273	.346	.373	619	169	28	5	8	58	70	53		.298	.373	.410	2204	656	111	13	37	275	269	193
vs. Left	.274	.338	.351	248	68	7	3	2	19	23	32		.283	.358	.401	729	206	34	8	12	99	84	92
vs. Right	.272	.351	.388	371	101	21	2	6	39	47	21		.305	.380	.415	1475	450	77	5	25	176	185	101
at Home	.289	.364	.398	322	93	18	1	5	32	38	28		.313	.392	.417	1138	356	58	5	17	146	149	89
on Road	.256	.327	.347	297	76	10	4	3	26	32	25		.281	.352	.402	1066	300	53	8	20	129	120	104
on Grass	.283	.352	.386	453	128	22	2	7	41	49	42		.304	.377	.409	1596	485	81	7	24	200	191	138
on Turf	.247	.332	.337	166	41	6	3	1	17	21	11		.281	.363	.414	608	171	30	6	13	75	78	55
Day Games	.281	.349	.391	317	89	12	1	7	39	33	30		.303	.384	.407	1188	360	60	5	18	145	157	101
Night Games	.265	.343	.354	302	80	16	4	1	19	37	23		.291	.359	.413	1016	296	51	8	19	130	112	92
April	.268	.365	.394	71	19	4	1	1	12	10	3		.286	.386	.392	217	62	12	1	3	27	35	16
May	.286	.348	.419	105	30	8	0	2	10	10	9		.293	.347	.390	413	121	20	1	6	44	34	39
June	.276	.339	.352	105	29	3	1	1	11	11	12		.292	.370	.383	332	97	13	4	3	39	43	26
July	.248	.347	.386	101	25	6	1	2	16	16	6		.295	.371	.434	369	109	22	1	9	46	47	26
August	.336	.385	.395	119	40	5	1	0	11	10	13		.330	.395	.473	446	147	23	4	11	64	49	45
Sept–Oct	.220	.301	.305	118	26	2	1	2	8	13	10		.281	.370	.375	427	120	21	2	5	55	61	39
Bases Empty	.251	.329	.339	375	94	13	1	6	6	42	38		.284	.358	.399	1248	354	62	5	24	24	141	128
Leadoff	.222	.289	.291	117	26	2	0	2	2	10	10		.320	.370	.446	428	137	19	1	11	11	33	36
Runners On Base	.307	.371	.426	244	75	15	4	2	52	28	15		.316	.391	.425	956	302	49	8	13	251	128	65
Scoring Position	.229	.333	.328	131	30	6	2	1	46	23	10		.291	.391	.395	574	167	27	6	7	230	104	48
Late and Close	.237	.345	.288	118	28	3	0	1	10	18	10		.300	.405	.387	357	107	14	1	5	40	62	28

MIKE GREENWELL — bats left — throws right — age 29 — BOS — *O/D — 7-YEAR TOTALS (1985–1991)

1991	BA	OBA	SA	AB	H	2B	3B	HR	RBI	BB	SO	BA	OBA	SA	AB	H	2B	3B	HR	RBI	BB	SO
Total	.300	.350	.419	544	163	26	6	9	83	43	35	.311	.378	.476	2800	870	165	26	82	471	294	211
vs. Left	.327	.357	.476	168	55	9	2	4	34	8	12	.296	.338	.415	849	251	43	5	16	126	45	68
vs. Right	.287	.347	.394	376	108	17	4	5	49	35	23	.317	.395	.503	1951	619	122	21	66	345	249	143
at Home	.302	.365	.451	255	77	17	3	5	42	27	13	.321	.389	.500	1391	446	105	15	38	251	153	94
on Road	.298	.337	.391	289	86	9	3	4	41	16	22	.301	.367	.453	1409	424	60	11	44	220	141	117
on Grass	.299	.358	.419	442	132	23	3	8	68	41	22	.312	.382	.474	2371	740	150	20	65	398	257	170
on Turf	.304	.314	.422	102	31	3	3	1	15	2	13	.303	.359	.485	429	130	15	6	17	73	37	41
Day Games	.297	.358	.401	172	51	9	0	3	28	18	12	.325	.393	.496	927	301	74	8	23	160	99	68
Night Games	.301	.347	.427	372	112	17	6	6	55	25	23	.304	.371	.466	1873	569	91	18	59	311	195	143
April	.300	.372	.529	70	21	3	2	3	8	8	4	.289	.388	.463	315	91	15	2	12	41	42	28
May	.282	.333	.379	103	29	5	1	1	19	9	8	.274	.358	.404	445	122	21	2	11	75	56	37
June	.364	.396	.424	99	36	3	0	1	14	6	6	.345	.396	.504	490	169	29	2	15	99	39	32
July	.266	.303	.372	94	25	2	1	2	8	5	2	.314	.376	.482	488	153	29	4	15	66	49	32
August	.327	.363	.436	101	33	6	1	1	21	8	8	.328	.394	.496	488	160	33	8	11	90	55	35
Sept–Oct	.247	.333	.403	77	19	7	1	1	13	7	7	.305	.364	.493	574	175	38	8	18	100	53	47
Bases Empty	.303	.357	.437	277	84	14	4	5	5	20	14	.307	.372	.482	1362	418	85	14	42	42	129	98
Leadoff	.353	.370	.517	116	41	6	2	3	3	3	5	.302	.354	.492	592	179	42	5	20	20	45	39
Runners On Base	.296	.343	.401	267	79	12	2	4	78	23	21	.314	.384	.470	1438	452	80	12	40	429	165	113
Scoring Position	.309	.353	.426	162	50	9	2	2	74	15	12	.296	.383	.443	845	250	46	9	20	374	128	73
Late and Close	.284	.349	.365	74	21	4	1	0	10	6	6	.292	.374	.474	418	122	25	6	13	65	51	42

KEN GRIFFEY JR. — bats left — throws left — age 23 — SEA — *O/D — 3-YEAR TOTALS (1989–1991)

1991	BA	OBA	SA	AB	H	2B	3B	HR	RBI	BB	SO	BA	OBA	SA	AB	H	2B	3B	HR	RBI	BB	SO
Total	.327	.399	.527	548	179	42	1	22	100	71	82	.299	.367	.479	1600	478	93	8	60	241	178	246
vs. Left	.314	.386	.472	159	50	10	0	5	26	20	30	.286	.347	.429	496	142	30	1	13	60	46	106
vs. Right	.332	.404	.550	389	129	32	1	17	74	51	52	.304	.376	.502	1104	336	63	7	47	181	132	140
at Home	.365	.432	.617	282	103	23	0	16	59	36	47	.309	.380	.512	805	249	53	4	34	136	94	116
on Road	.286	.364	.432	266	76	19	1	6	41	35	35	.288	.354	.447	795	229	40	4	26	105	84	130
on Grass	.277	.356	.413	206	57	14	1	4	33	27	29	.292	.358	.448	614	179	27	3	21	88	66	99
on Turf	.357	.425	.596	342	122	28	0	18	67	44	53	.303	.373	.499	986	299	66	5	39	153	112	147
Day Games	.301	.356	.500	156	47	14	1	5	24	15	34	.293	.348	.481	437	128	22	3	18	59	40	78
Night Games	.337	.415	.538	392	132	28	0	17	76	56	48	.301	.374	.479	1163	350	71	5	42	182	138	168
April	.293	.365	.427	75	22	4	0	2	7	9	12	.336	.391	.517	232	78	10	1	10	32	22	37
May	.300	.381	.511	90	27	7	0	4	15	13	14	.301	.371	.521	286	86	16	1	15	42	33	44
June	.226	.323	.333	84	19	6	0	1	10	13	16	.264	.351	.388	276	73	19	0	5	30	38	40
July	.434	.489	.735	83	36	8	1	5	25	9	11	.336	.398	.534	247	83	17	1	10	47	27	38
August	.377	.447	.660	106	40	12	0	6	17	14	13	.310	.372	.525	261	81	19	2	11	38	26	41
Sept–Oct	.318	.384	.473	110	35	5	0	4	26	13	16	.258	.331	.409	298	77	12	3	9	52	32	46
Bases Empty	.311	.373	.516	283	88	23	1	11	11	28	39	.296	.353	.485	881	261	50	4	36	36	77	122
Leadoff	.307	.351	.545	88	27	7	1	4	4	6	15	.272	.311	.438	320	87	11	3	12	12	17	37
Runners On Base	.343	.425	.540	265	91	19	0	11	89	43	43	.302	.383	.473	719	217	43	4	24	205	101	124
Scoring Position	.331	.426	.512	166	55	12	0	6	76	34	36	.315	.412	.468	410	129	26	2	11	171	78	84
Late and Close	.284	.410	.444	81	23	7	0	2	13	18	22	.242	.334	.391	248	60	9	2	8	33	35	63

ALFREDO GRIFFIN — bats both — throws right — age 35 — LA — *S — 8-YEAR TOTALS (1984–1991)

1991	BA	OBA	SA	AB	H	2B	3B	HR	RBI	BB	SO	BA	OBA	SA	AB	H	2B	3B	HR	RBI	BB	SO
Total	.243	.286	.271	350	85	6	2	0	27	22	49	.249	.286	.310	3754	936	124	30	15	322	191	377
vs. Left	.265	.314	.286	147	39	1	1	0	8	10	19	.254	.292	.304	1291	328	32	10	4	101	69	135
vs. Right	.227	.265	.261	203	46	5	1	0	19	12	30	.247	.282	.314	2463	608	92	20	11	221	122	242
at Home	.203	.247	.215	158	32	2	0	0	11	11	20	.236	.273	.282	1814	429	51	10	4	146	92	185
on Road	.276	.319	.318	192	53	4	2	0	16	11	29	.261	.298	.337	1940	507	73	20	11	176	99	192
on Grass	.237	.278	.265	249	59	5	1	0	18	15	33	.250	.289	.309	2784	697	97	18	10	246	151	296
on Turf	.257	.306	.287	101	26	1	1	0	9	7	16	.246	.276	.314	970	239	27	12	5	76	40	81
Day Games	.256	.297	.273	121	31	0	1	0	11	6	19	.252	.283	.319	1278	322	41	15	5	132	61	125
Night Games	.236	.280	.271	229	54	6	1	0	16	16	30	.248	.287	.306	2476	614	83	15	10	190	130	252
April	.213	.222	.213	61	13	0	0	0	3	1	9	.243	.276	.316	605	147	30	4	2	51	29	53
May	.263	.356	.342	38	10	1	1	0	5	6	4	.261	.305	.323	541	141	18	5	2	66	34	50
June	.239	.261	.250	88	21	1	0	0	5	3	13	.273	.309	.340	644	176	19	6	4	54	33	73
July	.268	.322	.329	82	22	3	1	0	6	6	13	.233	.274	.285	589	137	17	4	3	45	33	53
August	.214	.267	.214	14	3	0	0	0	1	1	2	.237	.274	.298	691	164	20	5	4	55	36	67
Sept–Oct	.239	.288	.254	67	16	1	0	0	6	5	8	.250	.277	.301	684	171	20	6	1	51	26	81
Bases Empty	.211	.247	.235	213	45	5	0	0	0	10	37	.234	.276	.291	2240	524	82	11	8	8	122	241
Leadoff	.170	.215	.193	88	15	2	0	0	0	5	16	.217	.266	.271	999	217	32	5	4	4	64	104
Runners On Base	.292	.342	.328	137	40	1	2	0	27	12	12	.272	.300	.339	1514	412	42	19	7	314	69	136
Scoring Position	.262	.319	.287	80	21	0	1	0	26	8	10	.254	.292	.323	902	229	25	14	3	298	58	90
Late and Close	.328	.358	.359	64	21	2	0	0	5	3	9	.245	.278	.299	628	154	15	5	3	56	28	75

MARQUIS GRISSOM — bats right — throws right — age 25 — MON — *O

1991 / **3-YEAR TOTALS (1989–1991)**

1991	BA	OBA	SA	AB	H	2B	3B	HR	RBI	BB	SO		BA	OBA	SA	AB	H	2B	3B	HR	RBI	BB	SO
Total	.267	.310	.373	558	149	23	9	6	39	34	89		.263	.318	.362	920	242	39	11	10	70	73	150
vs. Left	.284	.341	.389	211	60	11	1	3	18	18	35		.264	.328	.367	425	112	23	3	5	34	41	68
vs. Right	.256	.291	.363	347	89	12	8	3	21	16	54		.263	.309	.358	495	130	16	8	5	36	32	82
at Home	.279	.323	.373	233	65	7	3	3	18	15	41		.272	.333	.365	416	113	14	5	5	36	38	73
on Road	.258	.301	.372	325	84	16	6	3	21	19	48		.256	.305	.359	504	129	25	6	5	34	35	77
on Grass	.260	.291	.326	181	47	3	3	1	12	7	27		.247	.291	.307	267	66	4	3	2	14	16	41
on Turf	.271	.319	.395	377	102	20	6	5	27	27	62		.270	.328	.384	653	176	35	8	8	56	57	109
Day Games	.234	.285	.341	167	39	5	2	3	18	12	36		.222	.285	.326	270	60	9	2	5	25	24	59
Night Games	.281	.321	.386	391	110	18	7	3	21	22	53		.280	.331	.377	650	182	30	9	5	45	49	91
April	.229	.250	.371	35	8	2	0	1	6	1	9		.229	.282	.349	109	25	10	0	1	11	8	21
May	.305	.359	.466	118	36	5	1	4	9	10	19		.289	.340	.397	194	56	7	1	4	13	15	27
June	.268	.322	.313	112	30	3	1	0	7	9	17		.276	.333	.328	116	32	4	1	0	8	10	18
July	.198	.263	.242	91	18	2	1	0	7	7	18		.230	.296	.311	148	34	3	3	1	13	13	27
August	.242	.274	.429	91	22	6	4	1	4	4	12		.233	.271	.391	133	31	7	4	2	11	7	17
Sept–Oct	.315	.333	.396	111	35	5	2	0	6	3	14		.291	.349	.373	220	64	8	2	2	14	20	40
Bases Empty	.249	.292	.365	345	86	17	7	3	3	20	57		.249	.305	.357	558	139	26	6	6	6	44	95
Leadoff	.224	.287	.333	147	33	7	3	1	1	13	25		.257	.325	.376	226	58	10	4	3	3	23	39
Runners On Base	.296	.339	.385	213	63	6	2	3	36	14	32		.285	.337	.370	362	103	13	3	4	64	29	55
Scoring Position	.288	.355	.408	125	36	4	1	3	34	13	23		.274	.346	.377	215	59	8	1	4	59	24	42
Late and Close	.191	.239	.273	110	21	1	1	2	11	7	20		.226	.283	.321	190	43	4	1	4	22	15	39

KELLY GRUBER — bats right — throws right — age 30 — TOR — *3/D

1991 / **8-YEAR TOTALS (1984–1991)**

1991	BA	OBA	SA	AB	H	2B	3B	HR	RBI	BB	SO		BA	OBA	SA	AB	H	2B	3B	HR	RBI	BB	SO
Total	.252	.308	.443	429	108	18	2	20	65	31	70		.264	.312	.445	2647	698	128	21	103	391	169	421
vs. Left	.277	.323	.527	112	31	4	0	8	18	8	15		.268	.311	.448	857	230	44	10	30	120	56	139
vs. Right	.243	.303	.413	317	77	14	2	12	47	23	55		.261	.313	.443	1790	468	84	11	73	271	113	282
at Home	.262	.327	.398	221	58	6	0	8	31	18	34		.267	.313	.447	1328	355	55	12	53	196	81	217
on Road	.240	.288	.490	208	50	12	2	12	34	13	36		.260	.311	.443	1319	343	73	9	50	195	88	204
on Grass	.247	.301	.506	166	41	11	1	10	29	12	27		.260	.313	.455	1072	279	66	7	43	167	74	161
on Turf	.255	.313	.403	263	67	7	1	10	36	19	43		.266	.312	.437	1575	419	62	14	60	224	95	260
Day Games	.304	.353	.529	138	42	7	0	8	24	9	19		.249	.298	.428	853	212	39	6	34	129	52	140
Night Games	.227	.286	.402	291	66	11	2	12	41	22	51		.271	.318	.453	1794	486	89	15	69	262	117	281
April	.257	.321	.419	74	19	1	1	3	11	7	13		.300	.349	.516	337	101	13	3	18	62	22	63
May	.000	.333	.000	2	0	0	0	0	0	1	1		.273	.335	.446	417	114	27	3	13	55	37	66
June	.204	.317	.407	54	11	2	0	3	5	6	9		.295	.348	.515	478	141	27	3	24	78	33	73
July	.286	.329	.486	70	20	2	0	4	13	5	14		.228	.265	.371	447	102	15	2	15	51	18	71
August	.236	.286	.418	110	26	8	0	4	13	7	14		.224	.257	.350	451	101	23	2	10	51	19	63
Sept–Oct	.269	.302	.479	119	32	5	1	6	23	5	19		.269	.323	.478	517	139	23	8	23	94	40	85
Bases Empty	.251	.298	.454	227	57	8	1	12	12	13	39		.245	.294	.424	1492	366	69	9	60	60	86	261
Leadoff	.223	.255	.362	94	21	2	1	3	3	4	13		.239	.283	.385	553	132	22	4	17	17	28	85
Runners On Base	.252	.319	.431	202	51	10	1	8	53	18	31		.287	.334	.471	1155	332	59	12	43	331	83	160
Scoring Position	.238	.320	.369	130	31	6	1	3	42	15	23		.284	.336	.481	701	199	40	10	26	289	62	104
Late and Close	.224	.268	.368	76	17	2	0	3	11	5	21		.271	.320	.442	421	114	17	2	17	78	28	72

PEDRO GUERRERO — bats right — throws right — age 36 — SL — *1

1991 / **8-YEAR TOTALS (1984–1991)**

1991	BA	OBA	SA	AB	H	2B	3B	HR	RBI	BB	SO		BA	OBA	SA	AB	H	2B	3B	HR	RBI	BB	SO
Total	.272	.326	.361	427	116	12	1	8	70	37	46		.302	.375	.472	3485	1054	178	13	129	591	413	536
vs. Left	.256	.326	.300	160	41	5	1	0	15	17	14		.301	.379	.453	1167	351	62	4	36	171	155	179
vs. Right	.281	.327	.397	267	75	7	0	8	55	20	32		.303	.372	.481	2318	703	116	9	93	420	258	357
at Home	.282	.340	.370	216	61	7	0	4	42	21	23		.302	.371	.447	1791	540	91	5	53	307	207	283
on Road	.261	.311	.351	211	55	5	1	4	28	16	23		.303	.378	.499	1694	514	87	8	76	284	206	253
on Grass	.237	.289	.263	118	28	1	1	0	10	9	14		.312	.386	.492	1805	564	74	8	78	292	211	285
on Turf	.285	.340	.398	309	88	11	0	8	60	28	32		.292	.363	.451	1680	490	104	5	51	299	202	251
Day Games	.294	.348	.412	119	35	3	1	3	20	12	11		.304	.371	.475	1096	333	58	5	40	187	123	166
Night Games	.263	.318	.341	308	81	9	0	5	50	25	35		.302	.376	.470	2389	721	120	8	89	404	290	370
April	.278	.360	.392	79	22	3	0	2	13	10	7		.280	.363	.454	535	150	24	3	21	101	69	82
May	.300	.330	.400	90	27	4	1	1	18	5	6		.309	.366	.465	632	195	39	3	18	100	62	93
June	.244	.324	.278	90	22	0	0	1	13	12	9		.294	.368	.460	606	178	24	4	23	88	75	101
July	.367	.387	.700	30	11	1	0	3	9	1	3		.340	.421	.551	430	146	30	2	19	76	63	60
August	.175	.227	.175	40	7	0	0	0	2	3	9		.279	.350	.431	578	161	23	1	21	94	65	93
Sept–Oct	.276	.321	.347	98	27	4	0	1	15	6	12		.318	.387	.487	704	224	38	0	27	132	79	107
Bases Empty	.244	.313	.335	221	54	6	1	4	4	22	25		.298	.364	.478	1868	557	101	8	73	73	183	292
Leadoff	.248	.320	.345	113	28	3	1	2	2	12	17		.290	.353	.450	831	241	39	5	28	28	78	122
Runners On Base	.301	.341	.388	206	62	6	0	4	66	15	21		.307	.386	.465	1617	497	77	5	56	518	230	244
Scoring Position	.350	.394	.455	143	50	6	0	3	64	14	11		.317	.414	.488	955	303	52	3	35	461	190	147
Late and Close	.254	.308	.310	71	18	1	0	1	13	6	11		.274	.370	.431	536	147	23	2	19	95	84	79

OZZIE GUILLEN — bats left — throws right — age 28 — CHA — *S

1991	BA	OBA	SA	AB	H	2B	3B	HR	RBI	BB	SO		7-YEAR TOTALS (1985–1991) BA	OBA	SA	AB	H	2B	3B	HR	RBI	BB	SO
Total	.273	.284	.340	524	143	20	3	3	49	11	38		.267	.288	.333	3801	1013	139	42	10	331	123	303
vs. Left	.211	.213	.248	161	34	3	0	1	9	1	15		.241	.259	.279	1168	282	28	5	2	98	29	118
vs. Right	.300	.315	.380	363	109	17	3	2	40	10	23		.278	.301	.357	2633	731	111	37	8	233	94	185
at Home	.287	.291	.364	247	71	10	3	1	29	4	21		.273	.296	.344	1851	505	62	26	6	177	67	142
on Road	.260	.278	.318	277	72	10	0	2	20	7	17		.261	.281	.323	1950	508	77	16	4	154	56	161
on Grass	.274	.287	.347	449	123	18	3	3	44	11	34		.265	.287	.333	3241	858	120	37	9	282	107	263
on Turf	.267	.267	.293	75	20	2	0	0	5	0	4		.277	.295	.334	560	155	19	5	1	49	16	40
Day Games	.285	.305	.347	144	41	4	1	1	10	5	9		.273	.299	.339	1028	281	40	12	1	86	39	79
Night Games	.268	.276	.337	380	102	16	2	2	39	6	29		.264	.284	.331	2773	732	99	30	9	245	84	224
April	.283	.313	.317	60	17	2	0	0	5	3	4		.257	.289	.313	479	123	17	5	0	33	23	37
May	.289	.290	.320	97	28	3	0	0	7	1	9		.276	.302	.337	671	185	19	8	2	42	26	55
June	.250	.263	.333	96	24	4	2	0	6	2	5		.257	.268	.312	647	166	23	5	1	62	11	48
July	.242	.242	.264	91	22	2	0	0	9	0	7		.288	.307	.350	632	182	27	6	0	68	18	50
August	.266	.283	.415	94	25	6	1	2	13	3	6		.263	.284	.341	672	177	28	6	4	59	20	46
Sept–Oct	.314	.326	.384	86	27	3	0	1	9	2	7		.257	.281	.340	700	180	25	12	3	67	25	67
Bases Empty	.267	.283	.322	307	82	15	1	0	0	7	26		.252	.277	.312	2241	565	76	22	5	5	73	215
Leadoff	.296	.315	.380	108	32	9	0	0	0	3	12		.255	.280	.305	954	243	36	6	0	0	33	103
Runners On Base	.281	.285	.364	217	61	5	2	3	49	4	12		.287	.304	.363	1560	448	63	20	5	326	50	88
Scoring Position	.248	.257	.349	129	32	4	0	3	46	4	6		.293	.318	.379	902	264	36	15	4	315	46	51
Late and Close	.273	.296	.344	128	35	6	0	1	13	5	12		.287	.317	.354	704	202	24	7	3	71	33	59

TONY GWYNN — bats left — throws left — age 32 — SD — *O

1991	BA	OBA	SA	AB	H	2B	3B	HR	RBI	BB	SO		8-YEAR TOTALS (1984–1991) BA	OBA	SA	AB	H	2B	3B	HR	RBI	BB	SO
Total	.318	.357	.433	529	168	27	11	4	62	35	18		.331	.386	.440	4685	1550	224	68	51	497	424	237
vs. Left	.300	.341	.401	207	62	7	4	2	19	14	5		.312	.364	.401	1723	537	60	20	18	177	137	96
vs. Right	.329	.367	.453	322	106	20	7	2	43	21	13		.342	.398	.463	2962	1013	164	48	33	320	287	141
at Home	.307	.348	.406	244	75	13	4	1	21	17	12		.337	.393	.455	2297	774	107	40	28	228	215	120
on Road	.326	.364	.456	285	93	14	7	3	41	18	6		.325	.379	.426	2388	776	117	28	23	269	209	117
on Grass	.321	.367	.437	371	119	20	7	3	37	29	16		.330	.387	.439	3432	1132	160	53	36	339	319	175
on Turf	.310	.331	.424	158	49	7	4	1	25	6	2		.334	.382	.445	1253	418	64	15	15	158	105	62
Day Games	.295	.333	.423	149	44	7	6	0	15	9	4		.308	.368	.408	1464	451	65	17	16	160	142	77
Night Games	.326	.366	.437	380	124	20	5	4	47	26	14		.341	.394	.455	3221	1099	159	51	35	337	282	160
April	.341	.378	.463	82	28	4	3	0	13	6	3		.333	.383	.469	670	223	36	11	11	57	55	38
May	.362	.403	.560	116	42	9	4	2	21	8	3		.315	.385	.439	749	236	42	15	7	77	81	36
June	.364	.374	.436	110	40	6	1	0	12	3	4		.357	.409	.482	873	312	44	16	11	115	81	41
July	.255	.304	.309	94	24	3	1	0	5	7	3		.315	.362	.414	828	261	33	8	11	87	61	50
August	.288	.351	.423	104	30	4	2	2	11	10	5		.345	.396	.435	875	302	42	8	7	88	74	43
Sept–Oct	.174	.208	.217	23	4	1	0	0	0	1	0		.313	.376	.399	690	216	27	10	4	73	72	29
Bases Empty	.279	.313	.386	298	83	14	6	2	2	15	11		.317	.359	.424	2772	878	122	37	34	34	177	151
Leadoff	.224	.262	.296	98	22	4	0	1	1	5	4		.332	.366	.437	931	309	34	14	12	12	48	45
Runners On Base	.368	.410	.494	231	85	13	5	2	60	20	7		.351	.421	.464	1913	672	102	31	17	463	247	86
Scoring Position	.380	.433	.527	129	49	8	4	1	55	16	6		.336	.435	.445	1020	343	50	17	9	410	199	58
Late and Close	.348	.398	.438	89	31	3	1	1	9	8	4		.333	.402	.426	789	263	32	7	9	87	93	50

MEL HALL — bats left — throws left — age 32 — NYA — *OD

1991	BA	OBA	SA	AB	H	2B	3B	HR	RBI	BB	SO		8-YEAR TOTALS (1984–1991) BA	OBA	SA	AB	H	2B	3B	HR	RBI	BB	SO
Total	.285	.321	.455	492	140	23	2	19	80	26	40		.277	.317	.437	3128	867	167	15	101	472	189	396
vs. Left	.309	.353	.444	162	50	5	1	5	27	9	9		.229	.286	.330	433	99	15	1	9	58	34	60
vs. Right	.273	.305	.461	330	90	18	1	14	53	17	31		.285	.322	.454	2695	768	152	14	92	414	155	336
at Home	.273	.317	.478	245	67	9	1	13	48	16	17		.282	.321	.447	1547	437	78	9	53	244	93	168
on Road	.296	.324	.433	247	73	14	1	6	32	10	23		.272	.313	.427	1581	430	89	6	48	228	96	228
on Grass	.283	.317	.460	424	120	17	2	18	73	21	29		.274	.310	.433	2656	729	133	11	89	402	143	318
on Turf	.294	.342	.426	68	20	6	0	1	7	5	11		.292	.356	.458	472	138	34	4	12	70	46	78
Day Games	.296	.335	.457	162	48	6	1	6	30	10	11		.289	.332	.470	1071	309	70	5	38	176	76	129
Night Games	.279	.313	.455	330	92	17	1	13	50	16	29		.271	.308	.420	2057	558	97	10	63	296	113	267
April	.176	.171	.353	34	6	3	0	1	8	0	3		.258	.298	.399	383	99	23	2	9	59	23	59
May	.297	.329	.622	74	22	3	0	7	18	2	6		.263	.296	.456	471	124	31	3	18	64	22	61
June	.333	.385	.500	84	28	5	0	3	14	7	8		.308	.358	.497	577	178	30	2	25	102	46	68
July	.353	.380	.506	85	30	4	0	3	17	4	8		.298	.332	.458	541	161	27	3	18	88	30	77
August	.300	.338	.475	120	36	5	2	4	18	8	7		.279	.321	.398	606	169	33	3	11	84	40	75
Sept–Oct	.189	.230	.253	95	18	3	0	1	5	5	8		.247	.283	.405	550	136	23	2	20	75	28	56
Bases Empty	.295	.318	.466	234	69	14	1	8	8	7	25		.277	.310	.440	1688	467	87	6	59	59	76	236
Leadoff	.259	.279	.417	108	28	8	0	3	3	3	12		.262	.284	.420	722	189	39	3	23	23	22	96
Runners On Base	.275	.323	.446	258	71	9	1	11	72	19	15		.278	.325	.433	1440	400	80	9	42	413	113	160
Scoring Position	.250	.305	.396	144	36	4	1	5	59	14	9		.277	.330	.428	839	232	56	7	19	357	85	88
Late and Close	.218	.282	.449	78	17	3	0	5	15	6	8		.276	.324	.470	474	131	27	1	21	76	35	57

BRIAN HARPER — bats right — throws right — age 33 — MIN — *C/D1O

1991	BA	OBA	SA	AB	H	2B	3B	HR	RBI	BB	SO
Total	.311	.336	.447	441	137	28	1	10	69	14	22
vs. Left	.316	.344	.447	114	36	7	1	2	14	5	8
vs. Right	.309	.333	.446	327	101	21	0	8	55	9	14
at Home	.341	.364	.470	217	74	14	1	4	35	7	12
on Road	.281	.309	.424	224	63	14	0	6	34	7	10
on Grass	.275	.313	.443	167	46	10	0	6	32	7	7
on Turf	.332	.351	.449	274	91	18	1	4	37	7	15
Day Games	.272	.300	.417	103	28	6	0	3	15	3	5
Night Games	.322	.347	.456	338	109	22	1	7	54	11	17
April	.327	.370	.510	49	16	3	0	2	7	3	3
May	.346	.361	.487	78	27	8	0	1	18	3	3
June	.304	.333	.392	79	24	7	0	0	7	1	5
July	.288	.303	.411	73	21	3	0	2	8	2	2
August	.317	.341	.488	82	26	3	1	3	17	2	7
Sept–Oct	.287	.318	.412	80	23	4	0	2	12	3	2
Bases Empty	.273	.300	.351	231	63	15	0	1	1	6	11
Leadoff	.312	.333	.419	93	29	7	0	1	1	2	1
Runners On Base	.352	.374	.552	210	74	13	1	9	68	8	11
Scoring Position	.313	.351	.473	131	41	9	0	4	56	8	6
Late and Close	.324	.333	.515	68	22	2	1	3	17	1	1

8-YEAR TOTALS (1984–1991)

	BA	OBA	SA	AB	H	2B	3B	HR	RBI	BB	SO
	.298	.330	.424	1688	503	115	5	29	225	66	98
	.279	.316	.412	628	175	44	2	12	80	32	40
	.309	.338	.430	1060	328	71	3	17	145	34	58
	.299	.331	.412	823	246	55	4	10	104	35	46
	.297	.329	.435	865	257	60	1	19	121	31	52
	.277	.312	.418	638	177	42	0	16	91	26	42
	.310	.341	.427	1050	326	73	5	13	134	40	56
	.300	.335	.428	444	133	31	1	8	69	19	25
	.297	.328	.422	1244	370	84	4	21	156	47	73
	.307	.363	.484	153	47	12	0	5	25	9	6
	.283	.315	.426	258	73	19	0	6	46	12	17
	.296	.340	.375	277	82	17	1	1	26	13	21
	.315	.337	.414	314	99	19	0	4	37	10	13
	.307	.325	.474	342	105	24	3	9	54	6	18
	.282	.316	.392	344	97	24	1	4	37	16	23
	.285	.318	.399	873	249	56	2	13	13	29	48
	.306	.332	.442	369	113	29	0	7	7	10	11
	.312	.342	.450	815	254	59	3	16	212	37	50
	.299	.335	.426	458	137	32	1	8	185	26	30
	.309	.331	.446	269	83	11	1	8	49	8	14

LENNY HARRIS — bats left — throws right — age 28 — LA — *32S/O

1991	BA	OBA	SA	AB	H	2B	3B	HR	RBI	BB	SO
Total	.287	.349	.350	429	123	16	1	3	38	37	32
vs. Left	.235	.305	.271	85	20	0	0	1	9	6	8
vs. Right	.299	.360	.369	344	103	16	1	2	29	31	24
at Home	.275	.341	.318	211	58	6	0	1	17	18	18
on Road	.298	.357	.381	218	65	10	1	2	21	19	14
on Grass	.265	.323	.326	313	83	11	1	2	28	24	24
on Turf	.345	.417	.414	116	40	5	0	1	10	13	8
Day Games	.268	.329	.341	138	37	5	1	1	10	11	17
Night Games	.296	.358	.354	291	86	11	0	2	28	26	15
April	.256	.310	.256	39	10	0	0	0	3	3	2
May	.365	.444	.397	63	23	2	0	0	3	9	7
June	.278	.337	.356	90	25	2	1	1	11	7	7
July	.213	.284	.262	61	13	3	0	0	6	5	6
August	.318	.361	.432	88	28	7	0	1	7	6	5
Sept–Oct	.273	.340	.330	88	24	2	0	1	7	5	7
Bases Empty	.286	.348	.329	234	67	10	0	0	0	20	16
Leadoff	.309	.356	.319	94	29	1	0	0	0	6	8
Runners On Base	.287	.350	.374	195	56	6	1	3	38	17	16
Scoring Position	.280	.345	.360	100	28	0	1	2	32	11	11
Late and Close	.315	.414	.370	73	23	4	0	1	7	10	5

4-YEAR TOTALS (1988–1991)

	BA	OBA	SA	AB	H	2B	3B	HR	RBI	BB	SO
	.282	.334	.346	1238	349	43	6	8	101	91	100
	.228	.295	.264	197	45	2	1	1	18	13	22
	.292	.341	.361	1041	304	41	5	7	83	78	78
	.275	.326	.327	611	168	20	3	2	44	43	48
	.289	.342	.364	627	181	23	3	6	57	48	52
	.279	.327	.347	825	230	28	5	6	71	58	68
	.288	.347	.344	413	119	15	1	2	30	33	32
	.267	.333	.338	382	102	11	2	4	33	35	37
	.289	.334	.349	856	247	32	4	4	68	56	63
	.242	.284	.263	95	23	0	1	0	8	6	4
	.326	.392	.394	175	57	8	2	0	13	18	20
	.275	.312	.345	255	70	7	1	3	19	13	21
	.242	.301	.313	211	51	10	1	1	18	15	14
	.288	.329	.340	212	61	8	0	1	17	13	15
	.300	.359	.372	290	87	10	1	3	26	26	26
	.282	.336	.337	756	213	30	3	2	2	57	56
	.287	.332	.331	363	104	9	2	1	1	24	21
	.282	.330	.359	482	136	13	3	6	99	34	44
	.272	.320	.340	250	68	2	3	3	86	20	28
	.264	.341	.295	193	51	6	0	0	12	20	22

BILLY HATCHER — bats right — throws right — age 32 — CIN — *O

1991	BA	OBA	SA	AB	H	2B	3B	HR	RBI	BB	SO
Total	.262	.312	.360	442	116	25	3	4	41	26	55
vs. Left	.277	.324	.369	130	36	7	1	1	11	8	20
vs. Right	.256	.307	.356	312	80	18	2	3	30	18	35
at Home	.269	.323	.380	216	58	16	1	2	17	16	24
on Road	.257	.300	.341	226	58	9	2	2	24	10	31
on Grass	.264	.287	.341	129	34	5	1	1	12	4	19
on Turf	.262	.322	.367	313	82	20	2	3	29	22	36
Day Games	.211	.285	.341	123	26	8	1	2	9	11	16
Night Games	.282	.323	.367	319	90	17	2	2	32	15	39
April	.130	.184	.130	46	6	0	0	0	4	1	7
May	.313	.348	.453	64	20	4	1	1	7	3	6
June	.295	.346	.474	95	28	9	1	2	7	6	14
July	.304	.325	.392	79	24	4	0	1	11	3	14
August	.194	.275	.222	72	14	2	0	0	4	8	9
Sept–Oct	.279	.333	.372	86	24	6	1	0	8	5	5
Bases Empty	.242	.288	.335	281	68	15	1	3	3	13	40
Leadoff	.220	.289	.276	123	27	7	0	0	0	9	23
Runners On Base	.298	.352	.404	161	48	10	2	1	38	13	15
Scoring Position	.340	.387	.447	94	32	6	2	0	35	9	12
Late and Close	.325	.361	.416	77	25	3	2	0	12	3	8

8-YEAR TOTALS (1984–1991)

	BA	OBA	SA	AB	H	2B	3B	HR	RBI	BB	SO
	.265	.315	.366	3111	824	152	23	39	278	199	349
	.272	.317	.371	1163	316	50	10	15	109	77	125
	.261	.314	.363	1948	508	102	13	24	169	122	224
	.260	.313	.352	1545	401	75	13	14	129	107	180
	.270	.317	.380	1566	423	77	10	25	149	92	169
	.254	.302	.366	1011	257	40	8	19	93	62	111
	.270	.321	.366	2100	567	112	15	20	185	137	238
	.268	.327	.407	1004	269	61	8	21	113	75	95
	.263	.309	.346	2107	555	91	15	18	165	124	254
	.281	.321	.386	399	112	16	4	6	41	21	58
	.288	.338	.361	490	141	24	3	2	40	31	53
	.276	.324	.412	634	175	37	8	11	59	41	84
	.249	.304	.318	503	125	26	0	3	37	35	63
	.262	.312	.391	516	135	31	3	10	50	33	45
	.239	.294	.325	569	136	18	5	7	51	38	46
	.260	.307	.365	1974	514	103	13	26	26	107	220
	.264	.320	.357	899	237	51	6	7	7	62	111
	.273	.328	.368	1137	310	49	10	13	252	92	129
	.264	.330	.355	692	183	31	7	6	230	70	86
	.280	.336	.386	510	143	27	6	6	61	38	77

CHARLIE HAYES — bats right — throws right — age 27 — PHI — *3/S

1991

	BA	OBA	SA	AB	H	2B	3B	HR	RBI	BB	SO
Total	.230	.257	.363	460	106	23	1	12	53	16	75
vs. Left	.259	.284	.397	189	49	14	0	4	22	6	29
vs. Right	.210	.238	.339	271	57	9	1	8	31	10	46
at Home	.262	.292	.407	248	65	16	1	6	34	10	36
on Road	.193	.216	.311	212	41	7	0	6	19	6	39
on Grass	.178	.218	.305	118	21	3	0	4	11	6	20
on Turf	.249	.271	.383	342	85	20	1	8	42	10	55
Day Games	.210	.246	.355	124	26	7	1	3	14	6	19
Night Games	.238	.261	.366	336	80	16	0	9	39	10	56
April	.247	.266	.416	77	19	4	0	3	14	2	14
May	.165	.198	.278	97	16	3	1	2	7	4	16
June	.210	.242	.290	62	13	2	0	1	5	3	15
July	.143	.189	.200	35	5	2	0	0	1	2	4
August	.274	.274	.451	113	31	8	0	4	14	0	17
Sept–Oct	.289	.341	.421	76	22	4	0	2	12	5	9
Bases Empty	.236	.263	.364	242	57	8	1	7	7	9	38
Leadoff	.267	.292	.465	86	23	5	0	4	4	3	14
Runners On Base	.225	.251	.362	218	49	15	0	5	46	7	37
Scoring Position	.239	.263	.404	109	26	6	0	4	38	4	21
Late and Close	.320	.352	.530	100	32	7	1	4	11	5	15

4-YEAR TOTALS (1988–1991)

	BA	OBA	SA	AB	H	2B	3B	HR	RBI	BB	SO
Total	.247	.276	.361	1336	330	58	2	30	153	55	219
vs. Left	.274	.301	.398	493	135	31	0	10	58	19	73
vs. Right	.231	.262	.339	843	195	27	2	20	95	36	146
at Home	.246	.275	.353	691	170	34	2	12	84	29	116
on Road	.248	.278	.369	645	160	24	0	18	69	26	103
on Grass	.246	.277	.383	350	86	15	0	11	35	16	55
on Turf	.247	.276	.353	986	244	43	2	19	118	39	164
Day Games	.226	.254	.361	368	83	19	2	9	38	15	61
Night Games	.255	.285	.361	968	247	39	0	21	115	40	158
April	.239	.270	.345	142	34	6	0	3	19	6	24
May	.234	.276	.356	188	44	6	1	5	16	11	33
June	.270	.294	.365	178	48	8	0	3	18	6	31
July	.231	.272	.376	229	53	9	0	8	34	14	37
August	.253	.263	.383	324	82	21	0	7	35	4	46
Sept–Oct	.251	.287	.331	275	69	8	1	4	31	14	48
Bases Empty	.246	.278	.358	741	182	30	1	17	17	33	129
Leadoff	.259	.278	.415	294	76	16	0	10	10	8	41
Runners On Base	.249	.275	.365	595	148	28	1	13	136	22	90
Scoring Position	.237	.262	.356	337	80	14	1	8	120	14	58
Late and Close	.272	.303	.420	250	68	11	1	8	29	11	46

DAVE HENDERSON — bats right — throws right — age 34 — OAK — *O/D2

1991

	BA	OBA	SA	AB	H	2B	3B	HR	RBI	BB	SO
Total	.276	.346	.465	572	158	33	0	25	85	58	113
vs. Left	.354	.416	.618	144	51	14	0	8	24	15	23
vs. Right	.250	.322	.414	428	107	19	0	17	61	43	90
at Home	.259	.329	.450	282	73	9	0	15	39	29	57
on Road	.293	.362	.479	290	85	24	0	10	46	29	56
on Grass	.287	.357	.480	488	140	25	0	23	77	51	99
on Turf	.214	.283	.381	84	18	8	0	2	8	7	14
Day Games	.272	.348	.511	184	50	8	0	12	33	21	42
Night Games	.278	.345	.443	388	108	25	0	13	52	37	71
April	.387	.453	.747	75	29	9	0	6	18	9	12
May	.294	.345	.520	102	30	5	0	6	21	8	15
June	.269	.376	.495	93	25	3	0	6	11	16	20
July	.206	.280	.289	97	20	5	0	1	10	9	20
August	.297	.346	.466	118	35	5	0	5	15	7	21
Sept–Oct	.218	.289	.322	87	19	6	0	1	10	9	25
Bases Empty	.262	.340	.462	305	80	16	0	15	15	33	50
Leadoff	.286	.325	.496	119	34	7	0	6	6	6	17
Runners On Base	.292	.353	.468	267	78	17	0	10	70	25	63
Scoring Position	.281	.349	.464	153	43	10	0	6	58	17	44
Late and Close	.271	.327	.354	96	26	5	0	1	7	7	20

8-YEAR TOTALS (1984–1991)

	BA	OBA	SA	AB	H	2B	3B	HR	RBI	BB	SO
Total	.267	.332	.445	3553	949	208	10	135	505	335	763
vs. Left	.304	.365	.517	1043	317	72	3	48	157	96	169
vs. Right	.252	.318	.416	2510	632	136	7	87	348	239	594
at Home	.278	.341	.469	1807	502	99	6	78	273	167	380
on Road	.256	.322	.421	1746	447	109	4	57	232	168	383
on Grass	.266	.331	.440	2458	653	139	4	94	348	235	536
on Turf	.270	.334	.457	1095	296	69	6	41	157	100	227
Day Games	.277	.340	.474	1180	327	69	2	53	188	115	242
Night Games	.262	.327	.431	2373	622	139	8	82	317	220	521
April	.266	.351	.462	485	129	23	3	22	66	63	115
May	.277	.328	.474	622	172	35	2	28	98	45	120
June	.247	.321	.436	667	165	41	2	27	95	70	148
July	.271	.327	.429	634	172	33	2	21	82	52	131
August	.277	.332	.443	596	165	40	1	19	79	47	120
Sept–Oct	.266	.336	.430	549	146	36	0	18	85	58	129
Bases Empty	.263	.333	.460	1932	509	112	5	86	86	190	403
Leadoff	.290	.339	.504	756	219	53	2	35	35	53	140
Runners On Base	.271	.329	.428	1621	440	96	5	49	419	145	360
Scoring Position	.277	.345	.415	931	258	53	3	23	347	104	217
Late and Close	.262	.315	.446	558	146	21	2	26	72	43	126

RICKEY HENDERSON — bats right — throws left — age 34 — OAK — *OD

1991

	BA	OBA	SA	AB	H	2B	3B	HR	RBI	BB	SO
Total	.268	.400	.423	470	126	17	1	18	57	98	73
vs. Left	.289	.401	.526	114	33	3	0	8	17	21	19
vs. Right	.261	.399	.390	356	93	14	1	10	40	77	54
at Home	.278	.401	.415	248	69	10	0	8	28	48	36
on Road	.257	.399	.432	222	57	7	1	10	29	50	37
on Grass	.270	.395	.412	415	112	15	1	14	47	81	62
on Turf	.255	.432	.509	55	14	2	0	4	10	17	11
Day Games	.291	.409	.430	151	44	6	0	5	19	30	23
Night Games	.257	.395	.420	319	82	11	1	13	38	68	50
April	.273	.360	.273	22	6	0	0	0	1	2	3
May	.253	.410	.389	95	24	4	0	3	12	26	18
June	.321	.481	.407	81	26	2	1	1	8	24	7
July	.248	.367	.406	101	25	4	0	4	12	16	17
August	.238	.363	.452	84	20	3	0	5	10	16	14
Sept–Oct	.287	.388	.506	87	25	4	0	5	14	14	14
Bases Empty	.270	.381	.405	311	84	12	0	10	10	51	49
Leadoff	.292	.410	.454	185	54	9	0	7	7	35	26
Runners On Base	.264	.431	.459	159	42	5	1	8	47	47	24
Scoring Position	.231	.447	.473	91	21	2	1	6	41	36	12
Late and Close	.239	.400	.408	71	17	3	0	3	15	19	13

8-YEAR TOTALS (1984–1991)

	BA	OBA	SA	AB	H	2B	3B	HR	RBI	BB	SO
Total	.291	.404	.465	4069	1185	209	26	149	466	757	534
vs. Left	.304	.423	.513	1259	383	77	9	56	134	259	158
vs. Right	.285	.395	.444	2810	802	132	17	93	332	498	376
at Home	.286	.405	.451	1910	546	99	14	63	209	374	243
on Road	.296	.403	.478	2159	639	110	12	86	257	383	291
on Grass	.285	.400	.454	3399	968	169	21	121	383	638	451
on Turf	.324	.425	.524	670	217	40	5	28	83	119	83
Day Games	.295	.411	.463	1287	380	64	4	28	154	251	169
Night Games	.289	.401	.466	2782	805	145	22	101	312	506	365
April	.303	.399	.484	545	165	32	5	19	68	88	64
May	.285	.405	.453	751	214	41	5	25	80	146	102
June	.334	.441	.516	641	214	32	5	25	85	123	77
July	.304	.417	.486	695	211	40	3	27	88	132	84
August	.260	.361	.416	649	169	25	2	24	68	101	87
Sept–Oct	.269	.399	.444	788	212	39	6	29	77	167	120
Bases Empty	.293	.398	.474	2704	791	153	20	99	99	455	355
Leadoff	.291	.396	.488	1679	488	93	16	69	69	283	207
Runners On Base	.289	.414	.448	1365	394	56	6	50	367	302	179
Scoring Position	.251	.401	.389	810	203	27	2	27	301	213	123
Late and Close	.324	.439	.518	581	188	28	5	25	100	122	79

CHRIS HOILES — bats right — throws right — age 27 — BAL — CD/1

1991

	BA	OBA	SA	AB	H	2B	3B	HR	RBI	BB	SO
Total	.243	.304	.384	341	83	15	0	11	31	29	61
vs. Left	.257	.320	.469	113	29	6	0	6	8	11	16
vs. Right	.237	.296	.342	228	54	9	0	5	23	18	45
at Home	.229	.306	.373	153	35	7	0	5	12	16	26
on Road	.255	.302	.394	188	48	8	0	6	19	13	35
on Grass	.229	.295	.373	284	65	11	0	10	23	26	51
on Turf	.316	.350	.439	57	18	4	0	1	8	3	10
Day Games	.233	.269	.356	73	17	3	0	2	11	4	11
Night Games	.246	.313	.392	268	66	12	0	9	20	25	50
April	.147	.194	.176	34	5	1	0	0	0	1	8
May	.265	.393	.429	49	13	2	0	2	4	11	8
June	.240	.283	.360	50	12	3	0	1	5	3	6
July	.319	.338	.500	72	23	4	0	3	10	2	12
August	.260	.299	.411	73	19	5	0	2	6	4	15
Sept–Oct	.175	.268	.317	63	11	0	0	3	6	8	12
Bases Empty	.256	.313	.451	195	50	8	0	10	10	16	33
Leadoff	.222	.300	.444	81	18	3	0	5	5	9	14
Runners On Base	.226	.292	.295	146	33	7	0	1	21	13	28
Scoring Position	.227	.316	.303	66	15	2	0	1	19	9	14
Late and Close	.194	.265	.435	62	12	0	0	5	11	6	15

3-YEAR TOTALS (1989–1991)

	BA	OBA	SA	AB	H	2B	3B	HR	RBI	BB	SO
Total	.232	.293	.366	413	96	19	0	12	38	35	76
vs. Left	.219	.279	.377	151	33	6	0	6	8	13	23
vs. Right	.240	.302	.359	262	63	13	0	6	30	22	53
at Home	.233	.310	.376	189	44	9	0	6	15	20	32
on Road	.232	.279	.357	224	52	10	0	6	23	15	44
on Grass	.224	.290	.362	340	76	14	0	11	28	31	62
on Turf	.274	.312	.384	73	20	5	0	1	10	4	14
Day Games	.204	.250	.312	93	19	4	0	2	12	6	17
Night Games	.241	.306	.381	320	77	15	0	10	26	29	59
April	.135	.200	.162	37	5	1	0	0	0	2	9
May	.260	.387	.420	50	13	2	0	2	4	11	9
June	.213	.272	.347	75	16	4	0	2	10	6	12
July	.307	.333	.480	75	23	4	0	3	10	3	12
August	.223	.255	.340	94	21	5	0	2	7	4	21
Sept–Oct	.220	.297	.366	82	18	3	0	3	7	9	13
Bases Empty	.238	.292	.409	235	56	10	0	10	10	18	43
Leadoff	.224	.290	.429	98	22	5	0	5	5	9	18
Runners On Base	.225	.294	.309	178	40	9	0	2	28	17	33
Scoring Position	.214	.316	.333	84	18	4	0	2	26	13	19
Late and Close	.203	.289	.446	74	15	0	0	6	14	9	17

SAM HORN — bats left — throws left — age 29 — BAL — *D

1991

	BA	OBA	SA	AB	H	2B	3B	HR	RBI	BB	SO
Total	.233	.326	.502	317	74	16	0	23	61	41	99
vs. Left	.111	.158	.278	18	2	0	0	1	1	1	7
vs. Right	.241	.335	.515	299	72	16	0	22	60	40	92
at Home	.248	.356	.544	149	37	8	0	12	28	24	40
on Road	.220	.298	.464	168	37	8	0	11	33	17	59
on Grass	.248	.336	.552	270	67	13	0	23	59	34	80
on Turf	.149	.273	.213	47	7	3	0	0	2	7	19
Day Games	.190	.284	.417	84	16	4	0	5	18	9	30
Night Games	.249	.341	.532	233	58	12	0	18	43	32	69
April	.214	.327	.452	42	9	1	0	3	10	7	21
May	.239	.327	.478	46	11	2	0	3	7	6	14
June	.247	.360	.548	73	18	7	0	5	12	12	21
July	.254	.357	.492	59	15	2	0	4	12	9	16
August	.128	.209	.256	39	5	2	0	1	4	4	10
Sept–Oct	.276	.323	.672	58	16	2	0	7	16	3	17
Bases Empty	.177	.262	.359	181	32	6	0	9	9	20	59
Leadoff	.156	.235	.260	77	12	2	0	2	2	8	24
Runners On Base	.309	.406	.691	136	42	10	0	14	52	21	40
Scoring Position	.266	.372	.620	79	21	7	0	7	36	13	29
Late and Close	.234	.294	.553	47	11	6	0	3	12	3	16

5-YEAR TOTALS (1987–1991)

	BA	OBA	SA	AB	H	2B	3B	HR	RBI	BB	SO
Total	.234	.325	.470	836	196	38	0	53	152	109	252
vs. Left	.164	.247	.356	73	12	2	0	4	10	7	33
vs. Right	.241	.332	.481	763	184	36	0	49	142	102	219
at Home	.242	.344	.487	421	102	19	0	28	76	64	125
on Road	.227	.305	.453	415	94	19	0	25	76	45	127
on Grass	.234	.324	.471	715	167	32	0	46	130	93	219
on Turf	.240	.333	.463	121	29	6	0	7	22	16	33
Day Games	.215	.310	.405	247	53	8	0	13	45	32	70
Night Games	.243	.331	.497	589	143	30	0	40	107	77	182
April	.234	.327	.375	128	30	3	0	5	26	18	45
May	.172	.265	.343	134	23	5	0	6	14	17	40
June	.229	.360	.494	83	19	7	0	5	12	16	23
July	.286	.372	.635	126	36	5	0	13	30	18	35
August	.220	.319	.415	164	36	8	0	8	21	23	40
Sept–Oct	.259	.323	.547	201	52	10	0	16	49	17	69
Bases Empty	.223	.301	.445	443	99	17	0	27	27	48	139
Leadoff	.221	.272	.442	199	44	8	0	12	12	14	58
Runners On Base	.247	.351	.499	393	97	21	0	26	125	61	113
Scoring Position	.239	.342	.487	230	55	12	0	15	100	36	72
Late and Close	.225	.308	.399	138	31	6	0	6	30	15	43

THOMAS HOWARD — bats both — throws right — age 28 — SD — O

1991

	BA	OBA	SA	AB	H	2B	3B	HR	RBI	BB	SO
Total	.249	.309	.356	281	70	12	3	4	22	24	57
vs. Left	.286	.394	.464	28	8	0	1	1	2	5	5
vs. Right	.245	.299	.344	253	62	12	2	3	20	19	52
at Home	.257	.316	.386	140	36	4	1	4	14	11	29
on Road	.241	.303	.326	141	34	8	2	0	8	13	28
on Grass	.255	.306	.373	204	52	8	2	4	18	14	41
on Turf	.234	.318	.312	77	18	4	1	0	4	10	16
Day Games	.286	.353	.442	77	22	4	1	2	6	7	12
Night Games	.235	.293	.324	204	48	8	2	2	16	17	45
April	.000	.000	.000	1	0	0	0	0	0	0	0
May	.214	.261	.286	42	9	1	1	0	2	3	10
June	.295	.360	.397	78	23	3	1	1	6	7	7
July	.220	.328	.260	50	11	2	0	0		8	12
August	.200	.217	.333	45	9	3	0	1	5	1	10
Sept–Oct	.277	.329	.446	65	18	3	1	2	9	5	18
Bases Empty	.236	.281	.333	174	41	7	2	2	2	10	30
Leadoff	.202	.239	.274	84	17	4	1	0	0	4	14
Runners On Base	.271	.352	.393	107	29	5	1	2	20	14	27
Scoring Position	.286	.378	.414	70	20	3	0	2	19	11	20
Late and Close	.197	.246	.262	61	12	1	0	1	7	4	13

2-YEAR TOTALS (1990–1991)

	BA	OBA	SA	AB	H	2B	3B	HR	RBI	BB	SO
Total	.252	.305	.351	325	82	14	3	4	22	24	68
vs. Left	.256	.333	.372	43	11	0	1	1	2	5	11
vs. Right	.252	.300	.348	282	71	14	2	3	20	19	57
at Home	.265	.316	.377	162	43	4	1	4	14	11	35
on Road	.239	.294	.325	163	39	10	2	0	8	13	33
on Grass	.259	.304	.366	232	60	9	2	4	18	14	49
on Turf	.237	.308	.312	93	22	5	1	0	4	10	19
Day Games	.281	.337	.406	96	27	4	1	2	6	7	15
Night Games	.240	.291	.328	229	55	10	2	2	16	17	53
April	.000	.000	.000	1	0	0	0	0	0	0	0
May	.214	.261	.286	42	9	1	1	0	2	3	10
June	.295	.360	.397	78	23	3	1	1	6	7	7
July	.247	.307	.290	93	23	4	0	0	0	8	23
August	.196	.213	.326	46	9	3	0	1	5	1	10
Sept–Oct	.277	.329	.446	65	18	3	1	2	9	5	18
Bases Empty	.250	.289	.345	200	50	9	2	2	2	10	34
Leadoff	.214	.245	.286	98	21	5	1	0	0	4	17
Runners On Base	.256	.329	.360	125	32	5	1	2	20	14	34
Scoring Position	.250	.337	.363	80	20	3	0	2	19	11	26
Late and Close	.194	.237	.264	72	14	2	0	1	7	4	15

KENT HRBEK — bats left — throws right — age 32 — MIN — *1

1991	BA	OBA	SA	AB	H	2B	3B	HR	RBI	BB	SO		8-YEAR TOTALS (1984–1991) BA	OBA	SA	AB	H	2B	3B	HR	RBI	BB	SO
Total	.284	.373	.461	462	131	20	1	20	89	67	48		.287	.372	.494	4018	1155	203	8	203	709	543	497
vs. Left	.281	.357	.445	128	36	3	0	6	25	15	19		.267	.344	.413	1173	313	44	1	42	192	136	191
vs. Right	.284	.379	.467	334	95	17	1	14	64	52	29		.296	.383	.527	2845	842	159	7	161	517	407	306
at Home	.318	.407	.504	236	75	11	0	11	52	37	22		.304	.388	.531	2038	620	113	7	112	428	286	248
on Road	.248	.336	.416	226	56	9	1	9	37	30	26		.270	.354	.455	1980	535	90	1	91	281	257	249
on Grass	.258	.341	.440	182	47	9	0	8	32	23	24		.273	.356	.474	1493	408	72	0	76	226	190	186
on Turf	.300	.393	.475	280	84	11	1	12	57	44	24		.296	.381	.505	2525	747	131	8	127	483	353	311
Day Games	.284	.356	.396	134	38	6	0	3	21	15	11		.290	.368	.494	1184	343	64	2	58	204	149	140
Night Games	.284	.380	.488	328	93	14	1	17	68	52	37		.287	.373	.493	2834	812	139	6	145	505	394	357
April	.182	.250	.288	66	12	1	0	2	13	6	8		.267	.369	.446	572	153	31	1	23	99	89	65
May	.292	.414	.444	72	21	3	1	2	7	15	4		.284	.364	.507	659	187	28	1	39	117	86	74
June	.359	.414	.551	78	28	6	0	3	18	8	6		.312	.393	.508	600	187	36	2	26	101	79	76
July	.278	.370	.456	79	22	2	0	4	17	12	8		.275	.367	.518	705	194	30	0	47	137	99	83
August	.316	.391	.500	98	31	6	0	4	18	12	14		.302	.371	.513	787	238	38	1	42	139	92	106
Sept–Oct	.246	.373	.493	69	17	2	0	5	16	14	8		.282	.368	.460	695	196	40	3	26	116	98	93
Bases Empty	.250	.346	.371	224	56	10	1	5	5	33	25		.284	.361	.491	2109	599	122	4	102	102	241	262
Leadoff	.195	.295	.221	113	22	3	0	0	0	16	13		.280	.353	.483	897	251	49	2	43	43	96	101
Runners On Base	.315	.398	.546	238	75	10	0	15	84	34	23		.291	.383	.497	1909	556	81	4	101	607	302	235
Scoring Position	.310	.399	.516	126	39	5	0	7	64	20	17		.279	.389	.469	1039	290	52	2	47	480	209	141
Late and Close	.389	.450	.630	54	21	1	0	4	15	6	5		.301	.388	.476	584	176	24	0	26	94	86	77

JEFF HUSON — bats left — throws right — age 28 — TEX — *S/23

1991	BA	OBA	SA	AB	H	2B	3B	HR	RBI	BB	SO		4-YEAR TOTALS (1988–1991) BA	OBA	SA	AB	H	2B	3B	HR	RBI	BB	SO
Total	.213	.312	.287	268	57	8	3	2	26	39	32		.227	.311	.282	780	177	27	5	2	59	95	95
vs. Left	.074	.194	.074	27	2	0	0	0	0	4	6		.185	.262	.207	92	17	2	0	0	5	9	16
vs. Right	.228	.325	.311	241	55	8	3	2	26	35	26		.233	.317	.292	688	160	25	5	2	54	86	79
at Home	.177	.297	.234	141	25	1	2	1	15	24	18		.208	.300	.263	399	83	13	3	1	28	51	57
on Road	.252	.329	.346	127	32	7	1	1	11	15	14		.247	.323	.302	381	94	14	2	1	31	44	38
on Grass	.233	.332	.315	232	54	7	3	2	26	35	28		.234	.319	.293	590	138	19	5	2	52	73	79
on Turf	.083	.175	.111	36	3	1	0	0	0	4	4		.205	.286	.247	190	39	8	0	0	7	22	16
Day Games	.219	.311	.234	64	14	1	0	0	6	9	2		.230	.317	.248	161	37	3	0	0	13	21	13
Night Games	.211	.312	.304	204	43	7	3	2	20	30	30		.226	.309	.291	619	140	24	5	2	46	74	82
April	.244	.304	.317	41	10	1	1	0	6	4	6		.260	.352	.312	77	20	2	1	0	11	12	12
May	.170	.323	.264	53	9	3	1	0	2	12	10		.244	.338	.336	131	32	10	1	0	5	18	18
June	.218	.295	.327	55	12	1	1	1	7	6	6		.248	.329	.323	133	33	3	2	1	11	16	15
July	.200	.280	.267	45	9	0	1	0	2	5	5		.231	.305	.301	156	36	6	1	1	11	16	17
August	.423	.500	.500	26	11	2	0	0	4	4	3		.202	.286	.227	119	24	3	0	0	8	14	16
Sept–Oct	.125	.250	.146	48	6	1	0	0	5	8	2		.195	.279	.213	164	32	3	0	0	13	19	17
Bases Empty	.197	.315	.243	152	30	5	1	0	0	26	23		.222	.308	.269	468	104	20	1	0	0	57	58
Leadoff	.206	.333	.270	63	13	4	0	0	0	12	9		.226	.313	.290	221	50	14	0	0	0	27	30
Runners On Base	.233	.308	.345	116	27	3	2	2	26	13	9		.234	.315	.301	312	73	7	4	2	59	38	37
Scoring Position	.267	.357	.367	60	16	1	1	1	21	9	5		.236	.336	.292	178	42	3	2	1	52	28	22
Late and Close	.270	.386	.270	37	10	0	0	0	0	7	2		.262	.359	.270	122	32	1	0	0	7	19	12

PETE INCAVIGLIA — bats right — throws right — age 28 — DET — OD

1991	BA	OBA	SA	AB	H	2B	3B	HR	RBI	BB	SO		6-YEAR TOTALS (1986–1991) BA	OBA	SA	AB	H	2B	3B	HR	RBI	BB	SO
Total	.214	.290	.353	337	72	12	1	11	38	36	92		.244	.311	.447	2786	679	132	14	135	425	255	880
vs. Left	.206	.264	.258	97	20	3	1	0	5	8	20		.268	.338	.497	882	236	46	6	48	140	89	257
vs. Right	.217	.300	.392	240	52	9	0	11	33	28	72		.233	.298	.423	1904	443	86	8	87	285	166	623
at Home	.205	.283	.357	171	35	6	1	6	20	18	49		.253	.328	.471	1364	345	63	6	74	229	146	431
on Road	.223	.297	.349	166	37	6	0	5	18	18	43		.235	.294	.423	1422	334	69	8	61	196	109	449
on Grass	.219	.304	.377	292	64	11	1	11	35	35	80		.248	.317	.458	2348	583	114	11	119	370	225	733
on Turf	.178	.191	.200	45	8	1	0	0	3	1	12		.219	.278	.384	438	96	18	3	16	55	30	147
Day Games	.196	.308	.295	112	22	2	0	3	9	17	28		.210	.292	.375	587	123	19	3	24	75	63	198
Night Games	.222	.280	.382	225	50	10	1	8	29	19	64		.253	.316	.466	2199	556	113	11	111	350	192	682
April	.170	.228	.264	53	9	2	0	1	4	4	14		.230	.297	.434	396	91	16	1	21	63	36	133
May	.253	.318	.481	79	20	6	0	4	14	7	25		.264	.333	.500	526	139	35	4	27	87	50	164
June	.171	.231	.171	35	6	0	0	0	2	3	10		.240	.296	.406	466	112	21	4	16	61	34	143
July	.214	.267	.357	42	9	0	0	2	5	3	8		.258	.326	.492	476	123	26	2	26	88	48	147
August	.233	.377	.419	43	10	2	0	2	5	10	14		.219	.295	.371	480	105	12	2	19	54	45	163
Sept–Oct	.212	.287	.329	85	18	2	1	2	8	9	21		.247	.312	.471	442	109	22	1	25	72	42	130
Bases Empty	.202	.283	.326	178	36	5	1	5	5	19	40		.248	.318	.469	1455	361	77	8	76	76	132	455
Leadoff	.182	.270	.348	66	12	2	0	3	3	8	13		.256	.322	.467	629	161	36	2	31	31	55	189
Runners On Base	.226	.298	.384	159	36	7	0	6	33	17	52		.239	.304	.422	1331	318	55	6	59	349	123	425
Scoring Position	.169	.262	.270	89	15	3	0	2	23	12	29		.236	.310	.421	738	174	35	3	32	281	83	240
Late and Close	.152	.222	.212	66	10	4	0	0	4	6	20		.218	.284	.394	449	98	26	1	17	69	41	151

DARRIN JACKSON — bats right — throws right — age 30 — SD — O/P

1991	BA	OBA	SA	AB	H	2B	3B	HR	RBI	BB	SO	6-YEAR TOTALS (1985–1991) BA	OBA	SA	AB	H	2B	3B	HR	RBI	BB	SO
Total	.265	.317	.479	359	95	12	1	21	49	27	66	.256	.298	.427	844	216	34	4	34	98	50	155
vs. Left	.267	.314	.484	161	43	5	0	10	25	12	23	.273	.316	.459	425	116	21	2	18	58	29	63
vs. Right	.263	.319	.475	198	52	7	1	11	24	15	43	.239	.279	.394	419	100	13	2	16	40	21	92
at Home	.259	.317	.494	174	45	3	1	12	24	13	29	.256	.301	.433	383	98	13	2	17	44	22	65
on Road	.270	.317	.465	185	50	9	0	9	25	14	37	.256	.295	.421	461	118	21	2	17	54	28	90
on Grass	.277	.332	.529	274	76	7	1	20	44	21	47	.257	.298	.435	623	160	20	2	29	76	35	112
on Turf	.224	.269	.318	85	19	5	0	1	5	6	19	.253	.297	.403	221	56	14	2	5	22	15	43
Day Games	.250	.290	.569	116	29	5	1	10	19	7	20	.260	.295	.442	335	87	14	4	13	37	17	56
Night Games	.272	.330	.436	243	66	7	0	11	30	20	46	.253	.299	.417	509	129	20	0	21	61	33	99
April	.333	.375	.524	21	7	1	0	1	2	2	3	.288	.321	.462	52	15	3	0	2	6	3	11
May	.132	.283	.263	38	5	2	0	1	3	8	8	.203	.263	.297	158	32	6	0	3	8	13	31
June	.279	.289	.558	43	12	0	0	4	8	1	8	.263	.286	.466	118	31	3	3	5	16	5	19
July	.357	.400	.667	42	15	1	0	4	7	3	3	.276	.321	.474	76	21	3	0	4	11	4	5
August	.228	.268	.413	92	21	3	1	4	11	5	22	.229	.265	.407	140	32	5	1	6	17	7	34
Sept–Oct	.285	.336	.496	123	35	5	0	7	18	8	22	.283	.325	.470	300	85	14	0	14	40	18	55
Bases Empty	.264	.308	.506	235	62	10	1	15	15	15	47	.266	.296	.472	515	137	22	3	26	26	22	100
Leadoff	.309	.336	.561	123	38	7	0	8	8	5	18	.296	.321	.527	226	67	13	0	13	13	8	38
Runners On Base	.266	.333	.427	124	33	2	0	6	34	12	19	.240	.300	.356	329	79	12	1	8	72	28	55
Scoring Position	.269	.348	.449	78	21	2	0	4	30	9	12	.230	.303	.364	209	48	10	0	6	66	22	39
Late and Close	.169	.217	.323	65	11	1	0	3	7	4	13	.203	.250	.301	153	31	3	0	4	15	10	34

BROOK JACOBY — bats right — throws right — age 33 — CLE/OAK — 31

1991	BA	OBA	SA	AB	H	2B	3B	HR	RBI	BB	SO	8-YEAR TOTALS (1984–1991) BA	OBA	SA	AB	H	2B	3B	HR	RBI	BB	SO
Total	.224	.274	.308	419	94	21	1	4	44	27	54	.271	.335	.412	4210	1142	197	24	116	508	411	706
vs. Left	.250	.326	.328	116	29	4	1	1	13	12	14	.277	.350	.422	1182	328	52	7	35	130	132	176
vs. Right	.215	.252	.300	303	65	17	0	3	31	15	40	.269	.330	.408	3028	814	145	17	81	378	279	530
at Home	.216	.276	.300	190	41	10	0	2	27	15	16	.262	.335	.417	2042	536	96	14	64	272	222	325
on Road	.231	.272	.314	229	53	11	1	2	17	12	38	.280	.336	.407	2168	606	101	10	52	236	189	381
on Grass	.237	.287	.336	333	79	19	1	4	44	22	35	.272	.338	.418	3544	965	168	22	102	450	357	582
on Turf	.174	.220	.198	86	15	2	0	0	0	5	19	.266	.322	.378	666	177	29	2	14	58	54	124
Day Games	.204	.253	.283	152	31	7	1	1	14	8	21	.255	.313	.397	1369	349	64	7	39	170	115	252
Night Games	.236	.285	.322	267	63	14	0	3	30	19	33	.279	.346	.419	2841	793	133	17	77	338	296	454
April	.200	.246	.323	65	13	3	1	1	5	4	10	.271	.339	.412	558	151	32	4	13	60	57	94
May	.273	.310	.436	55	15	0	0	3	10	3	9	.251	.316	.392	737	185	23	3	25	83	72	149
June	.200	.264	.250	80	16	4	0	0	4	7	9	.272	.333	.431	771	210	35	3	27	95	70	118
July	.327	.383	.418	55	18	5	0	0	8	3	7	.280	.341	.401	671	188	29	2	16	92	65	111
August	.221	.265	.274	95	21	5	0	0	10	5	9	.276	.354	.398	758	209	41	5	14	81	90	114
Sept–Oct	.159	.208	.217	69	11	4	0	0	7	5	10	.278	.330	.438	715	199	37	7	14	97	57	120
Bases Empty	.219	.264	.307	228	50	11	0	3	3	13	27	.264	.324	.420	2351	621	111	12	77	77	204	389
Leadoff	.207	.242	.264	87	18	2	0	1	1	4	14	.274	.330	.426	952	261	46	3	31	31	77	147
Runners On Base	.230	.284	.309	191	44	10	1	1	41	14	27	.280	.349	.402	1859	521	86	12	39	431	207	317
Scoring Position	.250	.322	.346	104	26	5	1	1	39	11	15	.254	.348	.367	990	251	44	4	20	367	158	193
Late and Close	.188	.225	.271	85	16	1	0	0	4	2	14	.253	.305	.373	683	173	20	4	18	68	50	119

CHRIS JAMES — bats right — throws right — age 30 — CLE — DO1

1991	BA	OBA	SA	AB	H	2B	3B	HR	RBI	BB	SO	6-YEAR TOTALS (1986–1991) BA	OBA	SA	AB	H	2B	3B	HR	RBI	BB	SO
Total	.238	.273	.318	437	104	16	2	5	41	18	61	.263	.303	.405	2413	634	112	15	67	301	134	352
vs. Left	.198	.239	.298	131	26	5	1	2	12	7	20	.263	.308	.438	784	206	35	6	30	116	52	111
vs. Right	.255	.288	.327	306	78	11	1	3	29	11	41	.263	.301	.389	1629	428	77	9	37	185	82	241
at Home	.290	.328	.357	221	64	8	2	1	21	10	20	.281	.325	.428	1153	324	57	7	33	161	72	148
on Road	.185	.217	.278	216	40	8	0	4	20	8	41	.246	.283	.383	1260	310	55	8	34	140	62	204
on Grass	.246	.281	.319	354	87	10	2	4	33	15	46	.267	.304	.397	1321	353	53	7	35	169	67	187
on Turf	.205	.241	.313	83	17	6	0	1	8	3	15	.257	.302	.414	1092	281	59	8	32	132	67	165
Day Games	.273	.318	.392	143	39	7	2	2	17	8	20	.275	.315	.444	676	186	35	5	23	97	39	118
Night Games	.221	.251	.282	294	65	9	0	3	24	10	41	.258	.299	.390	1737	448	77	10	44	204	95	234
April	.239	.320	.299	67	16	1	0	1	4	7	8	.238	.276	.330	303	72	8	1	6	31	15	54
May	.303	.327	.414	99	30	3	1	2	18	4	15	.252	.289	.369	369	93	14	1	9	47	18	50
June	.243	.284	.340	103	25	5	1	1	10	5	14	.273	.316	.432	433	118	24	3	13	60	25	64
July	.139	.149	.181	72	10	3	0	0	3	0	12	.264	.307	.430	447	118	24	4	14	51	24	61
August	.266	.284	.354	79	21	4	0	1	6	2	11	.299	.337	.489	468	140	26	3	19	67	27	63
Sept–Oct	.118	.167	.118	17	2	0	0	0	0	0	1	.237	.282	.338	393	93	16	3	6	45	25	60
Bases Empty	.255	.288	.329	255	65	11	1	3	3	9	35	.268	.309	.423	1311	352	67	9	39	39	67	184
Leadoff	.191	.240	.223	94	18	3	0	0	0	4	13	.257	.295	.394	525	135	25	1	15	15	23	77
Runners On Base	.214	.253	.302	182	39	5	1	3	39	9	26	.256	.297	.384	1102	282	45	6	28	262	67	168
Scoring Position	.237	.296	.330	97	23	3	0	2	35	9	15	.254	.301	.391	668	170	26	4	19	237	49	106
Late and Close	.188	.226	.225	80	15	3	0	0	1	4	16	.244	.295	.334	398	97	13	1	7	37	28	66

GREGG JEFFERIES — bats both — throws right — age 25 — NYN — 23

1991   **5-YEAR TOTALS (1987–1991)**

1991	BA	OBA	SA	AB	H	2B	3B	HR	RBI	BB	SO	BA	OBA	SA	AB	H	2B	3B	HR	RBI	BB	SO
Total	.272	.336	.374	486	132	19	2	9	62	47	38	.276	.332	.416	1713	472	96	9	42	205	140	134
vs. Left	.287	.348	.374	171	49	10	1	1	18	15	9	.269	.317	.418	598	161	36	4	15	76	38	46
vs. Right	.263	.330	.375	315	83	9	1	8	44	32	29	.279	.340	.414	1115	311	60	5	27	129	102	88
at Home	.295	.371	.406	244	72	10	1	5	28	30	21	.306	.370	.469	863	264	59	5	24	106	85	62
on Road	.248	.300	.343	242	60	9	1	4	34	17	17	.245	.292	.361	850	208	37	4	18	99	55	72
on Grass	.277	.335	.379	364	101	14	1	7	44	33	30	.294	.349	.437	1250	367	79	5	30	143	103	89
on Turf	.254	.341	.361	122	31	5	1	2	18	14	8	.227	.287	.359	463	105	17	4	12	62	37	45
Day Games	.272	.312	.327	162	44	6	0	1	19	10	14	.277	.329	.391	603	167	36	3	9	68	43	48
Night Games	.272	.348	.398	324	88	13	2	8	43	37	24	.275	.334	.429	1110	305	60	6	33	137	97	86
April	.192	.333	.269	52	10	4	0	0	8	10	6	.210	.287	.297	195	41	14	0	1	20	18	20
May	.368	.379	.421	57	21	3	0	0	10	1	6	.289	.314	.444	232	67	18	0	6	30	8	20
June	.258	.324	.454	97	25	4	0	5	14	10	7	.298	.366	.456	285	85	16	1	9	38	29	16
July	.286	.354	.429	70	20	2	1	2	15	8	3	.272	.337	.437	254	69	12	3	8	41	24	19
August	.214	.248	.311	103	22	2	1	2	7	5	10	.275	.317	.385	309	85	16	3	4	29	18	27
Sept–Oct	.318	.397	.355	107	34	4	0	0	8	13	6	.285	.347	.436	438	125	20	2	14	47	43	32
Bases Empty	.258	.324	.364	264	68	11	1	5	5	24	19	.273	.329	.422	995	272	55	3	29	29	75	74
Leadoff	.320	.365	.454	97	31	4	0	3	3	7	3	.271	.328	.441	399	108	21	1	15	15	33	28
Runners On Base	.288	.351	.387	222	64	8	1	4	57	23	19	.279	.336	.407	718	200	41	6	13	176	65	60
Scoring Position	.306	.386	.395	124	38	6	1	1	50	18	8	.280	.347	.397	411	115	27	3	5	152	47	38
Late and Close	.271	.380	.365	85	23	2	0	2	10	14	6	.252	.317	.330	282	71	10	0	4	28	25	22

HOWARD JOHNSON — bats both — throws right — age 32 — NYN — *3OS

1991   **8-YEAR TOTALS (1984–1991)**

1991	BA	OBA	SA	AB	H	2B	3B	HR	RBI	BB	SO	BA	OBA	SA	AB	H	2B	3B	HR	RBI	BB	SO
Total	.259	.342	.535	564	146	34	4	38	117	78	120	.254	.340	.470	3738	951	201	17	190	610	498	772
vs. Left	.250	.315	.500	212	53	9	1	14	39	23	57	.236	.324	.427	1174	277	51	4	55	169	157	277
vs. Right	.264	.357	.557	352	93	25	3	24	78	55	63	.263	.347	.489	2564	674	150	13	135	441	341	495
at Home	.268	.347	.557	280	75	12	3	21	64	38	60	.247	.336	.451	1799	444	83	9	89	290	248	370
on Road	.250	.337	.514	284	71	22	1	17	53	40	60	.261	.344	.487	1939	507	118	8	101	320	250	402
on Grass	.255	.339	.525	400	102	19	4	27	82	56	81	.256	.344	.469	2669	684	136	14	135	433	361	532
on Turf	.268	.349	.561	164	44	15	0	11	35	22	39	.250	.332	.471	1069	267	65	3	55	177	137	240
Day Games	.238	.318	.519	185	44	11	1	13	41	24	37	.266	.352	.480	1295	345	75	3	65	219	180	249
Night Games	.269	.354	.544	379	102	23	3	25	76	54	83	.248	.334	.465	2443	606	126	14	125	391	318	523
April	.211	.290	.456	57	12	2	0	4	14	8	15	.237	.332	.412	430	102	15	0	20	71	64	96
May	.271	.324	.573	96	26	6	1	7	21	9	17	.241	.329	.443	609	147	30	3	29	95	81	130
June	.236	.384	.517	89	21	5	1	6	20	22	13	.275	.344	.541	639	176	39	4	41	113	69	127
July	.290	.386	.527	93	27	7	0	5	16	17	13	.263	.351	.488	688	181	42	1	37	116	99	127
August	.236	.277	.462	106	25	4	1	6	15	5	24	.257	.355	.471	678	174	33	5	34	99	103	136
Sept–Oct	.285	.364	.626	123	35	10	1	10	31	17	38	.246	.325	.444	694	171	42	4	29	116	82	156
Bases Empty	.262	.349	.577	298	78	19	3	23	23	39	56	.247	.324	.467	2098	519	101	12	112	112	230	411
Leadoff	.285	.356	.674	144	41	8	0	16	16	16	22	.264	.325	.524	884	233	45	4	59	59	76	160
Runners On Base	.256	.334	.489	266	68	15	1	15	94	39	64	.263	.359	.473	1640	432	100	5	78	498	268	361
Scoring Position	.276	.359	.467	152	42	11	0	6	74	28	30	.267	.389	.485	908	242	60	0	46	418	207	205
Late and Close	.247	.339	.515	97	24	8	0	6	19	15	27	.256	.350	.488	652	167	31	3	38	117	96	160

LANCE JOHNSON — bats left — throws left — age 29 — CHA — *O

1991   **5-YEAR TOTALS (1987–1991)**

1991	BA	OBA	SA	AB	H	2B	3B	HR	RBI	BB	SO	BA	OBA	SA	AB	H	2B	3B	HR	RBI	BB	SO
Total	.274	.304	.342	588	161	14	13	0	49	26	58	.271	.311	.339	1492	405	46	26	1	129	86	144
vs. Left	.244	.291	.274	164	40	3	1	0	8	10	21	.266	.307	.310	406	108	8	5	0	33	24	56
vs. Right	.285	.309	.368	424	121	11	12	0	41	16	37	.273	.312	.350	1086	297	38	21	1	96	62	88
at Home	.266	.298	.325	286	76	5	6	0	22	14	26	.269	.306	.338	740	199	21	15	0	61	42	68
on Road	.281	.310	.358	302	85	9	7	0	27	12	32	.274	.315	.340	752	206	25	11	1	68	44	76
on Grass	.277	.308	.338	506	140	11	10	0	43	23	48	.274	.312	.343	1214	333	36	22	1	104	67	119
on Turf	.256	.282	.366	82	21	3	3	0	6	3	10	.259	.306	.324	278	72	10	4	0	25	19	25
Day Games	.264	.297	.328	174	46	3	4	0	13	9	25	.265	.305	.328	427	113	13	7	0	41	26	49
Night Games	.278	.307	.348	414	115	11	9	0	36	17	33	.274	.313	.344	1065	292	33	19	1	88	60	95
April	.221	.254	.250	68	15	2	0	0	1	3	10	.220	.255	.262	191	42	6	1	0	12	9	23
May	.259	.273	.269	108	28	1	0	0	8	1	12	.272	.313	.298	228	62	6	0	0	16	13	19
June	.284	.308	.324	102	29	2	1	0	9	4	6	.281	.308	.346	185	52	6	3	0	19	8	15
July	.250	.269	.330	100	25	2	3	0	10	3	12	.246	.279	.320	203	50	4	4	0	20	10	20
August	.265	.286	.324	102	27	2	2	0	8	3	7	.275	.308	.366	284	78	10	8	0	30	14	27
Sept–Oct	.343	.405	.519	108	37	5	7	0	13	12	11	.302	.354	.387	401	121	14	10	0	32	32	40
Bases Empty	.289	.308	.371	342	99	10	9	0	0	9	37	.264	.306	.333	908	240	30	16	0	0	54	92
Leadoff	.262	.284	.354	130	34	4	4	0	0	4	11	.261	.302	.334	422	110	17	7	0	0	25	35
Runners On Base	.252	.300	.301	246	62	4	4	0	49	17	21	.283	.318	.349	584	165	16	10	1	129	32	52
Scoring Position	.248	.312	.299	137	34	3	2	0	47	13	12	.287	.333	.358	335	96	9	6	0	124	25	30
Late and Close	.212	.244	.257	113	24	1	2	0	12	4	12	.231	.281	.288	260	60	5	5	0	22	18	35

RICKY JORDAN — bats right — throws right — age 27 — PHI — 1

1991	BA	OBA	SA	AB	H	2B	3B	HR	RBI	BB	SO
Total	.272	.304	.452	301	82	21	3	9	49	14	49
vs. Left	.310	.338	.500	126	39	12	0	4	19	6	15
vs. Right	.246	.280	.417	175	43	9	3	5	30	8	34
at Home	.297	.317	.475	158	47	9	2	5	27	4	21
on Road	.245	.291	.427	143	35	12	1	4	22	10	28
on Grass	.256	.318	.500	78	20	7	0	4	15	7	17
on Turf	.278	.299	.435	223	62	14	3	5	34	7	32
Day Games	.307	.330	.515	101	31	7	1	4	20	3	16
Night Games	.255	.292	.420	200	51	14	2	5	29	11	33
April	.294	.351	.588	34	10	5	1	1	5	3	5
May	.292	.320	.483	89	26	3	1	4	18	4	13
June	.250	.307	.368	68	17	8	0	0	7	5	9
July	.256	.273	.488	43	11	2	1	2	6	1	6
August	.205	.220	.333	39	8	2	0	1	9	1	10
Sept–Oct	.357	.357	.500	28	10	1	0	1	4	0	6
Bases Empty	.250	.287	.423	156	39	10	1	5	5	7	24
Leadoff	.273	.294	.500	66	18	3	0	4	4	2	11
Runners On Base	.297	.323	.483	145	43	11	2	4	44	7	25
Scoring Position	.310	.343	.552	87	27	7	1	4	42	7	15
Late and Close	.200	.256	.253	75	15	2	1	0	7	5	14

4-YEAR TOTALS (1988–1991)

	BA	OBA	SA	AB	H	2B	3B	HR	RBI	BB	SO
Total	.277	.307	.421	1422	394	80	7	37	211	57	190
vs. Left	.303	.347	.475	524	159	36	3	16	77	35	54
vs. Right	.262	.283	.390	898	235	44	4	21	134	22	136
at Home	.284	.302	.426	712	202	35	3	20	111	18	103
on Road	.270	.311	.417	710	192	45	4	17	100	39	87
on Grass	.283	.308	.444	385	109	22	2	12	58	14	45
on Turf	.275	.306	.413	1037	285	58	5	25	153	43	145
Day Games	.304	.328	.465	437	133	30	2	12	80	16	52
Night Games	.265	.298	.402	985	261	50	5	25	131	41	138
April	.265	.311	.383	162	43	11	1	2	24	11	23
May	.267	.289	.391	243	65	7	1	7	33	7	30
June	.257	.317	.410	183	47	16	0	4	23	15	24
July	.270	.296	.399	248	67	12	1	6	38	7	35
August	.291	.311	.486	282	82	21	2	10	54	7	36
Sept–Oct	.296	.318	.431	304	90	13	2	8	39	10	42
Bases Empty	.275	.297	.401	731	201	41	3	15	15	19	85
Leadoff	.300	.321	.447	333	100	14	1	11	11	9	34
Runners On Base	.279	.317	.443	691	193	39	4	22	196	38	105
Scoring Position	.279	.330	.434	387	108	21	3	11	162	32	73
Late and Close	.273	.323	.412	245	67	12	2	6	43	15	41

FELIX JOSE — bats both — throws right — age 27 — SL — *O

1991	BA	OBA	SA	AB	H	2B	3B	HR	RBI	BB	SO
Total	.305	.360	.438	568	173	40	6	8	77	50	113
vs. Left	.298	.356	.407	258	77	18	2	2	30	23	51
vs. Right	.310	.363	.465	310	96	22	4	6	47	27	62
at Home	.296	.353	.421	280	83	16	5	3	39	25	48
on Road	.313	.367	.455	288	90	24	1	5	38	25	65
on Grass	.270	.294	.411	163	44	12	1	3	22	6	41
on Turf	.319	.385	.449	405	129	28	5	5	55	44	72
Day Games	.311	.349	.506	164	51	11	3	5	33	10	30
Night Games	.302	.364	.411	404	122	29	3	3	44	40	83
April	.354	.422	.595	79	28	9	2	2	15	9	5
May	.326	.421	.413	92	30	8	0	0	10	14	24
June	.319	.354	.407	91	29	6	1	0	14	5	17
July	.266	.311	.372	94	25	7	0	1	10	7	21
August	.292	.343	.354	96	28	6	0	0	9	8	21
Sept–Oct	.284	.323	.500	116	33	4	0	3	19	7	25
Bases Empty	.289	.338	.393	298	86	20	1	3	3	21	63
Leadoff	.280	.307	.379	132	37	10	0	1	1	5	24
Runners On Base	.322	.384	.489	270	87	20	5	5	74	29	50
Scoring Position	.343	.424	.538	143	49	13	3	3	68	23	31
Late and Close	.352	.417	.538	91	32	8	0	3	8	10	19

4-YEAR TOTALS (1988–1991)

	BA	OBA	SA	AB	H	2B	3B	HR	RBI	BB	SO
Total	.283	.334	.406	1057	299	59	7	19	135	78	208
vs. Left	.299	.353	.411	384	115	25	3	4	52	31	78
vs. Right	.273	.324	.403	673	184	34	4	15	83	47	130
at Home	.268	.323	.386	526	141	26	6	8	71	41	100
on Road	.298	.346	.426	531	158	33	1	11	64	37	108
on Grass	.264	.303	.366	541	143	26	1	9	60	27	113
on Turf	.302	.366	.448	516	156	33	6	10	75	51	95
Day Games	.264	.307	.408	363	96	19	3	9	53	22	71
Night Games	.293	.348	.405	694	203	40	4	10	82	56	137
April	.308	.371	.503	143	44	12	2	4	23	14	19
May	.275	.348	.363	160	44	8	0	2	19	17	36
June	.273	.304	.354	161	44	11	1	0	18	7	30
July	.277	.329	.410	188	52	10	0	5	24	13	43
August	.291	.336	.337	196	57	9	0	0	16	12	38
Sept–Oct	.278	.324	.474	209	58	9	4	8	35	15	42
Bases Empty	.260	.317	.355	558	145	28	2	7	7	44	118
Leadoff	.259	.303	.351	239	62	13	0	3	3	15	47
Runners On Base	.309	.354	.463	499	154	31	5	12	128	34	90
Scoring Position	.329	.380	.507	280	92	23	3	7	116	24	57
Late and Close	.299	.359	.435	154	46	9	0	4	16	14	40

WALLY JOYNER — bats left — throws left — age 30 — CAL — *1

1991	BA	OBA	SA	AB	H	2B	3B	HR	RBI	BB	SO
Total	.301	.360	.488	551	166	34	3	21	96	52	66
vs. Left	.275	.308	.444	189	52	15	1	5	28	9	31
vs. Right	.315	.384	.511	362	114	19	2	16	68	43	35
at Home	.276	.343	.448	268	74	14	1	10	39	29	30
on Road	.325	.375	.527	283	92	20	2	11	57	23	36
on Grass	.294	.353	.478	473	139	29	2	18	77	45	54
on Turf	.346	.400	.551	78	27	5	1	3	19	7	12
Day Games	.286	.327	.500	140	40	10	1	6	16	9	14
Night Games	.307	.370	.484	411	126	24	2	15	80	43	52
April	.333	.423	.439	66	22	4	0	1	11	11	7
May	.360	.435	.620	100	36	5	0	7	23	13	9
June	.292	.316	.451	113	33	8	2	2	17	4	15
July	.240	.308	.344	96	23	4	0	2	13	10	14
August	.282	.322	.591	110	31	8	1	8	22	7	15
Sept–Oct	.318	.378	.439	66	21	5	0	1	10	7	6
Bases Empty	.286	.341	.487	308	88	22	2	12	12	26	33
Leadoff	.300	.386	.490	100	30	7	0	4	4	14	7
Runners On Base	.321	.382	.490	243	78	12	1	9	84	26	33
Scoring Position	.331	.410	.518	139	46	9	1	5	73	21	18
Late and Close	.304	.377	.507	69	21	5	0	3	14	8	9

6-YEAR TOTALS (1986–1991)

	BA	OBA	SA	AB	H	2B	3B	HR	RBI	BB	SO
Total	.288	.353	.454	3208	925	169	11	114	518	323	332
vs. Left	.260	.310	.385	1106	288	50	2	28	165	76	129
vs. Right	.303	.374	.491	2102	637	119	9	86	353	247	203
at Home	.273	.342	.437	1580	432	74	4	59	237	170	162
on Road	.303	.363	.471	1628	493	95	7	55	281	153	170
on Grass	.281	.346	.444	2723	764	138	10	96	427	277	275
on Turf	.332	.390	.511	485	161	31	1	18	91	46	57
Day Games	.288	.362	.504	826	238	48	2	42	143	92	101
Night Games	.288	.349	.437	2382	687	121	9	72	375	231	231
April	.277	.351	.433	487	135	28	0	16	67	56	49
May	.309	.373	.506	583	180	24	2	29	109	61	56
June	.290	.349	.433	600	174	32	3	16	98	58	68
July	.305	.360	.473	514	157	30	4	16	93	44	54
August	.266	.340	.466	515	137	30	2	23	82	58	50
Sept–Oct	.279	.340	.411	509	142	25	0	14	69	46	55
Bases Empty	.272	.329	.443	1760	479	88	6	67	67	142	175
Leadoff	.267	.321	.432	674	180	31	1	26	26	53	63
Runners On Base	.308	.379	.468	1448	446	81	5	47	451	181	157
Scoring Position	.307	.392	.472	845	259	48	4	28	397	140	95
Late and Close	.273	.346	.418	517	141	29	2	14	78	59	51

DAVID JUSTICE — bats left — throws left — age 26 — ATL — *O

3-YEAR TOTALS (1989–1991)

1991	BA	OBA	SA	AB	H	2B	3B	HR	RBI	BB	SO		BA	OBA	SA	AB	H	2B	3B	HR	RBI	BB	SO
Total	.275	.377	.503	396	109	25	1	21	87	65	81		.277	.371	.510	886	245	51	3	50	168	132	182
vs. Left	.279	.331	.468	154	43	6	1	7	39	13	24		.314	.377	.543	293	92	14	1	17	71	31	46
vs. Right	.273	.403	.525	242	66	19	0	14	48	52	57		.258	.368	.494	593	153	37	2	33	97	101	136
at Home	.269	.371	.537	175	47	12	1	11	41	30	39		.293	.381	.590	437	128	33	2	31	91	64	95
on Road	.281	.382	.475	221	62	13	0	10	46	35	42		.261	.360	.432	449	117	18	1	19	77	68	87
on Grass	.289	.383	.538	273	79	18	1	16	61	42	55		.288	.374	.543	646	186	42	3	39	123	90	136
on Turf	.244	.365	.423	123	30	7	0	5	26	23	26		.246	.361	.421	240	59	9	0	11	45	42	46
Day Games	.211	.357	.456	90	19	1	0	7	23	20	16		.242	.358	.493	223	54	5	0	17	45	40	30
Night Games	.294	.384	.516	306	90	24	1	14	64	45	65		.288	.375	.516	663	191	46	3	33	123	92	152
April	.232	.299	.377	69	16	4	0	2	10	7	17		.232	.299	.377	69	16	4	0	2	10	7	17
May	.381	.450	.629	97	37	9	0	5	28	11	16		.333	.404	.544	171	57	15	0	7	38	19	31
June	.243	.361	.500	70	17	4	1	4	13	12	20		.230	.340	.410	161	37	7	2	6	22	26	39
July	.000	.000	.000	0	0	0	0	0	0	0	0		.213	.306	.400	75	16	2	0	4	9	10	21
August	.240	.345	.500	50	12	4	0	3	10	8	9		.282	.350	.607	163	46	11	0	14	39	17	33
Sept–Oct	.245	.386	.473	110	27	4	0	7	26	27	19		.296	.416	.559	247	73	12	1	17	50	53	41
Bases Empty	.235	.314	.450	200	47	13	0	10	10	22	44		.231	.321	.461	484	112	23	2	28	28	62	103
Leadoff	.234	.268	.495	107	25	7	0	7	7	5	22		.229	.286	.454	227	52	12	0	13	13	18	53
Runners On Base	.316	.435	.556	196	62	12	1	11	77	43	37		.331	.427	.570	402	133	28	1	22	140	70	79
Scoring Position	.347	.479	.589	124	43	10	1	6	66	34	24		.329	.445	.573	246	81	19	1	13	118	54	54
Late and Close	.259	.386	.466	58	15	4	1	2	13	12	15		.266	.365	.469	128	34	6	1	6	23	20	32

PAT KELLY — bats right — throws right — age 25 — NYA — 32

1-YEAR TOTALS (1991)

1991	BA	OBA	SA	AB	H	2B	3B	HR	RBI	BB	SO		BA	OBA	SA	AB	H	2B	3B	HR	RBI	BB	SO
Total	.242	.287	.339	298	72	12	4	3	23	15	52		.242	.287	.339	298	72	12	4	3	23	15	52
vs. Left	.263	.292	.343	99	26	5	0	1	7	4	13		.263	.292	.343	99	26	5	0	1	7	4	13
vs. Right	.231	.285	.337	199	46	7	4	2	16	11	39		.231	.285	.337	199	46	7	4	2	16	11	39
at Home	.253	.307	.380	150	38	6	2	3	12	10	26		.253	.307	.380	150	38	6	2	3	12	10	26
on Road	.230	.268	.297	148	34	6	2	0	11	5	26		.230	.268	.297	148	34	6	2	0	11	5	26
on Grass	.241	.289	.340	253	61	12	2	3	21	13	45		.241	.289	.340	253	61	12	2	3	21	13	45
on Turf	.244	.277	.333	45	11	0	2	0	2	2	7		.244	.277	.333	45	11	0	2	0	2	2	7
Day Games	.221	.264	.372	86	19	3	2	2	7	3	22		.221	.264	.372	86	19	3	2	2	7	3	22
Night Games	.250	.297	.325	212	53	9	2	1	16	12	30		.250	.297	.325	212	53	9	2	1	16	12	30
April	.000	.000	.000	0	0	0	0	0	0	0	0		.000	.000	.000	0	0	0	0	0	0	0	0
May	.188	.278	.375	32	6	4	1	0	6	3	6		.188	.278	.375	32	6	4	1	0	6	3	6
June	.260	.296	.377	77	20	1	1	2	4	2	12		.260	.296	.377	77	20	1	1	2	4	2	12
July	.232	.281	.341	82	19	6	0	1	8	5	14		.232	.281	.341	82	19	6	0	1	8	5	14
August	.265	.303	.313	83	22	0	2	0	5	4	16		.265	.303	.313	83	22	0	2	0	5	4	16
Sept–Oct	.208	.240	.250	24	5	1	0	0	0	1	4		.208	.240	.250	24	5	1	0	0	0	1	4
Bases Empty	.268	.307	.363	179	48	8	3	1	1	7	28		.268	.307	.363	179	48	8	3	1	1	7	28
Leadoff	.348	.357	.435	69	24	6	0	0	0	1	9		.348	.357	.435	69	24	6	0	0	0	1	9
Runners On Base	.202	.260	.303	119	24	4	1	2	22	8	24		.202	.260	.303	119	24	4	1	2	22	8	24
Scoring Position	.188	.280	.234	64	12	3	0	0	17	7	14		.188	.280	.234	64	12	3	0	0	17	7	14
Late and Close	.262	.326	.452	42	11	3	1	1	4	3	4		.262	.326	.452	42	11	3	1	1	4	3	4

ROBERTO KELLY — bats right — throws right — age 28 — NYA — *O

5-YEAR TOTALS (1987–1991)

1991	BA	OBA	SA	AB	H	2B	3B	HR	RBI	BB	SO		BA	OBA	SA	AB	H	2B	3B	HR	RBI	BB	SO
Total	.267	.333	.444	486	130	22	2	20	69	45	77		.282	.336	.422	1697	479	79	10	46	192	127	344
vs. Left	.296	.372	.503	159	47	4	1	9	26	20	18		.309	.367	.458	572	177	27	2	18	67	51	106
vs. Right	.254	.313	.416	327	83	18	1	11	43	25	59		.268	.319	.404	1125	302	52	8	28	125	76	238
at Home	.310	.369	.500	232	72	11	0	11	30	21	32		.302	.355	.436	830	251	46	4	19	87	64	140
on Road	.228	.301	.394	254	58	11	2	9	39	24	45		.263	.317	.408	867	228	33	6	27	105	63	204
on Grass	.284	.350	.467	398	113	20	1	17	58	38	63		.283	.338	.422	1401	396	66	6	39	156	108	280
on Turf	.193	.255	.341	88	17	2	1	3	11	7	14		.280	.324	.422	296	83	13	4	7	36	19	64
Day Games	.277	.354	.438	137	38	5	1	5	21	17	22		.297	.350	.434	516	153	25	2	14	61	40	99
Night Games	.264	.324	.447	349	92	17	1	15	48	28	55		.276	.329	.417	1181	326	54	8	32	131	87	245
April	.279	.378	.410	61	17	2	0	2	11	11	9		.298	.347	.399	238	71	13	1	3	29	18	46
May	.245	.298	.387	106	26	6	0	3	9	7	19		.261	.315	.381	291	76	13	2	6	29	23	69
June	.241	.277	.393	112	27	3	1	4	13	4	23		.273	.312	.413	293	80	8	3	9	25	14	65
July	.444	.444	.667	18	8	1	0	1	3	0	2		.313	.364	.474	230	72	14	1	7	36	17	43
August	.197	.275	.344	61	12	0	0	3	9	6	10		.298	.360	.462	299	89	17	1	10	31	26	62
Sept–Oct	.313	.395	.570	128	40	10	1	7	24	17	14		.263	.325	.410	346	91	14	2	11	42	29	59
Bases Empty	.246	.316	.428	276	68	9	1	13	13	27	44		.277	.332	.425	1027	284	42	4	34	34	78	227
Leadoff	.243	.284	.371	140	34	6	0	4	4	8	25		.274	.320	.431	485	133	26	1	16	16	27	104
Runners On Base	.295	.354	.467	210	62	13	1	7	56	18	33		.291	.341	.418	670	195	37	6	12	158	49	117
Scoring Position	.299	.365	.504	117	35	6	0	6	52	12	19		.275	.334	.403	375	103	17	2	9	141	33	75
Late and Close	.272	.352	.519	81	22	2	0	6	15	9	15		.277	.340	.453	289	80	11	2	12	42	26	70

CHUCK KNOBLAUCH — bats right — throws right — age 24 — MIN — *2/S

1991	BA	OBA	SA	AB	H	2B	3B	HR	RBI	BB	SO
Total	.281	.351	.350	565	159	24	6	1	50	59	40
vs. Left	.257	.325	.324	148	38	8	1	0	6	14	10
vs. Right	.290	.360	.360	417	121	16	5	1	44	45	30
at Home	.328	.391	.415	287	94	12	5	1	26	30	18
on Road	.234	.310	.284	278	65	12	1	0	24	29	22
on Grass	.241	.321	.283	212	51	9	0	0	17	24	14
on Turf	.306	.369	.391	353	108	15	6	1	33	35	26
Day Games	.295	.367	.378	156	46	5	4	0	20	19	15
Night Games	.276	.344	.340	409	113	19	2	1	30	40	25
April	.333	.393	.427	75	25	3	2	0	9	8	8
May	.233	.314	.289	90	21	5	0	0	6	11	7
June	.289	.360	.333	90	26	2	1	0	7	9	2
July	.237	.314	.333	93	22	5	2	0	8	11	10
August	.267	.325	.343	105	28	5	0	1	10	8	10
Sept—Oct	.330	.400	.384	112	37	4	1	0	10	12	3
Bases Empty	.276	.337	.359	351	97	16	5	1	1	29	27
Leadoff	.305	.368	.359	131	40	5	1	0	0	11	11
Runners On Base	.290	.372	.336	214	62	8	1	0	49	30	13
Scoring Position	.310	.388	.362	116	36	4	1	0	46	18	10
Late and Close	.269	.301	.321	78	21	4	0	0	5	4	3

1-YEAR TOTALS (1991)

	BA	OBA	SA	AB	H	2B	3B	HR	RBI	BB	SO
	.281	.351	.350	565	159	24	6	1	50	59	40
	.257	.325	.324	148	38	8	1	0	6	14	10
	.290	.360	.360	417	121	16	5	1	44	45	30
	.328	.391	.415	287	94	12	5	1	26	30	18
	.234	.310	.284	278	65	12	1	0	24	29	22
	.241	.321	.283	212	51	9	0	0	17	24	14
	.306	.369	.391	353	108	15	6	1	33	35	26
	.295	.367	.378	156	46	5	4	0	20	19	15
	.276	.344	.340	409	113	19	2	1	30	40	25
	.333	.393	.427	75	25	3	2	0	9	8	8
	.233	.314	.289	90	21	5	0	0	6	11	7
	.289	.360	.333	90	26	2	1	0	7	9	2
	.237	.314	.333	93	22	5	2	0	8	11	10
	.267	.325	.343	105	28	5	0	1	10	8	10
	.330	.400	.384	112	37	4	1	0	10	12	3
	.276	.337	.359	351	97	16	5	1	1	29	27
	.305	.368	.359	131	40	5	1	0	0	11	11
	.290	.372	.336	214	62	8	1	0	49	30	13
	.310	.388	.362	116	36	4	1	0	46	18	10
	.269	.301	.321	78	21	4	0	0	5	4	3

JOHN KRUK — bats left — throws left — age 31 — PHI — *10

1991	BA	OBA	SA	AB	H	2B	3B	HR	RBI	BB	SO
Total	.294	.367	.483	538	158	27	6	21	92	67	100
vs. Left	.303	.356	.444	198	60	12	2	4	34	18	37
vs. Right	.288	.374	.506	340	98	15	4	17	58	49	63
at Home	.286	.363	.442	276	79	17	1	8	48	35	50
on Road	.302	.372	.527	262	79	10	5	13	44	32	50
on Grass	.261	.323	.500	138	36	2	2	9	23	14	26
on Turf	.305	.383	.477	400	122	25	4	12	69	53	74
Day Games	.254	.300	.464	138	35	5	3	6	16	10	27
Night Games	.308	.389	.490	400	123	22	3	15	76	57	73
April	.312	.353	.494	77	24	2	0	4	20	6	9
May	.274	.350	.393	84	23	5	1	1	12	12	16
June	.283	.349	.535	99	28	2	4	5	22	10	15
July	.240	.313	.440	75	18	4	1	3	7	8	17
August	.305	.427	.463	82	25	4	0	3	14	18	17
Sept—Oct	.331	.393	.537	121	40	10	0	5	17	13	26
Bases Empty	.293	.360	.480	294	86	14	4	11	11	31	60
Leadoff	.333	.396	.489	135	45	7	1	4	4	14	25
Runners On Base	.295	.376	.488	244	72	13	2	10	81	36	40
Scoring Position	.275	.381	.435	131	36	6	0	5	65	27	27
Late and Close	.282	.375	.359	103	29	3	1	1	12	16	25

6-YEAR TOTALS (1986–1991)

	BA	OBA	SA	AB	H	2B	3B	HR	RBI	BB	SO
	.291	.383	.442	2441	711	112	25	69	376	378	442
	.264	.333	.375	723	191	29	6	13	114	78	153
	.303	.404	.471	1718	520	83	19	56	262	300	289
	.295	.395	.450	1188	351	65	10	33	196	204	211
	.287	.371	.435	1253	360	47	15	36	180	174	231
	.275	.379	.427	1197	329	44	6	42	179	208	245
	.307	.388	.457	1244	382	68	19	27	197	170	197
	.273	.362	.427	733	200	34	8	21	96	105	138
	.299	.392	.449	1708	511	78	17	48	280	273	304
	.257	.340	.403	300	77	9	1	11	48	39	48
	.307	.404	.461	362	111	21	4	9	56	64	73
	.283	.383	.407	427	121	15	7	8	69	70	68
	.290	.396	.466	307	89	17	2	11	41	55	53
	.308	.404	.470	526	162	24	5	17	85	88	90
	.291	.363	.439	519	151	26	6	13	77	62	110
	.282	.367	.416	1316	371	54	9	35	35	178	238
	.297	.369	.424	589	175	26	2	15	15	67	89
	.302	.401	.473	1125	340	58	16	34	341	200	204
	.281	.401	.462	662	186	33	6	17	286	148	142
	.299	.409	.418	421	126	14	3	10	69	80	83

RAY LANKFORD — bats left — throws left — age 25 — SL — *O

1991	BA	OBA	SA	AB	H	2B	3B	HR	RBI	BB	SO
Total	.251	.301	.392	566	142	23	15	9	69	41	114
vs. Left	.243	.297	.360	214	52	11	7	0	26	16	45
vs. Right	.256	.303	.412	352	90	12	8	9	43	25	69
at Home	.237	.294	.385	283	67	10	10	4	33	23	53
on Road	.265	.308	.399	283	75	13	5	5	36	18	61
on Grass	.273	.321	.441	143	39	9	3	3	25	10	32
on Turf	.243	.295	.376	423	103	14	12	6	44	31	82
Day Games	.258	.327	.477	151	39	11	5	4	22	16	23
Night Games	.248	.291	.361	415	103	12	10	5	47	25	91
April	.255	.305	.345	55	14	1	2	0	3	4	6
May	.242	.258	.295	95	23	5	0	0	10	2	13
June	.250	.327	.370	92	23	3	4	0	12	10	16
July	.262	.307	.412	80	21	2	2	2	13	6	18
August	.212	.238	.364	118	25	5	5	1	14	4	30
Sept—Oct	.286	.362	.516	126	36	7	2	6	17	15	31
Bases Empty	.222	.261	.331	338	75	11	4	6	6	18	78
Leadoff	.263	.305	.385	179	47	6	2	4	4	11	43
Runners On Base	.294	.357	.482	228	67	12	11	3	63	23	36
Scoring Position	.286	.359	.466	133	38	5	8	1	54	16	20
Late and Close	.253	.313	.352	91	23	2	2	1	14	7	20

2-YEAR TOTALS (1990–1991)

	BA	OBA	SA	AB	H	2B	3B	HR	RBI	BB	SO
	.257	.311	.403	692	178	33	16	12	81	54	141
	.256	.311	.372	258	66	14	8	0	27	20	57
	.258	.311	.422	434	112	19	8	12	54	34	84
	.239	.303	.402	326	78	13	11	6	39	30	62
	.273	.317	.404	366	100	20	5	6	42	24	79
	.290	.330	.437	183	53	12	3	3	28	11	37
	.246	.304	.391	509	125	21	13	9	53	43	104
	.237	.306	.441	186	44	13	5	5	24	19	31
	.265	.313	.389	506	134	20	11	7	57	35	110
	.255	.305	.345	55	14	1	2	0	3	4	6
	.242	.258	.295	95	23	5	0	0	10	2	13
	.250	.327	.370	92	23	3	4	0	12	10	16
	.262	.307	.412	80	21	2	2	2	13	6	18
	.226	.259	.361	155	35	8	5	1	15	7	40
	.288	.363	.507	215	62	14	3	9	28	25	48
	.233	.278	.354	407	95	17	4	8	8	25	92
	.250	.290	.367	196	49	7	2	4	4	11	46
	.291	.355	.474	285	83	16	12	4	73	29	49
	.283	.354	.470	166	47	7	9	2	64	19	30
	.261	.322	.342	111	29	2	2	1	15	9	25

BARRY LARKIN — bats right — throws right — age 28 — CIN — *S

1991	BA	OBA	SA	AB	H	2B	3B	HR	RBI	BB	SO	6-YEAR TOTALS (1986–1991) BA	OBA	SA	AB	H	2B	3B	HR	RBI	BB	SO
Total	.302	.378	.506	464	140	27	4	20	69	55	64	.294	.350	.426	2589	762	118	24	58	290	210	233
vs. Left	.326	.433	.585	135	44	7	2	8	22	27	15	.315	.389	.490	784	247	39	10	26	103	95	44
vs. Right	.292	.353	.474	329	96	20	2	12	47	28	49	.285	.332	.398	1805	515	79	14	32	187	115	189
at Home	.326	.404	.612	242	79	17	2	16	48	30	37	.294	.353	.447	1310	385	61	11	39	171	116	122
on Road	.275	.349	.392	222	61	10	2	4	21	25	27	.295	.347	.404	1279	377	57	13	19	119	94	111
on Grass	.266	.324	.367	128	34	5	1	2	11	10	17	.297	.345	.404	747	222	37	5	11	70	48	67
on Turf	.315	.397	.560	336	106	22	3	18	58	45	47	.293	.352	.434	1842	540	81	19	47	220	162	166
Day Games	.308	.378	.551	107	33	5	0	7	16	10	10	.297	.358	.402	792	235	31	2	16	83	70	76
Night Games	.300	.378	.493	357	107	22	4	13	53	45	54	.293	.347	.436	1797	527	87	22	42	207	140	157
April	.217	.260	.362	69	15	1	0	3	7	4	11	.300	.349	.433	323	97	10	3	9	40	21	31
May	.379	.424	.828	29	11	3	2	2	6	2	3	.305	.359	.430	400	122	17	6	7	48	31	30
June	.370	.496	.717	92	34	5	0	9	23	23	12	.316	.377	.484	471	149	23	1	18	68	45	44
July	.250	.313	.342	76	19	4	0	1	8	7	15	.272	.340	.395	397	108	24	2	7	25	35	38
August	.300	.368	.483	120	36	6	2	4	18	12	12	.264	.311	.376	500	132	22	8	6	48	34	47
Sept–Oct	.321	.376	.462	78	25	8	0	1	7	7	11	.309	.364	.436	498	154	22	4	11	61	44	43
Bases Empty	.290	.350	.500	272	79	17	0	12	12	23	39	.279	.328	.405	1601	446	72	10	37	37	102	146
Leadoff	.290	.349	.520	100	29	8	0	5	5	9	15	.282	.335	.409	702	198	32	3	17	17	48	63
Runners On Base	.318	.414	.516	192	61	10	2	8	57	32	25	.320	.383	.459	988	316	46	14	21	253	108	87
Scoring Position	.288	.377	.441	111	32	4	2	3	45	16	15	.301	.371	.442	591	178	23	9	14	230	75	56
Late and Close	.254	.321	.352	71	18	2	1	1	7	6	17	.312	.366	.402	420	131	15	4	5	48	35	42

MIKE LaVALLIERE — bats left — throws right — age 32 — PIT — *C

1991	BA	OBA	SA	AB	H	2B	3B	HR	RBI	BB	SO	8-YEAR TOTALS (1984–1991) BA	OBA	SA	AB	H	2B	3B	HR	RBI	BB	SO
Total	.289	.351	.360	336	97	11	2	3	41	33	27	.271	.356	.344	1841	499	84	4	14	214	244	179
vs. Left	.222	.259	.296	54	12	2	1	0	14	3	9	.237	.324	.317	334	79	16	1	3	46	41	62
vs. Right	.301	.368	.372	282	85	9	1	3	27	30	18	.279	.363	.350	1507	420	68	3	11	168	203	117
at Home	.331	.400	.393	163	54	5	1	1	22	20	13	.286	.372	.357	913	261	40	2	7	112	126	82
on Road	.249	.304	.329	173	43	6	1	2	19	13	14	.256	.340	.331	928	238	44	2	7	102	118	97
on Grass	.229	.286	.349	83	19	4	0	2	11	5	6	.248	.332	.322	463	115	20	1	4	48	57	47
on Turf	.308	.372	.364	253	78	7	2	1	30	28	21	.279	.364	.351	1378	384	64	3	10	166	187	132
Day Games	.353	.412	.431	102	36	5	0	1	15	10	10	.276	.359	.340	591	163	27	1	3	71	79	60
Night Games	.261	.324	.329	234	61	6	2	2	26	23	17	.269	.355	.346	1250	336	57	3	11	143	165	119
April	.204	.235	.286	49	10	1	0	1	10	2	2	.266	.358	.321	252	67	11	0	1	39	38	17
May	.291	.359	.345	55	16	1	1	0	5	7	5	.288	.379	.343	236	68	8	1	1	29	37	23
June	.347	.439	.449	49	17	2	0	1	1	7	4	.260	.360	.342	269	70	14	1	2	26	41	23
July	.294	.351	.397	68	20	4	0	1	10	5	6	.264	.353	.328	345	91	16	0	2	39	45	34
August	.286	.349	.286	56	16	0	0	0	5	6	6	.267	.345	.368	367	98	20	1	5	39	44	42
Sept–Oct	.305	.358	.390	59	18	3	1	0	10	6	4	.282	.350	.352	372	105	15	1	3	42	39	40
Bases Empty	.326	.385	.395	190	62	7	0	2	2	16	10	.269	.334	.335	1069	288	48	2	6	6	99	105
Leadoff	.261	.330	.307	88	23	4	0	0	0	8	5	.270	.342	.345	440	119	26	2	1	1	44	37
Runners On Base	.240	.310	.315	146	35	4	2	1	39	17	17	.273	.384	.356	772	211	36	2	8	208	145	74
Scoring Position	.263	.336	.379	95	25	4	2	1	39	13	12	.284	.404	.398	497	141	32	2	7	204	109	51
Late and Close	.108	.277	.135	37	4	1	0	0	3	8	5	.250	.345	.346	280	70	19	1	2	37	40	40

MANUEL LEE — bats both — throws right — age 27 — TOR — *S

1991	BA	OBA	SA	AB	H	2B	3B	HR	RBI	BB	SO	7-YEAR TOTALS (1985–1991) BA	OBA	SA	AB	H	2B	3B	HR	RBI	BB	SO
Total	.234	.274	.288	445	104	18	3	0	29	24	107	.252	.294	.325	1756	443	57	16	13	160	108	353
vs. Left	.285	.333	.347	144	41	9	0	0	11	10	25	.283	.319	.393	672	190	29	9	9	76	36	117
vs. Right	.209	.245	.259	301	63	9	3	0	18	14	82	.233	.279	.283	1084	253	28	7	4	84	72	236
at Home	.249	.306	.324	213	53	12	2	0	12	18	50	.255	.303	.333	852	217	29	10	6	74	61	166
on Road	.220	.242	.254	232	51	6	1	0	17	6	57	.250	.286	.317	904	226	28	6	7	86	47	187
on Grass	.222	.250	.267	176	39	6	1	0	13	6	43	.259	.296	.330	713	185	20	6	6	74	38	137
on Turf	.242	.289	.301	269	65	12	2	0	16	18	64	.247	.293	.322	1043	258	37	10	7	86	70	216
Day Games	.226	.263	.274	146	33	7	0	0	6	8	37	.249	.290	.343	563	140	17	6	8	54	34	109
Night Games	.237	.279	.294	299	71	11	3	0	23	16	70	.254	.296	.317	1193	303	40	10	5	106	74	244
April	.262	.377	.338	65	17	3	1	0	2	12	18	.253	.321	.302	225	57	9	1	0	17	23	49
May	.333	.369	.400	60	20	2	1	0	8	3	13	.268	.301	.435	138	37	2	3	5	17	6	31
June	.215	.227	.262	107	23	5	0	0	6	2	27	.280	.305	.347	354	99	12	3	2	31	14	68
July	.185	.214	.210	81	15	2	0	0	4	3	22	.225	.264	.271	325	73	11	1	2	27	18	75
August	.220	.241	.268	82	18	2	1	0	8	2	17	.249	.286	.331	366	91	10	4	4	41	20	71
Sept–Oct	.220	.250	.300	50	11	4	0	0	1	2	10	.247	.300	.319	348	86	14	4	1	27	27	59
Bases Empty	.239	.282	.291	268	64	10	2	0	0	16	62	.249	.299	.317	1007	251	29	9	9	9	71	199
Leadoff	.269	.319	.333	108	29	5	1	0	0	8	24	.259	.308	.338	397	103	15	2	4	4	28	88
Runners On Base	.226	.262	.282	177	40	8	1	0	29	8	45	.256	.288	.336	749	192	28	10	4	151	37	154
Scoring Position	.219	.259	.257	105	23	4	0	0	28	6	26	.259	.289	.349	433	112	16	7	3	145	23	92
Late and Close	.200	.270	.237	80	16	3	0	0	5	7	18	.232	.295	.270	319	74	5	2	1	30	28	67

MARK LEWIS — bats right — throws right — age 23 — CLE — 2S

1-YEAR TOTALS (1991)

1991	BA	OBA	SA	AB	H	2B	3B	HR	RBI	BB	SO		BA	OBA	SA	AB	H	2B	3B	HR	RBI	BB	SO
Total	.264	.293	.318	314	83	15	1	0	30	15	45		.264	.293	.318	314	83	15	1	0	30	15	45
vs. Left	.276	.305	.310	87	24	3	0	0	7	5	12		.276	.305	.310	87	24	3	0	0	7	5	12
vs. Right	.260	.289	.322	227	59	12	1	0	23	10	33		.260	.289	.322	227	59	12	1	0	23	10	33
at Home	.277	.302	.327	159	44	6	1	0	15	7	19		.277	.302	.327	159	44	6	1	0	15	7	19
on Road	.252	.285	.310	155	39	9	0	0	15	8	26		.252	.285	.310	155	39	9	0	0	15	8	26
on Grass	.274	.307	.332	277	76	14	1	0	27	15	42		.274	.307	.332	277	76	14	1	0	27	15	42
on Turf	.189	.184	.216	37	7	1	0	0	3	0	3		.189	.184	.216	37	7	1	0	0	3	0	3
Day Games	.365	.385	.435	85	31	6	0	0	15	4	10		.365	.385	.435	85	31	6	0	0	15	4	10
Night Games	.227	.259	.275	229	52	9	1	0	15	11	35		.227	.259	.275	229	52	9	1	0	15	11	35
April	.429	.467	.643	14	6	3	0	0	2	1	2		.429	.467	.643	14	6	3	0	0	2	1	2
May	.355	.381	.400	110	39	5	0	0	13	6	15		.355	.381	.400	110	39	5	0	0	13	6	15
June	.144	.179	.167	90	13	2	0	0	6	4	9		.144	.179	.167	90	13	2	0	0	6	4	9
July	.150	.167	.200	40	6	0	1	0	1	1	8		.150	.167	.200	40	6	0	1	0	1	1	8
August	.000	.000	.000	0	0	0	0	0	0	0	0		.000	.000	.000	0	0	0	0	0	0	0	0
Sept–Oct	.317	.344	.400	60	19	5	0	0	8	3	11		.317	.344	.400	60	19	5	0	0	8	3	11
Bases Empty	.228	.265	.290	162	37	8	1	0	0	8	24		.228	.265	.290	162	37	8	1	0	0	8	24
Leadoff	.233	.298	.349	43	10	3	1	0	0	4	4		.233	.298	.349	43	10	3	1	0	0	4	4
Runners On Base	.303	.323	.349	152	46	7	0	0	30	7	21		.303	.323	.349	152	46	7	0	0	30	7	21
Scoring Position	.324	.329	.378	74	24	4	0	0	30	3	10		.324	.329	.378	74	24	4	0	0	30	3	10
Late and Close	.197	.254	.242	66	13	3	0	0	8	5	13		.197	.254	.242	66	13	3	0	0	8	5	13

JOSE LIND — bats right — throws right — age 28 — PIT — *2

5-YEAR TOTALS (1987–1991)

1991	BA	OBA	SA	AB	H	2B	3B	HR	RBI	BB	SO		BA	OBA	SA	AB	H	2B	3B	HR	RBI	BB	SO
Total	.265	.306	.339	502	133	16	6	3	54	30	56		.259	.303	.329	2348	607	97	22	8	210	154	259
vs. Left	.269	.326	.329	167	45	2	1	2	15	14	20		.258	.311	.335	865	223	39	8	4	72	72	94
vs. Right	.263	.295	.343	335	88	14	5	1	39	16	36		.259	.298	.325	1483	384	58	14	4	138	82	165
at Home	.244	.290	.332	262	64	7	5	2	30	17	32		.261	.304	.339	1196	312	52	12	6	125	79	127
on Road	.287	.323	.346	240	69	9	1	1	24	13	24		.256	.302	.318	1152	295	45	10	2	85	75	132
on Grass	.277	.310	.307	137	38	4	0	0	12	6	12		.238	.279	.274	610	145	17	1	1	38	33	68
on Turf	.260	.304	.351	365	95	12	6	3	42	24	44		.266	.311	.348	1738	462	80	21	7	172	121	191
Day Games	.295	.348	.380	129	38	7	2	0	13	10	20		.256	.300	.319	673	172	26	7	1	64	42	95
Night Games	.255	.291	.324	373	95	9	4	3	41	20	36		.260	.304	.333	1675	435	71	15	7	146	112	164
April	.266	.294	.344	64	17	2	0	1	6	3	8		.241	.287	.294	320	77	11	0	0	24	22	34
May	.257	.284	.371	70	18	3	1	1	9	3	4		.274	.318	.359	368	101	20	4	1	44	23	35
June	.239	.299	.282	71	17	0	0	1	8	6	8		.259	.306	.332	382	99	15	2	3	40	27	43
July	.284	.337	.341	88	25	3	1	0	6	6	5		.259	.298	.332	367	95	13	4	2	27	20	37
August	.242	.271	.323	99	24	4	2	0	7	5	16		.206	.258	.265	408	84	16	4	0	28	31	55
Sept–Oct	.291	.336	.364	110	32	4	2	0	18	7	15		.300	.340	.376	503	151	22	8	0	47	31	55
Bases Empty	.263	.293	.320	259	68	5	2	2	2	11	32		.252	.292	.320	1320	333	58	7	6	6	73	140
Leadoff	.213	.234	.278	108	23	2	1	1	1	3	12		.237	.271	.308	426	101	18	3	2	2	20	44
Runners On Base	.267	.319	.358	243	65	11	4	1	52	19	24		.267	.317	.339	1028	274	39	15	2	204	81	119
Scoring Position	.280	.355	.364	118	33	5	1	1	47	15	8		.266	.334	.350	575	153	23	11	1	191	66	64
Late and Close	.250	.274	.250	80	20	0	0	0	4	3	12		.263	.306	.309	418	110	12	2	1	30	28	50

KEVIN MAAS — bats left — throws left — age 27 — NYA — *D1

2-YEAR TOTALS (1990–1991)

1991	BA	OBA	SA	AB	H	2B	3B	HR	RBI	BB	SO		BA	OBA	SA	AB	H	2B	3B	HR	RBI	BB	SO
Total	.220	.333	.390	500	110	14	1	23	63	83	128		.231	.344	.439	754	174	23	1	44	104	126	204
vs. Left	.221	.338	.409	181	40	7	0	9	31	30	51		.206	.323	.383	248	51	8	0	12	39	41	79
vs. Right	.219	.330	.379	319	70	7	1	14	32	53	77		.243	.355	.466	506	123	15	1	32	65	85	125
at Home	.178	.301	.314	236	42	8	0	8	25	40	55		.216	.333	.415	371	80	14	0	20	52	63	93
on Road	.258	.361	.458	264	68	6	1	15	38	43	73		.245	.355	.462	383	94	9	1	24	52	63	111
on Grass	.210	.328	.371	415	87	13	0	18	51	71	109		.228	.344	.434	632	144	22	0	36	89	107	172
on Turf	.271	.357	.482	85	23	1	1	5	12	12	19		.246	.345	.467	122	30	1	1	8	15	19	32
Day Games	.262	.404	.418	141	37	7	0	5	21	34	25		.252	.379	.448	210	53	8	0	11	34	42	46
Night Games	.203	.302	.379	359	73	7	1	18	42	49	103		.222	.330	.436	544	121	15	1	33	70	84	158
April	.231	.467	.385	52	12	0	1	2	8	23	12		.231	.467	.385	52	12	0	1	2	8	23	12
May	.300	.412	.550	100	30	4	0	7	11	18	28		.300	.412	.550	100	30	4	0	7	11	18	28
June	.210	.289	.380	100	21	5	0	4	14	11	19		.217	.298	.377	106	23	5	0	4	15	12	20
July	.151	.245	.221	86	13	3	0	1	5	10	24		.201	.310	.409	149	30	4	0	9	19	23	45
August	.158	.273	.316	76	12	0	0	4	14	11	19		.217	.312	.450	180	39	6	0	12	29	23	50
Sept–Oct	.256	.327	.453	86	22	2	0	5	11	10	26		.240	.348	.443	167	40	4	0	10	22	27	49
Bases Empty	.249	.342	.453	285	71	8	1	16	16	38	70		.262	.352	.516	428	112	14	1	31	31	57	111
Leadoff	.272	.357	.474	114	31	3	1	6	6	15	24		.256	.347	.494	172	44	6	1	11	11	24	40
Runners On Base	.181	.322	.307	215	39	6	0	7	47	45	58		.190	.334	.337	326	62	9	0	13	73	69	93
Scoring Position	.180	.318	.303	122	22	3	0	4	40	26	30		.189	.357	.317	180	34	5	0	6	58	47	48
Late and Close	.271	.376	.518	85	23	3	0	6	18	14	23		.236	.368	.472	127	30	3	0	9	23	26	42

MIKE MACFARLANE — bats right — throws right — age 28 — KC — C/D

	BA	OBA	SA	AB	H	2B	3B	HR	RBI	BB	SO		BA	OBA	SA	AB	H	2B	3B	HR	RBI	BB	SO
1991												**5-YEAR TOTALS (1987–1991)**											
Total	.277	.330	.506	267	74	18	2	13	41	17	52		.257	.311	.400	1054	271	64	6	25	147	72	187
vs. Left	.321	.372	.563	112	36	10	1	5	14	7	19		.249	.291	.391	409	102	26	4	8	40	20	72
vs. Right	.245	.301	.465	155	38	8	1	8	27	10	33		.262	.323	.406	645	169	38	2	17	107	52	115
at Home	.286	.348	.516	126	36	7	2	6	17	9	20		.269	.321	.410	490	132	32	5	9	67	32	73
on Road	.270	.314	.496	141	38	11	0	7	24	8	32		.246	.302	.392	564	139	32	1	16	80	40	114
on Grass	.268	.306	.482	112	30	9	0	5	20	6	26		.248	.306	.389	447	111	25	1	12	68	35	87
on Turf	.284	.347	.523	155	44	9	2	8	21	11	26		.264	.314	.409	607	160	39	5	13	79	37	100
Day Games	.344	.375	.607	61	21	4	0	4	10	3	10		.279	.338	.438	251	70	17	1	7	37	21	50
Night Games	.257	.317	.476	206	53	14	2	9	31	14	42		.250	.302	.389	803	201	47	5	18	110	51	137
April	.339	.383	.500	56	19	7	1	0	6	3	10		.333	.378	.478	138	46	18	1	0	14	9	25
May	.198	.275	.444	81	16	5	0	5	10	7	16		.230	.299	.387	243	56	13	2	7	30	20	46
June	.284	.310	.481	81	23	2	1	4	11	3	15		.246	.283	.353	252	62	11	2	4	33	12	38
July	.333	.406	.852	27	9	2	0	4	12	3	6		.294	.350	.518	197	58	14	0	10	41	16	33
August	.000	.000	.000	0	0	0	0	0	0	0	0		.234	.271	.374	107	25	3	0	4	23	6	22
Sept–Oct	.318	.375	.409	22	7	2	0	0	2	1	5		.205	.288	.265	117	24	5	1	0	6	9	23
Bases Empty	.267	.327	.562	146	39	9	2	10	10	11	30		.235	.285	.394	587	138	35	5	16	16	34	114
Leadoff	.262	.314	.600	65	17	5	1	5	5	4	11		.224	.273	.402	254	57	11	2	10	10	14	45
Runners On Base	.289	.333	.438	121	35	9	0	3	31	6	22		.285	.342	.409	467	133	29	1	9	131	38	73
Scoring Position	.278	.325	.458	72	20	7	0	2	29	6	17		.272	.337	.401	279	76	16	1	6	117	29	48
Late and Close	.208	.309	.333	48	10	3	0	1	4	5	11		.231	.303	.352	182	42	9	2	3	21	15	43

SHANE MACK — bats right — throws right — age 29 — MIN — *O/D

	BA	OBA	SA	AB	H	2B	3B	HR	RBI	BB	SO		BA	OBA	SA	AB	H	2B	3B	HR	RBI	BB	SO
1991												**4-YEAR TOTALS (1987–1991)**											
Total	.310	.363	.529	442	137	27	8	18	74	34	79		.292	.355	.446	1112	325	51	15	30	155	95	216
vs. Left	.350	.412	.701	137	48	13	4	9	29	14	19		.319	.386	.521	470	150	27	7	18	81	44	74
vs. Right	.292	.341	.452	305	89	14	4	9	45	20	60		.273	.331	.391	642	175	24	8	12	74	51	142
at Home	.333	.383	.531	213	71	16	7	4	34	15	35		.305	.366	.478	515	157	30	13	11	76	44	104
on Road	.288	.345	.528	229	66	11	1	14	40	19	44		.281	.345	.419	597	168	21	2	19	79	51	112
on Grass	.281	.345	.534	178	50	9	0	12	33	17	37		.279	.345	.418	567	158	23	4	16	80	54	109
on Turf	.330	.376	.527	264	87	18	8	6	41	17	42		.306	.364	.475	545	167	28	11	14	75	41	107
Day Games	.324	.401	.597	139	45	13	2	7	22	16	20		.322	.384	.481	370	119	23	3	10	58	30	65
Night Games	.304	.345	.498	303	92	14	6	11	52	18	59		.278	.340	.429	742	206	28	12	20	97	65	151
April	.143	.189	.343	35	5	2	1	1	3	2	9		.208	.300	.434	53	11	4	1	2	5	5	10
May	.333	.408	.524	42	14	2	0	2	9	5	2		.299	.376	.396	164	49	6	2	2	20	18	24
June	.256	.313	.477	86	22	4	0	5	17	8	14		.258	.320	.404	225	58	9	0	8	35	20	45
July	.366	.435	.622	82	30	6	3	3	12	9	14		.302	.367	.478	232	70	10	5	7	24	22	51
August	.343	.387	.637	102	35	7	4	5	20	7	22		.290	.336	.488	207	60	10	5	7	37	14	45
Sept–Oct	.326	.363	.453	95	31	6	0	2	13	3	18		.333	.390	.455	231	77	12	2	4	34	16	41
Bases Empty	.314	.366	.527	245	77	16	6	8	8	18	41		.283	.346	.435	619	175	27	8	17	17	52	114
Leadoff	.305	.330	.476	105	32	5	2	3	3	3	15		.300	.350	.458	260	78	9	4	8	8	18	40
Runners On Base	.305	.360	.533	197	60	11	2	10	66	16	38		.304	.365	.460	493	150	24	7	13	138	43	102
Scoring Position	.265	.313	.496	113	30	6	1	6	54	8	25		.284	.355	.446	271	77	16	5	6	117	28	62
Late and Close	.194	.224	.306	62	12	1	0	2	8	3	16		.246	.294	.339	171	42	5	1	4	23	13	37

DAVE MAGADAN — bats left — throws right — age 30 — NYN — *1

	BA	OBA	SA	AB	H	2B	3B	HR	RBI	BB	SO		BA	OBA	SA	AB	H	2B	3B	HR	RBI	BB	SO
1991												**6-YEAR TOTALS (1986–1991)**											
Total	.258	.378	.342	418	108	23	0	4	51	83	50		.294	.391	.393	1767	519	101	10	18	226	291	205
vs. Left	.248	.347	.275	149	37	4	0	0	12	23	13		.274	.358	.338	541	148	19	2	4	71	70	58
vs. Right	.264	.395	.379	269	71	19	0	4	39	60	37		.303	.405	.417	1226	371	82	8	14	155	221	147
at Home	.243	.358	.322	202	49	10	0	2	25	38	27		.295	.392	.387	869	256	42	4	10	122	148	103
on Road	.273	.398	.361	216	59	13	0	2	26	45	23		.293	.389	.399	898	263	59	6	8	104	143	102
on Grass	.247	.357	.333	300	74	17	0	3	39	54	35		.291	.385	.380	1237	360	61	5	13	163	198	148
on Turf	.288	.430	.364	118	34	6	0	1	12	29	15		.300	.404	.423	530	159	40	5	5	63	93	57
Day Games	.210	.337	.301	143	30	7	0	2	13	27	19		.283	.378	.389	612	173	35	3	8	72	100	71
Night Games	.284	.399	.364	275	78	16	0	2	38	56	31		.300	.398	.395	1155	346	66	7	10	154	191	134
April	.270	.427	.317	63	17	3	0	0	8	18	12		.248	.385	.345	145	36	6	1	2	14	34	23
May	.250	.340	.386	88	22	6	0	2	14	12	8		.295	.370	.384	258	76	12	1	3	29	32	40
June	.215	.363	.316	79	17	5	0	1	9	19	8		.315	.415	.450	378	119	24	3	7	55	65	34
July	.305	.420	.390	82	25	4	0	1	12	16	8		.296	.387	.389	368	109	23	1	6	46	57	30
August	.289	.383	.333	90	26	4	0	0	8	15	13		.283	.386	.335	343	97	16	1	3	41	58	40
Sept–Oct	.063	.211	.125	16	1	1	0	0	0	3	1		.298	.392	.425	275	82	20	3	3	41	45	38
Bases Empty	.239	.371	.325	234	56	14	0	2	2	48	33		.264	.371	.364	987	261	53	6	11	11	162	119
Leadoff	.288	.422	.370	73	21	6	0	0	0	16	9		.271	.377	.360	347	94	17	1	4	4	57	36
Runners On Base	.283	.388	.364	184	52	9	0	2	49	35	17		.331	.415	.429	780	258	48	4	7	215	129	86
Scoring Position	.291	.394	.379	103	30	6	0	1	45	21	8		.319	.409	.417	458	146	28	1	5	197	86	53
Late and Close	.179	.337	.209	67	12	2	0	0	9	16	12		.267	.369	.340	303	81	11	1	3	35	45	45

CANDY MALDONADO — bats right — throws right — age 32 — MIL/TOR — O/D | 8-YEAR TOTALS (1984–1991)

1991	BA	OBA	SA	AB	H	2B	3B	HR	RBI	BB	SO		BA	OBA	SA	AB	H	2B	3B	HR	RBI	BB	SO
Total	.250	.342	.427	288	72	15	0	12	48	36	76		.258	.317	.424	3036	782	173	11	103	470	251	592
vs. Left	.276	.398	.461	76	21	5	0	3	12	15	13		.268	.331	.421	1208	324	65	4	37	171	114	191
vs. Right	.241	.321	.415	212	51	10	0	9	36	21	63		.251	.308	.426	1828	458	108	7	66	299	137	401
at Home	.228	.340	.433	127	29	5	0	7	22	20	40		.237	.288	.385	1472	349	69	2	48	219	101	315
on Road	.267	.344	.422	161	43	10	0	5	26	16	36		.277	.344	.460	1564	433	104	9	55	251	150	277
on Grass	.243	.328	.412	177	43	12	0	6	28	22	35		.258	.312	.421	2245	579	124	6	77	357	172	438
on Turf	.261	.364	.450	111	29	3	0	6	20	14	41		.257	.331	.430	791	203	49	5	26	113	79	154
Day Games	.220	.333	.378	82	18	1	0	4	13	12	25		.264	.323	.431	1126	297	58	5	40	201	97	216
Night Games	.262	.346	.447	206	54	14	0	8	35	24	51		.254	.314	.419	1910	485	115	6	63	269	154	376
April	.200	.429	.400	5	1	1	0	0	2	2	2		.286	.346	.441	433	124	26	1	13	61	37	76
May	.000	.000	.000	0	0	0	0	0	0	0	0		.245	.300	.427	510	125	29	2	20	77	35	85
June	.300	.417	.900	10	3	0	0	2	6	2	2		.275	.340	.456	458	126	33	1	16	76	43	86
July	.224	.277	.368	76	17	5	0	2	10	6	15		.259	.316	.376	455	118	24	1	9	56	38	90
August	.224	.294	.378	98	22	3	0	4	11	8	24		.227	.288	.404	555	126	24	1	24	90	46	115
Sept–Oct	.293	.418	.475	99	29	6	0	4	19	18	33		.261	.342	.437	625	163	37	5	21	110	52	140
Bases Empty	.242	.314	.359	153	37	6	0	4	4	12	39		.245	.297	.413	1635	401	82	3	62	62	107	318
Leadoff	.266	.329	.453	64	17	3	0	3	3	5	15		.251	.299	.420	745	187	34	1	30	30	44	144
Runners On Base	.259	.372	.504	135	35	9	0	8	44	24	37		.272	.340	.436	1401	381	91	8	41	408	144	274
Scoring Position	.250	.388	.488	80	20	4	0	5	35	19	20		.267	.349	.435	843	225	60	5	24	354	115	167
Late and Close	.122	.232	.245	49	6	0	0	2	5	7	16		.247	.296	.404	555	137	28	1	19	81	39	118

CARLOS MARTINEZ — bats right — throws right — age 28 — CLE — D1 | 4-YEAR TOTALS (1988–1991)

1991	BA	OBA	SA	AB	H	2B	3B	HR	RBI	BB	SO		BA	OBA	SA	AB	H	2B	3B	HR	RBI	BB	SO
Total	.284	.310	.397	257	73	14	0	5	30	10	43		.266	.297	.367	934	248	43	5	14	86	41	152
vs. Left	.338	.367	.550	80	27	5	0	4	13	6	11		.268	.292	.377	385	103	14	2	8	36	15	58
vs. Right	.260	.283	.328	177	46	9	0	1	17	4	32		.264	.300	.361	549	145	29	3	6	50	26	94
at Home	.317	.338	.424	139	44	6	0	3	18	5	21		.268	.302	.369	477	128	21	3	7	49	23	77
on Road	.246	.278	.364	118	29	8	0	2	12	5	22		.263	.292	.365	457	120	22	2	7	37	18	75
on Grass	.296	.319	.417	223	66	12	0	5	28	9	35		.270	.301	.377	767	207	36	5	12	78	36	118
on Turf	.206	.250	.265	34	7	2	0	0	2	1	8		.246	.276	.323	167	41	7	0	2	8	5	34
Day Games	.270	.278	.432	74	20	3	0	2	10	1	11		.214	.248	.257	257	55	8	0	5	28	11	50
Night Games	.290	.323	.383	183	53	11	0	2	20	9	32		.285	.315	.383	677	193	35	5	7	58	30	102
April	.000	.000	.000	0	0	0	0	0	0	0	0		.230	.254	.393	61	14	2	1	2	10	2	9
May	.000	.000	.000	0	0	0	0	0	0	0	0		.194	.229	.299	134	26	6	1	2	17	5	23
June	.000	.000	.000	0	0	0	0	0	0	0	0		.276	.330	.322	87	24	4	0	0	6	7	15
July	.347	.367	.467	75	26	3	0	2	8	3	15		.319	.349	.479	163	52	7	2	5	15	8	22
August	.286	.318	.351	77	22	5	0	0	11	3	16		.292	.324	.363	226	66	11	1	1	19	10	41
Sept–Oct	.238	.264	.381	105	25	6	0	3	11	4	12		.251	.274	.346	263	66	13	0	4	19	9	42
Bases Empty	.279	.307	.422	147	41	9	0	4	4	4	28		.278	.306	.411	508	141	26	3	12	12	18	81
Leadoff	.250	.300	.411	56	14	3	0	2	2	2	11		.279	.300	.433	201	56	11	1	6	6	4	27
Runners On Base	.291	.314	.364	110	32	5	0	1	26	6	15		.251	.286	.315	426	107	17	2	2	74	23	71
Scoring Position	.360	.362	.420	50	18	3	0	0	24	3	8		.261	.302	.345	226	59	12	2	1	71	16	41
Late and Close	.209	.244	.256	43	9	2	0	0	4	2	12		.220	.264	.311	132	29	9	0	1	15	8	29

DAVE MARTINEZ — bats left — throws left — age 28 — MON — *O | 6-YEAR TOTALS (1986–1991)

1991	BA	OBA	SA	AB	H	2B	3B	HR	RBI	BB	SO		BA	OBA	SA	AB	H	2B	3B	HR	RBI	BB	SO
Total	.295	.332	.418	397	117	18	5	7	42	20	54		.272	.327	.389	2153	586	79	32	36	196	171	368
vs. Left	.242	.293	.330	91	22	6	1	0	8	5	22		.224	.292	.307	277	62	7	2	4	26	24	78
vs. Right	.310	.344	.444	306	95	12	4	7	34	15	32		.279	.332	.401	1876	524	72	30	32	170	147	290
at Home	.282	.315	.408	174	49	9	2	3	21	8	19		.255	.311	.362	1053	268	34	14	17	84	84	169
on Road	.305	.345	.426	223	68	9	3	4	21	12	35		.289	.342	.415	1100	318	45	18	19	112	87	199
on Grass	.291	.325	.445	110	32	2	3	3	13	5	19		.272	.334	.400	945	257	33	17	18	86	86	180
on Turf	.296	.334	.408	287	85	16	2	4	29	15	35		.272	.321	.380	1208	329	46	15	18	110	85	188
Day Games	.275	.323	.400	120	33	5	2	2	17	8	22		.262	.330	.389	928	243	30	14	20	88	93	178
Night Games	.303	.336	.426	277	84	13	3	5	25	12	32		.280	.324	.389	1225	343	49	18	16	108	78	190
April	.207	.258	.259	58	12	1	1	0	5	4	8		.226	.288	.310	248	56	6	3	3	29	20	32
May	.263	.300	.421	38	10	1	1	1	7	2	5		.265	.334	.349	298	79	11	4	2	33	33	58
June	.261	.281	.380	92	24	6	1	1	11	3	12		.291	.344	.442	437	127	20	8	10	45	35	63
July	.351	.385	.432	74	26	3	0	1	3	4	7		.285	.333	.409	372	106	12	2	10	24	25	66
August	.347	.382	.528	72	25	5	1	2	8	2	8		.283	.330	.412	410	116	20	6	7	38	27	73
Sept–Oct	.317	.371	.476	63	20	2	1	2	8	5	14		.263	.318	.366	388	102	10	7	4	27	31	76
Bases Empty	.293	.315	.439	246	72	11	2	7	7	7	36		.271	.320	.394	1379	374	46	20	28	28	95	224
Leadoff	.250	.284	.333	88	22	1	2	1	1	4	7		.263	.311	.366	634	167	20	6	11	11	41	98
Runners On Base	.298	.357	.384	151	45	7	3	0	35	12	18		.274	.338	.379	774	212	33	12	8	168	76	144
Scoring Position	.296	.366	.347	98	29	3	1	0	31	9	13		.273	.350	.376	466	127	22	7	4	153	57	90
Late and Close	.205	.259	.218	78	16	1	0	0	6	4	9		.231	.292	.302	368	85	11	6	1	34	31	77

EDGAR MARTINEZ — bats right — throws right — age 29 — SEA — *3/D · **5-YEAR TOTALS (1987–1991)**

1991	BA	OBA	SA	AB	H	2B	3B	HR	RBI	BB	SO	BA	OBA	SA	AB	H	2B	3B	HR	RBI	BB	SO
Total	.307	.405	.452	544	167	35	1	14	52	84	72	.298	.389	.428	1277	380	76	5	27	131	181	172
vs. Left	.359	.442	.481	156	56	13	0	2	12	24	11	.318	.403	.457	403	128	27	1	9	48	56	43
vs. Right	.286	.390	.441	388	111	22	1	12	40	60	61	.288	.383	.415	874	252	49	4	18	83	125	129
at Home	.320	.427	.480	250	80	14	1	8	28	45	33	.300	.399	.429	594	178	38	3	11	57	93	78
on Road	.296	.385	.429	294	87	21	0	6	24	39	39	.296	.380	.428	683	202	38	2	16	74	88	94
on Grass	.288	.383	.414	222	64	13	0	5	17	32	31	.288	.374	.421	503	145	24	2	13	52	65	69
on Turf	.320	.419	.478	322	103	22	1	9	35	52	41	.304	.398	.433	774	235	52	3	14	79	116	103
Day Games	.276	.364	.388	152	42	9	1	2	14	21	19	.264	.349	.397	330	87	19	2	7	38	45	40
Night Games	.319	.420	.477	392	125	26	0	12	38	63	53	.309	.403	.439	947	293	57	3	20	93	136	132
April	.412	.551	.574	68	28	5	0	2	10	18	8	.314	.417	.430	172	54	8	0	4	19	27	21
May	.276	.376	.368	87	24	2	0	2	9	14	15	.309	.405	.462	223	69	6	2	8	27	35	29
June	.267	.319	.337	86	23	3	0	1	5	6	12	.281	.369	.367	221	62	13	0	2	16	29	40
July	.333	.417	.563	87	29	6	1	4	11	11	11	.284	.371	.433	208	59	11	1	6	24	26	30
August	.263	.381	.432	95	25	7	0	3	7	17	9	.263	.372	.419	186	49	14	0	5	16	30	18
Sept–Oct	.314	.400	.463	121	38	12	0	2	10	18	17	.326	.400	.453	267	87	24	2	2	29	34	34
Bases Empty	.335	.419	.497	328	110	24	1	9	9	43	50	.313	.394	.461	737	231	54	5	15	15	90	110
Leadoff	.339	.417	.552	165	56	15	1	6	6	21	25	.307	.377	.484	339	104	29	2	9	9	37	47
Runners On Base	.264	.385	.384	216	57	11	0	5	43	41	22	.276	.382	.383	540	149	22	0	12	116	91	62
Scoring Position	.219	.390	.324	105	23	5	0	2	33	30	10	.247	.383	.336	283	70	10	0	5	95	62	33
Late and Close	.354	.522	.462	65	23	4	0	1	10	21	8	.301	.440	.435	193	58	11	0	5	33	45	34

DON MATTINGLY — bats left — throws left — age 31 — NYA — *1D · **8-YEAR TOTALS (1984–1991)**

1991	BA	OBA	SA	AB	H	2B	3B	HR	RBI	BB	SO	BA	OBA	SA	AB	H	2B	3B	HR	RBI	BB	SO
Total	.288	.339	.394	587	169	35	0	9	68	46	42	.316	.362	.497	4712	1489	308	11	174	794	367	268
vs. Left	.264	.321	.383	227	60	12	0	5	29	18	20	.306	.349	.477	1701	520	118	4	55	320	119	110
vs. Right	.303	.350	.400	360	109	23	0	4	39	28	22	.322	.370	.508	3011	969	190	7	119	474	248	158
at Home	.305	.356	.462	266	81	21	0	7	40	22	20	.317	.363	.523	2265	718	136	2	109	426	177	136
on Road	.274	.325	.336	321	88	14	0	2	28	24	22	.315	.362	.472	2447	771	172	9	65	368	190	132
on Grass	.293	.349	.413	484	142	31	0	9	63	43	37	.314	.362	.496	3942	1239	247	6	152	672	318	226
on Turf	.262	.287	.301	103	27	4	0	0	5	3	5	.325	.364	.503	770	250	61	5	22	122	49	42
Day Games	.270	.355	.352	159	43	10	0	1	18	23	13	.327	.381	.507	1494	489	107	4	51	245	139	77
Night Games	.294	.333	.409	428	126	25	0	8	50	23	29	.311	.353	.492	3218	1000	201	7	123	549	228	191
April	.265	.367	.324	68	18	1	0	1	4	11	5	.280	.351	.401	608	170	47	3	7	86	69	39
May	.311	.360	.433	90	28	5	0	2	13	8	8	.330	.381	.515	821	271	51	1	33	150	72	48
June	.337	.355	.462	104	35	4	0	3	13	4	6	.310	.348	.460	768	238	36	2	25	115	51	38
July	.265	.313	.353	102	27	9	0	0	10	6	8	.319	.356	.522	806	257	64	2	32	133	50	44
August	.343	.400	.475	99	34	10	0	1	17	9	7	.322	.369	.526	797	257	53	2	35	138	59	39
Sept–Oct	.218	.267	.315	124	27	6	0	2	11	8	8	.325	.364	.527	912	296	57	1	42	172	66	60
Bases Empty	.278	.325	.384	331	92	20	0	5	5	22	28	.309	.347	.490	2513	776	166	10	90	90	139	154
Leadoff	.266	.310	.330	109	29	4	0	1	1	6	5	.304	.334	.498	838	255	54	3	34	34	35	41
Runners On Base	.301	.356	.406	256	77	15	0	4	63	24	14	.324	.378	.504	2199	713	142	1	84	704	228	114
Scoring Position	.294	.386	.404	136	40	9	0	2	57	24	11	.321	.392	.504	1212	389	84	0	46	603	182	75
Late and Close	.303	.402	.494	89	27	5	0	4	15	14	11	.303	.378	.480	710	215	38	2	28	132	85	40

WILLIE McGEE — bats both — throws right — age 34 — SF — *O · **8-YEAR TOTALS (1984–1991)**

1991	BA	OBA	SA	AB	H	2B	3B	HR	RBI	BB	SO	BA	OBA	SA	AB	H	2B	3B	HR	RBI	BB	SO
Total	.312	.357	.408	497	155	30	3	4	43	34	74	.300	.339	.414	4172	1251	204	65	47	472	248	634
vs. Left	.342	.384	.454	152	52	11	0	2	20	10	23	.294	.326	.440	1428	420	71	25	29	186	72	271
vs. Right	.299	.345	.388	345	103	19	3	2	23	24	51	.303	.345	.400	2744	831	133	40	18	286	176	363
at Home	.270	.306	.351	222	60	12	0	2	20	12	29	.303	.336	.415	2049	620	97	32	23	232	109	301
on Road	.345	.397	.455	275	95	18	3	2	23	22	45	.297	.341	.413	2123	631	107	33	24	240	139	333
on Grass	.284	.323	.375	363	103	17	2	4	32	22	59	.292	.335	.394	1400	409	66	16	15	153	90	219
on Turf	.388	.446	.500	134	52	13	1	0	11	12	15	.304	.340	.424	2772	842	138	49	32	319	158	415
Day Games	.337	.357	.437	199	67	13	2	1	23	7	28	.320	.355	.444	1429	457	65	29	18	177	77	205
Night Games	.295	.357	.389	298	88	17	1	3	20	27	46	.289	.330	.398	2743	794	139	36	29	295	171	429
April	.333	.356	.491	57	19	1	1	2	4	2	11	.295	.333	.410	502	148	17	10	7	61	29	91
May	.297	.325	.423	111	33	9	1	1	10	5	16	.277	.318	.379	839	232	36	13	8	93	51	122
June	.352	.434	.451	91	32	6	0	1	5	13	9	.317	.362	.421	745	236	37	13	5	89	57	107
July	.000	.000	.000	1	0	0	0	0	0	0	0	.320	.349	.463	581	186	36	7	11	68	26	88
August	.272	.325	.351	114	31	7	1	0	15	8	15	.299	.339	.417	703	210	34	11	9	89	41	101
Sept–Oct	.325	.357	.382	123	40	7	0	0	9	6	23	.298	.333	.406	802	239	44	11	7	72	44	125
Bases Empty	.297	.330	.404	317	94	21	2	3	3	15	53	.301	.333	.411	2381	716	120	34	25	25	112	358
Leadoff	.236	.282	.355	110	26	7	0	2	2	6	21	.290	.321	.391	916	266	45	13	7	7	40	135
Runners On Base	.339	.401	.417	180	61	9	1	1	40	19	21	.299	.345	.417	1791	535	84	31	22	447	136	276
Scoring Position	.343	.427	.400	105	36	6	0	0	35	16	16	.292	.348	.410	1133	331	61	20	11	405	106	188
Late and Close	.329	.370	.424	85	28	5	0	1	8	6	19	.285	.326	.381	717	204	32	8	7	91	45	134

FRED McGRIFF — bats left — throws left — age 29 — SD — *1

1991	BA	OBA	SA	AB	H	2B	3B	HR	RBI	BB	SO
Total	.280	.396	.495	529	148	19	1	31	106	104	136
vs. Left	.276	.382	.514	210	58	6	1	14	47	38	57
vs. Right	.282	.405	.483	319	90	13	0	17	59	66	79
at Home	.280	.426	.536	239	67	7	0	18	53	60	68
on Road	.279	.369	.462	290	81	12	1	13	53	44	68
on Grass	.287	.405	.517	387	111	14	0	25	79	78	101
on Turf	.261	.371	.437	142	37	5	1	6	27	26	35
Day Games	.272	.390	.522	136	37	8	1	8	27	27	33
Night Games	.282	.397	.486	393	111	11	0	23	79	77	103
April	.319	.444	.431	72	23	2	0	2	8	17	22
May	.279	.372	.587	104	29	3	1	9	22	15	27
June	.218	.396	.410	78	17	3	0	4	20	23	16
July	.310	.400	.494	87	27	4	0	4	10	13	21
August	.229	.339	.469	96	22	2	0	7	24	18	31
Sept–Oct	.326	.438	.543	92	30	5	0	5	22	18	19
Bases Empty	.257	.350	.468	280	72	8	0	17	17	39	69
Leadoff	.213	.310	.449	136	29	2	0	10	10	19	37
Runners On Base	.305	.441	.526	249	76	11	1	14	89	65	67
Scoring Position	.271	.451	.493	144	39	6	1	8	73	52	38
Late and Close	.236	.423	.347	72	17	2	0	2	7	24	23

6-YEAR TOTALS (1986–1991)

	BA	OBA	SA	AB	H	2B	3B	HR	RBI	BB	SO
Total	.278	.391	.523	2473	688	119	9	156	411	456	631
vs. Left	.253	.343	.419	798	202	25	4	33	117	108	233
vs. Right	.290	.412	.573	1675	486	94	5	123	294	348	398
at Home	.268	.396	.515	1166	313	57	3	75	198	243	279
on Road	.287	.386	.529	1307	375	62	6	81	213	213	352
on Grass	.283	.392	.510	1190	337	54	3	70	189	217	320
on Turf	.274	.389	.535	1283	351	65	6	86	222	239	311
Day Games	.264	.373	.479	760	201	40	3	39	113	130	174
Night Games	.284	.398	.542	1713	487	79	6	117	298	326	457
April	.304	.437	.527	319	97	15	1	18	45	73	93
May	.267	.369	.504	419	112	25	1	24	71	66	103
June	.259	.377	.511	401	104	18	1	27	74	75	100
July	.287	.388	.581	418	120	18	0	35	81	69	114
August	.281	.397	.565	469	132	25	6	32	78	93	134
Sept–Oct	.275	.383	.450	447	123	18	0	20	62	80	87
Bases Empty	.287	.387	.553	1391	399	73	6	95	95	223	339
Leadoff	.289	.382	.539	610	176	35	5	36	36	90	145
Runners On Base	.267	.395	.484	1082	289	46	3	61	316	233	292
Scoring Position	.246	.402	.420	602	148	22	1	27	234	166	182
Late and Close	.248	.378	.413	375	93	22	2	12	43	78	108

MARK McGWIRE — bats right — throws right — age 29 — OAK — *1

1991	BA	OBA	SA	AB	H	2B	3B	HR	RBI	BB	SO
Total	.201	.330	.383	483	97	22	0	22	75	93	116
vs. Left	.200	.316	.354	130	26	5	0	5	19	23	28
vs. Right	.201	.336	.394	353	71	17	0	17	56	70	88
at Home	.185	.329	.412	243	45	10	0	15	48	52	55
on Road	.217	.332	.354	240	52	12	0	7	27	41	61
on Grass	.205	.339	.408	400	82	18	0	21	69	80	96
on Turf	.181	.289	.265	83	15	4	0	1	6	13	20
Day Games	.182	.300	.412	170	31	6	0	11	32	29	36
Night Games	.211	.346	.367	313	66	16	0	11	43	64	80
April	.209	.354	.299	67	14	6	0	0	5	15	15
May	.228	.426	.443	79	18	2	0	5	16	28	22
June	.176	.297	.482	85	15	2	0	8	19	14	27
July	.173	.292	.259	81	14	4	0	1	8	13	20
August	.255	.330	.479	94	24	3	0	6	18	11	17
Sept–Oct	.156	.275	.299	77	12	5	0	2	12	12	15
Bases Empty	.172	.306	.324	244	42	13	0	8	8	44	54
Leadoff	.167	.279	.385	96	16	6	0	5	5	14	17
Runners On Base	.230	.355	.444	239	55	9	0	14	67	49	62
Scoring Position	.240	.368	.473	129	31	3	0	9	57	29	31
Late and Close	.169	.337	.385	65	11	2	0	4	15	17	19

6-YEAR TOTALS (1986–1991)

	BA	OBA	SA	AB	H	2B	3B	HR	RBI	BB	SO
Total	.244	.351	.489	2655	647	106	5	178	504	437	592
vs. Left	.248	.362	.503	750	186	36	1	51	158	140	146
vs. Right	.242	.347	.483	1905	461	70	4	127	346	297	446
at Home	.233	.345	.454	1289	300	56	2	75	228	219	296
on Road	.254	.357	.521	1366	347	50	3	103	276	218	296
on Grass	.244	.352	.497	2247	549	90	3	157	437	372	505
on Turf	.240	.349	.444	408	98	16	2	21	67	65	87
Day Games	.255	.350	.531	1007	257	40	2	78	203	141	211
Night Games	.237	.352	.462	1648	390	66	3	100	301	296	381
April	.256	.366	.511	309	79	13	0	22	64	52	67
May	.236	.365	.515	445	105	15	2	35	88	92	85
June	.233	.331	.490	451	105	16	2	32	83	68	108
July	.240	.320	.442	480	115	16	0	27	85	52	103
August	.231	.349	.450	493	114	16	1	30	91	89	115
Sept–Oct	.270	.380	.535	477	129	30	0	32	93	84	114
Bases Empty	.227	.336	.462	1445	328	56	1	94	94	222	314
Leadoff	.238	.344	.528	617	147	29	0	50	50	95	129
Runners On Base	.264	.369	.520	1210	319	50	4	84	410	215	278
Scoring Position	.282	.396	.519	674	190	22	3	44	321	145	168
Late and Close	.255	.367	.483	385	98	8	1	26	82	66	96

BRIAN McRAE — bats both — throws right — age 25 — KC — *O

1991	BA	OBA	SA	AB	H	2B	3B	HR	RBI	BB	SO
Total	.261	.288	.372	629	164	28	9	8	64	24	99
vs. Left	.294	.326	.407	204	60	13	2	2	19	9	16
vs. Right	.245	.270	.355	425	104	15	7	6	45	15	83
at Home	.267	.305	.384	318	85	16	6	3	29	17	52
on Road	.254	.270	.360	311	79	12	3	5	35	7	47
on Grass	.270	.278	.371	237	64	9	3	3	25	3	33
on Turf	.255	.294	.372	392	100	19	6	5	39	21	66
Day Games	.229	.253	.376	170	39	8	4	3	18	6	30
Night Games	.272	.301	.370	459	125	20	5	5	46	18	69
April	.143	.137	.224	49	7	1	0	1	8	0	11
May	.282	.345	.447	103	29	4	2	3	15	10	13
June	.275	.296	.342	120	33	4	2	0	9	4	21
July	.298	.325	.421	114	34	6	1	2	15	5	18
August	.271	.295	.364	118	32	5	3	0	7	2	15
Sept–Oct	.232	.248	.360	125	29	8	1	2	10	3	21
Bases Empty	.273	.296	.378	399	109	21	6	3	3	12	64
Leadoff	.307	.335	.431	218	67	16	4	1	1	9	33
Runners On Base	.239	.274	.361	230	55	7	3	5	61	12	35
Scoring Position	.259	.299	.353	139	36	5	1	2	52	9	27
Late and Close	.247	.295	.351	97	24	3	2	1	8	7	12

2-YEAR TOTALS (1990–1991)

	BA	OBA	SA	AB	H	2B	3B	HR	RBI	BB	SO
Total	.266	.294	.379	797	212	36	12	10	87	33	128
vs. Left	.312	.340	.420	276	86	17	2	3	32	12	23
vs. Right	.242	.270	.357	521	126	19	10	7	55	21	105
at Home	.276	.314	.401	399	110	22	8	4	44	23	65
on Road	.256	.274	.357	398	102	14	4	6	43	10	63
on Grass	.268	.281	.361	299	80	10	3	4	31	6	46
on Turf	.265	.302	.390	498	132	26	9	6	56	27	82
Day Games	.230	.254	.378	217	50	9	4	5	28	8	39
Night Games	.279	.309	.379	580	162	27	8	5	59	25	89
April	.143	.137	.224	49	7	1	0	1	8	0	11
May	.282	.345	.447	103	29	4	2	3	15	10	13
June	.275	.296	.342	120	33	4	2	0	9	4	21
July	.298	.325	.421	114	34	6	1	2	15	5	18
August	.281	.308	.389	185	52	9	4	1	17	6	22
Sept–Oct	.252	.277	.372	226	57	12	3	3	23	8	43
Bases Empty	.274	.301	.380	503	138	27	7	4	4	18	83
Leadoff	.291	.319	.403	268	78	19	4	1	1	11	44
Runners On Base	.252	.284	.378	294	74	9	5	6	83	15	45
Scoring Position	.278	.314	.391	169	47	6	2	3	72	11	31
Late and Close	.280	.323	.373	118	33	4	2	1	11	8	15

KEVIN McREYNOLDS — bats right — throws right — age 33 — NYN — *O

1991 / 8-YEAR TOTALS (1984–1991)

1991	BA	OBA	SA	AB	H	2B	3B	HR	RBI	BB	SO	BA	OBA	SA	AB	H	2B	3B	HR	RBI	BB	SO
Total	.259	.322	.416	522	135	32	1	16	74	49	46	.270	.328	.457	4379	1184	223	28	179	681	386	540
vs. Left	.257	.309	.401	187	48	10	1	5	18	14	17	.276	.344	.476	1486	410	77	14	64	212	157	155
vs. Right	.260	.330	.424	335	87	22	0	11	56	35	29	.268	.319	.447	2893	774	146	14	115	469	229	385
at Home	.237	.289	.386	236	56	12	1	7	33	17	14	.268	.326	.452	2135	573	94	13	91	324	190	265
on Road	.276	.349	.441	286	79	20	0	9	41	32	32	.272	.330	.461	2244	611	129	15	88	357	196	275
on Grass	.244	.299	.391	361	88	21	1	10	48	29	32	.266	.321	.454	3158	839	153	18	135	476	270	399
on Turf	.292	.372	.472	161	47	11	0	6	26	20	14	.283	.343	.464	1221	345	70	10	44	205	116	141
Day Games	.220	.297	.335	164	36	10	1	3	15	18	19	.263	.320	.456	1477	389	72	10	64	234	122	202
Night Games	.277	.334	.453	358	99	22	1	13	59	31	27	.274	.332	.457	2902	795	151	18	115	447	264	338
April	.128	.180	.255	47	6	3	0	1	6	3	3	.274	.333	.450	525	144	22	2	22	78	50	71
May	.330	.394	.489	88	29	8	0	2	13	10	6	.272	.332	.441	744	202	39	3	27	114	67	84
June	.340	.398	.557	97	33	9	0	4	18	9	8	.278	.342	.474	770	214	44	7	31	121	76	84
July	.240	.301	.375	104	25	5	0	3	15	9	10	.262	.329	.440	762	200	52	4	25	119	78	98
August	.233	.283	.344	90	21	2	1	2	7	7	10	.264	.307	.454	764	202	24	5	37	120	53	96
Sept–Oct	.219	.306	.396	96	21	5	0	4	15	11	9	.273	.325	.478	814	222	42	7	37	129	62	107
Bases Empty	.252	.300	.387	302	76	18	1	7	7	21	28	.266	.314	.458	2436	649	114	17	106	106	165	287
Leadoff	.208	.259	.338	130	27	6	1	3	3	9	9	.271	.323	.463	980	266	46	11	40	40	71	102
Runners On Base	.268	.350	.455	220	59	14	0	9	67	28	18	.275	.343	.455	1943	535	109	11	73	575	221	253
Scoring Position	.308	.383	.538	143	44	12	0	7	62	19	14	.284	.361	.473	1187	337	62	8	49	504	168	164
Late and Close	.259	.323	.541	85	22	6	0	6	22	8	12	.264	.318	.431	796	210	33	2	32	132	66	117

ORLANDO MERCED — bats both — throws right — age 26 — PIT — *1/O

1991 / 2-YEAR TOTALS (1990–1991)

1991	BA	OBA	SA	AB	H	2B	3B	HR	RBI	BB	SO	BA	OBA	SA	AB	H	2B	3B	HR	RBI	BB	SO
Total	.275	.373	.399	411	113	17	2	10	50	64	81	.271	.367	.391	435	118	18	2	10	50	65	90
vs. Left	.208	.263	.302	53	11	3	1	0	6	3	10	.197	.246	.279	61	12	3	1	0	6	3	15
vs. Right	.285	.388	.413	358	102	14	1	10	44	61	71	.283	.384	.409	374	106	15	1	10	44	62	75
at Home	.255	.370	.391	192	49	9	1	5	22	35	41	.255	.367	.387	204	52	10	1	5	22	36	46
on Road	.292	.376	.406	219	64	8	1	5	28	29	40	.286	.366	.394	231	66	8	1	5	28	29	44
on Grass	.324	.368	.457	105	34	3	1	3	17	8	17	.316	.358	.439	114	36	3	1	3	17	8	20
on Turf	.258	.375	.379	306	79	14	1	7	33	56	64	.255	.369	.374	321	82	15	1	7	33	57	70
Day Games	.316	.419	.509	114	36	6	2	4	25	20	24	.305	.411	.492	118	36	6	2	4	25	21	26
Night Games	.259	.355	.357	297	77	11	0	6	25	44	57	.259	.349	.353	317	82	12	0	6	25	44	64
April	.318	.464	.409	22	7	0	1	0	3	6	5	.318	.464	.409	22	7	0	1	0	3	6	5
May	.362	.450	.623	69	25	6	0	4	12	10	14	.362	.450	.623	69	25	6	0	4	12	10	14
June	.152	.240	.167	66	10	1	0	0	2	8	16	.157	.241	.186	70	11	2	0	0	2	8	17
July	.317	.429	.451	82	26	3	1	2	12	16	14	.305	.405	.421	95	29	3	1	2	12	16	20
August	.267	.353	.367	90	24	6	0	1	11	12	17	.272	.356	.370	92	25	6	0	1	11	12	17
Sept–Oct	.256	.351	.378	82	21	1	0	3	10	12	15	.241	.340	.356	87	21	1	0	3	10	13	17
Bases Empty	.249	.368	.337	261	65	9	1	4	4	49	45	.251	.366	.338	275	69	10	1	4	4	50	50
Leadoff	.235	.350	.294	170	40	8	1	0	0	30	26	.240	.351	.297	175	42	8	1	0	0	30	28
Runners On Base	.320	.383	.507	150	48	8	1	6	46	15	36	.306	.367	.481	160	49	8	1	6	46	15	40
Scoring Position	.326	.387	.611	95	31	7	1	6	46	10	25	.317	.375	.584	101	32	7	1	6	46	10	28
Late and Close	.210	.359	.403	62	13	3	0	3	12	15	16	.232	.372	.420	69	16	4	0	3	12	16	19

KEITH MILLER — bats right — throws right — age 29 — NYN — 2O/3S

1991 / 5-YEAR TOTALS (1987–1991)

1991	BA	OBA	SA	AB	H	2B	3B	HR	RBI	BB	SO	BA	OBA	SA	AB	H	2B	3B	HR	RBI	BB	SO
Total	.280	.345	.411	275	77	22	1	4	23	23	44	.264	.323	.354	772	204	40	4	7	48	59	133
vs. Left	.252	.303	.350	143	36	11	0	1	7	9	26	.271	.323	.362	398	108	23	2	3	22	29	72
vs. Right	.311	.389	.477	132	41	11	1	3	16	14	18	.257	.323	.345	374	96	17	2	4	26	30	61
at Home	.291	.354	.405	158	46	12	0	2	10	13	23	.256	.323	.345	391	100	19	2	4	25	36	62
on Road	.265	.333	.419	117	31	10	1	2	13	10	21	.273	.323	.362	381	104	21	2	3	23	23	71
on Grass	.274	.346	.382	186	51	14	0	2	13	18	30	.248	.314	.333	483	120	22	2	5	30	44	83
on Turf	.292	.344	.472	89	26	8	1	2	10	5	14	.291	.338	.388	289	84	18	2	2	18	15	50
Day Games	.326	.390	.505	95	31	14	0	1	9	8	9	.275	.332	.399	276	76	23	1	3	18	21	38
Night Games	.256	.322	.361	180	46	8	1	3	14	15	35	.258	.317	.329	496	128	17	3	4	30	38	95
April	.235	.316	.353	17	4	2	0	0	0	2	2	.246	.342	.391	69	17	7	0	1	3	10	11
May	.458	.480	.667	24	11	2	0	1	2	1	6	.286	.297	.365	63	18	2	0	1	2	1	13
June	.333	.333	.333	6	2	0	0	0	0	0	1	.305	.341	.398	128	39	6	3	0	7	7	19
July	.280	.294	.380	50	14	5	0	0	5	0	6	.268	.299	.339	112	30	5	0	1	8	2	18
August	.172	.262	.241	58	10	1	0	1	4	6	13	.209	.271	.261	153	32	5	0	1	11	11	34
Sept–Oct	.300	.384	.467	120	36	12	1	2	12	14	16	.275	.355	.381	247	68	15	1	3	17	28	38
Bases Empty	.246	.308	.374	179	44	9	1	4	4	13	29	.257	.315	.345	513	132	23	2	6	6	37	90
Leadoff	.208	.276	.323	96	20	5	0	2	2	8	15	.241	.315	.326	261	63	10	0	4	4	25	45
Runners On Base	.344	.413	.479	96	33	13	0	0	19	10	15	.278	.338	.371	259	72	17	2	1	42	22	43
Scoring Position	.345	.400	.448	58	20	6	0	0	18	5	9	.248	.315	.315	149	37	8	1	0	38	14	29
Late and Close	.265	.432	.412	34	9	2	0	1	4	10	7	.263	.354	.325	114	30	4	0	1	6	16	23

RANDY MILLIGAN — bats right — throws right — age 31 — BAL — *1D/O

1991	BA	OBA	SA	AB	H	2B	3B	HR	RBI	BB	SO	5-YEAR TOTALS (1987–1991) BA	OBA	SA	AB	H	2B	3B	HR	RBI	BB	SO
Total	.263	.373	.406	483	127	17	2	16	70	84	108	.262	.390	.443	1293	339	65	8	51	183	267	276
vs. Left	.229	.347	.371	140	32	3	1	5	19	26	35	.245	.380	.446	466	114	25	3	21	67	102	93
vs. Right	.277	.384	.420	343	95	14	1	11	51	58	73	.272	.395	.441	827	225	40	5	30	116	165	183
at Home	.249	.362	.388	237	59	9	0	8	33	41	51	.260	.406	.446	624	162	32	3	26	87	152	125
on Road	.276	.384	.423	246	68	8	2	8	37	43	57	.265	.374	.441	669	177	33	5	25	96	115	151
on Grass	.252	.360	.381	409	103	12	1	13	55	68	91	.263	.390	.440	1042	274	50	6	41	145	215	219
on Turf	.324	.440	.541	74	24	5	1	3	15	16	17	.259	.389	.454	251	65	15	2	10	38	52	57
Day Games	.296	.397	.444	108	32	4	0	4	13	17	27	.288	.415	.471	306	88	15	1	13	47	67	69
Night Games	.253	.366	.395	375	95	13	2	12	57	67	81	.254	.382	.435	987	251	50	7	38	136	200	207
April	.196	.303	.232	56	11	2	0	0	2	9	17	.218	.349	.324	170	37	6	0	4	17	35	45
May	.271	.374	.424	85	23	2	1	3	13	14	23	.244	.393	.414	266	65	18	3	7	32	63	70
June	.341	.420	.591	88	30	4	0	6	22	12	18	.333	.455	.620	255	85	16	0	19	59	57	44
July	.235	.377	.388	85	20	2	1	3	17	19	11	.242	.377	.460	248	60	8	2	14	40	53	41
August	.261	.382	.337	92	24	4	0	1	12	18	18	.249	.374	.348	181	45	8	2	2	20	36	38
Sept–Oct	.247	.356	.403	77	19	3	0	3	4	12	21	.272	.359	.422	173	47	9	1	5	15	23	38
Bases Empty	.272	.383	.437	261	71	10	0	11	11	47	52	.259	.389	.474	700	181	33	5	36	36	147	147
Leadoff	.245	.357	.409	110	27	3	0	5	5	19	27	.260	.391	.457	269	70	15	1	12	12	58	58
Runners On Base	.252	.361	.369	222	56	7	2	5	59	37	56	.266	.390	.406	593	158	32	3	15	147	120	129
Scoring Position	.307	.438	.425	127	39	4	1	3	53	29	35	.272	.413	.423	331	90	15	1	11	131	81	80
Late and Close	.244	.363	.372	86	21	3	1	2	12	16	14	.275	.428	.450	211	58	11	1	8	34	55	42

KEVIN MITCHELL — bats right — throws right — age 30 — SF — *O/1

1991	BA	OBA	SA	AB	H	2B	3B	HR	RBI	BB	SO	7-YEAR TOTALS (1984–1991) BA	OBA	SA	AB	H	2B	3B	HR	RBI	BB	SO
Total	.256	.338	.515	371	95	13	3	27	69	43	57	.275	.351	.517	2748	756	138	20	162	481	317	496
vs. Left	.274	.373	.496	113	31	4	0	7	22	17	7	.288	.374	.539	952	274	60	4	57	161	131	133
vs. Right	.248	.322	.523	258	64	9	1	20	47	26	50	.268	.339	.505	1796	482	78	16	105	320	186	363
at Home	.242	.307	.432	190	46	7	1	9	30	17	26	.279	.354	.511	1333	372	74	14	69	240	156	230
on Road	.271	.370	.602	181	49	6	0	18	39	26	31	.271	.348	.522	1415	384	64	6	93	241	161	266
on Grass	.242	.314	.476	273	66	8	1	18	45	25	39	.280	.353	.512	2016	565	104	17	110	355	226	370
on Turf	.296	.402	.622	98	29	5	0	9	24	18	18	.261	.345	.529	732	191	34	3	52	126	91	126
Day Games	.236	.319	.442	165	39	7	0	9	26	18	33	.277	.358	.499	1095	303	66	6	55	176	138	196
Night Games	.272	.353	.573	206	56	6	1	18	43	25	24	.274	.346	.529	1653	453	72	14	107	305	179	300
April	.269	.346	.612	67	18	2	0	7	16	8	3	.282	.348	.529	412	116	25	4	23	75	44	78
May	.240	.397	.440	50	12	1	0	3	5	13	7	.264	.347	.516	440	116	21	6	26	70	55	70
June	.467	.529	1.200	15	7	2	0	3	8	2	2	.314	.394	.586	382	120	27	1	25	80	52	53
July	.261	.306	.478	92	24	2	0	6	18	6	19	.271	.343	.547	490	133	21	0	38	96	52	94
August	.267	.347	.505	105	28	5	1	6	18	11	17	.282	.357	.505	578	163	26	8	29	93	64	119
Sept–Oct	.143	.217	.310	42	6	1	0	2	4	3	9	.242	.321	.428	446	108	18	1	21	67	50	82
Bases Empty	.271	.346	.547	192	52	6	1	15	15	18	32	.277	.343	.546	1419	393	72	14	94	94	131	246
Leadoff	.287	.361	.563	87	25	3	0	7	7	8	15	.278	.335	.565	605	168	28	7	44	44	49	109
Runners On Base	.240	.330	.480	179	43	7	0	12	54	25	25	.273	.359	.485	1329	363	66	6	68	387	186	250
Scoring Position	.242	.358	.455	99	24	3	0	6	39	19	13	.266	.378	.467	763	203	39	3	36	309	146	150
Late and Close	.148	.284	.279	61	9	2	0	2	7	11	18	.252	.336	.464	444	112	16	0	26	69	55	100

PAUL MOLITOR — bats right — throws right — age 36 — MIL — *D1

1991	BA	OBA	SA	AB	H	2B	3B	HR	RBI	BB	SO	8-YEAR TOTALS (1984–1991) BA	OBA	SA	AB	H	2B	3B	HR	RBI	BB	SO
Total	.325	.399	.489	665	216	32	13	17	75	77	62	.310	.377	.459	3831	1187	222	43	88	420	414	470
vs. Left	.322	.405	.489	174	56	8	3	5	17	24	13	.309	.382	.460	1084	335	63	10	27	103	127	110
vs. Right	.326	.397	.489	491	160	24	10	12	58	53	49	.310	.376	.459	2747	852	159	33	61	317	287	360
at Home	.292	.374	.454	315	92	14	8	7	38	39	23	.319	.386	.477	1834	585	108	22	46	228	203	210
on Road	.354	.422	.520	350	124	18	5	10	37	38	39	.301	.370	.443	1997	602	114	21	42	192	211	260
on Grass	.318	.399	.487	556	177	25	12	15	67	71	47	.313	.383	.463	3204	1002	185	36	75	365	361	381
on Turf	.358	.402	.495	109	39	7	1	2	8	6	15	.295	.350	.439	627	185	37	7	13	55	53	89
Day Games	.348	.442	.490	198	69	9	2	5	20	31	17	.315	.386	.453	1095	345	69	5	24	109	127	137
Night Games	.315	.380	.488	467	147	23	11	12	55	46	45	.308	.374	.462	2736	842	153	38	64	311	287	333
April	.324	.378	.456	68	22	6	0	1	5	6	6	.320	.392	.467	460	147	30	1	12	57	54	61
May	.361	.414	.525	122	44	4	5	2	10	10	9	.291	.355	.424	611	178	31	7	12	59	63	62
June	.310	.410	.570	100	31	7	2	5	15	14	11	.330	.405	.509	525	173	36	8	14	64	66	70
July	.301	.373	.416	113	34	3	2	2	11	12	15	.295	.354	.418	550	162	27	7	9	46	49	62
August	.357	.420	.558	129	46	9	1	5	20	14	10	.303	.371	.463	719	218	43	6	20	88	77	90
Sept–Oct	.293	.391	.406	133	39	3	3	2	14	21	11	.320	.386	.471	966	309	55	14	21	106	105	125
Bases Empty	.320	.381	.494	431	138	22	7	13	13	37	38	.297	.357	.451	2549	756	149	32	60	60	231	314
Leadoff	.322	.373	.515	270	87	12	5	10	10	18	22	.305	.360	.472	1499	457	78	23	42	42	124	178
Runners On Base	.333	.431	.479	234	78	10	6	4	62	40	24	.336	.415	.476	1282	431	73	11	28	360	183	156
Scoring Position	.326	.450	.464	138	45	7	3	2	54	31	17	.345	.433	.486	760	262	46	5	17	322	131	103
Late and Close	.293	.435	.424	92	27	3	0	3	15	22	9	.319	.394	.475	530	169	29	3	16	77	69	70

MICKEY MORANDINI — bats left — throws right — age 26 — PHI — 2

2-YEAR TOTALS (1990–1991)

1991	BA	OBA	SA	AB	H	2B	3B	HR	RBI	BB	SO	BA	OBA	SA	AB	H	2B	3B	HR	RBI	BB	SO
Total	.249	.313	.317	325	81	11	4	1	20	29	45	.248	.309	.319	404	100	15	4	2	23	35	64
vs. Left	.180	.219	.180	61	11	0	0	0	3	3	9	.171	.213	.184	76	13	1	0	0	3	4	14
vs. Right	.265	.333	.348	264	70	11	4	1	17	26	36	.265	.331	.351	328	87	14	4	2	20	31	50
at Home	.235	.295	.313	166	39	4	3	1	10	14	22	.249	.305	.329	213	53	5	3	2	13	17	31
on Road	.264	.331	.321	159	42	7	1	0	10	15	23	.246	.314	.309	191	47	10	1	0	10	18	33
on Grass	.310	.356	.393	84	26	5	1	0	9	6	7	.303	.349	.394	99	30	7	1	0	9	7	12
on Turf	.228	.299	.290	241	55	6	3	1	11	23	38	.230	.297	.295	305	70	8	3	2	14	28	52
Day Games	.227	.280	.280	75	17	2	1	0	6	6	12	.245	.286	.306	98	24	4	1	0	6	6	17
Night Games	.256	.322	.328	250	64	9	3	1	14	23	33	.248	.317	.324	306	76	11	3	2	17	29	47
April	.267	.313	.267	15	4	0	0	0	0	1	4	.267	.313	.267	15	4	0	0	0	0	1	4
May	.283	.353	.304	46	13	1	0	0	3	4	4	.283	.353	.304	46	13	1	0	0	3	4	4
June	.242	.307	.308	91	22	3	0	1	12	9	15	.242	.307	.308	91	22	3	0	1	12	9	15
July	.230	.284	.328	61	14	4	1	0	3	5	4	.230	.284	.328	61	14	4	1	0	3	5	4
August	.245	.322	.302	53	13	1	1	0	0	5	7	.245	.322	.302	53	13	1	1	0	0	5	7
Sept–Oct	.254	.313	.356	59	15	2	2	0	2	5	11	.246	.302	.341	138	34	6	2	1	5	11	30
Bases Empty	.255	.332	.320	200	51	9	2	0	0	21	29	.252	.324	.327	254	64	12	2	1	1	25	44
Leadoff	.286	.362	.333	84	24	4	0	0	0	9	12	.305	.381	.352	105	32	5	0	0	0	12	18
Runners On Base	.240	.281	.312	125	30	2	2	1	20	8	16	.240	.284	.307	150	36	3	2	1	22	10	20
Scoring Position	.266	.300	.344	64	17	0	1	1	19	4	10	.260	.298	.325	77	20	0	1	1	21	5	14
Late and Close	.255	.328	.327	55	14	2	1	0	2	5	7	.284	.360	.373	67	19	4	1	0	2	7	8

HAL MORRIS — bats left — throws left — age 27 — CIN — *1/O

4-YEAR TOTALS (1988–1991)

1991	BA	OBA	SA	AB	H	2B	3B	HR	RBI	BB	SO	BA	OBA	SA	AB	H	2B	3B	HR	RBI	BB	SO
Total	.318	.374	.479	478	152	33	1	14	59	46	61	.320	.369	.473	825	264	55	4	21	99	68	106
vs. Left	.252	.288	.379	103	26	8	1	1	12	6	25	.231	.279	.301	186	43	8	1	1	17	13	42
vs. Right	.336	.397	.507	375	126	25	0	13	47	40	36	.346	.395	.523	639	221	47	3	20	82	55	64
at Home	.319	.370	.525	238	76	20	1	9	33	21	31	.318	.366	.495	406	129	32	2	12	55	34	50
on Road	.317	.378	.433	240	76	13	0	5	26	25	30	.322	.373	.451	419	135	23	2	9	44	34	56
on Grass	.369	.430	.538	130	48	10	0	4	20	15	15	.314	.368	.446	271	85	17	2	5	32	23	41
on Turf	.299	.352	.457	348	104	23	1	10	39	31	46	.323	.370	.486	554	179	38	2	16	67	45	65
Day Games	.326	.381	.518	141	46	12	0	5	20	14	11	.288	.340	.461	267	77	22	0	8	33	21	31
Night Games	.315	.371	.463	337	106	21	1	9	39	32	50	.335	.384	.478	558	187	33	4	13	66	47	75
April	.358	.352	.604	53	19	7	0	2	9	0	5	.328	.333	.522	67	22	7	0	2	10	1	9
May	.316	.365	.463	95	30	6	1	2	14	7	11	.307	.355	.439	114	35	7	1	2	17	8	14
June	.266	.302	.367	79	21	5	0	1	7	5	14	.299	.340	.402	97	29	7	0	1	10	6	16
July	.363	.453	.563	80	29	7	0	3	11	14	9	.395	.446	.599	157	62	10	2	6	24	17	15
August	.303	.349	.421	76	23	3	0	2	7	6	8	.285	.321	.430	179	51	11	0	5	15	10	22
Sept–Oct	.316	.400	.495	95	30	5	0	1	11	14	14	.308	.382	.450	211	65	13	1	5	23	26	30
Bases Empty	.335	.380	.535	275	92	19	0	12	12	19	25	.340	.382	.537	456	155	33	3	17	17	29	45
Leadoff	.323	.343	.444	99	32	6	0	2	2	3	13	.345	.366	.492	177	61	12	1	4	4	6	21
Runners On Base	.296	.367	.404	203	60	14	1	2	47	27	36	.295	.355	.393	369	109	22	1	4	82	39	61
Scoring Position	.284	.375	.388	116	33	7	1	1	41	21	20	.306	.379	.397	209	64	11	1	2	72	30	33
Late and Close	.333	.400	.403	72	24	2	0	1	5	8	14	.266	.315	.338	139	37	7	0	1	7	9	26

RANCE MULLINIKS — bats left — throws right — age 36 — TOR — D/3

8-YEAR TOTALS (1984–1991)

1991	BA	OBA	SA	AB	H	2B	3B	HR	RBI	BB	SO	BA	OBA	SA	AB	H	2B	3B	HR	RBI	BB	SO
Total	.250	.364	.333	240	60	12	1	2	24	44	44	.285	.369	.426	2336	666	145	11	54	305	321	373
vs. Left	.083	.083	.083	12	1	0	0	0	0	0	3	.256	.365	.376	117	30	8	0	2	10	20	26
vs. Right	.259	.376	.346	228	59	12	1	2	24	44	41	.287	.369	.429	2219	636	137	11	52	295	301	347
at Home	.250	.355	.333	120	30	5	1	1	11	20	25	.290	.372	.446	1117	324	84	6	26	160	149	192
on Road	.250	.372	.333	120	30	7	0	1	13	24	19	.281	.366	.408	1219	342	61	5	28	145	172	181
on Grass	.294	.425	.400	85	25	6	0	1	13	20	13	.282	.369	.413	967	273	49	4	23	120	138	143
on Turf	.226	.328	.297	155	35	6	1	1	11	24	31	.287	.369	.435	1369	393	96	7	31	185	183	230
Day Games	.232	.337	.268	82	19	3	0	0	7	13	18	.276	.358	.404	768	212	45	4	15	92	103	117
Night Games	.259	.377	.367	158	41	9	1	2	17	31	26	.290	.374	.437	1568	454	100	7	39	213	218	256
April	.212	.366	.364	33	7	0	1	1	2	8	4	.245	.333	.345	310	76	17	1	4	29	42	49
May	.400	.500	.600	5	2	1	0	0	0	1	0	.293	.376	.439	376	110	20	1	11	57	52	67
June	.315	.465	.389	54	17	4	0	0	8	16	9	.290	.386	.424	458	133	26	4	9	55	75	65
July	.246	.333	.344	61	15	3	0	1	4	8	11	.312	.382	.496	417	130	31	2	14	62	47	58
August	.208	.311	.245	53	11	2	0	0	3	8	12	.281	.361	.429	399	112	25	2	10	49	51	74
Sept–Oct	.235	.289	.294	34	8	2	0	0	7	3	8	.279	.365	.402	376	105	26	1	6	53	54	60
Bases Empty	.245	.353	.350	143	35	7	1	2	2	24	29	.277	.353	.421	1370	379	83	8	33	33	160	226
Leadoff	.189	.328	.264	53	10	2	1	0	0	11	10	.266	.343	.405	481	128	24	5	11	11	55	79
Runners On Base	.258	.378	.309	97	25	5	0	0	22	20	15	.297	.390	.433	966	287	62	3	21	272	161	147
Scoring Position	.400	.529	.480	50	20	4	0	0	21	16	7	.312	.419	.457	580	181	44	2	12	243	122	90
Late and Close	.220	.377	.317	41	9	1	0	1	5	11	9	.278	.387	.418	352	98	18	2	9	51	65	59

DALE MURPHY — bats right — throws right — age 36 — PHI — *O

1991	BA	OBA	SA	AB	H	2B	3B	HR	RBI	BB	SO	8-YEAR BA	OBA	SA	AB	H	2B	3B	HR	RBI	BB	SO
Total	.252	.309	.415	544	137	33	1	18	81	48	93	.263	.348	.471	4676	1231	227	24	232	725	607	1042
vs. Left	.297	.351	.443	192	57	13	0	5	25	17	33	.293	.407	.524	1415	415	72	9	79	227	277	270
vs. Right	.227	.286	.401	352	80	20	1	13	56	31	60	.250	.320	.448	3261	816	155	15	153	498	330	772
at Home	.280	.343	.452	279	78	21	0	9	54	29	48	.280	.374	.496	2292	641	115	10	120	384	344	470
on Road	.223	.272	.377	265	59	12	1	9	27	19	45	.247	.322	.447	2384	590	112	14	112	341	263	572
on Grass	.204	.257	.357	157	32	4	1	6	13	12	25	.270	.359	.490	3097	837	131	17	172	499	426	673
on Turf	.271	.329	.439	387	105	29	0	12	68	36	68	.250	.325	.433	1579	394	96	7	60	226	181	369
Day Games	.185	.271	.294	119	22	7	0	2	14	14	26	.263	.353	.470	1363	358	67	7	67	192	192	303
Night Games	.271	.320	.449	425	115	26	1	16	67	34	67	.264	.346	.471	3313	873	160	17	165	533	415	739
April	.293	.333	.480	75	22	2	0	4	13	5	16	.281	.360	.516	595	167	32	3	34	105	75	144
May	.233	.283	.389	90	21	5	0	3	11	7	15	.270	.366	.472	805	217	40	3	39	102	123	164
June	.265	.326	.482	83	22	4	1	4	13	8	14	.252	.339	.451	814	205	37	4	39	128	108	195
July	.198	.274	.291	86	17	5	0	1	9	9	14	.243	.335	.465	764	186	35	4	42	120	106	178
August	.235	.312	.429	98	23	7	0	4	13	11	19	.265	.336	.485	835	221	43	3	45	136	90	187
Sept–Oct	.286	.325	.429	112	32	10	0	2	22	8	15	.272	.353	.450	863	235	40	7	33	134	105	174
Bases Empty	.258	.315	.446	287	74	18	0	12	12	24	46	.261	.330	.463	2581	674	133	17	118	118	261	565
Leadoff	.270	.333	.500	126	34	11	0	6	6	12	18	.269	.326	.475	1119	301	60	9	51	51	93	239
Runners On Base	.245	.302	.381	257	63	15	1	6	69	24	47	.266	.368	.481	2095	557	94	7	114	607	346	477
Scoring Position	.239	.306	.381	155	37	10	0	4	63	18	30	.270	.397	.502	1198	324	51	5	72	503	265	309
Late and Close	.241	.291	.481	108	26	5	0	7	20	8	24	.244	.346	.436	803	196	38	4	36	128	126	208

8-YEAR TOTALS (1984–1991)

EDDIE MURRAY — bats both — throws right — age 36 — LA — *1/3

1991	BA	OBA	SA	AB	H	2B	3B	HR	RBI	BB	SO	8-YEAR BA	OBA	SA	AB	H	2B	3B	HR	RBI	BB	SO
Total	.260	.321	.403	576	150	23	1	19	96	55	74	.288	.372	.471	4615	1327	217	15	200	772	641	585
vs. Left	.218	.271	.331	248	54	10	0	6	40	20	29	.259	.338	.418	1582	410	74	3	57	238	190	203
vs. Right	.293	.358	.457	328	96	13	1	13	56	35	45	.302	.389	.499	3033	917	143	12	143	534	451	382
at Home	.270	.347	.426	282	76	9	1	11	50	35	41	.292	.383	.468	2258	660	91	7	97	376	339	293
on Road	.252	.295	.381	294	74	14	0	8	46	20	33	.283	.361	.474	2357	667	126	8	103	396	302	292
on Grass	.277	.343	.427	419	116	13	1	16	73	46	49	.291	.379	.480	3714	1082	169	7	173	638	540	473
on Turf	.217	.257	.338	157	34	10	0	3	23	9	25	.272	.344	.433	901	245	48	8	27	134	101	112
Day Games	.269	.328	.417	175	47	8	0	6	32	16	22	.276	.362	.455	1299	359	58	3	56	212	178	166
Night Games	.257	.318	.397	401	103	15	1	13	64	39	52	.292	.376	.477	3316	968	159	12	144	560	463	419
April	.300	.407	.480	50	15	3	0	2	5	9	2	.263	.342	.438	598	157	28	1	25	104	74	77
May	.300	.339	.470	100	30	5	0	4	22	7	14	.308	.397	.499	751	231	40	4	32	150	119	87
June	.229	.291	.343	105	24	6	0	2	20	10	12	.260	.348	.422	809	210	42	1	29	114	113	113
July	.172	.248	.242	99	17	4	0	1	12	11	20	.272	.358	.500	728	198	29	1	45	137	101	105
August	.261	.317	.396	111	29	3	0	4	13	9	16	.322	.402	.490	822	265	30	6	32	140	111	94
Sept–Oct	.315	.364	.514	111	35	2	1	6	24	9	10	.293	.377	.473	907	266	48	2	37	127	123	109
Bases Empty	.247	.283	.381	299	74	10	0	10	10	15	33	.274	.350	.431	2403	658	99	6	89	89	279	316
Leadoff	.221	.237	.342	149	33	0	0	5	5	3	17	.271	.338	.421	1179	319	46	4	41	41	117	141
Runners On Base	.274	.357	.426	277	76	13	1	9	86	40	41	.302	.394	.514	2212	669	118	9	111	683	362	269
Scoring Position	.263	.376	.417	156	41	9	0	5	75	33	23	.301	.420	.536	1121	337	60	6	64	563	261	161
Late and Close	.268	.357	.423	97	26	4	1	3	18	15	13	.284	.381	.482	708	201	32	3	34	134	116	108

8-YEAR TOTALS (1984–1991)

GREG MYERS — bats left — throws right — age 26 — TOR — *C

1991	BA	OBA	SA	AB	H	2B	3B	HR	RBI	BB	SO	4-YEAR BA	OBA	SA	AB	H	2B	3B	HR	RBI	BB	SO
Total	.262	.306	.411	309	81	22	0	8	36	21	45	.239	.288	.356	612	146	31	1	13	59	45	90
vs. Left	.171	.211	.286	35	6	1	0	1	3	2	7	.180	.235	.246	61	11	1	0	1	5	5	12
vs. Right	.274	.319	.427	274	75	21	0	7	33	19	38	.245	.294	.368	551	135	30	1	12	54	40	78
at Home	.290	.356	.490	145	42	14	0	5	20	16	21	.251	.315	.388	291	73	16	0	8	33	29	45
on Road	.238	.259	.341	164	39	8	0	3	16	5	24	.227	.262	.327	321	73	15	1	5	26	16	45
on Grass	.191	.210	.270	115	22	3	0	2	9	3	21	.211	.253	.310	232	49	9	1	4	17	14	36
on Turf	.304	.360	.495	194	59	19	0	6	27	18	24	.255	.308	.384	380	97	22	0	9	42	31	54
Day Games	.274	.317	.411	95	26	7	0	2	12	6	15	.229	.286	.341	170	39	7	0	4	18	14	28
Night Games	.257	.302	.411	214	55	15	0	6	24	15	30	.242	.288	.362	442	107	24	1	9	41	31	62
April	.245	.283	.347	49	12	2	0	1	5	3	7	.272	.330	.402	92	25	3	0	3	13	9	9
May	.305	.397	.475	59	18	7	0	1	6	9	7	.247	.345	.384	73	18	7	0	1	6	11	10
June	.303	.324	.439	66	20	6	0	1	7	2	7	.280	.308	.416	125	35	8	0	3	10	5	18
July	.200	.207	.345	55	11	5	0	1	5	1	12	.179	.201	.269	134	24	7	1	1	14	5	25
August	.250	.270	.500	36	9	0	0	3	5	1	5	.291	.317	.443	79	23	3	0	3	6	3	12
Sept–Oct	.250	.327	.364	44	11	2	0	1	8	5	7	.193	.273	.275	109	21	3	0	2	10	12	16
Bases Empty	.304	.335	.474	171	52	14	0	5	5	8	25	.270	.312	.405	326	88	20	0	8	8	20	50
Leadoff	.393	.414	.714	56	22	12	0	2	2	2	5	.339	.377	.565	115	39	14	0	4	4	7	14
Runners On Base	.210	.273	.333	138	29	8	0	3	31	13	20	.203	.261	.301	286	58	11	1	5	51	25	40
Scoring Position	.225	.293	.363	80	18	5	0	2	28	9	11	.187	.249	.307	166	31	5	1	4	48	16	27
Late and Close	.264	.291	.377	53	14	6	0	0	3	2	5	.290	.320	.409	93	27	8	0	1	6	4	14

4-YEAR TOTALS (1987–1991)

OTIS NIXON — bats both — throws right — age 33 — ATL — *O | **8-YEAR TOTALS (1984–1991)**

1991	BA	OBA	SA	AB	H	2B	3B	HR	RBI	BB	SO	BA	OBA	SA	AB	H	2B	3B	HR	RBI	BB	SO
Total	.297	.371	.327	401	119	10	1	0	26	47	40	.247	.321	.291	1526	377	39	8	4	101	168	205
vs. Left	.301	.404	.355	93	28	5	0	0	7	15	7	.239	.314	.292	602	144	18	4	2	40	65	67
vs. Right	.295	.360	.318	308	91	5	1	0	19	32	33	.252	.326	.290	924	233	21	4	2	61	103	138
at Home	.329	.404	.367	207	68	8	0	0	15	26	18	.251	.333	.298	752	189	22	5	1	48	92	93
on Road	.263	.335	.284	194	51	2	1	0	11	21	22	.243	.310	.284	774	188	17	3	3	53	76	112
on Grass	.321	.396	.357	280	90	10	0	0	20	35	30	.259	.325	.299	772	200	20	1	3	47	77	108
on Turf	.240	.311	.256	121	29	0	1	0	6	12	10	.235	.317	.282	754	177	19	7	1	54	91	97
Day Games	.351	.407	.396	111	39	3	0	0	11	10	12	.255	.313	.305	491	125	15	5	0	42	42	74
Night Games	.276	.358	.300	290	80	7	0	0	15	37	28	.243	.325	.284	1035	252	24	3	4	59	126	131
April	.238	.360	.238	21	5	0	0	0	2	4	1	.196	.271	.223	179	35	3	1	0	12	19	21
May	.391	.463	.464	69	27	5	0	0	5	10	4	.275	.345	.309	204	56	5	1	0	10	23	30
June	.292	.346	.302	96	28	1	0	0	3	6	11	.236	.316	.269	275	65	5	2	0	17	30	32
July	.363	.435	.382	102	37	2	0	0	6	13	13	.266	.334	.316	316	84	11	1	1	17	33	35
August	.141	.227	.154	78	11	1	0	0	5	9	8	.228	.287	.270	307	70	5	1	2	23	26	53
Sept–Oct	.314	.390	.400	35	11	1	1	0	5	5	3	.273	.366	.343	245	67	10	2	1	22	37	34
Bases Empty	.306	.381	.331	281	86	7	0	0	0	33	27	.250	.337	.285	1011	253	22	2	3	3	131	141
Leadoff	.331	.404	.343	172	57	2	0	0	0	20	16	.266	.354	.304	572	152	12	2	2	2	77	80
Runners On Base	.275	.348	.317	120	33	3	1	0	26	14	13	.241	.289	.303	515	124	17	6	1	98	37	64
Scoring Position	.312	.378	.377	77	24	3	1	0	26	9	9	.246	.302	.311	309	76	14	3	0	92	27	45
Late and Close	.352	.435	.444	54	19	3	1	0	4	8	5	.306	.375	.363	281	86	9	2	1	18	31	45

MATT NOKES — bats left — throws right — age 29 — NYA — *C/D | **7-YEAR TOTALS (1985–1991)**

1991	BA	OBA	SA	AB	H	2B	3B	HR	RBI	BB	SO	BA	OBA	SA	AB	H	2B	3B	HR	RBI	BB	SO
Total	.268	.308	.469	456	122	20	0	24	77	25	49	.263	.315	.446	1994	524	74	3	95	303	139	271
vs. Left	.261	.303	.459	111	29	1	0	7	23	6	12	.238	.286	.413	298	71	7	0	15	50	17	60
vs. Right	.270	.310	.472	345	93	19	0	17	54	19	37	.267	.320	.452	1696	453	67	3	80	253	122	211
at Home	.260	.300	.495	200	52	8	0	13	43	12	26	.267	.318	.454	925	247	25	2	48	150	66	138
on Road	.273	.315	.449	256	70	12	0	11	34	13	23	.259	.312	.439	1069	277	49	1	47	153	73	133
on Grass	.255	.295	.462	372	95	14	0	21	67	21	41	.266	.316	.449	1670	444	56	2	82	253	115	224
on Turf	.321	.367	.500	84	27	6	0	3	10	4	8	.247	.308	.429	324	80	18	1	13	50	24	47
Day Games	.242	.296	.450	149	36	4	0	9	23	11	12	.264	.312	.487	675	178	22	0	43	125	45	90
Night Games	.280	.314	.479	307	86	16	0	15	54	14	37	.262	.316	.425	1319	346	52	3	52	178	94	181
April	.319	.340	.553	47	15	5	0	2	9	2	4	.286	.334	.500	280	80	12	0	16	52	21	38
May	.276	.313	.500	76	21	2	0	5	11	3	7	.258	.304	.447	333	86	10	1	17	52	19	50
June	.270	.299	.473	74	20	3	0	4	12	3	5	.271	.308	.468	314	85	12	1	16	50	16	43
July	.273	.314	.584	77	21	3	0	7	23	5	10	.247	.323	.462	275	68	8	0	17	49	24	44
August	.247	.300	.432	81	20	3	0	4	10	6	9	.257	.319	.408	343	88	13	0	13	46	32	36
Sept–Oct	.248	.300	.347	101	25	4	0	2	12	6	14	.261	.308	.414	449	117	19	1	16	54	27	60
Bases Empty	.257	.294	.426	249	64	9	0	11	11	12	25	.252	.305	.446	1054	266	42	3	52	52	69	133
Leadoff	.268	.305	.473	112	30	2	0	7	7	6	14	.275	.324	.519	443	122	21	0	29	29	26	59
Runners On Base	.280	.325	.522	207	58	11	0	13	66	13	24	.274	.327	.446	940	258	32	0	43	251	70	138
Scoring Position	.254	.318	.444	126	32	6	0	6	49	12	14	.257	.324	.399	536	138	19	0	19	195	52	77
Late and Close	.280	.353	.387	75	21	2	0	2	13	8	15	.267	.326	.436	303	81	6	0	15	59	27	49

PETE O'BRIEN — bats left — throws left — age 34 — SEA — *1DO | **8-YEAR TOTALS (1984–1991)**

1991	BA	OBA	SA	AB	H	2B	3B	HR	RBI	BB	SO	BA	OBA	SA	AB	H	2B	3B	HR	RBI	BB	SO
Total	.248	.300	.402	560	139	29	3	17	88	44	61	.269	.344	.420	4240	1139	204	14	136	590	511	446
vs. Left	.235	.280	.363	179	42	11	0	4	27	11	22	.248	.312	.348	1309	325	59	1	23	165	124	189
vs. Right	.255	.309	.420	381	97	18	3	13	61	33	39	.278	.358	.452	2931	814	145	13	113	425	387	257
at Home	.238	.279	.441	290	69	17	3	12	53	19	30	.278	.354	.432	2058	572	112	5	65	322	259	209
on Road	.259	.321	.359	270	70	12	0	5	35	25	31	.260	.334	.408	2182	567	92	9	71	268	252	237
on Grass	.280	.335	.382	207	58	9	0	4	28	17	24	.276	.353	.420	3119	861	143	6	98	440	392	326
on Turf	.229	.279	.414	353	81	20	3	13	60	27	37	.248	.318	.418	1121	278	61	8	38	150	119	120
Day Games	.273	.305	.435	154	42	8	1	5	26	9	21	.268	.348	.403	988	265	41	4	28	123	124	105
Night Games	.239	.298	.389	406	97	21	2	12	62	35	40	.269	.343	.425	3252	874	163	10	108	467	387	341
April	.259	.307	.395	81	21	5	0	2	12	5	7	.285	.359	.464	554	158	29	2	22	80	67	50
May	.229	.296	.438	96	22	3	1	5	17	10	10	.241	.305	.401	701	169	28	3	26	97	68	73
June	.234	.294	.309	94	22	7	0	0	12	8	11	.286	.374	.431	700	200	40	1	20	99	100	76
July	.275	.276	.441	102	28	7	2	2	13	1	6	.272	.336	.418	791	215	41	3	23	108	81	72
August	.265	.333	.378	98	26	5	0	2	14	11	11	.282	.349	.424	769	217	37	3	22	111	81	84
Sept–Oct	.225	.290	.449	89	20	2	0	6	20	9	16	.248	.345	.389	725	180	29	2	23	95	114	91
Bases Empty	.221	.273	.371	294	65	14	3	8	8	20	33	.268	.336	.428	2362	633	111	6	85	85	236	261
Leadoff	.212	.252	.379	132	28	5	1	5	5	7	13	.278	.337	.438	917	255	48	3	31	31	81	90
Runners On Base	.278	.328	.436	266	74	15	0	9	80	24	28	.269	.354	.409	1878	506	93	8	51	505	275	185
Scoring Position	.286	.340	.469	175	50	11	0	7	75	19	22	.267	.365	.413	1085	290	55	5	31	442	198	124
Late and Close	.204	.259	.347	98	20	5	0	3	19	8	9	.246	.334	.391	699	172	30	1	23	85	94	81

JOHN OLERUD — bats left — throws left — age 24 — TOR — *1/D

1991	BA	OBA	SA	AB	H	2B	3B	HR	RBI	BB	SO	3-YEAR TOTALS (1989–1991) BA	OBA	SA	AB	H	2B	3B	HR	RBI	BB	SO
Total	.256	.353	.438	454	116	30	1	17	68	68	84	.261	.358	.434	820	214	45	2	31	116	125	160
vs. Left	.217	.358	.386	83	18	3	1	3	16	17	19	.274	.396	.452	157	43	8	1	6	31	32	38
vs. Right	.264	.352	.450	371	98	27	0	14	52	51	65	.258	.349	.430	663	171	37	1	25	85	93	122
at Home	.270	.374	.447	226	61	17	1	7	39	36	36	.274	.373	.469	420	115	24	2	18	65	65	79
on Road	.241	.332	.430	228	55	13	0	10	29	32	48	.248	.342	.398	400	99	21	0	13	51	60	81
on Grass	.256	.347	.448	172	44	12	0	7	24	25	35	.266	.363	.429	308	82	20	0	10	43	49	62
on Turf	.255	.357	.433	282	72	18	1	10	44	43	49	.258	.355	.438	512	132	25	2	21	73	76	98
Day Games	.243	.373	.429	140	34	8	0	6	29	28	23	.222	.346	.354	243	54	11	0	7	36	45	53
Night Games	.261	.343	.443	314	82	22	1	11	39	40	61	.277	.364	.468	577	160	34	2	24	80	80	107
April	.262	.375	.475	61	16	4	0	3	9	10	9	.257	.367	.450	109	28	6	0	5	14	18	16
May	.156	.258	.260	77	12	2	0	2	6	11	16	.196	.316	.311	148	29	3	1	4	16	27	35
June	.271	.346	.471	70	19	3	1	3	11	8	15	.303	.370	.517	145	44	8	1	7	26	16	31
July	.342	.395	.557	79	27	5	0	4	8	5	13	.315	.380	.514	146	46	8	0	7	15	13	24
August	.237	.347	.438	80	19	7	0	3	18	14	12	.226	.324	.404	146	33	11	0	5	25	22	26
Sept–Oct	.264	.394	.437	87	23	9	0	2	16	20	19	.270	.401	.413	126	34	9	0	3	20	20	28
Bases Empty	.238	.329	.435	260	62	15	0	12	12	31	50	.239	.337	.422	448	107	20	1	20	20	62	92
Leadoff	.293	.379	.560	116	34	10	0	7	7	15	23	.297	.395	.547	172	51	11	1	10	10	27	36
Runners On Base	.278	.383	.443	194	54	15	1	5	56	37	34	.288	.383	.449	372	107	25	1	11	96	63	68
Scoring Position	.233	.396	.362	116	27	6	0	3	45	36	24	.261	.399	.389	203	53	11	0	5	72	53	44
Late and Close	.258	.369	.427	89	23	9	0	2	13	16	20	.283	.374	.453	159	45	12	0	5	28	24	38

JOE OLIVER — bats right — throws right — age 27 — CIN — C

1991	BA	OBA	SA	AB	H	2B	3B	HR	RBI	BB	SO	3-YEAR TOTALS (1989–1991) BA	OBA	SA	AB	H	2B	3B	HR	RBI	BB	SO
Total	.216	.265	.379	269	58	11	0	11	41	18	53	.233	.290	.371	784	183	42	0	22	116	61	156
vs. Left	.229	.308	.450	131	30	5	0	8	27	15	24	.281	.344	.451	384	108	23	0	14	68	37	73
vs. Right	.203	.220	.312	138	28	6	0	3	14	3	29	.188	.237	.295	400	75	19	0	8	48	24	83
at Home	.200	.256	.386	145	29	6	0	7	17	11	27	.225	.283	.366	396	89	23	0	11	56	31	79
on Road	.234	.275	.371	124	29	5	0	4	24	7	26	.242	.298	.376	388	94	19	0	11	60	30	77
on Grass	.231	.268	.410	78	18	2	0	4	19	4	19	.242	.282	.410	227	55	14	0	8	41	13	50
on Turf	.209	.263	.366	191	40	9	0	7	22	14	34	.230	.293	.355	557	128	28	0	14	75	48	106
Day Games	.277	.333	.319	47	13	2	0	0	5	4	11	.301	.340	.437	183	55	13	0	4	29	11	36
Night Games	.203	.250	.392	222	45	9	0	11	36	14	42	.213	.275	.351	601	128	29	0	18	87	50	120
April	.156	.229	.219	32	5	2	0	0	1	3	9	.214	.298	.274	84	18	5	0	0	3	10	19
May	.194	.219	.226	31	6	1	0	0	0	1	7	.243	.325	.421	107	26	4	0	5	16	12	17
June	.286	.359	.457	35	10	3	0	1	3	4	6	.231	.314	.315	108	25	6	0	1	12	13	24
July	.232	.259	.429	56	13	2	0	4	10	2	7	.221	.265	.344	154	34	7	0	4	24	10	32
August	.167	.236	.379	66	11	2	0	4	14	6	15	.246	.282	.439	171	42	9	0	8	34	9	34
Sept–Oct	.265	.294	.469	49	13	1	0	3	13	2	9	.237	.278	.381	160	38	11	0	4	27	7	30
Bases Empty	.204	.247	.299	157	32	6	0	3	3	9	31	.217	.268	.321	433	94	18	0	9	9	28	88
Leadoff	.197	.219	.310	71	14	2	0	2	2	2	16	.198	.231	.326	187	37	6	0	6	6	7	41
Runners On Base	.232	.289	.491	112	26	5	0	8	38	9	22	.254	.317	.433	351	89	24	0	13	107	33	68
Scoring Position	.258	.343	.565	62	16	4	0	5	32	8	13	.274	.356	.481	208	57	19	0	8	95	27	40
Late and Close	.234	.294	.234	47	11	0	0	0	2	4	7	.258	.321	.359	128	33	7	0	2	12	11	21

GREG OLSON — bats right — throws right — age 32 — ATL — *C

1991	BA	OBA	SA	AB	H	2B	3B	HR	RBI	BB	SO	3-YEAR TOTALS (1989–1991) BA	OBA	SA	AB	H	2B	3B	HR	RBI	BB	SO
Total	.241	.316	.345	411	99	25	0	6	44	44	48	.250	.323	.360	711	178	37	1	13	80	74	99
vs. Left	.283	.342	.424	99	28	8	0	2	17	10	12	.302	.363	.460	252	76	17	1	7	42	25	38
vs. Right	.228	.308	.321	312	71	17	0	4	27	34	36	.222	.302	.305	459	102	20	0	6	38	49	61
at Home	.287	.330	.431	202	58	11	0	6	31	15	18	.287	.333	.425	355	102	17	1	10	52	27	38
on Road	.196	.303	.263	209	41	14	0	0	13	29	30	.213	.314	.295	356	76	20	0	3	28	47	61
on Grass	.248	.312	.366	306	76	18	0	6	34	29	34	.252	.317	.368	524	132	26	1	11	59	50	66
on Turf	.219	.328	.286	105	23	7	0	0	10	15	14	.246	.341	.337	187	46	11	0	2	21	24	33
Day Games	.223	.263	.339	112	25	7	0	2	8	6	14	.255	.323	.361	208	53	10	0	4	19	20	33
Night Games	.247	.334	.348	299	74	18	0	4	36	38	34	.249	.323	.360	503	125	27	1	9	61	54	66
April	.500	.522	.591	22	11	2	0	0	1	1	3	.424	.472	.515	33	14	3	0	0	2	3	6
May	.204	.279	.259	54	11	0	0	1	7	5	6	.250	.331	.402	112	28	2	0	5	18	11	18
June	.233	.300	.384	73	17	5	0	2	7	6	5	.270	.341	.395	152	41	7	0	4	19	16	13
July	.263	.337	.408	76	20	5	0	2	12	9	8	.224	.296	.308	143	32	6	0	2	14	15	20
August	.254	.333	.352	71	18	4	0	0	9	9	9	.306	.365	.452	124	38	10	1	2	18	12	19
Sept–Oct	.191	.282	.270	115	22	9	0	0	8	14	17	.170	.259	.231	147	25	9	0	0	9	17	23
Bases Empty	.215	.284	.319	251	54	14	0	4	4	23	33	.223	.292	.321	421	94	20	0	7	7	39	62
Leadoff	.233	.301	.369	103	24	5	0	3	3	10	14	.232	.310	.350	177	41	9	0	4	4	19	21
Runners On Base	.281	.364	.387	160	45	11	0	2	40	21	15	.290	.366	.417	290	84	17	1	6	73	35	37
Scoring Position	.287	.393	.372	94	27	5	0	1	33	19	11	.256	.363	.369	168	43	7	0	4	60	31	28
Late and Close	.187	.276	.227	75	14	3	0	0	6	9	10	.200	.280	.240	125	25	5	0	0	12	13	21

PAUL O'NEILL — bats left — throws left — age 29 — CIN — *O

1991	BA	OBA	SA	AB	H	2B	3B	HR	RBI	BB	SO	BA	OBA	SA	AB	H	2B	3B	HR	RBI	BB	SO
Total	.256	.346	.481	532	136	36	0	28	91	73	107	.262	.334	.444	2122	557	128	6	82	345	229	371
vs. Left	.204	.257	.311	167	34	9	0	3	15	11	51	.214	.271	.339	555	119	32	2	11	77	42	152
vs. Right	.279	.383	.559	365	102	27	0	25	76	62	56	.280	.356	.482	1567	438	96	4	71	268	187	219
at Home	.284	.361	.586	268	76	21	0	20	59	32	45	.280	.347	.505	1063	298	66	1	57	187	108	174
on Road	.227	.331	.375	264	60	15	0	8	32	41	62	.245	.322	.383	1059	259	62	5	25	158	121	197
on Grass	.286	.378	.491	161	46	9	0	8	26	24	38	.271	.348	.432	623	169	36	5	18	91	74	114
on Turf	.243	.332	.477	371	90	27	0	20	65	49	69	.259	.329	.450	1499	388	92	1	64	254	155	257
Day Games	.313	.377	.627	150	47	14	0	11	29	16	24	.255	.320	.447	682	174	47	3	26	108	67	114
Night Games	.233	.334	.424	382	89	22	0	17	62	57	83	.266	.341	.443	1440	383	81	3	56	237	162	257
April	.213	.324	.475	61	13	4	0	4	7	10	11	.268	.334	.431	269	72	17	0	9	46	27	51
May	.287	.380	.575	80	23	5	0	6	18	12	12	.255	.328	.430	365	93	19	0	15	61	38	67
June	.278	.364	.515	97	27	8	0	5	22	12	16	.282	.365	.510	390	110	23	0	22	72	49	52
July	.213	.284	.338	80	17	4	0	2	6	8	18	.246	.314	.389	337	83	16	1	10	41	32	59
August	.263	.381	.515	99	26	7	0	6	20	19	25	.274	.352	.495	307	84	23	0	15	51	39	62
Sept–Oct	.261	.328	.461	115	30	8	0	5	18	12	25	.253	.315	.414	454	115	30	5	11	74	44	80
Bases Empty	.246	.313	.450	280	69	21	0	12	12	26	55	.251	.307	.417	1129	283	73	2	37	37	88	205
Leadoff	.229	.306	.440	109	25	8	0	5	5	11	19	.244	.296	.438	479	117	28	1	21	21	33	78
Runners On Base	.266	.380	.516	252	67	15	0	16	79	47	52	.276	.363	.475	993	274	55	4	45	308	141	166
Scoring Position	.262	.403	.463	149	39	9	0	7	60	36	30	.271	.380	.460	598	162	37	2	24	255	112	108
Late and Close	.192	.366	.329	73	14	4	0	2	7	20	21	.233	.337	.367	360	84	22	1	8	48	54	71

7-YEAR TOTALS (1985–1991)

JOSE OQUENDO — bats both — throws right — age 29 — SL — *2S/1P

1991	BA	OBA	SA	AB	H	2B	3B	HR	RBI	BB	SO	BA	OBA	SA	AB	H	2B	3B	HR	RBI	BB	SO
Total	.240	.357	.301	366	88	11	4	1	26	67	48	.268	.359	.331	2417	647	84	18	11	204	356	268
vs. Left	.236	.363	.324	148	35	8	1	1	14	29	20	.262	.346	.352	904	237	39	6	10	84	120	91
vs. Right	.243	.353	.284	218	53	3	3	0	12	38	28	.271	.367	.319	1513	410	45	12	1	120	236	177
at Home	.261	.372	.299	184	48	3	2	0	14	32	19	.274	.362	.339	1195	328	40	11	5	100	170	124
on Road	.220	.342	.302	182	40	8	2	1	12	35	29	.261	.355	.323	1222	319	44	7	6	104	186	144
on Grass	.167	.331	.188	96	16	2	0	0	8	24	15	.270	.357	.316	730	197	22	3	2	50	102	87
on Turf	.267	.367	.341	270	72	9	4	1	18	43	33	.267	.360	.337	1687	450	62	15	9	154	254	181
Day Games	.263	.390	.326	95	25	3	0	1	12	21	11	.263	.357	.326	782	206	28	6	3	79	119	85
Night Games	.232	.345	.292	271	63	8	4	0	14	46	37	.270	.360	.333	1635	441	56	12	8	125	237	183
April	.200	.338	.300	60	12	2	2	0	5	13	8	.248	.355	.314	306	76	12	4	0	22	50	37
May	.146	.226	.250	48	7	0	1	1	1	5	5	.246	.337	.291	419	103	9	2	2	21	60	46
June	.274	.436	.288	73	20	1	0	0	4	21	9	.274	.356	.335	511	140	19	3	2	52	70	46
July	.328	.453	.410	61	20	3	1	0	1	13	8	.310	.393	.387	400	124	15	5	2	35	56	47
August	.277	.340	.337	83	23	5	0	0	13	9	14	.271	.351	.345	458	124	22	0	4	50	59	47
Sept–Oct	.146	.255	.146	41	6	0	0	0	2	6	4	.248	.362	.303	323	80	7	4	1	24	61	45
Bases Empty	.232	.312	.300	233	54	7	3	1	1	27	34	.258	.347	.322	1425	367	52	11	6	6	194	161
Leadoff	.219	.306	.260	96	21	4	0	0	0	12	12	.254	.341	.315	587	149	24	3	2	2	78	66
Runners On Base	.256	.424	.301	133	34	4	1	0	25	40	14	.282	.374	.344	992	280	32	7	5	198	162	107
Scoring Position	.250	.438	.313	80	20	3	1	0	25	29	12	.269	.376	.352	577	155	22	7	4	194	116	75
Late and Close	.297	.395	.375	64	19	2	0	1	6	10	8	.274	.381	.335	468	128	15	1	4	36	83	71

7-YEAR TOTALS (1984–1991)

JOE ORSULAK — bats left — throws left — age 30 — BAL — *O/D

1991	BA	OBA	SA	AB	H	2B	3B	HR	RBI	BB	SO	BA	OBA	SA	AB	H	2B	3B	HR	RBI	BB	SO
Total	.278	.321	.358	486	135	22	1	5	43	28	45	.277	.329	.381	2534	702	113	26	33	225	193	231
vs. Left	.234	.286	.281	64	15	3	0	0	6	4	8	.233	.284	.267	416	97	10	2	0	28	28	43
vs. Right	.284	.326	.370	422	120	19	1	5	37	24	37	.286	.338	.404	2118	605	103	24	33	197	165	188
at Home	.277	.322	.357	235	65	10	0	3	21	14	23	.281	.335	.384	1216	342	50	15	15	109	97	108
on Road	.279	.320	.359	251	70	12	1	2	22	14	22	.273	.324	.379	1318	360	63	11	18	116	96	123
on Grass	.281	.326	.365	406	114	20	1	4	29	25	37	.278	.334	.391	1621	451	78	9	29	159	132	150
on Turf	.262	.289	.325	80	21	2	0	1	14	3	8	.275	.321	.364	913	251	35	17	4	66	61	81
Day Games	.260	.317	.323	127	33	5	0	1	14	10	12	.269	.324	.373	681	183	33	4	10	54	54	63
Night Games	.284	.322	.370	359	102	17	1	4	29	18	33	.280	.331	.384	1853	519	80	22	23	171	139	168
April	.244	.306	.333	45	11	1	0	1	5	4	5	.274	.332	.397	317	87	21	3	4	29	26	31
May	.276	.304	.368	76	21	4	0	1	4	3	9	.271	.332	.378	373	101	18	2	6	41	31	36
June	.192	.243	.232	99	19	1	0	1	13	5	12	.260	.316	.322	488	127	18	3	2	41	38	33
July	.278	.298	.333	90	25	5	0	0	3	3	7	.284	.316	.397	426	121	16	7	6	34	23	37
August	.384	.419	.495	99	38	9	1	0	11	6	7	.302	.346	.435	496	150	29	5	9	50	35	47
Sept–Oct	.273	.345	.377	77	21	2	0	2	7	7	5	.267	.332	.362	434	116	11	6	6	30	40	47
Bases Empty	.304	.346	.388	263	80	14	1	2	2	15	21	.296	.341	.411	1549	458	76	21	20	20	99	145
Leadoff	.308	.337	.385	91	28	5	1	0	0	3	5	.312	.361	.433	679	212	38	7	10	10	48	62
Runners On Base	.247	.290	.323	223	55	8	0	3	41	13	24	.248	.312	.335	985	244	37	5	13	205	94	86
Scoring Position	.241	.315	.315	108	26	5	0	1	36	11	10	.248	.338	.346	544	135	24	4	7	187	77	46
Late and Close	.222	.273	.296	81	18	3	0	1	8	5	8	.249	.323	.330	421	105	16	3	4	42	45	38

7-YEAR TOTALS (1984–1991)

SPIKE OWEN — bats both — throws right — age 31 — MON — *S

1991	BA	OBA	SA	AB	H	2B	3B	HR	RBI	BB	SO		8-YEAR TOTALS (1984–1991) BA	OBA	SA	AB	H	2B	3B	HR	RBI	BB	SO
Total	.255	.321	.366	424	108	22	8	3	26	42	61		.244	.323	.341	3418	835	146	46	31	293	399	376
vs. Left	.303	.349	.424	198	60	17	2	1	12	14	25		.275	.341	.399	1126	310	72	11	15	107	111	134
vs. Right	.212	.297	.314	226	48	5	6	2	14	28	36		.229	.315	.313	2292	525	74	35	16	186	288	242
at Home	.211	.291	.280	161	34	6	1	1	7	19	26		.248	.330	.353	1635	406	72	24	17	150	199	184
on Road	.281	.339	.418	263	74	16	7	2	19	23	35		.241	.318	.330	1783	429	74	22	14	143	200	192
on Grass	.262	.323	.383	141	37	6	4	1	12	13	22		.238	.319	.325	1565	373	60	20	12	137	187	168
on Turf	.251	.320	.357	283	71	16	4	2	14	29	39		.249	.327	.355	1853	462	86	26	19	156	212	208
Day Games	.273	.329	.383	128	35	9	1	1	9	11	20		.262	.328	.378	1032	270	52	16	12	99	105	125
Night Games	.247	.317	.358	296	73	13	7	2	17	31	41		.237	.321	.325	2386	565	94	30	19	194	294	251
April	.236	.263	.309	55	13	2	1	0	3	2	6		.242	.312	.350	451	109	23	7	4	32	47	45
May	.203	.323	.278	79	16	3	0	1	6	13	14		.234	.340	.352	534	125	22	10	7	49	86	69
June	.175	.297	.302	63	11	4	2	0	1	11	8		.261	.345	.386	710	185	43	11	8	68	90	64
July	.286	.333	.413	63	18	5	0	1	5	5	6		.267	.340	.350	517	138	22	6	3	46	57	52
August	.296	.344	.407	54	16	2	2	0	5	5	13		.214	.290	.270	603	129	16	3	4	53	66	78
Sept–Oct	.309	.342	.445	110	34	6	3	1	6	6	14		.247	.309	.335	603	149	20	9	5	45	53	68
Bases Empty	.269	.329	.388	260	70	15	5	2	2	22	35		.241	.312	.332	2031	489	87	21	19	19	206	230
Leadoff	.293	.363	.435	92	27	4	3	1	1	10	10		.240	.315	.333	809	194	35	11	6	6	86	82
Runners On Base	.232	.309	.329	164	38	7	3	1	24	20	26		.249	.339	.354	1387	346	59	25	12	274	193	146
Scoring Position	.215	.330	.290	93	20	5	1	0	20	18	19		.241	.351	.327	781	188	28	12	5	235	140	95
Late and Close	.278	.348	.354	79	22	3	0	1	7	9	14		.227	.306	.323	585	133	17	6	9	49	67	81

MIKE PAGLIARULO — bats left — throws right — age 32 — MIN — *3/2

1991	BA	OBA	SA	AB	H	2B	3B	HR	RBI	BB	SO		8-YEAR TOTALS (1984–1991) BA	OBA	SA	AB	H	2B	3B	HR	RBI	BB	SO
Total	.279	.322	.384	365	102	20	0	6	36	21	55		.236	.305	.410	3185	753	161	14	121	425	301	670
vs. Left	.188	.316	.250	16	3	1	0	0	1	3	1		.206	.278	.328	676	139	28	2	17	85	61	193
vs. Right	.284	.323	.390	349	99	19	0	6	35	18	54		.245	.312	.432	2509	614	133	12	104	340	240	477
at Home	.284	.332	.405	190	54	11	0	4	27	13	32		.233	.309	.405	1513	353	61	8	61	219	157	346
on Road	.274	.312	.360	175	48	9	0	2	9	8	23		.239	.300	.414	1672	400	100	6	60	206	144	324
on Grass	.265	.299	.368	136	36	8	0	2	8	6	16		.232	.303	.413	2437	565	118	13	99	328	240	514
on Turf	.288	.336	.393	229	66	12	0	4	28	15	39		.251	.308	.400	748	188	43	1	22	97	61	156
Day Games	.288	.333	.452	104	30	8	0	3	11	5	11		.221	.301	.383	1005	222	43	3	38	122	107	219
Night Games	.276	.318	.356	261	72	12	0	3	25	16	44		.244	.306	.422	2180	531	118	11	83	303	194	451
April	.200	.200	.222	45	9	1	0	0	2	0	3		.194	.285	.339	345	67	15	1	11	47	42	80
May	.254	.275	.403	67	17	4	0	2	5	2	12		.241	.319	.417	523	126	31	2	19	73	57	99
June	.273	.344	.418	55	15	5	0	1	8	5	8		.243	.304	.418	564	137	34	1	21	69	49	118
July	.448	.508	.603	58	26	6	0	1	5	7	3		.292	.358	.494	520	152	30	3	23	78	51	98
August	.324	.352	.412	68	22	3	0	1	6	3	12		.231	.288	.426	615	142	24	6	28	79	49	136
Sept–Oct	.181	.237	.236	72	13	1	0	0	10	4	17		.209	.275	.348	618	129	27	1	19	79	53	139
Bases Empty	.297	.332	.410	212	63	12	0	4	4	8	33		.221	.284	.391	1787	395	87	11	65	65	143	381
Leadoff	.295	.319	.432	88	26	6	0	2	2	3	11		.214	.281	.384	716	153	25	5	29	29	64	148
Runners On Base	.255	.310	.346	153	39	8	0	2	32	13	22		.256	.330	.433	1398	358	74	3	56	360	158	289
Scoring Position	.195	.273	.264	87	17	3	0	1	25	10	18		.239	.331	.399	775	185	36	2	28	287	112	178
Late and Close	.245	.298	.283	53	13	2	0	0	5	4	11		.226	.304	.366	487	110	21	1	15	55	55	117

TOM PAGNOZZI — bats right — throws right — age 30 — SL — *C/1

1991	BA	OBA	SA	AB	H	2B	3B	HR	RBI	BB	SO		5-YEAR TOTALS (1987–1991) BA	OBA	SA	AB	H	2B	3B	HR	RBI	BB	SO
Total	.264	.319	.351	459	121	24	5	2	57	36	63		.257	.308	.336	1002	258	51	5	6	107	71	164
vs. Left	.256	.314	.362	199	51	11	2	2	25	18	28		.252	.311	.344	448	113	22	2	5	52	39	79
vs. Right	.269	.324	.342	260	70	13	3	0	32	18	35		.262	.305	.330	554	145	29	3	1	55	32	85
at Home	.226	.306	.321	221	50	11	2	2	23	23	29		.246	.316	.338	471	116	21	2	6	48	45	70
on Road	.298	.332	.378	238	71	13	3	0	34	13	34		.267	.300	.335	531	142	30	3	0	59	26	94
on Grass	.266	.311	.347	124	33	6	2	0	21	7	21		.253	.285	.323	257	65	14	2	0	35	11	49
on Turf	.263	.323	.352	335	88	18	3	2	36	29	42		.259	.315	.341	745	193	37	3	6	72	60	115
Day Games	.298	.369	.421	114	34	7	2	1	22	13	15		.254	.308	.350	351	89	18	2	4	49	29	53
Night Games	.252	.302	.328	345	87	17	3	1	35	23	48		.260	.308	.329	651	169	33	3	2	58	42	111
April	.238	.265	.254	63	15	1	0	0	4	3	9		.228	.266	.277	101	23	2	0	1	7	6	13
May	.278	.367	.418	79	22	6	1	1	14	9	8		.256	.326	.354	164	42	8	1	2	25	15	23
June	.236	.250	.326	89	21	3	1	1	13	2	11		.211	.243	.303	175	37	8	1	2	17	7	32
July	.237	.322	.316	76	18	2	2	0	8	9	12		.273	.350	.338	139	38	5	2	0	19	16	21
August	.253	.300	.361	83	21	7	1	0	6	6	13		.239	.278	.320	197	47	14	1	0	14	12	35
Sept–Oct	.348	.416	.420	69	24	5	0	0	12	7	10		.314	.361	.389	226	71	14	0	1	25	15	40
Bases Empty	.255	.310	.327	251	64	11	2	1	1	18	27		.257	.309	.337	552	142	28	2	4	4	37	75
Leadoff	.271	.333	.331	118	32	5	1	0	0	11	12		.243	.291	.323	235	57	11	1	2	2	15	29
Runners On Base	.274	.330	.380	208	57	13	3	1	56	18	36		.258	.307	.336	450	116	23	3	2	103	34	89
Scoring Position	.256	.320	.368	133	34	8	2	1	52	14	25		.259	.317	.348	270	70	14	2	2	96	26	56
Late and Close	.190	.266	.214	84	16	2	0	0	3	8	14		.207	.250	.232	198	41	5	0	0	18	10	43

RAFAEL PALMEIRO — bats left — throws left — age 28 — TEX — *1/D

1991	BA	OBA	SA	AB	H	2B	3B	HR	RBI	BB	SO
Total	.322	.389	.532	631	203	49	3	26	88	68	72
vs. Left	.274	.333	.473	186	51	8	1	9	26	14	26
vs. Right	.342	.411	.557	445	152	41	2	17	62	54	46
at Home	.339	.408	.540	298	101	22	1	12	43	34	36
on Road	.306	.372	.526	333	102	27	2	14	45	34	36
on Grass	.333	.402	.543	532	177	37	3	23	77	61	62
on Turf	.263	.315	.475	99	26	12	0	3	11	7	10
Day Games	.281	.345	.422	128	36	9	0	3	16	13	14
Night Games	.332	.400	.561	503	167	40	3	23	72	55	58
April	.318	.338	.485	66	21	5	0	2	11	3	6
May	.330	.376	.470	115	38	8	1	2	12	8	14
June	.304	.376	.527	112	34	10	0	5	10	13	11
July	.390	.456	.710	100	39	6	1	8	19	11	15
August	.322	.407	.537	121	39	9	1	5	21	16	11
Sept–Oct	.274	.365	.470	117	32	11	0	4	15	17	15
Bases Empty	.341	.401	.543	352	120	27	1	14	14	31	34
Leadoff	.336	.384	.500	140	47	8	0	5	5	10	15
Runners On Base	.297	.375	.520	279	83	22	2	12	74	37	38
Scoring Position	.231	.354	.371	143	33	12	1	2	49	29	21
Late and Close	.243	.317	.477	107	26	7	0	6	17	12	14

6-YEAR TOTALS (1986–1991)

	BA	OBA	SA	AB	H	2B	3B	HR	RBI	BB	SO
Total	.303	.360	.462	2662	806	168	19	73	337	233	245
vs. Left	.291	.335	.433	741	216	36	6	19	101	47	70
vs. Right	.307	.370	.474	1921	590	132	13	54	236	186	175
at Home	.298	.363	.466	1272	379	71	13	39	172	129	127
on Road	.307	.357	.459	1390	427	97	6	34	165	104	118
on Grass	.300	.360	.456	2110	632	111	18	61	283	194	204
on Turf	.315	.361	.487	552	174	57	1	12	54	39	41
Day Games	.292	.344	.456	878	256	57	6	25	119	69	79
Night Games	.308	.368	.466	1784	550	111	13	48	218	164	166
April	.318	.377	.502	299	95	24	2	9	46	30	26
May	.342	.382	.486	430	147	31	2	9	51	28	38
June	.296	.347	.432	477	141	28	2	11	56	33	38
July	.296	.353	.461	425	126	16	3	16	53	35	37
August	.287	.344	.448	498	143	32	6	12	61	44	53
Sept–Oct	.289	.365	.463	533	154	37	4	16	70	63	53
Bases Empty	.308	.356	.468	1486	457	96	8	42	42	103	134
Leadoff	.301	.346	.490	498	150	31	3	19	19	31	44
Runners On Base	.297	.365	.456	1176	349	72	11	31	295	130	111
Scoring Position	.268	.360	.391	649	174	40	5	10	236	101	75
Late and Close	.284	.334	.448	433	123	26	3	13	50	34	48

DEAN PALMER — bats right — throws right — age 24 — TEX — 3O/D

1991	BA	OBA	SA	AB	H	2B	3B	HR	RBI	BB	SO
Total	.187	.281	.403	268	50	9	2	15	37	32	98
vs. Left	.247	.337	.617	81	20	3	0	9	16	11	30
vs. Right	.160	.256	.310	187	30	6	2	6	21	21	68
at Home	.140	.279	.342	114	16	3	1	6	11	19	43
on Road	.221	.281	.448	154	34	6	1	9	26	13	55
on Grass	.175	.282	.377	228	40	8	1	12	28	31	80
on Turf	.250	.268	.550	40	10	1	1	3	9	1	18
Day Games	.271	.338	.557	70	19	6	1	4	11	7	26
Night Games	.157	.261	.348	198	31	3	1	11	26	25	72
April	.000	.000	.000	0	0	0	0	0	0	0	0
May	.000	.000	.000	0	0	0	0	0	0	0	0
June	.316	.381	.632	19	6	0	0	2	8	2	5
July	.219	.296	.438	73	16	2	1	4	8	6	22
August	.188	.261	.325	80	15	3	1	2	6	8	30
Sept–Oct	.135	.265	.396	96	13	4	0	7	15	16	41
Bases Empty	.171	.249	.354	164	28	8	2	6	6	16	61
Leadoff	.190	.281	.418	79	15	3	0	5	5	9	29
Runners On Base	.212	.328	.481	104	22	1	0	9	31	16	37
Scoring Position	.236	.364	.582	55	13	1	0	6	25	9	21
Late and Close	.283	.353	.696	46	13	2	1	5	11	5	20

2-YEAR TOTALS (1989–1991)

	BA	OBA	SA	AB	H	2B	3B	HR	RBI	BB	SO
Total	.181	.269	.390	287	52	11	2	15	38	32	110
vs. Left	.239	.320	.587	92	22	5	0	9	16	11	35
vs. Right	.154	.245	.297	195	30	6	2	6	22	21	75
at Home	.136	.264	.328	125	17	4	1	6	12	19	51
on Road	.216	.274	.438	162	35	7	1	9	26	13	59
on Grass	.171	.270	.366	246	42	10	1	12	29	31	92
on Turf	.244	.262	.537	41	10	1	1	3	9	1	18
Day Games	.256	.314	.526	78	20	7	1	4	12	7	31
Night Games	.153	.253	.340	209	32	4	1	11	26	25	79
April	.000	.000	.000	0	0	0	0	0	0	0	0
May	.000	.000	.000	0	0	0	0	0	0	0	0
June	.316	.381	.632	19	6	0	0	2	8	2	5
July	.219	.296	.438	73	16	2	1	4	8	6	22
August	.188	.261	.325	80	15	3	1	2	6	8	30
Sept–Oct	.130	.241	.365	115	15	6	0	7	16	16	53
Bases Empty	.165	.238	.341	176	29	9	2	6	6	16	69
Leadoff	.186	.271	.407	86	16	4	0	5	5	9	32
Runners On Base	.207	.315	.468	111	23	2	0	9	32	16	41
Scoring Position	.217	.333	.533	60	13	1	0	6	26	9	24
Late and Close	.271	.333	.667	48	13	2	1	5	12	5	22

DAVE PARKER — bats left — throws right — age 41 — CAL/TOR — *D

1991	BA	OBA	SA	AB	H	2B	3B	HR	RBI	BB	SO
Total	.239	.288	.365	502	120	26	2	11	59	33	98
vs. Left	.233	.259	.383	133	31	6	1	4	17	3	26
vs. Right	.241	.299	.358	369	89	20	1	7	42	30	72
at Home	.214	.273	.349	229	49	11	1	6	23	19	39
on Road	.260	.301	.377	273	71	15	1	5	36	14	59
on Grass	.233	.277	.356	404	94	18	1	10	49	25	78
on Turf	.265	.333	.398	98	26	8	1	1	10	8	20
Day Games	.283	.344	.392	120	34	8	1	1	12	9	28
Night Games	.225	.271	.356	382	86	18	1	10	47	24	70
April	.221	.250	.312	77	17	2	1	1	6	2	17
May	.189	.257	.253	95	18	3	0	1	10	8	22
June	.252	.295	.447	103	26	6	1	4	16	6	20
July	.287	.330	.426	94	27	4	0	3	13	6	16
August	.213	.263	.348	89	19	6	0	2	10	6	13
Sept–Oct	.295	.367	.409	44	13	5	0	0	4	5	10
Bases Empty	.230	.290	.370	270	62	16	2	6	6	20	60
Leadoff	.222	.282	.370	108	24	5	1	3	3	8	26
Runners On Base	.250	.286	.358	232	58	10	0	5	53	13	38
Scoring Position	.255	.303	.383	141	36	6	0	4	49	11	21
Late and Close	.275	.315	.522	69	19	5	0	4	10	4	9

8-YEAR TOTALS (1984–1991)

	BA	OBA	SA	AB	H	2B	3B	HR	RBI	BB	SO
Total	.273	.324	.445	4509	1233	230	13	173	735	337	760
vs. Left	.262	.289	.420	1345	352	59	5	48	240	46	257
vs. Right	.278	.337	.456	3164	881	171	8	125	495	291	503
at Home	.278	.331	.455	2185	607	113	5	88	370	179	349
on Road	.269	.317	.436	2324	626	117	8	85	365	158	411
on Grass	.266	.314	.428	2428	645	115	5	90	369	172	430
on Turf	.283	.335	.465	2081	588	115	8	83	366	165	330
Day Games	.259	.313	.441	1493	387	77	3	63	255	119	272
Night Games	.281	.329	.447	3016	846	153	10	110	480	218	488
April	.262	.300	.412	648	170	34	3	19	87	36	119
May	.305	.355	.490	776	237	44	3	31	137	61	132
June	.270	.325	.458	831	224	41	1	38	137	69	128
July	.266	.325	.447	696	185	32	2	30	126	59	113
August	.252	.299	.406	759	191	36	3	25	105	53	128
Sept–Oct	.283	.332	.452	799	226	43	1	30	143	59	140
Bases Empty	.250	.295	.409	2344	586	120	9	78	78	138	433
Leadoff	.284	.317	.499	940	267	52	6	46	46	44	154
Runners On Base	.299	.354	.485	2165	647	110	4	95	657	199	327
Scoring Position	.287	.363	.472	1228	353	62	3	53	547	163	211
Late and Close	.255	.321	.417	722	184	41	2	24	94	72	141

LANCE PARRISH — bats right — throws right — age 36 — CAL — *C/D1

8-YEAR TOTALS (1984–1991)

1991	BA	OBA	SA	AB	H	2B	3B	HR	RBI	BB	SO		BA	OBA	SA	AB	H	2B	3B	HR	RBI	BB	SO
Total	.216	.285	.388	402	87	12	0	19	51	35	117		.244	.310	.426	3653	892	125	7	175	557	337	819
vs. Left	.219	.297	.314	105	23	1	0	3	10	12	25		.270	.346	.454	1122	303	31	5	55	165	134	203
vs. Right	.215	.281	.414	297	64	11	0	16	41	23	92		.233	.293	.414	2531	589	94	2	120	392	203	616
at Home	.227	.280	.380	216	49	6	0	9	24	15	51		.255	.318	.431	1814	462	72	5	79	271	165	386
on Road	.204	.292	.398	186	38	6	0	10	27	20	66		.234	.302	.421	1839	430	53	2	96	286	172	433
on Grass	.203	.270	.355	335	68	9	0	14	41	27	93		.253	.319	.444	2538	642	81	5	131	405	236	546
on Turf	.284	.360	.552	67	19	3	0	5	10	8	24		.224	.289	.386	1115	250	44	2	44	152	101	273
Day Games	.268	.322	.427	82	22	1	0	4	11	6	29		.224	.287	.394	935	209	28	1	43	140	82	223
Night Games	.203	.276	.378	320	65	11	0	15	40	29	88		.251	.318	.437	2718	683	97	6	132	417	255	596
April	.250	.360	.422	64	16	2	0	3	6	9	16		.222	.297	.388	528	117	18	2	22	86	53	122
May	.192	.259	.346	78	15	3	0	3	11	6	24		.284	.344	.484	673	191	26	2	35	116	61	139
June	.333	.368	.583	36	12	3	0	2	6	2	6		.253	.314	.436	684	173	26	0	33	106	60	136
July	.171	.255	.293	82	14	1	0	3	10	9	25		.232	.302	.410	581	135	16	0	29	87	55	126
August	.208	.265	.390	77	16	2	0	4	9	5	29		.230	.305	.440	609	140	22	2	34	96	64	158
Sept–Oct	.215	.257	.415	65	14	1	0	4	9	4	17		.235	.289	.382	578	136	17	1	22	66	44	138
Bases Empty	.214	.284	.391	238	51	6	0	12	12	21	67		.234	.297	.412	1922	449	60	3	92	92	163	437
Leadoff	.265	.330	.554	83	22	3	0	7	7	6	23		.220	.282	.412	826	182	30	1	42	42	65	179
Runners On Base	.220	.288	.384	164	36	6	0	7	39	14	50		.256	.323	.442	1731	443	65	4	83	465	174	382
Scoring Position	.253	.321	.400	95	24	5	0	3	30	10	28		.241	.317	.395	1002	241	34	2	39	353	119	239
Late and Close	.105	.159	.175	57	6	1	0	1	4	4	22		.215	.295	.354	610	131	11	1	24	78	70	161

DAN PASQUA — bats left — throws left — age 31 — CHA — 10/D

7-YEAR TOTALS (1985–1991)

1991	BA	OBA	SA	AB	H	2B	3B	HR	RBI	BB	SO		BA	OBA	SA	AB	H	2B	3B	HR	RBI	BB	SO
Total	.259	.358	.465	417	108	22	5	18	66	62	86		.251	.337	.455	2156	541	101	13	104	333	273	525
vs. Left	.265	.379	.531	49	13	2	1	3	8	9	12		.190	.272	.310	358	68	14	1	9	44	35	102
vs. Right	.258	.355	.457	368	95	20	4	15	58	53	74		.263	.350	.483	1798	473	87	12	95	289	238	423
at Home	.291	.402	.531	196	57	11	3	10	29	26	34		.267	.359	.479	1047	280	48	9	52	157	149	248
on Road	.231	.317	.407	221	51	11	2	8	37	26	52		.235	.316	.431	1109	261	53	4	52	176	124	277
on Grass	.249	.355	.444	349	87	18	4	14	52	55	69		.246	.336	.440	1815	446	81	11	83	268	243	443
on Turf	.309	.373	.574	68	21	4	1	4	14	7	17		.279	.340	.534	341	95	20	2	21	65	30	82
Day Games	.303	.415	.569	109	33	5	3	6	20	19	22		.292	.378	.537	630	184	35	4	37	115	85	148
Night Games	.244	.337	.429	308	75	17	2	12	46	43	64		.234	.320	.421	1526	357	66	9	67	218	188	377
April	.250	.314	.438	32	8	0	0	2	5	3	7		.203	.290	.327	153	31	4	0	5	20	20	50
May	.220	.322	.340	50	11	3	0	1	5	8	5		.258	.372	.482	326	84	15	2	18	49	59	77
June	.268	.355	.512	82	22	4	2	4	13	11	18		.258	.337	.462	396	102	18	3	19	64	46	93
July	.330	.440	.577	97	32	7	1	5	21	17	17		.273	.342	.498	454	124	25	4	23	84	46	101
August	.169	.289	.229	83	14	2	0	1	5	13	21		.227	.314	.401	449	102	21	0	19	53	54	111
Sept–Oct	.288	.373	.630	73	21	6	2	5	17	10	18		.259	.345	.487	378	98	18	4	20	63	48	93
Bases Empty	.259	.335	.462	212	55	13	0	10	10	23	45		.250	.317	.465	1167	292	55	5	62	62	104	270
Leadoff	.272	.336	.563	103	28	6	0	8	8	9	21		.259	.317	.516	514	133	27	3	33	33	39	118
Runners On Base	.259	.381	.468	205	53	9	5	8	56	39	41		.252	.359	.442	989	249	46	8	42	271	169	255
Scoring Position	.241	.372	.438	112	27	3	5	3	43	22	27		.242	.354	.426	571	138	30	6	21	223	104	165
Late and Close	.295	.382	.462	78	23	4	0	3	11	11	17		.227	.333	.410	366	83	13	3	16	62	57	95

BILL PECOTA — bats right — throws right — age 32 — KC — *32/S1DPO

6-YEAR TOTALS (1986–1991)

1991	BA	OBA	SA	AB	H	2B	3B	HR	RBI	BB	SO		BA	OBA	SA	AB	H	2B	3B	HR	RBI	BB	SO
Total	.286	.356	.399	398	114	23	2	6	45	41	45		.254	.330	.370	1084	275	52	10	18	101	117	155
vs. Left	.336	.414	.461	128	43	10	0	2	17	17	13		.287	.364	.410	383	110	25	2	6	36	45	47
vs. Right	.263	.328	.370	270	71	13	2	4	28	24	32		.235	.312	.348	701	165	27	8	12	65	72	108
at Home	.296	.378	.414	203	60	12	0	4	25	25	20		.248	.332	.356	500	124	21	6	7	52	57	62
on Road	.277	.332	.385	195	54	11	2	2	20	16	25		.259	.329	.382	584	151	31	4	11	49	60	93
on Grass	.286	.336	.429	133	38	9	2	2	13	10	18		.252	.324	.375	408	103	20	3	8	34	41	72
on Turf	.287	.366	.385	265	76	14	0	4	32	31	27		.254	.334	.367	676	172	32	7	10	67	76	83
Day Games	.309	.375	.390	123	38	7	0	1	12	13	15		.268	.351	.372	339	91	16	2	5	31	41	58
Night Games	.276	.348	.404	275	76	16	2	5	33	28	30		.247	.321	.369	745	184	36	8	13	70	76	97
April	.235	.381	.235	17	4	0	0	0	1	4	3		.222	.333	.306	36	8	1	1	0	1	6	7
May	.241	.286	.367	79	19	4	0	2	12	5	8		.263	.311	.430	114	30	4	0	5	17	6	13
June	.414	.452	.724	29	12	3	0	2	8	2	4		.357	.400	.500	84	30	6	0	2	10	6	15
July	.338	.387	.365	74	25	2	0	0	7	4	9		.245	.311	.361	241	59	10	3	4	21	20	42
August	.271	.352	.417	96	26	9	1	1	6	12	11		.234	.316	.364	239	56	13	3	4	20	28	30
Sept–Oct	.272	.359	.369	103	28	5	1	1	11	14	10		.249	.342	.338	370	92	18	3	3	32	49	48
Bases Empty	.299	.354	.415	224	67	15	1	3	3	18	28		.266	.330	.394	635	169	37	4	12	12	56	95
Leadoff	.338	.386	.519	77	26	8	0	2	2	5	9		.276	.339	.394	221	61	14	0	4	4	19	36
Runners On Base	.270	.359	.379	174	47	8	1	3	42	23	17		.236	.330	.336	449	106	15	6	6	89	61	60
Scoring Position	.323	.440	.427	96	31	4	0	3	36	19	11		.253	.371	.337	261	66	9	2	3	75	48	37
Late and Close	.300	.387	.371	70	21	5	0	0	7	9	11		.205	.291	.248	161	33	7	0	0	10	19	29

TONY PENA — bats right — throws right — age 35 — BOS — *C

1991	BA	OBA	SA	AB	H	2B	3B	HR	RBI	BB	SO
Total	.231	.291	.321	464	107	23	2	5	48	37	53
vs. Left	.283	.336	.434	106	30	4	0	4	17	9	11
vs. Right	.215	.278	.288	358	77	19	2	1	31	28	42
at Home	.222	.290	.313	230	51	13	1	2	22	19	27
on Road	.239	.293	.329	234	56	10	1	3	26	18	26
on Grass	.226	.298	.307	381	86	18	2	3	40	36	44
on Turf	.253	.259	.386	83	21	5	0	2	8	1	9
Day Games	.199	.265	.298	151	30	8	2	1	21	13	20
Night Games	.246	.304	.332	313	77	15	0	4	27	24	33
April	.179	.191	.269	67	12	3	0	1	4	1	5
May	.337	.400	.453	86	29	5	1	1	10	7	3
June	.250	.321	.355	76	19	6	1	0	10	8	17
July	.179	.239	.333	84	15	4	0	3	9	6	11
August	.205	.221	.233	73	15	2	0	0	8	2	6
Sept–Oct	.218	.337	.256	78	17	3	0	0	7	13	11
Bases Empty	.245	.318	.361	241	59	17	1	3	3	23	31
Leadoff	.235	.322	.373	102	24	6	1	2	2	13	10
Runners On Base	.215	.261	.278	223	48	6	1	2	45	14	22
Scoring Position	.237	.295	.290	131	31	5	1	0	41	11	12
Late and Close	.127	.213	.155	71	9	2	0	0	4	8	11

8-YEAR TOTALS (1984–1991)

	BA	OBA	SA	AB	H	2B	3B	HR	RBI	BB	SO
	.258	.313	.363	3870	1000	175	16	66	426	302	486
	.295	.350	.425	1208	356	56	3	32	141	101	115
	.242	.296	.335	2662	644	119	13	34	285	201	371
	.256	.316	.352	1919	492	84	9	27	201	165	226
	.260	.309	.374	1951	508	91	7	39	225	137	260
	.243	.305	.333	1558	379	68	6	20	174	135	225
	.269	.318	.383	2312	621	107	10	46	252	167	261
	.255	.316	.351	1139	291	55	6	14	131	99	151
	.260	.311	.368	2731	709	120	10	52	295	203	335
	.265	.307	.389	486	129	24	0	12	40	28	63
	.255	.300	.372	648	165	26	4	14	80	37	84
	.272	.322	.377	713	194	34	7	9	88	54	91
	.246	.310	.337	686	169	28	2	10	60	63	83
	.247	.312	.333	664	164	23	2	10	77	62	84
	.266	.323	.377	673	179	40	1	11	81	58	81
	.257	.314	.375	2095	539	104	10	41	41	165	288
	.263	.320	.392	872	229	46	5	19	19	72	116
	.260	.312	.349	1775	461	71	6	25	385	137	198
	.254	.322	.340	1037	263	42	3	14	348	111	124
	.237	.289	.320	763	181	28	4	9	75	56	103

TERRY PENDLETON — bats both — throws right — age 32 — ATL — *3

1991	BA	OBA	SA	AB	H	2B	3B	HR	RBI	BB	SO
Total	.319	.363	.517	586	187	34	8	22	86	43	70
vs. Left	.301	.349	.460	176	53	10	3	4	23	14	9
vs. Right	.327	.369	.541	410	134	24	5	18	63	29	61
at Home	.340	.377	.561	285	97	18	3	13	48	18	30
on Road	.299	.350	.475	301	90	16	5	9	38	25	40
on Grass	.326	.367	.535	426	139	27	4	18	69	30	47
on Turf	.300	.351	.469	160	48	7	4	4	17	13	23
Day Games	.313	.349	.450	160	50	5	1	5	26	9	16
Night Games	.322	.368	.542	426	137	29	7	17	60	34	54
April	.234	.362	.426	47	11	3	0	2	6	10	4
May	.410	.446	.651	83	34	7	2	3	14	7	3
June	.302	.337	.448	96	29	6	1	2	12	5	17
July	.360	.385	.580	100	36	7	0	5	21	6	10
August	.254	.280	.405	126	32	3	2	4	14	5	18
Sept–Oct	.336	.386	.575	134	45	8	3	6	19	10	18
Bases Empty	.320	.364	.549	306	98	19	6	13	13	20	38
Leadoff	.377	.403	.658	114	43	11	3	5	5	5	12
Runners On Base	.318	.361	.482	280	89	15	2	9	73	23	32
Scoring Position	.320	.368	.509	169	54	9	1	7	66	17	19
Late and Close	.341	.392	.466	88	30	8	0	1	12	8	9

8-YEAR TOTALS (1984–1991)

	BA	OBA	SA	AB	H	2B	3B	HR	RBI	BB	SO
	.268	.316	.380	4018	1075	189	32	66	528	295	501
	.279	.316	.388	1367	381	78	10	17	184	80	114
	.262	.316	.376	2651	694	111	22	49	344	215	387
	.276	.322	.406	2029	559	109	21	38	279	146	227
	.259	.309	.353	1989	516	80	11	28	249	149	274
	.279	.326	.400	1281	357	55	5	30	169	96	167
	.262	.311	.370	2737	718	134	27	36	359	199	334
	.288	.337	.403	1331	383	60	5	28	183	99	165
	.258	.305	.368	2687	692	129	27	38	345	196	336
	.240	.305	.324	487	117	26	0	5	51	47	69
	.291	.344	.396	618	180	35	3	8	94	55	62
	.249	.304	.365	570	142	24	3	12	77	44	83
	.279	.311	.394	728	203	34	4	14	100	37	91
	.244	.295	.362	858	209	36	9	16	115	64	109
	.296	.336	.419	757	224	34	13	11	91	48	87
	.263	.308	.378	2122	559	98	16	38	38	134	263
	.293	.330	.419	819	240	49	9	12	12	45	93
	.272	.324	.381	1896	516	91	16	28	490	161	238
	.279	.337	.403	1170	327	63	15	17	456	118	156
	.256	.318	.363	699	179	39	6	7	75	63	116

TONY PHILLIPS — bats both — throws right — age 33 — DET — O32DS

1991	BA	OBA	SA	AB	H	2B	3B	HR	RBI	BB	SO
Total	.284	.371	.438	564	160	28	4	17	72	79	95
vs. Left	.357	.466	.617	154	55	7	0	11	25	32	18
vs. Right	.256	.333	.371	410	105	21	4	6	47	47	77
at Home	.295	.398	.438	292	86	13	1	9	42	50	43
on Road	.272	.341	.438	272	74	15	3	8	30	29	52
on Grass	.283	.378	.430	474	134	22	3	14	59	72	78
on Turf	.289	.333	.478	90	26	6	1	3	13	7	17
Day Games	.320	.400	.503	169	54	9	2	6	26	24	25
Night Games	.268	.359	.410	395	106	19	2	11	46	55	70
April	.293	.356	.493	75	22	4	1	3	11	9	13
May	.304	.430	.359	92	28	2	0	1	13	21	9
June	.268	.368	.423	97	26	4	1	3	13	15	19
July	.321	.368	.519	106	34	10	1	3	15	8	17
August	.291	.400	.519	79	23	3	0	5	10	14	20
Sept–Oct	.235	.313	.348	115	27	5	1	2	10	12	17
Bases Empty	.270	.359	.446	370	100	21	1	14	14	49	64
Leadoff	.259	.357	.407	216	56	9	1	7	7	32	39
Runners On Base	.309	.394	.423	194	60	7	3	3	58	30	31
Scoring Position	.322	.407	.441	118	38	5	3	1	52	20	22
Late and Close	.222	.347	.383	81	18	4	0	3	8	16	18

8-YEAR TOTALS (1984–1991)

	BA	OBA	SA	AB	H	2B	3B	HR	RBI	BB	SO
	.258	.350	.371	3230	834	144	29	54	343	459	574
	.298	.395	.432	1038	309	49	12	22	117	166	132
	.240	.329	.342	2192	525	95	17	32	226	293	442
	.253	.351	.360	1586	402	64	9	29	177	237	291
	.263	.350	.381	1644	432	80	20	25	166	222	283
	.257	.350	.364	2715	698	114	21	45	296	389	485
	.264	.353	.406	515	136	30	8	9	47	70	89
	.250	.336	.337	1126	281	42	9	13	112	148	201
	.263	.358	.389	2104	553	102	20	41	231	311	373
	.270	.368	.368	478	129	21	4	6	38	72	83
	.267	.361	.373	555	148	22	5	9	64	79	93
	.231	.332	.338	550	127	19	5	10	60	83	99
	.258	.356	.379	538	139	34	5	10	60	84	91
	.250	.341	.359	468	117	17	5	7	43	67	86
	.271	.345	.401	641	174	31	5	14	77	74	122
	.241	.338	.344	2008	484	82	13	33	33	286	367
	.243	.343	.335	999	243	41	3	15	15	147	174
	.286	.371	.415	1222	350	62	16	21	310	173	207
	.280	.367	.398	706	198	32	12	9	268	109	121
	.250	.361	.393	496	124	30	4	11	59	88	97

LUIS POLONIA — bats left — throws left — age 28 — CAL — *O/D

1991	BA	OBA	SA	AB	H	2B	3B	HR	RBI	BB	SO	5-YEAR TOTALS (1987–1991) BA	OBA	SA	AB	H	2B	3B	HR	RBI	BB	SO
Total	.296	.352	.379	604	179	28	8	2	50	52	74	.302	.347	.390	2164	653	79	37	13	207	155	265
vs. Left	.238	.283	.298	168	40	8	1	0	17	11	25	.254	.298	.319	398	101	12	7	0	36	25	65
vs. Right	.319	.377	.411	436	139	20	7	2	33	41	49	.313	.358	.407	1766	552	67	30	13	171	130	200
at Home	.261	.329	.333	303	79	11	4	1	20	30	36	.307	.358	.391	1078	331	40	16	6	103	83	128
on Road	.332	.374	.425	301	100	17	4	1	30	22	38	.297	.337	.390	1086	322	39	21	7	104	72	137
on Grass	.278	.337	.360	497	138	19	8	2	41	44	60	.298	.346	.383	1834	547	63	30	11	175	135	216
on Turf	.383	.419	.467	107	41	9	0	0	9	8	14	.321	.356	.430	330	106	16	7	2	32	20	49
Day Games	.331	.389	.459	148	49	11	4	0	16	14	14	.319	.366	.413	700	223	35	11	3	66	52	87
Night Games	.285	.339	.353	456	130	17	4	2	34	38	60	.294	.338	.380	1464	430	44	26	10	141	103	178
April	.333	.405	.387	75	25	2	1	0	7	8	8	.282	.333	.365	181	51	4	4	1	20	14	16
May	.314	.363	.438	105	33	5	4	0	10	8	12	.318	.356	.437	311	99	12	8	3	27	19	41
June	.263	.286	.307	114	30	3	1	0	15	4	16	.296	.344	.351	382	113	12	3	1	40	29	39
July	.259	.337	.358	81	21	3	1	1	5	10	8	.301	.336	.398	435	131	16	7	4	39	22	57
August	.327	.390	.445	110	36	8	1	0	9	12	14	.290	.329	.395	410	119	16	9	3	49	26	53
Sept–Oct	.286	.341	.345	119	34	7	0	0	4	10	16	.315	.377	.391	445	140	19	6	1	32	45	59
Bases Empty	.291	.357	.375	368	107	17	4	2	2	37	48	.299	.354	.384	1337	400	47	24	6	5	109	175
Leadoff	.264	.344	.364	220	58	10	3	2	2	26	33	.296	.355	.390	761	225	29	14	5	5	69	106
Runners On Base	.305	.343	.386	236	72	11	4	0	48	15	26	.306	.337	.401	827	253	32	13	7	201	46	90
Scoring Position	.333	.381	.394	132	44	4	2	0	44	12	17	.319	.351	.405	504	161	18	8	3	184	32	64
Late and Close	.299	.349	.325	77	23	2	0	0	1	6	11	.292	.326	.357	308	90	10	2	2	23	17	48

KIRBY PUCKETT — bats right — throws right — age 31 — MIN — *O

1991	BA	OBA	SA	AB	H	2B	3B	HR	RBI	BB	SO	8-YEAR TOTALS (1984–1991) BA	OBA	SA	AB	H	2B	3B	HR	RBI	BB	SO
Total	.319	.352	.460	611	195	29	6	15	89	31	78	.320	.357	.466	5006	1602	266	47	123	674	275	639
vs. Left	.406	.436	.658	155	63	8	5	7	24	8	19	.342	.379	.517	1417	484	83	21	41	186	85	165
vs. Right	.289	.324	.393	456	132	21	1	8	65	23	59	.312	.349	.446	3589	1118	183	26	82	488	190	474
at Home	.326	.356	.463	328	107	16	4	7	45	16	45	.349	.385	.512	2535	884	156	29	67	369	142	325
on Road	.311	.348	.456	283	88	13	2	8	44	15	33	.291	.328	.418	2471	718	110	18	56	305	133	314
on Grass	.323	.357	.484	217	70	10	2	7	38	10	26	.296	.334	.422	1883	558	84	12	43	245	104	250
on Turf	.317	.350	.447	394	125	19	4	8	51	21	52	.334	.371	.492	3123	1044	182	35	80	429	171	389
Day Games	.297	.323	.473	182	54	6	4	6	27	7	23	.317	.359	.464	1491	472	84	11	38	191	92	204
Night Games	.329	.364	.455	429	141	23	2	9	62	24	55	.321	.356	.466	3515	1130	182	36	85	483	183	435
April	.342	.369	.506	79	27	2	1	3	10	4	11	.332	.376	.537	587	195	34	7	24	90	38	76
May	.321	.339	.459	109	35	5	2	2	14	4	12	.340	.377	.507	864	294	48	9	26	136	48	93
June	.314	.376	.533	105	33	6	1	5	18	7	14	.309	.345	.436	865	267	44	9	16	101	43	102
July	.352	.387	.486	105	37	4	2	2	19	6	12	.313	.353	.457	852	267	45	10	19	116	53	118
August	.310	.322	.407	113	35	5	0	2	12	2	16	.308	.345	.423	863	266	44	5	15	96	46	127
Sept–Oct	.280	.324	.380	100	28	7	0	1	16	8	13	.321	.353	.458	975	313	51	7	23	135	47	123
Bases Empty	.336	.371	.514	327	110	20	4	10	10	14	38	.314	.348	.459	2910	914	154	21	75	75	133	368
Leadoff	.243	.291	.398	103	25	5	1	3	3	5	13	.322	.359	.451	1306	421	65	8	29	29	65	146
Runners On Base	.299	.331	.398	284	85	9	2	5	79	17	40	.328	.369	.475	2096	688	112	26	48	599	142	271
Scoring Position	.301	.341	.373	153	46	4	1	2	65	13	26	.323	.368	.470	1213	392	65	16	27	521	100	185
Late and Close	.378	.439	.581	74	28	4	1	3	15	6	14	.305	.354	.468	681	208	27	9	22	106	46	105

CARLOS QUINTANA — bats right — throws right — age 27 — BOS — *10/D

1991	BA	OBA	SA	AB	H	2B	3B	HR	RBI	BB	SO	4-YEAR TOTALS (1988–1991) BA	OBA	SA	AB	H	2B	3B	HR	RBI	BB	SO
Total	.295	.375	.412	478	141	21	1	11	71	61	66	.285	.359	.388	1073	306	54	1	18	146	122	155
vs. Left	.340	.436	.484	153	52	7	0	5	26	26	21	.338	.409	.461	373	126	22	0	8	56	44	48
vs. Right	.274	.345	.378	325	89	14	1	6	45	35	45	.257	.332	.349	700	180	32	1	10	90	78	107
at Home	.292	.382	.360	236	69	10	0	2	30	34	31	.290	.370	.364	503	146	22	0	5	62	62	70
on Road	.298	.368	.463	242	72	11	1	9	41	27	35	.281	.349	.409	570	160	32	1	13	84	60	85
on Grass	.291	.371	.392	398	116	20	1	6	56	50	54	.296	.370	.393	876	259	47	1	12	119	103	119
on Turf	.313	.396	.512	80	25	1	0	5	15	11	12	.239	.306	.365	197	47	7	0	6	27	19	36
Day Games	.356	.433	.509	163	58	8	1	5	36	23	23	.310	.393	.454	348	108	24	1	8	67	48	49
Night Games	.263	.345	.362	315	83	13	0	6	35	38	43	.273	.342	.356	725	198	30	0	10	79	74	106
April	.305	.317	.407	59	18	3	0	1	7	0	9	.321	.368	.420	81	26	5	0	1	7	5	13
May	.324	.384	.412	102	33	3	0	2	9	10	10	.316	.370	.418	177	56	9	0	3	23	14	15
June	.280	.416	.415	82	23	5	0	2	13	18	13	.288	.368	.394	198	57	9	0	4	27	24	36
July	.236	.305	.361	72	17	3	0	2	15	8	8	.277	.362	.436	188	52	12	0	6	35	27	25
August	.338	.411	.525	80	27	4	1	3	12	10	15	.276	.371	.378	185	51	8	1	3	23	27	33
Sept–Oct	.277	.384	.349	83	23	3	0	1	15	15	11	.262	.328	.320	244	64	11	0	1	31	25	33
Bases Empty	.308	.391	.405	247	76	9	0	5	5	32	45	.289	.369	.376	550	159	24	0	8	8	66	92
Leadoff	.413	.443	.587	92	38	7	0	3	3	5	13	.319	.365	.431	204	65	11	0	4	4	13	25
Runners On Base	.281	.357	.420	231	65	12	1	6	66	29	21	.281	.348	.400	523	147	30	1	10	138	56	63
Scoring Position	.277	.374	.415	130	36	6	0	4	58	22	13	.287	.366	.391	289	83	15	0	5	118	39	41
Late and Close	.394	.459	.470	66	26	2	0	1	14	8	8	.333	.383	.412	165	55	7	0	2	24	14	28

TIM RAINES — bats both — throws right — age 33 — CHA — *OD

1991	BA	OBA	SA	AB	H	2B	3B	HR	RBI	BB	SO	8-YEAR TOTALS (1984–1991) BA	OBA	SA	AB	H	2B	3B	HR	RBI	BB	SO
Total	.268	.359	.345	609	163	20	6	5	50	83	68	.302	.392	.438	4319	1303	216	64	81	450	635	444
vs. Left	.279	.343	.346	208	58	6	1	2	17	21	21	.302	.373	.433	1356	410	55	16	30	159	155	132
vs. Right	.262	.366	.344	401	105	14	5	3	33	62	47	.301	.400	.440	2963	893	161	48	51	291	480	312
at Home	.254	.348	.303	284	72	7	2	1	21	39	30	.301	.392	.434	2087	628	101	33	37	213	308	212
on Road	.280	.368	.382	325	91	13	4	4	29	44	38	.302	.391	.441	2232	675	115	31	44	237	327	232
on Grass	.277	.369	.349	519	144	15	5	4	40	73	57	.299	.393	.420	1546	462	68	15	30	161	239	171
on Turf	.211	.297	.322	90	19	5	1	1	10	10	11	.303	.391	.447	2773	841	148	49	51	289	396	273
Day Games	.251	.358	.333	171	43	6	1	2	15	29	19	.306	.405	.453	1361	417	64	26	28	146	232	148
Night Games	.274	.359	.349	438	120	14	5	3	35	54	49	.300	.385	.430	2958	886	152	38	53	304	403	296
April	.177	.261	.210	62	11	2	0	0	3	7	5	.270	.360	.389	537	145	25	9	7	61	79	50
May	.349	.454	.486	109	38	3	3	2	11	20	18	.310	.418	.472	778	241	34	16	20	93	139	94
June	.286	.360	.367	98	28	4	2	0	14	12	10	.318	.395	.452	713	227	48	7	11	90	93	68
July	.152	.288	.192	99	15	1	0	1	6	17	7	.281	.363	.399	676	190	25	8	13	60	85	71
August	.331	.409	.430	121	40	7	1	1	9	16	17	.311	.401	.465	850	264	49	11	20	90	129	89
Sept–Oct	.258	.326	.308	120	31	3	0	1	7	11	11	.308	.398	.427	765	236	35	13	10	56	110	72
Bases Empty	.279	.350	.345	426	119	13	3	3	3	43	49	.300	.374	.438	2811	843	154	44	49	49	317	286
Leadoff	.256	.326	.319	270	69	9	1	2	2	26	35	.294	.365	.430	1491	438	76	29	23	23	153	157
Runners On Base	.240	.377	.344	183	44	7	3	2	47	40	19	.305	.421	.436	1508	460	62	20	32	401	318	158
Scoring Position	.286	.447	.375	112	32	6	2	0	42	33	12	.302	.453	.419	881	266	36	11	15	349	265	100
Late and Close	.217	.331	.317	120	26	2	2	2	13	21	12	.319	.420	.441	778	248	34	8	15	100	136	80

WILLIE RANDOLPH — bats right — throws right — age 38 — MIL — *2/D

1991	BA	OBA	SA	AB	H	2B	3B	HR	RBI	BB	SO	8-YEAR TOTALS (1984–1991) BA	OBA	SA	AB	H	2B	3B	HR	RBI	BB	SO
Total	.327	.424	.374	431	141	14	3	0	54	75	38	.281	.378	.349	3774	1062	149	15	25	342	594	317
vs. Left	.358	.457	.405	148	53	5	1	0	21	27	10	.314	.409	.403	1266	398	62	7	12	111	205	79
vs. Right	.311	.407	.357	283	88	9	2	0	33	48	28	.265	.363	.321	2508	664	87	8	13	231	389	238
at Home	.336	.410	.400	220	74	10	2	0	31	28	20	.283	.385	.352	1849	524	73	10	11	165	309	149
on Road	.318	.438	.346	211	67	4	1	0	23	47	18	.279	.372	.346	1925	538	76	5	14	177	285	168
on Grass	.330	.428	.376	364	120	11	3	0	50	65	28	.284	.382	.351	3117	884	121	14	20	286	503	260
on Turf	.313	.403	.358	67	21	3	0	0	4	10	10	.271	.360	.339	657	178	28	1	5	56	91	57
Day Games	.317	.433	.341	123	39	3	0	0	13	26	6	.279	.385	.349	1142	319	46	5	8	104	196	90
Night Games	.331	.421	.386	308	102	11	3	0	41	49	32	.282	.376	.348	2632	743	103	10	17	238	398	227
April	.227	.346	.227	22	5	0	0	0	0	4	1	.258	.364	.303	531	137	18	0	2	34	87	53
May	.296	.390	.310	71	21	1	0	0	8	11	9	.290	.395	.365	732	212	27	5	6	76	128	53
June	.462	.533	.519	52	24	1	1	0	11	8	6	.287	.375	.357	655	188	33	2	3	68	94	64
July	.229	.373	.271	48	11	2	0	0	6	11	4	.279	.374	.341	581	162	26	2	2	51	90	38
August	.371	.449	.440	116	43	6	1	0	17	18	9	.272	.352	.342	588	160	21	4	4	48	75	49
Sept–Oct	.303	.411	.352	122	37	4	1	0	12	23	9	.295	.400	.371	687	203	24	2	8	65	120	60
Bases Empty	.281	.369	.326	224	63	10	0	0	0	31	17	.272	.368	.337	2265	617	87	9	14	14	335	194
Leadoff	.215	.292	.231	65	14	1	0	0	0	7	3	.284	.378	.346	912	259	35	5	4	4	137	62
Runners On Base	.377	.480	.425	207	78	4	3	0	54	44	21	.295	.393	.366	1509	445	62	6	11	328	259	123
Scoring Position	.373	.507	.445	110	41	2	3	0	52	33	10	.274	.395	.351	869	238	34	6	7	309	192	76
Late and Close	.291	.371	.367	79	23	1	0	0	9	10	7	.280	.373	.340	615	172	24	2	3	60	92	57

GARY REDUS — bats right — throws right — age 36 — PIT — 10

1991	BA	OBA	SA	AB	H	2B	3B	HR	RBI	BB	SO	8-YEAR TOTALS (1984–1991) BA	OBA	SA	AB	H	2B	3B	HR	RBI	BB	SO
Total	.246	.324	.393	252	62	12	2	7	24	28	39	.251	.343	.406	2546	638	140	33	63	249	362	490
vs. Left	.249	.302	.399	173	43	7	2	5	15	15	27	.260	.360	.426	1243	323	73	20	31	118	200	218
vs. Right	.241	.368	.380	79	19	5	0	2	9	13	12	.242	.327	.387	1303	315	67	13	32	131	162	272
at Home	.280	.353	.448	125	35	8	2	3	11	12	18	.263	.360	.426	1306	344	82	19	31	143	199	245
on Road	.213	.297	.339	127	27	4	0	4	13	16	21	.237	.325	.384	1240	294	58	14	32	106	163	245
on Grass	.213	.283	.387	80	17	2	0	4	9	9	11	.245	.329	.378	1091	267	52	15	21	112	146	210
on Turf	.262	.344	.395	172	45	10	2	3	15	19	28	.255	.354	.427	1455	371	88	18	42	137	216	280
Day Games	.150	.274	.250	60	9	0	0	2	5	11	11	.243	.343	.407	783	190	41	11	22	74	123	161
Night Games	.276	.341	.438	192	53	12	2	5	19	17	28	.254	.343	.405	1763	448	99	22	41	175	239	329
April	.231	.318	.282	39	9	2	0	0	1	4	3	.260	.372	.370	308	80	18	5	2	20	52	55
May	.179	.256	.179	39	7	0	0	0	1	4	5	.265	.326	.421	373	99	16	6	10	34	34	80
June	.289	.317	.553	38	11	4	0	2	4	4	7	.251	.350	.404	450	113	30	3	11	49	70	78
July	.311	.418	.556	45	14	3	1	2	8	8	7	.248	.331	.410	500	124	28	7	13	50	63	101
August	.229	.300	.486	35	8	0	0	3	6	4	8	.252	.350	.443	460	116	23	7	17	51	70	82
Sept–Oct	.232	.313	.321	56	13	3	1	0	4	7	9	.233	.336	.376	455	106	25	5	10	45	73	94
Bases Empty	.263	.332	.446	175	46	10	2	6	6	17	27	.260	.351	.425	1689	439	103	23	43	43	230	304
Leadoff	.280	.336	.439	107	30	6	1	3	3	9	14	.263	.351	.430	898	236	57	9	25	25	119	146
Runners On Base	.208	.309	.273	77	16	2	0	1	18	11	12	.232	.328	.369	857	199	37	10	20	206	132	186
Scoring Position	.143	.292	.204	49	7	0	0	1	18	10	7	.231	.326	.402	507	117	21	6	18	193	83	118
Late and Close	.275	.373	.353	51	14	1	0	1	6	7	9	.252	.347	.381	457	115	22	2	11	46	68	110

JODY REED — bats right — throws right — age 30 — BOS — *2/S

1991	BA	OBA	SA	AB	H	2B	3B	HR	RBI	BB	SO
Total	.283	.349	.382	618	175	42	2	5	60	60	53
vs. Left	.267	.328	.321	165	44	9	0	0	6	15	11
vs. Right	.289	.356	.404	453	131	33	2	5	54	45	42
at Home	.263	.336	.385	312	82	27	1	3	37	34	27
on Road	.304	.362	.379	306	93	15	1	2	23	26	26
on Grass	.287	.352	.392	530	152	39	1	5	59	54	45
on Turf	.261	.330	.318	88	23	3	1	0	1	6	8
Day Games	.240	.332	.304	204	49	13	0	0	16	27	21
Night Games	.304	.358	.420	414	126	29	2	5	44	33	32
April	.136	.197	.152	66	9	1	0	0	1	4	9
May	.315	.375	.407	108	34	5	1	1	16	11	5
June	.244	.306	.367	90	22	11	0	0	6	8	9
July	.268	.317	.366	112	30	5	0	2	11	9	10
August	.296	.341	.383	115	34	8	1	0	5	7	7
Sept–Oct	.362	.460	.504	127	46	12	0	2	21	21	13
Bases Empty	.256	.311	.333	351	90	19	1	2	2	25	31
Leadoff	.258	.305	.341	132	34	9	1	0	0	8	9
Runners On Base	.318	.395	.446	267	85	23	1	3	58	35	22
Scoring Position	.307	.402	.423	137	42	14	1	0	49	24	10
Late and Close	.256	.356	.282	78	20	2	0	0	7	10	12

5-YEAR TOTALS (1987–1991)

BA	OBA	SA	AB	H	2B	3B	HR	RBI	BB	SO
.288	.368	.386	2108	607	153	6	14	187	257	183
.289	.365	.370	581	168	42	1	1	48	71	44
.287	.368	.392	1527	439	111	5	13	139	186	139
.288	.366	.399	1085	312	90	2	9	106	130	105
.288	.369	.372	1023	295	63	4	5	81	127	78
.290	.371	.391	1827	530	135	4	14	175	230	154
.274	.345	.352	281	77	18	2	0	12	27	29
.288	.374	.380	698	201	53	1	3	64	93	58
.288	.364	.389	1410	406	100	5	11	123	164	125
.213	.300	.280	211	45	8	0	2	16	25	25
.296	.360	.391	338	100	25	2	1	30	34	32
.265	.348	.379	309	82	29	0	2	24	39	31
.319	.388	.434	392	125	36	0	3	37	46	32
.293	.362	.384	393	115	25	1	3	31	41	28
.301	.403	.398	465	140	30	3	3	49	72	35
.273	.346	.366	1206	329	82	3	8	8	128	103
.275	.350	.366	516	142	39	1	2	2	57	40
.308	.394	.414	902	278	71	3	6	179	129	80
.279	.386	.363	487	136	34	2	1	163	87	45
.285	.382	.346	298	85	15	0	1	35	45	29

KEVIN REIMER — bats left — throws right — age 28 — TEX — OD

1991	BA	OBA	SA	AB	H	2B	3B	HR	RBI	BB	SO
Total	.269	.332	.477	394	106	22	0	20	69	33	93
vs. Left	.222	.275	.333	36	8	1	0	1	4	2	9
vs. Right	.274	.338	.492	358	98	21	0	19	65	31	84
at Home	.272	.335	.565	184	50	15	0	13	41	16	56
on Road	.267	.329	.400	210	56	7	0	7	28	17	37
on Grass	.269	.329	.503	324	87	19	0	19	65	26	85
on Turf	.271	.346	.357	70	19	3	0	1	4	7	8
Day Games	.318	.388	.494	85	27	3	0	4	13	8	13
Night Games	.256	.316	.472	309	79	19	0	16	56	25	80
April	.256	.302	.462	39	10	2	0	2	6	2	12
May	.305	.369	.407	59	18	6	0	0	9	6	10
June	.262	.324	.338	65	17	2	0	1	8	6	12
July	.283	.321	.509	53	15	6	0	2	7	3	15
August	.267	.333	.564	101	27	3	0	9	25	8	23
Sept–Oct	.247	.330	.519	77	19	3	0	6	14	8	21
Bases Empty	.232	.284	.404	203	47	11	0	8	8	12	48
Leadoff	.284	.348	.519	81	23	7	0	4	4	6	20
Runners On Base	.309	.378	.555	191	59	11	0	12	61	21	45
Scoring Position	.287	.371	.614	101	29	6	0	9	53	16	33
Late and Close	.357	.438	.500	56	20	2	0	2	6	7	9

4-YEAR TOTALS (1988–1991)

BA	OBA	SA	AB	H	2B	3B	HR	RBI	BB	SO
.258	.320	.452	524	135	31	1	23	86	43	122
.205	.250	.295	44	9	1	0	1	4	2	12
.262	.326	.467	480	126	30	1	22	82	41	110
.265	.328	.521	238	63	22	0	13	50	20	68
.252	.313	.395	286	72	9	1	10	36	23	54
.262	.322	.478	427	112	27	1	21	81	34	108
.237	.308	.340	97	23	4	0	2	5	9	14
.282	.357	.436	110	31	5	0	4	16	11	22
.251	.309	.457	414	104	26	1	19	70	32	100
.256	.302	.462	39	10	2	0	2	6	2	12
.305	.369	.407	59	18	6	0	0	9	6	10
.244	.295	.349	86	21	3	0	2	12	6	17
.284	.344	.500	88	25	10	0	3	14	7	22
.258	.322	.508	128	33	5	0	9	25	10	31
.226	.300	.452	124	28	5	1	7	20	12	30
.230	.289	.398	256	59	13	0	10	10	18	58
.280	.337	.527	93	26	8	0	5	5	6	22
.284	.348	.504	268	76	18	1	13	76	25	64
.268	.341	.537	149	40	11	1	9	66	19	47
.320	.391	.485	97	31	5	1	3	13	10	18

GILBERTO REYES — bats right — throws right — age 29 — MON — C

1991	BA	OBA	SA	AB	H	2B	3B	HR	RBI	BB	SO
Total	.217	.285	.261	207	45	9	0	0	13	19	51
vs. Left	.186	.248	.206	97	18	2	0	0	4	8	26
vs. Right	.245	.317	.309	110	27	7	0	0	9	11	25
at Home	.221	.292	.256	86	19	3	0	0	6	9	23
on Road	.215	.280	.264	121	26	6	0	0	7	10	28
on Grass	.211	.243	.239	71	15	2	0	0	5	3	19
on Turf	.221	.305	.272	136	30	7	0	0	8	16	32
Day Games	.183	.262	.225	71	13	3	0	0	4	8	18
Night Games	.235	.297	.279	136	32	6	0	0	9	11	33
April	.424	.457	.485	33	14	2	0	0	2	2	3
May	.154	.233	.154	39	6	0	0	0	4	4	12
June	.200	.250	.233	30	6	1	0	0	4	2	5
July	.095	.130	.143	21	2	1	0	0	2	1	7
August	.182	.321	.227	44	8	2	0	0	1	8	14
Sept–Oct	.225	.262	.300	40	9	3	0	0	3	2	10
Bases Empty	.192	.248	.225	120	23	4	0	0	0	9	31
Leadoff	.262	.311	.333	42	11	3	0	0	0	3	9
Runners On Base	.253	.333	.310	87	22	5	0	0	13	10	20
Scoring Position	.255	.323	.345	55	14	5	0	0	13	6	14
Late and Close	.333	.366	.359	39	13	1	0	0	3	2	9

5-YEAR TOTALS (1984–1991)

BA	OBA	SA	AB	H	2B	3B	HR	RBI	BB	SO
.207	.276	.247	227	47	9	0	0	14	20	59
.174	.244	.193	109	19	2	0	0	5	9	32
.237	.305	.297	118	28	7	0	0	9	11	27
.196	.269	.227	97	19	3	0	0	6	9	28
.215	.282	.262	130	28	6	0	0	8	11	31
.184	.228	.207	87	16	2	0	0	5	4	26
.221	.304	.271	140	31	7	0	0	9	16	33
.171	.247	.211	76	13	3	0	0	4	8	20
.225	.291	.265	151	34	6	0	0	10	12	39
.424	.457	.485	33	14	2	0	0	2	2	3
.154	.233	.154	39	6	0	0	0	4	4	12
.200	.250	.233	30	6	1	0	0	4	2	5
.095	.130	.143	21	2	1	0	0	2	1	7
.182	.321	.227	44	8	2	0	0	1	8	14
.183	.234	.233	60	11	3	0	0	4	3	18
.180	.238	.211	133	24	4	0	0	0	10	37
.245	.288	.306	49	12	3	0	0	0	3	12
.245	.327	.298	94	23	5	0	0	14	10	22
.254	.318	.339	59	15	5	0	0	14	6	16
.310	.341	.333	42	13	1	0	0	3	2	11

HAROLD REYNOLDS — bats both — throws right — age 32 — SEA — *2/D

1991	BA	OBA	SA	AB	H	2B	3B	HR	RBI	BB	SO
Total	.254	.332	.341	631	160	34	6	3	57	72	63
vs. Left	.264	.326	.322	174	46	7	0	1	16	17	14
vs. Right	.249	.334	.348	457	114	27	6	2	41	55	49
at Home	.299	.387	.404	314	94	20	5	1	27	42	27
on Road	.208	.276	.278	317	66	14	1	2	30	30	36
on Grass	.197	.277	.252	238	47	10	0	1	24	26	29
on Turf	.288	.366	.394	393	113	24	6	2	33	46	34
Day Games	.186	.263	.234	167	31	5	0	1	14	17	23
Night Games	.278	.357	.379	464	129	29	6	2	43	55	40
April	.224	.272	.282	85	19	5	0	0	11	6	5
May	.373	.427	.445	110	41	6	1	0	9	12	10
June	.214	.342	.316	98	21	7	0	1	7	17	5
July	.211	.295	.312	109	23	6	1	1	12	12	12
August	.257	.333	.312	109	28	4	1	0	7	12	14
Sept—Oct	.233	.309	.358	120	28	6	3	1	11	13	17
Bases Empty	.226	.320	.310	371	84	18	5	1	1	49	38
Leadoff	.220	.324	.313	150	33	8	3	0	0	22	17
Runners On Base	.292	.349	.385	260	76	16	1	2	56	23	25
Scoring Position	.322	.379	.411	146	47	10	0	1	51	15	15
Late and Close	.309	.352	.412	97	30	5	1	1	15	7	12

8-YEAR TOTALS (1984–1991)

	BA	OBA	SA	AB	H	2B	3B	HR	RBI	BB	SO
	.263	.329	.348	3571	938	173	44	14	258	344	302
	.279	.330	.359	1052	293	55	6	6	82	81	77
	.256	.329	.343	2519	645	118	38	8	176	263	225
	.266	.338	.356	1749	465	84	26	7	123	185	134
	.260	.320	.340	1822	473	89	18	7	135	159	168
	.252	.313	.329	1406	354	65	14	5	110	123	127
	.270	.339	.360	2165	584	108	30	9	148	221	175
	.250	.321	.334	909	227	43	14	2	66	93	101
	.267	.332	.352	2662	711	130	30	12	192	251	201
	.244	.292	.337	454	111	18	9	2	42	31	32
	.293	.347	.379	564	165	36	5	1	49	51	49
	.245	.329	.313	571	140	26	5	1	26	65	46
	.257	.335	.331	637	164	22	8	3	54	73	50
	.259	.327	.339	661	171	41	6	0	31	64	55
	.273	.333	.380	684	187	30	11	7	56	60	70
	.254	.329	.342	2234	568	106	34	7	7	235	196
	.247	.329	.326	1120	277	53	16	1	1	126	102
	.277	.329	.358	1337	370	67	10	7	251	109	106
	.275	.337	.360	726	200	35	7	4	232	75	61
	.283	.350	.366	508	144	25	4	3	57	53	61

KARL RHODES — bats left — throws left — age 24 — HOU — O

1991	BA	OBA	SA	AB	H	2B	3B	HR	RBI	BB	SO
Total	.213	.289	.272	136	29	3	1	1	12	14	26
vs. Left	.242	.306	.303	33	8	2	0	0	4	3	7
vs. Right	.204	.284	.262	103	21	1	1	1	8	11	19
at Home	.243	.341	.271	70	17	2	0	0	6	11	10
on Road	.182	.229	.273	66	12	1	1	1	6	3	16
on Grass	.154	.214	.282	39	6	0	1	1	3	2	10
on Turf	.237	.318	.268	97	23	3	0	0	9	12	16
Day Games	.103	.156	.103	29	3	0	0	0	2	2	5
Night Games	.243	.325	.318	107	26	3	1	1	10	12	21
April	.263	.317	.351	57	15	2	0	1	6	5	11
May	.184	.279	.224	76	14	1	1	0	6	9	14
June	.000	.000	.000	3	0	0	0	0	0	0	1
July	.000	.000	.000	0	0	0	0	0	0	0	0
August	.000	.000	.000	0	0	0	0	0	0	0	0
Sept—Oct	.000	.000	.000	0	0	0	0	0	0	0	0
Bases Empty	.225	.319	.300	80	18	1	1	1	1	10	16
Leadoff	.194	.306	.323	31	6	1	0	1	1	4	9
Runners On Base	.196	.246	.232	56	11	2	0	0	11	4	10
Scoring Position	.233	.314	.300	30	7	2	0	0	11	4	5
Late and Close	.190	.261	.190	21	4	0	0	0	1	2	4

2-YEAR TOTALS (1990–1991)

	BA	OBA	SA	AB	H	2B	3B	HR	RBI	BB	SO
	.225	.310	.311	222	50	9	2	2	15	27	38
	.178	.229	.222	45	8	2	0	0	4	3	11
	.237	.328	.333	177	42	7	2	2	11	24	27
	.239	.336	.301	113	27	5	1	0	7	17	15
	.211	.281	.321	109	23	4	1	2	8	10	23
	.210	.265	.355	62	13	1	1	2	5	4	13
	.231	.326	.294	160	37	8	1	0	10	23	25
	.182	.217	.255	55	10	1	0	1	4	3	7
	.240	.339	.329	167	40	8	2	1	11	24	31
	.263	.317	.351	57	15	2	0	1	6	5	11
	.184	.279	.224	76	14	1	1	0	6	9	14
	.000	.000	.000	3	0	0	0	0	0	0	1
	.000	.000	.000	0	0	0	0	0	0	0	0
	.235	.333	.382	34	8	2	0	1	1	5	5
	.250	.344	.365	52	13	4	1	0	2	8	7
	.261	.353	.388	134	35	7	2	2	2	18	22
	.196	.302	.304	46	9	2	0	1	1	6	9
	.170	.242	.193	88	15	2	0	0	13	9	16
	.191	.310	.234	47	9	2	0	0	13	9	9
	.216	.348	.270	37	8	0	0	0	3	8	10

CAL RIPKEN — bats right — throws right — age 32 — BAL — *S

1991	BA	OBA	SA	AB	H	2B	3B	HR	RBI	BB	SO
Total	.323	.374	.566	650	210	46	5	34	114	53	46
vs. Left	.348	.411	.677	164	57	14	2	12	31	19	15
vs. Right	.315	.361	.529	486	153	32	3	22	83	34	31
at Home	.286	.343	.505	315	90	19	1	16	52	28	23
on Road	.358	.403	.624	335	120	27	4	18	62	25	23
on Grass	.315	.364	.562	550	173	35	4	31	96	41	42
on Turf	.370	.426	.590	100	37	11	1	3	18	12	4
Day Games	.304	.378	.547	161	49	7	1	10	34	20	7
Night Games	.329	.372	.573	489	161	39	4	24	80	33	39
April	.338	.408	.632	68	23	3	1	5	20	6	6
May	.349	.412	.613	106	37	7	0	7	15	12	6
June	.371	.417	.603	116	43	10	1	5	16	9	7
July	.245	.300	.436	110	27	6	0	5	15	8	7
August	.330	.370	.539	115	38	10	1	4	21	8	8
Sept—Oct	.311	.351	.593	135	42	10	2	8	27	10	12
Bases Empty	.324	.361	.575	358	116	23	2	21	21	19	24
Leadoff	.316	.345	.614	114	36	7	0	9	9	4	4
Runners On Base	.322	.388	.555	292	94	23	3	13	93	34	22
Scoring Position	.315	.410	.530	149	47	13	2	5	70	28	15
Late and Close	.347	.432	.564	101	35	8	1	4	13	16	5

8-YEAR TOTALS (1984–1991)

	BA	OBA	SA	AB	H	2B	3B	HR	RBI	BB	SO
	.277	.352	.462	5005	1388	261	26	204	746	583	547
	.290	.368	.506	1468	425	99	9	67	201	189	136
	.272	.345	.444	3537	963	162	17	137	545	394	411
	.262	.340	.447	2431	638	112	9	106	375	291	279
	.291	.363	.477	2574	750	149	17	98	371	292	268
	.271	.346	.451	4228	1144	204	22	171	618	496	478
	.314	.382	.525	777	244	57	4	33	128	87	69
	.285	.360	.481	1342	382	60	6	64	209	162	168
	.275	.348	.455	3663	1006	201	20	140	537	421	379
	.288	.380	.506	629	181	34	5	31	118	91	75
	.269	.352	.484	821	221	44	6	40	122	105	104
	.295	.366	.440	872	257	46	3	25	111	99	82
	.290	.364	.487	839	243	43	3	39	141	99	84
	.273	.340	.450	878	240	47	6	32	129	92	97
	.255	.319	.424	966	246	47	3	37	125	97	105
	.276	.345	.460	2753	760	135	10	117	117	277	303
	.299	.351	.512	951	284	49	2	50	50	70	94
	.279	.360	.465	2252	628	126	16	87	629	306	244
	.276	.376	.460	1227	339	62	7	50	523	226	146
	.294	.364	.483	751	221	41	4	31	118	85	94

BILLY RIPKEN — bats right — throws right — age 28 — BAL — *2

1991	BA	OBA	SA	AB	H	2B	3B	HR	RBI	BB	SO		5-YEAR TOTALS (1987–1991) BA	OBA	SA	AB	H	2B	3B	HR	RBI	BB	SO
Total	.216	.253	.261	287	62	11	1	0	14	15	31		.247	.296	.312	1757	434	77	5	9	132	119	213
vs. Left	.270	.302	.310	100	27	4	0	0	7	5	9		.277	.326	.341	618	171	29	1	3	45	47	69
vs. Right	.187	.227	.235	187	35	7	1	0	7	10	22		.231	.280	.296	1139	263	48	4	6	87	72	144
at Home	.214	.254	.270	126	27	5	1	0	8	7	18		.245	.293	.303	867	212	39	3	2	60	58	105
on Road	.217	.253	.255	161	35	6	0	0	6	8	13		.249	.299	.320	890	222	38	2	7	72	61	108
on Grass	.214	.248	.258	248	53	9	1	0	12	12	29		.245	.292	.303	1514	371	67	3	5	104	98	183
on Turf	.231	.286	.282	39	9	2	0	0	2	3	2		.259	.322	.366	243	63	10	2	4	28	21	30
Day Games	.230	.260	.257	74	17	2	0	0	0	3	7		.219	.272	.280	393	86	15	0	3	29	28	47
Night Games	.211	.251	.263	213	45	9	1	0	14	12	24		.255	.303	.321	1364	348	62	5	6	103	91	166
April	.190	.244	.190	42	8	0	0	0	2	3	4		.195	.248	.243	210	41	7	0	1	12	14	27
May	.203	.222	.246	69	14	3	0	0	4	2	7		.242	.292	.312	285	69	15	1	1	23	21	33
June	.294	.315	.353	51	15	3	0	0	4	2	7		.243	.281	.317	325	79	16	1	2	24	15	41
July	.143	.226	.179	28	4	1	0	0	0	3	2		.255	.313	.318	333	85	14	2	1	22	29	30
August	.242	.286	.273	33	8	1	0	0	1	2	7		.278	.324	.318	324	90	10	0	1	27	22	47
Sept–Oct	.203	.239	.281	64	13	3	1	0	3	3	4		.250	.302	.343	280	70	15	1	3	24	18	35
Bases Empty	.230	.275	.275	178	41	6	1	0	0	11	19		.242	.300	.312	1068	258	53	5	4	4	85	142
Leadoff	.234	.280	.273	77	18	3	0	0	0	5	6		.247	.304	.329	389	96	19	2	3	3	31	46
Runners On Base	.193	.217	.239	109	21	5	0	0	14	4	12		.255	.291	.312	689	176	24	0	5	128	34	71
Scoring Position	.207	.226	.259	58	12	3	0	0	13	2	7		.262	.295	.317	378	99	12	0	3	119	21	48
Late and Close	.161	.212	.161	31	5	0	0	0	0	2	2		.260	.316	.291	223	58	5	1	0	12	17	27

LUIS RIVERA — bats right — throws right — age 28 — BOS — *S

1991	BA	OBA	SA	AB	H	2B	3B	HR	RBI	BB	SO		6-YEAR TOTALS (1986–1991) BA	OBA	SA	AB	H	2B	3B	HR	RBI	BB	SO
Total	.258	.318	.384	414	107	22	3	8	40	35	86		.236	.290	.343	1652	390	89	8	24	158	122	314
vs. Left	.315	.356	.537	108	34	10	1	4	16	6	25		.241	.287	.368	568	137	34	4	14	97	36	112
vs. Right	.239	.305	.330	306	73	12	2	4	24	29	61		.233	.292	.330	1084	253	55	4	10	61	86	202
at Home	.255	.336	.377	204	52	13	0	4	16	23	43		.247	.299	.363	843	208	50	3	14	95	63	149
on Road	.262	.300	.390	210	55	9	3	4	24	12	43		.225	.281	.323	809	182	39	5	10	63	59	165
on Grass	.261	.328	.385	348	91	18	2	7	35	33	78		.243	.306	.357	1040	253	54	2	20	113	90	207
on Turf	.242	.261	.379	66	16	4	1	1	5	2	8		.224	.262	.320	612	137	35	6	4	45	32	107
Day Games	.274	.345	.411	124	34	8	0	3	14	13	22		.238	.302	.366	516	123	30	0	12	54	46	88
Night Games	.252	.306	.372	290	73	14	3	5	26	22	64		.235	.285	.333	1136	267	59	8	12	104	76	226
April	.154	.154	.154	13	2	0	0	0	1	0	2		.164	.193	.218	110	18	3	0	1	7	4	21
May	.293	.392	.537	82	24	7	2	3	14	13	17		.284	.343	.431	218	62	13	2	5	27	20	37
June	.274	.348	.387	62	17	4	0	1	4	7	12		.233	.280	.324	296	69	12	0	5	24	19	51
July	.300	.363	.456	90	27	6	1	2	7	10	16		.249	.303	.401	297	74	22	4	5	30	23	58
August	.187	.218	.253	75	14	2	0	1	4	2	18		.234	.297	.333	351	82	15	1	6	35	30	62
Sept–Oct	.250	.278	.315	92	23	3	0	1	10	3	21		.224	.277	.308	380	85	24	1	2	35	26	85
Bases Empty	.278	.332	.427	234	65	11	3	6	6	16	49		.235	.288	.341	919	216	44	4	15	15	62	184
Leadoff	.300	.369	.430	100	30	7	0	2	2	9	19		.227	.285	.298	406	92	21	1	2	2	30	87
Runners On Base	.233	.300	.328	180	42	11	0	2	34	19	37		.237	.292	.347	733	174	45	4	9	143	60	130
Scoring Position	.202	.300	.303	109	22	5	0	2	33	17	25		.215	.285	.315	447	96	24	3	5	129	47	86
Late and Close	.154	.228	.173	52	8	1	0	0	3	5	15		.219	.261	.309	269	59	11	2	3	21	16	58

BIP ROBERTS — bats both — throws right — age 29 — SD — 2O

1991	BA	OBA	SA	AB	H	2B	3B	HR	RBI	BB	SO		5-YEAR TOTALS (1986–1991) BA	OBA	SA	AB	H	2B	3B	HR	RBI	BB	SO
Total	.278	.340	.344	424	118	13	3	3	32	37	71		.291	.357	.386	1559	453	69	16	16	113	156	212
vs. Left	.246	.294	.288	118	29	3	1	0	8	7	13		.272	.329	.382	589	160	29	6	8	43	45	74
vs. Right	.291	.357	.366	306	89	10	2	3	24	30	58		.302	.374	.389	970	293	40	10	8	70	111	138
at Home	.287	.331	.354	223	64	4	1	3	17	12	32		.282	.338	.370	794	224	27	8	9	57	61	107
on Road	.269	.349	.333	201	54	9	2	0	15	25	39		.299	.376	.403	765	229	42	8	7	56	95	105
on Grass	.283	.328	.354	311	88	7	3	3	26	18	45		.282	.344	.365	1165	328	42	11	11	79	105	156
on Turf	.265	.368	.319	113	30	6	0	0	6	19	26		.317	.396	.449	394	125	27	5	5	34	51	56
Day Games	.310	.357	.405	116	36	2	0	3	10	8	19		.304	.380	.399	484	147	15	5	7	36	55	76
Night Games	.266	.333	.321	308	82	11	3	0	22	29	52		.285	.347	.380	1075	306	54	11	9	77	101	136
April	.263	.349	.316	76	20	2	1	0	6	9	12		.223	.286	.320	175	39	5	3	2	11	15	27
May	.270	.345	.330	100	27	4	1	0	6	10	16		.315	.389	.431	267	84	13	6	2	20	31	39
June	.260	.313	.312	77	20	2	1	0	7	6	17		.265	.330	.356	298	79	14	5	1	22	24	46
July	.292	.347	.369	65	19	2	0	1	7	6	11		.284	.354	.343	236	67	9	1	1	20	27	28
August	.346	.393	.500	52	18	2	0	2	3	4	12		.308	.365	.442	292	90	16	1	7	20	27	39
Sept–Oct	.259	.293	.278	54	14	1	0	0	3	3	3		.323	.391	.395	291	94	12	0	3	20	32	33
Bases Empty	.272	.340	.319	301	82	8	0	2	2	27	46		.280	.357	.357	1078	302	44	9	7	7	119	153
Leadoff	.277	.354	.328	177	49	6	0	1	1	18	26		.277	.352	.361	653	181	28	6	5	5	69	99
Runners On Base	.293	.338	.407	123	36	5	3	1	30	10	25		.314	.358	.451	481	151	25	7	9	106	37	59
Scoring Position	.316	.374	.443	79	25	1	0	1	28	9	18		.285	.334	.423	281	80	17	2	6	94	24	37
Late and Close	.279	.329	.368	68	19	1	1	1	7	4	13		.269	.354	.326	242	65	4	2	2	22	30	39

IVAN RODRIGUEZ — bats right — throws right — age 21 — TEX — C

1991 / 1-YEAR TOTALS (1991)

1991	BA	OBA	SA	AB	H	2B	3B	HR	RBI	BB	SO		BA	OBA	SA	AB	H	2B	3B	HR	RBI	BB	SO
Total	.264	.276	.354	280	74	16	0	3	27	5	42		.264	.276	.354	280	74	16	0	3	27	5	42
vs. Left	.239	.260	.366	71	17	6	0	1	9	2	9		.239	.260	.366	71	17	6	0	1	9	2	9
vs. Right	.273	.282	.349	209	57	10	0	2	18	3	33		.273	.282	.349	209	57	10	0	2	18	3	33
at Home	.237	.248	.370	135	32	9	0	3	18	2	23		.237	.248	.370	135	32	9	0	3	18	2	23
on Road	.290	.302	.338	145	42	7	0	0	9	3	19		.290	.302	.338	145	42	7	0	0	9	3	19
on Grass	.280	.291	.377	239	67	14	0	3	26	4	36		.280	.291	.377	239	67	14	0	3	26	4	36
on Turf	.171	.190	.220	41	7	2	0	0	1	1	6		.171	.190	.220	41	7	2	0	0	1	1	6
Day Games	.280	.294	.400	50	14	6	0	0	4	1	8		.280	.294	.400	50	14	6	0	0	4	1	8
Night Games	.261	.272	.343	230	60	10	0	3	23	4	34		.261	.272	.343	230	60	10	0	3	23	4	34
April	.000	.000	.000	0	0	0	0	0	0	0	0		.000	.000	.000	0	0	0	0	0	0	0	0
May	.000	.000	.000	0	0	0	0	0	0	0	0		.000	.000	.000	0	0	0	0	0	0	0	0
June	.378	.368	.432	37	14	2	0	0	4	0	5		.378	.368	.432	37	14	2	0	0	4	0	5
July	.265	.282	.337	83	22	6	0	0	6	2	8		.265	.282	.337	83	22	6	0	0	6	2	8
August	.237	.237	.325	80	19	4	0	1	8	0	15		.237	.237	.325	80	19	4	0	1	8	0	15
Sept–Oct	.237	.265	.363	80	19	4	0	2	9	3	14		.237	.265	.363	80	19	4	0	2	9	3	14
Bases Empty	.236	.245	.318	157	37	7	0	2	2	2	27		.236	.245	.318	157	37	7	0	2	2	2	27
Leadoff	.238	.238	.365	63	15	2	0	2	2	0	5		.238	.238	.365	63	15	2	0	2	2	0	5
Runners On Base	.301	.315	.398	123	37	9	0	1	25	3	15		.301	.315	.398	123	37	9	0	1	25	3	15
Scoring Position	.333	.340	.471	51	17	4	0	1	23	1	8		.333	.340	.471	51	17	4	0	1	23	1	8
Late and Close	.234	.265	.234	47	11	0	0	0	1	2	8		.234	.265	.234	47	11	0	0	0	1	2	8

CHRIS SABO — bats right — throws right — age 30 — CIN — *3

1991 / 4-YEAR TOTALS (1988–1991)

1991	BA	OBA	SA	AB	H	2B	3B	HR	RBI	BB	SO		BA	OBA	SA	AB	H	2B	3B	HR	RBI	BB	SO
Total	.301	.354	.505	582	175	35	3	26	88	44	79		.278	.334	.455	1992	553	134	8	68	232	159	222
vs. Left	.358	.412	.596	193	69	17	1	9	29	16	23		.319	.384	.529	645	206	48	3	27	81	63	57
vs. Right	.272	.325	.460	389	106	18	2	17	59	28	56		.258	.310	.420	1347	347	86	5	41	151	96	165
at Home	.339	.393	.584	298	101	24	2	15	45	25	37		.294	.356	.502	992	292	73	5	41	125	89	97
on Road	.261	.314	.423	284	74	11	1	11	43	19	42		.261	.312	.409	1000	261	61	3	27	107	70	125
on Grass	.284	.333	.449	176	50	6	1	7	28	12	25		.267	.317	.425	600	160	36	1	19	69	40	73
on Turf	.308	.363	.530	406	125	29	2	19	60	32	54		.282	.342	.468	1392	393	98	7	49	163	119	149
Day Games	.247	.317	.347	150	37	7	1	2	13	15	23		.239	.313	.407	578	138	34	3	19	56	58	67
Night Games	.319	.368	.560	432	138	28	2	24	75	29	56		.293	.344	.475	1414	415	100	5	49	176	101	155
April	.222	.291	.333	72	16	2	0	2	6	6	10		.271	.335	.455	303	82	23	0	11	28	28	32
May	.263	.339	.414	99	26	3	0	4	7	12	20		.265	.324	.440	377	100	21	0	15	49	32	46
June	.315	.404	.607	89	28	7	2	5	21	12	15		.326	.392	.560	405	132	35	6	16	54	41	49
July	.341	.383	.602	88	30	6	1	5	17	5	9		.229	.291	.380	284	65	17	1	8	33	22	29
August	.351	.375	.579	114	40	11	0	5	14	4	14		.291	.327	.448	326	95	19	1	10	29	14	32
Sept–Oct	.292	.325	.467	120	35	6	0	5	23	5	11		.266	.317	.411	297	79	19	0	8	39	22	34
Bases Empty	.292	.345	.488	322	94	17	2	14	14	24	48		.280	.332	.469	1204	337	79	7	45	45	86	127
Leadoff	.282	.356	.500	156	44	8	1	8	8	17	22		.284	.350	.478	517	147	27	2	23	23	50	45
Runners On Base	.312	.366	.527	260	81	18	1	12	74	20	31		.274	.339	.434	788	216	55	1	23	187	73	95
Scoring Position	.303	.377	.538	145	44	8	1	8	64	16	18		.273	.358	.452	458	125	32	1	16	168	59	56
Late and Close	.227	.289	.352	88	20	2	0	3	9	7	12		.249	.318	.416	317	79	15	1	12	38	30	40

LUIS SALAZAR — bats right — throws right — age 36 — CHN — 3/10

1991 / 8-YEAR TOTALS (1984–1991)

1991	BA	OBA	SA	AB	H	2B	3B	HR	RBI	BB	SO		BA	OBA	SA	AB	H	2B	3B	HR	RBI	BB	SO
Total	.258	.292	.432	333	86	14	1	14	38	15	45		.258	.292	.388	2275	588	83	11	63	260	103	363
vs. Left	.274	.312	.506	164	45	8	0	10	25	8	18		.277	.307	.442	1059	293	49	6	38	148	45	149
vs. Right	.243	.273	.361	169	41	6	1	4	13	7	27		.243	.279	.340	1216	295	34	5	25	112	58	214
at Home	.261	.278	.473	165	43	11	0	8	20	4	22		.261	.294	.394	1118	292	43	5	32	117	49	181
on Road	.256	.306	.393	168	43	3	1	6	18	11	23		.256	.290	.381	1157	296	40	6	31	143	54	182
on Grass	.267	.297	.466	236	63	12	1	11	30	10	29		.263	.295	.397	1738	457	62	9	51	209	78	271
on Turf	.237	.282	.351	97	23	2	0	3	8	5	16		.244	.281	.358	537	131	21	2	12	51	25	92
Day Games	.201	.217	.376	149	30	8	0	3	14	3	21		.255	.289	.384	850	217	31	3	24	100	36	124
Night Games	.304	.350	.478	184	56	6	1	8	24	12	24		.260	.294	.390	1425	371	52	8	39	160	67	239
April	.133	.188	.333	15	2	0	0	1	1	1	2		.241	.259	.336	241	58	5	0	6	22	6	34
May	.326	.370	.558	43	14	1	0	3	6	3	6		.257	.301	.374	350	90	8	0	11	36	22	61
June	.254	.333	.373	67	17	2	0	2	7	7	10		.299	.344	.438	388	116	14	2	12	51	26	58
July	.321	.321	.566	53	17	4	0	3	4	0	8		.256	.284	.426	387	99	15	3	15	49	13	59
August	.280	.289	.440	75	21	4	1	2	9	1	6		.244	.273	.374	454	111	22	2	11	48	16	68
Sept–Oct	.188	.217	.338	80	15	3	0	3	11	3	13		.251	.282	.363	455	114	19	4	8	54	20	83
Bases Empty	.267	.296	.446	195	52	6	1	9	9	7	22		.260	.284	.390	1300	338	46	9	35	35	39	200
Leadoff	.329	.338	.632	76	25	3	1	6	6	1	7		.286	.305	.445	521	149	19	5	18	18	14	73
Runners On Base	.246	.288	.413	138	34	8	0	5	29	8	23		.256	.302	.385	975	250	37	2	28	225	64	163
Scoring Position	.192	.224	.370	73	14	4	0	3	24	3	13		.258	.309	.390	566	146	25	1	16	195	43	92
Late and Close	.329	.372	.507	73	24	4	0	3	11	5	5		.298	.338	.416	409	122	15	3	9	60	24	63

JUAN SAMUEL — bats right — throws right — age 32 — LA — *2

1991	BA	OBA	SA	AB	H	2B	3B	HR	RBI	BB	SO	8-YEAR TOTALS (1984–1991) BA	OBA	SA	AB	H	2B	3B	HR	RBI	BB	SO
Total	.271	.328	.389	594	161	22	6	12	58	49	133	.259	.312	.417	4856	1259	234	79	125	545	328	1142
vs. Left	.252	.292	.398	246	62	11	2	7	26	13	59	.257	.310	.422	1531	394	78	21	44	171	108	350
vs. Right	.284	.352	.382	348	99	11	4	5	32	36	74	.260	.312	.415	3325	865	156	58	81	374	220	792
at Home	.254	.315	.342	295	75	12	1	4	26	25	67	.258	.319	.424	2372	611	122	43	62	278	187	548
on Road	.288	.342	.435	299	86	10	5	8	32	24	66	.261	.305	.411	2484	648	112	36	63	267	141	594
on Grass	.269	.322	.382	450	121	16	4	9	46	34	103	.258	.310	.391	1929	497	70	20	49	203	130	473
on Turf	.278	.348	.410	144	40	6	2	3	12	15	30	.260	.313	.435	2927	762	164	59	76	342	198	669
Day Games	.302	.337	.413	189	57	6	3	3	17	10	43	.268	.319	.442	1460	391	74	26	43	169	100	326
Night Games	.257	.324	.378	405	104	16	3	9	41	39	90	.256	.309	.406	3396	868	160	53	82	376	228	816
April	.301	.326	.518	83	25	4	1	4	15	3	14	.264	.318	.402	550	145	27	11	9	50	41	131
May	.351	.421	.447	94	33	6	0	1	12	12	22	.264	.312	.417	832	220	35	10	24	91	53	195
June	.309	.355	.409	110	34	2	0	3	12	9	24	.268	.324	.428	874	234	40	14	24	110	66	207
July	.221	.250	.317	104	23	2	1	2	6	4	20	.267	.322	.448	834	223	40	15	27	110	57	189
August	.209	.308	.264	91	19	1	2	0	7	12	26	.235	.289	.374	855	201	40	14	17	97	61	216
Sept–Oct	.241	.309	.393	112	27	7	2	2	6	9	27	.259	.307	.428	911	236	52	15	24	87	50	204
Bases Empty	.260	.316	.375	339	88	12	3	7	7	28	81	.253	.307	.403	2911	737	146	40	70	70	201	699
Leadoff	.229	.314	.352	105	24	2	1	3	3	13	22	.250	.312	.413	1352	338	70	21	36	36	108	304
Runners On Base	.286	.344	.408	255	73	10	3	5	51	21	52	.268	.319	.439	1945	522	88	39	55	475	127	443
Scoring Position	.248	.346	.357	129	32	6	1	2	41	19	28	.262	.320	.440	1166	305	49	27	35	416	96	275
Late and Close	.302	.382	.396	96	29	4	1	1	14	12	25	.255	.324	.410	752	192	32	12	20	103	70	199

RYNE SANDBERG — bats right — throws right — age 33 — CHN — *2

1991	BA	OBA	SA	AB	H	2B	3B	HR	RBI	BB	SO	8-YEAR TOTALS (1984–1991) BA	OBA	SA	AB	H	2B	3B	HR	RBI	BB	SO
Total	.291	.379	.485	585	170	32	2	26	100	87	89	.294	.355	.480	4822	1416	230	50	190	648	464	705
vs. Left	.357	.456	.565	207	74	19	0	8	27	39	23	.303	.378	.483	1335	404	79	12	46	157	165	170
vs. Right	.254	.336	.442	378	96	13	2	18	73	48	66	.290	.345	.479	3487	1012	151	38	144	491	299	535
at Home	.309	.394	.526	291	90	14	2	15	54	43	39	.310	.370	.526	2395	743	119	34	110	374	236	351
on Road	.272	.364	.446	294	80	18	0	11	46	44	50	.277	.339	.435	2427	673	111	16	80	274	228	354
on Grass	.303	.390	.528	409	124	22	2	22	78	62	57	.301	.360	.504	3428	1033	162	42	149	501	326	496
on Turf	.261	.353	.386	176	46	10	0	4	22	25	32	.275	.341	.423	1394	383	68	8	41	147	138	209
Day Games	.317	.384	.522	293	93	17	2	13	48	35	42	.305	.364	.499	2888	881	143	36	115	393	276	399
Night Games	.264	.375	.449	292	77	15	0	13	52	52	47	.277	.340	.452	1934	535	87	14	75	255	188	306
April	.202	.287	.274	84	17	3	0	1	2	10	9	.236	.295	.363	652	154	33	4	14	62	54	90
May	.340	.386	.602	103	35	9	0	6	20	9	15	.327	.383	.538	855	280	50	11	36	120	79	121
June	.320	.407	.534	103	33	5	1	5	18	15	10	.311	.374	.558	782	243	36	11	45	124	75	100
July	.329	.476	.544	79	26	5	0	4	19	22	13	.283	.345	.438	756	214	29	8	24	91	74	106
August	.236	.315	.391	110	26	2	0	5	17	13	26	.297	.358	.481	886	263	33	5	40	117	87	149
Sept–Oct	.311	.402	.547	106	33	8	1	5	24	18	16	.294	.359	.478	891	262	49	11	31	134	95	139
Bases Empty	.254	.331	.414	331	84	15	1	12	12	36	53	.284	.337	.476	2865	814	144	24	119	119	223	425
Leadoff	.273	.402	.511	88	24	7	1	4	4	18	16	.290	.343	.552	932	270	54	11	56	56	74	142
Runners On Base	.339	.436	.579	254	86	17	1	14	88	51	36	.308	.378	.487	1957	602	86	26	71	529	241	280
Scoring Position	.341	.440	.600	135	46	9	1	8	70	31	15	.283	.369	.446	1097	310	41	18	34	425	169	176
Late and Close	.252	.375	.387	111	28	4	1	3	19	23	23	.283	.353	.448	762	216	24	13	25	118	85	132

BENITO SANTIAGO — bats right — throws right — age 27 — SD — *C/O

1991	BA	OBA	SA	AB	H	2B	3B	HR	RBI	BB	SO	6-YEAR TOTALS (1986–1991) BA	OBA	SA	AB	H	2B	3B	HR	RBI	BB	SO
Total	.266	.295	.402	580	154	22	3	17	87	23	114	.265	.300	.409	2486	660	103	15	75	333	118	464
vs. Left	.279	.315	.475	204	57	12	2	8	34	10	41	.282	.320	.445	779	220	39	5	26	108	44	143
vs. Right	.258	.284	.362	376	97	10	1	9	53	13	73	.258	.290	.393	1707	440	64	10	49	225	74	321
at Home	.244	.267	.334	287	70	8	0	6	34	8	49	.259	.293	.398	1250	324	51	9	35	161	60	223
on Road	.287	.322	.468	293	84	14	3	11	53	15	65	.272	.306	.421	1236	336	52	6	40	172	58	241
on Grass	.277	.300	.429	441	122	16	3	15	68	14	83	.268	.300	.423	1846	494	73	12	63	259	83	349
on Turf	.230	.279	.317	139	32	6	0	2	19	9	31	.259	.299	.372	640	166	30	3	12	74	35	115
Day Games	.328	.365	.526	137	45	5	2	6	25	8	24	.290	.338	.429	611	177	23	4	18	80	43	107
Night Games	.246	.273	.363	443	109	17	1	11	62	15	90	.258	.287	.403	1875	483	80	11	57	253	75	357
April	.298	.306	.405	84	25	3	0	2	12	1	15	.286	.304	.448	377	108	15	2	14	51	9	62
May	.175	.204	.278	97	17	1	0	3	11	3	26	.227	.254	.316	449	102	12	2	8	47	15	86
June	.287	.308	.416	101	29	5	1	2	13	4	19	.274	.317	.390	369	101	15	2	8	46	23	83
July	.235	.264	.435	85	20	5	0	4	9	3	19	.275	.321	.433	305	84	20	2	8	36	19	59
August	.252	.294	.369	103	26	2	2	2	13	5	22	.270	.315	.430	437	118	15	5	15	63	29	75
Sept–Oct	.336	.378	.500	110	37	6	0	4	29	7	13	.268	.297	.443	549	147	26	2	22	90	23	99
Bases Empty	.262	.298	.400	290	76	8	1	10	10	11	58	.275	.309	.412	1333	366	53	8	38	38	57	261
Leadoff	.299	.342	.411	107	32	1	1	3	3	5	18	.276	.310	.381	540	149	19	1	12	12	24	105
Runners On Base	.269	.291	.403	290	78	14	2	7	77	12	56	.255	.289	.407	1153	294	50	7	37	295	61	203
Scoring Position	.273	.294	.436	172	47	8	1	6	72	8	40	.241	.281	.394	675	163	27	5	22	252	45	142
Late and Close	.321	.354	.491	106	34	4	1	4	20	6	16	.316	.349	.460	465	147	17	4	14	64	23	87

STEVE SAX — bats right — throws right — age 32 — NYA — *2/3D

1991	BA	OBA	SA	AB	H	2B	3B	HR	RBI	BB	SO		8-YR BA	OBA	SA	AB	H	2B	3B	HR	RBI	BB	SO
Total	.304	.345	.414	652	198	38	2	10	56	41	38		.287	.341	.365	4850	1393	204	30	38	398	391	394
vs. Left	.344	.390	.507	215	74	20	0	5	20	17	6		.300	.358	.398	1572	472	92	7	16	125	145	94
vs. Right	.284	.322	.368	437	124	18	2	5	36	24	32		.281	.332	.349	3278	921	112	23	22	273	246	300
at Home	.291	.340	.413	327	95	20	1	6	27	25	19		.280	.337	.354	2359	661	99	10	18	188	199	184
on Road	.317	.350	.415	325	103	18	1	4	29	16	19		.294	.345	.376	2491	732	105	20	20	210	192	210
on Grass	.299	.341	.420	555	166	33	2	10	48	36	32		.281	.336	.356	3729	1048	147	20	31	292	311	298
on Turf	.330	.368	.381	97	32	5	0	0	8	5	6		.308	.356	.395	1121	345	57	10	7	106	80	96
Day Games	.271	.338	.372	188	51	11	1	2	21	18	13		.282	.338	.358	1489	420	65	9	10	138	128	107
Night Games	.317	.348	.431	464	147	27	1	8	35	23	25		.289	.342	.368	3361	973	139	21	28	260	263	287
April	.284	.329	.338	74	21	1	0	1	11	5	7		.274	.330	.343	566	155	17	2	6	55	49	43
May	.216	.264	.297	111	24	6	0	1	8	8	6		.280	.342	.380	810	227	39	6	10	62	77	72
June	.348	.393	.438	112	39	7	0	1	8	8	5		.294	.351	.353	846	249	29	6	3	69	73	72
July	.326	.383	.512	86	28	7	0	3	8	7	4		.292	.336	.380	798	233	35	4	9	72	53	66
August	.310	.350	.381	126	39	7	1	0	9	8	8		.266	.315	.318	906	241	41	3	0	60	62	84
Sept—Oct	.329	.349	.497	143	47	10	1	4	12	5	8		.312	.366	.410	924	288	43	9	10	80	77	57
Bases Empty	.313	.353	.433	416	130	25	2	7	7	25	22		.287	.335	.369	3176	910	148	18	26	26	220	246
Leadoff	.337	.367	.476	187	63	12	1	4	4	9	6		.278	.324	.360	1677	466	72	9	16	16	108	124
Runners On Base	.288	.331	.381	236	68	13	0	3	49	16	16		.289	.352	.358	1674	483	56	12	12	372	171	148
Scoring Position	.318	.351	.424	132	42	8	0	2	44	10	11		.297	.367	.375	1015	301	37	11	7	353	126	97
Late and Close	.243	.252	.311	103	25	4	0	1	7	2	6		.320	.373	.407	757	242	32	5	8	83	69	61

8-YEAR TOTALS (1984–1991)

DICK SCHOFIELD — bats right — throws right — age 30 — CAL — *S

1991	BA	OBA	SA	AB	H	2B	3B	HR	RBI	BB	SO		8-YR BA	OBA	SA	AB	H	2B	3B	HR	RBI	BB	SO
Total	.225	.310	.260	427	96	9	3	0	31	50	69		.233	.306	.320	3341	777	102	27	45	275	323	501
vs. Left	.183	.314	.191	115	21	1	0	0	8	22	15		.246	.327	.341	1124	276	40	11	15	74	126	144
vs. Right	.240	.309	.285	312	75	8	3	0	23	28	54		.226	.295	.309	2217	501	62	16	30	201	197	357
at Home	.209	.286	.237	211	44	4	1	0	19	22	29		.223	.294	.300	1669	372	41	12	21	145	153	253
on Road	.241	.333	.282	216	52	5	2	0	12	28	40		.242	.317	.340	1672	405	61	15	24	130	170	248
on Grass	.229	.307	.268	358	82	8	3	0	29	37	53		.231	.303	.317	2822	652	81	24	38	238	266	421
on Turf	.203	.329	.217	69	14	1	0	0	2	13	16		.241	.320	.333	519	125	21	3	7	37	57	80
Day Games	.224	.321	.265	98	22	2	1	0	10	13	15		.242	.317	.342	884	214	33	11	11	87	91	126
Night Games	.225	.307	.258	329	74	7	2	0	21	37	54		.229	.302	.312	2457	563	69	16	34	188	232	375
April	.275	.403	.275	51	14	0	0	0	2	10	10		.246	.309	.374	422	104	14	2	12	48	35	64
May	.254	.319	.349	63	16	4	1	0	9	5	10		.216	.276	.310	513	111	20	5	6	45	34	85
June	.264	.369	.292	72	19	2	0	0	6	12	10		.212	.295	.282	652	138	17	4	7	52	72	98
July	.233	.291	.260	73	17	2	0	0	6	6	9		.229	.311	.326	525	120	10	4	11	40	60	73
August	.176	.278	.176	85	15	0	0	0	3	11	12		.262	.337	.346	596	156	23	3	7	57	62	85
Sept—Oct	.181	.236	.241	83	15	1	2	0	5	6	18		.234	.304	.300	633	148	18	9	2	33	60	96
Bases Empty	.178	.255	.219	242	43	4	3	0	0	23	45		.233	.296	.321	2005	468	58	17	28	28	163	290
Leadoff	.143	.231	.181	105	15	0	2	0	0	10	17		.238	.299	.326	877	209	22	8	13	13	68	116
Runners On Base	.286	.380	.314	185	53	5	0	0	31	27	24		.231	.319	.317	1336	309	44	10	17	247	160	211
Scoring Position	.255	.374	.282	110	28	3	0	0	31	21	15		.231	.327	.336	748	173	25	7	13	233	104	132
Late and Close	.200	.297	.215	65	13	1	0	0	3	8	11		.229	.306	.299	489	112	11	4	5	38	53	83

8-YEAR TOTALS (1984–1991)

MIKE SCIOSCIA — bats left — throws right — age 34 — LA — *C

1991	BA	OBA	SA	AB	H	2B	3B	HR	RBI	BB	SO		8-YR BA	OBA	SA	AB	H	2B	3B	HR	RBI	BB	SO
Total	.264	.353	.391	345	91	16	2	8	40	47	32		.265	.355	.373	3200	849	163	7	56	340	438	216
vs. Left	.194	.283	.301	103	20	2	0	3	13	11	11		.231	.312	.309	761	176	24	1	11	71	86	64
vs. Right	.293	.384	.430	242	71	14	2	5	27	36	21		.276	.368	.393	2439	673	139	6	45	269	352	152
at Home	.288	.380	.399	163	47	9	0	3	22	26	15		.269	.361	.348	1514	407	66	0	18	162	219	97
on Road	.242	.329	.385	182	44	7	2	5	18	21	17		.262	.349	.396	1686	442	97	7	38	178	219	119
on Grass	.292	.372	.424	250	73	14	2	5	33	34	21		.277	.365	.379	2318	641	119	4	37	241	325	155
on Turf	.189	.306	.305	95	18	2	0	3	7	13	11		.236	.328	.357	882	208	44	3	19	99	113	61
Day Games	.314	.404	.438	121	38	7	1	2	13	16	10		.279	.372	.387	996	278	54	4	15	96	140	63
Night Games	.237	.326	.366	224	53	9	1	6	27	31	22		.259	.347	.367	2204	571	109	3	41	244	298	153
April	.317	.380	.444	63	20	3	1	1	9	7	4		.308	.395	.424	484	149	28	2	8	60	70	35
May	.193	.361	.333	57	11	2	0	2	6	14	6		.243	.335	.347	556	135	20	1	12	50	74	39
June	.310	.388	.431	58	18	7	0	0	7	7	7		.250	.341	.322	484	121	20	0	5	54	65	34
July	.292	.333	.333	24	7	1	0	0	5	2	2		.279	.368	.384	451	126	35	0	6	56	67	28
August	.194	.308	.239	67	13	0	0	1	4	11	10		.264	.359	.373	592	156	28	2	11	58	87	48
Sept—Oct	.289	.345	.513	76	22	3	1	4	9	6	3		.256	.338	.389	633	162	32	2	16	62	75	32
Bases Empty	.256	.339	.427	199	51	8	1	8	8	23	17		.260	.343	.388	1872	486	97	6	44	44	224	131
Leadoff	.256	.323	.467	90	23	2	1	5	5	8	6		.246	.339	.397	740	182	36	2	24	24	100	48
Runners On Base	.274	.371	.342	146	40	8	1	0	32	24	15		.273	.370	.352	1328	363	66	1	12	296	214	85
Scoring Position	.276	.368	.368	87	24	6	1	0	31	15	9		.261	.377	.337	754	197	37	1	6	273	151	54
Late and Close	.317	.429	.413	63	20	0	0	2	9	11	10		.245	.349	.330	564	138	25	1	7	41	89	54

8-YEAR TOTALS (1984–1991)

TERRY SHUMPERT — bats right — throws right — age 26 — KC — *2

1991	BA	OBA	SA	AB	H	2B	3B	HR	RBI	BB	SO
Total	.217	.283	.322	369	80	16	4	5	34	30	75
vs. Left	.207	.277	.296	135	28	6	0	2	12	9	25
vs. Right	.222	.286	.338	234	52	10	4	3	22	21	50
at Home	.219	.282	.311	183	40	8	3	1	16	14	35
on Road	.215	.283	.333	186	40	8	1	4	18	16	40
on Grass	.208	.286	.333	144	30	6	0	4	15	15	32
on Turf	.222	.280	.316	225	50	10	4	1	19	15	43
Day Games	.155	.237	.223	103	16	2	1	1	7	10	30
Night Games	.241	.300	.361	266	64	14	3	4	27	20	45
April	.176	.218	.235	51	9	1	1	0	5	3	13
May	.255	.300	.364	55	14	4	1	0	4	3	9
June	.179	.253	.328	67	12	1	0	3	8	7	12
July	.240	.305	.333	75	18	2	1	1	8	6	9
August	.299	.397	.403	67	20	5	1	0	4	10	17
Sept–Oct	.130	.175	.241	54	7	3	0	1	5	1	15
Bases Empty	.222	.297	.362	207	46	11	3	4	4	19	45
Leadoff	.213	.307	.371	89	19	4	2	2	2	9	23
Runners On Base	.210	.264	.272	162	34	5	1	1	30	11	30
Scoring Position	.266	.333	.319	94	25	3	1	0	27	9	21
Late and Close	.214	.292	.357	42	9	2	2	0	2	5	8

2-YEAR TOTALS (1990–1991)

	BA	OBA	SA	AB	H	2B	3B	HR	RBI	BB	SO
Total	.228	.284	.330	460	105	22	5	5	42	32	92
vs. Left	.236	.291	.327	165	39	9	0	2	15	9	28
vs. Right	.224	.281	.332	295	66	13	5	3	27	23	64
at Home	.228	.282	.325	228	52	11	4	1	18	14	42
on Road	.228	.286	.336	232	53	11	1	4	24	18	50
on Grass	.226	.289	.337	190	43	9	0	4	21	17	42
on Turf	.230	.281	.326	270	62	13	5	1	21	15	50
Day Games	.157	.230	.243	115	18	3	2	1	8	10	32
Night Games	.252	.302	.359	345	87	19	3	4	34	22	60
April	.176	.218	.235	51	9	1	1	0	5	3	13
May	.273	.296	.371	143	39	10	2	0	12	5	25
June	.171	.244	.314	70	12	1	0	3	8	7	13
July	.240	.305	.333	75	18	2	1	1	8	6	9
August	.299	.397	.403	67	20	5	1	0	4	10	17
Sept–Oct	.130	.190	.241	54	7	3	0	1	5	1	15
Bases Empty	.227	.290	.358	260	59	14	3	4	4	20	53
Leadoff	.213	.292	.361	108	23	6	2	2	2	9	26
Runners On Base	.230	.277	.295	200	46	8	1	1	38	12	39
Scoring Position	.274	.333	.333	117	32	5	1	0	34	10	27
Late and Close	.302	.348	.460	63	19	4	3	0	4	5	10

RUBEN SIERRA — bats both — throws right — age 27 — TEX — *O

1991	BA	OBA	SA	AB	H	2B	3B	HR	RBI	BB	SO
Total	.307	.357	.502	661	203	44	5	25	116	56	91
vs. Left	.335	.393	.548	188	63	15	2	7	32	20	22
vs. Right	.296	.342	.484	473	140	29	3	18	84	36	69
at Home	.320	.353	.521	328	105	22	4	12	61	18	44
on Road	.294	.360	.483	333	98	22	1	13	55	38	47
on Grass	.302	.349	.507	556	168	35	5	23	98	43	76
on Turf	.333	.397	.476	105	35	9	0	2	18	13	15
Day Games	.307	.368	.488	127	39	11	0	4	21	14	16
Night Games	.307	.354	.506	534	164	33	5	21	95	42	75
April	.273	.304	.530	66	18	5	0	4	13	3	8
May	.386	.445	.561	114	44	4	2	4	21	13	11
June	.325	.408	.544	114	37	9	2	4	22	16	17
July	.224	.257	.364	107	24	6	0	3	16	5	19
August	.278	.315	.429	133	37	9	1	3	18	8	21
Sept–Oct	.339	.378	.591	127	43	11	0	7	26	11	15
Bases Empty	.281	.347	.469	320	90	23	2	11	11	32	56
Leadoff	.274	.353	.444	124	34	9	0	4	4	15	21
Runners On Base	.331	.366	.534	341	113	21	3	14	105	24	35
Scoring Position	.344	.385	.586	186	64	12	3	9	92	18	22
Late and Close	.289	.359	.456	114	33	7	0	4	20	13	17

6-YEAR TOTALS (1986–1991)

	BA	OBA	SA	AB	H	2B	3B	HR	RBI	BB	SO
Total	.280	.325	.474	3543	993	196	37	139	586	253	529
vs. Left	.301	.333	.497	1138	342	76	8	44	188	66	123
vs. Right	.271	.321	.463	2405	651	120	29	95	398	187	406
at Home	.287	.329	.510	1724	495	94	24	81	321	116	279
on Road	.274	.321	.440	1819	498	102	13	58	265	137	250
on Grass	.276	.321	.473	2926	808	159	30	119	499	209	439
on Turf	.300	.344	.480	617	185	37	7	20	87	44	90
Day Games	.262	.312	.432	702	184	43	2	24	120	57	99
Night Games	.285	.328	.485	2841	809	153	35	115	466	196	430
April	.259	.314	.482	359	93	23	3	17	68	30	62
May	.304	.355	.466	517	157	27	6	15	78	41	86
June	.288	.342	.491	687	198	46	8	25	103	55	100
July	.255	.289	.470	581	148	28	8	27	103	32	87
August	.286	.325	.489	665	190	38	3	27	107	45	99
Sept–Oct	.282	.321	.451	734	207	34	3	28	127	50	95
Bases Empty	.264	.309	.450	1818	480	95	20	68	68	112	293
Leadoff	.272	.316	.463	756	206	41	8	29	29	45	103
Runners On Base	.297	.341	.499	1725	513	101	17	71	518	141	236
Scoring Position	.291	.335	.501	970	282	52	13	42	441	89	151
Late and Close	.277	.335	.457	560	155	26	6	21	86	50	81

JOEL SKINNER — bats right — throws right — age 31 — CLE — C

1991	BA	OBA	SA	AB	H	2B	3B	HR	RBI	BB	SO
Total	.243	.279	.303	284	69	14	0	1	24	14	67
vs. Left	.307	.319	.341	88	27	3	0	0	7	2	19
vs. Right	.214	.262	.286	196	42	11	0	1	17	12	48
at Home	.261	.300	.324	142	37	9	0	0	15	7	32
on Road	.225	.258	.282	142	32	5	0	1	9	7	35
on Grass	.268	.308	.338	231	62	13	0	1	22	13	47
on Turf	.132	.148	.151	53	7	1	0	0	2	1	20
Day Games	.190	.242	.262	84	16	3	0	1	8	6	24
Night Games	.265	.295	.320	200	53	11	0	0	16	8	43
April	.300	.300	.400	10	3	1	0	0	2	0	4
May	.327	.333	.481	52	17	5	0	1	8	1	7
June	.209	.229	.254	67	14	3	0	0	4	2	19
July	.154	.214	.154	26	4	0	0	0	1	2	9
August	.215	.279	.253	79	17	3	0	0	8	6	17
Sept–Oct	.280	.321	.320	50	14	2	0	0	3	3	11
Bases Empty	.250	.292	.296	152	38	4	0	1	1	9	38
Leadoff	.234	.300	.328	64	15	3	0	1	1	6	20
Runners On Base	.235	.264	.311	132	31	10	0	0	23	5	29
Scoring Position	.176	.237	.221	68	12	3	0	0	19	5	17
Late and Close	.255	.309	.314	51	13	3	0	0	3	4	10

8-YEAR TOTALS (1984–1991)

	BA	OBA	SA	AB	H	2B	3B	HR	RBI	BB	SO
Total	.228	.269	.311	1430	326	62	3	17	135	80	386
vs. Left	.233	.280	.294	476	111	20	0	3	45	31	109
vs. Right	.225	.264	.320	954	215	42	3	14	90	49	277
at Home	.217	.260	.285	687	149	30	1	5	63	38	188
on Road	.238	.278	.335	743	177	32	2	12	72	42	198
on Grass	.232	.275	.316	1201	279	55	3	13	117	70	321
on Turf	.205	.242	.288	229	47	7	0	4	18	10	65
Day Games	.239	.284	.329	468	112	22	1	6	52	29	132
Night Games	.222	.262	.302	962	214	40	2	11	83	51	254
April	.131	.178	.204	137	18	5	1	1	13	7	43
May	.252	.278	.380	242	61	14	1	5	25	9	52
June	.235	.272	.290	293	69	13	0	1	21	15	78
July	.223	.282	.355	197	44	11	0	5	28	16	61
August	.198	.243	.244	242	48	8	0	1	20	14	73
Sept–Oct	.270	.312	.348	319	86	11	0	4	28	19	79
Bases Empty	.225	.267	.302	830	187	30	2	10	10	45	242
Leadoff	.212	.266	.283	353	75	19	0	2	2	25	101
Runners On Base	.232	.273	.323	600	139	32	1	7	125	35	144
Scoring Position	.236	.292	.346	301	71	16	1	5	115	25	73
Late and Close	.239	.287	.330	176	42	10	0	2	10	12	46

LONNIE SMITH — bats right — throws right — age 37 — ATL — O

1991	BA	OBA	SA	AB	H	2B	3B	HR	RBI	BB	SO	8-YEAR TOTALS (1984–1991) BA	OBA	SA	AB	H	2B	3B	HR	RBI	BB	SO
Total	.275	.377	.394	353	97	19	1	7	44	50	64	.278	.365	.409	3137	871	160	32	63	322	390	541
vs. Left	.342	.438	.439	114	39	9	1	0	11	18	22	.293	.376	.443	1084	318	68	14	22	106	140	169
vs. Right	.243	.347	.372	239	58	10	0	7	33	32	42	.269	.359	.392	2053	553	92	18	41	216	250	372
at Home	.290	.374	.435	193	56	10	0	6	31	23	35	.288	.376	.424	1539	444	86	19	28	172	199	255
on Road	.256	.380	.344	160	41	9	1	1	13	27	29	.267	.354	.395	1598	427	74	13	35	150	191	286
on Grass	.279	.376	.404	280	78	14	0	7	37	39	48	.287	.371	.435	1676	481	89	12	45	188	206	300
on Turf	.260	.379	.356	73	19	5	1	0	7	11	16	.267	.357	.380	1461	390	71	20	18	134	184	241
Day Games	.247	.354	.358	81	20	4	1	1	10	14	21	.279	.362	.411	864	241	43	10	17	74	107	168
Night Games	.283	.384	.404	272	77	15	0	6	34	36	43	.277	.366	.409	2273	630	117	22	46	248	283	373
April	.000	.000	.000	1	0	0	0	0	0	0	0	.281	.389	.416	310	87	14	5	6	33	48	64
May	.288	.432	.441	59	17	3	0	2	10	12	15	.254	.368	.368	402	102	17	4	7	37	64	78
June	.237	.311	.338	80	19	3	1	1	10	8	11	.267	.351	.441	506	135	24	11	14	66	61	73
July	.308	.430	.462	65	20	4	0	2	11	13	13	.301	.400	.439	554	167	29	4	13	53	84	94
August	.328	.391	.397	58	19	4	0	0	4	4	9	.277	.348	.379	665	184	35	3	9	60	65	111
Sept–Oct	.244	.349	.367	90	22	5	0	2	9	13	16	.280	.347	.413	700	196	41	5	14	73	68	121
Bases Empty	.266	.372	.388	214	57	12	1	4	4	30	42	.269	.351	.398	1994	536	95	12	46	46	222	346
Leadoff	.310	.400	.460	113	35	6	1	3	3	13	22	.272	.341	.393	918	250	42	6	19	19	86	157
Runners On Base	.288	.384	.403	139	40	7	0	3	40	20	22	.293	.387	.430	1143	335	65	20	17	276	168	195
Scoring Position	.299	.391	.381	97	29	5	0	1	36	15	16	.268	.378	.367	665	178	25	10	7	232	120	137
Late and Close	.232	.368	.286	56	13	3	0	0	1	8	10	.240	.358	.340	470	113	17	6	6	37	72	99

OZZIE SMITH — bats both — throws right — age 38 — SL — *S

1991	BA	OBA	SA	AB	H	2B	3B	HR	RBI	BB	SO	8-YEAR TOTALS (1984–1991) BA	OBA	SA	AB	H	2B	3B	HR	RBI	BB	SO
Total	.285	.380	.367	550	157	30	3	3	50	83	36	.276	.359	.349	4293	1184	209	29	16	428	562	256
vs. Left	.262	.355	.377	244	64	18	2	2	24	34	18	.275	.364	.370	1588	436	100	6	13	153	226	98
vs. Right	.304	.399	.359	306	93	12	1	1	26	49	18	.277	.356	.337	2705	748	109	23	3	275	336	158
at Home	.323	.416	.416	291	94	19	1	2	28	46	18	.281	.368	.357	2106	592	108	14	8	221	290	128
on Road	.243	.338	.313	259	63	11	2	1	22	37	18	.271	.350	.342	2187	592	101	15	8	207	272	128
on Grass	.197	.274	.265	132	26	7	1	0	7	14	11	.267	.335	.336	1153	308	58	9	1	105	120	73
on Turf	.313	.411	.400	418	131	23	2	3	43	69	25	.279	.367	.354	3140	876	151	20	15	323	442	183
Day Games	.280	.341	.373	150	42	10	2	0	12	13	7	.286	.360	.365	1418	406	73	10	6	148	163	74
Night Games	.287	.393	.365	400	115	20	1	3	38	70	29	.271	.358	.342	2875	778	136	19	10	280	399	182
April	.261	.373	.290	69	18	2	0	0	4	12	4	.250	.346	.308	519	130	17	2	3	51	80	31
May	.387	.467	.441	93	36	5	0	0	13	14	6	.286	.364	.358	776	222	44	3	2	76	93	42
June	.282	.390	.388	85	24	7	1	0	12	15	7	.281	.369	.351	769	216	38	5	2	92	110	47
July	.261	.375	.295	88	23	3	0	0	4	16	7	.289	.361	.366	662	191	35	5	2	65	74	37
August	.277	.371	.406	101	28	9	2	2	9	15	6	.255	.338	.326	749	191	32	6	3	67	95	50
Sept–Oct	.246	.312	.360	114	28	10	0	1	8	11	6	.286	.369	.373	818	234	43	8	4	77	110	49
Bases Empty	.276	.379	.339	333	92	16	1	1	1	55	23	.265	.347	.336	2544	673	128	14	9	9	316	170
Leadoff	.272	.405	.330	103	28	4	1	0	0	23	6	.278	.375	.355	849	236	47	6	2	2	130	42
Runners On Base	.300	.381	.410	217	65	14	2	2	49	28	13	.292	.376	.368	1749	511	81	15	7	419	246	86
Scoring Position	.273	.374	.367	139	38	6	2	1	43	23	9	.271	.374	.337	1112	301	45	7	5	385	199	61
Late and Close	.237	.379	.276	76	18	1	1	0	13	17	7	.268	.362	.349	714	191	28	7	5	90	108	42

LUIS SOJO — bats right — throws right — age 26 — CAL — *2/S3OD

1991	BA	OBA	SA	AB	H	2B	3B	HR	RBI	BB	SO	2-YEAR TOTALS (1990–1991) BA	OBA	SA	AB	H	2B	3B	HR	RBI	BB	SO
Total	.258	.295	.327	364	94	14	1	3	20	14	26	.252	.291	.322	444	112	17	1	4	29	19	31
vs. Left	.298	.328	.377	114	34	7	1	0	5	5	6	.280	.316	.353	150	42	9	1	0	7	8	9
vs. Right	.240	.280	.304	250	60	7	0	3	15	9	20	.238	.277	.306	294	70	8	0	4	22	11	22
at Home	.239	.287	.284	176	42	5	0	1	6	11	11	.236	.284	.283	191	45	6	0	1	8	12	11
on Road	.277	.303	.367	188	52	9	1	2	14	3	15	.265	.295	.352	253	67	11	1	3	21	7	20
on Grass	.256	.297	.298	305	78	10	0	1	12	14	21	.251	.294	.303	350	88	12	0	2	19	17	25
on Turf	.271	.283	.475	59	16	4	1	2	8	0	5	.255	.278	.394	94	24	5	1	2	10	2	6
Day Games	.269	.310	.373	67	18	4	0	1	5	3	6	.261	.309	.352	88	23	5	0	1	5	5	7
Night Games	.256	.292	.316	297	76	10	1	2	15	11	20	.250	.286	.315	356	89	12	1	3	24	14	24
April	.241	.268	.296	54	13	1	0	1	3	1	3	.241	.268	.296	54	13	1	1	0	3	1	3
May	.196	.224	.268	56	11	4	0	1	3	2	4	.196	.224	.268	56	11	4	0	1	3	2	4
June	.255	.314	.319	47	12	3	0	0	4	2	2	.255	.314	.319	47	12	3	0	0	4	2	2
July	.304	.314	.348	69	21	3	0	0	5	1	9	.286	.314	.316	98	28	3	0	0	4	2	2
August	.244	.289	.385	78	19	2	0	3	4	5	4	.236	.276	.382	110	26	4	0	4	10	6	9
Sept–Oct	.300	.354	.317	60	18	1	0	0	3	2	4	.278	.329	.304	79	22	2	0	0	3	5	5
Bases Empty	.268	.321	.356	194	52	8	0	3	3	11	16	.258	.311	.339	233	60	10	0	3	3	14	19
Leadoff	.259	.333	.309	81	21	4	0	0	0	7	5	.245	.327	.296	98	24	5	0	0	0	9	6
Runners On Base	.247	.294	.294	170	42	6	1	0	17	3	10	.246	.267	.303	211	52	7	1	1	26	5	12
Scoring Position	.225	.248	.284	102	23	6	0	0	16	3	6	.234	.263	.313	128	30	7	1	1	25	5	6
Late and Close	.318	.388	.341	44	14	1	0	0	4	2	2	.300	.373	.317	60	18	1	0	0	2	6	2

SAMMY SOSA — bats right — throws right — age 24 — CHA — *O/D

1991	BA	OBA	SA	AB	H	2B	3B	HR	RBI	BB	SO		3-YR BA	OBA	SA	AB	H	2B	3B	HR	RBI	BB	SO
Total	.203	.240	.335	316	64	10	1	10	33	14	98		.228	.273	.376	1031	235	44	11	29	116	58	295
vs. Left	.227	.277	.383	128	29	5	0	5	11	8	39		.267	.319	.465	439	117	24	3	19	57	35	117
vs. Right	.186	.214	.303	188	35	5	1	5	22	6	59		.199	.239	.311	592	118	20	8	10	59	23	178
at Home	.186	.222	.297	145	27	5	1	3	10	7	44		.238	.291	.406	478	114	22	8	14	51	33	140
on Road	.216	.256	.368	171	37	5	0	7	23	7	54		.219	.258	.351	553	121	22	3	15	65	25	155
on Grass	.205	.246	.330	264	54	7	1	8	25	13	84		.223	.271	.374	879	196	36	11	25	92	52	250
on Turf	.192	.208	.365	52	10	3	0	2	8	1	14		.257	.290	.388	152	39	8	0	4	24	6	45
Day Games	.192	.241	.385	78	15	3	0	4	9	3	21		.201	.246	.361	249	50	12	2	8	29	12	77
Night Games	.206	.240	.319	238	49	7	1	6	24	11	77		.237	.282	.381	782	185	32	9	21	87	46	218
April	.222	.288	.444	54	12	1	1	3	8	4	14		.261	.311	.477	111	29	3	3	5	17	8	30
May	.221	.245	.358	95	21	1	0	4	8	3	35		.217	.247	.339	189	41	5	0	6	14	7	63
June	.173	.209	.284	81	14	3	0	2	10	4	26		.253	.282	.419	229	58	10	5	6	25	8	62
July	.160	.160	.280	25	4	3	0	0	0	0	6		.185	.215	.325	157	29	12	2	2	17	6	44
August	.214	.313	.214	14	3	0	0	1	6	1	12		.231	.299	.350	143	33	5	0	4	18	13	36
Sept–Oct	.213	.245	.319	47	10	2	0	1	6	1	12		.223	.291	.366	202	45	9	1	6	25	16	60
Bases Empty	.179	.214	.283	184	33	7	0	4	4	6	60		.218	.266	.355	605	132	25	5	16	16	33	177
Leadoff	.161	.198	.218	87	14	2	0	1	1	3	24		.204	.254	.324	299	61	9	3	7	7	16	84
Runners On Base	.235	.277	.409	132	31	3	1	6	29	8	38		.242	.284	.406	426	103	19	6	13	100	25	118
Scoring Position	.237	.279	.463	80	19	1	1	5	27	5	25		.236	.287	.422	258	61	13	4	9	88	19	72
Late and Close	.275	.296	.493	69	19	4	1	3	6	2	16		.220	.274	.328	177	39	8	1	3	9	12	48

3-YEAR TOTALS (1989–1991)

BILL SPIERS — bats left — throws right — age 26 — MIL — *S/O

1991	BA	OBA	SA	AB	H	2B	3B	HR	RBI	BB	SO		3-YR BA	OBA	SA	AB	H	2B	3B	HR	RBI	BB	SO
Total	.283	.337	.401	414	117	13	6	8	54	34	55		.261	.305	.353	1122	293	37	12	14	123	71	163
vs. Left	.222	.305	.282	117	26	1	0	2	12	13	16		.239	.292	.310	268	64	6	2	3	28	19	48
vs. Right	.306	.350	.448	297	91	12	6	6	42	21	39		.268	.309	.367	854	229	31	10	11	95	52	115
at Home	.299	.370	.369	187	56	6	2	1	24	21	30		.280	.326	.363	535	150	20	6	4	63	37	82
on Road	.269	.309	.427	227	61	7	4	7	30	13	25		.244	.285	.344	587	143	17	6	10	60	34	81
on Grass	.302	.361	.420	348	105	11	6	6	47	32	45		.271	.314	.367	963	261	32	12	12	111	60	144
on Turf	.182	.203	.303	66	12	2	0	2	7	2	10		.201	.250	.270	159	32	5	0	2	12	11	19
Day Games	.260	.301	.378	127	33	7	1	2	14	8	19		.257	.301	.360	369	95	17	3	5	39	23	61
Night Games	.293	.352	.411	287	84	6	5	6	40	26	36		.263	.307	.349	753	198	20	9	9	84	48	102
April	.281	.339	.456	57	16	1	0	3	10	5	9		.241	.312	.398	83	20	1	0	4	15	9	13
May	.212	.255	.288	52	11	4	0	0	3	3	10		.214	.274	.269	145	31	8	0	0	9	11	26
June	.234	.319	.281	64	15	1	1	0	5	7	10		.270	.326	.360	178	48	9	2	1	15	14	25
July	.237	.265	.355	76	18	1	1	2	10	4	12		.265	.286	.340	200	53	4	1	3	24	8	33
August	.386	.450	.500	88	34	3	2	1	17	11	8		.254	.311	.320	244	62	7	3	1	32	20	30
Sept–Oct	.299	.341	.468	77	23	3	2	2	9	4	6		.290	.314	.419	272	79	8	6	5	28	9	36
Bases Empty	.256	.311	.353	238	61	6	4	3	3	17	31		.251	.294	.326	668	168	19	5	7	7	37	94
Leadoff	.184	.215	.243	103	19	4	1	0	0	4	14		.213	.246	.280	300	64	13	2	1	1	12	37
Runners On Base	.318	.371	.466	176	56	7	2	5	51	17	24		.275	.321	.392	454	125	18	7	7	116	34	69
Scoring Position	.324	.365	.529	102	33	5	2	4	49	9	12		.286	.331	.431	276	79	13	6	5	111	23	44
Late and Close	.347	.415	.500	72	25	2	3	1	14	8	8		.288	.335	.356	191	55	4	3	1	23	14	30

3-YEAR TOTALS (1989–1991)

TERRY STEINBACH — bats right — throws right — age 30 — OAK — *C/1D

1991	BA	OBA	SA	AB	H	2B	3B	HR	RBI	BB	SO		6-YR BA	OBA	SA	AB	H	2B	3B	HR	RBI	BB	SO
Total	.274	.312	.386	456	125	31	1	6	67	22	70		.270	.322	.396	2045	553	94	8	49	277	137	314
vs. Left	.266	.302	.410	139	37	11	0	3	15	7	17		.288	.339	.433	663	191	34	4	18	85	48	81
vs. Right	.278	.316	.375	317	88	20	1	3	52	15	53		.262	.313	.378	1382	362	60	4	31	192	89	233
at Home	.277	.314	.377	220	61	19	0	1	31	14	29		.269	.320	.376	970	261	39	1	21	130	70	131
on Road	.271	.310	.394	236	64	12	1	5	36	8	41		.272	.323	.414	1075	292	55	7	28	147	67	183
on Grass	.280	.315	.388	371	104	26	1	4	58	19	52		.277	.329	.406	1707	473	77	4	45	241	121	249
on Turf	.247	.297	.376	85	21	5	0	2	9	3	18		.237	.286	.346	338	80	17	4	4	36	16	65
Day Games	.306	.333	.448	134	41	10	0	3	28	6	20		.290	.334	.425	746	216	40	2	19	112	46	110
Night Games	.261	.303	.360	322	84	21	1	3	39	16	50		.259	.315	.380	1299	337	54	6	30	165	91	204
April	.286	.333	.381	63	18	3	0	1	11	2	17		.253	.323	.367	289	73	16	1	9	38	26	53
May	.291	.329	.468	79	23	8	0	2	13	4	7		.289	.335	.432	287	83	12	1	9	37	18	36
June	.302	.333	.460	63	19	4	0	2	7	2	6		.271	.312	.402	361	98	16	2	9	39	19	60
July	.326	.337	.449	89	29	9	1	1	17	3	11		.292	.321	.432	315	92	19	2	7	47	13	43
August	.241	.311	.354	79	19	6	0	1	10	9	12		.250	.305	.338	376	94	18	0	5	47	26	57
Sept–Oct	.205	.236	.217	83	17	1	0	0	9	2	17		.271	.334	.412	417	113	13	2	14	69	35	65
Bases Empty	.272	.307	.381	239	65	17	0	3	3	9	41		.265	.320	.387	1132	300	47	5	27	27	79	173
Leadoff	.225	.274	.315	89	20	5	0	1	1	5	14		.261	.325	.374	433	113	20	1	9	9	36	59
Runners On Base	.276	.317	.392	217	60	14	1	3	64	13	29		.277	.323	.407	913	253	47	3	22	250	58	141
Scoring Position	.285	.333	.400	130	37	7	1	3	60	12	18		.275	.330	.399	509	140	25	1	12	220	43	79
Late and Close	.291	.340	.326	86	25	3	0	0	10	5	17		.247	.305	.326	344	85	9	0	6	44	25	60

6-YEAR TOTALS (1986–1991)

KURT STILLWELL — bats both — throws right — age 27 — KC — *S

1991	BA	OBA	SA	AB	H	2B	3B	HR	RBI	BB	SO
Total	.265	.322	.361	385	102	17	1	6	51	33	56
vs. Left	.266	.304	.367	109	29	6	1	1	15	6	17
vs. Right	.264	.328	.359	276	73	11	0	5	36	27	39
at Home	.257	.324	.339	183	47	10	1	1	24	18	23
on Road	.272	.320	.381	202	55	7	0	5	27	15	33
on Grass	.287	.340	.412	136	39	5	0	4	18	12	25
on Turf	.253	.311	.333	249	63	12	1	2	33	21	31
Day Games	.257	.325	.385	109	28	8	0	2	11	11	19
Night Games	.268	.320	.351	276	74	9	1	4	40	22	37
April	.317	.380	.429	63	20	4	0	1	6	7	12
May	.216	.245	.278	97	21	1	1	1	11	4	15
June	.265	.333	.386	83	22	4	0	2	11	9	13
July	.189	.279	.324	37	7	2	0	1	6	5	6
August	.286	.286	.357	14	4	1	0	0	0	0	3
Sept–Oct	.308	.370	.396	91	28	5	0	1	17	8	7
Bases Empty	.246	.300	.333	195	48	9	1	2	2	14	31
Leadoff	.260	.333	.438	73	19	5	1	2	2	7	10
Runners On Base	.284	.343	.389	190	54	8	0	4	49	19	25
Scoring Position	.303	.387	.414	99	30	5	0	2	44	16	18
Late and Close	.187	.299	.213	75	14	2	0	0	4	12	10

6-YEAR TOTALS (1986–1991)

	BA	OBA	SA	AB	H	2B	3B	HR	RBI	BB	SO
Total	.253	.316	.360	2487	630	126	25	30	268	223	353
vs. Left	.239	.314	.324	661	158	28	8	4	73	68	92
vs. Right	.258	.317	.373	1826	472	98	17	26	195	155	261
at Home	.249	.313	.361	1204	300	64	16	13	137	110	175
on Road	.257	.319	.359	1283	330	62	9	17	131	113	178
on Grass	.242	.307	.329	933	226	46	4	9	79	84	127
on Turf	.260	.322	.379	1554	404	80	21	21	189	139	226
Day Games	.253	.321	.365	720	182	40	4	11	77	73	114
Night Games	.254	.314	.358	1767	448	86	21	19	191	150	239
April	.295	.352	.431	339	100	20	4	6	43	28	54
May	.256	.341	.352	480	123	17	4	7	52	62	72
June	.244	.300	.354	495	121	29	5	5	47	38	69
July	.220	.264	.320	350	77	17	3	4	36	21	48
August	.256	.323	.369	453	116	20	8	5	48	45	66
Sept–Oct	.251	.312	.343	370	93	23	1	3	42	29	44
Bases Empty	.225	.298	.316	1422	320	67	12	13	13	137	215
Leadoff	.220	.302	.328	551	121	31	4	7	7	62	83
Runners On Base	.291	.341	.419	1065	310	59	13	17	255	86	138
Scoring Position	.283	.350	.412	604	171	32	11	8	226	68	87
Late and Close	.224	.305	.271	406	91	12	2	1	31	47	71

DARRYL STRAWBERRY — bats left — throws left — age 30 — LA — *O

1991	BA	OBA	SA	AB	H	2B	3B	HR	RBI	BB	SO
Total	.265	.361	.491	505	134	22	4	28	99	75	125
vs. Left	.278	.373	.484	223	62	9	2	11	41	34	58
vs. Right	.255	.351	.496	282	72	13	2	17	58	41	67
at Home	.284	.374	.510	257	73	12	2	14	54	38	55
on Road	.246	.347	.472	248	61	10	2	14	45	37	70
on Grass	.270	.364	.499	367	99	18	3	20	71	55	85
on Turf	.254	.350	.471	138	35	4	1	8	28	20	40
Day Games	.247	.355	.425	146	36	6	1	6	32	23	38
Night Games	.273	.363	.518	359	98	16	3	22	67	52	87
April	.246	.357	.406	69	17	6	1	1	7	11	17
May	.207	.356	.451	82	17	2	0	6	17	19	27
June	.219	.286	.250	32	7	1	0	0	2	3	6
July	.290	.377	.548	93	27	2	2	6	17	13	21
August	.302	.395	.604	106	32	5	0	9	28	16	29
Sept–Oct	.276	.341	.488	123	34	6	1	6	28	13	25
Bases Empty	.229	.332	.443	253	58	11	2	13	13	38	62
Leadoff	.187	.295	.352	91	17	3	0	4	4	14	24
Runners On Base	.302	.389	.540	252	76	11	2	15	86	37	63
Scoring Position	.283	.374	.503	159	45	4	2	9	72	24	41
Late and Close	.264	.346	.407	91	24	4	0	3	20	12	29

8-YEAR TOTALS (1984–1991)

	BA	OBA	SA	AB	H	2B	3B	HR	RBI	BB	SO
Total	.264	.361	.517	3988	1051	194	27	254	759	608	958
vs. Left	.243	.317	.457	1557	378	60	8	86	277	169	412
vs. Right	.277	.388	.555	2431	673	134	19	168	482	439	546
at Home	.267	.361	.531	1907	510	94	14	127	394	281	452
on Road	.260	.361	.504	2081	541	100	13	127	365	327	506
on Grass	.263	.359	.512	2802	738	136	19	174	530	414	670
on Turf	.264	.366	.529	1186	313	58	8	80	229	194	288
Day Games	.266	.364	.509	1390	370	69	11	82	271	208	321
Night Games	.262	.360	.521	2598	681	125	16	172	488	400	637
April	.296	.385	.552	554	164	37	3	33	89	81	126
May	.227	.331	.443	634	144	26	3	35	96	98	168
June	.274	.395	.554	504	138	25	4	36	104	100	99
July	.271	.362	.544	750	203	36	8	51	154	106	191
August	.242	.344	.451	774	187	31	4	41	138	120	188
Sept–Oct	.278	.363	.567	772	215	39	5	58	178	103	186
Bases Empty	.247	.333	.494	2090	517	104	14	128	128	255	499
Leadoff	.243	.328	.503	949	231	42	9	62	62	115	215
Runners On Base	.281	.390	.542	1898	534	90	13	126	631	353	459
Scoring Position	.265	.395	.502	1099	291	50	13	69	491	256	283
Late and Close	.223	.335	.396	669	149	24	1	30	99	113	195

FRANKLIN STUBBS — bats left — throws left — age 32 — MIL — 1/OD

1991	BA	OBA	SA	AB	H	2B	3B	HR	RBI	BB	SO
Total	.213	.282	.359	362	77	16	2	11	38	35	71
vs. Left	.218	.236	.368	87	19	7	0	2	10	1	19
vs. Right	.211	.295	.356	275	58	9	2	9	28	34	52
at Home	.219	.304	.410	183	40	11	0	8	22	21	41
on Road	.207	.259	.307	179	37	5	2	3	16	14	30
on Grass	.205	.281	.350	297	61	13	0	10	33	31	63
on Turf	.246	.286	.400	65	16	3	2	1	5	4	8
Day Games	.253	.348	.455	99	25	5	0	5	14	14	19
Night Games	.198	.256	.323	263	52	11	2	6	24	21	52
April	.214	.274	.339	56	12	4	0	1	4	4	9
May	.221	.292	.302	86	19	4	0	1	9	9	17
June	.214	.267	.429	56	12	3	0	3	6	4	13
July	.216	.284	.405	74	16	1	2	3	10	7	16
August	.233	.314	.411	73	17	4	0	3	9	10	12
Sept–Oct	.059	.158	.059	17	1	0	0	0	0	1	4
Bases Empty	.215	.268	.390	195	42	9	2	7	7	14	37
Leadoff	.267	.300	.512	86	23	4	1	5	5	4	16
Runners On Base	.210	.297	.323	167	35	7	0	4	31	21	34
Scoring Position	.150	.286	.290	100	15	7	0	4	29	21	26
Late and Close	.181	.253	.222	72	13	4	0	0	1	6	16

8-YEAR TOTALS (1984–1991)

	BA	OBA	SA	AB	H	2B	3B	HR	RBI	BB	SO
Total	.232	.300	.409	2188	507	86	11	93	287	214	531
vs. Left	.221	.250	.351	515	114	20	1	15	54	18	117
vs. Right	.235	.315	.426	1673	393	66	10	78	233	196	414
at Home	.229	.299	.390	1122	257	46	3	43	147	113	272
on Road	.235	.301	.428	1066	250	40	8	50	140	101	259
on Grass	.214	.286	.373	1466	314	47	3	60	182	149	364
on Turf	.267	.329	.481	722	193	39	8	33	105	65	167
Day Games	.244	.315	.424	648	158	25	4	28	87	67	154
Night Games	.227	.294	.402	1540	349	61	7	65	200	147	377
April	.238	.298	.454	260	62	11	0	15	37	22	78
May	.246	.320	.397	358	88	15	3	11	41	39	91
June	.238	.306	.448	424	101	17	0	24	63	42	96
July	.229	.288	.415	494	113	14	6	22	66	40	113
August	.218	.295	.364	349	76	15	0	12	39	40	85
Sept–Oct	.221	.297	.370	303	67	14	2	9	41	31	68
Bases Empty	.230	.285	.406	1215	279	48	8	50	50	92	282
Leadoff	.271	.312	.473	491	133	21	3	24	24	27	94
Runners On Base	.234	.318	.412	973	228	38	3	43	237	122	249
Scoring Position	.208	.315	.407	558	116	21	3	28	199	91	163
Late and Close	.230	.320	.397	395	91	14	2	16	48	50	111

B.J. SURHOFF — bats left — throws right — age 28 — MIL — *C/D302

1991	BA	OBA	SA	AB	H	2B	3B	HR	RBI	BB	SO		5-YEAR TOTALS (1987–1991) BA	OBA	SA	AB	H	2B	3B	HR	RBI	BB	SO
Total	.289	.319	.372	505	146	19	4	5	68	26	33		.271	.315	.364	2304	625	100	15	28	290	158	178
vs. Left	.255	.291	.294	102	26	2	1	0	11	6	12		.275	.318	.373	491	135	18	3	8	68	32	46
vs. Right	.298	.326	.392	403	120	17	3	5	57	20	21		.270	.314	.362	1813	490	82	12	20	222	126	132
at Home	.267	.303	.364	236	63	8	3	3	34	14	13		.269	.323	.371	1122	302	47	8	17	154	91	85
on Road	.309	.332	.379	269	83	11	1	2	34	12	20		.273	.308	.358	1182	323	53	7	11	136	67	93
on Grass	.298	.326	.386	433	129	18	4	4	55	22	27		.274	.319	.369	1984	543	88	12	26	256	140	149
on Turf	.236	.273	.292	72	17	1	0	1	13	4	6		.256	.292	.331	320	82	12	3	2	34	18	29
Day Games	.273	.305	.350	143	39	6	1	1	21	8	10		.249	.297	.324	638	159	24	3	6	71	46	60
Night Games	.296	.324	.381	362	107	13	3	4	47	18	23		.280	.322	.379	1666	466	76	12	22	219	112	118
April	.153	.194	.153	59	9	0	0	0	3	3	6		.212	.262	.296	260	55	8	1	4	32	20	31
May	.254	.297	.299	67	17	1	1	0	10	5	3		.274	.321	.354	336	92	13	1	4	34	25	26
June	.262	.300	.287	80	21	2	0	0	8	6	5		.284	.311	.381	388	110	22	2	4	45	17	29
July	.306	.318	.376	85	26	6	0	0	14	2	5		.263	.299	.315	365	96	12	2	1	42	19	24
August	.343	.364	.520	102	35	7	1	3	14	4	6		.277	.328	.367	376	104	19	3	3	43	29	30
Sept–Oct	.339	.370	.455	112	38	3	2	2	19	6	8		.290	.340	.418	579	168	26	6	12	94	48	38
Bases Empty	.260	.294	.363	273	71	11	1	5	5	13	21		.251	.297	.344	1309	329	57	5	18	18	84	108
Leadoff	.235	.264	.324	102	24	3	0	2	2	4	6		.239	.271	.335	481	115	20	1	8	8	21	30
Runners On Base	.323	.346	.384	232	75	8	3	0	63	13	12		.297	.337	.391	995	296	43	10	10	272	74	70
Scoring Position	.316	.338	.406	133	42	6	3	0	62	9	9		.290	.336	.406	576	167	24	8	9	256	55	49
Late and Close	.284	.323	.398	88	25	4	0	2	13	6	8		.259	.313	.347	375	97	16	1	5	56	32	37

DANNY TARTABULL — bats right — throws right — age 30 — KC — *O/D

1991	BA	OBA	SA	AB	H	2B	3B	HR	RBI	BB	SO		8-YEAR TOTALS (1984–1991) BA	OBA	SA	AB	H	2B	3B	HR	RBI	BB	SO
Total	.316	.397	.593	484	153	35	3	31	100	65	121		.287	.372	.514	2919	838	174	16	152	535	396	766
vs. Left	.296	.408	.542	142	42	9	1	8	22	27	31		.302	.406	.524	821	248	54	4	40	133	146	198
vs. Right	.325	.392	.614	342	111	26	2	23	78	38	90		.281	.358	.510	2098	590	120	12	112	402	250	568
at Home	.314	.395	.571	226	71	15	2	13	35	30	54		.284	.372	.506	1411	401	78	11	71	234	199	349
on Road	.318	.398	.612	258	82	20	1	18	65	35	67		.290	.372	.521	1508	437	96	5	81	301	197	417
on Grass	.317	.394	.653	199	63	14	1	17	55	27	52		.290	.371	.521	1132	328	71	4	61	230	146	320
on Turf	.316	.399	.551	285	90	21	2	14	45	38	69		.285	.373	.509	1787	510	103	12	91	305	250	446
Day Games	.331	.414	.563	142	47	12	0	7	30	20	35		.284	.372	.516	736	209	45	3	40	144	101	204
Night Games	.310	.390	.605	342	106	23	3	24	70	45	86		.288	.372	.513	2183	629	129	13	112	391	295	562
April	.288	.321	.452	73	21	7	1	1	10	4	22		.290	.368	.459	379	110	26	1	12	61	47	100
May	.295	.337	.477	88	26	4	0	4	14	5	20		.259	.342	.481	451	117	17	4	25	73	55	116
June	.368	.421	.736	87	32	5	0	9	25	8	20		.313	.384	.557	467	146	25	1	29	87	57	111
July	.378	.489	.797	74	28	7	0	8	19	17	23		.271	.346	.490	451	122	27	3	22	87	51	125
August	.278	.361	.528	72	20	7	1	3	14	9	19		.280	.375	.517	547	153	36	2	30	107	86	158
Sept–Oct	.289	.429	.567	90	26	5	1	6	18	22	17		.304	.402	.553	624	190	43	5	34	120	100	156
Bases Empty	.285	.348	.554	267	76	17	2	17	17	26	71		.277	.361	.500	1517	420	88	8	78	78	195	409
Leadoff	.293	.344	.621	140	41	9	2	11	11	11	34		.279	.354	.505	707	197	46	6	34	34	81	180
Runners On Base	.355	.451	.641	217	77	18	1	14	83	39	50		.298	.384	.529	1402	418	86	8	74	457	201	357
Scoring Position	.380	.500	.694	121	46	12	1	8	68	32	32		.289	.389	.510	824	238	54	7	38	370	144	229
Late and Close	.316	.379	.557	79	25	5	1	4	14	8	16		.297	.370	.517	462	137	31	4	21	87	54	129

MICKEY TETTLETON — bats both — throws right — age 32 — DET — *CD/O1

1991	BA	OBA	SA	AB	H	2B	3B	HR	RBI	BB	SO		8-YEAR TOTALS (1984–1991) BA	OBA	SA	AB	H	2B	3B	HR	RBI	BB	SO
Total	.263	.387	.491	501	132	17	2	31	89	101	131		.242	.356	.424	2348	568	96	8	105	323	416	674
vs. Left	.248	.349	.532	109	27	4	0	9	25	17	32		.239	.336	.452	786	188	38	0	43	115	116	230
vs. Right	.268	.397	.480	392	105	13	2	22	64	84	99		.243	.367	.410	1562	380	58	8	62	208	300	444
at Home	.264	.402	.498	239	63	7	2	15	44	56	63		.258	.375	.456	1158	299	45	0	56	171	219	325
on Road	.263	.371	.485	262	69	10	0	16	45	45	68		.226	.338	.392	1190	269	51	0	49	152	197	349
on Grass	.271	.394	.496	425	115	14	2	26	81	87	113		.249	.362	.445	1947	484	82	8	95	287	347	553
on Turf	.224	.344	.461	76	17	3	0	5	8	14	18		.209	.329	.319	401	84	14	0	10	36	69	121
Day Games	.250	.343	.395	172	43	5	1	6	18	25	54		.254	.348	.414	756	192	31	3	28	89	108	231
Night Games	.271	.407	.541	329	89	12	1	25	71	76	77		.236	.360	.428	1592	376	65	5	77	234	308	443
April	.188	.344	.354	48	9	2	0	2	7	12	13		.174	.290	.298	258	45	11	0	7	32	43	85
May	.329	.430	.553	85	28	2	1	5	15	15	22		.269	.370	.496	353	95	12	1	22	64	56	91
June	.262	.396	.548	84	22	1	1	7	19	18	19		.267	.389	.497	439	117	21	4	24	70	89	115
July	.273	.354	.511	88	24	3	0	6	19	11	27		.246	.358	.405	467	115	18	1	18	56	80	142
August	.237	.409	.464	97	23	4	0	6	15	29	26		.231	.359	.394	363	84	12	1	15	49	72	99
Sept–Oct	.263	.365	.465	99	26	5	0	5	14	16	24		.239	.348	.412	468	112	22	1	19	52	76	142
Bases Empty	.255	.371	.456	294	75	13	2	14	14	52	80		.249	.341	.442	1341	334	57	8	62	62	179	378
Leadoff	.248	.359	.431	109	27	5	0	5	5	18	29		.250	.338	.444	577	144	26	4	26	26	74	150
Runners On Base	.275	.408	.541	207	57	4	0	17	75	49	51		.232	.376	.399	1007	234	39	0	43	261	237	296
Scoring Position	.283	.434	.508	120	34	3	0	8	57	35	37		.206	.379	.373	573	118	21	0	25	218	166	186
Late and Close	.240	.303	.440	100	24	2	0	6	18	8	32		.225	.319	.393	400	90	16	0	19	54	53	123

TIM TEUFEL — bats right — throws right — age 34 — NYN/SD — 23/1

8-YEAR TOTALS (1984–1991)

1991	BA	OBA	SA	AB	H	2B	3B	HR	RBI	BB	SO	BA	OBA	SA	AB	H	2B	3B	HR	RBI	BB	SO
Total	.217	.319	.370	341	74	16	0	12	44	51	76	.255	.338	.404	2587	660	157	9	70	317	326	438
vs. Left	.262	.370	.485	130	34	8	0	7	27	23	21	.263	.350	.416	1208	318	79	3	33	142	166	164
vs. Right	.190	.286	.299	211	40	8	0	5	17	28	55	.248	.328	.394	1379	342	78	6	37	175	160	274
at Home	.228	.344	.401	162	37	10	0	6	24	28	33	.249	.329	.391	1246	310	70	4	33	157	151	205
on Road	.207	.296	.341	179	37	6	0	6	20	23	43	.261	.347	.416	1341	350	87	5	37	160	175	233
on Grass	.191	.304	.337	246	47	12	0	8	34	40	57	.243	.332	.367	1438	349	82	2	31	160	195	262
on Turf	.284	.358	.453	95	27	4	0	4	10	11	19	.271	.347	.450	1149	311	75	7	39	157	131	176
Day Games	.208	.284	.333	96	20	6	0	2	12	10	24	.266	.341	.442	866	230	62	2	29	128	100	145
Night Games	.220	.332	.384	245	54	10	0	10	32	41	52	.250	.337	.385	1721	430	95	7	41	189	226	293
April	.077	.143	.077	13	1	0	0	0	0	1	0	.246	.344	.339	345	85	18	1	4	47	50	47
May	.143	.182	.286	21	3	0	0	1	2	1	8	.268	.356	.407	418	112	18	2	12	54	58	80
June	.321	.448	.462	78	25	5	0	2	14	18	15	.282	.357	.429	401	113	30	1	9	55	46	57
July	.149	.240	.194	67	10	3	0	0	2	8	14	.251	.333	.364	426	107	22	1	8	38	53	71
August	.276	.377	.569	58	16	2	0	5	13	10	15	.264	.351	.457	455	120	29	1	19	60	64	82
Sept–Oct	.183	.277	.356	104	19	6	0	4	13	13	24	.227	.300	.411	542	123	40	3	18	63	55	101
Bases Empty	.218	.323	.326	193	42	9	0	4	4	30	42	.251	.335	.401	1437	361	86	6	39	39	172	251
Leadoff	.235	.303	.346	81	19	3	0	2	2	8	18	.276	.342	.467	510	141	32	1	21	21	49	71
Runners On Base	.216	.314	.426	148	32	7	0	8	40	21	34	.260	.343	.408	1150	299	71	3	31	278	154	187
Scoring Position	.211	.313	.453	95	20	5	0	6	35	15	23	.238	.340	.390	672	160	40	1	20	241	115	127
Late and Close	.233	.317	.411	73	17	4	0	3	10	9	15	.243	.340	.372	457	111	23	0	12	57	68	77

FRANK THOMAS — bats right — throws right — age 24 — CHA — *D1

2-YEAR TOTALS (1990–1991)

1991	BA	OBA	SA	AB	H	2B	3B	HR	RBI	BB	SO	BA	OBA	SA	AB	H	2B	3B	HR	RBI	BB	SO
Total	.318	.453	.553	559	178	31	2	32	109	138	112	.321	.453	.547	750	241	42	5	39	140	182	166
vs. Left	.376	.500	.624	170	64	9	0	11	35	42	27	.386	.511	.656	241	93	15	1	16	47	63	44
vs. Right	.293	.432	.522	389	114	22	2	21	74	96	85	.291	.425	.495	509	148	27	4	23	93	119	122
at Home	.371	.509	.708	267	99	16	1	24	61	76	60	.365	.509	.671	340	124	20	3	26	74	102	84
on Road	.271	.399	.411	292	79	15	1	8	48	62	52	.285	.403	.444	410	117	22	2	13	66	80	82
on Grass	.343	.475	.596	470	161	28	2	29	95	119	94	.339	.472	.583	611	207	37	5	34	122	155	137
on Turf	.191	.333	.326	89	17	3	0	3	14	19	18	.245	.367	.388	139	34	5	0	5	18	27	29
Day Games	.340	.472	.627	153	52	11	0	11	37	39	32	.328	.463	.583	192	63	13	0	12	39	49	44
Night Games	.310	.446	.525	406	126	20	2	21	72	99	80	.319	.450	.534	558	178	29	5	27	101	133	122
April	.313	.413	.531	64	20	3	1	3	13	11	11	.313	.413	.531	64	20	3	1	3	13	11	11
May	.322	.492	.552	87	28	5	0	5	24	30	19	.322	.492	.552	87	28	5	0	5	24	30	19
June	.280	.412	.477	107	30	6	0	5	20	23	29	.280	.412	.477	107	30	6	0	5	20	23	29
July	.323	.460	.586	99	32	5	0	7	15	25	18	.323	.460	.586	99	32	5	0	7	15	25	18
August	.373	.481	.682	110	41	8	1	8	27	24	14	.342	.461	.608	199	68	15	4	10	40	45	36
Sept–Oct	.293	.444	.467	92	27	4	0	4	10	25	21	.325	.457	.505	194	63	8	0	9	28	48	53
Bases Empty	.314	.445	.557	296	93	16	1	18	18	70	58	.313	.442	.553	400	125	23	2	23	23	93	90
Leadoff	.287	.436	.575	87	25	7	0	6	6	23	16	.291	.428	.597	134	39	12	1	9	9	32	35
Runners On Base	.323	.461	.548	263	85	15	1	14	91	68	54	.331	.465	.540	350	116	19	3	16	117	89	76
Scoring Position	.347	.497	.571	147	51	10	1	7	75	45	32	.345	.483	.550	200	69	11	3	8	99	56	47
Late and Close	.295	.465	.442	95	28	5	0	3	17	31	25	.309	.456	.504	123	38	7	1	5	29	34	35

MILT THOMPSON — bats left — throws right — age 33 — SL — O

8-YEAR TOTALS (1984–1991)

1991	BA	OBA	SA	AB	H	2B	3B	HR	RBI	BB	SO	BA	OBA	SA	AB	H	2B	3B	HR	RBI	BB	SO
Total	.307	.368	.442	326	100	16	5	6	34	32	53	.280	.338	.382	2775	777	115	34	33	242	234	460
vs. Left	.216	.247	.297	74	16	3	0	1	6	3	17	.226	.271	.297	580	131	25	5	2	45	32	127
vs. Right	.333	.401	.484	252	84	13	5	5	28	29	36	.294	.355	.404	2195	646	90	29	31	197	202	333
at Home	.283	.347	.447	159	45	6	4	4	21	16	22	.288	.345	.406	1387	400	62	25	17	139	119	215
on Road	.329	.388	.437	167	55	10	1	2	13	16	31	.272	.330	.357	1388	377	53	9	16	103	115	245
on Grass	.376	.442	.505	101	38	8	1	1	9	12	18	.281	.338	.372	899	253	41	8	8	52	69	151
on Turf	.276	.333	.413	225	62	8	4	5	25	20	35	.279	.337	.386	1876	524	74	26	25	190	165	309
Day Games	.320	.383	.464	97	31	5	0	1	12	10	15	.268	.325	.366	922	247	40	10	10	85	74	157
Night Games	.301	.361	.432	229	69	11	2	5	22	22	38	.286	.344	.390	1853	530	75	24	23	157	160	303
April	.417	.548	.458	24	10	1	0	0	3	7	3	.282	.354	.356	337	95	15	2	2	24	37	55
May	.424	.472	.576	33	14	0	1	0	3	3	6	.222	.305	.325	415	92	11	7	6	28	47	68
June	.321	.365	.538	78	25	6	4	1	15	6	8	.287	.337	.422	436	125	21	10	6	55	35	66
July	.294	.321	.333	51	15	2	0	0	5	2	6	.287	.336	.395	415	119	15	4	6	34	29	71
August	.298	.385	.509	57	17	3	0	3	5	8	9	.329	.367	.435	538	177	26	5	7	62	30	94
Sept–Oct	.229	.281	.313	83	19	4	0	1	3	6	21	.267	.328	.350	634	169	27	1	8	39	56	106
Bases Empty	.346	.390	.516	182	63	12	2	5	5	13	25	.269	.321	.372	1713	460	75	17	23	23	124	281
Leadoff	.440	.481	.653	75	33	7	0	3	3	6	6	.279	.329	.377	735	205	33	3	11	11	51	111
Runners On Base	.257	.341	.347	144	37	4	3	1	29	19	28	.298	.364	.396	1062	317	40	17	10	219	110	179
Scoring Position	.221	.333	.326	86	19	3	3	0	26	15	18	.272	.357	.365	606	165	24	10	4	195	83	123
Late and Close	.282	.342	.437	71	20	4	2	1	11	7	14	.301	.365	.410	488	147	23	6	6	51	50	104

ROBBY THOMPSON — bats right — throws right — age 30 — SF — *2

1991	BA	OBA	SA	AB	H	2B	3B	HR	RBI	BB	SO
Total	.262	.352	.447	492	129	24	5	19	48	63	95
vs. Left	.284	.381	.515	134	38	8	1	7	16	20	26
vs. Right	.254	.342	.422	358	91	16	4	12	32	43	69
at Home	.295	.399	.519	241	71	13	4	11	26	38	43
on Road	.231	.305	.378	251	58	11	1	8	22	25	52
on Grass	.273	.369	.472	362	99	19	4	15	37	51	67
on Turf	.231	.303	.377	130	30	5	1	4	11	12	28
Day Games	.287	.391	.495	188	54	9	3	8	21	29	34
Night Games	.247	.327	.418	304	75	15	2	11	27	34	61
April	.233	.317	.452	73	17	3	2	3	6	8	16
May	.289	.388	.506	83	24	6	0	4	7	13	16
June	.232	.329	.377	69	16	4	0	2	9	7	12
July	.281	.347	.506	89	25	3	1	5	9	9	19
August	.305	.381	.476	105	32	7	1	3	10	13	16
Sept–Oct	.205	.333	.329	73	15	1	1	2	7	13	16
Bases Empty	.283	.370	.505	311	88	16	4	15	15	39	58
Leadoff	.232	.333	.416	125	29	6	1	5	5	16	27
Runners On Base	.227	.322	.348	181	41	8	1	4	33	24	37
Scoring Position	.229	.324	.333	96	22	4	0	2	28	13	22
Late and Close	.280	.398	.366	82	23	4	0	1	8	15	14

6-YEAR TOTALS (1986–1991)

	BA	OBA	SA	AB	H	2B	3B	HR	RBI	BB	SO
	.257	.327	.401	2983	768	149	33	71	293	270	638
	.294	.364	.475	958	282	64	14	27	108	94	179
	.240	.309	.366	2025	486	85	19	44	185	176	459
	.274	.351	.440	1449	397	82	19	40	166	153	297
	.242	.303	.364	1534	371	67	14	31	127	117	341
	.266	.341	.418	2185	582	111	26	56	231	220	456
	.233	.288	.355	798	186	38	7	15	62	50	182
	.273	.348	.435	1218	333	67	17	32	140	121	250
	.246	.312	.377	1765	435	82	16	39	153	149	388
	.239	.317	.354	443	106	20	5	7	38	47	100
	.300	.362	.478	494	148	30	5	16	56	43	94
	.254	.332	.407	504	128	23	6	14	57	52	106
	.250	.309	.391	517	129	25	6	12	50	35	118
	.269	.328	.401	579	156	33	5	11	46	46	121
	.226	.311	.368	446	101	18	6	11	46	47	99
	.254	.320	.404	1820	463	95	18	47	47	154	406
	.263	.331	.413	659	173	40	7	15	15	59	136
	.262	.337	.396	1163	305	54	15	24	246	116	232
	.242	.334	.366	653	158	26	5	15	205	81	156
	.263	.329	.380	502	132	26	3	9	59	45	110

DICKIE THON — bats right — throws right — age 34 — PHI — *S

1991	BA	OBA	SA	AB	H	2B	3B	HR	RBI	BB	SO
Total	.252	.283	.351	539	136	18	4	9	44	25	84
vs. Left	.256	.304	.340	203	52	7	2	2	14	14	22
vs. Right	.250	.271	.357	336	84	11	2	7	30	11	62
at Home	.270	.299	.359	270	73	8	2	4	19	12	40
on Road	.234	.268	.342	269	63	10	2	5	19	13	40
on Grass	.245	.278	.323	155	38	7	1	1	7	7	22
on Turf	.255	.286	.362	384	98	11	3	8	37	18	62
Day Games	.228	.257	.283	145	33	3	1	1	10	6	24
Night Games	.261	.293	.376	394	103	15	3	8	34	19	60
April	.267	.309	.350	60	16	2	0	1	5	5	15
May	.237	.268	.301	93	22	3	0	1	6	4	15
June	.247	.300	.387	93	23	1	3	2	5	7	15
July	.208	.247	.260	77	16	2	1	0	3	4	9
August	.298	.308	.447	114	34	8	0	3	20	2	13
Sept–Oct	.245	.267	.324	102	25	2	0	2	5	3	17
Bases Empty	.277	.307	.372	325	90	7	3	6	6	14	55
Leadoff	.269	.285	.388	134	36	2	1	4	4	3	21
Runners On Base	.215	.249	.318	214	46	11	1	3	38	11	29
Scoring Position	.218	.260	.294	119	26	9	0	0	29	8	12
Late and Close	.248	.265	.372	113	28	3	1	3	10	2	19

8-YEAR TOTALS (1984–1991)

	BA	OBA	SA	AB	H	2B	3B	HR	RBI	BB	SO
	.257	.311	.361	2396	615	88	17	43	224	191	407
	.263	.328	.368	1107	291	41	9	19	97	110	163
	.251	.296	.356	1289	324	47	8	24	127	81	244
	.247	.304	.338	1164	288	36	8	18	112	94	199
	.265	.318	.383	1232	327	52	9	25	112	97	208
	.258	.325	.340	770	199	30	3	9	62	77	155
	.256	.304	.371	1626	416	58	14	34	162	114	252
	.245	.303	.343	743	182	34	3	11	66	62	134
	.262	.315	.370	1653	433	54	14	32	158	129	273
	.226	.290	.280	314	71	10	2	1	22	28	60
	.250	.315	.347	424	106	15	4	6	40	41	75
	.230	.295	.324	392	90	10	3	7	30	37	79
	.294	.325	.407	364	107	16	2	7	35	16	56
	.252	.305	.376	428	108	20	3	9	52	33	66
	.281	.330	.411	474	133	17	3	13	45	36	71
	.263	.313	.363	1395	367	49	9	24	24	98	240
	.275	.317	.371	618	170	19	5	10	10	35	99
	.248	.309	.360	1001	248	39	8	19	200	93	167
	.263	.334	.384	555	146	26	4	11	176	66	95
	.261	.319	.348	425	111	9	2	8	32	37	78

ALAN TRAMMELL — bats right — throws right — age 34 — DET — S/D3

1991	BA	OBA	SA	AB	H	2B	3B	HR	RBI	BB	SO
Total	.248	.320	.373	375	93	20	0	9	55	37	39
vs. Left	.212	.268	.372	113	24	6	0	4	17	8	10
vs. Right	.263	.341	.374	262	69	14	0	5	38	29	29
at Home	.243	.318	.376	218	53	11	0	6	39	22	17
on Road	.255	.322	.369	157	40	9	0	3	16	15	22
on Grass	.244	.317	.370	324	79	17	0	8	49	33	34
on Turf	.275	.339	.392	51	14	3	0	1	6	4	5
Day Games	.248	.304	.387	137	34	7	0	4	19	10	14
Night Games	.248	.328	.366	238	59	13	0	5	36	27	25
April	.297	.375	.484	64	19	6	0	2	12	6	3
May	.214	.306	.286	98	21	7	0	0	9	12	11
June	.212	.272	.376	85	18	2	0	4	9	7	10
July	.429	.429	.619	21	9	1	0	1	4	0	2
August	.222	.288	.241	54	12	1	0	0	9	5	7
Sept–Oct	.264	.344	.434	53	14	3	0	2	12	7	6
Bases Empty	.246	.303	.350	183	45	7	0	4	4	14	23
Leadoff	.255	.293	.400	55	14	2	0	2	2	3	5
Runners On Base	.250	.335	.396	192	48	13	0	5	51	23	16
Scoring Position	.270	.333	.441	111	30	7	0	4	47	11	7
Late and Close	.157	.283	.196	51	8	2	0	0	3	9	5

8-YEAR TOTALS (1984–1991)

	BA	OBA	SA	AB	H	2B	3B	HR	RBI	BB	SO
	.290	.356	.441	4179	1211	223	27	119	563	426	422
	.296	.367	.474	1387	411	82	9	49	186	157	116
	.287	.350	.425	2792	800	141	18	70	377	269	306
	.295	.364	.441	2073	612	105	10	59	313	221	187
	.284	.347	.442	2106	599	118	17	60	250	205	235
	.288	.355	.439	3523	1013	184	21	102	484	369	352
	.302	.359	.457	656	198	39	6	17	79	57	70
	.295	.364	.449	1320	389	79	10	35	173	140	136
	.288	.352	.438	2859	822	144	17	84	390	286	286
	.301	.372	.478	581	175	36	8	17	81	63	60
	.288	.352	.403	775	223	39	1	16	89	79	77
	.284	.340	.429	763	217	30	4	24	104	65	80
	.263	.347	.391	581	153	33	4	11	63	72	61
	.294	.348	.476	819	241	45	7	30	133	70	78
	.306	.381	.471	660	202	40	3	21	93	77	66
	.285	.346	.448	2277	649	115	19	73	73	200	227
	.296	.338	.477	797	236	36	6	32	32	50	62
	.295	.368	.433	1902	562	108	8	46	490	226	195
	.291	.371	.425	1060	308	57	4	26	430	154	114
	.302	.382	.421	622	188	29	0	15	104	78	69

JEFF TREADWAY — bats left — throws right — age 29 — ATL — 2

5-YEAR TOTALS (1987–1991)

1991	BA	OBA	SA	AB	H	2B	3B	HR	RBI	BB	SO	BA	OBA	SA	AB	H	2B	3B	HR	RBI	BB	SO
Total	.320	.368	.418	306	98	17	2	3	32	23	19	.285	.329	.394	1638	467	78	11	26	158	107	135
vs. Left	.167	.167	.167	18	3	0	0	0	0	0	2	.245	.296	.319	282	69	7	1	4	33	19	32
vs. Right	.330	.380	.434	288	95	17	2	3	32	23	17	.294	.336	.409	1356	398	71	10	22	125	88	103
at Home	.264	.343	.340	159	42	7	1	1	12	18	8	.282	.336	.384	794	224	37	4	12	76	60	55
on Road	.381	.399	.503	147	56	10	1	2	20	5	11	.288	.322	.403	844	243	41	7	14	82	47	80
on Grass	.294	.353	.381	218	64	11	1	2	16	19	12	.278	.326	.366	1007	280	43	5	12	88	71	88
on Turf	.386	.409	.511	88	34	6	1	1	16	4	7	.296	.333	.437	631	187	35	6	14	70	36	47
Day Games	.303	.372	.342	76	23	3	0	0	10	9	7	.266	.315	.361	493	131	24	4	5	42	33	49
Night Games	.326	.367	.443	230	75	14	2	3	22	14	12	.293	.335	.408	1145	336	54	7	21	116	74	86
April	.327	.358	.490	49	16	0	1	2	9	3	1	.264	.296	.386	220	58	9	3	4	23	11	13
May	.359	.409	.436	39	14	1	1	0	2	3	1	.337	.388	.449	276	93	13	3	4	30	23	14
June	.340	.389	.420	50	17	4	0	0	3	4	8	.284	.326	.391	338	96	19	1	5	28	20	45
July	.316	.400	.456	57	18	5	0	1	9	8	1	.257	.313	.377	257	66	9	2	6	28	21	24
August	.299	.333	.358	67	20	4	0	0	5	4	5	.276	.310	.367	286	79	12	1	4	20	15	22
Sept–Oct	.295	.326	.364	44	13	3	0	0	4	1	3	.287	.332	.391	261	75	16	1	3	29	17	17
Bases Empty	.308	.357	.390	182	56	10	1	1	1	12	11	.274	.314	.381	996	273	46	6	16	16	52	88
Leadoff	.273	.322	.345	55	15	1	0	1	1	3	4	.285	.312	.413	358	102	19	3	7	7	11	31
Runners On Base	.339	.384	.460	124	42	7	1	2	31	11	8	.302	.351	.414	642	194	32	5	10	142	55	47
Scoring Position	.333	.390	.439	66	22	4	0	1	27	8	4	.301	.361	.406	342	103	17	2	5	125	41	27
Late and Close	.243	.275	.297	37	9	0	1	0	6	2	2	.272	.311	.370	265	72	9	4	3	35	16	27

JOSE URIBE — bats both — throws right — age 33 — SF — S

8-YEAR TOTALS (1984–1991)

1991	BA	OBA	SA	AB	H	2B	3B	HR	RBI	BB	SO	BA	OBA	SA	AB	H	2B	3B	HR	RBI	BB	SO
Total	.221	.283	.303	231	51	8	4	1	12	20	33	.241	.298	.313	2849	686	89	33	17	203	234	395
vs. Left	.250	.328	.317	60	15	2	1	0	3	7	8	.248	.303	.328	871	216	33	5	9	78	68	117
vs. Right	.211	.266	.298	171	36	6	3	1	9	13	25	.238	.297	.306	1978	470	56	28	8	125	166	278
at Home	.235	.290	.296	115	27	3	2	0	7	9	16	.240	.302	.314	1382	332	50	14	8	88	122	188
on Road	.207	.276	.310	116	24	5	2	1	5	11	17	.241	.295	.312	1467	354	39	19	9	115	112	207
on Grass	.188	.257	.244	160	30	5	2	0	8	15	22	.244	.303	.313	2035	496	69	21	10	150	173	282
on Turf	.296	.342	.437	71	21	3	2	1	4	5	11	.233	.287	.313	814	190	20	12	7	53	61	113
Day Games	.272	.324	.379	103	28	7	2	0	3	8	13	.244	.295	.318	1273	311	48	14	6	83	91	164
Night Games	.180	.250	.242	128	23	1	2	1	9	12	20	.238	.301	.309	1576	375	41	19	11	120	143	231
April	.091	.200	.091	22	2	0	0	0	0	3	4	.245	.294	.299	355	87	11	4	0	22	25	56
May	.182	.308	.273	33	6	0	0	1	3	6	10	.250	.309	.333	508	127	14	5	6	38	43	75
June	.200	.263	.343	35	7	1	2	0	2	3	3	.237	.285	.317	460	109	13	9	2	32	31	48
July	.208	.240	.333	24	5	1	1	0	1	1	2	.229	.285	.297	502	115	17	4	3	29	39	61
August	.316	.365	.418	79	25	6	1	0	5	6	6	.232	.294	.299	535	124	22	7	0	42	48	86
Sept–Oct	.158	.179	.158	38	6	0	0	0	1	1	8	.254	.321	.331	489	124	12	4	6	40	48	69
Bases Empty	.199	.245	.274	146	29	6	1	1	1	9	25	.227	.272	.296	1676	380	52	17	10	10	103	249
Leadoff	.214	.290	.321	56	12	3	0	1	1	6	11	.234	.282	.306	700	164	23	6	5	5	46	93
Runners On Base	.259	.344	.353	85	22	2	3	0	11	11	8	.261	.335	.338	1173	306	37	16	7	193	131	146
Scoring Position	.250	.350	.365	52	13	2	2	0	10	8	6	.251	.358	.325	653	164	26	8	2	171	111	95
Late and Close	.207	.324	.241	29	6	1	0	0	0	5	8	.232	.314	.295	440	102	13	3	3	23	52	61

DAVE VALLE — bats right — throws right — age 32 — SEA — *C/1

8-YEAR TOTALS (1984–1991)

1991	BA	OBA	SA	AB	H	2B	3B	HR	RBI	BB	SO	BA	OBA	SA	AB	H	2B	3B	HR	RBI	BB	SO
Total	.194	.286	.299	324	63	8	1	8	32	34	49	.228	.302	.367	1712	391	69	9	50	225	150	242
vs. Left	.232	.320	.402	112	26	1	0	6	17	10	14	.252	.319	.421	651	164	27	4	25	94	57	82
vs. Right	.175	.269	.245	212	37	7	1	2	15	24	35	.214	.291	.334	1061	227	42	5	25	131	93	160
at Home	.162	.238	.197	173	28	4	1	0	8	17	27	.224	.298	.347	872	195	40	4	20	108	79	116
on Road	.232	.339	.417	151	35	4	0	8	24	17	22	.233	.305	.387	840	196	29	5	30	117	71	126
on Grass	.277	.359	.500	112	31	4	0	7	21	11	16	.238	.303	.402	647	154	22	3	26	97	52	101
on Turf	.151	.248	.193	212	32	4	1	1	11	23	33	.223	.301	.346	1065	237	47	6	24	128	98	141
Day Games	.185	.280	.321	81	15	2	0	3	10	9	14	.216	.294	.346	408	88	16	2	11	43	38	62
Night Games	.198	.289	.292	243	48	6	1	5	22	25	35	.232	.304	.373	1304	303	53	7	39	182	112	180
April	.228	.333	.333	57	13	0	0	2	5	7	9	.213	.285	.375	301	64	8	1	13	40	25	43
May	.070	.221	.123	57	4	0	0	1	2	10	9	.238	.326	.377	244	58	10	3	6	36	30	30
June	.073	.174	.073	41	3	0	0	0	0	3	7	.232	.312	.392	181	42	8	3	6	19	17	28
July	.216	.237	.378	37	8	1	1	1	3	1	6	.216	.272	.383	264	57	15	1	9	39	15	30
August	.222	.295	.370	54	12	2	0	2	3	6	8	.221	.288	.332	253	56	7	0	7	20	21	34
Sept–Oct	.295	.374	.436	78	23	5	0	2	19	7	10	.243	.319	.356	469	114	21	1	10	71	42	77
Bases Empty	.216	.319	.319	185	40	5	1	4	4	22	29	.209	.288	.346	954	199	37	5	28	28	89	141
Leadoff	.205	.310	.301	73	15	2	1	1	1	7	14	.218	.294	.374	372	81	15	2	13	13	30	53
Runners On Base	.165	.242	.273	139	23	3	0	4	28	12	20	.253	.319	.393	758	192	32	4	22	197	61	101
Scoring Position	.161	.240	.264	87	14	3	0	2	24	8	11	.261	.324	.420	467	122	24	4	14	179	36	65
Late and Close	.214	.241	.393	56	12	2	1	2	5	2	8	.215	.281	.360	297	64	10	3	9	36	20	43

ANDY VAN SLYKE — bats left — throws right — age 32 — PIT — *O

1991

	BA	OBA	SA	AB	H	2B	3B	HR	RBI	BB	SO
Total	.265	.355	.446	491	130	24	7	17	83	71	85
vs. Left	.195	.287	.330	185	36	9	2	4	23	23	40
vs. Right	.307	.396	.516	306	94	15	5	13	60	48	45
at Home	.226	.319	.392	265	60	9	4	9	46	37	44
on Road	.310	.397	.509	226	70	15	3	8	37	34	41
on Grass	.277	.353	.429	119	33	4	1	4	16	14	22
on Turf	.261	.356	.452	372	97	20	6	13	67	57	63
Day Games	.298	.373	.510	151	45	9	1	7	28	19	25
Night Games	.250	.348	.418	340	85	15	6	10	55	52	60
April	.254	.321	.493	67	17	2	1	4	16	8	9
May	.221	.358	.360	86	19	2	2	2	10	18	11
June	.200	.273	.237	80	16	3	0	0	6	7	17
July	.352	.467	.704	71	25	4	3	5	25	18	14
August	.255	.317	.457	94	24	5	1	4	16	9	21
Sept–Oct	.312	.387	.462	93	29	5	1	0	11	11	13
Bases Empty	.243	.346	.401	267	65	16	1	8	8	41	48
Leadoff	.187	.288	.341	91	17	6	1	2	2	12	15
Runners On Base	.290	.366	.500	224	65	8	6	9	75	30	37
Scoring Position	.280	.365	.379	132	37	6	2	1	55	23	26
Late and Close	.268	.321	.380	71	19	2	0	2	11	8	13

8-YEAR TOTALS (1984–1991)

	BA	OBA	SA	AB	H	2B	3B	HR	RBI	BB	SO
Total	.270	.346	.450	3814	1028	191	65	122	561	454	732
vs. Left	.218	.293	.340	1178	257	45	24	17	147	125	267
vs. Right	.292	.370	.498	2636	771	146	41	105	414	329	465
at Home	.264	.350	.450	1839	485	90	36	60	291	250	342
on Road	.275	.343	.450	1975	543	101	29	62	270	204	390
on Grass	.282	.348	.465	1035	292	41	17	38	139	108	200
on Turf	.265	.346	.444	2779	736	150	48	84	422	346	532
Day Games	.280	.349	.474	1247	349	68	18	46	194	140	226
Night Games	.265	.345	.438	2567	679	123	47	76	367	314	506
April	.259	.346	.424	436	113	20	8	12	63	60	81
May	.279	.360	.448	605	169	21	9	21	96	78	108
June	.266	.342	.440	695	185	38	16	17	95	79	146
July	.244	.330	.429	636	155	27	14	21	86	83	125
August	.284	.348	.490	676	192	40	6	29	111	66	122
Sept–Oct	.279	.352	.456	766	214	45	12	22	110	88	150
Bases Empty	.261	.334	.431	2074	542	101	26	66	66	218	400
Leadoff	.262	.327	.450	760	199	47	9	26	26	72	133
Runners On Base	.279	.361	.472	1740	486	90	39	56	495	236	332
Scoring Position	.273	.369	.436	1024	280	47	25	23	401	174	215
Late and Close	.259	.326	.430	669	173	27	11	22	100	72	166

GREG VAUGHN — bats right — throws right — age 27 — MIL — *OD

1991

	BA	OBA	SA	AB	H	2B	3B	HR	RBI	BB	SO
Total	.244	.319	.456	542	132	24	5	27	98	62	125
vs. Left	.227	.307	.377	154	35	6	1	5	22	19	35
vs. Right	.250	.323	.487	388	97	18	4	22	76	43	90
at Home	.246	.332	.504	256	63	16	1	16	54	34	58
on Road	.241	.306	.413	286	69	8	4	11	44	28	67
on Grass	.256	.328	.495	461	118	23	3	27	92	52	100
on Turf	.173	.264	.235	81	14	1	2	0	6	10	25
Day Games	.287	.367	.549	164	47	9	2	10	44	22	41
Night Games	.225	.297	.415	378	85	15	3	17	54	40	84
April	.271	.375	.646	48	13	3	0	5	11	7	11
May	.256	.326	.453	86	22	6	1	3	11	9	20
June	.233	.313	.495	103	24	4	1	7	28	12	21
July	.181	.255	.325	83	15	1	1	3	9	9	24
August	.242	.342	.424	99	24	4	1	4	15	16	22
Sept–Oct	.276	.319	.463	123	34	6	1	5	22	9	27
Bases Empty	.226	.296	.429	301	68	13	3	14	14	29	70
Leadoff	.248	.318	.504	137	34	6	1	9	9	13	29
Runners On Base	.266	.345	.490	241	64	11	2	13	84	33	55
Scoring Position	.276	.348	.519	156	43	9	1	9	74	21	40
Late and Close	.212	.297	.384	99	21	2	0	5	18	12	24

3-YEAR TOTALS (1989–1991)

	BA	OBA	SA	AB	H	2B	3B	HR	RBI	BB	SO
Total	.237	.306	.444	1037	246	53	7	49	182	108	239
vs. Left	.215	.291	.370	303	65	16	2	9	39	35	69
vs. Right	.247	.313	.474	734	181	37	5	40	143	73	170
at Home	.230	.307	.453	499	115	29	2	26	91	57	112
on Road	.243	.306	.435	538	131	24	5	23	91	51	127
on Grass	.244	.312	.465	902	220	48	5	47	166	94	199
on Turf	.193	.267	.304	135	26	5	2	2	16	14	40
Day Games	.251	.328	.482	299	75	14	2	17	66	37	68
Night Games	.232	.297	.428	738	171	39	5	32	116	71	171
April	.234	.327	.453	128	30	8	1	6	22	18	29
May	.243	.306	.467	169	41	10	2	8	34	15	36
June	.194	.262	.383	175	34	5	2	8	27	17	51
July	.229	.297	.391	179	41	6	1	7	24	19	40
August											
Sept–Oct	.254	.313	.460	287	73	15	1	14	53	27	59
Bases Empty	.210	.271	.395	582	122	23	5	25	25	48	137
Leadoff	.208	.273	.417	259	54	10	1	14	14	22	52
Runners On Base	.273	.348	.505	455	124	30	2	24	157	60	102
Scoring Position	.296	.362	.544	274	81	21	1	15	134	37	70
Late and Close	.203	.276	.366	153	31	4	0	7	29	16	36

ROBIN VENTURA — bats left — throws right — age 25 — CHA — *31

1991

	BA	OBA	SA	AB	H	2B	3B	HR	RBI	BB	SO
Total	.284	.367	.442	606	172	25	1	23	100	80	67
vs. Left	.260	.364	.370	192	50	6	0	5	20	31	29
vs. Right	.295	.369	.476	414	122	19	1	18	80	49	38
at Home	.289	.368	.490	304	88	13	0	16	58	37	37
on Road	.278	.367	.394	302	84	12	1	7	42	43	30
on Grass	.284	.366	.463	518	147	22	1	23	93	66	57
on Turf	.284	.375	.318	88	25	3	0	0	7	14	10
Day Games	.289	.364	.398	166	48	3	0	5	17	20	20
Night Games	.282	.369	.459	440	124	22	1	18	83	60	47
April	.322	.429	.475	59	19	3	0	2	9	11	5
May	.208	.266	.218	101	21	1	0	0	5	7	15
June	.312	.387	.413	109	34	5	0	2	14	14	6
July	.357	.431	.739	115	41	8	0	12	33	14	9
August	.283	.358	.481	106	30	4	1	5	25	14	11
Sept–Oct	.233	.348	.319	116	27	4	0	2	14	20	21
Bases Empty	.268	.361	.416	339	91	15	1	11	11	45	41
Leadoff	.240	.301	.404	104	25	5	0	4	4	8	12
Runners On Base	.303	.375	.476	267	81	10	0	12	89	35	26
Scoring Position	.333	.406	.540	150	50	7	0	8	77	23	16
Late and Close	.284	.341	.457	116	33	6	1	4	20	10	10

3-YEAR TOTALS (1989–1991)

	BA	OBA	SA	AB	H	2B	3B	HR	RBI	BB	SO
Total	.265	.346	.381	1144	303	45	2	28	161	143	126
vs. Left	.244	.348	.314	353	86	8	1	5	32	56	56
vs. Right	.274	.345	.411	791	217	37	1	23	129	87	70
at Home	.278	.357	.409	565	157	18	1	18	86	68	64
on Road	.252	.336	.354	579	146	27	1	10	75	75	62
on Grass	.267	.346	.393	984	263	39	2	27	145	118	109
on Turf	.250	.346	.306	160	40	6	0	1	16	25	17
Day Games	.261	.337	.355	299	78	11	1	5	32	36	38
Night Games	.266	.349	.391	845	225	34	1	23	129	107	88
April	.257	.380	.406	101	26	4	1	3	12	19	15
May	.197	.276	.243	173	34	2	0	2	12	18	23
June	.305	.377	.384	203	62	10	0	2	25	24	21
July	.311	.370	.536	222	69	11	0	13	44	20	16
August	.238	.321	.365	181	43	6	1	5	32	24	19
Sept–Oct	.261	.351	.341	264	69	12	0	3	36	38	32
Bases Empty	.243	.333	.345	667	162	25	2	13	13	86	81
Leadoff	.238	.306	.346	214	51	8	0	5	5	20	23
Runners On Base	.296	.364	.432	477	141	20	0	15	148	57	45
Scoring Position	.313	.388	.440	284	89	12	0	8	127	42	33
Late and Close	.260	.324	.365	192	50	6	1	4	30	18	22

OMAR VIZQUEL — bats both — throws right — age 25 — SEA — *S/2

3-YEAR TOTALS (1989–1991)

1991	BA	OBA	SA	AB	H	2B	3B	HR	RBI	BB	SO	BA	OBA	SA	AB	H	2B	3B	HR	RBI	BB	SO
Total	.230	.302	.293	426	98	16	4	1	41	45	37	.230	.290	.283	1068	246	26	9	4	79	91	99
vs. Left	.230	.284	.276	87	20	4	0	0	11	7	5	.219	.256	.278	270	59	10	0	2	25	14	19
vs. Right	.230	.306	.298	339	78	12	4	1	30	38	32	.234	.300	.284	798	187	16	9	2	54	77	80
at Home	.252	.319	.359	206	52	11	4	1	24	21	21	.240	.291	.312	509	122	19	6	2	42	38	59
on Road	.209	.286	.232	220	46	5	0	0	17	24	16	.222	.288	.256	559	124	7	3	2	37	53	40
on Grass	.216	.286	.234	167	36	3	0	0	13	17	10	.226	.287	.255	424	96	5	2	1	25	37	26
on Turf	.239	.311	.332	259	62	13	4	1	28	28	27	.233	.291	.301	644	150	21	7	3	54	54	73
Day Games	.287	.371	.339	115	33	4	1	0	13	16	8	.256	.318	.303	297	76	7	2	1	23	28	20
Night Games	.209	.275	.277	311	65	12	3	1	28	29	29	.220	.279	.275	771	170	19	7	3	56	63	79
April	.200	.273	.260	50	10	1	1	0	4	5	1	.163	.241	.194	98	16	1	1	0	4	10	4
May	.203	.268	.284	74	15	2	2	0	7	7	6	.242	.287	.326	132	32	3	4	0	14	9	13
June	.237	.314	.289	76	18	4	0	0	6	9	6	.247	.322	.285	158	39	6	0	0	10	18	16
July	.292	.347	.323	65	19	2	0	0	5	6	4	.274	.317	.354	212	58	6	1	3	18	14	15
August	.200	.286	.267	75	15	2	0	1	8	9	11	.191	.246	.231	225	43	4	1	1	15	16	28
Sept–Oct	.244	.316	.326	86	21	5	1	0	11	9	9	.239	.306	.280	243	58	6	2	0	18	24	23
Bases Empty	.207	.281	.277	242	50	8	3	1	1	25	25	.226	.291	.282	610	138	13	6	3	3	55	61
Leadoff	.219	.317	.295	105	23	5	0	1	1	15	12	.254	.327	.333	240	61	7	3	2	2	26	26
Runners On Base	.261	.329	.315	184	48	8	1	0	40	20	12	.236	.287	.284	458	108	13	3	1	76	36	38
Scoring Position	.312	.371	.376	109	34	5	1	0	39	12	6	.230	.284	.290	269	62	9	2	1	73	23	22
Late and Close	.203	.262	.338	74	15	6	2	0	3	6	6	.225	.276	.296	169	38	8	2	0	4	12	12

CHICO WALKER — bats both — throws right — age 35 — CHN — 3O/2

6-YEAR TOTALS (1984–1991)

1991	BA	OBA	SA	AB	H	2B	3B	HR	RBI	BB	SO	BA	OBA	SA	AB	H	2B	3B	HR	RBI	BB	SO
Total	.257	.315	.337	374	96	10	1	6	34	33	57	.235	.296	.302	672	158	18	3	7	51	61	121
vs. Left	.210	.256	.319	119	25	2	0	3	12	8	17	.227	.277	.319	163	37	4	0	3	14	12	26
vs. Right	.278	.342	.345	255	71	8	0	3	22	25	40	.238	.302	.297	509	121	14	2	4	37	49	95
at Home	.270	.324	.365	200	54	5	1	4	19	17	27	.244	.306	.317	344	84	9	2	4	28	33	56
on Road	.241	.304	.305	174	42	5	0	2	15	16	30	.226	.285	.287	328	74	9	1	3	23	28	65
on Grass	.270	.328	.367	278	75	7	1	6	31	25	41	.233	.296	.304	481	112	12	2	6	42	46	83
on Turf	.219	.276	.250	96	21	3	0	0	3	8	16	.241	.295	.298	191	46	6	1	1	9	15	38
Day Games	.260	.319	.333	192	50	3	1	3	12	17	28	.238	.297	.306	369	88	9	2	4	24	33	67
Night Games	.253	.310	.341	182	46	7	0	3	22	16	29	.231	.294	.297	303	70	9	1	3	27	28	54
April	.200	.273	.200	10	2	0	0	0	0	1	0	.211	.279	.237	76	16	2	0	0	5	8	13
May	.342	.419	.421	38	13	0	0	1	4	5	8	.237	.315	.281	114	27	2	0	1	6	13	25
June	.235	.304	.294	51	12	3	0	0	3	5	11	.175	.218	.214	103	18	4	0	0	5	6	24
July	.333	.379	.419	93	31	3	1	1	12	8	13	.326	.371	.411	95	31	3	1	1	12	8	13
August	.210	.255	.300	100	21	3	0	2	8	6	9	.210	.255	.300	100	21	3	0	2	8	6	9
Sept–Oct	.207	.275	.293	82	17	1	0	2	7	8	16	.245	.316	.337	184	45	4	2	3	15	20	37
Bases Empty	.246	.281	.306	248	61	7	1	2	2	12	34	.235	.287	.299	422	99	14	2	3	3	31	69
Leadoff	.220	.259	.273	132	29	4	0	1	1	7	17	.210	.269	.263	224	47	9	0	1	1	18	36
Runners On Base	.278	.373	.397	126	35	3	0	4	32	21	23	.236	.310	.308	250	59	4	1	4	48	30	52
Scoring Position	.286	.400	.381	84	24	2	0	2	28	18	18	.223	.318	.277	148	33	2	0	2	42	24	34
Late and Close	.326	.398	.400	95	31	4	0	1	11	12	19	.266	.331	.318	154	41	5	0	1	12	16	31

LARRY WALKER — bats left — throws right — age 26 — MON — *O1

3-YEAR TOTALS (1989–1991)

1991	BA	OBA	SA	AB	H	2B	3B	HR	RBI	BB	SO	BA	OBA	SA	AB	H	2B	3B	HR	RBI	BB	SO
Total	.290	.351	.459	486	141	30	2	16	64	43	102	.263	.336	.434	952	250	48	5	35	119	97	227
vs. Left	.291	.360	.424	158	46	9	0	4	25	14	39	.253	.317	.415	277	70	15	0	10	43	22	69
vs. Right	.290	.347	.476	328	95	21	2	12	39	29	63	.267	.343	.441	675	180	33	5	25	76	75	158
at Home	.274	.335	.430	186	51	14	0	5	24	15	46	.258	.332	.420	419	108	22	2	14	55	41	105
on Road	.300	.361	.477	300	90	16	2	11	40	28	56	.266	.339	.445	533	142	26	3	21	64	56	122
on Grass	.288	.367	.481	156	45	4	1	8	26	21	28	.286	.374	.500	266	76	8	2	15	43	37	61
on Turf	.291	.343	.448	330	96	26	1	8	38	23	74	.254	.321	.408	686	174	40	3	20	76	60	166
Day Games	.250	.358	.397	136	34	4	2	4	21	21	33	.229	.331	.402	266	61	10	3	10	37	38	70
Night Games	.306	.348	.483	350	107	26	0	12	43	22	69	.276	.338	.446	686	189	38	2	25	82	59	157
April	.182	.258	.255	55	10	2	1	0	3	6	11	.213	.298	.333	108	23	8	1	1	8	13	31
May	.242	.320	.407	91	22	3	0	4	8	11	22	.256	.328	.423	156	40	6	1	6	14	17	35
June	.256	.356	.385	78	20	4	0	2	10	10	24	.258	.354	.457	151	39	9	0	7	22	21	38
July	.317	.364	.634	41	13	2	1	3	12	3	8	.205	.250	.393	117	24	2	1	6	18	6	37
August	.376	.427	.624	101	38	13	0	4	12	7	12	.323	.388	.530	198	64	14	0	9	28	17	35
Sept–Oct	.317	.349	.442	120	38	6	0	3	19	6	25	.270	.344	.410	222	60	9	2	6	29	23	51
Bases Empty	.285	.346	.426	291	83	18	1	7	7	25	66	.272	.342	.443	548	149	31	3	19	19	52	140
Leadoff	.323	.371	.489	133	43	11	1	3	3	10	28	.302	.351	.493	225	68	15	2	8	8	17	53
Runners On Base	.297	.359	.508	195	58	12	1	9	57	18	36	.250	.328	.421	404	101	17	2	16	100	45	87
Scoring Position	.271	.357	.415	118	32	9	1	2	41	16	26	.233	.336	.363	240	56	11	1	6	77	38	61
Late and Close	.292	.376	.521	96	28	6	2	4	13	11	20	.262	.345	.431	195	51	11	2	6	20	23	48

TIM WALLACH — bats right — throws right — age 35 — MON — *3

1991	BA	OBA	SA	AB	H	2B	3B	HR	RBI	BB	SO
Total	.225	.292	.334	577	130	22	1	13	73	50	100
vs. Left	.222	.293	.346	185	41	8	0	5	21	18	29
vs. Right	.227	.292	.329	392	89	14	1	8	52	32	71
at Home	.213	.303	.317	230	49	9	0	5	23	26	36
on Road	.233	.285	.346	347	81	13	1	8	50	24	64
on Grass	.236	.304	.333	165	39	4	0	4	22	15	36
on Turf	.221	.287	.335	412	91	18	1	9	51	35	64
Day Games	.264	.322	.374	163	43	3	0	5	25	14	34
Night Games	.210	.280	.319	414	87	19	1	8	48	36	66
April	.210	.220	.272	81	17	2	0	1	4	1	13
May	.220	.339	.310	100	22	3	0	2	11	16	19
June	.286	.360	.455	112	32	4	0	5	20	11	17
July	.227	.302	.360	75	17	4	0	2	12	9	14
August	.183	.241	.308	104	19	5	1	2	11	7	22
Sept–Oct	.219	.263	.286	105	23	4	0	1	15	6	15
Bases Empty	.228	.269	.347	320	73	14	0	8	8	17	50
Leadoff	.242	.265	.342	161	39	7	0	3	3	5	22
Runners On Base	.222	.318	.319	257	57	8	1	5	65	33	50
Scoring Position	.240	.348	.329	167	40	4	1	3	58	26	37
Late and Close	.233	.336	.284	116	27	3	0	1	10	17	21

8-YEAR TOTALS (1984–1991)

	BA	OBA	SA	AB	H	2B	3B	HR	RBI	BB	SO
Total	.263	.319	.422	4592	1207	258	23	143	665	357	700
vs. Left	.264	.326	.427	1339	354	87	7	39	178	124	170
vs. Right	.262	.316	.421	3253	853	171	16	104	487	233	530
at Home	.264	.328	.414	2180	576	130	16	55	307	196	325
on Road	.262	.310	.430	2412	631	128	7	88	358	161	375
on Grass	.262	.309	.437	1260	330	58	3	52	190	81	209
on Turf	.263	.323	.417	3332	877	200	20	91	475	276	491
Day Games	.271	.323	.451	1467	398	81	6	57	227	107	235
Night Games	.259	.317	.409	3125	809	177	17	86	438	250	465
April	.286	.331	.446	597	171	39	1	18	81	39	80
May	.268	.321	.444	825	221	52	6	27	122	56	124
June	.274	.351	.444	792	217	56	5	23	125	89	115
July	.261	.318	.449	770	201	42	5	31	128	64	131
August	.263	.311	.392	834	219	34	4	22	111	55	119
Sept–Oct	.230	.282	.366	774	178	35	2	22	98	54	131
Bases Empty	.261	.301	.419	2546	664	137	14	79	79	137	399
Leadoff	.289	.324	.469	1124	325	73	6	39	39	52	158
Runners On Base	.265	.340	.427	2046	543	121	9	64	586	220	301
Scoring Position	.266	.357	.429	1280	341	79	6	39	507	180	198
Late and Close	.254	.331	.393	853	217	38	1	26	118	92	138

JEROME WALTON — bats right — throws right — age 27 — CHN — *O

1991	BA	OBA	SA	AB	H	2B	3B	HR	RBI	BB	SO
Total	.219	.275	.330	270	59	13	1	5	17	19	55
vs. Left	.198	.264	.246	126	25	6	0	0	6	10	23
vs. Right	.236	.284	.403	144	34	7	1	5	11	9	32
at Home	.225	.286	.350	120	27	6	0	3	6	10	21
on Road	.213	.265	.313	150	32	7	1	2	11	9	34
on Grass	.223	.280	.337	166	37	7	0	4	8	11	32
on Turf	.212	.265	.317	104	22	6	1	1	9	8	23
Day Games	.227	.289	.297	128	29	4	1	1	7	10	22
Night Games	.211	.261	.359	142	30	9	0	4	10	9	33
April	.265	.288	.388	49	13	3	0	1	4	1	9
May	.230	.238	.311	61	14	5	0	0	2	1	13
June	.254	.319	.317	63	16	1	0	1	2	5	9
July	.200	.294	.400	30	6	3	0	1	3	3	8
August	.135	.175	.216	37	5	0	0	1	4	2	8
Sept–Oct	.167	.324	.367	30	5	1	1	1	2	4	8
Bases Empty	.232	.294	.381	181	42	12	0	5	5	14	37
Leadoff	.239	.270	.436	117	28	8	0	5	5	5	22
Runners On Base	.191	.235	.225	89	17	1	1	0	12	5	18
Scoring Position	.173	.233	.192	52	9	1	0	0	11	4	13
Late and Close	.161	.213	.268	56	9	1	1	1	1	6	13

3-YEAR TOTALS (1989–1991)

	BA	OBA	SA	AB	H	2B	3B	HR	RBI	BB	SO
Total	.265	.326	.353	1137	301	52	6	12	84	96	202
vs. Left	.270	.336	.354	396	107	18	3	3	37	37	67
vs. Right	.262	.321	.352	741	194	34	3	9	47	59	135
at Home	.281	.339	.377	551	155	21	4	8	38	48	84
on Road	.249	.315	.329	586	146	31	2	4	46	48	118
on Grass	.279	.344	.370	755	211	33	4	9	47	67	122
on Turf	.236	.292	.319	382	90	19	2	3	37	29	80
Day Games	.281	.340	.360	572	161	25	4	4	47	49	92
Night Games	.248	.313	.345	565	140	27	2	8	37	47	110
April	.267	.332	.379	195	52	11	1	3	13	15	32
May	.268	.317	.340	153	41	9	1	0	7	12	29
June	.268	.348	.351	205	55	11	0	2	14	23	37
July	.287	.316	.399	143	41	10	0	2	16	5	26
August	.277	.346	.353	235	65	5	2	3	22	23	36
Sept–Oct	.228	.290	.306	206	47	6	2	2	12	18	42
Bases Empty	.263	.324	.361	784	206	37	2	12	12	63	139
Leadoff	.283	.343	.413	487	138	26	2	11	11	39	79
Runners On Base	.269	.332	.334	353	95	15	4	0	72	33	63
Scoring Position	.267	.332	.336	217	58	9	3	0	71	24	46
Late and Close	.218	.285	.285	179	39	5	2	1	18	17	39

LOU WHITAKER — bats left — throws right — age 35 — DET — *2/D

1991	BA	OBA	SA	AB	H	2B	3B	HR	RBI	BB	SO
Total	.279	.391	.489	470	131	26	2	23	78	90	45
vs. Left	.247	.354	.340	97	24	3	0	2	14	15	15
vs. Right	.287	.400	.528	373	107	23	2	21	64	75	30
at Home	.304	.442	.557	237	72	13	1	15	51	61	23
on Road	.253	.335	.421	233	59	13	1	8	27	29	22
on Grass	.295	.409	.512	400	118	23	2	20	70	80	36
on Turf	.186	.289	.357	70	13	3	0	3	8	10	9
Day Games	.293	.411	.529	140	41	10	1	7	32	30	15
Night Games	.273	.382	.473	330	90	16	1	16	46	60	30
April	.294	.444	.706	34	10	2	0	4	8	10	3
May	.200	.337	.306	85	17	4	1	1	12	17	8
June	.264	.400	.471	87	23	1	1	5	14	20	10
July	.429	.486	.619	63	27	6	0	2	7	8	4
August	.271	.388	.594	96	26	7	0	8	22	19	14
Sept–Oct	.267	.358	.410	105	28	6	0	3	15	16	6
Bases Empty	.258	.365	.441	256	66	14	0	11	11	42	24
Leadoff	.231	.348	.333	78	18	2	0	2	2	14	8
Runners On Base	.304	.421	.547	214	65	12	2	12	67	48	21
Scoring Position	.284	.407	.486	109	31	7	0	5	47	28	12
Late and Close	.231	.396	.462	78	18	3	0	5	16	22	8

8-YEAR TOTALS (1984–1991)

	BA	OBA	SA	AB	H	2B	3B	HR	RBI	BB	SO
Total	.268	.357	.437	4208	1129	205	28	150	537	595	533
vs. Left	.216	.302	.316	1146	247	37	9	20	120	140	209
vs. Right	.288	.377	.483	3062	882	168	19	130	417	455	324
at Home	.267	.363	.451	2011	536	91	12	85	281	312	255
on Road	.270	.351	.425	2197	593	114	16	65	256	283	278
on Grass	.266	.357	.433	3532	941	158	24	128	460	513	443
on Turf	.278	.355	.457	676	188	47	4	22	77	82	90
Day Games	.262	.353	.433	1250	327	62	4	48	168	185	164
Night Games	.271	.358	.439	2958	802	143	24	102	369	410	369
April	.278	.375	.444	518	144	23	3	19	63	84	59
May	.272	.360	.443	743	202	28	3	31	95	103	98
June	.261	.346	.422	785	205	34	7	26	91	108	108
July	.295	.367	.468	712	210	42	6	33	85	84	85
August	.270	.373	.468	775	209	45	5	33	126	130	100
Sept–Oct	.236	.321	.376	675	159	33	4	18	77	86	83
Bases Empty	.268	.351	.421	2564	687	135	18	74	74	325	317
Leadoff	.278	.354	.426	1324	368	66	11	36	36	153	154
Runners On Base	.269	.365	.462	1644	442	70	10	76	463	270	216
Scoring Position	.249	.358	.413	908	226	37	5	34	361	176	126
Late and Close	.262	.368	.414	625	164	27	1	22	87	108	96

DEVON WHITE — bats both — throws right — age 30 — TOR — *O

1991	BA	OBA	SA	AB	H	2B	3B	HR	RBI	BB	SO	7-YEAR TOTALS (1985–1991) BA	OBA	SA	AB	H	2B	3B	HR	RBI	BB	SO
Total	.282	.342	.455	642	181	40	10	17	60	55	135	.255	.305	.403	2874	732	131	34	76	301	199	610
vs. Left	.302	.350	.518	199	60	15	2	8	20	16	32	.259	.310	.426	910	236	44	9	30	88	63	158
vs. Right	.273	.339	.427	443	121	25	8	9	40	39	103	.253	.303	.393	1964	496	87	25	46	213	136	452
at Home	.298	.355	.497	326	97	26	6	9	33	25	61	.250	.301	.406	1411	353	67	21	37	146	97	301
on Road	.266	.330	.411	316	84	14	4	8	27	30	74	.259	.309	.401	1463	379	64	13	39	155	102	309
on Grass	.255	.314	.398	251	64	11	2	7	22	22	63	.250	.299	.392	2094	524	90	19	56	219	140	452
on Turf	.299	.360	.491	391	117	29	8	10	38	33	72	.267	.323	.435	780	208	41	15	20	82	59	158
Day Games	.326	.374	.491	218	71	20	2	4	19	16	48	.273	.323	.421	799	218	49	9	17	75	55	178
Night Games	.259	.326	.436	424	110	20	8	13	41	39	87	.248	.299	.397	2075	514	82	25	59	226	144	432
April	.333	.386	.480	75	25	9	1	0	13	5	11	.272	.326	.464	412	112	26	7	13	54	29	77
May	.242	.339	.358	95	23	4	2	1	11	14	22	.258	.315	.411	431	111	23	8	9	45	35	80
June	.305	.359	.441	118	36	9	2	1	6	9	25	.265	.311	.421	475	126	22	5	14	49	30	116
July	.281	.317	.456	114	32	4	2	4	9	6	20	.272	.314	.405	474	129	16	4	13	54	28	100
August	.316	.385	.624	117	37	8	2	8	15	13	27	.239	.297	.407	548	131	24	7	18	61	45	116
Sept–Oct	.228	.280	.366	123	28	6	1	3	6	8	30	.230	.278	.330	534	123	20	3	9	38	32	121
Bases Empty	.301	.355	.500	418	126	29	6	14	14	28	84	.263	.307	.427	1710	450	85	21	51	51	98	371
Leadoff	.346	.392	.586	266	92	22	3	12	12	14	54	.300	.337	.476	797	239	45	10	25	25	38	153
Runners On Base	.246	.319	.371	224	55	11	4	3	46	27	51	.242	.304	.369	1164	282	46	13	25	250	101	239
Scoring Position	.172	.263	.250	128	22	5	1	1	37	18	34	.223	.290	.337	677	151	25	5	14	218	67	161
Late and Close	.306	.370	.370	108	33	5	1	0	8	11	30	.251	.315	.365	490	123	19	2	11	54	44	123

MARK WHITEN — bats both — throws right — age 26 — TOR/CLE — *O/D

1991	BA	OBA	SA	AB	H	2B	3B	HR	RBI	BB	SO	2-YEAR TOTALS (1990–1991) BA	OBA	SA	AB	H	2B	3B	HR	RBI	BB	SO
Total	.243	.297	.388	407	99	18	7	9	45	30	85	.248	.301	.386	495	123	19	8	11	52	37	99
vs. Left	.257	.311	.413	109	28	7	2	2	10	9	26	.272	.323	.429	147	40	8	3	3	14	12	35
vs. Right	.238	.291	.379	298	71	11	5	7	35	21	59	.239	.292	.368	348	83	11	5	8	38	25	64
at Home	.249	.310	.401	197	49	8	5	4	16	16	40	.248	.308	.398	226	56	9	5	5	19	18	46
on Road	.238	.284	.376	210	50	10	2	5	29	14	45	.249	.296	.375	269	67	10	3	6	33	19	53
on Grass	.258	.309	.396	283	73	13	4	6	31	21	51	.264	.316	.397	330	87	13	5	7	35	26	58
on Turf	.210	.269	.371	124	26	5	3	3	14	9	34	.218	.271	.364	165	36	6	3	4	17	11	41
Day Games	.210	.279	.303	119	25	4	2	1	12	12	30	.201	.265	.278	144	29	4	2	1	12	13	34
Night Games	.257	.304	.424	288	74	14	5	8	33	18	55	.268	.317	.430	351	94	15	6	10	40	24	65
April	.309	.339	.436	55	17	2	1	1	14	4	13	.309	.339	.436	55	17	2	1	1	14	4	13
May	.200	.257	.292	65	13	2	2	0	4	4	14	.200	.257	.292	65	13	2	2	0	4	4	14
June	.182	.250	.295	44	8	2	0	1	2	4	10	.182	.250	.295	44	8	2	0	1	2	4	10
July	.274	.324	.463	95	26	5	2	3	12	5	18	.260	.305	.409	154	40	5	3	4	14	8	29
August	.237	.307	.421	114	27	7	1	4	12	12	21	.242	.312	.419	124	30	8	1	4	14	13	21
Sept–Oct	.235	.250	.294	34	8	0	1	0	1	1	9	.283	.322	.377	53	15	0	1	0	1	4	12
Bases Empty	.250	.306	.419	236	59	10	3	8	8	17	45	.261	.309	.416	291	76	10	4	9	9	18	49
Leadoff	.309	.343	.532	94	29	6	0	5	5	4	17	.314	.346	.529	121	38	6	1	6	6	5	19
Runners On Base	.234	.284	.345	171	40	8	4	1	37	13	40	.230	.291	.343	204	47	9	4	2	43	19	50
Scoring Position	.232	.284	.305	95	22	5	1	0	31	9	23	.219	.280	.289	114	25	6	1	0	35	12	30
Late and Close	.203	.238	.342	79	16	3	1	2	9	3	15	.213	.265	.330	94	20	3	1	2	9	6	16

RICK WILKINS — bats left — throws right — age 25 — CHN — C

1991	BA	OBA	SA	AB	H	2B	3B	HR	RBI	BB	SO	1-YEAR TOTALS (1991) BA	OBA	SA	AB	H	2B	3B	HR	RBI	BB	SO
Total	.222	.307	.355	203	45	9	0	6	22	19	56	.222	.307	.355	203	45	9	0	6	22	19	56
vs. Left	.243	.333	.351	37	9	1	0	1	5	3	13	.243	.333	.351	37	9	1	0	1	5	3	13
vs. Right	.217	.301	.355	166	36	8	0	5	17	16	43	.217	.301	.355	166	36	8	0	5	17	16	43
at Home	.175	.248	.291	103	18	6	0	2	9	7	29	.175	.248	.291	103	18	6	0	2	9	7	29
on Road	.270	.365	.420	100	27	3	0	4	13	12	27	.270	.365	.420	100	27	3	0	4	13	12	27
on Grass	.206	.276	.310	155	32	7	0	3	14	12	43	.206	.276	.310	155	32	7	0	3	14	12	43
on Turf	.271	.397	.500	48	13	2	0	3	8	7	13	.271	.397	.500	48	13	2	0	3	8	7	13
Day Games	.164	.233	.255	110	18	4	0	2	9	9	29	.164	.233	.255	110	18	4	0	2	9	9	29
Night Games	.290	.389	.473	93	27	5	0	4	13	10	27	.290	.389	.473	93	27	5	0	4	13	10	27
April	.000	.000	.000	0	0	0	0	0	0	0	0	.000	.000	.000	0	0	0	0	0	0	0	0
May	.000	.000	.000	0	0	0	0	0	0	0	0	.000	.000	.000	0	0	0	0	0	0	0	0
June	.278	.350	.537	54	15	2	0	4	11	3	13	.278	.350	.537	54	15	2	0	4	11	3	13
July	.225	.286	.324	71	16	4	0	1	4	5	21	.225	.286	.324	71	16	4	0	1	4	5	21
August	.167	.306	.200	60	10	2	0	0	5	10	17	.167	.306	.200	60	10	2	0	0	5	10	17
Sept–Oct	.222	.263	.444	18	4	1	0	1	2	1	5	.222	.263	.444	18	4	1	0	1	2	1	5
Bases Empty	.237	.318	.381	118	28	5	0	4	4	10	29	.237	.318	.381	118	28	5	0	4	4	10	29
Leadoff	.226	.317	.264	53	12	2	0	0	0	4	13	.226	.317	.264	53	12	2	0	0	0	4	13
Runners On Base	.200	.292	.318	85	17	4	0	2	18	9	27	.200	.292	.318	85	17	4	0	2	18	9	27
Scoring Position	.233	.365	.442	43	10	3	0	2	17	7	14	.233	.365	.442	43	10	3	0	2	17	7	14
Late and Close	.304	.385	.500	46	14	6	0	1	5	5	14	.304	.385	.500	46	14	6	0	1	5	5	14

BERNIE WILLIAMS — bats both — throws right — age 24 — NYA — O

1991	BA	OBA	SA	AB	H	2B	3B	HR	RBI	BB	SO
Total	.237	.336	.350	320	76	19	4	3	34	48	57
vs. Left	.202	.309	.317	104	21	6	0	2	13	17	11
vs. Right	.255	.349	.366	216	55	13	4	1	21	31	46
at Home	.264	.355	.371	159	42	10	2	1	19	23	22
on Road	.211	.317	.329	161	34	9	2	2	15	25	35
on Grass	.246	.345	.359	276	68	17	4	2	31	42	43
on Turf	.182	.280	.295	44	8	2	0	1	3	6	14
Day Games	.301	.388	.456	103	31	9	2	1	19	15	19
Night Games	.207	.311	.300	217	45	10	2	2	15	33	38
April	.000	.000	.000	0	0	0	0	0	0	0	0
May	.000	.000	.000	0	0	0	0	0	0	0	0
June	.000	.000	.000	0	0	0	0	0	0	0	0
July	.254	.386	.423	71	18	4	1	2	11	15	14
August	.240	.331	.360	125	30	10	1	1	14	17	25
Sept–Oct	.226	.310	.298	124	28	5	2	0	9	16	18
Bases Empty	.207	.317	.328	198	41	9	3	3	3	31	31
Leadoff	.231	.355	.317	104	24	4	1	1	1	20	15
Runners On Base	.287	.366	.385	122	35	10	1	0	31	17	26
Scoring Position	.343	.405	.463	67	23	6	1	0	29	9	12
Late and Close	.218	.317	.273	55	12	3	0	0	8	7	13

1-YEAR TOTALS (1991)

	BA	OBA	SA	AB	H	2B	3B	HR	RBI	BB	SO
	.237	.336	.350	320	76	19	4	3	34	48	57
	.202	.309	.317	104	21	6	0	2	13	17	11
	.255	.349	.366	216	55	13	4	1	21	31	46
	.264	.355	.371	159	42	10	2	1	19	23	22
	.211	.317	.329	161	34	9	2	2	15	25	35
	.246	.345	.359	276	68	17	4	2	31	42	43
	.182	.280	.295	44	8	2	0	1	3	6	14
	.301	.388	.456	103	31	9	2	1	19	15	19
	.207	.311	.300	217	45	10	2	2	15	33	38
	.000	.000	.000	0	0	0	0	0	0	0	0
	.000	.000	.000	0	0	0	0	0	0	0	0
	.000	.000	.000	0	0	0	0	0	0	0	0
	.254	.386	.423	71	18	4	1	2	11	15	14
	.240	.331	.360	125	30	10	1	1	14	17	25
	.226	.310	.298	124	28	5	2	0	9	16	18
	.207	.317	.328	198	41	9	3	3	3	31	31
	.231	.355	.317	104	24	4	1	1	1	20	15
	.287	.366	.385	122	35	10	1	0	31	17	26
	.343	.405	.463	67	23	6	1	0	29	9	12
	.218	.317	.273	55	12	3	0	0	8	7	13

MATT WILLIAMS — bats right — throws right — age 27 — SF — *3/S

1991	BA	OBA	SA	AB	H	2B	3B	HR	RBI	BB	SO
Total	.268	.310	.499	589	158	24	5	34	98	33	128
vs. Left	.282	.318	.460	163	46	8	0	7	25	9	33
vs. Right	.263	.307	.514	426	112	16	5	27	73	24	95
at Home	.287	.327	.526	289	83	12	3	17	46	16	60
on Road	.250	.294	.473	300	75	12	2	17	52	17	68
on Grass	.284	.317	.502	444	126	19	3	24	71	20	92
on Turf	.221	.290	.490	145	32	5	2	10	27	13	36
Day Games	.291	.326	.574	251	73	11	3	18	46	13	49
Night Games	.251	.299	.444	338	85	13	2	16	52	20	79
April	.269	.310	.436	78	21	2	1	3	15	5	13
May	.180	.195	.288	111	20	4	1	2	8	1	19
June	.253	.310	.495	91	23	7	0	5	18	7	20
July	.341	.378	.758	91	31	3	1	11	21	4	24
August	.255	.304	.443	106	27	6	1	4	13	8	30
Sept–Oct	.321	.368	.598	112	36	2	1	9	23	8	22
Bases Empty	.261	.312	.516	310	81	14	4	19	19	19	65
Leadoff	.308	.366	.592	130	40	4	3	9	9	9	23
Runners On Base	.276	.308	.480	279	77	10	1	15	79	14	63
Scoring Position	.238	.287	.347	147	35	2	1	4	54	12	35
Late and Close	.217	.280	.391	92	20	4	0	4	13	7	17

5-YEAR TOTALS (1987–1991)

	BA	OBA	SA	AB	H	2B	3B	HR	RBI	BB	SO
	.245	.289	.461	1899	466	84	11	101	310	104	447
	.255	.305	.491	584	149	25	1	37	106	41	120
	.241	.281	.447	1315	317	59	10	64	204	63	327
	.252	.291	.497	945	238	45	5	59	167	49	217
	.239	.286	.425	954	228	39	6	42	143	55	230
	.260	.296	.482	1450	377	70	6	80	246	69	328
	.198	.265	.392	449	89	14	5	21	64	35	119
	.270	.302	.530	773	209	38	5	51	151	34	172
	.228	.280	.413	1126	257	46	6	50	159	70	275
	.226	.269	.365	266	60	6	2	9	39	16	74
	.224	.256	.378	304	68	13	2	10	35	12	57
	.262	.304	.511	309	81	17	0	20	63	18	73
	.280	.326	.547	225	63	9	3	15	43	12	56
	.245	.290	.509	383	94	20	3	25	57	21	90
	.243	.292	.454	412	100	19	1	22	73	25	97
	.239	.276	.463	1044	250	42	10	57	57	45	256
	.255	.297	.488	428	109	13	6	25	25	22	91
	.253	.303	.458	855	216	42	1	44	253	59	191
	.240	.306	.418	488	117	19	1	22	198	49	120
	.208	.254	.363	284	59	15	1	9	33	14	72

DAVE WINFIELD — bats right — throws right — age 41 — CAL — *OD

1991	BA	OBA	SA	AB	H	2B	3B	HR	RBI	BB	SO
Total	.262	.326	.472	568	149	27	4	28	86	56	109
vs. Left	.300	.381	.575	160	48	9	1	11	27	20	24
vs. Right	.248	.304	.431	408	101	18	3	17	59	36	85
at Home	.244	.305	.432	271	66	10	1	13	33	25	54
on Road	.279	.345	.508	297	83	17	3	15	53	31	55
on Grass	.251	.318	.421	475	119	21	3	18	53	48	89
on Turf	.323	.373	.731	93	30	6	1	10	33	8	20
Day Games	.260	.345	.455	123	32	6	0	6	25	16	28
Night Games	.263	.321	.476	445	117	21	4	22	61	40	81
April	.232	.224	.464	56	13	4	0	3	14	0	8
May	.283	.347	.528	106	30	7	2	5	15	11	17
June	.320	.372	.641	103	33	5	2	8	24	9	20
July	.245	.311	.383	94	23	4	0	3	7	8	12
August	.200	.280	.356	90	18	2	0	4	8	10	25
Sept–Oct	.269	.360	.437	119	32	5	0	5	18	18	27
Bases Empty	.249	.298	.464	317	79	13	2	17	17	21	72
Leadoff	.236	.304	.375	144	34	6	1	4	4	13	32
Runners On Base	.279	.360	.482	251	70	14	2	11	69	35	37
Scoring Position	.283	.371	.478	138	39	10	1	5	56	23	17
Late and Close	.216	.275	.378	74	16	3	0	3	7	6	22

7-YEAR TOTALS (1984–1991)

	BA	OBA	SA	AB	H	2B	3B	HR	RBI	BB	SO
	.286	.356	.480	3942	1129	206	24	170	685	435	647
	.298	.389	.531	1250	372	67	12	67	236	194	166
	.281	.339	.457	2692	757	139	12	103	449	241	481
	.287	.361	.482	1889	542	95	9	85	328	225	290
	.286	.351	.479	2053	587	111	15	85	357	210	357
	.283	.356	.473	3318	939	172	20	139	553	384	531
	.304	.357	.521	624	190	34	4	31	132	51	116
	.297	.366	.472	1177	349	49	7	48	210	136	186
	.282	.351	.484	2765	780	157	17	122	475	299	461
	.291	.377	.497	443	129	22	3	21	81	63	74
	.270	.331	.488	682	184	38	6	33	117	65	110
	.324	.387	.545	673	218	40	5	33	130	71	104
	.285	.352	.470	657	187	32	3	28	110	69	98
	.281	.360	.450	698	196	34	3	26	107	86	122
	.272	.337	.444	789	215	40	4	29	140	81	139
	.274	.339	.466	2031	556	111	6	89	89	196	365
	.283	.354	.455	877	248	50	1	33	33	92	148
	.300	.373	.496	1911	573	95	18	81	596	239	282
	.314	.396	.512	1081	339	56	10	46	508	168	161
	.275	.335	.444	612	168	25	2	25	96	57	116

ERIC YELDING — bats right — throws right — age 27 — HOU — S/O

3-YEAR TOTALS (1989–1991)

1991	BA	OBA	SA	AB	H	2B	3B	HR	RBI	BB	SO		BA	OBA	SA	AB	H	2B	3B	HR	RBI	BB	SO
Total	.243	.276	.301	276	67	11	1	1	20	13	46		.249	.294	.294	877	218	22	6	2	57	59	152
vs. Left	.295	.333	.347	95	28	3	1	0	4	6	15		.275	.320	.323	371	102	10	4	0	23	27	54
vs. Right	.215	.245	.276	181	39	8	0	1	16	7	31		.229	.275	.273	506	116	12	2	2	34	32	98
at Home	.226	.252	.248	137	31	3	0	0	10	5	28		.240	.290	.268	421	101	4	4	0	24	32	72
on Road	.259	.299	.353	139	36	8	1	1	10	8	18		.257	.298	.318	456	117	18	2	2	33	27	80
on Grass	.236	.286	.278	72	17	3	0	0	3	5	9		.275	.330	.325	265	73	11	1	0	20	22	43
on Turf	.245	.272	.309	204	50	8	1	1	17	8	37		.237	.278	.281	612	145	11	5	2	37	37	109
Day Games	.265	.296	.397	68	18	4	1	1	6	3	12		.254	.313	.311	244	62	7	2	1	18	20	45
Night Games	.236	.269	.269	208	49	7	0	0	14	10	34		.246	.287	.288	633	156	15	4	1	39	39	107
April	.191	.214	.265	68	13	3	1	0	0	2	12		.219	.236	.286	105	23	3	2	0	6	3	17
May	.306	.322	.400	85	26	5	0	1	10	2	16		.293	.325	.346	188	55	5	1	1	16	9	31
June	.226	.290	.250	84	19	2	0	0	9	8	13		.234	.309	.263	171	40	3	1	0	12	19	27
July	.231	.250	.256	39	9	1	0	0	1	1	5		.281	.317	.317	167	47	4	1	0	12	10	29
August	.000	.000	.000	0	0	0	0	0	0	0	0		.175	.221	.198	126	22	3	0	0	5	7	20
Sept–Oct	.000	.000	.000	0	0	0	0	0	0	0	0		.258	.321	.333	120	31	4	1	0	6	11	28
Bases Empty	.222	.257	.293	167	37	7	1	1	0	8	33		.242	.297	.287	571	138	16	2	2	2	44	116
Leadoff	.216	.266	.270	74	16	2	1	0	0	5	11		.241	.299	.275	324	78	6	1	1	1	26	58
Runners On Base	.275	.304	.312	109	30	4	0	0	19	5	13		.261	.289	.307	306	80	6	4	0	55	15	36
Scoring Position	.238	.279	.286	63	15	3	0	0	18	4	11		.250	.280	.293	188	47	4	2	0	52	11	23
Late and Close	.314	.364	.353	51	16	2	0	0	5	4	10		.274	.335	.288	146	40	2	0	0	12	13	26

ROBIN YOUNT — bats right — throws right — age 37 — MIL — *OD

8-YEAR TOTALS (1984–1991)

1991	BA	OBA	SA	AB	H	2B	3B	HR	RBI	BB	SO		BA	OBA	SA	AB	H	2B	3B	HR	RBI	BB	SO
Total	.260	.332	.376	503	131	20	4	10	77	54	79		.292	.363	.445	4572	1337	222	55	122	643	512	592
vs. Left	.256	.377	.341	129	33	5	0	2	18	26	16		.287	.369	.434	1305	374	60	14	35	172	178	165
vs. Right	.262	.314	.388	374	98	15	4	8	59	28	63		.295	.361	.449	3267	963	162	41	87	471	334	427
at Home	.236	.311	.396	250	59	10	3	2	42	26	43		.294	.365	.467	2259	664	110	32	72	354	251	289
on Road	.285	.352	.356	253	72	10	1	2	35	28	36		.291	.362	.424	2313	673	112	23	50	289	261	303
on Grass	.259	.338	.379	428	111	16	4	9	67	51	69		.293	.366	.450	3891	1142	178	47	112	561	444	504
on Turf	.267	.291	.360	75	20	4	0	1	10	3	10		.286	.349	.419	681	195	44	8	10	82	68	88
Day Games	.274	.344	.384	164	45	3	0	5	28	17	20		.285	.352	.455	1355	386	70	10	47	187	140	179
Night Games	.254	.326	.372	339	86	17	4	5	49	37	59		.296	.368	.441	3217	951	152	45	75	456	372	413
April	.342	.400	.632	76	26	5	1	5	17	7	8		.282	.357	.428	593	167	23	8	16	71	66	66
May	.252	.303	.402	107	27	4	0	4	16	9	14		.296	.358	.445	733	217	33	5	22	101	71	88
June	.200	.302	.250	100	20	3	1	0	10	13	24		.280	.356	.416	779	218	45	11	13	104	95	109
July	.353	.389	.529	17	6	1	1	0	0	1	1		.305	.379	.481	699	213	41	14	18	97	85	92
August	.327	.391	.406	101	33	6	1	0	17	11	15		.282	.353	.409	820	231	37	8	17	111	93	97
Sept–Oct	.186	.274	.225	102	19	1	0	1	17	13	17		.307	.375	.485	948	291	43	9	36	159	102	140
Bases Empty	.237	.287	.335	257	61	9	2	4	4	16	39		.274	.343	.420	2524	691	120	29	64	64	252	333
Leadoff	.222	.260	.325	117	26	6	0	2	2	5	18		.270	.321	.413	971	262	52	12	21	21	67	120
Runners On Base	.285	.373	.419	246	70	11	2	6	73	38	40		.315	.387	.476	2048	646	102	26	58	579	260	259
Scoring Position	.299	.385	.465	144	43	5	2	5	68	25	23		.307	.389	.457	1186	364	60	17	58	496	188	173
Late and Close	.240	.301	.467	75	18	3	1	4	13	6	12		.295	.371	.418	660	195	29	5	14	102	81	100

TODD ZEILE — bats right — throws right — age 27 — SL — *3

3-YEAR TOTALS (1989–1991)

1991	BA	OBA	SA	AB	H	2B	3B	HR	RBI	BB	SO		BA	OBA	SA	AB	H	2B	3B	HR	RBI	BB	SO
Total	.280	.353	.412	565	158	36	3	11	81	62	94		.263	.342	.402	1142	300	64	7	27	146	138	185
vs. Left	.297	.370	.418	232	69	14	1	4	30	26	43		.284	.361	.420	440	125	26	2	10	56	52	69
vs. Right	.267	.340	.408	333	89	22	2	7	51	36	51		.249	.330	.390	702	175	38	5	17	90	86	116
at Home	.297	.374	.459	279	83	20	2	7	50	33	40		.278	.361	.434	551	153	33	4	15	82	70	78
on Road	.262	.331	.367	286	75	16	1	4	31	29	54		.249	.325	.372	591	147	31	3	12	64	68	107
on Grass	.268	.325	.349	149	40	12	0	0	12	11	30		.236	.306	.336	292	69	20	0	3	24	29	62
on Turf	.284	.362	.435	416	118	24	3	11	69	51	64		.272	.355	.425	850	231	44	7	24	122	109	123
Day Games	.318	.379	.484	157	50	12	1	4	24	16	22		.291	.365	.458	299	87	21	1	9	45	38	50
Night Games	.265	.343	.385	408	108	24	2	7	57	46	72		.253	.334	.382	843	213	43	6	18	101	100	135
April	.317	.377	.444	63	20	3	1	1	12	5	10		.287	.359	.442	129	37	7	2	3	20	14	22
May	.323	.396	.452	93	30	7	1	1	10	11	19		.262	.344	.393	168	44	11	1	3	20	21	34
June	.235	.301	.333	102	24	7	0	1	10	9	14		.237	.320	.371	194	46	9	1	5	20	23	27
July	.260	.333	.450	100	26	5	1	4	14	11	15		.244	.311	.419	172	42	7	1	7	21	17	25
August	.287	.339	.380	108	31	4	0	2	18	8	14		.303	.352	.415	234	71	7	2	5	30	18	32
Sept–Oct	.273	.380	.434	99	27	10	0	2	17	18	22		.245	.362	.388	245	60	23	0	4	35	45	45
Bases Empty	.268	.338	.419	310	83	18	1	9	9	30	55		.258	.330	.411	635	164	29	4	20	20	64	107
Leadoff	.328	.408	.464	125	41	8	0	3	3	16	18		.290	.359	.468	297	86	17	0	12	12	31	47
Runners On Base	.294	.369	.404	255	75	18	2	2	72	32	39		.268	.357	.391	507	136	35	3	7	126	74	78
Scoring Position	.304	.402	.399	158	48	10	1	1	64	28	30		.242	.358	.342	310	75	20	1	3	106	60	57
Late and Close	.288	.375	.385	104	30	5	1	1	8	13	21		.244	.339	.325	209	51	9	1	2	14	29	39

PITCHERS

JIM ABBOTT — bats left — throws left — age 25 — CAL — P

3-YEAR TOTALS (1989–1991)

1991	G	IP	H	BB	SO	SB	CS	W	L	SV	ERA	G	IP	H	BB	SO	SB	CS	W	L	SV	ERA
Total	34	243.0	222	73	158	12	14	18	11	0	2.89	96	636.0	658	219	378	55	26	40	37	0	3.72
at Home	17	129.1	109	35	78	6	9	8	7	0	2.57	49	326.2	348	101	185	29	16	17	19	0	3.91
on Road	17	113.2	113	38	80	6	5	10	4	0	3.25	47	309.1	310	118	193	26	10	23	18	0	3.52
on Grass	29	211.0	184	59	139	8	14	15	9	0	2.60	80	534.0	538	175	324	41	22	33	28	0	3.56
on Turf	5	32.0	38	14	19	4	0	3	2	0	4.78	16	102.0	120	44	54	14	4	7	9	0	4.59
Day Games	11	73.0	74	29	48	5	5	9	2	0	3.21	25	164.0	174	56	102	15	9	13	12	0	3.29
Night Games	23	170.0	148	44	110	7	9	9	9	0	2.75	71	472.0	484	163	276	40	17	27	25	0	3.87
April	4	24.0	31	9	15	1	2	0	4	0	6.00	11	65.0	80	26	34	9	4	1	7	0	5.12
May	5	36.2	32	8	17	1	4	4	0	0	1.96	17	108.2	105	41	60	8	6	10	4	0	3.48
June	6	42.0	39	15	32	1	2	2	1	0	3.43	16	105.1	101	40	62	7	4	6	5	0	4.10
July	6	44.0	38	9	34	2	1	3	2	0	2.66	16	116.0	114	23	74	8	4	8	6	0	2.56
August	6	45.1	36	15	27	1	1	5	1	0	1.99	18	115.0	127	48	74	13	3	9	7	0	4.30
Sept–Oct	7	51.0	46	17	33	6	4	4	3	0	2.65	18	126.0	131	41	74	10	5	6	8	0	3.43

	BA	OBA	SA	AB	H	2B	3B	HR	RBI	BB	SO	BA	OBA	SA	AB	H	2B	3B	HR	RBI	BB	SO
Total	.244	.302	.336	909	222	35	3	14	75	73	158	.270	.332	.370	2436	658	97	9	43	244	219	378
vs. Left	.303	.348	.430	142	43	9	0	3	18	9	25	.315	.377	.443	375	118	22	1	8	57	38	67
vs. Right	.233	.293	.318	767	179	26	3	11	57	64	133	.262	.323	.357	2061	540	75	8	35	187	181	311
Bases Empty	.247	.305	.332	551	136	21	1	8	8	44	92	.273	.331	.378	1416	386	60	4	27	27	117	208
Leadoff	.245	.292	.342	237	58	11	0	4	4	16	40	.275	.330	.384	619	170	28	2	12	12	48	84
Runners On Base	.240	.297	.341	358	86	14	2	6	67	29	66	.267	.332	.360	1020	272	37	5	16	217	102	170
Scoring Position	.236	.295	.361	191	45	7	1	5	63	19	37	.252	.335	.340	544	137	18	3	8	197	74	96
Late and Close	.267	.320	.333	90	24	0	0	2	10	7	13	.289	.344	.363	204	59	1	1	4	23	17	24

RICK AGUILERA — bats right — throws right — age 31 — MIN — P

7-YEAR TOTALS (1985–1991)

1991	G	IP	H	BB	SO	SB	CS	W	L	SV	ERA	G	IP	H	BB	SO	SB	CS	W	L	SV	ERA
Total	63	69.0	44	30	61	7	0	4	5	42	2.35	244	683.0	644	203	530	50	20	49	40	81	3.33
at Home	34	36.0	14	12	36	4	0	2	0	23	1.00	126	338.0	296	94	282	23	9	25	14	42	3.01
on Road	29	33.0	30	18	25	3	0	2	5	19	3.82	118	345.0	348	109	248	27	11	24	26	39	3.65
on Grass	23	26.2	25	15	20	1	0	2	4	14	4.05	125	400.2	372	101	318	25	13	30	23	33	3.23
on Turf	40	42.1	19	15	41	6	0	2	1	28	1.28	119	282.1	272	102	212	25	7	19	17	48	3.47
Day Games	16	23.1	14	14	11	1	0	3	1	7	1.16	92	249.1	230	81	186	20	9	19	15	20	3.39
Night Games	47	45.2	30	16	50	6	0	1	4	35	2.96	152	433.2	414	122	344	30	11	30	25	61	3.30
April	7	7.2	6	3	10	2	0	0	1	4	1.17	28	77.1	83	23	72	5	3	6	8	4	4.42
May	11	16.1	10	11	13	3	0	1	1	6	2.20	41	91.2	82	31	92	4	3	4	5	19	2.85
June	12	11.2	10	8	8	0	0	1	1	10	4.63	45	75.0	70	38	59	10	1	5	6	17	3.84
July	11	10.2	9	1	10	1	0	0	1	7	2.53	46	127.1	116	33	92	9	6	11	8	13	2.83
August	11	11.0	5	2	10	1	0	2	0	9	0.82	37	140.1	139	30	102	7	4	16	7	12	3.72
Sept–Oct	11	11.2	4	5	10	0	0	0	1	6	2.31	47	171.1	154	48	113	13	3	7	12	7	2.94

	BA	OBA	SA	AB	H	2B	3B	HR	RBI	BB	SO	BA	OBA	SA	AB	H	2B	3B	HR	RBI	BB	SO
Total	.183	.274	.275	240	44	9	2	3	27	30	61	.250	.308	.374	2581	644	126	18	53	277	203	530
vs. Left	.185	.287	.274	135	25	4	1	2	14	19	36	.256	.320	.366	1284	329	61	13	18	119	117	240
vs. Right	.181	.256	.276	105	19	5	1	1	13	11	25	.243	.295	.382	1297	315	65	5	35	158	86	290
Bases Empty	.165	.254	.228	127	21	2	0	2	2	14	30	.249	.302	.369	1473	367	70	11	28	28	99	303
Leadoff	.104	.232	.125	48	5	1	0	0	0	8	10	.246	.301	.367	619	152	33	3	12	12	41	127
Runners On Base	.204	.295	.327	113	23	7	2	1	25	16	31	.250	.315	.381	1108	277	56	7	25	249	104	227
Scoring Position	.203	.316	.297	64	13	4	1	0	20	12	21	.240	.317	.355	647	155	29	5	12	205	76	150
Late and Close	.185	.268	.261	184	34	7	2	1	24	22	45	.225	.295	.316	591	133	20	2	10	69	58	149

ALLAN ANDERSON — bats left — throws left — age 28 — MIN — P

6-YEAR TOTALS (1986–1991)

1991	G	IP	H	BB	SO	SB	CS	W	L	SV	ERA	G	IP	H	BB	SO	SB	CS	W	L	SV	ERA
Total	29	134.1	148	42	51	14	6	5	11	0	4.96	148	818.2	900	211	339	54	38	49	55	0	4.11
at Home	14	67.2	69	16	30	9	2	2	4	0	4.52	75	411.0	464	106	182	33	19	23	27	0	4.77
on Road	15	66.2	79	26	21	5	4	3	7	0	5.40	73	407.2	436	105	157	21	19	26	28	0	3.44
on Grass	11	49.2	52	20	17	4	4	1	5	0	5.07	55	314.1	332	83	112	11	18	19	21	0	3.24
on Turf	18	84.2	96	22	34	10	2	4	6	0	4.89	93	504.1	568	128	227	43	20	30	34	0	4.66
Day Games	6	20.1	23	8	9	4	1	0	4	0	5.75	52	274.1	314	61	120	18	8	19	18	0	4.20
Night Games	23	114.0	125	34	42	10	5	5	7	0	4.82	96	544.1	586	150	219	36	30	30	37	0	4.07
April	5	31.0	27	12	6	2	1	1	2	0	4.06	16	94.2	96	32	26	7	6	7	6	0	3.71
May	5	24.1	34	7	10	6	0	0	0	0	6.66	26	136.2	166	40	55	12	6	4	10	0	5.86
June	6	37.2	40	6	14	4	3	3	2	0	2.87	30	186.0	217	37	81	17	14	11	13	0	3.68
July	5	13.1	19	6	6	1	0	0	2	0	8.77	21	153.0	180	37	70	8	3	9	12	0	4.82
August	2	9.0	12	3	6	0	1	0	0	0	8.00	21	123.0	112	28	48	2	4	9	6	0	2.85
Sept–Oct	6	19.0	16	8	9	1	1	1	3	0	4.26	26	125.1	129	31	59	8	5	9	8	0	3.52

	BA	OBA	SA	AB	H	2B	3B	HR	RBI	BB	SO	BA	OBA	SA	AB	H	2B	3B	HR	RBI	BB	SO
Total	.281	.336	.474	527	148	26	2	24	74	42	51	.282	.329	.425	3192	900	172	12	87	370	211	339
vs. Left	.225	.265	.315	111	25	4	0	2	9	6	5	.288	.346	.393	563	162	29	0	10	61	50	53
vs. Right	.296	.354	.517	416	123	22	2	22	65	36	46	.281	.325	.432	2629	738	143	12	77	309	161	286
Bases Empty	.276	.322	.451	337	93	15	1	14	14	20	40	.275	.323	.429	1870	514	100	6	59	59	115	217
Leadoff	.252	.284	.459	135	34	7	0	7	7	5	17	.284	.318	.424	813	231	48	3	20	20	36	80
Runners On Base	.289	.359	.516	190	55	11	1	10	60	22	11	.292	.336	.419	1322	386	72	6	28	311	96	122
Scoring Position	.245	.333	.453	106	26	4	0	6	47	15	7	.282	.337	.391	708	200	38	3	11	257	69	72
Late and Close	.326	.396	.535	43	14	3	0	2	3	4	3	.238	.297	.332	214	51	5	0	5	9	17	22

KEVIN APPIER — bats right — throws right — age 25 — KC — P

1991

1991	G	IP	H	BB	SO	SB	CS	W	L	SV	ERA
Total	34	207.2	205	61	158	10	8	13	10	0	3.42
at Home	15	96.2	83	28	74	7	5	5	5	0	2.79
on Road	19	111.0	122	33	84	3	3	8	5	0	3.97
on Grass	16	91.2	103	26	73	3	3	7	5	0	3.93
on Turf	18	116.0	102	35	85	7	5	6	5	0	3.03
Day Games	12	70.0	67	23	54	2	3	4	3	0	1.93
Night Games	22	137.2	138	38	104	8	5	9	7	0	4.18
April	4	21.1	30	7	13	0	1	1	3	0	4.64
May	6	34.0	29	6	16	0	1	2	2	0	3.18
June	6	39.1	36	12	28	2	0	1	2	0	3.89
July	5	32.0	31	7	31	3	3	3	0	0	3.09
August	6	39.2	35	13	34	4	1	3	2	0	2.72
Sept–Oct	7	41.1	44	16	36	1	2	3	1	0	3.48

	BA	OBA	SA	AB	H	2B	3B	HR	RBI	BB	SO
Total	.255	.307	.357	803	205	41	1	13	79	61	158
vs. Left	.268	.327	.396	399	107	25	1	8	41	37	60
vs. Right	.243	.287	.319	404	98	16	0	5	38	24	98
Bases Empty	.224	.277	.305	482	108	19	1	6	6	33	98
Leadoff	.208	.266	.292	202	42	11	0	2	2	15	38
Runners On Base	.302	.352	.436	321	97	22	0	7	73	28	60
Scoring Position	.285	.353	.397	179	51	11	0	3	61	22	37
Late and Close	.226	.244	.274	84	19	2	1	0	4	2	15

3-YEAR TOTALS (1989–1991)

	G	IP	H	BB	SO	SB	CS	W	L	SV	ERA
Total	72	415.0	418	127	295	26	11	26	22	0	3.43
at Home	32	186.2	177	50	135	13	6	13	10	0	3.09
on Road	40	228.1	241	77	160	13	5	13	12	0	3.71
on Grass	34	188.1	205	64	135	9	5	12	11	0	3.78
on Turf	38	226.2	213	63	160	17	6	14	11	0	3.14
Day Games	22	115.1	118	46	87	6	5	7	8	0	2.97
Night Games	50	299.2	300	81	208	20	6	19	14	0	3.60
April	6	23.2	32	9	17	0	1	1	3	0	4.18
May	13	58.0	41	14	28	0	1	3	2	0	3.41
June	17	94.0	96	35	61	9	1	3	8	0	4.31
July	12	79.2	75	21	68	4	4	7	2	0	3.62
August	11	73.2	64	20	54	6	1	8	2	0	2.32
Sept–Oct	13	86.0	89	28	67	7	3	4	5	0	3.03

	BA	OBA	SA	AB	H	2B	3B	HR	RBI	BB	SO
Total	.261	.315	.357	1603	418	63	2	29	158	127	295
vs. Left	.272	.336	.391	757	206	35	2	17	89	79	110
vs. Right	.251	.295	.326	846	212	28	0	12	69	48	185
Bases Empty	.242	.301	.325	935	226	31	1	15	15	75	181
Leadoff	.237	.296	.335	400	95	18	0	7	7	32	75
Runners On Base	.287	.333	.401	668	192	32	1	14	143	52	114
Scoring Position	.253	.320	.347	363	92	17	1	5	120	41	69
Late and Close	.234	.265	.291	141	33	3	1	1	11	6	27

LUIS AQUINO — bats right — throws right — age 28 — KC — P

1991

1991	G	IP	H	BB	SO	SB	CS	W	L	SV	ERA
Total	38	157.0	152	47	80	10	6	8	4	3	3.44
at Home	20	77.2	74	24	38	7	5	3	1	1	3.13
on Road	18	79.1	78	23	42	3	1	5	3	2	3.74
on Grass	15	71.1	74	20	40	2	1	4	3	2	3.79
on Turf	23	85.2	78	27	40	8	5	4	1	1	3.15
Day Games	14	49.2	42	19	24	3	1	2	0	2	2.72
Night Games	24	107.1	110	28	56	7	5	6	4	1	3.77
April	5	12.2	16	4	4	1	1	0	0	0	7.82
May	7	10.1	9	5	6	0	0	0	0	0	1.74
June	8	34.0	36	10	17	3	0	1	1	1	2.91
July	7	33.0	28	4	25	2	1	4	1	2	1.09
August	4	29.1	20	10	15	0	2	1	0	0	2.76
Sept–Oct	7	37.2	43	14	13	4	2	2	2	0	5.50

	BA	OBA	SA	AB	H	2B	3B	HR	RBI	BB	SO
Total	.253	.308	.374	601	152	33	5	10	67	47	80
vs. Left	.256	.311	.363	281	72	16	4	2	29	25	42
vs. Right	.250	.305	.384	320	80	17	1	8	38	22	38
Bases Empty	.246	.301	.345	354	87	20	3	3	3	27	53
Leadoff	.240	.293	.349	146	35	12	2	0	0	11	18
Runners On Base	.263	.318	.417	247	65	13	2	7	64	20	27
Scoring Position	.230	.293	.363	135	31	4	1	4	53	15	17
Late and Close	.203	.284	.291	79	16	4	0	1	6	9	16

5-YEAR TOTALS (1986–1991)

	G	IP	H	BB	SO	SB	CS	W	L	SV	ERA
Total	106	407.0	406	129	192	21	15	20	14	3	3.47
at Home	50	201.1	183	60	85	10	9	10	5	1	2.82
on Road	56	205.2	223	69	107	11	6	10	9	2	4.11
on Grass	45	176.0	186	53	100	7	4	8	8	2	3.78
on Turf	61	231.0	220	76	92	14	11	12	6	1	3.23
Day Games	31	117.2	96	47	50	6	3	8	0	2	2.07
Night Games	75	289.1	310	82	142	15	12	12	14	1	4.04
April	14	36.0	35	14	14	1	2	2	0	0	4.50
May	19	48.1	45	15	30	2	1	2	3	0	3.35
June	15	62.1	60	20	32	5	2	2	2	1	3.03
July	18	104.0	85	25	49	4	3	9	4	2	1.99
August	19	90.0	104	31	44	2	5	3	5	0	4.40
Sept–Oct	21	66.1	77	24	23	7	2	2	2	2	4.48

	BA	OBA	SA	AB	H	2B	3B	HR	RBI	BB	SO
Total	.261	.320	.372	1558	406	81	9	25	179	129	192
vs. Left	.272	.337	.391	740	201	42	8	10	81	74	97
vs. Right	.251	.304	.356	818	205	39	1	15	98	55	95
Bases Empty	.256	.314	.357	860	220	47	5	10	10	69	116
Leadoff	.243	.308	.320	366	89	21	2	1	1	33	43
Runners On Base	.266	.326	.391	698	186	34	4	15	169	60	76
Scoring Position	.252	.322	.366	393	99	18	3	7	146	45	47
Late and Close	.268	.333	.405	153	41	7	1	4	15	15	25

JACK ARMSTRONG — bats right — throws right — age 27 — CIN — P

1991

1991	G	IP	H	BB	SO	SB	CS	W	L	SV	ERA
Total	27	139.2	158	54	93	12	7	7	13	0	5.48
at Home	12	66.1	74	30	44	4	3	4	8	0	6.38
on Road	15	73.1	84	24	49	8	4	3	5	0	4.66
on Grass	10	50.1	57	17	29	3	3	3	3	0	4.47
on Turf	17	89.1	101	37	64	9	4	4	10	0	6.04
Day Games	6	32.2	34	12	24	4	2	2	3	0	3.31
Night Games	21	107.0	124	42	69	8	5	5	10	0	6.14
April	3	17.0	14	4	14	3	0	1	1	0	4.24
May	5	33.0	32	10	26	2	2	3	2	0	4.09
June	6	27.1	39	15	16	3	1	3	1	0	6.26
July	6	24.1	26	12	16	0	1	1	3	0	6.29
August	1	5.0	6	2	2	0	0	0	1	0	12.60
Sept–Oct	6	33.0	41	11	19	4	1	0	3	0	5.18

	BA	OBA	SA	AB	H	2B	3B	HR	RBI	BB	SO
Total	.293	.354	.491	540	158	24	4	25	84	54	93
vs. Left	.281	.357	.485	295	83	13	4	13	48	35	34
vs. Right	.306	.349	.498	245	75	11	0	12	36	19	59
Bases Empty	.266	.329	.446	334	89	13	1	15	15	30	60
Leadoff	.258	.329	.515	132	34	7	0	9	9	13	24
Runners On Base	.335	.392	.563	206	69	11	3	10	69	24	33
Scoring Position	.363	.409	.602	113	41	4	1	7	59	15	20
Late and Close	.278	.316	.389	18	5	0	1	0	1	1	5

4-YEAR TOTALS (1988–1991)

	G	IP	H	BB	SO	SB	CS	W	L	SV	ERA
Total	79	413.2	412	172	271	48	16	25	32	0	4.61
at Home	39	191.1	197	86	129	19	7	14	16	0	5.50
on Road	40	222.1	215	86	142	29	9	11	16	0	3.85
on Grass	23	126.1	132	50	71	12	6	6	9	0	4.42
on Turf	56	287.1	280	122	200	36	10	19	23	0	4.70
Day Games	23	126.1	116	53	97	25	4	9	8	0	3.56
Night Games	56	287.1	296	119	174	23	12	16	24	0	5.07
April	7	42.2	35	9	34	4	1	5	1	0	2.53
May	14	91.0	72	36	53	5	3	7	4	0	3.07
June	14	73.0	85	36	54	13	5	3	7	0	5.42
July	18	89.1	92	33	64	9	2	5	6	0	5.34
August	8	35.1	46	25	15	3	3	1	5	0	8.15
Sept–Oct	18	82.1	82	33	51	14	2	4	6	0	4.37

	BA	OBA	SA	AB	H	2B	3B	HR	RBI	BB	SO
Total	.262	.334	.417	1574	412	79	12	47	203	172	271
vs. Left	.274	.356	.432	891	244	48	9	25	123	116	114
vs. Right	.246	.303	.397	683	168	31	3	22	80	56	157
Bases Empty	.241	.316	.376	934	225	46	4	24	24	98	175
Leadoff	.249	.320	.414	394	98	24	1	13	13	38	75
Runners On Base	.292	.359	.477	640	187	33	8	23	179	74	96
Scoring Position	.281	.352	.465	381	107	18	5	14	152	51	68
Late and Close	.231	.306	.338	65	15	1	1	3	5	6	9

PAUL ASSENMACHER — bats left — throws left — age 32 — CHN — P

6-YEAR TOTALS (1986–1991)

1991	G	IP	H	BB	SO	SB	CS	W	L	SV	ERA		G	IP	H	BB	SO	SB	CS	W	L	SV	ERA
Total	75	102.2	85	31	117	8	5	7	8	15	3.24		389	484.2	440	177	457	32	20	33	25	39	3.34
at Home	43	61.0	44	13	69	5	2	4	2	8	2.07		209	261.0	236	82	253	20	8	24	12	21	3.28
on Road	32	41.2	41	18	48	3	3	3	6	7	4.97		180	223.2	204	95	204	12	12	9	13	18	3.42
on Grass	56	78.2	59	20	93	5	3	5	4	11	2.63		294	369.1	333	126	363	23	14	27	19	31	3.31
on Turf	19	24.0	26	11	24	3	2	2	4	4	5.25		95	115.1	107	51	94	9	6	6	6	8	3.43
Day Games	39	53.2	46	15	67	3	1	4	4	9	2.85		159	211.1	189	80	210	15	7	14	8	20	3.41
Night Games	36	49.0	39	16	50	5	4	3	7	6	3.67		230	273.1	251	97	247	17	13	19	17	19	3.29
April	11	15.2	8	3	17	0	2	0	0	3	2.30		52	65.2	40	23	63	5	6	1	4	5	2.19
May	13	16.0	17	5	19	3	0	2	2	1	5.06		75	87.0	73	31	75	7	1	6	5	6	3.00
June	17	16.0	13	13	21	2	1	1	2	2	3.94		69	83.2	100	45	94	8	7	4	5	7	5.81
July	10	13.1	15	1	17	1	0	0	0	5	2.70		65	78.0	73	25	76	4	2	6	4	7	3.00
August	11	22.1	15	5	25	1	2	4	1	1	2.01		54	75.1	54	22	73	1	3	7	1	5	2.03
Sept–Oct	13	19.1	17	4	18	1	0	0	3	3	3.72		63	95.0	100	31	94	7	1	9	6	9	3.60

	BA	OBA	SA	AB	H	2B	3B	HR	RBI	BB	SO		BA	OBA	SA	AB	H	2B	3B	HR	RBI	BB	SO
Total	.223	.284	.357	381	85	13	4	10	47	31	117		.243	.311	.358	1810	440	66	11	40	229	177	457
vs. Left	.179	.247	.261	134	24	6	1	1	14	10	49		.224	.285	.296	595	133	19	3	6	74	47	168
vs. Right	.247	.304	.409	247	61	7	3	9	33	21	68		.253	.323	.388	1215	307	47	8	34	155	130	289
Bases Empty	.221	.259	.369	217	48	7	2	7	7	11	71		.243	.294	.365	966	235	33	5	25	25	68	236
Leadoff	.217	.270	.373	83	18	2	1	3	3	6	33		.268	.320	.445	400	107	15	4	16	16	30	95
Runners On Base	.226	.314	.341	164	37	6	2	3	40	20	46		.243	.329	.350	844	205	33	6	15	204	109	221
Scoring Position	.262	.360	.388	103	27	5	1	2	36	16	27		.255	.358	.358	530	135	22	3	9	181	89	138
Late and Close	.219	.278	.344	279	61	10	2	7	35	21	83		.253	.322	.368	964	244	40	4	21	128	98	256

DON AUGUST — bats right — throws right — age 29 — MIL — P

4-YEAR TOTALS (1988–1991)

1991	G	IP	H	BB	SO	SB	CS	W	L	SV	ERA		G	IP	H	BB	SO	SB	CS	W	L	SV	ERA
Total	28	138.1	166	47	62	18	4	9	8	0	5.47		88	440.0	491	158	181	42	17	34	30	0	4.64
at Home	14	80.2	78	20	30	8	2	8	5	0	4.13		40	211.0	217	63	85	16	8	21	12	0	3.88
on Road	14	57.2	88	27	32	10	2	1	3	0	7.34		48	229.0	274	95	96	26	9	13	18	0	5.34
on Grass	23	116.2	130	33	48	12	3	9	6	0	4.86		74	367.0	408	121	144	31	13	31	25	0	4.46
on Turf	5	21.2	36	14	14	6	1	0	2	0	8.72		14	73.0	83	37	37	11	4	3	5	0	5.55
Day Games	6	23.0	35	9	12	3	0	1	2	0	8.22		24	124.1	145	33	47	13	3	9	9	0	4.42
Night Games	22	115.1	131	38	50	15	4	8	6	0	4.92		64	315.2	346	125	134	29	14	25	21	0	4.73
April	3	13.0	18	0	8	1	1	1	2	0	7.62		12	52.1	65	17	25	8	3	2	8	0	5.33
May	5	29.0	23	8	14	1	0	3	0	0	2.79		11	56.1	62	15	23	4	1	6	2	0	4.31
June	6	31.2	29	14	8	2	0	2	1	0	4.26		17	99.0	92	37	29	8	3	9	4	0	3.55
July	5	27.0	37	8	10	4	2	2	2	0	6.33		17	91.0	110	33	42	8	5	5	8	0	5.74
August	5	27.2	39	14	14	8	1	1	1	0	5.86		14	65.1	79	29	36	8	4	3	3	0	4.96
Sept–Oct	4	10.0	20	3	8	1	0	0	2	0	10.80		17	76.0	83	27	26	6	2	8	5	0	4.26

	BA	OBA	SA	AB	H	2B	3B	HR	RBI	BB	SO		BA	OBA	SA	AB	H	2B	3B	HR	RBI	BB	SO
Total	.301	.358	.450	551	166	22	3	18	79	47	62		.283	.343	.413	1733	491	65	9	47	211	158	181
vs. Left	.318	.378	.473	292	93	11	3	10	49	27	17		.293	.355	.418	888	260	33	6	22	113	88	64
vs. Right	.282	.335	.425	259	73	11	1	8	30	20	45		.273	.329	.407	845	231	32	3	25	98	70	117
Bases Empty	.316	.371	.443	307	97	11	2	8	8	24	31		.288	.341	.402	998	287	38	5	22	22	76	100
Leadoff	.340	.380	.482	141	48	6	1	4	4	8	16		.293	.348	.405	437	128	18	2	9	9	34	39
Runners On Base	.283	.341	.459	244	69	11	1	10	71	23	31		.278	.345	.427	735	204	27	4	25	189	82	81
Scoring Position	.328	.381	.557	131	43	7	1	7	62	13	17		.271	.335	.464	399	108	18	4	17	168	45	53
Late and Close	.342	.435	.579	38	13	0	0	3	8	6	5		.354	.418	.635	96	34	3	0	8	15	11	7

STEVE AVERY — bats left — throws left — age 22 — ATL — P

2-YEAR TOTALS (1990–1991)

1991	G	IP	H	BB	SO	SB	CS	W	L	SV	ERA		G	IP	H	BB	SO	SB	CS	W	L	SV	ERA
Total	35	210.1	189	65	137	21	11	18	8	0	3.38		56	309.1	310	110	212	41	19	21	19	0	4.10
at Home	18	105.2	100	33	66	12	8	9	5	0	3.75		29	165.0	165	60	109	22	14	12	9	0	3.87
on Road	17	104.2	89	32	71	9	3	9	3	0	3.01		27	144.1	145	50	103	19	5	9	10	0	4.36
on Grass	25	151.1	137	46	95	14	10	14	7	0	3.39		41	231.0	229	78	151	30	17	17	13	0	3.82
on Turf	10	59.0	52	19	42	7	1	4	1	0	3.36		15	78.1	81	32	61	11	2	4	6	0	4.94
Day Games	12	71.1	64	18	49	5	5	7	3	0	3.53		20	104.1	112	29	75	14	7	7	7	0	4.66
Night Games	23	139.0	125	47	88	16	6	11	5	0	3.30		36	205.0	198	81	137	27	12	14	12	0	3.82
April	4	22.0	17	9	12	3	1	2	1	0	2.86		4	22.0	17	9	12	3	1	2	1	0	2.86
May	6	37.1	36	15	23	2	3	4	1	0	3.38		6	37.1	36	15	23	2	3	4	1	0	3.38
June	6	32.1	38	11	20	4	2	3	0	0	4.73		9	46.1	56	21	30	10	2	2	4	0	5.24
July	6	37.2	24	11	21	2	4	4	0	0	2.87		12	72.2	62	27	39	5	6	4	4	0	3.72
August	6	29.0	39	9	27	6	1	3	3	0	4.97		12	62.0	73	22	60	11	5	5	6	0	4.65
Sept–Oct	7	52.0	35	10	34	4	0	4	0	0	2.25		13	69.0	66	16	48	10	2	4	3	0	4.04

	BA	OBA	SA	AB	H	2B	3B	HR	RBI	BB	SO		BA	OBA	SA	AB	H	2B	3B	HR	RBI	BB	SO
Total	.240	.299	.372	788	189	33	4	21	80	65	137		.261	.324	.392	1189	310	58	7	28	147	110	212
vs. Left	.184	.239	.288	163	30	4	2	3	10	12	33		.205	.260	.295	224	46	5	3	3	22	17	52
vs. Right	.254	.314	.394	625	159	29	2	18	70	53	104		.274	.338	.415	965	264	53	4	25	125	93	160
Bases Empty	.223	.279	.347	502	112	21	4	11	11	37	83		.237	.305	.353	697	165	35	5	12	12	65	117
Leadoff	.257	.300	.419	210	54	10	3	6	6	13	36		.266	.332	.415	301	80	19	4	6	6	29	51
Runners On Base	.269	.332	.416	286	77	12	0	10	69	28	54		.295	.350	.447	492	145	23	2	16	135	45	95
Scoring Position	.250	.321	.384	164	41	7	0	5	57	19	36		.277	.338	.393	300	83	14	0	7	112	32	66
Late and Close	.143	.211	.143	35	5	0	0	0	3	3	4		.217	.270	.261	69	15	1	1	0	8	5	10

JEFF BALLARD — bats left — throws left — age 29 — BAL — P

1991	G	IP	H	BB	SO	SB	CS	W	L	SV	ERA
Total	26	123.2	153	28	37	1	4	6	12	0	5.60
at Home	10	44.0	57	12	18	0	2	0	8	0	5.93
on Road	16	79.2	96	16	19	1	2	6	4	0	5.42
on Grass	21	104.1	126	22	31	0	4	5	11	0	5.35
on Turf	5	19.1	27	6	6	1	0	1	1	0	6.98
Day Games	7	37.1	41	5	11	0	1	2	3	0	5.06
Night Games	19	86.1	112	23	26	1	3	4	9	0	5.84
April	5	30.2	27	8	11	0	1	2	2	0	4.40
May	7	34.2	38	6	13	0	2	1	2	0	3.63
June	5	25.1	39	6	8	1	1	1	2	0	7.82
July	6	27.1	37	6	5	0	0	2	3	0	6.26
August	0	0.0	0	0	0	0	0	0	0	0	0.00
Sept–Oct	3	5.2	12	2	0	0	0	0	1	0	11.12

5-YEAR TOTALS (1987–1991)

	G	IP	H	BB	SO	SB	CS	W	L	SV	ERA
Total	144	695.1	812	204	217	44	34	36	51	0	4.63
at Home	70	345.0	401	99	116	30	18	17	28	0	4.46
on Road	74	350.1	411	105	101	14	16	19	23	0	4.80
on Grass	120	585.1	686	176	181	38	29	32	43	0	4.64
on Turf	24	110.0	126	28	36	6	5	4	8	0	4.58
Day Games	35	174.2	194	39	49	10	9	9	12	0	4.43
Night Games	109	520.2	618	165	168	34	25	27	39	0	4.70
April	14	93.0	83	17	27	0	3	7	5	0	3.10
May	24	131.0	155	36	41	8	8	8	9	0	3.98
June	24	128.2	179	50	48	10	8	5	13	0	6.44
July	27	100.0	116	18	28	11	4	4	10	0	5.31
August	23	108.1	116	32	27	5	3	7	4	0	3.66
Sept–Oct	32	134.1	163	51	46	10	8	5	10	0	4.89

	BA	OBA	SA	AB	H	2B	3B	HR	RBI	BB	SO
Total	.302	.340	.478	506	153	33	4	16	81	28	37
vs. Left	.182	.232	.284	88	16	4	1	1	9	6	13
vs. Right	.328	.363	.519	418	137	29	3	15	72	22	24
Bases Empty	.259	.297	.424	297	77	12	2	11	11	14	22
Leadoff	.260	.311	.480	123	32	7	1	6	6	7	5
Runners On Base	.364	.398	.555	209	76	21	2	5	70	14	15
Scoring Position	.384	.429	.616	112	43	9	1	5	65	11	10
Late and Close	.313	.421	.563	16	5	4	0	0	3	3	1

	BA	OBA	SA	AB	H	2B	3B	HR	RBI	BB	SO
Total	.295	.345	.453	2757	812	160	13	84	347	204	217
vs. Left	.274	.330	.406	485	133	18	2	14	56	38	74
vs. Right	.299	.348	.463	2272	679	142	11	70	291	166	143
Bases Empty	.294	.336	.446	1632	480	98	9	44	44	93	123
Leadoff	.311	.352	.491	694	216	42	4	25	25	40	46
Runners On Base	.295	.357	.464	1125	332	62	4	40	303	111	94
Scoring Position	.306	.390	.485	602	184	35	2	23	258	87	63
Late and Close	.267	.324	.369	187	50	10	0	3	18	16	21

BRIAN BARNES — bats left — throws left — age 25 — MON — P

1991	G	IP	H	BB	SO	SB	CS	W	L	SV	ERA
Total	28	160.0	135	84	117	20	8	5	8	0	4.22
at Home	12	68.0	57	32	59	11	2	1	5	0	4.24
on Road	16	92.0	78	52	58	9	6	4	3	0	4.21
on Grass	8	43.2	35	26	24	3	1	3	0	0	3.92
on Turf	20	116.1	100	58	93	17	7	2	8	0	4.33
Day Games	6	35.0	28	17	26	2	0	2	2	0	4.89
Night Games	22	125.0	107	67	91	18	8	3	6	0	4.03
April	0	0.0	0	0	0	0	0	0	0	0	0.00
May	4	19.1	23	11	14	3	1	0	2	0	8.38
June	6	37.0	31	18	34	6	2	0	1	0	3.65
July	4	22.0	21	13	15	1	0	2	0	0	4.09
August	7	41.0	25	17	25	4	1	1	2	0	2.63
Sept–Oct	7	40.2	35	25	29	6	4	2	3	0	4.43

2-YEAR TOTALS (1990–1991)

	G	IP	H	BB	SO	SB	CS	W	L	SV	ERA
Total	32	188.0	160	91	140	24	8	6	9	0	4.02
at Home	14	84.0	64	35	70	11	2	2	5	0	3.75
on Road	18	104.0	96	56	70	13	6	4	4	0	4.24
on Grass	9	49.2	43	29	28	4	1	3	0	0	3.99
on Turf	23	138.1	117	62	112	20	7	3	9	0	4.03
Day Games	7	41.0	36	20	30	3	0	2	2	0	4.83
Night Games	25	147.0	124	71	110	21	8	4	7	0	3.80
April	0	0.0	0	0	0	0	0	0	0	0	0.00
May	4	19.1	23	11	14	3	1	0	2	0	8.38
June	6	37.0	31	18	34	6	2	0	1	0	3.65
July	4	22.0	21	13	15	1	0	2	0	0	4.09
August	7	41.0	25	17	25	1	1	1	2	0	2.63
Sept–Oct	11	68.2	60	32	52	10	4	3	4	0	3.80

	BA	OBA	SA	AB	H	2B	3B	HR	RBI	BB	SO
Total	.233	.333	.371	580	135	24	4	16	70	84	117
vs. Left	.240	.380	.413	104	25	5	2	3	13	22	19
vs. Right	.231	.322	.361	476	110	19	2	13	57	62	98
Bases Empty	.227	.325	.349	344	78	13	1	9	9	46	64
Leadoff	.236	.323	.385	148	35	7	0	5	5	17	24
Runners On Base	.242	.345	.403	236	57	11	3	7	61	38	53
Scoring Position	.233	.318	.383	133	31	6	1	4	49	17	33
Late and Close	.241	.333	.310	29	7	2	0	0	3	4	8

	BA	OBA	SA	AB	H	2B	3B	HR	RBI	BB	SO
Total	.233	.326	.363	686	160	27	4	18	79	91	140
vs. Left	.240	.360	.440	125	30	6	2	5	16	22	21
vs. Right	.232	.318	.346	561	130	21	2	13	63	69	119
Bases Empty	.221	.314	.344	407	90	15	1	11	11	51	79
Leadoff	.236	.318	.385	174	41	8	0	6	6	19	29
Runners On Base	.251	.344	.391	279	70	12	3	7	68	40	61
Scoring Position	.241	.316	.364	162	39	6	1	4	55	18	39
Late and Close	.242	.324	.303	33	8	2	0	0	3	4	8

STEVE BEDROSIAN — bats right — throws right — age 35 — MIN — P

1991	G	IP	H	BB	SO	SB	CS	W	L	SV	ERA
Total	56	77.1	70	35	44	4	1	5	3	6	4.42
at Home	34	44.0	37	28	24	4	1	2	3	2	5.52
on Road	22	33.1	33	7	20	0	0	3	0	4	2.97
on Grass	17	28.2	28	4	17	0	0	3	0	4	3.45
on Turf	39	48.2	42	31	27	4	1	2	3	2	4.99
Day Games	16	19.0	28	12	12	0	0	1	1	2	10.42
Night Games	40	58.1	42	23	32	4	1	4	2	4	2.47
April	8	12.2	8	10	7	1	0	2	1	0	3.55
May	10	15.1	11	6	6	1	0	0	0	2	4.70
June	8	11.0	13	3	4	1	0	0	1	0	2.45
July	10	14.1	15	3	10	0	0	0	1	0	3.14
August	11	16.0	12	7	14	1	1	2	1	0	4.50
Sept–Oct	9	8.0	11	5	3	0	0	0	0	1	10.13

8-YEAR TOTALS (1984–1991)

	G	IP	H	BB	SO	SB	CS	W	L	SV	ERA
Total	458	783.1	694	349	573	116	18	52	55	153	3.50
at Home	230	397.0	353	153	290	51	11	28	25	74	3.51
on Road	228	386.1	341	196	283	65	7	24	30	79	3.49
on Grass	209	416.1	358	168	299	45	13	26	26	66	3.24
on Turf	249	367.0	336	181	274	71	5	26	29	87	3.80
Day Games	160	270.0	242	124	218	42	7	21	20	48	3.73
Night Games	298	513.1	452	225	355	74	11	31	35	105	3.38
April	54	88.2	83	46	55	11	1	7	9	12	4.57
May	76	131.2	102	57	102	18	5	7	6	27	2.32
June	93	159.2	146	72	120	32	3	12	14	32	3.16
July	81	137.0	119	63	98	19	2	7	9	27	3.74
August	83	149.2	133	61	110	15	5	10	7	24	3.19
Sept–Oct	71	116.2	111	50	88	21	2	9	10	31	4.63

	BA	OBA	SA	AB	H	2B	3B	HR	RBI	BB	SO
Total	.243	.327	.420	288	70	16	1	11	40	35	44
vs. Left	.267	.372	.450	120	32	8	1	4	17	22	21
vs. Right	.226	.292	.399	168	38	8	0	7	23	13	23
Bases Empty	.242	.314	.438	153	37	9	0	7	7	14	23
Leadoff	.213	.304	.492	61	13	5	0	4	4	7	8
Runners On Base	.244	.342	.400	135	33	7	1	4	33	21	21
Scoring Position	.205	.314	.361	83	17	2	1	3	29	14	16
Late and Close	.244	.345	.378	127	31	8	0	3	19	18	20

	BA	OBA	SA	AB	H	2B	3B	HR	RBI	BB	SO
Total	.237	.318	.364	2933	694	110	12	80	340	349	573
vs. Left	.257	.351	.418	1525	392	65	8	55	205	223	269
vs. Right	.214	.281	.305	1408	302	45	4	25	135	126	304
Bases Empty	.232	.304	.366	1604	372	62	6	47	47	161	323
Leadoff	.235	.305	.389	665	156	29	4	22	22	66	125
Runners On Base	.242	.334	.362	1329	322	48	6	33	293	188	250
Scoring Position	.209	.326	.317	826	173	20	3	21	257	148	179
Late and Close	.232	.310	.356	1379	320	45	6	38	174	158	292

TIM BELCHER — bats right — throws right — age 31 — LA — P

5-YEAR TOTALS (1987–1991)

1991	G	IP	H	BB	SO	SB	CS	W	L	SV	ERA	G	IP	H	BB	SO	SB	CS	W	L	SV	ERA
Total	33	209.1	189	75	156	17	10	10	9	0	2.62	138	806.0	680	261	633	65	44	50	38	5	2.99
at Home	17	121.1	111	34	102	8	4	7	4	0	2.67	67	427.0	355	113	342	35	22	33	15	2	2.53
on Road	16	88.0	78	41	54	9	6	3	5	0	2.56	71	379.0	325	148	291	30	22	17	23	3	3.51
on Grass	26	172.1	154	57	137	13	6	9	6	0	2.51	101	600.2	515	180	465	45	30	40	24	3	2.74
on Turf	7	37.0	35	18	19	4	4	1	3	0	3.16	37	205.1	165	81	168	20	14	10	14	2	3.73
Day Games	12	61.2	64	29	42	7	5	2	4	0	3.50	51	256.2	238	93	202	22	16	15	14	1	3.68
Night Games	21	147.2	125	46	114	10	5	8	5	0	2.26	87	549.1	442	168	431	43	28	35	24	4	2.67
April	4	29.2	20	7	21	1	0	3	1	0	0.91	20	119.1	92	30	95	9	3	7	6	1	2.64
May	6	28.1	38	17	17	5	2	2	3	0	4.76	21	132.2	121	49	103	14	10	9	7	0	3.73
June	6	43.1	32	17	36	3	3	2	0	0	1.45	26	129.0	122	52	108	12	7	5	9	2	3.70
July	5	29.0	36	10	17	3	2	1	0	0	5.90	26	134.0	115	43	94	10	7	10	6	2	3.02
August	6	46.2	34	11	37	2	2	2	1	0	1.16	21	134.2	118	45	108	10	8	7	5	0	3.14
Sept–Oct	6	32.1	29	13	28	3	1	1	1	0	3.06	24	156.1	112	42	125	10	9	12	5	0	1.90

	BA	OBA	SA	AB	H	2B	3B	HR	RBI	BB	SO	BA	OBA	SA	AB	H	2B	3B	HR	RBI	BB	SO
Total	.240	.306	.318	789	189	26	3	10	66	75	156	.228	.292	.327	2977	680	95	13	57	268	261	633
vs. Left	.272	.339	.339	449	122	16	1	4	33	45	82	.236	.304	.322	1600	378	53	6	24	124	153	328
vs. Right	.197	.263	.291	340	67	10	2	6	33	30	74	.219	.278	.332	1377	302	42	7	33	144	108	305
Bases Empty	.248	.309	.331	447	111	19	0	6	6	38	88	.227	.283	.319	1837	417	57	5	34	34	137	374
Leadoff	.255	.313	.340	200	51	8	0	3	3	16	35	.232	.290	.323	770	179	19	3	15	15	59	128
Runners On Base	.228	.303	.301	342	78	7	3	4	60	37	68	.231	.306	.339	1140	263	38	8	23	234	124	259
Scoring Position	.218	.297	.316	193	42	4	3	3	56	22	43	.236	.317	.356	615	145	23	6	13	206	77	154
Late and Close	.268	.339	.351	97	26	6	1	0	6	11	16	.226	.291	.297	323	73	12	1	3	20	31	61

STAN BELINDA — bats right — throws right — age 26 — PIT — P

3-YEAR TOTALS (1989–1991)

1991	G	IP	H	BB	SO	SB	CS	W	L	SV	ERA	G	IP	H	BB	SO	SB	CS	W	L	SV	ERA
Total	60	78.1	50	35	71	13	3	7	5	16	3.45	123	147.0	111	66	136	22	3	10	10	24	3.67
at Home	28	41.2	23	9	38	3	2	2	1	13	1.94	59	74.0	64	29	66	9	2	3	4	15	3.65
on Road	32	36.2	27	26	33	10	1	5	4	3	5.15	64	73.0	47	37	70	13	1	7	6	9	3.70
on Grass	16	18.2	14	13	19	4	1	2	2	1	5.30	29	34.0	18	19	31	4	1	2	2	2	3.18
on Turf	44	59.2	36	22	52	9	2	5	3	15	2.87	94	113.0	93	47	105	18	2	8	8	22	3.82
Day Games	15	21.0	17	9	18	6	1	2	2	4	4.71	31	38.1	41	21	33	9	1	2	4	7	6.34
Night Games	45	57.1	33	26	53	7	2	5	3	12	2.98	92	108.2	70	45	103	13	2	8	6	17	2.73
April	6	8.2	6	5	10	1	0	1	1	2	6.23	6	8.2	6	5	10	1	0	1	1	2	6.23
May	11	13.2	9	8	13	4	1	2	0	3	4.61	16	19.0	11	9	18	4	1	2	0	3	4.26
June	11	10.1	6	2	13	2	0	0	0	1	0.00	24	23.2	16	12	25	4	0	2	2	4	1.52
July	11	15.2	11	10	13	2	1	0	1	3	5.17	27	29.0	21	16	25	2	1	0	2	5	4.34
August	11	17.0	8	5	14	1	0	0	2	2	2.12	27	35.0	29	12	31	2	0	3	3	7	3.86
Sept–Oct	10	13.0	10	5	8	3	1	4	1	2	2.77	26	31.2	28	12	27	9	1	5	2	3	3.41

	BA	OBA	SA	AB	H	2B	3B	HR	RBI	BB	SO	BA	OBA	SA	AB	H	2B	3B	HR	RBI	BB	SO
Total	.184	.283	.327	272	50	5	2	10	38	35	71	.211	.302	.332	527	111	14	4	14	67	66	136
vs. Left	.195	.291	.317	123	24	3	0	4	12	14	26	.202	.295	.300	233	47	8	0	5	24	29	55
vs. Right	.174	.277	.336	149	26	2	2	6	26	21	45	.218	.307	.357	294	64	6	4	9	43	37	81
Bases Empty	.158	.253	.304	158	25	3	1	6	6	17	46	.182	.274	.306	291	53	6	3	8	8	33	83
Leadoff	.117	.197	.250	60	7	2	0	2	2	6	21	.179	.250	.308	117	21	4	1	3	3	11	36
Runners On Base	.219	.324	.360	114	25	2	1	4	32	18	25	.246	.335	.364	236	58	8	1	6	59	33	53
Scoring Position	.188	.306	.325	80	15	0	1	3	30	14	19	.218	.328	.327	156	34	3	1	4	53	27	37
Late and Close	.189	.282	.333	159	30	4	2	5	23	18	41	.203	.297	.321	296	60	11	3	6	38	37	75

ANDY BENES — bats right — throws right — age 25 — SD — P

3-YEAR TOTALS (1989–1991)

1991	G	IP	H	BB	SO	SB	CS	W	L	SV	ERA	G	IP	H	BB	SO	SB	CS	W	L	SV	ERA
Total	33	223.0	194	59	167	11	10	15	11	0	3.03	75	482.0	422	159	373	37	16	31	25	0	3.32
at Home	17	111.0	117	35	94	5	8	6	5	0	3.73	38	239.1	228	90	207	17	10	15	11	0	3.91
on Road	16	112.0	77	24	73	6	2	9	6	0	2.33	37	242.2	194	69	166	20	6	16	14	0	2.74
on Grass	23	154.0	142	39	121	6	9	10	7	0	3.16	56	361.2	321	116	285	25	14	22	17	0	3.26
on Turf	10	69.0	52	20	46	5	1	5	4	0	2.74	19	120.1	101	43	88	12	2	9	8	0	3.52
Day Games	11	71.2	68	18	56	3	2	7	2	0	2.76	22	139.2	130	46	118	14	4	10	5	0	2.64
Night Games	22	151.1	126	41	111	8	8	8	9	0	3.15	53	342.1	292	113	255	23	12	21	20	0	3.60
April	4	23.1	24	11	30	0	1	0	2	0	3.86	8	44.0	44	21	50	3	1	2	4	0	4.09
May	6	41.1	40	14	29	4	2	2	4	0	3.70	12	80.2	70	27	54	9	4	5	6	0	3.79
June	6	37.2	41	13	22	1	3	2	2	0	5.02	12	76.2	68	29	55	9	3	4	5	0	3.99
July	4	30.0	24	6	18	5	1	1	2	0	2.10	8	53.2	49	14	38	7	1	2	3	0	2.52
August	6	41.1	23	6	31	0	2	5	0	0	2.40	16	99.1	75	34	70	6	4	10	3	0	3.53
Sept–Oct	7	49.1	42	9	37	1	1	5	1	0	1.64	19	127.2	116	34	106	3	3	9	5	0	2.54

	BA	OBA	SA	AB	H	2B	3B	HR	RBI	BB	SO	BA	OBA	SA	AB	H	2B	3B	HR	RBI	BB	SO
Total	.232	.284	.357	838	194	24	6	23	70	59	167	.233	.296	.363	1808	422	58	16	48	167	159	373
vs. Left	.226	.278	.350	468	106	11	4	13	36	32	92	.236	.301	.366	1031	243	32	12	26	90	95	194
vs. Right	.238	.292	.365	370	88	13	2	10	34	27	75	.230	.289	.359	777	179	26	4	22	77	64	179
Bases Empty	.229	.274	.362	533	122	17	6	14	14	32	105	.227	.287	.364	1123	255	34	12	32	32	91	228
Leadoff	.237	.277	.370	219	52	4	5	5	5	11	32	.230	.288	.388	466	107	11	6	17	17	36	77
Runners On Base	.236	.302	.348	305	72	7	0	9	56	27	62	.244	.310	.361	685	167	24	4	16	135	68	145
Scoring Position	.197	.287	.280	157	31	4	0	3	43	18	34	.213	.287	.307	375	80	11	3	6	111	40	85
Late and Close	.239	.316	.284	88	21	6	0	0	6	10	26	.273	.333	.379	161	44	3	1	4	17	15	33

JUAN BERENGUER — bats right — throws right — age 38 — ATL — P

8-YEAR TOTALS (1984–1991)

1991	G	IP	H	BB	SO	SB	CS	W	L	SV	ERA		G	IP	H	BB	SO	SB	CS	W	L	SV	ERA
Total	49	64.1	43	20	53	3	1	0	3	17	2.24		368	822.2	712	406	708	85	35	51	35	30	3.65
at Home	26	32.2	22	8	30	2	0	0	1	9	2.76		187	442.2	382	207	394	48	15	32	16	15	3.62
on Road	23	31.2	21	12	23	1	1	0	2	8	1.71		181	380.0	330	199	314	37	20	19	19	15	3.69
on Grass	35	43.2	29	12	41	2	1	0	2	13	2.68		201	470.0	416	236	390	42	20	24	26	22	4.10
on Turf	14	20.2	14	8	12	1	0	0	1	4	1.31		167	352.2	296	170	318	43	15	27	9	8	3.06
Day Games	12	17.1	12	5	10	1	0	0	1	5	2.60		118	246.2	235	139	209	35	13	16	16	13	4.60
Night Games	37	47.0	31	15	43	2	1	0	2	12	2.11		250	576.0	477	267	499	50	22	35	19	17	3.25
April	9	11.1	10	6	9	1	0	0	0	1	2.38		44	97.1	84	54	97	10	5	6	4	2	3.79
May	13	19.2	14	8	16	2	0	0	1	5	2.29		68	167.1	152	76	142	16	5	12	8	6	3.66
June	12	14.1	8	4	8	0	1	0	2	5	2.51		73	164.0	127	86	146	14	7	10	6	11	2.91
July	9	12.0	3	2	10	0	0	0	0	4	0.75		66	108.2	89	44	82	13	5	6	6	5	3.73
August	6	7.0	8	0	10	0	0	0	0	2	3.86		61	137.0	128	67	117	16	6	6	2	4	4.34
Sept–Oct	0	0.0	0	0	0	0	0	0	0	0	0.00		56	148.1	132	79	124	16	7	11	9	2	3.70

	BA	OBA	SA	AB	H	2B	3B	HR	RBI	BB	SO		BA	OBA	SA	AB	H	2B	3B	HR	RBI	BB	SO
Total	.189	.261	.303	228	43	7	2	5	16	20	53		.234	.325	.359	3040	712	128	16	73	358	406	708
vs. Left	.202	.308	.260	104	21	3	0	1	2	15	22		.261	.359	.404	1514	395	71	8	43	177	231	319
vs. Right	.177	.218	.339	124	22	4	2	4	14	5	31		.208	.291	.315	1526	317	57	8	30	181	175	389
Bases Empty	.176	.260	.290	131	23	6	0	3	3	13	28		.227	.317	.342	1697	385	72	6	37	37	216	403
Leadoff	.208	.288	.321	53	11	3	0	1	1	6	12		.205	.297	.306	706	145	36	4	9	9	90	175
Runners On Base	.206	.262	.320	97	20	1	2	2	13	7	25		.243	.335	.380	1343	327	56	10	36	321	190	305
Scoring Position	.143	.231	.161	56	8	1	0	0	7	7	18		.240	.344	.379	776	186	33	6	21	279	133	185
Late and Close	.164	.269	.293	116	19	4	1	3	8	15	28		.220	.327	.325	782	172	30	5	14	80	125	192

MIKE BIELECKI — bats right — throws right — age 33 — CHN/ATL — P

8-YEAR TOTALS (1984–1991)

1991	G	IP	H	BB	SO	SB	CS	W	L	SV	ERA		G	IP	H	BB	SO	SB	CS	W	L	SV	ERA
Total	41	173.2	171	56	75	17	9	13	11	0	4.46		183	844.2	841	348	489	71	44	51	48	1	4.20
at Home	19	95.0	101	21	35	8	6	8	7	0	4.74		85	436.2	420	172	262	32	28	25	26	0	4.18
on Road	22	78.2	70	35	40	9	3	5	4	0	4.12		98	408.0	421	176	227	39	16	26	22	1	4.21
on Grass	28	124.2	127	33	50	10	6	9	9	0	4.76		104	481.1	467	188	287	28	26	31	28	0	4.15
on Turf	13	49.0	44	23	25	7	3	4	2	0	3.67		79	363.1	374	160	202	43	18	20	20	1	4.26
Day Games	19	84.2	86	26	31	8	4	6	7	0	4.89		83	370.2	374	155	211	28	23	20	23	1	4.69
Night Games	22	89.0	85	30	44	9	5	7	4	0	4.04		100	474.0	467	193	278	43	21	31	25	0	3.82
April	6	26.2	18	9	10	4	1	4	1	0	2.70		24	101.2	100	50	60	8	5	8	5	0	4.16
May	8	25.1	20	14	13	4	2	3	1	0	3.91		31	148.1	143	70	85	12	8	11	8	0	3.58
June	9	21.0	26	9	11	1	2	1	4	0	6.86		27	125.0	136	58	83	8	10	4	12	0	5.40
July	5	33.0	37	8	13	3	1	3	1	0	3.82		25	119.1	121	44	69	10	3	10	4	0	4.53
August	6	37.1	42	7	13	3	1	1	1	0	4.82		31	177.0	172	61	99	16	7	9	7	0	4.07
Sept–Oct	7	30.1	28	9	15	2	2	1	3	0	5.04		45	173.1	169	65	93	17	11	9	12	1	3.79

	BA	OBA	SA	AB	H	2B	3B	HR	RBI	BB	SO		BA	OBA	SA	AB	H	2B	3B	HR	RBI	BB	SO
Total	.262	.319	.420	653	171	31	9	18	83	56	75		.262	.334	.401	3213	841	160	36	72	369	348	489
vs. Left	.268	.337	.417	343	92	15	3	10	40	36	38		.264	.336	.406	1785	471	91	17	43	191	199	239
vs. Right	.255	.299	.423	310	79	16	6	8	43	20	37		.259	.330	.395	1428	370	69	19	29	178	149	250
Bases Empty	.257	.311	.429	385	99	17	5	13	13	28	38		.260	.326	.406	1860	484	95	21	45	45	173	255
Leadoff	.311	.369	.503	161	50	12	2	5	5	13	12		.274	.340	.415	796	218	43	6	19	19	75	104
Runners On Base	.269	.331	.407	268	72	14	4	5	70	28	37		.264	.344	.394	1353	357	65	15	27	324	175	234
Scoring Position	.262	.344	.375	160	42	9	3	1	59	23	22		.263	.361	.387	803	211	32	10	16	283	135	137
Late and Close	.292	.402	.444	72	21	3	1	2	14	13	12		.234	.341	.372	218	51	8	2	6	29	35	47

BUD BLACK — bats left — throws left — age 35 — SF — P

8-YEAR TOTALS (1984–1991)

1991	G	IP	H	BB	SO	SB	CS	W	L	SV	ERA		G	IP	H	BB	SO	SB	CS	W	L	SV	ERA
Total	34	214.1	201	71	104	14	11	12	16	0	3.99		284	1426.2	1340	419	750	90	58	81	84	11	3.67
at Home	16	112.0	92	31	48	4	7	8	7	0	2.81		146	751.2	697	197	380	51	37	46	40	7	3.42
on Road	18	102.1	109	40	56	10	4	4	9	0	5.28		138	675.0	643	222	370	39	21	35	44	4	3.95
on Grass	27	182.2	161	58	87	11	11	11	11	0	3.35		156	828.2	781	257	433	46	35	45	52	5	3.89
on Turf	7	31.2	40	13	17	3	0	1	5	0	7.67		128	598.0	559	162	317	44	23	36	32	6	3.37
Day Games	10	67.0	58	25	39	7	2	5	2	0	3.22		84	408.1	387	131	248	28	19	23	25	4	3.55
Night Games	24	147.1	143	46	65	7	9	7	14	0	4.34		200	1018.1	953	288	502	62	39	58	59	7	3.72
April	5	35.1	31	16	21	2	3	1	3	0	5.09		41	197.0	192	60	91	15	14	11	12	1	3.93
May	6	47.2	31	14	23	2	2	4	2	0	1.89		54	275.0	226	77	146	5	7	19	13	2	2.72
June	5	34.0	36	11	14	3	3	1	1	0	3.97		46	223.0	214	84	113	15	11	12	12	0	4.16
July	5	28.1	27	9	9	1	1	2	2	0	3.49		47	244.2	250	71	137	13	8	12	18	1	4.30
August	7	34.0	41	11	19	4	1	2	5	0	6.35		49	229.2	255	69	125	24	9	11	16	3	4.51
Sept–Oct	6	35.0	35	10	18	2	1	2	3	0	3.86		47	257.1	203	58	138	18	9	16	13	4	2.73

	BA	OBA	SA	AB	H	2B	3B	HR	RBI	BB	SO		BA	OBA	SA	AB	H	2B	3B	HR	RBI	BB	SO
Total	.251	.313	.396	800	201	31	5	25	92	71	104		.248	.304	.375	5411	1340	220	34	134	558	419	750
vs. Left	.281	.333	.415	171	48	5	0	6	27	15	18		.229	.286	.342	1129	258	32	6	28	124	89	153
vs. Right	.243	.307	.391	629	153	26	5	19	65	56	86		.253	.309	.384	4282	1082	188	28	106	434	330	597
Bases Empty	.239	.290	.348	511	122	18	1	12	12	34	72		.246	.295	.369	3292	810	142	22	73	73	210	437
Leadoff	.238	.293	.345	206	49	4	0	6	6	16	18		.240	.288	.361	1379	331	56	9	31	31	83	153
Runners On Base	.273	.350	.481	289	79	13	4	13	80	37	32		.250	.319	.385	2119	530	78	12	61	485	209	313
Scoring Position	.261	.355	.451	153	40	8	3	5	62	25	14		.247	.324	.378	1152	285	49	7	29	404	133	184
Late and Close	.219	.296	.266	64	14	1	1	0	7	7	8		.254	.322	.382	662	168	22	6	17	72	63	102

MIKE BODDICKER — bats right — throws right — age 35 — KC — P

8-YEAR TOTALS (1984–1991)

1991	G	IP	H	BB	SO	SB	CS	W	L	SV	ERA	G	IP	H	BB	SO	SB	CS	W	L	SV	ERA
Total	30	180.2	188	59	79	17	8	12	12	0	4.08	266	1765.1	1735	598	1113	195	63	113	98	0	3.78
at Home	17	110.2	111	29	50	9	3	7	8	0	4.07	133	899.1	886	289	573	93	38	57	52	0	3.65
on Road	13	70.0	77	30	29	8	5	5	4	0	4.11	133	866.0	849	309	540	102	25	56	46	0	3.92
on Grass	10	51.2	59	25	23	7	2	4	3	0	4.35	212	1392.1	1384	489	898	159	53	88	78	0	3.81
on Turf	20	129.0	129	34	56	10	6	8	9	0	3.98	54	373.0	351	109	215	36	10	25	20	0	3.69
Day Games	9	40.0	50	13	16	3	5	4	3	0	5.40	76	471.1	476	164	293	59	20	35	26	0	3.76
Night Games	21	140.2	138	46	63	14	3	8	9	0	3.71	190	1294.0	1259	434	820	136	43	78	72	0	3.79
April	4	31.0	20	9	10	2	0	2	2	0	2.03	37	223.2	211	93	150	29	8	12	16	0	3.98
May	4	22.2	24	11	9	1	3	1	2	0	5.56	43	305.0	264	115	191	28	13	23	12	0	3.19
June	6	36.1	28	9	16	2	1	3	2	0	2.48	48	335.2	315	104	190	35	9	21	18	0	3.91
July	5	30.0	41	8	11	2	0	2	1	0	6.30	44	300.0	322	87	187	36	10	21	14	0	4.08
August	6	39.0	49	13	21	6	3	3	2	0	3.00	47	314.0	316	99	206	41	10	20	19	0	3.67
Sept–Oct	5	21.2	26	9	12	4	1	1	3	0	7.06	47	287.0	307	100	189	26	16	16	19	0	3.92

	BA	OBA	SA	AB	H	2B	3B	HR	RBI	BB	SO	BA	OBA	SA	AB	H	2B	3B	HR	RBI	BB	SO
Total	.272	.340	.408	692	188	41	7	13	80	59	79	.258	.324	.385	6716	1735	293	40	160	702	598	1113
vs. Left	.301	.365	.470	349	105	28	5	7	42	29	22	.268	.331	.396	3615	968	168	24	83	386	315	448
vs. Right	.242	.314	.344	343	83	13	2	6	38	30	57	.247	.316	.372	3101	767	125	16	77	316	283	665
Bases Empty	.283	.358	.418	385	109	27	5	5	5	40	46	.261	.325	.392	3929	1026	183	26	93	93	334	631
Leadoff	.326	.386	.436	172	56	8	1	3	3	14	18	.274	.335	.409	1699	466	84	8	43	43	133	269
Runners On Base	.257	.316	.394	307	79	14	2	8	75	19	33	.254	.322	.376	2787	709	110	14	67	609	264	482
Scoring Position	.249	.318	.337	181	45	9	2	1	56	13	25	.235	.314	.352	1562	367	57	9	36	523	178	301
Late and Close	.270	.329	.333	63	17	1	0	1	6	3	6	.210	.293	.316	605	127	17	1	15	49	62	99

JOE BOEVER — bats right — throws right — age 32 — PHI — P

7-YEAR TOTALS (1985–1991)

1991	G	IP	H	BB	SO	SB	CS	W	L	SV	ERA	G	IP	H	BB	SO	SB	CS	W	L	SV	ERA
Total	68	98.1	90	54	89	12	2	3	5	0	3.84	255	345.2	322	167	285	47	15	11	25	36	3.70
at Home	35	54.0	45	28	46	6	1	2	1	0	3.17	139	204.0	180	88	159	23	10	8	12	15	3.40
on Road	33	44.1	45	26	43	6	1	1	4	0	4.67	116	141.2	142	79	126	24	5	3	13	21	4.13
on Grass	21	30.0	24	15	32	4	0	1	2	0	2.70	133	173.2	159	73	145	20	11	8	13	18	3.52
on Turf	47	68.1	66	39	57	8	2	2	3	0	4.35	122	172.0	163	94	140	27	4	3	12	18	3.87
Day Games	19	23.1	29	18	19	4	0	0	2	0	6.56	69	90.1	91	47	80	14	4	2	5	9	4.58
Night Games	49	75.0	61	36	70	8	2	3	3	0	3.00	186	255.1	231	120	205	33	11	9	20	27	3.38
April	12	18.1	16	11	17	5	2	1	1	0	3.44	29	44.0	37	24	40	9	5	2	3	5	3.48
May	12	21.2	19	9	22	1	0	2	3	0	3.74	33	47.1	40	21	43	5	1	4	5	8	2.85
June	13	18.2	18	16	14	3	0	0	1	0	5.30	35	44.0	44	38	42	4	1	0	2	6	5.93
July	9	11.1	10	6	6	1	0	0	0	0	1.59	40	46.2	34	19	24	5	1	2	1	9	2.51
August	12	16.1	16	10	17	2	0	0	0	0	3.86	57	76.0	84	40	65	14	3	1	5	5	4.38
Sept–Oct	10	12.0	11	2	13	0	0	0	0	0	4.50	61	87.2	83	25	71	10	4	2	9	3	3.18

	BA	OBA	SA	AB	H	2B	3B	HR	RBI	BB	SO	BA	OBA	SA	AB	H	2B	3B	HR	RBI	BB	SO
Total	.245	.336	.383	368	90	15	3	10	51	54	89	.248	.332	.374	1298	322	53	7	32	169	167	285
vs. Left	.256	.356	.378	172	44	7	1	4	25	29	41	.235	.336	.322	646	152	21	4	9	74	100	144
vs. Right	.235	.318	.388	196	46	8	2	6	26	25	48	.261	.329	.425	652	170	32	3	23	95	67	141
Bases Empty	.233	.304	.364	206	48	6	0	7	7	21	53	.254	.327	.401	693	176	26	2	24	24	74	147
Leadoff	.229	.289	.361	83	19	2	0	3	3	7	19	.240	.311	.410	288	69	12	2	11	11	29	54
Runners On Base	.259	.373	.407	162	42	9	3	3	44	33	36	.241	.339	.342	605	146	27	5	8	145	93	138
Scoring Position	.258	.405	.423	97	25	8	1	2	38	28	20	.236	.367	.346	364	86	21	2	5	130	80	80
Late and Close	.228	.348	.335	158	36	5	0	4	11	29	39	.233	.335	.345	605	141	22	2	14	64	92	145

CHRIS BOSIO — bats right — throws right — age 29 — MIL — P

6-YEAR TOTALS (1986–1991)

1991	G	IP	H	BB	SO	SB	CS	W	L	SV	ERA	G	IP	H	BB	SO	SB	CS	W	L	SV	ERA
Total	32	204.2	187	58	117	9	3	14	10	0	3.25	177	954.0	951	242	627	71	16	51	54	8	3.72
at Home	16	96.1	105	26	58	4	2	5	6	0	3.83	85	485.0	495	120	326	33	12	25	26	3	3.71
on Road	16	108.1	82	32	59	5	1	9	4	0	2.74	92	469.0	456	122	301	38	4	26	28	5	3.72
on Grass	29	183.0	165	50	108	8	3	13	9	0	3.30	154	845.2	831	210	557	60	16	46	46	8	3.66
on Turf	3	21.2	22	8	9	1	0	1	1	0	2.91	23	108.1	120	32	70	11	0	5	8	0	4.15
Day Games	10	69.1	66	23	38	2	1	4	3	0	3.50	50	282.0	251	75	181	18	4	14	15	5	2.87
Night Games	22	135.1	121	35	79	7	2	10	7	0	3.13	127	672.0	700	167	446	53	12	37	39	3	4.07
April	5	36.0	28	16	19	1	0	3	2	0	2.00	25	159.2	121	39	91	9	1	15	4	1	1.92
May	6	37.2	31	5	24	3	2	2	2	0	2.87	31	184.1	195	28	113	19	3	7	13	0	3.22
June	5	29.0	29	11	20	2	0	2	2	0	5.28	29	146.0	158	42	85	10	1	3	9	1	4.81
July	4	25.0	28	10	12	1	0	1	1	0	3.24	24	143.1	153	51	98	8	4	9	10	0	3.58
August	6	39.1	44	6	24	0	0	3	1	0	3.66	29	154.0	161	44	110	10	5	6	11	1	4.15
Sept–Oct	6	37.2	27	10	18	2	1	4	1	0	2.87	39	166.2	163	38	130	15	2	11	7	5	4.75

	BA	OBA	SA	AB	H	2B	3B	HR	RBI	BB	SO	BA	OBA	SA	AB	H	2B	3B	HR	RBI	BB	SO
Total	.244	.302	.350	766	187	28	4	15	72	58	117	.258	.305	.378	3683	951	146	19	86	394	242	627
vs. Left	.250	.302	.346	416	104	16	3	6	39	30	53	.259	.307	.382	1969	510	78	12	47	212	132	280
vs. Right	.237	.301	.354	350	83	12	1	9	33	28	64	.257	.303	.373	1714	441	68	7	39	182	110	347
Bases Empty	.238	.291	.349	470	112	17	4	9	9	31	76	.247	.291	.364	2196	542	78	13	51	51	126	385
Leadoff	.234	.280	.408	201	47	11	3	6	6	13	29	.251	.290	.378	927	233	38	8	21	21	50	149
Runners On Base	.253	.318	.351	296	75	11	0	6	63	27	41	.275	.326	.399	1487	409	68	6	35	343	116	242
Scoring Position	.267	.318	.353	150	40	14	0	2	52	12	20	.262	.321	.375	831	218	38	4	16	292	80	149
Late and Close	.297	.384	.391	64	19	0	0	2	6	8	3	.228	.282	.298	429	98	9	3	5	28	32	60

SHAWN BOSKIE — bats right — throws right — age 25 — CHN — P

	G	IP	H	BB	SO	SB	CS	W	L	SV	ERA	G	IP	H	BB	SO	SB	CS	W	L	SV	ERA
1991 / 2-YEAR TOTALS (1990–1991)																						
Total	28	129.0	150	52	62	4	2	4	9	0	5.23	43	226.2	249	83	111	10	8	9	15	0	4.57
at Home	17	64.2	85	34	27	2	1	3	5	0	5.43	26	124.1	149	50	54	4	4	5	10	0	4.78
on Road	11	64.1	65	18	35	2	1	1	4	0	5.04	17	102.1	100	33	57	6	4	4	5	0	4.31
on Grass	22	90.0	118	41	40	4	2	3	8	0	6.10	33	158.0	192	67	71	7	6	6	13	0	5.24
on Turf	6	39.0	32	11	22	0	0	1	1	0	3.23	10	68.2	57	16	40	3	2	3	2	0	3.01
Day Games	17	75.0	90	30	35	1	1	3	5	0	4.92	24	129.0	142	40	62	2	4	5	8	0	4.12
Night Games	11	54.0	60	22	27	3	1	1	4	0	5.67	19	97.2	107	43	49	8	4	4	7	0	5.16
April	4	28.0	25	9	10	0	0	2	1	0	2.25	4	28.0	25	9	10	0	0	2	1	0	2.25
May	6	33.0	41	12	19	3	1	0	3	0	5.73	9	57.0	64	17	30	3	1	1	5	0	4.74
June	6	31.0	36	12	12	1	0	1	3	0	5.81	11	59.0	65	25	33	3	2	2	5	0	5.34
July	1	3.0	11	1	1	0	0	0	1	0	24.00	7	42.2	51	13	17	1	2	2	3	0	4.85
August	5	10.2	6	4	8	0	0	1	0	0	0.00	6	16.2	13	5	9	2	0	2	0	0	0.54
Sept–Oct	6	23.1	31	14	12	0	1	0	1	0	7.33	6	23.1	31	14	12	0	1	0	1	0	7.33

	BA	OBA	SA	AB	H	2B	3B	HR	RBI	BB	SO	BA	OBA	SA	AB	H	2B	3B	HR	RBI	BB	SO
Total	.294	.361	.454	511	150	28	6	14	65	52	62	.282	.345	.430	884	249	49	8	22	98	83	111
vs. Left	.324	.396	.530	287	93	17	6	10	43	35	28	.302	.378	.473	493	149	32	8	12	59	62	50
vs. Right	.254	.313	.357	224	57	11	0	4	22	17	34	.256	.299	.376	391	100	17	0	10	39	21	61
Bases Empty	.303	.370	.494	271	82	20	4	8	8	26	39	.285	.346	.435	501	143	34	4	11	11	43	75
Leadoff	.350	.445	.650	117	41	12	4	5	5	18	14	.315	.386	.523	216	68	19	4	6	6	23	30
Runners On Base	.283	.350	.408	240	68	8	2	6	57	26	23	.277	.343	.423	383	106	15	4	11	87	40	36
Scoring Position	.250	.309	.375	144	36	4	1	4	49	14	14	.249	.311	.400	225	56	10	3	6	73	23	25
Late and Close	.321	.424	.500	28	9	2	0	1	3	4	1	.288	.391	.407	59	17	4	0	1	6	9	6

OIL CAN BOYD — bats right — throws right — age 33 — MON/TEX — P

	G	IP	H	BB	SO	SB	CS	W	L	SV	ERA	G	IP	H	BB	SO	SB	CS	W	L	SV	ERA
1991 / 8-YEAR TOTALS (1984–1991)																						
Total	31	182.1	196	57	115	14	12	8	15	0	4.59	196	1282.2	1313	343	753	99	73	74	68	0	4.09
at Home	16	100.1	92	27	69	5	8	5	5	0	3.23	101	678.2	708	172	413	45	47	42	35	0	3.93
on Road	15	82.0	104	30	46	9	4	3	10	0	6.26	95	604.0	605	171	340	54	26	32	33	0	4.28
on Grass	15	82.2	97	23	53	5	3	4	9	0	5.55	141	937.1	984	242	556	64	55	54	54	0	4.17
on Turf	16	99.2	99	34	62	9	9	4	6	0	3.79	55	345.1	329	101	197	35	18	20	14	0	3.88
Day Games	11	67.2	67	23	45	7	4	3	6	0	3.99	70	442.0	445	116	266	35	23	25	27	0	4.01
Night Games	20	114.2	129	34	70	7	8	5	9	0	4.94	126	840.2	868	227	487	64	50	49	41	0	4.13
April	4	23.0	30	9	9	3	4	0	3	0	6.26	28	177.1	188	57	93	19	10	7	12	0	4.92
May	6	38.2	31	8	30	4	2	2	3	0	2.79	32	210.0	199	57	131	19	8	16	10	0	3.43
June	5	30.1	34	15	22	3	2	2	1	0	3.86	37	251.0	269	73	149	18	18	14	13	0	3.91
July	6	35.2	31	14	27	2	1	2	3	0	3.79	35	215.2	210	55	132	14	13	13	12	0	4.47
August	4	24.1	36	7	13	1	1	0	2	0	7.77	29	198.2	221	45	107	11	15	8	10	0	4.39
Sept–Oct	6	30.1	34	4	14	1	2	2	3	0	4.75	35	230.0	226	56	141	18	9	16	11	0	3.64

	BA	OBA	SA	AB	H	2B	3B	HR	RBI	BB	SO	BA	OBA	SA	AB	H	2B	3B	HR	RBI	BB	SO
Total	.277	.329	.448	708	196	44	7	21	82	57	115	.266	.313	.426	4943	1313	257	36	155	559	343	753
vs. Left	.267	.326	.401	359	96	25	4	5	30	32	54	.253	.299	.383	2716	688	130	19	61	271	178	413
vs. Right	.287	.332	.496	349	100	19	3	16	52	25	61	.281	.329	.480	2227	625	127	17	94	288	165	340
Bases Empty	.277	.331	.436	422	117	28	3	11	11	34	66	.266	.317	.424	2992	796	154	20	93	93	213	460
Leadoff	.227	.284	.398	176	40	15	0	5	5	14	30	.262	.316	.420	1239	324	72	5	38	38	95	182
Runners On Base	.276	.326	.465	286	79	16	4	10	71	23	49	.265	.306	.430	1951	517	103	16	62	466	130	293
Scoring Position	.288	.351	.509	163	47	8	2	8	64	18	30	.254	.304	.427	1057	269	57	7	37	395	90	162
Late and Close	.286	.286	.543	35	10	4	1	1	5	0	5	.306	.349	.451	399	122	18	2	12	42	26	49

JEFF BRANTLEY — bats right — throws right — age 29 — SF — P

	G	IP	H	BB	SO	SB	CS	W	L	SV	ERA	G	IP	H	BB	SO	SB	CS	W	L	SV	ERA
1991 / 4-YEAR TOTALS (1988–1991)																						
Total	67	95.1	78	52	81	17	2	5	2	15	2.45	190	300.0	278	129	222	38	9	17	7	35	2.94
at Home	28	42.0	36	19	34	6	0	2	0	7	2.14	82	134.2	124	57	107	14	3	10	3	16	2.67
on Road	39	53.1	42	33	47	11	2	3	2	8	2.70	108	165.1	154	72	115	24	6	7	4	19	3.16
on Grass	47	66.0	60	31	58	11	0	4	0	10	2.45	137	213.2	211	87	160	26	3	12	5	23	2.99
on Turf	20	29.1	18	21	23	6	2	1	2	5	2.45	53	86.1	67	42	62	12	6	5	2	12	2.81
Day Games	29	37.2	35	23	32	5	0	3	0	6	2.39	75	114.1	102	51	85	12	1	10	3	13	2.20
Night Games	38	57.2	43	29	49	12	2	2	2	9	2.50	115	185.2	176	78	137	26	8	7	4	22	3.39
April	8	10.0	9	5	8	0	0	0	1	2	3.60	29	43.0	38	23	32	2	0	0	2	3	3.56
May	12	17.0	14	10	16	2	1	0	0	2	2.12	33	48.2	38	22	34	6	2	1	0	6	1.11
June	11	15.0	15	10	10	0	0	3	0	1	1.20	32	54.2	56	18	32	4	1	5	1	6	2.80
July	10	13.0	10	8	7	0	0	0	0	4	5.54	30	47.0	43	18	33	4	3	7	2	10	3.83
August	13	19.1	12	12	18	7	1	2	1	3	0.93	36	60.0	52	31	52	11	2	4	2	6	2.25
Sept–Oct	13	21.0	18	7	22	6	0	0	0	3	2.57	30	46.2	51	17	39	11	1	1	0	4	4.44

	BA	OBA	SA	AB	H	2B	3B	HR	RBI	BB	SO	BA	OBA	SA	AB	H	2B	3B	HR	RBI	BB	SO
Total	.225	.332	.338	346	78	13	1	8	36	52	81	.248	.329	.350	1120	278	41	2	23	116	129	222
vs. Left	.212	.341	.296	179	38	6	0	3	16	35	41	.258	.344	.338	589	152	23	0	8	51	79	100
vs. Right	.240	.321	.383	167	40	7	1	5	20	17	40	.237	.313	.363	531	126	18	2	15	65	50	122
Bases Empty	.264	.343	.429	182	48	9	0	7	7	20	42	.261	.331	.384	578	151	26	0	15	15	56	116
Leadoff	.203	.322	.405	74	15	6	0	3	3	11	13	.252	.337	.401	242	61	12	0	8	8	28	46
Runners On Base	.183	.320	.238	164	30	4	1	1	29	32	39	.234	.328	.314	542	127	15	2	8	101	73	106
Scoring Position	.162	.301	.214	117	19	3	0	1	28	23	31	.208	.313	.279	337	70	6	0	6	94	51	78
Late and Close	.234	.348	.319	235	55	5	0	5	19	41	46	.233	.329	.305	541	126	18	0	7	37	74	104

KEVIN BROWN — bats left — throws left — age 26 — MIL — P

1991	G	IP	H	BB	SO	SB	CS	W	L	SV	ERA	2-YEAR TOTALS (1990–1991) G	IP	H	BB	SO	SB	CS	W	L	SV	ERA
Total	15	63.2	66	34	30	5	4	2	4	0	5.51	22	86.2	82	42	42	6	4	3	5	0	4.67
at Home	7	26.0	29	17	11	3	2	1	2	0	6.92	9	34.0	30	19	15	3	2	2	2	0	5.29
on Road	8	37.2	37	17	19	2	2	1	2	0	4.54	13	52.2	52	23	27	3	2	1	3	0	4.27
on Grass	12	53.0	51	29	22	4	4	1	4	0	5.09	18	75.0	65	37	34	5	4	2	5	0	4.32
on Turf	3	10.2	15	5	8	1	0	1	0	0	7.59	4	11.2	17	5	8	1	0	1	1	0	6.94
Day Games	5	20.2	23	12	12	2	1	1	1	0	6.10	5	20.2	23	12	12	2	1	1	1	0	6.10
Night Games	10	43.0	43	22	18	3	3	1	3	0	5.23	17	66.0	59	30	30	4	3	2	4	0	4.23
April	3	15.2	17	7	9	1	0	1	0	0	5.17	3	15.2	17	7	9	1	0	1	0	0	5.17
May	6	36.1	33	20	18	4	3	1	2	0	4.71	6	36.1	33	20	18	4	3	1	2	0	4.71
June	6	11.2	16	7	3	0	1	0	2	0	8.49	6	11.2	16	7	3	0	1	0	2	0	8.49
July	0	0.0	0	0	0	0	0	0	0	0	0.00	1	1.0	0	1	0	0	0	0	0	0	0.00
August	0	0.0	0	0	0	0	0	0	0	0	0.00	1	1.0	2	0	0	0	0	0	0	0	0.00
Sept–Oct	0	0.0	0	0	0	0	0	0	0	0	0.00	5	21.0	14	7	12	1	0	1	1	0	2.57

	BA	OBA	SA	AB	H	2B	3B	HR	RBI	BB	SO	BA	OBA	SA	AB	H	2B	3B	HR	RBI	BB	SO
Total	.270	.361	.418	244	66	16	1	6	33	34	30	.249	.336	.374	329	82	18	1	7	40	42	42
vs. Left	.170	.264	.234	47	8	0	0	1	7	6	3	.162	.240	.206	68	11	0	0	1	8	7	4
vs. Right	.294	.383	.462	197	58	16	1	5	26	28	27	.272	.360	.418	261	71	18	1	6	32	35	38
Bases Empty	.258	.351	.402	132	34	11	1	2	2	18	13	.225	.324	.337	178	40	12	1	2	2	24	21
Leadoff	.293	.397	.431	58	17	5	0	1	1	9	8	.247	.363	.351	77	19	5	0	1	1	13	11
Runners On Base	.286	.372	.438	112	32	5	0	4	31	16	17	.278	.351	.417	151	42	6	0	5	38	18	21
Scoring Position	.313	.405	.522	67	21	2	0	4	31	11	11	.295	.373	.500	88	26	3	0	5	38	12	13
Late and Close	.133	.188	.133	15	2	0	0	0	0	1	2	.105	.190	.105	19	2	0	0	0	0	2	2

TOM BROWNING — bats left — throws left — age 32 — CIN — P

1991	G	IP	H	BB	SO	SB	CS	W	L	SV	ERA	8-YEAR TOTALS (1984–1991) G	IP	H	BB	SO	SB	CS	W	L	SV	ERA
Total	36	230.1	241	56	115	21	6	14	14	0	4.18	256	1670.2	1619	446	889	106	58	107	75	0	3.80
at Home	18	121.0	104	33	57	9	5	10	4	0	3.50	130	839.1	826	240	422	54	36	53	41	0	4.19
on Road	18	109.1	137	23	58	12	1	4	10	0	4.94	126	831.1	793	206	467	52	22	54	34	0	3.40
on Grass	11	73.1	79	15	35	7	1	3	4	0	3.68	78	527.1	497	121	289	31	11	31	17	0	3.23
on Turf	25	157.0	162	41	80	14	5	11	10	0	4.41	178	1143.1	1122	325	600	75	47	76	58	0	4.06
Day Games	14	91.0	90	23	45	8	4	6	6	0	3.66	96	606.1	619	169	325	46	19	41	29	0	3.87
Night Games	22	139.1	151	33	70	13	2	8	8	0	4.52	160	1064.1	1000	277	564	60	39	66	46	0	3.75
April	5	38.2	26	2	16	2	2	3	1	0	2.33	34	214.2	194	42	110	7	12	12	9	0	3.56
May	6	39.0	36	11	19	4	1	3	3	0	4.38	41	255.1	268	83	128	18	8	14	21	0	4.48
June	6	35.2	34	18	24	3	1	4	0	0	3.79	40	250.1	232	87	147	25	13	19	6	0	3.56
July	6	36.2	52	8	15	3	1	1	3	0	6.38	43	286.2	283	54	147	11	10	17	14	0	3.86
August	6	39.2	43	5	22	1	1	2	1	0	2.72	45	308.0	285	88	158	15	5	21	11	0	3.54
Sept–Oct	7	40.2	50	12	19	8	0	1	6	0	5.53	53	355.2	357	92	202	30	10	24	14	0	3.80

	BA	OBA	SA	AB	H	2B	3B	HR	RBI	BB	SO	BA	OBA	SA	AB	H	2B	3B	HR	RBI	BB	SO
Total	.266	.309	.427	906	241	40	5	32	114	56	115	.255	.304	.408	6357	1619	309	24	206	693	446	889
vs. Left	.203	.269	.344	212	43	14	2	2	22	19	41	.248	.315	.393	1068	265	51	4	32	118	106	208
vs. Right	.285	.321	.452	694	198	26	3	28	92	37	74	.256	.302	.411	5289	1354	258	20	174	575	340	681
Bases Empty	.254	.298	.417	556	141	21	2	22	22	33	68	.252	.299	.403	3970	1000	170	9	137	137	249	573
Leadoff	.247	.287	.410	227	56	3	2	10	10	12	26	.255	.298	.409	1634	416	68	5	58	58	91	224
Runners On Base	.286	.326	.443	350	100	19	3	10	92	23	47	.259	.311	.417	2387	619	139	15	69	556	197	316
Scoring Position	.320	.363	.457	175	56	10	1	4	74	17	25	.269	.341	.428	1191	320	73	9	33	454	154	172
Late and Close	.324	.355	.507	71	23	4	0	3	9	4	8	.239	.292	.358	523	125	26	0	12	44	39	71

TIM BURKE — bats right — throws right — age 33 — MON/NYN — P

1991	G	IP	H	BB	SO	SB	CS	W	L	SV	ERA	7-YEAR TOTALS (1985–1991) G	IP	H	BB	SO	SB	CS	W	L	SV	ERA
Total	72	101.2	96	26	59	8	1	6	7	6	3.36	460	655.2	572	201	429	70	18	46	29	102	2.62
at Home	34	50.0	40	12	27	2	1	2	2	4	2.16	219	318.1	275	99	204	26	5	27	11	41	2.49
on Road	38	51.2	56	14	32	6	0	4	5	2	4.53	241	337.1	297	102	225	44	13	19	18	61	2.75
on Grass	37	56.2	57	12	37	2	0	4	5	2	3.81	137	213.1	174	57	148	19	8	14	12	31	2.11
on Turf	35	45.0	39	14	22	6	1	2	2	4	2.80	323	442.1	398	144	281	51	10	32	17	71	2.87
Day Games	24	31.1	39	8	25	1	1	1	4	1	6.03	158	235.2	200	75	170	25	7	7	10	38	2.64
Night Games	48	70.1	57	18	34	7	0	5	3	5	2.18	302	420.0	372	126	259	45	11	39	19	64	2.61
April	10	11.1	9	4	4	0	0	1	0	2	3.97	63	80.1	74	30	58	11	5	5	3	20	3.25
May	12	17.1	13	6	13	0	1	0	1	2	3.63	80	117.2	101	35	70	10	6	6	3	21	2.52
June	11	13.1	16	2	6	0	0	0	1	0	5.40	75	101.1	88	30	60	15	2	8	3	9	2.66
July	11	14.0	17	4	9	2	0	1	2	1	3.21	75	106.2	100	42	60	15	3	8	5	16	2.53
August	14	23.1	23	4	12	0	0	0	2	1	3.47	83	124.1	108	30	83	7	4	11	9	15	2.32
Sept–Oct	14	22.1	18	6	15	0	0	2	0	0	1.61	84	125.1	101	34	98	12	3	8	6	21	2.66

	BA	OBA	SA	AB	H	2B	3B	HR	RBI	BB	SO	BA	OBA	SA	AB	H	2B	3B	HR	RBI	BB	SO
Total	.249	.301	.369	385	96	16	3	8	41	26	59	.236	.298	.338	2421	572	91	9	46	265	201	429
vs. Left	.296	.343	.413	189	56	12	2	2	26	14	20	.271	.338	.384	1194	324	52	4	25	146	126	160
vs. Right	.204	.262	.327	196	40	4	1	6	15	12	39	.202	.257	.293	1227	248	39	5	21	119	75	269
Bases Empty	.255	.291	.387	212	54	9	2	5	5	10	33	.236	.280	.347	1322	312	48	6	29	29	72	224
Leadoff	.312	.340	.484	93	29	5	1	3	3	4	11	.263	.304	.402	552	145	26	3	15	15	32	76
Runners On Base	.243	.313	.347	173	42	7	1	3	36	16	26	.226	.330	.313	718	162	28	1	11	214	114	143
Scoring Position	.270	.361	.420	100	27	6	0	3	35	13	17	.230	.291	.324	461	136	52	4	26	164	120	255
Late and Close	.231	.286	.337	208	48	11	1	3	23	15	30	.230	.291	.324	1461	336	52	4	26	164	120	255

JOHN BURKETT — bats right — throws right — age 28 — SF — P

1991	G	IP	H	BB	SO	SB	CS	W	L	SV	ERA		3-YEAR TOTALS (1987–1991) G	IP	H	BB	SO	SB	CS	W	L	SV	ERA
Total	36	206.2	223	60	131	17	15	12	11	0	4.18		72	416.2	431	124	254	35	22	26	18	1	4.00
at Home	17	109.1	102	25	72	5	4	6	6	0	3.54		35	217.1	208	60	144	18	8	12	8	0	3.81
on Road	19	97.1	121	35	59	12	11	6	5	0	4.90		37	199.1	223	64	110	17	14	14	10	1	4.20
on Grass	26	152.0	156	39	93	13	8	7	9	0	3.73		53	310.1	308	89	190	27	12	17	13	1	3.65
on Turf	10	54.2	67	21	38	4	7	5	2	0	5.43		19	106.1	123	35	64	8	10	9	5	0	4.99
Day Games	17	95.2	94	31	53	6	7	6	6	0	3.20		31	186.0	181	60	104	14	14	13	8	0	3.24
Night Games	19	111.0	129	29	78	11	8	6	5	0	5.03		41	230.2	250	64	150	21	8	13	10	1	4.60
April	5	32.0	33	9	18	1	5	2	2	0	3.66		6	39.0	40	10	21	2	5	3	2	0	3.46
May	6	36.0	39	12	27	5	4	0	1	0	3.50		12	69.1	76	28	41	7	8	3	2	0	4.15
June	6	37.1	26	14	18	2	3	2	1	0	2.41		12	81.0	60	26	49	4	5	5	2	0	2.56
July	7	39.1	44	9	23	2	0	3	1	0	3.89		13	76.1	83	17	46	8	1	6	2	0	3.77
August	6	29.0	43	7	18	5	2	2	3	0	7.45		12	65.1	77	18	37	8	1	4	5	0	5.51
Sept–Oct	6	33.0	38	9	27	2	1	3	3	0	4.91		17	85.2	95	25	60	6	1	6	5	1	4.52

	BA	OBA	SA	AB	H	2B	3B	HR	RBI	BB	SO		BA	OBA	SA	AB	H	2B	3B	HR	RBI	BB	SO
Total	.277	.332	.392	804	223	31	2	19	101	60	131		.268	.324	.387	1608	431	66	4	39	182	124	254
vs. Left	.293	.348	.434	461	135	24	1	13	59	39	70		.271	.326	.399	929	252	43	2	24	109	75	137
vs. Right	.257	.311	.335	343	88	7	1	6	42	21	61		.264	.321	.370	679	179	23	2	15	73	49	117
Bases Empty	.266	.331	.394	436	116	15	1	13	13	35	75		.262	.320	.384	912	239	33	3	24	24	68	152
Leadoff	.303	.352	.451	195	59	8	0	7	7	14	29		.294	.336	.415	402	118	17	1	10	10	25	57
Runners On Base	.291	.334	.389	368	107	16	1	6	88	25	56		.276	.329	.391	696	192	33	1	15	158	56	102
Scoring Position	.320	.360	.396	197	63	7	1	2	76	16	36		.279	.340	.379	377	105	17	1	8	135	39	64
Late and Close	.222	.283	.389	54	12	0	0	3	8	5	5		.265	.323	.381	113	30	4	0	3	13	9	12

GREG CADARET — bats left — throws left — age 30 — NYA — P

1991	G	IP	H	BB	SO	SB	CS	W	L	SV	ERA		5-YEAR TOTALS (1987–1991) G	IP	H	BB	SO	SB	CS	W	L	SV	ERA
Total	68	121.2	110	59	105	11	8	8	6	3	3.62		255	474.1	457	240	360	25	32	29	19	9	3.83
at Home	31	61.0	62	35	51	4	4	4	3	0	4.72		122	242.0	221	119	192	10	14	17	7	2	3.57
on Road	37	60.2	48	24	54	7	2	4	3	3	2.52		133	232.1	236	121	168	15	18	12	12	7	4.11
on Grass	55	100.0	86	54	82	10	7	7	5	2	3.78		212	394.1	366	206	297	18	27	26	14	7	3.81
on Turf	13	21.2	24	5	23	1	1	1	1	1	2.91		43	80.0	91	34	63	7	5	3	5	2	3.94
Day Games	24	55.1	53	28	50	2	4	4	2	2	4.39		96	188.1	189	99	150	7	12	15	10	7	4.01
Night Games	44	66.1	57	31	55	9	4	4	2	1	2.98		159	286.0	268	141	210	18	20	14	9	2	3.71
April	10	11.2	9	6	15	1	1	1	3	0	5.40		30	45.2	41	26	42	4	2	2	4	0	5.32
May	14	17.0	12	11	7	2	1	0	0	1	1.06		42	59.1	47	32	32	4	2	0	3	1	2.43
June	13	23.2	20	12	22	4	0	1	0	0	3.04		42	75.2	74	37	55	6	5	4	1	0	3.09
July	6	17.1	20	5	13	1	1	1	1	0	4.67		43	86.2	83	33	59	5	5	6	3	3	3.53
August	11	32.1	30	11	32	1	2	3	1	1	4.73		48	128.1	126	57	108	2	5	10	6	3	3.79
Sept–Oct	14	19.2	19	14	16	2	3	2	1	1	2.75		50	78.2	86	55	64	4	8	7	2	2	5.15

	BA	OBA	SA	AB	H	2B	3B	HR	RBI	BB	SO		BA	OBA	SA	AB	H	2B	3B	HR	RBI	BB	SO
Total	.246	.335	.365	447	110	21	4	8	54	59	105		.258	.346	.369	1771	457	86	9	31	218	240	360
vs. Left	.246	.313	.305	118	29	7	0	0	11	12	25		.236	.319	.308	529	125	20	0	6	55	63	99
vs. Right	.246	.342	.386	329	81	14	4	8	43	47	80		.267	.357	.395	1242	332	66	9	25	163	177	261
Bases Empty	.244	.335	.339	242	59	12	1	3	3	31	60		.245	.332	.358	923	226	47	3	17	17	114	193
Leadoff	.223	.322	.330	103	23	5	0	2	2	13	29		.240	.329	.340	400	96	22	0	6	6	50	82
Runners On Base	.249	.335	.395	205	51	9	3	5	51	28	45		.272	.361	.382	848	231	39	6	14	201	126	167
Scoring Position	.300	.394	.455	110	33	5	3	2	44	19	25		.281	.373	.393	506	142	22	4	9	182	84	104
Late and Close	.230	.340	.320	122	28	3	1	2	14	21	31		.247	.347	.334	425	105	17	4	4	42	67	94

TOM CANDIOTTI — bats right — throws right — age 35 — CLE/TOR — P

1991	G	IP	H	BB	SO	SB	CS	W	L	SV	ERA		7-YEAR TOTALS (1984–1991) G	IP	H	BB	SO	SB	CS	W	L	SV	ERA
Total	34	238.0	202	73	167	26	8	13	13	0	2.65		203	1349.0	1287	445	857	138	53	80	74	0	3.51
at Home	16	110.0	103	35	84	12	4	6	6	0	3.11		107	735.0	695	222	477	73	30	47	34	0	3.39
on Road	18	128.0	99	38	83	14	4	7	7	0	2.25		96	614.0	592	223	380	65	23	33	40	0	3.65
on Grass	18	128.2	101	35	88	10	2	9	7	0	2.80		166	1105.2	1044	358	687	105	42	69	59	0	3.48
on Turf	16	109.1	101	38	79	16	6	4	6	0	2.47		37	243.1	243	87	170	33	11	11	15	0	3.66
Day Games	11	77.0	59	30	56	7	4	6	4	0	2.10		64	437.0	438	130	284	39	24	26	25	0	3.62
Night Games	23	161.0	143	43	111	19	4	7	9	0	2.91		139	912.0	849	315	573	99	29	54	49	0	3.45
April	4	29.0	21	8	19	2	1	2	1	0	1.24		26	169.2	159	66	121	11	7	13	8	0	3.29
May	6	43.0	38	11	35	7	0	4	1	0	3.14		32	224.2	221	73	152	24	8	14	12	0	3.45
June	6	42.1	37	11	35	2	3	1	5	0	2.34		36	222.0	235	87	147	27	15	11	18	0	4.18
July	5	37.2	33	11	26	5	2	2	3	0	2.15		34	228.1	214	65	130	19	9	13	11	0	3.31
August	6	43.2	33	16	29	3	0	2	1	0	2.68		33	239.0	196	76	138	21	8	17	8	0	2.94
Sept–Oct	7	42.1	40	16	23	7	2	2	2	0	3.83		42	265.1	262	78	169	36	6	12	17	0	3.83

	BA	OBA	SA	AB	H	2B	3B	HR	RBI	BB	SO		BA	OBA	SA	AB	H	2B	3B	HR	RBI	BB	SO
Total	.228	.288	.337	887	202	41	10	12	67	73	167		.250	.312	.365	5142	1287	205	25	111	515	445	857
vs. Left	.241	.294	.351	439	106	16	7	6	40	34	59		.252	.314	.357	2672	674	93	20	49	259	248	370
vs. Right	.214	.282	.324	448	96	25	3	6	27	39	108		.248	.309	.373	2470	613	112	5	62	256	197	487
Bases Empty	.237	.297	.364	539	128	30	7	8	8	42	106		.253	.307	.374	3071	777	135	12	71	71	222	535
Leadoff	.205	.270	.308	224	46	12	1	3	3	19	46		.240	.289	.349	1308	314	58	3	26	26	86	230
Runners On Base	.213	.273	.296	348	74	11	3	4	59	31	61		.246	.319	.351	2071	510	70	13	40	444	223	322
Scoring Position	.190	.269	.275	211	40	7	1	3	55	25	36		.251	.338	.367	1175	295	43	9	25	403	165	188
Late and Close	.200	.274	.263	95	19	2	2	0	4	8	22		.255	.333	.357	498	127	19	4	8	42	55	74

NORM CHARLTON — bats both — throws left — age 29 — CIN — P

1991

	G	IP	H	BB	SO	SB	CS	W	L	SV	ERA
Total	39	108.1	92	34	77	10	7	3	5	1	2.91
at Home	15	42.2	43	16	27	4	2	0	4	1	4.01
on Road	24	65.2	49	18	50	6	5	3	1	0	2.19
on Grass	12	27.0	14	10	24	2	1	1	0	0	0.33
on Turf	27	81.1	78	24	53	8	6	2	5	1	3.76
Day Games	10	29.2	35	11	17	4	2	0	3	0	5.76
Night Games	29	78.2	57	23	60	6	5	3	2	1	1.83
April	4	29.1	22	11	23	1	3	1	2	0	2.45
May	5	24.1	30	9	6	3	1	1	3	0	6.29
June	2	12.0	13	2	8	1	1	0	0	0	4.50
July	4	6.0	4	1	7	1	1	0	0	0	1.50
August	11	19.0	13	7	17	0	0	0	0	1	1.42
Sept–Oct	13	17.2	10	4	16	4	1	0	0	0	0.00

4-YEAR TOTALS (1988–1991)

	G	IP	H	BB	SO	SB	CS	W	L	SV	ERA
Total	174	419.1	350	164	331	41	18	27	22	3	3.00
at Home	82	199.1	173	82	142	21	7	11	10	2	3.30
on Road	92	220.0	177	82	189	20	11	16	12	1	2.74
on Grass	51	110.1	81	46	90	10	7	12	7	0	2.28
on Turf	123	309.0	269	118	241	31	11	15	15	3	3.26
Day Games	54	134.0	114	44	110	20	5	7	9	1	2.75
Night Games	120	285.1	236	120	221	21	13	20	13	2	3.12
April	21	49.2	36	24	48	3	3	2	2	0	2.54
May	29	54.0	54	22	36	6	2	5	4	1	4.50
June	27	47.1	42	15	35	3	2	5	3	0	3.80
July	24	53.2	46	18	39	4	3	3	6	0	2.68
August	32	102.0	76	40	76	11	2	5	3	1	2.12
Sept–Oct	41	112.2	96	45	97	13	6	7	7	0	3.12

	BA	OBA	SA	AB	H	2B	3B	HR	RBI	BB	SO
Total	.236	.306	.336	390	92	13	4	6	46	34	77
vs. Left	.253	.359	.299	87	22	4	0	0	16	11	19
vs. Right	.231	.290	.347	303	70	9	4	6	30	23	58
Bases Empty	.228	.291	.287	237	54	4	2	2	2	17	45
Leadoff	.240	.296	.300	100	24	1	1	1	1	7	20
Runners On Base	.248	.329	.412	153	38	9	2	4	44	17	32
Scoring Position	.242	.296	.374	99	24	8	1	1	36	8	19
Late and Close	.234	.327	.309	94	22	2	1	1	14	11	31

	BA	OBA	SA	AB	H	2B	3B	HR	RBI	BB	SO
Total	.229	.308	.329	1531	350	55	9	27	149	164	331
vs. Left	.208	.317	.295	322	67	11	1	5	44	43	77
vs. Right	.234	.305	.338	1209	283	44	8	22	105	121	254
Bases Empty	.218	.296	.319	901	196	32	7	15	15	90	200
Leadoff	.241	.312	.350	386	93	18	3	6	6	37	76
Runners On Base	.244	.324	.344	630	154	23	2	12	134	74	131
Scoring Position	.227	.315	.310	374	85	14	1	5	112	50	82
Late and Close	.214	.296	.319	373	80	15	3	6	32	42	108

STEVE CHITREN — bats right — throws right — age 25 — OAK — P

1991

	G	IP	H	BB	SO	SB	CS	W	L	SV	ERA
Total	56	60.1	59	32	47	5	0	1	4	4	4.33
at Home	27	29.0	26	17	31	2	0	0	0	1	5.28
on Road	29	31.1	33	15	16	3	0	1	4	3	3.45
on Grass	45	48.2	45	28	43	4	0	1	3	3	4.25
on Turf	11	11.2	14	4	4	1	0	0	1	1	4.63
Day Games	18	18.1	20	11	20	2	0	0	1	0	6.38
Night Games	38	42.0	39	21	27	3	0	1	3	4	3.43
April	9	9.0	7	7	9	2	0	1	0	0	0.00
May	13	15.0	14	10	13	2	0	1	0	0	4.80
June	9	12.0	13	5	13	2	0	0	1	2	4.50
July	9	10.0	9	2	5	0	0	0	1	2	3.60
August	9	7.2	11	4	6	1	0	0	1	0	9.39
Sept–Oct	7	6.2	5	4	1	0	0	0	1	0	4.05

2-YEAR TOTALS (1990–1991)

	G	IP	H	BB	SO	SB	CS	W	L	SV	ERA
Total	64	78.0	66	36	66	5	0	2	4	4	3.58
at Home	30	38.2	28	17	42	2	0	0	4	3	3.96
on Road	34	39.1	38	19	24	3	0	2	4	3	3.20
on Grass	51	64.1	52	31	61	4	0	2	3	3	3.50
on Turf	13	13.2	14	5	5	1	0	0	1	1	3.95
Day Games	23	31.0	26	11	33	2	0	1	1	0	4.35
Night Games	41	47.0	40	25	33	3	0	1	3	4	3.06
April	9	9.0	7	7	9	2	0	1	0	0	0.00
May	13	15.0	14	10	13	2	0	1	0	0	4.80
June	9	12.0	13	5	13	2	0	0	1	2	4.50
July	9	10.0	9	2	5	0	0	0	1	2	3.60
August	9	7.2	11	4	6	0	0	0	1	0	9.39
Sept–Oct	15	24.1	12	8	20	0	0	0	1	0	1.85

	BA	OBA	SA	AB	H	2B	3B	HR	RBI	BB	SO
Total	.258	.356	.432	229	59	10	3	8	43	32	47
vs. Left	.290	.402	.484	93	27	4	1	4	16	15	15
vs. Right	.235	.323	.397	136	32	6	2	4	27	17	32
Bases Empty	.243	.328	.423	111	27	3	1	5	5	12	24
Leadoff	.227	.333	.341	44	10	2	0	1	1	6	8
Runners On Base	.271	.380	.441	118	32	7	2	3	38	20	23
Scoring Position	.296	.429	.451	71	21	4	2	1	32	16	17
Late and Close	.244	.371	.419	86	21	4	1	3	19	15	18

	BA	OBA	SA	AB	H	2B	3B	HR	RBI	BB	SO
Total	.228	.320	.374	289	66	12	3	8	46	36	66
vs. Left	.261	.364	.420	119	31	5	1	4	18	17	22
vs. Right	.206	.288	.341	170	35	7	2	4	28	19	44
Bases Empty	.192	.272	.327	156	30	4	1	5	5	15	40
Leadoff	.180	.265	.262	61	11	2	0	1	1	6	13
Runners On Base	.271	.373	.429	133	36	8	2	3	41	21	26
Scoring Position	.308	.429	.462	78	24	5	2	1	35	16	18
Late and Close	.245	.359	.418	98	24	6	1	3	21	15	21

ROGER CLEMENS — bats right — throws right — age 30 — BOS — P

1991

	G	IP	H	BB	SO	SB	CS	W	L	SV	ERA
Total	35	271.1	219	65	241	23	16	18	10	0	2.62
at Home	18	142.2	120	35	132	15	8	8	5	0	2.59
on Road	17	128.2	99	30	109	8	8	10	5	0	2.66
on Grass	30	235.2	182	53	213	19	11	16	8	0	2.52
on Turf	5	35.2	37	12	28	4	5	2	2	0	3.28
Day Games	9	73.0	59	10	70	8	3	6	2	0	2.22
Night Games	26	198.1	160	55	171	15	13	12	8	0	2.77
April	4	32.0	17	5	34	4	2	4	0	0	0.28
May	6	45.0	35	10	46	4	1	3	2	0	3.80
June	5	41.2	37	11	26	1	0	2	3	0	1.94
July	6	42.1	42	13	36	1	4	2	2	0	3.19
August	7	53.1	41	18	49	4	7	3	1	0	2.70
Sept–Oct	7	57.0	47	8	50	9	2	4	2	0	3.00

8-YEAR TOTALS (1984–1991)

	G	IP	H	BB	SO	SB	CS	W	L	SV	ERA
Total	241	1784.1	1499	490	1665	145	89	134	61	0	2.85
at Home	120	890.1	765	225	852	68	40	65	31	0	2.91
on Road	121	894.0	734	265	813	77	49	69	30	0	2.79
on Grass	206	1517.0	1295	418	1452	117	73	112	53	0	2.95
on Turf	35	267.1	204	72	213	28	16	22	8	0	2.29
Day Games	79	585.0	458	160	557	42	31	46	15	0	2.26
Night Games	162	1199.1	1041	330	1108	103	58	88	46	0	3.14
April	33	255.0	175	66	260	22	13	22	6	0	2.05
May	44	339.2	270	95	312	30	19	25	12	0	3.23
June	42	297.0	291	77	264	22	8	22	13	0	3.30
July	44	321.2	284	87	285	28	16	21	12	0	2.77
August	44	312.1	267	101	304	24	19	23	10	0	3.14
Sept–Oct	34	258.2	212	64	240	19	14	21	8	0	2.37

	BA	OBA	SA	AB	H	2B	3B	HR	RBI	BB	SO
Total	.221	.270	.328	993	219	46	8	15	82	65	241
vs. Left	.224	.286	.310	548	123	26	6	3	45	47	117
vs. Right	.216	.249	.351	445	96	20	2	12	37	18	124
Bases Empty	.208	.253	.307	635	132	31	4	8	8	35	168
Leadoff	.224	.258	.316	263	59	13	1	3	3	12	72
Runners On Base	.243	.299	.366	358	87	15	4	7	74	30	73
Scoring Position	.231	.306	.332	199	46	7	2	4	60	25	32
Late and Close	.224	.312	.320	125	28	6	3	0	8	16	29

	BA	OBA	SA	AB	H	2B	3B	HR	RBI	BB	SO
Total	.226	.282	.330	6627	1499	267	34	117	543	490	1665
vs. Left	.238	.298	.334	3629	864	175	20	44	296	297	809
vs. Right	.212	.263	.325	2998	635	92	14	73	247	193	856
Bases Empty	.227	.278	.328	4075	925	169	17	70	70	264	1032
Leadoff	.235	.282	.328	1718	403	70	6	26	26	105	423
Runners On Base	.225	.290	.332	2552	574	98	17	47	473	226	633
Scoring Position	.213	.285	.307	1402	299	47	11	21	398	143	364
Late and Close	.220	.286	.317	778	171	26	4	14	53	70	199

DAVID CONE — bats left — throws right — age 29 — NYN — P

6-YEAR TOTALS (1986–1991)

1991	G	IP	H	BB	SO	SB	CS	W	L	SV	ERA		G	IP	H	BB	SO	SB	CS	W	L	SV	ERA
Total	34	232.2	204	73	241	27	13	14	14	0	3.29		166	1017.1	858	349	966	115	57	67	41	1	3.18
at Home	17	115.0	112	36	118	12	5	6	7	0	3.91		78	510.2	429	163	490	51	30	34	19	0	3.07
on Road	17	117.2	92	37	123	15	8	8	7	0	2.68		88	506.2	429	186	476	64	27	33	22	1	3.30
on Grass	23	153.0	147	44	152	14	6	8	11	0	3.94		105	691.1	589	217	675	73	40	46	31	0	3.22
on Turf	11	79.2	57	29	89	13	7	6	3	0	2.03		61	326.0	269	132	291	42	17	21	10	1	3.12
Day Games	11	70.2	68	18	70	5	7	5	6	0	3.95		59	342.0	308	105	310	38	32	24	15	1	3.42
Night Games	23	162.0	136	55	171	22	6	9	8	0	3.00		107	675.1	550	244	656	77	25	43	26	0	3.07
April	4	24.0	32	12	18	3	4	2	1	0	5.25		25	111.1	120	60	97	17	9	6	7	0	5.09
May	6	45.0	36	7	43	3	2	3	2	0	2.20		25	167.2	138	50	148	18	15	12	5	0	2.74
June	5	35.2	28	13	38	7	2	2	2	0	2.52		26	150.1	129	50	141	25	4	8	5	0	3.53
July	6	43.0	33	9	45	3	0	3	2	0	3.14		22	158.0	122	48	150	16	5	11	4	0	3.02
August	6	34.0	45	12	33	3	4	2	3	0	5.03		27	188.0	157	53	177	17	12	14	8	0	2.78
Sept–Oct	7	51.0	30	20	64	8	1	2	4	0	2.82		41	242.0	192	88	253	22	12	16	12	1	2.83

	BA	OBA	SA	AB	H	2B	3B	HR	RBI	BB	SO		BA	OBA	SA	AB	H	2B	3B	HR	RBI	BB	SO
Total	.235	.296	.329	868	204	29	7	13	78	73	241		.228	.295	.344	3767	858	140	34	77	348	349	966
vs. Left	.249	.312	.342	535	133	19	5	7	47	49	121		.242	.315	.372	2107	510	97	25	42	190	219	437
vs. Right	.213	.270	.309	333	71	10	2	6	31	24	120		.210	.269	.310	1660	348	43	9	35	158	130	529
Bases Empty	.233	.295	.319	514	120	20	6	4	4	42	141		.224	.287	.332	2290	512	88	19	41	41	190	585
Leadoff	.261	.311	.356	222	58	9	3	2	2	15	63		.237	.295	.355	963	228	29	8	23	23	73	220
Runners On Base	.237	.297	.345	354	84	9	1	9	74	31	100		.234	.306	.363	1477	346	52	15	36	307	159	381
Scoring Position	.228	.305	.359	206	47	4	1	7	65	24	64		.211	.303	.336	869	183	25	9	22	260	121	256
Late and Close	.226	.258	.333	84	19	2	2	1	5	4	22		.233	.282	.349	416	97	10	7	8	33	30	105

CHUCK CRIM — bats right — throws right — age 31 — MIL — P

5-YEAR TOTALS (1987–1991)

1991	G	IP	H	BB	SO	SB	CS	W	L	SV	ERA		G	IP	H	BB	SO	SB	CS	W	L	SV	ERA
Total	66	91.1	115	25	39	12	1	8	5	3	4.63		332	531.2	548	155	252	39	13	33	31	42	3.45
at Home	37	49.2	65	15	26	8	1	5	2	2	5.07		175	279.0	290	71	131	26	9	18	16	24	3.39
on Road	29	41.2	50	10	13	4	0	3	3	1	4.10		157	252.2	258	84	121	13	4	15	15	18	3.53
on Grass	56	75.2	101	21	33	11	1	7	4	2	4.76		280	451.0	470	130	207	36	11	27	26	37	3.39
on Turf	10	15.2	14	4	6	1	0	1	1	1	4.02		52	80.2	78	25	45	3	2	6	5	5	3.79
Day Games	22	30.1	36	14	14	5	1	4	2	1	6.53		100	152.0	154	51	67	11	5	13	12	10	3.85
Night Games	44	61.0	79	11	25	7	0	4	3	2	3.69		232	379.2	394	104	185	28	8	20	19	32	3.29
April	11	16.0	13	4	7	3	0	1	1	2	4.50		45	70.1	69	23	25	3	0	4	5	6	3.97
May	12	17.0	20	9	8	4	0	2	2	1	7.41		56	75.2	80	20	38	7	2	6	4	3	4.28
June	11	11.2	15	1	3	2	1	1	1	0	1.54		56	89.0	88	32	37	5	5	4	11	8	4.15
July	10	12.0	22	2	5	0	0	1	1	0	6.00		45	74.1	76	16	44	5	0	4	3	4	2.91
August	12	20.1	23	6	8	3	0	2	0	0	5.31		52	85.1	87	22	41	5	2	9	1	8	2.95
Sept–Oct	10	14.1	22	3	8	0	0	1	0	0	1.88		78	137.0	148	42	67	14	4	6	7	13	2.89

	BA	OBA	SA	AB	H	2B	3B	HR	RBI	BB	SO		BA	OBA	SA	AB	H	2B	3B	HR	RBI	BB	SO
Total	.305	.351	.416	377	115	15	0	9	55	25	39		.268	.320	.383	2045	548	70	9	49	260	155	252
vs. Left	.302	.360	.458	179	54	7	0	7	29	15	19		.270	.335	.394	889	240	33	1	25	108	85	111
vs. Right	.308	.341	.379	198	61	8	0	2	26	10	20		.266	.309	.375	1156	308	37	8	24	152	70	141
Bases Empty	.275	.313	.400	200	55	10	0	5	5	10	20		.263	.306	.390	1095	288	44	4	29	29	63	131
Leadoff	.238	.264	.333	84	20	5	0	1	1	3	11		.264	.303	.424	462	122	25	2	15	15	24	60
Runners On Base	.339	.392	.435	177	60	5	0	4	50	15	19		.274	.336	.375	950	260	26	5	20	231	92	121
Scoring Position	.364	.441	.482	110	40	4	0	3	47	15	12		.273	.353	.395	557	152	16	5	14	216	74	74
Late and Close	.305	.361	.378	164	50	6	0	2	23	14	17		.260	.317	.350	904	235	28	4	15	94	77	126

RON DARLING — bats right — throws right — age 32 — NYN/MON/OAK — P

8-YEAR TOTALS (1984–1991)

1991	G	IP	H	BB	SO	SB	CS	W	L	SV	ERA		G	IP	H	BB	SO	SB	CS	W	L	SV	ERA
Total	32	194.1	185	71	129	24	5	8	15	0	4.26		267	1676.1	1531	640	1196	187	69	101	76	0	3.58
at Home	16	90.0	100	39	59	15	2	3	9	0	5.40		131	871.0	778	285	634	83	36	59	33	0	3.18
on Road	16	104.1	85	32	70	9	3	5	6	0	3.28		136	805.1	753	355	562	104	33	42	43	0	4.01
on Grass	24	143.1	141	54	100	22	3	6	11	0	4.52		190	1214.1	1099	439	897	120	45	76	51	0	3.55
on Turf	8	51.0	44	17	29	2	2	2	4	0	3.53		77	462.0	432	201	299	67	24	25	25	0	3.66
Day Games	11	66.0	77	18	42	7	3	1	6	0	4.91		87	527.1	496	215	350	61	22	28	28	0	3.79
Night Games	21	128.1	108	53	87	17	2	7	9	0	3.93		180	1149.0	1035	425	846	126	47	73	48	0	3.49
April	4	21.0	22	4	12	6	0	1	2	0	3.86		35	202.1	204	82	134	32	6	10	11	0	4.18
May	5	31.0	30	8	20	4	2	1	0	0	4.06		43	280.0	239	98	208	24	13	17	9	0	3.50
June	6	35.1	38	11	18	2	1	1	3	0	5.09		45	282.1	254	109	197	24	13	17	11	0	3.41
July	5	32.0	31	10	19	5	1	1	3	0	4.22		48	309.2	297	114	215	35	17	21	15	0	3.49
August	6	38.0	33	18	26	2	2	3	1	0	3.55		47	306.0	284	127	231	30	14	20	14	0	3.74
Sept–Oct	6	37.0	31	20	34	5	0	0	6	0	4.62		49	296.0	253	110	211	42	6	16	16	0	3.34

	BA	OBA	SA	AB	H	2B	3B	HR	RBI	BB	SO		BA	OBA	SA	AB	H	2B	3B	HR	RBI	BB	SO
Total	.254	.325	.414	727	185	30	10	22	89	71	129		.245	.316	.381	6259	1531	266	43	168	667	640	1196
vs. Left	.241	.307	.364	382	92	15	4	8	42	37	74		.245	.314	.369	3359	824	143	26	74	337	337	627
vs. Right	.270	.345	.470	345	93	15	6	14	47	34	55		.244	.319	.395	2900	707	123	17	94	330	303	569
Bases Empty	.246	.321	.411	423	104	20	4	14	14	41	75		.247	.315	.386	3751	926	153	24	107	107	350	702
Leadoff	.273	.332	.372	183	50	6	0	4	4	12	35		.252	.311	.379	1593	401	54	8	44	44	122	304
Runners On Base	.266	.330	.418	304	81	10	6	8	75	30	54		.241	.317	.374	2508	605	113	19	61	560	290	494
Scoring Position	.291	.363	.464	179	52	6	5	3	66	22	28		.233	.324	.363	1440	336	60	12	34	480	209	302
Late and Close	.267	.365	.467	45	12	1	1	2	6	7	10		.242	.323	.362	578	140	26	2	13	52	65	97

JOSE DeJESUS — bats right — throws right — age 27 — PHI — P

1991 — Pitching

1991	G	IP	H	BB	SO	SB	CS	W	L	SV	ERA
Total	31	181.2	147	128	118	20	10	10	9	1	3.42
at Home	12	77.0	67	54	52	9	5	4	5	0	3.39
on Road	19	104.2	80	74	66	11	5	6	4	1	3.44
on Grass	10	47.1	26	37	25	6	3	3	2	1	3.61
on Turf	21	134.1	121	91	93	14	7	7	7	0	3.35
Day Games	6	37.1	31	25	25	4	2	2	1	0	3.62
Night Games	25	144.1	116	103	93	16	8	8	8	1	3.37
April	4	20.0	15	20	9	4	1	0	1	0	5.40
May	3	15.2	14	13	10	1	0	1	1	0	3.45
June	7	39.0	34	23	24	0	3	4	1	1	3.00
July	5	34.1	25	18	19	4	2	2	1	0	2.10
August	6	38.2	34	28	36	4	2	3	0	0	3.49
Sept–Oct	6	34.0	25	26	20	7	2	0	5	0	3.97

4-YEAR TOTALS (1988–1991) — Pitching

	G	IP	H	BB	SO	SB	CS	W	L	SV	ERA
Total	58	322.1	257	214	209	34	16	17	18	1	3.77
at Home	27	154.2	134	96	105	19	8	6	11	0	3.96
on Road	31	167.2	123	118	104	15	8	11	7	1	3.60
on Grass	17	89.0	52	61	48	7	3	6	3	1	3.34
on Turf	41	233.1	205	153	161	27	13	11	15	0	3.93
Day Games	12	63.2	57	51	44	7	5	4	4	0	4.66
Night Games	46	258.2	200	163	165	27	11	13	14	1	3.55
April	4	20.0	15	20	9	4	1	0	1	0	5.40
May	3	15.2	14	13	10	1	0	1	1	0	3.45
June	10	56.0	47	37	32	1	4	4	2	1	2.89
July	11	66.1	54	35	44	6	4	4	2	0	2.98
August	12	79.2	59	44	65	8	4	5	3	0	3.28
Sept–Oct	18	84.2	68	65	49	14	3	3	9	0	5.10

1991 — Batting Against

	BA	OBA	SA	AB	H	2B	3B	HR	RBI	BB	SO
Total	.224	.353	.318	655	147	32	4	7	64	128	118
vs. Left	.230	.376	.306	379	87	20	3	1	41	90	67
vs. Right	.217	.319	.333	276	60	12	1	6	23	38	51
Bases Empty	.216	.345	.307	348	75	16	2	4	4	67	57
Leadoff	.230	.344	.348	161	37	9	2	2	2	27	22
Runners On Base	.235	.362	.329	307	72	16	2	3	60	61	61
Scoring Position	.204	.346	.293	191	39	9	1	2	55	41	42
Late and Close	.281	.354	.439	57	16	4	1	1	7	7	7

4-YEAR TOTALS (1988–1991) — Batting Against

	BA	OBA	SA	AB	H	2B	3B	HR	RBI	BB	SO
Total	.222	.345	.325	1158	257	51	7	18	123	214	209
vs. Left	.212	.353	.291	688	146	29	5	5	63	149	125
vs. Right	.236	.334	.374	470	111	22	2	13	60	65	84
Bases Empty	.216	.344	.319	620	134	26	4	10	10	108	108
Leadoff	.234	.366	.360	278	65	14	3	5	5	57	49
Runners On Base	.229	.347	.331	538	123	25	3	8	113	96	101
Scoring Position	.227	.347	.318	330	75	14	2	4	100	59	69
Late and Close	.242	.305	.347	95	23	5	1	1	8	9	16

JOSE DeLEON — bats right — throws right — age 32 — SL — P

1991 — Pitching

1991	G	IP	H	BB	SO	SB	CS	W	L	SV	ERA
Total	28	162.2	144	61	118	12	12	5	9	0	2.71
at Home	16	89.1	78	33	65	7	6	3	4	0	2.42
on Road	12	73.1	66	28	53	5	6	2	5	0	3.07
on Grass	5	31.2	26	4	22	2	1	1	3	0	2.56
on Turf	23	131.0	118	57	96	10	11	4	6	0	2.75
Day Games	7	46.2	38	10	42	3	3	2	3	0	2.51
Night Games	21	116.0	106	51	76	9	9	3	6	0	2.79
April	5	28.1	20	11	25	4	1	1	2	0	2.22
May	5	27.1	26	18	19	3	2	1	2	0	4.28
June	6	38.1	32	8	31	1	2	1	2	0	3.05
July	5	34.0	38	11	19	3	4	2	2	0	2.38
August	5	29.0	25	11	20	1	2	0	1	0	2.17
Sept–Oct	2	5.2	3	2	4	0	1	0	0	0	0.00

8-YEAR TOTALS (1984–1991) — Pitching

	G	IP	H	BB	SO	SB	CS	W	L	SV	ERA
Total	246	1472.0	1211	650	1225	171	80	66	102	4	3.74
at Home	126	767.1	619	314	656	83	44	34	55	2	3.78
on Road	120	704.2	592	336	569	88	36	32	47	2	3.70
on Grass	89	532.0	461	234	444	61	22	24	36	1	3.79
on Turf	157	940.0	750	416	781	110	58	42	66	3	3.71
Day Games	77	443.1	396	200	355	55	22	19	27	0	3.72
Night Games	169	1028.2	815	450	870	116	58	47	75	4	3.75
April	30	176.1	134	83	158	16	9	11	10	0	3.42
May	48	260.0	234	127	221	31	13	12	18	1	4.19
June	41	262.0	222	116	216	28	16	11	20	0	3.78
July	38	245.0	211	102	189	34	13	9	21	0	3.89
August	44	273.0	214	112	236	26	18	11	18	0	3.89
Sept–Oct	45	255.2	196	110	205	36	11	12	15	3	3.31

1991 — Batting Against

	BA	OBA	SA	AB	H	2B	3B	HR	RBI	BB	SO
Total	.239	.313	.378	603	144	29	5	15	46	61	118
vs. Left	.252	.339	.408	326	82	18	3	9	25	43	44
vs. Right	.224	.281	.343	277	62	11	2	6	21	18	74
Bases Empty	.244	.323	.411	377	92	19	4	12	12	40	73
Leadoff	.222	.289	.392	158	35	9	0	6	6	15	34
Runners On Base	.230	.296	.323	226	52	10	1	3	34	21	45
Scoring Position	.169	.241	.250	124	21	2	1	2	31	11	27
Late and Close	.324	.375	.541	37	12	3	1	1	5	3	4

8-YEAR TOTALS (1984–1991) — Batting Against

	BA	OBA	SA	AB	H	2B	3B	HR	RBI	BB	SO
Total	.225	.311	.345	5389	1211	222	38	117	550	650	1225
vs. Left	.256	.351	.387	2879	736	134	24	65	330	426	475
vs. Right	.189	.262	.298	2510	475	88	14	52	220	224	750
Bases Empty	.214	.304	.336	3216	689	132	21	73	73	387	734
Leadoff	.226	.317	.344	1362	308	61	8	28	28	172	296
Runners On Base	.240	.321	.358	2173	522	90	17	44	477	263	491
Scoring Position	.236	.327	.358	1261	297	61	12	23	416	179	288
Late and Close	.236	.328	.381	470	111	19	8	11	52	63	89

RICH DeLUCIA — bats right — throws right — age 28 — SEA — P

1991 — Pitching

1991	G	IP	H	BB	SO	SB	CS	W	L	SV	ERA
Total	32	182.0	176	78	98	4	9	12	13	0	5.09
at Home	15	89.2	80	31	48	2	4	7	4	0	4.72
on Road	17	92.1	96	47	50	2	5	5	9	0	5.46
on Grass	13	73.1	73	39	39	1	4	4	8	0	5.65
on Turf	19	108.2	103	39	59	3	5	8	5	0	4.72
Day Games	10	54.2	57	25	33	1	2	3	6	0	5.76
Night Games	22	127.1	119	53	65	3	7	9	7	0	4.81
April	4	25.2	26	14	16	0	3	2	3	0	5.26
May	6	33.2	35	12	25	0	0	3	0	0	3.74
June	6	30.0	22	22	17	3	1	1	3	0	5.40
July	5	32.2	28	10	16	0	2	3	0	0	3.86
August	5	32.0	29	5	13	1	2	2	2	0	3.38
Sept–Oct	6	28.0	36	15	11	0	1	1	5	0	9.64

2-YEAR TOTALS (1990–1991) — Pitching

	G	IP	H	BB	SO	SB	CS	W	L	SV	ERA
Total	37	218.0	206	87	118	4	10	13	15	0	4.58
at Home	16	97.2	88	32	54	2	4	8	4	0	4.52
on Road	21	120.1	118	55	64	2	6	5	11	0	4.64
on Grass	17	101.1	95	47	53	1	5	4	10	0	4.62
on Turf	20	116.2	111	40	65	3	5	9	5	0	4.55
Day Games	12	68.1	70	29	41	1	3	3	7	0	5.00
Night Games	25	149.2	136	58	77	3	7	10	8	0	4.39
April	4	25.2	26	14	16	0	3	2	3	0	5.26
May	6	33.2	35	12	25	0	0	3	0	0	3.74
June	6	30.0	22	22	17	3	1	1	3	0	5.40
July	5	32.2	28	10	16	0	2	3	0	0	3.86
August	5	32.0	29	5	13	1	2	2	2	0	3.38
Sept–Oct	11	64.0	66	24	31	0	2	2	7	0	5.34

1991 — Batting Against

	BA	OBA	SA	AB	H	2B	3B	HR	RBI	BB	SO
Total	.260	.333	.457	678	176	35	3	31	96	78	98
vs. Left	.286	.386	.454	315	90	14	3	11	42	54	33
vs. Right	.237	.284	.460	363	86	21	0	20	54	24	65
Bases Empty	.244	.307	.439	435	106	19	3	20	20	39	67
Leadoff	.264	.316	.500	182	48	9	2	10	10	14	28
Runners On Base	.288	.375	.490	243	70	16	0	11	76	39	31
Scoring Position	.272	.364	.464	125	34	6	0	4	63	26	21
Late and Close	.400	.423	1.000	25	10	3	0	4	5	1	4

2-YEAR TOTALS (1990–1991) — Batting Against

	BA	OBA	SA	AB	H	2B	3B	HR	RBI	BB	SO
Total	.254	.324	.436	811	206	39	5	33	101	87	118
vs. Left	.281	.373	.439	385	108	15	5	12	44	59	39
vs. Right	.230	.277	.434	426	98	24	0	21	57	28	79
Bases Empty	.241	.303	.424	519	125	21	4	22	22	45	80
Leadoff	.256	.306	.479	219	56	10	0	11	11	16	31
Runners On Base	.277	.359	.459	292	81	18	1	11	79	42	38
Scoring Position	.258	.347	.424	151	39	7	0	6	65	28	24
Late and Close	.375	.405	.825	40	15	3	0	5	6	2	5

JIM DESHAIES — bats left — throws left — age 32 — HOU — P

8-YEAR TOTALS (1984–1991)

1991	G	IP	H	BB	SO	SB	CS	W	L	SV	ERA		G	IP	H	BB	SO	SB	CS	W	L	SV	ERA
Total	28	161.0	156	72	98	21	14	5	12	0	4.98		183	1109.1	974	430	736	134	65	61	60	0	3.72
at Home	10	65.1	50	27	37	5	7	2	3	0	3.72		88	559.0	454	197	364	66	30	33	22	0	3.11
on Road	18	95.2	106	45	61	16	7	3	9	0	5.83		95	550.1	520	233	372	68	35	28	38	0	4.33
on Grass	10	51.1	61	28	30	8	3	2	6	0	6.66		52	305.1	295	121	210	32	18	16	21	0	4.48
on Turf	18	109.2	95	44	68	13	11	3	6	0	4.19		131	804.0	679	309	526	102	47	45	39	0	3.43
Day Games	4	19.0	24	8	14	2	1	0	3	0	7.11		48	276.1	260	95	175	32	18	16	16	0	4.07
Night Games	24	142.0	132	64	84	19	13	5	9	0	4.69		135	833.0	714	335	561	102	47	45	44	0	3.60
April	4	21.0	25	10	10	4	0	0	2	0	6.43		23	140.2	111	57	89	15	6	7	6	0	3.07
May	6	33.1	36	23	20	6	3	2	3	0	5.94		31	190.0	163	81	101	26	12	13	9	0	4.26
June	6	39.0	31	17	22	3	4	0	2	0	4.62		33	205.0	191	81	120	21	10	13	9	0	3.78
July	5	28.2	25	6	12	1	1	2	1	0	3.45		30	180.1	159	67	137	19	13	8	12	0	4.04
August	6	34.0	31	15	31	3	5	0	4	0	4.76		33	195.2	187	78	141	29	11	9	15	0	4.14
Sept–Oct	1	5.0	8	1	3	4	1	1	0	0	5.40		33	197.2	163	66	148	24	13	12	9	0	2.87

	BA	OBA	SA	AB	H	2B	3B	HR	RBI	BB	SO		BA	OBA	SA	AB	H	2B	3B	HR	RBI	BB	SO
Total	.259	.336	.430	602	156	36	5	19	78	72	98		.238	.310	.384	4096	974	197	29	114	423	430	736
vs. Left	.279	.386	.471	104	29	6	1	4	19	19	18		.268	.362	.424	668	179	39	7	17	71	99	113
vs. Right	.255	.324	.422	498	127	30	4	15	59	53	80		.232	.299	.376	3428	795	158	22	97	352	331	623
Bases Empty	.225	.303	.347	377	85	15	2	9	9	41	64		.237	.307	.380	2518	597	115	16	71	71	244	428
Leadoff	.240	.308	.351	154	37	6	1	3	3	14	17		.240	.304	.390	1056	253	51	6	32	32	94	163
Runners On Base	.316	.388	.569	225	71	21	3	10	69	31	34		.239	.314	.389	1578	377	82	13	43	352	186	308
Scoring Position	.265	.373	.515	132	35	14	2	5	56	27	24		.222	.314	.360	905	201	47	6	22	288	137	205
Late and Close	.250	.333	.308	52	13	3	0	0	3	7	5		.205	.261	.279	297	61	6	2	4	15	23	44

ROB DIBBLE — bats left — throws right — age 28 — CIN — P

4-YEAR TOTALS (1988–1991)

1991	G	IP	H	BB	SO	SB	CS	W	L	SV	ERA		G	IP	H	BB	SO	SB	CS	W	L	SV	ERA
Total	67	82.1	67	25	124	16	5	3	5	31	3.17		246	338.2	234	119	460	64	12	22	14	44	2.21
at Home	33	39.1	38	16	60	11	1	1	4	18	5.26		122	165.0	122	68	218	35	7	10	8	24	2.51
on Road	34	43.0	29	9	64	5	4	2	1	13	1.26		124	173.2	112	51	242	29	5	12	6	20	1.92
on Grass	20	27.2	22	7	39	3	2	2	1	5	1.95		75	108.0	76	29	147	14	3	6	5	8	2.33
on Turf	47	54.2	45	18	85	13	3	1	4	26	3.79		171	230.2	158	90	313	50	9	16	9	36	2.15
Day Games	14	20.0	14	4	28	2	1	1	0	8	1.35		68	98.0	62	39	126	20	3	9	2	10	2.20
Night Games	53	62.1	53	21	96	14	4	2	5	23	3.75		178	240.2	172	80	334	44	9	13	12	34	2.21
April	10	10.2	11	1	21	4	0	0	0	5	2.53		33	40.0	33	14	62	9	1	4	0	9	2.03
May	10	13.2	5	4	21	2	0	0	0	7	0.00		34	43.0	26	17	70	12	1	3	1	9	1.47
June	15	16.0	9	7	22	3	1	0	0	10	1.69		44	59.1	29	21	87	7	2	3	4	12	1.67
July	8	9.0	13	2	9	3	3	1	1	1	5.00		37	52.2	40	26	51	12	4	2	2	2	3.42
August	13	21.0	15	7	32	2	1	2	2	4	3.86		49	80.1	62	26	112	18	3	6	4	6	2.24
Sept–Oct	11	12.0	14	4	19	2	0	0	2	4	6.75		49	63.1	44	15	78	6	1	4	3	6	2.27

	BA	OBA	SA	AB	H	2B	3B	HR	RBI	BB	SO		BA	OBA	SA	AB	H	2B	3B	HR	RBI	BB	SO
Total	.223	.280	.322	301	67	9	3	5	34	25	124		.195	.267	.276	1201	234	44	6	14	117	119	460
vs. Left	.198	.257	.273	172	34	5	1	2	14	14	74		.195	.282	.273	605	118	26	3	5	52	74	241
vs. Right	.256	.310	.388	129	33	4	2	3	20	11	50		.195	.252	.280	596	116	18	3	9	65	45	219
Bases Empty	.213	.274	.316	155	33	4	3	2	2	13	67		.193	.262	.273	642	124	22	4	7	7	57	261
Leadoff	.233	.324	.300	60	14	2	1	0	0	8	25		.205	.266	.292	264	54	12	1	3	3	21	100
Runners On Base	.233	.286	.329	146	34	5	0	3	32	12	57		.197	.272	.281	559	110	22	2	7	110	62	199
Scoring Position	.221	.270	.337	104	23	3	0	3	32	8	39		.180	.258	.257	405	73	16	0	5	103	47	153
Late and Close	.247	.298	.349	215	53	8	1	3	30	17	84		.220	.285	.306	728	160	29	2	10	82	67	269

DOUG DRABEK — bats right — throws right — age 30 — PIT — P

6-YEAR TOTALS (1986–1991)

1991	G	IP	H	BB	SO	SB	CS	W	L	SV	ERA		G	IP	H	BB	SO	SB	CS	W	L	SV	ERA
Total	35	234.2	245	62	142	29	14	15	14	0	3.07		192	1237.2	1135	333	719	100	57	84	59	0	3.19
at Home	19	131.0	131	30	87	15	11	9	8	0	2.40		93	631.1	563	148	399	46	30	43	27	0	2.82
on Road	16	103.2	114	32	55	14	3	6	6	0	3.91		99	606.1	572	185	320	54	27	41	32	0	3.56
on Grass	8	48.1	59	16	27	7	2	2	4	0	5.77		67	373.0	375	121	194	29	16	22	25	0	4.32
on Turf	27	186.1	186	46	115	22	12	13	10	0	2.37		125	864.2	760	212	525	71	41	62	34	0	2.37
Day Games	13	83.0	87	22	54	11	4	5	5	0	3.69		58	358.0	321	95	207	25	14	25	16	0	3.12
Night Games	22	151.2	158	40	88	18	10	10	9	0	2.73		134	879.2	814	238	512	75	43	59	43	0	3.21
April	5	30.1	35	11	11	7	0	1	4	0	4.15		24	154.0	140	40	81	19	7	10	10	0	3.16
May	5	36.0	33	8	20	7	3	2	3	0	2.75		24	162.1	140	54	81	16	8	9	9	0	3.10
June	6	40.0	47	12	29	0	2	3	1	0	2.25		35	195.0	204	64	112	15	11	6	11	0	4.15
July	6	40.2	40	15	26	6	4	4	2	0	3.98		35	225.0	201	70	132	14	12	19	10	0	3.60
August	6	38.0	41	5	15	4	1	3	1	0	2.84		37	255.2	226	54	157	16	8	20	9	0	2.57
Sept–Oct	7	49.2	49	11	41	2	2	2	3	0	2.72		37	245.2	224	51	156	20	11	20	10	0	2.75

	BA	OBA	SA	AB	H	2B	3B	HR	RBI	BB	SO		BA	OBA	SA	AB	H	2B	3B	HR	RBI	BB	SO
Total	.274	.321	.385	894	245	41	5	16	79	62	142		.246	.297	.371	4623	1135	198	28	108	425	333	719
vs. Left	.290	.341	.396	520	151	29	1	8	49	41	59		.260	.316	.386	2511	654	121	15	55	239	209	317
vs. Right	.251	.293	.369	374	94	12	4	8	30	21	83		.228	.274	.352	2112	481	77	13	53	186	124	402
Bases Empty	.285	.332	.409	526	150	24	4	11	11	34	85		.241	.293	.366	2885	695	118	17	70	70	204	475
Leadoff	.305	.346	.407	226	69	12	1	3	3	14	36		.263	.309	.394	1202	316	55	6	30	30	79	179
Runners On Base	.258	.306	.351	368	95	17	1	5	68	28	57		.253	.304	.377	1738	440	80	11	38	355	129	244
Scoring Position	.244	.320	.325	209	51	8	2	3	61	26	35		.242	.304	.360	964	233	40	7	20	301	94	148
Late and Close	.319	.412	.444	72	23	3	0	2	8	10	10		.246	.320	.348	414	102	12	0	10	27	44	60

DENNIS ECKERSLEY — bats right — throws right — age 38 — OAK — P

1991	G	IP	H	BB	SO	SB	CS	W	L	SV	ERA		G	IP	H	BB	SO	SB	CS	W	L	SV	ERA
Total	67	76.0	60	9	87	8	1	5	4	43	2.96		386	990.2	878	155	766	88	28	54	46	185	3.16
at Home	35	39.1	23	7	49	6	1	5	1	18	1.83		191	471.0	395	79	416	44	16	37	21	89	3.08
on Road	32	36.2	37	2	38	2	0	0	3	25	4.17		195	519.2	483	76	350	44	12	17	25	96	3.24
on Grass	58	64.1	44	9	74	6	1	5	3	36	2.52		310	728.0	634	108	607	58	24	45	33	152	3.14
on Turf	9	11.2	16	0	13	2	0	0	1	7	5.40		76	262.2	244	47	159	30	4	9	13	33	3.22
Day Games	28	35.1	19	7	40	3	1	2	1	19	1.53		182	532.0	453	95	436	42	18	32	22	76	3.10
Night Games	39	40.2	41	2	47	5	0	3	3	24	4.20		204	458.2	425	60	330	46	10	22	24	109	3.24
April	8	9.0	6	0	6	0	1	0	1	7	4.00		57	163.0	134	21	121	6	6	8	7	32	3.15
May	11	12.2	15	0	16	1	0	1	0	6	2.13		64	184.2	188	24	136	15	7	12	10	27	4.09
June	10	13.0	6	1	13	1	0	0	0	9	0.69		55	157.1	133	33	103	15	2	5	8	27	3.32
July	11	13.0	14	3	17	2	0	1	1	5	4.85		62	156.2	120	24	139	11	5	8	7	28	2.59
August	14	13.1	9	3	16	3	0	2	0	9	1.35		67	153.0	145	26	118	16	3	9	4	37	2.41
Sept–Oct	13	15.0	11	2	19	1	0	2	2	7	4.80		81	176.0	158	27	149	21	5	12	10	34	3.22

	BA	OBA	SA	AB	H	2B	3B	HR	RBI	BB	SO		BA	OBA	SA	AB	H	2B	3B	HR	RBI	BB	SO
Total	.208	.235	.365	288	60	8	2	11	33	9	87		.236	.267	.367	3725	878	179	18	91	384	155	766
vs. Left	.228	.263	.356	149	34	4	0	5	18	6	34		.256	.292	.394	1889	483	104	11	45	210	97	274
vs. Right	.187	.204	.374	139	26	4	2	6	15	3	53		.215	.241	.339	1836	395	75	7	46	174	58	492
Bases Empty	.234	.251	.386	171	40	7	2	5	5	3	47		.241	.265	.364	2305	556	115	11	49	49	66	494
Leadoff	.266	.277	.469	64	17	2	1	3	3	1	16		.251	.269	.380	926	232	49	4	21	21	19	178
Runners On Base	.171	.211	.333	117	20	1	0	6	28	6	40		.227	.270	.370	1420	322	64	7	42	335	89	272
Scoring Position	.152	.202	.278	79	12	1	0	3	22	5	29		.224	.277	.355	842	189	42	4	20	284	69	171
Late and Close	.205	.232	.341	220	45	7	1	7	29	7	67		.197	.225	.313	1105	218	36	4	28	123	39	291

MARK EICHHORN — bats right — throws right — age 32 — CAL — P

1991	G	IP	H	BB	SO	SB	CS	W	L	SV	ERA		G	IP	H	BB	SO	SB	CS	W	L	SV	ERA
Total	70	81.2	63	13	49	3	3	3	3	1	1.98		370	586.0	525	179	457	69	21	34	28	29	2.89
at Home	37	41.2	29	5	23	3	2	2	2	1	1.30		183	300.1	267	82	232	34	13	18	16	10	2.79
on Road	33	40.0	34	8	26	0	1	1	1	0	2.70		187	285.2	258	97	225	35	8	16	12	19	2.99
on Grass	58	67.2	50	9	37	3	2	2	3	1	2.26		218	315.1	298	90	237	36	14	16	19	15	3.14
on Turf	12	14.0	13	4	12	0	1	1	0	0	0.64		152	270.2	227	89	220	33	7	18	9	14	2.59
Day Games	19	24.2	16	3	15	1	2	1	1	1	1.82		117	191.2	184	59	156	32	6	7	10	10	3.01
Night Games	51	57.0	47	10	34	2	1	2	2	0	2.05		253	394.1	341	120	301	37	15	27	18	19	2.83
April	7	10.1	8	0	4	1	0	0	0	0	0.87		50	98.2	72	29	76	11	2	5	6	5	2.37
May	11	17.1	10	0	9	1	0	0	0	0	0.00		57	98.2	81	32	72	10	4	6	6	10	2.28
June	15	15.0	16	1	11	0	0	0	1	0	1.80		68	91.1	92	21	76	10	4	5	4	3	2.56
July	9	12.1	8	2	6	0	0	0	1	0	2.19		63	100.1	118	37	80	15	2	5	4	4	4.40
August	13	11.2	7	4	11	1	0	0	1	0	2.31		68	107.2	80	30	83	8	5	8	5	5	2.76
Sept–Oct	15	15.0	14	6	8	0	0	1	1	0	4.80		64	89.1	82	30	70	15	4	4	4	2	2.92

	BA	OBA	SA	AB	H	2B	3B	HR	RBI	BB	SO		BA	OBA	SA	AB	H	2B	3B	HR	RBI	BB	SO
Total	.219	.255	.309	288	63	16	2	2	27	13	49		.243	.307	.346	2161	525	98	10	35	269	179	457
vs. Left	.258	.277	.371	124	32	8	0	2	13	4	15		.277	.345	.399	968	268	52	6	18	130	92	159
vs. Right	.189	.239	.262	164	31	8	2	0	14	9	34		.215	.275	.303	1193	257	46	4	17	139	87	298
Bases Empty	.226	.253	.317	164	37	7	1	2	2	6	23		.239	.282	.342	1139	272	52	6	18	18	58	237
Leadoff	.169	.182	.262	65	11	3	0	1	1	1	9		.244	.283	.341	472	115	25	3	5	5	21	87
Runners On Base	.210	.257	.298	124	26	9	1	0	25	7	26		.248	.332	.350	1022	253	46	4	17	251	121	220
Scoring Position	.211	.232	.303	76	16	7	0	0	22	2	19		.229	.324	.321	717	164	31	1	11	232	96	157
Late and Close	.207	.261	.290	145	30	10	1	0	13	10	23		.229	.297	.318	864	198	38	3	11	95	80	194

SCOTT ERICKSON — bats right — throws right — age 24 — MIN — P

1991	G	IP	H	BB	SO	SB	CS	W	L	SV	ERA		G	IP	H	BB	SO	SB	CS	W	L	SV	ERA
Total	32	204.0	189	71	108	4	10	20	8	0	3.18		51	317.0	297	122	161	10	13	28	12	0	3.07
at Home	15	97.0	97	29	51	1	4	10	3	0	3.53		28	175.1	180	53	95	7	5	17	5	0	3.49
on Road	17	107.0	92	42	57	3	6	10	5	0	2.86		23	141.2	117	69	66	3	8	11	7	0	2.54
on Grass	13	82.1	68	31	41	2	5	9	2	0	2.51		17	108.1	81	52	49	2	6	10	3	0	1.99
on Turf	19	121.2	121	40	67	2	5	11	6	0	3.62		34	208.2	216	70	112	8	7	18	9	0	3.62
Day Games	13	84.1	85	20	44	1	6	7	4	0	3.52		20	132.2	123	41	62	6	6	11	4	0	2.85
Night Games	19	119.2	104	51	64	3	4	13	4	0	2.93		31	184.1	174	81	99	4	7	17	8	0	3.22
April	4	31.0	29	12	15	1	4	2	2	0	2.03		4	31.0	29	12	15	1	4	2	2	0	2.03
May	6	46.1	35	13	29	1	2	5	0	0	1.36		6	46.1	35	13	29	1	2	5	0	0	1.36
June	6	45.1	37	11	30	0	2	5	0	0	2.18		8	57.2	46	19	39	0	0	6	2	0	2.34
July	4	19.2	24	11	5	2	1	2	0	0	5.49		10	48.0	60	24	18	4	1	3	1	0	4.50
August	5	20.0	30	7	9	0	0	2	3	0	9.45		10	45.2	66	16	19	1	2	3	5	0	6.70
Sept–Oct	7	41.2	34	17	20	0	3	4	2	0	3.02		13	88.1	61	38	41	2	4	9	2	0	2.14

	BA	OBA	SA	AB	H	2B	3B	HR	RBI	BB	SO		BA	OBA	SA	AB	H	2B	3B	HR	RBI	BB	SO
Total	.248	.314	.364	762	189	39	5	13	72	71	108		.251	.324	.365	1184	297	55	7	22	116	122	161
vs. Left	.293	.361	.425	409	120	26	2	8	36	44	39		.277	.350	.399	632	175	35	3	12	63	71	55
vs. Right	.195	.260	.292	353	69	13	3	5	36	27	69		.221	.294	.326	552	122	20	4	10	53	51	106
Bases Empty	.261	.335	.371	437	114	26	2	6	6	46	70		.253	.332	.363	677	171	35	2	12	12	75	102
Leadoff	.256	.313	.390	195	50	11	0	5	5	15	35		.241	.324	.378	294	71	16	0	8	8	33	49
Runners On Base	.231	.286	.354	325	75	13	3	7	66	25	38		.234	.316	.328	507	126	20	5	10	104	47	59
Scoring Position	.236	.316	.348	161	38	8	1	2	52	21	24		.235	.295	.383	265	62	10	3	3	85	35	41
Late and Close	.254	.277	.397	63	16	4	1	1	7	2	6		.235	.295	.383	81	19	4	1	2	9	7	8

STEVE FARR — bats right — throws right — age 36 — NYA — P

1991	G	IP	H	BB	SO	SB	CS	W	L	SV	ERA	8-YEAR TOTALS (1984–1991) G	IP	H	BB	SO	SB	CS	W	L	SV	ERA
Total	60	70.0	57	20	60	2	2	5	5	23	2.19	380	697.0	632	269	572	45	38	42	40	73	3.22
at Home	31	38.2	30	9	37	2	0	3	3	12	2.56	200	377.2	324	140	316	22	14	30	14	44	2.88
on Road	29	31.1	27	11	23	0	2	2	2	11	1.72	180	319.1	308	129	256	23	24	12	26	29	3.61
on Grass	54	62.2	52	16	54	2	2	5	4	21	2.15	182	341.1	324	135	273	23	18	13	29	36	3.85
on Turf	6	7.1	5	4	6	0	0	0	1	2	2.45	198	355.2	308	134	299	22	20	29	11	37	2.61
Day Games	14	18.2	16	9	21	1	0	2	1	6	0.96	97	194.1	186	76	169	14	12	9	14	14	3.66
Night Games	46	51.1	41	11	39	1	2	3	4	17	2.63	283	502.2	446	193	403	31	26	33	26	59	3.04
April	7	9.2	8	7	9	0	0	0	1	1	3.72	41	67.0	64	29	59	9	3	2	3	7	4.30
May	11	13.2	13	4	13	1	1	2	0	1	1.98	72	131.0	104	43	120	7	9		7	13	2.20
June	12	14.1	6	1	11	0	1	0	0	8	0.00	64	115.0	94	40	94	8	11		5	16	2.74
July	9	8.2	4	1	8	0	0	0	0	6	0.00	70	122.2	116	50	98	8	4		9	14	3.23
August	9	12.0	14	4	10	1	0	1	3	1	6.75	67	125.0	135	45	89	7	5	6	9	10	4.75
Sept–Oct	12	11.2	12	3	9	0	0	2	1	6	0.77	66	136.1	119	62	112	6	6	11	7	13	2.64

	BA	OBA	SA	AB	H	2B	3B	HR	RBI	BB	SO	BA	OBA	SA	AB	H	2B	3B	HR	RBI	BB	SO
Total	.219	.288	.312	260	57	12	0	4	25	20	60	.243	.319	.362	2596	632	113	15	55	310	269	572
vs. Left	.248	.341	.354	113	28	6	0	2	10	11	23	.247	.333	.360	1239	306	54	10	22	135	154	237
vs. Right	.197	.244	.279	147	29	6	0	2	15	9	37	.240	.305	.364	1357	326	59	5	33	175	115	335
Bases Empty	.219	.255	.288	146	32	7	0	1	1	6	33	.252	.321	.382	1393	351	72	8	31	31	128	297
Leadoff	.254	.279	.339	59	15	5	0	0	0	1	15	.259	.324	.410	595	154	37	4	15	15	53	112
Runners On Base	.219	.326	.342	114	25	5	0	3	24	14	27	.234	.316	.339	1203	281	41	7	24	279	141	275
Scoring Position	.190	.329	.317	63	12	2	0	2	20	10	16	.224	.326	.320	704	158	20	4	13	243	105	181
Late and Close	.216	.302	.310	171	37	7	0	3	19	17	40	.252	.329	.360	822	207	28	2	19	107	88	188

JEFF FASSERO — bats left — throws left — age 29 — MON — P

1991	G	IP	H	BB	SO	SB	CS	W	L	SV	ERA	1-YEAR TOTALS (1991) G	IP	H	BB	SO	SB	CS	W	L	SV	ERA
Total	51	55.0	40	17	40	3	1	2	5	8	2.45	51	55.0	40	17	40	3	1	2	5	8	2.45
at Home	24	28.2	16	13	22	2	1	2	2	3	2.20	24	28.2	16	13	22	2	1	2	2	3	2.20
on Road	27	26.1	24	4	18	1	0	0	3	5	2.73	27	26.1	24	4	18	1	0	0	3	5	2.73
on Grass	13	13.0	12	1	6	1	0	0	1	4	1.38	13	13.0	12	1	6	1	0	0	1	4	1.38
on Turf	38	42.0	28	16	34	2	1	2	4	4	2.79	38	42.0	28	16	34	2	1	2	4	4	2.79
Day Games	18	20.2	16	8	20	3	1	0	4	2	2.61	18	20.2	16	8	20	3	1	0	4	2	2.61
Night Games	33	34.1	24	9	20	0	0	2	1	6	2.36	33	34.1	24	9	20	0	0	2	1	6	2.36
April	0	0.0	0	0	0	0	0	0	0	0	0.00	0	0.0	0	0	0	0	0	0	0	0	0.00
May	1	2.0	2	1	1	1	1	0	1	0	4.50	1	2.0	2	1	1	1	1	0	1	0	4.50
June	12	15.0	7	3	14	0	0	1	0	2	1.20	12	15.0	7	3	14	0	0	1	0	2	1.20
July	11	14.2	6	4	9	0	0	0	2	2	1.23	11	14.2	6	4	9	0	0	0	2	2	1.23
August	15	13.0	12	5	9	1	0	1	3	2	2.77	15	13.0	12	5	9	1	0	1	3	2	2.77
Sept–Oct	12	10.1	13	4	7	1	0	0	1	2	5.23	12	10.1	13	4	7	1	0	0	1	2	5.23

	BA	OBA	SA	AB	H	2B	3B	HR	RBI	BB	SO	BA	OBA	SA	AB	H	2B	3B	HR	RBI	BB	SO
Total	.200	.266	.270	200	40	7	2	1	20	17	40	.200	.266	.270	200	40	7	2	1	20	17	40
vs. Left	.257	.307	.343	70	18	2	2	0	11	5	18	.257	.307	.343	70	18	2	2	0	11	5	18
vs. Right	.169	.245	.231	130	22	5	0	1	9	12	22	.169	.245	.231	130	22	5	0	1	9	12	22
Bases Empty	.198	.267	.250	96	19	5	0	0	0	9	18	.198	.267	.250	96	19	5	0	0	0	9	18
Leadoff	.273	.333	.341	44	12	3	0	0	0	4	6	.273	.333	.341	44	12	3	0	0	0	4	6
Runners On Base	.202	.265	.288	104	21	2	2	1	20	8	22	.202	.265	.288	104	21	2	2	1	20	8	22
Scoring Position	.211	.277	.303	76	16	2	1	1	19	7	16	.211	.277	.303	76	16	2	1	1	19	7	16
Late and Close	.225	.301	.250	120	27	1	1	0	14	12	25	.225	.301	.250	120	27	1	1	0	14	12	25

ALEX FERNANDEZ — bats right — throws right — age 23 — CHA — P

1991	G	IP	H	BB	SO	SB	CS	W	L	SV	ERA	2-YEAR TOTALS (1990–1991) G	IP	H	BB	SO	SB	CS	W	L	SV	ERA
Total	34	191.2	186	88	145	15	11	9	13	0	4.51	47	279.1	275	122	206	16	15	14	18	0	4.29
at Home	17	96.1	80	36	70	5	4	5	7	0	4.48	21	123.1	109	47	87	5	6	7	8	0	4.31
on Road	17	95.1	106	52	75	10	7	4	6	0	4.53	26	156.0	166	75	119	11	9	7	10	0	4.27
on Grass	31	171.1	167	72	132	12	10	8	13	0	4.78	40	234.0	228	97	175	13	14	11	17	0	4.50
on Turf	3	20.1	19	16	13	3	1	1	0	0	2.21	7	45.1	47	25	31	3	1	3	1	0	3.18
Day Games	8	39.1	49	17	31	3	3	2	4	0	7.32	11	63.1	67	24	50	3	3	3	6	0	5.12
Night Games	26	152.1	137	71	114	12	8	7	9	0	3.78	36	216.0	208	98	156	13	12	11	12	0	4.04
April	5	20.0	27	16	20	3	1	2	2	0	8.55	5	20.0	27	16	20	3	1	2	2	0	8.55
May	5	30.0	27	19	23	3	3	0	2	0	4.80	5	30.0	27	19	23	3	3	0	2	0	4.80
June	6	36.1	34	13	29	1	3	2	3	0	4.71	6	36.1	34	13	29	1	3	2	3	0	4.71
July	6	28.2	29	7	14	1	0	1	0	0	4.08	6	28.2	29	7	14	1	0	1	0	0	4.08
August	6	36.2	39	10	29	2	1	1	5	0	4.66	12	74.1	79	25	54	2	3	1	6	0	4.72
Sept–Oct	6	40.0	30	23	30	5	3	3	1	0	2.25	13	90.0	79	42	66	6	5	6	5	0	2.70

	BA	OBA	SA	AB	H	2B	3B	HR	RBI	BB	SO	BA	OBA	SA	AB	H	2B	3B	HR	RBI	BB	SO
Total	.259	.337	.388	719	186	33	6	16	86	88	145	.261	.337	.379	1055	275	43	8	22	119	122	206
vs. Left	.248	.329	.350	323	80	19	1	4	30	42	64	.258	.335	.359	496	128	25	2	7	42	59	93
vs. Right	.268	.343	.419	396	106	14	5	12	56	46	81	.263	.339	.397	559	147	18	6	15	77	63	113
Bases Empty	.240	.318	.363	421	101	18	5	8	8	46	81	.239	.320	.355	602	144	22	6	12	12	68	114
Leadoff	.275	.365	.401	182	50	7	2	4	4	24	31	.263	.352	.363	262	69	10	2	4	4	34	45
Runners On Base	.285	.362	.423	298	85	15	1	8	78	42	64	.289	.358	.411	453	131	21	2	10	107	54	92
Scoring Position	.268	.357	.382	157	42	6	0	4	67	28	35	.278	.364	.396	227	63	11	2	7	93	36	47
Late and Close	.226	.317	.302	53	12	1	0	1	4	7	11	.188	.270	.237	80	15	1	1	1	5	9	16

CHUCK FINLEY — bats left — throws left — age 30 — CAL — P

1991

	G	IP	H	BB	SO	SB	CS	W	L	SV	ERA
Total	34	227.1	205	101	171	15	15	18	9	0	3.80
at Home	17	124.2	99	50	103	7	11	9	3	0	3.03
on Road	17	102.2	106	51	68	8	4	9	6	0	4.73
on Grass	28	184.2	174	81	148	13	13	13	9	0	4.05
on Turf	6	42.2	31	20	23	2	2	5	0	0	2.74
Day Games	7	43.1	41	21	35	2	1	4	3	0	4.36
Night Games	27	184.0	164	80	136	13	14	14	6	0	3.67
April	4	29.1	16	12	24	2	0	4	0	0	2.45
May	6	41.2	46	20	41	4	5	4	2	0	4.54
June	6	35.1	31	21	31	0	4	3	1	0	3.82
July	6	41.0	40	16	26	2	2	3	2	0	4.39
August	5	34.2	31	11	19	3	1	2	2	0	3.38
Sept–Oct	7	45.1	41	21	30	4	3	2	2	0	3.77

6-YEAR TOTALS (1986–1991)

	G	IP	H	BB	SO	SB	CS	W	L	SV	ERA
Total	186	997.2	928	412	716	70	63	66	50	0	3.34
at Home	95	532.2	473	202	406	32	40	36	26	0	3.01
on Road	91	465.0	455	210	310	38	23	30	24	0	3.72
on Grass	160	851.2	800	354	644	61	56	52	46	0	3.40
on Turf	26	146.0	128	58	72	9	7	14	4	0	2.96
Day Games	45	244.2	218	114	182	17	12	16	16	0	3.27
Night Games	141	753.0	710	298	534	53	51	50	34	0	3.36
April	24	139.0	108	53	90	13	8	12	8	0	2.46
May	28	152.0	153	66	114	11	8	13	6	0	3.79
June	33	179.0	170	69	146	12	13	11	10	0	3.47
July	34	175.1	162	62	138	15	11	12	5	0	3.39
August	32	161.2	149	64	98	12	8	9	10	0	3.34
Sept–Oct	35	190.2	186	98	130	7	15	9	9	0	3.45

1991 Batting Against

	BA	OBA	SA	AB	H	2B	3B	HR	RBI	BB	SO
Total	.244	.330	.385	839	205	43	3	23	88	101	171
vs. Left	.257	.336	.422	109	28	6	0	4	8	13	22
vs. Right	.242	.329	.379	730	177	37	3	19	80	88	149
Bases Empty	.241	.320	.395	506	122	27	3	15	15	56	98
Leadoff	.227	.304	.333	216	49	6	1	5	5	21	35
Runners On Base	.249	.345	.369	333	83	16	0	8	73	45	73
Scoring Position	.261	.350	.408	184	48	12	0	5	66	26	42
Late and Close	.211	.292	.316	95	20	1	0	3	8	11	24

6-Year Batting Against

	BA	OBA	SA	AB	H	2B	3B	HR	RBI	BB	SO
Total	.250	.327	.369	3705	928	167	16	80	366	412	716
vs. Left	.254	.328	.325	676	172	30	0	6	58	71	110
vs. Right	.250	.327	.379	3029	756	137	16	74	308	341	606
Bases Empty	.250	.327	.373	2176	544	87	8	55	55	236	404
Leadoff	.244	.309	.342	954	233	34	4	17	17	81	155
Runners On Base	.251	.328	.363	1529	384	80	8	25	311	176	312
Scoring Position	.254	.344	.361	803	204	46	5	10	267	119	167
Late and Close	.260	.334	.376	481	125	24	1	10	42	53	93

MIKE FLANAGAN — bats left — throws left — age 41 — BAL — P

1991

	G	IP	H	BB	SO	SB	CS	W	L	SV	ERA
Total	64	98.1	84	25	55	6	3	2	7	3	2.38
at Home	33	45.1	46	10	32	4	2	0	5	0	3.18
on Road	31	53.0	38	15	23	2	1	2	2	3	1.70
on Grass	56	79.0	72	18	47	6	3	1	7	2	2.73
on Turf	8	19.1	12	7	8	0	0	1	0	1	0.93
Day Games	17	25.2	13	5	14	1	2	0	1	0	0.70
Night Games	47	72.2	71	20	41	5	1	2	6	3	2.97
April	9	17.0	11	5	10	2	1	0	0	0	1.59
May	11	14.0	19	4	10	2	0	1	3	1	5.79
June	9	22.0	18	6	5	1	0	0	0	0	1.23
July	14	21.0	11	2	12	0	1	0	0	0	0.86
August	12	13.1	15	3	8	1	0	1	0	2	3.38
Sept–Oct	9	11.0	10	5	10	1	0	1	0	2	3.27

8-YEAR TOTALS (1984–1991)

	G	IP	H	BB	SO	SB	CS	W	L	SV	ERA
Total	233	1126.2	1155	382	548	73	35	55	69	3	3.87
at Home	116	548.1	567	179	276	36	18	33	27	0	3.53
on Road	117	578.1	588	203	272	37	17	22	42	3	4.19
on Grass	159	708.2	715	248	370	44	22	31	43	2	4.04
on Turf	74	418.0	440	134	178	29	13	24	26	1	3.57
Day Games	68	326.1	333	131	172	35	8	15	25	0	3.83
Night Games	165	800.1	822	251	376	38	27	40	44	3	3.88
April	36	172.2	169	72	78	12	10	8	9	0	3.70
May	40	155.0	197	58	74	18	1	6	16	1	5.75
June	27	146.0	120	52	67	6	5	9	5	0	2.59
July	44	221.1	196	59	98	5	8	13	10	0	3.21
August	44	211.2	248	60	100	21	7	10	15	1	4.12
Sept–Oct	42	220.0	225	81	131	11	4	9	14	1	3.93

1991 Batting Against

	BA	OBA	SA	AB	H	2B	3B	HR	RBI	BB	SO
Total	.236	.289	.323	356	84	13	0	6	30	25	55
vs. Left	.181	.221	.236	127	23	1	0	2	10	6	27
vs. Right	.266	.327	.371	229	61	12	0	4	20	19	28
Bases Empty	.271	.310	.365	192	52	9	0	3	3	10	27
Leadoff	.317	.349	.415	82	26	2	0	2	2	4	7
Runners On Base	.195	.266	.274	164	32	4	0	3	27	15	28
Scoring Position	.188	.294	.282	85	16	2	0	2	25	13	15
Late and Close	.254	.325	.343	134	34	6	0	2	17	12	19

8-Year Batting Against

	BA	OBA	SA	AB	H	2B	3B	HR	RBI	BB	SO
Total	.268	.328	.405	4315	1155	228	21	107	465	382	548
vs. Left	.230	.284	.311	788	181	30	2	10	81	57	132
vs. Right	.276	.337	.426	3527	974	198	19	97	384	325	416
Bases Empty	.268	.339	.408	2463	661	134	11	63	63	255	310
Leadoff	.276	.328	.448	1097	303	61	7	38	38	84	122
Runners On Base	.267	.312	.400	1852	494	94	10	44	402	127	238
Scoring Position	.255	.317	.374	932	238	48	6	17	325	91	137
Late and Close	.245	.321	.342	421	103	16	2	7	39	46	57

JOHN FRANCO — bats left — throws left — age 32 — NYN — P

1991

	G	IP	H	BB	SO	SB	CS	W	L	SV	ERA
Total	52	55.1	61	18	45	4	2	5	9	30	2.93
at Home	28	27.0	32	10	20	1	2	1	4	18	3.00
on Road	24	28.1	29	8	25	3	0	4	5	12	2.86
on Grass	36	37.2	39	12	25	2	2	2	5	21	2.15
on Turf	16	17.2	22	6	20	2	0	3	4	9	4.58
Day Games	14	17.1	16	6	14	1	1	1	2	8	2.60
Night Games	38	38.0	45	12	31	3	1	4	7	22	3.08
April	7	6.0	4	5	5	0	0	1	0	5	1.50
May	9	12.0	12	3	7	1	0	0	1	5	0.00
June	8	6.0	13	3	7	1	0	0	3	5	12.00
July	9	8.0	9	2	7	0	1	0	1	5	0.00
August	10	13.1	11	0	12	1	0	1	2	3	2.03
Sept–Oct	9	10.0	12	5	7	2	0	1	2	6	5.40

8-YEAR TOTALS (1984–1991)

	G	IP	H	BB	SO	SB	CS	W	L	SV	ERA
Total	500	651.0	588	249	468	32	31	52	42	211	2.53
at Home	264	348.2	317	120	237	17	17	30	18	112	2.56
on Road	236	302.1	271	129	231	15	14	22	24	99	2.50
on Grass	188	227.2	215	91	181	14	7	17	17	87	2.53
on Turf	312	423.1	373	158	287	18	24	35	25	124	2.53
Day Games	161	206.1	181	84	161	9	11	17	11	68	2.75
Night Games	339	444.2	407	165	307	23	20	35	31	143	2.43
April	56	71.2	41	27	44	1	2	1	3	28	1.51
May	77	109.1	101	52	83	6	6	9	7	31	2.30
June	92	114.2	110	41	76	5	5	11	9	32	2.43
July	86	116.1	90	38	84	3	9	11	4	40	2.24
August	94	127.2	123	42	89	9	3	11	5	38	2.04
Sept–Oct	95	111.1	123	49	92	8	6	9	14	42	4.37

1991 Batting Against

	BA	OBA	SA	AB	H	2B	3B	HR	RBI	BB	SO
Total	.271	.328	.360	225	61	8	3	2	30	18	45
vs. Left	.340	.397	.415	53	18	2	1	0	6	4	7
vs. Right	.250	.306	.343	172	43	6	2	2	24	14	38
Bases Empty	.298	.327	.372	94	28	2	1	1	1	4	25
Leadoff	.244	.261	.311	45	11	0	0	1	1	1	12
Runners On Base	.252	.329	.351	131	33	6	2	1	29	14	20
Scoring Position	.244	.337	.360	86	21	5	1	2	29	14	42
Late and Close	.272	.326	.371	202	55	8	3	2	27	15	42

8-Year Batting Against

	BA	OBA	SA	AB	H	2B	3B	HR	RBI	BB	SO
Total	.244	.314	.322	2413	588	73	9	33	261	249	468
vs. Left	.219	.275	.275	494	108	13	3	3	58	37	94
vs. Right	.250	.324	.335	1919	480	60	6	30	203	212	374
Bases Empty	.242	.303	.320	1258	304	35	5	18	18	108	235
Leadoff	.246	.293	.343	548	135	16	2	11	11	35	82
Runners On Base	.246	.326	.325	1155	284	38	4	15	243	141	233
Scoring Position	.234	.341	.313	683	160	27	3	7	219	114	144
Late and Close	.237	.307	.314	1794	426	49	7	25	200	180	350

MIKE GARDINER — bats both throws right — age 27 — BOS — P

1991	G	IP	H	BB	SO	SB	CS	W	L	SV	ERA
Total	22	130.0	140	47	91	11	6	9	10	0	4.85
at Home	12	75.1	81	27	50	4	1	4	5	0	4.30
on Road	10	54.2	59	20	41	7	5	5	5	0	5.60
on Grass	19	112.1	120	41	79	6	4	7	9	0	4.73
on Turf	3	17.2	20	6	12	5	2	2	1	0	5.60
Day Games	7	46.2	39	12	32	4	2	4	2	0	3.86
Night Games	15	83.1	101	35	59	7	4	5	8	0	5.40
April	0	0.0	0	0	0	0	0	0	0	0	0.00
May	1	7.0	6	2	5	0	0	1	0	0	2.57
June	5	29.1	34	11	24	1	0	2	2	0	5.52
July	3	17.1	22	10	9	6	2	0	3	0	4.15
August	6	36.1	38	11	28	4	3	3	1	0	5.45
Sept–Oct	7	40.0	40	13	25	0	1	3	4	0	4.50

	BA	OBA	SA	AB	H	2B	3B	HR	RBI	BB	SO
Total	.274	.333	.438	511	140	26	2	18	64	47	91
vs. Left	.259	.316	.366	243	63	12	1	4	23	21	39
vs. Right	.287	.349	.504	268	77	14	1	14	41	26	52
Bases Empty	.258	.321	.418	299	77	16	1	10	10	28	61
Leadoff	.304	.392	.512	125	38	6	1	6	6	18	19
Runners On Base	.297	.350	.467	212	63	10	1	8	54	19	30
Scoring Position	.283	.333	.469	113	32	7	1	4	46	10	15
Late and Close	.400	.438	.667	15	6	1	0	1	3	1	2

2-YEAR TOTALS (1990–1991)

	G	IP	H	BB	SO	SB	CS	W	L	SV	ERA
	27	142.2	162	52	97	11	7	9	12	0	5.36
	15	83.2	99	31	54	4	1	4	7	0	5.49
	12	59.0	63	21	43	7	6	5	5	0	5.19
	20	112.2	121	41	80	6	4	7	9	0	4.71
	7	30.0	41	11	17	5	3	2	3	0	7.80
	9	52.1	45	15	36	4	2	4	3	0	4.47
	18	90.1	117	37	61	7	5	5	9	0	5.88
	0	0.0	0	0	0	0	0	0	0	0	0.00
	1	7.0	6	2	5	0	0	1	0	0	2.57
	5	29.1	34	11	24	1	0	2	2	0	5.52
	3	17.1	22	10	9	6	2	0	3	0	4.15
	6	36.1	38	11	28	4	3	3	1	0	5.45
	12	52.2	62	18	31	0	2	3	6	0	5.98

	BA	OBA	SA	AB	H	2B	3B	HR	RBI	BB	SO
	.285	.344	.450	569	162	29	4	19	77	52	97
	.271	.325	.394	269	73	14	2	5	29	23	43
	.297	.361	.500	300	89	15	2	14	48	29	54
	.265	.327	.415	328	87	17	1	10	10	30	64
	.299	.389	.489	137	41	6	1	6	6	20	19
	.311	.368	.498	241	75	12	3	9	67	22	33
	.297	.356	.484	128	38	8	3	4	56	13	18
	.400	.438	.667	15	6	1	0	1	3	1	2

MARK GARDNER — bats right — throws right — age 30 — MON — P

1991	G	IP	H	BB	SO	SB	CS	W	L	SV	ERA
Total	27	168.1	139	75	107	13	17	9	11	0	3.90
at Home	10	64.2	52	30	46	6	6	4	4	0	2.64
on Road	17	103.2	87	45	61	7	11	5	7	0	4.69
on Grass	10	56.1	61	23	36	3	6	1	6	0	6.39
on Turf	17	112.0	78	52	71	10	11	8	5	0	2.65
Day Games	11	63.1	62	30	49	6	5	2	7	0	4.83
Night Games	16	105.0	77	45	58	7	12	7	4	0	3.34
April	0	0.0	0	0	0	0	0	0	0	0	0.00
May	4	22.1	23	8	18	2	1	0	2	0	4.43
June	5	30.2	32	12	14	2	4	3	2	0	4.11
July	6	43.1	24	21	29	2	3	2	3	0	1.87
August	6	39.1	34	13	22	2	6	3	2	0	2.75
Sept–Oct	6	32.2	26	21	24	5	3	1	2	0	7.44

	BA	OBA	SA	AB	H	2B	3B	HR	RBI	BB	SO
Total	.230	.318	.356	604	139	21	2	17	68	75	107
vs. Left	.225	.315	.346	382	86	12	2	10	41	49	62
vs. Right	.239	.324	.374	222	53	9	0	7	27	26	45
Bases Empty	.208	.297	.289	370	77	10	1	6	6	45	63
Leadoff	.277	.371	.368	155	43	6	1	2	2	21	27
Runners On Base	.265	.351	.462	234	62	11	1	11	62	30	44
Scoring Position	.280	.374	.496	125	35	4	1	7	49	19	28
Late and Close	.216	.322	.314	51	11	2	0	1	2	8	9

3-YEAR TOTALS (1989–1991)

	G	IP	H	BB	SO	SB	CS	W	L	SV	ERA
	61	347.1	294	147	263	35	24	16	23	0	3.78
	27	154.2	119	61	131	15	10	9	8	0	2.27
	34	192.2	175	86	132	20	14	7	15	0	5.00
	21	115.0	123	50	88	15	8	3	10	0	5.79
	40	232.1	171	97	175	20	16	13	13	0	2.79
	21	111.1	117	52	90	17	7	3	12	0	5.25
	40	236.0	177	95	173	18	17	13	11	0	3.09
	3	11.1	12	5	8	1	1	0	2	0	3.18
	13	68.0	61	23	58	8	3	2	3	0	3.04
	11	66.0	61	28	37	7	5	5	4	0	3.82
	11	83.1	43	32	69	4	5	4	4	0	1.62
	11	61.2	63	25	47	5	6	4	4	0	4.23
	12	57.0	54	34	44	10	4	1	6	0	7.42

	BA	OBA	SA	AB	H	2B	3B	HR	RBI	BB	SO
	.232	.317	.355	1269	294	45	8	32	138	147	263
	.226	.319	.350	766	173	24	7	19	78	105	147
	.241	.313	.364	503	121	21	1	13	60	42	116
	.196	.276	.294	795	156	24	3	16	16	82	175
	.224	.290	.320	331	74	12	1	6	6	29	68
	.291	.382	.458	474	138	21	5	16	122	65	88
	.273	.376	.433	282	77	12	3	9	100	45	59
	.268	.349	.381	97	26	3	1	2	8	12	21

PAUL GIBSON — bats left — throws right — age 32 — DET — P

1991	G	IP	H	BB	SO	SB	CS	W	L	SV	ERA
Total	68	96.0	112	48	52	5	5	5	7	8	4.59
at Home	33	53.0	59	25	34	2	2	4	3	4	4.08
on Road	35	43.0	53	23	18	3	3	1	4	4	5.23
on Grass	55	72.2	91	37	42	3	4	4	6	5	4.83
on Turf	13	23.1	21	11	10	2	1	1	1	3	3.86
Day Games	23	28.1	36	18	16	2	2	2	2	1	4.45
Night Games	45	67.2	76	30	36	3	3	3	5	7	4.66
April	10	14.1	9	6	11	0	2	2	1	0	0.00
May	14	26.0	18	8	17	1	0	1	0	2	3.46
June	11	10.0	21	6	5	2	0	1	2	1	9.90
July	12	15.1	24	10	4	2	1	1	1	0	7.04
August	12	18.2	28	13	8	0	2	1	2	1	6.75
Sept–Oct	9	11.2	12	5	7	0	0	0	1	4	1.54

	BA	OBA	SA	AB	H	2B	3B	HR	RBI	BB	SO
Total	.297	.379	.424	377	112	10	4	10	59	48	52
vs. Left	.351	.411	.559	111	39	1	2	6	30	11	11
vs. Right	.274	.366	.368	266	73	9	2	4	29	37	41
Bases Empty	.280	.358	.390	182	51	6	1	4	4	20	30
Leadoff	.278	.360	.418	79	22	3	1	2	2	9	14
Runners On Base	.313	.398	.456	195	61	4	3	6	55	28	22
Scoring Position	.299	.396	.376	117	35	2	2	1	43	20	15
Late and Close	.276	.333	.431	174	48	4	1	7	26	16	24

4-YEAR TOTALS (1988–1991)

	G	IP	H	BB	SO	SB	CS	W	L	SV	ERA
	214	417.1	423	182	235	35	18	18	21	11	3.88
	105	227.0	206	98	146	19	8	12	8	6	3.17
	109	190.1	217	84	89	16	10	6	13	5	4.73
	171	349.1	353	142	198	30	16	17	17	7	3.66
	43	68.0	70	40	37	5	2	1	4	4	5.03
	61	112.0	121	48	64	8	7	6	4	3	3.86
	153	305.1	302	134	171	27	11	12	17	8	3.89
	27	46.1	48	25	27	0	5	4	2	1	3.11
	40	97.0	90	42	60	10	1	3	5	5	3.62
	34	61.0	65	23	36	5	3	3	4	1	4.13
	34	90.0	80	38	43	9	4	2	1	1	3.60
	43	70.1	92	28	34	6	2	2	8	1	5.25
	36	52.2	48	26	35	5	3	4	0	2	3.42

	BA	OBA	SA	AB	H	2B	3B	HR	RBI	BB	SO
	.266	.343	.398	1589	423	78	10	37	208	182	235
	.276	.335	.415	468	129	17	3	14	81	44	50
	.262	.346	.391	1121	294	61	7	23	127	138	185
	.272	.345	.404	815	222	44	3	19	19	85	127
	.279	.358	.425	348	97	25	1	8	8	39	60
	.260	.340	.391	774	201	34	7	18	189	97	108
	.252	.354	.368	457	115	18	4	9	162	81	63
	.273	.337	.420	374	102	13	3	12	44	37	55

TOM GLAVINE — bats left — throws left — age 26 — ATL — P

1991	G	IP	H	BB	SO	SB	CS	W	L	SV	ERA
Total	34	246.2	201	69	192	18	10	20	11	0	2.55
at Home	15	106.1	90	28	78	5	5	10	4	0	2.71
on Road	19	140.1	111	41	114	13	5	10	7	0	2.44
on Grass	24	176.2	148	45	125	7	6	17	6	0	2.55
on Turf	10	70.0	53	24	67	11	4	3	5	0	2.57
Day Games	11	75.2	68	27	67	3	3	7	4	0	3.21
Night Games	23	171.0	133	42	125	15	7	13	7	0	2.26
April	4	26.1	20	6	26	3	1	2	2	0	2.39
May	6	46.0	35	6	33	2	2	6	0	0	1.76
June	6	45.2	38	8	39	1	2	3	2	0	2.17
July	5	37.2	32	8	29	4	2	3	1	0	2.87
August	6	42.0	30	18	28	1	2	3	3	0	1.71
Sept—Oct	7	49.0	46	23	37	7	1	3	3	0	4.22

5-YEAR TOTALS (1987–1991)

G	IP	H	BB	SO	SB	CS	W	L	SV	ERA
139	892.2	861	283	515	70	44	53	52	0	3.81
65	415.0	414	119	229	22	25	25	25	0	4.12
74	477.2	447	164	286	48	19	28	27	0	3.54
96	616.1	612	174	350	28	31	39	34	0	3.87
43	276.1	249	109	165	42	13	14	18	0	3.68
38	231.2	244	89	155	12	10	14	15	0	4.70
101	661.0	617	194	360	58	34	39	37	0	3.50
17	116.0	105	26	62	5	4	6	7	0	3.10
23	140.2	120	50	91	17	4	11	5	0	3.45
23	146.2	163	36	95	5	5	9	10	0	4.23
20	134.1	127	34	82	11	11	6	6	0	3.62
28	170.0	181	62	85	16	11	9	15	0	4.45
28	185.0	165	75	100	16	9	12	9	0	3.75

	BA	OBA	SA	AB	H	2B	3B	HR	RBI	BB	SO
Total	.222	.277	.330	905	201	35	6	17	74	69	192
vs. Left	.284	.348	.408	169	48	8	2	3	17	17	38
vs. Right	.208	.260	.313	736	153	27	4	14	57	52	154
Bases Empty	.211	.254	.324	587	124	23	2	13	13	33	124
Leadoff	.196	.231	.321	240	47	10	1	6	6	10	45
Runners On Base	.242	.316	.343	318	77	12	4	4	61	36	68
Scoring Position	.249	.346	.329	173	43	4	2	2	51	28	35
Late and Close	.231	.268	.308	91	21	7	0	0	7	5	14

BA	OBA	SA	AB	H	2B	3B	HR	RBI	BB	SO
.255	.313	.373	3383	861	148	18	72	359	283	515
.243	.322	.333	573	139	20	4	8	50	64	112
.257	.311	.381	2810	722	128	14	64	309	219	403
.242	.285	.366	2087	505	87	8	52	52	117	319
.253	.291	.370	880	223	42	5	17	17	40	114
.275	.354	.383	1296	356	61	10	20	307	166	196
.270	.376	.373	732	198	35	5	10	272	134	121
.277	.325	.414	285	79	17	2	6	29	21	32

DWIGHT GOODEN — bats right — throws right — age 28 — NYN — P

1991	G	IP	H	BB	SO	SB	CS	W	L	SV	ERA
Total	27	190.0	185	56	150	34	17	13	7	0	3.60
at Home	15	106.1	98	29	85	18	12	9	3	0	3.55
on Road	12	83.2	87	27	65	16	5	4	4	0	3.66
on Grass	20	144.2	132	40	112	23	14	12	4	0	3.30
on Turf	7	45.1	53	16	38	11	3	1	3	0	4.57
Day Games	8	58.1	59	15	54	11	6	4	3	0	3.70
Night Games	19	131.2	126	41	96	23	11	9	4	0	3.55
April	5	37.0	27	8	39	4	3	3	1	0	4.75
May	6	41.2	53	11	29	8	2	2	3	0	5.80
June	6	40.1	47	10	24	10	5	2	2	0	2.15
July	5	37.2	29	13	36	5	4	4	0	0	2.43
August	5	33.1	29	14	22	7	3	2	1	0	2.43
Sept—Oct	0	0.0	0	0	0	0	0	0	0	0	0.00

8-YEAR TOTALS (1984–1991)

G	IP	H	BB	SO	SB	CS	W	L	SV	ERA
238	1713.2	1467	505	1541	306	81	132	53	1	2.91
121	895.2	707	263	832	147	49	74	23	0	2.57
117	818.0	760	242	709	159	32	58	30	1	3.28
173	1272.0	1055	374	1163	203	62	105	31	1	2.70
65	441.2	412	131	378	103	19	27	22	0	3.53
82	545.1	531	164	466	109	27	39	24	1	3.73
156	1168.1	936	341	1075	197	54	93	29	0	2.53
34	242.1	174	69	223	45	9	21	5	0	2.34
40	284.2	265	84	272	53	12	18	14	0	3.38
46	339.0	293	114	270	70	17	25	11	0	3.21
37	265.0	227	79	216	40	14	23	6	0	2.62
41	283.2	272	81	259	44	13	22	7	0	3.43
40	299.0	236	78	301	54	16	23	10	0	2.35

	BA	OBA	SA	AB	H	2B	3B	HR	RBI	BB	SO
Total	.257	.311	.369	721	185	33	6	12	73	56	150
vs. Left	.251	.319	.342	415	104	22	2	4	35	42	75
vs. Right	.265	.300	.405	306	81	11	4	8	38	14	75
Bases Empty	.259	.317	.378	413	107	22	3	7	7	33	81
Leadoff	.301	.347	.464	183	55	11	2	5	5	12	34
Runners On Base	.253	.304	.357	308	78	11	3	5	66	23	69
Scoring Position	.277	.335	.380	184	51	6	2	3	58	17	44
Late and Close	.210	.234	.258	62	13	0	0	1	4	2	17

BA	OBA	SA	AB	H	2B	3B	HR	RBI	BB	SO
.231	.289	.320	6361	1467	231	37	87	543	505	1541
.225	.289	.302	3519	791	127	20	35	272	315	791
.238	.288	.341	2842	676	104	17	52	271	190	750
.232	.293	.324	3762	872	147	24	51	51	309	883
.235	.298	.343	1602	376	61	13	29	29	136	351
.229	.283	.313	2599	595	84	13	36	492	196	658
.222	.289	.303	1552	345	47	9	20	444	152	434
.226	.283	.292	774	175	16	1	11	56	61	205

JEFF GRAY — bats right — throws right — age 29 — BOS — P

1991	G	IP	H	BB	SO	SB	CS	W	L	SV	ERA
Total	50	61.2	39	10	41	5	3	2	3	1	2.34
at Home	22	29.2	21	4	18	3	1	1	1	1	2.12
on Road	28	32.0	18	6	23	2	2	1	2	0	2.53
on Grass	38	49.1	30	5	35	3	1	1	1	1	1.64
on Turf	12	12.1	9	5	6	2	2	1	2	2	5.11
Day Games	13	17.1	13	3	9	1	0	0	1	1	2.60
Night Games	37	44.1	26	7	32	4	3	2	2	0	2.23
April	11	14.0	8	4	8	1	1	1	1	1	1.93
May	15	17.1	14	1	13	1	1	0	2	0	3.63
June	11	14.1	6	3	10	1	1	0	0	0	0.63
July	13	16.0	11	2	10	1	0	0	0	0	2.81
August	0	0.0	0	0	0	0	0	0	0	0	0.00
Sept—Oct	0	0.0	0	0	0	0	0	0	0	0	0.00

3-YEAR TOTALS (1988–1991)

G	IP	H	BB	SO	SB	CS	W	L	SV	ERA
96	121.2	104	29	96	12	4	4	7	10	3.33
45	62.0	55	11	42	8	2	3	3	7	2.90
51	59.2	49	18	54	4	2	1	4	3	3.77
71	91.1	75	16	72	6	2	3	5	8	2.56
25	30.1	29	13	24	6	2	1	2	2	5.64
29	37.1	30	7	27	4	1	1	1	5	2.89
67	84.1	74	22	69	8	3	3	6	5	3.52
11	14.0	8	4	8	1	1	1	1	1	1.93
15	17.1	14	1	13	2	1	0	2	0	3.63
24	35.1	24	9	25	2	2	1	1	2	2.04
23	28.0	35	6	18	2	0	0	0	0	5.46
12	15.0	6	4	17	1	0	1	0	6	0.60
11	12.0	7	5	15	1	0	0	1	1	6.75

	BA	OBA	SA	AB	H	2B	3B	HR	RBI	BB	SO
Total	.181	.219	.338	216	39	11	1	7	26	10	41
vs. Left	.202	.219	.319	94	19	5	0	2	12	2	15
vs. Right	.164	.220	.352	122	20	6	1	5	14	8	26
Bases Empty	.173	.192	.315	127	22	6	1	3	3	2	29
Leadoff	.208	.224	.438	48	10	5	0	2	2	1	11
Runners On Base	.191	.255	.371	89	17	4	0	3	23	8	12
Scoring Position	.191	.263	.368	68	13	3	0	3	21	7	6
Late and Close	.201	.252	.358	134	27	7	1	4	17	8	24

BA	OBA	SA	AB	H	2B	3B	HR	RBI	BB	SO
.231	.278	.360	450	104	22	3	10	54	29	96
.237	.273	.348	207	49	9	1	4	25	11	40
.226	.283	.370	243	55	13	2	6	29	18	56
.232	.262	.341	246	57	13	1	4	4	8	54
.282	.308	.437	103	29	10	0	2	2	2	20
.230	.297	.382	204	47	9	2	6	50	21	42
.229	.309	.357	140	32	7	1	3	43	18	28
.224	.272	.365	241	54	10	3	6	28	15	48

TOMMY GREENE — bats right — throws right — age 25 — PHI — P

3-YEAR TOTALS (1989–1991)

1991	G	IP	H	BB	SO	SB	CS	W	L	SV	ERA		G	IP	H	BB	SO	SB	CS	W	L	SV	ERA
Total	36	207.2	177	66	154	18	7	13	7	0	3.38		55	285.1	249	98	192	21	15	17	12	0	3.75
at Home	19	108.2	95	34	89	11	3	6	4	0	3.31		29	151.0	129	52	111	13	7	9	6	0	3.46
on Road	17	99.0	82	32	65	7	4	7	3	0	3.45		26	134.1	120	46	81	8	8	8	6	0	4.09
on Grass	8	31.0	29	13	17	3	1	2	1	0	4.94		15	60.1	59	22	33	5	3	3	3	0	5.22
on Turf	28	176.2	148	53	137	15	6	11	6	0	3.11		40	225.0	190	76	159	16	12	14	9	0	3.36
Day Games	12	69.1	48	32	54	7	2	6	3	0	3.38		15	85.1	58	37	66	7	4	7	3	0	3.38
Night Games	24	138.1	129	34	100	11	5	7	4	0	3.38		40	200.0	191	61	126	14	11	10	9	0	3.92
April	6	20.2	18	6	6	2	0	0	0	0	4.79		8	24.0	22	10	6	2	0	0	0	0	5.63
May	6	31.0	12	11	30	3	2	4	0	0	0.29		6	31.0	12	11	30	3	2	4	0	0	0.29
June	6	42.1	40	10	33	3	1	1	1	0	3.19		9	51.1	50	15	37	4	2	2	1	0	3.86
July	6	36.0	32	15	24	5	2	2	3	0	4.00		6	36.0	32	15	24	5	2	2	3	0	4.00
August	6	38.2	38	15	31	2	2	2	2	0	3.96		9	49.2	52	19	34	2	3	2	4	0	4.71
Sept–Oct	6	39.0	37	9	30	3	0	4	1	0	4.15		17	93.1	81	28	61	5	6	7	4	0	3.76

	BA	OBA	SA	AB	H	2B	3B	HR	RBI	BB	SO		BA	OBA	SA	AB	H	2B	3B	HR	RBI	BB	SO
Total	.230	.290	.361	768	177	35	4	19	82	66	154		.236	.299	.384	1057	249	49	6	32	121	98	192
vs. Left	.255	.320	.404	451	115	23	4	12	52	45	82		.269	.342	.438	603	162	32	5	20	76	69	98
vs. Right	.196	.246	.300	317	62	12	0	7	30	21	72		.192	.240	.313	454	87	17	1	12	45	29	94
Bases Empty	.208	.273	.336	491	102	19	1	14	14	41	107		.218	.288	.360	661	144	26	1	22	22	62	135
Leadoff	.177	.251	.281	192	34	8	0	4	4	18	40		.208	.286	.321	265	55	9	0	7	7	28	53
Runners On Base	.271	.319	.404	277	75	16	3	5	68	25	47		.265	.318	.424	396	105	23	5	10	99	36	57
Scoring Position	.279	.326	.409	154	43	10	2	2	58	16	29		.270	.328	.414	215	58	13	3	4	79	25	37
Late and Close	.220	.281	.305	59	13	2	0	1	4	5	16		.200	.273	.286	70	14	3	0	1	5	7	18

MARK GUBICZA — bats right — throws right — age 30 — KC — P

8-YEAR TOTALS (1984–1991)

1991	G	IP	H	BB	SO	SB	CS	W	L	SV	ERA		G	IP	H	BB	SO	SB	CS	W	L	SV	ERA
Total	26	133.0	168	42	89	18	6	9	12	0	5.68		241	1540.1	1476	582	1010	137	60	97	87	0	3.76
at Home	13	65.2	75	18	48	10	2	4	6	0	5.21		130	847.0	787	297	535	84	24	53	46	0	3.45
on Road	13	67.1	93	24	41	8	4	5	6	0	6.15		111	693.1	689	285	475	53	36	44	41	0	4.13
on Grass	8	42.2	55	17	23	0	1	3	3	0	6.12		82	520.1	501	215	352	36	26	33	29	0	3.89
on Turf	18	90.1	113	25	66	18	5	6	9	0	5.48		159	1020.0	975	367	658	101	34	64	58	0	3.69
Day Games	8	40.2	51	17	30	4	2	3	4	0	5.98		66	415.0	398	174	281	31	20	27	22	0	3.99
Night Games	18	92.1	117	25	59	14	4	6	8	0	5.56		175	1125.1	1078	408	729	106	40	70	65	0	3.67
April	0	0.0	0	0	0	0	0	0	0	0	0.00		27	171.1	166	74	92	21	7	6	15	0	3.89
May	4	23.0	27	6	18	5	0	1	3	0	4.70		45	291.2	293	110	182	35	6	16	18	0	4.07
June	4	17.2	23	6	8	1	0	2	1	0	5.60		42	276.0	235	109	196	12	8	24	10	0	2.93
July	6	30.0	39	9	22	1	3	1	1	0	6.00		39	234.0	236	76	153	23	13	12	11	0	3.65
August	6	36.0	38	8	24	1	1	2	2	0	4.25		43	279.1	265	104	192	15	7	16	16	0	4.06
Sept–Oct	6	26.1	41	13	17	8	4	1	5	0	8.20		45	288.0	281	109	195	31	19	20	17	0	3.94

	BA	OBA	SA	AB	H	2B	3B	HR	RBI	BB	SO		BA	OBA	SA	AB	H	2B	3B	HR	RBI	BB	SO
Total	.308	.361	.424	545	168	27	3	10	81	42	89		.254	.323	.358	5822	1476	256	44	89	600	582	1010
vs. Left	.331	.399	.445	254	84	14	3	3	36	28	40		.258	.335	.365	3058	789	130	25	49	303	347	478
vs. Right	.289	.326	.405	291	84	13	0	7	45	14	49		.249	.309	.351	2764	687	126	19	40	297	235	532
Bases Empty	.279	.342	.391	294	82	12	3	5	5	26	46		.251	.324	.360	3325	836	162	26	49	49	335	568
Leadoff	.282	.324	.412	131	37	7	2	2	2	7	17		.269	.333	.382	1463	393	80	13	20	20	129	206
Runners On Base	.343	.384	.462	251	86	15	0	5	76	16	43		.256	.322	.356	2497	640	94	18	40	551	247	442
Scoring Position	.313	.361	.433	150	47	9	0	5	67	11	30		.246	.319	.351	1442	355	52	9	27	491	168	285
Late and Close	.091	.167	.091	11	1	0	0	0	0	1	3		.256	.329	.370	519	133	25	5	8	39	56	106

LEE GUETTERMAN — bats left — throws left — age 34 — NYA — P

7-YEAR TOTALS (1984–1991)

1991	G	IP	H	BB	SO	SB	CS	W	L	SV	ERA		G	IP	H	BB	SO	SB	CS	W	L	SV	ERA
Total	64	88.0	91	25	35	4	3	3	4	6	3.68		287	518.0	552	158	231	34	11	31	26	21	4.03
at Home	33	51.2	55	17	25	2	3	2	1	4	4.18		155	289.1	305	86	137	15	7	21	10	13	4.14
on Road	31	36.1	36	8	10	2	0	1	3	2	2.97		132	228.2	247	72	94	19	4	10	16	8	3.90
on Grass	55	75.2	78	22	34	3	3	3	2	6	3.57		217	358.1	360	102	165	22	9	22	17	18	3.62
on Turf	9	12.1	13	3	1	1	0	0	2	0	4.38		70	159.2	192	56	66	12	2	9	9	3	4.96
Day Games	20	26.2	28	7	6	1	0	0	1	2	3.71		92	164.2	159	53	51	12	4	12	5	6	3.12
Night Games	44	61.1	63	18	29	3	3	3	3	4	3.67		195	353.1	393	105	180	22	7	19	21	15	4.46
April	6	6.2	6	1	3	0	0	0	0	0	1.35		36	56.1	55	15	31	2	0	1	1	3	2.40
May	12	12.2	9	3	2	2	0	1	0	3	1.42		46	77.1	68	24	31	7	0	4	1	7	3.26
June	10	10.0	12	2	1	0	0	1	1	0	3.60		50	100.2	110	25	44	7	1	8	6	2	3.67
July	9	17.1	15	3	4	0	0	0	0	2	2.60		41	94.1	111	33	33	7	3	7	7	3	4.96
August	13	16.1	24	9	2	0	2	0	1	1	8.27		60	91.1	104	29	44	6	4	4	4	3	5.32
Sept–Oct	14	25.0	25	7	17	0	1	1	1	0	3.24		54	98.0	104	32	48	5	3	7	7	3	3.86

	BA	OBA	SA	AB	H	2B	3B	HR	RBI	BB	SO		BA	OBA	SA	AB	H	2B	3B	HR	RBI	BB	SO
Total	.268	.320	.388	340	91	19	2	6	39	25	35		.278	.331	.397	1988	552	87	15	40	255	158	231
vs. Left	.175	.250	.289	97	17	5	0	2	8	7	13		.242	.308	.333	525	127	20	5	6	60	46	73
vs. Right	.305	.348	.428	243	74	14	2	4	31	18	22		.290	.339	.420	1463	425	67	10	34	195	112	158
Bases Empty	.283	.328	.417	180	51	13	1	3	3	9	17		.279	.323	.391	1045	292	46	7	19	19	61	125
Leadoff	.267	.304	.400	75	20	7	0	1	1	3	4		.310	.342	.454	452	140	22	2	13	13	20	54
Runners On Base	.250	.311	.356	160	40	6	1	3	36	16	18		.276	.339	.403	943	260	41	8	21	236	97	106
Scoring Position	.232	.300	.358	95	22	1	1	3	34	11	11		.252	.332	.375	563	142	20	5	13	210	76	74
Late and Close	.292	.331	.433	120	35	6	0	4	16	6	13		.282	.335	.399	567	160	16	4	14	75	41	62

BILL GULLICKSON — bats right — throws right — age 33 — DET — P

6-YEAR TOTALS (1984–1991)

1991	G	IP	H	BB	SO	SB	CS	W	L	SV	ERA	G	IP	H	BB	SO	SB	CS	W	L	SV	ERA
Total	35	226.1	256	44	91	15	8	20	9	0	3.90	200	1285.1	1357	299	570	126	52	85	69	0	3.84
at Home	17	103.2	123	23	47	10	2	10	4	0	4.95	104	678.2	696	149	324	62	22	53	28	0	3.81
on Road	18	122.2	133	21	44	5	6	10	5	0	3.01	96	606.2	661	150	246	64	30	32	41	0	3.89
on Grass	27	174.0	191	40	70	10	6	15	7	0	4.09	78	484.0	531	116	209	42	20	29	29	0	4.30
on Turf	8	52.1	65	4	21	5	2	5	2	0	3.27	122	801.1	826	183	361	84	32	56	40	0	3.57
Day Games	14	81.2	108	20	30	6	4	4	5	0	5.29	69	435.0	475	106	188	43	20	32	20	0	4.01
Night Games	21	144.2	148	24	61	9	4	16	4	0	3.11	131	850.1	882	193	382	83	32	53	49	0	3.76
April	4	22.2	27	7	8	2	1	2	0	0	4.37	24	136.2	145	37	57	14	10	9	8	0	4.15
May	6	36.0	50	5	11	1	2	3	2	0	5.00	36	225.0	248	53	103	29	13	17	13	0	4.12
June	6	46.1	48	9	16	5	2	4	2	0	2.91	30	205.0	216	44	86	19	7	11	10	0	3.47
July	6	35.0	48	8	15	2	0	4	1	0	5.40	33	216.0	236	55	92	16	6	15	10	0	3.96
August	6	36.0	35	7	17	5	1	3	1	0	2.75	37	252.0	234	47	121	23	8	18	13	0	2.89
Sept–Oct	7	50.1	48	8	24	0	2	4	2	0	3.58	40	250.2	278	63	111	25	8	15	15	0	4.60

	BA	OBA	SA	AB	H	2B	3B	HR	RBI	BB	SO	BA	OBA	SA	AB	H	2B	3B	HR	RBI	BB	SO
Total	.288	.321	.435	890	256	51	7	22	102	44	91	.273	.313	.424	4973	1357	251	38	142	564	299	570
vs. Left	.276	.314	.448	471	130	30	3	15	51	25	34	.279	.326	.432	2663	743	139	20	76	281	191	241
vs. Right	.301	.330	.420	419	126	21	4	7	51	19	57	.266	.297	.416	2310	614	112	18	66	283	108	329
Bases Empty	.280	.308	.425	543	152	34	3	13	13	18	60	.268	.306	.425	3052	817	150	20	97	97	159	378
Leadoff	.262	.274	.352	233	61	10	1	3	3	4	25	.270	.307	.406	1272	343	57	7	34	34	65	143
Runners On Base	.300	.341	.450	347	104	17	4	9	89	26	31	.281	.323	.423	1921	540	101	18	45	467	140	192
Scoring Position	.310	.375	.429	184	57	7	0	5	73	24	20	.266	.322	.405	1096	292	58	8	26	399	110	119
Late and Close	.306	.367	.431	72	22	4	1	1	12	6	9	.263	.315	.358	411	108	17	2	6	32	31	44

JOSE GUZMAN — bats right — throws right — age 29 — TEX — P

5-YEAR TOTALS (1985–1991)

1991	G	IP	H	BB	SO	SB	CS	W	L	SV	ERA	G	IP	H	BB	SO	SB	CS	W	L	SV	ERA
Total	25	169.2	152	84	125	12	13	13	7	0	3.08	125	785.0	745	320	533	87	27	50	51	0	3.93
at Home	9	60.2	57	27	42	2	5	5	3	0	3.86	65	405.0	381	149	270	46	13	29	26	0	3.73
on Road	16	109.0	95	57	83	10	8	8	4	0	2.64	60	380.0	364	171	263	41	14	21	25	0	4.14
on Grass	20	140.1	116	61	102	7	8	13	4	0	2.63	106	671.0	626	263	449	70	20	46	42	0	3.72
on Turf	5	29.1	36	23	23	5	5	0	3	0	5.22	19	114.0	119	57	84	17	7	4	9	0	5.21
Day Games	5	32.1	21	26	24	2	2	2	0	0	2.23	18	107.2	107	55	78	12	2	4	8	0	3.76
Night Games	20	137.1	131	58	101	10	11	11	7	0	3.28	107	677.1	638	265	455	75	25	46	43	0	3.96
April	0	0.0	0	0	0	0	0	0	0	0	0.00	12	72.0	68	14	44	9	1	5	6	0	4.00
May	2	11.1	13	10	3	1	2	0	1	0	3.97	19	116.0	127	60	80	11	7	6	8	0	4.34
June	6	43.1	37	18	35	3	2	3	2	0	2.91	24	166.1	146	60	120	16	4	12	9	0	3.79
July	5	34.2	29	21	28	3	2	3	1	0	2.08	21	135.2	131	57	86	20	8	8	9	0	3.45
August	6	32.2	39	14	26	1	2	3	1	0	4.13	22	109.2	120	47	68	12	5	8	6	0	4.84
Sept–Oct	6	47.2	34	21	33	4	5	4	2	0	3.02	27	185.1	153	82	135	19	6	11	13	0	3.59

	BA	OBA	SA	AB	H	2B	3B	HR	RBI	BB	SO	BA	OBA	SA	AB	H	2B	3B	HR	RBI	BB	SO
Total	.239	.330	.341	636	152	33	1	10	51	84	125	.250	.324	.387	2980	745	146	5	84	306	320	533
vs. Left	.248	.357	.374	278	69	15	1	6	29	46	51	.250	.323	.381	1503	375	74	3	39	160	160	247
vs. Right	.232	.308	.316	358	83	18	0	4	22	38	74	.251	.326	.393	1477	370	72	2	45	146	160	286
Bases Empty	.258	.342	.371	356	92	19	0	7	7	44	69	.248	.319	.382	1778	441	91	2	48	48	176	338
Leadoff	.270	.341	.384	159	43	6	0	4	4	16	29	.246	.311	.375	759	187	39	1	19	19	67	143
Runners On Base	.214	.316	.304	280	60	14	1	3	44	40	56	.253	.333	.394	1202	304	55	3	36	258	144	195
Scoring Position	.162	.283	.208	154	25	5	1	0	36	26	36	.218	.317	.323	674	147	22	2	15	207	102	124
Late and Close	.209	.274	.328	67	14	5	0	1	3	7	17	.237	.310	.369	274	65	14	2	6	16	29	45

ERIK HANSON — bats right — throws right — age 27 — SEA — P

4-YEAR TOTALS (1988–1991)

1991	G	IP	H	BB	SO	SB	CS	W	L	SV	ERA	G	IP	H	BB	SO	SB	CS	W	L	SV	ERA
Total	27	174.2	182	56	143	11	11	8	8	0	3.81	83	565.2	525	168	465	34	28	37	25	0	3.40
at Home	14	89.0	100	19	80	9	4	4	5	0	4.25	42	279.1	284	73	235	19	11	16	15	0	3.90
on Road	13	85.2	82	37	63	2	7	4	3	0	3.36	41	286.1	241	95	230	15	17	21	10	0	2.92
on Grass	10	66.2	61	29	53	2	6	3	2	0	2.97	32	224.1	179	78	190	14	15	16	7	0	2.81
on Turf	17	108.0	121	27	90	9	5	5	6	0	4.33	51	341.1	346	90	275	20	13	21	18	0	3.80
Day Games	8	50.1	50	17	37	4	4	1	3	0	4.29	21	138.1	132	44	106	10	8	6	7	0	3.45
Night Games	19	124.1	132	39	106	7	7	7	5	0	3.62	62	427.1	393	124	359	24	20	31	18	0	3.39
April	5	35.2	33	16	30	1	2	3	2	0	3.28	14	91.0	82	34	80	5	6	6	3	0	2.87
May	3	14.2	22	4	15	2	2	1	1	0	5.52	14	81.1	93	30	65	7	6	6	4	0	4.76
June	2	13.2	11	4	9	1	1	1	1	0	2.63	8	54.2	52	19	47	2	5	4	4	0	4.45
July	6	37.2	44	5	29	0	1	2	2	0	4.06	11	73.1	69	20	59	3	3	5	4	0	3.68
August	6	40.0	43	14	30	2	1	1	2	0	4.28	13	96.0	84	24	75	7	6	3	3	0	3.19
Sept–Oct	5	33.0	29	13	30	5	4	1	1	0	3.27	23	169.1	145	41	139	10	6	13	5	0	2.71

	BA	OBA	SA	AB	H	2B	3B	HR	RBI	BB	SO	BA	OBA	SA	AB	H	2B	3B	HR	RBI	BB	SO
Total	.269	.323	.414	676	182	36	7	16	69	56	143	.246	.302	.363	2134	525	97	13	42	195	168	465
vs. Left	.240	.276	.406	350	84	21	5	9	45	18	82	.228	.281	.336	1112	254	55	7	17	102	81	247
vs. Right	.301	.371	.423	326	98	15	2	7	24	38	61	.265	.325	.391	1022	271	42	6	25	93	87	218
Bases Empty	.271	.323	.421	399	108	22	4	10	10	31	82	.236	.289	.348	1319	311	53	7	27	27	93	292
Leadoff	.241	.275	.402	174	42	9	2	5	5	8	34	.199	.247	.298	554	110	22	3	9	9	35	126
Runners On Base	.267	.324	.404	277	74	14	3	6	59	25	61	.263	.323	.387	815	214	44	6	15	168	75	173
Scoring Position	.233	.309	.373	150	35	6	3	3	49	20	34	.230	.301	.351	444	102	21	4	8	140	49	103
Late and Close	.238	.315	.302	63	15	2	1	0	6	8	11	.217	.275	.288	198	43	7	1	5	15	16	49

PETE HARNISCH — bats both — throws right — age 26 — HOU — P

4-YEAR TOTALS (1988–1991)

1991	G	IP	H	BB	SO	SB	CS	W	L	SV	ERA	G	IP	H	BB	SO	SB	CS	W	L	SV	ERA
Total	33	216.2	169	83	172	27	6	12	9	0	2.70	84	521.2	468	242	374	61	16	28	31	0	3.74
at Home	17	119.1	87	34	102	10	3	7	4	0	2.41	38	243.0	201	86	191	22	7	17	11	0	3.37
on Road	16	97.1	82	49	70	17	3	5	5	0	3.05	46	278.2	267	156	183	39	9	11	20	0	4.07
on Grass	9	56.1	43	27	41	10	2	4	1	0	1.92	51	308.1	278	158	221	37	10	19	19	0	3.74
on Turf	24	160.1	126	56	131	17	4	8	8	0	2.98	33	213.1	190	84	153	24	6	9	12	0	3.75
Day Games	7	43.0	44	18	34	4	3	2	2	0	4.40	17	106.0	100	55	75	11	5	5	5	0	3.99
Night Games	26	173.2	125	65	138	23	3	10	7	0	2.28	67	415.2	368	187	299	50	11	23	26	0	3.68
April	4	25.2	14	17	21	4	0	1	0	0	1.05	10	59.0	46	37	40	8	0	3	1	0	2.75
May	6	39.1	31	14	23	5	0	2	3	0	3.43	12	79.2	68	30	43	5	5	5	5	0	3.50
June	6	43.2	31	15	34	7	4	2	3	0	2.06	11	74.0	58	30	60	10	4	3	5	0	2.80
July	5	36.0	33	12	24	4	1	1	1	0	3.00	16	95.1	99	39	61	13	4	4	5	0	5.00
August	6	40.0	31	17	39	4	1	2	1	0	2.70	19	124.2	113	66	100	10	4	5	9	0	3.32
Sept–Oct	6	32.0	29	8	31	3	0	4	1	0	3.66	16	89.0	84	40	70	10	1	7	6	0	4.65

	BA	OBA	SA	AB	H	2B	3B	HR	RBI	BB	SO	BA	OBA	SA	AB	H	2B	3B	HR	RBI	BB	SO
Total	.212	.288	.313	796	169	28	5	14	63	83	172	.239	.323	.359	1959	468	86	12	42	187	242	374
vs. Left	.232	.317	.349	453	105	15	4	10	35	55	87	.258	.347	.392	1088	281	56	9	24	104	143	182
vs. Right	.187	.249	.265	343	64	13	1	4	28	28	85	.215	.294	.318	871	187	30	3	18	83	99	192
Bases Empty	.219	.294	.342	465	102	16	4	11	11	45	101	.233	.320	.358	1121	261	46	8	26	26	135	213
Leadoff	.224	.304	.358	201	45	9	3	4	4	21	40	.234	.323	.367	491	115	26	3	11	11	60	84
Runners On Base	.202	.281	.272	331	67	12	1	3	52	38	71	.247	.328	.362	838	207	40	4	16	161	107	161
Scoring Position	.189	.295	.254	201	38	7	0	2	47	32	45	.216	.324	.323	477	103	20	2	9	138	83	99
Late and Close	.133	.232	.181	83	11	2	1	0	3	11	20	.186	.293	.295	156	29	2	3	3	10	24	26

GREG HARRIS — bats both — throws right — age 37 — BOS — P

8-YEAR TOTALS (1984–1991)

1991	G	IP	H	BB	SO	SB	CS	W	L	SV	ERA	G	IP	H	BB	SO	SB	CS	W	L	SV	ERA
Total	53	173.0	157	69	127	1	6	11	12	2	3.85	419	986.2	880	422	749	73	36	54	55	38	3.45
at Home	25	71.0	66	31	55	1	4	4	6	2	3.80	202	487.0	445	194	371	36	13	31	27	20	3.60
on Road	28	102.0	91	38	72	0	2	7	6	0	3.88	217	499.2	435	228	378	37	23	23	28	18	3.30
on Grass	46	132.0	127	55	100	1	5	10	9	2	3.95	287	712.0	631	285	555	45	24	43	36	32	3.51
on Turf	7	41.0	30	14	27	0	1	1	3	0	3.51	132	274.2	249	137	194	28	12	11	19	6	3.28
Day Games	16	46.0	43	27	40	1	3	4	2	0	2.93	112	253.1	209	130	205	21	10	16	9	10	2.88
Night Games	37	127.0	114	42	87	0	3	7	10	2	4.18	307	733.1	671	292	544	52	26	38	46	28	3.65
April	4	22.1	23	11	13	0	1	1	2	0	3.63	51	106.2	86	49	75	5	3	7	7	3	3.21
May	9	27.2	29	10	20	0	0	0	3	1	5.20	76	165.2	152	68	126	10	10	4	13	10	3.59
June	6	34.0	28	14	29	0	3	0	2	0	4.24	71	175.1	165	68	129	9	1	11	8	11	3.59
July	8	37.2	33	8	25	0	3	3	4	0	4.30	66	181.2	169	68	120	13	8	10	11	3	2.97
August	9	24.2	15	12	21	1	2	3	0	0	1.09	78	184.2	131	79	166	14	6	14	5	2	2.68
Sept–Oct	17	26.2	29	14	19	0	0	1	1	1	4.05	77	172.2	177	90	133	22	8	8	11	9	4.64

	BA	OBA	SA	AB	H	2B	3B	HR	RBI	BB	SO	BA	OBA	SA	AB	H	2B	3B	HR	RBI	BB	SO
Total	.243	.318	.363	645	157	30	4	13	75	69	127	.240	.321	.363	3663	880	168	20	81	422	422	749
vs. Left	.248	.326	.359	298	74	14	2	5	35	34	57	.231	.315	.342	1754	405	75	13	31	193	213	326
vs. Right	.239	.310	.366	347	83	16	2	8	40	35	70	.249	.326	.383	1909	475	93	7	50	229	209	423
Bases Empty	.227	.309	.326	374	85	15	2	6	6	40	71	.231	.311	.354	2045	473	93	13	44	44	217	425
Leadoff	.219	.316	.361	155	34	6	2	4	4	18	29	.218	.300	.346	856	187	39	5	20	20	89	157
Runners On Base	.266	.330	.413	271	72	15	2	7	69	29	56	.252	.333	.375	1618	407	75	7	37	378	205	324
Scoring Position	.293	.367	.443	140	41	8	2	3	56	20	28	.240	.343	.343	934	224	41	2	17	313	156	194
Late and Close	.190	.305	.264	121	23	3	0	3	9	20	25	.223	.310	.347	883	197	31	6	22	108	107	190

GREG HARRIS — bats right — throws right — age 29 — SD — P

4-YEAR TOTALS (1988–1991)

1991	G	IP	H	BB	SO	SB	CS	W	L	SV	ERA	G	IP	H	BB	SO	SB	CS	W	L	SV	ERA
Total	20	133.0	116	27	95	13	8	9	5	0	2.23	152	403.1	327	131	313	30	15	27	22	15	2.34
at Home	10	73.0	60	11	48	7	5	5	2	0	1.85	71	198.2	160	65	164	15	8	16	10	4	2.04
on Road	10	60.0	56	16	47	6	3	4	3	0	2.70	81	204.2	167	66	149	15	7	11	12	11	2.64
on Grass	16	109.0	93	20	73	9	7	8	4	0	2.15	111	302.2	242	94	236	20	12	22	15	10	1.99
on Turf	4	24.0	23	7	22	4	1	1	1	0	2.63	41	100.2	85	37	77	10	3	5	7	5	3.40
Day Games	5	38.1	24	7	26	5	3	4	0	0	1.64	46	132.0	96	40	97	13	7	13	7	5	2.11
Night Games	15	94.2	92	20	69	8	5	5	5	0	2.47	106	271.1	231	91	216	17	8	14	15	10	2.45
April	3	15.2	12	1	9	2	0	1	1	0	2.30	16	35.1	24	5	27	2	0	3	1	0	1.53
May	0	0.0	0	0	0	0	0	0	0	0	0.00	24	42.0	27	18	42	4	1	2	2	0	1.93
June	0	0.0	0	0	0	0	0	0	0	0	0.00	24	38.2	31	22	34	4	3	3	3	1	2.79
July	5	31.0	32	9	21	2	2	1	2	0	3.19	25	76.0	72	25	49	5	2	8	1	1	3.91
August	6	43.0	35	9	32	4	5	2	1	0	1.67	28	95.0	78	30	72	5	6	7	3	2	2.27
Sept–Oct	6	43.1	37	8	33	5	1	3	1	0	2.08	35	116.1	95	31	89	10	1	10	5	5	1.62

	BA	OBA	SA	AB	H	2B	3B	HR	RBI	BB	SO	BA	OBA	SA	AB	H	2B	3B	HR	RBI	BB	SO
Total	.233	.273	.363	498	116	17	0	16	40	27	95	.222	.286	.321	1475	327	49	4	30	126	131	313
vs. Left	.252	.286	.391	302	76	9	0	11	26	15	65	.240	.301	.335	840	202	30	2	15	72	73	165
vs. Right	.204	.252	.321	196	40	8	0	5	14	12	30	.197	.267	.304	635	125	19	2	15	54	58	148
Bases Empty	.244	.277	.375	328	80	13	0	10	10	15	59	.217	.267	.322	911	198	32	0	21	21	57	193
Leadoff	.223	.263	.392	130	29	7	0	5	5	7	23	.196	.251	.291	368	72	17	0	6	6	25	80
Runners On Base	.212	.265	.341	170	36	4	0	6	30	12	36	.229	.315	.321	564	129	17	4	9	105	74	120
Scoring Position	.156	.245	.229	96	15	1	0	2	21	11	27	.193	.309	.265	321	62	10	2	3	87	58	81
Late and Close	.148	.216	.185	81	12	3	0	0	1	7	18	.203	.296	.259	518	105	16	2	3	44	67	116

BRYAN HARVEY — bats right — throws right — age 29 — CAL — P

1991	G	IP	H	BB	SO	SB	CS	W	L	SV	ERA
Total	67	78.2	51	17	101	12	0	2	4	46	1.60
at Home	32	39.1	28	11	47	4	0	2	2	22	2.06
on Road	35	39.1	23	6	54	8	0	0	2	24	1.14
on Grass	54	63.1	38	16	78	11	0	2	3	36	1.99
on Turf	13	15.1	13	1	23	1	0	0	1	10	0.00
Day Games	18	22.2	11	6	31	3	0	0	0	11	0.79
Night Games	49	56.0	40	11	70	9	0	2	4	35	1.93
April	8	10.1	6	1	8	0	0	1	0	4	0.87
May	11	11.0	10	3	14	4	0	0	1	8	1.64
June	10	13.2	1	1	21	0	0	0	0	6	0.66
July	10	11.0	6	2	15	4	0	1	2	5	4.09
August	11	14.0	7	1	20	1	0	0	0	8	0.64
Sept–Oct	17	18.2	14	9	23	0	0	1	2	13	1.93

5-YEAR TOTALS (1987–1991)

	G	IP	H	BB	SO	SB	CS	W	L	SV	ERA
	225	279.0	197	115	331	32	5	15	16	113	2.45
	116	151.1	115	61	171	16	1	10	7	54	2.56
	109	127.2	82	54	160	16	4	5	9	59	2.33
	196	243.2	168	103	288	31	4	12	13	96	2.59
	29	35.1	29	12	43	1	1	3	3	17	1.53
	55	73.2	52	27	92	10	1	2	3	27	2.08
	170	205.1	145	88	239	22	4	13	13	86	2.59
	27	33.2	23	16	33	2	1	3	1	10	1.87
	40	56.2	41	19	58	7	1	3	3	14	2.22
	40	47.1	30	23	63	7	0	0	2	24	1.90
	36	45.0	40	19	48	6	1	5	5	15	3.80
	35	48.0	24	13	71	3	1	2	1	21	0.75
	47	48.1	39	25	58	7	1	2	4	29	4.10

	BA	OBA	SA	AB	H	2B	3B	HR	RBI	BB	SO
Total	.178	.225	.266	286	51	7	0	6	25	17	101
vs. Left	.181	.233	.294	160	29	6	0	4	14	11	61
vs. Right	.175	.216	.230	126	22	1	0	2	11	6	40
Bases Empty	.200	.231	.307	150	30	4	0	4	4	6	48
Leadoff	.190	.242	.362	58	11	4	0	2	2	4	16
Runners On Base	.154	.220	.221	136	21	3	0	2	21	11	53
Scoring Position	.144	.225	.222	90	13	1	0	2	20	9	36
Late and Close	.187	.245	.271	214	40	6	0	4	23	16	78

	BA	OBA	SA	AB	H	2B	3B	HR	RBI	BB	SO
	.196	.278	.288	1003	197	26	3	20	105	115	331
	.178	.268	.275	517	92	16	2	10	58	66	182
	.216	.288	.302	486	105	10	1	10	47	49	149
	.206	.264	.302	506	104	10	0	13	13	39	163
	.214	.285	.338	201	43	7	0	6	6	19	62
	.187	.291	.274	497	93	16	3	7	92	76	168
	.165	.298	.269	316	52	9	3	6	88	64	113
	.199	.287	.295	678	135	16	2	15	87	84	235

TOM HENKE — bats right — throws right — age 35 — TOR — P

1991	G	IP	H	BB	SO	SB	CS	W	L	SV	ERA
Total	49	50.1	33	11	53	2	0	0	0	32	2.32
at Home	22	23.1	17	5	25	1	0	0	1	14	2.31
on Road	27	27.0	16	6	28	1	0	0	1	18	2.33
on Grass	18	17.2	9	5	19	1	0	0	1	13	2.55
on Turf	31	32.2	24	6	34	1	0	0	0	19	2.20
Day Games	15	15.0	12	4	13	0	0	0	0	9	1.20
Night Games	34	35.1	21	7	40	2	0	0	2	23	2.80
April	2	2.0	2	0	1	0	0	0	0	2	0.00
May	4	4.1	0	1	4	0	0	0	0	3	0.00
June	13	12.1	7	3	11	0	0	0	0	9	2.19
July	10	10.0	8	1	8	1	0	0	0	7	1.80
August	13	14.0	9	2	21	0	0	0	2	10	4.50
Sept–Oct	7	7.2	7	4	8	1	0	0	0	1	1.17

8-YEAR TOTALS (1984–1991)

	G	IP	H	BB	SO	SB	CS	W	L	SV	ERA
	414	535.2	407	164	623	37	10	27	28	185	2.69
	206	257.2	194	76	298	22	5	16	8	84	2.55
	208	278.0	213	88	325	15	5	11	20	101	2.82
	178	231.1	178	72	268	15	5	10	14	82	2.65
	236	304.1	229	92	355	22	5	17	14	103	2.72
	127	158.0	131	57	177	18	2	8	7	44	2.79
	287	377.2	276	107	446	19	8	19	21	141	2.65
	51	51.2	47	24	54	2	2	3	4	17	4.01
	55	77.0	49	28	94	4	1	4	5	17	2.81
	66	82.0	59	26	88	6	2	5	1	34	1.98
	72	96.0	59	29	107	10	2	4	4	40	2.25
	83	120.1	93	21	149	5	2	4	4	44	2.09
	87	108.2	100	36	131	10	1	6	10	33	3.56

	BA	OBA	SA	AB	H	2B	3B	HR	RBI	BB	SO
Total	.184	.232	.307	179	33	8	1	4	16	11	53
vs. Left	.183	.248	.355	93	17	5	1	3	10	8	24
vs. Right	.186	.213	.256	86	16	3	0	1	6	3	29
Bases Empty	.179	.213	.265	117	21	5	1	1	1	5	36
Leadoff	.191	.208	.255	47	9	1	1	0	0	1	12
Runners On Base	.194	.265	.387	62	12	3	0	3	15	6	17
Scoring Position	.216	.293	.432	37	8	2	0	2	12	4	12
Late and Close	.153	.187	.254	118	18	4	1	1	11	5	38

	BA	OBA	SA	AB	H	2B	3B	HR	RBI	BB	SO
	.210	.271	.327	1941	407	80	9	43	229	164	623
	.215	.284	.330	997	214	38	4	23	117	98	309
	.204	.257	.323	944	193	42	5	20	112	66	314
	.206	.253	.304	1074	221	46	4	17	17	64	353
	.216	.262	.311	431	93	16	2	7	7	25	128
	.215	.291	.355	867	186	34	5	26	212	100	270
	.217	.307	.358	534	116	20	5	15	185	78	173
	.204	.267	.336	1264	258	53	6	34	179	111	434

MIKE HENNEMAN — bats right — throws right — age 31 — DET — P

1991	G	IP	H	BB	SO	SB	CS	W	L	SV	ERA
Total	60	84.1	81	34	61	3	2	10	2	21	2.88
at Home	38	50.2	43	17	41	0	0	7	0	15	1.95
on Road	22	33.2	38	17	20	3	2	3	2	6	4.28
on Grass	52	73.0	71	28	53	2	0	10	1	18	2.71
on Turf	8	11.1	10	6	8	1	2	0	1	3	3.97
Day Games	19	25.1	23	17	12	3	0	5	0	5	2.84
Night Games	41	59.0	58	17	49	0	2	5	2	16	2.90
April	9	13.0	10	5	8	1	0	2	0	4	0.69
May	13	20.2	21	9	11	0	1	2	1	2	2.18
June	12	15.0	15	9	9	0	0	0	1	5	6.00
July	11	15.2	13	5	13	0	1	0	0	4	1.72
August	8	11.2	14	5	11	0	0	1	0	4	3.09
Sept–Oct	7	8.1	8	1	9	0	1	0	0	2	4.32

5-YEAR TOTALS (1987–1991)

	G	IP	H	BB	SO	SB	CS	W	L	SV	ERA
	309	456.2	413	173	313	20	9	49	21	80	2.90
	162	240.2	191	72	182	8	5	34	6	41	2.66
	147	216.0	222	101	131	12	4	15	15	39	3.17
	265	396.0	361	145	276	17	7	46	16	65	2.80
	44	60.2	52	28	37	3	2	3	5	15	3.56
	90	130.1	133	49	74	8	3	15	7	24	3.66
	219	326.1	280	124	239	12	6	34	14	56	2.59
	37	46.0	33	16	27	1	2	4	1	12	1.96
	47	72.0	58	27	39	2	4	9	6	12	3.00
	57	80.0	75	39	59	5	1	8	2	15	2.93
	55	81.1	77	37	64	4	0	15	6	9	4.32
	52	84.0	88	28	60	3	2	7	2	12	2.04
	61	93.1	82	26	64	5	0	8	4	15	2.80

	BA	OBA	SA	AB	H	2B	3B	HR	RBI	BB	SO
Total	.258	.326	.344	314	81	17	2	2	35	34	61
vs. Left	.270	.375	.341	126	34	9	0	0	11	23	17
vs. Right	.250	.289	.346	188	47	8	2	2	24	11	44
Bases Empty	.281	.340	.336	146	41	6	1	0	0	13	28
Leadoff	.303	.333	.379	66	20	1	1	0	0	3	7
Runners On Base	.238	.314	.351	168	40	11	1	2	35	21	33
Scoring Position	.245	.317	.373	102	25	8	1	1	33	13	23
Late and Close	.232	.300	.286	224	52	9	0	1	25	23	47

	BA	OBA	SA	AB	H	2B	3B	HR	RBI	BB	SO
	.243	.316	.335	1698	413	67	7	25	185	173	313
	.250	.344	.347	747	187	37	4	9	69	104	113
	.238	.292	.326	951	226	30	3	16	116	69	200
	.247	.304	.331	882	218	33	4	11	11	65	162
	.235	.281	.329	374	88	14	3	5	5	22	60
	.239	.327	.339	816	195	34	3	14	174	108	151
	.207	.316	.295	498	103	20	0	6	151	85	106
	.233	.312	.313	977	228	32	2	14	99	109	188

JOE HESKETH — bats right — throws left — age 33 — BOS — P

1991	G	IP	H	BB	SO	SB	CS	W	L	SV	ERA	G	IP	H	BB	SO	SB	CS	W	L	SV	ERA
Total	39	153.1	142	53	104	7	8	12	4	0	3.29	256	645.2	606	245	504	53	23	41	29	19	3.46
at Home	19	70.2	60	24	53	2	6	7	1	0	2.04	128	322.0	315	125	270	25	13	21	13	8	3.49
on Road	20	82.2	82	29	51	5	2	5	3	0	4.35	128	323.2	291	120	234	28	10	20	16	11	3.42
on Grass	31	128.0	117	48	87	7	8	9	4	0	3.09	106	277.2	260	107	201	17	9	17	13	6	3.24
on Turf	8	25.1	25	5	17	0	0	3	0	0	4.26	150	368.0	346	138	303	36	14	24	16	13	3.62
Day Games	17	69.1	65	30	45	5	3	4	3	0	3.76	91	246.0	251	86	185	27	10	14	14	4	3.59
Night Games	22	84.0	77	23	59	2	5	8	1	0	2.89	165	399.2	355	159	319	26	13	27	15	15	3.38
April	7	9.1	7	5	9	0	0	0	0	0	3.86	25	57.1	59	25	44	12	2	6	4	1	4.55
May	8	17.1	15	13	9	2	2	2	0	0	4.15	49	121.1	105	51	101	8	5	10	4	2	3.78
June	7	17.2	19	11	16	1	1	0	1	0	4.08	50	116.1	121	51	84	12	4	3	4	6	4.10
July	5	30.2	32	5	22	1	4	2	1	0	2.93	40	105.0	92	33	81	8	7	8	5	3	2.91
August	6	38.0	33	6	20	1	0	5	1	0	3.55	46	126.2	120	41	90	9	4	8	5	3	3.41
Sept–Oct	6	40.1	36	13	28	2	1	3	1	0	2.45	46	119.0	109	44	104	4	1	6	7	4	2.50

	BA	OBA	SA	AB	H	2B	3B	HR	RBI	BB	SO	BA	OBA	SA	AB	H	2B	3B	HR	RBI	BB	SO
Total	.250	.313	.424	568	142	32	5	19	53	53	104	.251	.319	.388	2414	606	133	13	57	263	245	504
vs. Left	.244	.333	.395	86	21	7	0	2	8	12	18	.236	.324	.335	495	117	18	2	9	64	61	121
vs. Right	.251	.309	.429	482	121	25	5	17	45	41	86	.255	.318	.401	1919	489	115	11	48	199	184	383
Bases Empty	.291	.350	.486	333	97	23	3	12	12	30	56	.254	.318	.391	1395	355	73	8	34	34	126	283
Leadoff	.283	.329	.497	145	41	9	2	6	6	10	26	.243	.304	.383	596	145	31	5	14	14	51	110
Runners On Base	.191	.261	.336	235	45	9	2	7	41	23	48	.246	.322	.383	1019	251	60	5	23	229	119	221
Scoring Position	.140	.245	.272	136	19	4	1	4	33	20	34	.225	.323	.353	600	135	29	3	14	198	92	153
Late and Close	.175	.313	.275	40	7	2	1	0	1	8	8	.251	.339	.346	442	111	21	3	5	45	58	102

GREG HIBBARD — bats left — throws left — age 28 — CHA — P

1991	G	IP	H	BB	SO	SB	CS	W	L	SV	ERA	G	IP	H	BB	SO	SB	CS	W	L	SV	ERA
Total	32	194.0	196	57	71	6	7	11	11	0	4.31	88	542.1	540	153	218	26	21	31	27	0	3.58
at Home	15	91.2	92	28	29	4	7	4	5	0	3.44	45	281.2	260	85	107	13	14	16	13	0	3.10
on Road	17	102.1	104	29	42	2	0	7	6	0	5.10	43	260.2	280	68	111	13	7	15	14	0	4.11
on Grass	27	159.2	161	49	58	4	7	9	9	0	4.00	74	463.0	445	130	182	20	19	27	22	0	3.30
on Turf	5	34.1	35	8	13	2	0	2	2	0	5.77	14	79.1	95	23	36	6	2	4	5	0	5.22
Day Games	10	63.2	63	17	23	1	2	3	3	0	4.95	23	145.0	144	35	71	6	6	8	6	0	3.91
Night Games	22	130.1	133	40	48	5	5	8	8	0	4.01	65	397.1	396	118	147	20	15	23	21	0	3.47
April	4	29.0	19	13	14	0	3	2	0	0	1.55	7	47.2	36	17	24	3	4	4	1	0	2.08
May	6	40.2	43	12	12	1	1	1	3	0	4.43	13	87.1	80	24	33	4	3	3	5	0	3.30
June	6	41.2	54	7	14	3	2	3	3	0	5.18	16	102.1	116	25	40	7	2	5	6	0	3.87
July	5	30.2	30	8	11	2	1	1	2	0	5.58	16	93.2	98	23	40	5	2	5	3	0	4.23
August	4	19.2	22	12	7	0	0	1	2	0	6.41	17	101.2	106	34	36	2	6	6	8	0	3.98
Sept–Oct	7	32.1	28	5	13	0	0	3	1	0	3.06	19	109.2	104	30	45	5	4	8	4	0	3.28

	BA	OBA	SA	AB	H	2B	3B	HR	RBI	BB	SO	BA	OBA	SA	AB	H	2B	3B	HR	RBI	BB	SO
Total	.266	.320	.402	737	196	27	2	23	90	57	71	.262	.314	.374	2058	540	87	13	39	204	153	218
vs. Left	.250	.283	.392	120	30	2	0	5	19	4	10	.251	.304	.355	279	70	12	1	5	34	20	31
vs. Right	.269	.326	.404	617	166	25	2	18	71	53	61	.264	.316	.377	1779	470	75	12	34	170	133	187
Bases Empty	.244	.303	.352	454	111	11	1	12	12	37	39	.252	.307	.351	1252	316	46	6	22	22	92	133
Leadoff	.266	.325	.354	192	51	3	1	4	4	17	11	.233	.279	.332	545	127	19	4	9	9	34	49
Runners On Base	.300	.346	.481	283	85	16	1	11	78	20	32	.278	.326	.409	806	224	41	7	17	182	61	85
Scoring Position	.354	.403	.611	144	51	11	1	8	70	13	17	.287	.338	.440	414	119	27	6	8	156	37	43
Late and Close	.234	.290	.328	64	15	3	0	1	4	5	2	.251	.305	.328	183	46	8	0	2	7	12	17

KEN HILL — bats right — throws right — age 27 — SL — P

1991	G	IP	H	BB	SO	SB	CS	W	L	SV	ERA	G	IP	H	BB	SO	SB	CS	W	L	SV	ERA
Total	30	181.1	147	67	121	19	11	11	10	0	3.57	84	470.2	428	205	297	47	25	23	32	0	4.03
at Home	14	87.2	63	34	60	13	6	6	4	0	3.18	37	212.2	189	91	124	23	14	10	11	0	3.94
on Road	16	93.2	84	33	61	6	5	5	6	0	3.94	47	258.0	239	114	173	24	11	13	21	0	4.12
on Grass	10	60.1	50	18	39	5	3	4	3	0	3.28	23	142.0	121	49	92	10	6	8	8	0	3.42
on Turf	20	121.0	97	49	82	14	8	7	7	0	3.72	61	328.2	307	156	205	37	19	15	24	0	4.30
Day Games	10	67.1	47	19	43	7	3	6	2	0	2.14	30	180.1	160	72	123	22	10	9	12	0	3.49
Night Games	20	114.0	100	48	78	12	8	5	8	0	4.42	54	290.1	268	133	174	25	15	14	20	0	4.37
April	4	20.1	23	10	9	3	3	2	1	0	3.54	10	46.0	46	20	20	4	4	3	2	0	3.91
May	6	38.1	28	9	27	3	1	3	1	0	3.29	12	80.2	66	28	60	6	7	4	3	0	2.90
June	5	33.0	30	10	25	5	4	2	3	0	3.27	11	64.2	62	32	42	10	5	4	4	0	3.62
July	6	31.1	26	17	21	2	1	1	2	0	6.32	13	75.2	65	35	45	5	3	4	7	0	4.52
August	2	9.2	10	3	6	0	0	0	2	0	5.59	13	66.2	64	33	45	6	2	4	7	0	4.99
Sept–Oct	7	48.2	30	18	33	6	2	3	1	0	1.85	25	137.0	125	57	85	17	4	4	11	0	4.20

	BA	OBA	SA	AB	H	2B	3B	HR	RBI	BB	SO	BA	OBA	SA	AB	H	2B	3B	HR	RBI	BB	SO
Total	.224	.299	.346	656	147	23	6	15	69	67	121	.245	.325	.359	1750	428	74	17	31	194	205	297
vs. Left	.232	.304	.327	370	86	8	3	7	36	38	63	.256	.340	.357	966	247	34	11	14	101	125	147
vs. Right	.213	.293	.371	286	61	15	3	8	33	29	58	.231	.306	.362	784	181	40	6	17	93	80	150
Bases Empty	.204	.287	.301	402	82	8	2	9	9	43	76	.232	.317	.339	1009	234	37	7	19	19	118	168
Leadoff	.188	.283	.315	165	31	1	1	6	6	19	26	.237	.337	.377	427	101	13	4	13	13	59	60
Runners On Base	.256	.317	.417	254	65	15	4	6	60	24	45	.262	.336	.387	741	194	37	10	12	175	87	129
Scoring Position	.254	.325	.446	130	33	8	1	5	50	16	26	.265	.357	.404	411	109	20	5	9	155	66	81
Late and Close	.222	.310	.397	63	14	1	2	2	6	7	12	.342	.423	.500	120	41	4	3	3	17	14	19

SHAWN HILLEGAS — bats right — throws right — age 28 — CLE — P

1991	G	IP	H	BB	SO	SB	CS	W	L	SV	ERA
Total	51	83.0	67	46	66	6	2	3	4	7	4.34
at Home	30	55.2	38	30	47	4	1	3	2	5	3.07
on Road	21	27.1	29	16	19	2	1	0	2	2	6.91
on Grass	42	73.0	57	40	58	6	1	3	4	6	3.95
on Turf	9	10.0	10	6	8	0	1	0	0	1	7.20
Day Games	17	28.0	28	15	22	2	2	0	1	0	7.07
Night Games	34	55.0	39	31	44	4	0	3	3	7	2.95
April	3	7.2	4	2	7	0	0	0	0	0	1.17
May	9	13.1	10	6	14	1	0	0	0	3	2.03
June	7	12.2	5	11	13	1	0	2	1	1	2.13
July	13	14.0	14	12	9	2	1	0	1	1	9.00
August	11	17.0	17	8	14	0	1	1	1	1	4.76
Sept–Oct	8	18.1	17	7	9	2	0	0	1	1	4.91

5-YEAR TOTALS (1987–1991)

	G	IP	H	BB	SO	SB	CS	W	L	SV	ERA
	137	368.2	339	168	254	26	16	20	24	10	4.08
	73	198.2	177	87	138	16	8	12	12	6	3.85
	64	170.0	162	81	116	10	8	8	12	4	4.34
	113	301.1	272	133	205	23	12	16	19	8	3.85
	24	67.1	67	35	49	3	4	4	5	2	5.08
	43	111.1	112	49	76	7	6	6	7	0	5.09
	94	257.1	227	119	178	19	10	14	17	10	3.64
	8	32.2	30	16	19	2	2	0	3	0	4.13
	17	45.0	53	22	33	4	1	3	3	4	5.80
	19	45.1	34	21	31	1	1	4	2	2	2.38
	32	66.2	61	28	39	5	2	4	6	2	4.59
	29	66.1	68	35	56	5	5	3	4	1	4.75
	32	112.2	93	46	76	9	3	6	6	1	3.36

	BA	OBA	SA	AB	H	2B	3B	HR	RBI	BB	SO
Total	.223	.324	.340	300	67	12	1	7	43	46	66
vs. Left	.230	.321	.295	139	32	6	0	1	14	20	32
vs. Right	.217	.326	.379	161	35	6	1	6	29	26	34
Bases Empty	.200	.302	.280	150	30	4	1	2	2	22	32
Leadoff	.197	.254	.288	66	13	1	1	1	1	5	17
Runners On Base	.247	.344	.400	150	37	8	0	5	41	24	34
Scoring Position	.209	.324	.407	86	18	5	0	4	38	17	19
Late and Close	.216	.350	.344	125	27	4	0	4	19	28	30

	BA	OBA	SA	AB	H	2B	3B	HR	RBI	BB	SO
	.245	.327	.369	1386	339	53	10	33	169	168	254
	.267	.363	.379	663	177	24	4	14	83	101	112
	.224	.292	.360	723	162	29	6	19	86	67	142
	.232	.315	.356	775	180	26	8	18	18	90	138
	.230	.304	.382	330	76	12	4	10	10	34	59
	.260	.342	.385	611	159	27	2	15	151	78	116
	.253	.344	.395	352	89	18	1	10	136	54	70
	.254	.358	.362	287	73	11	1	6	34	48	50

BRIAN HOLMAN — bats right — throws right — age 27 — SEA — P

1991	G	IP	H	BB	SO	SB	CS	W	L	SV	ERA
Total	30	195.1	199	77	108	4	5	13	14	0	3.69
at Home	17	118.2	106	32	74	3	3	9	7	0	2.65
on Road	13	76.2	93	45	34	1	2	4	7	0	5.28
on Grass	10	57.0	72	35	23	1	1	3	5	0	5.05
on Turf	20	138.1	127	42	85	3	4	10	9	0	3.12
Day Games	12	79.2	83	32	44	3	4	3	8	0	3.50
Night Games	18	115.2	116	45	64	1	1	10	6	0	3.81
April	4	28.2	27	13	13	1	1	2	2	0	2.83
May	6	39.2	36	17	23	1	1	3	3	0	3.40
June	5	31.0	32	16	19	0	1	2	3	0	5.81
July	5	33.1	36	9	13	0	0	2	2	0	2.16
August	6	34.2	40	16	22	0	1	2	3	0	4.67
Sept–Oct	4	28.0	28	6	18	2	1	2	1	0	3.21

4-YEAR TOTALS (1988–1991)

	G	IP	H	BB	SO	SB	CS	W	L	SV	ERA
	109	676.2	682	254	392	37	21	37	45	0	3.71
	56	372.2	378	130	225	19	15	20	24	0	3.45
	53	304.0	304	124	167	18	6	17	21	0	4.03
	34	196.1	211	86	109	7	4	12	14	0	4.49
	75	480.1	471	168	283	30	17	25	31	0	3.39
	33	206.0	205	75	117	9	8	11	17	0	3.54
	76	470.2	477	179	275	28	13	26	28	0	3.79
	15	73.2	66	28	44	4	2	6	4	0	3.18
	17	100.1	105	47	62	8	3	6	7	0	4.49
	17	110.2	118	47	61	4	6	7	8	0	4.39
	22	142.0	131	46	75	6	2	6	6	0	2.73
	23	147.1	153	55	102	9	4	5	14	0	4.21
	15	102.2	109	31	48	6	4	7	6	0	3.24

	BA	OBA	SA	AB	H	2B	3B	HR	RBI	BB	SO
Total	.268	.343	.392	743	199	36	4	16	77	77	108
vs. Left	.285	.364	.396	389	111	21	2	6	42	46	48
vs. Right	.249	.321	.387	354	88	15	2	10	35	31	60
Bases Empty	.287	.364	.414	401	115	20	2	9	9	44	53
Leadoff	.297	.379	.412	182	54	6	0	5	5	21	20
Runners On Base	.246	.319	.365	342	84	16	2	7	68	33	55
Scoring Position	.227	.320	.326	172	39	6	1	3	57	23	31
Late and Close	.189	.259	.264	53	10	1	0	1	2	3	8

	BA	OBA	SA	AB	H	2B	3B	HR	RBI	BB	SO
	.264	.333	.375	2588	682	114	17	47	262	254	392
	.277	.355	.397	1327	368	66	9	25	133	155	164
	.249	.309	.352	1261	314	48	8	22	129	99	228
	.260	.324	.369	1479	385	56	9	29	29	131	226
	.285	.352	.387	646	184	20	2	14	14	63	84
	.268	.344	.383	1109	297	58	8	18	233	123	166
	.238	.331	.337	605	144	29	5	7	199	84	104
	.295	.354	.382	207	61	6	0	4	18	15	27

CHARLIE HOUGH — bats right — throws right — age 44 — CHA — P

1991	G	IP	H	BB	SO	SB	CS	W	L	SV	ERA
Total	31	199.1	167	94	107	10	8	9	10	0	4.02
at Home	15	106.2	89	41	59	5	6	5	5	0	3.38
on Road	16	92.2	78	53	48	5	2	4	5	0	4.76
on Grass	24	156.0	127	81	88	7	8	7	7	0	3.81
on Turf	7	43.1	40	13	19	3	0	2	3	0	4.78
Day Games	10	69.2	47	25	42	3	2	4	3	0	2.45
Night Games	21	129.2	120	69	65	7	6	5	7	0	4.86
April	2	5.2	5	8	7	0	1	0	1	0	7.94
May	5	33.2	31	12	22	1	1	1	1	0	4.01
June	6	46.0	28	24	22	0	1	4	3	0	3.13
July	6	42.2	33	17	17	3	2	1	3	0	3.16
August	6	30.2	39	18	15	1	2	1	0	0	7.04
Sept–Oct	6	40.2	31	15	24	5	1	2	2	0	3.10

8-YEAR TOTALS (1984–1991)

	G	IP	H	BB	SO	SB	CS	W	L	SV	ERA
	271	1889.1	1620	825	1166	194	68	111	104	0	3.77
	130	917.0	816	379	589	99	37	59	51	0	3.86
	141	972.1	804	446	577	95	31	52	53	0	3.68
	221	1537.2	1304	667	973	155	58	96	81	0	3.72
	50	351.2	316	158	193	39	10	15	23	0	3.99
	62	435.0	355	201	261	38	18	21	22	0	3.46
	209	1454.1	1265	624	905	156	50	90	82	0	3.86
	33	213.0	178	108	140	19	10	9	11	0	3.97
	45	290.1	287	122	171	32	8	20	18	0	4.56
	50	390.0	277	162	231	25	15	24	16	0	2.79
	44	309.1	267	144	209	31	9	14	23	0	4.07
	49	337.0	304	163	210	38	14	24	17	0	4.17
	50	349.2	307	126	205	49	12	20	19	0	3.42

	BA	OBA	SA	AB	H	2B	3B	HR	RBI	BB	SO
Total	.229	.320	.381	729	167	28	10	21	90	94	107
vs. Left	.233	.323	.367	343	80	10	6	8	43	44	47
vs. Right	.225	.317	.394	386	87	18	4	13	47	50	60
Bases Empty	.227	.329	.381	428	97	19	4	13	13	58	67
Leadoff	.232	.314	.389	185	43	8	3	5	5	18	23
Runners On Base	.233	.308	.382	301	70	9	6	8	77	36	40
Scoring Position	.201	.289	.336	149	30	4	2	4	62	23	19
Late and Close	.264	.368	.431	72	19	3	0	3	9	12	11

	BA	OBA	SA	AB	H	2B	3B	HR	RBI	BB	SO
	.231	.317	.373	7008	1620	277	40	212	797	825	1166
	.236	.322	.364	3469	819	122	25	90	395	417	552
	.226	.312	.382	3539	801	155	15	122	402	408	614
	.228	.306	.380	4298	982	180	23	142	142	441	707
	.231	.295	.382	1807	417	75	11	59	59	149	269
	.235	.332	.361	2710	638	97	17	70	655	384	459
	.229	.340	.347	1578	362	50	9	39	573	272	314
	.226	.308	.343	831	188	28	3	21	73	93	151

JAY HOWELL — bats right — throws right — age 37 — LA — P

8-YEAR TOTALS (1984–1991)

1991	G	IP	H	BB	SO	SB	CS	W	L	SV	ERA	G	IP	H	BB	SO	SB	CS	W	L	SV	ERA
Total	44	51.0	39	11	40	3	1	6	5	16	3.18	393	562.0	487	183	479	41	14	45	38	148	2.80
at Home	26	31.2	26	6	26	2	1	6	2	8	2.84	198	299.1	251	82	262	23	7	32	17	74	2.44
on Road	18	19.1	13	5	14	1	0	0	3	8	3.72	195	262.2	236	101	217	18	7	13	21	74	3.22
on Grass	35	43.1	32	7	37	2	1	6	2	13	2.28	320	458.1	394	150	395	30	11	39	29	123	2.79
on Turf	9	7.2	7	4	3	1	0	0	3	3	8.22	73	103.2	93	33	84	11	3	6	9	25	2.86
Day Games	12	14.0	16	1	15	0	0	0	1	5	4.50	132	190.2	155	59	161	13	6	13	10	53	2.17
Night Games	32	37.0	23	10	25	2	1	6	4	11	2.68	261	371.1	332	124	318	28	8	32	28	95	3.13
April	5	7.2	9	0	10	0	0	0	0	1	2.35	57	80.2	80	22	69	3	5	6	8	17	3.35
May	12	16.0	11	1	13	1	1	0	1	8	2.25	68	95.1	93	46	72	13	2	5	9	27	3.12
June	9	10.0	7	2	6	2	0	0	2	1	3.60	70	109.0	87	31	105	8	2	10	6	28	1.90
July	2	2.0	0	2	0	0	0	2	0	0	0.00	58	76.2	66	29	67	4	1	6	4	23	2.47
August	13	12.1	9	4	10	0	0	1	2	4	3.65	80	111.0	79	24	86	5	1	9	5	31	2.27
Sept–Oct	3	3.0	3	2	1	0	0	1	1	1	9.00	60	89.1	82	31	80	8	3	9	6	22	4.03

	BA	OBA	SA	AB	H	2B	3B	HR	RBI	BB	SO	BA	OBA	SA	AB	H	2B	3B	HR	RBI	BB	SO
Total	.213	.259	.328	183	39	8	2	3	19	11	40	.234	.297	.326	2083	487	79	10	31	223	183	479
vs. Left	.179	.231	.295	95	17	6	1	1	11	6	21	.231	.301	.316	1095	253	47	5	12	111	107	245
vs. Right	.250	.290	.364	88	22	2	1	2	8	5	19	.237	.292	.337	988	234	32	5	19	112	76	234
Bases Empty	.211	.246	.339	109	23	6	1	2	2	4	23	.228	.284	.329	1124	256	48	3	20	20	81	257
Leadoff	.311	.340	.533	45	14	2	1	2	2	2	9	.229	.277	.346	468	107	17	1	12	12	29	100
Runners On Base	.216	.277	.311	74	16	2	1	1	17	7	17	.241	.311	.322	959	231	31	7	11	203	102	222
Scoring Position	.204	.268	.327	49	10	1	1	1	16	5	12	.255	.334	.332	581	148	13	7	6	183	75	138
Late and Close	.182	.240	.263	137	25	3	1	2	14	10	28	.231	.296	.315	1531	354	55	8	19	174	137	343

BRUCE HURST — bats left — throws left — age 34 — SD — P

8-YEAR TOTALS (1984–1991)

1991	G	IP	H	BB	SO	SB	CS	W	L	SV	ERA	G	IP	H	BB	SO	SB	CS	W	L	SV	ERA
Total	31	221.2	201	59	141	11	6	15	8	0	3.29	256	1767.0	1708	537	1330	102	71	110	80	0	3.59
at Home	18	126.2	103	36	92	5	2	7	5	0	3.34	137	970.2	907	289	777	43	37	68	37	0	3.47
on Road	13	95.0	98	23	49	6	4	8	3	0	3.22	119	796.1	801	248	553	59	34	42	43	0	3.74
on Grass	24	170.1	154	47	111	7	2	10	6	0	3.54	210	1471.0	1411	450	1122	70	58	97	62	0	3.58
on Turf	7	51.1	47	12	30	4	4	5	2	0	2.45	46	296.0	297	87	208	32	13	13	18	0	3.65
Day Games	5	39.0	38	10	14	3	2	2	1	0	3.69	81	559.1	553	167	400	33	16	34	23	0	3.60
Night Games	26	182.2	163	49	127	8	4	13	7	0	3.20	175	1207.2	1155	370	930	69	55	76	57	0	3.58
April	4	29.0	21	8	26	0	0	2	0	0	2.17	38	262.1	236	80	205	13	13	16	12	0	3.53
May	6	43.1	47	14	27	2	3	3	2	0	3.95	45	316.2	303	92	254	23	14	20	15	0	3.35
June	6	47.0	36	12	20	0	2	4	2	0	2.49	41	273.2	289	80	182	15	9	17	12	0	3.91
July	5	35.0	30	9	24	1	0	3	1	0	3.86	39	265.0	259	77	199	16	7	18	11	0	4.01
August	6	46.2	43	11	32	3	1	3	1	0	3.28	46	334.2	317	108	246	18	10	22	12	0	3.50
Sept–Oct	4	20.2	24	5	12	5	0	0	2	0	4.35	47	314.2	304	100	244	17	18	17	18	0	3.35

	BA	OBA	SA	AB	H	2B	3B	HR	RBI	BB	SO	BA	OBA	SA	AB	H	2B	3B	HR	RBI	BB	SO
Total	.241	.292	.340	835	201	30	1	17	75	59	141	.254	.310	.390	6721	1708	322	21	184	667	537	1330
vs. Left	.176	.247	.221	136	24	3	0	1	10	13	31	.253	.316	.380	1109	281	58	2	26	123	99	234
vs. Right	.253	.301	.363	699	177	27	1	16	65	46	110	.254	.309	.393	5612	1427	264	19	158	544	438	1096
Bases Empty	.224	.281	.334	509	114	17	0	13	13	39	95	.251	.311	.391	4005	1006	167	14	122	122	333	809
Leadoff	.177	.242	.301	209	37	11	0	5	5	18	38	.245	.310	.393	1679	412	74	6	54	54	151	316
Runners On Base	.267	.310	.350	326	87	13	1	4	62	20	46	.258	.309	.389	2716	702	155	7	62	545	204	521
Scoring Position	.262	.308	.375	168	44	7	0	4	58	12	26	.253	.311	.384	1385	350	78	1	34	460	126	295
Late and Close	.211	.260	.267	90	19	3	1	0	4	5	14	.263	.315	.401	704	185	33	5	18	66	53	109

MIKE JACKSON — bats right — throws right — age 28 — SEA — P

6-YEAR TOTALS (1986–1991)

1991	G	IP	H	BB	SO	SB	CS	W	L	SV	ERA	G	IP	H	BB	SO	SB	CS	W	L	SV	ERA
Total	72	88.2	64	34	74	6	0	7	7	14	3.25	326	487.1	383	235	409	63	13	25	35	29	3.56
at Home	34	47.2	25	9	39	3	0	3	2	6	2.64	161	249.2	176	110	211	35	3	15	14	11	3.28
on Road	38	41.0	39	25	35	3	0	4	5	8	3.95	165	237.2	207	125	198	28	10	10	21	18	3.86
on Grass	28	31.0	23	19	31	2	0	3	2	6	3.77	118	166.2	146	93	147	21	6	8	11	14	3.89
on Turf	44	57.2	41	15	43	4	0	4	5	8	2.97	208	320.2	237	142	262	42	7	17	24	15	3.40
Day Games	17	16.2	14	12	12	3	0	2	1	0	6.48	91	126.2	96	76	97	30	2	6	10	5	4.05
Night Games	55	72.0	50	22	62	3	0	5	6	14	2.50	235	360.2	287	159	312	33	11	19	25	24	3.39
April	8	11.2	8	4	11	1	0	1	2	1	3.86	46	73.0	59	29	56	7	2	2	5	3	3.21
May	12	19.0	9	2	18	1	0	1	0	0	0.95	47	78.2	57	38	63	15	1	6	4	5	3.55
June	12	12.2	6	3	12	0	0	0	0	9	4.26	51	78.0	71	43	78	10	5	6	12		3.75
July	12	13.0	17	9	8	2	0	0	2	0	4.85	59	78.1	73	43	70	14	1	6	7	12	4.37
August	15	17.1	10	5	13	1	0	2	0	1	0.00	63	83.1	53	41	63	6	1	4	5	2	2.48
Sept–Oct	13	15.0	14	11	16	1	0	1	3	0	7.20	60	78.0	70	41	72	11	3	1	8	3	4.04

	BA	OBA	SA	AB	H	2B	3B	HR	RBI	BB	SO	BA	OBA	SA	AB	H	2B	3B	HR	RBI	BB	SO
Total	.201	.290	.298	319	64	10	3	5	33	34	74	.217	.313	.344	1765	383	69	4	49	253	235	409
vs. Left	.256	.360	.393	117	30	6	2	2	12	17	23	.251	.363	.400	753	189	37	3	23	120	130	116
vs. Right	.168	.247	.243	202	34	4	1	3	21	17	51	.192	.273	.302	1012	194	32	1	26	133	105	293
Bases Empty	.183	.239	.280	175	32	3	1	4	4	12	36	.213	.298	.338	917	195	32	1	27	27	100	205
Leadoff	.186	.260	.229	70	13	1	1	0	0	7	15	.235	.307	.368	383	90	12	1	12	12	37	75
Runners On Base	.222	.345	.319	144	32	7	2	1	29	22	38	.222	.328	.350	848	188	37	3	22	226	135	204
Scoring Position	.218	.376	.299	87	19	4	0	1	27	18	23	.225	.355	.350	546	123	27	1	13	204	114	135
Late and Close	.221	.296	.346	208	46	8	3	4	26	20	50	.230	.332	.343	778	179	34	3	16	121	113	181

RANDY JOHNSON — bats right — throws left — age 29 — SEA — P

1991	G	IP	H	BB	SO	SB	CS	W	L	SV	ERA
Total	33	201.1	151	152	228	18	9	13	10	0	3.98
at Home	17	105.2	85	72	114	8	5	6	5	0	3.92
on Road	16	95.2	66	80	114	10	4	7	5	0	4.05
on Grass	12	69.0	45	61	87	6	4	7	3	0	4.43
on Turf	21	132.1	106	91	141	12	5	6	7	0	3.74
Day Games	9	44.1	42	38	53	4	3	3	3	0	7.51
Night Games	24	157.0	109	114	175	14	6	10	7	0	2.98
April	4	27.1	24	22	22	3	1	2	2	0	4.94
May	6	34.1	28	32	44	5	1	1	3	0	4.46
June	5	29.1	17	29	36	2	1	3	1	0	3.38
July	6	39.1	25	25	46	3	2	3	1	0	2.97
August	5	33.0	26	12	40	2	2	3	2	0	3.00
Sept–Oct	7	38.0	31	32	40	3	2	1	1	0	5.21

3-YEAR TOTALS (1989–1991)

	G	IP	H	BB	SO	SB	CS	W	L	SV	ERA
	95	581.2	472	368	552	78	22	34	34	0	4.08
	44	278.0	210	174	261	30	12	16	15	0	3.76
	51	303.2	262	194	291	48	10	18	19	0	4.39
	37	233.2	187	146	225	34	9	17	11	0	4.04
	58	348.0	285	222	327	44	13	17	23	0	4.11
	28	156.1	135	110	152	32	7	11	9	0	5.24
	67	425.1	337	258	400	46	15	23	25	0	3.66
	13	70.1	63	49	56	8	4	4	6	0	5.12
	15	86.0	71	67	93	17	4	3	4	0	4.92
	15	94.0	64	67	89	7	2	10	3	0	3.06
	17	117.2	88	67	111	18	3	6	7	0	3.06
	17	113.0	89	55	104	17	5	8	6	0	3.74
	18	100.2	97	63	99	11	4	3	8	0	5.19

	BA	OBA	SA	AB	H	2B	3B	HR	RBI	BB	SO
Total	.213	.358	.325	708	151	32	1	15	81	152	228
vs. Left	.212	.337	.306	85	18	2	0	2	14	15	25
vs. Right	.213	.361	.327	623	133	30	1	13	67	137	203
Bases Empty	.189	.340	.296	392	74	16	1	8	8	81	132
Leadoff	.203	.357	.314	172	35	7	0	4	4	37	53
Runners On Base	.244	.379	.361	316	77	16	0	7	73	71	96
Scoring Position	.237	.370	.353	190	45	10	0	4	65	43	62
Late and Close	.246	.352	.311	61	15	4	0	0	3	9	20

	BA	OBA	SA	AB	H	2B	3B	HR	RBI	BB	SO
	.224	.341	.349	2107	472	86	8	54	246	368	552
	.201	.288	.291	254	51	11	0	4	32	30	67
	.227	.348	.357	1853	421	75	8	50	214	338	485
	.215	.338	.349	1191	256	44	7	34	34	211	302
	.237	.371	.360	511	121	21	3	12	12	104	129
	.236	.344	.349	916	216	42	1	20	212	157	250
	.234	.339	.347	551	129	27	1	11	188	96	159
	.206	.306	.271	170	35	5	0	2	7	24	47

JEFF JOHNSON — bats right — throws left — age 26 — NYA — P

1991	G	IP	H	BB	SO	SB	CS	W	L	SV	ERA
Total	23	127.0	156	33	62	18	4	6	11	0	5.95
at Home	11	64.2	83	9	26	5	1	2	6	0	5.57
on Road	12	62.1	73	24	36	13	3	4	5	0	6.35
on Grass	19	105.0	131	27	56	16	3	4	9	0	5.83
on Turf	4	22.0	25	6	6	2	1	2	2	0	6.55
Day Games	7	35.0	48	10	15	7	2	1	4	0	7.97
Night Games	16	92.0	108	23	47	11	2	5	7	0	5.18
April	0	0.0	0	0	0	0	0	0	0	0	0.00
May	0	0.0	0	0	0	0	0	0	0	0	0.00
June	5	29.2	29	7	11	4	0	1	3	0	4.25
July	5	32.1	33	5	13	4	3	3	0	0	2.78
August	6	25.2	43	7	16	7	0	1	5	0	10.87
Sept–Oct	7	39.1	51	14	22	3	1	1	3	0	6.64

1-YEAR TOTALS (1991)

	G	IP	H	BB	SO	SB	CS	W	L	SV	ERA
	23	127.0	156	33	62	18	4	6	11	0	5.95
	11	64.2	83	9	26	5	1	2	6	0	5.57
	12	62.1	73	24	36	13	3	4	5	0	6.35
	19	105.0	131	27	56	16	3	4	9	0	5.83
	4	22.0	25	6	6	2	1	2	2	0	6.55
	7	35.0	48	10	15	7	2	1	4	0	7.97
	16	92.0	108	23	47	11	2	5	7	0	5.18
	0	0.0	0	0	0	0	0	0	0	0	0.00
	0	0.0	0	0	0	0	0	0	0	0	0.00
	5	29.2	29	7	11	4	0	1	3	0	4.25
	5	32.1	33	5	13	4	3	3	0	0	2.78
	6	25.2	43	7	16	7	0	1	5	0	10.87
	7	39.1	51	14	22	3	1	1	3	0	6.64

	BA	OBA	SA	AB	H	2B	3B	HR	RBI	BB	SO
Total	.305	.351	.453	512	156	21	5	15	77	33	62
vs. Left	.231	.344	.308	52	12	1	0	1	7	7	7
vs. Right	.313	.352	.470	460	144	20	5	14	70	26	55
Bases Empty	.282	.318	.413	298	84	8	2	9	9	12	34
Leadoff	.281	.319	.453	128	36	4	0	6	6	7	15
Runners On Base	.336	.394	.509	214	72	13	3	6	68	21	28
Scoring Position	.328	.392	.469	128	42	5	2	3	58	15	16
Late and Close	.250	.308	.500	24	6	0	0	3	3	2	1

	BA	OBA	SA	AB	H	2B	3B	HR	RBI	BB	SO
	.305	.351	.453	512	156	21	5	15	77	33	62
	.231	.344	.308	52	12	1	0	1	7	7	7
	.313	.352	.470	460	144	20	5	14	70	26	55
	.282	.318	.413	298	84	8	2	9	9	12	34
	.281	.319	.453	128	36	4	0	6	6	7	15
	.336	.394	.509	214	72	13	3	6	68	21	28
	.328	.392	.469	128	42	5	2	3	58	15	16
	.250	.308	.500	24	6	0	0	3	3	2	1

BARRY JONES — bats right — throws right — age 29 — MON — P

1991	G	IP	H	BB	SO	SB	CS	W	L	SV	ERA
Total	77	88.2	76	33	46	8	6	4	9	13	3.35
at Home	35	40.0	30	15	23	8	4	1	2	6	2.70
on Road	42	48.2	46	18	23	0	2	3	7	7	3.88
on Grass	20	21.2	19	12	8	0	0	1	4	3	4.57
on Turf	57	67.0	57	21	38	8	6	3	5	10	2.96
Day Games	26	26.0	20	8	11	2	3	0	1	7	2.77
Night Games	51	62.2	56	25	35	6	3	4	8	6	3.59
April	11	13.0	12	8	5	0	0	0	0	1	2.77
May	14	20.2	9	7	9	3	1	2	2	1	2.61
June	12	14.0	19	2	9	4	0	1	3	0	6.43
July	11	10.2	8	6	5	1	2	0	2	2	4.22
August	15	16.1	10	5	10	0	2	0	1	3	0.00
Sept–Oct	14	14.0	18	5	8	0	1	1	1	3	5.14

6-YEAR TOTALS (1986–1991)

	G	IP	H	BB	SO	SB	CS	W	L	SV	ERA
	281	356.0	316	155	213	30	14	26	26	22	3.19
	143	185.1	172	77	105	19	10	15	9	8	3.25
	138	170.2	144	78	108	11	4	11	17	14	3.11
	136	173.0	133	80	109	13	2	15	12	9	2.65
	145	183.0	183	75	104	17	12	11	14	13	3.69
	80	92.1	86	37	57	7	3	5	6	9	3.02
	201	263.2	230	118	156	23	11	21	20	13	3.24
	40	54.0	48	25	31	3	0	4	3	2	3.17
	39	53.1	43	14	27	5	3	7	3	1	2.19
	40	47.2	57	20	34	5	1	6	5	5	5.29
	52	64.0	53	32	37	3	4	1	3	5	3.94
	51	68.0	62	30	38	7	3	1	5	5	2.25
	59	69.0	53	34	46	7	3	7	7	4	2.74

	BA	OBA	SA	AB	H	2B	3B	HR	RBI	BB	SO
Total	.246	.318	.369	309	76	10	2	8	44	33	46
vs. Left	.259	.348	.374	139	36	6	2	2	15	20	15
vs. Right	.235	.292	.365	170	40	4	0	6	29	13	31
Bases Empty	.206	.284	.273	165	34	5	0	2	2	18	26
Leadoff	.254	.333	.388	67	17	3	0	2	2	8	10
Runners On Base	.292	.356	.479	144	42	5	2	6	42	15	20
Scoring Position	.315	.366	.494	89	28	2	1	4	37	9	13
Late and Close	.286	.357	.427	185	53	7	2	5	34	21	27

	BA	OBA	SA	AB	H	2B	3B	HR	RBI	BB	SO
	.246	.325	.355	1286	316	43	8	27	178	155	213
	.268	.354	.382	552	148	20	5	11	81	78	66
	.229	.302	.334	734	168	23	3	16	97	77	147
	.227	.298	.321	670	152	20	2	13	13	67	123
	.257	.310	.413	288	74	13	1	10	10	22	50
	.266	.352	.391	616	164	23	6	14	165	88	90
	.263	.355	.398	407	107	17	4	10	154	68	66
	.261	.339	.359	735	192	24	6	12	106	90	120

DOUG JONES — bats right — throws right — age 35 — CLE — P

6-YEAR TOTALS (1986–1991)

1991	G	IP	H	BB	SO	SB	CS	W	L	SV	ERA		G	IP	H	BB	SO	SB	CS	W	L	SV	ERA
Total	36	63.1	87	17	48	4	0	4	8	7	5.54		272	421.0	417	98	339	10	3	26	32	128	3.04
at Home	13	26.2	38	5	24	1	0	1	4	1	6.41		145	217.1	226	49	168	2	2	17	17	59	3.60
on Road	23	36.2	49	12	24	3	0	3	4	6	4.91		127	203.2	191	49	171	8	1	9	15	69	2.43
on Grass	31	58.1	78	14	43	4	0	4	7	6	4.94		231	357.2	362	79	286	8	3	24	27	106	3.17
on Turf	5	5.0	9	3	5	0	0	0	1	1	12.60		41	63.1	55	19	53	2	0	2	5	22	2.27
Day Games	11	10.0	16	5	7	0	0	1	0	5	3.60		88	126.0	120	31	97	1	1	4	6	46	2.64
Night Games	25	53.1	71	12	41	4	0	3	8	2	5.91		184	295.0	297	67	242	9	2	22	26	82	3.20
April	9	9.0	12	1	8	1	0	0	2	5	5.00		37	48.1	51	16	45	1	0	1	4	20	2.98
May	9	7.2	16	3	7	0	0	1	2	0	11.74		41	55.2	51	11	39	0	0	3	5	24	3.56
June	9	8.2	11	3	5	0	0	0	2	1	6.23		37	47.1	46	8	36	0	0	4	4	20	3.23
July	4	6.0	6	4	4	0	0	0	1	0	7.50		49	75.2	62	19	60	2	0	5	6	18	2.62
August	0	0.0	0	0	0	0	0	0	0	0	0.00		45	71.2	64	17	53	1	1	3	5	23	3.01
Sept–Oct	5	32.0	42	6	24	3	0	3	1	1	3.66		63	122.1	143	27	106	6	1	10	8	23	3.02

	BA	OBA	SA	AB	H	2B	3B	HR	RBI	BB	SO		BA	OBA	SA	AB	H	2B	3B	HR	RBI	BB	SO
Total	.320	.357	.496	272	87	23	2	7	45	17	48		.257	.301	.349	1625	417	73	7	21	208	98	339
vs. Left	.344	.383	.534	131	45	11	1	4	25	9	20		.247	.291	.347	850	210	38	4	13	108	55	149
vs. Right	.298	.333	.461	141	42	12	1	3	20	8	28		.267	.312	.351	775	207	35	3	8	100	43	190
Bases Empty	.324	.357	.493	136	44	11	0	4	4	7	21		.253	.290	.338	782	198	37	1	9	9	36	164
Leadoff	.197	.222	.344	61	12	3	0	2	2	2	12		.262	.297	.354	336	88	19	0	4	4	16	68
Runners On Base	.316	.358	.500	136	43	12	2	3	41	10	27		.260	.310	.359	843	219	36	6	12	199	62	175
Scoring Position	.325	.364	.550	80	26	8	2	2	38	6	13		.258	.311	.379	515	133	24	4	10	189	43	111
Late and Close	.407	.433	.725	91	37	13	2	4	26	5	17		.263	.308	.353	1022	269	49	5	11	132	62	213

JIMMY KEY — bats right — throws left — age 31 — TOR — P

8-YEAR TOTALS (1984–1991)

1991	G	IP	H	BB	SO	SB	CS	W	L	SV	ERA		G	IP	H	BB	SO	SB	CS	W	L	SV	ERA
Total	33	209.1	207	44	125	6	2	16	12	0	3.05		284	1479.0	1419	345	827	51	35	103	68	10	3.41
at Home	18	110.1	120	27	66	2	1	7	8	0	3.43		149	799.2	778	183	444	28	21	53	40	3	3.55
on Road	15	99.0	87	17	59	4	1	9	4	0	2.64		135	679.1	641	162	383	23	14	50	28	7	3.25
on Grass	14	94.0	82	16	59	4	0	9	4	0	2.59		110	572.2	534	145	326	20	14	41	26	5	3.19
on Turf	19	115.1	125	28	66	2	2	7	8	0	3.43		174	906.1	885	200	501	31	21	62	42	5	3.55
Day Games	10	65.1	59	13	38	1	1	5	3	0	2.07		97	524.2	508	123	299	22	13	36	30	1	3.53
Night Games	23	144.0	148	31	87	5	1	11	9	0	3.50		187	954.1	911	222	528	29	22	67	38	9	3.34
April	4	29.0	18	8	16	0	0	4	0	0	1.86		37	185.2	172	46	105	4	5	16	9	1	3.83
May	6	37.2	38	11	32	3	0	3	2	0	2.87		49	224.2	214	58	130	10	5	17	9	3	3.93
June	6	39.0	43	3	20	0	0	3	1	0	2.08		43	229.2	211	48	130	8	3	13	12	0	2.67
July	5	31.1	37	4	17	2	1	1	3	0	4.88		50	283.1	285	62	146	4	8	16	15	0	3.62
August	6	35.2	37	9	20	1	0	3	3	0	3.03		48	243.0	243	55	129	14	8	20	13	3	3.41
Sept–Oct	6	36.2	34	9	20	1	0	2	3	0	3.68		57	313.1	294	76	187	11	6	21	10	3	3.13

	BA	OBA	SA	AB	H	2B	3B	HR	RBI	BB	SO		BA	OBA	SA	AB	H	2B	3B	HR	RBI	BB	SO
Total	.254	.293	.347	815	207	36	2	12	66	44	125		.253	.296	.388	5619	1419	277	31	141	557	345	827
vs. Left	.286	.325	.357	112	32	2	0	2	9	6	19		.237	.283	.329	1023	242	35	6	16	94	62	206
vs. Right	.249	.288	.346	703	175	34	2	10	57	38	106		.256	.299	.401	4596	1177	242	25	125	463	283	621
Bases Empty	.231	.269	.300	484	112	18	0	5	5	22	78		.245	.286	.371	3481	853	163	18	80	80	187	536
Leadoff	.242	.276	.304	207	50	10	0	1	1	9	27		.250	.283	.388	1460	365	72	9	37	37	62	207
Runners On Base	.287	.327	.417	331	95	18	2	7	61	22	47		.265	.312	.416	2138	566	114	13	61	477	158	291
Scoring Position	.207	.267	.316	174	36	6	2	3	49	16	26		.252	.314	.389	1117	281	57	9	26	381	113	156
Late and Close	.284	.324	.388	67	19	1	0	2	7	4	8		.264	.320	.383	598	158	17	3	16	74	49	85

DARRYL KILE — bats right — throws right — age 24 — HOU — P

1-YEAR TOTALS (1991)

1991	G	IP	H	BB	SO	SB	CS	W	L	SV	ERA		G	IP	H	BB	SO	SB	CS	W	L	SV	ERA
Total	37	153.2	144	84	100	12	3	7	11	0	3.69		37	153.2	144	84	100	12	3	7	11	0	3.69
at Home	18	77.2	68	45	49	6	1	4	5	0	3.36		18	77.2	68	45	49	6	1	4	5	0	3.36
on Road	19	76.0	76	39	51	6	2	3	6	0	4.03		19	76.0	76	39	51	6	2	3	6	0	4.03
on Grass	11	44.2	43	22	27	2	2	1	3	0	4.23		11	44.2	43	22	27	2	2	1	3	0	4.23
on Turf	26	109.0	101	62	73	10	1	6	8	0	3.47		26	109.0	101	62	73	10	1	6	8	0	3.47
Day Games	11	45.2	44	25	29	3	1	1	6	0	4.34		11	45.2	44	25	29	3	1	1	6	0	4.34
Night Games	26	108.0	100	59	71	9	2	6	5	0	3.42		26	108.0	100	59	71	9	2	6	5	0	3.42
April	7	14.1	16	9	9	1	0	0	1	0	8.16		7	14.1	16	9	9	1	0	0	1	0	8.16
May	6	11.2	12	10	3	3	1	0	0	0	3.09		6	11.2	12	10	3	3	1	0	0	0	3.09
June	7	35.0	25	19	18	2	0	2	1	0	1.80		7	35.0	25	19	18	2	0	2	1	0	1.80
July	6	25.2	30	11	22	2	1	2	4	0	3.86		6	25.2	30	11	22	2	1	2	4	0	3.86
August	5	30.1	30	18	21	1	0	2	2	0	3.86		5	30.1	30	18	21	1	0	2	2	0	3.86
Sept–Oct	6	36.2	31	17	27	3	1	1	3	0	3.68		6	36.2	31	17	27	3	1	1	3	0	3.68

	BA	OBA	SA	AB	H	2B	3B	HR	RBI	BB	SO		BA	OBA	SA	AB	H	2B	3B	HR	RBI	BB	SO
Total	.246	.344	.393	585	144	28	5	16	70	84	100		.246	.344	.393	585	144	28	5	16	70	84	100
vs. Left	.263	.364	.401	339	89	20	3	7	36	55	64		.263	.364	.401	339	89	20	3	7	36	55	64
vs. Right	.224	.316	.382	246	55	8	2	9	34	29	36		.224	.316	.382	246	55	8	2	9	34	29	36
Bases Empty	.244	.351	.403	303	74	17	2	9	9	48	57		.244	.351	.403	303	74	17	2	9	9	48	57
Leadoff	.231	.335	.388	134	31	5	2	4	4	21	26		.231	.335	.388	134	31	5	2	4	4	21	26
Runners On Base	.248	.336	.383	282	70	11	3	7	61	36	43		.248	.336	.383	282	70	11	3	7	61	36	43
Scoring Position	.220	.319	.357	182	40	8	3	5	53	29	31		.220	.319	.357	182	40	8	3	5	53	29	31
Late and Close	.226	.359	.452	31	7	2	1	1	6	7	5		.226	.359	.452	31	7	2	1	1	6	7	5

ERIC KING — bats right — throws right — age 28 — CLE — P

1991

	G	IP	H	BB	SO	SB	CS	W	L	SV	ERA
Total	25	150.2	166	44	59	8	3	6	11	0	4.60
at Home	12	65.0	89	22	26	5	1	2	7	0	5.95
on Road	13	85.2	77	22	33	3	2	4	4	0	3.57
on Grass	21	123.2	144	37	52	7	2	6	8	0	4.80
on Turf	4	27.0	22	7	7	1	1	0	3	0	3.67
Day Games	13	80.1	85	21	32	3	3	4	4	0	4.37
Night Games	12	70.1	81	23	27	5	0	2	7	0	4.86
April	4	27.2	30	1	14	1	0	2	2	0	4.55
May	6	35.2	38	13	17	1	1	2	2	0	6.06
June	3	13.2	19	7	0	2	0	0	1	0	5.93
July	1	8.0	6	0	4	0	0	0	1	0	2.25
August	5	33.0	34	10	17	0	0	1	2	0	3.55
Sept–Oct	6	32.2	39	13	7	4	2	1	3	0	4.13

6-YEAR TOTALS (1986–1991)

	G	IP	H	BB	SO	SB	CS	W	L	SV	ERA
Total	186	784.0	724	305	414	53	25	48	39	15	3.85
at Home	92	401.0	379	164	201	30	16	23	22	6	3.93
on Road	94	383.0	345	141	213	23	9	25	17	9	3.76
on Grass	157	671.0	624	270	359	44	20	41	32	12	3.88
on Turf	29	113.0	100	35	55	9	5	7	7	3	3.66
Day Games	61	247.2	261	95	114	15	10	14	16	3	4.94
Night Games	125	536.1	463	210	300	38	15	34	23	12	3.34
April	23	98.0	90	27	61	7	1	6	6	0	3.31
May	34	153.1	127	69	80	11	6	9	8	4	3.99
June	31	138.1	117	62	78	12	3	9	6	3	3.38
July	29	126.2	127	43	75	7	4	6	8	3	4.12
August	27	121.1	125	51	58	3	4	7	6	1	4.90
Sept–Oct	42	146.1	138	53	62	13	7	11	5	4	3.38

1991 (vs. batters)

	BA	OBA	SA	AB	H	2B	3B	HR	RBI	BB	SO
Total	.279	.328	.384	594	166	33	4	7	72	44	59
vs. Left	.287	.336	.396	321	92	12	4	5	43	26	33
vs. Right	.271	.319	.370	273	74	21	0	2	29	18	26
Bases Empty	.263	.306	.367	338	89	14	3	5	5	20	34
Leadoff	.253	.309	.380	150	38	7	3	2	2	11	17
Runners On Base	.301	.355	.406	256	77	19	1	2	67	24	25
Scoring Position	.292	.356	.401	137	40	12	0	1	63	16	11
Late and Close	.480	.567	.720	25	12	4	1	0	5	4	0

6-YEAR TOTALS (vs. batters)

	BA	OBA	SA	AB	H	2B	3B	HR	RBI	BB	SO
Total	.245	.320	.356	2956	724	116	14	61	314	305	414
vs. Left	.241	.320	.369	1476	356	52	13	37	164	165	205
vs. Right	.249	.320	.342	1480	368	64	1	24	150	140	209
Bases Empty	.240	.316	.355	1698	407	56	8	41	41	170	247
Leadoff	.241	.319	.369	731	176	22	6	20	20	77	106
Runners On Base	.252	.325	.357	1258	317	60	6	20	273	135	167
Scoring Position	.236	.321	.325	679	160	28	3	9	234	87	91
Late and Close	.263	.347	.362	365	96	15	3	5	43	45	59

LES LANCASTER — bats right — throws right — age 30 — CHN — P

1991

	G	IP	H	BB	SO	SB	CS	W	L	SV	ERA
Total	64	156.0	150	49	102	14	14	9	7	3	3.52
at Home	33	83.1	77	21	57	5	9	7	2	1	3.46
on Road	31	72.2	73	28	45	9	5	2	5	2	3.59
on Grass	46	111.2	110	34	77	10	14	8	4	1	3.63
on Turf	18	44.1	40	15	25	4	0	1	3	2	3.25
Day Games	29	74.2	69	21	52	4	11	6	1	1	3.62
Night Games	35	81.1	81	28	50	10	3	3	6	2	3.43
April	8	15.1	11	4	7	1	1	0	0	0	4.11
May	11	21.1	21	3	14	5	2	2	1	1	2.53
June	10	35.0	33	15	26	1	3	2	1	0	2.57
July	7	41.0	44	10	26	2	2	3	2	0	5.71
August	15	21.2	22	3	15	2	1	2	3	2	2.91
Sept–Oct	13	21.2	19	14	14	3	5	0	0	0	2.08

5-YEAR TOTALS (1987–1991)

	G	IP	H	BB	SO	SB	CS	W	L	SV	ERA
Total	232	555.2	558	188	337	37	29	34	23	22	3.82
at Home	123	298.0	309	92	187	18	18	22	11	10	4.02
on Road	109	257.2	249	96	150	19	11	12	12	12	3.60
on Grass	170	414.1	419	134	257	27	27	27	14	14	3.84
on Turf	62	141.1	139	54	80	10	2	7	9	8	3.76
Day Games	131	324.0	327	110	209	19	22	23	15	14	4.08
Night Games	101	231.2	231	78	128	18	7	11	8	8	3.46
April	31	51.0	46	25	29	2	4	2	3	1	4.24
May	28	83.2	92	18	42	6	5	6	4	3	3.23
June	42	98.2	96	46	62	7	3	7	3	5	3.28
July	45	113.0	116	36	77	6	5	8	5	4	5.26
August	43	95.1	106	27	66	7	3	5	5	4	4.44
Sept–Oct	43	114.0	102	36	61	9	9	6	3	4	2.61

1991 (vs. batters)

	BA	OBA	SA	AB	H	2B	3B	HR	RBI	BB	SO
Total	.256	.315	.376	587	150	26	3	13	72	49	102
vs. Left	.262	.338	.375	309	81	15	1	6	36	34	46
vs. Right	.248	.289	.378	278	69	11	2	7	36	15	56
Bases Empty	.257	.305	.357	350	90	15	1	6	6	22	62
Leadoff	.222	.273	.313	144	32	4	0	3	3	9	27
Runners On Base	.253	.330	.405	237	60	11	2	7	66	27	40
Scoring Position	.308	.385	.519	133	41	6	2	6	61	17	23
Late and Close	.289	.349	.370	135	39	6	1	1	15	13	30

5-YEAR TOTALS (vs. batters)

	BA	OBA	SA	AB	H	2B	3B	HR	RBI	BB	SO
Total	.263	.322	.382	2120	558	100	10	44	261	188	337
vs. Left	.274	.346	.391	1080	296	58	4	20	119	121	150
vs. Right	.252	.295	.373	1040	262	42	6	24	142	67	187
Bases Empty	.259	.312	.374	1192	309	61	5	22	22	88	200
Leadoff	.255	.308	.368	505	129	24	3	9	9	37	83
Runners On Base	.268	.333	.392	928	249	39	5	22	239	100	137
Scoring Position	.268	.336	.407	555	149	24	4	15	214	68	89
Late and Close	.276	.344	.371	590	163	20	3	10	73	63	97

BILL LANDRUM — bats right — throws right — age 35 — PIT — P

1991

	G	IP	H	BB	SO	SB	CS	W	L	SV	ERA
Total	61	76.1	76	19	45	9	1	4	4	17	3.18
at Home	30	35.0	26	6	23	5	0	1	1	9	1.80
on Road	31	41.1	50	13	22	4	1	3	3	8	4.35
on Grass	16	24.1	30	7	14	3	1	3	2	2	4.81
on Turf	45	52.0	46	12	31	6	0	1	2	15	2.42
Day Games	12	14.1	10	4	8	1	0	0	2	3	3.14
Night Games	49	62.0	66	15	37	8	1	4	2	14	3.19
April	9	10.1	6	1	7	1	0	0	0	0	0.00
May	12	14.2	11	2	7	1	0	0	0	6	2.45
June	10	10.1	18	1	5	0	0	0	1	0	3.48
July	10	14.2	19	6	8	3	1	0	2	0	5.52
August	11	15.0	7	4	12	1	0	0	2	2	1.80
Sept–Oct	9	11.1	15	5	6	3	0	0	2	0	5.56

6-YEAR TOTALS (1986–1991)

	G	IP	H	BB	SO	SB	CS	W	L	SV	ERA
Total	232	319.2	315	109	197	32	14	17	12	58	3.13
at Home	117	157.0	151	48	95	16	7	9	5	28	3.10
on Road	115	162.2	164	61	102	16	7	8	7	30	3.15
on Grass	65	95.0	86	32	60	5	8	7	3	16	3.60
on Turf	167	224.2	229	77	137	27	6	10	9	42	2.92
Day Games	69	94.0	93	28	56	4	7	5	4	14	2.97
Night Games	163	225.2	222	81	141	28	7	12	8	44	3.19
April	28	43.2	34	13	31	6	0	2	1	5	2.27
May	37	50.1	40	10	25	6	2	3	1	11	1.79
June	42	62.1	61	19	38	4	4	4	1	20	2.45
July	46	59.1	68	29	37	7	2	1	4	8	4.70
August	34	44.2	40	14	29	3	2	2	2	8	2.82
Sept–Oct	45	59.1	72	24	37	6	4	5	1	6	4.25

1991 (vs. batters)

	BA	OBA	SA	AB	H	2B	3B	HR	RBI	BB	SO
Total	.252	.296	.329	301	76	7	2	4	36	19	45
vs. Left	.273	.336	.360	139	38	4	1	2	18	13	19
vs. Right	.235	.260	.302	162	38	3	1	2	18	6	26
Bases Empty	.244	.258	.344	160	39	2	1	4	4	3	27
Leadoff	.231	.242	.415	65	15	1	1	3	3	1	7
Runners On Base	.262	.335	.312	141	37	5	1	0	32	16	18
Scoring Position	.280	.375	.354	82	23	4	1	0	32	13	9
Late and Close	.246	.305	.320	175	43	4	0	3	19	15	26

6-YEAR TOTALS (vs. batters)

	BA	OBA	SA	AB	H	2B	3B	HR	RBI	BB	SO
Total	.262	.322	.348	1200	315	38	11	14	143	109	197
vs. Left	.248	.315	.319	577	143	15	4	6	57	58	80
vs. Right	.276	.328	.374	623	172	23	7	8	86	51	117
Bases Empty	.268	.312	.359	624	167	20	5	9	9	40	99
Leadoff	.304	.338	.414	273	83	6	3	6	6	14	34
Runners On Base	.257	.332	.335	576	148	18	6	5	134	69	98
Scoring Position	.278	.370	.354	356	99	14	1	5	124	57	59
Late and Close	.227	.301	.288	559	127	17	1	5	58	60	85

MARK LANGSTON — bats right — throws left — age 32 — CAL — P

1991	G	IP	H	BB	SO	SB	CS	W	L	SV	ERA
Total	34	246.1	190	96	183	10	15	19	8	0	3.00
at Home	18	127.0	103	45	105	5	8	9	3	0	3.33
on Road	16	119.1	87	51	78	5	7	10	5	0	2.64
on Grass	29	211.0	167	82	162	6	14	15	7	0	3.07
on Turf	5	35.1	23	14	21	4	1	4	1	0	2.55
Day Games	10	66.2	61	26	57	2	4	3	3	0	3.51
Night Games	24	179.2	129	70	126	8	11	16	5	0	2.81
April	4	24.2	23	12	20	1	1	1	1	0	4.38
May	6	46.1	37	19	29	4	3	5	1	0	3.30
June	5	36.2	26	13	31	1	1	5	0	0	3.19
July	7	52.2	43	16	42	2	4	3	3	0	3.42
August	5	34.2	24	18	17	1	1	1	2	0	2.08
Sept–Oct	7	51.1	37	18	44	1	5	4	1	0	2.10

8-YEAR TOTALS (1984–1991)

	G	IP	H	BB	SO	SB	CS	W	L	SV	ERA
	266	1835.2	1604	866	1621	135	94	115	100	0	3.77
	129	912.0	787	414	853	71	45	54	47	0	3.97
	137	923.2	817	452	768	64	49	61	53	0	3.57
	138	934.2	827	449	785	58	52	58	52	0	3.65
	128	901.0	777	417	836	77	42	57	48	0	3.89
	76	480.0	468	243	449	42	28	26	34	0	4.57
	190	1355.2	1136	623	1172	93	66	89	66	0	3.48
	39	262.2	242	123	215	20	14	15	16	0	3.91
	45	318.0	283	141	260	15	15	21	17	0	3.91
	40	276.0	241	120	264	25	12	21	14	0	3.46
	42	287.2	251	123	268	21	15	14	18	0	4.19
	49	335.0	295	183	267	19	17	21	17	0	3.98
	51	356.1	292	176	347	35	21	23	18	0	3.23

	BA	OBA	SA	AB	H	2B	3B	HR	RBI	BB	SO
Total	.215	.291	.360	884	190	34	2	30	82	96	183
vs. Left	.217	.294	.295	129	28	5	1	1	7	14	27
vs. Right	.215	.291	.371	755	162	29	1	29	75	82	156
Bases Empty	.219	.306	.355	558	122	20	1	18	18	69	108
Leadoff	.235	.327	.354	226	53	9	0	6	6	31	43
Runners On Base	.209	.267	.368	326	68	14	1	12	64	27	75
Scoring Position	.228	.305	.443	149	34	8	0	8	54	19	43
Late and Close	.224	.300	.337	98	22	2	0	3	5	11	17

	BA	OBA	SA	AB	H	2B	3B	HR	RBI	BB	SO
Total	.237	.324	.379	6772	1604	304	45	189	755	866	1621
vs. Left	.200	.284	.299	1056	211	39	6	18	91	120	272
vs. Right	.244	.332	.393	5716	1393	265	39	171	664	746	1349
Bases Empty	.230	.328	.374	3928	903	163	23	119	119	556	954
Leadoff	.228	.323	.365	1682	384	70	8	48	48	233	388
Runners On Base	.246	.320	.385	2844	701	141	22	70	636	310	667
Scoring Position	.255	.334	.409	1532	391	79	15	42	560	194	377
Late and Close	.259	.332	.391	760	197	36	2	20	81	85	163

CRAIG LEFFERTS — bats left — throws left — age 35 — SD — P

1991	G	IP	H	BB	SO	SB	CS	W	L	SV	ERA
Total	54	69.0	74	14	48	6	4	1	6	23	3.91
at Home	28	41.2	41	9	29	1	2	0	5	10	3.46
on Road	26	27.1	33	5	19	5	2	1	1	13	4.61
on Grass	38	50.2	54	12	32	4	2	0	6	15	3.91
on Turf	16	18.1	20	2	16	2	2	1	0	8	3.93
Day Games	14	18.2	16	3	12	1	1	0	3	7	3.86
Night Games	40	50.1	58	11	36	5	3	1	3	16	3.93
April	8	8.1	9	2	6	1	0	0	1	5	4.32
May	11	18.2	18	7	11	2	2	0	1	5	4.82
June	8	11.2	12	0	4	1	1	0	2	3	4.63
July	7	7.1	6	3	5	1	0	0	0	2	3.68
August	10	9.2	16	0	6	0	0	1	1	3	4.66
Sept–Oct	10	13.1	13	2	16	1	1	0	1	4	1.35

8-YEAR TOTALS (1984–1991)

	G	IP	H	BB	SO	SB	CS	W	L	SV	ERA
	526	742.2	662	212	471	56	27	37	46	99	3.02
	259	373.0	308	89	258	30	18	24	21	45	2.58
	267	369.2	354	123	213	26	9	13	25	54	3.46
	389	554.2	472	150	364	38	21	32	30	72	2.76
	137	188.0	190	62	107	18	6	5	16	27	3.78
	182	259.1	200	70	174	22	8	14	21	33	2.74
	344	483.1	462	142	297	34	19	23	25	66	3.17
	73	99.0	66	23	70	8	4	7	2	11	1.64
	87	135.0	116	44	83	16	5	1	14	25	3.27
	90	144.1	131	41	87	7	4	13	7	16	3.55
	89	130.1	102	35	87	7	5	5	9	16	2.69
	99	130.2	148	34	67	10	3	4	7	18	3.72
	88	103.1	99	35	77	8	6	7	7	13	2.79

	BA	OBA	SA	AB	H	2B	3B	HR	RBI	BB	SO
Total	.285	.318	.408	260	74	11	3	5	42	14	48
vs. Left	.281	.309	.422	64	18	2	2	1	17	3	16
vs. Right	.286	.321	.403	196	56	9	1	4	25	11	32
Bases Empty	.317	.359	.458	120	38	8	0	3	3	8	21
Leadoff	.333	.370	.392	51	17	3	0	0	0	3	6
Runners On Base	.257	.283	.364	140	36	3	3	2	39	6	27
Scoring Position	.286	.321	.357	70	20	1	2	0	32	5	16
Late and Close	.269	.310	.382	186	50	7	1	4	33	12	27

	BA	OBA	SA	AB	H	2B	3B	HR	RBI	BB	SO
Total	.242	.295	.365	2738	662	114	16	64	313	212	471
vs. Left	.220	.268	.313	709	156	17	5	13	83	45	155
vs. Right	.249	.305	.383	2029	506	97	11	51	230	167	316
Bases Empty	.252	.296	.390	1476	372	74	5	40	40	89	244
Leadoff	.259	.297	.382	625	162	25	2	16	16	32	96
Runners On Base	.230	.294	.336	1262	290	40	11	24	273	123	227
Scoring Position	.220	.303	.331	759	167	24	6	16	243	98	137
Late and Close	.243	.295	.360	1500	364	53	9	35	181	112	250

CHARLIE LEIBRANDT — bats right — throws left — age 36 — ATL — P

1991	G	IP	H	BB	SO	SB	CS	W	L	SV	ERA
Total	36	229.2	212	56	128	35	10	15	13	0	3.49
at Home	16	101.1	105	28	55	13	7	6	8	0	4.35
on Road	20	128.1	107	28	73	22	3	9	5	0	2.81
on Grass	26	170.1	154	36	93	20	10	10	11	0	3.33
on Turf	10	59.1	58	20	35	15	0	5	2	0	3.94
Day Games	12	75.1	74	19	43	13	4	4	6	0	3.58
Night Games	24	154.1	138	37	85	22	6	11	7	0	3.44
April	5	33.1	33	9	21	4	2	2	2	0	2.97
May	6	39.0	38	6	20	7	3	2	2	0	2.77
June	5	35.1	23	10	20	7	1	2	2	0	2.55
July	6	32.0	47	9	18	7	1	2	4	0	7.31
August	6	41.0	34	7	29	2	1	4	2	0	2.63
Sept–Oct	8	49.0	37	15	30	8	2	2	2	0	3.31

8-YEAR TOTALS (1984–1991)

	G	IP	H	BB	SO	SB	CS	W	L	SV	ERA
	254	1649.0	1670	450	822	129	61	100	85	0	3.54
	115	754.1	792	187	337	49	35	50	35	0	3.39
	139	894.2	878	263	485	80	26	50	50	0	3.67
	124	806.2	790	226	424	69	24	46	49	0	3.60
	130	842.1	880	224	398	60	37	54	36	0	3.48
	68	428.0	425	114	212	46	20	27	23	0	3.20
	186	1221.0	1245	336	610	83	41	73	62	0	3.66
	31	210.2	195	74	103	14	9	15	10	0	2.95
	34	226.2	231	56	101	20	14	9	16	0	3.81
	45	318.2	306	77	145	24	13	18	16	0	3.13
	45	274.2	312	85	139	23	9	16	16	0	4.52
	45	291.1	299	69	161	19	6	21	13	0	3.46
	54	327.0	327	89	173	29	10	21	14	0	3.39

	BA	OBA	SA	AB	H	2B	3B	HR	RBI	BB	SO
Total	.245	.292	.363	864	212	38	5	18	91	56	128
vs. Left	.271	.317	.388	188	51	14	1	2	20	13	31
vs. Right	.238	.286	.357	676	161	24	4	16	71	43	97
Bases Empty	.234	.278	.317	546	128	17	2	8	8	31	77
Leadoff	.222	.262	.329	225	50	6	0	6	6	12	27
Runners On Base	.264	.316	.443	318	84	21	3	10	83	25	51
Scoring Position	.281	.348	.515	171	48	14	1	8	74	19	25
Late and Close	.260	.287	.312	77	20	1	0	1	4	3	7

	BA	OBA	SA	AB	H	2B	3B	HR	RBI	BB	SO
Total	.263	.312	.385	6347	1670	314	36	129	647	450	822
vs. Left	.267	.311	.366	1209	323	54	6	18	127	71	152
vs. Right	.262	.313	.389	5138	1347	260	30	111	520	379	670
Bases Empty	.263	.305	.386	3817	1004	191	21	79	79	219	492
Leadoff	.258	.294	.381	1621	418	79	8	35	35	79	172
Runners On Base	.263	.323	.383	2530	666	123	15	50	568	231	330
Scoring Position	.248	.319	.362	1434	356	61	12	26	495	159	186
Late and Close	.236	.300	.332	593	140	22	4	9	41	53	76

MARK LEITER — bats right — throws right — age 29 — DET — P

1991	G	IP	H	BB	SO	SB	CS	W	L	SV	ERA
Total	38	134.2	125	50	103	6	5	9	7	1	4.21
at Home	20	72.1	64	28	58	2	0	4	3	1	4.11
on Road	18	62.1	61	22	45	4	5	5	4	0	4.33
on Grass	32	123.1	115	43	96	5	4	8	5	1	4.01
on Turf	6	11.1	10	7	7	1	1	1	2	0	6.35
Day Games	10	45.0	42	8	39	2	0	4	3	1	3.80
Night Games	28	89.2	83	42	64	4	5	5	4	0	4.42
April	3	1.2	1	2	2	0	0	1	1	0	16.20
May	12	25.0	18	19	23	2	2	1	0	0	2.16
June	4	4.0	3	4	4	1	0	0	0	0	13.50
July	7	26.2	26	8	17	2	0	0	1	0	5.40
August	5	30.2	34	7	22	1	2	5	0	0	2.93
Sept–Oct	7	46.2	43	10	35	0	1	2	5	0	4.24

	BA	OBA	SA	AB	H	2B	3B	HR	RBI	BB	SO
Total	.245	.316	.397	511	125	20	5	16	67	50	103
vs. Left	.235	.319	.412	226	53	9	2	9	26	26	33
vs. Right	.253	.313	.386	285	72	11	3	7	41	24	70
Bases Empty	.228	.304	.401	302	69	14	4	10	10	31	66
Leadoff	.213	.289	.369	122	26	5	1	4	4	12	28
Runners On Base	.268	.332	.392	209	56	6	1	6	57	19	37
Scoring Position	.294	.371	.445	119	35	6	0	4	52	16	18
Late and Close	.317	.356	.415	41	13	2	1	0	6	2	5

2-YEAR TOTALS (1990–1991)

	G	IP	H	BB	SO	SB	CS	W	L	SV	ERA
Total	46	161.0	158	59	124	9	6	10	8	1	4.64
at Home	25	95.0	90	36	76	4	1	5	3	1	4.55
on Road	21	66.0	68	23	48	5	5	5	5	0	4.77
on Grass	40	149.2	148	52	117	8	5	9	6	1	4.51
on Turf	6	11.1	10	7	7	1	1	1	2	0	6.35
Day Games	11	47.0	46	8	42	2	0	4	3	1	4.21
Night Games	35	114.0	112	51	82	7	6	6	5	0	4.82
April	3	1.2	1	2	2	0	0	1	1	0	16.20
May	12	25.0	18	19	23	2	2	1	0	0	2.16
June	4	4.0	3	4	4	1	0	0	0	0	13.50
July	10	35.2	37	10	21	3	0	1	2	0	5.55
August	6	31.1	38	8	23	2	2	5	0	0	4.31
Sept–Oct	11	63.1	61	16	51	1	2	2	5	0	4.41

	BA	OBA	SA	AB	H	2B	3B	HR	RBI	BB	SO
Total	.256	.326	.417	616	158	26	5	21	85	59	124
vs. Left	.251	.331	.427	279	70	12	2	11	36	32	44
vs. Right	.261	.322	.409	337	88	14	3	10	49	27	80
Bases Empty	.237	.318	.395	354	84	18	4	10	10	38	78
Leadoff	.222	.313	.361	144	32	6	1	4	4	17	33
Runners On Base	.282	.337	.447	262	74	8	1	11	75	21	46
Scoring Position	.301	.366	.425	146	44	6	0	4	59	17	22
Late and Close	.354	.385	.500	48	17	2	1	2	8	2	5

GREG MADDUX — bats right — throws right — age 26 — CHN — P

1991	G	IP	H	BB	SO	SB	CS	W	L	SV	ERA
Total	37	263.0	232	66	198	25	7	15	11	0	3.35
at Home	18	127.2	118	36	94	9	6	7	5	0	3.45
on Road	19	135.1	114	30	104	16	1	8	6	0	3.26
on Grass	26	185.1	162	49	139	17	6	12	8	0	3.40
on Turf	11	77.2	70	17	59	8	1	3	3	0	3.24
Day Games	21	147.0	140	43	106	12	6	8	8	0	3.49
Night Games	16	116.0	92	23	92	13	1	7	3	0	3.18
April	4	26.1	23	7	20	0	0	2	1	0	3.76
May	6	48.0	38	13	31	5	0	3	2	0	3.00
June	7	42.2	39	14	43	7	1	3	3	0	4.01
July	6	43.1	47	7	33	4	0	2	0	0	3.95
August	6	41.1	43	16	30	5	2	3	2	0	3.92
Sept–Oct	8	61.1	42	9	41	4	1	4	3	0	2.20

	BA	OBA	SA	AB	H	2B	3B	HR	RBI	BB	SO
Total	.237	.288	.345	979	232	34	9	18	94	66	198
vs. Left	.256	.311	.385	577	148	18	7	14	65	44	109
vs. Right	.209	.256	.289	402	84	16	2	4	29	22	89
Bases Empty	.220	.273	.305	610	134	22	3	8	8	41	125
Leadoff	.234	.288	.333	252	59	8	1	5	5	16	45
Runners On Base	.266	.313	.412	369	98	12	6	10	86	25	73
Scoring Position	.262	.319	.400	210	55	5	6	4	70	18	46
Late and Close	.333	.385	.459	111	37	4	2	2	17	9	24

6-YEAR TOTALS (1986–1991)

	G	IP	H	BB	SO	SB	CS	W	L	SV	ERA
Total	178	1180.0	1161	385	745	106	38	75	65	0	3.64
at Home	85	572.2	571	191	366	42	24	34	30	0	3.69
on Road	93	607.1	590	194	379	64	14	41	35	0	3.59
on Grass	124	809.0	792	284	504	70	26	52	45	0	3.76
on Turf	54	371.0	369	101	241	36	12	23	20	0	3.37
Day Games	103	672.2	699	230	433	62	28	41	40	0	3.83
Night Games	75	507.1	462	155	312	44	10	34	25	0	3.39
April	23	150.2	142	50	86	11	2	11	8	0	3.46
May	29	204.0	175	59	126	17	6	14	11	0	3.22
June	29	191.2	176	74	130	22	5	8	12	0	3.52
July	31	206.1	212	61	126	24	10	14	7	0	3.97
August	29	188.2	193	76	119	14	9	13	9	0	3.77
Sept–Oct	37	238.2	263	65	158	18	6	15	18	0	3.81

	BA	OBA	SA	AB	H	2B	3B	HR	RBI	BB	SO
Total	.258	.320	.362	4498	1161	192	25	75	478	385	745
vs. Left	.274	.344	.380	2509	688	111	17	40	283	257	372
vs. Right	.238	.289	.339	1989	473	81	8	35	195	128	373
Bases Empty	.244	.305	.335	2613	638	105	11	37	37	207	480
Leadoff	.254	.306	.352	1139	289	43	6	19	19	76	193
Runners On Base	.277	.340	.399	1885	523	87	14	38	441	178	265
Scoring Position	.271	.351	.380	1082	293	44	10	18	384	136	179
Late and Close	.258	.319	.338	480	124	11	3	7	45	42	80

MIKE MADDUX — bats left — throws right — age 31 — SD — P

1991	G	IP	H	BB	SO	SB	CS	W	L	SV	ERA
Total	64	98.2	78	27	57	5	7	7	2	5	2.46
at Home	35	51.1	31	12	29	1	3	5	1	1	1.75
on Road	29	47.1	47	15	28	4	4	2	1	4	3.23
on Grass	47	72.1	57	19	43	3	6	6	1	4	2.86
on Turf	17	26.1	21	8	14	2	1	1	1	1	1.37
Day Games	14	27.0	25	8	13	4	1	2	0	1	2.33
Night Games	50	71.2	53	19	44	1	6	5	2	4	2.51
April	10	14.0	18	5	9	0	1	2	1	1	3.86
May	13	17.2	18	7	8	1	3	0	0	1	3.06
June	10	19.1	12	1	9	1	0	1	0	0	1.40
July	9	12.1	3	5	7	1	0	1	0	0	0.00
August	10	13.1	17	4	8	3	1	1	1	0	6.75
Sept–Oct	12	22.0	10	5	16	0	2	2	0	3	0.82

	BA	OBA	SA	AB	H	2B	3B	HR	RBI	BB	SO
Total	.221	.277	.300	353	78	10	3	4	26	27	57
vs. Left	.247	.297	.300	170	42	5	2	0	12	13	26
vs. Right	.197	.258	.301	183	36	5	1	4	14	14	31
Bases Empty	.221	.265	.324	213	47	6	2	4	4	12	35
Leadoff	.261	.316	.477	88	23	3	2	4	4	6	14
Runners On Base	.221	.293	.264	140	31	4	1	0	22	15	22
Scoring Position	.185	.260	.217	92	17	3	0	0	20	10	16
Late and Close	.225	.292	.255	102	23	3	0	0	13	9	17

6-YEAR TOTALS (1986–1991)

	G	IP	H	BB	SO	SB	CS	W	L	SV	ERA
Total	140	353.2	356	119	217	40	25	18	16	6	4.02
at Home	72	184.2	180	48	122	18	12	14	6	1	3.66
on Road	68	169.0	176	71	95	22	13	4	10	5	4.42
on Grass	73	158.1	149	60	89	16	12	7	6	5	4.09
on Turf	67	195.1	207	59	128	24	13	11	10	1	3.96
Day Games	42	133.0	127	45	81	15	10	7	5	1	4.13
Night Games	98	220.2	229	74	136	25	15	11	11	5	3.96
April	22	44.2	44	12	35	1	2	4	1	2	3.43
May	28	57.0	60	19	31	5	7	0	2	0	3.63
June	20	49.0	55	12	27	7	2	2	4	0	6.24
July	17	50.0	51	18	29	7	3	3	1	1	3.24
August	21	77.1	79	31	39	12	7	4	5	0	4.77
Sept–Oct	32	75.2	67	27	56	8	4	5	3	3	2.97

	BA	OBA	SA	AB	H	2B	3B	HR	RBI	BB	SO
Total	.266	.329	.369	1339	356	66	3	22	153	119	217
vs. Left	.266	.337	.352	696	185	32	2	8	74	70	104
vs. Right	.266	.320	.387	643	171	34	1	14	79	49	113
Bases Empty	.254	.309	.347	763	194	37	2	10	10	55	127
Leadoff	.287	.347	.440	327	94	22	2	8	8	25	53
Runners On Base	.281	.354	.398	576	162	29	1	12	143	64	90
Scoring Position	.266	.356	.394	353	94	21	0	8	128	52	62
Late and Close	.224	.284	.268	183	41	5	0	1	19	14	31

DENNIS MARTINEZ — bats right — throws right — age 37 — MON — P

1991	G	IP	H	BB	SO	SB	CS	W	L	SV	ERA		G	IP	H	BB	SO	SB	CS	W	L	SV	ERA
Total	31	222.0	187	62	123	22	5	14	11	0	2.39		243	1486.1	1415	385	835	152	46	88	72	0	3.49
at Home	13	96.0	86	21	51	9	0	7	4	0	2.16		115	725.2	689	179	416	68	21	41	39	0	3.52
on Road	18	126.0	101	41	72	13	5	7	7	0	2.57		128	760.2	726	206	419	84	25	47	33	0	3.45
on Grass	9	64.2	52	20	36	5	2	4	2	0	2.51		104	548.0	567	153	297	57	12	31	31	0	4.14
on Turf	22	157.1	135	42	87	17	3	10	9	0	2.35		139	938.1	848	232	538	95	34	57	41	0	3.11
Day Games	6	42.1	31	14	25	4	0	3	2	0	2.34		68	404.0	400	96	238	45	11	22	25	0	3.59
Night Games	25	179.2	156	48	98	18	5	11	9	0	2.40		175	1082.1	1015	289	597	107	35	66	47	0	3.45
April	5	36.2	23	11	23	6	0	3	2	0	1.23		34	184.1	162	51	103	20	5	11	7	0	2.73
May	6	41.1	46	8	23	0	0	3	2	0	3.48		35	198.2	212	52	112	14	4	11	13	0	3.53
June	6	46.0	38	15	27	5	2	3	1	0	1.37		43	277.0	242	83	138	36	8	17	8	0	2.89
July	5	38.1	30	9	17	4	1	2	1	0	2.11		43	278.1	278	61	164	25	9	20	9	0	3.94
August	5	33.0	29	12	19	3	1	1	3	0	4.09		46	305.1	280	63	176	29	13	18	17	0	3.24
Sept–Oct	4	26.2	21	7	14	4	1	2	2	0	2.36		42	242.2	241	75	142	28	7	11	18	0	4.49

8-YEAR TOTALS (1984–1991)

	BA	OBA	SA	AB	H	2B	3B	HR	RBI	BB	SO		BA	OBA	SA	AB	H	2B	3B	HR	RBI	BB	SO
Total	.226	.282	.311	829	187	32	6	9	62	62	123		.250	.301	.385	5659	1415	251	44	142	569	385	835
vs. Left	.233	.304	.301	489	114	17	2	4	34	51	73		.246	.303	.370	3177	783	135	24	70	306	262	476
vs. Right	.215	.247	.326	340	73	15	4	5	28	11	50		.255	.300	.405	2482	632	116	20	72	263	123	359
Bases Empty	.229	.266	.315	511	117	20	3	6	6	25	70		.250	.292	.383	3517	880	158	29	84	84	185	506
Leadoff	.225	.249	.289	218	49	7	2	1	1	7	28		.253	.287	.394	1465	370	65	14	38	38	62	196
Runners On Base	.220	.305	.305	318	70	12	3	3	56	37	53		.250	.316	.388	2142	535	93	15	58	485	200	329
Scoring Position	.197	.316	.285	193	38	8	3	1	50	33	38		.239	.319	.370	1261	302	47	8	34	407	149	226
Late and Close	.205	.246	.268	127	26	3	1	1	6	6	13		.240	.282	.371	596	143	23	5	15	57	31	76

RAMON MARTINEZ — bats right — throws right — age 24 — LA — P

1991	G	IP	H	BB	SO	SB	CS	W	L	SV	ERA		G	IP	H	BB	SO	SB	CS	W	L	SV	ERA
Total	33	220.1	190	69	150	15	9	17	13	0	3.27		90	589.0	487	199	485	44	35	44	26	0	3.15
at Home	15	105.0	82	37	85	8	8	9	4	0	2.91		46	310.0	229	119	286	24	26	24	12	0	2.90
on Road	18	115.1	108	32	65	7	1	8	9	0	3.59		44	279.0	258	80	199	20	9	20	14	0	3.42
on Grass	26	174.0	154	53	125	12	8	14	10	0	3.26		69	455.2	368	155	382	30	29	34	20	0	3.08
on Turf	7	46.1	36	16	25	3	1	3	3	0	3.30		21	133.1	119	44	103	14	6	10	6	0	3.38
Day Games	13	88.1	65	32	64	6	3	7	5	0	2.45		30	193.2	154	71	160	15	14	14	9	0	2.93
Night Games	20	132.0	125	37	86	9	6	10	8	0	3.82		60	395.1	333	128	325	29	21	30	17	0	3.26
April	4	29.0	21	5	21	1	0	3	1	0	2.17		8	57.0	41	10	49	3	1	5	1	0	2.21
May	6	41.0	36	12	28	5	1	5	1	0	3.07		12	75.0	70	25	69	11	6	8	4	0	3.84
June	5	38.0	29	13	26	2	5	2	1	0	2.61		12	93.0	71	29	91	4	8	7	1	0	1.94
July	6	43.2	36	8	21	4	1	4	2	0	1.24		14	97.0	77	27	70	12	2	9	3	0	2.60
August	5	29.2	35	8	21	0	0	1	4	0	6.37		21	135.0	126	50	99	4	8	6	10	0	3.93
Sept–Oct	7	39.0	33	23	33	3	2	2	4	0	4.85		23	132.0	102	58	107	10	8	9	7	0	3.61

4-YEAR TOTALS (1988–1991)

	BA	OBA	SA	AB	H	2B	3B	HR	RBI	BB	SO		BA	OBA	SA	AB	H	2B	3B	HR	RBI	BB	SO
Total	.229	.293	.337	828	190	33	1	18	79	69	150		.223	.292	.342	2179	487	86	10	51	205	199	485
vs. Left	.224	.301	.316	455	102	21	0	7	39	48	81		.240	.322	.357	1216	292	52	6	26	118	141	246
vs. Right	.236	.283	.362	373	88	12	1	11	40	21	69		.202	.252	.324	963	195	34	4	25	87	58	239
Bases Empty	.210	.276	.311	505	106	22	1	9	9	41	96		.213	.285	.335	1331	283	57	5	32	32	124	318
Leadoff	.217	.286	.329	207	45	11	0	4	4	17	37		.232	.307	.382	547	127	25	3	17	17	52	118
Runners On Base	.260	.319	.378	323	84	11	0	9	70	28	54		.241	.304	.354	848	204	29	5	19	173	75	167
Scoring Position	.237	.284	.332	190	45	6	0	4	60	13	36		.222	.293	.321	473	105	16	2	9	145	46	104
Late and Close	.121	.194	.182	66	8	1	0	1	2	5	13		.182	.252	.256	203	37	6	0	3	9	18	44

KIRK McCASKILL — bats right — throws right — age 31 — CAL — P

1991	G	IP	H	BB	SO	SB	CS	W	L	SV	ERA		G	IP	H	BB	SO	SB	CS	W	L	SV	ERA
Total	30	177.2	193	66	71	8	6	10	19	0	4.26		192	1221.0	1191	448	714	35	47	78	74	0	3.86
at Home	15	92.2	94	27	38	3	2	4	10	0	4.08		93	608.0	567	190	355	12	24	40	32	0	3.61
on Road	15	85.0	99	39	33	5	4	6	9	0	4.45		99	613.0	624	258	359	23	23	38	42	0	4.11
on Grass	25	149.1	155	56	55	5	5	7	17	0	4.10		165	1054.0	1013	390	624	29	37	66	65	0	3.77
on Turf	5	28.1	38	10	16	3	1	3	2	0	5.08		27	167.0	178	58	90	6	10	12	9	0	4.47
Day Games	4	27.2	23	13	14	0	2	2	2	0	2.28		44	285.0	277	99	203	6	11	21	11	0	3.79
Night Games	26	150.0	170	53	57	8	4	8	17	0	4.62		148	936.0	914	349	511	29	36	57	63	0	3.88
April	4	25.1	20	14	12	0	0	2	2	0	2.84		24	167.0	130	65	98	2	9	13	7	0	2.48
May	6	33.0	37	10	12	1	1	3	3	0	4.09		33	193.0	211	73	121	1	7	9	11	0	4.10
June	6	38.1	41	14	20	2	2	2	4	0	3.76		32	205.1	201	74	142	11	7	15	14	0	3.81
July	6	38.2	40	12	12	1	0	1	4	0	4.19		36	234.1	232	87	114	5	6	16	14	0	3.65
August	6	30.1	41	12	8	2	2	2	4	0	6.23		38	241.1	248	90	120	6	13	16	14	0	4.48
Sept–Oct	2	12.0	14	4	7	2	1	0	2	0	4.50		29	180.0	169	59	119	10	5	9	14	0	4.40

7-YEAR TOTALS (1985–1991)

	BA	OBA	SA	AB	H	2B	3B	HR	RBI	BB	SO		BA	OBA	SA	AB	H	2B	3B	HR	RBI	BB	SO
Total	.283	.347	.435	681	193	36	5	19	83	66	71		.257	.323	.380	4633	1191	182	30	109	506	448	714
vs. Left	.313	.356	.460	339	106	16	2	10	47	22	23		.266	.328	.396	2426	646	93	21	60	264	223	311
vs. Right	.254	.338	.409	342	87	20	3	9	36	44	48		.247	.318	.362	2207	545	89	9	49	242	225	403
Bases Empty	.274	.349	.413	390	107	20	2	10	10	44	34		.245	.316	.363	2711	663	112	17	58	58	270	427
Leadoff	.283	.357	.464	166	47	7	1	7	7	19	13		.260	.330	.372	1160	302	54	6	21	21	114	160
Runners On Base	.296	.343	.464	291	86	16	3	9	73	22	37		.275	.333	.404	1922	528	70	13	51	448	178	287
Scoring Position	.269	.337	.449	156	42	9	2	5	63	18	25		.268	.331	.400	1020	273	36	9	27	380	108	168
Late and Close	.200	.263	.371	35	7	0	0	2	4	3	5		.238	.298	.367	390	93	13	2	11	41	31	63

BEN McDONALD — bats right — throws right — age 25 — BAL — P

3-YEAR TOTALS (1989–1991)

1991	G	IP	H	BB	SO	SB	CS	W	L	SV	ERA		G	IP	H	BB	SO	SB	CS	W	L	SV	ERA
Total	21	126.1	126	43	85	14	3	6	8	0	4.56		48	252.1	222	82	153	25	5	15	13	0	3.67
at Home	10	73.0	75	12	50	6	3	2	4	0	3.21		26	151.2	140	33	95	13	5	6	7	0	3.09
on Road	11	53.1	51	31	35	8	0	4	4	0	6.41		22	100.2	82	49	58	12	0	9	6	0	4.56
on Grass	18	110.0	110	38	75	13	3	5	8	0	4.42		42	219.2	196	70	132	24	5	11	13	0	3.65
on Turf	3	16.1	16	5	10	1	0	1	0	0	5.51		6	32.2	26	12	21	1	0	4	0	0	3.86
Day Games	4	24.0	26	4	17	1	0	0	1	0	4.88		12	53.2	53	13	28	4	0	2	3	0	4.53
Night Games	17	102.1	100	39	68	13	3	6	7	0	4.49		36	198.2	169	69	125	21	5	13	10	0	3.44
April	2	7.1	15	4	4	1	0	0	1	0	12.27		2	7.1	15	4	4	1	0	0	1	0	12.27
May	5	24.2	18	12	15	3	1	2	2	0	5.47		5	24.2	18	12	15	3	1	2	2	0	5.47
June	0	0	0	0	0	0	0	0	0	0	0.00		0	0	0	0	0	0	0	0	0	0	0.00
July	6	38.2	39	10	31	4	0	2	2	0	3.72		15	71.0	64	16	50	5	2	5	2	0	2.66
August	6	42.2	43	16	24	6	2	1	3	0	3.80		11	74.2	71	27	39	9	2	3	6	0	3.98
Sept–Oct	2	13.0	11	1	11	0	0	1	0	0	3.46		15	74.2	54	23	45	7	0	5	2	0	2.89

	BA	OBA	SA	AB	H	2B	3B	HR	RBI	BB	SO		BA	OBA	SA	AB	H	2B	3B	HR	RBI	BB	SO
Total	.261	.321	.418	483	126	22	3	16	62	43	85		.236	.296	.368	940	222	37	3	27	101	82	153
vs. Left	.216	.281	.349	255	55	8	1	8	30	24	50		.202	.266	.299	485	98	15	1	10	39	44	89
vs. Right	.311	.365	.496	228	71	14	2	8	32	19	35		.273	.327	.442	455	124	22	2	17	62	38	64
Bases Empty	.225	.283	.362	307	69	11	2	9	9	25	58		.217	.276	.334	590	128	20	2	15	15	48	104
Leadoff	.194	.248	.355	124	24	9	2	3	3	9	24		.197	.259	.314	239	47	9	2	5	5	20	40
Runners On Base	.324	.384	.517	176	57	11	1	7	53	18	27		.269	.327	.426	350	94	17	1	12	86	34	49
Scoring Position	.318	.411	.511	88	28	6	1	3	43	16	18		.240	.316	.385	179	43	9	1	5	69	24	33
Late and Close	.259	.310	.556	27	7	2	0	2	6	2	6		.194	.250	.398	108	21	4	0	6	14	8	16

JACK McDOWELL — bats right — throws right — age 26 — CHA — P

4-YEAR TOTALS (1987–1991)

1991	G	IP	H	BB	SO	SB	CS	W	L	SV	ERA		G	IP	H	BB	SO	SB	CS	W	L	SV	ERA
Total	35	253.2	212	82	191	22	10	17	10	0	3.41		98	645.1	564	233	455	61	24	39	29	0	3.61
at Home	20	138.2	134	48	101	14	5	10	6	0	3.89		57	374.2	323	133	265	37	12	24	13	0	3.41
on Road	15	115.0	78	34	90	8	5	7	4	0	2.82		41	270.2	241	100	190	24	12	15	16	0	3.89
on Grass	31	226.2	186	76	177	19	9	15	8	0	3.22		88	579.0	499	213	423	54	21	35	24	0	3.53
on Turf	4	27.0	26	6	14	3	1	2	2	0	5.00		10	66.1	65	20	32	7	3	4	5	0	4.34
Day Games	12	86.1	60	35	66	10	3	5	4	0	3.44		28	187.1	150	69	126	18	6	12	8	0	3.70
Night Games	23	167.1	152	47	125	12	7	12	6	0	3.39		70	458.0	414	164	329	43	18	27	21	0	3.58
April	5	36.1	24	13	31	4	2	4	1	0	2.97		14	79.1	66	33	64	7	3	6	4	0	4.54
May	6	39.0	47	20	32	4	1	1	2	0	5.08		15	92.1	102	42	71	12	5	2	7	0	4.87
June	6	49.1	28	14	33	6	4	4	1	0	2.01		17	121.1	86	44	83	14	5	9	3	0	2.37
July	5	41.2	31	7	26	2	0	4	1	0	2.59		16	112.2	103	31	77	8	6	6	4	0	3.51
August	6	43.0	42	11	35	3	1	2	3	0	3.98		19	130.1	111	44	81	11	1	8	6	0	3.38
Sept–Oct	7	44.1	40	17	34	3	2	2	2	0	4.06		17	109.1	96	39	79	9	4	8	5	0	3.62

	BA	OBA	SA	AB	H	2B	3B	HR	RBI	BB	SO		BA	OBA	SA	AB	H	2B	3B	HR	RBI	BB	SO
Total	.228	.292	.347	930	212	44	5	19	89	82	191		.235	.306	.356	2400	564	107	14	52	240	233	455
vs. Left	.225	.289	.326	476	107	23	2	7	39	41	84		.237	.306	.350	1244	295	52	7	25	115	119	213
vs. Right	.231	.295	.370	454	105	21	3	12	50	41	107		.233	.307	.362	1156	269	55	7	27	125	114	242
Bases Empty	.203	.272	.300	577	117	23	3	9	9	52	123		.223	.295	.330	1473	329	57	11	26	26	139	279
Leadoff	.201	.259	.320	244	49	12	1	5	5	18	55		.216	.278	.318	625	135	31	3	9	9	49	124
Runners On Base	.269	.325	.425	353	95	21	2	10	80	30	68		.254	.324	.398	927	235	50	3	26	214	94	176
Scoring Position	.268	.330	.402	194	52	12	1	4	59	19	43		.239	.321	.385	514	123	28	1	15	174	65	113
Late and Close	.228	.297	.359	92	21	6	0	2	7	8	21		.232	.298	.364	220	51	15	1	4	20	19	46

ROGER McDOWELL — bats right — throws right — age 32 — PHI/LA — P

7-YEAR TOTALS (1985–1991)

1991	G	IP	H	BB	SO	SB	CS	W	L	SV	ERA		G	IP	H	BB	SO	SB	CS	W	L	SV	ERA
Total	71	101.1	100	48	50	12	4	9	9	10	2.93		467	712.1	661	260	350	59	19	51	49	135	3.03
at Home	36	51.2	60	21	24	6	2	5	5	4	3.48		217	344.2	310	110	167	25	9	31	24	60	2.82
on Road	35	49.2	40	27	26	6	2	4	4	6	2.36		250	367.2	351	150	183	34	10	20	25	75	3.23
on Grass	36	50.0	48	23	25	5	1	5	4	6	3.06		266	431.2	391	136	213	31	7	32	25	79	2.71
on Turf	35	51.1	52	25	25	7	3	4	5	4	2.81		201	280.2	270	124	137	28	12	19	24	56	3.53
Day Games	20	31.1	26	14	18	2	1	2	2	3	3.16		172	270.0	251	96	140	21	10	18	20	49	3.43
Night Games	51	70.0	74	34	32	10	3	7	7	7	2.83		295	442.1	410	164	210	38	9	33	29	86	2.79
April	11	18.1	13	6	9	1	0	3	0	0	0.98		47	74.0	59	28	38	7	2	11	0	11	3.04
May	10	14.1	11	8	5	0	1	0	1	2	1.88		77	129.2	121	41	66	6	4	7	7	24	3.05
June	13	21.1	30	16	11	5	0	0	4	1	5.48		78	127.0	139	67	67	10	2	7	13	14	3.76
July	4	5.0	7	2	3	0	0	0	1	0	5.40		72	114.1	98	37	53	9	3	4	9	25	2.05
August	16	22.0	19	7	13	2	2	2	2	2	3.27		102	141.0	114	38	66	13	4	14	11	30	3.06
Sept–Oct	17	20.1	20	9	9	4	1	4	1	5	1.77		91	126.1	130	49	60	14	4	7	9	31	3.13

	BA	OBA	SA	AB	H	2B	3B	HR	RBI	BB	SO		BA	OBA	SA	AB	H	2B	3B	HR	RBI	BB	SO
Total	.262	.346	.357	381	100	20	2	4	47	48	50		.248	.317	.328	2660	661	95	13	30	308	260	350
vs. Left	.276	.387	.378	196	54	10	2	2	26	36	25		.262	.348	.350	1336	350	48	12	15	165	174	145
vs. Right	.249	.296	.335	185	46	10	0	2	21	12	25		.235	.284	.306	1324	311	47	1	15	143	86	205
Bases Empty	.281	.330	.422	192	54	11	2	4	4	14	24		.242	.299	.321	1389	336	49	8	15	15	111	180
Leadoff	.276	.323	.402	87	24	9	1	0	0	6	12		.248	.307	.323	600	149	26	2	5	5	50	73
Runners On Base	.243	.360	.291	189	46	9	0	0	43	34	26		.256	.335	.335	1271	325	46	5	15	293	149	170
Scoring Position	.227	.367	.258	132	30	4	0	0	42	29	17		.255	.356	.342	774	197	28	5	10	277	123	118
Late and Close	.271	.367	.360	258	70	14	0	3	29	40	34		.260	.333	.342	1644	428	53	8	22	212	179	197

JOSE MESA — bats right — throws right — age 26 — BAL — P

1991 / **3-YEAR TOTALS (1987–1991)**

1991	G	IP	H	BB	SO	SB	CS	W	L	SV	ERA	G	IP	H	BB	SO	SB	CS	W	L	SV	ERA
Total	23	123.2	151	62	64	11	5	6	11	0	5.97	36	201.2	226	104	105	13	7	10	16	0	5.49
at Home	12	58.2	67	34	32	7	1	2	8	0	5.68	18	95.1	96	56	53	9	1	4	11	0	5.76
on Road	11	65.0	84	28	32	4	4	4	3	0	6.23	18	106.1	130	48	52	4	6	6	5	0	5.25
on Grass	19	101.2	121	50	57	8	3	5	10	0	5.58	30	169.0	180	87	93	10	4	8	14	0	5.22
on Turf	4	22.0	30	12	7	3	2	1	1	0	7.77	6	32.2	46	17	12	3	3	2	2	0	6.89
Day Games	6	34.2	41	15	24	4	3	2	1	0	4.41	9	51.2	57	21	34	4	3	2	3	0	4.35
Night Games	17	89.0	110	47	40	7	2	4	10	0	6.57	27	150.0	169	83	71	9	4	8	13	0	5.88
April	4	24.1	22	11	17	3	1	1	3	0	3.33	4	24.1	22	11	17	3	1	1	3	0	3.33
May	7	44.1	48	22	15	3	1	3	2	0	4.47	7	44.1	48	22	15	3	1	3	2	0	4.47
June	5	19.0	35	11	8	2	2	0	3	0	11.84	5	19.0	35	11	8	2	2	0	3	0	11.84
July	0	0.0	0	0	0	0	0	0	0	0	0.00	0	0.0	0	0	0	0	0	0	0	0	0.00
August	2	13.0	10	4	12	0	0	1	0	0	5.54	3	19.2	16	7	14	0	0	1	1	0	6.41
Sept–Oct	5	23.0	36	14	12	3	1	1	3	0	7.04	17	94.1	105	53	51	5	3	7	6	0	5.06

	BA	OBA	SA	AB	H	2B	3B	HR	RBI	BB	SO	BA	OBA	SA	AB	H	2B	3B	HR	RBI	BB	SO
Total	.307	.385	.449	492	151	33	2	11	64	62	64	.286	.369	.433	790	226	50	3	20	105	104	105
vs. Left	.303	.378	.406	254	77	14	0	4	27	32	23	.287	.369	.404	418	120	20	1	9	53	55	49
vs. Right	.311	.393	.496	238	74	19	2	7	37	30	41	.285	.370	.465	372	106	30	2	11	52	49	56
Bases Empty	.284	.370	.395	271	77	13	1	5	5	35	30	.275	.363	.398	437	120	25	1	9	9	58	56
Leadoff	.341	.409	.496	123	42	4	0	5	5	14	9	.309	.385	.479	194	60	9	0	8	8	24	21
Runners On Base	.335	.403	.516	221	74	20	1	6	59	27	34	.300	.377	.476	353	106	25	2	11	96	46	49
Scoring Position	.352	.428	.557	122	43	11	1	4	53	19	18	.326	.415	.542	190	62	13	2	8	86	33	26
Late and Close	.250	.357	.333	12	3	1	0	0	0	0	2	0	.256	.356	.385	39	10	2	0	1	3	6	1

BOB MILACKI — bats right — throws right — age 28 — BAL — P

1991 / **4-YEAR TOTALS (1988–1991)**

1991	G	IP	H	BB	SO	SB	CS	W	L	SV	ERA	G	IP	H	BB	SO	SB	CS	W	L	SV	ERA
Total	31	184.0	175	53	108	12	6	10	9	0	4.01	98	587.1	560	211	299	51	15	31	29	0	3.86
at Home	15	83.2	98	18	50	6	6	4	4	0	5.16	47	280.0	283	99	149	25	11	13	14	0	4.18
on Road	16	100.1	77	35	58	6	0	6	5	0	3.05	51	307.1	277	112	150	26	4	18	15	0	3.57
on Grass	26	147.0	143	46	83	11	6	8	6	0	4.04	81	489.0	457	185	247	45	14	25	25	0	3.74
on Turf	5	37.0	32	7	25	1	0	2	3	0	3.89	17	98.1	103	26	52	6	1	6	4	0	4.48
Day Games	6	32.2	22	16	20	3	1	2	2	0	3.03	22	128.0	101	48	68	7	3	7	6	0	3.38
Night Games	25	151.1	153	37	88	9	5	8	7	0	4.22	76	459.1	459	163	231	44	12	24	23	0	4.00
April	1	5.1	1	2	1	0	0	1	0	0	0.00	11	67.0	51	32	23	8	1	3	1	0	3.22
May	6	21.1	25	12	10	2	0	0	2	0	5.48	18	88.2	104	46	38	16	2	2	9	0	5.28
June	6	38.1	37	11	26	4	3	3	0	0	3.52	18	116.2	121	35	69	11	8	7	4	0	3.93
July	5	33.0	24	10	17	1	0	2	3	0	4.91	17	90.1	93	33	43	4	1	3	8	0	4.88
August	6	41.0	43	5	23	2	0	2	2	0	3.51	12	88.1	76	17	50	4	0	6	4	0	3.46
Sept–Oct	7	45.0	45	13	31	3	3	2	2	0	4.00	22	136.1	115	48	76	8	3	10	3	0	2.77

	BA	OBA	SA	AB	H	2B	3B	HR	RBI	BB	SO	BA	OBA	SA	AB	H	2B	3B	HR	RBI	BB	SO
Total	.253	.305	.383	692	175	39	0	17	82	53	108	.253	.316	.383	2216	560	106	6	57	243	211	299
vs. Left	.257	.308	.352	358	92	19	0	5	41	28	56	.250	.317	.362	1136	284	53	4	22	108	115	158
vs. Right	.249	.301	.416	334	83	20	0	12	41	25	52	.256	.315	.406	1080	276	53	2	35	135	96	141
Bases Empty	.246	.303	.380	418	103	23	0	11	11	33	67	.247	.318	.375	1332	329	66	3	33	33	136	191
Leadoff	.298	.352	.472	178	53	10	0	7	7	14	26	.257	.324	.413	569	146	25	2	20	20	55	74
Runners On Base	.263	.308	.387	274	72	16	0	6	71	20	41	.261	.314	.395	884	231	40	3	24	210	75	108
Scoring Position	.331	.381	.478	136	45	8	0	4	64	14	23	.278	.339	.406	446	124	20	2	11	173	49	58
Late and Close	.196	.288	.391	46	9	3	0	2	3	6	4	.213	.318	.351	202	43	8	1	6	11	30	24

JEFF MONTGOMERY — bats right — throws right — age 30 — KC — P

1991 / **5-YEAR TOTALS (1987–1991)**

1991	G	IP	H	BB	SO	SB	CS	W	L	SV	ERA	G	IP	H	BB	SO	SB	CS	W	L	SV	ERA
Total	67	90.0	83	28	77	4	0	4	4	33	2.90	262	358.1	309	126	325	34	13	26	16	76	2.66
at Home	37	49.2	49	12	46	2	0	3	3	15	3.44	141	190.1	161	53	178	8	9	20	8	39	2.22
on Road	30	40.1	34	16	31	2	0	1	1	18	2.23	121	168.0	148	73	147	26	4	6	8	37	3.16
on Grass	24	31.1	27	10	21	2	0	1	1	15	2.01	87	129.0	109	55	108	19	3	6	7	27	3.00
on Turf	43	58.2	56	18	56	2	0	3	3	18	3.38	175	229.1	200	71	217	15	10	20	9	49	2.47
Day Games	17	24.0	26	12	19	1	0	0	1	9	4.50	71	103.0	87	38	94	16	6	8	4	18	2.71
Night Games	50	66.0	57	16	58	3	0	4	3	24	2.32	191	255.1	222	88	231	18	7	18	12	58	2.64
April	8	10.1	9	0	13	0	0	1	1	5	1.74	26	36.1	33	7	34	5	3	4	3	5	2.48
May	11	14.2	15	6	14	0	0	0	0	4	4.91	33	54.2	38	14	56	7	1	7	2	8	2.47
June	12	18.2	28	6	11	0	0	0	2	6	6.27	44	62.1	65	23	59	5	2	0	3	11	3.90
July	13	17.0	16	6	15	3	0	0	0	6	1.59	50	77.2	59	30	70	5	4	4	2	18	1.51
August	11	13.1	8	4	11	0	0	2	0	6	0.68	54	69.1	59	28	66	3	3	8	2	19	2.86
Sept–Oct	12	16.0	7	6	13	1	0	1	0	7	1.13	55	58.0	55	24	40	9	0	3	4	15	2.95

	BA	OBA	SA	AB	H	2B	3B	HR	RBI	BB	SO	BA	OBA	SA	AB	H	2B	3B	HR	RBI	BB	SO
Total	.246	.305	.355	338	83	15	2	6	43	28	77	.230	.300	.331	1342	309	58	4	23	153	126	325
vs. Left	.268	.330	.409	164	44	9	1	4	31	15	31	.257	.328	.374	641	165	32	2	13	84	66	104
vs. Right	.224	.282	.305	174	39	6	1	2	12	13	46	.205	.275	.291	701	144	26	2	10	69	60	221
Bases Empty	.256	.324	.400	160	41	10	2	3	3	15	33	.234	.301	.347	692	162	36	3	12	12	60	154
Leadoff	.239	.320	.418	67	16	6	0	2	2	8	12	.224	.292	.337	294	66	15	0	6	6	25	68
Runners On Base	.236	.289	.315	178	42	5	0	3	40	13	44	.226	.299	.314	650	147	22	1	11	141	66	171
Scoring Position	.221	.276	.295	122	27	3	0	2	37	9	31	.219	.307	.302	411	90	14	1	6	127	51	114
Late and Close	.243	.296	.345	255	62	9	1	5	39	18	53	.238	.300	.346	769	183	35	3	14	102	66	183

MIKE MOORE — bats right — throws right — age 33 — OAK — P

1991	G	IP	H	BB	SO	SB	CS	W	L	SV	ERA		G	IP	H	BB	SO	SB	CS	W	L	SV	ERA
Total	33	210.0	176	105	153	19	12	17	8	0	2.96		279	1843.2	1789	670	1163	97	74	102	109	2	3.91
at Home	18	117.2	81	54	81	7	7	11	3	0	2.14		144	963.1	894	354	612	47	39	59	47	2	3.50
on Road	15	92.1	95	51	72	12	5	6	5	0	4.00		135	880.1	895	316	551	50	35	43	62	0	4.34
on Grass	28	177.0	147	91	122	15	11	14	8	0	3.00		152	1003.0	940	369	623	58	42	62	60	0	3.79
on Turf	5	33.0	29	14	31	4	1	3	0	0	2.73		127	840.2	849	301	540	39	32	40	49	2	4.05
Day Games	14	84.2	70	42	68	10	4	10	1	0	3.51		85	553.0	540	195	369	36	20	35	35	0	3.87
Night Games	19	125.1	106	63	85	9	8	7	7	0	2.59		194	1290.2	1249	475	794	61	54	67	74	2	3.92
April	4	25.0	24	14	16	1	2	3	0	0	2.52		39	259.1	252	118	147	14	13	14	12	0	4.06
May	6	32.2	39	19	24	7	2	4	2	0	6.06		43	265.1	248	117	149	21	10	14	22	0	4.27
June	7	46.2	33	27	29	1	2	2	4	0	3.09		49	295.1	292	101	177	14	9	14	18	1	3.99
July	3	15.0	9	10	10	2	1	0	1	0	2.40		45	297.1	303	99	181	6	16	16	20	0	4.18
August	6	41.1	37	11	36	4	3	3	1	0	2.61		50	356.2	338	102	262	19	13	19	19	1	3.33
Sept–Oct	7	49.1	34	24	38	4	2	5	0	0	1.46		53	369.2	356	133	247	23	13	25	18	0	3.80

	BA	OBA	SA	AB	H	2B	3B	HR	RBI	BB	SO		BA	OBA	SA	AB	H	2B	3B	HR	RBI	BB	SO
Total	.229	.324	.318	768	176	35	0	11	65	105	153		.256	.322	.379	6998	1789	329	37	154	756	670	1163
vs. Left	.231	.324	.310	390	90	19	0	4	32	56	65		.257	.328	.371	3796	977	182	23	68	391	404	560
vs. Right	.228	.324	.325	378	86	16	0	7	33	49	88		.254	.314	.389	3202	812	147	14	86	365	266	603
Bases Empty	.225	.320	.337	448	101	20	0	10	10	58	98		.245	.309	.366	4171	1021	192	22	90	90	369	752
Leadoff	.219	.327	.333	192	42	7	0	5	5	30	40		.247	.307	.372	1783	440	78	11	41	41	147	301
Runners On Base	.234	.331	.291	320	75	15	0	1	55	47	55		.272	.339	.399	2827	768	137	15	64	666	301	411
Scoring Position	.210	.329	.260	181	38	9	0	0	51	33	34		.266	.344	.386	1577	419	81	9	30	574	206	230
Late and Close	.296	.367	.389	54	16	5	0	0	4	5	11		.253	.324	.379	672	170	37	3	14	62	66	109

MIKE MORGAN — bats right — throws right — age 33 — LA — P

1991	G	IP	H	BB	SO	SB	CS	W	L	SV	ERA		G	IP	H	BB	SO	SB	CS	W	L	SV	ERA
Total	34	236.1	197	61	140	24	7	14	10	1	2.78		201	1098.0	1108	317	549	82	49	58	76	3	3.84
at Home	17	119.1	100	32	71	7	3	6	5	1	3.32		100	587.2	582	152	301	44	24	27	39	2	3.87
on Road	17	117.0	97	29	69	17	4	8	5	0	2.23		101	510.1	526	165	248	38	25	31	37	1	3.79
on Grass	24	172.2	141	43	97	17	4	11	6	1	2.97		118	645.1	593	170	321	43	29	32	37	3	3.21
on Turf	10	63.2	56	18	43	7	3	3	4	0	2.26		83	452.2	515	147	228	39	20	26	39	0	4.73
Day Games	11	72.2	58	16	47	7	1	5	4	1	1.98		48	264.2	260	78	137	17	8	17	19	2	3.30
Night Games	23	163.2	139	45	93	17	6	9	6	0	3.13		153	833.1	848	239	412	65	41	41	57	1	4.01
April	4	31.2	20	6	12	1	0	2	2	0	1.42		33	175.2	153	40	68	6	6	10	14	1	3.48
May	5	35.2	33	9	25	2	3	3	2	0	2.52		37	202.0	192	66	130	11	11	13	12	1	3.61
June	6	46.1	35	7	24	6	0	4	1	0	2.91		30	197.0	204	39	89	12	7	9	13	1	3.11
July	6	32.0	30	12	18	3	3	0	1	1	3.09		34	166.0	186	68	63	20	6	6	13	1	4.88
August	6	40.0	36	16	23	4	1	1	3	0	3.60		36	184.1	186	54	97	15	9	5	15	0	3.91
Sept–Oct	7	50.2	43	11	38	8	0	4	1	0	2.84		31	173.0	187	50	102	18	10	11	9	0	4.21

	BA	OBA	SA	AB	H	2B	3B	HR	RBI	BB	SO		BA	OBA	SA	AB	H	2B	3B	HR	RBI	BB	SO
Total	.226	.278	.307	871	197	22	6	12	70	61	140		.263	.316	.384	4207	1108	180	24	93	444	317	549
vs. Left	.223	.285	.307	489	109	11	3	8	40	43	77		.271	.328	.392	2271	616	102	11	50	242	192	289
vs. Right	.230	.268	.306	382	88	11	3	4	30	18	63		.254	.302	.374	1936	492	78	13	43	202	125	260
Bases Empty	.214	.250	.304	570	122	12	3	11	11	26	93		.256	.304	.383	2525	647	96	17	63	63	162	347
Leadoff	.224	.249	.338	237	53	7	1	6	6	8	37		.252	.303	.375	1060	267	35	7	27	27	73	132
Runners On Base	.249	.327	.312	301	75	10	3	1	59	35	47		.274	.335	.386	1682	461	84	7	30	381	155	202
Scoring Position	.252	.354	.319	163	41	7	2	0	55	27	34		.254	.332	.362	952	242	51	5	14	335	115	137
Late and Close	.256	.313	.367	90	23	3	2	1	8	7	10		.278	.336	.382	327	91	10	3	6	31	27	35

JACK MORRIS — bats right — throws right — age 37 — MIN — P

1991	G	IP	H	BB	SO	SB	CS	W	L	SV	ERA		G	IP	H	BB	SO	SB	CS	W	L	SV	ERA
Total	35	246.2	226	92	163	32	8	18	12	0	3.43		268	1932.0	1760	703	1377	216	62	128	98	0	3.72
at Home	18	133.1	120	42	85	24	3	13	3	0	3.31		134	952.0	887	319	657	111	34	65	45	0	3.81
on Road	17	113.1	106	50	78	8	5	5	9	0	3.57		134	980.0	873	384	720	105	28	63	53	0	3.64
on Grass	16	104.1	100	47	74	8	5	4	9	0	3.88		215	1540.2	1399	579	1085	155	49	98	84	0	3.73
on Turf	19	142.1	126	45	89	24	3	14	3	0	3.10		53	391.1	361	124	292	61	13	30	14	0	3.68
Day Games	15	100.1	99	39	66	16	2	9	4	0	3.59		87	630.1	575	218	443	76	22	47	28	0	3.50
Night Games	20	146.1	127	53	97	16	6	9	8	0	3.32		181	1301.2	1185	485	934	140	40	81	70	0	3.83
April	5	32.0	42	16	25	10	1	2	3	0	5.34		42	304.1	301	122	233	41	10	20	19	0	3.96
May	6	42.2	36	23	28	1	4	3	2	0	3.80		45	320.2	276	129	243	36	22	19	18	0	3.68
June	6	48.0	36	15	25	3	1	6	0	0	2.25		40	275.0	280	91	173	29	8	25	9	0	4.35
July	5	27.2	28	7	17	5	0	2	2	0	5.20		39	281.0	260	79	203	30	9	15	17	0	3.43
August	6	44.2	45	13	33	6	2	2	3	0	3.83		48	340.0	302	126	226	35	7	22	17	0	4.16
Sept–Oct	7	51.2	39	18	35	7	0	3	2	0	1.74		54	411.0	341	156	299	45	6	27	18	0	3.00

	BA	OBA	SA	AB	H	2B	3B	HR	RBI	BB	SO		BA	OBA	SA	AB	H	2B	3B	HR	RBI	BB	SO
Total	.245	.315	.347	922	226	28	6	18	97	92	163		.241	.308	.377	7297	1760	276	47	207	790	703	1377
vs. Left	.282	.357	.396	450	127	18	3	9	51	55	62		.248	.321	.385	3806	944	139	30	107	437	415	673
vs. Right	.210	.272	.301	472	99	10	3	9	46	37	101		.234	.294	.369	3491	816	137	17	100	353	288	704
Bases Empty	.246	.309	.345	556	137	21	5	8	8	47	106		.238	.304	.381	4366	1039	181	27	130	130	403	848
Leadoff	.247	.303	.340	235	58	9	2	3	3	18	41		.245	.303	.407	1835	450	75	16	64	64	151	326
Runners On Base	.243	.323	.350	366	89	7	1	10	89	45	57		.246	.314	.371	2931	721	95	20	77	660	300	529
Scoring Position	.268	.359	.408	213	57	3	0	9	83	33	37		.243	.327	.377	1628	396	57	10	47	571	216	340
Late and Close	.243	.317	.351	111	27	4	1	2	11	11	18		.250	.310	.378	873	218	30	2	26	97	78	158

TERRY MULHOLLAND — bats right — throws left — age 29 — PHI — P

5-YEAR TOTALS (1986–1991)

1991	G	IP	H	BB	SO	SB	CS	W	L	SV	ERA		G	IP	H	BB	SO	SB	CS	W	L	SV	ERA
Total	34	232.0	231	49	142	6	5	16	13	0	3.61		116	628.2	641	169	328	21	14	32	38	0	3.89
at Home	18	130.2	121	28	83	2	4	11	2	0	2.96		54	324.0	284	85	167	6	7	19	13	0	2.97
on Road	16	101.1	110	21	59	4	1	5	11	0	4.44		62	304.2	357	84	161	15	7	13	25	0	4.87
on Grass	11	67.1	83	11	42	3	1	3	8	0	4.81		49	236.1	267	71	127	8	5	11	22	0	4.42
on Turf	23	164.2	148	38	100	3	4	13	5	0	3.12		67	392.1	374	98	201	13	9	21	16	0	3.58
Day Games	10	73.2	72	11	41	2	1	6	4	0	3.18		39	205.0	212	56	119	9	6	10	15	0	4.26
Night Games	24	158.1	159	38	101	4	4	10	9	0	3.81		77	423.2	429	113	209	12	8	22	23	0	3.72
April	5	34.0	33	8	10	3	0	2	2	0	2.91		9	53.1	57	14	15	6	0	3	2	0	3.54
May	6	45.2	40	8	23	1	2	4	1	0	3.35		17	80.1	79	20	35	1	3	6	3	0	3.81
June	5	22.1	36	10	13	0	2	0	5	0	7.66		21	77.2	100	33	43	4	3	1	11	0	6.61
July	5	40.0	37	5	33	2	0	3	2	0	2.25		25	159.0	153	28	83	7	4	7	8	0	2.72
August	6	42.0	43	11	31	0	0	3	1	0	3.64		22	132.2	131	36	86	1	0	8	7	0	3.60
Sept–Oct	7	48.0	42	7	32	0	1	4	2	0	3.56		22	125.2	121	38	64	2	4	7	7	0	4.23

	BA	OBA	SA	AB	H	2B	3B	HR	RBI	BB	SO		BA	OBA	SA	AB	H	2B	3B	HR	RBI	BB	SO
Total	.260	.299	.374	887	231	42	7	15	89	49	142		.265	.314	.386	2416	641	127	16	44	263	169	328
vs. Left	.255	.280	.414	157	40	3	2	6	20	6	19		.254	.296	.372	406	103	15	3	9	46	25	61
vs. Right	.262	.303	.366	730	191	39	5	9	69	43	123		.268	.317	.389	2010	538	112	13	35	217	144	267
Bases Empty	.242	.282	.348	532	129	26	6	6	6	26	89		.257	.303	.374	1411	363	74	11	23	23	86	192
Leadoff	.252	.286	.365	230	58	14	3	2	2	9	34		.284	.331	.411	616	175	38	5	10	10	39	77
Runners On Base	.287	.326	.414	355	102	16	1	9	83	23	53		.277	.328	.402	1005	278	53	5	21	240	83	136
Scoring Position	.300	.344	.484	190	57	12	1	7	77	16	24		.272	.333	.411	562	153	33	3	13	215	58	75
Late and Close	.230	.263	.372	113	26	5	1	3	11	3	17		.289	.316	.482	228	66	18	4	6	23	6	30

RANDY MYERS — bats left — throws left — age 30 — CIN — P

7-YEAR TOTALS (1985–1991)

1991	G	IP	H	BB	SO	SB	CS	W	L	SV	ERA		G	IP	H	BB	SO	SB	CS	W	L	SV	ERA
Total	58	132.0	116	80	108	4	7	6	13	6	3.55		309	458.2	354	215	470	18	20	27	32	93	2.85
at Home	34	72.0	63	44	57	3	3	3	5	5	3.75		167	244.2	172	115	241	10	12	16	8	54	2.61
on Road	24	60.0	53	36	51	1	4	3	8	1	3.30		142	214.0	182	100	229	8	8	11	24	39	3.11
on Grass	13	34.0	34	17	27	1	1	1	4	1	3.44		164	227.0	163	97	246	7	8	14	12	52	2.70
on Turf	45	98.0	82	63	81	3	6	5	9	5	3.58		145	231.2	191	118	224	11	12	13	20	41	2.99
Day Games	16	32.1	22	24	29	0	2	2	2	1	3.06		106	138.1	109	75	154	8	7	4	8	26	3.38
Night Games	42	99.2	94	56	79	4	5	4	11	5	3.70		203	320.1	245	140	316	10	13	23	24	67	2.61
April	7	6.1	5	7	0	1	0	1	0	3	2.84		38	41.2	37	27	52	5	2	3	3	16	3.89
May	13	17.2	18	12	14	2	3	1	2	1	3.57		50	61.2	40	24	69	3	7	7	2	13	2.04
June	16	21.1	12	11	23	0	1	3	2	2	1.69		59	84.2	59	40	83	4	3	8	8	14	2.13
July	8	23.0	20	14	17	1	1	0	3	0	5.87		52	85.0	69	33	75	2	3	2	6	16	3.39
August	7	32.1	32	22	20	1	0	1	4	0	3.34		55	91.1	80	44	84	2	3	1	8	19	2.66
Sept–Oct	7	31.1	26	16	27	0	1	1	1	0	3.45		55	94.1	69	47	107	2	2	6	5	15	3.24

	BA	OBA	SA	AB	H	2B	3B	HR	RBI	BB	SO		BA	OBA	SA	AB	H	2B	3B	HR	RBI	BB	SO
Total	.242	.347	.342	480	116	18	3	8	58	80	108		.215	.306	.315	1644	354	50	12	30	171	215	470
vs. Left	.287	.407	.426	122	35	6	1	3	18	26	38		.207	.309	.320	406	84	12	5	8	42	62	152
vs. Right	.226	.326	.313	358	81	12	2	5	40	54	70		.218	.305	.313	1238	270	38	7	22	129	153	318
Bases Empty	.228	.329	.340	259	59	9	1	6	6	39	63		.224	.310	.337	854	191	30	5	19	19	105	247
Leadoff	.216	.300	.302	116	25	5	1	1	1	14	23		.224	.304	.358	366	82	13	3	10	10	41	108
Runners On Base	.258	.368	.344	221	57	9	2	2	52	41	45		.206	.301	.291	790	163	20	7	11	152	110	223
Scoring Position	.264	.369	.326	129	34	5	0	1	47	24	31		.192	.292	.285	474	91	12	4	8	140	72	150
Late and Close	.278	.396	.379	169	47	9	1	2	20	34	36		.200	.293	.292	894	179	24	5	16	89	118	268

CHRIS NABHOLZ — bats left — throws left — age 25 — MON — P

2-YEAR TOTALS (1990–1991)

1991	G	IP	H	BB	SO	SB	CS	W	L	SV	ERA		G	IP	H	BB	SO	SB	CS	W	L	SV	ERA
Total	24	153.2	134	57	99	15	10	8	7	0	3.63		35	223.2	177	89	152	22	13	14	9	0	3.38
at Home	11	75.0	59	29	51	11	5	3	5	0	3.36		17	114.2	81	49	79	14	7	6	7	0	3.14
on Road	13	78.2	75	28	48	4	5	5	2	0	3.89		18	109.0	96	40	73	8	6	8	2	0	3.63
on Grass	4	23.1	27	11	13	0	1	1	2	0	6.56		7	43.1	38	20	30	4	1	3	2	0	4.78
on Turf	20	130.1	107	46	86	15	9	7	5	0	3.11		28	180.1	139	69	122	18	12	11	7	0	3.04
Day Games	7	44.0	40	21	30	8	3	2	2	0	4.91		10	66.1	49	29	43	8	4	3	0	0	3.93
Night Games	17	109.2	94	36	69	7	7	6	5	0	3.12		25	157.1	128	60	109	14	9	10	8	0	3.15
April	4	25.2	23	12	11	0	3	0	3	0	4.56		4	25.2	23	12	11	0	3	0	3	0	4.56
May	4	24.1	16	11	22	1	0	2	0	0	3.33		4	24.1	16	11	22	1	0	2	0	0	3.33
June	4	21.1	25	8	13	7	2	0	1	0	4.64		5	26.1	30	10	18	7	2	0	1	0	4.44
July	0	0.0	0	0	0	0	0	0	0	0	0.00		0	0.0	0	0	0	0	0	0	0	0	0.00
August	5	32.0	31	10	15	3	2	0	3	0	4.78		9	57.1	41	21	36	9	3	3	0	0	3.77
Sept–Oct	7	50.1	39	16	38	4	3	6	0	0	2.15		13	90.0	67	35	65	5	5	9	2	0	2.50

	BA	OBA	SA	AB	H	2B	3B	HR	RBI	BB	SO		BA	OBA	SA	AB	H	2B	3B	HR	RBI	BB	SO
Total	.237	.307	.336	566	134	35	3	5	51	57	99		.218	.297	.324	811	177	43	5	11	70	89	152
vs. Left	.227	.299	.392	97	22	6	2	2	8	10	26		.191	.292	.333	141	27	7	2	3	11	19	39
vs. Right	.239	.308	.324	469	112	29	1	3	43	47	73		.224	.298	.322	670	150	36	3	8	59	70	113
Bases Empty	.235	.305	.338	340	80	16	2	5	5	34	67		.215	.301	.329	492	106	21	4	9	9	58	100
Leadoff	.255	.329	.407	145	37	9	2	3	3	16	27		.230	.312	.388	209	48	12	3	5	5	24	41
Runners On Base	.239	.310	.332	226	54	19	1	0	46	23	32		.223	.291	.317	319	71	22	1	2	61	31	52
Scoring Position	.260	.340	.350	123	32	11	0	0	43	15	16		.227	.309	.294	163	37	11	0	0	54	20	27
Late and Close	.200	.351	.233	30	6	1	0	0	2	7	2		.151	.297	.170	53	8	1	0	0	2	11	5

CHARLES NAGY — bats left — throws right — age 25 — CLE — P

1991	G	IP	H	BB	SO	SB	CS	W	L	SV	ERA
Total	33	211.1	228	66	109	23	8	10	15	0	4.13
at Home	13	93.2	92	25	55	14	4	6	5	0	3.56
on Road	20	117.2	136	41	54	9	4	4	10	0	4.59
on Grass	27	172.1	184	49	85	19	6	10	10	0	4.07
on Turf	6	39.0	44	17	24	4	2	0	5	0	4.38
Day Games	11	73.0	75	22	48	8	4	3	6	0	3.95
Night Games	22	138.1	153	44	61	15	4	7	9	0	4.23
April	4	28.2	19	10	17	0	2	1	1	0	1.57
May	6	33.2	39	15	15	6	0	0	4	0	6.42
June	6	37.0	46	12	26	4	3	2	4	0	3.41
July	5	38.0	34	10	9	0	2	3	1	0	1.42
August	6	33.0	46	12	22	5	1	2	1	0	6.82
Sept–Oct	6	41.0	44	7	20	8	0	2	4	0	5.05

	BA	OBA	SA	AB	H	2B	3B	HR	RBI	BB	SO
Total	.275	.330	.403	828	228	45	8	15	89	66	109
vs. Left	.288	.339	.416	452	130	25	6	7	47	36	62
vs. Right	.261	.319	.388	376	98	20	2	8	42	30	47
Bases Empty	.284	.336	.399	464	132	26	6	5		36	68
Leadoff	.272	.324	.393	206	56	10	3	3	3	16	35
Runners On Base	.264	.323	.409	364	96	19	2	10	84	30	41
Scoring Position	.238	.308	.379	206	49	9	1	6	71	21	29
Late and Close	.236	.291	.264	72	17	2	0	0	3	6	10

2-YEAR TOTALS (1990–1991)

	G	IP	H	BB	SO	SB	CS	W	L	SV	ERA
	42	257.0	286	87	135	25	10	12	19	0	4.45
	20	131.2	139	39	76	15	5	8	8	0	4.03
	22	125.1	147	48	59	10	5	4	11	0	4.88
	34	210.1	231	63	106	20	7	12	13	0	4.28
	8	46.2	55	24	29	5	3	0	6	0	5.21
	15	93.2	99	32	59	10	5	4	8	0	4.42
	27	163.1	187	55	76	15	5	8	11	0	4.46
	4	28.2	19	10	17	0	2	1	1	0	1.57
	6	33.2	39	15	15	6	0	0	4	0	6.42
	7	41.1	53	16	27	4	3	2	5	0	3.92
	7	46.1	46	14	13	1	2	3	3	0	2.91
	7	38.1	53	14	23	5	1	2	1	0	6.57
	11	68.2	76	18	40	9	2	4	5	0	4.85

	BA	OBA	SA	AB	H	2B	3B	HR	RBI	BB	SO
	.283	.341	.417	1012	286	54	8	22	118	87	135
	.295	.351	.421	556	164	28	6	10	63	48	79
	.268	.328	.412	456	122	26	2	12	55	39	56
	.282	.335	.406	574	162	32	6	9		46	86
	.270	.321	.381	252	68	13	3	3	3	19	39
	.283	.347	.432	438	124	22	2	13	109	41	49
	.259	.330	.404	255	66	11	1	8	94	28	37
	.225	.276	.250	80	18	2	0	0	3	6	12

JAIME NAVARRO — bats right — throws right — age 25 — MIL — P

1991	G	IP	H	BB	SO	SB	CS	W	L	SV	ERA
Total	34	234.0	237	73	114	23	7	15	12	0	3.92
at Home	16	113.0	111	34	60	10	3	9	3	0	3.58
on Road	18	121.0	126	39	54	13	4	6	9	0	4.24
on Grass	27	191.0	181	59	92	20	5	13	8	0	3.63
on Turf	7	43.0	56	14	22	3	2	2	4	0	5.23
Day Games	10	73.0	68	19	38	9	2	6	3	0	3.33
Night Games	24	161.0	169	54	76	14	5	9	9	0	4.19
April	4	18.2	30	7	13	0	1	1	0	0	6.27
May	6	48.2	43	7	26	4	1	4	2	0	2.59
June	5	36.0	35	14	18	1	2	2	2	0	4.25
July	6	43.0	51	15	21	4	2	1	4	0	4.19
August	6	34.1	37	15	14	3	0	4	2	0	6.03
Sept–Oct	7	53.1	41	15	22	4	2	3	2	0	2.53

	BA	OBA	SA	AB	H	2B	3B	HR	RBI	BB	SO
Total	.261	.318	.370	908	237	39	3	18	104	73	114
vs. Left	.261	.322	.380	463	121	14	1	13	57	43	51
vs. Right	.261	.313	.360	445	116	25	2	5	47	30	63
Bases Empty	.265	.318	.373	528	140	25	1	10	10	37	76
Leadoff	.241	.303	.357	224	54	8	0	6	6	17	38
Runners On Base	.255	.317	.366	380	97	14	2	8	94	36	38
Scoring Position	.252	.314	.379	214	54	10	1	5	84	22	19
Late and Close	.234	.279	.383	94	22	5	0	3	10	6	10

3-YEAR TOTALS (1989–1991)

	G	IP	H	BB	SO	SB	CS	W	L	SV	ERA
	85	493.0	532	146	245	46	16	30	27	1	3.91
	43	252.2	257	77	126	25	7	19	11	1	3.53
	42	240.1	275	69	119	21	9	11	16	0	4.31
	70	411.1	422	125	194	43	13	24	21	1	3.59
	15	81.2	110	21	51	3	3	6	6	0	5.51
	33	172.1	179	46	94	16	4	11	10	0	3.39
	52	320.2	353	100	151	30	12	19	17	1	4.18
	8	37.2	57	15	21	2	2	1	0	0	5.73
	10	65.0	73	11	32	4	1	5	3	0	4.15
	10	65.2	69	27	35	15	2	4	3	0	3.84
	19	86.0	94	27	45	7	4	7	7	1	3.35
	19	100.2	107	31	54	7	3	9	8	0	5.10
	19	138.0	132	35	58	11	4	9	6	0	2.80

	BA	OBA	SA	AB	H	2B	3B	HR	RBI	BB	SO
	.275	.327	.380	1938	532	80	10	35	207	146	245
	.277	.333	.376	971	269	33	3	19	102	84	114
	.272	.320	.385	967	263	47	7	16	105	62	131
	.270	.323	.375	1101	297	45	7	19	19	79	144
	.245	.304	.344	477	117	16	2	9	9	36	64
	.281	.332	.387	837	235	35	3	16	188	67	101
	.267	.326	.359	460	123	19	1	7	160	44	59
	.305	.341	.455	167	51	8	1	5	22	10	20

BOB OJEDA — bats left — throws left — age 35 — LA — P

1991	G	IP	H	BB	SO	SB	CS	W	L	SV	ERA
Total	31	189.1	181	70	120	23	15	12	9	0	3.18
at Home	15	98.2	95	34	67	11	6	6	4	0	3.01
on Road	16	90.2	86	36	53	12	9	6	5	0	3.38
on Grass	20	125.1	127	43	80	16	10	8	6	0	3.30
on Turf	11	64.0	54	27	40	7	5	4	3	0	2.95
Day Games	9	53.2	58	20	28	10	5	2	4	0	4.36
Night Games	22	135.2	123	50	92	13	10	10	5	0	2.72
April	4	22.0	31	5	10	3	2	1	3	0	5.32
May	6	39.0	38	18	23	3	3	3	1	0	3.23
June	4	30.1	22	7	17	2	1	2	1	0	1.19
July	5	29.1	32	13	16	4	2	2	3	0	4.60
August	6	30.0	24	15	21	3	1	1	1	0	3.30
Sept–Oct	6	38.2	34	12	33	2	4	3	1	0	2.33

	BA	OBA	SA	AB	H	2B	3B	HR	RBI	BB	SO
Total	.257	.323	.376	705	181	31	4	15	72	70	120
vs. Left	.257	.301	.324	136	35	4	1	1	11	7	36
vs. Right	.257	.328	.388	569	146	27	3	14	61	63	84
Bases Empty	.264	.327	.409	413	109	20	2	12	12	38	71
Leadoff	.249	.310	.381	181	45	7	1	5	5	15	29
Runners On Base	.247	.316	.329	292	72	11	2	3	60	32	49
Scoring Position	.231	.307	.283	173	40	5	2	0	52	23	30
Late and Close	.316	.435	.421	38	12	2	1	0	2	7	5

8-YEAR TOTALS (1984–1991)

	G	IP	H	BB	SO	SB	CS	W	L	SV	ERA
	243	1327.2	1248	427	818	136	80	84	72	1	3.39
	121	680.1	651	202	446	63	43	41	35	0	3.39
	122	647.1	597	225	372	73	37	43	37	1	3.39
	178	982.1	925	304	633	90	58	63	51	1	3.39
	65	345.1	323	123	185	46	22	21	21	0	3.39
	83	431.1	399	127	241	49	26	26	21	1	3.15
	160	896.1	849	300	577	87	54	58	51	0	3.50
	41	164.1	178	62	86	15	15	11	11	0	4.16
	45	239.1	200	79	162	29	16	15	15	1	2.78
	37	260.0	265	86	151	35	16	16	9	0	3.63
	37	205.1	188	61	129	22	9	12	13	0	3.51
	42	204.0	208	70	120	23	11	13	11	0	3.88
	41	254.2	209	69	120	12	13	17	12	0	2.72

	BA	OBA	SA	AB	H	2B	3B	HR	RBI	BB	SO
	.250	.309	.365	4997	1248	227	33	95	486	427	818
	.223	.277	.325	981	219	37	9	15	74	69	220
	.256	.316	.375	4016	1029	190	24	80	412	358	598
	.258	.313	.381	2946	760	145	17	61	61	227	465
	.255	.313	.377	1261	321	61	9	25	25	102	177
	.238	.303	.343	2051	488	82	16	34	425	200	353
	.244	.317	.343	1140	278	40	11	17	368	135	214
	.253	.331	.347	513	130	22	4	6	44	60	80

STEVE OLIN — bats right — throws right — age 27 — CLE — P

1991

	G	IP	H	BB	SO	SB	CS	W	L	SV	ERA
Total	48	56.1	61	23	38	3	2	3	6	17	3.36
at Home	19	21.1	20	10	11	0	0	0	1	7	3.80
on Road	29	35.0	41	13	27	3	2	3	5	10	3.09
on Grass	43	53.0	53	21	35	3	2	3	5	16	3.23
on Turf	5	3.1	8	2	3	0	0	0	1	1	5.40
Day Games	16	21.0	17	9	15	1	1	2	2	4	1.71
Night Games	32	35.1	44	14	23	2	1	1	4	13	4.33
April	8	12.2	10	3	5	0	1	2	1	0	2.84
May	6	6.2	11	3	4	0	0	0	2	0	10.80
June	0	0.0	0	0	0	0	0	0	0	0	0.00
July	8	11.2	9	4	11	2	1	0	0	4	1.54
August	12	11.0	17	4	11	0	0	0	3	5	3.27
Sept–Oct	14	14.1	14	9	7	1	0	0	1	8	1.88

	BA	OBA	SA	AB	H	2B	3B	HR	RBI	BB	SO
Total	.274	.344	.354	223	61	10	1	2	29	23	38
vs. Left	.333	.404	.422	102	34	4	1	1	11	12	10
vs. Right	.223	.293	.298	121	27	6	0	1	18	11	28
Bases Empty	.250	.306	.286	112	28	4	0	0		9	22
Leadoff	.208	.269	.229	48	10	1	0	0		4	10
Runners On Base	.297	.381	.423	111	33	6	1	2	29	14	16
Scoring Position	.328	.444	.418	67	22	3	0	1	24	13	10
Late and Close	.235	.318	.288	132	31	4	0	1	15	16	26

3-YEAR TOTALS (1989–1991)

	G	IP	H	BB	SO	SB	CS	W	L	SV	ERA
Total	123	184.2	192	63	126	16	6	8	14	19	3.46
at Home	53	76.1	83	34	51	7	1	1	3	7	4.48
on Road	70	108.1	109	29	75	9	5	7	11	12	2.74
on Grass	106	162.1	163	55	114	13	6	7	10	17	3.38
on Turf	17	22.1	29	8	12	3	0	1	4	2	4.03
Day Games	39	56.2	65	20	51	4	2	3	4	4	3.97
Night Games	84	128.0	127	43	75	12	4	5	10	15	3.23
April	13	20.2	20	4	14	0	1	2	2	0	2.61
May	16	22.2	26	6	11	3	1	1	3	0	5.96
June	4	4.1	8	2	3	0	0	0	0	0	8.31
July	17	29.1	27	8	22	3	2	0	0	4	2.76
August	31	51.2	56	17	38	3	1	2	6	6	3.14
Sept–Oct	42	56.0	55	26	38	7	1	3	3	9	3.05

	BA	OBA	SA	AB	H	2B	3B	HR	RBI	BB	SO
Total	.269	.333	.343	715	192	29	3	6	95	63	126
vs. Left	.317	.385	.413	293	93	15	2	3	36	31	33
vs. Right	.235	.296	.294	422	99	14	1	3	59	32	93
Bases Empty	.253	.306	.310	352	89	13	2	1	1	24	73
Leadoff	.233	.290	.293	150	35	7	1	0	0	10	33
Runners On Base	.284	.358	.375	363	103	16	1	5	94	39	53
Scoring Position	.303	.392	.373	228	69	10	0	2	83	33	36
Late and Close	.250	.333	.311	228	57	6	1	2	24	28	41

OMAR OLIVARES — bats right — throws right — age 25 — SL — P

1991

	G	IP	H	BB	SO	SB	CS	W	L	SV	ERA
Total	28	167.1	148	61	91	10	11	11	7	1	3.71
at Home	16	97.1	88	31	51	7	8	7	5	1	3.33
on Road	12	70.0	60	30	40	3	3	4	2	0	4.24
on Grass	6	38.0	36	17	22	1	1	1	1	0	5.68
on Turf	22	129.1	112	44	69	9	10	10	6	1	3.13
Day Games	6	38.0	39	12	25	3	1	2	2	0	4.74
Night Games	22	129.1	109	49	66	7	10	9	5	1	3.41
April	3	7.0	6	3	5	0	0	0	0	1	5.14
May	1	5.0	5	2	2	0	0	0	0	0	7.20
June	6	35.2	34	17	10	1	2	1	1	0	5.30
July	5	24.0	23	13	17	2	4	2	2	0	4.88
August	6	42.1	38	10	22	2	1	4	2	0	2.13
Sept–Oct	7	53.1	42	16	35	5	3	4	2	0	2.87

	BA	OBA	SA	AB	H	2B	3B	HR	RBI	BB	SO
Total	.243	.316	.356	609	148	22	4	13	64	61	91
vs. Left	.232	.319	.321	340	79	9	3	5	32	41	48
vs. Right	.257	.313	.401	269	69	13	1	8	32	20	43
Bases Empty	.233	.307	.342	377	88	13	2	8	8	36	61
Leadoff	.209	.259	.282	163	34	7	1	1	1	11	28
Runners On Base	.259	.331	.379	232	60	9	2	5	56	25	30
Scoring Position	.268	.352	.350	123	33	5	1	1	43	17	15
Late and Close	.232	.358	.357	56	13	2	1	1	1	10	8

2-YEAR TOTALS (1990–1991)

	G	IP	H	BB	SO	SB	CS	W	L	SV	ERA
Total	37	216.2	193	78	111	12	14	12	8	1	3.53
at Home	19	110.0	97	35	54	7	8	7	5	1	3.19
on Road	18	106.2	96	43	57	5	6	5	3	0	3.88
on Grass	8	49.2	55	20	23	1	4	1	1	0	5.62
on Turf	29	167.0	138	58	88	11	10	11	7	1	2.91
Day Games	7	43.0	47	15	25	3	2	2	2	0	5.02
Night Games	30	173.2	146	63	86	9	11	10	6	1	3.16
April	3	7.0	6	3	5	0	0	0	0	1	5.14
May	1	5.0	5	2	2	0	0	0	0	0	7.20
June	6	35.2	34	17	10	1	2	1	1	0	5.30
July	5	24.0	23	13	17	2	4	2	2	0	4.88
August	9	63.2	56	16	29	3	2	4	2	0	2.12
Sept–Oct	13	81.1	69	27	48	6	5	5	3	0	3.10

	BA	OBA	SA	AB	H	2B	3B	HR	RBI	BB	SO
Total	.244	.317	.351	790	193	29	5	15	78	78	111
vs. Left	.222	.314	.297	424	94	11	3	5	38	54	58
vs. Right	.270	.321	.413	366	99	18	2	10	40	24	53
Bases Empty	.237	.313	.345	481	114	16	3	10	10	47	75
Leadoff	.234	.286	.340	209	49	9	2	3	3	15	32
Runners On Base	.256	.324	.359	309	79	13	2	5	68	31	36
Scoring Position	.264	.341	.337	163	43	7	1	1	53	20	18
Late and Close	.211	.326	.316	76	16	3	1	1	1	12	10

GREGG OLSON — bats right — throws right — age 26 — BAL — P

1991

	G	IP	H	BB	SO	SB	CS	W	L	SV	ERA
Total	72	73.2	74	29	72	13	1	4	6	31	3.18
at Home	35	34.1	31	19	33	9	1	3	1	13	3.15
on Road	37	39.1	43	10	39	4	0	1	5	18	3.20
on Grass	61	58.2	54	23	55	11	1	3	3	28	2.76
on Turf	11	15.0	20	6	17	2	0	1	3	3	4.80
Day Games	20	22.1	32	14	21	1	1	1	5	7	7.25
Night Games	52	51.1	42	15	51	12	0	3	1	24	1.40
April	7	6.1	6	0	4	0	1	0	0	8	1.42
May	11	12.0	12	7	13	1	0	0	1	5	3.00
June	14	14.2	12	7	18	1	0	1	1	8	4.91
July	14	14.2	16	2	15	2	0	0	1	7	3.07
August	13	12.0	17	7	7	5	0	2	0	4	3.00
Sept–Oct	13	14.0	11	6	15	4	0	1	3	5	2.57

	BA	OBA	SA	AB	H	2B	3B	HR	RBI	BB	SO
Total	.261	.331	.304	283	74	5	2	1	36	29	72
vs. Left	.230	.316	.266	139	32	2	0	1	15	17	39
vs. Right	.292	.346	.340	144	42	3	2	0	21	12	33
Bases Empty	.246	.293	.304	138	34	3	1	1	1	8	35
Leadoff	.206	.219	.302	63	13	1	1	1	1	1	8
Runners On Base	.276	.365	.303	145	40	2	1	0	35	21	37
Scoring Position	.269	.384	.301	93	25	1	1	0	34	18	25
Late and Close	.268	.341	.320	194	52	3	2	1	29	21	50

4-YEAR TOTALS (1988–1991)

	G	IP	H	BB	SO	SB	CS	W	L	SV	ERA
Total	210	244.0	198	116	245	43	4	16	14	95	2.43
at Home	104	116.0	82	62	130	29	1	11	1	38	2.09
on Road	106	128.0	116	54	115	14	3	5	13	57	2.74
on Grass	172	196.0	140	92	201	36	3	13	8	82	2.11
on Turf	38	48.0	58	24	44	7	1	3	6	13	3.75
Day Games	51	63.0	59	29	51	8	2	2	7	26	4.29
Night Games	159	181.0	139	87	194	35	2	14	7	69	1.79
April	24	35.2	25	13	24	5	2	3	0	8	1.77
May	32	42.0	35	21	51	4	2	1	1	13	1.50
June	36	39.0	31	14	43	11	0	3	4	21	3.00
July	38	42.2	41	25	48	3	0	1	4	20	2.74
August	33	34.0	32	19	28	9	0	2	1	15	3.44
Sept–Oct	47	50.2	44	24	51	11	0	5	4	18	2.31

	BA	OBA	SA	AB	H	2B	3B	HR	RBI	BB	SO
Total	.221	.312	.278	896	198	29	2	6	86	116	245
vs. Left	.188	.291	.220	446	84	8	0	2	36	62	117
vs. Right	.253	.334	.336	450	114	21	2	4	50	54	128
Bases Empty	.229	.297	.303	433	99	18	1	4	4	39	117
Leadoff	.180	.261	.273	183	33	3	1	4	4	18	47
Runners On Base	.214	.326	.255	463	99	11	1	2	82	77	128
Scoring Position	.204	.337	.241	299	61	6	1	1	79	61	91
Late and Close	.217	.314	.271	608	132	17	2	4	65	84	168

AL OSUNA — bats right — throws left — age 27 — HOU — P

1991 | **2-YEAR TOTALS (1990–1991)**

1991	G	IP	H	BB	SO	SB	CS	W	L	SV	ERA	G	IP	H	BB	SO	SB	CS	W	L	SV	ERA
Total	71	81.2	59	46	68	2	0	7	6	12	3.42	83	93.0	69	52	74	2	1	9	6	12	3.58
at Home	37	41.1	29	23	32	2	0	4	3	5	4.35	43	45.2	37	25	35	2	1	5	3	5	4.93
on Road	34	40.1	30	23	36	0	0	3	3	7	2.45	40	47.1	32	27	39	0	0	4	3	7	2.28
on Grass	19	20.2	14	10	19	0	0	2	0	5	2.61	23	24.0	16	12	20	0	0	3	0	5	2.63
on Turf	52	61.0	45	36	49	2	0	5	6	7	3.69	60	69.0	53	40	54	2	1	6	6	7	3.91
Day Games	17	23.2	12	9	21	0	0	1	1	3	1.90	19	25.2	16	9	24	0	0	1	1	3	2.81
Night Games	54	58.0	47	37	47	2	0	6	5	9	4.03	64	67.1	53	43	50	2	1	8	5	9	3.88
April	10	9.0	7	3	3	0	0	1	0	0	1.00	10	9.0	7	3	3	0	0	1	0	0	1.00
May	11	12.2	7	6	13	0	0	0	2	4	3.55	11	12.2	7	6	13	0	0	0	2	4	3.55
June	13	13.2	14	9	8	2	0	3	0	1	2.63	13	13.2	14	9	8	2	0	3	0	1	2.63
July	11	17.1	8	14	17	0	0	2	1	2	1.56	11	17.1	8	14	17	0	0	2	1	2	1.56
August	13	15.0	13	7	11	0	0	1	2	2	3.60	13	15.0	13	7	11	0	0	1	2	2	3.60
Sept–Oct	13	14.0	10	7	16	0	0		1	3	7.71	25	25.1	20	13	22	0	1	2	1	3	6.39

	BA	OBA	SA	AB	H	2B	3B	HR	RBI	BB	SO	BA	OBA	SA	AB	H	2B	3B	HR	RBI	BB	SO
Total	.201	.311	.304	293	59	13	1	5	38	46	68	.209	.322	.324	330	69	16	2	6	42	52	74
vs. Left	.239	.298	.349	109	26	3	0	3	21	10	24	.232	.315	.328	125	29	3	0	3	21	13	28
vs. Right	.179	.318	.277	184	33	10	1	2	17	36	44	.195	.325	.322	205	40	13	2	3	21	39	46
Bases Empty	.159	.267	.261	157	25	7	0	3	3	23	41	.165	.280	.280	182	30	7	1	4	4	27	46
Leadoff	.152	.253	.242	66	10	3	0	1	1	9	18	.171	.284	.276	76	13	3	1	1	1	11	19
Runners On Base	.250	.359	.353	136	34	6	1	2	35	23	27	.264	.370	.378	148	39	9	1	2	38	25	28
Scoring Position	.266	.394	.392	79	21	2	1	2	34	19	17	.262	.389	.393	84	22	3	1	2	37	20	18
Late and Close	.206	.326	.322	199	41	9	1	4	32	35	40	.214	.335	.341	220	47	11	1	5	34	39	43

ALEJANDRO PENA — bats right — throws right — age 33 — NYN/ATL — P

1991 | **8-YEAR TOTALS (1984–1991)**

1991	G	IP	H	BB	SO	SB	CS	W	L	SV	ERA	G	IP	H	BB	SO	SB	CS	W	L	SV	ERA
Total	59	82.1	74	22	62	8	4	8	1	15	2.40	316	690.2	631	206	556	69	31	36	29	50	2.83
at Home	30	38.1	38	13	31	3	1	4	1	5	3.05	154	332.2	288	100	255	40	16	16	14	23	2.52
on Road	29	44.0	36	9	31	5	3	4	0	10	1.84	162	358.0	343	106	301	29	15	20	15	27	3.12
on Grass	43	59.2	52	19	47	5	3	6	1	10	2.26	224	482.2	432	138	372	49	24	27	21	38	2.69
on Turf	16	22.2	22	3	15	3	1	2	0	5	2.78	92	208.0	199	68	184	20	7	9	8	12	3.16
Day Games	13	16.2	15	7	14	2	0	2	0	3	3.24	91	199.2	173	53	150	16	7	11	5	17	2.75
Night Games	46	65.2	59	15	48	6	4	6	1	12	2.19	225	491.0	458	153	406	53	24	25	24	33	2.86
April	7	9.0	5	3	3	0	0	0	0	1	2.00	36	98.1	82	19	71	2	4	6	2	7	1.92
May	8	10.2	12	5	6	0	0	1	0	1	4.22	49	106.1	119	45	79	17	3	5	9	3	4.23
June	9	14.1	17	2	13	4	1	3	0	1	2.51	61	118.0	118	43	114	18	6	8	7	5	3.28
July	11	14.2	14	7	13	3	2	2	0	1	2.45	51	135.1	109	45	94	13	9	8	2	5	2.73
August	10	16.0	18	2	14	1	1	0	1	0	3.38	52	123.2	127	32	97	12	9	4	6	3	2.98
Sept–Oct	14	17.2	8	3	13	0	0	2	0	11	0.51	67	109.0	76	22	101	7	0	5	3	27	1.73

	BA	OBA	SA	AB	H	2B	3B	HR	RBI	BB	SO	BA	OBA	SA	AB	H	2B	3B	HR	RBI	BB	SO
Total	.245	.293	.341	302	74	9	1	6	30	22	62	.243	.298	.338	2599	631	101	9	43	244	206	556
vs. Left	.197	.261	.286	147	29	4	0	3	14	14	33	.249	.317	.334	1286	320	42	7	18	100	130	268
vs. Right	.290	.323	.394	155	45	5	1	3	16	9	29	.237	.279	.342	1313	311	59	2	25	144	76	288
Bases Empty	.244	.293	.313	176	43	5	0	3	3	12	29	.239	.292	.342	1495	357	49	5	32	32	110	302
Leadoff	.130	.167	.174	69	9	0	0	1	1	3	12	.220	.275	.325	628	138	23	2	13	13	47	132
Runners On Base	.246	.293	.381	126	31	6	1	3	27	10	33	.248	.307	.332	1104	274	52	4	11	212	96	254
Scoring Position	.271	.329	.471	70	19	3	1	3	27	8	20	.237	.313	.316	630	149	28	2	6	189	77	160
Late and Close	.231	.278	.299	147	34	4	0	2	19	11	32	.223	.286	.305	847	189	34	3	11	84	74	209

DAN PLESAC — bats left — throws left — age 30 — MIL — P

1991 | **6-YEAR TOTALS (1986–1991)**

1991	G	IP	H	BB	SO	SB	CS	W	L	SV	ERA	G	IP	H	BB	SO	SB	CS	W	L	SV	ERA
Total	45	92.1	92	39	61	4	4	2	7	8	4.29	321	445.1	396	151	394	27	12	24	33	132	3.25
at Home	22	48.0	49	27	38	2	2	0	4	5	5.63	158	225.0	204	78	210	19	7	12	13	62	3.84
on Road	23	44.1	43	12	23	2	2	2	3	3	2.84	163	220.1	192	73	184	8	5	12	20	70	2.66
on Grass	37	79.2	81	38	57	4	3	2	6	7	4.63	269	377.1	337	132	347	26	11	22	27	105	3.55
on Turf	8	12.2	11	1	4	0	1	0	1	1	2.13	52	68.0	59	19	47	1	1	2	6	27	1.59
Day Games	12	21.1	20	14	20	0	1	0	1	3	3.80	94	130.0	109	51	121	13	5	6	8	36	2.98
Night Games	33	71.0	72	25	41	4	3	2	6	5	4.44	227	315.1	287	100	273	14	7	18	25	96	3.37
April	8	9.1	14	1	5	0	0	0	1	0	4.82	42	56.2	48	16	55	3	1	2	4	14	3.18
May	5	5.0	2	3	3	0	0	0	0	1	0.00	46	65.0	60	18	68	1	2	4	4	28	2.91
June	11	11.1	7	3	8	2	0	0	0	3	3.18	66	67.2	64	29	45	4	5	7	6	27	3.46
July	10	14.2	11	8	10	1	0	0	2	1	2.45	56	74.2	72	29	59	13	1	4	8	24	3.62
August	4	19.0	17	9	11	0	1	1	1	0	4.74	50	82.2	53	26	68	3	1	4	3	17	2.40
Sept–Oct	7	33.0	41	15	24	1	1	1	2	0	5.73	61	98.2	99	33	71	3	2	3	8	22	3.83

	BA	OBA	SA	AB	H	2B	3B	HR	RBI	BB	SO	BA	OBA	SA	AB	H	2B	3B	HR	RBI	BB	SO
Total	.263	.336	.434	350	92	20	2	12	52	39	61	.238	.302	.357	1663	396	65	9	38	236	151	394
vs. Left	.286	.352	.508	63	18	2	0	4	13	7	12	.221	.283	.347	349	77	12	4	8	62	31	88
vs. Right	.258	.332	.418	287	74	18	2	8	39	32	49	.243	.307	.359	1314	319	53	5	30	174	120	306
Bases Empty	.293	.385	.511	174	51	6	1	10	10	25	29	.234	.305	.347	813	190	27	4	19	19	79	203
Leadoff	.300	.378	.512	80	24	3	1	4	4	9	13	.249	.313	.374	342	85	12	2	9	9	28	72
Runners On Base	.233	.286	.358	176	41	14	1	2	42	14	32	.242	.298	.366	850	206	38	5	19	217	72	191
Scoring Position	.235	.314	.353	85	20	8	1	1	36	11	14	.256	.320	.389	488	125	24	4	11	195	51	107
Late and Close	.295	.380	.557	61	18	4	0	4	15	8	7	.252	.316	.386	966	243	44	4	26	173	90	226

MARK PORTUGAL — bats right — throws right — age 30 — HOU — P

7-YEAR TOTALS (1985–1991)

1991	G	IP	H	BB	SO	SB	CS	W	L	SV	ERA	G	IP	H	BB	SO	SB	CS	W	L	SV	ERA
Total	32	168.1	163	59	120	12	6	10	12	1	4.49	156	711.1	695	268	480	58	30	39	42	5	4.20
at Home	16	79.1	71	24	58	7	3	4	5	1	3.06	77	339.2	330	121	241	28	15	22	16	3	3.58
on Road	16	89.0	92	35	62	5	3	6	7	0	5.76	79	371.2	365	147	239	30	15	17	26	2	4.77
on Grass	11	59.0	73	31	41	5	2	4	6	0	7.02	60	266.2	284	100	168	21	7	11	21	2	5.16
on Turf	21	109.1	90	28	79	7	4	6	6	1	3.13	96	444.2	411	168	312	37	23	28	21	3	3.62
Day Games	12	57.1	61	26	35	4	2	5	5	1	4.87	56	268.1	258	113	179	21	12	14	17	4	4.16
Night Games	20	111.0	102	33	85	8	4	5	7	0	4.30	100	443.0	437	155	301	37	18	25	25	1	4.23
April	3	17.0	19	3	13	2	1	2	1	0	5.82	16	63.2	79	22	43	11	3	4	7	1	5.94
May	6	37.2	34	13	31	2	2	3	1	0	3.82	27	120.1	135	44	73	14	5	4	8	0	5.24
June	5	36.0	29	8	27	3	1	1	2	0	3.25	25	129.0	115	46	90	8	5	3	8	0	4.33
July	4	19.0	21	9	12	1	0	2	1	0	3.79	24	98.0	93	37	72	2	2	7	4	2	3.58
August	4	25.0	22	9	21	2	1	2	1	0	5.04	24	137.0	130	53	98	13	6	10	3	0	3.22
Sept–Oct	10	33.2	38	17	16	2	1	0	6	1	5.88	40	163.1	143	66	104	10	9	11	12	2	3.86

	BA	OBA	SA	AB	H	2B	3B	HR	RBI	BB	SO	BA	OBA	SA	AB	H	2B	3B	HR	RBI	BB	SO
Total	.256	.318	.400	637	163	29	3	19	79	59	120	.259	.326	.403	2684	695	123	6	84	315	268	480
vs. Left	.243	.313	.380	366	89	14	3	10	45	37	79	.241	.317	.377	1483	357	64	6	42	168	166	295
vs. Right	.273	.326	.428	271	74	15	0	9	34	22	41	.281	.338	.435	1201	338	59	0	42	147	102	185
Bases Empty	.250	.301	.383	384	96	16	1	11	11	27	78	.268	.332	.406	1555	416	70	4	46	46	145	272
Leadoff	.278	.341	.449	158	44	7	1	6	6	15	26	.294	.368	.457	663	195	28	4	24	24	75	110
Runners On Base	.265	.342	.427	253	67	13	2	8	68	32	42	.247	.319	.399	1129	279	53	2	38	269	123	208
Scoring Position	.308	.379	.497	143	44	7	1	6	58	20	24	.244	.324	.398	615	150	30	1	21	224	80	116
Late and Close	.345	.415	.500	58	20	3	0	2	9	7	9	.317	.379	.449	243	77	11	0	7	26	24	33

SCOTT RADINSKY — bats left — throws left — age 24 — CHA — P

2-YEAR TOTALS (1990–1991)

1991	G	IP	H	BB	SO	SB	CS	W	L	SV	ERA	G	IP	H	BB	SO	SB	CS	W	L	SV	ERA
Total	67	71.1	53	23	49	1	0	5	5	8	2.02	129	123.2	100	59	95	3	0	11	6	12	3.20
at Home	37	41.2	29	8	31	0	0	1	2	6	1.51	68	67.2	46	24	54	2	0	3	3	9	2.66
on Road	30	29.2	24	15	18	1	0	4	3	2	2.73	61	56.0	54	35	41	1	0	8	3	3	3.86
on Grass	57	61.1	46	20	43	1	0	3	5	6	2.05	107	103.1	81	49	83	3	0	8	6	10	3.14
on Turf	10	10.0	7	3	6	0	0	2	0	2	1.80	22	20.1	19	10	12	0	0	3	0	2	3.54
Day Games	20	23.2	17	7	16	1	0	1	2	3	1.52	41	39.1	37	17	27	1	0	4	3	4	3.89
Night Games	47	47.2	36	16	33	0	0	4	3	5	2.27	88	84.1	63	42	68	2	0	7	3	8	2.88
April	8	6.1	6	2	7	0	0	1	1	0	1.42	16	12.1	10	6	11	0	0	2	1	0	1.46
May	9	13.0	12	3	8	1	0	1	1	0	3.46	23	26.0	16	9	22	1	0	4	1	2	2.77
June	11	12.2	5	3	10	0	0	0	0	3	0.71	23	23.0	15	9	17	1	0	1	0	4	1.57
July	13	13.2	14	5	10	0	0	1	1	0	3.29	26	24.1	27	13	22	1	0	0	2	2	4.81
August	11	11.2	9	4	6	0	0	1	1	2	0.77	20	21.0	18	9	14	0	0	1	1	3	2.57
Sept–Oct	15	14.0	7	6	8	0	0	1	1	3	1.93	21	17.0	14	13	9	0	0	2	1	3	5.82

	BA	OBA	SA	AB	H	2B	3B	HR	RBI	BB	SO	BA	OBA	SA	AB	H	2B	3B	HR	RBI	BB	SO
Total	.206	.270	.288	257	53	9	0	4	24	23	49	.221	.312	.292	452	100	15	1	5	51	59	95
vs. Left	.205	.220	.346	78	16	2	0	3	11	2	18	.194	.243	.295	139	27	3	1	3	19	9	37
vs. Right	.207	.291	.263	179	37	7	0	1	13	21	31	.233	.340	.291	313	73	12	0	2	32	50	58
Bases Empty	.254	.314	.357	126	32	4	0	3	3	11	19	.260	.323	.363	215	56	8	1	4	4	19	37
Leadoff	.294	.379	.451	51	15	2	0	2	2	7	5	.283	.371	.424	92	26	4	0	3	3	12	12
Runners On Base	.160	.230	.221	131	21	5	0	1	21	12	30	.186	.302	.228	237	44	7	0	1	47	40	58
Scoring Position	.116	.184	.140	86	10	2	0	0	18	8	21	.166	.297	.185	157	26	3	0	0	43	31	42
Late and Close	.210	.282	.280	157	33	5	0	2	15	14	31	.195	.287	.264	231	45	8	1	2	20	29	46

DENNIS RASMUSSEN — bats left — throws left — age 33 — SD — P

8-YEAR TOTALS (1984–1991)

1991	G	IP	H	BB	SO	SB	CS	W	L	SV	ERA	G	IP	H	BB	SO	SB	CS	W	L	SV	ERA
Total	24	146.2	155	49	75	21	5	6	13	0	3.74	230	1365.1	1329	484	792	99	73	86	73	0	4.12
at Home	10	60.1	62	18	30	10	3	4	5	0	3.88	102	612.2	573	225	386	37	36	44	33	0	3.92
on Road	14	86.1	93	31	45	11	2	2	8	0	3.65	128	752.2	756	259	406	62	37	42	40	0	4.28
on Grass	18	109.1	118	36	50	15	4	5	10	0	4.03	169	998.1	988	360	570	64	50	60	58	0	4.18
on Turf	6	37.1	37	13	25	6	1	1	3	0	2.89	61	367.0	341	124	222	35	23	26	15	0	3.95
Day Games	7	42.2	52	11	19	4	2	3	3	0	3.59	74	409.2	432	157	237	24	19	24	27	0	4.50
Night Games	17	104.0	103	38	56	17	3	3	10	0	3.81	156	955.2	897	327	555	75	54	62	46	0	3.96
April	0	0.0	0	0	0	0	0	0	0	0	0.00	24	143.1	154	46	78	10	11	7	9	0	4.14
May	2	14.0	11	2	11	2	1	1	0	0	0.64	39	237.2	205	89	151	17	15	14	11	0	3.75
June	5	36.0	37	9	17	2	2	2	2	0	2.00	41	256.0	250	91	141	15	12	10	10	0	3.90
July	6	36.1	37	20	14	8	1	0	6	0	4.95	41	237.1	234	105	134	14	18	15	15	0	4.44
August	6	31.2	34	11	17	5	1	1	3	0	4.26	41	244.0	213	80	141	20	7	15	17	0	3.95
Sept–Oct	5	28.2	36	7	16	4	0	2	2	0	5.34	44	247.0	273	73	147	23	10	20	11	0	4.55

	BA	OBA	SA	AB	H	2B	3B	HR	RBI	BB	SO	BA	OBA	SA	AB	H	2B	3B	HR	RBI	BB	SO
Total	.271	.328	.385	572	155	17	6	12	63	49	75	.256	.320	.409	5183	1329	226	35	165	589	484	792
vs. Left	.235	.291	.333	102	24	2	1	2	10	8	18	.262	.319	.406	890	233	31	8	27	112	74	140
vs. Right	.279	.335	.396	470	131	15	5	10	53	41	57	.255	.320	.410	4293	1096	195	27	138	477	410	652
Bases Empty	.276	.333	.387	323	89	10	4	6	6	27	43	.247	.315	.402	3153	779	141	23	100	100	300	474
Leadoff	.281	.342	.403	139	39	4	2	3	3	13	14	.258	.324	.416	1316	340	68	10	40	40	121	174
Runners On Base	.265	.320	.382	249	66	7	2	6	57	22	32	.271	.328	.421	2030	550	85	12	65	489	184	318
Scoring Position	.256	.324	.388	121	31	3	2	3	50	14	17	.261	.330	.423	1035	270	52	10	32	411	122	184
Late and Close	.278	.350	.333	36	10	2	0	0	2	4	6	.282	.349	.405	326	92	16	0	8	32	35	44

JEFF REARDON — bats right — throws right — age 37 — BOS — P

8-YEAR TOTALS (1984–1991)

1991	G	IP	H	BB	SO	SB	CS	W	L	SV	ERA		G	IP	H	BB	SO	SB	CS	W	L	SV	ERA
Total	57	59.1	54	16	44	3	1	1	4	40	3.03		488	600.2	520	178	476	54	9	37	47	264	3.43
at Home	31	32.1	29	9	25	1	1	1	2	19	3.62		251	308.0	269	97	246	31	5	27	27	137	3.54
on Road	26	27.0	25	7	19	2	0	0	2	21	2.33		237	292.2	251	81	230	23	4	10	20	127	3.32
on Grass	48	48.1	43	14	38	2	1	1	4	31	3.35		206	244.0	204	70	193	18	4	14	14	108	3.39
on Turf	9	11.0	11	2	6	1	0	0	0	9	1.64		282	356.2	316	108	283	36	5	23	33	156	3.46
Day Games	18	17.0	23	4	17	1	0	0	3	11	6.88		162	195.1	176	59	142	14	4	11	17	77	3.73
Night Games	39	42.1	31	12	27	2	1	1	1	29	1.49		326	405.1	344	119	334	40	5	26	30	187	3.29
April	9	8.2	7	5	5	0	0	0	0	8	1.04		66	88.2	66	36	58	8	2	5	6	32	2.64
May	11	10.1	8	1	7	1	0	0	1	6	4.35		94	119.0	92	27	97	13	0	7	7	50	3.03
June	8	9.0	8	1	6	0	0	0	1	5	3.00		88	110.1	92	28	94	10	0	8	8	50	3.43
July	9	10.1	7	1	8	0	0	0	0	5	3.48		74	83.0	94	24	65	9	3	2	8	36	4.66
August	10	12.0	16	4	12	2	0	0	1	9	3.75		80	97.2	91	39	77	9	3	6	12	48	4.52
Sept–Oct	10	9.0	8	4	6	0	0	1	1	7	2.00		86	102.0	85	24	85	5	1	9	6	48	2.56

	BA	OBA	SA	AB	H	2B	3B	HR	RBI	BB	SO		BA	OBA	SA	AB	H	2B	3B	HR	RBI	BB	SO
Total	.236	.286	.419	229	54	11	2	9	24	16	44		.232	.291	.367	2244	520	93	6	66	297	178	476
vs. Left	.304	.353	.536	125	38	6	1	7	17	10	17		.253	.321	.393	1161	294	45	3	37	167	115	191
vs. Right	.154	.205	.279	104	16	5	1	2	7	6	27		.209	.256	.339	1083	226	48	3	29	130	63	285
Bases Empty	.237	.259	.467	135	32	6	2	7	7	4	25		.225	.274	.360	1213	273	50	3	36	36	77	253
Leadoff	.125	.143	.229	48	6	3	1	0	0	1	7		.181	.233	.302	470	85	20	2	11	11	29	103
Runners On Base	.234	.321	.351	94	22	5	0	2	17	12	19		.240	.309	.374	1031	247	43	3	30	261	101	223
Scoring Position	.213	.315	.377	61	13	4	0	2	17	10	12		.236	.319	.377	674	159	28	2	21	235	83	150
Late and Close	.223	.279	.394	175	39	8	2	6	18	13	36		.235	.298	.370	1692	398	63	6	51	254	145	359

DAVE RIGHETTI — bats left — throws left — age 34 — SF — P

8-YEAR TOTALS (1984–1991)

1991	G	IP	H	BB	SO	SB	CS	W	L	SV	ERA		G	IP	H	BB	SO	SB	CS	W	L	SV	ERA
Total	61	71.2	64	28	51	8	4	2	7	24	3.39		501	685.2	629	278	557	37	16	43	45	247	2.98
at Home	32	37.0	32	11	32	4	1	1	4	14	4.14		253	347.2	294	116	309	20	7	28	16	124	2.59
on Road	29	34.2	32	17	19	4	3	1	3	10	2.60		248	338.0	335	162	248	17	9	15	29	123	3.38
on Grass	46	56.0	55	21	40	7	3	2	7	18	4.18		417	576.0	531	230	473	32	14	39	40	197	3.13
on Turf	15	15.2	9	7	11	1	1	0	0	6	0.57		84	109.2	98	48	84	5	2	4	5	50	2.22
Day Games	24	28.0	26	17	20	7	2	2	4	8	4.18		157	207.2	178	91	170	14	7	20	14	72	2.69
Night Games	37	43.2	38	11	31	1	2	0	3	16	2.89		344	478.0	451	187	387	23	9	23	31	175	3.11
April	6	8.1	7	3	7	1	0	2	0	1	3.24		68	96.0	98	48	72	4	4	9	4	32	3.66
May	12	15.2	22	6	10	4	2	0	2	0	5.74		78	110.1	92	36	93	9	4	6	6	35	2.37
June	12	14.2	11	8	6	0	1	0	1	9	3.07		88	116.2	121	62	85	9	3	10	9	39	4.32
July	10	9.1	6	3	5	0	1	0	1	6	1.93		83	110.2	92	45	85	2	2	5	6	40	2.20
August	11	13.2	4	2	13	1	0	0	2	4	1.32		94	129.1	105	49	101	6	1	8	10	45	2.51
Sept–Oct	10	10.0	14	6	10	2	0	0	2	4	4.50		90	122.2	121	38	121	7	2	5	10	56	2.93

	BA	OBA	SA	AB	H	2B	3B	HR	RBI	BB	SO		BA	OBA	SA	AB	H	2B	3B	HR	RBI	BB	SO
Total	.240	.317	.330	267	64	12	0	4	32	28	51		.244	.318	.336	2575	629	92	8	43	323	278	557
vs. Left	.167	.197	.167	72	12	0	0	0	9	2	13		.236	.314	.331	614	145	21	2	11	88	68	142
vs. Right	.267	.357	.390	195	52	12	0	4	23	26	38		.247	.320	.338	1961	484	71	6	32	235	210	415
Bases Empty	.217	.294	.319	138	30	5	0	3	3	13	25		.229	.302	.321	1235	283	40	4	22	22	120	274
Leadoff	.161	.277	.214	56	9	3	0	0	0	8	13		.220	.292	.341	513	113	21	1	13	13	48	124
Runners On Base	.264	.340	.341	129	34	7	0	1	29	15	26		.258	.333	.350	1340	346	52	4	21	301	158	283
Scoring Position	.296	.366	.383	81	24	4	0	2	29	9	16		.255	.336	.343	816	208	33	3	11	275	109	164
Late and Close	.241	.321	.342	187	45	7	0	4	26	21	36		.242	.317	.335	1965	476	64	5	36	265	218	429

JOSE RIJO — bats right — throws right — age 27 — CIN — P

8-YEAR TOTALS (1984–1991)

1991	G	IP	H	BB	SO	SB	CS	W	L	SV	ERA		G	IP	H	BB	SO	SB	CS	W	L	SV	ERA
Total	30	204.1	165	55	172	16	3	15	6	0	2.51		223	1076.0	946	454	925	109	38	68	58	3	3.40
at Home	15	99.1	73	35	74	8	2	9	0	0	2.99		104	517.1	429	232	469	62	23	33	23	1	3.24
on Road	15	105.0	92	20	98	8	1	6	6	0	2.06		119	558.2	517	222	456	47	15	35	35	2	3.54
on Grass	11	77.1	66	15	75	8	1	4	4	0	1.86		113	535.0	492	240	451	55	21	30	33	3	3.53
on Turf	19	127.0	99	40	97	8	2	11	2	0	2.91		110	541.0	454	214	474	54	17	38	25	0	3.26
Day Games	7	53.0	36	7	46	3	1	4	2	0	1.70		71	311.0	270	138	277	37	14	19	16	0	3.13
Night Games	23	151.1	129	48	126	13	2	11	4	0	2.80		152	765.0	676	316	648	72	24	49	42	3	3.51
April	4	27.0	17	7	21	3	1	1	1	0	2.67		43	158.2	140	77	150	19	10	7	9	1	3.63
May	6	38.0	39	11	33	1	1	3	1	0	3.08		44	192.1	162	90	164	22	7	13	5	0	2.99
June	5	36.2	22	8	32	1	1	2	0	0	2.21		47	197.0	183	78	161	19	8	10	17	2	4.39
July	2	13.0	12	1	7	1	0	1	0	0	2.77		23	142.2	127	50	122	12	5	9	7	0	2.65
August	6	42.2	31	14	39	6	0	4	2	0	2.11		31	181.0	161	86	148	20	4	12	12	0	3.83
Sept–Oct	7	47.0	44	14	40	2	0	4	2	0	2.49		35	204.1	173	73	180	17	4	17	8	0	2.77

	BA	OBA	SA	AB	H	2B	3B	HR	RBI	BB	SO		BA	OBA	SA	AB	H	2B	3B	HR	RBI	BB	SO
Total	.219	.272	.305	755	165	33	4	8	61	55	172		.236	.314	.351	4004	946	180	26	76	409	454	925
vs. Left	.253	.313	.355	434	110	21	4	5	45	38	93		.255	.348	.387	2172	554	104	18	49	253	309	482
vs. Right	.171	.213	.237	321	55	12	0	3	16	17	79		.214	.273	.308	1832	392	76	8	27	156	145	443
Bases Empty	.201	.249	.304	483	97	23	3	7	7	29	115		.229	.300	.356	2373	544	120	14	51	51	234	530
Leadoff	.190	.240	.277	195	37	9	1	2	2	11	47		.226	.302	.361	996	225	45	6	26	26	104	212
Runners On Base	.250	.309	.305	272	68	10	1	1	54	26	57		.246	.334	.344	1631	402	60	12	25	358	220	395
Scoring Position	.214	.285	.277	159	34	8	2	0	2	3	7		.247	.342	.331	986	244	35	7	11	317	151	268
Late and Close	.222	.282	.278	36	8	2	0	0	2	3	7		.259	.353	.381	386	100	16	5	7	40	54	80

DON ROBINSON — bats right — throws right — age 35 — SF — P

1991	G	IP	H	BB	SO	SB	CS	W	L	SV	ERA
Total	34	121.1	123	50	78	10	5	5	9	1	4.38
at Home	14	61.2	51	26	43	3	4	3	2	0	2.77
on Road	20	59.2	72	24	35	7	1	2	7	1	6.03
on Grass	23	86.1	78	35	61	4	4	4	5	1	3.44
on Turf	11	35.0	45	15	17	6	1	1	4	0	6.69
Day Games	16	57.1	47	23	32	4	2	2	3	1	3.77
Night Games	18	64.0	76	27	46	6	3	3	6	0	4.92
April	7	9.1	12	3	8	0	0	0	0	0	3.86
May	6	28.2	32	13	18	3	2	1	4	0	5.97
June	5	29.1	30	13	20	3	2	2	2	0	3.38
July	3	18.2	13	8	13	2	0	2	1	0	2.89
August	5	20.0	24	12	9	2	0	0	2	0	6.75
Sept–Oct	6	15.1	12	1	10	0	1	0	0	1	2.35

8-YEAR TOTALS (1984–1991)

	G	IP	H	BB	SO	SB	CS	W	L	SV	ERA
Total	358	1048.0	993	338	682	94	45	61	61	53	3.54
at Home	166	493.0	462	139	347	41	21	35	16	26	3.05
on Road	192	555.0	531	199	335	53	24	26	45	27	3.97
on Grass	169	566.2	530	165	347	43	27	34	28	19	3.37
on Turf	189	481.1	463	173	335	51	18	27	33	34	3.74
Day Games	142	398.2	384	134	269	40	14	19	19	24	3.59
Night Games	216	649.1	609	204	413	54	31	42	42	29	3.51
April	48	93.2	95	41	64	7	5	5	4	8	3.94
May	51	153.1	145	62	105	13	10	8	8	7	3.70
June	69	197.0	198	63	127	20	9	12	13	8	3.47
July	59	202.2	188	55	152	25	3	9	7	9	3.42
August	67	223.1	196	66	141	13	10	14	19	10	3.67
Sept–Oct	64	178.0	171	51	93	16	8	13	10	11	3.24

	BA	OBA	SA	AB	H	2B	3B	HR	RBI	BB	SO
Total	.265	.334	.417	465	123	25	5	12	62	50	78
vs. Left	.278	.369	.421	252	70	15	3	5	36	39	45
vs. Right	.249	.288	.413	213	53	10	2	7	26	11	33
Bases Empty	.245	.310	.427	274	67	17	3	9	9	25	47
Leadoff	.243	.298	.452	115	28	7	1	5	5	9	18
Runners On Base	.293	.367	.403	191	56	8	2	3	53	25	31
Scoring Position	.365	.447	.539	115	42	7	2	3	52	21	19
Late and Close	.306	.350	.444	36	11	2	0	1	3	3	5

	BA	OBA	SA	AB	H	2B	3B	HR	RBI	BB	SO
Total	.250	.308	.379	3965	993	200	24	87	446	338	682
vs. Left	.247	.317	.367	2049	507	100	12	40	205	212	335
vs. Right	.254	.299	.392	1916	486	100	12	47	241	126	347
Bases Empty	.241	.292	.368	2337	564	120	18	47	47	163	399
Leadoff	.241	.297	.368	969	234	48	6	21	21	74	152
Runners On Base	.264	.330	.394	1628	429	80	6	40	399	175	283
Scoring Position	.262	.344	.400	982	257	53	4	25	351	139	187
Late and Close	.240	.309	.348	1074	258	54	4	16	116	110	224

KENNY ROGERS — bats left — throws left — age 28 — TEX — P

1991	G	IP	H	BB	SO	SB	CS	W	L	SV	ERA
Total	63	109.2	121	61	73	1	4	10	10	5	5.42
at Home	34	46.2	50	31	36	0	1	6	5	3	5.59
on Road	29	63.0	71	30	37	1	3	4	5	2	5.29
on Grass	50	88.1	94	51	65	1	3	7	9	5	5.81
on Turf	13	21.1	27	10	8	0	1	3	1	0	3.80
Day Games	8	11.0	11	6	5	1	0	1	2	0	6.55
Night Games	55	98.2	110	55	68	0	4	9	8	5	5.29
April	3	11.2	19	8	8	1	2	0	3	0	13.11
May	7	29.1	40	20	13	0	1	4	1	0	4.60
June	10	20.0	26	10	13	0	0	0	3	1	8.10
July	15	17.0	10	6	18	0	0	1	2	0	2.65
August	16	21.0	17	9	16	0	0	3	1	1	3.00
Sept–Oct	12	10.2	9	8	5	0	0	1	2	1	3.38

3-YEAR TOTALS (1989–1991)

	G	IP	H	BB	SO	SB	CS	W	L	SV	ERA
Total	205	281.0	274	145	210	10	11	23	20	22	3.97
at Home	111	146.1	139	75	107	7	3	18	9	12	3.57
on Road	94	134.2	135	70	103	3	8	5	11	10	4.41
on Grass	169	233.1	221	122	181	10	6	20	16	21	3.90
on Turf	36	47.2	53	23	29	0	5	3	4	1	4.34
Day Games	33	37.1	38	23	27	1	3	3	4	5	4.10
Night Games	172	243.2	236	122	183	9	8	20	16	17	3.95
April	20	31.2	41	19	21	2	2	2	4	0	6.82
May	35	65.2	70	38	42	5	2	6	1	0	4.25
June	35	47.0	58	26	36	1	2	0	5	6	5.36
July	38	42.0	29	17	49	0	1	4	2	8	2.79
August	42	47.2	38	22	35	1	3	4	3	3	3.02
Sept–Oct	35	47.0	38	23	27	1	1	7	5	5	2.30

	BA	OBA	SA	AB	H	2B	3B	HR	RBI	BB	SO
Total	.281	.375	.444	430	121	22	3	14	66	61	73
vs. Left	.224	.342	.357	98	22	4	0	3	16	16	19
vs. Right	.298	.385	.470	332	99	18	3	11	50	45	54
Bases Empty	.288	.359	.460	226	65	14	2	7	7	24	39
Leadoff	.268	.330	.320	97	26	5	0	0	0	9	13
Runners On Base	.275	.390	.426	204	56	8	1	7	59	37	34
Scoring Position	.294	.444	.487	119	35	5	0	4	56	32	22
Late and Close	.210	.322	.355	124	26	4	0	4	9	18	22

	BA	OBA	SA	AB	H	2B	3B	HR	RBI	BB	SO
Total	.258	.349	.384	1063	274	56	6	22	149	145	210
vs. Left	.206	.309	.309	272	56	14	1	4	36	35	58
vs. Right	.276	.363	.410	791	218	42	5	18	113	110	152
Bases Empty	.260	.340	.390	503	131	24	4	11	11	58	99
Leadoff	.234	.317	.308	214	50	8	1	2	2	25	38
Runners On Base	.255	.357	.379	560	143	32	2	11	138	87	111
Scoring Position	.256	.371	.394	355	91	20	1	9	132	66	79
Late and Close	.227	.321	.336	431	98	21	1	8	53	57	89

BRUCE RUFFIN — bats both — throws left — age 29 — PHI — P

1991	G	IP	H	BB	SO	SB	CS	W	L	SV	ERA
Total	31	119.0	125	38	85	7	3	4	7	0	3.78
at Home	19	75.2	71	25	54	5	3	3	3	0	3.21
on Road	12	43.1	54	13	31	2	0	1	4	0	4.78
on Grass	5	20.0	24	7	15	1	0	1	2	0	5.40
on Turf	26	99.0	101	31	70	6	3	3	5	0	3.45
Day Games	9	20.0	30	11	10	3	1	0	1	0	7.65
Night Games	22	99.0	95	27	75	4	2	4	6	0	3.00
April	0	0.0	0	0	0	0	0	0	0	0	0.00
May	0	0.0	0	0	0	0	0	0	0	0	0.00
June	8	22.2	22	7	12	2	0	0	2	0	2.78
July	6	38.0	39	9	30	4	1	2	3	0	2.84
August	5	26.0	30	11	15	1	2	0	2	0	5.19
Sept–Oct	12	32.1	34	11	28	0	0	1	2	0	4.45

6-YEAR TOTALS (1986–1991)

	G	IP	H	BB	SO	SB	CS	W	L	SV	ERA
Total	199	891.0	981	360	480	62	37	42	58	4	4.15
at Home	108	488.1	528	202	267	30	23	28	27	3	4.05
on Road	91	402.2	453	158	213	32	14	14	31	1	4.27
on Grass	49	213.1	235	81	114	12	6	9	16	0	4.22
on Turf	150	677.2	746	279	366	50	31	33	42	4	4.13
Day Games	58	249.2	271	94	129	18	10	10	13	3	3.89
Night Games	141	641.1	710	266	351	44	27	32	45	1	4.25
April	14	79.1	104	29	42	3	8	4	4	1	5.22
May	18	99.0	112	39	44	5	2	6	9	0	4.91
June	34	150.1	169	49	84	9	5	5	7	1	4.07
July	44	214.2	213	89	107	14	9	15	12	3	3.40
August	46	169.1	183	83	100	21	8	6	10	0	4.73
Sept–Oct	43	178.1	200	71	103	10	10	6	10	0	3.68

	BA	OBA	SA	AB	H	2B	3B	HR	RBI	BB	SO
Total	.272	.327	.386	459	125	28	3	6	47	38	85
vs. Left	.250	.289	.333	108	27	6	0	1	12	6	21
vs. Right	.279	.338	.402	351	98	22	3	5	35	32	64
Bases Empty	.291	.342	.409	247	72	18	1	3	3	18	42
Leadoff	.307	.358	.404	114	35	9	1	0	0	8	26
Runners On Base	.250	.309	.358	212	53	10	2	3	44	20	43
Scoring Position	.241	.313	.362	116	28	4	2	2	40	16	24
Late and Close	.327	.383	.400	55	18	4	0	0	3	4	7

	BA	OBA	SA	AB	H	2B	3B	HR	RBI	BB	SO
Total	.284	.350	.405	3458	981	196	22	60	416	360	480
vs. Left	.257	.344	.342	631	162	28	4	6	83	85	116
vs. Right	.290	.351	.419	2827	819	168	18	54	333	275	364
Bases Empty	.281	.344	.407	1908	537	106	14	35	35	178	267
Leadoff	.286	.361	.406	835	239	48	8	12	12	93	114
Runners On Base	.286	.357	.403	1550	444	90	8	25	381	182	213
Scoring Position	.299	.377	.430	855	256	54	5	16	344	121	113
Late and Close	.290	.377	.387	297	86	17	0	4	34	42	38

JEFF RUSSELL — bats right — throws right — age 31 — TEX — P

1991	G	IP	H	BB	SO	SB	CS	W	L	SV	ERA
Total	68	79.1	71	26	52	1	0	6	4	30	3.29
at Home	34	39.0	33	9	29	0	0	2	1	18	3.00
on Road	34	40.1	38	17	23	1	0	4	3	12	3.57
on Grass	55	63.2	57	18	44	0	0	3	3	25	3.11
on Turf	13	15.2	14	8	8	1	0	3	1	5	4.02
Day Games	19	22.0	20	11	14	0	0	2	3	7	4.09
Night Games	49	57.1	51	15	38	1	0	4	1	23	2.98
April	8	10.0	3	0	9	0	0	0	0	5	0.00
May	14	16.1	16	4	7	0	0	1	0	7	4.41
June	10	15.0	15	7	7	0	0	1	1	3	4.20
July	12	13.2	7	6	14	0	0	1	2	5	1.98
August	12	12.1	12	4	7	0	0	0	1	5	2.92
Sept–Oct	12	12.0	18	5	8	1	0	3	0	5	5.25

8-YEAR TOTALS (1984–1991)

	G	IP	H	BB	SO	SB	CS	W	L	SV	ERA
Total	335	789.2	776	306	488	83	26	42	52	83	4.03
at Home	168	391.1	387	137	237	46	16	19	21	51	4.12
on Road	167	398.1	389	169	251	37	10	23	31	32	3.95
on Grass	269	583.0	563	226	366	58	20	29	37	73	3.87
on Turf	66	206.2	213	80	122	25	6	13	15	10	4.49
Day Games	76	163.2	162	69	111	18	5	13	13	17	4.18
Night Games	259	626.0	614	237	377	65	21	29	39	66	4.00
April	38	67.0	56	23	43	6	2	4	4	14	2.28
May	58	110.2	113	36	69	9	2	7	7	16	3.82
June	45	141.0	132	53	80	16	5	7	8	13	3.57
July	56	126.1	120	49	79	12	3	9	8	9	3.70
August	69	180.1	189	84	104	18	5	8	16	15	5.24
Sept–Oct	69	164.1	166	61	113	22	9	7	9	16	4.22

	BA	OBA	SA	AB	H	2B	3B	HR	RBI	BB	SO
Total	.236	.295	.365	301	71	6	0	11	52	26	52
vs. Left	.248	.321	.305	141	35	2	0	2	27	16	20
vs. Right	.225	.271	.419	160	36	4	0	9	25	10	32
Bases Empty	.223	.277	.311	148	33	1	0	4	4	10	29
Leadoff	.236	.311	.309	55	13	1	0	1	1	6	13
Runners On Base	.248	.312	.418	153	38	5	0	7	48	16	23
Scoring Position	.198	.248	.238	101	20	1	0	1	34	8	13
Late and Close	.208	.277	.327	226	47	3	0	8	37	22	39

	BA	OBA	SA	AB	H	2B	3B	HR	RBI	BB	SO
Total	.258	.328	.385	3007	776	134	10	76	420	306	488
vs. Left	.276	.350	.403	1433	395	68	3	36	214	166	217
vs. Right	.242	.308	.369	1574	381	66	7	40	206	140	271
Bases Empty	.240	.307	.351	1631	391	66	5	35	35	146	276
Leadoff	.238	.296	.340	680	162	20	2	15	15	53	109
Runners On Base	.280	.353	.426	1376	385	68	5	41	385	160	212
Scoring Position	.268	.350	.394	866	232	46	3	19	332	117	149
Late and Close	.218	.301	.325	795	173	35	1	16	112	92	164

NOLAN RYAN — bats right — throws right — age 45 — TEX — P

1991	G	IP	H	BB	SO	SB	CS	W	L	SV	ERA
Total	27	173.0	102	72	203	24	8	12	6	0	2.91
at Home	20	131.2	75	53	157	19	6	10	4	0	3.08
on Road	7	41.1	27	19	46	5	2	2	2	0	2.40
on Grass	22	144.0	80	56	172	19	6	11	4	0	2.81
on Turf	5	29.0	22	16	31	5	2	1	2	0	3.41
Day Games	7	48.2	28	22	59	6	1	3	0	0	2.03
Night Games	20	124.1	74	50	144	18	7	9	6	0	3.26
April	4	29.2	23	10	37	4	1	2	2	0	3.94
May	4	23.1	8	11	30	4	2	1	0	0	3.09
June	4	30.0	17	6	30	2	1	1	0	0	1.20
July	6	39.0	19	20	48	5	2	3	1	0	3.00
August	3	12.0	10	7	12	3	1	2	1	0	3.75
Sept–Oct	6	39.0	25	18	46	6	1	3	0	0	3.00

8-YEAR TOTALS (1984–1991)

	G	IP	H	BB	SO	SB	CS	W	L	SV	ERA
Total	251	1642.0	1208	663	1834	270	62	95	83	0	3.27
at Home	139	943.1	639	352	1067	143	31	60	38	0	2.95
on Road	112	698.2	569	311	767	127	31	35	45	0	3.70
on Grass	125	822.2	609	326	937	116	29	50	42	0	3.51
on Turf	126	819.1	599	337	897	154	33	45	41	0	3.02
Day Games	63	398.2	292	180	458	66	15	24	15	0	2.93
Night Games	188	1243.1	916	483	1376	204	47	71	68	0	3.37
April	38	255.2	179	91	290	35	14	18	12	0	3.27
May	43	276.2	201	124	294	47	13	15	13	0	3.48
June	37	239.1	193	84	262	46	9	15	19	0	3.42
July	45	287.2	213	138	330	58	6	17	19	0	3.57
August	43	285.2	219	109	316	43	14	13	17	0	3.34
Sept–Oct	45	297.0	203	117	342	41	6	17	8	0	2.58

	BA	OBA	SA	AB	H	2B	3B	HR	RBI	BB	SO
Total	.172	.263	.285	594	102	25	3	12	54	72	203
vs. Left	.182	.254	.282	340	62	13	3	5	27	32	104
vs. Right	.157	.275	.287	254	40	12	0	7	27	40	99
Bases Empty	.146	.242	.257	404	59	17	2	8	8	48	163
Leadoff	.160	.230	.276	163	26	8	1	3	3	15	64
Runners On Base	.226	.307	.342	190	43	8	1	4	46	24	40
Scoring Position	.227	.327	.378	119	27	4	1	4	44	20	28
Late and Close	.143	.222	.245	49	7	2	0	1	2	5	19

	BA	OBA	SA	AB	H	2B	3B	HR	RBI	BB	SO
Total	.203	.286	.312	5947	1208	214	40	117	589	663	1834
vs. Left	.206	.291	.300	3053	629	92	26	48	271	366	874
vs. Right	.200	.281	.323	2894	579	122	14	69	318	297	960
Bases Empty	.187	.269	.289	3671	687	121	28	66	66	387	1223
Leadoff	.204	.281	.308	1528	311	58	9	28	28	158	476
Runners On Base	.229	.313	.348	2276	521	93	12	51	523	276	611
Scoring Position	.214	.314	.315	1428	306	46	3	30	449	212	426
Late and Close	.195	.263	.298	590	115	21	2	12	54	51	194

BRET SABERHAGEN — bats right — throws right — age 28 — KC — P

1991	G	IP	H	BB	SO	SB	CS	W	L	SV	ERA
Total	28	196.1	165	45	136	9	9	13	8	0	3.07
at Home	14	94.2	70	25	62	6	5	7	3	0	2.76
on Road	14	101.2	95	20	74	3	4	6	5	0	3.36
on Grass	10	68.0	71	16	47	1	3	2	5	0	4.37
on Turf	18	128.1	94	29	89	8	6	11	3	0	2.38
Day Games	9	64.0	51	17	46	2	2	4	4	0	3.09
Night Games	19	132.1	114	28	90	7	7	9	4	0	3.06
April	5	32.1	36	9	19	1	2	1	3	0	3.34
May	6	47.0	37	7	25	1	2	5	0	0	2.30
June	2	12.0	13	4	8	0	0	0	2	0	4.50
July	4	22.0	25	11	18	3	1	1	2	0	6.55
August	5	41.0	20	7	31	1	2	3	1	0	0.88
Sept–Oct	6	42.0	34	7	35	3	2	3	2	0	3.64

8-YEAR TOTALS (1984–1991)

	G	IP	H	BB	SO	SB	CS	W	L	SV	ERA
Total	252	1660.1	1551	331	1092	72	57	110	78	1	3.21
at Home	123	850.1	791	145	553	43	29	54	35	1	3.07
on Road	129	810.0	760	186	539	29	28	56	43	0	3.37
on Grass	100	644.1	582	134	431	18	20	44	33	0	3.09
on Turf	152	1016.0	969	197	661	54	37	66	45	1	3.30
Day Games	70	421.2	376	102	299	22	15	23	24	0	3.50
Night Games	182	1238.2	1175	229	793	50	42	87	54	1	3.12
April	40	252.1	245	46	132	12	8	15	14	0	3.17
May	46	339.0	309	71	212	12	9	24	14	0	3.05
June	40	271.0	243	62	174	12	5	15	14	0	2.99
July	42	256.1	265	47	175	12	10	16	14	1	4.14
August	36	228.0	202	40	159	10	11	20	6	0	2.80
Sept–Oct	48	313.2	287	65	240	14	14	20	16	0	3.16

	BA	OBA	SA	AB	H	2B	3B	HR	RBI	BB	SO
Total	.228	.280	.327	724	165	28	4	12	63	45	136
vs. Left	.220	.276	.341	346	76	11	2	9	36	27	67
vs. Right	.235	.285	.315	378	89	17	2	3	27	18	69
Bases Empty	.216	.270	.323	449	97	15	3	9	9	28	86
Leadoff	.216	.279	.303	185	40	7	0	3	3	14	32
Runners On Base	.247	.298	.335	275	68	13	1	3	54	17	50
Scoring Position	.268	.310	.401	142	38	8	1	2	53	7	27
Late and Close	.225	.273	.333	102	23	5	0	2	9	6	25

	BA	OBA	SA	AB	H	2B	3B	HR	RBI	BB	SO
Total	.248	.286	.369	6265	1551	265	58	126	580	331	1092
vs. Left	.238	.283	.364	3305	786	124	34	75	307	213	648
vs. Right	.258	.290	.374	2960	765	141	24	51	273	118	444
Bases Empty	.246	.282	.366	3898	957	153	35	82	82	180	705
Leadoff	.252	.289	.380	1614	407	67	19	34	34	76	288
Runners On Base	.256	.304	.388	2367	594	112	23	44	498	151	387
Scoring Position	.230	.268	.366	1257	322	67	12	25	430	100	217
Late and Close	.230	.268	.366	734	169	21	8	21	61	34	124

SCOTT SANDERSON — bats right — throws right — age 36 — NYA — P

1991	G	IP	H	BB	SO	SB	CS	W	L	SV	ERA		G	IP	H	BB	SO	SB	CS	W	L	SV	ERA
Total	34	208.0	200	29	130	16	7	16	10	0	3.81		228	1152.0	1134	267	736	87	50	75	63	3	3.82
at Home	15	92.2	102	16	55	9	4	7	6	0	4.66		107	542.0	524	133	359	41	21	35	32	1	3.84
on Road	19	115.1	98	13	75	7	3	9	4	0	3.12		121	610.0	610	134	377	46	29	40	31	2	3.81
on Grass	29	174.2	173	26	105	13	7	14	9	0	3.97		172	891.2	878	205	588	58	40	60	48	2	3.71
on Turf	5	33.1	27	3	25	3	0	2	1	0	2.97		56	260.1	256	62	148	29	10	15	15	1	4.18
Day Games	10	66.2	57	11	44	6	2	3	5	0	3.65		115	582.1	540	152	402	44	24	31	34	1	3.65
Night Games	24	141.1	143	18	86	10	5	13	5	0	3.88		113	569.2	594	115	334	43	26	44	29	2	4.00
April	4	21.1	29	3	11	3	2	1	1	0	6.33		25	147.2	144	30	80	12	8	11	7	0	3.78
May	6	39.2	32	5	22	3	1	5	1	0	2.27		39	230.2	212	48	154	12	10	18	3	0	3.20
June	5	31.2	37	2	21	6	1	2	1	0	3.69		30	181.1	184	44	115	15	10	9	14	0	3.82
July	7	40.1	43	7	22	0	3	2	4	0	6.02		41	206.0	202	40	135	10	13	12	12	2	4.11
August	6	39.1	29	9	38	4	0	4	1	0	3.43		43	209.0	220	61	148	20	8	12	14	0	4.52
Sept–Oct	6	35.2	30	3	16	0	0	2	2	0	2.02		50	177.1	172	44	104	18	1	13	11	1	3.50

	BA	OBA	SA	AB	H	2B	3B	HR	RBI	BB	SO		BA	OBA	SA	AB	H	2B	3B	HR	RBI	BB	SO
Total	.252	.279	.405	795	200	46	5	22	89	29	130		.257	.299	.413	4406	1134	221	41	128	482	267	736
vs. Left	.265	.295	.446	426	113	24	4	15	53	17	72		.261	.308	.421	2416	631	119	26	72	262	168	359
vs. Right	.236	.260	.358	369	87	22	1	7	36	12	58		.253	.289	.404	1990	503	102	15	56	220	99	377
Bases Empty	.256	.285	.406	508	130	29	4	13	13	19	83		.254	.293	.408	2747	697	140	23	79	79	146	459
Leadoff	.257	.295	.408	206	53	9	2	6	6	9	28		.261	.293	.399	1143	298	56	12	26	26	50	164
Runners On Base	.244	.267	.404	287	70	17	1	9	76	10	47		.263	.309	.423	1659	437	81	18	49	403	121	277
Scoring Position	.272	.294	.437	151	41	11	1	4	62	6	29		.254	.312	.402	914	232	44	11	23	330	93	169
Late and Close	.188	.212	.219	32	6	1	0	0	1	1	3		.234	.287	.344	308	72	4	3	8	24	23	47

CURT SCHILLING — bats right — throws right — age 26 — HOU — P

1991	G	IP	H	BB	SO	SB	CS	W	L	SV	ERA		G	IP	H	BB	SO	SB	CS	W	L	SV	ERA
Total	56	75.2	79	39	71	3	4	3	5	8	3.81		100	145.0	149	71	113	7	5	4	11	11	4.16
at Home	32	47.0	50	26	46	3	3	3	3	3	3.64		55	91.1	99	47	68	7	4	4	6	5	4.24
on Road	24	28.2	29	13	25	0	1	0	2	5	4.08		45	53.2	50	24	45	0	1	0	5	6	4.02
on Grass	16	19.0	18	10	14	0	0	0	1	2	4.26		52	78.2	78	38	51	4	1	1	5	4	4.35
on Turf	40	56.2	61	29	57	3	4	3	4	6	3.65		48	66.1	71	33	62	3	4	3	6	7	3.93
Day Games	11	17.1	15	12	21	1	0	0	1	1	4.15		22	31.2	31	18	28	1	0	0	3	2	4.55
Night Games	45	58.1	64	27	50	2	4	3	4	7	3.70		78	113.1	118	53	85	6	5	4	8	9	4.05
April	8	12.0	11	5	12	0	1	0	1	3	3.75		8	12.0	11	5	12	0	1	0	1	3	3.75
May	12	12.1	20	7	15	1	1	1	2	2	5.11		12	12.1	20	7	15	1	1	1	2	2	5.11
June	9	9.0	10	4	9	1	2	0	2	0	6.00		9	11.1	11	4	13	0	1	0	2	1	4.76
July	0	0.0	0	0	0	0	0	0	0	0	0.00		10	15.0	16	2	10	0	0	0	1	1	3.00
August	13	20.1	20	13	15	1	0	0	0	1	3.10		24	37.1	28	26	28	2	0	0	1	1	1.69
Sept–Oct	15	22.0	18	10	20	1	0	0	0	2	2.86		37	57.0	63	27	35	4	2	0	6	3	5.84

	BA	OBA	SA	AB	H	2B	3B	HR	RBI	BB	SO		BA	OBA	SA	AB	H	2B	3B	HR	RBI	BB	SO
Total	.271	.356	.364	291	79	15	3	2	38	39	71		.269	.349	.384	554	149	30	5	8	82	71	113
vs. Left	.247	.362	.336	146	36	8	1	1	14	27	40		.277	.365	.406	256	71	15	3	4	34	38	51
vs. Right	.297	.350	.393	145	43	7	2	1	24	12	31		.262	.334	.366	298	78	15	2	4	48	33	62
Bases Empty	.271	.345	.368	133	36	5	1	2	2	15	26		.248	.325	.347	274	68	13	1	4	4	30	50
Leadoff	.344	.437	.393	61	21	3	0	0	0	10	10		.289	.363	.339	121	35	6	0	0	0	14	18
Runners On Base	.272	.366	.361	158	43	10	2	0	36	24	45		.289	.371	.421	280	81	17	4	4	78	41	63
Scoring Position	.264	.363	.358	106	28	8	1	0	34	17	33		.287	.377	.431	174	50	13	3	2	72	30	46
Late and Close	.283	.365	.384	138	39	5	3	1	20	18	34		.263	.346	.360	186	49	6	3	2	30	24	42

JOHN SMILEY — bats left — throws left — age 27 — PIT — P

1991	G	IP	H	BB	SO	SB	CS	W	L	SV	ERA		G	IP	H	BB	SO	SB	CS	W	L	SV	ERA
Total	33	207.2	194	44	129	18	13	20	8	0	3.08		196	854.0	788	230	534	91	37	60	42	4	3.57
at Home	16	99.2	90	24	60	6	9	10	5	0	2.98		96	415.0	350	128	258	43	20	31	22	2	3.10
on Road	17	108.0	104	20	69	12	4	10	3	0	3.17		100	439.0	438	102	276	48	17	29	20	2	4.02
on Grass	9	54.1	51	14	28	4	2	4	3	0	3.31		54	243.2	231	58	148	20	10	17	14	1	3.84
on Turf	24	153.1	143	30	101	14	11	16	5	0	2.99		142	610.1	557	172	386	71	27	43	28	3	3.47
Day Games	10	71.1	55	8	41	3	1	8	1	0	2.14		64	280.1	267	58	155	27	9	24	11	1	3.21
Night Games	23	136.1	139	36	88	15	12	12	7	0	3.56		132	573.2	521	172	379	64	28	36	31	3	3.75
April	4	27.2	20	12	10	1	0	4	0	0	2.28		27	127.2	106	29	75	11	3	10	5	0	2.75
May	5	27.0	31	6	18	4	4	3	1	0	3.67		32	144.2	143	35	95	20	11	12	6	1	3.86
June	6	37.0	36	4	29	4	1	2	4	0	3.65		29	119.2	108	31	92	15	3	8	8	0	3.61
July	5	32.1	31	13	24	3	3	3	2	0	3.62		36	173.2	138	63	113	14	6	7	12	1	3.21
August	6	39.1	41	8	24	2	2	4	1	0	3.43		30	139.1	155	38	74	18	7	9	8	1	4.00
Sept–Oct	7	44.1	35	8	24	0	3	4	0	0	2.03		42	149.0	138	34	85	13	7	14	7	0	3.99

	BA	OBA	SA	AB	H	2B	3B	HR	RBI	BB	SO		BA	OBA	SA	AB	H	2B	3B	HR	RBI	BB	SO
Total	.251	.292	.381	774	194	38	6	17	71	44	129		.245	.296	.375	3217	788	147	19	78	333	230	534
vs. Left	.199	.223	.325	151	30	4	3	3	12	5	29		.214	.271	.325	557	119	18	7	10	54	44	103
vs. Right	.263	.308	.395	623	164	34	3	14	59	39	100		.252	.301	.386	2660	669	129	12	68	279	186	431
Bases Empty	.244	.291	.363	491	120	23	4	9	9	29	88		.235	.287	.357	1982	465	90	9	45	45	137	342
Leadoff	.250	.298	.358	204	51	10	3	2	2	12	34		.240	.290	.369	824	198	39	5	19	19	53	135
Runners On Base	.261	.295	.413	283	74	15	2	8	62	15	41		.262	.309	.404	1235	323	57	10	33	288	93	192
Scoring Position	.265	.307	.377	151	40	9	1	4	46	11	22		.274	.332	.416	693	190	34	5	18	241	70	118
Late and Close	.233	.313	.267	60	14	2	0	0	3	7	8		.222	.301	.349	415	92	19	2	10	47	48	72

BRYN SMITH — bats right — throws right — age 37 — SL — P

1991	G	IP	H	BB	SO	SB	CS	W	L	SV	ERA	G	IP	H	BB	SO	SB	CS	W	L	SV	ERA
Total	31	198.2	188	45	94	19	8	12	9	0	3.85	237	1487.2	1412	346	847	174	55	93	72	0	3.49
at Home	16	107.1	95	25	46	11	3	5	4	0	3.52	120	779.1	710	202	473	86	32	49	31	0	3.21
on Road	15	91.1	93	20	48	8	5	7	5	0	4.24	117	708.1	702	144	374	88	23	44	41	0	3.80
on Grass	8	48.1	51	10	27	4	3	3	4	0	4.47	71	433.2	442	90	232	39	16	24	30	0	3.94
on Turf	23	150.1	137	35	67	15	5	9	5	0	3.65	166	1054.0	970	256	615	135	39	69	42	0	3.30
Day Games	8	49.1	42	16	26	8	2	3	2	0	3.47	73	448.2	417	119	235	46	16	26	22	0	3.45
Night Games	23	149.1	146	29	68	11	6	9	7	0	3.98	164	1039.0	995	227	612	128	39	67	50	0	3.51
April	4	27.0	23	5	15	2	2	3	0	0	3.00	30	198.1	178	48	102	17	6	16	7	0	3.18
May	6	38.1	44	8	20	4	4	1	3	0	5.63	46	292.2	304	61	173	25	23	17	15	0	3.75
June	5	34.0	30	9	9	2	0	2	1	0	2.38	42	256.0	256	64	138	43	6	16	13	0	3.90
July	6	38.1	34	7	18	4	1	3	3	0	3.52	43	285.2	239	57	180	31	12	18	12	0	2.71
August	6	35.2	36	10	16	3	1	2	1	0	5.05	37	228.1	222	56	122	23	4	11	13	0	3.98
Sept–Oct	4	25.1	21	6	16	4	0	1	1	0	2.84	39	226.2	213	60	132	35	4	15	12	0	3.45

	BA	OBA	SA	AB	H	2B	3B	HR	RBI	BB	SO	BA	OBA	SA	AB	H	2B	3B	HR	RBI	BB	SO
Total	.251	.297	.381	749	188	39	5	16	84	45	94	.250	.295	.369	5656	1412	235	45	116	584	346	847
vs. Left	.276	.321	.408	434	120	28	4	7	49	27	40	.262	.308	.370	3093	811	132	30	47	324	200	392
vs. Right	.216	.265	.343	315	68	11	1	9	35	18	54	.234	.280	.367	2563	601	103	15	69	260	146	455
Bases Empty	.245	.280	.345	473	116	21	4	6	6	20	56	.244	.289	.351	3429	838	129	27	61	61	198	500
Leadoff	.281	.309	.439	196	55	7	3	6	6	7	15	.260	.297	.387	1453	378	56	16	32	32	69	190
Runners On Base	.261	.324	.442	276	72	18	1	10	78	25	38	.258	.305	.396	2227	574	106	18	55	523	148	347
Scoring Position	.250	.323	.415	164	41	10	1	5	63	19	33	.249	.305	.395	1293	322	58	16	33	455	108	234
Late and Close	.280	.280	.480	25	7	3	1	0	2	0	2	.276	.315	.422	294	81	14	4	7	22	17	40

DAVE SMITH — bats right — throws right — age 37 — CHN — P

1991	G	IP	H	BB	SO	SB	CS	W	L	SV	ERA	G	IP	H	BB	SO	SB	CS	W	L	SV	ERA
Total	35	33.0	39	19	16	3	0	0	6	17	6.00	408	481.0	400	158	339	40	14	33	40	181	2.58
at Home	17	17.2	18	7	9	1	0	0	3	10	5.60	217	257.0	214	74	196	23	5	25	20	97	2.63
on Road	18	15.1	21	12	7	2	0	0	3	7	6.46	191	224.0	186	84	143	17	9	8	20	84	2.53
on Grass	26	26.0	31	13	13	2	0	0	4	12	5.88	128	149.2	139	59	96	14	5	5	18	57	3.31
on Turf	9	7.0	8	6	3	1	0	0	2	5	6.43	280	331.1	261	99	243	26	9	28	22	124	2.25
Day Games	19	18.1	23	11	9	2	0	0	3	10	6.38	112	122.0	104	53	80	11	2	5	14	50	3.17
Night Games	16	14.2	16	8	7	1	0	0	3	7	5.52	296	359.0	296	105	259	29	12	28	26	131	2.38
April	7	5.2	10	5	4	0	0	0	2	4	9.53	67	77.1	64	18	65	3	2	4	7	35	2.21
May	7	7.0	4	1	3	0	0	0	0	7	0.00	70	80.2	55	25	52	3	1	4	9	33	2.34
June	11	12.0	12	6	4	3	0	0	2	5	4.50	78	91.1	67	37	81	7	4	3	8	38	2.27
July	6	5.2	7	5	4	0	0	0	1	0	7.94	62	75.0	69	27	49	7	2	7	5	22	3.36
August	0	0.0	0	0	0	0	0	0	0	0	0.00	61	75.1	63	28	48	7	2	9	6	27	2.51
Sept–Oct	4	2.2	6	2	1	0	0	0	1	1	16.88	70	81.1	82	23	44	13	3	6	8	26	2.88

	BA	OBA	SA	AB	H	2B	3B	HR	RBI	BB	SO	BA	OBA	SA	AB	H	2B	3B	HR	RBI	BB	SO
Total	.302	.396	.535	129	39	4	4	6	28	19	16	.228	.293	.317	1758	400	48	17	25	198	158	339
vs. Left	.378	.459	.676	74	28	4	3	4	21	10	7	.231	.299	.311	872	201	24	8	10	98	83	134
vs. Right	.200	.313	.345	55	11	0	1	2	7	9	9	.225	.287	.323	886	199	24	9	15	100	75	205
Bases Empty	.279	.380	.426	61	17	1	1	2	2	10	8	.222	.287	.294	909	202	24	7	9	9	78	188
Leadoff	.379	.419	.690	29	11	1	1	2	2	2	4	.249	.319	.333	381	95	6	4	6	6	37	60
Runners On Base	.324	.410	.632	68	22	3	3	4	26	9	8	.233	.299	.342	849	198	24	10	16	189	80	151
Scoring Position	.302	.423	.535	43	13	2	1	2	20	9	4	.222	.312	.340	535	119	14	5	13	172	72	98
Late and Close	.333	.426	.576	99	33	3	3	5	24	15	11	.233	.301	.332	1281	299	35	14	21	166	121	239

LEE SMITH — bats right — throws right — age 35 — SL — P

1991	G	IP	H	BB	SO	SB	CS	W	L	SV	ERA	G	IP	H	BB	SO	SB	CS	W	L	SV	ERA
Total	67	73.0	70	13	67	9	2	6	3	47	2.34	521	683.1	604	254	732	88	27	50	44	265	2.98
at Home	39	45.2	39	7	39	8	2	6	1	26	1.38	281	379.2	347	119	414	50	15	35	20	136	3.15
on Road	28	27.1	31	6	28	1	0	0	2	21	3.95	240	303.2	257	135	318	38	12	15	24	129	2.76
on Grass	11	12.0	12	3	12	1	0	0	0	7	2.25	338	454.2	391	172	498	50	17	36	26	166	3.03
on Turf	56	61.0	58	10	55	8	2	6	3	40	2.36	183	228.2	213	82	234	38	10	14	18	99	2.87
Day Games	20	21.0	20	4	26	1	0	2	1	14	3.00	275	377.1	341	133	424	45	15	32	25	131	3.39
Night Games	47	52.0	50	9	41	8	2	4	2	33	2.08	246	306.0	263	121	308	43	12	18	19	134	2.47
April	10	13.0	6	2	14	0	0	2	0	8	1.38	64	86.0	73	40	111	11	5	9	8	33	2.62
May	9	7.1	10	2	6	2	0	0	2	4	6.14	87	117.0	102	35	113	16	4	11	7	39	3.38
June	13	15.2	13	3	16	2	0	1	0	7	1.72	98	129.0	113	59	134	15	7	5	10	43	3.28
July	11	13.1	16	1	12	0	1	2	0	7	2.70	90	129.1	108	41	145	9	3	12	6	53	2.78
August	12	12.0	13	3	8	1	1	1	1	10	1.50	92	113.2	104	35	106	19	5	10	6	45	2.22
Sept–Oct	12	11.2	12	2	11	4	0	0	0	10	2.31	90	108.1	104	44	123	18	3	3	7	52	3.49

	BA	OBA	SA	AB	H	2B	3B	HR	RBI	BB	SO	BA	OBA	SA	AB	H	2B	3B	HR	RBI	BB	SO
Total	.249	.281	.352	281	70	8	3	5	31	13	67	.237	.304	.343	2553	604	100	15	47	297	254	732
vs. Left	.256	.303	.366	164	42	5	2	3	19	11	42	.249	.331	.363	1387	345	61	8	27	172	174	382
vs. Right	.239	.250	.333	117	28	3	1	2	12	2	25	.222	.271	.319	1166	259	39	7	20	125	80	350
Bases Empty	.248	.277	.359	153	38	5	3	2	6	6	29	.239	.299	.348	1275	305	53	7	24	24	107	364
Leadoff	.246	.281	.377	61	15	2	0	2	2	3	13	.236	.297	.371	534	126	24	3	14	14	44	135
Runners On Base	.250	.287	.344	128	32	3	0	3	29	7	38	.234	.309	.337	1278	299	47	8	23	273	147	368
Scoring Position	.267	.312	.372	86	23	5	0	2	27	6	25	.215	.303	.315	820	176	31	6	13	243	111	251
Late and Close	.252	.288	.357	230	58	5	2	5	29	12	58	.240	.309	.355	1951	469	81	11	40	263	198	568

ZANE SMITH — bats left — throws left — age 32 — PIT — P

8-YEAR TOTALS (1984–1991)

1991	G	IP	H	BB	SO	SB	CS	W	L	SV	ERA	G	IP	H	BB	SO	SB	CS	W	L	SV	ERA
Total	35	228.0	234	29	120	26	8	16	10	0	3.20	258	1344.1	1335	464	772	159	49	67	78	3	3.58
at Home	19	129.1	132	14	69	20	3	11	3	0	2.78	132	717.0	725	232	434	83	19	38	34	2	3.48
on Road	16	98.2	102	15	51	6	5	5	7	0	3.74	126	627.1	610	232	338	76	30	29	44	1	3.70
on Grass	8	44.2	61	7	21	2	2	1	6	0	5.24	136	731.0	738	280	400	73	29	33	50	1	3.92
on Turf	27	183.1	173	22	99	24	6	15	4	0	2.70	122	613.1	597	184	372	86	20	34	28	2	3.18
Day Games	9	51.2	66	9	24	8	2	4	4	0	4.53	67	348.1	356	137	188	46	13	16	27	0	3.82
Night Games	26	176.1	168	20	96	18	6	12	6	0	2.81	191	996.0	979	327	584	113	36	51	51	3	3.50
April	4	26.2	33	5	14	5	0	2	1	0	2.70	38	207.1	194	55	120	22	0	10	12	0	3.08
May	6	43.1	33	3	27	1	0	5	1	0	1.87	44	241.0	265	93	156	29	5	13	14	0	4.03
June	6	36.1	43	8	13	6	4	1	4	0	3.96	41	252.2	258	98	133	41	16	11	18	0	3.49
July	5	24.1	32	5	14	5	1	2	2	0	5.92	41	206.0	205	88	119	25	13	9	15	1	4.11
August	6	43.1	45	2	20	4	2	2	1	0	2.70	39	206.1	197	57	100	11	8	11	8	1	3.49
Sept–Oct	8	54.0	48	6	32	5	1	4	1	0	3.17	55	231.0	216	73	144	31	7	13	11	1	3.27

	BA	OBA	SA	AB	H	2B	3B	HR	RBI	BB	SO	BA	OBA	SA	AB	H	2B	3B	HR	RBI	BB	SO
Total	.268	.292	.370	873	234	36	4	15	88	29	120	.264	.327	.365	5064	1335	222	31	77	566	464	772
vs. Left	.264	.288	.311	148	39	0	2	1	12	5	32	.219	.269	.275	804	176	22	4	5	79	55	195
vs. Right	.269	.292	.382	725	195	36	2	14	76	24	88	.272	.337	.382	4260	1159	200	27	72	487	409	577
Bases Empty	.256	.275	.350	554	142	20	4	8	8	14	81	.260	.320	.354	2923	760	127	20	36	36	246	437
Leadoff	.303	.309	.429	231	70	11	0	6	6	2	36	.264	.320	.370	1271	336	57	7	21	21	97	180
Runners On Base	.288	.320	.404	319	92	16	0	7	80	15	39	.269	.336	.381	2141	575	95	11	41	530	218	335
Scoring Position	.302	.340	.434	182	55	12	0	4	72	11	20	.284	.361	.409	1226	348	65	7	25	478	155	211
Late and Close	.263	.273	.316	76	20	1	0	1	8	1	10	.257	.318	.330	572	147	21	0	7	57	50	90

JOHN SMOLTZ — bats right — throws right — age 25 — ATL — P

4-YEAR TOTALS (1988–1991)

1991	G	IP	H	BB	SO	SB	CS	W	L	SV	ERA	G	IP	H	BB	SO	SB	CS	W	L	SV	ERA
Total	36	229.2	206	77	148	14	13	14	13	0	3.80	111	733.0	646	272	523	65	29	42	42	0	3.72
at Home	21	136.0	138	32	81	6	7	9	7	0	4.10	57	394.2	341	125	287	27	17	25	19	0	3.49
on Road	15	93.2	68	45	67	8	6	5	6	0	3.36	54	338.1	305	147	236	38	12	17	23	0	3.99
on Grass	28	174.0	165	53	105	7	8	10	11	0	4.24	82	545.1	484	189	384	48	19	31	29	0	3.83
on Turf	8	55.2	41	24	43	7	5	4	2	0	2.43	29	187.2	162	83	139	17	10	11	13	0	3.40
Day Games	5	35.1	30	9	21	1	1	1	2	0	3.31	25	178.1	137	50	124	16	2	10	9	0	3.23
Night Games	31	194.1	176	68	127	13	12	13	11	0	3.89	86	554.2	509	222	399	49	27	32	33	0	3.88
April	5	29.2	28	9	15	3	4	3	1	0	3.64	14	82.2	81	34	56	8	5	4	7	0	4.35
May	6	40.2	39	13	26	2	3	2	3	0	4.20	17	124.0	93	37	91	7	5	5	6	0	2.98
June	6	34.1	41	18	27	3	2	0	4	0	6.55	17	107.0	116	41	93	16	5	4	6	0	4.63
July	6	28.2	32	13	12	4	0	4	2	0	7.85	20	139.0	101	47	85	9	3	9	6	0	3.69
August	6	44.2	28	10	37	1	3	4	0	0	1.41	24	157.1	139	66	123	18	8	11	9	0	3.60
Sept–Oct	7	51.2	38	14	31	1	3	4	0	0	1.57	19	123.0	116	47	75	7	3	6	5	0	3.44

	BA	OBA	SA	AB	H	2B	3B	HR	RBI	BB	SO	BA	OBA	SA	AB	H	2B	3B	HR	RBI	BB	SO
Total	.243	.305	.360	849	206	38	7	16	89	77	148	.237	.306	.359	2723	646	114	17	61	290	272	523
vs. Left	.287	.362	.420	488	140	23	6	10	56	60	69	.262	.341	.384	1593	417	75	15	30	169	192	246
vs. Right	.183	.222	.280	361	66	15	1	6	33	17	79	.203	.255	.323	1130	229	39	2	31	121	80	277
Bases Empty	.242	.306	.357	499	121	20	2	11	11	45	89	.229	.296	.339	1628	372	64	7	34	34	152	327
Leadoff	.264	.329	.370	216	57	11	0	4	4	21	38	.240	.301	.346	696	167	26	3	14	14	58	132
Runners On Base	.243	.303	.366	350	85	18	5	5	78	32	59	.250	.320	.388	1095	274	50	10	27	256	120	196
Scoring Position	.262	.342	.424	191	50	9	5	5	71	26	37	.245	.339	.384	597	146	26	9	13	217	95	132
Late and Close	.214	.233	.238	42	9	1	0	0	3	1	11	.207	.270	.309	246	51	11	1	4	24	21	52

DAVE STEWART — bats right — throws right — age 35 — OAK — P

8-YEAR TOTALS (1984–1991)

1991	G	IP	H	BB	SO	SB	CS	W	L	SV	ERA	G	IP	H	BB	SO	SB	CS	W	L	SV	ERA
Total	35	226.0	245	105	144	23	9	11	11	0	5.18	296	1727.1	1631	669	1158	143	54	111	81	4	3.80
at Home	18	115.1	118	45	72	12	6	8	3	0	4.21	152	907.2	812	324	622	83	29	58	36	1	3.34
on Road	17	110.2	127	60	72	11	3	3	8	0	6.18	144	819.2	819	345	536	60	25	53	45	3	4.32
on Grass	29	192.0	192	85	120	18	9	11	6	0	4.59	241	1453.0	1349	551	976	123	44	92	65	4	3.62
on Turf	6	34.0	53	20	24	5	0	0	5	0	8.47	55	274.1	282	118	182	20	10	19	16	0	4.76
Day Games	11	76.1	87	21	51	8	2	6	4	0	4.95	102	632.1	575	220	441	48	18	46	29	1	3.25
Night Games	24	149.2	158	84	93	15	7	5	7	0	5.29	194	1095.0	1056	449	717	95	36	65	52	3	4.13
April	5	32.0	39	14	19	3	1	2	2	0	6.75	45	237.2	232	104	140	25	6	21	12	2	4.13
May	4	24.1	24	13	11	4	2	1	2	0	2.22	43	228.2	220	88	128	14	7	15	10	1	3.46
June	6	39.1	43	21	23	4	1	2	2	0	7.09	53	289.0	265	116	193	26	13	13	17	1	4.52
July	7	49.1	41	18	37	2	0	3	1	0	4.01	53	307.0	278	115	209	23	4	13	17	0	3.57
August	6	37.1	46	21	18	7	3	2	3	0	5.79	49	324.1	300	112	240	22	13	21	13	0	3.55
Sept–Oct	7	43.2	52	18	36	3	2	1	3	0	4.74	53	340.2	336	134	248	33	11	21	17	0	3.57

	BA	OBA	SA	AB	H	2B	3B	HR	RBI	BB	SO	BA	OBA	SA	AB	H	2B	3B	HR	RBI	BB	SO
Total	.278	.356	.428	880	245	44	8	24	126	105	144	.249	.319	.379	6548	1631	307	39	156	718	669	1158
vs. Left	.305	.361	.433	439	134	22	5	8	71	43	50	.253	.327	.378	3423	865	156	21	77	390	390	555
vs. Right	.252	.351	.424	441	111	22	3	16	55	62	94	.245	.311	.381	3125	766	151	18	79	328	279	603
Bases Empty	.266	.342	.406	500	133	25	3	13	13	54	72	.250	.315	.384	3834	959	177	25	95	95	344	678
Leadoff	.250	.319	.431	216	54	16	1	7	7	19	34	.246	.307	.391	1643	404	79	12	45	45	138	283
Runners On Base	.295	.373	.458	380	112	19	5	11	113	51	72	.248	.325	.373	2714	672	130	14	61	623	325	480
Scoring Position	.292	.370	.475	219	64	11	4	7	102	32	43	.228	.306	.347	1598	364	72	11	32	541	198	297
Late and Close	.311	.475	.378	45	14	0	0	1	7	14	11	.236	.323	.343	648	153	26	2	13	58	85	109

TODD STOTTLEMYRE — bats left — throws right — age 27 — TOR — P

1991

	G	IP	H	BB	SO	SB	CS	W	L	SV	ERA
Total	34	219.0	194	75	116	24	3	15	8	0	3.78
at Home	17	116.0	99	28	51	11	1	9	3	0	3.96
on Road	17	103.0	95	47	65	13	2	6	5	0	3.58
on Grass	13	78.1	71	37	48	11	2	4	4	0	3.68
on Turf	21	140.2	123	38	68	13	1	11	4	0	3.84
Day Games	12	71.1	68	28	29	10	1	3	3	0	4.54
Night Games	22	147.2	126	47	87	14	2	12	5	0	3.41
April	4	23.0	19	12	17	2	0	2	0	0	3.91
May	6	41.0	31	15	27	9	0	3	1	0	3.07
June	6	45.1	41	8	19	0	0	4	2	0	2.78
July	5	30.0	27	14	20	5	0	1	1	0	4.20
August	6	37.0	44	11	14	4	1	2	2	0	5.35
Sept–Oct	7	42.2	32	15	19	4	2	3	2	0	3.80

4-YEAR TOTALS (1988–1991)

G	IP	H	BB	SO	SB	CS	W	L	SV	ERA
122	647.2	654	234	361	78	26	39	40	0	4.27
59	336.2	349	112	180	35	11	21	18	0	4.33
63	311.0	305	122	181	43	15	18	22	0	4.20
44	227.1	218	83	135	32	9	13	15	0	3.88
78	420.1	436	151	226	46	17	26	25	0	4.48
39	203.0	224	80	115	28	7	7	17	0	5.19
83	444.2	430	154	246	50	19	32	23	0	3.85
22	83.1	85	47	54	20	6	5	7	0	4.97
20	107.0	102	36	71	19	1	5	9	0	4.54
19	127.0	119	30	51	4	4	10	4	0	2.76
20	98.1	116	45	65	11	4	5	7	0	5.58
17	111.0	111	32	58	9	5	6	6	0	3.81
24	121.0	121	44	62	15	6	8	7	0	4.46

	BA	OBA	SA	AB	H	2B	3B	HR	RBI	BB	SO
Total	.235	.305	.356	826	194	27	5	21	84	75	116
vs. Left	.244	.312	.357	414	101	8	3	11	33	39	50
vs. Right	.226	.298	.354	412	93	19	2	10	51	36	66
Bases Empty	.230	.308	.329	487	112	15	3	9	9	46	67
Leadoff	.251	.323	.382	207	52	5	2	6	6	18	24
Runners On Base	.242	.301	.395	339	82	12	2	12	75	29	49
Scoring Position	.238	.313	.375	168	40	9	1	4	57	21	22
Late and Close	.293	.339	.414	58	17	2	1	1	3	4	9

BA	OBA	SA	AB	H	2B	3B	HR	RBI	BB	SO
.264	.332	.402	2478	654	110	18	65	289	234	361
.292	.357	.436	1235	361	58	10	33	144	118	135
.236	.307	.368	1243	293	52	8	32	145	116	226
.268	.335	.396	1425	382	69	9	32	32	125	209
.300	.353	.443	621	186	27	4	18	18	45	83
.258	.328	.408	1053	272	41	9	33	257	109	152
.257	.342	.394	573	147	31	3	14	207	78	78
.278	.339	.364	162	45	9	1	1	13	14	25

BILL SWIFT — bats right — throws right — age 31 — SEA — P

1991

	G	IP	H	BB	SO	SB	CS	W	L	SV	ERA
Total	71	90.1	74	26	48	1	1	1	2	17	1.99
at Home	33	43.2	34	10	27	1	1	1	0	7	1.65
on Road	38	46.2	40	16	21	0	0	0	0	10	2.31
on Grass	28	37.0	29	9	17	0	0	0	0	9	1.70
on Turf	43	53.1	45	17	31	1	1	1	2	8	2.19
Day Games	17	20.1	19	4	13	0	1	0	0	4	1.77
Night Games	54	70.0	55	22	35	1	0	1	2	13	2.06
April	2	1.1	3	1	2	0	0	0	0	0	6.75
May	15	22.2	16	4	13	0	0	0	1	5	2.38
June	14	16.2	17	5	7	1	0	0	0	1	3.24
July	11	15.2	13	5	10	0	0	0	1	3	1.15
August	13	15.2	8	6	4	0	0	0	0	2	0.00
Sept–Oct	16	18.1	17	5	12	0	1	0	0	6	2.45

6-YEAR TOTALS (1985–1991)

G	IP	H	BB	SO	SB	CS	W	L	SV	ERA
253	759.0	827	253	292	37	26	30	40	24	4.04
123	384.0	413	125	143	22	9	16	18	9	3.73
130	375.0	414	128	149	15	17	14	22	15	4.37
96	272.1	299	100	115	10	15	10	16	13	4.49
157	486.2	528	153	177	27	11	20	24	11	3.79
68	206.0	236	59	70	11	8	10	12	6	3.80
185	553.0	591	194	222	26	18	20	28	18	4.13
23	58.1	71	29	30	4	2	1	0	1	3.70
45	140.2	153	39	64	7	5	8	7	5	3.97
43	151.1	169	48	46	11	0	7	7	4	4.46
36	128.0	147	40	49	2	2	6	10	4	4.36
44	138.2	142	53	40	6	1	2	8	4	3.70
62	142.0	145	44	63	7	6	6	8	6	3.87

	BA	OBA	SA	AB	H	2B	3B	HR	RBI	BB	SO
Total	.224	.283	.276	330	74	6	1	3	31	26	48
vs. Left	.238	.290	.279	122	29	2	0	1	9	9	15
vs. Right	.216	.279	.274	208	45	4	1	2	22	17	33
Bases Empty	.255	.312	.331	157	40	4	1	2	2	13	25
Leadoff	.274	.303	.370	73	20	2	1	1	1	3	13
Runners On Base	.197	.257	.225	173	34	2	0	1	29	13	23
Scoring Position	.182	.277	.222	99	18	1	0	1	28	12	13
Late and Close	.254	.304	.302	169	43	5	0	1	14	12	28

BA	OBA	SA	AB	H	2B	3B	HR	RBI	BB	SO
.281	.343	.373	2940	827	135	12	37	359	253	292
.313	.375	.423	1424	445	81	5	22	183	136	105
.252	.312	.327	1516	382	54	7	15	176	117	187
.270	.330	.356	1572	425	67	5	19	19	121	163
.271	.320	.355	705	191	31	2	8	8	46	80
.294	.357	.393	1368	402	68	7	18	340	132	129
.280	.362	.363	801	224	35	4	8	304	103	86
.254	.317	.335	465	118	12	1	8	40	39	52

GREG SWINDELL — bats right — throws left — age 27 — CLE — P

1991

	G	IP	H	BB	SO	SB	CS	W	L	SV	ERA
Total	33	238.0	241	31	169	9	10	9	16	0	3.48
at Home	20	153.1	139	18	107	5	8	7	9	0	2.52
on Road	13	84.2	102	13	62	4	2	2	7	0	5.21
on Grass	29	209.1	208	28	151	7	9	8	13	0	3.18
on Turf	4	28.2	33	3	18	2	1	1	3	0	5.65
Day Games	10	72.2	75	9	37	3	3	3	6	0	3.47
Night Games	23	165.1	166	22	132	6	7	6	10	0	3.48
April	5	34.0	34	8	28	1	0	3	1	0	2.91
May	5	39.2	39	7	25	1	1	2	2	0	2.72
June	6	49.0	49	6	33	4	2	2	1	0	2.94
July	6	35.2	35	4	36	0	1	1	3	0	4.04
August	5	35.2	37	5	19	1	4	2	2	0	3.79
Sept–Oct	6	44.0	47	6	28	1	1	1	4	0	4.50

6-YEAR TOTALS (1986–1991)

G	IP	H	BB	SO	SB	CS	W	L	SV	ERA
153	1043.0	1059	226	756	52	57	60	55	0	3.79
78	554.1	527	111	388	24	28	34	26	0	3.38
75	488.2	532	115	368	28	29	26	29	0	4.25
131	902.1	898	189	659	45	48	55	42	0	3.55
22	140.2	161	37	97	7	9	5	13	0	5.31
47	346.2	352	60	258	12	18	23	18	0	3.27
106	696.1	707	166	498	40	39	37	37	0	4.05
25	167.1	153	37	124	7	9	10	8	0	3.33
28	205.2	194	44	146	8	14	12	8	0	3.15
27	179.1	212	44	127	12	12	7	11	0	4.62
22	153.2	135	29	124	6	7	11	8	0	3.16
21	136.1	158	32	96	8	7	8	12	0	4.22
30	200.2	207	40	139	11	8	12	8	0	4.26

	BA	OBA	SA	AB	H	2B	3B	HR	RBI	BB	SO
Total	.263	.287	.393	916	241	48	4	21	102	31	169
vs. Left	.275	.309	.373	153	42	8	2	1	14	7	28
vs. Right	.261	.283	.397	763	199	40	2	20	88	24	141
Bases Empty	.247	.269	.344	578	143	30	1	8	8	14	116
Leadoff	.260	.272	.388	242	63	14	1	5	5	2	45
Runners On Base	.290	.317	.476	338	98	18	3	13	94	17	53
Scoring Position	.249	.286	.370	189	47	7	2	4	69	13	33
Late and Close	.252	.271	.331	139	35	8	0	1	7	4	24

BA	OBA	SA	AB	H	2B	3B	HR	RBI	BB	SO
.264	.302	.401	4015	1059	175	25	109	430	226	756
.265	.298	.381	637	169	31	2	13	73	31	105
.263	.303	.405	3378	890	144	23	96	357	195	651
.250	.287	.380	2502	625	102	15	65	65	127	501
.257	.287	.421	1046	269	49	10	34	34	40	201
.287	.326	.436	1513	434	73	10	44	365	99	255
.275	.324	.411	816	224	39	6	20	301	73	155
.281	.323	.397	463	130	26	2	8	42	29	81

FRANK TANANA — bats left — throws left — age 39 — DET — P

1991

	G	IP	H	BB	SO	SB	CS	W	L	SV	ERA
Total	33	217.1	217	78	107	17	14	13	12	0	3.77
at Home	18	120.2	122	49	62	12	12	7	5	0	4.10
on Road	15	96.2	95	29	45	5	2	6	7	0	3.35
on Grass	31	205.2	203	73	102	16	14	13	11	0	3.72
on Turf	2	11.2	14	5	5	1	0	0	1	0	4.63
Day Games	11	77.0	73	26	38	6	5	4	5	0	3.16
Night Games	22	140.1	144	52	69	11	9	9	7	0	4.10
April	5	34.0	40	9	15	5	2	1	2	0	3.71
May	5	22.0	31	14	10	4	1	1	2	0	7.77
June	6	44.2	29	14	30	0	4	3	2	0	1.21
July	4	24.2	28	8	11	2	1	2	1	0	4.38
August	6	41.0	43	14	16	2	2	4	1	0	3.73
Sept–Oct	7	51.0	46	19	25	4	4	2	1	0	4.06

8-YEAR TOTALS (1984–1991)

	G	IP	H	BB	SO	SB	CS	W	L	SV	ERA
Total	265	1686.0	1706	541	1056	116	70	100	92	1	3.98
at Home	140	889.2	885	289	573	60	40	54	49	0	4.12
on Road	125	796.1	821	252	483	56	30	46	43	1	3.82
on Grass	233	1484.2	1489	471	948	106	61	94	78	1	3.92
on Turf	32	201.1	217	70	108	10	9	6	14	0	4.38
Day Games	79	498.0	523	162	309	47	14	30	32	0	4.08
Night Games	186	1188.0	1183	379	747	69	56	70	60	1	3.93
April	37	240.2	253	77	133	19	14	17	13	0	4.19
May	45	274.1	285	93	164	29	9	15	17	0	4.76
June	44	309.2	286	107	202	15	17	20	14	0	3.31
July	42	257.2	269	86	171	18	5	12	16	0	4.02
August	47	281.0	308	78	162	17	7	20	14	1	4.29
Sept–Oct	50	322.2	305	100	224	18	18	16	18	0	3.49

	BA	OBA	SA	AB	H	2B	3B	HR	RBI	BB	SO
Total	.265	.327	.412	818	217	34	4	26	87	78	107
vs. Left	.233	.282	.371	159	37	5	1	5	17	11	25
vs. Right	.273	.338	.422	659	180	29	3	21	70	67	82
Bases Empty	.286	.342	.463	486	139	20	3	20	20	40	54
Leadoff	.308	.354	.548	208	64	9	1	13	13	15	23
Runners On Base	.235	.308	.337	332	78	14	1	6	67	38	53
Scoring Position	.204	.293	.290	186	38	7	0	3	58	26	30
Late and Close	.395	.479	.421	38	15	1	0	0	9	8	5

	BA	OBA	SA	AB	H	2B	3B	HR	RBI	BB	SO
Total	.262	.320	.414	6500	1706	290	41	205	751	541	1056
vs. Left	.252	.304	.381	1086	274	48	7	26	113	77	196
vs. Right	.264	.323	.421	5414	1432	242	34	179	638	464	860
Bases Empty	.260	.309	.418	3953	1028	184	25	130	130	253	637
Leadoff	.260	.298	.409	1663	432	79	8	51	51	84	270
Runners On Base	.266	.337	.409	2547	678	106	16	75	621	288	419
Scoring Position	.258	.349	.392	1373	354	53	10	37	521	216	250
Late and Close	.270	.348	.426	493	133	23	3	16	55	59	68

KEVIN TAPANI — bats right — throws right — age 28 — MIN — P

1991

	G	IP	H	BB	SO	SB	CS	W	L	SV	ERA
Total	34	244.0	225	40	135	18	3	16	9	0	2.99
at Home	18	132.1	117	25	80	10	2	10	5	0	2.79
on Road	16	111.2	108	15	55	8	1	6	4	0	3.22
on Grass	10	70.1	66	9	31	4	0	5	1	0	2.82
on Turf	24	173.2	159	31	104	14	3	11	8	0	3.06
Day Games	9	59.1	58	10	26	4	1	3	2	0	2.73
Night Games	25	184.2	167	30	109	14	2	13	7	0	3.07
April	4	30.0	26	4	23	2	1	2	0	0	2.10
May	6	38.2	46	10	22	6	0	0	6	0	5.35
June	6	40.1	29	2	19	2	0	3	0	0	1.56
July	7	45.2	48	6	17	2	0	3	0	0	2.76
August	6	48.0	35	10	20	3	1	5	0	0	2.63
Sept–Oct	6	41.1	41	8	34	5	1	3	2	0	3.48

3-YEAR TOTALS (1989–1991)

	G	IP	H	BB	SO	SB	CS	W	L	SV	ERA
Total	70	443.1	428	81	259	32	12	30	19	0	3.45
at Home	34	225.1	221	48	137	17	5	19	9	0	3.24
on Road	36	218.0	207	33	122	15	7	11	10	0	3.67
on Grass	26	148.0	144	22	84	9	4	9	6	0	3.71
on Turf	44	295.1	284	59	175	23	8	21	13	0	3.32
Day Games	19	117.0	106	24	67	7	4	7	4	0	2.85
Night Games	51	326.1	322	57	192	25	8	23	15	0	3.67
April	8	52.0	46	9	38	4	2	4	2	0	2.42
May	12	76.2	88	17	53	7	3	4	7	0	4.70
June	11	77.2	69	7	43	3	3	3	0	0	3.13
July	15	82.0	80	13	36	4	1	6	0	0	2.96
August	8	56.0	42	14	23	3	2	5	1	0	3.05
Sept–Oct	16	99.0	103	21	66	11	1	6	6	0	3.91

	BA	OBA	SA	AB	H	2B	3B	HR	RBI	BB	SO
Total	.245	.277	.382	917	225	48	4	23	76	40	135
vs. Left	.237	.259	.346	511	121	26	3	8	42	16	68
vs. Right	.256	.298	.426	406	104	22	1	15	34	24	67
Bases Empty	.258	.292	.419	582	150	34	3	18	18	26	94
Leadoff	.274	.312	.498	237	65	17	3	10	10	12	29
Runners On Base	.224	.251	.316	335	75	14	1	5	58	14	41
Scoring Position	.208	.234	.268	183	38	6	1	1	46	8	21
Late and Close	.257	.300	.378	74	19	3	0	2	6	5	13

	BA	OBA	SA	AB	H	2B	3B	HR	RBI	BB	SO
Total	.253	.287	.385	1692	428	83	13	38	154	81	259
vs. Left	.261	.294	.394	909	237	48	11	17	83	43	132
vs. Right	.244	.279	.374	783	191	35	2	21	71	38	127
Bases Empty	.246	.279	.389	1085	267	56	9	27	27	47	179
Leadoff	.252	.278	.440	445	112	26	8	14	14	15	70
Runners On Base	.265	.301	.377	607	161	27	4	11	127	34	80
Scoring Position	.256	.291	.350	340	87	13	2	5	108	22	47
Late and Close	.295	.328	.395	129	38	5	1	2	13	7	22

WADE TAYLOR — bats right — throws right — age 27 — NYA — P

1991

	G	IP	H	BB	SO	SB	CS	W	L	SV	ERA
Total	23	116.1	144	53	72	12	7	7	12	0	6.27
at Home	11	62.1	81	19	36	6	6	5	6	0	5.34
on Road	12	54.0	63	34	36	6	1	2	6	0	7.33
on Grass	21	103.0	131	48	62	12	7	7	11	0	6.55
on Turf	2	13.1	13	5	10	0	0	0	1	0	4.05
Day Games	6	29.2	40	17	21	6	3	2	3	0	7.58
Night Games	17	86.2	104	36	51	6	4	5	9	0	5.82
April	0	0.0	0	0	0	0	0	0	0	0	0.00
May	0	0.0	0	0	0	0	0	0	0	0	0.00
June	5	25.1	27	11	16	1	2	3	2	0	6.39
July	6	33.0	46	15	21	2	3	2	4	0	6.55
August	6	29.2	34	12	17	4	2	2	1	0	5.16
Sept–Oct	6	28.1	37	15	18	5	0	0	5	0	6.99

1-YEAR TOTALS (1991)

	G	IP	H	BB	SO	SB	CS	W	L	SV	ERA
Total	23	116.1	144	53	72	12	7	7	12	0	6.27
at Home	11	62.1	81	19	36	6	6	5	6	0	5.34
on Road	12	54.0	63	34	36	6	1	2	6	0	7.33
on Grass	21	103.0	131	48	62	12	7	7	11	0	6.55
on Turf	2	13.1	13	5	10	0	0	0	1	0	4.05
Day Games	6	29.2	40	17	21	6	3	2	3	0	7.58
Night Games	17	86.2	104	36	51	6	4	5	9	0	5.82
April	0	0.0	0	0	0	0	0	0	0	0	0.00
May	0	0.0	0	0	0	0	0	0	0	0	0.00
June	5	25.1	27	11	16	1	2	3	2	0	6.39
July	6	33.0	46	15	21	2	3	2	4	0	6.55
August	6	29.2	34	12	17	4	2	2	1	0	5.16
Sept–Oct	6	28.1	37	15	18	5	0	0	5	0	6.99

	BA	OBA	SA	AB	H	2B	3B	HR	RBI	BB	SO
Total	.314	.388	.477	459	144	28	4	13	73	53	72
vs. Left	.327	.414	.488	205	67	13	1	6	30	30	29
vs. Right	.303	.366	.469	254	77	15	3	7	43	23	43
Bases Empty	.305	.393	.449	236	72	16	3	4	29	40	40
Leadoff	.368	.429	.570	114	42	10	2	3	3	11	16
Runners On Base	.323	.383	.507	223	72	12	1	9	69	24	32
Scoring Position	.323	.363	.433	127	41	6	1	2	54	11	14
Late and Close	1.000	1.000	2.500	2	2	0	0	1	2	0	0

	BA	OBA	SA	AB	H	2B	3B	HR	RBI	BB	SO
Total	.314	.388	.477	459	144	28	4	13	73	53	72
vs. Left	.327	.414	.488	205	67	13	1	6	30	30	29
vs. Right	.303	.366	.469	254	77	15	3	7	43	23	43
Bases Empty	.305	.393	.449	236	72	16	3	4	29	40	40
Leadoff	.368	.429	.570	114	42	10	2	3	3	11	16
Runners On Base	.323	.383	.507	223	72	12	1	9	69	24	32
Scoring Position	.323	.363	.433	127	41	6	1	2	54	11	14
Late and Close	1.000	1.000	2.500	2	2	0	0	1	2	0	0

WALT TERRELL — bats left — throws right — age 34 — DET — P

1991	G	IP	H	BB	SO	SB	CS	W	L	SV	ERA
Total	35	218.2	257	79	80	6	5	12	14	0	4.24
at Home	19	111.2	138	36	38	3	3	9	7	0	4.84
on Road	16	107.0	119	43	42	3	2	3	7	0	3.62
on Grass	31	199.1	225	72	76	6	5	12	12	0	4.02
on Turf	4	19.1	32	7	4	0	0	0	2	0	6.52
Day Games	10	65.1	70	26	25	1	0	5	3	0	3.72
Night Games	25	153.1	187	53	55	5	5	7	11	0	4.46
April	5	30.0	38	9	13	0	1	0	3	0	3.60
May	6	34.2	47	14	10	3	0	2	2	0	5.45
June	6	40.2	46	11	14	2	1	1	2	0	3.98
July	6	33.0	38	12	12	0	0	3	1	0	3.82
August	6	39.2	40	20	18	1	1	3	1	0	4.31
Sept–Oct	6	40.2	48	13	13	0	2	2	4	0	4.20

8-YEAR TOTALS (1984–1991)

	G	IP	H	BB	SO	SB	CS	W	L	SV	ERA
Total	260	1693.0	1776	629	800	57	56	96	102	0	4.17
at Home	125	833.1	821	278	390	20	24	57	39	0	3.73
on Road	135	859.2	955	351	410	37	32	39	63	0	4.60
on Grass	203	1347.2	1380	484	632	44	41	81	74	0	3.93
on Turf	57	345.1	396	145	168	13	15	15	28	0	5.08
Day Games	72	460.0	483	170	238	15	19	23	30	0	4.15
Night Games	188	1233.0	1293	459	562	42	37	73	72	0	4.18
April	32	203.1	222	61	91	4	8	11	10	0	3.72
May	46	302.0	308	113	163	14	6	18	19	0	3.96
June	44	271.2	293	116	115	8	13	11	24	0	4.74
July	41	264.2	252	99	144	6	9	14	13	0	3.98
August	48	333.1	362	135	155	17	10	20	18	0	4.48
Sept–Oct	49	318.0	339	105	132	8	10	22	18	0	3.99

	BA	OBA	SA	AB	H	2B	3B	HR	RBI	BB	SO
Total	.301	.358	.433	853	257	48	8	16	99	79	80
vs. Left	.308	.374	.442	452	139	26	4	9	55	50	28
vs. Right	.294	.340	.421	401	118	22	4	7	44	29	52
Bases Empty	.300	.344	.456	487	146	36	5	10	10	32	53
Leadoff	.320	.352	.479	219	70	22	2	3	3	11	18
Runners On Base	.303	.376	.402	366	111	12	3	6	89	47	27
Scoring Position	.314	.398	.425	207	65	10	2	3	80	34	16
Late and Close	.303	.349	.408	76	23	5	0	1	8	6	7

	BA	OBA	SA	AB	H	2B	3B	HR	RBI	BB	SO
Total	.273	.338	.410	6505	1776	310	45	164	743	629	800
vs. Left	.274	.340	.405	3401	933	172	19	78	387	345	347
vs. Right	.272	.335	.416	3104	843	138	26	86	356	284	453
Bases Empty	.268	.334	.413	3739	1001	177	27	104	104	356	499
Leadoff	.265	.329	.402	1628	432	81	11	40	40	148	198
Runners On Base	.280	.343	.406	2766	775	133	18	60	639	273	301
Scoring Position	.277	.350	.407	1439	398	70	9	33	547	180	191
Late and Close	.284	.341	.462	634	180	29	3	26	81	53	72

BOB TEWKSBURY — bats right — throws right — age 32 — SL — P

1991	G	IP	H	BB	SO	SB	CS	W	L	SV	ERA
Total	30	191.0	206	38	75	10	9	11	12	0	3.25
at Home	14	94.1	93	18	34	3	7	6	3	0	3.24
on Road	16	96.2	113	20	41	7	2	5	9	0	3.26
on Grass	8	54.2	61	9	24	2	0	3	5	0	2.47
on Turf	22	136.1	145	29	51	8	9	8	7	0	3.56
Day Games	10	64.0	74	16	19	4	3	4	6	0	2.95
Night Games	20	127.0	132	22	56	6	6	7	6	0	3.40
April	4	25.0	21	7	17	3	1	2	1	0	3.24
May	4	21.0	30	5	3	1	3	1	1	0	4.29
June	6	43.1	37	8	18	2	1	3	2	0	1.66
July	5	31.0	31	5	15	2	3	1	3	0	2.32
August	5	29.0	40	6	8	0	0	1	2	0	5.90
Sept–Oct	6	41.2	47	7	14	2	1	3	3	0	3.24

6-YEAR TOTALS (1986–1991)

	G	IP	H	BB	SO	SB	CS	W	L	SV	ERA
Total	104	551.1	611	116	214	22	18	32	34	1	3.69
at Home	48	265.2	275	53	103	9	11	15	12	0	3.42
on Road	56	285.2	336	63	111	13	7	17	22	1	3.94
on Grass	46	256.0	299	61	98	6	6	15	18	0	3.83
on Turf	58	295.1	312	55	116	16	12	17	16	1	3.57
Day Games	42	233.1	249	53	88	6	6	14	18	0	3.66
Night Games	62	318.0	362	63	126	14	12	18	16	1	3.71
April	17	71.1	86	17	30	4	3	4	3	1	4.79
May	11	46.0	67	10	15	2	4	3	2	0	4.89
June	17	109.0	102	18	37	2	1	8	3	0	2.31
July	19	105.1	123	28	50	5	5	4	13	0	3.84
August	15	78.0	87	11	22	4	1	5	4	0	3.35
Sept–Oct	25	141.2	146	32	60	5	4	8	9	0	3.88

	BA	OBA	SA	AB	H	2B	3B	HR	RBI	BB	SO
Total	.281	.317	.413	733	206	42	8	13	79	38	75
vs. Left	.281	.328	.394	406	114	28	3	4	38	31	29
vs. Right	.281	.302	.437	327	92	14	5	9	41	7	46
Bases Empty	.287	.320	.423	442	127	28	4	8	8	18	50
Leadoff	.286	.325	.434	189	54	13	3	3	3	9	23
Runners On Base	.271	.313	.399	291	79	14	4	5	71	20	25
Scoring Position	.284	.328	.438	169	48	10	2	4	64	15	16
Late and Close	.233	.313	.372	43	10	1	1	1	3	5	7

	BA	OBA	SA	AB	H	2B	3B	HR	RBI	BB	SO
Total	.284	.322	.407	2150	611	116	18	37	235	116	214
vs. Left	.283	.323	.397	1179	334	65	9	17	114	74	88
vs. Right	.285	.320	.418	971	277	51	9	20	121	42	126
Bases Empty	.274	.309	.401	1286	352	78	10	22	22	56	138
Leadoff	.288	.318	.414	556	160	32	4	10	10	21	65
Runners On Base	.300	.340	.414	864	259	38	8	15	213	60	76
Scoring Position	.302	.345	.421	503	152	25	4	9	192	44	40
Late and Close	.275	.338	.450	120	33	5	2	4	11	12	9

BOBBY THIGPEN — bats right — throws right — age 29 — CHA — P

1991	G	IP	H	BB	SO	SB	CS	W	L	SV	ERA
Total	67	69.2	63	38	47	8	5	7	5	30	3.49
at Home	35	33.1	35	17	22	4	2	5	2	12	4.59
on Road	32	36.1	28	21	25	4	3	2	3	18	2.48
on Grass	61	61.1	53	34	43	6	2	6	4	27	3.67
on Turf	6	8.1	10	4	4	2	3	1	1	3	2.16
Day Games	18	18.0	15	13	15	3	1	1	1	6	2.00
Night Games	49	51.2	48	25	32	5	4	6	4	24	4.01
April	10	10.1	8	7	9	0	0	0	0	6	4.35
May	12	14.2	10	13	11	2	1	1	1	3	3.07
June	11	9.1	5	5	7	1	1	1	1	6	5.79
July	14	16.2	11	6	7	2	2	3	1	9	1.62
August	10	11.1	10	3	9	1	1	0	1	3	2.38
Sept–Oct	10	7.1	12	4	6	2	0	0	1	3	6.14

6-YEAR TOTALS (1986–1991)

	G	IP	H	BB	SO	SB	CS	W	L	SV	ERA
Total	344	452.0	393	179	298	24	8	27	30	178	2.89
at Home	184	246.1	235	94	164	13	5	19	13	87	3.00
on Road	160	205.2	158	85	134	11	3	8	17	91	2.76
on Grass	300	387.0	342	160	265	19	5	23	25	151	3.02
on Turf	44	65.0	51	19	33	5	3	4	5	27	2.08
Day Games	96	122.2	114	56	82	9	2	5	8	50	2.42
Night Games	248	329.1	279	123	216	15	6	22	22	128	3.06
April	46	67.0	58	28	37	0	0	1	3	19	3.09
May	59	70.2	66	37	46	2	1	7	9	22	4.33
June	46	52.1	42	22	37	2	1	5	2	30	2.75
July	55	72.1	60	26	48	7	2	4	9	29	2.12
August	65	94.1	83	33	69	6	1	1	2	36	2.39
Sept–Oct	73	95.1	84	33	61	4	2	6	4	42	2.83

	BA	OBA	SA	AB	H	2B	3B	HR	RBI	BB	SO
Total	.245	.348	.409	257	63	8	2	10	42	38	47
vs. Left	.261	.369	.479	119	31	4	2	6	23	21	18
vs. Right	.232	.329	.348	138	32	4	0	4	19	17	29
Bases Empty	.265	.346	.434	113	30	2	1	5	5	12	20
Leadoff	.174	.296	.239	46	8	0	0	1	1	7	8
Runners On Base	.229	.349	.389	144	33	6	1	5	37	26	27
Scoring Position	.216	.368	.341	88	19	1	2	2	30	21	19
Late and Close	.265	.385	.444	189	50	6	2	8	39	35	35

	BA	OBA	SA	AB	H	2B	3B	HR	RBI	BB	SO
Total	.236	.313	.346	1664	393	43	7	42	213	179	298
vs. Left	.248	.334	.351	809	201	18	4	19	106	107	125
vs. Right	.225	.292	.342	855	192	25	3	23	107	72	173
Bases Empty	.250	.328	.364	789	197	25	4	19	19	88	144
Leadoff	.240	.326	.350	329	79	10	1	8	8	41	55
Runners On Base	.224	.299	.330	875	196	18	3	23	194	91	154
Scoring Position	.227	.314	.343	498	113	13	3	13	171	62	93
Late and Close	.231	.311	.340	1216	281	32	5	30	168	138	227

RANDY TOMLIN — bats left — throws left — age 26 — PIT — P

1991	G	IP	H	BB	SO	SB	CS	W	L	SV	ERA		G	IP	H	BB	SO	SB	CS	W	L	SV	ERA
Total	31	175.0	170	54	104	17	12	8	7	0	2.98		43	252.2	232	66	146	19	18	12	11	0	2.85
at Home	16	92.1	86	25	64	9	7	5	4	0	2.83		24	143.0	126	29	90	9	13	7	7	0	2.90
on Road	15	82.2	84	29	40	8	5	3	3	0	3.16		19	109.2	106	37	56	10	5	5	4	0	2.79
on Grass	9	50.1	42	15	22	2	5	2	1	0	2.15		9	50.1	42	15	22	2	5	2	1	0	2.15
on Turf	22	124.2	128	39	82	15	7	6	6	0	3.32		34	202.1	190	51	124	17	13	10	10	0	3.02
Day Games	10	52.1	53	13	28	5	5	1	2	0	3.10		14	76.2	79	17	43	6	8	1	5	0	3.40
Night Games	21	122.2	117	41	76	12	7	7	5	0	2.93		29	176.0	153	49	103	13	10	11	6	0	2.61
April	3	20.0	16	5	5	2	3	2	0	0	2.70		3	20.0	16	5	5	2	3	2	0	0	2.70
May	5	18.1	18	7	12	5	3	1	1	0	2.45		5	18.1	18	7	12	5	3	1	1	0	2.45
June	5	24.0	20	9	18	2	0	0	2	0	3.38		5	24.0	20	9	18	2	0	0	2	0	3.38
July	4	30.2	23	11	17	2	1	3	0	0	0.88		4	30.2	23	11	17	2	1	3	0	0	0.88
August	7	43.0	40	11	26	3	4	2	1	0	3.77		12	77.1	67	15	46	3	7	3	3	0	3.26
Sept–Oct	7	39.0	53	11	26	3	1	0	3	0	3.92		14	82.1	88	19	48	5	4	3	5	0	3.17

2-YEAR TOTALS (1990–1991)

	BA	OBA	SA	AB	H	2B	3B	HR	RBI	BB	SO		BA	OBA	SA	AB	H	2B	3B	HR	RBI	BB	SO
Total	.254	.315	.354	669	170	28	6	9	63	54	104		.244	.297	.351	949	232	45	7	14	83	66	146
vs. Left	.176	.262	.221	131	23	3	0	1	10	12	29		.198	.265	.277	177	35	5	0	3	15	13	40
vs. Right	.273	.328	.387	538	147	25	6	8	53	42	75		.255	.305	.368	772	197	40	7	11	68	53	106
Bases Empty	.242	.318	.323	359	87	13	2	4	4	37	45		.236	.300	.339	554	131	26	2	9	9	46	79
Leadoff	.265	.350	.358	162	43	7	1	2	2	20	16		.235	.308	.319	238	56	9	1	3	3	23	30
Runners On Base	.268	.310	.390	310	83	15	4	5	59	17	59		.256	.294	.367	395	101	19	5	5	74	20	67
Scoring Position	.280	.347	.376	157	44	8	2	1	49	15	28		.273	.333	.364	198	54	11	2	1	63	18	33
Late and Close	.314	.375	.510	51	16	4	0	2	5	3	6		.313	.378	.537	67	21	6	0	3	6	5	8

FRANK VIOLA — bats left — throws left — age 32 — NYN — P

1991	G	IP	H	BB	SO	SB	CS	W	L	SV	ERA		G	IP	H	BB	SO	SB	CS	W	L	SV	ERA
Total	35	231.1	259	54	132	6	16	13	15	0	3.97		284	1999.2	1935	530	1386	85	89	139	100	0	3.44
at Home	19	122.2	142	28	65	3	8	8	8	0	4.26		137	998.2	959	239	724	40	46	74	41	0	3.22
on Road	16	108.2	117	26	67	3	8	5	7	0	3.64		147	1001.0	976	291	662	45	43	65	59	0	3.66
on Grass	26	171.0	184	38	93	3	12	10	12	0	3.84		143	975.2	957	256	652	46	43	71	56	0	3.53
on Turf	9	60.1	75	16	39	3	4	3	3	0	4.33		141	1024.0	978	274	734	39	46	68	44	0	3.35
Day Games	13	89.0	98	18	61	2	7	5	5	0	3.13		92	653.2	618	145	453	22	33	46	33	0	3.19
Night Games	22	142.1	161	36	71	4	9	8	10	0	4.49		192	1346.0	1317	385	933	63	56	93	67	0	3.56
April	4	31.1	28	5	17	0	2	3	0	0	0.86		40	283.2	263	83	202	13	13	17	14	0	3.30
May	6	41.2	45	10	23	1	5	3	2	0	3.46		47	324.0	330	78	225	13	17	24	17	0	3.75
June	6	43.1	49	14	22	1	4	2	1	0	4.15		45	323.0	321	83	209	20	19	25	12	0	3.09
July	6	40.2	33	7	24	0	1	3	2	0	2.66		47	341.2	284	103	224	14	11	25	16	0	3.11
August	6	31.1	48	10	25	1	1	1	5	0	8.33		50	348.0	361	90	235	11	15	21	23	0	3.80
Sept–Oct	7	43.0	56	8	21	3	3	1	3	0	4.60		55	379.1	376	93	291	14	14	27	18	0	3.54

8-YEAR TOTALS (1984–1991)

	BA	OBA	SA	AB	H	2B	3B	HR	RBI	BB	SO		BA	OBA	SA	AB	H	2B	3B	HR	RBI	BB	SO
Total	.286	.325	.423	905	259	41	4	25	99	54	132		.254	.303	.385	7632	1935	333	34	201	750	530	1386
vs. Left	.233	.277	.363	193	45	8	1	5	22	12	35		.257	.306	.387	1397	359	70	6	33	143	88	247
vs. Right	.301	.339	.440	712	214	33	3	20	77	42	97		.253	.302	.385	6235	1576	263	28	168	607	442	1139
Bases Empty	.279	.320	.431	531	148	24	3	17	17	32	73		.251	.302	.384	4609	1159	200	24	121	121	321	826
Leadoff	.275	.305	.437	229	63	12	2	7	7	10	31		.248	.298	.387	1936	481	83	10	55	55	132	329
Runners On Base	.297	.333	.412	374	111	17	1	8	82	22	59		.257	.304	.387	3023	776	133	10	80	629	209	560
Scoring Position	.272	.330	.366	202	55	7	0	4	69	19	34		.256	.307	.385	1555	398	63	6	42	522	126	319
Late and Close	.315	.360	.435	92	29	2	0	3	9	7	5		.240	.290	.351	732	176	22	4	17	62	49	105

DUANE WARD — bats right — throws right — age 28 — TOR — P

1991	G	IP	H	BB	SO	SB	CS	W	L	SV	ERA		G	IP	H	BB	SO	SB	CS	W	L	SV	ERA
Total	81	107.1	80	33	132	7	4	7	6	23	2.77		308	491.0	415	217	476	48	20	23	29	64	3.61
at Home	44	63.0	46	15	81	3	4	5	4	14	3.14		158	257.2	206	100	256	21	8	12	16	35	3.32
on Road	37	44.1	34	18	51	4	0	2	2	9	2.23		150	233.1	209	117	220	27	12	11	13	29	3.93
on Grass	26	33.1	27	13	33	2	0	1	2	5	2.16		116	178.1	155	91	168	17	9	10	11	17	4.04
on Turf	55	74.0	53	20	99	5	4	6	4	18	3.04		192	312.2	260	126	308	31	11	13	18	47	3.37
Day Games	30	40.2	21	8	57	3	1	4	2	10	1.99		99	159.1	122	71	166	19	7	12	9	17	3.56
Night Games	51	66.2	59	25	75	4	3	3	4	13	3.24		209	331.2	293	146	310	29	13	11	20	47	3.64
April	9	11.2	12	2	19	1	0	0	1	5	3.09		49	66.1	62	26	69	11	4	1	5	10	3.53
May	14	16.0	10	6	14	2	0	0	1	7	1.69		52	77.1	67	49	70	9	2	6	11	13	3.26
June	14	23.2	12	10	28	2	0	1	1	2	2.66		54	99.0	83	45	88	10	2	2	8	11	3.91
July	12	18.1	14	4	27	1	1	2	0	2	2.95		43	79.2	73	22	78	7	1	4	5	12	3.39
August	15	20.1	21	6	21	1	3	3	2	1	4.43		48	82.0	70	28	75	3	6	6	5	9	3.62
Sept–Oct	17	17.1	11	5	23	0	1	0	1	5	1.56		62	86.2	60	47	96	8	6	2	5	13	3.84

6-YEAR TOTALS (1986–1991)

	BA	OBA	SA	AB	H	2B	3B	HR	RBI	BB	SO		BA	OBA	SA	AB	H	2B	3B	HR	RBI	BB	SO
Total	.207	.271	.262	386	80	10	1	3	38	33	132		.233	.318	.318	1780	415	64	9	23	212	217	476
vs. Left	.192	.277	.280	182	35	5	1	3	18	21	74		.240	.350	.348	768	184	32	3	15	96	131	211
vs. Right	.221	.265	.245	204	45	5	0	0	20	12	58		.228	.291	.295	1012	231	32	6	8	116	86	265
Bases Empty	.190	.223	.237	232	44	8	0	1	1	10	93		.216	.290	.301	955	206	40	4	11	11	97	279
Leadoff	.213	.229	.277	94	20	3	0	1	1	2	38		.223	.310	.303	399	89	16	2	4	4	50	112
Runners On Base	.234	.333	.299	154	36	2	1	2	37	23	39		.253	.347	.338	825	209	24	5	12	201	120	197
Scoring Position	.280	.372	.370	100	28	1	1	2	37	15	23		.253	.353	.341	537	136	13	2	9	190	91	136
Late and Close	.211	.283	.266	237	50	5	1	2	25	23	76		.233	.318	.321	917	214	27	7	13	114	114	261

BILL WEGMAN — bats right — throws right — age 30 — MIL — P

1991	G	IP	H	BB	SO	SB	CS	W	L	SV	ERA		G	IP	H	BB	SO	SB	CS	W	L	SV	ERA
Total	28	193.1	176	40	89	10	7	15	7	0	2.84	**7-YEAR TOTALS (1985–1991)**	150	911.1	947	216	407	56	33	51	51	0	4.27
at Home	15	103.0	91	21	51	6	3	7	4	0	2.62		80	508.1	520	101	238	36	19	26	22	0	4.02
on Road	13	90.1	85	19	38	4	4	8	3	0	3.09		70	403.0	427	115	169	20	14	25	29	0	4.58
on Grass	25	174.1	155	36	80	8	6	14	5	0	2.53		128	793.1	812	188	353	49	28	43	40	0	4.14
on Turf	3	19.0	21	4	9	2	1	1	2	0	5.68		22	118.0	135	28	54	7	5	8	11	0	5.11
Day Games	10	71.2	68	13	23	2	1	6	1	0	1.63		43	249.1	286	56	107	20	8	13	13	0	4.11
Night Games	18	121.2	108	27	66	8	6	9	6	0	3.55		107	662.0	661	160	300	36	25	38	38	0	4.32
April	0	0.0	0	0	0	0	0	0	0	0	0.00		17	107.1	105	31	41	10	5	3	8	0	3.61
May	5	22.2	24	7	9	0	2	1	1	0	5.16		31	154.1	186	45	69	6	8	15	15	0	5.83
June	5	30.2	30	6	16	3	2	2	2	0	3.23		21	122.0	128	30	54	6	2	8	6	0	4.57
July	5	42.1	36	8	16	3	3	3	2	0	2.76		20	134.1	131	24	58	9	8	8	8	0	3.62
August	6	40.0	42	8	13	2	0	4	1	0	2.47		20	120.1	136	26	49	7	4	5	5	0	4.71
Sept–Oct	7	57.2	44	11	35	2	0	5	1	0	2.03		41	273.0	261	60	136	18	6	21	10	0	3.63

	BA	OBA	SA	AB	H	2B	3B	HR	RBI	BB	SO		BA	OBA	SA	AB	H	2B	3B	HR	RBI	BB	SO
Total	.242	.286	.356	728	176	29	3	16	62	40	89		.267	.311	.424	3544	947	170	16	118	414	216	407
vs. Left	.226	.277	.314	376	85	13	1	6	34	26	33		.264	.310	.414	1893	499	85	8	61	221	128	182
vs. Right	.259	.297	.401	352	91	16	2	10	28	14	56		.271	.313	.436	1651	448	85	8	57	193	88	225
Bases Empty	.249	.293	.386	466	116	22	3	12	12	24	55		.259	.303	.418	2205	571	108	10	74	74	123	249
Leadoff	.266	.299	.443	192	51	5	1	9	9	9	22		.265	.300	.447	910	241	37	3	41	41	44	92
Runners On Base	.229	.275	.302	262	60	7	0	4	50	16	34		.281	.324	.435	1339	376	62	6	44	340	93	158
Scoring Position	.231	.282	.293	147	34	3	0	2	46	11	24		.287	.323	.435	717	206	32	4	22	286	49	89
Late and Close	.219	.260	.411	73	16	2	0	4	8	3	17		.275	.316	.435	276	76	13	2	9	29	16	40

BOB WELCH — bats right — throws right — age 36 — OAK — P

1991	G	IP	H	BB	SO	SB	CS	W	L	SV	ERA		G	IP	H	BB	SO	SB	CS	W	L	SV	ERA
Total	35	220.0	220	91	101	12	16	12	13	0	4.58	**8-YEAR TOTALS (1984–1991)**	261	1746.0	1625	561	1124	129	84	122	75	0	3.37
at Home	18	125.0	112	43	65	5	11	8	7	0	3.60		135	950.1	856	255	635	63	50	72	36	0	2.87
on Road	17	95.0	108	48	36	7	5	4	6	0	5.87		126	795.2	769	306	489	66	34	50	39	0	3.96
on Grass	28	180.0	172	71	91	9	14	11	9	0	3.85		209	1431.2	1296	437	930	101	71	106	52	0	3.07
on Turf	7	40.0	48	20	10	3	2	1	4	0	7.88		52	314.1	329	124	194	28	13	16	23	0	4.70
Day Games	11	79.2	68	34	45	2	2	5	4	0	3.28		96	651.1	588	214	416	49	26	52	24	0	3.10
Night Games	24	140.1	152	57	56	7	14	7	9	0	5.32		165	1094.2	1037	347	708	80	58	70	51	0	3.53
April	5	40.0	31	6	13	2	2	3	1	0	1.80		37	264.1	214	82	159	16	12	20	11	0	2.28
May	6	38.1	39	21	16	4	1	1	2	0	5.63		39	262.2	254	94	166	20	2	18	11	0	3.94
June	5	35.1	26	12	13	0	3	3	2	0	3.82		44	282.2	293	93	160	24	16	19	12	0	3.92
July	6	34.1	45	10	24	3	2	1	1	0	4.98		44	288.0	271	81	207	21	20	17	14	0	3.31
August	6	40.1	39	15	15	1	4	3	3	0	4.69		49	335.1	307	111	235	22	19	26	15	0	3.30
Sept–Oct	7	31.2	40	27	20	2	4	1	4	0	7.11		48	313.0	286	100	197	26	15	22	12	0	3.42

	BA	OBA	SA	AB	H	2B	3B	HR	RBI	BB	SO		BA	OBA	SA	AB	H	2B	3B	HR	RBI	BB	SO
Total	.263	.341	.404	835	220	34	4	25	112	91	101		.247	.309	.373	6585	1625	294	46	148	632	561	1124
vs. Left	.275	.351	.382	422	116	17	2	8	57	50	48		.246	.311	.357	3412	839	150	30	56	294	319	519
vs. Right	.252	.332	.426	413	104	17	2	17	55	41	53		.248	.307	.390	3173	786	144	16	92	338	242	605
Bases Empty	.252	.328	.382	484	122	14	2	15	15	50	52		.249	.299	.379	4032	1005	186	30	92	92	268	641
Leadoff	.276	.364	.478	203	56	9	1	10	10	27	19		.246	.293	.376	1698	418	79	8	42	42	109	244
Runners On Base	.279	.359	.433	351	98	20	2	10	97	41	49		.243	.324	.363	2553	620	108	16	56	540	293	483
Scoring Position	.311	.396	.447	190	59	12	1	4	82	29	33		.249	.338	.364	1460	363	66	12	26	459	200	314
Late and Close	.244	.309	.419	86	21	4	1	3	9	6	12		.238	.290	.348	635	151	22	4	14	56	44	93

DAVID WELLS — bats left — throws left — age 29 — TOR — P

1991	G	IP	H	BB	SO	SB	CS	W	L	SV	ERA		G	IP	H	BB	SO	SB	CS	W	L	SV	ERA
Total	40	198.1	188	49	106	8	13	15	10	1	3.72	**5-YEAR TOTALS (1987–1991)**	197	568.0	522	165	387	36	30	40	28	11	3.44
at Home	18	86.0	89	24	49	3	7	6	5	0	4.81		95	262.2	243	80	175	19	14	17	13	5	3.46
on Road	22	112.1	99	25	57	5	6	9	5	1	2.88		102	305.1	279	85	212	17	16	23	15	6	3.42
on Grass	15	84.0	72	19	47	4	4	7	5	1	3.11		82	243.1	223	70	184	15	11	19	12	5	3.51
on Turf	25	114.1	116	30	59	4	9	8	5	0	4.17		115	324.2	299	95	203	21	19	21	16	6	3.38
Day Games	10	36.2	49	11	17	1	2	1	4	0	7.85		61	136.0	133	46	81	12	7	8	8	2	4.17
Night Games	30	161.2	139	38	89	7	11	14	6	1	2.78		136	432.0	389	119	306	24	23	32	20	9	3.21
April	4	22.2	26	6	7	1	1	1	3	0	5.16		30	68.0	61	22	50	9	2	4	6	3	4.37
May	6	41.2	28	9	31	0	5	5	1	0	1.73		41	94.1	64	30	81	6	7	7	6	3	2.10
June	5	34.0	26	9	20	3	0	1	3	0	2.91		34	110.2	109	37	85	6	4	7	6	3	4.07
July	6	38.1	32	13	15	2	3	3	1	0	3.52		24	100.0	89	27	53	5	8	4	4	0	3.15
August	5	30.1	41	7	17	2	0	1	4	0	6.23		20	80.1	94	25	41	7	4	6	4	0	4.71
Sept–Oct	14	31.1	35	5	16	0	2	2	1	1	4.02		48	114.2	105	24	77	1	5	9	4	2	2.75

	BA	OBA	SA	AB	H	2B	3B	HR	RBI	BB	SO		BA	OBA	SA	AB	H	2B	3B	HR	RBI	BB	SO
Total	.252	.297	.403	747	188	37	2	24	70	49	106		.245	.299	.385	2131	522	107	13	55	212	165	387
vs. Left	.208	.246	.315	130	27	3	1	3	9	6	14		.248	.304	.355	428	106	22	3	6	41	31	53
vs. Right	.261	.308	.421	617	161	34	1	21	61	43	92		.244	.298	.392	1703	416	85	10	49	171	134	334
Bases Empty	.255	.306	.387	463	118	23	1	12	12	33	70		.249	.305	.375	1247	311	63	5	28	28	97	242
Leadoff	.246	.298	.325	191	47	6	0	3	3	14	34		.247	.306	.367	515	127	19	2	13	13	44	98
Runners On Base	.246	.283	.430	284	70	14	1	12	58	16	36		.239	.292	.398	884	211	44	8	27	184	68	145
Scoring Position	.248	.307	.406	133	33	6	0	5	41	14	17		.228	.303	.363	479	109	27	4	10	141	55	82
Late and Close	.255	.284	.337	98	25	2	0	2	7	4	18		.253	.314	.407	513	130	23	4	16	55	47	111

WALLY WHITEHURST — bats right — throws right — age 28 — NYN — P

3-YEAR TOTALS (1989–1991)

1991	G	IP	H	BB	SO	SB	CS	W	L	SV	ERA	G	IP	H	BB	SO	SB	CS	W	L	SV	ERA
Total	36	133.1	142	25	87	9	8	7	12	1	4.18	83	213.0	222	39	142	14	11	8	13	3	3.93
at Home	18	61.0	68	12	44	5	4	3	7	0	4.43	41	96.0	93	23	68	8	4	3	7	1	3.56
on Road	18	72.1	74	13	43	4	4	4	5	1	3.98	42	117.0	129	16	74	6	7	5	6	2	4.23
on Grass	24	85.2	90	17	62	6	5	4	9	1	4.31	57	140.0	144	28	102	9	8	5	10	3	3.92
on Turf	12	47.2	52	8	25	3	3	3	3	0	3.97	26	73.0	78	11	40	5	3	3	3	0	3.95
Day Games	10	34.0	41	9	24	1	2	1	4	1	5.82	28	61.0	77	12	46	1	3	1	5	1	5.16
Night Games	26	99.1	101	16	63	8	6	6	8	0	3.62	55	152.0	145	27	96	13	8	7	8	2	3.43
April	4	20.0	20	2	7	0	3	1	1	0	3.60	9	26.1	26	3	8	0	3	1	1	0	3.42
May	7	17.0	14	4	15	2	0	2	1	0	3.18	14	30.1	24	7	25	2	2	2	1	2	2.08
June	6	31.2	34	5	23	3	1	1	2	0	3.41	9	35.2	37	6	29	3	1	1	2	0	3.53
July	4	23.2	22	6	16	2	2	1	3	0	4.94	13	44.1	48	9	28	5	2	2	4	0	5.68
August	4	16.0	26	4	12	1	0	0	3	0	7.31	13	30.1	38	7	19	3	1	0	3	0	5.64
Sept–Oct	11	25.0	26	4	14	1	2	2	2	1	3.60	25	46.0	49	7	33	1	2	2	2	1	2.93

	BA	OBA	SA	AB	H	2B	3B	HR	RBI	BB	SO	BA	OBA	SA	AB	H	2B	3B	HR	RBI	BB	SO
Total	.274	.311	.409	518	142	24	5	12	60	25	87	.268	.303	.393	827	222	34	6	19	95	39	142
vs. Left	.299	.336	.458	264	79	15	3	7	30	14	42	.274	.313	.401	416	114	21	4	8	39	23	76
vs. Right	.248	.285	.358	254	63	9	2	5	30	11	45	.263	.293	.384	411	108	13	2	11	56	16	66
Bases Empty	.261	.294	.374	318	83	16	1	6	6	13	48	.251	.279	.355	499	125	21	2	9	9	18	81
Leadoff	.267	.288	.422	135	36	7	1	4	4	3	16	.245	.270	.380	208	51	11	1	5	5	6	21
Runners On Base	.295	.336	.465	200	59	8	4	6	54	12	39	.296	.338	.451	328	97	13	4	10	86	21	61
Scoring Position	.265	.317	.389	113	30	2	3	2	41	9	30	.282	.332	.404	188	53	5	3	4	69	15	44
Late and Close	.326	.341	.465	43	14	3	0	1	4	0	3	.250	.258	.337	92	23	5	0	1	8	0	9

MITCH WILLIAMS — bats left — throws left — age 28 — PHI — P

6-YEAR TOTALS (1986–1991)

1991	G	IP	H	BB	SO	SB	CS	W	L	SV	ERA	G	IP	H	BB	SO	SB	CS	W	L	SV	ERA
Total	69	88.1	56	62	84	10	2	12	5	30	2.34	436	510.1	367	384	486	38	21	35	36	114	3.35
at Home	37	47.0	32	34	50	5	0	9	2	17	2.11	218	260.2	205	204	248	14	9	23	13	52	3.45
on Road	32	41.1	24	28	34	5	2	3	3	13	2.61	218	249.2	162	180	238	24	12	12	23	62	3.24
on Grass	20	24.2	15	15	19	1	1	1	2	8	3.65	304	357.1	265	281	328	20	18	20	24	66	3.58
on Turf	49	63.2	41	47	65	9	1	11	3	22	1.84	132	153.0	102	103	158	18	3	15	12	48	2.82
Day Games	24	30.0	20	20	23	4	0	2	4	11	2.10	143	144.2	122	113	117	15	3	7	10	41	3.67
Night Games	45	58.1	36	42	61	6	2	10	1	19	2.47	293	365.2	245	271	369	23	18	28	26	73	3.22
April	12	14.0	7	12	12	1	1	0	2	5	2.57	58	62.1	43	44	60	5	5	3	6	23	2.31
May	8	8.2	8	4	11	0	0	0	0	4	3.12	71	78.1	53	60	90	4	2	4	5	17	3.56
June	10	12.0	12	10	12	1	0	1	1	4	3.75	71	84.1	61	58	90	6	0	8	5	15	3.09
July	10	12.0	7	6	9	0	1	0	0	6	1.50	67	80.1	59	61	66	5	4	2	4	20	2.69
August	15	22.1	10	16	22	7	0	8	1	5	1.21	86	109.0	69	84	95	12	2	14	4	22	2.72
Sept–Oct	14	19.1	12	14	18	1	0	3	1	6	2.79	83	96.0	82	77	85	6	8	4	12	17	5.34

	BA	OBA	SA	AB	H	2B	3B	HR	RBI	BB	SO	BA	OBA	SA	AB	H	2B	3B	HR	RBI	BB	SO
Total	.182	.330	.266	308	56	12	1	4	27	62	84	.205	.353	.317	1794	367	74	11	35	243	384	486
vs. Left	.191	.353	.279	68	13	4	1	0	6	12	17	.196	.336	.295	511	100	23	2	8	73	94	159
vs. Right	.179	.323	.262	240	43	8	0	4	21	50	67	.208	.360	.325	1283	267	51	9	27	170	290	327
Bases Empty	.233	.393	.338	133	31	5	0	3	3	31	29	.203	.355	.306	798	162	29	4	15	15	170	196
Leadoff	.177	.354	.290	62	11	1	0	2	2	14	12	.188	.345	.279	341	64	7	0	8	8	72	78
Runners On Base	.143	.280	.211	175	25	7	1	1	24	31	55	.206	.352	.325	996	205	45	7	20	228	214	290
Scoring Position	.108	.269	.167	102	11	3	0	1	21	21	33	.189	.348	.295	630	119	23	4	12	199	152	187
Late and Close	.180	.337	.269	245	44	8	1	1	25	53	70	.202	.338	.302	1069	216	40	5	19	142	202	303

TREVOR WILSON — bats left — throws left — age 26 — SF — P

4-YEAR TOTALS (1988–1991)

1991	G	IP	H	BB	SO	SB	CS	W	L	SV	ERA	G	IP	H	BB	SO	SB	CS	W	L	SV	ERA
Total	44	202.0	173	77	139	8	11	13	11	0	3.56	89	373.2	313	158	242	12	20	23	23	0	3.83
at Home	20	119.2	91	43	78	4	6	8	4	0	2.71	43	222.2	170	93	136	8	11	14	10	0	3.07
on Road	24	82.1	82	34	61	4	5	5	7	0	4.81	46	151.0	143	65	106	4	9	9	13	0	4.95
on Grass	32	156.0	126	58	101	4	7	11	7	0	3.23	67	289.0	232	115	181	8	13	19	15	0	3.46
on Turf	12	46.0	47	19	38	4	4	2	4	0	4.70	22	84.2	81	43	61	4	7	4	8	0	5.10
Day Games	18	92.2	75	33	69	4	3	9	1	0	2.82	33	149.0	131	62	108	5	4	12	5	0	3.50
Night Games	26	109.1	98	44	70	4	8	4	10	0	4.20	56	224.2	182	96	134	7	16	11	18	0	4.05
April	9	13.0	13	11	12	0	0	0	2	0	6.92	9	13.0	13	11	12	0	0	0	2	0	6.92
May	9	31.1	22	10	20	3	2	1	2	0	2.87	9	31.1	22	10	20	3	2	1	2	0	2.87
June	7	39.0	38	15	19	2	2	3	2	0	3.23	17	82.1	67	32	49	4	6	7	3	0	2.95
July	6	35.2	29	14	25	3	3	3	3	0	4.29	19	94.1	80	48	57	4	7	6	7	0	4.48
August	6	41.0	36	12	35	0	3	2	0	0	2.63	12	65.0	56	26	49	0	3	4	4	0	4.02
Sept–Oct	7	42.0	35	14	28	0	1	4	2	0	3.64	23	87.2	75	31	55	1	2	5	5	0	3.70

	BA	OBA	SA	AB	H	2B	3B	HR	RBI	BB	SO	BA	OBA	SA	AB	H	2B	3B	HR	RBI	BB	SO
Total	.234	.308	.343	740	173	32	5	13	75	77	139	.230	.313	.341	1358	313	55	7	27	144	158	242
vs. Left	.172	.275	.217	157	27	2	1	1	13	22	37	.190	.277	.252	258	49	6	2	2	27	30	55
vs. Right	.250	.318	.377	583	146	30	4	12	62	55	102	.240	.322	.362	1100	264	49	5	25	117	128	187
Bases Empty	.222	.294	.314	433	96	17	1	7	7	42	79	.209	.300	.299	800	167	28	1	14	14	99	145
Leadoff	.219	.309	.262	183	40	5	0	1	1	23	31	.212	.318	.269	335	71	10	0	3	3	50	52
Runners On Base	.251	.329	.384	307	77	15	4	6	68	35	60	.262	.333	.401	558	146	27	6	13	130	59	97
Scoring Position	.264	.358	.416	178	47	9	3	4	63	26	34	.293	.378	.475	297	87	16	4	10	121	42	50
Late and Close	.209	.321	.269	67	14	1	0	1	4	10	14	.203	.298	.271	133	27	6	0	1	7	17	27

Part 2

Non-Regular Players' Situational Statistics

In this part are situational breakdowns for every major-league player who was not a regular in 1991. Players are listed alphabetically, separated into batters and pitchers.

Each player's statistics follow the same format. The first line gives the player's name, how he bats and throws, and his age, effective for the 1992 season. It also lists the team he played for and the positions he played in 1991.

On the left-hand side of the page are the player's situational statistics for 1991 for the most important breakdowns (vs. left/vs. right, home/road, bases empty/runners on base). On the right-hand side of the page are the player's situational statistics totals from 1984–1991. If a player played in the majors every year from 1984 to 1991, it will show "8-Year Totals." If he played in the majors for only part of that period, the header will list the actual number of years he played and the first year he played. For example, a player who played in 1989, 1990, and 1991 would have "3-Year Totals" listed.

BATTERS

SHAWN ABNER — bats right — throws right — age 26 — SD/CAL — O/D

1991	BA	OBA	SA	AB	H	2B	3B	HR	RBI	BB	SO
vs. Left	.181	.218	.337	83	15	4	0	3	8	3	14
vs. Right	.203	.246	.278	133	27	6	2	0	6	8	29
at Home	.192	.227	.308	104	20	6	0	2	9	4	23
on Road	.196	.244	.295	112	22	4	2	1	5	7	20
Bases Empty	.193	.232	.326	135	26	8	2	2	2	6	27
Runners On Base	.198	.241	.259	81	16	2	0	1	12	5	16

5-YEAR TOTALS (1987–1991)

BA	OBA	SA	AB	H	2B	3B	HR	RBI	BB	SO
.196	.233	.298	285	56	12	1	5	30	12	49
.222	.265	.326	347	77	17	2	5	25	19	69
.208	.249	.321	346	72	18	0	7	31	17	66
.213	.252	.304	286	61	11	3	3	24	14	52
.199	.240	.285	372	74	16	2	4	4	17	67
.227	.265	.354	260	59	13	1	6	51	14	51

TROY AFENIR — bats right — throws right — age 29 — OAK — /CD

1991	BA	OBA	SA	AB	H	2B	3B	HR	RBI	BB	SO
vs. Left	.000	.000	.000	1	0	0	0	0	0	0	0
vs. Right	.100	.100	.100	10	1	0	0	0	0	0	2
at Home	.091	.091	.091	11	1	0	0	0	0	0	2
on Road	.000	.000	.000	0	0	0	0	0	0	0	0
Bases Empty	.250	.250	.250	4	1	0	0	0	0	0	1
Runners On Base	.000	.000	.000	7	0	0	0	0	0	0	1

3-YEAR TOTALS (1987–1991)

BA	OBA	SA	AB	H	2B	3B	HR	RBI	BB	SO
.208	.200	.250	24	5	1	0	0	2	0	10
.190	.190	.190	21	4	0	0	0	1	0	10
.219	.212	.250	32	7	1	0	0	2	0	13
.154	.154	.154	13	2	0	0	0	1	0	7
.238	.238	.238	21	5	0	0	0	0	0	11
.167	.160	.208	24	4	1	0	0	3	0	9

MIKE ALDRETE — bats left — throws left — age 31 — SD/CLE — 1O/D

1991	BA	OBA	SA	AB	H	2B	3B	HR	RBI	BB	SO
vs. Left	.167	.154	.333	12	2	0	1	0	1	0	5
vs. Right	.247	.376	.296	186	46	6	0	1	19	39	36
at Home	.225	.355	.258	89	20	1	1	0	7	18	15
on Road	.257	.371	.330	109	28	5	0	1	13	21	26
Bases Empty	.169	.305	.229	118	20	2	1	1	1	23	29
Runners On Base	.350	.449	.400	80	28	4	0	0	19	16	12

6-YEAR TOTALS (1986–1991)

BA	OBA	SA	AB	H	2B	3B	HR	RBI	BB	SO
.262	.316	.355	214	56	11	3	1	16	19	40
.270	.374	.365	1243	335	61	5	16	160	208	211
.266	.383	.371	695	185	28	6	11	77	131	118
.270	.350	.357	762	206	44	2	6	99	96	133
.249	.344	.343	819	204	36	4	11	11	118	142
.293	.393	.390	638	187	36	4	6	165	109	109

LUIS ALICEA — bats both — throws right — age 27 — SL — 2/3S

1991	BA	OBA	SA	AB	H	2B	3B	HR	RBI	BB	SO
vs. Left	.250	.333	.313	16	4	1	0	0	0	2	3
vs. Right	.173	.259	.212	52	9	2	0	0	6	6	16
at Home	.179	.281	.214	28	5	1	0	0	4	4	7
on Road	.200	.273	.250	40	8	2	0	0	4	4	12
Bases Empty	.224	.321	.286	49	11	3	0	0	0	7	14
Runners On Base	.105	.150	.105	19	2	0	0	0	6	1	5

2-YEAR TOTALS (1988–1991)

BA	OBA	SA	AB	H	2B	3B	HR	RBI	BB	SO
.148	.212	.176	108	16	3	0	0	5	7	14
.233	.303	.315	257	60	10	4	1	19	26	37
.221	.298	.308	172	38	6	3	1	12	18	23
.197	.256	.244	193	38	7	1	0	12	15	28
.242	.303	.340	194	47	10	3	1	1	17	26
.170	.246	.199	171	29	3	1	0	23	16	25

ANDY ALLANSON — bats right — throws right — age 31 — DET — C/1D

1991	BA	OBA	SA	AB	H	2B	3B	HR	RBI	BB	SO
vs. Left	.217	.244	.278	115	25	7	0	0	10	4	26
vs. Right	.278	.333	.444	36	10	3	0	1	6	3	5
at Home	.254	.299	.286	63	16	2	0	0	5	4	8
on Road	.216	.242	.341	88	19	8	0	1	11	3	23
Bases Empty	.198	.238	.229	96	19	3	0	0	0	5	20
Runners On Base	.291	.316	.473	55	16	7	0	1	16	2	11

5-YEAR TOTALS (1986–1991)

BA	OBA	SA	AB	H	2B	3B	HR	RBI	BB	SO
.261	.298	.320	444	116	22	2	0	35	24	70
.236	.280	.306	911	215	21	2	13	93	54	137
.240	.288	.304	657	158	17	2	7	71	43	91
.248	.284	.317	698	173	26	2	6	57	35	116
.233	.275	.289	772	180	20	1	7	7	42	110
.259	.301	.340	583	151	23	3	6	121	36	97

BEAU ALLRED — bats left — throws left — age 27 — CLE — O/D

1991	BA	OBA	SA	AB	H	2B	3B	HR	RBI	BB	SO
vs. Left	.167	.375	.250	12	2	1	0	0	1	4	2
vs. Right	.239	.358	.336	113	27	2	0	3	11	21	33
at Home	.209	.349	.224	67	14	1	0	0	5	15	18
on Road	.259	.371	.448	58	15	2	0	3	7	10	17
Bases Empty	.274	.404	.411	73	20	1	0	3	3	15	23
Runners On Base	.173	.297	.212	52	9	2	0	0	9	10	12

3-YEAR TOTALS (1989–1991)

BA	OBA	SA	AB	H	2B	3B	HR	RBI	BB	SO
.154	.353	.231	13	2	1	0	0	1	4	2
.237	.344	.355	152	36	6	0	4	14	25	46
.215	.344	.253	79	17	3	0	0	6	16	24
.244	.347	.430	86	21	4	0	4	9	13	24
.237	.357	.371	97	23	4	0	3	3	17	34
.221	.329	.309	68	15	3	0	1	12	12	14

SANDY ALOMAR — bats right — throws right — age 26 — CLE — C/D

1991	BA	OBA	SA	AB	H	2B	3B	HR	RBI	BB	SO
vs. Left	.214	.283	.238	42	9	1	0	0	1	4	3
vs. Right	.218	.258	.275	142	31	8	0	0	6	4	21
at Home	.246	.316	.304	69	17	4	0	0	0	5	8
on Road	.200	.231	.243	115	23	5	0	0	7	3	16
Bases Empty	.237	.275	.299	97	23	6	0	0	0	4	11
Runners On Base	.195	.253	.230	87	17	3	0	0	7	4	13

4-YEAR TOTALS (1988–1991)

BA	OBA	SA	AB	H	2B	3B	HR	RBI	BB	SO
.323	.365	.396	164	53	6	0	2	19	13	17
.247	.288	.367	485	120	30	2	8	60	23	57
.283	.330	.395	314	89	17	0	6	36	21	32
.251	.287	.355	335	84	19	2	4	43	15	42
.261	.297	.382	356	93	15	2	8	8	15	44
.273	.321	.365	293	80	21	0	2	71	21	30

RICH AMARAL — bats right — throws right — age 30 — SEA — /23S1

1991	BA	OBA	SA	AB	H	2B	3B	HR	RBI	BB	SO
vs. Left	.143	.143	.143	7	1	0	0	0	0	0	3
vs. Right	.000	.182	.000	9	0	0	0	0	1	2	2
at Home	.000	.182	.000	9	0	0	0	0	1	2	2
on Road	.143	.143	.143	7	1	0	0	0	0	0	3
Bases Empty	.091	.167	.091	11	1	0	0	0	0	1	2
Runners On Base	.000	.167	.000	5	0	0	0	0	0	1	3

1-YEAR TOTALS (1991)

BA	OBA	SA	AB	H	2B	3B	HR	RBI	BB	SO
.143	.143	.143	7	1	0	0	0	0	0	3
.000	.182	.000	9	0	0	0	0	1	2	2
.000	.182	.000	9	0	0	0	0	1	2	2
.143	.143	.143	7	1	0	0	0	0	0	3
.091	.167	.091	11	1	0	0	0	0	1	2
.000	.167	.000	5	0	0	0	0	0	1	3

RUBEN AMARO — bats both — throws right — age 27 — CAL — /O2

1991	BA	OBA	SA	AB	H	2B	3B	HR	RBI	BB	SO
vs. Left	.000	.200	.000	4	0	0	0	0	0	1	0
vs. Right	.263	.333	.316	19	5	1	0	0	2	2	3
at Home	.167	.375	.167	6	1	0	0	0	0	2	0
on Road	.235	.278	.294	17	4	1	0	0	2	1	3
Bases Empty	.111	.111	.111	9	1	0	0	0	0	0	2
Runners On Base	.286	.412	.357	14	4	1	0	0	2	3	1

1-YEAR TOTALS (1991)

BA	OBA	SA	AB	H	2B	3B	HR	RBI	BB	SO
.000	.200	.000	4	0	0	0	0	0	1	0
.263	.333	.316	19	5	1	0	0	2	2	3
.167	.375	.167	6	1	0	0	0	0	2	0
.235	.278	.294	17	4	1	0	0	2	1	3
.111	.111	.111	9	1	0	0	0	0	0	2
.286	.412	.357	14	4	1	0	0	2	3	1

BRADY ANDERSON — bats left — throws left — age 28 — BAL — *O/D

4-YEAR TOTALS (1988–1991)

1991	BA	OBA	SA	AB	H	2B	3B	HR	RBI	BB	SO		BA	OBA	SA	AB	H	2B	3B	HR	RBI	BB	SO
vs. Left	.139	.347	.194	36	5	0	1	0	5	11	12		.160	.283	.224	237	38	4	4	1	13	36	59
vs. Right	.245	.336	.345	220	54	12	2	2	22	27	32		.236	.322	.329	844	199	38	7	9	75	99	151
at Home	.225	.336	.306	111	25	4	1	1	15	16	17		.203	.295	.284	546	111	19	5	5	48	61	111
on Road	.234	.339	.338	145	34	8	2	1	12	22	27		.236	.331	.329	535	126	23	6	5	40	74	99
Bases Empty	.233	.361	.327	159	37	8	2	1	1	29	29		.202	.295	.288	663	134	28	7	5	5	78	138
Runners On Base	.227	.297	.320	97	22	4	1	1	26	9	15		.246	.341	.335	418	103	14	4	5	83	57	72

DAVE ANDERSON — bats right — throws right — age 32 — SF — S13/2

8-YEAR TOTALS (1984–1991)

1991	BA	OBA	SA	AB	H	2B	3B	HR	RBI	BB	SO		BA	OBA	SA	AB	H	2B	3B	HR	RBI	BB	SO
vs. Left	.150	.209	.213	80	12	0	1	1	3	6	12		.245	.327	.317	650	159	21	4	6	51	79	101
vs. Right	.301	.329	.370	146	44	5	1	1	10	6	23		.245	.309	.315	1177	288	44	6	9	82	111	205
at Home	.197	.239	.268	127	25	2	2	1	9	7	18		.250	.322	.314	893	223	26	5	7	67	94	144
on Road	.313	.346	.374	99	31	3	0	1	4	5	17		.240	.310	.318	934	224	39	5	8	66	96	162
Bases Empty	.238	.278	.286	126	30	2	2	0	0	7	22		.239	.318	.316	1074	257	40	6	10	10	121	198
Runners On Base	.260	.295	.350	100	26	3	0	2	13	5	13		.252	.313	.316	753	190	25	4	5	123	69	108

ERIC ANTHONY — bats left — throws left — age 25 — HOU — O

3-YEAR TOTALS (1989–1991)

1991	BA	OBA	SA	AB	H	2B	3B	HR	RBI	BB	SO		BA	OBA	SA	AB	H	2B	3B	HR	RBI	BB	SO
vs. Left	.143	.250	.143	28	4	0	0	0	1	4	8		.190	.273	.293	116	22	3	0	3	11	13	33
vs. Right	.156	.220	.256	90	14	6	0	1	6	8	33		.175	.263	.338	302	53	13	0	12	32	37	102
at Home	.122	.182	.163	49	6	2	0	0	2	4	16		.190	.274	.342	184	35	7	0	7	20	21	56
on Road	.174	.260	.275	69	12	4	0	1	5	8	25		.171	.259	.312	234	40	9	0	8	23	29	79
Bases Empty	.147	.229	.240	75	11	4	0	1	1	8	28		.157	.245	.309	249	39	5	0	11	11	28	86
Runners On Base	.163	.224	.209	43	7	2	0	0	6	4	13		.213	.295	.349	169	36	11	0	4	32	22	49

OSCAR AZOCAR — bats left — throws left — age 27 — SD — O/1

2-YEAR TOTALS (1990–1991)

1991	BA	OBA	SA	AB	H	2B	3B	HR	RBI	BB	SO		BA	OBA	SA	AB	H	2B	3B	HR	RBI	BB	SO
vs. Left	.000	.000	.000	2	0	0	0	0	1	0	0		.194	.203	.274	62	12	2	0	1	8	1	2
vs. Right	.255	.276	.291	55	14	2	0	0	8	1	9		.263	.276	.359	209	55	8	0	4	20	2	22
at Home	.265	.297	.294	34	9	1	0	0	6	1	6		.280	.300	.385	143	40	6	0	3	17	3	12
on Road	.217	.217	.261	23	5	1	0	0	3	0	3		.211	.211	.289	128	27	4	0	2	11	0	12
Bases Empty	.276	.276	.345	29	8	2	0	0	0	0	3		.266	.275	.367	158	42	7	0	3	3	1	8
Runners On Base	.214	.258	.214	28	6	0	0	0	9	1	6		.221	.237	.301	113	25	3	0	2	25	2	16

WALLY BACKMAN — bats both — throws right — age 33 — PHI — 23

8-YEAR TOTALS (1984–1991)

1991	BA	OBA	SA	AB	H	2B	3B	HR	RBI	BB	SO		BA	OBA	SA	AB	H	2B	3B	HR	RBI	BB	SO
vs. Left	.087	.154	.130	23	2	1	0	0	3	2	2		.170	.267	.208	399	68	11	2	0	33	51	71
vs. Right	.265	.370	.333	162	43	11	0	0	12	28	28		.295	.361	.362	2337	690	110	13	7	167	248	316
at Home	.280	.367	.390	82	23	9	0	0	11	13	15		.287	.361	.349	1333	383	63	8	1	102	156	178
on Road	.214	.325	.243	103	22	3	0	0	4	17	15		.267	.334	.331	1403	375	58	7	6	98	143	209
Bases Empty	.243	.341	.296	115	28	6	0	0	0	17	16		.270	.334	.336	1755	473	81	10	5	5	167	244
Runners On Base	.243	.349	.329	70	17	6	0	0	15	13	14		.291	.370	.348	981	285	40	5	2	195	132	143

JEFF BANISTER — bats right — throws right — age 27 — PIT

1-YEAR TOTALS (1991)

1991	BA	OBA	SA	AB	H	2B	3B	HR	RBI	BB	SO		BA	OBA	SA	AB	H	2B	3B	HR	RBI	BB	SO
vs. Left	.000	.000	.000	0	0	0	0	0	0	0	0		.000	.000	.000	0	0	0	0	0	0	0	0
vs. Right	1.000	1.000	1.000	1	1	0	0	0	0	0	0		1.000	1.000	1.000	1	1	0	0	0	0	0	0
at Home	1.000	1.000	1.000	1	1	0	0	0	0	0	0		1.000	1.000	1.000	1	1	0	0	0	0	0	0
on Road	.000	.000	.000	0	0	0	0	0	0	0	0		.000	.000	.000	0	0	0	0	0	0	0	0
Bases Empty	1.000	1.000	1.000	1	1	0	0	0	0	0	0		1.000	1.000	1.000	1	1	0	0	0	0	0	0
Runners On Base	.000	.000	.000	0	0	0	0	0	0	0	0		.000	.000	.000	0	0	0	0	0	0	0	0

BRET BARBERIE — bats both — throws right — age 25 — MON — S23/1

1-YEAR TOTALS (1991)

1991	BA	OBA	SA	AB	H	2B	3B	HR	RBI	BB	SO		BA	OBA	SA	AB	H	2B	3B	HR	RBI	BB	SO
vs. Left	.250	.349	.389	36	9	2	0	1	4	6	5		.250	.349	.389	36	9	2	0	1	4	6	5
vs. Right	.390	.466	.560	100	39	10	2	1	14	14	17		.390	.466	.560	100	39	10	2	1	14	14	17
at Home	.268	.354	.415	41	11	0	0	2	4	6	7		.268	.354	.415	41	11	0	0	2	4	6	7
on Road	.389	.469	.558	95	37	12	2	0	14	14	15		.389	.469	.558	95	37	12	2	0	14	14	15
Bases Empty	.388	.441	.565	85	33	5	2	2	2	6	11		.388	.441	.565	85	33	5	2	2	2	6	11
Runners On Base	.294	.426	.431	51	15	7	0	0	16	14	11		.294	.426	.431	51	15	7	0	0	16	14	11

JESSE BARFIELD — bats right — throws right — age 33 — NYA — O

8-YEAR TOTALS (1984–1991)

1991	BA	OBA	SA	AB	H	2B	3B	HR	RBI	BB	SO		BA	OBA	SA	AB	H	2B	3B	HR	RBI	BB	SO
vs. Left	.315	.408	.602	108	34	4	0	9	24	17	22		.279	.377	.499	1314	366	64	5	72	191	208	335
vs. Right	.170	.250	.352	176	30	8	0	8	24	19	58		.252	.327	.461	2473	623	121	18	120	383	266	664
at Home	.231	.331	.538	130	30	7	0	11	30	20	31		.265	.348	.486	1880	498	106	14	94	299	236	480
on Road	.221	.294	.370	154	34	5	0	6	18	16	49		.257	.343	.463	1907	491	79	9	98	275	238	519
Bases Empty	.235	.320	.458	153	36	4	0	10	10	19	44		.261	.332	.486	2151	561	99	13	120	120	213	572
Runners On Base	.214	.302	.435	131	28	8	0	7	38	17	36		.262	.361	.458	1636	428	86	10	72	454	261	427

SKEETER BARNES — bats right — throws right — age 35 — DET — O3/12D

5-YEAR TOTALS (1984–1991)

1991	BA	OBA	SA	AB	H	2B	3B	HR	RBI	BB	SO		BA	OBA	SA	AB	H	2B	3B	HR	RBI	BB	SO
vs. Left	.282	.330	.506	85	24	6	2	3	11	6	12		.234	.279	.391	128	30	7	2	3	13	8	16
vs. Right	.297	.321	.473	74	22	7	0	2	6	3	12		.245	.277	.425	106	26	7	0	4	10	5	16
at Home	.276	.311	.397	58	16	2	1	1	5	3	9		.227	.272	.340	97	22	3	1	2	8	6	14
on Road	.297	.333	.545	101	30	11	1	4	12	6	15		.248	.283	.453	137	34	11	1	5	15	7	18
Bases Empty	.304	.333	.576	92	28	13	0	4	4	4	11		.231	.262	.434	143	33	14	0	5	5	6	15
Runners On Base	.269	.315	.373	67	18	0	2	1	13	5	13		.253	.303	.363	91	23	0	2	2	18	7	17

MARTY BARRETT — bats right — throws right — age 34 — SD — /23

1991	BA	OBA	SA	AB	H	2B	3B	HR	RBI	BB	SO
vs. Left	.167	.167	.667	6	1	0	0	1	3	0	2
vs. Right	.200	.273	.300	10	2	1	0	0	0	0	1
at Home	.400	.400	1.000	5	2	0	0	1	3	0	1
on Road	.091	.167	.182	11	1	1	0	0	0	0	2
Bases Empty	.222	.300	.333	9	2	1	0	0	0	0	1
Runners On Base	.143	.143	.571	7	1	0	0	1	3	0	2

8-YEAR TOTALS (1984–1991)

BA	OBA	SA	AB	H	2B	3B	HR	RBI	BB	SO
.295	.359	.380	974	287	53	3	8	97	103	40
.273	.331	.337	2341	640	108	5	10	215	198	168
.286	.349	.371	1613	461	95	3	12	162	156	116
.274	.330	.329	1702	466	66	5	6	150	145	92
.273	.327	.336	1899	518	91	3	8	8	145	124
.289	.355	.367	1416	409	70	5	10	304	156	84

KIM BATISTE — bats right — throws right — age 24 — PHI — /S

1991	BA	OBA	SA	AB	H	2B	3B	HR	RBI	BB	SO
vs. Left	.273	.273	.273	11	3	0	0	0	1	0	2
vs. Right	.188	.235	.188	16	3	0	0	0	0	1	6
at Home	.176	.176	.176	17	3	0	0	0	1	0	6
on Road	.300	.364	.300	10	3	0	0	0	0	1	2
Bases Empty	.235	.235	.235	17	4	0	0	0	0	0	6
Runners On Base	.200	.273	.200	10	2	0	0	0	1	1	2

1-YEAR TOTALS (1991)

BA	OBA	SA	AB	H	2B	3B	HR	RBI	BB	SO
.273	.273	.273	11	3	0	0	0	1	0	2
.188	.235	.188	16	3	0	0	0	0	1	6
.176	.176	.176	17	3	0	0	0	1	0	6
.300	.364	.300	10	3	0	0	0	0	1	2
.235	.235	.235	17	4	0	0	0	0	0	6
.200	.273	.200	10	2	0	0	0	1	1	2

DEREK BELL — bats right — throws right — age 24 — TOR — O

1991	BA	OBA	SA	AB	H	2B	3B	HR	RBI	BB	SO
vs. Left	.150	.292	.150	20	3	0	0	0	0	3	4
vs. Right	.125	.364	.125	8	1	0	0	0	1	3	1
at Home	.067	.222	.067	15	1	0	0	0	0	2	3
on Road	.231	.412	.231	13	3	0	0	0	1	4	2
Bases Empty	.158	.304	.158	19	3	0	0	0	0	4	3
Runners On Base	.111	.333	.111	9	1	0	0	0	1	2	2

1-YEAR TOTALS (1991)

BA	OBA	SA	AB	H	2B	3B	HR	RBI	BB	SO
.150	.292	.150	20	3	0	0	0	0	3	4
.125	.364	.125	8	1	0	0	0	1	3	1
.067	.222	.067	15	1	0	0	0	0	2	3
.231	.412	.231	13	3	0	0	0	1	4	2
.158	.304	.158	19	3	0	0	0	0	4	3
.111	.333	.111	9	1	0	0	0	1	2	2

JUAN BELL — bats right — throws right — age 24 — BAL — 2S/DO

1991	BA	OBA	SA	AB	H	2B	3B	HR	RBI	BB	SO
vs. Left	.104	.104	.125	48	5	1	0	0	0	0	16
vs. Right	.193	.228	.286	161	31	8	2	1	15	8	35
at Home	.155	.202	.227	110	17	4	2	0	9	7	27
on Road	.192	.200	.273	99	19	5	0	1	6	1	24
Bases Empty	.175	.189	.217	120	21	5	0	0	0	2	29
Runners On Base	.169	.216	.292	89	15	4	2	1	15	6	22

3-YEAR TOTALS (1989–1991)

BA	OBA	SA	AB	H	2B	3B	HR	RBI	BB	SO
.102	.102	.122	49	5	1	0	0	0	0	16
.187	.222	.277	166	31	8	2	1	15	8	37
.155	.202	.227	110	17	4	2	0	9	7	27
.181	.189	.257	105	19	5	0	1	6	1	26
.171	.184	.211	123	21	5	0	0	0	2	31
.163	.210	.283	92	15	4	2	1	15	6	22

MIKE BELL — bats left — throws left — age 24 — ATL — 1

1991	BA	OBA	SA	AB	H	2B	3B	HR	RBI	BB	SO
vs. Left	.000	.000	.000	3	0	0	0	0	0	0	1
vs. Right	.148	.207	.259	27	4	0	0	1	1	2	6
at Home	.211	.250	.368	19	4	0	0	1	1	1	2
on Road	.000	.083	.000	11	0	0	0	0	0	1	5
Bases Empty	.190	.261	.333	21	4	0	0	1	1	2	6
Runners On Base	.000	.000	.000	9	0	0	0	0	0	0	1

2-YEAR TOTALS (1990–1991)

BA	OBA	SA	AB	H	2B	3B	HR	RBI	BB	SO
.000	.100	.000	9	0	0	0	0	0	0	2
.227	.271	.424	66	15	5	1	2	6	4	14
.160	.222	.280	25	4	0	0	1	1	2	4
.220	.264	.420	50	11	5	1	1	5	2	12
.200	.265	.378	45	9	3	1	1	1	3	10
.200	.226	.367	30	6	2	0	1	5	1	6

ESTEBAN BELTRE — bats right — throws right — age 25 — CHA — /S

1991	BA	OBA	SA	AB	H	2B	3B	HR	RBI	BB	SO
vs. Left	.000	.000	.000	1	0	0	0	0	0	0	0
vs. Right	.200	.333	.200	5	1	0	0	0	0	1	1
at Home	.000	.000	.000	2	0	0	0	0	0	0	1
on Road	.250	.400	.250	4	1	0	0	0	0	1	0
Bases Empty	.000	.250	.000	3	0	0	0	0	0	1	1
Runners On Base	.333	.333	.333	3	1	0	0	0	0	0	0

1-YEAR TOTALS (1991)

BA	OBA	SA	AB	H	2B	3B	HR	RBI	BB	SO
.000	.000	.000	1	0	0	0	0	0	0	0
.200	.333	.200	5	1	0	0	0	0	1	1
.000	.000	.000	2	0	0	0	0	0	0	1
.250	.400	.250	4	1	0	0	0	0	1	1
.000	.250	.000	3	0	0	0	0	0	1	1
.333	.333	.333	3	1	0	0	0	0	0	0

FREDDIE BENAVIDES — bats right — throws right — age 26 — CIN — S/2

1991	BA	OBA	SA	AB	H	2B	3B	HR	RBI	BB	SO
vs. Left	.278	.316	.278	18	5	0	0	0	0	0	2
vs. Right	.289	.298	.311	45	13	1	0	0	3	1	13
at Home	.269	.269	.269	26	7	0	0	0	0	0	7
on Road	.297	.325	.324	37	11	1	0	0	3	1	8
Bases Empty	.293	.310	.317	41	12	1	0	0	0	0	7
Runners On Base	.273	.292	.273	22	6	0	0	0	3	1	8

1-YEAR TOTALS (1991)

BA	OBA	SA	AB	H	2B	3B	HR	RBI	BB	SO
.278	.316	.278	18	5	0	0	0	0	0	2
.289	.298	.311	45	13	1	0	0	3	1	13
.269	.269	.269	26	7	0	0	0	0	0	7
.297	.325	.324	37	11	1	0	0	3	1	8
.293	.310	.317	41	12	1	0	0	0	0	7
.273	.292	.273	22	6	0	0	0	3	1	8

MIKE BENJAMIN — bats right — throws right — age 27 — SF — S/3

1991	BA	OBA	SA	AB	H	2B	3B	HR	RBI	BB	SO
vs. Left	.167	.242	.300	30	5	1	0	1	1	3	6
vs. Right	.105	.167	.171	76	8	2	0	1	7	4	20
at Home	.065	.137	.065	46	3	0	0	0	1	4	10
on Road	.167	.227	.317	60	10	3	0	2	7	3	16
Bases Empty	.162	.197	.279	68	11	2	0	2	2	3	19
Runners On Base	.053	.174	.079	38	2	1	0	0	6	4	7

3-YEAR TOTALS (1989–1991)

BA	OBA	SA	AB	H	2B	3B	HR	RBI	BB	SO
.169	.222	.271	59	10	1	1	1	1	4	11
.147	.202	.275	109	16	5	0	3	10	6	26
.148	.205	.247	81	12	2	0	0	3	6	18
.161	.213	.299	87	14	4	1	2	8	4	19
.206	.234	.374	107	22	4	1	4	4	4	24
.066	.169	.098	61	4	2	0	0	7	6	13

DAVE BERGMAN — bats left — throws left — age 39 — DET — 1D/O

1991	BA	OBA	SA	AB	H	2B	3B	HR	RBI	BB	SO
vs. Left	.053	.182	.105	19	1	1	0	0	1	3	11
vs. Right	.257	.368	.440	175	45	9	1	7	28	32	29
at Home	.218	.346	.322	87	19	3	0	2	11	18	20
on Road	.252	.355	.477	107	27	7	1	5	18	17	20
Bases Empty	.210	.299	.420	119	25	5	1	6	6	15	23
Runners On Base	.280	.423	.387	75	21	5	0	1	23	20	17

8-YEAR TOTALS (1984–1991)

BA	OBA	SA	AB	H	2B	3B	HR	RBI	BB	SO
.201	.264	.256	164	33	7	1	0	15	13	36
.268	.358	.390	1622	434	63	11	38	193	234	193
.246	.344	.377	853	210	31	6	23	102	132	122
.275	.355	.378	933	257	39	6	15	106	115	107
.257	.343	.392	1023	263	43	7	27	27	131	131
.267	.358	.359	763	204	27	5	11	181	116	98

TONY BERNAZARD — bats both — throws right — age 36 — DET — /2D

1991	BA	OBA	SA	AB	H	2B	3B	HR	RBI	BB	SO
vs. Left	1.000	1.000	1.000	1	1	0	0	0	0	0	0
vs. Right	.091	.091	.091	11	1	0	0	0	0	0	4
at Home	.200	.200	.200	5	1	0	0	0	0	0	3
on Road	.143	.143	.143	7	1	0	0	0	0	0	1
Bases Empty	.167	.167	.167	6	1	0	0	0	0	0	3
Runners On Base	.167	.167	.167	6	1	0	0	0	0	0	1

5-YEAR TOTALS (1984–1991)

BA	OBA	SA	AB	H	2B	3B	HR	RBI	BB	SO
.269	.359	.392	554	149	31	2	11	61	78	71
.261	.327	.388	1465	383	64	11	33	158	142	231
.282	.354	.406	970	274	49	10	17	105	109	136
.246	.319	.373	1049	258	46	3	27	114	111	166
.260	.326	.406	1191	310	56	9	33	33	113	183
.268	.348	.365	828	222	39	4	11	186	107	119

SEAN BERRY — bats right — throws right — age 26 — KC — 3

1991	BA	OBA	SA	AB	H	2B	3B	HR	RBI	BB	SO
vs. Left	.167	.219	.200	30	5	1	0	0	0	2	10
vs. Right	.100	.206	.167	30	3	2	0	0	3	3	13
at Home	.136	.240	.227	22	3	2	0	0	1	2	13
on Road	.132	.195	.158	38	5	1	0	0	3	3	10
Bases Empty	.156	.250	.219	32	5	2	0	0	0	3	11
Runners On Base	.107	.167	.143	28	3	1	0	0	1	2	12

2-YEAR TOTALS (1990–1991)

BA	OBA	SA	AB	H	2B	3B	HR	RBI	BB	SO
.186	.239	.256	43	8	1	1	0	3	3	12
.125	.222	.200	40	5	3	0	0	2	4	16
.136	.240	.227	22	3	2	0	0	1	2	13
.164	.227	.230	61	10	2	1	0	4	5	15
.167	.231	.229	48	8	3	0	0	0	3	15
.143	.231	.229	35	5	1	1	0	5	4	13

DAMON BERRYHILL — bats both — throws right — age 29 — CHN/ATL

1991	BA	OBA	SA	AB	H	2B	3B	HR	RBI	BB	SO
vs. Left	.053	.075	.053	38	2	0	0	0	3	1	7
vs. Right	.230	.293	.410	122	28	7	0	5	11	10	35
at Home	.159	.225	.317	82	13	4	0	3	7	6	25
on Road	.218	.262	.333	78	17	3	0	2	7	5	17
Bases Empty	.214	.267	.367	98	21	6	0	3	3	6	22
Runners On Base	.145	.206	.258	62	9	1	0	2	11	5	20

5-YEAR TOTALS (1987–1991)

BA	OBA	SA	AB	H	2B	3B	HR	RBI	BB	SO
.250	.270	.354	240	60	10	0	5	27	8	28
.233	.282	.351	643	150	35	1	13	76	43	142
.260	.301	.399	446	116	27	1	11	62	26	90
.215	.256	.304	437	94	18	0	7	41	25	80
.229	.272	.354	475	109	29	0	10	10	26	100
.248	.286	.350	408	101	16	1	8	93	25	70

DANN BILARDELLO — bats right — throws right — age 33 — SD — C

1991	BA	OBA	SA	AB	H	2B	3B	HR	RBI	BB	SO
vs. Left	.167	.286	.167	6	1	0	0	0	0	1	0
vs. Right	.300	.364	.500	20	6	2	1	0	5	2	4
at Home	.333	.333	.583	12	4	1	1	0	3	0	3
on Road	.214	.353	.286	14	3	1	0	0	2	3	1
Bases Empty	.067	.176	.067	15	1	0	0	0	0	2	2
Runners On Base	.545	.583	.909	11	6	2	1	0	5	1	2

6-YEAR TOTALS (1984–1991)

BA	OBA	SA	AB	H	2B	3B	HR	RBI	BB	SO
.204	.263	.275	240	49	8	0	3	18	19	51
.185	.243	.270	378	70	12	1	6	34	27	62
.203	.254	.296	291	59	10	1	5	28	20	57
.183	.248	.251	327	60	10	0	4	24	26	56
.188	.238	.245	351	66	11	0	3	3	21	62
.199	.267	.307	267	53	9	1	6	49	25	51

LANCE BLANKENSHIP — bats right — throws right — age 29 — OAK — 2O3/D

1991	BA	OBA	SA	AB	H	2B	3B	HR	RBI	BB	SO
vs. Left	.222	.301	.302	63	14	2	0	1	10	8	9
vs. Right	.262	.355	.361	122	32	6	0	2	11	15	33
at Home	.193	.269	.229	83	16	3	0	0	6	9	18
on Road	.294	.388	.431	102	30	5	0	3	15	14	24
Bases Empty	.268	.393	.381	97	26	5	0	2	2	18	21
Runners On Base	.227	.268	.295	88	20	3	0	1	19	5	21

4-YEAR TOTALS (1988–1991)

BA	OBA	SA	AB	H	2B	3B	HR	RBI	BB	SO
.211	.282	.261	180	38	3	0	2	20	19	31
.234	.321	.312	269	63	13	1	2	15	32	66
.197	.262	.248	218	43	6	1	1	15	20	50
.251	.345	.333	231	58	10	0	3	20	31	47
.238	.336	.321	252	60	10	1	3	3	35	53
.208	.266	.254	197	41	6	0	1	32	16	44

JEFF BLAUSER — bats right — throws right — age 27 — ATL — S23

1991	BA	OBA	SA	AB	H	2B	3B	HR	RBI	BB	SO
vs. Left	.299	.408	.480	127	38	5	3	4	25	24	20
vs. Right	.236	.328	.369	225	53	9	0	7	29	30	39
at Home	.270	.382	.425	174	47	6	0	7	32	31	25
on Road	.247	.333	.393	178	44	8	3	4	22	23	34
Bases Empty	.209	.304	.346	191	40	5	0	7	7	26	33
Runners On Base	.317	.418	.484	161	51	9	3	4	47	28	26

5-YEAR TOTALS (1987–1991)

BA	OBA	SA	AB	H	2B	3B	HR	RBI	BB	SO
.289	.367	.455	532	154	32	7	14	71	66	87
.246	.315	.371	894	220	39	5	21	90	81	188
.273	.352	.423	681	186	36	6	18	85	79	121
.252	.318	.384	745	188	35	6	17	76	68	154
.246	.308	.393	861	212	38	5	26	26	72	162
.287	.373	.418	565	162	33	7	9	135	75	113

MIKE BLOWERS — bats right — throws right — age 27 — NYA — 3

1991	BA	OBA	SA	AB	H	2B	3B	HR	RBI	BB	SO
vs. Left	.250	.368	.438	16	4	0	0	1	3	3	1
vs. Right	.158	.200	.158	19	3	0	0	0	1	1	2
at Home	.222	.300	.222	18	4	0	0	0	0	2	2
on Road	.176	.263	.353	17	3	0	0	1	4	2	1
Bases Empty	.238	.273	.381	21	5	0	0	1	1	1	1
Runners On Base	.143	.294	.143	14	2	0	0	0	3	3	2

3-YEAR TOTALS (1989–1991)

BA	OBA	SA	AB	H	2B	3B	HR	RBI	BB	SO
.288	.381	.452	73	21	3	0	3	12	11	14
.160	.209	.229	144	23	1	0	3	13	8	52
.210	.288	.250	100	21	1	0	1	7	11	30
.197	.254	.350	117	23	3	0	5	18	8	36
.176	.243	.280	125	22	1	0	4	4	11	34
.239	.307	.337	92	22	3	0	2	21	8	32

ROD BOOKER — bats left — throws right — age 34 — PHI — S/3

1991	BA	OBA	SA	AB	H	2B	3B	HR	RBI	BB	SO
vs. Left	.000	.000	.000	5	0	0	0	0	0	0	3
vs. Right	.250	.260	.271	48	12	1	0	0	7	1	4
at Home	.161	.188	.161	31	5	0	0	0	3	1	5
on Road	.318	.304	.364	22	7	1	0	0	4	0	2
Bases Empty	.160	.160	.160	25	4	0	0	0	0	0	5
Runners On Base	.286	.300	.321	28	8	1	0	0	7	1	2

5-YEAR TOTALS (1987–1991)

BA	OBA	SA	AB	H	2B	3B	HR	RBI	BB	SO
.233	.303	.300	30	7	0	1	0	3	3	11
.250	.316	.307	244	61	10	2	0	25	24	33
.221	.301	.279	140	31	6	1	0	17	16	24
.276	.329	.336	134	37	4	2	0	11	11	20
.250	.314	.320	128	32	7	1	0	0	12	26
.247	.315	.295	146	36	3	2	0	28	15	18

PAT BORDERS — bats right — throws right — age 29 — TOR — *C

1991	BA	OBA	SA	AB	H	2B	3B	HR	RBI	BB	SO
vs. Left	.238	.271	.320	147	35	9	0	1	14	7	19
vs. Right	.250	.272	.389	144	36	8	0	4	22	4	26
at Home	.247	.268	.356	146	36	10	0	2	18	5	17
on Road	.241	.275	.352	145	35	7	0	3	18	6	28
Bases Empty	.193	.212	.259	166	32	8	0	1	1	4	32
Runners On Base	.312	.346	.480	125	39	9	0	4	35	7	13

4-YEAR TOTALS (1988–1991)

BA	OBA	SA	AB	H	2B	3B	HR	RBI	BB	SO
.272	.307	.431	636	173	38	6	17	83	33	98
.255	.273	.389	396	101	20	0	11	52	10	73
.263	.295	.437	487	128	34	3	15	64	24	69
.268	.292	.394	545	146	24	3	13	71	19	102
.263	.287	.409	574	151	33	3	15	15	18	101
.269	.302	.421	458	123	25	3	13	120	25	70

DARYL BOSTON — bats left — throws left — age 29 — NYN — *O

1991	BA	OBA	SA	AB	H	2B	3B	HR	RBI	BB	SO
vs. Left	.207	.207	.414	29	6	3	0	1	1	0	9
vs. Right	.283	.366	.416	226	64	13	4	3	20	30	33
at Home	.244	.338	.400	135	33	11	2	2	13	19	26
on Road	.308	.364	.433	120	37	5	2	2	8	11	16
Bases Empty	.287	.357	.443	167	48	11	3	3	3	18	27
Runners On Base	.250	.337	.364	88	22	5	1	1	18	12	15

8-YEAR TOTALS (1984–1991)

BA	OBA	SA	AB	H	2B	3B	HR	RBI	BB	SO
.225	.266	.317	284	64	14	3	2	23	17	70
.254	.315	.416	1688	429	86	16	52	166	150	262
.255	.314	.400	978	249	48	14	22	84	87	168
.245	.302	.404	994	244	52	5	32	105	80	164
.260	.313	.421	1206	313	69	12	34	34	92	212
.235	.301	.372	766	180	31	7	20	155	75	120

SCOTT BRADLEY — bats left — throws right — age 32 — SEA — C/3D1

1991	BA	OBA	SA	AB	H	2B	3B	HR	RBI	BB	SO
vs. Left	.182	.308	.182	11	2	0	0	0	2	2	2
vs. Right	.205	.278	.248	161	33	7	0	0	9	17	17
at Home	.202	.277	.238	84	17	3	0	0	6	9	10
on Road	.205	.283	.250	88	18	4	0	0	5	10	9
Bases Empty	.184	.257	.223	103	19	4	0	0	0	10	14
Runners On Base	.232	.313	.275	69	16	3	0	0	11	9	5

8-YEAR TOTALS (1984–1991)

BA	OBA	SA	AB	H	2B	3B	HR	RBI	BB	SO
.188	.225	.244	176	33	5	1	1	21	8	16
.265	.310	.355	1466	389	70	5	17	162	94	93
.269	.318	.385	784	211	41	4	14	97	56	49
.246	.286	.304	858	211	34	2	4	86	46	60
.246	.285	.323	923	227	44	3	7	7	46	66
.271	.321	.369	719	195	31	3	11	176	56	43

GLENN BRAGGS — bats right — throws right — age 30 — CIN — O

1991	BA	OBA	SA	AB	H	2B	3B	HR	RBI	BB	SO
vs. Left	.285	.355	.455	123	35	6	0	5	23	14	22
vs. Right	.236	.290	.409	127	30	4	0	6	16	9	24
at Home	.300	.346	.550	120	36	6	0	8	23	9	19
on Road	.223	.301	.323	130	29	4	0	3	16	14	27
Bases Empty	.254	.331	.469	130	33	4	0	8	8	13	28
Runners On Base	.267	.313	.392	120	32	6	0	3	31	10	18

6-YEAR TOTALS (1986–1991)

BA	OBA	SA	AB	H	2B	3B	HR	RBI	BB	SO
.282	.351	.451	723	204	35	3	27	114	77	129
.248	.303	.379	1347	334	51	10	35	169	98	296
.259	.323	.411	1038	269	41	9	33	156	93	214
.261	.318	.396	1032	269	45	4	29	127	82	211
.251	.316	.409	1178	296	44	8	42	42	99	255
.271	.326	.397	892	242	42	5	20	241	76	170

ROD BREWER — bats left — throws left — age 26 — SL — 1/O

1991	BA	OBA	SA	AB	H	2B	3B	HR	RBI	BB	SO
vs. Left	.200	.200	.200	5	1	0	0	0	1	0	3
vs. Right	.000	.000	.000	8	0	0	0	0	0	0	2
at Home	.000	.000	.000	2	0	0	0	0	0	0	2
on Road	.091	.091	.091	11	1	0	0	0	1	0	3
Bases Empty	.000	.000	.000	8	0	0	0	0	0	0	4
Runners On Base	.200	.200	.200	5	1	0	0	0	1	0	1

2-YEAR TOTALS (1990–1991)

BA	OBA	SA	AB	H	2B	3B	HR	RBI	BB	SO
.222	.222	.222	9	2	0	0	0	3	0	3
.172	.172	.207	29	5	1	0	0	0	0	6
.000	.000	.000	6	0	0	0	0	0	0	2
.219	.219	.250	32	7	1	0	0	3	0	7
.136	.136	.182	22	3	1	0	0	0	0	7
.250	.250	.250	16	4	0	0	0	3	0	2

GREG BROCK — bats left — throws right — age 35 — MIL — 1

1991	BA	OBA	SA	AB	H	2B	3B	HR	RBI	BB	SO
vs. Left	.400	.471	.667	15	6	1	0	1	4	2	1
vs. Right	.244	.404	.311	45	11	3	0	0	2	12	8
at Home	.278	.480	.389	18	5	2	0	0	1	7	3
on Road	.286	.388	.405	42	12	2	0	1	5	7	6
Bases Empty	.265	.405	.412	34	9	2	0	1	1	8	3
Runners On Base	.308	.438	.385	26	8	2	0	0	5	6	6

8-YEAR TOTALS (1984–1991)

BA	OBA	SA	AB	H	2B	3B	HR	RBI	BB	SO
.239	.306	.362	687	164	29	1	18	114	64	115
.258	.349	.414	2042	526	97	3	72	281	287	268
.256	.339	.388	1339	343	53	3	39	209	166	175
.250	.338	.414	1390	347	73	1	51	186	185	208
.231	.309	.372	1462	337	64	1	47	47	156	196
.279	.371	.434	1267	353	62	3	43	348	195	187

SCOTT BROSIUS — bats right — throws right — age 26 — OAK — 2O/3D

1991	BA	OBA	SA	AB	H	2B	3B	HR	RBI	BB	SO
vs. Left	.208	.296	.250	24	5	1	0	0	1	3	2
vs. Right	.250	.250	.477	44	11	4	0	2	3	0	9
at Home	.189	.211	.324	37	7	2	0	1	1	1	5
on Road	.290	.333	.484	31	9	3	0	1	3	2	6
Bases Empty	.262	.295	.476	42	11	3	0	2	2	2	8
Runners On Base	.192	.222	.269	26	5	2	0	0	2	1	3

1-YEAR TOTALS (1991)

BA	OBA	SA	AB	H	2B	3B	HR	RBI	BB	SO
.208	.296	.250	24	5	1	0	0	1	3	2
.250	.250	.477	44	11	4	0	2	3	0	9
.189	.211	.324	37	7	2	0	1	1	1	5
.290	.333	.484	31	9	3	0	1	3	2	6
.262	.295	.476	42	11	3	0	2	2	2	8
.192	.222	.269	26	5	2	0	0	2	1	3

JARVIS BROWN — bats right — throws right — age 25 — MIN — O/D

1991	BA	OBA	SA	AB	H	2B	3B	HR	RBI	BB	SO
vs. Left	.000	.000	.000	9	0	0	0	0	0	0	0
vs. Right	.286	.333	.286	28	8	0	0	0	0	2	8
at Home	.375	.375	.375	8	3	0	0	0	0	2	3
on Road	.172	.226	.172	29	5	0	0	0	0	1	5
Bases Empty	.200	.231	.200	25	5	0	0	0	0	1	5
Runners On Base	.250	.308	.250	12	3	0	0	0	0	1	3

1-YEAR TOTALS (1991)

BA	OBA	SA	AB	H	2B	3B	HR	RBI	BB	SO
.000	.000	.000	9	0	0	0	0	0	0	0
.286	.333	.286	28	8	0	0	0	0	2	8
.375	.375	.375	8	3	0	0	0	0	2	3
.172	.226	.172	29	5	0	0	0	0	1	5
.200	.231	.200	25	5	0	0	0	0	1	5
.250	.308	.250	12	3	0	0	0	0	1	3

JERRY BROWNE — bats both — throws right — age 26 — CLE — 2O3/D

1991	BA	OBA	SA	AB	H	2B	3B	HR	RBI	BB	SO
vs. Left	.231	.310	.244	78	18	1	0	0	6	8	9
vs. Right	.226	.285	.278	212	48	4	2	1	23	19	20
at Home	.259	.313	.304	135	35	3	0	1	16	10	12
on Road	.200	.274	.239	155	31	2	2	0	13	17	17
Bases Empty	.198	.272	.222	167	33	2	1	0	0	17	16
Runners On Base	.268	.319	.333	123	33	3	1	0	29	10	13

6-YEAR TOTALS (1986–1991)

BA	OBA	SA	AB	H	2B	3B	HR	RBI	BB	SO
.287	.362	.378	585	168	26	9	3	59	69	49
.263	.341	.340	1507	396	63	10	11	123	185	177
.297	.374	.382	1089	323	51	12	6	98	135	104
.240	.318	.316	1003	241	38	7	8	84	119	122
.267	.340	.353	1373	367	61	13	10	10	148	162
.274	.359	.346	719	197	28	6	4	172	106	64

MIKE BRUMLEY — bats both — throws right — age 29 — BOS — S3/2O

1991	BA	OBA	SA	AB	H	2B	3B	HR	RBI	BB	SO
vs. Left	.308	.357	.359	39	12	2	0	0	2	3	9
vs. Right	.165	.233	.203	79	13	3	0	0	3	7	13
at Home	.197	.258	.230	61	12	2	0	0	3	5	8
on Road	.228	.290	.281	57	13	3	0	0	2	5	14
Bases Empty	.232	.284	.246	69	16	1	0	0	0	5	14
Runners On Base	.184	.259	.265	49	9	4	0	0	5	5	8

4-YEAR TOTALS (1987–1991)

BA	OBA	SA	AB	H	2B	3B	HR	RBI	BB	SO
.239	.280	.296	159	38	4	1	1	9	9	30
.197	.260	.268	422	83	13	7	1	23	35	89
.209	.256	.280	296	62	10	4	1	20	18	60
.207	.274	.270	285	59	7	4	1	12	26	59
.220	.286	.287	327	72	8	7	0	29	30	56
.193	.239	.260	254	49	9	1	2	32	15	56

SCOTT BULLETT — bats both — throws left — age 24 — PIT — /O

1-YEAR TOTALS (1991)

1991	BA	OBA	SA	AB	H	2B	3B	HR	RBI	BB	SO		BA	OBA	SA	AB	H	2B	3B	HR	RBI	BB	SO
vs. Left	.000	.000	.000	0	0	0	0	0	0	0	0		.000	.000	.000	0	0	0	0	0	0	0	0
vs. Right	.000	.200	.000	4	0	0	0	0	0	0	3		.000	.200	.000	4	0	0	0	0	0	0	3
at Home	.000	.000	.000	1	0	0	0	0	0	0	0		.000	.000	.000	1	0	0	0	0	0	0	0
on Road	.000	.250	.000	3	0	0	0	0	0	0	3		.000	.250	.000	3	0	0	0	0	0	0	3
Bases Empty	.000	.250	.000	3	0	0	0	0	0	0	3		.000	.250	.000	3	0	0	0	0	0	0	3
Runners On Base	.000	.000	.000	1	0	0	0	0	0	0	0		.000	.000	.000	1	0	0	0	0	0	0	0

ERIC BULLOCK — bats left — throws left — age 32 — MON — /01

6-YEAR TOTALS (1985–1991)

1991	BA	OBA	SA	AB	H	2B	3B	HR	RBI	BB	SO		BA	OBA	SA	AB	H	2B	3B	HR	RBI	BB	SO
vs. Left	.500	.750	1.000	2	1	0	0	0	0	2	1		.111	.273	.222	9	1	1	0	0	0	2	4
vs. Right	.214	.282	.300	70	15	3	0	1	6	7	12		.220	.278	.280	132	29	5	0	1	12	11	18
at Home	.293	.388	.439	41	12	3	0	1	4	7	7		.242	.320	.319	91	22	4	0	1	8	11	13
on Road	.129	.182	.161	31	4	1	0	0	2	2	6		.160	.192	.200	50	8	2	0	0	4	2	9
Bases Empty	.200	.300	.257	35	7	2	0	0	0	5	6		.224	.280	.263	76	17	3	0	1	12	7	11
Runners On Base	.243	.310	.378	37	9	2	0	1	6	4	7		.200	.274	.292	65	13	3	0	1	12	7	11

RANDY BUSH — bats left — throws left — age 34 — MIN — O1D

8-YEAR TOTALS (1984–1991)

1991	BA	OBA	SA	AB	H	2B	3B	HR	RBI	BB	SO		BA	OBA	SA	AB	H	2B	3B	HR	RBI	BB	SO
vs. Left	.000	.000	.000	2	0	0	0	0	0	0	1		.178	.279	.288	73	13	6	1	0	7	10	20
vs. Right	.305	.403	.488	164	50	10	1	6	23	24	24		.258	.346	.429	2254	582	108	20	79	307	278	356
at Home	.246	.372	.385	65	16	3	0	2	9	12	15		.262	.361	.458	1128	295	62	14	44	171	158	184
on Road	.337	.417	.545	101	34	7	1	4	14	12	10		.250	.326	.393	1199	300	52	7	35	143	130	192
Bases Empty	.330	.404	.557	88	29	6	1	4	4	9	14		.240	.320	.401	1310	314	65	10	42	42	126	220
Runners On Base	.269	.394	.397	78	21	4	0	2	19	15	11		.276	.371	.455	1017	281	49	11	37	272	162	156

FRANCISCO CABRERA — bats right — throws right — age 26 — ATL — C1

3-YEAR TOTALS (1989–1991)

1991	BA	OBA	SA	AB	H	2B	3B	HR	RBI	BB	SO		BA	OBA	SA	AB	H	2B	3B	HR	RBI	BB	SO
vs. Left	.226	.250	.340	53	12	3	0	1	9	2	11		.258	.276	.433	178	46	8	1	7	30	5	25
vs. Right	.262	.326	.548	42	11	3	0	3	14	4	9		.250	.310	.475	80	20	6	0	4	18	7	22
at Home	.214	.267	.393	56	12	4	0	2	12	4	16		.264	.296	.458	144	38	10	0	6	29	7	27
on Road	.282	.310	.487	39	11	2	0	2	11	2	4		.246	.275	.430	114	28	4	1	5	19	5	20
Bases Empty	.209	.261	.372	43	9	1	0	2	2	3	7		.224	.257	.396	134	30	5	0	6	6	6	23
Runners On Base	.269	.304	.481	52	14	5	0	2	21	3	13		.290	.318	.500	124	36	9	1	5	42	6	24

SIL CAMPUSANO — bats right — throws right — age 27 — PHI — O

3-YEAR TOTALS (1988–1991)

1991	BA	OBA	SA	AB	H	2B	3B	HR	RBI	BB	SO		BA	OBA	SA	AB	H	2B	3B	HR	RBI	BB	SO
vs. Left	.053	.100	.053	19	1	0	0	0	0	1	4		.200	.248	.338	145	29	5	3	3	16	9	33
vs. Right	.188	.188	.375	16	3	0	0	1	2	0	6		.205	.273	.308	117	24	6	0	2	7	7	26
at Home	.107	.138	.107	28	3	0	0	0	1	1	7		.221	.279	.338	136	30	5	1	3	9	7	33
on Road	.143	.143	.571	7	1	0	0	1	1	0	3		.183	.239	.310	126	23	6	2	2	14	9	26
Bases Empty	.143	.182	.286	21	3	0	0	1	1	1	4		.208	.274	.375	144	30	8	2	4	4	9	26
Runners On Base	.071	.071	.071	14	1	0	0	0	1	0	6		.195	.242	.263	118	23	3	1	1	19	7	33

GEORGE CANALE — bats left — throws right — age 27 — MIL — 1

3-YEAR TOTALS (1989–1991)

1991	BA	OBA	SA	AB	H	2B	3B	HR	RBI	BB	SO		BA	OBA	SA	AB	H	2B	3B	HR	RBI	BB	SO
vs. Left	.000	.222	.000	6	0	0	0	0	1	2	0		.143	.278	.143	14	2	0	0	0	1	3	2
vs. Right	.214	.343	.607	28	6	2	0	3	9	6	6		.169	.275	.441	59	10	4	0	4	12	9	13
at Home	.133	.316	.400	15	2	1	0	1	3	4	4		.097	.243	.226	31	3	1	0	1	3	6	9
on Road	.211	.320	.579	19	4	1	0	2	7	4	2		.214	.300	.500	42	9	3	0	3	10	6	6
Bases Empty	.150	.320	.500	20	3	1	0	2	2	5	5		.116	.224	.302	43	5	2	0	2	2	6	11
Runners On Base	.214	.316	.500	14	3	1	0	1	8	3	1		.233	.342	.500	30	7	2	0	2	11	6	4

NICK CAPRA — bats right — throws right — age 34 — TEX — /O

3-YEAR TOTALS (1985–1991)

1991	BA	OBA	SA	AB	H	2B	3B	HR	RBI	BB	SO		BA	OBA	SA	AB	H	2B	3B	HR	RBI	BB	SO
vs. Left	.000	.000	.000	0	0	0	0	0	0	0	0		.100	.100	.100	10	1	0	0	0	0	0	0
vs. Right	.000	1.000	.000	0	0	0	0	0	0	1	0		.148	.233	.185	27	4	1	0	0	0	3	3
at Home	.000	.000	.000	0	0	0	0	0	0	0	0		.167	.211	.222	18	3	1	0	0	0	1	2
on Road	.000	1.000	.000	0	0	0	0	0	0	1	0		.105	.190	.105	19	2	0	0	0	0	2	1
Bases Empty	.000	1.000	.000	0	0	0	0	0	0	1	0		.182	.280	.227	22	4	1	0	0	0	3	3
Runners On Base	.000	.000	.000	0	0	0	0	0	0	0	0		.067	.067	.067	15	1	0	0	0	0	0	2

CHUCK CARR — bats both — throws right — age 25 — NYN — /O

2-YEAR TOTALS (1990–1991)

1991	BA	OBA	SA	AB	H	2B	3B	HR	RBI	BB	SO		BA	OBA	SA	AB	H	2B	3B	HR	RBI	BB	SO
vs. Left	.400	.400	.400	5	2	0	0	0	1	0	1		.333	.333	.333	6	2	0	0	0	1	0	2
vs. Right	.000	.000	.000	6	0	0	0	0	0	0	1		.000	.000	.000	7	0	0	0	0	0	0	2
at Home	.000	.000	.000	5	0	0	0	0	0	0	2		.000	.000	.000	5	0	0	0	0	0	0	2
on Road	.333	.333	.333	6	2	0	0	0	1	0	0		.250	.250	.250	8	2	0	0	0	1	0	2
Bases Empty	.167	.167	.167	6	1	0	0	0	0	0	0		.143	.143	.143	7	1	0	0	0	0	0	2
Runners On Base	.200	.200	.200	5	1	0	0	0	1	0	1		.167	.167	.167	6	1	0	0	0	1	0	2

MARK CARREON — bats right — throws left — age 29 — NYN — O

5-YEAR TOTALS (1987–1991)

1991	BA	OBA	SA	AB	H	2B	3B	HR	RBI	BB	SO		BA	OBA	SA	AB	H	2B	3B	HR	RBI	BB	SO
vs. Left	.247	.287	.327	162	40	4	0	3	14	7	15		.256	.304	.433	363	93	16	0	16	42	23	44
vs. Right	.283	.316	.337	92	26	2	0	1	7	5	11		.296	.355	.403	233	69	10	0	5	23	19	30
at Home	.252	.299	.335	155	39	4	0	3	15	9	15		.258	.317	.381	310	80	14	0	8	28	22	39
on Road	.273	.294	.323	99	27	2	0	1	6	3	11		.287	.333	.465	286	82	12	0	13	37	20	35
Bases Empty	.252	.286	.362	127	32	2	0	4	4	5	13		.261	.313	.465	318	83	14	0	17	17	23	37
Runners On Base	.268	.309	.299	127	34	4	0	0	17	7	14		.284	.338	.371	278	79	12	0	4	48	19	37

VINNY CASTILLA — bats right — throws right — age 25 — ATL — S

1991	BA	OBA	SA	AB	H	2B	3B	HR	RBI	BB	SO
vs. Left	.000	.000	.000	0	0	0	0	0	0	0	0
vs. Right	.200	.200	.200	5	1	0	0	0	0	0	2
at Home	.250	.250	.250	4	1	0	0	0	0	0	2
on Road	.000	.000	.000	1	0	0	0	0	0	0	0
Bases Empty	.250	.250	.250	4	1	0	0	0	0	0	2
Runners On Base	.000	.000	.000	1	0	0	0	0	0	0	0

1-YEAR TOTALS (1991)

	BA	OBA	SA	AB	H	2B	3B	HR	RBI	BB	SO
	.000	.000	.000	0	0	0	0	0	0	0	0
	.200	.200	.200	5	1	0	0	0	0	0	2
	.250	.250	.250	4	1	0	0	0	0	0	2
	.000	.000	.000	1	0	0	0	0	0	0	0
	.250	.250	.250	4	1	0	0	0	0	0	2
	.000	.000	.000	1	0	0	0	0	0	0	0

BRAULIO CASTILLO — bats right — throws right — age 24 — PHI — O

1991	BA	OBA	SA	AB	H	2B	3B	HR	RBI	BB	SO
vs. Left	.167	.200	.208	24	4	1	0	0	1	1	7
vs. Right	.179	.179	.250	28	5	2	0	0	1	0	8
at Home	.176	.176	.235	34	6	2	0	0	2	0	12
on Road	.167	.211	.222	18	3	1	0	0	0	1	3
Bases Empty	.194	.219	.226	31	6	1	0	0	0	1	8
Runners On Base	.143	.143	.238	21	3	2	0	0	2	0	7

1-YEAR TOTALS (1991)

	BA	OBA	SA	AB	H	2B	3B	HR	RBI	BB	SO
	.167	.200	.208	24	4	1	0	0	1	1	7
	.179	.179	.250	28	5	2	0	0	1	0	8
	.176	.176	.235	34	6	2	0	0	2	0	12
	.167	.211	.222	18	3	1	0	0	0	1	3
	.194	.219	.226	31	6	1	0	0	0	1	8
	.143	.143	.238	21	3	2	0	0	2	0	7

CARMEN CASTILLO — bats right — throws right — age 34 — MIN — /OD

1991	BA	OBA	SA	AB	H	2B	3B	HR	RBI	BB	SO
vs. Left	.111	.111	.111	9	1	0	0	0	0	0	2
vs. Right	.333	.500	1.000	3	1	0	1	0	0	0	0
at Home	.333	.333	1.000	3	1	0	1	0	0	0	1
on Road	.111	.200	.111	9	1	0	0	0	0	0	1
Bases Empty	.286	.375	.571	7	2	0	1	0	0	0	1
Runners On Base	.000	.000	.000	5	0	0	0	0	0	0	1

8-YEAR TOTALS (1984–1991)

	BA	OBA	SA	AB	H	2B	3B	HR	RBI	BB	SO
	.266	.314	.455	880	234	42	5	38	127	61	168
	.236	.271	.379	483	114	23	2	14	56	19	100
	.292	.336	.498	644	188	42	5	27	103	44	117
	.223	.266	.364	719	160	23	2	25	80	36	151
	.259	.304	.458	725	188	38	5	32	32	42	145
	.251	.293	.393	638	160	27	2	20	151	38	123

DAVE CLARK — bats left — throws right — age 30 — KC/OD

1991	BA	OBA	SA	AB	H	2B	3B	HR	RBI	BB	SO
vs. Left	.000	.000	.000	0	0	0	0	0	0	0	0
vs. Right	.200	.273	.200	10	2	0	0	0	1	1	1
at Home	.400	.400	.400	5	2	0	0	0	1	0	0
on Road	.000	.167	.000	5	0	0	0	0	0	1	1
Bases Empty	.250	.400	.250	4	1	0	0	0	0	1	0
Runners On Base	.167	.167	.167	6	1	0	0	0	1	0	1

6-YEAR TOTALS (1986–1991)

	BA	OBA	SA	AB	H	2B	3B	HR	RBI	BB	SO
	.194	.231	.222	36	7	1	0	0	2	2	15
	.252	.312	.390	703	177	25	3	22	87	63	153
	.251	.308	.389	375	94	13	3	11	47	32	86
	.247	.308	.374	364	90	13	0	11	42	33	82
	.259	.311	.409	425	110	17	1	15	15	32	91
	.236	.304	.344	314	74	9	2	7	74	33	77

ROYCE CLAYTON — bats right — throws right — age 22 — SF — /S

1991	BA	OBA	SA	AB	H	2B	3B	HR	RBI	BB	SO
vs. Left	.200	.200	.200	5	1	0	0	0	0	0	1
vs. Right	.095	.136	.143	21	2	1	0	0	2	1	5
at Home	.154	.154	.154	13	2	0	0	0	2	0	4
on Road	.077	.143	.154	13	1	1	0	0	0	1	2
Bases Empty	.133	.188	.200	15	2	1	0	0	0	1	5
Runners On Base	.091	.091	.091	11	1	0	0	0	2	0	1

1-YEAR TOTALS (1991)

	BA	OBA	SA	AB	H	2B	3B	HR	RBI	BB	SO
	.200	.200	.200	5	1	0	0	0	0	0	1
	.095	.136	.143	21	2	1	0	0	2	1	5
	.154	.154	.154	13	2	0	0	0	2	0	4
	.077	.143	.154	13	1	1	0	0	0	1	2
	.133	.188	.200	15	2	1	0	0	0	1	5
	.091	.091	.091	11	1	0	0	0	2	0	1

DAVE COCHRANE — bats both — throws right — age 29 — SEA — OC3/1D

1991	BA	OBA	SA	AB	H	2B	3B	HR	RBI	BB	SO
vs. Left	.245	.302	.347	49	12	5	0	0	10	3	3
vs. Right	.248	.279	.357	129	32	8	0	2	12	6	35
at Home	.288	.346	.425	73	21	7	0	1	15	7	19
on Road	.219	.241	.305	105	23	6	0	1	7	2	19
Bases Empty	.175	.210	.202	114	20	3	0	0	5	5	28
Runners On Base	.375	.414	.625	64	24	10	0	2	22	4	10

4-YEAR TOTALS (1986–1991)

	BA	OBA	SA	AB	H	2B	3B	HR	RBI	BB	SO
	.198	.261	.255	106	21	6	0	0	12	8	21
	.242	.299	.371	256	62	13	1	6	19	20	74
	.250	.317	.400	180	45	10	1	5	23	18	55
	.209	.258	.275	182	38	9	0	1	8	10	40
	.199	.258	.274	226	45	6	1	3	3	17	61
	.279	.336	.441	136	38	13	0	3	28	11	34

STU COLE — bats right — throws right — age 26 — KC — /2DS

1991	BA	OBA	SA	AB	H	2B	3B	HR	RBI	BB	SO
vs. Left	.000	.000	.000	4	0	0	0	0	0	0	1
vs. Right	.333	.600	.333	3	1	0	0	0	0	2	1
at Home	.333	.600	.333	3	1	0	0	0	0	2	0
on Road	.000	.000	.000	4	0	0	0	0	0	0	2
Bases Empty	.000	.200	.000	4	0	0	0	0	0	1	1
Runners On Base	.333	.500	.333	3	1	0	0	0	0	1	1

1-YEAR TOTALS (1991)

	BA	OBA	SA	AB	H	2B	3B	HR	RBI	BB	SO
	.000	.000	.000	4	0	0	0	0	0	0	1
	.333	.600	.333	3	1	0	0	0	0	2	1
	.333	.600	.333	3	1	0	0	0	0	2	0
	.000	.000	.000	4	0	0	0	0	0	0	2
	.000	.200	.000	4	0	0	0	0	0	1	1
	.333	.500	.333	3	1	0	0	0	0	1	1

DARNELL COLES — bats right — throws right — age 30 — SF — /O1

1991	BA	OBA	SA	AB	H	2B	3B	HR	RBI	BB	SO
vs. Left	.429	.429	.429	7	3	0	0	0	0	0	1
vs. Right	.000	.000	.000	7	0	0	0	0	0	0	1
at Home	.333	.333	.333	9	3	0	0	0	0	0	1
on Road	.000	.000	.000	5	0	0	0	0	0	0	1
Bases Empty	.286	.286	.286	7	2	0	0	0	0	0	0
Runners On Base	.143	.143	.143	7	1	0	0	0	0	0	2

8-YEAR TOTALS (1984–1991)

	BA	OBA	SA	AB	H	2B	3B	HR	RBI	BB	SO
	.239	.312	.384	813	194	40	3	24	111	87	109
	.243	.302	.377	1348	328	61	7	35	174	98	229
	.259	.328	.413	1058	274	46	3	37	159	101	159
	.225	.284	.347	1103	248	55	7	22	126	84	179
	.240	.309	.377	1213	291	48	8	34	34	105	202
	.244	.301	.383	948	231	53	2	25	251	80	136

SCOTT COOLBAUGH — bats right — throws right — age 26 — SD — 3

1991	BA	OBA	SA	AB	H	2B	3B	HR	RBI	BB	SO
vs. Left	.235	.322	.373	51	12	4	0	1	7	7	11
vs. Right	.209	.282	.279	129	27	4	1	1	8	12	34
at Home	.236	.317	.360	89	21	8	0	1	10	10	24
on Road	.198	.270	.253	91	18	0	1	1	5	9	21
Bases Empty	.235	.322	.324	102	24	6	0	1	1	12	26
Runners On Base	.192	.256	.282	78	15	2	1	1	14	7	19

3-YEAR TOTALS (1989–1991)

	BA	OBA	SA	AB	H	2B	3B	HR	RBI	BB	SO
	.262	.338	.352	122	32	8	0	1	14	15	22
	.197	.260	.280	289	57	7	1	5	21	23	82
	.229	.290	.333	201	46	12	0	3	18	16	57
	.205	.279	.271	210	43	3	1	3	17	22	47
	.240	.315	.341	229	55	11	0	4	4	23	61
	.187	.245	.253	182	34	4	1	2	31	15	43

GARY COOPER — bats right — throws right — age 28 — HOU — /3

1991	BA	OBA	SA	AB	H	2B	3B	HR	RBI	BB	SO
vs. Left	.000	.400	.000	3	0	0	0	0	0	2	1
vs. Right	.308	.357	.385	13	4	1	0	0	2	1	5
at Home	.125	.222	.125	8	1	0	0	0	0	1	4
on Road	.375	.500	.500	8	3	1	0	0	2	2	2
Bases Empty	.100	.100	.100	10	1	0	0	0	0	0	3
Runners On Base	.500	.667	.667	6	3	1	0	0	2	3	3

1-YEAR TOTALS (1991)

BA	OBA	SA	AB	H	2B	3B	HR	RBI	BB	SO
.000	.400	.000	3	0	0	0	0	0	2	1
.308	.357	.385	13	4	1	0	0	2	1	5
.125	.222	.125	8	1	0	0	0	0	1	4
.375	.500	.500	8	3	1	0	0	2	2	2
.100	.100	.100	10	1	0	0	0	0	0	3
.500	.667	.667	6	3	1	0	0	2	3	3

SCOTT COOPER — bats left — throws right — age 25 — BOS — 3

1991	BA	OBA	SA	AB	H	2B	3B	HR	RBI	BB	SO
vs. Left	.667	.714	1.000	6	4	0	1	0	2	1	1
vs. Right	.414	.433	.621	29	12	4	1	0	5	1	1
at Home	.560	.577	.880	25	14	4	2	0	7	1	0
on Road	.200	.273	.200	10	2	0	0	0	0	1	2
Bases Empty	.417	.462	.625	24	10	3	1	0	0	2	2
Runners On Base	.545	.545	.818	11	6	1	1	0	7	0	0

2-YEAR TOTALS (1990–1991)

BA	OBA	SA	AB	H	2B	3B	HR	RBI	BB	SO
.667	.714	1.000	6	4	0	1	0	2	1	1
.400	.419	.600	30	12	4	1	0	5	1	2
.538	.556	.846	26	14	4	2	0	7	1	1
.200	.273	.200	10	2	0	0	0	0	1	2
.400	.444	.600	25	10	3	1	0	0	2	3
.545	.545	.818	11	6	1	1	0	7	0	0

JOEY CORA — bats both — throws right — age 27 — CHA — 2/SD

1991	BA	OBA	SA	AB	H	2B	3B	HR	RBI	BB	SO
vs. Left	.298	.365	.298	57	17	0	0	0	1	5	6
vs. Right	.222	.295	.269	171	38	2	3	0	17	15	15
at Home	.319	.394	.372	113	36	2	2	0	10	10	6
on Road	.165	.233	.183	115	19	0	1	0	8	10	15
Bases Empty	.225	.299	.261	142	32	1	2	0	0	13	15
Runners On Base	.267	.333	.302	86	23	1	1	0	18	7	6

4-YEAR TOTALS (1987–1991)

BA	OBA	SA	AB	H	2B	3B	HR	RBI	BB	SO
.269	.332	.291	182	49	2	1	0	6	16	18
.236	.308	.283	406	96	11	4	0	28	39	38
.269	.350	.307	283	76	7	2	0	17	31	25
.226	.282	.266	305	69	6	3	0	17	24	31
.246	.318	.285	382	94	9	3	0	0	37	39
.248	.312	.286	206	51	4	2	0	34	18	17

HENRY COTTO — bats right — throws right — age 31 — SEA — O/D

1991	BA	OBA	SA	AB	H	2B	3B	HR	RBI	BB	SO
vs. Left	.323	.359	.490	96	31	2	1	4	13	5	15
vs. Right	.284	.333	.432	81	23	4	1	2	10	5	12
at Home	.301	.366	.438	73	22	2	1	2	13	6	10
on Road	.308	.333	.481	104	32	4	1	2	10	4	17
Bases Empty	.307	.358	.377	114	35	2	0	2	2	7	21
Runners On Base	.302	.328	.619	63	19	4	2	4	21	3	6

8-YEAR TOTALS (1984–1991)

BA	OBA	SA	AB	H	2B	3B	HR	RBI	BB	SO
.264	.301	.374	845	223	30	6	17	85	43	132
.262	.308	.378	801	210	38	2	17	77	45	132
.265	.310	.382	822	218	31	4	19	87	46	120
.261	.299	.370	824	215	37	4	15	75	42	144
.252	.292	.349	959	242	41	2	16	16	47	162
.278	.321	.413	687	191	27	6	18	146	41	102

WARREN CROMARTIE — bats left — throws left — age 39 — KC — 1/OD

1991	BA	OBA	SA	AB	H	2B	3B	HR	RBI	BB	SO
vs. Left	.313	.353	.313	16	5	0	0	0	4	1	3
vs. Right	.313	.385	.435	115	36	7	2	1	16	14	15
at Home	.291	.352	.342	79	23	4	0	0	12	8	11
on Road	.346	.424	.538	52	18	3	2	1	8	7	7
Bases Empty	.303	.338	.395	76	23	5	1	0	0	4	13
Runners On Base	.327	.433	.455	55	18	2	1	1	20	11	5

1-YEAR TOTALS (1991)

BA	OBA	SA	AB	H	2B	3B	HR	RBI	BB	SO
.313	.353	.313	16	5	0	0	0	4	1	3
.313	.385	.435	115	36	7	2	1	16	14	15
.291	.352	.342	79	23	4	0	0	12	8	11
.346	.424	.538	52	18	3	2	1	8	7	7
.303	.338	.395	76	23	5	1	0	0	4	13
.327	.433	.455	55	18	2	1	1	20	11	5

CHRIS CRON — bats right — throws right — age 28 — CAL — /1D

1991	BA	OBA	SA	AB	H	2B	3B	HR	RBI	BB	SO
vs. Left	.250	.333	.250	8	2	0	0	0	0	1	2
vs. Right	.000	.125	.000	7	0	0	0	0	0	1	3
at Home	.000	.167	.000	5	0	0	0	0	0	1	2
on Road	.200	.273	.200	10	2	0	0	0	0	1	3
Bases Empty	.143	.333	.143	7	1	0	0	0	0	2	1
Runners On Base	.125	.125	.125	8	1	0	0	0	0	0	4

1-YEAR TOTALS (1991)

BA	OBA	SA	AB	H	2B	3B	HR	RBI	BB	SO
.250	.333	.250	8	2	0	0	0	0	1	2
.000	.125	.000	7	0	0	0	0	0	1	3
.000	.167	.000	5	0	0	0	0	0	1	2
.200	.273	.200	10	2	0	0	0	0	1	3
.143	.333	.143	7	1	0	0	0	0	2	1
.125	.125	.125	8	1	0	0	0	0	0	4

DOUG DASCENZO — bats both — throws left — age 28 — CHN — O/P

1991	BA	OBA	SA	AB	H	2B	3B	HR	RBI	BB	SO
vs. Left	.274	.319	.321	84	23	4	0	0	7	5	7
vs. Right	.245	.331	.310	155	38	7	0	1	11	19	19
at Home	.232	.309	.272	125	29	5	0	0	8	13	12
on Road	.281	.346	.360	114	32	6	0	1	10	11	14
Bases Empty	.266	.335	.343	143	38	8	0	1	1	14	19
Runners On Base	.240	.315	.271	96	23	3	0	0	17	10	7

4-YEAR TOTALS (1988–1991)

BA	OBA	SA	AB	H	2B	3B	HR	RBI	BB	SO
.271	.317	.332	295	80	15	0	1	34	20	23
.203	.288	.266	399	81	9	5	2	26	47	38
.245	.312	.304	359	88	12	3	1	30	34	28
.218	.288	.284	335	73	12	2	2	30	33	33
.221	.288	.282	447	99	18	3	1	1	41	42
.251	.320	.316	247	62	6	2	2	59	26	19

JACK DAUGHERTY — bats both — throws left — age 32 — TEX — O1/D

1991	BA	OBA	SA	AB	H	2B	3B	HR	RBI	BB	SO
vs. Left	.233	.324	.333	30	7	1	1	0	2	4	7
vs. Right	.184	.256	.246	114	21	2	1	1	9	12	16
at Home	.190	.282	.238	63	12	1	1	0	2	8	13
on Road	.198	.261	.284	81	16	2	1	1	9	8	10
Bases Empty	.216	.289	.318	88	19	2	2	1	1	9	12
Runners On Base	.161	.242	.179	56	9	1	0	0	10	7	11

4-YEAR TOTALS (1987–1991)

BA	OBA	SA	AB	H	2B	3B	HR	RBI	BB	SO
.267	.338	.359	131	35	5	2	1	15	13	32
.271	.323	.390	439	119	23	4	7	54	36	64
.281	.342	.417	295	83	14	4	6	34	25	48
.258	.310	.345	275	71	14	2	2	35	24	48
.284	.342	.383	334	95	13	4	4	4	28	56
.250	.306	.381	236	59	15	2	4	65	21	40

MARK DAVIDSON — bats right — throws right — age 31 — HOU — O

1991	BA	OBA	SA	AB	H	2B	3B	HR	RBI	BB	SO
vs. Left	.179	.271	.274	95	17	6	0	1	12	10	16
vs. Right	.213	.245	.277	47	10	0	0	1	3	2	12
at Home	.213	.267	.300	80	17	4	0	1	8	5	19
on Road	.161	.257	.242	62	10	2	0	1	7	7	9
Bases Empty	.187	.265	.240	75	14	5	0	1	1	7	12
Runners On Base	.194	.260	.313	67	13	5	0	1	14	5	16

6-YEAR TOTALS (1986–1991)

BA	OBA	SA	AB	H	2B	3B	HR	RBI	BB	SO
.229	.291	.314	459	105	21	3	4	41	38	83
.218	.286	.277	202	44	6	0	2	16	20	45
.226	.294	.291	327	74	14	2	1	23	31	63
.225	.284	.314	334	75	13	1	5	34	27	65
.232	.300	.303	396	92	12	2	4	4	36	76
.215	.274	.302	265	57	15	1	2	53	22	52

GLENN DAVIS — bats right — throws right — age 31 — BAL — 1D

1991	BA	OBA	SA	AB	H	2B	3B	HR	RBI	BB	SO
vs. Left	.255	.314	.638	47	12	3	0	5	7	3	7
vs. Right	.217	.304	.395	129	28	6	1	5	21	13	22
at Home	.247	.304	.438	73	18	3	1	3	7	4	12
on Road	.214	.308	.476	103	22	6	0	7	21	12	17
Bases Empty	.223	.298	.511	94	21	4	1	7	7	6	13
Runners On Base	.232	.316	.402	82	19	5	0	3	21	10	16

8-YEAR TOTALS (1984–1991)

BA	OBA	SA	AB	H	2B	3B	HR	RBI	BB	SO
.259	.348	.517	1063	275	58	2	71	192	133	140
.261	.328	.463	2145	560	101	9	105	354	193	379
.281	.353	.485	1599	450	87	7	75	262	161	252
.239	.317	.477	1609	385	72	4	101	284	165	267
.259	.315	.480	1749	453	81	7	97	97	111	285
.262	.357	.483	1459	382	78	4	79	449	215	234

MARK DAVIS — bats right — throws right — age 28 — CAL — /O

1991	BA	OBA	SA	AB	H	2B	3B	HR	RBI	BB	SO
vs. Left	.000	.000	.000	0	0	0	0	0	0	0	0
vs. Right	.000	.000	.000	2	0	0	0	0	0	0	0
at Home	.000	.000	.000	2	0	0	0	0	0	0	0
on Road	.000	.000	.000	0	0	0	0	0	0	0	0
Bases Empty	.000	.000	.000	1	0	0	0	0	0	0	0
Runners On Base	.000	.000	.000	1	0	0	0	0	0	0	0

1-YEAR TOTALS (1991)

BA	OBA	SA	AB	H	2B	3B	HR	RBI	BB	SO
.000	.000	.000	0	0	0	0	0	0	0	0
.000	.000	.000	2	0	0	0	0	0	0	0
.000	.000	.000	2	0	0	0	0	0	0	0
.000	.000	.000	0	0	0	0	0	0	0	0
.000	.000	.000	1	0	0	0	0	0	0	0
.000	.000	.000	1	0	0	0	0	0	0	0

BUTCH DAVIS — bats right — throws right — age 34 — LA

1991	BA	OBA	SA	AB	H	2B	3B	HR	RBI	BB	SO
vs. Left	.000	.000	.000	0	0	0	0	0	0	0	0
vs. Right	.000	.000	.000	1	0	0	0	0	0	0	0
at Home	.000	.000	.000	1	0	0	0	0	0	0	0
on Road	.000	.000	.000	0	0	0	0	0	0	0	0
Bases Empty	.000	.000	.000	1	0	0	0	0	0	0	0
Runners On Base	.000	.000	.000	0	0	0	0	0	0	0	0

5-YEAR TOTALS (1984–1991)

BA	OBA	SA	AB	H	2B	3B	HR	RBI	BB	SO
.146	.174	.233	103	15	3	0	2	7	4	20
.192	.288	.250	52	10	3	0	0	5	7	13
.237	.298	.329	76	18	4	0	1	8	7	9
.089	.131	.152	79	7	2	0	1	4	4	24
.148	.207	.259	81	12	3	0	2	2	6	21
.176	.222	.216	74	13	3	0	0	10	5	12

LUIS De Los SANTOS — bats right — throws right — age 26 — DET — /DO13

1991	BA	OBA	SA	AB	H	2B	3B	HR	RBI	BB	SO
vs. Left	.167	.200	.250	24	4	2	0	0	0	1	2
vs. Right	.167	.286	.167	6	1	0	0	0	0	1	2
at Home	.100	.100	.100	10	1	0	0	0	0	0	1
on Road	.200	.273	.300	20	4	2	0	0	0	2	3
Bases Empty	.190	.261	.238	21	4	1	0	0	0	2	3
Runners On Base	.111	.111	.222	9	1	1	0	0	0	0	1

3-YEAR TOTALS (1988–1991)

BA	OBA	SA	AB	H	2B	3B	HR	RBI	BB	SO
.234	.289	.325	77	18	5	1	0	6	6	10
.177	.250	.226	62	11	1	1	0	1	6	12
.158	.238	.228	57	9	2	1	0	3	6	7
.244	.295	.317	82	20	4	1	0	4	6	15
.253	.317	.333	75	19	4	1	0	0	7	13
.156	.217	.219	64	10	2	1	0	7	5	9

RICK DEMPSEY — bats right — throws right — age 43 — MIL — C/P1

1991	BA	OBA	SA	AB	H	2B	3B	HR	RBI	BB	SO
vs. Left	.237	.330	.371	97	23	4	0	3	15	15	14
vs. Right	.220	.328	.300	50	11	1	0	1	6	8	6
at Home	.260	.364	.384	73	19	3	0	2	13	13	12
on Road	.203	.294	.311	74	15	2	0	2	8	10	8
Bases Empty	.195	.305	.220	82	16	2	0	0	0	13	10
Runners On Base	.277	.359	.508	65	18	3	0	4	21	10	10

8-YEAR TOTALS (1984–1991)

BA	OBA	SA	AB	H	2B	3B	HR	RBI	BB	SO
.241	.345	.406	849	205	48	1	30	122	137	167
.204	.300	.324	904	184	37	0	24	84	122	215
.225	.326	.368	827	186	37	0	27	108	126	189
.219	.318	.361	926	203	48	1	27	98	133	193
.223	.332	.367	965	215	44	1	31	31	153	211
.221	.310	.360	788	174	41	0	23	175	106	171

MARIO DIAZ — bats right — throws right — age 30 — TEX — S2/3

1991	BA	OBA	SA	AB	H	2B	3B	HR	RBI	BB	SO
vs. Left	.268	.333	.329	82	22	5	0	0	12	8	6
vs. Right	.260	.306	.310	100	26	2	0	1	10	7	12
at Home	.269	.333	.359	78	21	4	0	1	11	8	6
on Road	.260	.306	.288	104	27	3	0	0	11	7	12
Bases Empty	.225	.288	.294	102	23	4	0	1	1	9	12
Runners On Base	.313	.356	.350	80	25	3	0	0	21	6	6

5-YEAR TOTALS (1987–1991)

BA	OBA	SA	AB	H	2B	3B	HR	RBI	BB	SO
.234	.290	.275	171	40	7	0	0	18	14	18
.248	.284	.317	202	50	6	1	2	24	11	19
.216	.271	.284	162	35	6	1	1	15	13	15
.261	.299	.308	211	55	7	0	1	27	12	22
.218	.275	.277	206	45	7	1	1	1	16	24
.269	.302	.323	167	45	6	0	1	41	9	13

GARY DiSARCINA — bats right — throws right — age 25 — CAL — S/23

1991	BA	OBA	SA	AB	H	2B	3B	HR	RBI	BB	SO
vs. Left	.222	.222	.278	18	4	1	0	0	1	0	1
vs. Right	.205	.295	.231	39	8	1	0	0	2	3	3
at Home	.148	.258	.185	27	4	1	0	0	0	2	2
on Road	.267	.290	.300	30	8	1	0	0	3	1	2
Bases Empty	.200	.220	.250	40	8	2	0	0	0	1	3
Runners On Base	.235	.381	.235	17	4	0	0	0	3	2	1

2-YEAR TOTALS (1990–1991)

BA	OBA	SA	AB	H	2B	3B	HR	RBI	BB	SO
.133	.161	.167	30	4	1	0	0	1	1	2
.190	.253	.238	84	16	2	1	0	2	5	12
.094	.186	.113	53	5	1	0	0	0	4	6
.246	.270	.311	61	15	2	1	0	3	2	8
.176	.208	.243	74	13	3	1	0	0	3	8
.175	.267	.175	40	7	0	0	0	3	3	6

CHRIS DONNELS — bats left — throws right — age 26 — NYN — 13

1991	BA	OBA	SA	AB	H	2B	3B	HR	RBI	BB	SO
vs. Left	.281	.378	.281	32	9	0	0	0	2	5	6
vs. Right	.193	.303	.228	57	11	2	0	0	3	9	13
at Home	.211	.318	.211	38	8	0	0	0	1	6	10
on Road	.235	.339	.275	51	12	2	0	0	4	8	9
Bases Empty	.234	.357	.255	47	11	1	0	0	0	9	8
Runners On Base	.214	.298	.238	42	9	1	0	0	5	5	11

1-YEAR TOTALS (1991)

BA	OBA	SA	AB	H	2B	3B	HR	RBI	BB	SO
.281	.378	.281	32	9	0	0	0	2	5	6
.193	.303	.228	57	11	2	0	0	3	9	13
.211	.318	.211	38	8	0	0	0	1	6	10
.235	.339	.275	51	12	2	0	0	4	8	9
.234	.357	.255	47	11	1	0	0	0	9	8
.214	.298	.238	42	9	1	0	0	5	5	11

BRIAN DORSETT — bats right — throws right — age 31 — SD — /1

1991	BA	OBA	SA	AB	H	2B	3B	HR	RBI	BB	SO
vs. Left	.167	.167	.167	6	1	0	0	0	1	0	0
vs. Right	.000	.000	.000	6	0	0	0	0	0	0	3
at Home	.250	.250	.250	4	1	0	0	0	1	0	0
on Road	.000	.000	.000	8	0	0	0	0	0	0	3
Bases Empty	.000	.000	.000	5	0	0	0	0	0	0	1
Runners On Base	.143	.143	.143	7	1	0	0	0	1	0	2

5-YEAR TOTALS (1987–1991)

BA	OBA	SA	AB	H	2B	3B	HR	RBI	BB	SO
.152	.176	.182	33	5	1	0	0	1	0	3
.224	.274	.310	58	13	2	0	1	9	4	15
.289	.333	.422	45	13	3	0	1	6	2	5
.109	.146	.109	46	5	0	0	0	4	2	13
.136	.208	.182	44	6	2	0	0	0	3	11
.255	.271	.340	47	12	1	0	1	10	1	7

ROB DUCEY — bats left — throws right — age 27 — TOR — O/D

1991	BA	OBA	SA	AB	H	2B	3B	HR	RBI	BB	SO
vs. Left	.333	.385	.750	12	4	0	1	1	2	1	5
vs. Right	.214	.279	.286	56	12	2	1	0	2	5	21
at Home	.242	.265	.303	33	8	0	1	0	2	1	14
on Road	.229	.325	.429	35	8	2	1	1	2	5	12
Bases Empty	.281	.378	.500	32	9	2	1	1	1	5	12
Runners On Base	.194	.216	.250	36	7	0	1	0	3	1	14

5-YEAR TOTALS (1987–1991)

	BA	OBA	SA	AB	H	2B	3B	HR	RBI	BB	SO
	.284	.348	.407	81	23	2	1	2	11	8	23
	.234	.316	.317	218	51	14	2	0	19	27	60
	.232	.322	.318	151	35	6	2	1	16	20	40
	.264	.327	.365	148	39	10	1	1	14	15	43
	.230	.307	.323	161	37	8	2	1	1	18	45
	.268	.344	.362	138	37	8	1	1	29	17	38

JIM EISENREICH — bats left — throws left — age 33 — KC — *O1/D

1991	BA	OBA	SA	AB	H	2B	3B	HR	RBI	BB	SO
vs. Left	.322	.351	.402	87	28	2	1	1	16	4	12
vs. Right	.295	.328	.389	288	85	20	2	1	31	16	23
at Home	.311	.337	.409	193	60	9	2	2	25	9	14
on Road	.291	.330	.374	182	53	13	1	0	22	11	21
Bases Empty	.299	.329	.397	204	61	15	1	1	1	8	21
Runners On Base	.304	.339	.386	171	52	7	2	1	46	12	14

6-YEAR TOTALS (1984–1991)

	BA	OBA	SA	AB	H	2B	3B	HR	RBI	BB	SO
	.289	.320	.379	388	112	17	3	4	52	19	46
	.274	.320	.404	1297	355	84	17	17	148	95	132
	.281	.327	.416	836	235	50	15	11	112	63	76
	.273	.312	.380	849	232	51	5	10	88	51	102
	.269	.308	.394	954	257	63	13	10	10	52	101
	.287	.334	.404	731	210	38	7	11	190	62	77

JOSE ESCOBAR — bats right — throws right — age 32 — CLE — /S23

1991	BA	OBA	SA	AB	H	2B	3B	HR	RBI	BB	SO
vs. Left	.143	.250	.143	7	1	0	0	0	0	1	2
vs. Right	.250	.250	.250	8	2	0	0	0	1	0	2
at Home	.167	.167	.167	12	2	0	0	0	1	0	4
on Road	.333	.500	.333	3	1	0	0	0	0	1	0
Bases Empty	.182	.182	.182	11	2	0	0	0	0	0	3
Runners On Base	.250	.400	.250	4	1	0	0	0	1	1	1

1-YEAR TOTALS (1991)

	BA	OBA	SA	AB	H	2B	3B	HR	RBI	BB	SO
	.143	.250	.143	7	1	0	0	0	0	1	2
	.250	.250	.250	8	2	0	0	0	1	0	2
	.167	.167	.167	12	2	0	0	0	1	0	4
	.333	.500	.333	3	1	0	0	0	0	1	0
	.182	.182	.182	11	2	0	0	0	0	0	3
	.250	.400	.250	4	1	0	0	0	1	1	1

CECIL ESPY — bats both — throws right — age 29 — PIT — O

1991	BA	OBA	SA	AB	H	2B	3B	HR	RBI	BB	SO
vs. Left	.188	.188	.188	16	3	0	0	0	1	0	3
vs. Right	.258	.301	.364	66	17	4	0	1	10	5	14
at Home	.245	.263	.358	53	13	3	0	1	9	2	10
on Road	.241	.313	.276	29	7	1	0	0	2	3	7
Bases Empty	.216	.286	.275	51	11	3	0	0	0	5	11
Runners On Base	.290	.273	.419	31	9	1	0	1	11	0	6

5-YEAR TOTALS (1987–1991)

	BA	OBA	SA	AB	H	2B	3B	HR	RBI	BB	SO
	.254	.297	.360	197	50	7	1	4	21	13	44
	.238	.294	.309	786	187	26	12	2	61	61	178
	.267	.306	.374	479	128	16	10	5	45	28	105
	.216	.284	.268	504	109	17	3	1	37	46	117
	.238	.301	.326	601	143	22	11	3	3	51	138
	.246	.285	.309	382	94	11	2	3	79	23	84

TONY EUSEBIO — bats right — throws right — age 25 — HOU — /C

1991	BA	OBA	SA	AB	H	2B	3B	HR	RBI	BB	SO
vs. Left	.111	.111	.111	9	1	0	0	0	0	0	5
vs. Right	.100	.438	.200	10	1	1	0	0	6	6	3
at Home	.125	.364	.125	8	1	0	0	0	0	3	3
on Road	.091	.286	.182	11	1	1	0	0	0	3	5
Bases Empty	.167	.231	.250	12	2	1	0	0	0	1	5
Runners On Base	.000	.417	.000	7	0	0	0	0	0	5	3

1-YEAR TOTALS (1991)

	BA	OBA	SA	AB	H	2B	3B	HR	RBI	BB	SO
	.111	.111	.111	9	1	0	0	0	0	0	5
	.100	.438	.200	10	1	1	0	0	0	6	3
	.125	.364	.125	8	1	0	0	0	0	3	3
	.091	.286	.182	11	1	1	0	0	0	3	5
	.167	.231	.250	12	2	1	0	0	0	1	5
	.000	.417	.000	7	0	0	0	0	0	5	3

PAUL FARIES — bats right — throws right — age 27 — SD — 23/S

1991	BA	OBA	SA	AB	H	2B	3B	HR	RBI	BB	SO
vs. Left	.239	.300	.304	46	11	3	0	0	1	4	2
vs. Right	.143	.242	.167	84	12	0	1	0	6	10	19
at Home	.250	.302	.375	40	10	3	1	0	5	3	5
on Road	.144	.245	.144	90	13	0	0	0	2	11	16
Bases Empty	.095	.193	.108	74	7	1	0	0	0	9	14
Runners On Base	.286	.355	.357	56	16	2	1	0	7	5	7

2-YEAR TOTALS (1990–1991)

	BA	OBA	SA	AB	H	2B	3B	HR	RBI	BB	SO
	.267	.318	.333	60	16	4	0	0	3	5	3
	.131	.238	.150	107	14	0	1	0	6	13	25
	.237	.281	.339	59	14	4	1	0	6	3	8
	.148	.258	.148	108	16	0	0	0	3	15	20
	.139	.216	.158	101	14	2	0	0	0	10	20
	.242	.338	.303	66	16	2	1	0	9	8	8

MONTY FARISS — bats right — throws right — age 25 — TEX — /O2D

1991	BA	OBA	SA	AB	H	2B	3B	HR	RBI	BB	SO
vs. Left	.261	.414	.391	23	6	0	0	1	3	6	8
vs. Right	.250	.333	.375	8	2	1	0	0	3	1	3
at Home	.300	.333	.500	20	6	1	0	1	4	1	7
on Road	.182	.471	.182	11	2	0	0	0	2	6	4
Bases Empty	.261	.370	.391	23	6	0	0	1	1	4	8
Runners On Base	.250	.455	.375	8	2	1	0	0	5	3	3

1-YEAR TOTALS (1991)

	BA	OBA	SA	AB	H	2B	3B	HR	RBI	BB	SO
	.261	.414	.391	23	6	0	0	1	3	6	8
	.250	.333	.375	8	2	1	0	0	3	1	3
	.300	.333	.500	20	6	1	0	1	4	1	7
	.182	.471	.182	11	2	0	0	0	2	6	4
	.261	.370	.391	23	6	0	0	1	1	4	8
	.250	.455	.375	8	2	1	0	0	5	3	3

JUNIOR FELIX — bats both — throws right — age 25 — CAL — O

1991	BA	OBA	SA	AB	H	2B	3B	HR	RBI	BB	SO
vs. Left	.291	.286	.382	55	16	3	1	0	9	0	17
vs. Right	.280	.332	.366	175	49	7	1	2	17	11	38
at Home	.305	.351	.400	105	32	2	1	2	11	6	20
on Road	.264	.295	.344	125	33	8	1	0	15	5	35
Bases Empty	.285	.331	.392	130	37	6	1	2	2	8	37
Runners On Base	.280	.308	.340	100	28	4	1	0	24	3	18

3-YEAR TOTALS (1989–1991)

	BA	OBA	SA	AB	H	2B	3B	HR	RBI	BB	SO
	.220	.286	.387	336	74	15	4	11	46	30	97
	.285	.338	.418	772	220	32	13	15	91	59	158
	.259	.326	.415	540	140	19	13	13	56	50	112
	.271	.318	.403	568	154	28	4	13	81	39	143
	.268	.328	.421	649	174	28	13	15	15	56	159
	.261	.313	.392	459	120	19	4	11	122	33	96

MIKE FITZGERALD — bats right — throws right — age 32 — MON — C/1O

1991	BA	OBA	SA	AB	H	2B	3B	HR	RBI	BB	SO
vs. Left	.224	.295	.388	85	19	3	1	3	19	9	13
vs. Right	.186	.266	.248	113	21	2	1	1	9	13	22
at Home	.141	.187	.212	85	12	1	1	1	8	5	13
on Road	.248	.341	.381	113	28	4	1	3	20	17	22
Bases Empty	.185	.248	.252	119	22	3	1	1	1	10	21
Runners On Base	.228	.319	.392	79	18	2	1	3	27	12	14

8-YEAR TOTALS (1984–1991)

	BA	OBA	SA	AB	H	2B	3B	HR	RBI	BB	SO
	.234	.329	.332	819	192	27	4	15	97	117	142
	.242	.321	.361	1287	311	66	5	26	176	150	250
	.230	.311	.329	1037	238	41	7	16	123	121	195
	.248	.337	.361	1069	265	52	2	25	150	146	197
	.223	.297	.325	1186	265	45	6	22	22	121	236
	.259	.356	.382	920	238	48	4	19	251	146	156

DARRIN FLETCHER — bats left — throws right — age 26 — PHI — C

1991	BA	OBA	SA	AB	H	2B	3B	HR	RBI	BB	SO
vs. Left	.286	.286	.381	21	6	2	0	0	4	0	6
vs. Right	.217	.250	.296	115	25	6	0	0	8	5	9
at Home	.237	.262	.339	59	14	3	0	1	5	2	7
on Road	.221	.250	.286	77	17	5	0	0	7	3	8
Bases Empty	.190	.200	.241	79	15	4	0	0	0	1	8
Runners On Base	.281	.328	.404	57	16	4	0	1	12	4	7

3-YEAR TOTALS (1989–1991)

	BA	OBA	SA	AB	H	2B	3B	HR	RBI	BB	SO
	.280	.280	.360	25	7	2	0	0	4	0	6
	.218	.255	.310	142	31	7	0	2	11	7	15
	.216	.247	.338	74	16	3	0	2	6	3	11
	.237	.268	.301	93	22	6	0	0	9	4	10
	.194	.210	.276	98	19	5	0	1	1	2	10
	.275	.324	.377	69	19	4	0	1	14	5	11

KEVIN FLORA — bats right — throws right — age 23 — CAL — /2

1991	BA	OBA	SA	AB	H	2B	3B	HR	RBI	BB	SO
vs. Left	.000	.000	.000	1	0	0	0	0	0	0	1
vs. Right	.143	.250	.143	7	1	0	0	0	0	1	4
at Home	.000	.000	.000	0	0	0	0	0	0	0	0
on Road	.125	.222	.125	8	1	0	0	0	0	1	5
Bases Empty	.167	.286	.167	6	1	0	0	0	0	1	5
Runners On Base	.000	.000	.000	2	0	0	0	0	0	0	0

1-YEAR TOTALS (1991)

	BA	OBA	SA	AB	H	2B	3B	HR	RBI	BB	SO
	.000	.000	.000	1	0	0	0	0	0	0	1
	.143	.250	.143	7	1	0	0	0	0	1	4
	.000	.000	.000	0	0	0	0	0	0	0	0
	.125	.222	.125	8	1	0	0	0	0	1	5
	.167	.286	.167	6	1	0	0	0	0	1	5
	.000	.000	.000	2	0	0	0	0	0	0	0

TOM FOLEY — bats left — throws right — age 33 — MON — S1/32

1991	BA	OBA	SA	AB	H	2B	3B	HR	RBI	BB	SO
vs. Left	.150	.217	.200	20	3	1	0	0	2	1	5
vs. Right	.216	.276	.297	148	32	10	1	0	13	13	26
at Home	.188	.280	.262	80	15	6	0	0	4	11	14
on Road	.227	.258	.307	88	20	5	1	0	11	3	17
Bases Empty	.204	.241	.291	103	21	9	0	0	0	5	18
Runners On Base	.215	.308	.277	65	14	2	1	0	15	9	13

8-YEAR TOTALS (1984–1991)

	BA	OBA	SA	AB	H	2B	3B	HR	RBI	BB	SO
	.227	.265	.258	233	53	5	1	0	14	12	49
	.252	.313	.362	1921	484	102	16	26	196	173	253
	.251	.313	.366	1036	260	56	9	15	93	94	146
	.248	.304	.337	1118	277	51	8	11	117	91	156
	.247	.301	.341	1271	314	64	7	14	14	94	171
	.253	.318	.365	883	223	43	10	12	196	91	131

CARLOS GARCIA — bats right — throws right — age 25 — PIT — /S32

1991	BA	OBA	SA	AB	H	2B	3B	HR	RBI	BB	SO
vs. Left	.400	.500	1.200	5	2	0	2	0	1	1	2
vs. Right	.211	.211	.211	19	4	0	0	0	0	0	6
at Home	.286	.286	.571	7	2	0	1	0	1	0	1
on Road	.235	.278	.353	17	4	0	1	0	0	1	7
Bases Empty	.250	.250	.417	12	3	0	1	0	0	0	4
Runners On Base	.250	.308	.417	12	3	0	1	0	1	1	4

2-YEAR TOTALS (1990–1991)

	BA	OBA	SA	AB	H	2B	3B	HR	RBI	BB	SO
	.429	.500	1.000	7	3	0	2	0	1	1	3
	.238	.238	.238	21	5	0	0	0	0	0	7
	.300	.300	.500	10	3	0	1	0	1	0	3
	.278	.316	.389	18	5	0	1	0	0	1	7
	.286	.286	.429	14	4	0	1	0	0	0	5
	.286	.333	.429	14	4	0	1	0	1	1	5

JEFF GARDNER — bats left — throws right — age 28 — NYN — /S2

1991	BA	OBA	SA	AB	H	2B	3B	HR	RBI	BB	SO
vs. Left	.000	.000	.000	7	0	0	0	0	0	0	2
vs. Right	.200	.286	.200	30	6	0	0	0	1	4	4
at Home	.182	.269	.182	22	4	0	0	0	1	3	4
on Road	.133	.188	.133	15	2	0	0	0	0	1	2
Bases Empty	.111	.200	.111	27	3	0	0	0	0	3	5
Runners On Base	.300	.333	.300	10	3	0	0	0	1	1	1

1-YEAR TOTALS (1991)

	BA	OBA	SA	AB	H	2B	3B	HR	RBI	BB	SO
	.000	.000	.000	7	0	0	0	0	0	0	2
	.200	.286	.200	30	6	0	0	0	1	4	4
	.182	.269	.182	22	4	0	0	0	1	3	4
	.133	.188	.133	15	2	0	0	0	0	1	2
	.111	.200	.111	27	3	0	0	0	0	3	5
	.300	.333	.300	10	3	0	0	0	1	1	1

RICH GEDMAN — bats left — throws right — age 33 — SL — C

1991	BA	OBA	SA	AB	H	2B	3B	HR	RBI	BB	SO
vs. Left	.000	.091	.000	10	0	0	0	0	1	1	3
vs. Right	.119	.146	.238	84	10	1	0	3	7	3	12
at Home	.064	.132	.128	47	3	0	0	1	3	4	8
on Road	.149	.149	.298	47	7	1	0	2	5	0	7
Bases Empty	.092	.119	.185	65	6	0	0	2	2	2	9
Runners On Base	.138	.182	.276	29	4	1	0	1	6	2	6

8-YEAR TOTALS (1984–1991)

	BA	OBA	SA	AB	H	2B	3B	HR	RBI	BB	SO
	.228	.278	.352	435	99	20	2	10	72	27	87
	.252	.311	.418	1896	477	104	7	66	231	164	290
	.263	.322	.427	1135	298	67	6	36	171	101	168
	.232	.287	.385	1196	278	57	3	40	132	90	209
	.239	.286	.401	1308	313	53	4	50	50	76	219
	.257	.327	.413	1023	263	71	5	26	253	115	158

BOB GEREN — bats right — throws right — age 31 — NYA — C

1991	BA	OBA	SA	AB	H	2B	3B	HR	RBI	BB	SO
vs. Left	.257	.304	.333	105	27	2	0	2	11	7	21
vs. Right	.043	.120	.087	23	1	1	0	0	1	2	10
at Home	.138	.185	.195	87	12	2	0	1	5	5	22
on Road	.390	.444	.488	41	16	1	0	1	7	4	9
Bases Empty	.171	.203	.211	76	13	0	0	1	1	3	21
Runners On Base	.288	.362	.404	52	15	3	0	1	11	6	10

4-YEAR TOTALS (1988–1991)

	BA	OBA	SA	AB	H	2B	3B	HR	RBI	BB	SO
	.258	.308	.375	291	75	10	0	8	31	19	55
	.219	.263	.340	329	72	5	1	11	39	17	96
	.226	.261	.335	337	76	10	0	9	32	15	84
	.251	.311	.382	283	71	5	1	10	38	21	67
	.219	.275	.316	351	77	5	1	9	9	22	94
	.260	.296	.409	269	70	10	1	10	61	14	57

RAY GIANNELLI — bats left — throws right — age 26 — TOR — /3

1991	BA	OBA	SA	AB	H	2B	3B	HR	RBI	BB	SO
vs. Left	.500	.500	.500	2	1	0	0	0	0	0	0
vs. Right	.136	.296	.182	22	3	1	0	0	0	5	9
at Home	.188	.350	.250	16	3	1	0	0	0	4	5
on Road	.125	.222	.125	8	1	0	0	0	0	1	4
Bases Empty	.071	.188	.143	14	1	1	0	0	0	2	4
Runners On Base	.300	.462	.300	10	3	0	0	0	0	3	5

1-YEAR TOTALS (1991)

	BA	OBA	SA	AB	H	2B	3B	HR	RBI	BB	SO
	.500	.500	.500	2	1	0	0	0	0	0	0
	.136	.296	.182	22	3	1	0	0	0	5	9
	.188	.350	.250	16	3	1	0	0	0	4	5
	.125	.222	.125	8	1	0	0	0	0	1	4
	.071	.188	.143	14	1	1	0	0	0	2	4
	.300	.462	.300	10	3	0	0	0	0	3	5

JOE GIRARDI — bats right — throws right — age 28 — CHN — C

1991	BA	OBA	SA	AB	H	2B	3B	HR	RBI	BB	SO
vs. Left	.229	.325	.286	35	8	2	0	0	6	5	3
vs. Right	.083	.154	.083	12	1	0	0	0	0	1	3
at Home	.182	.270	.212	33	6	1	0	0	6	4	3
on Road	.214	.313	.286	14	3	1	0	0	0	2	3
Bases Empty	.194	.265	.258	31	6	2	0	0	0	3	5
Runners On Base	.188	.316	.188	16	3	0	0	0	6	3	1

3-YEAR TOTALS (1989–1991)

	BA	OBA	SA	AB	H	2B	3B	HR	RBI	BB	SO
	.286	.315	.400	220	63	20	1	1	27	10	21
	.243	.292	.295	403	98	16	1	1	31	24	61
	.262	.308	.323	313	82	14	1	1	39	20	39
	.255	.292	.342	310	79	22	1	1	19	14	43
	.245	.273	.320	359	88	22	1	1	1	11	46
	.277	.333	.348	264	73	14	1	1	57	23	36

RENE GONZALES — bats right — throws right — age 32 — TOR — S32/1

1991	BA	OBA	SA	AB	H	2B	3B	HR	RBI	BB	SO
vs. Left	.212	.366	.242	33	7	1	0	0	2	7	6
vs. Right	.188	.255	.247	85	16	2	0	1	4	5	16
at Home	.250	.412	.375	40	10	2	0	1	3	9	5
on Road	.167	.214	.179	78	13	1	0	0	3	3	17
Bases Empty	.242	.333	.288	66	16	0	0	1	1	7	13
Runners On Base	.135	.233	.192	52	7	3	0	0	5	5	9

7-YEAR TOTALS (1984–1991)

	BA	OBA	SA	AB	H	2B	3B	HR	RBI	BB	SO
	.238	.324	.298	252	60	8	2	1	21	31	40
	.201	.248	.254	488	98	11	0	5	32	25	81
	.226	.302	.303	340	77	12	1	4	23	32	58
	.203	.251	.240	400	81	7	1	2	30	24	63
	.203	.262	.260	438	89	7	0	6	6	31	73
	.228	.293	.281	302	69	12	2	0	47	25	48

JOSE GONZALEZ — bats right — throws right — age 28 — LA/PIT/CLE — O

1991	BA	OBA	SA	AB	H	2B	3B	HR	RBI	BB	SO
vs. Left	.059	.145	.103	68	4	1	1	0	2	6	20
vs. Right	.184	.286	.327	49	9	1	0	2	5	7	22
at Home	.179	.242	.304	56	10	2	1	1	4	4	16
on Road	.049	.171	.098	61	3	0	0	1	3	9	26
Bases Empty	.086	.220	.100	70	6	1	0	0	0	11	22
Runners On Base	.149	.180	.340	47	7	1	1	2	7	2	20

7-YEAR TOTALS (1985–1991)

	BA	OBA	SA	AB	H	2B	3B	HR	RBI	BB	SO
	.227	.281	.328	357	81	16	4	4	22	26	81
	.200	.273	.325	265	53	12	3	5	18	27	85
	.220	.291	.344	282	62	13	2	6	20	27	72
	.212	.266	.312	340	72	15	5	3	20	26	94
	.224	.289	.339	389	87	17	5	6	6	34	100
	.202	.258	.305	233	47	11	2	3	34	19	66

TOM GOODWIN — bats left — throws right — age 24 — LA — /O

1991	BA	OBA	SA	AB	H	2B	3B	HR	RBI	BB	SO
vs. Left	.000	.000	.000	2	0	0	0	0	0	0	0
vs. Right	.200	.200	.200	5	1	0	0	0	0	0	0
at Home	1.000	1.000	1.000	1	1	0	0	0	0	0	0
on Road	.000	.000	.000	6	0	0	0	0	0	0	0
Bases Empty	.250	.250	.250	4	1	0	0	0	0	0	0
Runners On Base	.000	.000	.000	3	0	0	0	0	0	0	0

1-YEAR TOTALS (1991)

	BA	OBA	SA	AB	H	2B	3B	HR	RBI	BB	SO
	.000	.000	.000	2	0	0	0	0	0	0	0
	.200	.200	.200	5	1	0	0	0	0	0	0
	1.000	1.000	1.000	1	1	0	0	0	0	0	0
	.000	.000	.000	6	0	0	0	0	0	0	0
	.250	.250	.250	4	1	0	0	0	0	0	0
	.000	.000	.000	3	0	0	0	0	0	0	0

CRAIG GREBECK — bats right — throws right — age 28 — CHA — 32S

1991	BA	OBA	SA	AB	H	2B	3B	HR	RBI	BB	SO
vs. Left	.304	.404	.539	115	35	8	2	5	21	20	22
vs. Right	.257	.367	.376	109	28	8	1	1	10	18	18
at Home	.294	.395	.450	109	32	8	0	3	12	19	19
on Road	.270	.378	.470	115	31	8	3	3	19	19	21
Bases Empty	.286	.379	.443	140	40	8	1	4	4	21	25
Runners On Base	.274	.398	.488	84	23	8	2	2	27	17	15

2-YEAR TOTALS (1990–1991)

	BA	OBA	SA	AB	H	2B	3B	HR	RBI	BB	SO
	.236	.319	.394	203	48	11	3	5	25	26	40
	.250	.354	.364	140	35	8	1	2	15	20	24
	.253	.332	.386	166	42	8	1	4	18	21	32
	.232	.335	.379	177	41	11	3	3	22	25	32
	.242	.322	.361	219	53	10	2	4	4	25	44
	.242	.351	.419	124	30	9	2	3	36	21	20

GARY GREEN — bats right — throws right — age 30 — TEX — /S

1991	BA	OBA	SA	AB	H	2B	3B	HR	RBI	BB	SO
vs. Left	.077	.143	.077	13	1	0	0	0	0	1	5
vs. Right	.286	.286	.429	7	2	1	0	0	1	0	1
at Home	.167	.167	.250	12	2	1	0	0	1	0	3
on Road	.125	.222	.125	8	1	0	0	0	0	1	3
Bases Empty	.182	.250	.182	11	2	0	0	0	0	1	4
Runners On Base	.111	.111	.222	9	1	1	0	0	1	0	2

4-YEAR TOTALS (1986–1991)

	BA	OBA	SA	AB	H	2B	3B	HR	RBI	BB	SO
	.215	.259	.266	79	17	4	0	0	3	5	15
	.213	.247	.258	89	19	4	0	0	8	4	21
	.239	.264	.307	88	21	6	0	0	8	3	16
	.188	.241	.213	80	15	2	0	0	3	6	20
	.231	.273	.269	104	24	4	0	0	0	6	24
	.188	.221	.250	64	12	4	0	0	11	3	12

TOMMY GREGG — bats left — throws left — age 29 — ATL — O1

1991	BA	OBA	SA	AB	H	2B	3B	HR	RBI	BB	SO
vs. Left	.000	.000	.000	5	0	0	0	0	0	0	4
vs. Right	.196	.287	.324	102	20	8	1	1	4	12	20
at Home	.161	.212	.290	62	10	3	1	1	3	3	12
on Road	.222	.352	.333	45	10	5	0	0	1	9	12
Bases Empty	.246	.317	.386	57	14	6	1	0	0	6	15
Runners On Base	.120	.228	.220	50	6	2	0	1	4	6	9

5-YEAR TOTALS (1987–1991)

	BA	OBA	SA	AB	H	2B	3B	HR	RBI	BB	SO
	.182	.258	.193	88	16	1	0	0	2	9	28
	.254	.307	.384	586	149	33	2	13	64	44	88
	.248	.294	.352	335	83	18	1	5	38	22	49
	.242	.306	.366	339	82	16	1	8	28	31	67
	.239	.281	.354	393	94	25	1	6	6	22	73
	.253	.326	.367	281	71	9	1	7	60	31	43

KEN GRIFFEY SR. — bats left — throws left — age 42 — SEA — O/D

1991	BA	OBA	SA	AB	H	2B	3B	HR	RBI	BB	SO
vs. Left	.333	.333	.667	3	1	1	0	0	0	0	1
vs. Right	.280	.381	.390	82	23	6	0	1	9	13	12
at Home	.318	.404	.500	44	14	5	0	1	8	6	5
on Road	.244	.354	.293	41	10	2	0	0	1	7	8
Bases Empty	.286	.386	.429	49	14	4	0	1	1	8	8
Runners On Base	.278	.372	.361	36	10	3	0	0	8	5	5

8-YEAR TOTALS (1984–1991)

	BA	OBA	SA	AB	H	2B	3B	HR	RBI	BB	SO
	.259	.300	.378	495	128	28	2	9	68	29	67
	.287	.350	.437	1934	555	91	10	60	267	195	231
	.287	.349	.453	1208	347	65	6	41	174	117	153
	.275	.331	.398	1221	336	54	6	28	161	107	145
	.296	.347	.454	1344	398	58	8	46	46	101	170
	.263	.331	.390	1085	285	61	4	23	289	123	128

CHRIS GWYNN — bats left — throws left — age 28 — LA — O

1991	BA	OBA	SA	AB	H	2B	3B	HR	RBI	BB	SO
vs. Left	.182	.182	.182	11	2	0	0	0	1	0	2
vs. Right	.258	.310	.430	128	33	5	1	5	21	10	21
at Home	.306	.371	.500	62	19	1	1	3	9	6	10
on Road	.208	.241	.338	77	16	4	0	2	13	4	13
Bases Empty	.215	.244	.329	79	17	3	0	2	2	3	12
Runners On Base	.300	.366	.517	60	18	2	1	3	20	7	11

5-YEAR TOTALS (1987–1991)

	BA	OBA	SA	AB	H	2B	3B	HR	RBI	BB	SO
	.170	.220	.191	47	8	1	0	0	4	3	12
	.267	.300	.404	344	92	11	3	10	49	18	57
	.271	.305	.349	166	45	2	1	3	13	8	27
	.244	.280	.400	225	55	10	2	7	40	13	42
	.236	.259	.351	225	53	7	2	5	5	7	38
	.283	.330	.416	166	47	5	1	5	48	14	31

DARRYL HAMILTON — bats left — throws right — age 28 — MIL — *O

1991	BA	OBA	SA	AB	H	2B	3B	HR	RBI	BB	SO
vs. Left	.276	.308	.322	87	24	2	1	0	11	4	12
vs. Right	.321	.374	.403	318	102	13	5	1	46	29	26
at Home	.344	.406	.436	195	67	10	4	0	24	21	21
on Road	.281	.317	.338	210	59	5	2	1	33	12	17
Bases Empty	.259	.322	.310	216	56	7	2	0	0	20	28
Runners On Base	.370	.405	.471	189	70	8	4	1	57	13	10

3-YEAR TOTALS (1988–1991)

	BA	OBA	SA	AB	H	2B	3B	HR	RBI	BB	SO
	.214	.267	.270	126	27	5	1	0	12	8	15
	.305	.357	.375	538	164	19	5	3	74	46	44
	.302	.363	.392	301	91	13	4	2	36	29	29
	.275	.321	.325	363	100	11	2	1	50	25	30
	.249	.313	.302	374	93	13	2	1	1	34	38
	.338	.376	.424	290	98	11	4	2	85	20	21

JEFF HAMILTON — bats right — throws right — age 28 — LA — 3/S

1991	BA	OBA	SA	AB	H	2B	3B	HR	RBI	BB	SO
vs. Left	.192	.222	.244	78	15	4	0	0	9	3	19
vs. Right	.375	.412	.563	16	6	0	0	1	5	1	2
at Home	.188	.204	.292	48	9	2	0	1	7	1	13
on Road	.261	.306	.304	46	12	2	0	0	7	3	8
Bases Empty	.109	.128	.109	46	5	0	0	0	0	1	10
Runners On Base	.333	.373	.479	48	16	4	0	1	14	3	11

6-YEAR TOTALS (1986–1991)

BA	OBA	SA	AB	H	2B	3B	HR	RBI	BB	SO
.214	.247	.293	495	106	21	0	6	48	20	82
.248	.274	.389	710	176	40	3	18	76	23	129
.246	.274	.381	577	142	29	2	15	66	18	97
.223	.253	.320	628	140	32	1	9	58	25	114
.217	.235	.333	702	152	30	2	16	16	12	132
.258	.300	.372	503	130	31	1	8	108	31	79

DAVE HANSEN — bats left — throws right — age 24 — LA — 3/S

1991	BA	OBA	SA	AB	H	2B	3B	HR	RBI	BB	SO
vs. Left	.167	.167	.333	6	1	1	0	0	0	0	2
vs. Right	.280	.308	.400	50	14	3	0	1	5	2	10
at Home	.286	.333	.357	28	8	2	0	0	1	2	7
on Road	.250	.250	.429	28	7	2	0	1	4	0	5
Bases Empty	.303	.324	.394	33	10	3	0	0	0	1	10
Runners On Base	.217	.250	.391	23	5	1	0	1	5	1	2

2-YEAR TOTALS (1990–1991)

BA	OBA	SA	AB	H	2B	3B	HR	RBI	BB	SO
.143	.143	.286	7	1	1	0	0	0	0	3
.268	.293	.375	56	15	3	0	1	6	2	12
.265	.306	.324	34	9	2	0	0	2	2	9
.241	.241	.414	29	7	2	0	1	4	0	6
.263	.282	.342	38	10	3	0	0	0	1	13
.240	.269	.400	25	6	1	0	1	6	1	2

SHAWN HARE — bats left — throws left — age 25 — DET — /OD

1991	BA	OBA	SA	AB	H	2B	3B	HR	RBI	BB	SO
vs. Left	.000	.000	.000	0	0	0	0	0	0	0	0
vs. Right	.053	.143	.105	19	1	1	0	0	0	2	1
at Home	.000	.167	.000	10	0	0	0	0	0	2	1
on Road	.111	.111	.222	9	1	1	0	0	0	0	0
Bases Empty	.111	.200	.222	9	1	1	0	0	0	1	1
Runners On Base	.000	.091	.000	10	0	0	0	0	0	1	0

1-YEAR TOTALS (1991)

BA	OBA	SA	AB	H	2B	3B	HR	RBI	BB	SO
.000	.000	.000	0	0	0	0	0	0	0	0
.053	.143	.105	19	1	1	0	0	0	2	1
.000	.167	.000	10	0	0	0	0	0	2	1
.111	.111	.222	9	1	1	0	0	0	0	0
.111	.200	.222	9	1	1	0	0	0	1	1
.000	.091	.000	10	0	0	0	0	0	1	0

DONALD HARRIS — bats right — throws right — age 25 — TEX — O/D

1991	BA	OBA	SA	AB	H	2B	3B	HR	RBI	BB	SO
vs. Left	.333	.500	.333	3	1	0	0	0	0	1	1
vs. Right	.400	.400	1.000	5	2	0	0	1	2	0	2
at Home	.000	.000	.000	1	0	0	0	0	0	0	0
on Road	.429	.500	.857	7	3	0	0	1	2	1	3
Bases Empty	.667	.667	.667	3	2	0	0	0	0	0	1
Runners On Base	.200	.333	.800	5	1	0	0	1	2	1	2

1-YEAR TOTALS (1991)

BA	OBA	SA	AB	H	2B	3B	HR	RBI	BB	SO
.333	.500	.333	3	1	0	0	0	0	1	1
.400	.400	1.000	5	2	0	0	1	2	0	2
.000	.000	.000	1	0	0	0	0	0	0	0
.429	.500	.857	7	3	0	0	1	2	1	3
.667	.667	.667	3	2	0	0	0	0	0	1
.200	.333	.800	5	1	0	0	1	2	1	2

RON HASSEY — bats left — throws right — age 39 — MON — C

1991	BA	OBA	SA	AB	H	2B	3B	HR	RBI	BB	SO
vs. Left	.333	.600	.333	3	1	0	0	0	1	2	1
vs. Right	.224	.289	.319	116	26	8	0	1	13	11	15
at Home	.231	.305	.365	52	12	7	0	0	6	6	6
on Road	.224	.297	.284	67	15	1	0	1	8	7	10
Bases Empty	.167	.224	.259	54	9	2	0	1	1	4	9
Runners On Base	.277	.360	.369	65	18	6	0	0	13	9	7

8-YEAR TOTALS (1984–1991)

BA	OBA	SA	AB	H	2B	3B	HR	RBI	BB	SO
.194	.266	.228	289	56	7	0	1	20	25	37
.272	.345	.413	1611	438	90	3	44	211	179	186
.263	.334	.377	914	240	49	1	18	108	97	109
.258	.333	.392	986	254	48	2	27	123	107	114
.259	.330	.408	1038	269	55	3	31	31	102	120
.261	.337	.358	862	225	42	0	14	200	102	103

VON HAYES — bats left — throws right — age 34 — PHI — O

1991	BA	OBA	SA	AB	H	2B	3B	HR	RBI	BB	SO
vs. Left	.273	.362	.341	88	24	4	1	0	8	11	15
vs. Right	.204	.275	.260	196	40	11	0	0	13	20	27
at Home	.202	.319	.242	99	20	4	0	0	5	17	14
on Road	.238	.294	.308	185	44	11	1	0	16	14	28
Bases Empty	.247	.323	.312	170	42	11	0	0	0	19	26
Runners On Base	.193	.276	.246	114	22	4	1	0	21	12	16

8-YEAR TOTALS (1984–1991)

BA	OBA	SA	AB	H	2B	3B	HR	RBI	BB	SO
.235	.323	.352	1188	279	48	5	27	161	151	225
.289	.383	.466	2767	801	175	20	91	375	432	397
.270	.371	.459	1850	500	93	17	74	280	302	273
.276	.359	.408	2105	580	130	8	44	256	281	349
.259	.349	.425	2196	569	128	12	71	71	298	387
.291	.384	.439	1759	511	95	13	47	465	285	235

MIKE HEATH — bats right — throws right — age 37 — ATL — C

1991	BA	OBA	SA	AB	H	2B	3B	HR	RBI	BB	SO
vs. Left	.167	.182	.259	54	9	2	0	1	3	1	11
vs. Right	.235	.290	.271	85	20	1	1	0	9	6	15
at Home	.227	.256	.320	75	17	2	1	1	2	3	15
on Road	.188	.243	.203	64	12	1	0	0	10	4	11
Bases Empty	.250	.250	.355	76	19	3	1	1	1	0	14
Runners On Base	.159	.250	.159	63	10	0	0	0	11	7	12

8-YEAR TOTALS (1984–1991)

BA	OBA	SA	AB	H	2B	3B	HR	RBI	BB	SO
.271	.319	.427	1171	317	58	10	35	140	83	157
.238	.291	.350	1422	338	52	9	30	159	100	273
.249	.300	.404	1251	311	52	10	41	141	89	203
.256	.307	.367	1342	344	58	9	24	158	94	227
.254	.298	.392	1484	377	66	9	40	40	85	237
.251	.311	.376	1109	278	44	10	25	259	98	193

DANNY HEEP — bats left — throws left — age 35 — ATL — /10

1991	BA	OBA	SA	AB	H	2B	3B	HR	RBI	BB	SO
vs. Left	.000	.000	.000	0	0	0	0	0	0	0	0
vs. Right	.417	.462	.500	12	5	1	0	0	3	1	4
at Home	.444	.444	.556	9	4	1	0	0	3	0	3
on Road	.333	.500	.333	3	1	0	0	0	0	1	1
Bases Empty	.400	.500	.400	5	2	0	0	0	0	1	3
Runners On Base	.429	.429	.571	7	3	1	0	0	3	0	1

8-YEAR TOTALS (1984–1991)

BA	OBA	SA	AB	H	2B	3B	HR	RBI	BB	SO
.212	.316	.257	113	24	5	0	0	13	17	20
.265	.338	.364	1199	318	54	5	18	154	134	127
.267	.349	.345	632	169	24	2	7	73	78	60
.254	.323	.363	680	173	35	3	11	94	73	87
.233	.308	.304	716	167	22	4	7	7	74	82
.294	.367	.414	596	175	37	1	11	160	77	65

SCOTT HEMOND — bats right — throws right — age 27 — OAK — /C2D3S

1991	BA	OBA	SA	AB	H	2B	3B	HR	RBI	BB	SO
vs. Left	.273	.333	.273	11	3	0	0	0	0	1	2
vs. Right	.167	.167	.167	12	2	0	0	0	0	0	5
at Home	.143	.143	.143	7	1	0	0	0	0	0	3
on Road	.250	.294	.250	16	4	0	0	0	0	1	4
Bases Empty	.133	.188	.133	15	2	0	0	0	0	1	5
Runners On Base	.375	.375	.375	8	3	0	0	0	0	0	2

2-YEAR TOTALS (1990–1991)

BA	OBA	SA	AB	H	2B	3B	HR	RBI	BB	SO
.222	.263	.222	18	4	0	0	0	0	1	5
.167	.167	.167	18	3	0	0	0	1	0	7
.150	.150	.150	20	3	0	0	0	1	0	8
.250	.294	.250	16	4	0	0	0	0	1	4
.125	.160	.125	24	3	0	0	0	0	1	8
.333	.333	.333	12	4	0	0	0	1	0	4

CARLOS HERNANDEZ — bats right — throws right — age 25 — LA — C/3

1991

1991	BA	OBA	SA	AB	H	2B	3B	HR	RBI	BB	SO
vs. Left	.333	.375	.500	6	2	1	0	0	1	0	1
vs. Right	.125	.125	.125	8	1	0	0	0	0	0	4
at Home	.000	.000	.000	2	0	0	0	0	0	0	1
on Road	.250	.286	.333	12	3	1	0	0	1	0	4
Bases Empty	.222	.222	.333	9	2	1	0	0	0	0	4
Runners On Base	.200	.286	.200	5	1	0	0	0	1	0	1

2-YEAR TOTALS (1990–1991)

	BA	OBA	SA	AB	H	2B	3B	HR	RBI	BB	SO
vs. Left	.300	.318	.400	20	6	2	0	0	2	0	2
vs. Right	.071	.071	.071	14	1	0	0	0	0	0	5
at Home	.211	.211	.263	19	4	1	0	0	1	0	2
on Road	.200	.235	.267	15	3	1	0	0	1	0	5
Bases Empty	.200	.200	.280	25	5	2	0	0	0	0	6
Runners On Base	.222	.273	.222	9	2	0	0	0	2	0	1

JOSE HERNANDEZ — bats right — throws right — age 23 — TEX — S/3

1991

1991	BA	OBA	SA	AB	H	2B	3B	HR	RBI	BB	SO
vs. Left	.241	.241	.345	29	7	1	1	0	2	0	4
vs. Right	.159	.194	.174	69	11	1	0	0	3	3	27
at Home	.225	.279	.300	40	9	1	1	0	3	3	9
on Road	.155	.155	.172	58	9	1	0	0	2	0	22
Bases Empty	.208	.236	.264	53	11	1	1	0	0	2	15
Runners On Base	.156	.174	.178	45	7	1	0	0	4	1	16

1-YEAR TOTALS (1991)

	BA	OBA	SA	AB	H	2B	3B	HR	RBI	BB	SO
vs. Left	.241	.241	.345	29	7	1	1	0	2	0	4
vs. Right	.159	.194	.174	69	11	1	0	0	3	3	27
at Home	.225	.279	.300	40	9	1	1	0	3	3	9
on Road	.155	.155	.172	58	9	1	0	0	2	0	22
Bases Empty	.208	.236	.264	53	11	1	1	0	0	2	15
Runners On Base	.156	.174	.178	45	7	1	0	0	4	1	16

TOM HERR — bats both — throws right — age 36 — NYN/SF — 2/30

1991

1991	BA	OBA	SA	AB	H	2B	3B	HR	RBI	BB	SO
vs. Left	.213	.357	.275	80	17	3	1	0	14	18	11
vs. Right	.207	.335	.267	135	28	5	0	1	7	27	17
at Home	.190	.322	.220	100	19	3	0	0	7	20	15
on Road	.226	.362	.313	115	26	5	1	1	14	25	13
Bases Empty	.195	.317	.268	123	24	6	0	1	1	22	18
Runners On Base	.228	.376	.272	92	21	2	1	0	20	23	10

8-YEAR TOTALS (1984–1991)

	BA	OBA	SA	AB	H	2B	3B	HR	RBI	BB	SO
vs. Left	.285	.359	.368	1393	397	67	6	12	160	159	126
vs. Right	.261	.341	.339	2507	654	128	13	14	285	311	322
at Home	.269	.350	.347	1900	511	92	10	12	226	234	207
on Road	.270	.345	.352	2000	540	103	9	14	219	234	241
Bases Empty	.255	.338	.332	2187	558	109	6	16	16	262	266
Runners On Base	.288	.360	.371	1713	493	86	13	10	429	208	182

DONNIE HILL — bats both — throws right — age 32 — CAL — 2S/1

1991

1991	BA	OBA	SA	AB	H	2B	3B	HR	RBI	BB	SO
vs. Left	.257	.395	.400	35	9	3	1	0	4	8	5
vs. Right	.236	.321	.282	174	41	5	0	1	16	22	16
at Home	.196	.281	.265	102	20	2	1	1	9	12	14
on Road	.280	.384	.336	107	30	6	0	0	11	18	7
Bases Empty	.194	.270	.226	124	24	4	0	0		13	14
Runners On Base	.306	.422	.412	85	26	4	1	1	20	17	7

7-YEAR TOTALS (1984–1991)

	BA	OBA	SA	AB	H	2B	3B	HR	RBI	BB	SO
vs. Left	.243	.311	.335	597	145	27	2	8	57	62	71
vs. Right	.261	.308	.345	1501	392	54	12	16	154	104	128
at Home	.250	.307	.316	1002	251	41	8	3	82	85	92
on Road	.261	.310	.366	1096	286	40	6	21	129	81	107
Bases Empty	.245	.295	.326	1194	293	45	6	13	13	82	119
Runners On Base	.270	.326	.364	904	244	36	8	11	198	84	80

GLENALLEN HILL — bats right — throws right — age 27 — TOR/CLE — OD

1991

1991	BA	OBA	SA	AB	H	2B	3B	HR	RBI	BB	SO
vs. Left	.281	.361	.500	96	27	7	1	4	12	12	17
vs. Right	.240	.295	.360	125	30	1	1	4	13	11	37
at Home	.296	.339	.454	108	32	6	1	3	9	7	22
on Road	.221	.311	.389	113	25	2	1	5	16	16	32
Bases Empty	.258	.336	.438	128	33	6	1	5	5	15	35
Runners On Base	.258	.308	.398	93	24	2	1	3	20	8	19

3-YEAR TOTALS (1989–1991)

	BA	OBA	SA	AB	H	2B	3B	HR	RBI	BB	SO
vs. Left	.248	.310	.433	270	67	12	4	10	29	24	61
vs. Right	.247	.297	.407	263	65	7	1	11	35	20	67
at Home	.261	.310	.444	268	70	14	1	11	30	19	55
on Road	.234	.297	.396	265	62	5	4	10	34	25	73
Bases Empty	.236	.287	.424	309	73	13	3	13	13	22	77
Runners On Base	.263	.325	.415	224	59	6	2	8	51	22	51

DAVE HOLLINS — bats both — throws right — age 26 — PHI — 3/1

1991

1991	BA	OBA	SA	AB	H	2B	3B	HR	RBI	BB	SO
vs. Left	.444	.510	.756	45	20	1	2	3	10	5	9
vs. Right	.236	.322	.406	106	25	9	0	3	11	12	17
at Home	.317	.440	.600	60	19	6	1	3	8	11	9
on Road	.286	.330	.451	91	26	4	1	3	13	6	17
Bases Empty	.280	.359	.500	82	23	7	1	3	3	9	19
Runners On Base	.319	.400	.522	69	22	3	1	3	18	8	7

2-YEAR TOTALS (1990–1991)

	BA	OBA	SA	AB	H	2B	3B	HR	RBI	BB	SO
vs. Left	.318	.375	.580	88	28	1	2	6	17	7	21
vs. Right	.215	.300	.350	177	38	9	0	5	19	20	33
at Home	.220	.324	.415	118	26	6	1	6	14	16	28
on Road	.272	.325	.435	147	40	4	1	6	22	11	26
Bases Empty	.220	.295	.380	150	33	7	1	5	5	15	38
Runners On Base	.287	.361	.487	115	33	3	1	6	31	12	16

WAYNE HOUSIE — bats both — throws right — age 27 — BOS — /OD

1991

1991	BA	OBA	SA	AB	H	2B	3B	HR	RBI	BB	SO
vs. Left	.500	.500	1.000	2	1	1	0	0	0	0	0
vs. Right	.167	.286	.167	6	1	0	0	0	0	1	3
at Home	.167	.286	.333	6	1	1	0	0	0	1	2
on Road	.500	.500	.500	2	1	0	0	0	0	0	1
Bases Empty	.000	.200	.000	4	0	0	0	0	0	1	2
Runners On Base	.500	.500	.750	4	2	1	0	0	0	0	1

1-YEAR TOTALS (1991)

	BA	OBA	SA	AB	H	2B	3B	HR	RBI	BB	SO
vs. Left	.500	.500	1.000	2	1	1	0	0	0	0	0
vs. Right	.167	.286	.167	6	1	0	0	0	0	1	3
at Home	.167	.286	.333	6	1	1	0	0	0	1	2
on Road	.500	.500	.500	2	1	0	0	0	0	0	1
Bases Empty	.000	.200	.000	4	0	0	0	0	0	1	2
Runners On Base	.500	.500	.750	4	2	1	0	0	0	0	1

CHRIS HOWARD — bats right — throws right — age 26 — SEA — /C

1991

1991	BA	OBA	SA	AB	H	2B	3B	HR	RBI	BB	SO
vs. Left	.200	.333	.400	5	1	1	0	0	0	1	1
vs. Right	.000	.000	.000	1	0	0	0	0	0	0	1
at Home	.000	.250	.000	3	0	0	0	0	0	1	1
on Road	.333	.333	.667	3	1	1	0	0	0	0	1
Bases Empty	.250	.400	.500	4	1	1	0	0	0	1	0
Runners On Base	.000	.000	.000	2	0	0	0	0	0	0	2

1-YEAR TOTALS (1991)

	BA	OBA	SA	AB	H	2B	3B	HR	RBI	BB	SO
vs. Left	.200	.333	.400	5	1	1	0	0	0	1	1
vs. Right	.000	.000	.000	1	0	0	0	0	0	0	1
at Home	.000	.250	.000	3	0	0	0	0	0	1	1
on Road	.333	.333	.667	3	1	1	0	0	0	0	1
Bases Empty	.250	.400	.500	4	1	1	0	0	0	1	0
Runners On Base	.000	.000	.000	2	0	0	0	0	0	0	2

DAVID HOWARD — bats both — throws right — age 25 — KC — S2/30D

1991

1991	BA	OBA	SA	AB	H	2B	3B	HR	RBI	BB	SO
vs. Left	.225	.276	.287	80	18	2	0	1	10	6	12
vs. Right	.212	.262	.244	156	33	5	0	0	7	10	33
at Home	.207	.271	.233	116	24	3	0	0	7	11	22
on Road	.225	.262	.283	120	27	4	0	1	10	5	23
Bases Empty	.194	.260	.224	134	26	4	0	0	0	11	29
Runners On Base	.245	.275	.304	102	25	3	0	1	17	5	16

1-YEAR TOTALS (1991)

	BA	OBA	SA	AB	H	2B	3B	HR	RBI	BB	SO
vs. Left	.225	.276	.287	80	18	2	0	1	10	6	12
vs. Right	.212	.262	.244	156	33	5	0	0	7	10	33
at Home	.207	.271	.233	116	24	3	0	0	7	11	22
on Road	.225	.262	.283	120	27	4	0	1	10	5	23
Bases Empty	.194	.260	.224	134	26	4	0	0	0	11	29
Runners On Base	.245	.275	.304	102	25	3	0	1	17	5	16

JACK HOWELL — bats left — throws right — age 31 — CAL/SD — 32/O1D

1991	BA	OBA	SA	AB	H	2B	3B	HR	RBI	BB	SO
vs. Left	.103	.133	.138	29	3	1	0	0	0	1	10
vs. Right	.222	.313	.363	212	47	4	1	8	23	28	34
at Home	.205	.295	.299	117	24	2	0	3	12	15	19
on Road	.210	.290	.371	124	26	3	1	5	11	14	25
Bases Empty	.172	.279	.306	134	23	4	1	4	4	20	25
Runners On Base	.252	.310	.374	107	27	1	0	4	19	9	19

7-YEAR TOTALS (1985–1991)

	BA	OBA	SA	AB	H	2B	3B	HR	RBI	BB	SO
vs. Left	.175	.247	.292	521	91	27	5	8	52	41	155
vs. Right	.254	.338	.444	1747	444	84	10	76	222	224	384
at Home	.233	.314	.401	1108	258	48	6	42	147	130	268
on Road	.239	.321	.417	1160	277	63	9	42	127	135	271
Bases Empty	.217	.293	.389	1295	281	66	8	47	47	137	313
Runners On Base	.261	.350	.436	973	254	45	7	37	227	128	226

DANN HOWITT — bats left — throws right — age 28 — OAK — O/1

1991	BA	OBA	SA	AB	H	2B	3B	HR	RBI	BB	SO
vs. Left	.000	.000	.000	2	0	0	0	0	0	0	1
vs. Right	.175	.190	.275	40	7	1	0	1	3	1	11
at Home	.048	.087	.048	21	1	0	0	0	2	1	3
on Road	.286	.286	.476	21	6	1	0	1	1	0	9
Bases Empty	.250	.280	.417	24	6	1	0	1	1	1	4
Runners On Base	.056	.053	.056	18	1	0	0	0	2	0	8

3-YEAR TOTALS (1989–1991)

	BA	OBA	SA	AB	H	2B	3B	HR	RBI	BB	SO
vs. Left	.000	.000	.000	6	0	0	0	0	0	0	3
vs. Right	.164	.212	.262	61	10	1	1	1	4	4	23
at Home	.071	.100	.071	28	2	0	0	0	2	1	8
on Road	.205	.262	.359	39	8	1	1	1	2	3	18
Bases Empty	.205	.279	.308	39	8	1	0	1	1	4	13
Runners On Base	.071	.069	.143	28	2	0	1	0	3	0	13

REX HUDLER — bats right — throws right — age 32 — SL — O1/2

1991	BA	OBA	SA	AB	H	2B	3B	HR	RBI	BB	SO
vs. Left	.255	.286	.359	153	39	9	2	1	10	7	21
vs. Right	.148	.190	.167	54	8	1	0	0	5	3	8
at Home	.238	.273	.352	105	25	7	1	1	9	5	13
on Road	.216	.248	.265	102	22	3	1	0	6	5	16
Bases Empty	.195	.233	.276	123	24	5	1	1	1	6	17
Runners On Base	.274	.300	.357	84	23	5	1	0	14	4	12

7-YEAR TOTALS (1984–1991)

	BA	OBA	SA	AB	H	2B	3B	HR	RBI	BB	SO
vs. Left	.248	.282	.384	537	133	24	5	13	43	26	80
vs. Right	.256	.292	.375	320	82	19	2	5	22	14	52
at Home	.251	.294	.379	406	102	23	4	7	33	22	64
on Road	.251	.278	.381	451	113	20	3	11	32	18	68
Bases Empty	.255	.278	.385	517	132	20	4	13	13	14	84
Runners On Base	.244	.298	.374	340	83	23	3	5	52	26	48

MIKE HUFF — bats right — throws right — age 29 — CLE/CHA — O/2D

1991	BA	OBA	SA	AB	H	2B	3B	HR	RBI	BB	SO
vs. Left	.231	.333	.355	121	28	4	1	3	9	16	21
vs. Right	.270	.388	.336	122	33	6	1	0	16	21	27
at Home	.264	.374	.376	125	33	7	2	1	10	17	24
on Road	.237	.348	.314	118	28	3	0	2	15	20	24
Bases Empty	.243	.366	.361	144	35	6	1	3	3	24	29
Runners On Base	.263	.353	.323	99	26	4	1	0	22	13	19

2-YEAR TOTALS (1989–1991)

	BA	OBA	SA	AB	H	2B	3B	HR	RBI	BB	SO
vs. Left	.237	.335	.374	139	33	5	1	4	10	17	23
vs. Right	.256	.378	.318	129	33	6	1	0	17	23	31
at Home	.264	.379	.372	129	34	7	2	1	11	19	26
on Road	.230	.335	.324	139	32	4	0	3	16	21	28
Bases Empty	.244	.356	.375	160	39	7	1	4	4	24	33
Runners On Base	.250	.357	.306	108	27	4	1	0	23	16	21

TIM HULETT — bats right — throws right — age 32 — BAL — 32D/S

1991	BA	OBA	SA	AB	H	2B	3B	HR	RBI	BB	SO
vs. Left	.139	.205	.250	72	10	2	0	2	8	5	17
vs. Right	.239	.282	.403	134	32	7	0	5	10	8	32
at Home	.154	.214	.244	78	12	4	0	1	3	6	24
on Road	.234	.279	.414	128	30	5	0	6	15	7	25
Bases Empty	.243	.300	.423	111	27	5	0	5	5	9	26
Runners On Base	.158	.200	.263	95	15	4	0	2	13	4	23

7-YEAR TOTALS (1984–1991)

	BA	OBA	SA	AB	H	2B	3B	HR	RBI	BB	SO
vs. Left	.244	.293	.406	606	148	21	7	21	67	42	115
vs. Right	.235	.278	.348	1012	238	45	3	21	94	58	209
at Home	.234	.283	.356	752	176	27	7	17	61	51	158
on Road	.242	.284	.381	866	210	39	3	25	100	49	166
Bases Empty	.243	.288	.401	935	227	39	8	31	31	55	175
Runners On Base	.233	.278	.327	683	159	27	2	11	130	45	149

MIKE HUMPHREYS — bats right — throws right — age 25 — NYA — /OD3

1991	BA	OBA	SA	AB	H	2B	3B	HR	RBI	BB	SO
vs. Left	.250	.423	.250	20	5	0	0	0	3	6	5
vs. Right	.150	.261	.150	20	3	0	0	0	0	3	2
at Home	.250	.375	.250	20	5	0	0	0	3	4	2
on Road	.150	.320	.150	20	3	0	0	0	0	5	5
Bases Empty	.111	.238	.111	18	2	0	0	0	0	3	4
Runners On Base	.273	.429	.273	22	6	0	0	0	3	6	3

1-YEAR TOTALS (1991)

	BA	OBA	SA	AB	H	2B	3B	HR	RBI	BB	SO
vs. Left	.250	.423	.250	20	5	0	0	0	3	6	5
vs. Right	.150	.261	.150	20	3	0	0	0	0	3	2
at Home	.250	.375	.250	20	5	0	0	0	3	4	2
on Road	.150	.320	.150	20	3	0	0	0	0	5	5
Bases Empty	.111	.238	.111	18	2	0	0	0	0	3	4
Runners On Base	.273	.429	.273	22	6	0	0	0	3	6	3

TODD HUNDLEY — bats both — throws right — age 23 — NYN — C

1991	BA	OBA	SA	AB	H	2B	3B	HR	RBI	BB	SO
vs. Left	.056	.182	.056	18	1	0	0	0	2	2	9
vs. Right	.167	.239	.286	42	7	0	1	1	5	4	5
at Home	.118	.205	.265	34	4	0	1	1	5	3	9
on Road	.154	.241	.154	26	4	0	0	0	2	3	5
Bases Empty	.103	.188	.207	29	3	0	0	1	1	3	5
Runners On Base	.161	.250	.226	31	5	0	1	0	6	3	9

2-YEAR TOTALS (1990–1991)

	BA	OBA	SA	AB	H	2B	3B	HR	RBI	BB	SO
vs. Left	.154	.244	.205	39	6	2	0	0	2	4	17
vs. Right	.182	.250	.284	88	16	4	1	1	7	8	15
at Home	.173	.267	.288	52	9	1	1	1	5	6	11
on Road	.173	.235	.240	75	13	5	0	0	4	6	21
Bases Empty	.149	.222	.230	74	11	3	0	1	1	7	17
Runners On Base	.208	.283	.302	53	11	3	1	0	8	5	15

BRIAN HUNTER — bats right — throws left — age 24 — ATL — 1/O

1991	BA	OBA	SA	AB	H	2B	3B	HR	RBI	BB	SO
vs. Left	.275	.307	.458	120	33	4	0	6	22	6	17
vs. Right	.232	.287	.444	151	35	12	1	6	28	11	31
at Home	.270	.331	.482	141	38	7	1	7	33	12	22
on Road	.231	.255	.415	130	30	9	0	5	17	5	26
Bases Empty	.203	.250	.392	143	29	6	0	7	7	9	27
Runners On Base	.305	.345	.516	128	39	10	1	5	43	8	21

1-YEAR TOTALS (1991)

	BA	OBA	SA	AB	H	2B	3B	HR	RBI	BB	SO
vs. Left	.275	.307	.458	120	33	4	0	6	22	6	17
vs. Right	.232	.287	.444	151	35	12	1	6	28	11	31
at Home	.270	.331	.482	141	38	7	1	7	33	12	22
on Road	.231	.255	.415	130	30	9	0	5	17	5	26
Bases Empty	.203	.250	.392	143	29	6	0	7	7	9	27
Runners On Base	.305	.345	.516	128	39	10	1	5	43	8	21

BO JACKSON — bats right — throws right — age 30 — CHA — D

1991	BA	OBA	SA	AB	H	2B	3B	HR	RBI	BB	SO
vs. Left	.231	.323	.500	26	6	1	0	2	6	4	13
vs. Right	.222	.340	.356	45	10	3	0	1	8	8	12
at Home	.200	.267	.475	40	8	2	0	3	10	4	13
on Road	.258	.410	.323	31	8	2	0	0	4	8	12
Bases Empty	.179	.289	.308	39	7	2	0	1	1	6	14
Runners On Base	.281	.385	.531	32	9	2	0	2	13	6	11

6-YEAR TOTALS (1986–1991)

	BA	OBA	SA	AB	H	2B	3B	HR	RBI	BB	SO
vs. Left	.258	.331	.493	554	143	18	5	34	92	57	205
vs. Right	.246	.300	.470	1354	333	52	9	78	235	100	458
at Home	.278	.335	.516	932	259	51	9	51	173	80	286
on Road	.222	.283	.440	976	217	19	5	61	154	77	377
Bases Empty	.256	.305	.487	1032	264	41	6	62	62	68	353
Runners On Base	.242	.313	.465	876	212	29	8	50	265	89	310

STAN JAVIER — bats both — throws right — age 28 — LA — O/1

7-YEAR TOTALS (1984–1991)

1991	BA	OBA	SA	AB	H	2B	3B	HR	RBI	BB	SO		BA	OBA	SA	AB	H	2B	3B	HR	RBI	BB	SO
vs. Left	.242	.311	.305	95	23	2	2	0	9	10	18		.237	.305	.305	524	124	12	6	4	40	50	88
vs. Right	.160	.216	.259	81	13	3	1	1	2	6	18		.250	.324	.327	940	235	37	10	5	78	104	167
at Home	.205	.292	.229	83	17	2	0	0	7	11	20		.248	.334	.301	707	175	19	5	3	56	92	116
on Road	.204	.245	.333	93	19	3	3	1	4	5	16		.243	.300	.336	757	184	30	11	6	62	62	139
Bases Empty	.228	.271	.347	101	23	5	2	1	1	6	24		.247	.314	.331	835	206	31	9	7	7	81	160
Runners On Base	.173	.264	.200	75	13	0	1	0	10	10	12		.243	.321	.304	629	153	18	7	2	111	73	95

REGGIE JEFFERSON — bats both — throws left — age 24 — CIN/CLE — 1

1-YEAR TOTALS (1991)

1991	BA	OBA	SA	AB	H	2B	3B	HR	RBI	BB	SO		BA	OBA	SA	AB	H	2B	3B	HR	RBI	BB	SO
vs. Left	.160	.160	.200	25	4	1	0	0	3	0	7		.160	.160	.200	25	4	1	0	0	3	0	7
vs. Right	.205	.239	.337	83	17	2	0	3	10	4	17		.205	.239	.337	83	17	2	0	3	10	4	17
at Home	.179	.220	.321	56	10	2	0	2	4	3	11		.179	.220	.321	56	10	2	0	2	4	3	11
on Road	.212	.222	.288	52	11	1	0	1	9	1	13		.212	.222	.288	52	11	1	0	1	9	1	13
Bases Empty	.238	.238	.365	63	15	2	0	2	2	0	15		.238	.238	.365	63	15	2	0	2	2	0	15
Runners On Base	.133	.200	.222	45	6	1	0	1	11	4	9		.133	.200	.222	45	6	1	0	1	11	4	9

STAN JEFFERSON — bats both — throws right — age 30 — CIN — /O

6-YEAR TOTALS (1986–1991)

1991	BA	OBA	SA	AB	H	2B	3B	HR	RBI	BB	SO		BA	OBA	SA	AB	H	2B	3B	HR	RBI	BB	SO
vs. Left	.000	.000	.000	5	0	0	0	0	0	0	0		.217	.275	.261	314	68	8	0	2	14	23	64
vs. Right	.071	.133	.071	14	1	0	0	0	0	1	3		.216	.276	.365	518	112	17	9	14	53	42	113
at Home	.077	.077	.077	13	1	0	0	0	0	0	2		.221	.298	.353	439	97	15	5	11	40	45	104
on Road	.000	.143	.000	6	0	0	0	0	0	1	1		.211	.250	.295	393	83	10	4	5	27	20	73
Bases Empty	.071	.133	.071	14	1	0	0	0	0	1	2		.230	.291	.353	527	121	18	7	11	11	40	130
Runners On Base	.000	.000	.000	5	0	0	0	0	0	0	1		.193	.249	.279	305	59	7	2	5	56	25	47

DOUG JENNINGS — bats left — throws left — age 28 — OAK — /O

4-YEAR TOTALS (1988–1991)

1991	BA	OBA	SA	AB	H	2B	3B	HR	RBI	BB	SO		BA	OBA	SA	AB	H	2B	3B	HR	RBI	BB	SO
vs. Left	.000	.000	.000	0	0	0	0	0	0	0	0		.214	.214	.357	14	3	1	0	0	0	0	2
vs. Right	.111	.273	.111	9	1	0	0	0	0	2	2		.191	.304	.285	256	49	13	1	3	29	40	78
at Home	.000	.333	.000	2	0	0	0	0	0	1	0		.157	.285	.214	140	22	5	0	1	9	24	44
on Road	.143	.250	.143	7	1	0	0	0	0	1	2		.231	.316	.369	130	30	8	2	2	20	16	36
Bases Empty	.167	.375	.167	6	1	0	0	0	0	2	1		.214	.320	.325	154	33	7	2	2	2	22	43
Runners On Base	.000	.000	.000	3	0	0	0	0	0	0	1		.164	.275	.241	116	19	6	0	1	27	18	37

CHRIS JONES — bats right — throws right — age 27 — CIN — O

1-YEAR TOTALS (1991)

1991	BA	OBA	SA	AB	H	2B	3B	HR	RBI	BB	SO		BA	OBA	SA	AB	H	2B	3B	HR	RBI	BB	SO
vs. Left	.283	.306	.413	46	13	1	1	1	5	2	20		.283	.306	.413	46	13	1	1	1	5	2	20
vs. Right	.302	.302	.419	43	13	0	1	1	1	0	11		.302	.302	.419	43	13	0	1	1	1	0	11
at Home	.273	.304	.273	44	12	0	0	0	0	2	18		.273	.304	.273	44	12	0	0	0	0	2	18
on Road	.311	.304	.556	45	14	1	2	2	6	0	13		.311	.304	.556	45	14	1	2	2	6	0	13
Bases Empty	.306	.328	.452	62	19	1	1	2	2	2	23		.306	.328	.452	62	19	1	1	2	2	2	23
Runners On Base	.259	.250	.333	27	7	0	1	0	4	0	8		.259	.250	.333	27	7	0	1	0	4	0	8

RON JONES — bats left — throws right — age 28 — PHI

4-YEAR TOTALS (1988–1991)

1991	BA	OBA	SA	AB	H	2B	3B	HR	RBI	BB	SO		BA	OBA	SA	AB	H	2B	3B	HR	RBI	BB	SO
vs. Left	.000	.000	.000	1	0	0	0	0	0	0	1		.333	.386	.588	51	17	1	0	4	12	5	7
vs. Right	.160	.222	.240	25	4	2	0	0	3	2	8		.255	.314	.457	188	48	9	1	8	28	17	26
at Home	.059	.111	.059	17	1	0	0	0	0	1	6		.272	.321	.483	147	40	5	1	8	25	11	22
on Road	.333	.400	.556	9	3	2	0	0	3	1	3		.272	.343	.489	92	25	5	0	4	15	11	11
Bases Empty	.000	.091	.000	10	0	0	0	0	0	1	2		.239	.297	.425	134	32	4	0	7	7	11	17
Runners On Base	.250	.294	.375	16	4	2	0	0	3	1	7		.314	.370	.562	105	33	6	1	6	33	11	16

TRACY JONES — bats right — throws right — age 31 — SEA — DO

6-YEAR TOTALS (1986–1991)

1991	BA	OBA	SA	AB	H	2B	3B	HR	RBI	BB	SO		BA	OBA	SA	AB	H	2B	3B	HR	RBI	BB	SO
vs. Left	.203	.289	.254	118	24	3	0	1	15	15	16		.298	.362	.420	674	201	31	3	15	91	65	61
vs. Right	.351	.393	.579	57	20	5	1	2	9	3	6		.247	.292	.354	628	155	25	3	12	73	35	80
at Home	.192	.276	.269	78	15	3	0	1	6	8	10		.272	.342	.384	622	169	30	2	12	71	58	65
on Road	.299	.358	.433	97	29	5	1	2	18	10	12		.275	.317	.391	680	187	26	4	15	93	42	76
Bases Empty	.325	.378	.458	83	27	5	0	2	2	7	11		.284	.336	.422	742	211	34	4	20	20	53	75
Runners On Base	.185	.274	.272	92	17	3	1	1	22	11	11		.259	.319	.343	560	145	22	2	7	144	47	66

TIM JONES — bats left — throws right — age 30 — SL — S/2

4-YEAR TOTALS (1988–1991)

1991	BA	OBA	SA	AB	H	2B	3B	HR	RBI	BB	SO		BA	OBA	SA	AB	H	2B	3B	HR	RBI	BB	SO
vs. Left	.000	.000	.000	3	0	0	0	0	1	0	1		.188	.276	.250	48	9	3	0	0	6	6	7
vs. Right	.190	.261	.286	21	4	2	0	0	1	2	5		.255	.315	.329	231	59	12	1	1	18	19	37
at Home	.100	.182	.100	10	1	0	0	0	1	1	3		.202	.273	.271	129	26	6	0	1	10	13	19
on Road	.214	.250	.357	14	3	2	0	0	1	1	3		.280	.337	.353	150	42	9	1	0	14	12	25
Bases Empty	.231	.231	.385	13	3	2	0	0	0	0	4		.247	.311	.315	162	40	8	0	1	1	14	27
Runners On Base	.091	.214	.091	11	1	0	0	0	2	2	2		.239	.303	.316	117	28	7	1	0	23	11	17

RON KARKOVICE — bats right — throws right — age 29 — CHA — C/O

6-YEAR TOTALS (1986–1991)

1991	BA	OBA	SA	AB	H	2B	3B	HR	RBI	BB	SO		BA	OBA	SA	AB	H	2B	3B	HR	RBI	BB	SO
vs. Left	.295	.368	.492	61	18	3	0	3	8	7	13		.225	.279	.369	347	78	18	1	10	47	27	111
vs. Right	.217	.276	.368	106	23	10	0	2	14	8	29		.220	.285	.357	482	106	25	1	13	48	37	146
at Home	.235	.295	.296	81	19	5	0	0	7	6	22		.198	.251	.282	393	78	22	1	3	30	27	126
on Road	.256	.323	.523	86	22	8	0	5	15	9	20		.243	.311	.433	436	106	21	1	20	65	37	131
Bases Empty	.263	.307	.400	95	25	10	0	1	1	6	24		.219	.283	.357	474	104	30	1	11	11	36	146
Runners On Base	.222	.313	.431	72	16	3	0	4	21	9	18		.225	.282	.369	355	80	13	1	12	84	28	111

ERIC KARROS — bats right — throws right — age 25 — LA — 1

1-YEAR TOTALS (1991)

1991	BA	OBA	SA	AB	H	2B	3B	HR	RBI	BB	SO		BA	OBA	SA	AB	H	2B	3B	HR	RBI	BB	SO
vs. Left	.000	.091	.000	10	0	0	0	0	0	1	4		.000	.091	.000	10	0	0	0	0	0	1	4
vs. Right	.250	.250	.500	4	1	1	0	0	1	0	2		.250	.250	.500	4	1	1	0	0	1	0	2
at Home	.167	.286	.333	6	1	1	0	0	1	1	3		.167	.286	.333	6	1	1	0	0	1	1	3
on Road	.000	.000	.000	8	0	0	0	0	0	0	3		.000	.000	.000	8	0	0	0	0	0	0	3
Bases Empty	.000	.000	.000	8	0	0	0	0	0	0	3		.000	.000	.000	8	0	0	0	0	0	0	3
Runners On Base	.167	.286	.333	6	1	1	0	0	1	1	3		.167	.286	.333	6	1	1	0	0	1	1	3

TERRY KENNEDY — bats left — throws right — age 36 — SF — C/1

8-YEAR TOTALS (1984–1991)

1991	BA	OBA	SA	AB	H	2B	3B	HR	RBI	BB	SO		BA	OBA	SA	AB	H	2B	3B	HR	RBI	BB	SO
vs. Left	.300	.273	.800	10	3	0	1	1	3	0	2		.219	.255	.335	704	154	24	2	18	86	32	183
vs. Right	.230	.283	.311	161	37	7	0	2	10	11	29		.260	.316	.369	2395	623	108	3	49	253	196	382
at Home	.240	.287	.413	75	18	5	1	2	11	5	16		.242	.297	.366	1535	371	63	4	40	182	120	295
on Road	.229	.279	.281	96	22	2	0	1	2	6	15		.260	.308	.357	1564	406	69	1	27	157	108	270
Bases Empty	.227	.250	.299	97	22	4	0	1	1	3	19		.249	.289	.362	1785	445	71	2	42	42	96	308
Runners On Base	.243	.321	.392	74	18	3	1	2	12	8	12		.253	.319	.361	1314	332	61	3	25	297	132	257

JEFF KING — bats right — throws right — age 28 — PIT — 3

3-YEAR TOTALS (1989–1991)

1991	BA	OBA	SA	AB	H	2B	3B	HR	RBI	BB	SO		BA	OBA	SA	AB	H	2B	3B	HR	RBI	BB	SO
vs. Left	.323	.500	.419	31	10	0	0	1	4	11	2		.249	.315	.406	374	93	21	4	10	48	38	43
vs. Right	.205	.241	.359	78	16	1	1	3	14	3	13		.206	.247	.364	321	66	10	1	13	42	17	56
at Home	.222	.310	.413	63	14	1	1	3	10	7	10		.235	.288	.421	361	85	16	3	15	50	27	48
on Road	.261	.352	.326	46	12	0	0	1	8	7	5		.222	.282	.350	334	74	15	2	8	40	28	51
Bases Empty	.194	.286	.242	62	12	0	0	1	1	8	12		.247	.299	.407	393	97	22	4	13	13	27	47
Runners On Base	.298	.382	.553	47	14	1	1	3	17	6	3		.205	.267	.361	302	62	9	4	10	77	28	52

MIKE KINGERY — bats left — throws left — age 31 — SF — O/1

6-YEAR TOTALS (1986–1991)

1991	BA	OBA	SA	AB	H	2B	3B	HR	RBI	BB	SO		BA	OBA	SA	AB	H	2B	3B	HR	RBI	BB	SO
vs. Left	.083	.154	.250	12	1	0	1	0	0	1	4		.191	.244	.255	110	21	2	1	1	7	7	22
vs. Right	.194	.295	.235	98	19	2	1	0	8	14	17		.263	.321	.380	969	255	49	11	14	106	85	128
at Home	.189	.283	.264	53	10	2	1	0	0	7	9		.262	.318	.398	558	146	33	8	9	54	45	72
on Road	.175	.277	.211	57	10	0	1	0	8	8	12		.250	.310	.334	521	130	18	4	6	59	47	78
Bases Empty	.170	.279	.245	53	9	2	1	0	0	8	12		.241	.303	.368	617	149	32	8	10	10	51	95
Runners On Base	.193	.281	.228	57	11	0	1	0	8	7	9		.275	.328	.366	462	127	19	4	5	103	41	55

WAYNE KIRBY — bats left — throws right — age 28 — CLE — O

1-YEAR TOTALS (1991)

1991	BA	OBA	SA	AB	H	2B	3B	HR	RBI	BB	SO		BA	OBA	SA	AB	H	2B	3B	HR	RBI	BB	SO
vs. Left	.000	.000	.000	7	0	0	0	0	1	0	3		.000	.000	.000	7	0	0	0	0	1	0	3
vs. Right	.250	.282	.306	36	9	2	0	0	4	2	3		.250	.282	.306	36	9	2	0	0	4	2	3
at Home	.172	.172	.207	29	5	1	0	0	2	0	4		.172	.172	.207	29	5	1	0	0	2	0	4
on Road	.286	.353	.357	14	4	1	0	0	3	2	2		.286	.353	.357	14	4	1	0	0	3	2	2
Bases Empty	.200	.231	.200	25	5	0	0	0	0	1	5		.200	.231	.200	25	5	0	0	0	0	1	5
Runners On Base	.222	.250	.333	18	4	2	0	0	5	1	1		.222	.250	.333	18	4	2	0	0	5	1	1

RON KITTLE — bats right — throws right — age 34 — CHA — 1

8-YEAR TOTALS (1984–1991)

1991	BA	OBA	SA	AB	H	2B	3B	HR	RBI	BB	SO		BA	OBA	SA	AB	H	2B	3B	HR	RBI	BB	SO
vs. Left	.188	.316	.375	16	3	0	0	1	2	2	2		.234	.318	.474	911	213	33	0	62	150	105	231
vs. Right	.194	.278	.290	31	6	0	0	1	5	3	7		.237	.294	.462	1248	296	46	0	78	203	89	351
at Home	.200	.273	.200	30	6	0	0	0	2	2	6		.228	.300	.450	1051	240	44	0	63	165	103	273
on Road	.176	.318	.529	17	3	0	0	2	5	3	3		.243	.308	.483	1108	269	35	0	77	188	91	309
Bases Empty	.150	.320	.150	20	3	0	0	0	0	3	5		.234	.307	.473	1190	278	45	0	80	80	106	313
Runners On Base	.222	.267	.444	27	6	0	0	2	7	2	4		.238	.300	.459	969	231	34	0	60	273	88	269

RANDY KNORR — bats right — throws right — age 24 — TOR — /C

1-YEAR TOTALS (1991)

1991	BA	OBA	SA	AB	H	2B	3B	HR	RBI	BB	SO		BA	OBA	SA	AB	H	2B	3B	HR	RBI	BB	SO
vs. Left	.000	.000	.000	1	0	0	0	0	0	0	1		.000	.000	.000	1	0	0	0	0	0	0	1
vs. Right	.000	1.000	.000	0	0	0	0	0	0	1	0		.000	1.000	.000	0	0	0	0	0	0	1	0
at Home	.000	.000	.000	0	0	0	0	0	0	0	0		.000	.000	.000	0	0	0	0	0	0	0	0
on Road	.000	.500	.000	1	0	0	0	0	0	1	1		.000	.500	.000	1	0	0	0	0	0	1	1
Bases Empty	.000	.500	.000	1	0	0	0	0	0	1	1		.000	.500	.000	1	0	0	0	0	0	1	1
Runners On Base	.000	.000	.000	0	0	0	0	0	0	0	0		.000	.000	.000	0	0	0	0	0	0	0	0

BRAD KOMMINSK — bats right — throws right — age 31 — OAK — O

7-YEAR TOTALS (1984–1991)

1991	BA	OBA	SA	AB	H	2B	3B	HR	RBI	BB	SO		BA	OBA	SA	AB	H	2B	3B	HR	RBI	BB	SO
vs. Left	.143	.143	.143	14	2	0	0	0	1	0	4		.200	.270	.312	420	84	14	3	9	38	39	117
vs. Right	.091	.231	.182	11	1	1	0	0	1	2	5		.233	.325	.359	529	123	21	2	14	63	70	134
at Home	.077	.143	.154	13	1	1	0	0	1	1	5		.216	.303	.356	481	104	20	4	13	58	60	125
on Road	.167	.231	.167	12	2	0	0	0	1	1	4		.220	.298	.321	468	103	15	1	10	43	49	126
Bases Empty	.000	.154	.000	11	0	0	0	0	0	2	4		.209	.289	.322	531	111	20	5	10	10	55	138
Runners On Base	.214	.214	.286	14	3	1	0	0	2	0	5		.230	.315	.359	418	96	15	0	13	91	54	113

CHAD KREUTER — bats both — throws right — age 28 — TEX — /C

3-YEAR TOTALS (1989–1991)

1991	BA	OBA	SA	AB	H	2B	3B	HR	RBI	BB	SO		BA	OBA	SA	AB	H	2B	3B	HR	RBI	BB	SO
vs. Left	.000	.000	.000	2	0	0	0	0	0	0	1		.173	.343	.385	52	9	2	0	3	6	14	14
vs. Right	.000	.000	.000	2	0	0	0	0	0	0	0		.121	.240	.182	132	16	2	0	2	5	21	36
at Home	.000	.000	.000	4	0	0	0	0	0	0	1		.151	.306	.233	86	13	1	0	2	6	20	24
on Road	.000	.000	.000	0	0	0	0	0	0	0	0		.122	.239	.245	98	12	3	0	3	5	15	26
Bases Empty	.000	.000	.000	0	0	0	0	0	0	0	0		.145	.291	.282	117	17	1	0	5	5	24	31
Runners On Base	.000	.000	.000	4	0	0	0	0	0	0	1		.119	.237	.164	67	8	3	0	0	6	11	19

STEVE LAKE — bats right — throws right — age 35 — PHI — C

8-YEAR TOTALS (1984–1991)

1991	BA	OBA	SA	AB	H	2B	3B	HR	RBI	BB	SO		BA	OBA	SA	AB	H	2B	3B	HR	RBI	BB	SO
vs. Left	.245	.259	.291	110	27	3	1	0	7	2	16		.256	.288	.340	468	120	17	2	6	48	20	60
vs. Right	.188	.188	.271	48	9	1	0	1	4	0	10		.213	.248	.291	399	85	12	2	5	39	16	66
at Home	.215	.225	.266	79	17	2	1	0	4	1	13		.246	.274	.329	395	97	14	2	5	37	14	54
on Road	.241	.250	.304	79	19	2	0	1	7	1	13		.229	.267	.307	472	108	15	2	6	50	22	72
Bases Empty	.225	.233	.258	89	20	1	1	0	0	1	13		.207	.229	.289	484	100	15	2	7	7	11	73
Runners On Base	.232	.243	.319	69	16	3	0	1	11	1	13		.274	.319	.352	383	105	14	2	4	80	25	53

TOM LAMPKIN — bats left — throws right — age 28 — SD — C

3-YEAR TOTALS (1988–1991)

1991	BA	OBA	SA	AB	H	2B	3B	HR	RBI	BB	SO		BA	OBA	SA	AB	H	2B	3B	HR	RBI	BB	SO
vs. Left	.000	.000	.000	0	0	0	0	0	0	0	0		.429	.429	.429	7	3	0	0	0	2	0	2
vs. Right	.190	.230	.276	58	11	3	1	0	3	3	9		.186	.238	.271	118	22	3	2	1	5	8	16
at Home	.250	.270	.361	36	9	2	1	0	2	1	6		.261	.292	.391	69	18	2	2	1	6	3	10
on Road	.091	.167	.136	22	2	1	0	0	1	2	3		.125	.197	.143	56	7	1	0	0	1	5	8
Bases Empty	.147	.147	.265	34	5	2	1	0	0	0	5		.181	.203	.306	72	13	2	1	1	1	2	11
Runners On Base	.250	.333	.292	24	6	1	0	0	3	3	4		.226	.305	.245	53	12	1	0	0	6	6	7

CED LANDRUM — bats left — throws right — age 29 — CHN — O

1-YEAR TOTALS (1991)

1991	BA	OBA	SA	AB	H	2B	3B	HR	RBI	BB	SO		BA	OBA	SA	AB	H	2B	3B	HR	RBI	BB	SO
vs. Left	.385	.467	.538	13	5	0	1	0	2	2	4		.385	.467	.538	13	5	0	1	0	2	2	4
vs. Right	.205	.284	.233	73	15	2	0	0	4	8	14		.205	.284	.233	73	15	2	0	0	4	8	14
at Home	.209	.292	.233	43	9	1	0	0	1	5	11		.209	.292	.233	43	9	1	0	0	1	5	11
on Road	.256	.333	.326	43	11	1	1	0	5	5	7		.256	.333	.326	43	11	1	1	0	5	5	7
Bases Empty	.206	.286	.238	63	13	1	0	0	0	7	14		.206	.286	.238	63	13	1	0	0	0	7	14
Runners On Base	.304	.385	.391	23	7	2	0	0	6	3	4		.304	.385	.391	23	7	2	0	0	6	3	4

CARNEY LANSFORD — bats right — throws right — age 35 — OAK — /3D

8-YEAR TOTALS (1984–1991)

1991	BA	OBA	SA	AB	H	2B	3B	HR	RBI	BB	SO		BA	OBA	SA	AB	H	2B	3B	HR	RBI	BB	SO
vs. Left	.000	.000	.000	9	0	0	0	0	0	0	2		.299	.357	.413	1124	336	43	8	23	98	101	83
vs. Right	.143	.143	.143	7	1	0	0	0	1	0	0		.287	.339	.399	2649	759	112	12	54	330	187	214
at Home	.091	.091	.091	11	1	0	0	0	1	0	2		.297	.352	.414	1816	540	83	10	36	221	142	134
on Road	.000	.000	.000	5	0	0	0	0	0	0	0		.284	.338	.393	1957	555	72	10	41	207	146	163
Bases Empty	.111	.111	.111	9	1	0	0	0	0	0	1		.285	.332	.403	2178	620	93	12	47	47	131	154
Runners On Base	.000	.000	.000	7	0	0	0	0	1	0	1		.298	.361	.403	1595	475	62	8	30	381	157	143

GENE LARKIN — bats both — throws right — age 30 — MIN — O1/D23

5-YEAR TOTALS (1987–1991)

1991	BA	OBA	SA	AB	H	2B	3B	HR	RBI	BB	SO		BA	OBA	SA	AB	H	2B	3B	HR	RBI	BB	SO
vs. Left	.273	.363	.398	88	24	8	0	1	6	13	7		.302	.377	.412	592	179	40	5	5	72	66	59
vs. Right	.293	.360	.359	167	49	6	1	1	13	17	14		.255	.344	.364	1248	318	66	5	20	134	153	159
at Home	.313	.387	.359	131	41	6	0	0	12	16	8		.283	.364	.396	935	265	56	5	13	118	111	95
on Road	.258	.333	.387	124	32	8	1	2	7	14	13		.256	.345	.362	905	232	50	5	12	88	108	123
Bases Empty	.329	.401	.421	140	46	10	0	1	1	17	11		.282	.368	.398	963	272	59	5	14	14	113	108
Runners On Base	.235	.313	.313	115	27	4	1	2	18	13	10		.257	.340	.359	877	225	47	5	11	192	106	110

VANCE LAW — bats right — throws right — age 36 — OAK — 3/SOP1

7-YEAR TOTALS (1984–1991)

1991	BA	OBA	SA	AB	H	2B	3B	HR	RBI	BB	SO		BA	OBA	SA	AB	H	2B	3B	HR	RBI	BB	SO
vs. Left	.259	.365	.352	54	14	5	0	0	7	9	11		.267	.348	.419	940	251	55	2	28	116	117	133
vs. Right	.175	.258	.225	80	14	2	1	0	2	9	16		.253	.323	.369	1954	495	95	15	34	224	208	345
at Home	.206	.286	.286	63	13	5	0	0	4	7	11		.266	.343	.401	1406	374	79	9	31	197	167	218
on Road	.211	.317	.268	71	15	2	1	0	5	11	16		.250	.321	.371	1488	372	71	8	31	143	158	260
Bases Empty	.162	.262	.230	74	12	3	1	0	0	10	14		.254	.322	.389	1623	412	82	10	39	39	161	266
Runners On Base	.267	.353	.333	60	16	4	0	0	9	8	13		.263	.343	.382	1271	334	68	7	23	301	164	212

TERRY LEE — bats right — throws right — age 30 — CIN — /1

2-YEAR TOTALS (1990–1991)

1991	BA	OBA	SA	AB	H	2B	3B	HR	RBI	BB	SO		BA	OBA	SA	AB	H	2B	3B	HR	RBI	BB	SO
vs. Left	.000	.000	.000	5	0	0	0	0	0	0	1		.182	.240	.227	22	4	1	0	0	3	2	3
vs. Right	.000	.000	.000	1	0	0	0	0	0	0	1		.000	.000	.000	3	0	0	0	0	0	0	1
at Home	.000	.000	.000	3	0	0	0	0	0	0	2		.100	.136	.100	20	2	0	0	0	1	1	4
on Road	.000	.000	.000	3	0	0	0	0	0	0	0		.400	.500	.600	5	2	1	0	0	2	1	0
Bases Empty	.000	.000	.000	3	0	0	0	0	0	0	2		.167	.286	.167	12	2	0	0	0	0	2	3
Runners On Base	.000	.000	.000	3	0	0	0	0	0	0	0		.154	.143	.231	13	2	1	0	0	3	0	1

SCOTT LEIUS — bats right — throws right — age 27 — MIN — 3S/O

2-YEAR TOTALS (1990–1991)

1991	BA	OBA	SA	AB	H	2B	3B	HR	RBI	BB	SO		BA	OBA	SA	AB	H	2B	3B	HR	RBI	BB	SO
vs. Left	.305	.427	.445	128	39	5	2	3	13	28	17		.301	.420	.455	143	43	6	2	4	17	30	18
vs. Right	.254	.274	.366	71	18	2	0	2	7	2	18		.247	.265	.346	81	20	2	0	2	7	2	19
at Home	.368	.435	.505	95	35	5	1	2	10	12	15		.369	.441	.505	103	38	6	1	2	13	14	15
on Road	.212	.328	.337	104	22	2	1	3	10	18	20		.207	.309	.339	121	25	2	1	4	11	18	22
Bases Empty	.313	.412	.500	112	35	5	2	4	4	19	16		.313	.405	.500	128	40	5	2	5	5	20	18
Runners On Base	.253	.333	.310	87	22	2	0	1	16	11	19		.240	.321	.302	96	23	3	0	1	19	12	19

MARK LEMKE — bats both — throws right — age 27 — ATL — *23

4-YEAR TOTALS (1988–1991)

1991	BA	OBA	SA	AB	H	2B	3B	HR	RBI	BB	SO		BA	OBA	SA	AB	H	2B	3B	HR	RBI	BB	SO
vs. Left	.252	.312	.333	111	28	7	1	0	11	11	7		.256	.313	.363	262	67	18	2	2	31	23	17
vs. Right	.222	.299	.297	158	35	4	1	2	12	18	20		.203	.274	.259	359	73	12	1	2	25	36	44
at Home	.280	.345	.386	132	37	8	0	2	14	14	13		.244	.303	.341	311	76	19	1	3	32	27	27
on Road	.190	.266	.241	137	26	3	2	0	9	15	14		.206	.277	.265	310	64	11	2	1	24	32	34
Bases Empty	.245	.319	.354	147	36	8	2	2	2	16	17		.198	.261	.278	363	72	18	1	3	3	31	42
Runners On Base	.221	.288	.262	122	27	3	1	0	21	13	10		.264	.329	.337	258	68	12	2	1	53	28	19

PATRICK LENNON — bats right — throws right — age 24 — SEA — /DO

1991	BA	OBA	SA	AB	H	2B	3B	HR	RBI	BB	SO
vs. Left	.125	.222	.250	8	1	1	0	0	1	1	1
vs. Right	.000	1.000	.000	0	0	0	0	0	0	2	0
at Home	.000	.333	.000	4	0	0	0	0	0	2	0
on Road	.250	.400	.500	4	1	1	0	0	1	1	1
Bases Empty	.000	.250	.000	3	0	0	0	0	0	1	1
Runners On Base	.200	.429	.400	5	1	1	0	0	1	2	0

1-YEAR TOTALS (1991)

BA	OBA	SA	AB	H	2B	3B	HR	RBI	BB	SO
.125	.222	.250	8	1	1	0	0	1	1	1
.000	1.000	.000	0	0	0	0	0	0	2	0
.000	.333	.000	4	0	0	0	0	0	2	0
.250	.400	.500	4	1	1	0	0	1	1	1
.000	.250	.000	3	0	0	0	0	0	1	1
.200	.429	.400	5	1	1	0	0	1	2	0

MARK LEONARD — bats left — throws right — age 28 — SF — O

1991	BA	OBA	SA	AB	H	2B	3B	HR	RBI	BB	SO
vs. Left	.000	.100	.000	9	0	0	0	0	0	1	2
vs. Right	.258	.321	.383	120	31	7	1	2	14	11	23
at Home	.167	.265	.217	60	10	3	0	0	5	8	13
on Road	.304	.342	.478	69	21	4	1	2	9	4	12
Bases Empty	.209	.274	.313	67	14	4	0	1	1	5	11
Runners On Base	.274	.338	.403	62	17	3	1	1	13	7	14

2-YEAR TOTALS (1990–1991)

BA	OBA	SA	AB	H	2B	3B	HR	RBI	BB	SO
.077	.143	.077	13	1	0	0	0	1	1	5
.248	.320	.391	133	33	8	1	3	15	14	28
.190	.292	.254	63	12	4	0	0	6	9	14
.265	.315	.446	83	22	4	1	3	10	6	19
.213	.289	.360	75	16	5	0	2	2	7	14
.254	.321	.366	71	18	3	1	1	14	8	19

DARREN LEWIS — bats right — throws right — age 25 — SF — O

1991	BA	OBA	SA	AB	H	2B	3B	HR	RBI	BB	SO
vs. Left	.284	.391	.405	74	21	4	1	1	6	12	7
vs. Right	.230	.341	.264	148	34	1	2	0	9	24	23
at Home	.231	.354	.248	121	28	2	0	0	6	21	15
on Road	.267	.362	.386	101	27	3	3	1	9	15	15
Bases Empty	.217	.333	.297	138	30	2	3	1	1	24	21
Runners On Base	.298	.398	.333	84	25	3	0	0	14	12	9

2-YEAR TOTALS (1990–1991)

BA	OBA	SA	AB	H	2B	3B	HR	RBI	BB	SO
.293	.402	.402	82	24	4	1	1	6	14	8
.223	.340	.251	175	39	1	2	0	10	29	26
.223	.341	.237	139	31	2	0	0	6	23	16
.271	.361	.373	118	32	3	3	1	10	20	18
.235	.361	.307	153	36	3	3	1	1	29	22
.260	.358	.288	104	27	3	0	0	15	14	12

JIM LEYRITZ — bats right — throws right — age 29 — NYA — 3/C1D

1991	BA	OBA	SA	AB	H	2B	3B	HR	RBI	BB	SO
vs. Left	.243	.333	.297	37	9	2	0	0	2	5	9
vs. Right	.125	.271	.150	40	5	1	0	0	2	8	6
at Home	.182	.379	.182	22	4	0	0	0	2	7	6
on Road	.182	.262	.236	55	10	3	0	0	2	6	9
Bases Empty	.173	.271	.231	52	9	3	0	0	0	7	9
Runners On Base	.200	.355	.200	25	5	0	0	0	4	6	6

2-YEAR TOTALS (1990–1991)

BA	OBA	SA	AB	H	2B	3B	HR	RBI	BB	SO
.279	.377	.400	140	39	9	1	2	9	20	24
.221	.293	.287	240	53	7	0	3	20	20	42
.255	.341	.340	188	48	11	1	1	15	22	31
.229	.308	.318	192	44	5	0	4	14	18	35
.250	.329	.346	228	57	11	1	3	3	21	38
.230	.318	.303	152	35	5	0	2	26	19	28

JIM LINDEMAN — bats right — throws right — age 30 — PHI — O/1

1991	BA	OBA	SA	AB	H	2B	3B	HR	RBI	BB	SO
vs. Left	.433	.514	.483	60	26	3	0	0	8	10	10
vs. Right	.171	.231	.229	35	6	2	0	0	4	3	4
at Home	.321	.400	.358	53	17	2	0	0	7	7	10
on Road	.357	.429	.429	42	15	3	0	0	5	6	4
Bases Empty	.315	.383	.370	54	17	3	0	0	0	6	10
Runners On Base	.366	.449	.415	41	15	2	0	0	12	7	4

6-YEAR TOTALS (1986–1991)

BA	OBA	SA	AB	H	2B	3B	HR	RBI	BB	SO
.253	.311	.374	281	71	10	0	8	41	26	74
.199	.236	.337	196	39	12	0	5	22	7	46
.223	.274	.322	233	52	11	0	4	31	16	68
.238	.287	.393	244	58	11	0	9	32	17	52
.234	.292	.426	244	57	14	0	11	11	17	63
.227	.270	.288	233	53	8	0	2	52	16	57

DOUG LINDSEY — bats right — throws right — age 25 — PHI — /C

1991	BA	OBA	SA	AB	H	2B	3B	HR	RBI	BB	SO
vs. Left	.000	.000	.000	0	0	0	0	0	0	0	0
vs. Right	.000	.000	.000	3	0	0	0	0	0	0	3
at Home	.000	.000	.000	3	0	0	0	0	0	0	3
on Road	.000	.000	.000	0	0	0	0	0	0	0	0
Bases Empty	.000	.000	.000	2	0	0	0	0	0	0	2
Runners On Base	.000	.000	.000	1	0	0	0	0	0	0	1

1-YEAR TOTALS (1991)

BA	OBA	SA	AB	H	2B	3B	HR	RBI	BB	SO
.000	.000	.000	0	0	0	0	0	0	0	0
.000	.000	.000	3	0	0	0	0	0	0	3
.000	.000	.000	3	0	0	0	0	0	0	3
.000	.000	.000	0	0	0	0	0	0	0	0
.000	.000	.000	2	0	0	0	0	0	0	2
.000	.000	.000	1	0	0	0	0	0	0	1

NELSON LIRIANO — bats both — throws right — age 28 — KC — 2

1991	BA	OBA	SA	AB	H	2B	3B	HR	RBI	BB	SO
vs. Left	.000	.000	.000	1	0	0	0	0	0	0	0
vs. Right	.429	.429	.429	21	9	0	0	0	1	0	2
at Home	.500	.500	.500	12	6	0	0	0	1	0	1
on Road	.300	.300	.300	10	3	0	0	0	0	0	1
Bases Empty	.375	.375	.375	16	6	0	0	0	0	0	0
Runners On Base	.500	.500	.500	6	3	0	0	0	1	0	2

5-YEAR TOTALS (1987–1991)

BA	OBA	SA	AB	H	2B	3B	HR	RBI	BB	SO
.237	.307	.321	312	74	11	3	3	36	32	60
.261	.318	.358	917	239	39	13	8	79	76	99
.262	.329	.368	608	159	26	12	5	66	62	88
.248	.302	.329	621	154	24	4	6	49	46	71
.245	.307	.342	717	176	34	7	7	7	60	87
.268	.327	.357	512	137	16	9	4	108	48	72

GREG LITTON — bats right — throws right — age 28 — SF — 123/SOPC

1991	BA	OBA	SA	AB	H	2B	3B	HR	RBI	BB	SO
vs. Left	.159	.213	.250	44	7	4	0	0	3	3	5
vs. Right	.193	.269	.289	83	16	3	1	1	12	8	20
at Home	.213	.275	.362	47	10	5	1	0	4	4	6
on Road	.162	.236	.225	80	13	2	0	1	11	7	19
Bases Empty	.181	.262	.278	72	13	4	1	0	0	8	15
Runners On Base	.182	.233	.273	55	10	3	0	1	14	3	10

3-YEAR TOTALS (1989–1991)

BA	OBA	SA	AB	H	2B	3B	HR	RBI	BB	SO
.258	.288	.392	283	73	15	4	5	30	12	50
.188	.262	.246	191	36	6	1	1	26	17	49
.283	.324	.426	223	63	13	5	3	31	12	48
.183	.236	.251	251	46	8	0	3	25	17	51
.224	.284	.343	254	57	9	3	5	5	20	55
.236	.269	.323	220	52	12	2	1	51	9	44

SCOTT LIVINGSTONE — bats left — throws right — age 27 — DET — 3

1991	BA	OBA	SA	AB	H	2B	3B	HR	RBI	BB	SO
vs. Left	.417	.500	.750	12	5	1	0	1	1	2	1
vs. Right	.278	.323	.339	115	32	4	0	1	10	8	24
at Home	.349	.408	.465	43	15	2	0	1	5	5	8
on Road	.262	.303	.333	84	22	3	0	1	6	5	17
Bases Empty	.324	.359	.459	74	24	4	0	2	2	4	18
Runners On Base	.245	.317	.264	53	13	1	0	0	9	6	7

1-YEAR TOTALS (1991)

BA	OBA	SA	AB	H	2B	3B	HR	RBI	BB	SO
.417	.500	.750	12	5	1	0	1	1	2	1
.278	.323	.339	115	32	4	0	1	10	8	24
.349	.408	.465	43	15	2	0	1	5	5	8
.262	.303	.333	84	22	3	0	1	6	5	17
.324	.359	.459	74	24	4	0	2	2	4	18
.245	.317	.264	53	13	1	0	0	9	6	7

KENNY LOFTON — bats left — throws left — age 25 — HOU — O

1991	BA	OBA	SA	AB	H	2B	3B	HR	RBI	BB	SO		BA	OBA	SA	AB	H	2B	3B	HR	RBI	BB	SO
vs. Left	.250	.318	.250	20	5	0	0	0	0	2	8		.250	.318	.250	20	5	0	0	0	0	2	8
vs. Right	.185	.228	.204	54	10	1	0	0	0	3	11		.185	.228	.204	54	10	1	0	0	0	3	11
at Home	.176	.222	.176	34	6	0	0	0	0	2	13		.176	.222	.176	34	6	0	0	0	0	2	13
on Road	.225	.279	.250	40	9	1	0	0	0	3	6		.225	.279	.250	40	9	1	0	0	0	3	6
Bases Empty	.180	.231	.180	61	11	0	0	0	0	4	14		.180	.231	.180	61	11	0	0	0	0	4	14
Runners On Base	.308	.357	.385	13	4	1	0	0	0	1	5		.308	.357	.385	13	4	1	0	0	0	1	5

LUIS LOPEZ — bats right — throws right — age 28 — CLE — C1/D3O

1991	BA	OBA	SA	AB	H	2B	3B	HR	RBI	BB	SO		BA	OBA	SA	AB	H	2B	3B	HR	RBI	BB	SO
vs. Left	.234	.275	.319	47	11	2	1	0	5	3	1		.208	.246	.283	53	11	2	1	0	5	3	3
vs. Right	.200	.243	.257	35	7	2	0	0	2	1	6		.200	.243	.257	35	7	2	0	0	2	1	6
at Home	.209	.255	.302	43	9	2	1	0	6	3	4		.209	.255	.289	45	9	2	1	0	6	3	4
on Road	.231	.268	.282	39	9	2	0	0	1	1	3		.209	.244	.256	43	9	2	0	0	1	1	5
Bases Empty	.255	.255	.298	47	12	2	0	0	0	0	5		.235	.235	.275	51	12	2	0	0	0	0	6
Runners On Base	.171	.268	.286	35	6	2	1	0	7	4	2		.162	.256	.270	37	6	2	1	0	7	4	3

TOREY LOVULLO — bats both — throws right — age 27 — NYA — 3

1991	BA	OBA	SA	AB	H	2B	3B	HR	RBI	BB	SO		BA	OBA	SA	AB	H	2B	3B	HR	RBI	BB	SO
vs. Left	.167	.167	.167	6	1	0	0	0	0	0	1		.114	.196	.182	44	5	0	0	1	4	5	7
vs. Right	.178	.260	.222	45	8	2	0	0	2	5	6		.191	.285	.278	115	22	5	1	1	4	15	22
at Home	.269	.321	.346	26	7	2	0	0	2	2	1		.206	.282	.254	63	13	3	0	0	1	7	8
on Road	.080	.179	.080	25	2	0	0	0	0	3	6		.146	.245	.250	96	14	2	1	2	7	13	21
Bases Empty	.200	.250	.200	30	6	0	0	0	0	2	5		.215	.277	.301	93	20	3	1	1	1	8	17
Runners On Base	.143	.250	.238	21	3	2	0	0	2	3	2		.106	.237	.182	66	7	2	0	1	7	12	12

SCOTT LUSADER — bats left — throws left — age 28 — NYA — O

1991	BA	OBA	SA	AB	H	2B	3B	HR	RBI	BB	SO		BA	OBA	SA	AB	H	2B	3B	HR	RBI	BB	SO
vs. Left	.000	.000	.000	0	0	0	0	0	0	0	0		.240	.269	.320	25	6	2	0	0	2	1	7
vs. Right	.143	.250	.143	7	1	0	0	0	0	1	3		.247	.317	.349	235	58	7	1	5	34	27	36
at Home	.167	.286	.167	6	1	0	0	0	0	1	3		.228	.308	.324	136	31	4	0	3	18	17	27
on Road	.000	.000	.000	1	0	0	0	0	0	0	0		.266	.319	.371	124	33	5	1	2	18	11	16
Bases Empty	.000	.000	.000	5	0	0	0	0	0	0	3		.235	.283	.272	162	38	6	0	0	0	11	30
Runners On Base	.500	.667	.500	2	1	0	0	0	1	1	0		.265	.355	.469	98	26	3	1	5	36	17	13

BARRY LYONS — bats right — throws right — age 32 — LA/CAL — /C1

1991	BA	OBA	SA	AB	H	2B	3B	HR	RBI	BB	SO		BA	OBA	SA	AB	H	2B	3B	HR	RBI	BB	SO
vs. Left	.000	.000	.000	8	0	0	0	0	0	0	2		.235	.275	.367	226	53	13	1	5	23	13	29
vs. Right	.167	.167	.167	6	1	0	0	0	0	0	0		.237	.269	.320	337	80	11	1	5	50	12	48
at Home	.000	.000	.000	5	0	0	0	0	0	0	2		.234	.275	.358	274	64	14	1	6	36	14	35
on Road	.111	.111	.111	9	1	0	0	0	0	0	0		.239	.269	.322	289	69	10	1	4	37	11	42
Bases Empty	.083	.083	.083	12	1	0	0	0	0	0	1		.230	.256	.318	305	70	10	1	5	5	10	39
Runners On Base	.000	.000	.000	2	0	0	0	0	0	0	1		.244	.289	.364	258	63	14	1	5	68	15	38

STEVE LYONS — bats left — throws right — age 32 — BOS — O23/1DPS

1991	BA	OBA	SA	AB	H	2B	3B	HR	RBI	BB	SO		BA	OBA	SA	AB	H	2B	3B	HR	RBI	BB	SO
vs. Left	.167	.231	.417	12	2	0	0	1	2	1	5		.241	.282	.324	395	95	8	5	5	42	25	90
vs. Right	.245	.280	.350	200	49	10	1	3	15	10	30		.258	.309	.349	1689	436	91	10	14	150	126	261
at Home	.217	.246	.317	120	26	6	0	2	9	8	14		.244	.293	.330	1046	255	44	11	8	94	73	161
on Road	.272	.316	.402	92	25	4	1	2	8	6	21		.266	.315	.358	1038	276	55	4	11	98	78	190
Bases Empty	.243	.293	.383	115	28	5	1	3	3	8	21		.253	.305	.342	1176	297	61	7	10	10	84	207
Runners On Base	.237	.257	.320	97	23	5	0	1	14	3	14		.258	.303	.347	908	234	38	8	9	182	67	144

EVER MAGALLANES — bats left — throws right — age 27 — CLE — /S

1991	BA	OBA	SA	AB	H	2B	3B	HR	RBI	BB	SO		BA	OBA	SA	AB	H	2B	3B	HR	RBI	BB	SO
vs. Left	.000	.000	.000	0	0	0	0	0	0	0	0		.000	.000	.000	0	0	0	0	0	0	0	0
vs. Right	.000	.333	.000	2	0	0	0	0	0	1	1		.000	.333	.000	2	0	0	0	0	0	1	1
at Home	.000	.333	.000	2	0	0	0	0	0	1	1		.000	.333	.000	2	0	0	0	0	0	1	1
on Road	.000	.000	.000	0	0	0	0	0	0	0	0		.000	.000	.000	0	0	0	0	0	0	0	0
Bases Empty	.000	.333	.000	2	0	0	0	0	0	1	1		.000	.333	.000	2	0	0	0	0	0	1	1
Runners On Base	.000	.000	.000	0	0	0	0	0	0	0	0		.000	.000	.000	0	0	0	0	0	0	0	0

FRED MANRIQUE — bats right — throws right — age 31 — OAK — /S2

1991	BA	OBA	SA	AB	H	2B	3B	HR	RBI	BB	SO		BA	OBA	SA	AB	H	2B	3B	HR	RBI	BB	SO
vs. Left	.100	.100	.100	10	1	0	0	0	0	0	1		.272	.315	.384	536	146	26	5	8	57	33	102
vs. Right	.182	.308	.182	11	2	0	0	0	0	2	0		.246	.279	.351	773	190	33	6	12	93	32	125
at Home	.167	.231	.167	12	2	0	0	0	0	1	0		.270	.319	.387	623	168	29	7	10	84	41	98
on Road	.111	.200	.111	9	1	0	0	0	0	1	1		.245	.271	.344	686	168	30	4	10	66	24	129
Bases Empty	.231	.286	.231	13	3	0	0	0	0	1	1		.240	.280	.334	779	187	30	8	9	9	36	151
Runners On Base	.000	.111	.000	8	0	0	0	0	0	1	0		.281	.315	.409	530	149	29	3	11	141	29	76

JEFF MANTO — bats right — throws right — age 28 — CLE — 31/CO

1991	BA	OBA	SA	AB	H	2B	3B	HR	RBI	BB	SO		BA	OBA	SA	AB	H	2B	3B	HR	RBI	BB	SO
vs. Left	.222	.280	.267	45	10	2	0	0	5	4	7		.236	.364	.292	72	17	4	0	0	8	15	13
vs. Right	.205	.320	.337	83	17	5	0	2	8	10	15		.205	.327	.371	132	27	8	1	4	19	20	27
at Home	.203	.324	.288	59	12	5	0	0	6	9	8		.222	.333	.342	117	26	9	1	1	16	24	24
on Road	.217	.289	.333	69	15	2	0	2	7	5	14		.207	.310	.345	87	18	3	0	3	11	11	16
Bases Empty	.205	.301	.329	73	15	3	0	0	0	8	16		.189	.318	.324	111	21	4	1	3	3	19	29
Runners On Base	.218	.313	.291	55	12	4	0	0	11	6	6		.247	.366	.366	93	23	8	0	1	24	16	11

KIRT MANWARING — bats right — throws right — age 27 — SF — C

1991	BA	OBA	SA	AB	H	2B	3B	HR	RBI	BB	SO		BA	OBA	SA	AB	H	2B	3B	HR	RBI	BB	SO
												5-YEAR TOTALS (1987–1991)											
vs. Left	.308	.333	.385	65	20	5	0	0	9	3	9		.234	.277	.283	244	57	8	2	0	20	12	34
vs. Right	.177	.236	.212	113	20	4	0	0	10	6	13		.211	.258	.274	270	57	12	1	1	33	10	41
at Home	.267	.305	.333	90	24	6	0	0	11	4	9		.239	.271	.287	251	60	10	1	0	29	6	35
on Road	.182	.237	.216	88	16	3	0	0	8	5	13		.205	.263	.270	263	54	10	2	1	24	16	40
Bases Empty	.218	.252	.282	110	24	7	0	0	0	3	13		.193	.226	.248	322	62	13	1	1	1	10	52
Runners On Base	.235	.299	.265	68	16	2	0	0	19	6	9		.271	.330	.328	192	52	7	2	0	52	12	23

MIKE MARSHALL — bats right — throws right — age 32 — BOS/CAL — /D10

1991	BA	OBA	SA	AB	H	2B	3B	HR	RBI	BB	SO		BA	OBA	SA	AB	H	2B	3B	HR	RBI	BB	SO
												8-YEAR TOTALS (1984–1991)											
vs. Left	.313	.313	.375	16	5	1	0	0	2	0	5		.258	.323	.455	994	256	57	2	45	140	96	210
vs. Right	.245	.245	.358	53	13	3	0	1	5	0	15		.276	.314	.448	2013	555	93	5	81	316	94	446
at Home	.237	.237	.368	38	9	2	0	1	5	0	9		.271	.316	.461	1502	407	79	3	67	226	91	312
on Road	.290	.290	.355	31	9	2	0	0	2	0	11		.268	.319	.439	1505	404	71	4	59	230	99	344
Bases Empty	.250	.250	.361	36	9	0	0	1	1	0	12		.261	.305	.433	1565	409	65	4	65	65	83	364
Runners On Base	.273	.273	.364	33	9	3	0	0	6	0	8		.279	.330	.469	1442	402	85	3	61	391	107	292

CARMELO MARTINEZ — bats right — throws right — age 32 — PIT/KC/CIN — 10/D

1991	BA	OBA	SA	AB	H	2B	3B	HR	RBI	BB	SO		BA	OBA	SA	AB	H	2B	3B	HR	RBI	BB	SO
												8-YEAR TOTALS (1984–1991)											
vs. Left	.223	.338	.323	130	29	7	0	2	16	23	32		.253	.364	.423	1110	281	62	2	41	168	198	184
vs. Right	.221	.311	.414	145	32	4	0	8	20	20	32		.240	.321	.393	1706	409	69	5	61	240	202	325
at Home	.215	.307	.362	130	28	4	0	5	15	18	28		.242	.343	.420	1375	333	55	3	61	215	212	253
on Road	.228	.339	.379	145	33	7	0	5	21	25	36		.248	.334	.391	1441	357	76	4	41	193	188	256
Bases Empty	.225	.347	.400	160	36	4	0	8	8	30	37		.231	.332	.392	1484	343	54	2	60	60	221	283
Runners On Base	.217	.290	.330	115	25	7	0	2	28	13	27		.261	.345	.420	1332	347	77	5	42	348	179	226

TINO MARTINEZ — bats left — throws right — age 25 — SEA — 1/D

1991	BA	OBA	SA	AB	H	2B	3B	HR	RBI	BB	SO		BA	OBA	SA	AB	H	2B	3B	HR	RBI	BB	SO
												2-YEAR TOTALS (1990–1991)											
vs. Left	.257	.333	.400	35	9	2	0	1	4	7	8		.260	.345	.380	50	13	3	0	1	2	7	8
vs. Right	.182	.244	.299	77	14	0	0	3	8	7	17		.192	.262	.285	130	25	3	0	3	12	13	25
at Home	.228	.290	.404	57	13	1	0	3	6	5	10		.203	.280	.338	74	15	1	0	3	6	8	12
on Road	.182	.254	.255	55	10	1	0	1	3	6	14		.217	.289	.292	106	23	5	0	1	8	12	21
Bases Empty	.241	.290	.466	58	14	1	0	4	4	4	11		.230	.300	.380	100	23	3	0	4	4	10	15
Runners On Base	.167	.254	.185	54	9	1	0	0	5	7	13		.188	.269	.225	80	15	3	0	0	10	10	18

CHITO MARTINEZ — bats left — throws left — age 27 — BAL — O/D1

1991	BA	OBA	SA	AB	H	2B	3B	HR	RBI	BB	SO		BA	OBA	SA	AB	H	2B	3B	HR	RBI	BB	SO
												1-YEAR TOTALS (1991)											
vs. Left	.207	.258	.345	29	6	1	0	1	1	2	10		.207	.258	.345	29	6	1	0	1	1	2	10
vs. Right	.278	.310	.540	187	52	11	1	12	32	9	41		.278	.310	.540	187	52	11	1	12	32	9	41
at Home	.276	.313	.562	105	29	6	0	8	19	6	22		.276	.313	.562	105	29	6	0	8	19	6	22
on Road	.261	.293	.468	111	29	6	1	5	14	5	29		.261	.293	.468	111	29	6	1	5	14	5	29
Bases Empty	.258	.310	.500	120	31	8	0	7	7	9	26		.258	.310	.500	120	31	8	0	7	7	9	26
Runners On Base	.281	.293	.531	96	27	4	1	6	26	2	25		.281	.293	.531	96	27	4	1	6	26	2	25

JOHN MARZANO — bats right — throws right — age 29 — BOS — C

1991	BA	OBA	SA	AB	H	2B	3B	HR	RBI	BB	SO		BA	OBA	SA	AB	H	2B	3B	HR	RBI	BB	SO
												5-YEAR TOTALS (1987–1991)											
vs. Left	.300	.333	.400	30	9	3	0	0	2	1	3		.244	.284	.317	123	30	9	0	0	8	6	23
vs. Right	.250	.247	.310	84	21	5	0	0	7	0	13		.253	.276	.378	288	73	18	0	6	35	8	49
at Home	.255	.250	.309	55	14	3	0	0	5	0	9		.234	.257	.361	205	48	11	0	5	24	4	41
on Road	.271	.290	.356	59	16	5	0	0	4	1	7		.267	.299	.359	206	55	16	0	1	19	10	31
Bases Empty	.226	.226	.258	62	14	2	0	0	0	0	8		.218	.229	.327	211	46	14	0	3	3	3	34
Runners On Base	.308	.321	.423	52	16	6	0	0	9	1	8		.285	.326	.395	200	57	13	0	3	40	11	38

ROB MAURER — bats left — throws left — age 25 — TEX — /1D

1991	BA	OBA	SA	AB	H	2B	3B	HR	RBI	BB	SO		BA	OBA	SA	AB	H	2B	3B	HR	RBI	BB	SO
												1-YEAR TOTALS (1991)											
vs. Left	.000	.000	.000	0	0	0	0	0	0	0	0		.000	.000	.000	0	0	0	0	0	0	0	0
vs. Right	.063	.211	.125	16	1	1	0	0	2	2	6		.063	.211	.125	16	1	1	0	0	2	2	6
at Home	.200	.429	.400	5	1	1	0	0	2	2	2		.200	.429	.400	5	1	1	0	0	2	2	2
on Road	.000	.083	.000	11	0	0	0	0	0	0	4		.000	.083	.000	11	0	0	0	0	0	0	4
Bases Empty	.000	.000	.000	10	0	0	0	0	0	0	3		.000	.000	.000	10	0	0	0	0	0	0	3
Runners On Base	.167	.444	.333	6	1	1	0	0	2	2	3		.167	.444	.333	6	1	1	0	0	2	2	3

DERRICK MAY — bats left — throws right — age 24 — CHN — /O

1991	BA	OBA	SA	AB	H	2B	3B	HR	RBI	BB	SO		BA	OBA	SA	AB	H	2B	3B	HR	RBI	BB	SO
												2-YEAR TOTALS (1990–1991)											
vs. Left	.000	.500	.000	1	0	0	0	0	0	1	0		.333	.500	.333	6	2	0	0	0	1	2	0
vs. Right	.238	.261	.476	21	5	2	0	1	3	1	1		.234	.250	.377	77	18	5	0	2	13	2	8
at Home	.250	.304	.500	20	5	2	0	1	3	2	1		.267	.320	.467	45	12	3	0	2	11	4	2
on Road	.000	.000	.000	2	0	0	0	0	0	0	0		.211	.211	.263	38	8	2	0	0	3	0	6
Bases Empty	.200	.250	.467	15	3	1	0	1	1	1	1		.204	.250	.286	49	10	2	0	1	1	3	5
Runners On Base	.286	.333	.429	7	2	1	0	0	2	0	0		.294	.306	.500	34	10	4	0	1	13	3	3

BRENT MAYNE — bats left — throws right — age 24 — KC — C/D

1991	BA	OBA	SA	AB	H	2B	3B	HR	RBI	BB	SO		BA	OBA	SA	AB	H	2B	3B	HR	RBI	BB	SO
												2-YEAR TOTALS (1990–1991)											
vs. Left	.091	.179	.091	22	2	0	0	0	3	3	8		.091	.179	.091	22	2	0	0	0	3	3	8
vs. Right	.268	.332	.349	209	56	8	0	3	28	20	34		.266	.335	.342	222	59	8	0	3	29	23	37
at Home	.269	.333	.346	130	35	4	0	2	19	13	23		.273	.336	.348	132	36	4	0	2	19	13	24
on Road	.228	.292	.297	101	23	4	0	1	12	10	19		.223	.299	.286	112	25	4	0	1	12	13	21
Bases Empty	.197	.255	.220	127	25	3	0	0	0	10	20		.197	.262	.219	137	27	3	0	0	0	12	21
Runners On Base	.317	.383	.452	104	33	5	0	3	31	13	22		.318	.387	.449	107	34	5	0	3	32	14	24

LLOYD McCLENDON — bats right — throws right — age 33 — PIT — O1/C

1991	BA	OBA	SA	AB	H	2B	3B	HR	RBI	BB	SO
vs. Left	.350	.429	.547	117	41	5	0	6	19	14	17
vs. Right	.130	.200	.239	46	6	2	0	1	5	4	6
at Home	.227	.301	.364	66	15	3	0	2	7	6	13
on Road	.330	.409	.526	97	32	4	0	5	17	12	10
Bases Empty	.366	.423	.606	71	26	5	0	4	4	7	7
Runners On Base	.228	.324	.348	92	21	2	0	3	20	11	16

5-YEAR TOTALS (1987–1991)

	BA	OBA	SA	AB	H	2B	3B	HR	RBI	BB	SO
	.273	.348	.431	432	118	20	0	16	62	51	66
	.214	.299	.353	309	66	11	1	10	41	37	47
	.239	.310	.371	356	85	14	0	11	46	36	55
	.257	.344	.423	385	99	17	1	15	57	52	58
	.272	.350	.431	390	106	18	1	14	14	47	57
	.222	.304	.362	351	78	13	0	12	89	41	56

RODNEY McCRAY — bats right — throws right — age 29 — CHA — /OD

1991	BA	OBA	SA	AB	H	2B	3B	HR	RBI	BB	SO
vs. Left	.000	.000	.000	1	0	0	0	0	0	0	0
vs. Right	.333	.333	.333	6	2	0	0	0	0	0	2
at Home	.500	.500	.500	2	1	0	0	0	0	0	0
on Road	.200	.200	.200	5	1	0	0	0	0	0	2
Bases Empty	.333	.333	.333	6	2	0	0	0	0	0	1
Runners On Base	.000	.000	.000	1	0	0	0	0	0	0	1

2-YEAR TOTALS (1990–1991)

	BA	OBA	SA	AB	H	2B	3B	HR	RBI	BB	SO
	.000	.000	.000	5	0	0	0	0	0	0	3
	.250	.333	.250	8	2	0	0	0	0	1	3
	.200	.333	.200	5	1	0	0	0	0	1	2
	.125	.125	.125	8	1	0	0	0	0	0	4
	.250	.250	.250	8	2	0	0	0	0	1	3
	.000	.167	.000	5	0	0	0	0	0	1	3

TERRY McDANIEL — bats right — throws right — age 26 — NYN — O

1991	BA	OBA	SA	AB	H	2B	3B	HR	RBI	BB	SO
vs. Left	.286	.333	.286	14	4	0	0	0	0	1	3
vs. Right	.133	.133	.200	15	2	1	0	0	2	0	8
at Home	.182	.217	.182	22	4	0	0	0	1	1	9
on Road	.286	.286	.429	7	2	1	0	0	2	0	2
Bases Empty	.133	.188	.133	15	2	0	0	0	0	1	6
Runners On Base	.286	.286	.357	14	4	1	0	0	2	0	5

1-YEAR TOTALS (1991)

	BA	OBA	SA	AB	H	2B	3B	HR	RBI	BB	SO
	.286	.333	.286	14	4	0	0	0	0	1	3
	.133	.133	.200	15	2	1	0	0	2	0	8
	.182	.217	.182	22	4	0	0	0	1	1	9
	.286	.286	.429	7	2	1	0	0	2	0	2
	.133	.188	.133	15	2	0	0	0	0	1	6
	.286	.286	.357	14	4	1	0	0	2	0	5

TIM McINTOSH — bats right — throws right — age 27 — MIL — /OD1

1991	BA	OBA	SA	AB	H	2B	3B	HR	RBI	BB	SO
vs. Left	.444	.444	.889	9	4	1	0	1	1	0	2
vs. Right	.000	.000	.000	2	0	0	0	0	0	0	2
at Home	.333	.333	.833	6	2	0	0	1	0	0	3
on Road	.400	.400	.600	5	2	1	0	0	0	0	1
Bases Empty	.500	.500	1.167	6	3	1	0	1	1	0	0
Runners On Base	.200	.200	.200	5	1	0	0	0	0	0	4

2-YEAR TOTALS (1990–1991)

	BA	OBA	SA	AB	H	2B	3B	HR	RBI	BB	SO
	.357	.357	.857	14	5	1	0	2	2	0	4
	.000	.000	.000	2	0	0	0	0	0	0	2
	.273	.273	.818	11	3	0	0	2	2	0	5
	.400	.400	.600	5	2	1	0	0	0	0	1
	.364	.364	1.000	11	4	1	0	2	2	0	2
	.200	.200	.200	5	1	0	0	0	0	0	4

JEFF McKNIGHT — bats both — throws right — age 29 — BAL — /OD1

1991	BA	OBA	SA	AB	H	2B	3B	HR	RBI	BB	SO
vs. Left	.150	.190	.150	20	3	0	0	0	1	1	3
vs. Right	.190	.227	.238	21	4	1	0	0	1	1	4
at Home	.190	.227	.238	21	4	1	0	0	2	1	4
on Road	.150	.190	.150	20	3	0	0	0	0	1	3
Bases Empty	.167	.250	.167	18	3	0	0	0	0	2	2
Runners On Base	.174	.174	.217	23	4	1	0	0	2	0	5

3-YEAR TOTALS (1989–1991)

	BA	OBA	SA	AB	H	2B	3B	HR	RBI	BB	SO
	.224	.274	.241	58	13	1	0	0	4	4	7
	.171	.237	.243	70	12	2	0	1	3	5	18
	.175	.217	.246	57	10	1	0	1	3	3	14
	.211	.282	.239	71	15	2	0	0	3	6	11
	.203	.267	.246	69	14	0	0	1	1	5	10
	.186	.238	.237	59	11	3	0	0	5	4	15

MARK McLEMORE — bats both — throws right — age 28 — HOU — 2

1991	BA	OBA	SA	AB	H	2B	3B	HR	RBI	BB	SO
vs. Left	.179	.233	.214	28	5	1	0	0	1	2	8
vs. Right	.121	.211	.121	33	4	0	0	0	1	4	5
at Home	.088	.158	.088	34	3	0	0	0	1	3	8
on Road	.222	.300	.259	27	6	1	0	0	1	3	5
Bases Empty	.158	.220	.184	38	6	1	0	0	0	3	8
Runners On Base	.130	.222	.130	23	3	0	0	0	2	3	5

6-YEAR TOTALS (1986–1991)

	BA	OBA	SA	AB	H	2B	3B	HR	RBI	BB	SO
	.225	.283	.286	276	62	10	2	1	23	23	38
	.225	.300	.290	618	139	20	4	4	52	68	111
	.221	.301	.292	425	94	12	3	1	38	50	68
	.228	.289	.286	469	107	18	3	1	37	41	81
	.234	.300	.298	516	121	18	3	3	3	47	84
	.212	.289	.275	378	80	12	3	2	72	44	65

LUIS MEDINA — bats right — throws left — age 29 — CLE — /D

1991	BA	OBA	SA	AB	H	2B	3B	HR	RBI	BB	SO
vs. Left	.000	.000	.000	10	0	0	0	0	0	0	6
vs. Right	.167	.286	.167	6	1	0	0	0	0	1	1
at Home	.000	.000	.000	6	0	0	0	0	0	0	5
on Road	.100	.182	.100	10	1	0	0	0	0	1	2
Bases Empty	.091	.167	.091	11	1	0	0	0	0	1	7
Runners On Base	.000	.000	.000	5	0	0	0	0	0	0	0

3-YEAR TOTALS (1988–1991)

	BA	OBA	SA	AB	H	2B	3B	HR	RBI	BB	SO
	.229	.270	.450	109	25	0	0	8	12	6	42
	.146	.239	.317	41	6	1	0	2	4	3	18
	.229	.280	.443	70	16	0	0	5	9	3	27
	.188	.244	.387	80	15	1	0	5	7	6	33
	.258	.310	.495	93	24	1	0	7	7	5	33
	.123	.180	.281	57	7	0	0	3	9	4	27

BOB MELVIN — bats right — throws right — age 31 — BAL — C/D

1991	BA	OBA	SA	AB	H	2B	3B	HR	RBI	BB	SO
vs. Left	.269	.348	.333	78	21	5	0	0	5	10	14
vs. Right	.240	.239	.293	150	36	5	0	1	18	1	32
at Home	.238	.258	.287	122	29	6	0	0	12	4	25
on Road	.264	.302	.330	106	28	4	0	1	11	7	21
Bases Empty	.255	.277	.314	137	35	5	0	1	1	4	29
Runners On Base	.242	.282	.297	91	22	5	0	0	22	7	17

7-YEAR TOTALS (1985–1991)

	BA	OBA	SA	AB	H	2B	3B	HR	RBI	BB	SO
	.280	.321	.409	707	198	42	2	15	82	45	98
	.196	.226	.286	968	190	31	4	16	97	40	232
	.216	.246	.315	802	173	31	2	15	84	35	162
	.246	.285	.359	873	215	42	4	16	95	50	168
	.205	.243	.307	954	196	36	2	19	19	47	198
	.266	.297	.379	721	192	37	4	12	160	38	132

LUIS MERCEDES — bats right — throws right — age 24 — BAL — O/D

1991	BA	OBA	SA	AB	H	2B	3B	HR	RBI	BB	SO
vs. Left	.212	.235	.212	33	7	0	0	0	0	1	8
vs. Right	.190	.292	.286	21	4	2	0	0	2	3	1
at Home	.172	.250	.241	29	5	2	0	0	2	3	4
on Road	.240	.269	.240	25	6	0	0	0	1	1	5
Bases Empty	.200	.263	.229	35	7	1	0	0	0	1	7
Runners On Base	.211	.250	.263	19	4	1	0	0	2	1	2

1-YEAR TOTALS (1991)

	BA	OBA	SA	AB	H	2B	3B	HR	RBI	BB	SO
	.212	.235	.212	33	7	0	0	0	0	1	8
	.190	.292	.286	21	4	2	0	0	2	3	1
	.172	.250	.241	29	5	2	0	0	2	3	4
	.240	.269	.240	25	6	0	0	0	1	1	5
	.200	.263	.229	35	7	1	0	0	0	3	7
	.211	.250	.263	19	4	1	0	0	2	1	2

MATT MERULLO — bats left — throws right — age 27 — CHA — C1/D

1991	BA	OBA	SA	AB	H	2B	3B	HR	RBI	BB	SO
vs. Left	.125	.222	.125	8	1	0	0	0	1	1	0
vs. Right	.235	.271	.356	132	31	1	0	5	20	8	18
at Home	.225	.256	.275	80	18	1	0	1	11	4	11
on Road	.233	.284	.433	60	14	0	0	4	10	5	7
Bases Empty	.211	.222	.380	71	15	0	0	4	4	1	13
Runners On Base	.246	.309	.304	69	17	1	0	1	17	8	5

2-YEAR TOTALS (1989–1991)

BA	OBA	SA	AB	H	2B	3B	HR	RBI	BB	SO
.200	.333	.400	15	3	0	0	1	2	3	2
.228	.265	.311	206	47	2	0	5	27	12	30
.213	.254	.268	127	27	1	0	2	15	8	21
.245	.291	.383	94	23	1	0	4	14	7	11
.207	.227	.336	116	24	0	0	5	5	3	22
.248	.311	.295	105	26	2	0	1	24	12	10

HENSLEY MEULENS — bats right — throws right — age 25 — NYA — OD/1

1991	BA	OBA	SA	AB	H	2B	3B	HR	RBI	BB	SO
vs. Left	.236	.297	.365	178	42	6	1	5	19	12	54
vs. Right	.200	.239	.245	110	22	2	0	1	10	6	43
at Home	.214	.261	.325	154	33	5	0	4	16	8	54
on Road	.231	.293	.313	134	31	3	1	2	13	10	43
Bases Empty	.194	.245	.267	180	35	4	0	3	3	10	61
Runners On Base	.269	.325	.407	108	29	4	1	3	26	8	36

3-YEAR TOTALS (1989–1991)

BA	OBA	SA	AB	H	2B	3B	HR	RBI	BB	SO
.243	.300	.379	214	52	9	1	6	24	14	64
.200	.270	.281	185	37	6	0	3	16	15	66
.231	.283	.358	229	53	11	0	6	22	14	73
.212	.289	.300	170	36	4	1	3	18	15	57
.204	.267	.306	245	50	10	0	5	5	18	83
.253	.316	.377	154	39	5	1	4	35	11	47

KEITH MITCHELL — bats right — throws right — age 23 — ATL — O

1991	BA	OBA	SA	AB	H	2B	3B	HR	RBI	BB	SO
vs. Left	.345	.424	.345	29	10	0	0	0	1	4	3
vs. Right	.297	.366	.459	37	11	0	0	2	4	4	9
at Home	.452	.500	.548	31	14	0	0	1	3	3	4
on Road	.200	.300	.286	35	7	0	0	1	2	5	8
Bases Empty	.348	.423	.478	46	16	0	0	2	2	6	7
Runners On Base	.250	.318	.250	20	5	0	0	0	3	2	5

1-YEAR TOTALS (1991)

BA	OBA	SA	AB	H	2B	3B	HR	RBI	BB	SO
.345	.424	.345	29	10	0	0	0	1	4	3
.297	.366	.459	37	11	0	0	2	4	4	9
.452	.500	.548	31	14	0	0	1	3	3	4
.200	.300	.286	35	7	0	0	1	2	5	8
.348	.423	.478	46	16	0	0	2	2	6	7
.250	.318	.250	20	5	0	0	0	3	2	5

BOBBY MOORE — bats right — throws right — age 27 — KC — O

1991	BA	OBA	SA	AB	H	2B	3B	HR	RBI	BB	SO
vs. Left	.455	.500	.545	11	5	1	0	0	0	1	0
vs. Right	.000	.000	.000	3	0	0	0	0	0	0	2
at Home	.200	.333	.200	5	1	0	0	0	0	1	1
on Road	.444	.444	.556	9	4	1	0	0	0	0	1
Bases Empty	.417	.462	.500	12	5	1	0	0	0	1	1
Runners On Base	.000	.000	.000	2	0	0	0	0	0	0	1

1-YEAR TOTALS (1991)

BA	OBA	SA	AB	H	2B	3B	HR	RBI	BB	SO
.455	.500	.545	11	5	1	0	0	0	1	0
.000	.000	.000	3	0	0	0	0	0	0	2
.200	.333	.200	5	1	0	0	0	0	1	1
.444	.444	.556	9	4	1	0	0	0	0	1
.417	.462	.500	12	5	1	0	0	0	1	1
.000	.000	.000	2	0	0	0	0	0	0	1

RUSS MORMAN — bats right — throws right — age 30 — KC — /1OD

1991	BA	OBA	SA	AB	H	2B	3B	HR	RBI	BB	SO
vs. Left	.238	.273	.238	21	5	0	0	0	1	1	5
vs. Right	.500	.500	.500	2	1	0	0	0	0	0	0
at Home	.200	.250	.200	15	3	0	0	0	1	1	4
on Road	.375	.375	.375	8	3	0	0	0	1	0	1
Bases Empty	.231	.231	.231	13	3	0	0	0	1	0	4
Runners On Base	.300	.364	.300	10	3	0	0	0	1	1	1

5-YEAR TOTALS (1986–1991)

BA	OBA	SA	AB	H	2B	3B	HR	RBI	BB	SO
.251	.295	.333	219	55	7	1	3	19	12	48
.241	.320	.346	133	32	6	1	2	13	17	29
.250	.310	.319	144	36	5	1	1	10	11	33
.245	.301	.351	208	51	8	1	4	22	18	44
.261	.310	.377	199	52	7	2	4	4	13	47
.229	.299	.288	153	35	6	0	1	28	16	30

JOHN MORRIS — bats left — throws left — age 31 — PHI — O

1991	BA	OBA	SA	AB	H	2B	3B	HR	RBI	BB	SO
vs. Left	.364	.462	.364	11	4	0	0	0	0	1	1
vs. Right	.207	.276	.267	116	24	2	1	1	6	11	24
at Home	.238	.324	.317	63	15	0	1	1	4	7	10
on Road	.203	.261	.234	64	13	2	0	0	2	5	15
Bases Empty	.244	.311	.317	82	20	1	1	0	1	8	18
Runners On Base	.178	.260	.200	45	8	1	0	0	5	4	7

6-YEAR TOTALS (1986–1991)

BA	OBA	SA	AB	H	2B	3B	HR	RBI	BB	SO
.270	.303	.302	63	17	2	0	0	9	2	14
.237	.289	.336	494	117	12	8	7	51	36	83
.233	.292	.372	253	59	8	6	5	32	20	44
.247	.290	.299	304	75	6	2	2	28	18	53
.237	.285	.339	316	75	7	5	2	5	20	57
.245	.299	.324	241	59	7	3	2	55	18	40

LLOYD MOSEBY — bats left — throws right — age 33 — DET — O/D

1991	BA	OBA	SA	AB	H	2B	3B	HR	RBI	BB	SO
vs. Left	.239	.340	.391	46	11	4	0	1	9	6	11
vs. Right	.266	.316	.397	214	57	11	1	5	26	15	32
at Home	.272	.335	.417	151	41	8	1	4	25	13	26
on Road	.248	.299	.367	109	27	7	0	2	10	8	17
Bases Empty	.255	.311	.376	149	38	7	1	3	3	10	29
Runners On Base	.270	.333	.423	111	30	8	0	3	32	11	14

8-YEAR TOTALS (1984–1991)

BA	OBA	SA	AB	H	2B	3B	HR	RBI	BB	SO
.240	.320	.359	1316	316	53	11	27	142	133	280
.265	.349	.446	2706	716	129	36	97	373	350	493
.254	.347	.428	1953	497	85	29	65	265	261	377
.259	.333	.408	2069	535	97	18	59	250	222	396
.253	.336	.407	2324	588	103	29	66	66	268	470
.261	.345	.432	1698	444	79	18	58	449	215	303

JOHN MOSES — bats both — throws left — age 35 — DET — O

1991	BA	OBA	SA	AB	H	2B	3B	HR	RBI	BB	SO
vs. Left	.000	.000	.000	3	0	0	0	0	1	0	1
vs. Right	.056	.150	.111	18	1	1	0	0	0	2	6
at Home	.000	.000	.000	4	0	0	0	0	0	0	2
on Road	.059	.158	.118	17	1	1	0	0	1	2	5
Bases Empty	.067	.176	.133	15	1	1	0	0	0	2	7
Runners On Base	.000	.000	.000	6	0	0	0	0	1	0	1

8-YEAR TOTALS (1984–1991)

BA	OBA	SA	AB	H	2B	3B	HR	RBI	BB	SO
.257	.321	.322	354	91	10	2	3	28	33	36
.259	.313	.340	1172	303	49	13	7	107	89	161
.242	.308	.331	741	179	32	11	4	70	66	96
.274	.321	.341	785	215	27	4	6	65	56	101
.247	.300	.323	963	238	38	10	5	5	67	133
.277	.339	.359	563	156	21	5	5	130	55	64

ANDY MOTA — bats right — throws right — age 26 — HOU — 2

1991	BA	OBA	SA	AB	H	2B	3B	HR	RBI	BB	SO
vs. Left	.114	.139	.114	35	4	0	0	0	1	1	11
vs. Right	.236	.236	.327	55	13	2	0	1	5	0	6
at Home	.159	.159	.182	44	7	1	0	0	3	0	9
on Road	.217	.234	.304	46	10	1	0	1	3	1	8
Bases Empty	.208	.224	.229	48	10	1	0	0	1	1	10
Runners On Base	.167	.167	.262	42	7	1	0	1	6	0	7

1-YEAR TOTALS (1991)

BA	OBA	SA	AB	H	2B	3B	HR	RBI	BB	SO
.114	.139	.114	35	4	0	0	0	1	1	11
.236	.236	.327	55	13	2	0	1	5	0	6
.159	.159	.182	44	7	1	0	0	3	0	9
.217	.234	.304	46	10	1	0	1	3	1	8
.208	.224	.229	48	10	1	0	0	1	1	10
.167	.167	.262	42	7	1	0	1	6	0	7

JOSE MOTA — bats both — throws right — age 27 — SD — 2/S

1991	BA	OBA	SA	AB	H	2B	3B	HR	RBI	BB	SO
vs. Left	.444	.444	.444	9	4	0	0	0	0	0	0
vs. Right	.148	.233	.148	27	4	0	0	0	2	2	7
at Home	.238	.304	.238	21	5	0	0	0	2	2	2
on Road	.200	.250	.200	15	3	0	0	0	0	0	5
Bases Empty	.182	.280	.182	22	4	0	0	0	0	2	4
Runners On Base	.286	.286	.286	14	4	0	0	0	2	0	3

1-YEAR TOTALS (1991)

BA	OBA	SA	AB	H	2B	3B	HR	RBI	BB	SO
.444	.444	.444	9	4	0	0	0	0	0	0
.148	.233	.148	27	4	0	0	0	2	2	7
.238	.304	.238	21	5	0	0	0	2	2	2
.200	.250	.200	15	3	0	0	0	0	0	5
.182	.280	.182	22	4	0	0	0	0	0	4
.286	.286	.286	14	4	0	0	0	2	0	3

PEDRO MUNOZ — bats right — throws right — age 24 — MIN — O/D

1991	BA	OBA	SA	AB	H	2B	3B	HR	RBI	BB	SO
vs. Left	.295	.333	.591	44	13	2	1	3	16	3	12
vs. Right	.277	.324	.457	94	26	5	0	4	10	6	19
at Home	.313	.356	.552	67	21	4	0	4	14	5	12
on Road	.254	.299	.451	71	18	3	1	3	12	4	19
Bases Empty	.320	.346	.520	75	24	6	0	3	3	3	17
Runners On Base	.238	.306	.476	63	15	1	1	4	23	6	14

2-YEAR TOTALS (1990–1991)

BA	OBA	SA	AB	H	2B	3B	HR	RBI	BB	SO
.328	.351	.567	67	22	3	2	3	18	4	13
.256	.291	.385	156	40	8	0	4	13	7	34
.275	.302	.459	109	30	6	1	4	17	5	24
.281	.317	.421	114	32	5	1	3	14	6	23
.302	.323	.457	129	39	9	1	3	3	3	26
.245	.292	.415	94	23	2	1	4	28	7	21

TIM NAEHRING — bats right — throws right — age 25 — BOS — S/32

1991	BA	OBA	SA	AB	H	2B	3B	HR	RBI	BB	SO
vs. Left	.125	.222	.125	16	2	0	0	0	0	2	6
vs. Right	.103	.186	.128	39	4	1	0	0	3	4	9
at Home	.063	.189	.063	32	2	0	0	0	1	5	11
on Road	.174	.208	.217	23	4	1	0	0	2	1	4
Bases Empty	.088	.205	.088	34	3	0	0	0	0	5	11
Runners On Base	.143	.182	.190	21	3	1	0	0	3	1	4

2-YEAR TOTALS (1990–1991)

BA	OBA	SA	AB	H	2B	3B	HR	RBI	BB	SO
.311	.404	.444	45	14	3	0	1	7	7	10
.158	.216	.232	95	15	4	0	1	8	7	20
.154	.254	.308	52	8	2	0	2	7	7	18
.239	.295	.295	88	21	5	0	0	8	7	12
.167	.247	.238	84	14	3	0	1	1	9	19
.268	.328	.393	56	15	4	0	1	14	5	11

AL NEWMAN — bats both — throws right — age 32 — MIN — S23/D10

1991	BA	OBA	SA	AB	H	2B	3B	HR	RBI	BB	SO
vs. Left	.242	.265	.303	66	16	4	0	0	8	2	7
vs. Right	.172	.259	.178	180	31	1	0	0	11	21	14
at Home	.179	.263	.205	117	21	3	0	0	10	13	8
on Road	.202	.257	.217	129	26	2	0	0	9	10	13
Bases Empty	.167	.252	.174	132	22	1	0	0	0	15	13
Runners On Base	.219	.270	.254	114	25	4	0	0	19	8	8

7-YEAR TOTALS (1985–1991)

BA	OBA	SA	AB	H	2B	3B	HR	RBI	BB	SO
.250	.327	.326	565	141	34	3	1	51	65	72
.217	.292	.245	1293	280	29	4	0	93	137	114
.233	.322	.275	918	214	30	4	0	78	121	85
.220	.282	.265	940	207	33	3	1	66	81	101
.212	.299	.247	1111	235	31	4	0	0	137	130
.249	.308	.304	747	186	32	3	1	144	65	56

WARREN NEWSON — bats left — throws left — age 28 — CHA — O/D

1991	BA	OBA	SA	AB	H	2B	3B	HR	RBI	BB	SO
vs. Left	.143	.250	.143	7	1	0	0	0	0	1	3
vs. Right	.304	.428	.440	125	38	5	0	4	25	27	31
at Home	.279	.364	.338	68	19	1	0	1	13	9	16
on Road	.313	.470	.516	64	20	4	0	3	12	19	18
Bases Empty	.262	.407	.431	65	17	2	0	3	3	16	18
Runners On Base	.328	.430	.418	67	22	3	0	1	22	12	16

1-YEAR TOTALS (1991)

BA	OBA	SA	AB	H	2B	3B	HR	RBI	BB	SO
.143	.250	.143	7	1	0	0	0	0	1	3
.304	.428	.440	125	38	5	0	4	25	27	31
.279	.364	.338	68	19	1	0	1	13	9	16
.313	.470	.516	64	20	4	0	3	12	19	18
.262	.407	.431	65	17	2	0	3	3	16	18
.328	.430	.418	67	22	3	0	1	22	12	16

CARL NICHOLS — bats right — throws right — age 30 — HOU — C

1991	BA	OBA	SA	AB	H	2B	3B	HR	RBI	BB	SO
vs. Left	.200	.310	.200	25	5	0	0	0	0	4	9
vs. Right	.192	.222	.308	26	5	3	0	0	1	1	8
at Home	.273	.333	.364	22	6	2	0	0	1	2	7
on Road	.138	.219	.172	29	4	1	0	0	1	3	10
Bases Empty	.194	.265	.258	31	6	2	0	0	0	3	11
Runners On Base	.200	.273	.250	20	4	1	0	0	1	2	6

6-YEAR TOTALS (1986–1991)

BA	OBA	SA	AB	H	2B	3B	HR	RBI	BB	SO
.198	.275	.231	121	24	4	0	0	17	14	29
.215	.271	.277	65	14	4	0	1	4	4	20
.232	.295	.284	95	22	5	0	0	11	8	25
.176	.252	.209	91	16	3	0	1	7	10	24
.176	.226	.222	108	19	5	0	0	0	7	30
.244	.333	.282	78	19	3	0	1	18	11	19

JUNIOR NOBOA — bats right — throws right — age 28 — MON — /023S1

1991	BA	OBA	SA	AB	H	2B	3B	HR	RBI	BB	SO
vs. Left	.256	.266	.333	78	20	3	0	1	2	1	7
vs. Right	.176	.176	.176	17	3	0	0	0	0	0	1
at Home	.213	.213	.234	47	10	1	0	0	0	0	5
on Road	.271	.286	.375	48	13	2	0	1	2	1	3
Bases Empty	.279	.279	.377	61	17	3	0	1	1	0	4
Runners On Base	.176	.200	.176	34	6	0	0	0	1	1	4

6-YEAR TOTALS (1984–1991)

BA	OBA	SA	AB	H	2B	3B	HR	RBI	BB	SO
.259	.284	.307	251	65	7	1	1	13	10	21
.221	.235	.282	149	33	5	2	0	11	2	13
.256	.274	.299	211	54	7	1	0	13	5	17
.233	.258	.296	189	44	5	2	1	11	7	17
.234	.250	.302	235	55	7	3	1	1	5	20
.261	.288	.291	165	43	5	0	0	23	7	14

KEN OBERKFELL — bats left — throws right — age 36 — HOU — 1/3

1991	BA	OBA	SA	AB	H	2B	3B	HR	RBI	BB	SO
vs. Left	.333	.333	.333	3	1	0	0	0	0	0	1
vs. Right	.224	.358	.284	67	15	4	0	0	14	14	7
at Home	.250	.486	.292	24	6	1	0	0	6	11	2
on Road	.217	.265	.283	46	10	3	0	0	8	3	6
Bases Empty	.219	.265	.250	32	7	1	0	0	0	2	2
Runners On Base	.237	.420	.316	38	9	3	0	0	14	12	6

8-YEAR TOTALS (1984–1991)

BA	OBA	SA	AB	H	2B	3B	HR	RBI	BB	SO
.250	.309	.323	585	146	25	6	2	67	50	63
.273	.351	.359	2013	549	104	11	16	171	239	140
.276	.353	.358	1272	351	57	10	9	134	154	87
.259	.330	.345	1326	344	72	7	9	104	135	116
.271	.337	.347	1538	417	79	5	9	9	140	121
.262	.347	.358	1060	278	50	12	9	229	149	82

CHARLIE O'BRIEN — bats right — throws right — age 32 — NYN — C

1991	BA	OBA	SA	AB	H	2B	3B	HR	RBI	BB	SO
vs. Left	.169	.235	.234	77	13	2	0	1	7	6	10
vs. Right	.198	.302	.275	91	18	4	0	1	7	11	15
at Home	.185	.292	.247	81	15	4	0	1	7	10	10
on Road	.184	.253	.264	87	16	4	0	1	7	7	15
Bases Empty	.182	.250	.253	99	18	4	0	1	1	8	16
Runners On Base	.188	.301	.261	69	13	2	0	1	13	9	9

6-YEAR TOTALS (1985–1991)

BA	OBA	SA	AB	H	2B	3B	HR	RBI	BB	SO
.191	.259	.305	341	65	20	1	5	26	26	41
.214	.308	.298	392	84	16	1	5	53	44	52
.203	.288	.319	335	68	14	2	7	37	36	38
.204	.284	.286	398	81	22	1	3	42	34	55
.164	.246	.239	426	70	15	1	5	5	38	59
.257	.339	.388	307	79	21	2	5	74	32	34

JOSE OFFERMAN — bats both — throws right — age 24 — LA — S

1991	BA	OBA	SA	AB	H	2B	3B	HR	RBI	BB	SO
vs. Left	.286	.375	.306	49	14	1	0	0	2	7	11
vs. Right	.125	.325	.141	64	8	1	0	0	1	18	21
at Home	.230	.390	.262	61	14	2	0	0	1	15	15
on Road	.154	.290	.154	52	8	0	0	0	2	10	17
Bases Empty	.194	.299	.224	67	13	2	0	0	0	9	18
Runners On Base	.196	.403	.196	46	9	0	0	0	3	16	14

2-YEAR TOTALS (1990–1991)

BA	OBA	SA	AB	H	2B	3B	HR	RBI	BB	SO
.253	.317	.267	75	19	1	0	0	4	7	15
.125	.294	.167	96	12	1	0	1	6	22	31
.198	.319	.250	96	19	2	0	1	4	16	23
.160	.284	.160	75	12	0	0	0	6	13	23
.194	.282	.245	98	19	2	0	1	1	11	23
.164	.330	.164	73	12	0	0	0	9	18	23

JIM OLANDER — bats right — throws right — age 29 — MIL — /OD

1991	BA	OBA	SA	AB	H	2B	3B	HR	RBI	BB	SO
vs. Left	.000	.200	.000	8	0	0	0	0	0	2	5
vs. Right	.000	.000	.000	1	0	0	0	0	0	0	0
at Home	.000	.125	.000	7	0	0	0	0	0	1	4
on Road	.000	.333	.000	2	0	0	0	0	0	1	1
Bases Empty	.000	.167	.000	5	0	0	0	0	0	1	2
Runners On Base	.000	.200	.000	4	0	0	0	0	0	1	3

1-YEAR TOTALS (1991)

BA	OBA	SA	AB	H	2B	3B	HR	RBI	BB	SO
.000	.200	.000	8	0	0	0	0	0	2	5
.000	.000	.000	1	0	0	0	0	0	0	0
.000	.125	.000	7	0	0	0	0	0	1	4
.000	.333	.000	2	0	0	0	0	0	1	1
.000	.167	.000	5	0	0	0	0	0	1	2
.000	.200	.000	4	0	0	0	0	0	1	3

JUNIOR ORTIZ — bats right — throws right — age 33 — MIN — C

1991	BA	OBA	SA	AB	H	2B	3B	HR	RBI	BB	SO
vs. Left	.143	.217	.190	42	6	0	1	0	5	4	5
vs. Right	.239	.327	.293	92	22	5	0	0	6	11	7
at Home	.188	.257	.234	64	12	1	1	0	7	6	5
on Road	.229	.325	.286	70	16	4	0	0	4	9	7
Bases Empty	.250	.363	.294	68	17	3	0	0	0	11	7
Runners On Base	.167	.214	.227	66	11	2	1	0	11	4	5

8-YEAR TOTALS (1984–1991)

BA	OBA	SA	AB	H	2B	3B	HR	RBI	BB	SO
.270	.327	.331	507	137	21	2	2	53	42	55
.261	.314	.319	609	159	22	2	3	68	46	70
.292	.352	.349	544	159	22	3	1	77	50	53
.240	.288	.301	572	137	21	1	4	44	38	72
.246	.299	.310	626	154	26	1	4	4	43	72
.290	.346	.343	490	142	17	3	1	117	45	53

JAVIER ORTIZ — bats right — throws right — age 29 — HOU — O

1991	BA	OBA	SA	AB	H	2B	3B	HR	RBI	BB	SO
vs. Left	.255	.386	.298	47	12	2	0	0	2	10	10
vs. Right	.306	.375	.500	36	11	2	1	1	3	4	4
at Home	.344	.382	.438	32	11	3	0	0	2	2	5
on Road	.235	.381	.353	51	12	1	1	1	3	12	9
Bases Empty	.357	.449	.524	42	15	2	1	1	1	7	8
Runners On Base	.195	.313	.244	41	8	2	0	0	4	7	6

2-YEAR TOTALS (1990–1991)

BA	OBA	SA	AB	H	2B	3B	HR	RBI	BB	SO
.291	.386	.419	86	25	6	1	1	7	14	15
.257	.360	.365	74	19	3	1	1	8	12	10
.286	.363	.400	70	20	5	0	1	11	9	9
.267	.383	.389	90	24	4	2	1	4	17	16
.313	.421	.475	80	25	3	2	2	2	15	14
.237	.326	.313	80	19	6	0	0	13	11	11

JOHN ORTON — bats right — throws right — age 27 — CAL — C

1991	BA	OBA	SA	AB	H	2B	3B	HR	RBI	BB	SO
vs. Left	.316	.381	.368	19	6	1	0	0	1	2	2
vs. Right	.160	.288	.220	50	8	3	0	0	2	8	15
at Home	.167	.231	.292	24	4	3	0	0	1	2	8
on Road	.222	.352	.244	45	10	1	0	0	2	8	9
Bases Empty	.184	.311	.211	38	7	1	0	0	0	7	8
Runners On Base	.226	.314	.323	31	7	3	0	0	3	3	9

3-YEAR TOTALS (1989–1991)

BA	OBA	SA	AB	H	2B	3B	HR	RBI	BB	SO
.211	.262	.246	57	12	2	0	0	2	4	16
.185	.267	.267	135	25	8	0	1	11	13	49
.145	.193	.193	83	12	4	0	0	5	4	31
.229	.317	.312	109	25	6	0	1	8	13	34
.179	.250	.239	117	21	4	0	1	1	11	38
.213	.289	.293	75	16	6	0	0	12	6	27

ERIK PAPPAS — bats right — throws right — age 26 — CHN — /C

1991	BA	OBA	SA	AB	H	2B	3B	HR	RBI	BB	SO
vs. Left	.100	.182	.100	10	1	0	0	0	1	1	3
vs. Right	.286	.286	.286	7	2	0	0	0	1	0	2
at Home	.500	.500	.500	2	1	0	0	0	0	0	0
on Road	.133	.188	.133	15	2	0	0	0	2	1	5
Bases Empty	.077	.143	.077	13	1	0	0	0	0	1	4
Runners On Base	.500	.500	.500	4	2	0	0	0	2	0	1

1-YEAR TOTALS (1991)

BA	OBA	SA	AB	H	2B	3B	HR	RBI	BB	SO
.100	.182	.100	10	1	0	0	0	1	1	3
.286	.286	.286	7	2	0	0	0	1	0	2
.500	.500	.500	2	1	0	0	0	0	0	0
.133	.188	.133	15	2	0	0	0	2	1	5
.077	.143	.077	13	1	0	0	0	0	1	4
.500	.500	.500	4	2	0	0	0	2	0	1

JOHNNY PAREDES — bats right — throws right — age 30 — DET — /2D3S

1991	BA	OBA	SA	AB	H	2B	3B	HR	RBI	BB	SO
vs. Left	.357	.357	.357	14	5	0	0	0	0	0	1
vs. Right	.250	.250	.250	4	1	0	0	0	0	0	0
at Home	.667	.667	.667	6	4	0	0	0	0	0	0
on Road	.167	.167	.167	12	2	0	0	0	0	0	1
Bases Empty	.308	.308	.308	13	4	0	0	0	0	0	1
Runners On Base	.400	.400	.400	5	2	0	0	0	0	0	1

3-YEAR TOTALS (1988–1991)

BA	OBA	SA	AB	H	2B	3B	HR	RBI	BB	SO
.319	.360	.362	47	15	2	0	0	4	3	3
.145	.253	.197	76	11	1	0	1	7	8	15
.220	.304	.244	41	9	1	0	0	2	5	5
.207	.286	.268	82	17	2	0	1	9	6	13
.239	.308	.282	71	17	3	0	0	0	5	11
.173	.271	.231	52	9	0	0	1	11	6	7

MARK PARENT — bats right — throws right — age 31 — TEX — /C

1991	BA	OBA	SA	AB	H	2B	3B	HR	RBI	BB	SO
vs. Left	.000	.000	.000	1	0	0	0	0	0	0	1
vs. Right	.000	.000	.000	0	0	0	0	0	0	0	0
at Home	.000	.000	.000	1	0	0	0	0	0	0	1
on Road	.000	.000	.000	0	0	0	0	0	0	0	0
Bases Empty	.000	.000	.000	0	0	0	0	0	0	0	0
Runners On Base	.000	.000	.000	0	0	0	0	0	0	0	0

6-YEAR TOTALS (1986–1991)

BA	OBA	SA	AB	H	2B	3B	HR	RBI	BB	SO
.239	.303	.388	201	48	9	0	7	20	19	37
.167	.198	.293	287	48	9	0	9	34	12	62
.210	.250	.410	205	43	8	0	11	27	12	47
.187	.237	.276	283	53	10	0	5	27	19	52
.211	.247	.364	275	58	12	0	10	10	13	56
.178	.237	.291	213	38	6	0	6	44	18	43

RICK PARKER — bats right — throws right — age 29 — SF — /O

1991	BA	OBA	SA	AB	H	2B	3B	HR	RBI	BB	SO
vs. Left	.000	.000	.000	3	0	0	0	0	0	0	1
vs. Right	.091	.167	.091	11	1	0	0	0	0	1	4
at Home	.000	.000	.000	9	0	0	0	0	0	0	3
on Road	.200	.333	.200	5	1	0	0	0	0	1	2
Bases Empty	.000	.000	.000	7	0	0	0	0	0	0	3
Runners On Base	.143	.250	.143	7	1	0	0	0	0	1	2

2-YEAR TOTALS (1990–1991)

BA	OBA	SA	AB	H	2B	3B	HR	RBI	BB	SO
.256	.322	.378	82	21	4	0	2	10	8	12
.154	.233	.179	39	6	1	0	0	5	3	8
.192	.250	.192	52	10	0	0	0	2	4	9
.246	.325	.406	69	17	5	0	2	13	7	11
.197	.269	.262	61	12	1	0	1	1	5	12
.250	.318	.367	60	15	4	0	1	14	6	8

JORGE PEDRE — bats right — throws right — age 26 — KC — /C1

1991	BA	OBA	SA	AB	H	2B	3B	HR	RBI	BB	SO
vs. Left	.231	.231	.462	13	3	1	1	0	2	0	4
vs. Right	.333	.556	.333	6	2	0	0	0	1	3	1
at Home	.333	.333	.667	9	3	1	1	0	2	0	1
on Road	.200	.385	.200	10	2	0	0	0	1	3	4
Bases Empty	.300	.417	.400	10	3	1	0	0	0	2	2
Runners On Base	.222	.300	.444	9	2	0	1	0	3	1	3

1-YEAR TOTALS (1991)

	BA	OBA	SA	AB	H	2B	3B	HR	RBI	BB	SO
	.231	.231	.462	13	3	1	1	0	2	0	4
	.333	.556	.333	6	2	0	0	0	1	3	1
	.333	.333	.667	9	3	1	1	0	2	0	1
	.200	.385	.200	10	2	0	0	0	1	3	4
	.300	.417	.400	10	3	1	0	0	0	2	2
	.222	.300	.444	9	2	0	1	0	3	1	3

GERONIMO PENA — bats both — throws right — age 25 — SL — 2/O

1991	BA	OBA	SA	AB	H	2B	3B	HR	RBI	BB	SO
vs. Left	.293	.352	.489	92	27	7	1	3	12	6	24
vs. Right	.194	.292	.312	93	18	1	2	2	5	12	21
at Home	.220	.333	.352	91	20	5	2	1	4	14	24
on Road	.266	.311	.447	94	25	3	1	4	13	4	21
Bases Empty	.254	.331	.465	114	29	5	2	5	5	11	28
Runners On Base	.225	.310	.296	71	16	3	1	0	12	7	17

2-YEAR TOTALS (1990–1991)

	BA	OBA	SA	AB	H	2B	3B	HR	RBI	BB	SO
	.295	.355	.467	105	31	7	1	3	13	8	27
	.200	.291	.304	125	25	3	2	2	6	14	32
	.224	.339	.336	107	24	5	2	1	4	16	29
	.260	.304	.415	123	32	5	1	4	15	6	30
	.257	.335	.431	144	37	6	2	5	5	14	35
	.221	.297	.291	86	19	4	1	0	14	8	24

TONY PEREZCHICA — bats right — throws right — age 26 — SF/CLE — S/23

1991	BA	OBA	SA	AB	H	2B	3B	HR	RBI	BB	SO
vs. Left	.250	.348	.300	20	5	1	0	0	1	3	4
vs. Right	.280	.308	.420	50	14	5	1	0	2	2	13
at Home	.238	.304	.333	21	5	2	0	0	0	2	7
on Road	.286	.327	.408	49	14	4	1	0	3	3	10
Bases Empty	.333	.381	.462	39	13	5	0	0	0	3	7
Runners On Base	.194	.242	.290	31	6	1	1	0	3	2	10

3-YEAR TOTALS (1988–1991)

	BA	OBA	SA	AB	H	2B	3B	HR	RBI	BB	SO
	.250	.345	.292	24	6	1	0	0	2	4	6
	.263	.311	.386	57	15	5	1	0	2	4	14
	.207	.294	.276	29	6	2	0	0	1	4	9
	.288	.339	.404	52	15	4	1	0	3	4	11
	.318	.362	.432	44	14	5	0	0	1	4	9
	.189	.279	.270	37	7	1	1	0	4	5	11

GERALD PERRY — bats left — throws right — age 32 — SL — 1/O

1991	BA	OBA	SA	AB	H	2B	3B	HR	RBI	BB	SO
vs. Left	.235	.275	.363	102	24	3	2	2	13	6	14
vs. Right	.243	.316	.393	140	34	5	2	4	23	16	20
at Home	.185	.246	.277	130	24	1	4	1	15	11	15
on Road	.304	.360	.500	112	34	7	0	5	21	11	19
Bases Empty	.183	.236	.298	131	24	3	0	4	4	9	16
Runners On Base	.306	.370	.477	111	34	5	4	2	32	13	18

8-YEAR TOTALS (1984–1991)

	BA	OBA	SA	AB	H	2B	3B	HR	RBI	BB	SO
	.255	.297	.368	793	202	33	3	17	93	47	114
	.267	.341	.375	1914	511	91	8	33	239	222	186
	.272	.337	.378	1384	376	73	7	20	183	141	141
	.255	.320	.367	1323	337	51	4	30	149	128	159
	.242	.304	.343	1475	357	57	4	28	28	124	169
	.289	.356	.408	1232	356	67	7	22	304	145	131

GENO PETRALLI — bats left — throws right — age 33 — TEX — C/3D

1991	BA	OBA	SA	AB	H	2B	3B	HR	RBI	BB	SO
vs. Left	.111	.100	.111	9	1	0	0	0	2	0	3
vs. Right	.279	.351	.363	190	53	8	1	2	18	21	22
at Home	.235	.298	.282	85	20	4	0	0	5	8	11
on Road	.298	.370	.404	114	34	4	1	2	15	13	14
Bases Empty	.257	.328	.319	113	29	4	0	1	1	12	11
Runners On Base	.291	.354	.395	86	25	4	1	1	19	9	14

8-YEAR TOTALS (1984–1991)

	BA	OBA	SA	AB	H	2B	3B	HR	RBI	BB	SO
	.195	.293	.204	113	22	1	0	0	9	17	21
	.283	.355	.389	1388	393	63	9	22	151	152	184
	.256	.347	.331	695	178	25	3	7	61	93	108
	.294	.353	.413	806	237	39	6	15	99	76	97
	.283	.349	.391	852	241	36	4	16	16	80	123
	.268	.352	.354	649	174	28	5	6	144	89	82

GARY PETTIS — bats both — throws right — age 34 — TEX — *O/D

1991	BA	OBA	SA	AB	H	2B	3B	HR	RBI	BB	SO
vs. Left	.195	.315	.234	77	15	1	1	0	6	14	17
vs. Right	.224	.351	.293	205	46	6	4	0	13	40	74
at Home	.212	.343	.299	137	29	2	5	0	8	28	41
on Road	.221	.339	.255	145	32	5	0	0	11	26	50
Bases Empty	.214	.370	.279	154	33	4	3	0		16	37
Runners On Base	.219	.303	.273	128	28	3	2	0	19	38	54

8-YEAR TOTALS (1984–1991)

	BA	OBA	SA	AB	H	2B	3B	HR	RBI	BB	SO
	.237	.319	.298	1127	267	34	13	3	78	136	230
	.235	.339	.309	2254	530	68	30	13	163	349	666
	.234	.332	.304	1621	379	43	25	7	120	239	417
	.237	.332	.307	1760	418	59	18	9	121	246	479
	.230	.329	.295	2139	491	66	24	9	9	311	589
	.246	.338	.323	1242	306	36	19	7	232	174	307

PHIL PLANTIER — bats left — throws right — age 23 — BOS — O/D

1991	BA	OBA	SA	AB	H	2B	3B	HR	RBI	BB	SO
vs. Left	.320	.367	.720	25	8	1	0	3	13	3	11
vs. Right	.333	.431	.593	123	41	6	1	8	22	20	27
at Home	.315	.366	.630	73	23	3	1	6	21	7	17
on Road	.347	.467	.600	75	26	4	0	5	14	16	21
Bases Empty	.338	.416	.676	68	23	2	0	7	7	9	12
Runners On Base	.325	.423	.563	80	26	5	1	4	28	14	26

2-YEAR TOTALS (1990–1991)

	BA	OBA	SA	AB	H	2B	3B	HR	RBI	BB	SO
	.320	.367	.720	25	8	1	0	3	13	3	11
	.312	.418	.551	138	43	7	1	8	25	24	33
	.295	.367	.590	78	23	3	1	6	21	10	20
	.329	.448	.565	85	28	5	0	5	17	17	24
	.320	.420	.627	75	24	2	0	7	7	13	15
	.307	.402	.534	88	27	5	1	4	31	14	29

ALONZO POWELL — bats right — throws right — age 28 — SEA — O/1D

1991	BA	OBA	SA	AB	H	2B	3B	HR	RBI	BB	SO
vs. Left	.250	.325	.456	68	17	5	0	3	7	8	16
vs. Right	.163	.229	.233	43	7	1	1	0	5	3	8
at Home	.161	.290	.250	56	9	2	0	1	4	10	11
on Road	.273	.286	.491	55	15	4	1	2	8	1	13
Bases Empty	.197	.274	.364	66	13	3	1	2	2	7	14
Runners On Base	.244	.308	.378	45	11	3	0	1	10	4	10

2-YEAR TOTALS (1987–1991)

	BA	OBA	SA	AB	H	2B	3B	HR	RBI	BB	SO
	.274	.354	.464	84	23	7	0	3	8	11	21
	.134	.203	.194	67	9	2	1	0	8	5	19
	.156	.282	.234	64	10	2	0	1	6	11	14
	.253	.293	.425	87	22	7	1	2	10	5	26
	.191	.262	.330	94	18	5	1	2	2	9	26
	.246	.328	.368	57	14	4	0	1	14	7	14

JIM PRESLEY — bats right — throws right — age 31 — SD — 3

1991	BA	OBA	SA	AB	H	2B	3B	HR	RBI	BB	SO
vs. Left	.130	.167	.261	23	3	0	0	1	1	1	6
vs. Right	.139	.220	.139	36	5	1	1	0	4	3	10
at Home	.128	.209	.128	39	5	0	0	0	3	3	12
on Road	.150	.182	.300	20	3	1	1	1	2	1	4
Bases Empty	.143	.167	.229	35	5	3	1	0	1	1	8
Runners On Base	.125	.241	.125	24	3	0	0	0	4	3	8

8-YEAR TOTALS (1984–1991)

	BA	OBA	SA	AB	H	2B	3B	HR	RBI	BB	SO
	.276	.321	.443	1071	296	62	4	36	135	72	227
	.234	.276	.410	2475	579	119	10	99	360	138	632
	.260	.303	.441	1838	478	113	8	68	252	106	434
	.232	.276	.397	1708	397	68	6	67	243	104	425
	.244	.279	.419	1950	475	91	7	79	79	88	471
	.251	.303	.421	1596	400	90	7	56	416	122	388

TOM PRINCE — bats right — throws right — age 28 — PIT — C/1

1991	BA	OBA	SA	AB	H	2B	3B	HR	RBI	BB	SO
vs. Left	.375	.500	.688	16	6	2	0	1	2	4	1
vs. Right	.167	.318	.222	18	3	1	0	0	0	3	2
at Home	.333	.455	.444	9	3	1	0	0	1	2	1
on Road	.240	.387	.440	25	6	2	0	1	1	5	2
Bases Empty	.438	.550	.813	16	7	3	0	1	1	3	1
Runners On Base	.111	.273	.111	18	2	0	0	0	1	4	2

5-YEAR TOTALS (1987–1991)

BA	OBA	SA	AB	H	2B	3B	HR	RBI	BB	SO
.175	.238	.278	97	17	4	0	2	7	8	18
.183	.277	.256	82	15	6	0	0	8	10	16
.145	.243	.194	62	9	3	0	0	4	8	12
.197	.264	.308	117	23	7	0	2	11	10	22
.186	.262	.268	97	18	5	0	1	1	9	19
.171	.250	.268	82	14	5	0	1	14	9	15

TERRY PUHL — bats left — throws right — age 36 — KC — /DO

1991	BA	OBA	SA	AB	H	2B	3B	HR	RBI	BB	SO
vs. Left	.000	.000	.000	2	0	0	0	0	0	0	0
vs. Right	.250	.368	.250	16	4	0	0	0	3	3	2
at Home	.111	.333	.111	9	1	0	0	0	2	3	2
on Road	.333	.333	.333	9	3	0	0	0	1	0	0
Bases Empty	.000	.250	.000	3	0	0	0	0	0	1	0
Runners On Base	.267	.353	.267	15	4	0	0	0	3	2	2

8-YEAR TOTALS (1984–1991)

BA	OBA	SA	AB	H	2B	3B	HR	RBI	BB	SO
.262	.323	.331	320	84	15	2	1	36	28	51
.284	.365	.401	1264	359	66	14	18	128	163	135
.282	.360	.379	808	228	35	11	7	83	99	85
.277	.353	.396	776	215	46	5	12	81	92	101
.284	.357	.391	937	266	51	5	13	13	104	97
.274	.356	.382	647	177	30	11	6	151	87	89

HARVEY PULLIAM — bats right — throws right — age 25 — KC — O

1991	BA	OBA	SA	AB	H	2B	3B	HR	RBI	BB	SO
vs. Left	.267	.333	.600	30	8	1	0	3	4	3	8
vs. Right	.333	.333	.333	3	1	0	0	0	0	0	1
at Home	.238	.304	.571	21	5	1	0	2	3	2	5
on Road	.333	.385	.583	12	4	0	0	1	1	1	4
Bases Empty	.304	.304	.609	23	7	1	0	2	2	0	6
Runners On Base	.200	.385	.500	10	2	0	0	1	2	3	3

1-YEAR TOTALS (1991)

BA	OBA	SA	AB	H	2B	3B	HR	RBI	BB	SO
.267	.333	.600	30	8	1	0	3	4	3	8
.333	.333	.333	3	1	0	0	0	0	0	1
.238	.304	.571	21	5	1	0	2	3	2	5
.333	.385	.583	12	4	0	0	1	1	1	4
.304	.304	.609	23	7	1	0	2	2	0	6
.200	.385	.500	10	2	0	0	1	2	3	3

LUIS QUINONES — bats both — throws right — age 30 — CIN — 23/S

1991	BA	OBA	SA	AB	H	2B	3B	HR	RBI	BB	SO
vs. Left	.175	.268	.254	63	11	2	0	1	4	8	9
vs. Right	.242	.309	.356	149	36	2	3	3	16	13	22
at Home	.258	.368	.427	89	23	3	3	2	14	14	11
on Road	.195	.238	.252	123	24	1	0	2	6	7	20
Bases Empty	.196	.293	.324	102	20	2	1	3	3	13	14
Runners On Base	.245	.300	.327	110	27	2	2	1	17	8	17

6-YEAR TOTALS (1986–1991)

BA	OBA	SA	AB	H	2B	3B	HR	RBI	BB	SO
.218	.282	.380	326	71	10	2	13	45	28	60
.234	.288	.326	629	147	24	8	6	56	46	90
.241	.299	.362	423	102	19	4	8	43	32	65
.218	.276	.331	532	116	15	6	11	58	42	85
.205	.268	.341	522	107	19	5	14	14	42	94
.256	.308	.349	433	111	15	5	5	87	32	56

JAMIE QUIRK — bats left — throws right — age 38 — OAK — C/13D

1991	BA	OBA	SA	AB	H	2B	3B	HR	RBI	BB	SO
vs. Left	.313	.421	.313	16	5	0	0	0	2	3	2
vs. Right	.257	.312	.294	187	48	4	0	1	15	13	26
at Home	.261	.333	.293	92	24	3	0	0	4	9	17
on Road	.261	.311	.297	111	29	1	0	1	13	7	11
Bases Empty	.243	.281	.296	115	28	3	0	1	1	5	19
Runners On Base	.284	.370	.295	88	25	1	0	0	16	11	9

8-YEAR TOTALS (1984–1991)

BA	OBA	SA	AB	H	2B	3B	HR	RBI	BB	SO
.310	.360	.360	100	31	5	0	0	19	8	23
.233	.305	.354	1080	252	43	3	27	124	109	208
.241	.314	.350	588	142	31	3	9	62	63	118
.238	.306	.358	592	141	17	0	18	81	54	113
.218	.285	.328	707	154	25	1	17	17	61	146
.273	.346	.393	473	129	23	2	10	126	56	85

RAFAEL RAMIREZ — bats right — throws right — age 34 — HOU — S2/3

1991	BA	OBA	SA	AB	H	2B	3B	HR	RBI	BB	SO
vs. Left	.245	.294	.309	110	27	4	0	1	14	8	20
vs. Right	.228	.256	.276	123	28	6	0	0	6	5	20
at Home	.242	.300	.308	91	22	6	0	0	10	8	15
on Road	.232	.257	.282	142	33	4	0	1	10	5	25
Bases Empty	.241	.273	.301	133	32	5	0	1	1	6	24
Runners On Base	.230	.275	.280	100	23	5	0	0	19	7	16

8-YEAR TOTALS (1984–1991)

BA	OBA	SA	AB	H	2B	3B	HR	RBI	BB	SO
.260	.294	.342	1253	326	57	9	9	122	63	136
.252	.282	.332	2362	596	102	10	22	209	96	285
.258	.297	.337	1699	438	77	11	12	169	96	192
.253	.276	.334	1916	484	82	8	19	162	63	229
.249	.277	.322	2149	535	80	10	19	19	76	271
.264	.300	.355	1466	387	79	9	12	312	83	150

JOHN RAMOS — bats right — throws right — age 27 — NYA — /CD

1991	BA	OBA	SA	AB	H	2B	3B	HR	RBI	BB	SO
vs. Left	.333	.375	.400	15	5	1	0	0	1	1	2
vs. Right	.273	.231	.273	11	3	0	0	0	2	0	1
at Home	.182	.154	.182	11	2	0	0	0	2	0	1
on Road	.400	.438	.467	15	6	1	0	0	1	1	2
Bases Empty	.300	.333	.300	20	6	0	0	0	0	1	3
Runners On Base	.333	.250	.500	6	2	1	0	0	3	0	0

1-YEAR TOTALS (1991)

BA	OBA	SA	AB	H	2B	3B	HR	RBI	BB	SO
.333	.375	.400	15	5	1	0	0	1	1	2
.273	.231	.273	11	3	0	0	0	2	0	1
.182	.154	.182	11	2	0	0	0	2	0	1
.400	.438	.467	15	6	1	0	0	1	1	2
.300	.333	.300	20	6	0	0	0	0	1	3
.333	.250	.500	6	2	1	0	0	3	0	0

RANDY READY — bats right — throws right — age 32 — PHI — 2

1991	BA	OBA	SA	AB	H	2B	3B	HR	RBI	BB	SO
vs. Left	.265	.418	.367	147	39	10	1	1	18	39	17
vs. Right	.207	.294	.207	58	12	0	0	0	2	8	8
at Home	.250	.414	.343	108	27	5	1	1	10	30	11
on Road	.247	.350	.299	97	24	5	0	0	10	17	14
Bases Empty	.246	.369	.322	118	29	6	0	1	1	22	11
Runners On Base	.253	.405	.322	87	22	4	1	0	19	25	14

8-YEAR TOTALS (1984–1991)

BA	OBA	SA	AB	H	2B	3B	HR	RBI	BB	SO
.273	.380	.428	919	251	59	10	21	112	161	105
.245	.330	.353	824	202	34	8	13	91	100	125
.266	.369	.401	830	221	43	9	17	102	134	107
.254	.345	.384	913	232	50	9	17	101	127	123
.248	.344	.390	992	246	61	7	22	22	140	125
.276	.372	.395	751	207	32	11	12	181	121	105

JOE REDFIELD — bats right — throws right — age 31 — PIT — /3

1991	BA	OBA	SA	AB	H	2B	3B	HR	RBI	BB	SO
vs. Left	.125	.176	.125	16	2	0	0	0	0	1	1
vs. Right	.000	.600	.000	2	0	0	0	0	0	3	0
at Home	.000	.000	.000	0	0	0	0	0	0	0	0
on Road	.111	.273	.111	18	2	0	0	0	0	4	1
Bases Empty	.000	.200	.000	8	0	0	0	0	0	2	0
Runners On Base	.200	.333	.200	10	2	0	0	0	0	2	1

2-YEAR TOTALS (1988–1991)

BA	OBA	SA	AB	H	2B	3B	HR	RBI	BB	SO
.111	.158	.111	18	2	0	0	0	0	1	1
.000	.600	.000	2	0	0	0	0	0	3	0
.000	.000	.000	0	0	0	0	0	0	0	0
.100	.250	.100	20	2	0	0	0	0	4	1
.000	.182	.000	9	0	0	0	0	0	2	0
.182	.308	.182	11	2	0	0	0	0	2	1

JEFF REED — bats left — throws right — age 30 — CIN — C

1991	BA	OBA	SA	AB	H	2B	3B	HR	RBI	BB	SO
vs. Left	.192	.281	.269	26	5	2	0	0	5	3	6
vs. Right	.275	.326	.381	244	67	13	2	3	26	20	32
at Home	.261	.336	.400	115	30	9	2	1	15	13	19
on Road	.271	.310	.348	155	42	6	0	2	16	10	19
Bases Empty	.285	.326	.382	165	47	11	1	1	1	10	23
Runners On Base	.238	.315	.352	105	25	4	1	2	30	13	15

8-YEAR TOTALS (1984–1991)

BA	OBA	SA	AB	H	2B	3B	HR	RBI	BB	SO
.223	.319	.325	157	35	10	0	2	22	20	34
.236	.301	.315	1243	293	53	6	11	95	119	165
.224	.296	.318	660	148	35	3	7	57	69	104
.243	.309	.314	740	180	28	3	6	60	70	95
.244	.299	.330	843	206	48	3	6	6	64	116
.219	.308	.294	557	122	15	3	7	111	75	83

JEFF RICHARDSON — bats right — throws right — age 27 — PIT — /3S

1991	BA	OBA	SA	AB	H	2B	3B	HR	RBI	BB	SO
vs. Left	.333	.333	.333	3	1	0	0	0	0	0	2
vs. Right	.000	.000	.000	1	0	0	0	0	0	0	1
at Home	.500	.500	.500	2	1	0	0	0	0	0	1
on Road	.000	.000	.000	2	0	0	0	0	0	0	2
Bases Empty	.333	.333	.333	3	1	0	0	0	0	0	2
Runners On Base	.000	.000	.000	1	0	0	0	0	0	0	1

2-YEAR TOTALS (1989–1991)

BA	OBA	SA	AB	H	2B	3B	HR	RBI	BB	SO
.200	.286	.340	50	10	1	0	2	5	6	8
.152	.200	.190	79	12	3	0	0	6	4	18
.129	.205	.186	70	9	1	0	1	4	6	14
.220	.270	.322	59	13	3	0	1	7	4	12
.147	.227	.235	68	10	3	0	1	1	7	14
.197	.242	.262	61	12	1	0	1	10	3	12

NIKCO RIESGO — bats right — throws right — age 25 — MON — /O

1991	BA	OBA	SA	AB	H	2B	3B	HR	RBI	BB	SO
vs. Left	.167	.444	.167	6	1	0	0	0	0	3	1
vs. Right	.000	.000	.000	1	0	0	0	0	0	0	0
at Home	.167	.444	.167	6	1	0	0	0	0	3	1
on Road	.000	.000	.000	1	0	0	0	0	0	0	0
Bases Empty	.000	.400	.000	3	0	0	0	0	0	2	0
Runners On Base	.250	.400	.250	4	1	0	0	0	0	1	1

1-YEAR TOTALS (1991)

BA	OBA	SA	AB	H	2B	3B	HR	RBI	BB	SO
.167	.444	.167	6	1	0	0	0	0	3	1
.000	.000	.000	1	0	0	0	0	0	0	0
.167	.444	.167	6	1	0	0	0	0	3	1
.000	.000	.000	1	0	0	0	0	0	0	0
.000	.400	.000	3	0	0	0	0	0	2	1
.250	.400	.250	4	1	0	0	0	0	1	1

ERNIE RILES — bats left — throws right — age 32 — OAK — 3S/21

1991	BA	OBA	SA	AB	H	2B	3B	HR	RBI	BB	SO
vs. Left	.143	.143	.143	21	3	0	0	0	1	0	2
vs. Right	.219	.301	.338	260	57	8	4	5	31	31	40
at Home	.236	.319	.358	148	35	7	1	3	18	18	25
on Road	.188	.258	.286	133	25	1	3	2	14	13	17
Bases Empty	.189	.249	.274	164	31	5	3	1	1	13	26
Runners On Base	.248	.343	.393	117	29	3	1	4	31	18	16

7-YEAR TOTALS (1985–1991)

BA	OBA	SA	AB	H	2B	3B	HR	RBI	BB	SO
.220	.286	.301	422	93	9	5	5	40	37	89
.267	.330	.381	1878	501	74	15	37	220	185	269
.279	.351	.408	1114	311	47	12	24	128	125	164
.239	.295	.328	1186	283	36	8	18	132	97	194
.251	.309	.356	1313	329	54	15	18	18	110	217
.268	.339	.381	987	265	29	5	24	242	112	141

CARLOS RODRIGUEZ — bats both — throws right — age 25 — NYA — S/2

1991	BA	OBA	SA	AB	H	2B	3B	HR	RBI	BB	SO
vs. Left	.500	.500	.500	8	4	0	0	0	1	0	0
vs. Right	.103	.133	.103	29	3	0	0	0	1	1	2
at Home	.333	.333	.333	9	3	0	0	0	2	0	0
on Road	.143	.172	.143	28	4	0	0	0	0	1	2
Bases Empty	.217	.250	.217	23	5	0	0	0	0	1	1
Runners On Base	.143	.143	.143	14	2	0	0	0	2	0	1

1-YEAR TOTALS (1991)

BA	OBA	SA	AB	H	2B	3B	HR	RBI	BB	SO
.500	.500	.500	8	4	0	0	0	1	0	0
.103	.133	.103	29	3	0	0	0	1	1	2
.333	.333	.333	9	3	0	0	0	2	0	0
.143	.172	.143	28	4	0	0	0	0	1	2
.217	.250	.217	23	5	0	0	0	0	1	1
.143	.143	.143	14	2	0	0	0	2	0	1

DAVE ROHDE — bats both — throws right — age 28 — HOU — /23S1

1991	BA	OBA	SA	AB	H	2B	3B	HR	RBI	BB	SO
vs. Left	.000	.056	.000	17	0	0	0	0	0	1	5
vs. Right	.208	.321	.208	24	5	0	0	0	0	4	3
at Home	.148	.258	.148	27	4	0	0	0	0	4	6
on Road	.071	.133	.071	14	1	0	0	0	0	1	2
Bases Empty	.120	.241	.120	25	3	0	0	0	0	4	3
Runners On Base	.125	.176	.125	16	2	0	0	0	0	1	5

2-YEAR TOTALS (1990–1991)

BA	OBA	SA	AB	H	2B	3B	HR	RBI	BB	SO
.153	.250	.203	59	9	3	0	0	3	6	15
.175	.275	.188	80	14	1	0	0	2	8	13
.225	.333	.268	71	16	3	0	0	2	7	10
.103	.187	.118	68	7	1	0	0	3	7	18
.178	.259	.219	73	13	3	0	0	0	8	12
.152	.269	.167	66	10	1	0	0	5	6	16

KEVIN ROMINE — bats right — throws right — age 31 — BOS — OD

1991	BA	OBA	SA	AB	H	2B	3B	HR	RBI	BB	SO
vs. Left	.176	.222	.206	34	6	1	0	0	3	2	4
vs. Right	.143	.182	.333	21	3	1	0	1	4	1	6
at Home	.125	.192	.125	24	3	0	0	0	0	2	8
on Road	.194	.219	.355	31	6	2	0	1	7	1	2
Bases Empty	.167	.219	.200	30	5	1	0	0	0	2	6
Runners On Base	.160	.192	.320	25	4	1	0	1	7	1	4

7-YEAR TOTALS (1985–1991)

BA	OBA	SA	AB	H	2B	3B	HR	RBI	BB	SO
.314	.358	.379	277	87	13	1	1	29	19	36
.201	.265	.283	353	71	17	0	4	26	30	88
.245	.304	.341	302	74	15	1	4	33	26	63
.256	.307	.311	328	84	15	0	1	22	23	61
.271	.325	.360	339	92	18	0	4	4	24	66
.227	.283	.285	291	66	12	1	1	51	25	58

BOBBY ROSE — bats right — throws right — age 25 — CAL — /2031

1991	BA	OBA	SA	AB	H	2B	3B	HR	RBI	BB	SO
vs. Left	.359	.381	.564	39	14	3	1	1	6	2	9
vs. Right	.154	.185	.231	26	4	2	0	0	2	1	4
at Home	.343	.395	.486	35	12	3	1	0	3	3	7
on Road	.200	.194	.367	30	6	2	0	1	5	0	6
Bases Empty	.226	.226	.323	31	7	1	1	0	0	0	2
Runners On Base	.324	.368	.529	34	11	4	0	1	8	3	11

3-YEAR TOTALS (1989–1991)

BA	OBA	SA	AB	H	2B	3B	HR	RBI	BB	SO
.329	.368	.571	70	23	4	2	3	9	5	15
.174	.261	.261	46	8	2	1	0	4	2	9
.344	.403	.590	61	21	3	3	2	7	6	11
.182	.207	.291	55	10	3	0	1	6	1	13
.259	.295	.466	58	15	2	2	2	2	2	8
.276	.328	.431	58	16	4	1	1	11	5	16

RICO ROSSY — bats right — throws right — age 28 — ATL — /S

1991	BA	OBA	SA	AB	H	2B	3B	HR	RBI	BB	SO
vs. Left	.000	.000	.000	0	0	0	0	0	0	0	0
vs. Right	.000	.000	.000	1	0	0	0	0	0	0	1
at Home	.000	.000	.000	1	0	0	0	0	0	0	1
on Road	.000	.000	.000	0	0	0	0	0	0	0	0
Bases Empty	.000	.000	.000	1	0	0	0	0	0	0	1
Runners On Base	.000	.000	.000	0	0	0	0	0	0	0	0

1-YEAR TOTALS (1991)

BA	OBA	SA	AB	H	2B	3B	HR	RBI	BB	SO
.000	.000	.000	0	0	0	0	0	0	0	0
.000	.000	.000	1	0	0	0	0	0	0	1
.000	.000	.000	1	0	0	0	0	0	0	1
.000	.000	.000	0	0	0	0	0	0	0	0
.000	.000	.000	1	0	0	0	0	0	0	1
.000	.000	.000	0	0	0	0	0	0	0	0

RICH ROWLAND — bats right — throws right — age 25 — DET — /CD

1991

1991	BA	OBA	SA	AB	H	2B	3B	HR	RBI	BB	SO
vs. Left	.333	.400	.333	3	1	0	0	0	1	1	1
vs. Right	.000	.000	.000	1	0	0	0	0	0	0	1
at Home	.000	.000	.000	0	0	0	0	0	1	0	0
on Road	.250	.400	.250	4	1	0	0	0	0	1	2
Bases Empty	.500	.667	.500	2	1	0	0	0	0	1	1
Runners On Base	.000	.000	.000	2	0	0	0	0	1	0	1

2-YEAR TOTALS (1990–1991)

	BA	OBA	SA	AB	H	2B	3B	HR	RBI	BB	SO
vs. Left	.267	.333	.333	15	4	1	0	0	1	2	2
vs. Right	.000	.111	.000	8	0	0	0	0	0	1	4
at Home	.167	.143	.167	6	1	0	0	0	1	0	1
on Road	.176	.300	.235	17	3	1	0	0	0	3	5
Bases Empty	.333	.429	.417	12	4	1	0	0	0	2	2
Runners On Base	.000	.077	.000	11	0	0	0	0	1	1	4

STAN ROYER — bats right — throws right — age 25 — SL — /3

1991

1991	BA	OBA	SA	AB	H	2B	3B	HR	RBI	BB	SO
vs. Left	.250	.250	.250	8	2	0	0	0	1	0	1
vs. Right	.308	.357	.385	13	4	1	0	0	0	1	1
at Home	.222	.300	.222	9	2	0	0	0	1	1	1
on Road	.333	.333	.417	12	4	1	0	0	0	0	1
Bases Empty	.300	.300	.400	10	3	1	0	0	0	0	1
Runners On Base	.273	.333	.273	11	3	0	0	0	1	1	1

1-YEAR TOTALS (1991)

	BA	OBA	SA	AB	H	2B	3B	HR	RBI	BB	SO
vs. Left	.250	.250	.250	8	2	0	0	0	1	0	1
vs. Right	.308	.357	.385	13	4	1	0	0	0	1	1
at Home	.222	.300	.222	9	2	0	0	0	1	1	1
on Road	.333	.333	.417	12	4	1	0	0	0	0	1
Bases Empty	.300	.300	.400	10	3	1	0	0	0	0	1
Runners On Base	.273	.333	.273	11	3	0	0	0	1	1	1

JOHN RUSSELL — bats right — throws right — age 31 — TEX — /OCD

1991

1991	BA	OBA	SA	AB	H	2B	3B	HR	RBI	BB	SO
vs. Left	.133	.133	.133	15	2	0	0	0	0	0	4
vs. Right	.083	.143	.083	12	1	0	0	0	1	1	3
at Home	.118	.111	.118	17	2	0	0	0	1	0	3
on Road	.100	.182	.100	10	1	0	0	0	0	1	4
Bases Empty	.154	.214	.154	13	2	0	0	0	0	0	3
Runners On Base	.071	.067	.071	14	1	0	0	0	1	0	4

8-YEAR TOTALS (1984–1991)

	BA	OBA	SA	AB	H	2B	3B	HR	RBI	BB	SO
vs. Left	.222	.288	.349	496	110	25	1	12	47	44	151
vs. Right	.231	.278	.394	559	129	24	2	21	77	37	190
at Home	.250	.302	.418	529	132	29	3	18	72	40	171
on Road	.203	.263	.327	526	107	20	0	15	52	41	170
Bases Empty	.198	.257	.349	576	114	25	1	20	20	43	207
Runners On Base	.261	.313	.401	479	125	24	2	13	104	38	134

MARK SALAS — bats left — throws right — age 31 — DET — C/D1

1991

1991	BA	OBA	SA	AB	H	2B	3B	HR	RBI	BB	SO
vs. Left	.000	.000	.000	3	0	0	0	0	2	0	1
vs. Right	.093	.125	.167	54	5	1	0	1	5	0	10
at Home	.111	.111	.167	18	2	1	0	0	1	0	3
on Road	.077	.119	.154	39	3	0	0	1	6	0	7
Bases Empty	.057	.083	.086	35	2	1	0	0	0	0	8
Runners On Base	.136	.167	.273	22	3	0	0	1	7	0	2

8-YEAR TOTALS (1984–1991)

	BA	OBA	SA	AB	H	2B	3B	HR	RBI	BB	SO
vs. Left	.239	.306	.321	109	26	4	1	1	17	10	21
vs. Right	.248	.299	.395	1182	293	45	9	37	126	78	142
at Home	.255	.306	.428	671	171	27	7	25	75	44	91
on Road	.239	.292	.347	620	148	22	3	13	68	44	72
Bases Empty	.236	.289	.366	721	170	32	4	18	18	46	85
Runners On Base	.261	.312	.418	570	149	17	6	20	125	42	78

REY SANCHEZ — bats right — throws right — age 25 — CHN — S/2

1991

1991	BA	OBA	SA	AB	H	2B	3B	HR	RBI	BB	SO
vs. Left	.000	.286	.000	5	0	0	0	0	1	2	1
vs. Right	.333	.400	.333	18	6	0	0	0	1	2	2
at Home	.111	.158	.111	18	2	0	0	0	1	1	3
on Road	.800	.875	.800	5	4	0	0	0	1	3	0
Bases Empty	.214	.353	.214	14	3	0	0	0	0	3	2
Runners On Base	.333	.400	.333	9	3	0	0	0	2	1	1

1-YEAR TOTALS (1991)

	BA	OBA	SA	AB	H	2B	3B	HR	RBI	BB	SO
vs. Left	.000	.286	.000	5	0	0	0	0	1	2	1
vs. Right	.333	.400	.333	18	6	0	0	0	1	2	2
at Home	.111	.158	.111	18	2	0	0	0	1	1	3
on Road	.800	.875	.800	5	4	0	0	0	1	3	0
Bases Empty	.214	.353	.214	14	3	0	0	0	0	3	2
Runners On Base	.333	.400	.333	9	3	0	0	0	2	1	1

DEION SANDERS — bats left — throws left — age 25 — ATL — O

1991

1991	BA	OBA	SA	AB	H	2B	3B	HR	RBI	BB	SO
vs. Left	.133	.278	.200	15	2	1	0	0	1	3	7
vs. Right	.200	.269	.368	95	19	0	2	4	12	9	16
at Home	.206	.286	.333	63	13	0	1	2	9	7	16
on Road	.170	.250	.362	47	8	1	1	2	4	5	7
Bases Empty	.123	.200	.315	73	9	1	2	3	3	7	14
Runners On Base	.324	.405	.405	37	12	0	0	1	10	5	9

3-YEAR TOTALS (1989–1991)

	BA	OBA	SA	AB	H	2B	3B	HR	RBI	BB	SO
vs. Left	.149	.216	.213	47	7	1	1	0	2	4	16
vs. Right	.189	.264	.342	243	46	4	3	9	27	24	42
at Home	.197	.281	.292	137	27	0	2	3	15	15	29
on Road	.170	.234	.346	153	26	5	2	6	14	13	29
Bases Empty	.145	.195	.291	179	26	3	4	5	5	10	33
Runners On Base	.243	.346	.369	111	27	2	0	4	24	18	25

REGGIE SANDERS — bats right — throws right — age 25 — CIN — /O

1991

1991	BA	OBA	SA	AB	H	2B	3B	HR	RBI	BB	SO
vs. Left	.125	.125	.125	16	2	0	0	0	1	0	3
vs. Right	.250	.250	.375	24	6	0	0	1	2	0	6
at Home	.000	.000	.000	11	0	0	0	0	0	0	3
on Road	.276	.276	.379	29	8	0	0	1	3	0	6
Bases Empty	.161	.161	.161	31	5	0	0	0	0	0	8
Runners On Base	.333	.333	.667	9	3	0	0	1	3	0	1

1-YEAR TOTALS (1991)

	BA	OBA	SA	AB	H	2B	3B	HR	RBI	BB	SO
vs. Left	.125	.125	.125	16	2	0	0	0	1	0	3
vs. Right	.250	.250	.375	24	6	0	0	1	2	0	6
at Home	.000	.000	.000	11	0	0	0	0	0	0	3
on Road	.276	.276	.379	29	8	0	0	1	3	0	6
Bases Empty	.161	.161	.161	31	5	0	0	0	0	0	8
Runners On Base	.333	.333	.667	9	3	0	0	1	3	0	1

NELSON SANTOVENIA — bats right — throws right — age 31 — MON — C/1

1991

1991	BA	OBA	SA	AB	H	2B	3B	HR	RBI	BB	SO
vs. Left	.265	.283	.429	49	13	2	0	2	8	2	7
vs. Right	.234	.224	.298	47	11	3	0	0	6	0	11
at Home	.250	.296	.458	24	6	2	0	1	5	2	3
on Road	.250	.240	.333	72	18	3	0	1	9	0	15
Bases Empty	.281	.281	.404	57	16	4	0	1	1	0	14
Runners On Base	.205	.222	.308	39	8	1	0	0	13	2	4

5-YEAR TOTALS (1987–1991)

	BA	OBA	SA	AB	H	2B	3B	HR	RBI	BB	SO
vs. Left	.251	.304	.390	295	74	13	2	8	40	23	41
vs. Right	.225	.269	.349	578	130	29	2	18	74	35	123
at Home	.277	.323	.457	411	114	25	2	15	72	30	65
on Road	.195	.242	.279	462	90	17	2	6	42	28	99
Bases Empty	.212	.265	.341	472	100	23	1	12	12	29	98
Runners On Base	.259	.299	.389	401	104	19	3	9	102	29	66

MACKEY SASSER — bats left — throws right — age 30 — NYN — CO1

1991

1991	BA	OBA	SA	AB	H	2B	3B	HR	RBI	BB	SO
vs. Left	.143	.138	.214	28	4	2	0	0	2	0	5
vs. Right	.290	.319	.445	200	58	12	2	5	33	9	14
at Home	.321	.350	.495	109	35	6	2	3	21	6	11
on Road	.227	.248	.345	119	27	8	0	2	14	3	8
Bases Empty	.230	.254	.357	126	29	6	2	2	2	4	9
Runners On Base	.324	.348	.490	102	33	8	0	3	33	5	10

5-YEAR TOTALS (1987–1991)

	BA	OBA	SA	AB	H	2B	3B	HR	RBI	BB	SO
vs. Left	.185	.222	.277	119	22	8	0	1	10	6	22
vs. Right	.304	.331	.430	711	216	44	5	12	107	31	42
at Home	.280	.310	.412	415	116	28	3	7	65	20	37
on Road	.294	.321	.405	415	122	24	2	6	52	17	27
Bases Empty	.268	.286	.373	440	118	30	2	4	4	10	31
Runners On Base	.308	.347	.449	390	120	22	3	9	113	27	33

JEFF SCHAEFER — bats right — throws right — age 32 — SEA — S32

1991	BA	OBA	SA	AB	H	2B	3B	HR	RBI	BB	SO
vs. Left	.263	.286	.347	95	25	5	0	1	4	3	14
vs. Right	.232	.254	.290	69	16	2	1	0	7	2	11
at Home	.232	.241	.280	82	19	2	1	0	7	1	14
on Road	.268	.302	.366	82	22	5	0	1	4	4	11
Bases Empty	.262	.290	.350	103	27	6	0	1	1	4	15
Runners On Base	.230	.242	.279	61	14	1	1	0	10	1	10

3-YEAR TOTALS (1989–1991)

BA	OBA	SA	AB	H	2B	3B	HR	RBI	BB	SO
.269	.294	.338	130	35	6	0	1	6	5	17
.192	.218	.232	151	29	4	1	0	11	3	21
.195	.220	.242	128	25	4	1	0	11	2	17
.255	.281	.314	153	39	6	0	1	6	6	21
.246	.271	.304	171	42	7	0	1	1	5	20
.200	.226	.245	110	22	3	1	0	16	3	18

RICK SCHU — bats right — throws right — age 30 — PHI — /31

1991	BA	OBA	SA	AB	H	2B	3B	HR	RBI	BB	SO
vs. Left	.143	.133	.143	14	2	0	0	0	1	0	5
vs. Right	.000	.111	.000	8	0	0	0	0	1	1	2
at Home	.000	.000	.000	12	0	0	0	0	0	0	4
on Road	.200	.250	.200	10	2	0	0	0	2	1	3
Bases Empty	.182	.182	.182	11	2	0	0	0	0	0	5
Runners On Base	.000	.077	.000	11	0	0	0	0	2	1	2

8-YEAR TOTALS (1984–1991)

BA	OBA	SA	AB	H	2B	3B	HR	RBI	BB	SO
.266	.318	.451	710	189	38	6	27	71	53	108
.231	.305	.331	853	197	29	7	14	63	86	174
.245	.311	.388	740	181	37	9	17	63	71	129
.249	.310	.383	823	205	30	4	24	71	68	153
.259	.320	.416	906	235	39	8	29	29	75	160
.230	.298	.342	657	151	28	5	12	105	64	122

JEFF SCHULZ — bats left — throws right — age 31 — PIT

1991	BA	OBA	SA	AB	H	2B	3B	HR	RBI	BB	SO
vs. Left	.000	.000	.000	0	0	0	0	0	0	0	0
vs. Right	.000	.000	.000	3	0	0	0	0	0	0	2
at Home	.000	.000	.000	2	0	0	0	0	0	0	1
on Road	.000	.000	.000	1	0	0	0	0	0	0	1
Bases Empty	.000	.000	.000	1	0	0	0	0	0	0	2
Runners On Base	.000	.000	.000	2	0	0	0	0	0	0	0

3-YEAR TOTALS (1989–1991)

BA	OBA	SA	AB	H	2B	3B	HR	RBI	BB	SO
.111	.111	.111	9	1	0	0	0	0	0	4
.261	.320	.362	69	18	5	1	0	7	6	13
.275	.341	.375	40	11	2	1	0	4	4	5
.211	.250	.289	38	8	3	0	0	3	2	12
.158	.200	.211	38	6	2	0	0	0	2	8
.325	.386	.450	40	13	3	1	0	7	4	9

DONNIE SCOTT — bats both — throws right — age 31 — CIN — /C

1991	BA	OBA	SA	AB	H	2B	3B	HR	RBI	BB	SO
vs. Left	.154	.154	.154	13	2	0	0	0	0	0	0
vs. Right	.167	.167	.167	6	1	0	0	0	0	0	2
at Home	.000	.000	.000	7	0	0	0	0	0	0	1
on Road	.250	.250	.250	12	3	0	0	0	0	0	1
Bases Empty	.214	.214	.214	14	3	0	0	0	0	0	2
Runners On Base	.000	.000	.000	5	0	0	0	0	0	0	0

3-YEAR TOTALS (1984–1991)

BA	OBA	SA	AB	H	2B	3B	HR	RBI	BB	SO
.213	.238	.313	80	17	5	0	1	8	3	13
.220	.280	.318	359	79	17	0	6	35	32	74
.224	.271	.312	237	53	12	0	3	26	17	43
.213	.275	.322	202	43	10	0	4	17	18	44
.219	.279	.319	251	55	16	0	3	3	21	46
.218	.264	.314	188	41	6	0	4	40	14	41

GARY SCOTT — bats right — throws right — age 24 — CHN — 3

1991	BA	OBA	SA	AB	H	2B	3B	HR	RBI	BB	SO
vs. Left	.167	.412	.250	24	4	2	0	0	0	10	4
vs. Right	.164	.246	.236	55	9	1	0	1	5	3	10
at Home	.167	.340	.262	42	7	1	0	1	5	9	8
on Road	.162	.262	.216	37	6	2	0	0	0	4	6
Bases Empty	.120	.254	.200	50	6	1	0	1	1	8	11
Runners On Base	.241	.389	.310	29	7	2	0	0	4	5	3

1-YEAR TOTALS (1991)

BA	OBA	SA	AB	H	2B	3B	HR	RBI	BB	SO
.167	.412	.250	24	4	2	0	0	0	10	4
.164	.246	.236	55	9	1	0	1	5	3	10
.167	.340	.262	42	7	1	0	1	5	9	8
.162	.262	.216	37	6	2	0	0	0	4	6
.120	.254	.200	50	6	1	0	1	1	8	11
.241	.389	.310	29	7	2	0	0	4	5	3

TONY SCRUGGS — bats right — throws right — age 26 — TEX — /O

1991	BA	OBA	SA	AB	H	2B	3B	HR	RBI	BB	SO
vs. Left	.000	.000	.000	5	0	0	0	0	0	0	1
vs. Right	.000	.000	.000	1	0	0	0	0	0	0	0
at Home	.000	.000	.000	6	0	0	0	0	0	0	1
on Road	.000	.000	.000	0	0	0	0	0	0	0	0
Bases Empty	.000	.000	.000	4	0	0	0	0	0	0	1
Runners On Base	.000	.000	.000	2	0	0	0	0	0	0	0

1-YEAR TOTALS (1991)

BA	OBA	SA	AB	H	2B	3B	HR	RBI	BB	SO
.000	.000	.000	5	0	0	0	0	0	0	1
.000	.000	.000	1	0	0	0	0	0	0	0
.000	.000	.000	6	0	0	0	0	0	0	1
.000	.000	.000	0	0	0	0	0	0	0	0
.000	.000	.000	4	0	0	0	0	0	0	1
.000	.000	.000	2	0	0	0	0	0	0	0

DAVID SEGUI — bats both — throws left — age 26 — BAL — 10/D

1991	BA	OBA	SA	AB	H	2B	3B	HR	RBI	BB	SO
vs. Left	.337	.363	.408	98	33	4	0	1	12	4	8
vs. Right	.228	.276	.281	114	26	3	0	1	10	8	11
at Home	.250	.279	.302	116	29	3	0	1	11	5	13
on Road	.313	.359	.385	96	30	4	0	1	11	7	6
Bases Empty	.267	.292	.328	116	31	4	0	1	4	4	8
Runners On Base	.292	.343	.354	96	28	3	0	1	21	8	11

2-YEAR TOTALS (1990–1991)

BA	OBA	SA	AB	H	2B	3B	HR	RBI	BB	SO
.312	.336	.413	138	43	8	0	2	18	5	13
.234	.300	.294	197	46	6	0	2	19	18	21
.249	.293	.314	185	46	6	0	2	20	12	22
.287	.340	.380	150	43	8	0	2	17	11	12
.265	.302	.323	189	50	8	0	1	1	10	19
.267	.329	.370	146	39	6	0	3	36	8	15

KEVIN SEITZER — bats right — throws right — age 30 — KC — 3/D

1991	BA	OBA	SA	AB	H	2B	3B	HR	RBI	BB	SO
vs. Left	.333	.429	.424	66	22	3	0	1	7	11	3
vs. Right	.238	.317	.321	168	40	8	3	0	18	18	18
at Home	.274	.344	.368	117	32	7	2	0	15	11	10
on Road	.256	.356	.333	117	30	4	1	1	10	18	11
Bases Empty	.242	.324	.326	132	32	8	0	1	1	15	15
Runners On Base	.294	.381	.382	102	30	3	3	0	24	14	6

6-YEAR TOTALS (1986–1991)

BA	OBA	SA	AB	H	2B	3B	HR	RBI	BB	SO
.299	.390	.427	793	237	42	12	12	76	118	83
.292	.375	.381	1956	572	86	12	21	190	251	243
.321	.402	.445	1363	437	80	16	19	152	181	142
.268	.358	.345	1386	372	48	8	14	114	188	184
.289	.367	.389	1690	488	77	13	22	22	197	207
.303	.399	.403	1059	321	51	11	11	244	172	119

SCOTT SERVAIS — bats right — throws right — age 25 — HOU — C

1991	BA	OBA	SA	AB	H	2B	3B	HR	RBI	BB	SO
vs. Left	.167	.286	.167	6	1	0	0	0	1	1	2
vs. Right	.161	.235	.258	31	5	3	0	0	5	3	6
at Home	.143	.250	.214	14	2	1	0	0	2	2	1
on Road	.174	.240	.261	23	4	2	0	0	4	2	7
Bases Empty	.100	.143	.200	20	2	1	0	0	0	1	5
Runners On Base	.235	.350	.294	17	4	1	0	0	6	3	3

1-YEAR TOTALS (1991)

BA	OBA	SA	AB	H	2B	3B	HR	RBI	BB	SO
.167	.286	.167	6	1	0	0	0	1	1	2
.161	.235	.258	31	5	3	0	0	5	3	6
.143	.250	.214	14	2	1	0	0	2	2	1
.174	.240	.261	23	4	2	0	0	4	2	7
.100	.143	.200	20	2	1	0	0	0	1	5
.235	.350	.294	17	4	1	0	0	6	3	3

MIKE SHARPERSON — bats right — throws right — age 31 — LA — 3S1/2

1991	BA	OBA	SA	AB	H	2B	3B	HR	RBI	BB	SO
vs. Left	.325	.394	.452	157	51	10	2	2	15	18	18
vs. Right	.153	.254	.169	59	9	1	0	0	5	7	6
at Home	.330	.409	.402	97	32	4	0	1	9	13	11
on Road	.235	.311	.353	119	28	7	2	1	11	12	13
Bases Empty	.277	.372	.387	119	33	7	0	2	2	18	13
Runners On Base	.278	.333	.361	97	27	4	2	0	18	7	11

5-YEAR TOTALS (1987–1991)

	BA	OBA	SA	AB	H	2B	3B	HR	RBI	BB	SO
	.312	.380	.393	433	135	20	3	3	41	48	55
	.236	.314	.309	356	84	16	2	2	34	39	47
	.288	.358	.351	385	111	14	2	2	37	42	51
	.267	.343	.359	404	108	22	3	3	38	45	51
	.265	.333	.348	457	121	24	1	4	4	46	60
	.295	.373	.364	332	98	12	4	1	71	41	42

GARY SHEFFIELD — bats right — throws right — age 24 — MIL — 3/D

1991	BA	OBA	SA	AB	H	2B	3B	HR	RBI	BB	SO
vs. Left	.140	.264	.233	43	6	2	1	0	4	7	2
vs. Right	.212	.282	.348	132	28	10	1	2	18	12	13
at Home	.257	.368	.459	74	19	7	1	2	7	11	6
on Road	.149	.209	.218	101	15	5	1	0	15	8	9
Bases Empty	.190	.296	.310	100	19	7	1	1	1	15	6
Runners On Base	.200	.253	.333	75	15	5	1	0	21	4	9

4-YEAR TOTALS (1988–1991)

	BA	OBA	SA	AB	H	2B	3B	HR	RBI	BB	SO
	.258	.322	.408	314	81	22	2	7	38	31	26
	.258	.317	.362	796	205	39	1	14	94	66	70
	.260	.328	.374	543	141	34	2	8	50	54	56
	.256	.308	.376	567	145	27	1	13	82	43	40
	.235	.304	.355	614	144	36	1	12	12	56	53
	.286	.336	.399	496	142	25	2	9	120	41	43

JOHN SHELBY — bats both — throws right — age 34 — DET — O/D

1991	BA	OBA	SA	AB	H	2B	3B	HR	RBI	BB	SO
vs. Left	.175	.212	.349	63	11	5	0	2	4	3	9
vs. Right	.136	.195	.235	81	11	3	1	1	4	5	14
at Home	.159	.221	.317	63	10	4	0	2	4	5	12
on Road	.148	.188	.259	81	12	4	1	1	4	3	11
Bases Empty	.161	.198	.287	87	14	6	1	1	1	3	12
Runners On Base	.140	.210	.281	57	8	2	0	2	7	5	11

8-YEAR TOTALS (1984–1991)

	BA	OBA	SA	AB	H	2B	3B	HR	RBI	BB	SO
	.231	.269	.367	1003	232	40	6	28	99	52	213
	.239	.284	.360	1726	412	70	16	36	185	112	388
	.228	.267	.339	1331	304	48	6	29	137	73	298
	.243	.289	.386	1398	340	62	16	35	147	91	303
	.230	.273	.349	1595	367	53	13	37	37	91	349
	.244	.287	.382	1134	277	57	9	27	247	73	252

PAT SHERIDAN — bats left — throws right — age 35 — NYA — O/D

1991	BA	OBA	SA	AB	H	2B	3B	HR	RBI	BB	SO
vs. Left	.200	.200	.200	15	3	0	0	0	1	0	6
vs. Right	.204	.297	.357	98	20	3	0	4	6	13	24
at Home	.288	.382	.424	59	17	2	0	2	5	9	12
on Road	.111	.172	.241	54	6	1	0	2	2	4	18
Bases Empty	.191	.276	.353	68	13	2	0	3	3	8	18
Runners On Base	.222	.300	.311	45	10	1	0	1	4	5	12

7-YEAR TOTALS (1984–1991)

	BA	OBA	SA	AB	H	2B	3B	HR	RBI	BB	SO
	.197	.247	.282	238	47	6	4	2	15	14	78
	.257	.329	.381	1847	474	73	15	42	206	202	358
	.253	.322	.385	986	249	47	9	22	106	102	202
	.247	.318	.355	1099	272	32	10	22	115	114	234
	.250	.324	.379	1195	299	39	14	29	29	128	238
	.249	.315	.356	890	222	40	5	15	192	88	198

CRAIG SHIPLEY — bats right — throws right — age 29 — SD — S2

1991	BA	OBA	SA	AB	H	2B	3B	HR	RBI	BB	SO
vs. Left	.326	.356	.442	43	14	2	0	1	2	2	7
vs. Right	.229	.245	.250	48	11	1	0	0	4	0	7
at Home	.222	.222	.267	45	10	2	0	0	2	0	9
on Road	.326	.367	.413	46	15	1	0	1	4	2	5
Bases Empty	.276	.288	.362	58	16	2	0	0	1	1	10
Runners On Base	.273	.314	.303	33	9	1	0	0	5	1	4

4-YEAR TOTALS (1986–1991)

	BA	OBA	SA	AB	H	2B	3B	HR	RBI	BB	SO
	.268	.297	.352	71	19	3	0	1	5	3	8
	.213	.239	.236	89	19	2	0	0	7	1	18
	.192	.203	.219	73	14	2	0	0	4	0	15
	.276	.315	.345	87	24	3	0	1	8	4	11
	.253	.269	.319	91	23	3	0	1	1	2	16
	.217	.260	.246	69	15	2	0	0	11	2	10

MIKE SIMMS — bats right — throws right — age 25 — HOU — O

1991	BA	OBA	SA	AB	H	2B	3B	HR	RBI	BB	SO
vs. Left	.196	.323	.353	51	10	2	0	2	8	10	19
vs. Right	.208	.284	.292	72	15	3	0	1	8	8	19
at Home	.194	.272	.278	72	14	3	0	0	9	8	28
on Road	.216	.339	.373	51	11	2	0	2	7	10	10
Bases Empty	.203	.298	.311	74	15	2	0	2	2	10	27
Runners On Base	.204	.305	.327	49	10	3	0	1	14	8	11

2-YEAR TOTALS (1990–1991)

	BA	OBA	SA	AB	H	2B	3B	HR	RBI	BB	SO
	.207	.319	.414	58	12	3	0	3	9	10	22
	.218	.287	.295	78	17	3	0	1	9	8	20
	.184	.259	.263	76	14	3	0	1	9	8	28
	.250	.352	.450	60	15	3	0	3	9	10	14
	.218	.307	.372	78	17	3	0	3	3	10	28
	.207	.294	.310	58	12	3	0	1	15	8	14

MATT SINATRO — bats right — throws right — age 32 — SEA — /C

1991	BA	OBA	SA	AB	H	2B	3B	HR	RBI	BB	SO
vs. Left	.000	.000	.000	3	0	0	0	0	0	0	1
vs. Right	.400	.500	.400	5	2	0	0	0	1	1	0
at Home	.400	.500	.400	5	2	0	0	0	1	1	0
on Road	.000	.000	.000	3	0	0	0	0	0	0	1
Bases Empty	.200	.333	.200	5	1	0	0	0	0	1	0
Runners On Base	.333	.333	.333	3	1	0	0	0	1	0	1

6-YEAR TOTALS (1984–1991)

	BA	OBA	SA	AB	H	2B	3B	HR	RBI	BB	SO
	.216	.273	.216	51	11	0	0	0	2	4	5
	.250	.288	.313	48	12	3	0	0	9	2	11
	.227	.271	.242	66	15	1	0	0	4	4	12
	.242	.297	.303	33	8	2	0	0	7	2	4
	.259	.286	.259	54	14	0	0	0	0	2	7
	.200	.275	.267	45	9	3	0	0	11	4	9

DON SLAUGHT — bats right — throws right — age 34 — PIT — C/3

1991	BA	OBA	SA	AB	H	2B	3B	HR	RBI	BB	SO
vs. Left	.262	.345	.341	126	33	10	0	0	11	14	20
vs. Right	.340	.388	.468	94	32	7	1	1	18	7	12
at Home	.322	.372	.415	118	38	11	0	0	15	9	19
on Road	.265	.353	.373	102	27	6	1	1	14	12	13
Bases Empty	.348	.411	.464	112	39	10	0	1	1	9	16
Runners On Base	.241	.314	.324	108	26	7	1	0	28	12	16

8-YEAR TOTALS (1984–1991)

	BA	OBA	SA	AB	H	2B	3B	HR	RBI	BB	SO
	.284	.346	.448	1002	285	72	10	24	126	92	168
	.259	.310	.390	1422	368	85	9	28	152	90	208
	.289	.342	.443	1218	352	92	9	26	139	94	174
	.250	.307	.385	1206	301	65	10	26	139	88	202
	.275	.329	.451	1388	382	101	13	39	39	96	221
	.262	.319	.365	1036	271	56	6	13	239	86	155

GREG SMITH — bats both — throws right — age 25 — LA — /2

1991	BA	OBA	SA	AB	H	2B	3B	HR	RBI	BB	SO
vs. Left	.000	.000	.000	0	0	0	0	0	0	0	0
vs. Right	.000	.000	.000	3	0	0	0	0	0	0	2
at Home	.000	.000	.000	1	0	0	0	0	0	0	0
on Road	.000	.000	.000	2	0	0	0	0	0	0	2
Bases Empty	.000	.000	.000	0	0	0	0	0	0	0	0
Runners On Base	.000	.000	.000	2	0	0	0	0	0	0	2

3-YEAR TOTALS (1989–1991)

	BA	OBA	SA	AB	H	2B	3B	HR	RBI	BB	SO
	.111	.111	.111	9	1	0	0	0	0	0	2
	.233	.277	.326	43	10	2	1	0	7	2	5
	.158	.158	.211	19	3	1	0	0	1	0	2
	.242	.297	.333	33	8	1	0	0	6	2	5
	.192	.222	.308	26	5	1	0	0	0	0	3
	.231	.276	.269	26	6	1	0	0	7	2	4

DWIGHT SMITH — bats left — throws right — age 29 — CHN — O

1991	BA	OBA	SA	AB	H	2B	3B	HR	RBI	BB	SO
vs. Left	.000	.167	.000	5	0	0	0	0	0	1	2
vs. Right	.235	.283	.358	162	38	7	2	3	21	10	30
at Home	.253	.297	.379	95	24	4	1	2	16	6	16
on Road	.194	.256	.306	72	14	3	1	1	5	5	16
Bases Empty	.167	.200	.260	96	16	2	2	1	1	4	19
Runners On Base	.310	.380	.465	71	22	5	0	2	20	7	13

3-YEAR TOTALS (1989–1991)

BA	OBA	SA	AB	H	2B	3B	HR	RBI	BB	SO
.221	.289	.368	68	15	2	1	2	7	6	20
.287	.347	.425	732	210	39	7	16	93	64	109
.298	.356	.446	383	114	21	3	10	56	34	58
.266	.328	.396	417	111	20	5	8	44	36	71
.263	.324	.409	445	117	20	6	11	11	39	68
.304	.364	.434	355	108	21	2	7	89	31	61

CORY SNYDER — bats right — throws right — age 30 — CHA/TOR — O1/3D

1991	BA	OBA	SA	AB	H	2B	3B	HR	RBI	BB	SO
vs. Left	.164	.192	.276	116	19	4	0	3	10	4	42
vs. Right	.200	.268	.240	50	10	0	1	0	7	5	18
at Home	.183	.227	.310	71	13	3	0	2	7	4	25
on Road	.168	.208	.232	95	16	1	1	1	10	5	35
Bases Empty	.189	.232	.311	90	17	2	0	3	3	5	30
Runners On Base	.158	.198	.211	76	12	2	1	0	14	4	30

6-YEAR TOTALS (1986–1991)

BA	OBA	SA	AB	H	2B	3B	HR	RBI	BB	SO
.250	.299	.454	807	202	43	2	39	119	56	224
.236	.270	.419	1788	422	74	8	79	237	86	478
.228	.271	.402	1245	284	58	3	51	157	73	336
.252	.288	.455	1350	340	59	7	67	199	69	366
.241	.277	.439	1444	348	62	7	70	70	69	389
.240	.283	.418	1151	276	55	3	48	286	73	313

PAUL SORRENTO — bats left — throws right — age 27 — MIN — 1/D

1991	BA	OBA	SA	AB	H	2B	3B	HR	RBI	BB	SO
vs. Left	.600	.600	1.400	5	3	1	0	1	2	0	0
vs. Right	.214	.283	.452	42	9	1	0	3	11	4	11
at Home	.333	.400	.722	18	6	1	0	2	7	2	5
on Road	.207	.258	.448	29	6	1	0	2	6	2	6
Bases Empty	.217	.280	.522	23	5	1	0	2	2	2	7
Runners On Base	.292	.346	.583	24	7	1	0	2	11	2	4

3-YEAR TOTALS (1989–1991)

BA	OBA	SA	AB	H	2B	3B	HR	RBI	BB	SO
.300	.417	.700	10	3	1	0	1	2	2	4
.218	.294	.391	179	39	5	1	8	25	19	42
.257	.315	.426	101	26	5	0	4	13	8	24
.182	.284	.386	88	16	1	1	5	14	13	22
.257	.328	.438	105	27	4	0	5	5	11	29
.179	.268	.369	84	15	2	1	4	22	10	17

TIM SPEHR — bats right — throws right — age 26 — KC — C

1991	BA	OBA	SA	AB	H	2B	3B	HR	RBI	BB	SO
vs. Left	.209	.314	.465	43	9	2	0	3	10	6	11
vs. Right	.161	.235	.258	31	5	3	0	0	4	3	7
at Home	.200	.394	.400	25	5	2	0	1	10	8	6
on Road	.184	.212	.367	49	9	3	0	2	4	1	12
Bases Empty	.270	.357	.514	37	10	3	0	2	2	4	10
Runners On Base	.108	.209	.243	37	4	2	0	1	12	5	8

1-YEAR TOTALS (1991)

BA	OBA	SA	AB	H	2B	3B	HR	RBI	BB	SO
.209	.314	.465	43	9	2	0	3	10	6	11
.161	.235	.258	31	5	3	0	0	4	3	7
.200	.394	.400	25	5	2	0	1	10	8	6
.184	.212	.367	49	9	3	0	2	4	1	12
.270	.357	.514	37	10	3	0	2	2	4	10
.108	.209	.243	37	4	2	0	1	12	5	8

ED SPRAGUE — bats right — throws right — age 25 — TOR — 31/CD

1991	BA	OBA	SA	AB	H	2B	3B	HR	RBI	BB	SO
vs. Left	.267	.347	.400	90	24	3	0	3	11	10	24
vs. Right	.286	.378	.386	70	20	4	0	1	9	9	19
at Home	.286	.329	.429	77	22	2	0	3	11	3	19
on Road	.265	.386	.361	83	22	5	0	1	9	16	24
Bases Empty	.250	.345	.323	96	24	4	0	1	1	13	26
Runners On Base	.313	.384	.500	64	20	3	0	3	19	6	17

1-YEAR TOTALS (1991)

BA	OBA	SA	AB	H	2B	3B	HR	RBI	BB	SO
.267	.347	.400	90	24	3	0	3	11	10	24
.286	.378	.386	70	20	4	0	1	9	9	19
.286	.329	.429	77	22	2	0	3	11	3	19
.265	.386	.361	83	22	5	0	1	9	16	24
.250	.345	.323	96	24	4	0	1	1	13	26
.313	.384	.500	64	20	3	0	3	19	6	17

MIKE STANLEY — bats right — throws right — age 29 — TEX — C1/3DO

1991	BA	OBA	SA	AB	H	2B	3B	HR	RBI	BB	SO
vs. Left	.277	.405	.479	94	26	8	1	3	15	21	21
vs. Right	.218	.333	.276	87	19	5	0	0	10	13	23
at Home	.281	.389	.406	96	27	7	1	1	17	16	17
on Road	.212	.352	.353	85	18	6	0	2	8	18	27
Bases Empty	.253	.378	.424	99	25	6	1	3	3	19	26
Runners On Base	.244	.364	.329	82	20	7	0	0	22	15	18

6-YEAR TOTALS (1986–1991)

BA	OBA	SA	AB	H	2B	3B	HR	RBI	BB	SO
.272	.369	.392	548	149	27	3	11	63	85	111
.225	.321	.300	440	99	16	1	5	57	62	104
.283	.370	.381	501	142	24	2	7	74	69	97
.218	.325	.320	487	106	19	2	9	46	78	118
.236	.331	.328	555	131	19	1	10	10	76	119
.270	.368	.381	433	117	24	3	6	110	71	96

RAY STEPHENS — bats right — throws right — age 30 — SL — /C

1991	BA	OBA	SA	AB	H	2B	3B	HR	RBI	BB	SO
vs. Left	.167	.167	.167	6	1	0	0	0	0	0	3
vs. Right	1.000	1.000	1.000	1	1	0	0	0	0	1	0
at Home	.167	.167	.167	6	1	0	0	0	0	0	3
on Road	1.000	1.000	1.000	1	1	0	0	0	0	1	0
Bases Empty	.250	.400	.250	4	1	0	0	0	0	1	2
Runners On Base	.333	.333	.333	3	1	0	0	0	0	0	1

2-YEAR TOTALS (1990–1991)

BA	OBA	SA	AB	H	2B	3B	HR	RBI	BB	SO
.154	.154	.385	13	2	0	0	1	1	0	5
.222	.300	.333	9	2	1	0	0	0	1	1
.222	.222	.556	9	2	0	0	1	1	0	4
.154	.214	.231	13	2	1	0	0	0	1	2
.200	.250	.467	15	3	1	0	1	1	0	5
.143	.143	.143	7	1	0	0	0	0	0	1

PHIL STEPHENSON — bats left — throws left — age 32 — SD

1991	BA	OBA	SA	AB	H	2B	3B	HR	RBI	BB	SO
vs. Left	.000	.000	.000	0	0	0	0	0	0	0	0
vs. Right	.286	.444	.286	7	2	0	0	0	0	2	3
at Home	.250	.250	.250	4	1	0	0	0	0	0	1
on Road	.333	.600	.333	3	1	0	0	0	0	2	2
Bases Empty	.500	.600	.500	4	2	0	0	0	0	1	1
Runners On Base	.000	.250	.000	3	0	0	0	0	0	1	2

3-YEAR TOTALS (1989–1991)

BA	OBA	SA	AB	H	2B	3B	HR	RBI	BB	SO
.278	.366	.417	36	10	3	1	0	5	5	8
.204	.317	.330	191	39	6	0	6	16	32	43
.238	.339	.390	105	25	4	0	4	11	16	18
.197	.313	.303	122	24	5	1	2	10	21	33
.207	.314	.356	135	28	5	0	5	5	21	30
.228	.339	.326	92	21	4	1	1	16	16	21

LEE STEVENS — bats left — throws left — age 25 — CAL — 1/O

1991	BA	OBA	SA	AB	H	2B	3B	HR	RBI	BB	SO
vs. Left	.294	.294	.353	17	5	1	0	0	5	0	3
vs. Right	.293	.375	.439	41	12	6	0	0	4	6	9
at Home	.333	.378	.424	33	11	3	0	0	8	3	6
on Road	.240	.321	.400	25	6	4	0	0	3	3	6
Bases Empty	.273	.351	.394	33	9	3	0	0	0	4	7
Runners On Base	.320	.357	.440	25	8	3	0	0	9	2	5

2-YEAR TOTALS (1990–1991)

BA	OBA	SA	AB	H	2B	3B	HR	RBI	BB	SO
.225	.273	.296	71	16	2	0	1	14	5	22
.230	.295	.370	235	54	15	0	6	27	23	65
.271	.326	.398	166	45	9	0	4	28	15	44
.179	.247	.300	140	25	8	0	3	13	13	43
.222	.282	.341	167	37	11	0	3	3	14	51
.237	.299	.367	139	33	6	0	4	38	14	36

DOUG STRANGE — bats both — throws right — age 28 — CHN — /3

1991	BA	OBA	SA	AB	H	2B	3B	HR	RBI	BB	SO
vs. Left	.400	.400	.400	5	2	0	0	0	0	0	0
vs. Right	.500	.500	.750	4	2	1	0	0	1	0	1
at Home	.444	.455	.556	9	4	1	0	0	1	0	1
on Road	.000	.000	.000	0	0	0	0	0	0	0	0
Bases Empty	.571	.625	.714	7	4	1	0	0	0	0	1
Runners On Base	.000	.000	.000	2	0	0	0	0	1	0	0

2-YEAR TOTALS (1989–1991)

BA	OBA	SA	AB	H	2B	3B	HR	RBI	BB	SO
.213	.245	.234	47	10	1	0	0	0	2	6
.228	.301	.285	158	36	4	1	1	15	15	31
.229	.311	.286	105	24	3	0	1	9	11	20
.220	.264	.260	100	22	2	1	0	6	6	17
.220	.278	.276	123	27	4	0	1	1	9	26
.232	.304	.268	82	19	1	1	0	14	8	11

GLENN SUTKO — bats right — throws right — age 24 — CIN — /C

1991	BA	OBA	SA	AB	H	2B	3B	HR	RBI	BB	SO
vs. Left	.250	.400	.250	4	1	0	0	0	1	1	2
vs. Right	.000	.143	.000	6	0	0	0	0	0	1	4
at Home	.167	.167	.167	6	1	0	0	0	1	0	4
on Road	.000	.333	.000	4	0	0	0	0	0	2	2
Bases Empty	.000	.000	.000	5	0	0	0	0	0	0	3
Runners On Base	.200	.429	.200	5	1	0	0	0	1	2	3

2-YEAR TOTALS (1990–1991)

BA	OBA	SA	AB	H	2B	3B	HR	RBI	BB	SO
.200	.333	.200	5	1	0	0	0	1	1	3
.000	.143	.000	6	0	0	0	0	0	1	4
.143	.143	.143	7	1	0	0	0	1	0	5
.000	.333	.000	4	0	0	0	0	0	2	2
.000	.000	.000	6	0	0	0	0	0	0	2
.200	.429	.200	5	1	0	0	0	1	2	3

DALE SVEUM — bats both — throws right — age 29 — MIL — S3/D2

1991	BA	OBA	SA	AB	H	2B	3B	HR	RBI	BB	SO
vs. Left	.246	.331	.364	118	29	6	1	2	16	15	35
vs. Right	.236	.312	.365	148	35	13	0	2	27	17	43
at Home	.219	.307	.349	146	32	10	0	3	21	19	42
on Road	.267	.336	.383	120	32	9	1	1	22	13	36
Bases Empty	.213	.319	.333	141	30	8	0	3	3	22	48
Runners On Base	.272	.321	.400	125	34	11	1	1	40	10	30

5-YEAR TOTALS (1986–1991)

BA	OBA	SA	AB	H	2B	3B	HR	RBI	BB	SO
.259	.317	.436	621	161	32	6	22	90	52	152
.233	.288	.352	1081	252	48	4	24	146	85	274
.249	.311	.378	873	217	44	6	19	109	79	210
.236	.286	.387	829	196	36	4	27	127	58	216
.224	.285	.339	959	215	32	3	24	24	78	253
.266	.317	.439	743	198	48	7	22	212	59	173

PAT TABLER — bats right — throws right — age 34 — TOR — D1/O

1991	BA	OBA	SA	AB	H	2B	3B	HR	RBI	BB	SO
vs. Left	.190	.275	.238	147	28	5	1	0	15	19	10
vs. Right	.316	.469	.395	38	12	0	0	1	6	10	11
at Home	.215	.286	.290	93	20	2	1	1	10	10	10
on Road	.217	.348	.250	92	20	3	0	0	11	19	11
Bases Empty	.217	.284	.245	106	23	3	0	0	0	10	10
Runners On Base	.215	.356	.304	79	17	2	1	1	21	19	11

8-YEAR TOTALS (1984–1991)

BA	OBA	SA	AB	H	2B	3B	HR	RBI	BB	SO
.309	.371	.417	1181	365	63	5	18	169	121	110
.272	.333	.363	1977	538	92	12	21	250	168	327
.307	.367	.418	1555	477	83	9	24	229	146	191
.266	.328	.349	1603	426	72	8	15	190	143	246
.264	.325	.356	1665	440	86	9	16	16	144	242
.310	.371	.413	1493	463	69	8	23	403	145	195

JEFF TACKETT — bats right — throws right — age 27 — BAL — /C

1991	BA	OBA	SA	AB	H	2B	3B	HR	RBI	BB	SO
vs. Left	.333	.500	.333	3	1	0	0	0	0	1	0
vs. Right	.000	.167	.000	5	0	0	0	0	0	1	2
at Home	.000	.250	.000	3	0	0	0	0	0	1	1
on Road	.200	.333	.200	5	1	0	0	0	0	1	1
Bases Empty	.143	.143	.143	7	1	0	0	0	0	0	2
Runners On Base	.000	.667	.000	1	0	0	0	0	0	2	0

1-YEAR TOTALS (1991)

BA	OBA	SA	AB	H	2B	3B	HR	RBI	BB	SO
.333	.500	.333	3	1	0	0	0	0	1	0
.000	.167	.000	5	0	0	0	0	0	1	2
.000	.250	.000	3	0	0	0	0	0	1	1
.200	.333	.200	5	1	0	0	0	0	1	1
.143	.143	.143	7	1	0	0	0	0	0	2
.000	.667	.000	1	0	0	0	0	0	2	0

EDDIE TAUBENSEE — bats left — throws right — age 24 — CLE — C

1991	BA	OBA	SA	AB	H	2B	3B	HR	RBI	BB	SO
vs. Left	.400	.455	.400	10	4	0	0	0	0	1	2
vs. Right	.214	.258	.286	56	12	2	1	0	8	4	14
at Home	.200	.244	.250	40	8	2	0	0	7	3	9
on Road	.308	.357	.385	26	8	0	1	0	1	2	7
Bases Empty	.220	.256	.268	41	9	0	1	0	0	2	13
Runners On Base	.280	.333	.360	25	7	2	0	0	8	3	3

1-YEAR TOTALS (1991)

BA	OBA	SA	AB	H	2B	3B	HR	RBI	BB	SO
.400	.455	.400	10	4	0	0	0	0	1	2
.214	.258	.286	56	12	2	1	0	8	4	14
.200	.244	.250	40	8	2	0	0	7	3	9
.308	.357	.385	26	8	0	1	0	1	2	7
.220	.256	.268	41	9	0	1	0	0	2	13
.280	.333	.360	25	7	2	0	0	8	3	3

GARRY TEMPLETON — bats both — throws right — age 36 — SD/NYN — S13/O

1991	BA	OBA	SA	AB	H	2B	3B	HR	RBI	BB	SO
vs. Left	.347	.382	.463	95	33	4	2	0	13	6	10
vs. Right	.155	.171	.221	181	28	6	0	2	13	4	28
at Home	.254	.299	.362	138	35	7	1	2	18	9	20
on Road	.188	.190	.246	138	26	3	1	1	8	1	18
Bases Empty	.239	.262	.296	159	38	4	1	2	1	5	25
Runners On Base	.197	.224	.316	117	23	6	1	2	25	5	13

8-YEAR TOTALS (1984–1991)

BA	OBA	SA	AB	H	2B	3B	HR	RBI	BB	SO
.265	.307	.349	1185	314	49	9	11	125	72	176
.242	.287	.330	2522	611	110	18	25	218	162	398
.245	.292	.348	1874	460	84	17	25	184	124	312
.254	.294	.324	1833	465	75	10	11	159	110	262
.247	.272	.325	2181	538	97	13	16	16	76	340
.254	.320	.352	1526	387	62	14	20	327	158	234

JIM THOME — bats left — throws right — age 22 — CLE — 3

1991	BA	OBA	SA	AB	H	2B	3B	HR	RBI	BB	SO
vs. Left	.050	.050	.050	20	1	0	0	0	0	0	5
vs. Right	.308	.357	.449	78	24	4	2	1	9	5	11
at Home	.245	.310	.358	53	13	2	2	0	1	4	6
on Road	.267	.283	.378	45	12	2	0	1	8	1	10
Bases Empty	.263	.311	.351	57	15	3	1	0	0	3	7
Runners On Base	.244	.279	.390	41	10	1	1	1	9	2	9

1-YEAR TOTALS (1991)

BA	OBA	SA	AB	H	2B	3B	HR	RBI	BB	SO
.050	.050	.050	20	1	0	0	0	0	0	5
.308	.357	.449	78	24	4	2	1	9	5	11
.245	.310	.358	53	13	2	2	0	1	4	6
.267	.283	.378	45	12	2	0	1	8	1	10
.263	.311	.351	57	15	3	1	0	0	3	7
.244	.279	.390	41	10	1	1	1	9	2	9

GARY THURMAN — bats right — throws right — age 28 — KC — O

1991	BA	OBA	SA	AB	H	2B	3B	HR	RBI	BB	SO
vs. Left	.267	.302	.350	120	32	7	0	1	9	6	23
vs. Right	.297	.352	.375	64	19	2	0	1	4	5	19
at Home	.200	.242	.278	90	18	4	0	1	3	4	16
on Road	.351	.392	.436	94	33	5	0	1	10	7	26
Bases Empty	.267	.315	.388	116	31	8	0	2	0	9	27
Runners On Base	.294	.329	.309	68	20	1	0	0	11	4	15

5-YEAR TOTALS (1987–1991)

BA	OBA	SA	AB	H	2B	3B	HR	RBI	BB	SO
.256	.309	.324	250	64	12	1	1	15	19	53
.232	.298	.268	228	53	5	0	1	13	21	67
.212	.271	.273	231	49	9	0	1	12	18	51
.275	.333	.320	247	68	8	0	1	16	22	69
.243	.307	.314	296	72	13	1	2	0	26	77
.247	.298	.269	182	45	4	0	0	26	14	43

RON TINGLEY — bats right — throws right — age 33 — CAL — C

1991	BA	OBA	SA	AB	H	2B	3B	HR	RBI	BB	SO
vs. Left	.212	.235	.273	33	7	2	0	0	3	1	7
vs. Right	.195	.267	.293	82	16	5	0	1	10	7	27
at Home	.255	.349	.418	55	14	6	0	1	11	8	17
on Road	.150	.164	.167	60	9	1	0	0	2	0	17
Bases Empty	.246	.313	.344	61	15	3	0	1	1	5	21
Runners On Base	.148	.193	.222	54	8	4	0	0	12	3	13

4-YEAR TOTALS (1988–1991)

BA	OBA	SA	AB	H	2B	3B	HR	RBI	BB	SO
.205	.239	.318	44	9	2	0	1	5	2	9
.188	.268	.267	101	19	5	0	1	10	10	34
.229	.333	.357	70	16	6	0	1	11	11	21
.160	.182	.213	75	12	1	0	1	4	1	22
.228	.299	.304	79	18	3	0	1	1	7	26
.152	.211	.258	66	10	4	0	1	14	5	17

JOSE TOLENTINO — bats left — throws left — age 31 — HOU — 1/O

1991	BA	OBA	SA	AB	H	2B	3B	HR	RBI	BB	SO
vs. Left	.500	.571	.833	6	3	2	0	0	1	1	0
vs. Right	.229	.269	.333	48	11	2	0	1	5	3	9
at Home	.194	.265	.387	31	6	3	0	1	3	3	5
on Road	.348	.360	.391	23	8	1	0	0	3	1	4
Bases Empty	.259	.310	.370	27	7	3	0	0	0	2	5
Runners On Base	.259	.300	.407	27	7	1	0	1	6	2	4

1-YEAR TOTALS (1991)

BA	OBA	SA	AB	H	2B	3B	HR	RBI	BB	SO
.500	.571	.833	6	3	2	0	0	1	1	0
.229	.269	.333	48	11	2	0	1	5	3	9
.194	.265	.387	31	6	3	0	1	3	3	5
.348	.360	.391	23	8	1	0	0	3	1	4
.259	.310	.370	27	7	3	0	0	0	2	5
.259	.300	.407	27	7	1	0	1	6	2	4

KELVIN TORVE — bats left — throws right — age 32 — NYN — /1

1991	BA	OBA	SA	AB	H	2B	3B	HR	RBI	BB	SO
vs. Left	.000	.000	.000	0	0	0	0	0	0	0	0
vs. Right	.000	.000	.000	8	0	0	0	0	0	0	1
at Home	.000	.000	.000	6	0	0	0	0	0	0	1
on Road	.000	.000	.000	2	0	0	0	0	0	0	0
Bases Empty	.000	.000	.000	3	0	0	0	0	0	0	0
Runners On Base	.000	.000	.000	5	0	0	0	0	0	0	1

3-YEAR TOTALS (1988–1991)

BA	OBA	SA	AB	H	2B	3B	HR	RBI	BB	SO
.500	.750	1.000	2	1	1	0	0	0	2	0
.217	.277	.317	60	13	3	0	1	4	3	12
.350	.435	.450	20	7	2	0	0	3	1	4
.167	.239	.286	42	7	2	0	1	1	4	8
.273	.333	.424	33	9	2	0	1	1	2	4
.172	.273	.241	29	5	2	0	0	3	3	8

SHANE TURNER — bats left — throws right — age 29 — BAL — /2

1991	BA	OBA	SA	AB	H	2B	3B	HR	RBI	BB	SO
vs. Left	.000	.000	.000	0	0	0	0	0	0	0	0
vs. Right	.000	.000	.000	1	0	0	0	0	0	0	0
at Home	.000	.000	.000	0	0	0	0	0	0	0	0
on Road	.000	.000	.000	1	0	0	0	0	0	0	0
Bases Empty	.000	.000	.000	0	0	0	0	0	0	0	0
Runners On Base	.000	.000	.000	1	0	0	0	0	0	0	0

2-YEAR TOTALS (1988–1991)

BA	OBA	SA	AB	H	2B	3B	HR	RBI	BB	SO
.000	.000	.000	0	0	0	0	0	0	0	0
.167	.268	.167	36	6	0	0	0	1	5	9
.167	.333	.167	12	2	0	0	0	0	3	3
.167	.231	.167	24	4	0	0	0	1	2	6
.143	.250	.143	21	3	0	0	0	0	3	4
.200	.294	.200	15	3	0	0	0	1	2	5

JOHN VANDERWAL — bats left — throws left — age 26 — MON — O

1991	BA	OBA	SA	AB	H	2B	3B	HR	RBI	BB	SO
vs. Left	.063	.059	.063	16	1	0	0	0	1	0	8
vs. Right	.267	.283	.467	45	12	4	1	1	7	1	10
at Home	.500	.500	1.000	4	2	0	1	0	1	0	0
on Road	.193	.203	.316	57	11	4	0	1	7	1	18
Bases Empty	.125	.125	.292	24	3	1	0	1	1	0	6
Runners On Base	.270	.282	.405	37	10	3	1	0	7	1	12

1-YEAR TOTALS (1991)

BA	OBA	SA	AB	H	2B	3B	HR	RBI	BB	SO
.063	.059	.063	16	1	0	0	0	1	0	8
.267	.283	.467	45	12	4	1	1	7	1	10
.500	.500	1.000	4	2	0	1	0	1	0	0
.193	.203	.316	57	11	4	0	1	7	1	18
.125	.125	.292	24	3	1	0	1	1	0	6
.270	.282	.405	37	10	3	1	0	7	1	12

GARY VARSHO — bats left — throws right — age 31 — PIT — O/1

1991	BA	OBA	SA	AB	H	2B	3B	HR	RBI	BB	SO
vs. Left	.200	.333	.200	5	1	0	0	0	0	0	1
vs. Right	.275	.345	.423	182	50	11	2	4	23	19	33
at Home	.242	.314	.347	95	23	5	1	1	8	8	13
on Road	.304	.375	.489	92	28	6	1	3	15	11	21
Bases Empty	.265	.303	.327	113	30	5	1	0	0	5	20
Runners On Base	.284	.400	.554	74	21	6	1	4	23	14	14

4-YEAR TOTALS (1988–1991)

BA	OBA	SA	AB	H	2B	3B	HR	RBI	BB	SO
.100	.143	.150	20	2	1	0	0	1	0	5
.258	.304	.367	376	97	21	4	4	34	25	54
.243	.288	.332	202	49	11	2	1	15	11	22
.258	.305	.381	194	50	11	2	3	20	14	37
.241	.268	.299	241	58	10	2	0	0	8	31
.265	.337	.445	155	41	12	2	4	35	17	28

JIM VATCHER — bats right — throws right — age 26 — SD — O

1991	BA	OBA	SA	AB	H	2B	3B	HR	RBI	BB	SO
vs. Left	.273	.333	.273	11	3	0	0	0	1	1	3
vs. Right	.111	.333	.111	9	1	0	0	0	0	3	3
at Home	.250	.308	.250	12	3	0	0	0	1	1	3
on Road	.125	.364	.125	8	1	0	0	0	0	3	3
Bases Empty	.091	.167	.091	11	1	0	0	0	0	1	5
Runners On Base	.333	.500	.333	9	3	0	0	0	2	3	1

2-YEAR TOTALS (1990–1991)

BA	OBA	SA	AB	H	2B	3B	HR	RBI	BB	SO
.300	.354	.417	60	18	2	1	1	6	5	13
.152	.243	.152	33	5	0	0	0	3	4	8
.268	.317	.357	56	15	2	0	1	6	4	10
.216	.310	.270	37	8	0	1	0	3	5	11
.160	.250	.220	50	8	1	1	0	0	6	13
.349	.391	.442	43	15	1	0	1	9	3	8

MO VAUGHN — bats left — throws right — age 25 — BOS — 1D

1991	BA	OBA	SA	AB	H	2B	3B	HR	RBI	BB	SO
vs. Left	.212	.257	.273	33	7	2	0	0	7	2	8
vs. Right	.269	.352	.387	186	50	10	0	4	25	24	35
at Home	.320	.421	.430	100	32	8	0	1	16	18	20
on Road	.210	.262	.319	119	25	4	0	3	16	8	23
Bases Empty	.205	.290	.316	117	24	4	0	3	3	13	25
Runners On Base	.324	.392	.431	102	33	8	0	1	29	13	18

1-YEAR TOTALS (1991)

BA	OBA	SA	AB	H	2B	3B	HR	RBI	BB	SO
.212	.257	.273	33	7	2	0	0	7	2	8
.269	.352	.387	186	50	10	0	4	25	24	35
.320	.421	.430	100	32	8	0	1	16	18	20
.210	.262	.319	119	25	4	0	3	16	8	23
.205	.290	.316	117	24	4	0	3	3	13	25
.324	.392	.431	102	33	8	0	1	29	13	18

RANDY VELARDE — bats right — throws right — age 30 — NYA — 3S/O

1991	BA	OBA	SA	AB	H	2B	3B	HR	RBI	BB	SO
vs. Left	.253	.349	.307	75	19	4	0	0	3	10	17
vs. Right	.239	.303	.349	109	26	7	1	1	12	8	26
at Home	.297	.381	.378	74	22	6	0	0	9	7	13
on Road	.209	.281	.300	110	23	5	1	1	6	11	30
Bases Empty	.306	.375	.417	108	33	7	0	1	1	10	22
Runners On Base	.158	.247	.211	76	12	4	0	0	14	8	21

5-YEAR TOTALS (1987–1991)

BA	OBA	SA	AB	H	2B	3B	HR	RBI	BB	SO
.249	.314	.341	205	51	9	2	2	11	17	46
.225	.289	.353	445	100	18	3	11	47	36	94
.253	.323	.362	304	77	17	2	4	33	26	57
.214	.273	.338	346	74	10	3	9	25	27	83
.245	.304	.355	400	98	17	3	7	7	30	87
.212	.285	.340	250	53	10	2	6	51	23	53

MAX VENABLE — bats left — throws right — age 35 — CAL — O/D

1991	BA	OBA	SA	AB	H	2B	3B	HR	RBI	BB	SO
vs. Left	.211	.286	.211	19	4	0	0	0	0	1	5
vs. Right	.250	.293	.375	168	42	8	2	3	21	10	25
at Home	.233	.286	.320	103	24	1	1	2	13	7	17
on Road	.262	.300	.405	84	22	7	1	1	8	4	13
Bases Empty	.271	.310	.393	107	29	5	1	2	2	5	16
Runners On Base	.213	.270	.313	80	17	3	1	1	19	6	14

7-YEAR TOTALS (1984–1991)

BA	OBA	SA	AB	H	2B	3B	HR	RBI	BB	SO
.225	.289	.250	80	18	2	0	0	10	7	17
.260	.312	.388	709	184	40	9	11	70	55	108
.247	.305	.359	393	97	16	5	6	39	33	56
.265	.314	.389	396	105	26	4	5	41	29	69
.258	.307	.398	457	118	25	6	9	9	30	70
.253	.313	.340	332	84	17	3	2	71	32	55

HECTOR VILLANUEVA — bats right — throws right — age 28 — CHN — C/1

1991	BA	OBA	SA	AB	H	2B	3B	HR	RBI	BB	SO
vs. Left	.283	.388	.535	99	28	5	1	6	16	17	16
vs. Right	.269	.296	.548	93	25	5	0	7	16	4	14
at Home	.324	.385	.686	105	34	3	1	11	24	11	17
on Road	.218	.299	.368	87	19	7	0	2	8	10	13
Bases Empty	.306	.389	.559	111	34	7	0	7	7	15	18
Runners On Base	.235	.284	.519	81	19	3	1	6	25	6	12

2-YEAR TOTALS (1990–1991)

BA	OBA	SA	AB	H	2B	3B	HR	RBI	BB	SO
.274	.356	.554	157	43	7	2	11	29	20	28
.275	.306	.503	149	41	7	0	9	21	5	29
.305	.365	.597	154	47	4	1	13	32	13	28
.243	.299	.461	152	37	10	1	7	18	12	29
.294	.356	.503	177	52	11	1	8	8	17	33
.248	.300	.566	129	32	3	1	12	42	8	24

JOSE VIZCAINO — bats both — throws right — age 24 — CHN — 3S/2

1991	BA	OBA	SA	AB	H	2B	3B	HR	RBI	BB	SO
vs. Left	.222	.237	.222	36	8	0	0	0	2	1	5
vs. Right	.275	.298	.321	109	30	5	0	0	8	4	13
at Home	.235	.256	.284	81	19	4	0	0	10	3	9
on Road	.297	.318	.313	64	19	1	0	0	0	2	9
Bases Empty	.207	.225	.230	87	18	2	0	0	0	2	12
Runners On Base	.345	.365	.397	58	20	3	0	0	10	3	6

3-YEAR TOTALS (1989–1991)

BA	OBA	SA	AB	H	2B	3B	HR	RBI	BB	SO
.255	.311	.255	55	14	0	0	0	3	5	8
.265	.282	.318	151	40	6	1	0	9	4	19
.250	.276	.310	116	29	5	1	0	11	5	12
.278	.309	.289	90	25	1	0	0	1	4	15
.238	.261	.277	130	31	3	1	0	0	4	19
.303	.337	.342	76	23	3	0	0	12	5	8

DON WAKAMATSU — bats right — throws right — age 29 — CHA — C

1991	BA	OBA	SA	AB	H	2B	3B	HR	RBI	BB	SO
vs. Left	.313	.313	.313	16	5	0	0	0	0	0	2
vs. Right	.133	.188	.133	15	2	0	0	0	0	1	4
at Home	.273	.333	.273	11	3	0	0	0	0	1	2
on Road	.200	.200	.200	20	4	0	0	0	0	0	4
Bases Empty	.174	.208	.174	23	4	0	0	0	0	1	5
Runners On Base	.375	.375	.375	8	3	0	0	0	0	0	1

1-YEAR TOTALS (1991)

BA	OBA	SA	AB	H	2B	3B	HR	RBI	BB	SO
.313	.313	.313	16	5	0	0	0	0	0	2
.133	.188	.133	15	2	0	0	0	0	1	4
.273	.333	.273	11	3	0	0	0	0	1	2
.200	.200	.200	20	4	0	0	0	0	0	4
.174	.208	.174	23	4	0	0	0	0	1	5
.375	.375	.375	8	3	0	0	0	0	0	1

DENNY WALLING — bats left — throws right — age 38 — TEX — 3/O

1991	BA	OBA	SA	AB	H	2B	3B	HR	RBI	BB	SO
vs. Left	.000	.000	.000	6	0	0	0	0	0	0	1
vs. Right	.105	.209	.132	38	4	1	0	0	2	3	7
at Home	.000	.208	.000	19	0	0	0	0	0	3	4
on Road	.160	.160	.200	25	4	1	0	0	2	0	4
Bases Empty	.048	.130	.048	21	1	0	0	0	0	1	5
Runners On Base	.130	.231	.174	23	3	1	0	0	2	2	3

8-YEAR TOTALS (1984–1991)

BA	OBA	SA	AB	H	2B	3B	HR	RBI	BB	SO
.214	.264	.257	206	44	6	0	1	21	14	39
.280	.338	.414	1579	442	95	13	30	199	144	143
.279	.336	.386	874	244	51	6	10	109	76	82
.266	.324	.405	911	242	50	7	21	111	82	100
.273	.317	.390	977	267	66	6	12	12	62	93
.271	.344	.402	808	219	35	7	19	208	96	89

KEVIN WARD — bats right — throws right — age 31 — SD — O

1991	BA	OBA	SA	AB	H	2B	3B	HR	RBI	BB	SO
vs. Left	.299	.356	.552	67	20	7	2	2	7	5	16
vs. Right	.150	.227	.150	40	6	0	0	0	1	4	11
at Home	.167	.224	.278	54	9	2	2	0	4	3	12
on Road	.321	.390	.528	53	17	5	0	2	4	6	15
Bases Empty	.250	.344	.429	56	14	4	0	2	2	8	10
Runners On Base	.235	.264	.373	51	12	3	2	0	6	1	17

1-YEAR TOTALS (1991)

BA	OBA	SA	AB	H	2B	3B	HR	RBI	BB	SO
.299	.356	.552	67	20	7	2	2	7	5	16
.150	.227	.150	40	6	0	0	0	1	4	11
.167	.224	.278	54	9	2	2	0	4	3	12
.321	.390	.528	53	17	5	0	2	4	6	15
.250	.344	.429	56	14	4	0	2	2	8	10
.235	.264	.373	51	12	3	2	0	6	1	17

TURNER WARD — bats both — throws right — age 27 — CLE/TOR — O

1991	BA	OBA	SA	AB	H	2B	3B	HR	RBI	BB	SO
vs. Left	.250	.351	.313	32	8	2	0	0	3	5	4
vs. Right	.235	.287	.296	81	19	5	0	0	4	6	14
at Home	.146	.222	.220	41	6	3	0	0	2	4	10
on Road	.292	.354	.347	72	21	4	0	0	5	7	8
Bases Empty	.194	.254	.242	62	12	3	0	0	0	5	10
Runners On Base	.294	.368	.373	51	15	4	0	0	7	6	8

2-YEAR TOTALS (1990–1991)

BA	OBA	SA	AB	H	2B	3B	HR	RBI	BB	SO
.273	.347	.318	44	12	2	0	0	4	5	5
.270	.323	.374	115	31	7	1	1	13	9	21
.186	.238	.254	59	11	4	0	0	3	4	13
.320	.382	.420	100	32	5	1	1	14	10	13
.228	.291	.278	79	18	4	0	0	0	7	10
.313	.368	.438	80	25	5	1	1	17	7	16

LENNY WEBSTER — bats right — throws right — age 27 — MIN — C

1991	BA	OBA	SA	AB	H	2B	3B	HR	RBI	BB	SO
vs. Left	.400	.462	.400	10	4	0	0	0	2	2	1
vs. Right	.250	.357	.667	24	6	1	0	3	6	4	9
at Home	.286	.304	.476	21	6	1	0	1	5	1	6
on Road	.308	.500	.769	13	4	0	0	2	3	5	4
Bases Empty	.250	.294	.500	16	4	1	0	1	1	1	3
Runners On Base	.333	.458	.667	18	6	0	0	2	7	5	7

3-YEAR TOTALS (1989–1991)

BA	OBA	SA	AB	H	2B	3B	HR	RBI	BB	SO
.316	.391	.316	19	6	0	0	0	2	3	1
.293	.396	.610	41	12	4	0	3	7	7	12
.273	.306	.424	33	9	2	0	1	6	2	8
.333	.486	.630	27	9	2	0	2	1	8	5
.281	.324	.469	32	9	3	0	1	1	2	5
.321	.459	.571	28	9	1	0	2	8	8	8

MITCH WEBSTER — bats both — throws left — age 33 — CLE/PIT/LA — O/1

1991	BA	OBA	SA	AB	H	2B	3B	HR	RBI	BB	SO
vs. Left	.238	.313	.366	101	24	1	3	2	12	11	26
vs. Right	.176	.250	.284	102	18	7	2	0	7	10	35
at Home	.197	.321	.364	66	13	3	1	2	8	12	21
on Road	.212	.260	.307	137	29	5	4	0	11	9	40
Bases Empty	.200	.290	.327	110	22	4	2	2	2	14	30
Runners On Base	.215	.270	.323	93	20	4	3	0	17	7	31

8-YEAR TOTALS (1984–1991)

BA	OBA	SA	AB	H	2B	3B	HR	RBI	BB	SO
.286	.333	.441	1025	293	50	11	29	121	68	147
.254	.333	.383	1811	460	77	36	28	157	207	330
.259	.330	.393	1365	354	56	24	26	146	139	216
.271	.336	.414	1471	399	71	23	31	132	136	261
.259	.323	.403	1673	434	76	34	23	34	144	289
.274	.346	.405	1163	319	51	16	23	244	131	188

ERIC WEDGE — bats right — throws right — age 24 — BOS — /D

1991	BA	OBA	SA	AB	H	2B	3B	HR	RBI	BB	SO
vs. Left	.000	.000	.000	0	0	0	0	0	0	0	0
vs. Right	1.000	1.000	1.000	1	1	0	0	0	0	0	0
at Home	1.000	1.000	1.000	1	1	0	0	0	0	0	0
on Road	.000	.000	.000	0	0	0	0	0	0	0	0
Bases Empty	1.000	1.000	1.000	1	1	0	0	0	0	0	0
Runners On Base	.000	.000	.000	0	0	0	0	0	0	0	0

1-YEAR TOTALS (1991)

BA	OBA	SA	AB	H	2B	3B	HR	RBI	BB	SO
.000	.000	.000	0	0	0	0	0	0	0	0
1.000	1.000	1.000	1	1	0	0	0	0	0	0
1.000	1.000	1.000	1	1	0	0	0	0	0	0
.000	.000	.000	0	0	0	0	0	0	0	0
1.000	1.000	1.000	1	1	0	0	0	0	0	0
.000	.000	.000	0	0	0	0	0	0	0	0

JOHN WEHNER — bats right — throws right — age 25 — PIT — 3

1991	BA	OBA	SA	AB	H	2B	3B	HR	RBI	BB	SO
vs. Left	.346	.370	.404	52	18	3	0	0	1	2	7
vs. Right	.333	.390	.407	54	18	4	0	0	6	5	10
at Home	.380	.392	.480	50	19	5	0	0	5	1	7
on Road	.304	.371	.339	56	17	2	0	0	2	6	10
Bases Empty	.387	.424	.468	62	24	5	0	0	0	4	11
Runners On Base	.273	.319	.318	44	12	2	0	0	7	3	6

1-YEAR TOTALS (1991)

BA	OBA	SA	AB	H	2B	3B	HR	RBI	BB	SO
.346	.370	.404	52	18	3	0	0	1	2	7
.333	.390	.407	54	18	4	0	0	6	5	10
.380	.392	.480	50	19	5	0	0	5	1	7
.304	.371	.339	56	17	2	0	0	2	6	10
.387	.424	.468	62	24	5	0	0	0	4	11
.273	.319	.318	44	12	2	0	0	7	3	6

WALT WEISS — bats both — throws right — age 29 — OAK — S

1991	BA	OBA	SA	AB	H	2B	3B	HR	RBI	BB	SO
vs. Left	.194	.219	.258	31	6	2	0	0	1	1	0
vs. Right	.235	.304	.294	102	24	4	1	0	12	11	14
at Home	.167	.233	.192	78	13	2	0	0	4	7	10
on Road	.309	.361	.418	55	17	4	1	0	9	5	4
Bases Empty	.246	.297	.304	69	17	4	0	0	0	5	8
Runners On Base	.203	.274	.266	64	13	2	1	0	13	7	6

5-YEAR TOTALS (1987–1991)

BA	OBA	SA	AB	H	2B	3B	HR	RBI	BB	SO
.233	.271	.284	313	73	14	1	0	24	17	28
.260	.334	.335	979	255	41	4	8	85	99	136
.231	.296	.282	657	152	22	1	3	44	55	100
.277	.343	.365	635	176	33	4	5	65	61	64
.247	.319	.321	725	179	40	1	4	4	69	95
.263	.319	.325	567	149	15	4	4	105	47	69

ERNIE WHITT — bats left — throws right — age 40 — BAL — C/D

1991	BA	OBA	SA	AB	H	2B	3B	HR	RBI	BB	SO
vs. Left	.200	.200	.200	5	1	0	0	0	0	0	1
vs. Right	.246	.338	.281	57	14	2	0	0	3	8	11
at Home	.276	.344	.310	29	8	1	0	0	3	3	5
on Road	.212	.316	.242	33	7	1	0	0	0	5	7
Bases Empty	.294	.368	.353	34	10	2	0	0	0	4	6
Runners On Base	.179	.281	.179	28	5	0	0	0	3	4	6

8-YEAR TOTALS (1984–1991)

BA	OBA	SA	AB	H	2B	3B	HR	RBI	BB	SO
.232	.312	.340	315	73	8	1	8	37	35	80
.253	.332	.427	2279	576	112	8	90	340	278	248
.239	.337	.419	1238	296	64	6	49	190	186	171
.260	.322	.414	1356	353	56	3	49	187	127	157
.246	.318	.413	1428	352	75	2	53	53	147	179
.255	.342	.421	1166	297	45	7	45	324	166	149

CURTIS WILKERSON — bats both — throws right — age 31 — PIT — 2S3

1991	BA	OBA	SA	AB	H	2B	3B	HR	RBI	BB	SO
vs. Left	.224	.286	.306	49	11	4	0	0	5	5	6
vs. Right	.176	.227	.268	142	25	5	1	2	13	10	34
at Home	.180	.255	.326	89	16	5	1	2	8	9	19
on Road	.196	.232	.235	102	20	4	0	0	10	6	21
Bases Empty	.167	.231	.281	96	16	6	1	1	1	8	21
Runners On Base	.211	.255	.274	95	20	3	0	1	17	7	19

8-YEAR TOTALS (1984–1991)

BA	OBA	SA	AB	H	2B	3B	HR	RBI	BB	SO
.230	.289	.292	465	107	17	3	2	33	38	74
.251	.288	.312	1628	409	51	18	4	116	79	271
.253	.293	.321	992	251	33	11	4	78	51	158
.241	.284	.296	1101	265	35	10	2	71	66	187
.250	.287	.314	1266	316	48	9	5	5	61	219
.242	.290	.299	827	200	20	12	1	144	56	126

JERRY WILLARD — bats left — throws right — age 32 — ATL — /C

1991	BA	OBA	SA	AB	H	2B	3B	HR	RBI	BB	SO
vs. Left	.000	.000	.000	0	0	0	0	0	0	0	0
vs. Right	.214	.313	.429	14	3	0	0	1	4	2	5
at Home	.200	.333	.800	5	1	0	0	1	2	1	2
on Road	.222	.300	.222	9	2	0	0	0	2	1	3
Bases Empty	.143	.333	.143	7	1	0	0	0	0	2	2
Runners On Base	.286	.286	.714	7	2	0	0	1	4	0	3

6-YEAR TOTALS (1984–1991)

BA	OBA	SA	AB	H	2B	3B	HR	RBI	BB	SO
.204	.276	.257	113	23	3	0	1	13	11	39
.259	.333	.405	617	160	25	1	21	90	69	111
.261	.333	.393	364	95	12	0	12	55	39	80
.240	.315	.372	366	88	16	1	10	48	41	70
.251	.322	.373	402	101	14	1	11	11	41	86
.250	.326	.393	328	82	14	0	11	92	39	64

KENNY WILLIAMS — bats right — throws right — age 28 — TOR/MON — O/D

1991	BA	OBA	SA	AB	H	2B	3B	HR	RBI	BB	SO
vs. Left	.267	.309	.427	75	20	5	2	1	4	4	19
vs. Right	.208	.321	.292	24	5	2	0	0	3	8	8
at Home	.195	.250	.317	41	8	3	1	0	1	2	12
on Road	.293	.354	.448	58	17	4	1	1	3	5	15
Bases Empty	.292	.333	.492	65	19	6	2	1	1	2	15
Runners On Base	.176	.275	.206	34	6	1	0	0	3	3	12

6-YEAR TOTALS (1986–1991)

BA	OBA	SA	AB	H	2B	3B	HR	RBI	BB	SO
.234	.282	.379	589	138	25	6	16	58	31	149
.200	.255	.299	545	109	17	2	11	59	25	138
.228	.281	.347	556	127	25	4	11	65	32	140
.208	.258	.334	578	120	17	4	16	52	24	147
.216	.268	.333	658	142	26	6	15	15	29	149
.221	.271	.351	476	105	16	5	12	102	27	138

CRAIG WILSON — bats right — throws right — age 28 — SL — 3/012

1991	BA	OBA	SA	AB	H	2B	3B	HR	RBI	BB	SO
vs. Left	.216	.263	.255	51	11	2	0	0	10	4	8
vs. Right	.097	.152	.097	31	3	0	0	0	3	2	8
at Home	.154	.211	.192	52	8	2	0	0	8	4	8
on Road	.200	.242	.200	30	6	0	0	0	5	2	2
Bases Empty	.097	.176	.129	31	3	1	0	0	0	3	3
Runners On Base	.216	.250	.235	51	11	1	0	0	13	3	7

3-YEAR TOTALS (1989–1991)

BA	OBA	SA	AB	H	2B	3B	HR	RBI	BB	SO
.248	.300	.272	125	31	3	0	0	18	11	18
.171	.209	.183	82	14	1	0	0	3	4	8
.184	.261	.214	103	19	3	0	0	11	11	18
.250	.270	.260	104	26	1	0	0	10	4	8
.273	.340	.295	88	24	2	0	0	0	9	8
.176	.209	.193	119	21	2	0	0	21	6	18

MOOKIE WILSON — bats both — throws right — age 36 — TOR — OD

1991	BA	OBA	SA	AB	H	2B	3B	HR	RBI	BB	SO
vs. Left	.209	.209	.256	43	9	2	0	0	1	0	8
vs. Right	.247	.291	.369	198	49	10	4	2	27	8	27
at Home	.270	.298	.383	115	31	8	1	1	14	3	20
on Road	.214	.259	.317	126	27	4	3	1	14	5	15
Bases Empty	.202	.244	.306	124	25	6	2	1	1	5	23
Runners On Base	.282	.312	.393	117	33	6	2	1	27	3	12

8-YEAR TOTALS (1984–1991)

BA	OBA	SA	AB	H	2B	3B	HR	RBI	BB	SO
.268	.314	.396	1382	371	65	24	21	119	92	238
.278	.318	.395	2002	557	99	21	31	195	108	345
.267	.308	.378	1628	434	85	15	22	142	93	293
.281	.324	.412	1756	494	79	30	30	172	107	290
.279	.321	.406	2078	580	100	28	36	36	116	378
.266	.309	.378	1306	348	64	17	16	278	84	205

WILLIE WILSON — bats both — throws right — age 37 — OAK — O/D

1991	BA	OBA	SA	AB	H	2B	3B	HR	RBI	BB	SO
vs. Left	.253	.302	.293	99	25	4	0	0	6	6	13
vs. Right	.231	.284	.323	195	45	10	4	0	22	12	30
at Home	.250	.303	.341	132	33	8	2	0	16	9	19
on Road	.228	.280	.290	162	37	6	2	0	12	9	24
Bases Empty	.223	.283	.277	166	37	9	0	0	0	11	25
Runners On Base	.258	.299	.359	128	33	5	4	0	28	7	18

8-YEAR TOTALS (1984–1991)

BA	OBA	SA	AB	H	2B	3B	HR	RBI	BB	SO
.282	.312	.381	1187	335	55	19	8	96	53	213
.269	.318	.363	2775	747	93	58	17	215	174	406
.284	.328	.384	1984	564	72	49	9	162	118	280
.262	.304	.353	1978	518	76	28	16	149	109	339
.289	.329	.384	1470	425	63	28	7	293	85	216

HERM WINNINGHAM — bats left — throws right — age 31 — CIN — O

1991	BA	OBA	SA	AB	H	2B	3B	HR	RBI	BB	SO
vs. Left	.154	.214	.154	13	2	0	0	0	0	1	2
vs. Right	.231	.277	.301	156	36	6	1	1	4	10	38
at Home	.238	.289	.321	84	20	4	0	1	2	6	19
on Road	.212	.256	.259	85	18	2	1	0	2	5	21
Bases Empty	.257	.294	.336	113	29	6	0	1	1	6	29
Runners On Base	.161	.230	.196	56	9	0	1	0	3	5	11

8-YEAR TOTALS (1984–1991)

BA	OBA	SA	AB	H	2B	3B	HR	RBI	BB	SO
.242	.266	.342	219	53	6	2	4	23	9	61
.240	.305	.339	1435	344	55	23	14	110	138	303
.230	.299	.307	835	192	25	12	5	65	83	190
.250	.302	.374	819	205	36	13	13	68	64	174
.233	.290	.335	1030	240	45	12	12	68	83	220
.252	.316	.348	624	157	16	13	6	121	64	144

RON WITMEYER — bats left — throws left — age 25 — OAK — /1

1991	BA	OBA	SA	AB	H	2B	3B	HR	RBI	BB	SO
vs. Left	.000	.000	.000	1	0	0	0	0	0	0	0
vs. Right	.056	.056	.056	18	1	0	0	0	0	0	5
at Home	.000	.000	.000	6	0	0	0	0	0	0	4
on Road	.077	.077	.077	13	1	0	0	0	0	0	1
Bases Empty	.100	.100	.100	10	1	0	0	0	0	0	2
Runners On Base	.000	.000	.000	9	0	0	0	0	0	0	3

1-YEAR TOTALS (1991)

BA	OBA	SA	AB	H	2B	3B	HR	RBI	BB	SO
.000	.000	.000	1	0	0	0	0	0	0	0
.056	.056	.056	18	1	0	0	0	0	0	5
.000	.000	.000	6	0	0	0	0	0	0	4
.077	.077	.077	13	1	0	0	0	0	0	1
.100	.100	.100	10	1	0	0	0	0	0	2
.000	.000	.000	9	0	0	0	0	0	0	3

TED WOOD — bats left — throws left — age 25 — SF — /O

1991	BA	OBA	SA	AB	H	2B	3B	HR	RBI	BB	SO
vs. Left	.333	.333	.333	3	1	0	0	0	0	0	0
vs. Right	.091	.167	.091	22	2	0	0	0	1	2	11
at Home	.125	.222	.125	8	1	0	0	0	1	1	3
on Road	.118	.167	.118	17	2	0	0	0	0	1	8
Bases Empty	.118	.167	.118	17	2	0	0	0	0	1	5
Runners On Base	.125	.222	.125	8	1	0	0	0	1	1	6

1-YEAR TOTALS (1991)

BA	OBA	SA	AB	H	2B	3B	HR	RBI	BB	SO
.333	.333	.333	3	1	0	0	0	0	0	0
.091	.167	.091	22	2	0	0	0	1	2	11
.125	.222	.125	8	1	0	0	0	1	1	3
.118	.167	.118	17	2	0	0	0	0	1	8
.118	.167	.118	17	2	0	0	0	0	1	5
.125	.222	.125	8	1	0	0	0	1	1	6

CRAIG WORTHINGTON — bats right — throws right — age 27 — BAL — 3

1991	BA	OBA	SA	AB	H	2B	3B	HR	RBI	BB	SO
vs. Left	.258	.343	.419	31	8	2	0	1	4	4	3
vs. Right	.211	.300	.352	71	15	1	0	3	8	8	11
at Home	.239	.314	.326	46	11	1	0	1	3	4	7
on Road	.214	.313	.411	56	12	2	0	3	9	8	7
Bases Empty	.255	.339	.418	55	14	3	0	2	2	7	10
Runners On Base	.191	.283	.319	47	9	0	0	2	10	5	4

4-YEAR TOTALS (1988–1991)

BA	OBA	SA	AB	H	2B	3B	HR	RBI	BB	SO
.250	.362	.355	344	86	15	0	7	36	59	63
.225	.307	.351	761	171	30	0	22	94	86	185
.244	.340	.365	542	132	18	0	16	65	76	117
.222	.310	.339	563	125	27	0	13	65	69	131
.223	.317	.369	610	136	29	0	20	20	81	136
.244	.335	.331	495	121	16	0	9	110	64	112

GERALD YOUNG — bats both — throws right — age 28 — HOU — O

1991	BA	OBA	SA	AB	H	2B	3B	HR	RBI	BB	SO
vs. Left	.244	.326	.333	78	19	2	1	1	4	10	8
vs. Right	.188	.329	.203	64	12	1	0	0	7	14	9
at Home	.230	.333	.270	74	17	1	1	0	5	12	10
on Road	.206	.321	.279	68	14	2	0	1	6	12	7
Bases Empty	.213	.278	.270	89	19	0	1	1	1	8	13
Runners On Base	.226	.394	.283	53	12	3	0	0	10	16	4

5-YEAR TOTALS (1987–1991)

BA	OBA	SA	AB	H	2B	3B	HR	RBI	BB	SO
.274	.346	.341	580	159	22	4	3	37	62	71
.236	.325	.287	1098	259	32	12	0	68	148	122
.254	.332	.312	866	220	29	9	1	54	101	91
.244	.332	.299	812	198	25	7	2	51	109	102
.236	.315	.291	1153	272	32	11	3	3	131	139
.278	.368	.339	525	146	22	5	0	102	79	54

EDDIE ZOSKY — bats right — throws right — age 24 — TOR — S

1991	BA	OBA	SA	AB	H	2B	3B	HR	RBI	BB	SO
vs. Left	.167	.167	.333	6	1	1	0	0	0	0	2
vs. Right	.143	.143	.238	21	3	0	1	0	2	0	6
at Home	.167	.167	.278	18	3	0	1	0	2	0	6
on Road	.111	.111	.222	9	1	1	0	0	0	0	2
Bases Empty	.200	.200	.400	15	3	1	1	0	0	0	4
Runners On Base	.083	.083	.083	12	1	0	0	0	2	0	4

1-YEAR TOTALS (1991)

BA	OBA	SA	AB	H	2B	3B	HR	RBI	BB	SO
.167	.167	.333	6	1	1	0	0	0	0	2
.143	.143	.238	21	3	0	1	0	2	0	6
.167	.167	.278	18	3	0	1	0	2	0	6
.111	.111	.222	9	1	1	0	0	0	0	2
.200	.200	.400	15	3	1	1	0	0	0	4
.083	.083	.083	12	1	0	0	0	2	0	4

BOB ZUPCIC — bats right — throws right — age 26 — BOS — O

1991	BA	OBA	SA	AB	H	2B	3B	HR	RBI	BB	SO
vs. Left	.182	.250	.182	11	2	0	0	0	2	1	1
vs. Right	.143	.143	.357	14	2	0	0	1	1	0	5
at Home	.231	.286	.462	13	3	0	0	1	2	1	3
on Road	.083	.083	.083	12	1	0	0	0	1	0	3
Bases Empty	.214	.267	.429	14	3	0	0	1	1	1	4
Runners On Base	.091	.091	.091	11	1	0	0	0	2	0	2

1-YEAR TOTALS (1991)

BA	OBA	SA	AB	H	2B	3B	HR	RBI	BB	SO
.182	.250	.182	11	2	0	0	0	2	1	1
.143	.143	.357	14	2	0	0	1	1	0	5
.231	.286	.462	13	3	0	0	1	2	1	3
.083	.083	.083	12	1	0	0	0	1	0	3
.214	.277	.429	14	3	0	0	1	1	1	4
.091	.091	.091	11	1	0	0	0	2	0	2

PAUL ZUVELLA — bats right — throws right — age 34 — KC — /3

1991	BA	OBA	SA	AB	H	2B	3B	HR	RBI	BB	SO
vs. Left	.000	.000	.000	0	0	0	0	0	0	0	0
vs. Right	.000	.000	.000	0	0	0	0	0	0	0	0
at Home	.000	.000	.000	0	0	0	0	0	0	0	0
on Road	.000	.000	.000	0	0	0	0	0	0	0	0
Bases Empty	.000	.000	.000	0	0	0	0	0	0	0	0
Runners On Base	.000	.000	.000	0	0	0	0	0	0	0	0

6-YEAR TOTALS (1984–1991)

BA	OBA	SA	AB	H	2B	3B	HR	RBI	BB	SO
.225	.282	.258	151	34	5	0	0	4	12	11
.225	.270	.290	334	75	12	2	2	16	20	38
.211	.265	.269	242	51	6	1	2	8	17	22
.239	.283	.292	243	58	11	1	2	12	15	27
.236	.281	.285	284	67	6	1	2	18	18	28
.209	.264	.274	201	42	11	1	0	18	14	21

PITCHERS

KYLE ABBOTT — bats left — throws left — age 24 — CAL — P

1991

	G	IP	H	BB	SO	SB	CS	W	L	SV	ERA
at Home	2	10.2	14	5	6	0	0	0	2	0	5.06
on Road	3	9.0	8	8	6	1	2	1	0	0	4.00

	BA	OBA	SA	AB	H	2B	3B	HR	RBI	BB	SO
Total	.301	.414	.438	73	22	4	0	2	9	13	12
vs. Left	.308	.400	.308	13	4	0	0	0	2	2	3
vs. Right	.300	.417	.467	60	18	4	0	2	7	11	9
Bases Empty	.297	.422	.351	37	11	2	0	0		8	8
Runners On Base	.306	.405	.528	36	11	2	0	2	9	5	4

1-YEAR TOTALS (1991)

G	IP	H	BB	SO	SB	CS	W	L	SV	ERA
2	10.2	14	5	6	0	0	0	2	0	5.06
3	9.0	8	8	6	1	2	1	0	0	4.00

BA	OBA	SA	AB	H	2B	3B	HR	RBI	BB	SO
.301	.414	.438	73	22	4	0	2	9	13	12
.308	.400	.308	13	4	0	0	0	2	2	3
.300	.417	.467	60	18	4	0	2	7	11	9
.297	.422	.351	37	11	2	0	0		8	8
.306	.405	.528	36	11	2	0	2	9	5	4

PAUL ABBOTT — bats right — throws right — age 25 — MIN — P

1991

	G	IP	H	BB	SO	SB	CS	W	L	SV	ERA
at Home	7	21.2	16	11	22	2	0	2	0	0	2.49
on Road	8	25.2	22	25	21	4	1	1	1	0	6.66

	BA	OBA	SA	AB	H	2B	3B	HR	RBI	BB	SO
Total	.232	.365	.396	164	38	10	1	5	26	36	43
vs. Left	.186	.367	.356	59	11	1	0	3	12	18	15
vs. Right	.257	.363	.419	105	27	9	1	2	14	18	28
Bases Empty	.261	.375	.386	88	23	8	0	1	1	16	26
Runners On Base	.197	.354	.408	76	15	2	1	4	25	20	17

2-YEAR TOTALS (1990–1991)

G	IP	H	BB	SO	SB	CS	W	L	SV	ERA
9	28.1	24	17	26	5	0	2	2	0	4.76
13	53.2	51	47	42	11	3	1	4	0	5.53

BA	OBA	SA	AB	H	2B	3B	HR	RBI	BB	SO
.254	.385	.390	295	75	19	3	5	43	64	68
.218	.385	.316	133	29	2	1	3	22	37	33
.284	.384	.451	162	46	17	2	2	21	27	35
.267	.412	.377	146	39	13	0	1	1	35	39
.242	.357	.403	149	36	6	3	4	42	29	29

JIM ACKER — bats right — throws right — age 34 — TOR — P

1991

	G	IP	H	BB	SO	SB	CS	W	L	SV	ERA
at Home	29	53.0	49	18	24	3	2	2	2	0	4.92
on Road	25	35.1	28	18	20	6	1	1	3	1	5.60

	BA	OBA	SA	AB	H	2B	3B	HR	RBI	BB	SO
Total	.238	.314	.424	323	77	10	1	16	57	36	44
vs. Left	.303	.383	.475	122	37	6	0	5	18	17	10
vs. Right	.199	.271	.393	201	40	4	1	11	39	19	34
Bases Empty	.188	.261	.322	202	38	4	1	7	7	18	28
Runners On Base	.322	.396	.595	121	39	6	0	9	50	18	16

8-YEAR TOTALS (1984–1991)

G	IP	H	BB	SO	SB	CS	W	L	SV	ERA
207	405.2	385	138	209	36	23	15	18	13	3.84
205	370.2	385	141	218	32	16	13	30	16	3.91

BA	OBA	SA	AB	H	2B	3B	HR	RBI	BB	SO
.264	.330	.389	2922	770	127	14	71	394	279	427
.283	.355	.397	1384	392	62	9	26	182	155	142
.246	.307	.382	1538	378	65	5	45	212	124	285
.253	.316	.373	1615	408	69	7	37	37	138	236
.277	.346	.410	1307	362	58	7	34	357	141	191

JUAN AGOSTO — bats left — throws left — age 34 — SL — P

1991

	G	IP	H	BB	SO	SB	CS	W	L	SV	ERA
at Home	36	47.0	42	22	18	2	1	3	2	2	4.21
on Road	36	39.0	50	17	16	5	3	2	1	0	5.54

	BA	OBA	SA	AB	H	2B	3B	HR	RBI	BB	SO
Total	.291	.380	.408	316	92	17	4	4	56	39	34
vs. Left	.271	.393	.375	96	26	6	2	0	14	14	12
vs. Right	.300	.373	.423	220	66	11	2	4	42	25	22
Bases Empty	.289	.376	.362	152	44	8	0	1	1	20	15
Runners On Base	.293	.383	.451	164	48	9	4	3	55	19	19

8-YEAR TOTALS (1984–1991)

G	IP	H	BB	SO	SB	CS	W	L	SV	ERA
232	287.0	253	124	146	22	4	22	12	14	2.98
224	234.0	259	101	100	29	4	14	15	8	4.62

BA	OBA	SA	AB	H	2B	3B	HR	RBI	BB	SO
.264	.344	.356	1943	512	76	16	24	258	225	246
.216	.305	.275	684	148	20	4	4	86	73	118
.289	.366	.400	1259	364	56	12	20	172	152	128
.259	.327	.339	1003	260	40	5	10	10	95	121
.268	.362	.374	940	252	36	11	14	248	130	125

DARREL AKERFELDS — bats right — throws right — age 30 — PHI — P

1991

	G	IP	H	BB	SO	SB	CS	W	L	SV	ERA
at Home	13	22.2	20	12	15	3	0	1	1	0	5.16
on Road	17	27.0	29	15	16	3	3	1	0	0	5.33

	BA	OBA	SA	AB	H	2B	3B	HR	RBI	BB	SO
Total	.257	.354	.382	191	49	5	2	5	28	27	31
vs. Left	.239	.349	.341	88	21	4	1	1	11	14	13
vs. Right	.272	.359	.417	103	28	1	1	4	17	13	18
Bases Empty	.245	.360	.372	94	23	2	1	3	3	14	13
Runners On Base	.268	.348	.392	97	26	3	1	2	25	13	18

5-YEAR TOTALS (1986–1991)

G	IP	H	BB	SO	SB	CS	W	L	SV	ERA
61	109.2	101	60	58	11	3	6	2	1	4.76
64	124.0	115	67	71	20	6	3	9	2	5.37

BA	OBA	SA	AB	H	2B	3B	HR	RBI	BB	SO
.246	.346	.424	878	216	34	7	36	137	127	129
.246	.342	.461	423	104	18	5	21	77	60	59
.246	.349	.389	455	112	16	2	15	60	67	70
.261	.355	.445	467	122	21	4	19	19	62	61
.229	.335	.399	411	94	13	3	17	118	65	68

SCOTT ALDRED — bats left — throws left — age 24 — DET — P

1991

	G	IP	H	BB	SO	SB	CS	W	L	SV	ERA
at Home	6	33.1	39	17	23	4	1	1	3	0	7.02
on Road	5	24.0	19	13	12	1	1	1	1	0	2.63

	BA	OBA	SA	AB	H	2B	3B	HR	RBI	BB	SO
Total	.266	.352	.427	218	58	6	1	9	29	30	35
vs. Left	.242	.359	.364	33	8	1	0	1	3	6	2
vs. Right	.270	.351	.438	185	50	5	1	8	26	24	33
Bases Empty	.297	.375	.492	128	38	4	1	7	7	16	20
Runners On Base	.222	.321	.333	90	20	2	0	2	22	14	15

2-YEAR TOTALS (1990–1991)

G	IP	H	BB	SO	SB	CS	W	L	SV	ERA
8	42.0	47	22	28	5	1	1	5	0	6.86
7	29.2	24	18	14	3	1	2	1	0	2.12

BA	OBA	SA	AB	H	2B	3B	HR	RBI	BB	SO
.266	.360	.404	267	71	8	1	9	34	40	42
.286	.388	.381	42	12	1	0	1	4	7	2
.262	.355	.409	225	59	7	1	8	30	33	40
.293	.380	.473	150	44	6	0	7	7	21	24
.231	.336	.316	117	27	2	1	2	27	19	18

GERALD ALEXANDER — bats right — throws right — age 24 — TEX — P

1991

	G	IP	H	BB	SO	SB	CS	W	L	SV	ERA
at Home	15	47.0	47	19	24	1	2	4	2	0	4.79
on Road	15	42.1	46	29	26	6	1	1	1	0	5.74

	BA	OBA	SA	AB	H	2B	3B	HR	RBI	BB	SO
Total	.272	.364	.430	342	93	15	3	11	54	48	50
vs. Left	.225	.323	.356	160	36	2	2	5	22	24	18
vs. Right	.313	.400	.495	182	57	13	1	6	32	24	32
Bases Empty	.271	.358	.412	177	48	8	1	5	5	23	26
Runners On Base	.273	.369	.448	165	45	7	2	6	49	25	24

2-YEAR TOTALS (1990–1991)

G	IP	H	BB	SO	SB	CS	W	L	SV	ERA
18	54.0	61	24	32	1	2	4	2	0	5.17
15	42.1	46	29	26	6	1	1	1	0	5.74

BA	OBA	SA	AB	H	2B	3B	HR	RBI	BB	SO
.286	.377	.439	374	107	16	4	11	60	53	58
.237	.337	.356	177	42	2	2	5	25	27	24
.330	.414	.513	197	65	14	2	6	35	26	34
.284	.367	.426	190	54	8	1	5	5	29	30
.288	.386	.451	184	53	8	3	6	55	24	28

DANA ALLISON — bats right — throws left — age 26 — OAK — P

1991	G	IP	H	BB	SO	SB	CS	W	L	SV	ERA
at Home	4	4.2	6	1	2	0	0	1	0	0	1.93
on Road	7	6.1	10	4	2	0	0	0	1	0	11.37

	BA	OBA	SA	AB	H	2B	3B	HR	RBI	BB	SO
Total	.381	.438	.476	42	16	2	1	0	9	5	4
vs. Left	.421	.429	.526	19	8	2	0	0	4	1	0
vs. Right	.348	.444	.435	23	8	0	1	0	5	4	4
Bases Empty	.500	.538	.583	12	6	1	0	0	0	1	1
Runners On Base	.333	.400	.433	30	10	1	1	0	9	4	3

1-YEAR TOTALS (1991)

G	IP	H	BB	SO	SB	CS	W	L	SV	ERA
4	4.2	6	1	2	0	0	1	0	0	1.93
7	6.1	10	4	2	0	0	0	1	0	11.37

BA	OBA	SA	AB	H	2B	3B	HR	RBI	BB	SO
.381	.438	.476	42	16	2	1	0	9	5	4
.421	.429	.526	19	8	2	0	0	4	1	0
.348	.444	.435	23	8	0	1	0	5	4	4
.500	.538	.583	12	6	1	0	0	0	1	1
.333	.400	.433	30	10	1	1	0	9	4	3

WILSON ALVAREZ — bats left — throws left — age 22 — CHA — P

1991	G	IP	H	BB	SO	SB	CS	W	L	SV	ERA
at Home	3	19.1	14	8	8	0	2	1	1	0	2.79
on Road	7	37.0	33	21	24	0	2	2	1	0	3.89

	BA	OBA	SA	AB	H	2B	3B	HR	RBI	BB	SO
Total	.230	.325	.407	204	47	7	1	9	18	29	32
vs. Left	.222	.263	.222	18	4	0	0	0	0	1	3
vs. Right	.231	.330	.425	186	43	7	1	9	18	28	29
Bases Empty	.238	.317	.462	130	31	6	1	7	7	15	22
Runners On Base	.216	.337	.311	74	16	1	0	2	11	14	10

2-YEAR TOTALS (1989–1991)

G	IP	H	BB	SO	SB	CS	W	L	SV	ERA
4	19.1	17	10	8	0	2	1	2	0	4.19
7	37.0	33	21	24	0	2	2	1	0	3.89

BA	OBA	SA	AB	H	2B	3B	HR	RBI	BB	SO
.242	.339	.444	207	50	7	1	11	21	31	32
.222	.300	.222	18	4	0	0	0	0	2	3
.243	.342	.466	189	46	7	1	11	21	29	29
.250	.331	.492	132	33	6	1	8	8	16	22
.227	.352	.360	75	17	1	0	3	13	15	10

LARRY ANDERSEN — bats right — throws right — age 39 — SD — P

1991	G	IP	H	BB	SO	SB	CS	W	L	SV	ERA
at Home	21	24.2	21	4	20	2	1	3	0	8	2.19
on Road	17	22.1	18	9	20	4	1	0	4	5	2.42

	BA	OBA	SA	AB	H	2B	3B	HR	RBI	BB	SO
Total	.232	.284	.268	168	39	6	0	0	16	13	40
vs. Left	.281	.340	.337	89	25	5	0	0	10	9	13
vs. Right	.177	.217	.190	79	14	1	0	0	6	4	27
Bases Empty	.212	.271	.253	99	21	4	0	0	0	8	23
Runners On Base	.261	.303	.290	69	18	2	0	0	16	5	17

8-YEAR TOTALS (1984–1991)

G	IP	H	BB	SO	SB	CS	W	L	SV	ERA
236	338.2	294	89	289	44	14	20	11	18	2.02
216	317.1	310	113	236	39	10	11	19	23	3.43

BA	OBA	SA	AB	H	2B	3B	HR	RBI	BB	SO
.246	.303	.327	2452	604	87	17	26	288	202	525
.273	.344	.357	1178	322	43	7	14	144	129	194
.221	.262	.300	1274	282	44	10	12	144	73	331
.248	.294	.329	1302	323	47	7	15	15	81	282
.244	.312	.325	1150	281	40	10	11	273	121	243

BRAD ARNSBERG — bats right — throws right — age 29 — TEX — P

1991	G	IP	H	BB	SO	SB	CS	W	L	SV	ERA
at Home	3	5.1	6	1	7	0	0	0	0	0	10.13
on Road	6	4.1	4	4	1	0	0	0	1	0	6.23

	BA	OBA	SA	AB	H	2B	3B	HR	RBI	BB	SO
Total	.256	.341	.641	39	10	0	0	5	9	5	8
vs. Left	.200	.273	.500	10	2	0	0	1	2	1	2
vs. Right	.276	.364	.690	29	8	0	0	4	7	4	6
Bases Empty	.208	.345	.333	24	5	0	0	1	1	5	5
Runners On Base	.333	.333	1.133	15	5	0	0	4	8	0	3

5-YEAR TOTALS (1986–1991)

G	IP	H	BB	SO	SB	CS	W	L	SV	ERA
45	77.0	76	32	52	1	0	6	1	2	3.86
41	70.2	70	42	43	3	3	3	5	4	3.57

BA	OBA	SA	AB	H	2B	3B	HR	RBI	BB	SO
.255	.342	.407	573	146	22	1	21	82	74	95
.290	.362	.463	214	62	8	1	9	36	24	27
.234	.331	.373	359	84	14	0	12	46	50	68
.271	.361	.425	306	83	15	1	10	10	40	52
.236	.321	.386	267	63	7	0	11	72	34	43

ANDY ASHBY — bats right — throws right — age 25 — PHI — P

1991	G	IP	H	BB	SO	SB	CS	W	L	SV	ERA
at Home	5	26.1	29	10	18	0	1	0	3	0	6.49
on Road	3	15.2	12	9	8	0	0	1	2	0	5.17

	BA	OBA	SA	AB	H	2B	3B	HR	RBI	BB	SO
Total	.256	.341	.431	160	41	9	2	5	25	19	26
vs. Left	.247	.317	.409	93	23	2	2	3	14	10	15
vs. Right	.269	.370	.463	67	18	7	0	2	11	9	11
Bases Empty	.213	.327	.371	89	19	4	2	2	2	14	16
Runners On Base	.310	.358	.507	71	22	5	0	3	23	5	10

1-YEAR TOTALS (1991)

G	IP	H	BB	SO	SB	CS	W	L	SV	ERA
5	26.1	29	10	18	0	1	0	3	0	6.49
3	15.2	12	9	8	0	0	1	2	0	5.17

BA	OBA	SA	AB	H	2B	3B	HR	RBI	BB	SO
.256	.341	.431	160	41	9	2	5	25	19	26
.247	.317	.409	93	23	2	2	3	14	10	15
.269	.370	.463	67	18	7	0	2	11	9	11
.213	.327	.371	89	19	4	2	2	2	14	16
.310	.358	.507	71	22	5	0	3	23	5	10

JIM AUSTIN — bats right — throws right — age 29 — MIL — P

1991	G	IP	H	BB	SO	SB	CS	W	L	SV	ERA
at Home	2	3.2	3	5	1	0	0	0	0	0	9.82
on Road	3	5.0	5	6	2	0	0	0	0	0	7.20

	BA	OBA	SA	AB	H	2B	3B	HR	RBI	BB	SO
Total	.276	.500	.448	29	8	2	0	1	7	11	3
vs. Left	.231	.583	.231	13	3	0	0	0	4	8	1
vs. Right	.313	.400	.625	16	5	2	0	1	3	3	2
Bases Empty	.375	.643	.625	8	3	2	0	0	0	6	1
Runners On Base	.238	.433	.381	21	5	0	0	1	7	5	2

1-YEAR TOTALS (1991)

G	IP	H	BB	SO	SB	CS	W	L	SV	ERA
2	3.2	3	5	1	0	0	0	0	0	9.82
3	5.0	5	6	2	0	0	0	0	0	7.20

BA	OBA	SA	AB	H	2B	3B	HR	RBI	BB	SO
.276	.500	.448	29	8	2	0	1	7	11	3
.231	.583	.231	13	3	0	0	0	4	8	1
.313	.400	.625	16	5	2	0	1	3	3	2
.375	.643	.625	8	3	2	0	0	0	6	1
.238	.433	.381	21	5	0	0	1	7	5	2

SCOTT BAILES — bats left — throws left — age 31 — CAL — P

1991	G	IP	H	BB	SO	SB	CS	W	L	SV	ERA
at Home	15	21.1	12	11	12	0	1	0	2	0	3.80
on Road	27	30.1	29	11	29	2	1	1	0	0	4.45

	BA	OBA	SA	AB	H	2B	3B	HR	RBI	BB	SO
Total	.218	.310	.346	188	41	7	1	5	25	22	41
vs. Left	.247	.318	.416	77	19	4	0	3	16	6	13
vs. Right	.198	.305	.297	111	22	3	1	2	9	16	28
Bases Empty	.212	.316	.293	99	21	4	0	1	1	11	23
Runners On Base	.225	.304	.404	89	20	4	0	4	24	11	18

6-YEAR TOTALS (1986–1991)

G	IP	H	BB	SO	SB	CS	W	L	SV	ERA
112	296.0	298	92	142	22	5	22	20	6	4.41
129	282.2	322	115	140	19	7	12	23	7	5.16

BA	OBA	SA	AB	H	2B	3B	HR	RBI	BB	SO
.274	.336	.427	2260	620	98	11	75	338	207	282
.264	.321	.356	576	152	17	0	12	97	44	81
.278	.341	.451	1684	468	81	11	63	241	163	201
.274	.332	.421	1227	336	48	8	39	39	97	148
.275	.340	.434	1033	284	50	3	36	299	110	134

SCOTT BANKHEAD — bats right — throws right — age 29 — SEA — P

1991	G	IP	H	BB	SO	SB	CS	W	L	SV	ERA
at Home	8	24.1	35	11	11	1	0	1	2	0	4.44
on Road	9	36.1	38	10	17	7	0	2	4	0	5.20

	BA	OBA	SA	AB	H	2B	3B	HR	RBI	BB	SO
Total	.297	.354	.467	246	73	16	1	8	35	21	28
vs. Left	.313	.366	.455	112	35	10	0	2	17	9	11
vs. Right	.284	.345	.478	134	38	6	1	6	18	12	17
Bases Empty	.264	.316	.417	144	38	8	1	4	4	10	16
Runners On Base	.343	.405	.539	102	35	8	0	4	31	11	12

6-YEAR TOTALS (1986–1991)

	G	IP	H	BB	SO	SB	CS	W	L	SV	ERA
	64	336.2	341	95	231	28	10	20	21	0	4.57
	62	352.2	340	108	238	29	10	21	21	0	3.93

	BA	OBA	SA	AB	H	2B	3B	HR	RBI	BB	SO
	.256	.309	.425	2658	681	138	26	86	305	203	469
	.259	.310	.421	1405	364	78	15	40	163	107	237
	.253	.308	.429	1253	317	60	11	46	142	96	232
	.243	.291	.413	1654	402	83	15	56	56	106	283
	.278	.338	.444	1004	279	55	11	30	249	97	186

WILLIE BANKS — bats right — throws right — age 23 — MIN — P

1991	G	IP	H	BB	SO	SB	CS	W	L	SV	ERA
at Home	3	9.1	12	8	5	1	0	0	1	0	7.71
on Road	2	8.0	9	4	11	0	0	1	0	0	3.38

	BA	OBA	SA	AB	H	2B	3B	HR	RBI	BB	SO
Total	.288	.388	.356	73	21	2	0	1	11	12	16
vs. Left	.313	.353	.344	32	10	1	0	0	7	2	7
vs. Right	.268	.412	.366	41	11	1	0	1	4	10	9
Bases Empty	.310	.429	.310	29	9	0	0	0	0	6	5
Runners On Base	.273	.360	.386	44	12	2	0	1	11	6	11

1-YEAR TOTALS (1991)

	G	IP	H	BB	SO	SB	CS	W	L	SV	ERA
	3	9.1	12	8	5	1	0	0	1	0	7.71
	2	8.0	9	4	11	0	0	1	0	0	3.38

	BA	OBA	SA	AB	H	2B	3B	HR	RBI	BB	SO
	.288	.388	.356	73	21	2	0	1	11	12	16
	.313	.353	.344	32	10	1	0	0	7	2	7
	.268	.412	.366	41	11	1	0	1	4	10	9
	.310	.429	.310	29	9	0	0	0	0	6	5
	.273	.360	.386	44	12	2	0	1	11	6	11

FLOYD BANNISTER — bats left — throws left — age 37 — CAL — P

1991	G	IP	H	BB	SO	SB	CS	W	L	SV	ERA
at Home	7	12.0	11	3	7	0	0	0	0	0	2.25
on Road	9	13.0	14	7	9	0	1	0	0	0	5.54

	BA	OBA	SA	AB	H	2B	3B	HR	RBI	BB	SO
Total	.266	.337	.500	94	25	3	2	5	12	10	16
vs. Left	.258	.343	.484	31	8	1	0	2	4	4	5
vs. Right	.270	.333	.508	63	17	2	2	3	8	6	11
Bases Empty	.295	.317	.492	61	18	1	1	3	3	2	11
Runners On Base	.212	.366	.515	33	7	2	1	2	9	8	5

7-YEAR TOTALS (1984–1991)

	G	IP	H	BB	SO	SB	CS	W	L	SV	ERA
	89	542.1	509	185	367	49	18	28	28	0	3.85
	102	570.0	585	188	363	37	14	38	36	0	4.66

	BA	OBA	SA	AB	H	2B	3B	HR	RBI	BB	SO
	.256	.316	.423	4272	1094	205	29	150	504	373	730
	.256	.317	.405	739	189	44	3	20	84	66	124
	.256	.316	.427	3533	905	161	26	130	420	307	606
	.251	.306	.416	2623	658	120	18	92	92	201	449
	.264	.332	.435	1649	436	85	11	58	412	172	281

JOHN BARFIELD — bats left — throws left — age 28 — TEX — P

1991	G	IP	H	BB	SO	SB	CS	W	L	SV	ERA
at Home	15	46.2	59	13	12	1	0	2	2	0	5.01
on Road	13	36.2	37	9	15	0	2	2	2	1	3.93

	BA	OBA	SA	AB	H	2B	3B	HR	RBI	BB	SO
Total	.289	.330	.464	332	96	19	3	11	43	22	27
vs. Left	.269	.273	.346	52	14	4	0	0	7	1	5
vs. Right	.293	.340	.486	280	82	15	3	11	36	21	22
Bases Empty	.284	.324	.438	201	57	9	2	6	6	12	12
Runners On Base	.298	.338	.504	131	39	10	1	5	37	10	15

3-YEAR TOTALS (1989–1991)

	G	IP	H	BB	SO	SB	CS	W	L	SV	ERA
	32	72.2	87	21	21	1	1	4	2	0	5.08
	33	66.2	66	18	32	2	4	4	6	2	4.32

	BA	OBA	SA	AB	H	2B	3B	HR	RBI	BB	SO
	.285	.330	.433	536	153	32	4	13	79	39	53
	.269	.308	.333	108	29	7	0	0	12	6	13
	.290	.336	.458	428	124	25	4	13	67	33	40
	.252	.296	.374	318	80	14	2	7	7	19	30
	.335	.378	.518	218	73	18	2	6	72	20	23

JOSE BAUTISTA — bats right — throws right — age 28 — BAL — P

1991	G	IP	H	BB	SO	SB	CS	W	L	SV	ERA
at Home	2	1.0	2	2	1	0	0	0	0	0	9.00
on Road	3	4.1	11	3	2	0	0	0	0	0	18.69

	BA	OBA	SA	AB	H	2B	3B	HR	RBI	BB	SO
Total	.464	.559	.750	28	13	5	0	1	11	5	3
vs. Left	.400	.500	.533	15	6	2	0	0	5	3	3
vs. Right	.538	.625	1.000	13	7	3	0	1	6	2	0
Bases Empty	.364	.462	.909	11	4	3	0	1	1	2	1
Runners On Base	.529	.619	.647	17	9	2	0	0	10	3	2

4-YEAR TOTALS (1988–1991)

	G	IP	H	BB	SO	SB	CS	W	L	SV	ERA
	39	153.0	158	35	62	21	3	6	10	0	4.65
	36	128.2	138	37	62	15	6	4	10	0	4.97

	BA	OBA	SA	AB	H	2B	3B	HR	RBI	BB	SO
	.269	.317	.447	1102	296	46	11	43	153	72	124
	.279	.327	.480	542	151	26	7	23	70	35	53
	.259	.308	.416	560	145	20	4	20	83	37	71
	.255	.309	.385	660	168	25	8	15	15	46	74
	.290	.330	.541	442	128	21	3	28	138	26	50

CHRIS BEASLEY — bats right — throws right — age 30 — CAL — P

1991	G	IP	H	BB	SO	SB	CS	W	L	SV	ERA
at Home	9	14.2	9	4	10	0	0	0	0	0	1.23
on Road	13	12.0	17	6	4	0	1	0	1	0	6.00

	BA	OBA	SA	AB	H	2B	3B	HR	RBI	BB	SO
Total	.257	.327	.366	101	26	5	0	2	15	10	14
vs. Left	.275	.326	.525	40	11	4	0	2	8	3	5
vs. Right	.246	.329	.262	61	15	1	0	0	7	7	9
Bases Empty	.244	.346	.356	45	11	2	0	1	1	7	8
Runners On Base	.268	.311	.375	56	15	3	0	1	14	3	6

1-YEAR TOTALS (1991)

	G	IP	H	BB	SO	SB	CS	W	L	SV	ERA
	9	14.2	9	4	10	0	0	0	0	0	1.23
	13	12.0	17	6	4	0	1	0	1	0	6.00

	BA	OBA	SA	AB	H	2B	3B	HR	RBI	BB	SO
	.257	.327	.366	101	26	5	0	2	15	10	14
	.275	.326	.525	40	11	4	0	2	8	3	5
	.246	.329	.262	61	15	1	0	0	7	7	9
	.244	.346	.356	45	11	2	0	1	1	7	8
	.268	.311	.375	56	15	3	0	1	14	3	6

BLAINE BEATTY — bats left — throws left — age 28 — NYN — P

1991	G	IP	H	BB	SO	SB	CS	W	L	SV	ERA
at Home	4	6.2	8	3	5	2	0	0	0	0	4.05
on Road	1	3.0	1	1	2	0	0	0	0	0	0.00

	BA	OBA	SA	AB	H	2B	3B	HR	RBI	BB	SO
Total	.250	.317	.333	36	9	3	0	0	4	4	7
vs. Left	.500	.538	.600	10	5	1	0	0	1	0	2
vs. Right	.154	.214	.231	26	4	2	0	0	3	4	5
Bases Empty	.417	.500	.583	12	5	2	0	0	1	2	3
Runners On Base	.167	.222	.208	24	4	1	0	0	4	2	4

2-YEAR TOTALS (1989–1991)

	G	IP	H	BB	SO	SB	CS	W	L	SV	ERA
	4	6.2	8	3	5	2	0	0	0	0	4.05
	3	9.0	6	3	5	1	0	0	0	0	1.00

	BA	OBA	SA	AB	H	2B	3B	HR	RBI	BB	SO
	.237	.303	.356	59	14	4	0	0	5	6	10
	.313	.368	.375	16	5	1	0	0	1	1	4
	.209	.277	.349	43	9	3	0	0	4	4	6
	.333	.375	.533	30	10	3	0	0	1	2	4
	.138	.235	.172	29	4	1	0	0	4	4	6

ROD BECK — bats right — throws right — age 24 — SF — P

1991	G	IP	H	BB	SO	SB	CS	W	L	SV	ERA
at Home	15	25.2	26	4	23	1	3	0	1	1	3.86
on Road	16	26.2	27	9	15	1	0	1	0	0	3.71

	BA	OBA	SA	AB	H	2B	3B	HR	RBI	BB	SO
Total	.273	.319	.412	194	53	11	2	4	26	13	38
vs. Left	.312	.354	.538	93	29	7	1	4	15	6	19
vs. Right	.238	.288	.297	101	24	4	1	0	11	7	19
Bases Empty	.243	.250	.409	115	28	5	1	4	4	1	25
Runners On Base	.316	.404	.418	79	25	6	1	0	22	12	13

1-YEAR TOTALS (1991)

G	IP	H	BB	SO	SB	CS	W	L	SV	ERA
15	25.2	26	4	23	1	3	0	1	1	3.86
16	26.2	27	9	15	1	0	1	0	0	3.71

BA	OBA	SA	AB	H	2B	3B	HR	RBI	BB	SO
.273	.319	.412	194	53	11	2	4	26	13	38
.312	.354	.538	93	29	7	1	4	15	6	19
.238	.288	.297	101	24	4	1	0	11	7	19
.243	.250	.409	115	28	5	1	4	4	1	25
.316	.404	.418	79	25	6	1	0	22	12	13

ERIC BELL — bats left — throws left — age 29 — CLE — P

1991	G	IP	H	BB	SO	SB	CS	W	L	SV	ERA
at Home	5	12.0	3	5	4	2	0	2	0	0	0.75
on Road	5	6.0	2	0	3	0	0	2	0	0	0.00

	BA	OBA	SA	AB	H	2B	3B	HR	RBI	BB	SO
Total	.091	.180	.091	55	5	0	0	0	0	5	7
vs. Left	.045	.125	.045	22	1	0	0	0	0	2	4
vs. Right	.121	.216	.121	33	4	0	0	0	0	3	3
Bases Empty	.079	.146	.079	38	3	0	0	0	0	2	2
Runners On Base	.118	.250	.118	17	2	0	0	0	0	3	5

4-YEAR TOTALS (1985–1991)

G	IP	H	BB	SO	SB	CS	W	L	SV	ERA
21	88.0	89	42	59	6	2	5	7	0	5.42
30	124.0	117	59	81	10	7	10	8	0	4.65

BA	OBA	SA	AB	H	2B	3B	HR	RBI	BB	SO
.255	.339	.461	807	206	47	4	37	109	101	140
.264	.340	.438	144	38	7	0	6	21	17	19
.253	.339	.466	663	168	40	4	31	88	84	121
.236	.308	.440	509	120	31	2	23	23	50	88
.289	.389	.497	298	86	16	2	14	86	51	52

JOE BITKER — bats right — throws right — age 28 — TEX — P

1991	G	IP	H	BB	SO	SB	CS	W	L	SV	ERA
at Home	6	10.2	14	4	11	0	1	0	0	0	6.75
on Road	3	4.0	3	4	5	1	0	0	0	0	6.75

	BA	OBA	SA	AB	H	2B	3B	HR	RBI	BB	SO
Total	.274	.357	.532	62	17	4	0	4	11	8	16
vs. Left	.346	.393	.808	26	9	3	0	3	8	2	6
vs. Right	.222	.333	.333	36	8	1	0	1	3	6	10
Bases Empty	.303	.361	.515	33	10	1	0	2	2	3	10
Runners On Base	.241	.353	.552	29	7	3	0	2	9	5	6

2-YEAR TOTALS (1990–1991)

G	IP	H	BB	SO	SB	CS	W	L	SV	ERA
10	19.2	21	6	18	0	1	0	0	0	4.12
5	7.0	4	6	6	1	0	0	0	0	6.43

BA	OBA	SA	AB	H	2B	3B	HR	RBI	BB	SO
.240	.322	.452	104	25	6	2	4	15	12	24
.283	.321	.604	53	15	4	2	3	10	3	12
.196	.323	.294	51	10	2	0	1	5	9	12
.294	.379	.490	51	15	2	1	2	2	6	14
.189	.267	.415	53	10	4	1	2	13	6	10

WILLIE BLAIR — bats right — throws right — age 27 — CLE — P

1991	G	IP	H	BB	SO	SB	CS	W	L	SV	ERA
at Home	8	22.2	40	7	11	0	1	1	0	0	6.75
on Road	3	13.1	18	3	2	0	1	1	2	0	6.75

	BA	OBA	SA	AB	H	2B	3B	HR	RBI	BB	SO
Total	.377	.413	.565	154	58	8	0	7	27	10	13
vs. Left	.397	.436	.603	73	29	6	0	3	11	4	7
vs. Right	.358	.393	.531	81	29	2	0	4	16	6	6
Bases Empty	.395	.456	.543	81	32	6	0	2	2	8	8
Runners On Base	.356	.364	.589	73	26	2	0	5	25	2	5

2-YEAR TOTALS (1990–1991)

G	IP	H	BB	SO	SB	CS	W	L	SV	ERA
26	55.0	65	22	32	3	1	4	3	0	5.07
12	49.2	59	16	24	3	1	1	5	0	4.89

BA	OBA	SA	AB	H	2B	3B	HR	RBI	BB	SO
.297	.353	.450	418	124	23	4	11	59	38	56
.294	.353	.452	197	58	12	2	5	25	18	26
.299	.354	.448	221	66	11	2	6	34	20	30
.268	.337	.390	231	62	11	1	5	5	22	34
.332	.373	.524	187	62	12	3	6	54	16	22

BRIAN BOHANON — bats left — throws left — age 24 — TEX — P

1991	G	IP	H	BB	SO	SB	CS	W	L	SV	ERA
at Home	4	21.1	30	8	11	4	0	1	2	0	5.91
on Road	7	40.0	36	15	23	1	0	3	1	0	4.28

	BA	OBA	SA	AB	H	2B	3B	HR	RBI	BB	SO
Total	.274	.336	.378	241	66	13	0	4	32	23	34
vs. Left	.265	.286	.324	34	9	2	0	0	5	1	2
vs. Right	.275	.343	.386	207	57	11	0	4	27	22	32
Bases Empty	.258	.329	.386	132	34	8	0	3	3	13	18
Runners On Base	.294	.344	.367	109	32	5	0	1	29	10	16

2-YEAR TOTALS (1990–1991)

G	IP	H	BB	SO	SB	CS	W	L	SV	ERA
11	38.2	52	20	18	5	1	1	4	0	6.52
11	56.2	54	21	31	1	1	3	2	0	4.76

BA	OBA	SA	AB	H	2B	3B	HR	RBI	BB	SO
.283	.353	.419	375	106	19	1	10	56	41	49
.224	.270	.293	58	13	2	1	0	9	4	7
.293	.367	.442	317	93	17	0	10	47	37	42
.262	.345	.383	206	54	10	0	5	5	24	28
.308	.362	.462	169	52	9	1	5	51	17	21

TOM BOLTON — bats left — throws left — age 30 — BOS — P

1991	G	IP	H	BB	SO	SB	CS	W	L	SV	ERA
at Home	14	65.1	84	24	33	4	2	5	5	0	4.68
on Road	11	44.2	52	27	31	1	0	3	4	0	6.04

	BA	OBA	SA	AB	H	2B	3B	HR	RBI	BB	SO
Total	.308	.378	.485	441	136	22	4	16	60	51	64
vs. Left	.247	.295	.395	81	20	6	0	2	10	5	11
vs. Right	.322	.396	.506	360	116	16	4	14	50	46	53
Bases Empty	.314	.366	.457	258	81	12	2	7	7	21	39
Runners On Base	.301	.394	.525	183	55	10	2	9	53	30	25

5-YEAR TOTALS (1987–1991)

G	IP	H	BB	SO	SB	CS	W	L	SV	ERA
46	166.0	191	59	98	8	6	13	7	1	3.96
61	173.1	195	90	110	12	5	7	14	0	5.09

BA	OBA	SA	AB	H	2B	3B	HR	RBI	BB	SO
.290	.361	.414	1331	386	64	7	29	178	149	208
.275	.338	.374	342	94	18	2	4	52	32	57
.295	.368	.428	989	292	46	5	25	126	117	151
.276	.344	.388	722	199	29	2	16	16	72	117
.307	.380	.445	609	187	35	5	13	162	77	91

RICKY BONES — bats right — throws right — age 23 — SD — P

1991	G	IP	H	BB	SO	SB	CS	W	L	SV	ERA
at Home	7	33.1	38	9	20	1	1	3	3	0	5.40
on Road	4	20.2	19	9	11	2	0	1	3	0	3.92

	BA	OBA	SA	AB	H	2B	3B	HR	RBI	BB	SO
Total	.269	.321	.354	212	57	7	1	3	30	18	31
vs. Left	.274	.331	.354	113	31	3	0	2	19	11	13
vs. Right	.263	.308	.354	99	26	4	1	1	11	7	18
Bases Empty	.224	.276	.248	125	28	4	0	0	9	9	20
Runners On Base	.333	.380	.506	87	29	6	0	3	30	9	11

1-YEAR TOTALS (1991)

G	IP	H	BB	SO	SB	CS	W	L	SV	ERA
7	33.1	38	9	20	1	1	3	3	0	5.40
4	20.2	19	9	11	2	0	1	3	0	3.92

BA	OBA	SA	AB	H	2B	3B	HR	RBI	BB	SO
.269	.321	.354	212	57	7	1	3	30	18	31
.274	.331	.354	113	31	3	0	2	19	11	13
.263	.308	.354	99	26	4	1	1	11	7	18
.224	.276	.248	125	28	4	0	0	9	9	20
.333	.380	.506	87	29	6	0	3	30	9	11

DENIS BOUCHER — bats right — throws left — age 24 — TOR/CLE — P

1991	G	IP	H	BB	SO	SB	CS	W	L	SV	ERA
at Home	5	22.1	32	8	11	1	1	0	2	0	7.25
on Road	7	35.2	42	16	18	2	0	1	5	0	5.30

	BA	OBA	SA	AB	H	2B	3B	HR	RBI	BB	SO
Total	.308	.375	.554	240	74	21	1	12	35	24	29
vs. Left	.344	.400	.531	32	11	3	0	1	1	3	1
vs. Right	.303	.371	.558	208	63	18	1	11	34	21	28
Bases Empty	.326	.382	.598	132	43	13	1	7	7	12	14
Runners On Base	.287	.366	.500	108	31	8	0	5	28	12	15

1-YEAR TOTALS (1991)

G	IP	H	BB	SO	SB	CS	W	L	SV	ERA
5	22.1	32	8	11	1	1	0	2	0	7.25
7	35.2	42	16	18	2	0	1	5	0	5.30

BA	OBA	SA	AB	H	2B	3B	HR	RBI	BB	SO
.308	.375	.554	240	74	21	1	12	35	24	29
.344	.400	.531	32	11	3	0	1	1	3	1
.303	.371	.558	208	63	18	1	11	34	21	28
.326	.382	.598	132	43	13	1	7	7	12	14
.287	.366	.500	108	31	8	0	5	28	12	15

RYAN BOWEN — bats right — throws right — age 24 — HOU — P

1991	G	IP	H	BB	SO	SB	CS	W	L	SV	ERA
at Home	7	42.2	39	18	25	5	1	3	2	0	3.16
on Road	7	29.0	34	18	24	7	1	3	2	0	8.07

	BA	OBA	SA	AB	H	2B	3B	HR	RBI	BB	SO
Total	.268	.353	.360	272	73	13	0	4	34	36	49
vs. Left	.287	.366	.382	157	45	9	0	2	24	22	30
vs. Right	.243	.336	.330	115	28	4	0	2	10	14	19
Bases Empty	.283	.363	.355	152	43	8	0	1	1	18	21
Runners On Base	.250	.342	.367	120	30	5	0	3	33	18	28

1-YEAR TOTALS (1991)

G	IP	H	BB	SO	SB	CS	W	L	SV	ERA
7	42.2	39	18	25	5	1	3	2	0	3.16
7	29.0	34	18	24	7	1	3	2	0	8.07

BA	OBA	SA	AB	H	2B	3B	HR	RBI	BB	SO
.268	.353	.360	272	73	13	0	4	34	36	49
.287	.366	.382	157	45	9	0	2	24	22	30
.243	.336	.330	115	28	4	0	2	10	14	19
.283	.363	.355	152	43	8	0	1	1	18	21
.250	.342	.367	120	30	5	0	3	33	18	28

CLIFF BRANTLEY — bats right — throws right — age 24 — PHI — P

1991	G	IP	H	BB	SO	SB	CS	W	L	SV	ERA
at Home	4	20.0	18	12	13	5	1	1	1	0	3.60
on Road	2	11.2	8	7	12	1	1	1	1	0	3.09

	BA	OBA	SA	AB	H	2B	3B	HR	RBI	BB	SO
Total	.228	.341	.281	114	26	4	1	0	11	19	25
vs. Left	.222	.337	.236	72	16	1	0	0	4	13	13
vs. Right	.238	.346	.357	42	10	3	1	0	7	6	12
Bases Empty	.224	.348	.276	58	13	1	1	0	0	10	12
Runners On Base	.232	.333	.286	56	13	3	0	0	11	9	13

1-YEAR TOTALS (1991)

G	IP	H	BB	SO	SB	CS	W	L	SV	ERA
4	20.0	18	12	13	5	1	1	1	0	3.60
2	11.2	8	7	12	1	1	1	1	0	3.09

BA	OBA	SA	AB	H	2B	3B	HR	RBI	BB	SO
.228	.341	.281	114	26	4	1	0	11	19	25
.222	.337	.236	72	16	1	0	0	4	13	13
.238	.346	.357	42	10	3	1	0	7	6	12
.224	.348	.276	58	13	1	1	0	0	10	12
.232	.333	.286	56	13	3	0	0	11	9	13

JOHN BRISCOE — bats right — throws right — age 25 — OAK — P

1991	G	IP	H	BB	SO	SB	CS	W	L	SV	ERA
at Home	4	4.1	9	4	4	0	0	0	0	0	16.62
on Road	7	9.2	3	6	5	0	0	0	0	0	2.79

	BA	OBA	SA	AB	H	2B	3B	HR	RBI	BB	SO
Total	.235	.355	.471	51	12	3	0	3	14	10	9
vs. Left	.235	.409	.294	17	4	1	0	0	3	5	3
vs. Right	.235	.325	.559	34	8	2	0	3	11	5	6
Bases Empty	.143	.357	.476	21	3	1	0	2	2	7	7
Runners On Base	.300	.353	.467	30	9	2	0	1	12	3	2

1-YEAR TOTALS (1991)

G	IP	H	BB	SO	SB	CS	W	L	SV	ERA
4	4.1	9	4	4	0	0	0	0	0	16.62
7	9.2	3	6	5	0	0	0	0	0	2.79

BA	OBA	SA	AB	H	2B	3B	HR	RBI	BB	SO
.235	.355	.471	51	12	3	0	3	14	10	9
.235	.409	.294	17	4	1	0	0	3	5	3
.235	.325	.559	34	8	2	0	3	11	5	6
.143	.357	.476	21	3	1	0	2	2	7	7
.300	.353	.467	30	9	2	0	1	12	3	2

TERRY BROSS — bats right — throws right — age 26 — NYN — P

1991	G	IP	H	BB	SO	SB	CS	W	L	SV	ERA
at Home	6	8.0	7	2	5	0	0	0	0	0	2.25
on Road	2	2.0	0	1	0	0	0	0	0	0	0.00

	BA	OBA	SA	AB	H	2B	3B	HR	RBI	BB	SO
Total	.200	.263	.314	35	7	1	0	1	2	3	5
vs. Left	.125	.176	.125	16	2	0	0	0	0	1	3
vs. Right	.263	.333	.474	19	5	1	0	1	2	2	2
Bases Empty	.200	.304	.250	20	4	1	0	0	0	3	3
Runners On Base	.200	.200	.400	15	3	0	0	1	2	0	2

1-YEAR TOTALS (1991)

G	IP	H	BB	SO	SB	CS	W	L	SV	ERA
6	8.0	7	2	5	0	0	0	0	0	2.25
2	2.0	0	1	0	0	0	0	0	0	0.00

BA	OBA	SA	AB	H	2B	3B	HR	RBI	BB	SO
.200	.263	.314	35	7	1	0	1	2	3	5
.125	.176	.125	16	2	0	0	0	0	1	3
.263	.333	.474	19	5	1	0	1	2	2	2
.200	.304	.250	20	4	1	0	0	0	3	3
.200	.200	.400	15	3	0	0	1	2	0	2

KEVIN BROWN — bats right — throws right — age 27 — TEX — P

1991	G	IP	H	BB	SO	SB	CS	W	L	SV	ERA
at Home	17	111.0	124	45	45	2	9	4	5	0	4.14
on Road	16	99.2	109	45	51	3	3	5	7	0	4.70

	BA	OBA	SA	AB	H	2B	3B	HR	RBI	BB	SO
Total	.284	.362	.404	821	233	40	4	17	100	90	96
vs. Left	.276	.349	.399	406	112	22	2	8	52	45	51
vs. Right	.292	.374	.410	415	121	18	2	9	48	45	45
Bases Empty	.280	.358	.420	436	122	22	3	11	11	46	55
Runners On Base	.288	.367	.387	385	111	18	1	6	89	44	41

5-YEAR TOTALS (1986–1991)

G	IP	H	BB	SO	SB	CS	W	L	SV	ERA
44	296.0	295	113	146	13	18	17	13	0	3.47
48	314.0	319	115	158	10	6	18	19	0	4.16

BA	OBA	SA	AB	H	2B	3B	HR	RBI	BB	SO
.262	.331	.367	2340	614	106	6	42	249	228	304
.259	.324	.364	1152	298	55	3	20	120	113	147
.266	.338	.370	1188	316	51	3	22	129	115	157
.263	.334	.373	1309	344	64	4	24	24	130	175
.262	.327	.359	1031	270	42	2	18	225	98	129

KEITH BROWN — bats both — throws right — age 28 — CIN — P

1991	G	IP	H	BB	SO	SB	CS	W	L	SV	ERA
at Home	8	10.1	10	4	2	1	2	0	0	0	0.00
on Road	3	1.2	5	2	2	0	0	0	0	0	16.20

	BA	OBA	SA	AB	H	2B	3B	HR	RBI	BB	SO
Total	.306	.382	.408	49	15	3	1	0	7	6	4
vs. Left	.238	.385	.238	21	5	0	0	0	1	5	2
vs. Right	.357	.379	.536	28	10	3	1	0	6	1	2
Bases Empty	.350	.435	.400	20	7	1	0	0	0	3	2
Runners On Base	.276	.344	.414	29	8	2	1	0	7	3	2

3-YEAR TOTALS (1988–1991)

G	IP	H	BB	SO	SB	CS	W	L	SV	ERA
18	33.2	33	9	13	1	5	2	1	0	2.41
5	6.0	8	4	5	2	0	0	0	0	7.50

BA	OBA	SA	AB	H	2B	3B	HR	RBI	BB	SO
.273	.331	.387	150	41	6	1	3	18	13	18
.247	.337	.356	73	18	2	0	2	8	10	10
.299	.325	.416	77	23	4	1	1	10	3	8
.247	.319	.318	85	21	3	0	1	1	9	13
.308	.348	.477	65	20	3	1	2	17	4	5

DAVE BURBA — bats right — throws right — age 26 — SEA — P

1991	G	IP	H	BB	SO	SB	CS	W	L	SV	ERA
at Home	12	15.1	16	6	9	0	1	1	1	1	5.28
on Road	10	21.1	18	8	7	1	0	1	1	0	2.53

	BA	OBA	SA	AB	H	2B	3B	HR	RBI	BB	SO
Total	.245	.314	.453	139	34	7	2	6	15	14	16
vs. Left	.288	.373	.441	59	17	3	0	2	4	8	5
vs. Right	.213	.267	.463	80	17	4	2	4	11	6	11
Bases Empty	.253	.301	.506	87	22	3	2	5	5	6	7
Runners On Base	.231	.333	.365	52	12	4	0	1	10	8	9

2-YEAR TOTALS (1990–1991)

G	IP	H	BB	SO	SB	CS	W	L	SV	ERA
15	20.2	19	8	13	1	1	1	1	1	3.92
13	24.0	23	8	7	1	0	1	1	0	3.75

BA	OBA	SA	AB	H	2B	3B	HR	RBI	BB	SO
.249	.317	.420	169	42	7	2	6	17	16	20
.265	.359	.397	68	18	3	0	2	4	9	7
.238	.287	.436	101	24	4	2	4	13	7	13
.280	.327	.500	100	28	3	2	5	5	7	7
.203	.304	.304	69	14	4	0	1	12	9	13

TODD BURNS — bats right — throws right — age 29 — OAK — P

1991	G	IP	H	BB	SO	SB	CS	W	L	SV	ERA
at Home	5	7.2	8	4	2	1	0	1	0	0	4.70
on Road	4	5.2	2	4	1	0	0	0	0	0	1.59

	BA	OBA	SA	AB	H	2B	3B	HR	RBI	BB	SO
Total	.217	.321	.413	46	10	3	0	2	11	8	3
vs. Left	.087	.160	.130	23	2	1	0	0	0	2	2
vs. Right	.348	.452	.696	23	8	2	0	2	11	6	1
Bases Empty	.136	.321	.227	22	3	2	0	0	0	6	2
Runners On Base	.292	.321	.583	24	7	1	0	2	11	2	1

4-YEAR TOTALS (1988–1991)

G	IP	H	BB	SO	SB	CS	W	L	SV	ERA
63	161.2	131	50	80	4	8	12	3	7	2.39
56	129.1	116	52	73	6	5	6	7	5	3.34

BA	OBA	SA	AB	H	2B	3B	HR	RBI	BB	SO
.232	.298	.347	1066	247	44	8	21	108	102	153
.226	.301	.343	499	113	20	7	8	36	53	61
.236	.295	.351	567	134	24	1	13	72	49	92
.248	.313	.365	608	151	29	3	12	12	56	87
.210	.279	.323	458	96	15	5	9	96	46	66

KEVIN CAMPBELL — bats right — throws right — age 28 — OAK — P

1991	G	IP	H	BB	SO	SB	CS	W	L	SV	ERA
at Home	6	7.2	6	5	6	1	0	0	0	0	3.52
on Road	8	15.1	7	9	10	0	0	1	0	0	2.35

	BA	OBA	SA	AB	H	2B	3B	HR	RBI	BB	SO
Total	.167	.301	.359	78	13	3	0	4	10	14	16
vs. Left	.129	.325	.258	31	4	1	0	1	2	9	5
vs. Right	.191	.283	.426	47	9	2	0	3	8	5	11
Bases Empty	.140	.302	.395	43	6	2	0	3	3	9	11
Runners On Base	.200	.300	.314	35	7	1	0	1	7	5	5

1-YEAR TOTALS (1991)

G	IP	H	BB	SO	SB	CS	W	L	SV	ERA
6	7.2	6	5	6	1	0	0	0	0	3.52
8	15.1	7	9	10	0	0	1	0	0	2.35

BA	OBA	SA	AB	H	2B	3B	HR	RBI	BB	SO
.167	.301	.359	78	13	3	0	4	10	14	16
.129	.325	.258	31	4	1	0	1	2	9	5
.191	.283	.426	47	9	2	0	3	8	5	11
.140	.302	.395	43	6	2	0	3	3	9	11
.200	.300	.314	35	7	1	0	1	7	5	5

JOHN CANDELARIA — bats left — throws left — age 39 — LA — P

1991	G	IP	H	BB	SO	SB	CS	W	L	SV	ERA
at Home	27	15.0	14	5	20	1	1	1	0	1	3.60
on Road	32	18.2	17	6	18	0	2	0	1	1	3.86

	BA	OBA	SA	AB	H	2B	3B	HR	RBI	BB	SO
Total	.252	.307	.415	123	31	9	1	3	18	11	38
vs. Left	.138	.206	.207	58	8	1	0	1	4	5	25
vs. Right	.354	.392	.600	65	23	8	1	2	14	6	13
Bases Empty	.293	.349	.517	58	17	5	1	2	2	5	22
Runners On Base	.215	.270	.323	65	14	4	0	1	16	6	16

8-YEAR TOTALS (1984–1991)

G	IP	H	BB	SO	SB	CS	W	L	SV	ERA
138	470.1	471	101	388	10	21	33	24	13	3.87
137	396.1	381	90	283	14	14	32	21	6	3.25

BA	OBA	SA	AB	H	2B	3B	HR	RBI	BB	SO
.258	.297	.416	3302	852	161	34	98	387	191	671
.200	.236	.282	595	119	19	3	8	45	31	194
.271	.311	.446	2707	733	142	31	90	342	160	477
.255	.292	.407	2000	509	102	19	55	55	95	384
.263	.305	.431	1302	343	59	15	43	332	96	287

MIKE CAPEL — bats right — throws right — age 31 — HOU — P

1991	G	IP	H	BB	SO	SB	CS	W	L	SV	ERA
at Home	10	9.2	12	3	10	2	1	0	1	1	4.66
on Road	15	23.0	21	12	13	1	2	1	2	2	2.35

	BA	OBA	SA	AB	H	2B	3B	HR	RBI	BB	SO
Total	.266	.343	.419	124	33	10	0	3	18	15	23
vs. Left	.278	.376	.431	72	20	5	0	2	15	12	11
vs. Right	.250	.291	.404	52	13	5	0	1	3	3	12
Bases Empty	.314	.368	.529	70	22	6	0	3	3	6	14
Runners On Base	.204	.313	.278	54	11	4	0	0	15	9	9

3-YEAR TOTALS (1988–1991)

G	IP	H	BB	SO	SB	CS	W	L	SV	ERA
29	33.1	50	17	28	4	2	1	1	1	6.75
20	29.0	23	12	15	1	1	1	3	2	2.17

BA	OBA	SA	AB	H	2B	3B	HR	RBI	BB	SO
.296	.377	.466	247	73	16	1	8	43	29	43
.304	.397	.440	125	38	6	1	3	23	20	18
.287	.356	.492	122	35	10	0	5	20	9	25
.331	.380	.535	127	42	8	0	6	6	10	19
.258	.375	.392	120	31	8	1	2	37	19	24

DON CARMAN — bats left — throws left — age 33 — CIN — P

1991	G	IP	H	BB	SO	SB	CS	W	L	SV	ERA
at Home	14	20.1	26	11	8	1	0	0	2	0	7.08
on Road	14	15.2	14	8	7	1	2	1	0	1	2.87

	BA	OBA	SA	AB	H	2B	3B	HR	RBI	BB	SO
Total	.286	.373	.514	140	40	8	0	8	23	19	15
vs. Left	.306	.375	.429	49	15	3	0	1	8	5	6
vs. Right	.275	.371	.560	91	25	5	0	7	15	14	9
Bases Empty	.275	.375	.594	69	19	7	0	5	5	10	7
Runners On Base	.296	.370	.437	71	21	1	0	3	18	9	8

8-YEAR TOTALS (1984–1991)

G	IP	H	BB	SO	SB	CS	W	L	SV	ERA
163	463.2	404	190	310	39	17	33	22	5	3.94
174	447.2	439	186	283	41	24	19	32	5	4.30

BA	OBA	SA	AB	H	2B	3B	HR	RBI	BB	SO
.246	.322	.406	3424	843	162	20	115	413	376	593
.243	.305	.405	704	171	30	3	26	94	55	117
.247	.326	.406	2720	672	132	17	89	319	321	476
.242	.304	.416	2040	493	105	11	76	76	173	361
.253	.346	.392	1384	350	57	9	39	337	203	232

CRIS CARPENTER — bats right — throws right — age 27 — SL — P

1991	G	IP	H	BB	SO	SB	CS	W	L	SV	ERA
at Home	28	34.2	26	10	26	2	3	5	1	0	3.38
on Road	31	31.1	27	10	21	1	1	5	0	0	5.17

	BA	OBA	SA	AB	H	2B	3B	HR	RBI	BB	SO
Total	.220	.278	.365	241	53	17	0	6	30	20	47
vs. Left	.230	.307	.336	122	28	13	0	0	13	14	21
vs. Right	.210	.246	.395	119	25	4	0	6	17	6	26
Bases Empty	.184	.211	.313	147	27	10	0	3	3	5	30
Runners On Base	.277	.369	.447	94	26	7	0	3	27	15	17

4-YEAR TOTALS (1988–1991)

G	IP	H	BB	SO	SB	CS	W	L	SV	ERA
51	91.0	95	31	54	8	5	6	5	0	4.35
56	98.2	89	26	58	6	4	10	6	0	3.65

BA	OBA	SA	AB	H	2B	3B	HR	RBI	BB	SO
.253	.307	.393	726	184	42	1	15	92	57	112
.285	.348	.413	358	102	25	3	5	43	36	44
.223	.265	.372	368	82	17	4	10	49	21	68
.237	.278	.351	430	102	22	3	7	7	23	72
.277	.345	.453	296	82	20	4	8	85	34	40

AMALIO CARRENO — bats right — throws right — age 28 — PHI — P

1991	G	IP	H	BB	SO	SB	CS	W	L	SV	ERA
at Home	3	3.1	5	3	2	1	0	0	0	0	16.20
on Road	0	0.0	0	0	0	0	0	0	0	0	0.00

	BA	OBA	SA	AB	H	2B	3B	HR	RBI	BB	SO
Total	.333	.500	.733	15	5	1	1	1	8	3	2
vs. Left	.222	.364	.556	9	2	0	0	1	5	2	0
vs. Right	.500	.667	1.000	6	3	1	1	0	3	1	2
Bases Empty	.500	.750	1.500	2	1	0	1	0	0	1	0
Runners On Base	.308	.438	.615	13	4	1	0	1	8	2	2

1-YEAR TOTALS (1991)

G	IP	H	BB	SO	SB	CS	W	L	SV	ERA
3	3.1	5	3	2	1	0	0	0	0	16.20
0	0.0	0	0	0	0	0	0	0	0	0.00

BA	OBA	SA	AB	H	2B	3B	HR	RBI	BB	SO
.333	.500	.733	15	5	1	1	1	8	3	2
.222	.364	.556	9	2	0	0	1	5	2	0
.500	.667	1.000	6	3	1	1	0	3	1	2
.500	.750	1.500	2	1	0	1	0	0	1	0
.308	.438	.615	13	4	1	0	1	8	2	2

JEFF CARTER — bats right — throws right — age 28 — CHA — P

1991	G	IP	H	BB	SO	SB	CS	W	L	SV	ERA
at Home	3	6.2	3	1	1	0	0	0	0	0	2.70
on Road	2	5.1	5	4	1	1	0	0	1	0	8.44

	BA	OBA	SA	AB	H	2B	3B	HR	RBI	BB	SO
Total	.182	.265	.318	44	8	3	0	1	6	5	2
vs. Left	.158	.273	.368	19	3	1	0	1	2	3	1
vs. Right	.200	.259	.280	25	5	2	0	0	4	2	1
Bases Empty	.154	.241	.231	26	4	2	0	0	0	3	2
Runners On Base	.222	.300	.444	18	4	1	0	1	6	2	0

1-YEAR TOTALS (1991)

G	IP	H	BB	SO	SB	CS	W	L	SV	ERA
3	6.2	3	1	1	0	0	0	0	0	2.70
2	5.1	5	4	1	1	0	0	1	0	8.44

BA	OBA	SA	AB	H	2B	3B	HR	RBI	BB	SO
.182	.265	.318	44	8	3	0	1	6	5	2
.158	.273	.368	19	3	1	0	1	2	3	1
.200	.259	.280	25	5	2	0	0	4	2	1
.154	.241	.231	26	4	2	0	0	0	3	2
.222	.300	.444	18	4	1	0	1	6	2	0

CHUCK CARY — bats left — throws left — age 32 — NYA — P

1991	G	IP	H	BB	SO	SB	CS	W	L	SV	ERA
at Home	4	21.2	21	9	14	4	0	1	2	0	4.98
on Road	6	31.2	40	23	20	3	1	0	4	0	6.54

	BA	OBA	SA	AB	H	2B	3B	HR	RBI	BB	SO
Total	.285	.378	.439	214	61	13	1	6	32	32	34
vs. Left	.324	.479	.541	37	12	2	0	2	9	11	8
vs. Right	.277	.354	.418	177	49	11	1	4	23	21	26
Bases Empty	.279	.385	.423	104	29	7	1	2	2	18	20
Runners On Base	.291	.371	.455	110	32	6	0	4	30	14	14

7-YEAR TOTALS (1985–1991)

G	IP	H	BB	SO	SB	CS	W	L	SV	ERA
59	214.1	190	68	173	18	7	8	9	2	3.53
58	174.1	178	79	139	15	7	5	17	1	4.85

BA	OBA	SA	AB	H	2B	3B	HR	RBI	BB	SO
.248	.316	.415	1483	368	81	10	49	197	147	312
.266	.335	.413	312	83	15	2	9	48	31	62
.243	.311	.416	1171	285	66	8	40	149	116	250
.231	.298	.386	889	205	55	7	23	23	81	195
.274	.343	.460	594	163	26	3	26	174	66	117

LARRY CASIAN — bats right — throws left — age 27 — MIN — P

1991	G	IP	H	BB	SO	SB	CS	W	L	SV	ERA
at Home	11	10.1	21	4	3	0	0	0	0	0	12.19
on Road	4	8.0	7	3	3	0	0	0	0	0	1.13

	BA	OBA	SA	AB	H	2B	3B	HR	RBI	BB	SO
Total	.354	.414	.620	79	28	9	0	4	14	7	6
vs. Left	.138	.138	.207	29	4	2	0	0	2	0	5
vs. Right	.480	.552	.860	50	24	7	0	4	12	7	1
Bases Empty	.469	.528	.781	32	15	4	0	2	2	3	4
Runners On Base	.277	.333	.511	47	13	5	0	2	12	4	2

2-YEAR TOTALS (1990–1991)

G	IP	H	BB	SO	SB	CS	W	L	SV	ERA
15	27.2	41	6	12	0	0	2	1	0	6.18
5	13.0	13	5	5	0	0	0	0	0	2.77

BA	OBA	SA	AB	H	2B	3B	HR	RBI	BB	SO
.329	.373	.537	164	54	16	0	6	22	11	17
.184	.200	.237	38	7	2	0	0	3	1	8
.373	.423	.627	126	47	14	0	6	19	10	9
.386	.427	.614	83	32	10	0	3	3	5	13
.272	.318	.457	81	22	6	0	3	19	6	4

TONY CASTILLO — bats left — throws left — age 29 — ATL/NYN — P

1991	G	IP	H	BB	SO	SB	CS	W	L	SV	ERA
at Home	8	17.1	25	4	12	3	0	0	1	0	3.63
on Road	9	15.0	15	7	6	0	1	2	0	0	3.00

	BA	OBA	SA	AB	H	2B	3B	HR	RBI	BB	SO
Total	.299	.349	.425	134	40	5	0	4	15	11	18
vs. Left	.176	.171	.324	34	6	2	0	1	3	0	9
vs. Right	.340	.405	.460	100	34	3	0	3	12	11	9
Bases Empty	.387	.441	.516	62	24	2	0	2	2	6	6
Runners On Base	.222	.269	.347	72	16	3	0	2	13	5	12

4-YEAR TOTALS (1988–1991)

G	IP	H	BB	SO	SB	CS	W	L	SV	ERA
49	68.1	83	20	53	11	2	2	1	1	4.21
63	82.2	91	27	58	11	3	7	3	1	3.92

BA	OBA	SA	AB	H	2B	3B	HR	RBI	BB	SO
.291	.339	.392	597	174	27	0	11	92	47	111
.262	.297	.360	172	45	8	0	3	27	9	42
.304	.356	.405	425	129	19	0	8	65	38	69
.294	.337	.389	293	86	13	0	5	5	18	47
.289	.342	.395	304	88	14	0	6	87	29	64

FRANK CASTILLO — bats right — throws right — age 23 — CHN — P

1991	G	IP	H	BB	SO	SB	CS	W	L	SV	ERA
at Home	8	50.2	42	12	43	5	1	3	3	0	3.73
on Road	10	61.0	65	21	30	2	3	3	4	0	4.87

	BA	OBA	SA	AB	H	2B	3B	HR	RBI	BB	SO
Total	.252	.304	.351	425	107	23	2	5	44	33	73
vs. Left	.283	.345	.392	265	75	10	2	5	26	26	48
vs. Right	.200	.232	.281	160	32	13	0	0	18	7	25
Bases Empty	.220	.261	.343	254	56	15	2	4	4	14	51
Runners On Base	.298	.363	.363	171	51	8	0	1	40	19	22

1-YEAR TOTALS (1991)

G	IP	H	BB	SO	SB	CS	W	L	SV	ERA
8	50.2	42	12	43	5	1	3	3	0	3.73
10	61.0	65	21	30	2	3	3	4	0	4.87

BA	OBA	SA	AB	H	2B	3B	HR	RBI	BB	SO
.252	.304	.351	425	107	23	2	5	44	33	73
.283	.345	.392	265	75	10	2	5	26	26	48
.200	.232	.281	160	32	13	0	0	18	7	25
.220	.261	.343	254	56	15	2	4	4	14	51
.298	.363	.363	171	51	8	0	1	40	19	22

JOHN CERUTTI — bats left — throws left — age 32 — DET — P

1991	G	IP	H	BB	SO	SB	CS	W	L	SV	ERA
at Home	16	40.1	35	22	12	1	0	3	1	0	4.24
on Road	22	48.1	59	17	4	1	0	5	4	0	4.84

	BA	OBA	SA	AB	H	2B	3B	HR	RBI	BB	SO
Total	.276	.348	.412	340	94	11	4	9	60	37	29
vs. Left	.191	.278	.338	68	13	2	1	2	16	9	8
vs. Right	.298	.366	.430	272	81	9	3	7	44	28	21
Bases Empty	.215	.282	.288	191	41	5	0	3	3	17	19
Runners On Base	.356	.428	.570	149	53	6	4	6	57	20	10

7-YEAR TOTALS (1985–1991)

G	IP	H	BB	SO	SB	CS	W	L	SV	ERA
114	405.2	416	138	194	24	15	21	19	1	4.24
115	455.2	478	153	204	25	24	28	24	3	3.67

BA	OBA	SA	AB	H	2B	3B	HR	RBI	BB	SO
.271	.331	.440	3302	894	145	28	119	416	291	398
.235	.288	.391	685	161	27	7	22	89	51	106
.280	.342	.452	2617	733	118	21	97	327	240	292
.274	.332	.446	1967	539	88	13	75	75	163	228
.266	.330	.430	1335	355	57	15	44	341	128	170

DARRIN CHAPIN — bats right — throws right — age 26 — NYA — P

1991	G	IP	H	BB	SO	SB	CS	W	L	SV	ERA
at Home	1	3.1	3	3	3	1	0	0	1	0	5.40
on Road	2	2.0	0	3	2	0	0	0	0	0	4.50

	BA	OBA	SA	AB	H	2B	3B	HR	RBI	BB	SO
Total	.158	.360	.263	19	3	2	0	0	2	6	5
vs. Left	.071	.071	.071	14	1	0	0	0	0	0	4
vs. Right	.400	.727	.800	5	2	2	0	0	2	6	1
Bases Empty	.111	.273	.222	9	1	1	0	0	0	2	3
Runners On Base	.200	.429	.300	10	2	1	0	0	2	4	2

1-YEAR TOTALS (1991)

G	IP	H	BB	SO	SB	CS	W	L	SV	ERA
1	3.1	3	3	3	1	0	0	1	0	5.40
2	2.0	0	3	2	0	0	0	0	0	4.50

BA	OBA	SA	AB	H	2B	3B	HR	RBI	BB	SO
.158	.360	.263	19	3	2	0	0	2	6	5
.071	.071	.071	14	1	0	0	0	0	0	4
.400	.727	.800	5	2	2	0	0	2	6	1
.111	.273	.222	9	1	1	0	0	0	2	3
.200	.429	.300	10	2	1	0	0	2	4	2

SCOTT CHIAMPARINO — bats right — throws right — age 26 — TEX — P

1991	G	IP	H	BB	SO	SB	CS	W	L	SV	ERA
at Home	2	12.2	13	3	5	1	0	1	0	0	2.13
on Road	3	9.2	13	9	3	1	0	0	0	0	6.52

	BA	OBA	SA	AB	H	2B	3B	HR	RBI	BB	SO
Total	.295	.380	.375	88	26	2	1	1	9	12	8
vs. Left	.387	.486	.452	31	12	0	1	0	2	6	2
vs. Right	.246	.317	.333	57	14	2	0	1	7	6	6
Bases Empty	.359	.468	.538	39	14	2	1	1	1	8	4
Runners On Base	.245	.302	.245	49	12	0	0	0	8	4	4

2-YEAR TOTALS (1990–1991)

G	IP	H	BB	SO	SB	CS	W	L	SV	ERA
5	31.1	31	11	15	1	3	2	1	0	3.16
6	28.2	31	13	12	3	0	0	1	0	3.14

BA	OBA	SA	AB	H	2B	3B	HR	RBI	BB	SO
.267	.340	.341	232	62	9	1	2	22	24	27
.264	.345	.302	106	28	2	1	0	8	13	11
.270	.336	.373	126	34	7	0	2	14	11	16
.248	.333	.336	125	31	6	1	1	1	15	17
.290	.347	.346	107	31	3	0	1	21	9	10

MIKE CHRISTOPHER — bats right — throws right — age 29 — LA — P

1991	G	IP	H	BB	SO	SB	CS	W	L	SV	ERA
at Home	0	0.0	0	0	0	0	0	0	0	0	0.00
on Road	3	4.0	2	3	2	0	0	0	0	0	0.00

	BA	OBA	SA	AB	H	2B	3B	HR	RBI	BB	SO
Total	.167	.333	.250	12	2	1	0	0	0	3	2
vs. Left	.000	.143	.000	6	0	0	0	0	0	1	1
vs. Right	.333	.500	.500	6	2	1	0	0	0	2	1
Bases Empty	.286	.500	.429	7	2	1	0	0	0	3	1
Runners On Base	.000	.000	.000	5	0	0	0	0	0	0	1

1-YEAR TOTALS (1991)

G	IP	H	BB	SO	SB	CS	W	L	SV	ERA
0	0.0	0	0	0	0	0	0	0	0	0.00
3	4.0	2	3	2	0	0	0	0	0	0.00

BA	OBA	SA	AB	H	2B	3B	HR	RBI	BB	SO
.167	.333	.250	12	2	1	0	0	0	3	2
.000	.143	.000	6	0	0	0	0	0	1	1
.333	.500	.500	6	2	1	0	0	0	2	1
.286	.500	.429	7	2	1	0	0	0	3	1
.000	.000	.000	5	0	0	0	0	0	0	1

JIM CLANCY — bats right — throws right — age 37 — HOU/ATL — P

1991	G	IP	H	BB	SO	SB	CS	W	L	SV	ERA
at Home	26	40.0	33	18	26	2	1	2	3	3	4.28
on Road	28	49.2	40	16	24	3	0	1	2	5	3.62

	BA	OBA	SA	AB	H	2B	3B	HR	RBI	BB	SO
Total	.223	.295	.373	327	73	17	4	8	39	34	50
vs. Left	.224	.305	.367	147	33	11	2	2	21	17	22
vs. Right	.222	.286	.378	180	40	6	2	6	18	17	28
Bases Empty	.181	.262	.302	182	33	9	2	3	3	20	34
Runners On Base	.276	.335	.462	145	40	8	2	5	36	14	16

8-YEAR TOTALS (1984–1991)

G	IP	H	BB	SO	SB	CS	W	L	SV	ERA
127	562.0	597	177	348	51	14	35	37	4	4.69
159	756.0	740	271	445	53	25	39	49	6	4.19

BA	OBA	SA	AB	H	2B	3B	HR	RBI	BB	SO
.263	.323	.410	5076	1337	243	41	139	597	448	793
.277	.341	.413	2676	740	143	22	59	301	269	392
.249	.303	.406	2400	597	100	19	80	296	179	401
.252	.313	.396	2985	752	137	20	84	84	255	507
.280	.338	.429	2091	585	106	21	55	513	193	286

MARK CLARK — bats right — throws right — age 24 — SL — P

1991	G	IP	H	BB	SO	SB	CS	W	L	SV	ERA
at Home	4	15.2	15	7	6	2	1	1	1	0	3.45
on Road	3	6.2	2	4	7	3	0	0	0	0	5.40

	BA	OBA	SA	AB	H	2B	3B	HR	RBI	BB	SO
Total	.215	.301	.354	79	17	2	0	3	9	11	13
vs. Left	.222	.321	.378	45	10	1	0	2	5	7	9
vs. Right	.206	.275	.324	34	7	1	0	1	4	4	4
Bases Empty	.236	.288	.364	55	13	1	0	2	2	4	9
Runners On Base	.167	.324	.333	24	4	1	0	1	7	7	4

1-YEAR TOTALS (1991)

G	IP	H	BB	SO	SB	CS	W	L	SV	ERA
4	15.2	15	7	6	2	1	1	1	0	3.45
3	6.2	2	4	7	3	0	0	0	0	5.40

BA	OBA	SA	AB	H	2B	3B	HR	RBI	BB	SO
.215	.301	.354	79	17	2	0	3	9	11	13
.222	.321	.378	45	10	1	0	2	5	7	9
.206	.275	.324	34	7	1	0	1	4	4	4
.236	.288	.364	55	13	1	0	2	2	4	9
.167	.324	.333	24	4	1	0	1	7	7	4

PAT CLEMENTS — bats right — throws left — age 30 — SD — P

1991	G	IP	H	BB	SO	SB	CS	W	L	SV	ERA
at Home	7	7.1	4	4	5	0	0	0	0	0	1.23
on Road	5	7.0	9	5	3	0	0	1	0	0	6.43

	BA	OBA	SA	AB	H	2B	3B	HR	RBI	BB	SO
Total	.255	.349	.314	51	13	3	0	0	10	9	8
vs. Left	.174	.240	.261	23	4	2	0	0	4	2	6
vs. Right	.321	.421	.357	28	9	1	0	0	6	7	2
Bases Empty	.182	.250	.227	22	4	1	0	0	2	4	4
Runners On Base	.310	.410	.379	29	9	2	0	0	10	7	4

7-YEAR TOTALS (1985–1991)

G	IP	H	BB	SO	SB	CS	W	L	SV	ERA
124	167.1	154	68	77	5	2	6	3	8	2.85
114	144.2	161	69	61	8	5	7	7	4	5.10

BA	OBA	SA	AB	H	2B	3B	HR	RBI	BB	SO
.273	.350	.374	1153	315	57	4	17	163	137	138
.232	.324	.334	380	88	19	1	6	64	48	71
.294	.363	.393	773	227	38	3	11	99	89	67
.266	.330	.362	591	157	27	3	8	8	53	71
.281	.369	.386	562	158	30	1	9	155	84	67

PAT COMBS — bats left — throws left — age 26 — PHI — P

1991	G	IP	H	BB	SO	SB	CS	W	L	SV	ERA
at Home	8	31.1	28	27	20	4	2	1	2	0	6.03
on Road	6	33.0	36	16	21	8	0	1	4	0	3.82

	BA	OBA	SA	AB	H	2B	3B	HR	RBI	BB	SO
Total	.254	.365	.389	252	64	13	0	7	30	43	41
vs. Left	.195	.377	.293	41	8	1	0	1	2	10	6
vs. Right	.265	.362	.408	211	56	12	0	6	28	33	35
Bases Empty	.301	.423	.398	113	34	5	0	2	2	13	13
Runners On Base	.216	.315	.381	139	30	8	0	5	28	20	28

3-YEAR TOTALS (1989–1991)

G	IP	H	BB	SO	SB	CS	W	L	SV	ERA
24	136.0	116	64	81	10	6	7	4	0	3.44
28	150.1	163	71	98	16	7	9	12	0	4.49

BA	OBA	SA	AB	H	2B	3B	HR	RBI	BB	SO
.255	.338	.373	1093	279	56	5	21	121	135	179
.246	.347	.380	187	46	5	1	6	22	27	32
.257	.336	.372	906	233	51	4	15	99	108	147
.250	.337	.342	597	149	29	4	6	6	75	88
.262	.339	.411	496	130	27	1	15	115	60	91

KEITH COMSTOCK — bats left — throws left — age 37 — SEA — P

1991	G	IP	H	BB	SO	SB	CS	W	L	SV	ERA
at Home	0	0.0	0	0	0	0	0	0	0	0	0.00
on Road	1	0.1	2	1	0	0	0	0	0	0	54.00

	G	IP	H	BB	SO	SB	CS	W	L	SV	ERA
	73	84.0	78	37	73	9	5	5	4	3	3.86
	71	69.0	56	38	69	2	4	5	3	0	4.30

	BA	OBA	SA	AB	H	2B	3B	HR	RBI	BB	SO
Total	.667	.750	1.000	3	2	1	0	0	1	1	0
vs. Left	1.000	1.000	2.000	1	1	1	0	0	0	0	0
vs. Right	.500	.667	.500	2	1	0	0	0	1	1	0
Bases Empty	1.000	1.000	2.000	1	1	1	0	0	0	0	0
Runners On Base	.500	.667	.500	2	1	0	0	0	1	1	0

	BA	OBA	SA	AB	H	2B	3B	HR	RBI	BB	SO
	.241	.327	.357	555	134	20	1	14	86	75	142
	.282	.342	.374	206	58	7	0	4	39	21	36
	.218	.319	.347	349	76	13	1	10	47	54	106
	.196	.294	.281	281	55	9	0	5	5	39	81
	.288	.361	.434	274	79	11	1	9	81	36	61

DENNIS COOK — bats left — throws left — age 30 — LA — P

1991	G	IP	H	BB	SO	SB	CS	W	L	SV	ERA
at Home	7	3.1	2	2	2	0	0	0	0	0	2.70
on Road	13	14.1	10	5	6	1	1	0	0	0	0.00

	G	IP	H	BB	SO	SB	CS	W	L	SV	ERA
	46	182.0	144	58	95	11	6	11	6	1	3.02
	48	134.2	142	54	57	13	7	8	7	0	4.34

	BA	OBA	SA	AB	H	2B	3B	HR	RBI	BB	SO
Total	.203	.279	.254	59	12	3	0	0	6	7	8
vs. Left	.160	.214	.200	25	4	1	0	0	3	2	5
vs. Right	.235	.325	.294	34	8	2	0	0	3	5	3
Bases Empty	.242	.265	.303	33	8	2	0	0	0	1	5
Runners On Base	.154	.294	.192	26	4	1	0	0	6	6	3

	BA	OBA	SA	AB	H	2B	3B	HR	RBI	BB	SO
	.244	.308	.395	1174	286	49	6	39	140	112	152
	.261	.338	.430	230	60	11	2	8	35	26	32
	.239	.301	.387	944	226	38	4	31	105	86	120
	.236	.284	.383	760	179	31	3	25	25	48	101
	.258	.349	.418	414	107	18	3	14	115	64	51

ARCHIE CORBIN — bats right — throws right — age 25 — KC — P

1991	G	IP	H	BB	SO	SB	CS	W	L	SV	ERA
at Home	2	2.1	3	2	1	0	0	0	0	0	3.86
on Road	0	0.0	0	0	0	0	0	0	0	0	0.00

	G	IP	H	BB	SO	SB	CS	W	L	SV	ERA
	2	2.1	3	2	1	0	0	0	0	0	3.86
	0	0.0	0	0	0	0	0	0	0	0	0.00

	BA	OBA	SA	AB	H	2B	3B	HR	RBI	BB	SO
Total	.300	.417	.300	10	3	0	0	0	1	2	1
vs. Left	.250	.400	.250	4	1	0	0	0	0	1	0
vs. Right	.333	.429	.333	6	2	0	0	0	1	1	1
Bases Empty	.400	.400	.400	5	2	0	0	0	0	0	1
Runners On Base	.200	.429	.200	5	1	0	0	0	1	2	1

	BA	OBA	SA	AB	H	2B	3B	HR	RBI	BB	SO
	.300	.417	.300	10	3	0	0	0	1	2	1
	.250	.400	.250	4	1	0	0	0	0	1	0
	.333	.429	.333	6	2	0	0	0	1	1	1
	.400	.400	.400	5	2	0	0	0	0	0	1
	.200	.429	.200	5	1	0	0	0	1	2	1

RHEAL CORMIER — bats left — throws left — age 25 — SL — P

1991	G	IP	H	BB	SO	SB	CS	W	L	SV	ERA
at Home	6	39.2	47	3	18	1	1	4	2	0	4.08
on Road	5	28.0	27	5	20	0	2	0	3	0	4.18

	G	IP	H	BB	SO	SB	CS	W	L	SV	ERA
	6	39.2	47	3	18	1	1	4	2	0	4.08
	5	28.0	27	5	20	0	2	0	3	0	4.18

	BA	OBA	SA	AB	H	2B	3B	HR	RBI	BB	SO
Total	.277	.300	.401	267	74	16	1	5	27	8	38
vs. Left	.146	.163	.146	48	7	0	0	0	2	1	10
vs. Right	.306	.329	.457	219	67	16	1	5	25	7	28
Bases Empty	.269	.301	.391	156	42	8	1	3	3	5	25
Runners On Base	.288	.299	.414	111	32	8	0	2	24	3	13

	BA	OBA	SA	AB	H	2B	3B	HR	RBI	BB	SO
	.277	.300	.401	267	74	16	1	5	27	8	38
	.146	.163	.146	48	7	0	0	0	2	1	10
	.306	.329	.457	219	67	16	1	5	25	7	28
	.269	.301	.391	156	42	8	1	3	3	5	25
	.288	.299	.414	111	32	8	0	2	24	3	13

JIM CORSI — bats right — throws right — age 31 — HOU — P

1991	G	IP	H	BB	SO	SB	CS	W	L	SV	ERA
at Home	24	38.2	34	6	28	5	1	0	3	0	4.66
on Road	23	39.0	42	17	25	3	2	0	2	0	2.77

	G	IP	H	BB	SO	SB	CS	W	L	SV	ERA
	38	65.2	55	13	42	11	2	1	4	0	4.39
	42	71.2	67	26	42	3	2	0	4	0	2.13

	BA	OBA	SA	AB	H	2B	3B	HR	RBI	BB	SO
Total	.259	.310	.357	294	76	9	1	6	34	23	53
vs. Left	.289	.353	.434	152	44	5	1	5	18	15	25
vs. Right	.225	.263	.275	142	32	4	0	1	16	8	28
Bases Empty	.230	.295	.267	161	37	3	0	1	1	15	34
Runners On Base	.293	.329	.466	133	39	6	1	5	33	8	19

	BA	OBA	SA	AB	H	2B	3B	HR	RBI	BB	SO
	.242	.293	.331	505	122	14	2	9	59	39	84
	.239	.296	.336	238	57	6	1	5	21	19	35
	.243	.291	.326	267	65	8	1	4	38	20	49
	.218	.283	.256	289	63	5	0	2	2	25	55
	.273	.308	.431	216	59	9	2	7	57	14	29

JOHN COSTELLO — bats right — throws right — age 32 — SD — P

1991	G	IP	H	BB	SO	SB	CS	W	L	SV	ERA
at Home	13	18.1	18	10	11	0	0	0	0	0	1.96
on Road	14	16.2	19	7	13	4	0	0	0	0	4.32

	G	IP	H	BB	SO	SB	CS	W	L	SV	ERA
	62	78.1	62	35	41	10	4	9	2	1	1.61
	57	79.1	79	28	63	10	3	2	4	3	4.31

	BA	OBA	SA	AB	H	2B	3B	HR	RBI	BB	SO
Total	.276	.353	.366	134	37	4	1	2	18	17	24
vs. Left	.246	.384	.351	57	14	1	1	1	9	14	8
vs. Right	.299	.325	.377	77	23	3	0	1	9	3	16
Bases Empty	.315	.351	.425	73	23	2	0	2	2	4	14
Runners On Base	.230	.355	.295	61	14	2	1	0	16	13	10

	BA	OBA	SA	AB	H	2B	3B	HR	RBI	BB	SO
	.239	.312	.367	589	141	28	4	13	77	63	104
	.254	.350	.381	236	60	9	3	5	24	37	34
	.229	.284	.357	353	81	19	1	8	53	26	70
	.235	.282	.360	353	83	19	2	7	7	22	68
	.246	.351	.377	236	58	9	2	6	70	41	36

DANNY COX — bats right — throws right — age 33 — PHI — P

1991	G	IP	H	BB	SO	SB	CS	W	L	SV	ERA
at Home	11	49.0	44	19	25	3	1	2	4	0	4.41
on Road	12	53.1	54	20	21	8	6	2	2	0	4.72

	G	IP	H	BB	SO	SB	CS	W	L	SV	ERA
	85	554.2	533	146	265	22	19	32	26	0	3.23
	78	450.1	464	167	238	43	28	25	30	0	3.90

	BA	OBA	SA	AB	H	2B	3B	HR	RBI	BB	SO
Total	.258	.323	.426	380	98	16	3	14	53	39	46
vs. Left	.266	.343	.447	188	50	11	1	7	31	24	15
vs. Right	.250	.303	.406	192	48	5	2	7	22	15	31
Bases Empty	.238	.327	.396	227	54	7	1	9	9	30	26
Runners On Base	.288	.318	.471	153	44	9	2	5	44	9	20

	BA	OBA	SA	AB	H	2B	3B	HR	RBI	BB	SO
	.264	.321	.393	3778	997	192	29	79	382	313	503
	.282	.342	.423	1872	528	106	16	42	207	177	191
	.246	.299	.363	1906	469	86	13	37	175	136	312
	.262	.324	.397	2233	586	116	16	51	51	194	297
	.266	.315	.386	1545	411	76	13	28	331	119	206

STEVE CRAWFORD — bats right — throws right — age 34 — KC — P

1991	G	IP	H	BB	SO	SB	CS	W	L	SV	ERA
at Home	18	25.1	33	11	19	5	1	3	2	0	8.17
on Road	15	21.1	27	4	11	4	1	0	0	1	3.38

	BA	OBA	SA	AB	H	2B	3B	HR	RBI	BB	SO
Total	.311	.367	.440	193	60	8	4	3	29	18	38
vs. Left	.360	.412	.494	89	32	5	2	1	15	8	16
vs. Right	.269	.331	.394	104	28	3	2	2	14	10	22
Bases Empty	.300	.333	.400	100	30	5	2	1	1	5	22
Runners On Base	.323	.400	.484	93	30	5	2	2	28	13	16

7-YEAR TOTALS (1984–1991)

	G	IP	H	BB	SO	SB	CS	W	L	SV	ERA
	137	240.2	270	80	155	14	10	19	6	11	4.71
	115	223.0	248	80	124	15	4	8	12	8	3.55

	BA	OBA	SA	AB	H	2B	3B	HR	RBI	BB	SO
	.286	.344	.416	1814	518	92	11	41	282	160	279
	.320	.386	.463	845	270	54	5	19	137	95	98
	.256	.307	.376	969	248	38	6	22	145	65	181
	.270	.318	.391	911	246	41	3	21	21	61	146
	.301	.369	.442	903	272	51	8	20	261	99	133

TIM CREWS — bats right — throws right — age 31 — LA — P

1991	G	IP	H	BB	SO	SB	CS	W	L	SV	ERA
at Home	32	36.2	38	9	19	6	2	2	1	4	2.95
on Road	28	39.1	37	10	34	4	0	0	2	2	3.89

	BA	OBA	SA	AB	H	2B	3B	HR	RBI	BB	SO
Total	.256	.299	.392	293	75	17	1	7	36	19	53
vs. Left	.303	.336	.465	142	43	12	1	3	19	8	9
vs. Right	.212	.265	.325	151	32	5	0	4	17	11	44
Bases Empty	.255	.272	.376	165	42	9	1	3	3	4	30
Runners On Base	.258	.331	.414	128	33	8	0	4	33	15	23

5-YEAR TOTALS (1987–1991)

	G	IP	H	BB	SO	SB	CS	W	L	SV	ERA
	116	174.0	196	40	118	20	6	7	6	7	3.57
	116	171.2	153	49	132	14	7	4	4	8	2.52

	BA	OBA	SA	AB	H	2B	3B	HR	RBI	BB	SO
	.261	.307	.388	1336	349	65	10	28	157	89	250
	.267	.317	.389	660	176	32	8	11	69	50	90
	.256	.298	.386	676	173	33	2	17	88	39	160
	.260	.280	.371	774	201	37	5	13	13	21	146
	.263	.341	.411	562	148	28	5	15	144	68	104

MIKE DALTON — bats right — throws left — age 29 — DET — P

1991	G	IP	H	BB	SO	SB	CS	W	L	SV	ERA
at Home	1	1.2	1	0	1	0	0	0	0	0	0.00
on Road	3	6.1	11	2	3	0	0	0	0	0	4.26

	BA	OBA	SA	AB	H	2B	3B	HR	RBI	BB	SO
Total	.333	.368	.583	36	12	1	1	2	3	2	4
vs. Left	.286	.333	.643	14	4	0	1	1	2	1	2
vs. Right	.364	.391	.545	22	8	1	0	1	1	1	2
Bases Empty	.474	.474	.947	19	9	1	1	2	2	0	1
Runners On Base	.176	.263	.176	17	3	0	0	0	1	2	3

1-YEAR TOTALS (1991)

	G	IP	H	BB	SO	SB	CS	W	L	SV	ERA
	1	1.2	1	0	1	0	0	0	0	0	0.00
	3	6.1	11	2	3	0	0	0	0	0	4.26

	BA	OBA	SA	AB	H	2B	3B	HR	RBI	BB	SO
	.333	.368	.583	36	12	1	1	2	3	2	4
	.286	.333	.643	14	4	0	1	1	2	1	2
	.364	.391	.545	22	8	1	0	1	1	1	2
	.474	.474	.947	19	9	1	1	2	2	0	1
	.176	.263	.176	17	3	0	0	0	1	2	3

DANNY DARWIN — bats right — throws right — age 37 — BOS — P

1991	G	IP	H	BB	SO	SB	CS	W	L	SV	ERA
at Home	8	44.2	50	8	33	4	0	2	4	0	4.84
on Road	4	23.1	21	7	9	1	1	1	2	0	5.79

	BA	OBA	SA	AB	H	2B	3B	HR	RBI	BB	SO
Total	.263	.309	.500	270	71	17	1	15	33	15	42
vs. Left	.240	.301	.395	129	31	11	0	3	12	10	21
vs. Right	.284	.318	.596	141	40	6	1	12	21	5	21
Bases Empty	.273	.312	.517	176	48	11	1	10	10	8	26
Runners On Base	.245	.305	.468	94	23	6	0	5	23	7	16

8-YEAR TOTALS (1984–1991)

	G	IP	H	BB	SO	SB	CS	W	L	SV	ERA
	161	676.0	648	195	460	75	18	30	39	7	3.25
	157	690.1	655	164	425	69	24	39	38	7	3.68

	BA	OBA	SA	AB	H	2B	3B	HR	RBI	BB	SO
	.250	.300	.385	5209	1303	224	28	140	564	359	885
	.272	.331	.421	2722	741	142	19	75	303	233	411
	.226	.266	.345	2487	562	82	9	65	261	126	474
	.241	.288	.383	3120	751	143	15	90	90	189	536
	.264	.318	.387	2089	552	81	13	50	474	170	349

STORM DAVIS — bats right — throws right — age 31 — KC — P

1991	G	IP	H	BB	SO	SB	CS	W	L	SV	ERA
at Home	25	54.2	60	18	18	0	0	2	3	0	4.12
on Road	26	59.2	80	28	35	2	2	1	6	2	5.73

	BA	OBA	SA	AB	H	2B	3B	HR	RBI	BB	SO
Total	.306	.367	.437	458	140	21	3	11	73	46	53
vs. Left	.336	.404	.493	223	75	13	2	6	43	26	29
vs. Right	.277	.332	.383	235	65	8	1	5	30	20	24
Bases Empty	.303	.348	.432	234	71	13	1	5	5	15	29
Runners On Base	.308	.386	.442	224	69	8	2	6	68	31	24

8-YEAR TOTALS (1984–1991)

	G	IP	H	BB	SO	SB	CS	W	L	SV	ERA
	127	652.1	684	232	379	38	26	43	38	1	3.99
	125	590.0	621	245	312	38	27	38	32	2	4.27

	BA	OBA	SA	AB	H	2B	3B	HR	RBI	BB	SO
	.272	.337	.392	4799	1305	221	31	97	552	477	691
	.277	.353	.400	2429	673	121	18	47	290	297	377
	.267	.320	.383	2370	632	100	13	50	262	180	314
	.266	.329	.390	2702	718	127	19	57	57	250	381
	.280	.346	.393	2097	587	94	12	40	495	227	310

MARK DAVIS — bats left — throws left — age 32 — KC — P

1991	G	IP	H	BB	SO	SB	CS	W	L	SV	ERA
at Home	12	29.0	29	19	17	0	2	4	1	0	4.66
on Road	17	33.2	26	20	30	4	1	2	2	1	4.28

	BA	OBA	SA	AB	H	2B	3B	HR	RBI	BB	SO
Total	.240	.347	.376	229	55	11	1	6	36	39	47
vs. Left	.304	.394	.339	56	17	2	0	0	6	8	11
vs. Right	.220	.332	.387	173	38	9	1	6	30	31	36
Bases Empty	.240	.326	.352	125	30	8	0	2	2	15	25
Runners On Base	.240	.368	.404	104	25	3	1	4	34	24	22

8-YEAR TOTALS (1984–1991)

	G	IP	H	BB	SO	SB	CS	W	L	SV	ERA
	223	411.2	354	171	384	27	20	26	27	46	3.28
	245	419.0	387	181	375	38	13	15	40	46	4.21

	BA	OBA	SA	AB	H	2B	3B	HR	RBI	BB	SO
	.241	.320	.370	3076	741	125	14	81	401	352	759
	.205	.280	.307	698	143	24	4	13	87	66	199
	.251	.332	.388	2378	598	101	10	68	314	286	560
	.233	.304	.352	1655	386	69	5	39	39	154	425
	.250	.338	.391	1421	355	56	9	42	362	198	334

KEN DAYLEY — bats left — throws left — age 33 — TOR — P

1991	G	IP	H	BB	SO	SB	CS	W	L	SV	ERA
at Home	3	2.1	4	0	3	0	0	0	0	0	0.00
on Road	5	2.0	3	5	0	2	0	0	0	0	13.50

	BA	OBA	SA	AB	H	2B	3B	HR	RBI	BB	SO
Total	.368	.500	.368	19	7	0	0	0	3	5	3
vs. Left	.300	.467	.300	10	3	0	0	0	3	3	2
vs. Right	.444	.545	.444	9	4	0	0	0	0	2	1
Bases Empty	.800	.875	.800	5	4	0	0	0	0	3	1
Runners On Base	.214	.333	.214	14	3	0	0	0	3	2	2

8-YEAR TOTALS (1984–1991)

	G	IP	H	BB	SO	SB	CS	W	L	SV	ERA
	176	208.0	217	73	146	12	7	13	13	22	3.20
	163	188.2	167	86	153	16	4	10	18	17	3.43

	BA	OBA	SA	AB	H	2B	3B	HR	RBI	BB	SO
	.257	.328	.363	1495	384	72	12	21	201	159	299
	.269	.333	.353	484	130	22	2	5	64	46	110
	.251	.326	.368	1011	254	50	10	16	137	113	189
	.232	.296	.338	754	175	30	7	12	12	66	172
	.282	.359	.389	741	209	42	5	9	189	93	127

FRANCISCO De La ROSA — bats both — throws right — age 26 — BAL — P

1991	G	IP	H	BB	SO	SB	CS	W	L	SV	ERA
at Home	1	1.1	2	1	0	0	0	0	0	0	0.00
on Road	1	2.2	4	1	1	0	0	0	0	0	6.75

	BA	OBA	SA	AB	H	2B	3B	HR	RBI	BB	SO
Total	.353	.400	.471	17	6	2	0	0	2	2	1
vs. Left	.500	.500	.625	8	4	1	0	0	0	0	0
vs. Right	.222	.333	.333	9	2	1	0	0	2	2	1
Bases Empty	.250	.500	.250	4	1	0	0	0	0	2	0
Runners On Base	.385	.357	.538	13	5	2	0	0	2	0	1

1-YEAR TOTALS (1991)

G	IP	H	BB	SO	SB	CS	W	L	SV	ERA
1	1.1	2	1	0	0	0	0	0	0	0.00
1	2.2	4	1	1	0	0	0	0	0	6.75

BA	OBA	SA	AB	H	2B	3B	HR	RBI	BB	SO
.353	.400	.471	17	6	2	0	0	2	2	1
.500	.500	.625	8	4	1	0	0	0	0	0
.222	.333	.333	9	2	1	0	0	2	2	1
.250	.500	.250	4	1	0	0	0	0	2	0
.385	.357	.538	13	5	2	0	0	2	0	1

JOHN DOPSON — bats left — throws right — age 29 — BOS — P

1991	G	IP	H	BB	SO	SB	CS	W	L	SV	ERA
at Home	1	1.0	2	1	0	0	0	0	0	0	18.00
on Road	0	0.0	0	0	0	0	0	0	0	0	0.00

	BA	OBA	SA	AB	H	2B	3B	HR	RBI	BB	SO
Total	.500	.500	.750	4	2	1	0	0	2	1	0
vs. Left	.000	.333	.000	1	0	0	0	0	1	1	0
vs. Right	.667	.667	1.000	3	2	1	0	0	1	0	0
Bases Empty	.000	1.000	.000	0	0	0	0	0	0	1	0
Runners On Base	.500	.400	.750	4	2	1	0	0	2	0	0

5-YEAR TOTALS (1985–1991)

G	IP	H	BB	SO	SB	CS	W	L	SV	ERA
35	205.1	201	85	118	37	10	7	12	0	3.68
29	164.1	155	56	91	27	3	8	9	0	3.83

BA	OBA	SA	AB	H	2B	3B	HR	RBI	BB	SO
.251	.318	.370	1420	356	50	7	35	150	141	209
.253	.324	.350	700	177	19	2	15	65	77	93
.249	.312	.389	720	179	31	5	20	85	64	116
.254	.324	.374	832	211	26	4	22	22	84	135
.247	.310	.364	588	145	24	3	13	128	57	74

KELLY DOWNS — bats right — throws right — age 32 — SF — P

1991	G	IP	H	BB	SO	SB	CS	W	L	SV	ERA
at Home	21	55.1	47	24	32	8	1	5	2	0	3.90
on Road	24	56.1	52	29	30	7	3	5	2	0	4.47

	BA	OBA	SA	AB	H	2B	3B	HR	RBI	BB	SO
Total	.239	.326	.373	415	99	16	2	12	57	53	62
vs. Left	.267	.340	.410	217	58	9	2	6	31	24	19
vs. Right	.207	.312	.333	198	41	7	0	6	26	29	43
Bases Empty	.240	.324	.338	225	54	10	0	4	4	27	34
Runners On Base	.237	.329	.416	190	45	6	2	8	53	26	28

6-YEAR TOTALS (1986–1991)

G	IP	H	BB	SO	SB	CS	W	L	SV	ERA
77	346.2	287	121	231	25	11	25	14	1	3.43
81	353.0	354	122	230	34	12	21	22	0	3.90

BA	OBA	SA	AB	H	2B	3B	HR	RBI	BB	SO
.243	.308	.355	2640	641	129	7	51	281	243	461
.249	.311	.356	1451	361	75	6	23	150	131	214
.235	.304	.353	1189	280	54	1	28	131	112	247
.236	.297	.333	1538	363	63	4	26	26	124	271
.252	.323	.386	1102	278	66	3	25	255	119	190

BRIAN DRAHMAN — bats right — throws right — age 26 — CHA — P

1991	G	IP	H	BB	SO	SB	CS	W	L	SV	ERA
at Home	12	11.1	11	7	9	0	1	2	2	0	5.56
on Road	16	19.1	10	6	9	0	0	1	0	0	1.86

	BA	OBA	SA	AB	H	2B	3B	HR	RBI	BB	SO
Total	.193	.276	.349	109	21	3	1	4	20	13	18
vs. Left	.250	.324	.563	32	8	2	1	2	7	4	1
vs. Right	.169	.256	.260	77	13	1	0	2	13	9	17
Bases Empty	.196	.237	.357	56	11	1	1	2	2	3	9
Runners On Base	.189	.313	.340	53	10	2	0	2	18	10	9

1-YEAR TOTALS (1991)

G	IP	H	BB	SO	SB	CS	W	L	SV	ERA
12	11.1	11	7	9	0	1	2	2	0	5.56
16	19.1	10	6	9	0	0	1	0	0	1.86

BA	OBA	SA	AB	H	2B	3B	HR	RBI	BB	SO
.193	.276	.349	109	21	3	1	4	20	13	18
.250	.324	.563	32	8	2	1	2	7	4	1
.169	.256	.260	77	13	1	0	2	13	9	17
.196	.237	.357	56	11	1	1	2	2	3	9
.189	.313	.340	53	10	2	0	2	18	10	9

TOM DREES — bats both — throws left — age 29 — CHA — P

1991	G	IP	H	BB	SO	SB	CS	W	L	SV	ERA
at Home	2	2.1	6	2	1	1	0	0	0	0	23.14
on Road	2	5.0	4	4	1	0	0	0	0	0	7.20

	BA	OBA	SA	AB	H	2B	3B	HR	RBI	BB	SO
Total	.345	.444	.793	29	10	1	0	4	11	6	2
vs. Left	.286	.333	1.143	7	2	0	0	2	5	1	1
vs. Right	.364	.481	.682	22	8	1	0	2	6	5	1
Bases Empty	.417	.563	1.000	12	5	1	0	2	2	4	0
Runners On Base	.294	.350	.647	17	5	0	0	2	9	2	2

1-YEAR TOTALS (1991)

G	IP	H	BB	SO	SB	CS	W	L	SV	ERA
2	2.1	6	2	1	1	0	0	0	0	23.14
2	5.0	4	4	1	0	0	0	0	0	7.20

BA	OBA	SA	AB	H	2B	3B	HR	RBI	BB	SO
.345	.444	.793	29	10	1	0	4	11	6	2
.286	.333	1.143	7	2	0	0	2	5	1	1
.364	.481	.682	22	8	1	0	2	6	5	1
.417	.563	1.000	12	5	1	0	2	2	4	0
.294	.350	.647	17	5	0	0	2	9	2	2

KIRK DRESSENDORFER — bats right — throws right — age 23 — OAK — P

1991	G	IP	H	BB	SO	SB	CS	W	L	SV	ERA
at Home	3	13.1	15	9	9	1	1	1	2	0	8.10
on Road	4	21.1	18	12	8	2	1	2	1	0	3.90

	BA	OBA	SA	AB	H	2B	3B	HR	RBI	BB	SO
Total	.244	.344	.407	135	33	7	0	5	26	21	17
vs. Left	.271	.370	.386	70	19	5	0	1	12	11	12
vs. Right	.215	.316	.431	65	14	2	0	4	14	10	5
Bases Empty	.188	.316	.313	80	15	4	0	2	2	15	13
Runners On Base	.327	.387	.545	55	18	3	0	3	24	6	4

1-YEAR TOTALS (1991)

G	IP	H	BB	SO	SB	CS	W	L	SV	ERA
3	13.1	15	9	9	1	1	1	2	0	8.10
4	21.1	18	12	8	2	1	2	1	0	3.80

BA	OBA	SA	AB	H	2B	3B	HR	RBI	BB	SO
.244	.344	.407	135	33	7	0	5	26	21	17
.271	.370	.386	70	19	5	0	1	12	11	12
.215	.316	.431	65	14	2	0	4	14	10	5
.188	.316	.313	80	15	4	0	2	2	15	13
.327	.387	.545	55	18	3	0	3	24	6	4

TOM EDENS — bats right — throws right — age 31 — MIN — P

1991	G	IP	H	BB	SO	SB	CS	W	L	SV	ERA
at Home	4	10.0	11	2	6	0	0	0	1	0	6.30
on Road	4	23.0	23	8	13	1	2	1	2	1	3.13

	BA	OBA	SA	AB	H	2B	3B	HR	RBI	BB	SO
Total	.256	.308	.391	133	34	8	2	2	14	10	19
vs. Left	.250	.304	.406	64	16	3	2	1	4	5	11
vs. Right	.261	.311	.377	69	18	5	0	1	10	5	8
Bases Empty	.284	.321	.473	74	21	4	2	2	2	6	11
Runners On Base	.220	.292	.288	59	13	4	0	0	12	6	11

3-YEAR TOTALS (1987–1991)

G	IP	H	BB	SO	SB	CS	W	L	SV	ERA
21	52.2	67	16	19	3	3	3	4	0	6.15
24	77.1	71	31	44	8	5	3	3	2	3.38

BA	OBA	SA	AB	H	2B	3B	HR	RBI	BB	SO
.271	.335	.403	509	138	23	4	12	62	47	63
.279	.339	.425	226	63	10	4	5	25	21	28
.265	.332	.385	283	75	13	0	7	37	26	35
.265	.321	.427	279	74	15	3	8	8	23	38
.278	.351	.374	230	64	8	1	4	54	24	25

WAYNE EDWARDS — bats left — throws left — age 28 — CHA — P

1991	G	IP	H	BB	SO	SB	CS	W	L	SV	ERA
at Home	7	13.0	8	8	4	1	0	0	0	0	2.77
on Road	6	10.1	14	9	8	1	0	0	2	0	5.23

	BA	OBA	SA	AB	H	2B	3B	HR	RBI	BB	SO
Total	.259	.375	.376	85	22	4	0	2	14	17	12
vs. Left	.308	.419	.308	26	8	0	0	0	4	5	1
vs. Right	.237	.356	.407	59	14	4	0	2	10	12	11
Bases Empty	.217	.308	.326	46	10	2	0	1	1	6	4
Runners On Base	.308	.442	.436	39	12	2	0	1	13	11	8

3-YEAR TOTALS (1989–1991)

G	IP	H	BB	SO	SB	CS	W	L	SV	ERA
32	67.0	50	27	48	2	4	4	1	1	2.55
30	58.2	60	34	36	9	1	1	4	1	4.30

BA	OBA	SA	AB	H	2B	3B	HR	RBI	BB	SO
.241	.331	.341	457	110	17	1	9	57	61	84
.209	.297	.248	129	27	0	1	1	17	17	22
.253	.344	.378	328	83	17	0	8	40	44	62
.213	.304	.311	244	52	9	0	5	5	29	36
.272	.360	.376	213	58	8	1	4	52	32	48

BRUCE EGLOFF — bats right — throws right — age 27 — CLE — P

1991	G	IP	H	BB	SO	SB	CS	W	L	SV	ERA
at Home	3	2.0	4	0	3	0	0	0	0	0	4.50
on Road	3	3.2	4	4	5	0	0	0	0	0	4.91

	BA	OBA	SA	AB	H	2B	3B	HR	RBI	BB	SO
Total	.333	.429	.417	24	8	2	0	0	3	4	8
vs. Left	.300	.364	.400	10	3	1	0	0	1	1	5
vs. Right	.357	.471	.429	14	5	1	0	0	2	3	3
Bases Empty	.400	.500	.500	10	4	1	0	0	0	2	3
Runners On Base	.286	.375	.357	14	4	1	0	0	3	2	5

1-YEAR TOTALS (1991)

G	IP	H	BB	SO	SB	CS	W	L	SV	ERA
3	2.0	4	0	3	0	0	0	0	0	4.50
3	3.2	4	4	5	0	0	0	0	0	4.91

BA	OBA	SA	AB	H	2B	3B	HR	RBI	BB	SO
.333	.429	.417	24	8	2	0	0	3	4	8
.300	.364	.400	10	3	1	0	0	1	1	5
.357	.471	.429	14	5	1	0	0	2	3	3
.400	.500	.500	10	4	1	0	0	0	2	3
.286	.375	.357	14	4	1	0	0	3	2	5

DAVE EILAND — bats right — throws right — age 26 — NYA — P

1991	G	IP	H	BB	SO	SB	CS	W	L	SV	ERA
at Home	10	44.1	46	14	11	3	0	2	2	0	4.67
on Road	8	28.1	41	9	7	3	1	0	3	0	6.35

	BA	OBA	SA	AB	H	2B	3B	HR	RBI	BB	SO
Total	.302	.356	.510	288	87	20	5	10	49	23	18
vs. Left	.267	.312	.432	146	39	9	3	3	15	10	7
vs. Right	.338	.400	.592	142	48	11	2	7	34	13	11
Bases Empty	.299	.357	.455	167	50	11	0	5	5	14	7
Runners On Base	.306	.356	.587	121	37	9	5	5	44	9	11

4-YEAR TOTALS (1988–1991)

G	IP	H	BB	SO	SB	CS	W	L	SV	ERA
18	84.2	96	25	34	4	2	4	4	0	5.42
14	65.1	81	20	18	7	3	1	5	0	4.82

BA	OBA	SA	AB	H	2B	3B	HR	RBI	BB	SO
.297	.351	.497	595	177	34	8	23	88	45	52
.293	.346	.505	321	94	17	6	13	42	26	17
.303	.358	.489	274	83	17	2	10	46	19	35
.290	.349	.476	355	103	19	1	15	15	29	30
.308	.355	.529	240	74	15	7	8	73	16	22

CAL ELDRED — bats right — throws right — age 25 — MIL — P

1991	G	IP	H	BB	SO	SB	CS	W	L	SV	ERA
at Home	2	9.2	13	4	5	2	0	1	0	0	6.52
on Road	1	6.1	7	2	5	1	1	1	0	0	1.42

	BA	OBA	SA	AB	H	2B	3B	HR	RBI	BB	SO
Total	.299	.356	.403	67	20	1	0	2	7	6	10
vs. Left	.222	.243	.306	36	8	0	0	1	2	1	7
vs. Right	.387	.472	.516	31	12	1	0	1	5	5	3
Bases Empty	.289	.357	.447	38	11	0	0	2	2	4	5
Runners On Base	.310	.355	.345	29	9	1	0	0	5	2	5

1-YEAR TOTALS (1991)

G	IP	H	BB	SO	SB	CS	W	L	SV	ERA
2	9.2	13	4	5	2	0	1	0	0	6.52
1	6.1	7	2	5	1	1	1	0	0	1.42

BA	OBA	SA	AB	H	2B	3B	HR	RBI	BB	SO
.299	.356	.403	67	20	1	0	2	7	6	10
.222	.243	.306	36	8	0	0	1	2	1	7
.387	.472	.516	31	12	1	0	1	5	5	3
.289	.357	.447	38	11	0	0	2	2	4	5
.310	.355	.345	29	9	1	0	0	5	2	5

HECTOR — FAJARDO — bats right — throws right — age 22 — PIT/TEX — P

1991	G	IP	H	BB	SO	SB	CS	W	L	SV	ERA
at Home	4	11.1	21	10	15	6	2	0	1	0	9.53
on Road	2	14.0	14	1	8	1	0	0	1	0	4.50

	BA	OBA	SA	AB	H	2B	3B	HR	RBI	BB	SO
Total	.337	.395	.471	104	35	6	1	2	10	11	23
vs. Left	.311	.385	.422	45	14	3	1	0	3	6	10
vs. Right	.356	.403	.508	59	21	3	0	2	7	5	13
Bases Empty	.431	.473	.647	51	22	6	1	1	1	4	6
Runners On Base	.245	.328	.302	53	13	0	0	1	9	7	17

1-YEAR TOTALS (1991)

G	IP	H	BB	SO	SB	CS	W	L	SV	ERA
4	11.1	21	10	15	6	2	0	1	0	9.53
2	14.0	14	1	8	1	0	0	1	0	4.50

BA	OBA	SA	AB	H	2B	3B	HR	RBI	BB	SO
.337	.395	.471	104	35	6	1	2	10	11	23
.311	.385	.422	45	14	3	1	0	3	6	10
.356	.403	.508	59	21	3	0	2	7	5	13
.431	.473	.647	51	22	6	1	1	1	4	6
.245	.328	.302	53	13	0	0	1	9	7	17

SID FERNANDEZ — bats left — throws left — age 30 — NYN — P

1991	G	IP	H	BB	SO	SB	CS	W	L	SV	ERA
at Home	3	19.0	12	2	21	2	1	1	1	0	1.42
on Road	5	25.0	24	7	10	1	0	0	2	0	3.96

	BA	OBA	SA	AB	H	2B	3B	HR	RBI	BB	SO
Total	.222	.262	.327	162	36	3	1	4	16	9	31
vs. Left	.394	.412	.485	33	13	0	0	1	3	1	7
vs. Right	.178	.225	.287	129	23	3	1	3	13	8	24
Bases Empty	.224	.245	.280	107	24	3	0	1	1	3	22
Runners On Base	.218	.290	.418	55	12	0	1	3	15	6	9

8-YEAR TOTALS (1984–1991)

G	IP	H	BB	SO	SB	CS	W	L	SV	ERA
103	664.0	422	251	675	82	19	49	25	1	2.51
103	586.1	500	242	500	85	18	30	36	0	4.05

BA	OBA	SA	AB	H	2B	3B	HR	RBI	BB	SO
.204	.284	.331	4522	922	183	32	109	427	493	1175
.220	.297	.335	674	148	33	3	13	62	71	206
.201	.282	.330	3848	774	150	29	96	365	422	969
.198	.278	.318	2836	562	108	19	65	65	295	780
.214	.295	.352	1686	360	75	13	44	362	198	395

MIKE FETTERS — bats right — throws right — age 28 — CAL — P

1991	G	IP	H	BB	SO	SB	CS	W	L	SV	ERA
at Home	7	11.0	12	6	5	1	0	2	1	0	6.55
on Road	12	33.2	41	22	19	5	4	0	4	0	4.28

	BA	OBA	SA	AB	H	2B	3B	HR	RBI	BB	SO
Total	.305	.410	.414	174	53	7	0	4	27	28	24
vs. Left	.279	.361	.337	86	24	2	0	1	13	11	10
vs. Right	.330	.454	.489	88	29	5	0	3	14	17	14
Bases Empty	.299	.396	.368	87	26	6	0	0	0	13	9
Runners On Base	.310	.423	.460	87	27	1	0	4	27	15	15

3-YEAR TOTALS (1989–1991)

G	IP	H	BB	SO	SB	CS	W	L	SV	ERA
19	43.2	50	15	18	5	0	2	2	1	3.92
27	72.0	85	34	45	7	1	1	4	0	4.88

BA	OBA	SA	AB	H	2B	3B	HR	RBI	BB	SO
.295	.370	.420	457	135	13	1	14	69	49	63
.319	.378	.474	213	68	7	1	8	39	18	22
.275	.363	.373	244	67	6	0	6	30	31	41
.280	.345	.391	243	68	4	1	6	6	21	31
.313	.398	.453	214	67	4	1	8	63	28	32

DAVE FLEMING — bats left — throws left — age 23 — SEA — P

1991	G	IP	H	BB	SO	SB	CS	W	L	SV	ERA
at Home	5	8.2	6	1	3	1	0	1	0	0	0.00
on Road	4	9.0	13	2	8	0	1	0	0	0	13.00

	BA	OBA	SA	AB	H	2B	3B	HR	RBI	BB	SO
Total	.284	.342	.537	67	19	6	1	3	13	3	11
vs. Left	.333	.455	.667	9	3	3	0	0	2	1	0
vs. Right	.276	.323	.517	58	16	3	1	3	11	2	11
Bases Empty	.205	.255	.364	44	9	4	0	1	1	2	7
Runners On Base	.435	.500	.870	23	10	2	1	2	12	1	4

1-YEAR TOTALS (1991)

	G	IP	H	BB	SO	SB	CS	W	L	SV	ERA
	5	8.2	6	1	3	1	0	1	0	0	0.00
	4	9.0	13	2	8	0	1	0	0	0	13.00

	BA	OBA	SA	AB	H	2B	3B	HR	RBI	BB	SO
	.284	.342	.537	67	19	6	1	3	13	3	11
	.333	.455	.667	9	3	3	0	0	2	1	0
	.276	.323	.517	58	16	3	1	3	11	2	11
	.205	.255	.364	44	9	4	0	1	1	2	7
	.435	.500	.870	23	10	2	1	2	12	1	4

TONY FOSSAS — bats left — throws left — age 35 — BOS — P

1991	G	IP	H	BB	SO	SB	CS	W	L	SV	ERA
at Home	26	22.0	20	14	12	2	0	1	0	1	2.45
on Road	38	35.0	29	14	17	3	2	2	2	0	4.11

	BA	OBA	SA	AB	H	2B	3B	HR	RBI	BB	SO
Total	.236	.335	.327	208	49	10	0	3	31	28	29
vs. Left	.190	.277	.298	84	16	3	0	2	13	8	15
vs. Right	.266	.372	.347	124	33	7	0	1	18	20	14
Bases Empty	.247	.341	.390	77	19	5	0	2	2	9	8
Runners On Base	.229	.331	.290	131	30	5	0	1	29	19	21

4-YEAR TOTALS (1988–1991)

	G	IP	H	BB	SO	SB	CS	W	L	SV	ERA
	74	80.1	81	31	55	5	3	3	0	2	3.25
	78	72.2	80	31	40	4	2	4	7	0	5.08

	BA	OBA	SA	AB	H	2B	3B	HR	RBI	BB	SO
	.273	.344	.385	590	161	25	4	11	100	62	95
	.211	.288	.282	209	44	3	0	4	32	20	53
	.307	.375	.441	381	117	22	4	7	68	42	42
	.257	.321	.379	253	65	11	4	4	4	21	36
	.285	.360	.389	337	96	14	0	7	96	41	59

STEVE FOSTER — bats right — throws right — age 26 — CIN — P

1991	G	IP	H	BB	SO	SB	CS	W	L	SV	ERA
at Home	6	9.0	5	3	6	0	0	0	0	0	2.00
on Road	5	5.0	2	1	5	0	0	0	0	0	1.80

	BA	OBA	SA	AB	H	2B	3B	HR	RBI	BB	SO
Total	.143	.208	.224	49	7	1	0	1	3	4	11
vs. Left	.192	.250	.308	26	5	0	0	1	3	2	2
vs. Right	.087	.160	.130	23	2	1	0	0	0	2	9
Bases Empty	.114	.162	.229	35	4	1	0	1	1	2	9
Runners On Base	.214	.313	.214	14	3	0	0	0	2	2	2

1-YEAR TOTALS (1991)

	G	IP	H	BB	SO	SB	CS	W	L	SV	ERA
	6	9.0	5	3	6	0	0	0	0	0	2.00
	5	5.0	2	1	5	0	0	0	0	0	1.80

	BA	OBA	SA	AB	H	2B	3B	HR	RBI	BB	SO
	.143	.208	.224	49	7	1	0	1	3	4	11
	.192	.250	.308	26	5	0	0	1	3	2	2
	.087	.160	.130	23	2	1	0	0	0	2	9
	.114	.162	.229	35	4	1	0	1	1	2	9
	.214	.313	.214	14	3	0	0	0	2	2	2

WILLIE FRASER — bats right — throws right — age 28 — TOR/SL — P

1991	G	IP	H	BB	SO	SB	CS	W	L	SV	ERA
at Home	23	37.1	38	16	20	6	1	1	3	0	4.82
on Road	25	38.1	39	16	17	5	4	2	2	0	5.87

	BA	OBA	SA	AB	H	2B	3B	HR	RBI	BB	SO
Total	.265	.346	.447	291	77	12	1	13	53	32	37
vs. Left	.248	.331	.391	133	33	2	1	5	19	15	15
vs. Right	.278	.359	.494	158	44	10	0	8	34	17	22
Bases Empty	.203	.292	.348	158	32	5	0	6	6	16	26
Runners On Base	.338	.409	.564	133	45	7	1	7	47	16	11

6-YEAR TOTALS (1986–1991)

	G	IP	H	BB	SO	SB	CS	W	L	SV	ERA
	97	292.2	274	111	161	26	9	15	18	3	4.12
	111	326.1	321	112	148	28	12	19	21	2	4.63

	BA	OBA	SA	AB	H	2B	3B	HR	RBI	BB	SO
	.252	.321	.419	2361	595	123	13	82	332	223	309
	.254	.329	.448	1128	287	60	10	46	169	122	125
	.250	.312	.393	1233	308	63	3	36	163	101	184
	.233	.306	.395	1370	319	66	6	48	48	130	175
	.279	.340	.453	991	276	57	7	34	284	93	134

MARVIN FREEMAN — bats right — throws right — age 29 — ATL — P

1991	G	IP	H	BB	SO	SB	CS	W	L	SV	ERA
at Home	23	33.1	21	7	21	1	2	1	0	1	1.08
on Road	11	14.2	16	6	13	1	0	0	0	0	7.36

	BA	OBA	SA	AB	H	2B	3B	HR	RBI	BB	SO
Total	.214	.275	.283	173	37	6	0	2	20	13	34
vs. Left	.259	.333	.296	81	21	3	0	0	9	9	10
vs. Right	.174	.222	.272	92	16	3	0	2	11	4	24
Bases Empty	.184	.250	.223	103	19	4	0	0	0	8	19
Runners On Base	.257	.312	.371	70	18	2	0	2	20	5	15

5-YEAR TOTALS (1986–1991)

	G	IP	H	BB	SO	SB	CS	W	L	SV	ERA
	40	80.1	68	40	54	5	3	1	2	2	4.26
	34	86.1	73	48	63	18	6	5	3	0	4.38

	BA	OBA	SA	AB	H	2B	3B	HR	RBI	BB	SO
	.229	.331	.318	616	141	20	4	9	74	88	117
	.268	.389	.363	317	85	13	4	3	43	62	44
	.187	.265	.271	299	56	7	0	6	31	26	73
	.202	.315	.279	341	69	10	2	4	4	53	63
	.262	.352	.367	275	72	10	2	5	70	35	54

STEVE FREY — bats right — throws left — age 29 — MON — P

1991	G	IP	H	BB	SO	SB	CS	W	L	SV	ERA
at Home	15	14.2	19	10	9	2	0	0	0	0	5.52
on Road	16	25.0	24	13	12	1	0	0	1	1	4.68

	BA	OBA	SA	AB	H	2B	3B	HR	RBI	BB	SO
Total	.281	.374	.373	153	43	5	0	3	23	23	21
vs. Left	.273	.359	.364	55	15	2	0	1	11	7	15
vs. Right	.286	.383	.378	98	28	3	0	2	12	16	6
Bases Empty	.184	.326	.250	76	14	2	0	1	1	15	9
Runners On Base	.377	.425	.494	77	29	3	0	2	22	8	12

3-YEAR TOTALS (1989–1991)

	G	IP	H	BB	SO	SB	CS	W	L	SV	ERA
	52	54.2	49	29	32	9	2	5	1	7	2.63
	50	62.0	67	34	33	2	2	6	4	3	4.65

	BA	OBA	SA	AB	H	2B	3B	HR	RBI	BB	SO
	.262	.354	.385	442	116	19	1	11	55	63	65
	.273	.365	.385	143	39	7	1	3	25	21	33
	.258	.349	.385	299	77	12	1	8	30	42	32
	.232	.341	.379	224	52	10	1	7	7	34	34
	.294	.368	.390	218	64	9	0	4	48	29	31

TODD FROHWIRTH — bats right — throws right — age 30 — BAL — P

1991	G	IP	H	BB	SO	SB	CS	W	L	SV	ERA
at Home	27	54.1	39	13	48	7	3	4	1	1	2.48
on Road	24	42.0	25	16	29	2	1	3	2	2	1.07

	BA	OBA	SA	AB	H	2B	3B	HR	RBI	BB	SO
Total	.190	.255	.267	337	64	14	3	2	36	29	77
vs. Left	.223	.320	.315	130	29	8	2	0	16	18	26
vs. Right	.169	.211	.237	207	35	6	1	2	20	11	51
Bases Empty	.185	.243	.262	195	36	8	2	1	1	14	58
Runners On Base	.197	.272	.275	142	28	6	1	1	35	15	19

5-YEAR TOTALS (1987–1991)

	G	IP	H	BB	SO	SB	CS	W	L	SV	ERA
	65	102.0	81	27	82	13	4	6	1	1	2.82
	58	81.0	70	39	55	7	3	4	5	2	2.89

	BA	OBA	SA	AB	H	2B	3B	HR	RBI	BB	SO
	.227	.299	.320	665	151	26	6	8	84	66	137
	.287	.379	.414	261	75	16	4	3	41	37	37
	.188	.245	.260	404	76	10	2	5	43	29	100
	.225	.268	.310	374	84	14	3	4	4	21	83
	.230	.336	.333	291	67	12	3	4	80	45	54

DAN GAKELER — bats right — throws right — age 28 — DET — P

1991	G	IP	H	BB	SO	SB	CS	W	L	SV	ERA
at Home	17	36.0	36	13	28	3	0	0	1	1	6.00
on Road	14	37.2	37	26	15	4	1	1	3	1	5.50

	BA	OBA	SA	AB	H	2B	3B	HR	RBI	BB	SO
Total	.256	.345	.358	285	73	12	1	5	41	39	43
vs. Left	.310	.406	.425	113	35	5	1	2	14	19	17
vs. Right	.221	.303	.314	172	38	7	0	3	27	20	26
Bases Empty	.219	.313	.290	155	34	5	0	2	2	20	26
Runners On Base	.300	.382	.438	130	39	7	1	3	39	19	17

1-YEAR TOTALS (1991)

G	IP	H	BB	SO	SB	CS	W	L	SV	ERA
17	36.0	36	13	28	3	0	0	1	1	6.00
14	37.2	37	26	15	4	1	1	3	1	5.50

BA	OBA	SA	AB	H	2B	3B	HR	RBI	BB	SO
.256	.345	.358	285	73	12	1	5	41	39	43
.310	.406	.425	113	35	5	1	2	14	19	17
.221	.303	.314	172	38	7	0	3	27	20	26
.219	.313	.290	155	34	5	0	2	2	20	26
.300	.382	.438	130	39	7	1	3	39	19	17

RAMON GARCIA — bats right — throws right — age 23 — CHA — P

1991	G	IP	H	BB	SO	SB	CS	W	L	SV	ERA
at Home	10	45.0	47	19	20	2	1	2	2	0	6.40
on Road	6	33.1	32	12	20	2	3	2	2	0	4.05

	BA	OBA	SA	AB	H	2B	3B	HR	RBI	BB	SO
Total	.269	.340	.449	294	79	14	0	13	38	31	40
vs. Left	.275	.358	.427	131	36	8	0	4	15	18	16
vs. Right	.264	.326	.466	163	43	6	0	9	23	13	24
Bases Empty	.267	.333	.466	191	51	11	0	9	9	18	31
Runners On Base	.272	.353	.417	103	28	3	0	4	29	13	9

1-YEAR TOTALS (1991)

G	IP	H	BB	SO	SB	CS	W	L	SV	ERA
10	45.0	47	19	20	2	1	2	2	0	6.40
6	33.1	32	12	20	2	3	2	2	0	4.05

BA	OBA	SA	AB	H	2B	3B	HR	RBI	BB	SO
.269	.340	.449	294	79	14	0	13	38	31	40
.275	.358	.427	131	36	8	0	4	15	18	16
.264	.326	.466	163	43	6	0	9	23	13	24
.267	.333	.466	191	51	11	0	9	9	18	31
.272	.353	.417	103	28	3	0	4	29	13	9

CHRIS GARDNER — bats right — throws right — age 23 — HOU — P

1991	G	IP	H	BB	SO	SB	CS	W	L	SV	ERA
at Home	2	10.2	9	8	4	0	0	0	1	0	5.91
on Road	3	14.0	10	6	8	0	0	1	1	0	2.57

	BA	OBA	SA	AB	H	2B	3B	HR	RBI	BB	SO
Total	.218	.327	.414	87	19	2	0	5	10	14	12
vs. Left	.100	.308	.275	40	4	1	0	2	2	12	7
vs. Right	.319	.347	.532	47	15	1	0	3	8	2	5
Bases Empty	.194	.265	.355	62	12	1	0	3	3	6	10
Runners On Base	.280	.455	.560	25	7	1	0	2	7	8	2

1-YEAR TOTALS (1991)

G	IP	H	BB	SO	SB	CS	W	L	SV	ERA
2	10.2	9	8	4	0	0	0	1	0	5.91
3	14.0	10	6	8	0	0	1	1	0	2.57

BA	OBA	SA	AB	H	2B	3B	HR	RBI	BB	SO
.218	.327	.414	87	19	2	0	5	10	14	12
.100	.308	.275	40	4	1	0	2	2	12	7
.319	.347	.532	47	15	1	0	3	8	2	5
.194	.265	.355	62	12	1	0	3	3	6	10
.280	.455	.560	25	7	1	0	2	7	8	2

WES GARDNER — bats right — throws right — age 31 — SD/KC — P

1991	G	IP	H	BB	SO	SB	CS	W	L	SV	ERA
at Home	7	11.2	19	4	3	2	0	0	1	0	7.71
on Road	10	14.1	13	10	9	0	0	0	0	1	4.40

	BA	OBA	SA	AB	H	2B	3B	HR	RBI	BB	SO
Total	.291	.371	.373	110	32	2	2	1	13	14	12
vs. Left	.405	.519	.619	42	17	2	1	1	8	10	3
vs. Right	.221	.264	.221	68	15	0	0	0	5	4	9
Bases Empty	.290	.353	.339	62	18	1	1	0	0	6	6
Runners On Base	.292	.393	.417	48	14	1	1	1	13	8	6

8-YEAR TOTALS (1984–1991)

G	IP	H	BB	SO	SB	CS	W	L	SV	ERA
89	232.0	212	99	175	25	5	10	10	11	4.07
100	234.1	264	119	183	20	7	8	20	4	5.72

BA	OBA	SA	AB	H	2B	3B	HR	RBI	BB	SO
.265	.344	.414	1795	476	94	9	52	247	218	358
.293	.387	.436	837	245	51	6	19	128	135	148
.241	.305	.396	958	231	43	3	33	119	83	210
.249	.332	.394	983	245	51	5	27	27	119	207
.284	.360	.440	812	231	43	4	25	220	99	151

SCOTT GARRELTS — bats right — throws right — age 31 — SF — P

1991	G	IP	H	BB	SO	SB	CS	W	L	SV	ERA
at Home	3	6.0	11	3	2	1	1	0	1	0	12.00
on Road	5	13.2	14	6	6	3	0	1	0	0	3.95

	BA	OBA	SA	AB	H	2B	3B	HR	RBI	BB	SO
Total	.313	.378	.563	80	25	3	1	5	14	9	8
vs. Left	.390	.435	.634	41	16	2	1	2	10	4	2
vs. Right	.231	.318	.487	39	9	1	0	3	4	5	6
Bases Empty	.364	.429	.614	44	16	2	0	3	3	5	5
Runners On Base	.250	.317	.500	36	9	1	1	2	11	4	3

8-YEAR TOTALS (1984–1991)

G	IP	H	BB	SO	SB	CS	W	L	SV	ERA
172	481.1	385	192	359	55	17	39	29	24	2.97
174	440.1	394	199	324	58	11	28	22	24	3.64

BA	OBA	SA	AB	H	2B	3B	HR	RBI	BB	SO
.231	.311	.339	3372	779	117	19	70	380	391	683
.249	.331	.354	1718	427	67	14	29	197	213	291
.213	.289	.323	1654	352	50	5	41	183	178	392
.224	.293	.325	1953	437	67	14	34	34	188	373
.241	.333	.359	1419	342	50	5	36	346	203	310

CHRIS GEORGE — bats right — throws right — age 26 — MIL — P

1991	G	IP	H	BB	SO	SB	CS	W	L	SV	ERA
at Home	0	0.0	0	0	0	0	0	0	0	0	0.00
on Road	2	6.0	8	0	2	1	0	0	0	0	3.00

	BA	OBA	SA	AB	H	2B	3B	HR	RBI	BB	SO
Total	.333	.320	.458	24	8	3	0	0	2	0	2
vs. Left	.429	.400	.643	14	6	3	0	0	2	0	1
vs. Right	.200	.200	.200	10	2	0	0	0	0	0	1
Bases Empty	.429	.429	.571	14	6	2	0	0	0	0	1
Runners On Base	.200	.182	.300	10	2	1	0	0	2	0	1

1-YEAR TOTALS (1991)

G	IP	H	BB	SO	SB	CS	W	L	SV	ERA
2	6.0	8	0	2	1	0	0	0	0	3.00
2	6.0	8	0	2	1	0	0	0	0	3.00

BA	OBA	SA	AB	H	2B	3B	HR	RBI	BB	SO
.333	.320	.458	24	8	3	0	0	2	0	2
.429	.400	.643	14	6	3	0	0	2	0	1
.200	.200	.200	10	2	0	0	0	0	0	1
.429	.429	.571	14	6	2	0	0	0	0	1
.200	.182	.300	10	2	1	0	0	2	0	1

JERRY GLEATON — bats left — throws left — age 35 — DET — P

1991	G	IP	H	BB	SO	SB	CS	W	L	SV	ERA
at Home	20	34.1	28	15	19	3	1	2	1	0	4.46
on Road	27	41.0	46	24	28	5	5	1	1	2	3.73

	BA	OBA	SA	AB	H	2B	3B	HR	RBI	BB	SO
Total	.269	.355	.415	275	74	11	4	7	39	39	47
vs. Left	.263	.301	.395	76	20	1	3	1	12	5	14
vs. Right	.271	.374	.422	199	54	10	1	6	27	34	33
Bases Empty	.282	.346	.415	142	40	6	2	3	3	14	24
Runners On Base	.256	.364	.414	133	34	5	2	4	36	25	23

7-YEAR TOTALS (1984–1991)

G	IP	H	BB	SO	SB	CS	W	L	SV	ERA
123	157.0	130	65	108	9	6	3	6	14	4.18
128	151.2	154	69	103	7	10	7	9	12	3.74

BA	OBA	SA	AB	H	2B	3B	HR	RBI	BB	SO
.252	.330	.365	1129	284	43	8	23	161	134	211
.249	.306	.352	369	92	12	4	6	63	29	70
.253	.342	.371	760	192	31	4	17	98	105	141
.274	.350	.394	541	148	24	4	11	11	62	96
.231	.313	.338	588	136	19	4	12	150	72	115

TOM GORDON — bats right — throws right — age 25 — KC — P

1991	G	IP	H	BB	SO	SB	CS	W	L	SV	ERA
at Home	22	92.1	77	46	93	8	6	2	8	1	4.00
on Road	23	65.2	52	41	74	1	1	7	6	0	3.70

	BA	OBA	SA	AB	H	2B	3B	HR	RBI	BB	SO
Total	.221	.324	.357	585	129	16	8	16	63	87	167
vs. Left	.253	.343	.350	297	75	7	5	4	31	41	80
vs. Right	.188	.305	.365	288	54	9	3	12	32	46	87
Bases Empty	.246	.325	.402	333	82	13	3	11	11	38	88
Runners On Base	.187	.322	.298	252	47	3	5	5	52	49	79

4-YEAR TOTALS (1988–1991)

	G	IP	H	BB	SO	SB	CS	W	L	SV	ERA
	68	290.1	243	138	275	16	13	20	19	1	3.60
	63	241.2	216	141	238	13	10	18	17	1	4.02

	BA	OBA	SA	AB	H	2B	3B	HR	RBI	BB	SO
	.233	.329	.353	1972	459	68	19	44	225	279	513
	.241	.338	.333	993	239	32	9	14	103	145	228
	.225	.320	.374	979	220	36	10	30	122	134	285
	.234	.324	.369	1099	257	39	11	29	29	145	280
	.231	.335	.334	873	202	29	8	15	196	134	233

RICH GOSSAGE — bats right — throws right — age 41 — TEX — P

1991	G	IP	H	BB	SO	SB	CS	W	L	SV	ERA
at Home	24	22.1	17	6	16	1	1	2	0	1	2.01
on Road	20	18.0	16	10	12	1	1	2	2	0	5.50

	BA	OBA	SA	AB	H	2B	3B	HR	RBI	BB	SO
Total	.228	.317	.366	145	33	6	1	4	31	16	28
vs. Left	.178	.260	.311	45	8	3	0	1	7	5	5
vs. Right	.250	.342	.390	100	25	3	1	3	24	11	23
Bases Empty	.237	.308	.339	59	14	3	0	1	1	4	9
Runners On Base	.221	.323	.384	86	19	3	1	3	30	12	19

7-YEAR TOTALS (1984–1991)

	G	IP	H	BB	SO	SB	CS	W	L	SV	ERA
	162	210.2	183	55	159	14	6	22	12	55	2.65
	167	229.0	201	99	171	26	13	14	15	47	3.66

	BA	OBA	SA	AB	H	2B	3B	HR	RBI	BB	SO
	.238	.306	.341	1615	384	63	10	28	221	154	330
	.250	.328	.365	765	191	35	7	13	107	95	137
	.227	.284	.320	850	193	28	3	15	114	59	193
	.219	.283	.297	844	185	31	4	9	9	69	193
	.258	.329	.389	771	199	32	6	19	212	85	137

JIM GOTT — bats right — throws right — age 33 — LA — P

1991	G	IP	H	BB	SO	SB	CS	W	L	SV	ERA
at Home	27	37.0	23	21	41	5	1	1	0	1	2.68
on Road	28	39.0	40	11	32	3	0	3	3	1	3.23

	BA	OBA	SA	AB	H	2B	3B	HR	RBI	BB	SO
Total	.223	.304	.312	282	63	6	2	5	24	32	73
vs. Left	.194	.282	.273	139	27	1	2	2	9	17	34
vs. Right	.252	.325	.350	143	36	5	0	3	15	15	39
Bases Empty	.238	.284	.279	172	41	4	0	1	1	11	42
Runners On Base	.200	.331	.364	110	22	2	2	4	23	21	31

8-YEAR TOTALS (1984–1991)

	G	IP	H	BB	SO	SB	CS	W	L	SV	ERA
	149	307.1	238	125	255	18	15	16	13	29	2.90
	149	266.2	287	117	189	17	7	12	19	26	4.49

	BA	OBA	SA	AB	H	2B	3B	HR	RBI	BB	SO
	.244	.321	.357	2149	525	91	16	40	243	242	444
	.244	.332	.358	1070	261	45	10	19	114	142	213
	.245	.309	.357	1079	264	46	6	21	129	100	231
	.232	.305	.339	1208	280	51	8	21	21	120	252
	.260	.340	.380	941	245	40	8	19	222	122	192

MAURO GOZZO — bats right — throws right — age 26 — CLE — P

1991	G	IP	H	BB	SO	SB	CS	W	L	SV	ERA
at Home	1	1.2	4	4	1	0	0	0	0	0	27.00
on Road	1	3.0	5	3	2	1	0	0	0	0	15.00

	BA	OBA	SA	AB	H	2B	3B	HR	RBI	BB	SO
Total	.450	.571	.700	20	9	5	0	0	6	7	3
vs. Left	.357	.471	.571	14	5	3	0	0	4	3	2
vs. Right	.667	.727	1.000	6	4	2	0	0	2	4	1
Bases Empty	.429	.636	.571	7	3	1	0	0	0	4	1
Runners On Base	.462	.529	.769	13	6	4	0	0	6	3	2

3-YEAR TOTALS (1989–1991)

	G	IP	H	BB	SO	SB	CS	W	L	SV	ERA
	8	22.1	26	12	8	0	0	2	1	0	7.66
	5	17.0	20	6	7	2	0	2	0	0	4.24

	BA	OBA	SA	AB	H	2B	3B	HR	RBI	BB	SO
	.303	.374	.428	152	46	14	1	1	21	18	15
	.339	.394	.435	62	21	6	0	1	10	7	6
	.278	.359	.422	90	25	8	1	1	11	11	9
	.294	.407	.397	68	20	5	1	0	0	13	9
	.310	.344	.452	84	26	9	0	1	21	5	6

JOE GRAHE — bats right — throws right — age 25 — CAL — P

1991	G	IP	H	BB	SO	SB	CS	W	L	SV	ERA
at Home	9	43.1	42	16	20	6	3	1	3	0	3.53
on Road	9	29.2	42	17	20	3	2	2	4	0	6.67

	BA	OBA	SA	AB	H	2B	3B	HR	RBI	BB	SO
Total	.288	.365	.397	292	84	20	3	2	41	33	40
vs. Left	.303	.367	.430	142	43	13	1	1	20	15	22
vs. Right	.273	.363	.367	150	41	7	2	1	21	18	18
Bases Empty	.240	.312	.331	154	37	8	0	2	2	14	23
Runners On Base	.341	.421	.471	138	47	12	3	0	39	19	17

2-YEAR TOTALS (1990–1991)

	G	IP	H	BB	SO	SB	CS	W	L	SV	ERA
	13	62.1	71	24	33	8	3	2	5	0	4.76
	13	54.0	64	32	32	4	3	4	6	0	5.00

	BA	OBA	SA	AB	H	2B	3B	HR	RBI	BB	SO
	.290	.372	.412	466	135	32	5	5	67	56	65
	.327	.389	.493	223	73	19	3	4	36	22	30
	.255	.358	.337	243	62	13	2	1	31	34	35
	.266	.328	.371	248	66	14	0	4	4	21	39
	.317	.419	.459	218	69	18	5	1	63	35	26

MARK GRATER — bats right — throws right — age 28 — SL — P

1991	G	IP	H	BB	SO	SB	CS	W	L	SV	ERA
at Home	1	0.2	0	0	0	0	0	0	0	0	0.00
on Road	2	2.1	5	2	0	0	1	0	0	0	0.00

	BA	OBA	SA	AB	H	2B	3B	HR	RBI	BB	SO
Total	.385	.467	.385	13	5	0	0	0	1	2	0
vs. Left	.333	.400	.333	9	3	0	0	0	0	1	0
vs. Right	.500	.600	.500	4	2	0	0	0	1	1	0
Bases Empty	.750	.800	.750	4	3	0	0	0	0	1	0
Runners On Base	.222	.300	.222	9	2	0	0	0	1	1	0

1-YEAR TOTALS (1991)

	G	IP	H	BB	SO	SB	CS	W	L	SV	ERA
	1	0.2	0	0	0	0	0	0	0	0	0.00
	2	2.1	5	2	0	0	1	0	0	0	0.00

	BA	OBA	SA	AB	H	2B	3B	HR	RBI	BB	SO
	.385	.467	.385	13	5	0	0	0	1	2	0
	.333	.400	.333	9	3	0	0	0	0	1	0
	.500	.600	.500	4	2	0	0	0	1	1	0
	.750	.800	.750	4	3	0	0	0	0	1	0
	.222	.300	.222	9	2	0	0	0	1	1	0

JASON GRIMSLEY — bats right — throws right — age 25 — PHI — P

1991	G	IP	H	BB	SO	SB	CS	W	L	SV	ERA
at Home	4	23.1	17	15	15	6	0	1	2	0	3.47
on Road	8	37.2	37	26	27	8	1	0	5	0	5.73

	BA	OBA	SA	AB	H	2B	3B	HR	RBI	BB	SO
Total	.242	.364	.368	223	54	12	2	4	23	41	42
vs. Left	.262	.398	.369	130	34	6	1	2	11	29	29
vs. Right	.215	.315	.366	93	20	6	1	2	12	12	13
Bases Empty	.286	.393	.429	119	34	8	0	3	3	20	24
Runners On Base	.192	.333	.298	104	20	4	2	1	20	21	18

3-YEAR TOTALS (1989–1991)

	G	IP	H	BB	SO	SB	CS	W	L	SV	ERA
	11	58.2	47	40	38	8	0	1	5	0	4.14
	16	78.0	73	63	52	11	6	4	7	0	4.50

	BA	OBA	SA	AB	H	2B	3B	HR	RBI	BB	SO
	.240	.373	.345	501	120	22	5	7	47	103	90
	.239	.380	.337	297	71	11	3	4	26	66	54
	.240	.361	.358	204	49	11	2	3	21	37	36
	.255	.365	.373	271	69	15	1	5	5	46	47
	.222	.381	.313	230	51	7	4	2	42	57	43

KEVIN GROSS — bats right — throws right — age 31 — LA — P

8-YEAR TOTALS (1984–1991)

1991	G	IP	H	BB	SO	SB	CS	W	L	SV	ERA
at Home	22	61.1	59	21	58	10	4	7	3	1	2.79
on Road	24	54.1	64	29	37	5	2	3	8	2	4.47

	BA	OBA	SA	AB	H	2B	3B	HR	RBI	BB	SO
Total	.275	.348	.380	447	123	13	2	10	48	50	95
vs. Left	.312	.396	.443	237	74	9	2	6	32	34	44
vs. Right	.233	.291	.310	210	49	4	0	4	16	16	51
Bases Empty	.256	.320	.380	266	68	7	1	8	8	25	61
Runners On Base	.304	.387	.381	181	55	6	1	2	40	25	34

G	IP	H	BB	SO	SB	CS	W	L	SV	ERA
147	759.1	715	290	549	106	40	47	44	1	3.72
147	729.2	754	308	476	120	37	39	51	3	4.32

BA	OBA	SA	AB	H	2B	3B	HR	RBI	BB	SO
.259	.333	.386	5677	1469	229	53	130	631	598	1025
.268	.357	.404	3122	838	142	37	69	355	413	539
.247	.302	.365	2555	631	87	16	61	276	185	486
.257	.327	.400	3258	837	124	25	97	97	307	597
.261	.341	.369	2419	632	105	28	33	534	291	428

KIP GROSS — bats right — throws right — age 28 — CIN — P

2-YEAR TOTALS (1990–1991)

1991	G	IP	H	BB	SO	SB	CS	W	L	SV	ERA
at Home	13	36.1	45	18	15	3	2	1	3	0	4.71
on Road	16	49.1	48	22	25	5	1	5	1	0	2.55

	BA	OBA	SA	AB	H	2B	3B	HR	RBI	BB	SO
Total	.279	.355	.393	333	93	12	1	8	41	40	40
vs. Left	.306	.385	.421	183	56	3	0	6	26	24	21
vs. Right	.247	.317	.360	150	37	9	1	2	15	16	19
Bases Empty	.266	.335	.359	184	49	6	1	3	3	19	22
Runners On Base	.295	.378	.436	149	44	6	0	5	38	21	18

G	IP	H	BB	SO	SB	CS	W	L	SV	ERA
16	40.1	49	20	17	3	3	1	3	0	4.69
18	51.2	50	22	26	6	1	5	1	0	2.61

BA	OBA	SA	AB	H	2B	3B	HR	RBI	BB	SO
.279	.352	.386	355	99	12	1	8	44	42	43
.297	.373	.406	192	57	3	0	6	26	24	23
.258	.328	.362	163	42	9	1	2	18	18	20
.260	.324	.345	200	52	6	1	3	3	19	25
.303	.387	.439	155	47	6	0	5	41	23	18

ERIC GUNDERSON — bats right — throws left — age 26 — SF — P

2-YEAR TOTALS (1990–1991)

1991	G	IP	H	BB	SO	SB	CS	W	L	SV	ERA
at Home	0	0.0	0	0	0	0	0	0	0	0	0.00
on Road	2	3.1	6	1	2	0	0	0	0	1	5.40

	BA	OBA	SA	AB	H	2B	3B	HR	RBI	BB	SO
Total	.353	.389	.471	17	6	2	0	0	5	1	2
vs. Left	.000	.333	.000	2	0	0	0	0	0	1	0
vs. Right	.400	.400	.533	15	6	2	0	0	5	0	2
Bases Empty	.286	.286	.429	7	2	1	0	0	0	0	0
Runners On Base	.400	.455	.500	10	4	1	0	0	5	1	2

G	IP	H	BB	SO	SB	CS	W	L	SV	ERA
4	13.1	16	7	11	0	2	0	1	0	4.05
5	9.2	14	5	5	2	0	1	1	1	7.45

BA	OBA	SA	AB	H	2B	3B	HR	RBI	BB	SO
.303	.378	.414	99	30	5	0	2	19	12	16
.263	.364	.263	19	5	0	0	0	4	3	2
.313	.382	.450	80	25	5	0	2	15	9	14
.208	.276	.264	53	11	3	0	0	0	5	6
.413	.491	.587	46	19	2	0	2	19	7	10

MARK GUTHRIE — bats both — throws right — age 27 — MIN — P

3-YEAR TOTALS (1989–1991)

1991	G	IP	H	BB	SO	SB	CS	W	L	SV	ERA
at Home	20	44.2	60	17	40	4	2	1	4	1	6.25
on Road	21	53.1	56	24	32	5	3	6	1	1	2.70

	BA	OBA	SA	AB	H	2B	3B	HR	RBI	BB	SO
Total	.303	.369	.465	383	116	19	5	11	46	41	72
vs. Left	.337	.383	.500	86	29	2	0	4	10	7	14
vs. Right	.293	.365	.455	297	87	17	5	7	36	34	58
Bases Empty	.365	.432	.548	197	72	14	2	6	6	22	30
Runners On Base	.237	.303	.376	186	44	5	3	5	40	19	42

G	IP	H	BB	SO	SB	CS	W	L	SV	ERA
37	146.0	164	45	121	11	11	5	9	1	4.44
41	154.0	172	56	90	20	12	11	9	1	3.80

BA	OBA	SA	AB	H	2B	3B	HR	RBI	BB	SO
.288	.344	.415	1166	336	58	6	26	131	101	211
.332	.365	.459	229	76	8	0	7	28	12	32
.277	.339	.404	937	260	50	6	19	103	89	179
.308	.368	.433	656	202	39	2	13	13	61	110
.263	.314	.392	510	134	19	4	13	118	40	101

JUAN GUZMAN — bats right — throws right — age 26 — TOR — P

1-YEAR TOTALS (1991)

1991	G	IP	H	BB	SO	SB	CS	W	L	SV	ERA
at Home	11	63.2	47	34	62	8	4	5	1	0	3.82
on Road	12	75.0	51	32	61	4	2	5	2	0	2.28

	BA	OBA	SA	AB	H	2B	3B	HR	RBI	BB	SO
Total	.197	.294	.268	497	98	13	2	6	45	66	123
vs. Left	.188	.290	.235	234	44	6	1	1	14	34	49
vs. Right	.205	.297	.297	263	54	7	1	5	31	32	74
Bases Empty	.193	.308	.251	275	53	7	0	3	3	43	67
Runners On Base	.203	.275	.288	222	45	6	2	3	42	23	56

G	IP	H	BB	SO	SB	CS	W	L	SV	ERA
11	63.2	47	34	62	8	4	5	1	0	3.82
12	75.0	51	32	61	4	2	5	2	0	2.28

BA	OBA	SA	AB	H	2B	3B	HR	RBI	BB	SO
.197	.294	.268	497	98	13	2	6	45	66	123
.188	.290	.235	234	44	6	1	1	14	34	49
.205	.297	.297	263	54	7	1	5	31	32	74
.193	.308	.251	275	53	7	0	3	3	43	67
.203	.275	.288	222	45	6	2	3	42	23	56

JOHNNY GUZMAN — bats right — throws left — age 21 — OAK — P

1-YEAR TOTALS (1991)

1991	G	IP	H	BB	SO	SB	CS	W	L	SV	ERA
at Home	4	3.0	4	2	0	0	0	1	0	0	6.00
on Road	1	2.0	7	0	3	0	0	0	0	0	13.50

	BA	OBA	SA	AB	H	2B	3B	HR	RBI	BB	SO
Total	.500	.542	.682	22	11	4	0	0	5	2	3
vs. Left	.500	.500	.667	6	3	1	0	0	3	0	1
vs. Right	.500	.556	.688	16	8	3	0	0	2	2	2
Bases Empty	1.000	1.000	1.750	4	4	3	0	0	0	0	0
Runners On Base	.389	.450	.444	18	7	1	0	0	5	2	3

G	IP	H	BB	SO	SB	CS	W	L	SV	ERA
4	3.0	4	2	0	0	0	1	0	0	6.00
1	2.0	7	0	3	0	0	0	0	0	13.50

BA	OBA	SA	AB	H	2B	3B	HR	RBI	BB	SO
.500	.542	.682	22	11	4	0	0	5	2	3
.500	.500	.667	6	3	1	0	0	3	0	1
.500	.556	.688	16	8	3	0	0	2	2	2
1.000	1.000	1.750	4	4	3	0	0	0	0	0
.389	.450	.444	18	7	1	0	0	5	2	3

DAVE HAAS — bats right — throws right — age 27 — DET — P

1-YEAR TOTALS (1991)

1991	G	IP	H	BB	SO	SB	CS	W	L	SV	ERA
at Home	6	7.1	5	6	4	0	1	0	0	0	2.45
on Road	5	3.1	3	6	2	0	0	1	0	0	16.20

	BA	OBA	SA	AB	H	2B	3B	HR	RBI	BB	SO
Total	.242	.438	.364	33	8	1	0	1	8	12	6
vs. Left	.167	.286	.167	6	1	0	0	0	1	1	0
vs. Right	.259	.463	.407	27	7	1	0	1	7	11	6
Bases Empty	.143	.368	.429	14	2	1	0	1	1	5	3
Runners On Base	.316	.483	.316	19	6	0	0	0	7	7	3

G	IP	H	BB	SO	SB	CS	W	L	SV	ERA
6	7.1	5	6	4	0	1	0	0	0	2.45
5	3.1	3	6	2	0	0	1	0	0	16.20

BA	OBA	SA	AB	H	2B	3B	HR	RBI	BB	SO
.242	.438	.364	33	8	1	0	1	8	12	6
.167	.286	.167	6	1	0	0	0	1	1	0
.259	.463	.407	27	7	1	0	1	7	11	6
.143	.368	.429	14	2	1	0	1	1	5	3
.316	.483	.316	19	6	0	0	0	7	7	3

JOHN HABYAN — bats right — throws right — age 29 — NYA — P

1991	G	IP	H	BB	SO	SB	CS	W	L	SV	ERA
at Home	30	47.1	32	9	35	2	1	3	0	2	1.33
on Road	36	42.2	41	11	35	2	0	1	2	0	3.38

	BA	OBA	SA	AB	H	2B	3B	HR	RBI	BB	SO
Total	.225	.274	.315	324	73	17	3	2	35	20	70
vs. Left	.268	.303	.348	112	30	7	1	0	16	6	16
vs. Right	.203	.259	.297	212	43	10	2	2	19	14	54
Bases Empty	.211	.257	.278	180	38	7	1	1	1	9	40
Runners On Base	.243	.295	.361	144	35	10	2	1	34	11	30

6-YEAR TOTALS (1985–1991)

	G	IP	H	BB	SO	SB	CS	W	L	SV	ERA
	53	134.0	126	35	76	12	5	5	2	5	3.83
	61	124.2	116	49	82	11	3	5	7	1	3.61

	BA	OBA	SA	AB	H	2B	3B	HR	RBI	BB	SO
	.249	.310	.405	971	242	50	10	27	120	84	158
	.265	.323	.417	465	123	25	8	10	49	41	53
	.235	.298	.393	506	119	25	2	17	71	43	105
	.253	.298	.413	574	145	29	3	19	19	35	93
	.244	.326	.393	397	97	21	7	8	101	49	65

ATLEE HAMMAKER — bats both — throws left — age 34 — SD — P

1991	G	IP	H	BB	SO	SB	CS	W	L	SV	ERA
at Home	1	4.2	8	3	1	1	0	0	1	0	5.79
on Road	0	0.0	0	0	0	0	0	0	0	0	0.00

	BA	OBA	SA	AB	H	2B	3B	HR	RBI	BB	SO
Total	.364	.440	.409	22	8	1	0	0	4	3	1
vs. Left	.250	.250	.250	4	1	0	0	0	0	0	0
vs. Right	.389	.476	.444	18	7	1	0	0	4	3	1
Bases Empty	.600	.750	.600	5	3	0	0	0	0	3	1
Runners On Base	.294	.294	.353	17	5	1	0	0	4	0	0

7-YEAR TOTALS (1984–1991)

	G	IP	H	BB	SO	SB	CS	W	L	SV	ERA
	88	383.1	341	100	208	34	12	23	17	2	3.31
	84	301.1	318	106	163	40	13	13	30	3	4.24

	BA	OBA	SA	AB	H	2B	3B	HR	RBI	BB	SO
	.253	.307	.373	2603	659	96	11	65	273	206	371
	.214	.273	.286	462	99	12	3	5	32	34	87
	.262	.315	.392	2141	560	84	8	60	241	172	284
	.244	.290	.374	1596	389	57	8	45	45	102	234
	.268	.333	.372	1007	270	39	3	20	228	104	137

CHRIS HAMMOND — bats left — throws left — age 26 — CIN — P

1991	G	IP	H	BB	SO	SB	CS	W	L	SV	ERA
at Home	10	45.2	46	26	26	6	2	3	0	0	4.73
on Road	10	54.0	46	22	24	2	1	4	4	0	3.50

	BA	OBA	SA	AB	H	2B	3B	HR	RBI	BB	SO
Total	.250	.339	.340	368	92	17	2	4	42	48	50
vs. Left	.188	.291	.260	96	18	2	1	1	11	13	14
vs. Right	.272	.356	.368	272	74	15	1	3	31	35	36
Bases Empty	.237	.326	.318	211	50	9	1	2	2	27	33
Runners On Base	.268	.356	.369	157	42	8	1	2	40	21	17

2-YEAR TOTALS (1990–1991)

	G	IP	H	BB	SO	SB	CS	W	L	SV	ERA
	12	52.2	56	33	29	7	3	3	4	0	4.96
	11	58.1	49	27	25	2	1	4	5	0	3.70

	BA	OBA	SA	AB	H	2B	3B	HR	RBI	BB	SO
	.255	.352	.358	411	105	20	2	6	49	60	54
	.211	.323	.339	109	23	3	1	3	14	17	15
	.272	.363	.364	302	82	17	1	3	35	43	39
	.238	.337	.345	235	56	11	1	4	4	34	37
	.278	.373	.375	176	49	9	1	2	45	26	17

CHRIS HANEY — bats left — throws left — age 24 — MON — P

1991	G	IP	H	BB	SO	SB	CS	W	L	SV	ERA
at Home	7	44.1	40	16	27	2	1	3	2	0	2.44
on Road	9	40.0	54	27	24	6	5	0	5	0	5.85

	BA	OBA	SA	AB	H	2B	3B	HR	RBI	BB	SO
Total	.281	.363	.406	335	94	20	2	6	41	43	51
vs. Left	.183	.347	.250	60	11	2	1	0	6	14	13
vs. Right	.302	.367	.440	275	83	18	1	6	35	29	38
Bases Empty	.282	.365	.397	174	49	12	1	2	2	22	28
Runners On Base	.280	.361	.416	161	45	8	1	4	39	21	23

1-YEAR TOTALS (1991)

	G	IP	H	BB	SO	SB	CS	W	L	SV	ERA
	7	44.1	40	16	27	2	1	3	2	0	2.44
	9	40.0	54	27	24	6	5	0	5	0	5.85

	BA	OBA	SA	AB	H	2B	3B	HR	RBI	BB	SO
	.281	.363	.406	335	94	20	2	6	41	43	51
	.183	.347	.250	60	11	2	1	0	6	14	13
	.302	.367	.440	275	83	18	1	6	35	29	38
	.282	.365	.397	174	49	12	1	2	2	22	28
	.280	.361	.416	161	45	8	1	4	39	21	23

MIKE HARKEY — bats right — throws right — age 26 — CHN — P

1991	G	IP	H	BB	SO	SB	CS	W	L	SV	ERA
at Home	2	10.1	15	3	6	2	0	0	1	0	6.10
on Road	2	8.1	6	3	9	0	0	0	1	0	4.32

	BA	OBA	SA	AB	H	2B	3B	HR	RBI	BB	SO
Total	.273	.321	.442	77	21	4	0	4	11	6	15
vs. Left	.263	.333	.395	38	10	2	0	1	7	4	10
vs. Right	.282	.310	.487	39	11	2	0	3	4	2	5
Bases Empty	.238	.304	.429	42	10	2	0	2	2	4	11
Runners On Base	.314	.342	.457	35	11	2	0	2	9	2	4

3-YEAR TOTALS (1988–1991)

	G	IP	H	BB	SO	SB	CS	W	L	SV	ERA
	17	117.1	114	37	63	5	9	5	4	0	2.76
	19	109.2	93	43	64	8	2	7	7	0	3.94

	BA	OBA	SA	AB	H	2B	3B	HR	RBI	BB	SO
	.240	.309	.364	863	207	40	8	17	83	80	127
	.243	.310	.359	510	124	27	4	8	46	49	71
	.235	.309	.371	353	83	13	4	9	37	31	56
	.243	.293	.389	522	127	29	4	13	13	33	81
	.235	.332	.326	341	80	11	4	4	70	47	46

REGGIE HARRIS — bats right — throws right — age 24 — OAK — P

1991	G	IP	H	BB	SO	SB	CS	W	L	SV	ERA
at Home	0	0.0	0	0	0	0	0	0	0	0	0.00
on Road	2	3.0	5	3	2	1	0	0	0	0	12.00

	BA	OBA	SA	AB	H	2B	3B	HR	RBI	BB	SO
Total	.455	.533	.545	11	5	1	0	0	3	3	2
vs. Left	.500	.500	.500	4	2	0	0	0	2	1	0
vs. Right	.429	.556	.571	7	3	1	0	0	1	2	2
Bases Empty	.400	.500	.400	5	2	0	0	0	0	1	1
Runners On Base	.500	.556	.667	6	3	1	0	0	3	2	1

2-YEAR TOTALS (1990–1991)

	G	IP	H	BB	SO	SB	CS	W	L	SV	ERA
	7	20.0	9	8	13	2	0	0	0	0	0.90
	11	24.1	21	16	20	2	0	1	0	0	6.66

	BA	OBA	SA	AB	H	2B	3B	HR	RBI	BB	SO
	.196	.308	.327	153	30	5	0	5	19	24	33
	.232	.333	.391	69	16	2	0	3	10	11	16
	.167	.287	.274	84	14	3	0	2	9	13	17
	.165	.304	.294	85	14	2	0	3	3	15	18
	.235	.313	.368	68	16	3	0	2	16	9	15

GENE HARRIS — bats right — throws right — age 28 — SEA — P

1991	G	IP	H	BB	SO	SB	CS	W	L	SV	ERA
at Home	6	12.1	11	8	5	0	0	0	0	1	2.19
on Road	2	1.0	4	2	1	0	0	0	0	0	27.00

	BA	OBA	SA	AB	H	2B	3B	HR	RBI	BB	SO
Total	.273	.385	.400	55	15	4	0	1	4	10	6
vs. Left	.227	.414	.364	22	5	3	0	0	2	7	3
vs. Right	.303	.361	.424	33	10	1	0	1	2	3	3
Bases Empty	.231	.355	.423	26	6	2	0	1	1	5	2
Runners On Base	.310	.412	.379	29	9	2	0	0	3	5	4

3-YEAR TOTALS (1989–1991)

	G	IP	H	BB	SO	SB	CS	W	L	SV	ERA
	28	61.2	53	36	44	5	1	3	2	1	3.94
	26	43.0	56	29	30	6	2	0	5	1	7.12

	BA	OBA	SA	AB	H	2B	3B	HR	RBI	BB	SO
	.275	.374	.431	397	109	24	4	10	66	65	74
	.306	.423	.472	180	55	16	1	4	30	38	23
	.249	.332	.396	217	54	8	3	6	36	27	51
	.268	.374	.448	194	52	11	3	6	6	32	37
	.281	.374	.414	203	57	13	1	4	60	33	37

MIKE HARTLEY — bats right — throws right — age 31 — LA/PHI — P

1991	G	IP	H	BB	SO	SB	CS	W	L	SV	ERA
at Home	31	43.0	44	23	37	7	1	3	0	0	4.19
on Road	27	40.1	30	24	26	6	0	1	1	2	4.24

	BA	OBA	SA	AB	H	2B	3B	HR	RBI	BB	SO
Total	.237	.347	.388	312	74	10	2	11	44	47	63
vs. Left	.239	.342	.384	159	38	4	2	5	18	25	24
vs. Right	.235	.352	.392	153	36	6	0	6	26	22	39
Bases Empty	.261	.360	.416	161	42	4	0	7	7	21	34
Runners On Base	.212	.333	.358	151	32	6	2	4	37	26	29

3-YEAR TOTALS (1989–1991)

G	IP	H	BB	SO	SB	CS	W	L	SV	ERA
49	90.1	66	35	82	14	2	7	1	1	2.69
46	78.1	68	42	61	13	0	3	4	2	4.48

BA	OBA	SA	AB	H	2B	3B	HR	RBI	BB	SO
.215	.309	.349	622	134	19	5	18	74	77	143
.217	.322	.337	323	70	8	5	7	28	49	66
.214	.295	.361	299	64	11	0	11	46	28	77
.202	.294	.302	361	73	8	2	8	8	42	90
.234	.329	.414	261	61	11	3	10	66	35	53

ANDY HAWKINS — bats right — throws right — age 32 — NYA/OAK — P

1991	G	IP	H	BB	SO	SB	CS	W	L	SV	ERA
at Home	9	46.2	45	18	23	3	3	1	4	0	5.21
on Road	10	43.0	46	24	22	4	3	3	2	0	5.86

	BA	OBA	SA	AB	H	2B	3B	HR	RBI	BB	SO
Total	.262	.348	.418	347	91	16	4	10	53	42	45
vs. Left	.244	.363	.375	176	43	7	2	4	22	33	14
vs. Right	.281	.330	.462	171	48	9	2	6	31	9	31
Bases Empty	.220	.322	.312	205	45	8	1	3	3	27	24
Runners On Base	.324	.385	.570	142	46	8	3	7	50	15	21

8-YEAR TOTALS (1984–1991)

G	IP	H	BB	SO	SB	CS	W	L	SV	ERA
131	777.0	781	280	341	48	35	42	46	0	3.93
113	598.1	621	256	281	42	31	35	33	0	4.87

BA	OBA	SA	AB	H	2B	3B	HR	RBI	BB	SO
.267	.336	.410	5258	1402	264	34	140	631	536	622
.292	.373	.440	2636	770	150	21	66	309	347	254
.241	.296	.379	2622	632	114	13	74	322	189	368
.262	.324	.406	3127	819	160	22	82	82	275	380
.274	.352	.415	2131	583	104	12	58	549	261	242

NEAL HEATON — bats left — throws left — age 32 — PIT — P

1991	G	IP	H	BB	SO	SB	CS	W	L	SV	ERA
at Home	17	31.1	37	11	15	2	1	1	2	0	5.17
on Road	25	37.1	35	10	19	7	1	2	1	0	3.62

	BA	OBA	SA	AB	H	2B	3B	HR	RBI	BB	SO
Total	.275	.334	.401	262	72	15	0	6	36	21	34
vs. Left	.350	.379	.463	80	28	3	0	2	12	4	15
vs. Right	.242	.315	.374	182	44	12	0	4	24	17	19
Bases Empty	.243	.309	.365	148	36	9	0	3	3	11	13
Runners On Base	.316	.367	.447	114	36	6	0	3	33	10	21

8-YEAR TOTALS (1984–1991)

G	IP	H	BB	SO	SB	CS	W	L	SV	ERA
138	657.1	672	216	303	49	36	34	39	1	3.75
147	600.1	651	214	261	68	26	31	47	2	5.01

BA	OBA	SA	AB	H	2B	3B	HR	RBI	BB	SO
.274	.334	.424	4829	1323	248	29	140	583	430	564
.267	.320	.415	950	254	51	7	25	114	72	141
.276	.337	.427	3879	1069	197	22	115	469	358	423
.274	.330	.424	2858	784	141	17	84	84	221	331
.273	.340	.425	1971	539	107	12	56	499	209	233

DWAYNE HENRY — bats right — throws right — age 30 — HOU — P

1991	G	IP	H	BB	SO	SB	CS	W	L	SV	ERA
at Home	28	38.2	29	26	32	5	2	3	1	2	3.26
on Road	24	29.0	22	13	19	1	1	0	1	0	3.10

	BA	OBA	SA	AB	H	2B	3B	HR	RBI	BB	SO
Total	.219	.333	.361	233	51	10	1	7	39	39	51
vs. Left	.227	.352	.371	132	30	5	1	4	23	25	30
vs. Right	.208	.308	.347	101	21	5	0	3	16	14	21
Bases Empty	.199	.283	.360	136	27	5	1	5	5	16	41
Runners On Base	.247	.395	.361	97	24	5	0	2	34	23	10

8-YEAR TOTALS (1984–1991)

G	IP	H	BB	SO	SB	CS	W	L	SV	ERA
79	99.1	86	60	88	7	4	7	4	5	4.71
73	84.1	80	63	69	7	3	1	6	2	4.48

BA	OBA	SA	AB	H	2B	3B	HR	RBI	BB	SO
.245	.362	.373	678	166	31	4	16	120	123	157
.231	.363	.352	324	75	15	3	6	52	68	75
.257	.362	.393	354	91	16	1	10	68	55	82
.196	.311	.313	342	67	11	1	9	9	55	99
.295	.412	.435	336	99	20	3	7	111	68	58

DOUG HENRY — bats right — throws right — age 29 — MIL — P

1991	G	IP	H	BB	SO	SB	CS	W	L	SV	ERA
at Home	15	17.0	6	7	20	0	1	1	0	7	0.53
on Road	17	19.0	10	7	8	0	0	1	1	8	1.42

	BA	OBA	SA	AB	H	2B	3B	HR	RBI	BB	SO
Total	.133	.221	.208	120	16	6	0	1	7	14	28
vs. Left	.119	.221	.203	59	7	5	0	0	2	8	14
vs. Right	.148	.221	.213	61	9	1	0	1	5	6	14
Bases Empty	.157	.234	.257	70	11	4	0	1	1	7	19
Runners On Base	.100	.203	.140	50	5	2	0	0	6	7	9

1-YEAR TOTALS (1991)

G	IP	H	BB	SO	SB	CS	W	L	SV	ERA
15	17.0	6	7	20	0	1	1	0	7	0.53
17	19.0	10	7	8	0	0	1	1	8	1.42

BA	OBA	SA	AB	H	2B	3B	HR	RBI	BB	SO
.133	.221	.208	120	16	6	0	1	7	14	28
.119	.221	.203	59	7	5	0	0	2	8	14
.148	.221	.213	61	9	1	0	1	5	6	14
.157	.234	.257	70	11	4	0	1	1	7	19
.100	.203	.140	50	5	2	0	0	6	7	9

PAT HENTGEN — bats right — throws right — age 24 — TOR — P

1991	G	IP	H	BB	SO	SB	CS	W	L	SV	ERA
at Home	2	2.1	2	2	1	0	0	0	0	0	3.86
on Road	1	5.0	3	1	2	1	0	0	0	0	1.80

	BA	OBA	SA	AB	H	2B	3B	HR	RBI	BB	SO
Total	.208	.345	.417	24	5	2	0	1	2	3	3
vs. Left	.333	.500	.833	6	2	0	0	1	2	1	0
vs. Right	.167	.286	.278	18	3	2	0	0	0	2	3
Bases Empty	.235	.350	.529	17	4	2	0	1	1	1	3
Runners On Base	.143	.333	.143	7	1	0	0	0	1	2	0

1-YEAR TOTALS (1991)

G	IP	H	BB	SO	SB	CS	W	L	SV	ERA
2	2.1	2	2	1	0	0	0	0	0	3.86
1	5.0	3	1	2	1	0	0	0	0	1.80

BA	OBA	SA	AB	H	2B	3B	HR	RBI	BB	SO
.208	.345	.417	24	5	2	0	1	2	3	3
.333	.500	.833	6	2	0	0	1	2	1	0
.167	.286	.278	18	3	2	0	0	0	2	3
.235	.350	.529	17	4	2	0	1	1	1	3
.143	.333	.143	7	1	0	0	0	1	2	0

GIL HEREDIA — bats right — throws right — age 27 — SF — P

1991	G	IP	H	BB	SO	SB	CS	W	L	SV	ERA
at Home	5	25.0	18	4	11	1	1	0	2	0	3.96
on Road	2	8.0	9	3	2	1	1	0	0	0	3.38

	BA	OBA	SA	AB	H	2B	3B	HR	RBI	BB	SO
Total	.233	.274	.379	116	27	3	1	4	13	7	13
vs. Left	.224	.257	.358	67	15	1	1	2	5	3	5
vs. Right	.245	.296	.408	49	12	2	0	2	8	4	8
Bases Empty	.210	.247	.383	81	17	2	0	4	4	4	10
Runners On Base	.286	.333	.371	35	10	1	0	0	9	3	3

1-YEAR TOTALS (1991)

G	IP	H	BB	SO	SB	CS	W	L	SV	ERA
5	25.0	18	4	11	1	1	0	2	0	3.96
2	8.0	9	3	2	1	1	0	0	0	3.38

BA	OBA	SA	AB	H	2B	3B	HR	RBI	BB	SO
.233	.274	.379	116	27	3	1	4	13	7	13
.224	.257	.358	67	15	1	1	2	5	3	5
.245	.296	.408	49	12	2	0	2	8	4	8
.210	.247	.383	81	17	2	0	4	4	4	10
.286	.333	.371	35	10	1	0	0	9	3	3

XAVIER HERNANDEZ — bats left — throws right — age 27 — HOU — P

1991	G	IP	H	BB	SO	SB	CS	W	L	SV	ERA
at Home	14	28.1	21	13	22	2	0	1	3	1	3.18
on Road	18	34.2	45	19	33	5	2	1	4	2	5.97

	BA	OBA	SA	AB	H	2B	3B	HR	RBI	BB	SO
Total	.263	.345	.382	251	66	12	0	6	31	32	55
vs. Left	.215	.320	.277	130	28	5	0	1	17	20	31
vs. Right	.314	.373	.496	121	38	7	0	5	14	12	24
Bases Empty	.248	.333	.376	125	31	10	0	2	2	16	26
Runners On Base	.278	.357	.389	126	35	2	0	4	29	16	29

3-YEAR TOTALS (1989–1991)

G	IP	H	BB	SO	SB	CS	W	L	SV	ERA
34	68.1	50	23	39	7	3	3	3	1	2.90
39	79.2	101	41	47	9	2	5	5	2	6.21

BA	OBA	SA	AB	H	2B	3B	HR	RBI	BB	SO
.263	.338	.397	575	151	27	1	16	76	64	86
.265	.365	.366	279	74	11	1	5	37	43	37
.260	.311	.426	296	77	16	0	11	39	21	49
.261	.339	.399	303	79	15	0	9	9	33	46
.265	.337	.393	272	72	12	1	7	67	31	40

JEREMY HERNANDEZ — bats right — throws right — age 26 — SD — P

1991	G	IP	H	BB	SO	SB	CS	W	L	SV	ERA
at Home	5	9.0	6	3	6	0	0	0	0	2	0.00
on Road	4	5.1	2	2	3	0	0	0	0	0	0.00

	BA	OBA	SA	AB	H	2B	3B	HR	RBI	BB	SO
Total	.157	.232	.196	51	8	2	0	0	2	5	9
vs. Left	.115	.233	.115	26	3	0	0	0	1	4	4
vs. Right	.200	.231	.280	25	5	2	0	0	1	1	5
Bases Empty	.176	.222	.235	34	6	2	0	0	0	2	4
Runners On Base	.118	.250	.118	17	2	0	0	0	2	3	5

1-YEAR TOTALS (1991)

G	IP	H	BB	SO	SB	CS	W	L	SV	ERA
5	9.0	6	3	6	0	0	0	0	2	0.00
4	5.1	2	2	3	0	0	0	0	0	0.00

BA	OBA	SA	AB	H	2B	3B	HR	RBI	BB	SO
.157	.232	.196	51	8	2	0	0	2	5	9
.115	.233	.115	26	3	0	0	0	1	4	4
.200	.231	.280	25	5	2	0	0	1	1	5
.176	.222	.235	34	6	2	0	0	0	2	4
.118	.250	.118	17	2	0	0	0	2	3	5

ROBERTO HERNANDEZ — bats right — throws right — age 28 — CHA — P

1991	G	IP	H	BB	SO	SB	CS	W	L	SV	ERA
at Home	5	9.0	7	3	4	0	0	1	0	0	3.00
on Road	4	6.0	11	4	2	2	0	0	0	0	15.00

	BA	OBA	SA	AB	H	2B	3B	HR	RBI	BB	SO
Total	.290	.362	.403	62	18	4	0	1	12	7	6
vs. Left	.212	.278	.333	33	7	1	0	1	7	3	5
vs. Right	.379	.455	.483	29	11	3	0	0	5	4	1
Bases Empty	.162	.225	.216	37	6	2	0	0	0	3	4
Runners On Base	.480	.552	.680	25	12	2	0	1	12	4	2

1-YEAR TOTALS (1991)

G	IP	H	BB	SO	SB	CS	W	L	SV	ERA
5	9.0	7	3	4	0	0	1	0	0	3.00
4	6.0	11	4	2	2	0	0	0	0	15.00

BA	OBA	SA	AB	H	2B	3B	HR	RBI	BB	SO
.290	.362	.403	62	18	4	0	1	12	7	6
.212	.278	.333	33	7	1	0	1	7	3	5
.379	.455	.483	29	11	3	0	0	5	4	1
.162	.225	.216	37	6	2	0	0	0	3	4
.480	.552	.680	25	12	2	0	1	12	4	2

OREL HERSHISER — bats right — throws right — age 34 — LA — P

1991	G	IP	H	BB	SO	SB	CS	W	L	SV	ERA
at Home	12	63.1	61	22	37	8	2	3	2	0	3.27
on Road	9	48.2	51	10	36	3	0	4	0	0	3.70

	BA	OBA	SA	AB	H	2B	3B	HR	RBI	BB	SO
Total	.259	.316	.330	433	112	18	2	3	40	32	73
vs. Left	.295	.358	.386	210	62	9	2	2	21	18	27
vs. Right	.224	.276	.278	223	50	9	0	1	19	14	46
Bases Empty	.275	.319	.347	236	65	10	2	1	1	13	36
Runners On Base	.239	.314	.310	197	47	8	0	2	39	19	37

8-YEAR TOTALS (1984–1991)

G	IP	H	BB	SO	SB	CS	W	L	SV	ERA
126	830.1	697	235	574	63	31	59	32	0	2.56
122	756.0	674	229	521	47	18	47	35	4	2.99

BA	OBA	SA	AB	H	2B	3B	HR	RBI	BB	SO
.232	.291	.317	5909	1371	212	28	78	488	464	1095
.249	.311	.342	3155	785	129	20	42	279	279	479
.213	.268	.288	2754	586	83	8	36	209	185	616
.234	.281	.320	3584	837	130	17	49	49	217	647
.230	.305	.312	2325	534	82	11	29	439	247	448

BRYAN HICKERSON — bats left — throws left — age 29 — SF — P

1991	G	IP	H	BB	SO	SB	CS	W	L	SV	ERA
at Home	9	21.2	19	5	23	4	1	1	1	0	3.74
on Road	8	28.1	34	12	20	2	3	1	1	0	3.49

	BA	OBA	SA	AB	H	2B	3B	HR	RBI	BB	SO
Total	.275	.333	.378	193	53	11	0	3	16	17	43
vs. Left	.234	.294	.255	47	11	1	0	0	2	4	10
vs. Right	.288	.346	.418	146	42	10	0	3	14	13	33
Bases Empty	.314	.363	.467	105	33	7	0	3	3	8	23
Runners On Base	.227	.299	.273	88	20	4	0	0	13	9	20

1-YEAR TOTALS (1991)

G	IP	H	BB	SO	SB	CS	W	L	SV	ERA
9	21.2	19	5	23	4	1	1	1	0	3.74
8	28.1	34	12	20	2	3	1	1	0	3.49

BA	OBA	SA	AB	H	2B	3B	HR	RBI	BB	SO
.275	.333	.378	193	53	11	0	3	16	17	43
.234	.294	.255	47	11	1	0	0	2	4	10
.288	.346	.418	146	42	10	0	3	14	13	33
.314	.363	.467	105	33	7	0	3	3	8	23
.227	.299	.273	88	20	4	0	0	13	9	20

KEVIN HICKEY — bats left — throws left — age 35 — BAL — P

1991	G	IP	H	BB	SO	SB	CS	W	L	SV	ERA
at Home	10	6.0	4	4	5	0	0	0	0	0	7.50
on Road	9	8.0	11	2	5	0	0	0	1	0	10.13

	BA	OBA	SA	AB	H	2B	3B	HR	RBI	BB	SO
Total	.278	.339	.593	54	15	4	2	3	12	6	10
vs. Left	.321	.355	.714	28	9	1	2	2	9	2	7
vs. Right	.231	.323	.462	26	6	3	0	1	3	4	3
Bases Empty	.269	.296	.538	26	7	2	1	1	1	1	6
Runners On Base	.286	.371	.643	28	8	2	1	2	11	5	4

3-YEAR TOTALS (1989–1991)

G	IP	H	BB	SO	SB	CS	W	L	SV	ERA
54	46.1	42	26	33	6	2	1	6	2	4.66
53	43.1	37	16	22	3	2	3	0	1	4.36

BA	OBA	SA	AB	H	2B	3B	HR	RBI	BB	SO
.243	.329	.388	325	79	12	4	9	43	42	55
.250	.301	.450	140	35	7	3	5	26	10	27
.238	.349	.341	185	44	5	1	4	17	32	28
.253	.311	.373	166	42	6	1	5	4	14	31
.233	.346	.403	159	37	6	3	4	39	28	24

TEDDY HIGUERA — bats both — throws left — age 34 — MIL — P

1991	G	IP	H	BB	SO	SB	CS	W	L	SV	ERA
at Home	4	20.0	18	6	17	1	0	2	0	0	4.50
on Road	3	16.1	19	4	16	4	0	1	2	0	4.41

	BA	OBA	SA	AB	H	2B	3B	HR	RBI	BB	SO
Total	.262	.314	.362	141	37	8	0	2	18	10	33
vs. Left	.219	.242	.281	32	7	2	0	0	3	1	11
vs. Right	.275	.333	.385	109	30	6	0	2	15	9	22
Bases Empty	.227	.301	.320	75	17	4	0	1	1	7	18
Runners On Base	.303	.329	.409	66	20	4	0	1	17	3	15

7-YEAR TOTALS (1985–1991)

G	IP	H	BB	SO	SB	CS	W	L	SV	ERA
98	690.0	581	197	558	50	21	54	22	0	3.13
90	601.1	564	194	461	40	25	38	34	0	3.65

BA	OBA	SA	AB	H	2B	3B	HR	RBI	BB	SO
.238	.295	.359	4819	1145	209	16	114	470	391	1019
.241	.281	.351	838	202	35	3	17	82	45	192
.237	.298	.360	3981	943	174	13	97	388	346	827
.225	.288	.352	2942	663	114	8	78	78	247	651
.257	.305	.369	1877	482	95	8	36	392	144	368

MILT HILL — bats right — throws right — age 27 — CIN — P

1991	G	IP	H	BB	SO	SB	CS	W	L	SV	ERA
at Home	17	26.2	24	7	12	4	2	0	1	0	3.38
on Road	5	6.2	12	1	8	0	1	0	1	0	5.40

	BA	OBA	SA	AB	H	2B	3B	HR	RBI	BB	SO
Total	.295	.331	.402	122	36	8	1	1	16	8	20
vs. Left	.274	.329	.339	62	17	4	0	0	6	6	11
vs. Right	.317	.333	.467	60	19	4	1	1	10	2	9
Bases Empty	.339	.391	.458	59	20	4	0	1	1	5	10
Runners On Base	.254	.275	.349	63	16	4	1	0	15	3	10

1-YEAR TOTALS (1991)

G	IP	H	BB	SO	SB	CS	W	L	SV	ERA
17	26.2	24	7	12	4	2	0	1	0	3.38
5	6.2	12	1	8	0	1	0	1	0	5.40

BA	OBA	SA	AB	H	2B	3B	HR	RBI	BB	SO
.295	.331	.402	122	36	8	1	1	16	8	20
.274	.329	.339	62	17	4	0	0	6	6	11
.317	.333	.467	60	19	4	1	1	10	2	9
.339	.391	.458	59	20	4	0	1	1	5	10
.254	.275	.349	63	16	4	1	0	15	3	10

DARREN HOLMES — bats right — throws right — age 26 — MIL — P

1991	G	IP	H	BB	SO	SB	CS	W	L	SV	ERA
at Home	21	40.1	51	14	33	1	2	0	1	1	4.91
on Road	19	36.0	39	13	26	0	1	1	3	2	4.50

	BA	OBA	SA	AB	H	2B	3B	HR	RBI	BB	SO
Total	.295	.351	.410	305	90	15	1	6	49	27	59
vs. Left	.274	.340	.370	146	40	8	0	2	20	14	27
vs. Right	.314	.362	.447	159	50	7	1	4	29	13	32
Bases Empty	.277	.314	.345	148	41	4	0	2	2	8	28
Runners On Base	.312	.383	.471	157	49	11	1	4	47	19	31

2-YEAR TOTALS (1990–1991)

G	IP	H	BB	SO	SB	CS	W	L	SV	ERA
28	50.0	61	17	42	3	3	0	2	1	5.22
26	43.2	44	21	36	2	2	1	3	2	4.33

BA	OBA	SA	AB	H	2B	3B	HR	RBI	BB	SO
.285	.350	.397	368	105	18	1	7	57	38	78
.274	.335	.363	179	49	10	0	2	21	16	36
.296	.363	.429	189	56	8	1	5	36	22	42
.264	.306	.330	182	48	6	0	2	2	11	36
.306	.388	.462	186	57	12	1	5	55	27	42

RICK HONEYCUTT — bats left — throws left — age 40 — OAK — P

1991	G	IP	H	BB	SO	SB	CS	W	L	SV	ERA
at Home	23	21.0	18	10	14	4	1	0	2	0	2.14
on Road	20	16.2	19	10	12	1	0	2	2	0	5.40

	BA	OBA	SA	AB	H	2B	3B	HR	RBI	BB	SO
Total	.261	.358	.394	142	37	6	2	3	14	20	26
vs. Left	.204	.306	.315	54	11	3	0	1	4	8	11
vs. Right	.295	.388	.443	88	26	3	2	2	10	12	15
Bases Empty	.284	.368	.343	67	19	2	1	0	0	8	13
Runners On Base	.240	.348	.440	75	18	4	1	3	14	12	13

8-YEAR TOTALS (1984–1991)

G	IP	H	BB	SO	SB	CS	W	L	SV	ERA
173	476.1	437	125	267	26	19	23	26	14	2.76
178	417.1	418	166	241	27	22	18	30	13	4.03

BA	OBA	SA	AB	H	2B	3B	HR	RBI	BB	SO
.252	.312	.363	3397	855	167	19	58	342	291	508
.201	.252	.315	751	151	26	6	11	84	49	147
.266	.328	.382	2646	704	141	13	47	258	242	361
.245	.294	.348	1985	487	90	10	31	31	130	290
.261	.334	.385	1412	368	77	9	27	311	161	218

VINCE HORSMAN — bats right — throws left — age 25 — TOR — P

1991	G	IP	H	BB	SO	SB	CS	W	L	SV	ERA
at Home	1	1.0	0	1	0	0	0	0	0	0	0.00
on Road	3	3.0	2	2	2	0	0	0	0	0	0.00

	BA	OBA	SA	AB	H	2B	3B	HR	RBI	BB	SO
Total	.167	.333	.167	12	2	0	0	0	2	3	2
vs. Left	.333	.600	.333	3	1	0	0	0	2	2	0
vs. Right	.111	.200	.111	9	1	0	0	0	0	1	2
Bases Empty	.143	.250	.143	7	1	0	0	0	0	1	1
Runners On Base	.200	.429	.200	5	1	0	0	0	2	2	1

1-YEAR TOTALS (1991)

G	IP	H	BB	SO	SB	CS	W	L	SV	ERA
1	1.0	0	1	0	0	0	0	0	0	0.00
3	3.0	2	2	2	0	0	0	0	0	0.00

BA	OBA	SA	AB	H	2B	3B	HR	RBI	BB	SO
.167	.333	.167	12	2	0	0	0	2	3	2
.333	.600	.333	3	1	0	0	0	2	2	0
.111	.200	.111	9	1	0	0	0	0	1	2
.143	.250	.143	7	1	0	0	0	0	1	1
.200	.429	.200	5	1	0	0	0	2	2	1

STEVE HOWE — bats left — throws left — age 34 — NYA — P

1991	G	IP	H	BB	SO	SB	CS	W	L	SV	ERA
at Home	16	23.2	20	3	17	0	0	2	1	0	2.28
on Road	21	24.2	19	4	17	1	0	1	0	3	1.09

	BA	OBA	SA	AB	H	2B	3B	HR	RBI	BB	SO
Total	.222	.262	.284	176	39	8	0	1	11	7	34
vs. Left	.128	.160	.149	47	6	1	0	0	2	1	13
vs. Right	.256	.299	.333	129	33	7	0	1	9	6	21
Bases Empty	.232	.255	.273	99	23	4	0	0	0	1	19
Runners On Base	.208	.271	.299	77	16	4	0	1	11	6	15

3-YEAR TOTALS (1985–1991)

G	IP	H	BB	SO	SB	CS	W	L	SV	ERA
45	65.0	67	13	41	3	3	7	3	2	3.32
48	55.2	63	14	33	2	0	2	5	5	4.04

BA	OBA	SA	AB	H	2B	3B	HR	RBI	BB	SO
.275	.320	.364	472	130	22	1	6	64	27	74
.247	.287	.322	146	36	6	1	1	14	5	26
.288	.335	.383	326	94	16	0	5	50	22	48
.231	.277	.290	238	55	8	0	5	2	10	41
.321	.363	.440	234	75	14	1	4	62	17	33

MARK HUISMANN — bats right — throws right — age 34 — PIT — P

1991	G	IP	H	BB	SO	SB	CS	W	L	SV	ERA
at Home	4	5.0	6	2	5	0	0	0	0	0	7.20
on Road	1	0.0	1	0	0	0	0	0	0	0	0.00

	BA	OBA	SA	AB	H	2B	3B	HR	RBI	BB	SO
Total	.304	.360	.435	23	7	1	1	0	6	2	5
vs. Left	.455	.455	.636	11	5	0	1	0	2	0	2
vs. Right	.167	.286	.250	12	2	1	0	0	4	2	3
Bases Empty	.125	.222	.125	8	1	0	0	0	0	1	3
Runners On Base	.400	.438	.600	15	6	1	1	0	6	1	2

8-YEAR TOTALS (1984–1991)

G	IP	H	BB	SO	SB	CS	W	L	SV	ERA
76	149.0	145	36	111	13	5	6	5	5	3.81
63	117.0	131	30	88	11	3	5	5	6	4.85

BA	OBA	SA	AB	H	2B	3B	HR	RBI	BB	SO
.267	.311	.434	1032	276	50	7	36	153	66	199
.298	.338	.459	503	150	24	6	15	68	31	57
.238	.285	.410	529	126	26	1	21	85	35	142
.278	.324	.463	540	150	28	3	22	22	35	108
.256	.296	.402	492	126	22	4	14	131	31	91

JIM HUNTER — bats right — throws right — age 28 — MIL — P

1991	G	IP	H	BB	SO	SB	CS	W	L	SV	ERA
at Home	2	8.0	12	7	3	0	0	0	1	0	9.00
on Road	6	23.0	33	10	11	4	0	0	4	0	6.65

	BA	OBA	SA	AB	H	2B	3B	HR	RBI	BB	SO
Total	.349	.437	.481	129	45	8	0	3	25	17	14
vs. Left	.370	.459	.438	73	27	5	0	0	13	11	8
vs. Right	.321	.409	.536	56	18	3	0	3	12	6	6
Bases Empty	.286	.412	.357	56	16	4	0	0	0	9	6
Runners On Base	.397	.458	.575	73	29	4	0	3	25	8	8

1-YEAR TOTALS (1991)

G	IP	H	BB	SO	SB	CS	W	L	SV	ERA
2	8.0	12	7	3	0	0	0	1	0	9.00
6	23.0	33	10	11	4	0	0	4	0	6.65

BA	OBA	SA	AB	H	2B	3B	HR	RBI	BB	SO
.349	.437	.481	129	45	8	0	3	25	17	14
.370	.459	.438	73	27	5	0	0	13	11	8
.321	.409	.536	56	18	3	0	3	12	6	6
.286	.412	.357	56	16	4	0	0	0	9	6
.397	.458	.575	73	29	4	0	3	25	8	8

MIKE IGNASIAK — bats both — throws right — age 26 — MIL — P

1991

	G	IP	H	BB	SO	SB	CS	W	L	SV	ERA
at Home	1	5.0	2	3	6	1	0	0	1	0	5.40
on Road	3	7.2	5	5	4	1	0	2	0	0	5.87

	BA	OBA	SA	AB	H	2B	3B	HR	RBI	BB	SO
Total	.163	.294	.349	43	7	0	1	2	6	8	10
vs. Left	.150	.320	.300	20	3	0	0	1	2	5	1
vs. Right	.174	.269	.391	23	4	0	1	1	4	3	9
Bases Empty	.136	.321	.136	22	3	0	0	0	0	6	6
Runners On Base	.190	.261	.571	21	4	0	1	2	6	2	4

1-YEAR TOTALS (1991)

	G	IP	H	BB	SO	SB	CS	W	L	SV	ERA
	1	5.0	2	3	6	1	0	0	1	0	5.40
	3	7.2	5	5	4	1	0	2	0	0	5.87

BA	OBA	SA	AB	H	2B	3B	HR	RBI	BB	SO
.163	.294	.349	43	7	0	1	2	6	8	10
.150	.320	.300	20	3	0	0	1	2	5	1
.174	.269	.391	23	4	0	1	1	4	3	9
.136	.321	.136	22	3	0	0	0	0	6	6
.190	.261	.571	21	4	0	1	2	6	2	4

JEFF INNIS — bats right — throws right — age 30 — NYN — P

1991

	G	IP	H	BB	SO	SB	CS	W	L	SV	ERA
at Home	36	48.2	30	12	27	3	2	0	2	0	2.59
on Road	33	36.0	36	11	20	3	2	0	0	0	2.75

	BA	OBA	SA	AB	H	2B	3B	HR	RBI	BB	SO
Total	.219	.270	.291	302	66	10	3	2	35	23	47
vs. Left	.254	.306	.336	122	31	5	1	1	14	10	17
vs. Right	.194	.245	.261	180	35	5	2	1	21	13	30
Bases Empty	.212	.243	.306	170	36	6	2	2	2	7	26
Runners On Base	.227	.301	.273	132	30	4	1	0	33	16	21

5-YEAR TOTALS (1987–1991)

	G	IP	H	BB	SO	SB	CS	W	L	SV	ERA
	74	98.2	73	24	60	12	2	2	6	1	2.10
	71	96.2	98	23	57	18	3	0	2	0	3.35

BA	OBA	SA	AB	H	2B	3B	HR	RBI	BB	SO
.237	.283	.334	722	171	35	3	13	73	47	117
.294	.342	.445	272	80	15	1	8	33	21	28
.202	.246	.267	450	91	10	2	5	40	26	89
.246	.274	.379	414	102	15	2	12	12	14	70
.224	.293	.273	308	69	10	1	1	61	33	47

DARYL IRVINE — bats right — throws right — age 28 — BOS — P

1991

	G	IP	H	BB	SO	SB	CS	W	L	SV	ERA
at Home	5	13.0	14	4	6	1	0	0	0	0	4.15
on Road	4	5.0	11	5	2	0	0	0	1	0	10.80

	BA	OBA	SA	AB	H	2B	3B	HR	RBI	BB	SO
Total	.321	.404	.526	78	25	8	1	2	19	9	8
vs. Left	.273	.368	.455	33	9	4	1	0	6	5	6
vs. Right	.356	.431	.578	45	16	4	0	2	13	4	2
Bases Empty	.324	.378	.441	34	11	4	0	0	0	2	4
Runners On Base	.318	.423	.591	44	14	4	1	2	19	7	4

2-YEAR TOTALS (1990–1991)

	G	IP	H	BB	SO	SB	CS	W	L	SV	ERA
	11	24.0	23	8	9	1	0	0	0	0	3.75
	9	11.1	17	11	8	0	0	1	1	0	8.74

BA	OBA	SA	AB	H	2B	3B	HR	RBI	BB	SO
.288	.374	.417	139	40	10	1	2	29	19	17
.283	.361	.383	60	17	4	1	0	12	9	9
.291	.385	.443	79	23	6	0	2	17	10	8
.273	.342	.348	66	18	5	0	0	0	6	11
.301	.400	.479	73	22	5	1	2	29	13	6

DANNY JACKSON — bats right — throws left — age 30 — CHN — P

1991

	G	IP	H	BB	SO	SB	CS	W	L	SV	ERA
at Home	9	40.0	53	20	20	3	2	0	2	0	7.20
on Road	8	30.2	36	28	11	5	0	1	3	0	6.16

	BA	OBA	SA	AB	H	2B	3B	HR	RBI	BB	SO
Total	.309	.407	.451	288	89	15	1	8	49	48	31
vs. Left	.300	.417	.383	60	18	3	1	0	12	12	7
vs. Right	.311	.404	.469	228	71	12	0	8	37	36	24
Bases Empty	.283	.396	.406	138	39	8	0	3	3	26	14
Runners On Base	.333	.417	.493	150	50	7	1	5	46	22	17

8-YEAR TOTALS (1984–1991)

	G	IP	H	BB	SO	SB	CS	W	L	SV	ERA
	104	624.1	600	249	359	34	17	37	33	1	3.63
	105	633.2	625	266	400	39	33	35	45	0	3.89

BA	OBA	SA	AB	H	2B	3B	HR	RBI	BB	SO
.257	.331	.364	4767	1225	201	40	77	526	515	759
.269	.341	.366	855	230	36	10	9	94	93	180
.254	.329	.364	3912	995	165	30	68	432	422	579
.243	.319	.343	2715	661	110	24	37	37	292	451
.275	.346	.393	2052	564	91	16	40	489	223	308

MIKE JEFFCOAT — bats left — throws left — age 33 — TEX — P

1991

	G	IP	H	BB	SO	SB	CS	W	L	SV	ERA
at Home	33	37.1	52	15	26	3	1	4	0	1	4.82
on Road	37	42.1	52	10	17	2	1	1	3	0	4.46

	BA	OBA	SA	AB	H	2B	3B	HR	RBI	BB	SO
Total	.321	.373	.466	324	104	13	5	8	46	25	43
vs. Left	.289	.323	.413	121	35	3	3	2	15	7	17
vs. Right	.340	.401	.498	203	69	10	2	6	31	18	26
Bases Empty	.335	.389	.466	161	54	5	2	4	4	12	25
Runners On Base	.307	.357	.466	163	50	8	3	4	42	13	18

7-YEAR TOTALS (1984–1991)

	G	IP	H	BB	SO	SB	CS	W	L	SV	ERA
	119	221.1	247	61	129	9	7	14	5	5	3.50
	115	223.2	265	70	97	6	6	10	17	2	5.07

BA	OBA	SA	AB	H	2B	3B	HR	RBI	BB	SO
.291	.342	.436	1758	512	92	15	44	238	131	226
.271	.315	.380	495	134	19	4	9	76	31	73
.299	.352	.458	1263	378	73	11	35	162	100	153
.291	.334	.416	963	280	42	8	21	21	56	133
.292	.350	.459	795	232	50	7	23	217	75	93

DAVE JOHNSON — bats right — throws right — age 33 — BAL — P

1991

	G	IP	H	BB	SO	SB	CS	W	L	SV	ERA
at Home	11	42.0	65	9	26	2	1	2	4	0	6.43
on Road	11	42.0	62	15	12	1	2	2	4	0	7.71

	BA	OBA	SA	AB	H	2B	3B	HR	RBI	BB	SO
Total	.349	.394	.563	364	127	20	2	18	68	24	38
vs. Left	.405	.440	.631	195	79	10	2	10	41	13	17
vs. Right	.284	.342	.485	169	48	10	0	8	27	11	21
Bases Empty	.332	.372	.550	202	67	10	2	10	10	12	26
Runners On Base	.370	.421	.580	162	60	10	0	8	58	12	12

4-YEAR TOTALS (1987–1991)

	G	IP	H	BB	SO	SB	CS	W	L	SV	ERA
	35	186.2	215	51	76	2	7	10	13	0	4.44
	36	173.0	211	46	60	2	6	11	11	0	5.46

BA	OBA	SA	AB	H	2B	3B	HR	RBI	BB	SO
.297	.344	.490	1433	426	80	8	60	186	97	136
.331	.379	.541	708	234	50	6	29	95	58	51
.265	.310	.440	725	192	30	2	31	91	39	85
.301	.343	.510	870	262	58	5	38	38	52	86
.291	.346	.458	563	164	22	3	22	148	45	50

JOEL JOHNSTON — bats right — throws right — age 25 — KC — P

1991

	G	IP	H	BB	SO	SB	CS	W	L	SV	ERA
at Home	5	11.1	4	2	10	0	0	0	0	0	0.00
on Road	8	11.0	5	7	11	1	1	1	0	0	0.82

	BA	OBA	SA	AB	H	2B	3B	HR	RBI	BB	SO
Total	.120	.214	.133	75	9	1	0	0	1	9	21
vs. Left	.133	.188	.167	30	4	1	0	0	0	2	6
vs. Right	.111	.231	.111	45	5	0	0	0	1	7	15
Bases Empty	.171	.227	.195	41	7	1	0	0	0	3	10
Runners On Base	.059	.200	.059	34	2	0	0	0	1	6	11

1-YEAR TOTALS (1991)

	G	IP	H	BB	SO	SB	CS	W	L	SV	ERA
	11	11.1	4	2	10	0	0	0	0	0	0.00
	8	11.0	5	7	11	1	1	1	0	0	0.82

BA	OBA	SA	AB	H	2B	3B	HR	RBI	BB	SO
.120	.214	.133	75	9	1	0	0	1	9	21
.133	.188	.167	30	4	1	0	0	0	2	6
.111	.231	.111	45	5	0	0	0	1	7	15
.171	.227	.195	41	7	1	0	0	0	3	10
.059	.200	.059	34	2	0	0	0	1	6	11

CALVIN JONES — bats right — throws right — age 29 — SEA — P

1991	G	IP	H	BB	SO	SB	CS	W	L	SV	ERA
at Home	15	25.0	18	12	15	2	2	2	1	0	1.44
on Road	12	21.1	15	17	27	3	0	0	1	2	3.80

	BA	OBA	SA	AB	H	2B	3B	HR	RBI	BB	SO
Total	.209	.335	.247	158	33	4	1	0	15	29	42
vs. Left	.164	.309	.194	67	11	2	0	0	4	14	17
vs. Right	.242	.355	.286	91	22	2	1	0	11	15	25
Bases Empty	.153	.280	.200	85	13	2	1	0	0	15	24
Runners On Base	.274	.398	.301	73	20	2	0	0	15	14	18

1-YEAR TOTALS (1991)

G	IP	H	BB	SO	SB	CS	W	L	SV	ERA
15	25.0	18	12	15	2	2	2	1	0	1.44
12	21.1	15	17	27	3	0	0	1	2	3.80

BA	OBA	SA	AB	H	2B	3B	HR	RBI	BB	SO
.209	.335	.247	158	33	4	1	0	15	29	42
.164	.309	.194	67	11	2	0	0	4	14	17
.242	.355	.286	91	22	2	1	0	11	15	25
.153	.280	.200	85	13	2	1	0	0	15	24
.274	.398	.301	73	20	2	0	0	15	14	18

JIMMY JONES — bats right — throws right — age 28 — HOU — P

1991	G	IP	H	BB	SO	SB	CS	W	L	SV	ERA
at Home	16	96.1	82	35	64	13	5	4	3	0	3.08
on Road	10	39.0	61	16	24	5	1	2	5	0	7.62

	BA	OBA	SA	AB	H	2B	3B	HR	RBI	BB	SO
Total	.270	.336	.374	530	143	18	5	9	59	51	88
vs. Left	.302	.371	.414	348	105	13	4	6	40	37	57
vs. Right	.209	.268	.297	182	38	5	1	3	19	14	31
Bases Empty	.270	.335	.361	296	80	9	0	6	6	27	51
Runners On Base	.269	.337	.389	234	63	9	5	3	53	24	37

6-YEAR TOTALS (1986–1991)

G	IP	H	BB	SO	SB	CS	W	L	SV	ERA
66	333.1	341	104	171	30	11	15	17	0	3.75
50	242.1	286	87	115	23	9	14	15	0	5.35

BA	OBA	SA	AB	H	2B	3B	HR	RBI	BB	SO
.278	.335	.406	2254	627	96	16	53	293	191	286
.291	.352	.414	1228	357	54	11	25	140	117	151
.263	.315	.396	1026	270	42	5	28	153	74	135
.260	.317	.375	1297	337	47	9	28	28	103	167
.303	.359	.447	957	290	49	7	25	265	88	119

STACY JONES — bats right — throws right — age 25 — BAL — P

1991	G	IP	H	BB	SO	SB	CS	W	L	SV	ERA
at Home	3	9.0	11	5	5	0	0	0	0	0	5.00
on Road	1	2.0	0	0	2	0	0	0	0	0	0.00

	BA	OBA	SA	AB	H	2B	3B	HR	RBI	BB	SO
Total	.256	.327	.465	43	11	6	0	1	8	5	10
vs. Left	.333	.407	.625	24	8	4	0	1	5	3	4
vs. Right	.158	.227	.263	19	3	2	0	0	3	2	6
Bases Empty	.200	.259	.360	25	5	1	0	1	1	2	5
Runners On Base	.333	.409	.611	18	6	5	0	0	7	3	5

1-YEAR TOTALS (1991)

G	IP	H	BB	SO	SB	CS	W	L	SV	ERA
3	9.0	11	5	5	0	0	0	0	0	5.00
1	2.0	0	0	2	0	0	0	0	0	0.00

BA	OBA	SA	AB	H	2B	3B	HR	RBI	BB	SO
.256	.327	.465	43	11	6	0	1	8	5	10
.333	.407	.625	24	8	4	0	1	5	3	4
.158	.227	.263	19	3	2	0	0	3	2	6
.200	.259	.360	25	5	1	0	1	1	2	5
.333	.409	.611	18	6	5	0	0	7	3	5

JEFF JUDEN — bats right — throws right — age 21 — HOU — P

1991	G	IP	H	BB	SO	SB	CS	W	L	SV	ERA
at Home	2	11.1	10	2	8	1	0	0	1	0	4.76
on Road	2	6.2	9	5	3	2	1	0	1	0	8.10

	BA	OBA	SA	AB	H	2B	3B	HR	RBI	BB	SO
Total	.275	.329	.449	69	19	3	0	3	13	7	11
vs. Left	.222	.268	.389	36	8	0	0	2	4	3	8
vs. Right	.333	.395	.515	33	11	3	0	1	9	4	3
Bases Empty	.195	.283	.366	41	8	1	0	2	2	5	8
Runners On Base	.393	.394	.571	28	11	2	0	1	11	2	3

1-YEAR TOTALS (1991)

G	IP	H	BB	SO	SB	CS	W	L	SV	ERA
2	11.1	10	2	8	1	0	0	1	0	4.76
2	6.2	9	5	3	2	1	0	1	0	8.10

BA	OBA	SA	AB	H	2B	3B	HR	RBI	BB	SO
.275	.329	.449	69	19	3	0	3	13	7	11
.222	.268	.389	36	8	0	0	2	4	3	8
.333	.395	.515	33	11	3	0	1	9	4	3
.195	.283	.366	41	8	1	0	2	2	5	8
.393	.394	.571	28	11	2	0	1	11	2	3

JEFF KAISER — bats right — throws left — age 32 — DET — P

1991	G	IP	H	BB	SO	SB	CS	W	L	SV	ERA
at Home	6	3.2	5	4	3	0	0	0	1	1	9.82
on Road	4	1.1	1	1	1	0	0	0	1	0	6.75

	BA	OBA	SA	AB	H	2B	3B	HR	RBI	BB	SO
Total	.286	.423	.476	21	6	1	0	1	5	5	4
vs. Left	.375	.444	.750	8	3	0	0	1	4	1	2
vs. Right	.231	.412	.308	13	3	1	0	0	1	4	2
Bases Empty	.182	.250	.182	11	2	0	0	0	0	1	1
Runners On Base	.400	.571	.800	10	4	1	0	1	5	4	3

6-YEAR TOTALS (1985–1991)

G	IP	H	BB	SO	SB	CS	W	L	SV	ERA
23	22.2	24	18	17	3	1	0	2	1	7.54
18	21.1	34	23	12	0	0	0	0	0	11.39

BA	OBA	SA	AB	H	2B	3B	HR	RBI	BB	SO
.317	.437	.568	183	58	9	2	11	59	41	29
.361	.506	.541	61	22	3	1	2	22	16	8
.295	.401	.582	122	36	6	1	9	37	25	21
.239	.356	.375	88	21	4	1	2	2	14	16
.389	.504	.747	95	37	5	1	9	57	27	13

SCOTT KAMIENIECKI — bats right — throws right — age 28 — NYA — P

1991	G	IP	H	BB	SO	SB	CS	W	L	SV	ERA
at Home	4	26.1	22	5	17	1	1	2	2	0	3.76
on Road	5	29.0	32	17	17	3	1	2	2	0	4.03

	BA	OBA	SA	AB	H	2B	3B	HR	RBI	BB	SO
Total	.256	.333	.455	211	54	12	3	8	23	22	34
vs. Left	.272	.346	.491	114	31	6	2	5	13	13	21
vs. Right	.237	.318	.412	97	23	6	1	3	10	9	13
Bases Empty	.308	.357	.562	130	40	8	2	7	7	9	20
Runners On Base	.173	.299	.284	81	14	4	1	1	16	13	14

1-YEAR TOTALS (1991)

G	IP	H	BB	SO	SB	CS	W	L	SV	ERA
4	26.1	22	5	17	1	1	2	2	0	3.76
5	29.0	32	17	17	3	1	2	2	0	4.03

BA	OBA	SA	AB	H	2B	3B	HR	RBI	BB	SO
.256	.333	.455	211	54	12	3	8	23	22	34
.272	.346	.491	114	31	6	2	5	13	13	21
.237	.318	.412	97	23	6	1	3	10	9	13
.308	.357	.562	130	40	8	2	7	7	9	20
.173	.299	.284	81	14	4	1	1	16	13	14

DANA KIECKER — bats right — throws right — age 31 — BOS — P

1991	G	IP	H	BB	SO	SB	CS	W	L	SV	ERA
at Home	12	28.2	38	18	13	4	2	1	1	0	7.22
on Road	6	11.2	18	5	8	3	1	1	2	0	7.71

	BA	OBA	SA	AB	H	2B	3B	HR	RBI	BB	SO
Total	.344	.429	.503	163	56	8	0	6	34	23	21
vs. Left	.311	.407	.365	74	23	1	0	1	11	12	6
vs. Right	.371	.447	.618	89	33	7	0	5	23	11	15
Bases Empty	.347	.456	.467	75	26	0	0	3	3	15	8
Runners On Base	.341	.404	.534	88	30	8	0	3	31	8	13

2-YEAR TOTALS (1990–1991)

G	IP	H	BB	SO	SB	CS	W	L	SV	ERA
29	92.1	117	42	43	7	4	4	6	0	6.73
21	100.0	84	35	71	15	5	6	6	0	2.79

BA	OBA	SA	AB	H	2B	3B	HR	RBI	BB	SO
.273	.349	.388	735	201	39	3	13	94	77	114
.310	.375	.411	377	117	19	2	5	44	41	29
.235	.321	.363	358	84	20	1	8	50	36	85
.254	.325	.360	422	107	22	1	7	7	42	63
.300	.378	.425	313	94	17	2	6	87	35	51

JOHN KIELY — bats right — throws right — age 28 — DET — P

1991

	G	IP	H	BB	SO	SB	CS	W	L	SV	ERA
at Home	1	1.0	1	2	0	0	0	0	0	0	0.00
on Road	6	5.2	12	7	1	0	0	0	1	0	17.47

	BA	OBA	SA	AB	H	2B	3B	HR	RBI	BB	SO
Total	.448	.575	.586	29	13	4	0	0	9	9	1
vs. Left	.444	.643	.556	9	4	1	0	0	4	5	0
vs. Right	.450	.538	.600	20	9	3	0	0	5	4	1
Bases Empty	.667	.750	1.000	6	4	2	0	0	0	2	0
Runners On Base	.391	.531	.478	23	9	2	0	0	9	7	1

1-YEAR TOTALS (1991)

	G	IP	H	BB	SO	SB	CS	W	L	SV	ERA
at Home	1	1.0	1	2	0	0	0	0	0	0	0.00
on Road	6	5.2	12	7	1	0	0	0	1	0	17.47

	BA	OBA	SA	AB	H	2B	3B	HR	RBI	BB	SO
Total	.448	.575	.586	29	13	4	0	0	9	9	1
vs. Left	.444	.643	.556	9	4	1	0	0	4	5	0
vs. Right	.450	.538	.600	20	9	3	0	0	5	4	1
Bases Empty	.667	.750	1.000	6	4	2	0	0	0	2	0
Runners On Base	.391	.531	.478	23	9	2	0	0	9	7	1

PAUL KILGUS — bats left — throws left — age 30 — BAL — P

1991

	G	IP	H	BB	SO	SB	CS	W	L	SV	ERA
at Home	19	32.2	39	13	15	2	1	0	2	0	7.44
on Road	19	29.1	21	11	17	0	1	0	0	1	2.45

	BA	OBA	SA	AB	H	2B	3B	HR	RBI	BB	SO
Total	.256	.328	.415	234	60	13	0	8	39	24	32
vs. Left	.237	.308	.350	80	19	6	0	1	16	7	12
vs. Right	.266	.339	.448	154	41	7	0	7	23	17	20
Bases Empty	.259	.338	.397	116	30	4	0	4	4	11	17
Runners On Base	.254	.319	.432	118	30	9	0	4	35	13	15

5-YEAR TOTALS (1987–1991)

	G	IP	H	BB	SO	SB	CS	W	L	SV	ERA
at Home	70	281.0	288	91	121	15	10	10	17	1	4.39
on Road	70	235.2	240	91	109	13	9	10	17	2	4.39

	BA	OBA	SA	AB	H	2B	3B	HR	RBI	BB	SO
Total	.263	.329	.400	2007	528	98	12	51	249	182	230
vs. Left	.240	.312	.381	420	101	17	3	12	63	36	57
vs. Right	.269	.333	.405	1587	427	81	9	39	186	146	173
Bases Empty	.253	.323	.371	1139	288	48	4	26	26	105	128
Runners On Base	.276	.336	.439	868	240	50	8	25	223	77	102

BOB KIPPER — bats right — throws left — age 28 — PIT — P

1991

	G	IP	H	BB	SO	SB	CS	W	L	SV	ERA
at Home	24	30.2	38	15	19	2	4	1	1	1	6.75
on Road	28	29.1	28	7	19	5	0	1	1	3	2.45

	BA	OBA	SA	AB	H	2B	3B	HR	RBI	BB	SO
Total	.276	.335	.431	239	66	12	2	7	32	22	38
vs. Left	.325	.346	.506	77	25	2	0	4	15	3	19
vs. Right	.253	.330	.395	162	41	10	2	3	17	19	19
Bases Empty	.244	.301	.363	135	33	7	0	3	3	11	20
Runners On Base	.317	.376	.519	104	33	5	2	4	29	11	18

7-YEAR TOTALS (1985–1991)

	G	IP	H	BB	SO	SB	CS	W	L	SV	ERA
at Home	120	269.2	250	108	190	29	22	12	18	2	4.37
on Road	126	253.2	237	95	157	35	7	12	16	9	4.29

	BA	OBA	SA	AB	H	2B	3B	HR	RBI	BB	SO
Total	.246	.316	.420	1983	487	97	15	73	262	203	347
vs. Left	.240	.293	.330	500	120	19	4	6	58	35	96
vs. Right	.247	.323	.450	1483	367	78	11	67	204	168	251
Bases Empty	.231	.304	.390	1173	271	52	7	40	40	114	211
Runners On Base	.267	.332	.464	810	216	45	8	33	222	89	136

GARLAND KISER — bats left — throws left — age 24 — CLE — P

1991

	G	IP	H	BB	SO	SB	CS	W	L	SV	ERA
at Home	3	2.2	4	1	2	0	0	0	0	0	3.38
on Road	4	2.0	3	3	1	1	0	0	0	0	18.00

	BA	OBA	SA	AB	H	2B	3B	HR	RBI	BB	SO
Total	.368	.500	.368	19	7	0	0	0	3	4	3
vs. Left	.308	.438	.308	13	4	0	0	0	3	2	3
vs. Right	.500	.625	.500	6	3	0	0	0	0	2	0
Bases Empty	.500	.625	.500	6	3	0	0	0	0	2	1
Runners On Base	.308	.438	.308	13	4	0	0	0	3	2	2

1-YEAR TOTALS (1991)

	G	IP	H	BB	SO	SB	CS	W	L	SV	ERA
at Home	3	2.2	4	1	2	0	0	0	0	0	3.38
on Road	4	2.0	3	3	1	1	0	0	0	0	18.00

	BA	OBA	SA	AB	H	2B	3B	HR	RBI	BB	SO
Total	.368	.500	.368	19	7	0	0	0	3	4	3
vs. Left	.308	.438	.308	13	4	0	0	0	3	2	3
vs. Right	.500	.625	.500	6	3	0	0	0	0	2	0
Bases Empty	.500	.625	.500	6	3	0	0	0	0	2	1
Runners On Base	.308	.438	.308	13	4	0	0	0	3	2	2

JOE KLINK — bats left — throws left — age 30 — OAK — P

1991

	G	IP	H	BB	SO	SB	CS	W	L	SV	ERA
at Home	33	32.1	27	8	18	4	0	4	1	1	3.34
on Road	29	29.2	33	13	16	0	2	6	2	1	5.46

	BA	OBA	SA	AB	H	2B	3B	HR	RBI	BB	SO
Total	.260	.335	.364	231	60	10	1	4	29	21	34
vs. Left	.224	.276	.337	98	22	3	1	2	9	5	18
vs. Right	.286	.375	.383	133	38	7	0	2	20	16	16
Bases Empty	.252	.295	.374	115	29	5	0	3	3	4	19
Runners On Base	.267	.370	.353	116	31	5	1	1	26	17	15

3-YEAR TOTALS (1987–1991)

	G	IP	H	BB	SO	SB	CS	W	L	SV	ERA
at Home	7	63.0	59	14	34	6	0	4	1	1	2.86
on Road	57	61.2	72	36	36	1	2	6	3	2	5.25

	BA	OBA	SA	AB	H	2B	3B	HR	RBI	BB	SO
Total	.273	.347	.379	480	131	20	2	9	56	50	70
vs. Left	.245	.313	.367	196	48	10	1	4	21	18	37
vs. Right	.292	.370	.387	284	83	10	1	5	35	32	33
Bases Empty	.265	.314	.378	238	63	10	1	5	5	14	39
Runners On Base	.281	.377	.380	242	68	10	1	4	51	36	31

MARK KNUDSON — bats right — throws right — age 32 — MIL — P

1991

	G	IP	H	BB	SO	SB	CS	W	L	SV	ERA
at Home	7	23.2	37	12	17	4	1	0	3	0	9.51
on Road	5	11.1	17	3	6	0	0	0	1	0	4.76

	BA	OBA	SA	AB	H	2B	3B	HR	RBI	BB	SO
Total	.355	.409	.605	152	54	12	1	8	31	15	23
vs. Left	.357	.385	.619	84	30	8	1	4	19	5	12
vs. Right	.353	.438	.588	68	24	4	0	4	12	10	11
Bases Empty	.330	.371	.549	91	30	5	0	5	5	6	17
Runners On Base	.393	.459	.689	61	24	7	1	3	26	9	6

7-YEAR TOTALS (1985–1991)

	G	IP	H	BB	SO	SB	CS	W	L	SV	ERA
at Home	58	235.1	291	63	100	21	13	12	15	0	4.82
on Road	59	244.0	261	60	94	12	10	12	14	0	4.17

	BA	OBA	SA	AB	H	2B	3B	HR	RBI	BB	SO
Total	.288	.330	.437	1918	552	91	12	57	239	123	194
vs. Left	.283	.326	.423	944	267	54	6	22	110	65	94
vs. Right	.293	.334	.451	974	285	37	6	35	129	58	100
Bases Empty	.299	.337	.450	1116	334	58	7	32	32	61	111
Runners On Base	.272	.321	.419	802	218	33	5	25	207	62	83

TOM KRAMER — bats both — throws right — age 24 — CLE — P

1991

	G	IP	H	BB	SO	SB	CS	W	L	SV	ERA
at Home	1	1.2	6	1	0	0	0	0	0	0	27.00
on Road	3	3.0	4	5	4	0	0	0	0	0	12.00

	BA	OBA	SA	AB	H	2B	3B	HR	RBI	BB	SO
Total	.476	.533	.857	21	10	3	1	1	11	6	4
vs. Left	.455	.500	.727	11	5	1	1	0	6	3	1
vs. Right	.500	.571	1.000	10	5	2	0	1	5	3	3
Bases Empty	.400	.455	.900	10	4	1	0	1	1	2	2
Runners On Base	.545	.579	.818	11	6	2	1	0	10	5	2

1-YEAR TOTALS (1991)

	G	IP	H	BB	SO	SB	CS	W	L	SV	ERA
	1	1.2	6	1	0	0	0	0	0	0	27.00
	3	3.0	4	5	4	0	0	0	0	0	12.00

	BA	OBA	SA	AB	H	2B	3B	HR	RBI	BB	SO
	.476	.533	.857	21	10	3	1	1	11	6	4
	.455	.500	.727	11	5	1	1	0	6	3	1
	.500	.571	1.000	10	5	2	0	1	5	3	3
	.400	.455	.900	10	4	1	0	1	1	2	2
	.545	.579	.818	11	6	2	1	0	10	5	2

BILL KRUEGER — bats left — throws left — age 34 — SEA — P

1991

1991	G	IP	H	BB	SO	SB	CS	W	L	SV	ERA
at Home	19	94.0	100	31	52	5	2	7	3	0	3.73
on Road	16	81.0	94	29	39	5	3	4	5	0	3.44

	BA	OBA	SA	AB	H	2B	3B	HR	RBI	BB	SO
Total	.289	.346	.418	672	194	34	4	15	72	60	91
vs. Left	.307	.351	.414	140	43	7	1	2	16	10	19
vs. Right	.284	.345	.419	532	151	27	3	13	56	50	72
Bases Empty	.297	.339	.446	397	118	18	1	13	13	23	58
Runners On Base	.276	.356	.378	275	76	16	3	2	59	37	33

8-YEAR TOTALS (1984–1991)

G	IP	H	BB	SO	SB	CS	W	L	SV	ERA
90	404.1	424	165	209	54	15	25	22	2	4.16
90	331.1	380	160	150	37	15	15	21	2	4.45

BA	OBA	SA	AB	H	2B	3B	HR	RBI	BB	SO
.281	.353	.402	2858	804	132	17	60	361	325	359
.273	.341	.372	608	166	22	4	10	77	63	85
.284	.356	.411	2250	638	110	13	50	284	262	274
.279	.351	.411	1538	429	63	7	42	42	164	186
.284	.355	.392	1320	375	69	10	18	319	161	173

MIKE LaCOSS — bats right — throws right — age 36 — SF — P

1991

1991	G	IP	H	BB	SO	SB	CS	W	L	SV	ERA
at Home	10	28.1	32	11	19	2	0	1	2	0	5.40
on Road	8	19.0	29	13	11	3	2	0	3	0	9.95

	BA	OBA	SA	AB	H	2B	3B	HR	RBI	BB	SO
Total	.314	.392	.448	194	61	10	2	4	29	24	30
vs. Left	.327	.395	.478	113	37	4	2	3	16	14	16
vs. Right	.296	.387	.407	81	24	6	0	1	13	10	14
Bases Empty	.308	.363	.442	104	32	4	2	2	2	9	18
Runners On Base	.322	.422	.456	90	29	6	0	2	27	15	12

8-YEAR TOTALS (1984–1991)

G	IP	H	BB	SO	SB	CS	W	L	SV	ERA
113	500.1	458	186	273	42	19	34	24	7	3.24
118	438.0	464	206	221	56	29	21	31	3	4.60

BA	OBA	SA	AB	H	2B	3B	HR	RBI	BB	SO
.261	.336	.357	3531	922	140	21	52	408	392	494
.259	.342	.353	1926	499	70	16	26	209	243	263
.264	.328	.362	1605	423	70	5	26	199	149	231
.249	.314	.335	2029	505	75	12	25	25	186	308
.278	.364	.387	1502	417	65	9	27	383	206	186

DENNIS LAMP — bats right — throws right — age 40 — BOS — P

1991

1991	G	IP	H	BB	SO	SB	CS	W	L	SV	ERA
at Home	24	41.0	52	19	21	3	0	3	3	0	6.59
on Road	27	51.0	48	12	36	7	0	3	0	0	3.18

	BA	OBA	SA	AB	H	2B	3B	HR	RBI	BB	SO
Total	.275	.335	.420	364	100	21	4	8	60	31	57
vs. Left	.328	.415	.445	128	42	5	2	2	19	18	22
vs. Right	.246	.289	.407	236	58	16	2	6	41	13	35
Bases Empty	.271	.327	.420	181	49	9	3	4	4	14	28
Runners On Base	.279	.343	.421	183	51	12	1	4	56	17	29

8-YEAR TOTALS (1984–1991)

G	IP	H	BB	SO	SB	CS	W	L	SV	ERA
179	367.2	399	114	197	44	7	24	13	10	4.06
191	342.1	359	100	195	42	7	18	19	5	3.92

BA	OBA	SA	AB	H	2B	3B	HR	RBI	BB	SO
.275	.327	.382	2753	758	109	16	51	396	214	392
.299	.365	.388	1190	356	39	8	17	155	127	147
.257	.297	.377	1563	402	70	8	34	241	87	245
.248	.299	.342	1431	355	50	9	22	22	97	217
.305	.357	.426	1322	403	59	7	29	374	117	175

DAVE LaPOINT — bats left — throws left — age 33 — PHI — P

1991

1991	G	IP	H	BB	SO	SB	CS	W	L	SV	ERA
at Home	1	1.1	5	3	1	2	0	0	1	0	40.50
on Road	1	3.2	5	3	2	1	0	0	0	0	7.36

	BA	OBA	SA	AB	H	2B	3B	HR	RBI	BB	SO
Total	.435	.548	.565	23	10	3	0	0	9	6	3
vs. Left	.000	.000	.000	0	0	0	0	0	0	0	0
vs. Right	.435	.548	.565	23	10	3	0	0	9	6	3
Bases Empty	.222	.417	.333	9	2	1	0	0	0	2	2
Runners On Base	.571	.632	.714	14	8	2	0	0	9	4	1

8-YEAR TOTALS (1984–1991)

G	IP	H	BB	SO	SB	CS	W	L	SV	ERA
100	580.0	586	221	304	42	28	32	28	0	3.55
106	530.0	619	185	292	45	19	24	46	0	4.72

BA	OBA	SA	AB	H	2B	3B	HR	RBI	BB	SO
.278	.339	.406	4340	1205	200	37	94	486	406	596
.277	.327	.395	683	189	23	5	16	66	52	70
.278	.341	.408	3657	1016	177	32	78	420	354	526
.274	.332	.415	2493	684	109	26	63	63	212	334
.282	.347	.394	1847	521	91	11	31	423	194	262

TIM LAYANA — bats right — throws right — age 28 — CIN — P

1991

1991	G	IP	H	BB	SO	SB	CS	W	L	SV	ERA
at Home	11	10.0	17	7	5	3	0	0	0	0	9.90
on Road	11	10.2	6	4	9	2	1	0	2	0	4.22

	BA	OBA	SA	AB	H	2B	3B	HR	RBI	BB	SO
Total	.277	.362	.325	83	23	1	0	1	15	11	14
vs. Left	.324	.390	.351	37	12	1	0	0	9	4	6
vs. Right	.239	.340	.304	46	11	0	0	1	6	7	8
Bases Empty	.282	.333	.308	39	11	1	0	0	0	3	7
Runners On Base	.273	.385	.341	44	12	0	0	1	15	8	7

2-YEAR TOTALS (1990–1991)

G	IP	H	BB	SO	SB	CS	W	L	SV	ERA
39	55.1	53	28	30	10	3	4	2	1	4.88
38	45.1	41	27	37	4	3	1	3	1	3.38

BA	OBA	SA	AB	H	2B	3B	HR	RBI	BB	SO
.251	.348	.369	374	94	20	0	8	49	55	67
.274	.379	.405	168	46	13	0	3	26	28	28
.233	.322	.340	206	48	7	0	5	23	27	39
.268	.353	.399	198	53	14	0	4	4	26	38
.233	.343	.335	176	41	6	0	4	45	29	29

TERRY LEACH — bats right — throws right — age 38 — MIN — P

1991

1991	G	IP	H	BB	SO	SB	CS	W	L	SV	ERA
at Home	25	39.0	46	5	15	6	0	0	0	0	2.54
on Road	25	28.1	36	9	17	4	2	1	2	0	5.08

	BA	OBA	SA	AB	H	2B	3B	HR	RBI	BB	SO
Total	.299	.332	.401	274	82	19	0	3	40	14	32
vs. Left	.373	.394	.492	126	47	12	0	1	20	5	5
vs. Right	.236	.280	.324	148	35	7	0	2	20	9	27
Bases Empty	.271	.306	.357	140	38	9	0	1	1	9	16
Runners On Base	.328	.359	.448	134	44	10	0	2	39	7	16

7-YEAR TOTALS (1985–1991)

G	IP	H	BB	SO	SB	CS	W	L	SV	ERA
127	242.1	254	56	122	33	4	9	2	4	3.34
142	287.1	290	89	138	35	15	20	18	2	3.29

BA	OBA	SA	AB	H	2B	3B	HR	RBI	BB	SO
.267	.317	.376	2034	544	106	9	32	239	145	260
.297	.353	.422	890	264	61	6	13	105	78	69
.245	.288	.339	1144	280	45	3	19	134	67	191
.265	.308	.391	1119	296	62	4	24	24	66	139
.271	.326	.356	915	248	44	5	8	215	79	121

TIM LEARY — bats right — throws right — age 34 — NYA — P

1991

1991	G	IP	H	BB	SO	SB	CS	W	L	SV	ERA
at Home	12	56.1	62	26	39	6	3	1	4	0	5.75
on Road	16	64.1	88	31	44	4	2	3	6	0	7.13

	BA	OBA	SA	AB	H	2B	3B	HR	RBI	BB	SO
Total	.312	.388	.511	481	150	32	2	20	75	57	83
vs. Left	.303	.372	.487	261	79	19	1	9	38	30	42
vs. Right	.323	.406	.541	220	71	13	1	11	37	27	41
Bases Empty	.283	.359	.496	272	77	20	1	12	12	31	52
Runners On Base	.349	.425	.531	209	73	12	1	8	63	26	31

8-YEAR TOTALS (1984–1991)

G	IP	H	BB	SO	SB	CS	W	L	SV	ERA
111	579.0	600	186	383	62	27	27	44	0	4.04
113	568.1	595	188	370	44	19	30	41	1	4.18

BA	OBA	SA	AB	H	2B	3B	HR	RBI	BB	SO
.270	.329	.401	4431	1195	198	27	110	487	374	753
.280	.346	.417	2228	624	104	16	56	249	221	326
.259	.312	.385	2203	571	94	11	54	238	153	427
.262	.315	.400	2617	686	118	16	70	70	183	447
.281	.350	.403	1814	509	80	11	40	417	191	306

MARK LEE — bats left — throws left — age 28 — MIL — P

1991	G	IP	H	BB	SO	SB	CS	W	L	SV	ERA
at Home	28	40.0	40	15	26	1	2	1	3	1	3.83
on Road	34	27.2	32	16	17	5	1	1	2	0	3.90

	BA	OBA	SA	AB	H	2B	3B	HR	RBI	BB	SO
Total	.283	.362	.453	254	72	11	1	10	44	31	43
vs. Left	.308	.382	.440	91	28	3	0	3	18	10	10
vs. Right	.270	.351	.460	163	44	8	1	7	26	21	33
Bases Empty	.314	.394	.512	121	38	6	0	6	6	16	20
Runners On Base	.256	.333	.398	133	34	5	1	4	38	15	23

3-YEAR TOTALS (1988–1991)

G	IP	H	BB	SO	SB	CS	W	L	SV	ERA
35	55.0	56	18	31	3	2	1	3	1	3.76
42	39.0	42	18	26	5	2	2	2	0	3.00

BA	OBA	SA	AB	H	2B	3B	HR	RBI	BB	SO
.278	.344	.440	352	98	18	3	11	54	36	57
.305	.368	.424	118	36	5	0	3	25	12	13
.265	.332	.449	234	62	13	3	8	29	24	44
.322	.379	.523	174	56	12	1	7	7	16	29
.236	.312	.360	178	42	6	2	4	47	20	28

AL LEITER — bats left — throws left — age 27 — TOR — P

1991	G	IP	H	BB	SO	SB	CS	W	L	SV	ERA
at Home	2	1.2	1	3	1	0	0	0	0	0	5.40
on Road	1	0.0	2	2	0	0	0	0	0	0	0.00

	BA	OBA	SA	AB	H	2B	3B	HR	RBI	BB	SO
Total	.429	.667	.714	7	3	2	0	0	3	5	1
vs. Left	.333	.429	.500	6	2	1	0	0	2	1	1
vs. Right	1.000	1.000	2.000	1	1	1	0	0	1	4	0
Bases Empty	.000	.750	.000	1	0	0	0	0	0	3	0
Runners On Base	.500	.625	.833	6	3	2	0	0	3	2	1

5-YEAR TOTALS (1987–1991)

G	IP	H	BB	SO	SB	CS	W	L	SV	ERA
16	71.1	61	43	77	9	4	3	5	0	4.54
14	50.0	48	35	43	1	3	4	3	0	5.76

BA	OBA	SA	AB	H	2B	3B	HR	RBI	BB	SO
.240	.359	.361	454	109	20	1	11	54	78	120
.192	.315	.205	78	15	1	0	0	5	13	30
.250	.368	.394	376	94	19	1	11	49	65	90
.202	.356	.332	238	48	10	0	7	7	51	65
.282	.363	.394	216	61	10	1	4	47	27	55

JIM LEWIS — bats right — throws right — age 28 — SD — P

1991	G	IP	H	BB	SO	SB	CS	W	L	SV	ERA
at Home	7	7.2	8	7	7	1	0	0	0	0	3.52
on Road	5	5.1	6	4	3	0	0	0	0	0	5.06

	BA	OBA	SA	AB	H	2B	3B	HR	RBI	BB	SO
Total	.275	.403	.490	51	14	3	1	2	7	11	10
vs. Left	.200	.385	.300	20	4	0	1	0	2	6	6
vs. Right	.323	.417	.613	31	10	3	0	2	5	5	4
Bases Empty	.269	.387	.462	26	7	2	0	1	1	5	7
Runners On Base	.280	.419	.520	25	7	1	1	1	6	6	3

1-YEAR TOTALS (1991)

G	IP	H	BB	SO	SB	CS	W	L	SV	ERA
7	7.2	8	7	7	1	0	0	0	0	3.52
5	5.1	6	4	3	0	0	0	0	0	5.06

BA	OBA	SA	AB	H	2B	3B	HR	RBI	BB	SO
.275	.403	.490	51	14	3	1	2	7	11	10
.200	.385	.300	20	4	0	1	0	2	6	6
.323	.417	.613	31	10	3	0	2	5	5	4
.269	.387	.462	26	7	2	0	1	1	5	7
.280	.419	.520	25	7	1	1	1	6	6	3

SCOTT LEWIS — bats right — throws right — age 27 — CAL — P

1991	G	IP	H	BB	SO	SB	CS	W	L	SV	ERA
at Home	7	31.0	43	12	14	4	2	3	3	0	6.39
on Road	9	29.1	38	9	23	2	0	1	2	0	6.14

	BA	OBA	SA	AB	H	2B	3B	HR	RBI	BB	SO
Total	.316	.373	.484	256	81	16	0	9	42	21	37
vs. Left	.293	.356	.415	123	36	9	0	2	20	11	15
vs. Right	.338	.389	.549	133	45	7	0	7	22	10	22
Bases Empty	.299	.360	.460	137	41	10	0	4	4	12	21
Runners On Base	.336	.388	.513	119	40	6	0	5	38	9	16

2-YEAR TOTALS (1990–1991)

G	IP	H	BB	SO	SB	CS	W	L	SV	ERA
8	40.0	46	13	19	4	3	2	4	0	5.40
10	36.2	45	10	27	2	0	2	2	0	5.40

BA	OBA	SA	AB	H	2B	3B	HR	RBI	BB	SO
.290	.342	.455	314	91	19	0	11	46	23	46
.255	.314	.366	161	41	9	0	3	22	13	19
.327	.372	.549	153	50	10	0	8	24	10	27
.262	.318	.426	183	48	12	0	6	6	14	27
.328	.376	.496	131	43	7	0	5	40	9	19

DEREK LILLIQUIST — bats left — throws left — age 26 — SD — P

1991	G	IP	H	BB	SO	SB	CS	W	L	SV	ERA
at Home	3	5.2	9	1	4	0	0	0	1	0	11.12
on Road	2	8.2	16	3	3	0	1	0	1	0	7.27

	BA	OBA	SA	AB	H	2B	3B	HR	RBI	BB	SO
Total	.379	.414	.606	66	25	6	0	3	12	4	7
vs. Left	.333	.368	.611	18	6	2	0	1	4	1	2
vs. Right	.396	.431	.604	48	19	4	0	3	8	3	5
Bases Empty	.400	.417	.771	35	14	4	0	3	3	1	5
Runners On Base	.355	.412	.419	31	11	2	0	0	9	3	2

3-YEAR TOTALS (1989–1991)

G	IP	H	BB	SO	SB	CS	W	L	SV	ERA
35	160.2	189	36	85	6	3	7	12	0	4.09
31	141.1	174	44	64	12	7	6	11	0	5.48

BA	OBA	SA	AB	H	2B	3B	HR	RBI	BB	SO
.299	.343	.445	1215	363	67	3	35	144	80	149
.300	.347	.462	210	63	11	1	7	27	13	43
.299	.342	.442	1005	300	56	2	28	117	67	106
.282	.322	.435	717	202	41	3	21	21	39	97
.323	.370	.460	498	161	26	0	14	123	41	52

BILL LONG — bats right — throws right — age 32 — MON — P

1991	G	IP	H	BB	SO	SB	CS	W	L	SV	ERA
at Home	0	0.0	0	0	0	0	0	0	0	0	0.00
on Road	3	1.2	4	4	0	0	0	0	0	0	10.80

	BA	OBA	SA	AB	H	2B	3B	HR	RBI	BB	SO
Total	.500	.667	.750	8	4	2	0	0	4	4	0
vs. Left	.000	.600	.000	2	0	0	0	0	0	3	0
vs. Right	.667	.714	1.000	6	4	2	0	0	4	1	0
Bases Empty	.500	.600	1.000	4	2	2	0	0	0	1	0
Runners On Base	.500	.714	.500	4	2	0	0	0	4	3	0

6-YEAR TOTALS (1985–1991)

G	IP	H	BB	SO	SB	CS	W	L	SV	ERA
78	239.0	278	66	108	22	9	11	15	5	4.71
82	286.2	293	76	142	21	12	17	12	4	3.99

BA	OBA	SA	AB	H	2B	3B	HR	RBI	BB	SO
.279	.327	.446	2048	571	110	22	63	274	142	250
.294	.346	.476	1019	300	54	16	33	135	78	116
.263	.307	.417	1029	271	56	6	30	139	64	134
.275	.319	.430	1191	328	71	10	31	31	66	157
.284	.336	.469	857	243	39	12	32	243	76	93

ROB MacDONALD — bats left — throws left — age 27 — TOR — P

1991	G	IP	H	BB	SO	SB	CS	W	L	SV	ERA
at Home	25	31.2	31	14	12	4	3	1	1	0	2.84
on Road	20	22.0	20	11	12	2	1	2	2	0	2.86

	BA	OBA	SA	AB	H	2B	3B	HR	RBI	BB	SO
Total	.252	.332	.361	202	51	7	0	5	35	25	24
vs. Left	.325	.416	.455	77	25	4	0	2	18	12	9
vs. Right	.208	.279	.304	125	26	3	0	3	17	13	15
Bases Empty	.223	.298	.309	94	21	2	0	2	2	10	9
Runners On Base	.278	.360	.407	108	30	5	0	3	33	15	15

2-YEAR TOTALS (1990–1991)

G	IP	H	BB	SO	SB	CS	W	L	SV	ERA
26	32.0	31	14	12	4	3	1	1	0	2.81
23	24.0	20	13	12	2	1	2	2	0	2.63

BA	OBA	SA	AB	H	2B	3B	HR	RBI	BB	SO
.245	.329	.351	208	51	7	0	5	35	27	24
.316	.413	.443	79	25	4	0	2	18	13	9
.202	.276	.295	129	26	3	0	3	17	14	15
.214	.294	.296	98	21	2	0	3	2	11	9
.273	.359	.400	110	30	5	0	3	33	16	15

JULIO MACHADO — bats right — throws right — age 27 — MIL — P

1991

	G	IP	H	BB	SO	SB	CS	W	L	SV	ERA
at Home	27	45.2	32	32	51	1	3	1	1	1	2.76
on Road	27	43.0	33	23	47	4	2	2	2	2	4.19

	BA	OBA	SA	AB	H	2B	3B	HR	RBI	BB	SO
Total	.211	.334	.364	308	65	11	0	12	44	55	98
vs. Left	.218	.335	.415	147	32	5	0	8	24	25	47
vs. Right	.205	.333	.317	161	33	6	0	4	20	30	51
Bases Empty	.216	.356	.399	148	32	6	0	7	7	31	45
Runners On Base	.206	.314	.331	160	33	5	0	5	37	24	53

3-YEAR TOTALS (1989–1991)

G	IP	H	BB	SO	SB	CS	W	L	SV	ERA
48	72.0	49	43	83	4	6	2	2	3	2.13
53	75.0	66	40	68	9	3	5	3	3	4.08

BA	OBA	SA	AB	H	2B	3B	HR	RBI	BB	SO
.219	.328	.356	526	115	18	3	16	74	83	151
.217	.332	.377	244	53	8	2	9	39	41	71
.220	.324	.337	282	62	10	1	7	35	42	80
.224	.343	.382	254	57	10	0	10	10	44	72
.213	.313	.331	272	58	8	3	6	64	39	79

MIKE MAGNANTE — bats left — throws left — age 27 — KC — P

1991

	G	IP	H	BB	SO	SB	CS	W	L	SV	ERA
at Home	20	30.1	31	10	31	0	1	0	0	0	3.26
on Road	18	24.2	24	13	11	1	1	0	1	0	1.46

	BA	OBA	SA	AB	H	2B	3B	HR	RBI	BB	SO
Total	.262	.333	.386	210	55	15	1	3	24	23	42
vs. Left	.260	.337	.384	73	19	6	0	1	9	9	15
vs. Right	.263	.331	.387	137	36	9	1	2	15	14	27
Bases Empty	.269	.361	.442	104	28	9	0	3	3	15	18
Runners On Base	.255	.304	.330	106	27	6	1	0	21	8	24

1-YEAR TOTALS (1991)

G	IP	H	BB	SO	SB	CS	W	L	SV	ERA
20	30.1	31	10	31	0	1	0	0	0	3.26
18	24.2	24	13	11	1	1	0	1	0	1.46

BA	OBA	SA	AB	H	2B	3B	HR	RBI	BB	SO
.262	.333	.386	210	55	15	1	3	24	23	42
.260	.337	.384	73	19	6	0	1	9	9	15
.263	.331	.387	137	36	9	1	2	15	14	27
.269	.361	.442	104	28	9	0	3	3	15	18
.255	.304	.330	106	27	6	1	0	21	8	24

RICK MAHLER — bats right — throws right — age 39 — MON/ATL — P

1991

	G	IP	H	BB	SO	SB	CS	W	L	SV	ERA
at Home	12	31.2	33	13	15	4	2	2	1	0	4.26
on Road	11	34.1	37	15	12	5	4	0	3	0	4.72

	BA	OBA	SA	AB	H	2B	3B	HR	RBI	BB	SO
Total	.276	.351	.398	254	70	15	2	4	39	28	27
vs. Left	.254	.324	.377	130	33	11	1	1	18	14	10
vs. Right	.298	.379	.419	124	37	4	1	3	21	14	17
Bases Empty	.281	.348	.391	128	36	9	1	1	1	12	14
Runners On Base	.270	.354	.405	126	34	6	1	3	38	16	13

8-YEAR TOTALS (1984–1991)

G	IP	H	BB	SO	SB	CS	W	L	SV	ERA
146	782.1	846	228	370	55	41	42	37	1	4.10
146	811.1	855	252	403	66	40	37	58	3	3.94

BA	OBA	SA	AB	H	2B	3B	HR	RBI	BB	SO
.277	.330	.403	6151	1701	279	41	138	729	480	773
.289	.341	.419	3368	974	174	28	69	386	265	376
.261	.317	.383	2783	727	105	13	69	343	215	397
.266	.308	.391	3701	985	166	21	85	85	213	464
.292	.361	.420	2450	716	113	20	53	644	267	309

CARLOS MALDONADO — bats both — throws right — age 26 — KC — P

1991

	G	IP	H	BB	SO	SB	CS	W	L	SV	ERA
at Home	3	4.2	8	5	0	0	0	0	0	0	11.57
on Road	2	3.0	3	4	1	0	0	0	0	0	3.00

	BA	OBA	SA	AB	H	2B	3B	HR	RBI	BB	SO
Total	.333	.476	.424	33	11	3	0	0	6	9	1
vs. Left	.353	.450	.412	17	6	1	0	0	4	3	0
vs. Right	.313	.500	.438	16	5	2	0	0	2	6	1
Bases Empty	.231	.375	.308	13	3	1	0	0	0	3	0
Runners On Base	.400	.538	.500	20	8	2	0	0	6	6	1

2-YEAR TOTALS (1990–1991)

G	IP	H	BB	SO	SB	CS	W	L	SV	ERA
5	6.1	11	6	3	0	0	0	0	0	11.37
4	7.1	9	7	7	1	0	0	0	0	6.14

BA	OBA	SA	AB	H	2B	3B	HR	RBI	BB	SO
.339	.452	.475	59	20	6	1	0	10	13	10
.387	.474	.548	31	12	3	1	0	6	6	4
.286	.429	.393	28	8	3	0	0	4	7	6
.292	.393	.333	24	7	1	0	0	4	4	4
.371	.489	.571	35	13	5	1	0	10	9	6

ROB MALLICOAT — bats left — throws left — age 28 — HOU — P

1991

	G	IP	H	BB	SO	SB	CS	W	L	SV	ERA
at Home	10	7.1	12	4	6	0	0	0	1	0	8.59
on Road	14	16.0	10	9	12	1	1	0	1	1	1.69

	BA	OBA	SA	AB	H	2B	3B	HR	RBI	BB	SO
Total	.259	.363	.388	85	22	5	0	2	16	13	18
vs. Left	.263	.378	.395	38	10	2	0	1	9	6	7
vs. Right	.255	.351	.383	47	12	3	0	1	7	7	11
Bases Empty	.179	.360	.308	39	7	2	0	1	1	11	8
Runners On Base	.326	.365	.457	46	15	3	0	1	15	2	10

2-YEAR TOTALS (1987–1991)

G	IP	H	BB	SO	SB	CS	W	L	SV	ERA
12	9.0	17	9	6	4	0	0	1	0	11.00
16	21.0	13	10	16	1	3	0	1	1	1.71

BA	OBA	SA	AB	H	2B	3B	HR	RBI	BB	SO
.273	.383	.373	110	30	5	0	2	21	19	22
.227	.358	.341	44	10	2	0	1	9	8	9
.303	.400	.394	66	20	3	0	1	12	11	13
.173	.338	.269	52	9	2	0	1	1	13	10
.362	.426	.466	58	21	3	0	1	20	6	12

BARRY MANUEL — bats right — throws right — age 27 — TEX — P

1991

	G	IP	H	BB	SO	SB	CS	W	L	SV	ERA
at Home	4	9.1	3	4	2	0	0	0	0	0	0.96
on Road	4	6.2	4	2	3	0	0	1	0	0	1.35

	BA	OBA	SA	AB	H	2B	3B	HR	RBI	BB	SO
Total	.143	.224	.163	49	7	1	0	0	4	6	5
vs. Left	.091	.200	.136	22	2	1	0	0	1	3	2
vs. Right	.185	.242	.185	27	5	0	0	0	3	3	3
Bases Empty	.133	.235	.133	30	4	0	0	0	0	4	2
Runners On Base	.158	.208	.211	19	3	1	0	0	4	2	2

1-YEAR TOTALS (1991)

G	IP	H	BB	SO	SB	CS	W	L	SV	ERA
4	9.1	3	4	2	0	0	0	0	0	0.96
4	6.2	4	2	3	0	0	1	0	0	1.35

BA	OBA	SA	AB	H	2B	3B	HR	RBI	BB	SO
.143	.224	.163	49	7	1	0	0	4	6	5
.091	.200	.136	22	2	1	0	0	1	3	2
.185	.242	.185	27	5	0	0	0	3	3	3
.133	.235	.133	30	4	0	0	0	0	4	2
.158	.208	.211	19	3	1	0	0	4	2	2

JOSIAS MANZANILLO — bats right — throws right — age 25 — BOS — P

1991

	G	IP	H	BB	SO	SB	CS	W	L	SV	ERA
at Home	1	1.0	2	3	1	0	0	0	0	0	18.00
on Road	0	0.0	0	0	0	0	0	0	0	0	0.00

	BA	OBA	SA	AB	H	2B	3B	HR	RBI	BB	SO
Total	.400	.625	.600	5	2	1	0	0	2	3	1
vs. Left	.500	.667	1.000	2	1	1	0	0	2	3	1
vs. Right	.333	.600	.333	3	1	0	0	0		2	1
Bases Empty	.000	1.000	.000	2	0	0	0	0		2	1
Runners On Base	.400	.571	.600	5	2	1	0	0	2		1

1-YEAR TOTALS (1991)

G	IP	H	BB	SO	SB	CS	W	L	SV	ERA
1	1.0	2	3	1	0	0	0	0	0	18.00
0	0.0	0	0	0	0	0	0	0	0	0.00

BA	OBA	SA	AB	H	2B	3B	HR	RBI	BB	SO
.400	.625	.600	5	2	1	0	0	2	3	1
.500	.667	1.000	2	1	1	0	0	2	3	1
.333	.600	.333	3	1	0	0	0		2	1
.000	1.000	.000	2	0	0	0	0		2	1
.400	.571	.600	5	2	1	0	0	2		1

ROGER MASON — bats right — throws right — age 34 — PIT — P

6-YEAR TOTALS (1984–1991)

1991	G	IP	H	BB	SO	SB	CS	W	L	SV	ERA
at Home	14	16.2	13	2	11	0	2	2	1	2	3.24
on Road	10	13.0	8	4	10	0	0	1	1		2.77
	25	93.0	70	31	67	3	7	7	4	2	2.61
	27	75.2	90	38	59	6	4	7	2	7	5.83

	BA	OBA	SA	AB	H	2B	3B	HR	RBI	BB	SO
Total	.200	.248	.305	105	21	3	1	2	10	6	21
vs. Left	.220	.286	.340	50	11	1	1	1	6	5	8
vs. Right	.182	.211	.273	55	10	2	0	1	4	1	13
Bases Empty	.143	.194	.222	63	9	0	1	1		4	13
Runners On Base	.286	.326	.429	42	12	3	0	1	9	2	8
	.252	.327	.377	634	160	34	3	13	70	69	126
	.285	.360	.420	333	95	15	3	8	40	41	60
	.216	.290	.329	301	65	19	0	5	30	28	66
	.238	.302	.359	365	87	18	1	8	8	32	68
	.271	.359	.401	269	73	16	2	5	62	37	58

TERRY MATHEWS — bats left — throws right — age 28 — TEX — P

1-YEAR TOTALS (1991)

1991	G	IP	H	BB	SO	SB	CS	W	L	SV	ERA
at Home	17	26.1	20	12	24	5	2	2	0	1	3.42
on Road	17	31.0	34	6	27	3	2	2	0	0	3.77
	17	26.1	20	12	24	5	2	2	0	1	3.42
	17	31.0	34	6	27	3	2	2	0	0	3.77

	BA	OBA	SA	AB	H	2B	3B	HR	RBI	BB	SO
Total	.251	.312	.419	215	54	19	1	5	22	18	51
vs. Left	.291	.385	.468	79	23	6	1	2	8	11	14
vs. Right	.228	.266	.390	136	31	13	0	3	14	7	37
Bases Empty	.262	.321	.413	126	33	8	1	3	3	11	28
Runners On Base	.236	.299	.427	89	21	11	0	2	19	7	23
	.251	.312	.419	215	54	19	1	5	22	18	51
	.291	.385	.468	79	23	6	1	2	8	11	14
	.228	.266	.390	136	31	13	0	3	14	7	37
	.262	.321	.413	126	33	8	1	3	3	11	28
	.236	.299	.427	89	21	11	0	2	19	7	23

TIM MAUSER — bats right — throws right — age 26 — PHI — P

1-YEAR TOTALS (1991)

1991	G	IP	H	BB	SO	SB	CS	W	L	SV	ERA
at Home	3	10.2	18	3	6	0	0	0	0	0	7.59
on Road	0	0.0	0	0	0	0	0	0	0	0	0.00
	3	10.2	18	3	6	0	0	0	0	0	7.59
	0	0.0	0	0	0	0	0	0	0	0	0.00

	BA	OBA	SA	AB	H	2B	3B	HR	RBI	BB	SO
Total	.367	.404	.633	49	18	4	0	3	10	3	6
vs. Left	.500	.550	.778	18	9	2	0	1	4	2	0
vs. Right	.290	.313	.548	31	9	2	0	2	6	1	6
Bases Empty	.417	.462	.750	24	10	2	0	2	2	2	3
Runners On Base	.320	.346	.520	25	8	2	0	1	8	1	3
	.367	.404	.633	49	18	4	0	3	10	3	6
	.500	.550	.778	18	9	2	0	1	4	2	0
	.290	.313	.548	31	9	2	0	2	6	1	6
	.417	.462	.750	24	10	2	0	2	2	2	3
	.320	.346	.520	25	8	2	0	1	8	1	3

SCOTT MAY — bats right — throws right — age 31 — CHN — P

2-YEAR TOTALS (1988–1991)

1991	G	IP	H	BB	SO	SB	CS	W	L	SV	ERA
at Home	1	0.0	2	1	0	0	0	0	0	0	0.00
on Road	1	2.0	4	0	1	0	0	0	0	0	4.50
	2	3.0	4	2	2	0	0	0	0	0	12.00
	3	6.1	10	3	3	0	0	0	0	0	9.95

	BA	OBA	SA	AB	H	2B	3B	HR	RBI	BB	SO
Total	.545	.583	.727	11	6	2	0	0	1	1	1
vs. Left	.667	.667	1.000	3	2	1	0	0	1	0	0
vs. Right	.500	.556	.625	8	4	1	0	0	1	0	1
Bases Empty	.600	.600	.800	5	3	1	0	0	0	0	0
Runners On Base	.500	.571	.667	6	3	1	0	0	1	1	1
	.368	.422	.711	38	14	4	0	3	8	5	5
	.294	.381	.588	17	5	2	0	1	3	3	3
	.429	.458	.810	21	9	2	0	2	5	2	2
	.320	.370	.640	25	8	2	0	2	2	2	4
	.462	.500	.846	13	6	2	0	1	6	3	1

PAUL McCLELLAN — bats right — throws right — age 26 — SF — P

2-YEAR TOTALS (1990–1991)

1991	G	IP	H	BB	SO	SB	CS	W	L	SV	ERA
at Home	7	35.1	34	12	28	6	4	2	2	0	4.33
on Road	6	35.2	34	13	16	6	1	1	4	0	4.79
	8	35.2	39	14	28	6	4	2	2	0	5.30
	9	43.0	43	17	18	6	1	1	5	0	5.23

	BA	OBA	SA	AB	H	2B	3B	HR	RBI	BB	SO
Total	.252	.316	.437	270	68	12	1	12	35	25	44
vs. Left	.273	.350	.462	143	39	6	0	7	20	16	19
vs. Right	.228	.277	.409	127	29	6	1	5	15	9	25
Bases Empty	.259	.311	.441	170	44	10	0	7	7	12	25
Runners On Base	.240	.325	.430	100	24	2	1	5	28	13	19
	.268	.338	.480	306	82	18	1	15	45	31	46
	.279	.353	.473	165	46	11	0	7	23	18	20
	.255	.321	.489	141	36	7	1	8	22	13	26
	.269	.330	.500	186	50	13	0	10	10	15	27
	.267	.350	.450	120	32	5	1	5	35	16	19

BOB McCLURE — bats right — throws left — age 40 — CAL/SL — P

8-YEAR TOTALS (1984–1991)

1991	G	IP	H	BB	SO	SB	CS	W	L	SV	ERA
at Home	28	19.1	21	10	12	0	1	1	0	0	3.72
on Road	17	13.1	16	3	8	0	1	0	1	0	6.75
	165	243.1	259	87	145	10	8	20	9	8	3.85
	166	235.0	223	87	147	12	5	9	12	13	3.94

	BA	OBA	SA	AB	H	2B	3B	HR	RBI	BB	SO
Total	.294	.359	.429	126	37	3	1	4	21	13	20
vs. Left	.230	.319	.311	61	14	0	1	1	10	8	13
vs. Right	.354	.397	.538	65	23	3	0	3	11	5	7
Bases Empty	.246	.300	.431	65	16	1	1	3	3	8	12
Runners On Base	.344	.413	.426	61	21	2	0	1	18	5	8
	.265	.329	.398	1820	482	85	17	41	248	174	292
	.218	.285	.326	579	126	17	8	10	78	58	120
	.287	.349	.431	1241	356	68	9	31	170	116	172
	.259	.312	.377	979	254	45	9	18	18	69	134
	.271	.346	.422	841	228	40	9	23	230	105	158

CHUCK McELROY — bats left — throws left — age 25 — CHN — P

3-YEAR TOTALS (1989–1991)

1991	G	IP	H	BB	SO	SB	CS	W	L	SV	ERA
at Home	36	58.2	43	27	53	4	6	3	1	3	1.53
on Road	35	42.2	30	30	39	8	4	3	1	0	2.53
	53	73.2	70	38	69	6	6	3	2	3	2.69
	45	52.0	39	33	47	9	4	3	1	0	2.42

	BA	OBA	SA	AB	H	2B	3B	HR	RBI	BB	SO
Total	.210	.317	.305	347	73	10	1	7	38	57	92
vs. Left	.174	.282	.273	121	21	3	0	1	15	19	41
vs. Right	.230	.336	.323	226	52	7	1	6	23	38	51
Bases Empty	.209	.327	.294	187	39	7	0	3	3	33	49
Runners On Base	.213	.305	.319	160	34	3	1	4	35	24	43
	.240	.338	.344	454	109	21	1	8	56	71	116
	.200	.301	.307	150	30	7	0	3	19	23	45
	.260	.357	.362	304	79	14	1	5	37	48	71
	.242	.353	.352	227	55	13	0	4	4	39	54
	.238	.323	.335	227	54	8	1	4	52	32	62

ANDY McGAFFIGAN — bats right — throws right — age 36 — KC — P

1991	G	IP	H	BB	SO	SB	CS	W	L	SV	ERA
at Home	3	7.2	13	1	2	0	0	0	0	0	4.70
on Road	1	0.1	1	1	0	0	0	0	0	0	0.00

	BA	OBA	SA	AB	H	2B	3B	HR	RBI	BB	SO
Total	.389	.410	.500	36	14	2	1	0	4	2	3
vs. Left	.471	.474	.647	17	8	1	1	0	3	1	1
vs. Right	.316	.350	.368	19	6	1	0	0	1	1	2
Bases Empty	.412	.444	.529	17	7	2	0	0	0	1	2
Runners On Base	.368	.381	.474	19	7	0	1	0	4	1	1

8-YEAR TOTALS (1984–1991)

G	IP	H	BB	SO	SB	CS	W	L	SV	ERA
155	333.1	306	114	236	41	9	17	10	8	3.16
159	350.2	326	137	275	46	11	17	14	14	3.34

BA	OBA	SA	AB	H	2B	3B	HR	RBI	BB	SO
.246	.315	.347	2569	632	110	19	37	280	251	511
.239	.321	.337	1331	318	55	12	17	138	164	258
.254	.308	.358	1238	314	55	7	20	142	87	253
.240	.305	.341	1436	345	60	9	22	22	128	277
.253	.326	.355	1133	287	50	10	15	258	123	234

RUSTY MEACHAM — bats right — throws right — age 24 — DET — P

1991	G	IP	H	BB	SO	SB	CS	W	L	SV	ERA
at Home	4	13.1	20	7	7	1	0	1	0	0	6.75
on Road	6	14.1	15	4	7	0	0	1	1	0	3.77

	BA	OBA	SA	AB	H	2B	3B	HR	RBI	BB	SO
Total	.315	.368	.495	111	35	8	0	4	16	11	14
vs. Left	.404	.444	.660	47	19	3	0	4	12	5	3
vs. Right	.250	.310	.375	64	16	5	0	1	4	6	11
Bases Empty	.284	.333	.478	67	19	7	0	2	2	5	11
Runners On Base	.364	.415	.523	44	16	1	0	2	14	6	3

1-YEAR TOTALS (1991)

G	IP	H	BB	SO	SB	CS	W	L	SV	ERA
4	13.1	20	7	7	1	0	1	0	0	6.75
6	14.1	15	4	7	0	0	1	1	0	3.77

BA	OBA	SA	AB	H	2B	3B	HR	RBI	BB	SO
.315	.368	.495	111	35	8	0	4	16	11	14
.404	.444	.660	47	19	3	0	4	12	5	3
.250	.310	.375	64	16	5	0	1	4	6	11
.284	.333	.478	67	19	7	0	2	2	5	11
.364	.415	.523	44	16	1	0	2	14	6	3

JOSE MELENDEZ — bats right — throws right — age 27 — SD — P

1991	G	IP	H	BB	SO	SB	CS	W	L	SV	ERA
at Home	14	46.1	36	9	28	0	3	5	3	1	3.30
on Road	17	47.1	41	15	32	1	3	3	2	2	3.23

	BA	OBA	SA	AB	H	2B	3B	HR	RBI	BB	SO
Total	.221	.269	.368	348	77	16	1	11	32	24	60
vs. Left	.226	.283	.362	177	40	6	0	6	17	16	33
vs. Right	.216	.254	.374	171	37	10	1	5	15	8	27
Bases Empty	.224	.275	.399	228	51	11	1	9	9	15	39
Runners On Base	.217	.259	.308	120	26	5	0	2	23	9	21

2-YEAR TOTALS (1990–1991)

G	IP	H	BB	SO	SB	CS	W	L	SV	ERA
17	51.2	44	12	35	1	3	5	3	1	4.18
17	47.1	41	15	32	1	3	3	2	2	3.23

BA	OBA	SA	AB	H	2B	3B	HR	RBI	BB	SO
.228	.280	.384	372	85	17	1	13	39	27	67
.234	.297	.367	188	44	7	0	6	18	19	36
.223	.262	.402	184	41	10	1	7	21	8	31
.221	.278	.387	240	53	11	1	9	9	17	44
.242	.284	.379	132	32	6	0	4	30	10	23

KENT MERCKER — bats left — throws left — age 24 — ATL — P

1991	G	IP	H	BB	SO	SB	CS	W	L	SV	ERA
at Home	27	36.1	30	19	30	2	0	4	1	5	2.48
on Road	23	37.0	26	16	32	8	0	1	2	1	2.68

	BA	OBA	SA	AB	H	2B	3B	HR	RBI	BB	SO
Total	.211	.303	.316	266	56	9	2	5	24	35	62
vs. Left	.197	.321	.254	71	14	1	0	1	6	13	20
vs. Right	.215	.295	.338	195	42	8	2	4	18	22	42
Bases Empty	.217	.337	.322	143	31	8	2	1	1	26	38
Runners On Base	.203	.259	.309	123	25	1	0	4	23	9	24

3-YEAR TOTALS (1989–1991)

G	IP	H	BB	SO	SB	CS	W	L	SV	ERA
44	59.2	54	29	47	4	2	7	3	10	2.87
44	66.1	53	36	58	12	2	2	7	3	3.39

BA	OBA	SA	AB	H	2B	3B	HR	RBI	BB	SO
.229	.324	.350	468	107	18	3	11	52	65	105
.215	.333	.289	121	26	3	0	2	8	22	32
.233	.321	.372	347	81	15	3	9	44	43	73
.217	.323	.354	254	55	11	3	6	6	39	59
.243	.325	.346	214	52	7	0	5	46	26	46

PAUL MILLER — bats right — throws right — age 27 — PIT — P

1991	G	IP	H	BB	SO	SB	CS	W	L	SV	ERA
at Home	0	0.0	0	0	0	0	0	0	0	0	0.00
on Road	1	5.0	4	3	2	0	0	0	0	0	5.40

	BA	OBA	SA	AB	H	2B	3B	HR	RBI	BB	SO
Total	.222	.333	.333	18	4	2	0	0	0	3	2
vs. Left	.500	.667	.833	6	3	2	0	0	0	3	0
vs. Right	.083	.083	.083	12	1	0	0	0	0	0	2
Bases Empty	.333	.455	.556	9	3	2	0	0	0	2	0
Runners On Base	.111	.200	.111	9	1	0	0	0	0	1	2

1-YEAR TOTALS (1991)

G	IP	H	BB	SO	SB	CS	W	L	SV	ERA
0	0.0	0	0	0	0	0	0	0	0	0.00
1	5.0	4	3	2	0	0	0	0	0	5.40

BA	OBA	SA	AB	H	2B	3B	HR	RBI	BB	SO
.222	.333	.333	18	4	2	0	0	0	3	2
.500	.667	.833	6	3	2	0	0	0	3	0
.083	.083	.083	12	1	0	0	0	0	0	2
.333	.455	.556	9	3	2	0	0	0	2	0
.111	.200	.111	9	1	0	0	0	0	1	2

ALAN MILLS — bats right — throws right — age 26 — NYA — P

1991	G	IP	H	BB	SO	SB	CS	W	L	SV	ERA
at Home	3	8.1	6	2	5	3	0	0	0	0	1.08
on Road	3	8.0	10	6	6	0	0	1	1	0	7.88

	BA	OBA	SA	AB	H	2B	3B	HR	RBI	BB	SO
Total	.254	.333	.333	63	16	2	0	1	8	8	11
vs. Left	.333	.408	.452	42	14	2	0	1	6	6	6
vs. Right	.095	.174	.095	21	2	0	0	0	2	2	5
Bases Empty	.235	.297	.353	34	8	2	0	1	1	3	7
Runners On Base	.276	.371	.310	29	8	1	0	0	7	5	4

2-YEAR TOTALS (1990–1991)

G	IP	H	BB	SO	SB	CS	W	L	SV	ERA
19	30.1	36	16	17	5	1	0	4	0	3.56
23	27.2	28	25	18	2	0	2	2	0	4.88

BA	OBA	SA	AB	H	2B	3B	HR	RBI	BB	SO
.286	.396	.424	224	64	12	2	5	34	41	35
.308	.418	.410	117	36	6	0	2	12	22	19
.262	.370	.439	107	28	6	2	3	22	19	16
.323	.422	.516	93	30	7	1	3	3	16	12
.260	.377	.359	131	34	5	1	2	31	25	23

GINO MINUTELLI — bats left — throws left — age 28 — CIN — P

1991	G	IP	H	BB	SO	SB	CS	W	L	SV	ERA
at Home	10	17.0	21	11	13	1	0	0	1	0	3.18
on Road	6	8.1	9	7	8	1	0	0	1	0	11.88

	BA	OBA	SA	AB	H	2B	3B	HR	RBI	BB	SO
Total	.288	.387	.519	104	30	5	1	5	14	18	21
vs. Left	.333	.459	.630	27	9	3	1	1	5	8	6
vs. Right	.273	.356	.481	77	21	2	1	4	9	10	15
Bases Empty	.286	.365	.554	56	16	4	1	3	3	7	9
Runners On Base	.292	.410	.479	48	14	1	1	2	11	11	12

2-YEAR TOTALS (1990–1991)

G	IP	H	BB	SO	SB	CS	W	L	SV	ERA
12	18.0	21	13	13	1	0	0	1	0	3.50
6	8.1	9	7	8	1	0	0	1	0	11.88

BA	OBA	SA	AB	H	2B	3B	HR	RBI	BB	SO
.280	.392	.505	107	30	5	2	5	14	20	21
.333	.487	.630	27	9	3	1	1	5	10	6
.262	.352	.463	80	21	2	1	4	9	10	15
.271	.358	.525	59	16	4	1	3	3	8	9
.292	.429	.479	48	14	1	1	2	11	12	12

RICH MONTELEONE — bats right — throws right — age 29 — NYA — P

1991	G	IP	H	BB	SO	SB	CS	W	L	SV	ERA
at Home	14	23.0	19	9	17	1	0	2	0	0	3.52
on Road	12	24.0	23	10	17	1	2	1	1	0	3.75

	BA	OBA	SA	AB	H	2B	3B	HR	RBI	BB	SO
Total	.236	.307	.376	178	42	10	0	5	28	19	34
vs. Left	.306	.351	.431	72	22	3	0	2	12	5	6
vs. Right	.189	.279	.340	106	20	7	0	3	16	14	28
Bases Empty	.244	.323	.349	86	21	6	0	1	10	18
Runners On Base	.228	.291	.402	92	21	4	0	4	27	9	16

5-YEAR TOTALS (1987–1991)

G	IP	H	BB	SO	SB	CS	W	L	SV	ERA
27	49.0	43	17	30	2	1	2	1	0	3.31
34	56.1	60	22	44	1	3	3	3	0	3.99

BA	OBA	SA	AB	H	2B	3B	HR	RBI	BB	SO
.253	.320	.383	407	103	21	1	10	59	39	74
.273	.333	.383	183	50	9	1	3	21	16	21
.237	.310	.384	224	53	12	0	7	38	23	53
.245	.304	.344	212	52	10	1	3	3	17	43
.262	.336	.426	195	51	11	0	7	56	22	31

KEVIN MORTON — bats right — throws left — age 24 — BOS — P

1991	G	IP	H	BB	SO	SB	CS	W	L	SV	ERA
at Home	9	44.0	52	21	29	0	1	4	2	0	4.91
on Road	7	42.1	41	19	16	4	1	2	3	0	4.25

	BA	OBA	SA	AB	H	2B	3B	HR	RBI	BB	SO
Total	.284	.356	.448	328	93	23	2	9	41	40	45
vs. Left	.268	.375	.463	41	11	2	0	2	5	6	8
vs. Right	.286	.354	.446	287	82	21	2	7	36	34	37
Bases Empty	.307	.361	.505	192	59	15	1	7	7	15	22
Runners On Base	.250	.351	.368	136	34	8	1	2	34	25	23

1-YEAR TOTALS (1991)

G	IP	H	BB	SO	SB	CS	W	L	SV	ERA
9	44.0	52	21	29	0	1	4	2	0	4.91
7	42.1	41	19	16	4	1	2	3	0	4.25

BA	OBA	SA	AB	H	2B	3B	HR	RBI	BB	SO
.284	.356	.448	328	93	23	2	9	41	40	45
.268	.375	.463	41	11	2	0	2	5	6	8
.286	.354	.446	287	82	21	2	7	36	34	37
.307	.361	.505	192	59	15	1	7	7	15	22
.250	.351	.368	136	34	8	1	2	34	25	23

JAMIE MOYER — bats left — throws left — age 30 — SL — P

1991	G	IP	H	BB	SO	SB	CS	W	L	SV	ERA
at Home	3	13.1	17	6	6	1	1	0	1	0	6.07
on Road	5	18.0	21	10	14	7	2	0	4	0	5.50

	BA	OBA	SA	AB	H	2B	3B	HR	RBI	BB	SO
Total	.319	.399	.529	119	38	8	1	5	20	16	20
vs. Left	.520	.556	1.000	25	13	3	0	3	8	2	4
vs. Right	.266	.360	.404	94	25	5	1	2	12	14	16
Bases Empty	.257	.358	.457	70	18	3	1	3	3	10	15
Runners On Base	.408	.456	.633	49	20	5	0	2	17	6	5

6-YEAR TOTALS (1986–1991)

G	IP	H	BB	SO	SB	CS	W	L	SV	ERA
72	389.0	412	151	257	36	27	17	23	0	4.35
69	311.0	354	131	178	48	18	17	31	0	4.83

BA	OBA	SA	AB	H	2B	3B	HR	RBI	BB	SO
.283	.351	.431	2710	766	134	15	79	346	282	435
.245	.325	.404	428	105	19	2	15	56	48	72
.290	.356	.436	2282	661	115	13	64	290	234	363
.282	.348	.429	1534	432	75	8	45	45	145	259
.284	.355	.433	1176	334	59	7	34	301	137	176

MIKE MUNOZ — bats left — throws left — age 27 — DET — P

1991	G	IP	H	BB	SO	SB	CS	W	L	SV	ERA
at Home	4	5.1	11	3	2	0	0	0	0	0	11.81
on Road	2	4.0	3	2	1	0	0	0	0	0	6.75

	BA	OBA	SA	AB	H	2B	3B	HR	RBI	BB	SO
Total	.350	.413	.400	40	14	2	0	0	10	5	3
vs. Left	.357	.400	.500	14	5	2	0	0	6	1	1
vs. Right	.346	.419	.346	26	9	0	0	0	4	4	2
Bases Empty	.278	.350	.278	18	5	0	0	0	0	2	2
Runners On Base	.409	.462	.500	22	9	2	0	0	10	3	1

3-YEAR TOTALS (1989–1991)

G	IP	H	BB	SO	SB	CS	W	L	SV	ERA
7	8.0	13	3	5	0	1	0	0	0	7.88
10	9.2	12	7	3	0	0	0	1	0	9.31

BA	OBA	SA	AB	H	2B	3B	HR	RBI	BB	SO
.347	.422	.431	72	25	3	0	1	18	10	8
.333	.400	.407	27	9	2	0	0	8	3	3
.356	.434	.444	45	16	1	0	1	10	7	5
.379	.419	.483	29	11	0	0	1	1	2	4
.326	.423	.395	43	14	3	0	0	17	8	4

ROB MURPHY — bats left — throws left — age 32 — SEA — P

1991	G	IP	H	BB	SO	SB	CS	W	L	SV	ERA
at Home	27	25.2	19	10	16	1	0	0	0	3	1.40
on Road	30	22.1	28	9	18	4	0	0	1	1	4.84

	BA	OBA	SA	AB	H	2B	3B	HR	RBI	BB	SO
Total	.250	.322	.410	188	47	12	3	4	28	19	34
vs. Left	.203	.224	.351	74	15	3	1	2	11	1	9
vs. Right	.281	.379	.447	114	32	9	2	2	17	18	25
Bases Empty	.205	.286	.330	88	18	5	1	2	2	9	13
Runners On Base	.290	.355	.480	100	29	7	3	2	26	10	21

7-YEAR TOTALS (1985–1991)

G	IP	H	BB	SO	SB	CS	W	L	SV	ERA
202	233.1	213	90	214	16	8	9	10	10	3.01
196	215.1	204	95	191	22	8	10	15	17	3.30

BA	OBA	SA	AB	H	2B	3B	HR	RBI	BB	SO
.249	.323	.366	1677	417	80	10	32	205	185	405
.222	.275	.299	519	115	23	1	5	49	37	120
.261	.343	.396	1158	302	57	9	27	156	148	285
.242	.310	.366	868	210	43	1	21	21	84	200
.256	.336	.365	809	207	37	9	11	184	101	205

MIKE MUSSINA — bats right — throws right — age 24 — BAL — P

1991	G	IP	H	BB	SO	SB	CS	W	L	SV	ERA
at Home	6	42.2	36	11	30	4	1	3	1	0	2.74
on Road	6	45.0	41	10	22	0	3	1	4	0	3.00

	BA	OBA	SA	AB	H	2B	3B	HR	RBI	BB	SO
Total	.239	.286	.354	322	77	14	1	7	29	21	52
vs. Left	.214	.273	.302	182	39	7	0	3	17	14	29
vs. Right	.271	.304	.421	140	38	7	1	4	12	7	23
Bases Empty	.224	.287	.346	205	46	10	0	5	5	17	38
Runners On Base	.265	.285	.368	117	31	4	1	2	24	4	14

1-YEAR TOTALS (1991)

G	IP	H	BB	SO	SB	CS	W	L	SV	ERA
6	42.2	36	11	30	4	1	3	1	0	2.74
6	45.0	41	10	22	0	3	1	4	0	3.00

BA	OBA	SA	AB	H	2B	3B	HR	RBI	BB	SO
.239	.286	.354	322	77	14	1	7	29	21	52
.214	.273	.302	182	39	7	0	3	17	14	29
.271	.304	.421	140	38	7	1	4	12	7	23
.224	.287	.346	205	46	10	0	5	5	17	38
.265	.285	.368	117	31	4	1	2	24	4	14

JEFF MUTIS — bats left — throws left — age 26 — CLE — P

1991	G	IP	H	BB	SO	SB	CS	W	L	SV	ERA
at Home	2	7.1	18	3	1	0	0	0	2	0	15.95
on Road	1	5.0	5	4	5	0	0	0	1	0	5.40

	BA	OBA	SA	AB	H	2B	3B	HR	RBI	BB	SO
Total	.397	.455	.603	58	23	5	2	1	11	7	6
vs. Left	.000	.250	.000	3	0	0	0	0	0	1	1
vs. Right	.418	.468	.636	55	23	5	2	1	11	6	5
Bases Empty	.400	.400	.667	30	12	3	1	1	1	0	2
Runners On Base	.393	.500	.536	28	11	2	1	0	10	7	4

1-YEAR TOTALS (1991)

G	IP	H	BB	SO	SB	CS	W	L	SV	ERA
2	7.1	18	3	1	0	0	0	2	0	15.95
1	5.0	5	4	5	0	0	0	1	0	5.40

BA	OBA	SA	AB	H	2B	3B	HR	RBI	BB	SO
.397	.455	.603	58	23	5	2	1	11	7	6
.000	.250	.000	3	0	0	0	0	0	1	1
.418	.468	.636	55	23	5	2	1	11	6	5
.400	.400	.667	30	12	3	1	1	1	0	2
.393	.500	.536	28	11	2	1	0	10	7	4

DENNY NEAGLE — bats left — throws left — age 24 — MIN — P

1991	G	IP	H	BB	SO	SB	CS	W	L	SV	ERA
at Home	6	18.0	27	7	13	1	1	0	1	0	4.50
on Road	1	2.0	1	0	1	1	0	0	0	0	0.00

	BA	OBA	SA	AB	H	2B	3B	HR	RBI	BB	SO
Total	.329	.380	.553	85	28	8	1	3	7	7	14
vs. Left	.238	.238	.429	21	5	4	0	0	2	0	5
vs. Right	.359	.423	.594	64	23	4	1	3	5	7	9
Bases Empty	.370	.431	.696	46	17	4	1	3	3	5	5
Runners On Base	.282	.317	.385	39	11	4	0	0	4	2	9

1-YEAR TOTALS (1991)

G	IP	H	BB	SO	SB	CS	W	L	SV	ERA
6	18.0	27	7	13	1	1	0	1	0	4.50
1	2.0	1	0	1	1	0	0	0	0	0.00

BA	OBA	SA	AB	H	2B	3B	HR	RBI	BB	SO
.329	.380	.553	85	28	8	1	3	7	7	14
.238	.238	.429	21	5	4	0	0	2	0	5
.359	.423	.594	64	23	4	1	3	5	7	9
.370	.431	.696	46	17	4	1	3	3	5	5
.282	.317	.385	39	11	4	0	0	4	2	9

GENE NELSON — bats right — throws right — age 32 — OAK — P

1991	G	IP	H	BB	SO	SB	CS	W	L	SV	ERA
at Home	22	27.1	30	13	14	3	0	0	1	0	5.27
on Road	22	21.1	30	10	9	1	1	1	4	0	8.86

	BA	OBA	SA	AB	H	2B	3B	HR	RBI	BB	SO
Total	.306	.381	.577	196	60	9	4	12	52	23	23
vs. Left	.360	.457	.627	75	27	5	3	3	18	15	5
vs. Right	.273	.326	.545	121	33	4	1	9	34	8	18
Bases Empty	.333	.394	.567	90	30	7	1	4	4	8	8
Runners On Base	.283	.370	.585	106	30	2	3	8	48	15	15

8-YEAR TOTALS (1984–1991)

G	IP	H	BB	SO	SB	CS	W	L	SV	ERA
174	382.2	335	142	269	19	13	24	21	7	3.65
199	391.0	387	126	230	19	11	17	24	16	3.94

BA	OBA	SA	AB	H	2B	3B	HR	RBI	BB	SO
.247	.313	.400	2923	722	136	32	82	370	268	499
.258	.323	.404	1329	343	64	17	32	156	129	201
.238	.306	.396	1594	379	72	15	50	214	139	298
.251	.312	.415	1635	411	82	19	49	49	128	277
.241	.315	.380	1288	311	54	13	33	321	140	222

ROD NICHOLS — bats right — throws right — age 28 — CLE — P

1991	G	IP	H	BB	SO	SB	CS	W	L	SV	ERA
at Home	15	75.0	87	22	35	10	6	1	7	0	4.08
on Road	16	62.1	58	8	41	6	2	1	4	1	2.89

	BA	OBA	SA	AB	H	2B	3B	HR	RBI	BB	SO
Total	.273	.316	.344	532	145	18	1	6	60	30	76
vs. Left	.297	.351	.376	266	79	13	1	2	34	20	33
vs. Right	.248	.281	.312	266	66	5	0	4	26	10	43
Bases Empty	.274	.313	.333	303	83	9	0	3	3	11	46
Runners On Base	.271	.321	.358	229	62	9	1	3	57	19	30

4-YEAR TOTALS (1988–1991)

G	IP	H	BB	SO	SB	CS	W	L	SV	ERA
31	164.1	174	48	84	22	9	3	13	0	3.83
30	130.0	149	35	68	13	6	4	14	1	4.98

BA	OBA	SA	AB	H	2B	3B	HR	RBI	BB	SO
.280	.333	.400	1154	323	48	8	25	146	83	152
.298	.356	.410	563	168	27	3	10	70	46	65
.262	.309	.391	591	155	21	5	15	76	37	87
.284	.331	.393	656	186	27	3	13	13	38	87
.275	.334	.410	498	137	21	5	12	133	45	65

ERIC NOLTE — bats left — throws left — age 28 — SD/TEX — P

1991	G	IP	H	BB	SO	SB	CS	W	L	SV	ERA
at Home	5	11.0	19	5	8	3	1	1	1	0	9.00
on Road	4	13.2	21	8	8	6	0	2	1	0	11.20

	BA	OBA	SA	AB	H	2B	3B	HR	RBI	BB	SO
Total	.367	.424	.596	109	40	5	1	6	28	13	16
vs. Left	.276	.314	.552	29	8	2	0	2	9	3	2
vs. Right	.400	.467	.613	80	32	3	1	4	19	10	14
Bases Empty	.333	.403	.500	60	20	2	1	2	2	7	8
Runners On Base	.408	.448	.714	49	20	3	0	4	26	6	8

4-YEAR TOTALS (1987–1991)

G	IP	H	BB	SO	SB	CS	W	L	SV	ERA
12	43.0	51	30	31	8	1	2	3	0	5.86
14	61.0	64	28	38	10	1	3	5	0	5.46

BA	OBA	SA	AB	H	2B	3B	HR	RBI	BB	SO
.279	.367	.437	412	115	21	1	14	64	58	69
.278	.355	.506	79	22	3	0	5	16	9	9
.279	.370	.420	333	93	18	1	9	48	49	60
.281	.373	.424	217	61	8	1	7	7	30	34
.277	.360	.451	195	54	13	0	7	57	28	35

EDWIN NUNEZ — bats right — throws right — age 29 — MIL — P

1991	G	IP	H	BB	SO	SB	CS	W	L	SV	ERA
at Home	13	14.1	17	9	15	0	0	2	1	2	6.28
on Road	10	11.0	11	4	9	2	0	0	0	6	5.73

	BA	OBA	SA	AB	H	2B	3B	HR	RBI	BB	SO
Total	.277	.353	.525	101	28	5	1	6	25	13	24
vs. Left	.300	.390	.580	50	15	3	1	3	18	8	12
vs. Right	.255	.316	.471	51	13	2	0	3	7	5	12
Bases Empty	.204	.295	.444	54	11	1	0	4	4	7	14
Runners On Base	.362	.418	.617	47	17	4	1	2	21	6	10

8-YEAR TOTALS (1984–1991)

G	IP	H	BB	SO	SB	CS	W	L	SV	ERA
147	230.1	216	98	187	18	7	14	10	28	3.79
138	199.2	196	83	137	16	5	9	11	22	3.92

BA	OBA	SA	AB	H	2B	3B	HR	RBI	BB	SO
.254	.328	.412	1625	412	78	9	54	243	181	324
.255	.339	.423	740	189	32	4	28	116	96	140
.252	.318	.403	885	223	46	5	26	127	85	184
.240	.305	.402	855	205	44	4	29	29	76	176
.269	.352	.423	770	207	34	5	25	214	105	148

FRANCISCO OLIVERAS — bats right — throws right — age 29 — SF — P

1991	G	IP	H	BB	SO	SB	CS	W	L	SV	ERA
at Home	27	33.1	30	12	20	5	5	2	3	3	3.51
on Road	28	46.0	39	10	28	5	4	1	4	0	4.11

	BA	OBA	SA	AB	H	2B	3B	HR	RBI	BB	SO
Total	.242	.296	.400	285	69	7	1	12	38	22	48
vs. Left	.265	.331	.422	147	39	6	1	5	21	15	24
vs. Right	.217	.257	.377	138	30	1	0	7	17	7	24
Bases Empty	.239	.290	.389	180	43	4	1	7	7	13	32
Runners On Base	.248	.305	.419	105	26	3	0	5	31	9	16

3-YEAR TOTALS (1989–1991)

G	IP	H	BB	SO	SB	CS	W	L	SV	ERA
55	97.2	100	33	51	10	7	7	6	5	4.33
45	92.2	80	25	62	6	5	4	6	0	3.11

BA	OBA	SA	AB	H	2B	3B	HR	RBI	BB	SO
.253	.310	.402	711	180	23	4	25	90	58	113
.253	.320	.428	367	93	14	4	14	50	37	51
.253	.299	.375	344	87	9	0	11	40	21	62
.250	.305	.409	416	104	16	4	14	14	32	67
.258	.317	.393	295	76	7	0	11	76	26	46

JESSE OROSCO — bats right — throws left — age 35 — CLE — P

1991	G	IP	H	BB	SO	SB	CS	W	L	SV	ERA
at Home	20	23.2	21	3	19	1	0	1	0	0	1.90
on Road	27	22.0	31	12	17	4	0	1	0	0	5.73

	BA	OBA	SA	AB	H	2B	3B	HR	RBI	BB	SO
Total	.286	.338	.396	182	52	8	0	4	30	15	36
vs. Left	.286	.313	.381	63	18	3	0	1	8	3	14
vs. Right	.286	.351	.403	119	34	5	0	3	22	12	22
Bases Empty	.241	.286	.342	79	19	5	0	1	1	4	17
Runners On Base	.320	.376	.437	103	33	3	0	3	29	11	19

8-YEAR TOTALS (1984–1991)

G	IP	H	BB	SO	SB	CS	W	L	SV	ERA
210	281.0	244	105	262	19	5	21	20	42	2.82
246	284.1	227	137	244	33	6	21	17	57	3.20

BA	OBA	SA	AB	H	2B	3B	HR	RBI	BB	SO
.226	.307	.338	2085	471	77	6	48	253	242	506
.205	.269	.260	551	113	15	0	5	56	51	150
.233	.320	.366	1534	358	62	6	43	197	191	356
.245	.321	.379	1007	247	46	4	27	27	108	239
.208	.294	.299	1078	224	31	2	21	226	134	267

DAVE OTTO — bats left — throws left — age 28 — CLE — P

1991	G	IP	H	BB	SO	SB	CS	W	L	SV	ERA
at Home	9	59.0	63	11	31	1	3	1	6	0	4.12
on Road	9	41.0	45	16	16	3	1	1	2	0	4.39

	BA	OBA	SA	AB	H	2B	3B	HR	RBI	BB	SO
Total	.283	.333	.395	382	108	14	4	7	42	27	47
vs. Left	.304	.347	.333	69	21	2	0	0	11	4	3
vs. Right	.278	.330	.409	313	87	12	4	7	31	23	44
Bases Empty	.295	.338	.401	217	64	10	2	3	3	12	24
Runners On Base	.267	.328	.388	165	44	4	2	4	39	15	23

5-YEAR TOTALS (1987–1991)

G	IP	H	BB	SO	SB	CS	W	L	SV	ERA
15	75.2	81	17	43	2	4	1	6	0	4.04
12	49.1	52	22	20	5	1	1	2	0	4.56

BA	OBA	SA	AB	H	2B	3B	HR	RBI	BB	SO
.280	.337	.389	475	133	20	4	8	56	39	63
.287	.333	.319	94	27	3	0	0	16	6	7
.278	.338	.407	381	106	17	4	8	40	33	56
.283	.330	.387	269	76	15	2	3	3	17	33
.277	.346	.393	206	57	5	2	5	53	22	30

VICENTE PALACIOS — bats right — throws right — age 29 — PIT — P

1991	G	IP	H	BB	SO	SB	CS	W	L	SV	ERA
at Home	19	48.1	34	25	36	1	4	1	0	2.05	
on Road	17	33.1	35	13	28	1	3	2	2	3	6.21

	BA	OBA	SA	AB	H	2B	3B	HR	RBI	BB	SO
Total	.228	.315	.386	303	69	10	1	12	37	38	64
vs. Left	.234	.321	.321	137	32	6	0	2	13	18	24
vs. Right	.223	.310	.440	166	37	4	1	10	24	20	40
Bases Empty	.202	.290	.320	178	36	6	0	5	5	22	36
Runners On Base	.264	.350	.480	125	33	4	1	7	32	16	28

4-YEAR TOTALS (1987–1991)

G	IP	H	BB	SO	SB	CS	W	L	SV	ERA
30	85.1	61	40	53	7	3	6	2	2	2.95
26	65.0	67	24	47	6	4	3	4	4	5.26

BA	OBA	SA	AB	H	2B	3B	HR	RBI	BB	SO
.231	.312	.363	554	128	19	3	16	68	64	100
.227	.314	.340	256	58	10	2	5	32	32	38
.235	.310	.383	298	70	9	1	11	36	32	62
.202	.290	.301	322	65	9	1	7	7	39	59
.272	.342	.448	232	63	10	2	9	61	25	41

DONN PALL — bats right — throws right — age 30 — CHA — P

1991	G	IP	H	BB	SO	SB	CS	W	L	SV	ERA
at Home	26	37.0	29	11	23	2	4	5	0	0	2.19
on Road	25	34.0	30	9	17	1	2	2	2	0	2.65

	BA	OBA	SA	AB	H	2B	3B	HR	RBI	BB	SO
Total	.231	.295	.337	255	59	6	0	7	25	20	40
vs. Left	.188	.261	.248	101	19	3	0	1	4	10	17
vs. Right	.260	.317	.396	154	40	3	0	6	21	10	23
Bases Empty	.195	.253	.312	154	30	3	0	5	5	10	29
Runners On Base	.287	.357	.376	101	29	3	0	2	20	10	11

4-YEAR TOTALS (1988–1991)

G	IP	H	BB	SO	SB	CS	W	L	SV	ERA
89	131.1	126	33	86	10	5	6	5	4	3.36
88	131.1	125	38	67	8	3	8	9	4	2.81

BA	OBA	SA	AB	H	2B	3B	HR	RBI	BB	SO
.256	.315	.383	979	251	42	5	24	124	71	153
.252	.310	.369	420	106	20	4	7	47	33	68
.259	.319	.394	559	145	22	1	17	77	38	85
.257	.317	.403	494	127	19	4	15	15	33	84
.256	.313	.363	485	124	23	1	9	109	38	69

JEFF PARRETT — bats right — throws right — age 31 — ATL — P

1991	G	IP	H	BB	SO	SB	CS	W	L	SV	ERA
at Home	13	15.2	27	8	12	1	0	1	2	0	8.04
on Road	5	5.2	4	4	2	0	0	0	0	1	1.59

	BA	OBA	SA	AB	H	2B	3B	HR	RBI	BB	SO
Total	.326	.402	.453	95	31	4	1	2	14	12	14
vs. Left	.362	.434	.489	47	17	4	1	0	11	6	6
vs. Right	.292	.370	.417	48	14	0	0	2	3	6	8
Bases Empty	.424	.500	.636	33	14	1	0	2	2	5	8
Runners On Base	.274	.348	.355	62	17	3	1	0	12	7	6

6-YEAR TOTALS (1986–1991)

G	IP	H	BB	SO	SB	CS	W	L	SV	ERA
133	219.1	186	110	166	15	7	18	15	13	3.82
142	190.1	192	89	171	25	12	19	14	8	3.78

BA	OBA	SA	AB	H	2B	3B	HR	RBI	BB	SO
.250	.335	.390	1509	378	71	13	38	207	199	337
.246	.346	.364	783	193	35	9	13	105	122	157
.255	.324	.419	726	185	36	4	25	102	77	180
.253	.332	.393	810	205	42	4	21	21	95	183
.247	.339	.388	699	173	29	9	17	186	104	154

KEN PATTERSON — bats left — throws left — age 28 — CHA — P

1991	G	IP	H	BB	SO	SB	CS	W	L	SV	ERA
at Home	22	32.1	26	18	13	2	1	3	0	1	2.51
on Road	21	31.2	22	17	19	3	2	0	0	0	3.13

	BA	OBA	SA	AB	H	2B	3B	HR	RBI	BB	SO
Total	.214	.321	.330	224	48	7	2	5	32	35	32
vs. Left	.270	.360	.413	63	17	2	1	2	12	10	7
vs. Right	.193	.305	.298	161	31	5	1	4	20	25	25
Bases Empty	.228	.353	.307	114	26	3	0	2	2	21	15
Runners On Base	.200	.286	.355	110	22	4	2	3	30	14	17

4-YEAR TOTALS (1988–1991)

G	IP	H	BB	SO	SB	CS	W	L	SV	ERA
73	111.0	99	48	61	8	2	5	3	3	3.81
72	105.2	96	56	62	8	6	6	1	1	3.58

BA	OBA	SA	AB	H	2B	3B	HR	RBI	BB	SO
.244	.331	.390	798	195	30	7	24	119	104	123
.256	.343	.367	215	55	5	2	5	39	31	34
.240	.327	.398	583	140	25	5	19	80	73	89
.267	.353	.421	409	109	18	3	13	13	53	65
.221	.308	.357	389	86	12	4	11	106	51	58

BOB PATTERSON — bats right — throws right — age 33 — PIT — P

1991	G	IP	H	BB	SO	SB	CS	W	L	SV	ERA
at Home	23	27.1	30	6	29	0	1	2	2	0	4.94
on Road	31	38.1	37	9	28	1	4	2	1	2	3.52

	BA	OBA	SA	AB	H	2B	3B	HR	RBI	BB	SO
Total	.267	.306	.406	251	67	12	1	7	36	15	57
vs. Left	.267	.308	.380	150	40	9	1	2	16	9	38
vs. Right	.267	.303	.446	101	27	3	0	5	20	6	19
Bases Empty	.239	.291	.384	138	33	8	0	4	4	10	31
Runners On Base	.301	.325	.434	113	34	4	1	3	32	5	26

6-YEAR TOTALS (1985–1991)

G	IP	H	BB	SO	SB	CS	W	L	SV	ERA
76	156.2	160	45	114	5	8	11	7	3	4.54
74	113.2	129	29	81	4	6	8	11	5	4.35

BA	OBA	SA	AB	H	2B	3B	HR	RBI	BB	SO
.276	.324	.417	1046	289	57	6	26	147	74	195
.259	.307	.361	540	140	29	4	6	60	36	111
.294	.341	.476	506	149	28	2	20	87	38	84
.256	.305	.396	579	148	37	4	12	12	38	116
.302	.346	.443	467	141	20	2	14	135	36	79

DAVE PAVLAS — bats right — throws right — age 30 — CHN — P

1991	G	IP	H	BB	SO	SB	CS	W	L	SV	ERA
at Home	1	1.0	3	0	0	0	0	0	0	0	18.00
on Road	0	0.0	0	0	0	0	0	0	0	0	0.00

	BA	OBA	SA	AB	H	2B	3B	HR	RBI	BB	SO
Total	.750	.750	1.500	4	3	0	0	0	0	0	0
vs. Left	.500	.500	.500	2	1	0	0	0	0	0	0
vs. Right	1.000	1.000	2.500	2	2	0	0	0	0	0	0
Bases Empty	1.000	1.000	2.500	2	2	0	0	0	0	0	0
Runners On Base	.500	.500	.500	2	1	0	0	0	0	0	0

2-YEAR TOTALS (1990–1991)

G	IP	H	BB	SO	SB	CS	W	L	SV	ERA
7	12.0	15	0	4	0	0	2	0	0	3.00
7	10.1	11	6	8	1	0	0	0	0	2.61

BA	OBA	SA	AB	H	2B	3B	HR	RBI	BB	SO
.292	.330	.472	89	26	5	1	3	10	6	12
.348	.385	.587	46	16	3	1	2	7	4	3
.233	.267	.349	43	10	2	0	1	3	2	9
.306	.320	.551	49	15	4	1	2	2	1	9
.275	.340	.375	40	11	1	0	1	8	5	3

MELIDO PEREZ — bats right — throws right — age 26 — CHA — P

1991

	G	IP	H	BB	SO	SB	CS	W	L	SV	ERA
at Home	25	62.0	57	23	56	6	3	2	3	0	3.63
on Road	24	73.1	54	29	72	9	2	6	4	1	2.70

	BA	OBA	SA	AB	H	2B	3B	HR	RBI	BB	SO
Total	.224	.299	.352	495	111	16	1	15	50	52	128
vs. Left	.205	.283	.336	220	45	9	1	6	25	24	66
vs. Right	.240	.311	.364	275	66	7	0	9	25	28	62
Bases Empty	.225	.299	.370	284	64	9	1	10	10	29	77
Runners On Base	.223	.298	.327	211	47	7	0	5	40	23	51

5-YEAR TOTALS (1987–1991)

G	IP	H	BB	SO	SB	CS	W	L	SV	ERA
70	323.2	324	128	239	25	19	18	18	0	4.45
80	399.1	355	177	334	34	21	27	28	1	4.12

BA	OBA	SA	AB	H	2B	3B	HR	RBI	BB	SO
.248	.324	.397	2735	679	112	27	80	321	305	573
.244	.319	.394	1403	343	62	20	36	167	156	289
.252	.328	.399	1332	336	50	7	44	154	149	284
.240	.321	.393	1593	383	60	12	53	53	184	338
.259	.328	.402	1142	296	52	15	27	268	121	235

MIKE PEREZ — bats right — throws right — age 28 — SL — P

1991

	G	IP	H	BB	SO	SB	CS	W	L	SV	ERA
at Home	6	9.0	9	3	3	0	0	0	2	0	4.00
on Road	8	8.0	10	4	4	2	1	0	0	0	7.88

	BA	OBA	SA	AB	H	2B	3B	HR	RBI	BB	SO
Total	.288	.365	.455	66	19	6	1	1	7	7	7
vs. Left	.333	.429	.500	24	8	2	1	0	2	4	2
vs. Right	.262	.326	.429	42	11	4	0	1	5	3	5
Bases Empty	.313	.371	.563	32	10	3	1	1	1	2	4
Runners On Base	.265	.359	.353	34	9	3	0	0	6	5	3

2-YEAR TOTALS (1990–1991)

G	IP	H	BB	SO	SB	CS	W	L	SV	ERA
11	15.1	16	3	6	0	0	1	2	1	4.11
16	15.1	15	7	6	4	1	0	0	0	5.87

BA	OBA	SA	AB	H	2B	3B	HR	RBI	BB	SO
.267	.326	.388	116	31	9	1	1	14	10	12
.294	.373	.431	51	15	5	1	0	4	7	4
.246	.286	.354	65	16	4	0	1	10	3	8
.258	.300	.424	66	17	6	1	1	1	3	8
.280	.356	.340	50	14	3	0	0	13	7	4

PASCUAL PEREZ — bats right — throws right — age 35 — NYA — P

1991

	G	IP	H	BB	SO	SB	CS	W	L	SV	ERA
at Home	9	43.1	37	19	24	4	2	1	3	0	3.53
on Road	5	30.1	31	5	17	0	2	1	1	0	2.67

	BA	OBA	SA	AB	H	2B	3B	HR	RBI	BB	SO
Total	.250	.311	.371	272	68	6	3	7	25	24	41
vs. Left	.283	.349	.457	138	39	5	2	5	15	14	24
vs. Right	.216	.271	.284	134	29	1	1	2	10	10	17
Bases Empty	.251	.301	.351	171	43	5	3	2	2	12	24
Runners On Base	.248	.327	.406	101	25	1	0	5	23	12	17

7-YEAR TOTALS (1984–1991)

G	IP	H	BB	SO	SB	CS	W	L	SV	ERA
72	452.2	382	125	319	32	16	24	28	0	3.22
67	398.2	380	115	277	43	23	22	20	0	3.63

BA	OBA	SA	AB	H	2B	3B	HR	RBI	BB	SO
.239	.294	.366	3188	762	118	26	78	315	240	596
.250	.311	.394	1704	426	64	16	50	176	150	294
.226	.275	.333	1484	336	54	10	28	139	90	302
.233	.277	.354	2017	470	73	17	46	46	114	394
.249	.322	.385	1171	292	45	9	32	269	126	202

YORKIS PEREZ — bats left — throws left — age 25 — CHN — P

1991

	G	IP	H	BB	SO	SB	CS	W	L	SV	ERA
at Home	2	4.0	2	2	2	0	0	1	0	0	2.25
on Road	1	0.1	0	0	1	0	0	0	0	0	0.00

	BA	OBA	SA	AB	H	2B	3B	HR	RBI	BB	SO
Total	.167	.250	.333	12	2	2	0	0	3	2	3
vs. Left	.167	.143	.333	6	1	1	0	0	2	0	3
vs. Right	.167	.333	.333	6	1	1	0	0	1	2	0
Bases Empty	.200	.333	.400	5	1	1	0	0	0	1	1
Runners On Base	.143	.200	.286	7	1	1	0	0	3	1	2

1-YEAR TOTALS (1991)

G	IP	H	BB	SO	SB	CS	W	L	SV	ERA
2	4.0	2	2	2	0	0	1	0	0	2.25
1	0.1	0	0	1	0	0	0	0	0	0.00

BA	OBA	SA	AB	H	2B	3B	HR	RBI	BB	SO
.167	.250	.333	12	2	2	0	0	3	2	3
.167	.143	.333	6	1	1	0	0	2	0	3
.167	.333	.333	6	1	1	0	0	1	2	0
.200	.333	.400	5	1	1	0	0	0	1	1
.143	.200	.286	7	1	1	0	0	3	1	2

ADAM PETERSON — bats right — throws right — age 27 — SD — P

1991

	G	IP	H	BB	SO	SB	CS	W	L	SV	ERA
at Home	7	29.1	23	17	23	1	4	1	2	0	2.76
on Road	6	25.1	27	11	14	1	0	2	2	0	6.39

	BA	OBA	SA	AB	H	2B	3B	HR	RBI	BB	SO
Total	.242	.329	.449	207	50	7	3	10	31	28	37
vs. Left	.278	.349	.591	115	32	6	3	8	20	13	16
vs. Right	.196	.306	.272	92	18	1	0	2	11	15	21
Bases Empty	.276	.364	.577	123	34	6	2	9	9	17	15
Runners On Base	.190	.278	.262	84	16	1	1	1	22	11	22

5-YEAR TOTALS (1987–1991)

G	IP	H	BB	SO	SB	CS	W	L	SV	ERA
19	73.1	76	40	40	7	6	2	4	0	4.79
20	81.2	91	25	35	2	3	3	7	0	6.06

BA	OBA	SA	AB	H	2B	3B	HR	RBI	BB	SO
.277	.347	.460	602	167	22	8	24	91	65	75
.321	.374	.577	293	94	15	6	16	51	25	24
.236	.322	.350	309	73	7	2	8	40	40	51
.285	.357	.513	337	96	13	5	18	18	36	36
.268	.333	.392	265	71	9	3	6	73	29	39

MARK PETKOVSEK — bats right — throws right — age 27 — TEX — P

1991

	G	IP	H	BB	SO	SB	CS	W	L	SV	ERA
at Home	3	4.2	11	2	3	0	0	0	0	0	15.43
on Road	1	4.2	10	2	3	1	0	0	1	0	13.50

	BA	OBA	SA	AB	H	2B	3B	HR	RBI	BB	SO
Total	.438	.472	.750	48	21	3	0	4	16	4	6
vs. Left	.476	.542	.905	21	10	3	0	2	7	3	0
vs. Right	.407	.414	.630	27	11	0	0	2	9	1	6
Bases Empty	.320	.370	.600	25	8	1	0	2	2	1	5
Runners On Base	.565	.577	.913	23	13	2	0	2	14	2	1

1-YEAR TOTALS (1991)

G	IP	H	BB	SO	SB	CS	W	L	SV	ERA
3	4.2	11	2	3	0	0	0	0	0	15.43
1	4.2	10	2	3	1	0	0	1	0	13.50

BA	OBA	SA	AB	H	2B	3B	HR	RBI	BB	SO
.438	.472	.750	48	21	3	0	4	16	4	6
.476	.542	.905	21	10	3	0	2	7	3	0
.407	.414	.630	27	11	0	0	2	9	1	6
.320	.370	.600	25	8	1	0	2	2	1	5
.565	.577	.913	23	13	2	0	2	14	2	1

DAN PETRY — bats right — throws right — age 34 — DET/ATL/BOS — P

1991

	G	IP	H	BB	SO	SB	CS	W	L	SV	ERA
at Home	24	61.2	70	27	21	8	1	1	1	0	4.96
on Road	16	39.2	46	18	18	5	4	1	2	1	4.99

	BA	OBA	SA	AB	H	2B	3B	HR	RBI	BB	SO
Total	.289	.362	.463	402	116	22	3	14	69	45	39
vs. Left	.292	.362	.482	168	49	9	1	7	29	19	14
vs. Right	.286	.363	.449	234	67	13	2	7	40	26	25
Bases Empty	.269	.342	.413	208	56	10	1	6	6	21	18
Runners On Base	.309	.384	.515	194	60	12	2	8	63	24	21

8-YEAR TOTALS (1984–1991)

G	IP	H	BB	SO	SB	CS	W	L	SV	ERA
123	619.2	590	249	313	59	33	33	36	0	4.12
108	545.0	559	227	290	57	24	33	24	1	4.26

BA	OBA	SA	AB	H	2B	3B	HR	RBI	BB	SO
.259	.332	.408	4443	1149	213	23	135	538	476	603
.254	.333	.398	2244	570	98	12	67	260	267	288
.263	.332	.418	2199	579	115	11	68	278	209	315
.249	.324	.387	2576	642	121	8	73	73	270	343
.272	.343	.437	1867	507	92	15	62	465	206	260

DOUG PIATT — bats left — throws right — age 27 — MON — P

1-YEAR TOTALS (1991)

1991	G	IP	H	BB	SO	SB	CS	W	L	SV	ERA
at Home	8	12.2	8	6	7	2	1	0	0	0	1.42
on Road	13	22.0	21	11	22	1	0	0	0	0	3.27

	BA	OBA	SA	AB	H	2B	3B	HR	RBI	BB	SO
Total	.230	.322	.357	126	29	7	0	3	15	17	29
vs. Left	.321	.415	.536	56	18	3	0	3	9	9	13
vs. Right	.157	.244	.214	70	11	4	0	0	6	8	16
Bases Empty	.254	.342	.358	67	17	4	0	1	1	9	14
Runners On Base	.203	.299	.356	59	12	3	0	2	14	8	15

1-YEAR TOTALS (1991)

G	IP	H	BB	SO	SB	CS	W	L	SV	ERA
8	12.2	8	6	7	2	1	0	0	0	1.42
13	22.0	21	11	22	1	0	0	0	0	3.27

BA	OBA	SA	AB	H	2B	3B	HR	RBI	BB	SO
.230	.322	.357	126	29	7	0	3	15	17	29
.321	.415	.536	56	18	3	0	3	9	9	13
.157	.244	.214	70	11	4	0	0	6	8	16
.254	.342	.358	67	17	4	0	1	1	9	14
.203	.299	.356	59	12	3	0	2	14	8	15

ERIC PLUNK — bats right — throws right — age 29 — NYA — P

1991	G	IP	H	BB	SO	SB	CS	W	L	SV	ERA
at Home	23	62.0	68	37	51	13	2	2	2	0	4.35
on Road	20	49.2	60	25	52	15	1	0	3	0	5.26

	BA	OBA	SA	AB	H	2B	3B	HR	RBI	BB	SO
Total	.286	.371	.478	448	128	22	5	18	70	62	103
vs. Left	.294	.388	.507	221	65	9	4	10	30	35	44
vs. Right	.278	.354	.449	227	63	13	1	8	40	27	59
Bases Empty	.293	.377	.524	229	67	12	4	11	11	30	42
Runners On Base	.279	.365	.429	219	61	10	1	7	59	32	61

6-YEAR TOTALS (1986–1991)

G	IP	H	BB	SO	SB	CS	W	L	SV	ERA
113	283.1	256	193	246	33	16	19	11	5	4.38
134	298.2	256	179	277	46	16	18	18	3	3.86

BA	OBA	SA	AB	H	2B	3B	HR	RBI	BB	SO
.238	.351	.372	2149	512	75	13	62	292	372	523
.253	.371	.385	1030	261	35	10	27	121	196	239
.224	.333	.359	1119	251	40	3	35	176	284
.242	.358	.378	1126	273	37	10	32	32	199	265
.234	.344	.365	1023	239	38	3	30	260	173	258

JEFF PLYMPTON — bats right — throws right — age 27 — BOS — P

1991	G	IP	H	BB	SO	SB	CS	W	L	SV	ERA
at Home	3	5.0	5	4	1	0	0	0	0	0	0.00
on Road	1	0.1	0	0	1	0	0	0	0	0	0.00

	BA	OBA	SA	AB	H	2B	3B	HR	RBI	BB	SO
Total	.263	.375	.316	19	5	1	0	0	1	4	2
vs. Left	.167	.143	.167	6	1	0	0	0	0	0	0
vs. Right	.308	.471	.385	13	4	1	0	0	0	4	2
Bases Empty	.429	.429	.571	7	3	1	0	0	0	0	0
Runners On Base	.167	.353	.167	12	2	0	0	0	1	4	2

1-YEAR TOTALS (1991)

G	IP	H	BB	SO	SB	CS	W	L	SV	ERA
3	5.0	5	4	1	0	0	0	0	0	0.00
1	0.1	0	0	1	0	0	0	0	0	0.00

BA	OBA	SA	AB	H	2B	3B	HR	RBI	BB	SO
.263	.375	.316	19	5	1	0	0	1	4	2
.167	.143	.167	6	1	0	0	0	0	0	0
.308	.471	.385	13	4	1	0	0	0	4	2
.429	.429	.571	7	3	1	0	0	0	0	0
.167	.353	.167	12	2	0	0	0	1	4	2

JIM POOLE — bats left — throws left — age 26 — TEX/BAL — P

1991	G	IP	H	BB	SO	SB	CS	W	L	SV	ERA
at Home	16	29.0	13	6	23	0	1	3	1	1	1.55
on Road	13	13.0	16	6	15	0	0	0	1	0	4.15

	BA	OBA	SA	AB	H	2B	3B	HR	RBI	BB	SO
Total	.196	.252	.284	148	29	4	0	3	16	12	38
vs. Left	.188	.200	.275	69	13	0	0	2	10	1	18
vs. Right	.203	.290	.291	79	16	4	0	1	6	11	20
Bases Empty	.185	.241	.259	81	15	3	0	1	1	6	16
Runners On Base	.209	.263	.313	67	14	1	0	2	15	6	22

2-YEAR TOTALS (1990–1991)

G	IP	H	BB	SO	SB	CS	W	L	SV	ERA
25	36.0	18	11	26	0	1	3	1	1	1.75
20	16.2	18	9	18	0	0	0	1	0	4.86

BA	OBA	SA	AB	H	2B	3B	HR	RBI	BB	SO
.194	.268	.290	186	36	6	0	4	22	20	44
.188	.198	.313	80	15	1	0	3	13	1	20
.198	.313	.274	106	21	5	0	1	9	19	24
.182	.250	.263	99	18	5	0	1	1	9	20
.207	.287	.322	87	18	1	0	3	21	11	24

TED POWER — bats right — throws right — age 37 — CIN — P

1991	G	IP	H	BB	SO	SB	CS	W	L	SV	ERA
at Home	40	50.1	43	18	29	4	4	5	0	2	3.04
on Road	28	36.2	44	13	22	0	0	3	1	1	4.42

	BA	OBA	SA	AB	H	2B	3B	HR	RBI	BB	SO
Total	.265	.329	.387	328	87	18	2	6	36	31	51
vs. Left	.288	.374	.447	170	49	13	1	4	19	23	23
vs. Right	.241	.276	.323	158	38	5	1	2	17	8	28
Bases Empty	.255	.310	.372	188	48	8	1	4	4	13	32
Runners On Base	.279	.352	.407	140	39	10	1	2	32	18	19

8-YEAR TOTALS (1984–1991)

G	IP	H	BB	SO	SB	CS	W	L	SV	ERA
210	430.0	435	161	266	37	19	29	21	27	3.93
179	426.1	404	160	278	39	12	27	31	22	3.93

BA	OBA	SA	AB	H	2B	3B	HR	RBI	BB	SO
.259	.324	.387	3241	839	163	17	73	407	321	544
.277	.354	.416	1573	436	88	11	36	205	193	247
.242	.295	.360	1668	403	75	6	37	202	128	297
.253	.311	.374	1776	450	92	9	35	35	143	282
.266	.339	.403	1465	389	71	8	38	372	178	262

RICK REED — bats right — throws right — age 28 — PIT — P

1991	G	IP	H	BB	SO	SB	CS	W	L	SV	ERA
at Home	0	0.0	0	0	0	0	0	0	0	0	0.00
on Road	1	4.1	8	1	2	0	0	0	0	0	10.38

	BA	OBA	SA	AB	H	2B	3B	HR	RBI	BB	SO
Total	.400	.429	.700	20	8	3	0	1	4	1	2
vs. Left	.417	.417	.750	12	5	1	0	1	3	0	1
vs. Right	.375	.444	.625	8	3	2	0	0	1	1	1
Bases Empty	.500	.545	.700	10	5	2	0	0	0	1	0
Runners On Base	.300	.300	.700	10	3	1	0	1	4	0	2

4-YEAR TOTALS (1988–1991)

G	IP	H	BB	SO	SB	CS	W	L	SV	ERA
14	62.2	62	12	30	11	1	2	4	0	3.16
17	62.0	80	14	39	6	0	2	3	1	6.82

BA	OBA	SA	AB	H	2B	3B	HR	RBI	BB	SO
.285	.321	.427	499	142	28	2	13	67	26	69
.258	.307	.378	283	73	15	2	5	36	20	32
.319	.341	.491	216	69	13	0	8	31	6	37
.262	.286	.377	305	80	15	1	6	6	9	45
.320	.373	.505	194	62	13	1	7	61	17	24

MIKE REMLINGER — bats left — throws left — age 26 — SF — P

1991	G	IP	H	BB	SO	SB	CS	W	L	SV	ERA
at Home	3	21.2	17	9	10	0	1	1	1	0	2.49
on Road	5	13.1	19	11	9	1	0	1	1	0	7.43

	BA	OBA	SA	AB	H	2B	3B	HR	RBI	BB	SO
Total	.271	.364	.451	133	36	9	0	5	14	20	19
vs. Left	.250	.375	.400	20	5	0	0	1	2	4	2
vs. Right	.274	.362	.460	113	31	9	0	4	12	16	17
Bases Empty	.268	.395	.507	71	19	5	0	4	4	15	12
Runners On Base	.274	.324	.387	62	17	4	0	1	10	5	7

1-YEAR TOTALS (1991)

G	IP	H	BB	SO	SB	CS	W	L	SV	ERA
3	21.2	17	9	10	0	1	1	1	0	2.49
5	13.1	19	11	9	1	0	1	1	0	7.43

BA	OBA	SA	AB	H	2B	3B	HR	RBI	BB	SO
.271	.364	.451	133	36	9	0	5	14	20	19
.274	.362	.460	113	31	9	0	4	12	16	17
.268	.395	.507	71	19	9	0	4	4	15	12
.274	.324	.387	62	17	4	0	1	10	5	7

LADDIE RENFROE — bats both — throws right — age 30 — CHN — P

1991

	G	IP	H	BB	SO	SB	CS	W	L	SV	ERA
at Home	2	2.0	2	1	2	0	0	0	0	0	9.00
on Road	2	2.2	9	1	2	0	0	0	1	0	16.88

	BA	OBA	SA	AB	H	2B	3B	HR	RBI	BB	SO
Total	.440	.481	.640	25	11	2	0	1	9	2	4
vs. Left	.182	.250	.455	11	2	0	0	1	3	1	2
vs. Right	.643	.667	.786	14	9	2	0	0	6	1	2
Bases Empty	.143	.200	.214	14	2	1	0	0	1	1	4
Runners On Base	.818	.833	1.182	11	9	1	0	1	9	1	0

1-YEAR TOTALS (1991)

G	IP	H	BB	SO	SB	CS	W	L	SV	ERA
2	2.0	2	1	2	0	0	0	0	0	9.00
2	2.2	9	1	2	0	0	0	1	0	16.88

BA	OBA	SA	AB	H	2B	3B	HR	RBI	BB	SO
.440	.481	.640	25	11	2	0	1	9	2	4
.182	.250	.455	11	2	0	0	1	3	1	2
.643	.667	.786	14	9	2	0	0	6	1	2
.143	.200	.214	14	2	1	0	0	1	1	4
.818	.833	1.182	11	9	1	0	1	9	1	0

RICK REUSCHEL — bats right — throws right — age 43 — SF — P

1991

	G	IP	H	BB	SO	SB	CS	W	L	SV	ERA
at Home	3	4.2	8	4	2	0	0	0	1	0	3.86
on Road	1	6.0	9	3	2	0	0	0	1	0	4.50

	BA	OBA	SA	AB	H	2B	3B	HR	RBI	BB	SO
Total	.370	.453	.478	46	17	5	0	0	8	7	4
vs. Left	.417	.517	.583	24	10	4	0	0	5	5	3
vs. Right	.318	.375	.364	22	7	1	0	0	3	2	1
Bases Empty	.400	.526	.533	15	6	2	0	0	0	4	3
Runners On Base	.355	.412	.452	31	11	3	0	0	8	3	1

8-YEAR TOTALS (1984–1991)

G	IP	H	BB	SO	SB	CS	W	L	SV	ERA
104	650.0	626	145	346	28	23	47	28	0	3.10
102	630.0	644	163	323	23	25	33	37	2	3.53

BA	OBA	SA	AB	H	2B	3B	HR	RBI	BB	SO
.260	.305	.374	4876	1270	236	33	84	477	308	669
.282	.329	.398	2609	737	144	26	35	245	186	245
.235	.278	.347	2267	533	92	7	49	232	122	424
.254	.293	.373	2940	748	135	24	55	55	146	403
.270	.322	.376	1936	522	101	9	29	422	162	266

ARMANDO REYNOSO — bats right — throws right — age 26 — ATL — P

1991

	G	IP	H	BB	SO	SB	CS	W	L	SV	ERA
at Home	3	11.0	10	5	4	1	0	1	0	0	4.09
on Road	3	12.1	16	5	6	0	1	1	1	0	8.03

	BA	OBA	SA	AB	H	2B	3B	HR	RBI	BB	SO
Total	.299	.390	.552	87	26	4	3	4	16	10	10
vs. Left	.286	.362	.643	42	12	3	3	2	9	4	6
vs. Right	.311	.415	.467	45	14	1	0	2	7	6	4
Bases Empty	.260	.383	.480	50	13	1	2	2	2	7	9
Runners On Base	.351	.400	.649	37	13	3	1	2	14	3	1

1-YEAR TOTALS (1991)

G	IP	H	BB	SO	SB	CS	W	L	SV	ERA
3	11.0	10	5	4	1	0	1	0	0	4.09
3	12.1	16	5	6	0	1	1	1	0	8.03

BA	OBA	SA	AB	H	2B	3B	HR	RBI	BB	SO
.299	.390	.552	87	26	4	3	4	16	10	10
.286	.362	.643	42	12	3	3	2	9	4	6
.311	.415	.467	45	14	1	0	2	7	6	4
.260	.383	.480	50	13	1	2	2	2	7	9
.351	.400	.649	37	13	3	1	2	14	3	1

ARTHUR LEE RHODES — bats left — throws left — age 23 — BAL — P

1991

	G	IP	H	BB	SO	SB	CS	W	L	SV	ERA
at Home	3	14.2	14	10	13	1	1	0	1	0	6.14
on Road	5	21.1	33	13	10	6	1	0	2	0	9.28

	BA	OBA	SA	AB	H	2B	3B	HR	RBI	BB	SO
Total	.320	.405	.469	147	47	8	1	4	28	23	23
vs. Left	.154	.313	.154	13	2	0	0	0	1	3	3
vs. Right	.336	.414	.500	134	45	8	1	4	27	20	20
Bases Empty	.231	.348	.321	78	18	4	0	1	1	14	14
Runners On Base	.420	.469	.638	69	29	4	1	3	27	9	9

1-YEAR TOTALS (1991)

G	IP	H	BB	SO	SB	CS	W	L	SV	ERA
3	14.2	14	10	13	1	1	0	1	0	6.14
5	21.1	33	13	10	6	1	0	2	0	9.28

BA	OBA	SA	AB	H	2B	3B	HR	RBI	BB	SO
.320	.405	.469	147	47	8	1	4	28	23	23
.154	.313	.154	13	2	0	0	0	1	3	3
.336	.414	.500	134	45	8	1	4	27	20	20
.231	.348	.321	78	18	4	0	1	1	14	14
.420	.469	.638	69	29	4	1	3	27	9	9

PAT RICE — bats right — throws right — age 29 — SEA — P

1991

	G	IP	H	BB	SO	SB	CS	W	L	SV	ERA
at Home	5	11.1	9	8	4	0	1	0	1	0	4.76
on Road	2	9.2	9	2	8	0	0	1	0	0	0.93

	BA	OBA	SA	AB	H	2B	3B	HR	RBI	BB	SO
Total	.234	.319	.351	77	18	0	0	3	11	10	12
vs. Left	.222	.317	.222	36	8	0	0	0	1	5	4
vs. Right	.244	.320	.463	41	10	0	0	3	10	5	8
Bases Empty	.233	.313	.302	43	10	0	0	1	1	4	7
Runners On Base	.235	.326	.412	34	8	0	0	2	10	6	5

1-YEAR TOTALS (1991)

G	IP	H	BB	SO	SB	CS	W	L	SV	ERA
5	11.1	9	8	4	0	1	0	1	0	4.76
2	9.2	9	2	8	0	0	1	0	0	0.93

BA	OBA	SA	AB	H	2B	3B	HR	RBI	BB	SO
.234	.319	.351	77	18	0	0	3	11	10	12
.222	.317	.222	36	8	0	0	0	1	5	4
.244	.320	.463	41	10	0	0	3	10	5	8
.233	.313	.302	43	10	0	0	1	1	4	7
.235	.326	.412	34	8	0	0	2	10	6	5

WALLY RITCHIE — bats left — throws left — age 27 — PHI — P

1991

	G	IP	H	BB	SO	SB	CS	W	L	SV	ERA
at Home	22	31.0	27	15	10	6	0	1	2	0	2.03
on Road	17	19.1	17	2	16	4	0	0	0	0	3.26

	BA	OBA	SA	AB	H	2B	3B	HR	RBI	BB	SO
Total	.234	.299	.346	188	44	7	1	4	20	17	26
vs. Left	.161	.221	.274	62	10	2	1	1	7	4	13
vs. Right	.270	.336	.381	126	34	5	0	3	13	13	13
Bases Empty	.234	.268	.364	107	25	5	0	3	3	4	12
Runners On Base	.235	.333	.321	81	19	2	1	1	17	13	14

3-YEAR TOTALS (1987–1991)

G	IP	H	BB	SO	SB	CS	W	L	SV	ERA
54	77.1	75	38	43	10	1	2	3	2	3.61
53	61.1	48	25	36	9	1	2	1	1	2.64

BA	OBA	SA	AB	H	2B	3B	HR	RBI	BB	SO
.238	.321	.380	516	123	24	5	13	64	63	79
.243	.308	.408	152	37	5	4	4	24	14	27
.236	.326	.368	364	86	19	1	9	40	49	52
.254	.309	.395	276	70	12	3	7	7	20	42
.221	.333	.363	240	53	12	2	6	57	43	37

KEVIN RITZ — bats right — throws right — age 27 — DET — P

1991

	G	IP	H	BB	SO	SB	CS	W	L	SV	ERA
at Home	4	6.1	7	9	4	0	0	0	1	0	7.11
on Road	7	9.0	10	13	5	3	0	0	2	0	15.00

	BA	OBA	SA	AB	H	2B	3B	HR	RBI	BB	SO
Total	.288	.482	.390	59	17	3	0	1	14	22	9
vs. Left	.348	.559	.435	23	8	2	0	0	3	11	3
vs. Right	.250	.431	.361	36	9	1	0	1	11	11	6
Bases Empty	.292	.469	.333	24	7	0	0	0	8	11	5
Runners On Base	.286	.491	.429	35	10	2	0	1	14	14	4

3-YEAR TOTALS (1989–1991)

G	IP	H	BB	SO	SB	CS	W	L	SV	ERA
11	48.0	52	34	34	6	1	4	4	0	4.13
16	48.2	54	46	34	5	4	0	9	0	7.95

BA	OBA	SA	AB	H	2B	3B	HR	RBI	BB	SO
.281	.405	.369	377	106	18	3	3	56	80	68
.292	.433	.409	171	50	10	2	3	21	43	30
.272	.380	.335	206	56	8	1	1	35	37	38
.258	.355	.354	198	51	11	1	2	2	30	31
.307	.452	.385	179	55	7	2	1	54	50	37

JEFF ROBINSON — bats right — throws right — age 32 — CAL — P

8-YEAR TOTALS (1984–1991)

1991	G	IP	H	BB	SO	SB	CS	W	L	SV	ERA
at Home	19	31.1	21	10	40	1	0	0	1	1	2.30
on Road	20	25.2	35	19	17	3	0	0	2	2	9.12

	G	IP	H	BB	SO	SB	CS	W	L	SV	ERA
	204	394.1	369	139	307	37	15	16	22	17	3.38
	200	428.1	434	168	275	47	19	26	31	21	4.31

	BA	OBA	SA	AB	H	2B	3B	HR	RBI	BB	SO
Total	.259	.349	.444	216	56	13	0	9	33	29	57
vs. Left	.272	.327	.467	92	25	6	0	4	16	8	21
vs. Right	.250	.365	.427	124	31	7	0	5	17	21	36
Bases Empty	.287	.363	.465	101	29	9	0	3	3	11	22
Runners On Base	.235	.338	.426	115	27	4	0	6	30	18	35

	BA	OBA	SA	AB	H	2B	3B	HR	RBI	BB	SO
	.257	.324	.381	3121	803	140	18	70	379	307	582
	.265	.325	.392	1567	416	72	12	34	188	141	248
	.249	.323	.370	1554	387	68	6	36	191	166	334
	.252	.306	.379	1776	447	88	12	38	38	133	325
	.265	.346	.384	1345	356	52	6	32	341	174	257

JEFF ROBINSON — bats right — throws right — age 31 — BAL — P

5-YEAR TOTALS (1987–1991)

1991	G	IP	H	BB	SO	SB	CS	W	L	SV	ERA
at Home	11	69.0	72	28	40	6	3	3	3	0	3.78
on Road	10	35.1	47	23	25	4	2	1	6	0	7.90

	G	IP	H	BB	SO	SB	CS	W	L	SV	ERA
	62	361.1	299	170	232	15	15	24	13	0	3.94
	55	265.1	290	141	161	22	13	16	22	0	5.83

	BA	OBA	SA	AB	H	2B	3B	HR	RBI	BB	SO
Total	.289	.375	.434	412	119	22	1	12	50	51	65
vs. Left	.343	.432	.567	210	72	14	0	11	31	31	27
vs. Right	.233	.314	.297	202	47	8	1	1	19	20	38
Bases Empty	.275	.364	.398	236	65	11	0	6	6	28	36
Runners On Base	.307	.390	.483	176	54	11	1	6	44	23	29

	BA	OBA	SA	AB	H	2B	3B	HR	RBI	BB	SO
	.248	.339	.407	2376	589	113	12	80	303	311	393
	.247	.344	.425	1214	300	65	8	45	148	177	188
	.249	.333	.387	1162	289	48	4	35	155	134	205
	.232	.322	.382	1420	329	59	5	48	48	175	242
	.272	.363	.444	956	260	54	7	32	255	136	151

RON ROBINSON — bats right — throws right — age 30 — MIL — P

8-YEAR TOTALS (1984–1991)

1991	G	IP	H	BB	SO	SB	CS	W	L	SV	ERA
at Home	0	0.0	0	0	0	0	0	0	0	0	0.00
on Road	1	4.1	6	3	0	1	0	0	1	0	6.23

	G	IP	H	BB	SO	SB	CS	W	L	SV	ERA
	110	366.1	376	107	215	31	23	20	19	9	3.73
	114	398.1	392	133	246	34	30	27	16	10	3.37

	BA	OBA	SA	AB	H	2B	3B	HR	RBI	BB	SO
Total	.353	.476	.588	17	6	2	1	0	2	3	0
vs. Left	.357	.438	.571	14	5	1	1	0	1	2	0
vs. Right	.333	.600	.667	3	1	1	0	0	1	1	0
Bases Empty	.667	.714	1.167	6	4	1	1	0	0	1	0
Runners On Base	.182	.357	.273	11	2	1	0	0	2	2	0

	BA	OBA	SA	AB	H	2B	3B	HR	RBI	BB	SO
	.263	.320	.387	2917	768	142	23	58	320	240	461
	.282	.347	.404	1442	407	70	17	24	155	144	156
	.245	.292	.371	1475	361	72	6	34	165	96	305
	.259	.309	.388	1717	444	88	12	37	37	118	300
	.270	.334	.386	1200	324	54	11	21	283	122	161

RICH RODRIGUEZ — bats left — throws left — age 29 — SD — P

2-YEAR TOTALS (1990–1991)

1991	G	IP	H	BB	SO	SB	CS	W	L	SV	ERA
at Home	33	37.1	35	28	25	3	0	1	1	0	4.58
on Road	31	42.2	30	16	17	3	4	2	0	0	2.11

	G	IP	H	BB	SO	SB	CS	W	L	SV	ERA
	51	65.1	64	38	42	5	1	2	1	0	3.72
	45	62.1	53	22	22	5	5	2	1	1	2.45

	BA	OBA	SA	AB	H	2B	3B	HR	RBI	BB	SO
Total	.231	.333	.363	281	65	11	1	8	34	44	42
vs. Left	.223	.342	.362	94	21	4	0	3	12	17	14
vs. Right	.235	.329	.364	187	44	7	1	5	22	27	28
Bases Empty	.246	.340	.423	142	35	4	0	7	7	20	24
Runners On Base	.216	.327	.302	139	30	7	1	1	27	24	18

	BA	OBA	SA	AB	H	2B	3B	HR	RBI	BB	SO
	.253	.338	.368	462	117	21	1	10	56	60	64
	.226	.324	.314	159	36	5	0	3	19	23	26
	.267	.346	.396	303	81	16	1	7	37	37	38
	.272	.347	.409	232	63	8	0	8	8	26	33
	.235	.330	.326	230	54	13	1	2	48	34	31

ROSARIO RODRIGUEZ — bats right — throws left — age 23 — PIT — P

3-YEAR TOTALS (1989–1991)

1991	G	IP	H	BB	SO	SB	CS	W	L	SV	ERA
at Home	7	8.1	9	2	5	0	0	1	1	1	6.48
on Road	11	7.0	5	6	5	0	1	1	0	5	1.29

	G	IP	H	BB	SO	SB	CS	W	L	SV	ERA
	18	19.0	20	3	12	0	0	1	1	1	4.74
	16	11.0	12	10	6	0	2	1	1	1	4.91

	BA	OBA	SA	AB	H	2B	3B	HR	RBI	BB	SO
Total	.246	.348	.333	57	14	2	0	1	6	8	10
vs. Left	.263	.300	.263	19	5	0	0	0	0	1	4
vs. Right	.237	.370	.368	38	9	2	0	1	6	7	6
Bases Empty	.276	.344	.310	29	8	1	0	0	0	3	4
Runners On Base	.214	.353	.357	28	6	1	0	1	6	5	6

	BA	OBA	SA	AB	H	2B	3B	HR	RBI	BB	SO
	.278	.359	.426	115	32	3	1	4	16	13	18
	.289	.319	.356	45	13	0	0	1	3	2	8
	.271	.381	.471	70	19	3	1	3	13	11	10
	.279	.343	.393	61	17	1	0	2	2	5	7
	.278	.375	.463	54	15	2	1	2	14	8	11

MEL ROJAS — bats right — throws right — age 26 — MON — P

2-YEAR TOTALS (1990–1991)

1991	G	IP	H	BB	SO	SB	CS	W	L	SV	ERA
at Home	13	17.1	13	3	10	1	0	1	2	2	3.12
on Road	24	30.2	29	10	27	4	1	2	1	4	4.11

	G	IP	H	BB	SO	SB	CS	W	L	SV	ERA
	23	31.0	29	11	21	4	1	1	2	3	4.65
	37	57.0	47	26	42	5	2	5	2	4	3.16

	BA	OBA	SA	AB	H	2B	3B	HR	RBI	BB	SO
Total	.228	.280	.375	184	42	9	3	4	22	13	37
vs. Left	.262	.326	.476	84	22	6	3	2	15	9	15
vs. Right	.200	.238	.290	100	20	3	0	2	7	4	22
Bases Empty	.258	.301	.402	97	25	6	1	2	4	5	18
Runners On Base	.195	.258	.345	87	17	3	2	2	20	8	19

	BA	OBA	SA	AB	H	2B	3B	HR	RBI	BB	SO
	.231	.313	.380	329	76	16	3	9	40	37	63
	.231	.335	.405	173	40	9	3	5	25	28	28
	.231	.286	.353	156	36	7	0	4	15	9	35
	.292	.360	.447	161	47	11	1	4	4	16	31
	.173	.269	.315	168	29	5	2	5	36	21	32

STEVE ROSENBERG — bats left — throws left — age 28 — SD — P

4-YEAR TOTALS (1988–1991)

1991	G	IP	H	BB	SO	SB	CS	W	L	SV	ERA
at Home	5	5.0	3	1	1	0	0	0	0	0	1.80
on Road	5	6.2	8	4	5	0	1	1	1	0	10.80

	G	IP	H	BB	SO	SB	CS	W	L	SV	ERA
	41	100.2	113	36	54	0	4	2	8	1	4.83
	46	109.0	109	51	61	15	5	4	7	0	5.04

	BA	OBA	SA	AB	H	2B	3B	HR	RBI	BB	SO
Total	.250	.327	.477	44	11	1	0	3	11	5	6
vs. Left	.308	.357	.615	13	4	1	0	1	5	1	4
vs. Right	.226	.314	.419	31	7	0	0	2	6	4	2
Bases Empty	.154	.241	.154	26	4	0	0	0	3	5	3
Runners On Base	.389	.450	.944	18	7	1	0	3	11	2	1

	BA	OBA	SA	AB	H	2B	3B	HR	RBI	BB	SO
	.277	.344	.443	802	222	45	8	24	121	87	115
	.296	.363	.458	179	53	12	1	5	28	19	30
	.271	.338	.438	623	169	33	7	19	93	68	85
	.261	.341	.421	437	114	21	5	13	13	52	71
	.296	.347	.468	365	108	24	3	11	108	35	44

WAYNE ROSENTHAL — bats right — throws right — age 27 — TEX — P

1991	G	IP	H	BB	SO	SB	CS	W	L	SV	ERA
at Home	17	34.2	34	15	34	4	1	0	2	0	4.15
on Road	19	35.2	38	21	27	2	0	1	2	1	6.31

	BA	OBA	SA	AB	H	2B	3B	HR	RBI	BB	SO
Total	.257	.341	.425	280	72	16	2	9	47	36	61
vs. Left	.272	.346	.421	114	31	4	2	3	18	13	21
vs. Right	.247	.337	.428	166	41	12	0	6	29	23	40
Bases Empty	.240	.321	.467	150	36	8	1	8	8	17	32
Runners On Base	.277	.362	.377	130	36	8	1	1	39	19	29

1-YEAR TOTALS (1991)

G	IP	H	BB	SO	SB	CS	W	L	SV	ERA
17	34.2	34	15	34	4	1	0	2	0	4.15
19	35.2	38	21	27	2	0	1	2	1	6.31

BA	OBA	SA	AB	H	2B	3B	HR	RBI	BB	SO
.257	.341	.425	280	72	16	2	9	47	36	61
.272	.346	.421	114	31	4	2	3	18	13	21
.247	.337	.428	166	41	12	0	6	29	23	40
.240	.321	.467	150	36	8	1	8	8	17	32
.277	.362	.377	130	36	8	1	1	39	19	29

SCOTT RUSKIN — bats right — throws left — age 29 — MON — P

1991	G	IP	H	BB	SO	SB	CS	W	L	SV	ERA
at Home	26	28.0	24	7	18	3	3	3	2	2	1.93
on Road	38	35.2	33	23	28	4	0	1	2	4	6.06

	BA	OBA	SA	AB	H	2B	3B	HR	RBI	BB	SO
Total	.241	.333	.371	237	57	15	2	4	27	30	46
vs. Left	.275	.347	.363	91	25	6	1	0	10	10	18
vs. Right	.219	.325	.377	146	32	9	1	4	17	20	28
Bases Empty	.232	.303	.341	138	32	7	1	2	2	14	27
Runners On Base	.253	.373	.414	99	25	8	1	2	25	16	19

2-YEAR TOTALS (1990–1991)

G	IP	H	BB	SO	SB	CS	W	L	SV	ERA
58	69.1	59	29	48	14	5	5	2	4	1.56
73	69.2	73	39	55	13	0	2	4	4	5.30

BA	OBA	SA	AB	H	2B	3B	HR	RBI	BB	SO
.251	.341	.357	526	132	26	3	8	54	68	103
.277	.349	.369	206	57	8	1	3	23	23	44
.234	.336	.350	320	75	18	2	5	31	45	59
.243	.325	.336	280	68	13	2	3	3	32	53
.260	.359	.382	246	64	13	1	5	51	36	50

RANDY ST.CLAIRE — bats right — throws right — age 32 — ATL — P

1991	G	IP	H	BB	SO	SB	CS	W	L	SV	ERA
at Home	12	18.2	20	4	23	1	0	0	0	0	4.82
on Road	7	10.0	11	5	7	0	3	0	0	0	2.70

	BA	OBA	SA	AB	H	2B	3B	HR	RBI	BB	SO
Total	.282	.333	.445	110	31	6	0	4	13	9	30
vs. Left	.238	.319	.357	42	10	2	0	1	3	5	13
vs. Right	.309	.342	.500	68	21	4	0	3	10	4	17
Bases Empty	.317	.338	.524	63	20	4	0	3	3	2	20
Runners On Base	.234	.327	.340	47	11	2	0	1	10	7	10

7-YEAR TOTALS (1984–1991)

G	IP	H	BB	SO	SB	CS	W	L	SV	ERA
73	113.0	120	46	91	11	1	5	4	2	5.10
77	121.2	110	37	60	8	3	7	2	7	2.96

BA	OBA	SA	AB	H	2B	3B	HR	RBI	BB	SO
.257	.320	.395	896	230	33	5	27	116	83	151
.260	.329	.374	404	105	14	4	8	43	45	74
.254	.312	.413	492	125	19	1	19	73	38	77
.261	.311	.408	495	129	17	4	16	16	33	84
.252	.330	.379	401	101	16	1	11	100	50	67

BILL SAMPEN — bats right — throws right — age 29 — MON — P

1991	G	IP	H	BB	SO	SB	CS	W	L	SV	ERA
at Home	16	35.1	35	19	26	2	2	4	2	0	3.31
on Road	27	57.0	61	27	26	14	6	5	3	0	4.42

	BA	OBA	SA	AB	H	2B	3B	HR	RBI	BB	SO
Total	.273	.358	.452	352	96	22	1	13	50	46	52
vs. Left	.257	.358	.441	179	46	10	1	7	25	30	23
vs. Right	.289	.358	.462	173	50	12	0	6	25	16	29
Bases Empty	.276	.370	.486	181	50	11	0	9	9	26	29
Runners On Base	.269	.345	.415	171	46	11	1	4	41	20	23

2-YEAR TOTALS (1990–1991)

G	IP	H	BB	SO	SB	CS	W	L	SV	ERA
48	81.0	88	31	61	12	5	11	6	0	3.11
54	101.2	102	48	60	19	6	10	6	2	3.81

BA	OBA	SA	AB	H	2B	3B	HR	RBI	BB	SO
.270	.345	.407	703	190	34	1	20	89	79	121
.249	.333	.365	353	88	15	1	8	43	47	49
.291	.357	.449	350	102	19	0	12	46	32	72
.272	.351	.434	371	101	18	0	14	14	43	74
.268	.339	.377	332	89	16	1	6	75	36	47

MO SANFORD — bats right — throws right — age 26 — CIN — P

1991	G	IP	H	BB	SO	SB	CS	W	L	SV	ERA
at Home	3	15.0	12	9	18	1	0	0	1	0	6.00
on Road	2	13.0	7	6	13	3	0	1	1	0	1.38

	BA	OBA	SA	AB	H	2B	3B	HR	RBI	BB	SO
Total	.186	.297	.294	102	19	2	0	3	12	15	31
vs. Left	.207	.352	.310	58	12	0	0	2	6	13	13
vs. Right	.159	.213	.273	44	7	2	0	1	6	2	18
Bases Empty	.138	.254	.259	58	8	1	0	2	2	8	14
Runners On Base	.250	.353	.341	44	11	1	0	1	10	7	17

1-YEAR TOTALS (1991)

G	IP	H	BB	SO	SB	CS	W	L	SV	ERA
3	15.0	12	9	18	1	0	0	1	0	6.00
2	13.0	7	6	13	3	0	1	1	0	1.38

BA	OBA	SA	AB	H	2B	3B	HR	RBI	BB	SO
.186	.297	.294	102	19	2	0	3	12	15	31
.207	.352	.310	58	12	0	0	2	6	13	13
.159	.213	.273	44	7	2	0	1	6	2	18
.138	.254	.259	58	8	1	0	2	2	8	14
.250	.353	.341	44	11	1	0	1	10	7	17

RICH SAUVEUR — bats left — throws left — age 29 — NYN — P

1991	G	IP	H	BB	SO	SB	CS	W	L	SV	ERA
at Home	4	1.1	5	0	2	0	0	0	0	0	13.50
on Road	2	2.0	2	2	2	0	0	0	0	0	9.00

	BA	OBA	SA	AB	H	2B	3B	HR	RBI	BB	SO
Total	.467	.529	.867	15	7	1	1	1	5	2	4
vs. Left	.500	.500	.750	4	2	1	0	0	0	0	1
vs. Right	.455	.538	.909	11	5	0	1	1	5	2	3
Bases Empty	.600	.667	.800	5	3	0	0	1	1	1	1
Runners On Base	.400	.455	.900	10	4	1	1	1	5	1	3

3-YEAR TOTALS (1986–1991)

G	IP	H	BB	SO	SB	CS	W	L	SV	ERA
8	9.0	14	5	4	2	3	0	0	0	6.00
5	9.1	13	5	9	2	0	0	0	0	7.71

BA	OBA	SA	AB	H	2B	3B	HR	RBI	BB	SO
.360	.448	.653	75	27	5	1	5	16	10	13
.267	.421	.333	15	4	1	0	0	1	3	4
.383	.456	.733	60	23	4	1	5	15	7	9
.341	.413	.512	41	14	4	0	1	1	3	7
.382	.488	.824	34	13	1	1	4	15	7	6

BOB SCANLAN — bats right — throws right — age 26 — CHN — P

1991	G	IP	H	BB	SO	SB	CS	W	L	SV	ERA
at Home	23	59.0	75	24	22	4	6	5	5	1	5.49
on Road	17	52.0	39	16	22	1	1	2	3	0	2.08

	BA	OBA	SA	AB	H	2B	3B	HR	RBI	BB	SO
Total	.269	.332	.373	424	114	19	5	5	55	40	44
vs. Left	.262	.327	.371	221	58	12	3	2	25	21	18
vs. Right	.276	.338	.374	203	56	7	2	3	30	19	26
Bases Empty	.245	.308	.336	229	56	10	1	4	3	19	20
Runners On Base	.297	.359	.415	195	58	9	4	2	52	21	24

1-YEAR TOTALS (1991)

G	IP	H	BB	SO	SB	CS	W	L	SV	ERA
23	59.0	75	24	22	4	6	5	5	1	5.49
17	52.0	39	16	22	1	1	2	3	0	2.08

BA	OBA	SA	AB	H	2B	3B	HR	RBI	BB	SO
.269	.332	.373	424	114	19	5	5	55	40	44
.262	.327	.371	221	58	12	3	2	25	21	18
.276	.338	.374	203	56	7	2	3	30	19	26
.245	.308	.336	229	56	10	1	4	3	19	20
.297	.359	.415	195	58	9	4	2	52	21	24

DAN SCHATZEDER — bats left — throws left — age 38 — KC — P

8-YEAR TOTALS (1984–1991)

1991	G	IP	H	BB	SO	SB	CS	W	L	SV	ERA
at Home	5	4.2	8	4	2	0	0	0	0	0	9.64
on Road	3	2.0	3	3	2	0	0	0	0	0	9.00
	149	315.0	297	103	217	31	3	15	14	2	3.17
	142	254.2	275	96	147	21	10	12	12	5	4.42

	BA	OBA	SA	AB	H	2B	3B	HR	RBI	BB	SO
Total	.367	.486	.467	30	11	3	0	0	12	7	4
vs. Left	.455	.500	.545	11	5	1	0	0	6	1	0
vs. Right	.316	.480	.421	19	6	2	0	0	6	6	4
Bases Empty	.250	.455	.375	8	2	1	0	0	0	3	2
Runners On Base	.409	.500	.500	22	9	2	0	0	12	4	2
	.264	.325	.406	2170	572	104	15	58	288	199	364
	.272	.318	.355	595	162	25	3	6	82	40	117
	.260	.327	.425	1575	410	79	12	52	206	159	247
	.250	.316	.392	1206	301	57	8	33	33	115	211
	.281	.335	.422	964	271	47	7	25	255	84	153

CALVIN SCHIRALDI — bats right — throws right — age 30 — TEX — P

8-YEAR TOTALS (1984–1991)

1991	G	IP	H	BB	SO	SB	CS	W	L	SV	ERA
at Home	1	0.0	1	2	0	1	0	0	0	0	0.00
on Road	2	4.2	4	3	1	0	0	0	1	0	9.64
	113	264.2	273	113	224	37	14	15	18	10	4.32
	121	288.1	250	155	247	26	13	17	21	11	4.25

	BA	OBA	SA	AB	H	2B	3B	HR	RBI	BB	SO
Total	.263	.417	.737	19	5	0	0	3	7	5	1
vs. Left	.286	.286	.714	7	2	0	0	1	4	0	1
vs. Right	.250	.471	.750	12	3	0	0	2	3	5	1
Bases Empty	.167	.333	.417	12	2	0	0	1	1	3	1
Runners On Base	.429	.556	1.286	7	3	0	0	2	6	2	0
	.249	.334	.396	2103	523	91	16	62	291	268	471
	.267	.360	.419	1102	294	44	8	36	153	161	197
	.229	.306	.370	1001	229	47	8	26	138	107	274
	.241	.329	.353	1139	274	45	7	23	23	145	260
	.258	.341	.446	964	249	46	9	39	268	123	211

DAVE SCHMIDT — bats right — throws right — age 35 — MON — P

8-YEAR TOTALS (1984–1991)

1991	G	IP	H	BB	SO	SB	CS	W	L	SV	ERA
at Home	1	2.0	1	1	1	0	0	0	0	0	0.00
on Road	3	2.1	8	1	2	0	0	0	1	0	19.29
	147	361.0	385	92	209	38	13	22	19	26	4.04
	149	351.1	383	95	158	29	8	25	27	15	3.97

	BA	OBA	SA	AB	H	2B	3B	HR	RBI	BB	SO
Total	.429	.478	.762	21	9	1	0	2	5	2	3
vs. Left	.800	.800	1.500	10	8	1	0	2	5	0	0
vs. Right	.091	.231	.091	11	1	0	0	0	0	2	3
Bases Empty	.429	.429	.714	14	6	0	0	1	1	0	1
Runners On Base	.429	.556	.857	7	3	0	0	1	4	2	2
	.276	.322	.417	2782	768	120	24	75	346	187	367
	.283	.327	.433	1375	389	63	16	37	178	92	182
	.269	.317	.402	1407	379	57	8	38	168	95	185
	.283	.319	.445	1549	438	75	12	51	51	79	187
	.268	.325	.382	1233	330	45	12	24	295	108	180

MIKE SCHOOLER — bats right — throws right — age 30 — SEA — P

4-YEAR TOTALS (1988–1991)

1991	G	IP	H	BB	SO	SB	CS	W	L	SV	ERA
at Home	19	18.1	10	4	19	2	0	2	1	4	2.45
on Road	15	16.0	15	6	12	1	0	1	2	3	5.06
	101	114.2	105	30	108	10	2	6	10	48	2.83
	89	101.0	93	39	91	12	2	4	12	37	3.12

	BA	OBA	SA	AB	H	2B	3B	HR	RBI	BB	SO
Total	.198	.255	.278	126	25	2	1	2	16	10	31
vs. Left	.179	.258	.286	56	10	1	1	1	7	6	10
vs. Right	.214	.253	.271	70	15	1	0	1	9	4	21
Bases Empty	.171	.227	.243	70	12	2	0	1	1	5	19
Runners On Base	.232	.290	.321	56	13	0	1	1	15	5	12
	.241	.301	.335	821	198	28	5	13	97	69	199
	.250	.325	.369	412	103	17	4	8	60	47	89
	.232	.274	.301	409	95	11	1	5	37	22	110
	.214	.268	.305	416	89	11	3	7	7	30	103
	.269	.333	.365	405	109	17	2	6	90	39	96

PETE SCHOUREK — bats left — throws left — age 23 — NYN — P

1-YEAR TOTALS (1991)

1991	G	IP	H	BB	SO	SB	CS	W	L	SV	ERA
at Home	17	49.0	42	27	40	6	0	4	1	0	3.31
on Road	18	37.1	40	16	27	6	0	1	3	2	5.54
	17	49.0	42	27	40	6	0	4	1	0	3.31
	18	37.1	40	16	27	6	0	1	3	2	5.54

	BA	OBA	SA	AB	H	2B	3B	HR	RBI	BB	SO
Total	.248	.334	.390	331	82	14	6	7	53	43	67
vs. Left	.266	.339	.394	109	29	4	2	2	18	13	17
vs. Right	.239	.332	.387	222	53	10	4	5	35	30	50
Bases Empty	.220	.314	.363	168	37	7	4	3	3	23	37
Runners On Base	.276	.354	.417	163	45	7	2	4	50	20	30
	.248	.334	.390	331	82	14	6	7	53	43	67
	.266	.339	.394	109	29	4	2	2	18	13	17
	.239	.332	.387	222	53	10	4	5	35	30	50
	.220	.314	.363	168	37	7	4	3	3	23	37
	.276	.354	.417	163	45	7	2	4	50	20	30

MIKE SCOTT — bats right — throws right — age 37 — HOU — P

8-YEAR TOTALS (1984–1991)

1991	G	IP	H	BB	SO	SB	CS	W	L	SV	ERA
at Home	1	3.0	6	3	2	1	1	0	1	0	15.00
on Road	1	4.0	5	1	1	1	0	0	1	0	11.25
	123	838.2	632	219	685	121	27	59	32	0	2.55
	116	720.1	669	240	560	127	25	41	43	0	4.09

	BA	OBA	SA	AB	H	2B	3B	HR	RBI	BB	SO
Total	.367	.457	.667	30	11	3	0	2	10	4	3
vs. Left	.417	.500	.583	12	5	2	0	0	4	2	0
vs. Right	.333	.429	.722	18	6	1	0	2	6	2	3
Bases Empty	.333	.375	.600	15	5	1	0	1	1	1	1
Runners On Base	.400	.526	.733	15	6	2	0	1	9	3	2
	.225	.283	.348	5787	1301	221	42	136	564	459	1245
	.232	.295	.344	3122	724	125	27	57	283	280	525
	.217	.268	.353	2665	577	96	15	79	281	179	720
	.215	.267	.337	3649	783	132	27	87	87	251	758
	.242	.308	.367	2138	518	89	15	49	477	208	487

TIM SCOTT — bats right — throws right — age 26 — SD — P

1-YEAR TOTALS (1991)

1991	G	IP	H	BB	SO	SB	CS	W	L	SV	ERA
at Home	0	0.0	0	0	0	0	0	0	0	0	0.00
on Road	2	1.0	2	0	1	0	1	0	0	0	9.00
	0	0.0	0	0	0	0	0	0	0	0	0.00
	2	1.0	2	0	1	0	1	0	0	0	9.00

	BA	OBA	SA	AB	H	2B	3B	HR	RBI	BB	SO
Total	.400	.400	.600	5	2	1	0	0	1	0	1
vs. Left	.000	.000	.000	2	0	0	0	0	0	0	1
vs. Right	.667	.667	1.000	3	2	1	0	0	1	0	0
Bases Empty	1.000	1.000	1.000	1	1	0	0	0	0	0	0
Runners On Base	.250	.250	.500	4	1	1	0	0	1	0	1
	.400	.400	.600	5	2	1	0	0	1	0	1
	.000	.000	.000	2	0	0	0	0	0	0	1
	.667	.667	1.000	3	2	1	0	0	1	0	0
	1.000	1.000	1.000	1	1	0	0	0	0	0	0
	.250	.250	.500	4	1	1	0	0	1	0	1

SCOTT SCUDDER — bats right — throws right — age 24 — CIN — P

1991	G	IP	H	BB	SO	SB	CS	W	L	SV	ERA
at Home	14	55.2	52	33	29	5	4	3	6	0	5.34
on Road	13	45.2	39	23	22	7	2	3	3	1	3.15

	BA	OBA	SA	AB	H	2B	3B	HR	RBI	BB	SO
Total	.246	.352	.362	370	91	19	3	6	41	56	51
vs. Left	.254	.371	.385	213	54	13	3	3	23	38	29
vs. Right	.236	.324	.331	157	37	6	0	3	18	18	22
Bases Empty	.249	.346	.354	209	52	12	2	2	2	26	28
Runners On Base	.242	.359	.373	161	39	7	1	4	39	30	23

3-YEAR TOTALS (1989–1991)

G	IP	H	BB	SO	SB	CS	W	L	SV	ERA
39	139.2	137	72	87	13	5	8	12	0	5.16
32	133.2	119	75	72	24	6	7	11	1	3.91

BA	OBA	SA	AB	H	2B	3B	HR	RBI	BB	SO
.249	.346	.405	1029	256	49	8	32	128	147	159
.254	.353	.392	564	143	31	7	11	58	84	75
.243	.339	.422	465	113	18	1	21	70	63	84
.248	.339	.395	585	145	25	5	17	17	76	92
.250	.356	.419	444	111	24	3	15	111	71	67

RUDY SEANEZ — bats right — throws right — age 24 — CLE — P

1991	G	IP	H	BB	SO	SB	CS	W	L	SV	ERA
at Home	5	5.0	10	7	7	0	0	0	0	0	16.20
on Road	0	0.0	0	0	0	0	0	0	0	0	0.00

	BA	OBA	SA	AB	H	2B	3B	HR	RBI	BB	SO
Total	.385	.515	.692	26	10	2	0	2	10	7	7
vs. Left	.455	.538	.545	11	5	0	0	0	4	2	1
vs. Right	.333	.500	.800	15	5	1	0	2	6	5	6
Bases Empty	.286	.545	.429	7	2	1	0	0	0	4	3
Runners On Base	.421	.500	.789	19	8	1	0	2	10	3	4

3-YEAR TOTALS (1989–1991)

G	IP	H	BB	SO	SB	CS	W	L	SV	ERA
16	18.1	18	21	19	5	0	0	0	0	9.33
18	19.0	15	15	19	2	1	2	1	0	4.26

BA	OBA	SA	AB	H	2B	3B	HR	RBI	BB	SO
.236	.389	.364	140	33	4	1	4	32	36	38
.309	.452	.418	55	17	1	1	1	15	15	6
.188	.346	.329	85	16	3	0	3	17	21	32
.220	.443	.360	50	11	1	0	2	2	20	15
.244	.355	.367	90	22	3	1	2	30	16	23

STEVE SEARCY — bats left — throws left — age 28 — DET/PHI — P

1991	G	IP	H	BB	SO	SB	CS	W	L	SV	ERA
at Home	15	34.2	34	17	25	5	1	2	1	0	4.93
on Road	19	36.1	47	27	28	2	0	1	2	0	8.17

	BA	OBA	SA	AB	H	2B	3B	HR	RBI	BB	SO
Total	.288	.379	.466	281	81	14	3	10	50	44	53
vs. Left	.242	.358	.379	66	16	1	1	2	9	13	13
vs. Right	.302	.386	.493	215	65	13	2	8	41	31	40
Bases Empty	.271	.382	.443	140	38	5	2	5	5	25	28
Runners On Base	.305	.376	.489	141	43	9	1	5	45	19	25

4-YEAR TOTALS (1988–1991)

G	IP	H	BB	SO	SB	CS	W	L	SV	ERA
28	85.2	88	47	58	7	5	4	4	0	5.04
32	91.0	104	64	77	9	3	2	9	0	6.23

BA	OBA	SA	AB	H	2B	3B	HR	RBI	BB	SO
.281	.376	.450	684	192	33	4	25	112	111	135
.266	.360	.374	139	37	4	1	3	19	22	21
.284	.380	.470	545	155	29	3	22	93	89	114
.248	.361	.394	363	90	14	3	11	11	64	78
.318	.393	.514	321	102	19	1	14	101	47	57

JOSE SEGURA — bats right — throws right — age 29 — SF — P

1991	G	IP	H	BB	SO	SB	CS	W	L	SV	ERA
at Home	4	4.1	6	4	2	1	1	0	0	0	6.23
on Road	7	12.0	14	1	8	2	1	0	1	0	3.75

	BA	OBA	SA	AB	H	2B	3B	HR	RBI	BB	SO
Total	.303	.352	.379	66	20	0	1	1	11	5	10
vs. Left	.400	.419	.567	30	12	0	1	1	9	1	3
vs. Right	.222	.300	.222	36	8	0	0	0	2	4	7
Bases Empty	.323	.400	.323	31	10	0	0	0	0	4	7
Runners On Base	.286	.306	.429	35	10	0	1	1	11	1	3

3-YEAR TOTALS (1988–1991)

G	IP	H	BB	SO	SB	CS	W	L	SV	ERA
10	8.2	16	6	5	1	1	0	0	0	11.42
12	22.1	36	10	11	2	1	0	2	0	8.06

BA	OBA	SA	AB	H	2B	3B	HR	RBI	BB	SO
.377	.439	.500	138	52	3	1	4	35	16	16
.492	.541	.692	65	32	2	1	3	23	8	6
.274	.346	.329	73	20	1	0	1	12	8	10
.279	.362	.328	61	17	0	0	1	1	8	10
.455	.500	.636	77	35	3	1	3	34	8	6

JEFF SHAW — bats right — throws right — age 26 — CLE — P

1991	G	IP	H	BB	SO	SB	CS	W	L	SV	ERA
at Home	13	41.1	36	7	17	0	3	0	3	1	2.61
on Road	16	31.0	36	20	14	1	0	0	2	0	4.35

	BA	OBA	SA	AB	H	2B	3B	HR	RBI	BB	SO
Total	.262	.332	.371	275	72	10	1	6	40	27	31
vs. Left	.288	.345	.385	104	30	2	1	2	12	9	8
vs. Right	.246	.325	.363	171	42	8	0	4	28	18	23
Bases Empty	.287	.353	.404	136	39	5	1	3	3	12	12
Runners On Base	.237	.313	.338	139	33	5	0	3	37	15	19

2-YEAR TOTALS (1990–1991)

G	IP	H	BB	SO	SB	CS	W	L	SV	ERA
21	75.2	84	21	33	1	4	2	6	1	4.76
20	45.1	61	26	23	4	0	1	3	0	4.57

BA	OBA	SA	AB	H	2B	3B	HR	RBI	BB	SO
.302	.364	.471	480	145	26	2	17	69	47	56
.324	.378	.464	222	72	11	1	6	25	20	21
.283	.353	.477	258	73	15	1	11	44	27	35
.347	.404	.565	248	86	17	2	11	11	22	26
.254	.323	.371	232	59	9	0	6	58	25	30

TIM SHERRILL — bats left — throws left — age 27 — SL — P

1991	G	IP	H	BB	SO	SB	CS	W	L	SV	ERA
at Home	6	9.0	6	3	3	1	0	0	0	0	6.00
on Road	4	5.1	14	0	1	1	0	0	0	0	11.81

	BA	OBA	SA	AB	H	2B	3B	HR	RBI	BB	SO
Total	.339	.379	.458	59	20	1	0	2	13	3	4
vs. Left	.294	.381	.294	17	5	0	0	0	3	2	1
vs. Right	.357	.378	.524	42	15	1	0	2	10	1	3
Bases Empty	.233	.281	.267	30	7	1	0	0	0	2	3
Runners On Base	.448	.471	.655	29	13	0	0	2	13	1	1

2-YEAR TOTALS (1990–1991)

G	IP	H	BB	SO	SB	CS	W	L	SV	ERA
11	11.2	10	4	4	1	0	0	0	0	5.40
7	7.0	20	2	3	2	1	0	0	0	11.57

BA	OBA	SA	AB	H	2B	3B	HR	RBI	BB	SO
.375	.422	.500	80	30	4	0	2	20	6	7
.346	.419	.423	26	9	2	0	0	8	3	3
.389	.424	.537	54	21	2	0	2	12	3	4
.257	.316	.314	35	9	2	0	0	0	3	4
.467	.500	.644	45	21	2	0	2	20	3	3

ERIC SHOW — bats right — throws right — age 36 — OAK — P

1991	G	IP	H	BB	SO	SB	CS	W	L	SV	ERA
at Home	12	26.1	28	9	10	1	1	0	2	0	6.84
on Road	11	25.1	34	8	10	3	0	1	0	0	4.97

	BA	OBA	SA	AB	H	2B	3B	HR	RBI	BB	SO
Total	.300	.346	.464	207	62	17	1	5	31	17	20
vs. Left	.358	.436	.621	95	34	11	1	4	17	14	9
vs. Right	.250	.263	.330	112	28	6	0	1	14	3	11
Bases Empty	.277	.333	.454	119	33	10	1	3	3	10	13
Runners On Base	.330	.364	.477	88	29	7	0	2	28	7	7

8-YEAR TOTALS (1984–1991)

G	IP	H	BB	SO	SB	CS	W	L	SV	ERA
118	647.0	584	249	411	46	36	37	34	0	3.62
117	634.2	608	230	330	42	24	38	34	1	3.80

BA	OBA	SA	AB	H	2B	3B	HR	RBI	BB	SO
.249	.319	.389	4794	1192	213	28	134	516	479	741
.271	.352	.416	2543	690	127	24	64	249	320	328
.223	.280	.358	2251	502	86	4	70	267	159	413
.251	.311	.398	2958	743	133	19	88	88	242	459
.245	.331	.373	1836	449	80	9	46	428	237	282

DOUG SIMONS — bats left — throws left — age 26 — NYN — P

1-YEAR TOTALS (1991)

1991	G	IP	H	BB	SO	SB	CS	W	L	SV	ERA
at Home	24	36.2	37	10	24	3	3	1	1	0	4.91
on Road	18	24.0	18	9	14	2	1	1	2	1	5.63

	BA	OBA	SA	AB	H	2B	3B	HR	RBI	BB	SO
Total	.246	.305	.379	224	55	13	1	5	34	19	38
vs. Left	.195	.250	.253	87	17	3	1	0	9	7	23
vs. Right	.277	.340	.460	137	38	10	0	5	25	12	15
Bases Empty	.211	.242	.306	147	31	9	1	1	6	6	26
Runners On Base	.312	.406	.519	77	24	4	0	4	33	13	12

1-YEAR TOTALS side:

G	IP	H	BB	SO	SB	CS	W	L	SV	ERA
24	36.2	37	10	24	3	3	1	1	0	4.91
18	24.0	18	9	14	2	1	1	2	1	5.63

BA	OBA	SA	AB	H	2B	3B	HR	RBI	BB	SO
.246	.305	.379	224	55	13	1	5	34	19	38
.195	.250	.253	87	17	3	1	0	9	7	23
.277	.340	.460	137	38	10	0	5	25	12	15
.211	.242	.306	147	31	9	1	1	6	6	26
.312	.406	.519	77	24	4	0	4	33	13	12

DOUG SISK — bats right — throws right — age 35 — ATL — P

7-YEAR TOTALS (1984–1991)

1991	G	IP	H	BB	SO	SB	CS	W	L	SV	ERA
at Home	9	10.0	15	6	4	0	0	1	0	0	4.50
on Road	5	4.1	6	2	1	2	0	1	1	0	6.23

	BA	OBA	SA	AB	H	2B	3B	HR	RBI	BB	SO
Total	.333	.403	.476	63	21	2	2	1	14	8	5
vs. Left	.394	.475	.667	33	13	2	2	1	11	6	3
vs. Right	.267	.313	.267	30	8	0	0	0	3	2	2
Bases Empty	.321	.367	.429	28	9	1	1	0	0	2	2
Runners On Base	.343	.429	.514	35	12	1	1	1	14	6	3

7-YEAR TOTALS side:

G	IP	H	BB	SO	SB	CS	W	L	SV	ERA
127	200.0	205	95	75	8	4	6	6	10	3.15
129	209.1	225	106	83	17	11	11	8	11	3.78

BA	OBA	SA	AB	H	2B	3B	HR	RBI	BB	SO
.276	.362	.348	1560	430	56	9	13	212	201	158
.286	.387	.364	706	202	32	4	5	97	116	57
.267	.340	.335	854	228	24	5	8	115	85	101
.254	.340	.305	753	191	24	6	1	1	93	87
.296	.382	.388	807	239	32	3	12	211	108	71

HEATHCLIFF SLOCUMB — bats right — throws right — age 26 — CHN — P

1-YEAR TOTALS (1991)

1991	G	IP	H	BB	SO	SB	CS	W	L	SV	ERA
at Home	28	33.0	28	11	20	3	1	2	0	1	3.00
on Road	24	29.2	25	19	14	9	0	0	1	0	3.94

	BA	OBA	SA	AB	H	2B	3B	HR	RBI	BB	SO
Total	.231	.321	.323	229	53	10	1	3	30	30	34
vs. Left	.291	.364	.437	103	30	4	1	3	14	12	10
vs. Right	.183	.287	.230	126	23	6	0	0	16	18	24
Bases Empty	.202	.297	.240	104	21	4	0	0	0	12	14
Runners On Base	.256	.340	.392	125	32	6	1	3	30	18	20

1-YEAR TOTALS side:

G	IP	H	BB	SO	SB	CS	W	L	SV	ERA
28	33.0	28	11	20	3	1	2	0	1	3.00
24	29.2	25	19	14	9	0	0	1	0	3.94

BA	OBA	SA	AB	H	2B	3B	HR	RBI	BB	SO
.231	.321	.323	229	53	10	1	3	30	30	34
.291	.364	.437	103	30	4	1	3	14	12	10
.183	.287	.230	126	23	6	0	0	16	18	24
.202	.297	.240	104	21	4	0	0	0	12	14
.256	.340	.392	125	32	6	1	3	30	18	20

JOE SLUSARSKI — bats right — throws right — age 26 — OAK — P

1-YEAR TOTALS (1991)

1991	G	IP	H	BB	SO	SB	CS	W	L	SV	ERA
at Home	7	43.2	46	17	24	1	2	2	3	0	5.36
on Road	13	65.2	75	35	36	4	3	3	4	0	5.07

	BA	OBA	SA	AB	H	2B	3B	HR	RBI	BB	SO
Total	.283	.364	.436	427	121	17	3	14	53	52	60
vs. Left	.298	.351	.449	245	73	10	3	7	25	21	27
vs. Right	.264	.381	.418	182	48	7	0	7	28	31	33
Bases Empty	.265	.346	.422	249	66	9	3	8	8	30	32
Runners On Base	.309	.388	.455	178	55	8	0	6	45	22	28

1-YEAR TOTALS side:

G	IP	H	BB	SO	SB	CS	W	L	SV	ERA
7	43.2	46	17	24	1	2	2	3	0	5.36
13	65.2	75	35	36	4	3	3	4	0	5.07

BA	OBA	SA	AB	H	2B	3B	HR	RBI	BB	SO
.283	.364	.436	427	121	17	3	14	53	52	60
.298	.351	.449	245	73	10	3	7	25	21	27
.264	.381	.418	182	48	7	0	7	28	31	33
.265	.346	.422	249	66	9	3	8	8	30	32
.309	.388	.455	178	55	8	0	6	45	22	28

ROY SMITH — bats right — throws right — age 31 — BAL — P

8-YEAR TOTALS (1984–1991)

1991	G	IP	H	BB	SO	SB	CS	W	L	SV	ERA
at Home	11	49.2	60	19	15	6	4	4	1	0	5.44
on Road	6	30.2	39	5	10	0	1	1	3	0	5.87

	BA	OBA	SA	AB	H	2B	3B	HR	RBI	BB	SO
Total	.311	.358	.465	318	99	18	2	9	41	24	25
vs. Left	.275	.325	.444	153	42	10	2	4	23	12	14
vs. Right	.345	.390	.485	165	57	8	0	5	18	12	11
Bases Empty	.306	.352	.464	196	60	11	1	6	6	14	18
Runners On Base	.320	.368	.467	122	39	7	1	3	35	10	7

8-YEAR TOTALS side:

G	IP	H	BB	SO	SB	CS	W	L	SV	ERA
69	332.0	359	103	168	24	21	20	13	1	4.17
67	286.1	348	99	152	33	15	10	18	0	5.09

BA	OBA	SA	AB	H	2B	3B	HR	RBI	BB	SO
.289	.343	.449	2446	707	121	15	80	317	202	320
.307	.366	.476	1213	372	67	12	38	178	116	150
.272	.320	.423	1233	335	54	3	42	139	86	170
.288	.343	.436	1416	408	66	4	45	45	110	187
.290	.343	.467	1030	299	55	11	35	272	92	133

PETE SMITH — bats right — throws right — age 26 — ATL — P

5-YEAR TOTALS (1987–1991)

1991	G	IP	H	BB	SO	SB	CS	W	L	SV	ERA
at Home	7	23.1	31	13	9	6	1	0	2	0	6.94
on Road	7	24.2	17	9	20	7	0	1	1	0	3.28

	BA	OBA	SA	AB	H	2B	3B	HR	RBI	BB	SO
Total	.262	.335	.437	183	48	13	2	5	27	22	29
vs. Left	.309	.364	.515	97	30	9	1	3	15	10	13
vs. Right	.209	.303	.349	86	18	4	1	2	12	12	16
Bases Empty	.262	.350	.456	103	27	8	0	4	4	14	17
Runners On Base	.262	.315	.412	80	21	5	2	1	23	8	12

5-YEAR TOTALS side:

G	IP	H	BB	SO	SB	CS	W	L	SV	ERA
50	278.0	282	122	177	46	20	12	22	0	4.47
43	216.0	209	83	158	26	9	7	18	0	4.25

BA	OBA	SA	AB	H	2B	3B	HR	RBI	BB	SO
.260	.330	.389	1885	491	83	9	47	225	205	335
.282	.360	.412	1053	297	52	5	25	126	135	152
.233	.292	.359	832	194	31	4	22	99	70	183
.242	.310	.360	1146	277	47	1	29	29	113	212
.290	.361	.433	739	214	36	8	18	196	92	123

MIKE STANTON — bats left — throws left — age 25 — ATL — P

3-YEAR TOTALS (1989–1991)

1991	G	IP	H	BB	SO	SB	CS	W	L	SV	ERA
at Home	36	40.2	30	8	20	3	6	1	1	4	2.21
on Road	38	37.1	32	13	34	6	0	4	4	3	3.62

	BA	OBA	SA	AB	H	2B	3B	HR	RBI	BB	SO
Total	.217	.273	.325	286	62	9	2	6	35	21	54
vs. Left	.194	.252	.233	103	20	1	0	1	4	8	26
vs. Right	.230	.284	.377	183	42	8	2	5	31	13	28
Bases Empty	.226	.257	.323	164	37	7	0	3	3	7	28
Runners On Base	.205	.292	.328	122	25	2	2	3	32	14	26

3-YEAR TOTALS side:

G	IP	H	BB	SO	SB	CS	W	L	SV	ERA
49	59.0	54	11	40	6	6	1	3	8	3.66
52	50.0	41	22	48	6	0	4	6	8	3.42

BA	OBA	SA	AB	H	2B	3B	HR	RBI	BB	SO
.235	.296	.334	404	95	11	4	7	57	33	88
.200	.270	.248	125	25	1	1	1	11	11	34
.251	.308	.373	279	70	10	3	6	46	22	54
.226	.261	.307	212	48	8	0	3	3	9	44
.245	.332	.365	192	47	3	4	4	54	24	44

DAVE STIEB — bats right — throws right — age 35 — TOR — P

1991	G	IP	H	BB	SO	SB	CS	W	L	SV	ERA
at Home	3	18.0	15	5	10	2	0	1	2	0	5.50
on Road	6	41.2	37	18	19	3	5	3	1	0	2.16

	BA	OBA	SA	AB	H	2B	3B	HR	RBI	BB	SO
Total	.243	.321	.346	214	52	8	1	4	21	23	29
vs. Left	.239	.318	.333	117	28	5	0	2	11	13	15
vs. Right	.247	.324	.361	97	24	3	1	2	10	10	14
Bases Empty	.254	.348	.331	118	30	4	1	1	1	15	15
Runners On Base	.229	.286	.365	96	22	4	0	3	20	8	14

8-YEAR TOTALS (1984–1991)

	G	IP	H	BB	SO	SB	CS	W	L	SV	ERA
	119	779.0	692	286	497	42	40	56	35	0	3.37
	127	821.2	674	309	509	45	35	49	30	1	3.13

	BA	OBA	SA	AB	H	2B	3B	HR	RBI	BB	SO
	.232	.309	.347	5895	1366	242	31	126	557	595	1006
	.241	.319	.359	3160	761	123	18	72	314	345	441
	.221	.298	.333	2735	605	119	13	54	243	250	565
	.220	.306	.348	3486	768	139	22	87	87	381	605
	.248	.314	.347	2409	598	103	9	39	470	214	401

RICK SUTCLIFFE — bats left — throws right — age 36 — CHN — P

1991	G	IP	H	BB	SO	SB	CS	W	L	SV	ERA
at Home	10	56.2	47	18	37	13	1	3	1	0	3.18
on Road	9	40.0	49	27	15	8	1	3	4	0	5.40

	BA	OBA	SA	AB	H	2B	3B	HR	RBI	BB	SO
Total	.264	.338	.379	364	96	20	5	4	44	45	52
vs. Left	.287	.363	.426	216	62	12	3	4	30	29	23
vs. Right	.230	.301	.311	148	34	8	2	0	14	16	29
Bases Empty	.262	.336	.393	206	54	10	4	3	3	23	25
Runners On Base	.266	.340	.361	158	42	10	1	1	41	22	27

8-YEAR TOTALS (1984–1991)

	G	IP	H	BB	SO	SB	CS	W	L	SV	ERA
	100	655.0	627	267	484	70	31	40	29	0	3.82
	108	706.2	670	260	483	97	21	46	41	0	3.86

	BA	OBA	SA	AB	H	2B	3B	HR	RBI	BB	SO
	.253	.322	.381	5123	1297	233	43	112	538	527	967
	.257	.330	.383	2847	732	145	25	54	283	312	520
	.248	.313	.379	2276	565	88	18	58	255	215	447
	.245	.303	.373	3108	763	133	27	70	70	249	578
	.265	.349	.393	2015	534	100	16	42	468	278	389

RUSS SWAN — bats left — throws left — age 28 — SEA — P

1991	G	IP	H	BB	SO	SB	CS	W	L	SV	ERA
at Home	28	30.2	43	9	18	2	0	1	2	0	5.28
on Road	35	48.0	38	19	15	5	1	5	0	2	2.25

	BA	OBA	SA	AB	H	2B	3B	HR	RBI	BB	SO
Total	.269	.330	.405	301	81	17	0	8	33	28	33
vs. Left	.195	.256	.229	118	23	1	0	1	9	10	12
vs. Right	.317	.378	.519	183	58	16	0	7	24	18	21
Bases Empty	.313	.360	.469	160	50	10	0	5	5	12	15
Runners On Base	.220	.297	.333	141	31	7	0	3	28	16	18

3-YEAR TOTALS (1989–1991)

	G	IP	H	BB	SO	SB	CS	W	L	SV	ERA
	36	58.1	72	22	30	6	0	2	3	0	4.94
	42	76.1	68	32	21	6	2	6	5	2	3.07

	BA	OBA	SA	AB	H	2B	3B	HR	RBI	BB	SO
	.272	.339	.419	515	140	27	2	15	69	54	51
	.203	.254	.234	158	32	2	0	1	16	12	14
	.303	.375	.501	357	108	25	2	14	53	42	37
	.283	.347	.424	276	78	15	0	8	8	27	23
	.259	.330	.414	239	62	12	2	7	61	27	28

ANTHONY TELFORD — bats right — throws right — age 26 — BAL — P

1991	G	IP	H	BB	SO	SB	CS	W	L	SV	ERA
at Home	4	12.2	12	4	11	0	0	0	0	0	2.84
on Road	5	14.0	15	2	13	1	0	0	0	0	5.14

	BA	OBA	SA	AB	H	2B	3B	HR	RBI	BB	SO
Total	.265	.303	.402	102	27	5	0	3	15	6	24
vs. Left	.271	.300	.354	48	13	1	0	1	6	2	10
vs. Right	.259	.305	.444	54	14	4	0	2	9	4	14
Bases Empty	.271	.306	.390	59	16	1	0	2	2	3	13
Runners On Base	.256	.298	.419	43	11	4	0	1	13	3	11

2-YEAR TOTALS (1990–1991)

	G	IP	H	BB	SO	SB	CS	W	L	SV	ERA
	10	44.1	42	21	29	2	2	3	2	0	3.05
	7	18.2	28	4	15	2	1	0	1	0	8.20

	BA	OBA	SA	AB	H	2B	3B	HR	RBI	BB	SO
	.282	.347	.423	248	70	14	0	7	32	25	44
	.291	.328	.444	117	34	6	0	4	18	7	19
	.275	.362	.405	131	36	8	0	3	14	18	25
	.285	.355	.460	137	39	6	0	6	6	15	21
	.279	.336	.378	111	31	8	0	1	26	10	23

SCOTT TERRY — bats right — throws right — age 33 — SL — P

1991	G	IP	H	BB	SO	SB	CS	W	L	SV	ERA
at Home	34	45.1	38	15	31	4	4	4	1	0	1.19
on Road	31	35.0	38	17	21	3	0	0	3	1	4.89

	BA	OBA	SA	AB	H	2B	3B	HR	RBI	BB	SO
Total	.249	.320	.308	305	76	11	2	1	31	32	52
vs. Left	.241	.332	.306	170	41	6	1	1	18	23	29
vs. Right	.259	.306	.311	135	35	5	1	0	13	9	23
Bases Empty	.262	.302	.313	160	42	6	1	0	0	9	29
Runners On Base	.234	.339	.303	145	34	5	1	1	31	23	23

6-YEAR TOTALS (1986–1991)

	G	IP	H	BB	SO	SB	CS	W	L	SV	ERA
	125	277.2	259	80	144	25	15	17	12	3	3.08
	111	221.2	232	96	118	18	6	7	16	5	4.55

	BA	OBA	SA	AB	H	2B	3B	HR	RBI	BB	SO
	.258	.321	.378	1901	491	95	14	35	233	176	262
	.269	.339	.397	927	249	46	8	19	121	101	137
	.248	.304	.360	974	242	49	6	16	112	75	125
	.236	.294	.334	1069	252	56	8	11	11	85	152
	.287	.355	.435	832	239	39	6	24	222	91	110

MIKE TIMLIN — bats right — throws right — age 26 — TOR — P

1991	G	IP	H	BB	SO	SB	CS	W	L	SV	ERA
at Home	33	61.1	59	24	41	11	3	7	2	1	2.35
on Road	30	47.0	35	26	44	0	2	4	4	2	4.21

	BA	OBA	SA	AB	H	2B	3B	HR	RBI	BB	SO
Total	.233	.317	.297	404	94	6	1	6	52	50	85
vs. Left	.296	.392	.373	169	50	2	1	3	22	27	27
vs. Right	.187	.260	.243	235	44	4	0	3	30	23	58
Bases Empty	.181	.260	.217	226	41	2	0	2	2	24	49
Runners On Base	.298	.386	.399	178	53	4	1	4	50	26	36

1-YEAR TOTALS (1991)

	G	IP	H	BB	SO	SB	CS	W	L	SV	ERA
	33	61.1	59	24	41	11	3	7	2	1	2.35
	30	47.0	35	26	44	0	2	4	4	2	4.21

	BA	OBA	SA	AB	H	2B	3B	HR	RBI	BB	SO
	.233	.317	.297	404	94	6	1	6	52	50	85
	.296	.392	.373	169	50	2	1	3	22	27	27
	.187	.260	.243	235	44	4	0	3	30	23	58
	.181	.260	.217	226	41	2	0	2	2	24	49
	.298	.386	.399	178	53	4	1	4	50	26	36

EFRAIN VALDEZ — bats left — throws left — age 26 — CLE — P

1991	G	IP	H	BB	SO	SB	CS	W	L	SV	ERA
at Home	4	3.1	3	1	0	0	0	0	0	0	0.00
on Road	3	2.2	2	2	1	0	0	0	0	0	3.38

	BA	OBA	SA	AB	H	2B	3B	HR	RBI	BB	SO
Total	.238	.346	.238	21	5	0	0	0	1	3	1
vs. Left	.444	.615	.444	9	4	0	0	0	0	0	3
vs. Right	.083	.077	.083	12	1	0	0	0	1	0	1
Bases Empty	.364	.417	.364	11	4	0	0	0	0	1	0
Runners On Base	.100	.286	.100	10	1	0	0	0	1	2	1

2-YEAR TOTALS (1990–1991)

	G	IP	H	BB	SO	SB	CS	W	L	SV	ERA
	10	14.2	13	7	6	2	1	0	0	0	1.84
	10	15.0	12	10	8	1	1	0	0	0	3.60

	BA	OBA	SA	AB	H	2B	3B	HR	RBI	BB	SO
	.234	.333	.336	107	25	5	0	2	12	17	14
	.244	.360	.293	41	10	2	0	0	5	7	4
	.227	.316	.364	66	15	3	0	2	7	10	10
	.267	.333	.417	60	16	3	0	2	2	6	7
	.191	.333	.234	47	9	2	0	0	10	11	7

SERGIO VALDEZ — bats right — throws right — age 28 — CLE — P

1991	G	IP	H	BB	SO	SB	CS	W	L	SV	ERA
at Home	2	8.0	5	2	6	0	0	1	0	0	4.50
on Road	4	8.1	10	3	5	2	0	0	0	0	6.48

	BA	OBA	SA	AB	H	2B	3B	HR	RBI	BB	SO
Total	.238	.290	.397	63	15	1	0	3	8	5	11
vs. Left	.267	.353	.400	30	8	1	0	1	3	4	3
vs. Right	.212	.229	.394	33	7	0	0	2	5	1	8
Bases Empty	.200	.256	.375	40	8	1	0	2	2	3	9
Runners On Base	.304	.346	.435	23	7	0	0	1	6	2	2

4-YEAR TOTALS (1986–1991)

G	IP	H	BB	SO	SB	CS	W	L	SV	ERA
31	96.2	99	30	65	5	2	4	6	0	4.38
29	85.0	101	41	58	7	3	4	6	0	6.56

BA	OBA	SA	AB	H	2B	3B	HR	RBI	BB	SO
.280	.344	.454	714	200	41	1	27	104	71	123
.262	.344	.415	340	89	17	1	11	43	44	48
.297	.344	.489	374	111	24	0	16	61	27	75
.263	.328	.432	403	106	20	0	16	16	38	74
.302	.365	.482	311	94	21	1	11	88	33	49

FERNANDO VALENZUELA — bats left — throws left — age 32 — CAL — P

1991	G	IP	H	BB	SO	SB	CS	W	L	SV	ERA
at Home	2	6.2	14	3	5	0	0	0	2	0	12.15
on Road	0	0.0	0	0	0	0	0	0	0	0	0.00

	BA	OBA	SA	AB	H	2B	3B	HR	RBI	BB	SO
Total	.452	.486	.839	31	14	3	0	3	7	3	5
vs. Left	.500	.500	1.000	6	3	0	0	1	1	0	0
vs. Right	.440	.483	.800	25	11	3	0	2	6	3	5
Bases Empty	.556	.556	1.000	18	10	2	0	2	2	0	2
Runners On Base	.308	.412	.615	13	4	1	0	1	5	3	3

8-YEAR TOTALS (1984–1991)

G	IP	H	BB	SO	SB	CS	W	L	SV	ERA
112	807.2	724	316	578	51	40	43	41	1	3.20
114	795.2	749	354	602	70	39	49	47	0	3.79

BA	OBA	SA	AB	H	2B	3B	HR	RBI	BB	SO
.245	.320	.354	6011	1473	272	18	115	616	670	1180
.258	.317	.374	1082	279	53	5	21	104	98	221
.242	.321	.349	4929	1194	219	13	94	512	572	959
.231	.307	.332	3448	795	152	8	61	61	373	747
.265	.337	.382	2563	678	120	10	54	555	297	433

JULIO VALERA — bats right — throws right — age 24 — NYN — P

1991	G	IP	H	BB	SO	SB	CS	W	L	SV	ERA
at Home	2	2.0	1	4	3	1	0	0	0	0	0.00
on Road	0	0.0	0	0	0	0	0	0	0	0	0.00

	BA	OBA	SA	AB	H	2B	3B	HR	RBI	BB	SO
Total	.143	.455	.143	7	1	0	0	0	1	4	3
vs. Left	.500	.800	.500	2	1	0	0	0	0	3	1
vs. Right	.000	.167	.000	5	0	0	0	0	1	1	2
Bases Empty	.000	1.000	.000	0	0	0	0	0	0	1	0
Runners On Base	.143	.400	.143	7	1	0	0	0	3	3	3

2-YEAR TOTALS (1990–1991)

G	IP	H	BB	SO	SB	CS	W	L	SV	ERA
4	13.0	13	9	6	1	2	1	0	0	4.15
1	2.0	8	2	1	1	0	0	1	0	18.00

BA	OBA	SA	AB	H	2B	3B	HR	RBI	BB	SO
.328	.427	.453	64	21	5	0	1	10	11	7
.368	.467	.474	38	14	4	0	1	4	7	2
.269	.367	.423	26	7	1	0	0	6	4	5
.267	.389	.400	30	8	1	0	1	1	6	2
.382	.462	.500	34	13	4	0	0	9	5	5

TODD VanPOPPEL — bats right — throws right — age 21 — OAK — P

1991	G	IP	H	BB	SO	SB	CS	W	L	SV	ERA
at Home	1	4.2	7	2	6	1	1	0	0	0	9.64
on Road	0	0.0	0	0	0	0	0	0	0	0	0.00

	BA	OBA	SA	AB	H	2B	3B	HR	RBI	BB	SO
Total	.368	.429	.632	19	7	0	1	1	5	2	6
vs. Left	.385	.429	.538	13	5	0	1	0	2	1	3
vs. Right	.333	.429	.833	6	2	0	0	1	3	1	3
Bases Empty	.182	.308	.182	11	2	0	0	0	0	2	5
Runners On Base	.625	.625	1.250	8	5	0	1	1	5	0	1

1-YEAR TOTALS (1991)

G	IP	H	BB	SO	SB	CS	W	L	SV	ERA
1	4.2	7	2	6	1	1	0	0	0	9.64
0	0.0	0	0	0	0	0	0	0	0	0.00

BA	OBA	SA	AB	H	2B	3B	HR	RBI	BB	SO
.368	.429	.632	19	7	0	1	1	5	2	6
.385	.429	.538	13	5	0	1	0	2	1	3
.333	.429	.833	6	2	0	0	1	3	1	3
.182	.308	.182	11	2	0	0	0	0	2	5
.625	.625	1.250	8	5	0	1	1	5	0	1

HECTOR WAGNER — bats right — throws right — age 24 — KC — P

1991	G	IP	H	BB	SO	SB	CS	W	L	SV	ERA
at Home	1	4.0	12	3	1	0	0	0	1	0	15.75
on Road	1	6.0	4	0	4	0	0	1	0	0	1.50

	BA	OBA	SA	AB	H	2B	3B	HR	RBI	BB	SO
Total	.348	.388	.587	46	16	5	0	2	8	3	5
vs. Left	.320	.370	.480	25	8	1	0	1	3	2	3
vs. Right	.381	.409	.714	21	8	4	0	1	5	1	2
Bases Empty	.333	.407	.625	24	8	4	0	1	1	3	4
Runners On Base	.364	.364	.545	22	8	1	0	1	7	0	1

2-YEAR TOTALS (1990–1991)

G	IP	H	BB	SO	SB	CS	W	L	SV	ERA
4	18.2	35	10	8	2	0	0	2	0	8.20
3	14.2	13	4	11	2	0	1	1	0	7.36

BA	OBA	SA	AB	H	2B	3B	HR	RBI	BB	SO
.331	.385	.524	145	48	10	0	6	26	14	19
.286	.340	.396	91	26	4	0	2	11	8	13
.407	.459	.741	54	22	6	0	4	15	6	6
.319	.395	.583	72	23	7	0	4	4	9	12
.342	.375	.466	73	25	3	0	2	22	5	7

DAVE WAINHOUSE — bats left — throws right — age 25 — MON — P

1991	G	IP	H	BB	SO	SB	CS	W	L	SV	ERA
at Home	1	2.0	1	1	0	0	0	0	0	0	4.50
on Road	1	0.2	1	3	1	0	0	0	1	0	13.50

	BA	OBA	SA	AB	H	2B	3B	HR	RBI	BB	SO
Total	.222	.429	.222	9	2	0	0	0	2	4	1
vs. Left	.000	.500	.000	2	0	0	0	0	0	2	0
vs. Right	.286	.400	.286	7	2	0	0	0	2	2	1
Bases Empty	.000	.400	.000	3	0	0	0	0	0	2	0
Runners On Base	.333	.444	.333	6	2	0	0	0	2	2	1

1-YEAR TOTALS (1991)

G	IP	H	BB	SO	SB	CS	W	L	SV	ERA
1	2.0	1	1	0	0	0	0	0	0	4.50
1	0.2	1	3	1	0	0	0	1	0	13.50

BA	OBA	SA	AB	H	2B	3B	HR	RBI	BB	SO
.222	.429	.222	9	2	0	0	0	2	4	1
.000	.500	.000	2	0	0	0	0	0	2	0
.286	.400	.286	7	2	0	0	0	2	2	1
.000	.400	.000	3	0	0	0	0	0	2	0
.333	.444	.333	6	2	0	0	0	2	2	1

BOB WALK — bats right — throws right — age 36 — PIT — P

1991	G	IP	H	BB	SO	SB	CS	W	L	SV	ERA
at Home	12	62.0	56	18	39	6	2	4	2	0	3.48
on Road	13	53.0	48	17	28	1	2	5	0	0	3.74

	BA	OBA	SA	AB	H	2B	3B	HR	RBI	BB	SO
Total	.240	.302	.363	433	104	21	1	10	48	35	67
vs. Left	.256	.322	.384	242	62	14	1	5	23	21	29
vs. Right	.220	.276	.335	191	42	7	0	5	25	14	38
Bases Empty	.209	.285	.316	263	55	13	0	5	25	14	41
Runners On Base	.288	.328	.435	170	49	8	1	5	43	10	26

8-YEAR TOTALS (1984–1991)

G	IP	H	BB	SO	SB	CS	W	L	SV	ERA
104	482.2	457	152	257	44	19	29	21	2	3.43
106	498.1	478	186	253	40	25	30	20	1	3.70

BA	OBA	SA	AB	H	2B	3B	HR	RBI	BB	SO
.252	.316	.373	3714	935	170	25	77	391	338	510
.264	.331	.381	2014	531	94	17	36	188	200	234
.238	.298	.364	1700	404	76	8	41	203	138	276
.244	.307	.355	2211	539	98	16	39	39	188	291
.263	.329	.399	1503	396	72	9	38	352	150	219

MIKE WALKER — bats right — throws right — age 26 — CLE — P

1991

1991	G	IP	H	BB	SO	SB	CS	W	L	SV	ERA
at Home	1	1.0	0	0	0	0	0	0	0	0	0.00
on Road	4	3.1	6	2	2	0	0	1	0	0	2.70

	BA	OBA	SA	AB	H	2B	3B	HR	RBI	BB	SO
Total	.316	.409	.421	19	6	2	0	0	1	2	2
vs. Left	.500	.500	.750	4	2	1	0	0	0	0	0
vs. Right	.267	.389	.333	15	4	1	0	0	1	2	2
Bases Empty	.429	.500	.714	7	3	2	0	0	0	0	1
Runners On Base	.250	.357	.250	12	3	0	0	0	1	2	1

3-YEAR TOTALS (1988–1991)

	G	IP	H	BB	SO	SB	CS	W	L	SV	ERA
	11	35.0	40	19	14	3	1	1	3	0	5.40
	15	53.2	56	35	29	3	1	1	5	0	4.70

	BA	OBA	SA	AB	H	2B	3B	HR	RBI	BB	SO
	.277	.384	.396	346	96	19	2	6	44	54	43
	.261	.368	.385	161	42	9	1	3	18	26	23
	.292	.397	.405	185	54	10	1	3	26	28	20
	.291	.402	.453	172	50	11	1	5	5	30	24
	.264	.366	.339	174	46	8	1	1	39	24	19

BRUCE WALTON — bats right — throws right — age 30 — OAK — P

1991

1991	G	IP	H	BB	SO	SB	CS	W	L	SV	ERA
at Home	4	4.2	3	2	3	1	0	1	0	0	9.64
on Road	8	8.1	8	4	7	1	0	0	0	0	4.32

	BA	OBA	SA	AB	H	2B	3B	HR	RBI	BB	SO
Total	.229	.321	.458	48	11	2	0	3	9	6	10
vs. Left	.071	.188	.071	14	1	0	0	0	0	1	2
vs. Right	.294	.375	.618	34	10	2	0	3	9	5	8
Bases Empty	.200	.333	.360	25	5	1	0	1	1	4	5
Runners On Base	.261	.308	.565	23	6	1	0	2	8	2	5

1-YEAR TOTALS (1991)

	G	IP	H	BB	SO	SB	CS	W	L	SV	ERA
	4	4.2	3	2	3	1	0	1	0	0	9.64
	8	8.1	8	4	7	1	0	0	0	0	4.32

	BA	OBA	SA	AB	H	2B	3B	HR	RBI	BB	SO
	.229	.321	.458	48	11	2	0	3	9	6	10
	.071	.188	.071	14	1	0	0	0	0	1	2
	.294	.375	.618	34	10	2	0	3	9	5	8
	.200	.333	.360	25	5	1	0	1	1	4	5
	.261	.308	.565	23	6	1	0	2	8	2	5

STEVE WAPNICK — bats right — throws right — age 27 — CHA — P

1991

1991	G	IP	H	BB	SO	SB	CS	W	L	SV	ERA
at Home	4	3.2	1	3	1	0	0	0	0	0	0.00
on Road	2	1.1	1	0	0	0	0	0	1	0	6.75

	BA	OBA	SA	AB	H	2B	3B	HR	RBI	BB	SO
Total	.111	.273	.167	18	2	1	0	0	0	4	1
vs. Left	.250	.250	.375	8	2	1	0	0	0	0	0
vs. Right	.000	.286	.000	10	0	0	0	0	0	4	1
Bases Empty	.222	.222	.333	9	2	1	0	0	0	0	0
Runners On Base	.000	.308	.000	9	0	0	0	0	0	4	1

2-YEAR TOTALS (1990–1991)

	G	IP	H	BB	SO	SB	CS	W	L	SV	ERA
	5	5.1	3	5	4	0	1	0	0	0	0.00
	5	6.2	7	9	3	1	0	0	1	0	8.10

	BA	OBA	SA	AB	H	2B	3B	HR	RBI	BB	SO
	.222	.407	.289	45	10	3	0	0	4	14	7
	.368	.400	.474	19	7	2	0	0	2	1	1
	.115	.410	.154	26	3	1	0	0	2	13	6
	.467	.600	.600	15	7	2	0	0	0	5	0
	.100	.308	.133	30	3	1	0	0	4	9	7

GARY WAYNE — bats left — throws left — age 30 — MIN — P

1991

1991	G	IP	H	BB	SO	SB	CS	W	L	SV	ERA
at Home	4	3.2	5	3	0	0	0	1	0	0	14.73
on Road	4	8.2	6	1	7	0	0	0	0	1	1.04

	BA	OBA	SA	AB	H	2B	3B	HR	RBI	BB	SO
Total	.244	.314	.378	45	11	3	0	1	7	4	7
vs. Left	.308	.333	.462	13	4	2	0	0	3	0	4
vs. Right	.219	.306	.344	32	7	1	0	1	4	4	3
Bases Empty	.208	.296	.250	24	5	1	0	0	0	2	6
Runners On Base	.286	.333	.524	21	6	2	0	1	7	2	1

3-YEAR TOTALS (1989–1991)

	G	IP	H	BB	SO	SB	CS	W	L	SV	ERA
	57	61.1	50	32	40	2	2	4	0	2	3.82
	49	60.2	54	21	36	5	1	1	5	1	3.71

	BA	OBA	SA	AB	H	2B	3B	HR	RBI	BB	SO
	.230	.311	.362	453	104	28	1	10	68	53	76
	.194	.272	.324	139	27	6	0	4	26	14	28
	.245	.329	.379	314	77	22	1	6	42	39	48
	.230	.306	.343	230	53	15	1	3	3	24	39
	.229	.317	.381	223	51	13	0	7	65	29	37

DAVE WEATHERS — bats right — throws right — age 23 — TOR — P

1991

1991	G	IP	H	BB	SO	SB	CS	W	L	SV	ERA
at Home	8	6.1	8	10	4	0	0	0	0	0	5.68
on Road	7	8.1	7	7	9	4	1	1	0	0	4.32

	BA	OBA	SA	AB	H	2B	3B	HR	RBI	BB	SO
Total	.263	.442	.386	57	15	4	0	1	10	17	13
vs. Left	.294	.455	.588	17	5	2	0	1	1	5	4
vs. Right	.250	.436	.300	40	10	2	0	0	9	12	9
Bases Empty	.250	.444	.550	20	5	3	0	1	1	6	7
Runners On Base	.270	.440	.297	37	10	1	0	0	9	11	6

1-YEAR TOTALS (1991)

	G	IP	H	BB	SO	SB	CS	W	L	SV	ERA
	8	6.1	8	10	4	0	0	0	0	0	5.68
	7	8.1	7	7	9	4	1	1	0	0	4.32

	BA	OBA	SA	AB	H	2B	3B	HR	RBI	BB	SO
	.263	.442	.386	57	15	4	0	1	10	17	13
	.294	.455	.588	17	5	2	0	1	1	5	4
	.250	.436	.300	40	10	2	0	0	9	12	9
	.250	.444	.550	20	5	3	0	1	1	6	7
	.270	.440	.297	37	10	1	0	0	9	11	6

DAVID WEST — bats left — throws left — age 28 — MIN — P

1991

1991	G	IP	H	BB	SO	SB	CS	W	L	SV	ERA
at Home	7	25.1	25	12	23	1	0	1	3	0	7.46
on Road	8	46.0	41	16	29	2	1	3	1	0	2.93

	BA	OBA	SA	AB	H	2B	3B	HR	RBI	BB	SO
Total	.244	.314	.458	271	66	17	1	13	36	28	52
vs. Left	.343	.415	.600	35	12	1	1	2	4	5	8
vs. Right	.229	.298	.436	236	54	16	1	11	32	23	44
Bases Empty	.224	.289	.454	174	39	11	1	9	9	16	29
Runners On Base	.278	.354	.464	97	27	6	0	4	27	12	23

4-YEAR TOTALS (1988–1991)

	G	IP	H	BB	SO	SB	CS	W	L	SV	ERA
	32	129.0	131	68	103	4	3	6	10	0	6.84
	35	158.1	156	74	94	5	4	9	7	0	4.04

	BA	OBA	SA	AB	H	2B	3B	HR	RBI	BB	SO
	.261	.347	.453	1100	287	68	7	43	166	142	197
	.238	.333	.360	172	41	6	3	3	20	24	33
	.265	.349	.470	928	246	62	4	40	146	118	164
	.237	.324	.393	649	154	37	5	18	18	81	111
	.295	.379	.539	451	133	31	2	25	148	61	86

MICKEY WESTON — bats right — throws right — age 31 — TOR — P

1991

1991	G	IP	H	BB	SO	SB	CS	W	L	SV	ERA
at Home	1	1.0	0	0	1	0	0	0	0	0	0.00
on Road	1	1.0	1	1	1	0	0	0	0	0	0.00

	BA	OBA	SA	AB	H	2B	3B	HR	RBI	BB	SO
Total	.143	.250	.286	7	1	1	0	0	0	1	1
vs. Left	.000	1.000	.000	0	0	0	0	0	0	1	0
vs. Right	.143	.143	.286	7	1	1	0	0	0	0	1
Bases Empty	.167	.167	.333	6	1	1	0	0	0	0	1
Runners On Base	.000	.500	.000	1	0	0	0	0	0	1	0

3-YEAR TOTALS (1989–1991)

	G	IP	H	BB	SO	SB	CS	W	L	SV	ERA
	8	19.1	17	6	8	0	0	0	0	1	3.26
	10	16.2	30	3	9	0	0	1	1	0	10.26

	BA	OBA	SA	AB	H	2B	3B	HR	RBI	BB	SO
	.322	.365	.514	146	47	5	1	7	28	9	17
	.344	.408	.531	64	22	1	1	3	10	7	5
	.305	.329	.500	82	25	4	0	4	18	2	12
	.266	.318	.468	79	21	4	0	3	4	5	9
	.388	.423	.567	67	26	3	0	3	24	4	8

JOHN WETTELAND — bats right — throws right — age 26 — LA — P

1991	G	IP	H	BB	SO	SB	CS	W	L	SV	ERA
at Home	2	2.0	1	3	1	0	0	1	0	0	0.00
on Road	4	7.0	4	8	0	0	0	0	0	0	0.00

	BA	OBA	SA	AB	H	2B	3B	HR	RBI	BB	SO
Total	.161	.250	.194	31	5	1	0	0	3	3	9
vs. Left	.188	.263	.250	16	3	1	0	0	2	1	6
vs. Right	.133	.235	.133	15	2	0	0	0	1	2	3
Bases Empty	.154	.313	.231	13	2	1	0	0	0	2	6
Runners On Base	.167	.200	.167	18	3	0	0	0	3	1	3

3-YEAR TOTALS (1989–1991)

G	IP	H	BB	SO	SB	CS	W	L	SV	ERA
28	65.2	57	21	60	7	3	6	5	1	3.56
31	89.0	73	33	81	9	3	2	7	0	4.04

BA	OBA	SA	AB	H	2B	3B	HR	RBI	BB	SO
.228	.299	.344	569	130	22	1	14	78	54	141
.229	.304	.328	293	67	9	1	6	36	27	68
.228	.294	.362	276	63	13	0	8	42	27	73
.213	.291	.320	328	70	9	1	8	8	33	88
.249	.310	.378	241	60	13	0	6	70	21	53

ED WHITSON — bats right — throws right — age 37 — SD — P

1991	G	IP	H	BB	SO	SB	CS	W	L	SV	ERA
at Home	5	33.0	35	9	19	6	1	0	3	0	5.18
on Road	8	45.2	58	8	21	2	1	4	3	0	4.93

	BA	OBA	SA	AB	H	2B	3B	HR	RBI	BB	SO
Total	.299	.332	.479	311	93	11	3	13	43	17	40
vs. Left	.283	.326	.439	180	51	7	3	5	15	12	18
vs. Right	.321	.341	.534	131	42	4	0	8	28	5	22
Bases Empty	.289	.320	.407	194	56	5	3	4	4	9	28
Runners On Base	.316	.352	.598	117	37	6	0	9	39	8	12

8-YEAR TOTALS (1984–1991)

G	IP	H	BB	SO	SB	CS	W	L	SV	ERA
120	729.0	703	176	437	44	26	44	38	0	3.68
120	676.1	723	190	365	47	17	43	37	0	4.05

BA	OBA	SA	AB	H	2B	3B	HR	RBI	BB	SO
.265	.311	.404	5387	1426	235	33	149	587	366	802
.276	.326	.411	2966	820	138	20	74	305	220	378
.250	.292	.394	2421	606	97	13	75	282	146	424
.258	.307	.386	3255	841	128	17	85	85	218	478
.274	.316	.430	2132	585	107	16	64	502	148	324

DEAN WILKINS — bats right — throws right — age 26 — HOU — P

1991	G	IP	H	BB	SO	SB	CS	W	L	SV	ERA
at Home	6	7.2	14	8	4	1	2	2	1	1	9.39
on Road	1	0.1	2	2	0	0	0	0	0	0	54.00

	BA	OBA	SA	AB	H	2B	3B	HR	RBI	BB	SO
Total	.410	.531	.590	39	16	5	1	0	12	10	4
vs. Left	.440	.533	.600	25	11	2	1	0	6	5	2
vs. Right	.357	.526	.571	14	5	3	0	0	6	5	2
Bases Empty	.455	.571	.818	11	5	2	0	0	0	3	1
Runners On Base	.393	.514	.500	28	11	3	0	0	12	7	3

3-YEAR TOTALS (1989–1991)

G	IP	H	BB	SO	SB	CS	W	L	SV	ERA
21	29.0	35	19	19	1	3	3	1	1	6.52
4	2.0	5	7	2	0	0	0	0	1	22.50

BA	OBA	SA	AB	H	2B	3B	HR	RBI	BB	SO
.310	.429	.504	129	40	14	1	3	29	26	21
.314	.422	.457	70	22	8	1	0	10	13	13
.305	.438	.559	59	18	6	0	3	19	13	8
.315	.393	.630	54	17	9	1	2	2	6	7
.307	.453	.413	75	23	5	0	1	27	20	14

BRIAN WILLIAMS — bats right — throws right — age 23 — HOU — P

1991	G	IP	H	BB	SO	SB	CS	W	L	SV	ERA
at Home	1	5.0	5	1	2	0	0	0	0	0	3.60
on Road	1	7.0	6	3	2	1	2	0	1	0	3.86

	BA	OBA	SA	AB	H	2B	3B	HR	RBI	BB	SO
Total	.250	.327	.386	44	11	0	0	2	5	4	4
vs. Left	.222	.323	.333	27	6	0	0	1	3	4	2
vs. Right	.294	.333	.471	17	5	0	0	1	2	0	2
Bases Empty	.280	.400	.280	25	7	0	0	0	0	4	2
Runners On Base	.211	.211	.526	19	4	0	0	2	5	0	2

1-YEAR TOTALS (1991)

G	IP	H	BB	SO	SB	CS	W	L	SV	ERA
1	5.0	5	1	2	0	0	0	0	0	3.60
1	7.0	6	3	2	1	2	0	1	0	3.86

BA	OBA	SA	AB	H	2B	3B	HR	RBI	BB	SO
.250	.327	.386	44	11	0	0	2	5	4	4
.222	.323	.333	27	6	0	0	1	3	4	2
.294	.333	.471	17	5	0	0	1	2	0	2
.280	.400	.280	25	7	0	0	0	0	4	2
.211	.211	.526	19	4	0	0	2	5	0	2

MARK WILLIAMSON — bats right — throws right — age 33 — BAL — P

1991	G	IP	H	BB	SO	SB	CS	W	L	SV	ERA
at Home	35	44.0	34	16	30	3	0	3	4	1	2.66
on Road	30	36.1	53	19	23	7	3	2	1	3	6.69

	BA	OBA	SA	AB	H	2B	3B	HR	RBI	BB	SO
Total	.275	.343	.424	316	87	16	2	9	51	35	53
vs. Left	.252	.331	.353	119	30	4	1	2	16	15	21
vs. Right	.289	.350	.467	197	57	12	1	7	35	20	32
Bases Empty	.255	.316	.389	157	40	6	0	5	5	14	29
Runners On Base	.296	.368	.459	159	47	10	2	4	46	21	24

5-YEAR TOTALS (1987–1991)

G	IP	H	BB	SO	SB	CS	W	L	SV	ERA
144	275.0	234	81	158	16	9	22	15	9	2.95
133	240.2	270	93	152	19	10	14	14	10	4.71

BA	OBA	SA	AB	H	2B	3B	HR	RBI	BB	SO
.259	.319	.389	1948	504	93	10	47	291	174	310
.257	.315	.381	869	223	34	7	20	117	76	134
.260	.322	.396	1079	281	59	3	27	174	98	176
.235	.283	.354	1050	247	47	6	22	22	65	165
.286	.358	.430	898	257	46	4	25	269	109	145

CARL WILLIS — bats left — throws right — age 32 — MIN — P

1991	G	IP	H	BB	SO	SB	CS	W	L	SV	ERA
at Home	23	50.2	48	3	36	4	2	7	2	0	2.84
on Road	17	38.1	28	16	17	1	1	1	2	2	2.35

	BA	OBA	SA	AB	H	2B	3B	HR	RBI	BB	SO
Total	.232	.273	.311	328	76	12	1	4	29	19	53
vs. Left	.289	.333	.367	128	37	8	1	0	10	9	14
vs. Right	.195	.234	.275	200	39	4	0	4	19	10	39
Bases Empty	.245	.279	.314	188	46	7	0	2	2	8	34
Runners On Base	.214	.265	.307	140	30	5	1	2	27	11	19

5-YEAR TOTALS (1984–1991)

G	IP	H	BB	SO	SB	CS	W	L	SV	ERA
55	106.1	117	32	62	7	5	9	5	1	4.82
48	86.1	85	38	34	7	3	1	4	3	3.86

BA	OBA	SA	AB	H	2B	3B	HR	RBI	BB	SO
.275	.336	.412	735	202	41	6	16	104	70	96
.306	.369	.428	304	93	19	3	4	40	31	30
.253	.313	.401	431	109	22	3	12	64	39	66
.288	.341	.405	385	111	15	3	8	8	29	55
.260	.331	.420	350	91	26	3	8	96	41	41

FRANK WILLS — bats right — throws right — age 34 — TOR — P

1991	G	IP	H	BB	SO	SB	CS	W	L	SV	ERA
at Home	1	2.0	4	3	1	0	0	0	0	0	13.50
on Road	3	2.1	4	2	1	0	0	0	1	0	19.29

	BA	OBA	SA	AB	H	2B	3B	HR	RBI	BB	SO
Total	.421	.560	.789	19	8	1	0	2	8	5	2
vs. Left	.333	.600	.500	6	2	1	0	0	1	4	2
vs. Right	.462	.533	.923	13	6	0	0	2	7	1	0
Bases Empty	.429	.600	.857	7	3	0	0	1	1	2	1
Runners On Base	.417	.533	.750	12	5	1	0	1	7	3	1

8-YEAR TOTALS (1984–1991)

G	IP	H	BB	SO	SB	CS	W	L	SV	ERA
80	234.2	219	95	146	18	15	12	12	5	4.45
67	165.2	183	88	112	9	7	8	13	1	6.14

BA	OBA	SA	AB	H	2B	3B	HR	RBI	BB	SO
.264	.342	.418	1523	402	73	9	48	234	183	258
.271	.366	.421	717	194	39	6	19	99	109	95
.258	.319	.416	806	208	34	3	29	135	74	163
.257	.331	.407	809	208	33	5	26	26	85	160
.272	.353	.431	714	194	40	4	22	208	98	98

STEVE WILSON — bats left — throws left — age 28 — CHN/LA — P

1991	G	IP	H	BB	SO	SB	CS	W	L	SV	ERA
at Home	10	7.2	6	8	4	0	0	0	0	2	5.87
on Road	9	13.0	8	1	10	1	0	0	0	0	0.69

	BA	OBA	SA	AB	H	2B	3B	HR	RBI	BB	SO
Total	.197	.284	.282	71	14	3	0	1	11	9	14
vs. Left	.167	.300	.208	24	4	1	0	0	6	5	6
vs. Right	.213	.275	.319	47	10	2	0	1	5	4	8
Bases Empty	.189	.268	.216	37	7	1	0	0	0	4	8
Runners On Base	.206	.300	.353	34	7	2	0	1	11	5	6

4-YEAR TOTALS (1988–1991)

	G	IP	H	BB	SO	SB	CS	W	L	SV	ERA
	58	123.1	132	48	90	5	5	5	8	4	5.33
	62	129.2	112	40	85	8	8	5	5	1	3.68

	BA	OBA	SA	AB	H	2B	3B	HR	RBI	BB	SO
	.254	.316	.399	961	244	40	12	25	124	88	175
	.238	.306	.352	261	62	10	4	4	35	25	57
	.260	.320	.416	700	182	30	8	21	89	63	118
	.247	.306	.388	554	137	19	4	17	17	46	107
	.263	.329	.413	407	107	21	8	8	107	42	68

MIKE WITT — bats right — throws right — age 32 — NYA — P

1991	G	IP	H	BB	SO	SB	CS	W	L	SV	ERA
at Home	1	5.0	6	0	0	0	0	0	0	0	5.40
on Road	1	0.1	2	1	0	1	0	0	1	0	81.00

	BA	OBA	SA	AB	H	2B	3B	HR	RBI	BB	SO
Total	.320	.346	.520	25	8	2	0	1	6	1	0
vs. Left	.385	.385	.538	13	5	2	0	0	1	0	0
vs. Right	.250	.308	.500	12	3	0	0	1	5	1	0
Bases Empty	.250	.250	.313	16	4	1	0	0	0	0	0
Runners On Base	.444	.500	.889	9	4	1	0	1	6	1	0

8-YEAR TOTALS (1984–1991)

	G	IP	H	BB	SO	SB	CS	W	L	SV	ERA
	113	819.1	736	243	553	32	28	49	42	1	3.36
	120	782.1	809	279	552	42	32	43	42	0	4.15

	BA	OBA	SA	AB	H	2B	3B	HR	RBI	BB	SO
	.253	.313	.379	6095	1545	268	35	142	656	522	1105
	.259	.319	.382	3342	866	145	18	77	340	290	532
	.247	.306	.375	2753	679	123	17	65	316	232	573
	.246	.302	.365	3665	900	162	19	79	79	283	691
	.265	.328	.400	2430	645	106	16	63	577	239	414

BOBBY WITT — bats right — throws right — age 28 — TEX — P

1991	G	IP	H	BB	SO	SB	CS	W	L	SV	ERA
at Home	8	40.0	42	30	40	8	4	0	5	0	6.30
on Road	9	48.2	42	44	42	10	1	3	2	0	5.92

	BA	OBA	SA	AB	H	2B	3B	HR	RBI	BB	SO
Total	.254	.388	.356	331	84	18	2	4	54	74	82
vs. Left	.233	.376	.333	150	35	5	2	2	21	35	40
vs. Right	.271	.397	.376	181	49	13	0	2	33	39	42
Bases Empty	.250	.400	.341	164	41	7	1	2	2	40	41
Runners On Base	.257	.376	.371	167	43	11	1	2	52	34	41

6-YEAR TOTALS (1986–1991)

	G	IP	H	BB	SO	SB	CS	W	L	SV	ERA
	75	466.2	404	309	437	94	18	26	26	0	4.15
	85	513.2	437	373	514	95	11	33	33	0	5.06

	BA	OBA	SA	AB	H	2B	3B	HR	RBI	BB	SO
	.233	.353	.340	3617	841	144	16	71	454	682	951
	.236	.363	.343	1854	438	74	11	34	234	372	451
	.229	.343	.337	1763	403	70	5	37	220	310	500
	.218	.349	.324	1942	424	69	5	42	42	381	521
	.249	.358	.359	1675	417	75	11	29	412	301	430

MARK WOHLERS — bats right — throws right — age 22 — ATL — P

1991	G	IP	H	BB	SO	SB	CS	W	L	SV	ERA
at Home	7	11.0	5	4	7	3	0	1	0	1	1.64
on Road	10	8.2	12	9	6	2	0	2	1	1	5.19

	BA	OBA	SA	AB	H	2B	3B	HR	RBI	BB	SO
Total	.239	.368	.380	71	17	5	1	1	11	13	13
vs. Left	.321	.457	.536	28	9	1	1	1	4	7	5
vs. Right	.186	.308	.279	43	8	4	0	0	7	6	8
Bases Empty	.214	.389	.393	28	6	0	1	1	1	7	3
Runners On Base	.256	.353	.372	43	11	5	0	0	10	6	10

1-YEAR TOTALS (1991)

	G	IP	H	BB	SO	SB	CS	W	L	SV	ERA
	7	11.0	5	4	7	3	0	1	0	1	1.64
	10	8.2	12	9	6	2	0	2	1	1	5.19

	BA	OBA	SA	AB	H	2B	3B	HR	RBI	BB	SO
	.239	.368	.380	71	17	5	1	1	11	13	13
	.321	.457	.536	28	9	1	1	1	4	7	5
	.186	.308	.279	43	8	4	0	0	7	6	8
	.214	.389	.393	28	6	0	1	1	1	7	3
	.256	.353	.372	43	11	5	0	0	10	6	10

MIKE YORK — bats right — throws right — age 28 — CLE — P

1991	G	IP	H	BB	SO	SB	CS	W	L	SV	ERA
at Home	6	18.0	24	13	8	3	2	1	1	0	7.00
on Road	8	16.2	21	6	11	1	0	0	3	0	6.48

	BA	OBA	SA	AB	H	2B	3B	HR	RBI	BB	SO
Total	.333	.412	.489	135	45	7	4	2	25	19	19
vs. Left	.304	.393	.391	69	21	4	1	0	12	11	7
vs. Right	.364	.434	.591	66	24	3	3	2	13	8	12
Bases Empty	.390	.471	.644	59	23	3	3	2	2	8	9
Runners On Base	.289	.370	.368	76	22	4	1	0	23	11	10

2-YEAR TOTALS (1990–1991)

	G	IP	H	BB	SO	SB	CS	W	L	SV	ERA
	8	21.2	28	15	10	3	2	1	2	0	6.65
	10	25.2	30	9	13	1	0	1	3	0	4.91

	BA	OBA	SA	AB	H	2B	3B	HR	RBI	BB	SO
	.319	.397	.434	182	58	7	4	2	30	24	23
	.313	.386	.375	96	30	4	1	0	15	13	7
	.326	.410	.500	86	28	3	3	2	15	11	16
	.375	.457	.563	80	30	3	3	2	2	11	10
	.275	.352	.333	102	28	4	1	0	28	13	13

ANTHONY YOUNG — bats right — throws right — age 26 — NYN — P

1991	G	IP	H	BB	SO	SB	CS	W	L	SV	ERA
at Home	6	28.2	34	5	15	2	0	1	3	0	3.77
on Road	4	20.2	14	7	5	1	1	1	2	0	2.18

	BA	OBA	SA	AB	H	2B	3B	HR	RBI	BB	SO
Total	.257	.303	.374	187	48	8	1	4	19	12	20
vs. Left	.287	.322	.444	108	31	6	1	3	10	6	10
vs. Right	.215	.279	.278	79	17	2	0	1	9	6	10
Bases Empty	.241	.290	.336	116	28	3	1	2	2	7	15
Runners On Base	.282	.325	.437	71	20	5	0	2	17	5	5

1-YEAR TOTALS (1991)

	G	IP	H	BB	SO	SB	CS	W	L	SV	ERA
	6	28.2	34	5	15	2	0	1	3	0	3.77
	4	20.2	14	7	5	1	1	1	2	0	2.18

	BA	OBA	SA	AB	H	2B	3B	HR	RBI	BB	SO
	.257	.303	.374	187	48	8	1	4	19	12	20
	.287	.322	.444	108	31	6	1	3	10	6	10
	.215	.279	.278	79	17	2	0	1	9	6	10
	.241	.290	.336	116	28	3	1	2	2	7	15
	.282	.325	.437	71	20	5	0	2	17	5	5

CLIFF YOUNG — bats left — throws left — age 28 — CAL — P

1991	G	IP	H	BB	SO	SB	CS	W	L	SV	ERA
at Home	4	6.1	7	3	4	1	0	1	0	0	7.11
on Road	7	6.1	5	0	2	1	0	0	0	0	1.42

	BA	OBA	SA	AB	H	2B	3B	HR	RBI	BB	SO
Total	.261	.306	.478	46	12	1	0	3	7	3	6
vs. Left	.250	.333	.625	8	2	0	0	1	2	1	1
vs. Right	.263	.300	.447	38	10	1	0	2	5	2	5
Bases Empty	.318	.375	.364	22	7	0	1	0	2	0	3
Runners On Base	.208	.240	.583	24	5	0	0	3	7	1	3

2-YEAR TOTALS (1990–1991)

	G	IP	H	BB	SO	SB	CS	W	L	SV	ERA
	13	21.1	36	6	13	1	1	1	0	0	6.33
	15	22.0	16	4	12	0	2	1	1	0	1.23

	BA	OBA	SA	AB	H	2B	3B	HR	RBI	BB	SO
	.308	.342	.456	169	52	8	1	5	29	10	25
	.366	.400	.488	41	15	2	0	1	10	3	8
	.289	.324	.445	128	37	6	1	4	19	7	17
	.343	.403	.514	70	24	4	0	3	2	6	12
	.283	.299	.414	99	28	4	0	3	27	4	13

CURT YOUNG — bats right — throws left — age 32 — OAK — P

8-YEAR TOTALS (1984–1991)

1991	G	IP	H	BB	SO	SB	CS	W	L	SV	ERA
at Home	19	29.2	32	15	13	3	0	1	1	0	4.55
on Road	22	38.2	42	19	14	1	3	3	1	0	5.35

	BA	OBA	SA	AB	H	2B	3B	HR	RBI	BB	SO
Total	.278	.363	.425	266	74	11	2	8	28	34	27
vs. Left	.229	.298	.321	109	25	2	1	2	10	9	19
vs. Right	.312	.407	.497	157	49	9	1	6	18	25	8
Bases Empty	.321	.379	.536	140	45	8	2	6	6	13	12
Runners On Base	.230	.347	.302	126	29	3	0	2	22	21	15

G	IP	H	BB	SO	SB	CS	W	L	SV	ERA
108	527.1	493	176	274	39	31	28	22	0	3.75
109	488.1	529	162	233	29	22	36	27	0	4.74

BA	OBA	SA	AB	H	2B	3B	HR	RBI	BB	SO
.262	.323	.424	3903	1022	184	15	139	457	338	507
.232	.284	.323	809	188	26	1	15	81	44	107
.270	.334	.450	3094	834	158	14	124	376	294	400
.256	.315	.422	2367	606	114	10	86	86	189	324
.271	.336	.426	1536	416	70	5	53	371	149	183

MATT YOUNG — bats left — throws left — age 34 — BOS — P

7-YEAR TOTALS (1984–1991)

1991	G	IP	H	BB	SO	SB	CS	W	L	SV	ERA
at Home	9	45.2	42	30	33	5	2	2	3	0	4.53
on Road	10	43.0	50	23	36	3	1	1	4	0	5.86

	BA	OBA	SA	AB	H	2B	3B	HR	RBI	BB	SO
Total	.266	.365	.335	346	92	12	0	4	37	53	69
vs. Left	.255	.356	.353	51	13	2	0	1	4	7	8
vs. Right	.268	.366	.332	295	79	10	0	3	33	46	61
Bases Empty	.266	.352	.330	188	50	6	0	2	2	25	41
Runners On Base	.266	.379	.342	158	42	6	0	2	35	28	28

G	IP	H	BB	SO	SB	CS	W	L	SV	ERA
131	488.0	462	214	363	38	22	30	32	14	3.73
119	352.2	423	174	242	24	19	13	38	11	5.84

BA	OBA	SA	AB	H	2B	3B	HR	RBI	BB	SO
.272	.351	.384	3258	885	129	18	67	420	388	605
.230	.309	.293	622	143	17	2	6	66	63	147
.281	.361	.406	2636	742	112	16	61	354	325	458
.264	.341	.382	1729	456	70	10	38	38	196	318
.281	.362	.387	1529	429	59	8	29	382	192	287

Part 3

Team and League Statistics

This part contains batting and pitching situational totals for the 1991 season for both leagues and for all 26 teams. The reports are presented in exactly the same fashion as for regular batters and pitchers.

Also included are the 1991 official batting, pitching, and fielding statistics totals for both leagues and all 26 teams.

Following the team batting and pitching totals are three other interesting team breakdowns.

The first report separates team pitching totals by Starting Pitching and Relief Pitching, allowing you to see how effective or ineffective each team's rotation and bullpen were.

The second report lists each team's batting statistics by Lineup Order, allowing you to see which slots in the batting order were carrying their weight and which were not.

The third report lists each team's batting statistics by Defensive Position, allowing you to see which positions were producing offensively and which were not.

TEAM AND LEAGUE SITUATIONAL STATISTICS

AMERICAN LEAGUE BATTING

	BA	OBA	SA	AB	H	2B	3B	HR	RBI	BB	SO
Totals	.260	.329	.395	77603	20195	3680	453	1953	9610	7730	12944
vs. Left	.265	.335	.405	22460	5956	1070	121	612	2782	2304	3574
vs. Right	.258	.327	.391	55143	14239	2610	332	1341	6828	5426	9370
at Home	.263	.336	.402	37862	9962	1848	252	965	4796	4021	6138
on Road	.257	.322	.388	39741	10233	1832	201	988	4814	3709	6806
on Grass	.259	.329	.394	55263	14334	2556	277	1444	6915	5603	9218
on Turf	.262	.329	.397	22340	5861	1124	176	509	2695	2127	3726
Day Games	.260	.331	.395	22821	5938	1122	123	570	2917	2380	3863
Night Games	.260	.328	.395	54782	14257	2558	330	1383	6693	5350	9081
April	.253	.327	.380	8792	2223	398	52	204	1036	932	1467
May	.261	.333	.394	13079	3415	591	80	329	1631	1399	2130
June	.258	.326	.391	13230	3410	604	66	343	1639	1292	2150
July	.267	.330	.412	12877	3436	629	76	362	1646	1178	2091
August	.264	.329	.407	14076	3720	710	94	371	1770	1332	2370
Sept–Oct	.257	.327	.382	15549	3991	748	85	344	1888	1597	2736
Bases Empty	.254	.320	.385	43914	11167	2065	243	1068	1068	3953	7448
Leadoff	.255	.319	.392	18668	4754	898	101	488	488	1644	2979
Runners On Base	.268	.340	.407	33689	9028	1615	210	885	8542	3777	5496
Scoring Position	.266	.351	.402	19169	5093	913	138	477	7372	2721	3368
Late and Close	.244	.320	.362	12875	3143	509	65	295	1532	1392	2418

Baltimore Batting

	BA	OBA	SA	AB	H	2B	3B	HR	RBI	BB	SO
Totals	.254	.319	.401	5604	1421	256	29	170	660	528	974
vs. Left	.256	.331	.406	1487	381	62	10	47	157	167	254
vs. Right	.253	.315	.399	4117	1040	194	19	123	503	361	720
at Home	.244	.311	.387	2701	659	121	12	80	318	258	463
on Road	.262	.327	.414	2903	762	135	17	90	342	270	511
on Grass	.250	.316	.398	4704	1178	207	24	147	549	440	817
on Turf	.270	.337	.412	900	243	49	5	23	111	88	157
Day Games	.238	.311	.362	1410	336	58	6	35	152	141	267
Night Games	.259	.322	.413	4194	1085	198	23	135	508	387	707
April	.231	.315	.365	589	136	21	2	18	66	67	128
May	.252	.327	.388	917	231	39	1	28	100	104	164
June	.267	.337	.416	1001	267	50	6	29	129	100	154
July	.253	.314	.394	942	238	43	3	28	105	84	152
August	.257	.311	.404	1007	259	57	8	25	127	80	171
Sept–Oct	.253	.311	.418	1148	290	46	9	42	133	93	205
Bases Empty	.256	.319	.406	3226	826	147	16	102	102	283	558
Leadoff	.243	.308	.392	1348	328	59	5	44	44	119	225
Runners On Base	.250	.319	.393	2378	595	109	13	68	558	245	416
Scoring Position	.252	.337	.389	1262	318	61	8	32	461	173	248
Late and Close	.237	.305	.363	970	230	29	3	29	109	94	171

Boston Batting

	BA	OBA	SA	AB	H	2B	3B	HR	RBI	BB	SO
Totals	.269	.340	.401	5530	1486	305	25	126	691	593	820
vs. Left	.288	.354	.433	1481	426	81	9	39	212	158	197
vs. Right	.262	.335	.389	4049	1060	224	16	87	479	435	623
at Home	.277	.352	.428	2749	762	183	12	69	359	316	389
on Road	.260	.328	.375	2781	724	122	13	57	332	277	431
on Grass	.267	.340	.399	4646	1242	261	18	105	580	512	686
on Turf	.276	.339	.413	884	244	44	7	21	111	81	134
Day Games	.271	.347	.400	1921	521	107	6	43	266	219	296
Night Games	.267	.337	.402	3609	965	198	19	83	425	374	524
April	.239	.315	.371	607	145	28	2	16	58	62	93
May	.282	.357	.411	968	273	52	5	21	132	114	123
June	.250	.322	.379	879	220	49	2	20	107	94	144
July	.262	.330	.408	961	252	49	5	27	113	99	139
August	.282	.346	.410	996	281	57	8	18	123	97	138
Sept–Oct	.282	.357	.414	1119	315	70	3	24	158	127	183
Bases Empty	.266	.335	.397	3001	799	155	14	70	70	287	445
Leadoff	.275	.337	.410	1316	362	81	6	28	28	117	177
Runners On Base	.272	.346	.406	2529	687	150	11	56	621	306	375
Scoring Position	.264	.357	.400	1436	379	80	7	34	553	232	221
Late and Close	.225	.303	.307	805	181	33	3	9	76	87	165

California Batting

	BA	OBA	SA	AB	H	2B	3B	HR	RBI	BB	SO
Totals	.255	.314	.374	5470	1396	245	29	115	607	448	928
vs. Left	.254	.309	.375	1561	397	77	8	32	182	120	254
vs. Right	.256	.316	.373	3909	999	168	21	83	425	328	674
at Home	.243	.307	.355	2650	645	94	13	59	266	235	438
on Road	.266	.321	.391	2820	751	151	16	56	341	213	490
on Grass	.251	.310	.362	4514	1131	188	23	90	475	371	749
on Turf	.277	.333	.428	956	265	57	6	25	132	77	179
Day Games	.268	.325	.403	1375	368	77	8	31	172	110	236
Night Games	.251	.311	.364	4095	1028	168	21	84	435	338	692
April	.270	.336	.380	679	183	27	6	12	78	62	112
May	.259	.316	.395	919	238	43	8	22	118	71	152
June	.270	.323	.389	941	254	43	6	19	117	68	152
July	.254	.308	.361	871	221	35	2	18	97	68	148
August	.232	.293	.381	960	223	41	3	32	93	79	173
Sept–Oct	.252	.315	.343	1100	277	56	4	12	104	100	191
Bases Empty	.243	.302	.370	3124	760	140	18	73	73	244	555
Leadoff	.241	.310	.355	1314	317	54	7	27	27	118	207
Runners On Base	.271	.330	.379	2346	636	105	11	42	534	204	373
Scoring Position	.276	.345	.390	1356	374	66	7	25	482	150	209
Late and Close	.231	.297	.316	746	172	23	1	13	57	67	138

Chicago Batting

	BA	OBA	SA	AB	H	2B	3B	HR	RBI	BB	SO
Totals	.262	.336	.391	5594	1464	226	39	139	722	610	896
vs. Left	.258	.330	.379	1782	459	63	6	47	194	186	305
vs. Right	.264	.339	.396	3812	1005	163	33	92	528	424	591
at Home	.271	.346	.407	2713	735	108	20	74	361	305	426
on Road	.253	.326	.375	2881	729	118	19	65	361	305	470
on Grass	.267	.342	.396	4765	1271	195	33	119	622	526	756
on Turf	.233	.303	.357	829	193	31	6	20	100	84	140
Day Games	.265	.339	.390	1563	414	53	10	41	199	175	260
Night Games	.260	.335	.391	4031	1050	173	29	98	523	435	636
April	.271	.337	.389	601	163	26	3	13	75	57	83
May	.251	.319	.334	963	242	26	3	16	95	95	177
June	.258	.324	.378	996	257	38	9	21	121	94	151
July	.262	.345	.425	944	247	43	6	33	143	113	133
August	.275	.344	.427	1016	279	46	8	31	150	107	153
Sept–Oct	.257	.346	.389	1074	276	47	10	25	138	144	199
Bases Empty	.256	.323	.371	3207	821	129	18	68	68	298	526
Leadoff	.242	.306	.357	1353	327	61	7	27	27	114	227
Runners On Base	.269	.352	.417	2387	643	97	21	71	654	312	370
Scoring Position	.272	.368	.410	1404	382	64	12	35	557	223	236
Late and Close	.264	.340	.390	1109	293	45	7	27	144	124	172

Cleveland Batting

	BA	OBA	SA	AB	H	2B	3B	HR	RBI	BB	SO
Totals	.254	.313	.350	5470	1390	236	26	79	546	449	888
vs. Left	.262	.321	.362	1504	394	66	9	22	160	127	233
vs. Right	.251	.310	.346	3966	996	170	17	57	386	322	655
at Home	.262	.321	.343	2693	705	122	15	22	253	221	393
on Road	.247	.306	.357	2777	685	114	11	57	293	228	495
on Grass	.259	.319	.359	4670	1209	201	25	72	490	395	729
on Turf	.226	.278	.299	800	181	35	1	7	56	54	159
Day Games	.247	.314	.354	1736	429	74	9	31	182	165	289
Night Games	.257	.313	.348	3734	961	162	17	48	364	284	599
April	.235	.300	.328	583	137	21	3	9	44	48	99
May	.271	.335	.384	912	247	40	6	17	118	83	146
June	.230	.294	.295	933	215	32	2	8	65	82	125
July	.259	.315	.367	911	236	36	4	18	91	71	150
August	.260	.316	.368	1028	267	49	6	18	114	78	185
Sept–Oct	.261	.315	.351	1103	288	58	7	9	114	87	183
Bases Empty	.249	.312	.344	3127	780	130	13	47	47	259	529
Leadoff	.254	.326	.357	1323	336	57	8	21	21	130	209
Runners On Base	.260	.315	.358	2343	610	106	13	32	499	190	359
Scoring Position	.255	.322	.347	1277	325	54	8	16	443	134	224
Late and Close	.218	.279	.286	1043	227	28	5	11	91	84	209

Detroit Batting

	BA	OBA	SA	AB	H	2B	3B	HR	RBI	BB	SO
Totals	.247	.333	.416	5547	1372	259	26	209	778	699	1185
vs. Left	.255	.337	.434	1529	390	79	7	60	206	182	307
vs. Right	.244	.331	.410	4018	982	180	19	149	572	517	878
at Home	.251	.349	.425	2680	673	110	14	109	416	399	554
on Road	.244	.316	.409	2867	699	149	12	100	362	300	631
on Grass	.249	.337	.417	4683	1168	218	22	174	666	615	995
on Turf	.236	.306	.414	864	204	41	4	35	112	84	190
Day Games	.251	.336	.423	1764	443	89	10	65	255	223	374
Night Games	.246	.331	.413	3783	929	170	16	144	523	476	811
April	.229	.318	.396	637	146	32	4	22	90	80	132
May	.246	.344	.407	920	226	41	4	33	142	139	186
June	.234	.318	.400	926	217	27	6	38	119	111	194
July	.270	.333	.472	915	247	56	3	41	131	85	199
August	.235	.339	.415	1033	243	52	4	42	153	160	263
Sept—Oct	.263	.337	.406	1116	293	51	5	33	143	124	211
Bases Empty	.241	.322	.397	3154	760	147	14	106	106	364	679
Leadoff	.227	.309	.371	1301	295	52	8	40	40	151	268
Runners On Base	.256	.345	.442	2393	612	112	12	103	672	335	506
Scoring Position	.257	.353	.423	1344	345	65	7	48	538	217	305
Late and Close	.218	.308	.355	911	199	38	1	28	114	115	221

Minnesota Batting

	BA	OBA	SA	AB	H	2B	3B	HR	RBI	BB	SO
Totals	.280	.344	.420	5556	1557	270	42	140	733	526	747
vs. Left	.291	.360	.465	1511	440	82	21	46	214	164	191
vs. Right	.276	.338	.403	4045	1117	188	21	94	519	362	556
at Home	.302	.366	.440	2764	834	139	29	62	383	276	354
on Road	.259	.322	.399	2792	723	131	13	78	350	250	393
on Grass	.265	.329	.423	2159	572	106	8	67	289	198	293
on Turf	.290	.354	.423	3397	985	164	34	73	444	328	454
Day Games	.278	.347	.426	1677	467	86	13	45	220	170	210
Night Games	.281	.343	.417	3879	1090	184	29	95	513	356	537
April	.262	.336	.395	656	172	25	7	16	77	71	93
May	.277	.340	.409	965	267	51	7	21	108	92	115
June	.279	.340	.432	962	268	45	5	31	137	83	120
July	.300	.363	.446	914	274	45	10	23	131	93	117
August	.289	.347	.431	1006	291	54	10	23	134	84	139
Sept—Oct	.271	.337	.398	1053	285	50	3	26	146	103	163
Bases Empty	.280	.341	.413	3066	858	155	24	68	68	260	400
Leadoff	.270	.331	.393	1316	355	56	8	30	30	110	156
Runners On Base	.281	.348	.428	2490	699	115	18	72	665	266	347
Scoring Position	.263	.344	.400	1431	376	66	10	30	556	192	230
Late and Close	.283	.355	.421	769	218	34	3	22	118	81	122

Kansas City Batting

	BA	OBA	SA	AB	H	2B	3B	HR	RBI	BB	SO
Totals	.264	.328	.394	5584	1475	290	41	117	689	523	969
vs. Left	.264	.330	.388	1820	481	95	11	36	211	171	297
vs. Right	.264	.328	.396	3764	994	195	30	81	478	352	672
at Home	.265	.333	.388	2767	732	143	29	47	328	273	437
on Road	.264	.324	.399	2817	743	147	12	70	361	250	532
on Grass	.266	.322	.408	2154	572	115	7	59	284	182	412
on Turf	.263	.332	.385	3430	903	175	34	58	405	341	557
Day Games	.258	.321	.382	1708	441	87	11	34	200	158	309
Night Games	.267	.332	.399	3876	1034	203	30	83	489	365	660
April	.250	.299	.361	637	159	34	5	9	68	45	126
May	.247	.313	.367	897	222	37	5	20	98	82	148
June	.272	.333	.426	982	267	51	5	30	145	93	157
July	.303	.368	.452	945	286	55	7	24	148	93	143
August	.263	.328	.394	972	256	56	13	15	101	91	174
Sept—Oct	.248	.321	.357	1151	285	57	6	19	129	119	221
Bases Empty	.258	.317	.389	3173	819	176	22	65	65	253	575
Leadoff	.270	.322	.436	1364	368	88	14	37	37	95	252
Runners On Base	.272	.343	.400	2411	656	114	19	52	624	270	394
Scoring Position	.290	.376	.423	1405	408	73	12	30	554	210	257
Late and Close	.236	.319	.349	938	221	37	12	15	91	114	1747

New York Batting

	BA	OBA	SA	AB	H	2B	3B	HR	RBI	BB	SO
Totals	.256	.316	.387	5541	1418	249	19	147	630	473	861
vs. Left	.271	.336	.410	2002	542	89	3	61	257	189	289
vs. Right	.248	.305	.375	3539	876	160	16	86	373	284	572
at Home	.258	.320	.385	2685	692	129	7	82	333	242	394
on Road	.254	.313	.373	2856	726	120	12	65	297	231	467
on Grass	.255	.317	.387	4687	1193	211	13	128	548	414	715
on Turf	.263	.314	.389	854	225	38	6	19	82	59	146
Day Games	.260	.334	.390	1646	428	76	9	40	210	182	239
Night Games	.254	.308	.386	3895	990	173	10	107	420	291	622
April	.254	.342	.369	574	146	21	3	13	75	79	96
May	.239	.304	.405	927	222	46	1	35	102	80	169
June	.273	.314	.410	967	264	38	2	30	119	55	145
July	.255	.320	.400	868	221	44	2	26	101	79	138
August	.263	.323	.376	1044	275	44	7	20	126	88	154
Sept—Oct	.250	.305	.364	1161	290	56	4	23	107	92	159
Bases Empty	.254	.310	.386	3216	818	134	14	87	87	243	500
Leadoff	.264	.313	.392	1363	360	57	3	37	37	94	191
Runners On Base	.258	.325	.389	2325	600	115	5	60	543	230	361
Scoring Position	.257	.334	.389	1296	333	66	3	33	470	160	210
Late and Close	.244	.318	.381	881	215	35	1	28	112	89	162

Milwaukee Batting

	BA	OBA	SA	AB	H	2B	3B	HR	RBI	BB	SO
Totals	.271	.336	.396	5611	1523	247	53	116	750	556	802
vs. Left	.260	.337	.364	1614	420	59	11	29	196	189	240
vs. Right	.276	.336	.409	3997	1103	188	42	87	554	367	562
at Home	.270	.343	.410	2698	729	136	27	62	376	299	394
on Road	.273	.330	.384	2913	794	111	26	54	374	257	408
on Grass	.276	.343	.404	4729	1303	208	46	102	654	496	660
on Turf	.249	.296	.357	882	220	39	7	14	96	60	142
Day Games	.280	.350	.415	1725	483	82	14	41	248	191	242
Night Games	.268	.330	.388	3886	1040	165	39	75	502	365	560
April	.252	.316	.402	650	164	36	2	19	86	60	93
May	.267	.330	.401	971	259	44	10	22	116	94	141
June	.253	.326	.373	897	227	34	7	20	129	94	159
July	.261	.320	.377	907	237	40	10	15	109	80	134
August	.305	.364	.431	1045	319	51	10	20	152	104	125
Sept—Oct	.278	.347	.392	1141	317	42	14	20	158	124	150
Bases Empty	.257	.318	.379	3123	802	140	25	64	64	269	442
Leadoff	.262	.315	.402	1363	357	57	10	38	38	98	170
Runners On Base	.290	.357	.418	2488	721	107	28	52	686	287	360
Scoring Position	.284	.362	.438	1446	410	64	23	38	636	209	228
Late and Close	.270	.343	.391	959	259	37	8	21	139	103	151

Oakland Batting

	BA	OBA	SA	AB	H	2B	3B	HR	RBI	BB	SO
Totals	.248	.331	.389	5410	1342	246	19	159	716	642	981
vs. Left	.261	.338	.410	1336	349	71	1	42	167	154	218
vs. Right	.244	.328	.382	4074	993	175	18	117	549	488	763
at Home	.241	.328	.379	2627	633	121	7	76	342	336	473
on Road	.255	.333	.398	2783	709	125	12	83	374	306	508
on Grass	.249	.330	.390	4531	1126	211	15	133	599	538	810
on Turf	.246	.332	.383	879	216	35	4	26	117	104	171
Day Games	.255	.335	.405	1842	470	87	6	59	265	213	341
Night Games	.244	.328	.380	3568	872	159	13	100	451	429	640
April	.254	.349	.382	646	164	34	5	13	84	89	125
May	.263	.358	.408	923	243	42	4	28	142	137	150
June	.255	.344	.422	906	231	42	2	35	114	119	158
July	.246	.323	.378	952	234	47	2	25	139	100	161
August	.236	.303	.388	950	224	40	3	33	105	86	167
Sept—Oct	.238	.314	.356	1033	246	41	3	25	132	111	220
Bases Empty	.239	.321	.372	3047	728	142	6	84	84	338	545
Leadoff	.241	.322	.387	1292	311	59	2	42	42	145	216
Runners On Base	.260	.343	.410	2363	614	104	13	75	632	304	436
Scoring Position	.261	.357	.420	1352	353	52	11	47	556	217	260
Late and Close	.241	.329	.384	843	203	33	5	26	122	107	176

Seattle Batting

	BA	OBA	SA	AB	H	2B	3B	HR	RBI	BB	SO
Totals	.255	.328	.383	5494	1400	268	29	126	665	588	811
vs. Left	.262	.334	.389	1651	432	80	4	41	211	175	233
vs. Right	.252	.325	.380	3843	968	188	25	85	454	413	578
at Home	.259	.337	.400	2706	701	137	19	69	353	314	411
on Road	.251	.319	.366	2788	699	131	10	57	312	274	400
on Grass	.256	.323	.372	2127	544	93	7	47	248	211	308
on Turf	.254	.331	.390	3367	856	175	22	79	417	377	503
Day Games	.256	.317	.377	1506	385	72	6	33	174	139	251
Night Games	.255	.332	.385	3988	1015	196	23	93	491	449	560
April	.257	.340	.374	708	182	28	2	17	81	85	96
May	.245	.318	.365	913	224	34	6	21	107	99	133
June	.237	.316	.339	894	212	45	2	14	100	98	131
July	.275	.326	.431	924	254	48	9	26	122	69	124
August	.257	.333	.402	927	238	54	3	25	107	108	139
Sept–Oct	.257	.333	.383	1128	290	59	7	23	148	129	188
Bases Empty	.247	.318	.365	3126	773	145	17	63	63	306	486
Leadoff	.246	.312	.367	1337	329	60	9	28	28	120	194
Runners On Base	.265	.339	.407	2368	627	123	12	63	602	282	325
Scoring Position	.265	.351	.388	1339	355	62	9	28	505	199	200
Late and Close	.246	.320	.378	928	228	51	6	20	117	100	154

Texas Batting

	BA	OBA	SA	AB	H	2B	3B	HR	RBI	BB	SO
Totals	.270	.341	.424	5703	1539	288	31	177	774	596	1039
vs. Left	.275	.353	.464	1516	417	76	11	63	219	180	268
vs. Right	.268	.337	.410	4187	1122	212	20	114	555	416	771
at Home	.270	.344	.424	2734	738	143	21	79	368	292	508
on Road	.270	.339	.424	2969	801	145	10	98	406	304	531
on Grass	.273	.346	.431	4757	1299	239	27	153	663	512	869
on Turf	.254	.316	.390	946	240	49	4	24	111	84	170
Day Games	.266	.342	.416	1131	301	64	5	32	156	124	187
Night Games	.271	.341	.426	4572	1238	224	26	145	618	472	852
April	.254	.323	.382	532	135	25	2	13	63	51	81
May	.306	.379	.463	992	304	54	7	29	152	117	148
June	.256	.336	.390	987	253	47	5	25	130	118	183
July	.268	.332	.443	920	247	44	6	35	122	80	178
August	.285	.344	.453	1115	318	56	7	39	164	96	213
Sept–Oct	.244	.325	.398	1157	282	62	4	36	143	134	236
Bases Empty	.258	.328	.399	3144	810	158	15	86	86	309	595
Leadoff	.256	.329	.405	1333	341	67	3	42	42	136	244
Runners On Base	.285	.357	.455	2559	729	130	16	91	688	287	444
Scoring Position	.274	.360	.435	1452	398	66	12	48	573	203	271
Late and Close	.265	.340	.404	993	263	36	3	32	138	109	183

Toronto Batting

	BA	OBA	SA	AB	H	2B	3B	HR	RBI	BB	SO
Totals	.257	.322	.400	5489	1412	295	45	133	649	499	1043
vs. Left	.257	.316	.408	1666	428	90	10	47	196	142	288
vs. Right	.257	.325	.397	3823	984	205	35	86	453	357	755
at Home	.269	.337	.432	2695	724	162	27	75	340	255	504
on Road	.246	.308	.369	2794	688	133	18	58	309	244	539
on Grass	.246	.309	.370	2137	526	103	9	48	248	193	419
on Turf	.264	.331	.419	3352	886	192	36	85	401	306	624
Day Games	.249	.315	.386	1817	452	110	10	40	218	170	362
Night Games	.261	.326	.407	3672	960	185	35	93	431	329	681
April	.276	.347	.411	693	191	40	6	14	91	76	110
May	.243	.318	.373	892	217	42	13	16	101	92	178
June	.269	.331	.421	959	258	58	7	23	107	83	177
July	.268	.322	.409	903	242	44	7	23	94	64	175
August	.253	.307	.411	977	247	53	6	30	121	74	176
Sept–Oct	.241	.316	.378	1065	257	53	6	27	135	110	227
Bases Empty	.256	.314	.405	3180	813	167	27	85	85	240	613
Leadoff	.274	.329	.462	1345	368	90	11	47	47	97	243
Runners On Base	.259	.333	.393	2309	599	128	18	48	564	259	430
Scoring Position	.246	.336	.370	1369	337	74	9	26	488	202	269
Late and Close	.239	.323	.347	980	234	50	7	14	104	118	220

NATIONAL LEAGUE BATTING

	BA	OBA	SA	AB	H	2B	3B	HR	RBI	BB	SO
Totals	.250	.317	.373	65365	16363	2819	441	1430	7438	6254	11446
vs. Left	.253	.318	.375	22911	5788	1029	142	497	2633	2174	3933
vs. Right	.249	.316	.371	42454	10575	1790	299	933	4805	4080	7513
at Home	.254	.323	.382	31952	8124	1424	215	744	3778	3168	5456
on Road	.247	.311	.363	33413	8239	1395	226	686	3660	3086	5990
on Grass	.252	.315	.376	33090	8334	1316	191	807	3835	3025	5734
on Turf	.249	.318	.369	32275	8029	1503	250	623	3603	3229	5712
Day Games	.252	.317	.380	20679	5207	912	145	482	2413	1934	3630
Night Games	.250	.317	.369	44686	11156	1907	296	948	5025	4320	7816
April	.242	.312	.356	7994	1938	327	59	155	882	803	1329
May	.253	.320	.379	10801	2732	451	79	252	1244	1041	1854
June	.255	.325	.374	11259	2876	509	77	224	1284	1134	1898
July	.254	.319	.384	10208	2595	435	62	254	1222	960	1732
August	.250	.314	.374	11888	2973	525	81	263	1338	1090	2202
Sept–Oct	.246	.311	.366	13215	3249	572	83	282	1468	1226	2431
Bases Empty	.243	.306	.362	37756	9173	1594	217	822	822	3236	6668
Leadoff	.251	.313	.377	15992	4008	705	98	374	374	1359	2634
Runners On Base	.260	.331	.387	27609	7190	1225	224	608	6616	3018	4778
Scoring Position	.258	.342	.384	16197	4183	721	143	341	5787	2241	3007
Late and Close	.247	.325	.354	11499	2843	453	73	211	1341	1299	2185

Atlanta Batting

	BA	OBA	SA	AB	H	2B	3B	HR	RBI	BB	SO
Totals	.258	.328	.393	5456	1407	255	30	141	704	563	906
vs. Left	.267	.332	.399	1567	418	81	11	35	220	155	235
vs. Right	.254	.327	.391	3889	989	174	19	106	484	408	671
at Home	.273	.340	.424	2709	739	127	12	83	388	275	427
on Road	.243	.317	.366	2747	668	128	18	58	316	288	479
on Grass	.264	.332	.406	4008	1058	189	19	114	529	403	641
on Turf	.241	.319	.358	1448	349	66	11	27	175	160	265
Day Games	.261	.328	.386	1460	381	57	7	37	184	145	251
Night Games	.257	.328	.396	3996	1026	198	23	104	520	418	655
April	.237	.305	.360	603	143	28	5	12	71	61	95
May	.287	.360	.439	882	253	41	6	27	139	98	132
June	.254	.316	.379	987	251	46	7	21	110	83	165
July	.281	.345	.436	866	243	43	4	28	130	86	136
August	.255	.320	.384	1009	257	42	2	28	121	97	177
Sept–Oct	.234	.321	.362	1109	260	55	6	25	133	138	201
Bases Empty	.249	.315	.382	3098	772	137	16	81	81	283	527
Leadoff	.267	.328	.418	1324	354	55	9	42	42	112	204
Runners On Base	.269	.345	.408	2358	635	118	14	60	623	280	379
Scoring Position	.286	.368	.429	1444	413	80	9	36	550	205	236
Late and Close	.242	.327	.345	823	199	34	6	13	106	100	145

Chicago Batting

	BA	OBA	SA	AB	H	2B	3B	HR	RBI	BB	SO
Totals	.253	.309	.390	5522	1395	232	26	159	654	442	879
vs. Left	.258	.318	.408	1995	514	81	10	66	238	175	280
vs. Right	.250	.304	.381	3527	881	151	16	93	416	267	599
at Home	.258	.313	.409	2829	731	126	10	93	362	217	425
on Road	.247	.305	.371	2693	664	106	16	66	292	225	454
on Grass	.261	.315	.407	3945	1031	165	16	126	497	301	605
on Turf	.231	.296	.349	1577	364	67	10	33	157	141	274
Day Games	.254	.309	.394	2795	711	115	12	84	340	217	437
Night Games	.251	.310	.387	2727	684	117	14	75	314	225	442
April	.231	.298	.365	698	161	31	3	19	81	63	99
May	.265	.311	.436	909	241	42	4	35	107	57	147
June	.270	.325	.392	967	261	35	4	25	110	76	160
July	.247	.311	.390	885	219	45	3	16	116	80	145
August	.257	.304	.367	1023	263	38	7	20	117	69	167
Sept–Oct	.240	.305	.390	1040	250	41	5	35	123	97	161
Bases Empty	.244	.302	.376	3268	799	133	12	91	91	243	527
Leadoff	.245	.300	.398	1354	332	63	6	44	44	95	208
Runners On Base	.264	.320	.411	2254	596	99	14	68	563	199	352
Scoring Position	.249	.319	.398	1285	320	51	9	41	482	146	213
Late and Close	.257	.321	.382	1134	292	49	7	26	138	101	206

Cincinnati Batting

	BA	OBA	SA	AB	H	2B	3B	HR	RBI	BB	SO
Totals	.258	.320	.403	5501	1419	250	27	164	654	488	1006
vs. Left	.256	.321	.400	1744	446	86	9	49	212	166	358
vs. Right	.259	.319	.404	3757	973	164	18	115	442	322	648
at Home	.273	.336	.455	2704	737	151	15	104	361	257	476
on Road	.244	.304	.352	2797	682	99	12	60	293	231	530
on Grass	.259	.314	.386	1699	440	56	9	47	197	132	326
on Turf	.257	.323	.410	3802	979	194	18	117	457	356	680
Day Games	.269	.330	.429	1467	395	68	8	50	179	129	248
Night Games	.254	.316	.393	4034	1024	182	19	114	475	359	758
April	.230	.300	.350	634	146	30	2	14	59	60	115
May	.242	.306	.390	884	214	31	8	28	95	75	146
June	.292	.372	.464	955	279	53	6	33	141	118	183
July	.274	.324	.406	849	233	41	1	23	101	64	153
August	.250	.312	.390	1055	264	47	5	30	121	93	203
Sept—Oct	.252	.301	.399	1124	283	48	5	36	137	78	206
Bases Empty	.256	.311	.400	3219	823	145	11	99	99	241	608
Leadoff	.254	.313	.406	1331	338	64	3	44	44	107	249
Runners On Base	.261	.331	.407	2282	596	105	16	65	555	247	398
Scoring Position	.255	.338	.394	1311	334	56	15	32	471	178	245
Late and Close	.236	.308	.327	890	210	25	7	14	84	90	1889

Houston Batting

	BA	OBA	SA	AB	H	2B	3B	HR	RBI	BB	SO
Totals	.244	.309	.347	5504	1345	240	43	79	570	502	1027
vs. Left	.243	.311	.332	1946	472	83	8	25	196	190	368
vs. Right	.245	.308	.355	3558	873	157	35	54	374	312	659
at Home	.253	.318	.354	2725	690	136	29	27	285	255	524
on Road	.236	.300	.339	2779	655	104	14	52	285	247	503
on Grass	.239	.301	.341	1655	396	53	7	34	175	141	301
on Turf	.247	.313	.349	3849	949	187	36	45	395	361	726
Day Games	.240	.308	.347	1347	323	67	7	21	134	129	253
Night Games	.246	.310	.347	4157	1022	173	36	58	436	373	774
April	.221	.291	.306	637	141	24	6	6	46	62	129
May	.260	.322	.376	945	246	44	10	15	102	87	150
June	.230	.299	.316	953	219	39	2	13	76	94	169
July	.267	.332	.400	834	223	41	11	16	111	76	139
August	.245	.318	.351	1013	248	50	8	14	130	104	208
Sept—Oct	.239	.292	.327	1122	268	42	6	15	105	79	232
Bases Empty	.237	.298	.334	3164	749	134	24	42	42	253	594
Leadoff	.247	.304	.346	1363	336	64	12	16	16	102	243
Runners On Base	.255	.324	.364	2340	596	106	19	37	528	249	433
Scoring Position	.255	.341	.367	1348	344	66	11	21	473	188	288
Late and Close	.253	.322	.330	988	250	40	3	10	113	96	198

Los Angeles Batting

	BA	OBA	SA	AB	H	2B	3B	HR	RBI	BB	SO
Totals	.253	.326	.359	5408	1366	191	29	108	605	583	957
vs. Left	.242	.312	.340	2285	554	73	13	41	252	227	437
vs. Right	.260	.336	.372	3123	812	118	16	67	353	356	520
at Home	.254	.334	.357	2625	667	82	8	57	309	315	464
on Road	.251	.318	.360	2783	699	109	21	51	296	268	493
on Grass	.255	.328	.364	3985	1018	138	18	86	461	432	691
on Turf	.245	.319	.344	1423	348	53	11	22	144	151	266
Day Games	.253	.318	.348	1774	448	62	10	29	190	166	328
Night Games	.253	.330	.364	3634	918	129	19	79	415	417	629
April	.250	.306	.345	661	165	24	3	11	78	54	108
May	.242	.332	.346	881	213	29	3	19	105	118	176
June	.271	.334	.369	932	253	33	5	16	104	89	144
July	.251	.323	.365	857	215	32	6	18	100	89	158
August	.251	.338	.348	963	242	29	5	18	95	124	184
Sept—Oct	.250	.318	.372	1114	278	44	7	26	123	109	187
Bases Empty	.241	.310	.338	3114	750	108	12	57	57	300	550
Leadoff	.250	.313	.342	1333	333	39	6	24	24	119	219
Runners On Base	.269	.347	.386	2294	616	83	17	51	548	283	407
Scoring Position	.259	.354	.382	1322	342	42	11	33	485	211	246
Late and Close	.268	.355	.367	961	258	36	7	15	128	128	185

Montreal Batting

	BA	OBA	SA	AB	H	2B	3B	HR	RBI	BB	SO
Totals	.246	.308	.357	5412	1329	236	42	95	536	484	1056
vs. Left	.247	.312	.365	1866	461	81	10	40	192	170	385
vs. Right	.245	.307	.353	3546	868	155	32	55	344	314	671
at Home	.242	.308	.344	2217	536	95	13	35	193	213	436
on Road	.248	.308	.367	3195	793	141	29	60	343	271	620
on Grass	.248	.307	.364	1611	400	56	17	33	177	137	329
on Turf	.244	.309	.354	3801	929	180	25	62	359	347	727
Day Games	.242	.310	.346	1636	396	60	13	28	171	163	352
Night Games	.247	.308	.362	3776	933	176	29	67	365	321	704
April	.244	.296	.333	652	159	24	5	8	52	48	120
May	.240	.318	.360	934	224	35	4	23	99	107	181
June	.251	.326	.361	952	239	52	7	13	104	104	192
July	.228	.288	.319	806	184	27	5	12	69	69	150
August	.247	.310	.390	943	233	50	11	21	89	79	180
Sept—Oct	.258	.305	.366	1125	290	48	10	18	123	77	233
Bases Empty	.242	.301	.358	3207	775	147	24	59	59	256	629
Leadoff	.240	.300	.367	1350	324	65	13	27	27	111	250
Runners On Base	.251	.319	.357	2205	554	89	18	36	477	228	427
Scoring Position	.244	.329	.344	1350	330	58	10	19	420	182	290
Late and Close	.246	.322	.347	1060	261	39	7	18	101	115	212

New York Batting

	BA	OBA	SA	AB	H	2B	3B	HR	RBI	BB	SO
Totals	.244	.317	.365	5359	1305	250	24	117	605	578	789
vs. Left	.249	.313	.348	2015	502	93	4	33	191	186	283
vs. Right	.240	.320	.374	3344	803	157	20	84	414	392	506
at Home	.246	.322	.354	2670	657	123	12	57	307	300	390
on Road	.241	.313	.364	2689	648	127	12	60	298	278	399
on Grass	.244	.316	.360	3787	925	176	15	78	425	398	558
on Turf	.242	.322	.375	1572	380	74	9	39	180	180	231
Day Games	.235	.310	.358	1752	411	89	8	37	193	186	261
Night Games	.248	.321	.368	3607	894	161	16	80	412	392	528
April	.223	.327	.348	646	144	34	4	13	74	100	95
May	.263	.328	.397	859	226	41	4	22	110	85	138
June	.247	.332	.392	908	224	49	4	25	123	117	111
July	.244	.317	.349	893	218	41	1	17	103	95	115
August	.231	.283	.329	966	223	31	5	18	82	68	155
Sept—Oct	.248	.321	.370	1087	270	54	6	22	113	113	175
Bases Empty	.240	.308	.368	3095	743	142	15	75	75	293	434
Leadoff	.253	.320	.391	1313	332	66	4	36	36	126	172
Runners On Base	.248	.330	.360	2264	562	108	9	42	530	285	355
Scoring Position	.256	.346	.364	1353	347	69	5	22	472	202	224
Late and Close	.234	.328	.368	913	214	44	3	24	109	128	158

Philadelphia Batting

	BA	OBA	SA	AB	H	2B	3B	HR	RBI	BB	SO
Totals	.241	.303	.358	5521	1332	248	33	111	590	490	1026
vs. Left	.262	.326	.381	2001	525	103	13	36	224	185	358
vs. Right	.229	.290	.346	3520	807	145	20	75	366	305	668
at Home	.251	.316	.376	2782	697	133	16	61	325	261	509
on Road	.232	.290	.341	2739	635	115	17	50	265	229	517
on Grass	.238	.296	.364	1473	350	56	7	35	154	126	276
on Turf	.243	.306	.359	4048	982	192	26	76	436	364	750
Day Games	.232	.295	.342	1572	365	67	8	30	161	142	296
Night Games	.245	.306	.365	3949	967	181	25	81	429	348	730
April	.248	.317	.363	735	182	34	3	15	90	77	134
May	.233	.290	.324	891	208	37	4	12	84	71	149
June	.250	.306	.368	971	243	39	9	19	110	79	183
July	.214	.285	.332	799	171	30	5	18	74	75	147
August	.243	.319	.396	986	240	49	7	29	125	111	191
Sept—Oct	.253	.301	.361	1139	288	59	5	18	107	77	222
Bases Empty	.242	.302	.355	3163	764	133	18	63	63	266	593
Leadoff	.254	.314	.380	1354	344	58	7	33	33	113	235
Runners On Base	.241	.304	.363	2358	568	115	15	48	527	224	433
Scoring Position	.239	.314	.362	1317	315	66	6	28	457	160	251
Late and Close	.235	.305	.343	1099	258	44	6	21	108	110	219

Pittsburgh Batting

	BA	OBA	SA	AB	H	2B	3B	HR	RBI	BB	SO
Totals	.263	.338	.398	5449	1433	259	50	126	725	620	901
vs. Left	.258	.333	.406	1894	489	89	19	51	255	210	297
vs. Right	.266	.341	.394	3555	944	170	31	75	470	410	604
at Home	.258	.334	.394	2702	697	131	27	61	359	304	445
on Road	.268	.343	.402	2747	736	128	23	65	366	316	456
on Grass	.262	.325	.391	1501	393	60	13	36	183	140	232
on Turf	.263	.344	.401	3948	1040	199	37	90	542	480	669
Day Games	.271	.347	.423	1558	422	83	14	42	231	184	279
Night Games	.260	.335	.388	3891	1011	176	36	84	494	436	622
April	.252	.321	.372	651	164	28	4	14	90	64	88
May	.261	.336	.403	821	214	35	8	22	112	93	132
June	.228	.310	.339	870	198	38	7	15	80	102	153
July	.301	.371	.475	968	291	44	13	33	168	110	143
August	.260	.328	.393	982	255	58	5	21	123	105	189
Sept—Oct	.269	.352	.394	1157	311	56	13	21	152	146	196
Bases Empty	.255	.330	.377	2988	761	142	23	59	59	318	486
Leadoff	.261	.332	.386	1301	339	74	13	21	21	131	176
Runners On Base	.273	.349	.424	2461	672	117	27	67	666	302	415
Scoring Position	.270	.355	.413	1447	390	72	14	36	569	217	258
Late and Close	.248	.338	.374	855	212	41	5	19	117	117	158

San Diego Batting

	BA	OBA	SA	AB	H	2B	3B	HR	RBI	BB	SO
Totals	.244	.310	.362	5408	1321	204	36	121	591	501	1069
vs. Left	.252	.316	.400	1777	447	70	13	56	221	167	311
vs. Right	.241	.307	.344	3631	874	134	23	65	370	334	758
at Home	.245	.312	.366	2640	646	97	14	65	293	247	512
on Road	.244	.308	.359	2768	675	107	22	56	298	254	557
on Grass	.246	.310	.369	3983	979	145	25	99	459	360	796
on Turf	.240	.309	.343	1425	342	59	11	22	132	141	273
Day Games	.242	.305	.383	1534	371	69	15	39	172	134	307
Night Games	.245	.312	.354	3874	950	135	21	82	419	367	762
April	.253	.315	.345	704	178	21	7	10	78	63	140
May	.236	.305	.364	952	225	35	12	21	100	90	193
June	.266	.338	.377	942	251	42	4	18	105	100	157
July	.217	.281	.315	787	171	30	1	15	55	68	157
August	.242	.300	.384	983	238	34	6	31	117	79	212
Sept—Oct	.248	.317	.375	1040	258	42	6	26	136	101	210
Bases Empty	.229	.293	.339	3177	728	114	16	68	68	272	622
Leadoff	.239	.303	.355	1327	317	43	6	33	33	115	250
Runners On Base	.266	.333	.395	2231	593	90	20	53	523	229	447
Scoring Position	.267	.347	.412	1301	348	54	13	36	470	169	282
Late and Close	.252	.319	.369	932	235	31	6	22	112	89	181

St. Louis Batting

	BA	OBA	SA	AB	H	2B	3B	HR	RBI	BB	SO
Totals	.255	.322	.357	5362	1366	239	53	68	599	532	857
vs. Left	.251	.318	.349	2242	563	117	21	20	238	217	372
vs. Right	.257	.325	.363	3120	803	122	32	48	361	315	485
at Home	.252	.325	.355	2707	682	116	34	32	313	290	394
on Road	.258	.319	.359	2655	684	123	19	36	286	242	463
on Grass	.250	.307	.344	1438	360	72	10	14	154	119	263
on Turf	.256	.327	.362	3924	1006	167	43	54	445	413	594
Day Games	.265	.328	.398	1537	408	79	19	29	202	149	219
Night Games	.250	.319	.341	3825	958	160	34	39	397	383	638
April	.260	.345	.359	691	180	26	9	8	75	88	84
May	.273	.339	.363	873	238	44	7	7	109	88	136
June	.261	.327	.363	928	242	43	14	8	117	94	128
July	.248	.315	.356	856	212	31	7	16	89	84	142
August	.255	.311	.348	924	236	39	10	9	96	76	162
Sept—Oct	.237	.303	.354	1090	258	56	6	20	113	102	205
Bases Empty	.242	.305	.343	3052	739	128	19	47	47	269	496
Leadoff	.260	.324	.368	1314	341	60	7	23	23	124	199
Runners On Base	.271	.343	.376	2310	627	111	34	21	552	263	361
Scoring Position	.271	.360	.375	1424	386	66	26	10	505	215	241
Late and Close	.251	.332	.344	926	232	34	7	13	110	110	159

San Francisco Batting

	BA	OBA	SA	AB	H	2B	3B	HR	RBI	BB	SO
Totals	.246	.309	.381	5463	1345	215	48	141	605	471	973
vs. Left	.251	.308	.396	1579	397	72	11	45	194	126	249
vs. Right	.244	.309	.374	3884	948	143	37	96	411	345	724
at Home	.244	.308	.382	2642	645	107	25	69	283	234	454
on Road	.248	.309	.379	2821	700	108	23	72	322	237	519
on Grass	.246	.307	.379	4005	984	150	35	105	424	336	716
on Turf	.248	.315	.384	1458	361	65	13	36	181	135	257
Day Games	.256	.318	.395	2247	576	96	24	56	256	190	399
Night Games	.239	.302	.370	3216	769	119	24	85	349	281	574
April	.257	.320	.424	682	175	23	8	25	88	63	122
May	.237	.291	.359	970	230	37	9	21	82	72	174
June	.242	.307	.365	894	216	40	8	18	104	78	153
July	.266	.324	.438	808	215	30	5	33	106	64	147
August	.263	.322	.407	1041	274	58	10	24	122	85	174
Sept—Oct	.220	.296	.316	1068	235	27	8	20	103	109	203
Bases Empty	.240	.298	.373	3211	770	131	27	81	81	242	602
Leadoff	.239	.302	.368	1328	318	54	12	31	31	104	229
Runners On Base	.255	.325	.391	2252	575	84	21	60	524	229	371
Scoring Position	.242	.326	.358	1295	314	41	14	27	433	168	233
Late and Close	.242	.327	.353	918	222	36	9	16	115	115	176

AMERICAN LEAGUE PITCHING

	G	IP	H	BB	SO	SB	CS	W	L	S	ERA
Totals	7048	20382.0	20195	7730	12944	1469	758	1134	1134	618	4.10
at Home	3538	10469.0	10233	3709	6806	754	414	598	536	293	4.00
on Road	3510	9913.0	9962	4021	6138	715	344	536	598	325	4.21
on Grass	5009	14529.0	14334	5603	9218	1001	561	810	810	434	4.11
on Turf	2039	5853.0	5861	2127	3726	468	197	324	324	184	4.08
Day Games	2071	5988.0	5938	2380	3863	428	226	332	332	166	4.20
Night Games	4977	14394.0	14257	5350	9081	1041	532	802	802	452	4.06
April	783	2345.1	2223	932	1467	161	95	131	131	73	3.86
May	1198	3421.1	3415	1399	2130	280	123	190	190	96	4.15
June	1163	3474.2	3410	1292	2150	238	119	193	193	115	4.09
July	1150	3351.1	3436	1178	2091	216	129	186	186	102	4.24
August	1243	3681.2	3720	1332	2370	263	143	206	206	110	4.21
Sept–Oct	1511	4107.2	3991	1597	2736	311	149	228	228	122	4.00

	BA	OBA	SA	AB	H	2B	3B	HR	RBI	BB	SO
Totals	.260	.329	.395	77603	20195	3680	453	1953	9610	7730	12944
vs. Left	.264	.333	.391	31521	8334	1486	218	687	3860	3243	4777
vs. Right	.257	.326	.398	46082	11861	2194	235	1266	5750	4487	8167
Home	.257	.322	.388	39741	10233	1832	201	988	4814	3709	6806
Road	.263	.336	.402	37862	9962	1848	252	965	4796	4021	6138
Bases Empty	.254	.320	.385	43914	11167	2065	243	1068	1068	3953	7448
Leadoff	.255	.319	.392	18668	4754	898	101	488	488	1644	2979
Runners On Base	.268	.340	.407	33689	9028	1615	210	885	8542	3777	5496
Scoring Position	.266	.351	.402	19169	5093	913	138	477	7372	2721	3368
Late and Close	.244	.320	.362	12875	3143	509	65	295	1532	1392	2418

Baltimore Pitching

	G	IP	H	BB	SO	SB	CS	W	L	S	ERA
Totals	534	1457.2	1534	504	868	111	51	67	95	42	4.59
at Home	273	744.0	775	245	478	63	30	33	48	15	4.33
on Road	261	713.2	759	259	390	48	21	34	47	27	4.86
on Grass	455	1238.0	1284	428	732	96	46	58	80	36	4.45
on Turf	79	219.2	250	76	136	15	5	9	15	6	5.37
Day Games	134	372.1	374	123	217	19	19	17	24	14	4.40
Night Games	400	1085.1	1160	381	651	92	32	50	71	28	4.65
April	55	159.2	170	61	76	9	7	6	12	3	4.85
May	91	236.0	250	92	131	15	5	10	17	6	4.69
June	102	257.0	284	96	148	26	14	14	14	11	5.01
July	89	245.1	252	66	135	16	7	10	17	8	4.77
August	96	260.0	269	86	165	22	6	13	16	6	4.29
Sept–Oct	101	299.2	309	103	213	23	12	14	19	8	4.11

	BA	OBA	SA	AB	H	2B	3B	HR	RBI	BB	SO
Totals	.273	.333	.412	5626	1534	294	25	147	757	504	868
vs. Left	.264	.327	.390	2485	656	116	11	58	325	236	399
vs. Right	.280	.338	.430	3141	878	178	14	89	432	268	469
Home	.270	.328	.398	2871	775	138	7	72	371	245	478
Road	.275	.338	.427	2755	759	156	18	75	386	259	390
Bases Empty	.255	.316	.387	3202	818	144	12	84	84	263	514
Leadoff	.255	.310	.410	1353	345	62	5	46	46	99	190
Runners On Base	.295	.356	.446	2424	716	150	13	63	673	241	354
Scoring Position	.303	.379	.460	1338	406	79	10	37	593	186	221
Late and Close	.241	.315	.355	912	220	44	6	16	99	96	157

Boston Pitching

	G	IP	H	BB	SO	SB	CS	W	L	S	ERA
Totals	490	1439.2	1405	530	999	97	53	84	78	45	4.02
at Home	248	749.0	757	285	523	50	29	43	38	23	3.91
on Road	242	690.2	648	245	476	47	24	41	40	22	4.14
on Grass	417	1225.2	1200	454	863	77	42	70	67	36	4.05
on Turf	73	214.0	205	76	136	20	11	14	11	9	3.87
Day Games	167	502.2	498	201	340	35	16	28	28	12	4.15
Night Games	323	937.0	907	329	659	62	37	56	50	33	3.95
April	60	163.0	125	70	115	11	7	11	7	9	2.76
May	91	244.0	249	99	180	22	6	15	13	7	4.94
June	73	236.0	229	80	157	9	3	11	16	5	3.66
July	85	250.0	266	83	166	15	14	11	16	5	4.39
August	74	254.0	239	87	190	20	13	18	11	9	3.72
Sept–Oct	107	292.2	297	111	191	20	10	18	15	10	4.18

	BA	OBA	SA	AB	H	2B	3B	HR	RBI	BB	SO
Totals	.257	.323	.402	5477	1405	286	34	147	664	530	999
vs. Left	.249	.318	.367	2052	511	108	13	36	226	204	362
vs. Right	.261	.326	.422	3425	894	178	21	111	438	326	637
Home	.264	.331	.406	2865	757	149	14	76	343	285	523
Road	.248	.314	.397	2612	648	137	20	71	321	245	476
Bases Empty	.255	.315	.397	3131	799	162	20	81	81	256	593
Leadoff	.259	.323	.412	1318	342	70	10	37	37	116	236
Runners On Base	.258	.334	.408	2346	606	124	14	66	583	274	406
Scoring Position	.253	.346	.395	1358	344	74	10	33	497	206	235
Late and Close	.235	.317	.369	839	197	42	10	17	85	95	150

California Pitching

	G	IP	H	BB	SO	SB	CS	W	L	S	ERA
Totals	472	1441.2	1351	543	990	89	72	81	81	50	3.69
at Home	225	748.0	649	251	520	41	38	40	41	24	3.30
on Road	247	693.2	702	292	470	48	34	41	40	26	4.11
on Grass	386	1208.2	1125	449	830	69	64	64	71	39	3.70
on Turf	86	233.0	226	94	160	20	8	17	10	11	3.63
Day Games	115	354.0	347	133	266	21	19	22	18	13	3.81
Night Games	357	1087.2	1004	410	724	68	53	59	63	37	3.65
April	56	180.0	158	64	117	9	5	10	10	5	3.35
May	79	238.2	229	81	165	17	14	16	11	9	3.62
June	86	242.1	251	104	195	5	13	15	12	8	4.53
July	64	230.0	220	73	154	13	8	11	15	6	3.95
August	83	255.0	240	92	147	17	13	11	18	9	3.49
Sept–Oct	104	295.2	253	129	212	28	19	18	15	13	3.23

	BA	OBA	SA	AB	H	2B	3B	HR	RBI	BB	SO
Totals	.250	.321	.383	5399	1351	250	21	141	609	543	990
vs. Left	.272	.330	.406	1639	446	89	4	41	213	138	271
vs. Right	.241	.318	.372	3760	905	161	17	100	396	405	719
Home	.237	.303	.366	2744	649	122	5	74	281	251	520
Road	.264	.340	.400	2655	702	128	16	67	328	292	470
Bases Empty	.248	.319	.373	3105	771	143	10	75	75	307	535
Leadoff	.249	.321	.369	1305	325	60	2	31	31	132	211
Runners On Base	.253	.324	.395	2294	580	107	11	66	534	236	455
Scoring Position	.253	.336	.405	1269	321	67	6	38	459	168	271
Late and Close	.220	.288	.326	860	189	26	1	21	92	81	199

Chicago Pitching

	G	IP	H	BB	SO	SB	CS	W	L	S	ERA
Totals	500	1478.0	1302	601	923	96	67	87	75	40	3.80
at Home	258	750.0	668	281	452	46	38	46	35	19	3.72
on Road	242	728.0	634	320	471	50	29	41	40	21	3.88
on Grass	431	1265.1	1104	521	807	80	59	74	64	35	3.74
on Turf	69	212.2	198	80	116	16	8	13	11	5	4.15
Day Games	135	412.2	330	175	261	25	16	24	20	9	3.55
Night Games	365	1065.1	972	426	662	71	51	63	55	31	3.89
April	61	157.0	139	84	125	11	8	11	6	6	4.30
May	82	252.0	236	126	161	21	9	10	17	3	4.11
June	74	264.0	214	84	153	17	17	17	12	9	3.34
July	81	251.0	220	80	124	13	12	19	8	10	3.48
August	85	261.2	245	101	175	13	10	12	18	5	4.23
Sept–Oct	117	292.1	248	126	185	21	11	18	14	7	3.57

	BA	OBA	SA	AB	H	2B	3B	HR	RBI	BB	SO
Totals	.239	.315	.374	5448	1302	215	30	154	648	601	923
vs. Left	.234	.310	.361	2117	495	87	15	51	246	234	359
vs. Right	.242	.319	.382	3331	807	128	15	103	402	367	564
Home	.241	.312	.378	2767	668	113	14	79	324	281	452
Road	.236	.319	.370	2681	634	102	16	75	324	320	471
Bases Empty	.229	.305	.360	3178	728	118	17	88	88	328	542
Leadoff	.236	.314	.380	1330	314	56	9	39	39	142	205
Runners On Base	.253	.329	.394	2270	574	97	13	66	560	273	381
Scoring Position	.257	.342	.396	1250	321	49	7	37	478	181	224
Late and Close	.231	.319	.348	985	228	33	2	26	109	121	174

Cleveland Pitching

	G	IP	H	BB	SO	SB	CS	W	L	S	ERA
Totals	451	1441.1	1551	441	862	102	47	57	105	33	4.24
at Home	212	747.0	788	207	447	51	29	30	52	14	4.10
on Road	239	694.1	763	234	415	51	18	27	53	19	4.39
on Grass	383	1241.0	1323	369	746	86	41	53	85	30	4.15
on Turf	68	200.1	228	72	116	16	6	4	20	3	4.81
Day Games	146	454.1	482	144	274	31	14	19	32	9	4.12
Night Games	305	987.0	1069	297	588	71	33	38	73	24	4.29
April	44	155.1	136	37	104	6	5	7	10	5	2.61
May	77	238.2	256	72	162	20	4	10	17	3	4.64
June	70	248.0	260	83	155	21	9	7	21	4	3.99
July	85	239.2	266	80	142	14	10	9	18	5	4.21
August	78	265.1	299	81	151	15	15	10	20	6	4.71
Sept–Oct	97	294.1	334	88	148	26	4	14	19	10	4.59

	BA	OBA	SA	AB	H	2B	3B	HR	RBI	BB	SO
Totals	.276	.329	.398	5623	1551	279	38	110	708	441	862
vs. Left	.292	.348	.401	2270	662	111	21	32	282	199	304
vs. Right	.265	.316	.395	3353	889	168	17	78	426	242	558
Home	.272	.321	.373	2900	788	128	22	41	346	207	447
Road	.280	.337	.423	2723	763	151	16	69	362	234	415
Bases Empty	.271	.320	.382	3118	844	154	22	50	50	205	492
Leadoff	.262	.309	.392	1357	356	68	12	28	28	80	221
Runners On Base	.282	.340	.417	2505	707	125	16	60	658	236	370
Scoring Position	.274	.345	.405	1421	390	70	11	31	574	177	220
Late and Close	.266	.340	.372	927	247	45	4	15	117	105	156

Detroit Pitching

	G	IP	H	BB	SO	SB	CS	W	L	S	ERA
Totals	488	1450.1	1570	593	739	88	56	84	78	38	4.54
at Home	245	740.0	784	295	405	44	23	49	32	22	4.60
on Road	243	710.1	786	298	334	44	33	35	46	16	4.47
on Grass	417	1235.1	1321	503	642	72	48	74	63	32	4.55
on Turf	71	215.0	249	90	97	16	8	10	15	6	4.48
Day Games	153	456.0	523	187	236	26	14	26	25	10	4.86
Night Games	335	994.1	1047	406	503	62	42	58	53	28	4.39
April	57	170.2	174	67	85	14	7	10	9	6	3.43
May	88	244.1	303	110	111	16	13	13	14	6	5.27
June	77	249.0	253	108	125	18	8	14	14	7	4.45
July	86	227.0	284	100	110	13	4	14	12	5	5.91
August	83	272.1	288	106	148	21	13	18	12	8	4.23
Sept–Oct	97	287.0	268	102	160	6	11	15	17	6	3.86

	BA	OBA	SA	AB	H	2B	3B	HR	RBI	BB	SO
Totals	.281	.348	.422	5596	1570	257	45	148	752	593	739
vs. Left	.282	.351	.436	2088	589	101	19	61	285	227	215
vs. Right	.280	.347	.413	3508	981	156	26	87	467	366	524
Home	.274	.340	.421	2860	784	124	14	89	388	295	405
Road	.287	.357	.423	2736	786	133	31	59	364	298	334
Bases Empty	.273	.333	.419	3129	854	156	21	86	86	271	429
Leadoff	.277	.329	.421	1347	373	66	7	38	38	102	163
Runners On Base	.290	.367	.426	2467	716	101	24	62	666	322	310
Scoring Position	.288	.379	.416	1411	406	64	12	31	580	238	190
Late and Close	.272	.346	.391	882	240	36	6	19	128	105	142

Kansas City Pitching

	G	IP	H	BB	SO	SB	CS	W	L	S	ERA
Totals	457	1466.0	1473	529	1004	94	56	82	80	41	3.92
at Home	234	765.0	746	257	513	54	31	40	41	17	3.92
on Road	223	701.0	727	272	491	40	25	42	39	24	3.93
on Grass	168	534.2	557	211	371	26	16	31	31	19	3.96
on Turf	289	931.1	916	318	633	68	40	51	49	22	3.90
Day Games	140	440.0	446	178	318	21	21	23	25	12	3.91
Night Games	317	1026.0	1027	351	686	73	35	59	55	29	3.93
April	48	167.0	166	53	104	5	6	8	11	5	3.66
May	68	238.0	228	79	145	10	11	13	14	5	3.74
June	82	255.2	282	95	164	16	3	12	15	8	4.47
July	80	241.1	263	92	180	19	9	16	10	9	4.40
August	69	266.0	234	83	192	15	13	18	11	7	2.64
Sept–Oct	110	298.0	300	127	219	29	14	15	19	7	4.50

	BA	OBA	SA	AB	H	2B	3B	HR	RBI	BB	SO
Totals	.261	.327	.380	5640	1473	271	42	105	672	529	1004
vs. Left	.281	.346	.406	2651	744	141	27	46	337	264	424
vs. Right	.244	.310	.357	2989	729	130	15	59	335	265	580
Home	.255	.319	.367	2927	746	150	29	40	345	257	513
Road	.268	.336	.394	2713	727	121	13	65	327	272	491
Bases Empty	.254	.317	.372	3142	798	159	25	54	54	272	562
Leadoff	.252	.314	.365	1347	340	71	10	20	20	111	219
Runners On Base	.270	.339	.390	2498	675	112	17	51	618	257	442
Scoring Position	.263	.340	.380	1470	386	66	13	27	541	177	282
Late and Close	.254	.321	.343	934	237	30	4	15	106	87	185

Milwaukee Pitching

	G	IP	H	BB	SO	SB	CS	W	L	S	ERA
Totals	503	1463.2	1498	527	859	115	47	83	79	41	4.18
at Home	251	746.0	762	275	468	52	26	43	37	19	4.26
on Road	252	717.2	736	252	391	63	21	40	42	22	4.09
on Grass	427	1246.2	1257	450	742	93	40	75	62	34	4.06
on Turf	76	217.0	241	77	117	22	7	8	17	7	4.81
Day Games	158	456.1	481	182	273	35	12	28	21	11	4.26
Night Games	345	1007.1	1017	345	586	80	35	55	58	30	4.14
April	66	174.0	179	61	118	16	5	10	9	5	4.34
May	80	257.1	243	86	150	17	10	12	15	7	3.74
June	90	238.2	237	88	142	29	8	12	15	4	4.30
July	77	234.1	286	102	115	18	12	9	18	3	5.38
August	93	264.0	281	97	145	16	5	19	10	10	4.30
Sept–Oct	97	295.1	272	93	189	19	7	21	12	12	3.29

	BA	OBA	SA	AB	H	2B	3B	HR	RBI	BB	SO
Totals	.266	.332	.398	5623	1498	254	22	147	725	527	859
vs. Left	.265	.331	.392	2618	694	106	10	69	356	253	339
vs. Right	.268	.332	.403	3005	804	148	12	78	369	274	520
Home	.266	.332	.390	2866	762	126	6	73	389	275	468
Road	.267	.332	.406	2757	736	128	16	74	336	252	391
Bases Empty	.265	.330	.399	3129	829	142	13	84	84	278	481
Leadoff	.264	.330	.407	1338	353	59	6	40	40	124	223
Runners On Base	.268	.334	.396	2494	669	112	9	63	641	249	378
Scoring Position	.280	.352	.421	1409	394	65	7	40	574	168	228
Late and Close	.257	.330	.409	930	239	33	0	36	135	101	148

Minnesota Pitching

	G	IP	H	BB	SO	SB	CS	W	L	S	ERA
Totals	453	1449.1	1402	488	876	118	43	95	67	53	3.69
at Home	243	743.0	725	224	469	72	18	51	30	26	3.90
on Road	210	706.1	677	264	407	46	25	44	37	27	3.48
on Grass	162	543.0	518	204	316	30	21	35	27	21	3.50
on Turf	291	906.1	884	284	560	88	22	60	40	32	3.81
Day Games	136	431.0	434	142	248	34	14	27	21	11	3.63
Night Games	317	1018.1	968	346	628	84	29	68	46	42	3.72
April	54	176.1	184	73	99	21	8	9	11	4	3.98
May	75	252.0	240	97	152	26	9	14	14	8	3.82
June	64	252.2	237	64	133	16	4	22	6	12	2.81
July	79	230.2	237	68	142	15	7	16	10	10	3.71
August	81	258.2	245	89	154	17	6	17	12	11	4.52
Sept–Oct	100	279.0	259	97	196	23	9	17	14	8	3.42

	BA	OBA	SA	AB	H	2B	3B	HR	RBI	BB	SO
Totals	.255	.317	.392	5491	1402	273	31	139	616	488	876
vs. Left	.268	.328	.389	2329	625	122	14	44	243	213	319
vs. Right	.246	.308	.394	3162	777	151	17	95	373	275	557
Home	.257	.313	.402	2821	725	149	18	75	322	224	469
Road	.254	.320	.382	2670	677	124	13	64	294	264	407
Bases Empty	.263	.321	.403	3184	837	169	17	81	81	256	526
Leadoff	.270	.323	.436	1348	364	73	8	45	45	98	196
Runners On Base	.245	.310	.378	2307	565	104	14	58	535	232	350
Scoring Position	.237	.318	.360	1310	310	55	8	30	450	173	230
Late and Close	.239	.307	.357	852	204	39	5	17	95	81	143

New York Pitching

	G	IP	H	BB	SO	SB	CS	W	L	S	ERA
Totals	539	1444.0	1510	506	936	134	51	71	91	37	4.43
at Home	260	739.0	761	243	466	65	29	39	42	18	4.31
on Road	279	705.0	749	263	470	69	22	32	49	19	4.56
on Grass	459	1235.2	1271	442	797	116	47	64	74	33	4.36
on Turf	80	208.1	239	64	139	18	4	7	17	4	4.84
Day Games	161	433.1	467	189	296	51	20	22	27	11	4.98
Night Games	378	1010.2	1043	317	640	83	31	49	64	26	4.19
April	56	149.0	162	62	102	14	6	6	11	1	5.19
May	97	245.1	227	102	139	32	9	14	13	6	3.49
June	97	241.1	255	65	153	26	6	13	14	10	4.25
July	80	231.0	250	63	142	10	12	13	13	9	4.36
August	101	274.2	300	102	215	27	8	12	19	3	5.54
Sept–Oct	108	302.2	316	112	185	25	10	13	21	8	4.01

	BA	OBA	SA	AB	H	2B	3B	HR	RBI	BB	SO
Totals	.271	.334	.421	5574	1510	295	42	152	736	506	936
vs. Left	.273	.339	.429	2266	618	122	18	65	282	219	361
vs. Right	.270	.331	.415	3308	892	173	24	87	454	287	575
Home	.269	.329	.415	2831	761	137	12	84	363	243	466
Road	.273	.339	.427	2743	749	158	30	68	373	263	470
Bases Empty	.268	.326	.409	3142	841	169	23	76	76	248	521
Leadoff	.264	.326	.415	1325	350	79	8	35	35	111	211
Runners On Base	.275	.344	.436	2432	669	126	19	76	660	258	415
Scoring Position	.281	.358	.444	1409	396	76	15	41	561	180	257
Late and Close	.252	.323	.365	819	206	34	4	17	91	80	152

Oakland Pitching

	G	IP	H	BB	SO	SB	CS	W	L	S	ERA
Totals	559	1444.1	1425	655	892	116	60	84	78	49	4.57
at Home	278	744.0	678	306	474	60	35	47	34	20	4.05
on Road	281	700.1	747	349	418	56	25	37	44	29	5.13
on Grass	466	1224.2	1149	552	758	96	52	76	60	41	4.21
on Turf	93	219.2	276	103	134	20	8	8	18	8	6.60
Day Games	189	500.2	479	210	340	37	20	33	23	20	4.51
Night Games	370	943.2	946	445	552	79	40	51	55	29	4.61
April	62	176.1	165	80	88	14	12	13	7	8	3.73
May	100	239.2	260	115	143	26	6	15	12	7	5.41
June	82	244.0	226	118	147	10	10	13	15	11	4.91
July	98	251.1	239	93	150	18	10	15	12	7	4.30
August	102	259.1	262	107	146	23	12	15	14	9	4.44
Sept–Oct	115	273.2	273	142	218	25	10	13	18	7	4.47

	BA	OBA	SA	AB	H	2B	3B	HR	RBI	BB	SO
Totals	.260	.342	.405	5481	1425	253	38	155	750	655	892
vs. Left	.266	.345	.390	2649	704	122	21	55	339	325	373
vs. Right	.255	.339	.419	2832	721	131	17	100	411	330	519
Home	.245	.323	.373	2772	678	119	18	67	342	306	474
Road	.276	.361	.437	2709	747	134	20	88	408	349	418
Bases Empty	.249	.330	.391	3043	758	138	17	87	87	339	493
Leadoff	.248	.328	.398	1295	321	64	7	39	39	143	202
Runners On Base	.274	.356	.422	2438	667	115	21	68	663	316	399
Scoring Position	.280	.370	.436	1405	393	70	18	38	580	218	255
Late and Close	.251	.335	.406	914	229	41	7	29	133	106	184

Seattle Pitching

	G	IP	H	BB	SO	SB	CS	W	L	S	ERA
Totals	545	1464.1	1387	628	1003	84	44	83	79	48	3.79
at Home	274	760.0	697	273	534	41	22	45	36	22	3.46
on Road	271	704.1	690	355	469	43	22	38	43	26	4.15
on Grass	204	537.2	510	273	370	33	18	32	30	22	3.92
on Turf	341	926.2	877	355	633	51	26	51	49	26	3.72
Day Games	151	393.1	386	173	271	23	17	16	29	7	4.67
Night Games	394	1071.0	1001	455	732	61	27	67	50	41	3.47
April	53	185.0	185	90	116	10	8	10	11	4	3.94
May	86	247.0	235	108	176	13	6	15	12	8	3.50
June	91	234.0	198	114	166	19	7	14	13	11	4.04
July	84	244.0	224	87	166	12	6	15	12	6	2.80
August	107	253.1	255	95	175	16	9	13	15	8	3.84
Sept–Oct	124	301.0	290	134	204	14	8	16	16	11	4.51

	BA	OBA	SA	AB	H	2B	3B	HR	RBI	BB	SO
Totals	.253	.332	.386	5486	1387	258	32	136	630	628	1003
vs. Left	.257	.332	.379	2072	533	100	15	41	237	230	316
vs. Right	.250	.332	.390	3414	854	158	17	95	393	398	687
Home	.246	.314	.376	2833	697	130	16	69	301	273	534
Road	.260	.351	.396	2653	690	128	16	67	329	355	469
Bases Empty	.249	.322	.388	3104	772	139	17	86	86	311	563
Leadoff	.242	.315	.382	1325	320	58	7	38	38	132	227
Runners On Base	.258	.345	.384	2382	615	119	15	50	544	317	440
Scoring Position	.246	.351	.360	1340	330	58	10	25	468	229	266
Late and Close	.246	.319	.354	956	235	40	6	17	96	99	187

Texas Pitching

	G	IP	H	BB	SO	SB	CS	W	L	S	ERA
Totals	548	1479.0	1486	662	1022	107	58	85	77	41	4.47
at Home	278	749.0	741	312	553	55	35	46	35	25	4.31
on Road	270	730.0	745	350	469	52	23	39	42	16	4.64
on Grass	453	1245.0	1252	542	877	84	50	71	66	35	4.58
on Turf	95	234.0	234	120	145	23	8	14	11	6	3.88
Day Games	105	287.1	268	147	206	22	9	17	14	8	4.26
Night Games	443	1191.2	1218	515	816	85	49	68	63	33	4.52
April	50	144.0	117	60	106	13	7	8	8	5	4.00
May	105	249.1	257	138	156	19	9	18	9	9	4.26
June	89	261.2	265	117	153	10	9	13	14	4	4.26
July	89	238.1	224	110	196	15	8	13	14	9	4.38
August	101	276.2	305	111	187	20	11	15	16	8	4.91
Sept–Oct	114	309.0	318	126	224	30	14	18	16	6	4.72

	BA	OBA	SA	AB	H	2B	3B	HR	RBI	BB	SO
Totals	.262	.341	.402	5669	1486	278	31	151	761	662	1022
vs. Left	.250	.331	.371	2273	569	98	18	47	291	275	398
vs. Right	.270	.348	.423	3396	917	180	13	104	470	387	624
Home	.259	.333	.399	2857	741	133	17	77	376	312	553
Road	.265	.349	.405	2812	745	145	14	74	385	350	469
Bases Empty	.256	.333	.394	3117	797	148	18	82	82	341	600
Leadoff	.260	.328	.389	1349	351	66	6	32	32	130	240
Runners On Base	.270	.350	.412	2552	689	130	13	69	679	321	422
Scoring Position	.253	.349	.377	1509	382	72	5	35	576	232	274
Late and Close	.235	.322	.370	1036	243	43	5	29	126	129	207

Toronto Pitching

	G	IP	H	BB	SO	SB	CS	W	L	S	ERA
Totals	509	1462.2	1301	523	971	118	53	91	71	60	3.50
at Home	259	745.0	702	255	504	60	31	46	35	29	3.83
on Road	250	717.2	599	268	467	58	22	45	36	31	3.16
on Grass	181	547.2	463	205	367	43	17	33	30	21	3.39
on Turf	328	915.0	838	318	604	75	36	58	41	39	3.57
Day Games	181	494.0	423	196	317	48	15	30	25	19	3.66
Night Games	328	968.2	878	327	654	70	38	61	46	41	3.42
April	61	188.0	163	70	112	8	4	12	9	7	3.97
May	79	239.0	202	94	159	26	12	15	12	12	2.97
June	86	250.1	219	76	159	16	8	16	12	11	3.27
July	73	237.1	205	81	169	25	10	15	11	10	3.45
August	90	260.2	258	95	180	21	9	15	14	11	3.97
Sept–Oct	120	287.1	254	107	192	22	10	18	13	9	3.45

	BA	OBA	SA	AB	H	2B	3B	HR	RBI	BB	SO
Totals	.238	.307	.352	5470	1301	217	22	121	582	523	971
vs. Left	.243	.320	.347	2012	488	63	12	41	198	226	337
vs. Right	.235	.299	.355	3458	813	154	10	80	384	297	634
Home	.248	.313	.371	2827	702	114	9	72	323	255	504
Road	.227	.300	.331	2643	599	103	13	49	259	268	467
Bases Empty	.226	.294	.323	3190	721	124	11	54	54	278	597
Leadoff	.225	.297	.311	1331	300	46	4	20	20	124	235
Runners On Base	.254	.325	.393	2280	580	93	11	67	528	245	374
Scoring Position	.247	.338	.375	1270	314	48	6	34	441	188	215
Late and Close	.223	.297	.316	1029	229	23	5	21	120	106	234

NATIONAL LEAGUE PITCHING

	G	IP	H	BB	SO	SB	CS	W	L	S	ERA
Totals	6123	17387.2	16363	6254	11446	1651	808	970	970	514	3.69
at Home	3089	8940.0	8239	3086	5990	798	432	533	437	268	3.51
on Road	3034	8447.2	8124	3168	5456	853	376	437	533	246	3.87
on Grass	3061	8747.1	8334	3025	5734	765	405	489	489	255	3.76
on Turf	3062	8640.1	8029	3229	5712	886	403	481	481	259	3.61
Day Games	1913	5463.2	5207	1934	3630	520	254	307	307	160	3.77
Night Games	4210	11924.0	11156	4320	7816	1131	554	663	663	354	3.65
April	764	2150.0	1938	803	1329	196	95	120	120	69	3.57
May	989	2864.2	2732	1041	1854	310	148	159	159	86	3.79
June	1067	3000.1	2876	1134	1898	304	164	167	167	97	3.65
July	920	2695.2	2595	960	1732	253	124	152	152	71	3.81
August	1113	3164.0	2973	1090	2202	250	144	175	175	81	3.68
Sept–Oct	1270	3513.0	3249	1226	2431	338	133	197	197	110	3.62

	BA	OBA	SA	AB	H	2B	3B	HR	RBI	BB	SO
Totals	.250	.317	.373	65365	16363	2819	441	1430	7438	6254	11446
vs. Left	.256	.330	.376	28462	7289	1235	236	569	3244	3125	4850
vs. Right	.246	.307	.370	36903	9074	1584	205	861	4194	3129	6596
Home	.247	.311	.363	33413	8239	1395	226	686	3660	3086	5990
Road	.254	.323	.382	31952	8124	1424	215	744	3778	3168	5456
Bases Empty	.243	.306	.362	37756	9173	1594	217	822	822	3236	6668
Leadoff	.251	.313	.377	15992	4008	705	98	374	374	1359	2634
Runners On Base	.260	.331	.387	27609	7190	1225	224	608	6616	3018	4778
Scoring Position	.258	.342	.384	16197	4183	721	143	341	5787	2241	3007
Late and Close	.247	.325	.354	11499	2843	453	73	211	1341	1299	2185

Atlanta Pitching

	G	IP	H	BB	SO	SB	CS	W	L	S	ERA
Totals	507	1452.2	1304	481	969	149	59	94	68	48	3.49
at Home	267	740.0	711	227	461	64	32	48	33	25	3.81
on Road	240	712.2	593	254	508	85	27	46	35	23	3.17
on Grass	369	1075.1	969	331	683	92	44	70	50	36	3.55
on Turf	138	377.1	335	150	286	57	15	24	18	12	3.34
Day Games	128	383.0	334	121	268	38	17	25	18	10	3.36
Night Games	379	1069.2	970	360	701	111	42	69	50	38	3.54
April	65	164.2	141	63	114	16	8	8	10	3	2.95
May	77	235.0	222	60	153	21	11	17	9	8	3.18
June	93	258.0	250	93	164	27	13	12	17	6	4.12
July	78	225.2	205	80	138	31	10	16	10	8	4.31
August	90	269.0	242	86	196	17	12	19	11	10	3.31
Sept–Oct	104	300.1	244	99	204	37	5	22	11	13	3.06

	BA	OBA	SA	AB	H	2B	3B	HR	RBI	BB	SO
Totals	.240	.303	.364	5429	1304	235	41	118	597	481	969
vs. Left	.262	.334	.388	1867	489	91	21	34	211	205	319
vs. Right	.229	.287	.351	3562	815	144	20	84	386	276	650
Home	.254	.311	.391	2801	711	127	19	73	340	227	461
Road	.226	.295	.335	2628	593	108	22	45	257	254	508
Bases Empty	.233	.294	.348	3198	744	135	18	66	66	262	572
Leadoff	.246	.301	.385	1349	332	66	7	36	36	101	226
Runners On Base	.251	.317	.386	2231	560	100	23	52	531	219	397
Scoring Position	.259	.341	.405	1295	336	60	13	34	464	169	241
Late and Close	.217	.290	.306	903	196	31	5	13	83	89	167

Chicago Pitching

	G	IP	H	BB	SO	SB	CS	W	L	S	ERA
Totals	520	1456.2	1415	542	927	139	64		83	40	4.05
at Home	277	773.0	763	257	501	64	42	46	37	24	4.02
on Road	243	683.2	652	285	426	75	22	31	46	16	4.08
on Grass	380	1048.2	1039	377	679	97	55	59	56	29	4.16
on Turf	140	408.0	376	165	248	42	9	18	27	11	3.75
Day Games	270	753.2	749	264	493	65	41	44	39	23	4.26
Night Games	250	703.0	666	278	434	74	23	33	44	17	3.82
April	68	188.1	158	68	107	13	5	10	11	7	3.68
May	84	236.2	220	83	141	34	9	14	12	11	3.95
June	102	249.1	254	117	164	27	16	10	18	7	4.08
July	76	235.1	274	61	159	18	8	14	11	6	4.86
August	86	269.2	249	98	179	23	13	17	12	4	3.50
Sept–Oct	104	277.1	260	115	177	24	13	12	19	5	4.19

	BA	OBA	SA	AB	H	2B	3B	HR	RBI	BB	SO
Totals	.257	.324	.384	5499	1415	245	50	117	686	542	927
vs. Left	.269	.338	.404	2791	750	124	31	64	361	295	442
vs. Right	.246	.309	.363	2708	665	121	19	53	325	247	485
Home	.260	.319	.397	2931	763	124	26	75	373	257	501
Road	.254	.329	.369	2568	652	121	24	42	313	285	426
Bases Empty	.244	.308	.365	3111	760	141	23	63	63	273	536
Leadoff	.263	.340	.399	1311	345	64	12	30	30	142	200
Runners On Base	.274	.343	.408	2388	655	104	27	54	623	269	391
Scoring Position	.275	.354	.407	1443	397	60	19	31	548	200	240
Late and Close	.269	.346	.402	1083	291	44	11	26	149	126	229

Cincinnati Pitching

	G	IP	H	BB	SO	SB	CS	W	L	S	ERA
Totals	516	1440.0	1372	560	997	140	60	74	88	43	3.83
at Home	273	737.0	696	321	482	68	32	39	42	26	4.24
on Road	243	703.0	676	239	515	72	28	35	46	17	3.41
on Grass	139	421.1	403	141	312	44	16	22	26	7	3.33
on Turf	377	1018.2	969	419	685	96	44	52	62	36	4.04
Day Games	135	381.0	373	148	256	36	19	20	23	11	3.92
Night Games	381	1059.0	999	412	741	104	41	54	65	32	3.80
April	55	174.0	144	46	119	16	9	11	8	9	2.95
May	80	234.0	227	94	159	25	11	12	15	8	4.08
June	98	251.0	233	113	171	22	13	18	10	13	3.69
July	81	210.2	226	82	125	25	12	8	16	3	4.57
August	93	281.2	250	112	213	20	7	15	16	5	3.55
Sept–Oct	109	288.2	292	113	210	32	8	10	23	5	4.02

	BA	OBA	SA	AB	H	2B	3B	HR	RBI	BB	SO
Totals	.253	.323	.379	5420	1372	231	35	127	647	560	997
vs. Left	.256	.339	.379	2264	579	105	18	46	280	284	432
vs. Right	.251	.312	.379	3156	793	126	17	81	367	276	565
Home	.252	.329	.389	2758	696	113	17	77	358	321	482
Road	.254	.317	.368	2662	676	118	18	50	289	239	515
Bases Empty	.240	.307	.365	3152	757	128	18	77	77	284	591
Leadoff	.247	.314	.373	1315	325	44	7	36	36	120	237
Runners On Base	.271	.345	.398	2268	615	103	17	50	570	276	406
Scoring Position	.270	.351	.379	1334	360	65	9	21	492	192	274
Late and Close	.269	.345	.371	825	222	33	6	13	99	97	199

Houston Pitching

	G	IP	H	BB	SO	SB	CS	W	L	S	ERA
Totals	527	1453.0	1347	651	1033	143	61	65	97	36	4.00
at Home	266	754.0	648	318	551	71	31	37	44	15	3.55
on Road	261	699.0	699	333	482	72	30	28	53	21	4.49
on Grass	152	410.0	399	205	283	39	20	18	30	12	4.26
on Turf	375	1043.0	948	446	750	104	41	47	67	24	3.90
Day Games	127	350.2	323	164	261	29	11	14	26	8	4.03
Night Games	400	1102.1	1024	487	772	114	50	51	71	28	3.99
April	64	172.2	156	73	104	17	5	8	11	5	3.96
May	84	246.0	235	122	169	32	10	10	18	7	4.28
June	88	258.0	214	109	168	29	16	11	17	6	3.28
July	75	219.1	220	96	152	15	5	12	13	5	3.94
August	96	265.0	256	122	221	25	14	12	17	4	4.38
Sept–Oct	120	292.0	266	129	219	25	11	12	21	9	4.13

	BA	OBA	SA	AB	H	2B	3B	HR	RBI	BB	SO
Totals	.247	.328	.374	5454	1347	248	30	129	665	651	1033
vs. Left	.254	.343	.379	2781	707	122	19	62	345	378	539
vs. Right	.239	.311	.370	2673	640	126	11	67	320	273	494
Home	.234	.313	.339	2775	648	126	18	44	306	318	551
Road	.261	.343	.411	2679	699	122	12	85	359	333	482
Bases Empty	.235	.314	.356	3063	721	129	12	72	72	340	606
Leadoff	.246	.330	.378	1295	318	61	7	32	32	158	226
Runners On Base	.262	.344	.398	2391	626	119	18	57	593	311	427
Scoring Position	.259	.359	.400	1438	373	77	10	35	521	246	276
Late and Close	.249	.345	.368	951	237	45	7	18	141	140	188

Los Angeles Pitching

	G	IP	H	BB	SO	SB	CS	W	L	S	ERA
Totals	529	1458.0	1312	500	1028	145	60	93	69	40	3.07
at Home	262	750.0	671	256	566	74	33	54	27	21	3.04
on Road	267	708.0	641	244	462	71	27	39	42	19	3.10
on Grass	392	1097.0	985	366	788	110	41	75	45	33	3.04
on Turf	137	361.0	327	134	240	35	19	18	24	7	3.14
Day Games	169	465.2	432	173	325	48	19	28	25	11	3.17
Night Games	360	992.1	880	327	703	97	41	65	44	29	3.02
April	56	176.0	157	47	128	10	6	10	10	2	2.97
May	85	237.0	230	97	166	26	11	17	10	11	3.11
June	83	252.1	213	90	177	37	16	18	9	9	2.75
July	85	229.2	220	84	139	25	8	13	13	3	3.45
August	102	264.1	234	81	186	18	7	13	16	6	3.37
Sept–Oct	118	298.2	258	101	232	29	12	22	11	9	2.80

	BA	OBA	SA	AB	H	2B	3B	HR	RBI	BB	SO
Totals	.241	.306	.341	5448	1312	202	28	96	529	500	1028
vs. Left	.247	.318	.342	2643	653	97	17	40	244	270	476
vs. Right	.235	.295	.340	2805	659	105	11	56	285	230	552
Home	.240	.303	.328	2799	671	90	9	46	265	256	566
Road	.242	.309	.355	2649	641	112	19	50	264	244	462
Bases Empty	.242	.297	.348	3191	771	124	14	63	63	236	608
Leadoff	.245	.296	.352	1365	335	50	6	28	28	90	253
Runners On Base	.240	.318	.331	2257	541	78	14	33	466	264	420
Scoring Position	.232	.326	.321	1322	307	42	12	17	421	194	273
Late and Close	.232	.311	.326	969	225	39	8	12	102	110	196

Montreal Pitching

	G	IP	H	BB	SO	SB	CS	W	L	S	ERA
Totals	528	1440.1	1304	584	909	149	81	71	90	39	3.64
at Home	223	639.0	530	238	425	69	36	33	35	16	2.86
on Road	305	801.1	774	346	484	80	45	38	55	23	4.27
on Grass	153	401.0	393	171	230	34	20	19	27	14	4.49
on Turf	375	1039.1	911	413	679	115	61	52	63	25	3.32
Day Games	168	434.2	399	173	292	52	19	19	30	12	3.95
Night Games	360	1005.2	905	411	617	97	62	52	60	27	3.51
April	67	175.0	160	80	82	18	14	7	13	4	3.75
May	89	249.0	217	87	164	16	11	13	14	5	3.76
June	97	258.0	259	99	172	41	15	13	15	8	3.70
July	76	222.1	194	85	142	16	10	10	15	6	3.08
August	93	248.1	216	106	151	20	13	9	19	6	3.77
Sept–Oct	106	287.2	258	127	198	38	18	19	14	10	3.75

	BA	OBA	SA	AB	H	2B	3B	HR	RBI	BB	SO
Totals	.244	.320	.368	5345	1304	254	39	111	600	584	909
vs. Left	.251	.333	.380	2255	565	113	24	44	259	282	366
vs. Right	.239	.311	.360	3090	739	141	15	67	341	302	543
Home	.229	.302	.334	2318	530	106	20	33	214	238	425
Road	.256	.334	.394	3027	774	148	19	78	386	346	484
Bases Empty	.239	.312	.353	3058	731	141	16	58	58	311	514
Leadoff	.250	.316	.367	1318	330	68	7	24	24	121	220
Runners On Base	.251	.331	.390	2287	573	113	23	53	542	273	395
Scoring Position	.248	.342	.388	1377	342	63	15	33	474	198	258
Late and Close	.241	.322	.336	1044	252	47	8	12	120	119	173

New York Pitching

	G	IP	H	BB	SO	SB	CS	W	L	S	ERA
Totals	475	1437.1	1403	410	1028	134	74	77	84	39	3.56
at Home	255	750.0	760	215	554	71	41	40	42	21	3.74
on Road	220	687.1	643	195	474	63	33	37	42	18	3.37
on Grass	345	1036.1	1013	292	735	94	53	54	61	28	3.58
on Turf	130	401.0	390	118	293	40	21	23	23	11	3.52
Day Games	153	471.1	470	131	349	39	29	24	29	12	3.69
Night Games	322	966.0	933	279	679	95	45	53	55	27	3.50
April	56	178.0	164	52	120	14	12	12	8	7	3.03
May	68	226.0	227	64	160	25	12	14	11	7	3.58
June	81	247.2	263	72	174	31	12	13	15	6	4.22
July	71	236.0	200	62	189	16	15	16	11	7	2.86
August	101	257.1	284	83	189	20	11	8	21	4	4.27
Sept–Oct	98	292.1	265	77	196	28	12	14	18	8	3.26

	BA	OBA	SA	AB	H	2B	3B	HR	RBI	BB	SO
Totals	.257	.309	.374	5466	1403	226	46	108	601	410	1028
vs. Left	.258	.313	.364	2410	622	106	21	36	237	197	448
vs. Right	.256	.306	.382	3056	781	0	25	72	364	213	580
Home	.263	.314	.380	2886	760	113	29	55	327	215	554
Road	.249	.303	.368	2580	643	113	17	53	274	195	474
Bases Empty	.252	.302	.365	3151	793	139	25	56	56	214	580
Leadoff	.272	.313	.400	1359	369	63	12	29	29	76	243
Runners On Base	.263	.319	.387	2315	610	87	21	52	545	196	448
Scoring Position	.254	.327	.372	1365	347	42	13	31	471	159	288
Late and Close	.258	.308	.362	921	238	36	7	15	99	67	167

Philadelphia Pitching

	G	IP	H	BB	SO	SB	CS	W	L	S	ERA
Totals	483	1463.0	1346	670	988	151	47	78	84	35	3.86
at Home	252	773.0	702	347	536	79	22	47	36	18	3.64
on Road	231	690.0	644	323	452	72	25	31	48	17	4.11
on Grass	134	369.0	342	174	243	40	13	17	25	10	4.05
on Turf	349	1094.0	1004	496	745	111	34	61	59	25	3.80
Day Games	144	410.2	390	192	277	46	10	20	26	12	4.32
Night Games	339	1052.1	956	478	711	105	37	58	58	23	3.69
April	73	194.0	161	118	113	33	5	9	12	5	4.31
May	74	238.1	199	95	164	21	7	13	13	6	2.83
June	87	249.0	264	135	161	24	10	10	18	6	4.99
July	64	220.0	212	82	144	21	8	10	15	6	3.44
August	88	265.2	254	122	190	28	8	20	9	6	3.69
Sept–Oct	97	296.0	256	118	216	24	9	16	17	6	3.92

	BA	OBA	SA	AB	H	2B	3B	HR	RBI	BB	SO
Totals	.246	.329	.367	5480	1346	261	36	111	634	670	988
vs. Left	.247	.344	.368	2236	552	102	18	44	273	330	381
vs. Right	.245	.319	.367	3244	794	159	18	67	361	340	607
Home	.244	.328	.358	2877	702	140	14	53	319	347	536
Road	.247	.331	.378	2603	644	121	22	58	315	323	452
Bases Empty	.242	.324	.363	3027	732	137	19	64	64	342	537
Leadoff	.233	.316	.347	1307	304	67	10	21	21	148	213
Runners On Base	.250	.336	.372	2453	614	124	17	47	570	328	451
Scoring Position	.241	.338	.367	1454	350	77	10	29	508	234	283
Late and Close	.237	.341	.345	1028	244	48	3	19	106	156	199

Pittsburgh Pitching

	G	IP	H	BB	SO	SB	CS	W	L	S	ERA
Totals	515	1456.2	1411	401	919	142	73	98	64	51	3.44
at Home	250	765.0	721	196	508	73	43	52	32	26	3.14
on Road	265	691.2	690	205	411	69	30	46	32	25	3.77
on Grass	147	372.2	379	121	218	30	20	20	22	12	4.27
on Turf	368	1084.0	1032	280	701	112	53	78	42	39	3.15
Day Games	139	408.1	404	98	247	39	18	26	20	15	3.79
Night Games	376	1048.1	1007	303	672	103	55	72	44	36	3.31
April	60	178.0	156	53	93	20	5	13	7	5	3.29
May	81	225.0	207	61	146	27	13	17	8	9	3.28
June	88	237.0	243	60	152	19	8	15	12	11	3.15
July	82	242.2	232	91	161	31	16	15	12	5	3.86
August	91	264.0	251	59	161	20	17	17	12	10	3.14
Sept—Oct	113	310.0	322	77	206	25	14	21	13	11	3.80

	BA	OBA	SA	AB	H	2B	3B	HR	RBI	BB	SO
Totals	.256	.308	.373	5522	1411	236	32	117	592	401	919
vs. Left	.262	.318	.367	2012	528	81	11	36	205	159	336
vs. Right	.252	.302	.377	3510	883	155	21	81	387	242	583
Home	.251	.302	.366	2870	721	122	21	55	295	196	508
Road	.260	.314	.382	2652	690	114	11	62	297	205	411
Bases Empty	.243	.296	.353	3239	788	133	17	63	63	226	533
Leadoff	.260	.309	.378	1363	354	62	6	29	29	91	214
Runners On Base	.273	.323	.402	2283	623	103	15	54	529	175	386
Scoring Position	.269	.335	.390	1310	352	60	9	27	456	137	220
Late and Close	.252	.321	.367	979	247	34	3	24	116	91	168

San Diego Pitching

	G	IP	H	BB	SO	SB	CS	W	L	S	ERA
Totals	496	1452.2	1385	457	921	109	65	84	78	47	3.58
at Home	254	744.0	691	232	501	49	34	42	39	22	3.48
on Road	242	708.2	694	225	420	60	31	42	39	25	3.68
on Grass	361	1080.1	1027	336	676	72	47	62	58	34	3.67
on Turf	135	372.1	358	121	245	37	18	22	20	13	3.34
Day Games	134	407.2	416	127	245	34	18	26	20	15	3.84
Night Games	362	1045.0	969	330	676	75	47	58	58	32	3.48
April	68	188.1	197	63	126	10	5	11	10	8	4.25
May	92	257.0	263	103	152	26	18	13	15	4	4.20
June	75	246.2	231	71	131	11	14	14	14	5	3.47
July	70	213.2	190	78	125	23	8	10	14	5	3.45
August	86	263.0	235	64	186	20	15	15	14	9	3.35
Sept—Oct	105	284.0	269	78	201	19	5	21	11	14	2.98

	BA	OBA	SA	AB	H	2B	3B	HR	RBI	BB	SO
Totals	.252	.308	.375	5499	1385	197	32	139	607	457	921
vs. Left	.245	.305	.372	2234	548	74	18	58	245	201	389
vs. Right	.256	.310	.377	3265	837	123	14	81	362	256	532
Home	.246	.304	.366	2808	691	95	13	72	297	232	501
Road	.258	.313	.385	2691	694	102	19	67	310	225	420
Bases Empty	.249	.302	.377	3270	814	117	20	87	87	242	560
Leadoff	.243	.295	.392	1357	330	49	12	43	43	96	208
Runners On Base	.256	.317	.373	2229	571	80	12	52	520	215	361
Scoring Position	.251	.326	.361	1204	302	44	7	25	446	152	211
Late and Close	.237	.302	.324	972	230	34	3	15	114	93	185

St. Louis Pitching

	G	IP	H	BB	SO	SB	CS	W	L	S	ERA
Totals	531	1435.1	1367	454	822	121	81	84	78	51	3.69
at Home	275	771.0	693	229	426	66	45	52	32	29	3.15
on Road	256	664.1	674	225	396	55	36	32	46	22	4.31
on Grass	132	354.2	372	113	210	24	16	15	27	7	4.62
on Turf	399	1080.2	995	341	612	97	65	69	51	44	3.38
Day Games	143	402.0	379	120	235	42	19	25	21	14	3.29
Night Games	388	1033.1	988	334	587	79	62	59	57	37	3.84
April	75	188.0	163	65	117	22	12	13	8	10	3.02
May	86	220.0	231	73	124	24	14	11	14	5	4.99
June	91	251.1	233	74	136	16	14	16	12	8	3.19
July	85	229.0	239	83	129	19	16	13	13	7	4.40
August	93	248.1	236	62	137	8	13	16	12	10	3.37
Sept—Oct	101	298.2	265	97	179	32	12	15	19	11	3.28

	BA	OBA	SA	AB	H	2B	3B	HR	RBI	BB	SO
Totals	.255	.315	.381	5368	1367	251	42	114	615	454	822
vs. Left	.254	.323	.369	2731	695	128	24	46	287	272	376
vs. Right	.255	.307	.392	2637	672	123	18	68	328	182	446
Home	.244	.305	.353	2840	693	134	26	41	275	229	426
Road	.267	.327	.412	2528	674	117	16	73	340	225	396
Bases Empty	.245	.302	.364	3172	778	137	24	64	64	235	497
Leadoff	.245	.301	.372	1332	326	57	10	31	31	96	197
Runners On Base	.268	.333	.405	2196	589	114	18	50	551	219	325
Scoring Position	.267	.343	.407	1279	341	71	11	29	477	165	208
Late and Close	.259	.328	.382	930	241	34	10	20	108	93	160

San Francisco Pitching

	G	IP	H	BB	SO	SB	CS	W	L	S	ERA
Totals	496	1442.0	1397	544	905	129	83	75	87	45	4.03
at Home	235	744.0	653	250	479	50	41	43	38	25	3.41
on Road	261	698.0	744	294	426	79	42	32	49	20	4.69
on Grass	357	1081.0	1013	398	677	89	60	58	62	33	3.75
on Turf	139	361.0	384	146	228	40	23	17	25	12	4.86
Day Games	203	595.0	538	223	382	52	34	36	30	17	3.48
Night Games	293	847.0	859	321	523	77	49	39	57	28	4.42
April	57	173.0	181	75	106	7	9	8	12	4	4.63
May	89	260.2	254	102	156	33	21	8	20	3	4.14
June	84	242.0	219	101	128	20	17	17	10	12	3.12
July	77	211.1	183	76	129	13	8	15	9	10	3.53
August	94	267.2	266	95	193	31	14	14	16	7	4.51
Sept—Oct	95	287.1	294	95	193	25	14	13	20	9	4.26

	BA	OBA	SA	AB	H	2B	3B	HR	RBI	BB	SO
Totals	.257	.326	.390	5435	1397	233	30	143	665	544	905
vs. Left	.269	.341	.401	2238	601	92	14	59	297	252	346
vs. Right	.249	.315	.382	3197	796	141	16	84	368	292	559
Home	.237	.303	.353	2750	653	105	14	62	291	250	479
Road	.277	.350	.427	2685	744	128	16	81	374	294	426
Bases Empty	.251	.315	.386	3124	784	133	11	89	89	271	534
Leadoff	.257	.322	.381	1321	340	54	2	35	35	120	197
Runners On Base	.265	.341	.395	2311	613	100	19	54	576	273	371
Scoring Position	.273	.357	.402	1376	376	60	15	29	509	195	235
Late and Close	.246	.335	.362	894	220	28	2	24	104	118	154

1991 AMERICAN LEAGUE TEAM STATISTICS

BATTING

TEAM	AB	R	H	2B	3B	HR	RBI	SH	SF	HP	BB	IBB	SO	SB	CS	GDP	SHO	BA	SA	OBA
BALTIMORE	5604	686	1421	256	29	170	660	47	45	33	528	33	974	50	33	147	6	.254	.319	.401
BOSTON	5530	731	1486	305	25	126	691	50	51	32	593	49	820	59	39	143	12	.269	.340	.401
CALIFORNIA	5470	653	1396	245	29	115	607	63	31	38	448	28	928	94	56	114	15	.255	.314	.374
CHICAGO	5594	758	1464	226	39	139	722	76	41	37	610	45	896	134	74	132	12	.262	.336	.391
CLEVELAND	5470	576	1390	236	26	79	546	62	46	43	449	24	888	84	58	146	18	.254	.313	.350
DETROIT	5547	817	1372	259	26	209	778	38	44	31	699	40	1185	109	47	90	7	.247	.333	.416
KANSAS CITY	5584	727	1475	290	41	117	689	53	47	35	523	47	969	119	68	126	9	.264	.328	.394
MILWAUKEE	5611	799	1523	247	53	116	750	52	66	23	556	48	802	106	68	137	11	.271	.336	.396
MINNESOTA	5556	776	1557	270	42	140	733	37	49	40	526	38	747	107	68	157	8	.280	.344	.420
NEW YORK	5541	674	1418	249	19	147	630	37	50	39	473	38	861	109	36	125	10	.256	.316	.387
OAKLAND	5410	760	1342	246	19	159	716	41	49	50	642	55	981	151	64	131	14	.248	.331	.389
SEATTLE	5494	702	1400	268	29	126	665	55	62	37	588	57	811	97	44	139	10	.255	.328	.383
TEXAS	5703	829	1539	288	31	177	774	59	41	42	596	51	1039	102	50	128	9	.270	.341	.424
TORONTO	5489	684	1412	295	45	133	649	56	65	58	499	49	1043	148	53	108	9	.257	.322	.400
TOTALS	**77603**	**10172**	**20195**	**3680**	**453**	**1953**	**9610**	**733**	**687**	**538**	**7730**	**602**	**12944**	**1469**	**758**	**1823**	**150**	**.260**	**.329**	**.395**

PITCHING

TEAM	W	L	ERA	G	CG	SHO	REL	SV	IP	H	R	ER	HR	HB	BB	IBB	SO	WP	BK	O/BA
BALTIMORE	67	95	4.59	162	8	8	372	42	1457.2	1534	796	743	147	28	504	40	868	49	8	.273
BOSTON	84	78	4.01	162	15	13	328	45	1439.2	1405	712	642	147	31	530	59	999	42	4	.257
CALIFORNIA	81	81	3.69	162	18	10	310	50	1441.2	1351	649	591	141	38	543	29	990	49	11	.250
CHICAGO	87	75	3.79	162	28	8	338	40	1478.0	1302	681	622	154	31	601	25	923	44	6	.239
CLEVELAND	57	105	4.23	162	22	8	289	33	1441.1	1551	759	678	110	39	441	61	862	48	6	.276
DETROIT	84	78	4.51	162	18	8	326	38	1450.1	1570	794	726	148	24	593	88	739	50	5	.281
KANSAS CITY	82	80	3.92	162	17	12	295	41	1466.0	1473	722	639	105	43	529	44	1004	47	5	.261
MILWAUKEE	83	79	4.14	162	23	11	341	41	1463.2	1498	744	674	147	45	527	31	859	53	5	.266
MINNESOTA	95	67	3.69	162	21	12	291	53	1449.1	1402	652	595	139	27	488	38	876	57	5	.255
NEW YORK	71	91	4.42	162	3	11	377	37	1444.0	1510	777	709	152	42	506	29	936	53	14	.271
OAKLAND	84	78	4.57	162	14	10	397	49	1444.1	1425	776	734	155	55	655	30	892	60	7	.260
SEATTLE	83	79	3.79	162	10	13	383	48	1464.1	1387	674	616	136	47	628	50	1003	82	7	.253
TEXAS	85	77	4.47	162	9	10	386	41	1479.0	1486	814	734	151	45	662	37	1022	77	12	.262
TORONTO	91	71	3.50	162	10	16	347	60	1462.2	1301	622	569	121	43	523	41	971	55	8	.238
TOTALS	**1134**	**1134**	**4.09**	**1134**	**216**	**150**	**4780**	**618**	**20382.0**	**20195**	**10172**	**9272**	**1953**	**538**	**7730**	**602**	**12944**	**766**	**103**	**.260**

FIELDING

TEAM	FA	G	PO	A	E	TC	DP	TP	PB
BALTIMORE	.985	162	4373	1809	91	6273	172	0	8
BOSTON	.981	162	4319	1768	116	6203	165	0	11
CALIFORNIA	.984	162	4325	1858	102	6285	156	0	23
CHICAGO	.982	162	4434	1740	116	6290	151	0	20
CLEVELAND	.976	162	4324	1710	149	6183	150	0	19
DETROIT	.983	162	4351	1796	104	6251	171	0	12
KANSAS CITY	.980	162	4398	1694	125	6217	141	0	11
MILWAUKEE	.981	162	4391	1770	118	6279	176	0	16
MINNESOTA	.985	162	4348	1779	95	6222	161	0	12
NEW YORK	.979	162	4332	1752	133	6217	181	0	13
OAKLAND	.982	162	4333	1608	107	6048	150	0	8
SEATTLE	.983	162	4393	1783	110	6286	187	2	24
TEXAS	.979	162	4437	1711	134	6282	138	0	15
TORONTO	.980	162	4388	1686	127	6201	115	0	21
TOTALS	**.981**	**1134**	**61146**	**24464**	**1627**	**87237**	**2214**	**2**	**213**

1991 NATIONAL LEAGUE TEAM STATISTICS

BATTING

TEAM	AB	R	H	2B	3B	HR	RBI	SH	SF	HP	BB	IBB	SO	SB	CS	GDP	SHO	BA	SA	OBA
ATLANTA	5456	749	1407	255	30	141	704	86	45	32	563	55	906	165	76	104	9	.258	.328	.393
CHICAGO	5522	695	1395	232	26	159	654	75	55	36	442	41	879	123	64	87	4	.253	.309	.390
CINCINNATI	5501	689	1419	250	27	164	654	72	41	32	488	54	1006	124	56	85	9	.258	.320	.403
HOUSTON	5504	605	1345	240	43	79	570	63	43	35	502	45	1027	125	68	87	16	.244	.309	.347
LOS ANGELES	5408	665	1366	191	29	108	605	94	46	28	583	50	957	126	68	109	8	.253	.326	.359
MONTREAL	5412	579	1329	236	42	95	536	64	47	28	484	51	1056	221	100	97	10	.246	.308	.357
NEW YORK	5359	640	1305	250	24	117	605	60	52	27	578	53	789	153	70	97	9	.244	.317	.365
PHILADELPHIA	5521	629	1332	248	33	111	590	52	49	21	490	48	1026	92	30	114	12	.241	.303	.358
PITTSBURGH	5449	768	1433	259	50	126	725	99	66	35	620	62	901	124	46	111	6	.263	.338	.398
SAN DIEGO	5408	636	1321	204	36	121	591	78	38	32	501	60	1069	101	64	122	12	.244	.310	.362
SAN FRANCISCO	5463	649	1345	215	48	141	605	90	33	40	471	59	973	95	57	91	13	.246	.309	.381
ST. LOUIS	5362	651	1366	239	53	68	599	58	47	21	532	48	857	202	110	94	14	.255	.322	.357
TOTALS	**65365**	**7955**	**16363**	**2819**	**441**	**1430**	**7438**	**891**	**562**	**367**	**6254**	**626**	**11446**	**1651**	**809**	**1198**	**122**	**.250**	**.317**	**.373**

PITCHING

TEAM	W	L	ERA	G	CG	SHO	REL	SV	IP	H	R	ER	HR	HB	BB	IBB	SO	WP	BK	O/BA
ATLANTA	94	68	3.49	162	18	7	345	48	1452.2	1304	644	563	118	28	481	39	969	66	13	.240
CHICAGO	77	83	4.03	160	12	4	360	40	1456.2	1415	734	653	117	28	542	64	927	48	12	.257
CINCINNATI	74	88	3.83	162	7	11	354	43	1440.0	1372	691	613	127	28	560	41	997	60	9	.253
HOUSTON	65	97	4.00	162	7	13	365	36	1453.0	1347	717	646	129	29	651	62	1033	46	17	.247
LOS ANGELES	93	69	3.06	162	15	14	367	40	1458.0	1312	565	496	96	28	500	77	1028	48	12	.241
MONTREAL	71	90	3.64	161	12	14	367	39	1440.1	1304	655	583	111	32	584	42	909	51	9	.244
NEW YORK	77	84	3.56	161	12	11	314	39	1437.1	1403	646	568	108	25	410	41	1028	59	14	.257
PHILADELPHIA	78	84	3.86	162	16	11	321	35	1463.0	1346	680	628	111	43	670	58	988	81	6	.246
PITTSBURGH	98	64	3.44	162	18	11	353	51	1456.2	1411	632	557	117	30	401	34	919	40	12	.256
SAN FRANCISCO	75	87	4.03	162	10	10	334	45	1442.0	1397	697	646	143	36	544	60	905	44	14	.257
SAN DIEGO	84	78	3.57	162	14	11	334	47	1452.2	1385	646	577	139	13	457	56	921	49	13	.252
ST. LOUIS	84	78	3.69	162	9	5	369	51	1435.1	1367	648	588	114	47	454	52	822	33	7	.255
TOTALS	**970**	**970**	**3.68**	**970**	**150**	**122**	**4183**	**514**	**17387.2**	**16363**	**7955**	**7118**	**1430**	**367**	**6254**	**626**	**11446**	**625**	**138**	**.250**

FIELDING

TEAM	FA	G	PO	A	E	TC	DP	TP	PB
ATLANTA	.978	162	4358	1834	138	6330	122	0	14
CHICAGO	.982	160	4370	1829	113	6312	120	0	19
CINCINNATI	.979	162	4320	1615	125	6060	131	0	20
HOUSTON	.974	162	4359	1617	161	6137	129	2	16
LOS ANGELES	.980	162	4374	1795	123	6292	126	0	8
MONTREAL	.979	161	4321	1796	133	6250	128	1	22
NEW YORK	.977	161	4312	1766	143	6221	112	0	12
PHILADELPHIA	.981	162	4389	1623	119	6131	111	1	9
PITTSBURGH	.981	162	4370	1846	120	6336	134	0	9
SAN DIEGO	.982	162	4358	1731	113	6202	130	0	9
SAN FRANCISCO	.982	162	4326	1753	109	6188	151	0	9
ST. LOUIS	.982	162	4306	1689	107	6102	133	1	8
TOTALS	**.980**	**970**	**52163**	**20894**	**1504**	**74561**	**1527**	**5**	**155**

TEAM AND LEAGUE STARTING PITCHING/RELIEF PITCHING STATISTICS

		G	IP	H	BB	SO	SB	CS	W	L	S	ERA
AMERICAN LEAGUE	SP	2268	13728.1	13918	5011	8285	1062	590	809	839	0	4.26
	RP	4784	6653.2	6277	2719	4659	407	168	325	295	618	3.77
BALTIMORE	SP	162	900.0	1025	318	479	75	36	42	69	0	5.29
	RP	372	557.2	509	186	389	36	15	25	26	42	3.45
BOSTON	SP	162	984.1	984	341	711	70	41	65	61	0	4.22
	RP	328	455.1	421	189	288	27	12	19	17	45	3.58
CALIFORNIA	SP	162	1042.0	1009	404	660	69	64	70	67	0	3.81
	RP	310	399.2	342	139	330	20	8	11	14	50	3.38
CHICAGO	SP	162	1014.1	927	411	621	71	48	54	55	0	4.23
	RP	338	463.2	375	190	302	25	19	33	20	40	2.85
CLEVELAND	SP	162	1032.1	1124	261	596	76	39	42	79	0	4.21
	RP	289	409.0	427	180	266	26	8	15	26	33	4.31
DETROIT	SP	162	961.1	1074	333	436	63	39	60	60	0	4.46
	RP	328	489.0	496	260	303	25	17	24	18	38	4.69
KANSAS CITY	SP	162	1002.2	990	327	638	67	48	63	59	0	3.98
	RP	295	463.1	483	202	366	27	8	19	21	41	3.81
MILWAUKEE	SP	162	974.2	1012	314	502	84	29	62	52	0	4.17
	RP	341	489.0	486	213	357	31	18	21	27	41	4.18
MINNESOTA	SP	162	1000.2	982	324	582	90	33	71	51	0	3.77
	RP	291	448.2	420	164	294	28	10	24	16	53	3.53
NEW YORK	SP	162	892.0	984	304	528	89	37	45	68	0	5.07
	RP	377	552.0	526	202	408	45	14	26	23	37	3.41
OAKLAND	SP	162	986.2	965	460	585	82	54	56	56	0	4.50
	RP	398	457.2	460	195	307	34	6	28	22	49	4.74
SEATTLE	SP	162	974.2	961	432	688	60	38	60	59	0	4.11
	RP	383	489.2	426	196	315	24	6	23	20	48	3.16
TEXAS	SP	162	948.0	968	442	653	83	44	52	53	0	4.63
	RP	387	531.0	518	220	369	24	14	33	24	41	4.19
TORONTO	SP	162	1014.2	913	340	606	83	40	67	50	0	3.49
	RP	347	448.0	388	183	365	35	13	24	21	60	3.52

		G	IP	H	BB	SO	SB	CS	W	L	S	ERA
NATIONAL LEAGUE	SP	1940	11854.1	11252	4002	7512	1148	596	686	691	0	3.73
	RP	4183	5533.1	5111	2252	3934	503	212	284	279	514	3.60
ATLANTA	SP	162	1009.0	897	310	661	105	50	72	49	0	3.46
	RP	345	443.2	407	171	308	44	9	22	19	48	3.57
CHICAGO	SP	160	957.0	972	331	542	89	43	48	54	0	4.35
	RP	360	499.2	443	211	385	50	21	29	29	40	3.46
CINCINNATI	SP	162	966.0	930	359	614	83	34	59	65	0	3.98
	RP	354	474.0	442	201	383	57	26	15	23	43	3.53
HOUSTON	SP	162	956.1	884	402	666	108	42	45	63	0	4.07
	RP	365	496.2	463	249	367	35	19	20	34	36	3.86
LOS ANGELES	SP	162	1023.0	926	332	679	99	49	65	48	0	3.06
	RP	367	435.0	386	168	349	46	11	28	21	40	3.08
MONTREAL	SP	161	998.2	892	403	622	110	64	49	59	0	3.56
	RP	367	441.2	412	181	287	39	17	22	31	39	3.83
NEW YORK	SP	161	1017.2	1007	277	748	106	59	57	65	0	3.71
	RP	314	419.2	396	133	280	28	15	20	19	39	3.22
PHILADELPHIA	SP	162	964.0	900	419	631	95	39	51	63	0	3.99
	RP	321	499.0	446	251	357	56	8	27	21	35	3.63
PITTSBURGH	SP	162	1005.0	991	244	594	103	56	67	44	0	3.27
	RP	353	451.2	420	157	325	39	17	31	20	51	3.83
ST. LOUIS	SP	162	1001.1	942	300	557	86	61	54	57	0	3.54
	RP	369	434.0	425	154	265	35	20	30	21	51	4.02
SAN DIEGO	SP	162	1011.1	978	285	636	82	42	65	61	0	3.68
	RP	334	441.1	407	172	285	27	23	19	17	47	3.36
SAN FRANCISCO	SP	162	945.0	933	340	562	82	57	54	63	0	4.18
	RP	334	497.0	464	204	343	47	26	21	24	45	3.75

TEAM BATTING BY LINEUP ORDER

AMERICAN LEAGUE

TEAM	POS	AB	H	2B	3B	HR	RBI	BB	SO	BA	OBA	SA
BALTIMORE	P1	688	176	32	11	16	58	63	130	.256	.318	.404
	P2	667	163	29	3	10	61	59	102	.244	.309	.342
	P3	660	212	46	5	34	114	54	50	.321	.372	.561
	P4	624	163	30	1	28	108	74	122	.261	.345	.447
	P5	582	145	24	3	17	74	96	110	.249	.359	.388
	P6	615	167	23	1	28	88	58	123	.272	.336	.449
	P7	598	133	26	2	19	61	50	120	.222	.282	.368
	P8	596	144	24	0	11	52	40	114	.242	.288	.337
	P9	574	118	22	3	7	44	34	103	.206	.250	.291
BOSTON	P1	670	216	49	5	12	52	92	53	.322	.403	.464
	P2	661	178	43	1	9	72	69	74	.269	.339	.378
	P3	629	179	30	4	20	95	87	89	.285	.369	.440
	P4	605	146	27	2	28	103	98	157	.241	.348	.431
	P5	624	191	36	3	13	94	53	62	.306	.364	.436
	P6	609	147	34	2	24	98	58	95	.241	.305	.422
	P7	591	163	35	4	7	71	55	103	.276	.339	.384
	P8	587	134	29	1	6	56	38	70	.228	.278	.312
	P9	554	132	22	3	7	50	43	117	.238	.296	.327
CLEVELAND	P1	637	175	28	4	5	36	93	95	.275	.368	.355
	P2	656	152	26	2	1	54	47	88	.232	.285	.282
	P3	640	185	25	3	7	70	48	94	.289	.340	.370
	P4	637	169	32	2	28	103	39	134	.265	.313	.454
	P5	621	148	28	3	14	69	43	102	.238	.288	.361
	P6	597	156	29	5	13	67	49	92	.261	.319	.392
	P7	581	143	30	1	7	58	50	103	.246	.311	.337
	P8	554	119	20	3	3	44	41	104	.215	.278	.278
	P9	547	143	18	3	1	45	39	76	.261	.309	.311
DETROIT	P1	675	182	31	6	13	69	87	121	.270	.354	.391
	P2	653	187	41	4	26	101	92	70	.286	.374	.481
	P3	654	155	39	1	25	97	74	119	.237	.317	.414
	P4	634	164	26	0	44	134	79	153	.259	.344	.508
	P5	593	154	18	2	36	94	106	153	.260	.371	.479
	P6	606	133	25	3	27	90	77	165	.219	.307	.404
	P7	594	142	30	3	18	76	63	162	.239	.314	.391
	P8	576	110	29	2	13	71	68	134	.191	.276	.316
	P9	562	145	20	5	7	46	53	108	.258	.324	.349
MILWAUKEE	P1	683	218	32	13	18	78	79	63	.319	.394	.483
	P2	662	210	31	7	4	91	78	49	.317	.387	.403
	P3	663	164	24	7	6	99	50	83	.247	.295	.332
	P4	633	152	29	2	17	94	69	124	.240	.312	.373
	P5	620	157	28	2	23	101	62	108	.253	.320	.416
	P6	616	164	24	9	13	68	56	106	.266	.327	.398
	P7	608	161	26	4	17	84	47	92	.265	.317	.415
	P8	574	150	27	3	10	55	59	81	.261	.329	.371
	P9	552	147	26	6	8	80	56	96	.266	.333	.379
NEW YORK	P1	677	176	37	3	11	58	63	97	.260	.325	.372
	P2	671	191	32	3	12	64	48	62	.285	.331	.395
	P3	641	182	38	0	12	86	60	61	.284	.347	.399
	P4	617	168	25	3	26	87	74	93	.272	.349	.449
	P5	622	153	25	2	33	100	53	118	.246	.304	.452
	P6	611	146	24	0	20	76	41	109	.239	.294	.376
	P7	574	126	18	0	20	69	57	124	.220	.290	.355
	P8	572	131	22	2	8	43	41	107	.229	.285	.316
	P9	556	145	28	6	5	47	36	90	.261	.311	.360
TORONTO	P1	680	189	41	10	17	61	57	142	.278	.337	.443
	P2	658	189	41	11	10	76	55	94	.287	.344	.429
	P3	646	172	35	5	30	99	51	108	.266	.327	.475
	P4	617	158	36	1	22	88	66	102	.256	.332	.425
	P5	590	146	31	4	13	76	81	104	.247	.340	.380
	P6	595	146	27	4	19	80	56	125	.245	.312	.400
	P7	592	145	38	3	7	62	51	128	.245	.307	.355
	P8	570	139	22	2	13	65	45	132	.244	.298	.358
	P9	541	128	24	5	2	42	37	108	.237	.293	.311

TEAM	POS	AB	H	2B	3B	HR	RBI	BB	SO	BA	OBA	SA
CALIFORNIA	P1	671	197	29	8	4	58	61	79	.294	.352	.379
	P2	651	173	35	3	14	86	53	88	.266	.322	.393
	P3	635	189	35	6	23	103	60	85	.298	.356	.480
	P4	635	140	27	2	21	82	49	139	.220	.276	.369
	P5	619	156	28	1	20	80	46	112	.252	.308	.397
	P6	598	136	22	2	15	58	53	137	.227	.297	.346
	P7	595	158	27	2	11	53	28	111	.266	.302	.373
	P8	544	121	26	3	6	49	50	94	.222	.295	.314
	P9	522	126	16	2	1	38	48	83	.241	.314	.285
CHICAGO	P1	667	177	22	6	6	55	91	76	.265	.356	.343
	P2	669	177	23	1	21	98	72	80	.265	.338	.396
	P3	605	178	28	1	29	95	129	113	.294	.419	.488
	P4	630	157	34	6	24	110	82	116	.249	.340	.437
	P5	618	157	27	4	22	104	82	128	.254	.342	.417
	P6	624	167	25	6	14	80	53	123	.268	.326	.394
	P7	618	145	21	9	11	57	39	131	.235	.283	.351
	P8	582	140	22	2	7	57	40	85	.241	.289	.321
	P9	581	166	24	4	5	66	22	44	.286	.314	.367
KANSAS CITY	P1	705	188	34	5	7	59	44	113	.267	.311	.359
	P2	670	183	37	8	12	81	58	113	.273	.337	.406
	P3	646	172	47	4	14	79	72	104	.266	.336	.416
	P4	624	190	39	3	33	114	80	132	.304	.382	.535
	P5	636	172	37	5	12	87	54	88	.270	.328	.401
	P6	608	169	21	7	10	79	61	91	.278	.349	.385
	P7	581	148	34	1	12	72	52	104	.255	.317	.379
	P8	569	132	20	2	9	62	55	117	.232	.300	.322
	P9	545	121	21	6	8	56	47	107	.222	.287	.327
MINNESOTA	P1	687	180	24	11	12	73	62	92	.262	.325	.381
	P2	659	183	29	5	5	66	71	52	.278	.351	.360
	P3	670	211	33	7	20	104	34	85	.315	.349	.475
	P4	606	172	30	1	29	116	94	73	.284	.377	.480
	P5	615	181	40	1	23	95	67	118	.294	.364	.475
	P6	608	178	34	9	16	84	53	73	.293	.353	.457
	P7	588	167	28	2	18	80	48	86	.284	.342	.430
	P8	566	146	28	4	9	58	56	84	.258	.326	.369
	P9	557	139	24	2	8	57	41	84	.250	.301	.343
OAKLAND	P1	629	165	25	3	18	66	117	96	.262	.383	.397
	P2	680	172	36	0	23	88	56	135	.253	.316	.407
	P3	638	167	32	1	46	129	85	167	.262	.354	.531
	P4	613	168	33	1	20	108	90	91	.274	.364	.429
	P5	606	158	32	2	15	80	70	106	.261	.335	.394
	P6	594	124	24	3	10	73	58	111	.209	.283	.310
	P7	567	133	32	2	10	72	62	91	.235	.311	.351
	P8	551	126	18	4	13	56	52	97	.229	.297	.347
	P9	532	129	14	3	4	44	52	87	.242	.316	.303
SEATTLE	P1	668	172	39	3	14	58	79	74	.257	.338	.388
	P2	653	172	29	7	8	60	70	86	.263	.337	.366
	P3	632	211	45	1	24	115	79	90	.334	.404	.522
	P4	621	171	35	2	16	95	67	103	.275	.346	.415
	P5	623	137	18	2	18	78	56	101	.220	.283	.342
	P6	583	140	31	4	18	71	79	121	.240	.334	.400
	P7	590	140	27	5	18	80	55	94	.237	.301	.392
	P8	569	129	24	2	1	49	53	80	.227	.294	.281
	P9	555	128	20	3	9	59	50	62	.231	.299	.326
TEXAS	P1	679	163	20	6	23	71	88	138	.240	.334	.389
	P2	671	211	40	4	17	85	79	90	.314	.390	.462
	P3	685	216	49	4	21	108	56	86	.315	.364	.491
	P4	656	196	37	4	28	111	71	114	.299	.367	.495
	P5	648	179	34	1	33	115	60	131	.276	.342	.485
	P6	617	145	30	5	22	88	68	134	.235	.315	.407
	P7	599	152	28	2	22	80	65	138	.254	.330	.417
	P8	602	152	31	2	8	68	39	104	.253	.298	.351
	P9	546	125	19	3	3	48	70	104	.229	.317	.291

AMERICAN LEAGUE TOTALS	POS	AB	H	2B	3B	HR	RBI	BB	SO	BA	OBA	SA
	P1	9416	2574	443	94	176	852	1076	1369	.273	.350	.396
	P2	9281	2541	472	59	172	1083	907	1183	.274	.341	.393
	P3	9044	2593	506	49	311	1393	939	1334	.287	.353	.457
	P4	8752	2314	440	30	364	1453	1032	1653	.264	.343	.446
	P5	8617	2234	406	35	292	1247	929	1541	.259	.332	.416
	P6	8481	2118	373	60	249	1100	820	1605	.250	.318	.396
	P7	8276	2056	400	40	197	975	722	1587	.248	.311	.378
	P8	8012	1873	342	32	117	785	677	1403	.234	.295	.328
	P9	7724	1892	298	54	75	722	628	1269	.245	.305	.327

NATIONAL LEAGUE

TEAM	POS	AB	H	2B	3B	HR	RBI	BB	SO	BA	OBA	SA
CHICAGO	P1	672	163	22	2	8	41	55	100	.243	.303	.317
	P2	650	184	30	6	12	58	69	68	.283	.349	.403
	P3	604	169	31	1	21	105	89	76	.280	.370	.439
	P4	649	175	22	1	33	109	34	94	.270	.304	.459
	P5	643	179	33	4	25	100	35	79	.278	.320	.459
	P6	625	152	33	2	24	78	40	120	.243	.290	.418
	P7	594	148	25	4	15	58	36	103	.249	.290	.380
	P8	558	128	24	3	12	55	51	81	.229	.305	.348
	P9	527	97	12	3	9	50	33	158	.184	.233	.269
MONTREAL	P1	641	149	21	9	10	48	92	153	.232	.329	.340
	P2	667	191	32	6	7	56	45	109	.286	.332	.384
	P3	619	193	30	8	20	90	67	91	.312	.378	.483
	P4	628	144	26	0	17	86	49	110	.229	.291	.352
	P5	618	164	39	4	12	74	42	113	.265	.313	.400
	P6	604	155	22	6	10	49	46	102	.257	.310	.363
	P7	576	124	25	2	11	58	47	128	.215	.273	.323
	P8	537	130	32	6	6	47	61	97	.242	.317	.358
	P9	522	79	9	1	2	28	35	153	.151	.206	.184
NEW YORK	P1	668	171	36	7	6	43	71	107	.256	.330	.358
	P2	615	167	34	3	10	70	92	80	.272	.366	.385
	P3	627	163	27	4	19	90	71	79	.260	.332	.407
	P4	615	163	40	1	25	94	67	90	.265	.338	.455
	P5	599	144	27	3	27	95	68	83	.240	.314	.431
	P6	595	148	16	2	12	67	55	74	.249	.314	.343
	P7	554	138	26	2	3	55	72	74	.249	.334	.320
	P8	555	118	26	2	8	55	54	81	.213	.288	.310
	P9	531	93	18	0	7	36	28	121	.175	.218	.249
PHILADELPHIA	P1	665	177	32	9	4	28	78	78	.266	.345	.359
	P2	643	159	27	3	5	62	67	107	.247	.318	.322
	P3	646	169	28	8	19	83	62	114	.262	.325	.418
	P4	634	174	33	3	24	96	63	126	.274	.338	.450
	P5	621	153	42	3	16	95	58	103	.246	.311	.401
	P6	599	149	36	3	22	101	54	103	.249	.311	.429
	P7	598	132	23	2	10	54	35	111	.221	.264	.316
	P8	583	141	17	2	8	46	36	88	.242	.284	.319
	P9	532	78	10	0	3	25	37	196	.147	.204	.182
PITTSBURGH	P1	663	174	31	4	16	71	86	121	.262	.351	.394
	P2	655	180	38	8	17	72	56	108	.275	.334	.435
	P3	624	164	29	8	18	94	86	111	.263	.349	.421
	P4	604	180	45	6	19	104	95	69	.298	.390	.487
	P5	577	173	30	5	29	129	106	80	.300	.404	.520
	P6	614	148	24	7	14	78	57	110	.241	.308	.371
	P7	587	165	26	3	6	69	63	71	.281	.351	.366
	P8	588	152	23	6	3	64	40	77	.259	.305	.333
	P9	537	97	13	3	4	44	31	154	.181	.227	.238
ST. LOUIS	P1	676	167	31	11	10	67	56	119	.247	.305	.370
	P2	615	177	35	3	4	59	92	49	.288	.382	.374
	P3	636	163	28	11	11	80	63	111	.256	.324	.387
	P4	622	167	23	1	12	98	62	71	.268	.331	.367
	P5	617	184	42	7	9	81	46	112	.298	.344	.433
	P6	589	144	25	5	11	59	54	106	.244	.309	.360
	P7	571	139	26	9	5	65	39	85	.243	.296	.347
	P8	515	125	15	4	4	46	83	72	.243	.346	.311
	P9	521	100	14	2	2	44	37	132	.192	.244	.238

TEAM	POS	AB	H	2B	3B	HR	RBI	BB	SO	BA	OBA	SA
ATLANTA	P1	667	199	20	4	12	61	74	88	.298	.371	.394
	P2	663	183	30	5	12	73	57	76	.276	.333	.391
	P3	643	185	37	6	20	90	61	94	.288	.353	.457
	P4	608	164	36	3	37	133	84	120	.270	.361	.521
	P5	599	171	40	1	24	111	77	100	.285	.366	.476
	P6	584	134	21	5	20	84	81	73	.229	.321	.385
	P7	590	140	34	2	11	77	50	90	.237	.299	.358
	P8	575	141	21	2	4	48	39	96	.245	.294	.310
	P9	527	90	16	2	1	27	40	169	.171	.231	.214
CINCINNATI	P1	680	180	28	1	14	59	57	103	.265	.323	.371
	P2	641	184	28	5	24	76	70	92	.287	.358	.459
	P3	634	179	34	4	18	84	69	94	.282	.355	.434
	P4	605	173	41	1	28	98	81	123	.286	.373	.496
	P5	616	163	32	3	25	100	51	103	.265	.320	.448
	P6	614	164	26	5	16	77	41	108	.267	.316	.404
	P7	590	142	26	5	16	71	52	115	.241	.302	.383
	P8	575	138	21	3	14	58	43	97	.240	.293	.360
	P9	546	96	14	0	9	31	24	171	.176	.211	.251
HOUSTON	P1	684	175	30	9	8	51	54	98	.256	.309	.361
	P2	658	171	18	7	4	55	55	82	.260	.318	.327
	P3	631	177	30	6	13	77	66	98	.281	.354	.409
	P4	627	153	28	5	13	80	58	124	.244	.316	.367
	P5	610	162	41	4	11	91	66	124	.266	.338	.400
	P6	610	145	24	3	11	68	53	134	.238	.300	.341
	P7	596	151	28	5	11	68	50	125	.253	.311	.372
	P8	572	131	26	4	5	51	49	97	.229	.288	.315
	P9	516	80	15	0	3	29	51	145	.155	.234	.202
LOS ANGELES	P1	640	190	14	5	2	39	110	83	.297	.400	.344
	P2	655	191	30	6	10	68	59	113	.292	.351	.402
	P3	634	156	22	4	23	97	74	138	.246	.320	.402
	P4	622	156	29	1	25	110	70	110	.251	.325	.421
	P5	599	162	17	3	23	86	77	115	.270	.352	.424
	P6	599	159	27	4	7	59	47	67	.265	.323	.359
	P7	561	136	24	1	11	54	61	90	.242	.324	.348
	P8	554	129	16	2	1	47	60	92	.233	.308	.274
	P9	544	87	12	3	6	45	25	149	.160	.199	.226
SAN DIEGO	P1	673	176	23	6	9	52	52	110	.262	.317	.354
	P2	647	168	30	7	8	44	64	95	.260	.326	.365
	P3	648	202	32	12	7	78	47	37	.312	.355	.431
	P4	577	158	21	1	33	113	105	142	.274	.385	.485
	P5	623	163	22	2	19	100	50	130	.262	.317	.395
	P6	611	138	25	3	19	64	38	140	.226	.276	.370
	P7	567	117	23	2	13	63	53	132	.206	.276	.323
	P8	543	132	18	2	8	41	54	100	.243	.319	.328
	P9	519	67	10	1	5	36	38	183	.129	.193	.181
SAN FRANCISCO	P1	661	165	23	12	5	36	64	93	.250	.321	.343
	P2	668	183	38	5	10	64	46	115	.274	.322	.391
	P3	659	204	35	7	31	133	49	105	.310	.357	.525
	P4	615	159	23	3	38	105	65	107	.259	.335	.491
	P5	610	153	20	6	28	89	56	123	.251	.316	.441
	P6	599	141	21	5	16	45	57	107	.235	.305	.367
	P7	570	131	25	2	9	62	44	87	.230	.291	.328
	P8	567	110	15	8	3	39	46	98	.194	.254	.265
	P9	514	99	15	0	1	32	44	138	.193	.260	.228
NATIONAL LEAGUE TOTALS	P1	7990	2086	311	79	104	596	849	1253	.261	.334	.359
	P2	7777	2138	370	64	123	757	772	1094	.275	.341	.386
	P3	7605	2124	363	79	220	1101	804	1148	.279	.348	.435
	P4	7406	1966	367	26	304	1226	833	1286	.265	.341	.445
	P5	7332	1971	385	45	248	1151	732	1265	.269	.335	.435
	P6	7243	1777	300	50	182	829	623	1244	.245	.307	.376
	P7	6954	1663	311	39	121	754	602	1211	.239	.301	.347
	P8	6722	1575	254	44	76	597	616	1076	.234	.300	.319
	P9	6336	1063	158	15	52	427	423	1869	.168	.222	.222

TEAM BATTING BY DEFENSIVE POSITION

AMERICAN LEAGUE

TEAM	POS	AB	H	2B	3B	HR	RBI	BB	SO	BA	OBA	SA
BALTIMORE	C	566	139	26	0	10	50	40	109	.246	.294	.345
	1B	605	162	24	3	20	86	78	100	.268	.355	.417
	2B	522	106	22	3	4	34	27	90	.203	.241	.280
	3B	582	134	24	2	24	66	55	114	.230	.297	.402
	SS	661	211	46	5	34	114	54	50	.319	.370	.558
	LF	629	151	29	2	6	55	55	80	.240	.306	.321
	CF	685	182	31	12	19	67	62	128	.266	.327	.429
	RF	613	159	24	2	15	71	59	108	.259	.325	.378
BOSTON	C	575	135	30	2	5	56	38	68	.235	.286	.320
	1B	592	172	24	1	12	77	79	92	.291	.374	.395
	2B	660	189	43	2	6	65	63	61	.286	.351	.385
	3B	638	207	48	4	8	58	93	44	.324	.407	.450
	SS	531	126	25	3	8	47	47	115	.237	.301	.341
	LF	634	190	32	6	15	104	52	58	.300	.352	.440
	CF	619	152	42	4	17	70	47	102	.246	.303	.409
	RF	594	140	29	2	24	94	63	102	.236	.309	.412
CLEVELAND	C	548	129	28	2	1	44	28	108	.235	.278	.299
	1B	598	141	20	3	10	74	45	108	.236	.287	.329
	2B	629	151	23	4	3	64	38	85	.240	.285	.304
	3B	592	159	27	3	11	62	60	71	.269	.340	.380
	SS	572	160	23	2	0	48	38	54	.280	.325	.327
	LF	593	164	28	2	27	93	57	126	.277	.343	.467
	CF	617	165	23	3	7	40	87	93	.267	.361	.348
	RF	561	133	31	5	8	49	54	109	.237	.308	.353
DETROIT	C	565	140	23	2	24	83	90	131	.248	.351	.423
	1B	602	158	24	1	38	121	85	139	.262	.358	.495
	2B	621	176	34	2	28	89	110	68	.283	.388	.480
	3B	614	164	31	1	15	81	46	129	.267	.319	.394
	SS	651	172	40	3	21	98	57	119	.264	.326	.432
	LF	628	136	30	3	18	79	52	130	.217	.277	.360
	CF	569	146	22	8	4	37	58	107	.257	.331	.344
	RF	574	109	23	2	26	72	100	190	.190	.309	.373
MILWAUKEE	C	603	165	22	4	8	85	45	47	.274	.318	.363
	1B	607	156	30	5	20	78	81	89	.257	.343	.422
	2B	603	188	25	4	0	63	90	49	.312	.401	.367
	3B	626	161	34	4	7	66	39	70	.257	.301	.358
	SS	540	145	25	7	8	79	53	93	.269	.333	.385
	LF	630	152	26	5	26	106	63	137	.241	.308	.422
	CF	640	182	28	4	12	97	65	92	.284	.349	.397
	RF	636	158	24	7	15	83	31	128	.248	.281	.379
NEW YORK	C	580	153	24	0	26	90	33	80	.264	.306	.440
	1B	643	184	34	0	14	80	54	65	.286	.343	.404
	2B	665	199	39	2	10	59	42	46	.299	.344	.409
	3B	540	121	21	4	6	39	47	89	.224	.291	.311
	SS	568	141	26	3	4	36	20	76	.248	.275	.326
	LF	602	163	24	2	28	98	47	107	.271	.327	.457
	CF	637	157	32	5	14	71	71	117	.246	.323	.378
	RF	612	141	24	2	22	73	54	123	.230	.292	.384
TORONTO	C	575	147	38	0	13	67	30	86	.256	.291	.390
	1B	563	135	31	2	19	77	87	99	.240	.342	.403
	2B	647	190	41	11	9	69	60	88	.294	.356	.433
	3B	602	150	22	2	23	82	44	117	.249	.307	.407
	SS	539	120	22	4	0	36	32	128	.223	.270	.278
	LF	588	158	34	5	16	74	57	122	.269	.344	.425
	CF	679	189	41	10	17	61	57	141	.278	.338	.443
	RF	625	159	31	5	30	109	44	135	.254	.308	.464
CALIFORNIA	C	553	119	23	0	19	65	50	156	.215	.287	.360
	1B	631	185	40	4	21	105	58	87	.293	.351	.469
	2B	558	137	22	2	3	31	45	50	.246	.308	.308
	3B	629	151	22	1	19	69	35	110	.240	.287	.369
	SS	537	124	14	3	1	45	62	81	.231	.316	.274
	LF	659	192	31	8	4	57	60	84	.291	.349	.381
	CF	587	158	29	3	6	64	34	118	.269	.313	.359
	RF	610	165	34	6	23	88	53	103	.270	.328	.459

TEAM	POS	AB	H	2B	3B	HR	RBI	BB	SO	BA	OBA	SA
CHICAGO	C	607	160	36	0	22	92	42	118	.264	.317	.432
	1B	606	157	28	2	25	90	93	119	.259	.364	.436
	2B	546	125	17	5	1	49	51	60	.229	.302	.284
	3B	636	179	27	2	24	104	84	72	.281	.364	.443
	SS	584	165	25	3	6	62	19	51	.283	.302	.366
	LF	636	165	19	5	7	58	94	82	.259	.358	.338
	CF	639	171	16	13	2	57	26	71	.268	.297	.343
	RF	578	136	22	5	18	84	55	156	.235	.303	.384
KANSAS CITY	C	551	140	29	3	18	82	51	109	.254	.320	.416
	1B	609	165	32	5	4	71	60	92	.271	.338	.360
	2B	506	113	20	4	5	46	44	103	.223	.292	.308
	3B	577	150	30	4	7	56	62	75	.260	.335	.362
	SS	565	146	24	1	6	67	43	82	.258	.310	.336
	LF	630	169	28	7	13	68	64	116	.268	.341	.397
	CF	702	191	39	9	8	73	26	107	.272	.297	.387
	RF	618	195	41	3	34	122	79	140	.316	.391	.557
MINNESOTA	C	600	172	33	2	13	87	34	42	.287	.329	.413
	1B	600	168	27	1	23	102	81	65	.280	.364	.443
	2B	642	173	26	6	1	60	69	42	.269	.341	.333
	3B	537	147	25	2	11	55	47	77	.274	.334	.389
	SS	539	130	26	3	8	47	37	90	.241	.292	.345
	LF	651	166	23	9	13	73	48	90	.255	.311	.378
	CF	664	197	29	7	17	92	36	93	.297	.334	.438
	RF	585	192	41	9	17	87	54	95	.328	.386	.516
OAKLAND	C	613	163	34	1	7	75	35	93	.266	.309	.359
	1B	552	110	23	0	21	82	97	123	.199	.321	.355
	2B	517	131	20	3	13	54	64	95	.253	.342	.379
	3B	568	125	28	3	4	58	53	86	.220	.285	.301
	SS	515	113	13	4	3	42	47	74	.219	.286	.278
	LF	618	158	29	3	16	74	104	93	.256	.369	.390
	CF	648	179	37	1	25	91	63	130	.276	.345	.452
	RF	632	160	29	2	41	111	78	156	.253	.339	.500
SEATTLE	C	508	105	17	1	8	46	52	70	.207	.288	.291
	1B	617	144	28	2	18	78	48	73	.233	.286	.373
	2B	648	166	35	6	3	57	72	67	.256	.332	.343
	3B	614	183	40	2	14	62	89	87	.298	.391	.438
	SS	536	128	22	4	2	48	50	54	.239	.303	.306
	LF	598	158	29	3	14	60	51	83	.264	.322	.393
	CF	625	203	46	1	26	117	76	96	.325	.393	.526
	RF	594	141	22	7	27	86	62	151	.237	.313	.434
TEXAS	C	576	153	31	2	8	62	39	87	.266	.312	.368
	1B	658	205	50	4	26	91	74	80	.312	.383	.518
	2B	657	217	29	3	16	87	74	90	.330	.401	.457
	3B	582	131	23	4	25	83	66	134	.225	.309	.407
	SS	508	118	18	4	3	49	52	76	.232	.303	.301
	LF	627	154	27	1	25	102	59	135	.246	.317	.411
	CF	589	146	25	5	19	77	79	153	.248	.337	.404
	RF	678	206	43	5	25	115	55	97	.304	.352	.493
AMERICAN LEAGUE TOTALS	C	8020	2020	394	19	182	984	607	1304	.252	.307	.374
	1B	8483	2242	415	33	271	1212	1020	1331	.264	.344	.417
	2B	8421	2261	396	57	102	827	849	994	.268	.338	.365
	3B	8337	2162	402	38	198	941	820	1275	.259	.328	.388
	SS	7846	1999	349	49	104	818	611	1143	.255	.310	.352
	LF	8723	2276	389	61	228	1101	863	1443	.261	.331	.398
	CF	8900	2418	440	85	193	1014	787	1548	.272	.332	.405
	RF	8510	2194	418	62	325	1244	841	1793	.258	.325	.436

TEAM	POS	AB	H	2B	3B	HR	RBI	BB	SO	BA	OBA	SA
CHICAGO	C	571	131	27	0	23	69	54	127	.229	.303	.398
	1B	636	169	28	5	8	59	72	52	.266	.340	.363
	2B	617	178	33	1	26	101	89	90	.288	.375	.472
	3B	619	158	20	1	16	55	38	93	.255	.302	.368
	SS	592	154	27	7	12	60	28	79	.260	.292	.390
	LF	639	180	30	1	24	92	41	71	.282	.324	.444
	CF	634	150	28	2	10	47	61	107	.237	.306	.334
	RF	650	174	25	5	31	111	29	93	.268	.302	.465
MONTREAL	C	554	120	26	2	4	55	47	108	.217	.276	.292
	1B	607	143	22	4	15	64	43	132	.236	.288	.359
	2B	624	151	20	5	10	55	98	151	.242	.344	.338
	3B	620	147	26	2	13	80	56	105	.237	.305	.348
	SS	557	145	34	8	5	41	56	85	.260	.325	.377
	LF	618	175	29	6	20	90	63	99	.283	.349	.447
	CF	662	180	24	10	10	53	40	101	.272	.315	.384
	RF	623	180	42	4	13	59	41	113	.289	.336	.432
NEW YORK	C	531	120	27	2	5	48	54	63	.226	.304	.313
	1B	585	146	28	1	5	62	95	75	.250	.352	.326
	2B	629	161	36	2	13	71	69	66	.256	.331	.382
	3B	594	159	25	4	22	94	77	85	.268	.350	.434
	SS	577	133	30	3	15	67	58	91	.231	.298	.371
	LF	624	167	31	2	14	83	47	56	.268	.322	.391
	CF	638	170	29	8	8	48	75	95	.266	.343	.375
	RF	611	150	29	2	26	88	65	123	.245	.317	.427
PHILADELPHIA	C	577	122	24	1	14	63	48	108	.211	.273	.329
	1B	631	180	36	6	25	105	57	114	.285	.343	.480
	2B	608	149	24	5	2	43	80	80	.245	.332	.311
	3B	633	158	37	3	17	74	38	107	.250	.295	.398
	SS	613	153	20	4	9	53	28	95	.250	.280	.339
	LF	629	153	27	6	18	88	62	112	.243	.310	.391
	CF	616	155	29	6	4	33	71	89	.252	.331	.338
	RF	627	160	36	2	18	86	58	108	.255	.315	.405
PITTSBURGH	C	572	172	30	2	5	70	57	58	.301	.367	.386
	1B	646	176	31	4	15	69	90	103	.272	.363	.402
	2B	596	148	22	6	3	63	37	83	.248	.291	.320
	3B	623	178	31	4	16	85	62	99	.286	.351	.425
	SS	648	174	35	9	16	68	56	109	.269	.329	.424
	LF	570	159	30	5	31	132	109	87	.279	.390	.512
	CF	625	155	30	8	19	95	82	120	.248	.334	.413
	RF	584	162	34	10	14	88	84	84	.277	.365	.442
ST. LOUIS	C	552	132	25	5	5	64	41	81	.239	.294	.330
	1B	637	163	20	4	13	92	52	73	.256	.309	.361
	2B	527	122	19	7	6	38	79	92	.231	.336	.328
	3B	609	164	37	3	11	84	64	99	.269	.341	.394
	SS	611	173	32	3	3	55	93	45	.283	.377	.360
	LF	612	151	24	5	10	42	66	95	.247	.319	.351
	CF	662	169	28	16	9	75	44	119	.255	.301	.387
	RF	616	185	40	8	9	87	53	121	.300	.355	.435
ATLANTA	C	590	141	32	1	12	74	54	81	.239	.304	.358
	1B	593	139	30	1	21	93	48	86	.234	.292	.395
	2B	610	174	33	7	10	77	67	49	.285	.355	.411
	3B	643	199	37	8	23	89	50	75	.309	.356	.499
	SS	544	135	14	2	5	48	49	104	.248	.313	.309
	LF	624	164	23	4	11	73	85	106	.263	.358	.365
	CF	628	164	37	3	33	110	77	110	.261	.344	.487
	RF	618	179	29	2	23	98	87	106	.290	.377	.455
CINCINNATI	C	554	133	25	2	14	73	43	93	.240	.294	.368
	1B	614	183	37	2	17	77	64	89	.298	.361	.448
	2B	634	166	18	7	15	63	56	86	.262	.322	.383
	3B	635	186	36	3	27	93	50	87	.293	.349	.487
	SS	634	189	30	5	22	84	58	95	.298	.360	.465
	LF	640	165	26	3	17	80	40	122	.258	.305	.388
	CF	619	142	23	2	13	45	66	138	.229	.310	.336
	RF	597	150	42	1	31	98	82	119	.251	.342	.481

TEAM	POS	AB	H	2B	3B	HR	RBI	BB	SO	BA	OBA	SA
HOUSTON	C	623	171	28	4	4	49	66	94	.274	.344	.352
	1B	594	172	30	4	14	85	84	119	.290	.385	.424
	2B	601	139	22	4	5	56	46	89	.231	.285	.306
	3B	629	160	31	3	13	87	50	92	.254	.312	.375
	SS	643	157	30	3	11	63	27	139	.244	.274	.351
	LF	621	161	32	12	15	77	47	121	.259	.318	.422
	CF	651	173	29	10	8	51	55	81	.266	.322	.378
	RF	585	131	22	3	6	57	59	133	.224	.296	.303
LOS ANGELES	C	558	145	29	2	14	62	60	56	.260	.338	.394
	1B	627	158	25	1	18	94	60	83	.252	.315	.381
	2B	643	179	26	6	13	63	56	136	.278	.339	.398
	3B	570	158	23	3	5	55	44	69	.277	.331	.354
	SS	527	126	12	2	0	36	55	82	.239	.312	.269
	LF	599	152	16	4	21	85	80	142	.254	.339	.399
	CF	633	187	14	5	2	39	108	82	.295	.398	.343
	RF	607	158	30	4	29	106	83	141	.260	.348	.466
SAN DIEGO	C	636	166	26	4	17	92	27	122	.261	.292	.395
	1B	569	156	20	1	32	112	109	149	.274	.389	.482
	2B	585	156	22	4	10	57	66	109	.267	.346	.369
	3B	571	111	15	3	14	52	65	128	.194	.278	.305
	SS	633	174	31	5	4	46	55	84	.275	.334	.359
	LF	593	136	23	2	15	64	49	125	.229	.291	.351
	CF	619	157	24	3	18	52	43	107	.254	.304	.389
	RF	636	194	32	12	6	75	43	49	.305	.347	.421
SAN FRANCISCO	C	564	122	22	2	8	54	35	93	.216	.268	.305
	1B	646	187	33	7	31	124	53	105	.289	.344	.506
	2B	595	155	30	6	19	61	74	113	.261	.348	.427
	3B	628	166	25	6	34	100	40	135	.264	.311	.486
	SS	543	111	19	7	4	32	39	96	.204	.258	.287
	LF	614	158	22	6	30	93	66	97	.257	.335	.459
	CF	652	185	29	6	5	38	64	86	.284	.350	.370
	RF	642	156	22	5	9	58	55	99	.243	.304	.335
NATIONAL LEAGUE TOTALS	C	6882	1675	321	27	125	773	586	1084	.243	.305	.352
	1B	7385	1972	340	40	214	1036	827	1180	.267	.341	.411
	2B	7269	1878	305	60	132	748	817	1144	.258	.334	.371
	3B	7374	1944	343	43	211	948	634	1174	.264	.324	.408
	SS	7122	1824	314	58	106	653	602	1104	.256	.314	.361
	LF	7383	1921	313	56	226	999	755	1233	.260	.330	.410
	CF	7639	1987	324	79	139	686	786	1235	.260	.330	.378
	RF	7396	1979	383	58	215	1011	739	1289	.268	.334	.422

Part 4 Special Reports

This part presents special reports on Starting Pitching, Relief Pitching, Fielding, and Basestealing. Each report gives information not contained in the official statistics, information that is very useful when analyzing player performance.

The Starting Pitching report includes all pitchers who had at least one game started in 1991. The pitchers are listed alphabetically by league; pitchers who played on more than one team are listed separately for each team for which they started a game. This report tells you how well each pitcher was supported by his offense, what his team's record was in the games he started, and his endurance by innings in each start.

The Relief Pitching report includes all pitchers who had at least one relief appearance in 1991, listed alphabetically by league. This report tells you how often a pitcher was used in save situations, how effective he was, when he entered games, how many inherited runners he allowed to score, and how he did against the first batter he faced in each appearance.

Special introductions precede each of the last two reports, whose tables present a lot of new material not normally available in this form.

The Fielding Range reports analyze players at each position in both leagues by calculating adjusted fielding ranges. By counting the number of batted balls each player fields and by calculating how many game equivalents he played at a position, a more accurate measure can be made of each fielder's prowess.

The last Fielding report details the games started at each position for all players who started at least one game in 1991. Players are listed separately by position for each team.

The Basestealing reports give much more information than the traditional stolen base/caught stealing stats. There are separate reports by league for pitchers, catchers, and baserunners. For baserunners, they tell how many opportunities they had to steal, how often they attempted to steal, and how successful they were. For pitchers and catchers, the same information is given for opposing runners, showing how effective they were at containing the opposition's running game.

STARTING PITCHING REPORT

AMERICAN LEAGUE

	GS	R/GS	W	L	TM/W	TM/L	1I	2I	3I	4I	5I	6I	7I	8I	9I	XI
Jim Abbott	34	4.2	18	11	20	14	0	0	0	0	2	3	6	12	10	1
Kyle Abbott	3	2.3	1	2	1	2	0	0	0	0	1	0	1	1	0	0
Paul Abbott	3	4.0	0	1	1	2	0	1	0	0	1	0	1	0	0	0
Jim Acker	4	5.2	1	2	1	3	0	0	0	0	2	1	1	0	0	0
Scott Aldred	11	5.2	2	4	5	6	1	0	1	1	2	0	3	2	1	0
Gerald Alexander	9	5.7	2	1	5	4	0	0	2	1	1	1	1	3	0	0
Wilson Alvarez	9	5.5	3	2	4	5	0	0	0	1	3	2	1	0	2	0
Allan Anderson	22	3.6	5	9	9	13	0	1	1	4	2	2	5	5	2	0
Kevin Appier	31	4.7	13	9	18	13	0	0	1	2	1	8	5	5	9	0
Luis Aquino	18	4.7	6	4	9	9	0	0	1	0	1	4	3	5	3	1
Don August	23	5.3	8	7	11	12	0	1	1	3	2	3	8	3	2	0
Jeff Ballard	22	3.8	6	12	6	16	1	0	2	2	2	3	8	2	2	0
Scott Bankhead	9	3.3	2	5	4	5	0	0	2	1	1	2	2	1	0	0
Willie Banks	3	5.3	1	1	2	1	0	0	0	2	0	0	1	0	0	0
John Barfield	9	5.8	2	3	5	4	0	0	1	2	1	0	2	3	0	0
Willie Blair	5	3.4	2	2	2	3	0	0	1	0	1	0	0	1	2	0
Mike Boddicker	29	4.2	11	12	13	16	1	0	0	1	3	5	7	5	7	0
Brian Bohanon	11	6.7	4	3	7	4	0	1	1	2	0	0	3	2	2	0
Tom Bolton	19	4.1	7	9	9	10	0	1	2	4	2	3	3	2	1	0
Chris Bosio	32	4.9	14	10	19	13	0	0	1	2	1	6	7	8	7	0
Denis Boucher (TOR)	7	4.2	0	3	2	5	0	0	1	0	1	3	1	1	0	0
Denis Boucher (CLE)	5	2.4	1	4	1	4	0	0	1	1	1	1	0	1	0	0
OilCan Boyd	12	3.0	2	7	2	10	0	0	2	0	1	4	3	2	0	0
Kevin D. Brown (MIL)	10	5.1	2	3	5	5	0	0	0	1	2	3	3	0	0	1
J. Kevin Brown (TEX)	33	4.9	9	12	17	16	0	1	1	1	1	2	3	7	12	5	1
Dave Burba	2	4.0	1	1	1	1	0	0	0	0	0	0	2	0	0	0
Greg Cadaret	5	7.5	3	1	3	2	0	0	0	1	0	1	1	1	1	0
Tom Candiotti (TOR)	19	3.6	6	7	10	9	1	0	0	0	1	1	3	7	5	1
Tom Candiotti (CLE)	15	3.5	7	6	8	7	0	0	0	0	0	1	3	5	6	0
Jeff Carter	2	7.0	0	1	1	1	0	0	0	1	0	1	0	0	0	0
Chuck Cary	9	3.4	1	6	3	6	0	0	1	1	0	3	3	0	1	0
John Cerutti	8	4.2	1	4	2	6	1	1	0	0	1	0	3	1	1	0
Scott Chiamparino	5	5.4	1	0	3	2	1	0	0	1	0	1	1	1	0	0
Roger Clemens	35	4.4	18	10	23	12	0	0	0	0	1	2	2	10	19	1
Ron Darling	12	2.5	3	7	4	8	0	0	0	1	1	2	1	6	1	0
Danny Darwin	12	3.5	3	6	4	8	0	1	0	0	1	4	3	3	0	0
Mark Davis	5	4.1	3	1	4	1	0	0	0	0	0	2	3	0	0	0
Storm Davis	9	3.6	2	5	3	6	0	0	1	1	0	2	3	1	1	0
Rich DeLucia	31	5.0	11	13	15	16	0	0	3	2	3	4	8	9	2	0
Kirk Dressendorfer	7	6.5	3	3	4	3	0	0	0	1	2	3	0	1	0	0
Tom Edens	6	5.0	2	2	3	3	0	1	0	0	0	2	2	1	0	0
Dave Eiland	13	3.3	2	5	4	9	0	0	2	1	2	6	0	2	0	0
Cal Eldred	3	4.3	2	0	3	0	0	0	0	1	1	1	0	0	0	0
Scott Erickson	32	5.3	20	8	23	9	1	0	1	2	2	3	6	10	7	0
Hector Fajardo	3	5.0	0	2	1	2	0	0	0	0	1	0	1	1	0	0
Alex Fernandez	32	3.6	9	13	16	16	0	3	1	0	3	6	5	10	4	0
Mike Fetters	4	4.2	0	4	0	4	0	1	0	0	2	1	0	0	0	0
Chuck Finley	34	4.7	18	9	22	12	1	0	0	3	1	1	6	13	9	0
Mike Flanagan	1	3.0	0	1	0	1	0	0	0	0	1	0	0	0	0	0
Dave Fleming	3	6.0	1	0	3	0	0	0	0	1	0	1	1	0	0	0
Willie Fraser	1	8.0	0	1	0	1	0	0	0	1	0	0	0	0	0	0
Dan Gakeler	7	4.5	1	3	2	5	0	1	0	2	0	1	1	2	0	0
Ramon Garcia	15	5.6	4	4	10	5	1	2	0	1	0	3	3	4	1	0
Mike Gardiner	22	4.8	9	10	11	11	0	0	0	0	2	9	6	4	1	0
Chris George	1	2.0	0	0	0	1	0	0	0	0	0	0	0	1	0	0
Tom Gordon	14	4.5	5	7	5	9	0	0	0	1	2	2	2	3	4	0
Mauro Gozzo	2	7.5	0	0	0	2	0	1	0	1	0	0	0	0	0	0
Joe Grahe	10	2.9	2	7	2	8	1	0	1	0	1	1	3	2	1	0
Mark Gubicza	26	4.1	9	12	11	15	1	0	0	3	3	12	5	1	1	0
Bill Gullickson	35	5.6	20	9	24	11	0	1	1	1	2	5	8	13	3	1
Mark Guthrie	12	5.5	5	4	8	4	0	1	3	1	0	2	3	2	0	0
Jose Guzman	25	4.9	13	7	15	10	0	0	1	2	0	1	8	6	7	0
Juan Guzman	23	4.7	10	3	14	9	0	0	0	3	3	2	5	6	4	0

	GS	R/GS	W	L	TM/W	TM/L	1I	2I	3I	4I	5I	6I	7I	8I	9I	XI
Erik Hanson	27	4.6	8	8	12	15	0	0	1	1	5	1	3	8	8	0
Greg Harris	21	3.7	7	10	8	13	0	0	1	1	3	3	8	4	1	0
Andy Hawkins (NY)	3	4.0	0	2	0	3	0	0	1	1	0	0	1	0	0	0
Andy Hawkins (OAK)	14	5.0	4	4	8	6	0	0	0	2	2	4	4	1	1	0
Pat Hentgen	1	3.0	0	0	1	0	0	0	0	0	0	1	0	0	0	0
Roberto Hernandez	3	6.6	1	0	2	1	0	0	1	0	0	0	0	1	0	0
Joe Hesketh	17	4.8	10	4	11	6	0	0	0	0	1	4	5	5	2	0
Greg Hibbard	29	4.9	10	11	13	16	0	0	0	5	3	4	3	8	5	1
Teddy Higuera	6	6.0	3	2	3	3	0	0	0	0	1	2	2	1	0	0
Shawn Hillegas	3	3.3	0	0	3	0	0	0	0	0	1	2	0	0	0	0
Brian Holman	30	3.4	13	14	16	14	0	0	0	1	3	5	8	6	7	0
Charlie Hough	29	4.1	9	10	18	11	0	0	2	2	0	4	2	12	7	0
Jim Hunter	6	3.8	0	4	0	6	0	0	0	3	1	2	0	0	0	0
Mike Ignasiak	1	4.0	0	0	0	1	0	0	0	1	0	0	0	0	0	0
Dave Johnson	14	3.9	2	8	4	10	0	1	2	1	3	3	4	0	0	0
Jeff Johnson	23	4.0	6	11	10	13	0	1	3	1	0	8	1	5	4	0
Randy Johnson	33	4.6	13	10	17	16	0	2	0	1	4	5	7	6	8	0
Doug Jones	4	4.5	3	1	3	1	0	0	0	0	0	0	0	2	2	0
Stacy Jones	1	8.0	0	0	1	0	0	0	0	1	0	0	0	0	0	0
Scott Kamieniecki	9	3.6	4	4	5	4	0	0	0	1	0	1	4	3	0	0
Jimmy Key	33	4.1	16	12	20	13	0	0	1	0	2	7	8	11	4	0
Dana Kiecker	5	6.4	2	1	4	1	0	1	0	1	0	3	0	0	0	0
Eric King	24	4.5	6	11	10	14	0	0	1	1	4	2	8	4	4	0
Mark Knudson	7	5.1	1	3	4	3	0	0	1	3	2	1	0	0	0	0
Bill Krueger	25	4.0	10	7	14	11	0	0	1	0	2	4	12	4	2	0
Mark Langston	34	4.2	19	8	21	13	0	0	0	0	2	2	5	16	7	2
Tim Leary	18	4.7	4	8	9	9	0	1	0	1	4	4	3	3	2	0
Mark Leiter	15	4.9	7	6	8	7	0	0	0	1	2	3	4	2	3	0
Scott Lewis	11	5.4	2	5	5	6	0	0	0	3	4	1	1	2	0	0
Terry Mathews	2	10.0	0	0	2	0	0	0	1	0	0	1	0	0	0	0
Kirk McCaskill	30	2.9	10	19	10	20	0	0	1	2	5	4	5	10	3	0
Ben McDonald	21	4.6	6	8	9	12	0	1	2	1	2	2	4	3	5	1
Jack McDowell	35	5.0	17	10	20	15	0	1	2	0	1	2	4	9	16	0
Rusty Meacham	4	6.7	2	1	3	1	0	0	1	0	1	1	0	1	0	0
Jose Mesa	23	4.8	6	11	11	12	0	1	2	1	4	3	6	4	2	0
Bob Milacki	26	4.0	9	9	13	13	1	0	2	0	1	5	5	7	4	1
Alan Mills	2	2.0	0	1	0	2	0	0	0	1	0	1	0	0	0	0
Mike Moore	33	3.9	17	8	19	14	0	0	0	3	0	5	12	9	4	0
Jack Morris	35	4.8	18	12	20	15	0	1	1	0	2	4	2	13	12	0
Kevin Morton	15	6.0	6	5	8	7	1	0	1	0	1	4	4	3	1	0
Mike Mussina	12	4.1	4	5	5	7	0	0	0	1	0	1	1	3	5	1
Jeff Mutis	3	3.0	0	3	0	3	0	0	1	0	0	2	0	0	0	0
Charles Nagy	33	3.2	10	15	12	21	0	1	1	2	0	8	7	4	9	1
Jaime Navarro	34	4.5	15	12	15	19	0	1	2	1	0	3	7	9	10	1
Denny Neagle	3	4.6	0	1	2	1	0	0	0	1	1	1	0	0	0	0
Rod Nichols	16	2.2	2	10	2	14	0	0	0	2	2	4	2	2	4	0
Dave Otto	14	3.5	2	8	4	10	0	0	2	0	0	0	4	4	4	0
Melido Perez	8	3.7	1	4	3	5	0	0	0	1	1	3	1	1	1	0
Pascual Perez	14	3.7	2	4	9	5	1	0	0	0	2	4	6	0	1	0
Mark Petkovsek	1	7.0	0	1	0	1	0	0	0	1	0	0	0	0	0	0
Dan Petry (DET)	6	5.0	2	3	2	4	0	1	0	1	1	0	1	1	1	0
Dan Plesac	10	5.3	2	3	5	5	0	1	0	1	2	3	2	0	1	0
Eric Plunk	8	3.1	0	3	1	7	0	0	0	1	0	2	5	0	0	0
ArthurLee Rhodes	8	3.8	0	3	4	4	0	0	0	2	4	0	1	1	0	0
Pat Rice	2	3.5	1	1	1	1	0	0	1	0	0	1	0	0	0	0
Kevin Ritz	5	5.4	0	3	1	4	2	2	0	0	0	1	0	0	0	0
Jeff M. Robinson (BAL)	19	3.5	4	9	6	13	2	0	1	2	3	3	2	5	1	0
Ron Robinson	1	3.0	0	1	0	1	0	0	0	0	1	0	0	0	0	0
Kenny Rogers	9	5.3	4	4	4	5	0	1	1	0	2	2	1	1	1	0
Nolan Ryan	27	4.7	12	6	16	11	0	1	0	0	2	6	4	8	5	1
Bret Saberhagen	28	4.6	13	8	18	10	0	0	1	0	2	3	1	12	9	0
Scott Sanderson	34	4.5	16	10	19	15	0	1	1	0	0	11	8	8	5	0
Steve Searcy	5	4.5	1	1	3	2	0	1	2	0	1	0	0	0	0	0
Jeff Shaw	1	0.0	0	1	0	1	0	0	0	0	1	0	0	0	0	0

	GS	R/GS	W	L	TM/W	TM/L	1I	2I	3I	4I	5I	6I	7I	8I	9I	XI
Eric Show	5	4.8	1	2	3	2	0	0	0	1	0	1	2	1	0	0
Joe Slusarski	19	5.2	5	7	9	10	0	0	1	1	4	4	4	5	0	0
Roy Smith	14	4.7	5	3	7	7	0	2	0	1	2	2	3	3	1	0
Dave Stewart	35	5.6	11	11	18	17	0	1	0	1	0	8	6	13	6	0
Dave Stieb	9	3.6	4	3	4	5	0	0	0	0	0	1	5	2	1	0
Todd Stottlemyre	34	4.2	15	8	21	13	0	0	0	0	3	7	6	13	5	0
Greg Swindell	33	3.4	9	16	11	22	0	1	0	0	3	0	9	5	12	3
Frank Tanana	33	4.7	13	12	19	14	1	0	1	0	0	7	9	7	8	0
Kevin Tapani	34	4.8	16	9	20	14	0	0	0	0	1	4	4	12	13	0
Wade Taylor	22	4.1	7	12	7	15	1	1	0	2	3	4	6	4	1	0
Anthony Telford	1	5.0	0	0	1	0	0	0	0	0	0	1	0	0	0	0
Walt Terrell	33	4.7	11	14	15	18	0	0	0	3	4	4	7	8	7	0
Mike Timlin	3	2.0	1	1	2	1	0	0	0	1	0	1	1	0	0	0
Fernando Valenzuela	2	0.0	0	2	0	2	0	1	0	0	0	0	1	0	0	0
Todd VanPoppel	1	6.0	0	0	1	0	0	0	0	0	1	0	0	0	0	0
Hector Wagner	2	9.5	1	1	1	1	0	0	0	0	1	0	1	0	0	0
Bill Wegman	28	5.0	15	7	18	10	1	0	1	0	1	4	3	5	13	0
Bob Welch	35	4.3	12	13	18	17	0	1	2	3	2	5	5	7	10	0
Dave Wells	28	4.3	14	10	16	12	0	0	2	1	2	5	3	5	10	0
David West	12	4.2	4	4	7	5	0	0	1	1	2	3	2	2	1	0
Bobby Witt	16	5.3	3	7	8	8	0	2	1	3	0	1	4	2	3	0
Mike Witt	2	4.0	0	1	1	1	1	0	0	0	0	1	0	0	0	0
Mike York	4	6.7	0	2	1	3	0	0	0	1	2	1	0	0	0	0
Curt Young	1	3.0	0	1	0	1	0	0	0	0	0	1	0	0	0	0
Matt Young	16	3.9	3	6	6	10	0	0	1	3	2	3	4	2	0	1

NATIONAL LEAGUE

	GS	R/GS	W	L	TM/W	TM/L	1I	2I	3I	4I	5I	6I	7I	8I	9I	XI
Jack Armstrong	24	3.8	7	13	7	17	0	0	3	0	2	8	4	5	2	0
Andy Ashby	8	3.0	1	5	3	5	0	0	0	1	2	3	0	2	0	0
Steve Avery	35	5.2	18	8	24	11	0	0	2	3	4	6	6	7	7	0
Brian Barnes	27	3.4	5	8	8	19	0	0	0	1	4	8	7	5	2	0
Tim Belcher	33	3.7	10	9	19	14	1	2	1	2	0	1	7	10	9	0
Andy Benes	33	3.2	15	11	17	16	0	0	0	1	3	1	9	11	8	0
Mike Bielecki (CHI)	25	4.7	10	8	15	10	0	0	1	1	3	6	4	6	4	0
Bud Black	34	3.7	12	16	15	19	0	1	1	2	0	6	7	11	6	0
Ricky Bones	11	5.9	4	6	5	6	0	2	0	1	2	1	2	3	0	0
Shawn Boskie	20	4.0	3	9	7	13	0	0	2	2	2	4	7	4	0	0
Ryan Bowen	13	4.4	5	4	6	7	0	1	0	0	2	5	2	2	1	0
OilCan Boyd	19	3.7	6	8	9	10	0	0	0	2	5	4	5	3	0	0
Cliff Brantley	5	4.1	2	2	3	2	0	0	0	2	1	0	2	0	0	0
Tom Browning	36	4.8	14	14	20	16	0	0	1	1	2	5	11	9	7	0
John Burkett	34	3.7	12	11	17	17	0	0	3	2	2	8	4	5	10	0
Frank Castillo	18	3.8	6	7	8	10	2	0	0	1	2	1	3	1	8	0
Tony Castillo (NY)	3	3.0	1	0	3	0	0	0	0	0	1	1	1	0	0	0
Norm Charlton	11	2.7	3	5	4	7	0	1	0	0	1	0	5	2	2	0
Mark Clark	2	3.5	0	0	0	2	0	0	0	0	0	1	1	0	0	1
Pat Combs	13	4.1	2	6	5	8	2	1	0	1	2	3	1	0	2	1
David Cone	34	3.8	14	14	15	19	0	0	1	0	2	4	6	8	13	0
Dennis Cook	1	2.0	1	0	1	0	0	0	0	0	1	0	0	0	0	0
Rheal Cormier	10	3.2	4	5	4	6	0	0	0	0	0	2	4	3	1	0
Danny Cox	17	4.8	4	6	9	8	0	1	0	1	3	5	3	4	0	0
Ron Darling (NY)	17	3.9	5	6	8	9	0	1	1	0	0	2	6	5	2	0
Ron Darling (MON)	3	3.6	0	2	0	3	0	0	0	0	0	1	2	0	0	0
Jose DeJesus	29	3.7	10	9	13	16	0	2	2	1	1	3	4	9	7	0
Jose DeLeon	28	4.0	5	9	13	15	1	0	1	0	3	5	9	7	2	0
Jim Deshaies	28	3.3	5	12	10	18	1	0	2	1	3	6	3	8	3	1
Kelly Downs	11	2.9	3	4	3	8	1	0	0	0	0	2	4	3	1	0
Doug Drabek	35	4.3	15	14	19	16	0	0	1	0	2	4	8	12	6	0
Hector Fajardo	2	7.5	0	0	1	1	0	0	1	0	1	0	0	0	0	0
Sid Fernandez	8	3.7	1	3	3	5	0	0	0	1	1	0	5	1	0	0

NATIONAL LEAGUE (continued)

	GS	R/GS	W	L	TM/W	TM/L	1I	2I	3I	4I	5I	6I	7I	8I	9I	XI
Chris Gardner	4	3.0	1	2	2	2	0	0	0	0	1	2	0	1	0	0
Mark Gardner	27	3.5	9	11	14	13	0	0	2	3	1	11	6	3	1	0
Scott Garrelts	3	8.0	1	1	1	2	0	0	1	1	0	0	1	0	0	0
Tom Glavine	34	4.5	20	11	21	13	0	0	0	1	1	2	6	11	13	0
Dwight Gooden	27	5.0	13	7	16	11	0	0	0	0	2	1	6	8	10	0
Tommy Greene	27	4.1	12	7	16	11	1	0	1	0	0	2	6	10	7	0
Jason Grimsley	12	3.0	1	7	2	10	1	0	0	0	3	3	3	2	0	0
Kevin Gross	10	3.7	4	5	5	5	0	1	0	1	2	0	3	3	0	0
Kip Gross	9	5.4	4	4	4	5	0	0	1	0	2	2	2	0	2	0
Atlee Hammaker	1	1.0	0	1	0	1	0	0	0	0	1	0	0	0	0	0
Chris Hammond	18	3.2	7	7	8	10	0	1	1	1	3	0	8	4	0	0
Chris Haney	16	3.1	3	7	5	11	0	0	0	2	3	4	5	2	0	0
Mike Harkey	4	5.2	0	2	1	3	0	0	0	1	1	1	1	0	0	0
Pete Harnisch	33	3.4	12	9	16	17	0	0	1	0	1	4	10	11	6	0
Greg Harris	20	3.6	9	5	13	7	1	0	0	0	2	1	4	6	6	0
Neal Heaton	1	1.0	0	1	0	1	0	0	0	0	1	0	0	0	0	0
Gil Heredia	4	3.5	0	2	2	2	0	0	0	0	0	0	1	3	0	0
Xavier Hernandez	6	1.6	0	5	1	5	0	0	0	2	0	1	2	1	0	0
Orel Hershiser	21	5.6	7	2	16	5	0	1	0	1	4	3	9	3	0	0
Bryan Hickerson	6	3.6	2	2	3	3	0	0	1	0	0	2	2	1	0	0
Ken Hill	30	3.8	11	10	16	14	0	1	2	2	1	3	10	3	8	0
Bruce Hurst	31	4.3	15	8	19	12	0	1	0	0	0	1	9	7	12	1
Danny Jackson	14	5.1	1	5	4	10	0	1	1	3	1	3	3	2	0	0
Jimmy Jones	22	3.5	5	7	7	15	0	0	1	3	2	2	6	5	3	0
Jeff Juden	3	2.3	0	2	0	3	0	0	0	0	0	2	1	0	0	0
Darryl Kile	22	4.1	7	9	8	14	0	0	1	2	2	2	5	9	1	0
Mike LaCoss	5	4.1	1	2	3	2	0	1	1	0	0	1	0	1	1	0
Les Lancaster	11	4.9	5	3	6	5	0	0	0	0	0	4	2	4	1	0
Dave LaPoint	2	6.5	0	1	1	1	0	1	0	1	0	0	0	0	0	0
Charlie Leibrandt	36	4.0	15	13	18	18	0	0	1	1	4	6	5	12	7	0
Derek Lilliquist	2	4.5	0	2	0	2	0	0	0	1	0	1	0	0	0	0
Greg Maddux	37	4.2	15	11	20	17	0	0	0	1	2	2	9	9	13	1
Mike Maddux	1	11.0	1	0	1	0	0	0	0	0	0	0	1	0	0	0
Rick Mahler (ATL)	2	7.5	1	0	2	0	0	0	1	0	0	0	1	0	0	0
Rick Mahler (MON)	6	2.8	1	3	2	4	0	0	0	0	2	1	2	1	0	0
Dennis Martinez	31	3.4	14	11	16	15	0	0	0	2	1	2	4	10	12	0
Ramon Martinez	33	4.4	17	13	19	14	0	0	1	2	0	6	4	12	7	1
Paul McClellan	12	4.9	3	6	5	7	0	0	0	0	4	2	2	3	1	0
Jose Melendez	9	3.5	5	3	6	3	0	0	0	0	1	2	2	3	1	0
Kent Mercker	4	3.7	1	0	3	1	0	0	0	0	2	1	1	0	0	0
Paul Miller	1	3.0	0	0	0	1	0	0	0	0	0	1	0	0	0	0
Gino Minutelli	3	4.0	0	1	1	2	0	1	0	0	1	1	0	0	0	0
Mike Morgan	33	3.6	14	10	17	16	0	0	1	0	0	1	12	8	10	1
Jamie Moyer	7	2.5	0	5	1	6	0	0	3	0	2	1	1	0	0	0
Terry Mulholland	34	3.7	16	13	18	16	0	1	2	1	2	5	2	5	15	1
Randy Myers	12	3.3	2	6	3	9	0	1	1	0	1	1	4	2	2	0
Chris Nabholz	24	4.1	8	7	12	12	0	0	0	0	2	5	6	8	3	0
Eric Nolte	6	5.3	3	2	4	2	1	1	1	0	0	2	1	0	0	0
Bob Ojeda	31	3.8	12	9	16	15	0	0	2	1	2	3	12	9	2	0
Omar Olivares	24	4.2	11	7	14	10	0	0	0	2	0	3	6	7	6	0
Francisco Oliveras	1	3.0	0	1	0	1	0	0	0	0	0	1	0	0	0	0
Vicente Palacios	7	4.5	2	2	5	2	0	0	0	1	2	0	2	1	1	0
Bob Patterson	1	4.0	0	0	1	0	0	0	0	1	0	0	0	0	0	0
Adam Peterson	11	3.8	3	4	5	6	0	1	0	1	2	3	3	1	0	0
Mark Portugal	27	4.7	10	10	15	12	1	0	1	1	2	4	4	10	3	1
Dennis Rasmussen	24	3.5	6	13	9	15	1	1	0	1	1	2	5	10	3	0
Rick Reed	1	6.0	0	0	0	1	0	0	0	0	1	0	0	0	0	0
Mike Remlinger	6	7.3	2	1	5	1	0	0	1	1	0	1	2	0	0	0
Rick Reuschel	1	2.0	0	1	0	1	0	0	0	0	0	0	1	0	0	0
Armando Reynoso	5	6.0	2	1	4	1	0	0	0	1	1	0	1	1	0	0
Jose Rijo	30	5.0	15	6	19	11	0	0	0	0	0	1	14	10	5	0
Don Robinson	16	3.9	5	8	7	9	0	0	0	2	3	2	2	3	1	3
Rich Rodriguez	1	1.0	0	0	0	1	0	0	0	0	0	0	1	0	0	0
Bruce Ruffin	15	3.4	3	7	8	7	1	2	0	0	0	1	2	6	3	0

	GS	R/GS	W	L	TM/W	TM/L	1I	2I	3I	4I	5I	6I	7I	8I	9I	XI
Bill Sampen	8	4.0	3	2	5	3	0	0	1	0	0	5	1	1	0	0
Mo Sanford	5	3.7	1	2	2	3	0	0	0	0	1	1	2	1	0	0
Bob Scanlan	13	3.5	2	4	7	6	0	2	0	1	0	4	2	4	0	0
Pete Schourek	8	5.2	3	3	5	3	0	1	0	0	1	0	4	1	1	0
Mike Scott	2	2.0	0	2	0	2	0	0	0	1	1	0	0	0	0	0
Scott Scudder	14	4.2	6	7	6	8	1	0	1	0	0	4	5	3	0	0
Doug Simons	1	5.0	0	1	0	1	0	0	1	0	0	0	0	0	0	0
John Smiley	32	4.6	19	8	22	10	0	0	1	0	1	9	7	8	6	0
Bryn Smith	31	4.6	12	9	18	13	0	0	0	0	4	2	12	9	4	0
Pete Smith	10	4.6	1	3	4	6	1	1	1	0	3	0	3	1	0	0
Zane Smith	35	4.5	16	10	20	15	0	0	1	3	3	4	5	8	11	0
John Smoltz	36	4.4	14	13	18	18	0	1	1	1	4	6	8	9	6	1
Rick Sutcliffe	18	4.2	6	5	9	9	0	1	1	1	3	3	5	2	2	0
Bob Tewksbury	30	4.0	11	12	18	12	0	0	1	2	3	2	5	10	7	0
Randy Tomlin	27	5.1	8	7	15	12	0	1	0	1	3	3	7	7	5	0
Frank Viola	35	3.4	13	15	17	18	0	0	0	2	2	3	9	10	9	0
Bob Walk	20	5.3	7	2	15	5	0	1	0	0	4	7	4	3	1	0
Wally Whitehurst	20	3.8	5	11	8	12	0	0	1	0	4	8	2	4	1	0
Ed Whitson	12	3.6	4	6	5	7	0	0	0	1	0	1	6	1	3	0
Brian Williams	2	4.0	0	1	0	2	0	0	0	0	0	1	0	1	0	0
Trevor Wilson	29	3.8	13	8	14	15	0	3	0	1	0	5	6	5	9	0
Anthony Young	8	3.0	2	5	2	6	0	0	0	1	1	1	4	1	0	0

RELIEF PITCHING REPORT

AMERICAN LEAGUE

	GR	SVS	SV	BSV	SC%	SV%	<6I	6I	7I	8I	9I	XI	IR	IRS	IRP	BA	OBA
Abbott, Kyle	2	0	0	0	.000	.000	0	1	1	0	0	0	0	0	.000	.000	.000
Abbott, Paul	13	1	0	0	.000	.000	6	4	1	2	0	0	11	5	.455	.167	.167
Acker, Jim	50	10	1	2	.100	.333	6	10	7	17	6	4	31	14	.452	.205	.280
Aguilera, Rick	63	51	42	9	.824	.824	0	0	0	16	43	4	37	10	.270	.127	.238
Alexander, Gerald	21	4	0	0	.000	.000	8	5	4	1	1	2	25	9	.360	.118	.250
Allison, Dana	12	2	0	0	.000	.000	3	3	2	1	3	0	15	4	.267	.200	.273
Alvarez, Wilson	1	0	0	0	.000	.000	1	0	0	0	0	0	0	0	.000	.000	.000
Anderson, Allan	7	0	0	0	.000	.000	2	1	0	0	3	1	3	0	.000	.286	.286
Appier, Kevin	3	1	0	0	.000	.000	1	1	1	0	0	0	2	0	.000	.000	.000
Aquino, Luis	20	5	3	1	.600	.750	5	6	3	3	2	1	16	7	.438	.278	.300
Arnsberg, Brad	9	0	0	0	.000	.000	2	1	3	0	2	1	4	2	.500	.250	.333
August, Don	5	0	0	0	.000	.000	2	0	0	1	0	2	1	0	.000	.600	.600
Austin, Jim	5	0	0	0	.000	.000	3	1	0	0	1	0	8	1	.125	.000	.200
Bailes, Scott	42	9	0	1	.000	.000	8	8	9	10	3	4	33	10	.303	.194	.268
Ballard, Jeff	4	0	0	0	.000	.000	2	0	1	1	0	0	5	1	.200	.333	.500
Bankhead, Scott	8	0	0	0	.000	.000	4	0	2	1	0	1	9	4	.444	.250	.250
Banks, Willie	2	0	0	0	.000	.000	0	0	1	1	0	0	0	0	.000	.000	.000
Bannister, Floyd	16	0	0	0	.000	.000	7	4	0	3	1	1	15	4	.267	.286	.375
Barfield, John	19	1	1	0	1.000	1.000	7	1	5	4	1	1	23	5	.217	.235	.316
Bautista, Jose	5	1	0	0	.000	.000	0	2	1	0	1	1	2	2	1.000	.250	.400
Beasley, Chris	22	2	0	0	.000	.000	5	1	7	7	2	0	20	5	.250	.158	.273
Bedrosian, Steve	56	18	6	1	.333	.857	0	3	13	31	8	1	43	10	.233	.135	.179
Bell, Eric	10	2	0	0	.000	.000	2	2	0	5	1	0	7	1	.143	.000	.100
Bitker, Joe	9	2	0	0	.000	.000	2	2	1	1	1	2	4	2	.500	.500	.556
Blair, Willie	6	1	0	1	.000	.000	1	1	2	1	1	0	8	4	.500	.500	.500
Boddicker, Mike	1	0	0	0	.000	.000	0	0	0	0	0	1	0	0	.000	.000	.000
Bohanon, Brian	1	1	0	0	.000	.000	0	0	1	0	0	0	0	0	.000	.000	.000
Bolton, Tom	6	0	0	0	.000	.000	3	0	1	1	1	0	3	3	1.000	.333	.333
Briscoe, John	11	0	0	0	.000	.000	1	1	0	7	2	0	9	5	.556	.200	.273
Brown, Kevin D.	5	1	0	1	.000	.000	2	2	0	1	0	0	7	3	.429	.250	.400
Burba, Dave	20	1	1	0	1.000	1.000	3	4	2	2	6	3	10	5	.500	.316	.350
Burns, Todd	9	1	0	0	.000	.000	2	0	2	4	0	1	6	6	1.000	.286	.375
Cadaret, Greg	63	19	3	4	.158	.429	5	18	15	18	6	1	44	15	.341	.192	.323
Campbell, Kevin	14	4	0	1	.000	.000	4	3	1	3	2	1	15	6	.400	.182	.357
Carter, Jeff	3	0	0	0	.000	.000	2	0	0	1	0	0	4	1	.250	.667	.667
Cary, Chuck	1	0	0	0	.000	.000	1	0	0	0	0	0	1	1	1.000	.000	.000
Casian, Larry	15	2	0	0	.000	.000	2	1	4	4	2	2	15	3	.200	.385	.467
Cerutti, John	30	7	2	3	.286	.400	7	6	8	4	3	2	39	19	.487	.360	.448
Chapin, Darrin	3	0	0	0	.000	.000	0	0	1	1	1	0	1	0	.000	.500	.667
Chitren, Steve	56	23	4	3	.174	.571	4	12	12	18	9	1	50	20	.400	.306	.393
Comstock, Keith	1	0	0	0	.000	.000	0	0	0	1	0	0	0	0	.000	1.000	1.000
Corbin, Archie	2	0	0	0	.000	.000	0	0	0	1	1	0	1	0	.000	.000	.000
Crawford, Steve	33	5	1	0	.200	1.000	4	6	5	11	2	5	22	6	.273	.290	.312
Crim, Chuck	66	19	3	2	.158	.600	3	10	18	20	13	2	46	15	.326	.333	.354
Dalton, Mike	5	0	0	0	.000	.000	2	2	0	1	0	0	6	4	.667	.000	.200
Davis, Mark	24	4	1	1	.250	.500	5	0	6	5	8	0	19	8	.421	.118	.375
Davis, Storm	42	8	2	1	.250	.667	1	7	11	14	6	3	31	11	.355	.286	.390
Dayley, Ken	8	2	0	0	.000	.000	1	0	1	5	0	1	6	2	.333	.667	.750
DelaRosa, Francisco	2	0	0	0	.000	.000	1	0	0	1	0	0	3	0	.000	.500	.500
DeLucia, Rich	1	0	0	0	.000	.000	1	0	0	0	0	0	0	0	.000	.000	.000
Dopson, John	1	0	0	0	.000	.000	0	0	0	0	1	0	0	0	.000	.000	1.000
Drahman, Brian	28	4	0	2	.000	.000	5	6	2	9	3	3	36	14	.389	.192	.250
Drees, Tom	4	0	0	0	.000	.000	2	0	1	1	0	0	2	2	1.000	.000	1.000
Eckersley, Dennis	68	52	43	8	.827	.843	0	0	0	22	41	5	31	9	.290	.209	.221
Edens, Tom	2	0	0	0	.000	.000	1	0	0	1	0	0	1	0	.000	.000	.000
Edwards, Wayne	13	3	0	0	.000	.000	5	3	1	0	1	3	18	7	.389	.125	.333
Egloff, Bruce	6	0	0	0	.000	.000	0	1	3	1	1	0	7	2	.286	.333	.333
Eichhorn, Mark	70	30	1	3	.033	.250	2	4	16	35	12	1	54	14	.259	.188	.246
Eiland, Dave	5	0	0	0	.000	.000	1	1	0	2	1	0	2	2	1.000	.400	.400
Fajardo, Hector	1	0	0	0	.000	.000	0	0	0	0	1	0	0	0	.000	1.000	1.000
Farr, Steve	60	32	23	6	.719	.793	0	0	7	16	35	2	31	8	.258	.232	.283
Fernandez, Alex	2	1	0	0	.000	.000	0	1	0	1	0	0	1	0	.000	.000	.000
Fetters, Mike	15	1	0	1	.000	.000	4	2	3	0	3	3	7	2	.286	.167	.333
Flanagan, Mike	64	21	3	2	.143	.600	7	3	11	28	12	3	47	12	.255	.293	.344
Fleming, Dave	6	2	0	0	.000	.000	1	0	1	2	2	0	3	0	.000	.000	.000

AMERICAN LEAGUE (continued)

	GR	SVS	SV	BSV	SC%	SV%	<6I	6I	7I	8I	9I	XI	IR	IRS	IRP	BA	OBA
Fossas, Tony	64	22	1	1	.045	.500	2	8	17	26	11	0	71	22	.310	.130	.230
Fraser, Willie	12	1	0	0	.000	.000	3	3	0	3	2	1	5	1	.200	.333	.500
Frohwirth, Todd	51	15	3	2	.200	.600	13	10	10	11	6	1	58	21	.362	.109	.160
Gakeler, Dan	24	6	2	2	.333	.500	4	2	7	7	4	0	25	7	.280	.292	.292
Garcia, Ramon	1	0	0	0	.000	.000	0	0	1	0	0	0	0	0	.000	.000	.000
Gardner, Wes	3	1	0	0	.000	.000	0	1	1	1	0	0	2	0	.000	.000	.333
George, Chris	1	0	0	0	.000	.000	0	0	0	0	1	0	0	0	.000	.000	.000
Gibson, Paul	68	25	8	5	.320	.615	8	5	22	20	10	3	71	27	.380	.350	.403
Gleaton, Jerry	47	9	2	1	.222	.667	9	4	12	14	5	3	46	12	.261	.205	.298
Gordon, Tom	31	11	1	3	.091	.250	3	11	7	7	1	2	17	7	.412	.192	.300
Gossage, Rich	44	12	1	4	.083	.200	0	2	17	13	8	4	53	22	.415	.308	.372
Grahe, Joe	8	1	0	0	.000	.000	3	2	0	0	2	1	7	3	.429	.429	.500
Gray, Jeff	50	23	1	3	.043	.250	0	1	22	19	6	2	36	12	.333	.200	.229
Guetterman, Lee	64	17	6	3	.353	.667	2	11	10	22	18	1	33	10	.303	.276	.328
Gullickson, Bill	1	1	0	0	.000	.000	0	0	1	0	0	0	0	0	.000	.000	.000
Guthrie, Mark	29	9	2	0	.222	1.000	3	4	6	11	5	0	11	4	.364	.346	.414
Guzman, Johnny	5	0	0	0	.000	.000	0	1	1	3	0	0	7	3	.429	.600	.600
Haas, David	11	1	0	1	.000	.000	2	0	6	2	0	1	13	9	.692	.800	.909
Habyan, John	66	24	2	2	.083	.500	5	13	20	19	6	3	49	18	.367	.200	.262
Harris, Gene	8	2	1	0	.500	1.000	1	1	3	2	1	0	0	0	.000	.286	.375
Harris, Greg	32	12	2	3	.167	.400	0	7	9	11	3	2	27	9	.333	.300	.344
Harris, Reggie	2	0	0	0	.000	.000	1	0	1	0	0	0	0	0	.000	.500	.500
Harvey, Bryan	67	52	46	6	.885	.885	0	0	0	28	37	2	37	10	.270	.203	.239
Hawkins, Andy	2	0	0	0	.000	.000	0	0	0	1	1	0	1	0	.000	.000	.500
Henke, Tom	49	37	32	3	.865	.914	0	1	1	6	38	3	15	3	.200	.188	.204
Henneman, Mike	62	27	21	3	.778	.875	0	0	6	31	19	6	41	8	.195	.236	.311
Henry, Doug	32	19	15	1	.789	.938	1	0	2	9	19	1	18	3	.167	.143	.226
Hentgen, Pat	2	0	0	0	.000	.000	0	0	0	1	1	0	0	0	.000	.000	.500
Hernandez, Roberto	6	0	0	0	.000	.000	2	0	1	0	3	0	3	3	1.000	.200	.333
Hesketh, Joe	22	4	0	0	.000	.000	5	7	5	4	0	1	26	11	.423	.235	.350
Hibbard, Greg	3	0	0	0	.000	.000	2	0	0	0	1	0	2	0	.000	.235	.316
Hickey, Kevin	19	5	0	1	.000	.000	1	6	5	4	3	0	18	5	.278	.235	.316
Higuera, Teddy	1	0	0	0	.000	.000	0	0	0	1	0	0	0	0	.000	1.000	1.000
Hillegas, Shawn	48	14	7	2	.500	.778	2	3	8	18	16	1	46	17	.370	.189	.354
Holmes, Darren	40	10	3	4	.300	.429	13	11	8	4	2	2	44	17	.386	.382	.447
Honeycutt, Rick	43	18	0	4	.000	.000	1	2	12	17	10	1	23	9	.391	.190	.209
Horsman, Vince	4	1	0	0	.000	.000	0	0	3	1	0	0	6	2	.333	.333	.333
Hough, Charlie	2	0	0	0	.000	.000	0	0	1	0	0	1	0	0	.000	.000	.000
Howe, Steve	37	11	3	0	.273	1.000	3	5	14	7	8	0	26	6	.231	.167	.189
Hunter, Jim	2	0	0	0	.000	.000	2	0	0	0	0	0	3	2	.667	.000	1.000
Ignasiak, Mike	3	0	0	0	.000	.000	3	0	0	0	0	0	2	0	.000	.000	.000
Irvine, Daryl	9	0	0	0	.000	.000	1	3	2	3	0	0	16	10	.625	.500	.500
Jackson, Michael	73	33	14	8	.424	.636	2	5	15	21	25	5	52	10	.192	.145	.264
Jeffcoat, Mike	70	16	1	4	.062	.200	7	5	16	24	14	4	40	19	.475	.350	.420
Johnson, Dave	8	0	0	0	.000	.000	4	1	1	1	0	1	11	9	.818	.250	.250
Johnston, Joel	13	3	0	0	.000	.000	2	5	3	3	0	0	10	0	.000	.273	.385
Jones, Calvin	27	4	2	1	.500	.667	8	3	7	3	4	2	16	6	.375	.211	.423
Jones, Doug	32	12	7	5	.583	.583	0	2	0	8	15	7	13	9	.692	.200	.219
Jones, Stacy	3	0	0	0	.000	.000	2	1	0	0	0	0	5	2	.400	.333	.333
Kaiser, Jeff	10	2	2	0	1.000	1.000	1	1	2	2	4	0	10	2	.200	.125	.300
Kiecker, Dana	13	0	0	0	.000	.000	3	4	2	2	1	1	16	9	.562	.364	.462
Kiely, John	7	0	0	0	.000	.000	1	2	2	2	0	0	8	4	.500	.600	.571
Kilgus, Paul	38	4	1	0	.250	1.000	10	4	12	6	4	2	36	11	.306	.156	.250
King, Eric	1	0	0	0	.000	.000	1	0	0	0	0	0	3	3	1.000	.000	.000
Kiser, Garland	7	0	0	0	.000	.000	1	2	3	0	1	0	15	4	.267	.333	.429
Klink, Joe	62	23	2	2	.087	.500	3	10	16	21	8	4	46	12	.261	.236	.300
Knudson, Mark	5	1	0	0	.000	.000	1	0	1	2	1	0	2	1	.500	.600	.600
Kramer, Tom	4	0	0	0	.000	.000	1	1	0	1	1	0	5	5	1.000	.500	.500
Krueger, Bill	10	0	0	0	.000	.000	3	3	1	2	0	1	5	1	.200	.500	.500
Lamp, Dennis	51	7	0	0	.000	.000	21	11	8	7	2	2	57	19	.333	.244	.306
Leach, Terry	50	9	0	2	.000	.000	5	7	10	20	6	2	38	14	.368	.312	.312
Leary, Tim	10	0	0	0	.000	.000	4	0	2	3	1	0	5	1	.200	.444	.500
Lee, Mark	62	22	1	6	.045	.143	5	7	23	20	4	3	56	20	.357	.294	.419
Leiter, Al	3	0	0	0	.000	.000	0	0	2	1	0	0	.000	.000	.667
Leiter, Mark	23	5	1	1	.200	.500	10	4	3	4	2	0	35	16	.457	.294	.478
Lewis, Scott	5	0	0	0	.000	.000	3	0	2	0	0	0	9	3	.333	.200	.200
MacDonald, Rob	45	9	0	4	.000	.000	5	11	11	10	6	2	49	21	.429	.225	.273
Machado, Julio	54	18	3	3	.167	.500	9	14	17	8	4	2	54	16	.296	.156	.296

	GR	SVS	SV	BSV	SC%	SV%	<6I	6I	7I	8I	9I	XI	IR	IRS	IRP	BA	OBA
Magnante, Mike	38	5	0	0	.000	.000	8	10	9	4	6	1	36	13	.361	.286	.342
Maldonado, Carlos	5	0	0	0	.000	.000	1	0	3	1	0	0	1	0	.000	.000	.600
Manuel, Barry	8	0	0	0	.000	.000	3	0	1	3	0	1	6	2	.333	.000	.125
Manzanillo, Jose	1	0	0	0	.000	.000	0	0	0	0	1	0	0	0	.000	.000	1.000
Mathews, Terry	32	5	1	2	.200	.333	4	4	7	14	2	1	21	9	.429	.226	.250
McClure, Bob	13	1	0	0	.000	.000	1	0	5	4	3	0	11	5	.455	.200	.385
McGaffigan, Andy	4	0	0	0	.000	.000	2	0	2	0	0	0	2	0	.000	.000	.250
Meacham, Rusty	6	2	0	0	.000	.000	3	0	2	1	0	0	4	1	.250	.000	.167
Milacki, Bob	5	0	0	0	.000	.000	4	0	0	1	0	0	9	6	.667	.600	.600
Mills, Alan	4	0	0	0	.000	.000	1	0	1	0	1	1	5	2	.400	.250	.250
Monteleone, Rich	26	1	0	0	.000	.000	5	5	5	6	4	1	26	12	.462	.286	.400
Montgomery, Jeff	67	42	33	6	.786	.846	0	1	1	24	35	6	41	18	.439	.311	.373
Morton, Kevin	1	0	0	0	.000	.000	1	0	0	0	0	0	1	1	1.000	1.000	1.000
Munoz, Mike	6	0	0	0	.000	.000	1	1	2	0	2	0	2	0	.000	.200	.333
Murphy, Rob	57	15	4	0	.267	1.000	1	1	10	24	21	0	46	15	.326	.302	.327
Neagle, Denny	4	0	0	0	.000	.000	1	1	1	0	1	0	0	0	.000	.000	.250
Nelson, Gene	44	12	0	5	.000	.000	3	9	13	13	3	3	46	17	.370	.225	.295
Nichols, Rod	15	3	1	1	.333	.500	5	2	5	3	0	0	17	11	.647	.357	.400
Nolte, Eric	3	0	0	0	.000	.000	0	0	0	1	2	0	1	1	1.000	.667	.667
Nunez, Edwin	23	10	8	1	.800	.889	0	0	1	7	12	3	7	5	.714	.111	.304
Olin, Steve	48	24	17	5	.708	.773	1	1	5	12	24	5	28	14	.500	.375	.479
Olson, Gregg	72	40	31	8	.775	.795	0	0	0	16	47	9	30	12	.400	.182	.229
Orosco, Jesse	47	3	0	0	.000	.000	2	2	16	13	12	2	60	27	.450	.326	.340
Otto, Dave	4	0	0	0	.000	.000	3	1	0	0	0	0	7	4	.571	.500	.500
Pall, Donn	51	14	0	1	.000	.000	12	9	8	14	6	2	46	17	.370	.213	.245
Patterson, Ken	43	5	1	1	.200	.500	11	7	15	7	1	2	49	18	.367	.270	.333
Perez, Melido	41	14	1	4	.071	.200	5	8	9	12	6	1	36	15	.417	.382	.421
Petkovsek, Mark	3	0	0	0	.000	.000	0	0	1	2	0	0	2	1	.500	1.000	1.000
Petry, Dan	24	6	1	0	.167	1.000	6	6	4	6	1	1	31	12	.387	.087	.125
Plesac, Dan	35	14	8	4	.571	.667	2	1	2	15	12	3	22	4	.182	.188	.235
Plunk, Eric	35	2	0	0	.000	.000	14	5	7	8	1	0	24	11	.458	.294	.314
Plympton, Jeff	4	1	0	0	.000	.000	0	0	1	2	1	0	2	1	.500	.667	.750
Poole, Jim	30	5	0	0	.000	.000	8	4	6	9	0	3	33	11	.333	.148	.138
Radinsky, Scott	67	30	8	7	.267	.533	0	3	8	40	13	3	63	20	.317	.186	.246
Reardon, Jeff	57	49	40	9	.816	.816	0	0	0	12	44	1	18	4	.222	.222	.246
Rice, Pat	5	0	0	0	.000	.000	5	0	0	0	0	0	6	3	.500	.000	.200
Ritz, Kevin	6	1	0	1	.000	.000	0	2	1	2	1	0	3	2	.667	.250	.500
Robinson, Jeff D.	39	12	3	2	.250	.600	4	7	7	13	7	1	36	9	.250	.270	.308
Robinson, Jeff M.	2	0	0	0	.000	.000	1	1	0	0	0	0	0	0	.000	.500	.500
Rogers, Kenny	54	18	5	1	.278	.833	2	6	18	15	9	4	50	11	.220	.196	.288
Rosenthal, Wayne	37	5	0	1	.000	.000	13	5	9	6	1	3	34	16	.471	.300	.432
Russell, Jeff	68	40	30	10	.750	.750	0	0	0	25	32	11	45	18	.400	.390	.448
Schatzeder, Dan	8	0	0	0	.000	.000	2	1	1	1	3	0	11	8	.727	.625	.625
Schiraldi, Calvin	3	0	0	0	.000	.000	1	0	1	0	0	1	2	1	.500	.333	.333
Schooler, Mike	34	12	7	3	.583	.700	0	1	1	8	20	4	14	5	.357	.242	.242
Seanez, Rudy	5	1	0	1	.000	.000	0	0	2	3	0	0	1	1	1.000	.000	.200
Searcy, Steve	11	2	0	0	.000	.000	4	4	1	0	1	1	7	3	.429	.222	.364
Shaw, Jeff	28	4	1	3	.250	.250	11	5	5	5	1	1	40	21	.525	.333	.357
Show, Eric	19	2	0	0	.000	.000	1	4	5	5	3	1	7	3	.429	.222	.222
Slusarski, Joe	2	0	0	0	.000	.000	1	0	0	1	0	0	0	0	.000	.000	.000
Smith, Roy	3	1	0	0	.000	.000	2	0	1	0	0	0	2	0	.000	.333	.333
Swan, Russ	63	18	2	3	.111	.400	9	12	14	11	11	6	58	14	.241	.328	.344
Swift, Bill	73	34	17	1	.500	.944	6	6	19	20	17	5	61	17	.279	.239	.282
Tanana, Frank	1	1	0	0	.000	.000	0	0	1	0	0	0	0	0	.000	.000	.000
Taylor, Wade	1	0	0	0	.000	.000	0	0	0	1	0	0	0	0	.000	1.000	1.000
Telford, Anthony	8	0	0	0	.000	.000	4	2	1	1	0	0	9	3	.333	.375	.375
Terrell, Walt	2	1	0	0	.000	.000	0	0	1	1	0	0	1	1	1.000	.000	.000
Thigpen, Bobby	67	39	30	9	.769	.769	0	0	0	13	41	13	42	12	.286	.220	.288
Timlin, Mike	60	19	3	5	.158	.375	11	7	16	17	6	3	44	20	.455	.294	.390
Valdez, Efrain	7	1	0	0	.000	.000	1	4	1	1	0	0	7	7	1.000	.750	.857
Valdez, Sergio	6	0	0	0	.000	.000	4	1	1	0	0	0	9	2	.222	.000	.000
Walker, Mike	5	0	0	0	.000	.000	0	0	2	3	0	0	3	0	.000	.200	.200
Walton, Bruce	12	3	0	1	.000	.000	2	1	1	6	2	0	10	3	.300	.000	.000
Wapnick, Steve	6	0	0	0	.000	.000	1	0	0	1	4	0	5	1	.200	.000	.167
Ward, Duane	81	44	23	4	.523	.852	0	4	14	30	29	4	36	10	.278	.231	.237
Wayne, Gary	9	3	1	0	.333	1.000	0	1	1	5	2	0	6	0	.000	.250	.333

	GR	SVS	SV	BSV	SC%	SV%	<6I	6I	7I	8I	9I	XI	IR	IRS	IRP	BA	OBA
Weathers, David	15	1	0	0	.000	.000	3	4	1	2	4	1	18	7	.389	.333	.400
Wells, Dave	12	5	1	1	.200	.500	1	1	2	5	3	0	7	1	.143	.300	.417
West, David	3	0	0	0	.000	.000	1	1	1	0	0	0	0	0	.000	.000	.000
Weston, Mickey	2	0	0	0	.000	.000	0	0	0	1	1	0	0	0	.000	.000	.000
Williamson, Mark	65	21	4	3	.190	.571	7	5	29	15	6	3	62	22	.355	.263	.308
Willis, Carl	40	8	2	1	.250	.667	16	10	7	3	0	4	28	7	.250	.114	.150
Wills, Frank	4	0	0	0	.000	.000	0	0	1	2	0	1	0	0	.000	.250	.250
Witt, Bobby	1	0	0	0	.000	.000	1	0	0	0	0	0	1	0	.000	.000	.000
York, Mike	10	0	0	0	.000	.000	2	1	4	2	0	1	11	4	.364	.167	.500
Young, Cliff	11	0	0	0	.000	.000	1	1	2	7	0	0	9	1	.111	.364	.364
Young, Curt	41	8	0	0	.000	.000	13	10	10	6	1	1	25	10	.400	.189	.268
Young, Matt	3	1	0	0	.000	.000	0	1	1	0	0	1	3	0	.000	.000	.667

NATIONAL LEAGUE

	GR	SVS	SV	BSV	SC%	SV%	<6I	6I	7I	8I	9I	XI	IR	IRS	IRP	BA	OBA
Agosto, Juan	72	16	2	5	.125	.286	6	10	19	27	9	1	39	21	.538	.322	.423
Akerfelds, Darrel	30	2	0	0	.000	.000	8	10	3	5	2	2	19	3	.158	.296	.367
Andersen, Larry	38	22	13	3	.591	.812	0	0	7	15	14	2	23	6	.261	.250	.263
Armstrong, Jack	3	0	0	0	.000	.000	2	0	0	1	0	0	1	1	1.000	.333	.333
Assenmacher, Paul	75	39	15	9	.385	.625	0	4	13	37	17	4	51	20	.392	.209	.293
Barnes, Brian	1	0	0	0	.000	.000	0	0	1	0	0	0	2	2	1.000	.000	.000
Beatty, Blaine	5	0	0	0	.000	.000	2	0	2	0	0	1	3	2	.667	.250	.400
Beck, Rodney	31	2	1	0	.500	1.000	9	5	4	10	2	1	14	5	.357	.200	.226
Belinda, Stan	60	28	16	4	.571	.800	0	4	14	26	15	1	38	13	.342	.120	.267
Berenguer, Juan	49	22	17	1	.773	.944	0	0	11	20	16	2	27	3	.111	.170	.204
Bielecki, Mike	16	1	0	1	.000	.000	3	2	3	3	2	3	12	7	.583	.286	.375
Boever, Joe	68	11	0	2	.000	.000	8	11	16	19	9	5	35	15	.429	.271	.353
Boskie, Shawn	8	0	0	0	.000	.000	5	0	1	1	0	1	11	1	.091	.000	.250
Bowen, Ryan	1	0	0	0	.000	.000	1	0	0	0	0	0	0	0	.000	.000	.000
Brantley, Cliff	1	0	0	0	.000	.000	1	0	0	0	0	0	3	1	.333	.000	.000
Brantley, Jeff	67	32	15	4	.469	.789	0	6	16	30	13	2	39	11	.282	.190	.269
Bross, Terry	8	0	0	0	.000	.000	1	1	1	3	2	0	3	0	.000	.250	.250
Brown, Keith	11	0	0	0	.000	.000	0	2	5	2	2	0	8	4	.500	.273	.273
Burke, Tim	72	28	6	10	.214	.375	4	3	20	29	14	2	39	11	.282	.308	.375
Burkett, John	2	1	0	0	.000	.000	0	0	2	0	0	0	4	2	.500	.000	.500
Candelaria, John	59	27	2	3	.074	.400	0	0	17	25	15	2	60	18	.300	.179	.203
Capel, Mike	25	6	3	1	.500	.750	2	6	5	3	5	4	18	5	.278	.261	.320
Carman, Don	28	1	1	0	1.000	1.000	3	6	6	7	4	2	17	5	.294	.348	.429
Carpenter, Cris	59	13	0	0	.000	.000	5	8	12	23	8	3	37	10	.270	.273	.310
Carreno, Amalio	3	0	0	0	.000	.000	2	0	0	0	1	0	5	2	.400	.000	.333
Castillo, Tony	14	2	0	0	.000	.000	2	1	4	3	3	1	8	0	.000	.385	.429
Charlton, Norm	28	8	1	3	.125	.250	2	3	11	10	2	0	16	12	.750	.346	.370
Christopher, Mike	3	1	0	0	.000	.000	0	0	1	2	0	0	0	0	.000	.000	.667
Clancy, Jim	54	14	8	3	.571	.727	15	7	8	10	12	2	26	7	.269	.239	.333
Clark, Mark	5	1	0	0	.000	.000	1	2	0	2	0	0	2	0	.000	.000	.000
Clements, Pat	12	2	0	0	.000	.000	5	0	4	2	1	0	9	3	.333	.364	.333
Combs, Pat	1	0	0	0	.000	.000	1	0	0	0	0	0	1	0	.000	.000	.000
Cook, Dennis	19	4	0	1	.000	.000	3	4	4	1	5	2	28	11	.393	.364	.526
Cormier, Rheal	1	0	0	0	.000	.000	0	0	0	1	0	0	0	0	.000	1.000	1.000
Corsi, Jim	47	7	0	3	.000	.000	11	13	8	7	4	4	22	4	.182	.167	.255
Costello, John	27	9	0	1	.000	.000	5	3	10	5	4	0	13	4	.308	.423	.444
Cox, Danny	6	1	0	0	.000	.000	2	0	1	2	1	0	6	1	.167	.000	.000
Crews, Tim	60	17	6	2	.353	.750	13	8	14	12	11	2	49	16	.327	.250	.271
DeJesus, Jose	2	1	1	0	1.000	1.000	1	0	0	0	0	1	0	0	.000	.000	.000
Dibble, Rob	67	36	31	5	.861	.861	0	0	2	28	31	6	42	8	.190	.259	.343
Downs, Kelly	34	3	0	2	.000	.000	12	11	5	5	1	0	32	13	.406	.219	.235
Fassero, Jeff	51	19	8	3	.421	.727	0	2	11	23	7	8	38	11	.289	.200	.294
Foster, Steve	11	0	0	0	.000	.000	1	1	3	4	2	0	3	0	.000	.182	.182
Franco, John	52	35	30	5	.857	.857	0	0	0	9	35	8	25	8	.320	.200	.216
Fraser, Willie	35	4	0	0	.000	.000	7	2	10	9	5	2	20	9	.450	.276	.400
Freeman, Marvin	34	11	1	0	.091	1.000	10	9	8	7	0	0	18	8	.444	.161	.212
Frey, Steve	31	7	1	1	.143	.500	6	3	9	6	4	3	17	9	.529	.240	.355
Gardner, Chris	1	0	0	0	.000	.000	1	0	0	0	0	0	0	0	.000	.000	.000
Gardner, Wes	14	2	1	0	.500	1.000	5	3	1	2	1	2	6	3	.500	.462	.500
Garrelts, Scott	5	0	0	0	.000	.000	1	1	1	2	0	0	1	0	.000	.600	.600
Gott, Jim	55	14	2	3	.143	.400	5	4	18	21	4	3	21	7	.333	.319	.400

	GR	SVS	SV	BSV	SC%	SV%	<6I	6I	7I	8I	9I	XI	IR	IRS	IRP	BA	OBA
Grater, Mark	3	0	0	0	.000	.000	1	0	1	1	0	0	4	2	.500	.333	.333
Greene, Tommy	9	0	0	0	.000	.000	5	2	0	1	0	1	14	8	.571	.125	.111
Gross, Kevin	36	11	3	3	.273	.500	5	3	9	7	8	4	8	3	.375	.375	.444
Gross, Kip	20	1	0	0	.000	.000	9	3	3	2	3	0	14	10	.714	.389	.450
Gunderson, Eric	2	2	1	0	.500	1.000	0	1	1	0	0	0	2	2	1.000	1.000	1.000
Hammond, Chris	2	0	0	0	.000	.000	1	0	1	0	0	0	0	0	.000	.500	.500
Hartley, Mike	58	13	2	2	.154	.500	10	10	14	13	7	4	38	16	.421	.255	.328
Heaton, Neal	41	9	0	1	.000	.000	11	8	14	5	2	1	12	5	.417	.282	.300
Henry, Dwayne	52	5	2	0	.400	1.000	5	5	13	15	9	5	35	18	.514	.250	.353
Heredia, Gil	3	0	0	0	.000	.000	0	2	0	1	0	0	0	0	.000	.500	.667
Hernandez, Jeremy	9	3	2	0	.667	1.000	0	1	2	4	2	0	3	1	.333	.143	.333
Hernandez, Xavier	26	12	3	3	.250	.500	1	8	5	6	5	1	21	8	.381	.318	.423
Hickerson, Bryan	11	1	0	0	.000	.000	3	3	1	1	3	0	6	0	.000	.250	.455
Hill, Milt	22	1	0	1	.000	.000	6	3	2	7	3	1	19	7	.368	.300	.318
Howell, Jay	44	20	16	2	.800	.889	0	0	0	10	26	8	15	5	.333	.238	.273
Huismann, Mark	5	1	0	0	.000	.000	1	1	0	3	0	0	3	2	.667	.500	.600
Innis, Jeff	69	8	0	3	.000	.000	11	8	12	22	12	4	57	21	.368	.222	.275
Jackson, Danny	3	0	0	0	.000	.000	2	0	0	1	0	0	2	1	.500	1.000	1.000
Jones, Barry	77	26	13	8	.500	.619	0	4	11	30	29	3	51	16	.314	.290	.333
Jones, Jimmy	4	1	0	0	.000	.000	2	1	1	0	0	0	3	0	.000	.250	.250
Juden, Jeff	1	0	0	0	.000	.000	1	0	0	0	0	0	0	0	.000	.000	.000
Kile, Darryl	15	1	0	1	.000	.000	6	2	2	5	0	0	6	2	.333	.200	.467
Kipper, Bob	52	14	4	2	.286	.667	5	5	9	19	8	6	32	11	.344	.234	.308
LaCoss, Mike	13	2	0	1	.000	.000	3	2	2	1	2	3	2	0	.000	.250	.308
Lancaster, Les	53	10	3	3	.300	.500	7	10	11	16	5	4	43	22	.512	.319	.385
Landrum, Bill	61	27	17	5	.630	.773	0	2	5	18	32	4	35	10	.286	.155	.197
Layana, Tim	22	3	1	1	.333	.500	6	3	4	4	4	1	15	4	.267	.300	.364
Lefferts, Craig	54	35	23	7	.657	.767	0	0	0	26	24	4	30	9	.300	.333	.346
Lewis, Jim	12	3	0	0	.000	.000	2	3	1	5	1	0	5	3	.600	.400	.500
Lilliquist, Derek	4	0	0	0	.000	.000	2	0	0	2	0	0	0	0	.000	.000	.250
Long, Bill	3	1	0	0	.000	.000	0	0	2	1	0	0	2	2	1.000	.500	.667
Maddux, Mike	63	16	5	2	.312	.714	10	7	14	20	9	3	46	11	.239	.196	.262
Mahler, Rick	15	2	0	2	.000	.000	6	6	1	2	0	0	15	7	.467	.214	.267
Mallicoat, Rob	24	13	1	0	.077	1.000	2	1	13	8	0	0	20	10	.500	.250	.304
Mason, Roger	24	6	3	0	.500	1.000	4	2	8	6	3	1	21	2	.095	.174	.208
Mauser, Tim	3	0	0	0	.000	.000	2	1	0	0	0	0	2	0	.000	.333	.333
May, Scott	2	1	0	0	.000	.000	0	1	1	0	0	0	0	0	.000	1.000	1.000
McClellan, Paul	1	0	0	0	.000	.000	0	0	0	0	1	0	0	0	.000	1.000	1.000
McClure, Bob	32	12	0	4	.000	.000	0	0	6	15	10	1	31	12	.387	.280	.355
McDowell, Roger	72	27	10	5	.370	.667	1	1	17	30	18	5	43	16	.372	.348	.394
McElroy, Chuck	71	18	3	3	.167	.500	9	18	20	13	6	5	58	23	.397	.246	.324
Melendez, Jose	22	6	3	1	.500	.750	3	2	7	5	2	3	9	3	.333	.250	.227
Mercker, Kent	46	12	6	2	.500	.750	2	2	6	19	15	2	13	7	.538	.216	.370
Minutelli, Gino	13	2	0	0	.000	.000	3	2	3	4	0	1	10	7	.700	.125	.462
Morgan, Mike	1	1	1	0	1.000	1.000	0	0	1	0	0	0	2	0	.000	.000	.000
Moyer, Jamie	1	0	0	0	.000	.000	0	0	0	1	0	0	0	0	.000	.000	.000
Myers, Randy	46	19	6	4	.316	.600	1	3	19	11	11	1	38	8	.211	.275	.348
Olivares, Omar	4	1	1	0	1.000	1.000	2	0	1	1	0	0	2	1	.500	.250	.250
Oliveras, Francisco	54	16	3	1	.188	.750	6	9	12	18	7	2	31	8	.258	.167	.226
Osuna, Al	71	33	12	9	.364	.571	0	3	14	36	13	5	57	24	.421	.233	.333
Palacios, Vicente	29	10	3	2	.300	.600	6	8	4	5	5	1	15	9	.600	.259	.286
Parrett, Jeff	18	1	1	0	1.000	1.000	1	3	1	7	3	3	5	4	.800	.688	.722
Patterson, Bob	53	16	2	1	.125	.667	4	5	10	19	12	3	29	7	.241	.294	.321
Pavlas, Dave	1	0	0	0	.000	.000	0	0	0	0	1	0	0	0	.000	1.000	1.000
Pena, Alejandro	59	21	15	5	.714	.750	2	1	14	19	20	3	28	8	.286	.170	.220
Perez, Mike	14	2	0	0	.000	.000	1	2	6	3	1	1	6	2	.333	.170	.220
Perez, Yorkis	3	1	0	1	.000	.000	1	2	0	0	0	0	5	2	.400	.462	.500
Peterson, Adam	2	0	0	0	.000	.000	0	1	0	0	0	1	0	0	.000	.000	.333
Petry, Dan	10	0	0	0	.000	.000	4	2	2	2	0	0	4	4	1.000	.000	.500
Piatt, Doug	21	3	0	0	.000	.000	3	8	6	2	2	0	14	6	.429	.333	.556
Portugal, Mark	5	3	1	1	.333	.500	0	0	0	3	1	1	6	4	.667	.368	.429
Power, Ted	68	17	3	1	.176	.750	2	12	22	19	10	3	33	10	.303	.262	.324
Remlinger, Mike	2	0	0	0	.000	.000	0	1	0	1	0	0	0	0	.000	.000	.500
Renfroe, Laddie	4	1	0	1	.000	.000	0	1	0	1	1	1	3	3	1.000	.500	.500
Reuschel, Rick	3	1	0	1	.000	.000	0	1	1	1	0	0	5	3	.600	.667	.667

	GR	SVS	SV	BSV	SC%	SV%	<6I	6I	7I	8I	9I	XI	IR	IRS	IRP	BA	OBA
Reynoso, Armando	1	0	0	0	.000	.000	0	0	0	0	1	0	0	0	.000	.000	.000
Righetti, Dave	61	34	24	5	.706	.828	0	0	2	18	37	4	32	5	.156	.071	.148
Ritchie, Wally	39	11	0	3	.000	.000	3	5	12	12	7	0	28	7	.250	.062	.184
Robinson, Don	18	2	1	0	.500	1.000	7	1	2	5	3	0	10	3	.300	.250	.278
Rodriguez, Rich	63	13	0	2	.000	.000	7	12	18	15	8	3	49	15	.306	.232	.306
Rodriguez, Rosario	18	10	6	0	.600	1.000	0	1	3	9	5	0	7	1	.143	.235	.278
Rojas, Mel	37	17	6	3	.353	.667	4	7	10	13	2	1	18	6	.333	.265	.297
Rosenberg, Steve	10	3	0	1	.000	.000	0	1	3	3	2	1	7	3	.429	.333	.400
Ruffin, Bruce	16	5	0	0	.000	.000	5	8	1	1	0	1	14	4	.286	.083	.250
Ruskin, Scott	64	21	6	5	.286	.545	1	7	16	24	13	3	42	10	.238	.186	.250
Sampen, Bill	35	5	0	0	.000	.000	10	8	7	5	1	4	21	7	.333	.242	.286
Sauveur, Rich	6	4	0	2	.000	.000	1	2	0	2	1	0	7	2	.286	.500	.500
Scanlan, Bob	27	4	1	1	.250	.500	4	2	3	8	6	4	15	5	.333	.333	.462
Schilling, Curt	56	17	8	3	.471	.727	2	1	13	21	17	2	29	11	.379	.396	.482
Schmidt, Dave	4	0	0	0	.000	.000	0	1	2	0	0	1	0	0	.000	.500	.500
Schourek, Pete	27	7	2	1	.286	.667	4	5	11	4	1	2	19	9	.474	.250	.385
Scott, Tim	2	0	0	0	.000	.000	1	0	1	0	0	0	2	0	.000	.500	.500
Scudder, Scott	13	2	1	0	.500	1.000	4	1	6	0	1	1	2	1	.500	.333	.385
Searcy, Steve	18	1	0	0	.000	.000	6	1	4	5	2	0	10	3	.300	.471	.471
Segura, Jose	11	1	0	1	.000	.000	4	1	5	0	1	0	7	2	.286	.300	.364
Sherrill, Tim	10	0	0	0	.000	.000	2	1	4	1	2	0	1	0	.000	.200	.200
Simons, Doug	41	5	1	0	.200	1.000	6	6	10	12	5	2	17	9	.529	.306	.350
Sisk, Doug	14	4	0	0	.000	.000	1	3	4	2	1	3	14	5	.357	.286	.286
Slocumb, Heathcliff	52	9	1	2	.111	.333	6	4	12	16	10	4	40	14	.350	.146	.308
Smiley, John	1	0	0	0	.000	.000	1	0	0	0	0	0	0	0	.000	.000	.000
Smith, Dave	35	25	17	6	.680	.739	0	0	1	11	19	4	21	9	.429	.375	.429
Smith, Lee	67	53	47	6	.887	.887	0	0	0	15	47	5	26	12	.462	.270	.299
Smith, Pete	4	0	0	0	.000	.000	1	1	0	2	0	0	6	2	.333	.500	.500
St.Claire, Randy	19	0	0	0	.000	.000	5	2	4	4	2	2	11	4	.364	.444	.474
Stanton, Mike	74	26	7	3	.269	.700	2	8	25	23	15	1	58	15	.259	.171	.216
Sutcliffe, Rick	1	0	0	0	.000	.000	1	0	0	0	0	0	1	1	1.000	1.000	1.000
Terry, Scott	65	19	1	2	.053	.333	7	8	19	22	7	2	33	12	.364	.291	.400
Tomlin, Randy	4	0	0	0	.000	.000	2	0	1	1	0	0	0	0	.000	.000	.250
Valera, Julio	2	0	0	0	.000	.000	0	0	1	0	1	0	3	1	.333	.000	.000
Wainhouse, Dave	2	0	0	0	.000	.000	0	0	0	2	0	0	0	0	.000	.000	.500
Walk, Bob	5	1	0	1	.000	.000	2	1	1	1	0	0	1	1	1.000	.600	.600
Wetteland, John	6	0	0	0	.000	.000	2	0	0	2	1	1	5	3	.600	.333	.500
Whitehurst, Wally	16	4	1	0	.250	1.000	3	4	6	0	2	1	8	4	.500	.200	.250
Whitson, Ed	1	0	0	0	.000	.000	0	0	1	0	0	0	0	0	.000	1.000	1.000
Wilkins, Dean	7	3	1	1	.333	.500	0	1	2	2	1	1	7	0	.000	.333	.429
Williams, Mitch	69	40	30	9	.750	.769	0	0	2	25	34	8	24	7	.292	.145	.319
Wilson, Steve	19	7	2	0	.286	1.000	5	1	5	6	2	0	23	6	.261	.308	.526
Wilson, Trevor	15	5	0	1	.000	.000	3	4	4	3	0	1	9	3	.333	.231	.333
Wohlers, Mark	17	6	2	2	.333	.500	0	5	4	4	4	0	8	5	.625	.250	.294
Young, Anthony	2	0	0	0	.000	.000	0	0	2	0	0	0	2	0	.000	.000	.000

The Fielding Range Reports

These tables show a new and more accurate method of measuring a fielder's range, based on balls actually fielded by players. What really matters for fielders is their ability to position themselves properly to catch batted balls and turn them into outs. There are many ways to do this: by catching fly balls, pop-ups, or line drives; by fielding ground balls and putting out the batter or a runner unassisted; or by fielding ground balls and throwing to another player, putting out the batter or a runner. (Note that only one player can be credited in this way on each play.)

Infielders, especially, get putouts in various ways that have nothing to do with their range and everything to do with their position (e.g., receiving a throw at first base). Traditional ways of measuring fielding range are much less accurate, since they are based simply on putouts, assists or total chances, not on balls fielded.

For outfielders, the major problem with traditional fielding statistics is different, since putouts are clearly related to their range while assists equally clearly are not. Here the problem is that official fielding statistics add all plays in left, center, or right fields together, giving one total for three different positions. The fielding reports that follow separate each player's defensive statistics in left field, center field, and right field, making meaningful range calculations possible.

The first step in calculating fielding range is to credit a "Ball Fielded" (BF) to each player when he is the first to handle a batted ball put into play that results in an out. Thus, the player who catches a fly ball or who starts a ground out or double play gets credit for fielding that ball.

The second step is to get a more accurate measure of just how much time a player puts in at a fielding position. Official fielding statistics tally "Games at Position," but these can't easily be used to determine range accurately (because a player gets credit for one game at position whether he plays the whole game there or only the 9th inning). Therefore, to determine a player's opportunities to field batted balls, we count the number of balls put into play by opposing batters when he is in the field. A "Ball in Play" is defined as a hit, an error, or an out, except that home runs are not counted because they usually cannot be fielded.

In the third step, "Defensive Equivalent Games" (DEG) are computed for all players by counting the balls put into play while they are on the field and dividing by the league average of balls put into play per game. (Theoretically, a player could have more than 162 DEG if he plays almost every game for a team whose pitching staff allows a lot of hits and/or strikes out few batters.)

Using these numbers, a player's fielding range is computed by dividing his balls fielded at a position by his DEG at that position. Then one final adjustment is made to this range figure to get the Adjusted Fielding Range (AFR), which is the basis for the fielding reports for infielders and outfielders.

Players on different teams face different numbers of right- and left-handed batters due to the composition of their pitching staff. This can have a substantial effect on their range numbers, for right-handed batters hit many more ground balls to shortstop and third base than left-handed batters do, for example. (The converse is true for balls hit to the right side of the infield.) Therefore, each player's range is adjusted to reflect a league-average percentage of left- and right-handed hitters facing his team.

For outfielders, the reports give information for each outfield position played, treating left, center, and right fields separately. Note that an outfielder's total games in LF+CF+RF will frequently be greater than his total official games in the outfield, because he may have played more than one outfield position in some games.

For catchers, the reports change format to show the wild pitches and passed balls they allowed. Because there are relatively few wild pitches and even fewer passed balls, we compute the rates per full season for catchers based on their defensive equivalent games. Balls put into play are not particularly relevant, so catchers' DEG are defined simply as their defensive innings divided by nine. The column heads become: Innings (Innings Caught); Inn/9 (Innings Caught/9); WP (Wild Pitches allowed); WP/162 (Wild Pitches per 162 games); PB (Passed Balls); PB/162 (Passed Balls per 162 games).

FIELDING RANGE REPORTS

AMERICAN LEAGUE

CATCHER	Innings	Inn/9	WP	WP/162	PB	PB/162
Afenir, Troy	27.0	3.0	1	54.0	0	0.0
Allanson, Andy	396.2	44.1	9	33.1	3	11.0
Alomar, Sandy	395.1	43.9	11	40.6	5	18.4
Borders, Pat	699.2	77.7	34	70.9	13	27.1
Bradley, Scott	406.2	45.2	36	129.1	3	10.8
Cochrane, Dave	78.1	8.7	6	111.7	6	111.7
Dempsey, Rick	407.2	45.3	13	46.5	5	17.9
Fisk, Carlton	795.1	88.4	27	49.5	11	20.2
Geren, Bob	375.2	41.7	16	62.1	1	3.9
Harper, Brian	991.0	110.1	36	53.0	9	13.2
Hemond, Scott	31.0	3.4	1	47.0	0	0.0
Hoiles, Chris	728.2	81.0	18	36.0	3	6.0
Howard, Chris	30.0	3.3	0	0.0	0	0.0
Karkovice, Ron	455.1	50.6	11	35.2	2	6.4
Knorr, Randy	4.0	0.4	1	364.5	0	0.0
Kreuter, Chad	5.0	0.6	0	0.0	0	0.0
Leyritz, Jim	25.2	2.9	1	56.8	0	0.0
Lopez, Luis	59.0	6.6	3	74.1	2	49.4
Macfarlane, Mike	579.2	64.4	28	70.4	4	10.1
Manto, Jeff	16.0	1.8	1	91.1	2	182.2
Marzano, John	280.0	31.1	8	41.7	6	31.2
Mayne, Brent	606.0	67.3	15	36.1	2	4.8
Melvin, Bob	580.2	64.5	23	57.8	3	7.5
Merullo, Matt	135.2	15.1	4	43.0	3	32.2
Myers, Greg	753.0	83.7	20	38.7	9	17.4
Nokes, Matt	1001.2	111.3	33	48.0	11	16.0
Ortiz, Junior	369.2	41.1	18	71.0	3	11.8
Orton, John	205.2	22.9	10	70.9	1	7.1
Parent, Mark	5.0	0.6	0	0.0	0	0.0
Parrish, Lance	912.2	101.4	23	36.7	19	30.4
Pedre, Jorge	50.0	5.6	2	58.3	0	0.0
Pena, Tony	1159.2	128.9	34	42.7	5	6.3
Petralli, Geno	403.0	44.8	20	72.4	3	10.9
Quirk, Jamie	437.0	48.6	20	66.7	2	6.7
Ramos, John	41.0	4.6	3	106.7	1	35.6
Rodriguez, Ivan	686.0	76.2	39	82.9	8	17.0
Rowland, Rick	2.0	0.2	0	0.0	0	0.0
Russell, John	25.0	2.8	1	58.3	1	58.3
Salas, Mark	38.0	4.2	2	76.7	0	0.0
Sinatro, Matt	25.0	2.8	2	116.6	0	0.0
Skinner, Joel	790.0	87.8	26	48.0	6	11.1
Spehr, Tim	230.1	25.6	2	12.7	5	31.6
Sprague, Ed	6.0	0.7	0	0.0	0	0.0
Stanley, Mike	355.0	39.4	17	69.8	4	16.4
Steinbach, Terry	949.1	105.5	38	58.4	6	9.2
Surhoff, B.J.	1056.0	117.3	40	55.2	11	15.2
Tackett, Jeff	30.1	3.4	2	96.1	1	48.1
Taubensee, Eddie	181.0	20.1	7	56.4	4	32.2
Tettleton, Mickey	1013.2	112.6	39	56.1	9	12.9
Tingley, Ron	323.1	35.9	16	72.1	3	13.5

CATCHER (contd.)	Innings	Inn/9	WP	WP/162	PB	PB/162
Valle, Dave	924.1	102.7	38	59.9	15	23.7
Wakamatsu, Don	91.2	10.2	2	31.8	4	63.6
Webster, Lenny	88.2	9.9	3	49.3	0	0.0
Whitt, Ernie	118.0	13.1	6	74.1	1	12.4
American League	**20382.0**	**2264.7**	**766**	**54.8**	**215**	**15.4**

FIRST BASE	G	DEG	AFR
Aldrete, Mike	46	33.87	1.83
Allanson, Andy	2	0.46	2.07
Amaral, Richard	1	0.35	2.35
Barnes, Skeeter	9	2.44	1.59
Benzinger, Todd	75	69.85	2.09
Bergman, Dave	49	44.12	1.68
Bradley, Scott	1	0.25	3.92
Brett, George	10	9.72	1.55
Brock, Greg	25	17.85	1.91
Buhner, Jay	1	0.14	0.00
Bush, Randy	12	5.23	1.79
Canale, George	19	12.80	3.64
Cochrane, Dave	5	2.30	2.18
Cromartie, Warren	29	25.98	1.34
Cron, Chris	5	3.89	4.65
Daugherty, Jack	11	7.28	2.03
Davis, Alvin	13	10.85	2.49
Davis, Glenn	37	34.86	2.12
DelosSantos, Luis	1	0.07	0.00
Dempsey, Rick	1	0.00	0.00
Eisenreich, Jim	15	11.35	2.21
Fielder, Cecil	122	123.05	1.80
Fisk, Carlton	12	10.43	2.18
Gomez, Leo	3	1.48	1.41
Gonzales, Rene	2	0.25	11.03
Harper, Brian	1	0.18	0.00
Hill, Donnie	3	1.77	0.75
Hoiles, Chris	2	1.17	0.94
Howell, Jack	3	1.48	2.87
Howitt, Dann	1	0.95	4.17
Hrbek, Kent	129	119.87	2.10
Jacoby, Brook	57	50.09	1.82
James, Chris	15	12.97	1.39
Jefferson, Reggie	26	28.39	2.06
Joyner, Wally	141	132.00	2.32
Kittle, Ron	15	10.64	1.73
Larkin, Gene	39	27.57	2.18
Law, Vance	2	0.46	4.13
Leyritz, Jim	3	0.53	1.65
Lopez, Luis	10	8.24	2.84
Lyons, Barry	2	1.10	2.35
Lyons, Steve	2	0.21	0.00

FIRST BASE (contd.)	G	DEG	AFR
Maas, Kevin	36	35.10	2.19
Manto, Jeff	14.	8.70	0.81
Marshall, Mike	6	5.44	1.50
Martinez, Carlos	32	28.88	1.54
Martinez, Carmelo	43	36.87	2.21
Martinez, Chito	1	0.18	3.31
Martinez, Tino	29	27.26	2.19
Mattingly, Don	127	122.52	1.97
Maurer, Rob	4	0.99	5.88
McGwire, Mark	152	139.99	2.21
McIntosh, Tim	1	0.18	0.00
McKnight, Jeff	2	1.91	3.33
Merullo, Matt	16	7.71	2.02
Meulens, Hensley	7	3.57	2.06
Milligan, Randy	105	103.54	2.00
Molitor, Paul	46	46.41	2.16
Morman, Russ	8	4.84	3.09
Newman, Al	1	0.67	1.74
O'Brien, Pete	133	113.51	2.08
Olerud, John	135	122.03	2.21
Palmeiro, Rafael	157	149.60	1.90
Parrish, Lance	3	1.63	0.41
Pasqua, Dan	83	58.05	1.98
Pecota, Bill	8	4.28	1.03
Pedre, Jorge	1	0.67	0.00
Powell, Alonzo	6	2.19	1.96
Quintana, Carlos	138	112.66	2.17
Quirk, Jamie	8	5.34	1.94
Riles, Ernie	5	2.83	3.52
Rose, Bobby	3	2.33	1.49
Salas, Mark	5	0.78	2.65
Segui, David	42	23.08	2.17
Snyder, Cory	22	12.73	3.01
Sorrento, Paul	13	8.17	1.53
Sprague, Ed	22	15.77	1.87
Stanley, Mike	12	4.98	2.62
Steinbach, Terry	9	5.27	2.18
Stevens, Lee	11	8.34	2.41
Stubbs, Franklin	92	89.75	2.04
Tabler, Pat	20	18.31	2.81
Tettleton, Mickey	1	0.18	0.00
Thomas, Frank	56	51.36	1.65
Valle, Dave	2	0.42	0.00
Vaughn, Mo	49	39.10	2.13
Ventura, Robin	31	9.65	2.04
Witmeyer, Ron	8	3.75	1.39
American League	**2268**	**2268.00**	**2.05**

SECOND BASE	G	DEG	AFR
Alomar, Roberto	160	153.84	3.66
Amaral, Richard	5	2.19	6.95
Amaro Jr., Ruben	4	2.40	1.68
Baerga, Carlos	75	76.39	3.14
Barnes, Skeeter	7	4.63	2.86
Bell, Juan	77	58.01	3.26
Bernazard, Tony	2	1.17	2.89

SECOND BASE (contd.)	G	DEG	AFR
Blankenship, Lance	45	30.33	3.64
Bordick, Mike	8	4.67	2.88
Briley, Greg	1	0.25	0.00
Brosius, Scott	18	2.16	1.74
Browne, Jerry	47	39.03	3.43
Brumley, Mike	7	4.49	4.44
Buechele, Steve	13	10.75	3.41
Cole, Stu	5	1.13	3.24
Cora, Joey	80	60.77	3.19
Diaz, Mario	20	8.70	3.91
Disarcina, Gary	7	5.51	2.40
Escobar, Jose	4	2.19	3.56
Fariss, Monty	4	2.83	2.95
Fletcher, Scott	86	68.44	3.24
Flora, Kevin	3	2.58	1.56
Franco, Julio	146	140.13	3.04
Gallego, Mike	132	115.49	3.29
Gantner, Jim	59	52.50	3.70
Gonzales, Rene	11	4.49	3.10
Grebeck, Craig	36	29.23	3.90
Hernond, Scott	7	2.93	5.10
Henderson, Dave	1	0.21	0.00
Hill, Donnie	39	29.87	3.41
Howard, David	27	17.89	3.60
Howell, Jack	12	9.37	4.73
Huff, Mike	4	1.63	2.64
Hulett, Tim	26	12.73	2.61
Huson, Jeff	2	0.46	3.92
Kelly, Pat	18	12.90	3.62
Knoblauch, Chuck	148	138.22	3.45
Larkin, Gene	1	0.11	0.00
Lewis, Mark	50	48.89	3.10
Liriano, Nelson	10	6.29	3.50
Lyons, Steve	16	7.78	3.62
Manrique, Fred	2	1.13	4.28
Naehring, Tim	1	0.57	3.92
Newman, Al	35	23.30	3.65
Pagliarulo, Mike	1	0.07	0.00
Paredes, Johnny	7	4.60	2.09
Pecota, Bill	33	16.47	2.51
Perezchica, Tony	2	1.06	4.73
Phillips, Tony	36	36.55	3.52
Randolph, Willie	121	113.33	3.30
Reed, Jody	152	143.45	3.42
Reynolds, Harold	159	150.84	3.25
Riles, Ernie	7	3.75	3.22
Ripken, Billy	103	95.37	3.01
Rodriguez, Carlos	3	0.71	1.50
Rose, Bobby	8	7.81	3.14
Sax, Steve	149	146.84	3.15
Schaefer, Jeff	11	3.85	2.85
Shumpert, Terry	144	121.78	3.21
Sojo, Luis	107	96.12	3.88
Surhoff, B.J.	1	0.21	0.00
Sveum, Dale	2	0.95	5.21
Turner, Shane	1	0.11	5.88

SECOND BASE (contd.)	G	DEG	AFR
Velarde, Randy	1	1.27	4.71
Vizquel, Omar	1	0.14	0.00
Whitaker, Lou	134	124.15	3.21
American League	**2268**	**2268.00**	**3.33**

THIRD BASE	G	DEG	AFR
Amaral, Richard	2	0.14	8.27
Baerga, Carlos	89	79.61	2.78
Barnes, Skeeter	17	11.06	2.30
Berry, Sean	30	18.77	3.42
Bichette, Dante	1	0.21	0.00
Blankenship, Lance	14	9.40	2.64
Blowers, Mike	14	9.93	2.11
Boggs, Wade	141	128.75	2.47
Bordick, Mike	1	0.21	0.00
Bradley, Scott	4	1.73	1.18
Briley, Greg	1	0.21	0.00
Brosius, Scott	7	6.33	2.39
Browne, Jerry	15	13.11	2.81
Brumley, Mike	17	9.01	3.24
Buechele, Steve	111	101.10	2.92
Cochrane, Dave	13	10.32	2.19
Cooper, Scott	13	9.83	2.72
DelosSantos, Luis	2	1.10	0.72
Diaz, Mario	8	3.61	2.23
Disarcina, Gary	2	1.38	3.22
Escobar, Jose	1	0.11	0.00
Espinoza, Alvaro	2	1.87	2.72
Fletcher, Scott	4	0.60	1.18
Fryman, Travis	86	84.88	2.15
Gaetti, Gary	152	143.17	2.74
Gantner, Jim	90	85.55	2.27
Giannelli, Ray	9	6.58	1.84
Gomez, Leo	105	103.75	2.28
Gonzales, Rene	26	12.02	3.63
Grebeck, Craig	49	19.51	3.27
Gruber, Kelly	111	106.16	2.72
Hemond, Scott	2	1.17	1.02
Hernandez, Jose	1	0.35	6.09
Howard, David	1	0.21	0.00
Howell, Jack	8	6.29	2.75
Hulett, Tim	39	32.20	2.37
Humphreys, Mike	.6	3.85	2.36
Huson, Jeff	1	0.14	5.51
Jacoby, Brook	67	59.57	2.42
Kelly, Pat	81	75.97	2.39
Lansford, Carney	4	2.79	1.27
Larkin, Gene	1	0.07	0.00
Law, Vance	66	40.41	2.22
Leius, Scott	79	51.82	2.60
Leyritz, Jim	18	15.38	2.03
Livingstone, Scott	43	36.69	2.45
Lopez, Luis	1	0.39	0.00
Lovullo, Torey	22	15.62	3.26
Lyons, Steve	12	7.11	3.35
Manto, Jeff	32	31.21	2.40
Martinez, Edgar	144	133.80	2.65
Mulliniks, Rance	5	2.90	2.96

THIRD BASE (contd.)	G	DEG	AFR
Naehring, Tim	2	1.59	1.84
Newman, Al	35	9.79	2.60
Pagliarulo, Mike	118	100.01	2.93
Palmer, Dean	50	44.26	2.16
Paredes, Johnny	1	0.04	0.00
Pecota, Bill	102	84.03	2.66
Perezchica, Tony	3	1.17	0.83
Petralli, Geno	7	3.36	1.43
Phillips, Tony	44	37.19	2.55
Quirk, Jamie	1	0.11	0.00
Riles, Ernie	69	54.40	2.70
Rose, Bobby	4	1.80	2.11
Sax, Steve	5	4.91	2.24
Schaefer, Jeff	30	11.06	2.00
Seitzer, Kevin	68	60.31	2.92
Sheffield, Gary	43	43.30	2.11
Snyder, Cory	3	1.94	2.90
Sojo, Luis	1	1.03	2.91
Sprague, Ed	35	28.74	2.43
Stanley, Mike	6	2.76	2.03
Surhoff, B.J.	5	2.47	3.45
Sveum, Dale	38	35.46	2.51
Thome, Jim	27	29.73	2.32
Velarde, Randy	48	34.18	3.00
Ventura, Robin	151	138.47	2.71
Walling, Denny	14	7.28	2.09
Whitaker, Lou	1	0.14	0.00
Worthington, Craig	30	30.26	2.28
Zuvella, Paul	2	0.25	0.00
American League	**2268**	**2268.00**	**2.58**

SHORTSTOP	G	DEG	AFR
Amaral, Richard	2	1.94	2.06
Baerga, Carlos	2	1.06	0.00
Bell, Juan	15	3.04	3.38
Beltre, Esteban	8	2.19	1.70
Bordick, Mike	81	71.83	3.63
Brumley, Mike	31	21.92	3.36
Buechele, Steve	4	0.53	1.96
Cole, Stu	1	0.67	0.97
Cora, Joey	5	2.19	3.56
Diaz, Mario	65	40.02	3.13
Disarcina, Gary	10	9.86	3.02
Escobar, Jose	5	3.08	3.07
Espinoza, Alvaro	147	134.90	3.33
Fermin, Felix	129	127.97	3.39
Fryman, Travis	70	69.60	3.30
Gagne, Greg	137	118.60	3.62
Gallego, Mike	58	33.48	3.02
Gonzales, Rene	36	23.19	3.75
Grebeck, Craig	26	15.55	2.39
Green, Gary	8	5.59	4.31
Guillen, Ozzie	149	138.64	3.63

SHORTSTOP (contd.)	G	DEG	AFR
Hemond, Scott	1	0.07	5.88
Hernandez, Jose	44	33.51	3.44
Hill, Donnie	29	21.60	4.30
Howard, David	63	56.91	4.19
Hulett, Tim	1	0.11	0.00
Huson, Jeff	116	83.21	3.79
Knoblauch, Chuck	2	0.32	0.00
Law, Vance	3	1.10	3.33
Lee, Manuel	138	126.09	3.29
Leius, Scott	19	8.27	3.48
Lewis, Mark	36	33.83	3.20
Lyons, Steve	1	0.14	4.13
Magallanes, Everardo	2	0.39	2.36
Manrique, Fred	7	6.36	2.20
Naehring, Tim	17	13.50	3.84
Newman, Al	55	34.50	3.20
Paredes, Johnny	1	0.07	0.00
Pecota, Bill	10	3.75	5.81
Perezchica, Tony	6	2.72	2.40
Phillips, Tony	13	10.39	3.59
Reed, Jody	6	1.24	4.09
Riles, Ernie	20	11.77	2.50
Ripken, Cal	162	163.07	3.79
Rivera, Luis	129	119.48	3.38
Rodriguez, Carlos	11	9.23	3.33
Schaefer, Jeff	46	34.47	3.00
Schofield, Dick	133	121.18	3.34
Sojo, Luis	2	1.03	4.45
Spiers, Bill	128	125.88	3.10
Stillwell, Kurt	118	102.23	3.12
Sveum, Dale	51	41.11	3.60
Trammell, Alan	92	91.03	3.52
Velarde, Randy	31	17.60	3.86
Vizquel, Omar	138	120.86	3.73
Weiss, Walt	40	36.06	3.33
Zosky, Eddie	18	9.05	2.97
American League	**2268**	**2268.00**	**3.45**

LEFT FIELD	G	DEG	AFR
Aldrete, Mike	16	14.00	1.42
Allred, Beau	20	13.68	3.05
Amaro Jr., Ruben	3	2.58	1.38
Anderson, Brady	75	44.54	1.83
Baines, Harold	1	0.67	0.00
Barfield, Jesse	1	0.85	1.31
Barnes, Skeeter	13	10.96	2.19
Bell, Derek	7	6.15	1.62
Bell, Juan	1	0.07	0.00
Belle, Albert	88	83.85	2.03
Bergman, Dave	4	0.60	2.94
Bichette, Dante	1	0.88	1.07
Blankenship, Lance	18	9.40	3.41
Briley, Greg	94	56.45	2.19
Brosius, Scott	5	2.12	3.35
Brown, Jarvis	3	1.20	4.59

LEFT FIELD (contd.)	G	DEG	AFR
Browne, Jerry	17	13.93	1.84
Buhner, Jay	1	0.25	2.94
Bush, Randy	7	3.29	2.44
Capra, Nick	1	0.21	2.94
Carrillo, Matias	3	0.35	0.00
Carter, Joe	57	49.91	1.91
Castillo, Carmen	1	0.14	4.13
Cochrane, Dave	23	14.67	1.75
Cole, Alex	8	5.13	1.98
Cotto, Henry	38	19.51	2.64
Cromartie, Warren	4	1.41	1.99
Cuyler, Milt	1	0.14	8.27
Daugherty, Jack	34	24.89	2.00
Davis, Chili	2	0.28	8.27
DelosSantos, Luis	3	2.30	2.26
Devereaux, Mike	1	0.32	4.13
Ducey, Rob	18	11.52	1.91
Eisenreich, Jim	59	42.03	1.79
Fariss, Monty	8	5.20	3.96
Gallagher, Dave	7	5.59	1.65
Gibson, Kirk	91	84.91	1.76
Gladden, Dan	126	111.14	2.13
Gonzalez, Jose	5	4.10	1.72
Gonzalez, Juan	92	55.54	1.96
Greenwell, Mike	143	131.29	2.02
Griffey Sr., Ken	26	19.16	1.62
Hall, Mel	62	53.45	2.04
Hamilton, Darryl	25	15.31	2.02
Harper, Brian	1	0.11	0.00
Harris, Donald	2	0.32	0.00
Henderson, Dave	4	3.18	2.44
Henderson, Rickey	119	110.19	2.19
Hill, Glenallen	21	14.25	2.94
Howell, Jack	1	0.64	1.95
Howitt, Dann	5	1.91	3.76
Huff, Mike	17	5.94	3.21
Humphreys, Mike	8	3.22	2.16
Incaviglia, Pete	50	46.52	2.02
James, Chris	25	21.92	2.10
Jennings, Doug	6	2.83	2.99
Jones, Tracy	35	20.61	2.43
Karkovice, Ron	1	0.04	0.00
Kelly, Roberto	52	50.87	1.93
Kirby, Wayne	5	0.88	0.84
Komminsk, Brad	7	2.30	1.92
Larkin, Gene	2	0.57	1.31
Law, Vance	3	0.42	0.00
Lennon, Pat	1	0.21	5.88
Lopez, Luis	1	0.21	0.00
Lusader, Scott	1	0.07	0.00
Lyons, Steve	8	2.58	1.95
Mack, Shane	48	37.79	2.59
Maldonado, Candy	65	62.68	2.08
Manto, Jeff	1	0.39	0.00
Marshall, Mike	1	0.67	0.00
Martinez, Chito	1	0.71	5.60
McCray, Rodney	4	0.85	5.41
McIntosh, Tim	4	0.64	0.00
McKnight, Jeff	6	4.84	1.62
Mercedes, Luis	13	10.61	1.0
Meulens, Hensley	61	51.19	2.24
Milligan, Randy	9	7.46	2.64

LEFT FIELD (contd.)	G	DEG	AFR
Moore, Bobby	9	1.66	2.16
Morman, Russ	2	1.34	2.23
Moseby, Lloyd	64	61.72	2.05
Moses, John	11	6.61	1.96
Munoz, Pedro	10	6.54	2.32
Newman, Al	1	0.64	0.00
Newson, Warren	16	10.29	1.48
O'Brien, Pete	13	10.22	1.68
Olander, Jim	2	0.71	7.07
Orsulak, Joe	85	74.02	2.07
Palmer, Dean	29	19.90	2.16
Pasqua, Dan	9	6.93	1.90
Pecota, Bill	1	0.71	1.07
Phillips, Tony	25	20.43	2.60
Plantier, Phil	16	13.86	1.95
Polonia, Luis	143	131.93	1.99
Powell, Alonzo	24	16.19	1.90
Puhl, Terry	1	0.11	0.00
Pulliam, Harvey	11	4.77	1.26
Quintana, Carlos	1	0.85	4.70
Raines, Tim	134	126.20	2.21
Reimer, Kevin	61	51.40	2.14
Romine, Kevin	10	5.73	1.18
Rose, Bobby	6	4.74	1.86
Russell, John	6	2.55	1.08
Scruggs, Tony	5	0.78	4.12
Segui, David	28	23.65	2.04
Shelby, John	25	21.42	2.05
Sheridan, Pat	3	1.45	0.53
Snyder, Cory	13	9.76	1.85
Sojo, Luis	1	1.03	1.81
Stanley, Mike	1	0.07	0.00
Stevens, Lee	1	0.99	4.44
Stubbs, Franklin	4	3.54	1.35
Tabler, Pat	1	0.11	5.88
Tettleton, Mickey	2	0.39	0.00
Thurman, Gary	39	26.62	2.43
Vaughn, Greg	134	132.14	2.26
Velarde, Randy	2	0.64	1.68
Venable, Max	13	6.19	3.10
Walling, Denny	3	2.01	2.24
Ward, Turner	1	0.39	0.00
Webster, Mitch	6	3.46	2.79
Williams, Kenny	1	0.18	0.00
Wilson, Mookie	36	32.66	1.92
Wilson, Willie	40	27.64	2.74
Zupcic, Bob	3	1.31	2.34
American League	**2268**	**2268.00**	**2.10**

CENTER FIELD	G	DEG	AFR
Abner, Shawn	31	25.13	2.82
Anderson, Brady	26	21.71	2.51
Barnes, Skeeter	5	3.57	2.49
Bell, Derek	6	3.11	2.01
Bichette, Dante	7	5.06	3.98
Briley, Greg	4	3.04	1.96
Brown, Jarvis	11	5.69	2.43

CENTER FIELD (contd.)	G	DEG	AFR
Brumley, Mike	4	2.30	2.19
Brunansky, Tom	1	0.14	0.00
Buhner, Jay	3	0.92	0.92
Burks, Ellis	126	114.61	2.47
Capra, Nick	1	0.35	10.23
Cole, Alex	101	93.82	2.61
Cotto, Henry	19	14.67	2.71
Cromartie, Warren	1	0.07	0.00
Cuyler, Milt	150	145.75	2.84
Devereaux, Mike	148	144.12	2.77
Ducey, Rob	1	0.11	0.00
Eisenreich, Jim	13	8.66	3.09
Felix, Junior	63	54.72	2.28
Gallagher, Dave	61	51.65	2.58
Gonzalez, Jose	10	6.12	2.62
Gonzalez, Juan	93	73.78	2.56
Griffey Jr., Ken	152	135.25	2.66
Hall, Mel	1	0.00	0.00
Hamilton, Darryl	55	45.11	2.34
Harris, Donald	7	2.30	2.71
Henderson, Dave	135	130.41	2.75
Hill, Glenallen	26	25.17	2.75
Housie, Wayne	4	2.09	1.35
Howitt, Dann	7	2.93	4.32
Huff, Mike	53	41.47	2.58
Johnson, Lance	157	143.24	2.98
Kelly, Roberto	73	72.04	2.33
Kirby, Wayne	1	0.25	5.51
Komminsk, Brad	8	2.83	3.69
Leius, Scott	2	0.18	0.00
Lusader, Scott	3	1.20	1.60
Lyons, Steve	36	28.81	2.78
Mack, Shane	36	19.97	2.68
McCray, Rodney	2	0.81	7.97
McRae, Brian	150	145.40	2.76
Moore, Bobby	5	2.12	3.77
Newson, Warren	1	0.11	0.00
Olander, Jim	6	1.31	1.76
Orsulak, Joe	1	0.39	2.94
Pettis, Gary	126	83.85	2.91
Phillips, Tony	9	5.69	2.74
Polonia, Luis	1	0.64	0.97
Powell, Alonzo	6	3.39	2.37
Puckett, Kirby	144	135.85	2.53
Raines, Tim	1	0.04	0.00
Romine, Kevin	4	3.54	2.73
Scruggs, Tony	1	0.95	1.23
Shelby, John	26	16.08	3.52
Sheridan, Pat	6	4.17	3.64
Sierra, Ruben	3	1.63	2.45
Sosa, Sammy	13	8.24	2.18
Spiers, Bill	1	0.28	0.00
Surhoff, B.J.	1	0.53	3.75

CENTER FIELD (contd.)	G	DEG	AFR
Thurman, Gary	9	7.32	3.14
Venable, Max	27	21.53	1.51
Ward, Turner	2	1.98	1.48
Webster, Mitch	1	0.67	1.07
White, Devon	156	150.10	2.91
Whiten, Mark	8	5.73	3.16
Williams, Bernie	85	84.31	2.73
Williams, Kenny	1	0.53	3.68
Wilson, Mookie	5	4.49	2.63
Wilson, Willie	33	24.50	2.65
Yount, Robin	117	114.71	2.70
Zupcic, Bob	7	4.81	1.71
American League	**2268**	**2268.00**	**2.69**

RIGHT FIELD	G	DEG	AFR
Abner, Shawn	7	1.38	0.66
Allred, Beau	27	23.83	2.64
Amaro Jr., Ruben	2	0.25	0.00
Anderson, Brady	9	4.84	2.27
Baines, Harold	10	5.76	1.88
Barfield, Jesse	81	75.19	2.34
Barnes, Skeeter	17	8.84	2.55
Belle, Albert	2	1.41	1.44
Bichette, Dante	120	110.26	2.35
Blankenship, Lance	11	3.68	2.82
Briley, Greg	46	32.73	1.79
Brosius, Scott	10	7.28	2.31
Brown, Jarvis	19	5.13	1.18
Brunansky, Tom	136	119.55	2.18
Buhner, Jay	131	109.73	2.20
Bush, Randy	32	22.06	1.93
Canseco, Jose	131	120.72	2.14
Carter, Joe	100	94.88	1.92
Castillo, Carmen	3	1.03	3.01
Clark, Dave	1	0.04	0.00
Cochrane, Dave	3	1.98	1.31
Cotto, Henry	8	4.88	2.46
Cromartie, Warren	1	0.14	20.45
Daugherty, Jack	3	0.74	0.87
Davis, Mark	3	0.71	1.50
Deer, Rob	132	135.43	2.24
Ducey, Rob	6	4.49	1.75
Eisenreich, Jim	42	24.11	1.72
Evans, Dwight	67	59.85	1.99
Felix, Junior	2	1.70	0.00
Gallagher, Dave	23	16.58	2.08
Gibson, Kirk	3	2.12	2.97
Gonzalez, Jose	17	14.53	2.01
Gonzalez, Juan	8	3.18	1.92
Hall, Mel	65	55.78	1.97
Hamilton, Darryl	49	44.68	2.15
Hare, Shawn	6	2.97	2.71
Harris, Donald	5	0.95	0.97
Henderson, Dave	1	0.25	0.00
Hill, Glenallen	5	3.46	1.38
Howard, David	1	0.07	0.00

RIGHT FIELD (contd.)	G	DEG	AFR
Howell, Jack	4	2.12	1.59
Howitt, Dann	10	4.81	1.70
Huff, Mike	40	19.69	2.28
Humphreys, Mike	2	1.24	2.92
Incaviglia, Pete	4	4.10	3.46
James, Chris	18	16.12	1.97
Johnson, Lance	2	0.32	0.00
Jones, Tracy	3	0.85	2.49
Kirby, Wayne	17	14.14	2.63
Komminsk, Brad	8	3.54	0.95
Larkin, Gene	48	33.55	1.83
Lyons, Steve	3	2.62	2.11
Mack, Shane	81	60.73	2.23
Maldonado, Candy	14	10.11	1.53
Marshall, Mike	3	1.45	1.65
Martinez, Chito	53	48.18	2.25
McCray, Rodney	2	0.53	3.75
McKnight, Jeff	1	0.92	2.54
Mercedes, Luis	3	2.12	4.01
Meulens, Hensley	13	11.70	2.39
Moses, John	1	0.35	0.00
Munoz, Pedro	39	29.52	2.49
Newson, Warren	34	19.09	1.71
Olander, Jim	1	0.99	2.36
Orsulak, Joe	68	45.96	2.39
Pasqua, Dan	51	34.93	1.74
Phillips, Tony	23	16.26	2.75
Plantier, Phil	27	18.24	2.40
Powell, Alonzo	15	7.11	1.43
Puckett, Kirby	19	9.69	2.92
Pulliam, Harvey	5	4.31	3.98
Quintana, Carlos	12	7.81	1.80
Reimer, Kevin	6	1.20	0.79
Romine, Kevin	10	4.56	2.64
Rose, Bobby	1	0.07	0.00
Russell, John	2	0.46	0.00
Segui, David	5	4.35	2.79
Shelby, John	3	2.83	3.37
Sheridan, Pat	26	17.82	1.66
Sierra, Ruben	161	154.62	1.95
Snyder, Cory	31	19.20	2.40
Sosa, Sammy	102	74.94	2.54
Stevens, Lee	8	6.15	1.39
Surhoff, B.J.	1	0.07	0.00
Tartabull, Dan	124	117.29	1.65
Tettleton, Mickey	1	0.32	8.24
Thurman, Gary	29	15.48	2.34
Vaughn, Greg	1	0.88	1.07
Venable, Max	30	17.68	1.87
Walling, Denny	2	1.70	0.00
Ward, Turner	41	31.18	2.03
Webster, Mitch	6	5.37	2.48
Whiten, Mark	105	101.21	2.30
Williams, Kenny	8	6.65	2.07
Wilson, Willie	19	14.63	1.96
Winfield, Dave	115	107.04	1.75
Zupcic, Bob	6	2.05	1.79
American League	**2268**	**2268.00**	**2.11**

NATIONAL LEAGUE

CATCHER	Innings	Inn/9	WP	WP/162	PB	PB/162
Berryhill, Damon	350.2	39.0	7	29.1	8	33.3
Biggio, Craig	1175.1	130.6	37	45.9	11	13.6
Bilardello, Dann	67.1	7.5	1	21.7	0	0.0
Cabrera, Francisco	111.0	12.3	5	65.7	3	39.4
Carter, Gary	497.1	55.3	16	46.9	4	11.7
Cerone, Rick	573.0	63.7	27	68.7	5	12.7
Daulton, Darren	717.0	79.7	38	77.3	2	4.1
Decker, Steve	578.1	64.3	26	65.5	7	17.6
Eusebio, Tony	58.0	6.4	4	100.6	1	25.1
Fitzgerald, Mike	421.2	46.9	25	86.4	2	6.9
Fletcher, Darrin	334.0	37.1	16	69.8	1	4.4
Gedman, Rich	251.0	27.9	3	17.4	3	17.4
Girardi, Joe	134.0	14.9	6	65.3	1	10.9
Hassey, Ron	275.1	30.6	3	15.9	4	21.2
Heath, Mike	324.1	36.0	14	62.9	6	27.0
Hernandez, Carlos	37.2	4.2	0	0.0	1	38.7
Hundley, Todd	150.0	16.7	5	48.6	1	9.7
Kennedy, Terry	390.1	43.4	11	41.1	2	7.5
Lake, Steve	403.0	44.8	24	86.8	5	18.1
Lampkin, Tom	78.0	8.7	0	0.0	1	18.7
LaValliere, Mike	852.2	94.7	27	46.2	5	8.5
Lindsey, Doug	9.0	1.0	3	486.0	1	162.0
Litton, Greg	2.0	0.2	0	0.0	0	0.0
Lyons, Barry	15.2	1.7	1	93.1	0	0.0
Manwaring, Kirt	471.1	52.4	7	21.7	0	0.0
McClendon, Lloyd	7.1	0.8	0	0.0	0	0.0
Nichols, Carl	125.2	14.0	2	23.2	2	23.2
O'Brien, Charlie	488.0	54.2	16	47.8	2	6.0
Oliver, Joe	676.1	75.1	27	58.2	10	21.6
Olson, Greg	1010.1	112.3	47	67.8	6	8.7
Pagnozzi, Tom	1156.1	128.5	28	35.3	5	6.3
Pappas, Erik	36.2	4.1	3	119.3	0	0.0
Prince, Tom	87.2	9.7	4	66.5	1	16.6
Reed, Jeff	690.2	76.7	31	65.4	7	14.8
Reyes, Gilberto	567.1	63.0	16	41.1	11	28.3
Santiago, Benito	1307.1	145.3	48	53.5	8	8.9
Santovenia, Nelson	176.0	19.6	7	58.0	6	49.7
Sasser, Mackey	226.1	25.1	11	70.9	3	19.3
Scioscia, Mike	907.1	100.8	31	49.8	3	4.8
Scott, Donnie	41.0	4.6	1	35.6	2	71.1
Servais, Scott	94.0	10.4	3	46.5	0	0.0
Slaught, Don	509.0	56.6	9	25.8	3	8.6
Stephens, Ray	28.0	3.1	2	104.1	0	0.0
Sutko, Glenn	32.0	3.6	1	45.6	1	45.6
Villanueva, Hector	399.0	44.3	13	47.5	4	14.6
Wilkins, Rich	539.1	59.9	19	51.4	6	16.2
Willard, Jerry	4.0	0.4	0	0.0	0	0.0
National League	**17387.2**	**1932.0**	**625**	**52.4**	**154**	**12.9**

FIRST BASE	G	DEG	AFR
Anderson, Dave	16	9.85	2.60
Azocar, Oscar	1	0.40	0.00
Bagwell, Jeff	155	146.06	2.13
Barberie, Bret	1	0.68	0.00
Bell, Mike	14	7.69	1.69
Benzinger, Todd	21	15.75	2.11
Bonilla, Bobby	4	3.20	0.98
Bream, Sid	85	69.56	2.21
Brewer, Rod	15	3.38	2.05
Bullock, Eric	3	1.58	2.39
Cabrera, Francisco	14	7.12	2.43
Calderon, Ivan	4	2.77	1.04
Carter, Gary	10	6.15	1.85
Clark, Jerald	16	10.82	1.59
Clark, Will	144	138.62	2.35
Coles, Darnell	1	0.40	1.53
Donnels, Chris	15	13.01	3.55
Doran, Bill	4	2.19	0.32
Dorsett, Brian	2	0.58	2.03
Fitzgerald, Mike	3	2.73	1.81
Foley, Tom	31	14.74	1.56
Galarraga, Andres	105	95.48	2.07
Grace, Mark	160	159.97	2.61
Gregg, Tommy	13	10.32	2.29
Guerrero, Pedro	112	105.22	2.03
Heep, Danny	1	0.07	0.00
Hollins, Dave	6	4.49	2.64
Hudler, Rex	12	3.74	0.98
Hunter, Brian	85	65.43	2.26
Javier, Stan	2	2.01	1.44
Jefferson, Reggie	2	1.33	2.91
Jordan, Ricky	72	67.48	2.44
Karros, Eric	10	3.09	1.86
Kennedy, Terry	2	0.36	8.05
Kingery, Mike	6	2.77	2.56
Kruk, John	103	89.12	2.26
Lee, Terry	2	1.29	2.71
Lindeman, Jim	1	0.40	0.00
Litton, Greg	15	9.67	1.75
Magadan, Dave	122	115.61	1.97
Martinez, Carmelo	33	25.96	1.80
McClendon, Lloyd	22	15.78	1.91
McGriff, Fred	153	152.17	1.89
Merced, Orlando	105	98.25	1.77
Mitchell, Kevin	1	0.40	0.00
Morris, Hal	128	117.23	2.13
Murray, Eddie	149	141.86	2.31
Noboa, Junior	1	0.18	0.00
Oberkfell, Ken	13	6.94	2.87
Oquendo, Jose	3	0.40	0.00
Pagnozzi, Tom	3	0.86	4.36
Perry, Gerald	61	49.25	1.90
Prince, Tom	1	0.11	0.00
Redus, Gary	47	41.31	1.81
Rohde, Dave	1	0.29	3.05

FIRST BASE (contd.)

	G	DEG	AFR		G	DEG	AFR
Salazar, Luis	7	3.88	1.26	Ramirez, Rafael	27	17.87	3.18
Santovenia, Nelson	7	3.45	1.19	Ready, Randy	66	53.71	3.19
Sasser, Mackey	10	8.77	2.18	Roberts, Bip	68	63.67	3.22
Schu, Rick	1	1.08	1.02	Rohde, Dave	4	3.34	4.41
Sharperson, Mike	10	6.36	3.39				
				Samuel, Juan	153	144.08	3.28
Templeton, Garry	25	18.41	1.94	Sanchez, Rey	2	1.11	6.93
Teufel, Tim	6	4.42	1.49	Sandberg, Ryne	157	156.34	3.42
Tolentino, Jose	10	5.39	2.22	Sharperson, Mike	6	1.76	6.70
Torve, Kelvin	1	0.11	8.13	Shipley, Craig	14	9.81	3.78
				Smith, Greg	1	0.11	0.00
Varsho, Gary	3	1.37	1.62				
Villanueva, Hector	6	1.91	1.58	Teufel, Tim	66	50.72	3.06
				Thompson, Rob	144	136.86	3.23
Walker, Larry	39	37.50	2.03	Treadway, Jeff	93	69.67	3.52
Webster, Mitch	1	0.07	0.00				
Wilson, Craig	4	1.19	1.72	Vizcaino, Jose	9	4.17	3.78
				Walker, Chico	6	4.13	4.51
National League	**1940**	**1940.00**	**2.15**	Wilkerson, Curtis	30	24.55	3.72
				Wilson, Craig	3	0.36	8.13
				National League	**1940**	**1940.00**	**3.35**

SECOND BASE

	G	DEG	AFR
Alicea, Luis	11	6.94	4.42
Anderson, Dave	6	2.09	1.95
Backman, Wally	36	24.19	2.56
Barberie, Bret	10	9.67	2.99
Barrett, Marty	2	1.19	4.82
Benavides, Freddie	3	1.80	3.92
Biggio, Craig	3	2.66	2.86
Blauser, Jeff	33	25.16	3.20
Candaele, Casey	109	93.65	3.37
DeShields, Delino	148	143.01	3.13
Doran, Bill	88	78.48	2.94
Duncan, Mariano	64	53.31	3.62
Faries, Paul	36	28.29	3.73
Felder, Mike	1	0.14	13.91
Foley, Tom	2	1.51	5.28
Garcia, Carlos	1	0.47	0.00
Gardner, Jeff	3	2.48	4.05
Harris, Lenny	26	13.59	3.73
Herr, Tom	72	50.47	3.13
Hudler, Rex	4	0.86	2.22
Jefferies, Gregg	77	69.92	3.12
Jones, Tim	4	1.29	1.41
Lemke, Mark	109	65.36	3.68
Lind, Jose	149	139.70	3.76
Litton, Greg	15	9.49	2.72
McLemore, Mark	19	17.36	3.27
Miller, Keith	60	47.38	3.74
Morandini, Mickey	97	84.66	3.42
Mota, Andy	27	23.80	3.03
Mota, Jose	13	10.64	2.60
Noboa, Junior	6	4.93	3.56
Oquendo, Jose	118	102.96	3.68
Pena, Geronimo	83	51.62	2.91
Perezchica, Tony	6	3.20	2.53
Quinones, Luis	31	25.45	2.86

THIRD BASE

	G	DEG	AFR
Alicea, Luis	2	0.25	4.07
Anderson, Dave	11	5.46	2.57
Backman, Wally	20	14.34	2.41
Barberie, Bret	10	8.59	2.93
Barrett, Marty	2	0.93	2.60
Benjamin, Mike	1	0.22	0.00
Blauser, Jeff	17	12.94	2.79
Bonilla, Bobby	67	58.38	2.67
Booker, Rod	3	1.04	3.49
Buechele, Steve	31	29.77	2.44
Caminiti, Ken	152	144.26	2.83
Candaele, Casey	11	6.47	2.81
Coolbaugh, Scott	54	51.30	2.37
Cooper, Gary	4	2.80	1.85
Donnels, Chris	11	8.77	3.30
Faries, Paul	12	6.36	2.68
Felder, Mike	3	1.01	4.78
Foley, Tom	6	2.62	1.95
Garcia, Carlos	2	2.26	3.53
Hamilton, Jeff	33	23.04	2.55
Hansen, Dave	21	8.02	2.45
Harris, Lenny	114	85.70	2.55
Hayes, Charlie	138	115.33	2.57
Hernandez, Carlos	1	0.07	0.00
Herr, Tom	3	1.55	2.71
Hollins, Dave	36	30.02	2.50
Howell, Jack	54	41.09	2.86
Jefferies, Gregg	51	47.78	2.42
Johnson, Howard	104	98.50	2.07
King, Jeff	33	32.50	2.16
Lemke, Mark	16	6.18	2.25
Litton, Greg	11	6.00	2.71
Miller, Keith	2	1.11	1.59
Murray, Eddie	1	0.07	0.00
Noboa, Junior	2	1.80	1.04

	G	DEG	AFR			G	DEG	AFR
Oberkfell, Ken	4	3.74	2.28		Johnson, Howard	28	24.09	4.01
					Jones, Tim	14	5.86	2.56
Pendleton, Terry	149	141.06	2.73					
Presley, Jim	16	15.96	2.25		Larkin, Barry	120	112.56	3.96
					Litton, Greg	9	4.75	2.83
Quinones, Luis	19	15.06	1.91					
					Miller, Keith	2	0.97	4.48
Ramirez, Rafael	2	0.22	0.00		Mota, Jose	3	1.33	2.53
Redfield, Joe	9	5.25	2.13					
Richardson, Jeff	3	0.29	0.00		Noboa, Junior	2	0.72	3.12
Rohde, Dave	2	1.19	1.69					
Royer, Stan	5	3.52	2.28		Offerman, Jose	50	38.07	3.85
					Oquendo, Jose	22	14.60	2.68
Sabo, Chris	151	143.98	2.16		Owen, Spike	133	118.49	3.43
Salazar, Luis	86	75.57	2.59					
Schu, Rick	3	1.83	1.15		Perezchica, Tony	13	9.17	3.05
Scott, Gary	31	27.29	2.40					
Sharperson, Mike	68	42.64	2.41		Quinones, Luis	7	6.36	4.11
Slaught, Don	1	0.14	0.00					
Strange, Doug	3	3.24	1.22		Ramirez, Rafael	45	29.80	3.16
					Richardson, Jeff	2	0.58	1.30
Templeton, Garry	17	12.29	2.36		Rohde, Dave	3	1.98	5.92
Teufel, Tim	53	40.19	2.47		Rossy, Rico	1	0.11	0.00
	G	**DEG**	**AFR**			**G**	**DEG**	**AFR**
Vizcaino, Jose	57	16.90	2.26		Sanchez, Rey	10	6.94	3.34
					Sharperson, Mike	16	5.93	3.08
Walker, Chico	57	42.78	2.13		Shipley, Craig	19	15.28	2.80
Wallach, Tim	150	146.10	2.60		Smith, Ozzie	150	143.44	3.30
Wehner, John	36	26.39	2.97					
Wilkerson, Curtis	14	9.74	3.33		Templeton, Garry	41	30.66	3.90
Williams, Matt	155	147.82	2.66		Thon, Dickie	146	141.50	3.34
Wilson, Craig	12	8.38	2.12					
					Uribe, Jose	87	69.27	3.49
Zeile, Todd	154	151.89	2.74					
					Vizcaino, Jose	33	22.43	3.67
National League	**1940**	**1940.00**	**2.53**					
					Wilkerson, Curtis	15	6.72	3.03
					Williams, Matt	4	1.94	1.03
SHORTSTOP	**G**	**DEG**	**AFR**		Yelding, Eric	72	65.07	3.25
Alicea, Luis	1	0.14	0.00		**National League**	**1940**	**1940.00**	**3.44**
Anderson, Dave	63	36.06	3.01					
Barberie, Bret	19	14.49	3.17		**LEFT FIELD**	**G**	**DEG**	**AFR**
Batiste, Kim	7	6.15	4.01					
Bell, Jay	156	152.39	3.53		Aldrete, Mike	5	3.34	2.40
Belliard, Rafael	145	109.00	3.61		Azocar, Oscar	12	6.65	2.06
Benavides, Freddie	20	16.39	3.75					
Benjamin, Mike	51	34.15	4.05		Bass, Kevin	23	18.48	1.89
Blauser, Jeff	85	48.03	2.93		Bell, George	146	135.82	1.78
Booker, Rod	20	13.62	2.89		Benzinger, Todd	15	10.53	2.36
					Biggio, Craig	1	0.04	0.00
Castilla, Vinny	12	3.06	3.33		Bonds, Barry	150	147.00	2.23
Cedeno, Andujar	66	61.83	2.64		Boston, Daryl	9	5.57	2.86
Clayton, Royce	8	6.72	2.62		Braggs, Glenn	55	44.33	2.28
					Bullett, Scott	1	0.07	12.20
Duncan, Mariano	30	23.73	3.30		Bullock, Eric	6	3.09	1.72
Dunston, Shawon	142	136.39	3.44					
					Calderon, Ivan	122	115.50	2.22
Elster, Kevin	107	98.03	3.45		Campusano, Sil	1	0.47	0.00
					Candaele, Casey	18	12.11	2.30
Faries, Paul	8	4.67	3.21		Carreon, Mark	43	34.94	2.03
Fernandez, Tony	145	142.18	3.44		Chamberlain, Wes	95	92.93	2.07
Foley, Tom	43	25.42	3.31		Clark, Jerald	85	77.65	1.83
Garcia, Carlos	9	5.03	2.63		Daniels, Kal	132	112.92	1.89
Gardner, Jeff	8	7.08	2.57		Dascenzo, Doug	32	7.98	1.83
Griffin, Alfredo	109	103.07	3.96		Davidson, Mark	32	15.42	2.24
					Davis, Eric	7	4.85	2.69
Hamilton, Jeff	1	0.07	0.00		Doran, Bill	6	5.43	2.04
Hansen, Dave	1	0.07	0.00		Duncan, Mariano	6	2.98	1.57
Harris, Lenny	20	12.33	3.91					
Hayes, Charlie	2	1.29	2.97					

LEFT FIELD (contd.)	G	DEG	AFR
Espy, Cecil	2	0.36	1.74
Felder, Mike	45	26.57	2.28
Finley, Steve	1	0.22	0.00
Gilkey, Bernard	74	67.80	2.31
Gonzalez, Jose	15	4.53	3.21
Gonzalez, Luis	133	119.57	2.39
Goodwin, Tom	2	0.25	0.00
Gregg, Tommy	9	6.40	1.44
Grissom, Marquis	3	0.65	1.42
Gwynn, Chris	31	14.09	1.75
Harris, Lenny	1	0.11	0.00
Hatcher, Billy	81	60.83	2.13
Hayes, Von	20	20.53	2.79
Heep, Danny	1	0.14	0.00
Howard, Thomas	34	20.31	2.56
Hudler, Rex	28	20.49	2.07
Hunter, Brian	5	1.94	1.17
Jackson, Darrin	21	16.72	1.94
Javier, Stan	49	17.65	2.20
Jefferson, Stan	4	2.12	0.98
Jones, Chris	18	11.43	1.86
Kingery, Mike	14	3.02	2.38
Kruk, John	36	35.66	2.25
Landrum, Ced	25	8.56	2.09
Leonard, Mark	24	18.41	1.57
Lindeman, Jim	14	8.34	1.69
Litton, Greg	2	0.40	0.00
Martinez, Carmelo	16	12.47	2.82
Martinez, Dave	36	19.63	1.54
May, Derrick	7	4.31	2.46
McClendon, Lloyd	14	5.79	1.33
McDaniel, Terry	7	2.12	3.43
McDowell, Roger	2	0.11	0.00
McReynolds, Kevin	125	106.34	2.12
Miller, Keith	14	6.79	1.63
Mitchell, Keith	24	7.73	2.46
Mitchell, Kevin	100	93.43	2.02
Morris, Hal	1	1.04	0.00
Morris, John	11	4.64	1.62
Nixon, Otis	55	38.03	2.31
Noboa, Junior	1	0.22	0.00
Ortiz, Javier	15	8.41	2.29
Parker, Rick	4	1.76	2.91
Pena, Geronimo	4	2.23	2.69
Perry, Gerald	4	4.17	1.21
Redus, Gary	11	5.28	1.51
Roberts, Bip	19	14.24	2.72
Salazar, Luis	1	0.07	0.00
Sanders, Deion	41	26.35	2.05
Sasser, Mackey	7	4.57	2.01
Simms, Mike	1	0.04	0.00
Smith, Dwight	5	3.49	2.28
Smith, Lonnie	99	79.59	1.77
Thompson, Milt	72	66.61	2.36
Tolentino, Jose	1	1.01	4.25
Vanderwal, John	17	13.30	2.66
Varsho, Gary	5	4.24	3.67
Vatcher, Jim	2	0.40	0.00

	G	DEG	AFR
Walker, Chico	20	5.54	1.82
Ward, Kevin	31	24.66	2.11
Webster, Mitch	31	11.86	2.08
Williams, Kenny	9	6.72	2.96
Wilson, Craig	5	2.73	2.83
Winningham, Herm	12	3.02	2.86
Young, Gerald	6	1.87	3.76
National League	**1940**	**1940.00**	**2.11**

CENTER FIELD	G	DEG	AFR
Abner, Shawn	36	29.44	2.82
Biggio, Craig	1	0.11	0.00
Bonds, Barry	4	1.19	5.28
Boston, Daryl	74	47.70	2.47
Bullett, Scott	1	1.04	0.60
Butler, Brett	161	154.19	2.42
Campusano, Sil	15	9.42	2.64
Candaele, Casey	5	3.09	1.64
Carr, Chuck	9	2.44	4.08
Carreon, Mark	22	14.52	1.31
Castillo, Braulio	24	15.06	2.58
Coleman, Vince	70	66.11	2.02
Dascenzo, Doug	59	45.84	2.30
Davidson, Mark	4	0.68	0.00
Davis, Eric	77	70.57	2.54
Duncan, Mariano	2	0.90	3.19
Dykstra, Lenny	63	61.33	2.70
Espy, Cecil	25	15.10	2.70
Felder, Mike	38	25.67	2.65
Finley, Steve	124	105.62	2.55
Gant, Ron	148	141.60	2.35
Gonzalez, Jose	7	3.34	3.19
Goodwin, Tom	4	1.47	5.43
Grissom, Marquis	125	121.87	2.68
Gwynn, Chris	2	0.86	0.81
Hatcher, Billy	54	45.26	2.73
Hayes, Von	49	47.13	2.86
Herr, Tom	1	0.25	0.00
Howard, Thomas	41	36.49	3.01
Hudler, Rex	21	17.72	2.53
Jackson, Darrin	79	73.44	2.84
Javier, Stan	7	2.23	3.16
Jefferson, Stan	1	1.11	1.81
Jones, Chris	3	0.47	0.00
Kingery, Mike	2	0.22	5.21
Kruk, John	11	9.10	2.09
Landrum, Ced	18	15.17	2.60
Lankford, Ray	149	138.62	2.62
Lewis, Darren	68	57.81	2.79
Lindeman, Jim	6	3.56	1.54
Lofton, Kenny	20	16.36	2.45
Martinez, Dave	34	32.03	2.49
McDaniel, Terry	5	3.74	2.06
McGee, Willie	89	78.33	2.45
McReynolds, Kevin	33	25.09	1.98
Miller, Keith	2	0.47	3.05

	G	DEG	AFR		G	DEG	AFR
Mitchell, Keith	1	1.04	0.00	Gwynn, Tony	134	132.87	2.18
Morris, John	27	16.97	2.71				
				Hayes, Von	6	2.95	3.58
Nixon, Otis	17	15.24	2.97	Howard, Thomas	14	12.73	2.11
				Hudler, Rex	10	4.96	2.18
Parker, Rick	1	0.04	0.00	Hunter, Brian	1	0.18	0.00
Redus, Gary	12	5.64	2.64	Javier, Stan	18	14.56	1.83
Roberts, Bip	29	24.59	3.00	Jefferson, Stan	1	0.07	0.00
				Johnson, Howard	30	30.13	1.99
Sanders, Deion	5	2.30	1.71	Jones, Chris	9	3.99	1.54
Sanders, Reggie	9	8.23	2.66	Jose, Felix	153	149.80	1.84
Smith, Dwight	13	8.81	2.54	Justice, Dave	106	104.68	1.83
Thompson, Milt	12	7.69	3.12	Kingery, Mike	22	12.98	2.37
				Kruk, John	6	4.24	3.60
VanSlyke, Andy	135	128.02	2.11				
Varsho, Gary	5	3.06	1.64	Landrum, Ced	8	1.19	1.72
				Leonard, Mark	12	8.34	1.71
Walker, Chico	36	29.30	2.03	Lindeman, Jim	10	6.26	1.57
Walker, Larry	5	3.42	1.71	Litton, Greg	4	1.37	1.62
Walton, Jerome	100	66.65	2.48				
Webster, Mitch	13	8.12	2.58	Martinez, Dave	54	45.08	2.19
Williams, Kenny	4	1.80	2.82	McClendon, Lloyd	18	12.01	1.53
Winningham, Herm	55	32.50	2.73	McDaniel, Terry	4	0.68	2.93
				McGee, Willie	48	40.16	1.67
Yelding, Eric	3	0.61	1.53	McReynolds, Kevin	2	2.01	0.60
Young, Gerald	76	32.21	2.72	Merced, Orlando	7	1.40	3.37
				Miller, Keith	17	8.74	2.39
National League	**1940**	**1940.00**	**2.52**	Mitchell, Keith	10	7.48	1.38
				Morris, John	24	8.63	2.86
				Murphy, Dale	147	137.94	2.08
RIGHT FIELD	**G**	**DEG**	**AFR**				
				Nixon, Otis	48	44.72	1.86
Abner, Shawn	3	0.97	1.95	Noboa, Junior	6	4.85	1.63
Anthony, Eric	37	31.38	2.02				
Azocar, Oscar	1	1.19	0.95	O'Neill, Paul	150	139.12	2.12
				Ortiz, Javier	11	7.26	1.08
Bass, Kevin	79	66.83	1.83				
Bonilla, Bobby	104	92.25	1.84	Perry, Gerald	1	0.14	6.10
Boston, Daryl	37	12.08	1.67				
Braggs, Glenn	27	15.46	2.32	Redus, Gary	11	2.70	1.10
Brewer, Rod	3	0.83	3.69	Rhodes, Karl	44	39.22	2.25
Brooks, Hubie	100	88.36	1.95	Riesgo, Nikco	2	2.09	0.00
Bullett, Scott	1	0.11	0.00				
Bullock, Eric	3	1.40	2.17	Sanders, Deion	1	1.19	0.00
				Sasser, Mackey	14	11.43	1.39
Candaele, Casey	4	2.19	1.78	Simms, Mike	41	28.83	1.70
Carreon, Mark	22	6.51	1.15	Smith, Dwight	28	21.61	2.09
Castillo, Braulio	2	0.93	2.03	Strawberry, Darryl	136	130.17	1.61
Chamberlain, Wes	3	1.62	2.84				
Clark, Jerald	13	9.92	2.05	Templeton, Garry	2	0.40	0.00
Coles, Darnell	3	1.26	0.00	Thompson, Milt	12	8.30	2.59
Dascenzo, Doug	16	5.43	1.72	Varsho, Gary	45	32.28	2.08
Davidson, Mark	32	14.85	2.29	Vatcher, Jim	9	4.89	1.64
Dawson, Andre	138	134.77	1.89				
				Walker, Chico	8	2.62	0.37
Espy, Cecil	11	6.18	2.21	Walker, Larry	99	85.99	2.49
				Walton, Jerome	1	0.14	0.00
Felder, Mike	44	25.09	2.31	Ward, Kevin	2	1.40	0.79
Finley, Steve	69	33.43	1.65	Webster, Mitch	27	19.30	1.88
Fitzgerald, Mike	3	2.48	4.03	Williams, Kenny	11	8.74	2.06
				Winningham, Herm	1	0.40	1.74
Gonzalez, Jose	20	5.18	2.51	Wood, Ted	8	6.04	1.66
Gregg, Tommy	5	1.94	3.71				
Grissom, Marquis	11	8.48	2.53	Yelding, Eric	1	0.22	0.00
Gwynn, Chris	14	8.12	1.13	Young, Gerald	5	1.29	3.55
				National League	**1940**	**1940.00**	**1.97**

GAMES STARTED AT POSITION REPORT

Starting P/BAL
J. Ballard	22
J. Mesa	23
J. Robinson	19
B. McDonald	21
D. Johnson	14
B. Milacki	26
R. Smith	14
M. Mussina	12
S. Jones	1
A. Rhodes	8
A. Telford	1
M. Flanagan	1

Starting C/BAL
B. Melvin	67
C. Hoiles	80
E. Whitt	12
J. Tackett	3

Starting 1B/BAL
G. Davis	37
R. Milligan	102
L. Gomez	1
D. Segui	19
C. Hoiles	1
J. McKnight	2

Starting 2B/BAL
B. Ripken	98
J. Bell	54
T. Hulett	10

Starting 3B/BAL
C. Worthington	30
L. Gomez	102
T. Hulett	30

Starting SS/BAL
C. Ripken	162

Starting LF/BAL
R. Milligan	9
J. Orsulak	78
B. Anderson	33
J. McKnight	5
D. Segui	25
L. Mercedes	12

Starting CF/BAL
M. Devereaux	138
B. Anderson	24

Starting RF/BAL
D. Evans	59
J. Orsulak	40
J. McKnight	1
B. Anderson	3
C. Martinez	53
L. Mercedes	2
D. Segui	4

Starting DH/BAL
S. Horn	92
L. Gomez	6
J. McKnight	2
C. Hoiles	10
R. Milligan	21
D. Evans	9
T. Hulett	8
C. Martinez	4
G. Davis	9
B. Melvin	1

Starting P/BOS
G. Harris	21
D. Darwin	12
J. Hesketh	17
M. Gardiner	22
R. Clemens	35
M. Young	16
T. Bolton	19
D. Kiecker	5
K. Morton	15

Starting C/BOS
T. Pena	132
J. Marzano	30

Starting 1B/BOS
M. Vaughn	47
C. Quintana	110
M. Marshall	5

Starting 2B/BOS
J. Reed	150
S. Lyons	8
M. Brumley	4

Starting 3B/BOS
W. Boggs	140
T. Naehring	1
M. Brumley	6
S. Lyons	7
S. Cooper	8

Starting SS/BOS
L. Rivera	128
M. Brumley	18
T. Naehring	15
J. Reed	1

Starting LF/BOS
M. Greenwell	141
K. Romine	5
C. Quintana	1
P. Plantier	12
B. Zupcic	1
S. Lyons	1
M. Marshall	1

Starting CF/BOS
E. Burks	123
S. Lyons	29
K. Romine	3
M. Brumley	3
B. Zupcic	3
W. Housie	1

Starting RF/BOS
T. Brunansky	122
C. Quintana	10
P. Plantier	24
M. Marshall	2
K. Romine	1
S. Lyons	3

Starting DH/BOS
J. Clark	134
M. Vaughn	16
M. Marshall	6
P. Plantier	4
E. Burks	1
M. Greenwell	1

Starting P/CLE
T. Candiotti	15
C. Nagy	33
R. Nichols	16
D. Otto	14
G. Swindell	33
E. King	24
J. Shaw	1
J. Mutis	3
M. York	4
D. Boucher	5
M. Gozzo	2
W. Blair	5
D. Jones	4
S. Hillegas	3

Starting C/CLE
J. Skinner	90
S. Alomar	45
L. Lopez	6
E. Taubensee	20
J. Manto	1

Starting 1B/CLE
B. Jacoby	47
R. Jefferson	26
M. Aldrete	32
L. Lopez	8
C. Martinez	29
C. James	13
J. Manto	7

Starting 2B/CLE
M. Lewis	48
C. Baerga	73
T. Perezchica	1
J. Browne	36
J. Escobar	2
M. Huff	2

Starting 3B/CLE
C. Baerga	77
J. Thome	27
J. Manto	30
B. Jacoby	14
J. Browne	14

Starting SS/CLE
F. Fermin	127
M. Lewis	30
J. Escobar	2
T. Perezchica	2
C. Baerga	1

Starting LF/CLE
A. Belle	87
J. Browne	14
B. Allred	13
M. Aldrete	14
C. James	20
M. Webster	3
G. Hill	4
A. Cole	5
J. Gonzalez	2

Starting CF/CLE
A. Cole	90
M. Huff	32
G. Hill	26
M. Whiten	6
J. Gonzalez	5
T. Ward	2
M. Webster	1

Starting RF/CLE
B. Allred	25
T. Ward	27
J. Gonzalez	12
M. Webster	5
M. Whiten	61
C. James	17
W. Kirby	13
M. Huff	1
A. Belle	1

Starting DH/CLE
C. James	58
A. Belle	31
C. Martinez	40
A. Cole	4
L. Lopez	5
L. Medina	5
M. Aldrete	7
S. Alomar	4
J. Browne	4
G. Hill	1
M. Whiten	3

Starting P/DET
D. Gakeler	7
B. Gullickson	35
F. Tanana	33
S. Aldred	11
M. Leiter	15
R. Meacham	4
W. Terrell	33
K. Ritz	5
S. Searcy	5
D. Petry	6
J. Cerutti	8

Starting C/DET
M. Tettleton	116
A. Allanson	44
M. Salas	2

Starting 1B/DET
D. Bergman	42
C. Fielder	120

Starting 2B/DET
L. Whitaker	119
T. Phillips	35
J. Paredes	4
S. Barnes	4

Starting 3B/DET
T. Phillips	33
S. Barnes	9
S. Livingstone	36
T. Fryman	84

Starting SS/DET
T. Fryman	63
T. Phillips	10
A. Trammell	89

Starting LF/DET
J. Shelby	17
L. Moseby	59
P. Incaviglia	48
S. Barnes	12
T. Phillips	20
L. DelosSantos	2
J. Moses	4

Starting CF/DET
M. Cuyler	136
T. Phillips	6
J. Shelby	16
S. Barnes	4

Starting RF/DET
R. Deer	129
S. Barnes	6
P. Incaviglia	4
S. Hare	4
T. Phillips	17
J. Shelby	2

Starting DH/DET
C. Fielder	42
M. Tettleton	23
M. Salas	8
P. Incaviglia	40
R. Rowland	1
D. Bergman	9
A. Trammell	5
T. Phillips	17
L. DelosSantos	6
L. Whitaker	3
J. Shelby	1
S. Hare	1
S. Barnes	1
T. Bernazard	1
L. Moseby	4

Starting P/MIL
K. Brown	10
D. August	23
J. Navarro	34
J. Hunter	6
B. Wegman	28
C. Bosio	32
C. Eldred	3
D. Plesac	10
M. Knudson	7
C. George	1
T. Higuera	6
R. Robinson	1
M. Ignasiak	1

Starting C/MIL
B. Surhoff	118
R. Dempsey	44

Starting 1B/MIL
F. Stubbs	88
P. Molitor	46
G. Brock	16
G. Canale	12

Starting 2B/MIL
J. Gantner	53
W. Randolph	108
D. Sveum	1

Starting 3B/MIL
G. Sheffield	43
J. Gantner	83
D. Sveum	34
B. Surhoff	2

Starting SS/MIL
B. Spiers	125
D. Sveum	37

Starting LF/MIL
G. Vaughn	129
C. Maldonado	13
D. Hamilton	14
F. Stubbs	4
J. Olander	1
D. Bichette	1

Starting CF/MIL
R. Yount	116
D. Hamilton	42
D. Bichette	4

Starting RF/MIL
D. Bichette	104
D. Hamilton	47
C. Maldonado	9
J. Olander	1
G. Vaughn	1

Starting DH/MIL
P. Molitor	112
R. Yount	13
C. Maldonado	7
W. Randolph	2
F. Stubbs	3
T. McIntosh	2
G. Vaughn	10
G. Sheffield	5
D. Sveum	3
B. Surhoff	5

Starting P/NYA
S. Sanderson	34
P. Perez	14
C. Cary	9
E. Plunk	8
W. Taylor	22
T. Leary	18
D. Eiland	13
J. Johnson	23
A. Mills	2
S. Kamieniecki	9
A. Hawkins	3
M. Witt	2
G. Cadaret	5

Starting C/NYA
M. Nokes	112
B. Geren	42
J. Ramos	5
J. Leyritz	3

Starting 1B/NYA
D. Mattingly	124
K. Maas	35
H. Meulens	3

Starting 2B/NYA
P. Kelly	13
S. Sax	148
R. Velarde	1

Starting 3B/NYA
S. Sax	5
P. Kelly	78
R. Velarde	32
M. Humphreys	4
J. Leyritz	16
T. Lovullo	15
M. Blowers	10
A. Espinoza	2

Starting SS/NYA
A. Espinoza	136
R. Velarde	17
C. Rodriguez	9

Starting LF/NYA
M. Hall	54
H. Meulens	52
R. Kelly	52
M. Humphreys	2
P. Sheridan	1
J. Barfield	1

Starting CF/NYA
R. Kelly	72
B. Williams	85
P. Sheridan	4
S. Lusader	1

Starting RF/NYA
J. Barfield	75
M. Hall	58
H. Meulens	11
M. Humphreys	2
P. Sheridan	16

Starting DH/NYA
K. Maas	103
D. Mattingly	22
S. Sax	4
H. Meulens	12
J. Leyritz	1
J. Ramos	3
M. Humphreys	2
M. Nokes	3
M. Hall	11
P. Sheridan	1

Starting P/TOR
J. Acker	4
J. Guzman	23
J. Key	33
T. Stottlemyre	34
T. Candiotti	19
D. Wells	28
D. Boucher	7
D. Stieb	9
M. Timlin	3
W. Fraser	1
P. Hentgen	1

Starting C/TOR
G. Myers	91
P. Borders	71

Starting 1B/TOR
J. Olerud	124
P. Tabler	19
E. Sprague	18
C. Snyder	1

Starting 2B/TOR
R. Alomar	159
R. Gonzales	3

Starting 3B/TOR
E. Sprague	31
K. Gruber	109
R. Gonzales	10
R. Giannelli	8
R. Mulliniks	3
C. Snyder	1

Starting SS/TOR
M. Lee	134
R. Gonzales	22
E. Zosky	6

Starting LF/TOR
M. Wilson	34
G. Hill	8
C. Maldonado	52
J. Carter	53
D. Bell	6
R. Ducey	9

Starting CF/TOR
D. White	156
M. Wilson	5
D. Bell	1

Starting RF/TOR
J. Carter	99
M. Whiten	39
C. Snyder	8
G. Hill	4
K. Williams	7
R. Ducey	4
T. Ward	1

Starting DH/TOR
R. Mulliniks	70
J. Carter	10
P. Tabler	28
G. Hill	17
E. Sprague	2
M. Wilson	21
K. Gruber	2
R. Ducey	1
D. Parker	10

Starting P/CAL
S. Lewis	11
C. Finley	34
K. McCaskill	30
J. Abbott	34
M. Langston	34
M. Fetters	4
J. Grahe	10
F. Valenzuela	2
K. Abbott	3

Starting C/CAL
L. Parrish	102
R. Tingley	38
J. Orton	22

Starting 1B/CAL
W. Joyner	140
B. Rose	2
D. Hill	2
C. Cron	5
L. Stevens	9
M. Marshall	1
B. Lyons	1
L. Parrish	1
J. Howell	1

Starting 2B/CAL
D. Hill	29
L. Sojo	103
B. Rose	8
J. Howell	10
G. Disarcina	7
K. Flora	3
R. Amaro. Jr.,2	

Starting 3B/CAL
G. Gaetti	151
J. Howell	7
B. Rose	2
G. Disarcina	1
L. Sojo	1

Starting SS/CAL
D. Schofield	128
D. Hill	23
L. Sojo	1
G. Disarcina	10

Starting LF/CAL
L. Polonia	140
D. Gallagher	6
M. Venable	5
B. Rose	5
L. Sojo	1
L. Stevens	1
R. Amaro. Jr.,3	
J. Howell	1

Starting CF/CAL
M. Venable	23
J. Felix	62
D. Gallagher	50
S. Abner	26
L. Polonia	1

Starting RF/CAL
D. Winfield	115
D. Gallagher	17
M. Venable	16
S. Abner	1
J. Howell	3
J. Felix	2
L. Stevens	8

Starting DH/CAL
D. Parker	119
D. Winfield	34
L. Parrish	5
L. Polonia	4

Starting P/CHA
J. McDowell	35
G. Hibbard	29
C. Hough	29
R. Garcia	15
W. Alvarez	9
M. Perez	8
A. Fernandez	32
J. Carter	2
R. Hernandez	3

Starting C/CHA
C. Fisk	91
R. Karkovice	49
M. Merullo	13
D. Wakamatsu	9

Starting 1B/CHA
F. Thomas	56
D. Pasqua	54
R. Kittle	14
C. Snyder	9
R. Ventura	7
C. Fisk	12
M. Merullo	10

Starting 2B/CHA
S. Fletcher	68
J. Cora	63
C. Grebeck	31

Starting 3B/CHA
R. Ventura	146
C. Grebeck	16

Starting SS/CHA
O. Guillen	144
C. Grebeck	15
J. Cora	2
E. Beltre	1

Starting LF/CHA
C. Snyder	8
T. Raines	132
W. Newson	11
D. Pasqua	7
M. Huff	4

Starting CF/CHA
L. Johnson	146
S. Sosa	9
M. Huff	7

Starting RF/CHA
S. Sosa	67
M. Huff	12
W. Newson	25
D. Pasqua	46
C. Snyder	12

Starting DH/CHA
T. Raines	18
D. Pasqua	7
F. Thomas	101
C. Fisk	12
M. Merullo	3
B. Jackson	21

Starting P/KC
M. Gubicza	26
B. Saberhagen	28
K. Appier	31
L. Aquino	18
S. Davis	9
M. Boddicker	29
T. Gordon	14
M. Davis	5
H. Wagner	2

Starting C/KC
M. Macfarlane	66
B. Mayne	63
J. Pedre	6
T. Spehr	27

Starting 1B/KC
C. Martinez	34
T. Benzinger	70
G. Brett	10
W. Cromartie	26
R. Morman	4
J. Eisenreich	14
J. Pedre	1
B. Pecota	3

Starting 2B/KC
T. Shumpert	125
B. Pecota	10
D. Howard	21
N. Liriano	6

Starting 3B/KC
K. Seitzer	55
B. Pecota	88
S. Berry	19

Starting SS/KC
K. Stillwell	98
D. Howard	60
B. Pecota	3
S. Cole	1

Starting LF/KC
K. Gibson	89
J. Eisenreich	39
R. Morman	2
H. Pulliam	5
G. Thurman	24
B. Pecota	1
W. Cromartie	1
B. Moore	1

Starting CF/KC
B. McRae	142
G. Thurman	9
J. Eisenreich	9
B. Moore	2

Starting RF/KC
J. Eisenreich	20
D. Tartabull	124
G. Thurman	11
K. Gibson	2
H. Pulliam	5

Starting DH/KC
G. Brett	118
K. Gibson	29
D. Tartabull	6
T. Puhl	2
T. Benzinger	1
M. Macfarlane	4
J. Eisenreich	1
C. Martinez	1

Starting P/MIN
A. Anderson	22
S. Erickson	32
J. Morris	35
T. Edens	6
D. West	12
K. Tapani	34
M. Guthrie	12
P. Abbott	3
W. Banks	3
D. Neagle	3

Starting C/MIN
B. Harper	114
J. Ortiz	41
L. Webster	7

Starting 1B/MIN
K. Hrbek	126
G. Larkin	24
R. Bush	4
P. Sorrento	7
A. Newman	1

Starting 2B/MIN
C. Knoblauch	141
A. Newman	21

Starting 3B/MIN
M. Pagliarulo	112
S. Leius	46
A. Newman	4

Starting SS/MIN
A. Newman	29
G. Gagne	127
S. Leius	6

Starting LF/MIN
S. Mack	37
D. Gladden	110
R. Bush	4
J. Brown	1
P. Munoz	8
A. Newman	1
G. Larkin	1

Starting CF/MIN
K. Puckett	143
S. Mack	16
J. Brown	3

Starting RF/MIN
P. Munoz	27
S. Mack	62
G. Larkin	39
R. Bush	24
K. Puckett	9
C. Castillo	1

Starting DH/MIN
C. Davis	149
R. Bush	6
C. Castillo	1
P. Munoz	1
P. Sorrento	2
B. Harper	1
G. Larkin	2

Starting P/OAK
J. Slusarski	19
B. Welch	35
K. Dressendorfer	7
D. Stewart	35
M. Moore	33
E. Show	5
A. Hawkins	14
R. Darling	12
C. Young	1
T. VanPoppel	1

Starting C/OAK
J. Quirk	49
T. Steinbach	108
T. Afenir	3
S. Hemond	2

Starting 1B/OAK
M. McGwire	142
J. Quirk	5
T. Steinbach	6
R. Witmeyer	3
E. Riles	3
D. Howitt	1
B. Jacoby	2

Starting 2B/OAK
M. Gallego	123
L. Blankenship	28
M. Bordick	4
S. Hemond	3
F. Manrique	1
E. Riles	3

Starting 3B/OAK
E. Riles	59
V. Law	36
B. Jacoby	47
C. Lansford	3
S. Brosius	7
L. Blankenship	9
S. Hemond	1

Starting SS/OAK
W. Weiss	37
M. Gallego	29
M. Bordick	79
E. Riles	10
F. Manrique	6
V. Law	1

Starting LF/OAK
R. Henderson	118
W. Wilson	26
D. Jennings	1
D. Howitt	2
L. Blankenship	7
D. Henderson	3
S. Brosius	2
B. Komminsk	2
H. Baines	1

Starting CF/OAK
D. Henderson	135
D. Howitt	2
W. Wilson	23
B. Komminsk	2

Starting RF/OAK
J. Canseco	126
H. Baines	6
W. Wilson	14
L. Blankenship	2
S. Brosius	8
B. Komminsk	3
D. Howitt	3

Starting DH/OAK
H. Baines	123
J. Canseco	22
R. Henderson	8
D. Henderson	4
T. Steinbach	1
W. Wilson	1
L. Blankenship	1
C. Lansford	1
S. Brosius	1

Starting P/SEA
R. DeLucia	31
E. Hanson	27
R. Johnson	33
B. Krueger	25
B. Holman	30
S. Bankhead	9
P. Rice	2
D. Burba	2
D. Fleming	3

Starting C/SEA
D. Valle	106
S. Bradley	47
M. Sinatro	2
D. Cochrane	6
C. Howard	1

Starting 1B/SEA
P. O'Brien	119
D. Cochrane	3
A. Powell	2
T. Martinez	26
A. Davis	12

Starting 2B/SEA
H. Reynolds	158
J. Schaefer	3
R. Amaral	1

Starting 3B/SEA
E. Martinez	143
D. Cochrane	12
J. Schaefer	5
S. Bradley	2

Starting SS/SEA
O. Vizquel	123
J. Schaefer	37
R. Amaral	2

Starting LF/SEA
K. Griffey, Sr.,25	
H. Cotto	20
G. Briley	49
D. Cochrane	17
T. Jones	22
A. Powell	17
P. O'Brien	12

Starting CF/SEA
K. Griffey, Jr.,145	
H. Cotto	12
A. Powell	3
G. Briley	2

Starting RF/SEA
G. Briley	40
J. Buhner	110
H. Cotto	6
D. Cochrane	1
T. Jones	1
A. Powell	4

Starting DH/SEA
A. Davis	115
T. Jones	19
P. O'Brien	16
H. Reynolds	1
D. Cochrane	1
E. Martinez	2
P. Lennon	2
T. Martinez	3
H. Cotto	1
K. Griffey, Jr.,1	
A. Powell	1

Starting P/TEX
K. Rogers	9
N. Ryan	27
B. Bohanon	11
J. Guzman	25
G. Alexander	9
O. Boyd	12
S. Chiamparino	5
B. Witt	16
K. Brown	33
M. Petkovsek	1
J. Barfield	9
H. Fajardo	3
T. Mathews	2

Starting C/TEX
G. Petralli	45
I. Rodriguez	81
M. Stanley	34
J. Russell	2

Starting 1B/TEX
R. Palmeiro	152
J. Daugherty	5
M. Stanley	5

Starting 2B/TEX
J. Franco	144
S. Buechele	12
M. Diaz	4
M. Fariss	2

Starting 3B/TEX
S. Buechele	101
D. Palmer	45
D. Walling	7
M. Diaz	2
M. Stanley	4
G. Petralli	3

Starting SS/TEX
J. Huson	85
J. Hernandez	35
M. Diaz	36
G. Green	6

Starting LF/TEX
K. Reimer	56
J. Gonzalez	44
J. Daugherty	25
D. Palmer	24
J. Russell	3
M. Fariss	8
D. Walling	2

Starting CF/TEX
G. Pettis	73
J. Gonzalez	87
D. Harris	1
T. Scruggs	1

Starting RF/TEX
R. Sierra	160
J. Gonzalez	2

Starting DH/TEX
B. Downing	98
K. Reimer	48
D. Palmer	4
J. Gonzalez	4
M. Stanley	1
G. Petralli	2
R. Palmeiro	2
R. Maurer	2
M. Fariss	1

Starting P/CHN
D. Jackson	14
G. Maddux	37
M. Harkey	4
S. Boskie	20
M. Bielecki	25
R. Sutcliffe	18
B. Scanlan	13
L. Lancaster	11
F. Castillo	18

Starting C/CHN
D. Berryhill	37
J. Girardi	14
H. Villanueva	51
R. Wilkins	54
E. Pappas	4

Starting 1B/CHN
M. Grace	155
H. Villanueva	1
L. Salazar	4

Starting 2B/CHN
R. Sandberg	154
J. Vizcaino	3
R. Sanchez	1
C. Walker	2

Starting 3B/CHN
G. Scott	27
J. Vizcaino	5
L. Salazar	78
C. Walker	47
D. Strange	3

Starting SS/CHN
S. Dunston	131
J. Vizcaino	22
R. Sanchez	7

Starting LF/CHN
G. Bell 145
C. Walker 2
D. Smith 3
D. May 4
C. Landrum 6

Starting CF/CHN
J. Walton 59
D. Dascenzo 43
C. Walker 29
C. Landrum 16
D. Smith 13

Starting RF/CHN
A. Dawson 137
D. Smith 19
D. Dascenzo 4

Starting P/MON
M. Gardner 27
R. Mahler 6
D. Martinez 31
B. Barnes 27
C. Haney 16
B. Sampen 8
O. Boyd 19
C. Nabholz 24
R. Darling 3

Starting C/MON
G. Reyes 63
R. Hassey 34
M. Fitzgerald 47
N. Santovenia 17

Starting 1B/MON
A. Galarraga 99
T. Foley 13
L. Walker 39
E. Bullock 1
M. Fitzgerald 3
I. Calderon 3
N. Santovenia 3

Starting 2B/MON
D. DeShields 145
B. Barberie 10
T. Foley 1
J. Noboa 5

Starting 3B/MON
T. Wallach 150
B. Barberie 9
J. Noboa 1
T. Foley 1

Starting SS/MON
T. Foley 26
S. Owen 119
B. Barberie 15
J. Noboa 1

Starting LF/MON
D. Martinez 16
I. Calderon 119
J. Vanderwal 17
E. Bullock 3
K. Williams 6

Starting CF/MON
M. Grissom 122
D. Martinez 34
K. Williams 2
L. Walker 3

Starting RF/MON
L. Walker 87
D. Martinez 44
N. Riesgo 2
M. Grissom 9
J. Noboa 6
E. Bullock 2
K. Williams 9
M. Fitzgerald 2

Starting P/NYN
F. Viola 35
R. Darling 17
D. Cone 34
W. Whitehurst 20
S. Fernandez 8
D. Gooden 27
T. Castillo 3
A. Young 8
P. Schourek 8
D. Simons 1

Starting C/NYN
R. Cerone 63
C. O'Brien 56
M. Sasser 25
T. Hundley 17

Starting 1B/NYN
D. Magadan 115
C. Donnels 14
T. Teufel 5
G. Templeton 18
M. Sasser 9

Starting 2B/NYN
G. Jefferies 74
K. Miller 45
T. Herr 40
J. Gardner 2

Starting 3B/NYN
H. Johnson 99
G. Jefferies 49
C. Donnels 8
G. Templeton 2
K. Miller 1
T. Teufel 2

Starting SS/NYN
K. Elster 98
G. Templeton 30
J. Gardner 8
H. Johnson 25

Starting LF/NYN
K. McReynolds 110
M. Sasser 6
M. Carreon 33
D. Boston 5
K. Miller 6
T. McDaniel 1

Starting CF/NYN
V. Coleman 70
K. McReynolds 25
D. Boston 46
M. Carreon 16
T. McDaniel 3
C. Carr 1

Starting RF/NYN
H. Brooks 97
D. Boston 6
M. Sasser 12
H. Johnson 30
M. Carreon 4

K. McReynolds 2
K. Miller 10

Starting P/PHI
J. Grimsley 12
J. DeJesus 29
P. Combs 13
B. Ruffin 15
T. Mulholland 34
D. Cox 17
A. Ashby 8
T. Greene 27
C. Brantley 5
D. LaPoint 2

Starting C/PHI
D. Daulton 80
D. Fletcher 36
S. Lake 45
D. Lindsey 1

Starting 1B/PHI
J. Kruk 89
R. Jordan 67
D. Hollins 5
R. Schu 1

Starting 2B/PHI
W. Backman 23
R. Ready 54
M. Morandini 85

Starting 3B/PHI
C. Hayes 109
D. Hollins 33
R. Booker 1
W. Backman 17
R. Schu 2

Starting SS/PHI
D. Thon 143
R. Booker 11
K. Batiste 7
C. Hayes 1

Starting LF/PHI
V. Hayes 20
W. Chamberlain 95
J. Kruk 36
J. Lindeman 7
J. Morris 4

Starting CF/PHI
L. Dykstra 62
B. Castillo 14
V. Hayes 48
J. Morris 16
S. Campusano 8
J. Lindeman 3
J. Kruk 11

Starting RF/PHI
D. Murphy 141
J. Morris 6
J. Lindeman 6
J. Kruk 4
B. Castillo 1
V. Hayes 3
W. Chamberlain 1

Starting P/PIT
J. Smiley 32
D. Drabek 35
B. Walk 20
Z. Smith 35
R. Tomlin 27
V. Palacios 7

H. Fajardo 2
N. Heaton 1
P. Miller 1
R. Reed 1
B. Patterson 1

Starting C/PIT
M. LaValliere 100
D. Slaught 53
T. Prince 8
L. McClendon 1

Starting 1B/PIT
G. Varsho 2
G. Redus 43
C. Martinez 4
O. Merced 95
L. McClendon 15
B. Bonilla 3

Starting 2B/PIT
J. Lind 139
C. Wilkerson 23

Starting 3B/PIT
J. King 32
B. Bonilla 60
S. Buechele 31
J. Wehner 25
C. Garcia 1
C. Wilkerson 8
J. Redfield 5

Starting SS/PIT
J. Bell 153
C. Wilkerson 6
C. Garcia 3

Starting LF/PIT
B. Bonds 146
L. McClendon 4
G. Redus 6
G. Varsho 4
J. Gonzalez 1
M. Webster 1

Starting CF/PIT
A. VanSlyke 129
G. Varsho 4
G. Redus 7
B. Bonds 1
C. Espy 11
S. Bullett 1
M. Webster 7
J. Gonzalez 2

Starting RF/PIT
B. Bonilla 92
M. Webster 15
G. Varsho 36
L. McClendon 12
O. Merced 1
C. Espy 6

Starting P/SL
B. Smith 31
J. DeLeon 28
K. Hill 30
O. Olivares 24
B. Tewksbury 30
M. Clark 2
J. Moyer 7
R. Cormier 10

Starting C/SL
T. Pagnozzi 133
R. Gedman 27
R. Stephens 2

Starting 1B/SL
P. Guerrero 111
G. Perry 46
R. Brewer 1
R. Hudler 3
C. Wilson 1

Starting 2B/SL
J. Oquendo 114
T. Jones 3
L. Alicea 6
G. Pena 39

Starting 3B/SL
T. Zeile 154
S. Royer 4
C. Wilson 4

Starting SS/SL
O. Smith 148
T. Jones 4
J. Oquendo 10

Starting LF/SL
B. Gilkey 71
M. Thompson 64
R. Hudler 20
G. Pena 2
C. Wilson 1
G. Perry 4

Starting CF/SL
R. Hudler 21
M. Thompson 6
R. Lankford 135

Starting RF/SL
F. Jose 152
R. Hudler 4
M. Thompson 6

Starting P/ATL
T. Glavine 34
J. Smoltz 36
C. Leibrandt 36
S. Avery 35
P. Smith 10
K. Mercker 4
A. Reynoso 5
R. Mahler 2

Starting C/ATL
G. Olson 113
M. Heath 37
F. Cabrera 11
J. Willard 1

Starting 1B/ATL
S. Bream 72
B. Hunter 63
F. Cabrera 9
T. Gregg 12
M. Bell 6

Starting 2B/ATL
J. Blauser 27
J. Treadway 85
M. Lemke 50

Starting 3B/ATL
T. Pendleton	148
J. Blauser	12
M. Lemke	2

Starting SS/ATL
R. Belliard	110
J. Blauser	51
V. Castilla	1

Starting LF/ATL
O. Nixon	33
L. Smith	98
T. Gregg	6
D. Sanders	23
K. Mitchell	1
B. Hunter	1

Starting CF/ATL
R. Gant	145
O. Nixon	14
D. Sanders	2
K. Mitchell	1

Starting RF/ATL
D. Justice	106
O. Nixon	46
D. Sanders	1
K. Mitchell	8
T. Gregg	1

Starting P/CIN
T. Browning	36
J. Rijo	30
J. Armstrong	24
R. Myers	12
N. Charlton	11
C. Hammond	18
S. Scudder	14
K. Gross	9
G. Minutelli	3
M. Sanford	5

Starting C/CIN
J. Reed	77
J. Oliver	78
G. Sutko	3
D. Scott	4

Starting 1B/CIN
H. Morris	120
T. Benzinger	16
C. Martinez	21
T. Lee	2
B. Doran	2
R. Jefferson	1

Starting 2B/CIN
B. Doran	78
M. Duncan	59
L. Quinones	23
F. Benavides	2

Starting 3B/CIN
C. Sabo	149
L. Quinones	13

Starting SS/CIN
B. Larkin	120
M. Duncan	21
F. Benavides	16
L. Quinones	5

Starting LF/CIN
T. Benzinger	11
B. Hatcher	58
C. Martinez	16
G. Braggs	47
C. Jones	12
S. Jefferson	2
M. Duncan	4
H. Winningham	1
E. Davis	5
H. Morris	1
B. Doran	5

Starting CF/CIN
E. Davis	74
B. Hatcher	47
H. Winningham	30
R. Sanders	9
S. Jefferson	1
M. Duncan	1

Starting RF/CIN
P. O'Neill	145
G. Braggs	14
C. Jones	3

Starting P/HOU
M. Portugal	27
J. Deshaies	28
P. Harnisch	33
D. Kile	22
J. Jones	22
R. Bowen	13
X. Hernandez	6
J. Juden	3
M. Scott	2
C. Gardner	4
B. Williams	2

Starting C/HOU
C. Biggio	131
C. Nichols	14
T. Eusebio	7
S. Servais	10

Starting 1B/HOU
J. Bagwell	151
K. Oberkfell	7
J. Tolentino	4

Starting 2B/HOU
C. Candaele	95
M. McLemore	17
R. Ramirez	18
A. Mota	26
D. Rohde	3
C. Biggio	3

Starting 3B/HOU
K. Caminiti	150
K. Oberkfell	4
C. Candaele	5
G. Cooper	3

Starting SS/HOU
E. Yelding	67
R. Ramirez	27
A. Cedeno	66
D. Rohde	2

Starting LF/HOU
L. Gonzalez	124
M. Davidson	12
C. Candaele	14
J. Tolentino	1
J. Ortiz	10
G. Young	1

Starting CF/HOU
S. Finley	122
G. Young	20
K. Lofton	18
C. Candaele	2

Starting RF/HOU
K. Rhodes	40
E. Anthony	36
J. Ortiz	8
M. Simms	38
C. Candaele	2
S. Finley	23
M. Davidson	15

Starting P/LA
M. Morgan	33
T. Belcher	33
O. Hershiser	21
R. Martinez	33
B. Ojeda	31
K. Gross	10
D. Cook	1

Starting C/LA
M. Scioscia	104
G. Carter	55
C. Hernandez	2
B. Lyons	1

Starting 1B/LA
E. Murray	148
G. Carter	4
M. Sharperson	6
S. Javier	2
E. Karros	2

Starting 2B/LA
J. Samuel	151
L. Harris	10
M. Sharperson	1

Starting 3B/LA
L. Harris	89
M. Sharperson	45
J. Hamilton	22
D. Hansen	6

Starting SS/LA
A. Griffin	107
J. Offerman	37
M. Sharperson	5
L. Harris	13

Starting LF/LA
K. Daniels	132
C. Gwynn	13
S. Javier	10
M. Webster	6
J. Gonzalez	1

Starting CF/LA
B. Butler	160
C. Gwynn	1
S. Javier	1

Starting RF/LA
S. Javier	14
D. Strawberry	136
J. Gonzalez	2
C. Gwynn	9
M. Webster	1

Starting P/SD
A. Benes	33
D. Rasmussen	24
J. Melendez	9
B. Hurst	31
E. Nolte	6
E. Whitson	12
A. Peterson	11
D. Lilliquist	2
G. Harris	20
M. Maddux	1
R. Bones	11
R. Rodriguez	1
A. Hammaker	1

Starting C/SD
B. Santiago	148
T. Lampkin	8
D. Bilardello	6

Starting 1B/SD
F. McGriff	153
J. Clark	9

Starting 2B/SD
T. Teufel	48
J. Mota	10
C. Shipley	10
B. Roberts	64
M. Barrett	2
P. Faries	28

Starting 3B/SD
S. Coolbaugh	51
J. Howell	39
T. Teufel	40
P. Faries	6
J. Presley	16
G. Templeton	8
M. Barrett	2

Starting SS/SD
T. Fernandez	143
C. Shipley	15
P. Faries	4

Starting LF/SD
D. Jackson	13
J. Clark	84
K. Ward	23
M. Aldrete	2
B. Roberts	14
T. Howard	18
O. Azocar	8

Starting CF/SD
T. Howard	37
D. Jackson	71
S. Abner	27
B. Roberts	27

Starting RF/SD
T. Gwynn	133
J. Clark	11
T. Howard	13
J. Vatcher	3
K. Ward	1
O. Azocar	1

Starting P/SF
B. Black	34
D. Robinson	16
T. Wilson	29
B. Hickerson	6
P. McClellan	12
K. Downs	11
J. Burkett	34
M. LaCoss	5
M. Remlinger	6
F. Oliveras	1
S. Garrelts	3
R. Reuschel	1
G. Heredia	4

Starting C/SF
T. Kennedy	40
S. Decker	65
K. Manwaring	57

Starting 1B/SF
G. Litton	8
M. Kingery	2
W. Clark	143
D. Anderson	9

Starting 2B/SF
T. Perezchica	2
R. Thompson	142
T. Herr	10
D. Anderson	2
G. Litton	6

Starting 3B/SF
M. Williams	152
G. Litton	6
T. Herr	1
D. Anderson	3

Starting SS/SF
J. Uribe	75
D. Anderson	32
T. Perezchica	8
M. Benjamin	34
G. Litton	4
M. Williams	1
R. Clayton	8

Starting LF/SF
M. Leonard	20
K. Mitchell	99
M. Felder	23
K. Bass	18
G. Litton	1
R. Parker	1

Starting CF/SF
W. McGee	84
D. Lewis	54
M. Felder	24

Starting RF/SF
K. Bass	72
M. Felder	23
T. Wood	7
W. McGee	40
M. Kingery	9
M. Leonard	9
G. Litton	1
D. Coles	1

The Basestealing Reports

These special reports are designed to give more insight into basestealing. They do so in two ways: first, by showing opportunities for basestealing; second, by showing the defensive aspects of basestealing. The reports are presented for pitchers and catchers (minimum 10 opposition stolen base attempts) and baserunners (minimum 10 stolen base attempts). Players are listed alphabetically by league in each category.

Counting stolen base opportunities is almost as important as knowing the traditional stolen base success rate. (Imagine if you knew only how many base hits a player made, without knowing how many at-bats it took him to accumulate them!) Looking at how well pitchers and catchers defend against the steal is just as important as looking at how baserunners do offensively—they are mirror images of the same part of the game. The league averages and totals are given after the pitcher listings; note the large difference between the leagues in the frequency of basestealing attempts and the smaller difference in success rates.

Calculating stolen base opportunities defensively shows the effect pitchers and catchers have on their opponents' running game, both by preventing basestealing attempts as well as by throwing runners out. For pitchers and baserunners, individual success rates vary even more than they do for catchers. In each case, exactly the same things are being counted—an opportunity for a runner is also an opportunity "against" the pitcher and the catcher.

A stolen base opportunity (for second base) is defined as a plate appearance that occurs with first base occupied and second base not occupied, or an attempt to steal second even if it is occupied (i.e., part of a double steal). If Rickey Henderson walks to lead off an inning, stays put while Mike Gallego pops up and Jose Canseco strikes out, then steals second with Harold Baines at bat with two out, he is charged with three opportunities: one each for being on first base with second base unoccupied during Gallego's, Canseco's, and Baines's at-bats. The definition for opportunities to steal third base is analogous to that for stealing second base, but no opportunities are calculated for the rare attempts to steal home.

Once we know how many opportunities there were to steal a base, we calculate the Attempt Percentage for both second base and third base. "Attempts" are simply stolen bases plus caught stealings; attempt percentages (Att2%, Att3%) show the rate of attempts per 100 basestealing opportunities of second and third bases, respectively.

Shown after the attempt percentages are the actual totals of stolen bases and caught stealings of second base (SB2, CS2) and third base (SB3, CS3). Note that all caught stealings are counted here, whether they were initiated by the pitcher (e.g., scored "1-3-6") or the catcher (e.g., scored "2-6").

The next columns in each report show the total stolen bases and caught stealings for each runner or against each pitcher or catcher, including steals and caught stealings at home plate. (These are quite rare events, as there were only 15 successful steals of home plate in 1991.) For baserunners, the last column shows the traditional stolen base percentage (SB%—stolen bases divided by attempts); for pitchers and catchers, the last column is their opponents' stolen base percentage (OSB%, calculated the same way). Obviously, the higher the SB% for runners, the better they were at theft on the basepaths. The lower the OSB% for pitchers and catchers, the better they were at foiling attempted larcenies.

All things considered, the most important stat for pitchers and catchers is the percentage of times opposing baserunners attempted to steal second base (Att2%). Why? Because stealing second base puts a runner in scoring position, which is critical to his chances of scoring; stealing third base merely advances a runner who was already in scoring position. It's safe to say that managers would almost always gladly trade the certainty of keeping a runner at first—and keeping the double play in order—than take their chances on throwing the runner out at second.

BASESTEALING REPORTS

PITCHERS

AMERICAN LEAGUE

NAME	TEAM	Att2%	SB2	CS2	Att3%	SB3	CS3	Total SB	Total CS	OSB%
Abbott, Jim	CAL	9.1	9	13	2.7	3	1	12	14	46.2
Anderson, Allan	MIN	12.8	12	4	4.5	2	2	14	6	70
Appier, Kevin	KC	7.9	9	7	1.4	1	1	10	8	55.6
Aquino, Luis	KC	9	9	5	2.1	1	1	10	6	62.5
August, Don	MIL	11	15	4	3.2	3	0	18	4	81.8
Boddicker, Mike	KC	12	15	8	2.8	2	2	17	10	63
Bosio, Chris	MIL	5.4	8	3	1.8	1	1	9	4	69.2
Brown, Kevin	TEX	4.8	3	8	2.5	2	2	5	11	31.2
Cadaret, Greg	NYA	10.4	8	6	4.7	3	1	11	8	57.9
Candiotti, Tom	CLE	10.1	7	3	3.7	3	0	10	3	76.9
Candiotti, Tom	TOR	18	15	5	1.1	1	0	16	5	76.2
Clemens, Roger	BOS	15.7	22	14	1.9	1	2	23	16	59
Crawford, Steve	KC	20.4	9	2	0	0	0	9	2	81.8
Crim, Chuck	MIL	10.7	10	1	2.4	2	0	12	1	92.3
DeLucia, Rich	SEA	7.4	4	9	0	0	0	4	9	30.8
Erickson, Scott	MIN	6.1	4	9	0	0	0	4	10	28.6
Fernandez, Alex	CHA	11.1	14	8	3.4	1	3	15	11	57.7
Finley, Chuck	CAL	10.6	11	12	3.2	4	1	15	14	51.7
Frohwirth, Todd	BAL	16.9	9	3	3.3	1	1	10	4	71.4
Gardiner, Mike	BOS	10.3	11	4	1.4	0	1	11	5	68.8
Gleaton, Jerry	DET	11.1	5	5	7.1	3	1	8	8	50
Gordon, Tom	KC	8.1	8	6	0	0	0	8	7	53.3
Grahe, Joe	CAL	14.6	8	4	3.2	1	1	9	5	64.3
Gubicza, Mark	KC	12.7	17	3	1.9	1	1	18	6	75
Gullickson, Bill	DET	10	14	8	.7	1	0	15	8	65.2
Guthrie, Mark	MIN	8.3	5	5	4.7	4	0	9	5	64.3
Guzman, Jose	TEX	12.2	11	13	.9	1	0	12	13	48
Guzman, Juan	TOR	11.3	11	6	0	0	0	11	6	64.7
Hanson, Erik	SEA	9.1	9	8	1.8	1	1	11	10	52.4
Harvey, Bryan	CAL	14.1	10	0	3.8	2	0	12	0	100
Hawkins, Andy	OAK	13.6	7	4	2.1	0	1	7	5	58.3
Hibbard, Greg	CHA	7.1	6	7	0	0	0	6	8	42.9
Hough, Charlie	CHA	8.1	10	8	.9	0	1	10	9	52.6
Johnson, Jeff	NYA	10.6	12	3	7.6	6	1	18	4	81.8
Johnson, Randy	SEA	10.6	14	9	2.6	4	0	18	9	66.7
King, Eric	CLE	5.8	7	3	1.1	1	0	8	3	72.7
Krueger, Bill	SEA	5.9	7	4	4.5	4	1	11	5	68.8
Lamp, Dennis	BOS	10.3	10	0	0	0	0	10	0	100
Langston, Mark	CAL	8.2	9	10	4.8	1	5	10	15	40
Leary, Tim	NYA	9	9	3	1.9	1	1	10	5	66.7
McCaskill, Kirk	CAL	6.9	8	5	.9	0	1	8	6	57.1
McDonald, Ben	BAL	11.2	11	2	5.2	3	1	14	3	82.4
McDowell, Jack	CHA	13	21	10	.6	1	0	22	11	66.7
Mesa, Jose	BAL	11.3	11	5	1	1	0	12	5	70.6
Milacki, Bob	BAL	8.1	9	6	3.1	3	0	12	6	66.7
Moore, Mike	OAK	13.4	19	11	.8	0	1	19	12	61.3
Morris, Jack	MIN	15.8	30	8	1.1	2	0	32	8	80
Nagy, Charles	CLE	11.3	21	6	1.5	2	0	23	7	76.7
Navarro, Jaime	MIL	10.2	20	6	1.8	3	0	23	7	76.7
Nichols, Rod	CLE	14.2	15	7	2.2	1	1	16	8	66.7
Olson, Gregg	BAL	14.9	12	1	1.4	1	0	13	1	92.9
Perez, Melido	CHA	11.3	12	4	4.7	3	1	15	5	75
Plunk, Eric	NYA	18.4	23	3	4.5	5	0	28	3	90.3

NAME	TEAM	Att2%	SB2	CS2	Att3%	SB3	CS3	Total SB	Total CS	OSB%
Robinson, Jeff	BAL	8.8	7	4	5.6	3	1	10	5	66.7
Ryan, Nolan	TEX	22	22	7	2.9	2	1	24	8	75
Saberhagen, Bret	KC	7	5	9	2.1	2	0	9	9	50
Sanderson, Scott	NYA	11.2	13	7	2.8	3	0	16	7	69.6
Smith, Roy	BAL	12.2	6	5	0	0	0	6	5	54.5
Stewart, Dave	OAK	11.6	21	9	1.3	2	0	23	9	71.9
Stottlemyre, Todd	TOR	11.8	23	3	0	0	0	24	3	88.9
Swindell, Greg	CLE	8.7	9	9	1.3	0	2	9	11	45
Tanana, Frank	DET	11	11	12	4.8	6	1	17	13	56.7
Tapani, Kevin	MIN	9.9	17	3	.8	1	0	18	3	85.7
Taylor, Wade	NYA	10.8	9	7	3.1	3	0	12	7	63.2
Terrell, Walt	DET	4.8	6	5	0	0	0	6	5	54.5
Thigpen, Bobby	CHA	13.4	8	5	0	0	0	8	5	61.5
Timlin, Mike	TOR	14.6	11	4	1.2	0	1	11	5	68.8
Wegman, Bill	MIL	9.8	10	6	.9	0	1	10	7	58.8
Welch, Bob	OAK	10.1	11	14	2.1	1	2	12	16	42.9
Wells, Dave	TOR	9.4	6	13	1.8	2	0	8	13	38.1
Williamson, Mark	BAL	12.2	9	3	1.3	1	0	10	3	76.9
Witt, Bobby	TEX	17.9	17	4	1.2	1	0	18	4	81.8
AMERICAN LEAGUE AVERAGE		**8.9**	**1259**	**646**	**1.9**	**202**	**78**	**1468**	**758**	**65.9**

NATIONAL LEAGUE

NAME	TEAM	Att2%	SB2	CS2	Att3%	SB3	CS3	Total SB	Total CS	OSB%
Armstrong, Jack	CIN	12.4	10	8	2.3	2	0	12	8	60
Assenmacher, Paul	CHN	10.9	6	5	2.8	2	0	8	5	61.5
Avery, Steve	ATL	14.1	16	10	4.5	5	1	21	11	65.6
Barnes, Brian	MON	13.5	18	5	5	2	3	20	8	71.4
Belcher, Tim	LA	10.4	15	8	2.9	2	2	17	10	63
Belinda, Stan	PIT	18.8	10	3	5.7	3	0	13	3	81.2
Benes, Andy	SD	8.5	9	8	2.5	1	2	10	11	47.6
Bielecki, Mike	CHN	14	16	8	1.9	1	1	17	9	65.4
Black, Buddy	SF	8.8	9	9	4.3	5	0	14	11	56
Boever, Joe	PHI	12.5	10	2	2.2	2	0	12	2	85.7
Bowen, Ryan	HOU	14.1	10	1	4.5	2	1	12	2	85.7
Boyd, Oil Can	MON	16.5	11	9	0	0	0	11	9	55
Brantley, Jeff	SF	19.1	16	2	1.2	1	0	17	2	89.5
Browning, Tom	CIN	8.8	17	4	3.8	4	1	21	6	77.8
Burkett, John	SF	11.7	16	15	1.5	1	1	17	16	51.5
Charlton, Norm	CIN	12.2	6	5	8	4	2	10	7	58.8
Combs, Pat	PHI	12	10	1	5.5	2	1	12	2	85.7
Cone, David	NYN	16.7	25	13	1.2	2	0	27	13	67.5
Corsi, Jim	HOU	11.8	7	3	2.2	1	0	8	3	72.7
Cox, Danny	PHI	16.5	11	7	0	0	0	11	7	61.1
Crews, Tim	LA	13.7	8	2	3.3	2	0	10	2	83.3
Darling, Ron	NYN	11.8	10	2	1.3	1	0	12	2	85.7
DeJesus, Jose	PHI	12.1	15	9	4.1	4	2	19	11	63.3
DeLeon, Jose	SL	13.8	11	11	1.2	1	1	12	12	50
Deshaies, Jim	HOU	19.1	17	13	2.8	3	0	21	14	60
Dibble, Rob	CIN	24.1	14	5	2.7	2	0	16	5	76.2
Downs, Kelly	SF	15.7	15	3	0	0	0	15	4	78.9
Drabek, Doug	PIT	16.8	28	14	.7	1	0	29	14	67.4
Gardner, Mark	MON	16.4	13	15	.9	0	1	13	17	43.3
Glavine, Tom	ATL	11.4	16	9	2.3	2	1	18	10	64.3
Gooden, Dwight	NYN	21.9	30	13	3.8	3	2	33	16	67.3
Greene, Tommy	PHI	11.5	17	5	2.6	1	2	18	7	72
Grimsley, Jason	PHI	18.8	14	1	0	0	0	14	1	93.3
Gross, Kevin	LA	13.9	13	6	3.3	2	0	15	6	71.4
Gross, Kip	CIN	10.2	7	3	0	0	0	8	3	72.7
Hammond, Chris	CIN	9.6	7	3	1.4	1	0	8	3	72.7
Haney, Chris	MON	12.4	7	6	1.6	1	0	8	6	57.1

NAME	TEAM	Att2%	SB2	CS2	Att3%	SB3	CS3	Total SB	Total CS	OSB%
Harnisch, Pete	HOU	16.4	27	6	0	0	0	27	6	81.8
Harris, Greg	SD	18.6	13	8	0	0	0	13	8	61.9
Hartley, Mike	LA	15.4	9	1	1.6	1	0	10	1	90.9
Hershiser, Orel	LA	9.3	10	2	1.4	1	0	11	2	84.6
Hickerson, Bryan	SF	17.2	6	4	0	0	0	6	4	60
Hill, Ken	SL	14.2	18	9	1.1	1	0	19	11	63.3
Hurst, Bruce	SD	7.5	10	6	.8	1	0	11	6	64.7
Jones, Barry	MON	12.2	5	6	3.1	2	0	8	6	57.1
Jones, Jimmy	HOU	13.5	16	5	3	2	1	18	6	75
Kile, Darryl	HOU	8.3	10	3	1.5	2	0	12	3	80
Kipper, Bob	PIT	16.4	6	4	2	1	0	7	4	63.6
Lancaster, Lester	CHN	15.3	12	13	2.1	2	0	14	14	50
Leibrandt, Charlie	ATL	15.9	26	11	6.2	9	0	35	11	76.1
Maddux, Greg	CHN	11.6	21	7	2.7	4	0	25	7	78.1
Maddux, Mike	SD	14.1	5	6	1.5	0	1	5	7	41.7
Martinez, Dennis	MON	12.8	21	4	.7	1	0	22	4	84.6
Martinez, Ramon	LA	10.6	15	7	0	0	0	16	9	64
McClellan, Paul	SF	21.9	11	5	2.2	1	0	12	5	70.6
McElroy, Chuck	CHN	14	9	8	7.2	3	2	12	10	54.5
Mercker, Kent	ATL	12.5	10	0	0	0	0	10	0	100
Morgan, Mike	LA	13.5	24	5	1.6	0	2	24	7	77.4
Nabholz, Chris	MON	14	11	9	5.9	4	2	15	11	57.7
Ojeda, Bobby	LA	16.8	20	12	4.2	3	3	23	15	60.5
Oliveras, Francisco	SF	19.7	5	9	0	0	0	5	9	35.7
Olivares, Omar	SL	12.7	10	10	2	1	1	11	11	50
Pena, Alejandro	NYN	15.2	7	3	2.4	1	0	8	4	66.7
Portugal, Mark	HOU	11.3	12	7	0	0	0	12	7	63.2
Power, Ted	CIN	13.3	8	4	6	4	0	12	4	75
Rasmussen, Dennis	SD	12.6	17	4	5	3	2	21	6	77.8
Righetti, Dave	SF	12.5	7	4	1.8	1	0	8	4	66.7
Rijo, Jose	CIN	9.5	15	1	2.9	1	2	16	3	84.2
Robinson, Don	SF	11.6	9	4	2.1	1	1	10	5	66.7
Sampen, Bill	MON	20	15	6	2.2	1	1	16	8	66.7
Scanlan, R.	CHN	8.5	5	5	1.1	0	1	5	7	41.7
Scudder, Scott	CIN	15.4	12	6	0	0	0	12	6	66.7
Smiley, John	PIT	14.1	14	12	4.3	4	1	18	13	58.1
Smith, Bryn	SL	14.5	17	8	1.6	2	0	19	8	70.4
Smith, Lee	SL	14.1	8	2	1.9	1	0	9	2	81.8
Smith, Pete	ATL	29.2	13	1	0	0	0	13	1	92.9
Smith, Zane	PIT	13.6	20	8	4.7	6	0	26	8	76.5
Smoltz, John	ATL	9.4	13	9	2	1	2	14	13	51.9
Sutcliffe, Rick	CHN	21.2	19	2	2.6	2	0	21	2	91.3
Terry, Scott	SL	12	7	3	0	0	0	7	3	70
Tewksbury, Bob	SL	10.1	8	10	1.6	2	0	10	10	50
Tomlin, Randy	PIT	12.4	14	12	2.7	3	0	17	12	58.6
Viola, Frank	NYN	8.6	6	15	.7	0	1	6	16	27.3
Walk, Bob	PIT	9.3	6	4	1.4	1	0	7	4	63.6
Whitehurst, Wally	NYN	9	7	5	5.8	2	2	9	8	52.9
Williams, Mitch	PHI	9.1	9	2	3.8	3	0	12	2	85.7
Wilson, Trevor	SF	9	8	11	.8	0	1	8	12	40
NATIONAL LEAGUE AVERAGE		**12.1**	**1433**	**708**	**2.3**	**210**	**65**	**1651**	**808**	**67.1**

CATCHERS

AMERICAN LEAGUE

NAME	TEAM	Att2%	SB2	CS2	Att3%	SB3	CS3	Total SB	Total CS	OSB%
Allanson, Andy	DET	7.2	17	13	1.8	3	2	20	16	62.7
Alomar, Sandy	CLE	7.1	20	9	1	1	2	21	12	64.7
Borders, Pat	TOR	9.6	46	22	1.2	3	3	50	28	73.1
Bradley, Scott	SEA	8.6	29	6	2.8	7	1	37	7	59.2
Dempsey, Rick	MIL	9	27	11	1.1	2	1	29	12	71.1
Fisk, Carlton	CHA	10.4	50	33	1	4	1	54	38	55.3
Geren, Bob	NYA	10.1	25	14	2.2	6	0	31	14	72.8
Harper, Brian	MIN	11.3	83	24	2.2	14	2	98	28	62.4
Hoiles, Chris	BAL	8.7	43	22	2.1	6	4	49	26	64.7
Karkovice, Ron	CHA	8.3	23	16	1.4	2	2	25	19	50
Macfarlane, Mike	KC	6.1	21	16	.2	0	1	21	17	58.9
Marzano, John	BOS	7	14	7	3.6	2	6	16	13	66.9
Mayne, Brent	KC	9.5	43	19	1.6	7	1	52	23	55.3
Melvin, Bob	BAL	9.1	40	17	2.2	8	1	48	19	65.3
Merullo, Matt	CHA	13.4	14	7	1.8	1	1	15	8	58.7
Myers, Greg	TOR	10.8	61	21	2.1	7	3	68	25	72.4
Nokes, Matt	NYA	10.2	78	30	3.6	21	5	99	37	71
Ortiz, Junior	MIN	6.6	14	11	.8	1	1	15	13	77.8
Orton, John	CAL	9.6	14	8	3	2	3	16	11	57.6
Parrish, Lance	CAL	8.4	45	31	2.6	8	7	53	39	69
Pena, Tony	BOS	9.1	72	32	1.6	8	5	81	40	68.5
Petralli, Gene	TEX	11.9	33	16	1.2	3	1	36	17	0
Quirk, Jamie	OAK	11.3	34	21	2.3	4	3	38	24	68.5
Rodriguez, Ivan	TEX	8.2	32	30	1.5	4	3	36	34	65.6
Skinner, Joel	CLE	8.2	47	25	1.9	7	3	54	28	63.6
Spehr, Tim	KC	9.9	12	10	2.4	1	3	13	14	69.3
Stanley, Mike	TEX	8	25	7	3	9	0	34	7	67.9
Steinbach, Terry	OAK	9.6	69	32	1.5	7	3	76	35	73.3
Surhoff, B.J.	MIL	8.2	72	27	2.6	14	6	86	35	61.1
Taubensee, Ed	CLE	9.9	17	3	1.4	2	0	19	3	62.5
Tettleton, Mickey	DET	7.8	50	36	1.8	14	0	64	38	68.5
Tingley, Ron	CAL	9.5	14	20	3.2	6	1	20	22	59.3
Valle, Dave	SEA	6.5	36	28	1.6	9	1	45	31	65.9
Whitt, Ernie	BAL	11	7	6	4.5	4	0	11	6	67.1

NATIONAL LEAGUE

NAME	TEAM	Att2%	SB2	CS2	Att3%	SB3	CS3	Total SB	Total CS	OSB%
Berryhill, Damon	CHN	10.8	28	9	2.6	5	1	33	10	65.9
Biggio, Craig	HOU	12.6	109	41	2.1	16	3	126	46	70
Cabrera, Francisco	ATL	8.3	8	3	3.4	2	1	10	4	72
Carter, Gary	LA	15.3	54	21	2.9	4	6	59	28	73.2
Cerone, Rick	NYN	11.3	34	29	1.9	5	2	39	32	70.6
Daulton, Darren	PHI	11	71	16	2.6	12	2	84	18	64.4
Decker, Steve	SF	11.4	44	24	1.3	5	1	49	28	55.7
Fitzgerald, Mike	MON	15.1	54	16	3.7	7	5	61	21	68
Fletcher, Darrin	PHI	11.8	28	12	2.5	5	1	33	13	68
Gedman, Rich	SL	14.3	27	8	2	3	0	30	10	55.1
Girardi, Joe	CHN	11.8	12	6	2.2	2	0	14	6	72.4
Hassey, Ron	MON	16.8	31	8	.6	1	0	33	9	74.4

NAME	TEAM	Att2%	SB2	CS2	Att3%	SB3	CS3	Total SB	Total CS	OSB%
Heath, Mike	ATL	15.7	39	12	3.5	5	4	44	18	59.9
Hundley, Todd	NYN	15.4	16	6	0	0	0	16	6	54.9
Kennedy, Terry	SF	16.6	38	35	2.3	6	0	44	35	62.6
Lake, Steve	PHI	9.6	29	13	2.4	5	3	34	16	82.4
Lampkin, Tom	SD	11.7	8	3	3.4	2	0	10	3	60
LaValliere, Mike	PIT	12.9	76	38	2.7	14	1	90	39	76.3
Manwaring, Kirt	SF	10.5	34	16	1	1	2	35	20	63.6
Nichols, Carl	HOU	13.3	8	9	0	0	0	8	9	73.3
O'Brien, Charlie	NYN	12.3	45	21	3.4	9	3	55	26	64.8
Oliver, Joe	CIN	12.2	60	25	2.7	10	2	70	28	55.6
Olson, Greg	ATL	11.8	82	33	2.4	13	3	95	37	71
Pagnozzi, Tom	SL	12.2	74	65	1.8	12	2	86	70	66
Prince, Tom	PIT	15.9	7	7	2.9	1	1	8	8	69.8
Reed, Jeff	CIN	10.4	48	23	2	7	3	57	28	71.6
Reyes, Gil	MON	12.7	36	39	1	2	2	38	43	68.5
Santiago, Benito	SD	9.8	82	48	2	10	7	93	58	70.7
Santovenia, Nelson	MON	12.1	13	7	3.9	4	1	17	8	46.9
Sasser, Mackey	NYN	14.2	23	9	1.3	1	1	24	10	67.9
Scioscia, Mike	LA	10.4	72	24	2.2	10	3	82	30	70.1
Slaught, Don	PIT	12.2	35	25	2.6	7	1	42	26	50
Villanueva, Hector	CHN	13.3	37	15	2.1	5	1	42	16	60.5
Wilkins, Rick	CHN	10	36	25	3.1	10	2	46	30	66.7

BASERUNNERS

AMERICAN LEAGUE

NAME	TEAM	Att2%	SB2	CS2	Att3%	SB3	CS3	Total SB	Total CS	SB%
Alomar, Roberto	TOR	22	32	10	14.2	21	1	53	11	82.8
Anderson, Brady	BAL	14.6	11	4	2.8	1	1	12	5	70.6
Bichette, Dante	MIL	25.9	13	8	1.9	1	0	14	8	63.6
Blankenship, Lance	OAK	14.9	8	3	6.9	4	0	12	3	80
Briley, Greg	SEA	29.7	20	10	4.5	3	1	23	11	67.6
Burks, Ellis	BOS	12.8	5	9	2.3	1	1	6	11	35.3
Canseco, Jose	OAK	18.9	21	6	3.4	4	0	26	6	81.2
Carter, Joe	TOR	18.1	18	9	1.7	2	0	20	9	69
Cole, Alex	CLE	24.2	22	15	7.4	5	2	27	17	61.4
Cora, Joey	CHA	16.5	10	6	1.9	1	0	11	6	64.7
Cotto, Henry	SEA	25	14	2	5.8	2	1	16	3	84.2
Cuyler, Milt	DET	26.7	31	9	9.4	10	1	41	10	80.4
Devereaux, Mike	BAL	12.3	13	8	3	3	1	16	9	64
Felix, Junior	CAL	15.4	5	5	3.4	2	0	7	5	58.3
Franco, Julio	TEX	17.4	32	6	4	4	2	36	9	80
Fryman, Travis	DET	12.2	10	5	2.2	2	0	12	5	70.6
Gaetti, Gary	CAL	7.3	5	5	0	0	0	5	5	50
Gagne, Greg	MIN	18	11	7	1.5	0	1	11	9	55
Gallego, Mike	OAK	8.4	5	8	1.1	0	1	6	9	40
Gibson, Kirk	KC	14.1	14	4	4.7	4	0	18	4	81.8
Gladden, Dan	MIN	17.7	14	9	1.3	1	0	15	9	62.5
Greenwell, Mike	BOS	11.3	14	4	2.1	1	1	15	5	75
Griffe, George Kenneth	SEA	13.4	18	4	1.9	0	2	18	6	75
Gruber, Kelly	TOR	17.3	10	7	2.6	2	0	12	7	63.2
Guillen, Ozzie	CHA	29.5	21	15	0	0	0	21	15	58.3
Hamilton, Darryl	MIL	14.6	15	5	2.5	1	1	16	6	72.7
Henderson, Dave	OAK	7.3	6	6	0	0	0	6	6	50
Henderson, Rickey	OAK	28.1	37	11	20.5	21	6	58	18	76.3
Huff, Mike	CLE	18	9	2	4.3	2	0	11	2	84.6
Huson, Jeff	TEX	13.7	7	3	2	1	0	8	3	72.7

NAME	TEAM	Att2%	SB2	CS2	Att3%	SB3	CS3	Total SB	Total CS	OSB%
Johnson, Lance	CHA	22.4	24	11	1	1	0	26	11	70.3
Kelly, Bobby	NYA	33	28	9	3.8	4	0	32	9	78
Kelly, Pat	NYA	14.3	9	1	6.1	3	0	12	1	92.3
Knoblauch, Chuck	MIN	14.6	25	5	0	0	0	25	5	83.3
Lyons, Steve	BOS	18.9	8	2	9.1	2	1	10	3	76.9
Mack, Shane	MIN	15.5	12	6	2.2	1	1	13	9	59.1
McRae, Brian	KC	18.9	20	10	0	0	0	20	11	64.5
Molitor, Paul	MIL	10.4	16	6	1.8	2	1	19	8	70.4
Pecota, Bill	KC	15.8	14	5	3.1	2	1	16	7	69.6
Pena, Tony	BOS	12.4	8	3	0	0	0	8	3	72.7
Pettis, Gary	TEX	32	24	9	9.5	5	2	29	13	69
Phillips, Tony	DET	7.6	10	5	0	0	0	10	5	66.7
Polonia, Luis	CAL	25.6	31	19	14.7	17	3	48	23	67.6
Puckett, Kirby	MIN	8.3	11	4	.8	0	1	11	5	68.8
Raines, Tim	CHA	30	49	15	1.4	2	0	51	15	77.3
Reed, Jody	BOS	6	6	5	0	0	0	6	5	54.5
Reynolds, Harold	SEA	16.5	24	8	2.9	4	0	28	8	77.8
Sax, Steve	NYA	17	26	9	5.3	5	2	31	11	73.8
Schofield, Dick	CAL	7.1	6	4	2.9	2	0	8	4	66.7
Shumpert, Terry	KC	29.5	14	9	6.3	3	1	17	11	60.7
Sierra, Ruben	TEX	11.4	16	4	0	0	0	16	4	80
Sosa, Sammy	CHA	26.7	13	3	2	0	1	13	6	68.4
Spiers III, Bill	MIL	17.6	14	8	0	0	0	14	8	63.6
Stubbs, Franklin	MIL	19.5	11	4	2.9	2	0	13	4	76.5
Surhoff, B.J.	MIL	7.5	5	7	1.2	0	1	5	8	38.5
Thurman, Gary	KC	28.6	14	4	6.1	1	1	15	5	75
Trammell, Alan	DET	12.1	11	2	0	0	0	11	2	84.6
White, Devon	TOR	24.1	28	10	3.4	5	0	33	10	76.7
Williams, Bernie	NYA	11.5	8	4	3.2	2	0	10	5	66.7
Wilson, Mookie	TOR	24.6	11	3	0	0	0	11	3	78.6
Wilson, Willie	OAK	25.3	18	5	2.6	2	0	20	5	80

NATIONAL LEAGUE

NAME	TEAM	Att2%	SB2	CS2	Att3%	SB3	CS3	Total SB	Total CS	SB%
Bagwell, Jeff	HOU	5.8	7	4	0	0	0	7	4	63.6
Bell, Jay	PIT	7.6	7	6	2.6	3	0	10	6	62.5
Biggio, Craig	HOU	11.6	16	6	2.4	3	0	19	6	76
Blauser, Jeff	ATL	10.5	5	6	0	0	0	5	6	45.5
Bonds, Barry	PIT	31.2	33	12	8.3	9	0	43	13	76.8
Boston, Daryl	NYN	29.3	14	8	1.4	1	0	15	8	65.2
Braggs, Glenn	CIN	17.6	10	3	2.1	1	0	11	3	78.6
Butler, Brett	LA	23.2	35	27	2.5	3	1	38	28	57.6
Calderon, Ivan	MON	28.9	28	15	4.8	3	1	31	16	66
Candaele, Casey	HOU	7.8	7	3	2.1	2	0	9	3	75
Chamberlain, Wes	PHI	13.3	8	4	1.6	1	0	9	4	69.2
Coleman, Vince	NYN	42.9	31	11	12.5	6	2	37	14	72.5
Dascenzo, Doug	CHN	20.9	13	6	1.4	1	0	14	7	66.7
Davis, Eric	CIN	15.9	12	2	3.5	2	0	14	2	87.5
DeShields, Delino	MON	34.7	48	18	9.2	8	4	56	23	70.9
Dunston, Shawon	CHN	18	18	4	5	3	2	21	6	77.8
Dykstra, Lenny	PHI	25.8	19	4	6.3	5	0	24	4	85.7
Felder, Mike	SF	23.2	20	6	1.2	1	0	21	6	77.8
Fernandez, Tony	SD	17.6	19	9	4.4	4	0	23	9	71.9
Finley, Steve	HOU	25	32	14	3.1	2	3	34	18	65.4

NAME	TEAM	Att2%	SB2	CS2	Att3%	SB3	CS3	Total SB	Total CS	SB%
Gant, Ron	ATL	37.3	32	15	1.8	2	0	34	15	69.4
Gilkey, Bernard	SL	32.3	14	7	1.9	0	1	14	8	63.6
Gonzalez, Luis	HOU	15.2	10	5	1.1	0	1	10	7	58.8
Grissom, Marquis	MON	45	58	14	15.4	18	3	76	17	81.7
Gwynn, Tony	SD	7.1	5	6	3.6	3	1	8	8	50
Harris, Lenny	LA	9.1	10	2	2.4	2	0	12	3	80
Hatcher, Billy	CIN	13.7	9	8	2.1	2	0	11	9	55
Howard, Thomas	SD	22.1	9	6	3.6	1	1	10	7	58.8
Hudler, Rex	SL	31.4	8	8	10.8	4	0	12	8	60
Jefferies, Gregg	NYN	19.1	23	4	2.5	2	1	26	5	83.9
Johnson, Howard	NYN	31.1	23	15	7.4	7	1	30	16	65.2
Jose, Felix	SL	18.4	18	11	2.7	2	1	20	12	62.5
Justice, Dave	ATL	15.7	8	8	0	0	0	8	8	50
Landrum, Ced	CHN	44.2	18	5	22	9	0	27	5	84.4
Lankford, Ray	SL	44.3	41	17	4.7	3	2	44	20	68.8
Larkin, Barry	CIN	14.8	14	6	9.5	10	0	24	6	80
Lewis, Darren	SF	24.4	12	7	0	0	0	13	7	65
Lind, Jose	PIT	7.9	7	3	1.2	0	1	7	4	63.6
Martinez, Dave	MON	14.8	11	7	6.1	5	0	16	7	69.6
McGee, Willie	SF	14.2	14	9	2.7	3	0	17	9	65.4
McReynolds, Kevin	NYN	9.4	6	6	0	0	0	6	6	50
Merced, Orlando	PIT	7.4	7	4	1	1	0	8	4	66.7
Miller, Keith	NYN	18.1	11	4	4.1	3	0	14	4	77.8
Morandini, Mickey	PHI	10.4	10	2	4.8	3	0	13	2	86.7
Morris, Hal	CIN	8.3	9	3	2	1	1	10	4	71.4
Murray, Eddie	LA	7.1	7	3	3.1	3	0	10	3	76.9
Nixon, Otis	ATL	45.1	59	19	9.8	13	2	72	21	77.4
O'Neill, Paul	CIN	14.2	11	6	2.4	1	1	12	7	63.2
Pagnozzi, Tom	SL	16.2	9	12	1	0	1	9	13	40.9
Pena, Geronimo	SL	22.2	13	5	3.8	2	0	15	5	75
Pendleton, Terry	ATL	7	10	1	.7	0	1	10	2	83.3
Perry, Gerald	SL	39.2	12	8	7.5	3	0	15	8	65.2
Redus, Gary	PIT	25	16	2	2.9	1	1	17	3	85
Roberts, Bip	SD	25.5	26	10	.8	0	1	26	11	70.3
Sabo, Chris	CIN	14.6	16	5	3.2	3	0	19	6	76
Samuel, Juan	LA	16.3	23	8	0	0	0	23	8	74.2
Sanders, Deion	ATL	41.2	11	3	0	0	0	11	3	78.6
Sandberg, Ryne	CHN	17	22	8	0	0	0	22	8	73.3
Smith, Lonnie	ATL	11.5	9	4	1.2	0	1	9	5	64.3
Smith, Ozzie	SL	18.7	32	8	3	3	1	35	9	79.5
Strawberry, Darryl	LA	13.6	10	8	0	0	0	10	8	55.6
Thompson, Milt	SL	25.6	15	8	2.6	1	1	16	9	64
Thompson, Robbie	SF	12.6	11	7	2.9	3	0	14	7	66.7
Thon, Dickie	PHI	11	10	5	1	1	0	11	5	68.8
VanSlyke, Andy	PIT	7.1	10	2	1.1	0	1	10	3	76.9
Varsho, Gary	PIT	15.6	9	1	2.3	0	1	9	2	81.8
Walker, Chico	CHN	15.5	13	4	1.2	0	1	13	5	72.2
Walker, Larry	MON	13.8	12	6	3.3	2	2	14	9	60.9
Williams, Matt	SF	8.1	5	5	0	0	0	5	5	50
Yelding, Eric	HOU	33.9	10	9	2.1	1	0	11	9	55
Young, Gerald	HOU	34	15	3	4.1	1	1	16	5	76.2
Zeile, Todd	SL	15.3	17	10	0	0	0	17	11	60.7

Part 5   Career Records

This part includes year-by-year, career major-league batting and pitching information for all 1,034 players who played in the majors in 1991 (plus the 20 players who were on major-league disabled lists in 1991 but didn't get into a game). Each team for every year is listed separately, and if a player played for more than one major-league team in the same season, a totals line for the year is also included.

The career records are separated into alphabetical batter and pitcher registers. Every official batting and pitching category is included. (Note that batting stats for pitchers are not shown in the batter register, nor are pitching stats for non-pitchers shown in the pitcher register.)

In addition to the major-leaguers, career information is given for many top prospects for 1992 who did not play in the majors in 1991. These prospects were selected after careful analysis of data from several sources and after consulting with Jim Keller of Howe Sportsdata International, the official statisticians for the minor leagues.

For all players in this section, complete minor-league records are included back through the 1984 season. Prior to 1984, Howe Sportsdata's minor-league records are not completely computerized, so 1983 and earlier data are not available for all players.

The first line for each player lists his full name, followed by his "use" name in quotes. A player's use name is the name he is commonly called (if different from his given name). Additional surnames for Hispanic players are shown in parentheses. Shown after the player's name are how he bats and throws and his date of birth. The last entry on the name line for major-leaguers shows how many games they played at each position in 1991. For minor-leaguers, the last entries show their primary position and the major-league organization they played in last season.

The career statistics are organized so that similar types of stats are grouped together from left to right across the page:

- The first columns show the year, team, and league.

- The second group is usage—how often they played, pitched, and batted.

- Third are the ways players reach base. For batters, these show their base hits and walks; for pitchers, how many hits and walks they allowed. Hit batters are placed next to walks, since they have the same effect.

- Next come ways of making outs—strikeouts, double plays, and sacrifices.

- Next are basestealing stats for batters and the pitcher statistics that advance baserunners (wild pitches and balks).

- The last group of categories is the most important, showing the results of all the others. For batters, their runs scored and driven in are shown, followed by their batting, on-base, and slugging averages. For pitchers, their runs allowed are shown, followed by wins, losses, saves, and earned-run averages.

Abner, Shawn Wesley — bats right — throws right — b.6/17/66 — 1991 positions: OF 77, DH 3

YR	TM/LG	CL	G	TPA	AB	H	2B	3B	HR	TB	BB	IBB	HB	SO	GDP	SH	SF	SB	CS	R	RBI	BA	OBA	SA
84	KIN/APP	R+	46	197	183	50	8	0	10	88	10	1	2	24	4	0	2	9	6	32	35	.273	.315	.481
	LF/NYP	A–	18	74	68	18	2	0	1	23	5	0	0	16	0	0	1	3	6	7	5	.265	.311	.338
85	LYN/CAR	A+	139	586	542	163	30	11	16	263	28	1	9	77	14	0	7	8	7	71	89	.301	.341	.485
86	JAC/TEX	AA	134	550	511	136	29	8	14	223	23	1	7	76	10	2	7	8	6	80	76	.266	.303	.436
87	LV/PCL	AAA	105	447	406	122	14	11	11	191	26	2	8	68	5	2	5	11	11	60	85	.300	.351	.470
	SD/NL		16	49	47	13	3	1	2	24	2	0	0	8	0	0	0	1	0	5	7	.277	.306	.511
88	SD/NL		37	89	83	15	3	0	2	24	4	1	1	19	1	0	1	0	1	6	5	.181	.225	.289
	LV/PCL	AAA	63	268	252	64	16	2	4	96	11	0	1	39	4	0	4	0	1	35	34	.254	.284	.381
89	LV/PCL	AAA	56	244	223	60	11	2	8	99	17	0	1	53	2	2	1	3	3	31	31	.269	.322	.444
	SD/NL		57	108	102	18	4	0	2	28	5	2	0	20	1	0	1	0	1	13	14	.176	.213	.275
90	SD/NL		91	198	184	45	9	0	1	57	9	1	2	28	3	2	1	2	3	17	15	.245	.286	.310
91	SD/NL		53	125	115	19	4	1	1	28	7	4	1	25	3	1	1	0	0	15	5	.165	.218	.243
	CAL/AL		41	105	101	23	6	1	2	37	4	0	0	18	3	0	0	1	2	12	9	.228	.257	.366
	YEAR		94	230	216	42	10	2	3	65	11	4	1	43	6	1	1	1	2	27	14	.194	.236	.301
5 YR TOTALS			**295**	**674**	**632**	**133**	**29**	**3**	**10**	**198**	**31**	**8**	**4**	**118**	**11**	**3**	**4**	**5**	**6**	**68**	**55**	**.210**	**.250**	**.313**

Afenir, Michael Troy "Troy" — bats right — throws right — b.9/21/63 — 1991 positions: C 4, DH 1

YR	TM/LG	CL	G	TPA	AB	H	2B	3B	HR	TB	BB	IBB	HB	SO	GDP	SH	SF	SB	CS	R	RBI	BA	OBA	SA
84	AST/GCL	R	27	111	89	26	5	1	5	48	17	0	2	34	1	1	2	2	3	16	24	.292	.409	.539
	AUB/NYP	A–	7	26	26	3	0	0	0	3	0	0	0	15	0	0	0	0	0	2	0	.115	.115	.115
	ASH/SAL	A	115	409	358	69	16	0	16	133	39	1	2	125	9	4	6	1	2	44	69	.193	.272	.372
85	OSC/FSL	A+	99	347	323	80	19	1	6	119	20	1	0	86	4	2	2	3	1	38	41	.248	.290	.368
86	COL/SOU	AA	91	345	313	68	15	3	14	131	22	0	3	90	6	4	3	0	5	50	45	.217	.273	.419
87	COL/SOU	AA	31	107	99	20	8	0	2	34	6	0	0	20	0	2	0	0	0	15	11	.202	.248	.343
	OSC/FSL	A+	79	337	294	81	20	1	14	145	33	1	2	75	5	0	8	1	0	60	68	.276	.344	.493
	HOU/NL		10	20	20	6	1	0	0	7	0	0	0	12	0	0	0	0	0	1	1	.300	.300	.350
88	COL/SOU	AA	137	549	494	122	21	5	16	201	45	0	5	131	6	0	5	11	6	61	66	.247	.313	.407
89	HUN/SOU	AA	65	258	225	57	15	1	13	113	28	0	1	63	3	0	4	1	3	31	45	.253	.333	.502
90	TAC/PCL	AAA	88	325	289	72	14	2	15	135	30	0	1	81	5	4	1	1	1	44	47	.249	.321	.467
	OAK/AL		14	15	14	2	0	0	0	2	0	0	0	7	0	0	1	0	0	0	2	.143	.133	.143
91	OAK/AL		5	11	11	1	0	0	0	1	0	0	0	2	1	0	0	0	0	0	0	.091	.091	.091
	TAC/PCL	AAA	80	296	262	64	12	3	10	112	22	1	3	59	5	3	6	0	0	35	38	.244	.304	.427
3 YR TOTALS			**29**	**46**	**45**	**9**	**1**	**0**	**0**	**10**	**0**	**0**	**0**	**20**	**1**	**0**	**1**	**0**	**0**	**1**	**3**	**.200**	**.196**	**.222**

Aldrete, Michael Peter "Mike" — bats left — throws left — b.1/29/61 — 1991 positions: 1B 47, OF 21, DH 7

YR	TM/LG	CL	G	TPA	AB	H	2B	3B	HR	TB	BB	IBB	HB	SO	GDP	SH	SF	SB	CS	R	RBI	BA	OBA	SA
84	FRE/CAL	A+	136	572	457	155	28	3	12	225	109	5	1	77	5	1	4	14	5	89	72	.339	.464	.492
85	SHR/TEX	AA	127	541	441	147	32	1	15	226	94	9	0	57	11	2	4	16	7	80	77	.333	.447	.512
	PHO/PCL	AAA	3	8	8	1	1	0	0	2	0	0	0	3	0	0	0	0	0	0	1	.125	.125	.250
86	PHO/PCL	AAA	47	200	159	59	14	0	6	91	36	3	0	24	1	1	4	0	0	36	35	.371	.477	.572
	SF/NL		84	256	216	54	18	3	2	84	33	4	2	34	3	4	1	1	3	27	25	.250	.353	.389
87	SF/NL		126	406	357	116	18	2	9	165	43	5	0	50	6	4	2	6	0	50	51	.325	.396	.462
88	SF/NL		139	449	389	104	15	0	3	128	56	13	0	65	10	1	3	6	5	44	50	.267	.357	.329
89	IND/AMA	AAA	10	39	31	4	1	0	0	5	8	0	0	10	0	0	0	0	1	4	2	.129	.308	.161
	MON/NL		76	159	136	30	8	1	1	43	19	0	1	30	4	1	0	0	1	12	12	.221	.316	.316
90	MON/NL		96	200	161	39	7	1	1	51	37	2	1	31	2	2	0	1	2	22	18	.242	.385	.317
91	SD/NL		12	18	15	0	0	0	0	0	3	0	0	4	1	0	0	0	0	2	1	.000	.167	.000
	CS/PCL	AAA	23	84	76	22	5	0	0	27	8	1	0	17	2	0	0	0	0	4	8	.289	.357	.355
	CLE/AL		85	222	183	48	6	1	1	59	36	1	0	37	1	1	2	1	2	22	19	.262	.380	.322
	YEAR		97	240	198	48	6	1	1	59	39	1	0	41	1	1	2	1	3	24	20	.242	.364	.298
6 YR TOTALS			**618**	**1710**	**1457**	**391**	**72**	**8**	**17**	**530**	**227**	**25**	**4**	**251**	**26**	**11**	**11**	**16**	**16**	**179**	**176**	**.268**	**.366**	**.364**

Alicea, Luis Rene (De Jesus) — bats both — throws right — b.7/29/65 — 1991 positions: 2B 11, 3B 2, SS 1

YR	TM/LG	CL	G	TPA	AB	H	2B	3B	HR	TB	BB	IBB	HB	SO	GDP	SH	SF	SB	CS	R	RBI	BA	OBA	SA
86	ERI/NYP	A–	47	201	163	46	6	1	3	63	37	2	1	20	0	0	0	27	4	40	18	.282	.418	.387
	ARK/TEX	AA	25	77	68	16	3	0	0	19	5	0	0	11	2	2	2	0	3	8	3	.235	.280	.279
87	ARK/TEX	AA	101	398	337	91	14	3	4	123	49	2	2	28	7	5	5	13	8	57	47	.270	.361	.365
	LOU/AMA	AAA	29	117	105	32	10	2	2	52	9	1	1	9	2	1	1	4	2	18	20	.305	.362	.495
88	LOU/AMA	AAA	49	209	191	53	11	6	1	79	11	1	1	21	5	3	3	8	4	21	21	.277	.316	.414
	STL/NL		93	330	297	63	10	4	1	84	25	4	2	32	12	4	2	1	1	20	24	.212	.276	.283
89	LOU/AMA	AAA	124	482	412	102	20	3	8	152	59	1	4	55	10	3	4	13	5	53	48	.248	.344	.369
90	SP/FSL	A+	29	121	95	22	1	4	0	31	20	2	5	14	1	0	1	9	3	14	12	.232	.388	.326
	ARK/TEX	AA	14	57	49	14	3	1	0	19	7	0	1	8	0	0	0	2	2	11	4	.286	.386	.388
	LOU/AMA	AAA	25	98	92	32	6	3	0	44	5	0	1	12	4	0	0	0	4	10	10	.348	.388	.478
91	LOU/AMA	AAA	31	132	112	44	6	3	4	68	14	1	2	8	2			2	2	26	16	.393	.462	.607
	STL/NL		56	76	68	13	3	0	0	16	8	0	0	19	0	0	0	0	1	5	0	.191	.276	.235
2 YR TOTALS			**149**	**406**	**365**	**76**	**13**	**4**	**1**	**100**	**33**	**4**	**2**	**51**	**12**	**4**	**2**	**1**	**2**	**25**	**24**	**.208**	**.276**	**.274**

Allanson, Andrew Neal "Andy" — bats right — throws right — b.12/22/61 — 1991 positions: C 56, 1B 2, DH 1

YR	TM/LG	CL	G	TPA	AB	H	2B	3B	HR	TB	BB	IBB	HB	SO	GDP	SH	SF	SB	CS	R	RBI	BA	OBA	SA
83	WAT/MID	A	17	57	50	10	1	0	0	10	7	0	0	10	1	0	0	1	1	4	0	.200	.298	.200
	BAT/NYP	A–	51	174	145	38	3	0	0	41	25	0	0	16	5	4	0	3	0	27	6	.262	.371	.283
84	WAT/MID	A	46	165	144	39	5	0	0	44	20	0	0	16	3	1	0	6	5	14	10	.271	.360	.306

Allanson, Andrew Neal "Andy" (continued)

YR	TM/LG	CL	G	TPA	AB	H	2B	3B	HR	TB	BB	IBB	HB	SO	GDP	SH	SF	SB	CS	R	RBI	BA	OBA	SA
	BUF/EAS	AA	39	127	111	28	4	0	0	32	15	0	0	18	3	1	0	0	5	12	11	.252	.341	.288
85	WAT/EAS	AA	120	487	420	131	17	1	0	150	52	1	3	25	13	8	4	22	9	69	47	.312	.388	.357
86	CLE/AL		101	323	293	66	7	3	1	82	14	0	1	36	7	11	4	10	1	30	29	.225	.260	.280
87	BUF/AMA	AAA	76	289	276	75	8	0	4	95	9	0	1	36	10	1	2	2	4	21	39	.272	.295	.344
	CLE/AL		50	172	154	41	6	0	3	56	9	0	0	30	2	4	5	1	1	17	16	.266	.298	.364
88	CLE/AL		133	474	434	114	11	0	5	140	25	2	3	63	6	4	5	9	4	44	50	.263	.305	.323
89	CLE/AL		111	359	323	75	9	1	3	95	23	2	4	47	7	6	3	4	4	30	17	.232	.289	.294
90	OC/AMA	AAA	13	47	40	4	0	0	0	4	6	0	0	7	2	1	0	0	0	3	4	.100	.217	.100
	SAL/CAL	A+	36	150	127	37	6	1	3	54	19	0	2	22	4	0	2	6	5	21	18	.291	.387	.425
91	DET/AL		60	160	151	35	10	0	1	48	7	0	0	31	3	2	0	0	0	10	16	.232	.266	.318
5 YR TOTALS			**455**	**1488**	**1355**	**331**	**43**	**4**	**13**	**421**	**78**	**4**	**8**	**207**	**25**	**31**	**16**	**20**	**16**	**131**	**128**	**.244**	**.286**	**.311**

Allred, Dale Le Beau "Beau" — bats left — throws left — b.6/4/65 — 1991 positions: OF 42, DH 1

YR	TM/LG	CL	G	TPA	AB	H	2B	3B	HR	TB	BB	IBB	HB	SO	GDP	SH	SF	SB	CS	R	RBI	BA	OBA	SA
87	BUR/APP	R+	54	209	167	57	14	1	10	103	35	3	1	33	1	2	4	4	0	39	38	.341	.449	.617
88	KIN/CAR	A+	126	469	397	100	23	3	15	174	59	4	5	112	5	0	8	6	0	66	74	.252	.350	.438
89	CAN/EAS	AA	118	480	412	125	23	5	14	200	56	2	2	88	8	2	8	0	0	67	75	.303	.383	.485
	CS/PCL	AAA	11	49	47	13	3	0	1	19	2	0	0	10	2	0	0	0	3	8	4	.277	.306	.405
	CLE/AL		13	26	24	6	3	0	0	9	2	0	0	10	0	0	0	0	0	0	1	.250	.308	.375
90	CLE/AL		4	18	16	3	1	0	1	7	2	0	0	3	0	0	0	0	0	2	2	.188	.278	.438
	CS/PCL	AAA	115	451	378	105	23	6	13	179	60	1	4	54	5	2	7	6	3	79	74	.278	.376	.474
91	CLE/AL		48	156	125	29	3	0	3	41	25	1	3	35	1	3	2	2	2	17	12	.232	.359	.328
	CS/PCL	AAA	53	187	148	37	12	3	6	73	34	1	3	55	0	2	1	1	1	39	21	.250	.396	.493
3 YR TOTALS			**65**	**200**	**165**	**38**	**7**	**0**	**4**	**57**	**29**	**2**	**1**	**48**	**1**	**3**	**2**	**2**	**2**	**19**	**15**	**.230**	**.345**	**.345**

Alomar, Roberto (Velazquez) — bats both — throws right — b.2/5/68 — 1991 positions: 2B 160

YR	TM/LG	CL	G	TPA	AB	H	2B	3B	HR	TB	BB	IBB	HB	SO	GDP	SH	SF	SB	CS	R	RBI	BA	OBA	SA
85	CHA/SAL	A	137	623	546	160	14	3	0	180	61	3	3	73	9	12	4	36	19	89	54	.293	.362	.330
86	REN/CAL	A+	90	404	356	123	16	4	4	159	32	2	3	38	7	6	7	14	8	53	49	.346	.397	.447
87	WIC/TEX	AA	130	595	536	171	41	4	12	256	49	5	2	74	9	1	7	43	15	88	68	.319	.374	.478
88	LV/PCL	AAA	9	41	37	10	1	0	2	17	1	0	0	2	0	2	1	3	0	5	14	.270	.282	.459
	SD/NL		143	611	545	145	24	6	9	208	47	5	3	83	15	16	0	24	6	84	41	.266	.328	.382
89	SD/NL		158	702	623	184	27	1	7	234	53	4	1	76	10	17	8	42	17	82	56	.295	.347	.376
90	SD/NL		147	646	586	168	27	5	6	223	48	1	2	72	16	5	5	24	7	80	60	.287	.340	.381
91	TOR/AL		161	719	637	188	41	11	9	278	57	3	4	86	5	16	5	53	11	88	69	.295	.354	.436
4 YR TOTALS			**609**	**2678**	**2391**	**685**	**119**	**23**	**31**	**943**	**205**	**13**	**10**	**317**	**46**	**54**	**18**	**143**	**41**	**334**	**226**	**.286**	**.343**	**.394**

Alomar, Santos Jr. (Velazquez) "Sandy" — bats right — throws right — b.6/18/66 — 1991 positions: C 46, DH 4

YR	TM/LG	CL	G	TPA	AB	H	2B	3B	HR	TB	BB	IBB	HB	SO	GDP	SH	SF	SB	CS	R	RBI	BA	OBA	SA
84	SPO/NWL	A–	59	239	219	47	5	0	0	52	13	0	1	20	7	4	2	3	0	13	21	.215	.260	.237
85	CHA/SAL	A	100	393	352	73	7	0	3	89	31	1	3	30	9	5	2	3	1	38	43	.207	.276	.253
86	BEA/TEX	AA	100	367	346	83	15	1	4	112	15	2	1	35	16	2	3	2	6	36	27	.240	.271	.324
87	WIC/TEX	AA	103	411	375	115	19	1	8	160	21	1	5	37	12	3	7	1	5	50	65	.307	.346	.427
88	LV/PCL	AAA	93	374	337	100	9	5	16	167	28	1	4	35	11	1	4	1	1	59	71	.297	.354	.496
	SD/NL		1	1	1	0	0	0	0	0	0	0	0	1	0	0	0	0	0	0	0	.000	.000	.000
89	LV/PCL	AAA	131	572	523	160	33	8	13	248	42	5	2	58	23	2	3	3	1	88	101	.306	.358	.474
	SD/NL		7	22	19	4	1	0	1	8	3	1	0	3	1	0	0	0	0	1	6	.211	.318	.421
90	CLE/AL		132	483	445	129	26	2	9	186	25	2	2	46	10	5	6	4	1	60	66	.290	.326	.418
91	CLE/AL		51	199	184	40	9	0	0	49	8	1	4	24	4	2	1	0	0	10	7	.217	.264	.266
	CS/PCL	AAA	12	41	35	14	2	0	1	19	5	2	0	0	0	1	0	1	0	5	10	.400	.463	.543
4 YR TOTALS			**191**	**705**	**649**	**173**	**36**	**2**	**10**	**243**	**36**	**4**	**6**	**74**	**15**	**7**	**7**	**4**	**5**	**71**	**79**	**.267**	**.308**	**.374**

Alou, Moises Rojas — bats right — throws right — b.7/3/66 — 1991 positions: OF

YR	TM/LG	CL	G	TPA	AB	H	2B	3B	HR	TB	BB	IBB	HB	SO	GDP	SH	SF	SB	CS	R	RBI	BA	OBA	SA
86	WAT/NYP	A–	69	277	254	60	9	8	6	103	22	1	1	72	5	0	0	14	8	30	35	.236	.300	.406
87	MAC/SAL	A	4	10	8	1	0	0	0	1	2	0	0	4	0	0	0	0	0	1	0	.125	.300	.125
	WAT/NYP	A–	39	139	117	25	6	2	4	47	16	0	4	36	0	0	2	6	3	20	18	.214	.324	.402
88	AUG/SAL	A	105	421	358	112	23	5	7	166	51	4	5	84	5	0	7	24	12	58	62	.313	.399	.464
89	SAL/CAR	A+	86	361	321	97	29	2	14	172	35	2	3	69	6	0	2	12	5	50	53	.302	.374	.536
	HAR/EAS	AA	54	224	205	60	5	2	3	78	17	1	0	38	1	0	2	8	4	36	19	.293	.344	.380
90	HAR/EAS	AA	36	150	132	39	12	2	3	64	16	3	1	21	5	0	1	7	4	19	22	.295	.373	.485
	PIT/NL		2	5	5	1	0	0	0	1	0	0	0	0	0	0	0	0	0	0	0	.200	.200	.200
	BUF/AMA	AAA	75	309	271	74	4	6	5	105	30	0	0	43	8	2	4	9	4	38	31	.273	.345	.387
	IND/AMA	AAA	15	59	55	12	1	0	0	13	3	0	0	3	0	0	1	4	3	6	6	.218	.254	.236
	MON/NL		14	16	15	3	0	1	0	6	0	0	0	3	1	1	0	0	0	4	0	.200	.200	.400
	YEAR		16	21	20	4	0	1	0	6	0	0	0	3	1	1	0	0	0	4	0	.200	.200	.300
1 YR TOTALS			**16**	**21**	**20**	**4**	**0**	**1**	**0**	**6**	**0**	**0**	**0**	**3**	**1**	**1**	**0**	**0**	**0**	**4**	**0**	**.200**	**.200**	**.300**

Amaral, Richard Louis "Rich" — bats right — throws right — b.4/1/62 — 1991 positions: 2B 5, 3B 2, SS 2, 1B 1

YR	TM/LG	CL	G	TPA	AB	H	2B	3B	HR	TB	BB	IBB	HB	SO	GDP	SH	SF	SB	CS	R	RBI	BA	OBA	SA
83	GEN/NYP	A–	67	318	269	68	17	3	1	94	45	2	2	47	5	1	1	22	7	63	24	.253	.363	.349
84	QC/MID	A	34	144	119	25	1	0	0	26	24	0	1	29	0	1	0	12	0	21	7	.210	.343	.218
85	WIN/CAR	A+	124	495	428	116	15	5	3	150	59	1	2	68	11	5	1	26	6	62	36	.271	.361	.350
86	PIT/EAS	AA	114	405	355	89	12	0	0	101	39	1	4	65	5	5	2	25	8	43	24	.251	.330	.285
87	PIT/EAS	AA	104	368	315	80	8	5	0	98	43	2	3	50	1	6	1	28	6	45	28	.254	.348	.311

(continued)

Amaral, Richard Louis "Rich" (continued)

YR	TM/LG	CL	G	TPA	AB	H	2B	3B	HR	TB	BB	IBB	HB	SO	GDP	SH	SF	SB	CS	R	RBI	BA	OBA	SA
88	PIT/EAS	AA	122	489	422	117	15	4	4	152	56	1	1	53	2	5	5	54	5	66	47	.277	.360	.360
89	BIR/SOU	AA	122	533	432	123	15	6	4	162	88	2	2	66	6	7	4	57	14	90	48	.285	.405	.375
90	VAN/PCL	AAA	130	567	462	139	39	5	4	200	88	3	4	68	4	9	4	20	14	87	56	.301	.414	.433
91	CAL/PCL	AAA	86	409	347	120	26	2	3	159	53	0	3	37	6	3	3	30	8	79	36	.346	.433	.458
	SEA/AL		14	18	16	1	0	0	0	1	1	0	1	5	1	0	0	0	0	2	0	.063	.167	.063

Amaro, Ruben Jr. — bats both — throws right — b.2/12/65 — 1991 positions: OF 5, 2B 4

YR	TM/LG	CL	G	TPA	AB	H	2B	3B	HR	TB	BB	IBB	HB	SO	GDP	SH	SF	SB	CS	R	RBI	BA	OBA	SA
87	SAL/NWL	A–	71	306	241	68	7	3	3	90	49	5	7	28	5	3	6	27	11	51	31	.282	.409	.373
88	MID/TEX	AA	13	36	31	4	1	0	0	5	4	0	1	5	1	0	0	4	0	5	2	.129	.250	.161
	PS/CAL	A+	115	537	417	111	13	3	4	142	105	2	8	61	13	5	2	44	20	96	50	.266	.421	.341
89	QC/MID	A	59	250	200	72	9	4	3	98	42	4	7	25	5	0	1	20	8	50	27	.360	.484	.490
	MID/TEX	AA	29	125	110	42	9	2	3	64	10	1	1	19	0	2	2	7	1	28	9	.382	.431	.582
90	MID/TEX	AA	57	266	224	80	15	6	4	119	29	1	9	23	4	2	2	8	5	50	38	.357	.447	.531
	EDM/PCL	AAA	82	373	318	92	15	4	3	124	40	2	7	43	2	5	3	32	14	53	32	.289	.378	.390
91	EDM/PCL	AAA	121	552	472	154	42	6	3	217	63	2	6	50	6	9	2	36	18	95	42	.326	.411	.460
	CAL/AL		10	26	23	5	0	0	0	5	3	0	0	3	1	0	0	0	0	0	2	.217	.308	.261

Anderson, Brady Kevin — bats left — throws left — b.1/18/64 — 1991 positions: OF 101, DH 2

YR	TM/LG	CL	G	TPA	AB	H	2B	3B	HR	TB	BB	IBB	HB	SO	GDP	SH	SF	SB	CS	R	RBI	BA	OBA	SA
85	ELM/NYP	A–	71	285	215	55	7	6	5	89	67	0	2	32	2	1	0	13	9	36	21	.256	.437	.414
86	WH/FSL	A+	126	543	417	133	19	11	12	210	107	5	6	47	2	7	6	44	19	86	87	.319	.459	.504
87	NB/EAS	AA	52	219	170	50	4	3	6	78	45	3	2	24	5	1	1	7	3	30	35	.294	.445	.459
	PAW/INT	AAA	23	95	79	30	4	0	2	40	16	3	0	8	0	0	0	2	1	18	8	.380	.484	.506
88	BOS/AL		41	172	148	34	5	3	0	45	15	0	4	35	2	4	1	4	2	14	12	.230	.315	.304
	PAW/INT	AAA	49	196	167	48	6	1	4	68	26	3	3	33	2	0	0	8	3	27	19	.287	.393	.407
	BAL/AL		53	192	177	35	8	1	1	48	8	0	0	40	1	7	0	6	4	17	9	.198	.232	.271
	YEAR		94	364	325	69	13	4	1	93	23	0	4	75	3	11	1	10	6	31	21	.212	.272	.286
89	ROC/INT	AAA	21	84	70	14	1	2	1	22	12	1	1	13	0	0	0	2	2	14	8	.200	.333	.314
	BAL/AL		94	317	266	55	12	2	4	83	43	6	3	45	4	5	0	16	4	44	16	.207	.324	.312
90	FRE/CAR	A+	2	8	7	3	1	0	0	4	1	0	0	1	0	0	0	0	0	2	3	.429	.500	.571
	HAG/EAS	AA	9	41	34	13	0	2	1	20	5	1	0	5	1	1	1	2	1	8	5	.382	.450	.588
	BAL/AL		89	279	234	54	5	2	3	72	31	2	5	46	4	4	5	15	2	24	24	.231	.327	.308
91	ROC/INT	AAA	7	33	25	10	3	0	0	13	8	0	0	4	0	0	0	4	1	5	2	.400	.545	.520
	BAL/AL		113	313	256	59	12	3	2	83	38	0	5	44	1	11	3	12	5	40	27	.230	.338	.324
4 YR TOTALS			**390**	**1273**	**1081**	**237**	**42**	**11**	**10**	**331**	**135**	**8**	**17**	**210**	**12**	**31**	**9**	**53**	**17**	**139**	**88**	**.219**	**.313**	**.306**

Anderson, David Carter "Dave" — bats right — throws right — b.8/1/60 — 1991 positions: SS 63, 1B 16, 3B 11, 2B 6

YR	TM/LG	CL	G	TPA	AB	H	2B	3B	HR	TB	BB	IBB	HB	SO	GDP	SH	SF	SB	CS	R	RBI	BA	OBA	SA
83	LA/NL		61	131	115	19	4	2	1	30	12	1	0	15	1	4	0	6	3	12	2	.165	.244	.261
84	LA/NL		121	433	374	94	16	2	3	123	45	4	2	55	8	7	5	15	5	51	34	.251	.331	.329
85	ALB/PCL	AAA	28	121	97	28	7	0	3	44	22	0	1	17	0	0	1	10	4	23	16	.289	.421	.454
	LA/NL		77	262	221	44	6	0	4	62	35	3	1	42	4	4	1	5	4	24	18	.199	.310	.281
86	LA/NL		92	241	216	53	9	0	1	65	22	1	0	39	11	2	1	5	1	31	15	.245	.314	.301
87	LA/NL		108	297	265	62	12	3	1	83	24	1	1	43	2	6	1	9	5	32	13	.234	.299	.313
88	LA/NL		116	325	285	71	10	2	2	91	32	4	1	45	9	5	2	4	2	31	20	.249	.325	.319
89	LA/NL		87	163	140	32	2	0	1	37	17	1	0	26	1	5	1	2	0	15	14	.229	.310	.264
90	SF/NL		60	104	100	35	5	1	1	45	3	0	0	20	2	1	0	1	1	14	6	.350	.369	.450
91	SF/NL		100	240	226	56	5	2	2	71	12	2	0	35	8	2	0	2	4	24	13	.248	.286	.314
9 YR TOTALS			**822**	**2196**	**1942**	**466**	**69**	**12**	**16**	**607**	**202**	**17**	**5**	**320**	**46**	**36**	**11**	**49**	**26**	**234**	**135**	**.240**	**.312**	**.313**

Anthony, Eric Todd — bats left — throws left — b.11/8/67 — 1991 positions: OF 37

YR	TM/LG	CL	G	TPA	AB	H	2B	3B	HR	TB	BB	IBB	HB	SO	GDP	SH	SF	SB	CS	R	RBI	BA	OBA	SA
86	AST/GCL	R	13	18	12	3	0	0	0	3	5	0	1	5	1	0	0	2	0	2	0	.250	.500	.250
87	AST/GCL	R	60	245	216	57	11	6	10	110	26	3	2	58	4	0	1	2	2	38	46	.264	.347	.509
88	ASH/SAL	A	115	485	439	120	36	1	29	245	40	5	3	101	10	0	3	10	4	73	89	.273	.336	.558
89	COL/SOU		107	444	403	121	16	2	28	225	35	5	3	127	3	0	3	14	9	67	79	.300	.358	.558
	TUC/PCL	AAA	12	52	46	10	3	0	3	22	6	0	0	11	2	0	0	0	0	10	11	.217	.308	.478
	HOU/NL		25	70	61	11	2	0	4	25	9	2	0	16	1	0	0	0	0	7	7	.180	.286	.410
90	COL/SOU	AA	4	15	12	2	0	0	1	5	3	0	0	4	0	0	0	0	0	2	3	.167	.333	.417
	TUC/PCL	AAA	40	182	161	46	10	2	6	78	17	0	1	41	4	0	3	8	3	28	26	.286	.352	.484
	HOU/NL		84	277	239	46	8	0	10	84	29	3	2	78	4	1	6	5	0	26	29	.192	.279	.351
91	HOU/NL		39	132	118	18	6	0	1	27	12	1	0	41	0	2	1	0	1	11	7	.153	.227	.229
	TUC/PCL	AAA	79	349	318	107	22	2	9	160	25	6	3	58	13	0	3	11	5	57	63	.336	.387	.503
3 YR TOTALS			**148**	**479**	**418**	**75**	**16**	**0**	**15**	**136**	**50**	**6**	**2**	**135**	**7**	**1**	**8**	**6**	**0**	**44**	**43**	**.179**	**.266**	**.325**

Azocar, Oscar Gregorio (Azocar) — bats left — throws left — b.2/21/65 — 1991 positions: OF 13, 1B 1

YR	TM/LG	CL	G	TPA	AB	H	2B	3B	HR	TB	BB	IBB	HB	SO	GDP	SH	SF	SB	CS	R	RBI	BA	OBA	SA
87	FL/FSL	A+	53	195	192	69	11	3	6	104	3	0	0	18	6	0	0	5	5	25	39	.359	.369	.542
88	ALB/EAS	AA	138	565	543	148	22	9	6	206	12	6	2	48	15	4	4	21	6	60	66	.273	.289	.379
89	ALB/EAS	AA	92	384	362	101	15	2	4	132	10	4	1	31	6	8	4	11	6	50	47	.279	.295	.365
	COL/INT	AAA	37	139	130	38	9	3	1	56	7	0	1	10	1	1	2	3	1	14	12	.292	.333	.431
90	COL/INT	AAA	94	396	374	109	20	5	5	154	9	2	2	26	15	1	4	7	8	49	52	.291	.306	.412
	NY/AL		65	218	214	53	8	0	5	76	2	0	1	15	1	0	1	7	0	18	19	.248	.257	.355
91	LV/PCL	AAA	107	389	361	107	23	3	7	157	21	3	1	26	12	1	5	4	4	51	50	.296	.332	.435

Azocar, Oscar Gregorio (Azocar) (continued)

YR	TM/LG	CL	G	TPA	AB	H	2B	3B	HR	TB	BB	IBB	HB	SO	GDP	SH	SF	SB	CS	R	RBI	BA	OBA	SA
	SD/NL		38	60	57	14	2	0	0	16	1	1	1	9	1	0	1	2	0	5	9	.246	.267	.281
2 YR TOTALS			103	278	271	67	10	0	5	92	3	1	2	24	2	0	2	9	0	23	28	.247	.259	.339

Backman, Walter Wayne "Wally" — bats both — throws right — b.9/22/59 — 1991 positions: 2B 36, 3B 20

YR	TM/LG	CL	G	TPA	AB	H	2B	3B	HR	TB	BB	IBB	HB	SO	GDP	SH	SF	SB	CS	R	RBI	BA	OBA	SA
80	NY/NL		27	110	93	30	1	1	0	33	11	1	1	14	3	4	1	2	3	12	9	.323	.396	.355
81	NY/NL		26	42	36	10	2	0	0	12	4	0	0	7	0	2	0	1	0	5	0	.278	.350	.333
82	NY/NL		96	312	261	71	13	2	3	97	49	1	0	47	6	2	0	8	7	37	22	.272	.387	.372
83	NY/NL		26	45	42	7	0	1	0	9	2	0	0	8	2	1	0	0	0	6	3	.167	.205	.214
84	NY/NL		128	499	436	122	19	2	1	148	56	0	0	63	13	5	2	32	9	68	26	.280	.360	.339
85	NY/NL		145	574	520	142	24	5	1	179	36	1	1	72	3	14	3	30	12	77	38	.273	.320	.344
86	NY/NL		124	440	387	124	18	2	1	149	36	1	0	32	3	14	3	13	7	67	27	.320	.376	.385
87	NY/NL		94	335	300	75	6	1	1	86	25	0	0	43	5	9	1	11	3	43	23	.250	.307	.287
88	NY/NL		99	347	294	89	12	0	0	101	41	1	1	49	6	9	2	9	5	44	17	.303	.388	.344
89	MIN/AL		87	337	299	69	9	2	1	85	32	0	1	45	4	4	1	1	1	33	26	.231	.306	.284
90	PIT/NL		104	361	315	92	21	3	2	125	42	1	1	53	5	0	3	6	3	62	28	.292	.374	.397
91	PHI/NL		94	220	185	45	12	0	0	57	30	0	0	30	1	2	2	0	3	20	15	.243	.344	.308
12 YR TOTALS			1050	3622	3168	876	137	19	10	1081	364	8	5	463	52	66	19	116	52	474	234	.277	.350	.341

Baerga, Carlos Obed (Ortiz) — bats both — throws right — b.11/4/68 — 1991 positions: 3B 89, 2B 75, SS 2

YR	TM/LG	CL	G	TPA	AB	H	2B	3B	HR	TB	BB	IBB	HB	SO	GDP	SH	SF	SB	CS	R	RBI	BA	OBA	SA
86	CHA/SAL	A	111	416	378	102	14	4	7	145	26	1	5	60	4	2	5	6	1	57	41	.270	.321	.384
87	CHS/SAL	A	134	573	515	157	23	9	7	219	38	7	12	107	10	6	2	26	21	83	50	.305	.365	.425
88	WIC/TEX	AA	122	487	444	121	28	1	12	187	31	2	9	83	10	0	3	4	4	63	74	.273	.331	.421
89	LV/PCL	AAA	132	562	520	143	28	2	10	205	30	5	6	98	10	0	6	6	6	63	74	.275	.319	.394
90	CS/PCL	AAA	12	55	50	19	2	1	1	26	5	2	0	4	4	0	0	1	0	11	11	.380	.436	.520
	CLE/AL		108	338	312	81	17	2	7	123	16	2	4	57	4	1	5	0	2	46	47	.260	.300	.394
91	CLE/AL		158	654	593	171	28	2	11	236	48	5	6	74	12	4	3	3	2	80	69	.288	.346	.398
2 YR TOTALS			266	992	905	252	45	4	18	359	64	7	10	131	16	5	8	3	4	126	116	.278	.330	.397

Bagwell, Jeffery Robert "Jeff" — bats right — throws right — b.5/27/68 — 1991 positions: 1B 155

YR	TM/LG	CL	G	TPA	AB	H	2B	3B	HR	TB	BB	IBB	HB	SO	GDP	SH	SF	SB	CS	R	RBI	BA	OBA	SA
89	RS/GCL	R	5	22	19	6	1	0	0	7	3	0	0	0	1	0	0	0	0	3	3	.316	.409	.368
	WH/FSL	A+	64	240	210	65	13	2	2	88	23	0	3	25	7	3	1	1	1	27	19	.310	.384	.419
90	NB/EAS	AA	136	569	481	160	34	7	4	220	72	12	7	57	15	3	6	5	7	63	61	.333	.422	.457
91	HOU/NL		156	650	554	163	26	4	15	242	75	5	13	116	12	1	7	7	4	79	82	.294	.387	.437

Baines, Harold Douglass — bats left — throws left — b.3/15/59 — 1991 positions: DH125, OF12

YR	TM/LG	CL	G	TPA	AB	H	2B	3B	HR	TB	BB	IBB	HB	SO	GDP	SH	SF	SB	CS	R	RBI	BA	OBA	SA
80	CHI/AL		141	518	491	125	23	6	13	199	19	7	1	65	15	2	5	2	4	55	49	.255	.281	.405
81	CHI/AL		82	296	280	80	11	7	10	135	12	4	2	41	6	0	2	6	2	42	41	.286	.318	.482
82	CHI/AL		161	668	608	165	29	8	25	285	49	10	0	95	12	2	9	10	3	89	105	.271	.321	.469
83	CHI/AL		156	655	596	167	33	2	20	264	49	13	1	85	15	3	6	7	5	76	99	.280	.333	.443
84	CHI/AL		147	629	569	173	28	10	29	308	54	9	1	75	12	1	5	1	2	72	94	.304	.361	.541
85	CHI/AL		160	693	640	198	29	3	22	299	42	8	1	89	16	0	10	1	1	86	113	.309	.348	.467
86	CHI/AL		145	618	570	169	29	2	21	265	38	2	1	82	12	0	8	2	1	72	88	.296	.338	.465
87	CHI/AL		132	554	505	148	26	4	20	242	46	9	1	89	21	0	2	0	0	59	93	.293	.352	.479
88	CHI/AL		158	674	599	166	39	1	13	246	67	14	1	109	21	0	7	0	0	55	81	.277	.347	.411
89	CHI/AL		96	397	333	107	20	1	13	168	60	13	1	52	11	0	3	0	1	55	56	.321	.423	.505
	TEX/AL		50	186	172	49	9	0	3	67	13	0	0	27	4	0	1	0	2	18	16	.285	.333	.390
	YEAR		146	583	505	156	29	1	16	235	73	13	1	79	15	0	4	0	3	73	72	.309	.395	.465
90	TEX/AL		103	371	321	93	10	1	13	144	47	9	0	63	13	0	3	0	1	41	44	.290	.377	.449
	OAK/AL		32	118	94	25	5	0	3	39	20	1	0	17	4	0	4	0	2	11	21	.266	.381	.415
	YEAR		135	489	415	118	15	1	16	183	67	10	0	80	17	0	7	0	3	52	65	.284	.378	.441
91	OAK/AL		141	566	488	144	25	1	20	231	72	22	1	67	12	0	5	0	1	76	90	.295	.383	.473
12 YR TOTALS			1704	6943	6266	1809	316	46	225	2892	588	121	11	956	174	8	70	29	25	807	990	.289	.347	.462

Banister, Jeffery Todd "Jeff" — bats right — throws right — b.1/15/65 — 1991 positions: C

YR	TM/LG	CL	G	TPA	AB	H	2B	3B	HR	TB	BB	IBB	HB	SO	GDP	SH	SF	SB	CS	R	RBI	BA	OBA	SA
86	WAT/NYP	A-	41	138	124	18	4	0	0	22	12	0	1	27	9	0	1	4	0	9	8	.145	.225	.177
87	MAC/SAL	A	101	342	307	78	20	0	6	116	27	0	2	70	7	3	3	1	0	35	37	.254	.316	.378
88	HAR/EAS	AA	71	220	205	53	6	0	6	77	10	4	1	38	4	0	0	0	1	9	26	.259	.296	.376
89	HAR/EAS	AA	102	373	336	80	13	0	12	129	30	0	4	57	11	1	2	2	1	48	48	.238	.306	.384
90	BUF/AMA	AAA	12	29	25	8	2	0	1	13	3	1	0	4	0	0	1	2	0	3	3	.320	.384	.520
	HAR/EAS	AA	101	399	368	99	13	0	10	142	23	0	3	30	6	0	5	0	0	43	57	.269	.313	.386
91	PIT/NL		1	1	1	1	0	0	0	1	0	0	0	0	0	0	0	0	0	0	0	1.000	1.000	1.000
	BUF/AMA	AAA	79	263	234	57	7	1	2	72	28	2	1	57	7	0	0	1	2	23	21	.244	.327	.308

Barberie, Bret Edward — bats both — throws right — b.8/16/67 — 1991 positions: SS 19, 2B 10, 3B 10, 1B 1

YR	TM/LG	CL	G	TPA	AB	H	2B	3B	HR	TB	BB	IBB	HB	SO	GDP	SH	SF	SB	CS	R	RBI	BA	OBA	SA
89	WPB/FSL	A+	124	540	457	122	16	4	4	158	64	7	10	39	9	5	4	10	4	63	34	.267	.366	.346
90	JAC/SOU	AA	133	537	431	112	18	3	7	157	87	6	11	64	3	3	5	20	7	71	56	.260	.393	.364
91	IND/AMA	AAA	71	283	218	68	14	2	10	116	59	2	3	47	4	1	2	10	5	45	48	.312	.461	.532
	MON/NL		57	162	136	48	12	2	2	70	20	2	2	22	4	1	1	0	0	16	18	.353	.435	.515

Barfield, Jesse Lee — bats right — throws right — b.10/29/59 — 1991 positions: OF81

YR	TM/LG	CL	G	TPA	AB	H	2B	3B	HR	TB	BB	IBB	HB	SO	GDP	SH	SF	SB	CS	R	RBI	BA	OBA	SA
81	TOR/AL		25	100	95	22	3	2	2	35	4	0	1	19	4	0	0	4	3	7	9	.232	.270	.368
82	TOR/AL		139	446	394	97	13	2	18	168	42	3	3	79	7	6	1	1	4	54	58	.246	.323	.426
83	TOR/AL		128	420	388	98	13	3	27	198	22	0	4	110	8	1	5	2	4	58	68	.253	.296	.510
84	TOR/AL		110	360	320	91	14	1	14	149	35	5	2	81	5	1	2	8	2	51	49	.284	.357	.466
85	TOR/AL		155	612	539	156	34	9	27	289	66	5	4	143	14	0	3	22	8	94	84	.289	.369	.536
86	TOR/AL		158	671	589	170	35	2	40	329	69	5	8	146	9	0	5	8	8	107	108	.289	.368	.559
87	TOR/AL		159	654	590	155	25	3	28	270	58	7	3	141	13	1	2	3	5	89	84	.263	.331	.458
88	TOR/AL		137	520	468	114	21	5	18	199	41	6	1	108	10	4	6	7	3	62	56	.244	.302	.425
89	TOR/AL		21	86	80	16	4	0	5	35	5	0	1	28	0	0	0	0	2	8	11	.200	.256	.438
	NY/AL		129	529	441	106	19	1	18	181	82	6	3	122	8	1	3	5	3	71	56	.240	.360	.410
	YEAR		150	615	521	122	23	1	23	216	87	6	3	150	8	1	3	5	5	79	67	.234	.345	.415
90	NY/AL		153	570	476	117	21	2	25	217	82	4	5	150	6	2	5	4	3	69	78	.246	.359	.456
91	NY/AL		84	321	284	64	12	0	17	127	36	6	0	80	11	0	1	1	0	37	48	.225	.312	.447
11 YR TOTALS			**1398**	**5289**	**4664**	**1206**	**214**	**30**	**239**	**2197**	**542**	**47**	**34**	**1207**	**95**	**16**	**33**	**65**	**46**	**707**	**709**	**.259**	**.338**	**.471**

Barker, Timothy Neal "Tim" — bats right — throws right — b.6/30/68 — 1991 positions: SS System LA/NL

YR	TM/LG	CL	G	TPA	AB	H	2B	3B	HR	TB	BB	IBB	HB	SO	GDP	SH	SF	SB	CS	R	RBI	BA	OBA	SA
89	GF/PIO	R+	59	242	201	63	9	6	5	99	37	0	2	55	2	1	1	25	9	54	36	.313	.423	.493
90	BAK/CAL	A+	125	527	443	120	22	6	8	178	71	1	5	116	1	4	4	33	14	83	62	.271	.375	.402
91	SA/TEX	AA	119	500	401	117	20	4	2	151	80	2	6	61	6	8	5	32	13	70	46	.292	.413	.377

Barnes, William Henry "Skeeter" — bats right — throws right — b.3/3/57 — 1991 positions: OF 33, 3B 17, 1B 9, 2B 7, DH 3

YR	TM/LG	CL	G	TPA	AB	H	2B	3B	HR	TB	BB	IBB	HB	SO	GDP	SH	SF	SB	CS	R	RBI	BA	OBA	SA
78	BIL/PIO	R+	68	314	277	102	22	5	3	143	29	5	1	27	1	1	6	21	3	66	76	.368	.422	.516
79	NAS/SOU	AA	145	542	500	133	19	4	12	196	27	1	4	64	18	4	7	5	3	54	77	.266	.305	.392
80	WAT/EAS	AA	138	571	533	156	27	6	4	207	24	0	1	54	18	6	7	18	10	62	64	.293	.320	.388
81	WAT/EAS	AA	96	406	363	93	17	0	6	128	33	6	4	29	9	3	3	15	4	45	49	.256	.323	.353
	IND/AMA	AAA	36	129	118	31	6	1	1	42	9	4	1	10	6	1	0	1	1	10	11	.263	.320	.356
82	IND/AMA	AAA	18	62	59	18	5	1	1	28	1	0	0	6	0	2	0	1	2	8	3	.305	.317	.475
	WAT/EAS	AA	112	470	418	128	24	6	12	200	44	5	1	32	6	5	2	31	9	67	72	.306	.372	.478
83	CIN/NL		15	43	34	7	0	0	1	10	7	0	2	3	0	0	0	2	2	5	4	.206	.372	.294
	IND/AMA	AAA	109	408	377	127	19	6	7	179	26	2	0	42	3	3	2	10	5	67	56	.337	.378	.475
84	WIC/AMA	AAA	92	393	360	118	23	4	14	191	26	3	1	30	13	1	5	24	5	59	67	.328	.370	.531
	CIN/NL		32	46	42	5	0	0	1	8	4	0	0	6	1	0	0	0	0	5	3	.119	.196	.190
85	DEN/AMA	AAA	12	49	41	9	0	0	2	15	6	1	1	7	3	1	0	2	3	6	8	.220	.333	.366
	MON/NL		19	26	26	4	1	0	0	5	0	0	0	1	0	0	0	0	0	0	0	.154	.154	.192
	IND/AMA	AAA	83	340	299	86	16	0	6	120	32	2	4	38	6	2	3	18	5	45	55	.288	.361	.401
86	JAC/SOU	AA	3	10	8	4	0	0	0	4	1	0	0	1	0	0	1	0	1	1	1	.500	.500	.500
	IND/AMA	AAA	85	338	300	80	18	5	5	123	26	0	5	28	5	4	3	16	10	40	40	.267	.332	.410
	POR/PCL	AAA	38	157	141	52	8	4	1	71	7	2	3	9	1	0	6	3	4	21	29	.369	.395	.504
87	STL/NL		4	4	4	1	0	0	0	4	0	0	0	0	0	0	0	0	0	1	3	.250	.250	1.000
	LOU/AMA	AAA	62	271	242	68	19	2	5	106	23	1	1	18	5	1	4	7	2	38	34	.281	.341	.438
	DEN/AMA	AAA	48	211	189	63	14	3	11	116	18	0	1	20	0	1	2	10	3	41	42	.333	.390	.614
88	BUF/AMA	AAA	21	51	51	11	1	0	2	18	0	0	0	7	0	0	0	0	1	4	5	.216	.216	.353
	NAS/AMA	AAA	101	354	328	85	15	0	4	112	17	0	3	40	1	0	3	15	3	43	34	.259	.299	.341
89	CIN/NL		5	3	3	0	0	0	0	0	0	0	0	0	0	0	0	0	0	1	0	.000	.000	.000
	NAS/AMA	AAA	124	522	472	143	39	3	6	206	32	2	5	59	7	5	8	15	6	57	55	.303	.348	.436
90	NAS/AMA	AAA	144	615	548	156	21	2	7	202	47	2	11	57	15	3	6	34	11	83	66	.285	.350	.369
91	TOL/INT	AAA	62	264	233	77	14	0	9	118	23	1	4	26	6	0	2	27	7	48	40	.330	.397	.506
	DET/AL		75	171	159	46	13	2	5	78	9	1	0	24	1	1	2	10	7	28	17	.289	.325	.491
6 YR TOTALS			**150**	**293**	**268**	**63**	**14**	**2**	**8**	**105**	**20**	**2**	**2**	**35**	**3**	**2**	**1**	**12**	**11**	**40**	**27**	**.235**	**.292**	**.392**

Barrett, Martin Glenn "Marty" — bats right — throws right — b.6/23/58 — 1991 positions: 2B 2, 3B 2

YR	TM/LG	CL	G	TPA	AB	H	2B	3B	HR	TB	BB	IBB	HB	SO	GDP	SH	SF	SB	CS	R	RBI	BA	OBA	SA
82	BOS/AL		8	18	18	1	0	0	0	1	0	0	0	1	0	0	0	0	0	0	0	.056	.056	.056
83	BOS/AL		33	48	44	10	1	1	0	13	3	0	0	1	1	0	1	0	0	7	2	.227	.271	.295
84	BOS/AL		139	526	475	144	23	3	3	182	42	1	1	25	9	4	4	5	3	56	45	.303	.358	.383
85	BOS/AL		156	608	534	142	26	0	5	183	56	3	2	50	14	12	4	7	5	59	56	.266	.336	.343
86	BOS/AL		158	713	625	179	39	4	4	238	65	0	1	31	13	18	4	15	7	94	60	.286	.353	.381
87	BOS/AL		137	638	559	164	23	0	3	196	51	0	1	38	11	22	5	15	7	72	43	.293	.351	.351
88	BOS/AL		150	687	612	173	28	1	1	206	40	1	7	35	16	20	8	7	3	83	65	.283	.330	.337
89	PAW/INT	AAA	11	42	35	10	1	1	0	13	5	0	1	1	1	0	1	0	0	4	4	.286	.390	.371
	BOS/AL		86	390	336	86	18	0	1	107	32	0	2	12	12	15	5	4	1	31	27	.256	.320	.318
90	BOS/AL		62	188	159	36	4	0	0	40	15	1	1	13	4	4	0	0	1	15	13	.226	.294	.252
91	SD/NL		12	17	16	3	1	0	1	7	0	0	1	3	0	0	0	0	0	1	3	.188	.235	.438
	LV/PCL	AAA	16	59	47	15	4	1	0	21	11	3	0	3	0	0	0	0	0	5	4	.319	.441	.447
10 YR TOTALS			**941**	**3833**	**3378**	**938**	**163**	**9**	**18**	**1173**	**304**	**7**	**16**	**209**	**81**	**102**	**33**	**57**	**21**	**418**	**314**	**.278**	**.337**	**.347**

Bass, Kevin Charles — bats both — throws right — b.5/12/59 — 1991 positions: OF 101

YR	TM/LG	CL	G	TPA	AB	H	2B	3B	HR	TB	BB	IBB	HB	SO	GDP	SH	SF	SB	CS	R	RBI	BA	OBA	SA
82	MIL/AL		18	11	9	0	0	0	0	0	1	0	0	1	0	0	1	0	0	4	0	.000	.100	.000
	HOU/NL		12	24	24	1	0	0	0	1	0	0	0	8	1	0	0	0	0	2	1	.042	.042	.042
	YEAR		30	35	33	1	0	0	0	1	1	0	0	9	1	0	1	0	0	6	1	.030	.059	.030
83	HOU/NL		88	206	195	46	7	3	2	65	6	1	0	27	2	4	1	2	2	25	18	.236	.257	.333
84	HOU/NL		121	342	331	86	17	5	2	119	6	1	3	57	4	2	0	5	5	33	29	.260	.279	.360

Bass, Kevin Charles (continued)

YR	TM/LG	CL	G	TPA	AB	H	2B	3B	HR	TB	BB	IBB	HB	SO	GDP	SH	SF	SB	CS	R	RBI	BA	OBA	SA
85	HOU/NL		150	582	539	145	27	5	16	230	31	1	6	63	10	4	2	19	8	72	68	.269	.315	.427
86	HOU/NL		157	640	591	184	33	5	20	287	38	11	6	72	15	1	4	22	13	83	79	.311	.357	.486
87	HOU/NL		157	654	592	168	31	5	19	266	53	13	4	77	15	0	5	21	8	83	85	.284	.344	.449
88	HOU/NL		157	595	541	138	27	2	14	211	42	10	6	65	16	3	3	31	6	57	72	.255	.314	.390
89	TUC/PCL	AAA	6	19	17	5	1	0	0	6	1	0	0	2	0	0	0	1	0	1	2	.294	.316	.353
	HOU/NL		87	348	313	94	19	4	5	136	29	3	1	44	2	1	4	11	4	42	44	.300	.357	.435
90	SJ/CAL	A+	6	23	22	8	1	0	0	9	0	0	1	1	0	0	0	0	0	2	4	.364	.391	.409
	PHO/PCL	AAA	8	33	33	2	0	0	0	10	0	0	0	4	3	0	0	1	1	2	4	.242	.242	.303
	SF/NL		61	233	214	54	9	1	7	86	14	3	2	26	5	2	1	2	2	25	32	.252	.303	.402
91	SJ/CAL	A+	5	22	19	2	2	0	0	4	2	1	1	3	0	0	0	1	0	1	1	.105	.227	.211
	PHO/PCL	AAA	10	44	41	13	3	1	2	24	2	0	0	4	0	0	1	1	0	8	7	.317	.341	.585
	SF/NL		124	406	361	84	10	4	10	132	36	8	4	56	12	2	3	7	4	43	40	.233	.307	.366
10 YR TOTALS			1132	4041	3710	1000	180	34	95	1533	256	51	32	496	80	20	23	120	52	469	468	.270	.320	.413

Batiste, Kimothy Emil "Kim" — bats right — throws right — b.3/15/68 — 1991 positions: SS 7

YR	TM/LG	CL	G	TPA	AB	H	2B	3B	HR	TB	BB	IBB	HB	SO	GDP	SH	SF	SB	CS	R	RBI	BA	OBA	SA
87	UTI/NYP	A–	46	157	150	26	8	1	2	42	7	3	0	65	3	0	0	4	0	15	10	.173	.210	.280
88	SPA/SAL	A	122	451	430	107	19	6	6	156	14	1	1	101	13	5	1	16	9	51	52	.249	.274	.363
89	CLE/FSL	A+	114	418	385	90	12	4	3	119	17	1	4	67	7	11	1	13	7	36	33	.234	.273	.309
90	REA/EAS	AA	125	508	486	134	14	4	6	174	13	1	2	73	11	5	2	28	14	57	33	.276	.296	.358
91	SCR/INT	AAA	122	491	462	135	25	6	1	175	11	0	4	72	5	10	4	18	12	54	41	.292	.312	.379
	PHI/NL		10	28	27	6	0	0	0	6	1	1	0	8	0	0	1	0	1	2	1	.222	.250	.222

Bell, Derek Nathaniel — bats right — throws right — b.12/11/68 — 1991 positions: OF 13

YR	TM/LG	CL	G	TPA	AB	H	2B	3B	HR	TB	BB	IBB	HB	SO	GDP	SH	SF	SB	CS	R	RBI	BA	OBA	SA
87	SC/NYP	A–	74	302	273	72	11	3	10	119	18	1	6	60	5	2	3	12	4	46	42	.264	.320	.436
88	MB/SAL	A	91	377	352	121	29	5	12	196	15	3	6	67	9	0	4	18	6	55	60	.344	.377	.557
	KNO/SOU	AA	14	53	52	13	3	1	0	18	1	0	0	14	1	0	0	4	1	9	3	.250	.264	.346
89	KNO/SOU	AA	136	549	513	124	22	6	16	206	26	4	4	92	6	0	4	15	7	72	75	.242	.284	.402
90	SYR/INT	AAA	109	434	402	105	13	5	7	149	23	0	3	75	8	0	6	21	7	57	56	.261	.302	.371
91	SYR/INT	AAA	119	528	457	158	22	12	13	243	57	7	9	69	16	0	5	27	11	89	93	.346	.424	.532
	TOR/AL		18	35	28	4	0	0	0	4	6	0	1	5	0	0	0	3	2	5	1	.143	.314	.143

Bell, Jay Stuart — bats right — throws right — b.12/11/65 — 1991 positions: SS 156

YR	TM/LG	CL	G	TPA	AB	H	2B	3B	HR	TB	BB	IBB	HB	SO	GDP	SH	SF	SB	CS	R	RBI	BA	OBA	SA
84	ELI/APP	R+	66	290	245	54	12	1	6	86	42	0	1	50	5	0	2	4	2	43	30	.220	.334	.351
85	VIS/CAL	A+	106	432	376	106	16	6	9	161	41	0	4	73	6	4	7	10	6	56	59	.282	.353	.428
	WAT/EAS	AA	29	124	114	34	11	2	1	52	9	1	0	16	3	1	0	3	3	13	14	.298	.350	.456
86	WAT/EAS	AA	138	593	494	137	28	4	7	194	87	0	1	65	7	1	11	11	7	86	74	.277	.378	.393
	CLE/AL		5	16	14	5	2	0	1	10	2	0	0	3	0	0	0	0	0	3	4	.357	.438	.714
87	BUF/AMA	AAA	110	440	362	94	15	4	17	168	70	1	2	84	3	3	3	6	5	71	60	.260	.380	.464
	CLE/AL		38	137	125	27	9	1	2	44	8	0	1	31	0	3	0	2	0	14	13	.216	.269	.352
88	CS/PCL	AAA	49	209	181	50	12	2	7	87	26	0	0	27	8	0	1	3	1	23	21	.276	.368	.481
	CLE/AL		73	236	211	46	5	1	2	59	21	0	1	53	3	1	2	4	2	23	21	.218	.289	.280
89	BUF/AMA	AAA	86	344	298	85	15	3	10	136	38	1	1	55	6	3	2	5	3	49	54	.285	.370	.456
	PIT/NL		78	303	271	70	13	3	2	95	19	0	1	47	9	10	2	5	3	33	27	.258	.307	.351
90	PIT/NL		159	696	583	148	28	7	7	211	65	0	3	109	14	39	6	10	6	93	52	.254	.329	.362
91	PIT/NL		157	697	608	164	32	8	16	260	52	1	4	99	15	30	3	10	10	96	67	.270	.330	.428
6 YR TOTALS			510	2085	1812	460	89	20	30	679	167	1	10	342	41	83	13	31	17	262	184	.254	.318	.375

Bell, Jorge (Mathey) "George" — bats right — throws right — b.10/21/59 — 1991 positions: OF 146

YR	TM/LG	CL	G	TPA	AB	H	2B	3B	HR	TB	BB	IBB	HB	SO	GDP	SH	SF	SB	CS	R	RBI	BA	OBA	SA
81	TOR/AL		60	168	163	38	2	1	5	57	5	1	0	27	1	0	0	3	2	19	12	.233	.256	.350
83	TOR/AL		39	118	112	30	5	4	2	49	4	1	2	17	4	0	0	1	1	5	17	.268	.305	.438
84	TOR/AL		159	641	606	177	39	4	26	302	24	2	8	86	14	0	3	11	2	85	87	.292	.326	.498
85	TOR/AL		157	666	607	167	28	6	28	291	43	6	8	90	8	0	8	21	6	87	95	.275	.327	.479
86	TOR/AL		159	690	641	198	38	6	31	341	41	3	2	62	15	0	5	7	8	101	108	.309	.349	.532
87	BAK/CAL	A+	134	531	473	116	15	3	4	149	43	3	3	91	4	7	5	21	1	54	58	.245	.309	.315
	TOR/AL		156	665	610	188	32	4	47	369	39	9	7	75	17	0	9	5	1	111	134	.308	.352	.605
88	TOR/AL		156	657	614	165	27	5	24	274	34	5	1	66	21	0	8	4	2	78	97	.269	.304	.446
89	TOR/AL		153	664	613	182	41	2	18	281	33	3	4	60	18	0	14	4	3	88	104	.297	.330	.458
90	TOR/AL		142	608	562	149	25	0	21	237	32	7	3	80	14	0	11	3	2	67	86	.265	.303	.422
91	CHI/NL		149	603	558	159	27	0	25	261	32	6	4	62	10	0	9	2	4	63	86	.285	.323	.468
10 YR TOTALS			1330	5480	5086	1453	264	32	227	2462	287	43	39	625	122		68	61	33		704	826	.286	.325	.484

Bell, Juan (Mathey) — bats right — throws right — b.3/29/68 — 1991 positions: 2B77, SS 15, DH 4, OF 1

YR	TM/LG	CL	G	TPA	AB	H	2B	3B	HR	TB	BB	IBB	HB	SO	GDP	SH	SF	SB	CS	R	RBI	BA	OBA	SA
85	DOD/GCL	R	42	121	106	17	0	0	0	17	12	0	1	20	1	2	0	2	1	11	8	.160	.252	.160
86	DOD/GCL	R	59	250	217	52	6	2	0	62	29	1	1	28	2	0	3	12	2	38	26	.240	.328	.286
88	SA/TEX	AA	61	237	215	60	4	2	5	83	16	2	2	37	3	3	1	13	7	42	45	.279	.333	.386
	ALB/PCL	AAA	73	283	257	77	9	3	8	116	16	1	1	92	8	2	4	17	10	50	32	.300	.339	.451
89	ROC/INT	AAA	116	454	408	107	15	6	6	140	39	1	0	92	8	2	4	17	10	50	32	.262	.325	.343
	BAL/AL		8	4	4	0	0	0	0	0	0	0	0	1	0	0	0	0	0	2	0	.000	.000	.000
90	ROC/INT	AAA	82	367	326	93	12	5	6	133	36	1	3	59	9	0	1	16	12	59	35	.285	.360	.408
	BAL/AL		5	2	2	0	0	0	0	0	0	0	0	0	0	0	0	0	0	1	0	.000	.000	.000

(continued)

Bell, Juan (Mathey) (continued)

YR	TM/LG	CL	G	TPA	AB	H	2B	3B	HR	TB	BB	IBB	HB	SO	GDP	SH	SF	SB	CS	R	RBI	BA	OBA	SA
91	BAL/AL		100	223	209	36	9	2	1	52	8	0	0	51	1	4	2	0		26	15	.172	.201	.249
	3 YR TOTALS		113	229	215	36	9	2	1	52	8	0	0	53	1	4	2	1	0	29	15	**.167**	**.196**	**.242**

Bell, Michael Allen "Mike" — bats left — throws left — b.4/22/68 — 1991 positions: 1B 14

YR	TM/LG	CL	G	TPA	AB	H	2B	3B	HR	TB	BB	IBB	HB	SO	GDP	SH	SF	SB	CS	R	RBI	BA	OBA	SA
87	SUM/SAL	A	133	501	443	108	17	3	5	146	54	3	3	95	10	0	1	11	9	54	51	.244	.329	.330
88	DUR/CAR	A+	126	512	440	113	18	3	17	188	58	3	6	91	5	2	6	11	3	72	84	.257	.347	.427
	GRE/SOU	AA	4	13	12	3	1	0	0	4	1	0	0	1	0	0	0	0	0	1	4	.250	.308	.333
89	GRE/SOU	AA	132	538	472	115	26	3	6	165	62	6	2	91	8	1	1	10	5	63	57	.244	.333	.350
90	GRE/SOU	AA	106	457	405	118	24	2	6	164	41	6	5	63	3	4	2	10	4	50	42	.291	.362	.405
	ATL/NL		36	48	45	11	5	1	1	21	2	0	0	9	0	0	0	0	1	8	5	.244	.292	.467
91	RIC/INT	AAA	91	373	341	85	12	2	5	116	26	2	2	68	8	2	2	2	3	37	29	.249	.305	.340
	ATL/NL		17	32	30	4	0	0	1	7	2	0	0	7	0	0	0	1	0	4	1	.133	.188	.233
	2 YR TOTALS		53	80	75	15	5	1	2	28	4	0	1	16	6	0	0	1	1	12	6	**.200**	**.250**	**.373**

Belle, Albert Jojuan "Albert" or "Joey" — bats right — throws right — b.8/25/66 — 1991 positions: OF 89, DH32

YR	TM/LG	CL	G	TPA	AB	H	2B	3B	HR	TB	BB	IBB	HB	SO	GDP	SH	SF	SB	CS	R	RBI	BA	OBA	SA
87	KIN/CAR	A+	10	45	37	12	2	0	3	23	8	0	0	16	1	0	0	0	1	5	9	.324	.444	.622
88	KIN/CAR	A+	41	171	153	46	16	0	8	86	18	1	0	45	4	0	0	2	0	21	39	.301	.374	.562
	WAT/MID	A	9	29	28	7	1	0	1	11	1	0	0	9	1	0	0	0	0	2	2	.250	.276	.393
89	CAN/EAS	AA	89	350	312	88	20	0	20	168	32	5	0	82	6	0	2	8	4	48	69	.282	.354	.538
	CLE/AL		62	234	218	49	8	4	7	86	12	0	0	55	4	0	2	2	2	22	37	.225	.269	.394
90	CLE/AL		9	25	23	4	0	0	1	7	1	0	0	6	1	0	1	0	0	1	3	.174	.208	.304
	CS/PCL	AAA	24	101	96	33	3	1	5	53	5	0	0	16	4	0	0	4	3	16	19	.344	.376	.552
	CAN/EAS	AA	9	35	32	8	1	0	0	9	3	1	0	7	2	0	0	4	3	4	3	.250	.314	.281
91	CS/PCL	AAA	16	66	61	20	3	2	2	33	2	0	1	8	1	0	2	1	1	9	16	.328	.348	.541
	CLE/AL		123	496	461	130	31	2	28	249	25	2	5	99	24	0	5	3	1	60	95	.282	.323	.540
	3 YR TOTALS		194	755	702	183	39	6	36	342	38	2	7	160	29	1	7	5	3	83	135	**.261**	**.302**	**.487**

Belliard, Rafael Leonidas (Matias) — bats right — throws right — b.10/24/61 — 1991 positions: SS145

YR	TM/LG	CL	G	TPA	AB	H	2B	3B	HR	TB	BB	IBB	HB	SO	GDP	SH	SF	SB	CS	R	RBI	BA	OBA	SA
82	PIT/NL		9	2	2	1	0	0	0	1	0	0	0	0	0	0	0	0	0	3	0	.500	.500	.500
83	PIT/NL		4	1	1	0	0	0	0	0	0	0	0	1	0	0	0	0	0	0	0	.000	.000	.000
84	PIT/NL		20	22	22	5	0	0	0	5	0	0	0	1	0	0	0	1	0	3	0	.227	.227	.227
85	HAW/PCL	AAA	100	350	341	84	12	4	1	107	4	0	1	49	6	3	1	9	7	35	18	.246	.256	.314
	PIT/NL		17	20	20	4	0	0	0	4	0	0	0	5	0	0	0	0	1	1	1	.200	.200	.200
86	PIT/NL		117	350	309	72	5	2	0	81	26	8	0	54	8	11	1	12	2	33	31	.233	.298	.262
87	HAR/EAS	AA	37	153	145	49	5	2	0	58	6	0	0	16	2	2	0	7	5	24	9	.338	.364	.400
	PIT/NL		81	229	203	42	4	3	1	55	20	6	3	25	4	2	1	5	1	26	15	.207	.286	.271
88	PIT/NL		122	321	286	61	0	4	0	69	26	3	4	47	10	5	0	7	1	28	11	.213	.288	.241
89	PIT/NL		67	165	154	33	4	0	0	37	8	2	0	22	1	3	0	5	5	10	8	.214	.253	.240
90	PIT/NL		47	61	54	11	3	0	0	14	5	0	1	13	2	1	0	1	2	10	6	.204	.283	.259
91	ATL/NL		149	385	353	88	9	2	0	101	22	2	2	63	4	7	1	3	1	36	27	.249	.296	.286
	10 YR TOTALS		633	1556	1404	317	25	11	1	367	107	19	13	231	29	29	3	38	10	151	99	**.226**	**.286**	**.261**

Beltre, Esteban (Valera) — bats right — throws right — b.12/26/67 — 1991 positions: SS8

YR	TM/LG	CL	G	TPA	AB	H	2B	3B	HR	TB	BB	IBB	HB	SO	GDP	SH	SF	SB	CS	R	RBI	BA	OBA	SA
84	CAL/PIO	R+	18	22	20	4	0	0	0	4	2	0	0	1	0	0	0	1	0	1	2	.200	.273	.200
85	UTI/NYP	A−	72	271	241	48	6	2	0	58	18	0	3	58	4	8	1	8	7	19	22	.199	.262	.241
86	WPB/FSL	A+	97	306	285	69	11	1	1	85	16	2	0	59	9	4	1	4	2	24	20	.242	.281	.298
87	JAC/SOU	AA	142	544	491	104	15	4	4	139	40	0	3	98	7	10	0	9	8	55	34	.212	.275	.283
88	JAC/SOU	AA	35	116	113	17	2	0	0	19	3	0	0	28	1	0	0	1	0	5	6	.150	.172	.168
	WPB/FSL	A+	69	250	226	63	5	6	0	80	11	0	1	38	4	11	1	9	3	23	15	.279	.314	.354
89	ROC/MID	A	104	414	375	80	15	3	2	107	33	1	0	83	8	5	1	9	3	42	33	.213	.276	.285
90	IND/AMA	AAA	133	450	407	92	11	2	1	110	32	1	0	77	9	5	4	8	2	33	37	.226	.283	.270
91	DEN/AMA	AAA	27	87	78	14	1	3	0	21	9	0	0	16	5	0	0	3	2	11	9	.179	.264	.269
	VAN/PCL	AAA	88	378	347	94	11	3	0	111	23	0	0	61	4	7	1	8	7	48	30	.271	.315	.320
	CHI/AL		8	7	6	1	0	0	0	1	1	0	0	1	0	0	0	0	0	0	0	.167	.286	.167

Benavides, Alfredo "Freddie" — bats right — throws right — b.4/7/66 — 1991 positions: SS 20, 2B 3

YR	TM/LG	CL	G	TPA	AB	H	2B	3B	HR	TB	BB	IBB	HB	SO	GDP	SH	SF	SB	CS	R	RBI	BA	OBA	SA
87	CR/MID	A	5	15	15	2	1	0	0	3	0	0	0	7	1	0	0	0	1	2	0	.133	.133	.200
88	CR/MID	A	88	359	314	70	9	2	1	86	35	3	2	75	7	4	4	18	7	38	32	.223	.301	.274
89	CHT/SOU	AA	88	313	284	71	14	3	0	91	22	0	2	46	2	2	3	1	4	25	27	.250	.305	.320
	NAS/AMA	AAA	31	101	94	16	4	0	1	23	6	0	0	24	1	1	0	0	0	9	12	.170	.220	.245
90	CHT/SOU	AA	55	215	197	51	10	1	1	66	11	0	2	25	4	3	2	4	2	20	28	.259	.302	.335
	NAS/AMA	AAA	77	286	266	56	7	3	2	75	12	3	3	50	4	4	1	7	7	30	20	.211	.252	.282
91	NAS/AMA	AAA	94	350	331	80	8	0	0	88	16	3	0	55	10	3	0	3	7	24	21	.242	.277	.266
	CIN/NL		24	67	63	18	1	0	0	19	1	1	1	15	1	1	1	0	1	11	3	.286	.303	.302

Benjamin, Michael Paul "Mike" — bats right — throws right — b.11/22/65 — 1991 positions: SS 51, 3B 1

YR	TM/LG	CL	G	TPA	AB	H	2B	3B	HR	TB	BB	IBB	HB	SO	GDP	SH	SF	SB	CS	R	RBI	BA	OBA	SA
87	FRE/CAL	A+	64	240	212	51	6	4	6	83	24	1	0	71	1	2	0	6	2	25	24	.241	.324	.392
88	SHR/TEX	AA	89	338	309	73	19	5	6	120	22	1	0	63	5	5	2	6	2	48	37	.236	.285	.388
	PHO/PCL	AAA	37	124	106	18	4	1	0	24	13	0	2	32	3	2	1	1	1	13	6	.170	.270	.226

Benjamin, Michael Paul "Mike" (continued)

YR	TM/LG	CL	G	TPA	AB	H	2B	3B	HR	TB	BB	IBB	HB	SO	GDP	SH	SF	SB	CS	R	RBI	BA	OBA	SA
89	PHO/PCL	AAA	113	401	363	94	17	6	3	132	18	1	6	82	6	12	2	10	4	44	36	.259	.303	.364
	SF/NL		14	6	6	1	0	0	0	1	0	0	0	1	0	0	0	0	0	6	0	.167	.167	.167
90	PHO/PCL	AAA	118	456	419	105	21	7	5	155	25	3	5	89	6	2	5	13	7	61	39	.251	.297	.370
	SF/NL		22	59	56	12	3	1	2	23	3	1	0	10	2	0	0	1	0	7	3	.214	.254	.411
91	PHO/PCL	AAA	64	253	226	46	13	2	6	81	20	3	2	67	5	1	4	3	2	34	31	.204	.270	.358
	SF/NL		54	120	106	13	3	0	2	22	7	2	2	26	1	3	2	3	0	12	8	.123	.188	.208
3 YR TOTALS			**90**	**185**	**168**	**26**	**6**	**1**	**4**	**46**	**10**	**3**	**2**	**37**	**3**	**3**	**2**	**4**	**0**	**25**	**11**	**.155**	**.209**	**.274**

Benzinger, Todd Eric — bats both — throws right — b.2/11/63 — 1991 positions: 1B 96, DH 1

YR	TM/LG	CL	G	TPA	AB	H	2B	3B	HR	TB	BB	IBB	HB	SO	GDP	SH	SF	SB	CS	R	RBI	BA	OBA	SA
84	NB/EAS	AA	110	430	391	101	25	5	10	166	33	4	1	89	10	3	2	0	1	49	60	.258	.316	.425
85	PAW/INT	AAA	70	273	256	64	13	1	11	112	12	1	0	49	13	2	3	0	0	31	47	.250	.280	.438
86	PAW/INT	AAA	90	342	314	79	13	2	11	129	23	2	1	76	6	1	3	7	5	41	32	.252	.302	.411
87	PAW/INT	AAA	65	278	257	83	17	3	13	145	16	1	2	41	5	0	3	7	2	47	49	.323	.363	.564
	BOS/AL		73	253	223	62	11	1	8	99	22	3	2	41	4	5	3	5	4	36	43	.278	.344	.444
88	BOS/AL		120	436	405	103	28	1	13	172	22	4	1	80	8	6	2	2	3	47	70	.254	.293	.425
89	CIN/NL		161	686	628	154	28	3	17	239	44	13	2	120	5	4	8	3	7	79	76	.245	.293	.381
90	CIN/NL		118	408	376	95	14	2	5	128	19	4	4	69	3	2	7	3	4	35	46	.253	.291	.340
91	CIN/NL		51	136	123	23	3	2	1	33	10	2	2	20	2	1	0	2	2	7	11	.187	.244	.268
	KC/AL		78	315	293	86	15	3	2	113	17	2	3	46	5	1	1	2	6	29	40	.294	.338	.386
	YEAR		129	451	416	109	18	5	3	146	27	4	3	66	7	2	3	4	6	36	51	.262	.310	.351
5 YR TOTALS			**601**	**2234**	**2048**	**523**	**99**	**12**	**46**	**784**	**134**	**28**	**12**	**376**	**28**	**17**	**23**	**17**	**24**	**233**	**286**	**.255**	**.302**	**.383**

Bergman, David Bruce "Dave" — bats left — throws left — b.6/6/53 — 1991 positions: 1B 49, DH 13, OF 4

YR	TM/LG	CL	G	TPA	AB	H	2B	3B	HR	TB	BB	IBB	HB	SO	GDP	SH	SF	SB	CS	R	RBI	BA	OBA	SA
75	NY/AL		7	19	17	0	0	0	0	0	2	0	0	4	0	0	0	0	0	0	0	.000	.105	.000
77	NY/AL		5	5	4	1	0	0	0	1	0	0	0	0	0	0	1	0	0	1	1	.250	.200	.250
78	HOU/NL		104	228	186	43	5	1	0	50	39	9	0	32	5	1	2	2	0	15	12	.231	.361	.269
79	HOU/NL		13	15	15	6	0	0	0	9	0	0	0	0	0	0	0	0	0	4	2	.400	.400	.600
80	HOU/NL		90	91	78	20	6	1	0	28	10	2	0	10	1	3	0	1	0	12	1	.256	.341	.359
81	HOU/NL		6	6	6	1	0	0	0	1	0	0	0	0	0	0	0	0	0	1	1	.167	.167	.167
	SF/NL		63	167	145	37	9	0	3	55	19	3	0	18	4	2	1	2	2	16	13	.255	.339	.379
	YEAR		69	173	151	38	9	0	4	59	19	3	0	18	4	2	1	2	2	17	14	.252	.333	.391
82	SF/NL		100	140	121	33	3	1	4	50	18	3	0	11	1	0	1	0	3	22	14	.273	.364	.413
83	SF/NL		90	167	140	40	4	1	6	64	24	2	1	21	2	1	1	0	2	16	24	.286	.394	.457
84	DET/AL		120	316	271	74	8	5	7	113	33	2	3	40	4	3	6	1	1	42	44	.273	.351	.417
85	NAS/AMA	AAA	11	45	39	9	1	0	1	13	6	0	0	6	1	0	2	0	0	8	7	.231	.311	.333
	DET/AL		69	157	140	25	2	0	3	36	14	0	0	15	6	1	2	0	0	14	6	.179	.250	.257
86	DET/AL		65	151	130	30	6	1	1	41	21	0	0	23	1	1	3	0	0	25	22	.231	.338	.315
87	DET/AL		91	207	172	47	7	3	6	78	30	4	1	23	1	3	2	1	2	37	35	.273	.379	.453
88	DET/AL		116	333	289	85	14	0	5	114	38	2	1	34	7	2	4	0	2	38	37	.294	.372	.394
89	DET/AL		137	436	385	103	13	1	7	139	44	3	0	44	5	4	1	1	3	21	26	.268	.345	.361
90	DET/AL		100	241	205	57	10	1	2	75	33	3	0	17	7	1	2	3	2	23	29	.278	.375	.366
91	DET/AL		86	231	194	46	10	1	7	79	35	2	0	40	2	0	2	1	1	8	12	.237	.351	.407
16 YR TOTALS			**1262**	**2910**	**2498**	**648**	**97**	**16**	**53**	**936**	**360**	**35**	**7**	**328**	**51**	**20**	**25**	**18**	**14**	**295**	**279**	**.259**	**.351**	**.375**

Bernazard, Antonio (Garcia) "Tony" — bats both — throws right — b.8/24/56 — 1991 positions: 2B 2, DH 2

YR	TM/LG	CL	G	TPA	AB	H	2B	3B	HR	TB	BB	IBB	HB	SO	GDP	SH	SF	SB	CS	R	RBI	BA	OBA	SA
79	MON/NL		22	58	40	12	2	0	1	17	15	2	0	12	2	2	0	1	2	11	8	.300	.500	.425
80	MON/NL		82	202	183	41	7	1	5	65	17	4	0	41	3	1	1	9	2	26	18	.224	.289	.355
81	CHI/AL		106	450	384	106	14	4	6	146	54	6	2	66	7	9	1	4	4	53	34	.276	.367	.380
82	CHI/AL		137	630	540	138	25	9	11	214	67	9	2	88	9	16	5	11	0	90	56	.256	.337	.396
83	CHI/AL		59	259	233	61	16	2	2	87	17	0	0	45	4	5	2	1	0	30	26	.262	.306	.373
	SEA/AL		80	347	300	80	18	1	6	118	38	3	2	52	4	5	2	21	8	35	30	.267	.332	.393
	YEAR		139	606	533	141	34	3	8	205	55	3	2	97	8	9	7	23	9	65	56	.265	.332	.385
84	CLE/AL		140	497	439	97	15	4	2	126	43	0	2	70	10	7	6	20	13	44	38	.221	.290	.287
85	CLE/AL		153	579	500	137	26	3	11	202	69	2	1	72	11	5	4	17	9	88	73	.274	.361	.404
86	CLE/AL		146	636	562	169	28	4	17	256	53	5	5	77	6	7	8	17	8	73	59	.301	.362	.456
87	CLE/AL		79	324	293	70	12	1	11	117	25	2	1	49	4	3	2	3	4	39	30	.239	.300	.399
	OAK/AL		61	249	214	57	14	1	3	82	30	2	1	30	6	3	2	4	4	34	19	.266	.354	.383
	YEAR		140	573	507	127	26	2	14	199	55	2	1	79	10	7	3	11	8	73	49	.250	.323	.393
91	DET/AL		6	12	12	2	0	0	0	2	0	0	0	4	0	0	0	0	0	0	0	.167	.167	.167
10 YR TOTALS			**1071**	**4243**	**3700**	**970**	**177**	**30**	**75**	**1432**	**428**	**22**	**17**	**606**	**67**	**63**	**35**	**113**	**55**	**523**	**391**	**.262**	**.339**	**.387**

Berry, Sean Robert — bats right — throws right — b.3/22/66 — 1991 positions: 3B 30

YR	TM/LG	CL	G	TPA	AB	H	2B	3B	HR	TB	BB	IBB	HB	SO	GDP	SH	SF	SB	CS	R	RBI	BA	OBA	SA
86	EUG/NWL	A—	65	290	238	76	20	2	5	115	44	0	5	73	1	2	2	10	1	53	44	.319	.433	.483
87	FM/FSL	A+	66	253	205	52	7	2	2	69	43	2	3	65	1	1	1	4	4	26	30	.254	.389	.337
88	BC/FSL	A+	94	343	304	71	6	4	4	97	31	1	2	62	3	3	3	24	11	34	30	.234	.306	.319
89	BC/FSL	A+	116	459	399	106	19	1	4	151	44	1	6	68	6	5	5	37	11	67	44	.266	.344	.378
90	MEM/SOU	AA	135	548	487	142	25	4	14	217	44	1	6	89	10	7	0	18	9	73	77	.292	.353	.446
	KC/AL		8	25	23	5	1	1	0	8	2	0	0	6	0	0	0	0	0	2	4	.217	.280	.348
91	OMA/AMA	AAA	103	424	368	97	21	9	11	169	48	2	3	70	6	5	5	18	9	62	54	.264	.349	.459
	KC/AL		31	66	60	8	2	0	0	11	5	0	0	23	1	0	0	0	0	5	1	.133	.212	.183
2 YR TOTALS			**39**	**91**	**83**	**13**	**4**	**1**	**0**	**19**	**7**	**0**	**1**	**28**	**1**	**0**	**0**	**0**	**0**	**7**	**5**	**.157**	**.231**	**.229**

Berryhill, Damon Scott — bats both — throws right — b.12/3/63 — 1991 positions: C 48

YR	TM/LG	CL	G	TPA	AB	H	2B	3B	HR	TB	BB	IBB	HB	SO	GDP	SH	SF	SB	CS	R	RBI	BA	OBA	SA
84	QC/MID	A	62	235	217	60	14	0	0	74	16	0	1	44	3	1	0	4	4	30	31	.276	.329	.341
85	WIN/CAR	A+	117	430	386	90	25	1	9	144	32	3	1	90	6	4	7	4	4	31	50	.233	.289	.373
86	PIT/EAS	AA	112	391	345	71	13	1	6	104	37	3	1	54	8	1	7	2	5	33	35	.206	.279	.301
87	IOW/AMA	AAA	121	470	429	123	22	1	18	201	32	3	0	58	6	1	8	5	4	54	67	.287	.330	.469
	CHI/NL		12	31	28	5	1	0	0	6	3	0	0	5	1	0	0	0	1	2	1	.179	.258	.214
88	IOW/AMA	AAA	21	81	73	16	5	1	2	29	7	1	0	21	0	0	1	0	0	11	11	.219	.284	.397
	CHI/NL		95	332	309	80	19	1	7	122	17	5	0	56	11	3	1	0	0	19	38	.259	.295	.395
89	IOW/AMA	AAA	7	31	30	6	1	0	2	13	1	0	0	6	0	0	0	0	0	4	4	.200	.226	.433
	CHI/NL		91	361	334	86	13	0	5	114	16	4	0	54	13	4	5	1	0	37	41	.257	.291	.341
90	PEO/MID	A	7	30	26	10	2	0	3	21	3	1	1	6	0	0	0	0	1	10	8	.385	.467	.808
	IOW/AMA	AAA	22	83	79	17	1	0	3	27	4	1	0	18	1	0	0	0	0	8	6	.215	.253	.342
	CHI/NL		17	59	53	10	4	0	1	17	5	1	0	14	3	0	0	0	2	8	6	.189	.254	.321
91	IOW/AMA	AAA	26	111	97	32	4	1	8	62	12	0	0	25	2	0	2	0	2	20	24	.330	.396	.639
	CHI/NL		62	172	159	30	7	0	5	52	11	1	1	41	2	0	1	1	2	13	14	.189	.244	.327
	ATL/NL		1	1	1	0	0	0	0	0	0	0	0	1	0	0	0	0	0	0	0	.000	.000	.000
	YEAR		63	173	160	30	7	0	5	52	11	1	1	42	2	0	1	1	2	13	14	.188	.243	.325
5 YR TOTALS			**278**	**956**	**884**	**211**	**44**	**1**	**18**	**311**	**52**	**11**	**3**	**171**	**30**	**7**	**10**	**3**	**3**	**77**	**103**	**.239**	**.280**	**.352**

Bichette, Alphonse Dante "Dante" — bats right — throws right — b.11/18/63 — 1991 positions: OF 127, 3B 1

YR	TM/LG	CL	G	TPA	AB	H	2B	3B	HR	TB	BB	IBB	HB	SO	GDP	SH	SF	SB	CS	R	RBI	BA	OBA	SA
84	SAL/NWL	A−	64	263	250	58	9	2	4	83	6	0	3	53	6	3	1	6	2	27	30	.232	.258	.332
85	QC/MID	A	137	582	547	145	28	4	11	214	25	1	3	89	11	0	7	25	11	58	78	.265	.297	.391
86	PS/CAL	A+	68	318	290	79	15	0	10	124	21	1	3	53	7	0	4	2	0	39	73	.272	.324	.428
	MID/TEX	AA	62	266	243	69	16	2	12	125	18	0	2	50	5	0	3	3	0	43	36	.284	.335	.514
87	EDM/PCL	AAA	92	392	360	108	20	3	13	173	26	4	4	68	8	0	2	3	3	54	50	.300	.352	.481
88	EDM/PCL	AAA	132	537	509	136	29	10	14	227	25	2	0	80	12	0	1	8	1	64	81	.267	.304	.446
	CAL/AL		21	50	46	12	2	0	0	14	0	0	0	7	0	0	4	0	0	1	8	.261	.240	.304
89	EDM/PCL	AAA	61	255	226	55	11	2	11	103	24	0	2	39	12	1	2	4	5	39	40	.243	.319	.456
	CAL/AL		48	146	138	29	7	0	3	45	6	0	0	24	3	0	2	3	0	13	15	.210	.240	.326
90	CAL/AL		109	371	349	89	15	1	15	151	16	1	3	79	9	1	2	5	2	40	53	.255	.292	.433
91	MIL/AL		134	475	445	106	18	3	15	175	22	4	1	107	9	1	6	14	8	53	59	.238	.272	.393
4 YR TOTALS			**312**	**1042**	**978**	**236**	**42**	**4**	**33**	**385**	**44**	**5**	**4**	**217**	**21**	**2**	**14**	**22**	**10**	**107**	**135**	**.241**	**.273**	**.394**

Biggio, Craig Alan — bats right — throws right — b.12/14/65 — 1991 positions: C 139, 2B 3, OF 2

YR	TM/LG	CL	G	TPA	AB	H	2B	3B	HR	TB	BB	IBB	HB	SO	GDP	SH	SF	SB	CS	R	RBI	BA	OBA	SA
87	ASH/SAL	A	64	260	216	81	17	2	9	129	39	0	2	33	5	1	2	31	10	59	49	.375	.471	.597
88	TUC/PCL	AAA	77	329	281	90	21	4	3	128	40	1	3	39	2	3	2	19	4	60	41	.320	.408	.456
	HOU/NL		50	131	123	26	6	1	3	43	7	2	0	29	1	1	0	6	1	14	5	.211	.254	.350
89	HOU/NL		134	509	443	114	21	2	13	178	49	8	6	64	7	6	5	21	3	64	60	.257	.336	.402
90	HOU/NL		150	621	555	153	24	2	4	193	53	1	3	79	11	9	1	25	11	53	42	.276	.342	.348
91	HOU/NL		149	609	546	161	23	4	4	204	53	3	2	71	2	5	3	19	6	79	46	.295	.358	.374
4 YR TOTALS			**483**	**1870**	**1667**	**454**	**74**	**9**	**24**	**618**	**162**	**14**	**11**	**243**	**21**	**21**	**9**	**71**	**21**	**210**	**153**	**.272**	**.339**	**.371**

Bilardello, Dann James — bats right — throws right — b.5/26/59 — 1991 positions: C 13

YR	TM/LG	CL	G	TPA	AB	H	2B	3B	HR	TB	BB	IBB	HB	SO	GDP	SH	SF	SB	CS	R	RBI	BA	OBA	SA
78	LET/PIO	R+	42	148	133	33	8	1	2	49	9	0	0	17	3	3	3	0	0	21	20	.248	.290	.368
79	CLI/MID	A	52	163	142	34	4	0	2	44	18	0	1	11	5	1	1	2	6	18	15	.239	.327	.310
80	LOD/CAL	A+	41	132	117	36	4	0	6	58	11	2	1	12	4	1	2	6	6	22	15	.308	.372	.496
81	SA/TEX	AA	6	22	19	1	0	0	0	1	1	0	0	9	0	1	1	0	0	1	0	.053	.095	.053
	LOD/CAL	A+	105	394	352	108	19	2	21	194	36	1	1	55	6	1	4	1	3	72	80	.307	.369	.551
82	SA/TEX	AA	103	380	347	99	14	2	17	168	27	3	2	40	7	1	3	2	2	49	48	.285	.338	.484
83	CIN/NL		109	320	298	71	18	0	9	116	15	3	1	49	9	1	2	2	1	27	38	.238	.274	.389
84	WIC/AMA	AAA	49	192	167	40	9	0	5	64	22	0	1	29	5	0	2	2	1	21	17	.240	.328	.383
	CIN/NL		68	206	182	38	7	0	2	51	19	3	1	34	6	4	0	0	0	16	10	.209	.287	.280
85	DEN/AMA	AAA	67	265	236	57	5	3	10	98	25	1	2	37	7	0	2	4	5	41	37	.242	.317	.415
	CIN/NL		42	108	102	17	0	0	1	20	4	1	1	15	1	0	1	0	0	6	9	.167	.206	.196
86	IND/AMA	AAA	2	5	5	3	0	0	1	6	0	0	0	0	0	0	0	0	0	1	0	.600	.600	1.000
	MON/NL		79	212	191	37	5	0	4	54	14	3	0	32	5	7	0	0	0	12	17	.194	.249	.283
87	VAN/PCL	AAA	37	108	97	21	3	0	1	27	8	0	0	15	0	2	0	0	0	7	11	.216	.283	.278
	OMA/AMA	AAA	22	77	71	13	5	1	2	26	4	0	0	15	2	0	2	0	0	7	11	.183	.227	.366
88	OMA/AMA	AAA	71	255	235	57	14	0	6	95	7	0	1	35	4	4	8	0	0	27	45	.243	.259	.404
89	BUF/AMA	AAA	66	201	180	37	6	0	3	54	14	3	5	26	8	5	1	3	2	11	17	.206	.265	.300
	PIT/NL		33	83	80	18	6	0	2	30	2	0	0	18	1	1	1	0	0	11	8	.225	.244	.375
90	BUF/AMA	AAA	52	168	154	44	8	0	5	69	7	2	2	20	3	0	5	0	0	19	26	.286	.325	.448
	PIT/NL		19	43	37	2	0	0	0	2	4	1	0	10	0	2	0	0	0	1	3	.054	.146	.054
91	LV/PCL	AAA	44	151	140	44	13	1	4	71	9	3	0	21	2	0	0	0	2	17	29	.314	.351	.507
	SD/NL		15	29	26	7	2	0	0	11	3	0	0	10	0	0	0	0	0	4	5	.269	.345	.423
7 YR TOTALS			**365**	**1001**	**916**	**190**	**38**	**1**	**18**	**284**	**61**	**11**	**3**	**162**	**26**	**17**	**4**	**4**	**4**	**77**	**90**	**.207**	**.258**	**.310**

Blankenship, Lance Robert — bats right — throws right — b.12/6/63 — 1991 positions: 2B 45, OF 28, 3B 14, DH 6

YR	TM/LG	CL	G	TPA	AB	H	2B	3B	HR	TB	BB	IBB	HB	SO	GDP	SH	SF	SB	CS	R	RBI	BA	OBA	SA
86	MED/NWL	A−	14	74	52	21	4	0	2	30	17	1	0	9	0	1	4	10	1	22	17	.404	.521	.577
	MOD/CAL	A+	55	217	171	50	5	5	6	79	41	0	4	39	1	0	1	14	5	47	25	.292	.440	.462
87	MOD/CAL	A+	22	98	84	23	9	2	0	36	12	1	1	29	0	1	0	12	3	14	17	.274	.371	.429
	HUN/SOU	AA	107	471	390	99	21	3	4	138	67	0	6	60	5	3	5	34	7	64	39	.254	.368	.354

Blankenship, Lance Robert (continued)

YR	TM/LG	CL	G	TPA	AB	H	2B	3B	HR	TB	BB	IBB	HB	SO	GDP	SH	SF	SB	CS	R	RBI	BA	OBA	SA
88	TAC/PCL	AAA	131	545	437	116	21	8	9	180	96	0	2	74	10	6	4	40	12	84	52	.265	.397	.412
	OAK/AL		10	3	3	0	0	0	0	0	0	0	0	1	0	0	0	0	1	1	0	.000	.000	.000
89	TAC/PCL	AAA	25	121	98	29	8	2	2	47	19	0	1	15	4	2	1	5	3	25	9	.296	.412	.480
	OAK/AL		58	137	125	29	5	1	1	39	8	0	0	31	0	3	1	5	1	22	4	.232	.276	.312
90	TAC/PCL	AAA	24	108	93	24	7	1	1	36	14	0	0	16	3	0	0	7	3	18	9	.258	.361	.387
	OAK/AL		86	162	136	26	3	0	0	29	20	0	1	23	6	6	0	3	1	18	10	.191	.295	.213
91	TAC/PCL	AAA	30	136	109	32	7	0	1	42	22	0	2	27	2	0	3	9	1	19	11	.294	.412	.385
	OAK/AL		90	216	185	46	8	0	3	63	23	0	3	42	2	2	3	12	3	33	21	.249	.336	.341
4 YR TOTALS			**244**	**518**	**449**	**101**	**16**	**1**	**4**	**131**	**51**	**0**	**3**	**97**	**8**	**11**	**4**	**20**	**6**	**74**	**35**	**.225**	**.306**	**.292**

Blauser, Jeffrey Michael "Jeff" — bats right — throws right — b.11/8/65 — 1991 positions: SS 85, 2B 32, 3B 18

YR	TM/LG	CL	G	TPA	AB	H	2B	3B	HR	TB	BB	IBB	HB	SO	GDP	SH	SF	SB	CS	R	RBI	BA	OBA	SA
84	PUL/APP	R+	62	262	217	54	6	1	3	71	38	0	3	47	4	3	1	14	2	41	24	.249	.367	.327
85	SUM/SAL	A	125	520	422	99	19	0	5	133	82	1	9	94	3	2	5	36	6	74	49	.235	.367	.315
86	DUR/CAR	A+	123	544	447	128	27	3	13	200	81	2	7	92	5	2	7	12	9	94	52	.286	.399	.447
87	RIC/INT	AAA	33	127	113	20	1	0	1	24	11	2	0	24	1	0	3	3	2	11	12	.177	.244	.212
	GRE/SOU	AA	72	311	265	66	13	3	4	97	34	0	3	49	3	5	3	5	3	35	32	.249	.338	.366
	ATL/NL		51	187	165	40	6	3	2	58	18	1	3	34	4	1	0	7	6	40	23	.284	.340	.417
88	RIC/INT	AAA	69	300	271	77	19	1	5	113	19	3	0	53	3	3	3	5	3	7	7	.239	.268	.403
	ATL/NL		18	74	67	16	3	1	2	27	2	0	1	11	1	3	1	0	1	7	7	.239	.268	.403
89	ATL/NL		142	507	456	123	24	2	12	187	38	2	8	101	7	8	4	5	5	63	46	.270	.325	.410
90	ATL/NL		115	429	386	104	24	3	8	158	35	1	5	70	4	3	0	3	5	46	39	.269	.338	.409
91	ATL/NL		129	415	352	91	14	3	11	144	54	4	2	59	4	4	3	0	7	49	54	.259	.358	.409
5 YR TOTALS			**455**	**1612**	**1426**	**374**	**71**	**12**	**35**	**574**	**147**	**8**	**12**	**275**	**20**	**19**	**8**	**20**	**17**	**176**	**161**	**.262**	**.335**	**.403**

Blowers, Michael Roy "Mike" — bats right — throws right — b.4/24/65 — 1991 positions: 3B 14

YR	TM/LG	CL	G	TPA	AB	H	2B	3B	HR	TB	BB	IBB	HB	SO	GDP	SH	SF	SB	CS	R	RBI	BA	OBA	SA
86	JAM/NYP	A−	32	117	95	24	9	2	1	40	17	2	3	18	4	2	0	3	2	13	6	.253	.383	.421
	EXP/GCL	R	31	132	115	25	3	1	2	36	15	0	0	25	4	2	0	2	0	14	17	.217	.308	.313
87	WPB/FSL	A+	136	542	491	124	30	3	16	208	48	0	3	118	11	0	3	4	4	58	60	.250	.349	.417
88	JAC/SOU	AA	137	531	460	115	20	6	15	192	41	4	2	109	10	1	3	3	2	49	56	.267	.327	.447
89	IND/AMA	AAA	131	508	461	123	29	6	14	206	41	4	2	109	10	1	3	3	2	49	56	.267	.327	.447
	NY/AL		13	41	38	10	0	0	0	10	3	0	0	13	1	0	0	0	0	2	3	.263	.317	.263
90	COL/INT	AAA	62	264	230	78	20	6	6	128	29	1	1	40	8	0	4	3	0	30	50	.339	.409	.557
	NY/AL		48	157	144	27	4	0	5	46	12	1	1	50	0	0	0	0	0	16	21	.188	.255	.319
91	NY/AL		15	40	35	7	0	0	1	10	4	0	0	3	1	1	0	0	0	3	1	.200	.282	.286
	CAL/PCL	AAA	90	379	329	95	20	2	9	146	40	1	3	74	11	1	6	3	1	56	59	.289	.365	.444
3 YR TOTALS			**76**	**238**	**217**	**44**	**4**	**0**	**6**	**66**	**19**	**1**	**1**	**66**	**5**	**1**	**0**	**1**	**0**	**21**	**25**	**.203**	**.270**	**.304**

Boggs, Wade Anthony — bats left — throws right — b.6/15/58 — 1991 positions: 3B 140

YR	TM/LG	CL	G	TPA	AB	H	2B	3B	HR	TB	BB	IBB	HB	SO	GDP	SH	SF	SB	CS	R	RBI	BA	OBA	SA
82	BOS/AL		104	381	338	118	14	1	5	149	35	4	0	21	9	4	4	1	0	51	44	.349	.406	.441
83	BOS/AL		153	685	582	210	44	7	5	283	92	2	1	36	15	3	7	3	3	100	74	.361	.444	.486
84	BOS/AL		158	726	625	203	31	4	6	260	89	6	0	44	13	8	4	3	2	109	55	.325	.407	.416
85	BOS/AL		161	758	653	240	42	3	8	312	96	5	4	61	20	3	2	2	1	107	78	.368	.450	.478
86	BOS/AL		149	693	580	207	47	2	8	282	105	14	0	44	11	4	4	0	4	107	71	.357	.453	.486
87	BOS/AL		147	667	551	200	40	6	24	324	105	19	2	48	13	1	9	1	3	108	89	.363	.461	.588
88	BOS/AL		155	719	584	214	45	6	5	286	125	18	3	34	23	0	6	2	3	128	58	.366	.476	.490
89	BOS/AL		156	742	621	205	51	7	3	279	107	19	7	51	19	0	6	2	6	113	54	.330	.430	.449
90	BOS/AL		155	713	619	187	44	5	6	259	87	19	1	68	14	0	7	0	0	89	63	.302	.386	.418
91	BOS/AL		144	641	546	181	42	2	8	251	89	25	0	32	16	1	6	1	2	93	51	.332	.421	.460
10 YR TOTALS			**1482**	**6725**	**5699**	**1965**	**400**	**43**	**78**	**2685**	**930**	**131**	**18**	**439**	**153**	**23**	**55**	**15**	**24**	**1005**	**637**	**.345**	**.435**	**.471**

Bonds, Barry Lamar — bats left — throws left — b.7/24/64 — 1991 positions: OF 150

YR	TM/LG	CL	G	TPA	AB	H	2B	3B	HR	TB	BB	IBB	HB	SO	GDP	SH	SF	SB	CS	R	RBI	BA	OBA	SA
85	PW/CAR	A+	71	296	254	76	16	4	13	139	37	0	0	52	3	1	4	15	3	49	37	.299	.383	.547
86	HAW/PCL	AAA	44	186	148	46	7	2	7	78	33	0	2	31	1	0	3	16	5	30	37	.311	.435	.527
	PIT/NL		113	484	413	92	26	3	16	172	65	2	2	102	4	2	2	36	7	72	48	.223	.330	.416
87	PIT/NL		150	611	551	144	34	9	25	271	54	3	3	88	4	0	3	32	10	99	59	.261	.329	.492
88	PIT/NL		144	614	538	152	30	5	24	264	72	14	2	82	3	0	2	17	11	97	58	.283	.368	.491
89	PIT/NL		159	679	580	144	34	6	19	247	93	22	1	93	9	1	4	32	10	96	58	.248	.351	.426
90	PIT/NL		151	621	519	156	32	3	33	293	93	15	3	83	8	0	6	52	13	104	114	.301	.406	.565
91	PIT/NL		153	634	510	149	28	5	25	262	107	25	4	73	8	0	13	43	13	95	116	.292	.410	.514
6 YR TOTALS			**870**	**3643**	**3111**	**837**	**184**	**31**	**142**	**1509**	**484**	**81**	**15**	**521**	**36**	**3**	**30**	**212**	**64**	**563**	**453**	**.269**	**.367**	**.485**

Bonilla, Roberto Martin Antonio "Bobby" — bats both — throws right — b.2/23/63 — 1991 positions: OF 104, 3B 67, 1B 4

YR	TM/LG	CL	G	TPA	AB	H	2B	3B	HR	TB	BB	IBB	HB	SO	GDP	SH	SF	SB	CS	R	RBI	BA	OBA	SA
84	NAS/EAS	AA	136	544	484	128	19	5	11	190	49	7	3	89	9	1	7	15	7	74	71	.264	.331	.393
85	PW/CAR	A+	39	147	130	34	4	1	3	49	16	2	0	29	5	0	1	1	1	27	26	.262	.340	.377
86	CHI/AL		75	271	234	63	10	2	2	83	33	2	1	49	4	2	1	4	4	28	17	.269	.361	.355
	PIT/NL		63	225	192	46	6	2	1	59	29	1	1	39	5	3	0	4	4	27	26	.240	.342	.307
	YEAR		138	496	426	109	16	4	3	142	62	2	2	88	9	5	1	8	8	55	43	.256	.352	.333
87	PIT/NL		141	515	466	140	33	3	15	224	39	4	0	64	8	0	8	3	5	58	77	.300	.351	.481
88	PIT/NL		159	681	584	160	32	7	24	278	85	19	4	82	4	0	8	3	5	87	100	.274	.366	.476

(continued)

Bonilla, Roberto Martin Antonio "Bobby" (continued)

YR	TM/LG	CL	G	TPA	AB	H	2B	3B	HR	TB	BB	IBB	HB	SO	GDP	SH	SF	SB	CS	R	RBI	BA	OBA	SA
89	PIT/NL		163	698	616	173	37	10	24	302	76	20	1	93	10	0	5	8	8	96	86	.281	.358	.490
90	PIT/NL		160	686	625	175	39	7	32	324	45	9	1	103	11	0	15	4	3	112	120	.280	.322	.518
91	PIT/NL		157	680	577	174	44	6	18	284	90	8	2	67	14	0	11	2	1	102	100	.302	.391	.492
6 YR TOTALS			**918**	**3756**	**3294**	**931**	**201**	**37**	**116**	**1554**	**397**	**63**	**12**	**497**	**56**	**5**	**48**	**28**	**30**	**510**	**526**	**.283**	**.357**	**.472**

Booker, Roderick Stewart "Rod" — bats left — throws right — b.9/4/58 — 1991 positions: SS 20, 3B 3

YR	TM/LG	CL	G	TPA	AB	H	2B	3B	HR	TB	BB	IBB	HB	SO	GDP	SH	SF	SB	CS	R	RBI	BA	OBA	SA
84	LOU/AMA	AAA	63	216	185	47	3	1	0	52	22	0	0	13	5	9	0	3	7	19	14	.254	.333	.281
	ARK/TEX	AA	52	239	209	43	4	3	0	53	24	2	1	28	1	4	1	8	3	10	22	.206	.289	.254
85	ARK/TEX	AA	129	534	466	123	18	3	1	150	55	4	1	43	8	8	4	13	5	59	47	.264	.340	.322
86	ARK/TEX	AA	36	159	151	48	7	2	0	59	7	1	0	17	1	0	1	8	5	20	20	.318	.346	.391
	LOU/AMA	AAA	78	324	289	81	11	5	1	105	32	1	0	27	4	2	1	18	6	51	30	.280	.351	.363
87	LOU/AMA	AAA	34	157	135	47	3	1	1	55	20	0	0	24	0	1	1	5	7	25	21	.348	.429	.407
	STL/NL		44	56	47	13	1	1	0	16	7	1	0	2	0	2	0	2	2	9	8	.277	.370	.340
88	LOU/AMA	AAA	111	419	370	96	12	1	4	122	45	3	0	44	1	2	2	15	7	50	31	.259	.338	.330
	STL/NL		18	39	35	12	3	0	0	15	4	0	0	3	0	0	0	2	2	6	3	.343	.410	.429
89	LOU/AMA	AAA	94	320	276	64	9	2	0	83	38	0	0	39	4	5	1	9	1	37	30	.232	.324	.301
	STL/NL		10	8	8	2	0	0	0	2	0	0	0	0	0	0	0	1	0	1	0	.250	.250	.250
90	PHI/NL		73	148	131	29	5	2	0	38	15	7	0	26	7	1	1	0	3	19	10	.221	.301	.290
91	PHI/NL		28	56	53	12	1	0	0	13	1	1	0	7	1	1	1	0	1	3	7	.226	.236	.245
5 YR TOTALS			**173**	**307**	**274**	**68**	**10**	**3**	**0**	**84**	**27**	**9**	**0**	**44**	**8**	**5**	**1**	**7**	**3**	**38**	**28**	**.248**	**.315**	**.307**

Boone, Bret Robert — bats right — throws right — b.4/6/69 — 1991 positions: 2B System SEA/AL

YR	TM/LG	CL	G	TPA	AB	H	2B	3B	HR	TB	BB	IBB	HB	SO	GDP	SH	SF	SB	CS	R	RBI	BA	OBA	SA
90	PEN/CAR	A+	74	303	255	68	13	2	8	109	47	0	1	57	1	0	0	5	2	42	38	.267	.383	.427
91	JAC/SOU	AA	139	556	475	121	18	1	19	198	72	2	5	123	21	1	3	9	6	64	75	.255	.357	.417

Borders, Patrick Lance "Pat" — bats right — throws right — b.5/14/63 — 1991 positions: C 102

YR	TM/LG	CL	G	TPA	AB	H	2B	3B	HR	TB	BB	IBB	HB	SO	GDP	SH	SF	SB	CS	R	RBI	BA	OBA	SA
84	FLO/SAL	A	131	527	467	129	32	5	12	207	56	0	1	109	6	0	3	3	4	69	85	.276	.353	.443
85	KIN/CAR	A+	127	508	460	120	16	1	10	168	45	1	1	116	11	0	2	6	5	43	60	.261	.327	.365
86	FLO/SAL	A	16	42	40	15	7	0	3	31	2	0	0	9	0	0	0	0	0	8	9	.375	.405	.775
	KNO/SOU	AA	12	37	34	12	1	0	2	19	1	0	0	6	2	2	0	0	3	3	5	.353	.371	.559
	KIN/CAR	A+	49	186	174	57	10	0	6	85	10	1	0	42	5	0	1	0	0	24	26	.328	.366	.489
87	DUN/FSL	A+	3	11	11	4	0	0	0	4	0	0	0	0	0	0	0	0	0	0	1	.364	.364	.364
	KNO/SOU	AA	94	374	349	102	14	1	11	151	20	1	2	56	13	0	3	2	5	44	51	.292	.332	.433
88	SYR/INT	AAA	35	138	120	29	8	0	3	46	16	0	0	22	1	0	2	0	0	11	14	.242	.326	.383
	TOR/AL		56	160	154	42	6	3	5	69	3	0	0	24	5	2	1	0	0	15	21	.273	.285	.448
89	TOR/AL		94	256	241	62	11	1	3	84	11	2	2	45	7	1	1	2	1	22	29	.257	.290	.349
90	TOR/AL		125	368	346	99	24	2	15	172	18	2	0	57	17	1	3	0	0	36	49	.286	.319	.497
91	TOR/AL		105	312	291	71	17	0	5	103	11	1	1	45	8	6	3	0	0	22	36	.244	.271	.354
4 YR TOTALS			**380**	**1096**	**1032**	**274**	**58**	**6**	**28**	**428**	**43**	**5**	**2**	**171**	**37**	**10**	**9**	**2**	**2**	**95**	**135**	**.266**	**.294**	**.415**

Bordick, Michael Todd "Mike" — bats right — throws right — b.7/21/65 — 1991 positions: SS 84, 2B 5, 3B 1

YR	TM/LG	CL	G	TPA	AB	H	2B	3B	HR	TB	BB	IBB	HB	SO	GDP	SH	SF	SB	CS	R	RBI	BA	OBA	SA
86	MED/NWL	A–	46	230	187	48	3	1	0	53	40	0	1	21	5	1	1	6	0	30	19	.257	.389	.283
87	MOD/CAL	A+	133	601	497	133	17	0	3	159	87	3	5	92	13	4	8	8	8	73	75	.268	.377	.320
88	HUN/SOU	AA	132	584	481	130	13	2	0	147	87	0	4	50	11	9	3	7	9	48	38	.270	.384	.306
89	TAC/PCL	AAA	136	569	487	117	11	1	1	139	58	0	7	51	14	15	2	4	9	55	43	.240	.329	.285
90	TAC/PCL	AAA	111	406	348	79	16	1	2	103	46	0	3	40	6	7	2	3	0	49	30	.227	.321	.296
	OAK/AL		25	15	14	1	0	0	0	1	0	0	0	4	0	0	0	0	0	0	0	.071	.133	.071
91	TAC/PCL	AAA	26	100	81	22	4	1	2	34	17	0	1	10	0	1	0	0	1	15	14	.272	.404	.420
	OAK/AL		90	265	235	56	5	1	0	63	14	0	3	37	3	12	1	3	4	21	21	.238	.289	.268
2 YR TOTALS			**115**	**280**	**249**	**57**	**5**	**1**	**0**	**64**	**15**	**0**	**3**	**41**	**3**	**12**	**1**	**3**	**4**	**21**	**21**	**.229**	**.280**	**.257**

Boston, Daryl Lamont — bats left — throws left — b.1/4/63 — 1991 positions: OF 115

YR	TM/LG	CL	G	TPA	AB	H	2B	3B	HR	TB	BB	IBB	HB	SO	GDP	SH	SF	SB	CS	R	RBI	BA	OBA	SA
84	DEN/AMA	AAA	127	550	471	147	21	19	15	251	65	1	2	82	10	1	11	40	17	94	82	.312	.390	.533
	CHI/AL		35	87	83	14	3	1	0	19	4	0	0	20	0	0	0	6	0	8	3	.169	.207	.229
85	BUF/AMA	AAA	63	281	241	66	12	1	10	110	33	0	4	48	4	2	1	15	5	45	36	.274	.369	.456
	CHI/AL		95	248	232	53	13	1	3	77	14	1	0	44	3	1	1	8	6	20	15	.228	.271	.332
86	BUF/AMA	AAA	96	411	360	109	16	3	5	146	42	4	1	45	3	1	5	38	10	57	41	.303	.374	.406
	CHI/AL		56	224	199	53	11	3	5	85	21	3	0	33	4	3	1	9	5	29	22	.266	.335	.427
87	HAW/PCL	AAA	21	88	77	23	3	0	5	41	10	1	1	10	0	0	0	10	6	14	13	.299	.386	.532
	CHI/AL		103	369	337	87	21	2	10	142	25	2	0	68	5	4	3	12	6	51	29	.258	.307	.421
88	CHI/AL		105	305	281	61	12	2	15	122	21	5	0	44	1	2	1	9	3	37	31	.217	.271	.434
89	CHI/AL		101	247	218	55	3	4	5	81	24	3	0	31	4	1	4	7	2	34	23	.252	.325	.372
90	CHI/AL		5	1	0	0	0	0	0	0	0	0	0	0	0	1	0	0	0	0	0	.000	.000	.000
	NY/NL		115	396	366	100	21	2	12	161	28	2	2	50	7	0	0	18	7	65	45	.273	.328	.440
	YEAR		120	397	367	100	21	2	12	161	28	2	2	50	7	0	0	19	7	65	45	.272	.327	.439
91	NY/NL		137	286	255	70	16	4	4	106	30	0	0	42	0	0	1	15	8	40	21	.275	.350	.416
8 YR TOTALS			**752**	**2163**	**1972**	**493**	**100**	**19**	**54**	**793**	**167**	**16**	**2**	**332**	**27**	**14**	**8**	**85**	**37**	**284**	**189**	**.250**	**.308**	**.402**

Bowie, James R. "Jim" — bats left — throws left — b.2/17/65 — 1991 positions: 1B System SEA/AL

YR	TM/LG	CL	G	TPA	AB	H	2B	3B	HR	TB	BB	IBB	HB	SO	GDP	SH	SF	SB	CS	R	RBI	BA	OBA	SA
86	BEL/NWL	A–	72	325	274	76	12	1	5	105	38	1	2	53	6	0	11	4	1	47	68	.277	.357	.383

Bowie, James R. "Jim" (continued)

YR	TM/LG	CL	G	TPA	AB	H	2B	3B	HR	TB	BB	IBB	HB	SO	GDP	SH	SF	SB	CS	R	RBI	BA	OBA	SA
87	WAU/MID	A	127	515	448	119	26	0	10	175	56	3	3	67	14	3	5	8	3	56	66	.266	.348	.391
88	SB/CAL	A+	139	599	529	154	28	0	15	227	58	5	1	84	14	1	10	8	5	76	102	.291	.356	.429
89	CAL/PCL	AAA	100	359	336	90	12	0	4	114	17	0	2	45	6	0	4	2	2	28	37	.268	.304	.339
	WIL/EAS	AA	11	47	42	11	5	0	0	16	5	0	0	7	0	0	0	0	0	3	1	.262	.340	.381
90	WIL/EAS	AA	128	504	446	122	18	0	5	155	51	6	3	47	15	1	3	0	2	45	48	.274	.350	.348
91	JAC/SOU	AA	123	491	448	139	25	0	10	194	36	2	1	67	16	1	6	3	3	51	67	.310	.357	.433
	CAL/PCL	AAA	14	52	50	17	3	0	1	23	2	0	0	8	1	0	0	0	0	9	7	.340	.365	.460

Bradley, Scott William — bats left — throws right — b.3/22/60 — 1991 positions: C 65, 3B 4, DH 2, 1B 1

YR	TM/LG	CL	G	TPA	AB	H	2B	3B	HR	TB	BB	IBB	HB	SO	GDP	SH	SF	SB	CS	R	RBI	BA	OBA	SA
84	COL/INT	AAA	138	584	538	180	31	2	6	233	33	7	2	31	15	5	6	1	2	84	84	.335	.371	.433
	NY/AL		9	22	21	6	1	0	0	7	1	0	0	1	0	0	0	0	0	3	2	.286	.318	.333
85	ALB/EAS	AA	6	26	24	3	1	0	0	4	2	0	0	1	0	0	0	0	0	4	1	.125	.192	.167
	NY/AL		19	51	49	8	2	1	0	12	1	0	1	5	2	0	0	0	0	2	2	.163	.196	.245
	COL/INT	AAA	43	176	163	49	10	0	4	71	8	2	1	12	5	0	4	2	0	17	27	.301	.330	.436
86	BUF/AMA	AAA	33	134	126	42	3	3	5	66	6	0	0	6	2	1	0	0	0	14	20	.333	.358	.524
	CHI/AL		9	24	21	6	0	0	0	6	1	0	0	2	1	0	0	0	0	3	0	.286	.375	.286
	SEA/AL		68	217	199	60	8	3	5	89	12	4	2	7	12	2	2	1	0	17	28	.302	.344	.447
	YEAR		77	241	220	66	8	3	5	95	13	4	2	9	13	2	2	1	0	20	28	.300	.347	.432
87	SEA/AL		102	366	342	95	15	1	5	127	15	1	5	18	13	2	4	0	1	34	43	.278	.310	.371
88	SEA/AL		103	359	335	86	17	1	4	117	17	1	2	16	11	3	2	1	1	45	33	.257	.295	.349
89	SEA/AL		103	299	270	74	16	0	3	99	21	4	1	23	5	1	6	1	1	21	37	.274	.322	.367
90	SEA/AL		101	257	233	52	9	0	1	64	15	0	3	20	6	3	6	0	1	11	28	.223	.264	.275
91	SEA/AL		83	198	172	35	7	0	0	42	19	2	0	19	2	5	2	0	0	10	11	.203	.280	.244
8 YR TOTALS			**597**	**1793**	**1642**	**422**	**75**	**6**	**18**	**563**	**102**	**14**	**11**	**109**	**52**	**16**	**22**	**3**	**6**	**148**	**183**	**.257**	**.301**	**.343**

Braggs, Glenn Erick — bats right — throws right — b.10/17/62 — 1991 positions: OF 74

YR	TM/LG	CL	G	TPA	AB	H	2B	3B	HR	TB	BB	IBB	HB	SO	GDP	SH	SF	SB	CS	R	RBI	BA	OBA	SA
84	STO/CAL	A+	108	479	399	118	29	2	15	196	66	4	6	87	4	0	8	9	1	76	86	.296	.397	.491
85	EP/TEX	AA	117	530	448	139	26	4	20	233	68	4	10	77	16	0	4	20	7	105	103	.310	.409	.520
86	VAN/PCL	AAA	90	377	325	117	26	6	15	200	45	2	5	32	8	0	2	22	7	80	75	.360	.443	.615
	MIL/AL		58	232	215	51	8	2	4	75	11	0	1	47	6	2	3	1	1	19	18	.237	.274	.349
87	MIL/AL		132	565	505	136	28	7	13	217	47	7	4	96	20	2	7	12	5	67	77	.269	.332	.430
88	MIL/AL		72	294	272	71	14	0	10	115	14	0	1	60	6	1	2	6	4	30	42	.261	.307	.423
89	MIL/AL		144	570	514	127	12	3	15	190	42	4	4	111	13	3	7	17	5	77	66	.247	.305	.370
90	MIL/AL		37	131	113	28	5	0	3	42	12	2	3	21	1	0	3	5	3	17	13	.248	.328	.372
	CIN/NL		72	231	201	60	9	1	6	89	26	1	3	43	3	0	1	3	4	22	28	.299	.385	.443
	YEAR		109	362	314	88	14	1	9	131	38	3	6	64	4	0	4	8	7	39	41	.280	.365	.417
91	CIN/NL		85	279	250	65	10	0	11	108	23	3	2	46	4	0	4	11	5	36	39	.260	.323	.432
6 YR TOTALS			**600**	**2302**	**2070**	**538**	**86**	**13**	**62**	**836**	**175**	**17**	**22**	**424**	**53**	**8**	**27**	**55**	**25**	**268**	**283**	**.260**	**.320**	**.404**

Bream, Sidney Eugene "Sid" — bats left — throws left — b.8/3/60 — 1991 positions: 1B 85

YR	TM/LG	CL	G	TPA	AB	H	2B	3B	HR	TB	BB	IBB	HB	SO	GDP	SH	SF	SB	CS	R	RBI	BA	OBA	SA
83	LA/NL		15	13	11	2	0	0	0	2	2	0	0	2	1	0	0	0	0	0	2	.182	.308	.182
84	ALB/PCL	AAA	114	506	429	147	25	4	20	240	67	7	1	62	8	1	8	2	2	82	90	.343	.426	.559
	LA/NL		27	58	49	9	3	0	0	12	6	2	0	9	1	1	2	1	0	2	6	.184	.263	.245
85	ALB/PCL	AAA	85	333	297	110	25	3	17	192	35	1	0	38	9	1	0	1	0	51	57	.370	.437	.646
	LA/NL		24	63	53	7	0	0	3	16	7	3	0	10	0	2	1	0	0	4	6	.132	.230	.302
	PIT/NL		26	108	95	27	7	0	3	43	11	2	0	14	4	1	1	0	0	14	15	.284	.355	.453
	YEAR		50	171	148	34	7	0	6	59	18	5	0	24	4	3	2	0	0	18	21	.230	.310	.399
86	PIT/NL		154	591	522	140	37	5	16	235	60	5	1	73	14	0	4	13	7	73	77	.268	.341	.450
87	PIT/NL		149	572	516	142	25	3	13	212	49	11	0	69	19	3	4	9	9	64	65	.275	.336	.411
88	PIT/NL		148	522	462	122	37	0	10	189	47	6	1	64	11	4	8	9	9	50	65	.264	.328	.409
89	PIT/NL		19	50	36	8	3	0	0	11	12	0	0	10	0	2	0	0	4	3	4	.222	.417	.306
90	PIT/NL		147	448	389	105	23	2	15	177	48	5	2	65	6	4	5	8	8	39	67	.270	.349	.455
91	ATL/NL		91	298	265	67	12	0	11	112	25	5	0	31	6	4	4	0	4	32	45	.253	.313	.423
9 YR TOTALS			**800**	**2723**	**2398**	**629**	**147**	**10**	**71**	**1009**	**267**	**39**	**4**	**347**	**64**	**22**	**32**	**40**	**37**	**281**	**352**	**.262**	**.333**	**.421**

Brett, George Howard — bats left — throws right — b.5/15/53 — 1991 positions: DH 118, 1B 10

YR	TM/LG	CL	G	TPA	AB	H	2B	3B	HR	TB	BB	IBB	HB	SO	GDP	SH	SF	SB	CS	R	RBI	BA	OBA	SA
73	KC/AL		13	41	40	5	2	0	0	7	0	0	0	5	0	1	0	0	0	2	0	.125	.125	.175
74	KC/AL		133	486	457	129	21	5	2	166	21	3	0	38	9	6	2	8	5	49	47	.282	.313	.363
75	KC/AL		159	697	634	195	35	13	11	289	46	6	2	49	8	9	6	13	10	84	89	.308	.353	.456
76	KC/AL		159	705	645	215	34	14	7	298	49	4	1	36	8	2	8	21	11	94	67	.333	.377	.462
77	KC/AL		139	627	564	176	32	13	22	300	55	9	2	24	12	3	3	14	12	105	88	.312	.373	.532
78	KC/AL		128	558	510	150	45	8	9	238	39	6	1	35	4	1	4	23	7	79	62	.294	.342	.467
79	KC/AL		154	701	645	212	42	20	23	363	51	14	0	36	8	1	4	17	10	119	107	.329	.376	.563
80	KC/AL		117	515	449	175	33	9	24	298	58	16	1	22	11	0	7	15	6	87	118	.390	.454	.664
81	KC/AL		89	379	347	109	27	7	6	168	27	7	1	23	7	0	4	14	6	42	43	.314	.361	.484
82	KC/AL		144	629	552	166	32	9	21	279	71	14	1	51	12	0	5	6	1	101	82	.301	.378	.505
83	KC/AL		123	525	464	144	38	2	25	261	57	13	1	39	9	0	5	0	1	90	93	.310	.385	.563
84	KC/AL		104	422	377	107	21	3	13	173	38	8	0	37	11	0	7	0	2	42	69	.284	.344	.459
85	KC/AL		155	665	550	184	38	5	30	322	103	31	3	49	12	0	4	9	1	108	112	.335	.436	.585
86	KC/AL		124	529	441	128	28	4	16	212	80	18	1	45	6	0	1	1	2	70	73	.290	.401	.481
87	KC/AL		115	508	427	124	18	2	22	212	72	14	1	47	10	0	8	6	3	71	78	.290	.388	.496

(continued)

Brett, George Howard (continued)

YR	TM/LG	CL	G	TPA	AB	H	2B	3B	HR	TB	BB	IBB	HB	SO	GDP	SH	SF	SB	CS	R	RBI	BA	OBA	SA
88	KC/AL		157	681	589	180	42	3	24	300	82	15	3	51	15	0	7	14	3	90	103	.306	.389	.509
89	KC/AL		124	528	457	129	26	3	12	197	59	14	3	47	18	0	9	14	4	67	80	.282	.362	.431
90	KC/AL		142	607	544	179	45	7	14	280	56	14	0	63	18	0	7	9	2	82	87	.329	.387	.515
91	KC/AL		131	572	505	129	40	2	10	203	58	10	0	75	20	1	8	2	0	77	61	.255	.327	.402
19 YR TOTALS			**2410**	**10375**	**9197**	**2836**	**599**	**129**	**291**	**4566**	**1022**	**214**	**24**	**772**	**200**	**26**	**106**	**186**	**86**	**1459**	**1459**	**.308**	**.375**	**.496**

Brewer, Rodney Lee "Rod" — bats left — throws left — b.2/24/66 — 1991 positions: 1B 15, OF 3

YR	TM/LG	CL	G	TPA	AB	H	2B	3B	HR	TB	BB	IBB	HB	SO	GDP	SH	SF	SB	CS	R	RBI	BA	OBA	SA
87	JC/APP	R+	67	279	238	60	11	2	10	105	36	5	3	40	4	0	2	2	2	33	42	.252	.355	.441
88	SPR/MID	A	133	530	457	136	25	2	8	189	63	7	5	52	22	1	4	6	4	57	64	.298	.386	.414
89	ARK/TEX	AA	128	526	470	130	25	2	10	189	46	3	7	46	8	0	3	2	3	71	93	.277	.348	.402
90	LOU/AMA	AAA	144	583	514	129	15	5	12	190	54	7	9	62	9	0	6	0	2	60	83	.251	.329	.370
	STL/NL		14	25	25	6	1	0	0	7	0	0	0	4	1	0	0	0	0	4	2	.240	.240	.280
91	LOU/AMA	AAA	104	424	382	86	21	1	8	133	35	1	6	57	10	0	1	4	0	39	52	.225	.300	.348
	STL/NL		19	13	13	1	0	0	0	1	0	0	0	5	0	0	0	0	0	0	1	.077	.077	.077
2 YR TOTALS			**33**	**38**	**38**	**7**	**1**	**0**	**0**	**8**	**0**	**0**	**0**	**9**	**1**	**0**	**0**	**0**	**0**	**4**	**3**	**.184**	**.184**	**.211**

Briley, Gregory "Greg" or "Peewee" — bats left — throws right — b.5/24/65 — 1991 positions: OF 125, DH 2, 2B 1, 3B 1

YR	TM/LG	CL	G	TPA	AB	H	2B	3B	HR	TB	BB	IBB	HB	SO	GDP	SH	SF	SB	CS	R	RBI	BA	OBA	SA
86	BEL/NWL	A–	63	278	218	65	12	4	7	106	50	1	3	29	1	0	7	26	5	52	46	.298	.424	.486
87	CHT/SOU	AA	137	592	539	148	21	5	7	200	41	1	2	58	10	2	8	34	14	81	61	.275	.324	.371
88	SEA/AL		13	42	36	9	2	0	1	14	5	1	0	6	0	0	1	0	1	6	4	.250	.333	.389
	CAL/PCL	AAA	112	497	445	139	29	9	11	219	40	5	3	51	2	2	7	27	10	74	66	.312	.368	.492
89	CAL/PCL	AAA	25	109	94	32	8	1	4	54	13	1	2	10	8	0	0	14	1	27	20	.340	.431	.574
	SEA/AL		115	444	394	105	22	4	13	174	39	1	5	82	9	1	5	11	5	52	52	.266	.336	.442
90	SEA/AL		125	380	337	83	18	2	5	120	37	0	1	48	4	1	4	16	4	40	29	.246	.319	.356
91	SEA/AL		139	412	381	99	17	3	2	128	27	0	0	51	7	1	3	23	11	39	26	.260	.307	.336
4 YR TOTALS			**392**	**1278**	**1148**	**296**	**59**	**9**	**21**	**436**	**108**	**2**	**6**	**187**	**22**	**3**	**13**	**50**	**21**	**137**	**111**	**.258**	**.322**	**.380**

Brito, Bernardo — bats right — throws right — b.12/4/63 — 1991 positions: DH System MIN/AL

YR	TM/LG	CL	G	TPA	AB	H	2B	3B	HR	TB	BB	IBB	HB	SO	GDP	SH	SF	SB	CS	R	RBI	BA	OBA	SA
81	BAT/NYP	A–	12	33	29	6	0	0	0	6	2	0	1	9	1	0	1	0	0	1	2	.207	.281	.207
82	BAT/NYP	A–	41	136	123	29	2	0	4	43	8	0	1	34	3	1	2	1	0	10	15	.236	.289	.350
83	WAT/MID	A	35	132	119	24	4	0	4	40	10	1	1	40	2	1	1	3	2	13	17	.202	.267	.336
	BAT/NYP	A–	60	229	206	50	10	3	7	87	15	1	5	65	6	2	1	5	1	18	34	.243	.308	.422
84	BAT/NYP	A–	76	314	297	89	19	3	19	171	14	1	1	67	7	2	0	3	4	41	57	.300	.333	.576
85	WAT/MID	A	135	529	498	128	27	1	29	244	24	1	4	133	15	0	3	1	4	66	78	.257	.295	.490
86	WAT/EAS	AA	129	510	479	118	17	1	18	191	22	0	2	127	10	3	2	1	2	61	75	.246	.282	.399
87	WIL/EAS	AA	124	487	452	125	20	4	24	225	24	2	5	121	15	0	6	2	6	64	79	.277	.316	.498
88	ORL/SOU	AA	135	538	508	122	20	4	24	222	20	2	1	138	12	0	9	2	2	55	76	.240	.266	.437
89	POR/PCL	AAA	111	394	355	90	12	7	22	182	31	4	4	111	7	2	2	1	3	51	74	.254	.319	.513
90	POR/PCL	AAA	113	411	376	106	26	3	25	213	27	3	2	102	13	2	4	1	4	48	79	.282	.330	.566
91	POR/PCL	AAA	115	470	428	111	17	2	21	213	28	2	7	110	9	0	7	1	0	65	83	.259	.311	.498

Brock, Gregory Allen "Greg" — bats left — throws right — b.6/14/57 — 1991 positions: 1B 25

YR	TM/LG	CL	G	TPA	AB	H	2B	3B	HR	TB	BB	IBB	HB	SO	GDP	SH	SF	SB	CS	R	RBI	BA	OBA	SA
82	LA/NL		18	18	17	2	1	0	0	3	1	1	0	5	0	0	0	0	0	1	1	.118	.167	.176
83	LA/NL		146	543	455	102	14	2	20	180	83	12	1	81	13	0	4	5	1	64	66	.224	.343	.396
84	ALB/PCL	AAA	24	107	93	29	7	0	6	54	14	4	0	9	4	0	0	2	1	19	15	.312	.402	.581
	LA/NL		88	313	271	61	6	0	14	109	39	3	0	37	6	0	3	8	0	33	34	.225	.319	.402
85	LA/NL		129	496	438	110	19	0	21	192	54	4	0	72	9	2	2	4	2	64	66	.251	.332	.438
86	LA/NL		115	367	325	76	13	0	16	137	37	5	0	60	5	1	4	2	5	33	52	.234	.309	.422
87	MIL/AL		141	602	532	159	29	3	13	233	57	4	6	63	9	4	5	4	5	81	85	.299	.371	.438
88	MIL/AL		115	437	364	77	16	1	6	113	63	16	3	48	11	3	4	6	2	53	50	.212	.329	.310
89	BEL/MID	A	16	65	52	18	2	0	2	26	11	0	1	5	0	0	1	0	0	10	10	.346	.477	.500
	MIL/AL		107	422	373	99	16	0	12	151	43	7	2	49	10	2	2	6	1	40	52	.265	.345	.405
90	MIL/AL		123	422	367	91	23	0	7	135	43	9	2	45	6	2	8	4	4	42	50	.248	.324	.368
91	MIL/AL		31	75	60	17	4	0	1	24	14	1	0	9	1	1	0	1	1	9	6	.283	.419	.400
	VAN/PCL	AAA	2	8	7	1	0	0	0	1	1	0	0	1	0	0	0	0	0	0	0	.143	.250	.143
10 YR TOTALS			**1013**	**3695**	**3202**	**794**	**141**	**6**	**110**	**1277**	**434**	**63**	**15**	**469**	**70**	**15**	**29**	**41**	**18**	**420**	**462**	**.248**	**.338**	**.399**

Brogna, Rico Joseph — bats left — throws left — b.4/18/70 — 1991 positions: 1B System DET/AL

YR	TM/LG	CL	G	TPA	AB	H	2B	3B	HR	TB	BB	IBB	HB	SO	GDP	SH	SF	SB	CS	R	RBI	BA	OBA	SA
88	BRI/APP	R+	60	239	209	53	11	2	7	89	25	2	2	42	3	2	1	3	4	37	33	.254	.338	.426
89	LAK/FSL	A+	128	505	459	108	20	7	5	157	38	6	2	82	10	3	3	2	4	47	51	.235	.295	.342
90	LON/EAS	AA	137	549	488	128	21	3	21	218	50	8	3	100	13	3	5	1	2	70	77	.262	.332	.447
91	LON/EAS	AA	77	326	293	80	13	1	13	134	25	2	2	59	7	3	5	0	1	40	51	.273	.325	.457
	TOL/INT	AAA	41	138	132	29	5	1	2	42	4	2	1	26	9	1	0	0	1	13	13	.220	.248	.318

Brooks, Hubert "Hubie" — bats right — throws right — b.9/24/56 — 1991 positions: OF 100

YR	TM/LG	CL	G	TPA	AB	H	2B	3B	HR	TB	BB	IBB	HB	SO	GDP	SH	SF	SB	CS	R	RBI	BA	OBA	SA
80	NY/NL		24	89	81	25	2	1	1	32	5	0	2	9	1	1	0	1	1	8	10	.309	.364	.395
81	NY/NL		98	389	358	110	21	2	4	147	23	2	1	65	9	1	1	9	1	34	38	.307	.345	.411
82	NY/NL		126	498	457	114	21	2	2	145	28	5	5	76	11	3	5	3	5	40	40	.249	.297	.317
83	NY/NL		150	624	586	147	18	4	5	188	24	2	4	96	14	7	3	6	4	53	58	.251	.284	.321

Brooks, Hubert "Hubie" (continued)

YR	TM/LG	CL	G	TPA	AB	H	2B	3B	HR	TB	BB	IBB	HB	SO	GDP	SH	SF	SB	CS	R	RBI	BA	OBA	SA
84	NY/NL		153	613	561	159	23	2	16	234	48	15	2	79	17	0	2	6	5	61	73	.283	.341	.417
85	MON/NL		156	652	605	163	34	7	13	250	34	6	5	79	20	0	8	6	9	67	100	.269	.310	.413
86	MON/NL		80	338	306	104	18	5	14	174	25	3	2	60	11	0	5	4	2	50	58	.340	.388	.569
87	MON/NL		112	459	430	113	22	3	14	183	24	2	1	72	7	0	4	4	3	57	72	.263	.301	.426
88	MON/NL		151	628	588	164	35	2	20	263	35	3	1	108	21	0	4	7	3	61	90	.279	.318	.447
89	MON/NL		148	593	542	145	30	1	14	219	39	2	4	108	15	0	8	6	11	56	70	.268	.317	.404
90	LA/NL		153	618	568	151	28	1	20	241	33	10	6	108	13	0	11	2	5	74	91	.266	.307	.424
91	NY/NL		103	407	357	85	11	1	16	146	44	8	3	62	7	0	3	3	1	48	50	.238	.324	.409
12 YR TOTALS			1454	5908	5439	1480	263	31	139	2222	362	58	36	922	146	12	59	60	52	609	750	**.272**	**.319**	**.409**

Brosius, Scott David — bats right — throws right — b.8/15/66 — 1991 positions: 2B 18, OF 13, 3B 7, DH 1

YR	TM/LG	CL	G	TPA	AB	H	2B	3B	HR	TB	BB	IBB	HB	SO	GDP	SH	SF	SB	CS	R	RBI	BA	OBA	SA
87	MED/NWL	A–	65	289	255	73	18	1	3	102	26	0	0	36	7	1	7	5	2	34	49	.286	.344	.400
88	MAD/MID	A	132	571	504	153	28	2	9	212	56	1	3	67	7	4	4	13	12	82	58	.304	.374	.421
89	HUN/SOU	AA	128	536	461	125	22	2	7	172	58	3	5	62	11	6	6	4	6	68	60	.271	.355	.373
90	HUN/SOU	AA	142	645	547	162	39	2	23	274	81	2	7	81	8	7	9	12	3	94	88	.296	.382	.501
	TAC/PCL	AAA	3	8	7	1	0	0	0	3	1	0	0	3	0	0	0	0	0	2	0	.143	.250	.429
91	TAC/PCL	AAA	65	268	245	70	16	3	8	116	18	0	2	29	7	1	2	4	2	28	31	.286	.337	.473
	OAK/AL		36	72	68	16	5	0	2	27	3	0	0	11	2	1	0	3	1	9	4	.235	.268	.397

Brown, Jarvis Ardel — bats right — throws right — b.3/26/67 — 1991 positions: OF 32, DH 4

YR	TM/LG	CL	G	TPA	AB	H	2B	3B	HR	TB	BB	IBB	HB	SO	GDP	SH	SF	SB	CS	R	RBI	BA	OBA	SA
86	ELI/APP	R+	49	208	180	41	4	0	3	54	18	0	4	41	3	5	1	15	3	28	23	.228	.310	.300
87	ELI/APP	R+	67	314	258	63	9	1	1	77	48	1	5	50	3	3	0	30	2	52	15	.244	.373	.298
88	KEN/MID	A	43	141	117	22	4	1	3	37	19	0	2	24	2	1	2	6	2	17	16	.188	.307	.316
	KEN/MID	A	138	624	531	156	25	7	7	216	71	0	10	89	10	7	5	72	15	108	45	.294	.384	.407
89	VIS/CAL	A+	141	639	545	131	21	6	4	176	73	0	13	112	12	4	4	49	13	95	46	.240	.342	.323
90	ORL/SOU	AA	135	623	527	137	22	7	14	215	80	1	9	79	13	5	2	33	19	104	57	.260	.366	.408
91	POR/PCL	AAA	108	482	436	126	5	8	3	156	36	1	6	66	0	1	3	26	12	62	37	.289	.351	.358
	MIN/AL		38	40	37	8	0	0	0	8	2	0	0	8	0	0	1	1	0	10	0	.216	.256	.216

Browne, Jerome Austin "Jerry" — bats both — throws right — b.2/13/66 — 1991 positions: 2B 47, OF 17, 3B 15, DH 7

YR	TM/LG	CL	G	TPA	AB	H	2B	3B	HR	TB	BB	IBB	HB	SO	GDP	SH	SF	SB	CS	R	RBI	BA	OBA	SA
84	BUR/MID	A	127	501	420	99	10	1	0	111	71	0	1	76	7	7	2	31	8	70	18	.236	.346	.264
85	SAL/CAR	A+	122	545	460	123	18	4	3	158	82	2	1	62	8	1	1	24	16	69	58	.267	.379	.343
86	TUL/TEX	AA	128	559	491	149	15	7	2	184	62	1	0	61	10	5	1	39	11	82	57	.303	.381	.375
	TEX/AL		12	25	24	10	2	0	0	12	1	0	0	4	0	0	0	0	2	6	3	.417	.440	.500
87	TEX/AL		132	526	454	123	16	6	1	154	61	0	2	50	7	7	2	27	17	63	38	.271	.358	.339
88	OC/AMA	AAA	76	329	286	72	15	2	5	106	37	2	4	29	9	4	2	14	5	26	17	.252	.335	.371
	TEX/AL		73	243	214	49	9	2	1	65	25	0	2	32	5	3	1	7	5	26	17	.229	.308	.304
89	CLE/AL		153	685	598	179	31	4	5	233	68	10	1	64	9	14	4	14	6	83	45	.299	.370	.390
90	CLE/AL		140	610	513	137	26	5	6	191	72	1	2	46	12	12	11	12	7	92	50	.267	.353	.372
91	CLE/AL		107	334	290	66	15	2	1	78	27	0	1	29	5	12	4	2	4	28	29	.228	.292	.269
6 YR TOTALS			617	2423	2093	564	89	19	14	733	254	11	6	225	37	48	22	62	41	298	182	**.269**	**.347**	**.350**

Bruett, Joseph Timothy "J.T." — bats left — throws left — b.10/8/67 — 1991 positions: OF System MIN/AL

YR	TM/LG	CL	G	TPA	AB	H	2B	3B	HR	TB	BB	IBB	HB	SO	GDP	SH	SF	SB	CS	R	RBI	BA	OBA	SA
88	ELI/APP	R+	28	110	91	27	3	0	0	30	19	0	0	15	3	0	0	17	4	23	3	.297	.418	.330
	KEN/MID	A	3	13	10	2	0	0	0	2	3	0	0	0	0	0	0	1	1	2	0	.200	.385	.200
89	KEN/MID	A	120	537	445	119	9	1	3	139	89	2	0	64	6	2	1	61	27	82	29	.267	.389	.312
90	POR/PCL	AAA	10	46	34	8	2	0	0	10	11	0	0	4	0	0	1	2	1	8	3	.235	.413	.294
	VIS/CAL	A+	123	553	437	134	15	3	1	158	101	4	4	60	8	1	9	50	21	86	33	.307	.439	.362
91	POR/PCL	AAA	99	397	345	98	6	3	0	110	40	1	3	41	10	9	0	21	9	51	35	.284	.363	.319

Brumley, Anthony Michael "Mike" — bats both — throws right — b.4/9/63 — 1991 positions: SS 31, 3B 17, 2B 7, OF 4

YR	TM/LG	CL	G	TPA	AB	H	2B	3B	HR	TB	BB	IBB	HB	SO	GDP	SH	SF	SB	CS	R	RBI	BA	OBA	SA
83	WH/FSL	A+	44	177	153	48	6	4	1	65	16	0	3	31	2	2	3	4	3	25	18	.314	.383	.425
84	NB/EAS	AA	34	142	121	28	6	2	0	38	18	0	1	33	5	2	1	3	0	14	9	.231	.329	.314
	MID/TEX	AA	73	305	255	55	11	3	6	90	48	3	1	49	2	1	1	5	2	37	21	.216	.339	.353
85	PIT/EAS	AA	131	545	460	127	23	14	3	187	74	5	2	95	8	2	9	29	7	66	58	.276	.370	.407
86	IOW/AMA	AAA	139	530	458	103	21	5	10	164	63	3	0	102	5	5	4	35	14	74	44	.225	.316	.358
87	IOW/AMA	AAA	92	360	319	81	20	5	6	129	35	1	1	61	4	3	2	27	10	44	42	.254	.328	.404
	CHI/NL		39	117	104	21	2	2	1	30	10	1	1	30	2	1	1	7	1	8	9	.202	.276	.288
88	LV/PCL	AAA	113	486	425	134	16	7	3	173	56	2	0	84	6	3	2	41	14	77	41	.315	.393	.407
89	TOL/INT	AAA	8	30	26	6	2	2	0	12	3	0	1	3	1	0	0	0	0	4	1	.231	.333	.462
	DET/AL		92	230	212	42	5	2	1	54	14	0	1	45	4	1	1	8	4	33	11	.198	.251	.255
90	CAL/PCL	AAA	8	29	28	9	1	0	0	10	1	0	0	3	1	0	0	0	0	4	1	.321	.345	.357
	SEA/AL		62	162	147	33	5	4	0	46	10	0	1	22	5	4	1	8	0	19	7	.224	.272	.313
91	PAW/INT	AAA	32	134	108	29	2	3	4	47	24	2	0	22	2	2	0	8	0	25	16	.269	.406	.435
	BOS/AL		63	132	118	25	5	0	0	30	10	0	1	22	0	2	1	2	0	16	5	.212	.273	.254
4 YR TOTALS			256	641	581	121	17	8	2	160	44	1	2	119	11	12	2	19	5	76	32	**.208**	**.266**	**.275**

Brunansky, Thomas Andrew "Tom" — bats right — throws right — b.8/20/60 — 1991 positions: OF 137, DH 1

YR	TM/LG	CL	G	TPA	AB	H	2B	3B	HR	TB	BB	IBB	HB	SO	GDP	SH	SF	SB	CS	R	RBI	BA	OBA	SA
81	CAL/AL		11	41	33	5	0	0	3	14	8	0	0	10	0	0	0	0	0	7	6	.152	.317	.424

(continued)

Brunansky, Thomas Andrew "Tom" (continued)

YR	TM/LG	CL	G	TPA	AB	H	2B	3B	HR	TB	BB	IBB	HB	SO	GDP	SH	SF	SB	CS	R	RBI	BA	OBA	SA
82	MIN/AL		127	545	463	126	30	1	20	218	71	0	8	101	12	1	2	1	2	77	46	.272	.377	.471
83	MIN/AL		151	611	542	123	24	5	28	241	61	4	4	95	13	1	3	2	5	70	82	.227	.308	.445
84	MIN/AL		155	628	567	144	21	0	32	261	57	2	0	94	15	0	4	4	5	75	85	.254	.320	.460
85	MIN/AL		157	651	567	137	28	4	27	254	71	7	0	86	12	0	13	5	3	71	90	.242	.320	.448
86	MIN/AL		157	655	593	152	28	1	23	251	53	4	1	98	15	1	7	12	4	69	75	.256	.315	.423
87	MIN/AL		155	614	532	138	22	2	32	260	74	5	0	104	12	0	4	11	11	83	85	.259	.352	.489
88	MIN/AL		14	56	49	9	1	0	1	13	7	0	0	11	0	0	0	1	2	5	6	.184	.286	.265
	STL/NL		143	613	523	128	22	4	22	224	79	6	4	82	17	1	6	16	6	69	79	.245	.345	.428
	YEAR		157	669	572	137	23	4	23	237	86	6	4	93	17	1	6	17	6	74	85	.240	.340	.414
89	STL/NL		158	622	556	133	29	3	20	228	59	3	2	107	10	0	5	5	5	67	85	.239	.312	.410
90	STL/NL		19	71	57	9	3	0	1	15	12	0	1	10	1	0	1	0	0	5	2	.158	.310	.263
	BOS/AL		129	526	461	123	24	5	15	202	54	7	3	105	12	0	8	5	10	61	71	.267	.342	.438
	YEAR		148	597	518	132	27	5	16	217	66	7	4	115	13	0	9	5	10	66	73	.255	.338	.419
91	BOS/AL		142	519	459	105	24	1	16	179	49	2	3	72	8	0	8	1	2	54	70	.229	.303	.390
11 YR TOTALS			**1518**	**6152**	**5402**	**1332**	**256**	**26**	**240**	**2360**	**655**	**40**	**30**	**975**	**127**	**4**	**61**	**64**	**59**	**713**	**782**	**.247**	**.328**	**.437**

Bryant, Scott Walter — bats right — throws right — b.10/31/67 — 1991 positions: OF System CIN/NL

YR	TM/LG	CL	G	TPA	AB	H	2B	3B	HR	TB	BB	IBB	HB	SO	GDP	SH	SF	SB	CS	R	RBI	BA	OBA	SA
89	CR/MID	A	49	218	186	47	7	0	9	81	30	0	0	46	7	1	1	2	4	26	39	.253	.355	.435
90	CR/MID	A	67	266	212	56	10	3	14	114	50	5	1	47	7	0	3	6	4	40	48	.264	.402	.538
	CHT/SOU	AA	44	155	131	41	10	3	6	75	22	0	1	28	5	0	0	1	1	23	30	.313	.419	.573
91	CHT/SOU	AA	91	345	306	93	14	6	8	143	34	1	3	77	8	0	2	3	1	42	43	.304	.377	.467

Buechele, Steven Bernard "Steve" — bats right — throws right — b.9/26/61 — 1991 positions: 3B 142

YR	TM/LG	CL	G	TPA	AB	H	2B	3B	HR	TB	BB	IBB	HB	SO	GDP	SH	SF	SB	CS	R	RBI	BA	OBA	SA
84	OC/AMA	AAA	131	499	447	118	25	3	7	170	36	3	4	71	14	7	5	7	2	48	59	.264	.321	.380
85	OC/AMA	AAA	89	389	350	104	20	7	9	165	33	2	4	62	11	0	2	6	3	56	64	.297	.362	.471
	TEX/AL		69	236	219	48	6	3	6	78	14	2	2	38	11	0	1	3	3	22	21	.219	.271	.356
86	TEX/AL		153	513	461	112	19	2	18	189	35	1	5	98	10	9	3	5	8	54	54	.243	.302	.410
87	TEX/AL		136	400	363	86	20	0	13	145	28	3	1	66	7	4	4	1	2	45	50	.237	.290	.399
88	TEX/AL		155	579	503	126	21	4	16	203	65	6	5	79	8	4	2	2	2	68	58	.250	.342	.404
89	TEX/AL		155	530	486	114	22	2	16	188	36	6	5	107	21	2	1	1	2	60	59	.235	.294	.387
90	OC/AMA	AAA	6	23	21	3	0	0	1	6	2	0	0	4	1	0	0	0	0	1	1	.143	.217	.286
	TEX/AL		91	289	251	54	10	0	7	85	27	1	2	63	5	7	2	1	0	30	30	.215	.294	.339
91	TEX/AL		121	472	416	111	17	2	18	186	39	4	5	69	11	10	2	0	4	58	66	.267	.335	.447
	PIT/NL		31	128	114	28	5	1	4	47	10	0	2	28	3	1	1	0	1	16	19	.246	.315	.412
	YEAR		152	600	530	139	22	3	22	233	49	4	7	97	14	11	3	0	5	74	85	.262	.331	.440
7 YR TOTALS			**911**	**3147**	**2813**	**679**	**120**	**14**	**98**	**1121**	**254**	**17**	**27**	**548**	**76**	**39**	**14**	**14**	**24**	**353**	**357**	**.241**	**.309**	**.399**

Buhner, Jay Campbell — bats right — throws right — b.8/13/64 — 1991 positions: OF 131

YR	TM/LG	CL	G	TPA	AB	H	2B	3B	HR	TB	BB	IBB	HB	SO	GDP	SH	SF	SB	CS	R	RBI	BA	OBA	SA
84	WAT/NYP	A−	65	274	229	74	16	3	9	123	42	4	1	58	3	0	2	3	1	43	58	.323	.427	.537
85	FL/FSL	A+	117	481	409	121	18	10	11	192	65	4	2	76	12	1	4	6	4	65	76	.296	.392	.469
86	FL/FSL	A+	36	155	139	42	9	1	7	74	15	1	1	30	5	0	1	1	0	24	31	.302	.368	.532
87	COL/INT	AAA	134	563	502	140	23	1	31	258	55	6	2	124	14	2	2	4	2	83	85	.279	.351	.514
	NY/AL		7	23	22	5	2	0	0	7	1	0	0	6	1	0	0	0	0	0	1	.227	.261	.318
88	NY/AL		25	76	69	13	0	0	3	22	3	0	3	25	1	1	0	0	0	8	13	.188	.250	.319
	COL/INT	AAA	38	152	129	33	5	0	8	62	19	3	3	33	2	0	1	1	1	26	18	.256	.362	.481
	SEA/AL		60	223	192	43	13	1	10	88	25	1	3	68	4	1	2	1	1	28	25	.224	.320	.458
	YEAR		85	299	261	56	13	1	13	110	28	1	6	93	5	1	2	1	1	36	38	.215	.302	.421
89	CAL/PCL	AAA	56	243	196	61	12	1	11	108	44	1	0	56	1	0	3	4	4	43	45	.311	.432	.551
	SEA/AL		58	226	204	56	15	1	9	100	19	0	2	55	5	0	0	1	1	27	33	.275	.341	.490
90	CAL/PCL	AAA	13	42	34	7	1	0	1	11	7	0	0	11	0	0	1	1	4	6	5	.206	.333	.412
	SEA/AL		51	185	163	45	12	0	7	78	17	1	4	50	6	0	1	0	2	16	33	.276	.357	.479
91	SEA/AL		137	471	406	99	14	4	27	202	53	5	6	117	10	0	1	2	4	64	77	.244	.337	.498
5 YR TOTALS			**338**	**1204**	**1056**	**261**	**56**	**6**	**56**	**497**	**118**	**7**	**18**	**321**	**22**	**3**	**9**	**4**	**8**	**143**	**182**	**.247**	**.331**	**.471**

Bullett, Scott Douglas — bats both — throws left — b.12/25/68 — 1991 positions: OF 3

YR	TM/LG	CL	G	TPA	AB	H	2B	3B	HR	TB	BB	IBB	HB	SO	GDP	SH	SF	SB	CS	R	RBI	BA	OBA	SA
88	PIR/GCL	R	21	70	61	11	1	0	0	12	7	1	0	9	0	1	1	2	5	6	8	.180	.261	.197
89	PIR/GCL	R	46	183	165	42	7	3	1	58	12	1	2	31	2	1	1	15	5	24	16	.255	.324	.352
90	WEL/NYP	A−	74	272	256	77	11	4	3	105	13	2	2	50	1	1	0	30	6	46	33	.301	.339	.410
91	AUG/SAL	A	95	415	384	109	21	6	1	145	27	2	2	79	1	1	1	48	17	61	36	.284	.333	.378
	SAL/CAR	A+	39	164	156	52	7	5	2	75	8	1	0	29	0	0	0	15	7	22	15	.333	.366	.481
	PIT/NL		11	5	4	0	0	0	0	0	0	0	0	3	0	0	0	1	1	2	0	.000	.200	.000

Bullock, Eric Gerald — bats left — throws left — b.2/16/60 — 1991 positions: OF 9, 1B 3

YR	TM/LG	CL	G	TPA	AB	H	2B	3B	HR	TB	BB	IBB	HB	SO	GDP	SH	SF	SB	CS	R	RBI	BA	OBA	SA
81	AST/GCL	R	56	218	184	54	8	3	1	0	34	0	0	23	0	0	0	24	0	38	15	.293	.404	.000
	DB/FSL	A+	1	3	2	1	1	0	0	0	0	0	0	0	0	0	0	0	0	1	1	.500	.667	.000
82	DB/FSL	A+	117	486	442	150	24	11	5	0	44	0	0	55	0	0	0	45	0	90	85	.339	.399	.000
	COL/SOU	AA	18	73	66	20	1	0	2	0	7	0	0	10	0	0	0	6	0	6	13	.303	.370	.000
83	COL/SOU	AA	130	544	475	131	15	6	9	0	69	0	0	63	0	0	0	53	0	65	59	.276	.368	.000
84	COL/SOU	AA	71	307	265	77	15	2	3	105	36	4	1	23	11	3	4	41	7	47	41	.291	.373	.396
	TUC/PCL	AAA	60	208	185	51	6	2	1	64	20	1	0	18	2	2	0	7	4	22	16	.276	.350	.346

Bullock, Eric Gerald (continued)

YR	TM/LG	CL	G	TPA	AB	H	2B	3B	HR	TB	BB	IBB	HB	SO	GDP	SH	SF	SB	CS	R	RBI	BA	OBA	SA
85	TUC/PCL	AAA	124	523	467	149	26	8	4	203	45	7	7	50	7	1	3	48	14	81	57	.319	.385	.435
	HOU/NL		18	26	25	7	2	0	0	9	1	0	0	3	0	0	0	0	1	3	2	.280	.308	.360
86	HOU/NL		6	21	21	1	0	0	0	1	0	0	0	3	0	0	0	2	0	0	1	.048	.048	.048
	TUC/PCL	AAA	42	177	151	58	8	2	3	79	22	5	1	15	4	1	2	14	8	28	21	.384	.460	.523
87	TUC/PCL	AAA	39	131	115	28	5	3	0	39	14	0	1	11	2	0	1	7	2	15	10	.243	.328	.339
	POR/PCL	AAA	67	246	215	60	8	3	2	80	28	7	1	16	10	1	1	7	5	27	24	.279	.363	.372
88	POR/PCL	AAA	117	483	434	134	20	8	2	176	40	2	1	43	11	2	6	51	18	69	46	.309	.364	.406
	MIN/AL		16	20	17	5	0	0	0	5	3	0	0	1	0	0	0	1	0	1	0	.294	.400	.294
89	PHI/NL		6	4	4	0	0	0	0	0	0	0	0	2	0	0	0	0	0	0	0	.000	.000	.000
	SCR/INT	AAA	80	305	281	77	10	8	3	112	18	5	1	30	7	2	3	16	7	37	40	.274	.317	.399
90	MON/NL		4	2	2	1	0	0	0	1	0	0	0	0	0	0	0	1	0	0	0	.500	.500	.500
	IND/AMA	AAA	107	470	434	122	19	7	3	164	32	4	2	43	8	0	2	40	16	62	32	.281	.332	.378
91	MON/NL		73	82	72	16	4	0	1	23	9	0	0	13	3	0	1	6	1	6	6	.222	.305	.319
6 YR TOTALS			**123**	**155**	**141**	**30**	**6**	**0**	**1**	**39**	**13**	**0**	**0**	**22**	**3**	**0**	**1**	**9**	**2**	**13**	**12**	**.213**	**.277**	**.277**

Burks, Ellis Rena — bats right — throws right — b.9/11/64 — 1991 positions: OF 126, DH 2

YR	TM/LG	CL	G	TPA	AB	H	2B	3B	HR	TB	BB	IBB	HB	SO	GDP	SH	SF	SB	CS	R	RBI	BA	OBA	SA
84	WH/FSL	A+	112	425	375	96	15	4	6	137	42	1	5	68	8	1	2	29	8	52	43	.256	.337	.365
85	NB/EAS	AA	133	527	476	121	25	7	10	190	42	0	3	85	5	2	4	17	14	66	61	.254	.316	.399
86	NB/EAS	AA	124	513	462	126	20	3	14	194	44	3	2	75	4	3	2	31	9	70	55	.273	.337	.420
87	PAW/INT	AAA	11	47	40	9	3	1	3	23	7	0	0	7	1	0	0	1	0	11	6	.225	.340	.575
	BOS/AL		133	606	558	152	30	2	20	246	41	0	2	98	4	1	4	27	6	94	59	.272	.324	.441
88	BOS/AL		144	615	540	159	37	5	18	260	62	1	3	89	8	4	6	25	9	93	92	.294	.367	.481
89	PAW/INT	AAA	5	23	21	3	1	0	0	4	2	0	0	1	0	0	0	0	0	4	0	.143	.217	.190
	BOS/AL		97	446	399	121	19	6	12	188	36	2	5	52	8	2	4	21	5	73	61	.303	.365	.471
90	BOS/AL		152	641	588	174	33	8	21	286	48	4	1	82	18	2	2	9	11	89	89	.296	.349	.486
91	BOS/AL		130	524	474	119	33	3	14	200	39	2	6	81	4	2	3	6	11	56	56	.251	.314	.422
5 YR TOTALS			**656**	**2832**	**2559**	**725**	**152**	**24**	**85**	**1180**	**226**	**9**	**17**	**402**	**42**	**14**	**16**	**88**	**42**	**405**	**357**	**.283**	**.344**	**.461**

Burnitz, Jeromy Neal — bats left — throws right — b.4/14/69 — 1991 positions: OF System NY/NL

YR	TM/LG	CL	G	TPA	AB	H	2B	3B	HR	TB	BB	IBB	HB	SO	GDP	SH	SF	SB	CS	R	RBI	BA	OBA	SA
90	PIT/NYP	A–	51	225	173	52	6	5	6	86	45	5	3	39	3	0	4	12	5	37	22	.301	.444	.497
	SL/FSL	A+	11	43	32	5	1	0	0	6	7	0	4	12	0	0	0	1	0	6	3	.156	.372	.188
91	WIL/EAS	AA	135	573	457	103	16	10	31	232	104	4	4	127	1	0	8	31	13	80	85	.225	.368	.508

Bush, Robert Randall "Randy" — bats left — throws left — b.10/5/58 — 1991 positions: OF 38, 1B 12, DH 10

YR	TM/LG	CL	G	TPA	AB	H	2B	3B	HR	TB	BB	IBB	HB	SO	GDP	SH	SF	SB	CS	R	RBI	BA	OBA	SA
82	MIN/AL		55	131	119	29	6	1	4	49	8	0	3	28	1	0	1	0	0	13	13	.244	.305	.412
83	MIN/AL		124	415	373	93	24	3	11	156	34	8	7	51	7	0	1	0	1	43	56	.249	.323	.418
84	MIN/AL		113	356	311	69	17	1	11	121	31	6	4	60	1	0	10	1	2	46	43	.222	.292	.389
85	MIN/AL		97	265	234	56	13	3	10	105	24	1	5	30	3	0	2	3	0	26	35	.239	.321	.449
86	MIN/AL		130	402	357	96	19	7	7	150	39	2	4	63	7	1	1	5	3	50	45	.269	.347	.420
87	MIN/AL		122	349	293	74	10	2	11	121	43	5	3	49	6	0	5	10	3	46	46	.253	.349	.413
88	MIN/AL		136	466	394	103	20	3	14	171	58	14	9	49	8	0	5	8	6	51	51	.261	.365	.434
89	MIN/AL		141	444	391	103	17	4	14	170	48	6	3	73	16	0	2	5	8	60	54	.263	.347	.435
90	POR/PCL	AAA	3	12	9	2	2	0	0	4	3	1	0	0	0	0	0	0	3	17	18	.243	.338	.387
	MIN/AL		73	210	181	44	8	2	6	70	21	2	6	27	2	0	0	0	2	21	23	.303	.401	.485
91	MIN/AL		93	192	165	50	10	1	6	80	24	3	3	25	5	0	0	0	2	21	23	.303	.401	.485
10 YR TOTALS			**1084**	**3230**	**2818**	**717**	**144**	**25**	**94**	**1193**	**330**	**47**	**47**	**455**	**56**	**6**	**29**	**32**	**28**	**373**	**384**	**.254**	**.339**	**.423**

Butler, Brett Morgan — bats left — throws left — b.6/15/57 — 1991 positions: OF 161

YR	TM/LG	CL	G	TPA	AB	H	2B	3B	HR	TB	BB	IBB	HB	SO	GDP	SH	SF	SB	CS	R	RBI	BA	OBA	SA
81	ATL/NL		40	145	126	32	2	3	0	40	19	0	0	17	0	0	0	9	1	17	4	.254	.352	.317
82	ATL/NL		89	268	240	52	2	0	0	54	25	0	0	35	1	3	0	21	8	35	7	.217	.291	.225
83	ATL/NL		151	613	549	154	21	13	5	216	54	3	2	56	5	3	4	39	23	84	37	.281	.344	.393
84	CLE/AL		159	709	602	162	25	9	3	214	86	1	4	62	6	11	6	52	22	108	49	.269	.361	.355
85	CLE/AL		152	666	591	184	28	14	5	255	63	2	1	42	8	8	3	47	20	106	50	.311	.377	.431
86	CLE/AL		161	683	587	163	17	14	4	220	70	1	4	65	8	17	5	32	15	92	51	.278	.356	.375
87	CLE/AL		137	618	522	154	25	8	9	222	91	0	2	55	3	2	2	33	16	91	41	.295	.399	.425
88	SF/NL		157	679	568	163	27	9	6	226	97	4	4	64	2	8	2	43	20	109	43	.287	.393	.398
89	SF/NL		154	672	594	168	22	4	4	210	59	2	3	69	4	13	3	31	16	100	36	.283	.349	.354
90	SF/NL		160	732	622	192	20	9	3	239	90	1	6	62	3	7	7	51	19	108	44	.309	.397	.384
91	LA/NL		161	730	615	182	13	5	2	211	108	4	1	79	3	4	2	38	28	112	38	.296	.401	.343
11 YR TOTALS			**1521**	**6515**	**5616**	**1606**	**202**	**88**	**41**	**2107**	**762**	**18**	**26**	**606**	**43**	**76**	**35**	**396**	**188**	**962**	**400**	**.286**	**.372**	**.375**

Cabrera, Francisco (Paulino) — bats right — throws right — b.10/10/66 — 1991 positions: C 17, 1B 14

YR	TM/LG	CL	G	TPA	AB	H	2B	3B	HR	TB	BB	IBB	HB	SO	GDP	SH	SF	SB	CS	R	RBI	BA	OBA	SA
86	VEN/CAL	A+	6	12	12	2	1	0	0	3	0	0	0	4	0	0	0	0	1	2	3	.167	.167	.250
	SC/NYP	A–	68	268	246	73	13	2	6	108	16	1	4	48	6	1	1	7	4	31	35	.297	.348	.439
87	MB/SAL	A	129	498	449	124	27	2	14	195	40	6	3	82	12	0	0	0	6	61	72	.276	.335	.434
88	DUN/FSL	A+	9	36	35	14	4	0	1	21	1	0	0	2	1	0	0	0	0	2	9	.400	.417	.600
	KNO/SOU	AA	119	464	429	122	19	1	20	203	26	2	3	75	13	2	5	4	3	59	54	.284	.325	.473
89	TOR/AL		3	13	12	2	1	0	0	3	0	0	0	3	0	0	0	1	0	1	0	.167	.231	.250
	SYR/INT	AAA	113	459	428	128	30	2	9	195	20	2	3	72	11	1	7	4	2	59	71	.299	.330	.456
	RIC/INT	AAA	3	7	6	2	1	0	0	3	0	0	0	0	0	0	0	0	0			.333	.286	.500

(continued)

Cabrera, Francisco (Paulino) (continued)

YR	TM/LG	CL	G	TPA	AB	H	2B	3B	HR	TB	BB	IBB	HB	SO	GDP	SH	SF	SB	CS	R	RBI	BA	OBA	SA
	ATL/NL		4	14	14	3	2	0	0	5	0	0	0	3	0	0	0	0	0	0	0	.214	.214	.357
	YEAR		7	27	26	5	3	0	0	8	1	0	0	6	0	0	0	0	0	1	0	.192	.222	.308
90	RIC/INT	AAA	35	142	132	30	3	1	7	56	7	0	1	23	3	0	2	2	0	12	20	.227	.268	.424
	ATL/NL		63	143	137	38	5	1	7	66	5	0	0	21	4	0	1	1	0	14	25	.277	.301	.482
91	RIC/INT	AAA	32	133	119	31	7	1	7	61	10	0	3	21	6	0	1	0	1	22	24	.261	.331	.513
	ATL/NL		44	102	95	23	6	0	4	41	6	0	0	20	5	0	1	1	1	7	23	.242	.284	.432
3 YR TOTALS			**114**	**272**	**258**	**66**	**14**	**1**	**11**	**115**	**12**	**0**	**0**	**47**	**9**	**0**	**2**	**2**	**1**	**22**	**48**	**.256**	**.287**	**.446**

Calderon, Ivan (Perez) — bats right — throws right — b.3/19/62 — 1991 positions: OF 122, 1B 4

YR	TM/LG	CL	G	TPA	AB	H	2B	3B	HR	TB	BB	IBB	HB	SO	GDP	SH	SF	SB	CS	R	RBI	BA	OBA	SA
84	SLC/PCL	AAA	66	281	255	93	7	9	4	130	21	1	1	32	4	1	3	18	6	61	45	.365	.411	.510
	SEA/AL		11	26	24	5	1	0	1	9	2	0	0	5	3	0	0	1	0	2	1	.208	.269	.375
85	SEA/AL		67	233	210	60	16	4	8	108	19	1	2	45	10	1	1	4	2	37	28	.286	.349	.514
86	SEA/AL		37	138	131	31	5	0	2	42	6	0	1	33	1	0	0	3	1	13	13	.237	.275	.321
	CAL/PCL	AAA	24	99	81	27	3	0	3	39	15	1	0	8	1	0	3	5	1	17	18	.333	.424	.481
	CHI/AL		13	36	33	10	2	1	0	14	3	1	0	6	0	0	0	0	0	3	2	.303	.361	.424
	YEAR		50	174	164	41	7	1	2	56	9	1	1	39	1	0	0	3	1	16	15	.250	.293	.341
	BUF/AMA	AAA	27	118	105	23	9	0	5	47	9	2	2	28	2	2	0	0	0	11	22	.219	.288	.448
87	CHI/AL		144	607	542	159	38	2	28	285	60	6	1	109	13	0	4	10	4	93	83	.293	.362	.526
88	CHI/AL		73	301	264	56	14	0	14	112	34	4	0	66	6	0	3	4	5	40	35	.212	.299	.424
89	CHI/AL		157	676	622	178	34	9	14	272	43	7	3	94	20	2	6	7	1	83	87	.286	.332	.437
90	CHI/AL		158	667	607	166	44	2	14	256	51	7	1	79	26	0	8	32	16	85	74	.273	.327	.422
91	MON/NL		134	537	470	141	22	3	19	226	53	4	3	64	7	1	10	31	16	69	75	.300	.368	.481
8 YR TOTALS			**794**	**3221**	**2903**	**806**	**176**	**21**	**100**	**1324**	**271**	**28**	**11**	**501**	**86**	**4**	**32**	**92**	**45**	**425**	**398**	**.278**	**.338**	**.456**

Caminiti, Kenneth Gene "Ken" — bats both — throws right — b.4/21/63 — 1991 positions: 3B 152

YR	TM/LG	CL	G	TPA	AB	H	2B	3B	HR	TB	BB	IBB	HB	SO	GDP	SH	SF	SB	CS	R	RBI	BA	OBA	SA
85	OSC/FSL	A+	126	527	468	133	26	9	4	189	51	5	1	54	13	1	6	14	4	83	73	.284	.352	.404
86	COL/SOU	AA	137	582	513	154	29	3	12	225	56	6	1	78	13	2	10	5	3	82	81	.300	.364	.439
87	COL/SOU	AA	95	407	375	122	25	2	15	196	25	4	0	58	8	0	7	11	5	66	69	.325	.361	.523
	HOU/NL		63	218	203	50	7	1	3	68	12	1	0	44	6	2	1	0	0	10	23	.246	.287	.335
88	TUC/PCL	AAA	109	457	416	113	24	7	5	166	29	4	3	54	14	1	8	13	5	54	66	.272	.318	.399
	HOU/NL		30	89	83	15	2	0	1	20	5	0	0	18	3	0	1	0	0	5	7	.181	.225	.241
89	HOU/NL		161	646	585	149	31	3	10	216	51	9	3	93	8	3	4	4	1	71	72	.255	.316	.369
90	HOU/NL		153	596	541	131	20	2	4	167	48	7	0	97	15	3	4	9	4	52	51	.242	.302	.309
91	HOU/NL		152	632	574	145	30	3	13	220	46	7	5	85	18	3	4	4	5	65	80	.253	.312	.383
5 YR TOTALS			**559**	**2181**	**1986**	**490**	**90**	**9**	**31**	**691**	**162**	**24**	**8**	**337**	**50**	**11**	**14**	**17**	**10**	**203**	**233**	**.247**	**.304**	**.348**

Campanis, James Alexander "Jim" — bats right — throws right — b.8/27/67 — 1991 positions: C System SEA/AL

YR	TM/LG	CL	G	TPA	AB	H	2B	3B	HR	TB	BB	IBB	HB	SO	GDP	SH	SF	SB	CS	R	RBI	BA	OBA	SA
89	SB/CAL	A+	133	523	455	116	26	0	11	175	51	1	14	96	12	0	3	0	2	49	58	.255	.346	.385
90	PEN/CAR	A+	112	429	364	91	22	0	14	155	40	1	18	76	16	0	7	3	3	47	60	.250	.347	.426
91	JAC/SOU	AA	118	435	387	96	10	0	15	151	37	2	7	64	13	0	4	0	0	36	49	.248	.322	.390

Campusano, Silvestre (Diaz) "Sil" — bats right — throws right — b.12/31/65 — 1991 positions: OF 15

YR	TM/LG	CL	G	TPA	AB	H	2B	3B	HR	TB	BB	IBB	HB	SO	GDP	SH	SF	SB	CS	R	RBI	BA	OBA	SA
84	BJ/GCL	R	63	260	236	63	17	2	0	84	20	0	3	40	3	0	1	21	4	42	22	.267	.331	.356
85	FLO/SAL	A	88	416	348	109	31	1	15	187	58	0	3	84	3	3	4	21	14	80	56	.313	.412	.537
	KNO/SOU	AA	45	196	178	54	9	0	6	81	14	0	0	32	6	1	1	10	4	30	29	.303	.352	.455
86	KNO/SOU	AA	132	564	493	126	32	6	14	212	61	2	6	110	3	0	4	18	10	89	59	.256	.342	.430
87	SYR/INT	AAA	129	538	481	127	28	10	14	217	47	1	4	110	4	0	2	26	15	70	63	.264	.333	.451
88	SYR/INT	AAA	17	64	62	13	3	0	0	16	2	0	0	20	1	0	0	1	2	8	3	.210	.234	.258
	TOR/AL		73	158	142	31	10	2	2	51	9	1	0	33	0	2	1	0	1	14	12	.218	.282	.359
89	SYR/INT	AAA	112	406	356	86	19	4	6	131	44	0	1	81	9	3	2	17	4	46	30	.242	.325	.368
90	PHI/NL		66	93	85	18	1	1	2	27	6	0	1	16	3	0	1	1	0	10	9	.212	.269	.318
91	PHI/NL		15	37	35	4	0	0	1	7	1	0	1	10	0	1	0	0	0	2	2	.114	.139	.200
	SCR/INT	AAA	94	333	305	80	12	1	8	118	23	2	2	63	4	0	3	9	7	44	47	.262	.315	.387
3 YR TOTALS			**154**	**288**	**262**	**53**	**11**	**3**	**5**	**85**	**16**	**1**	**1**	**59**	**1**	**3**	**2**	**1**	**0**	**26**	**23**	**.202**	**.260**	**.324**

Canale, George Anthony — bats left — throws right — b.8/11/65 — 1991 positions: 1B 19

YR	TM/LG	CL	G	TPA	AB	H	2B	3B	HR	TB	BB	IBB	HB	SO	GDP	SH	SF	SB	CS	R	RBI	BA	OBA	SA
86	HEL/PIO	R+	65	282	221	72	19	0	9	118	54	0	0	65	2	2	5	6	4	48	49	.326	.450	.534
87	STO/CAL	A+	66	289	246	69	18	1	7	110	38	3	1	59	8	2	2	5	4	42	48	.280	.376	.447
	EP/TEX	AA	65	275	253	65	10	2	7	100	20	1	2	69	4	0	0	3	2	38	36	.257	.316	.395
88	EP/TEX	AA	132	559	496	120	23	2	23	216	59	5	2	152	12	0	2	9	3	77	93	.242	.324	.435
89	DEN/AMA	AAA	144	584	503	140	33	9	18	245	71	5	2	134	3	2	6	5	8	80	71	.278	.366	.487
	MIL/AL		13	29	26	5	1	0	1	9	2	0	0	10	0	1	0	0	1	5	3	.192	.250	.346
90	DEN/AMA	AAA	134	544	468	119	18	6	12	185	69	4	1	103	10	3	3	12	5	76	60	.254	.349	.395
	MIL/AL		10	15	13	1	1	0	0	2	2	0	0	5	0	0	0	1	0	4	0	.077	.200	.154
91	DEN/AMA	AAA	88	330	274	64	10	2	10	108	51	0	0	49	6	0	3	6	2	36	47	.234	.355	.394
	MIL/AL		21	44	34	6	2	0	3	17	8	0	0	14	5	0	2	0	1	6	10	.176	.318	.500
3 YR TOTALS			**44**	**88**	**73**	**12**	**4**	**0**	**4**	**28**	**12**	**0**	**0**	**14**	**5**	**1**	**2**	**0**	**2**	**15**	**13**	**.164**	**.276**	**.384**

Candaele, Casey Todd — bats both — throws right — b.1/12/61 — 1991 positions: 2B 109, OF 26, 3B 11

YR	TM/LG	CL	G	TPA	AB	H	2B	3B	HR	TB	BB	IBB	HB	SO	GDP	SH	SF	SB	CS	R	RBI	BA	OBA	SA
84	JAC/SOU	AA	132	574	532	145	23	2	2	178	30	1	1	35	13	5	6	26	18	68	53	.273	.309	.335
85	IND/AMA	AAA	127	446	390	101	13	5	0	124	44	2	0	33	15	11	1	13	10	55	35	.259	.333	.318
86	IND/AMA	AAA	119	540	480	145	32	6	2	195	46	6	1	29	8	11	2	16	10	77	42	.302	.363	.406
	MON/NL		30	110	104	24	4	1	0	30	5	0	0	15	3	0	1	3	5	9	6	.231	.264	.288
87	MON/NL		138	495	449	122	23	4	1	156	38	3	2	28	5	4	2	7	10	62	23	.272	.330	.347
88	MON/NL		36	128	116	20	5	1	0	27	10	1	0	11	7	2	0	1	0	9	4	.172	.238	.233
	IND/AMA	AAA	60	259	239	63	11	6	2	92	12	0	0	20	5	1	7	5	1	23	36	.264	.291	.385
	TUC/PCL	AAA	17	70	66	17	3	0	0	20	4	0	0	6	5	0	0	4	2	8	5	.258	.300	.303
	HOU/NL		21	33	31	5	3	0	0	8	1	0	0	6	0	1	0	0	1	2	1	.161	.188	.258
	YEAR		57	161	147	25	8	1	0	35	11	1	0	17	7	3	0	1	1	11	5	.170	.228	.238
89	TUC/PCL	AAA	68	231	206	45	6	1	0	53	20	4	0	37	3	1	1	6	3	22	17	.218	.286	.257
90	TUC/PCL	AAA	7	33	28	6	1	0	0	7	3	1	1	2	1	1	0	1	2	2	2	.214	.313	.250
	HOU/NL		130	298	262	75	8	6	3	104	11	5	1	42	4	4	0	7	5	30	22	.286	.364	.397
91	HOU/NL		151	505	461	121	20	7	4	167	40	7	0	49	5	1	3	9	3	44	50	.262	.319	.362
5 YR TOTALS			**506**	**1569**	**1423**	**367**	**63**	**19**	**8**	**492**	**125**	**16**	**3**	**151**	**24**	**12**	**6**	**27**	**24**	**156**	**106**	**.258**	**.318**	**.346**

Canseco, Jose (Capas) — bats right — throws right — b.7/2/64 — 1991 positions: OF 131, DH 24

YR	TM/LG	CL	G	TPA	AB	H	2B	3B	HR	TB	BB	IBB	HB	SO	GDP	SH	SF	SB	CS	R	RBI	BA	OBA	SA
84	MOD/CAL	A+	116	500	410	113	21	2	15	183	74	5	6	127	3	3	7	10	6	61	73	.276	.388	.446
85	HUN/SOU	AA	58	251	211	67	10	2	25	156	30	5	6	55	2	0	5	6	0	47	80	.318	.406	.739
	TAC/PCL	AAA	60	277	233	81	16	1	11	132	40	5	1	66	5	0	3	5	0	41	47	.348	.440	.567
	OAK/AL		29	100	96	29	3	0	5	47	4	0	0	31	1	0	0	1	1	16	13	.302	.330	.490
86	OAK/AL		157	682	600	144	29	1	33	274	65	1	8	175	12	0	9	15	7	85	117	.240	.318	.457
87	OAK/AL		159	691	630	162	35	3	31	296	50	2	2	157	16	0	9	15	3	81	113	.257	.310	.470
88	OAK/AL		158	705	610	187	34	0	42	347	78	10	10	128	15	1	6	40	16	120	124	.307	.391	.569
89	HUN/SOU	AA	9	34	29	6	0	0	0	6	5	0	0	11	0	0	0	1	0	2	3	.207	.324	.207
	OAK/AL		65	258	227	61	9	1	17	123	23	4	2	69	4	0	6	6	3	40	57	.269	.333	.542
90	OAK/AL		131	563	481	132	14	2	37	261	72	8	5	158	9	0	5	19	10	83	101	.274	.371	.543
91	OAK/AL		154	665	572	152	32	1	44	318	78	7	9	152	16	0	6	26	6	115	122	.266	.359	.556
7 YR TOTALS			**853**	**3664**	**3216**	**867**	**156**	**8**	**209**	**1666**	**370**	**32**	**36**	**870**	**73**	**1**	**41**	**122**	**46**	**540**	**647**	**.270**	**.348**	**.518**

Capra, Nick Lee — bats right — throws right — b.3/8/58 — 1991 positions: OF 2

YR	TM/LG	CL	G	TPA	AB	H	2B	3B	HR	TB	BB	IBB	HB	SO	GDP	SH	SF	SB	CS	R	RBI	BA	OBA	SA
79	TUL/TEX	AA	66	240	212	59	7	0	3	75	23	1	2	32	8	2	1	16	5	29	26	.278	.353	.354
80	TUL/TEX	AA	117	506	440	127	25	9	6	188	57	0	4	69	5	2	3	55	14	90	53	.289	.373	.427
81	WIC/TEX	AA	123	488	398	104	16	4	4	140	76	0	0	61	5	8	6	41	15	74	38	.261	.375	.352
82	TEX/AL		13	19	15	4	0	0	1	7	3	0	1	4	1	0	0	2	1	2	1	.267	.421	.467
	DEN/AMA	AAA	121	492	416	117	15	10	9	179	71	1	0	72	1	4	1	29	13	82	40	.281	.385	.430
83	TEX/AL		8	2	2	0	0	0	0	0	0	0	0	0	0	0	0	0	0	2	0	.000	.000	.000
	OC/AMA	AAA	124	518	441	113	17	4	13	177	69	0	3	66	9	2	3	27	10	84	41	.256	.359	.401
84	OC/AMA	AAA	123	531	442	113	18	1	2	139	76	1	12	67	4	12	1	47	18	68	21	.256	.364	.314
85	TEX/AL		8	8	8	1	0	0	0	1	0	0	0	0	0	0	0	0	0	1	0	.125	.125	.125
	OC/AMA	AAA	97	428	353	96	17	1	0	115	68	1	4	45	5	2	1	25	16	53	27	.272	.394	.326
86	BUF/AMA	AAA	36	147	123	25	2	0	2	33	20	1	0	13	2	2	2	6	9	14	9	.203	.310	.268
	OC/AMA	AAA	72	339	283	80	16	2	5	115	46	0	2	36	5	6	2	26	6	54	22	.283	.384	.406
87	OC/AMA	AAA	97	424	353	107	18	3	1	134	62	3	6	53	6	6	3	21	13	69	39	.303	.404	.380
88	KC/AL		14	31	29	4	1	0	0	5	2	0	0	3	0	0	0	2	0	2	0	.138	.194	.172
	OMA/AMA	AAA	93	403	346	100	11	6	1	126	50	0	4	49	9	4	2	28	9	53	43	.289	.378	.364
89	OMA/AMA	AAA	128	580	500	145	27	3	7	199	70	1	4	67	4	6	1	31	18	84	44	.290	.381	.398
90	OC/AMA	AAA	122	530	451	125	26	3	5	172	68	0	3	61	4	7	1	34	14	80	45	.277	.375	.381
91	TEX/AL		2	1	0	0	0	0	0	0	1	0	0	0	0	0	0	0	0	1	0	.000	1.000	.000
	OC/AMA	AAA	127	585	485	132	33	4	5	188	87	1	8	58	7	8	1	27	13	74	38	.272	.386	.388
5 YR TOTALS			**45**	**61**	**54**	**9**	**1**	**0**	**1**	**13**	**6**	**0**	**1**	**7**	**4**	**0**	**0**	**3**	**1**	**9**	**1**	**.167**	**.262**	**.241**

Carey, Paul Stephen — bats left — throws right — b.1/8/68 — 1991 positions: OF System BAL/AL

YR	TM/LG	CL	G	TPA	AB	H	2B	3B	HR	TB	BB	IBB	HB	SO	GDP	SH	SF	SB	CS	R	RBI	BA	OBA	SA
90	MIA/FSL	A+	49	199	153	50	5	3	4	73	43	1	2	39	2	0	1	4	3	23	20	.327	.477	.477
91	HAG/EAS	AA	114	452	373	94	29	1	12	161	68	8	4	109	11	2	5	5	4	63	65	.252	.369	.432

Carr, Charles Lee Glenn "Chuck" — bats both — throws right — b.8/10/67 — 1991 positions: OF 9

YR	TM/LG	CL	G	TPA	AB	H	2B	3B	HR	TB	BB	IBB	HB	SO	GDP	SH	SF	SB	CS	R	RBI	BA	OBA	SA
86	RED/GCL	R	44	140	123	21	5	0	0	26	10	0	0	27	2	5	2	9	1	13	10	.171	.230	.211
87	BEL/NWL	A-	44	181	165	40	1	1	1	46	12	0	1	38	2	3	0	20	1	31	11	.242	.298	.279
88	WAU/MID	A	82	327	304	91	14	2	6	127	14	0	1	49	3	3	1	41	11	58	30	.299	.327	.418
	VER/EAS	AA	41	171	159	39	4	2	1	50	8	0	0	33	0	3	1	21	9	26	13	.245	.280	.314
89	JAC/TEX	AA	116	481	444	107	13	1	0	122	27	2	1	66	3	7	2	47	20	45	22	.241	.285	.275
90	TID/INT	AAA	20	87	81	21	5	1	0	28	4	0	0	12	0	0	0	6	4	13	8	.259	.287	.346
	NY/NL		4	2	2	0	0	0	0	0	0	0	0	2	0	0	0	1	0	0	0	.000	.000	.000
	JAC/TEX	AA	93	411	360	93	20	9	3	140	44	2	2	77	2	3	2	47	15	60	24	.258	.341	.389
91	TID/INT	AAA	64	266	246	48	6	1	1	59	18	0	1	37	3	0	2	27	8	34	11	.195	.253	.240
	NY/NL		12	11	11	2	0	0	0	2	0	0	0	2	0	0	0	2	0	1	1	.182	.182	.182
2 YR TOTALS			**16**	**13**	**13**	**2**	**0**	**0**	**0**	**2**	**0**	**0**	**0**	**4**	**0**	**0**	**0**	**2**	**0**	**1**	**1**	**.154**	**.154**	**.154**

Carreon, Mark Steven — bats right — throws left — b.7/19/63 — 1991 positions: OF 77

YR	TM/LG	CL	G	TPA	AB	H	2B	3B	HR	TB	BB	IBB	HB	SO	GDP	SH	SF	SB	CS	R	RBI	BA	OBA	SA
84	JAC/TEX	AA	119	490	435	122	14	3	1	145	38	1	5	24	10	7	5	12	8	64	43	.280	.342	.333
85	TID/INT	AAA	7	17	15	2	1	0	1	6	2	0	0	5	0	0	0	0	0	1	2	.133	.235	.400
	JAC/TEX	AA	123	547	447	140	23	5	6	191	87	3	6	32	8	3	4	23	6	96	51	.313	.428	.427
86	TID/INT	AAA	115	482	426	123	23	2	10	180	50	5	3	42	9	1	2	12	4	62	64	.289	.366	.423
87	TID/INT	AAA	133	563	525	164	41	5	10	245	34	2	0	48	16	0	4	31	6	83	89	.312	.352	.467
	NY/NL		9	13	12	3	0	0	0	3	1	0	0	1	0	0	0	0	1	0	1	.250	.308	.250
88	TID/INT	AAA	102	409	365	96	13	3	14	157	40	2	2	53	10	0	2	11	6	48	55	.263	.337	.430
	NY/NL		7	11	9	5	2	0	1	10	2	0	0	1	0	0	0	0	0	5	1	.556	.636	1.111
89	TID/INT	AAA	32	139	122	34	4	0	1	41	13	1	0	20	5	0	4	8	3	22	21	.279	.338	.336
	NY/NL		68	146	133	41	6	0	6	65	12	0	1	17	1	0	0	2	3	20	16	.308	.370	.489
90	NY/NL		82	205	188	47	12	0	10	89	15	1	0	2	29	1	0	0	1	0	30	26	.250	.312	.473
91	NY/NL		106	270	254	66	6	0	4	84	12	2	2	26	13	1	1	2	1	18	21	.260	.297	.331
5 YR TOTALS			**272**	**645**	**596**	**162**	**26**	**0**	**21**	**251**	**42**	**2**	**5**	**74**	**15**	**1**	**1**	**5**	**5**	**73**	**65**	**.272**	**.325**	**.421**

Carrillo, Matias (Garcia) — bats left — throws left — b.2/24/63 — 1991 positions: OF 3

YR	TM/LG	CL	G	TPA	AB	H	2B	3B	HR	TB	BB	IBB	HB	SO	GDP	SH	SF	SB	CS	R	RBI	BA	OBA	SA
86	NAS/EAS	AA	15	56	52	8	1	0	0	9	4	1	0	13	0	0	0	2	4	3	0	.154	.214	.173
87	SAL/CAR	A+	90	309	284	77	11	3	8	118	19	1	2	41	2	0	4	15	4	42	37	.271	.317	.415
88	EP/TEX	AA	106	428	396	118	17	2	12	175	26	1	0	81	10	2	4	11	11	76	55	.298	.338	.442
89	DEN/AMA	AAA	125	435	400	104	14	4	10	156	24	1	2	90	7	7	2	22	6	46	43	.260	.304	.390
90	DEN/AMA	AAA	21	78	75	20	6	2	2	36	2	0	0	16	2	0	1	0	2	15	10	.267	.282	.480
91	MIL/AL		3	0	0	0	0	0	0	0	0	0	0	0	0	0	0	0	0	0	0	.000	.000	.000
	DEN/AMA	AAA	120	461	421	116	18	5	8	168	32	2	0	84	11	5	3	11	13	56	56	.276	.325	.399

Carter, Gary Edmund — bats right — throws right — b.4/8/54 — 1991 positions: C 68, 1B 10

YR	TM/LG	CL	G	TPA	AB	H	2B	3B	HR	TB	BB	IBB	HB	SO	GDP	SH	SF	SB	CS	R	RBI	BA	OBA	SA
74	MON/NL		9	29	27	11	0	1	1	16	1	0	0	2	0	0	1	2	0	5	6	.407	.414	.593
75	MON/NL		144	590	503	136	20	1	17	209	72	8	1	83	7	10	4	5	2	58	68	.270	.360	.416
76	MON/NL		91	347	311	68	8	1	6	96	30	2	1	43	7	2	3	0	2	31	38	.219	.287	.309
77	MON/NL		154	595	522	148	29	2	31	274	58	5	5	103	9	3	7	5	5	86	84	.284	.356	.525
78	MON/NL		157	607	533	136	27	1	20	225	62	11	5	70	10	2	5	10	6	76	72	.255	.336	.422
79	MON/NL		141	559	505	143	26	5	22	245	40	3	5	62	11	2	7	3	2	74	75	.283	.338	.485
80	MON/NL		154	617	549	145	25	5	29	267	58	11	1	78	9	1	8	3	2	76	101	.264	.331	.486
81	MON/NL		100	419	374	94	20	2	16	166	35	4	1	35	6	3	6	1	5	48	68	.251	.313	.444
82	MON/NL		154	653	557	163	32	1	29	284	78	11	6	64	16	4	8	2	5	91	97	.293	.381	.510
83	MON/NL		145	609	541	146	37	3	17	240	51	7	6	57	14	2	8	1	1	63	79	.270	.336	.444
84	MON/NL		159	669	596	175	32	1	27	290	64	9	6	57	8	0	3	2	2	75	106	.294	.366	.487
85	NY/NL		149	633	555	156	17	1	32	271	69	16	6	46	18	0	3	1	1	83	100	.281	.365	.488
86	NY/NL		132	573	490	125	14	2	24	215	62	9	6	63	21	0	15	1	1	81	105	.255	.337	.439
87	NY/NL		139	573	523	123	18	2	20	205	42	1	1	73	14	1	6	0	0	55	83	.235	.290	.392
88	NY/NL		130	503	455	110	16	2	11	163	34	1	7	52	8	1	6	0	2	39	46	.242	.301	.358
89	TID/INT	AAA	5	18	16	3	0	0	1	6	2	0	0	1	0	0	0	0	0	2	3	.188	.278	.375
	NY/NL		50	166	153	28	8	0	2	42	12	0	1	15	5	0	1	0	0	14	15	.183	.241	.275
90	SF/NL		92	272	244	62	10	0	9	99	25	3	1	31	2	0	2	1	1	24	27	.254	.324	.406
91	LA/NL		101	280	248	61	14	0	6	93	22	1	7	26	11	1	2	2	2	22	26	.246	.323	.375
18 YR TOTALS			**2201**	**8694**	**7686**	**2030**	**353**	**30**	**319**	**3400**	**815**	**102**	**66**	**960**	**176**	**32**	**95**	**39**	**38**	**1001**	**1196**	**.264**	**.336**	**.442**

Carter, Joseph "Joe" — bats right — throws right — b.3/7/60 — 1991 positions: OF 151, DH 11

YR	TM/LG	CL	G	TPA	AB	H	2B	3B	HR	TB	BB	IBB	HB	SO	GDP	SH	SF	SB	CS	R	RBI	BA	OBA	SA
83	CHI/NL		23	52	51	9	1	1	0	12	0	0	0	21	1	1	0	1	0	6	1	.176	.176	.235
84	IOW/AMA	AAA	61	273	248	77	12	7	14	145	20	5	3	31	4	0	2	11	6	45	67	.310	.366	.585
	CLE/AL		66	257	244	67	6	1	13	114	11	0	1	48	2	0	1	2	4	32	41	.275	.307	.467
85	CLE/AL		143	523	489	128	27	0	15	200	25	2	2	74	9	3	4	24	6	64	59	.262	.298	.409
86	CLE/AL		162	709	663	200	36	9	29	341	32	3	5	95	8	1	8	29	7	108	121	.302	.335	.514
87	CLE/AL		149	629	588	155	27	2	32	282	27	6	9	105	8	1	4	31	6	83	106	.264	.304	.480
88	CLE/AL		157	670	621	168	36	6	27	297	35	6	7	82	6	1	6	27	5	85	98	.271	.314	.478
89	CLE/AL		162	705	651	158	32	4	35	303	39	8	8	112	6	2	5	13	6	84	105	.243	.292	.465
90	SD/NL		162	697	634	147	27	1	24	248	48	18	7	93	12	0	8	22	6	79	115	.232	.290	.391
91	TOR/AL		162	706	638	174	42	3	33	321	49	12	10	112	6	0	9	20	6	89	108	.273	.330	.503
9 YR TOTALS			**1186**	**4948**	**4579**	**1206**	**234**	**27**	**208**	**2118**	**266**	**55**	**49**	**742**	**58**	**9**	**45**	**169**	**48**	**630**	**754**	**.263**	**.308**	**.463**

Castilla, Vinicio (Soria) "Vinny" — bats right — throws right — b.7/4/67 — 1991 positions: SS 12

YR	TM/LG	CL	G	TPA	AB	H	2B	3B	HR	TB	BB	IBB	HB	SO	GDP	SH	SF	SB	CS	R	RBI	BA	OBA	SA
90	SUM/SAL	A	93	381	339	91	15	2	9	137	28	1	8	54	8	1	5	2	5	47	53	.268	.334	.404
	GRE/SOU	AA	46	186	170	40	5	1	4	59	13	3	2	23	7	0	1	4	4	20	16	.235	.296	.347
91	GRE/SOU	AA	66	276	259	70	17	3	7	114	9	1	2	35	4	2	4	0	1	34	44	.270	.296	.440
	RIC/INT	AAA	67	262	240	54	7	4	7	90	14	2	3	31	4	0	5	1	1	25	36	.225	.271	.375
	ATL/NL		12	6	5	1	0	0	0	1	0	0	0	2	0	0	0	0	0	1	0	.200	.200	.200

Castillo, Braulio Robinson (Medrano) — bats right — throws right — b.5/13/68 — 1991 positions: OF 26

YR	TM/LG	CL	G	TPA	AB	H	2B	3B	HR	TB	BB	IBB	HB	SO	GDP	SH	SF	SB	CS	R	RBI	BA	OBA	SA
87	DOD/GCL	R	49	162	140	28	4	2	1	39	16	1	4	41	2	1	1	7	2	21	19	.200	.298	.279

Castillo, Braulio Robinson (Medrano) (continued)

YR	TM/LG	CL	G	TPA	AB	H	2B	3B	HR	TB	BB	IBB	HB	SO	GDP	SH	SF	SB	CS	R	RBI	BA	OBA	SA
88	VB/FSL	A+	2	1	1	0	0	0	0	0	0	0	0	1	0	0	0	0	0	0	0	.000	.000	.000
	SAL/NWL	A–	73	340	306	86	20	5	8	140	22	1	7	72	6	1	4	16	4	51	40	.281	.339	.458
89	BAK/CAL	A+	126	556	494	147	28	8	18	245	42	1	15	132	7	0	5	31	22	83	82	.298	.367	.496
90	SA/TEX	AA	75	258	241	55	11	3	3	81	14	2	2	72	5	0	1	11	6	34	24	.228	.275	.336
91	SA/TEX	AA	87	339	297	89	19	3	8	138	32	2	6	73	7	1	3	22	10	49	48	.300	.376	.465
	SCR/INT	AAA	16	67	60	21	9	1	0	32	6	0	0	7	0	1	2	1	1	14	15	.350	.403	.533
	PHI/NL		28	53	52	9	3	0	0	12	1	0	0	15	1	0	0	1	1	3	2	.173	.189	.231

Castillo, Monte Carmelo "Carmen" — bats right — throws right — b.6/8/58 — 1991 positions: OF 4, DH 2

YR	TM/LG	CL	G	TPA	AB	H	2B	3B	HR	TB	BB	IBB	HB	SO	GDP	SH	SF	SB	CS	R	RBI	BA	OBA	SA
82	CLE/AL		47	129	120	25	4	0	2	35	6	0	2	17	2	1	0	0	0	11	11	.208	.258	.292
83	CLE/AL		23	41	36	10	2	1	1	17	4	0	0	6	0	0	0	1	1	9	3	.278	.366	.472
84	CLE/AL		87	237	211	55	9	2	10	98	21	0	2	32	7	0	3	1	3	36	36	.261	.329	.464
85	MAI/INT	AAA	26	107	96	23	2	2	2	35	9	0	0	13	2	0	2	2	1	12	18	.240	.299	.365
	CLE/AL		67	198	184	45	5	1	11	85	11	0	3	40	6	0	0	3	0	27	25	.245	.298	.462
86	CLE/AL		85	217	205	57	9	0	8	90	9	0	1	48	1	1	1	2	1	34	32	.278	.310	.439
87	CLE/AL		89	241	220	55	17	0	11	105	16	0	0	52	0	1	4	1	1	27	31	.250	.296	.477
88	CLE/AL		66	182	176	48	8	0	4	68	5	1	1	31	4	0	0	6	2	12	14	.273	.297	.386
89	MIN/AL		94	240	218	56	13	3	8	99	15	1	1	40	5	4	2	1	2	23	33	.257	.305	.454
90	MIN/AL		64	142	137	34	4	0	0	34	3	1	1	23	1	0	1	0	0	11	12	.219	.239	.248
91	MIN/AL		9	13	12	2	0	1	0	4	0	0	1	2	0	0	0	0	0	0	0	.167	.231	.333
	DEN/AMA	AAA	92	359	334	101	19	4	14	170	17	1	4	80	6	1	3	2	0	41	72	.302	.341	.509
10 YR TOTALS			**631**	**1640**	**1519**	**383**	**71**	**8**	**55**	**635**	**90**	**5**	**13**	**291**	**34**	**7**	**11**	**15**	**11**	**190**	**197**	**.252**	**.298**	**.418**

Cedeno, Andujar (Domastorg) — bats right — throws right — b.8/21/69 — 1991 positions: SS 66

YR	TM/LG	CL	G	TPA	AB	H	2B	3B	HR	TB	BB	IBB	HB	SO	GDP	SH	SF	SB	CS	R	RBI	BA	OBA	SA
88	AST/GCL	R	46	181	165	47	5	2	1	59	11	0	1	34	1	0	4	10	4	25	20	.285	.326	.358
89	ASH/SAL	A	126	524	487	146	23	6	14	223	29	0	1	124	10	2	5	23	10	76	93	.300	.337	.458
90	COL/SOU	AA	132	546	495	119	21	11	19	219	33	1	6	135	11	7	5	6	10	57	64	.240	.293	.442
	HOU/NL		7	8	8	0	0	0	0	0	0	0	0	5	0	0	0	0	0	0	0	.000	.000	.000
91	TUC/PCL	AAA	93	381	347	105	19	6	7	157	19	2	5	67	9	3	7	5	3	49	55	.303	.341	.452
	HOU/NL		67	264	251	61	13	2	9	105	9	1	1	74	3	1	2	4	3	27	36	.243	.270	.418
2 YR TOTALS			**74**	**272**	**259**	**61**	**13**	**2**	**9**	**105**	**9**	**1**	**1**	**79**	**3**	**1**	**2**	**4**	**3**	**27**	**36**	**.236**	**.262**	**.405**

Cerone, Richard Aldo "Rick" — bats right — throws right — b.5/19/54 — 1991 positions: C 81

YR	TM/LG	CL	G	TPA	AB	H	2B	3B	HR	TB	BB	IBB	HB	SO	GDP	SH	SF	SB	CS	R	RBI	BA	OBA	SA
75	CLE/AL		7	14	12	3	1	0	0	4	1	0	0	0	0	1	0	0	0	1	0	.250	.308	.333
76	CLE/AL		7	16	16	2	0	0	0	2	0	0	0	2	0	0	0	0	0	1	1	.125	.125	.125
77	TOR/AL		31	107	100	20	4	0	1	27	6	0	0	12	3	1	0	0	0	7	10	.200	.245	.270
78	TOR/AL		88	310	282	63	8	2	3	84	23	0	1	32	7	4	0	0	3	25	20	.223	.284	.298
79	TOR/AL		136	514	469	112	27	4	7	168	37	1	1	40	5	3	4	1	4	47	61	.239	.294	.358
80	NY/AL		147	575	519	144	30	4	14	224	32	2	6	56	14	8	10	1	3	70	85	.277	.321	.432
81	NY/AL		71	254	234	57	13	2	2	80	12	0	0	24	10	4	4	0	2	23	21	.244	.276	.342
82	NY/AL		89	329	300	68	10	0	5	93	19	1	1	27	12	4	5	0	2	29	28	.227	.271	.310
83	NY/AL		80	266	246	54	7	0	2	67	15	1	1	29	5	4	0	0	0	18	22	.220	.267	.272
84	COL/INT	AAA	8	27	25	5	2	0	0	7	2	0	0	3	0	0	0	0	0	2	1	.200	.259	.280
	NY/AL		38	132	120	25	3	0	2	34	9	0	1	15	1	0	2	0	0	8	13	.208	.269	.283
85	ATL/NL		96	316	282	61	9	0	3	79	29	1	0	25	15	0	5	1	1	15	25	.216	.288	.280
86	MIL/AL		68	242	216	56	14	0	4	82	15	0	4	28	5	5	5	1	1	22	18	.259	.304	.380
87	NY/AL		113	327	284	69	12	1	4	95	30	0	4	46	8	5	4	0	1	28	23	.243	.320	.335
88	BOS/AL		84	289	264	71	13	1	3	95	20	0	3	32	4	1	1	0	0	31	27	.269	.326	.360
89	BOS/AL		102	341	296	72	16	1	4	102	34	1	2	40	10	4	5	0	1	28	48	.243	.320	.345
90	YAN/GCL	R	3	8	7	1	0	0	0	1	0	0	1	0	0	0	0	0	0	0	0	.143	.250	.143
	COL/INT	AAA	4	13	11	1	0	0	0	1	2	0	0	0	0	0	0	0	0	0	0	.091	.231	.091
	NY/AL		49	146	139	42	6	0	2	54	5	0	1	13	4	1	1	0	0	12	11	.302	.324	.388
91	NY/NL		90	258	227	62	13	0	2	81	30	2	1	24	9	0	1	1	1	18	16	.273	.360	.357
17 YR TOTALS			**1296**	**4436**	**4006**	**981**	**186**	**15**	**58**	**1371**	**317**	**9**	**23**	**445**	**118**	**47**	**43**	**5**	**20**	**383**	**429**	**.245**	**.301**	**.342**

Chamberlain, Wesley Polk "Wes" — bats right — throws right — b.4/13/66 — 1991 positions: OF 98

YR	TM/LG	CL	G	TPA	AB	H	2B	3B	HR	TB	BB	IBB	HB	SO	GDP	SH	SF	SB	CS	R	RBI	BA	OBA	SA
87	WAT/NYP	A–	66	287	258	67	13	4	5	103	25	2	1	48	6	0	3	22	7	50	35	.260	.324	.399
88	AUG/SAL	A	27	121	107	36	7	2	1	50	11	0	1	11	4	2	0	1	3	22	17	.336	.403	.467
	SAL/CAR	A+	92	405	365	100	15	1	11	150	38	2	0	59	7	0	2	14	4	66	50	.274	.341	.411
89	HAR/EAS	AA	129	512	471	144	26	3	21	239	32	4	2	82	14	0	7	11	10	65	87	.306	.348	.507
90	BUF/AMA	AAA	123	465	416	104	24	2	6	150	34	1	8	58	9	1	2	5	14	19	43	52	.250	.315	.361
	PHI/NL		18	47	46	13	3	0	2	22	1	0	0	9	0	0	0	4	0	9	4	.283	.298	.478
91	SCR/INT	AAA	39	156	144	37	7	2	2	54	8	1	0	13	6	0	4	7	4	12	20	.257	.288	.375
	PHI/NL		101	417	383	92	16	3	13	153	31	0	2	73	8	1	0	9	4	51	50	.240	.300	.399
2 YR TOTALS			**119**	**464**	**429**	**105**	**19**	**3**	**15**	**175**	**32**	**0**	**2**	**82**	**8**	**1**	**0**	**13**	**4**	**60**	**54**	**.245**	**.300**	**.408**

Clark, David Earl "Dave" — bats left — throws right — b.9/3/62 — 1991 positions: OF 1, DH 1

YR	TM/LG	CL	G	TPA	AB	H	2B	3B	HR	TB	BB	IBB	HB	SO	GDP	SH	SF	SB	CS	R	RBI	BA	OBA	SA
84	WAT/MID	A	110	438	363	112	16	3	15	179	57	4	10	68	6	4	4	20	5	74	63	.309	.412	.493
	BUF/EAS	AA	17	68	56	10	1	0	3	20	9	0	1	13	1	0	2	1	1	12	10	.179	.294	.357
85	WAT/EAS	AA	132	555	463	140	24	7	12	214	86	8	1	79	11	1	4	27	12	75	64	.302	.410	.462

(continued)

Clark, David Earl "Dave" (continued)

YR	TM/LG	CL	G	TPA	AB	H	2B	3B	HR	TB	BB	IBB	HB	SO	GDP	SH	SF	SB	CS	R	RBI	BA	OBA	SA
86	MAI/INT	AAA	106	414	355	99	17	2	19	177	52	5	3	70	8	2	2	6	5	56	58	.279	.374	.499
	CLE/AL		18	68	58	16	1	0	3	26	7	0	0	11	1	2	1	1	0	10	9	.276	.348	.448
87	BUF/AMA	AAA	108	481	420	143	22	3	30	261	52	7	3	62	13	1	5	14	11	83	80	.340	.412	.621
	CLE/AL		29	89	87	18	5	0	3	32	2	0	0	24	4	0	0	1	0	11	12	.207	.225	.368
88	CS/PCL	AAA	47	197	165	49	10	2	4	75	27	1	2	38	5	1	2	4	5	27	31	.297	.398	.455
	CLE/AL		63	174	156	41	4	1	3	56	17	2	0	28	8	0	1	0	2	11	18	.263	.333	.359
89	CLE/AL		102	285	253	60	12	0	8	96	30	5	0	63	7	1	1	0	2	21	29	.237	.317	.379
90	CHI/NL		84	181	171	47	4	2	5	70	8	1	0	40	4	0	2	7	1	22	20	.275	.304	.409
91	OMA/AMA	AAA	104	391	359	108	24	3	13	177	30	1	0	53	13	0	2	6	5	45	64	.301	.353	.493
	KC/AL		11	11	10	2	0	0	0	2	1	0	0	1	0	0	0	0	0	1	1	.200	.273	.200
6 YR TOTALS			307	808	735	184	26	3	22	282	65	8	0	167	24	3	5	9	5	76	89	**.250**	**.309**	**.384**

Clark, Jack Anthony — bats right — throws right — b.11/10/55 — 1991 positions: DH 135

YR	TM/LG	CL	G	TPA	AB	H	2B	3B	HR	TB	BB	IBB	HB	SO	GDP	SH	SF	SB	CS	R	RBI	BA	OBA	SA
75	SF/NL		8	19	17	4	0	0	0	4	1	0	0	2	0	0	1	1	0	3	2	.235	.263	.235
76	SF/NL		26	115	102	23	6	2	2	39	8	0	0	18	0	3	2	6	2	14	10	.225	.277	.382
77	SF/NL		136	468	413	104	17	4	13	168	49	2	2	73	7	1	3	12	4	64	51	.252	.332	.407
78	SF/NL		156	657	592	181	46	8	25	318	50	8	3	72	15	3	9	15	11	90	98	.306	.358	.537
79	SF/NL		143	598	527	144	25	2	26	251	63	6	1	95	9	1	6	11	8	84	86	.273	.348	.476
80	SF/NL		127	524	437	124	20	8	22	226	74	13	2	52	12	1	10	2	5	77	82	.284	.382	.517
81	SF/NL		99	437	385	103	19	2	17	177	45	6	1	45	12	0	6	1	1	60	53	.268	.341	.460
82	SF/NL		157	659	563	154	30	3	27	271	90	7	1	91	20	0	5	6	9	90	103	.274	.372	.481
83	SF/NL		135	574	492	132	25	0	20	217	74	6	1	79	14	0	7	5	3	82	66	.268	.361	.441
84	SF/NL		57	249	203	65	9	1	11	109	43	7	0	29	9	0	3	1	1	33	44	.320	.434	.537
85	STL/NL		126	532	442	124	26	3	22	222	83	14	2	88	10	0	5	1	4	71	87	.281	.393	.502
86	STL/NL		65	279	232	55	12	2	9	98	45	4	1	61	4	0	1	1	1	34	23	.237	.362	.422
87	STL/NL		131	558	419	120	23	1	35	250	136	13	0	139	5	0	3	1	2	93	106	.286	.459	.597
88	NY/AL		150	616	496	120	14	0	27	215	113	6	2	141	14	0	5	3	2	81	93	.242	.381	.433
89	SD/NL		142	593	455	110	19	1	26	209	132	18	1	145	11	0	5	6	2	76	94	.242	.410	.459
90	SD/NL		115	442	334	89	12	1	25	178	104	11	2	91	10	0	5	4	3	59	62	.266	.441	.533
91	BOS/AL		140	585	481	120	18	1	28	224	96	3	3	133	11	0	2	5	2	75	87	.249	.374	.466
17 YR TOTALS			1913	7905	6590	1772	321	39	335	3176	1206	124	22	1354	170	9	78	76	60	1086	1147	**.269**	**.380**	**.482**

Clark, Jerald Dwayne — bats right — throws right — b.8/10/63 — 1991 positions: OF 96, 1B 16

YR	TM/LG	CL	G	TPA	AB	H	2B	3B	HR	TB	BB	IBB	HB	SO	GDP	SH	SF	SB	CS	R	RBI	BA	OBA	SA
85	SPO/NWL	A–	73	328	283	92	24	3	2	128	34	0	4	38	7	1	6	9	4	45	50	.325	.398	.452
86	REN/CAL	A+	95	434	389	118	34	3	7	179	29	3	9	46	8	0	7	5	4	76	58	.303	.359	.460
	BEA/TEX	AA	16	65	56	18	4	1	0	24	5	0	3	9	2	1	0	1	2	9	6	.321	.406	.429
87	WIC/TEX	AA	132	584	531	165	36	8	18	271	40	6	7	82	11	0	6	6	5	86	95	.311	.363	.510
88	LV/PCL	AAA	107	438	408	123	27	7	9	191	17	2	9	66	7	2	2	6	2	65	67	.301	.342	.468
	SD/NL		6	15	15	3	1	0	0	4	0	0	0	4	0	0	0	0	0	0	3	.200	.200	.267
89	LV/PCL	AAA	107	467	419	131	27	4	22	232	38	3	5	81	11	0	5	5	2	84	83	.313	.373	.554
	SD/NL		17	44	41	8	2	0	1	13	3	0	0	9	0	0	0	0	0	5	7	.195	.250	.317
90	LV/PCL	AAA	40	168	161	49	7	4	12	100	5	0	0	35	1	0	2	2	0	30	32	.304	.321	.621
	SD/NL		53	107	101	27	4	1	5	48	5	0	0	24	3	0	1	0	0	12	11	.267	.299	.475
91	SD/NL		118	411	369	84	16	0	10	130	31	2	6	90	10	1	4	2	1	26	47	.228	.295	.352
4 YR TOTALS			194	577	526	122	23	1	16	195	39	2	6	127	13	1	5	2	2	43	68	**.232**	**.290**	**.371**

Clark, William Nuschler "Will" — bats left — throws left — b.3/13/64 — 1991 positions: 1B 144

YR	TM/LG	CL	G	TPA	AB	H	2B	3B	HR	TB	BB	IBB	HB	SO	GDP	SH	SF	SB	CS	R	RBI	BA	OBA	SA
85	FRE/CAL	A+	65	289	217	67	14	0	10	111	62	2	2	46	4	3	5	11	2	41	48	.309	.458	.512
86	PHO/PCL	AAA	6	24	20	5	0	0	0	5	4	0	0	2	0	0	0	1	1	3	1	.250	.375	.250
	SF/NL		111	458	408	117	27	2	11	181	34	10	3	76	3	9	4	4	7	66	41	.287	.343	.444
87	SF/NL		150	588	529	163	29	5	35	307	49	11	5	98	3	3	2	5	17	89	91	.308	.371	.580
88	SF/NL		162	689	575	162	31	6	29	292	100	27	4	129	9	0	10	9	1	102	109	.282	.386	.508
89	SF/NL		159	675	588	196	38	9	23	321	74	14	5	103	6	0	8	8	3	104	111	.333	.407	.546
90	SF/NL		154	678	600	177	25	5	19	269	62	9	3	97	7	0	13	8	2	91	95	.295	.357	.448
91	SF/NL		148	622	565	170	32	7	29	303	51	12	2	91	5	0	4	4	2	84	116	.301	.359	.536
6 YR TOTALS			884	3710	3265	985	182	34	146	1673	370	83	22	594	32	12	41	38	32	536	563	**.302**	**.372**	**.512**

Clayton, Royce Spencer — bats right — throws right — b.1/2/70 — 1991 positions: SS 8

YR	TM/LG	CL	G	TPA	AB	H	2B	3B	HR	TB	BB	IBB	HB	SO	GDP	SH	SF	SB	CS	R	RBI	BA	OBA	SA
88	EVE/NWL	A–	60	245	212	55	4	0	3	68	27	0	3	54	8	1	2	10	4	35	29	.259	.348	.321
89	CLI/MID	A	104	437	385	91	13	3	0	110	39	0	4	101	6	4	5	28	16	39	24	.236	.309	.286
	SJ/CAL	A+	28	106	92	11	2	0	0	13	13	0	1	27	5	0	0	10	1	5	4	.120	.236	.141
90	SJ/CAL	A+	123	536	460	123	15	10	7	179	68	3	4	98	13	0	4	33	15	80	71	.267	.364	.389
91	SHR/TEX	AA	126	557	485	136	22	8	5	189	61	7	3	102	7	3	5	36	10	84	68	.280	.361	.390
	SF/NL		9	27	26	3	1	0	0	4	1	0	0	6	1	0	0	0	0	0	0	.115	.148	.154

Cochrane, David Carter "Dave" — bats both — throws right — b.1/31/63 — 1991 positions: OF 26, C 19, 3B 13, 1B 4, DH 1

YR	TM/LG	CL	G	TPA	AB	H	2B	3B	HR	TB	BB	IBB	HB	SO	GDP	SH	SF	SB	CS	R	RBI	BA	OBA	SA
82	LF/NYP	A–	70	316	269	81	16	2	22	167	39	0	7	117	0	0	1	3	0	51	62	.301	.402	.621
83	LYN/CAR	A+	120	520	445	117	16	1	25	210	71	11	2	146	11	0	2	4	2	73	102	.263	.365	.472
84	JAC/TEX	AA	129	519	454	121	29	3	14	222	61	9	1	133	8	1	2	3	1	66	77	.267	.353	.489
85	JAC/TEX	AA	33	127	103	23	1	0	4	36	20	3	0	45	1	1	3	0	2	14	20	.223	.341	.350

Cochrane, David Carter "Dave" (continued)

YR	TM/LG	CL	G	TPA	AB	H	2B	3B	HR	TB	BB	IBB	HB	SO	GDP	SH	SF	SB	CS	R	RBI	BA	OBA	SA
86	BIR/SOU	AA	93	418	349	95	23	5	17	179	61	4	2	102	4	0	6	4	4	66	74	.272	.378	.513
	BUF/AMA	AAA	38	139	124	28	7	0	6	53	11	1	0	45	2	2	2	0	1	15	16	.226	.285	.427
	CHI/AL		19	68	62	12	2	0	1	17	5	1	0	22	2	1	0	0	0	4	2	.194	.254	.274
87	HAW/PCL	AAA	129	499	451	122	23	3	15	196	35	2	8	121	11	0	5	7	7	60	66	.271	.331	.435
88	CAL/PCL	AAA	120	461	406	116	27	3	15	194	49	8	2	96	8	3	1	4	5	55	61	.286	.365	.478
89	CAL/PCL	AAA	32	139	125	34	10	0	6	62	11	0	1	36	1	0	2	2	1	22	35	.272	.331	.496
	SEA/AL		54	117	102	24	4	1	3	39	14	0	1	27	0	0	0	0	2	13	7	.235	.333	.382
90	SEA/AL		15	20	20	3	0	0	0	3	0	0	0	8	0	0	0	0	0	0	0	.150	.150	.150
	CAL/PCL	AAA	69	288	262	72	14	4	8	118	23	1	1	62	6	1	2	2	0	43	36	.275	.333	.450
91	CAL/PCL	AAA	47	202	190	61	11	0	3	81	8	1	1	36	5	0	3	2	0	25	37	.321	.347	.426
	SEA/AL		65	190	178	44	13	0	2	63	9	0	1	38	3	1	1	0	1	16	22	.247	.286	.354
4 YR TOTALS			**153**	**395**	**362**	**83**	**19**	**1**	**6**	**122**	**28**	**1**	**2**	**95**	**7**	**2**	**1**	**0**	**3**	**33**	**31**	**.229**	**.288**	**.337**

Colbrunn, Gregory Joseph "Greg" — bats right — throws right — b.7/26/69 — 1991 positions: C System MON/NL

YR	TM/LG	CL	G	TPA	AB	H	2B	3B	HR	TB	BB	IBB	HB	SO	GDP	SH	SF	SB	CS	R	RBI	BA	OBA	SA
88	ROC/MID	A	115	455	417	111	18	2	7	154	22	2	11	60	5	2	3	5	3	55	46	.266	.318	.369
89	WPB/FSL	A+	59	238	228	54	8	0	0	62	6	1	2	29	5	0	2	3	1	20	25	.237	.261	.272
	JAC/SOU	AA	55	194	178	49	11	1	3	71	13	0	2	33	9	0	1	0	1	21	18	.275	.330	.399
90	JAC/SOU	AA	125	511	458	138	29	1	13	208	38	4	6	78	8	3	6	1	2	57	76	.301	.358	.454

Cole, Alexander "Alex" — bats left — throws left — b.8/17/65 — 1991 positions: OF 107, DH 6

YR	TM/LG	CL	G	TPA	AB	H	2B	3B	HR	TB	BB	IBB	HB	SO	GDP	SH	SF	SB	CS	R	RBI	BA	OBA	SA
85	JC/APP	R+	66	264	232	61	5	1	1	71	30	0	1	27	4	0	1	46	8	60	13	.263	.348	.306
86	SP/FSL	A+	74	345	286	98	9	1	0	109	54	1	2	37	2	2	1	56	22	76	26	.343	.449	.381
	LOU/AMA	AAA	63	219	200	50	2	4	1	63	17	0	1	30	3	0	1	24	13	25	16	.250	.311	.315
87	ARK/TEX	AA	125	527	477	122	12	4	2	148	44	5	0	55	3	3	5	68	29	68	27	.256	.318	.310
88	LOU/AMA	AAA	120	442	392	91	7	8	0	114	42	1	1	59	2	6	1	40	15	44	24	.232	.307	.291
89	SP/FSL	A+	8	35	32	6	0	0	0	6	3	0	0	7	1	0	0	4	1	2	1	.188	.257	.188
	LOU/AMA	AAA	127	532	455	128	5	5	2	149	71	1	1	76	3	4	1	47	19	75	29	.281	.379	.327
90	LV/PCL	AAA	90	399	341	99	7	4	0	114	47	3	4	62	4	6	1	32	15	58	28	.290	.376	.334
	CS/PCL	AAA	14	57	49	21	2	0	0	23	8	0	0	7	1	0	0	6	4	13	3	.429	.509	.469
	CLE/AL		63	256	227	68	5	4	0	81	28	0	1	47	2	0	0	40	9	43	13	.300	.379	.357
91	CS/PCL	AAA	8	37	32	6	0	1	0	8	4	0	1	3	0	0	0	1	3	6	3	.188	.297	.250
	CLE/AL		122	452	387	114	17	3	0	137	58	2	1	47	8	4	2	27	17	58	21	.295	.386	.354
2 YR TOTALS			**185**	**708**	**614**	**182**	**22**	**7**	**0**	**218**	**86**	**2**	**2**	**85**	**10**	**4**	**2**	**67**	**26**	**101**	**34**	**.296**	**.384**	**.355**

Cole, Stewart Bryan "Stu" — bats right — throws right — b.2/7/66 — 1991 positions: 2B 5, DH 2, SS 1

YR	TM/LG	CL	G	TPA	AB	H	2B	3B	HR	TB	BB	IBB	HB	SO	GDP	SH	SF	SB	CS	R	RBI	BA	OBA	SA
87	EUG/NWL	A−	63	285	243	74	17	1	3	102	34	1	1	45	3	3	4	3	1	42	51	.305	.387	.420
88	VIR/CAR	A+	70	295	257	70	10	0	1	83	32	0	4	52	6	0	2	10	5	41	22	.272	.359	.323
	BC/FSL	A+	15	52	41	6	0	0	0	6	9	0	0	10	4	1	2	1	1	7	4	.146	.294	.146
89	MEM/SOU	AA	90	330	299	64	8	3	6	96	25	0	4	67	7	4	2	11	3	30	32	.214	.273	.321
90	MEM/SOU	AA	113	422	357	110	18	2	1	135	55	2	3	55	8	4	3	20	5	61	49	.308	.402	.378
91	OMA/AMA	AAA	120	491	441	115	13	7	3	151	42	0	1	60	12	5	2	11	10	64	39	.261	.325	.342
	KC/AL		9	9	7	1	0	0	0	1	2	0	0	2	0	0	0	0	0	1	0	.143	.333	.143

Coleman, Vincent Maurice "Vince" — bats both — throws right — b.9/22/60 — 1991 positions: OF 70

YR	TM/LG	CL	G	TPA	AB	H	2B	3B	HR	TB	BB	IBB	HB	SO	GDP	SH	SF	SB	CS	R	RBI	BA	OBA	SA
84	LOU/AMA	AAA	152	671	608	156	21	7	4	203	55	1	5	112	7	2	1	101	36	97	48	.257	.323	.334
85	LOU/AMA	AAA	5	22	21	3	0	0	0	3	0	0	0	3	0	1	0	0	1	1	0	.143	.143	.143
	STL/NL		151	692	636	170	20	10	1	213	50	1	0	115	3	5	1	110	25	107	40	.267	.320	.335
86	STL/NL		154	670	600	139	13	8	0	168	60	0	2	98	4	3	5	107	14	94	29	.232	.301	.280
87	STL/NL		151	702	623	180	14	10	3	223	70	0	3	126	7	5	1	109	22	121	43	.289	.363	.358
88	STL/NL		153	679	616	160	20	10	3	209	49	4	8	111	4	7	2	81	27	77	38	.260	.313	.339
89	STL/NL		145	624	563	143	21	9	2	188	50	0	2	90	4	7	2	65	10	94	28	.254	.316	.334
90	STL/NL		124	539	497	145	18	9	6	199	35	2	2	88	6	4	1	77	17	73	39	.292	.340	.400
91	NY/NL		72	318	278	71	7	5	1	91	39	0	0	47	3	1	0	37	14	45	17	.255	.347	.327
7 YR TOTALS			**950**	**4224**	**3813**	**1008**	**113**	**61**	**16**	**1291**	**353**	**6**	**10**	**675**	**31**	**33**	**15**	**586**	**129**	**611**	**234**	**.264**	**.327**	**.339**

Coles, Darnell — bats right — throws right — b.6/2/62 — 1991 positions: OF 3, 1B 1

YR	TM/LG	CL	G	TPA	AB	H	2B	3B	HR	TB	BB	IBB	HB	SO	GDP	SH	SF	SB	CS	R	RBI	BA	OBA	SA
83	SEA/AL		27	100	92	26	7	0	1	36	7	0	0	12	8	1	0	0	3	9	6	.283	.333	.391
84	SLC/PCL	AAA	69	304	242	77	22	3	14	147	48	2	2	41	4	6	6	7	2	57	68	.318	.426	.607
	SEA/AL		48	165	143	23	3	1	0	28	17	0	2	26	5	3	0	2	1	15	6	.161	.259	.196
85	SEA/AL		27	71	59	14	4	0	1	21	9	0	1	17	0	2	1	0	1	8	5	.237	.338	.356
	CAL/PCL	AAA	31	118	97	31	8	0	4	51	17	0	2	15	2	1	1	2	1	16	24	.320	.427	.526
86	DET/AL		142	587	521	142	30	2	20	236	45	3	6	84	8	7	8	6	3	67	86	.273	.333	.453
87	TOL/INT	AAA	10	41	37	12	5	0	1	20	4	1	0	0	0	0	0	0	0	7	8	.324	.390	.541
	DET/AL		53	169	149	27	5	1	4	46	15	1	2	23	1	2	1	0	1	14	15	.181	.263	.309
	PIT/NL		40	144	119	27	8	0	6	53	19	2	1	20	3	3	2	1	3	20	24	.227	.333	.445
	YEAR		93	313	268	54	13	1	10	99	34	3	4	43	4	5	3	1	4	34	39	.201	.295	.369
88	PIT/NL		68	241	211	49	13	1	5	79	20	1	3	41	3	0	7	1	1	20	36	.232	.299	.374
	SEA/AL		55	221	195	57	10	1	10	99	17	1	3	26	5	2	3	2	3	32	34	.292	.356	.508
	YEAR		123	462	406	106	23	2	15	178	37	2	6	67	8	2	10	4	3	52	70	.261	.326	.438
89	SEA/AL		146	573	535	135	21	3	10	192	27	1	6	61	13	2	3	5	4	54	59	.252	.294	.359

(continued)

Coles, Darnell (continued)

YR	TM/LG	CL	G	TPA	AB	H	2B	3B	HR	TB	BB	IBB	HB	SO	GDP	SH	SF	SB	CS	R	RBI	BA	OBA	SA
90	SEA/AL		37	113	107	23	5	1	2	36	4	1	1	17	1	0	1	0	0	9	16	.215	.248	.336
	DET/AL		52	122	108	22	2	0	1	27	12	1	0	21	3	1	1	0	4	13	4	.204	.281	.250
	YEAR		89	235	215	45	7	1	3	63	16	2	1	38	4	1	2	0	4	22	20	.209	.265	.293
91	SF/NL		11	14	14	3	0	0	0	3	0	0	0	2	1	0	0	0	0	1	0	.214	.214	.214
	PHO/PCL	AAA	83	365	328	95	23	2	6	140	27	2	6	43	10	1	3	0	0	43	65	.290	.352	.427
9 YR TOTALS			706	2520	2253	548	108	10	60	856	192	10	26	350	51	21	28	18	22	262	291	**.243**	**.307**	**.380**

Conine, Jeffrey Guy "Jeff" — bats right — throws right — b.6/27/66 — 1991 positions: 1B System KC/AL

YR	TM/LG	CL	G	TPA	AB	H	2B	3B	HR	TB	BB	IBB	HB	SO	GDP	SH	SF	SB	CS	R	RBI	BA	OBA	SA
88	BC/FSL	A+	118	470	415	113	23	9	10	184	46	1	0	77	6	5	4	26	12	63	59	.272	.342	.443
89	BC/FSL	A+	113	471	425	116	12	7	14	184	40	2	3	91	14	0	3	32	13	68	60	.273	.338	.433
90	MEM/SOU	AA	137	590	487	156	37	8	15	254	94	6	1	88	10	0	8	21	6	89	95	.320	.425	.522
	KC/AL		9	22	20	5	2	0	0	7	2	0	0	5	1	0	0	0	0	3	2	.250	.318	.350
91	OMA/AMA	AAA	51	198	171	44	9	1	3	64	26	2	0	39	3	0	0	0	6	23	15	.257	.359	.374
1 YR TOTALS			9	22	20	5	2	0	0	7	2	0	0	5	1	0	0	0	0	3	2	**.250**	**.318**	**.350**

Coolbaugh, Scott Robert — bats right — throws right — b.6/13/66 — 1991 positions: 3B 54

YR	TM/LG	CL	G	TPA	AB	H	2B	3B	HR	TB	BB	IBB	HB	SO	GDP	SH	SF	SB	CS	R	RBI	BA	OBA	SA
87	CHA/FSL	A+	66	260	233	64	21	0	2	91	24	1	0	56	5	1	2	0	1	27	20	.275	.340	.391
88	TUL/TEX	A	136	557	470	127	15	4	13	189	76	4	1	79	14	2	8	2	4	52	75	.270	.368	.402
89	OC/AMA	AAA	144	591	527	137	28	6	18	219	57	5	2	93	13	2	3	1	2	66	74	.260	.333	.416
	TEX/AL		25	57	51	14	1	0	2	21	4	0	0	12	2	1	1	0	0	7	7	.275	.321	.412
90	OC/AMA	AAA	76	324	293	66	17	2	6	105	27	2	1	62	6	0	3	0	1	39	30	.225	.290	.358
	TEX/AL		67	201	180	36	6	0	2	48	15	0	1	47	4	1	1	0	0	21	13	.200	.264	.267
91	SD/NL		60	205	180	39	8	1	2	55	19	2	1	45	4	0	1	0	3	12	15	.217	.294	.306
	LV/PCL	AAA	60	245	209	60	9	2	7	94	34	2	0	53	9	0	2	2	2	29	29	.287	.384	.450
3 YR TOTALS			152	463	411	89	15	1	6	124	38	2	2	104	12	9	3	1	3	40	35	**.217**	**.284**	**.302**

Cooper, Gary Clifton — bats right — throws right — b.8/13/64 — 1991 positions: 3B 4

YR	TM/LG	CL	G	TPA	AB	H	2B	3B	HR	TB	BB	IBB	HB	SO	GDP	SH	SF	SB	CS	R	RBI	BA	OBA	SA
86	AUB/NYP	A—	76	326	275	86	16	3	11	141	47	0	2	47	5	0	2	16	4	52	54	.313	.414	.513
87	OSC/FSL	A+	123	507	427	119	17	4	4	156	66	2	5	69	12	4	5	14	5	66	74	.279	.378	.365
88	COL/SOU	AA	140	576	474	128	25	7	7	188	87	0	4	87	20	4	7	13	7	65	69	.270	.383	.397
89	TUC/PCL	AAA	118	434	376	102	23	3	1	134	48	2	4	69	2	1	5	5	7	51	50	.271	.356	.356
90	OSC/FSL	A+	8	31	26	4	4	0	0	8	3	0	1	3	1	0	1	0	0	4	2	.154	.258	.308
	COL/SOU	AA	54	192	160	42	7	0	8	73	30	0	1	32	5	0	1	1	2	29	30	.262	.380	.456
91	TUC/PCL	AAA	120	482	406	124	25	6	14	203	66	5	3	108	11	2	5	7	8	86	75	.305	.402	.500
	HOU/NL		9	19	16	4	1	0	0	5	3	0	0	1	0	0	0	0	0	1	2	.250	.368	.313

Cooper, Scott Kendrick — bats left — throws right — b.10/13/67 — 1991 positions: 3B 13

YR	TM/LG	CL	G	TPA	AB	H	2B	3B	HR	TB	BB	IBB	HB	SO	GDP	SH	SF	SB	CS	R	RBI	BA	OBA	SA
86	ELM/NYP	A—	51	215	191	55	9	0	9	91	19	2	0	32	6	1	4	1	4	23	43	.288	.346	.476
87	GRE/SAL	A	119	436	370	93	21	2	15	163	58	7	2	69	5	0	6	1	0	52	63	.251	.351	.441
88	LYN/CAR	A+	130	563	497	148	45	7	9	234	58	0	2	74	11	2	4	0	0	90	73	.298	.371	.471
89	NB/EAS	AA	124	492	421	104	24	2	7	153	55	2	6	84	15	5	5	1	1	50	39	.247	.339	.363
90	PAW/INT	AAA	124	486	433	115	17	1	12	170	39	3	7	75	9	4	3	2	0	56	44	.266	.334	.393
	BOS/AL		2	1	1	0	0	0	0	0	0	0	0	1	0	0	0	0	0	0	0	.000	.000	.000
91	PAW/INT	AAA	137	550	483	134	21	2	15	204	50	11	7	58	13	4	6	3	4	55	72	.277	.350	.422
	BOS/AL		14	37	35	16	4	2	0	24	2	0	0	2	0	0	0	0	0	6	7	.457	.486	.686
2 YR TOTALS			16	38	36	16	4	2	0	24	2	0	0	3	0	0	0	0	0	6	7	**.444**	**.474**	**.667**

Cora, Jose Manuel (Amaro) "Joey" — bats both — throws right — b.5/14/65 — 1991 positions: 2B 80, SS 5, DH 2

YR	TM/LG	CL	G	TPA	AB	H	2B	3B	HR	TB	BB	IBB	HB	SO	GDP	SH	SF	SB	CS	R	RBI	BA	OBA	SA
85	SPO/NWL	A—	43	210	170	55	11	2	3	79	27	0	8	24	4	4	1	13	2	48	26	.324	.437	.465
86	BEA/TEX	AA	81	371	315	96	5	5	3	120	47	3	3	28	6	3	3	24	11	54	41	.305	.397	.381
87	LV/PCL	AAA	81	363	293	81	9	1	1	95	62	2	2	39	5	5	1	12	7	50	24	.276	.405	.324
	SD/NL		77	276	241	57	7	2	0	68	28	1	1	26	4	5	1	15	11	23	13	.237	.317	.282
88	LV/PCL	AAA	127	517	460	136	15	3	3	166	44	3	2	19	6	6	5	31	7	73	55	.296	.356	.361
89	LV/PCL	AAA	119	562	507	157	25	3	0	190	42	3	8	31	4	4	1	40	15	79	37	.310	.371	.375
	SD/NL		12	20	19	6	1	0	0	7	1	0	0	0	0	0	1	0	1	5	1	.316	.350	.368
90	LV/PCL	AAA	51	249	211	74	13	9	0	105	29	2	4	16	2	1	4	15	7	41	24	.351	.431	.498
	SD/NL		51	106	100	27	3	0	0	30	6	1	0	9	1	0	0	8	3	12	2	.270	.311	.300
91	SB/MID	A	1	5	5	1	0	0	0	1	0	0	0	0	0	0	0	1	0	1	0	.200	.200	.200
	CHI/AL		100	264	228	55	2	3	0	63	20	0	5	21	1	8	3	11	6	37	18	.241	.313	.276
4 YR TOTALS			240	666	588	145	13	5	0	168	55	2	6	56	6	13	4	35	20	77	34	**.247**	**.315**	**.286**

Cordero, Wilfredo "Wil" — bats right — throws right — b.10/3/71 — 1991 positions: SS System MON/NL

YR	TM/LG	CL	G	TPA	AB	H	2B	3B	HR	TB	BB	IBB	HB	SO	GDP	SH	SF	SB	CS	R	RBI	BA	OBA	SA
88	JAM/NYP	A—	52	211	190	49	3	0	2	58	15	0	4	44	2	0	2	3	3	18	22	.258	.322	.305
89	WPB/FSL	A+	78	328	289	80	12	2	6	114	33	2	3	58	6	1	2	2	5	37	29	.277	.355	.394
	JAC/SOU	AA	39	137	121	26	6	1	3	43	12	0	0	33	3	3	1	1	2	9	17	.215	.284	.355
90	JAC/SOU	AA	131	509	444	104	18	4	7	151	56	0	5	122	5	3	1	9	4	63	40	.234	.326	.340
91	IND/AMA	AAA	98	391	360	94	16	4	11	151	26	2	3	89	4	0	2	8	3	48	52	.261	.315	.419

Costo, Timothy Roger "Tim" — bats right — throws right — b.2/16/69 — 1991 positions: 1B System CIN/NL

YR	TM/LG	CL	G	TPA	AB	H	2B	3B	HR	TB	BB	IBB	HB	SO	GDP	SH	SF	SB	CS	R	RBI	BA	OBA	SA
90	KIN/CAR	A+	56	243	206	65	13	1	4	92	23	0	6	47	3	0	8	4	0	34	42	.316	.387	.447
91	CAN/EAS	AA	52	213	192	52	10	3	1	71	15	0	0	44	10	0	6	2	1	28	24	.271	.315	.370
	CHT/SOU	AA	85	319	293	82	19	3	5	122	20	0	4	65	5	0	2	11	4	31	29	.280	.332	.416

Cotto, Henry — bats right — throws right — b.1/5/61 — 1991 positions: OF 56, DH 6

YR	TM/LG	CL	G	TPA	AB	H	2B	3B	HR	TB	BB	IBB	HB	SO	GDP	SH	SF	SB	CS	R	RBI	BA	OBA	SA
84	IOW/AMA	AAA	8	33	30	6	2	0	0	8	2	0	1	3	2	0	0	1	2	3	0	.200	.273	.267
	CHI/NL		105	160	146	40	5	0	0	45	10	2	1	23	1	3	0	9	3	24	8	.274	.325	.308
85	COL/INT	AAA	75	297	272	70	16	2	7	111	19	0	2	61	4	1	3	10	4	38	36	.257	.307	.408
	NY/AL		34	60	56	17	1	0	1	21	3	0	0	12	1	1	0	1	1	4	6	.304	.339	.375
86	COL/INT	AAA	97	384	359	89	17	6	7	139	19	1	4	53	10	1	1	16	6	45	48	.248	.292	.387
	NY/AL		35	83	80	17	3	0	1	23	2	0	0	17	3	0	1	3	0	11	6	.213	.229	.287
87	COL/INT	AAA	34	141	129	39	13	2	3	65	10	0	1	16	3	0	1	14	2	26	20	.302	.355	.504
	NY/AL		68	156	149	35	10	0	5	60	6	0	1	35	7	0	4	2	2	21	20	.235	.269	.403
88	SEA/AL		133	418	386	100	18	1	8	144	23	0	2	53	8	4	3	27	3	50	33	.259	.302	.373
89	SEA/AL		100	310	295	78	11	2	9	120	12	3	3	44	4	0	0	10	4	44	33	.264	.300	.407
90	SEA/AL		127	390	355	92	14	3	4	124	22	0	6	52	13	6	3	21	3	40	33	.259	.307	.349
91	SEA/AL		66	192	177	54	6	2	6	82	10	0	2	27	7	2	1	16	3	35	23	.305	.347	.463
8 YR TOTALS			**668**	**1769**	**1644**	**433**	**68**	**8**	**34**	**619**	**88**	**7**	**13**	**263**	**44**	**16**	**8**	**91**	**19**	**229**	**162**	**.263**	**.305**	**.377**

Cromartie, Warren Livingston — bats left — throws left — b.9/29/53 — 1991 positions: 1B 29, OF 6, DH 1

YR	TM/LG	CL	G	TPA	AB	H	2B	3B	HR	TB	BB	IBB	HB	SO	GDP	SH	SF	SB	CS	R	RBI	BA	OBA	SA
74	MON/NL		8	20	17	3	0	0	0	3	3	0	0	3	0	0	0	1	0	2	0	.176	.300	.176
76	MON/NL		33	82	81	17	1	0	0	18	1	0	0	5	2	0	0	1	2	8	2	.210	.220	.222
77	MON/NL		155	662	620	175	41	7	5	245	33	3	4	40	15	2	3	10	3	64	50	.282	.321	.395
78	MON/NL		159	655	607	180	32	6	10	254	33	5	7	60	15	2	6	8	3	77	56	.297	.337	.418
79	MON/NL		158	710	659	181	46	5	8	261	38	19	6	78	11	6	6	8	7	84	46	.275	.313	.396
80	MON/NL		162	657	597	172	33	5	14	257	51	24	4	64	24	4	3	8	8	74	70	.288	.345	.430
81	MON/NL		99	400	358	109	19	2	6	150	39	12	0	27	8	0	3	2	3	41	42	.304	.370	.419
82	MON/NL		144	574	497	126	24	3	14	198	69	15	3	60	10	1	4	3	0	59	62	.254	.346	.398
83	MON/NL		120	410	360	100	26	2	3	139	43	7	1	48	11	1	5	8	3	37	43	.278	.352	.386
91	KC/AL		69	148	131	41	7	2	1	55	15	0	0	18	3	1	1	1	3	13	20	.313	.381	.420
10 YR TOTALS			**1107**	**4318**	**3927**	**1104**	**229**	**32**	**61**	**1580**	**325**	**85**	**18**	**403**	**99**	**17**	**31**	**50**	**37**	**459**	**391**	**.281**	**.336**	**.402**

Cron, Christopher John "Chris" — bats right — throws right — b.3/31/64 — 1991 positions: 1B 5, DH 1

YR	TM/LG	CL	G	TPA	AB	H	2B	3B	HR	TB	BB	IBB	HB	SO	GDP	SH	SF	SB	CS	R	RBI	BA	OBA	SA
84	PUL/APP	R+	32	139	114	42	8	0	7	71	17	1	6	20	2	0	2	2	0	22	37	.368	.468	.623
85	SUM/SAL	A	119	495	425	102	20	0	7	143	51	2	18	98	8	0	1	5	2	53	59	.240	.345	.336
86	DUR/CAR	A+	90	304	265	55	10	0	7	86	29	0	6	60	2	2	2	0	2	26	34	.208	.298	.325
87	QC/MID	A	111	460	398	110	20	1	11	165	44	2	17	88	5	0	1	1	3	53	62	.276	.372	.415
	PS/CAL	A+	26	106	92	25	3	0	2	34	9	0	2	27	3	1	2	2	2	6	9	.272	.343	.370
88	PS/CAL	A+	127	570	467	117	28	3	14	193	68	1	27	147	10	2	6	4	3	71	84	.251	.373	.413
89	MID/TEX	AA	128	551	491	148	33	2	22	253	39	5	14	126	10	1	6	0	1	80	103	.301	.365	.515
90	EDM/PCL	AAA	104	440	401	115	31	0	17	197	28	1	5	92	9	1	5	7	5	54	75	.287	.337	.491
91	EDM/PCL	AAA	123	531	461	134	21	1	22	223	47	3	10	103	12	2	11	6	5	74	91	.291	.361	.484
	CAL/AL		6	17	15	2	0	0	0	2	2	0	0	5	0	0	0	0	0	0	0	.133	.235	.133

Curtis, Chad David — bats right — throws right — b.11/6/68 — 1991 positions: 3B System CAL/AL

YR	TM/LG	CL	G	TPA	AB	H	2B	3B	HR	TB	BB	IBB	HB	SO	GDP	SH	SF	SB	CS	R	RBI	BA	OBA	SA
89	ANG/ARI	R	32	141	122	37	4	4	3	58	14	2	2	20	3	1	2	17	2	30	20	.303	.379	.475
	QC/MID	A	23	86	78	19	3	0	2	28	6	0	0	17	1	1	1	7	5	7	11	.244	.294	.359
90	QC/MID	A	135	568	492	151	28	1	14	223	57	3	12	76	8	4	3	63	21	87	65	.307	.390	.453
91	EDM/PCL	AAA	115	493	431	136	28	7	9	205	51	1	3	58	10	4	4	46	11	81	61	.316	.389	.476

Cuyler, Milton "Milt" — bats both — throws right — b.10/7/68 — 1991 positions: OF 151

YR	TM/LG	CL	G	TPA	AB	H	2B	3B	HR	TB	BB	IBB	HB	SO	GDP	SH	SF	SB	CS	R	RBI	BA	OBA	SA
86	BRI/APP	R+	45	196	174	40	3	5	1	56	15	0	5	35	1	2	0	12	4	24	11	.230	.309	.322
87	FAY/SAL	A	94	426	366	107	8	4	2	129	34	4	7	78	3	17	2	27	13	65	34	.292	.362	.352
88	LAK/FSL	A+	132	573	483	143	11	3	2	166	71	2	4	83	3	14	1	50	25	100	32	.296	.390	.344
89	TOL/INT	AAA	24	95	83	14	3	2	0	21	8	0	0	27	1	3	1	4	1	4	6	.169	.239	.253
	LON/EAS	AA	98	421	366	96	8	7	7	139	47	2	4	74	2	4	0	32	5	69	34	.262	.353	.380
90	TOL/INT	AAA	124	535	461	119	11	8	2	152	60	1	5	77	6	7	2	52	14	77	42	.258	.348	.330
	DET/AL		19	59	51	13	3	1	0	18	5	0	0	10	1	2	1	1	2	8	8	.255	.316	.353
91	DET/AL		154	546	475	122	15	7	3	160	52	0	5	92	4	12	2	41	10	77	33	.257	.335	.337
2 YR TOTALS			**173**	**605**	**526**	**135**	**18**	**8**	**3**	**178**	**57**	**0**	**5**	**102**	**5**	**14**	**3**	**42**	**12**	**85**	**41**	**.257**	**.333**	**.338**

Daniels, Kalvoski "Kal" — bats left — throws right — b.8/20/63 — 1991 positions: OF 132

YR	TM/LG	CL	G	TPA	AB	H	2B	3B	HR	TB	BB	IBB	HB	SO	GDP	SH	SF	SB	CS	R	RBI	BA	OBA	SA
84	VER/EAS	AA	122	491	415	130	29	4	17	218	73	5	2	59	4	0	1	43	11	81	62	.313	.418	.525
85	DEN/AMA	AAA	76	326	285	86	12	9	15	161	37	1	2	34	9	1	1	10	11	59	43	.302	.385	.565
86	DEN/AMA	AAA	42	169	132	49	12	2	8	89	34	3	2	20	2	1	1	6	2	33	32	.371	.503	.674
	CIN/NL		74	207	181	58	10	4	6	94	22	1	2	30	4	1	1	15	2	34	23	.320	.398	.519
87	CIN/NL		108	430	368	123	24	1	26	227	60	11	3	62	6	1	0	26	7	73	64	.334	.429	.617
88	CIN/NL		140	589	495	144	29	1	18	229	87	10	3	94	11	0	4	27	6	95	64	.291	.397	.463

(continued)

Daniels, Kalvoski "Kal" (continued)

YR	TM/LG	CL	G	TPA	AB	H	2B	3B	HR	TB	BB	IBB	HB	SO	GDP	SH	SF	SB	CS	R	RBI	BA	OBA	SA
89	CIN/NL		44	172	133	29	11	0	2	46	36	1	2	28	1	0	1	6	4	26	9	.218	.390	.346
	LA/NL		11	46	38	13	2	0	2	21	7	0	0	5	1	0	1	3	0	7	8	.342	.435	.553
	YEAR		55	218	171	42	13	0	4	67	43	1	2	33	2	0	2	9	4	33	17	.246	.399	.392
90	LA/NL		130	526	450	133	23	1	27	239	68	1	3	104	9	2	3	4	3	81	94	.296	.389	.531
91	LA/NL		137	531	461	115	15	1	17	183	63	4	1	116	9	0	6	6	1	54	73	.249	.337	.397
6 YR TOTALS			**644**	**2501**	**2126**	**615**	**114**	**8**	**98**	**1039**	**343**	**28**	**12**	**439**	**41**	**4**	**16**	**87**	**24**	**370**	**335**	**.289**	**.388**	**.489**

Dascenzo, Douglas Craig "Doug" — bats both — throws left — b.6/30/64 — 1991 positions: OF 86, P 3

YR	TM/LG	CL	G	TPA	AB	H	2B	3B	HR	TB	BB	IBB	HB	SO	GDP	SH	SF	SB	CS	R	RBI	BA	OBA	SA
85	GEN/NYP	A−	70	320	252	84	15	1	3	110	61	4	2	20	1	1	4	33	9	59	23	.333	.461	.437
86	WIN/CAR	A+	138	627	545	178	29	11	6	247	63	5	2	44	9	12	5	57	13	107	83	.327	.395	.453
87	PIT/EAS	AA	134	582	496	152	32	6	3	205	73	5	1	38	5	7	5	36	7	84	56	.306	.393	.413
88	IOW/AMA	AAA	132	556	505	149	22	5	6	199	37	4	2	41	7	7	5	30	14	73	49	.295	.342	.394
	CHI/NL		26	85	75	16	3	0	0	19	9	1	0	4	2	1	0	6	1	9	4	.213	.298	.253
89	IOW/AMA	AAA	111	493	431	121	18	4	4	159	51	3	0	41	7	9	2	34	21	59	33	.281	.355	.369
	CHI/NL		47	157	139	23	1	0	1	27	13	0	0	13	2	3	2	6	3	20	12	.165	.234	.194
90	CHI/NL		113	271	241	61	9	5	1	83	21	2	1	18	3	5	3	15	6	27	26	.253	.312	.344
91	CHI/NL		118	272	239	61	11	0	1	75	24	2	2	26	3	6	1	14	7	40	18	.255	.327	.314
4 YR TOTALS			**304**	**785**	**694**	**161**	**24**	**5**	**3**	**204**	**67**	**5**	**3**	**61**	**10**	**15**	**6**	**41**	**17**	**96**	**60**	**.232**	**.300**	**.294**

Daugherty, John Michael "Jack" — bats both — throws left — b.7/3/60 — 1991 positions: OF 37, 1B 11, DH 1

YR	TM/LG	CL	G	TPA	AB	H	2B	3B	HR	TB	BB	IBB	HB	SO	GDP	SH	SF	SB	CS	R	RBI	BA	OBA	SA
84	HEL/PIO	R+	66	315	259	104	26	2	15	179	52	10	2	48	2	0	2	16	3	77	82	.402	.502	.691
85	WPB/FSL	A+	133	561	481	152	25	3	10	213	75	11	1	58	14	0	5	33	6	76	87	.316	.405	.443
86	JAC/SOU	AA	138	595	502	159	37	4	4	216	79	1	4	58	14	7	3	15	6	87	63	.317	.412	.430
87	IND/AMA	AAA	117	469	420	131	35	3	7	193	42	5	1	54	12	2	4	11	0	65	50	.312	.373	.460
	MON/NL		11	12	10	1	0	0	0	2	0	0	0	2	0	2	0	0	0	1	1	.100	.100	.200
88	IND/AMA	AAA	137	552	481	137	33	2	6	192	56	4	1	50	14	7	7	18	6	82	67	.285	.356	.399
89	OC/AMA	AAA	82	355	311	78	15	3	3	108	39	5	0	35	9	2	3	2	2	28	32	.251	.331	.347
	TEX/AL		52	121	106	32	4	2	1	43	11	0	1	21	1	0	3	2	1	15	10	.302	.364	.406
90	TEX/AL		125	339	310	93	20	2	6	135	22	0	2	49	4	2	3	0	0	36	47	.300	.347	.435
91	OC/AMA	AAA	22	85	77	11	2	0	0	13	8	2	0	14	1	0	0	1	0	4	4	.143	.224	.169
	TEX/AL		58	167	144	28	3	2	1	38	16	1	0	23	2	4	3	1	0	8	11	.194	.270	.264
4 YR TOTALS			**246**	**639**	**570**	**154**	**28**	**6**	**8**	**218**	**49**	**1**	**3**	**96**	**7**	**8**	**9**	**3**	**1**	**60**	**69**	**.270**	**.326**	**.382**

Daulton, Darren Arthur — bats left — throws right — b.1/3/62 — 1991 positions: C 88

YR	TM/LG	CL	G	TPA	AB	H	2B	3B	HR	TB	BB	IBB	HB	SO	GDP	SH	SF	SB	CS	R	RBI	BA	OBA	SA
83	PHI/NL		2	4	3	1	0	0	0	1	1	0	0	1	0	0	0	0	0	1	0	.333	.500	.333
84	POR/PCL	AAA	80	313	252	75	19	4	7	123	57	3	0	49	4	3	1	3	3	45	38	.298	.426	.488
85	POR/PCL	AAA	23	82	64	19	5	3	2	36	16	0	1	13	1	0	1	6	1	13	10	.297	.439	.563
	PHI/NL		36	119	103	21	3	1	4	38	16	0	0	37	1	0	0	3	0	14	11	.204	.311	.369
86	PHI/NL		49	181	138	31	4	0	8	59	38	3	1	41	1	2	2	2	3	18	21	.225	.391	.428
87	CLE/FSL	A+	9	27	22	5	3	0	1	11	4	0	0	3	1	0	1	0	0	1	5	.227	.333	.500
	MAI/INT	AAA	20	87	70	15	1	1	3	27	16	1	0	15	5	0	1	5	1	9	10	.214	.356	.386
	PHI/NL		53	150	129	25	6	0	3	40	16	1	0	37	0	4	1	0	0	10	13	.194	.281	.310
88	PHI/NL		58	163	144	30	6	0	1	39	17	1	0	26	2	0	2	2	1	13	12	.208	.288	.271
89	PHI/NL		131	424	368	74	12	2	8	114	52	8	1	58	4	1	1	2	1	29	44	.201	.303	.310
90	PHI/NL		143	540	459	123	30	1	12	191	72	9	2	72	6	3	4	7	1	62	57	.268	.367	.416
91	SCR/INT	AAA	2	9	9	2	0	0	0	5	0	0	0	0	0	0	0	0	0	1	1	.222	.222	.556
	REA/EAS	AA	1	5	4	1	0	0	0	1	1	0	0	0	0	0	0	0	0	0	0	.250	.400	.250
	PHI/NL		89	335	285	56	12	0	12	104	41	4	2	66	4	2	5	5	0	36	42	.196	.297	.365
8 YR TOTALS			**561**	**1916**	**1629**	**361**	**73**	**4**	**48**	**586**	**253**	**26**	**7**	**338**	**18**	**12**	**15**	**21**	**6**	**183**	**200**	**.222**	**.326**	**.360**

Davidson, John Mark "Mark" — bats right — throws right — b.2/15/61 — 1991 positions: OF 63

YR	TM/LG	CL	G	TPA	AB	H	2B	3B	HR	TB	BB	IBB	HB	SO	GDP	SH	SF	SB	CS	R	RBI	BA	OBA	SA
84	ORL/SOU	AA	114	407	348	99	11	6	4	134	52	1	3	57	7	0	4	15	4	55	37	.284	.378	.385
85	ORL/SOU	AA	134	563	453	137	17	2	25	233	92	1	10	92	4	2	6	13	5	93	106	.302	.426	.514
86	TOL/INT	AAA	108	429	383	95	16	1	10	143	37	0	4	91	4	1	4	4	6	55	38	.248	.318	.373
	MIN/AL		36	77	68	8	3	0	0	11	6	0	0	22	1	3	0	2	3	5	2	.118	.189	.162
87	MIN/AL		102	169	150	40	4	1	1	49	13	1	0	26	4	2	2	9	2	32	14	.267	.321	.327
88	POR/PCL	AAA	15	68	56	18	4	2	0	26	10	0	0	8	0	1	1	1	0	6	5	.321	.418	.464
	MIN/AL		100	119	106	23	7	0	1	33	10	0	1	20	3	1	1	3	3	22	10	.217	.288	.311
89	POR/PCL	AAA	30	109	96	17	2	0	1	22	11	0	1	27	2	0	1	2	0	8	8	.177	.266	.229
	TUC/PCL	AAA	39	160	141	41	7	2	4	64	16	0	2	19	3	1	0	0	2	18	16	.291	.371	.454
	HOU/NL		33	73	65	13	2	1	1	20	7	0	0	14	1	0	1	1	0	7	5	.200	.278	.308
90	TUC/PCL	AAA	56	215	182	61	13	1	6	94	22	0	4	35	4	2	6	5	1	35	46	.335	.404	.516
	HOU/NL		57	142	130	38	7	1	0	48	10	1	0	18	1	1	1	0	3	12	11	.292	.340	.369
91	HOU/NL		85	156	142	27	6	0	2	39	12	0	2	28	2	0	0	0		10	15	.190	.263	.275
6 YR TOTALS			**413**	**736**	**661**	**149**	**27**	**3**	**6**	**200**	**58**	**2**	**3**	**128**	**12**	**10**	**4**	**15**	**11**	**88**	**57**	**.225**	**.289**	**.303**

Davis, Alvin Glenn — bats left — throws right — b.9/9/60 — 1991 positions: DH 126, 1B 14

YR	TM/LG	CL	G	TPA	AB	H	2B	3B	HR	TB	BB	IBB	HB	SO	GDP	SH	SF	SB	CS	R	RBI	BA	OBA	SA
84	SLC/PCL	AAA	1	4	3	2	0	0	0	2	1	0	0	1	0	0	0	0	0	2	1	.667	.750	.667
	SEA/AL		152	678	567	161	34	3	27	282	97	16	7	78	7	0	7	5	4	80	116	.284	.391	.497

Davis, Alvin Glenn (continued)

YR	TM/LG	CL	G	TPA	AB	H	2B	3B	HR	TB	BB	IBB	HB	SO	GDP	SH	SF	SB	CS	R	RBI	BA	OBA	SA
85	SEA/AL		155	677	578	166	33	1	18	255	90	7	2	71	14	0	7	1	2	78	78	.287	.381	.441
86	SEA/AL		135	562	479	130	18	1	18	204	76	10	3	68	11	2	2	0	3	66	72	.271	.373	.426
87	SEA/AL		157	662	580	171	37	2	29	299	72	6	2	84	17	0	8	0	0	86	100	.295	.370	.516
88	SEA/AL		140	582	478	141	24	1	18	221	95	13	4	53	14	0	5	1	1	67	69	.295	.412	.462
89	SEA/AL		142	611	498	152	30	1	21	247	101	15	6	49	15	0	6	0	1	84	95	.305	.424	.496
90	SEA/AL		140	592	494	140	21	0	17	212	85	10	4	68	9	0	9	0	2	63	68	.283	.387	.429
91	SEA/AL		145	528	462	102	15	1	12	155	56	9	0	78	8	0	10	0	3	39	69	.221	.299	.335
8 YR TOTALS			1166	4892	4136	1163	212	10	160	1875	672	86	28	549	95	2	54	7	16	563	667	**.281**	**.381**	**.453**

Davis, Charles Theodore "Chili" — bats both — throws right — b.1/17/60 — 1991 positions: DH 150, OF 2

YR	TM/LG	CL	G	TPA	AB	H	2B	3B	HR	TB	BB	IBB	HB	SO	GDP	SH	SF	SB	CS	R	RBI	BA	OBA	SA
81	SF/NL		8	16	15	2	0	0	0	2	1	0	0	2	1	0	0	2	0	1	0	.133	.188	.133
82	SF/NL		154	701	641	167	27	6	19	263	45	2	2	115	13	7	6	24	13	86	76	.261	.308	.410
83	SF/NL		137	553	486	113	21	2	11	171	55	6	0	108	9	3	9	10	12	54	59	.233	.305	.352
84	SF/NL		137	546	499	157	21	6	21	253	42	6	1	74	13	2	2	12	8	87	81	.315	.368	.507
85	SF/NL		136	551	481	130	25	2	13	198	62	12	0	74	16	1	7	15	7	53	56	.270	.349	.412
86	SF/NL		153	618	526	146	28	3	13	219	84	23	1	96	11	2	5	16	13	71	70	.278	.375	.416
87	SF/NL		149	578	500	125	22	1	24	221	72	15	2	109	8	0	4	16	9	80	76	.250	.344	.442
88	CAL/AL		158	667	600	161	29	3	21	259	56	14	1	118	13	1	10	9	10	81	93	.268	.326	.432
89	CAL/AL		154	630	560	152	24	1	22	244	61	12	0	109	21	3	6	3	0	81	90	.271	.340	.436
90	CAL/AL		113	476	412	109	17	1	12	164	61	4	0	89	14	0	3	1	2	58	58	.265	.357	.398
91	MIN/AL		153	634	534	148	34	1	29	271	95	13	1	117	9	0	4	5	6	84	93	.277	.385	.507
11 YR TOTALS			1452	5970	5254	1410	248	26	185	2265	634	107	7	1011	128	19	56	113	80	736	752	**.268**	**.345**	**.431**

Davis, Eric Keith — bats right — throws right — b.5/29/62 — 1991 positions: OF 81

YR	TM/LG	CL	G	TPA	AB	H	2B	3B	HR	TB	BB	IBB	HB	SO	GDP	SH	SF	SB	CS	R	RBI	BA	OBA	SA
84	WIC/AMA	AAA	52	223	194	61	9	5	14	122	25	1	2	55	2	1	1	27	10	42	34	.314	.396	.629
	CIN/NL		57	200	174	39	10	1	10	81	24	0	0	48	1	0	1	10	2	33	30	.224	.320	.466
85	DEN/AMA	AAA	64	239	206	57	10	2	15	116	29	0	1	67	2	0	3	35	5	48	38	.277	.364	.563
	CIN/NL		56	131	122	30	3	3	8	63	7	0	0	39	1	2	0	16	3	26	18	.246	.287	.516
86	CIN/NL		132	487	415	115	15	3	27	217	68	6	1	100	6	0	3	80	11	97	71	.277	.378	.523
87	CIN/NL		129	562	474	139	23	4	37	281	84	8	1	134	6	0	3	50	6	120	100	.293	.399	.593
88	CIN/NL		135	543	472	129	18	3	26	231	65	10	3	124	11	0	3	35	3	81	93	.273	.363	.489
89	CIN/NL		131	542	462	130	14	2	34	250	68	12	1	116	16	0	11	21	7	74	101	.281	.367	.541
90	CIN/NL		127	518	453	118	26	2	24	220	60	6	2	100	7	0	3	21	3	84	86	.260	.347	.486
91	CIN/NL		89	340	285	67	10	0	11	110	48	5	5	92	4	0	2	14	2	39	33	.235	.353	.386
8 YR TOTALS			856	3323	2857	767	119	18	177	1453	424	46	14	753	52	2	26	247	37	554	532	**.268**	**.363**	**.509**

Davis, Glenn Earle — bats right — throws right — b.3/28/61 — 1991 positions: 1B 36, DH 12

YR	TM/LG	CL	G	TPA	AB	H	2B	3B	HR	TB	BB	IBB	HB	SO	GDP	SH	SF	SB	CS	R	RBI	BA	OBA	SA
84	TUC/PCL	AAA	131	535	471	140	28	7	16	230	49	3	5	88	14	1	9	3	2	66	94	.297	.363	.488
	HOU/NL		18	68	61	13	5	0	2	24	4	0	0	12	0	2	1	0	0	6	8	.213	.258	.393
85	TUC/PCL	AAA	60	239	220	67	24	2	5	110	13	3	3	23	7	0	3	1	0	22	35	.305	.347	.500
	HOU/NL		100	390	350	95	11	0	20	166	27	6	7	68	12	2	4	0	0	51	64	.271	.332	.474
86	HOU/NL		158	654	574	152	32	3	31	283	64	6	9	72	11	0	7	3	1	91	101	.265	.344	.493
87	HOU/NL		151	635	578	145	35	2	27	265	47	10	5	84	16	0	5	4	1	70	93	.251	.310	.458
88	HOU/NL		152	634	561	152	26	0	30	268	53	20	11	77	11	0	9	4	3	78	99	.271	.341	.478
89	HOU/NL		158	663	581	156	26	1	34	286	69	17	7	123	9	0	6	4	2	87	89	.269	.350	.492
90	COL/SOU	AA	12	40	37	11	0	0	1	14	2	0	1	9	0	0	0	1	0	3	8	.297	.350	.378
	HOU/NL		93	381	327	82	15	4	22	171	46	17	8	54	5	0	0	8	3	44	64	.251	.357	.523
91	HAG/EAS	AA	7	26	24	6	1	0	1	10	1	0	0	2	1	0	1	0	0	4	3	.250	.269	.417
	BAL/AL		49	199	176	40	9	1	10	81	16	0	5	29	2	0	2	4	0	29	28	.227	.307	.460
8 YR TOTALS			879	3624	3208	835	159	11	176	1544	326	76	52	519	66	4	34	27	10	456	546	**.260**	**.335**	**.481**

Davis, Mark Anthony — bats right — throws right — b.11/25/64 — 1991 positions: OF 3

YR	TM/LG	CL	G	TPA	AB	H	2B	3B	HR	TB	BB	IBB	HB	SO	GDP	SH	SF	SB	CS	R	RBI	BA	OBA	SA
86	APP/MID	A	77	331	272	62	10	4	3	89	54	0	4	70	4	1	0	19	8	37	22	.228	.364	.327
87	PEN/CAR	A+	134	583	507	149	24	6	16	233	63	2	6	115	8	2	5	37	11	91	72	.294	.375	.460
88	BIR/SOU	AA	66	293	248	72	18	3	6	114	38	0	7	55	6	0	0	32	13	52	27	.290	.399	.460
	VAN/PCL	AAA	68	278	241	51	9	2	4	76	28	0	6	65	4	8	1	8	10	24	29	.212	.298	.315
89	VAN/PCL	AAA	39	141	123	16	4	1	0	22	13	0	5	38	4	0	0	6	2	13	8	.130	.241	.179
	BIR/SOU	AA	56	221	192	49	10	3	5	80	25	1	1	52	3	3	0	16	7	35	26	.255	.344	.417
	MID/TEX	AA	19	68	58	14	1	0	1	18	6	0	1	18	1	3	0	6	1	9	7	.241	.323	.310
90	MID/TEX	AA	92	413	353	94	16	1	12	148	48	2	6	96	4	3	3	16	8	66	41	.266	.361	.419
	EDM/PCL	AAA	35	154	133	49	10	5	9	96	17	0	2	23	3	2	2	7	8	30	34	.368	.434	.722
91	CAL/AL		3	2	2	0	0	0	0	0	0	0	0	0	0	0	0	0	0	0	0	.000	.000	.000
	EDM/PCL	AAA	115	509	421	117	20	6	13	188	70	0	8	112	8	8	2	32	13	86	56	.278	.389	.447

Davis, Wallace McArthur "Butch" — bats right — throws right — b.6/19/58 — 1991 positions: OF

YR	TM/LG	CL	G	TPA	AB	H	2B	3B	HR	TB	BB	IBB	HB	SO	GDP	SH	SF	SB	CS	R	RBI	BA	OBA	SA
80	ROY/GCL	R	61	270	235	74	17	4	2	105	29	2	1	36	4	0	5	31	4	46	35	.315	.385	.447
81	FM/FSL	A+	126	527	464	139	17	10	13	215	54	2	3	99	8	1	5	44	3	89	70	.300	.373	.463
82	JAC/SOU	AA	122	505	450	115	18	4	10	171	46	1	3	101	6	3	3	17	9	64	57	.256	.327	.380
83	JAC/SOU	AA	90	375	331	105	15	7	14	176	36	2	0	78	4	2	6	29	7	51	63	.317	.378	.532
	OMA/AMA	AAA	46	191	171	54	10	3	5	85	18	0	1	36	4	1	0	13	5	27	21	.316	.384	.497

(continued)

Davis, Wallace McArthur "Butch" (continued)

YR	TM/LG	CL	G	TPA	AB	H	2B	3B	HR	TB	BB	IBB	HB	SO	GDP	SH	SF	SB	CS	R	RBI	BA	OBA	SA
	KC/AL		33	130	122	42	2	6	2	62	4	0	0	19	3	2	2	4	3	13	18	.344	.359	.508
84	KC/AL		41	128	116	17	3	0	2	26	10	0	0	19	2	0	2	4	3	11	12	.147	.211	.224
	OMA/AMA	AAA	83	342	314	102	15	5	7	148	24	4	1	56	9	2	1	9	7	45	43	.325	.374	.471
85	OMA/AMA	AAA	109	436	403	106	26	10	6	170	26	0	1	89	6	3	3	15	6	58	34	.263	.307	.422
87	PIT/NL		7	8	7	1	1	0	0	2	1	0	0	3	0	0	0	0	0	3	0	.143	.250	.286
	VAN/PCL	AAA	111	454	424	115	17	7	7	167	22	1	1	73	6	1	6	22	6	58	57	.271	.305	.394
88	ROC/INT	AAA	8	31	28	4	0	2	0	8	0	0	2	2	0	1	0	0	0	4	0	.143	.200	.286
	CHA/SOU	AA	101	440	412	124	23	7	13	200	24	2	1	40	12	2	1	17	5	62	82	.301	.340	.485
	BAL/AL		13	25	25	6	1	0	0	7	0	0	0	8	2	0	0	1	0	2	0	.240	.240	.280
89	ROC/INT	AAA	127	520	479	145	29	9	10	222	28	4	6	57	12	2	5	19	8	81	64	.303	.346	.463
	BAL/AL		5	6	6	1	1	0	0	2	0	0	0	3	0	0	0	0	0	1	0	.167	.167	.333
90	ALB/PCL	AAA	124	519	480	164	31	9	10	243	24	5	4	53	18	0	11	25	14	87	85	.342	.370	.506
91	ALB/PCL	AAA	91	306	284	89	19	10	7	149	18	6	2	51	5	0	2	12	5	55	44	.313	.356	.525
	LA/NL		1	1	1	0	0	0	0	0	0	0	0	0	0	0	0	0	0	0	0	.000	.000	.000
6 YR TOTALS			**100**	**298**	**277**	**67**	**8**	**6**	**4**	**99**	**15**	**0**	**0**	**52**	**7**	**2**	**4**	**9**	**6**	**30**	**30**	**.242**	**.277**	**.357**

Dawson, Andre Fernando — bats right — throws right — b.7/10/54 — 1991 positions: OF 137

YR	TM/LG	CL	G	TPA	AB	H	2B	3B	HR	TB	BB	IBB	HB	SO	GDP	SH	SF	SB	CS	R	RBI	BA	OBA	SA
76	MON/NL		24	92	85	20	4	1	0	26	5	1	0	13	0	2	0	1	2	9	7	.235	.278	.306
77	MON/NL		139	566	525	148	26	9	19	249	34	4	2	93	6	1	4	21	7	64	65	.282	.326	.474
78	MON/NL		157	660	609	154	24	8	25	269	30	3	12	128	7	4	5	28	11	84	72	.253	.299	.442
79	MON/NL		155	684	639	176	24	12	25	299	27	5	6	115	10	8	4	35	10	90	92	.275	.309	.468
80	MON/NL		151	638	577	178	41	7	17	284	44	7	6	69	9	1	10	34	9	96	87	.308	.358	.492
81	MON/NL		103	441	394	119	21	3	24	218	35	14	7	50	6	0	5	26	4	71	64	.302	.365	.553
82	MON/NL		148	660	608	183	37	7	23	303	34	4	8	96	8	4	6	39	10	107	83	.301	.343	.498
83	MON/NL		159	698	633	189	36	10	32	341	38	12	9	81	14	0	18	25	11	104	113	.299	.338	.539
84	MON/NL		138	583	533	132	23	6	17	218	41	2	2	80	12	1	6	13	5	73	86	.248	.301	.409
85	MON/NL		139	570	529	135	27	2	23	235	29	8	4	92	12	1	7	13	4	65	91	.255	.295	.444
86	MON/NL		130	546	496	141	32	2	20	237	37	11	6	79	13	1	6	18	12	65	78	.284	.338	.478
87	CHI/NL		153	662	621	178	24	2	49	353	32	7	7	103	15	0	2	11	3	90	137	.287	.328	.568
88	CHI/NL		157	640	591	179	31	8	24	298	37	12	4	73	13	0	7	12	4	78	79	.303	.344	.504
89	CHI/NL		118	459	416	105	18	6	21	198	35	13	1	62	16	0	7	8	5	62	77	.252	.307	.476
90	CHI/NL		147	581	529	164	28	5	27	283	42	21	2	65	12	0	8	16	2	72	100	.310	.358	.535
91	CHI/NL		149	596	563	153	21	4	31	275	22	3	5	80	10	0	6	4	5	69	104	.272	.302	.488
16 YR TOTALS			**2167**	**9076**	**8348**	**2354**	**417**	**92**	**377**	**4086**	**522**	**127**	**81**	**1279**	**163**	**24**	**101**	**304**	**104**	**1199**	**1335**	**.282**	**.327**	**.489**

Decker, Steven Michael "Steve" — bats right — throws right — b.10/25/65 — 1991 positions: C 78

YR	TM/LG	CL	G	TPA	AB	H	2B	3B	HR	TB	BB	IBB	HB	SO	GDP	SH	SF	SB	CS	R	RBI	BA	OBA	SA
88	EVE/NWL	A−	13	53	42	22	2	0	2	30	7	0	1	5	1	0	3	0	0	11	13	.524	.566	.714
	SJ/CAL	A+	47	198	175	56	9	0	4	77	21	1	1	21	4	1	0	0	2	31	34	.320	.396	.440
89	SJ/CAL	A+	64	274	225	65	12	0	3	86	44	3	0	36	9	0	5	8	5	27	46	.289	.398	.382
	SHR/TEX	AA	44	155	142	46	8	0	1	57	11	0	0	24	5	1	1	0	3	19	18	.324	.370	.401
90	SHR/TEX	AA	116	452	403	118	22	1	15	187	40	2	2	64	11	0	7	3	7	52	80	.293	.354	.464
	SF/NL		15	56	54	16	2	0	3	27	1	0	0	10	1	1	0	0	0	5	8	.296	.309	.500
91	PHO/PCL	AAA	31	125	111	28	5	1	6	53	13	0	1	29	1	0	0	0	0	20	14	.252	.336	.477
	SF/NL		79	258	233	48	7	1	5	72	16	1	3	44	7	2	4	0	1	11	24	.206	.262	.309
2 YR TOTALS			**94**	**314**	**287**	**64**	**9**	**1**	**8**	**99**	**17**	**1**	**3**	**54**	**8**	**3**	**4**	**0**	**1**	**16**	**32**	**.223**	**.270**	**.345**

Deer, Robert George "Rob" — bats right — throws right — b.9/29/60 — 1991 positions: OF 132, DH 2

YR	TM/LG	CL	G	TPA	AB	H	2B	3B	HR	TB	BB	IBB	HB	SO	GDP	SH	SF	SB	CS	R	RBI	BA	OBA	SA
84	PHO/PCL	AAA	133	551	449	102	21	1	31	218	96	4	2	175	7	2	2	9	3	88	69	.227	.364	.486
	SF/NL		13	32	24	4	0	0	3	13	7	0	1	10	0	0	0	1	1	5	3	.167	.375	.542
85	SF/NL		78	187	162	30	5	1	8	61	23	0	0	71	0	0	2	0	1	22	20	.185	.283	.377
86	MIL/AL		134	546	466	108	17	3	33	230	72	3	3	179	4	2	3	5	2	75	86	.232	.336	.494
87	MIL/AL		134	566	474	113	15	2	28	216	86	6	5	186	4	1	1	12	4	71	80	.238	.360	.456
88	MIL/AL		135	555	492	124	24	0	23	217	51	4	7	153	4	0	5	9	5	71	85	.252	.328	.441
89	MIL/AL		130	532	466	98	18	2	26	198	60	5	4	158	8	0	2	4	8	72	65	.210	.305	.425
90	MIL/AL		134	511	440	92	15	1	27	190	64	6	4	147	0	0	3	2	3	57	69	.209	.313	.432
91	DET/AL		134	539	448	80	14	2	25	173	89	1	0	175	3	0	2	1	3	64	64	.179	.314	.386
8 YR TOTALS			**892**	**3468**	**2972**	**649**	**108**	**11**	**173**	**1298**	**452**	**25**	**24**	**1079**	**23**	**2**	**18**	**34**	**27**	**437**	**472**	**.218**	**.325**	**.437**

De los Santos, Luis Manuel (Martinez) — bats right — throws right — b.12/29/66 — 1991 positions: DH 9, OF 3, 1B 2, 3B 2

YR	TM/LG	CL	G	TPA	AB	H	2B	3B	HR	TB	BB	IBB	HB	SO	GDP	SH	SF	SB	CS	R	RBI	BA	OBA	SA
84	EUG/NWL	A−	67	273	257	69	10	2	2	89	13	1	1	33	8	0	2	5	3	27	30	.268	.304	.346
85	FM/FSL	A+	123	497	454	120	18	2	0	142	37	2	0	53	12	0	6	2	2	44	48	.264	.316	.313
86	MEM/SOU	AA	135	586	525	159	21	5	3	199	46	1	3	65	12	5	5	5	1	72	84	.303	.358	.379
87	OMA/AMA	AAA	135	557	518	152	29	6	2	199	29	0	2	80	20	3	5	2	4	53	67	.293	.330	.384
88	OMA/AMA	AAA	136	584	535	164	25	4	6	215	40	3	2	79	17	0	7	2	2	62	87	.307	.353	.402
	KC/AL		11	26	22	2	1	1	0	5	4	0	0	4	3	0	0	0	0	1	1	.091	.231	.227
89	OMA/AMA	AAA	99	423	387	115	31	3	3	161	29	1	0	53	19	1	6	1	4	45	62	.297	.341	.416
	KC/AL		28	92	87	22	3	1	0	27	5	0	0	14	2	0	0	0	0	6	6	.253	.293	.310
90	OMA/AMA	AAA	135	572	521	146	23	1	5	186	34	3	1	82	21	4	12	2	5	55	74	.280	.319	.357
91	DET/AL		16	32	30	5	2	0	0	7	1	0	0	1	9	0	1	0	0	1	0	.167	.219	.233
	TOL/INT	AAA	41	160	141	40	8	0	2	54	16	0	1	19	7	0	2	0	0	12	22	.284	.356	.383
3 YR TOTALS			**55**	**150**	**139**	**29**	**6**	**2**	**0**	**39**	**11**	**0**	**0**	**22**	**7**	**0**	**0**	**0**	**0**	**8**	**7**	**.209**	**.267**	**.281**

Dempsey, John Rikard "Rick" — bats right — throws right — b.9/13/49 — 1991 positions: C 56, P 2, 1B 1

YR	TM/LG	CL	G	TPA	AB	H	2B	3B	HR	TB	BB	IBB	HB	SO	GDP	SH	SF	SB	CS	R	RBI	BA	OBA	SA
69	MIN/AL		5	7	6	3	1	0	0	4	1	0	0	0	0	0	0	0	0	1	0	.500	.571	.667
70	MIN/AL		5	8	7	0	0	0	0	0	1	0	0	1	1	0	0	0	0	1	0	.000	.125	.000
71	MIN/AL		6	14	13	4	1	0	0	5	1	0	0	1	1	0	0	0	0	2	0	.308	.357	.385
72	MIN/AL		25	47	40	8	1	0	0	9	6	0	0	8	2	1	0	0	0	0	0	.200	.304	.225
73	NY/AL		6	13	11	2	0	0	0	2	1	0	0	3	1	1	0	0	0	0	0	.182	.250	.182
74	NY/AL		43	119	109	26	3	0	2	35	8	0	0	7	5	1	1	1	1	0	12	12	.239	.288	.321
75	NY/AL		71	170	145	38	8	0	1	49	21	1	0	15	5	3	1	0	1	0	18	11	.262	.353	.338
76	NY/AL		21	48	42	5	0	0	0	5	5	0	0	4	0	1	0	0	0	0	1	2	.119	.213	.119
	BAL/AL		59	192	174	37	2	0	0	39	13	0	2	17	2	3	0	1	1		11	10	.213	.275	.224
	YEAR		80	240	216	42	2	0	0	44	18	0	2	21	2	4	0	1	1		12	12	.194	.263	.204
77	BAL/AL		91	314	270	61	7	4	3	85	34	1	2	34	9	5	3	2	3		27	34	.226	.314	.315
78	BAL/AL		136	498	441	114	25	0	6	157	48	2	0	54	11	3	6	7	3		41	32	.259	.327	.356
79	BAL/AL		124	413	368	88	23	0	6	129	38	1	0	37	12	3	4	0	1		48	41	.239	.307	.351
80	BAL/AL		119	406	362	95	26	3	9	154	36	1	3	45	11	4	1	3	1		51	40	.262	.333	.425
81	BAL/AL		92	287	251	54	10	1	6	84	32	1	1	36	5	3	0	0			24	15	.215	.306	.335
82	BAL/AL		125	402	344	88	15	1	5	120	46	1	0	37	10	7	5	0	3		35	36	.256	.339	.349
83	BAL/AL		128	400	347	80	16	2	4	112	40	1	3	54	9	5	5	1	1		33	32	.231	.311	.323
84	BAL/AL		109	380	330	76	11	0	11	120	40	1	1	58	11	5	4	1	2		37	34	.230	.312	.364
85	BAL/AL		132	420	362	92	19	0	12	147	50	0	1	87	2	5	1	0	1		54	52	.254	.345	.406
86	BAL/AL		122	382	327	68	15	1	13	124	45	0	3	78	5	7	0	1	0		42	29	.208	.309	.379
87	CLE/AL		60	170	141	25	10	1	1	38	23	0	1	29	4	4	1	0	0		16	9	.177	.295	.270
88	LA/NL		77	198	167	42	13	0	7	76	25	0	0	44	4	0	6	1	0		25	30	.251	.338	.455
89	LA/NL		79	183	151	27	7	0	4	46	30	3	1	37	5	1	0	1	0		16	16	.179	.319	.305
90	LA/NL		62	151	128	25	5	0	2	36	23	0	0	29	8	0	0	1	0		13	15	.195	.318	.281
91	MIL/AL		61	174	147	34	5	0	4	51	23	1	0	20	7	1	3	0	2		15	21	.231	.329	.347
23 YR TOTALS			**1758**	**5396**	**4683**	**1092**	**223**	**12**	**96**	**1627**	**590**	**13**	**18**	**735**	**130**	**63**	**42**	**20**	**19**		**523**	**471**	**.233**	**.319**	**.347**

DeShields, Delino Lamont — bats left — throws right — b.1/15/69 — 1991 positions: 2B 148

YR	TM/LG	CL	G	TPA	AB	H	2B	3B	HR	TB	BB	IBB	HB	SO	GDP	SH	SF	SB	CS	R	RBI	BA	OBA	SA
87	EXP/GCL	R	31	134	111	24	5	2	1	36	21	0	2	30	0	0	0	16	5	17	4	.216	.351	.324
	JAM/NYP	A–	34	124	96	21	1	2	1	29	24	1	1	28	0	2	1	14	4	16	5	.219	.377	.302
88	ROC/MID	A	129	562	460	116	26	6	12	190	95	3	2	110	4	2	3	59	18	97	46	.252	.380	.413
89	JAC/SOU	AA	93	391	307	83	10	6	3	114	76	0	1	80	3	4	3	37	12	55	35	.270	.413	.371
	IND/AMA	AAA	47	198	181	47	8	4	2	69	16	0	0	53	0	1	0	16	7	29	14	.260	.320	.381
90	MON/NL		129	572	499	144	28	6	4	196	66	3	4	96	10	1	2	42	22	69	45	.289	.375	.393
91	MON/NL		151	673	563	134	15	4	10	187	95	2	2	151	6	8	5	56	23	83	51	.238	.347	.332
2 YR TOTALS			**280**	**1245**	**1062**	**278**	**43**	**10**	**14**	**383**	**161**	**5**	**6**	**247**	**16**	**9**	**7**	**98**	**45**	**152**	**96**	**.262**	**.360**	**.361**

Devereaux, Michael "Mike" — bats right — throws right — b.4/10/63 — 1991 positions: OF 149

YR	TM/LG	CL	G	TPA	AB	H	2B	3B	HR	TB	BB	IBB	HB	SO	GDP	SH	SF	SB	CS	R	RBI	BA	OBA	SA
85	GF/PIO	R+	70	329	289	103	17	10	4	152	32	1	2	29	6	0	6	40	9	73	67	.356	.416	.526
86	SA/TEX	AA	115	497	431	130	22	2	10	186	58	2	3	47	6	1	4	31	8	69	53	.302	.385	.432
87	SA/TEX	AA	135	624	562	169	28	9	26	293	48	8	2	65	8	1	11	33	18	90	91	.301	.352	.521
	ALB/PCL	AAA	3	11	11	3	1	0	1	7	0	0	0	2	0	0		1	0	2	1	.273	.273	.636
	LA/NL		19	58	54	12	3	0	0	15	3	0	0	10	0	1	0	3	1	7	4	.222	.263	.278
88	ALB/PCL	AAA	109	477	423	144	26	4	13	217	44	2	2	46	1	1	7	33	9	88	76	.340	.399	.513
	LA/NL		30	45	43	5	1	0	0	6	2	0	0	10	0	0	0	0	1	3	2	.116	.156	.140
89	BAL/AL		122	434	391	104	14	3	8	148	36	0	2	60	7	2	3	22	11	55	46	.266	.329	.379
90	FRE/CAR	A+	2	9	8	4	0	0	1	7	1	0	0	0	0	0	0			3	3	.500	.556	.875
	HAG/EAS	AA	4	20	20	5	3	0	0	8	0	0	0	1	2	0	0	0	1	4	3	.250	.250	.400
	BAL/AL		108	403	367	88	18	1	12	144	28	0	0	48	10	4	4	13	12	48	49	.240	.291	.392
91	BAL/AL		149	668	608	158	27	10	19	262	47	2	2	115	13	7	4	16	9	82	59	.260	.313	.431
5 YR TOTALS			**428**	**1608**	**1463**	**367**	**63**	**14**	**39**	**575**	**116**	**2**	**4**	**243**	**30**	**14**	**11**	**54**	**34**	**196**	**160**	**.251**	**.306**	**.393**

Diaz, Mario Rafael (Torres) — bats right — throws right — b.1/10/62 — 1991 positions: SS 65, 2B 20, 3B 8

YR	TM/LG	CL	G	TPA	AB	H	2B	3B	HR	TB	BB	IBB	HB	SO	GDP	SH	SF	SB	CS	R	RBI	BA	OBA	SA
79	BEL/NWL	A–	32	105	96	19	2	0	1	24	5	0	1	17	2	3	0	0	3	12	5	.198	.245	.250
80	WAU/MID	A	110	375	349	63	5	0	3	77	19	0	1	37	17	4	2	5	6	28	21	.181	.224	.221
81	LYN/EAS	AA	106	344	314	63	8	1	1	76	16	0	1	42	16	7	6	1	1	16	22	.201	.237	.242
82	SLC/PCL	AAA	5	20	19	7	1	0	0	8	0	0	0	1	0	1	0	1	0	2	2	.368	.368	.421
	LYN/EAS	AA	53	188	162	35	7	0	0	47	19	0	1	24	3	5	1	2	1	19	13	.216	.301	.290
83	BAK/CAL	A+	51	185	171	41	5	1	0	48	10	0	0	26	4	4	0	3	1	23	10	.240	.282	.281
	CHT/SOU	AA	33	116	111	30	6	5	2	52	5	0	0	15	5	0	0	0	1	18	13	.270	.302	.468
84	CHT/SOU	AA	108	361	322	67	7	1	1	79	21	0	0	18	14	13	5	6	5	23	19	.208	.253	.245
85	CHT/SOU	AA	115	442	400	101	6	7	0	121	21	2	0	20	15	14	7	3	3	38	38	.253	.285	.303
86	CAL/PCL	AAA	109	401	379	107	17	6	1	139	13	0	1	29	13	5	1	3	1	40	41	.282	.303	.367
87	CAL/PCL	AAA	108	407	376	106	17	3	4	141	19	2	1	25	13	10	1	1	5	52	52	.282	.317	.375
	SEA/AL		11	23	23	7	0	0	0	9	0	0	0	4	0	0	0	0	0	4	3	.304	.304	.391
88	CAL/PCL	AAA	46	180	164	54	18	0	1	75	9	0	3	10	5	1	3	1	2	16	30	.329	.369	.457
	SEA/AL		28	76	72	22	5	0	0	27	3	0	0	5	3	0	0	0		6	9	.306	.329	.375
89	CAL/PCL	AAA	37	137	127	43	8	1	2	59	8	0	1	7	2	0	1	0	4	22	9	.339	.380	.465
	SEA/AL		52	86	74	10	2	0	0	13	7	0	0	8	4	0	1	0	1	9	7	.135	.210	.176
90	CAL/PCL	AAA	32	108	105	35	5	1	0	45	1	0	0	3	0	0	0	1	0	10	19	.333	.343	.429
	NY/NL		16	23	22	3	0	0	0	3	1	0	0	3	0	0	0	0	0	1	0	.136	.130	.182
	TID/INT	AAA	29	111	104	33	8	0	1	44	6	0	1	6	3	0	0	1	2	15	9	.317	.360	.423

(continued)

Diaz, Mario Rafael (Torres) (continued)

YR	TM/LG	CL	G	TPA	AB	H	2B	3B	HR	TB	BB	IBB	HB	SO	GDP	SH	SF	SB	CS	R	RBI	BA	OBA	SA
91	TEX/AL		96	202	182	48	7	0	1	58	15	0	0	18	5	4	1	0	1	24	22	.264	.318	.319
5 YR TOTALS			**203**	**410**	**373**	**90**	**13**	**1**	**2**	**111**	**25**	**0**	**0**	**37**	**10**	**9**	**3**	**0**	**1**	**43**	**42**	**.241**	**.287**	**.298**

DiSarcina, Gary Thomas — bats right — throws right — b.11/19/67 — 1991 positions: SS 10, 2B 7, 3B 2

YR	TM/LG	CL	G	TPA	AB	H	2B	3B	HR	TB	BB	IBB	HB	SO	GDP	SH	SF	SB	CS	R	RBI	BA	OBA	SA
88	BEN/NWL	A—	71	332	295	90	11	5	2	117	27	1	2	34	6	4	4	7	4	40	39	.305	.363	.397
89	MID/TEX	AA	126	481	441	126	18	7	4	170	24	3	4	54	17	7	5	11	6	65	54	.286	.325	.385
	CAL/AL		2	0	0	0	0	0	0	0	0	0	0	0	0	0	0	0	0	0	0	.000	.000	.000
90	EDM/PCL	AAA	97	366	330	70	12	2	4	98	25	0	4	46	6	5	2	5	3	46	37	.212	.274	.297
	CAL/AL		18	61	57	8	1	1	0	11	3	0	0	10	3	1	0	1	0	8	0	.140	.183	.193
91	EDM/PCL	AAA	119	435	390	121	21	4	4	162	29	1	9	32	12	4	3	16	5	61	58	.310	.369	.415
	CAL/AL		18	64	57	12	2	0	0	14	3	0	2	4	0	2	0	0	0	5	3	.211	.274	.246
3 YR TOTALS			**38**	**125**	**114**	**20**	**3**	**1**	**0**	**25**	**6**	**0**	**2**	**14**	**3**	**3**	**0**	**1**	**0**	**13**	**3**	**.175**	**.230**	**.219**

Donnels, Chris Barton — bats left — throws right — b.4/21/66 — 1991 positions: 1B 15, 3B 11

YR	TM/LG	CL	G	TPA	AB	H	2B	3B	HR	TB	BB	IBB	HB	SO	GDP	SH	SF	SB	CS	R	RBI	BA	OBA	SA
87	KIN/APP	R+	26	106	86	26	4	0	3	39	17	1	1	17	1	0	2	4	1	18	16	.302	.415	.453
	COL/SAL	A	41	162	136	35	7	0	2	48	24	1	1	27	1	0	1	3	1	20	17	.257	.370	.353
88	SL/FSL	A+	65	235	198	43	14	2	3	70	32	1	2	53	4	2	1	4	3	25	22	.217	.330	.354
	COL/SAL	A	42	167	133	32	6	0	2	44	30	2	1	25	3	2	1	5	0	19	13	.241	.382	.331
89	SL/FSL	A+	117	480	386	121	23	1	17	197	83	15	6	65	5	2	3	18	4	70	78	.313	.439	.510
90	JAC/TEX	AA	130	543	419	114	24	0	12	174	111	5	1	81	12	5	7	11	8	66	63	.272	.420	.415
91	TID/INT	AAA	84	353	287	87	18	2	8	133	62	3	1	55	13	0	3	1	4	45	56	.303	.425	.463
	NY/NL		37	104	89	20	2	0	0	22	14	1	0	19	0	1	0	1	1	7	5	.225	.330	.247

Doran, William Donald "Bill" — bats both — throws right — b.5/28/58 — 1991 positions: 2B 88, OF 6, 1B 4

YR	TM/LG	CL	G	TPA	AB	H	2B	3B	HR	TB	BB	IBB	HB	SO	GDP	SH	SF	SB	CS	R	RBI	BA	OBA	SA
82	HOU/NL		26	102	97	27	3	0	0	30	4	0	0	11	0	0	1	5	0	11	6	.278	.304	.309
83	HOU/NL		154	629	535	145	12	7	8	195	86	11	0	67	6	7	1	12	12	70	39	.271	.371	.364
84	HOU/NL		147	626	548	143	18	11	4	195	66	7	2	69	6	7	3	21	12	92	41	.261	.341	.356
85	HOU/NL		148	657	578	166	31	6	14	251	71	6	0	69	10	3	5	23	15	84	59	.287	.362	.434
86	HOU/NL		145	642	550	152	29	3	6	205	81	7	2	57	10	4	5	42	19	92	37	.276	.368	.373
87	HOU/NL		162	719	625	177	23	3	16	254	82	3	3	64	11	2	7	31	11	82	79	.283	.365	.406
88	HOU/NL		132	552	480	119	18	1	7	160	65	3	1	60	7	4	2	17	4	66	53	.248	.338	.333
89	HOU/NL		142	574	507	111	25	2	8	164	59	2	3	63	8	3	3	22	3	65	58	.219	.301	.323
90	HOU/NL		109	421	344	99	21	2	6	142	71	2	1	53	2	1	5	18	9	49	32	.288	.405	.413
	CIN/NL		17	67	59	22	8	0	1	33	8	1	0	5	1	0	0	5	0	10	5	.373	.448	.559
	YEAR		126	488	403	121	29	2	7	175	79	2	1	58	3	1	5	23	9	59	37	.300	.411	.434
91	CIN/NL		111	410	361	101	12	2	6	135	46	1	0	39	4	0	3	5	4	51	35	.280	.359	.374
10 YR TOTALS			**1293**	**5399**	**4684**	**1262**	**200**	**37**	**76**	**1764**	**639**	**42**	**10**	**557**	**65**	**31**	**35**	**201**	**89**	**672**	**444**	**.269**	**.356**	**.377**

Dorsett, Brian Richard — bats right — throws right — b.4/9/61 — 1991 positions: 1B 2

YR	TM/LG	CL	G	TPA	AB	H	2B	3B	HR	TB	BB	IBB	HB	SO	GDP	SH	SF	SB	CS	R	RBI	BA	OBA	SA
83	MED/NWL	A—	14	53	48	13	2	1	1	20	5	0	0	5	1	0	0	0	0	11	10	.271	.340	.417
	MAD/MID	A	58	223	204	52	7	0	3	68	17	1	0	35	4	0	2	2	1	16	27	.255	.309	.333
84	MOD/CAL	A+	99	407	375	99	19	0	8	142	23	1	2	93	7	0	7	0	1	39	52	.264	.305	.379
85	MAD/MID	A	40	178	161	43	11	0	2	60	12	1	2	23	5	1	2	0	2	15	30	.267	.322	.373
	HUN/SOU	AA	88	354	313	84	18	3	11	141	38	1	0	61	11	3	0	2	0	38	43	.268	.348	.450
86	TAC/PCL	AAA	117	460	426	111	33	1	10	176	26	1	3	82	16	0	5	0	1	49	51	.261	.304	.413
87	TAC/PCL	AAA	78	324	282	66	14	1	6	100	33	3	3	50	12	1	6	0	1	31	39	.234	.316	.355
	BUF/AMA	AAA	26	90	86	22	5	1	4	41	3	1	0	21	2	0	1	0	0	9	14	.256	.278	.477
	CLE/AL		5	12	11	3	0	0	1	6	0	0	1	3	0	0	0	0	0	2	3	.273	.333	.545
88	EDM/PCL	AAA	53	194	163	43	7	0	11	83	28	1	0	29	3	1	2	1	2	21	32	.264	.368	.509
	CAL/AL		7	12	11	1	0	0	0	1	1	0	0	5	0	0	0	0	0	0	2	.091	.167	.091
89	COL/INT	AAA	110	431	388	97	21	0	17	171	31	2	5	87	10	2	5	2	2	45	62	.250	.310	.441
	NY/AL		8	23	22	8	1	0	0	9	1	0	0	3	0	0	0	0	0	3	4	.364	.391	.409
90	COL/INT	AAA	114	473	415	113	28	1	14	185	49	6	5	71	12	1	3	1	1	44	67	.272	.354	.446
	NY/AL		14	37	35	5	2	0	0	7	2	0	0	4	2	0	0	0	0	2	0	.143	.189	.200
91	SD/NL		11	12	12	1	0	0	0	1	0	0	0	3	0	0	0	0	0	0	1	.083	.083	.083
	LV/PCL	AAA	62	234	215	66	13	1	13	120	17	0	1	43	2	0	0	0	0	36	38	.307	.359	.558
	BUF/AMA	AAA	29	116	103	28	6	0	2	40	8	1	1	19	1	0	4	0	0	17	18	.272	.319	.388
5 YR TOTALS			**45**	**96**	**91**	**18**	**3**	**0**	**1**	**24**	**4**	**0**	**1**	**18**	**2**	**0**	**0**	**0**	**0**	**7**	**10**	**.198**	**.240**	**.264**

Downing, Brian Jay — bats right — throws right — b.10/9/50 — 1991 positions: DH 109

YR	TM/LG	CL	G	TPA	AB	H	2B	3B	HR	TB	BB	IBB	HB	SO	GDP	SH	SF	SB	CS	R	RBI	BA	OBA	SA
73	CHI/AL		34	85	73	13	1	0	2	20	10	1	0	17	3	2	0	0	0	5	4	.178	.277	.274
74	CHI/AL		108	350	293	66	12	0	10	110	51	3	2	72	11	4	0	0	1	41	39	.225	.344	.375
75	CHI/AL		138	516	420	101	12	1	7	136	76	5	3	75	12	11	6	13	4	58	41	.240	.356	.324
76	CHI/AL		104	365	317	81	14	0	3	104	40	0	1	55	2	4	3	7	3	38	30	.256	.338	.328
77	CHI/AL		69	214	169	48	4	2	4	68	34	0	2	21	3	5	4	1	2	28	25	.284	.402	.402
78	CAL/AL		133	476	412	105	15	1	7	141	52	2	6	47	14	4	2	3	2	42	46	.255	.345	.342
79	CAL/AL		148	596	509	166	27	3	12	235	77	4	5	57	17	3	2	3	3	87	75	.326	.418	.462
80	CAL/AL		30	108	93	27	6	0	2	39	12	1	0	12	5	1	2	0	2	5	25	.290	.364	.419
81	CAL/AL		93	370	317	79	14	0	9	120	46	1	4	35	11	3	1	0	1	47	41	.249	.351	.379

Downing, Brian Jay (continued)

YR	TM/LG	CL	G	TPA	AB	H	2B	3B	HR	TB	BB	IBB	HB	SO	GDP	SH	SF	SB	CS	R	RBI	BA	OBA	SA
82	CAL/AL		158	725	623	175	37	2	28	300	86	1	5	58	14	3	8	2	1	109	84	.281	.368	.482
83	CAL/AL		113	473	403	99	15	1	19	173	62	4	5	59	8	1	2	1	2	68	53	.246	.352	.429
84	CAL/AL		156	628	539	148	28	2	23	249	70	3	7	66	18	3	9	0	4	65	91	.275	.360	.462
85	CAL/AL		150	620	520	137	23	1	20	222	78	3	13	61	13	5	4	5	3	80	85	.263	.371	.427
86	CAL/AL		152	631	513	137	27	4	20	232	90	2	17	84	14	3	8	4	4	90	95	.267	.389	.452
87	CAL/AL		155	695	567	154	29	3	29	276	106	6	17	85	10	2	3	5	5	110	77	.272	.400	.487
88	CAL/AL		135	590	484	117	18	2	25	214	81	5	14	63	12	5	6	3	4	80	64	.242	.362	.442
89	CAL/AL		142	610	544	154	25	2	14	225	56	3	6	87	6	0	4	0	2	59	59	.283	.354	.414
90	CAL/AL		96	390	330	90	18	2	14	154	50	2	6	45	11	0	4	0	0	47	51	.273	.374	.467
91	TEX/AL		123	476	407	113	17	2	17	185	58	7	8	70	7	1	2	1	1	76	49	.278	.377	.455
19 YR TOTALS			2237	8918	7533	2010	342	28	265	3203	1135	53	121	1069	191	60	69	49	44	1135	1034	.267	.369	.425

Dozier, William Henry "D.J." — bats right — throws right — b.9/21/65 — 1991 positions: OF System NY/NL

YR	TM/LG	CL	G	TPA	AB	H	2B	3B	HR	TB	BB	IBB	HB	SO	GDP	SH	SF	SB	CS	R	RBI	BA	OBA	SA
90	SL/FSL	A+	93	366	317	94	11	3	13	150	45	0	1	76	5	0	3	33	5	56	57	.297	.383	.473
	JAC/TEX	AA	29	124	102	33	5	7	2	58	16	0	0	28	5	0	6	3	1	20	23	.324	.395	.569
91	WIL/EAS	AA	74	300	259	72	11	6	8	119	39	2	1	88	3	0	1	25	6	49	30	.278	.373	.459
	TID/INT	AAA	43	192	171	46	7	5	1	66	13	0	4	41	3	2	2	8	6	19	22	.269	.332	.386

Ducey, Robert Thomas "Rob" — bats left — throws right — b.5/24/65 — 1991 positions: OF 24, DH 2

YR	TM/LG	CL	G	TPA	AB	H	2B	3B	HR	TB	BB	IBB	HB	SO	GDP	SH	SF	SB	CS	R	RBI	BA	OBA	SA
84	MH/PIO	R+	63	279	235	71	10	3	12	123	41	0	1	61	4	1	1	13	6	49	49	.302	.406	.523
85	FLO/SAL	A	134	589	529	133	22	2	13	198	49	2	1	103	3	3	7	12	4	78	86	.251	.312	.374
86	VEN/CAL	A+	47	203	178	60	11	3	12	113	21	2	1	24	1	0		17	5	36	38	.337	.406	.635
	KNO/SOU	AA	88	377	344	106	22	3	11	167	29	3	0	59	2	0	4	7	7	49	58	.308	.358	.485
87	SYR/INT	AAA	100	428	359	102	14	10	10	166	61	5	3	88	6	0	5	7	7	62	60	.284	.388	.462
	TOR/AL		34	57	48	9	1	0	1	13	8	0	0	10	0	0	1	2	0	12	6	.188	.298	.271
88	SYR/INT	AAA	90	369	317	81	14	4	7	124	43	0	3	81	3	2	4	7	6	40	42	.256	.346	.391
	TOR/AL		27	63	54	17	4	1	0	23	5	0	0	7	1	2	1	1	0	15	6	.315	.361	.426
89	SYR/INT	AAA	10	40	29	3	0	1	0	5	9	0	1	13	0	0	1	0	0	0	3	.103	.325	.172
	TOR/AL		41	86	76	16	4	0	0	20	9	1	0	25	2	1	0	2	1	5	7	.211	.294	.263
90	SYR/INT	AAA	127	504	438	117	32	7	7	184	60	6	4	87	10	0	5	13	9	53	47	.267	.360	.420
	TOR/AL		19	62	53	16	5	0	0	21	7	0	0	15	0	0	1	1	1	7	7	.302	.387	.396
91	SYR/INT	AAA	72	323	266	78	10	3	8	118	51	4	0	58	1	4	2	5	7	53	40	.293	.404	.444
	TOR/AL		39	75	68	16	2	1	2	25	6	0	1	26	1	1	0	2	0	8	4	.235	.297	.368
5 YR TOTALS			160	343	299	74	16	3	2	102	35	1	1	83	4	4	4	8	2	47	30	.247	.324	.341

Duncan, Mariano (Nalasco) — bats both — throws right — b.3/13/63 — 1991 positions: 2B 62, SS 32, OF 7

YR	TM/LG	CL	G	TPA	AB	H	2B	3B	HR	TB	BB	IBB	HB	SO	GDP	SH	SF	SB	CS	R	RBI	BA	OBA	SA
84	SA/TEX	AA	125	554	502	127	14	11	2	169	41	0	5	110	8	4	2	41	13	80	44	.253	.315	.337
85	LA/NL		142	620	562	137	24	6	6	191	38	4	3	113	9	13	4	38	8	74	39	.244	.293	.340
86	LA/NL		109	445	407	93	7	0	8	124	30	1	2	78	6	5	1	48	13	47	30	.229	.284	.305
87	ALB/PCL	AAA	6	24	22	6	0	0	0	6	2	0	0	5	0	0	0	3	0	6	0	.273	.333	.273
	LA/NL		76	287	261	56	8	1	6	84	17	1	2	62	4	6	1	11	1	31	18	.215	.267	.322
88	ALB/PCL	AAA	56	250	227	65	4	8	0	85	10	0	8	40	2	0	3	33	7	48	25	.286	.335	.374
89	LA/NL		49	87	84	21	5	1	0	28	0	0	2	15	1	1	0	3	3	9	8	.250	.267	.333
	CIN/NL		45	186	174	43	10	1	3	64	8	0	3	36	2	1	0	6	2	23	13	.247	.292	.368
	YEAR		94	273	258	64	15	2	3	92	8	0	5	51	3	2	0	9	5	32	21	.248	.284	.357
90	CIN/NL		125	471	435	133	22	11	10	207	24	4	4	67	10	4	4	13	7	67	55	.306	.345	.476
91	CIN/NL		100	356	333	86	7	4	12	137	12	0	3	57	0	5	3	5	4	46	40	.258	.288	.411
6 YR TOTALS			646	2452	2256	569	83	24	45	835	129	10	19	428	32	35	13	124	38	297	203	.252	.297	.370

Dunston, Shawon Donnell — bats right — throws right — b.3/21/63 — 1991 positions: SS 142

YR	TM/LG	CL	G	TPA	AB	H	2B	3B	HR	TB	BB	IBB	HB	SO	GDP	SH	SF	SB	CS	R	RBI	BA	OBA	SA
84	MID/TEX	AA	73	318	298	98	13	3	3	126	11	2	3	38	9	2	4	11	8	44	34	.329	.354	.423
	IOW/AMA	AAA	61	217	210	49	11	1	7	83	4	0	0	40	4	2	1	9	3	25	27	.233	.247	.395
85	IOW/AMA	AAA	73	284	272	73	9	6	2	100	5	0	1	49	5	5	1	17	12	24	28	.268	.283	.368
	CHI/NL		74	272	250	65	12	4	4	97	19	3	0	42	3	1	2	11	3	40	18	.260	.310	.388
86	CHI/NL		150	611	581	145	37	3	17	239	21	5	3	114	5	4	2	13	11	66	68	.250	.278	.411
87	IOW/AMA	AAA	5	19	19	8	1	0	0	9	0	0	0	3	0	0	0	1	1	1	3	.421	.421	.474
	CHI/NL		95	359	346	85	18	3	5	124	10	1	1	68	6	0	2	12	3	40	22	.246	.267	.358
88	CHI/NL		155	599	575	143	23	6	9	205	16	8	2	108	9	0	4	30	9	69	56	.249	.271	.357
89	CHI/NL		138	512	471	131	20	6	9	190	30	15	1	86	7	6	4	19	11	52	60	.278	.320	.403
90	CHI/NL		146	573	545	143	22	8	17	232	15	1	9	87	9	4	6	25	5	73	66	.262	.283	.426
91	CHI/NL		142	534	492	128	22	7	12	200	23	1	1	64	9	4	11	21	6	59	50	.260	.292	.407
7 YR TOTALS			900	3460	3260	840	154	37	73	1287	134	38	14	569	45	23	29	131	48	399	340	.258	.287	.395

Dykstra, Leonard Kyle "Lenny" — bats left — throws left — b.2/10/63 — 1991 positions: OF 63

YR	TM/LG	CL	G	TPA	AB	H	2B	3B	HR	TB	BB	IBB	HB	SO	GDP	SH	SF	SB	CS	R	RBI	BA	OBA	SA
84	JAC/TEX	AA	131	581	501	138	25	7	6	195	73	6	5	45	6	1	1	53	17	100	52	.275	.372	.389
85	TID/INT	AAA	58	264	229	71	8	6	1	94	31	0	1	20	2	1	2	26	6	44	25	.310	.392	.410
	NY/NL		83	273	236	60	9	3	1	78	30	0	1	24	4	4	2	15	7	40	19	.254	.338	.331
86	NY/NL		147	498	431	127	27	7	8	192	58	1	0	55	4	7	2	31	7	77	45	.295	.377	.445
87	NY/NL		132	479	431	123	37	3	10	196	40	3	4	67	1	4	0	27	7	86	43	.285	.352	.455
88	NY/NL		126	466	429	116	19	3	8	165	30	2	3	43	3	2	2	30	8	57	33	.270	.321	.385

(continued)

Dykstra, Leonard Kyle "Lenny" (continued)

YR	TM/LG	CL	G	TPA	AB	H	2B	3B	HR	TB	BB	IBB	HB	SO	GDP	SH	SF	SB	CS	R	RBI	BA	OBA	SA
89	NY/NL		56	192	159	43	12	1	3	66	23	0	2	15	2	4	4	13	1	27	13	.270	.362	.415
	PHI/NL		90	392	352	78	20	3	4	116	37	1	1	38	5	1	1	17	11	39	19	.222	.297	.330
	YEAR		146	584	511	121	32	4	7	182	60	1	3	53	7	5	5	30	12	66	32	.237	.318	.356
90	PHI/NL		149	691	590	192	35	3	9	260	89	14	7	48	5	2	3	33	5	106	60	.325	.418	.441
91	PHI/NL		63	284	246	73	13	5	3	105	37	1	1	20	1	0	0	24	4	48	12	.297	.391	.427
7 YR TOTALS			**846**	**3275**	**2874**	**812**	**172**	**28**	**46**	**1178**	**344**	**22**	**19**	**310**	**25**	**24**	**14**	**190**	**45**	**480**	**244**	**.283**	**.361**	**.410**

Eisenreich, James Michael "Jim" — bats left — throws left — b.4/18/59 — 1991 positions: OF 105, 1B 15, DH 1

YR	TM/LG	CL	G	TPA	AB	H	2B	3B	HR	TB	BB	IBB	HB	SO	GDP	SH	SF	SB	CS	R	RBI	BA	OBA	SA
82	MIN/AL		34	111	99	30	6	0	2	42	11	0	1	13	1	0	0	0	0	10	9	.303	.378	.424
83	MIN/AL		2	8	7	2	1	0	0	3	1	0	0	1	0	0	0	0	0	1	0	.286	.375	.429
84	MIN/AL		12	36	32	7	1	0	0	8	2	1	0	4	1	0	2	2	0	1	3	.219	.250	.250
87	MEM/SOU	AA	70	324	275	105	36	10	11	194	47	3	0	44	8	0	2	13	4	60	57	.382	.469	.705
	KC/AL		44	115	105	25	8	2	4	49	7	2	0	13	2	0	3	1	1	10	21	.238	.278	.467
88	OMA/AMA	AAA	36	156	142	41	8	3	4	67	9	0	1	20	1	0	4	9	1	28	14	.289	.327	.472
	KC/AL		82	214	202	44	8	1	1	57	6	1	0	31	2	2	4	9	3	26	19	.218	.236	.282
89	KC/AL		134	519	475	139	33	7	9	213	37	9	0	44	8	3	4	27	8	64	59	.293	.341	.448
90	KC/AL		142	545	496	139	29	7	5	197	42	2	1	51	7	2	4	12	14	61	51	.280	.335	.397
91	KC/AL		135	405	375	113	22	3	2	147	20	1	1	35	10	3	6	5	3	47	47	.301	.333	.392
8 YR TOTALS			**585**	**1953**	**1791**	**499**	**108**	**20**	**23**	**716**	**126**	**16**	**3**	**192**	**31**	**10**	**23**	**56**	**29**	**220**	**209**	**.279**	**.323**	**.400**

Elster, Kevin Daniel — bats right — throws right — b.8/3/64 — 1991 positions: SS 107

YR	TM/LG	CL	G	TPA	AB	H	2B	3B	HR	TB	BB	IBB	HB	SO	GDP	SH	SF	SB	CS	R	RBI	BA	OBA	SA
84	LF/NYP	A−	71	298	257	66	7	3	3	88	35	1	1	41	5	0	5	13	2	35	35	.257	.342	.342
85	LYN/CAR	A+	59	260	224	66	9	0	7	96	33	2	2	21	5	0	0	8	2	41	26	.295	.388	.429
	JAC/TEX	AA	59	235	214	55	13	0	2	74	19	1	2	27	6	0	0	2	3	30	22	.257	.323	.346
86	JAC/TEX	AA	127	512	435	117	19	3	2	148	61	3	4	46	9	4	8	7	8	69	52	.269	.358	.340
	NY/NL		19	33	30	5	1	0	0	6	3	1	0	8	0	0	0	0	0	3	0	.167	.242	.200
87	TID/INT	AAA	134	591	549	170	33	7	8	241	35	.4	1	62	11	3	3	7	3	83	74	.310	.350	.439
	NY/NL		5	10	10	4	2	0	0	6	0	0	0	1	1	0	0	0	0	1	1	.400	.400	.600
88	NY/NL		149	450	406	87	11	1	9	127	35	12	3	47	5	6	0	2	0	41	37	.214	.282	.313
89	NY/NL		151	508	458	106	25	2	10	165	34	11	2	77	13	6	8	4	3	52	55	.231	.283	.360
90	NY/NL		92	352	314	65	20	1	9	114	30	2	1	54	4	1	6	2	0	36	45	.207	.274	.363
91	NY/NL		115	394	348	84	16	2	6	122	40	6	1	53	4	1	4	2	3	33	36	.241	.318	.351
6 YR TOTALS			**531**	**1747**	**1566**	**351**	**75**	**6**	**34**	**540**	**142**	**32**	**7**	**240**	**27**	**14**	**18**	**10**	**6**	**166**	**174**	**.224**	**.289**	**.345**

Esasky, Nicholas Andrew "Nick" bats right — throws right — b.2/24/60 — 1991 positions: 1B

YR	TM/LG	CL	G	TPA	AB	H	2B	3B	HR	TB	BB	IBB	HB	SO	GDP	SH	SF	SB	CS	R	RBI	BA	OBA	SA
83	CIN/NL		85	335	302	80	10	3	12	136	27	1	3	99	5	0	3	6	2	41	46	.265	.328	.450
84	CIN/NL		113	382	322	62	10	5	10	112	52	3	0	103	6	3	5	1	2	30	45	.193	.301	.348
85	CIN/NL		125	464	413	108	21	0	21	192	41	3	4	102	9	3	3	3	4	61	66	.262	.332	.465
86	CIN/NL		102	383	330	76	17	2	12	133	47	0	1	97	8	1	4	0	2	35	41	.230	.325	.403
87	NAS/AMA	AAA	13	58	52	23	6	0	5	44	5	0	0	11	0	0	1	0	0	13	18	.442	.483	.846
	CIN/NL		100	378	346	94	19	2	22	183	29	3	0	76	10	2	1	0	0	48	59	.272	.327	.529
88	CIN/NL		122	450	391	95	17	2	15	161	48	4	4	104	6	0	7	7	2	40	62	.243	.327	.412
89	BOS/AL		154	633	564	156	26	5	30	282	66	9	3	117	11	0	0	1	2	79	108	.277	.355	.500
90	ATL/NL		9	39	35	6	0	0	0	6	4	0	0	14	0	0	0	0	0	2	0	.171	.256	.171
8 YR TOTALS			**810**	**3064**	**2703**	**677**	**120**	**21**	**122**	**1205**	**314**	**23**	**15**	**712**	**55**	**9**	**23**	**18**	**14**	**336**	**427**	**.250**	**.329**	**.446**

Escobar, Jose Elias (Sanchez) — bats right — throws right — b.10/30/60 — 1991 positions: SS 5, 2B 4, 3B 1

YR	TM/LG	CL	G	TPA	AB	H	2B	3B	HR	TB	BB	IBB	HB	SO	GDP	SH	SF	SB	CS	R	RBI	BA	OBA	SA
84	KNO/SOU	AA	96	362	340	80	13	4	1	104	14	0	2	56	4	2	4	6	2	40	45	.235	.267	.306
85	REA/EAS	AA	40	135	122	31	4	0	1	38	11	1	0	17	2	1	1	3	2	17	8	.254	.313	.311
	POR/PCL	AAA	46	120	109	35	4	2	1	46	8	0	0	16	1	2	1	4	0	21	8	.321	.364	.422
86	KNO/SOU	AA	19	77	66	16	1	1	0	19	5	1	1	6	1	4	1	1	1	9	5	.242	.301	.288
	SYR/INT	AAA	62	153	143	35	5	0	2	46	4	0	1	14	4	5	0	2	1	12	14	.245	.270	.322
87	SYR/INT	AAA	37	68	68	24	2	2	0	30	0	0	0	8	1	0	0	0	0	12	14	.353	.353	.441
	KNO/SOU	AA	26	98	92	13	3	0	0	16	4	0	1	11	2	0	0	2	1	4	4	.141	.186	.174
88	KNO/SOU	AA	11	26	24	7	1	0	0	8	2	0	0	3	1	0	0	1		1	2	.292	.346	.333
	SYR/INT	AAA	46	136	124	26	1	1	0	29	9	0	0	20	3	1	2	2	0	8	12	.210	.259	.234
89	OMA/AMA	AAA	23	79	76	6	0	0	0	6	2	0	0	19	2	0	1	3		1		.079	.101	.079
	SYR/INT	AAA	46	156	142	33	3	1	0	38	7	0	0	27	1	5	2	2	0	12	14	.232	.265	.268
90	SYR/INT	AAA	79	278	252	68	6	2	0	78	18	0	1	35	3	7	0	3	0	16	17	.270	.321	.310
91	CLE/AL		10	17	15	3	0	0	0	3	1	0	0	4	0	1	0	0	0	0	1	.200	.250	.200
	CS/PCL	AAA	33	98	93	19	5	1	0	26	4	0	0	16	5	0	1	0	0	12	11	.204	.235	.280
	CAN/EAS	AA	12	37	34	2	1	0	0	3	1	0	0	7	0	2	0	0	0	0	1	.059	.086	.088

Espinoza, Alvaro Alberto — bats right — throws right — b.2/19/62 — 1991 positions: SS 147, 3B 2, P 1

YR	TM/LG	CL	G	TPA	AB	H	2B	3B	HR	TB	BB	IBB	HB	SO	GDP	SH	SF	SB	CS	R	RBI	BA	OBA	SA
84	TOL/INT	AAA	104	368	344	80	12	5	0	102	3	0	3	49	13	16	2	3	1	22	30	.233	.244	.297
	MIN/AL		1	0	0	0	0	0	0	0	0	0	0	0	0	0	0	0	0	0	0	.000	.000	.000
85	TOL/INT	AAA	82	293	266	61	11	0	1	75	14	0	3	30	10	8	2	1	3	24	33	.229	.274	.282
	MIN/AL		32	62	57	15	2	0	0	17	1	0	1	9	1	3	0	0	1	5	9	.263	.288	.298
86	TOL/INT	AAA	73	267	253	71	8	1	2	87	6	1	0	30	3	7	1	1	1	18	27	.281	.296	.344
	MIN/AL		37	45	42	9	1	0	0	10	1	0	0	10	0	2	0	0	1	4	1	.214	.233	.238

Espinoza, Alvaro Alberto (continued)

YR	TM/LG	CL	G	TPA	AB	H	2B	3B	HR	TB	BB	IBB	HB	SO	GDP	SH	SF	SB	CS	R	RBI	BA	OBA	SA
87	POR/PCL	AAA	91	309	291	80	3	2	4	99	12	1	2	37	12	4	0	2	1	28	28	.275	.308	.340
88	NY/AL		3	3	3	0	0	0	0	0	0	0	0	0	0	0	0	0	0	0	0	.000	.000	.000
	COL/INT	AAA	119	456	435	107	10	5	2	133	7	1	3	53	11	9	2	4	3	42	30	.246	.262	.306
89	NY/AL		146	544	503	142	23	1	0	167	14	1	1	60	14	23	3	3	3	51	41	.282	.301	.332
90	NY/AL		150	472	438	98	12	2	2	120	16	0	5	54	13	11	2	1	2	31	20	.224	.258	.274
91	NY/AL		148	509	480	123	23	2	5	165	16	0	2	57	10	9	2	4	1	51	33	.256	.282	.344
7 YR TOTALS			**517**	**1635**	**1523**	**387**	**61**	**5**	**7**	**479**	**48**	**1**	**9**	**190**	**39**	**48**	**7**	**8**	**8**	**142**	**104**	**.254**	**.280**	**.315**

Espy, Cecil Edward — bats both — throws right — b.1/20/63 — 1991 positions: OF 35

YR	TM/LG	CL	G	TPA	AB	H	2B	3B	HR	TB	BB	IBB	HB	SO	GDP	SH	SF	SB	CS	R	RBI	BA	OBA	SA
80	WS/GCL	R	58	243	212	58	7	3	0	71	26	1	0	38	5	2	3	23	6	33	26	.274	.349	.335
81	WS/GCL	R	43	158	142	40	3	1	0	45	11	1	1	13	4	3	1	9	4	24	16	.282	.335	.317
	APP/MID	A	72	312	273	55	2	2	1	64	30	2	1	54	2	8	0	11	3	37	19	.201	.283	.234
82	VB/FSL	A+	131	585	523	166	14	7	1	197	58	4	1	70	4	3	0	74	15	100	34	.317	.387	.377
83	SA/TEX	AA	133	611	564	151	16	11	4	201	39	2	1	77	11	3	4	51	16	88	38	.268	.314	.356
	LA/NL		20	12	11	3	1	0	0	4	1	0	0	2	0	0	0	0	0	4	1	.273	.333	.364
84	SA/TEX	AA	133	602	535	146	19	8	8	205	54	5	1	75	11	5	7	48	16	99	60	.273	.337	.383
85	SA/TEX	AA	124	517	461	129	24	3	5	174	47	1	0	59	10	4	3	20	17	64	49	.280	.347	.377
86	HAW/PCL	AAA	106	412	384	101	19	3	4	138	24	1	0	83	6	3	1	41	13	49	38	.263	.306	.359
87	OC/AMA	AAA	118	482	443	134	18	6	1	167	31	2	1	66	8	4	3	46	14	76	37	.302	.347	.377
	TEX/AL		14	9	8	0	0	0	0	0	1	0	0	3	1	0	0	2	0	1	0	.000	.111	.000
88	TEX/AL		123	376	347	86	17	6	2	121	20	1	1	83	2	5	3	33	10	46	39	.248	.288	.349
89	TEX/AL		142	527	475	122	12	7	3	157	38	2	10	99	2	2	10	2	45	20	65	31	.257	.313	.331
90	TEX/AL		52	82	71	9	0	0	0	9	10	0	1	20	1	1	0	11	5	10	1	.127	.235	.127
	OC/AMA	AAA	34	147	126	34	4	1	2	46	15	0	1	29	0	1	4	7	4	15	20	.270	.342	.365
91	BUF/AMA	AAA	102	442	398	124	27	10	2	177	36	2	0	65	2	4	4	22	10	69	43	.312	.365	.445
	PIT/NL		43	92	82	20	4	0	1	27	5	0	0	17	0	3	2	4	0	7	11	.244	.281	.329
6 YR TOTALS			**394**	**1098**	**994**	**240**	**34**	**13**	**6**	**318**	**75**	**3**	**3**	**224**	**6**	**19**	**7**	**95**	**35**	**133**	**83**	**.241**	**.295**	**.320**

Eusebio, Raul Antonio "Tony" — bats right — throws right — b.4/27/67 — 1991 positions: C 9

YR	TM/LG	CL	G	TPA	AB	H	2B	3B	HR	TB	BB	IBB	HB	SO	GDP	SH	SF	SB	CS	R	RBI	BA	OBA	SA
85	AST/GCL	R	1	1	1	0	0	0	0	0	0	0	0	0	0	0	0	0	0	0	0	.000	.000	.000
87	AST/GCL	R	42	150	125	26	1	2	1	34	18	0	7	19	4	0	0	8	2	26	15	.208	.340	.272
88	OSC/FSL	A+	118	442	392	96	6	3	0	108	40	2	6	69	18	1	3	20	13	45	40	.245	.322	.276
89	COL/SOU	AA	65	244	203	38	6	1	0	46	38	1	3	47	7	0	0	7	3	20	18	.187	.324	.227
	OSC/FSL	A+	52	199	175	50	6	3	0	62	19	0	1	27	10	1	3	5	3	22	30	.286	.354	.354
90	COL/SOU	AA	92	345	318	90	18	0	4	120	21	0	4	80	4	1	1	6	2	36	37	.283	.334	.377
91	TUC/PCL	AAA	5	23	20	8	1	0	0	9	3	0	0	3	2	0	0	1	1	5	2	.400	.478	.450
	JAC/TEX	AA	66	257	222	58	8	3	2	78	25	5	4	54	7	4	2	3	3	27	31	.261	.344	.351
	HOU/NL		10	25	19	2	1	0	0	3	6	0	0	8	1	0	0	0	0	4	0	.105	.320	.158

Evans, Dwight Michael "Dwight" or "Dewey" — bats right — throws right — b.11/3/51 — 1991 positions: OF 67, DH 21

YR	TM/LG	CL	G	TPA	AB	H	2B	3B	HR	TB	BB	IBB	HB	SO	GDP	SH	SF	SB	CS	R	RBI	BA	OBA	SA
72	BOS/AL		18	64	57	15	3	1	1	23	7	0	0	13	2	0	0	0	0	2	6	.263	.344	.404
73	BOS/AL		119	328	282	63	13	1	10	108	40	2	1	52	8	3	2	5	0	46	32	.223	.320	.383
74	BOS/AL		133	514	463	130	19	8	10	195	38	2	2	77	9	6	5	4	4	60	70	.281	.335	.421
75	BOS/AL		128	470	412	113	24	6	13	188	47	3	4	60	10	5	2	3	4	61	56	.274	.353	.456
76	BOS/AL		146	571	501	121	34	5	17	216	57	4	6	92	11	3	4	6	7	61	62	.242	.324	.431
77	BOS/AL		73	265	230	66	9	2	14	121	28	0	0	58	3	6	1	4	2	39	36	.287	.363	.526
78	BOS/AL		147	572	497	123	24	2	24	223	65	2	2	119	15	6	2	8	5	75	63	.247	.336	.449
79	BOS/AL		152	563	489	134	24	1	21	223	69	7	0	76	14	3	1	6	9	69	58	.274	.364	.456
80	BOS/AL		148	542	463	123	37	5	18	224	64	6	5	98	8	6	4	3	1	72	60	.266	.358	.484
81	BOS/AL		108	504	412	122	19	4	22	215	85	1	1	85	8	3	3	3	2	84	71	.296	.415	.522
82	BOS/AL		162	727	609	178	37	7	32	325	112	1	1	125	17	3	2	3	2	122	98	.292	.402	.534
83	BOS/AL		126	544	470	112	19	4	22	205	70	5	2	97	12	0	2	3	0	74	58	.238	.338	.436
84	BOS/AL		162	738	630	186	37	8	32	335	96	2	4	115	19	1	7	3	1	121	104	.295	.388	.532
85	BOS/AL		159	744	617	162	29	1	29	280	114	4	5	105	16	1	7	7	2	110	78	.263	.378	.454
86	BOS/AL		152	640	529	137	33	2	26	252	97	4	6	117	11	2	6	3	3	86	97	.259	.376	.476
87	BOS/AL		154	657	541	165	37	2	34	308	106	6	3	98	10	0	7	4	5	109	123	.305	.417	.569
88	BOS/AL		149	645	559	164	31	7	21	272	76	3	3	99	16	2	5	5	1	96	111	.293	.375	.487
89	BOS/AL		146	630	520	148	27	3	20	241	99	1	3	84	16	1	7	3	3	82	100	.285	.397	.463
90	BOS/AL		123	522	445	111	18	3	13	174	67	5	4	73	18	0	6	3	4	66	63	.249	.349	.391
91	BAL/AL		101	329	270	73	9	1	6	102	54	2	2	54	7	1	2	2	3	35	38	.270	.393	.378
20 YR TOTALS			**2606**	**10569**	**8996**	**2446**	**483**	**73**	**385**	**4230**	**1391**	**60**	**53**	**1697**	**227**	**52**	**77**	**78**	**59**	**1470**	**1384**	**.272**	**.370**	**.470**

Faries, Paul Tyrrell — bats right — throws right — b.2/20/65 — 1991 positions: 2B 36, 3B 12, SS 8

YR	TM/LG	CL	G	TPA	AB	H	2B	3B	HR	TB	BB	IBB	HB	SO	GDP	SH	SF	SB	CS	R	RBI	BA	OBA	SA
87	SPO/NWL	A−	74	330	280	86	9	3	0	101	36	0	5	25	7	4	5	30	9	67	27	.307	.390	.361
88	RIV/CAL	A+	141	673	579	183	39	4	2	236	72	1	8	79	14	7	7	65	30	108	77	.316	.395	.408
89	WIC/TEX	AA	130	565	513	136	25	8	6	195	47	0	2	52	13	2	1	41	13	79	52	.265	.329	.380
90	LV/PCL	AAA	137	641	552	172	29	3	5	222	75	1	6	60	16	7	1	48	15	109	64	.312	.399	.402
	SD/NL		14	45	37	7	1	0	0	8	4	0	1	7	0	2	1	0	1	4	2	.189	.279	.216
91	HD/CAL	A+	10	46	42	13	2	2	0	19	2	1	0	3	2	1	1	1	0	6	5	.310	.333	.452
	LV/PCL	AAA	20	90	75	23	2	1	1	30	12	0	0	5	2	1	1	7	3	16	12	.307	.398	.400

(continued)

Faries, Paul Tyrrell (continued)

YR	TM/LG	CL	G	TPA	AB	H	2B	3B	HR	TB	BB	IBB	HB	SO	GDP	SH	SF	SB	CS	R	RBI	BA	OBA	SA
	SD/NL		57	149	130	23	3	1	0	28	14	0	1	21				3		13	7	.177	.262	.215
2 YR TOTALS			**71**	**194**	**167**	**30**	**4**	**1**	**0**	**36**	**18**	**0**	**2**	**28**	**5**	**6**	**1**	**3**	**2**	**17**	**9**	**.180**	**.266**	**.216**

Fariss, Monty Ted — bats right — throws right — b.10/13/67 — 1991 positions: OF 8, 2B 4, DH 4

YR	TM/LG	CL	G	TPA	AB	H	2B	3B	HR	TB	BB	IBB	HB	SO	GDP	SH	SF	SB	CS	R	RBI	BA	OBA	SA
88	BUT/PIO	R+	17	77	53	21	1	0	4	34	20	2	2	7	1	0	2	2	0	16	22	.396	.558	.642
	TUL/TEX	AA	49	189	165	37	6	6	3	64	22	0	0	39	2	1	1	2	0	21	31	.224	.314	.388
89	TUL/TEX	AA	132	575	497	135	27	2	5	181	64	0	0	112	13	8	6	12	6	72	52	.272	.351	.364
90	TUL/TEX	AA	71	282	244	73	15	6	7	121	36	0	1	60	9	1	0	8	5	45	34	.299	.391	.496
	OC/AMA	AAA	62	261	225	68	12	3	4	98	34	0	0	48	7	0	2	1	1	30	31	.302	.391	.436
91	OC/AMA	AAA	137	590	494	134	31	9	13	222	91	1	0	143	11	3	2	4	7	84	73	.271	.383	.449
	TEX/AL		19	38	31	8	1	0	1	12	7	0	0	11	0	0	0	0	0	6	6	.258	.395	.387

Felder, Michael Otis "Mike" — bats both — throws right — b.11/18/61 — 1991 positions: OF 107, 3B 3, 2B 1

YR	TM/LG	CL	G	TPA	AB	H	2B	3B	HR	TB	BB	IBB	HB	SO	GDP	SH	SF	SB	CS	R	RBI	BA	OBA	SA
84	EP/TEX	AA	122	571	496	144	19	2	9	194	63	2	1	57	4	2	9	58	16	98	72	.290	.366	.391
85	VAN/PCL	AAA	137	628	563	177	16	11	2	221	55	1	2	70	14	3	5	61	12	91	43	.314	.374	.393
	MIL/AL		15	62	56	11	1	0	0	12	5	0	0	6	2	1	0	4	1	8	0	.196	.262	.214
86	EP/TEX	AA	8	38	31	14	3	0	0	17	5	1	0	3	1	1	1	7	0	10	2	.452	.514	.548
	MIL/AL		44	174	155	37	2	4	1	50	13	0	0	16	2	1	5	16	2	24	13	.239	.289	.323
	VAN/PCL	AAA	39	173	153	40	3	4	1	54	17	2	0	15	2	0	3	4	3	21	15	.261	.329	.353
87	DEN/AMA	AAA	27	130	113	41	6	2	0	57	14	1	1	6	0	1	1	17	1	26	20	.363	.434	.504
	MIL/AL		108	328	289	77	5	7	2	102	28	0	0	23	3	9	2	34	8	48	31	.266	.329	.353
88	DEN/AMA	AAA	20	84	78	21	4	1	0	27	5	0	0	10	2	0	1	8	1	10	5	.269	.310	.346
	MIL/AL		50	85	81	14	1	0	0	15	0	0	0	11	1	3	0	8	2	14	5	.173	.183	.185
89	MIL/AL		117	345	315	76	11	3	3	102	23	0	0	38	4	7	0	26	5	50	23	.241	.293	.324
90	MIL/AL		121	272	237	65	7	2	3	85	22	0	0	17	0	8	5	20	9	38	27	.274	.330	.359
91	SF/NL		132	383	348	92	10	6	0	114	30	2	1	31	1	4	0	21	6	51	18	.264	.325	.328
7 YR TOTALS			**587**	**1649**	**1481**	**372**	**37**	**22**	**9**	**480**	**121**	**5**	**2**	**142**	**13**	**33**	**12**	**129**	**33**	**233**	**117**	**.251**	**.306**	**.324**

Felix, Junior Francisco (Sanchez) — bats both — throws right — b.10/3/67 — 1991 positions: OF 65

YR	TM/LG	CL	G	TPA	AB	H	2B	3B	HR	TB	BB	IBB	HB	SO	GDP	SH	SF	SB	CS	R	RBI	BA	OBA	SA
86	MH/PIO	R+	67	304	263	75	9	3	4	102	35	1	6	84	4	0	0	37	9	57	28	.285	.382	.388
87	MB/SAL	A	124	523	466	135	15	9	12	204	43	8	10	124	2	2	2	64	28	70	51	.290	.361	.438
88	KNO/SOU	AA	93	386	360	91	16	5	3	126	20	2	3	82	4	2	1	40	16	52	25	.253	.297	.350
89	SYR/INT	AAA	21	98	87	24	4	2	1	35	9	0	0	18	2	1	1	13	3	17	10	.276	.340	.402
	TOR/AL		110	454	415	107	14	8	9	164	33	2	3	101	5	0	3	18	12	62	46	.258	.315	.395
90	TOR/AL		127	517	463	122	23	7	15	204	45	0	2	99	4	2	5	13	8	73	65	.263	.328	.441
91	PS/CAL	A+	18	80	64	23	3	0	2	32	16	1	0	11	2	0	0	8	2	12	10	.359	.488	.500
	CAL/AL		66	246	230	65	10	2	2	85	11	0	3	55	5	0	2	7	5	32	26	.283	.321	.370
3 YR TOTALS			**303**	**1217**	**1108**	**294**	**47**	**17**	**26**	**453**	**89**	**2**	**8**	**255**	**14**	**2**	**10**	**38**	**25**	**167**	**137**	**.265**	**.322**	**.409**

Fermin, Felix Jose (Minaya) — bats right — throws right — b.10/9/63 — 1991 positions: SS 129

YR	TM/LG	CL	G	TPA	AB	H	2B	3B	HR	TB	BB	IBB	HB	SO	GDP	SH	SF	SB	CS	R	RBI	BA	OBA	SA
84	PW/CAR	A+	119	423	382	94	13	1	0	109	29	0	5	32	13	5	2	32	10	34	41	.246	.306	.285
85	NAS/EAS	AA	137	495	443	100	10	2	0	114	37	0	3	30	14	10	2	29	15	32	27	.226	.289	.257
86	PW/CAR	A+	84	355	322	90	10	1	0	102	25	0	4	19	4	3	1	40	12	58	26	.280	.338	.317
	HAW/PCL	AAA	39	133	125	32	5	0	0	37	7	0	0	13	3	1	0	1	1	13	9	.256	.295	.296
87	HAR/EAS	AA	100	438	399	107	9	5	0	126	27	1	2	22	12	7	3	22	13	62	35	.268	.316	.316
	PIT/NL		23	75	68	17	0	0	0	17	4	1	1	9	3	2	0	0	0	6	4	.250	.301	.250
88	BUF/AMA	AAA	87	375	352	92	11	1	0	105	17	0	1	18	15	4	1	8	6	38	31	.261	.296	.298
	PIT/NL		43	100	87	24	0	2	0	28	8	1	3	10	3	1	1	3	1	9	2	.276	.354	.322
89	CLE/AL		156	562	484	115	9	1	0	126	41	0	4	27	15	32	1	6	4	50	21	.238	.302	.260
90	CLE/AL		148	458	414	106	13	2	1	126	26	0	0	22	13	13	5	3	3	47	40	.256	.297	.304
91	CS/PCL	AAA	2	8	8	2	0	0	0	2	0	0	0	0	0	0	0	0	0	1	1	.250	.250	.250
	CLE/AL		129	469	424	111	13	2	0	128	26	0	3	27	17	13	3	5	4	30	31	.262	.307	.302
5 YR TOTALS			**499**	**1664**	**1477**	**373**	**35**	**7**	**1**	**425**	**105**	**2**	**11**	**95**	**51**	**61**	**10**	**17**	**12**	**142**	**98**	**.253**	**.305**	**.288**

Fernandez, Octavio Antonio (Castro) "Tony"— bats both — throws right — b.8/6/62 — 1991 positions: SS 145

YR	TM/LG	CL	G	TPA	AB	H	2B	3B	HR	TB	BB	IBB	HB	SO	GDP	SH	SF	SB	CS	R	RBI	BA	OBA	SA
83	TOR/AL		15	38	34	9	1	1	0	12	2	0	1	2	1	1	0	0	1	5	2	.265	.324	.353
84	SYR/INT	AAA	26	109	94	24	1	0	0	25	13	0	0	9	4	1	1	1	3	12	6	.255	.343	.266
	TOR/AL		88	254	233	63	5	3	3	83	17	0	0	15	3	0	2	5	7	29	19	.270	.317	.356
85	TOR/AL		161	618	564	163	31	10	2	220	43	2	2	41	12	7	2	13	6	71	51	.289	.340	.390
86	TOR/AL		163	727	687	213	33	9	10	294	27	0	4	52	9	5	4	25	12	91	65	.310	.338	.428
87	TOR/AL		146	642	578	186	29	8	5	246	51	3	5	48	14	4	4	32	12	90	67	.322	.379	.426
88	TOR/AL		154	704	648	186	41	4	5	250	45	3	4	65	9	3	4	15	5	76	70	.287	.335	.386
89	TOR/AL		140	617	573	147	25	9	11	223	29	1	3	51	9	2	10	22	6	64	64	.257	.291	.389
90	TOR/AL		161	721	635	175	27	17	4	248	71	4	7	70	17	2	6	26	13	84	66	.276	.352	.391
91	SD/NL		145	621	558	152	27	5	4	201	55	0	0	74	12	7	1	23	9	81	38	.272	.337	.360
9 YR TOTALS			**1173**	**4942**	**4510**	**1294**	**219**	**66**	**44**	**1777**	**340**	**13**	**26**	**418**	**85**	**33**	**33**	**161**	**71**	**591**	**442**	**.287**	**.338**	**.394**

Fielder, Cecil Grant — bats right — throws right — b.9/21/63 — 1991 positions: 1B 122, DH 42

YR	TM/LG	CL	G	TPA	AB	H	2B	3B	HR	TB	BB	IBB	HB	SO	GDP	SH	SF	SB	CS	R	RBI	BA	OBA	SA
84	KIN/CAR	A+	61	255	222	63	12	1	19	134	28	7	1	44	8	1	3	2	1	42	49	.284	.362	.604

Fielder, Cecil Grant (continued)

YR	TM/LG	CL	G	TPA	AB	H	2B	3B	HR	TB	BB	IBB	HB	SO	GDP	SH	SF	SB	CS	R	RBI	BA	OBA	SA
	KNO/SOU	AA	64	262	236	60	12	2	9	103	22	3	1	48	6	0	3	0	0	33	44	.254	.317	.436
85	KNO/SOU	AA	96	414	361	106	26	2	18	190	45	3	3	83	5	0	5	0	0	52	81	.294	.372	.526
	TOR/AL		30	81	74	23	4	0	4	39	6	0	0	16	2	0	1	0	0	6	16	.311	.358	.527
86	SYR/INT	AAA	88	363	325	91	13	3	18	164	32	3	3	91	11	0	3	0	0	47	68	.280	.347	.505
	TOR/AL		34	90	83	13	2	0	4	27	6	0	1	27	3	0	0	0	0	7	13	.157	.222	.325
87	TOR/AL		82	197	175	47	7	1	14	98	20	2	1	48	6	0	1	0	1	30	32	.269	.345	.560
88	TOR/AL		74	190	174	40	6	1	9	75	14	0	1	53	6	0	1	0	1	24	23	.230	.289	.431
90	DET/AL		159	673	573	159	25	1	51	339	90	11	5	182	15	0	5	0	1	104	132	.277	.377	.592
91	DET/AL		162	712	624	163	25	0	44	320	78	12	6	151	17	0	4	0	0	102	133	.261	.347	.513
6 YR TOTALS			**541**	**1943**	**1703**	**445**	**69**	**3**	**126**	**898**	**214**	**25**	**14**	**477**	**49**	**0**	**12**	**0**	**3**	**273**	**349**	**.261**	**.346**	**.527**

Finley, Steven Allen "Steve" — bats left — throws left — b.3/12/65 — 1991 positions: OF 153

YR	TM/LG	CL	G	TPA	AB	H	2B	3B	HR	TB	BB	IBB	HB	SO	GDP	SH	SF	SB	CS	R	RBI	BA	OBA	SA
87	NEW/NYP	A−	54	249	222	65	13	2	3	91	22	0	2	24	4	1	2	26	5	40	33	.293	.359	.410
	HAG/CAR	A+	15	66	65	22	3	2	1	32	1	0	0	6	2	0	0	7	2	9	5	.338	.348	.492
88	HAG/CAR	A+	8	32	28	6	2	0	0	8	4	0	0	3	2	0	0	4	0	2	3	.214	.313	.286
	CHA/SOU	AA	10	45	40	12	4	2	1	23	4	0	1	3	1	0	0	2	0	9	5	.300	.378	.575
	ROC/INT	AAA	120	494	456	143	19	7	5	191	28	5	0	55	4	8	2	20	11	61	54	.314	.352	.419
89	ROC/INT	AAA	7	26	25	4	0	0	0	4	1	0	0	5	0	0	0	3	0	2	2	.160	.192	.160
	HAG/EAS	AA	11	53	48	20	3	1	0	25	4	0	0	3	0	0	1	4	0	11	7	.417	.453	.521
	BAL/AL		81	241	217	54	5	2	2	69	15	1	1	30	3	6	2	17	3	35	25	.249	.298	.318
90	BAL/AL		142	513	464	119	16	4	3	152	32	3	2	53	8	10	5	22	9	46	37	.256	.304	.328
91	HOU/NL		159	656	596	170	28	10	8	242	42	5	5	65	8	10	6	34	18	84	54	.285	.331	.406
3 YR TOTALS			**382**	**1410**	**1277**	**343**	**49**	**16**	**13**	**463**	**89**	**9**	**5**	**148**	**19**	**26**	**13**	**73**	**30**	**165**	**116**	**.269**	**.316**	**.363**

Fisk, Carlton Ernest "Carlton" or "Pudge" — bats right — throws right — b.12/26/47 — 1991 positions: C 106, DH 13, 1B 12

YR	TM/LG	CL	G	TPA	AB	H	2B	3B	HR	TB	BB	IBB	HB	SO	GDP	SH	SF	SB	CS	R	RBI	BA	OBA	SA
69	BOS/AL		2	5	5	0	0	0	0	0	0	0	0	2	0	0	0	0	0	0	0	.000	.000	.000
71	BOS/AL		14	49	48	15	2	1	2	25	1	0	0	10	1	0	0	0	0	7	6	.313	.327	.521
72	BOS/AL		131	514	457	134	28	9	22	246	52	6	4	83	11	1	0	5	2	74	61	.293	.370	.538
73	BOS/AL		135	558	508	125	21	0	26	224	37	2	10	99	11	1	2	7	2	65	71	.246	.309	.441
74	BOS/AL		52	216	187	56	12	1	11	103	24	2	2	23	5	2	1	5	1	36	26	.299	.383	.551
75	BOS/AL		79	294	263	87	14	4	10	139	27	4	2	32	7	0	2	4	3	47	52	.331	.395	.529
76	BOS/AL		134	557	487	124	17	5	17	202	56	3	6	71	11	3	5	12	5	76	58	.255	.336	.415
77	BOS/AL		152	632	536	169	26	3	26	279	75	3	9	85	9	2	10	7	6	106	102	.315	.402	.521
78	BOS/AL		157	658	571	162	39	5	20	271	71	6	7	83	10	3	6	7	2	94	88	.284	.366	.475
79	BOS/AL		91	340	320	87	23	2	10	144	10	0	6	38	9	1	3	3	0	49	42	.272	.304	.450
80	BOS/AL		131	530	478	138	25	3	18	223	36	6	13	62	12	0	3	11	5	73	62	.289	.353	.467
81	CHI/AL		96	394	338	89	12	0	7	122	38	3	12	37	9	1	5	3	2	44	45	.263	.354	.361
82	CHI/AL		135	536	476	127	17	3	14	192	46	7	6	60	12	4	4	17	2	66	65	.267	.336	.403
83	CHI/AL		138	545	488	141	26	4	26	253	46	3	6	88	8	2	3	9	6	85	86	.289	.355	.518
84	CHI/AL		102	395	359	83	20	1	21	168	26	4	5	60	7	1	4	6	0	54	43	.231	.289	.468
85	CHI/AL		153	620	543	129	23	1	37	265	52	12	17	81	9	2	6	17	9	85	107	.238	.320	.488
86	CHI/AL		125	491	457	101	11	0	14	154	22	2	6	92	10	0	6	2	4	42	63	.221	.263	.337
87	CHI/AL		135	508	454	116	22	1	23	209	39	8	8	72	9	1	6	1	4	68	71	.256	.321	.460
88	CHI/AL		76	298	253	70	8	1	19	137	37	9	5	40	6	1	2	0	0	37	50	.277	.377	.542
89	CHI/AL		103	419	375	110	19	2	13	178	36	8	3	60	15	0	5	1	0	47	68	.293	.356	.475
90	CHI/AL		137	521	452	129	21	0	18	204	61	8	7	73	12	0	1	7	2	65	65	.285	.378	.451
91	CHI/AL		134	501	460	111	25	0	18	190	32	4	7	86	19	0	2	1	2	42	74	.241	.299	.413
22 YR TOTALS			**2412**	**9581**	**8515**	**2303**	**417**	**46**	**372**	**3928**	**824**	**100**	**141**	**1337**	**202**	**25**	**76**	**125**	**57**	**1262**	**1305**	**.270**	**.342**	**.461**

Fitzgerald, Michael Roy "Mike" — bats right — throws right — b.7/13/60 — 1991 positions: C 54, 1B 3, OF 3

YR	TM/LG	CL	G	TPA	AB	H	2B	3B	HR	TB	BB	IBB	HB	SO	GDP	SH	SF	SB	CS	R	RBI	BA	OBA	SA
79	LYN/CAR	A+	117	448	368	93	16	4	13	156	54	2	8	84	8	7	11	0	2	55	75	.253	.351	.424
80	LYN/CAR	A+	105	408	338	71	10	2	10	115	54	1	2	62	7	8	6	5	7	36	44	.210	.318	.340
81	JAC/TEX	AA	66	250	218	68	14	2	4	98	24	1	4	44	4	3	1	1	1	28	29	.312	.386	.450
	TID/INT	AAA	24	65	58	9	2	0	1	14	5	0	0	13	0	1	1	2	0	9	3	.155	.219	.241
82	TID/INT	AAA	94	354	302	74	9	2	4	99	41	1	1	55	11	8	2	9	4	33	36	.245	.335	.328
83	TID/INT	AAA	111	452	370	105	17	1	14	166	73	3	3	57	10	3	3	2	3	64	65	.284	.403	.449
	NY/NL		8	23	20	2	0	0	1	5	3	1	0	6	0	0	0	0	0	1	2	.100	.217	.250
84	NY/NL		112	394	360	87	15	1	2	110	24	7	1	71	17	5	4	1	0	20	33	.242	.288	.306
85	MON/NL		108	341	295	61	7	1	5	85	38	12	2	55	8	1	5	0	3	25	34	.207	.297	.288
86	IND/AMA	AAA	10	37	32	11	3	0	0	14	5	0	0	1	0	0	0	0	0	4	4	.344	.432	.438
	MON/NL		73	243	209	59	13	1	6	92	27	6	1	34	10	3	1	3	4	32	36	.282	.364	.440
87	MON/NL		107	334	287	69	11	0	3	89	42	0	0	54	10	3	1	3	0	12	13	.240	.336	.310
88	IND/AMA	AAA	32	110	96	26	6	1	1	35	9	0	0	22	2	2	3	1	0	17	23	.271	.347	.419
	MON/NL		63	180	155	37	6	1	5	60	19	0	2	22	4	4	2	2	2	17	23	.238	.322	.386
89	MON/NL		100	331	290	69	18	2	7	112	35	8	2	61	8	2	3	4	3	36	41	.243	.365	.393
90	MON/NL		111	383	313	76	18	1	9	123	60	5	3	60	5	3	3	0	1	36	41	.222	.343	.370
91	IND/AMA	AAA	10	35	27	6	1	0	1	10	6	0	0	3	5	0	1	3	4	2	17	28	.202	.278	.308
	MON/NL		71	224	198	40	6	1	5	61	22	0	0	35	5	1	3	4	2	17	28	.237	.323	.349
9 YR TOTALS			**753**	**2453**	**2127**	**505**	**93**	**9**	**42**	**742**	**270**	**42**	**9**	**398**	**61**	**25**	**22**	**29**	**18**	**201**	**276**	**.237**	**.323**	**.349**

Fletcher, Darrin Glen — bats left — throws right — b.10/3/66 — 1991 positions: C 45

YR	TM/LG	CL	G	TPA	AB	H	2B	3B	HR	TB	BB	IBB	HB	SO	GDP	SH	SF	SB	CS	R	RBI	BA	OBA	SA
87	VB/FSL	A+	43	151	124	33	7	0	0	40	22	3	1	12	6	0	4	0	2	13	15	.266	.371	.323
88	SA/TEX	AA	89	307	279	58	8	0	1	69	17	5	3	42	6	6	2	2	2	19	20	.208	.259	.247
89	ALB/PCL	AAA	100	355	315	86	16	1	5	119	30	0	2	38	12	2	6	1	5	34	44	.273	.334	.378
	LA/NL		5	9	8	4	0	0	1	7	1	0	0	0	0	0	0	0	0	1	2	.500	.556	.875
90	ALB/PCL	AAA	105	404	350	102	23	1	13	166	40	6	5	37	11	3	6	1	1	58	65	.291	.367	.474
	LA/NL		2	1	1	0	0	0	0	0	0	0	1	0	0	0	0	0	0	0	0	.000	.000	.000
	PHI/NL		9	23	22	3	1	0	0	4	1	0	0	5	0	0	0	0	0	3	1	.136	.174	.182
	YEAR		11	24	23	3	1	0	0	4	1	0	0	6	0	0	0	0	0	3	1	.130	.167	.174
91	SCR/INT	AAA	90	339	306	87	13	1	8	126	23	4	3	29	7	1	6	1	2	39	50	.284	.334	.412
	PHI/NL		46	142	136	31	8	0	2	42	5	0	0	15	2	1	0	0	1	5	12	.228	.255	.309
3 YR TOTALS			**62**	**175**	**167**	**38**	**9**	**0**	**2**	**53**	**7**	**0**	**0**	**21**	**2**	**1**	**0**	**0**	**1**	**9**	**15**	**.228**	**.259**	**.317**

Fletcher, Scott Brian — bats right — throws right — b.7/30/58 — 1991 positions: 2B 86, 3B 4

YR	TM/LG	CL	G	TPA	AB	H	2B	3B	HR	TB	BB	IBB	HB	SO	GDP	SH	SF	SB	CS	R	RBI	BA	OBA	SA
81	CHI/NL		19	48	46	10	4	0	0	14	2	0	0	4	0	0	0	0	0	6	1	.217	.250	.304
82	CHI/NL		11	28	24	4	0	0	0	4	4	0	0	5	0	0	0	0	1	4	1	.167	.286	.167
83	CHI/AL		114	302	262	62	16	5	3	97	29	0	2	22	8	7	2	5	1	42	31	.237	.315	.370
84	CHI/AL		149	521	456	114	13	3	3	142	46	2	8	46	5	9	2	10	4	46	35	.250	.328	.311
85	CHI/AL		119	348	301	77	8	1	2	93	35	0	0	47	9	11	1	5	5	38	31	.256	.332	.309
86	TEX/AL		147	594	530	159	34	5	3	212	47	0	4	59	10	10	3	12	11	82	50	.300	.360	.400
87	TEX/AL		156	668	588	169	28	4	5	220	61	3	5	66	14	12	2	13	12	82	63	.287	.358	.374
88	TEX/AL		140	609	515	142	19	4	0	169	62	1	12	34	13	15	5	8	5	59	47	.276	.364	.328
89	TEX/AL		83	358	314	75	14	1	1	91	38	1	2	41	8	2	2	1	0	47	22	.239	.323	.290
	CHI/AL		59	271	232	63	11	1	1	79	26	0	1	19	4	9	3	1	1	30	21	.272	.344	.341
	YEAR		142	629	546	138	25	2	1	170	64	1	3	60	12	11	5	2	1	77	43	.253	.332	.311
90	CHI/AL		151	573	509	123	18	3	4	159	45	3	3	63	10	11	5	1	3	54	56	.242	.304	.312
91	CHI/AL		90	277	248	51	10	1	0	66	17	0	3	26	3	6	3	0	2	14	28	.206	.262	.266
11 YR TOTALS			**1238**	**4597**	**4025**	**1049**	**175**	**28**	**22**	**1346**	**412**	**10**	**40**	**432**	**84**	**92**	**28**	**57**	**44**	**504**	**386**	**.261**	**.333**	**.334**

Flora, Kevin Scot — bats right — throws right — b.6/10/69 — 1991 positions: 2B 3

YR	TM/LG	CL	G	TPA	AB	H	2B	3B	HR	TB	BB	IBB	HB	SO	GDP	SH	SF	SB	CS	R	RBI	BA	OBA	SA
87	SAL/NWL	A−	35	112	88	24	5	1	0	31	21	0	0	14	2	3	0	8	4	17	12	.273	.413	.352
88	QC/MID	A	48	171	152	33	3	4	0	44	18	4	0	33	4	1	0	5	3	19	15	.217	.300	.289
89	QC/MID	A	120	443	372	81	8	4	1	100	57	2	6	107	3	5	3	30	10	46	21	.218	.329	.269
90	MID/TEX	AA	71	259	232	53	16	5	5	94	23	0	6	53	6	3	3	11	5	35	32	.228	.297	.405
91	MID/TEX	AA	124	530	484	138	14	15	12	218	37	2	3	92	2	3	3	40	14	97	67	.285	.338	.450
	CAL/AL		3	10	8	1	0	0	0	1	1	0	0	5	1	1	0	1	0	1	0	.125	.222	.125

Foley, Thomas Michael "Tom" — bats left — throws right — b.9/9/59 — 1991 positions: SS 43, 1B 31, 3B 6, 2B 2

YR	TM/LG	CL	G	TPA	AB	H	2B	3B	HR	TB	BB	IBB	HB	SO	GDP	SH	SF	SB	CS	R	RBI	BA	OBA	SA
83	CIN/NL		68	113	98	20	4	1	0	26	13	2	0	17	1	2	0	1	0	7	9	.204	.297	.265
84	CIN/NL		106	304	277	70	8	3	5	99	24	7	0	36	2	1	2	3	0	26	27	.253	.310	.357
85	CIN/NL		43	98	92	18	5	1	0	25	6	1	0	16	0	0	0	1	2	7	6	.196	.245	.272
	PHI/NL		46	171	158	42	8	0	3	59	13	7	0	18	2	0	0	1	3	17	17	.266	.322	.373
	YEAR		89	269	250	60	13	1	3	84	19	8	0	34	2	0	0	2	3	24	23	.240	.294	.336
86	REA/EAS	AA	3	12	11	2	2	0	0	4	0	0	0	0	0	0	0	0	0	2	0	.182	.250	.364
	PHI/NL		39	72	61	18	2	1	0	22	10	1	0	11	1	0	0	1	0	7	7	.295	.389	.361
	MON/NL		64	227	202	52	13	2	1	72	20	5	0	26	3	2	3	8	3	18	18	.257	.320	.356
	YEAR		103	299	263	70	15	3	1	94	30	6	0	37	4	2	3	10	3	26	23	.266	.337	.357
87	MON/NL		106	293	280	82	18	3	5	121	11	0	1	46	1	0	6	10	4	35	28	.293	.322	.432
88	MON/NL		127	411	377	100	21	3	5	142	30	10	1	49	11	0	3	6	2	33	43	.265	.319	.377
89	MON/NL		122	431	375	86	19	2	7	130	45	4	3	53	2	4	4	2	3	34	39	.229	.314	.347
90	MON/NL		73	178	164	35	2	1	0	39	12	2	0	22	4	1	1	2	1	11	12	.213	.266	.238
91	MON/NL		86	187	168	35	11	1	0	48	14	4	1	30	4	1	3	2	0	12	15	.208	.269	.286
9 YR TOTALS			**880**	**2485**	**2252**	**558**	**111**	**18**	**26**	**783**	**198**	**43**	**6**	**318**	**36**	**12**	**17**	**28**	**29**	**208**	**219**	**.248**	**.308**	**.348**

Franco, Julio Cesar — bats right — throws right — b.8/23/58 — 1991 positions: 2B 146

YR	TM/LG	CL	G	TPA	AB	H	2B	3B	HR	TB	BB	IBB	HB	SO	GDP	SH	SF	SB	CS	R	RBI	BA	OBA	SA
82	PHI/NL		16	32	29	8	1	0	0	9	2	0	1	4	1	1	0	0	2	3	3	.276	.323	.310
83	CLE/AL		149	598	560	153	24	8	8	217	27	1	2	50	21	3	6	32	12	68	80	.273	.306	.387
84	CLE/AL		160	718	658	188	22	5	3	229	43	1	6	68	23	1	10	19	10	82	79	.286	.331	.348
85	CLE/AL		160	703	636	183	33	4	6	242	54	2	4	74	26	0	9	13	9	97	90	.288	.343	.381
86	CLE/AL		149	636	599	183	30	5	10	253	32	1	0	66	28	0	5	10	9	80	74	.306	.338	.422
87	CLE/AL		128	560	495	158	24	3	8	212	57	2	3	56	23	0	5	32	9	86	52	.319	.389	.428
88	CLE/AL		152	676	613	186	23	6	10	251	56	4	2	72	17	1	4	25	11	88	54	.303	.361	.409
89	TEX/AL		150	621	548	173	31	5	13	253	66	11	1	69	27	0	6	21	11	80	92	.316	.386	.462
90	TEX/AL		157	670	582	172	27	1	11	234	82	3	2	83	12	2	2	31	10	96	69	.296	.383	.402
91	TEX/AL		146	659	589	201	27	3	15	279	65	8	3	78	13	0	2	36	9	108	78	.341	.408	.474
10 YR TOTALS			**1367**	**5873**	**5309**	**1605**	**242**	**40**	**84**	**2179**	**484**	**34**	**23**	**620**	**191**	**8**	**49**	**219**	**82**	**788**	**671**	**.302**	**.360**	**.410**

Fryman, David Travis "Travis" — bats right — throws right — b.4/25/69 — 1991 positions: 3B 85, SS 71

YR	TM/LG	CL	G	TPA	AB	H	2B	3B	HR	TB	BB	IBB	HB	SO	GDP	SH	SF	SB	CS	R	RBI	BA	OBA	SA
87	BRI/APP	R+	67	273	248	58	9	0	2	73	22	0	1	40	12	0	2	5	5	25	20	.234	.297	.294
88	FAY/SAL	A	123	458	411	96	17	4	0	121	24	0	10	83	6	8	5	18	5	44	47	.234	.289	.294
89	LON/EAS	AA	118	459	426	113	30	1	9	172	19	0	8	78	5	2	4	5	3	52	56	.265	.306	.404

Fryman, David Travis "Travis" (continued)

YR	TM/LG	CL	G	TPA	AB	H	2B	3B	HR	TB	BB	IBB	HB	SO	GDP	SH	SF	SB	CS	R	RBI	BA	OBA	SA
90	TOL/INT	AAA	87	351	327	84	22	2	10	140	17	0	2	59	7	2	3	4	7	38	53	.257	.295	.428
	DET/AL		66	251	232	69	11	1	9	109	17	0	1	51	3	1	0	3	3	32	27	.297	.348	.470
91	DET/AL		149	612	557	144	36	3	21	249	40	0	3	149	13	6	6	12	5	65	91	.259	.309	.447
2 YR TOTALS			**215**	**863**	**789**	**213**	**47**	**4**	**30**	**358**	**57**	**0**	**4**	**200**	**16**	**7**	**6**	**15**	**8**	**97**	**118**	**.270**	**.320**	**.454**

Gaetti, Gary Joseph — bats right — throws right — b.8/19/58 — 1991 positions: 3B 152

YR	TM/LG	CL	G	TPA	AB	H	2B	3B	HR	TB	BB	IBB	HB	SO	GDP	SH	SF	SB	CS	R	RBI	BA	OBA	SA
81	MIN/AL		9	26	26	5	0	0	2	11	0	0	0	6	1	0	0	0	0	4	3	.192	.192	.423
82	MIN/AL		145	565	508	117	25	4	25	225	37	2	3	107	16	4	13	8	4	59	84	.230	.280	.443
83	MIN/AL		157	650	584	143	30	3	21	242	54	2	4	121	18	0	8	7	1	81	78	.245	.309	.414
84	MIN/AL		162	644	588	154	29	4	5	206	44	1	4	81	9	3	1	13	5	71	63	.262	.315	.350
85	MIN/AL		160	608	560	138	31	0	20	229	37	3	7	89	15	3	1	13	5	55	65	.246	.301	.409
86	MIN/AL		157	661	596	171	34	4	34	309	52	4	6	108	18	1	6	14	15	91	108	.287	.347	.518
87	MIN/AL		154	628	584	150	36	2	31	283	37	7	3	92	25	1	3	10	7	95	109	.257	.303	.485
88	MIN/AL		133	516	468	141	29	2	28	258	36	5	5	85	10	1	6	7	4	66	88	.301	.353	.551
89	MIN/AL		130	536	498	125	11	4	19	201	25	1	5	87	12	1	6	6	1	63	75	.251	.286	.404
90	MIN/AL		154	625	577	132	27	5	16	217	36	3	8	104	13	2	5	5	5	61	85	.229	.274	.376
91	CAL/AL		152	634	586	144	22	1	18	222	33	3	8	101	13	6	5	5	5	58	66	.246	.293	.379
11 YR TOTALS			**1513**	**6093**	**5575**	**1420**	**274**	**26**	**219**	**2403**	**391**	**33**	**46**	**981**	**159**	**17**	**64**	**79**	**49**	**704**	**824**	**.255**	**.306**	**.431**

Gagne, Gregory Carpenter "Greg" — bats right — throws right — b.11/12/61 — 1991 positions: SS 137

YR	TM/LG	CL	G	TPA	AB	H	2B	3B	HR	TB	BB	IBB	HB	SO	GDP	SH	SF	SB	CS	R	RBI	BA	OBA	SA
83	MIN/AL		10	29	27	3	1	0	0	4	0	0	0	6	0	0	0	2	0	2	3	.111	.103	.148
84	TOL/INT	AAA	70	274	236	66	7	2	9	104	34	2	1	52	6	2	1	2	3	31	27	.280	.371	.441
	MIN/AL		2	1	1	0	0	0	0	0	0	0	0	0	0	0	0	0	0	0	0	.000	.000	.000
85	MIN/AL		114	322	293	66	15	3	2	93	20	0	3	57	5	3	3	10	4	37	23	.225	.279	.317
86	MIN/AL		156	524	472	118	22	6	12	188	30	0	6	108	4	13	3	12	10	63	54	.250	.301	.398
87	MIN/AL		137	478	437	116	28	7	10	188	25	0	7	84	3	10	2	6	7	70	48	.265	.310	.430
88	MIN/AL		149	507	461	109	20	6	14	183	27	2	7	110	13	11	1	15	7	70	48	.236	.288	.397
89	MIN/AL		149	491	460	125	29	7	9	195	17	0	2	80	10	7	5	11	4	69	48	.272	.298	.424
90	MIN/AL		138	423	388	91	22	3	7	140	24	0	1	76	5	8	2	8	8	38	38	.235	.280	.361
91	MIN/AL		139	447	408	108	23	3	8	161	26	0	3	72	15	5	5	11	9	52	42	.265	.310	.395
9 YR TOTALS			**994**	**3222**	**2947**	**736**	**160**	**35**	**62**	**1152**	**169**	**2**	**26**	**593**	**55**	**57**	**23**	**73**	**48**	**399**	**296**	**.250**	**.294**	**.391**

Galarraga, Andres Jose — bats right — throws right — b.6/18/61 — 1991 positions: 1B 105

YR	TM/LG	CL	G	TPA	AB	H	2B	3B	HR	TB	BB	IBB	HB	SO	GDP	SH	SF	SB	CS	R	RBI	BA	OBA	SA
84	JAC/SOU	AA	143	606	533	154	28	4	27	271	59	10	9	122	10	1	4	2	8	81	87	.289	.367	.508
85	IND/AMA	AAA	121	494	439	118	15	8	25	224	45	4	7	103	12	0	3	3	0	75	87	.269	.344	.510
	MON/NL		24	79	75	14	1	0	2	21	3	0	1	18	0	0	0	1	2	9	4	.187	.228	.280
86	MON/NL		105	356	321	87	13	0	10	130	30	5	3	79	8	1	1	6	5	39	42	.271	.338	.405
87	MON/NL		147	606	551	168	40	3	13	253	41	13	10	127	11	0	4	7	10	72	90	.305	.361	.459
88	MON/NL		157	661	609	184	42	8	29	329	39	9	10	153	12	0	3	13	4	99	92	.302	.352	.540
89	MON/NL		152	636	572	147	30	1	23	248	48	10	13	158	12	0	3	12	5	76	85	.257	.327	.434
90	MON/NL		155	628	579	148	29	0	20	237	40	8	4	169	14	0	5	10	5	65	87	.256	.306	.409
91	MON/NL		107	400	375	82	13	2	9	126	23	5	2	86	6	0	0	5	6	34	33	.219	.268	.336
7 YR TOTALS			**847**	**3366**	**3082**	**830**	**168**	**14**	**106**	**1344**	**224**	**50**	**43**	**790**	**63**	**1**	**16**	**54**	**33**	**394**	**433**	**.269**	**.326**	**.436**

Gallagher, David Thomas "Dave" — bats right — throws right — b.9/20/60 — 1991 positions: OF 87, DH 2

YR	TM/LG	CL	G	TPA	AB	H	2B	3B	HR	TB	BB	IBB	HB	SO	GDP	SH	SF	SB	CS	R	RBI	BA	OBA	SA
84	MAI/INT	AAA	116	451	380	94	19	5	6	141	49	0	3	42	9	10	9	4	1	49	55	.247	.331	.371
85	MAI/INT	AAA	132	575	488	118	22	3	9	173	65	0	3	38	12	11	8	16	12	71	55	.242	.330	.355
86	MAI/INT	AAA	132	553	497	145	23	5	8	202	41	1	1	41	7	12	2	19	12	59	44	.292	.346	.406
87	CLE/AL		15	39	36	4	1	1	0	7	2	0	0	5	1	1	0	2	0	2	1	.111	.158	.194
	BUF/AMA	AAA	12	60	46	12	4	0	0	16	11	0	0	3	2	1	2	1	1	10	6	.261	.390	.348
	CAL/PCL	AAA	75	316	268	82	27	2	3	122	37	1	0	36	10	3	3	12	4	45	46	.306	.386	.455
88	VAN/PCL	AAA	34	147	131	44	8	1	4	66	12	0	1	21	1	1	2	5	1	23	27	.336	.390	.504
	CHI/AL		101	384	347	105	15	3	5	141	29	3	0	40	8	6	2	5	6	59	31	.303	.354	.406
89	CHI/AL		161	667	601	160	22	2	1	189	46	1	2	79	9	16	2	5	6	74	46	.266	.320	.314
90	CHI/AL		45	84	75	21	3	1	0	26	3	0	0	9	3	0	1	0	1	7	2	.280	.316	.347
	BAL/AL		23	58	51	11	1	0	0	12	4	0	0	3	0	1	1	1	2	5	5	.216	.268	.235
	YEAR		68	142	126	32	4	1	0	38	7	0	0	12	3	1	1	1	2	12	7	.254	.296	.302
91	CAL/AL		90	306	270	79	17	0	1	99	24	0	2	43	6	10	0	5	16	32	30	.293	.355	.367
5 YR TOTALS			**435**	**1538**	**1380**	**380**	**59**	**7**	**7**	**474**	**108**	**4**	**5**	**179**	**27**	**40**	**5**	**15**	**16**	**179**	**115**	**.275**	**.329**	**.343**

Gallego, Michael Anthony "Mike" — bats right — throws right — b.10/31/60 — 1991 positions: 2B 135, SS 55

YR	TM/LG	CL	G	TPA	AB	H	2B	3B	HR	TB	BB	IBB	HB	SO	GDP	SH	SF	SB	CS	R	RBI	BA	OBA	SA
84	TAC/PCL	AAA	101	324	288	70	8	1	1	80	27	0	0	39	7	7	2	7	5	29	18	.243	.306	.278
85	MOD/CAL	A+	6	27	25	5	1	0	0	6	2	0	0	8	1	0	0	1	1	1	2	.200	.259	.240
	OAK/AL		76	93	77	16	5	1	1	26	12	0	0	14	2	1	3	1	1	13	9	.208	.319	.338
86	TAC/PCL	AAA	132	505	443	122	16	5	4	160	39	0	0	58	9	8	7	3	3	58	46	.275	.340	.361
	OAK/AL		20	40	37	10	2	0	0	12	1	0	0	6	0	0	2	0	0	2	4	.270	.289	.324
87	TAC/PCL	AAA	10	51	41	11	1	0	1	15	10	0	0	7	1	0	0	1	1	6	6	.268	.412	.366
	OAK/AL		72	143	124	31	6	0	2	43	12	1	0	21	5	5	1	0	1	18	14	.250	.319	.347
88	OAK/AL		129	320	277	58	8	0	2	72	34	0	0	53	6	3	8	2	3	38	20	.209	.298	.260
89	OAK/AL		133	409	357	90	14	2	3	117	35	0	4	43	10	3	3	7	5	45	30	.252	.327	.328

Gallego, Michael Anthony "Mike" (continued)

YR	TM/LG	CL	G	TPA	AB	H	2B	3B	HR	TB	BB	IBB	HB	SO	GDP	SH	SF	SB	CS	R	RBI	BA	OBA	SA
90	OAK/AL		140	447	389	80	13	2	3	106	35	0	4	50	13	17	2	5	5	36	34	.206	.277	.272
91	OAK/AL		159	567	482	119	15	4	12	178	67	3	5	84	8	10	3	6	9	67	49	.247	.343	.369
7 YR TOTALS			**729**	**2019**	**1743**	**404**	**63**	**9**	**23**	**554**	**196**	**3**	**18**	**271**	**44**	**52**	**10**	**21**	**26**	**219**	**160**	**.232**	**.314**	**.318**

Gant, Ronald Edwin "Ron" — bats right — throws right — b.3/2/65 — 1991 positions: OF 148

YR	TM/LG	CL	G	TPA	AB	H	2B	3B	HR	TB	BB	IBB	HB	SO	GDP	SH	SF	SB	CS	R	RBI	BA	OBA	SA
84	AND/SAL	A	105	395	359	85	14	6	3	120	29	0	1	65	6	0	6	13	5	44	38	.237	.291	.334
85	SUM/SAL	A	102	341	305	78	14	4	7	121	33	2	2	59	8	1	0	19	10	46	37	.256	.332	.397
86	DUR/CAR	A+	137	601	512	142	31	10	26	271	78	0	3	85	12	2	6	35	9	108	102	.277	.372	.529
87	GRE/SOU	AA	140	598	527	130	27	3	14	205	59	0	2	92	8	3	7	24	4	78	82	.247	.321	.389
	ATL/NL		21	86	83	22	4	0	2	32	1	0	0	11	3	1	1	4	2	9	9	.265	.271	.386
88	RIC/INT	AAA	12	48	45	14	2	2	0	20	2	0	0	10	0	0	1	1	1	3	4	.311	.333	.444
	ATL/NL		146	618	563	146	28	8	19	247	46	4	3	118	7	2	4	19	10	85	60	.259	.317	.439
89	SUM/SAL	A	12	50	39	15	4	1	1	24	11	2	0	3	0	0	0	4	2	13	5	.385	.520	.615
	RIC/INT	AAA	63	255	225	59	13	2	11	109	29	1	0	42	6	0	1	7	2	42	27	.262	.345	.484
	ATL/NL		75	285	260	46	8	3	9	87	20	1	0	63	0	2	2	9	6	26	25	.177	.237	.335
90	ATL/NL		152	631	575	174	34	3	32	310	50	3	1	86	8	1	4	33	16	107	84	.303	.357	.539
91	ATL/NL		154	642	561	141	35	3	32	278	71	8	5	104	6	0	5	34	15	101	105	.251	.338	.496
5 YR TOTALS			**548**	**2262**	**2042**	**529**	**109**	**17**	**94**	**954**	**188**	**12**	**10**	**382**	**24**	**6**	**16**	**99**	**49**	**328**	**283**	**.259**	**.322**	**.467**

Gantner, James Elmer "Jim" — bats left — throws right — b.1/5/53 — 1991 positions: 3B 90, 2B 59

YR	TM/LG	CL	G	TPA	AB	H	2B	3B	HR	TB	BB	IBB	HB	SO	GDP	SH	SF	SB	CS	R	RBI	BA	OBA	SA
76	MIL/AL		26	79	69	17	1	0	0	18	6	0	1	11	1	3	0	1	0	6	7	.246	.316	.261
77	MIL/AL		14	49	47	14	1	0	1	18	2	0	0	0	0	0	0	2	1	4	2	.298	.327	.383
78	MIL/AL		43	105	97	21	1	0	1	25	5	0	1	10	0	1	0	2	0	14	8	.216	.269	.258
79	MIL/AL		70	234	208	59	10	3	2	81	16	1	2	17	3	5	3	3	5	29	22	.284	.336	.389
80	MIL/AL		132	457	415	117	21	3	4	156	30	5	1	29	8	8	3	11	10	47	40	.282	.330	.376
81	MIL/AL		107	397	352	94	14	1	2	116	29	5	3	29	6	9	4	3	6	35	33	.267	.325	.330
82	MIL/AL		132	485	447	132	17	2	4	165	26	3	2	36	6	7	3	6	3	48	43	.295	.335	.369
83	MIL/AL		161	662	603	170	23	8	11	242	38	5	6	46	10	11	4	5	6	85	74	.282	.329	.401
84	MIL/AL		153	658	613	173	27	1	3	211	30	5	3	51	16	2	10	6	5	61	56	.282	.314	.344
85	MIL/AL		143	573	523	133	15	4	5	171	33	7	3	42	13	10	4	11	8	63	44	.254	.300	.327
86	MIL/AL		139	542	497	136	25	1	7	184	26	2	6	50	13	6	7	13	7	58	38	.274	.313	.370
87	MIL/AL		81	294	265	72	14	0	4	98	19	2	5	22	7	4	1	6	2	37	30	.272	.331	.370
88	MIL/AL		155	596	539	149	28	2	0	181	34	1	3	50	9	18	2	20	8	67	47	.276	.322	.336
89	MIL/AL		116	453	409	112	18	0	0	136	21	2	10	33	10	8	5	20	8	51	34	.274	.321	.333
90	BEL/MID	A	9	36	29	11	1	0	2	18	7	1	0	1	2	0	0	6	0	10	6	.379	.500	.621
	DEN/AMA	AAA	6	25	22	8	1	0	0	9	2	0	1	1	1	0	0	1	0	1	1	.364	.440	.409
	MIL/AL		88	358	323	85	8	5	0	103	29	0	2	19	10	4	0	18	3	36	25	.263	.328	.319
91	MIL/AL		140	567	526	149	27	4	2	190	27	5	3	34	13	7	4	4	6	63	47	.283	.320	.361
16 YR TOTALS			**1700**	**6509**	**5933**	**1633**	**250**	**37**	**46**	**2095**	**371**	**38**	**52**	**484**	**126**	**103**	**50**	**131**	**76**	**704**	**550**	**.275**	**.321**	**.353**

Garcia, Carlos Jesus (Guerrero) — bats right — throws right — b.10/15/67 — 1991 positions: SS 9, 3B 2, 2B 1

YR	TM/LG	CL	G	TPA	AB	H	2B	3B	HR	TB	BB	IBB	HB	SO	GDP	SH	SF	SB	CS	R	RBI	BA	OBA	SA
87	MAC/SAL	A	110	406	373	95	14	3	3	124	23	2	6	80	6	2	2	20	10	44	38	.255	.307	.332
88	AUG/SAL	A	73	295	269	78	13	2	1	98	22	0	1	46	5	2	1	11	6	32	45	.290	.345	.364
	SAL/CAR	A+	62	250	236	65	9	3	1	83	10	0	1	32	9	0	3	8	2	21	28	.275	.304	.352
89	SAL/CAR	A+	81	332	304	86	12	4	7	127	18	0	4	51	3	1	5	19	6	45	49	.283	.326	.418
	HAR/EAS	AA	54	197	188	53	5	5	3	77	8	0	0	36	4	0	1	6	4	28	25	.282	.310	.410
90	HAR/EAS	AA	65	263	242	67	11	2	5	97	16	0	3	36	6	1	1	12	1	36	25	.277	.328	.401
	BUF/AMA	AAA	63	218	197	52	10	0	5	77	16	2	2	40	1	2	2	7	4	23	18	.264	.323	.391
	PIT/NL		4	4	4	2	0	0	0	2	0	0	0	2	0	0	0	0	0	1	0	.500	.500	.500
91	PIT/NL		12	25	24	6	0	2	0	10	1	0	0	10	1	0	0	0	0	2	1	.250	.280	.417
	BUF/AMA	AAA	127	512	463	123	21	6	7	177	33	5	7	78	6	3	0	30	7	62	60	.266	.322	.382
2 YR TOTALS			**16**	**29**	**28**	**8**	**0**	**2**	**0**	**12**	**1**	**0**	**0**	**10**	**1**	**0**	**0**	**0**	**0**	**3**	**1**	**.286**	**.310**	**.429**

Garcia, Jose Antonio "Cheo" — bats right — throws right — b.4/27/68 — 1991 positions: 3B System MIN/AL

YR	TM/LG	CL	G	TPA	AB	H	2B	3B	HR	TB	BB	IBB	HB	SO	GDP	SH	SF	SB	CS	R	RBI	BA	OBA	SA
88	ELI/APP	R+	59	251	228	59	9	3	2	80	15	0	5	46	2	2	1	9	5	31	27	.259	.317	.351
89	KEN/MID	A	123	498	468	110	24	4	6	160	18	2	6	69	11	1	3	16	8	58	49	.235	.270	.342
90	VIS/CAL	A+	137	553	486	133	29	4	10	200	56	1	7	68	22	1	3	10	5	68	71	.274	.355	.412
91	ORL/SOU	AA	137	559	496	140	24	4	9	199	45	3	10	49	14	1	7	13	4	57	75	.282	.349	.401

Gardner, Jeffrey Scott "Jeff" — bats left — throws right — b.2/4/64 — 1991 positions: SS 8, 2B 3

YR	TM/LG	CL	G	TPA	AB	H	2B	3B	HR	TB	BB	IBB	HB	SO	GDP	SH	SF	SB	CS	R	RBI	BA	OBA	SA
85	COL/SAL	A	123	559	401	118	9	1	0	129	142	0	1	40	9	10	1	31	5	80	50	.294	.483	.322
86	LYN/CAR	A+	111	430	334	91	11	2	1	109	81	3	4	33	10	8	3	6	4	59	39	.272	.417	.326
87	JAC/TEX	AA	119	467	399	109	10	3	0	125	58	1	3	55	7	5	2	1	5	55	30	.273	.368	.313
88	JAC/TEX	AA	134	517	432	109	15	2	0	128	69	7	1	52	6	14	1	13	8	46	33	.252	.356	.296
	TID/INT	AAA	2	9	8	3	1	0	0	6	1	0	0	1	0	0	0	0	0	3	2	.375	.444	.750
89	TID/INT	AAA	101	301	269	75	11	0	0	86	25	1	0	27	7	4	0	0	0	28	24	.279	.337	.320
90	TID/INT	AAA	138	553	463	125	11	1	0	138	84	3	1	33	12	4	1	3	3	55	33	.270	.383	.298
91	TID/INT	AAA	136	603	504	147	23	4	1	181	84	4	3	48	8	5	4	6	5	73	56	.292	.393	.359
	NY/NL		13	42	37	6	0	0	0	6	4	0	0	6	1	0	1	0	1	3	1	.162	.238	.162

Gedman, Richard Leo "Rich" — bats left — throws right — b.9/26/59 — 1991 positions: C 43

YR	TM/LG	CL	G	TPA	AB	H	2B	3B	HR	TB	BB	IBB	HB	SO	GDP	SH	SF	SB	CS	R	RBI	BA	OBA	SA
78	WH/FSL	A+	98	348	297	89	17	3	3	121	43	6	4	29	7	2	2	0	0	35	32	.300	.393	.407
	WH/FSL	A+	98	348	297	89	17	3	3	121	43	6	4	29	7	2	2	0	0	35	32	.300	.393	.407
79	BRI/EAS	AA	130	528	470	129	25	1	12	192	49	9	4	95	13	3	2	0	2	48	63	.274	.347	.409
80	PAW/AMA	AAA	111	383	347	82	18	2	11	137	30	4	5	64	11	0	1	0	1	43	29	.236	.305	.395
	BOS/AL		9	24	24	5	0	0	0	5	0	0	0	5	1	0	0	0	0	2	1	.208	.208	.208
81	PAW/AMA	AAA	25	91	81	24	3	0	2	33	9	3	1	11	9	0	0	0	0	8	11	.296	.374	.407
	BOS/AL		62	219	205	59	15	0	5	89	9	1	1	31	9	1	3	0	0	22	26	.288	.317	.434
82	BOS/AL		92	305	289	72	17	2	4	105	10	2	2	37	13	4	0	0	1	30	26	.249	.279	.363
83	BOS/AL		81	223	204	60	16	1	2	84	15	6	1	37	4	3	0	0	1	21	18	.294	.345	.412
84	BOS/AL		133	486	449	121	26	4	24	227	29	5	2	72	5	2	5	0	0	54	72	.269	.312	.506
85	BOS/AL		144	556	498	147	30	5	18	241	50	11	3	79	12	3	2	0	0	66	80	.295	.362	.484
86	BOS/AL		135	509	462	119	29	0	16	196	37	13	4	61	15	1	5	1	0	49	65	.258	.315	.424
87	BOS/AL		52	165	151	31	8	0	1	42	10	2	0	24	2	1	3	0	0	11	13	.205	.250	.278
88	PAW/INT	AAA	4	17	15	7	1	0	1	11	1	0	1	4	0	0	0	0	0	2	1	.467	.529	.733
	BOS/AL		95	332	299	69	14	0	9	110	18	2	3	49	6	9	3	0	0	33	39	.231	.279	.368
89	BOS/AL		93	289	260	55	9	0	4	76	23	1	0	47	8	3	3	0	0	24	16	.212	.273	.292
90	BOS/AL		10	21	15	3	0	0	0	3	5	0	1	6	1	0	0	0	0	2	1	.200	.429	.200
	HOU/NL		40	122	104	21	7	0	1	31	15	6	0	24	2	2	1	0	0	5	9	.202	.319	.286
	YEAR		50	143	119	24	7	0	1	34	20	6	1	30	3	2	1	0	0	7	10	.202	.319	.286
91	STL/NL		46	100	94	10	1	0	3	20	4	0	0	15	2	0	2	0	1	7	8	.106	.140	.213
12 YR TOTALS			**992**	**3351**	**3054**	**772**	**172**	**12**	**87**	**1229**	**225**	**52**	**16**	**487**	**80**	**29**	**27**	**3**	**4**	**326**	**374**	**.253**	**.305**	**.402**

Geren, Robert Peter "Bob" — bats right — throws right — b.9/22/61 — 1991 positions: C 63

YR	TM/LG	CL	G	TPA	AB	H	2B	3B	HR	TB	BB	IBB	HB	SO	GDP	SH	SF	SB	CS	R	RBI	BA	OBA	SA
84	ARK/TEX	AA	86	331	292	72	12	0	15	129	34	1	1	69	10	3	1	1	0	39	40	.247	.326	.442
	LOU/AMA	AAA	15	45	40	7	1	0	0	8	5	0	0	8	1	0	0	0	0	3	3	.175	.267	.200
85	LOU/AMA	AAA	5	14	14	5	2	0	1	10	0	0	0	1	0	0	0	0	0	2	3	.357	.357	.714
	ARK/TEX	AA	103	359	315	71	18	1	5	106	31	2	1	74	10	7	5	3	1	38	40	.225	.293	.337
86	ALB/EAS	AA	11	33	27	4	1	0	0	5	6	0	0	12	0	0	0	0	0	3	3	.148	.303	.185
	COL/INT	AAA	68	229	205	52	15	3	7	94	21	0	2	60	8	1	0	1	2	24	25	.254	.329	.459
87	COL/INT	AAA	5	21	20	3	0	0	1	6	0	0	0	9	0	1	0	0	0	1	3	.150	.150	.300
	ALB/EAS	AA	78	245	213	47	7	2	11	91	21	2	2	42	6	4	5	1	1	33	31	.221	.290	.427
88	COL/INT	AAA	95	363	321	87	13	2	8	128	33	0	1	69	10	4	4	0	0	37	35	.271	.337	.399
	NY/AL		10	12	10	1	0	0	0	1	2	0	0	3	0	0	0	0	0	0	0	.100	.250	.100
89	COL/INT	AAA	27	104	95	24	4	1	2	36	5	0	1	25	2	2	1	1	0	11	13	.253	.294	.379
	NY/AL		65	225	205	59	5	1	9	93	12	0	1	44	10	6	1	0	0	26	27	.288	.329	.454
90	NY/AL		110	303	277	59	7	0	8	90	13	1	5	73	7	6	2	0	0	21	31	.213	.259	.325
91	NY/AL		64	140	128	28	3	0	2	37	9	0	0	31	5	3	0	0	0	7	12	.219	.270	.289
4 YR TOTALS			**249**	**680**	**620**	**147**	**15**	**1**	**19**	**221**	**36**	**1**	**6**	**151**	**22**	**15**	**3**	**0**	**1**	**54**	**70**	**.237**	**.284**	**.356**

Giannelli, Raymond John "Ray" — bats left — throws right — b.2/5/66 — 1991 positions: 3B 9

YR	TM/LG	CL	G	TPA	AB	H	2B	3B	HR	TB	BB	IBB	HB	SO	GDP	SH	SF	SB	CS	R	RBI	BA	OBA	SA
88	MH/PIO	R+	47	146	123	30	8	3	4	56	19	2	0	22	6	1	3	0	0	17	28	.244	.338	.455
89	MB/SAL	A	127	550	458	138	17	1	18	211	78	4	5	53	10	1	8	2	6	76	84	.301	.403	.461
90	DUN/FSL	A+	118	487	416	120	18	1	18	194	66	7	1	56	12	1	3	4	8	64	57	.288	.385	.466
91	TOR/AL		9	29	24	4	1	0	0	5	5	0	0	9	0	0	0	0	0	2	0	.167	.310	.208
	KNO/SOU	AA	112	435	362	100	14	3	7	141	64	6	2	66	6	2	8	5	5	53	37	.276	.386	.390

Gibson, Kirk Harold — bats left — throws left — b.5/28/57 — 1991 positions: OF 94, DH 30

YR	TM/LG	CL	G	TPA	AB	H	2B	3B	HR	TB	BB	IBB	HB	SO	GDP	SH	SF	SB	CS	R	RBI	BA	OBA	SA
79	DET/AL		12	39	38	9	3	0	1	15	1	0	0	3	0	0	0	3	3	3	4	.237	.256	.395
80	DET/AL		51	189	175	46	2	1	9	77	10	0	1	45	0	1	2	4	7	23	16	.263	.303	.440
81	DET/AL		83	313	290	95	11	3	9	139	25	2	1	64	2	1	2	9	7	41	40	.328	.369	.479
82	DET/AL		69	294	266	74	16	2	8	118	25	2	1	41	2	1	1	14	3	34	35	.278	.341	.444
83	DET/AL		128	467	401	91	12	9	15	166	53	3	4	96	3	3	6	14	9	60	51	.227	.320	.414
84	DET/AL		149	611	531	150	23	10	27	274	63	6	8	103	4	3	6	29	9	92	91	.282	.363	.516
85	DET/AL		154	670	581	167	37	5	29	301	71	16	5	137	5	3	10	30	6	96	97	.287	.364	.518
86	DET/AL		119	521	441	118	11	2	28	217	68	4	7	107	8	1	4	34	6	84	86	.268	.371	.492
87	TOL/INT	AAA	6	21	17	4	1	0	0	4	4	0	0	3	0	0	0	3	1	2	3	.235	.381	.235
	DET/AL		128	568	487	135	25	3	24	238	71	5	5	117	5	1	4	26	7	95	79	.277	.372	.489
88	LA/NL		150	632	542	157	28	1	25	262	73	14	7	120	8	1	2	31	4	106	76	.290	.377	.483
89	LA/NL		71	292	253	54	8	2	9	93	35	5	2	55	5	1	1	12	3	35	28	.213	.312	.368
90	ALB/PCL	AAA	5	18	14	6	2	0	1	11	4	0	0	1	0	0	0	2	2	6	4	.429	.556	.786
	LA/NL		89	359	315	82	20	0	8	126	39	0	3	65	9	1	2	26	2	59	38	.260	.345	.400
91	KC/AL		132	540	462	109	17	6	16	186	69	3	6	103	9	1	2	18	4	81	55	.236	.341	.403
13 YR TOTALS			**1335**	**5495**	**4782**	**1287**	**213**	**44**	**208**	**2212**	**596**	**62**	**51**	**1056**	**61**	**20**	**46**	**253**	**64**	**809**	**696**	**.269**	**.353**	**.463**

Gilkey, Otis Bernard "Bernard" — bats right — throws right — b.9/24/66 — 1991 positions: OF 74

YR	TM/LG	CL	G	TPA	AB	H	2B	3B	HR	TB	BB	IBB	HB	SO	GDP	SH	SF	SB	CS	R	RBI	BA	OBA	SA
85	ERI/NYP	A−	77	358	294	60	9	1	7	92	55	1	3	57	4	4	2	34	10	57	27	.204	.333	.313
86	SAV/SAL	A	105	466	374	88	15	4	6	129	84	1	2	57	3	2	3	32	15	64	36	.235	.376	.345
87	SPR/MID	A	46	207	162	37	5	0	0	42	39	1	2	28	3	2	2	18	5	30	9	.228	.380	.259
88	SPR/MID	A	125	564	491	120	18	7	6	170	65	1	4	53	10	2	5	56	18	84	36	.244	.336	.346
89	ARK/TEX	AA	131	585	500	139	25	3	6	188	70	3	2	54	9	8	5	53	22	104	57	.278	.366	.376
90	LOU/AMA	AAA	132	578	499	147	26	8	3	198	75	3	2	49	11	1	4	45	32	83	46	.295	.388	.397

Gilkey, Otis Bernard "Bernard" (continued)

YR	TM/LG	CL	G	TPA	AB	H	2B	3B	HR	TB	BB	IBB	HB	SO	GDP	SH	SF	SB	CS	R	RBI	BA	OBA	SA
	STL/NL		18	72	64	19	5	2	1	31	8	0	0	5	1	0	0	6	1	11	3	.297	.375	.484
91	LOU/AMA	AAA	11	47	41	6	2	0	0	8	6	0	0	10	0	1	0	1	3	5	2	.146	.255	.195
	STL/NL		81	311	268	58	7	2	5	84	39	0	1	33	14	1	2	14	8	28	20	.216	.316	.313
2 YR TOTALS			**99**	**383**	**332**	**77**	**12**	**4**	**6**	**115**	**47**	**0**	**1**	**38**	**15**	**1**	**2**	**20**	**9**	**39**	**23**	**.232**	**.327**	**.346**

Girardi, Joseph Elliott "Joe" — bats right — throws right — b.10/14/64 — 1991 positions: C 21

YR	TM/LG	CL	G	TPA	AB	H	2B	3B	HR	TB	BB	IBB	HB	SO	GDP	SH	SF	SB	CS	R	RBI	BA	OBA	SA
86	PEO/MID	A	68	255	230	71	13	1	3	95	17	1	3	36	8	2	3	6	3	36	28	.309	.360	.413
87	WIN/CAR	A+	99	402	364	102	9	8	8	151	33	2	2	64	11	2	1	9	2	51	46	.280	.343	.415
88	PIT/EAS	AA	104	393	357	97	14	1	7	134	29	2	3	51	10	2	2	7	4	44	41	.272	.330	.375
89	IOW/AMA	AAA	32	115	110	27	4	2	2	41	5	1	0	19	0	0	0	3	1	12	11	.245	.278	.373
	CHI/NL		59	172	157	39	10	0	1	52	11	5	2	26	4	1	1	2	1	15	14	.248	.304	.331
90	CHI/NL		133	447	419	113	24	2	1	144	17	11	3	50	13	4	4	8	3	36	38	.270	.300	.344
91	IOW/AMA	AAA	12	41	36	8	1	0	0	9	4	0	0	8	0	1	0	2	0	3	4	.222	.300	.250
	CHI/NL		21	54	47	9	2	0	0	11	6	1	0	6	0	1	0	0	0	3	6	.191	.283	.234
3 YR TOTALS			**213**	**673**	**623**	**161**	**36**	**2**	**2**	**207**	**34**	**17**	**5**	**82**	**17**	**6**	**5**	**10**	**4**	**54**	**58**	**.258**	**.300**	**.332**

Gladden, Clinton Daniel "Dan" — bats right — throws right — b.7/7/57 — 1991 positions: OF 126

YR	TM/LG	CL	G	TPA	AB	H	2B	3B	HR	TB	BB	IBB	HB	SO	GDP	SH	SF	SB	CS	R	RBI	BA	OBA	SA
83	SF/NL		18	72	63	14	2	0	1	19	5	0	0	11	3	3	1	4	3	6	9	.222	.275	.302
84	PHO/PCL	AAA	59	280	234	93	11	7	3	127	45	2	0	23	4	0	1	32	11	70	27	.397	.493	.543
	SF/NL		86	384	342	120	17	2	4	153	33	2	2	37	3	6	1	31	16	71	31	.351	.410	.447
85	SF/NL		142	561	502	122	15	8	7	174	40	1	7	78	10	10	2	32	15	64	41	.243	.307	.347
86	PHO/PCL	AAA	7	29	27	9	4	0	0	13	2	0	0	2	0	0	0	0	0	5	0	.333	.379	.481
	SF/NL		102	402	351	97	16	1	4	127	39	2	5	59	5	7	0	27	10	55	29	.276	.357	.362
87	MIN/AL		121	482	438	109	21	2	8	158	38	2	3	72	8	1	2	25	9	69	38	.249	.312	.361
88	MIN/AL		141	633	576	155	32	6	11	232	46	4	4	74	9	2	5	28	8	91	62	.269	.325	.403
89	MIN/AL		121	501	461	136	23	3	8	189	23	3	5	53	6	3	5	23	7	69	46	.295	.331	.410
90	MIN/AL		136	571	534	147	27	6	5	201	26	5	6	67	17	1	4	25	9	64	40	.275	.314	.376
91	MIN/AL		126	511	461	114	14	9	6	164	36	1	5	60	13	5	3	15	9	65	52	.247	.306	.356
9 YR TOTALS			**993**	**4117**	**3728**	**1014**	**167**	**37**	**54**	**1417**	**286**	**18**	**37**	**511**	**74**	**40**	**26**	**210**	**86**	**554**	**348**	**.272**	**.328**	**.380**

Glanville, Douglas M. "Doug" — bats right — throws right — b.8/25/70 — 1991 positions: OF System CHI/NL

YR	TM/LG	CL	G	TPA	AB	H	2B	3B	HR	TB	BB	IBB	HB	SO	GDP	SH	SF	SB	CS	R	RBI	BA	OBA	SA
91	GEN/NYP	A–	36	168	152	46	8	0	2	60	11	0	1	25	1	3	1	17	3	29	12	.303	.352	.395

Gomez, Leonardo (Velez) "Leo" — bats right — throws right — b.3/2/66 — 1991 positions: 3B 105, DH 10, 1B 3

YR	TM/LG	CL	G	TPA	AB	H	2B	3B	HR	TB	BB	IBB	HB	SO	GDP	SH	SF	SB	CS	R	RBI	BA	OBA	SA
86	BLU/APP	R+	27	117	88	31	7	1	7	61	25	0	1	27	1	0	3	1	0	23	28	.352	.487	.693
87	HAG/CAR	A+	131	574	466	152	38	2	19	251	95	3	2	85	8	1	10	6	2	94	110	.326	.435	.539
88	CHA/SOU	AA	24	99	89	26	5	0	1	34	10	0	0	17	2	0	0	1	2	6	10	.292	.364	.382
89	HAG/EAS	AA	134	547	448	126	23	3	18	209	89	6	5	102	8	0	5	2	2	71	78	.281	.402	.467
90	ROC/INT	AAA	131	532	430	119	26	4	26	231	89	4	6	89	11	0	7	2	2	97	97	.277	.402	.537
	BAL/AL		12	48	39	9	0	0	0	9	8	0	0	7	2	1	0	0	0	3	1	.231	.362	.231
91	ROC/INT	AAA	28	119	101	26	6	0	6	50	16	0	0	18	1	0	0	0	0	13	19	.257	.370	.495
	BAL/AL		118	445	391	91	17	2	16	160	40	0	2	82	11	5	7	1	1	40	45	.233	.302	.409
2 YR TOTALS			**130**	**493**	**430**	**100**	**17**	**2**	**16**	**169**	**48**	**0**	**2**	**89**	**13**	**6**	**7**	**1**	**1**	**43**	**46**	**.233**	**.308**	**.393**

Gonzales, Rene Adrian — bats right — throws right — b.9/3/60 — 1991 positions: SS 36, 3B 26, 2B 11, 1B 2

YR	TM/LG	CL	G	TPA	AB	H	2B	3B	HR	TB	BB	IBB	HB	SO	GDP	SH	SF	SB	CS	R	RBI	BA	OBA	SA
84	IND/AMA	AAA	114	395	359	84	12	2	2	106	20	0	2	33	9	10	4	10	4	41	32	.234	.275	.295
	MON/NL		29	33	30	7	1	0	0	8	2	0	1	5	0	0	0	0	0	5	2	.233	.303	.267
85	IND/AMA	AAA	130	367	340	77	11	1	0	90	22	0	0	49	4	4	1	3	5	21	25	.226	.273	.265
86	IND/AMA	AAA	116	449	395	108	14	2	3	135	41	0	2	47	7	7	4	8	5	57	43	.273	.342	.342
	MON/NL		11	28	26	3	0	0	0	3	2	0	0	7	0	0	0	0	2	1	0	.115	.179	.115
87	ROC/INT	AAA	42	192	170	51	9	3	0	66	13	2	1	17	4	4	4	4	2	20	24	.300	.346	.388
	BAL/AL		37	65	60	16	2	1	1	23	3	0	0	11	2	2	0	1	0	14	7	.267	.302	.383
88	BAL/AL		92	260	237	51	5	0	2	63	13	0	3	32	5	5	2	2	0	13	15	.215	.263	.266
89	BAL/AL		71	185	166	36	4	0	1	43	12	1	0	30	6	4	2	2	0	16	11	.217	.268	.259
90	BAL/AL		67	121	103	22	3	1	1	30	12	0	0	14	0	5	1	2	3	13	12	.214	.296	.291
91	TOR/AL		71	141	118	23	3	0	1	29	12	0	4	22	5	6	1	0	0	16	6	.195	.289	.246
7 YR TOTALS			**378**	**833**	**740**	**158**	**19**	**2**	**6**	**199**	**56**	**0**	**8**	**121**	**21**	**25**	**4**	**9**	**7**	**78**	**53**	**.214**	**.275**	**.269**

Gonzalez, Jose Rafael (Gutierrez) — bats right — throws right — b.11/23/64 — 1991 positions: OF 73

YR	TM/LG	CL	G	TPA	AB	H	2B	3B	HR	TB	BB	IBB	HB	SO	GDP	SH	SF	SB	CS	R	RBI	BA	OBA	SA
84	BAK/CAL	A+	129	554	484	107	26	1	11	168	58	4	4	126	11	5	3	49	15	86	59	.221	.308	.347
85	SA/TEX	AA	128	516	448	137	22	6	13	210	60	4	4	80	7	1	3	34	17	82	62	.306	.390	.469
	LA/NL		23	12	11	3	2	0	0	5	1	0	0	3	1	0	0	1	1	6	0	.273	.333	.455
86	ALB/PCL	AAA	89	331	303	84	20	3	6	128	16	2	4	70	5	3	5	11	8	39	37	.277	.317	.422
	LA/NL		57	102	93	20	5	1	2	33	7	0	0	29	0	0	4	3	1	15	6	.215	.270	.355
87	ALB/PCL	AAA	116	402	339	95	22	3	13	162	55	2	4	94	3	2	2	19	10	67	61	.280	.385	.478
	LA/NL		19	18	16	3	2	0	0	5	1	0	0	5	0	1	0	0	0	7	0	.188	.222	.313
88	ALB/PCL	AAA	84	329	288	88	15	2	5	122	36	1	3	66	1	1	1	44	15	57	22	.306	.387	.424
	LA/NL		37	26	24	2	1	0	0	3	2	0	0	10	0	0	0	3	0	7	0	.083	.154	.125
89	ALB/PCL	AAA	50	200	180	48	12	4	4	80	16	0	3	39	0	0	1	10	0	32	31	.267	.337	.444

Gonzalez, Jose Rafael (Gutierrez) (continued)

YR	TM/LG	CL	G	TPA	AB	H	2B	3B	HR	TB	BB	IBB	HB	SO	GDP	SH	SF	SB	CS	R	RBI	BA	OBA	SA
	LA/NL		95	286	261	70	11	2	3	94	23	5	0	53	2	1	1	9	3	31	18	.268	.326	.360
90	LA/NL		106	108	99	23	5	3	2	40	6	1	1	27	1	1	1	3	1	15	8	.232	.280	.404
91	LA/NL		42	30	28	0	0	0	0	0	2	0	0	9	0	0	0	0	0	3	0	.000	.067	.000
	PIT/NL		16	23	20	2	0	0	1	5	0	0	0	6	0	2	1	0	0	2	3	.100	.095	.250
	CLE/AL		33	81	69	11	2	1	1	18	11	0	0	27	2	0	0	8	0	10	4	.159	.284	.261
	YEAR		91	134	117	13	2	1	2	23	13	0	2	42	2	2	1	8	0	15	7	.111	.205	.197
7 YR TOTALS			**428**	**686**	**621**	**134**	**28**	**7**	**9**	**203**	**53**	**6**	**2**	**166**	**6**	**6**	**4**	**33**	**8**	**91**	**40**	**.216**	**.278**	**.327**

Gonzalez, Juan Alberto (Vazquez) — bats right — throws right — b.10/20/69 — 1991 positions: OF 136, DH 4

YR	TM/LG	CL	G	TPA	AB	H	2B	3B	HR	TB	BB	IBB	HB	SO	GDP	SH	SF	SB	CS	R	RBI	BA	OBA	SA
86	RAN/GCL	R	60	259	233	56	4	1	0	62	21	0	1	57	9	1	3	7	5	24	36	.240	.302	.266
87	GAS/SAL	A	127	549	509	135	21	2	14	202	30	2	5	92	14	1	4	9	4	69	74	.265	.310	.397
88	CHA/FSL	A+	77	308	277	71	14	3	8	115	25	3	4	64	7	1	2	5	2	25	43	.256	.325	.415
89	TUL/TEX	AA	133	547	502	147	30	7	21	254	31	3	3	98	8	1	4	1	8	73	85	.293	.342	.506
	TEX/AL		24	68	60	9	3	0	1	15	6	0	0	17	4	2	0	0	0	6	7	.150	.227	.250
90	OC/AMA	AAA	128	537	496	128	29	4	29	252	32	2	1	109	11	0	8	2	2	78	101	.258	.300	.508
	TEX/AL		25	95	90	26	7	1	4	47	2	0	2	18	2	0	1	0	1	11	12	.289	.316	.522
91	TEX/AL		142	595	545	144	34	1	27	261	42	5	5	118	10	0	4	4	5	78	102	.264	.321	.479
3 YR TOTALS			**191**	**758**	**695**	**179**	**44**	**2**	**32**	**323**	**50**	**7**	**7**	**153**	**16**	**2**	**4**	**4**	**5**	**95**	**121**	**.258**	**.312**	**.465**

Gonzalez, Luis Emilio — bats left — throws right — b.9/3/67 — 1991 positions: OF 133

YR	TM/LG	CL	G	TPA	AB	H	2B	3B	HR	TB	BB	IBB	HB	SO	GDP	SH	SF	SB	CS	R	RBI	BA	OBA	SA
88	AUB/NYP	A−	39	176	157	49	10	3	5	80	12	1	1	19	1	1	5	2	0	32	27	.312	.354	.510
	ASH/SAL	A	31	129	115	29	7	1	2	44	12	0	2	17	4	0	0	2	1	13	14	.252	.333	.383
89	OSC/FSL	A+	86	333	287	82	16	7	6	130	37	5	4	49	6	1	4	2	1	46	38	.286	.370	.453
90	COL/SOU	AA	138	568	495	131	30	6	24	245	54	9	6	100	6	1	12	27	9	86	89	.265	.337	.495
	HOU/NL		12	23	21	4	2	0	0	6	2	1	0	5	0	0	0	0	0	1	0	.190	.261	.286
91	HOU/NL		137	526	473	120	28	9	13	205	40	4	8	101	9	1	4	10	7	51	69	.254	.320	.433
2 YR TOTALS			**149**	**549**	**494**	**124**	**30**	**9**	**13**	**211**	**42**	**5**	**8**	**106**	**9**	**1**	**4**	**10**	**7**	**52**	**69**	**.251**	**.318**	**.427**

Goodwin, Thomas Jones "Tom" — bats left — throws right — b.7/27/68 — 1991 positions: OF 5

YR	TM/LG	CL	G	TPA	AB	H	2B	3B	HR	TB	BB	IBB	HB	SO	GDP	SH	SF	SB	CS	R	RBI	BA	OBA	SA
89	GF/PIO	R+	63	273	240	74	12	3	2	98	28	1	2	30	3	1	2	60	8	55	33	.308	.382	.408
90	BAK/C3AL	A+	32	146	134	39	6	2	0	49	11	0	1	22	0	1	0	22	4	24	13	.291	.345	.366
	SA/TEX3	AA	102	478	428	119	14	4	0	141	38	2	1	72	3	8	3	60	11	76	28	.278	.336	.329
91	ALB/PCL	AAA	132	583	509	139	19	4	1	169	59	0	2	83	5	10	3	48	22	84	45	.273	.349	.332
	LA/NL		16	7	7	1	0	0	0	1	0	0	0	0	0	0	0	1	1	3	0	.143	.143	.143

Grace, Mark Eugene — bats left — throws left — b.6/28/64 — 1991 positions: 1B 160

YR	TM/LG	CL	G	TPA	AB	H	2B	3B	HR	TB	BB	IBB	HB	SO	GDP	SH	SF	SB	CS	R	RBI	BA	OBA	SA
86	PEO/MID	A	126	537	465	159	30	4	15	242	60	6	4	28	11	2	6	6	5	81	95	.342	.417	.520
87	PIT/EAS	AA	123	513	453	151	29	8	17	247	48	11	2	24	3	3	7	5	5	81	101	.333	.394	.545
88	IOW/AMA	AAA	21	83	67	17	4	0	0	21	13	1	0	4	0	0	3	1	0	11	14	.254	.361	.313
	CHI/NL		134	550	486	144	23	4	7	196	60	5	0	43	12	0	4	3	3	65	57	.296	.371	.403
89	CHI/NL		142	596	510	160	28	3	13	233	80	13	0	42	13	3	3	14	7	74	79	.314	.405	.457
90	CHI/NL		157	662	589	182	32	1	9	243	59	5	5	54	10	1	8	15	6	72	82	.309	.372	.413
91	CHI/NL		160	703	619	169	28	5	8	231	70	7	3	50	6	4	7	3	4	87	58	.273	.346	.373
4 YR TOTALS			**593**	**2511**	**2204**	**655**	**111**	**13**	**37**	**903**	**269**	**30**	**8**	**192**	**41**	**8**	**22**	**35**	**20**	**298**	**276**	**.297**	**.372**	**.410**

Grebeck, Craig Allen — bats right — throws right — b.12/29/64 — 1991 positions: 3B 49, 2B 36, SS 26

YR	TM/LG	CL	G	TPA	AB	H	2B	3B	HR	TB	BB	IBB	HB	SO	GDP	SH	SF	SB	CS	R	RBI	BA	OBA	SA
87	PEN/CAR	A+	104	422	378	106	22	3	15	179	37	0	1	62	8	2	4	3	6	63	67	.280	.343	.474
88	BIR/SOU	AA	133	527	450	126	21	1	9	176	65	3	2	72	10	7	3	5	7	57	53	.280	.371	.391
89	BIR/SOU	AA	143	618	533	153	25	4	5	201	63	4	4	77	15	11	7	14	15	85	80	.287	.362	.377
90	VAN/PCL	AAA	12	47	41	8	0	0	1	11	6	0	0	7	2	0	0	1	0	8	3	.195	.298	.268
	CHI/AL		59	135	119	20	3	1	1	28	8	0	2	24	2	3	3	0	0	7	9	.168	.227	.235
91	CHI/AL		107	268	224	63	16	3	6	103	38	0	4	40	4	1	1	1	3	37	31	.281	.386	.460
2 YR TOTALS			**166**	**403**	**343**	**83**	**19**	**4**	**7**	**131**	**46**	**0**	**6**	**64**	**6**	**4**	**4**	**1**	**3**	**44**	**40**	**.242**	**.333**	**.382**

Green, Gary Allan — bats right — throws right — b.1/14/62 — 1991 positions: SS 8

YR	TM/LG	CL	G	TPA	AB	H	2B	3B	HR	TB	BB	IBB	HB	SO	GDP	SH	SF	SB	CS	R	RBI	BA	OBA	SA
85	BEA/TEX	AA	119	456	409	105	17	1	1	127	27	2	1	54	11	15	4	8	7	44	51	.257	.302	.311
86	LV/PCL	AAA	129	454	416	104	11	3	0	121	29	1	1	46	12	5	3	3	0	42	41	.250	.298	.291
	SD/NL		13	35	33	7	1	0	0	8	1	0	0	11	0	1	0	0	0	2	2	.212	.235	.242
87	LV/PCL	AAA	111	391	337	80	8	2	1	95	35	2	1	58	9	14	4	2	4	39	37	.237	.308	.282
88	LV/PCL	AAA	88	327	302	82	16	2	0	102	16	0	1	50	7	3	5	4	1	32	32	.272	.306	.338
89	SD/NL		15	28	27	7	3	0	0	10	1	0	0	1	0	0	0	0	0	4	0	.259	.286	.370
	LV/PCL	AAA	62	217	191	40	6	0	0	46	20	0	0	32	4	2	4	2	1	19	25	.209	.279	.241
90	OC/AMA	AAA	55	193	167	39	11	0	4	62	22	0	0	43	6	2	2	1	2	18	18	.234	.319	.371
	TEX/AL		62	99	88	19	3	0	0	22	6	0	0	18	2	1	1	0	1	10	8	.216	.263	.250
91	TEX/AL		8	23	20	3	1	0	0	4	3	0	0	3	0	0	0	0	0	0	1	.150	.190	.200
	OC/AMA	AAA	100	360	308	67	8	3	0	81	35	9	0	36	2	7	1	1	2	36	30	.218	.299	.263
4 YR TOTALS			**98**	**185**	**168**	**36**	**8**	**0**	**0**	**44**	**11**	**0**	**0**	**33**	**2**	**2**	**2**	**0**	**2**	**16**	**11**	**.214**	**.253**	**.262**

Greenwell, Michael Lewis "Mike" — bats left — throws right — b.7/18/63 — 1991 positions: OF 143, DH 1

YR	TM/LG	CL	G	TPA	AB	H	2B	3B	HR	TB	BB	IBB	HB	SO	GDP	SH	SF	SB	CS	R	RBI	BA	OBA	SA
84	WIN/CAR	A+	130	527	454	139	23	6	16	222	56	4	15	40	10	1	1	9	5	70	84	.306	.399	.489
85	PAW/INT	AAA	117	467	418	107	21	1	13	169	38	2	6	45	10	1	4	3	4	47	52	.256	.324	.404
	BOS/AL		17	34	31	10	1	0	4	23	3	1	0	4	0	0	1	0	0	7	8	.323	.382	.742
86	PAW/INT	AAA	89	372	320	96	21	1	18	173	43	4	2	20	6	0	7	6	2	62	59	.300	.379	.541
	BOS/AL		31	40	35	11	2	0	0	13	5	0	0	7	1	0	0	0	0	4	4	.314	.400	.371
87	BOS/AL		125	456	412	135	31	6	19	235	35	1	6	40	7	0	3	5	4	71	89	.328	.386	.570
88	BOS/AL		158	693	590	192	39	8	22	313	87	18	9	38	11	0	7	16	8	86	119	.325	.416	.531
89	BOS/AL		145	641	578	178	36	0	14	256	56	15	3	44	21	0	4	13	5	87	95	.308	.370	.443
90	BOS/AL		159	682	610	181	30	6	14	265	65	12	4	43	19	0	3	8	7	71	73	.297	.367	.434
91	BOS/AL		147	598	544	163	26	6	9	228	43	6	3	35	11	1	7	15	5	76	83	.300	.350	.419
7 YR TOTALS			**782**	**3144**	**2800**	**870**	**165**	**26**	**82**	**1333**	**294**	**53**	**25**	**211**	**70**	**1**	**24**	**58**	**29**	**402**	**471**	**.311**	**.378**	**.476**

Gregg, William Thomas "Tommy" — bats left — throws left — b.7/29/63 — 1991 positions: OF 14, 1B 13

YR	TM/LG	CL	G	TPA	AB	H	2B	3B	HR	TB	BB	IBB	HB	SO	GDP	SH	SF	SB	CS	R	RBI	BA	OBA	SA
85	MAC/SAL	A	72	309	259	81	14	2	1	102	49	3	0	38	6	1	0	16	7	43	18	.313	.422	.394
86	NAS/EAS	AA	126	497	421	113	13	4	1	137	66	3	3	48	12	6	1	11	8	55	29	.268	.371	.325
87	HAR/EAS	AA	133	550	461	171	22	9	10	241	84	14	1	47	9	0	4	35	10	99	82	.371	.465	.523
	PIT/NL		10	8	8	2	1	0	0	3	0	0	0	2	2	0	0	0	0	3	0	.250	.250	.375
88	PIT/NL		14	17	15	3	1	0	0	7	1	0	0	4	0	0	1	0	0	4	3	.200	.235	.467
	BUF/AMA	AAA	72	282	252	74	12	0	6	104	25	4	0	26	3	0	4	7	9	34	27	.294	.355	.413
	ATL/NL		11	31	29	10	3	0	0	13	2	0	0	2	1	0	0	0	0	1	4	.345	.387	.448
	YEAR		25	48	44	13	4	0	1	20	3	0	0	6	1	0	1	0	1	5	7	.295	.333	.455
89	ATL/NL		102	298	276	67	8	0	6	93	18	2	0	45	4	3	1	3	4	24	23	.243	.288	.337
90	ATL/NL		124	261	239	63	13	1	5	93	20	2	1	39	1	0	1	3	4	18	32	.264	.322	.389
91	RIC/INT	AAA	3	14	13	6	0	0	1	9	1	0	0	2	0	0	0	1	1	3	4	.462	.500	.692
	ATL/NL		72	120	107	20	8	1	1	33	12	2	1	24	1	0	0	2	2	13	4	.187	.275	.308
5 YR TOTALS			**333**	**735**	**674**	**165**	**34**	**2**	**13**	**242**	**53**	**9**	**2**	**116**	**9**	**3**	**3**	**9**	**10**	**63**	**66**	**.245**	**.301**	**.359**

Griffey, George Kenneth Jr. "Ken" — bats left — throws left — b.11/21/69 — 1991 positions: OF 152, DH 1

YR	TM/LG	CL	G	TPA	AB	H	2B	3B	HR	TB	BB	IBB	HB	SO	GDP	SH	SF	SB	CS	R	RBI	BA	OBA	SA
87	BEL/NWL	A–	54	228	182	57	9	1	14	110	44	3	0	42	1	1	1	13	6	43	40	.313	.445	.604
88	SB/CAL	A+	58	256	219	74	13	3	11	126	34	2	2	39	3	1	0	32	6	50	42	.338	.431	.575
	VER/EAS	AA	17	68	61	17	5	1	2	30	5	0	2	12	3	0	0	4	2	10	10	.279	.353	.492
89	SEA/AL		127	506	455	120	23	0	16	191	44	8	2	83	4	1	4	16	7	61	61	.264	.329	.420
90	SEA/AL		155	666	597	179	28	7	22	287	63	12	2	81	12	0	4	16	11	91	80	.300	.366	.481
91	SEA/AL		154	633	548	179	42	1	22	289	71	21	1	82	10	4	9	18	6	76	100	.327	.399	.527
3 YR TOTALS			**436**	**1805**	**1600**	**478**	**93**	**8**	**60**	**767**	**178**	**41**	**5**	**246**	**26**	**5**	**17**	**50**	**24**	**228**	**241**	**.299**	**.367**	**.479**

Griffey, George Kenneth Sr. "Ken" — bats left — throws left — b.4/10/50 — 1991 positions: OF 26, DH 1

YR	TM/LG	CL	G	TPA	AB	H	2B	3B	HR	TB	BB	IBB	HB	SO	GDP	SH	SF	SB	CS	R	RBI	BA	OBA	SA
73	CIN/NL		25	92	86	33	5	1	3	49	6	0	0	10	0	0	0	4	2	19	14	.384	.424	.570
74	CIN/NL		88	256	227	57	9	5	2	82	27	2	1	43	2	1	0	9	4	24	19	.251	.333	.361
75	CIN/NL		132	540	463	141	15	9	4	186	67	2	1	67	10	6	3	16	7	95	46	.305	.391	.402
76	CIN/NL		148	628	562	189	28	9	6	253	62	0	1	65	3	0	3	34	11	111	74	.336	.401	.450
77	CIN/NL		154	657	585	186	35	8	12	273	69	2	0	84	12	1	2	17	8	117	57	.318	.389	.467
78	CIN/NL		158	680	614	177	33	8	10	256	54	1	0	70	6	9	3	23	5	90	63	.288	.344	.417
79	CIN/NL		95	420	380	120	27	4	8	179	36	3	1	39	7	0	3	12	5	62	32	.316	.374	.471
80	CIN/NL		146	615	544	160	28	10	13	247	62	6	1	77	4	0	3	23	1	89	85	.294	.364	.454
81	CIN/NL		101	442	396	123	21	6	2	162	39	6	1	42	9	2	4	23	1	65	34	.311	.370	.409
82	NY/AL		127	527	484	134	23	2	12	197	39	1	0	58	10	1	3	10	4	70	54	.277	.329	.407
83	NY/AL		118	499	458	140	21	3	11	200	34	3	2	45	3	3	2	6	1	60	46	.306	.355	.437
84	NY/AL		120	436	399	109	20	1	7	152	29	2	1	32	7	3	4	6	1	60	46	.273	.321	.381
85	NY/AL		127	487	438	120	28	4	10	186	41	4	0	51	2	0	4	2	2	44	56	.274	.331	.425
86	NY/AL		59	219	198	60	7	0	9	94	15	0	1	24	7	1	4	2	2	33	26	.303	.349	.475
	ATL/NL		80	313	292	90	15	3	12	147	20	4	0	43	2	0	2	12	7	36	32	.308	.349	.503
	YEAR		139	532	490	150	22	3	21	241	35	4	1	67	9	1	5	14	9	69	58	.306	.350	.492
87	ATL/NL		122	451	399	114	24	1	14	182	46	11	1	54	12	1	4	4	7	65	64	.286	.358	.456
88	ATL/NL		69	212	193	48	5	0	2	59	17	2	1	26	5	0	2	1	3	21	19	.249	.307	.306
	CIN/NL		25	52	50	14	1	0	2	21	2	1	0	5	0	0	0	0	0	5	4	.280	.308	.420
	YEAR		94	264	243	62	6	0	4	80	19	3	1	31	5	0	2	1	3	26	23	.255	.307	.329
89	CIN/NL		106	266	236	62	8	3	8	100	29	3	1	42	2	0	4	2	3	26	30	.263	.346	.424
90	CIN/NL		46	68	63	13	2	0	1	18	2	0	1	5	0	0	1	0		6	8	.206	.235	.286
	SEA/AL		21	88	77	29	2	0	3	40	10	0	0	5	3	1	0	1	0	13	18	.377	.443	.519
	YEAR		67	156	140	42	4	0	4	58	12	0	1	8	1	0	3	2	1	19	26	.300	.353	.414
91	SEA/AL		30	100	85	24	7	0	1	34	13	0	0	13	2						10	9	.282	.380	.400
19 YR TOTALS			**2097**	**8048**	**7229**	**2143**	**364**	**77**	**152**	**3117**	**719**	**51**	**14**	**898**	**106**	**31**	**55**	**200**	**83**	**1129**	**859**	**.296**	**.359**	**.431**

Griffin, Alfredo Claudino — bats both — throws right — b.10/6/57 — 1991 positions: SS 109

YR	TM/LG	CL	G	TPA	AB	H	2B	3B	HR	TB	BB	IBB	HB	SO	GDP	SH	SF	SB	CS	R	RBI	BA	OBA	SA
76	CLE/AL		12	4	4	1	0	0	0	1	0	0	0	2	0	0	0	0	0	0	0	.250	.250	.250
77	CLE/AL		14	44	41	6	1	0	0	7	3	0	0	2	0	0	0	0	0	5	3	.146	.205	.171
78	CLE/AL		5	6	4	2	1	0	0	3	0	0	0	1	0	1	0	0	2	0	5	3	.500	.667	.750
79	TOR/AL		153	689	624	179	22	10	2	227	40	0	5	59	10	16	4	21	16	81	31	.287	.333	.364
80	TOR/AL		155	696	653	166	26	15	2	228	24	2	4	58	7	10	5	18	23	63	41	.254	.283	.349
81	TOR/AL		101	414	388	81	19	6	0	112	17	1	1	38	6	6	2	8	12	30	21	.209	.243	.289

Griffin, Alfredo Claudino (continued)

YR	TM/LG	CL	G	TPA	AB	H	2B	3B	HR	TB	BB	IBB	HB	SO	GDP	SH	SF	SB	CS	R	RBI	BA	OBA	SA
82	TOR/AL		162	576	539	130	20	8	1	169	22	0	0	48	7	11	4	10	8	57	48	.241	.269	.314
83	TOR/AL		162	572	528	132	22	9	4	184	27	0	3	44	5	11	3	8	11	62	47	.250	.289	.348
84	TOR/AL		140	441	419	101	8	2	4	125	4	0	1	33	5	13	4	11	3	53	30	.241	.248	.298
85	OAK/AL		162	646	614	166	18	7	2	204	20	1	0	50	6	5	7	24	9	75	64	.270	.290	.332
86	OAK/AL		162	649	594	169	23	6	4	216	35	0	2	52	5	12	6	33	16	74	51	.285	.323	.364
87	OAK/AL		144	539	494	130	23	5	3	172	28	2	4	41	9	10	3	26	13	69	60	.263	.306	.348
88	LA/NL		95	354	316	63	8	3	1	80	24	7	2	30	3	11	1	7	5	39	27	.199	.259	.253
89	LA/NL		136	547	506	125	27	2	0	156	29	2	0	57	5	11	1	10	7	49	29	.247	.287	.308
90	LA/NL		141	502	461	97	11	3	1	117	29	11	2	65	5	6	4	6	3	38	35	.210	.258	.254
91	LA/NL		109	385	350	85	6	2	0	95	22	5	7	49	5	7	5	5	4	27	27	.243	.286	.271
16 YR TOTALS			1853	7064	6535	1633	235	78	24	2096	326	37	25	632	79	129	49	189	133	723	514	**.250**	**.286**	**.321**

Grissom, Marquis Deon — bats right — throws right — b.4/17/67 — 1991 positions: OF 138

YR	TM/LG	CL	G	TPA	AB	H	2B	3B	HR	TB	BB	IBB	HB	SO	GDP	SH	SF	SB	CS	R	RBI	BA	OBA	SA
88	JAM/NYP	A—	74	335	291	94	14	7	8	146	35	2	2	39	2	2	5	23	7	69	39	.323	.393	.502
89	JAC/SOU	AA	78	313	278	83	15	4	3	115	24	1	7	31	1	1	3	24	6	43	31	.299	.365	.414
	IND/AMA	AAA	49	202	187	52	10	4	2	76	14	0	0	23	0	1	1	16	4	28	21	.278	.327	.406
	MON/NL		26	87	74	19	2	0	1	24	12	0	0	21	1	0	0	1	0	3	3	.257	.360	.324
90	IND/AMA	AAA	5	22	22	4	0	0	2	10	0	0	0	5	0	0	0	1	0	3	3	.182	.182	.455
	MON/NL		98	320	288	74	14	2	3	101	27	0	1	40	3	4	1	22	2	42	29	.257	.320	.351
91	MON/NL		148	597	558	149	23	9	6	208	34	0	1	89	8	4	0	76	17	73	39	.267	.310	.373
3 YR TOTALS			272	1004	920	242	39	11	10	333	73	2	1	150	12	9	1	99	19	131	70	**.263**	**.318**	**.362**

Gruber, Kelly Wayne — bats right — throws right — b.2/26/62 — 1991 positions: 3B 111, DH 2

YR	TM/LG	CL	G	TPA	AB	H	2B	3B	HR	TB	BB	IBB	HB	SO	GDP	SH	SF	SB	CS	R	RBI	BA	OBA	SA
84	SYR/INT	AAA	97	373	342	92	12	2	21	171	23	0	7	67	6	0	1	12	2	53	55	.269	.327	.500
	TOR/AL		15	16	16	1	0	0	1	4	0	0	0	5	1	0	0	0	0	1	2	.063	.063	.250
85	SYR/INT	AAA	121	514	473	118	16	5	21	207	28	2	7	92	17	1	5	20	8	71	69	.249	.298	.438
	TOR/AL		5	13	13	3	0	0	0	3	0	0	0	3	0	0	0	0	0	0	1	.231	.231	.231
86	TOR/AL		87	152	143	28	4	1	5	49	5	0	0	27	4	2	2	2	2	20	15	.196	.220	.343
87	TOR/AL		138	368	341	80	14	3	12	136	17	2	7	70	11	1	2	12	2	50	36	.235	.283	.399
88	TOR/AL		158	623	569	158	33	5	16	249	38	1	7	92	20	5	4	23	5	75	81	.278	.328	.438
89	TOR/AL		135	583	545	158	24	4	18	244	30	0	3	60	13	0	5	10	5	83	73	.290	.328	.448
90	TOR/AL		150	662	592	162	36	6	31	303	48	2	8	94	14	1	13	14	2	92	118	.274	.330	.512
91	TOR/AL		113	474	429	108	18	2	20	190	31	5	3	70	7	3	12	12	7	58	65	.252	.308	.443
8 YR TOTALS			801	2891	2648	698	129	21	103	1178	169	10	31	421	70	12	31	73	26	379	391	**.264**	**.312**	**.445**

Guerrero, Pedro — bats right — throws right — b.6/29/56 — 1991 positions: 1B 112

YR	TM/LG	CL	G	TPA	AB	H	2B	3B	HR	TB	BB	IBB	HB	SO	GDP	SH	SF	SB	CS	R	RBI	BA	OBA	SA
78	LA/NL		5	8	8	5	0	1	0	7	0	0	0	0	0	0	0	0	0	3	1	.625	.625	.875
79	LA/NL		25	64	62	15	2	0	2	23	1	0	1	14	0	0	1	2	0	7	9	.242	.250	.371
80	LA/NL		75	199	183	59	9	1	7	91	12	3	0	31	2	1	3	2	1	27	31	.322	.359	.497
81	LA/NL		98	387	347	104	17	2	12	161	34	3	2	57	12	3	1	5	9	46	48	.300	.365	.464
82	LA/NL		150	652	575	175	27	5	32	308	65	16	5	89	7	4	3	22	5	87	100	.304	.378	.536
83	LA/NL		160	664	584	174	28	6	32	310	72	12	2	110	11	0	6	23	7	87	103	.298	.373	.531
84	LA/NL		144	594	535	162	29	4	16	247	49	7	1	68	13	1	8	9	8	85	72	.303	.358	.462
85	LA/NL		137	581	487	156	22	2	33	281	83	14	6	68	13	1	3	12	4	99	87	.320	.422	.577
86	LA/NL		31	64	61	15	3	0	5	33	3	0	0	19	1	0	0	0	0	7	10	.246	.281	.541
87	LA/NL		152	630	545	184	25	2	27	294	74	18	4	85	16	1	7	9	7	89	89	.338	.416	.539
88	ALB/PCL	AAA	5	17	12	5	0	0	1	8	5	2	0	3	0	0	0	0	0	3	4	.417	.588	.667
	LA/NL		59	246	215	64	7	1	5	88	25	2	0	33	2	1	3	2	1	24	35	.298	.374	.409
	STL/NL		44	176	149	40	7	1	5	64	21	7	2	26	3	0	7	4	1	36	30	.268	.358	.430
	YEAR		103	422	364	104	14	2	10	152	46	9	2	59	5	1	10	6	2	60	65	.286	.355	.418
89	STL/NL		162	665	570	177	42	1	17	272	79	13	4	84	17	0	12	2	0	60	117	.311	.391	.477
90	STL/NL		136	554	498	140	31	1	13	212	44	14	1	70	14	0	11	1	2	42	80	.281	.334	.426
91	LOU/AMA	AAA	3	11	11	5	0	0	1	8	0	0	0	0	0	0	0	0	0	2	2	.455	.455	.727
	STL/NL		115	472	427	116	12	1	8	154	37	2	2	46	12	0	7	2	0	41	70	.272	.326	.361
14 YR TOTALS			1493	5956	5246	1586	261	28	214	2545	598	112	32	837	118	9	71	95	45	720	882	**.302**	**.373**	**.485**

Guillen, Oswaldo Jose (Barrios) "Ozzie" — bats left — throws right — b.1/20/64 — 1991 positions: SS 149

YR	TM/LG	CL	G	TPA	AB	H	2B	3B	HR	TB	BB	IBB	HB	SO	GDP	SH	SF	SB	CS	R	RBI	BA	OBA	SA
85	CHI/AL		150	513	491	134	21	9	1	176	12	1	1	36	5	8	1	7	4	71	33	.273	.291	.358
86	CHI/AL		159	577	547	137	19	4	2	170	12	1	1	52	14	12	5	8	4	58	47	.250	.265	.311
87	CHI/AL		149	604	560	156	22	7	2	198	22	2	1	52	10	13	8	25	13	64	51	.279	.303	.354
88	CHI/AL		156	606	566	148	16	7	0	178	25	3	0	40	14	11	4	25	17	58	39	.261	.294	.314
89	CHI/AL		155	626	597	151	9	8	1	190	15	3	0	48	8	11	3	36	17	63	54	.253	.270	.318
90	CHI/AL		160	563	516	144	21	4	1	176	26	1	1	37	6	13	7	13	15	61	58	.279	.312	.341
91	CHI/AL		154	555	524	143	20	3	3	178	11	1	1	38	7	14	4	21	8	52	49	.273	.284	.340
7 YR TOTALS			1083	4044	3801	1013	139	42	10	1266	123	19	6	303	64	82	32	135	78	427	331	**.267**	**.288**	**.333**

Gwynn, Anthony Keith "Tony" — bats left — throws left — b.5/9/60 — 1991 positions: OF 134

YR	TM/LG	CL	G	TPA	AB	H	2B	3B	HR	TB	BB	IBB	HB	SO	GDP	SH	SF	SB	CS	R	RBI	BA	OBA	SA
82	SD/NL		54	209	190	55	12	2	1	74	14	0	0	16	5	4	1	8	3	33	17	.289	.337	.389
83	SD/NL		86	334	304	94	12	2	1	113	23	5	0	21	9	4	3	7	4	34	37	.309	.355	.372
84	SD/NL		158	675	606	213	21	10	5	269	59	13	2	23	15	6	2	33	18	88	71	.351	.410	.444

(continued)

Gwynn, Anthony Keith "Tony" (continued)

YR	TM/LG	CL	G	TPA	AB	H	2B	3B	HR	TB	BB	IBB	HB	SO	GDP	SH	SF	SB	CS	R	RBI	BA	OBA	SA
85	SD/NL		154	671	622	197	29	5	6	254	45	4	2	33	17	1	1	14	11	90	46	.317	.364	.408
86	SD/NL		160	701	642	211	33	7	14	300	52	11	3	35	20	2	2	37	9	107	59	.329	.381	.467
87	SD/NL		157	680	589	218	36	13	7	301	82	26	3	35	13	2	4	56	12	119	54	.370	.447	.511
88	SD/NL		133	578	521	163	22	5	7	216	51	13	0	40	11	4	2	26	11	64	70	.313	.373	.415
89	SD/NL		158	679	604	203	27	7	4	256	56	16	1	30	12	11	7	40	16	82	62	.336	.389	.424
90	SD/NL		141	629	573	177	29	10	4	238	44	20	1	23	13	7	4	17	8	79	72	.309	.357	.415
91	SD/NL		134	569	530	168	27	11	4	229	34	8	0	19	11	0	6	8	8	69	62	.317	.355	.432
10 YR TOTALS			**1335**	**5725**	**5181**	**1699**	**248**	**72**	**53**	**2250**	**460**	**116**	**12**	**275**	**126**	**41**	**31**	**246**	**100**	**765**	**550**	**.328**	**.382**	**.434**

Gwynn, Christopher Karlton "Chris" — bats left — throws left — b.10/13/64 — 1991 positions: OF 41

YR	TM/LG	CL	G	TPA	AB	H	2B	3B	HR	TB	BB	IBB	HB	SO	GDP	SH	SF	SB	CS	R	RBI	BA	OBA	SA
85	VB/FSL	A+	52	199	179	46	8	6	0	66	16	0	2	34	4	1	1	2	2	19	17	.257	.323	.369
86	SA/TEX	AA	111	427	401	115	22	1	6	157	16	7	3	44	8	1	6	2	2	46	67	.287	.315	.392
87	ALB/PCL	AAA	110	400	362	101	12	3	6	134	36	5	1	38	5	1	0	5	7	54	41	.279	.346	.370
	LA/NL		17	34	32	7	1	0	0	8	1	0	1	0	0	1	0	0	0	2	2	.219	.242	.250
88	ALB/PCL	AAA	112	465	411	123	22	10	5	180	39	6	2	39	4	4	9	1	2	57	61	.299	.356	.438
	LA/NL		12	12	11	2	0	0	0	2	1	0	0	2	0	0	0	0	0	1	0	.182	.250	.182
89	LA/NL		32	73	68	16	4	1	0	22	2	0	0	9	1	2	1	1	0	8	7	.235	.254	.324
	ALB/PCL	AAA	26	100	89	29	9	2	1	40	7	1	2	1	1	0	1	0	0	14	12	.326	.384	.449
90	LA/NL		101	151	141	40	2	1	5	59	7	2	0	28	2	0	3	0	1	19	22	.284	.311	.418
91	LA/NL		94	154	139	35	5	1	5	57	10	1	1	23	5	1	3	1	0	18	22	.252	.301	.410
5 YR TOTALS			**256**	**424**	**391**	**100**	**12**	**3**	**10**	**148**	**21**	**3**	**1**	**69**	**8**	**4**	**7**	**2**	**1**	**48**	**53**	**.256**	**.290**	**.379**

Hall, Melvin "Mel" — bats left — throws left — b.9/16/60 — 1991 positions: OF 120, DH 10

YR	TM/LG	CL	G	TPA	AB	H	2B	3B	HR	TB	BB	IBB	HB	SO	GDP	SH	SF	SB	CS	R	RBI	BA	OBA	SA
81	CHI/NL		10	12	11	1	0	0	0	4	0	0	0	4	0	0	0	0	0	1	2	.091	.167	.364
82	CHI/NL		24	88	80	21	3	2	0	28	5	1	2	17	0	0	1	0	1	6	4	.262	.318	.350
83	CHI/NL		112	458	410	116	23	5	17	200	42	6	3	101	4	1	2	6	6	60	56	.283	.352	.488
84	CHI/NL		48	164	150	42	11	3	4	71	12	3	0	23	2	1	1	2	1	25	22	.280	.329	.473
	CLE/AL		83	299	257	66	13	1	7	102	35	5	2	55	3	0	2	5	1	43	30	.257	.344	.397
	YEAR		131	463	407	108	24	4	11	173	47	8	2	78	5	1	3	7	2	68	52	.265	.344	.425
85	CLE/AL		23	75	66	21	6	0	0	27	8	0	2	12	0	1	0	1	0	7	12	.318	.387	.409
86	CLE/AL		140	480	442	131	29	2	18	218	33	8	2	65	8	0	1	0	2	68	77	.296	.346	.493
87	CLE/AL		142	508	485	136	21	1	18	213	20	6	1	68	7	0	2	5	4	57	76	.280	.309	.439
88	CLE/AL		150	553	515	144	32	4	6	202	28	12	0	50	8	0	7	8	3	69	71	.280	.312	.392
89	NY/AL		113	391	361	94	9	0	17	154	21	4	2	50	8	1	1	8	7	54	58	.260	.295	.427
90	NY/AL		113	371	360	93	23	2	12	156	6	2	2	46	7	0	3	0	0	41	46	.258	.272	.433
91	NY/AL		141	527	492	140	23	2	19	224	26	6	3	40	6	0	6	0	1	67	80	.285	.321	.455
11 YR TOTALS			**1099**	**3926**	**3629**	**1005**	**193**	**22**	**119**	**1599**	**237**	**53**	**15**	**518**	**56**	**4**	**41**	**27**	**20**	**498**	**534**	**.277**	**.320**	**.441**

Hamilton, Darryl Quinn — bats left — throws right — b.12/3/64 — 1991 positions: OF 117

YR	TM/LG	CL	G	TPA	AB	H	2B	3B	HR	TB	BB	IBB	HB	SO	GDP	SH	SF	SB	CS	R	RBI	BA	OBA	SA
86	HEL/PIO	R+	65	302	248	97	12	6	0	121	51	3	1	18	3	1	1	34	8	72	35	.391	.495	.488
87	STO/CAL	A+	125	586	494	162	17	6	8	215	74	9	6	59	2	5	7	43	12	102	61	.328	.417	.435
88	DEN/AMA	AAA	72	323	277	90	11	4	0	109	39	0	1	28	4	1	5	23	7	55	32	.325	.404	.394
	MIL/AL		44	117	103	19	4	0	1	26	12	0	1	9	2	0	1	7	3	14	11	.184	.274	.252
89	DEN/AMA	AAA	129	554	497	142	24	4	2	180	42	3	5	58	13	5	7	20	13	72	40	.286	.344	.362
90	MIL/AL		89	168	156	46	5	0	1	54	9	0	0	12	2	3	0	10	3	27	18	.295	.333	.346
91	MIL/AL		122	448	405	126	15	6	1	156	33	2	0	38	10	7	3	16	6	64	57	.311	.361	.385
3 YR TOTALS			**255**	**733**	**664**	**191**	**24**	**6**	**3**	**236**	**54**	**2**	**1**	**59**	**14**	**10**	**4**	**33**	**12**	**105**	**86**	**.288**	**.340**	**.355**

Hamilton, Jeffrey Robert "Jeff" — bats right — throws right — b.3/19/64 — 1991 positions: 3B 33, SS 1

YR	TM/LG	CL	G	TPA	AB	H	2B	3B	HR	TB	BB	IBB	HB	SO	GDP	SH	SF	SB	CS	R	RBI	BA	OBA	SA
84	VB/FSL	A+	127	516	466	121	31	4	5	172	41	2	4	78	8	2	3	7	7	51	59	.260	.323	.369
85	SA/TEX	AA	101	408	377	125	14	3	13	184	28	6	0	52	9	1	2	1	2	48	59	.332	.376	.488
86	ALB/PCL	AAA	71	301	288	90	21	3	10	147	12	2	0	44	6	0	1	1	1	40	42	.313	.339	.510
	LA/NL		71	151	147	33	5	0	5	53	2	1	0	43	3	0	2	0	0	22	19	.224	.232	.361
87	ALB/PCL	AAA	65	267	236	85	17	1	12	140	26	2	2	26	4	1	2	0	0	52	48	.360	.425	.593
	LA/NL		35	91	83	18	3	0	0	21	7	2	2	26	1	0	1	0	0	5	1	.217	.286	.253
88	LA/NL		111	327	309	73	14	2	6	109	10	1	4	51	8	2	2	0	2	34	33	.236	.268	.353
89	LA/NL		151	581	548	134	35	1	12	207	20	1	5	71	10	4	6	0	0	45	56	.245	.272	.378
90	LA/NL		7	24	24	3	0	0	0	3	0	0	0	3	1	0	0	0	0	1	1	.125	.125	.125
91	ALB/PCL	AAA	2	7	7	0	0	0	0	0	0	0	0	2	1	0	0	0	0	1	1	.000	.000	.000
	LA/NL		41	99	94	21	4	0	1	28	4	0	0	21	2	1	0	0	0	4	14	.223	.255	.298
6 YR TOTALS			**416**	**1273**	**1205**	**282**	**61**	**3**	**24**	**421**	**43**	**9**	**8**	**211**	**24**	**7**	**10**	**0**	**3**	**111**	**124**	**.234**	**.263**	**.349**

Hansen, David Andrew "Dave" — bats left — throws right — b.11/24/68 — 1991 positions: 3B 21, SS 1

YR	TM/LG	CL	G	TPA	AB	H	2B	3B	HR	TB	BB	IBB	HB	SO	GDP	SH	SF	SB	CS	R	RBI	BA	OBA	SA
86	GF/PIO	R+	61	232	204	61	7	3	1	77	27	0	1	28	6	1	0	9	5	39	36	.299	.381	.377
87	BAK/CAL	A+	132	508	432	113	22	1	3	146	65	4	4	61	11	6	1	4	2	68	38	.262	.363	.338
88	VB/FSL	A+	135	582	512	149	28	6	7	210	56	6	4	46	9	1	9	2	2	68	81	.291	.360	.410
89	SA/TEX	AA	121	521	464	138	21	4	7	185	50	6	4	44	18	0	5	3	2	72	52	.297	.365	.399
	ALB/PCL	AAA	6	32	30	8	1	0	2	15	2	0	0	3	0	0	0	0	0	6	10	.267	.313	.500
90	ALB/PCL	AAA	135	589	487	154	20	3	11	213	90	4	3	54	12	0	9	4	4	90	92	.316	.419	.437
	LA/NL		5	7	7	1	0	0	0	1	0	0	0	3	0	0	0	0	0	0	1	.143	.143	.143

Hansen, David Andrew "Dave" (continued)

YR	TM/LG	CL	G	TPA	AB	H	2B	3B	HR	TB	BB	IBB	HB	SO	GDP	SH	SF	SB	CS	R	RBI	BA	OBA	SA
91	ALB/PCL	AAA	68	310	254	77	11	1	5	105	49	3	0	33	7	0	7	4	3	42	40	.303	.406	.413
	LA/NL		53	58	56	15	4	0	1	22	2	0	0	12	2	0	0	1	0	3	5	.268	.293	.393
2 YR TOTALS			**58**	**65**	**63**	**16**	**4**	**0**	**1**	**23**	**2**	**0**	**0**	**15**	**2**	**0**	**0**	**1**	**0**	**3**	**6**	**.254**	**.277**	**.365**

Hansen, Terrel Ernest — bats right — throws right — b.9/25/66 — 1991 positions: OF System NY/NL

YR	TM/LG	CL	G	TPA	AB	H	2B	3B	HR	TB	BB	IBB	HB	SO	GDP	SH	SF	SB	CS	R	RBI	BA	OBA	SA
87	JAM/NYP	A—	29	79	67	16	3	0	1	22	10	1	0	20	3	0	2	1	2	8	14	.239	.329	.328
88	WPB/FSL	A+	58	208	190	49	9	0	4	70	10	1	6	38	5	0	2	2	2	17	28	.258	.313	.368
89	ROC/MID	A	125	524	468	126	24	3	16	204	25	4	23	120	8	1	7	5	2	60	81	.269	.333	.436
90	JAC/SOU	AA	123	491	420	109	26	2	24	211	43	2	24	88	14	1	3	3	4	72	83	.260	.359	.502
91	TID/INT	AAA	107	431	368	100	19	2	12	159	40	2	20	82	20	0	3	0	0	54	62	.272	.371	.432

Hare, Shawn Robert — bats left — throws left — b.3/26/67 — 1991 positions: OF 6, DH 2

YR	TM/LG	CL	G	TPA	AB	H	2B	3B	HR	TB	BB	IBB	HB	SO	GDP	SH	SF	SB	CS	R	RBI	BA	OBA	SA
89	LAK/FSL	A+	93	336	290	94	16	4	2	124	41	4	2	32	7	2	1	11	5	32	36	.324	.410	.428
90	TOL/INT	AAA	127	485	429	109	25	4	9	169	49	9	4	77	10	0	3	9	6	53	55	.254	.334	.394
91	LON/EAS	AA	31	138	125	34	12	1	4	58	12	1	1	23	5	0	0	2	2	20	28	.272	.341	.464
	TOL/INT	AAA	80	290	252	78	18	2	9	127	30	1	2	53	6	1	5	1	2	44	40	.310	.381	.504
	DET/AL		9	21	19	1	1	0	0	2	2	0	0	3	0	0	0	0	0	0	0	.053	.143	.105

Harper, Brian David — bats right — throws right — b.10/16/59 — 1991 positions: C 119, DH 2, 1B 1, OF 1

YR	TM/LG	CL	G	TPA	AB	H	2B	3B	HR	TB	BB	IBB	HB	SO	GDP	SH	SF	SB	CS	R	RBI	BA	OBA	SA
79	CAL/AL		1	2	2	0	0	0	0	0	0	0	0	1	0	0	0	0	0	0	1	.000	.000	.000
81	CAL/AL		4	12	11	3	0	0	0	3	0	0	0	0	0	0	1	1	0	0	1	.273	.250	.273
82	PIT/NL		20	31	29	8	1	0	2	15	1	1	0	4	1	1	1	0	0	4	4	.276	.300	.517
83	PIT/NL		61	140	131	29	4	1	7	56	2	0	1	15	3	2	4	0	0	16	20	.221	.232	.427
84	PIT/NL		46	121	112	29	4	0	2	39	5	2	0	11	4	1	1	0	0	4	11	.259	.300	.348
85	STL/NL		43	55	52	13	4	0	0	17	2	0	0	8	2	0	1	0	0	3	9	.250	.273	.327
86	DET/AL		19	41	36	5	1	0	0	6	3	0	1	6	0	0	1	0	0	2	4	.139	.200	.167
	NAS/AMA	AAA	95	351	317	83	11	1	11	129	26	1	2	27	9	1	5	3	8	41	45	.262	.317	.407
87	SJ/CAL	A+	8	32	29	9	0	0	3	18	2	0	0	0	0	0	1	0	1	5	8	.310	.344	.621
	TAC/PCL	AAA	94	371	323	100	17	0	9	144	28	7	4	23	13	4	12	1	2	41	62	.310	.360	.446
	OAK/AL		11	19	17	4	1	0	0	5	0	0	0	4	1	0	1	0	1	1	3	.235	.222	.294
88	POR/PCL	AAA	46	191	170	60	10	1	13	111	14	3	3	7	6	0	4	2	0	34	42	.353	.403	.653
	MIN/AL		60	182	166	49	11	1	3	71	10	1	3	12	12	1	3	0	0	15	20	.295	.344	.428
89	MIN/AL		126	412	385	125	24	0	8	173	13	3	6	16	11	4	4	2	4	43	57	.325	.353	.449
90	MIN/AL		134	509	479	141	42	3	6	207	19	2	7	27	20	0	4	3	2	61	54	.294	.328	.432
91	MIN/AL		123	469	441	137	28	1	10	197	14	3	6	22	14	2	6	1	2	54	69	.311	.336	.447
12 YR TOTALS			**648**	**1993**	**1861**	**543**	**120**	**6**	**38**	**789**	**69**	**10**	**25**	**118**	**69**	**14**	**24**	**7**	**11**	**206**	**250**	**.292**	**.322**	**.424**

Harris, Donald — bats right — throws right — b.11/12/67 — 1991 positions: OF 12, DH 3

YR	TM/LG	CL	G	TPA	AB	H	2B	3B	HR	TB	BB	IBB	HB	SO	GDP	SH	SF	SB	CS	R	RBI	BA	OBA	SA
89	BUT/PIO	R+	65	285	264	75	7	8	6	116	12	0	6	54	6	0	3	14	4	50	37	.284	.326	.439
90	TUL/TEX	AA	64	226	213	34	5	1	1	44	7	0	3	69	0	3	0	7	3	16	15	.160	.197	.207
	GAS/SAL	A	58	241	221	46	10	0	3	65	14	0	2	63	2	4	0	15	8	27	13	.208	.262	.294
91	TUL/TEX	AA	130	492	450	102	17	8	11	168	26	1	7	118	11	7	2	9	6	47	53	.227	.278	.373
	TEX/AL		18	9	8	3	0	0	1	6	1	0	0	3	0	0	0	1	0	4	2	.375	.444	.750

Harris, Leonard Anthony "Lenny" — bats left — throws right — b.10/28/64 — 1991 positions: 3B 113, 2B 27, SS 20, OF 1

YR	TM/LG	CL	G	TPA	AB	H	2B	3B	HR	TB	BB	IBB	HB	SO	GDP	SH	SF	SB	CS	R	RBI	BA	OBA	SA
84	CR/MID	A	132	521	468	115	15	3	6	154	42	4	3	59	14	2	6	31	10	52	53	.246	.308	.329
85	TAM/FSL	A+	132	549	499	129	11	8	3	165	37	2	1	57	9	5	7	15	8	66	51	.259	.307	.331
86	VER/EAS	AA	119	492	450	114	17	2	10	165	29	4	6	43	10	2	2	30	12	45	31	.253	.303	.367
87	NAS/AMA	AAA	120	439	403	100	12	3	2	124	27	4	5	43	10	2	2	36	12	45	31	.248	.302	.308
88	GF/EAS	AA	17	75	65	22	5	1	1	32	9	0	0	6	1	1	0	6	2	9	7	.338	.419	.492
	NAS/AMA	AAA	107	446	422	117	20	2	0	141	22	2	0	36	13	2	2	41	22	46	35	.277	.313	.334
	CIN/NL		16	51	43	16	1	0	0	17	5	0	0	4	0	1	2	4	1	7	8	.372	.420	.395
89	NAS/AMA	AAA	8	34	34	9	2	0	3	20	0	0	0	4	0	0	0	2	2	6	6	.265	.265	.588
	CIN/NL		61	199	188	42	4	0	2	52	9	1	0	20	5	1	0	10	6	17	11	.223	.263	.277
	LA/NL		54	159	147	37	4	0	1	48	11	0	1	13	9	0	0	4	3	19	15	.252	.308	.327
	YEAR		115	358	335	79	8	0	3	100	20	1	1	33	14	1	0	14	9	36	26	.236	.283	.299
90	LA/NL		137	465	431	131	16	4	2	161	29	2	3	31	8	1	1	15	10	61	29	.304	.348	.374
91	LA/NL		145	485	429	123	16	1	3	150	37	5	5	32	16	12	2	12	13	59	38	.287	.349	.350
4 YR TOTALS			**413**	**1359**	**1238**	**349**	**43**	**6**	**8**	**428**	**91**	**7**	**8**	**100**	**38**	**17**	**5**	**45**	**23**	**163**	**101**	**.282**	**.334**	**.346**

Hassey, Ronald William "Ron" — bats left — throws right — b.2/27/53 — 1991 positions: C 34

YR	TM/LG	CL	G	TPA	AB	H	2B	3B	HR	TB	BB	IBB	HB	SO	GDP	SH	SF	SB	CS	R	RBI	BA	OBA	SA
78	CLE/AL		25	83	74	15	0	0	2	21	5	0	1	7	1	1	2	2	0	5	9	.203	.256	.284
79	CLE/AL		75	249	223	64	14	0	4	90	19	2	0	19	8	4	3	1	0	20	32	.287	.339	.404
80	CLE/AL		130	447	390	124	18	4	8	174	49	5	1	51	13	3	3	0	1	8	25	.232	.297	.268
81	CLE/AL		61	215	190	44	4	0	1	51	17	0	2	11	5	3	2	0	1	33	34	.251	.356	.353
82	CLE/AL		113	382	323	81	18	0	5	114	53	1	0	32	10	3	2	0	2	48	42	.270	.342	.384
83	CLE/AL		117	388	341	92	21	0	6	131	38	2	0	35	11	4	5	0	1	41	19	.255	.321	.302
84	CLE/AL		48	165	149	38	5	0	4	45	15	2	0	26	4	0	1	0	0	5	5	.333	.405	.515
	CHI/NL		19	37	33	11	2	0	2	17	4	1	0	6	1	0	0	0	0	5	5	.333	.405	.515

(continued)

Hassey, Ronald William "Ron" (continued)

YR	TM/LG	CL	G	TPA	AB	H	2B	3B	HR	TB	BB	IBB	HB	SO	GDP	SH	SF	SB	CS	R	RBI	BA	OBA	SA
	YEAR		67	202	182	49	5	1	2	62	19	3	0	32	5	0	1	1	1	16	24	.269	.337	.341
85	NY/AL		92	298	267	79	16	1	13	136	28	4	3	21	7	0	0	0	0	31	42	.296	.369	.509
86	NY/AL		64	219	191	57	14	0	6	89	24	1	2	16	8	1	1	1	1	23	29	.298	.381	.466
	CHI/AL		49	174	150	53	11	1	3	75	22	2	1	11	7	0	1	0	0	22	20	.353	.437	.500
	YEAR		113	393	341	110	25	1	9	164	46	3	3	27	15	1	2	1	1	45	49	.323	.406	.481
87	HAW/PCL	AAA	6	23	21	3	2	0	0	5	2	0	0	1	0	0	0	0	0	3	4	.143	.217	.238
	CHI/AL		49	165	145	31	9	0	3	49	17	2	2	11	9	0	0	0	0	15	12	.214	.303	.338
88	OAK/AL		107	365	323	83	15	0	7	119	30	1	4	42	9	3	5	2	0	32	45	.257	.323	.368
89	OAK/AL		97	298	268	61	12	0	5	88	24	2	1	45	9	1	4	1	0	29	23	.228	.290	.328
90	OAK/AL		94	286	254	54	7	0	5	76	27	3	1	29	3	1	3	0	0	18	22	.213	.288	.299
91	MON/NL		52	135	119	27	8	0	1	38	13	1	0	16	5	2	1	1	1	5	14	.227	.301	.319
14 YR TOTALS			**1192**	**3906**	**3440**	**914**	**172**	**7**	**71**	**1313**	**385**	**31**	**21**	**378**	**110**	**22**	**38**	**14**	**10**	**348**	**438**	**.266**	**.340**	**.382**

Hatcher, William Augustus "Billy" — bats right — throws right — b.10/4/60 — 1991 positions: OF 121

YR	TM/LG	CL	G	TPA	AB	H	2B	3B	HR	TB	BB	IBB	HB	SO	GDP	SH	SF	SB	CS	R	RBI	BA	OBA	SA
84	IOW/AMA	AAA	150	659	595	164	27	18	9	254	51	4	9	54	8	1	3	56	18	96	59	.276	.340	.427
	CHI/NL		8	10	9	1	0	0	0	1	1	0	0	4	0	0	0	2	0	1	0	.111	.200	.111
85	IOW/AMA	AAA	67	309	279	78	14	5	5	117	24	0	2	40	5	2	2	17	11	39	19	.280	.339	.419
	CHI/NL		53	178	163	40	12	1	2	60	8	0	3	12	9	2	2	2	4	24	10	.245	.290	.368
86	HOU/NL		127	453	419	108	15	4	6	149	22	1	5	52	3	6	1	38	14	55	36	.258	.302	.356
87	HOU/NL		141	627	564	167	28	3	11	234	42	1	9	70	11	7	5	53	9	96	63	.296	.352	.415
88	HOU/NL		145	591	530	142	25	4	7	196	37	4	8	56	6	8	8	32	13	79	52	.268	.321	.370
89	HOU/NL		108	433	395	90	15	3	3	120	30	2	1	53	3	3	4	22	6	49	44	.228	.281	.304
	PIT/NL		27	87	86	21	4	0	1	28	0	0	1	9	1	0	0	2	1	10	7	.244	.253	.326
	YEAR		135	520	481	111	19	3	4	148	30	2	2	62	4	3	4	24	7	59	51	.231	.277	.308
90	CIN/NL		139	545	504	139	28	5	5	192	33	2	6	42	4	1	1	30	10	68	25	.276	.327	.381
91	CIN/NL		138	482	442	116	25	3	4	159	26	4	7	55	9	4	3	11	9	45	41	.262	.312	.360
8 YR TOTALS			**886**	**3406**	**3112**	**824**	**152**	**23**	**39**	**1139**	**199**	**18**	**40**	**349**	**46**	**31**	**24**	**192**	**66**	**427**	**278**	**.265**	**.315**	**.366**

Hayes, Charles Dewayne "Charlie" — bats right — throws right — b.5/29/65 — 1991 positions: 3B 138, SS 2

YR	TM/LG	CL	G	TPA	AB	H	2B	3B	HR	TB	BB	IBB	HB	SO	GDP	SH	SF	SB	CS	R	RBI	BA	OBA	SA
84	CLI/MID	A	116	435	392	96	17	2	2	123	34	1	1	110	7	5	3	4	1	41	51	.245	.305	.314
85	FRE/CAL	A+	131	534	467	132	17	2	4	165	56	0	6	95	9	1	4	7	8	73	68	.283	.364	.353
86	SHR/TEX	AA	121	472	434	107	23	2	5	149	28	3	2	83	11	4	4	1	4	52	45	.247	.293	.343
87	SHR/TEX	AA	128	524	487	148	33	3	14	229	26	6	3	76	12	1	7	5	9	66	75	.304	.338	.470
88	PHO/PCL	AAA	131	533	492	151	26	4	7	206	34	1	0	91	19	2	5	9	9	71	71	.307	.348	.419
	SF/NL		7	11	11	1	0	0	0	1	0	0	0	1	0	0	0	0	0	0	0	.091	.091	.091
89	SF/NL		3	5	5	1	0	0	0	1	0	0	0	1	0	0	0	0	0	0	0	.200	.200	.200
	PHO/PCL	AAA	61	246	229	65	15	1	7	103	15	1	0	48	2	0	2	5	5	25	27	.284	.325	.450
	SCR/INT	AAA	7	28	27	11	3	1	1	19	0	0	1	3	0	0	0	0	0	4	3	.407	.429	.704
	PHI/NL		84	315	299	77	15	1	8	118	11	0	0	49	6	2	3	3	1	26	43	.258	.281	.395
	YEAR		87	320	304	78	15	1	8	119	11	1	0	50	6	2	3	3	1	26	43	.257	.280	.391
90	PHI/NL		152	597	561	145	20	0	10	195	28	3	2	91	12	0	6	4	4	56	57	.258	.293	.348
91	PHI/NL		142	480	460	106	23	1	12	167	16	3	1	75	13	2	1	3	3	34	53	.230	.257	.363
4 YR TOTALS			**388**	**1408**	**1336**	**330**	**58**	**2**	**30**	**482**	**55**	**7**	**3**	**219**	**31**	**4**	**10**	**10**	**8**	**116**	**153**	**.247**	**.276**	**.361**

Hayes, Von Francis — bats left — throws right — b.8/31/58 — 1991 positions: OF 72

YR	TM/LG	CL	G	TPA	AB	H	2B	3B	HR	TB	BB	IBB	HB	SO	GDP	SH	SF	SB	CS	R	RBI	BA	OBA	SA
81	CLE/AL		43	131	109	28	8	2	1	43	14	1	2	10	2	4	2	8	1	21	17	.257	.346	.394
82	CLE/AL		150	583	527	132	25	3	14	205	42	3	4	63	10	8	2	32	13	65	82	.250	.310	.389
83	PHI/NL		124	392	351	93	9	5	6	130	36	7	3	55	11	0	2	20	12	45	32	.265	.337	.370
84	PHI/NL		152	622	561	164	27	6	16	251	59	4	0	84	10	0	2	48	13	85	67	.292	.359	.447
85	PHI/NL		152	637	570	150	30	4	13	227	61	6	0	99	6	2	4	21	8	76	70	.263	.332	.398
86	PHI/NL		158	690	610	186	46	2	19	293	74	9	1	77	14	1	4	24	12	107	98	.305	.379	.480
87	PHI/NL		158	681	556	154	36	5	21	263	121	12	0	77	12	0	4	16	7	84	84	.277	.404	.473
88	PHI/NL		104	423	367	100	28	2	6	150	49	5	1	59	7	1	5	20	9	43	45	.272	.355	.409
89	PHI/NL		154	652	540	140	27	2	26	249	101	14	4	103	7	0	7	28	7	93	78	.259	.376	.461
90	CLE/FSL	A+	2	8	6	1	1	0	0	2	1	0	1	1	0	0	0	0	0	0	0	.167	.375	.333
	PHI/NL		129	568	467	122	14	3	17	193	87	16	4	81	10	0	10	16	7	70	73	.261	.375	.413
91	SCR/INT	AAA	2	10	8	2	1	0	0	3	2	0	0	3	0	0	0	0	0	2	0	.250	.400	.375
	PHI/NL		77	323	284	64	15	1	0	81	31	1	3	42	6	0	5	9	2	43	21	.225	.303	.285
11 YR TOTALS			**1401**	**5702**	**4942**	**1333**	**265**	**35**	**139**	**2085**	**675**	**78**	**22**	**750**	**91**	**16**	**47**	**242**	**91**	**732**	**667**	**.270**	**.357**	**.422**

Heath, Michael Thomas "Mike" — bats right — throws right — b.2/5/55 — 1991 positions: C 45

YR	TM/LG	CL	G	TPA	AB	H	2B	3B	HR	TB	BB	IBB	HB	SO	GDP	SH	SF	SB	CS	R	RBI	BA	OBA	SA
78	NY/AL		33	99	92	21	3	1	0	26	4	0	1	9	1	1	1	0	0	6	8	.228	.265	.283
79	OAK/AL		74	286	258	66	8	0	3	83	17	1	3	18	14	1	5	1	0	19	27	.256	.304	.322
80	OAK/AL		92	329	305	74	10	2	1	91	16	2	0	28	7	7	1	3	3	27	33	.243	.280	.298
81	OAK/AL		84	321	301	71	7	1	8	104	13	1	1	36	9	5	1	3	3	26	30	.236	.269	.346
82	OAK/AL		101	351	318	77	18	4	3	112	27	3	0	36	8	2	4	8	3	43	39	.242	.298	.352
83	OAK/AL		96	366	345	97	17	0	6	132	16	4	1	59	9	1	1	3	4	45	33	.281	.318	.383
84	OAK/AL		140	508	475	118	21	5	13	188	26	2	1	72	14	2	4	7	4	49	64	.248	.287	.396
85	OAK/AL		138	492	436	109	18	6	13	178	41	0	4	63	13	10	4	7	7	71	55	.205	.313	.408
86	STL/NL		65	216	190	39	8	1	4	61	23	4	1	36	5	1	2	1	2	19	25	.205	.293	.321
	DET/AL		30	103	98	26	3	0	4	41	4	0	0	17	1	0	1	0	1	11	11	.265	.291	.418

Heath, Michael Thomas "Mike" (continued)

YR	TM/LG	CL	G	TPA	AB	H	2B	3B	HR	TB	BB	IBB	HB	SO	GDP	SH	SF	SB	CS	R	RBI	BA	OBA	SA
	YEAR		95	319	288	65	11	1	8	102	27	4	1	53	6	1	2	6	4	30	36	.226	.292	.354
87	DET/AL		93	296	270	76	16	0	3	116	21	0	3	42	5	1	1	1	5	34	33	.281	.339	.430
88	DET/AL		86	241	219	54	7	2	5	80	18	0	0	32	6	3	0	1	0	24	18	.247	.307	.365
89	DET/AL		122	429	396	104	16	2	10	154	24	2	4	71	18	1	4	7	1	38	43	.263	.308	.389
90	DET/AL		122	398	370	100	18	2	7	143	19	0	4	71	12	2	3	7	6	46	38	.270	.311	.386
91	ATL/NL		49	150	139	29	3	1	1	37	7	5	1	26	4	2	1	0	0	4	12	.209	.250	.266
14 YR TOTALS			**1325**	**4585**	**4212**	**1061**	**173**	**27**	**86**	**1546**	**278**	**24**	**22**	**616**	**121**	**41**	**32**	**54**	**40**	**462**	**469**	**.252**	**.300**	**.367**

Heep, Daniel William "Danny" — bats left — throws left — b.7/3/57 — 1991 positions: 1B 1, OF 1

YR	TM/LG	CL	G	TPA	AB	H	2B	3B	HR	TB	BB	IBB	HB	SO	GDP	SH	SF	SB	CS	R	RBI	BA	OBA	SA
79	HOU/NL		14	17	14	2	0	0	0	2	1	1	0	4	0	0	2	0	0	0	2	.143	.176	.143
80	HOU/NL		33	97	87	24	8	0	0	32	8	0	1	9	0	0	1	0	0	6	6	.276	.340	.368
81	HOU/NL		33	106	96	24	3	0	0	27	10	2	0	11	3	0	1	0	0	6	11	.250	.321	.281
82	HOU/NL		85	222	198	47	14	1	4	75	21	3	1	31	5	0	2	0	2	16	22	.237	.311	.379
83	NY/NL		115	289	253	64	12	0	8	100	29	6	1	40	5	1	5	3	3	36	21	.253	.326	.395
84	NY/NL		99	233	199	46	9	0	0	62	27	3	1	22	9	1	5	3	3	26	42	.231	.319	.312
85	NY/NL		95	305	271	76	17	0	7	114	27	1	1	27	12	0	6	1	2	24	33	.280	.341	.421
86	NY/NL		86	227	195	55	8	0	7	82	30	5	0	31	3	0	1	0	0	6	9	.282	.379	.421
87	SA/TEX	AA	11	52	47	16	1	0	2	23	4	0	1	10	6	1	0	1	0	7	9	.340	.404	.489
	LA/NL		60	107	98	16	4	0	0	20	8	0	1	13	4	0	1	0	1	14	11	.163	.226	.204
88	LA/NL		95	173	149	36	2	0	0	38	22	0	0	13	4	0	2	0	2	14	11	.242	.341	.255
89	BOS/AL		113	355	320	96	17	0	5	128	29	4	1	26	13	0	4	0	1	36	49	.300	.356	.400
90	BOS/AL		41	78	69	12	1	1	0	15	7	0	0	14	4	0	1	1	1	2	10	.174	.256	.217
91	VAN/PCL	AAA	20	75	70	17	6	0	0	23	4	0	0	4	0	0	0	0	0	4	3	.243	.280	.329
	ATL/NL		14	13	12	5	1	0	0	6	1	0	0	4	0	0	0	0	0			.417	.462	.500
13 YR TOTALS			**883**	**2222**	**1961**	**503**	**96**	**6**	**30**	**701**	**220**	**25**	**9**	**242**	**60**	**4**	**28**	**12**	**14**	**208**	**229**	**.257**	**.330**	**.357**

Hemond, Scott Mathew — bats right — throws right — b.11/18/65 — 1991 positions: C 8, 2B 7, DH 4, 3B 2, SS 1

YR	TM/LG	CL	G	TPA	AB	H	2B	3B	HR	TB	BB	IBB	HB	SO	GDP	SH	SF	SB	CS	R	RBI	BA	OBA	SA
86	MAD/MID	A	22	91	85	26	2	0	2	34	5	0	1	19	0	0	1	2	1	9	13	.306	.341	.400
87	MAD/MID	A	90	386	343	99	21	4	8	152	40	1	1	79	10	0	2	27	12	60	52	.289	.363	.443
	HUN/SOU	AA	33	115	110	20	3	1	1	28	4	0	0	30	3	1	0	5	1	10	8	.182	.211	.255
88	HUN/SOU	AA	133	541	482	106	22	4	9	163	48	1	3	114	7	1	7	29	8	51	53	.220	.291	.338
89	HUN/SOU	AA	132	578	490	130	26	6	5	183	62	0	7	77	11	13	6	45	17	89	62	.265	.352	.373
	OAK/AL		4	0	0	0	0	0	0	0	0	0	0	0	0	0	0	0	0	2	0	.000	.000	.000
90	OAK/AL		7	13	13	2	0	0	0	2	0	0	0	5	0	0	0	0	0	2	1	.154	.154	.154
	TAC/PCL	AAA	72	249	218	53	11	0	8	88	24	3	1	52	7	3	3	10	5	32	35	.243	.317	.404
91	TAC/PCL	AAA	92	379	327	89	19	5	3	127	39	1	7	69	11	1	1	11	8	50	31	.272	.361	.388
	OAK/AL		23	24	23	5	0	0	0	5	1	0	0	12	0	0	0	1	2	6	1	.217	.250	.217
3 YR TOTALS			**34**	**37**	**36**	**7**	**0**	**0**	**0**	**7**	**1**	**0**	**0**	**12**	**0**	**0**	**0**	**1**	**2**	**6**	**1**	**.194**	**.216**	**.194**

Henderson, David Lee "Dave" — bats right — throws right — b.7/21/58 — 1991 positions: OF 140, DH 7, 2B 1

YR	TM/LG	CL	G	TPA	AB	H	2B	3B	HR	TB	BB	IBB	HB	SO	GDP	SH	SF	SB	CS	R	RBI	BA	OBA	SA
81	SEA/AL		59	145	126	21	3	0	6	42	16	1	1	24	4	0	1	2	2	17	13	.167	.264	.333
82	SEA/AL		104	362	324	82	17	1	14	143	36	2	0	67	5	1	5	2	5	47	48	.253	.327	.441
83	SEA/AL		137	521	484	130	24	5	17	215	28	3	1	93	5	2	6	9	3	50	55	.269	.306	.444
84	SEA/AL		112	374	350	98	23	0	14	163	19	0	2	56	4	2	1	5	5	42	43	.280	.310	.388
85	SEA/AL		139	556	502	121	28	2	14	195	48	11	1	104	11	1	2	6	1	70	68	.241	.310	.388
86	SEA/AL		103	378	337	93	19	4	14	162	37	4	2	95	5	1	1	1	3	51	44	.276	.350	.481
	BOS/AL		36	54	51	10	3	0	1	16	2	0	0	15	1	0	1	1	0	8	3	.196	.226	.314
	YEAR		139	432	388	103	22	4	15	178	39	4	2	110	6	1	2	2	3	59	47	.265	.335	.459
87	BOS/AL		75	209	184	43	10	0	8	77	22	0	2	48	3	1	1	1	0	30	25	.234	.313	.418
	SF/NL		15	29	21	5	2	0	0	7	8	0	0	8	0	0	0	0	0	2	1	.238	.448	.333
	YEAR		90	238	205	48	12	0	8	84	30	0	2	53	3	1	1	1	0	32	26	.234	.329	.410
88	OAK/AL		146	570	507	154	38	1	24	266	47	1	4	92	14	5	7	2	4	100	94	.304	.363	.525
89	OAK/AL		152	643	579	145	24	3	15	220	54	1	3	131	13	1	6	8	5	77	80	.250	.315	.380
90	OAK/AL		127	494	450	122	28	0	20	210	40	1	1	105	5	1	2	3	6	65	63	.271	.331	.467
91	OAK/AL		150	637	572	158	33	0	25	266	58	3	4	113	9	1	2	3	6	86	85	.263	.327	.442
11 YR TOTALS			**1355**	**4972**	**4487**	**1182**	**252**	**16**	**172**	**1982**	**415**	**18**	**21**	**948**	**79**	**18**	**31**	**48**	**35**	**645**	**622**	**.263**	**.327**	**.442**

Henderson, Rickey Henley — bats right — throws left — b.12/25/58 — 1991 positions: OF 119, DH 10

YR	TM/LG	CL	G	TPA	AB	H	2B	3B	HR	TB	BB	IBB	HB	SO	GDP	SH	SF	SB	CS	R	RBI	BA	OBA	SA
79	OAK/AL		89	398	351	96	13	3	1	118	34	0	2	39	4	8	3	33	11	49	26	.274	.338	.336
80	OAK/AL		158	722	591	179	22	4	9	236	117	7	5	54	6	6	3	100	26	111	53	.303	.420	.399
81	OAK/AL		108	493	423	135	18	7	6	185	64	4	2	68	7	0	4	56	22	89	35	.319	.408	.437
82	OAK/AL		149	656	536	143	24	4	10	205	116	1	2	94	5	0	2	130	42	119	51	.267	.398	.382
83	OAK/AL		145	622	513	150	25	7	9	216	103	8	4	80	11	1	1	108	19	105	48	.292	.414	.421
84	OAK/AL		142	597	502	147	27	4	16	230	86	1	5	81	7	1	3	66	18	113	58	.293	.399	.458
85	FL/FSL	A+	3	11	6	1	0	0	0	1	5	0	0	3	0	0	0	0	0			.167	.545	.167
	NY/AL		143	654	547	172	28	5	24	282	99	1	3	65	8	0	5	80	10	146	72	.314	.419	.516
86	NY/AL		153	701	608	160	31	5	28	285	89	1	3	81	12	0	2	87	18	130	74	.263	.358	.469
87	NY/AL		95	440	358	104	17	3	17	178	80	1	3	52	10	0	0	41	8	78	37	.291	.423	.497
88	NY/AL		140	647	554	169	30	2	6	221	82	1	3	54	2	6	2	93	13	118	50	.305	.394	.399
89	NY/AL		65	293	235	58	13	1	3	82	56	0	5	29	6	0	3	25	8	41	35	.247	.392	.349
	OAK/AL		85	381	306	90	13	2	9	134	70	5	3	52	6	0	3	52	6	72	35	.294	.425	.438

(continued)

Henderson, Rickey Henley (continued)

YR	TM/LG	CL	G	TPA	AB	H	2B	3B	HR	TB	BB	IBB	HB	SO	GDP	SH	SF	SB	CS	R	RBI	BA	OBA	SA
	YEAR		150	674	541	148	26	3	12	216	126	5	3	68	8	0	4	77	14	113	57	.274	.411	.399
90	OAK/AL		136	594	489	159	33	3	28	282	97	2	4	60	13	2	2	65	10	119	61	.325	.439	.577
91	OAK/AL		134	578	470	126	17	1	18	199	98	7	7	73	14	1	3	58	18	105	57	.268	.400	.423
	13 YR TOTALS		1742	7776	6483	1888	311	51	184	2853	1191	40	44	869	104	20	38	994	229	1395	679	.291	.403	.440

Hernandez, Carlos Alberto (Almeida) — bats right — throws right — b.5/24/67 — 1991 positions: C 13, 3B 1

YR	TM/LG	CL	G	TPA	AB	H	2B	3B	HR	TB	BB	IBB	HB	SO	GDP	SH	SF	SB	CS	R	RBI	BA	OBA	SA
85	DOD/GCL	R	22	52	49	12	1	0	0	13	3	0	0	8	4	0	0	0	0	3	6	.245	.288	.265
86	DOD/GCL	R	57	214	205	64	7	0	1	74	5	2	2	18	7	1	1	1	2	19	31	.312	.333	.361
87	BAK/CAL	A+	48	182	162	37	6	1	3	54	14	0	3	23	6	1	2	8	4	22	22	.228	.298	.333
88	BAK/CAL	A+	92	357	333	103	15	2	5	137	16	2	1	39	18	3	4	3	2	37	52	.309	.339	.411
	ALB/PCL	AAA	3	8	8	1	0	0	0	1	0	0	0	0	1	0	0	0	0	0	1	.125	.125	.125
89	SA/TEX	AA	99	393	370	111	16	3	8	157	12	0	7	46	12	1	3	2	3	37	41	.300	.332	.424
	ALB/PCL	AAA	4	16	14	3	0	0	0	3	2	1	0	1	0	0	0	0	0	1	1	.214	.313	.214
90	ALB/PCL	AAA	52	155	143	45	8	1	0	55	8	1	1	25	5	0	3	2	0	11	16	.315	.348	.385
	LA/NL		10	20	20	4	1	0	0	5	0	0	0	2	0	0	0	0	0	2	1	.200	.200	.250
91	ALB/PCL	AAA	95	372	345	119	24	2	8	171	24	1	0	36	10	0	2	5	5	60	44	.345	.387	.496
	LA/NL		15	16	14	3	1	0	0	4	0	0	1	5	2	0	1	1	0	1	1	.214	.250	.286
	2 YR TOTALS		25	36	34	7	2	0	0	9	0	0	1	7	2	0	1	1	0	3	2	.206	.222	.265

Hernandez, Keith — bats left — throws left — b.10/20/53 — 1991 positions: 1B

YR	TM/LG	CL	G	TPA	AB	H	2B	3B	HR	TB	BB	IBB	HB	SO	GDP	SH	SF	SB	CS	R	RBI	BA	OBA	SA
74	STL/NL		14	41	34	10	1	2	0	15	7	0	0	8	1	0	0	0	0	3	2	.294	.415	.441
75	STL/NL		64	207	188	47	8	2	3	68	17	2	0	26	5	0	2	0	1	20	20	.250	.309	.362
76	STL/NL		129	428	374	108	21	5	7	160	49	5	3	53	8	2	0	4	2	54	46	.289	.376	.428
77	STL/NL		161	645	560	163	41	4	15	257	79	11	1	88	17	3	2	7	2	90	91	.291	.379	.459
78	STL/NL		159	633	542	138	32	4	11	211	82	11	2	68	12	1	6	13	5	90	64	.255	.351	.389
79	STL/NL		161	698	610	210	48	11	11	313	80	5	1	78	9	0	7	11	6	116	105	.344	.417	.513
80	STL/NL		159	690	595	191	39	8	16	294	86	4	4	73	14	1	4	14	8	111	99	.321	.408	.494
81	STL/NL		103	444	376	115	27	4	8	174	61	6	4	45	9	0	4	12	5	65	48	.306	.401	.463
82	STL/NL		160	694	579	173	33	6	7	239	100	19	2	67	10	1	12	19	11	79	94	.299	.397	.413
83	STL/NL		55	244	218	62	15	4	3	94	24	5	0	30	2	0	2	1	1	34	26	.284	.352	.431
	NY/NL		95	389	320	98	8	3	9	139	64	9	2	42	5	2	1	8	4	43	37	.306	.424	.434
	YEAR		150	633	538	160	23	7	12	233	88	14	2	72	7	2	3	9	5	77	63	.297	.396	.433
84	NY/NL		154	657	550	171	31	0	15	247	97	12	1	89	9	0	9	2	3	83	94	.311	.409	.449
85	NY/NL		158	682	593	183	34	4	10	255	77	15	2	59	14	0	10	3	3	87	91	.309	.384	.430
86	NY/NL		149	652	551	171	34	1	13	246	94	6	4	69	14	0	3	2	1	94	83	.310	.413	.446
87	NY/NL		154	676	587	170	28	2	18	256	81	4	4	104	15	0	4	0	2	87	89	.290	.377	.436
88	NY/NL		95	384	348	96	16	0	11	145	31	3	1	57	11	0	4	2	1	43	55	.276	.333	.417
89	SL/FSL	A+	4	17	16	6	1	0	0	7	1	0	0	4	0	0	0	0	0	1	1	.375	.412	.438
	NY/NL		75	244	215	50	8	0	4	70	27	3	2	39	4	0	0	0	0	18	19	.233	.324	.326
90	IND/GCL	R	5	12	11	5	1	0	1	9	1	0	0	2	0	0	0	0	3	3	2	.455	.500	.818
	CLE/AL		43	145	130	26	2	0	1	31	14	3	1	17	2	0	0	0	0	3	2	.200	.283	.238
	17 YR TOTALS		2088	8553	7370	2182	426	60	162	3214	1070	127	32	1012	161	10	71	98	63	1124	1071	.296	.384	.436

Hernandez, Jose (Figueroa) — bats right — throws right — b.7/14/69 — 1991 positions: SS 44, 3B 1

YR	TM/LG	CL	G	TPA	AB	H	2B	3B	HR	TB	BB	IBB	HB	SO	GDP	SH	SF	SB	CS	R	RBI	BA	OBA	SA
87	RAN/GCL	R	24	63	52	9	1	1	0	12	9	0	1	25	1	1	0	2	1	5	2	.173	.306	.231
88	RAN/GCL	R	55	175	162	26	7	1	1	38	12	0	0	36	5	0	1	4	1	19	13	.160	.217	.235
89	GAS/SAL	A	91	256	215	47	7	6	1	69	33	0	0	67	3	8	0	9	2	35	13	.219	.323	.321
90	CHA/FSL	A+	121	455	388	99	14	7	1	130	50	4	4	122	8	11	2	11	8	43	44	.255	.345	.335
91	OC/AMA	AAA	14	54	46	14	1	1	1	20	4	0	0	10	1	3	1	0	0	6	3	.304	.353	.435
	TUL/TEX	AA	91	337	301	72	17	4	1	100	26	0	1	75	6	5	4	4	3	36	20	.239	.298	.332
	TEX/AL		45	107	98	18	2	1	0	22	3	0	1	31	2	0	0	0	0	8	4	.184	.208	.224

Herr, Thomas Mitchell "Tom" — bats both — throws right — b.4/4/56 — 1991 positions: 2B 72, 3B 3, OF 1

YR	TM/LG	CL	G	TPA	AB	H	2B	3B	HR	TB	BB	IBB	HB	SO	GDP	SH	SF	SB	CS	R	RBI	BA	OBA	SA
79	STL/NL		14	12	10	2	0	0	0	2	2	0	0	2	0	0	0	1	0	4	1	.200	.333	.200
80	STL/NL		76	242	222	55	12	5	0	77	16	5	1	21	8	1	2	9	2	29	15	.248	.299	.347
81	STL/NL		103	462	411	110	14	9	0	142	39	3	1	30	9	6	5	23	7	50	46	.268	.329	.345
82	STL/NL		135	560	493	131	19	4	0	158	57	2	2	56	5	3	5	25	12	83	36	.266	.341	.320
83	STL/NL		89	368	313	101	14	4	2	129	43	2	1	27	7	8	3	6	6	43	31	.323	.403	.412
84	STL/NL		145	622	558	154	23	2	4	193	49	2	2	56	11	10	3	13	7	67	49	.276	.335	.346
85	STL/NL		159	696	596	180	38	3	8	248	80	5	5	55	6	5	13	31	3	97	110	.302	.379	.416
86	STL/NL		152	647	559	141	30	4	2	185	73	10	5	75	8	6	4	22	8	48	61	.252	.342	.331
87	STL/NL		141	597	510	134	29	2	2	169	68	3	5	62	12	4	12	19	4	73	83	.263	.346	.331
88	STL/NL		15	63	50	13	0	0	1	16	11	3	0	4	1	2	0	1	0	4	3	.260	.393	.320
	MIN/AL		86	345	304	80	16	0	1	99	40	1	0	47	9	1	0	10	3	42	21	.263	.346	.326
	YEAR		101	408	354	93	16	0	2	115	51	4	1	51	10	3	0	13	3	46	24	.263	.349	.326
89	PHI/NL		151	626	561	161	25	6	2	204	54	2	2	63	9	6	2	10	7	65	37	.287	.352	.364
90	PHI/NL		119	493	447	118	21	3	4	157	36	2	6	47	10	6	2	7	1	39	50	.264	.320	.351
	NY/NL		27	114	100	25	5	0	3	33	14	0	0	11	1	0	1	2	1	9	10	.250	.342	.330
	YEAR		146	607	547	143	26	3	5	190	50	4	2	58	11	6	2	7	1	48	60	.261	.342	.330
91	NY/NL		70	191	155	30	7	1	1	40	32	1	0	21	1	2	2	7	1	17	14	.194	.328	.258
	SF/NL		32	73	60	15	1	1	0	18	13	1	0	7	3	0	0	2	0	6	7	.250	.384	.300

Herr, Thomas Mitchell "Tom" (continued)

YR	TM/LG	CL	G	TPA	AB	H	2B	3B	HR	TB	BB	IBB	HB	SO	GDP	SH	SF	SB	CS	R	RBI	BA	OBA	SA
YEAR			102	264	215	45	8	1	1	58	45	5	0	28	4	2	2	9		23	21	.209	.344	.270
13 YR TOTALS			**1514**	**6111**	**5349**	**1450**	**254**	**41**	**28**	**1870**	**627**	**47**	**22**	**584**	**100**	**60**	**53**	**188**	**64**	**676**	**574**	**.271**	**.347**	**.350**

Hiatt, Philip Farrell "Phil" — bats right — throws right — b.5/1/69 — 1991 positions: 3B System KC/AL

YR	TM/LG	CL	G	TPA	AB	H	2B	3B	HR	TB	BB	IBB	HB	SO	GDP	SH	SF	SB	CS	R	RBI	BA	OBA	SA
90	EUG/NWL	A–	73	312	289	85	18	5	2	119	17	1	1	69	1	1	4	15	4	33	44	.294	.331	.412
91	BC/FSL	A+	81	343	315	94	21	6	5	142	22	4	3	70	8	1	2	28	14	41	33	.298	.348	.451
	MEM/SOU	AA	56	224	206	47	7	1	6	74	9	1	3	63	3	0	6	6	1	29	33	.228	.263	.359

Hill, Donald Earl "Donnie" — bats both — throws right — b.11/12/60 — 1991 positions: 2B 39, SS 29, 1B 3

YR	TM/LG	CL	G	TPA	AB	H	2B	3B	HR	TB	BB	IBB	HB	SO	GDP	SH	SF	SB	CS	R	RBI	BA	OBA	SA
83	OAK/AL		53	169	158	42	7	0	2	55	4	0	0	21	3	5	2	1	1	20	15	.266	.280	.348
84	TAC/PCL	AAA	42	163	141	46	12	3	2	70	18	0	1	15	2	1	2	7	2	28	24	.326	.401	.496
	OAK/AL		73	185	174	40	6	0	2	52	5	0	0	12	3	4	2	1	1	21	16	.230	.249	.299
85	OAK/AL		123	436	393	112	13	2	3	138	23	2	3	33	7	16	4	9	4	45	48	.285	.321	.351
86	OAK/AL		108	366	339	96	16	2	4	128	23	1	0	38	4	0	5	2	5	37	29	.283	.329	.378
87	HAW/PCL	AAA	7	25	23	9	2	0	2	17	2	0	0	1	0	0	0	0	0	5	7	.391	.440	.739
	CHI/AL		111	449	410	98	14	6	9	151	30	1	1	35	11	4	4	1	0	57	46	.239	.290	.368
88	VAN/PCL	AAA	7	31	26	9	4	0	0	13	3	1	1	5	1	0	1	1	0	5	7	.346	.419	.500
	CHI/AL		83	253	221	48	6	1	2	62	26	1	0	32	3	3	3	3	1	17	20	.217	.296	.281
89	TAC/PCL	AAA	58	218	180	47	7	2	4	70	33	1	2	18	0	1	2	4	2	26	23	.261	.378	.389
90	CAL/AL		103	392	352	93	18	2	3	124	29	1	1	27	10	6	1	0	0	36	32	.264	.319	.352
91	CAL/AL		77	242	209	50	8	1	1	63	30	1	1	21	3	0	1	0	0	36	20	.239	.335	.301
8 YR TOTALS			**731**	**2492**	**2256**	**579**	**88**	**14**	**26**	**773**	**170**	**7**	**2**	**219**	**47**	**45**	**19**	**22**	**11**	**269**	**226**	**.257**	**.307**	**.343**

Hill, Glenallen — bats right — throws right — b.3/22/65 — 1991 positions: OF 33, DH 17

YR	TM/LG	CL	G	TPA	AB	H	2B	3B	HR	TB	BB	IBB	HB	SO	GDP	SH	SF	SB	CS	R	RBI	BA	OBA	SA
83	MH/PIO	R+	46	153	133	34	3	4	6	63	17	0	1	49	3	2	0	4	4	26	27	.256	.344	.474
84	FLO/SAL	A	129	512	440	105	19	5	16	182	63	3	3	150	1	0	6	30	15	75	64	.239	.334	.414
85	KIN/CAR	A+	131	530	466	98	13	0	20	171	57	0	1	211	7	2	4	42	15	57	56	.210	.295	.367
86	KNO/SOU	AA	141	623	570	159	23	6	31	287	39	3	1	153	10	0	13	18	18	87	96	.279	.319	.504
87	SYR/INT	AAA	137	568	536	126	25	6	16	211	25	1	1	152	10	1	5	22	9	65	77	.235	.268	.394
88	SYR/INT	AAA	51	192	172	40	7	0	4	59	15	3	2	59	2	0	3	3	2	21	19	.233	.297	.343
	KNO/SOU	AA	79	302	269	71	13	2	12	124	28	1	2	75	4	3	0	10	7	86	72	.264	.334	.461
89	SYR/INT	AAA	125	529	483	155	31	15	21	279	34	0	5	107	4	3	4	21	7	37	38	.321	.369	.578
	TOR/AL		19	55	52	15	0	0	1	18	3	0	0	12	0	0	0	2	1	4	7	.288	.327	.346
90	TOR/AL		84	278	260	60	11	3	12	113	18	0	0	62	6	0	0	8	3	47	32	.231	.281	.435
91	TOR/AL		35	108	99	25	5	2	3	43	7	0	0	24	0	1	2	1	1	15	14	.253	.296	.434
	CLE/AL		37	140	122	32	3	0	5	50	16	0	0	54	7	1	1	4	4	15	11	.262	.345	.410
	YEAR		72	248	221	57	8	2	8	93	23	0	0	78	7	1	3	5	5	29	25	.258	.324	.421
3 YR TOTALS			**175**	**581**	**533**	**132**	**19**	**5**	**21**	**224**	**44**	**0**	**0**	**128**	**12**	**1**	**3**	**16**	**8**	**80**	**64**	**.248**	**.303**	**.420**

Hoiles, Christopher Allen "Chris" — bats right — throws right — b.3/20/65 — 1991 positions: C 89, DH 13, 1B 2

YR	TM/LG	CL	G	TPA	AB	H	2B	3B	HR	TB	BB	IBB	HB	SO	GDP	SH	SF	SB	CS	R	RBI	BA	OBA	SA
86	BRI/APP	R+	68	286	253	81	19	2	13	143	30	3	1	20	9	0	2	10	1	42	57	.320	.392	.565
87	GF/EAS	AA	108	425	380	105	12	0	13	156	35	4	3	37	10	4	3	1	5	47	53	.276	.340	.411
88	TOL/INT	AAA	22	73	69	11	1	0	2	18	2	0	2	12	4	0	0	1	0	4	6	.159	.205	.261
	GF/EAS	AA	103	423	360	102	21	3	17	180	50	4	7	57	5	3	3	4	3	67	73	.283	.379	.500
89	ROC/INT	AAA	96	363	322	79	19	1	10	130	31	1	4	58	10	2	4	1	2	41	51	.245	.316	.404
	BAL/AL		6	10	9	1	1	0	0	2	1	0	0	3	0	0	0	0	0	0	1	.111	.200	.222
90	ROC/INT	AAA	74	294	247	86	20	1	18	162	44	4	1	48	7	1	1	0	0	52	56	.348	.447	.656
	BAL/AL		23	68	63	12	3	0	1	18	5	1	0	12	0	0	0	0	0	7	6	.190	.250	.286
91	BAL/AL		107	372	341	83	15	0	11	131	29	1	1	61	11	0	1	0	2	36	31	.243	.304	.384
3 YR TOTALS			**136**	**450**	**413**	**96**	**19**	**0**	**12**	**151**	**35**	**2**	**1**	**76**	**11**	**0**	**1**	**0**	**2**	**43**	**38**	**.232**	**.293**	**.366**

Hollins, David Michaels "Dave" — bats both — throws right — b.5/25/66 — 1991 positions: 3B 36, 1B 6

YR	TM/LG	CL	G	TPA	AB	H	2B	3B	HR	TB	BB	IBB	HB	SO	GDP	SH	SF	SB	CS	R	RBI	BA	OBA	SA
87	SPO/NWL	A–	75	340	278	86	14	4	2	114	53	7	2	36	3	3	4	20	5	52	44	.309	.418	.410
88	RIV/CAL	A+	139	608	516	157	32	1	9	218	82	2	1	67	15	0	9	13	11	90	92	.304	.395	.422
89	WIC/TEX	AA	131	538	459	126	29	4	9	190	63	4	1	88	4	1	10	8	3	69	79	.275	.361	.414
90	PHI/NL		72	127	114	21	0	0	5	36	10	3	1	28	1	0	2	0	0	14	15	.184	.252	.316
91	SCR/INT	AAA	72	278	229	61	11	6	6	108	43	3	4	42	7	0	2	1	1	37	35	.266	.388	.472
	PHI/NL		56	172	151	45	10	2	6	77	17	1	0	26	2	0	3	1	1	18	21	.298	.378	.510
2 YR TOTALS			**128**	**299**	**265**	**66**	**10**	**2**	**11**	**113**	**27**	**4**	**4**	**54**	**3**	**0**	**3**	**1**	**1**	**32**	**36**	**.249**	**.324**	**.426**

Horn, Samuel Lee "Sam" — bats left — throws left — b.11/2/63 — 1991 positions: DH 102

YR	TM/LG	CL	G	TPA	AB	H	2B	3B	HR	TB	BB	IBB	HB	SO	GDP	SH	SF	SB	CS	R	RBI	BA	OBA	SA
84	WIN/CAR	A+	127	487	403	126	22	3	21	217	76	5	4	107	3	1	3	5	4	67	89	.313	.424	.538
85	NB/EAS	AA	134	535	457	129	32	0	11	194	64	14	4	107	5	1	9	4	6	64	82	.282	.369	.425
86	PAW/INT	AAA	20	82	77	15	2	0	3	26	5	1	0	23	1	0	0	1	0	8	14	.195	.244	.338
	NB/EAS	AA	100	400	345	85	13	0	8	122	49	4	1	80	6	1	5	1	0	41	46	.246	.338	.354
87	PAW/INT	AAA	94	373	333	107	19	0	30	216	33	3	5	88	9	0	2	0	0	57	84	.321	.389	.649
	BOS/AL		46	177	158	44	7	0	14	93	17	0	0	55	2	0	2	0	0	31	34	.278	.356	.589
88	BOS/AL		24	73	61	9	0	0	2	15	11	1	0	20	1	0	1	0	0	4	8	.148	.274	.246
	PAW/INT	AAA	83	324	279	65	10	0	10	105	44	10	0	82	9	0	1	0	0	33	31	.233	.333	.376

(continued)

Horn, Samuel Lee "Sam" (continued)

YR	TM/LG	CL	G	TPA	AB	H	2B	3B	HR	TB	BB	IBB	HB	SO	GDP	SH	SF	SB	CS	R	RBI	BA	OBA	SA
89	PAW/INT	AAA	51	187	164	38	9	1	8	73	20	2	0	46	4	0	3	0	0	15	27	.232	.310	.445
	BOS/AL		33	62	54	8	2	0	0	10	8	1	0	16	4	0	0	0	0	1	4	.148	.258	.185
90	HAG/EAS	AA	7	29	23	6	2	0	1	11	6	1	0	5	0	0	0	0	1	2	3	.261	.414	.478
	ROC/INT	AAA	17	67	58	24	4	0	9	55	9	1	0	13	2	0	0	0	1	16	26	.414	.493	.948
	BAL/AL		79	280	246	61	13	0	14	116	32	1	0	62	8	0	2	0	0	30	45	.248	.332	.472
91	BAL/AL		121	362	317	74	16	0	23	159	41	3	3	99	10	0	1	0	0	45	61	.233	.326	.502
5 YR TOTALS			**303**	**954**	**836**	**196**	**38**	**0**	**53**	**393**	**109**	**9**	**5**	**252**	**28**	**0**	**4**	**0**	**1**	**111**	**152**	**.234**	**.325**	**.470**

Hosey, Steven Bernard "Steve" — bats right — throws right — b.4/2/69 — 1991 positions: OF System SF/NL

YR	TM/LG	CL	G	TPA	AB	H	2B	3B	HR	TB	BB	IBB	HB	SO	GDP	SH	SF	SB	CS	R	RBI	BA	OBA	SA
89	EVE/NWL	A–	73	327	288	83	14	3	13	142	27	2	10	84	3	0	2	15	3	44	59	.288	.367	.493
90	SJ/CAL	A+	139	560	479	111	13	6	16	184	71	2	5	139	7	1	4	16	17	85	78	.232	.335	.384
91	SHR/TEX	AA	126	480	409	120	21	5	17	202	56	5	6	87	7	5	4	24	11	79	74	.293	.383	.494

Housie, Wayne Tyrone — bats both — throws right — b.5/20/65 — 1991 positions: OF 4, DH 2

YR	TM/LG	CL	G	TPA	AB	H	2B	3B	HR	TB	BB	IBB	HB	SO	GDP	SH	SF	SB	CS	R	RBI	BA	OBA	SA
86	GAS/SAL	A	90	388	336	87	10	6	2	115	43	0	4	85	4	4	1	38	13	55	29	.259	.349	.342
87	LAK/FSL	A+	125	512	458	118	12	7	1	147	39	2	3	74	7	6	6	26	11	58	45	.258	.316	.321
88	GF/EAS	AA	63	240	202	38	4	2	1	49	28	1	3	34	2	5	2	9	5	26	16	.188	.294	.243
	LAK/FSL	A+	55	231	212	57	11	3	0	74	13	0	3	40	1	2	1	24	6	31	23	.269	.319	.349
89	LON/EAS	AA	127	496	434	103	17	2	5	139	52	3	4	90	5	3	3	23	14	56	28	.237	.323	.320
90	SAL/CAL	AA	92	401	367	99	20	6	5	146	22	1	4	72	5	5	3	27	11	51	49	.270	.316	.398
	NB/EAS	AA	30	125	113	31	8	3	1	48	6	0	1	33	0	5	0	7	2	13	12	.274	.317	.425
91	NB/EAS	AA	113	508	444	123	24	2	6	169	55	2	3	86	5	6	0	43	14	58	26	.277	.361	.381
	PAW/INT	AAA	21	86	79	26	9	0	2	41	6	1	0	20	0	0	0	2	2	14	8	.329	.384	.519
	BOS/AL		11	10	8	2	1	0	0	3	1	0	0	3	1	0	1	0	1	2	0	.250	.333	.375

Howard, Christopher Hugh "Chris" — bats right — throws right — b.2/27/66 — 1991 positions: C 9

YR	TM/LG	CL	G	TPA	AB	H	2B	3B	HR	TB	BB	IBB	HB	SO	GDP	SH	SF	SB	CS	R	RBI	BA	OBA	SA
88	BEL/NWL	A–	2	10	9	3	0	0	1	6	1	0	0	2	0	0	0	0	0	3	3	.333	.400	.667
	WAU/MID	A	61	209	187	45	10	1	7	78	18	0	3	60	4	0	1	0	0	20	20	.241	.316	.417
89	WAU/MID	A	36	140	125	30	8	0	4	50	13	1	1	35	2	0	1	1	3	13	32	.240	.314	.400
	WIL/EAS	AA	86	331	296	75	13	0	9	115	28	0	5	79	10	2	0	0	1	30	36	.253	.328	.389
90	WIL/EAS	AA	118	449	401	95	19	1	5	131	37	1	3	91	16	4	4	3	1	48	49	.237	.303	.327
91	CAL/PCL	AAA	82	315	293	72	12	1	8	110	16	1	2	56	10	1	3	1	1	32	36	.246	.288	.375
	SEA/AL		9	7	6	1	1	0	0	2	1	0	0	2	0	0	0	0	0	1	0	.167	.286	.333

Howard, David Wayne — bats both — throws right — b.2/26/67 — 1991 positions: SS 63, 2B 26, 3B 1, OF 1, DH 1

YR	TM/LG	CL	G	TPA	AB	H	2B	3B	HR	TB	BB	IBB	HB	SO	GDP	SH	SF	SB	CS	R	RBI	BA	OBA	SA
87	FM/FSL	A+	89	326	289	56	9	4	1	76	30	0	0	68	3	7	0	11	10	26	19	.194	.270	.263
88	APP/MID	A	110	402	368	82	9	4	1	102	25	0	2	80	3	4	3	7	5	48	22	.223	.274	.277
89	BC/FSL	A+	83	296	267	63	7	3	3	85	23	1	1	44	1	3	2	12	2	36	30	.236	.297	.318
90	MEM/SOU	AA	116	440	384	96	10	4	5	129	39	0	1	73	8	10	6	15	4	41	44	.250	.316	.336
91	OMA/AMA	AAA	14	51	41	5	0	0	0	5	7	0	1	11	0	2	0	1	1	20	17	.122	.265	.122
	KC/AL		94	264	236	51	7	0	1	61	16	0	0	45	1	9	2	3	2	20	17	.216	.267	.258

Howard, Thomas Sylvester — bats both — throws right — b.12/11/64 — 1991 positions: OF 86

YR	TM/LG	CL	G	TPA	AB	H	2B	3B	HR	TB	BB	IBB	HB	SO	GDP	SH	SF	SB	CS	R	RBI	BA	OBA	SA
86	SPO/NWL	A–	13	59	55	23	3	3	2	38	3	0	1	9	0	0	0	2	1	16	17	.418	.458	.691
	REN/CAL	A+	61	261	223	57	7	3	10	100	34	1	1	49	3	1	3	10	2	35	39	.256	.350	.448
87	WIC/TEX	AA	113	447	401	133	27	4	14	210	36	9	1	72	8	8	1	26	8	72	60	.332	.387	.524
88	LV/PCL	AAA	44	181	167	42	9	1	0	53	12	2	1	31	5	1	0	3	4	29	15	.251	.306	.317
	WIC/TEX	AA	29	116	103	31	9	2	0	44	13	0	0	6	3	0	0	6	3	15	16	.301	.379	.427
89	LV/PCL	AAA	80	337	303	91	18	3	3	124	30	1	0	56	6	1	1	22	11	45	31	.300	.362	.409
90	SD/NL		20	45	44	12	2	0	0	14	0	0	1	11	1	1	0	0	1	4	0	.273	.273	.318
	LV/PCL	AAA	89	393	341	112	26	8	5	169	44	1	0	63	5	4	4	27	5	58	51	.328	.401	.496
91	LV/PCL	AAA	25	107	94	29	3	1	2	40	10	0	1	16	1	1	2	11	5	22	16	.309	.368	.426
	SD/NL		106	309	281	70	12	3	4	100	24	4	1	57	4	1	1	10	8	30	22	.249	.309	.356
2 YR TOTALS			**126**	**354**	**325**	**82**	**14**	**3**	**4**	**114**	**24**	**4**	**1**	**68**	**5**	**3**	**1**	**10**	**8**	**34**	**22**	**.252**	**.305**	**.351**

Howell, Jack Robert — bats left — throws right — b.8/18/61 — 1991 positions: 3B 62, 2B 12

YR	TM/LG	CL	G	TPA	AB	H	2B	3B	HR	TB	BB	IBB	HB	SO	GDP	SH	SF	SB	CS	R	RBI	BA	OBA	SA
84	RED/CAL	A+	135	509	451	111	21	5	5	157	44	3	3	95	9	5	6	12	4	62	64	.246	.313	.348
85	EDM/PCL	AAA	79	336	284	106	22	3	13	173	52	3	0	57	8	0	0	3	2	55	48	.373	.470	.609
	CAL/AL		43	158	137	27	4	0	5	46	16	2	0	33	1	4	1	1	1	19	18	.197	.279	.336
86	EDM/PCL	AAA	44	196	156	56	17	3	3	88	38	2	0	29	3	0	2	2	0	39	28	.359	.490	.564
	CAL/AL		63	175	151	41	14	2	4	71	19	0	2	28	1	3	2	2	0	26	21	.272	.349	.470
87	CAL/AL		138	511	449	110	18	5	23	207	57	4	2	118	7	1	2	4	3	64	64	.245	.331	.461
88	CAL/AL		154	558	500	127	32	2	16	211	46	8	6	130	4	4	4	2	6	59	63	.254	.323	.422
89	CAL/AL		144	533	474	108	19	4	20	195	52	9	3	125	3	1	3	0	3	56	52	.228	.308	.411
90	EDM/PCL	AAA	20	83	75	25	7	1	2	40	7	0	0	13	1	0	1	3	0	14	15	.333	.386	.533
	CAL/AL		105	366	316	72	19	1	8	117	46	1	1	61	1	1	3	2	0	35	33	.228	.326	.370
91	CAL/AL		32	92	81	17	2	1	2	25	11	0	0	11	1	0	0	0	0	11	7	.210	.304	.309
	SD/NL		58	179	160	33	3	1	6	56	18	1	0	33	1	0	1	0	0	24	16	.206	.287	.350

Howell, Jack Robert (continued)

YR	TM/LG	CL	G	TPA	AB	H	2B	3B	HR	TB	BB	IBB	HB	SO	GDP	SH	SF	SB	CS	R	RBI	BA	OBA	SA
	YEAR		90	271	241	50	5	1	8	81	29	1	0	44	2	1	0	1	1	35	23	.207	.293	.336
7 YR TOTALS			737	2572	2268	535	111	15	84	928	265	29	12	539	30	17	10	13	14	294	274	.236	.318	.409

Howitt, Dann Paul John — bats left — throws right — b.2/13/64 — 1991 positions: OF 20, 1B 1

YR	TM/LG	CL	G	TPA	AB	H	2B	3B	HR	TB	BB	IBB	HB	SO	GDP	SH	SF	SB	CS	R	RBI	BA	OBA	SA
86	MED/NWL	A–	66	260	208	66	9	2	6	97	49	3	1	37	7	1	1	5	1	36	37	.317	.448	.466
87	MOD/CAL	A+	109	405	336	70	11	2	8	109	59	1	4	110	8	3	3	7	9	44	42	.208	.331	.324
88	MOD/CAL	A+	132	565	480	121	20	2	18	199	81	3	2	106	9	0	2	11	5	75	86	.252	.361	.415
	TAC/PCL	AAA	4	15	15	2	1	0	0	3	0	0	0	4	0	0	0	0	0	1	0	.133	.133	.200
89	HUN/SOU	AA	138	588	509	143	28	2	26	253	68	7	3	107	6	2	6	2	1	78	111	.281	.365	.497
	OAK/AL		3	3	3	0	0	0	0	0	0	0	0	2	0	0	0	0	0	0	0	.000	.000	.000
90	TAC/PCL	AAA	118	481	437	116	30	1	11	181	38	3	2	95	16	0	4	4	4	58	69	.265	.324	.414
	OAK/AL		14	25	22	3	0	1	0	5	3	0	0	12	0	0	0	0	0	3	1	.136	.240	.227
91	TAC/PCL	AAA	122	506	449	120	28	6	14	202	49	2	2	92	14	1	5	5	2	58	73	.267	.339	.450
	OAK/AL		21	44	42	7	1	0	1	11	1	0	0	12	1	0	1	0	0	5	3	.167	.182	.262
3 YR TOTALS			38	72	67	10	1	1	1	16	4	0	0	26	1	0	1	0	0	8	4	.149	.194	.239

Hrbek, Kent Alan — bats left — throws right — b.5/21/60 — 1991 positions: 1B 128

YR	TM/LG	CL	G	TPA	AB	H	2B	3B	HR	TB	BB	IBB	HB	SO	GDP	SH	SF	SB	CS	R	RBI	BA	OBA	SA
81	MIN/AL		24	73	67	16	5	0	1	24	5	1	1	9	0	0	0	0	0	5	7	.239	.301	.358
82	MIN/AL		140	591	532	160	21	4	23	258	54	12	1	80	17	1	4	3	1	82	92	.301	.363	.485
83	MIN/AL		141	582	515	153	41	5	16	252	57	5	3	71	12	0	7	4	6	75	84	.297	.366	.489
84	MIN/AL		149	635	559	174	31	3	27	292	65	15	4	87	17	1	6	1	1	80	107	.311	.383	.522
85	MIN/AL		158	666	593	165	31	2	21	263	67	12	2	87	15	0	7	2	2	78	93	.278	.351	.444
86	MIN/AL		149	634	550	147	27	1	29	263	71	9	6	81	15	0	7	2	2	85	91	.267	.353	.478
87	MIN/AL		143	566	477	136	20	1	34	260	84	12	2	60	13	0	5	5	2	85	90	.285	.389	.545
88	MIN/AL		143	586	510	159	31	0	25	265	67	7	2	54	9	2	7	0	3	75	76	.312	.387	.520
89	MIN/AL		109	434	375	102	17	0	25	194	53	4	1	35	6	1	4	3	0	59	84	.272	.360	.517
90	MIN/AL		143	578	492	141	26	0	22	233	69	8	7	45	17	3	2	5	4	61	79	.287	.377	.474
91	MIN/AL		132	534	462	131	20	1	20	213	67	4	0	48	15	3	2	4	4	72	89	.284	.373	.461
11 YR TOTALS			1431	5879	5132	1484	270	17	243	2517	659	89	24	657	133	10	54	28	22	757	892	.289	.369	.490

Hudler, Rex Allen — bats right — throws right — b.9/2/60 — 1991 positions: OF 58, 1B 12, 2B 5

YR	TM/LG	CL	G	TPA	AB	H	2B	3B	HR	TB	BB	IBB	HB	SO	GDP	SH	SF	SB	CS	R	RBI	BA	OBA	SA
84	COL/INT	AAA	114	416	394	115	26	1	1	146	16	1	3	61	1	2	1	11	7	49	35	.292	.324	.371
	NY/AL		9	9	7	1	1	0	0	2	1	0	1	5	0	0	0	0	0	2	0	.143	.333	.286
85	COL/INT	AAA	106	404	380	95	13	4	3	125	17	1	2	51	9	5	0	29	7	62	18	.250	.286	.329
	NY/AL		20	57	51	8	0	1	0	10	1	0	0	9	0	5	0	0	1	4	1	.157	.173	.196
86	BAL/AL		14	1	1	0	0	0	0	0	0	0	0	0	0	0	0	1	0	1	0	.000	.000	.000
	ROC/INT	AAA	77	238	219	57	12	3	2	81	16	1	0	32	2	3	0	12	4	29	13	.260	.311	.370
87	ROC/INT	AAA	31	110	106	27	5	1	5	49	2	0	1	15	2	1	0	9	2	22	10	.255	.275	.462
88	IND/AMA	AAA	67	248	234	71	11	3	7	109	10	0	0	35	2	1	3	14	6	36	25	.303	.328	.466
	MON/NL		77	229	216	59	14	2	4	89	10	6	0	34	2	1	2	29	7	38	14	.273	.303	.412
89	MON/NL		92	162	155	38	7	0	6	63	6	2	1	23	2	0	0	15	4	21	13	.245	.278	.406
90	MON/NL		4	3	3	1	0	0	0	1	0	0	0	1	0	0	0	1	0	1	0	.333	.333	.333
	STL/NL		89	234	217	61	11	2	7	97	12	1	2	31	3	2	1	18	10	30	22	.281	.323	.447
	YEAR		93	237	220	62	11	2	7	98	12	1	2	32	3	2	1	18	10	31	22	.282	.323	.445
91	STL/NL		101	221	207	47	10	2	1	64	10	1	2	29	1	2	2	12	8	21	15	.227	.260	.309
7 YR TOTALS			406	916	857	215	43	7	18	326	40	10	4	132	8	10	5	75	30	118	65	.251	.286	.380

Huff, Michael Kale "Mike" — bats right — throws right — b.8/11/63 — 1991 positions: OF 96, 2B 2, DH 2

YR	TM/LG	CL	G	TPA	AB	H	2B	3B	HR	TB	BB	IBB	HB	SO	GDP	SH	SF	SB	CS	R	RBI	BA	OBA	SA
85	GF/PIO	R+	70	310	247	78	6	6	0	96	56	0	4	44	3	2	1	28	6	70	35	.316	.448	.389
86	VB/FSL	A+	113	439	362	106	6	8	2	134	67	1	5	67	10	3	2	28	13	73	32	.293	.408	.370
87	SA/TEX	AA	31	149	135	42	4	1	3	58	9	0	3	21	3	2	0	2	2	23	18	.311	.367	.430
88	SA/TEX	AA	102	443	395	120	18	10	2	164	37	2	5	55	3	5	1	34	10	68	40	.304	.370	.415
	ALB/PCL	AAA	2	4	4	1	1	0	0	2	0	0	0	0	0	0	0	0	0	0	0	.250	.250	.500
89	LA/NL		12	30	25	5	1	0	1	9	3	0	1	6	0	1	0	1	1	4	2	.200	.310	.360
	ALB/PCL	AAA	115	520	471	150	29	6	10	223	38	0	2	75	6	4	4	32	10	75	78	.318	.368	.473
90	ALB/PCL	AAA	138	575	474	154	28	11	7	225	82	5	3	68	11	6	10	27	13	99	84	.325	.420	.475
91	CLE/AL		51	179	146	35	6	1	2	49	25	0	4	30	2	3	1	11	2	28	10	.240	.364	.336
	CHI/AL		51	115	97	26	4	1	1	35	12	2	2	18	5	3	1	3	2	14	15	.268	.357	.361
	YEAR		102	294	243	61	10	2	3	84	37	2	6	48	7	6	2	14	4	42	25	.251	.361	.346
2 YR TOTALS			114	324	268	66	11	2	4	93	40	2	7	54	7	7	2	14	5	46	27	.246	.356	.347

Hulett, Timothy Craig "Tim" — bats right — throws right — b.1/12/60 — 1991 positions: 3B 39, 2B 26, DH 15, SS 1

YR	TM/LG	CL	G	TPA	AB	H	2B	3B	HR	TB	BB	IBB	HB	SO	GDP	SH	SF	SB	CS	R	RBI	BA	OBA	SA
80	GF/EAS		6	26	23	4	0	0	0	4	3	0	0	5	0	0	0	0	1	2	0	.174	.269	.174
	IOW/AMA	AAA	3	8	8	2	0	0	0	2	0	0	0	0	0	0	0	0	0	1	0	.250	.250	.250
81	GF/EAS	AA	134	511	437	99	27	1	10	158	66	1	6	87	4	1	1	4	0	59	55	.227	.329	.362
82	GF/EAS	AA	140	641	536	145	28	5	22	249	95	1	3	135	10	1	6	3	8	113	87	.271	.380	.465
83	DEN/AMA	AAA	133	551	477	130	19	4	21	220	61	3	1	64	20	2	9	5	3	77	88	.273	.352	.461
	CHI/AL		6	5	5	1	0	0	0	1	0	0	0	4	0	0	0	0	0	0	0	.200	.200	.200
84	CHI/AL		8	8	7	0	0	0	0	0	0	0	0	4	0	1	0	0	0	1	0	.000	.125	.000
	DEN/AMA	AAA	139	554	475	125	32	6	16	217	67	3	0	88	5	3	9	3	4	72	80	.263	.348	.457

(continued)

Hulett, Timothy Craig "Tim" (continued)

YR	TM/LG	CL	G	TPA	AB	H	2B	3B	HR	TB	BB	IBB	HB	SO	GDP	SH	SF	SB	CS	R	RBI	BA	OBA	SA
85	CHI/AL		141	436	395	106	19	4	5	148	30	1	4	81	8	4	3	6	4	52	37	.268	.324	.375
86	CHI/AL		150	552	520	120	16	5	17	197	21	0	1	91	11	6	4	4	1	53	44	.231	.260	.379
87	CHI/AL		68	257	240	52	10	0	7	83	10	1	0	41	6	5	2	0	2	20	28	.217	.246	.346
	HAW/PCL	AAA	42	170	157	37	5	2	1	49	9	0	0	28	7	1	3	4	1	13	24	.236	.272	.312
88	IND/AMA	AAA	126	471	427	100	29	2	7	154	34	1	0	106	11	1	9	2	0	36	59	.234	.285	.361
89	ROC/INT	AAA	122	514	461	129	32	12	3	194	38	1	9	81	9	1	5	2	5	61	50	.280	.343	.421
	BAL/AL		33	109	97	27	5	0	3	41	10	0	0	17	3	1	1	0	0	12	18	.278	.343	.423
90	ROC/INT	AAA	14	55	43	16	2	1	2	26	11	0	0	7	2	1	0	0	1	10	4	.372	.500	.605
	BAL/AL		53	169	153	39	7	1	3	57	15	0	0	41	2	1	0	1	0	16	16	.255	.321	.373
91	BAL/AL		79	221	206	42	9	0	7	72	13	0	1	49	3	1	0	0	1	29	18	.204	.255	.350
8 YR TOTALS			**538**	**1757**	**1623**	**387**	**66**	**10**	**42**	**599**	**100**	**2**	**6**	**324**	**33**	**18**	**10**	**13**	**8**	**183**	**161**	**.238**	**.283**	**.369**

Humphreys, Michael Butler "Mike" — bats right — throws right — b.4/10/67 — 1991 positions: OF 9, DH 7, 3B 6

YR	TM/LG	CL	G	TPA	AB	H	2B	3B	HR	TB	BB	IBB	HB	SO	GDP	SH	SF	SB	CS	R	RBI	BA	OBA	SA
88	SPO/NWL	A–	76	353	303	93	16	5	6	137	46	1	0	57	9	0	4	21	4	67	59	.307	.394	.452
89	RIV/CAL	A+	117	507	420	121	26	1	13	188	72	4	7	79	9	3	5	23	10	77	66	.288	.397	.448
90	WIC/TEX	AA	116	499	421	116	21	4	17	196	67	4	2	79	6	2	4	37	9	92	79	.276	.378	.466
	LV/PCL	AAA	12	49	42	10	1	0	2	17	4	0	1	11	4	2	0	1	0	7	6	.238	.319	.405
91	COL/INT	AAA	117	486	413	117	23	5	9	177	63	3	3	61	10	1	6	34	9	71	53	.283	.377	.429
	NY/AL		25	50	40	8	0	0	0	8	9	0	0	12	2	0	1	0	0	9	3	.200	.347	.200

Hundley, Todd Randolph — bats both — throws right — b.5/27/69 — 1991 positions: C 20

YR	TM/LG	CL	G	TPA	AB	H	2B	3B	HR	TB	BB	IBB	HB	SO	GDP	SH	SF	SB	CS	R	RBI	BA	OBA	SA
87	LF/NYP	A–	34	118	103	15	4	0	1	22	12	1	2	27	2	0	0	0	0	12	10	.146	.254	.214
88	LF/NYP	A–	52	199	176	33	8	0	2	47	16	1	4	31	2	2	1	1	1	23	18	.188	.269	.267
	SL/FSL	A+	1	3	1	0	0	0	0	0	2	0	0	1	0	0	0	0	0	0	0	.000	.667	.000
89	COL/SAL	A	125	507	439	118	23	4	11	182	54	10	8	67	20	1	5	6	3	67	66	.269	.356	.415
90	JAC/TEX	AA	81	317	279	74	12	2	1	93	34	3	1	44	5	0	3	5	3	27	35	.265	.344	.333
	NY/NL		36	74	67	14	6	0	0	20	6	0	0	18	1	1	0	0	0	8	2	.209	.274	.299
91	TID/INT	AAA	125	519	454	124	24	4	14	198	51	2	2	95	12	4	8	1	2	62	66	.273	.344	.436
	NY/NL		21	69	60	8	0	1	1	13	6	0	1	14	3	1	1	0	0	5	7	.133	.221	.217
2 YR TOTALS			**57**	**143**	**127**	**22**	**6**	**1**	**1**	**33**	**12**	**0**	**1**	**32**	**4**	**2**	**1**	**0**	**0**	**13**	**9**	**.173**	**.248**	**.260**

Hunter, Brian Ronald — bats right — throws left — b.3/4/68 — 1991 positions: 1B 85, OF 6

YR	TM/LG	CL	G	TPA	AB	H	2B	3B	HR	TB	BB	IBB	HB	SO	GDP	SH	SF	SB	CS	R	RBI	BA	OBA	SA
87	PUL/APP	R+	65	275	251	58	10	2	8	96	18	0	5	47	7	0	1	3	2	38	30	.231	.295	.382
88	BUR/MID	A	117	478	417	108	17	0	22	191	45	2	8	90	7	1	7	7	2	58	71	.259	.338	.458
	DUR/CAR	A+	13	56	49	17	3	0	3	29	7	0	0	8	0	0	0	2	0	13	9	.347	.429	.592
89	GRE/SOU	AA	124	501	451	114	19	2	19	194	33	2	7	61	4	1	9	5	4	57	82	.253	.308	.430
90	RIC/INT	AAA	43	157	137	27	4	0	5	46	18	0	1	37	0	0	1	2	1	13	16	.197	.288	.336
	GRE/SOU	AA	88	370	320	77	13	1	14	134	43	1	3	62	6	0	4	4	4	45	55	.241	.332	.419
91	RIC/INT	AAA	48	198	181	47	7	0	10	84	11	1	1	24	6	2	3	3	2	28	30	.260	.301	.464
	ATL/NL		97	291	271	68	16	1	12	122	17	0	1	48	6	0	3	0	2	32	50	.251	.296	.450

Huson, Jeffrey Kent "Jeff" — bats left — throws right — b.8/15/64 — 1991 positions: SS 116, 2B 2, 3B 1

YR	TM/LG	CL	G	TPA	AB	H	2B	3B	HR	TB	BB	IBB	HB	SO	GDP	SH	SF	SB	CS	R	RBI	BA	OBA	SA
86	BUR/MID	A	133	540	457	132	19	1	16	201	76	4	2	68	13	1	3	32	6	85	72	.289	.390	.440
	JAC/SOU	AA	1	4	4	0	0	0	0	0	0	0	0	0	0	0	0	0	0	0	0	.000	.000	.000
87	WPB/FSL	A+	131	520	455	130	15	4	1	156	50	1	4	30	9	6	4	33	9	54	53	.286	.352	.343
88	JAC/SOU	AA	128	546	471	117	18	1	0	137	59	3	3	45	15	10	3	56	13	72	34	.248	.334	.291
	MON/NL		20	46	42	13	2	0	0	15	4	2	0	3	2	0	0	2	1	7	3	.310	.370	.357
89	IND/AMA	AAA	102	433	378	115	17	4	3	149	50	1	1	26	10	2	2	30	17	70	35	.304	.385	.394
	MON/NL		32	83	74	12	5	0	0	17	6	3	0	6	3	0	3	0	1	1	2	.162	.225	.230
90	TEX/AL		145	454	396	95	12	2	0	111	46	2	0	54	8	7	3	12	4	57	28	.240	.320	.280
91	OC/AMA	AAA	2	6	6	3	1	0	0	4	0	0	0	1	0	0	0	0	0	0	2	.500	.500	.667
	TEX/AL		119	317	268	57	8	3	2	77	39	0	0	32	6	9	1	8	3	36	26	.213	.312	.287
4 YR TOTALS			**316**	**900**	**780**	**177**	**27**	**5**	**2**	**220**	**95**	**5**	**2**	**95**	**22**	**19**	**4**	**25**	**8**	**101**	**59**	**.227**	**.311**	**.282**

Incaviglia, Peter Joseph "Pete" — bats right — throws right — b.4/2/64 — 1991 positions: OF 54, DH 41

YR	TM/LG	CL	G	TPA	AB	H	2B	3B	HR	TB	BB	IBB	HB	SO	GDP	SH	SF	SB	CS	R	RBI	BA	OBA	SA
86	TEX/AL		153	606	540	135	21	2	30	250	55	2	4	185	9	0	7	3	2	82	88	.250	.320	.463
87	TEX/AL		139	563	509	138	26	4	27	253	48	1	1	168	8	0	5	9	3	85	80	.271	.332	.497
88	TEX/AL		116	467	418	104	19	3	22	195	39	3	7	153	6	0	3	6	4	59	54	.249	.321	.467
89	TEX/AL		133	495	453	107	27	4	21	205	32	0	6	136	12	0	4	5	7	48	81	.236	.293	.453
90	TEX/AL		153	587	529	123	27	0	24	222	45	5	9	146	18	0	4	3	4	59	85	.233	.302	.420
91	DET/AL		97	377	337	72	12	1	11	119	36	0	1	92	6	1	2	1	3	38	38	.214	.290	.353
6 YR TOTALS			**791**	**3095**	**2786**	**679**	**132**	**14**	**135**	**1244**	**255**	**11**	**28**	**880**	**59**	**1**	**25**	**27**	**23**	**371**	**426**	**.244**	**.311**	**.447**

Jackson, Darrin Jay — bats right — throws right — b.8/22/62 — 1991 positions: OF 98, P–1

YR	TM/LG	CL	G	TPA	AB	H	2B	3B	HR	TB	BB	IBB	HB	SO	GDP	SH	SF	SB	CS	R	RBI	BA	OBA	SA
81	CUB/GCL	R	62	244	210	39	5	0	1	47	28	0	1	53	5	3	2	18	4	29	15	.186	.282	.224
82	QC/MID	A	132	590	529	146	23	5	6	194	47	0	4	106	6	7	3	58	17	86	48	.276	.338	.367
83	SAL/CAL	A+	129	564	509	126	18	5	6	172	38	0	4	111	4	9	4	36	12	70	54	.248	.303	.338
84	MID/TEX	AA	132	555	496	134	18	2	15	201	49	2	2	103	4	5	3	13	8	63	54	.270	.337	.405
85	IOW/AMA	AAA	10	43	40	7	2	1	0	11	3	0	0	10	0	0	0	1	0	5	1	.175	.233	.275

YR	TM/LG	CL	G	TPA	AB	H	2B	3B	HR	TB	BB	IBB	HB	SO	GDP	SH	SF	SB	CS	R	RBI	BA	OBA	SA
	CHI/NL		5	11	11	1	0	0	0	1	0	0	0	3	0	0	0	0	0	0	0	.091	.091	.091
	PIT/EAS	AA	91	367	325	82	10	1	3	103	34	3	0	64	2	5	3	8	7	38	30	.252	.320	.317
86	PIT/EAS	AA	137	574	520	139	28	2	15	216	43	1	1	115	6	2	8	42	10	82	64	.267	.320	.415
87	IOW/AMA	AAA	132	510	474	130	32	5	23	241	26	3	2	110	6	5	3	13	10	81	81	.274	.313	.508
	CHI/NL		7	5	5	4	1	0	0	5	0	0	0	0	0	0	0	0	0	2	0	.800	.800	1.000
88	CHI/NL		100	197	188	50	11	3	6	85	5	1	1	28	3	2	1	4	1	29	20	.266	.287	.452
89	IOW/AMA	AAA	30	129	120	31	4	1	7	58	7	2	2	22	3	0	0	1	0	18	17	.258	.310	.483
	CHI/NL		45	89	83	19	4	0	1	26	6	1	0	17	1	0	0	1	2	7	8	.229	.281	.313
	SD/NL		25	96	87	18	3	0	3	30	7	4	0	17	0	0	2	0	2	10	12	.207	.260	.345
	YEAR		70	185	170	37	7	0	4	56	13	5	0	34	2	0	2	1	4	17	20	.218	.270	.329
90	LV/PCL	AAA	29	109	98	27	4	0	5	46	9	0	0	21	5	0	2	3	0	14	15	.276	.330	.469
	SD/NL		58	120	113	29	3	0	3	41	5	1	0	24	1	1	1	3	0	10	9	.257	.286	.363
91	SD/NL		122	394	359	94	12	1	21	171	27	2	2	66	5	3	5	3	3	51	49	.262	.315	.476
6 YR TOTALS			**362**	**912**	**846**	**215**	**34**	**4**	**34**	**359**	**50**	**9**	**3**	**155**	**11**	**6**	**7**	**13**	**8**	**109**	**98**	**.254**	**.296**	**.424**

Jackson, Vincent Edward "Bo" — bats right — throws right — b.11/30/62 — 1991 positions: DH 21

YR	TM/LG	CL	G	TPA	AB	H	2B	3B	HR	TB	BB	IBB	HB	SO	GDP	SH	SF	SB	CS	R	RBI	BA	OBA	SA
86	MEM/SOU	AA	53	212	184	51	9	3	7	87	22	0	5	81	1	0	1	3	6	30	25	.277	.368	.473
	KC/AL		25	91	82	17	2	1	2	27	7	0	2	34	1	0	0	3	1	9	9	.207	.286	.329
87	KC/AL		116	434	396	93	17	2	22	180	30	0	5	158	3	1	2	10	4	46	53	.235	.296	.455
88	KC/AL		124	468	439	108	16	4	25	207	25	6	1	146	6	1	2	27	6	63	68	.246	.287	.472
89	KC/AL		135	561	515	132	15	6	32	255	39	8	3	172	10	0	4	26	9	86	105	.256	.310	.495
90	KC/AL		111	456	405	110	16	1	28	212	44	2	2	128	10	0	5	15	9	74	78	.272	.342	.523
91	SAR/FSL	A+	2	7	6	2	0	0	0	2	0	0	0	0	0	0	1	0	0	1	2	.333	.286	.333
	BIR/SOU	AA	4	17	13	4	0	0	0	4	4	0	0	2	2	0	0	1	0	2	0	.308	.471	.308
	CHI/AL		23	84	71	16	4	0	3	29	12	1	0	25	3	0	1	0	1	8	14	.225	.333	.408
6 YR TOTALS			**534**	**2094**	**1908**	**476**	**70**	**14**	**112**	**910**	**157**	**17**	**13**	**663**	**33**	**2**	**14**	**81**	**30**	**286**	**327**	**.249**	**.309**	**.477**

Jacoby, Brook Wallace — bats right — throws right — b.11/23/59 — 1991 positions: 1B 58, 3B 52

YR	TM/LG	CL	G	TPA	AB	H	2B	3B	HR	TB	BB	IBB	HB	SO	GDP	SH	SF	SB	CS	R	RBI	BA	OBA	SA
81	ATL/NL		11	10	10	2	0	0	0	2	0	0	0	3	1	0	0	0	0	0	1	.200	.200	.200
83	ATL/NL		4	9	8	0	0	0	0	0	0	0	0	1	0	1	0	0	0	0	0	.000	.000	.000
84	CLE/AL		126	483	439	116	19	3	7	162	32	0	3	73	13	2	7	3	2	64	40	.264	.314	.369
85	CLE/AL		161	662	606	166	26	3	20	258	48	3	0	120	17	1	7	2	3	72	87	.274	.324	.426
86	CLE/AL		158	641	583	168	30	4	17	257	56	5	0	137	15	1	1	2	1	83	80	.288	.350	.441
87	CLE/AL		155	620	540	162	26	4	32	292	75	2	3	73	19	0	2	2	3	59	49	.300	.387	.541
88	CLE/AL		152	606	552	133	25	0	9	185	48	2	1	101	12	0	5	2	3	49	64	.241	.300	.335
89	CLE/AL		147	592	519	141	26	5	13	216	62	3	3	90	15	0	8	2	5	77	75	.272	.348	.416
90	CLE/AL		155	624	553	162	24	4	14	236	63	6	2	58	20	2	4	1	4	59	49	.293	.365	.427
91	CLE/AL		66	249	231	54	9	1	4	77	16	2	2	32	7	0	2	0	1	14	20	.234	.289	.333
	OAK/AL		56	204	188	40	12	0	0	52	11	1	1	22	6	0	4	2	1	28	44	.213	.255	.277
	YEAR		122	453	419	94	21	1	4	129	27	3	3	54	13	0	6	2	2	42	64	.224	.274	.308
10 YR TOTALS			**1191**	**4700**	**4229**	**1144**	**197**	**24**	**116**	**1737**	**411**	**24**	**15**	**710**	**125**	**7**	**38**	**16**	**22**	**505**	**509**	**.271**	**.335**	**.411**

Jaha, John Emile — bats right — throws right — b.5/27/66 — 1991 positions: 1B System MIL/AL

YR	TM/LG	CL	G	TPA	AB	H	2B	3B	HR	TB	BB	IBB	HB	SO	GDP	SH	SF	SB	CS	R	RBI	BA	OBA	SA
85	HEL/PIO	R+	24	83	68	18	3	0	2	27	14	0	0	23	0	0	1	4	0	13	14	.265	.386	.397
86	TRI/NWL	A−	73	335	258	82	13	2	15	144	70	4	5	75	2	0	9	4	9	65	67	.318	.469	.558
87	BEL/MID	A	122	487	376	101	22	0	7	144	102	2	4	86	11	2	3	10	5	68	47	.269	.427	.383
88	STO/CAL	A+	99	376	302	77	14	6	8	127	69	0	2	85	10	2	1	10	6	58	54	.255	.396	.421
89	STO/CAL	A+	140	611	479	140	26	5	25	251	112	6	5	115	15	2	13	8	11	83	91	.292	.422	.524
90	STO/CAL	A+	26	104	84	22	5	0	4	39	18	0	2	25	1	0	0	1	0	12	19	.262	.404	.464
91	EP/TEX	AA	130	578	486	167	38	3	30	301	78	6	8	101	9	1	2	5	6	121	134	.344	.438	.619

James, Donald Chris "Chris" — bats right — throws right — b.10/4/62 — 1991 positions: DH 60, OF 39, 1B 15

YR	TM/LG	CL	G	TPA	AB	H	2B	3B	HR	TB	BB	IBB	HB	SO	GDP	SH	SF	SB	CS	R	RBI	BA	OBA	SA
84	REA/EAS	AA	128	507	457	117	19	12	8	184	40	1	3	74	12	3	4	19	5	66	57	.256	.317	.403
85	POR/PCL	AAA	135	555	507	160	35	8	11	244	33	1	7	72	12	5	3	23	10	78	73	.316	.364	.481
86	POR/PCL	AAA	69	288	266	64	6	4	12	110	17	1	0	45	9	3	2	3	6	30	41	.241	.284	.414
	PHI/NL		16	48	46	13	3	0	1	19	1	0	0	13	1	0	0	2	0	5	3	.283	.298	.413
87	MAI/INT	AAA	13	45	40	9	2	1	0	13	3	1	0	9	0	0	2	0	0	5	3	.225	.267	.325
	PHI/NL		115	391	358	105	20	6	17	188	27	0	2	67	4	1	3	3	1	48	54	.293	.344	.525
88	PHI/NL		150	605	566	137	24	1	19	220	31	2	3	73	15	0	5	7	4	57	66	.242	.283	.389
89	PHI/NL		45	185	179	37	4	0	2	47	4	0	2	23	9	1	1	3	0	14	19	.207	.223	.263
	SD/NL		87	331	303	80	13	2	11	130	22	2	1	45	11	2	3	4	2	41	46	.264	.314	.429
	YEAR		132	516	482	117	17	2	13	177	26	2	3	68	20	3	4	7	2	55	65	.243	.281	.367
90	CLE/AL		140	569	528	158	32	4	12	234	31	4	2	71	11	3	3	4	3	62	70	.299	.341	.443
91	CLE/AL		115	463	437	104	16	2	5	139	18	0	4	61	9	2	4	2	4	31	41	.238	.273	.318
6 YR TOTALS			**668**	**2592**	**2417**	**634**	**112**	**15**	**67**	**977**	**134**	**10**	**14**	**353**	**60**	**11**	**16**	**22**	**14**	**258**	**301**	**.262**	**.303**	**.404**

Javier, Stanley Julian Antonio (De Javier) "Stan" — bats both — throws right — b.1/9/64 — 1991 positions: OF 69, 1B 2

YR	TM/LG	CL	G	TPA	AB	H	2B	3B	HR	TB	BB	IBB	HB	SO	GDP	SH	SF	SB	CS	R	RBI	BA	OBA	SA
84	NY/AL		7	7	7	1	0	0	0	1	0	0	0	3	1	0	0	0	0	1	0	.143	.143	.143
	NAS/SOU	AA	76	304	262	76	17	4	7	122	39	1	1	57	3	1	1	17	5	40	38	.290	.383	.466
	COL/INT	AAA	32	114	99	22	3	1	0	27	12	1	0	26	3	1	2	1	1	12	7	.222	.301	.273

(continued)

Javier, Stanley Julian Antonio (De Javier) "Stan" (continued)

YR	TM/LG	CL	G	TPA	AB	H	2B	3B	HR	TB	BB	IBB	HB	SO	GDP	SH	SF	SB	CS	R	RBI	BA	OBA	SA
85	HUN/SOU	AA	140	613	486	138	22	8	9	203	112	6	5	92	8	4	6	61	15	105	64	.284	.419	.418
86	TAC/PCL	AAA	69	302	248	81	16	2	4	113	47	2	2	46	2	0	5	18	8	50	51	.327	.430	.456
	OAK/AL		59	131	114	23	8	0	0	31	16	0	1	27	2	0	0	8	0	13	8	.202	.305	.272
87	TAC/PCL	AAA	15	55	51	11	2	0	0	13	4	0	0	12	2	0	0	3	1	6	2	.216	.273	.255
	OAK/AL		81	176	151	28	3	1	2	39	19	3	0	33	2	6	0	3	2	22	9	.185	.276	.258
88	OAK/AL		125	440	397	102	13	3	2	127	32	1	2	63	13	6	3	20	1	49	35	.257	.313	.320
89	OAK/AL		112	348	310	77	12	3	1	98	31	1	1	45	6	4	2	12	2	42	28	.248	.317	.316
90	OAK/AL		19	36	33	8	0	2	0	12	3	0	0	6	0	0	0	0	0	4	3	.242	.306	.364
	LA/NL		104	321	276	84	9	4	3	110	37	2	0	44	6	6	2	15	7	56	24	.304	.384	.399
	YEAR		123	357	309	92	9	6	3	122	40	2	0	50	6	6	2	15	7	60	27	.298	.376	.395
91	LA/NL		121	197	176	36	5	3	1	50	16	0	0	36	4	3	2	7	1	21	11	.205	.268	.284
7 YR TOTALS			**628**	**1656**	**1464**	**359**	**50**	**16**	**9**	**468**	**154**	**7**	**4**	**255**	**33**	**25**	**9**	**65**	**13**	**208**	**118**	**.245**	**.317**	**.320**

Jefferies, Gregory Scott "Gregg" — bats both — throws right — b.8/1/67 — 1991 positions: 2B 77, 3B 51

YR	TM/LG	CL	G	TPA	AB	H	2B	3B	HR	TB	BB	IBB	HB	SO	GDP	SH	SF	SB	CS	R	RBI	BA	OBA	SA
85	KIN/APP	R+	47	182	166	57	18	2	3	88	14	2	1	16	1	0	1	21	1	27	29	.343	.396	.530
	COL/SAL	A	20	68	64	18	2	2	1	27	4	0	0	4	1	0	0	7	0	7	12	.281	.324	.422
86	COL/SAL	A	25	122	112	38	6	1	5	61	9	0	0	10	1	0	1	13	1	29	24	.339	.385	.545
	LYN/CAR	A+	95	430	390	138	25	9	11	214	33	3	2	29	6	0	5	43	8	66	80	.354	.402	.549
	JAC/TEX	AA	5	21	19	8	1	1	0	11	2	1	0	2	0	0	0	1	0	1	7	.421	.476	.579
87	JAC/TEX	AA	134	570	510	187	48	5	20	305	49	18	5	43	12	0	6	26	10	81	101	.367	.423	.598
	NY/NL		6	6	6	3	1	0	0	4	0	0	0	0	0	0	0	0	0	0	2	.500	.500	.667
88	TID/INT	AAA	132	543	504	142	28	4	7	199	32	10	1	34	12	0	6	32	6	62	61	.282	.322	.395
	NY/NL		29	118	109	35	8	2	6	65	8	0	0	10	1	0	1	5	1	19	17	.321	.364	.596
89	NY/NL		141	559	508	131	28	2	12	199	39	8	5	46	16	2	5	21	6	72	56	.258	.314	.392
90	NY/NL		153	659	604	171	40	3	15	262	46	2	5	40	12	0	4	11	2	96	68	.283	.337	.434
91	NY/NL		136	539	486	132	19	2	9	182	47	2	2	38	12	3	1	26	5	59	62	.272	.336	.374
5YR TOTALS			**465**	**1881**	**1713**	**472**	**96**	**9**	**42**	**712**	**140**	**12**	**12**	**134**	**41**	**3**	**13**	**63**	**14**	**246**	**205**	**.276**	**.332**	**.416**

Jefferson, Reginald Jirod "Reggie" — bats both — throws left — b.9/25/68 — 1991 positions: 1B 28

YR	TM/LG	CL	G	TPA	AB	H	2B	3B	HR	TB	BB	IBB	HB	SO	GDP	SH	SF	SB	CS	R	RBI	BA	OBA	SA
86	RED/GCL	R	59	237	208	54	4	5	3	77	24	1	2	40	3	1	2	10	9	28	33	.260	.339	.370
87	CR/MID	A	15	58	54	12	5	0	3	26	1	0	3	12	2	0	0	1	1	9	11	.222	.276	.481
	BIL/PIO	R+	8	27	22	8	1	0	1	12	4	1	1	2	1	0	0	1	0	10	9	.364	.481	.545
88	CR/MID	A	135	575	517	149	26	2	18	233	40	6	13	89	12	0	5	2	1	76	90	.288	.351	.451
89	CHT/SOU	AA	135	541	487	140	19	3	17	216	43	5	7	73	11	0	4	2	3	66	80	.287	.351	.444
90	NAS/AMA	AAA	37	141	126	34	11	2	5	64	14	1	1	30	3	0	0	1	0	24	23	.270	.348	.508
91	NAS/AMA	AAA	28	117	103	33	3	1	3	47	10	1	4	22	3	0	0	3	1	15	20	.320	.402	.456
	CAN/EAS	AA	6	26	25	7	1	0	0	8	1	0	0	5	2	0	0	0	0	2	4	.280	.308	.320
	CS/PCL	AAA	39	155	136	42	11	0	3	62	16	1	1	28	1	0	2	0	0	29	21	.309	.381	.456
	CIN/NL		5	8	7	1	0	0	1	4	1	0	0	2	0	0	0	0	0	1	1	.143	.250	.571
	CLE/AL		26	105	101	20	3	0	2	29	3	0	0	22	1	0	1	0	0	10	12	.198	.219	.287
	YEAR		31	113	108	21	3	0	3	33	4	0	0	24	1	0	1	0	0	11	13	.194	.221	.306
1 YR TOTALS			**31**	**113**	**108**	**21**	**3**	**0**	**3**	**33**	**4**	**0**	**0**	**24**	**1**	**0**	**1**	**0**	**0**	**11**	**13**	**.194**	**.221**	**.306**

Jefferson, Stanley "Stan" — bats both — throws right — b.12/4/62 — 1991 positions: OF 5

YR	TM/LG	CL	G	TPA	AB	H	2B	3B	HR	TB	BB	IBB	HB	SO	GDP	SH	SF	SB	CS	R	RBI	BA	OBA	SA
84	LYN/CAR	A+	128	583	493	142	20	9	5	195	84	3	3	73	6	0	3	45	15	113	47	.288	.393	.396
85	JAC/TEX	AA	133	602	524	145	21	6	8	202	72	2	1	79	2	5	0	39	16	97	30	.277	.365	.385
86	TID/INT	AAA	95	415	369	107	19	4	2	140	41	4	2	65	4	2	1	25	7	60	37	.290	.363	.379
	NY/NL		14	27	24	5	1	0	1	9	2	0	1	8	1	0	0	0	0	6	3	.208	.296	.375
87	SD/NL		116	469	422	97	8	7	8	143	39	2	2	92	6	3	3	34	11	59	29	.230	.296	.339
88	LV/PCL	AAA	74	319	278	88	14	6	4	126	36	0	2	43	5	1	2	19	7	60	33	.317	.396	.453
	SD/NL		49	125	111	16	2	1	1	24	9	0	1	22	3	2	2	5	1	16	4	.144	.211	.216
89	NY/AL		10	12	12	1	0	0	0	1	0	0	0	4	0	0	0	1	1	1	1	.083	.083	.083
	COL/INT	AAA	68	291	257	68	10	6	2	96	30	0	1	40	3	2	1	15	7	34	24	.265	.343	.374
	ROC/INT	AAA	16	71	64	15	4	3	1	28	5	0	0	9	1	0	2	3	1	9	12	.234	.282	.438
	BAL/AL		35	134	127	33	7	0	4	52	4	0	1	22	1	0	2	9	3	19	20	.260	.284	.409
	YEAR		45	146	139	34	7	0	4	53	4	0	1	26	1	0	2	10	4	20	21	.245	.267	.381
90	BAL/AL		10	21	19	0	0	0	0	0	1	0	0	8	0	1	0	0	0	1	0	.000	.095	.000
	CS/PCL	AAA	33	140	119	41	9	3	3	65	20	1	0	22	1	0	0	8	6	27	17	.345	.436	.546
	CLE/AL		49	112	98	27	8	0	2	41	8	0	2	18	2	1	3	8	4	21	10	.276	.333	.418
	YEAR		59	133	117	27	8	0	2	41	10	0	2	26	2	1	3	9	4	22	10	.231	.295	.350
91	CS/PCL	AAA	28	81	74	21	2	1	2	31	5	0	0	9	1	1	1	3	2	11	9	.284	.325	.419
	NAS/AMA	AAA	27	83	78	19	4	3	2	35	4	0	1	19	1	0	0	2	0	10	5	.244	.289	.449
	CIN/NL		13	20	19	1	0	0	0	1	1	0	0	3	0	0	0	0	0	2	0	.053	.100	.053
6 YR TOTALS			**296**	**920**	**832**	**180**	**25**	**9**	**16**	**271**	**65**	**2**	**7**	**177**	**13**	**6**	**10**	**60**	**20**	**125**	**67**	**.216**	**.276**	**.326**

Jennings, James Douglas "Doug" — bats left — throws left — b.9/30/64 — 1991 positions: OF 6

YR	TM/LG	CL	G	TPA	AB	H	2B	3B	HR	TB	BB	IBB	HB	SO	GDP	SH	SF	SB	CS	R	RBI	BA	OBA	SA
84	SAL/NWL	A−	52	221	173	45	7	1	1	57	40	1	3	45	2	1	4	12	12	29	17	.260	.400	.329
85	QC/MID	A	95	394	319	81	17	7	5	127	62	1	5	76	7	2	6	10	8	50	54	.254	.378	.398
86	PS/CAL	A+	129	566	429	136	31	6	17	236	117	7	10	103	6	2	8	7	11	95	89	.317	.466	.550
87	MID/TEX	AA	126	577	464	157	33	1	30	282	94	11	13	136	8	2	4	7	3	106	104	.338	.459	.608
88	TAC/PCL	AAA	16	71	49	16	1	0	0	17	18	1	2	13	1	2	0	5	1	12	9	.327	.522	.347

Jennings, James Douglas "Doug" (continued)

YR	TM/LG	CL	G	TPA	AB	H	2B	3B	HR	TB	BB	IBB	HB	SO	GDP	SH	SF	SB	CS	R	RBI	BA	OBA	SA
	OAK/AL		71	128	101	21	6	0	1	30	21	1	2	28	1	1	3	0	1	9	15	.208	.346	.297
89	TAC/PCL	AAA	137	616	497	136	35	5	11	214	93	7	16	95	8	2	8	10	12	99	64	.274	.399	.431
	OAK/AL		4	4	4	0	0	0	0	0	0	0	0	2	0	0	0	0	0	0	0	.000	.000	.000
90	TAC/PCL	AAA	60	245	208	72	19	1	6	111	31	4	2	36	1	1	3	4	2	32	30	.346	.430	.534
	OAK/AL		64	180	156	30	7	2	2	47	17	0	2	48	1	2	3	0	3	19	14	.192	.275	.301
91	OAK/AL		8	11	9	1	0	0	0	1	2	0	0	2	1	0	0	0	1	0	0	.111	.273	.111
	TAC/PCL	AAA	95	400	332	89	17	2	3	119	47	1	11	65	6	1	9	5	1	43	44	.268	.368	.358
4 YR TOTALS			147	323	270	52	13	2	3	78	40	1	4	80	3	3	6	0	5	28	29	.193	.300	.289

Johnson, Howard Michael — bats both — throws right — b.11/29/60 — 1991 positions: 3B 104, OF 30, SS 28

YR	TM/LG	CL	G	TPA	AB	H	2B	3B	HR	TB	BB	IBB	HB	SO	GDP	SH	SF	SB	CS	R	RBI	BA	OBA	SA
82	DET/AL		54	173	155	49	5	0	4	66	16	1	1	30	3	1	0	7	4	23	14	.316	.384	.426
83	DET/AL		27	74	66	14	0	0	3	23	7	0	1	10	1	0	0	0	5	11	5	.212	.297	.348
84	DET/AL		116	402	355	88	14	1	12	140	40	1	1	67	6	4	2	10	6	43	50	.248	.324	.394
85	NY/NL		126	428	389	94	18	4	11	153	34	10	0	78	6	1	4	6	4	38	46	.242	.300	.393
86	NY/NL		88	253	220	54	14	0	10	98	31	8	1	64	2	1	0	8	1	30	39	.245	.341	.445
87	NY/NL		157	645	554	147	22	1	36	279	83	18	5	113	8	0	3	32	10	93	99	.265	.364	.504
88	NY/NL		148	594	495	114	21	1	24	209	86	25	3	104	6	2	8	23	7	85	68	.230	.343	.422
89	NY/NL		153	655	571	164	41	3	36	319	77	8	1	126	4	0	6	41	8	104	101	.287	.369	.559
90	NY/NL		154	668	590	144	37	3	23	256	69	12	0	100	4	0	9	34	8	89	90	.244	.319	.434
91	NY/NL		156	658	564	146	34	4	38	302	78	12	1	120	4	0	15	30	16	108	117	.259	.342	.535
10 YR TOTALS			1179	4550	3959	1014	206	17	197	1845	521	95	14	812	47	9	47	191	64	624	629	.256	.341	.466

Johnson, Kenneth Lance "Lance" — bats left — throws left — b.7/6/63 — 1991 positions: OF 157

YR	TM/LG	CL	G	TPA	AB	H	2B	3B	HR	TB	BB	IBB	HB	SO	GDP	SH	SF	SB	CS	R	RBI	BA	OBA	SA
84	ERI/NYP	A–	71	332	283	96	7	5	1	116	45	0	0	20	6	1	3	29	10	63	28	.339	.426	.410
85	SP/FSL	A+	129	566	497	134	17	10	2	177	58	5	0	39	7	2	9	33	19	68	55	.270	.340	.356
86	ARK/TEX	AA	127	510	445	128	24	6	2	170	59	2	1	57	6	3	2	49	13	82	33	.288	.371	.382
87	LOU/AMA	AAA	116	531	477	159	21	11	5	217	49	7	0	45	9	3	2	42	16	89	50	.333	.394	.455
	STL/NL		33	63	59	13	2	1	0	17	4	1	0	6	2	0	0	6	1	4	7	.220	.270	.288
88	VAN/PCL	AAA	100	460	411	126	12	6	2	156	42	4	0	52	7	2	5	49	16	71	36	.307	.367	.380
	CHI/AL		33	132	124	23	4	1	0	29	6	0	0	11	1	2	0	6	2	11	6	.185	.223	.234
89	VAN/PCL	AAA	106	458	408	124	11	7	0	149	46	0	0	36	4	0	4	33	18	69	28	.304	.371	.365
	CHI/AL		50	199	180	54	8	2	0	66	17	0	2	24	1	2	0	16	3	28	16	.300	.360	.367
90	CHI/AL		151	587	541	154	18	9	1	193	33	2	1	45	12	8	4	36	22	76	51	.285	.325	.357
91	CHI/AL		159	624	588	161	14	13	0	201	26	2	1	58	14	6	3	26	11	72	49	.274	.304	.342
5 YR TOTALS			426	1605	1492	405	46	26	1	506	86	5	2	144	30	18	7	90	39	191	129	.271	.311	.339

Jones, Christopher Carlos "Chris" — bats right — throws right — b.12/16/65 — 1991 positions: OF 26

YR	TM/LG	CL	G	TPA	AB	H	2B	3B	HR	TB	BB	IBB	HB	SO	GDP	SH	SF	SB	CS	R	RBI	BA	OBA	SA
84	BIL/PIO	R+	21	76	73	11	2	0	2	19	2	0	0	24	0	0	1	4	0	8	13	.151	.171	.260
85	BIL/PIO	R+	63	262	240	62	12	5	4	96	19	0	1	72	3	1	1	13	0	43	33	.258	.314	.400
86	CR/MID	A	128	500	473	117	13	9	20	208	20	1	3	126	7	0	4	23	17	65	78	.247	.280	.440
87	VER/EAS		113	415	383	88	11	4	10	137	23	4	4	99	12	2	3	13	10	50	39	.230	.278	.358
88	CHT/SOU	AA	116	448	410	111	20	7	4	157	29	1	2	102	4	0	7	11	9	50	61	.271	.317	.383
89	NAS/AMA	AAA	21	50	49	8	1	0	2	15	0	0	0	16	0	1	0	2	1	8	5	.163	.163	.306
	CHT/SOU	AA	103	405	378	95	18	2	10	147	23	1	3	68	13	0	1	10	2	47	54	.251	.299	.389
90	NAS/AMA	AAA	134	467	436	114	23	3	10	173	23	3	2	86	18	0	5	11	8	53	52	.261	.301	.397
91	NAS/AMA	AAA	73	289	267	65	5	4	9	105	19	1	2	65	6	0	4	10	5	29	33	.243	.298	.393
	CIN/NL		52	92	89	26	1	2	2	37	2	0	0	31	2	0	1	2	1	14	6	.292	.304	.416

Jones, Larry Wayne "Chipper" — bats right — throws right — b.4/24/72 — 1991 positions: SS System ATL/NL

YR	TM/LG	CL	G	TPA	AB	H	2B	3B	HR	TB	BB	IBB	HB	SO	GDP	SH	SF	SB	CS	R	RBI	BA	OBA	SA
90	BRA/GCL	R	44	164	140	32	1	1	1	38	14	1	6	25	3	2	2	5	3	20	18	.229	.321	.271
91	MAC/SAL	A	136	556	473	153	24	11	15	244	69	4	3	70	6	1	10	39	11	104	98	.323	.405	.516

Jones, Ronald Glen "Ron" — bats left — throws right — b.6/11/64 — 1991 positions: OF

YR	TM/LG	CL	G	TPA	AB	H	2B	3B	HR	TB	BB	IBB	HB	SO	GDP	SH	SF	SB	CS	R	RBI	BA	OBA	SA
85	BEN/NWL	A–	73	328	286	90	13	1	10	135	34	2	4	28	0	0	4	9	7	54	60	.315	.390	.472
86	CLE/FSL	A+	108	467	412	153	18	12	7	216	40	4	4	30	0	2	9	33	12	76	73	.371	.424	.524
	POR/PCL		11	35	34	4	1	0	0	5	0	0	0	1	0	0	0	0	0	4	2	.118	.143	.147
87	MAI/INT	AAA	90	359	316	78	13	4	7	120	38	1	3	50	4	0	1	13	4	33	32	.247	.332	.380
88	MAI/INT	AAA	125	508	445	119	15	3	16	188	49	8	4	53	9	2	8	16	3	64	75	.267	.340	.422
	PHI/NL		33	129	124	36	6	1	8	68	2	0	0	14	0	0	3	0	0	15	26	.290	.295	.548
89	PHI/NL		12	40	31	9	0	0	2	15	9	1	0	7	0	0	0	1	0	7	4	.290	.450	.484
90	SCR/INT	AAA	44	171	148	39	4	1	3	54	19	1	1	18	2	0	3	0	1	13	26	.264	.345	.365
	PHI/NL		24	67	58	16	2	0	3	27	9	0	0	9	1	0	0	0	0	5	7	.276	.373	.466
91	CLE/FSL	A+	12	51	38	6	4	0	1	13	13	2	0	8	1	0	0	2	0	8	6	.158	.373	.342
	SCR/INT	AAA	48	171	150	38	7	0	4	57	19	5	1	20	6	0	1	3	1	17	26	.253	.339	.380
	PHI/NL		28	28	26	4	2	0	0	6	2	0	0	13	0	0	0	1	1	0	2	.154	.214	.231
4 YR TOTALS			97	264	239	65	10	1	13	116	22	1	0	33	6	0	3	1	1	27	40	.272	.330	.485

Jones, Tracy Donald — bats right — throws right — b.3/31/61 — 1991 positions: DH 37, OF 36

YR	TM/LG	CL	G	TPA	AB	H	2B	3B	HR	TB	BB	IBB	HB	SO	GDP	SH	SF	SB	CS	R	RBI	BA	OBA	SA
84	TAM/FSL	A+	86	347	307	95	14	3	4	127	32	3	2	30	14	1	5	24	1	50	41	.309	.373	.414

(continued)

YR	TM/LG	CL	G	TPA	AB	H	2B	3B	HR	TB	BB	IBB	HB	SO	GDP	SH	SF	SB	CS	R	RBI	BA	OBA	SA
85	VER/EAS	AA	75	315	284	90	12	3	4	120	26	3	2	23	7	0	3	26	3	40	31	.317	.375	.423
	DEN/AMA	AAA	51	226	205	69	12	0	10	111	15	0	3	16	5	2	1	20	1	43	31	.337	.388	.541
86	CIN/NL		46	96	86	30	3	0	2	39	9	1	0	5	2	0	1	7	1	16	10	.349	.406	.453
87	CIN/NL		117	390	359	104	17	3	10	157	23	0	3	40	10	0	5	31	8	53	44	.290	.333	.437
88	NAS/AMA	AAA	2	7	6	3	1	0	0	4	1	0	0	0	1	0	0	0	0	2	1	.500	.571	.667
	CIN/NL		37	92	83	19	1	0	1	23	8	2	1	6	4	0	0	9	0	9	9	.229	.304	.277
	MON/NL		53	157	141	47	5	1	2	60	12	1	1	12	1	3	0	9	6	20	15	.333	.390	.426
	YEAR		90	249	224	66	6	1	3	83	20	3	2	18	5	3	0	18	6	29	24	.295	.358	.371
89	SF/NL		40	103	97	18	4	0	0	22	5	3	1	14	4	0	0	2	1	5	12	.186	.233	.227
	DET/AL		46	179	158	41	10	0	3	60	16	1	1	16	1	1	3	1	1	17	26	.259	.326	.380
	YEAR		86	282	255	59	14	0	3	82	21	4	2	30	5	1	3	3	2	22	38	.231	.292	.322
90	DET/AL		50	128	118	27	4	1	4	45	6	0	3	13	3	1	0	1	1	15	9	.229	.283	.381
	SEA/AL		25	92	86	26	4	0	2	36	3	0	2	12	4	1	0	0	1	8	15	.302	.341	.419
	YEAR		75	220	204	53	8	1	6	81	9	0	5	25	7	2	0	1	2	23	24	.260	.307	.397
91	SEA/AL		79	197	175	44	8	1	3	63	18	2	1	22	8	1	2	2	0	30	24	.251	.321	.360
6 YR TOTALS			493	1434	1303	356	56	6	27	505	100	10	13	140	37	7	11	62	19	173	164	**.273**	**.329**	**.388**

Jones, William Timothy "Tim" — bats left — throws right — b.12/1/62 — 1991 positions: SS 14, 2B 4

YR	TM/LG	CL	G	TPA	AB	H	2B	3B	HR	TB	BB	IBB	HB	SO	GDP	SH	SF	SB	CS	R	RBI	BA	OBA	SA
85	JC/APP	R+	68	267	235	75	10	1	3	96	27	1	0	19	1	0	5	28	6	33	48	.319	.382	.409
86	SP/FSL	A+	39	176	142	36	3	2	0	43	30	1	1	8	3	0	3	8	6	19	27	.254	.381	.303
	ARK/TEX	AA	96	333	284	76	15	1	2	99	42	2	2	32	7	3	2	7	5	36	27	.268	.364	.349
87	ARK/TEX	AA	61	213	176	58	12	0	3	79	29	4	2	16	3	3	3	16	10	23	26	.330	.424	.449
	LOU/AMA	AAA	73	307	276	78	14	3	4	110	29	1	0	27	4	2	0	11	3	48	43	.283	.351	.399
88	LOU/AMA	AAA	103	415	370	95	21	2	6	138	36	1	3	56	5	5	1	39	12	63	38	.257	.327	.373
	STL/NL		31	56	52	14	0	0	0	14	4	0	0	10	0	0	0	4	1	2	3	.269	.321	.269
89	STL/NL		42	86	75	22	6	0	0	28	7	1	1	8	2	1	2	1	0	11	7	.293	.353	.373
90	STL/NL		67	145	128	28	7	1	1	40	12	1	1	20	1	4	0	3	4	9	12	.219	.291	.313
91	LOU/AMA	AAA	86	349	305	78	9	1	5	104	37	1	0	59	2	4	3	19	5	34	29	.256	.333	.341
	STL/NL		16	27	24	4	2	0	0	6	2	1	0	6	0	0	1	0	1	1	2	.167	.222	.250
4 YR TOTALS			156	314	279	68	15	1	1	88	25	3	2	44	4	5	3	8	6	23	24	**.244**	**.307**	**.315**

Jordan, Paul Scott "Ricky" — bats right — throws right — b.5/26/65 — 1991 positions: 1B 72

YR	TM/LG	CL	G	TPA	AB	H	2B	3B	HR	TB	BB	IBB	HB	SO	GDP	SH	SF	SB	CS	R	RBI	BA	OBA	SA
84	SPA/SAL	A	128	531	490	143	23	4	10	204	32	2	4	63	14	0	5	8	2	72	76	.292	.337	.416
85	CLE/FSL	A+	139	560	528	146	22	8	7	205	25	3	1	59	10	2	4	26	8	60	62	.277	.308	.388
86	REA/EAS	AA	133	507	478	131	19	3	2	162	21	3	3	44	5	1	4	17	7	44	60	.274	.306	.339
87	REA/EAS	AA	132	515	475	151	28	3	16	233	28	4	3	22	18	0	9	15	9	78	95	.318	.353	.491
88	MAI/INT	AAA	87	345	338	104	23	1	7	150	6	0	0	30	15	0	1	10	0	42	36	.308	.319	.444
	PHI/NL		69	281	273	84	15	1	11	134	7	2	0	39	5	0	1	1	1	41	43	.308	.324	.491
89	PHI/NL		144	559	523	149	22	3	12	213	23	5	5	62	19	0	8	4	3	63	75	.285	.317	.407
90	SCR/INT	AAA	27	111	104	29	1	0	2	36	5	0	1	18	6	0	1	0	0	8	11	.279	.315	.346
	PHI/NL		92	346	324	78	21	0	5	114	13	6	5	39	9	0	4	2	0	32	44	.241	.277	.352
91	PHI/NL		101	322	301	82	21	3	9	136	14	2	2	49	11	0	5	0	2	38	49	.272	.304	.452
4 YR TOTALS			406	1508	1421	393	79	7	37	597	57	15	12	189	44	0	18	7	6	174	211	**.277**	**.306**	**.420**

Jorgensen, Terry Allen — bats right — throws right — b.9/2/66 — 1991 positions: 3B System MIN/AL

YR	TM/LG	CL	G	TPA	AB	H	2B	3B	HR	TB	BB	IBB	HB	SO	GDP	SH	SF	SB	CS	R	RBI	BA	OBA	SA
87	KEN/MID	A	67	275	254	80	17	0	7	118	18	0	2	43	7	0	1	1	0	37	33	.315	.364	.465
88	ORL/SOU	AA	135	526	472	116	27	4	3	160	40	3	6	62	11	2	6	4	1	53	43	.246	.309	.339
89	ORL/SOU	AA	135	604	514	135	27	5	13	211	76	4	5	78	6	0	9	4	1	84	101	.263	.358	.411
	MIN/AL		10	27	23	4	1	0	0	5	4	0	0	5	1	0	0	0	0	1	2	.174	.296	.217
90	POR/PCL	AAA	123	489	440	114	28	3	10	178	44	2	0	83	11	1	4	0	4	43	50	.259	.324	.405
91	POR/PCL	AAA	126	518	456	136	29	3	11	198	54	1	4	41	22	2	1	1	0	74	59	.298	.376	.434
1 YR TOTALS			10	27	23	4	1	0	0	5	4	0	0	5	1	0	0	0	0	1	2	**.174**	**.296**	**.217**

Jose, Domingo Felix Andujar "Felix" — bats both — throws right — b.5/2/65 — 1991 positions: OF 153

YR	TM/LG	CL	G	TPA	AB	H	2B	3B	HR	TB	BB	IBB	HB	SO	GDP	SH	SF	SB	CS	R	RBI	BA	OBA	SA
84	IF/PIO	R+	45	173	152	33	6	0	1	42	18	1	1	37	4	0	2	5	1	16	18	.217	.301	.276
85	MAD/MID	A	117	450	409	89	13	3	3	117	33	2	5	82	8	1	2	6	6	46	33	.218	.283	.286
86	MOD/CAL	A+	127	559	516	147	22	8	14	227	36	5	2	89	5	3	2	14	9	77	77	.285	.333	.440
87	HUN/SOU	AA	91	330	296	67	11	1	5	95	28	1	2	61	11	1	3	3	3	29	42	.226	.295	.321
88	TAC/PCL	AAA	134	568	508	161	29	5	12	236	53	9	1	77	10	2	4	16	8	72	83	.317	.380	.465
	OAK/AL		8	6	6	2	1	0	0	3	0	0	0	1	0	0	0	1	0	2	1	.333	.333	.500
89	TAC/PCL	AAA	104	434	387	111	26	0	14	179	41	8	3	82	14	1	2	11	7	59	63	.287	.358	.463
	OAK/AL		20	61	57	11	2	0	0	13	4	0	0	12	1	0	0	0	1	3	5	.193	.246	.228
90	OAK/AL		101	365	341	90	12	0	8	126	16	0	5	65	8	2	1	8	2	42	39	.264	.306	.370
	STL/NL		25	93	85	23	4	1	3	38	8	0	0	16	1	0	0	4	4	12	13	.271	.333	.447
	YEAR		126	458	426	113	16	1	11	164	24	0	5	81	9	2	1	12	6	54	52	.265	.311	.385
91	STL/NL		154	625	568	173	40	6	8	249	50	8	2	113	12	0	5	20	12	69	77	.305	.360	.438
4 YR TOTALS			308	1150	1057	299	59	7	19	429	78	8	7	208	23	2	6	33	19	128	135	**.283**	**.334**	**.406**

Joyner, Wallace Keith "Wally" — bats left — throws left — b.6/16/62 — 1991 positions: 1B 141

YR	TM/LG	CL	G	TPA	AB	H	2B	3B	HR	TB	BB	IBB	HB	SO	GDP	SH	SF	SB	CS	R	RBI	BA	OBA	SA
84	WAT/EAS	AA	134	548	467	148	24	7	12	222	67	8	1	60	8	5	8	0	5	81	72	.317	.398	.475

Joyner, Wallace Keith "Wally" (continued)

YR	TM/LG	CL	G	TPA	AB	H	2B	3B	HR	TB	BB	IBB	HB	SO	GDP	SH	SF	SB	CS	R	RBI	BA	OBA	SA
85	EDM/PCL	AAA	126	545	477	135	29	5	12	210	60	2	2	64	9	3	3	2	2	68	73	.283	.363	.440
86	CAL/AL		154	674	593	172	27	3	22	271	57	8	2	58	11	10	12	5	2	82	100	.290	.348	.457
87	CAL/AL		149	653	564	161	33	1	34	298	72	12	5	64	14	2	10	8	2	100	117	.285	.366	.528
88	CAL/AL		158	663	597	176	31	2	13	250	55	14	5	51	16	0	6	8	2	81	85	.295	.356	.419
89	CAL/AL		159	654	593	167	30	2	16	249	46	7	6	58	15	1	8	3	2	78	79	.282	.335	.420
90	CAL/AL		83	358	310	83	15	0	8	122	41	4	1	34	10	1	5	2	1	35	41	.268	.350	.394
91	CAL/AL		143	611	551	166	34	3	21	269	52	4	1	66	11	2	5	2	0	79	96	.301	.360	.488
6 YR TOTALS			**846**	**3613**	**3208**	**925**	**170**	**11**	**114**	**1459**	**323**	**49**	**20**	**331**	**77**	**16**	**46**	**28**	**9**	**455**	**518**	**.288**	**.353**	**.455**

Justice, David Christopher — bats left — throws left — b.4/14/66 — 1991 positions: OF 106

YR	TM/LG	CL	G	TPA	AB	H	2B	3B	HR	TB	BB	IBB	HB	SO	GDP	SH	SF	SB	CS	R	RBI	BA	OBA	SA
85	PUL/APP	R+	66	249	204	50	8	0	10	88	40	0	0	30	5	0	5	0	1	39	46	.245	.361	.431
86	SUM/SAL	A	61	280	220	66	16	0	10	112	48	2	5	28	7	0	7	10	2	48	61	.300	.425	.509
	DUR/CAR	A+	67	284	229	64	9	1	12	111	46	5	7	24	4	1	1	2	4	47	44	.279	.413	.485
87	GRE/SOU	AA	93	405	348	79	12	4	6	117	53	6	0	48	9	1	3	3	2	38	40	.227	.327	.336
88	RIC/INT	AAA	70	275	227	46	9	1	8	81	39	9	0	55	3	2	7	4	3	27	28	.203	.311	.357
	GRE/SOU	AA	58	237	198	55	13	1	9	97	36	4	2	43	6	0	1	6	2	34	37	.278	.392	.490
89	RIC/INT	AAA	115	457	391	102	24	3	12	168	59	4	3	66	4	1	3	12	8	47	58	.261	.360	.430
	ATL/NL		16	56	51	12	3	0	1	18	3	1	1	9	1	0	1	2	1	7	3	.235	.291	.353
90	RIC/INT	AAA	12	52	45	16	5	1	2	29	7	2	0	6	2	0	0	0	0	7	7	.356	.442	.644
	ATL/NL		127	504	439	124	23	2	28	235	64	4	0	92	2	0	1	11	6	76	78	.282	.373	.535
91	MAC/SAL	A	3	13	10	2	0	0	2	8	2	1	0	1	0	0	1	0	0	2	5	.200	.308	.800
	ATL/NL		109	469	396	109	25	1	21	199	65	9	3	81	4	0	5	8	5	67	87	.275	.377	.503
3 YR TOTALS			**252**	**1029**	**886**	**245**	**51**	**3**	**50**	**452**	**132**	**14**	**4**	**182**	**7**	**1**	**6**	**21**	**15**	**150**	**168**	**.277**	**.371**	**.510**

Karkovice, Ronald Joseph "Ron" — bats right — throws right — b.8/8/63 — 1991 positions: C 69, OF 1

YR	TM/LG	CL	G	TPA	AB	H	2B	3B	HR	TB	BB	IBB	HB	SO	GDP	SH	SF	SB	CS	R	RBI	BA	OBA	SA
84	DEN/AMA	AAA	31	99	86	19	1	0	2	26	8	0	1	25	4	1	3	1	0	7	10	.221	.286	.302
	GF/EAS	AA	88	287	260	56	9	1	13	106	25	1	1	102	1	0	3	1	3	37	39	.215	.287	.408
85	GF/EAS	AA	99	375	324	70	9	3	11	118	49	1	2	105	1	0	6	2	2	37	37	.216	.323	.364
86	BIR/SOU	AA	97	395	319	90	13	1	20	165	61	3	4	109	3	2	9	2	2	63	53	.282	.394	.517
	CHI/AL		37	109	97	24	7	0	4	43	9	0	1	37	3	1	1	1	0	13	13	.247	.315	.443
87	CHI/AL		39	95	85	6	0	0	2	12	7	0	2	40	2	1	0	3	0	7	7	.071	.160	.141
	HAW/PCL	AAA	34	112	104	19	3	0	4	34	8	0	0	37	4	0	0	3	0	15	11	.183	.241	.327
88	CHI/AL		46	126	115	20	4	0	3	33	7	0	1	30	1	0	4	2	0	10	9	.174	.228	.287
	VAN/PCL	AAA	39	129	116	29	10	0	2	45	8	0	2	26	2	3	1	0	0	21	24	.250	.302	.388
89	CHI/AL		71	203	182	48	9	2	3	70	10	0	2	56	7	2	0	0	0	21	24	.264	.306	.385
90	CHI/AL		68	208	183	45	10	0	6	73	16	1	1	52	1	7	1	2	0	30	20	.246	.308	.399
91	CHI/AL		75	193	167	41	13	0	5	69	15	1	1	42	2	9	2	1	0	25	22	.246	.310	.413
6 YR TOTALS			**336**	**934**	**829**	**184**	**43**	**2**	**23**	**300**	**64**	**2**	**8**	**257**	**9**	**28**	**5**	**10**	**2**	**106**	**95**	**.222**	**.283**	**.362**

Karros, Eric Peter — bats right — throws right — b.11/4/67 — 1991 positions: 1B 10

YR	TM/LG	CL	G	TPA	AB	H	2B	3B	HR	TB	BB	IBB	HB	SO	GDP	SH	SF	SB	CS	R	RBI	BA	OBA	SA
88	GF/PIO	R+	66	307	268	98	12	1	12	148	32	0	3	35	7	0	4	9	2	68	55	.366	.433	.552
89	BAK/CAL	A+	142	614	545	165	40	1	15	252	63	3	2	99	15	0	4	18	7	86	86	.303	.375	.462
90	SA/TEX	AA	131	579	509	179	45	2	18	282	57	5	6	80	18	1	6	8	10	90	78	.352	.419	.554
91	ALB/PCL	AAA	132	557	488	154	33	8	22	269	58	8	6	80	6	0	5	3	2	88	101	.316	.391	.551
	LA/NL		14	15	14	1	1	0	0	2	1	0	0	6	0	0	0	0	0	0	1	.071	.133	.143

Kelly, Michael Raymond "Mike" — bats right — throws right — b.6/2/70 — 1991 positions: OF System ATL/NL

YR	TM/LG	CL	G	TPA	AB	H	2B	3B	HR	TB	BB	IBB	HB	SO	GDP	SH	SF	SB	CS	R	RBI	BA	OBA	SA
91	DUR/CAR	A+	35	146	124	31	6	1	6	57	19	0	2	47	0	0	1	6	2	29	17	.250	.356	.460

Kelly, Patrick Franklin "Pat" — bats right — throws right — b.10/14/67 — 1991 positions: 3B 80, 2B 19

YR	TM/LG	CL	G	TPA	AB	H	2B	3B	HR	TB	BB	IBB	HB	SO	GDP	SH	SF	SB	CS	R	RBI	BA	OBA	SA
88	ONE/NYP	A-	71	307	280	92	11	6	2	121	16	0	5	45	0	5	1	25	6	49	34	.329	.374	.432
89	PW/CAR	A+	124	487	436	116	21	7	3	160	32	1	8	79	3	4		31	9	61	45	.266	.323	.367
90	ALB/EAS	AA	126	470	418	113	19	6	8	168	37	1	6	79	7	5	4	31	14	67	44	.270	.335	.402
91	COL/INT	AAA	31	126	116	39	9	2	3	61	9	1	0	16	1	1	0	8	2	27	19	.336	.384	.526
	NY/AL		96	322	298	72	12	4	3	101	15	0	5	52	6	3	2	12	1	35	23	.242	.287	.339

Kelly, Roberto Conrado (Gray) — bats right — throws right — b.10/1/64 — 1991 positions: OF 125

YR	TM/LG	CL	G	TPA	AB	H	2B	3B	HR	TB	BB	IBB	HB	SO	GDP	SH	SF	SB	CS	R	RBI	BA	OBA	SA
84	GRE/SAL	A	111	423	361	86	13	2	1	106	57	0	1	49	1	1	3	42	10	68	26	.238	.341	.294
85	FL/FSL	A+	114	487	417	103	4	13	3	142	58	1	3	70	6	3	6	49	14	86	38	.247	.339	.341
86	ALB/EAS	AA	86	334	299	87	11	4	2	112	29	0	0	63	5	1	5	10	5	42	43	.291	.348	.375
87	COL/INT	AAA	118	516	471	131	19	8	13	205	33	0	3	116	5	1	8	51	10	77	62	.278	.324	.435
	NY/AL		23	59	52	14	3	0	1	20	5	0	0	15	0	1	0	9	3	12	7	.269	.328	.385
88	COL/INT	AAA	30	128	120	40	8	1	3	59	6	1	1	29	3	0	0	11	3	25	16	.333	.370	.492
	NY/AL		38	84	77	19	4	1	1	28	3	0	0	15	0	3	1	5	2	9	7	.247	.272	.364
89	NY/AL		137	496	441	133	18	3	9	184	41	1	4	89	8	8	0	35	12	65	48	.302	.369	.417
90	NY/AL		162	686	641	183	32	4	15	268	33	0	4	148	7	4	4	42	17	85	61	.285	.323	.418
91	NY/AL		126	543	486	130	22	4	20	216	45	2	5	77	14	2	5	32	9	68	69	.267	.333	.444
5 YR TOTALS			**486**	**1868**	**1697**	**479**	**79**	**10**	**46**	**716**	**127**	**5**	**15**	**344**	**30**	**18**	**11**	**123**	**43**	**239**	**192**	**.282**	**.336**	**.422**

Kennedy, Terrence Edward "Terry" — bats left — throws right — b.6/4/56 — 1991 positions: C 58, 1B 2

YR	TM/LG	CL	G	TPA	AB	H	2B	3B	HR	TB	BB	IBB	HB	SO	GDP	SH	SF	SB	CS	R	RBI	BA	OBA	SA
78	STL/NL		10	33	29	5	0	0	0	5	4	2	0	3	2	0	0	0	0	0	2	.172	.273	.172
79	STL/NL		33	116	109	31	7	0	2	44	6	2	0	20	2	0	1	0	0	11	17	.284	.319	.404
80	STL/NL		84	281	248	63	12	3	4	93	28	3	0	34	9	1	4	0	0	28	34	.254	.325	.375
81	SD/NL		101	412	382	115	24	1	2	147	22	6	2	53	7	4	2	0	2	32	41	.301	.341	.385
82	SD/NL		153	604	562	166	42	1	21	273	26	9	5	91	7	3	8	1	0	75	97	.295	.328	.486
83	SD/NL		149	612	549	156	27	2	17	238	51	15	2	89	10	1	9	1	3	47	98	.284	.342	.434
84	SD/NL		148	570	530	127	16	1	14	187	33	8	0	99	16	0	5	1	2	54	57	.240	.284	.353
85	SD/NL		143	565	532	139	27	1	10	198	31	10	0	102	19	0	2	0	0	54	74	.261	.301	.372
86	SD/NL		141	476	432	114	22	1	12	174	37	7	7	74	10	4	1	0	3	46	57	.264	.324	.403
87	BAL/AL		143	549	512	128	13	1	18	197	35	6	1	112	13	1	0	1	0	51	62	.250	.299	.385
88	BAL/AL		85	285	265	60	10	0	3	79	15	1	0	53	13	2	2	0	0	20	16	.226	.269	.298
89	SF/NL		125	395	355	85	15	0	5	115	35	7	0	56	6	3	2	0	3	19	34	.239	.306	.324
90	SF/NL		107	339	303	84	22	0	2	112	31	7	0	38	7	3	2	1	2	25	26	.277	.342	.370
91	SF/NL		69	184	171	40	7	1	3	58	11	4	1	31	4	0	1	0	0	12	13	.234	.283	.339
14 YR TOTALS			**1491**	**5421**	**4979**	**1313**	**244**	**12**	**113**	**1920**	**365**	**86**	**16**	**855**	**125**	**22**	**39**	**6**	**15**	**474**	**628**	**.264**	**.314**	**.386**

King, Jeffrey Wayne "Jeff" — bats right — throws right — b.12/26/64 — 1991 positions: 3B 33

YR	TM/LG	CL	G	TPA	AB	H	2B	3B	HR	TB	BB	IBB	HB	SO	GDP	SH	SF	SB	CS	R	RBI	BA	OBA	SA
86	PW/CAR	A+	37	152	132	31	4	1	6	55	19	2	1	34	4	0	0	1	1	18	20	.235	.336	.417
87	SAL/CAR	A+	90	374	310	86	9	1	26	175	61	2	1	88	7	0	2	6	2	68	71	.277	.396	.565
	HAR/EAS	AA	26	108	100	24	7	0	2	37	4	0	0	27	2	0	4	0	1	12	25	.240	.259	.370
88	HAR/EAS	AA	117	467	411	105	21	1	14	170	46	3	0	87	5	2	8	5	4	49	66	.255	.325	.414
89	BUF/AMA	AAA	51	189	169	43	5	2	6	70	13	0	0	22	5	2	5	7	1	26	29	.254	.299	.414
	PIT/NL		75	243	215	42	13	3	5	76	20	1	2	34	3	2	4	4	2	31	19	.195	.266	.353
90	PIT/NL		127	402	371	91	17	1	14	152	21	1	1	50	12	2	7	3	3	46	53	.245	.283	.410
91	BUF/AMA	AAA	9	24	18	4	1	1	0	7	6	0	0	3	0	0	0	1	0	3	2	.222	.417	.389
	PIT/NL		33	125	109	26	1	1	4	41	14	3	1	15	3	0	1	3	1	16	18	.239	.328	.376
3 YR TOTALS			**235**	**770**	**695**	**159**	**31**	**5**	**23**	**269**	**55**	**5**	**4**	**99**	**18**	**4**	**12**	**10**	**6**	**93**	**90**	**.229**	**.285**	**.387**

Kingery, Michael Scott "Mike" — bats left — throws left — b.3/29/61 — 1991 positions: OF 38, 1B 6

YR	TM/LG	CL	G	TPA	AB	H	2B	3B	HR	TB	BB	IBB	HB	SO	GDP	SH	SF	SB	CS	R	RBI	BA	OBA	SA
84	MEM/SOU	AA	139	560	455	135	19	3	4	172	93	6	0	61	12	7	5	18	11	65	58	.297	.412	.378
85	OMA/AMA	AAA	132	512	444	113	25	6	2	156	61	9	0	59	13	5	2	16	12	51	49	.255	.343	.351
86	OMA/AMA	AAA	79	344	298	99	14	8	3	138	39	8	2	30	4	1	4	22	7	47	47	.332	.408	.463
	KC/AL		62	223	209	54	8	5	3	81	12	2	0	30	4	0	2	7	3	25	14	.258	.296	.388
87	SEA/AL		120	390	354	99	25	4	9	159	27	0	1	43	4	1	6	7	9	38	52	.280	.329	.449
88	CAL/PCL	AAA	47	207	170	54	12	2	1	73	33	1	1	23	3	1	2	6	10	29	14	.318	.427	.429
	SEA/AL		57	145	123	25	6	0	1	34	19	1	1	23	1	1	1	3	1	21	9	.203	.313	.276
89	CAL/PCL	AAA	107	449	396	115	22	9	4	167	47	2	2	52	8	2	2	7	4	72	47	.290	.367	.422
	SEA/AL		31	84	76	17	3	0	2	26	7	0	0	14	2	0	1	1	1	14	6	.224	.286	.342
90	PHO/PCL	AAA	35	122	100	24	9	2	1	40	18	0	1	15	3	0	3	2	4	12	16	.240	.352	.400
	SF/NL		105	226	207	61	7	1	0	70	12	0	1	19	1	5	1	6	1	24	24	.295	.335	.338
91	PHO/PCL	AAA	13	52	44	15	3	0	1	21	6	0	0	6	3	0	2	0	1	8	13	.341	.404	.477
	SF/NL		91	125	110	20	2	2	0	26	15	1	0	21	3	0	0	1	0	13	8	.182	.280	.236
6 YR TOTALS			**466**	**1193**	**1079**	**276**	**51**	**12**	**15**	**396**	**92**	**4**	**4**	**150**	**15**	**7**	**11**	**25**	**15**	**135**	**113**	**.256**	**.314**	**.367**

Kirby, Wayne Leonard — bats left — throws right — b.1/22/64 — 1991 positions: OF 21

YR	TM/LG	CL	G	TPA	AB	H	2B	3B	HR	TB	BB	IBB	HB	SO	GDP	SH	SF	SB	CS	R	RBI	BA	OBA	SA
83	DOD/GCL	R	60	256	216	63	7	1	0	72	34	0	1	19	3	4	1	23	8	43	13	.292	.389	.333
84	VB/FSL	A+	76	258	224	61	6	3	0	73	21	2	6	30	3	5	2	11	9	39	21	.272	.348	.326
	GF/PIO	R+	20	98	84	26	2	2	1	35	12	2	0	9	2	1	1	19	3	19	11	.310	.392	.417
	BAK/CAL	A+	23	91	84	23	3	0	0	26	4	0	0	5	0	2	1	8	3	14	10	.274	.303	.310
85	VB/FSL	A+	122	488	437	123	9	3	0	138	41	1	3	41	3	4	3	31	14	70	28	.281	.345	.316
86	VB/FSL	A+	114	429	387	101	9	4	2	124	37	3	1	30	5	2	2	28	14	60	31	.261	.326	.320
87	SA/TEX	AA	24	87	80	19	1	2	1	27	4	0	0	7	0	3	0	6	4	7	9	.237	.274	.338
	BAK/CAL	A+	105	475	416	112	14	3	0	132	49	1	3	41	3	5	2	56	21	77	34	.269	.349	.317
88	BAK/CAL	A+	12	58	47	13	0	1	0	15	11	0	0	4	0	0	0	9	2	12	4	.277	.414	.319
	SA/TEX	AA	100	369	334	80	9	2	0	93	21	2	3	42	1	10	1	26	10	50	21	.240	.290	.278
89	SA/TEX	AA	44	162	140	30	3	1	0	35	18	0	1	17	4	2	1	11	6	14	7	.214	.306	.250
	ALB/PCL	AAA	78	343	310	106	18	8	0	140	26	1	1	36	2	5	1	29	14	62	30	.342	.393	.452
90	ALB/PCL	AAA	119	380	342	95	14	5	0	119	28	1	3	36	2	4	3	29	7	56	30	.278	.335	.348
91	CS/PCL	AAA	118	429	385	113	14	4	1	138	34	2	2	36	3	5	3	29	14	66	39	.294	.351	.358
	CLE/AL		21	47	43	9	2	0	0	11	2	0	0	6	2	1	1	1	2	4	5	.209	.239	.256

Kittle, Ronald Dale "Ron" — bats right — throws right — b.1/5/58 — 1991 positions: 1B 15

YR	TM/LG	CL	G	TPA	AB	H	2B	3B	HR	TB	BB	IBB	HB	SO	GDP	SH	SF	SB	CS	R	RBI	BA	OBA	SA
82	CHI/AL		20	32	29	7	2	0	1	12	3	0	0	12	0	0	0	0	0	3	7	.241	.313	.414
83	CHI/AL		145	570	520	132	19	3	35	262	39	8	8	150	10	0	3	8	3	75	100	.254	.314	.504
84	CHI/AL		139	525	466	100	15	0	32	211	49	5	6	137	7	0	4	3	6	67	74	.215	.295	.453
85	BUF/AMA	AAA	6	27	21	7	2	0	2	15	5	0	1	3	2	0	0	0	0	3	5	.333	.481	.714
	CHI/AL		116	417	379	87	12	0	26	177	31	1	5	92	12	0	2	1	4	51	58	.230	.295	.467
86	CHI/AL		86	333	296	63	11	0	17	125	28	0	3	87	10	0	2	2	1	34	48	.213	.282	.422
	NY/AL		30	89	80	19	2	0	4	33	7	1	0	23	0	0	2	6	0	8	12	.237	.292	.412
	YEAR		116	422	376	82	13	0	21	158	35	1	3	110	10	0	4	8	1	42	60	.218	.284	.420
87	COL/INT	AAA	4	19	18	4	0	0	0	4	1	0	0	5	0	0	0	0	0	3	1	.222	.263	.222
	NY/AL		59	173	159	44	5	0	12	85	10	1	1	36	4	0	3	0	1	21	28	.277	.318	.535

Kittle, Ronald Dale "Ron"(continued)

YR	TM/LG	CL	G	TPA	AB	H	2B	3B	HR	TB	BB	IBB	HB	SO	GDP	SH	SF	SB	CS	R	RBI	BA	OBA	SA
88	CLE/AL		75	254	225	58	8	0	18	120	16	1	8	65	0	0	5	0	0	31	43	.258	.323	.533
89	CHI/AL		51	196	169	51	10	0	11	94	22	1	1	42	2	0	4	0	1	26	37	.302	.378	.556
90	CHI/AL		83	305	277	68	14	0	16	130	24	2	3	77	3	0	1	0	0	29	43	.245	.311	.469
	BAL/AL		22	64	61	10	2	0	2	18	2	0	1	14	3	0	0	0	0	4	3	.164	.203	.295
	YEAR		105	369	338	78	16	0	18	148	26	2	4	91	6	0	1	0	0	33	46	.231	.293	.438
91	VAN/PCL	AAA	17	77	71	22	4	1	4	38	6	0	0	13	1	0	0	1	1	9	21	.310	.364	.535
	CHI/AL		17	55	47	9	0	0	2	15	5	0	0	9	2	0	0	0	0	7	7	.191	.291	.319
10 YR TOTALS			**843**	**3013**	**2708**	**648**	**100**	**3**	**176**	**1282**	**236**	**20**	**38**	**744**	**53**	**0**	**31**	**16**	**16**	**356**	**460**	**.239**	**.306**	**.473**

Klesko, Ryan Anthony — bats left — throws left — b.6/12/71 — 1991 positions: 1B System ATL/NL

YR	TM/LG	CL	G	TPA	AB	H	2B	3B	HR	TB	BB	IBB	HB	SO	GDP	SH	SF	SB	CS	R	RBI	BA	OBA	SA
89	BRA/GCL	R	17	64	57	23	5	4	1	39	6	2	0	6	2	0	1	4	3	14	16	.404	.453	.684
	SUM/SAL	A	25	103	90	26	6	0	1	35	11	1	0	14	5	1	1	1	0	17	12	.289	.363	.389
90	SUM/SAL	A	63	268	231	85	15	1	10	132	31	1	5	30	6	0	5	13	1	41	38	.368	.437	.571
	DUR/CAR	A+	77	332	292	80	16	1	7	119	32	4	2	53	8	0	6	10	5	40	47	.274	.343	.408
91	GRE/SOU	AA	126	506	419	122	22	3	14	192	75	14	6	60	5	3	3	14	17	64	67	.291	.404	.458

Knoblauch, Edward Charles "Chuck" — bats right — throws right — b.7/7/68 — 1991 positions: 2B 148, SS 2

YR	TM/LG	CL	G	TPA	AB	H	2B	3B	HR	TB	BB	IBB	HB	SO	GDP	SH	SF	SB	CS	R	RBI	BA	OBA	SA
89	KEN/MID	A	51	231	196	56	13	1	2	77	32	0	1	23	5	1	1	9	7	29	19	.286	.387	.393
	VIS/CAL	A+	18	86	77	28	10	0	0	38	6	0	1	11	0	1	1	4	0	20	21	.364	.412	.494
90	ORL/SOU	AA	118	509	432	125	24	6	2	167	63	0	9	31	13	2	3	23	7	74	53	.289	.389	.387
91	MIN/AL		151	634	565	159	24	6	1	198	59	0	4	40	8	1	5	25	5	78	50	.281	.351	.350

Knorr, Randy Duane — bats right — throws right — b.11/12/68 — 1991 positions: C 3

YR	TM/LG	CL	G	TPA	AB	H	2B	3B	HR	TB	BB	IBB	HB	SO	GDP	SH	SF	SB	CS	R	RBI	BA	OBA	SA
86	MH/PIO	R+	55	238	215	58	13	0	4	83	17	0	0	53	6	3	3	0	0	21	32	.270	.319	.386
87	MH/PIO	R+	26	115	106	31	7	0	10	68	5	3	1	26	1	0	3	0	0	21	24	.292	.322	.642
	MB/SAL	A	46	137	129	34	4	0	6	56	6	0	0	46	1	1	0	2	0	17	21	.264	.292	.434
88	MB/SAL	A	117	416	364	85	13	0	9	125	41	0	9	91	7	9	2	0	1	43	42	.234	.310	.343
89	DUN/FSL	A+	33	130	122	32	6	0	6	56	6	0	0	21	0	0	2	0	2	13	23	.262	.292	.459
90	KNO/SOU	AA	116	435	392	108	12	1	13	161	31	2	2	83	7	4	6	0	3	51	64	.276	.327	.411
91	KNO/SOU	AA	24	86	74	13	4	0	0	17	10	1	1	18	0	0	1	2	0	7	4	.176	.279	.230
	SYR/INT	AAA	91	372	342	89	20	0	5	124	23	3	3	58	17	0	4	1	0	29	44	.260	.309	.363
	TOR/AL		3	2	1	0	0	0	0	0	1	0	0	1	0	0	0	0	0	0	0	.000	.500	.000

Komminsk, Brad Lynn — bats right — throws right — b.4/4/61 — 1991 positions: OF 22

YR	TM/LG	CL	G	TPA	AB	H	2B	3B	HR	TB	BB	IBB	HB	SO	GDP	SH	SF	SB	CS	R	RBI	BA	OBA	SA
79	KIN/APP	R+	59	238	185	41	9	1	7	73	48	1	3	74	3	1	1	20	2	37	34	.222	.388	.395
80	AND/SAL	A	121	514	425	111	17	5	20	198	74	2	7	102	8	3	5	27	9	86	67	.261	.376	.466
81	DUR/CAR	A+	132	581	459	148	27	2	33	278	110	8	8	101	24	0	4	35	12	108	104	.322	.458	.606
82	RIC/INT	AAA	5	19	17	6	1	0	2	13	2	0	0	5	0	0	0	0	1	4	5	.353	.421	.765
	SAV/SOU	AA	133	532	454	124	18	7	26	234	72	3	4	114	8	1	1	14	3	88	78	.273	.377	.515
83	RIC/INT	AAA	117	501	413	138	24	6	24	246	78	3	0	70	8	2	8	26	5	94	103	.334	.433	.596
	ATL/NL		19	41	36	8	2	0	0	10	5	0	0	7	1	0	0	0	0	2	4	.222	.317	.278
84	RIC/INT	AAA	42	177	144	37	11	3	5	69	31	1	0	20	3	0	2	8	2	23	28	.257	.384	.479
	ATL/NL		90	334	301	61	10	0	8	95	29	0	2	77	5	1	1	18	6	37	36	.203	.276	.316
85	ATL/NL		106	343	300	68	12	3	4	98	38	1	1	71	4	2	2	10	8	52	21	.227	.314	.327
86	RIC/INT	AAA	133	542	465	109	22	4	13	178	69	1	2	124	12	1	5	29	3	67	65	.234	.333	.383
	ATL/NL		5	5	5	2	0	0	0	2	0	0	0	1	0	0	0	0	1	0	0	.400	.400	.400
87	DEN/AMA	AAA	135	569	494	147	31	4	32	282	66	2	4	127	6	0	5	18	9	110	95	.298	.381	.571
	MIL/AL		7	17	15	1	0	0	0	1	1	0	0	7	0	1	0	1	0	0	0	.067	.125	.067
88	DEN/AMA	AAA	105	406	348	83	18	3	16	155	49	1	5	96	8	1	3	7	1	55	57	.239	.338	.445
89	CS/PCL	AAA	54	214	190	55	17	0	9	99	18	0	2	40	2	0	4	7	1	30	34	.289	.350	.521
	CLE/AL		71	227	198	47	8	2	6	83	24	0	1	55	4	1	3	8	2	27	33	.237	.319	.419
90	SF/NL		8	6	5	1	0	0	0	1	1	0	0	2	0	0	0	2	0	0	0	.200	.333	.200
	BAL/AL		46	119	101	24	4	0	3	37	14	1	2	29	2	2	0	1	1	18	8	.238	.342	.366
	YEAR		54	125	106	25	4	0	3	38	15	1	2	31	2	2	0	1	1	20	8	.236	.341	.358
	ROC/INT	AAA	28	93	79	23	2	0	1	28	10	2	1	16	1	1	2	0	3	7	8	.291	.370	.354
91	TAC/PCL	AAA	74	304	270	79	15	4	5	117	29	0	3	49	6	1	1	11	1	38	43	.293	.366	.433
	OAK/AL		24	27	25	3	1	0	0	4	2	0	0	6	1	0	0	1	2	1	2	.120	.185	.160
8 YR TOTALS			**376**	**1119**	**986**	**215**	**37**	**5**	**23**	**331**	**114**	**2**	**6**	**258**	**16**	**7**	**6**	**39**	**20**	**140**	**105**	**.218**	**.301**	**.336**

Koslofski, Kevin Craig — bats left — throws right — b.9/24/66 — 1991 positions: OF System KC/AL

YR	TM/LG	CL	G	TPA	AB	H	2B	3B	HR	TB	BB	IBB	HB	SO	GDP	SH	SF	SB	CS	R	RBI	BA	OBA	SA
84	EUG/NWL	A—	53	182	155	29	2	2	1	38	25	0	0	37	3	1	1	10	2	23	10	.187	.298	.245
85	ROY/GCL	R	33	125	108	27	4	2	0	35	12	0	3	19	1	2	0	7	2	17	11	.250	.341	.324
86	FM/FSL	A+	103	391	331	84	13	5	0	107	47	2	2	59	6	7	4	12	6	44	29	.254	.346	.323
87	FM/FSL	A+	109	388	330	80	12	3	0	98	46	3	7	64	4	3	2	25	9	46	25	.242	.345	.297
88	BC/FSL	A+	108	422	368	97	7	8	3	129	44	5	4	71	4	4	2	32	11	52	30	.264	.347	.351
89	BC/FSL	A+	116	407	343	89	10	3	4	117	51	2	5	57	9	5	3	41	14	65	33	.259	.361	.341
90	MEM/SOU	AA	118	433	367	78	11	5	3	108	54	4	2	89	4	4	2	12	7	52	32	.213	.315	.294
91	MEM/SOU	AA	81	332	287	93	15	3	7	135	33	3	4	56	2	1	4	10	13	41	39	.324	.396	.470
	OMA/AMA	AAA	25	113	94	28	3	2	2	41	15	0	1	19	1	2	1	4	3	13	19	.298	.396	.436

(continued)

Kreuter, Chadden Michael "Chad" — bats both — throws right — b.8/26/64 — 1991 positions: C 1

YR	TM/LG	CL	G	TPA	AB	H	2B	3B	HR	TB	BB	IBB	HB	SO	GDP	SH	SF	SB	CS	R	RBI	BA	OBA	SA
85	BUR/MID	A	69	246	199	53	9	0	4	74	38	0	1	48	4	5	3	3	2	25	26	.266	.382	.372
86	SAL/CAR	A+	125	465	387	85	21	2	6	128	67	2	3	82	14	4	4	5	5	55	49	.220	.336	.331
87	CHA/FSL	A+	85	316	281	61	18	1	9	108	31	2	1	32	5	2	1	1	1	36	40	.217	.296	.384
88	TUL/TEX	AA	108	422	358	95	24	6	3	140	55	1	2	66	12	2	5	2	2	46	51	.265	.362	.391
	TEX/AL		16	58	51	14	2	1	1	21	7	0	0	13	1	0	0	0	0	3	5	.275	.362	.412
89	OC/AMA	AAA	26	102	87	22	3	0	0	25	13	0	0	11	2	1	1	1	1	10	6	.253	.347	.287
	TEX/AL		87	192	158	24	3	0	5	42	27	0	0	40	4	6	1	0	1	16	9	.152	.274	.266
90	OC/AMA	AAA	92	347	291	65	17	1	7	105	52	0	2	80	8	2	0	0	3	41	35	.223	.345	.361
	TEX/AL		22	32	22	1	1	0	0	2	8	0	0	9	0	1	1	0	0	2	2	.045	.290	.091
91	TEX/AL		3	4	4	0	0	0	0	0	0	0	0	1	0	0	0	0	0	0	0	.000	.000	.000
	OC/AMA	AAA	24	89	70	19	6	0	1	28	18	0	0	16	4	0	1	2	0	14	12	.271	.416	.400
	TUL/TEX	AA	42	158	128	30	6	1	2	44	29	4	1	23	3	0	0	1	0	23	10	.234	.380	.344
4 YR TOTALS			**128**	**286**	**235**	**39**	**6**	**1**	**6**	**65**	**42**	**0**	**0**	**63**	**5**	**7**	**2**	**0**	**1**	**21**	**16**	**.166**	**.290**	**.277**

Kruk, John Martin — bats left — throws left — b.2/9/61 — 1991 positions: 1B 102, OF 52

YR	TM/LG	CL	G	TPA	AB	H	2B	3B	HR	TB	BB	IBB	HB	SO	GDP	SH	SF	SB	CS	R	RBI	BA	OBA	SA
84	LV/PCL	AAA	115	392	340	111	25	6	11	181	45	4	1	37	8	2	4	2	6	56	57	.326	.403	.532
85	LV/PCL	AAA	123	493	422	148	29	4	7	206	67	12	1	48	13	0	3	2	4	61	59	.351	.438	.488
86	LV/PCL	AAA	6	32	28	13	3	1	0	18	4	2	0	5	0	0	0	0	1	6	9	.464	.531	.643
	SD/NL		122	327	278	86	16	2	4	118	45	0	0	58	11	2	2	2	4	33	38	.309	.403	.424
87	SD/NL		138	527	447	140	14	2	20	218	73	15	0	93	6	3	4	18	10	72	91	.313	.406	.488
88	SD/NL		120	466	378	91	17	1	9	137	80	12	0	68	7	3	5	5	3	54	44	.241	.369	.362
89	SD/NL		31	94	76	14	0	0	3	23	17	0	0	14	5	1	0	0	0	7	6	.184	.333	.303
	PHI/NL		81	312	281	93	13	6	5	133	27	2	0	39	5	1	3	3	0	46	38	.331	.386	.473
	YEAR		112	406	357	107	13	6	8	156	44	2	0	53	10	2	3	3	0	53	44	.300	.374	.437
90	PHI/NL		142	515	443	129	25	8	7	191	69	16	0	70	11	2	1	10	5	52	67	.291	.386	.431
91	PHI/NL		152	615	538	158	27	6	21	260	67	16	1	100	11	0	9	7	0	84	92	.294	.367	.483
6 YR TOTALS			**786**	**2856**	**2441**	**711**	**112**	**25**	**69**	**1080**	**378**	**61**	**1**	**442**	**56**	**12**	**24**	**45**	**22**	**348**	**376**	**.291**	**.383**	**.442**

Kunkel, Jeffrey William "Jeff" — bats right — throws right — b.3/25/62 — 1991 positions: SS

YR	TM/LG	CL	G	TPA	AB	H	2B	3B	HR	TB	BB	IBB	HB	SO	GDP	SH	SF	SB	CS	R	RBI	BA	OBA	SA
84	TUL/TEX	AA	47	188	177	56	16	1	4	86	6	0	4	32	4	0	1	7	2	30	22	.316	.351	.486
	TEX/AL		50	150	142	29	2	3	3	46	2	0	1	35	2	3	2	4	3	13	7	.204	.218	.324
85	OC/AMA	AAA	99	400	370	72	8	6	5	107	20	0	3	81	15	2	5	8	9	40	43	.195	.239	.289
	TEX/AL		2	4	4	1	0	0	0	1	0	0	0	3	0	0	0	0	0	1	0	.250	.250	.250
86	OC/AMA	AAA	111	442	409	100	16	4	11	157	18	0	5	101	15	6	4	10	6	50	51	.244	.282	.384
	TEX/AL		8	13	13	3	0	0	1	6	0	0	0	2	0	0	0	0	0	3	2	.231	.231	.462
87	TEX/AL		15	34	32	7	0	0	1	10	0	0	0	10	0	1	0	0	0	1	2	.219	.242	.313
	OC/AMA	AAA	58	219	193	49	9	3	9	91	20	0	5	58	7	0	1	2	4	31	34	.254	.338	.472
88	OC/AMA	AAA	56	220	203	44	11	4	5	78	12	0	1	50	4	0	5	7	2	28	21	.217	.255	.384
	TEX/AL		55	161	154	35	8	3	2	55	4	1	1	35	5	1	1	0	1	14	15	.227	.250	.357
89	TEX/AL		108	326	293	79	21	2	8	128	20	0	3	75	6	10	0	3	2	39	29	.270	.323	.437
90	OC/AMA	AAA	4	19	19	8	1	0	0	9	0	0	0	2	0	0	0	0	0	0	3	.421	.421	.474
	TEX/AL		99	218	200	34	11	1	3	56	11	0	2	66	7	5	0	2	1	17	17	.170	.221	.280
7 YR TOTALS			**337**	**906**	**838**	**188**	**42**	**9**	**18**	**302**	**37**	**1**	**8**	**226**	**20**	**20**	**3**	**9**	**8**	**88**	**72**	**.224**	**.263**	**.360**

Lake, Steven Michael "Steve" — bats right — throws right — b.3/14/57 — 1991 positions: C 58

YR	TM/LG	CL	G	TPA	AB	H	2B	3B	HR	TB	BB	IBB	HB	SO	GDP	SH	SF	SB	CS	R	RBI	BA	OBA	SA
83	CHI/NL		38	88	85	22	4	1	1	31	2	2	1	6	4	0	0	0	0	9	7	.259	.284	.365
84	MID/TEX	AA	9	26	25	4	0	0	0	4	0	0	1	5	1	0	0	0	0	2	1	.160	.192	.160
	CHI/NL		25	57	54	12	4	0	2	22	0	0	1	7	0	1	1	0	0	4	7	.222	.232	.407
85	CHI/NL		58	128	119	18	2	0	1	23	3	1	1	21	3	4	1	1	0	5	11	.151	.177	.193
86	IOW/AMA	AAA	17	52	49	10	4	0	0	14	0	0	2	13	1	1	0	0	0	3	2	.204	.235	.286
	CHI/NL		10	21	19	8	1	0	0	9	1	0	1	2	1	0	0	0	0	4	4	.421	.450	.474
	LOU/AMA	AAA	16	51	49	14	2	0	0	16	2	0	0	7	1	0	0	0	0	2	11	.286	.314	.327
	STL/NL		26	51	49	12	1	0	2	19	2	0	0	5	2	0	0	0	0	4	10	.245	.275	.388
	YEAR		36	72	68	20	2	0	2	28	3	1	0	7	3	1	0	0	0	8	14	.294	.324	.412
87	STL/NL		74	195	179	45	7	2	2	62	10	4	0	18	2	5	1	0	0	19	19	.251	.289	.346
88	STL/NL		36	59	54	15	3	0	1	21	3	0	0	15	0	0	0	0	0	5	4	.278	.339	.389
89	PHI/NL		58	169	155	39	5	1	4	52	12	4	0	20	6	1	1	0	0	9	14	.252	.304	.335
90	PHI/NL		29	84	80	20	2	0	0	22	3	1	1	12	1	0	0	0	0	4	6	.250	.286	.275
91	PHI/NL		58	164	158	36	4	1	1	45	2	1	0	26	5	4	0	0	0	12	11	.228	.237	.321
9 YR TOTALS			**412**	**1016**	**952**	**227**	**33**	**5**	**12**	**306**	**38**	**14**	**6**	**132**	**24**	**16**	**4**	**1**	**0**	**75**	**93**	**.238**	**.271**	**.321**

Lampkin, Thomas Michael "Tom" — bats left — throws right — b.3/4/64 — 1991 positions: C 11

YR	TM/LG	CL	G	TPA	AB	H	2B	3B	HR	TB	BB	IBB	HB	SO	GDP	SH	SF	SB	CS	R	RBI	BA	OBA	SA
86	BAT/NYP	A-	63	223	190	49	5	1	1	59	31	3	0	14	4	1	1	4	3	24	20	.258	.360	.311
87	WAT/MID	A	118	441	398	106	19	2	7	150	34	2	2	41	7	1	6	5	0	49	55	.266	.323	.377
88	WIL/EAS	AA	80	291	263	71	10	0	2	90	25	0	3	20	6	0	0	1	2	38	23	.270	.340	.342
	CS/PCL	AAA	34	119	107	30	5	0	0	35	9	1	2	12	3	1	0	0	0	14	7	.280	.347	.327
	CLE/AL		4	5	4	0	0	0	0	0	1	0	0	0	1	0	0	0	0	0	0	.000	.200	.000

Lampkin, Thomas Michael "Tom" (continued)

YR	TM/LG	CL	G	TPA	AB	H	2B	3B	HR	TB	BB	IBB	HB	SO	GDP	SH	SF	SB	CS	R	RBI	BA	OBA	SA
89	CS/PCL	AAA	63	224	209	67	10	3	4	95	10	1	2	18	5	2	1	4	2	26	32	.321	.356	.455
90	CS/PCL	AAA	69	221	199	44	7	5	1	64	19	0	2	19	2	0	1	7	2	32	18	.221	.294	.322
	LV/PCL	AAA	1	2	2	1	0	0	0	1	0	0	0	1	0	0	0	0	0	0	0	.500	.500	.500
	SD/NL		26	67	63	14	0	1	1	19	4	1	0	9	2	0	0	0	1	4	4	.222	.269	.302
91	LV/PCL	AAA	45	177	164	52	11	1	2	71	10	1	2	20	4	0	1	2	1	25	29	.317	.362	.433
	SD/NL		38	61	58	11	3	1	0	16	3	0	0	9	0	0	0	0	0	4	3	.190	.230	.276
3 YR TOTALS			**68**	**133**	**125**	**25**	**3**	**2**	**1**	**35**	**8**	**1**	**0**	**18**	**3**	**0**	**0**	**0**	**1**	**8**	**7**	**.200**	**.248**	**.280**

Landrum, Cedric Bernard "Ced" — bats left — throws right — b.9/3/63 — 1991 positions: OF 44

YR	TM/LG	CL	G	TPA	AB	H	2B	3B	HR	TB	BB	IBB	HB	SO	GDP	SH	SF	SB	CS	R	RBI	BA	OBA	SA
86	GEN/NYP	A−	64	263	213	67	6	2	3	86	40	1	3	33	1	4	3	49	10	51	16	.315	.425	.404
87	WIN/CAR	A+	126	547	458	129	13	7	4	168	78	3	6	50	6	1	4	79	18	82	49	.282	.390	.367
88	PIT/EAS	AA	128	522	445	109	15	8	1	143	55	2	8	63	4	10	4	69	17	82	39	.245	.336	.321
89	CHA/SOU	AA	123	421	361	92	11	2	6	125	48	0	5	54	4	5	2	45	9	72	37	.255	.349	.346
90	IOW/AMA	AAA	123	424	372	110	10	4	0	128	43	1	1	63	4	5	3	46	16	71	24	.296	.368	.344
91	IOW/AMA	AAA	38	138	131	44	8	2	1	59	5	0	0	21	2	2	0	13	4	14	11	.336	.360	.450
	CHI/NL		56	99	86	20	2	1	0	24	10	0	0	18	2	3	0	27	5	28	6	.233	.313	.279

Lankford, Raymond Lewis "Ray" — bats left — throws left — b.6/5/67 — 1991 positions: OF 149

YR	TM/LG	CL	G	TPA	AB	H	2B	3B	HR	TB	BB	IBB	HB	SO	GDP	SH	SF	SB	CS	R	RBI	BA	OBA	SA
87	JC/APP	R+	66	278	253	78	17	4	3	112	19	0	5	43	5	0	1	14	11	45	32	.308	.367	.443
88	SPR/MID	A	135	605	532	151	26	16	11	242	60	2	10	92	4	1	2	33	17	90	66	.284	.366	.455
89	ARK/TEX	AA	134	574	498	158	28	12	11	243	65	6	4	57	7	0	7	38	10	98	98	.317	.395	.488
90	LOU/AMA	AAA	132	552	473	123	25	8	10	194	72	9	5	81	8	0	2	29	7	61	72	.260	.362	.410
	STL/NL		39	139	126	36	10	1	3	57	13	0	0	27	1	0	0	8	2	12	12	.286	.353	.452
91	STL/NL		151	615	566	142	23	15	9	222	41	1	1	114	4	4	3	44	20	83	69	.251	.301	.392
2 YR TOTALS			**190**	**754**	**692**	**178**	**33**	**16**	**12**	**279**	**54**	**1**	**1**	**141**	**5**	**4**	**3**	**52**	**22**	**95**	**81**	**.257**	**.311**	**.403**

Lansford, Carney Ray — bats right — throws right — b.2/7/57 — 1991 positions: 3B 4, DH 1

YR	TM/LG	CL	G	TPA	AB	H	2B	3B	HR	TB	BB	IBB	HB	SO	GDP	SH	SF	SB	CS	R	RBI	BA	OBA	SA
78	CAL/AL		121	500	453	133	23	2	8	184	31	2	4	67	4	5	7	20	9	63	52	.294	.339	.406
79	CAL/AL		157	712	654	188	30	5	19	285	39	2	3	115	16	12	4	20	8	114	79	.287	.329	.436
80	CAL/AL		151	670	602	157	27	3	15	235	50	2	0	93	12	7	11	14	5	87	80	.261	.312	.390
81	BOS/AL		102	438	399	134	23	3	4	175	34	3	2	28	6	1	2	15	10	61	52	.336	.389	.439
82	BOS/AL		128	539	482	145	28	4	11	214	46	2	2	48	15	1	8	9	4	65	63	.301	.359	.444
83	OAK/AL		80	328	299	92	16	2	10	142	22	4	3	33	8	0	4	3	8	43	45	.308	.357	.475
84	OAK/AL		151	651	597	179	31	5	14	262	40	6	3	62	12	2	9	9	3	70	74	.300	.342	.439
85	OAK/AL		98	432	401	111	18	2	13	172	18	1	4	27	6	4	5	2	3	51	46	.277	.311	.429
86	OAK/AL		151	640	591	168	16	4	19	249	39	2	5	51	16	1	4	16	7	80	72	.284	.332	.421
87	OAK/AL		151	631	554	160	27	4	19	252	60	11	9	44	9	5	3	27	8	89	76	.289	.366	.455
88	OAK/AL		150	607	556	155	20	2	7	200	35	4	7	35	17	5	4	29	8	80	57	.279	.327	.360
89	OAK/AL		148	616	551	185	28	2	2	223	51	2	9	25	21	1	4	37	15	81	52	.336	.398	.405
90	OAK/AL		134	564	507	136	15	1	3	162	45	4	6	50	10	2	4	16	14	58	50	.268	.333	.320
91	TAC/PCL	AAA	8	25	23	7	1	1	0	10	2	0	0	1	2	0	0	0	0	1	1	.304	.360	.435
	OAK/AL		5	16	16	1	0	0	0	1	0	0	0	2	0	0	0	0	0	0	1	.063	.063	.063
14 YR TOTALS			**1727**	**7344**	**6662**	**1944**	**302**	**39**	**144**	**2756**	**510**	**45**	**57**	**680**	**152**	**46**	**69**	**217**	**102**	**942**	**799**	**.292**	**.344**	**.414**

Larkin, Barry Louis — bats right — throws right — b.4/28/64 — 1991 positions: SS 119

YR	TM/LG	CL	G	TPA	AB	H	2B	3B	HR	TB	BB	IBB	HB	SO	GDP	SH	SF	SB	CS	R	RBI	BA	OBA	SA
85	VER/EAS	AA	72	288	255	68	13	2	1	88	23	1	3	21	13	4	3	12	1	42	31	.267	.331	.345
86	DEN/AMA	AAA	103	457	413	136	31	10	10	217	31	1	2	43	1	4	7	19	6	67	51	.329	.373	.525
	CIN/NL		41	169	159	45	4	3	3	64	9	1	0	21	2	0	1	8	0	27	19	.283	.320	.403
87	CIN/NL		125	488	439	107	16	2	12	163	36	3	5	52	8	5	3	21	6	64	43	.244	.306	.371
88	CIN/NL		151	652	588	174	32	5	12	252	41	7	10	24	7	10	5	40	7	91	56	.296	.347	.429
89	NAS/AMA	AAA	2	5	5	5	1	0	0	6	0	0	0	0	0	0	0	0	0	2	0	1.000	1.000	1.200
	CIN/NL		97	357	325	111	14	4	4	145	20	5	2	23	7	2	8	10	5	47	36	.342	.375	.446
90	CIN/NL		158	681	614	185	25	6	7	243	49	3	7	49	14	7	4	30	5	85	67	.301	.358	.396
91	CIN/NL		123	527	464	140	27	4	20	235	55	1	3	64	7	3	2	24	4	88	69	.302	.378	.506
6 YR TOTALS			**695**	**2874**	**2589**	**762**	**118**	**24**	**58**	**1102**	**210**	**16**	**25**	**233**	**45**	**27**	**23**	**133**	**29**	**402**	**290**	**.294**	**.350**	**.426**

Larkin, Eugene Thomas "Gene" — bats both — throws right — b.10/24/62 — 1991 positions: OF 47, 1B 39, DH 4, 2B 1, 3B 1

YR	TM/LG	CL	G	TPA	AB	H	2B	3B	HR	TB	BB	IBB	HB	SO	GDP	SH	SF	SB	CS	R	RBI	BA	OBA	SA
84	ELI/APP	R+	57	227	193	63	13	1	6	96	29	1	2	18	2	0	3	1	1	29	37	.326	.414	.497
85	VIS/CAL	A+	142	625	528	161	25	3	13	231	81	5	2	61	8	0	14	0	0	90	106	.305	.390	.438
86	ORL/SOU	AA	142	632	529	170	29	6	15	256	84	2	5	50	9	1	13	1	0	85	104	.321	.410	.484
87	POR/PCL	AAA	35	150	129	39	9	0	1	51	20	0	1	11	3	0	0	0	0	17	14	.302	.400	.395
	MIN/AL		85	262	233	62	11	2	4	89	25	3	2	31	4	0	2	1	2	23	28	.266	.340	.382
88	MIN/AL		149	594	505	135	30	2	8	193	68	8	15	55	12	.1	5	5	2	56	70	.267	.368	.382
89	MIN/AL		136	520	446	119	25	1	6	164	54	6	9	57	13	5	6	5	2	61	46	.267	.353	.368
90	MIN/AL		119	457	401	108	26	4	5	157	42	2	5	55	4	5	4	5	3	46	42	.269	.343	.392
91	MIN/AL		98	291	255	73	14	1	2	95	-30	3	1	21	9	3	2	2	1	34	19	.286	.361	.373
5 YR TOTALS			**587**	**2124**	**1840**	**497**	**106**	**10**	**25**	**698**	**219**	**22**	**32**	**219**	**44**	**14**	**19**	**16**	**14**	**220**	**205**	**.270**	**.355**	**.379**

Laureano, Francisco (Santana) "Frank" — bats right — throws right — b.10/4/67 — 1991 positions: 2B System KC/AL

YR	TM/LG	CL	G	TPA	AB	H	2B	3B	HR	TB	BB	IBB	HB	SO	GDP	SH	SF	SB	CS	R	RBI	BA	OBA	SA
86	BUR/MID	A	130	525	465	128	31	1	7	182	51	2	3	64	8	2	4	7	6	79	37	.275	.348	.391
87	APP/MID	A	139	580	498	161	25	1	16	236	70	0	1	81	5	0	11	19	9	86	87	.323	.400	.474
88	BC/FSL	A+	20	90	78	16	1	2	1	24	10	0	1	12	2	1	0	6	1	11	6	.205	.303	.308
	VIR/CAR	A+	117	460	387	87	9	2	2	106	65	1	4	50	11	1	3	21	9	47	37	.225	.340	.274
89	BC/FSL	A+	132	563	457	119	17	3	2	148	88	2	2	63	12	9	7	25	13	71	66	.260	.377	.324
90	MEM/SOU	AA	108	393	320	77	14	2	4	107	57	1	4	51	7	6	6	7	9	44	36	.241	.357	.334
91	OMA/AMA	AAA	6	22	19	3	0	0	1	6	2	0	0	5	1	0	1	0	0	2	5	.158	.227	.316
	MEM/SOU	AA	99	434	359	107	17	2	3	137	61	1	7	51	8	2	5	12	4	58	34	.298	.405	.382

LaValliere, Michael Eugene "Mike" — bats left — throws right — b.8/18/60 — 1991 positions: C 105

YR	TM/LG	CL	G	TPA	AB	H	2B	3B	HR	TB	BB	IBB	HB	SO	GDP	SH	SF	SB	CS	R	RBI	BA	OBA	SA
84	REA/EAS	AA	55	189	147	37	6	0	6	61	36	3	1	15	2	3	2	0	1	19	22	.252	.398	.415
	POR/PCL	AAA	37	140	122	38	6	3	5	65	15	1	1	11	4	1	1	0	0	20	21	.311	.388	.533
	PHI/NL		6	9	7	0	0	0	0	0	2	0	0	2	0	0	0	0	0	0	0	.000	.222	.000
85	STL/NL		12	44	34	5	1	0	0	6	7	0	0	3	2	0	3	0	0	2	6	.147	.273	.176
	LOU/AMA	AAA	83	289	231	47	12	1	4	73	48	2	1	20	9	3	6	0	1	19	26	.203	.336	.316
86	STL/NL		110	350	303	71	10	2	3	94	36	5	1	37	7	10	0	0	1	18	30	.234	.318	.310
87	PIT/NL		121	390	340	102	19	0	1	124	43	9	1	32	4	3	3	0	0	33	36	.300	.377	.365
88	PIT/NL		120	409	352	92	18	0	2	116	50	10	2	34	8	1	4	3	2	24	47	.261	.353	.330
89	BUF/AMA	AAA	7	22	18	2	0	0	0	2	3	0	0	4	1	0	1	0	0	0	1	.111	.227	.111
	PIT/NL		68	223	190	60	10	2	0	76	29	7	0	24	4	4	0	0	3	15	23	.316	.406	.400
90	PIT/NL		96	330	279	72	15	0	3	96	44	8	2	20	6	4	1	0	3	27	31	.258	.362	.344
91	PIT/NL		108	377	336	97	11	2	3	121	33	4	2	27	10	1	5	2	1	25	41	.289	.351	.360
8 YR TOTALS			**641**	**2132**	**1841**	**499**	**84**	**4**	**14**	**633**	**244**	**43**	**8**	**179**	**41**	**23**	**16**	**5**	**9**	**144**	**214**	**.271**	**.356**	**.344**

Law, Vance Aaron — bats right — throws right — b.10/1/56 — 1991 positions: 3B 67, SS 3, OF 3, 1B 1, P-1

YR	TM/LG	CL	G	TPA	AB	H	2B	3B	HR	TB	BB	IBB	HB	SO	GDP	SH	SF	SB	CS	R	RBI	BA	OBA	SA
80	PIT/NL		25	78	74	17	2	2	0	23	3	0	0	15	2	1	0	2	0	11	3	.230	.260	.311
81	PIT/NL		30	71	67	9	0	1	0	11	2	0	0	15	2	1	1	1	1	1	3	.134	.157	.164
82	CHI/AL		114	398	359	101	20	1	5	138	26	1	1	46	10	7	5	4	2	40	54	.281	.327	.384
83	CHI/AL		145	471	408	99	21	5	4	142	51	1	1	56	7	6	5	3	1	55	42	.243	.325	.348
84	CHI/AL		151	533	481	121	18	2	17	194	41	2	1	75	13	6	4	4	1	60	59	.252	.309	.403
85	MON/NL		147	621	519	138	30	6	10	210	86	0	2	96	11	8	6	6	5	75	52	.266	.369	.405
86	MON/NL		112	402	360	81	17	2	5	117	37	1	1	66	9	2	2	3	5	37	44	.225	.298	.325
87	MON/NL		133	492	436	119	27	1	12	184	51	5	0	62	8	2	3	8	5	52	56	.273	.347	.422
88	CHI/NL		151	621	556	163	29	2	11	229	55	4	3	79	15	4	3	1	4	73	78	.293	.358	.412
89	CHI/NL		130	454	408	96	22	3	0	145	38	0	0	73	11	1	7	2	2	38	42	.235	.296	.355
91	TAC/PCL	AAA	18	77	65	13	1	0	0	14	12	0	0	12	2	0	0	0	0	7	6	.200	.325	.215
	OAK/AL		74	157	134	28	7	1	0	37	18	0	0	27	4	5	0	0	0	11	9	.209	.303	.276
11 YR TOTALS			**1212**	**4298**	**3802**	**972**	**193**	**26**	**71**	**1430**	**408**	**14**	**9**	**602**	**92**	**43**	**36**	**34**	**26**	**453**	**442**	**.256**	**.326**	**.376**

Lee, Derek Gerald — bats left — throws right — b.7/28/66 — 1991 positions: OF System CHI/AL

YR	TM/LG	CL	G	TPA	AB	H	2B	3B	HR	TB	BB	IBB	HB	SO	GDP	SH	SF	SB	CS	R	RBI	BA	OBA	SA
88	UTI/NYP	A–	76	312	252	86	7	5	2	109	50	5	3	48	2	3	4	54	15	51	47	.341	.450	.433
89	SB/MID	A	125	550	448	128	24	7	11	199	87	4	9	83	5	4	2	45	26	89	48	.286	.410	.444
90	BIR/SOU	AA	126	496	411	105	21	3	7	153	71	5	6	93	8	3	5	14	10	68	75	.255	.369	.372
91	BIR/SOU	AA	45	207	154	50	10	2	5	79	46	5	6	23	1	0	1	9	7	36	16	.325	.493	.513
	VAN/PCL	AAA	87	360	319	94	28	5	6	150	35	2	2	62	1	3	1	4	2	54	44	.295	.367	.470

Lee, Manuel Lora "Manuel" or "Manny" — bats both — throws right — b.6/17/65 — 1991 positions: SS 138

YR	TM/LG	CL	G	TPA	AB	H	2B	3B	HR	TB	BB	IBB	HB	SO	GDP	SH	SF	SB	CS	R	RBI	BA	OBA	SA
84	COL/SAL	A	102	411	346	114	12	5	2	142	60	2	0	42	5	1	4	24	6	84	33	.329	.424	.410
85	TOR/AL		64	43	40	8	0	0	0	8	2	0	0	9	2	1	0	1	4	9	0	.200	.238	.200
86	KNO/SOU		41	179	158	43	1	2	0	48	20	1	0	29	1	0	1	8	4	21	11	.272	.352	.304
	SYR/INT	AAA	76	260	236	58	6	1	1	69	21	0	0	39	5	3	0	7	9	34	19	.246	.307	.292
	TOR/AL		35	85	78	16	0	1	1	21	4	0	0	10	5	2	1	0	1	8	7	.205	.241	.269
87	SYR/INT	AAA	74	274	251	71	9	5	3	99	18	0	0	50	9	3	2	2	2	25	26	.283	.328	.394
	TOR/AL		56	129	121	31	2	3	1	42	6	0	0	13	1	1	1	2	0	14	11	.256	.289	.347
88	TOR/AL		116	415	381	111	16	2	3	139	26	1	0	64	13	4	4	3	3	38	38	.291	.333	.365
89	TOR/AL		99	322	300	78	9	2	3	100	20	1	0	60	8	1	1	4	2	27	34	.260	.305	.333
90	TOR/AL		117	421	391	95	12	4	6	128	26	0	0	90	9	1	3	3	1	45	41	.243	.288	.340
91	TOR/AL		138	485	445	104	18	2	0	128	24	0	0	107	11	10	4	7	2	41	29	.234	.274	.288
7 YR TOTALS			**625**	**1900**	**1756**	**443**	**57**	**16**	**13**	**571**	**108**	**2**	**2**	**353**	**49**	**20**	**14**	**20**	**13**	**182**	**160**	**.252**	**.294**	**.325**

Lee, Terry James — bats right — throws right — b.3/13/62 — 1991 positions: 1B 2

YR	TM/LG	CL	G	TPA	AB	H	2B	3B	HR	TB	BB	IBB	HB	SO	GDP	SH	SF	SB	CS	R	RBI	BA	OBA	SA
83	CR/MID	A	123	453	405	106	31	1	19	196	40	4	4	86	16	2	2	11	5	60	67	.262	.333	.484
84	VER/EAS	AA	134	475	422	102	10	2	11	149	44	1	3	91	13	2	4	2	4	56	47	.242	.315	.353
85	VER/EAS	AA	121	464	409	118	20	1	12	178	48	2	3	51	9	0	4	4	0	56	62	.289	.364	.435
86	DEN/AMA	AAA	34	110	104	25	2	1	2	35	4	0	0	24	3	0	2	0	1	10	10	.240	.264	.337
88	GRE/SAL	A	25	67	56	18	5	0	2	29	11	2	0	11	2	0	0	0	0	8	9	.321	.433	.518
89	CHT/SOU	AA	51	196	177	46	13	0	5	74	13	0	1	32	10	1	4	0	0	23	27	.260	.308	.418
	NAS/AMA	AAA	13	52	47	11	4	0	0	15	3	0	0	8	2	1	0	0	0	5	3	.234	.294	.319

Lee, Terry James (continued)

YR	TM/LG	CL	G	TPA	AB	H	2B	3B	HR	TB	BB	IBB	HB	SO	GDP	SH	SF	SB	CS	R	RBI	BA	OBA	SA
90	CHT/SOU	AA	43	181	156	51	8	1	8	85	20	1	2	27	5	1	2	4	1	25	20	.327	.406	.545
	NAS/AMA	AAA	72	303	260	79	18	1	15	144	31	1	4	47	10	1	7	3	1	38	67	.304	.377	.554
	CIN/NL		12	22	19	4	1	0	0	5	2	0	0	2	1	0	1	0	0	1	3	.211	.273	.263
91	CIN/NL		3	6	6	0	0	0	0	0	0	0	0	2	0	0	0	0	0	0	0	.000	.000	.000
	NAS/AMA	AAA	126	508	437	133	21	4	15	207	62	1	5	80	9	0	4	12	6	70	67	.304	.394	.474
2 YR TOTALS			**15**	**28**	**25**	**4**	**1**	**0**	**0**	**5**	**2**	**0**	**0**	**4**	**1**	**0**	**1**	**0**	**0**	**1**	**3**	**.160**	**.214**	**.200**

Leius, Scott Thomas — bats right — throws right — b.9/24/65 — 1991 positions: 3B 79, SS 19, OF 2

YR	TM/LG	CL	G	TPA	AB	H	2B	3B	HR	TB	BB	IBB	HB	SO	GDP	SH	SF	SB	CS	R	RBI	BA	OBA	SA
86	ELI/APP	R+	61	269	237	66	14	1	4	94	26	0	3	45	6	2	1	5		37	23	.278	.356	.397
87	KEN/MID	A	126	476	414	99	16	4	8	147	50	0	3	88	2	5	4	6	4	65	51	.239	.323	.355
88	VIS/CAL	A+	93	362	308	73	14	4	3	104	42	0	5	50	11	8	1	3	1	44	46	.237	.333	.338
89	ORL/SOU	AA	99	389	346	105	22	2	4	143	38	0	4	74	4	3	2	3	2	49	45	.303	.370	.413
90	POR/PCL	AAA	103	392	353	81	13	5	2	110	35	0	0	66	8	4	0	5	3	34	23	.229	.299	.312
	MIN/AL		14	28	25	6	1	0	1	10	2	0	0	2	2	1	0	0	0	4	4	.240	.296	.400
91	MIN/AL		109	235	199	57	7	2	5	83	30	1	0	35	4	5	1	5	5	35	20	.286	.378	.417
2 YR TOTALS			**123**	**263**	**224**	**63**	**8**	**2**	**6**	**93**	**32**	**1**	**0**	**37**	**6**	**6**	**1**	**5**	**5**	**39**	**24**	**.281**	**.370**	**.415**

Lemke, Mark Alan — bats both — throws right — b.8/13/65 — 1991 positions: 2B 110, 3B 15

YR	TM/LG	CL	G	TPA	AB	H	2B	3B	HR	TB	BB	IBB	HB	SO	GDP	SH	SF	SB	CS	R	RBI	BA	OBA	SA
83	BRA/GCL	R	53	244	209	55	6	0	0	61	30	0	0	19	4	3	2	10	4	37	19	.263	.353	.292
84	AND/SAL	A	42	138	121	18	2	0	0	20	14	0	1	14	6	0	2	3	1	18	5	.149	.239	.165
	BRA/GCL	R	63	280	243	67	11	0	3	87	29	0	2	14	1	2	4	2	2	41	32	.276	.353	.358
85	SUM/SAL	A	90	274	231	50	6	0	0	56	34	2	6	22	6	2	1	2	2	25	20	.216	.331	.242
86	SUM/SAL	A	126	551	448	122	24	2	18	204	87	3	7	31	9	5	4	11	7	99	66	.272	.396	.455
87	DUR/CAR	A+	127	559	489	143	28	3	20	237	54	3	5	45	10	4	7	10	7	75	68	.292	.364	.485
	GRE/SOU	AA	6	27	26	6	0	0	0	6	0	0	0	4	0	0	1	0	0	0	4	.231	.231	.231
88	GRE/SOU	AA	143	628	567	153	30	4	16	239	52	5	2	92	8	1	6	18	7	81	80	.270	.330	.422
	ATL/NL		16	64	58	13	4	0	0	17	4	0	0	5	1	2	0	0	0	8	2	.224	.274	.293
89	RIC/INT	AAA	146	595	518	143	22	7	5	194	66	8	0	45	12	5	6	4	·8	69	61	.276	.354	.375
	ATL/NL		14	60	55	10	2	1	2	20	5	0	0	7	1	0	0	0	1	4	10	.182	.250	.364
90	BRA/GCL	R	4	13	11	4	0	0	1	7	1	0	0	3	0	0	1	0	0	2	5	.364	.385	.636
	ATL/NL		102	266	239	54	13	0	0	67	21	3	0	22	6	4	2	0	1	22	21	.226	.286	.280
91	ATL/NL		136	308	269	63	11	2	2	84	29	2	0	27	9	6	4	1	2	36	23	.234	.305	.312
4 YR TOTALS			**268**	**698**	**621**	**140**	**30**	**3**	**4**	**188**	**59**	**5**	**0**	**61**	**17**	**12**	**6**	**1**	**6**	**70**	**56**	**.225**	**.290**	**.303**

Lennon, Patrick Orlando — bats right — throws right — b.4/27/68 — 1991 positions: DH 5, OF 1

YR	TM/LG	CL	G	TPA	AB	H	2B	3B	HR	TB	BB	IBB	HB	SO	GDP	SH	SF	SB	CS	R	RBI	BA	OBA	SA
86	BEL/NWL	A–	51	207	169	41	5	2	3	59	36	0	0	50	3	1	1	8	6	35	27	.243	.374	.349
87	WAU/MID	A	98	369	319	80	21	3	7	128	46	1	1	82	10	1	2	25	8	54	34	.251	.345	.401
88	VER/EAS	AA	95	352	321	83	9	3	9	125	21	1	3	87	9	3	4	15	6	44	40	.259	.307	.389
89	WIL/EAS	AA	66	276	248	65	14	2	3	92	23	2	0	53	9	0	5	7	4	32	31	.262	.319	.371
90	SB/CAL	A+	44	179	163	47	6	2	8	81	15	1	0	51	4	0	1	6	0	29	30	.288	.346	.497
	WIL/EAS	AA	49	182	167	49	6	4	5	78	10	0	2	37	2	0	3	10	4	24	22	.293	.335	.467
91	CAL/PCL	AAA	112	468	416	137	29	5	15	221	46	4	4	68	9	1	1	12	5	75	74	.329	.400	.531
	SEA/AL		9	11	8	1	1	0	0	2	3	0	0	1	0	0	0	0	0	2	1	.125	.364	.250

Leonard, Mark David — bats left — throws right — b.8/14/64 — 1991 positions: OF 34

YR	TM/LG	CL	G	TPA	AB	H	2B	3B	HR	TB	BB	IBB	HB	SO	GDP	SH	SF	SB	CS	R	RBI	BA	OBA	SA
86	EVE/NWL	A–	2	11	8	1	0	0	0	1	2	0	0	2	0	0	1	0	0	0	2	.125	.273	.125
	TRI/NWL	A–	36	146	120	32	6	0	4	50	25	0	1	19	7	0	0	4	2	21	15	.267	.397	.417
87	CLI/MID	A	128	492	413	132	31	2	15	212	71	3	5	61	7	0	3	5	8	57	80	.320	.423	.513
88	SJ/CAL	A+	142	644	510	176	50	6	15	283	118	13	5	82	10	0	11	11	6	102	118	.345	.464	.555
89	SHR/TEX	AA	63	258	219	68	15	3	10	119	33	8	3	40	7	0	1	1	5	29	52	.311	.403	.543
	PHO/PCL	AAA	27	88	78	21	4	0	0	25	9	1	0	15	3	0	1	1	1	7	6	.269	.341	.321
90	PHO/PCL	AAA	109	474	390	130	22	2	19	213	76	1	4	81	7	0	4	6	3	76	82	.333	.443	.546
	SF/NL		11	20	17	3	1	0	1	7	3	0	0	8	0	0	0	0	0	3	2	.176	.300	.412
91	PHO/PCL	AAA	41	169	146	37	7	0	8	68	21	1	0	29	5	0	2	1	0	27	25	.253	.343	.466
	SF/NL		64	145	129	31	7	1	2	46	12	1	1	25	3	1	2	0	1	14	14	.240	.306	.357
2 YR TOTALS			**75**	**165**	**146**	**34**	**8**	**1**	**3**	**53**	**15**	**1**	**1**	**33**	**3**	**1**	**2**	**0**	**1**	**17**	**16**	**.233**	**.305**	**.363**

Lewis, Darren Joel — bats right — throws right — b.8/28/67 — 1991 positions: OF 68

YR	TM/LG	CL	G	TPA	AB	H	2B	3B	HR	TB	BB	IBB	HB	SO	GDP	SH	SF	SB	CS	R	RBI	BA	OBA	SA
88	ATH/ARI	R	5	24	15	5	3	0	0	8	6	0	1	5	1	1	1	4	0	8	4	.333	.522	.533
	MAD/MID	A	60	256	199	49	4	1	0	55	46	0	4	37	3	4	3	21	10	38	11	.246	.393	.276
89	MOD/CAL	A+	129	579	503	150	23	5	1	195	59	0	11	84	4	2	4	27	22	74	39	.298	.381	.388
	HUN/SOU	AA	9	36	31	10	1	1	1	16	2	0	1	6	1	2	0	0	1	7	7	.323	.382	.516
90	HUN/SOU	AA	71	330	284	84	11	3	3	110	36	3	7	28	8	0	3	21	7	52	23	.296	.385	.387
	TAC/PCL	AAA	60	270	247	72	5	2	2	87	16	0	1	35	4	2	4	16	6	32	26	.291	.335	.352
	OAK/AL		25	46	35	8	0	0	0	8	7	0	1	4	1	3	0	2	0	4	1	.229	.372	.229
91	PHO/PCL	AAA	81	367	315	107	12	10	2	145	41	1	2	36	11	4	5	32	10	63	52	.340	.413	.460
	SF/NL		72	267	222	55	5	3	1	69	36	0	2	30	1	0	3	13	7	41	15	.248	.358	.311
2 YR TOTALS			**97**	**313**	**257**	**63**	**5**	**3**	**1**	**77**	**43**	**0**	**3**	**34**	**3**	**10**	**0**	**15**	**7**	**45**	**16**	**.245**	**.360**	**.300**

Lewis, Mark David — bats right — throws right — b.11/30/69 — 1991 positions: 2B 50, SS 36

YR	TM/LG	CL	G	TPA	AB	H	2B	3B	HR	TB	BB	IBB	HB	SO	GDP	SH	SF	SB	CS	R	RBI	BA	OBA	SA
88	BUR/APP	R+	61	262	227	60	13	1	7	96	25	0	5	44	2	0	5	14	6	39	43	.264	.344	.423
89	KIN/CAR	A+	93	393	349	94	16	3	1	119	34	4	2	50	7	3	5	17	9	50	32	.269	.333	.341
	CAN/EAS	AA	7	26	25	5	1	0	0	6	1	0	0	3	1	0	0	0	0	4	1	.200	.231	.240
90	CAN/EAS	AA	102	424	390	106	19	3	10	161	23	3	4	49	10	2	5	8	7	55	60	.272	.315	.413
	CS/PCL	AAA	34	135	124	38	8	1	1	51	9	0	0	13	4	1	1	2	3	16	21	.306	.351	.411
91	CS/PCL	AAA	46	203	179	50	10	3	2	72	18	0	0	23	4	0	6	2	1	29	31	.279	.335	.402
	CLE/AL		84	336	314	83	15	1	0	100	15	0	0	45	12	2	5	2	2	29	30	.264	.293	.318

Leyritz, James Joseph "Jim" — bats right — throws right — b.12/27/63 — 1991 positions: 3B 18, C 5, 1B 3, DH 1

YR	TM/LG	CL	G	TPA	AB	H	2B	3B	HR	TB	BB	IBB	HB	SO	GDP	SH	SF	SB	CS	R	RBI	BA	OBA	SA
86	FL/FSL	A+	12	39	34	10	1	1	0	13	4	1	1	5	1	0	0	0	0	3	1	.294	.385	.382
	ONE/NYP	A—	23	101	91	33	3	1	4	50	5	1	0	10	0	2	3	1	0	12	15	.363	.384	.549
87	FL/FSL	A+	102	429	374	115	22	0	6	155	38	1	6	54	8	7	4	2	1	48	51	.307	.377	.414
88	ALB/EAS	AA	112	436	382	92	18	3	5	131	43	5	6	60	8	3	2	3	3	40	50	.241	.326	.343
89	ALB/EAS	AA	114	456	375	118	18	2	10	170	65	5	9	51	8	2	5	2	1	53	66	.315	.423	.453
90	COL/INT	AAA	59	247	204	59	11	1	8	96	37	1	3	33	6	2	1	4	2	36	32	.289	.404	.471
	NY/AL		92	339	303	78	13	1	5	108	27	1	7	51	11	1	1	2	3	28	25	.257	.331	.356
91	COL/INT	AAA	79	320	270	72	24	1	11	131	38	1	8	49	5	1	3	1	2	50	48	.267	.370	.485
	NY/AL		32	91	77	14	3	0	0	17	13	0	0	15	0	1	0	0	1	8	4	.182	.300	.221
2 YR TOTALS			**124**	**430**	**380**	**92**	**16**	**1**	**5**	**125**	**40**	**1**	**7**	**66**	**11**	**2**	**1**	**2**	**4**	**36**	**29**	**.242**	**.325**	**.329**

Lind, Jose (Salgado) — bats right — throws right — b.5/1/64 — 1991 positions: 2B 149

YR	TM/LG	CL	G	TPA	AB	H	2B	3B	HR	TB	BB	IBB	HB	SO	GDP	SH	SF	SB	CS	R	RBI	BA	OBA	SA
84	MAC/SAL	A	121	430	396	82	5	2	0	91	29	3	0	48	9	2	3	17	7	39	30	.207	.259	.230
85	PW/CAR	A+	105	409	377	104	9	4	0	121	32	1	0	42	9	0	0	11	7	42	28	.276	.333	.321
86	NAS/EAS	AA	134	568	520	137	18	5	1	168	43	5	1	28	17	2	2	29	12	58	33	.263	.320	.323
87	VAN/PCL	AAA	128	575	533	143	16	3	3	174	35	0	3	52	14	3	1	21	9	75	30	.268	.316	.326
	PIT/NL		35	157	143	46	8	4	0	62	8	1	0	12	5	6	0	2	1	21	11	.322	.358	.434
88	PIT/NL		154	668	611	160	24	4	2	198	42	0	0	75	11	12	3	15	4	82	49	.262	.308	.324
89	PIT/NL		153	637	578	134	21	3	2	167	39	7	2	64	13	13	5	15	1	52	48	.232	.280	.289
90	PIT/NL		152	561	514	134	28	5	1	175	35	19	1	52	20	4	7	8	0	46	48	.261	.305	.340
91	PIT/NL		150	545	502	133	16	6	3	170	30	10	2	56	20	5	6	7	4	53	54	.265	.306	.339
5 YR TOTALS			**644**	**2568**	**2348**	**607**	**97**	**22**	**8**	**772**	**154**	**37**	**5**	**259**	**69**	**40**	**21**	**47**	**10**	**254**	**210**	**.259**	**.303**	**.329**

Lindeman, James William "Jim" — bats right — throws right — b.1/10/62 — 1991 positions: OF 30, 1B 1

YR	TM/LG	CL	G	TPA	AB	H	2B	3B	HR	TB	BB	IBB	HB	SO	GDP	SH	SF	SB	CS	R	RBI	BA	OBA	SA
83	SP/FSL	A+	70	264	232	64	13	1	8	103	27	2	0	51	6	3	2	9	2	45	37	.276	.349	.444
84	SPR/MID	A	94	407	354	96	15	2	18	169	47	2	3	81	6	2	1	6	3	69	66	.271	.360	.477
	ARK/TEX	AA	40	151	137	26	4	3	0	36	10	0	1	34	2	2	1	3	1	14	13	.190	.248	.263
85	ARK/TEX	AA	128	502	450	127	30	6	10	199	41	1	6	82	13	2	3	11	13	54	63	.282	.348	.442
86	LOU/AMA	AAA	139	556	509	128	38	5	20	236	39	2	4	97	9	0	4	9	6	82	96	.251	.308	.464
	STL/NL		19	58	55	14	1	0	1	18	2	0	0	10	2	0	1	1	1	7	6	.255	.276	.327
87	LOU/AMA	AAA	20	86	78	24	3	1	4	41	8	1	0	15	1	0	0	0	0	11	10	.308	.372	.526
	STL/NL		75	227	207	43	13	0	8	80	11	0	3	56	4	2	4	3	1	20	28	.208	.253	.386
88	LOU/AMA	AAA	73	298	261	66	18	4	2	98	33	0	2	59	5	0	2	2	0	32	30	.253	.339	.375
	STL/NL		17	46	43	9	1	0	2	16	2	0	0	9	1	1	0	0	0	3	7	.209	.244	.372
89	LOU/AMA	AAA	29	123	109	33	8	1	5	58	14	2	0	17	5	0	0	3	0	18	20	.303	.382	.532
	STL/NL		73	50	45	5	1	0	0	6	3	0	0	18	2	1	0	0	0	8	2	.111	.163	.133
90	DET/AL		12	34	32	7	1	0	2	14	2	0	0	13	0	0	0	0	0	5	8	.219	.265	.438
	TOL/INT	AAA	109	410	374	85	17	2	12	142	26	2	6	83	16	1	3	2	3	48	50	.227	.286	.380
91	SCR/INT	AAA	11	45	40	11	1	1	2	20	5	0	0	6	1	0	0	0	0	7	7	.275	.356	.500
	PHI/NL		65	111	95	32	5	0	0	37	13	1	0	14	1	2	1	0	1	13	12	.337	.413	.389
6 YR TOTALS			**261**	**526**	**477**	**110**	**22**	**0**	**13**	**171**	**33**	**1**	**3**	**120**	**10**	**6**	**7**	**4**	**3**	**56**	**63**	**.231**	**.281**	**.358**

Lindsey, Michael Douglas "Doug" — bats right — throws right — b.9/22/67 — 1991 positions: C 1

YR	TM/LG	CL	G	TPA	AB	H	2B	3B	HR	TB	BB	IBB	HB	SO	GDP	SH	SF	SB	CS	R	RBI	BA	OBA	SA
87	UTI/NYP	A—	52	195	169	41	7	0	1	51	22	2	1	34	2	0	3	1	3	23	25	.243	.328	.302
88	SPA/SAL	A	90	362	324	76	19	0	4	107	29	1	4	68	5	2	3	4	2	29	46	.235	.303	.330
89	SPA/SAL	A	39	161	136	31	7	0	3	47	23	2	0	31	7	1	1	2	2	14	17	.228	.338	.346
	CLE/FSL	A+	36	125	118	23	3	0	0	26	5	0	0	18	4	0	2	0	0	8	9	.195	.224	.220
90	REA/EAS	AA	107	359	323	56	11	0	1	70	26	1	1	78	10	6	3	2	1	16	32	.173	.235	.217
91	REA/EAS	AA	94	344	313	81	13	0	1	97	21	0	2	49	12	4	4	1	0	26	34	.259	.306	.310
	PHI/NL		1	3	3	0	0	0	0	0	0	0	0	3	0	0	0	0	0	0	0	.000	.000	.000

Liriano, Nelson Arturo (Bonilla) — bats both — throws right — b.6/3/64 — 1991 positions: 2B 10

YR	TM/LG	CL	G	TPA	AB	H	2B	3B	HR	TB	BB	IBB	HB	SO	GDP	SH	SF	SB	CS	R	RBI	BA	OBA	SA
84	KIN/CAR	A+	132	571	512	126	22	4	5	171	46	4	4	86	13	7	2	10	9	68	50	.246	.312	.334
85	KIN/CAR	A+	134	496	451	130	23	1	6	173	39	1	2	55	11	4	0	25	11	68	36	.288	.348	.384
86	KNO/SOU	AA	135	617	557	159	25	15	7	235	48	2	3	63	11	4	5	35	14	88	59	.285	.343	.422
87	SYR/INT	AAA	130	588	531	133	19	10	10	202	44	3	2	76	5	5	6	36	10	72	55	.250	.307	.380
	TOR/AL		37	176	158	38	6	2	2	54	16	2	0	22	3	2	0	13	2	29	10	.241	.310	.342

Liriano, Nelson Arturo (Bonilla) (continued)

YR	TM/LG	CL	G	TPA	AB	H	2B	3B	HR	TB	BB	IBB	HB	SO	GDP	SH	SF	SB	CS	R	RBI	BA	OBA	SA
88	SYR/INT	AAA	8	33	31	6	1	1	0	9	2	0	0	4	1	0	0	2	1	2	1	.194	.242	.290
	TOR/AL		99	295	276	73	6	2	3	92	11	0	2	40	4	5	1	12	5	36	23	.264	.297	.333
89	TOR/AL		132	478	418	110	26	3	5	157	43	0	2	51	10	10	5	16	7	51	53	.263	.331	.376
90	TOR/AL		50	189	170	36	7	2	1	50	16	0	1	20	5	1	1	3	5	16	15	.212	.282	.294
	MIN/AL		53	211	185	47	5	7	0	66	22	0	0	24	3	3	1	5	2	30	13	.254	.332	.357
	YEAR		103	400	355	83	12	9	1	116	38	0	1	44	8	4	2	8	7	46	28	.234	.308	.327
91	KC/AL		10	23	22	9	0	0	0	9	0	0	0	2	1	0	0	1	1	5	1	.409	.409	.409
	OMA/AMA	AAA	86	331	292	80	16	9	2	120	31	3	2	39	8	3	3	6	8	50	36	.274	.345	.411
5 YR TOTALS			**381**	**1372**	**1229**	**313**	**50**	**16**	**11**	**428**	**108**	**2**	**5**	**159**	**25**	**22**	**8**	**49**	**22**	**167**	**115**	**.255**	**.316**	**.348**

Litton, Jon Gregory "Greg" — bats right — throws right — b.7/13/64 — 1991 positions: 1B 15, 2B 15, 3B 11, SS 9, OF 6, C 1, P–1

YR	TM/LG	CL	G	TPA	AB	H	2B	3B	HR	TB	BB	IBB	HB	SO	GDP	SH	SF	SB	CS	R	RBI	BA	OBA	SA
84	EVE/NWL	A–	62	271	243	57	12	2	4	85	27	0	1	47	4	0	0	2	1	29	26	.235	.314	.350
85	FRE/CAL	A+	141	626	564	150	33	7	12	233	50	0	3	86	8	2	7	8	4	88	103	.266	.325	.413
86	SHR/TEX	AA	131	518	455	112	30	3	10	178	52	4	4	77	13	5	2	1	2	46	55	.246	.327	.391
87	SHR/TEX	AA	72	282	254	66	6	3	8	102	22	2	2	51	2	2	2	2	4	34	33	.260	.321	.402
	PHO/PCL	AAA	60	228	203	44	8	2	1	59	18	1	2	40	5	2	3	0	1	24	22	.217	.283	.291
88	SHR/TEX	AA	116	482	432	120	35	5	11	198	37	2	5	84	8	1	7	2	2	58	64	.278	.337	.458
89	PHO/PCL	AAA	30	99	89	16	4	2	2	30	8	0	0	24	3	0	2	1	3	6	6	.180	.242	.337
	SF/NL		71	155	143	36	5	3	4	59	7	0	1	29	3	4	0	0	1	12	17	.252	.291	.413
90	PHO/PCL	AAA	6	25	22	6	1	0	0	7	2	0	0	7	0	0	1	0	0	3	4	.273	.320	.318
	SF/NL		93	220	204	50	9	1	1	64	11	0	1	45	5	2	2	1	0	17	24	.245	.284	.314
91	PHO/PCL	AAA	8	35	27	11	1	0	4	24	8	0	0	5	0	0	0	0	0	9	9	.407	.543	.889
	SF/NL		59	143	127	23	7	1	1	35	11	0	1	25	2	3	1	0	3	13	15	.181	.250	.276
3 YR TOTALS			**223**	**518**	**474**	**109**	**21**	**5**	**6**	**158**	**29**	**0**	**3**	**99**	**10**	**9**	**3**	**1**	**4**	**42**	**56**	**.230**	**.277**	**.333**

Livingstone, Scott Louis — bats left — throws right — b.7/15/65 — 1991 positions: 3B 43

YR	TM/LG	CL	G	TPA	AB	H	2B	3B	HR	TB	BB	IBB	HB	SO	GDP	SH	SF	SB	CS	R	RBI	BA	OBA	SA
88	LAK/FSL	A+	53	198	180	51	8	1	2	67	11	3	3	25	3	2	2	1	1	28	25	.283	.332	.372
89	LON/EAS	AA	124	512	452	98	18	1	14	160	52	4	2	67	4	0	6	1	1	46	71	.217	.297	.354
90	TOL/INT	AAA	103	368	345	94	19	0	6	131	21	0	1	40	7	0	1	1	5	44	36	.272	.315	.380
91	TOL/INT	AAA	92	382	331	100	13	3	3	128	40	3	2	52	9	3	6	2	1	48	62	.302	.375	.387
	DET/AL		44	139	127	37	5	0	2	48	10	0	1	25	0	1	1	2	1	19	11	.291	.341	.378

Lofton, Kenneth "Kenny" — bats left — throws left — b.5/31/67 — 1991 positions: OF 20

YR	TM/LG	CL	G	TPA	AB	H	2B	3B	HR	TB	BB	IBB	HB	SO	GDP	SH	SF	SB	CS	R	RBI	BA	OBA	SA
88	AUB/NYP	A–	48	207	187	40	6	1	1	51	19	0	0	51	3	1	0	26	4	23	14	.214	.286	.273
89	AUB/NYP	A–	34	129	110	29	3	1	0	34	14	0	0	30	1	1	4	26	5	21	8	.264	.336	.309
	ASH/SAL	A	22	97	82	27	2	0	1	32	12	0	1	10	1	2	0	14	6	14	9	.329	.421	.390
90	OSC/FSL	A+	124	556	481	159	15	5	2	190	61	4	3	77	4	8	3	62	16	98	35	.331	.407	.395
91	TUC/PCL	AAA	130	607	545	168	19	17	2	227	52	5	0	95	2	8	2	40	23	93	50	.308	.367	.417
	HOU/NL		20	79	74	15	1	0	0	16	5	0	0	19	0	0	0	2	0	9	0	.203	.253	.216

Lopez, Luis Antonio — bats right — throws right — b.9/1/64 — 1991 positions: C 12, 1B 10, DH 6, 3B 1, OF 1

YR	TM/LG	CL	G	TPA	AB	H	2B	3B	HR	TB	BB	IBB	HB	SO	GDP	SH	SF	SB	CS	R	RBI	BA	OBA	SA
84	GF/PIO	R+	68	310	275	90	15	5	6	133	27	1	5	15	10	1	2	4	4	60	61	.327	.395	.484
85	VB/FSL	A+	120	419	382	106	18	2	1	131	25	3	6	41	19	3	3	2	2	47	43	.277	.329	.343
86	VB/FSL	A+	122	475	434	124	21	3	1	154	33	2	2	25	21	2	4	5	7	52	60	.286	.336	.355
87	BAK/CAL	A+	142	608	550	181	43	2	16	276	38	3	9	49	9	5	6	6	6	89	96	.329	.378	.502
88	SA/TEX	AA	124	527	470	116	16	3	7	159	32	5	13	33	12	5	7	3	4	56	65	.247	.308	.338
89	SA/TEX	AA	99	372	327	87	17	0	10	134	38	4	5	39	14	0	2	1	0	46	51	.266	.349	.410
	ALB/PCL	AAA	19	84	75	37	7	0	2	50	6	0	1	7	1	0	2	1	0	17	16	.493	.524	.667
90	ALB/PCL	AAA	128	501	448	158	23	2	11	218	47	4	4	49	12	0	2	3	3	65	81	.353	.417	.487
	LA/NL		6	6	6	0	0	0	0	0	0	0	0	0	0	0	0	0	0	0	0	0	.000	.000	.000
91	CS/PCL	AAA	41	188	176	61	11	4	1	83	9	0	3	10	4	0	0	0	0	29	31	.347	.388	.472
	CLE/AL		35	89	82	18	4	1	0	24	4	1	1	7	0	1	1	0	0	7	7	.220	.261	.293
2 YR TOTALS			**41**	**95**	**88**	**18**	**4**	**1**	**0**	**24**	**4**	**1**	**1**	**9**	**0**	**1**	**1**	**0**	**0**	**7**	**7**	**.205**	**.245**	**.273**

Lovullo, Salvatore Anthony "Torey" — bats both — throws right — b.7/25/65 — 1991 positions: 3B 22

YR	TM/LG	CL	G	TPA	AB	H	2B	3B	HR	TB	BB	IBB	HB	SO	GDP	SH	SF	SB	CS	R	RBI	BA	OBA	SA
87	FAY/SAL	A	55	233	191	49	13	0	8	86	37	4	2	30	3	2	1	6	0	34	32	.257	.381	.450
	LAK/FSL	A+	18	73	60	16	3	0	1	22	10	0	0	8	3	0	3	0	0	11	16	.267	.356	.367
88	GF/EAS	AA	78	313	270	74	17	1	9	120	36	3	1	44	5	0	6	2	0	37	50	.274	.355	.444
	TOL/INT	AAA	57	194	177	41	8	1	5	66	9	0	1	24	1	7	1	2	1	18	20	.232	.267	.373
	DET/AL		12	23	21	8	1	1	1	14	1	0	1	2	1	0	0	0	2	2	2	.381	.409	.667
89	DET/AL		29	104	87	10	2	0	1	15	14	0	0	20	3	1	2	0	0	8	4	.115	.233	.172
	TOL/INT	AAA	112	465	409	94	23	2	10	151	44	10	1	57	10	7	4	2	1	48	52	.230	.303	.369
90	TOL/INT	AAA	141	557	486	131	38	1	14	213	61	6	4	74	12	2	4	4	1	71	58	.270	.353	.438
91	COL/INT	AAA	106	462	395	107	24	5	10	171	59	4	0	56	10	2	6	4	4	74	75	.271	.361	.433
	NY/AL		22	59	51	9	2	0	0	11	5	1	0	7	0	3	0	0	0	0	2	.176	.250	.216
3 YR TOTALS			**63**	**186**	**159**	**27**	**5**	**1**	**2**	**40**	**20**	**1**	**1**	**29**	**4**	**5**	**2**	**0**	**0**	**10**	**8**	**.170**	**.260**	**.252**

Lusader, Scott Edward — bats left — throws left — b.9/30/64 — 1991 positions: OF 4

YR	TM/LG	CL	G	TPA	AB	H	2B	3B	HR	TB	BB	IBB	HB	SO	GDP	SH	SF	SB	CS	R	RBI	BA	OBA	SA
85	LAK/FSL	A+	27	110	97	28	5	1	2	41	12	1	0	22	0	0	1	0	1	16	22	.289	.364	.423

(continued)

Lusader, Scott Edward (continued)

YR	TM/LG	CL	G	TPA	AB	H	2B	3B	HR	TB	BB	IBB	HB	SO	GDP	SH	SF	SB	CS	R	RBI	BA	OBA	SA
	BIR/SOU	AA	21	83	77	26	3	4	2	43	5	1	0	12	4	1	0	0	0	13	14	.338	.373	.558
86	GF/EAS	AA	136	552	479	134	23	3	11	196	69	3	0	87	13	1	3	13	5	74	59	.280	.368	.409
87	TOL/INT	AAA	136	562	505	136	29	8	17	232	50	2	1	93	7	2	4	19	5	78	80	.269	.334	.459
	DET/AL		23	54	47	15	3	1	1	23	5	1	0	7	0	1	1	1	0	8	8	.319	.377	.489
88	TOL/INT	AAA	89	367	329	86	11	5	4	119	30	1	3	56	5	1	4	22	8	38	46	.261	.325	.362
	DET/AL		16	18	16	1	0	0	1	4	1	0	0	4	1	0	1	0	0	3	3	.063	.111	.250
89	TOL/INT	AAA	44	180	153	37	9	1	2	54	23	0	0	31	2	1	3	6	3	17	15	.242	.335	.353
	TUC/PCL	AAA	33	141	121	30	3	1	2	41	17	0	1	24	3	1	1	5	4	15	13	.248	.343	.339
	DET/AL		40	113	103	26	4	0	1	33	9	0	0	21	2	0	1	3	0	15	8	.252	.310	.320
90	DET/AL		45	102	87	21	2	0	2	29	12	0	0	8	2	0	3	0	0	13	16	.241	.324	.333
	TOL/INT	AAA	76	306	268	67	12	1	4	93	34	2	1	51	5	2	1	15	9	35	25	.250	.336	.347
91	NY/AL		11	8	7	1	0	0	0	1	1	0	0	3	0	0	0	0	1	2	1	.143	.250	.143
	COL/INT	AAA	76	314	284	80	13	6	7	126	27	4	1	54	7	1	1	7	4	48	32	.282	.345	.444
5 YR TOTALS			135	295	260	64	9	1	5	90	28	1	0	43	5	1	6	4	1	41	36	.246	.313	.346

Lyons, Barry Stephen — bats right — throws right — b.6/3/60 — 1991 positions: C 6, 1B 2

YR	TM/LG	CL	G	TPA	AB	H	2B	3B	HR	TB	BB	IBB	HB	SO	GDP	SH	SF	SB	CS	R	RBI	BA	OBA	SA
84	LYN/CAR	A+	115	467	412	130	17	3	12	189	45	1	2	40	11	1	7	1	3	59	87	.316	.380	.459
85	JAC/TEX	AA	126	519	486	149	34	6	11	228	25	2	5	67	19	0	3	3	0	69	108	.307	.345	.469
86	NY/NL		6	10	9	0	0	0	0	0	1	1	0	2	0	0	0	0	0	1	2	.000	.100	.000
	TID/INT	AAA	61	262	234	69	16	0	4	97	18	2	1	32	6	2	7	0	0	28	46	.295	.338	.415
87	NY/NL		53	143	130	33	4	1	4	51	8	1	2	24	1	0	3	0	0	15	24	.254	.301	.392
88	NY/NL		50	98	91	21	7	1	0	30	3	0	0	12	3	3	1	0	0	5	11	.231	.253	.330
89	TID/INT	AAA	5	20	20	2	0	1	0	4	0	0	0	4	1	0	0	0	0	1	2	.100	.100	.200
	NY/NL		79	252	235	58	13	0	3	80	11	1	1	28	7	1	3	0	0	15	27	.247	.283	.340
90	NY/NL		24	83	80	19	0	0	2	25	2	0	1	9	2	0	0	0	0	8	7	.237	.265	.313
	TID/INT	AAA	57	183	164	28	5	0	0	33	16	1	1	25	3	0	1	0	0	8	17	.171	.251	.201
	LA/NL		3	5	5	1	0	0	0	4	0	0	0	1	0	0	0	0	0	1	2	.200	.200	.800
	YEAR		27	88	85	20	0	0	3	29	2	0	1	10	2	0	0	0	0	9	9	.235	.261	.341
91	LA/NL		9	9	9	0	0	0	0	0	0	0	0	2	0	0	0	0	0	0	0	.000	.000	.000
	EDM/PCL	AAA	47	179	165	51	13	0	2	70	10	1	3	11	5	0	1	0	0	15	23	.309	.358	.424
	CAL/AL		2	5	5	1	0	0	0	1	0	0	0	0	0	0	0	0	0	0	0	.200	.200	.200
	YEAR		11	14	14	1	0	0	0	1	0	0	0	2	0	0	0	0	0	0	0	.071	.071	.071
6 YR TOTALS			226	605	564	133	24	2	10	191	25	3	5	78	13	4	7	0	1	45	73	.236	.271	.339

Lyons, Stephen John "Steve" — bats left — throws right — b.6/3/60 — 1991 positions: OF 45, 2B 16, 3B 12, 1B 2, DH 2, SS 1, P–1

YR	TM/LG	CL	G	TPA	AB	H	2B	3B	HR	TB	BB	IBB	HB	SO	GDP	SH	SF	SB	CS	R	RBI	BA	OBA	SA
84	PAW/INT	AAA	131	520	444	119	21	2	17	195	66	3	1	71	9	3	6	35	14	80	62	.268	.360	.439
85	BOS/AL		133	409	371	98	14	3	5	133	32	0	1	64	2	2	3	12	9	52	30	.264	.322	.358
86	BOS/AL		59	139	124	31	7	2	1	45	12	2	0	23	3	1	2	2	3	20	14	.250	.312	.363
	BUF/AMA	AAA	20	92	74	22	5	1	3	38	16	1	1	14	1	1	0	5	1	18	8	.297	.429	.514
	CHI/AL		42	136	123	25	2	1	0	29	7	0	1	24	1	3	2	2	3	10	6	.203	.248	.236
	YEAR		101	275	247	56	9	3	1	74	19	2	1	47	4	4	4	4	6	30	20	.227	.280	.300
87	HAW/PCL	AAA	47	192	167	48	11	0	2	65	22	1	1	27	2	1	1	7	5	26	16	.287	.372	.389
	CHI/AL		76	210	193	54	11	1	1	70	12	0	1	37	4	4	1	3	1	26	19	.280	.320	.363
88	CHI/AL		146	526	472	127	28	3	5	176	32	1	1	59	6	15	6	1	2	59	45	.269	.313	.373
89	CHI/AL		140	494	443	117	21	3	2	150	35	3	1	68	3	12	3	9	6	51	50	.264	.317	.339
90	CHI/AL		94	163	146	28	6	1	1	39	10	1	1	41	1	4	2	1	0	22	11	.192	.245	.267
91	BOS/AL		87	227	212	51	10	1	4	75	11	2	1	35	1	3	1	10	3	15	17	.241	.277	.354
7 YR TOTALS			777	2304	2084	531	99	15	19	717	151	9	5	351	21	44	20	40	27	255	192	.255	.304	.344

Maas, Kevin Christian — bats left — throws left — b.1/20/65 — 1991 positions: DH 109, 1B 36

YR	TM/LG	CL	G	TPA	AB	H	2B	3B	HR	TB	BB	IBB	HB	SO	GDP	SH	SF	SB	CS	R	RBI	BA	OBA	SA
86	ONE/NYP	A–	28	109	101	36	10	0	0	46	7	1	0	9	1	0	1	5	1	14	18	.356	.394	.455
87	FL/FSL	A+	116	502	439	122	28	4	11	191	53	4	2	108	5	0	8	14	4	77	73	.278	.353	.435
88	PW/CAR	A+	29	133	108	32	7	0	12	75	17	1	4	28	0	0	4	3	1	24	35	.296	.398	.694
	ALB/EAS	AA	109	445	372	98	14	3	16	166	64	4	3	103	5	3	2	5	1	66	55	.263	.376	.446
89	COL/INT	AAA	83	336	291	93	23	2	6	138	40	0	1	73	3	0	4	2	3	42	45	.320	.399	.474
90	COL/INT	AAA	57	228	194	55	15	2	13	113	34	1	0	45	5	0	0	2	2	37	38	.284	.390	.582
	NY/AL		79	300	254	64	9	0	21	136	43	10	3	76	2	0	0	1	2	42	41	.252	.367	.535
91	NY/AL		148	592	500	110	14	1	23	195	83	3	4	128	4	0	5	5	1	69	63	.220	.333	.390
2 YR TOTALS			227	892	754	174	23	1	44	331	126	13	7	204	6	0	5	6	3	111	104	.231	.344	.439

Macfarlane, Michael Andrew "Mike" — bats right — throws right — b.4/12/64 — 1991 positions: C 69, DH 4

YR	TM/LG	CL	G	TPA	AB	H	2B	3B	HR	TB	BB	IBB	HB	SO	GDP	SH	SF	SB	CS	R	RBI	BA	OBA	SA
85	MEM/SOU	AA	65	243	223	60	15	4	8	107	11	1	5	30	6	2	2	0	0	29	39	.269	.315	.480
86	MEM/SOU	AA	40	154	141	34	7	2	12	81	10	0	2	26	7	0	1	0	1	26	29	.241	.299	.574
87	KC/AL		8	21	19	4	1	0	0	5	2	0	0	2	1	0	0	0	0	0	3	.211	.286	.263
	OMA/AMA	AAA	87	330	302	79	25	1	13	145	22	1	6	50	7	0	0	0	1	53	50	.262	.324	.480
88	KC/AL		70	236	211	56	15	0	4	83	21	2	1	37	6	1	2	0	0	25	26	.265	.332	.393
	OMA/AMA	AAA	21	83	76	18	7	2	2	35	4	0	2	15	1	1	0	0	0	8	8	.237	.293	.461
89	KC/AL		69	167	157	35	6	0	2	47	7	0	2	27	8	0	1	0	0	13	19	.223	.263	.299
90	KC/AL		124	439	400	102	24	4	6	152	25	2	1	69	9	1	6	1	0	37	58	.255	.306	.380
91	KC/AL		84	295	267	74	18	2	13	135	17	0	1	52	4	1	4	1	0	34	41	.277	.330	.506
5 YR TOTALS			355	1158	1054	271	64	6	25	422	72	4	16	187	27	3	13	2	0	109	147	.257	.311	.400

Mack, Shane Lee — bats right — throws right — b.12/7/63 — 1991 positions: OF 140, DH 1

YR	TM/LG	CL	G	TPA	AB	H	2B	3B	HR	TB	BB	IBB	HB	SO	GDP	SH	SF	SB	CS	R	RBI	BA	OBA	SA
85	BEA/TEX	AA	125	479	430	112	23	3	6	159	38	2	3	89	11	7	1	12	5	59	55	.260	.324	.370
86	BEA/TEX	AA	115	485	452	127	26	3	15	204	21	2	7	79	10	2	3	14	9	61	68	.281	.321	.451
	LV/PCL	AAA	19	72	69	25	1	6	0	38	2	0	1	13	0	0	0	3	4	13	6	.362	.389	.551
87	LV/PCL	AAA	39	173	152	51	11	1	5	79	19	0	1	32	2	0	1	13	0	38	26	.336	.410	.520
	SD/NL		105	267	238	57	11	3	4	86	18	0	3	47	11	6	2	4	5	28	25	.239	.299	.361
88	SD/NL		56	140	119	29	3	0	0	32	14	0	3	21	2	3	1	5	1	13	12	.244	.336	.269
	LV/PCL	AAA	55	230	196	68	7	1	10	107	29	4	3	44	3	0	2	7	1	43	40	.347	.435	.546
89	LV/PCL	AAA	24	96	80	18	3	1	1	26	14	0	1	19	1	0	1	4	2	10	8	.225	.344	.325
90	MIN/AL		125	353	313	102	10	4	8	144	29	1	5	69	7	4	0	13	6	50	44	.326	.392	.460
91	MIN/AL		143	489	442	137	27	8	18	234	34	1	6	79	11	2	5	13	9	79	74	.310	.363	.529
4 YR TOTALS			429	1249	1112	325	51	15	30	496	95	2	17	216	31	17	8	35	20	170	155	.292	.355	.446

Magadan, David Joseph "Dave" — bats left — throws right — b.9/30/62 — 1991 positions: 1B 122

YR	TM/LG	CL	G	TPA	AB	H	2B	3B	HR	TB	BB	IBB	HB	SO	GDP	SH	SF	SB	CS	R	RBI	BA	OBA	SA
84	LYN/CAR	A+	112	486	371	130	22	4	0	160	104	10	6	43	12	0	5	2	1	78	62	.350	.494	.431
85	JAC/TEX	AA	134	582	466	144	22	0	0	166	106	2	5	57	16	4	1	0	3	84	76	.309	.441	.356
86	TID/INT	AAA	133	571	473	147	33	6	1	195	84	5	3	45	10	2	9	2	2	68	64	.311	.411	.412
	NY/NL		10	21	18	8	0	0	0	8	3	0	0	1	1	0	0	0	0	3	3	.444	.524	.444
87	NY/NL		85	216	192	61	13	1	3	85	22	2	0	22	5	1	1	0	0	21	24	.318	.386	.443
88	NY/NL		112	380	314	87	15	0	1	105	60	4	2	39	9	1	3	0	1	39	35	.277	.393	.334
89	NY/NL		127	429	374	107	22	3	4	147	49	6	1	37	2	1	4	1	0	47	41	.286	.367	.393
90	NY/NL		144	541	451	148	28	6	6	206	74	4	2	55	11	4	10	2	1	74	72	.328	.417	.457
91	NY/NL		124	517	418	108	23	0	4	143	83	3	2	50	5	7	1	1	1	58	51	.258	.378	.342
6 YR TOTALS			602	2104	1767	519	101	10	18	694	291	19	7	204	33	14	25	4	3	242	226	.294	.391	.393

Magallanes, Everado "Ever" — bats left — throws right — b.11/6/65 — 1991 positions: SS 2

YR	TM/LG	CL	G	TPA	AB	H	2B	3B	HR	TB	BB	IBB	HB	SO	GDP	SH	SF	SB	CS	R	RBI	BA	OBA	SA
87	KIN/CAR	A+	58	224	205	50	4	3	2	66	16	0	1	18	7	2	0	2	0	20	23	.244	.302	.322
88	KIN/CAR	A+	119	480	396	104	13	3	1	126	76	3	2	48	16	3	3	12	6	67	45	.263	.382	.318
89	CAN/EAS	AA	74	286	241	67	5	0	0	72	37	0	1	24	5	4	3	1	6	26	18	.278	.372	.299
	CS/PCL	AAA	12	49	44	11	1	0	1	15	4	0	0	3	2	1	0	1	0	2	3	.250	.313	.341
90	CS/PCL	AAA	125	432	377	116	17	3	1	142	43	0	1	49	13	5	6	3	2	60	63	.308	.375	.377
91	CLE/AL		3	3	2	0	0	0	0	0	1	0	0	0	0	0	0	0	0	0	0	.000	.333	.000
	CS/PCL	AAA	94	332	305	87	13	1	1	105	23	1	2	36	9	1	1	1	2	37	33	.285	.338	.344

Maldonado, Candido (Guadarrama) "Candy" — bats right — throws right — b.9/5/60 — 1991 positions: OF 76, DH 9

YR	TM/LG	CL	G	TPA	AB	H	2B	3B	HR	TB	BB	IBB	HB	SO	GDP	SH	SF	SB	CS	R	RBI	BA	OBA	SA
81	LA/NL		11	12	12	1	0	0	0	1	0	0	0	5	0	0	0	0	0	0	0	.083	.083	.083
82	LA/NL		6	5	4	0	0	0	0	0	1	0	0	1	1	0	0	0	0	0	0	.000	.200	.000
83	LA/NL		42	68	62	12	1	1	1	18	5	0	0	14	1	1	0	0	0	5	6	.194	.254	.290
84	LA/NL		116	278	254	68	14	0	5	97	19	0	1	29	6	1	3	0	3	25	28	.268	.318	.382
85	LA/NL		121	235	213	48	7	1	5	72	19	4	0	40	3	2	1	1	1	20	19	.225	.288	.338
86	SF/NL		133	432	405	102	31	3	18	193	20	4	3	77	12	0	4	4	4	49	85	.252	.289	.477
87	SF/NL		118	489	442	129	28	4	20	225	34	4	6	78	9	0	7	8	8	69	85	.292	.346	.509
88	SF/NL		142	552	499	127	23	1	12	188	37	1	7	89	13	3	6	6	5	53	68	.255	.311	.377
89	SF/NL		129	389	345	75	23	0	9	125	37	8	1	69	8	1	3	4	1	39	41	.217	.296	.362
90	CLE/AL		155	651	590	161	32	2	22	263	49	4	5	134	13	0	7	3	5	76	95	.273	.330	.446
91	MIL/AL		34	125	111	23	6	0	5	44	13	0	1	23	4	0	1	0	1	11	20	.207	.288	.396
	TOR/AL		52	208	177	49	9	0	7	79	23	4	6	53	4	0	3	1	0	26	28	.277	.375	.446
	YEAR		86	333	288	72	15	0	12	123	36	4	7	76	8	0	3	4	0	37	48	.250	.342	.427
11 YR TOTALS			1059	3444	3114	795	174	12	104	1305	257	26	31	613	73	8	34	30	27	373	475	.255	.315	.419

Manahan, Anthony Charles "Tony" — bats right — throws right — b.12/15/68 — 1991 positions: SS System SEA/AL

YR	TM/LG	CL	G	TPA	AB	H	2B	3B	HR	TB	BB	IBB	HB	SO	GDP	SH	SF	SB	CS	R	RBI	BA	OBA	SA
90	SB/CAL	A+	51	228	198	63	10	2	7	98	24	0	2	34	4	1	3	8	1	46	30	.318	.392	.495
91	JAC/SOU	AA	113	475	410	104	23	2	7	152	54	0	8	81	8	2	3	11	5	67	45	.254	.347	.371

Manrique, Fred Eloy (Reyes) — bats right — throws right — b.5/11/61 — 1991 positions: SS 7, 2B 2

YR	TM/LG	CL	G	TPA	AB	H	2B	3B	HR	TB	BB	IBB	HB	SO	GDP	SH	SF	SB	CS	R	RBI	BA	OBA	SA
81	TOR/AL		14	29	28	4	0	0	0	4	0	0	1	12	0	0	0	0	1	1	1	.143	.172	.143
84	SYR/INT	AAA	129	557	517	146	15	5	6	189	29	0	2	61	14	6	3	14	7	63	45	.282	.321	.366
	TOR/AL		10	9	9	3	0	0	0	3	0	0	0	1	1	0	0	0	0	0	1	.333	.333	.333
85	IND/AMA	AAA	123	440	409	98	21	5	8	153	20	1	2	71	10	3	0	2	8	46	37	.240	.276	.374
	MON/NL		9	14	13	4	1	0	1	10	1	0	0	3	0	0	0	0	0	5	1	.308	.357	.769
86	LOU/AMA	AAA	133	554	520	148	19	6	9	206	24	4	3	85	19	5	2	15	6	79	51	.285	.319	.396
	STL/NL		13	18	17	3	0	0	1	6	1	0	0	1	1	0	0	0	0		3	.176	.222	.353
87	CHI/AL		115	330	298	77	13	3	4	108	19	1	9	69	4	9	3	5	3	30	29	.258	.302	.362
88	CHI/AL		140	387	345	81	10	6	5	118	21	1	3	54	7	16	2	6	4	43	37	.235	.283	.342
89	CHI/AL		65	202	187	56	13	1	2	77	8	1	2	30	6	4	1	1	1	23	22	.288	.318	.382
	TEX/AL		54	210	191	55	12	0	2	73	9	0	0	33	3	9	1	4	1	23	22	.288	.318	.382
	YEAR		119	412	378	111	25	1	4	150	17	1	2	63	9	13	2	5	5	46	52	.294	.326	.397
90	MIN/AL		69	237	228	54	10	1	1	79	4	0	2	35	8	1	2	0	1	22	29	.237	.254	.346
	POR/PCL	AAA	1	1	1	1	0	0	0	1	0	0	0	0	0	0	0	0	0	1	1	1.000	1.000	1.000

(continued)

Manrique, Fred Eloy (Reyes) (continued)

YR	TM/LG	CL	G	TPA	AB	H	2B	3B	HR	TB	BB	IBB	HB	SO	GDP	SH	SF	SB	CS	R	RBI	BA	OBA	SA
91	OAK/AL		9	23	21	3	0	0	0	3	2		1	1	0	1	0	0	0	2	0	.143	.217	.143
	TAC/PCL	AAA	12	46	41	11	0	0	1	14	3	0	1	9	1	0	1	0	0	6	4	.268	.326	.341
9 YR TOTALS			498	1459	1337	340	59	11	20	481	65	3	9	239	31	39	9	18	14	151	151	.254	.292	.360

Manto, Jeffrey Paul "Jeff" — bats right — throws right — b.8/23/64 — 1991 positions: 3B 32, 1B 14, C 5, OF 1

YR	TM/LG	CL	G	TPA	AB	H	2B	3B	HR	TB	BB	IBB	HB	SO	GDP	SH	SF	SB	CS	R	RBI	BA	OBA	SA
85	QC/MID	A	74	282	233	46	5	2	11	88	40	0	5	74	7	1	3	3	1	34	34	.197	.324	.378
86	QC/MID	A	73	283	239	59	13	0	8	96	37	0	4	70	2	1	2	2	1	31	49	.247	.355	.402
87	PS/CAL	A+	112	497	375	96	21	4	7	146	102	1	8	85	7	5	7	8	2	61	63	.256	.419	.389
88	MID/TEX	AA	120	485	408	123	23	3	24	224	62	5	8	76	17	3	4	7	5	88	101	.301	.400	.549
89	EDM/PCL	AAA	127	515	408	113	25	3	23	213	91	5	9	81	12	3	4	4	4	89	67	.277	.416	.522
90	CS/PCL	AAA	96	407	316	94	27	1	18	177	78	2	9	65	9	1	3	10	3	73	82	.297	.446	.560
	CLE/AL		30	97	76	17	5	1	2	30	21	1	0	18	0	0	0	0	1	12	14	.224	.392	.395
91	CS/PCL	AAA	43	192	153	49	16	0	6	83	33	2	3	24	3	0	3	1	0	36	36	.320	.443	.542
	CLE/AL		47	148	128	27	7	0	2	40	14	0	4	22	3	1	1	2	0	15	13	.211	.306	.313
2 YR TOTALS			77	245	204	44	12	1	4	70	35	1	4	40	3	1	1	2	1	27	27	.216	.340	.343

Manwaring, Kirt Dean — bats right — throws right — b.7/15/65 — 1991 positions: C 67

YR	TM/LG	CL	G	TPA	AB	H	2B	3B	HR	TB	BB	IBB	HB	SO	GDP	SH	SF	SB	CS	R	RBI	BA	OBA	SA
86	CLI/MID	A	49	167	147	36	7	1	2	51	14	1	1	26	0	4	1	1	2	18	16	.245	.313	.347
87	SHR/TEX	AA	98	336	307	82	13	2	2	105	19	3	8	33	6	2	0	1	2	27	22	.267	.326	.342
	SF/NL		6	8	7	1	0	0	0	1	0	0	0	1	1	0	0	0	0	0	0	.143	.250	.143
88	PHO/PCL	AAA	81	293	273	77	12	2	2	99	14	1	3	32	9	1	2	3	4	29	35	.282	.322	.363
	SF/NL		40	123	116	29	7	0	1	39	2	0	3	21	1	1	1	0	1	12	15	.250	.279	.336
89	SF/NL		85	223	200	42	4	2	0	50	11	1	4	28	5	7	1	2	1	14	18	.210	.264	.250
90	PHO/PCL	AAA	74	274	247	58	10	2	3	81	24	1	3	34	4	0	0	0	3	20	14	.235	.310	.328
	SF/NL		8	13	13	2	0	1	0	4	0	0	0	3	0	0	0	0	0	0	1	.154	.154	.308
91	PHO/PCL	AAA	24	90	81	18	0	0	4	30	8	0	0	15	2	0	1	0	0	8	14	.222	.289	.370
	SJ/CAL	A+	1	4	3	0	0	0	0	0	1	0	0	1	0	0	0	0	0	0	0	.000	.250	.000
	SF/NL		67	199	178	40	9	0	0	49	9	0	3	22	2	7	2	1	1	16	19	.225	.271	.275
5 YR TOTALS			206	566	514	114	20	3	1	143	22	1	11	75	9	15	4	3	3	42	53	.222	.267	.278

Marshall, Michael Allen "Mike" — bats right — throws right — b.1/12/60 — 1991 positions: 1B 6, DH 1

YR	TM/LG	CL	G	TPA	AB	H	2B	3B	HR	TB	BB	IBB	HB	SO	GDP	SH	SF	SB	CS	R	RBI	BA	OBA	SA
81	LA/NL		14	27	25	5	3	0	0	8	1	0	1	4	1	0	0	0	0	2	1	.200	.259	.320
82	LA/NL		49	110	95	23	3	0	5	41	13	1	1	23	1	0	1	2	0	10	9	.242	.336	.432
83	LA/NL		140	518	465	132	17	1	17	202	43	4	5	127	8	0	5	7	3	47	65	.284	.347	.434
84	LA/NL		134	541	495	127	27	0	21	217	40	6	3	93	12	1	2	4	3	68	65	.257	.315	.438
85	LA/NL		135	564	518	152	27	2	28	267	37	6	3	137	8	2	4	3	10	72	95	.293	.342	.515
86	LA/NL		103	362	330	77	11	0	19	145	27	3	4	90	5	0	1	4	4	47	53	.233	.298	.439
87	LA/NL		104	428	402	118	19	0	16	185	18	2	4	79	13	0	4	0	5	45	72	.294	.327	.460
88	LA/NL		144	577	542	150	27	2	20	241	24	7	7	93	17	0	4	4	1	63	82	.277	.314	.445
89	LA/NL		105	419	377	98	21	1	11	154	33	4	5	78	8	0	4	2	5	41	42	.260	.325	.408
90	NY/NL		53	176	163	39	8	1	6	67	7	0	3	40	2	0	3	0	2	24	27	.239	.278	.411
	PAW/INT	AAA	6	26	23	7	0	0	2	13	3	0	0	3	0	0	0	0	0	5	4	.304	.385	.565
	BOS/AL		30	117	112	32	6	1	4	52	4	0	1	26	2	0	0	0	2	10	12	.286	.316	.464
	YEAR		83	293	275	71	14	2	10	119	11	0	4	66	4	0	3	0	2	34	39	.258	.294	.433
91	BOS/AL		22	62	62	18	4	0	1	25	0	0	0	19	2	0	0	0	0	4	7	.290	.290	.403
	PS/CAL	A+	3	11	8	2	1	0	0	3	2	0	0	3	0	0	1	0	0	1	2	.250	.364	.375
	CAL/AL		2	7	7	0	0	0	0	0	0	0	0	1	0	0	0	0	0	0	0	.000	.000	.000
	YEAR		24	69	69	18	4	0	1	25	0	0	0	20	2	0	0	0	0	4	7	.261	.261	.362
11 YR TOTALS			1035	3908	3593	971	173	8	148	1604	247	33	37	810	79	3	28	26	33	433	530	.270	.321	.446

Martinez, Carlos Alberto Escobar — bats right — throws right — b.8/11/64 — 1991 positions: DH 41, 1B 31

YR	TM/LG	CL	G	TPA	AB	H	2B	3B	HR	TB	BB	IBB	HB	SO	GDP	SH	SF	SB	CS	R	RBI	BA	OBA	SA
84	YAN/GCL	R	31	100	91	14	1	1	0	17	6	0	0	15	1	2	1	3	0	9	4	.154	.204	.187
85	FL/FSL	A+	93	333	311	77	15	7	6	124	14	1	2	65	9	4	2	8	4	39	44	.248	.283	.399
86	FL/FSL	A+	5	16	16	1	0	0	0	1	0	0	0	6	1	0	0	0	0	1	0	.063	.063	.063
	ALB/EAS	AA	69	264	253	70	18	2	8	116	6	0	3	46	4	0	2	2	3	34	39	.277	.299	.458
	BUF/AMA	AAA	17	60	54	16	1	0	2	23	2	0	2	12	1	0	2	0	0	6	6	.296	.333	.426
87	HAW/PCL	AAA	83	322	304	75	15	1	3	101	14	1	0	50	8	1	3	3	2	32	36	.247	.277	.332
	BIR/SOU	AA	9	31	30	7	1	0	0	8	1	0	0	6	1	0	0	2	2	2	0	.233	.258	.267
88	BIR/SOU	AA	133	544	498	138	22	3	14	208	36	2	2	82	10	2	6	25	7	67	73	.277	.325	.418
	CHI/AL		17	55	55	9	1	0	0	10	0	0	0	12	1	0	0	1	0	5	0	.164	.164	.182
89	VAN/PCL	AAA	18	71	64	25	3	1	2	36	5	0	0	14	0	0	2	2	0	12	9	.391	.423	.563
	SB/MID	A	3	12	11	6	3	0	0	9	1	0	0	1	0	0	0	2	0	2	3	.545	.583	.818
	CHI/AL		109	379	350	105	22	0	5	142	21	2	1	57	14	6	1	4	4	44	32	.300	.340	.406
90	CHI/AL		92	283	272	61	6	5	4	89	10	2	0	40	8	1	0	0	4	18	24	.224	.252	.327
91	CAN/EAS	AA	80	326	295	97	22	2	11	156	22	3	2	47	7	0	7	11	4	48	73	.329	.371	.529
	CLE/AL		72	275	257	73	14	0	5	102	10	2	2	43	10	1	5	3	2	22	30	.284	.310	.397
4 YR TOTALS			290	992	934	248	43	5	14	343	41	6	3	152	33	8	6	8	7	89	86	.266	.297	.367

Martinez, Carmelo (Salgado) — bats right — throws right — b.7/28/60 — 1991 positions: 1B 76, OF 16

YR	TM/LG	CL	G	TPA	AB	H	2B	3B	HR	TB	BB	IBB	HB	SO	GDP	SH	SF	SB	CS	R	RBI	BA	OBA	SA
83	CHI/NL		29	94	89	23	3	0	6	44	4	0	0	19	3	0	0	0	0	8	16	.258	.287	.494
84	SD/NL		149	570	488	122	28	2	13	193	68	4	4	82	7	0	10	1	3	64	66	.250	.340	.395
85	SD/NL		150	610	514	130	28	1	21	223	87	4	3	82	10	2	4	0	4	64	72	.253	.362	.434
86	SD/NL		113	283	244	58	10	0	9	95	35	2	1	46	9	1	2	1	1	28	25	.238	.333	.389
87	SD/NL		139	525	447	122	21	2	15	192	70	5	3	82	11	1	4	5	5	59	70	.273	.372	.430
88	SD/NL		121	405	365	86	12	0	18	152	35	3	0	57	10	3	2	1	1	48	65	.236	.301	.416
89	SD/NL		111	301	267	59	12	2	6	93	32	3	0	54	12	0	2	0	0	23	39	.221	.302	.348
90	PHI/NL		71	227	198	48	8	0	8	80	29	0	0	37	3	0	0	2	1	23	31	.242	.339	.404
	PIT/NL		12	20	19	4	1	0	2	11	1	0	0	5	0	0	0	0	0	3	4	.211	.250	.579
	YEAR		83	247	217	52	9	0	10	91	30	0	0	42	3	0	0	2	1	26	35	.240	.332	.419
91	PIT/NL		11	17	16	4	0	0	0	4	1	0	0	2	0	0	0	0	0	1	0	.250	.294	.250
	KC/AL		44	148	121	25	6	0	4	43	27	3	0	25	4	0	0	0	0	17	17	.207	.351	.355
	CIN/NL		53	156	138	32	5	0	6	55	15	1	0	37	1	0	3	0	0	12	19	.232	.301	.399
	YEAR		108	321	275	61	11	0	10	102	43	4	0	64	7	0	3	0	0	30	36	.222	.324	.371
9 YR TOTALS			1003	3356	2906	713	134	7	108	1185	404	25	11	528	72	7	28	10	16	350	424	**.245**	**.337**	**.408**

Martinez, Constantino "Tino" — bats left — throws right — b.12/7/67 — 1991 positions: 1B 29, DH 5

YR	TM/LG	CL	G	TPA	AB	H	2B	3B	HR	TB	BB	IBB	HB	SO	GDP	SH	SF	SB	CS	R	RBI	BA	OBA	SA
89	WIL/EAS	AA	137	577	509	131	29	2	13	203	59	13	0	54	11	1	8	7	1	51	64	.257	.330	.399
90	CAL/PCL	AAA	128	540	453	145	28	1	17	226	74	11	3	37	9	2	8	8	5	83	93	.320	.413	.499
	SEA/AL		24	78	68	15	4	0	0	19	9	0	0	9	0	0	1	0	0	4	5	.221	.308	.279
91	CAL/PCL	AAA	122	535	442	144	34	5	18	242	82	7	3	44	5	0	8	3	3	94	86	.326	.428	.548
	SEA/AL		36	125	112	23	2	0	4	37	11	0	0	24	2	0	3	0	0	15	14	.211	.286	.311
2 YR TOTALS			60	203	180	38	6	0	4	56	20	0	0	33	2	0	3	0	0	15	14	**.211**	**.286**	**.311**

Martinez, David "Dave" — bats left — throws left — b.9/26/64 — 1991 positions: OF 112

YR	TM/LG	CL	G	TPA	AB	H	2B	3B	HR	TB	BB	IBB	HB	SO	GDP	SH	SF	SB	CS	R	RBI	BA	OBA	SA
84	QC/MID	A	12	51	41	9	2	2	0	15	9	0	1	13	1	0	0	3	4	6	5	.220	.373	.366
85	WIN/CAR	A+	115	454	386	132	14	4	5	169	62	5	3	35	9	1	2	38	14	52	54	.342	.435	.438
86	CHI/NL		53	116	108	15	1	1	1	21	6	0	1	22	1	0	0	1	4	13	7	.139	.190	.194
	IOW/AMA	AAA	83	362	318	92	11	5	5	128	36	1	1	34	2	4	3	42	5	52	32	.289	.360	.403
87	CHI/NL		142	520	459	134	18	8	8	192	57	4	2	96	4	1	1	16	8	70	36	.292	.372	.418
88	CHI/NL		75	283	256	65	10	1	4	89	21	5	2	46	2	0	4	7	3	27	34	.254	.311	.348
	MON/NL		63	211	191	49	3	5	2	68	17	3	0	48	1	2	1	16	6	24	12	.257	.316	.356
	YEAR		138	494	447	114	13	6	6	157	38	8	2	94	3	2	5	23	9	51	46	.255	.313	.351
89	MON/NL		126	396	361	99	16	7	3	138	27	2	0	57	1	1	7	23	4	41	27	.274	.324	.382
90	MON/NL		118	421	391	109	13	5	11	165	24	2	1	48	8	3	2	13	11	60	39	.279	.321	.422
91	MON/NL		124	427	396	117	18	5	7	166	20	3	3	54	5	3	3	16	7	47	42	.295	.332	.419
6 YR TOTALS			701	2374	2162	588	79	32	36	839	172	19	9	371	20	18	13	95	41	282	197	**.272**	**.326**	**.388**

Martinez, Edgar — bats right — throws right — b.1/2/63 — 1991 positions: 3B 144, DH 2

YR	TM/LG	CL	G	TPA	AB	H	2B	3B	HR	TB	BB	IBB	HB	SO	GDP	SH	SF	SB	CS	R	RBI	BA	OBA	SA
84	WAU/MID	A	126	533	433	131	32	2	15	212	84	2	3	57	7	7	6	11	9	72	66	.303	.414	.490
85	CHT/SOU	AA	111	455	357	92	15	5	3	126	71	2	5	30	16	10	12	1	3	43	47	.258	.378	.353
	CAL/PCL	AAA	20	80	68	24	7	1	0	33	12	1	0	7	2	0	0	1	2	8	14	.353	.450	.485
86	CHT/SOU	AA	132	553	451	119	29	5	1	176	89	2	2	35	8	5	5	2	5	71	74	.264	.383	.390
87	CAL/PCL	AAA	129	531	438	144	31	4	10	207	82	2	2	48	10	6	3	3	5	75	66	.329	.434	.473
	SEA/AL		13	46	43	16	5	2	0	25	2	0	1	5	0	0	0	0	0	0	5	.372	.413	.581
88	CAL/PCL	AAA	95	407	331	120	19	4	8	171	66	6	3	40	7	5	5	9	1	63	64	.363	.467	.517
	SEA/AL		14	38	32	9	4	0	0	13	4	0	0	7	1	0	1	0	0	0	5	.281	.351	.406
89	CAL/PCL	AAA	32	141	113	39	11	0	3	59	22	1	3	13	1	1	2	2	1	30	23	.345	.457	.522
	SEA/AL		65	196	171	41	5	0	2	52	17	1	3	26	3	2	3	2	1	20	20	.240	.314	.304
90	SEA/AL		144	570	487	147	27	2	11	211	74	3	5	62	13	1	3	1	4	71	49	.302	.397	.433
91	SEA/AL		150	642	544	167	35	1	14	246	84	9	8	72	19	2	4	0	3	98	52	.307	.405	.452
5 YR TOTALS			386	1492	1277	380	76	5	27	547	181	13	17	172	35	6	11	3	8	195	131	**.298**	**.389**	**.428**

Martinez, Reyenaldo Ignacio "Chito" — bats left — throws left — b.12/19/65 — 1991 positions: OF 54, DH 4, 1B 1

YR	TM/LG	CL	G	TPA	AB	H	2B	3B	HR	TB	BB	IBB	HB	SO	GDP	SH	SF	SB	CS	R	RBI	BA	OBA	SA
84	EUG/NWL	A—	59	201	176	53	12	3	0	71	24	3	0	38	1	3	1	0	4	18	26	.301	.385	.403
85	FM/FSL	A+	76	284	248	65	9	5	0	84	31	3	1	42	8	1	3	11	5	35	29	.262	.343	.339
86	MEM/SOU	AA	93	330	283	86	16	5	11	145	42	4	2	58	2	2	1	4	4	14	14	.304	.396	.512
87	OMA/AMA	AAA	35	132	121	26	10	1	2	44	11	0	0	43	0	0	0	0	0	34	43	.215	.280	.364
	MEM/SOU	AA	78	319	283	74	10	3	9	117	33	4	0	94	4	0	2	20	3	67	65	.261	.339	.413
88	MEM/SOU	AA	141	560	485	110	16	4	13	173	66	4	7	130	6	2	6	3	3	55	62	.227	.317	.357
89	MEM/SOU	AA	127	471	399	97	12	4	23	190	63	7	4	137	8	4	4	2	3	59	67	.243	.345	.476
90	OMA/AMA	AAA	122	424	364	96	12	4	21	187	54	5	3	129	3	3	3	6	6	42	50	.264	.361	.514
91	ROC/INT	AAA	60	239	211	68	8	1	20	138	26	5	3	69	3	3	3	1	2	32	33	.322	.393	.654
	BAL/AL		67	228	216	58	12	1	13	111	11	0	1	51	2	0	0	1	1	32	33	.269	.303	.514

Marzano, John Robert — bats right — throws right — b.2/14/63 — 1991 positions: C 48

YR	TM/LG	CL	G	TPA	AB	H	2B	3B	HR	TB	BB	IBB	HB	SO	GDP	SH	SF	SB	CS	R	RBI	BA	OBA	SA
85	NB/EAS	AA	103	388	350	86	14	6	4	124	19	0	3	43	14	7	9	4	3	36	51	.246	.283	.354
86	NB/EAS	AA	118	487	445	126	28	2	10	188	24	2	12	66	10	0	6	2	0	55	62	.283	.333	.422
87	PAW/INT	AAA	70	284	255	72	22	0	10	124	21	0	5	50	10	2	1	3	3	46	35	.282	.348	.486
	BOS/AL		52	182	168	41	11	0	5	67	7	0	2	41	3	2	1	0	1	20	24	.244	.283	.399

(continued)

Marzano, John Robert (continued)

YR	TM/LG	CL	G	TPA	AB	H	2B	3B	HR	TB	BB	IBB	HB	SO	GDP	SH	SF	SB	CS	R	RBI	BA	OBA	SA
88	PAW/INT	AAA	33	122	111	22	2	1	0	26	8	0	0	17	4	2	1	1	1	7	5	.198	.250	.234
	NB/EAS	AA	35	127	112	23	6	1	0	31	10	2	3	13	6	1	1	1	0	11	5	.205	.286	.277
	BOS/AL		10	30	29	4	1	0	0	5	1	0	0	3	1	0	0	0	0	3	1	.138	.167	.172
89	PAW/INT	AAA	106	347	322	68	11	0	8	103	15	1	4	53	7	4	2	1	4	27	36	.211	.254	.320
	BOS/AL		7	20	18	8	3	0	1	14	0	0	0	2	1	1	0	0	0	5	3	.444	.421	.778
90	PAW/INT	AAA	26	86	75	24	4	1	2	36	11	0	0	9	2	0	0	6	3	16	8	.320	.407	.480
	BOS/AL		32	91	83	20	4	0	0	24	5	0	0	10	0	2	1	0	1	8	6	.241	.281	.289
91	BOS/AL		49	119	114	30	8	0	0	38	1	0	1	16	5	1	2	0	0	10	9	.263	.271	.333
5 YR TOTALS			**150**	**442**	**412**	**103**	**27**	**0**	**6**	**148**	**14**	**0**	**4**	**72**	**10**	**6**	**6**	**0**	**2**	**46**	**43**	**.250**	**.278**	**.359**

Mattingly, Donald Arthur "Don" — bats left — throws left — b.4/20/61 — 1991 positions: 1B 127, DH 22

YR	TM/LG	CL	G	TPA	AB	H	2B	3B	HR	TB	BB	IBB	HB	SO	GDP	SH	SF	SB	CS	R	RBI	BA	OBA	SA
82	NY/AL		7	13	12	2	0	0	0	2	0	0	0	1	2	0	1	0	0	0	1	.167	.154	.167
83	NY/AL		91	305	279	79	15	4	4	114	21	5	1	31	8	2	2	0	0	34	32	.283	.333	.409
84	NY/AL		153	662	603	207	44	2	23	324	41	8	1	33	15	8	9	1	1	91	110	.343	.381	.537
85	NY/AL		159	727	652	211	48	3	35	370	56	13	2	41	15	2	15	2	2	107	145	.324	.371	.567
86	NY/AL		162	742	677	238	53	2	31	388	53	11	1	35	17	1	10	0	0	117	113	.352	.394	.573
87	NY/AL		141	629	569	186	38	2	30	318	51	13	1	38	16	0	9	1	4	93	115	.327	.378	.559
88	NY/AL		144	651	599	186	37	0	18	277	41	14	3	29	13	0	8	1	0	94	88	.311	.353	.462
89	NY/AL		158	693	631	191	37	2	23	301	51	18	1	30	15	0	10	3	0	79	113	.303	.351	.477
90	NY/AL		102	428	394	101	16	0	5	132	28	13	3	20	13	0	3	1	0	40	42	.256	.308	.335
91	NY/AL		152	646	587	169	35	0	9	231	46	11	4	42	21	0	9	2	0	64	68	.288	.339	.394
10 YR TOTALS			**1269**	**5496**	**5003**	**1570**	**323**	**15**	**178**	**2457**	**388**	**106**	**17**	**300**	**135**	**13**	**75**	**11**	**7**	**719**	**827**	**.314**	**.360**	**.491**

Maurer, Robert John "Rob" — bats left — throws left — b.1/7/67 — 1991 positions: 1B 4, DH 2

YR	TM/LG	CL	G	TPA	AB	H	2B	3B	HR	TB	BB	IBB	HB	SO	GDP	SH	SF	SB	CS	R	RBI	BA	OBA	SA
88	BUT/PIO	R+	63	273	233	91	18	3	8	139	35	3	3	33	2	0	2	0	0	65	60	.391	.473	.597
89	CHA/FSL	A+	132	554	456	126	18	9	6	180	86	6	6	109	9	0	4	3	4	69	51	.276	.397	.395
90	TUL/TEX	AA	104	429	367	110	31	4	21	212	54	6	6	112	5	0	2	4	2	55	78	.300	.396	.578
91	OC/AMA	AAA	132	564	459	138	41	3	20	245	96	8	3	134	5	0	6	2	3	76	77	.301	.420	.534
	TEX/AL		13	19	16	1	1	0	0	2	2	0	1	6	0	0	0	0	0	0	2	.063	.211	.125

May, Derrick Brant — bats left — throws right — b.7/14/68 — 1991 positions: OF 7

YR	TM/LG	CL	G	TPA	AB	H	2B	3B	HR	TB	BB	IBB	HB	SO	GDP	SH	SF	SB	CS	R	RBI	BA	OBA	SA
86	WYT/APP	R+	54	197	178	57	6	1	0	65	16	1	2	15	3	0	1	17	4	25	23	.320	.381	.365
87	PEO/MID	A	128	487	439	131	19	8	9	193	42	4	1	106	5	0	5	5	7	60	52	.298	.357	.440
88	WIN/CAR	A+	130	532	485	148	29	9	8	219	37	4	5	82	3	0	5	13	8	76	65	.305	.357	.452
89	CHA/SOU	AA	136	530	491	145	26	5	9	208	33	4	5	76	8	1	0	19	7	72	70	.295	.346	.424
90	IOW/AMA	AAA	119	489	459	136	27	1	8	189	23	4	0	50	11	1	6	5	6	55	69	.296	.326	.412
	CHI/NL		17	63	61	15	3	0	1	21	2	0	0	9	0	0	0	1	0	8	11	.246	.270	.344
91	IOW/AMA	AAA	82	337	310	92	18	4	3	127	19	4	4	38	9	1	3	7	9	47	49	.297	.342	.410
	CHI/NL		15	25	22	5	2	0	1	10	2	0	0	1	1	0	1	0	0	4	3	.227	.280	.455
2 YR TOTALS			**32**	**88**	**83**	**20**	**5**	**0**	**2**	**31**	**4**	**0**	**0**	**8**	**2**	**0**	**1**	**1**	**0**	**12**	**14**	**.241**	**.273**	**.373**

Mayne, Brent Danem — bats left — throws right — b.4/19/68 — 1991 positions: C 80, DH 1

YR	TM/LG	CL	G	TPA	AB	H	2B	3B	HR	TB	BB	IBB	HB	SO	GDP	SH	SF	SB	CS	R	RBI	BA	OBA	SA
89	BC/FSL	A+	7	24	24	13	3	1	0	18	0	0	0	3	0	0	0	0	1	5	8	.542	.542	.750
90	MEM/SOU	AA	115	481	412	110	16	3	2	138	52	1	2	51	13	7	8	5	2	48	61	.267	.346	.335
	KC/AL		5	16	13	3	0	0	0	3	3	0	0	3	0	0	0	0	1	2	1	.231	.375	.231
91	KC/AL		85	259	231	58	8	0	3	75	23	4	0	42	6	2	3	2	4	22	31	.251	.315	.325
2 YR TOTALS			**90**	**275**	**244**	**61**	**8**	**0**	**3**	**78**	**26**	**4**	**0**	**45**	**6**	**2**	**3**	**2**	**5**	**24**	**32**	**.250**	**.319**	**.320**

McCarty, David A. — bats right — throws left — b.11/23/69 — 1991 positions: OF System MIN/AL

YR	TM/LG	CL	G	TPA	AB	H	2B	3B	HR	TB	BB	IBB	HB	SO	GDP	SH	SF	SB	CS	R	RBI	BA	OBA	SA
91	VIS/CAL	A+	15	66	50	19	3	0	3	31	13	0	3	7	0	0	0	3	1	16	8	.380	.530	.620
	ORL/SOU	AA	28	100	88	23	4	0	3	36	10	0	2	20	1	0	0	0	1	18	11	.261	.350	.409

McClendon, Lloyd Glenn — bats right — throws right — b.1/11/59 — 1991 positions: OF 32, 1B 22, C 2

YR	TM/LG	CL	G	TPA	AB	H	2B	3B	HR	TB	BB	IBB	HB	SO	GDP	SH	SF	SB	CS	R	RBI	BA	OBA	SA
84	VER/EAS	AA	60	233	202	56	16	0	7	93	28	0	2	28	5	0	1	2	2	36	27	.277	.369	.460
	WIC/AMA	AAA	48	174	152	45	13	1	6	78	21	0	0	33	3	0	1	2	0	28	28	.296	.379	.513
85	DEN/AMA	AAA	114	436	379	105	18	5	16	181	51	4	3	56	6	0	3	4	4	57	79	.277	.365	.478
86	DEN/AMA	AAA	132	509	433	112	30	1	24	216	70	1	2	75	6	0	4	2	4	75	88	.259	.361	.499
87	NAS/AMA	AAA	26	105	84	24	6	0	3	39	17	0	2	15	1	0	2	1	1	11	14	.286	.410	.464
	CIN/NL		45	77	72	15	5	0	2	26	4	0	0	15	1	0	0	1	1	8	13	.208	.247	.361
88	NAS/AMA	AAA	2	8	7	1	0	0	0	1	1	0	0	1	0	0	0	0	0		1	.143	.250	.143
	CIN/NL		72	157	137	30	4	0	3	43	15	1	2	22	6	1	2	4	0	9	14	.219	.301	.314
89	IOW/AMA	AAA	34	131	109	35	10	0	4	57	21	1	0	19	3	0	1	4	1	18	13	.321	.427	.523
	CHI/NL		92	305	259	74	12	1	12	124	37	3	1	31	4	0	7	6	4	47	40	.286	.368	.479
90	IOW/AMA	AAA	25	102	91	26	2	0	2	34	8	1	2	19	3	0	1	3	1	14	10	.286	.353	.374
	CHI/NL		49	122	107	17	3	0	1	23	14	2	0	21	2	0	1	0	2	5	10	.159	.254	.215
	PIT/NL		4	3	3	1	0	0	0	4	0	0	0	0	0	0	0	0	0	1	2	.333	.333	1.333
	YEAR		53	125	110	18	3	0	2	27	14	2	0	22	2	0	1	0	2	6	12	.164	.256	.245
91	PIT/NL		85	183	163	47	7	0	5	75	18	0	2	23	2	0	0	0	2	24	24	.288	.366	.460
5 YR TOTALS			**347**	**847**	**741**	**184**	**31**	**1**	**26**	**295**	**88**	**6**	**5**	**113**	**14**	**2**	**11**	**14**	**5**	**94**	**103**	**.248**	**.328**	**.398**

McCray, Rodney Duncan — bats right — throws right — b.9/13/63 — 1991 positions: OF 8, DH 6

YR	TM/LG	CL	G	TPA	AB	H	2B	3B	HR	TB	BB	IBB	HB	SO	GDP	SH	SF	SB	CS	R	RBI	BA	OBA	SA
84	SPO/NWL	A–	71	315	244	50	6	1	1	61	65	0	2	50	8	0	4	25	5	40	20	.205	.371	.250
85	CHA/SAL	A	117	465	373	77	8	1	1	90	80	2	6	88	6	5	1	49	7	81	27	.206	.354	.241
86	CHA/SAL	A	123	538	417	107	13	3	4	138	108	2	5	80	3	6	2	81	32	88	33	.257	.414	.331
87	REN/CAL	A+	117	504	413	87	11	5	0	108	69	3	10	96	4	9	3	65	16	69	26	.211	.335	.262
88	SB/MID	A	107	381	306	65	10	2	1	82	56	0	10	72	5	7	2	55	12	48	24	.212	.350	.268
89	SAR/FSL	A+	124	533	422	112	19	4	1	142	96	3	9	81	6	4	2	44	22	36	16	.265	.410	.336
90	BIR/SOU	AA	60	237	188	37	2	2	1	46	36	0	5	42	2	6	2	25	10	7	6	.197	.338	.245
	VAN/PCL	AAA	19	66	53	12	4	2	0	20	10	0	1	4	0	1	0	6	0	8	0	.226	.369	.377
	CHI/AL		32	7	6	0	0	0	0	0	1	0	0	4	0	0	0	0	0	8	0	.000	.143	.000
91	VAN/PCL	AAA	83	260	222	51	9	5	0	70	26	0	8	48	4	2	2	14	10	37	13	.230	.329	.315
	CHI/AL		17	7	7	2	0	0	0	2	0	0	0	6	0	0	0	1	1	2	0	.286	.286	.286
2 YR TOTALS			49	14	13	2	0	0	0	2	1	0	0	10	0	0	0	1	1	10	0	**.154**	**.214**	**.154**

McDaniel, Terrence Keith "Terry" — bats right — throws right — b.12/6/66 — 1991 positions: OF 14

YR	TM/LG	CL	G	TPA	AB	H	2B	3B	HR	TB	BB	IBB	HB	SO	GDP	SH	SF	SB	CS	R	RBI	BA	OBA	SA
86	KIN/APP	R+	41	151	114	28	5	1	6	53	32	0	1	29	1	1	3	14	3	24	21	.246	.407	.465
87	LF/NYP	A–	70	294	237	57	4	2	5	80	52	0	1	82	1	3	1	20	10	51	31	.241	.378	.338
88	COL/SAL	A	127	536	449	111	16	6	5	154	74	5	3	173	4	3	3	41	10	76	43	.247	.360	.343
	SL/FSL	A+	4	14	12	3	0	0	0	3	1	0	1	3	0	0	0	0	0	1	0	.250	.357	.250
89	SL/FSL	A+	105	435	351	81	17	11	7	141	71	1	8	106	3	0	5	43	19	70	43	.231	.368	.402
90	JAC/TEX	AA	67	275	234	67	15	2	5	101	31	0	3	70	4	0	3	18	9	34	37	.286	.382	.432
91	TID/INT	AAA	118	456	399	99	23	6	9	161	50	4	5	117	8	2	0	17	4	63	42	.248	.339	.404
	NY/NL		23	30	29	6	1	0	0	7	1	0	0	11	0	0	0	0	0	3	2	.207	.233	.241

McFarlin, Jason Lamar — bats left — throws left — b.6/28/70 — 1991 positions: OF System SF/NL

YR	TM/LG	CL	G	TPA	AB	H	2B	3B	HR	TB	BB	IBB	HB	SO	GDP	SH	SF	SB	CS	R	RBI	BA	OBA	SA
89	EVE/NWL	A–	37	141	131	34	4	3	0	44	5	1	1	25	3	2	2	7	3	17	12	.260	.288	.336
90	CLI/MID	A	129	540	476	108	9	5	0	127	47	2	9	79	7	7	1	72	19	68	31	.227	.308	.267
91	SJ/CAL	A+	103	480	407	95	10	5	2	121	47	2	14	72	6	10	2	46	20	65	33	.233	.332	.297

McGee, Willie Dean — bats both — throws right — b.11/2/58 — 1991 positions: OF 128

YR	TM/LG	CL	G	TPA	AB	H	2B	3B	HR	TB	BB	IBB	HB	SO	GDP	SH	SF	SB	CS	R	RBI	BA	OBA	SA
82	STL/NL		123	439	422	125	12	8	4	165	12	2	1	58	9	2	1	24	12	43	56	.296	.318	.391
83	STL/NL		147	631	601	172	22	8	5	225	26	2	0	98	8	1	3	39	8	75	75	.286	.314	.374
84	STL/NL		145	604	571	166	19	11	6	225	29	2	1	80	12	0	1	43	10	82	50	.291	.325	.394
85	STL/NL		152	652	612	216	26	18	10	308	34	2	0	86	3	1	5	56	16	114	82	.353	.384	.503
86	STL/NL		124	539	497	127	22	7	7	184	37	7	1	82	8	0	4	19	16	65	48	.256	.306	.370
87	STL/NL		153	652	620	177	37	11	11	269	24	5	2	90	24	1	5	16	4	76	105	.285	.312	.434
88	STL/NL		137	600	562	164	24	6	3	209	32	5	2	84	10	2	3	41	6	73	50	.292	.329	.372
89	LOU/AMA	AAA	8	32	27	11	4	0	0	15	3	1	0	4	0	0	2	3	0	5	4	.407	.438	.556
	STL/NL		58	211	199	47	10	2	3	70	10	1	1	34	2	0	2	8	1	23	17	.236	.275	.352
90	STL/NL		125	542	501	168	32	5	2	219	38	6	1	86	9	0	2	28	9	76	62	.335	.382	.437
	OAK/AL		29	123	113	31	3	2	0	38	10	0	0	18	4	0	0	3	0	23	15	.274	.333	.336
	YEAR		154	665	614	199	35	7	2	257	48	6	1	104	13	0	2	31	9	99	77	.324	.373	.419
91	PHO/PCL	AAA	4	13	10	5	1	0	0	6	3	0	0	1	0	0	0	2	0	4	1	.500	.615	.600
	SF/NL		131	543	497	155	30	3	4	203	34	3	1	74	11	8	2	17	9	67	43	.312	.357	.408
10 YR TOTALS			1324	5536	5195	1548	237	81	56	2115	286	34	11	790	100	15	29	294	96	717	603	**.298**	**.334**	**.407**

McGriff, Frederick Stanley "Fred" — bats left — throws left — b.10/31/63 — 1991 positions: 1B 153

YR	TM/LG	CL	G	TPA	AB	H	2B	3B	HR	TB	BB	IBB	HB	SO	GDP	SH	SF	SB	CS	R	RBI	BA	OBA	SA
84	KNO/SOU	AA	56	222	189	47	13	2	9	91	29	3	1	55	2	0	3	0	2	29	25	.249	.347	.481
	SYR/INT	AAA	70	266	238	56	10	1	13	107	26	0	0	89	3	1	1	0	1	19	20	.235	.309	.450
85	SYR/INT	AAA	51	204	176	40	8	2	5	67	23	0	4	53	2	1	0	0	0	19	20	.227	.330	.381
86	TOR/AL		3	5	5	1	0	0	0	1	0	0	0	2	0	0	0	0	0	0	0	.200	.200	.200
	SYR/INT	AAA	133	563	468	121	23	4	19	209	83	8	4	119	16	0	8	0	3	69	74	.259	.369	.447
87	TOR/AL		107	356	295	73	16	0	20	149	60	4	1	104	6	0	0	3	0	58	43	.247	.376	.505
88	TOR/AL		154	623	536	151	35	4	34	296	79	3	4	149	15	0	4	6	7	100	82	.282	.376	.552
89	TOR/AL		161	680	551	148	27	3	36	289	119	12	4	132	14	1	5	7	4	98	92	.269	.399	.525
90	TOR/AL		153	658	557	167	21	1	35	295	94	12	2	135	14	0	7	4	3	91	88	.300	.400	.530
91	SD/NL		153	642	528	147	19	1	31	261	105	26	2	135	14	0	7	4	1	84	106	.278	.391	.494
6 YR TOTALS			731	2964	2472	687	118	9	156	1291	457	57	13	630	53	2	20	25	11	432	411	**.278**	**.391**	**.522**

McGwire, Mark David — bats right — throws right — b.10/1/63 — 1991 positions: 1B 152

YR	TM/LG	CL	G	TPA	AB	H	2B	3B	HR	TB	BB	IBB	HB	SO	GDP	SH	SF	SB	CS	R	RBI	BA	OBA	SA
84	MOD/CAL	A+	16	63	55	11	3	0	1	17	8	0	0	21	2	0	0	0	0	7	1	.200	.302	.309
85	MOD/CAL	A+	138	596	489	134	23	3	24	235	96	0	4	108	9	0	7	1	2	95	106	.274	.393	.481
86	HUN/SOU	AA	55	249	195	59	10	3	10	104	46	0	1	45	10	0	3	0	0	40	53	.303	.427	.533
	TAC/PCL	AAA	78	330	280	89	21	5	13	159	42	4	2	67	10	0	3	0	1	42	59	.318	.405	.568
	OAK/AL		18	58	53	10	1	0	3	20	4	0	1	18	0	0	0	0	0	10	9	.189	.259	.377
87	OAK/AL		151	641	557	161	28	4	49	344	71	8	5	131	6	0	7	1	1	97	118	.289	.370	.618
88	OAK/AL		155	635	550	143	22	1	32	263	76	4	3	117	15	0	11	0	0	87	99	.260	.352	.478
89	OAK/AL		143	587	490	113	17	0	33	229	83	12	3	94	23	0	11	1	1	74	95	.231	.339	.467
90	OAK/AL		156	650	523	123	16	0	39	256	110	13	6	116	13	0	7	2	2	62	75	.235	.370	.489
91	OAK/AL		154	585	483	97	22	0	22	185	93	3	7	116	13	0	3	2	2	62	75	.201	.330	.383
6 YR TOTALS			777	3156	2656	647	106	5	178	1297	437	29	23	592	70	3	37	6	5	417	504	**.244**	**.351**	**.488**

McIntosh, Timothy Allen "Tim" — bats right — throws right — b.3/21/65 — 1991 positions: OF 4, DH 2, 1B 1

YR	TM/LG	CL	G	TPA	AB	H	2B	3B	HR	TB	BB	IBB	HB	SO	GDP	SH	SF	SB	CS	R	RBI	BA	OBA	SA
86	BEL/MID	A	49	196	173	45	3	3	4	64	18	0	2	33	3	0	3	0	0	26	21	.260	.332	.370
87	BEL/MID	A	130	521	461	139	30	3	20	235	49	2	7	96	4	1	3	7	4	83	85	.302	.375	.510
88	STO/CAL	A+	138	598	519	147	32	6	15	236	57	1	11	96	6	6	5	10	5	81	92	.283	.363	.455
89	EP/TEX	AA	120	511	463	139	30	3	17	226	29	3	8	72	8	2	9	5	4	72	93	.300	.346	.488
90	DEN/AMA	AAA	116	466	416	120	20	3	18	200	26	0	14	58	9	3	7	6	2	72	74	.288	.346	.481
	MIL/AL		5	5	5	1	0	0	1	4	0	0	0	2	0	0	0	0	0	1	1	.200	.200	.800
91	DEN/AMA	AAA	122	517	462	135	19	9	18	226	37	4	11	59	13	0	7	2	5	69	91	.292	.354	.489
	MIL/AL		7	11	11	4	1	0	1	8	0	0	0	4	0	0	0	2	1	2	1	.364	.364	.727
2 YR TOTALS			**12**	**16**	**16**	**5**	**1**	**0**	**2**	**12**	**0**	**0**	**0**	**6**	**0**	**0**	**0**	**0**	**0**	**3**	**2**	**.313**	**.313**	**.750**

McKnight, Jefferson Alan "Jeff" — bats both — throws right — b.2/18/63 — 1991 positions: OF 7, DH 4, 1B 2

YR	TM/LG	CL	G	TPA	AB	H	2B	3B	HR	TB	BB	IBB	HB	SO	GDP	SH	SF	SB	CS	R	RBI	BA	OBA	SA
84	COL/SAL	A	95	280	251	64	10	1	1	79	26	2	1	17	5	1	1	9	1	31	27	.255	.326	.315
85	COL/SAL	A	67	183	159	42	6	1	1	53	21	2	1	18	2	0	2	6	2	26	24	.264	.350	.333
	LYN/CAR	A+	49	186	150	33	6	1	0	41	29	0	0	19	1	4	3	0	0	19	21	.220	.341	.273
86	JAC/TEX	AA	132	562	469	118	24	3	4	160	76	3	3	58	10	5	9	5	2	71	55	.252	.354	.341
87	JAC/TEX	AA	16	64	59	12	3	0	2	21	4	0	1	12	3	0	0	1	0	5	8	.203	.266	.356
	TID/INT	AAA	87	214	184	47	7	3	2	66	24	1	1	22	6	1	4	0	1	21	25	.255	.338	.359
88	TID/INT	AAA	113	385	345	88	14	0	2	108	36	5	0	32	1	3	0	6	1	36	25	.255	.323	.313
89	NY/NL		6	14	12	3	0	0	0	3	2	0	0	1	1	0	0	0	0	3	0	.250	.357	.250
	TID/INT	AAA	116	509	425	106	19	2	9	156	79	1	1	56	13	3	1	3	0	84	48	.249	.368	.367
90	ROC/INT	AAA	100	390	339	95	21	3	7	143	41	3	0	58	4	4	6	7	5	56	45	.280	.352	.422
	BAL/AL		29	84	75	15	2	0	1	20	5	0	1	17	0	3	0	0	0	11	4	.200	.259	.267
91	ROC/INT	AAA	22	96	81	31	7	2	1	45	14	0	0	10	3	0	1	1	2	19	18	.383	.469	.556
	BAL/AL		16	43	41	7	1	0	0	8	2	0	0	7	3	0	1	1	2	2	2	.171	.209	.195
3 YR TOTALS			**51**	**141**	**128**	**25**	**3**	**0**	**1**	**31**	**9**	**0**	**1**	**25**	**3**	**3**	**0**	**1**	**0**	**15**	**6**	**.195**	**.254**	**.242**

McLemore, Mark Tremell — bats both — throws right — b.10/4/64 — 1991 positions: 2B 19

YR	TM/LG	CL	G	TPA	AB	H	2B	3B	HR	TB	BB	IBB	HB	SO	GDP	SH	SF	SB	CS	R	RBI	BA	OBA	SA
82	SAL/NWL	A-	55	210	165	49	6	2	0	59	39	0	2	38	2	1	3	14	6	42	25	.297	.431	.358
83	PEO/MID	A	95	393	329	79	7	3	0	92	53	0	3	64	3	6	3	15	11	42	18	.240	.346	.280
84	RED/CAL	A+	134	603	482	142	8	3	0	156	106	1	1	75	2	11	3	59	15	102	45	.295	.421	.324
85	MID/TEX	AA	117	534	458	124	17	6	2	159	66	4	1	59	4	6	3	31	16	80	46	.271	.362	.347
86	MID/TEX	AA	63	291	237	75	9	1	1	89	48	1	1	18	5	1	4	38	8	54	29	.316	.428	.376
	EDM/PCL	AAA	73	333	286	79	13	1	0	94	39	2	0	30	0	4	4	29	9	41	23	.276	.359	.329
	CAL/AL		5	6	4	0	0	0	0	0	1	0	0	0	0	0	0	0	0	0	0	.000	.200	.000
87	CAL/AL		138	499	433	102	13	3	3	130	48	0	0	72	7	15	3	25	8	61	41	.236	.310	.300
88	PS/CAL	A+	11	57	44	15	3	1	0	20	11	0	1	7	1	0	1	7	3	9	6	.341	.474	.455
	EDM/PCL	AAA	12	51	45	12	3	0	0	15	4	0	0	4	1	2	0	2	1	7	6	.267	.327	.333
	CAL/AL		77	265	233	56	11	2	2	77	25	0	0	28	6	5	2	13	7	38	16	.240	.312	.330
89	EDM/PCL	AAA	114	485	430	105	13	2	2	128	49	1	1	67	14	2	3	26	11	60	34	.244	.321	.298
	CAL/AL		32	115	103	25	3	1	0	30	7	0	2	19	2	3	1	6	1	12	14	.243	.295	.291
90	CAL/AL		20	53	48	7	2	0	0	9	4	0	0	9	1	1	0	1	0	4	2	.146	.212	.188
	EDM/PCL	AAA	9	45	39	10	2	0	0	12	6	0	0	10	1	0	0	0	3	4	3	.256	.356	.308
	PS/CAL	A+	6	25	22	6	0	0	0	6	3	0	0	7	0	0	0	0	2	3	2	.273	.360	.273
	CS/PCL	AAA	14	65	54	15	2	0	1	20	11	0	0	8	2	0	0	5	0	11	7	.278	.400	.370
	CLE/AL		8	12	12	2	0	0	0	2	0	0	0	2	1	0	0	0	0	2	0	.167	.167	.167
	YEAR		28	65	60	9	2	0	0	11	4	0	0	15	1	0	0	1	0	6	2	.150	.203	.183
91	TUC/PCL	AAA	4	16	14	5	1	0	0	6	2	0	0	1	1	0	0	0	0	2	0	.357	.438	.429
	JAC/TEX	AA	7	28	22	5	3	0	1	11	6	0	0	3	0	0	0	1	0	2	0	.227	.393	.500
	HOU/NL		21	68	61	9	1	0	0	10	6	0	0	13	1	0	0	1	0	6	4	.148	.221	.164
	ROC/INT	AAA	57	259	228	64	11	4	1	86	27	0	1	29	5	2	1	0	1	6	2	.148	.221	.164
6 YR TOTALS			**301**	**1018**	**894**	**201**	**30**	**6**	**5**	**258**	**91**	**0**	**1**	**149**	**17**	**25**	**7**	**45**	**18**	**123**	**75**	**.225**	**.295**	**.289**

McRae, Brian Wesley — bats both — throws right — b.8/27/67 — 1991 positions: OF 150

YR	TM/LG	CL	G	TPA	AB	H	2B	3B	HR	TB	BB	IBB	HB	SO	GDP	SH	SF	SB	CS	R	RBI	BA	OBA	SA
85	ROY/GCL	R	60	253	217	58	6	5	0	74	28	0	2	34	7	4	2	27	12	40	23	.267	.353	.341
86	EUG/NWL	A-	72	355	306	82	10	3	1	101	41	1	5	49	6	1	2	28	4	66	29	.268	.362	.330
87	FM/FSL	A+	131	509	481	121	14	1	1	140	22	1	6	70	4	0	0	33	18	62	31	.252	.293	.291
88	BC/FSL	A+	30	121	107	33	2	0	1	38	9	0	3	11	2	2	0	8	5	18	11	.308	.378	.355
	MEM/SOU	AA	91	316	288	58	13	1	4	85	16	0	2	60	8	10	0	13	5	33	15	.201	.248	.295
89	MEM/SOU	AA	138	592	533	121	18	8	5	170	43	1	8	94	5	7	1	23	8	72	42	.227	.294	.319
90	MEM/SOU	AA	116	532	470	126	24	6	10	192	44	1	3	66	9	14	1	21	10	78	64	.268	.334	.409
	KC/AL		46	182	168	48	8	3	2	68	9	0	2	29	5	3	2	4	3	21	23	.286	.318	.405
91	KC/AL		152	663	629	164	28	9	8	234	24	1	2	99	12	3	2	20	11	86	64	.261	.288	.372
2 YR TOTALS			**198**	**845**	**797**	**212**	**36**	**12**	**10**	**302**	**33**	**1**	**2**	**128**	**17**	**6**	**7**	**24**	**14**	**107**	**87**	**.266**	**.294**	**.379**

McReynolds, Walter Kevin "Kevin" — bats right — throws right — b.10/16/59 — 1991 positions: OF 141

YR	TM/LG	CL	G	TPA	AB	H	2B	3B	HR	TB	BB	IBB	HB	SO	GDP	SH	SF	SB	CS	R	RBI	BA	OBA	SA
83	SD/NL		39	155	140	31	3	1	4	48	12	1	0	29	1	0	3	2	1	15	14	.221	.277	.343
84	SD/NL		147	571	525	146	26	6	20	244	34	8	0	69	14	3	9	3	6	68	75	.278	.317	.465
85	SD/NL		152	616	564	132	24	4	15	209	43	6	3	81	17	3	9	4	8	61	75	.234	.290	.371
86	SD/NL		158	641	560	161	31	6	26	282	66	6	1	83	9	5	9	8	6	89	96	.287	.358	.504
87	NY/NL		151	639	590	163	32	5	29	292	39	5	4	70	13	1	5	14	1	86	95	.276	.318	.495
88	NY/NL		147	600	552	159	30	2	27	274	38	3	4	56	6	1	5	21	0	82	99	.288	.336	.496

McReynolds, Walter Kevin "Kevin" (continued)

YR	TM/LG	CL	G	TPA	AB	H	2B	3B	HR	TB	BB	IBB	HB	SO	GDP	SH	SF	SB	CS	R	RBI	BA	OBA	SA
89	NY/NL		148	599	545	148	25	3	22	245	46	10	1	74	8	0	7	15	7	74	85	.272	.326	.450
90	NY/NL		147	601	521	140	23	1	24	237	71	11	1	61	8	0	8	9	2	75	82	.269	.353	.455
91	NY/NL		143	578	522	135	32	1	16	217	49	7	2	46	8	1	4	6	6	65	74	.259	.322	.416
9 YR TOTALS			**1232**	**5000**	**4519**	**1215**	**226**	**29**	**183**	**2048**	**398**	**57**	**13**	**569**	**84**	**13**	**57**	**82**	**29**	**615**	**695**	**.269**	**.326**	**.453**

Meadows, Gregory Scott "Scott" — bats right — throws right — b.11/2/66 — 1991 positions: OF System BAL/AL

YR	TM/LG	CL	G	TPA	AB	H	2B	3B	HR	TB	BB	IBB	HB	SO	GDP	SH	SF	SB	CS	R	RBI	BA	OBA	SA
88	HAG/CAR	A+	8	8	8	3	2	0	0	5	0	0	0	2	1	0	0	0	1	3	0	.375	.375	.625
89	WAT/MID	A	19	73	62	25	5	1	0	32	8	0	0	13	1	0	1	0	0	14	6	.403	.479	.516
	FRE/CAR	A+	99	424	371	101	17	4	2	132	42	0	1	56	10	1	7	12	7	59	41	.272	.345	.356
90	HAG/EAS	AA	138	579	495	145	29	3	6	198	66	5	9	70	10	2	7	9	11	60	75	.293	.381	.400
91	HAG/EAS	AA	33	156	120	36	7	1	1	48	34	0	1	22	4	0	1	1	4	18	11	.300	.455	.400
	ROC/INT	AAA	74	300	249	82	11	5	5	115	41	1	5	38	5	5	5	0	3	45	42	.329	.434	.462

Medina, Luis Main — bats right — throws left — b.3/26/63 — 1991 positions: DH 5

YR	TM/LG	CL	G	TPA	AB	H	2B	3B	HR	TB	BB	IBB	HB	SO	GDP	SH	SF	SB	CS	R	RBI	BA	OBA	SA
85	BAT/NYP	A-	76	325	290	77	16	0	12	129	32	1	3	72	3	0	3	0	7	43	43	.266	.345	.445
86	WAT/MID	A	136	587	505	160	25	5	35	300	75	4	4	109	15	0	3	6	5	107	110	.317	.407	.594
87	WIL/EAS	AA	96	402	341	109	15	6	16	184	48	6	5	75	7	0	8	10	2	61	68	.320	.403	.540
88	CS/PCL	AAA	111	451	406	126	28	6	28	250	42	4	0	107	4	0	3	1	2	81	81	.310	.373	.616
	CLE/AL		16	56	51	13	0	0	6	31	2	0	1	18	0	1	0	0	0	10	8	.255	.309	.608
89	CLE/AL		30	89	83	17	1	0	4	30	6	0	0	35	0	0	0	0	1	8	8	.205	.258	.361
	CS/PCL	AAA	51	186	166	29	8	0	3	46	19	0	0	50	4	0	3	7	3	17	19	.175	.258	.277
90	CS/PCL	AAA	94	359	320	87	15	0	18	156	33	0	3	68	13	0	3	7	3	58	53	.272	.343	.488
91	CLE/AL		5	18	16	1	0	0	0	1	1	0	0	7	0	1	0	0	0	0	0	.063	.118	.063
	CS/PCL	AAA	117	507	450	146	28	6	27	267	47	2	2	100	7	0	8	0	1	81	98	.324	.385	.593
3 YR TOTALS			**51**	**163**	**150**	**31**	**1**	**0**	**10**	**62**	**9**	**0**	**2**	**60**	**3**	**2**	**0**	**0**	**1**	**18**	**16**	**.207**	**.261**	**.413**

Melvin, Robert Paul "Bob" — bats right — throws right — b.10/28/61 — 1991 positions: C 72, DH 4

YR	TM/LG	CL	G	TPA	AB	H	2B	3B	HR	TB	BB	IBB	HB	SO	GDP	SH	SF	SB	CS	R	RBI	BA	OBA	SA
84	EVA/AMA	AAA	44	145	141	35	13	0	0	48	3	0	0	32	3	1	0	0	1	12	11	.248	.264	.340
	BIR/SOU	AA	69	293	271	73	14	1	2	95	18	2	0	47	12	2	2	1	0	34	33	.269	.313	.351
85	NAS/AMA	AAA	53	197	177	48	7	1	9	84	16	1	1	38	5	1	2	3	1	27	24	.271	.332	.475
	DET/AL		41	87	82	18	4	1	1	24	3	0	0	21	1	2	0	0	0	10	10	.220	.247	.293
86	SF/NL		89	289	268	60	14	2	5	93	15	1	0	69	7	1	3	3	2	24	25	.224	.262	.347
87	SF/NL		84	265	246	49	8	0	11	90	17	3	0	44	7	0	2	0	4	31	31	.199	.249	.366
88	PHO/PCL	AAA	21	84	75	23	5	0	2	34	8	0	0	13	4	0	1	0	0	11	9	.307	.381	.453
	SF/NL		92	288	273	64	13	1	8	103	13	0	0	46	5	1	1	0	2	23	27	.234	.268	.377
89	BAL/AL		85	301	278	67	10	1	1	82	15	3	0	53	10	1	3	0	1	22	32	.241	.279	.295
90	BAL/AL		93	318	301	73	14	1	5	104	11	1	0	53	8	3	3	0	0	30	37	.243	.267	.346
91	BAL/AL		79	245	228	57	10	0	1	70	11	2	0	46	5	1	5	0	0	11	23	.250	.279	.307
7 YR TOTALS			**563**	**1793**	**1676**	**388**	**73**	**6**	**31**	**566**	**85**	**10**	**0**	**332**	**43**	**17**	**15**	**4**	**13**	**151**	**179**	**.232**	**.266**	**.338**

Merced, Orlando Luis (Villanueva) — bats both — throws right — b.11/2/66 — 1991 positions: 1B 105, OF 7

YR	TM/LG	CL	G	TPA	AB	H	2B	3B	HR	TB	BB	IBB	HB	SO	GDP	SH	SF	SB	CS	R	RBI	BA	OBA	SA
85	PIR/GCL	R	40	146	136	31	6	0	1	40	9	0	1	9	3	0	0	3	1	16	13	.228	.281	.294
86	MAC/SAL	A	65	188	173	34	4	1	2	46	12	0	1	38	3	0	2	5	3	20	24	.197	.250	.266
	WAT/NYP	A-	27	106	89	16	0	1	3	27	14	2	2	21	2	0	1	6	2	12	9	.180	.302	.303
87	MAC/SAL	A	4	5	4	0	0	0	0	0	1	0	0	3	0	0	0	0	0	1	0	.000	.200	.000
	WAT/NYP	A-	4	14	12	5	0	1	0	7	1	0	0	1	0	0	0	0	0	4	3	.417	.500	.583
88	AUG/SAL	A	37	146	136	36	6	3	1	51	7	1	2	20	2	0	1	2	0	19	17	.265	.308	.375
	SAL/CAR	A+	80	332	298	87	12	7	7	134	27	1	1	64	7	1	5	13	3	47	42	.292	.347	.450
89	HAR/EAS	AA	95	380	341	82	16	4	6	124	32	1	6	66	4	1	2	1	0	43	48	.240	.306	.364
	BUF/AMA	AAA	35	139	129	44	5	3	1	58	7	1	0	26	2	2	1	0		18	16	.341	.372	.450
90	BUF/AMA	AAA	101	426	378	99	12	6	9	150	46	3	0	63	8	1	0	14	5	52	55	.262	.341	.397
	PIT/NL		25	25	24	5	1	0	0	6	1	0	0	9	0	0	0	0	1	3	0	.208	.240	.250
91	BUF/AMA	AAA	3	13	12	2	0	0	0	2	1	0	0	1	0	0	0	1	1	1	0	.167	.231	.167
	PIT/NL		120	478	411	113	17	2	10	164	64	4	1	81	6	1	1	8	4	83	50	.275	.373	.399
2 YR TOTALS			**145**	**503**	**435**	**118**	**18**	**2**	**10**	**170**	**65**	**4**	**1**	**90**	**7**	**1**	**1**	**8**	**4**	**86**	**50**	**.271**	**.367**	**.391**

Mercedes, Luis Roberto — bats right — throws right — b.2/20/68 — 1991 positions: OF 15, DH 1

YR	TM/LG	CL	G	TPA	AB	H	2B	3B	HR	TB	BB	IBB	HB	SO	GDP	SH	SF	SB	CS	R	RBI	BA	OBA	SA
88	BLU/APP	R+	59	253	215	59	8	4	0	75	32	0	3	39	6	3	1	16	11	36	20	.274	.372	.349
89	FRE/CAR	A+	108	438	401	124	12	5	3	155	30	2	3	62	7	2	2	38	14	62	36	.309	.360	.387
90	HAG/EAS	AA	108	464	416	139	12	4	3	168	34	2	6	70	13	6	4	23	14	71	37	.334	.391	.404
91	ROC/INT	AAA	102	454	374	125	14	5	0	155	65	0	6	63	10	6	4	10	2	68	36	.334	.435	.414
	BAL/AL		19	59	54	11	2	0	0	13	4	0	0	9	1	1	0	0	0	10	2	.204	.259	.241

Merullo, Matthew Bates "Matt" — bats left — throws right — b.8/4/65 — 1991 positions: C 27, 1B 16, DH 6

YR	TM/LG	CL	G	TPA	AB	H	2B	3B	HR	TB	BB	IBB	HB	SO	GDP	SH	SF	SB	CS	R	RBI	BA	OBA	SA
86	PEN/CAR	A+	64	231	208	63	12	2	3	88	19	3	1	16	5	0	3	1	0	21	35	.303	.359	.423
87	DB/FSL	A+	70	276	250	65	11	6	4	100	20	0	0	18	6	0	6	1	1	26	47	.260	.308	.400
	BIR/SOU	AA	48	173	167	46	7	0	2	59	6	0	0	20	5	0	0	1	0	13	17	.275	.301	.353
88	BIR/SOU	AA	125	496	449	117	26	0	6	161	40	3	3	60	9	1	3	3	2	58	60	.261	.323	.359

(continued)

Merullo, Matthew Bates "Matt" (continued)

YR	TM/LG	CL	G	TPA	AB	H	2B	3B	HR	TB	BB	IBB	HB	SO	GDP	SH	SF	SB	CS	R	RBI	BA	OBA	SA
89	VAN/PCL	AAA	3	12	9	2	1	0	0	3	2	0	0	1	1	1	0	0	0	0	2	.222	.364	.333
	CHI/AL		31	90	81	18	1	0	1	22	6	0	0	14	2	1	0	1	0	5	8	.222	.273	.272
	BIR/SOU	AA	33	140	119	35	6	0	3	50	16	2	0	15	3	2	3	0	1	19	23	.294	.370	.420
90	BIR/SOU	AA	102	420	378	110	26	1	8	162	34	6	3	49	6	3	2	2	4	57	50	.291	.353	.429
91	BIR/SOU	AA	8	30	28	6	0	0	2	12	2	0	0	4	1	0	0	0	0	5	3	.214	.267	.429
	CHI/AL		80	154	140	32	1	0	5	48	9	1	0	18	1	1	4	0	0	8	21	.229	.268	.343
2 YR TOTALS			**111**	**244**	**221**	**50**	**2**	**0**	**6**	**70**	**15**	**1**	**0**	**32**	**3**	**2**	**4**	**1**	**0**	**13**	**29**	**.226**	**.270**	**.317**

Meulens, Hensley Filemon Acasio "Hensley" or "Bam-Bam" — bats right — throws right — b.6/23/67 — 1991 positions: OF 73, DH 13, 1B 7

YR	TM/LG	CL	G	TPA	AB	H	2B	3B	HR	TB	BB	IBB	HB	SO	GDP	SH	SF	SB	CS	R	RBI	BA	OBA	SA
86	YAN/GCL	R	59	253	219	51	10	4	4	81	28	0	4	66	7	1	1	4	2	36	31	.233	.329	.370
87	PW/CAR	A+	116	498	430	129	23	2	28	240	53	3		124	7	0	6	14	3	76	103	.300	.384	.558
	FL/FSL	A+	17	65	58	10	3	0	0	13	7	0	0	25	0	0	0	0	0	2	2	.172	.262	.224
88	ALB/EAS	AA	79	316	278	68	9	1	13	118	37	2	1	97	7	0	0	3	0	50	40	.245	.335	.424
	COL/INT	AAA	55	224	209	48	9	1	6	77	14	1	0	61	5	0	1	2	0	27	22	.230	.277	.368
89	ALB/EAS	AA	104	406	335	86	8	2	11	131	61	1	9	108	6	0	1	3	2	55	45	.257	.384	.391
	COL/INT	AAA	14	53	45	13	4	0	1	20	8	0	0	13	2	0	0	0	0	2	1	.289	.396	.444
	NY/AL		8	30	28	5	0	0	0	5	2	0	0	8	2	0	0	0	0	2	1	.179	.233	.179
90	COL/INT	AAA	136	559	480	137	20	5	26	245	66	4	7	132	12	1	0	5	6	81	96	.285	.376	.510
	NY/AL		23	95	83	20	7	0	3	36	9	0	3	25	3	0	0	1	0	12	10	.241	.337	.434
91	NY/AL		96	313	288	64	8	1	6	92	18	1	4	97	7	1	2	3	0	37	29	.222	.276	.319
3 YR TOTALS			**127**	**438**	**399**	**89**	**15**	**1**	**9**	**133**	**29**	**1**	**7**	**130**	**12**	**1**	**2**	**4**	**1**	**51**	**40**	**.223**	**.286**	**.333**

Miller, Keith Alan — bats right — throws right — b.6/12/63 — 1991 positions: 2B 60, OF 28, 3B 2, SS 2

YR	TM/LG	CL	G	TPA	AB	H	2B	3B	HR	TB	BB	IBB	HB	SO	GDP	SH	SF	SB	CS	R	RBI	BA	OBA	SA
85	LYN/CAR	A+	89	369	325	98	16	5	7	145	39	0	4	52	6	1	1	14	2	51	54	.302	.383	.446
	JAC/TEX	AA	46	180	165	37	8	1	3	56	12	0	1	38	6	1	1	8	1	17	22	.224	.279	.339
86	JAC/TEX	AA	94	424	353	116	23	4	5	162	62	1	7	55	5	2	0	28	5	80	36	.329	.438	.459
87	TID/INT	AAA	53	220	202	50	9	1	6	79	14	1	1	36	5	3	0	14	2	29	22	.248	.300	.391
	NY/NL		25	57	51	19	2	2	0	25	2	0	1	5	3	3	0			14	1	.373	.407	.490
88	TID/INT	AAA	42	187	171	48	11	1	1	64	12	1	2	20	0	1	3	8	4	23	15	.281	.332	.374
	NY/NL		40	79	70	15	1	1	1	21	6	0	0	10	1	0	3	0	0	9	5	.214	.276	.300
89	TID/INT	AAA	48	204	184	49	8	2	1	64	18	0	2	24	2	0	0	12	2	33	15	.266	.338	.348
	NY/NL		57	152	143	33	7	0	1	43	5	0	1	27	3	3	0	6	0	15	7	.231	.262	.301
90	NY/NL		88	262	233	60	8	0	1	71	23	1	2	46	2	2	1	16	3	42	12	.258	.327	.305
91	NY/NL		98	304	275	77	22	1	4	113	23	0	2	44	2	2	1	14	3	41	23	.280	.345	.411
5 YR TOTALS			**308**	**854**	**772**	**204**	**40**	**4**	**7**	**273**	**59**	**1**	**9**	**133**	**9**	**11**	**3**	**44**	**13**	**121**	**48**	**.264**	**.323**	**.354**

Milligan, Randy Andre — bats right — throws right — b.11/27/61 — 1991 positions: 1B 106, DH 25, OF 9

YR	TM/LG	CL	G	TPA	AB	H	2B	3B	HR	TB	BB	IBB	HB	SO	GDP	SH	SF	SB	CS	R	RBI	BA	OBA	SA
84	JAC/TEX	AA	62	252	193	53	5	0	9	85	53	4	4	39	4	0	2	15	7	32	34	.275	.437	.440
85	JAC/TEX	AA	119	453	391	121	22	2	13	186	53	5	4	78	12	1	4	11	6	60	77	.309	.394	.476
86	JAC/TEX	AA	78	332	269	85	11	3	7	123	60	5	2	42	10	0	1	13	6	53	53	.316	.443	.457
	TID/INT	AAA	21	69	60	5	0	0	0	5	9	0	0	15	2	0	0	0	0	3	3	.083	.203	.083
87	TID/INT	AAA	136	557	457	149	28	4	29	272	91	10	4	77	18	0	5	8	4	99	103	.326	.438	.595
	NY/NL		3	2	1	0	0	0	0	0	0	0	0	1	0	0	0	0	0	0	0	.000	.500	.000
88	PIT/NL		40	103	82	18	5	0	3	32	20	0	1	24	2	0	0	0	0	10	8	.220	.379	.390
	BUF/AMA	AAA	63	263	221	61	15	3	2	88	36	2	1	40	7	0	5	2	1	37	30	.276	.373	.398
89	BAL/AL		124	444	365	98	23	5	12	167	74	2	3	75	10	1	1	1	2	56	45	.268	.373	.458
90	BAL/AL		109	456	362	96	20	1	20	178	88	3	2	68	11	0	4	6	3	64	60	.265	.408	.492
91	BAL/AL		141	571	483	127	17	2	16	196	84	4	2	108	23	0	4	6	3	57	70	.263	.373	.406
5 YR TOTALS			**417**	**1576**	**1293**	**339**	**65**	**8**	**51**	**573**	**267**	**9**	**8**	**276**	**48**	**0**	**8**	**16**	**15**	**187**	**183**	**.262**	**.390**	**.443**

Mitchell, Keith Alexander — bats right — throws right — b.8/6/69 — 1991 positions: OF 34

YR	TM/LG	CL	G	TPA	AB	H	2B	3B	HR	TB	BB	IBB	HB	SO	GDP	SH	SF	SB	CS	R	RBI	BA	OBA	SA
87	BRA/GCL	R	57	241	208	50	12	1	2	70	29	0	2	50	4	0	2	7	2	24	21	.240	.336	.337
88	SUM/SAL	A	98	391	341	85	16	1	5	118	41	0	4	50	8	3	2	9	6	35	33	.249	.335	.346
89	BUR/MID	A	127	527	448	117	23	0	10	170	70	1	5	65	9	0	4	12	7	64	49	.261	.364	.379
90	DUR/CAR	A+	129	560	456	134	24	3	6	182	92	2	4	48	16	0	4	18	17	81	48	.294	.411	.399
91	GRE/SOU	AA	60	252	214	70	15	3	10	121	29	1	5	29	5	3	5	12	8	46	47	.327	.402	.565
	RIC/INT	AAA	25	110	95	31	6	1	2	45	9	0	1	13	3	0	5	3	1	16	17	.326	.402	.474
	ATL/NL		48	74	66	21	0	0	2	27	8	0	0	12	1	0	0	3	1	11	5	.318	.380	.409

Mitchell, Kevin Darnell — bats right — throws right — b.1/13/62 — 1991 positions: OF 100, 1B 1

YR	TM/LG	CL	G	TPA	AB	H	2B	3B	HR	TB	BB	IBB	HB	SO	GDP	SH	SF	SB	CS	R	RBI	BA	OBA	SA
84	TID/INT	AAA	120	471	432	105	21	3	10	162	25	0	3	89	16	2	9	1	2	51	54	.243	.284	.375
	NY/NL		7	14	14	3	0	0	0	3	0	0	0	3	0	0	0	0	1	0	1	.214	.214	.214
85	TID/INT	AAA	95	385	348	101	24	2	9	156	32	1	2	60	14	0	3	3	1	44	43	.290	.351	.448
86	NY/NL		108	364	328	91	22	2	12	153	33	0	1	61	6	0	2	3	3	51	43	.277	.344	.466
87	SD/NL		62	217	196	48	7	1	7	78	20	3	0	38	5	0	1	3	3	19	26	.245	.313	.398
	SF/NL		69	298	268	82	13	1	15	142	28	1	1	50	5	0	0	9	6	30	18	.306	.376	.530
	YEAR		131	515	464	130	20	2	22	220	48	4	2	88	10	0	1	12	9	49	44	.280	.349	.474
88	SF/NL		148	566	505	127	25	7	19	223	48	7	5	85	6	0	1	5	5	68	70	.251	.319	.442
89	SF/NL		154	640	543	158	34	6	47	345	87	32	3	115	6	0	7	3	5	100	125	.291	.387	.635

Mitchell, Kevin Darnell (continued)

YR	TM/LG	CL	G	TPA	AB	H	2B	3B	HR	TB	BB	IBB	HB	SO	GDP	SH	SF	SB	CS	R	RBI	BA	OBA	SA
90	SF/NL		140	589	524	152	24	2	35	285	58	9	2	87	8	0	5	4	7	90	93	.290	.360	.544
91	SF/NL		113	423	371	95	13	1	27	191	43	8	5	57	6	0	4	2	3	52	69	.256	.338	.515
7 YR TOTALS			**801**	**3111**	**2749**	**756**	**138**	**20**	**162**	**1420**	**317**	**60**	**18**	**496**	**45**	**2**	**25**	**26**	**29**	**421**	**481**	**.275**	**.351**	**.517**

Molitor, Paul Leo — bats right — throws right — b.8/22/56 — 1991 positions: DH 112, 1B 46

YR	TM/LG	CL	G	TPA	AB	H	2B	3B	HR	TB	BB	IBB	HB	SO	GDP	SH	SF	SB	CS	R	RBI	BA	OBA	SA
78	MIL/AL		125	556	521	142	26	4	6	194	19	2	4	54	6	7	5	30	12	73	45	.273	.301	.372
79	MIL/AL		140	645	584	188	27	16	9	274	48	5	2	48	9	6	5	33	13	88	62	.322	.372	.469
80	MIL/AL		111	512	450	137	29	2	9	197	48	4	3	48	9	6	5	34	7	81	37	.304	.372	.438
81	MIL/AL		64	284	251	67	11	0	2	84	25	1	3	29	3	5	0	10	6	45	19	.267	.341	.335
82	MIL/AL		160	751	666	201	26	8	19	300	69	1	9	93	9	10	5	41	9	136	71	.302	.366	.450
83	MIL/AL		152	682	608	164	28	6	15	249	59	4	2	74	12	7	6	41	8	95	47	.270	.333	.410
84	MIL/AL		13	49	46	10	1	0	0	11	2	0	0	8	1	0	1	1	0	3	6	.217	.245	.239
85	MIL/AL		140	642	576	171	28	3	10	235	54	6	1	80	12	7	4	21	7	93	48	.297	.356	.408
86	MIL/AL		105	482	437	123	24	6	9	186	40	0	2	81	9	2	3	20	5	62	55	.281	.340	.426
87	MIL/AL		118	542	465	164	41	5	16	263	69	4	5	67	4	5	1	45	10	114	75	.353	.438	.566
88	MIL/AL		154	690	609	190	34	6	13	275	71	8	2	54	10	3	9	41	10	115	60	.312	.384	.452
89	MIL/AL		155	696	615	194	35	4	11	270	64	4	4	67	11	4	9	27	11	84	56	.315	.379	.439
90	BEL/MID	A	1	4	4	2	0	0	1	5	0	0	0	0	0	0	0	0	0	1	1	.500	.500	1.250
	MIL/AL		103	458	418	119	27	6	12	194	37	4	1	51	7	0	2	18	3	64	45	.285	.343	.464
91	MIL/AL		158	749	665	216	32	13	17	325	77	16	6	62	11	0	1	19	8	133	75	.325	.399	.489
14 YR TOTALS			**1698**	**7738**	**6911**	**2086**	**369**	**79**	**148**	**3057**	**682**	**57**	**31**	**816**	**112**	**64**	**50**	**381**	**109**	**1186**	**701**	**.302**	**.365**	**.442**

Mondesi, Raul Ramon — bats right — throws right — b.3/12/71 — 1991 positions: OF System LA/NL

YR	TM/LG	CL	G	TPA	AB	H	2B	3B	HR	TB	BB	IBB	HB	SO	GDP	SH	SF	SB	CS	R	RBI	BA	OBA	SA
90	GF/PIO	R+	44	189	175	53	10	4	8	95	11	1	2	30	0	0	1	30	6	35	31	.303	.349	.543
91	BAK/CAL	A+	28	115	106	30	7	2	3	50	5	1	3	21	1	0	1	9	4	23	13	.283	.330	.472
	SA/TEX	AA	53	228	213	58	10	5	5	93	8	0	4	47	1	0	3	7	3	32	26	.272	.307	.437
	ALB/PCL	AAA	2	9	9	3	0	1	0	5	0	0	0	1	0	0	0	1	0	3	0	.333	.333	.556

Moore, Robert Vincent "Bobby" — bats right — throws right — b.10/27/65 — 1991 positions: OF 13

YR	TM/LG	CL	G	TPA	AB	H	2B	3B	HR	TB	BB	IBB	HB	SO	GDP	SH	SF	SB	CS	R	RBI	BA	OBA	SA
87	EUG/NWL	A−	57	253	235	88	13	4	1	112	14	2	1	22	5	2	1	23	1	40	25	.374	.410	.477
88	BC/FSL	A+	60	247	224	52	4	2	0	60	17	0	2	20	4	4	0	12	7	25	10	.232	.292	.268
89	BC/FSL	A+	131	549	483	131	21	5	0	162	51	1	6	35	6	6	3	34	19	93	36	.271	.346	.335
90	MEM/SOU	AA	112	492	422	128	20	6	2	166	37	0	3	41	10	13	2	35	15	65	34	.303	.384	.393
91	OMA/AMA	AAA	130	549	494	120	13	3	0	139	47	0	3	53	9	2	3	16	8	65	43	.243	.309	.281
	KC/AL		18	15	14	5	1	0	0	6	1	0	0	2	0	0	0	3	2	3	0	.357	.400	.429

Morandini, Michael Robert "Mickey" — bats left — throws right — b.4/22/66 — 1991 positions: 2B 97

YR	TM/LG	CL	G	TPA	AB	H	2B	3B	HR	TB	BB	IBB	HB	SO	GDP	SH	SF	SB	CS	R	RBI	BA	OBA	SA
89	SPA/SAL	A	63	275	231	78	19	1	1	102	35	1	3	45	3	4	2	18	9	43	30	.338	.428	.442
	CLE/FSL	A+	17	72	63	19	4	1	0	25	7	1	1	8	0	1	0	3	1	14	4	.302	.375	.397
	REA/EAS	AA	48	213	188	66	12	1	5	95	23	4	1	32	2	1	0	5	5	39	29	.351	.425	.505
90	SCR/INT	AAA	138	577	502	131	24	10	1	178	60	0	5	90	11	10	0	16	6	77	31	.261	.346	.355
	PHI/NL		25	87	79	19	4	0	1	26	6	0	0	19	1	2	0	3	0	7	9	.241	.294	.329
91	SCR/INT	AAA	12	52	46	12	4	0	1	19	5	0	0	2	0	0	1	3	1	8	5	.261	.327	.413
	PHI/NL		98	364	325	81	11	4	1	103	29	0	2	45	7	6	2	13	2	40	14	.249	.313	.317
2 YR TOTALS			**123**	**451**	**404**	**100**	**15**	**4**	**2**	**129**	**35**	**0**	**2**	**64**	**8**	**8**	**2**	**16**	**2**	**47**	**23**	**.248**	**.309**	**.319**

Morman, Russell Lee "Russ" — bats right — throws right — b.4/28/62 — 1991 positions: 1B 8, OF 2, DH 1

YR	TM/LG	CL	G	TPA	AB	H	2B	3B	HR	TB	BB	IBB	HB	SO	GDP	SH	SF	SB	CS	R	RBI	BA	OBA	SA
84	APP/MID	A	122	520	424	111	17	7	7	163	80	3	8	93	17	4	4	29	6	68	80	.262	.386	.384
85	GF/EAS	AA	119	496	422	131	24	5	17	216	65	3	5	51	8	1	3	11	10	64	81	.310	.406	.512
	BUF/AMA	AAA	21	76	64	19	3	1	7	45	10	0	2	16	2	0	0	2	0	16	14	.297	.408	.703
86	BUF/AMA	AAA	106	427	365	97	17	2	13	157	54	4	5	58	5	0	3	3	1	52	57	.266	.365	.430
	CHI/AL		49	180	159	40	5	0	4	57	16	0	2	36	5	1	2	1	0	18	17	.252	.324	.358
87	HAW/PCL	AAA	89	358	294	79	19	2	9	129	60	3	1	56	4	0	3	3	3	52	53	.269	.391	.439
88	VAN/PCL	AAA	69	292	257	77	8	1	5	102	32	3	0	48	3	0	2	6	0	40	45	.300	.377	.397
	CHI/AL		40	80	75	18	4	0	0	20	3	0	0	17	2	2	0	0	1	8	3	.240	.269	.267
89	VAN/PCL	AAA	61	236	216	60	14	1	1	79	18	2	1	41	5	1	1	1	6	18	23	.278	.335	.366
	CHI/AL		37	67	58	13	2	0	0	15	6	1	0	16	1	0	0	1	0	5	8	.224	.292	.259
90	OMA/AMA	AAA	121	495	436	130	14	9	13	201	51	2	3	78	7	0	1	5	21	67	81	.298	.372	.461
	KC/AL		12	41	37	10	4	2	1	21	3	0	0	3	0	0	0	1	0	5	3	.270	.317	.568
91	KC/AL		12	24	23	6	0	0	0	6	1	1	0	5	3	0	0	0	0	1	1	.261	.292	.261
	OMA/AMA	AAA	88	368	316	83	15	3	5	119	43	2	2	53	12	1	6	10	6	46	50	.263	.349	.377
5 YR TOTALS			**150**	**392**	**352**	**87**	**13**	**2**	**5**	**119**	**29**	**2**	**2**	**77**	**11**	**5**	**4**	**2**	**0**	**37**	**32**	**.247**	**.305**	**.338**

Morris, John Daniel — bats left — throws left — b.2/23/61 — 1991 positions: OF 57

YR	TM/LG	CL	G	TPA	AB	H	2B	3B	HR	TB	BB	IBB	HB	SO	GDP	SH	SF	SB	CS	R	RBI	BA	OBA	SA
82	FM/FSL	A+	45	172	137	39	7	2	2	56	33	3	1	27	1	0	2	11	3	21	17	.285	.424	.409
83	JAC/SOU	AA	140	605	490	141	27	8	23	253	109	3	4	107	4	0	2	30	4	96	92	.288	.420	.516
84	OMA/AMA	AAA	148	567	492	133	24	4	15	210	65	2	3	96	10	3	3	18	5	77	60	.270	.358	.427
85	OMA/AMA	AAA	23	103	93	24	4	4	1	39	10	2	0	11	1	0	0	1	0	13	6	.258	.330	.419
	LOU/AMA	AAA	107	442	373	93	21	4	2	130	62	3	3	46	9	3	1	20	7	51	44	.249	.360	.349

(continued)

Morris, John Daniel (continued)

YR	TM/LG	CL	G	TPA	AB	H	2B	3B	HR	TB	BB	IBB	HB	SO	GDP	SH	SF	SB	CS	R	RBI	BA	OBA	SA
86	LOU/AMA	AAA	60	246	213	50	13	7	1	80	23	0	7	33	4	0	3	11	3	30	24	.235	.325	.376
	STL/NL		39	108	100	24	0	1	1	29	7	2	0	15	2	0	1	6	2	8	14	.240	.287	.290
87	LOU/AMA	AAA	14	59	47	16	5	2	3	34	11	1	0	3	0	1	2	3	3	13	12	.340	.458	.723
	STL/NL		101	170	157	41	6	4	3	64	11	4	1	22	2	1	0	5	2	22	23	.261	.314	.408
88	LOU/AMA	AAA	13	42	40	4	0	0	0	4	2	0	0	8	2	0	0	0	0	3	0	.100	.143	.100
	STL/NL		20	39	38	11	2	1	0	15	1	0	0	7	0	0	0	0	0	3	3	.289	.308	.395
89	STL/NL		96	124	117	28	4	1	2	40	4	0	0	22	4	3	0	1	0	8	14	.239	.264	.342
90	STL/NL		18	21	18	2	0	0	0	2	3	0	0	6	0	0	0	0	0	0	0	.111	.238	.111
91	PHI/NL		85	140	127	28	2	1	1	35	12	4	1	25	1	0	0	2	0	15	6	.220	.293	.276
6 YR TOTALS			**359**	**602**	**557**	**134**	**14**	**8**	**7**	**185**	**38**	**10**	**2**	**97**	**9**	**4**	**1**	**14**	**4**	**56**	**60**	**.241**	**.291**	**.332**

Morris, William Harold "Hal" — bats left — throws left — b.4/9/65 — 1991 positions: 1B 128, OF 1

YR	TM/LG	CL	G	TPA	AB	H	2B	3B	HR	TB	BB	IBB	HB	SO	GDP	SH	SF	SB	CS	R	RBI	BA	OBA	SA
86	ONE/NYP	A–	36	149	127	48	9	2	3	70	18	2	1	15	3	2	1	1	1	26	30	.378	.456	.551
	ALB/EAS	AA	25	85	79	17	5	0	0	22	4	0	1	10	3	1	0	0	1	7	4	.215	.262	.278
87	ALB/EAS	AA	135	580	530	173	31	4	5	227	36	2	4	43	12	5	5	7	4	65	73	.326	.370	.428
88	COL/INT	AAA	121	502	452	134	19	4	3	170	36	6	4	62	12	7	4	8	5	41	38	.296	.349	.376
	NY/AL		15	20	20	2	0	0	0	2	0	0	0	9	0	0	0	0	0	1	0	.100	.100	.100
89	COL/INT	AAA	111	456	417	136	24	1	17	213	28	2	4	47	5	3	4	5	3	70	66	.326	.371	.511
	NY/AL		15	19	18	5	0	0	0	5	1	0	0	4	2	0	0	0	0	2	4	.278	.316	.278
90	NAS/AMA	AAA	16	72	64	22	5	0	1	30	5	1	2	10	2	0	1	4	1	8	10	.344	.403	.469
	CIN/NL		107	336	309	105	22	3	7	154	21	4	1	32	12	3	2	9	3	50	36	.340	.381	.498
91	CIN/NL		136	537	478	152	33	1	14	229	46	7	1	61	18	4	5	7	10	72	59	.318	.374	.479
4 YR TOTALS			**273**	**912**	**825**	**264**	**55**	**4**	**21**	**390**	**68**	**11**	**2**	**106**	**18**	**8**	**9**	**19**	**7**	**125**	**99**	**.320**	**.369**	**.473**

Moseby, Lloyd Anthony — bats left — throws right — b.11/5/59 — 1991 positions: OF 64, DH 7

YR	TM/LG	CL	G	TPA	AB	H	2B	3B	HR	TB	BB	IBB	HB	SO	GDP	SH	SF	SB	CS	R	RBI	BA	OBA	SA
80	TOR/AL		114	430	389	89	24	1	9	142	25	4	4	85	11	10	2	4	6	44	46	.229	.281	.365
81	TOR/AL		100	412	378	88	16	2	9	135	24	3	1	86	4	5	4	11	8	36	43	.233	.278	.357
82	TOR/AL		147	533	487	115	20	9	9	180	33	3	8	106	10	3	2	11	7	51	52	.236	.294	.370
83	TOR/AL		151	604	539	170	31	7	18	269	51	4	5	85	10	0	3	27	8	104	81	.315	.376	.499
84	TOR/AL		158	688	592	166	28	15	18	278	78	9	8	122	8	3	7	39	9	97	92	.280	.368	.470
85	TOR/AL		152	670	584	151	30	7	18	249	76	4	4	91	12	1	5	37	15	92	70	.259	.345	.426
86	TOR/AL		152	668	589	149	24	5	21	246	64	3	6	122	7	2	7	32	11	89	86	.253	.329	.418
87	TOR/AL		155	670	592	167	27	4	26	280	70	4	2	124	11	8	3	39	7	106	96	.282	.358	.473
88	TOR/AL		128	552	472	113	17	7	10	174	70	6	6	93	10	3	1	31	7	77	42	.239	.343	.369
89	TOR/AL		135	572	502	111	25	3	11	175	56	1	6	101	7	7	1	24	7	72	43	.221	.306	.349
90	DET/AL		122	487	431	107	16	5	14	175	48	3	5	77	14	1	2	17	5	64	51	.248	.329	.406
91	DET/AL		74	288	260	68	15	1	6	103	21	2	3	43	3	1	3	8	1	37	35	.262	.321	.396
12 YR TOTALS			**1588**	**6574**	**5815**	**1494**	**273**	**66**	**169**	**2406**	**616**	**46**	**58**	**1135**	**105**	**40**	**45**	**280**	**92**	**869**	**737**	**.257**	**.332**	**.414**

Moses, John William — bats both — throws left — b.8/9/57 — 1991 positions: OF 12

YR	TM/LG	CL	G	TPA	AB	H	2B	3B	HR	TB	BB	IBB	HB	SO	GDP	SH	SF	SB	CS	R	RBI	BA	OBA	SA
82	SEA/AL		22	48	44	14	5	1	1	24	4	0	0	5	0	0	0	5	1	7	3	.318	.375	.545
83	SEA/AL		93	143	130	27	4	1	0	33	12	0	1	20	4	0	0	11	5	19	6	.208	.280	.254
84	CHT/SOU	AA	53	221	182	46	6	3	0	58	34	4	1	18	3	3	1	19	9	27	12	.253	.372	.319
	SLC/PCL	AAA	70	316	276	76	11	5	0	97	24	0	2	38	8	10	4	21	9	45	27	.275	.333	.351
	SEA/AL		19	39	35	12	1	1	0	15	2	0	0	5	0	1	0	1	0	3	2	.343	.395	.429
85	CAL/PCL	AAA	113	527	473	152	37	1	5	206	46	4	0	56	13	3	5	35	11	75	47	.321	.378	.436
	SEA/AL		33	65	62	12	0	0	0	12	2	0	0	8	3	1	0	5	2	4	3	.194	.219	.194
86	CAL/PCL	AAA	39	176	148	48	3	1	3	62	25	0	1	17	1	2	1	15	2	31	18	.324	.420	.419
	SEA/AL		103	442	399	102	16	3	3	133	34	3	0	65	7	5	4	25	18	56	34	.256	.311	.333
87	SEA/AL		116	433	390	96	16	4	3	129	29	2	3	49	6	3	5	23	15	58	38	.246	.301	.331
88	POR/PCL	AAA	17	71	66	23	3	1	0	28	5	2	0	2	1	0	0	5	1	13	6	.348	.394	.424
	MIN/AL		105	225	206	65	10	3	0	87	15	2	2	21	4	1	1	11	6	33	12	.316	.366	.422
89	MIN/AL		129	267	242	68	12	3	1	89	19	1	1	23	5	3	2	14	7	33	31	.281	.333	.368
90	MIN/AL		115	195	172	38	3	1	1	46	19	1	0	32	4	0	2	2	3	26	14	.221	.303	.267
91	CS/PCL	AAA	74	342	298	88	18	3	1	121	36	1	1	32	4	3	3	11	7	58	31	.295	.370	.406
	BUF/AMA	AAA	3	12	11	3	0	0	0	3	1	0	0	1	0	0	0	2	0	2	0	.273	.333	.273
	DET/AL		13	24	21	1	1	0	0	2	2	0	0	7	0	1	0	4	0	5	1	.048	.130	.095
10 YR TOTALS			**748**	**1881**	**1701**	**435**	**68**	**17**	**11**	**570**	**138**	**9**	**10**	**222**	**33**	**20**	**12**	**101**	**57**	**244**	**144**	**.256**	**.313**	**.335**

Mota, Andres Alberto (Matos) "Andy" — bats right — throws right — b.3/4/66 — 1991 positions: 2B 27

YR	TM/LG	CL	G	TPA	AB	H	2B	3B	HR	TB	BB	IBB	HB	SO	GDP	SH	SF	SB	CS	R	RBI	BA	OBA	SA
87	AUB/NYP	A–	70	282	255	67	9	1	4	90	16	0	5	42	7	5	1	6	5	26	14	.263	.318	.353
88	AUB/NYP	A–	72	318	271	95	15	3	3	125	38	2	5	34	4	0	4	31	6	56	47	.351	.434	.461
89	OSC/FSL	A+	131	571	505	161	21	4	4	202	42	3	11	61	9	3	10	28	9	68	69	.319	.377	.400
90	COL/SOU	AA	111	466	413	118	21	1	11	174	28	2	10	81	5	9	6	17	9	59	62	.286	.341	.421
91	TUC/PCL	AAA	123	497	462	138	19	4	2	171	22	3	7	76	6	4	2	14	9	65	46	.299	.339	.370
	HOU/NL		27	91	90	17	2	0	1	22	1	0	0	17	0	0	0	2	0	4	6	.189	.198	.244

Mota, Jose Manuel (Matos) — bats both — throws right — b.3/16/65 — 1991 positions: 2B 13, SS 3

YR	TM/LG	CL	G	TPA	AB	H	2B	3B	HR	TB	BB	IBB	HB	SO	GDP	SH	SF	SB	CS	R	RBI	BA	OBA	SA
85	BUF/AMA	AAA	6	20	18	5	0	0	0	5	2	0	0	0	1	0	0	0	0	3	1	.278	.350	.278
	NF/NYP	A–	65	291	254	77	9	2	0	90	28	3	2	29	1	5	2	8	5	35	27	.303	.374	.354

Mota, Jose Manuel (Matos) (continued)

YR	TM/LG	CL	G	TPA	AB	H	2B	3B	HR	TB	BB	IBB	HB	SO	GDP	SH	SF	SB	CS	R	RBI	BA	OBA	SA
86	TUL/TEX	AA	41	184	158	51	7	3	1	67	22	0	0	13	0	3	1	14	8	26	11	.323	.403	.424
	OC/AMA	AAA	71	287	255	71	9	1	0	82	24	1	3	43	7	5	0	7	5	38	20	.278	.348	.322
87	TUL/TEX	AA	21	85	71	15	2	0	0	17	13	0	0	12	0	0	1	2	2	11	4	.211	.329	.239
	SA/TEX	AA	54	218	190	50	4	3	0	60	21	1	2	34	3	5	0	3	4	23	11	.263	.343	.316
88	ALB/PCL	AAA	6	19	15	5	0	0	0	5	3	0	0	3	1	1	0	1	0	4	1	.333	.444	.333
	SA/TEX	AA	82	245	214	56	11	1	1	72	27	1	0	35	7	3	1	10	4	32	18	.262	.343	.336
89	HUN/SOU	AA	27	118	81	11	1	0	0	12	30	0	1	15	0	5	1	3	2	15	6	.136	.372	.148
	WIC/TEX	AA	41	130	109	35	5	1	1	45	17	0	0	21	1	4	0	3	2	17	9	.321	.413	.413
90	LV/PCL	AAA	92	296	247	74	4	4	4	98	42	2	3	35	0	3	1	2	1	44	21	.300	.406	.397
91	SD/NL		17	41	36	8	0	0	0	8	2	0	1	7	0	2	0	0	0	4	2	.222	.282	.222
	LV/PCL	AAA	107	442	377	109	10	2	1	126	54	2	2	48	10	6	3	15	10	56	37	.289	.378	.334

Mulliniks, Steven Rance "Rance" — bats left — throws right — b.1/15/56 — 1991 positions: DH 81, 3B 5

YR	TM/LG	CL	G	TPA	AB	H	2B	3B	HR	TB	BB	IBB	HB	SO	GDP	SH	SF	SB	CS	R	RBI	BA	OBA	SA
77	CAL/AL		78	303	271	73	13	3	2	99	23	1	1	36	2	8	0	1	1	36	21	.269	.329	.365
78	CAL/AL		50	130	119	22	3	1	1	30	8	0	1	23	3	0	2	2	0	6	6	.185	.238	.252
79	CAL/AL		22	78	68	10	0	0	1	13	4	0	1	14	2	0	5	0	0	7	8	.147	.192	.191
80	KC/AL		36	62	54	14	3	0	0	17	7	0	0	10	2	0	1	0	0	6	5	.259	.339	.315
81	KC/AL		24	46	44	10	3	0	0	13	2	0	0	7	2	0	0	0	1	8	6	.227	.261	.295
82	TOR/AL		112	353	311	76	25	0	4	113	37	1	1	49	10	3	1	3	2	54	49	.244	.326	.363
83	TOR/AL		129	427	364	100	34	3	10	170	57	5	1	43	13	3	2	0	2	41	42	.275	.373	.467
84	TOR/AL		125	379	343	111	21	5	3	151	33	3	1	44	7	0	2	2	3	55	57	.324	.383	.440
85	TOR/AL		129	427	366	108	26	1	10	166	55	1	0	54	10	1	5	2	0	55	45	.295	.383	.454
86	TOR/AL		117	395	348	90	22	0	11	145	43	1	1	55	10	1	2	1	1	37	44	.259	.340	.417
87	TOR/AL		124	372	332	103	28	1	11	166	34	1	0	55	10	3	3	1	1	49	48	.310	.371	.500
88	TOR/AL		119	399	337	101	21	1	12	160	56	3	0	57	10	2	4	1	0	25	29	.300	.395	.475
89	TOR/AL		103	309	273	65	11	2	3	89	34	6	0	45	12	0	2	0	0	11	27	.238	.320	.326
90	TOR/AL		57	120	97	28	4	0	2	38	22	2	0	19	2	0	1	2	0	27	24	.289	.417	.392
91	TOR/AL		97	286	240	60	12	1	2	80	44	0	0	45	9	0	2	0	0	27	24	.250	.364	.333
15 YR TOTALS			**1322**	**4086**	**3567**	**971**	**226**	**17**	**73**	**1450**	**459**	**28**	**7**	**555**	**104**	**21**	**32**	**15**	**12**	**444**	**435**	**.272**	**.354**	**.407**

Munoz, Pedro Javier (Gonzalez) — bats right — throws right — b.9/19/68 — 1991 positions: OF 44, DH 2

YR	TM/LG	CL	G	TPA	AB	H	2B	3B	HR	TB	BB	IBB	HB	SO	GDP	SH	SF	SB	CS	R	RBI	BA	OBA	SA
85	BJ/GCL	R	40	160	145	38	3	0	2	47	9	0	4	20	4	1	1	4	1	14	17	.262	.321	.324
86	FLO/SAL	A	122	508	445	131	16	5	14	199	54	4	5	100	12	2	2	9	5	69	82	.294	.375	.447
87	DUN/FSL	A+	92	382	341	80	11	5	8	125	34	0	2	74	7	1	4	13	4	55	44	.235	.304	.367
88	DUN/FSL	A+	133	544	481	141	21	7	8	200	52	5	4	87	23	0	7	15	4	59	73	.293	.362	.416
89	KNO/SOU	AA	122	468	442	118	15	4	19	198	20	2	2	85	11	0	4	10	4	54	65	.267	.299	.448
90	SYR/INT	AAA	86	346	317	101	22	3	7	150	24	3	1	64	12	1	3	16	7	41	56	.319	.365	.473
	POR/PCL	AAA	30	129	110	35	4	0	5	54	15	0	4	18	1	0	0	8	3	19	21	.318	.419	.491
	MIN/AL		22	90	85	23	4	1	0	29	2	0	0	16	3	1	2	3	0	13	5	.271	.281	.341
91	POR/PCL	AAA	56	233	212	67	19	2	7	105	19	3	1	42	6	0	1	9	9	33	28	.316	.373	.495
	MIN/AL		51	151	138	39	7	1	7	69	9	0	1	31	2	1	2	3	0	15	26	.283	.327	.500
2 YR TOTALS			**73**	**241**	**223**	**62**	**11**	**2**	**7**	**98**	**11**	**0**	**1**	**47**	**5**	**2**	**4**	**6**	**0**	**28**	**31**	**.278**	**.310**	**.439**

Murphy, Dale Bryan — bats right — throws right — b.3/12/56 — 1991 positions: OF 147

YR	TM/LG	CL	G	TPA	AB	H	2B	3B	HR	TB	BB	IBB	HB	SO	GDP	SH	SF	SB	CS	R	RBI	BA	OBA	SA
76	ATL/NL		19	72	65	17	6	0	0	23	7	0	0	9	3	0	0	0	0	3	9	.262	.333	.354
77	ATL/NL		18	76	76	24	8	1	2	40	0	0	0	8	3	0	0	0	1	5	14	.316	.316	.526
78	ATL/NL		151	583	530	120	14	3	23	209	42	3	3	145	15	3	5	11	7	66	79	.226	.284	.394
79	ATL/NL		104	429	384	106	7	2	21	180	38	5	2	67	12	1	6	6	6	53	57	.276	.340	.469
80	ATL/NL		156	633	569	160	27	2	33	290	59	9	1	133	10	2	2	9	14	98	89	.281	.349	.510
81	ATL/NL		104	416	369	91	12	1	13	144	44	8	0	72	10	0	3	14	5	43	50	.247	.325	.390
82	ATL/NL		162	698	598	168	23	2	36	303	93	12	2	134	15	2	3	23	11	113	109	.281	.378	.507
83	ATL/NL		162	687	589	178	34	4	36	318	90	20	2	110	13	0	6	30	4	131	121	.302	.393	.540
84	ATL/NL		162	691	607	176	32	8	36	332	79	13	2	134	13	0	3	19	7	94	100	.290	.372	.547
85	ATL/NL		162	712	616	185	32	2	37	332	90	15	2	141	14	0	4	10	7	118	111	.300	.388	.539
86	ATL/NL		160	692	614	163	29	7	29	293	75	5	2	141	11	0	1	7	5	89	83	.265	.347	.477
87	ATL/NL		159	693	566	167	27	1	44	328	115	29	7	136	24	0	5	16	6	115	105	.295	.417	.580
88	ATL/NL		156	671	592	134	35	4	24	249	74	16	2	125	14	0	3	3	5	77	77	.226	.313	.421
89	ATL/NL		154	647	574	131	16	0	20	207	65	11	2	142	11	0	6	3	9	60	84	.228	.306	.361
90	ATL/NL		97	394	349	81	14	0	17	146	41	11	1	84	11	0	3	9	2	38	55	.232	.312	.418
	PHI/NL		57	235	214	57	9	1	7	89	20	3	0	46	11	0	1	0	0	22	28	.266	.328	.416
	YEAR		154	629	563	138	23	1	24	235	61	14	1	130	22	0	4	9	2	60	83	.245	.318	.417
91	PHI/NL		153	599	544	137	33	1	18	226	48	3	1	93	20	0	6	1	0	66	81	.252	.309	.415
16 YR TOTALS			**2136**	**8928**	**7856**	**2095**	**348**	**39**	**396**	**3709**	**980**	**158**	**28**	**1720**	**201**	**6**	**58**	**161**	**68**	**1191**	**1252**	**.267**	**.348**	**.472**

Murray, Eddie Clarence — bats both — throws right — b.2/24/56 — 1991 positions: 1B 149, 3B 1

YR	TM/LG	CL	G	TPA	AB	H	2B	3B	HR	TB	BB	IBB	HB	SO	GDP	SH	SF	SB	CS	R	RBI	BA	OBA	SA
77	BAL/AL		160	666	611	173	29	2	27	287	48	6	1	104	22	0	6	0	1	81	88	.283	.333	.470
78	BAL/AL		161	690	610	174	32	3	27	293	70	7	1	97	15	1	8	6	5	85	95	.285	.356	.480
79	BAL/AL		159	687	606	179	30	2	25	288	72	9	2	78	16	1	6	10	2	90	99	.295	.369	.475
80	BAL/AL		158	683	621	186	36	2	32	322	54	10	2	71	18	0	6	7	2	100	116	.300	.354	.519
81	BAL/AL		99	422	378	111	21	2	22	202	40	10	1	43	10	0	3	2	3	57	78	.294	.360	.534
82	BAL/AL		151	627	550	174	30	1	32	302	70	18	1	82	17	0	6	7	2	87	110	.316	.391	.549

(continued)

Murray, Eddie Clarence (continued)

YR	TM/LG	CL	G	TPA	AB	H	2B	3B	HR	TB	BB	IBB	HB	SO	GDP	SH	SF	SB	CS	R	RBI	BA	OBA	SA
83	BAL/AL		156	680	582	178	30	3	33	313	86	13	3	90	1	0	9	5	1	115	111	.306	.393	.538
84	BAL/AL		162	705	588	180	26	3	29	299	107	25	2	87	9	0	8	10	2	97	110	.306	.410	.509
85	BAL/AL		156	677	583	173	37	1	31	305	84	12	2	68	8	0	8	5	2	111	124	.297	.383	.523
86	BAL/AL		137	578	495	151	25	1	17	229	78	7	0	49	17	0	5	3	0	61	84	.305	.396	.463
87	BAL/AL		160	694	618	171	28	3	30	295	73	6	0	80	15	0	3	1	2	89	91	.277	.352	.477
88	BAL/AL		161	681	603	171	27	2	28	286	75	8	0	78	20	0	3	5	2	75	84	.284	.361	.474
89	LA/NL		160	690	594	147	29	1	20	238	87	24	2	85	11	0	7	7	2	66	88	.247	.342	.401
90	LA/NL		155	645	558	184	22	3	26	290	82	21	1	64	19	0	4	8	5	96	95	.330	.414	.520
91	LA/NL		153	639	576	150	23	1	19	232	55	17	0	74	17	0	8	10	3	69	96	.260	.321	.403
15 YR TOTALS			2288	9764	8573	2502	425	30	398	4181	1081	193	18	1150	215	2	90	86	34	1279	1469	**.292**	**.369**	**.488**

Myers, Gregory Richard "Greg" — bats left — throws right — b.4/14/66 — 1991 positions: C 104

YR	TM/LG	CL	G	TPA	AB	H	2B	3B	HR	TB	BB	IBB	HB	SO	GDP	SH	SF	SB	CS	R	RBI	BA	OBA	SA
84	MH/PIO	R+	38	153	133	42	9	0	2	57	16		0	6		3	1	0	0	20	20	.316	.387	.429
85	FLO/SAL	A	134	539	489	109	19	2	5	147	39	0	2	54	12	2	7	0	0	52	62	.223	.279	.301
86	VEN/CAL	A+	124	502	451	133	23	4	20	224	43	5	2	46	10	1	5	9	4	65	79	.295	.355	.497
87	SYR/INT	AAA	107	370	342	84	19	1	10	135	22	1	1	46	5	3	2	3	3	35	47	.246	.292	.395
	TOR/AL		7	9	9	1	0	0	0	1	0	0	0	3	2	0	0	0	0	1	0	.111	.111	.111
88	SYR/INT	AAA	34	128	120	34	7	1	7	64	8	1	0	24	1	0	0	1	0	18	21	.283	.328	.533
89	KNO/SOU	AA	29	94	90	30	10	0	5	55	3	0	0	16	2	0	1	1	0	11	19	.333	.351	.611
	SYR/INT	AAA	24	94	89	24	6	0	1	33	4	0	1	9	2	0	0	0	0	8	11	.270	.301	.371
	TOR/AL		17	46	44	5	2	0	0	7	2	0	0	9	2	0	0	0	1	0	2	.114	.152	.159
90	SYR/INT	AAA	3	13	11	2	1	0	0	3	1	0	0	3	0	0	1	0	1	0	1	.182	.231	.273
	TOR/AL		87	277	250	59	7	1	5	83	22	0	0	33	12	1	4	0	1	33	22	.236	.293	.332
91	TOR/AL		107	333	309	81	22	1	8	127	21	4	0	45	13	0	3	0	0	25	36	.262	.306	.411
4 YR TOTALS			218	665	612	146	31	1	13	218	45	4	0	90	29	1	7	0	2	59	59	**.239**	**.288**	**.356**

Naehring, Timothy James "Tim" — bats right — throws right — b.2/1/67 — 1991 positions: SS 17, 3B 2, 2B 1

YR	TM/LG	CL	G	TPA	AB	H	2B	3B	HR	TB	BB	IBB	HB	SO	GDP	SH	SF	SB	CS	R	RBI	BA	OBA	SA
88	ELM/NYP	A–	19	73	59	18	3	0	1	24	8	0	1	11	1	1	4	0	0	6	13	.305	.375	.407
	WH/FSL	A+	42	164	141	32	7	0	1	39	19	0	3	24	1	0	1	4	0	17	10	.227	.329	.277
89	LYN/CAR	A+	56	236	209	63	7	1	4	84	23	0	1	30	7	1	3	2	0	24	37	.301	.366	.402
	PAW/INT	AAA	79	312	273	75	16	1	3	102	27	1	3	41	6	2	7	2	3	32	31	.275	.339	.374
90	PAW/INT	AAA	82	335	290	78	16	1	15	141	37	2	3	56	6	2	3	0	1	45	47	.269	.354	.486
	BOS/AL		24	93	85	23	6	0	2	35	8	1	0	15	2	0	0	0	0	10	12	.271	.333	.412
91	BOS/AL		20	65	55	6	1	0	0	7	6	0	0	15	0	4	0	0	0	1	3	.109	.197	.127
2 YR TOTALS			44	158	140	29	7	0	2	42	14	1	0	30	2	4	0	0	0	11	15	**.207**	**.279**	**.300**

Navarro, Norberto (Rodriguez) "Tito" — bats right — throws right — b.9/12/70 — 1991 positions: SS System NY/NL

YR	TM/LG	CL	G	TPA	AB	H	2B	3B	HR	TB	BB	IBB	HB	SO	GDP	SH	SF	SB	CS	R	RBI	BA	OBA	SA
88	KIN/APP	R+	54	210	172	42	3	2	0	49	30	0	3	27	4	2	3	3	4	26	23	.244	.361	.285
89	PIT/NYP	A–	46	179	157	44	6	2	0	54	18	0	0	30	8	3	1	13	3	26	14	.280	.352	.344
90	COL/SAL	A	136	582	497	156	25	4	0	189	69	1	2	56	4	7	7	50	14	87	54	.314	.395	.380
	JAC/TEX	AA	3	13	11	2	1	0	0	3	2	0	0	0	0	0	0	1	0	0	1	.182	.308	.273
91	WIL/EAS	AA	128	572	482	139	9	4	2	162	73	2	1	63	10	12	4	42	19	69	42	.288	.380	.336

Newman, Albert Dwayne "Al" — bats both — throws right — b.6/30/60 — 1991 positions: SS 55, 2B 35, 3B 35, DH 3, 1B 1, OF 1

YR	TM/LG	CL	G	TPA	AB	H	2B	3B	HR	TB	BB	IBB	HB	SO	GDP	SH	SF	SB	CS	R	RBI	BA	OBA	SA
84	BEA/TEX	AA	88	402	318	80	8	0	0	88	64	4	2	21	5	14	4	33	10	69	23	.252	.376	.277
	IND/AMA	AAA	37	132	123	37	3	0	0	40	6	0	0	9	3	3	0	11	5	13	11	.301	.333	.325
85	IND/AMA	AAA	87	353	301	85	16	2	0	105	46	1	2	27	7	3	1	31	11	42	23	.282	.380	.349
	MON/NL		25	32	29	5	1	0	0	6	3	0	0	4	0	0	0	2	1	7	1	.172	.250	.207
86	MON/NL		95	212	185	37	3	0	1	43	21	2	0	20	4	4	2	11	11	23	8	.200	.279	.232
87	MIN/AL		110	349	.307	68	15	5	0	93	34	0	0	27	5	7	1	15	11	44	29	.221	.298	.303
88	MIN/AL		105	295	260	58	7	0	0	65	29	0	0	34	4	6	0	13	4	35	19	.223	.301	.250
89	MIN/AL		141	521	446	113	18	2	0	135	59	0	2	46	3	10	4	25	12	62	38	.253	.341	.303
90	MIN/AL		144	433	388	94	14	0	0	108	33	0	2	34	7	9	1	13	6	43	30	.242	.304	.278
91	MIN/AL		118	278	246	47	5	0	0	52	21	0	3	21	5	4	4	3	4	25	19	.191	.260	.211
7 YR TOTALS			738	2120	1861	422	63	7	1	502	202	2	5	186	28	40	12	82	49	239	144	**.227**	**.302**	**.270**

Newson, Warren Dale — bats left — throws left — b.7/3/64 — 1991 positions: OF 50, DH 3

YR	TM/LG	CL	G	TPA	AB	H	2B	3B	HR	TB	BB	IBB	HB	SO	GDP	SH	SF	SB	CS	R	RBI	BA	OBA	SA
86	SPO/NWL	A–	54	208	159	37	8	1	2	53	47	1	0	37	5	1	1	3	1	29	31	.233	.406	.333
87	CHS/SAL	A	58	246	191	66	12	2	7	103	52	1	0	35	5	2	1	13	7	50	32	.346	.484	.539
	REN/CAL	A+	51	207	165	51	7	2	6	80	39	0	0	34	1	2	1	2	6	44	28	.309	.439	.485
88	RIV/CAL	A+	130	548	438	130	23	7	22	233	107	3	0	102	11	0	3	36	19	99	91	.297	.432	.532
89	WIC/TEX	AA	128	536	427	130	20	6	18	216	103	10	0	99	9	1	5	20	9	94	70	.304	.436	.506
90	LV/PCL	AAA	123	492	404	123	20	3	13	188	83	3	0	110	10	1	4	13	5	80	58	.304	.420	.465
91	VAN/PCL	AAA	33	143	111	41	12	1	2	61	30	1	0	26	2	1	1	5	4	19	19	.369	.497	.550
	CHI/AL		71	160	132	39	5	0	4	56	28	1	0	34	4	0	0	5	2	20	25	.295	.419	.424

Nichols, Carl Edward — bats right — throws right — b.10/14/62 — 1991 positions: C 17

YR	TM/LG	CL	G	TPA	AB	H	2B	3B	HR	TB	BB	IBB	HB	SO	GDP	SH	SF	SB	CS	R	RBI	BA	OBA	SA
80	BLU/APP	R+	37	107	85	18	2	0	2	24	18	0	3	12	0	0	1	4	1	24	10	.212	.364	.282
81	MIA/FSL	A+	16	36	31	6	0	0	0	6	3	0	0	5	0	1	1	0	0	0	3	.194	.257	.194

Nichols, Carl Edward (continued)

YR	TM/LG	CL	G	TPA	AB	H	2B	3B	HR	TB	BB	IBB	HB	SO	GDP	SH	SF	SB	CS	R	RBI	BA	OBA	SA
	HAG/CAR	A+	38	94	81	22	4	0	1	29	12	1	0	19	2	1	0	3	4	8	6	.272	.366	.358
82	MAC/SAL	A	84	290	257	55	10	2	0	69	27	0	2	50	5	1	3	7	1	33	30	.214	.291	.268
83	SJ/CAL	A+	54	179	152	31	4	0	1	38	21	1	3	42	3	0	3	2	0	16	12	.204	.307	.250
	NEW/NYP	A—	66	261	217	63	14	0	5	92	36	1	4	59	4	1	3	4	3	40	26	.290	.396	.424
84	SJ/CAL	A+	58	226	187	37	5	1	4	44	35	1	1	43	3	2	1	1	1	18	11	.198	.326	.235
	RED/CAL	A+	63	228	202	51	9	1	4	74	19	0	3	38	10	1	3	8	1	35	33	.252	.322	.366
85	CHA/SOU	AA	115	399	331	78	11	2	2	99	48	2	9	51	15	4	7	7	4	45	37	.236	.342	.299
86	CHA/SOU	AA	118	512	439	118	26	1	14	188	61	1	8	78	16	2	2	8	2	63	72	.269	.367	.428
	BAL/AL		5	6	5	0	0	0	0	0	1	1	0	4	0	0	0	0	0	0	0	.000	.167	.000
87	ROC/INT	AAA	108	415	364	93	15	3	11	147	42	1	3	76	17	6	0	0	3	45	52	.255	.337	.404
	BAL/AL		13	23	21	8	1	0	0	9	1	0	0	4	0	0	1	0	0	4	3	.381	.409	.429
88	ROC/INT	AAA	75	218	193	44	7	1	3	62	21	1	1	50	6	2	1	1	0	20	16	.228	.306	.321
	BAL/AL		18	52	47	9	1	0	0	10	3	0	1	10	3	1	1	0	0	2	1	.191	.235	.213
89	TUC/PCL	AAA	104	381	340	87	27	1	4	128	35	3	1	76	15	3	2	0	0	45	27	.256	.325	.376
	HOU/NL		8	13	13	1	0	0	0	1	0	0	0	3	0	0	0	0	0	0	2	.077	.077	.077
90	TUC/PCL	AAA	58	205	170	43	11	0	4	66	30	7	2	39	3	1	1	0	0	24	33	.253	.369	.388
	HOU/NL		32	61	49	10	3	0	0	13	8	1	1	11	3	0	2	0	0	7	11	.204	.317	.265
91	HOU/NL		20	56	51	10	3	0	0	13	5	1	0	17	0	0	0	0	0	13	17	.196	.268	.255
	TUC/PCL	AAA	36	141	121	26	4	1	3	41	17	0	1	26	3	2	3	0	0	16	18	.215	.317	.339
6 YR TOTALS			**96**	**211**	**186**	**38**	**8**	**0**	**0**	**46**	**18**	**3**	**1**	**49**	**4**	**3**	**3**	**0**	**0**	**16**	**18**	**.204**	**.274**	**.247**

Nilsson, David Wayne "Dave" — bats left — throws right — b.12/14/69 — 1991 positions: C System MIL/AL

YR	TM/LG	CL	G	TPA	AB	H	2B	3B	HR	TB	BB	IBB	HB	SO	GDP	SH	SF	SB	CS	R	RBI	BA	OBA	SA
87	HEL/PIO	R+	55	213	188	74	13	0	1	90	22	2	0	14	4	1	2	0	1	36	21	.394	.453	.479
88	BEL/MID	A	95	364	332	74	15	2	4	105	25	2	2	49	10	0	5	2	5	28	41	.223	.277	.316
89	STO/CAL	A+	125	532	472	115	16	6	5	158	51	1	1	75	20	0	4	2	1	59	56	.244	.316	.335
90	STO/CAL	A+	107	406	359	104	22	3	7	153	43	3	0	36	6	0	4	6	5	70	47	.290	.362	.426
91	EP/TEX	AA	65	279	249	104	24	3	5	149	27	4	1	14	4	0	0	2	1	52	57	.418	.473	.598
	DEN/AMA	AAA	28	112	95	22	8	0	1	33	17	0	0	16	2	0	0	1	1	10	14	.232	.348	.347

Nixon, Otis Junior — bats both — throws right — b.1/9/59 — 1991 positions: OF 115

YR	TM/LG	CL	G	TPA	AB	H	2B	3B	HR	TB	BB	IBB	HB	SO	GDP	SH	SF	SB	CS	R	RBI	BA	OBA	SA
83	NY/AL		13	15	14	2	0	0	0	2	1	0	0	5	0	0	0	2	0	2	0	.143	.200	.143
84	CLE/AL		49	103	91	14	0	0	0	14	8	0	0	11	2	3	1	12	6	16	1	.154	.220	.154
	MAI/INT	AAA	72	305	253	70	5	1	0	77	44	0	0	45	2	6	2	39	10	42	22	.277	.381	.304
85	CLE/AL		104	174	162	38	4	0	0	42	13	0	0	12	1	2	0	23	6	33	8	.235	.271	.315
86	CLE/AL		105	110	95	25	4	1	0	31	8	0	0	12	1	2	0	2	1	2	1	.263	.352	.326
87	CLE/AL		19	20	17	1	0	0	0	1	3	0	0	4	0	0	0	2	3	2	1	.059	.200	.059
	BUF/AMA	AAA	59	283	249	71	13	4	2	98	34	0	0	30	3	1	1	36	14	51	19	.285	.371	.394
88	IND/AMA	AAA	67	282	235	67	6	3	0	79	43	1	0	28	1	3	1	46	13	47	15	.285	.394	.336
	MON/NL		90	305	271	66	8	2	0	78	28	0	0	36	4	2	0	37	12	41	21	.244	.312	.288
89	MON/NL		126	293	258	56	7	2	0	67	33	0	0	33	2	3	0	50	13	46	20	.217	.306	.260
90	MON/NL		119	263	231	58	6	2	1	71	28	0	0	33	2	3	1	50	13	46	20	.251	.331	.307
91	ATL/NL		124	460	401	119	10	1	0	131	47	3	2	40	5	7	3	72	21	81	26	.297	.371	.327
9 YR TOTALS			**749**	**1743**	**1540**	**379**	**39**	**8**	**4**	**446**	**169**	**4**	**2**	**210**	**16**	**25**	**7**	**264**	**85**	**302**	**101**	**.246**	**.320**	**.290**

Noboa, Miliciades Arturo (Diaz) "Junior" — bats right — throws right — b.11/10/64 — 1991 positions: OF 7, 2B 6, 3B 2, SS 2, 1B 1

YR	TM/LG	CL	G	TPA	AB	H	2B	3B	HR	TB	BB	IBB	HB	SO	GDP	SH	SF	SB	CS	R	RBI	BA	OBA	SA
81	BAT/NYP	A—	50	178	162	49	8	0	0	57	11	0	2	19	2	2	1	11	4	15	6	.302	.352	.352
82	WAT/MID	A	121	471	385	86	12	5	0	118	62	1	2	61	7	19	3	44	12	68	23	.223	.332	.306
83	WAT/MID	A	132	522	449	115	22	3	1	146	48	1	1	71	3	18	2	47	20	64	29	.256	.333	.325
84	BUF/EAS	AA	117	436	383	97	18	4	1	126	31	0	1	28	7	17	3	12	7	55	45	.253	.310	.329
	CLE/AL		23	12	11	4	0	0	0	4	0	0	0	1	1	0	0	0	0	3	0	.364	.364	.364
85	MAI/INT	AAA	122	453	403	116	11	2	5	146	34	0	3	28	3	10	3	14	15	62	32	.288	.345	.362
86	MAI/INT	AAA	108	427	399	114	21	2	4	149	15	0	2	33	8	8	3	10	14	44	32	.286	.313	.373
87	BUF/AMA	AAA	43	169	149	47	6	2	0	57	18	0	0	16	3	1	1	2	2	26	14	.315	.387	.383
	CLE/AL		39	88	80	18	2	1	0	22	3	0	0	6	1	5	0	0	0	7	7	.225	.253	.275
88	CAL/AL		21	16	16	1	0	0	0	1	0	0	0	0	1	0	0	0	0	4	0	.063	.063	.063
	EDM/PCL	AAA	50	173	159	47	6	1	0	55	11	0	0	12	1	3	0	0	5	24	17	.296	.341	.346
89	IND/AMA	AAA	117	506	467	159	21	8	2	202	21	4	3	34	8	7	8	14	11	61	62	.340	.367	.433
	MON/NL		21	45	44	10	0	0	0	10	1	0	0	3	0	0	0	0	0	3	1	.227	.244	.227
90	MON/NL		81	173	158	42	7	2	0	53	7	0	0	14	2	3	4	4	1	15	14	.266	.294	.335
91	MON/NL		67	96	95	23	3	0	1	29	1	0	0	8	1	0	0	2	3	5	2	.242	.250	.305
6 YR TOTALS			**252**	**430**	**404**	**98**	**12**	**3**	**1**	**119**	**12**	**4**	**2**	**34**		**9**	**4**	**8**	**4**	**37**	**24**	**.243**	**.264**	**.295**

Nokes, Matthew Dodge "Matt" — bats left — throws right — b.10/31/63 — 1991 positions: C 130, DH 3

YR	TM/LG	CL	G	TPA	AB	H	2B	3B	HR	TB	BB	IBB	HB	SO	GDP	SH	SF	SB	CS	R	RBI	BA	OBA	SA
84	SHR/TEX	AA	97	340	308	89	19	2	11	145	30	0	0	34	9	0	2	0	2	32	61	.289	.350	.471
85	SHR/TEX	AA	105	396	344	101	24	1	14	169	41	2	2	47	11	2	7	2	0	52	61	.294	.365	.491
	SF/NL		19	55	53	11	2	0	2	19	2	0	0	9	2	0	0	3	5	3	5	.208	.236	.358
86	NAS/AMA	AAA	125	466	428	122	25	4	10	185	30	1	5	41	12	0	3	2	0	55	71	.285	.337	.432
	DET/AL		7	25	24	8	1	0	1	12	1	1	0	4	1	0	0	0	0	2	2	.333	.360	.500
87	DET/AL		135	508	461	133	14	2	32	247	35	3	2	70	13	3	3	2	1	69	87	.289	.345	.536
88	DET/AL		122	425	382	96	18	0	16	162	34	3	2	58	11	6	2	0	0	53	53	.251	.313	.424
89	DET/AL		87	290	268	67	10	0	9	104	17	1	2	37	7	1	2	0	0	15	39	.250	.298	.388

(continued)

YR	TM/LG	CL	G	TPA	AB	H	2B	3B	HR	TB	BB	IBB	HB	SO	GDP	SH	SF	SB	CS	R	RBI	BA	OBA	SA
90	DET/AL		44	118	111	30	5	1	3	46	4	3	2	14	5	0	1	0	0	12	8	.270	.305	.414
	NY/AL		92	264	240	57	4	0	8	85	20	3	4	33	6	0	0	2	2	21	32	.237	.307	.354
	YEAR		136	382	351	87	9	1	11	131	24	6	6	47	11	0	1	2	2	33	40	.248	.306	.373
91	NY/AL		135	493	456	122	20	0	24	214	25	5	5	49	6	0	7	3	2	52	77	.268	.308	.469
7 YR TOTALS			**641**	**2178**	**1995**	**524**	**74**	**3**	**95**	**889**	**137**	**18**	**21**	**271**	**51**	**10**	**15**	**8**	**6**	**227**	**303**	**.263**	**.315**	**.446**

Oberkfell, Kenneth Ray "Ken" — bats left — throws right — b.5/4/56 — 1991 positions: 1B 13, 3B 4

YR	TM/LG	CL	G	TPA	AB	H	2B	3B	HR	TB	BB	IBB	HB	SO	GDP	SH	SF	SB	CS	R	RBI	BA	OBA	SA
77	STL/NL		9	9	9	1	0	0	0	1	0	0	0	3	0	0	0	0	0	0	1	.111	.111	.111
78	STL/NL		24	54	50	6	1	0	0	7	3	0	0	1	1	1	0	0	0	7	0	.120	.170	.140
79	STL/NL		135	435	369	111	19	5	1	143	57	9	4	35	9	1	4	4	1	53	35	.301	.396	.388
80	STL/NL		116	486	422	128	27	4	3	176	51	8	1	23	11	9	3	4	4	58	46	.303	.377	.417
81	STL/NL		102	420	376	110	12	6	2	140	37	6	0	28	11	3	4	13	5	43	45	.293	.353	.372
82	STL/NL		137	516	470	136	22	5	2	174	40	6	1	31	11	3	2	11	9	55	34	.289	.345	.370
83	STL/NL		151	557	488	143	26	5	3	188	61	5	1	27	12	4	3	12	6	62	38	.293	.371	.385
84	STL/NL		50	169	152	47	11	1	0	60	16	2	1	10	3	0	0	1	2	17	11	.309	.379	.395
	ATL/NL		50	193	172	40	8	1	1	53	15	1	0	17	4	3	3	1	3	21	10	.233	.289	.308
	YEAR		100	362	324	87	19	2	1	113	31	3	1	27	7	3	3	2	5	38	21	.269	.331	.349
85	ATL/NL		134	472	412	112	19	4	3	148	51	6	6	38	10	1	2	1	2	30	35	.272	.359	.359
86	ATL/NL		151	596	503	136	24	3	5	181	83	6	2	40	11	4	4	7	4	62	48	.270	.373	.360
87	ATL/NL		135	566	508	142	29	2	3	184	48	5	2	29	13	5	3	3	3	59	48	.280	.342	.362
88	ATL/NL		120	469	422	117	20	4	1	154	32	6	2	28	6	5	8	4	5	42	40	.277	.325	.365
	PIT/NL		20	60	54	12	2	0	0	14	5	1	0	6	2	1	0	0	0	7	2	.222	.288	.259
	YEAR		140	529	476	129	22	4	1	168	37	7	2	34	8	6	8	4	5	49	42	.271	.321	.353
89	PIT/NL		14	44	40	5	1	0	0	6	2	0	0	2	0	1	1	0	0	2	2	.125	.163	.150
	SF/NL		83	129	116	37	5	1	2	50	8	0	2	8	4	1	2	0	1	17	15	.319	.367	.431
	YEAR		97	173	156	42	6	1	2	56	10	0	2	10	4	2	3	0	1	19	17	.269	.316	.359
90	HOU/NL		77	168	150	31	6	1	1	42	15	1	1	17	2	1	1	1	1	10	12	.207	.281	.280
91	HOU/NL		53	84	70	16	4	0	0	20	14	4	0	8	0	0	0	0	0	7	14	.229	.357	.286
15 YR TOTALS			**1561**	**5427**	**4783**	**1330**	**236**	**44**	**29**	**1741**	**538**	**66**	**23**	**351**	**110**	**43**	**40**	**62**	**46**	**552**	**436**	**.278**	**.351**	**.364**

O'Brien, Charles Hugh "Charlie" — bats right — throws right — b.5/1/60 — 1991 positions: C 67

YR	TM/LG	CL	G	TPA	AB	H	2B	3B	HR	TB	BB	IBB	HB	SO	GDP	SH	SF	SB	CS	R	RBI	BA	OBA	SA
84	MOD/CAL	A+	9	37	32	9	2	0	1	14	2	0	3	4	1	0	0	1	0	8	5	.281	.378	.438
	TAC/PCL	AAA	69	237	195	44	11	0	9	82	28	0	6	31	1	8	0	0	1	33	22	.226	.341	.421
85	HUN/SOU	AA	33	135	115	24	5	0	7	50	16	0	2	20	6	1	1	0	1	20	16	.209	.313	.435
	MOD/CAL	A+	9	29	27	8	4	1	1	17	2	1	0	5	0	0	0	0	0	5	2	.296	.345	.630
	TAC/PCL	AAA	18	65	57	9	4	0	0	13	6	0	1	17	0	0	1	0	0	5	7	.158	.246	.228
	OAK/AL		16	14	11	3	1	0	0	4	3	0	0	3	0	0	0	0	0	3	1	.273	.429	.364
86	VAN/PCL	AAA	6	21	17	2	0	0	0	2	4	0	0	4	0	0	0	0	0	1	1	.118	.286	.118
	EP/TEX	AA	92	399	336	109	20	3	15	180	50	0	6	30	7	1	6	0	0	72	75	.324	.415	.536
87	MIL/AL		10	40	35	7	3	1	0	12	4	0	0	4	0	1	0	0	0	2	0	.200	.282	.343
	DEN/AMA	AAA	80	318	266	75	12	1	8	113	42	2	2	33	5	6	2	5	5	37	35	.282	.381	.425
88	DEN/AMA	AAA	48	182	153	43	5	0	4	60	19	1	4	19	6	5	1	1	2	16	25	.281	.373	.392
	MIL/AL		40	127	118	26	6	0	2	38	5	0	0	16	3	4	0	0	1	12	9	.220	.252	.322
89	MIL/AL		62	226	188	44	10	0	6	72	21	1	9	11	11	8	0	0	1	22	35	.234	.339	.383
90	MIL/AL		46	166	145	27	7	2	0	38	11	1	2	26	3	1	0	0	0	11	11	.186	.253	.262
	NY/NL		28	83	68	11	3	0	0	14	10	2	1	8	1	2	2	0	0	6	9	.162	.272	.206
	YEAR		74	249	213	38	10	2	0	52	21	3	3	34	4	10	2	0	0	17	20	.178	.259	.244
91	NY/NL		69	191	168	31	6	0	2	43	17	1	4	25	5	0	2	0	2	16	14	.185	.272	.256
6 YR TOTALS			**271**	**847**	**733**	**149**	**36**	**3**	**10**	**221**	**71**	**5**	**16**	**93**	**23**	**23**	**4**	**0**	**4**	**72**	**79**	**.203**	**.286**	**.302**

O'Brien, Peter Michael "Pete" — bats left — throws left — b.2/9/58 — 1991 positions: 1B 132, DH 18, OF 13

YR	TM/LG	CL	G	TPA	AB	H	2B	3B	HR	TB	BB	IBB	HB	SO	GDP	SH	SF	SB	CS	R	RBI	BA	OBA	SA
82	TEX/AL		20	74	67	16	4	1	4	34	6	0	0	8	0	0	0	1	0	13	13	.239	.297	.507
83	TEX/AL		154	588	524	124	24	5	8	182	58	2	1	62	12	3	2	5	4	53	53	.237	.313	.347
84	TEX/AL		142	581	520	149	26	2	18	233	53	8	0	50	11	1	7	3	5	57	80	.287	.348	.448
85	TEX/AL		159	655	573	153	34	3	22	259	69	4	1	53	18	3	9	5	10	69	92	.267	.342	.452
86	TEX/AL		156	641	551	160	23	3	23	258	87	11	0	66	19	0	3	4	4	86	90	.290	.385	.468
87	TEX/AL		159	638	569	163	26	1	23	260	59	6	0	61	9	0	10	0	4	84	88	.286	.348	.457
88	TEX/AL		156	628	547	149	24	1	16	223	72	9	0	73	12	1	8	1	4	57	71	.272	.352	.408
89	CLE/AL		155	646	554	144	24	1	12	206	83	17	2	48	10	2	5	3	1	75	55	.260	.356	.372
90	SEA/AL		108	417	366	82	18	0	5	115	44	1	2	33	12	1	4	0	0	32	27	.224	.308	.314
91	SEA/AL		152	617	560	139	29	3	17	225	44	7	1	61	14	3	9	0	0	58	88	.248	.300	.402
10 YR TOTALS			**1361**	**5485**	**4831**	**1279**	**232**	**20**	**148**	**1995**	**575**	**65**	**7**	**515**	**117**	**14**	**58**	**22**	**33**	**584**	**657**	**.265**	**.340**	**.413**

Offerman, Jose Antonio (Dono) — bats both — throws right — b.11/8/68 — 1991 positions: SS 50

YR	TM/LG	CL	G	TPA	AB	H	2B	3B	HR	TB	BB	IBB	HB	SO	GDP	SH	SF	SB	CS	R	RBI	BA	OBA	SA
88	VB/FSL	A+	4	16	14	4	2	0	0	6	2	0	0	0	0	0	0	0	0	4	2	.286	.375	.429
	GF/PIO	R+	60	293	251	83	11	5	2	110	38	1	2	42	3	1	1	57	10	75	28	.331	.421	.438
89	BAK/CAL	A+	62	283	245	75	9	4	2	98	35	2	2	48	5	0	1	37	13	53	22	.306	.396	.400
	SA/TEX	AA	68	322	278	80	6	3	2	98	40	4	1	39	1	3	0	32	13	47	22	.288	.379	.353
90	ALB/PCL	AAA	117	535	454	148	16	11	0	186	71	2	2	81	7	4	4	60	19	104	56	.326	.416	.410
	LA/NL		29	63	58	9	0	0	1	12	4	1	0	14	0	1	0	1	0	7	7	.155	.210	.207

Offerman, Jose Antonio (Dono) (continued)

YR	TM/LG	CL	G	TPA	AB	H	2B	3B	HR	TB	BB	IBB	HB	SO	GDP	SH	SF	SB	CS	R	RBI	BA	OBA	SA
91	ALB/PCL	AAA	79	340	289	86	8	4	0	102	47	3	0	58	5	4	0	32	15	58	29	.298	.396	.353
	LA/NL		52	140	113	22	2	0	0	24	25	2	1	32	5	1	0	3	2	10	3	.195	.345	.212
2 YR TOTALS			**81**	**203**	**171**	**31**	**2**	**0**	**1**	**36**	**29**	**3**	**1**	**46**	**5**	**2**	**0**	**4**	**2**	**17**	**10**	**.181**	**.303**	**.211**

Olander, James Bentley "Jim" — bats right — throws right — b.2/21/63 — 1991 positions: OF 9, DH 2

YR	TM/LG	CL	G	TPA	AB	H	2B	3B	HR	TB	BB	IBB	HB	SO	GDP	SH	SF	SB	CS	R	RBI	BA	OBA	SA
81	HEL/PIO	R+	61	239	222	72	10	3	6		17	0	0	59	0	0	0	5	0	37	37	.324	.372	.000
82	SPA/SAL	A	121	484	423	129	25	6	12		61	0	0	86	0	0	0	12	0	77	63	.305	.393	.000
83	PEN/CAR	A+	126	546	503	125	21	3	15		43	0	0	146	0	0	0	12	0	62	79	.249	.308	.000
84	REA/EAS	AA	117	399	362	95	12	2	8	135	29	0	2	62	10	0	5	10	10	44	47	.262	.317	.373
85	POR/PCL	AAA	44	76	72	16	2	0	0	18	2	0	0	17	0	3	0	0	2	8	8	.222	.243	.250
	REA/EAS	AA	64	243	208	67	15	2	4	98	29	1	0	45	3	2	1	2	2	30	39	.322	.397	.471
86	REA/EAS	AA	129	530	464	151	33	4	8	216	56	3	2	84	5	1	0	2	2	77	68	.325	.397	.466
87	MAI/INT	AAA	43	159	145	31	7	0	1	41	13	1	0	30	5	1	0	2	2	17	8	.214	.278	.283
88	MAI/INT	AAA	25	77	71	15	3	0	0	18	4	1	1	18	1	0	0	0	0	5	4	.211	.263	.254
89	SCR/INT	AAA	111	314	274	69	17	4	3	103	27	1	3	69	5	1	3	8	2	35	29	.252	.324	.376
90	TUC/PCL	AAA	33	114	98	23	8	2	1	38	14	1	1	24	4	3	0	6	2	12	12	.235	.336	.388
	DEN/AMA	AAA	74	272	233	67	12	4	3	96	20	0	5	83	10	3	9	6	2	33	36	.288	.346	.412
91	DEN/AMA	AAA	134	571	498	162	32	10	9	241	64	0	5	2	0	0	0	0	0	89	78	.325	.405	.484
	MIL/AL		12		9	0	0	0	0	0	2	0	0	5	0	0	0	0	0	2	0	.000	.182	.000

Olerud, John Garrett — bats left — throws left — b.8/5/68 — 1991 positions: 1B 135, DH 1

YR	TM/LG	CL	G	TPA	AB	H	2B	3B	HR	TB	BB	IBB	HB	SO	GDP	SH	SF	SB	CS	R	RBI	BA	OBA	SA
89	TOR/AL		6	8	8	3	0	0	0	3	0	0	0	1	0	0	0	0	0	2	0	.375	.375	.375
90	TOR/AL		111	421	358	95	15	1	14	154	57	6	1	75	5	1	4	0	2	43	48	.265	.364	.430
91	TOR/AL		139	541	454	116	30	1	17	199	68	9	6	84	12	3	10	0	2	64	68	.256	.353	.438
3 YR TOTALS			**256**	**970**	**820**	**214**	**45**	**2**	**31**	**356**	**125**	**15**	**7**	**160**	**17**	**4**	**14**	**0**	**4**	**109**	**116**	**.261**	**.358**	**.434**

Oliver, Joseph Melton "Joe" — bats right — throws right — b.7/24/65 — 1991 positions: C 90

YR	TM/LG	CL	G	TPA	AB	H	2B	3B	HR	TB	BB	IBB	HB	SO	GDP	SH	SF	SB	CS	R	RBI	BA	OBA	SA
84	CR/MID	A	102	363	335	73	11	0	3	93	17	1	4	83	11	4	3	2	2	34	29	.218	.262	.278
85	TAM/FSL	A+	112	428	386	104	23	2	7	152	32	3	1	75	9	4	5	1	5	38	62	.269	.323	.394
86	VER/EAS	AA	84	308	282	78	18	1	6	116	21	1	0	47	12	0	2	1	2	31	60	.277	.321	.411
87	VER/EAS	AA	66	264	236	72	13	2	10	119	17	2	3	30	2	1	7	0	3	19	24	.305	.350	.504
88	NAS/AMA	AAA	73	244	220	45	7	2	4	68	18	1	4	39	9	1	0	1	0	15	20	.205	.276	.309
	CHT/SOU	AA	28	112	105	26	6	0	3	41	5	0	3	19	3	0	1	0	0	9	12	.248	.295	.390
89	NAS/AMA	AAA	71	255	233	68	13	0	3	99	13	1	3	35	3	1	1	1	0	22	31	.292	.331	.425
	CIN/NL		49	161	151	41	8	0	3	58	6	1	1	28	3	1	1	0	0	13	23	.272	.300	.384
90	CIN/NL		121	409	364	84	23	0	8	131	37	15	0	75	6	5	1	0	0	34	52	.231	.304	.360
91	CIN/NL		94	291	269	58	11	0	11	102	18	5	2	53	14	4	1	3	1	21	41	.216	.265	.379
3 YR TOTALS			**264**	**861**	**784**	**183**	**42**	**0**	**22**	**291**	**61**	**21**	**3**	**156**	**23**	**10**	**3**	**1**	**1**	**68**	**116**	**.233**	**.290**	**.371**

Olson, Gregory William "Greg" — bats right — throws right — b.9/6/60 — 1991 positions: C 127

YR	TM/LG	CL	G	TPA	AB	H	2B	3B	HR	TB	BB	IBB	HB	SO	GDP	SH	SF	SB	CS	R	RBI	BA	OBA	SA
84	JAC/TEX	AA	74	272	234	55	9	0	0	64	30	5	1	16	10	5	2	1	1	27	22	.235	.322	.274
85	JAC/TEX	AA	69	240	211	57	7	0	1	67	23	1	1	20	4	3	1	0	3	21	32	.270	.342	.318
86	JAC/TEX	AA	64	231	196	39	5	1	2	52	30	1	0	16	4	1	1	0	0	28	16	.199	.307	.265
	TID/INT	AAA	19	62	55	18	1	0	0	19	5	0	0	4	1	1	2	0	0	11	7	.327	.377	.345
87	TID/INT	AAA	47	138	120	34	8	1	0	50	14	1	0	13	1	2	2	0	0	15	15	.283	.353	.417
88	TID/INT	AAA	115	397	344	92	19	1	6	131	42	2	4	42	12	1	6	0	0	39	48	.267	.348	.381
89	MIN/AL		3	2	2	1	0	0	0	1	0	0	0	0	0	0	0	0	0	0	0	.500	.500	.500
	POR/PCL	AAA	79	303	247	58	12	1	2	88	45	2	4	51	8	3	5	3	2	38	38	.235	.353	.356
90	RIC/INT	AAA	3	7	7	0	0	0	0	0	0	0	0	0	0	0	0	0	0	0	0	.000	.000	.000
	ATL/NL		100	332	298	78	12	1	7	113	30	4	2	51	8	1	1	1	1	36	36	.262	.332	.379
91	ATL/NL		133	464	411	99	25	0	6	142	44	3	3	48	13	2	4	1	1	46	44	.241	.316	.345
3 YR TOTALS			**236**	**798**	**711**	**178**	**37**	**1**	**13**	**256**	**74**	**7**	**5**	**99**	**21**	**3**	**5**	**2**	**2**	**82**	**80**	**.250**	**.323**	**.360**

O'Neill, Paul Andrew — bats left — throws left — b.2/25/63 — 1991 positions: OF 150

YR	TM/LG	CL	G	TPA	AB	H	2B	3B	HR	TB	BB	IBB	HB	SO	GDP	SH	SF	SB	CS	R	RBI	BA	OBA	SA
84	VER/EAS	AA	134	536	475	126	31	5	16	215	52	6	2	72	4	0	7	29	11	70	76	.265	.336	.453
85	DEN/AMA	AAA	137	545	509	155	32	3	7	214	28	4	1	73	11	1	6	5	7	63	74	.305	.338	.420
	CIN/NL		5	12	12	4	1	0	0	5	0	0	0	2	0	0	0	0	0	1	1	.333	.333	.417
86	CIN/NL		3	3	2	0	0	0	0	0	1	0	0	1	0	0	0	0	0	0	0	.000	.333	.000
	DEN/AMA	AAA	55	206	193	49	9	2	5	77	9	3	2	28	6	0	1	1	1	20	27	.254	.291	.399
87	NAS/AMA	AAA	11	43	37	11	1	0	3	20	6	0	0	5	0	0	0	2	1	12	6	.297	.372	.541
	CIN/NL		84	178	160	41	14	1	7	78	18	1	0	29	7	0	0	2	0	24	28	.256	.331	.488
88	CIN/NL		145	533	485	122	25	3	16	201	38	3	2	65	3	0	2	8	7	58	73	.252	.306	.414
89	NAS/AMA	AAA	4	15	12	4	0	0	0	4	3	0	0	0	0	0	0	2	0	1	4	.333	.467	.333
	CIN/NL		117	480	428	118	24	2	15	191	46	8	2	64	7	0	4	20	5	49	74	.276	.346	.446
90	CIN/NL		145	564	503	136	28	0	16	212	53	13	2	103	12	0	1	13	11	59	78	.270	.339	.421
91	CIN/NL		152	607	532	136	36	0	28	256	73	14	1	107	8	0	1	12	7	71	91	.256	.346	.481
7 YR TOTALS			**651**	**2377**	**2122**	**557**	**128**	**6**	**82**	**943**	**229**	**41**	**7**	**371**	**37**	**4**	**15**	**55**	**30**	**262**	**345**	**.262**	**.334**	**.444**

Oquendo, Jose Manuel (Contreras) — bats both — throws right — b.7/4/63 — 1991 positions: 2B 118, SS 22, 1B 3, P–1

YR	TM/LG	CL	G	TPA	AB	H	2B	3B	HR	TB	BB	IBB	HB	SO	GDP	SH	SF	SB	CS	R	RBI	BA	OBA	SA
83	NY/NL		120	353	328	70	7	0	1	80	19	2	2	60	10	3	1	8	9	29	17	.213	.260	.244
84	TID/INT	AAA	38	120	113	18	1	0	1	22	5	0	1	14	3	1	0	8	0	8	8	.159	.202	.195
	NY/NL		81	211	189	42	5	0	0	47	15	2	2	26	2	3	2	10	1	23	10	.222	.284	.249
85	LOU/AMA	AAA	133	432	384	81	8	1	1	94	24	0	5	41	9	15	4	13	4	38	30	.211	.264	.245
86	STL/NL		76	158	138	41	4	1	0	47	15	4	0	20	3	2	3	2	3	20	13	.297	.359	.341
87	STL/NL		116	312	248	71	9	0	1	83	54	6	0	29	6	6	4	4	3	43	24	.286	.408	.335
88	STL/NL		148	518	451	125	10	1	7	158	52	7	0	40	8	12	3	4	6	36	46	.277	.350	.350
89	STL/NL		163	650	556	162	28	7	1	207	79	7	0	59	12	7	8	3	5	59	48	.291	.375	.372
90	STL/NL		156	553	469	118	17	5	1	148	74	8	0	46	7	5	5	1	1	38	37	.252	.350	.316
91	STL/NL		127	441	366	88	11	4	1	110	67	13	1	48	5	4	3	1	2	37	26	.240	.357	.301
8 YR TOTALS			**987**	**3196**	**2745**	**717**	**91**	**18**	**12**	**880**	**375**	**49**	**5**	**328**	**53**	**42**	**29**	**33**	**31**	**285**	**221**	**.261**	**.348**	**.321**

Orsulak, Joseph Michael "Joe" — bats left — throws left — b.5/31/62 — 1991 positions: OF 132, DH 2

YR	TM/LG	CL	G	TPA	AB	H	2B	3B	HR	TB	BB	IBB	HB	SO	GDP	SH	SF	SB	CS	R	RBI	BA	OBA	SA
83	PIT/NL		7	12	11	2	0	0	0	2	0	0	0	2	0	1	0	1	0	0	1	.182	.167	.182
84	HAW/PCL	AAA	98	425	388	110	19	12	3	162	29	5	2	38	4	3	3	14	12	51	53	.284	.334	.418
	PIT/NL		32	73	67	17	1	2	0	22	1	0	1	7	0	3	1	3	1	12	3	.254	.271	.328
85	PIT/NL		121	436	397	119	14	6	0	145	26	3	1	27	5	9	3	24	11	54	21	.300	.342	.365
86	PIT/NL		138	437	401	100	19	6	2	137	28	3	1	38	4	6	1	24	11	60	19	.249	.299	.342
87	VAN/PCL	AAA	39	165	143	33	6	1	1	44	17	5	2	21	4	2	1	2	4	20	12	.231	.319	.308
88	BAL/AL		125	416	379	109	21	3	8	160	23	2	3	30	7	8	3	9	8	48	27	.288	.331	.422
89	BAL/AL		123	446	390	111	22	5	7	164	41	6	2	35	8	7	6	5	3	59	55	.285	.351	.421
90	BAL/AL		124	465	413	111	14	3	11	164	46	9	1	48	7	4	1	6	8	49	57	.269	.343	.397
91	BAL/AL		143	521	486	135	22	1	5	174	28		1	4	45	9	7	3	6	2	57	43	.278	.321	.358
8 YR TOTALS			**813**	**2806**	**2544**	**704**	**113**	**26**	**33**	**968**	**193**	**23**	**13**	**232**	**40**	**37**	**19**	**77**	**45**	**339**	**226**	**.277**	**.329**	**.381**

Ortiz, Adalberto Colon "Junior" — bats right — throws right — b.10/24/59 — 1991 positions: C 60

YR	TM/LG	CL	G	TPA	AB	H	2B	3B	HR	TB	BB	IBB	HB	SO	GDP	SH	SF	SB	CS	R	RBI	BA	OBA	SA
82	PIT/NL		7	16	15	3	1	0	0	4	1	0	0	3	1	0	0	0	0	1	0	.200	.250	.267
83	PIT/NL		5	10	8	1	0	0	0	1	1	0	0	0	1	0	0	0	0	1	0	.125	.222	.125
	NY/NL		68	190	185	47	5	0	0	52	3	0	1	34	1	1	0	1	0	10	12	.254	.270	.281
	YEAR		73	200	193	48	5	0	0	53	4	0	1	34	1	1	0	1	0	11	12	.249	.268	.275
84	NY/NL		40	98	91	18	3	0	0	21	5	0	0	15	2	0	2	1	0	6	11	.198	.235	.231
85	PIT/NL		23	76	72	21	2	0	0	26	3	1	0	17	1	1	0	1	0	4	5	.292	.320	.361
86	PIT/NL		49	122	110	37	6	0	0	43	9	1	0	13	6	1	2	0	0	11	14	.336	.380	.391
87	PIT/NL		75	213	192	52	8	1	1	65	15	1	0	23	6	5	1	0	2	16	22	.271	.322	.339
88	PIT/NL		49	132	118	33	6	0	2	45	9	0	2	9	6	5	1	0	2	8	18	.280	.336	.381
89	PIT/NL		91	258	230	50	6	1	1	61	20	4	2	20	9	3	3	2	1	16	22	.217	.282	.265
90	MIN/AL		71	187	170	57	7	1	0	66	12	0	2	16	4	2	1	0	4	18	18	.335	.384	.388
91	MIN/AL		61	151	134	28	5	1	0	35	15	0	1	12	6	1	0	0	1	9	11	.209	.293	.261
10 YR TOTALS			**539**	**1453**	**1325**	**347**	**49**	**4**	**5**	**419**	**93**	**6**	**8**	**162**	**40**	**16**	**11**	**6**	**14**	**100**	**133**	**.262**	**.312**	**.316**

Ortiz, Javier Victor — bats right — throws right — b.1/22/63 — 1991 positions: OF 24

YR	TM/LG	CL	G	TPA	AB	H	2B	3B	HR	TB	BB	IBB	HB	SO	GDP	SH	SF	SB	CS	R	RBI	BA	OBA	SA
83	BUR/MID	A	101	427	378	133	23	4	16	212	42	3	2	94	14	2	3	10	6	72	79	.352	.416	.561
84	TUL/TEX	AA	94	385	325	97	21	3	8	148	47	2	5	67	8	4	4	4	5	42	53	.298	.391	.455
85	TUL/TEX	AA	86	361	304	75	12	3	5	108	52	2	4	75	10	0	1	11	3	47	31	.247	.363	.355
86	TUL/TEX	AA	110	443	378	114	29	3	14	191	54	1	1	94	4	1	4	15	10	52	65	.302	.398	.505
87	OC/AMA	AAA	119	454	381	105	23	7	15	187	58	2	4	99	6	1	10	5	4	58	69	.276	.369	.491
88	SA/TEX	AA	51	214	182	53	13	2	8	94	22	0	5	38	5	0	5	6	3	35	33	.291	.374	.516
89	ALB/PCL	AAA	70	259	220	59	10	5	11	102	34	1	4	54	4	1	0	2	2	42	36	.268	.376	.464
	TUC/PCL	AAA	11	42	40	7	0	0	0	7	2	0	0	9	1	0	0	0	0	5	0	.175	.214	.175
90	TUC/PCL	AAA	49	205	179	63	16	2	5	98	21	1	2	36	6	0	3	2	3	36	39	.352	.420	.547
	HOU/NL		30	90	77	21	5	1	1	31	12	0	0	11	1	0	2	0	0	7	10	.273	.367	.403
91	TUC/PCL	AAA	34	139	127	41	13	0	3	63	10	0	0	22	4	0	2	0	1	20	22	.323	.367	.496
	HOU/NL		47	97	83	23	4	1	1	32	14	0	0	14	3	0	0	0	0	7	5	.277	.381	.386
2 YR TOTALS			**77**	**187**	**160**	**44**	**9**	**2**	**2**	**63**	**26**	**0**	**0**	**25**	**4**	**0**	**1**	**1**	**1**	**14**	**15**	**.275**	**.374**	**.394**

Orton, John Andrew — bats right — throws right — b.12/8/65 — 1991 positions: C 28

YR	TM/LG	CL	G	TPA	AB	H	2B	3B	HR	TB	BB	IBB	HB	SO	GDP	SH	SF	SB	CS	R	RBI	BA	OBA	SA
87	SAL/NWL	A–	51	218	176	46	8	1	8	80	32	1	7	61	5	1	2	6	2	31	36	.261	.392	.455
	MID/TEX	AA	5	16	13	2	1	0	0	3	2	0	1	3	0	0	0	0	0	1	0	.154	.313	.231
88	PS/CAL	A+	68	287	230	46	6	1	1	57	45	0	10	79	4	2	0	0	0	42	28	.200	.354	.248
89	MID/TEX	AA	99	401	344	80	20	6	10	142	37	1	7	102	5	6	7	5	2	51	53	.233	.314	.413
	CAL/AL		16	42	39	7	1	0	0	8	2	0	0	17	0	1	0	0	0	4	4	.179	.220	.205
90	EDM/PCL	AAA	50	195	174	42	8	0	6	68	19	1	0	63	7	1	1	4	2	29	26	.241	.314	.391
	CAL/AL		31	92	84	16	5	0	1	24	5	0	1	31	2	2	0	1	0	8	6	.190	.244	.286
91	EDM/PCL	AAA	76	287	245	55	14	1	5	86	31	1	5	66	4	4	2	5	0	39	32	.224	.322	.351
	CAL/AL		29	84	69	14	4	0	0	18	10	0	1	17	2	0	0	0	2	7	3	.203	.313	.261
3 YR TOTALS			**76**	**218**	**192**	**37**	**10**	**0**	**1**	**50**	**17**	**0**	**2**	**65**	**4**	**7**	**0**	**0**	**2**	**19**	**13**	**.193**	**.265**	**.260**

Owen, Spike Dee — bats both — throws right — b.4/19/61 — 1991 positions: SS 133

YR	TM/LG	CL	G	TPA	AB	H	2B	3B	HR	TB	BB	IBB	HB	SO	GDP	SH	SF	SB	CS	R	RBI	BA	OBA	SA
83	SEA/AL		80	340	306	60	11	3	2	83	24	0	2	44	2	5	3	10	6	36	21	.196	.257	.271

Owen, Spike Dee (continued)

YR	TM/LG	CL	G	TPA	AB	H	2B	3B	HR	TB	BB	IBB	HB	SO	GDP	SH	SF	SB	CS	R	RBI	BA	OBA	SA
84	SEA/AL		152	590	530	130	18	8	3	173	46	0	3	63	5	9	2	16	8	67	43	.245	.308	.326
85	SEA/AL		118	393	352	91	10	6	6	131	34	0	0	27	5	5	2	11	5	41	37	.259	.322	.372
86	SEA/AL		112	446	402	99	22	6	0	133	34	1	1	42	11	7	2	1	3	46	35	.246	.305	.331
	BOS/AL		42	147	126	23	2	1	1	30	17	0	1	9	2	2	1	3	1	21	10	.183	.283	.238
	YEAR		154	593	528	122	24	7	1	163	51	1	2	51	13	9	3	4	4	67	45	.231	.300	.309
87	BOS/AL		132	504	437	113	17	7	2	150	53	2	1	43	9	9	4	11	8	50	48	.259	.337	.343
88	BOS/AL		89	294	257	64	14	1	5	95	27	0	2	27	7	7	1	0	1	40	18	.249	.324	.370
89	MON/NL		142	522	437	102	17	4	6	145	76	25	3	44	11	3	3	3	2	52	41	.233	.349	.332
90	MON/NL		149	533	453	106	24	5	5	155	70	12	0	60	6	5	5	8	6	55	35	.234	.333	.342
91	MON/NL		139	475	424	108	22	8	3	155	42	11	1	61	11	4	4	2	6	39	26	.255	.321	.366
9 YR TOTALS			1155	4244	3724	896	157	49	33	1250	423	51	14	420	69	56	27	65	46	447	314	.241	.318	.336

Pagliarulo, Michael Timothy "Mike" — bats left — throws right — b.3/15/60 — 1991 positions: 3B 118, 2B 1

YR	TM/LG	CL	G	TPA	AB	H	2B	3B	HR	TB	BB	IBB	HB	SO	GDP	SH	SF	SB	CS	R	RBI	BA	OBA	SA
84	COL/INT	AAA	58	169	146	31	5	1	7	59	18	0	0	30	2	2	3	0	0	24	25	.212	.293	.404
	NY/AL		67	219	201	48	15	3	7	90	15	0	0	46	5	0	3	0	0	24	34	.239	.288	.448
85	NY/AL		138	435	380	91	16	2	19	168	45	4	4	86	6	3	3	0	0	55	62	.239	.324	.442
86	NY/AL		149	565	504	120	24	3	28	234	54	10	4	120	10	1	2	4	1	71	71	.238	.316	.464
87	NY/AL		150	582	522	122	26	3	32	250	53	9	2	111	9	2	3	1	3	76	87	.234	.305	.479
88	NY/AL		125	490	444	96	20	1	15	163	37	9	2	104	5	1	6	1	0	46	67	.216	.276	.367
89	NY/AL		74	244	223	44	10	0	4	66	19	4	2	43	2	0	0	0	1	19	16	.197	.266	.296
	SD/NL		50	168	148	29	7	0	3	45	18	4	1	39	3	1	0	2	0	12	14	.196	.287	.304
	YEAR		124	412	371	73	17	0	7	111	37	8	3	82	5	1	0	3	1	31	30	.197	.275	.299
90	SD/NL		128	446	398	101	23	2	7	149	39	3	3	66	12	2	4	1	3	29	38	.254	.322	.374
91	MIN/AL		121	393	365	102	20	0	6	140	21	3	3	55	9	2	2	1	2	38	36	.279	.322	.384
8 YR TOTALS			1002	3542	3185	753	161	14	121	1305	301	42	21	670	61	12	23	11	10	370	425	.236	.305	.410

Pagnozzi, Thomas Alan "Tom" — bats right — throws right — b.7/30/62 — 1991 positions: C 139, 1B 3

YR	TM/LG	CL	G	TPA	AB	H	2B	3B	HR	TB	BB	IBB	HB	SO	GDP	SH	SF	SB	CS	R	RBI	BA	OBA	SA
84	SPR/MID	A	114	442	396	112	20	4	10	170	31	3	4	75	9	4	7	3	4	57	68	.283	.336	.429
85	ARK/TEX	AA	41	153	139	43	7	1	5	67	13	1	0	21	8	1	0	0	0	15	29	.309	.368	.482
	LOU/AMA	AAA	76	296	268	72	13	2	5	104	21	1	3	47	11	0	4	0	0	29	40	.269	.324	.388
86	LOU/AMA	AAA	30	113	106	31	4	0	1	38	6	0	1	21	3	0	0	0	0	12	18	.292	.336	.358
87	LOU/AMA	AAA	84	359	320	100	20	2	14	166	30	3	3	50	16	0	6	0	0	53	71	.313	.370	.519
	STL/NL		27	53	48	9	1	0	2	16	4	2	0	13	0	1	0	1	0	17	15	.188	.250	.333
88	STL/NL		81	209	195	55	9	0	0	64	11	2	0	32	5	2	1	0	0	3	3	.282	.319	.328
89	STL/NL		52	88	80	12	2	0	0	14	6	2	1	19	7	0	1	0	0	3	3	.150	.216	.175
90	STL/NL		69	237	220	61	15	0	2	82	14	1	1	37	0	0	2	1	1	20	23	.277	.321	.373
91	STL/NL		140	510	459	121	24	5	2	161	36	6	4	63	10	6	5	9	13	38	57	.264	.319	.351
5 YR TOTALS			369	1097	1002	258	51	5	6	337	71	12	6	164	22	9	9	11	14	86	107	.257	.308	.336

Palmeiro, Rafael (Corrales) — bats left — throws left — b.9/24/64 — 1991 positions: 1B 157, DH 2

YR	TM/LG	CL	G	TPA	AB	H	2B	3B	HR	TB	BB	IBB	HB	SO	GDP	SH	SF	SB	CS	R	RBI	BA	OBA	SA
85	PEO/MID	A	73	315	279	83	22	4	5	128	31	2	2	34	4	1	2	9	3	34	51	.297	.369	.459
86	PIT/EAS	AA	140	579	509	156	29	2	12	225	54	13	2	32	8	1	13	15	7	66	95	.306	.367	.442
	CHI/NL		22	78	73	18	4	0	3	31	4	0	1	6	4	0	1	1	1	9	12	.247	.295	.425
87	IOW/AMA	AAA	57	244	214	64	14	3	11	117	22	1	3	22	2	1	4	4	2	36	30	.299	.366	.547
	CHI/NL		84	244	221	61	15	1	14	120	20	1	1	26	4	0	2	2	2	32	30	.276	.336	.543
88	CHI/NL		152	629	580	178	41	5	8	253	38	6	3	34	11	2	6	12	2	75	53	.307	.349	.436
89	TEX/AL		156	632	559	154	23	4	8	209	63	3	6	48	18	2	2	4	3	76	64	.275	.354	.374
90	TEX/AL		154	651	598	191	35	6	14	280	40	6	3	59	24	2	8	3	3	72	89	.319	.361	.468
91	TEX/AL		159	714	631	203	49	3	26	336	68	10	6	72	17	2	7	4	3	115	88	.322	.389	.532
6 YR TOTALS			727	2948	2662	805	167	19	73	1229	233	26	20	245	78	8	25	26	14	379	336	.302	.360	.462

Palmer, Dean William — bats right — throws right — b.12/27/68 — 1991 positions: 3B 50, OF 29, DH 5

YR	TM/LG	CL	G	TPA	AB	H	2B	3B	HR	TB	BB	IBB	HB	SO	GDP	SH	SF	SB	CS	R	RBI	BA	OBA	SA
86	RAN/GCL	R	50	192	163	34	7	1	0	43	22	0	5	34	3	0	2	6	3	19	12	.209	.318	.264
87	GAS/SAL	A	128	527	484	104	16	0	9	147	36	1	6	126	16	0	1	4	4	51	54	.215	.277	.304
88	CHA/FSL	A+	74	324	305	81	12	1	4	107	15	1	1	69	12	0	3	0	0	38	35	.266	.299	.351
89	TUL/TEX	AA	133	550	498	125	32	5	25	242	41	4	0	152	6	3	4	15	5	82	90	.251	.311	.486
	TEX/AL		16	20	19	2	0	0	0	2	0	0	0	12	0	0	0	0	0	0	1	.105	.100	.211
90	TUL/TEX	AA	7	29	24	7	0	1	3	18	4	1	0	10	0	0	1	0	1	4	9	.292	.414	.750
	OC/AMA	AAA	88	343	316	69	17	4	12	130	20	0	4	106	0	0	3	1	4	33	39	.218	.271	.411
91	OC/AMA	AAA	60	259	234	70	11	2	22	151	20	2	2	61	2	0	1	2	4	45	59	.299	.357	.645
	TEX/AL		81	304	268	50	9	2	15	108	32	0	3	98	4	1	0	0	2	38	37	.187	.281	.403
2 YR TOTALS			97	324	287	52	11	2	15	112	32	0	3	110	4	1	1	0	2	38	38	.181	.269	.390

Pappas, Erik Daniel — bats right — throws right — b.4/25/66 — 1991 positions: C 6

YR	TM/LG	CL	G	TPA	AB	H	2B	3B	HR	TB	BB	IBB	HB	SO	GDP	SH	SF	SB	CS	R	RBI	BA	OBA	SA
84	SAL/NWL	A−	56	215	177	43	3	3	1	55	31	0	3	26	1	3	1	10	5	24	15	.243	.363	.311
85	QC/MID	A	100	385	317	76	8	4	2	98	61	1	3	56	3	3	1	16	6	53	29	.240	.366	.309
86	PS/CAL	A+	74	310	248	61	16	2	5	96	56	1	0	58	7	1	4	9	5	40	38	.246	.382	.387
87	PS/CAL	A+	119	471	395	96	17	3	4	131	66	0	7	77	8	4	16	14	6	40	38	.243	.346	.332
88	MID/TEX	AA	83	314	275	76	17	1	4	109	29	0	2	53	6	4	2	7	3	40	34	.276	.345	.396
89	CHA/SOU	AA	119	434	354	106	31	1	16	187	66	1	8	50	8	4	2	7	8	69	49	.299	.419	.528

(continued)

Pappas, Erik Daniel (continued)

YR	TM/LG	CL	G	TPA	AB	H	2B	3B	HR	TB	BB	IBB	HB	SO	GDP	SH	SF	SB	CS	R	RBI	BA	OBA	SA
90	IOW/AMA	AAA	131	487	405	101	19	2	16	172	65	1	8	84	13	6	3	6	5	56	55	.249	.362	.425
91	CHI/NL		7	18	17	3	0	0	0	3	1	0	0	5	0	0	0	0	0	1	2	.176	.222	.176
	IOW/AMA	AAA	88	340	284	78	19	1	7	120	45	4	4	47	12	4	3	5	3	41	48	.275	.378	.423

Paredes, Johnny Alfonso (Isambert) — bats right — throws right — b.9/2/62 — 1991 positions: 2B 7, DH 2, 3B 1, SS 1

YR	TM/LG	CL	G	TPA	AB	H	2B	3B	HR	TB	BB	IBB	HB	SO	GDP	SH	SF	SB	CS	R	RBI	BA	OBA	SA
82	HEL/PIO	R+	34	118	105	32	2	1	1	41	13	1	0	10	3	0	0	6	1	17	7	.305	.381	.390
83	SPA/SAL	A	46	143	130	31	0	3	0	37	12	0	1	22	5	0	0	10	4	14	11	.238	.308	.285
84	WPB/FSL	A+	112	496	438	111	11	1	0	124	43	2	5	47	14	8	2	23	11	64	32	.253	.326	.283
85	JAC/SOU	AA	21	83	73	23	2	0	0	25	6	0	2	7	2	2	0	3	4	11	5	.315	.383	.342
	WPB/FSL	A+	101	391	322	84	7	4	2	105	49	2	9	49	6	9	2	31	11	65	34	.261	.372	.326
86	JAC/SOU	AA	122	533	472	135	15	5	6	178	51	0	5	44	11	4	1	22	10	86	34	.286	.361	.377
87	IND/AMA	AAA	130	552	493	154	19	6	8	209	44	0	3	57	13	10	2	30	11	80	47	.312	.371	.424
88	IND/AMA	AAA	101	442	400	118	17	3	4	153	30	2	4	56	3	4	4	43	6	69	46	.295	.347	.382
	MON/NL		35	104	91	17	2	0	0	22	9	0	3	17	1	1	0	5	2	6	10	.187	.282	.242
90	DET/AL		6	9	8	1	0	0	0	1	1	0	0	0	0	0	0	0	0	2	0	.125	.222	.125
	IND/AMA	AAA	94	378	322	84	7	1	3	102	42	0	1	38	3	6	2	20	7	46	17	.261	.355	.317
	MON/NL		3	7	6	2	1	0	0	3	1	0	0	0	0	0	0	0	0	0	1	.333	.429	.500
	YEAR		9	16	14	3	1	0	0	4	2	0	0	0	0	0	0	0	0	2	1	.214	.313	.286
91	TOL/INT	AAA	135	590	514	146	25	6	1	186	47	3	11	51	11	16	2	36	15	82	53	.284	.355	.362
	DET/AL		16	18	18	6	0	0	0	6	0	0	0	1	0	0	0	0	0	4	0	.333	.333	.333
3 YR TOTALS			**60**	**138**	**123**	**26**	**3**	**0**	**1**	**32**	**11**	**1**	**3**	**18**	**1**	**1**	**0**	**6**	**3**	**12**	**11**	**.211**	**.292**	**.260**

Parent, Mark Allen — bats right — throws right — b.9/16/61 — 1991 positions: C 3

YR	TM/LG	CL	G	TPA	AB	H	2B	3B	HR	TB	BB	IBB	HB	SO	GDP	SH	SF	SB	CS	R	RBI	BA	OBA	SA
84	BEA/TEX	AA	111	430	380	109	24	3	7	160	38	5	1	39	18	4	7	1	4	52	60	.287	.347	.421
85	LV/PCL	AAA	105	392	361	87	23	3	7	137	29	2	0	58	10	1	1	1	3	36	45	.241	.297	.380
86	LV/PCL	AAA	86	295	267	77	10	4	5	110	23	2	0	25	10	1	4	0	3	29	40	.288	.340	.412
	SD/NL		8	15	14	2	0	0	0	2	1	0	0	3	1	0	0	0	0	1	0	.143	.200	.143
87	LV/PCL	AAA	105	429	387	113	23	2	4	152	38	3	1	53	16	1	2	2	1	50	43	.292	.355	.393
	SD/NL		12	25	25	2	0	0	0	2	0	0	0	9	0	0	0	0	0	0	2	.080	.080	.080
88	SD/NL		41	125	118	23	3	0	6	44	6	0	0	23	1	0	1	0	0	9	15	.195	.232	.373
89	SD/NL		52	154	141	27	4	0	7	52	8	2	0	34	5	1	4	1	0	12	21	.191	.229	.369
90	SD/NL		65	208	189	42	11	0	3	62	16	3	0	29	2	3	0	1	0	13	16	.222	.283	.328
91	OC/AMA	AAA	5	9	8	2	0	0	0	2	1	0	0	0	1	0	0	0	0	0	1	.250	.222	.250
	TEX/AL		3	1	1	0	0	0	0	0	0	0	0	0	0	0	0	0	0	0	0	.000	.000	.000
6 YR TOTALS			**181**	**528**	**488**	**96**	**18**	**0**	**16**	**162**	**31**	**5**	**0**	**99**	**9**	**4**	**5**	**2**	**0**	**35**	**54**	**.197**	**.242**	**.332**

Parker, David Gene "Dave" — bats left — throws right — b.6/9/51 — 1991 positions: DH 130

YR	TM/LG	CL	G	TPA	AB	H	2B	3B	HR	TB	BB	IBB	HB	SO	GDP	SH	SF	SB	CS	R	RBI	BA	OBA	SA
73	PIT/NL		54	144	139	40	9	1	4	63	2	1	2	27	2	1	0	1	1	17	14	.288	.308	.453
74	PIT/NL		73	233	220	62	10	3	4	90	10	1	3	53	3	0	0	3	3	27	29	.282	.322	.409
75	PIT/NL		148	602	558	172	35	10	25	302	38	4	5	89	18	0	1	8	6	75	101	.308	.357	.541
76	PIT/NL		138	573	537	168	28	10	13	255	30	6	2	80	16	0	4	19	7	82	90	.313	.349	.475
77	PIT/NL		159	706	637	215	44	8	21	338	58	13	7	107	7	0	4	17	19	107	88	.338	.397	.531
78	PIT/NL		148	642	581	194	32	12	30	340	57	23	2	92	8	0	2	20	7	102	117	.334	.394	.585
79	PIT/NL		158	707	622	193	45	7	25	327	67	14	9	101	9	0	9	20	4	109	94	.310	.380	.526
80	PIT/NL		139	550	518	153	31	1	17	237	25	5	2	69	8	0	5	10	7	71	79	.295	.327	.458
81	PIT/NL		67	254	240	62	14	3	9	109	9	3	2	25	5	0	3	6	2	29	48	.258	.287	.454
82	PIT/NL		73	270	244	66	19	3	6	109	22	2	1	45	7	0	3	7	5	41	29	.270	.330	.447
83	PIT/NL		144	586	552	154	29	4	12	227	28	6	0	89	11	0	6	12	9	68	69	.279	.311	.411
84	CIN/NL		156	655	607	173	28	0	16	249	41	10	1	89	8	0	6	11	10	73	94	.285	.328	.410
85	CIN/NL		160	694	635	198	42	4	34	350	52	24	3	80	26	0	4	5	13	88	125	.312	.365	.551
86	CIN/NL		162	700	637	174	31	3	31	304	56	18	0	126	18	0	6	1	6	89	116	.273	.330	.477
87	CIN/NL		153	647	589	149	28	0	26	255	44	13	1	104	14	0	6	7	3	77	97	.253	.311	.433
88	OAK/AL		101	411	377	97	18	1	12	153	32	2	0	70	3	0	6	0	3	43	55	.257	.314	.406
89	OAK/AL		144	600	553	146	27	0	22	239	38	13	1	91	21	0	8	0	0	56	97	.264	.308	.432
90	MIL/AL		157	669	610	176	30	3	21	275	41	11	4	102	18	0	14	4	7	71	92	.289	.330	.451
91	CAL/AL		119	501	466	108	22	2	11	167	29	3	3	91	9	0	3	3	2	45	56	.232	.279	.358
	TOR/AL		13	40	36	12	4	0	0	16	4	0	0	7	0	0	0	0	0	2	3	.333	.400	.444
	YEAR		132	541	502	120	26	2	11	183	33	3	3	98	9	0	3	3	3	47	59	.239	.288	.365
19 YR TOTALS			**2466**	**10184**	**9358**	**2712**	**526**	**75**	**339**	**4405**	**683**	**170**	**56**	**1537**	**209**	**1**	**86**	**154**	**113**	**1272**	**1493**	**.290**	**.339**	**.471**

Parker, Richard Allen "Rick" — bats right — throws right — b.3/20/63 — 1991 positions: OF 4

YR	TM/LG	CL	G	TPA	AB	H	2B	3B	HR	TB	BB	IBB	HB	SO	GDP	SH	SF	SB	CS	R	RBI	BA	OBA	SA
85	BEN/NWL	A–	55	252	205	51	9	1	2	68	40	0	4	42	2	0	3	14	7	45	20	.249	.377	.332
86	SPA/SAL	A	62	273	233	69	7	3	5	97	36	0	2	39	7	2	0	14	9	39	28	.296	.395	.416
	CLE/FSL	A+	63	246	218	51	10	2	0	65	21	1	2	29	2	1	3	8	9	24	15	.234	.305	.298
87	CLE/FSL	A+	101	369	330	83	13	3	3	111	31	3	3	36	4	2	3	6	4	56	34	.252	.319	.336
88	REA/EAS	AA	116	408	362	93	13	3	3	121	36	2	3	50	6	1	6	24	6	50	47	.257	.324	.334
89	REA/EAS	AA	103	440	388	92	7	3	3	126	42	0	5	62	8	2	3	17	13	59	32	.237	.317	.325
	PHO/PCL	AAA	18	72	68	18	2	0	0	24	2	0	1	14	1	1	0	1	0	5	11	.265	.296	.353
90	PHO/PCL	AAA	44	195	173	58	7	4	1	76	20	0	0	25	1	1	0	18	10	38	18	.335	.410	.439
	SF/NL		54	121	107	26	5	0	2	37	10	0	1	25	0	1	0	8	6	19	14	.243	.314	.346

Parker, Richard Allen "Rick" (continued)

YR	TM/LG	CL	G	TPA	AB	H	2B	3B	HR	TB	BB	IBB	HB	SO	GDP	SH	SF	SB	CS	R	RBI	BA	OBA	SA
91	PHO/PCL	AAA	85	331	297	89	10	9	6	135	26	1	2	35	7	0	6	16	3	41	41	.300	.353	.455
	SF/NL		13	15	14	1	0	0	0	1	1	0	0	5	0	0	0	0	0	0	1	.071	.133	.071
2 YR TOTALS			**67**	**136**	**121**	**27**	**5**	**0**	**2**	**38**	**11**	**0**	**1**	**20**	**1**	**0**	**3**	**6**	**1**	**19**	**15**	**.223**	**.293**	**.314**

Parrish, Lance Michael — bats right — throws right — b.6/15/56 — 1991 positions: C 111, DH 5, 1B 3

YR	TM/LG	CL	G	TPA	AB	H	2B	3B	HR	TB	BB	IBB	HB	SO	GDP	SH	SF	SB	CS	R	RBI	BA	OBA	SA
77	DET/AL		12	51	46	9	2	0	3	20	5	0	0	12	2	0	0	0	0	10	7	.196	.275	.435
78	DET/AL		85	304	288	63	11	3	14	122	11	0	3	71	8	1	1	0	0	37	41	.219	.254	.424
79	DET/AL		143	548	493	136	26	3	19	225	49	2	2	105	15	3	1	6	7	65	65	.276	.343	.456
80	DET/AL		144	592	553	158	34	6	24	276	31	3	3	109	24	2	3	6	4	79	82	.286	.325	.499
81	DET/AL		96	384	348	85	18	2	10	137	34	4	1	52	16	1	1	2	3	39	46	.244	.311	.394
82	DET/AL		133	529	486	138	19	2	32	257	40	5	1	99	5	0	2	3	4	75	87	.284	.338	.529
83	DET/AL		155	663	605	163	42	3	27	292	44	7	1	106	21	0	13	1	3	80	114	.269	.314	.483
84	DET/AL		147	629	578	137	16	2	33	256	41	6	1	120	12	2	6	2	3	75	98	.237	.287	.443
85	DET/AL		140	600	549	150	27	1	28	263	41	5	2	90	10	3	5	2	6	64	98	.273	.323	.479
86	DET/AL		91	374	327	84	6	1	22	158	38	3	5	83	3	1	3	0	0	53	62	.257	.340	.483
87	PHI/NL		130	518	466	114	21	0	17	186	47	2	1	104	23	1	3	0	0	42	67	.245	.313	.399
88	PHI/NL		123	478	424	91	17	2	15	157	47	7	2	93	11	0	5	0	0	44	60	.215	.293	.370
89	CAL/AL		124	482	433	103	12	1	17	168	42	6	2	104	10	1	4	1	1	48	50	.238	.306	.388
90	CAL/AL		133	523	470	126	14	0	24	212	46	4	5	107	12	0	2	2	2	54	70	.268	.338	.451
91	CAL/AL		119	445	402	87	12	0	19	156	35	2	5	117	7	0	3	0	1	38	51	.216	.285	.388
15 YR TOTALS			**1775**	**7120**	**6468**	**1644**	**277**	**26**	**304**	**2885**	**551**	**58**	**34**	**1372**	**179**	**15**	**52**	**25**	**35**	**803**	**998**	**.254**	**.314**	**.446**

Pasqua, Daniel Anthony "Dan" — bats left — throws left — b.10/17/61 — 1991 positions: 1B 83, OF 59, DH 8

YR	TM/LG	CL	G	TPA	AB	H	2B	3B	HR	TB	BB	IBB	HB	SO	GDP	SH	SF	SB	CS	R	RBI	BA	OBA	SA
84	NAS/SOU	AA	136	561	460	112	14	3	33	231	95	7	3	148	8	0	3	5	2	78	91	.243	.374	.502
85	COL/INT	AAA	78	339	287	92	16	5	18	172	48	2	2	62	10	0	2	5	0	52	69	.321	.419	.599
	NY/AL		60	166	148	31	3	1	9	63	16	0	1	38	1	0	1	0	0	17	25	.209	.289	.426
86	COL/INT	AAA	32	142	110	32	3	3	6	59	32	0	0	29	2	0	1	1	1	25	20	.291	.451	.536
	NY/AL		102	332	280	82	17	0	16	147	47	3	3	78	4	1	1	2	0	44	45	.293	.399	.525
87	COL/INT	AAA	23	92	85	29	6	0	6	53	5	0	1	21	1	1	1	0	2	16	15	.341	.385	.624
	NY/AL		113	362	318	74	7	1	17	134	40	3	2	99	7	2	1	0	2	42	42	.233	.319	.421
88	CHI/AL		129	475	422	96	16	2	20	176	46	5	3	100	10	2	2	1	2	48	50	.227	.307	.417
89	CHI/AL		73	277	246	61	9	1	11	105	25	1	1	58	0	1	4	1	2	26	47	.248	.315	.427
90	CHI/AL		112	369	325	89	27	3	13	161	37	7	2	66	4	0	5	1	1	43	58	.274	.347	.495
91	CHI/AL		134	484	417	108	22	5	18	194	62	4	3	86	9	1	1	0	1	71	66	.259	.358	.465
7 YR TOTALS			**723**	**2465**	**2156**	**541**	**101**	**13**	**104**	**980**	**273**	**27**	**14**	**525**	**35**	**7**	**15**	**5**	**7**	**291**	**333**	**.251**	**.337**	**.455**

Patterson, John Allen bats right — throws right — b.2/11/67 — 1991 positions: 2B System SF/NL

YR	TM/LG	CL	G	TPA	AB	H	2B	3B	HR	TB	BB	IBB	HB	SO	GDP	SH	SF	SB	CS	R	RBI	BA	OBA	SA
88	EVE/NWL	A–	58	251	232	58	10	4	0	76	18	0	0	27	1	0	1	21	3	37	26	.250	.303	.328
90	SJ/CAL	A+	131	596	530	160	23	6	4	207	46	2	9	74	7	5	6	29	17	91	66	.302	.364	.391
91	SHR/TEX	AA	117	511	464	137	31	13	4	206	30	3	11	63	9	3	3	40	19	81	56	.295	.350	.444

Pecota, William Joseph "Bill" — bats right — throws right — b.2/16/60 — 1991 positions: 3B 102, 2B 34, SS 9, 1B 8, DH 2, OF 1, P–1

YR	TM/LG	CL	G	TPA	AB	H	2B	3B	HR	TB	BB	IBB	HB	SO	GDP	SH	SF	SB	CS	R	RBI	BA	OBA	SA
84	MEM/SOU	AA	145	655	543	131	19	2	9	181	99	2	3	72	11	7	3	43	15	84	50	.241	.360	.333
85	OMA/AMA	AAA	130	478	409	98	17	3	1	124	57	0	5	55	14	2	5	21	10	47	34	.240	.336	.303
86	OMA/AMA	AAA	139	529	474	125	26	2	4	167	37	3	8	45	8	7	3	21	8	48	54	.264	.326	.352
	KC/AL		12	34	29	6	2	0	0	8	3	0	1	3	1	0	1	0	2	3	2	.207	.294	.276
87	OMA/AMA	AAA	35	144	126	39	8	1	2	55	15	0	1	15	1	1	0	7	1	31	16	.310	.392	.437
	KC/AL		66	172	156	43	5	1	3	59	15	0	0	25	3	0	1	2	2	22	14	.276	.343	.378
88	KC/AL		90	206	178	37	3	1	1	49	18	0	2	34	1	7	1	5	2	25	15	.208	.286	.275
89	KC/AL		64	285	248	63	12	1	3	86	29	2	2	21	5	1	5	10	5	34	40	.254	.331	.347
	OMA/AMA	AAA	65	92	83	17	4	2	3	34	7	1	1	9	4	1	0	5	0	21	5	.205	.275	.410
90	OMA/AMA	AAA	29	137	116	35	6	0	4	53	17	1	3	17	3	0	1	11	1	30	13	.302	.401	.457
	KC/AL		87	280	240	58	15	2	5	92	33	0	1	39	5	6	0	8	5	43	20	.242	.336	.383
91	KC/AL		125	448	398	114	23	2	6	159	41	6	2	45	12	7	0	16	7	53	45	.286	.356	.399
6 YR TOTALS			**445**	**1232**	**1084**	**275**	**52**	**10**	**18**	**401**	**117**	**7**	**8**	**155**	**26**	**21**	**2**	**41**	**16**	**167**	**101**	**.254**	**.330**	**.370**

Pedre, Jorge Enrique — bats right — throws right — b.10/12/66 — 1991 positions: C 9, 1B 1

YR	TM/LG	CL	G	TPA	AB	H	2B	3B	HR	TB	BB	IBB	HB	SO	GDP	SH	SF	SB	CS	R	RBI	BA	OBA	SA
87	EUG/NWL	A–	64	262	233	63	15	0	13	117	16	2	12	48	10	0	1	2	1	28	66	.270	.347	.502
88	APP/MID	A	111	445	412	112	20	2	6	154	23	1	4	76	7	0	6	4	2	44	54	.272	.312	.374
89	BC/FSL	A+	55	228	208	68	17	2	5	104	13	1	4	31	2	0	3	1	2	39	40	.327	.373	.500
	MEM/SOU	AA	38	153	141	33	4	1	0	44	9	0	0	18	4	1	0	2	0	17	16	.234	.276	.312
90	MEM/SOU	AA	99	400	360	93	14	1	9	136	27	1	6	47	10	0	7	6	1	55	54	.258	.315	.378
91	MEM/SOU	AA	100	398	363	92	28	1	9	149	24	4	7	72	12	3	1	5	2	43	59	.253	.310	.410
	OMA/AMA	AAA	31	120	116	25	4	0	1	32	4	0	0	18	1	0	0	0	0	12	6	.216	.242	.276
	KC/AL		10	22	19	5	1	0	0	8	3	0	0	6	0	0	0	0	3	2	3	.263	.364	.421

Peguero, Julio Cesar — bats right — throws right — b.9/7/68 — 1991 positions: OF System PHI/NL

YR	TM/LG	CL	G	TPA	AB	H	2B	3B	HR	TB	BB	IBB	HB	SO	GDP	SH	SF	SB	CS	R	RBI	BA	OBA	SA
87	MAC/SAL	A	132	582	520	148	11	6	4	183	56	3	1	76	5	1	4	23	9	88	53	.285	.353	.352
88	SAL/CAR	A+	128	589	517	135	17	5	5	177	64	3	5	81	11	2	1	43	11	89	50	.261	.348	.342

(continued)

Peguero, Julio Cesar (continued)

YR	TM/LG	CL	G	TPA	AB	H	2B	3B	HR	TB	BB	IBB	HB	SO	GDP	SH	SF	SB	CS	R	RBI	BA	OBA	SA
89	HAR/EAS	AA	76	316	284	70	14	1	2	92	29	0	2	39	5	1	0	14	12	34	21	.246	.321	.324
90	HAR/EAS	AA	104	442	411	116	14	9	1	151	29	1	0	53	17	0	2	8	12	40	26	.282	.328	.367
	REA/EAS	AA	3	14	12	1	0	0	0	1	2	0	0	1	0	0	0	0	0	0	2	.083	.214	.083
91	SCR/INT	AAA	133	554	506	138	20	9	2	182	40	3	1	71	12	5	2	21	14	71	39	.273	.326	.360

Pena, Antonio Francisco (Padilla) "Tony" — bats right — throws right — b.6/4/57 — 1991 positions: C 140

YR	TM/LG	CL	G	TPA	AB	H	2B	3B	HR	TB	BB	IBB	HB	SO	GDP	SH	SF	SB	CS	R	RBI	BA	OBA	SA
80	PIT/NL		8	21	21	9	1	1	0	12	0	0	0	4	1	0	0	0	1	1	1	.429	.429	.571
81	PIT/NL		66	223	210	63	9	1	2	80	8	2	1	23	4	2	2	1	2	16	17	.300	.326	.381
82	PIT/NL		138	523	497	147	28	4	11	216	17	3	4	57	17	3	2	2	5	53	63	.296	.323	.435
83	PIT/NL		151	580	542	163	22	3	15	236	31	8	6	73	13	6	1	6	7	51	70	.301	.338	.435
84	PIT/NL		147	592	546	156	27	2	15	232	36	5	4	79	14	4	2	12	8	77	78	.286	.333	.425
85	PIT/NL		147	587	546	136	27	2	10	197	29	4	0	67	19	7	5	12	8	53	59	.249	.284	.361
86	PIT/NL		144	565	510	147	26	2	10	207	53	6	0	69	21	0	1	9	10	56	52	.288	.356	.406
87	LOU/AMA	AAA	2	8	8	3	0	0	0	3	0	0	0	2	0	0	0	0	0	0	0	.375	.375	.375
	STL/NL		116	425	384	82	13	4	5	118	36	9	1	54	19	2	2	6	1	40	44	.214	.281	.307
88	STL/NL		149	546	505	133	23	1	10	188	33	11	1	60	12	3	4	6	2	55	51	.263	.308	.372
89	STL/NL		141	464	424	110	17	2	4	143	35	19	1	33	19	2	1	5	3	36	37	.259	.318	.337
90	BOS/AL		143	540	491	129	19	1	7	171	43	3	1	71	23	2	3	8	6	62	56	.263	.322	.348
91	BOS/AL		141	512	464	107	23	2	5	149	37	1	4	53	23	4	3	8	5	45	48	.231	.291	.321
12 YR TOTALS			**1491**	**5578**	**5140**	**1382**	**235**	**25**	**94**	**1949**	**358**	**71**	**19**	**643**	**185**	**35**	**26**	**75**	**56**	**545**	**576**	**.269**	**.317**	**.379**

Pena, Geronimo (Martinez) — bats both — throws right — b.3/29/67 — 1991 positions: 2B 83, OF 4

YR	TM/LG	CL	G	TPA	AB	H	2B	3B	HR	TB	BB	IBB	HB	SO	GDP	SH	SF	SB	CS	R	RBI	BA	OBA	SA
86	JC/APP	R+	56	259	202	60	7	4	3	84	46	4	7	33	1	1	3	27	3	55	20	.297	.438	.416
87	SAV/SAL	A	134	590	505	136	28	3	9	197	73	6	8	98	6	1	3	80	21	95	51	.269	.368	.390
88	SP/FSL	A+	130	593	484	125	25	10	4	182	88	3	8	103	5	8	5	35	35	82	35	.258	.378	.376
89	SP/FSL	A+	6	27	21	4	1	0	0	5	3	0	3	6	0	0	0	2	3	2	2	.190	.370	.238
	ARK/TEX	AA	77	320	267	79	16	8	9	138	38	3	3	68	0	3	4	14	6	61	44	.296	.394	.517
90	LOU/AMA	AAA	118	484	390	97	24	6	6	151	69	0	18	116	3	3	4	24	12	65	35	.249	.383	.387
	STL/NL		18	51	45	11	2	0	0	13	4	0	1	14	0	0	1	1	1	5	2	.244	.314	.289
91	STL/NL		104	212	185	45	8	3	5	74	18	1	5	45	0	1	3	15	5	38	17	.243	.322	.400
2 YR TOTALS			**122**	**263**	**230**	**56**	**10**	**3**	**5**	**87**	**22**	**1**	**6**	**59**	**0**	**1**	**4**	**16**	**6**	**43**	**19**	**.243**	**.321**	**.378**

Pendleton, Terry Lee — bats both — throws right — b.7/16/60 — 1991 positions: 3B 148

YR	TM/LG	CL	G	TPA	AB	H	2B	3B	HR	TB	BB	IBB	HB	SO	GDP	SH	SF	SB	CS	R	RBI	BA	OBA	SA
84	LOU/AMA	AAA	91	358	330	98	23	5	4	143	24	1	0	51	4	1	3	6	7	52	44	.297	.342	.433
	STL/NL		67	283	262	85	16	3	1	110	16	3	0	32	7	0	5	20	5	37	33	.324	.357	.420
85	STL/NL		149	602	559	134	16	3	5	171	37	4	0	75	18	3	3	17	12	56	69	.240	.285	.306
86	STL/NL		159	626	578	138	26	5	1	177	34	10	1	59	12	6	7	24	6	56	59	.239	.279	.306
87	STL/NL		159	667	583	167	29	4	12	240	70	6	2	74	18	3	9	19	12	82	96	.286	.360	.412
88	STL/NL		110	421	391	99	20	2	6	141	21	4	2	51	9	4	3	3	3	44	53	.253	.293	.361
89	STL/NL		162	661	613	162	28	5	13	239	44	3	0	81	16	2	2	9	5	83	74	.264	.313	.390
90	STL/NL		121	484	447	103	20	2	6	145	30	8	1	58	12	0	6	7	5	46	58	.230	.277	.324
91	ATL/NL		153	644	586	187	34	8	22	303	43	8	1	70	16	7	7	10	2	94	86	.319	.363	.517
8 YR TOTALS			**1080**	**4388**	**4019**	**1075**	**189**	**32**	**66**	**1526**	**295**	**46**	**7**	**500**	**108**	**25**	**42**	**109**	**50**	**498**	**528**	**.267**	**.316**	**.380**

Perezchica, Antonio Llamas (Gonzales) "Tony" — bats right — throws right — b.4/20/66 — 1991 positions: SS 19, 3B 3, 2B 2

YR	TM/LG	CL	G	TPA	AB	H	2B	3B	HR	TB	BB	IBB	HB	SO	GDP	SH	SF	SB	CS	R	RBI	BA	OBA	SA
84	EVE/NWL	A-	33	129	119	23	6	1	0	31	6	0	1	24	4	1	2	0	0	10	10	.193	.234	.261
85	CLI/MID	A	127	500	452	109	21	8	4	158	28	0	9	77	9	6	5	23	7	54	40	.241	.296	.350
86	FRE/CAL	A+	126	513	452	126	30	8	9	199	35	0	14	91	11	10	2	18	6	65	54	.279	.348	.440
87	SHR/TEX	AA	89	361	332	106	24	1	11	165	19	4	4	74	10	3	3	3	3	44	47	.319	.360	.497
88	PHO/PCL	AAA	134	574	517	158	18	10	9	223	44	1	3	125	16	7	3	10	13	79	64	.306	.362	.431
	SF/NL		7	11	8	1	0	0	0	1	2	0	0	1	0	0	1	0	0	1	1	.125	.273	.125
89	PHO/PCL	AAA	94	336	307	71	11	3	8	112	15	0	5	65	8	2	7	5	4	40	33	.231	.272	.365
90	SF/NL		4	4	3	1	0	0	0	1	1	0	0	2	0	0	0	0	0	1	0	.333	.500	.333
	PHO/PCL	AAA	105	437	392	105	22	6	9	166	34	3	7	76	8	0	4	8	5	55	49	.268	.334	.423
91	PHO/PCL	AAA	51	219	191	56	10	4	8	98	18	0	6	43	4	1	3	1	0	41	34	.293	.367	.513
	SF/NL		23	50	48	11	4	1	0	17	2	0	0	12	0	1	0	1	0	2	3	.229	.260	.354
	CLE/AL		17	25	22	8	2	0	0	10	3	0	0	5	0	0	0	0	0	4	0	.364	.440	.455
	YEAR		40	75	70	19	6	1	0	27	5	0	0	17	0	1	0	1	0	6	3	.271	.320	.386
3 YR TOTALS			**51**	**90**	**81**	**21**	**6**	**1**	**0**	**29**	**8**	**0**	**0**	**20**	**0**	**0**	**1**	**0**	**1**	**8**	**4**	**.259**	**.322**	**.358**

Perry, Gerald June — bats left — throws right — b.10/30/60 — 1991 positions: 1B 61, OF 5

YR	TM/LG	CL	G	TPA	AB	H	2B	3B	HR	TB	BB	IBB	HB	SO	GDP	SH	SF	SB	CS	R	RBI	BA	OBA	SA
83	ATL/NL		27	45	39	14	2	0	1	19	5	0	0	4	1	0	1	0	1	5	6	.359	.422	.487
84	ATL/NL		122	419	347	92	12	2	7	129	61	5	2	38	9	2	7	15	12	52	47	.265	.372	.372
85	ATL/NL		110	262	238	51	5	0	3	65	23	1	0	28	7	0	1	9	5	22	13	.214	.282	.273
86	RIC/INT	AAA	107	449	384	125	30	5	10	195	58	8	4	41	13	0	3	22	11	69	75	.326	.416	.508
	ATL/NL		29	80	70	19	2	0	2	27	8	1	0	4	4	1	1	0	1	6	11	.271	.342	.386
87	ATL/NL		142	590	533	144	35	2	12	219	48	1	1	63	18	0	5	42	16	77	74	.270	.329	.411
88	ATL/NL		141	595	547	164	29	1	8	219	36	9	3	49	18	0	10	29	14	61	74	.300	.338	.400
89	ATL/NL		72	303	266	67	11	0	4	90	32	5	3	28	5	0	2	10	6	24	21	.252	.337	.338

Perry, Gerald June (continued)

YR	TM/LG	CL	G	TPA	AB	H	2B	3B	HR	TB	BB	IBB	HB	SO	GDP	SH	SF	SB	CS	R	RBI	BA	OBA	SA
90	KC/AL		133	512	465	118	22	2	8	168	39	4	3	56	14	0	5	17	4	57	57	.254	.313	.361
91	STL/NL		109	267	242	58	8	4	6	92	22	1	0	34	2	0	3	15	8	29	36	.240	.300	.380
9 YR TOTALS			**885**	**3073**	**2747**	**727**	**126**	**11**	**51**	**1028**	**274**	**27**	**10**	**304**	**78**	**7**	**35**	**137**	**67**	**333**	**339**	**.265**	**.330**	**.374**

Petralli, Eugene James "Geno" — bats left — throws right — b.9/25/59 — 1991 positions: C 66, 3B 7, DH 5

YR	TM/LG	CL	G	TPA	AB	H	2B	3B	HR	TB	BB	IBB	HB	SO	GDP	SH	SF	SB	CS	R	RBI	BA	OBA	SA
82	TOR/AL		16	49	44	16	2	0	0	18	4	0	0	6	1	1	0	0	0	3	1	.364	.417	.409
83	TOR/AL		6	5	4	0	0	0	0	0	1	0	0	1	0	0	0	0	0	0	0	.000	.200	.000
84	TOR/AL		3	3	3	0	0	0	0	0	0	0	0	0	0	0	0	0	0	0	0	.000	.000	.000
	MAI/INT	AAA	23	96	83	18	3	0	0	21	13	2	0	10	5	0	0	0	0	9	5	.217	.323	.253
85	MAI/INT	AAA	2	8	7	1	0	0	0	1	0	0	0	0	1	0	0	0	0	0	1	.143	.143	.143
	OC/AMA	AAA	27	91	80	21	8	0	1	32	10	1	0	9	3	1	0	0	0	11	5	.262	.344	.400
	TEX/AL		42	116	100	27	2	0	0	29	8	0	1	12	4	3	4	0	1	7	11	.270	.319	.290
86	TEX/AL		69	142	137	35	9	3	2	56	5	0	0	14	7	0	0	3	0	17	18	.255	.282	.409
87	TEX/AL		101	232	202	61	11	2	7	97	27	2	2	29	4	0	1	0	2	28	31	.302	.388	.480
88	TEX/AL		129	400	351	99	14	2	7	138	41	5	2	52	12	1	5	0	1	35	36	.282	.356	.393
89	TUL/TEX	AA	5	15	13	3	0	0	1	6	2	0	0	2	1	0	0	0	0	2	1	.231	.333	.462
	TEX/AL		70	205	184	56	7	0	4	75	17	1	2	24	5	1	1	0	0	18	23	.304	.368	.408
90	TEX/AL		133	382	325	83	13	1	0	98	50	3	3	49	12	1	3	0	2	28	21	.255	.357	.302
91	OC/AMA	AAA	4	17	15	4	1	0	0	5	2	0	0	1	1	0	0	0	0	1	2	.267	.353	.333
	TEX/AL		87	228	199	54	8	1	2	70	21	1	0	25	4	7	1	2	1	21	20	.271	.339	.352
10 YR TOTALS			**656**	**1762**	**1549**	**431**	**66**	**9**	**22**	**581**	**174**	**12**	**10**	**212**	**49**	**14**	**15**	**6**	**6**	**157**	**161**	**.278**	**.352**	**.375**

Pettis, Gary George — bats both — throws right — b.4/3/58 — 1991 positions: OF 126, DH 3

YR	TM/LG	CL	G	TPA	AB	H	2B	3B	HR	TB	BB	IBB	HB	SO	GDP	SH	SF	SB	CS	R	RBI	BA	OBA	SA
82	CAL/AL		10	5	5	1	0	0	1	4	0	0	0	0	0	0	0	0	0	5	1	.200	.200	.800
83	CAL/AL		22	93	85	25	2	3	3	42	7	0	0	15	1	1	0	8	3	19	6	.294	.348	.494
84	CAL/AL		140	466	397	90	11	6	2	119	60	1	3	115	4	5	1	48	15	63	29	.227	.332	.300
85	CAL/AL		125	516	443	114	10	8	1	143	62	0	1	125	5	9	2	56	9	67	32	.257	.347	.323
86	CAL/AL		154	628	539	139	23	4	5	185	69	2	0	132	7	15	5	50	13	93	58	.258	.339	.343
87	EDM/PCL	AAA	8	19	16	2	1	0	0	3	3	0	0	5	0	0	0	3	1	6	1	.125	.263	.188
	CAL/AL		133	448	394	82	13	2	1	102	52	0	1	124	8	1	0	24	5	49	17	.208	.302	.259
88	DET/AL		129	512	458	96	14	4	3	127	47	0	1	85	3	6	0	44	10	65	36	.210	.285	.277
89	TOL/INT	AAA	6	28	21	7	1	0	1	11	7	0	0	2	0	0	0	4	3	6	3	.333	.500	.524
	DET/AL		119	536	444	114	8	6	1	137	84	0	0	106	14	8	0	43	15	77	18	.257	.375	.309
90	TEX/AL		136	498	423	101	16	8	3	142	57	0	4	118	6	11	3	38	15	66	31	.239	.333	.336
91	TEX/AL		137	343	282	61	7	5	0	78	54	0	0	91	4	6	1	29	13	37	19	.216	.341	.277
10 YR TOTALS			**1105**	**4045**	**3470**	**823**	**104**	**46**	**20**	**1079**	**492**	**3**	**9**	**913**	**52**	**62**	**12**	**340**	**100**	**541**	**247**	**.237**	**.332**	**.311**

Phillips, Keith Anthony "Tony" — bats both — throws right — b.4/25/59 — 1991 positions: OF 56, 3B 46, 2B 36, DH 18, SS 13

YR	TM/LG	CL	G	TPA	AB	H	2B	3B	HR	TB	BB	IBB	HB	SO	GDP	SH	SF	SB	CS	R	RBI	BA	OBA	SA
82	OAK/AL		40	100	81	17	2	2	0	23	12	0	2	26	0	5	0	2	3	11	8	.210	.326	.284
83	OAK/AL		148	476	412	102	12	3	4	132	48	0	2	70	5	11	3	16	5	54	35	.248	.327	.320
84	OAK/AL		154	505	451	120	24	3	4	162	42	1	0	86	5	7	5	10	6	62	37	.266	.325	.359
85	TAC/PCL	AAA	20	78	69	9	1	0	0	10	8	1	0	28	1	0	1	3	0	9	5	.130	.218	.145
	OAK/AL		42	178	161	45	12	2	4	73	13	0	3	34	1	3	1	3	2	23	17	.280	.331	.453
86	OAK/AL		118	532	441	113	14	5	5	152	76	0	3	82	2	9	3	15	10	76	52	.256	.367	.345
87	TAC/PCL	AAA	7	30	26	9	2	1	1	16	4	0	0	3	0	0	0	1	0	5	6	.346	.433	.615
	OAK/AL		111	441	379	91	20	0	10	141	57	1	0	76	9	2	3	7	6	48	46	.240	.337	.372
88	TAC/PCL	AAA	16	73	59	16	0	0	2	22	12	0	0	13	0	2	0	0	3	10	8	.271	.394	.373
	OAK/AL		79	251	212	43	8	4	2	65	36	0	1	50	6	1	1	0	2	32	17	.203	.320	.307
89	OAK/AL		143	524	451	118	15	6	4	157	58	2	3	66	17	5	7	3	3	48	47	.262	.345	.348
90	DET/AL		152	687	573	144	23	5	8	201	99	0	4	85	10	9	2	19	9	97	55	.251	.364	.351
91	DET/AL		146	655	564	160	28	4	17	247	79	3	6	95	8	3	6	10	5	87	72	.284	.371	.438
10 YR TOTALS			**1133**	**4349**	**3725**	**953**	**158**	**34**	**58**	**1353**	**520**	**10**	**18**	**670**	**63**	**55**	**31**	**85**	**56**	**538**	**386**	**.256**	**.347**	**.363**

Plantier, Phillip Alan "Phil" — bats left — throws right — b.1/27/69 — 1991 positions: OF 40, DH 5

YR	TM/LG	CL	G	TPA	AB	H	2B	3B	HR	TB	BB	IBB	HB	SO	GDP	SH	SF	SB	CS	R	RBI	BA	OBA	SA
87	ELM/NYP	A–	28	91	80	14	2	0	2	22	9	0	0	9	4	1	1	0	0	7	9	.175	.256	.275
88	WH/FSL	A+	111	399	337	81	13	1	4	108	51	6	5	62	4	3	3	0	2	29	32	.240	.346	.320
89	LYN/CAR	A+	131	528	443	133	26	1	27	242	74	7	7	122	2	0	4	4	5	73	105	.300	.405	.546
90	PAW/INT	AAA	123	507	430	109	22	3	33	236	62	3	9	148	4	3	3	1	8	83	79	.253	.357	.549
	BOS/AL		14	21	15	2	1	0	0	3	4	0	1	6	1	0	1	0	0	1	3	.133	.333	.200
91	PAW/INT	AAA	84	368	298	91	19	4	16	166	65	2	5	64	4	0	0	2	1	69	61	.305	.438	.557
	BOS/AL		53	174	148	49	7	1	11	91	23	2	1	38	2	0	2	1	0	28	38	.313	.410	.577
2 YR TOTALS			**67**	**195**	**163**	**51**	**8**	**1**	**11**	**94**	**27**	**2**	**2**	**44**	**3**	**0**	**3**	**1**	**0**	**28**	**38**	**.313**	**.410**	**.577**

Polonia, Luis Andrew (Almonte) — bats left — throws left — b.12/10/64 — 1991 positions: OF 143, DH 4

YR	TM/LG	CL	G	TPA	AB	H	2B	3B	HR	TB	BB	IBB	HB	SO	GDP	SH	SF	SB	CS	R	RBI	BA	OBA	SA
84	MAD/MID	A	135	601	528	162	21	10	8	227	57	7	5	95	5	9	2	55	24	103	64	.307	.378	.430
85	HUN/SOU	AA	130	584	515	149	15	18	2	206	59	3	0	54	5	6	4	39	20	82	36	.289	.360	.400
86	TAC/PCL	AAA	134	610	549	165	20	4	3	202	52	2	3	60	12	2	4	36	21	98	63	.301	.362	.368
87	TAC/PCL	AAA	14	71	56	18	1	2	0	23	14	1	0	6	1	0	1	4	2	18	8	.321	.451	.411
	OAK/AL		125	469	435	125	16	10	4	173	32	1	0	64	4	1	1	29	7	78	49	.287	.335	.398

(continued)

Polonia, Luis Andrew (Almonte) (continued)

YR	TM/LG	CL	G	TPA	AB	H	2B	3B	HR	TB	BB	IBB	HB	SO	GDP	SH	SF	SB	CS	R	RBI	BA	OBA	SA
88	TAC/PCL	AAA	65	287	254	85	13	5	2	114	29	1	1	28	0	0	3	31	15	58	27	.335	.401	.449
	OAK/AL		84	313	288	84	11	4	2	109	21	0	0	40	3	2	2	24	9	51	27	.292	.338	.378
89	OAK/AL		59	218	206	59	6	4	1	76	9	0	0	15	5	2	1	13	4	31	17	.286	.315	.369
	NY/AL		66	248	227	71	11	2	2	92	16	1	2	29	8	0	3	9	4	39	29	.313	.359	.405
	YEAR		125	466	433	130	17	6	3	168	25	1	2	44	13	2	4	22	8	70	46	.300	.338	.388
90	NY/AL		11	23	22	7	0	0	0	7	0	0	0	1	1	0	1	1	0	2	3	.318	.304	.318
	CAL/AL		109	413	381	128	7	9	2	159	25	1	1	42	8	3	3	20	14	50	32	.336	.376	.417
	YEAR		120	436	403	135	7	9	2	166	25	1	1	43	9	3	4	21	14	52	35	.335	.372	.412
91	CAL/AL		150	662	604	179	28	8	2	229	52	4	1	74	11	2	3	48	23	92	50	.296	.352	.379
5 YR TOTALS			**604**	**2346**	**2163**	**653**	**79**	**37**	**13**	**845**	**155**	**7**	**4**	**265**	**40**	**10**	**14**	**144**	**61**	**343**	**207**	**.302**	**.348**	**.391**

Powell, Alonzo Sidney — bats right — throws right — b.12/12/64 — 1991 positions: OF 40, 1B 7, DH 7

YR	TM/LG	CL	G	TPA	AB	H	2B	3B	HR	TB	BB	IBB	HB	SO	GDP	SH	SF	SB	CS	R	RBI	BA	OBA	SA
83	CLI/MID	A	36	132	113	22	5	1	0	29	15	1	2	27	2	2	0	2	1	14	9	.195	.300	.257
	GF/PIO	R+	51	164	149	33	2	2	1	42	12	1	1	34	1	2	0	10	4	13	16	.221	.284	.282
84	EVE/NWL	A-	6	20	17	3	1	0	1	7	1	0	0	3	1	0	2	0	0	2	4	.176	.200	.412
	CLI/MID	A	47	170	149	37	3	2	1	47	19	0	0	31	3	2	0	0	0	22	10	.248	.333	.315
85	SJ/CAL	A+	136	556	473	122	27	6	9	188	71	3	3	118	11	3	6	34	11	79	62	.258	.354	.397
86	WPB/FSL	A+	23	99	76	25	7	1	4	46	22	0	0	16	2	0	1	5	1	20	18	.329	.475	.605
	JAC/SOU	AA	105	460	402	121	21	5	15	197	49	3	4	78	10	2	3	15	11	67	80	.301	.380	.490
87	MON/NL		14	46	41	8	3	0	0	11	5	0	0	17	0	0	0	0	0	3	4	.195	.283	.268
	IND/AMA	AAA	90	370	331	99	14	10	19	190	32	1	1	68	7	3	3	12	8	64	74	.299	.360	.574
88	IND/AMA	AAA	88	315	282	74	18	3	4	110	28	0	0	72	7	2	3	10	8	31	39	.262	.326	.390
89	WPB/FSL	A+	12	49	41	13	4	3	1	26	7	2	0	3	1	0	1	1	1	7	8	.317	.408	.634
	IND/AMA	AAA	121	467	423	98	26	5	13	173	38	2	2	106	6	1	3	9	6	50	59	.232	.296	.409
90	POR/PCL	AAA	107	423	376	121	25	3	8	176	40	1	6	79	9	0	3	23	11	56	62	.322	.390	.468
91	CAL/PCL	AAA	53	228	192	72	18	7	7	125	31	2	0	33	3	0	5	2	6	45	43	.375	.452	.651
	SEA/AL		57	125	111	24	6	1	3	41	11	0	1	24	1	0	2	0	2	16	12	.216	.288	.369
2 YR TOTALS			**71**	**171**	**152**	**32**	**9**	**1**	**3**	**52**	**16**	**0**	**1**	**41**	**1**	**0**	**2**	**0**	**2**	**19**	**16**	**.211**	**.287**	**.342**

Presley, James Arthur "Jim" — bats right — throws right — b.10/23/61 — 1991 positions: 3B 16

YR	TM/LG	CL	G	TPA	AB	H	2B	3B	HR	TB	BB	IBB	HB	SO	GDP	SH	SF	SB	CS	R	RBI	BA	OBA	SA
84	SLC/PCL	AAA	69	287	265	84	13	4	13	144	15	1	1	46	8	0	6	1	1	43	56	.317	.348	.543
	SEA/AL		70	259	251	57	12	1	10	101	6	1	1	63	4	0	1	1	1	27	36	.227	.247	.402
85	SEA/AL		155	625	570	157	33	1	28	276	44	9	1	100	29	1	9	2	2	71	84	.275	.324	.484
86	SEA/AL		155	660	616	163	33	4	27	285	32	3	4	172	18	3	5	0	4	83	107	.265	.303	.463
87	SEA/AL		152	622	575	142	23	6	24	249	38	1	4	157	15	1	4	2	0	78	88	.247	.296	.433
88	SEA/AL		150	592	544	125	26	0	14	193	36	1	4	114	14	3	5	3	5	50	62	.230	.280	.355
89	SEA/AL		117	417	390	92	20	1	12	150	21	2	1	107	12	3	2	0	0	42	41	.236	.275	.385
90	ATL/NL		140	577	541	131	34	1	19	224	29	0	3	130	10	0	4	1	1	59	72	.242	.282	.414
91	SD/NL		20	66	59	8	0	0	1	11	4	1	1	16	2	1	0	1	1	3	5	.136	.200	.186
	OC/AMA	AAA	51	228	207	56	10	2	6	88	16	0	2	64	5	2	1	1	0	30	29	.271	.327	.425
8 YR TOTALS			**959**	**3818**	**3546**	**875**	**181**	**14**	**135**	**1489**	**210**	**18**	**19**	**859**	**104**	**12**	**31**	**9**	**14**	**413**	**495**	**.247**	**.290**	**.420**

Prince, Thomas Albert "Tom" — bats right — throws right — b.8/13/64 — 1991 positions: C 19, 1B 1

YR	TM/LG	CL	G	TPA	AB	H	2B	3B	HR	TB	BB	IBB	HB	SO	GDP	SH	SF	SB	CS	R	RBI	BA	OBA	SA
84	PIR/GCL	R	18	57	48	11	0	0	1	14	8	0	1	10	0	0	0	1	0	4	6	.229	.351	.292
	WAT/NYP	A-	23	80	69	14	3	0	2	23	9	0	1	13	1	1	0	0	0	6	13	.203	.304	.333
85	MAC/SAL	A	124	474	360	75	20	1	10	127	96	1	12	92	8	1	5	13	3	60	42	.208	.387	.353
86	PW/CAR	A+	121	457	395	100	34	1	10	166	50	1	7	74	5	3	2	4	5	59	47	.253	.346	.420
87	HAR/EAS	AA	113	430	365	112	23	2	6	157	51	2	8	46	16	4	2	6	3	41	54	.307	.401	.430
	PIT/NL		4	9	9	2	1	0	1	6	0	0	0	2	0	0	0	0	0	1	2	.222	.222	.667
88	BUF/AMA	AAA	86	338	304	79	16	0	14	137	23	2	7	53	6	3	1	3	6	35	42	.260	.325	.451
	PIT/NL		29	80	74	13	2	0	0	15	4	0	0	15	5	2	0	0	0	3	6	.176	.218	.203
89	PIT/NL		21	59	52	7	4	0	0	11	6	1	0	12	1	0	1	1	1	1	5	.135	.220	.212
	BUF/AMA	AAA	65	212	183	37	8	1	6	65	22	1	2	30	4	1	4	2	3	21	33	.202	.289	.355
90	BUF/AMA	AAA	94	334	284	64	13	0	7	98	39	0	5	47	6	3	3	4	7	38	37	.225	.326	.345
	PIT/NL		4	11	10	1	0	0	0	1	1	0	0	2	0	0	0	0	1	1	0	.100	.182	.100
91	BUF/AMA	AAA	80	270	221	46	8	3	6	78	37	1	7	30	4	2	3	3	4	29	32	.208	.336	.353
	PIT/NL		26	42	34	9	3	0	1	15	7	0	1	3	3	0	0	0	0	4	2	.265	.405	.441
5 YR TOTALS			**84**	**201**	**179**	**32**	**10**	**0**	**2**	**48**	**18**	**1**	**1**	**34**	**9**	**2**	**1**	**1**	**2**	**10**	**15**	**.179**	**.256**	**.268**

Puckett, Kirby — bats right — throws right — b.3/14/61 — 1991 positions: OF 152

YR	TM/LG	CL	G	TPA	AB	H	2B	3B	HR	TB	BB	IBB	HB	SO	GDP	SH	SF	SB	CS	R	RBI	BA	OBA	SA
84	TOL/INT	AAA	21	87	80	21	2	0	1	26	4	0	0	14	4	2	1	8	2	9	5	.262	.294	.325
	MIN/AL		128	583	557	165	12	5	0	187	16	1	4	69	11	4	2	14	7	63	31	.296	.320	.336
85	MIN/AL		161	744	691	199	29	13	4	266	41	0	4	87	9	5	3	21	12	80	74	.288	.330	.385
86	MIN/AL		161	723	680	223	37	6	31	365	34	4	7	99	14	2	0	20	12	119	96	.328	.366	.537
87	MIN/AL		157	668	624	207	32	5	28	333	32	7	6	91	16	0	6	12	7	96	99	.332	.367	.534
88	MIN/AL		158	691	657	234	42	5	24	358	23	4	2	83	17	0	9	6	7	109	121	.356	.375	.545
89	MIN/AL		159	684	635	215	45	4	9	295	41	9	3	59	21	0	5	11	4	75	85	.339	.379	.465
90	MIN/AL		146	615	551	164	40	3	12	246	57	11	3	73	15	1	3	5	4	82	80	.298	.365	.446
91	MIN/AL		152	661	611	195	29	6	15	281	31	4	4	78	14	8	7	11	5	92	89	.319	.352	.460
8 YR TOTALS			**1222**	**5369**	**5006**	**1602**	**266**	**47**	**123**	**2331**	**275**	**40**	**33**	**639**	**130**	**20**	**35**	**100**	**58**	**716**	**675**	**.320**	**.357**	**.466**

Puhl, Terry Stephen — bats left — throws right — b.7/8/56 — 1991 positions: DH 2, OF 1

YR	TM/LG	CL	G	TPA	AB	H	2B	3B	HR	TB	BB	IBB	HB	SO	GDP	SH	SF	SB	CS	R	RBI	BA	OBA	SA
77	HOU/NL		60	265	229	69	13	5	0	92	30	0	1	31	3	5	0	10	1	40	10	.301	.385	.402
78	HOU/NL		149	647	585	169	25	6	3	215	48	5	4	46	11	3	7	32	14	87	35	.289	.343	.368
79	HOU/NL		157	672	600	172	22	4	4	226	58	8	8	46	7	8	2	30	22	87	49	.287	.352	.377
80	HOU/NL		141	608	535	151	24	5	13	224	60	3	4	52	3	6	3	27	11	75	55	.282	.357	.419
81	HOU/NL		96	394	350	88	19	4	3	124	31	5	4	49	3	4	5	22	4	43	28	.251	.315	.354
82	HOU/NL		145	567	507	133	17	9	8	192	51	2	2	49	6	5	2	17	9	64	50	.262	.331	.379
83	HOU/NL		137	512	465	136	25	7	8	199	36	2	2	48	4	1	4	24	11	66	44	.292	.343	.428
84	HOU/NL		132	519	449	135	19	7	9	195	59	12	1	45	5	6	4	13	8	66	55	.301	.380	.434
85	HOU/NL		57	220	194	55	14	3	2	81	18	4	1	23	0	4	3	6	2	34	23	.284	.343	.418
86	HOU/NL		81	193	172	42	10	0	3	61	15	1	0	24	6	4	2	3	2	17	14	.244	.302	.355
87	HOU/NL		90	134	122	28	5	0	2	39	11	0	0	16	3	1	0	1	1	9	15	.230	.293	.320
88	HOU/NL		113	272	234	71	7	2	3	91	35	3	1	30	0	1	1	22	4	42	19	.303	.395	.389
89	HOU/NL		121	406	354	96	25	4	0	129	45	3	1	39	7	4	2	9	8	41	27	.271	.353	.364
90	HOU/NL		37	49	41	12	1	0	0	13	5	0	1	7	0	1	1	1	2	5	8	.293	.375	.317
91	KC/AL		15	21	18	4	0	0	0	4	3	1	0	2	1	0	0	0	0	0	3	.222	.333	.222
15 YR TOTALS			1531	5479	4855	1361	226	56	62	1885	505	49	26	507	59	57	36	217	99	676	435	**.280**	**.349**	**.388**

Pulliam, Harvey Jerome — bats right — throws right — b.10/20/67 — 1991 positions: OF 15

YR	TM/LG	CL	G	TPA	AB	H	2B	3B	HR	TB	BB	IBB	HB	SO	GDP	SH	SF	SB	CS	R	RBI	BA	OBA	SA
86	ROY/GCL	R	48	184	168	35	3	0	4	50	8	1	3	33	9	2	3	3	2	14	23	.208	.253	.298
87	APP/MID	A	110	428	395	109	20	1	9	158	26	0	3	79	10	1	3	21	7	54	55	.276	.323	.400
88	BC/FSL	A+	132	501	457	111	19	4	4	150	34	3	2	87	13	2	3	21	11	56	42	.243	.301	.328
89	OMA/AMA	AAA	7	25	22	4	2	0	0	6	3	0	0	6	0	0	0	0	0	3	2	.182	.280	.273
	MEM/SOU	AA	116	469	417	121	28	8	10	195	44	4	5	65	12	0	3	5	5	67	67	.290	.362	.468
90	OMA/AMA	AAA	123	494	436	117	18	5	16	193	49	1	4	82	16	2	4	9	3	72	72	.268	.343	.443
91	OMA/AMA	AAA	104	382	346	89	18	2	6	129	31	0	1	62	4	1	3	2	4	35	39	.257	.318	.373
	KC/AL		18	37	33	9	1	0	3	19	3	1	0	9	1	1	0	0	0	4	4	.273	.333	.576

Quinones, Luis Raul — bats both — throws right — b.4/28/62 — 1991 positions: 2B 33, 3B 19, SS 5

YR	TM/LG	CL	G	TPA	AB	H	2B	3B	HR	TB	BB	IBB	HB	SO	GDP	SH	SF	SB	CS	R	RBI	BA	OBA	SA
83	OAK/AL		19	45	42	8	2	1	0	12	1	0	0	4	0	1	1	1	1	5	4	.190	.205	.286
84	MAI/INT	AAA	131	519	473	127	27	3	8	184	39	3	1	73	5	1	5	5	6	71	60	.268	.322	.389
85	MAI/INT	AAA	14	51	45	8	2	1	1	15	6	0	0	5	0	0	0	0	0	4	2	.178	.275	.333
	PHO/PCL	AAA	85	342	304	78	13	7	8	129	28	5	1	41	8	4	5	4	1	46	47	.257	.317	.424
86	PHO/PCL	AAA	14	62	55	14	4	1	0	20	4	0	1	8	1	0	2	0	1	7	7	.255	.306	.364
	SF/NL		71	115	106	19	1	3	0	26	3	1	1	17	4	4	1	1	3	13	11	.179	.207	.245
87	IOW/AMA	AAA	77	308	287	91	14	12	11	162	16	1	1	30	5	0	4	2	3	44	62	.317	.351	.564
	CHI/NL		49	111	101	22	6	0	0	28	10	0	0	16	0	0	0	0	0	12	8	.218	.288	.277
88	NAS/AMA	AAA	114	454	417	115	28	6	9	182	29	3	3	51	8	3	5	3	7	42	53	.276	.319	.436
	CIN/NL		23	57	52	12	3	0	1	18	2	1	0	11	1	2	1	4	1	4	11	.231	.255	.346
89	NAS/AMA	AAA	45	193	176	40	9	2	4	65	8	1	1	22	2	4	4	2	4	19	24	.227	.258	.369
	CIN/NL		97	378	340	83	13	4	12	140	25	0	3	46	3	8	2	2	4	43	34	.244	.300	.412
90	CIN/NL		83	164	145	35	7	0	2	48	13	3	1	29	3	1	4	1	0	10	17	.241	.301	.331
91	CIN/NL		97	237	212	47	4	3	4	69	21	3	2	31	2	1	1	1	2	15	20	.222	.297	.325
7 YR TOTALS			439	1107	998	226	36	11	19	341	75	8	7	154	9	17	10	9	9	102	105	**.226**	**.283**	**.342**

Quintana, Carlos Narcis (Hernandez) — bats right — throws right — b.8/26/65 — 1991 positions: 1B 138, OF 13, DH 1

YR	TM/LG	CL	G	TPA	AB	H	2B	3B	HR	TB	BB	IBB	HB	SO	GDP	SH	SF	SB	CS	R	RBI	BA	OBA	SA
85	ELM/NYP	A-	65	254	220	61	8	0	4	81	29	0	3	31	6	0	2	3	0	27	35	.277	.366	.368
86	GRE/SAL	A	126	546	443	144	19	4	11	204	90	1	4	54	16	3	6	26	9	97	81	.325	.438	.460
87	NB/EAS	AA	56	235	206	64	11	3	2	87	24	3	1	33	9	0	4	3	3	31	31	.311	.379	.422
88	PAW/INT	AAA	131	517	471	134	25	3	16	213	38	1	3	72	15	2	3	3	5	67	66	.285	.340	.452
	BOS/AL		5	8	6	2	0	0	0	2	2	0	0	3	0	0	0	0	0	1	2	.333	.500	.333
89	PAW/INT	AAA	82	330	272	78	11	2	11	126	53	1	0	39	7	0	5	6	0	45	52	.287	.397	.463
	BOS/AL		34	84	77	16	5	0	0	21	7	0	0	12	5	0	0	0	0	6	6	.208	.274	.273
90	BOS/AL		149	572	512	147	28	0	7	196	52	0	2	74	19	4	2	1	2	56	67	.287	.354	.383
91	BOS/AL		149	550	478	141	21	1	11	197	61	2	2	66	17	6	3	1	0	69	71	.295	.375	.412
4 YR TOTALS			337	1214	1073	306	54	1	18	416	122	2	4	155	41	10	5	2	2	132	146	**.285**	**.359**	**.388**

Quirk, James Patrick "Jamie" — bats left — throws right — b.10/22/54 — 1991 positions: C 54, 1B 8, 3B 1, DH 1

YR	TM/LG	CL	G	TPA	AB	H	2B	3B	HR	TB	BB	IBB	HB	SO	GDP	SH	SF	SB	CS	R	RBI	BA	OBA	SA
75	KC/AL		14	41	39	10	0	0	1	13	2	0	0	7	1	0	0	0	0	2	5	.256	.293	.333
76	KC/AL		64	119	114	28	6	0	1	37	2	0	0	22	5	0	3	0	0	11	15	.246	.252	.325
77	MIL/AL		93	233	221	48	14	1	3	73	8	2	1	47	4	2	0	0	1	16	13	.217	.251	.330
78	KC/AL		17	34	29	6	2	0	0	8	5	0	0	13	0	0	0	0	0	3	11	.207	.324	.276
79	KC/AL		51	85	79	24	6	1	1	35	5	0	1	13	0	0	0	0	0	8	11	.304	.353	.443
80	KC/AL		62	177	163	45	5	0	5	65	7	2	1	24	7	3	3	2	2	13	21	.276	.305	.399
81	KC/AL		46	107	100	25	7	0	0	32	6	1	1	17	5	0	0	0	0	8	10	.250	.299	.320
82	KC/AL		36	82	78	18	3	0	1	24	3	0	0	15	2	0	1	0	0	8	5	.231	.256	.308
83	STL/NL		48	93	86	18	2	1	2	28	6	0	0	27	2	0	1	3	1	8	11	.209	.269	.326
84	CHI/AL		3	3	2	0	0	0	0	0	0	0	0	0	0	0	0	0	0	0	0	.000	.000	.000
	DEN/AMA	AAA	70	225	201	42	6	3	2	60	21	1	1	39	4	0	2	1	1	23	24	.209	.284	.299
	CLE/AL		1	1	1	1	0	0	1	4	0	0	0	0	0	0	0	0	0	1	2	1.000	1.000	4.000
	YEAR		4	4	3	1	0	0	1	4	0	0	0	2	0	0	0	0	0	1	2	.333	.250	1.333

(continued)

Quirk, James Patrick "Jamie" (continued)

YR	TM/LG	CL	G	TPA	AB	H	2B	3B	HR	TB	BB	IBB	HB	SO	GDP	SH	SF	SB	CS	R	RBI	BA	OBA	SA
85	OMA/AMA	AAA	104	365	324	79	5	1	8	110	35	4	0	56	6	0	6	0	5	33	48	.244	.312	.340
	KC/AL		19	59	57	16	3	1	0	21	2	0	0	9	1	0	0	0	0	3	4	.281	.305	.368
86	KC/AL		80	238	219	47	10	0	8	81	17	3	1	41	4	0	1	0	1	24	26	.215	.273	.370
87	KC/AL		109	334	296	70	17	0	5	102	28	1	4	56	8	2	4	1	0	24	33	.236	.307	.345
88	KC/AL		84	232	196	47	7	1	8	80	28	2	1	41	2	4	3	1	5	22	25	.240	.333	.408
89	NY/AL		13	27	24	2	0	0	0	2	3	0	0	5	1	0	0	0	1	0	0	.083	.185	.083
	TAC/PCL	AAA	14	50	47	8	2	0	1	13	3	0	0	12	1	0	0	0	0	5	5	.170	.220	.277
	OAK/AL		9	10	10	2	0	0	1	5	0	0	0	4	0	0	0	0	0	1	1	.200	.200	.500
	BAL/AL		25	62	51	11	2	0	0	13	9	0	0	11	3	1	1	0	1	5	9	.216	.328	.255
	YEAR		47	99	85	15	2	0	1	20	12	0	0	20	4	1	1	0	2	6	10	.176	.276	.235
90	OAK/AL		56	144	121	34	5	1	3	50	14	1	1	34	1	5	3	0	0	12	26	.281	.353	.413
91	OAK/AL		76	224	203	53	4	0	1	60	16	1	2	28	7	3	0	0	3	16	17	.261	.321	.296
17 YR TOTALS			**906**	**2305**	**2089**	**505**	**93**	**6**	**41**	**733**	**161**	**14**	**15**	**407**	**53**	**20**	**20**	**5**	**16**	**180**	**236**	**.242**	**.298**	**.351**

Raines, Timothy "Tim" or "Rock" — bats both — throws right — b.9/16/59 — 1991 positions: OF 133, DH 19

YR	TM/LG	CL	G	TPA	AB	H	2B	3B	HR	TB	BB	IBB	HB	SO	GDP	SH	SF	SB	CS	R	RBI	BA	OBA	SA
79	MON/NL		6	0	0	0	0	0	0	0	0	0	0	0	0	0	0	2	0	3	0	.000	.000	.000
80	MON/NL		15	27	20	1	0	0	0	1	6	0	0	3	0	1	0	5	0	5	0	.050	.269	.050
81	MON/NL		88	363	313	95	13	7	5	137	45	5	2	31	7	0	3	71	11	61	37	.304	.391	.438
82	MON/NL		156	731	647	179	32	8	4	239	75	9	2	83	6	1		78	16	90	43	.277	.353	.369
83	MON/NL		156	720	615	183	32	8	11	264	97	9	2	70	12	2	4	90	14	133	71	.298	.393	.429
84	MON/NL		160	718	622	192	38	9	8	272	87	7	2	69	7	3	4	75	10	106	60	.309	.393	.437
85	MON/NL		150	665	575	184	30	13	11	273	81	13	3	60	9	3		70	9	115	41	.320	.405	.475
86	MON/NL		151	664	580	194	35	10	9	276	78	9	2	60	6	1		70	9	91	62	.334	.413	.476
87	MON/NL		139	627	530	175	34	8	18	279	90	26	1	52	9	0	4	50	5	123	68	.330	.429	.526
88	MON/NL		109	488	429	116	19	7	12	185	53	14	2	44	8	0	4	33	7	66	48	.270	.350	.431
89	MON/NL		145	618	517	148	29	6	9	216	93	18	3	48	8	0	5	41	9	76	60	.286	.395	.418
90	MON/NL		130	538	457	131	11	5	9	179	70	8	3	43	9	0	8	49	16	65	62	.287	.379	.392
91	CHI/AL		155	709	609	163	20	6	5	210	83	9	3	68	7	9	3	51	15	102	50	.268	.359	.345
13 YR TOTALS			**1560**	**6868**	**5914**	**1761**	**293**	**87**	**101**	**2531**	**858**	**127**	**30**	**631**	**88**	**25**	**41**	**685**	**121**	**1036**	**602**	**.298**	**.387**	**.428**

Ramirez, Rafael Emilio (Peguero) — bats right — throws right — b.2/18/58 — 1991 positions: SS 45, 2B 27, 3B 2

YR	TM/LG	CL	G	TPA	AB	H	2B	3B	HR	TB	BB	IBB	HB	SO	GDP	SH	SF	SB	CS	R	RBI	BA	OBA	SA
80	ATL/NL		50	174	165	44	6	1	2	58	2	0	4	33	2	3	0	2	1	17	11	.267	.292	.352
81	ATL/NL		95	342	307	67	16	2	2	93	24	3	1	47	3	9	1	7	3	30	20	.218	.276	.303
82	ATL/NL		157	669	609	169	24	4	10	231	36	7	3	49	10	16	5	27	14	74	52	.278	.319	.379
83	ATL/NL		152	668	622	185	13	5	7	229	36	4	2	48	8	6	2	16	12	82	58	.297	.337	.368
84	ATL/NL		145	629	591	157	22	4	2	193	26	1	0	70	9	5	6	14	14	51	48	.266	.295	.327
85	ATL/NL		138	595	568	141	25	4	5	189	20	1	0	63	21	2	5	2	6	54	58	.248	.272	.333
86	ATL/NL		134	530	496	119	21	1	8	166	21	1	3	60	16	7	3	19	8	57	33	.240	.273	.335
87	ATL/NL		56	194	179	47	12	0	1	62	8	0	2	16	3	4	1	6	3	22	21	.263	.300	.346
88	HOU/NL		155	597	566	156	30	5	6	214	18	1	3	61	16	4	6	3	2	51	59	.276	.298	.378
89	HOU/NL		151	575	537	132	20	2	6	174	29	3	0	64	9	2	4	6	3	46	54	.246	.283	.324
90	HOU/NL		132	480	445	116	19	3	2	147	24	9	1	46	9	9	1	10	5	44	37	.261	.299	.330
91	HOU/NL		101	249	233	55	10	0	1	68	13	1	0	40	3	1	2	3	3	17	20	.236	.274	.292
12 YR TOTALS			**1466**	**5702**	**5318**	**1388**	**218**	**31**	**52**	**1824**	**257**	**36**	**20**	**597**	**108**	**72**	**35**	**112**	**75**	**545**	**471**	**.261**	**.296**	**.343**

Ramos, John Joseph — bats right — throws right — b.8/6/65 — 1991 positions: C 5, DH 4

YR	TM/LG	CL	G	TPA	AB	H	2B	3B	HR	TB	BB	IBB	HB	SO	GDP	SH	SF	SB	CS	R	RBI	BA	OBA	SA
86	FL/FSL	A+	54	217	184	49	10	1	2	67	26	0	1	23	5	4	2	8	3	25	28	.266	.357	.364
	ONE/NYP	A–	3	10	8	4	2	1	0	8	2	0	0	1	0	0	0	0	0	3	1	.500	.600	1.000
87	PW/CAR	A+	76	271	235	51	6	1	2	65	28	3	2	30	10	3	3	8	5	26	27	.217	.302	.277
88	PW/CAR	A+	109	454	391	119	18	2	8	165	49	1	7	34	7	2	5	8	2	47	57	.304	.387	.422
	ALB/EAS	AA	21	87	72	16	1	3	1	26	12	0	1	9	1	0	2	2	1	11	13	.222	.333	.361
89	ALB/EAS	AA	105	410	359	98	21	0	9	146	40	2	7	65	14	2	7	7	5	55	60	.273	.355	.407
90	COL/INT	AAA	2	6	6	0	0	0	0	0	0	0	0	0	0	0	0	0	0	0	1	.000	.000	.000
	ALB/EAS	AA	84	331	287	90	20	1	4	124	36	0	3	39	10	0	5	1	0	38	45	.314	.390	.432
91	COL/INT	AAA	104	446	377	116	18	3	10	170	56	3	3	54	15	1	9	1	5	52	63	.308	.393	.451
	NY/AL		10	29	26	8	1	0	0	9	1	0	0	3	1	0	2	0	0	4	3	.308	.310	.346

Randolph, Willie Larry — bats right — throws right — b.7/6/54 — 1991 positions: 2B 121, DH 2

YR	TM/LG	CL	G	TPA	AB	H	2B	3B	HR	TB	BB	IBB	HB	SO	GDP	SH	SF	SB	CS	R	RBI	BA	OBA	SA
75	PIT/NL		30	70	61	10	1	0	0	11	7	1	0	6	3	1	1	1	0	9	3	.164	.246	.180
76	NY/AL		125	500	430	115	15	4	1	141	58	5	3	39	10	6	3	37	12	59	40	.267	.356	.328
77	NY/AL		147	624	551	151	28	11	4	213	64	1	1	53	11	2	6	13	6	91	40	.274	.347	.387
78	NY/AL		134	596	499	139	18	6	3	178	82	1	4	51	12	6	5	36	7	87	42	.279	.381	.357
79	NY/AL		153	682	574	155	15	13	5	211	95	4	3	39	23	5	5	33	12	98	61	.270	.374	.368
80	NY/AL		138	642	513	151	23	7	7	209	119	4	2	45	6	5	3	30	5	99	46	.294	.427	.407
81	NY/AL		93	422	357	83	14	3	2	109	57	0	0	24	10	5	3	14	5	59	24	.232	.336	.305
82	NY/AL		144	643	553	155	21	4	3	193	75	3	3	35	13	10	2	16	9	85	36	.280	.368	.349
83	NY/AL		104	477	420	117	21	1	2	146	53	0	1	32	11	3	0	12	4	73	38	.279	.361	.348
84	NY/AL		142	664	564	162	24	2	2	196	86	4	0	42	7	7	6	10	6	86	31	.287	.377	.348
85	NY/AL		143	597	497	137	21	2	5	177	85	4	4	39	24	5	6	16	8	75	40	.276	.382	.356
86	NY/AL		141	601	492	136	15	2	5	170	94	0	3	49	11	8	4	15	2	76	50	.276	.393	.346
87	NY/AL		120	543	449	137	24	2	7	186	82	1	2	25	15	5	5	11	1	96	67	.305	.411	.414

Randolph, Willie Larry (continued)

YR	TM/LG	CL	G	TPA	AB	H	2B	3B	HR	TB	BB	IBB	HB	SO	GDP	SH	SF	SB	CS	R	RBI	BA	OBA	SA
88	NY/AL		110	474	404	93	20	1	2	121	55	2	2	39	10	8	5	8	4	43	34	.230	.322	.300
89	LA/NL		145	633	549	155	18	0	2	179	71	2	4	51	11	4	5	7	6	62	36	.282	.366	.326
90	LA/NL		26	113	96	26	4	0	1	33	13	0	1	9	3	3	0	1	0	15	9	.271	.364	.344
	OAK/AL		93	333	292	75	9	3	1	93	32	1	1	25	11	7	1	6	1	37	21	.257	.331	.318
	YEAR		119	446	388	101	13	3	2	126	45	1	2	34	14	10	1	7	1	52	30	.260	.339	.325
91	MIL/AL		124	512	431	141	14	3	0	161	75	3	0	38	14	3	3	4	2	60	54	.327	.424	.374
17 YR TOTALS			**2112**	**9126**	**7732**	**2138**	**305**	**64**	**52**	**2727**	**1203**	**36**	**34**	**641**	**213**	**93**	**64**	**270**	**91**	**1210**	**672**	**.277**	**.374**	**.353**

Ready, Randy Max — bats right — throws right — b.1/8/60 — 1991 positions: 2B 66

YR	TM/LG	CL	G	TPA	AB	H	2B	3B	HR	TB	BB	IBB	HB	SO	GDP	SH	SF	SB	CS	R	RBI	BA	OBA	SA
83	MIL/AL		12	43	37	15	3	2	1	25	6	1	0	3	0	0	0	0	1	8	6	.405	.488	.676
84	MIL/AL		37	140	123	23	6	1	3	40	14	0	0	18	2	3	0	0	0	13	13	.187	.270	.325
	VAN/PCL	AAA	43	201	151	49	7	4	3	73	43	2	5	21	4	2	0	10	4	48	18	.325	.487	.483
85	VAN/PCL	AAA	52	222	190	62	12	3	4	92	30	2	0	14	3	0	2	14	3	33	29	.326	.414	.484
	MIL/AL		48	200	181	48	9	5	1	70	14	0	1	23	6	2	2	0	0	29	21	.265	.318	.387
86	MIL/AL		23	89	79	15	4	0	1	22	9	0	0	9	3	1	0	2	0	8	4	.190	.273	.278
	SD/NL		1	3	3	0	0	0	0	0	0	0	0	1	0	0	0	0	0	0	0	.000	.000	.000
	YEAR		24	92	82	15	4	0	1	22	9	0	0	10	3	1	0	2	0	8	4	.183	.264	.268
	LV/PCL	AAA	10	44	38	14	4	0	1	21	6	0	0	2	0	0	0	1	1	5	8	.368	.455	.553
87	SD/NL		124	423	350	108	26	6	12	182	67	2	3	44	7	2	1	7	3	69	54	.309	.423	.520
88	SD/NL		114	380	331	88	16	2	7	129	39	1	3	38	3	4	3	6	2	43	39	.266	.346	.390
89	SD/NL		28	80	67	17	2	1	0	21	11	0	0	6	2	1	1	0	0	4	5	.254	.354	.313
	PHI/NL		72	223	187	50	11	1	8	87	31	0	2	31	2	0	3	4	3	33	21	.267	.372	.465
	YEAR		100	303	254	67	13	2	8	108	42	0	2	37	4	1	4	4	3	37	26	.264	.368	.425
90	PHI/NL		101	253	217	53	9	1	1	67	29	0	1	35	3	3	3	3	2	26	26	.244	.332	.309
91	PHI/NL		76	258	205	51	10	1	1	66	47	3	1	25	5	1	4	2	1	32	20	.249	.385	.322
9 YR TOTALS			**636**	**2092**	**1780**	**468**	**96**	**20**	**35**	**709**	**267**	**7**	**11**	**233**	**33**	**17**	**17**	**24**	**12**	**265**	**209**	**.263**	**.360**	**.398**

Redfield, Joseph Randall "Joe" — bats right — throws right — b.1/14/61 — 1991 positions: 3B 9

YR	TM/LG	CL	G	TPA	AB	H	2B	3B	HR	TB	BB	IBB	HB	SO	GDP	SH	SF	SB	CS	R	RBI	BA	OBA	SA
82	LF/NYP	A—	54	237	206	59	14	5	8	0	31	0	0	46	0	0	0	11	0	44	57	.286	.380	.000
83	LYN/CAR	A+	62	217	192	39	4	7	4	0	25	0	0	44	0	0	0	5	0	32	27	.203	.295	.000
	JAC/TEX	AA	36	144	127	25	4	1	2	0	17	0	0	43	0	0	0	0	0	16	12	.197	.292	.000
84	LYN/CAR	A+	122	501	428	115	18	7	11	180	64	1	4	81	12	2	3	14	7	80	58	.269	.367	.421
85	TID/INT	AAA	4	11	10	3	1	0	0	4	1	0	0	1	0	0	0	0	0	0	0	.300	.364	.400
	JAC/TEX	AA	39	90	73	10	4	0	1	17	15	0	0	23	3	2	0	0	0	12	5	.137	.284	.233
	LYN/CAR	A+	41	169	132	32	8	0	3	49	33	0	4	29	5	0	0	10	3	22	18	.242	.408	.371
86	JAC/TEX	AA	15	64	60	17	1	2	0	22	4	0	0	10	0	0	0	2	0	8	3	.283	.328	.367
	CHA/SOU	AA	95	391	344	102	16	4	14	168	38	1	7	62	4	1	1	8	4	65	49	.297	.377	.488
87	MID/TEX	AA	128	579	498	160	31	7	30	295	67	2	6	83	11	4	4	17	4	108	108	.321	.405	.592
88	CAL/AL		1	2	2	0	0	0	0	0	0	0	0	0	0	0	0	0	0	0	0	.000	.000	.000
	EDM/PCL	AAA	118	466	417	121	38	1	3	170	36	0	6	83	9	4	3	11	4	67	52	.290	.353	.408
89	SCR/INT	AAA	123	482	428	103	13	6	9	155	40	0	6	74	11	4	4	21	8	45	49	.241	.312	.362
90	DEN/AMA	AAA	137	602	525	144	23	10	17	238	57	0	10	76	8	5	5	34	18	87	71	.274	.353	.453
91	PIT/NL		11	23	18	2	0	0	0	2	4	0	0	1	0	1	0	0	1	1	0	.111	.273	.111
	BUF/AMA	AAA	105	436	356	98	20	6	7	151	54	2	15	50	4	10	1	21	4	60	50	.275	.392	.424
2 YR TOTALS			**12**	**25**	**20**	**2**	**0**	**0**	**0**	**2**	**4**	**0**	**0**	**1**	**0**	**1**	**0**	**0**	**1**	**1**	**0**	**.100**	**.250**	**.100**

Redus, Gary Eugene — bats right — throws right — b.11/1/56 — 1991 positions: 1B 47, OF 33

YR	TM/LG	CL	G	TPA	AB	H	2B	3B	HR	TB	BB	IBB	HB	SO	GDP	SH	SF	SB	CS	R	RBI	BA	OBA	SA
82	CIN/NL		20	89	83	18	3	2	1	28	5	0	0	21	0	0	1	11	2	12	7	.217	.258	.337
83	CIN/NL		125	531	453	112	20	9	17	201	71	4	3	111	6	2	2	39	14	90	51	.247	.352	.444
84	CIN/NL		123	455	394	100	21	3	7	148	52	3	1	71	4	3	5	48	11	69	22	.254	.338	.376
85	CIN/NL		101	294	246	62	14	4	6	102	44	2	1	52	0	2	1	48	12	51	28	.252	.366	.415
86	REA/EAS	AA	6	26	24	6	1	0	0	7	2	0	0	6	0	0	0	1	1	4	0	.250	.308	.292
	PHI/NL		90	392	340	84	22	4	11	147	47	4	3	78	2	1	1	25	7	62	33	.247	.343	.432
87	CHI/AL		130	554	475	112	26	6	12	186	69	0	0	90	7	3	7	52	11	78	48	.236	.328	.392
88	CHI/AL		77	304	262	69	10	4	6	105	33	1	2	52	5	0	7	26	2	42	34	.263	.342	.401
	PIT/NL		30	88	71	14	2	0	2	22	15	0	1	19	0	0	1	5	2	12	4	.197	.341	.310
	YEAR		107	392	333	83	12	4	8	127	48	1	3	71	6	0	8	31	4	54	38	.249	.342	.381
89	PIT/NL		98	324	279	79	18	7	6	129	40	3	1	51	5	1	3	25	6	42	33	.283	.372	.462
90	PIT/NL		96	268	227	56	15	3	6	95	33	0	2	38	1	1	5	11	5	32	23	.247	.341	.419
91	PIT/NL		98	288	252	62	12	2	7	99	28	2	3	39	0	1	4	17	3	45	24	.246	.324	.393
10 YR TOTALS			**988**	**3587**	**3082**	**768**	**163**	**44**	**81**	**1262**	**437**	**19**	**17**	**622**	**31**	**14**	**37**	**307**	**75**	**535**	**307**	**.249**	**.342**	**.409**

Reed, Darren Douglas — bats right — throws right — b.10/16/65 — 1991 positions: OF

YR	TM/LG	CL	G	TPA	AB	H	2B	3B	HR	TB	BB	IBB	HB	SO	GDP	SH	SF	SB	CS	R	RBI	BA	OBA	SA
84	ONE/NYP	A—	40	125	113	26	7	0	2	39	10	0	0	19	2	1	1	2	1	17	9	.230	.290	.345
85	FL/FSL	A+	100	419	369	117	21	4	10	176	36	3	7	56	9	0	7	13	3	63	61	.317	.382	.477
86	ALB/EAS	AA	51	218	196	45	11	1	4	70	15	0	1	24	2	1	5	1	0	22	27	.230	.281	.357
87	COL/INT	AAA	21	83	79	26	3	3	8	59	4	0	0	9	2	0	0	0	0	15	16	.329	.361	.747
	ALB/EAS	AA	107	466	404	129	23	4	20	220	51	9	8	50	10	0	3	9	6	68	79	.319	.403	.545
88	TID/INT	AAA	101	387	345	83	26	0	9	136	32	2	3	66	9	3	4	0	3	31	47	.241	.307	.394
89	TID/INT	AAA	133	520	444	119	30	6	4	173	60	1	11	70	15	1	4	11	2	57	50	.268	.366	.390

(continued)

Reed, Darren Douglas (continued)

YR	TM/LG	CL	G	TPA	AB	H	2B	3B	HR	TB	BB	IBB	HB	SO	GDP	SH	SF	SB	CS	R	RBI	BA	OBA	SA
90	TID/INT	AAA	104	420	359	95	21	6	17	179	51	4	6	62	11	0	4	15	4	58	74	.265	.362	.499
	NY/NL		26	42	39	8	4	1	1	17	3	0	0	11	0	0	0	1	0	5	2	.205	.262	.436
1 YR TOTALS			26	42	39	8	4	1	1	17	3	0	0	11	0	0	0	1	0	5	2	.205	.262	.436

Reed, Jeffrey Scott "Jeff" — bats left — throws right — b.11/12/62 — 1991 positions: C 89

YR	TM/LG	CL	G	TPA	AB	H	2B	3B	HR	TB	BB	IBB	HB	SO	GDP	SH	SF	SB	CS	R	RBI	BA	OBA	SA
84	TOL/INT	AAA	94	345	301	80	16	3	3	111	37	3	2	35	7	4	1	1	3	30	35	.266	.349	.369
	MIN/AL		18	24	21	3	3	0	0	6	2	0	0	6	0	1	0	0	0	3	1	.143	.217	.286
85	TOL/INT	AAA	122	483	404	100	15	3	5	136	59	3	5	49	13	9	6	1	1	53	36	.248	.346	.337
	MIN/AL		7	10	10	2	0	0	0	2	0	0	0	3	0	0	0	0	0	2	0	.200	.200	.200
86	TOL/INT	AAA	25	92	71	22	5	3	1	36	17	0	0	9	3	3	1	0	0	10	14	.310	.438	.507
	MIN/AL		68	185	165	39	6	1	1	53	16	0	0	19	2	3	0	1	0	13	9	.236	.308	.321
87	IND/AMA	AAA	5	19	17	3	0	0	0	3	1	0	0	2	0	1	0	0	0	1	0	.176	.222	.176
	MON/NL		75	228	207	44	11	0	1	58	12	1	1	20	8	4	4	0	0	15	21	.213	.254	.280
88	MON/NL		43	138	123	27	3	2	0	34	13	1	0	22	3	1	1	1	0	10	9	.220	.292	.276
	IND/AMA	AAA	8	24	22	7	3	0	0	10	2	0	0	2	0	0	0	0	0	1	1	.318	.375	.455
	CIN/NL		49	157	142	33	6	0	1	42	15	0	0	19	2	0	0	0	0	10	7	.232	.306	.296
	YEAR		92	295	265	60	9	2	1	76	28	1	0	41	5	1	1	1	0	20	16	.226	.299	.287
89	CIN/NL		102	330	287	64	11	0	3	84	34	5	2	46	6	3	4	0	0	16	23	.223	.306	.293
90	CIN/NL		72	205	175	44	8	1	3	63	24	5	0	26	4	5	1	0	0	12	16	.251	.340	.360
91	CIN/NL		91	300	270	72	15	2	3	100	23	3	1	38	6	1	5	0	1	20	31	.267	.321	.370
8 YR TOTALS			525	1577	1400	328	63	6	13	442	139	15	5	199	31	18	15	2	2	101	117	.234	.303	.316

Reed, Jody Eric — bats right — throws right — b.7/26/62 — 1991 positions: 2B 152, SS 6

YR	TM/LG	CL	G	TPA	AB	H	2B	3B	HR	TB	BB	IBB	HB	SO	GDP	SH	SF	SB	CS	R	RBI	BA	OBA	SA
84	WH/FSL	A+	77	334	273	74	14	1	0	90	52	3	0	19	5	6	3	9	8	46	20	.271	.384	.330
85	WH/FSL	A+	134	592	489	157	25	1	0	184	94	2	1	26	9	4	4	16	11	95	45	.321	.429	.376
86	NB/EAS	AA	60	275	218	50	12	1	0	64	52	1	0	9	5	3	2	10	5	33	11	.229	.375	.294
	PAW/INT	AAA	69	270	227	64	11	0	1	78	31	0	1	18	3	7	4	8	2	27	30	.282	.365	.344
87	PAW/INT	AAA	136	594	510	151	22	2	7	198	69	0	2	23	12	8	5	9	7	77	51	.296	.379	.388
	BOS/AL		9	35	30	9	1	1	0	12	4	0	0	0	0	0	1	1	1	4	8	.300	.382	.400
88	BOS/AL		109	400	338	99	23	1	1	127	45	1	4	21	5	11	2	1	3	60	28	.293	.380	.376
89	BOS/AL		146	619	524	151	42	2	3	206	73	0	4	44	12	13	5	4	5	76	40	.288	.376	.393
90	BOS/AL		155	691	598	173	45	0	5	233	75	4	4	65	19	11	3	4	4	70	51	.289	.371	.390
91	BOS/AL		153	696	618	175	42	2	5	236	60	2	4	53	15	11	3	6	5	87	60	.283	.349	.382
5 YR TOTALS			572	2441	2108	607	153	6	14	814	257	7	16	183	51	47	13	16	18	297	187	.288	.368	.386

Reimer, Kevin Michael — bats left — throws right — b.6/28/64 — 1991 positions: OF 66, DH 56

YR	TM/LG	CL	G	TPA	AB	H	2B	3B	HR	TB	BB	IBB	HB	SO	GDP	SH	SF	SB	CS	R	RBI	BA	OBA	SA
85	BUR/MID	A	80	323	292	67	12	0	8	103	22	0	8	43	10	0	1	0	4	25	33	.229	.300	.353
86	SAL/CAR	A+	133	525	453	111	21	2	16	184	61	6	7	71	15	2	2	4	5	57	76	.245	.342	.406
87	CHA/FSL	A+	74	304	271	66	13	7	6	111	29	2	2	48	6	0	2	2	1	36	34	.244	.319	.410
88	TUL/TEX	AA	133	534	486	147	30	11	21	262	38	9	5	95	9	0	5	4	4	74	76	.302	.356	.539
	TEX/AL		12	26	25	3	0	0	1	6	0	0	0	6	0	0	1	0	0	2	2	.120	.115	.240
89	TEX/AL		3	5	5	0	0	0	0	0	0	0	0	1	1	0	0	0	0	0	0	.000	.000	.000
	OC/AMA	AAA	133	554	514	137	37	7	10	218	33	3	2	91	13	1	4	4	1	59	73	.267	.311	.424
90	OC/AMA	AAA	51	217	198	56	18	2	4	90	18	3	0	25	7	0	1	2	0	24	33	.283	.341	.455
	TEX/AL		64	111	100	26	9	1	2	43	10	0	1	22	3	0	0	0	1	5	15	.260	.333	.430
91	TEX/AL		136	440	394	106	22	0	20	188	33	6	7	93	10	0	6	0	3	46	69	.269	.332	.477
4 YR TOTALS			215	582	524	135	31	1	23	237	43	6	8	122	14	0	7	0	4	53	86	.258	.320	.452

Reyes, Gilberto R. (Polanco) — bats right — throws right — b.12/10/63 — 1991 positions: C 80

YR	TM/LG	CL	G	TPA	AB	H	2B	3B	HR	TB	BB	IBB	HB	SO	GDP	SH	SF	SB	CS	R	RBI	BA	OBA	SA
80	LET/PIO	R+	6	13	11	2	0	0	0	2	2	0	0	5	0	0	0	0	0	0	1	.182	.308	.182
81	LET/PIO	R+	44	172	155	40	9	0	6	67	15	0	1	0	1	0	1	29	0	28	24	.258	.326	.432
	VB/FSL	A+	21	63	58	12	3	0	1	18	4	0	0	20	3	0	1	0	1	3	6	.207	.254	.310
82	LOD/CAL	A+	127	473	424	119	18	1	15	184	39	0	2	74	12	5	3	5	6	65	55	.281	.342	.434
83	SA/TEX	AA	33	130	124	35	7	0	1	45	3	0	0	18	6	0	3	0	1	10	16	.282	.292	.363
	ALB/PCL	AAA	20	68	62	19	1	2	2	30	2	0	0	13	3	2	2	1	0	8	15	.306	.318	.484
	LA/NL		19	32	31	5	2	0	0	7	0	0	1	5	3	0	0	0	1	1	0	.161	.188	.226
84	SA/TEX	AA	120	471	433	131	16	2	10	181	29	2	2	50	17	2	5	1	4	55	78	.303	.345	.418
	LA/NL		4	5	5	0	0	0	0	0	0	0	0	0	0	0	0	0	0	0	0	.000	.000	.000
85	ALB/PCL	AAA	111	394	366	97	20	0	6	135	15	1	3	74	6	2	8	0	0	35	54	.265	.293	.369
	LA/NL		6	3	1	0	0	0	0	0	1	0	0	1	0	0	0	0	0	0	0	.000	.667	.000
86	ALB/PCL	AAA	104	336	306	70	13	0	7	106	23	2	0	54	5	3	2	1	1	36	36	.229	.285	.346
87	ALB/PCL	AAA	89	304	265	72	18	2	5	109	30	0	6	57	7	1	2	0	1	42	46	.272	.356	.411
	LA/NL		1	0	0	0	0	0	0	0	0	0	0	0	0	0	0	0	0	0	0	.000	.000	.000
88	ALB/PCL	AAA	98	354	318	93	14	0	12	143	27	0	5	63	6	1	3	2	1	40	66	.292	.354	.450
	LA/NL		5	9	9	1	0	0	0	1	0	0	0	3	0	0	0	0	0	1	0	.111	.111	.111
89	IND/AMA	AAA	106	350	314	71	8	0	9	106	30	4	3	69	11	2	1	0	2	35	35	.226	.299	.338
	MON/NL		4	5	5	1	0	0	0	1	0	0	0	1	0	0	0	0	0	0	1	.200	.200	.200
90	IND/AMA	AAA	89	341	309	72	14	1	9	115	24	2	1	79	10	0	6	2	2	22	45	.233	.287	.372
91	MON/NL		83	229	207	45	9	0	0	54	19	2	1	51	3	1	1	2	4	11	13	.217	.285	.261
7 YR TOTALS			122	283	258	52	11	0	0	63	20	2	3	64	6	1	1	2	4	13	14	.202	.266	.244

Reynolds, Harold Craig — bats both — throws right — b.11/26/60 — 1991 positions: 2B 159, DH 1

YR	TM/LG	CL	G	TPA	AB	H	2B	3B	HR	TB	BB	IBB	HB	SO	GDP	SH	SF	SB	CS	R	RBI	BA	OBA	SA
83	SEA/AL		20	63	59	12	4	1	0	18	2	0	0	9	1	1	0	1	0	2	8	1	.203	.226	.305
84	SLC/PCL	AAA	135	646	558	165	22	6	3	208	73	2	3	72	9	1	9	3	37	17	94	54	.296	.378	.373
	SEA/AL		10	12	10	3	0	0	0	3	0	0	1	1	0	1	0	1	1	3	0	.300	.364	.300
85	CAL/PCL	AAA	52	248	212	77	11	3	5	109	28	1	1	18	2	3	4	9	13	36	30	.363	.433	.514
	SEA/AL		67	122	104	15	3	1	0	20	17	0	0	14	0	1	0	3	2	15	6	.144	.264	.192
86	CAL/PCL	AAA	29	139	118	37	7	0	0	47	20	1	1	12	1	1	0	10	8	20	7	.314	.413	.398
	SEA/AL		126	486	445	99	19	4	1	129	29	0	3	42	6	9	0	30	12	46	24	.222	.275	.290
87	SEA/AL		160	584	530	146	31	8	1	196	39	0	2	34	7	8	5	60	20	73	35	.275	.325	.370
88	SEA/AL		158	663	598	169	26	11	4	229	51	1	2	51	9	10	2	35	29	61	41	.283	.340	.383
89	SEA/AL		153	677	613	184	24	9	0	226	55	1	3	45	4	3	3	25	18	87	43	.300	.359	.369
90	SEA/AL		160	737	642	162	36	5	5	223	81	3	3	52	9	5	6	31	16	100	55	.252	.336	.347
91	SEA/AL		161	728	631	160	34	5	3	215	72	2	5	63	11	14	6	28	8	95	57	.254	.332	.341
9 YR TOTALS			**1015**	**4072**	**3632**	**950**	**177**	**45**	**14**	**1259**	**346**	**7**	**19**	**311**	**47**	**52**	**23**	**213**	**108**	**488**	**262**	**.262**	**.327**	**.347**

Rhodes, Karl Derrick — bats left — throws left — b.8/21/68 — 1991 positions: OF 44

YR	TM/LG	CL	G	TPA	AB	H	2B	3B	HR	TB	BB	IBB	HB	SO	GDP	SH	SF	SB	CS	R	RBI	BA	OBA	SA
86	AST/GCL	R	62	261	222	65	10	3	0	81	32	3	0	33	1	5	2	14	6	36	22	.293	.379	.365
87	ASH/SAL	A	129	501	413	104	16	4	3	137	77	6	0	82	4	3	8	43	14	62	50	.252	.363	.332
88	OSC/FSL	A+	132	546	452	128	4	2	1	139	81	4	2	58	7	6	5	65	23	69	34	.283	.391	.308
89	COL/SOU	AA	143	619	520	134	25	5	4	181	93	3	3	105	13	0	3	18	12	81	63	.258	.372	.348
90	TUC/PCL	AAA	107	440	385	106	24	11	3	161	47	2	0	75	9	3	5	24	4	68	59	.275	.350	.418
	HOU/NL		39	101	86	21	6	1	1	32	13	3	0	12	1	1	1	4	1	12	3	.244	.340	.372
91	HOU/NL		44	152	136	29	3	1	1	37	14	3	1	26	3	0	1	2	2	7	12	.213	.289	.272
	TUC/PCL	AAA	84	355	308	80	17	1	1	102	38	1	0	48	10	3	6	5	3	45	46	.260	.337	.331
2 YR TOTALS			**83**	**253**	**222**	**50**	**9**	**2**	**2**	**69**	**27**	**6**	**1**	**38**	**4**	**1**	**2**	**6**	**3**	**19**	**15**	**.225**	**.310**	**.311**

Richardson, Jeffrey Scott "Jeff" — bats right — throws right — b.8/26/65 — 1991 positions: 3B 3, SS 2

YR	TM/LG	CL	G	TPA	AB	H	2B	3B	HR	TB	BB	IBB	HB	SO	GDP	SH	SF	SB	CS	R	RBI	BA	OBA	SA
86	BIL/PIO	R+	47	180	162	51	14	4	0	73	17	0	1	23	0	0	0	12	1	42	20	.315	.383	.451
87	TAM/FSL	A+	100	415	374	112	9	2	0	125	30	5	3	35	16	1	7	10	4	44	37	.299	.350	.334
	VER/EAS	AA	35	142	134	28	4	0	0	32	5	0	1	25	4	2	0	5	0	24	8	.209	.243	.239
88	CHT/SOU	AA	122	447	399	100	17	1	1	122	23	0	9	56	7	12	4	8	1	50	37	.251	.303	.306
89	NAS/AMA	AAA	88	313	286	78	19	2	1	104	17	4	1	42	13	6	3	3	1	36	25	.273	.313	.364
	CIN/NL		53	140	125	21	4	0	2	31	10	1	0	23	1	3	1	1	0	10	11	.168	.234	.248
90	BUF/AMA	AAA	66	183	164	34	4	0	1	41	14	0	2	21	6	3	0	0	0	15	15	.207	.278	.250
91	PIT/NL		6	4	4	1	0	0	0	1	0	0	0	3	0	0	0	0	0	0	0	.250	.250	.250
	BUF/AMA	AAA	62	218	186	48	16	2	1	71	18	7	2	29	3	9	3	5	3	21	24	.258	.325	.382
2 YR TOTALS			**59**	**144**	**129**	**22**	**4**	**0**	**2**	**32**	**10**	**0**	**1**	**26**	**3**	**3**	**1**	**1**	**0**	**10**	**11**	**.171**	**.234**	**.248**

Riesgo, Damon Nikco "Nikco" — bats right — throws right — b.1/11/67 — 1991 positions: OF 2

YR	TM/LG	CL	G	TPA	AB	H	2B	3B	HR	TB	BB	IBB	HB	SO	GDP	SH	SF	SB	CS	R	RBI	BA	OBA	SA
88	SPO/NWL	A-	65	272	219	55	8	3	7	90	44	1	6	59	5	0	3	24	4	45	51	.251	.386	.411
89	CHS/SAL	A	119	491	402	96	25	1	13	162	73	3	10	81	5	3	3	34	13	74	53	.239	.367	.403
90	SL/FSL	A+	131	543	456	136	35	3	14	219	74	10	8	77	16	0	5	46	14	93	94	.298	.401	.480
91	WPB/FSL	A+	5	22	18	5	1	0	1	9	4	1	0	5	0	0	0	0	0	4	1	.278	.409	.500
	MON/NL		4	10	7	1	0	0	0	1	3	0	0	1	1	0	0	0	0	1	0	.143	.400	.143
	REA/EAS	AA	98	408	356	92	18	2	14	156	48	3	1	71	10	0	2	7	9	61	66	.258	.343	.438

Riles, Ernest "Ernie" — bats left — throws right — b.10/2/60 — 1991 positions: 3B 69, SS 20, 2B 7, 1B 5

YR	TM/LG	CL	G	TPA	AB	H	2B	3B	HR	TB	BB	IBB	HB	SO	GDP	SH	SF	SB	CS	R	RBI	BA	OBA	SA
84	VAN/PCL	AAA	123	501	424	113	19	7	3	155	67	8	1	67	15	1	8	1	2	59	54	.267	.362	.366
85	VAN/PCL	AAA	30	138	118	41	7	1	2	56	17	4	1	13	1	0	2	2	2	19	20	.347	.428	.475
	MIL/AL		116	495	448	128	12	7	5	169	36	0	2	54	16	6	3	2	7	54	45	.286	.339	.377
86	MIL/AL		145	588	524	132	24	2	9	187	54	0	1	80	14	6	3	7	7	69	47	.252	.321	.357
87	EP/TEX	AA	41	183	153	52	10	0	6	80	28	1	0	24	4	0	2	1	1	45	24	.340	.437	.523
	MIL/AL		83	316	276	72	11	1	4	97	30	0	1	47	6	3	6	3	4	38	38	.261	.329	.351
88	MIL/AL		41	135	127	32	6	1	1	43	7	0	0	26	0	0	2	0	2	7	9	.252	.291	.339
	SF/NL		79	201	187	55	7	2	6	75	10	2	0	33	5	0	4	1	2	26	28	.294	.323	.401
	YEAR		120	336	314	87	13	3	7	118	17	2	0	59	8	1	4	3	4	33	37	.277	.339	.404
89	SF/NL		122	337	302	84	13	2	7	122	28	2	3	50	7	1	6	1	0	43	40	.278	.339	.404
90	SF/NL		92	184	155	31	2	1	8	59	26	3	0	26	2	2	1	0	0	22	21	.200	.313	.381
91	OAK/AL		108	321	281	60	8	4	5	91	31	3	1	42	8	4	4	3	3	30	32	.214	.290	.324
7 YR TOTALS			**786**	**2577**	**2300**	**594**	**83**	**20**	**42**	**843**	**222**	**12**	**7**	**358**	**61**	**23**	**25**	**18**	**25**	**289**	**260**	**.258**	**.322**	**.367**

Ripken, Calvin Edwin Jr. "Cal" — bats right — throws right — b.8/24/60 — 1991 positions: SS 162

YR	TM/LG	CL	G	TPA	AB	H	2B	3B	HR	TB	BB	IBB	HB	SO	GDP	SH	SF	SB	CS	R	RBI	BA	OBA	SA
81	BAL/AL		23	40	39	5	0	0	0	5	1	0	0	8	4	0	0	0	0	1	0	.128	.150	.128
82	BAL/AL		160	655	598	158	32	5	28	284	46	3	3	95	16	2	6	3	3	90	93	.264	.317	.475
83	BAL/AL		162	726	663	211	47	2	27	343	58	0	0	97	24	0	5	0	4	121	102	.318	.371	.517
84	BAL/AL		162	716	641	195	37	7	27	327	71	1	2	89	16	0	2	2	1	103	86	.304	.374	.510
85	BAL/AL		161	718	642	181	32	5	26	301	67	1	1	68	32	0	8	2	3	116	110	.282	.355	.469
86	BAL/AL		162	707	627	177	35	1	25	289	70	5	0	60	19	0	6	4	2	98	81	.282	.355	.461
87	BAL/AL		162	717	624	157	28	3	27	272	81	3	0	77	19	0	11	3	5	97	98	.252	.333	.436
88	BAL/AL		161	689	575	152	25	1	23	248	102	7	2	69	10	0	10	2	1	87	81	.264	.372	.431
89	BAL/AL		162	712	646	166	30	0	21	259	57	5	3	72	22	0	6	3	2	80	93	.257	.317	.401

(continued)

Ripken, Calvin Edwin Jr. "Cal" (continued)

YR	TM/LG	CL	G	TPA	AB	H	2B	3B	HR	TB	BB	IBB	HB	SO	GDP	SH	SF	SB	CS	R	RBI	BA	OBA	SA
90	BAL/AL		161	695	600	150	28	4	21	249	82	17	5	66	12	1	7	3	1	78	84	.250	.341	.415
91	BAL/AL		162	717	650	210	46	5	34	368	53	15	5	46	19	0	9	6	1	99	114	.323	.374	.566
11 YR TOTALS			1638	7092	6305	1762	340	33	259	2945	688	54	26	747	193	3	70	28	24	970	942	**.279**	**.349**	**.467**

Ripken, William Oliver "Billy" — bats right — throws right — b.12/16/64 — 1991 positions: 2B 103

YR	TM/LG	CL	G	TPA	AB	H	2B	3B	HR	TB	BB	IBB	HB	SO	GDP	SH	SF	SB	CS	R	RBI	BA	OBA	SA
84	HAG/CAR	A+	115	451	409	94	15	3	2	121	36	1	4	64	11	2	0	3	5	48	40	.230	.298	.296
85	CHA/SOU	AA	18	58	51	7	1	0	0	8	6	0	0	4	1	1	0	0	0	2	3	.137	.228	.157
	DB/FSL	A+	67	250	222	51	11	0	0	62	22	1	0	24	6	5	1	7	4	23	18	.230	.298	.279
	HAG/CAR	A+	14	50	47	12	0	1	0	14	1	0	2	2	0	0	0	0	2	9	0	.255	.300	.298
86	CHA/SOU	AA	141	564	530	142	20	3	5	183	24	2	1	47	21	7	2	9	4	58	62	.268	.300	.345
87	ROC/INT	AAA	74	266	238	68	15	0	0	83	21	0	0	23	9	7	0	7	2	32	11	.286	.344	.349
	BAL/AL		58	257	234	72	9	0	2	87	21	0	0	23	3	1	1	4	1	27	20	.308	.363	.372
88	BAL/AL		150	559	512	106	18	1	2	132	33	0	5	63	14	6	3	8	2	52	34	.207	.260	.258
89	BAL/AL		115	364	318	76	11	2	2	97	22	0	1	53	12	19	5	1	2	31	26	.239	.284	.305
90	BAL/AL		129	456	406	118	28	1	3	157	28	2	4	43	7	17	1	5	2	48	38	.291	.342	.387
91	FRE/CAR	A+	1	4	4	1	0	0	0	1	0	0	0	1	0	0	0	0	0	2	1	.250	.250	.250
	HAG/EAS	AA	1	5	5	3	0	0	0	3	0	0	0	0	0	0	0	1	0	1	0	.600	.600	.600
	BAL/AL		104	315	287	62	11	1	0	75	15	0	0	31	14	11	2	0	1	24	14	.216	.253	.261
5 YR TOTALS			556	1951	1757	434	77	5	9	548	119	2	9	213	50	54	12	18	8	182	132	**.247**	**.296**	**.312**

Rivera, Luis Antonio (Pedraza) — bats right — throws right — b.1/3/64 — 1991 positions: SS 129

YR	TM/LG	CL	G	TPA	AB	H	2B	3B	HR	TB	BB	IBB	HB	SO	GDP	SH	SF	SB	CS	R	RBI	BA	OBA	SA
84	WPB/FSL	A+	124	497	439	100	23	0	6	141	50	5	5	79	16	0	3	14	2	54	43	.228	.312	.321
85	JAC/SOU	AA	138	598	538	129	20	2	16	201	44	1	7	69	7	3	6	18	15	74	72	.240	.303	.374
86	IND/AMA	AAA	108	447	407	100	17	5	7	148	29	0	4	68	12	1	6	18	8	60	43	.246	.298	.364
	MON/NL		55	187	166	34	11	1	0	47	17	0	2	33	1	1	1	1	1	20	13	.205	.285	.283
87	IND/AMA	AAA	108	473	433	135	26	3	8	191	32	2	2	73	4	3	3	24	11	73	53	.312	.360	.441
	MON/NL		18	33	32	5	2	0	0	7	1	0	0	8	0	0	0	0	0	0	1	.156	.182	.219
88	MON/NL		123	402	371	83	17	3	4	118	24	1	1	69	9	3	3	3	4	35	30	.224	.271	.318
89	PAW/INT	AAA	43	191	175	44	9	0	1	56	11	0	1	23	3	4	0	5	3	22	13	.251	.299	.320
	BOS/AL		93	349	323	83	17	1	5	117	20	1	1	60	7	4	1	2	3	35	29	.257	.301	.362
90	BOS/AL		118	385	346	78	20	0	7	119	25	0	1	58	10	12	1	4	3	38	45	.225	.279	.344
91	BOS/AL		129	468	414	107	22	3	8	159	35	0	3	86	10	12	4	4	4	64	40	.258	.318	.384
6 YR TOTALS			536	1824	1652	390	89	8	24	567	122	5	8	314	37	32	10	14	15	192	158	**.236**	**.290**	**.343**

Roberts, Leon Joseph "Bip" — bats both — throws right — b.10/27/63 — 1991 positions: 2B 68, OF 46

YR	TM/LG	CL	G	TPA	AB	H	2B	3B	HR	TB	BB	IBB	HB	SO	GDP	SH	SF	SB	CS	R	RBI	BA	OBA	SA
84	PW/CAR	A+	134	552	498	150	25	5	8	209	44	3	3	63	4	2	5	50	13	81	77	.301	.358	.420
85	NAS/EAS	AA	105	442	401	109	19	5	1	141	29	2	6	43	6	4	2	40	12	64	23	.272	.329	.352
86	SD/NL		101	258	241	61	5	2	1	73	14	1	0	29	2	2	1	14	12	34	12	.253	.293	.303
87	LV/PCL	AAA	98	406	359	110	18	10	1	151	37	3	3	39	11	6	1	27	14	66	38	.306	.375	.421
88	LV/PCL	AAA	100	383	343	121	21	8	7	179	32	1	0	45	5	6	2	29	7	73	51	.353	.406	.522
	SD/NL		5	10	9	3	0	0	0	3	1	0	0	2	0	0	0	0	2	1	0	.333	.400	.333
89	SD/NL		117	387	329	99	15	8	3	139	49	0	1	45	3	6	2	21	11	81	25	.301	.391	.422
90	SD/NL		149	629	556	172	36	3	9	241	55	1	6	65	8	8	4	46	12	104	44	.309	.375	.433
91	SD/NL		117	472	424	119	13	3	3	147	37	0	4	71	6	4	3	26	11	66	32	.281	.342	.347
5 YR TOTALS			489	1756	1559	454	69	16	16	603	156	2	11	212	19	20	10	107	48	286	113	**.291**	**.358**	**.387**

Rodriguez, Carlos (Marquez) — bats both — throws right — b.11/1/67 — 1991 positions: SS 11, 2B 3

YR	TM/LG	CL	G	TPA	AB	H	2B	3B	HR	TB	BB	IBB	HB	SO	GDP	SH	SF	SB	CS	R	RBI	BA	OBA	SA
87	YAN/GCL	R	50	146	115	18	0	0	0	18	23	0	1	8	1	6	1	2	1	15	11	.157	.300	.157
88	FL/FSL	A+	124	510	461	110	15	1	0	127	23	2	2	30	16	20	4	3	2	39	36	.239	.276	.275
89	FL/FSL	A+	102	429	353	85	15	1	0	102	49	1	3	25	7	21	3	9	8	48	26	.241	.336	.289
	ALB/EAS	AA	36	124	107	27	4	2	0	35	13	0	0	4	3	3	1	1	1	15	8	.252	.331	.327
90	ALB/EAS	AA	18	78	75	21	4	0	0	25	2	0	1	2	2	0	0	1	1	10	7	.280	.308	.333
	COL/INT	AAA	71	256	220	60	12	0	0	72	30	2	2	8	5	2	2	3	1	31	16	.273	.362	.327
91	NY/AL		15	39	37	7	0	0	0	7	1	0	0	2	3	1	0	0	0	1	2	.189	.211	.189
	COL/INT	AAA	73	265	212	54	9	3	0	69	42	1	1	13	10	5	1	9	4	32	21	.255	.373	.325

Rodriguez, Henry Anderson (Lorenzo) — bats left — throws left — b.11/8/67 — 1991 positions: OF System LA/NL

YR	TM/LG	CL	G	TPA	AB	H	2B	3B	HR	TB	BB	IBB	HB	SO	GDP	SH	SF	SB	CS	R	RBI	BA	OBA	SA
87	DOD/GCL	R	49	170	148	49	7	3	0	62	16	7	3	15	5	1	2	3	1	23	15	.331	.402	.419
88	SAL/NWL	A−	72	323	291	84	14	4	2	112	21	1	4	42	7	1	6	14	2	47	39	.289	.339	.385
89	VB/FSL	A+	126	490	433	123	33	1	10	188	48	11	2	58	12	1	6	7	6	53	73	.284	.354	.434
	BAK/CAL	A+	3	9	9	2	0	0	1	5	0	0	0	3	0	0	0	0	0	2	2	.222	.222	.556
90	SA/TEX	AA	129	573	495	144	21	9	28	267	61	9	2	66	10	1	14	5	4	82	109	.291	.362	.539
91	ALB/PCL	AAA	121	478	446	121	22	5	10	183	25	3	1	62	11	1	5	4	5	61	67	.271	.308	.410

Rodriguez, Ivan (Torres) — bats right — throws right — b.11/30/71 — 1991 positions: C 88

YR	TM/LG	CL	G	TPA	AB	H	2B	3B	HR	TB	BB	IBB	HB	SO	GDP	SH	SF	SB	CS	R	RBI	BA	OBA	SA
89	GAS/SAL	A	112	418	386	92	22	1	7	137	21	0	2	58	6	5	4	2	5	38	42	.238	.278	.355
90	CHA/FSL	A+	109	432	408	117	17	7	2	154	12	2	1	50	6	1	4	1	0	48	55	.287	.316	.377
91	TUL/TEX	AA	50	188	175	48	7	2	3	68	6	0	1	27	5	1	5	1	2	16	24	.274	.294	.389
	TEX/AL		88	288	280	74	16	0	3	99	5	0	0	42	10	2	1	0	1	24	27	.264	.276	.354

Rohde, David Grant "Dave" — bats both — throws right — b.5/8/64 — 1991 positions: 2B 4, 3B 3, SS 3, 1B 1

YR	TM/LG	CL	G	TPA	AB	H	2B	3B	HR	TB	BB	IBB	HB	SO	GDP	SH	SF	SB	CS	R	RBI	BA	OBA	SA
86	AUB/NYP	A–	61	247	207	54	6	4	2	74	37	1	0	37	2	1	2	28	9	41	42	.261	.370	.357
87	OSC/FSL	A+	103	441	377	108	15	1	5	140	50	1	4	58	4	10	0	12	6	57	42	.286	.376	.371
88	COL/SOU	AA	142	583	486	130	20	2	4	166	81	1	5	62	14	4	7	36	4	76	53	.267	.373	.342
89	COL/SOU	AA	67	303	254	71	5	2	2	86	41	0	1	25	6	5	2	15	5	40	27	.280	.379	.339
	TUC/PCL	AAA	75	279	234	68	7	3	1	84	32	1	1	30	4	7	5	11	5	35	30	.291	.371	.359
90	TUC/PCL	AAA	47	212	170	60	10	2	0	74	40	0	1	20	7	1	0	5	2	42	20	.353	.479	.435
	HOU/NL		58	117	98	18	4	0	0	22	9	2	5	20	3	4	1	0	0	8	5	.184	.283	.224
91	HOU/NL		29	48	41	5	0	0	0	5	5	0	0	8	1	2	0	0	0	3	0	.122	.217	.122
	TUC/PCL	AAA	73	317	253	94	10	4	1	115	52	3	5	34	4	2	5	15	6	36	40	.372	.479	.455
2 YR TOTALS			**87**	**165**	**139**	**23**	**4**	**0**	**0**	**27**	**14**	**2**	**5**	**28**	**4**	**6**	**1**	**0**	**0**	**11**	**5**	**.165**	**.264**	**.194**

Romine, Kevin Andrew — bats right — throws right — b.5/23/61 — 1991 positions: OF 23, DH 14

YR	TM/LG	CL	G	TPA	AB	H	2B	3B	HR	TB	BB	IBB	HB	SO	GDP	SH	SF	SB	CS	R	RBI	BA	OBA	SA
84	PAW/INT	AAA	113	425	336	85	10	1	12	133	83	4	0	66	13	1	5	13	7	62	72	.253	.396	.396
85	PAW/INT	AAA	106	450	403	98	20	1	5	135	43	0	0	76	15	2	1	19	4	43	33	.243	.317	.335
	BOS/AL		24	31	28	6	2	0	0	8	1	0	0	4	1	2	0	1	0	3	1	.214	.241	.286
86	PAW/INT	AAA	71	277	257	75	8	3	4	101	15	0	1	30	5	1	3	11	4	30	32	.292	.330	.393
	BOS/AL		35	39	35	9	2	0	0	11	3	0	0	6	1	1	0	2	0	6	2	.257	.316	.314
87	PAW/INT	AAA	129	558	491	131	24	1	11	190	64	0	0	70	16	0	3	21	6	72	52	.267	.349	.387
	BOS/AL		9	26	24	7	2	0	0	9	2	0	0	6	0	0	0	0	0	5	2	.292	.346	.375
88	PAW/INT	AAA	41	158	148	53	6	1	4	73	8	0	1	21	2	0	1	3	0	18	26	.358	.392	.493
	BOS/AL		57	85	78	15	2	1	1	22	7	0	0	15	3	0	0	2	0	17	6	.192	.259	.282
89	PAW/INT	AAA	27	105	90	27	3	0	2	36	15	0	1	13	7	0	0	0	0	9	7	.300	.400	.400
	BOS/AL		92	303	274	75	13	0	1	91	21	1	2	53	11	3	3	1	1	30	23	.274	.327	.332
90	BOS/AL		70	151	136	37	7	0	2	50	12	0	1	27	7	0	2	4	0	21	14	.272	.331	.368
91	BOS/AL		44	58	55	9	2	0	1	14	3	0	0	10	1	0	0	1	1	7	7	.164	.207	.255
7 YR TOTALS			**331**	**693**	**630**	**158**	**30**	**1**	**5**	**205**	**49**	**1**	**3**	**124**	**24**	**6**	**5**	**11**	**2**	**89**	**55**	**.251**	**.306**	**.325**

Rose, Robert Richard "Bobby" — bats right — throws right — b.3/15/67 — 1991 positions: 2B 8, OF 7, 3B 4, 1B 3

YR	TM/LG	CL	G	TPA	AB	H	2B	3B	HR	TB	BB	IBB	HB	SO	GDP	SH	SF	SB	CS	R	RBI	BA	OBA	SA
85	SAL/NWL	A–	50	182	167	37	6	2	0	47	14	0	0	43	3	1	0	8	2	15	16	.222	.282	.281
86	QC/MID	A	129	539	467	118	21	5	7	170	66	2	2	116	11	2	4	13	9	67	56	.253	.343	.364
88	QC/MID	A	135	574	483	137	23	3	13	205	78	3	7	92	9	3	3	14	7	75	78	.284	.389	.424
	PS/CAL	A+	1	3	3	1	0	0	0	1	0	0	0	1	0	0	0	0	0	0	1	.333	.333	.333
89	MID/TEX	AA	99	418	351	126	21	5	11	190	50	3	6	62	6	3	8	3	2	64	73	.359	.439	.541
	CAL/AL		14	42	38	8	1	2	1	16	2	0	1	10	2	1	0	0	0	4	3	.211	.268	.421
90	EDM/PCL	AAA	134	575	502	142	27	10	9	216	56	0	4	83	14	7	6	6	3	84	68	.283	.356	.430
	CAL/AL		7	16	13	5	0	0	1	8	2	0	0	1	0	1	0	0	0	5	2	.385	.467	.615
91	CAL/AL		22	69	65	18	5	1	1	28	3	0	0	13	1	0	1	0	0	5	8	.277	.304	.431
	EDM/PCL	AAA	62	277	242	72	14	5	6	114	21	1	5	41	7	1	8	3	0	35	56	.298	.355	.471
3 YR TOTALS			**43**	**127**	**116**	**31**	**6**	**3**	**3**	**52**	**7**	**0**	**1**	**24**	**3**	**2**	**1**	**0**	**0**	**14**	**13**	**.267**	**.312**	**.448**

Rossy, Elam Jose "Rico" — bats right — throws right — b.2/16/64 — 1991 positions: SS 1

YR	TM/LG	CL	G	TPA	AB	H	2B	3B	HR	TB	BB	IBB	HB	SO	GDP	SH	SF	SB	CS	R	RBI	BA	OBA	SA
85	NEW/NYP	A–	73	283	246	53	14	2	3	80	32	1	1	22	13	3	1	17	7	38	25	.215	.307	.325
86	MIA/FSL	A+	38	166	134	34	7	1	1	46	24	0	1	8	4	6	1	10	6	26	9	.254	.369	.343
	CHA/SOU	AA	77	269	232	68	16	2	3	97	26	0	2	19	2	3	1	13	5	40	50	.293	.368	.418
87	CHA/SOU	AA	127	521	471	135	22	3	4	175	43	0	3	38	20	3	1	20	9	69	50	.287	.349	.372
88	BUF/AMA	AAA	68	201	187	46	4	0	1	53	13	0	0	17	4	0	1	1	5	12	20	.246	.294	.283
89	HAR/EAS	AA	78	270	238	60	16	1	2	84	27	0	0	19	5	0	2	2	4	20	25	.252	.333	.353
	BUF/AMA	AAA	38	131	109	21	5	0	0	26	18	1	1	11	4	1	2	4	0	11	2	.193	.308	.239
90	BUF/AMA	AAA	8	23	17	3	1	0	0	5	4	0	0	2	0	1	1	1	0	3	2	.176	.318	.294
	GRE/SOU	AA	5	22	21	4	1	0	0	5	1	0	0	2	1	0	0	0	0	4	0	.190	.227	.238
	RIC/INT	AAA	107	461	380	88	13	0	4	113	69	1	3	43	12	7	2	11	6	58	32	.232	.352	.297
91	RIC/INT	AAA	139	570	482	124	25	1	2	157	67	1	5	46	12	13	3	4	8	58	48	.257	.352	.326
	ATL/NL		5	1	1	0	0	0	0	0	0	0	0	1	0	0	0	0	0	0	0	.000	.000	.000

Rowland, Richard Garnet "Rich" — bats right — throws right — b.2/25/67 — 1991 positions: C 2, DH 1

YR	TM/LG	CL	G	TPA	AB	H	2B	3B	HR	TB	BB	IBB	HB	SO	GDP	SH	SF	SB	CS	R	RBI	BA	OBA	SA
88	BRI/APP	R+	56	217	186	51	10	1	4	75	27	1	1	39	2	0	3	1	2	29	41	.274	.364	.403
89	FAY/SAL	A	108	438	375	102	17	1	9	148	54	2	3	98	8	3	3	4	1	43	59	.272	.366	.395
90	LON/EAS	AA	47	185	161	46	10	0	8	80	20	1	0	33	7	0	1	1	1	22	30	.286	.373	.497
	TOL/INT	AAA	62	213	192	50	12	0	7	83	15	0	1	33	3	3	2	2	3	28	22	.260	.314	.432
	DET/AL		7	21	19	3	1	0	0	4	2	0	0	4	1	0	0	0	0	3	0	.158	.238	.211
91	TOL/INT	AAA	109	447	383	104	25	0	13	168	60	0	3	77	8	0	1	4	2	56	68	.272	.374	.439
	DET/AL		4	6	4	1	0	0	0	1	1	1	0	2	0	0	1	0	0	0	1	.250	.333	.250
2 YR TOTALS			**11**	**27**	**23**	**4**	**1**	**0**	**0**	**5**	**3**	**1**	**0**	**6**	**1**	**0**	**1**	**0**	**0**	**3**	**1**	**.174**	**.259**	**.217**

Royer, Stanley Dean "Stan" — bats right — throws right — b.8/31/67 — 1991 positions: 3B 5

YR	TM/LG	CL	G	TPA	AB	H	2B	3B	HR	TB	BB	IBB	HB	SO	GDP	SH	SF	SB	CS	R	RBI	BA	OBA	SA
88	SO/NWL	A–	73	326	286	91	19	3	6	134	33	1	2	71	6	1	4	1	0	47	48	.318	.388	.469
89	TAC/PCL	AAA	6	21	19	5	1	0	0	6	2	0	0	6	1	0	0	0	0	2	2	.263	.333	.316
	MOD/CAL	A+	127	539	476	120	28	1	11	183	58	3	2	132	11	1	2	3	2	54	69	.252	.333	.384
90	HUN/SOU	AA	137	585	527	136	29	3	14	213	43	0	3	113	13	8	4	4	1	69	89	.258	.315	.404
	LOU/AMA	AAA	4	17	15	4	1	1	0	7	2	0	0	5	0	0	0	0	0	1	4	.267	.353	.467

(continued)

Royer, Stanley Dean "Stan" (continued)

YR	TM/LG	CL	G	TPA	AB	H	2B	3B	HR	TB	BB	IBB	HB	SO	GDP	SH	SF	SB	CS	R	RBI	BA	OBA	SA
91	LOU/AMA	AAA	138	575	523	133	29	6	14	216	43	1	3	126	13	0	6	1	2	48	74	.254	.311	.413
	STL/NL		9	22	21	6	1	0	0	7	1	0	0	2	0	0	0	0	0	1	1	.286	.318	.333

Russell, John William — bats right — throws right — b.1/5/61 — 1991 positions: OF 8, C 5, DH 5

YR	TM/LG	CL	G	TPA	AB	H	2B	3B	HR	TB	BB	IBB	HB	SO	GDP	SH	SF	SB	CS	R	RBI	BA	OBA	SA
82	REA/EAS	AA	77	295	263	53	10	5	6	91	23	3	4	84	8	2	3	3	2	26	30	.202	.273	.346
83	POR/PCL	AAA	128	491	445	113	23	3	27	223	42	1	2	109	3	0	2	3	3	71	76	.254	.320	.501
84	POR/PCL	AAA	93	403	350	101	22	5	19	190	44	0	6	91	10	0	3	1	0	75	77	.289	.375	.543
	PHI/NL		39	114	99	28	8	1	2	44	12	2	0	33	2	0	3	0	0	11	11	.283	.351	.444
85	POR/PCL	AAA	16	63	49	15	2	2	4	33	13	3	1	15	0	0	0	0	0	8	11	.306	.460	.673
	PHI/NL		81	234	216	47	12	0	9	86	18	0	0	72	5	0	0	2	0	22	23	.218	.278	.398
86	PHI/NL		93	348	315	76	21	2	13	140	25	2	3	103	6	1	4	0	1	35	60	.241	.300	.444
87	MAI/INT	AAA	44	167	143	29	6	1	7	58	22	0	0	37	7	1	1	2	3	15	24	.203	.307	.406
	PHI/NL		24	65	62	9	1	0	3	19	3	0	0	17	4	0	0	0	1	5	8	.145	.185	.306
88	MAI/INT	AAA	110	430	394	90	18	0	13	147	29	2	4	108	5	0	3	4	2	50	52	.228	.286	.373
	PHI/NL		22	53	49	12	1	0	2	19	3	0	1	15	0	0	0	0	0	5	4	.245	.302	.388
89	ATL/NL		74	169	159	29	2	0	2	37	8	1	1	53	0	0	1	0	0	14	9	.182	.225	.233
90	OC/AMA	AAA	6	24	22	9	4	0	2	19	2	0	0	3	2	0	0	0	0	7	6	.409	.458	.864
	TEX/AL		68	140	128	35	4	0	2	45	11	0	0	41	3	1	0	1	0	16	8	.273	.331	.352
91	TEX/AL		22	29	27	3	0	0	0	3	1	0	0	7	0	0	1	0	0	3	1	.111	.138	.111
8 YR TOTALS			**423**	**1152**	**1055**	**239**	**49**	**3**	**33**	**393**	**81**	**7**	**5**	**341**	**26**	**2**	**9**	**3**	**3**	**111**	**124**	**.227**	**.283**	**.373**

Sabo, Christopher Andrew "Chris" — bats right — throws right — b.1/19/62 — 1991 positions: 3B 151

YR	TM/LG	CL	G	TPA	AB	H	2B	3B	HR	TB	BB	IBB	HB	SO	GDP	SH	SF	SB	CS	R	RBI	BA	OBA	SA
84	VER/EAS	AA	125	495	441	94	19	1	5	130	44	1	4	62	11	2	4	10	5	44	38	.213	.288	.295
85	VER/EAS	AA	124	495	428	119	19	0	11	171	50	1	7	39	6	6	4	7	5	66	46	.278	.360	.400
86	DEN/AMA	AAA	129	492	432	118	26	2	10	178	48	2	3	53	9	3	6	9	2	83	60	.273	.346	.412
87	NAS/AMA	AAA	91	360	315	92	19	3	7	138	37	4	1	25	9	1	6	23	4	56	51	.292	.362	.438
88	CIN/NL		137	582	538	146	40	2	11	223	29	1	6	52	12	5	4	46	14	74	44	.271	.314	.414
89	NAS/AMA	AAA	7	30	30	5	2	0	0	7	0	0	0	0	4	0	0	0	0	0	3	.167	.167	.233
	CIN/NL		82	336	304	79	21	1	6	120	25	2	1	33	2	4	2	14	9	40	29	.260	.316	.395
90	CIN/NL		148	636	567	153	38	2	25	270	61	7	4	58	8	1	3	25	10	95	71	.270	.343	.476
91	CIN/NL		153	640	582	175	35	3	26	294	44	3	6	79	13	5	3	19	6	91	88	.301	.354	.505
4 YR TOTALS			**520**	**2194**	**1991**	**553**	**134**	**8**	**68**	**907**	**159**	**13**	**17**	**222**	**35**	**15**	**12**	**104**	**39**	**300**	**232**	**.278**	**.335**	**.456**

Salas, Mark Bruce — bats left — throws right — b.3/8/61 — 1991 positions: C 11, DH 8, 1B 5

YR	TM/LG	CL	G	TPA	AB	H	2B	3B	HR	TB	BB	IBB	HB	SO	GDP	SH	SF	SB	CS	R	RBI	BA	OBA	SA
84	STL/NL		14	21	20	2	1	0	0	3	0	0	0	3	0	1	0	0	0	1	1	.100	.100	.150
	LOU/AMA	AAA	95	340	316	77	20	2	12	137	20	1	0	43	9	1	3	2	1	28	48	.244	.286	.434
85	MIN/AL		120	382	360	108	20	5	9	165	18	5	1	37	7	0	3	0	1	51	41	.300	.332	.458
86	MIN/AL		91	285	258	60	7	4	8	99	18	2	1	32	8	5	3	3	1	28	33	.233	.282	.384
87	MIN/AL		22	51	45	17	2	0	3	28	5	1	0	6	0	0	1	0	1	8	9	.378	.431	.622
	COL/INT	AAA	12	48	43	10	1	0	2	17	5	0	0	8	0	0	1	0	0	5	4	.233	.313	.395
	NY/AL		50	130	115	23	4	0	3	36	10	0	3	17	2	1	1	0	0	13	12	.200	.279	.313
	YEAR		72	181	160	40	6	0	6	64	15	1	3	23	2	1	2	0	1	21	21	.250	.322	.400
88	CHI/AL		75	211	196	49	7	0	3	65	12	2	3	17	3	0	0	0	0	17	9	.250	.303	.332
89	CLE/AL		30	83	77	17	4	1	2	29	5	1	1	13	2	0	0	0	0	4	7	.221	.277	.377
	CS/PCL	AAA	46	166	146	46	10	2	6	78	16	6	1	16	3	2	1	0	0	27	20	.315	.384	.534
90	DET/AL		74	187	164	38	3	0	9	68	21	2	1	28	3	1	0	0	0	18	24	.232	.323	.415
91	DET/AL		33	60	57	5	1	0	1	9	0	0	2	10	0	0	1	0	0	2	7	.088	.117	.158
8 YR TOTALS			**509**	**1410**	**1292**	**319**	**49**	**10**	**38**	**502**	**89**	**13**	**12**	**163**	**25**	**8**	**9**	**3**	**3**	**142**	**143**	**.247**	**.300**	**.389**

Salazar, Luis Ernesto (Garcia) — bats right — throws right — b.5/19/56 — 1991 positions: 3B 86, 1B 7, OF 1

YR	TM/LG	CL	G	TPA	AB	H	2B	3B	HR	TB	BB	IBB	HB	SO	GDP	SH	SF	SB	CS	R	RBI	BA	OBA	SA
80	SD/NL		44	183	169	57	4	7	1	78	9	1	1	25	4	3	1	11	2	28	25	.337	.372	.462
81	SD/NL		109	424	400	121	19	6	3	161	16	2	1	72	7	5	2	11	8	37	38	.303	.329	.403
82	SD/NL		145	559	524	127	15	5	8	176	23	10	2	80	10	5	5	32	9	55	62	.242	.274	.336
83	SD/NL		134	510	481	124	16	2	14	186	17	8	2	80	3	8	2	24	9	52	45	.258	.285	.387
84	SD/NL		93	236	228	55	7	2	3	75	6	1	0	38	5	2	0	11	7	20	17	.241	.261	.329
85	CHI/AL		122	353	327	80	18	2	10	132	12	2	4	60	5	9	5	14	4	39	45	.245	.267	.404
86	APP/MID	A	21	84	79	16	1	0	2	23	4	0	1	18	2	0	1	0	0	9	4	.203	.250	.291
	CHI/AL		4	8	7	1	0	0	0	1	1	0	0	3	0	0	0	0	0	1	0	.143	.250	.143
87	LV/PCL	AAA	4	18	17	5	2	0	1	10	1	0	0	4	2	0	0	1	0	2	3	.294	.333	.588
	SD/NL		84	206	189	48	5	0	3	62	14	2	0	30	2	1	2	3	3	13	17	.254	.302	.328
88	DET/AL		130	489	452	122	14	1	12	174	21	2	3	70	13	10	3	6	0	61	62	.270	.305	.385
89	SD/NL		95	265	246	66	7	2	8	101	11	3	1	44	4	7	0	1	3	27	22	.268	.302	.411
	CHI/NL		26	84	80	26	5	0	1	34	4	0	0	13	2	0	0	0	1	7	12	.325	.357	.425
	YEAR		121	349	326	92	12	2	9	135	15	3	1	57	6	7	0	1	4	34	34	.282	.316	.414
90	CHI/NL		115	434	410	104	13	3	12	159	19	3	4	59	4	0	1	3	1	44	47	.254	.293	.388
91	CHI/NL		103	351	333	86	14	1	14	144	15	2	0	45	8	2	0	0	3	34	38	.258	.292	.432
12 YR TOTALS			**1204**	**4102**	**3846**	**1017**	**137**	**31**	**89**	**1483**	**168**	**35**	**15**	**619**	**67**	**52**	**21**	**116**	**50**	**418**	**430**	**.264**	**.296**	**.386**

Salmon, Timothy James "Tim" — bats right — throws right — b.8/24/68 — 1991 positions: OF System CAL/AL

YR	TM/LG	CL	G	TPA	AB	H	2B	3B	HR	TB	BB	IBB	HB	SO	GDP	SH	SF	SB	CS	R	RBI	BA	OBA	SA
89	BEN/NWL	A−	55	238	196	48	6	5	6	82	33	0	6	61	2	1	2	2	4	37	31	.245	.367	.418
90	PS/CAL	A+	36	143	118	34	6	0	2	46	21	0	4	44	1	0	0	11	1	19	21	.288	.413	.390
	MID/TEX	AA	27	117	97	26	3	1	3	40	18	0	1	38	1	0	1	1	0	17	16	.268	.385	.412
91	MID/TEX	AA	131	565	465	114	26	4	23	217	89	1	6	166	6	3	2	12	6	100	94	.245	.372	.467

Samuel, Juan Milton — bats right — throws right — b.12/9/60 — 1991 positions: 2B 152

YR	TM/LG	CL	G	TPA	AB	H	2B	3B	HR	TB	BB	IBB	HB	SO	GDP	SH	SF	SB	CS	R	RBI	BA	OBA	SA
83	PHI/NL		18	71	65	18	1	2	2	29	4	1	1	16	1	0	1	3	2	14	5	.277	.324	.446
84	PHI/NL		160	737	701	191	36	19	15	310	28	2	7	168	6	0	1	72	15	105	69	.272	.307	.442
85	PHI/NL		161	709	663	175	31	13	19	289	33	2	6	141	8	2	5	53	19	101	74	.264	.303	.436
86	PHI/NL		145	633	591	157	36	12	16	265	26	3	8	142	8	1	7	42	14	90	78	.266	.302	.448
87	PHI/NL		160	726	655	178	37	15	28	329	60	5	5	162	12	0	6	35	15	113	100	.272	.335	.502
88	PHI/NL		157	685	629	153	32	9	12	239	39	6	12	151	8	0	5	33	10	68	67	.243	.298	.380
89	PHI/NL		51	219	199	49	3	1	8	78	18	1	1	45	2	0	1	11	3	32	20	.246	.311	.392
	NY/NL		86	370	333	76	13	1	3	100	24	1	10	75	5	2	1	31	9	37	28	.228	.299	.300
	YEAR		137	589	532	125	16	2	11	178	42	2	11	120	7	2	2	42	12	69	48	.235	.303	.335
90	LA/NL		143	558	492	119	24	3	13	188	51	5	5	126	8	5	5	38	20	62	52	.242	.316	.382
91	LA/NL		153	659	594	161	22	6	12	231	49	4	3	133	8	10	3	23	8	74	58	.271	.328	.389
9 YR TOTALS			**1234**	**5367**	**4922**	**1277**	**235**	**81**	**128**	**2058**	**332**	**30**	**58**	**1159**	**66**	**20**	**35**	**341**	**115**	**696**	**551**	**.259**	**.312**	**.418**

Sanchez, Rey Francisco (Guadalupe) — bats right — throws right — b.10/5/67 — 1991 positions: SS 10, 2B 2

YR	TM/LG	CL	G	TPA	AB	H	2B	3B	HR	TB	BB	IBB	HB	SO	GDP	SH	SF	SB	CS	R	RBI	BA	OBA	SA
86	RAN/GCL	R	52	217	169	49	3	1	0	54	41	0	3	18	3	3	1	10	10	27	23	.290	.435	.320
87	GAS/SAL	A	50	187	160	35	1	2	1	43	22	0	2	17	9	3	0	6	3	19	10	.219	.321	.269
	BUT/PIO	R+	49	217	189	69	10	6	0	91	21	1	2	11	6	3	2	22	6	36	25	.365	.430	.481
88	CHA/FSL	A+	128	462	418	128	6	5	0	144	35	4	5	24	14	1	3	29	11	60	38	.306	.364	.344
89	OC/AMA	AAA	134	495	464	104	10	4	1	125	21	0	2	50	14	5	3	4	4	38	39	.224	.259	.269
91	IOW/AMA	AAA	126	474	417	121	16	5	2	153	37	1	7	27	11	11	2	13	7	60	46	.290	.356	.367
	CHI/NL		13	27	23	6	0	0	0	6	4	0	0	3	0	0	0	0	0	1	2	.261	.370	.261

Sandberg, Ryne Dee — bats right — throws right — b.9/18/59 — 1991 positions: 2B 157

YR	TM/LG	CL	G	TPA	AB	H	2B	3B	HR	TB	BB	IBB	HB	SO	GDP	SH	SF	SB	CS	R	RBI	BA	OBA	SA
81	PHI/NL		13	6	6	1	0	0	0	1	0	0	0	1	0	0	0	0	0	2	0	.167	.167	.167
82	CHI/NL		156	687	635	172	33	5	7	236	36	3	4	90	7	7	5	32	12	103	54	.271	.312	.372
83	CHI/NL		158	699	633	165	25	4	8	222	51	3	3	79	8	7	5	37	11	94	48	.261	.316	.351
84	CHI/NL		156	700	636	200	36	19	19	331	52	3	3	101	7	5	4	32	7	114	84	.314	.367	.520
85	CHI/NL		153	673	609	186	31	6	26	307	57	5	1	97	10	2	4	54	11	113	83	.305	.364	.504
86	CHI/NL		154	682	627	178	28	5	14	258	46	6	3	79	11	3	6	34	11	68	76	.284	.330	.411
87	CHI/NL		132	587	523	154	25	2	16	231	59	4	2	79	11	1	2	21	2	81	59	.294	.367	.442
88	CHI/NL		155	679	618	163	23	8	19	259	54	3	1	91	14	1	5	25	10	77	69	.264	.322	.419
89	CHI/NL		157	672	606	176	25	5	30	301	59	4	2	85	9	1	2	15	5	104	76	.290	.356	.497
90	CHI/NL		155	675	615	188	30	3	40	344	50	8	0	84	8	0	9	25	7	116	100	.306	.354	.559
91	CHI/NL		158	684	585	170	32	2	26	284	87	4	2	89	9	1	9	22	8	104	100	.291	.379	.485
11 YR TOTALS			**1547**	**6744**	**6093**	**1753**	**288**	**59**	**205**	**2774**	**551**	**47**	**21**	**875**	**94**	**28**	**51**	**297**	**84**	**976**	**749**	**.288**	**.346**	**.455**

Sanders, Deion Luwynn — bats left — throws left — b.8/9/67 — 1991 positions: OF 44

YR	TM/LG	CL	G	TPA	AB	H	2B	3B	HR	TB	BB	IBB	HB	SO	GDP	SH	SF	SB	CS	R	RBI	BA	OBA	SA
88	YAN/GCL	R	17	79	75	21	4	2	0	29	2	0	1	10	1	0	1	11	2	7	6	.280	.304	.387
	FL/FSL	A+	6	23	21	9	2	0	0	11	1	0	0	3	1	1	0	2	0	5	2	.429	.455	.524
	COL/INT	AAA	5	24	20	3	1	0	0	4	1	0	2	4	1	1	0	1	0	3	0	.150	.261	.200
89	ALB/EAS	AA	33	138	119	34	2	2	1	43	11	1	1	20	1	1	0	17	5	28	6	.286	.380	.361
	COL/INT	AAA	70	289	259	72	12	7	5	113	22	1	1	48	8	4	3	16	7	38	30	.278	.333	.436
	NY/AL		14	50	47	11	2	0	2	19	3	0	0	8	0	0	0	1	0	7	7	.234	.280	.404
90	COL/INT	AAA	22	105	84	27	7	1	2	42	17	0	2	15	1	1	1	9	1	21	10	.321	.442	.500
	NY/AL		57	149	133	21	2	2	3	36	13	0	1	27	2	1	1	8	2	24	9	.158	.236	.271
91	RIC/INT	AAA	29	141	130	34	6	3	5	61	10	0	0	28	0	0	1	12	4	20	16	.262	.312	.469
	ATL/NL		54	122	110	21	1	2	4	38	12	0	0	23	3	0	0	11	3	16	13	.191	.270	.345
3 YR TOTALS			**125**	**321**	**290**	**53**	**5**	**4**	**9**	**93**	**28**	**0**	**1**	**58**	**5**	**1**	**1**	**20**	**5**	**47**	**29**	**.183**	**.256**	**.321**

Sanders, Reginald Lavern "Reggie" — bats right — throws right — b.12/1/67 — 1991 positions: OF 9

YR	TM/LG	CL	G	TPA	AB	H	2B	3B	HR	TB	BB	IBB	HB	SO	GDP	SH	SF	SB	CS	R	RBI	BA	OBA	SA
88	BIL/PIO	R+	17	72	64	15	1	1	0	18	6	0	0	4	1	1	1	10	2	11	3	.234	.296	.281
89	GRE/SAL	A	81	349	315	91	18	5	9	146	29	2	3	63	3	1	1	21	7	53	53	.289	.353	.463
90	CR/MID	A	127	532	466	133	21	4	17	213	59	2	4	95	8	2	1	40	15	89	63	.285	.370	.457
91	CHT/SOU	AA	86	349	302	95	15	8	8	150	41	5	1	67	5	1	0	15	5	50	49	.315	.394	.497
	CIN/NL		9	40	40	8	0	0	1	11	0	0	0	8	0	0	0	1	1	6	3	.200	.200	.275

Santana, Andres Confesor — bats right — throws right — b.3/19/68 — 1991 positions: 2B System SF/NL

YR	TM/LG	CL	G	TPA	AB	H	2B	3B	HR	TB	BB	IBB	HB	SO	GDP	SH	SF	SB	CS	R	RBI	BA	OBA	SA
87	POC/PIO	R+	67	294	256	67	2	3	0	75	36	0	1	37	2	1	0	45	10	51	9	.262	.355	.293
88	CLI/MID	A	118	504	450	126	4	1	0	132	42	1	2	83	2	7	2	88	23	77	24	.280	.344	.293
	SHR/TEX	AA	11	41	36	6	0	0	0	6	4	0	0	9	0	1	0	3	2	3	3	.167	.250	.167
89	SJ/CAL	A+	18	78	69	18	3	0	0	21	8	1	0	16	2	1	0	10	6	14	3	.261	.333	.304
90	SHR/TEX	AA	92	376	336	98	5	4	0	111	31	0	1	41	3	7	1	31	18	50	24	.292	.352	.330
	SF/NL		6	2	2	0	0	0	0	0	0	0	0	0	0	0	0	0	0	0	1	.000	.000	.000

(continued)

Santana, Andres Confesor (continued)

YR	TM/LG	CL	G	TPA	AB	H	2B	3B	HR	TB	BB	IBB	HB	SO	GDP	SH	SF	SB	CS	R	RBI	BA	OBA	SA
91	PHO/PCL	AAA	113	499	456	144	7	5	1	164	36	0	4	46	3	2	1	45	19	84	35	.316	.370	.360
1 YR TOTALS			**6**	**2**	**2**	**0**	**0**	**0**	**0**	**0**	**0**	**0**	**0**	**0**	**0**	**0**	**0**	**0**	**0**	**0**	**1**	**.000**	**.000**	**.000**

Santiago, Benito (Rivera) — bats right — throws right — b.3/9/65 — 1991 positions: C 151, OF 1

YR	TM/LG	CL	G	TPA	AB	H	2B	3B	HR	TB	BB	IBB	HB	SO	GDP	SH	SF	SB	CS	R	RBI	BA	OBA	SA
84	REN/CAL	A+	114	464	416	116	20	6	16	196	36	4	4	75	11	2	6	5	2	64	83	.279	.338	.471
85	BEA/TEX	AA	101	401	372	111	16	6	5	154	16	1	2	59	6	8	3	12	2	55	52	.298	.328	.414
86	LV/PCL	AAA	117	461	437	125	26	3	17	208	17	1	1	81	12	2	4	19	7	55	71	.286	.312	.476
	SD/NL		17	65	62	18	2	0	3	29	2	0	0	12	0	0	1	0	1	10	6	.290	.308	.468
87	SD/NL		146	572	546	164	33	2	18	255	16	2	5	112	12	1	4	21	12	64	79	.300	.324	.467
88	SD/NL		139	527	492	122	22	2	10	178	24	2	1	82	18	5	5	15	7	49	46	.248	.282	.362
89	SD/NL		129	494	462	109	16	3	16	179	26	6	0	89	9	3	2	11	6	50	62	.236	.277	.387
90	LV/PCL	AAA	6	24	20	6	2	0	1	11	3	1	0	1	1	0	1	0	0	5	8	.300	.375	.550
	SD/NL		100	382	344	93	8	5	11	144	27	2	3	55	4	1	7	5	5	42	53	.270	.323	.419
91	SD/NL		152	614	580	155	22	3	17	234	23	5	4	114	21	0	7	8	10	60	87	.267	.296	.403
6 YR TOTALS			**683**	**2654**	**2486**	**661**	**103**	**15**	**75**	**1019**	**118**	**17**	**14**	**464**	**64**	**10**	**26**	**60**	**41**	**275**	**333**	**.266**	**.300**	**.410**

Santovenia, Nelson Gil (Mayol) — bats right — throws right — b.7/27/61 — 1991 positions: C 30, 1B 7

YR	TM/LG	CL	G	TPA	AB	H	2B	3B	HR	TB	BB	IBB	HB	SO	GDP	SH	SF	SB	CS	R	RBI	BA	OBA	SA
84	JAC/SOU	AA	90	305	255	55	9	0	5	79	44	2	0	30	12	4	2	0	3	27	29	.216	.329	.310
85	IND/AMA	AAA	28	83	75	16	2	0	0	18	7	0	0	11	0	0	1	1	1	5	4	.213	.277	.240
	JAC/SOU	AA	57	206	184	40	6	0	2	52	14	1	1	18	10	4	3	2	0	15	15	.217	.272	.283
86	JAC/SOU	AA	31	94	72	22	7	0	4	41	19	0	1	7	2	2	0	0	1	15	11	.306	.457	.569
	IND/AMA	AAA	18	63	57	12	1	0	1	16	5	0	0	13	1	1	0	0	0	6	2	.211	.274	.281
87	JAC/SOU	AA	117	439	394	110	17	0	19	184	36	1	5	58	13	1	3	3	4	56	63	.279	.345	.467
	MON/NL		2	1	1	0	0	0	0	0	0	0	0	0	0	0	0	0	0	0	0	.000	.000	.000
88	IND/AMA	AAA	27	98	91	28	5	0	2	39	4	0	1	16	2	1	1	0	0	9	13	.308	.340	.429
	MON/NL		92	344	309	73	20	2	8	121	24	3	4	77	4	4	3	2	3	26	41	.236	.294	.392
89	MON/NL		97	337	304	76	14	1	5	107	24	2	3	37	12	2	4	2	1	30	31	.250	.307	.352
90	IND/AMA	AAA	11	47	44	14	2	0	1	19	1	0	1	7	3	0	1	0	0	3	10	.318	.340	.432
	MON/NL		59	176	163	31	3	1	6	54	8	0	0	31	5	0	5	0	3	13	28	.190	.222	.331
91	IND/AMA	AAA	61	217	194	51	7	1	6	78	21	1	0	24	10	0	2	0	2	23	26	.263	.332	.402
	MON/NL		41	102	96	24	5	0	2	35	2	2	0	18	4	0	4	0	0	7	14	.250	.255	.365
5 YR TOTALS			**291**	**960**	**873**	**204**	**42**	**4**	**21**	**317**	**58**	**7**	**6**	**163**	**25**	**6**	**17**	**4**	**7**	**76**	**114**	**.234**	**.281**	**.363**

Sasser, Mack Daniel "Mackey" — bats left — throws right — b.8/3/62 — 1991 positions: C 43, OF 21, 1B 10

YR	TM/LG	CL	G	TPA	AB	H	2B	3B	HR	TB	BB	IBB	HB	SO	GDP	SH	SF	SB	CS	R	RBI	BA	OBA	SA
84	CLI/MID	A	118	471	428	125	20	5	6	173	30	3	2	46	11	4	7	15	2	57	65	.292	.336	.404
	FRE/CAL	A+	16	67	62	17	1	1	0	20	3	0	0	6	1	1	1	1	0	8	6	.274	.303	.323
85	FRE/CAL	A+	133	548	497	168	27	4	14	245	36	4	3	35	12	3	9	3	3	79	102	.338	.380	.493
86	SHR/TEX	AA	120	498	441	129	29	5	5	183	44	13	2	36	12	2	9	4	0	52	72	.293	.353	.415
87	SF/NL		2	4	4	0	0	0	0	0	0	0	0	0	0	0	0	0	0	0	0	.000	.000	.000
	PHO/PCL	AAA	87	335	307	101	21	0	1	125	22	2	2	13	4	1	3	2	3	45	42	.329	.374	.407
	VAN/PCL	AAA	28	106	93	26	3	1	2	37	10	1	1	6	1	1	1	1	0	8	14	.280	.352	.398
	PIT/NL		12	23	23	5	0	0	0	5	0	0	0	2	1	0	0	0	0	2	2	.217	.217	.217
	YEAR		14	27	27	5	0	0	0	5	0	0	0	2	1	0	0	0	0	2	2	.185	.185	.185
88	NY/NL		60	131	123	35	10	1	1	50	6	4	0	9	4	0	2	0	0	9	17	.285	.313	.407
89	NY/NL		72	191	182	53	14	2	1	74	7	4	0	15	3	1	1	0	1	17	22	.291	.316	.407
90	NY/NL		100	288	270	83	14	0	6	115	15	9	1	19	7	0	2	0	0	31	41	.307	.344	.426
91	NY/NL		96	243	228	62	14	2	5	95	9	2	1	19	6	1	4	0	2	18	35	.272	.298	.417
5 YR TOTALS			**342**	**880**	**830**	**238**	**52**	**5**	**13**	**339**	**37**	**19**	**2**	**64**	**21**	**2**	**9**	**0**	**3**	**77**	**117**	**.287**	**.315**	**.408**

Sax, Stephen Louis "Steve" — bats right — throws right — b.1/29/60 — 1991 positions: 2B 149, 3B 5, DH 4

YR	TM/LG	CL	G	TPA	AB	H	2B	3B	HR	TB	BB	IBB	HB	SO	GDP	SH	SF	SB	CS	R	RBI	BA	OBA	SA
81	LA/NL		31	127	119	33	2	0	2	41	7	1	0	14	0	1	0	5	7	15	9	.277	.317	.345
82	LA/NL		150	699	638	180	23	7	4	229	49	1	2	53	10	10	0	49	19	88	47	.282	.335	.359
83	LA/NL		155	692	623	175	18	5	5	218	58	3	1	73	8	8	2	56	30	94	41	.281	.342	.350
84	LA/NL		145	622	569	138	24	4	1	173	47	3	1	53	12	2	3	34	19	70	35	.243	.300	.304
85	LA/NL		136	551	488	136	8	4	1	155	54	12	3	43	15	3	3	27	11	62	42	.279	.352	.318
86	LA/NL		157	704	633	210	43	4	6	279	59	5	3	58	12	6	3	40	17	91	56	.332	.390	.441
87	LA/NL		157	663	610	171	22	7	6	225	44	5	3	61	13	5	1	37	11	84	46	.280	.331	.369
88	LA/NL		160	687	632	175	19	4	5	217	45	6	1	51	11	7	2	42	12	70	57	.277	.325	.343
89	NY/AL		158	717	651	205	26	3	5	252	52	2	1	44	19	4	5	43	17	88	63	.315	.364	.387
90	NY/AL		155	680	615	160	24	2	4	200	49	3	4	46	13	6	6	43	9	70	42	.260	.316	.325
91	NY/AL		158	707	652	198	38	2	10	270	41	2	3	38	15	5	6	31	11	85	56	.304	.345	.414
11 YR TOTALS			**1562**	**6849**	**6230**	**1781**	**247**	**42**	**49**	**2259**	**505**	**43**	**22**	**534**	**128**	**61**	**31**	**407**	**163**	**817**	**494**	**.286**	**.340**	**.363**

Schaefer, Jeffrey Scott "Jeff" — bats right — throws right — b.5/31/60 — 1991 positions: SS 46, 3B 30, 2B 11

YR	TM/LG	CL	G	TPA	AB	H	2B	3B	HR	TB	BB	IBB	HB	SO	GDP	SH	SF	SB	CS	R	RBI	BA	OBA	SA
81	BLU/APP	R+	62	292	250	67	8	2	1	81	35	0	0	26	3	3	4	17	9	45	31	.268	.353	.324
82	HAG/CAR	A+	18	69	60	6	0	0	0	6	8	0	0	16	0	1	1	1	1	4	7	.100	.203	.100
	CHA/SOU	AA	106	384	331	83	15	0	3	107	32	0	3	35	5	17	1	16	13	35	32	.251	.322	.323
83	HAG/CAR	A+	68	244	229	61	15	4	1	87	9	0	1	20	4	2	3	8	2	32	16	.266	.293	.380
	CHA/SOU	AA	51	191	182	43	7	2	2	60	5	0	0	25	7	3	1	4	4	20	28	.236	.255	.330

Schaefer, Jeffrey Scott "Jeff" (continued)

YR	TM/LG	CL	G	TPA	AB	H	2B	3B	HR	TB	BB	IBB	HB	SO	GDP	SH	SF	SB	CS	R	RBI	BA	OBA	SA
84	ROC/INT	AAA	31	103	91	24	5	1	0	31	9		0	20	5	3	0	0	0	10	3	.264	.330	.341
	CHA/SOU	AA	99	421	383	90	8	0	4	110	23	1	6	45	12	6	3	8	3	47	31	.235	.287	.287
85	CHA/SOU	AA	49	197	181	47	7	1	2	62	12	0	0	14	2	3	1	6	5	19	19	.260	.304	.343
	ROC/INT	AAA	68	196	187	37	4	0	2	47	6	0	0	21	5	2	1	1	2	17	12	.198	.222	.251
86	MID/TEX	AA	114	432	406	109	17	1	6	146	14	0	2	40	11	6	4	1	4	50	41	.268	.292	.360
87	SA/TEX	AA	101	395	368	112	18	2	0	134	13	0	3	49	8	7	4	2	4	39	37	.304	.330	.364
	ALB/PCL	AAA	8	28	27	7	1	0	0	8	1	0	0	3	2	0	0	0	0	3	3	.259	.286	.296
88	VAN/PCL	AAA	131	485	450	111	30	2	1	148	21	0	4	53	8	4	6	7	4	53	59	.247	.283	.329
89	CHI/AL		15	11	10	1	0	0	0	1	0	0	0	2	0	1	0	1	1	2	0	.100	.100	.100
	VAN/PCL	AAA	88	322	294	67	13	2	3	93	21	0	1	29	4	5	1	10	10	32	22	.228	.281	.316
90	CAL/PCL	AAA	49	199	170	41	9	2	0	54	18	0	0	15	3	9	2	4	1	24	19	.241	.311	.318
	SEA/AL		55	115	107	22	3	0	0	25	3	0	2	11	1	2	1	4	1	11	6	.206	.239	.234
91	SEA/AL		84	175	164	41	7	1	1	53	5	0	0	25	7	6	0	3	1	19	11	.250	.272	.323
3 YR TOTALS			**154**	**301**	**281**	**64**	**10**	**1**	**1**	**79**	**8**	**0**	**2**	**38**	**8**	**9**	**1**	**8**	**3**	**32**	**17**	**.228**	**.253**	**.281**

Schofield, Richard Craig "Dick" — bats right — throws right — b.11/21/62 — 1991 positions: SS 133

YR	TM/LG	CL	G	TPA	AB	H	2B	3B	HR	TB	BB	IBB	HB	SO	GDP	SH	SF	SB	CS	R	RBI	BA	OBA	SA
83	CAL/AL		21	62	54	11	2	0	3	22	6	0	1	8	2	1	0	0	0	4	4	.204	.295	.407
84	CAL/AL		140	452	400	77	10	3	4	105	33	0	6	79	7	13	0	5	2	39	21	.192	.264	.262
85	CAL/AL		147	496	438	96	19	3	8	145	35	0	8	70	8	12	3	11	4	50	41	.219	.287	.331
86	CAL/AL		139	529	458	114	17	6	13	182	48	2	5	55	8	9	9	23	5	67	57	.249	.321	.397
87	CAL/AL		134	531	479	120	17	3	9	170	37	0	2	63	4	10	3	19	3	52	46	.251	.305	.355
88	CAL/AL		155	589	527	126	11	6	6	167	40	0	9	57	5	11	2	20	5	61	34	.239	.303	.317
89	CAL/AL		91	346	302	69	11	2	4	96	28	0	3	47	4	11	2	9	3	42	26	.228	.299	.318
90	EDM/PCL	AAA	5	21	18	7	1	0	1	11	3	0	0	4	0	0	0	0	0	4	4	.389	.476	.611
	CAL/AL		99	379	310	79	8	1	1	92	52	3	3	61	3	13	2	3	4	41	18	.255	.363	.297
91	CAL/AL		134	487	427	96	9	3	0	111	50	2	3	69	3	7	0	8	3	44	31	.225	.310	.260
9 YR TOTALS			**1060**	**3871**	**3395**	**788**	**104**	**27**	**48**	**1090**	**329**	**7**	**39**	**509**	**44**	**87**	**21**	**98**	**30**	**400**	**278**	**.232**	**.305**	**.321**

Schu, Rick Spencer — bats right — throws right — b.1/26/62 — 1991 positions: 3B 3, 1B 1

YR	TM/LG	CL	G	TPA	AB	H	2B	3B	HR	TB	BB	IBB	HB	SO	GDP	SH	SF	SB	CS	R	RBI	BA	OBA	SA
81	BEN/NWL	A–	68	301	258	69	10	0	2	85	35	0	1	53	4	2	5	15	5	41	42	.267	.351	.329
82	SPA/SAL	A	125	490	429	117	28	1	12	183	55	1	1	66	4	0	5	37	12	78	60	.273	.353	.427
	ALB/PCL	AAA	26	85	73	24	4	0	2	34	10	0	2	12	1	0	0	1	3	15	10	.329	.424	.466
83	PEN/CAR	A+	122	499	444	119	22	3	14	189	48	1	3	83	7	1	3	29	8	69	63	.268	.341	.426
	POR/PCL	AAA	9	33	29	11	2	1	1	18	3	0	1	1	2	0	0	0	1	7	3	.379	.455	.621
84	POR/PCL	AAA	140	607	552	166	35	14	12	265	43	3	3	83	9	1	8	7	4	70	82	.301	.350	.480
	PHI/NL		17	36	29	8	2	1	2	18	6	0	0	6	0	0	1	0	0	12	5	.276	.389	.621
85	POR/PCL	AAA	42	166	150	42	8	3	4	68	14	0	2	20	2	0	0	1	6	19	22	.280	.349	.453
	PHI/NL		112	457	416	105	21	4	7	155	38	3	2	78	7	1	0	8	6	54	24	.252	.318	.373
86	PHI/NL		92	233	208	57	10	1	8	93	18	1	2	44	1	3	2	2	2	32	25	.274	.335	.447
87	PHI/NL		92	219	196	46	6	3	7	79	20	1	0	36	1	0	1	0	2	24	23	.235	.311	.403
88	BAL/AL		89	294	270	69	9	4	4	98	21	0	3	49	7	0	0	6	4	22	20	.256	.316	.363
89	ROC/INT	AAA	28	113	94	21	6	1	1	32	16	1	1	21	1	0	2	3	2	11	10	.223	.336	.340
	BAL/AL		1	0	0	0	0	0	0	0	0	0	0	0	0	0	0	0	0	0	0	.000	.000	.000
	DET/AL		98	293	266	57	11	0	7	89	24	0	0	37	6	2	1	1	2	25	21	.214	.278	.335
	YEAR		99	293	266	57	11	0	7	89	24	0	0	37	6	2	1	1	2	25	21	.214	.278	.335
90	EDM/PCL	AAA	18	69	60	18	7	0	1	28	6	0	1	3	2	0	2	0	0	8	8	.300	.362	.467
	CAL/AL		61	169	157	42	8	0	6	68	11	0	0	25	4	0	1	0	0	19	14	.268	.314	.433
91	SCR/INT	AAA	106	413	355	114	30	5	14	196	50	2	4	38	9	0	4	7	1	69	57	.321	.407	.552
	PHI/NL		17	24	22	2	0	0	0	2	1	0	0	7	1	0	1	0	0	2	1	.091	.125	.091
8 YR TOTALS			**579**	**1725**	**1564**	**386**	**67**	**13**	**41**	**602**	**139**	**5**	**9**	**282**	**27**	**6**	**7**	**17**	**16**	**189**	**134**	**.247**	**.311**	**.385**

Schulz, Jeffrey Alan "Jeff" — bats left — throws right — b.6/2/61 — 1991 positions: OF

YR	TM/LG	CL	G	TPA	AB	H	2B	3B	HR	TB	BB	IBB	HB	SO	GDP	SH	SF	SB	CS	R	RBI	BA	OBA	SA
83	BUT/PIO	R+	61	242	211	69	12	2	7	106	26	4	1	25	5	1	3	8	1	44	55	.327	.398	.502
84	CHA/SAL	A	69	302	265	89	14	3	5	124	34	3	1	20	1	0	2	4	2	52	54	.336	.411	.468
	FM/FSL	A+	59	227	204	64	10	0	0	74	18	0	1	23	7	2	2	8	5	23	26	.314	.369	.363
85	MEM/SOU	AA	136	559	488	149	15	5	4	186	59	5	0	42	15	4	8	8	4	73	53	.305	.375	.381
86	OMA/AMA	AAA	123	449	400	121	19	4	2	154	37	9	2	51	15	2	8	0	2	40	61	.303	.358	.385
87	OMA/AMA	AAA	99	345	316	81	12	7	4	119	24	1	2	56	12	1	2	1	0	25	36	.256	.311	.377
88	OMA/AMA	AAA	101	379	359	103	20	3	5	144	17	7	0	47	8	0	3	1	3	37	41	.287	.317	.401
89	OMA/AMA	AAA	95	363	331	92	19	5	2	127	28	6	2	47	10	1	1	2	0	31	37	.278	.337	.384
	KC/AL		7	9	9	2	0	0	0	2	0	0	0	1	0	0	0	0	0	0	1	.222	.222	.222
90	OMA/AMA	AAA	69	252	231	69	16	1	4	99	16	4	1	46	4	1	3	2	0	35	27	.299	.343	.429
	KC/AL		30	73	66	17	5	1	0	24	6	0	0	13	2	1	0	0	0	5	6	.258	.319	.364
91	PIT/NL		3	3	3	0	0	0	0	0	0	0	0	2	0	0	0	0	0	0	0	.000	.000	.000
	BUF/AMA	AAA	122	490	437	131	20	4	2	165	42	8	1	41	14	2	8	7	2	55	54	.300	.357	.378
3 YR TOTALS			**40**	**85**	**78**	**19**	**5**	**1**	**0**	**26**	**6**	**2**	**0**	**17**	**2**	**1**	**0**	**0**	**0**	**5**	**7**	**.244**	**.298**	**.333**

Scioscia, Michael Lorri "Mike" — bats left — throws right — b.11/27/58 — 1991 positions: C 115

YR	TM/LG	CL	G	TPA	AB	H	2B	3B	HR	TB	BB	IBB	HB	SO	GDP	SH	SF	SB	CS	R	RBI	BA	OBA	SA
80	LA/NL		54	152	134	34	5	1	1	44	12	2	0	9	2	5	1	1	0	8	8	.254	.313	.328
81	LA/NL		93	335	290	80	10	0	2	96	36	8	1	18	8	4	4	0	2	27	29	.276	.353	.331

(continued)

Scioscia, Michael Lorri "Mike" (continued)

YR	TM/LG	CL	G	TPA	AB	H	2B	3B	HR	TB	BB	IBB	HB	SO	GDP	SH	SF	SB	CS	R	RBI	BA	OBA	SA
82	LA/NL		129	419	365	80	11	1	5	108	44	11	1	31	8	5	4	2	0	31	38	.219	.302	.296
83	LA/NL		12	40	35	11	3	0	1	17	5	1	0	2	1	0	0	0	0	3	7	.314	.400	.486
84	LA/NL		114	399	341	93	18	0	5	126	52	10	1	26	10	1	4	2	1	29	38	.273	.367	.370
85	LA/NL		141	525	429	127	26	3	7	180	77	9	5	21	10	11	3	3	3	47	53	.296	.407	.420
86	LA/NL		122	449	374	94	18	1	5	129	62	4	3	23	11	6	4	3	3	36	26	.251	.359	.345
87	LA/NL		142	523	461	122	26	1	6	168	55	9	1	23	13	4	2	7	4	44	38	.265	.343	.364
88	LA/NL		130	452	408	105	18	0	3	132	38	12	0	31	14	3	3	0	3	29	35	.257	.318	.324
89	LA/NL		133	471	408	102	16	0	10	148	52	14	3	29	4	7	1	0	2	40	44	.250	.338	.363
90	LA/NL		135	498	435	115	25	0	12	176	55	14	3	31	11	1	4	4	1	46	66	.264	.348	.405
91	LA/NL		119	404	345	91	16	2	8	135	47	3	3	32	5	5	4	4	3	39	40	.264	.353	.391
12 YR TOTALS			1324	4667	4025	1054	192	9	65	1459	535	97	21	276	97	52	34	26	22	379	422	**.262**	**.349**	**.362**

Scott, Donald Malcolm "Donnie" — bats both — throws right — b.8/16/61 — 1991 positions: C 8

YR	TM/LG	CL	G	TPA	AB	H	2B	3B	HR	TB	BB	IBB	HB	SO	GDP	SH	SF	SB	CS	R	RBI	BA	OBA	SA
79	RAN/GCL	R	45	183	146	45	7	1	1	57	31	4	0	17	3	1	5	4	1	18	29	.308	.418	.390
80	ASH/SAL	A	115	481	421	124	22	1	13	187	54	3	0	53	11	1	5	5	0	57	78	.295	.371	.444
81	TUL/TEX	AA	114	439	385	91	16	2	5	126	42	6	3	78	7	6	3	4	6	44	41	.236	.314	.327
82	TUL/TEX	AA	108	429	367	104	19	3	12	165	57	5	1	71	9	3	1	1	0	55	61	.283	.380	.450
83	OC/AMA	AAA	112	432	371	94	14	3	4	126	45	3	1	67	15	8	7	0	1	44	54	.253	.330	.340
	TEX/AL		2	4	4	0	0	0	0	0	0	0	0	0	0	0	0	0	0	0	0	.000	.000	.000
84	OC/AMA	AAA	46	185	168	55	14	2	3	82	12	1	0	20	7	3	2	0	1	25	25	.327	.368	.488
	TEX/AL		81	263	235	52	9	0	3	70	20	1	0	44	5	6	2	0	1	16	20	.221	.280	.298
85	CAL/PCL	AAA	7	31	26	12	3	1	0	17	4	0	0	0	1	0	1	0	0	6	9	.462	.516	.654
	SEA/AL		80	205	185	41	13	0	4	66	15	0	0	41	3	1	4	1	1	18	23	.222	.275	.357
86	ROC/INT	AAA	59	194	173	47	7	1	1	59	16	2	1	18	5	2	1	1	1	17	16	.272	.333	.341
87	EP/TEX	AA	5	25	20	9	0	0	0	9	5	0	0	2	0	0	0	0	0	4	1	.450	.560	.450
	DEN/AMA	AAA	65	228	196	44	8	4	3	69	28	2	0	26	5	0	4	0	1	21	33	.224	.316	.352
88	EP/TEX	AA	13	59	50	17	0	1	1	22	7	0	0	7	0	1	1	0	0	15	7	.340	.414	.440
	DEN/AMA	AAA	29	78	68	14	2	0	0	16	8	0	1	4	1	1	0	0	0	3	3	.206	.299	.235
89	DEN/AMA	AAA	111	380	330	84	15	0	3	108	42	4	1	37	10	4	3	4	1	36	31	.255	.338	.327
90	NAS/AMA	AAA	78	274	243	55	12	3	0	73	24	3	0	30	4	5	2	0	7	18	21	.226	.294	.300
91	NAS/AMA	AAA	84	256	225	40	8	0	3	57	25	4	0	41	7	3	3	0	2	19	18	.178	.257	.253
	CIN/NL		10	19	19	3	0	0	0	3	0	0	0	2	0	0	0	0	0	0	0	.158	.158	.158
4 YR TOTALS			173	491	443	96	22	0	7	139	35	1	0	87	8	7	6	1	2	34	43	**.217**	**.271**	**.314**

Scott, Gary Thomas — bats right — throws right — b.8/22/68 — 1991 positions: 3B 31

YR	TM/LG	CL	G	TPA	AB	H	2B	3B	HR	TB	BB	IBB	HB	SO	GDP	SH	SF	SB	CS	R	RBI	BA	OBA	SA
89	GEN/NYP	A-	48	208	175	49	10	1	10	91	22	1	9	23	2	0	2	4	1	33	42	.280	.385	.520
90	WIN/CAR	A+	102	434	380	112	22	0	12	170	29	4	14	66	7	5	6	17	3	63	70	.295	.361	.447
	CHA/SOU	AA	35	153	143	44	9	0	4	65	7	1	0	17	3	0	3	3	4	21	17	.308	.333	.455
91	CHI/NL		31	96	79	13	3	0	1	19	13	4	3	14	2	1	0	0	1	8	5	.165	.305	.241
	IOW/AMA	AAA	63	262	231	48	10	2	3	71	26	2	0	45	11	4	2	0	6	21	34	.208	.286	.307

Scruggs, Anthony Raymond "Tony" — bats right — throws right — b.3/19/66 — 1991 positions: OF 5

YR	TM/LG	CL	G	TPA	AB	H	2B	3B	HR	TB	BB	IBB	HB	SO	GDP	SH	SF	SB	CS	R	RBI	BA	OBA	SA
87	RAN/GCL	R	30	133	119	41	5	0	6	64	12	3	2	22	3	0	0	12	5	24	24	.345	.414	.538
	CHA/FSL	A+	23	93	86	28	4	0	3	41	4	0	2	17	2	1	0	4	2	14	11	.326	.370	.477
88	RAN/GCL	R	5	16	12	1	0	0	0	1	3	0	1	4	1	0	0	0	0	1	0	.083	.313	.083
	CHA/FSL	A+	67	270	240	70	11	4	6	107	23	0	3	52	1	3	6	3	3	35	42	.292	.357	.446
89	TUL/TEX	AA	60	222	195	38	3	3	1	50	22	0	2	60	6	2	1	3	1	19	21	.195	.282	.256
	CHA/FSL	A+	60	243	197	58	9	4	3	84	38	1	2	50	9	2	4	15	5	29	34	.294	.407	.426
90	GAS/SAL	A	75	309	274	84	16	0	8	124	26	1	7	57	4	1		20	2	50	48	.307	.380	.453
	TUL/TEX		53	215	195	67	5	6	4	96	15	1	2	50	2	2	1	4	5	28	38	.344	.394	.492
91	TEX/AL		5	6	6	0	0	0	0	0	0	0	0	1	1	0	0	0	0	1	0	.000	.000	.000
	OC/AMA	AAA	53	212	182	37	4	0	3	50	20	0	4	41	6	1	0	3	4	19	21	.203	.292	.275

Segui, David Vincent — bats both — throws left — b.7/19/66 — 1991 positions: 1B 42, OF 33, DH 4

YR	TM/LG	CL	G	TPA	AB	H	2B	3B	HR	TB	BB	IBB	HB	SO	GDP	SH	SF	SB	CS	R	RBI	BA	OBA	SA
88	HAG/CAR	A+	60	219	190	51	12	4	3	80	22	3	3	23	7	0	4	0	0	35	31	.268	.347	.421
89	FRE/CAR	A+	83	332	284	90	19	0	10	139	41	3	4	32	4	0	3	2	1	43	50	.317	.407	.489
	HAG/EAS	AA	44	194	173	56	14	1	1	75	16	0	2	16	6	1	0	1	0	22	27	.324	.383	.434
90	ROC/INT	AAA	86	357	307	103	28	0	2	137	45	4	0	28	15	0	5	5	4	55	51	.336	.415	.446
	BAL/AL		40	136	123	30	7	0	2	43	11	2	1	15	12	1	0	0	0	14	15	.244	.311	.350
91	ROC/INT	AAA	28	115	96	26	2	0	1	31	15	1	1	6	6	0	3	1	1	9	10	.271	.365	.323
	BAL/AL		86	228	212	59	7	0	2	72	12	2	0	19	7	3	1	1	1	15	22	.278	.316	.340
2 YR TOTALS			126	364	335	89	14	0	4	115	23	4	1	34	19	4	1	1	1	29	37	**.266**	**.314**	**.343**

Seitzer, Kevin Lee — bats right — throws right — b.3/26/62 — 1991 positions: 3B 68, DH 3

YR	TM/LG	CL	G	TPA	AB	H	2B	3B	HR	TB	BB	IBB	HB	SO	GDP	SH	SF	SB	CS	R	RBI	BA	OBA	SA
84	CHA/SAL	A	141	617	489	145	26	5	8	205	118	2	3	70	15	1	6	23	5	96	79	.297	.432	.419
85	FM/FSL	A+	90	382	290	91	10	5	3	120	85	4	2	30	6	0	5	28	7	61	46	.314	.466	.414
	MEM/SOU	AA	52	218	187	65	6	2	1	78	25	1	5	21	2	1	5	9	3	26	20	.348	.438	.417
86	MEM/SOU	AA	4	18	11	3	0	0	0	3	7	0	0	1	0	0	0	2	1	4	1	.273	.556	.273
	OMA/AMA	AAA	129	540	432	138	20	11	13	219	89	4	9	57	6	1	9	20	13	86	74	.319	.438	.507
	KC/AL		28	116	96	31	4	1	2	43	19	0	1	14	0	0	0	0	0	16	11	.323	.440	.448

Seitzer, Kevin Lee (continued)

YR	TM/LG	CL	G	TPA	AB	H	2B	3B	HR	TB	BB	IBB	HB	SO	GDP	SH	SF	SB	CS	R	RBI	BA	OBA	SA
87	KC/AL		161	725	641	207	33	8	15	301	80	0	2	85	18	1	1	12	7	105	83	.323	.399	.470
88	KC/AL		149	643	559	170	32	5	5	227	72	4	6	64	15	3	3	10	8	90	60	.304	.387	.406
89	KC/AL		160	715	597	168	17	2	4	201	102	7	5	76	16	4	7	17	8	78	48	.281	.387	.337
90	KC/AL		158	697	622	171	31	5	6	230	67	2	5	66	11	4	2	7	5	91	38	.275	.346	.370
91	KC/AL		85	267	234	62	11	3	3	82	29	3	2	21	4	1	1	4	1	28	25	.265	.350	.350
6 YR TOTALS			**741**	**3163**	**2749**	**809**	**128**	**24**	**33**	**1084**	**369**	**16**	**18**	**326**	**64**	**13**	**14**	**50**	**29**	**408**	**265**	**.294**	**.380**	**.394**

Servais, Scott Daniel — bats right — throws right — b.6/4/67 — 1991 positions: C 14

YR	TM/LG	CL	G	TPA	AB	H	2B	3B	HR	TB	BB	IBB	HB	SO	GDP	SH	SF	SB	CS	R	RBI	BA	OBA	SA
89	OSC/FSL	A+	46	176	153	41	9	0	2	56	16	2	3	35	1	0	5	0	2	16	23	.268	.335	.366
	COL/SOU	AA	63	226	199	47	5	0	1	55	19	0	3	42	5	1	4	0	3	20	22	.236	.307	.276
90	TUC/PCL	AAA	89	332	303	66	11	3	5	98	18	1	4	61	6	3	4	0	0	37	37	.218	.267	.323
91	TUC/PCL	AAA	60	242	219	71	12	0	2	89	13	2	6	19	9	3	1	0	4	34	27	.324	.377	.406
	HOU/NL		16	42	37	6	3	0	0	9	4	0	0	8	0	1	0	0	0	0	6	.162	.244	.243

Sharperson, Michael Tyrone "Mike" — bats right — throws right — b.10/4/61 — 1991 positions: 3B 68, SS 16, 1B 10, 2B 5

YR	TM/LG	CL	G	TPA	AB	H	2B	3B	HR	TB	BB	IBB	HB	SO	GDP	SH	SF	SB	CS	R	RBI	BA	OBA	SA
84	KNO/SOU		140	596	542	165	25	7	4	216	48	2	1	66	10	4	1	20	13	86	48	.304	.361	.399
85	SYR/INT	AAA	134	616	536	155	19	7	1	191	71	1	2	75	5	3	4	14	15	86	59	.289	.372	.356
86	SYR/INT	AAA	133	600	519	150	18	9	4	198	69	1	7	67	15	4	1	17	13	86	45	.289	.379	.382
87	TOR/AL		32	105	96	20	4	1	0	26	7	0	1	15	2	1	0	2	1	4	9	.208	.269	.271
	SYR/INT	AAA	88	382	338	101	21	5	5	147	40	0	1	41	5	2	1	14	10	67	26	.299	.374	.435
	LA/NL		10	37	33	9	2	0	0	11	4	1	0	5	1	0	0	0	0	7	1	.273	.351	.333
	YEAR		42	142	129	29	6	1	0	37	11	1	1	20	3	1	0	2	1	11	10	.225	.291	.287
88	ALB/PCL	AAA	56	244	210	67	10	2	0	81	31	0	1	25	7	1	1	19	6	55	30	.319	.407	.386
	LA/NL		46	64	59	16	1	0	0	17	1	0	1	12	1	2	1	0	1	8	4	.271	.290	.288
89	ALB/PCL	AAA	98	434	359	111	15	7	3	149	66	2	2	46	9	4	3	17	12	81	48	.309	.416	.415
	LA/NL		27	34	28	7	3	0	0	10	4	1	0	7	1	1	1	0	1	2	5	.250	.333	.357
90	LA/NL		129	415	357	106	14	2	3	133	46	6	1	39	5	8	3	15	6	42	36	.297	.376	.373
91	LA/NL		105	252	216	60	11	2	2	81	25	0	1	24	2	10	0	1	3	24	20	.278	.355	.375
5 YR TOTALS			**349**	**907**	**789**	**218**	**35**	**5**	**5**	**278**	**87**	**8**	**4**	**102**	**12**	**22**	**5**	**18**	**12**	**87**	**75**	**.276**	**.349**	**.352**

Sheffield, Gary Antonian — bats right — throws right — b.11/18/68 — 1991 positions: 3B 43, DH 5

YR	TM/LG	CL	G	TPA	AB	H	2B	3B	HR	TB	BB	IBB	HB	SO	GDP	SH	SF	SB	CS	R	RBI	BA	OBA	SA
86	HEL/PIO	R+	57	253	222	81	12	2	15	142	20	2	3	14	3	1	7	14	4	53	71	.365	.413	.640
87	STO/CAL	A+	129	570	469	130	23	3	17	210	81	8	8	48	7	6	6	25	15	84	103	.277	.388	.448
88	EP/TEX	AA	77	343	296	93	19	3	19	175	35	0	3	41	9	4	5	5	4	70	65	.314	.386	.591
	DEN/AMA	AAA	57	244	212	73	9	5	9	119	21	1	5	22	3	1	5	8	4	42	54	.344	.407	.561
	MIL/AL		24	89	80	19	1	0	4	32	7	0	0	7	5	1	3	1	1	12	12	.237	.295	.400
89	DEN/AMA	AAA	7	32	29	4	1	1	0	7	2	0	0	1	1	0	0	0	3	0	2	.138	.194	.241
	MIL/AL		95	405	368	91	18	0	5	124	27	0	4	33	4	3	3	10	6	34	32	.247	.303	.337
90	MIL/AL		125	547	487	143	30	1	10	205	44	1	3	41	11	4	9	25	10	67	67	.294	.350	.421
91	MIL/AL		50	203	175	34	12	2	2	56	19	1	3	15	3	1	5	5	5	25	22	.194	.277	.320
4 YR TOTALS			**294**	**1244**	**1110**	**287**	**61**	**3**	**21**	**417**	**97**	**2**	**10**	**96**	**23**	**9**	**18**	**43**	**22**	**138**	**133**	**.259**	**.319**	**.376**

Shelby, John T. — bats both — throws right — b.2/23/58 — 1991 positions: OF 47, DH 4

YR	TM/LG	CL	G	TPA	AB	H	2B	3B	HR	TB	BB	IBB	HB	SO	GDP	SH	SF	SB	CS	R	RBI	BA	OBA	SA
81	BAL/AL		7	2	2	0	0	0	0	0	0	0	0	1	0	0	0	2	0	2	0	.000	.000	.000
82	BAL/AL		26	35	35	11	3	0	1	17	0	0	0	5	0	0	0	0	1	8	2	.314	.314	.486
83	BAL/AL		126	349	325	84	15	2	5	118	18	2	0	64	2	6	0	15	2	52	27	.258	.297	.363
84	BAL/AL		128	415	383	80	12	5	6	120	20	0	0	71	4	12	0	12	4	44	30	.209	.248	.313
85	ROC/INT	AAA	52	229	206	59	16	4	6	107	19	2	0	35	8	1	3	14	4	31	21	.286	.342	.519
	BAL/AL		69	214	205	58	6	2	7	89	7	0	0	44	4	2	0	5	1	28	27	.283	.307	.434
86	BAL/AL		135	428	404	92	14	4	11	147	18	0	2	75	3	2	2	18	6	54	49	.228	.263	.364
87	BAL/AL		21	34	32	6	0	0	1	9	1	0	0	13	0	1	0	0	1	4	3	.188	.212	.281
	ROC/INT	AAA	6	30	24	6	2	0	1	11	5	1	0	4	0	0	1	1	1	5	2	.250	.400	.458
	LA/NL		120	518	476	132	26	6	21	221	31	2	0	97	9	1	9	16	7	61	69	.277	.317	.464
	YEAR		141	552	508	138	26	6	22	230	32	2	1	110	9	2	9	16	7	65	64	.272	.311	.453
88	LA/NL		140	545	494	130	23	6	10	195	44	5	0	128	13	1	6	16	5	65	64	.263	.320	.395
89	LA/NL		108	371	345	63	11	1	1	79	25	5	0	92	6	0	1	10	7	28	12	.183	.237	.229
	ALB/PCL	AAA	32	135	126	36	7	3	4	61	6	0	2	33	2	0	1	12	3	20	21	.286	.326	.484
90	LA/NL		25	24	24	6	1	0	0	7	0	0	0	7	1	0	0	2	0	2	1	.250	.250	.292
	TOL/INT	AAA	5	21	19	6	1	0	0	7	2	0	0	6	0	0	0	3	5	2	1	.316	.381	.368
	DET/AL		78	238	222	55	9	3	4	82	10	0	0	51	6	6	0	4	5	22	20	.248	.280	.369
	YEAR		103	262	246	61	10	3	4	89	10	0	0	58	7	6	0	6	5	24	22	.248	.277	.362
91	DET/AL		53	153	143	22	8	1	3	41	8	1	1	23	3	1	0	0	2	19	8	.154	.204	.287
11 YR TOTALS			**1036**	**3326**	**3090**	**739**	**128**	**24**	**70**	**1125**	**182**	**15**	**4**	**671**	**51**	**32**	**18**	**98**	**40**	**389**	**313**	**.239**	**.281**	**.364**

Sheridan, Patrick Arthur "Pat" — bats left — throws right — b.12/4/57 — 1991 positions: OF 34, DH 2

YR	TM/LG	CL	G	TPA	AB	H	2B	3B	HR	TB	BB	IBB	HB	SO	GDP	SH	SF	SB	CS	R	RBI	BA	OBA	SA
81	KC/AL		3	1	1	0	0	0	0	0	0	0	0	0	0	0	0	0	0	0	0	.000	.000	.000
83	KC/AL		109	357	333	90	12	2	7	127	20	0	0	64	3	4	0	12	3	43	36	.270	.312	.381
84	KC/AL		138	531	481	136	24	4	8	192	41	3	1	91	6	5	3	19	6	64	53	.283	.338	.399
85	OMA/AMA	AAA	8	34	28	10	1	0	0	11	5	0	1	6	0	0	0	0	1	1	1	.357	.471	.393
	KC/AL		78	234	206	47	9	2	3	69	23	2	1	38	4	3	1	11	3	18	17	.228	.307	.335

(continued)

Sheridan, Patrick Arthur "Pat" (continued)

YR	TM/LG	CL	G	TPA	AB	H	2B	3B	HR	TB	BB	IBB	HB	SO	GDP	SH	SF	SB	CS	R	RBI	BA	OBA	SA
86	NAS/AMA	AAA	9	40	35	10	2	0	1	15	5	0	0	7	0	0	0	2	0	4	5	.286	.375	.429
	DET/AL		98	262	236	56	9	1	6	85	21	4	1	57	3	2	2	9	2	41	19	.237	.300	.360
87	DET/AL		141	473	421	109	19	3	6	152	44	4	1	90	7	2	5	18	13	57	49	.259	.327	.361
88	DET/AL		127	402	347	88	9	5	11	140	44	4	2	64	6	7	2	8	6	47	47	.254	.339	.403
89	DET/AL		50	139	120	29	3	0	3	41	17	0	0	21	2	1	1	4	0	16	15	.242	.333	.342
	SF/NL		70	174	161	33	3	4	3	53	13	1	0	45	1	0	0	4	1	20	14	.205	.264	.329
	YEAR		120	313	281	62	6	4	6	94	30	1	0	66	3	1	1	8	1	36	29	.221	.295	.335
90	IOW/AMA	AAA	23	81	70	23	3	0	4	38	11	0	0	18	1	0	0	2	2	16	10	.329	.420	.543
91	COL/INT	AAA	21	80	70	19	3	2	2	32	10	0	0	26	0	0	0	2	0	15	12	.271	.363	.457
	NY/AL		62	127	113	23	3	0	4	38	13	1	0	30	6	1	0	1	1	13	7	.204	.286	.336
9 YR TOTALS			**876**	**2700**	**2419**	**611**	**91**	**21**	**51**	**897**	**236**	**19**	**6**	**501**	**38**	**25**	**14**	**86**	**35**	**319**	**257**	**.253**	**.319**	**.371**

Shipley, Craig Barry — bats right — throws right — b.1/7/63 — 1991 positions: SS 19, 2B 14

YR	TM/LG	CL	G	TPA	AB	H	2B	3B	HR	TB	BB	IBB	HB	SO	GDP	SH	SF	SB	CS	R	RBI	BA	OBA	SA
84	VB/FSL	A+	85	351	293	82	11	2	0	97	52	6	4	44	9	1	1	18	7	56	28	.280	.394	.331
85	ALB/PCL	AAA	124	443	414	100	9	2	0	113	22	3	1	43	12	3	3	24	6	50	30	.242	.280	.273
86	LA/NL		12	31	27	3	1	0	0	4	2	1	1	5	1	1	0	0	0	3	4	.111	.200	.148
	ALB/PCL	AAA	61	220	203	59	8	2	0	71	11	0	2	23	3	3	1	6	7	33	16	.291	.332	.350
87	ALB/PCL	AAA	49	154	139	31	6	1	1	42	13	0	1	19	3	1	0	6	2	17	15	.223	.294	.302
	SA/TEX	AA	33	134	127	30	5	3	2	47	5	0	1	17	0	0	1	2	1	14	9	.236	.269	.370
	LA/NL		26	35	35	9	1	0	0	10	0	0	0	6	2	0	0	0	0	3	2	.257	.257	.286
88	JAC/TEX	AA	89	363	335	88	14	3	6	126	24	2	0	40	9	4	0	6	5	41	41	.263	.317	.376
	TID/INT	AAA	40	159	151	41	5	0	1	49	7	0	0	15	3	2	0	0	0	12	13	.272	.287	.325
89	TID/INT	AAA	44	142	131	27	1	0	2	34	7	0	0	22	3	2	2	0	0	6	9	.206	.243	.260
	NY/NL		4	7	7	1	0	0	0	1	0	0	0	1	0	0	0	0	0	3	0	.143	.143	.143
90	TID/INT	AAA	4	3	3	0	0	0	0	0	0	0	0	1	0	0	0	0	0	1	0	.000	.000	.000
91	LV/PCL	AAA	65	248	230	69	9	5	5	103	10	1	4	32	7	4	0	2	2	27	34	.300	.340	.448
	SD/NL		37	95	91	25	3	0	1	31	2	0	1	14	1	0	0	0	1	6	6	.275	.298	.341
4 YR TOTALS			**79**	**168**	**160**	**38**	**5**	**0**	**1**	**46**	**4**	**1**	**2**	**26**	**4**	**2**	**0**	**0**	**1**	**15**	**12**	**.237**	**.265**	**.287**

Shumpert, Terrance Darnell "Terry" — bats right — throws right — b.8/16/66 — 1991 positions: 2B 144

YR	TM/LG	CL	G	TPA	AB	H	2B	3B	HR	TB	BB	IBB	HB	SO	GDP	SH	SF	SB	CS	R	RBI	BA	OBA	SA
87	EUG/NWL	A–	48	218	186	54	16	1	4	84	27	0	3	41	0	0	2	16	4	38	21	.290	.385	.452
88	APP/MID	A	114	486	422	102	37	2	7	164	56	1	3	90	1	0	5	36	3	64	38	.242	.331	.389
89	OMA/AMA	AAA	113	398	355	88	29	2	4	133	25	0	10	63	5	7	1	23	7	54	22	.248	.315	.375
90	OMA/AMA	AAA	39	175	153	39	6	4	2	59	14	0	3	28	3	4	1	18	0	24	12	.255	.327	.386
	KC/AL		32	96	91	25	6	1	0	33	2	0	1	17	4	0	2	3	3	7	8	.275	.292	.363
91	KC/AL		144	417	369	80	16	4	5	119	30	0	5	75	10	10	3	17	11	45	34	.217	.283	.322
2 YR TOTALS			**176**	**513**	**460**	**105**	**22**	**5**	**5**	**152**	**32**	**0**	**6**	**92**	**14**	**10**	**5**	**20**	**14**	**52**	**42**	**.228**	**.284**	**.330**

Sierra, Ruben Angel (Garcia) — bats both — throws right — b.10/6/65 — 1991 positions: OF 161

YR	TM/LG	CL	G	TPA	AB	H	2B	3B	HR	TB	BB	IBB	HB	SO	GDP	SH	SF	SB	CS	R	RBI	BA	OBA	SA
84	BUR/MID	A	138	541	482	127	33	5	6	188	49	5	1	97	9	6	3	13	9	55	75	.263	.331	.390
85	TUL/TEX	AA	137	587	545	138	34	8	13	227	35	6	1	111	8	1	5	22	7	63	74	.253	.297	.417
86	OC/AMA	AAA	46	209	189	56	11	2	9	98	15	3	0	27	5	1	4	8	2	31	41	.296	.341	.519
	TEX/AL		113	411	382	101	13	10	16	182	22	3	1	65	8	1	5	7	8	50	55	.264	.302	.476
87	TEX/AL		158	696	643	169	35	4	30	302	39	4	2	114	18	0	12	16	11	97	109	.263	.302	.470
88	TEX/AL		156	668	615	156	32	2	23	261	44	10	1	91	15	0	8	18	4	77	91	.254	.301	.424
89	TEX/AL		162	689	634	194	35	14	29	344	43	2	2	82	7	0	10	8	2	101	119	.306	.347	.543
90	TEX/AL		159	666	608	170	37	2	16	259	49	13	1	86	15	0	8	9	0	70	96	.280	.330	.426
91	TEX/AL		161	726	661	203	44	5	25	332	56	7	0	91	17	0	9	16	4	110	116	.307	.357	.502
6 YR TOTALS			**909**	**3856**	**3543**	**993**	**196**	**37**	**139**	**1680**	**253**	**39**	**7**	**529**	**80**	**1**	**52**	**74**	**29**	**505**	**586**	**.280**	**.325**	**.474**

Silvestri, David Joseph "Dave" — bats right — throws right — b.9/29/67 — 1991 positions: SS System NY/AL

YR	TM/LG	CL	G	TPA	AB	H	2B	3B	HR	TB	BB	IBB	HB	SO	GDP	SH	SF	SB	CS	R	RBI	BA	OBA	SA
89	OSC/FSL	A+	129	529	437	111	20	1	2	139	68	1	6	72	15	8	10	28	13	67	50	.254	.355	.318
90	PW/CAR	A+	131	558	465	120	30	7	5	179	77	0	6	90	9	5	5	37	13	74	56	.258	.367	.385
	ALB/EAS	AA	2	7	7	2	0	0	2	0	0	0	1	0	0	0	0	0	0	2	.286	.286	.286
91	ALB/EAS	AA	140	601	512	134	31	8	19	238	83	3	2	126	18	2	3	20	13	97	83	.262	.366	.465

Simms, Michael Howard "Mike" — bats right — throws right — b.1/12/67 — 1991 positions: OF 41

YR	TM/LG	CL	G	TPA	AB	H	2B	3B	HR	TB	BB	IBB	HB	SO	GDP	SH	SF	SB	CS	R	RBI	BA	OBA	SA
85	AST/GCL	R	21	83	70	19	2	1	3	32	6	0	4	26	1	0	3	0	0	10	18	.271	.349	.457
86	AST/GCL	R	54	211	181	47	14	1	4	75	22	1	4	48	4	0	4	2	1	33	37	.260	.346	.414
87	ASH/SAL	A	133	554	469	128	19	0	39	264	73	5	9	167	4	1	3	0	0	93	100	.273	.379	.563
88	OSC/FSL	A+	123	511	428	104	19	1	16	173	76	3	1	130	6	0	6	6	6	63	73	.243	.354	.404
89	COL/SOU	AA	109	452	378	97	21	3	20	184	66	4	2	110	2	0	6	12	6	64	81	.257	.365	.487
90	TUC/PCL	AAA	124	512	421	115	34	5	13	198	74	3	8	135	5	1	8	3	6	75	72	.273	.386	.470
	HOU/NL		12	13	13	4	1	0	1	8	0	0	0	4	1	0	0	0	0	3	2	.308	.308	.615
91	TUC/PCL	AAA	85	345	297	73	20	2	15	142	36	0	4	94	3	1	7	2	2	53	59	.246	.328	.478
	HOU/NL		49	143	123	25	5	0	3	39	18	0	0	38	2	0	2	1	0	18	16	.203	.301	.317
2 YR TOTALS			**61**	**156**	**136**	**29**	**6**	**0**	**4**	**47**	**18**	**0**	**0**	**42**	**3**	**0**	**2**	**1**	**0**	**21**	**18**	**.213**	**.301**	**.346**

Sinatro, Matthew Stephen "Matt" — bats right — throws right — b.3/22/60 — 1991 positions: C 5

YR	TM/LG	CL	G	TPA	AB	H	2B	3B	HR	TB	BB	IBB	HB	SO	GDP	SH	SF	SB	CS	R	RBI	BA	OBA	SA
78	KIN/APP	R+	35	130	112	23	7	0	0	30	14	1	2	12	0	1	1	4	1	15	6	.205	.302	.268
79	GRE/WCL	A	120	441	385	97	16	4	7	142	42	5	6	59	6	4	4	25	15	54	57	.252	.332	.369
80	SAV/SOU	AA	122	512	449	125	16	1	11	176	48	1	5	57	5	6	4	17	10	76	50	.278	.352	.392
81	ATL/NL		12	37	32	9	1	1	0	12	5	1	0	4	0	0	0	1	0	4	4	.281	.378	.375
	RIC/INT	AAA	121	484	430	101	13	2	6	136	42	0	5	58	14	3	4	18	13	43	53	.235	.308	.316
82	RIC/INT	AAA	72	280	246	62	7	1	8	95	30	0	1	45	8	2	1	13	4	39	29	.252	.335	.386
	ATL/NL		37	87	81	11	2	0	1	16	4	0	0	9	3	2	0	0	1	10	4	.136	.176	.198
83	ATL/NL		7	14	12	2	0	0	0	2	2	0	0	1	0	0	0	0	0	0	2	.167	.286	.167
	RIC/INT	AAA	110	402	365	77	11	1	4	102	28	1	1	61	13	6	2	6	6	36	41	.211	.268	.279
84	ATL/NL		2	4	4	0	0	0	0	0	0	0	0	0	0	0	0	0	0	0	0	.000	.000	.000
	GRE/SOU	AA	101	399	352	80	16	1	5	113	36	1	2	43	14	5	4	8	5	36	49	.227	.299	.321
85	GRE/SOU	AA	49	194	172	48	4	1	6	72	15	0	1	13	5	5	2	4	2	25	28	.279	.333	.419
	RIC/INT	AAA	24	71	67	19	3	0	1	25	3	1	0	10	0	0	1	1	0	7	8	.284	.310	.373
86	RIC/INT	AAA	28	74	66	13	2	0	2	21	5	0	0	12	3	2	1	0	2	8	7	.197	.250	.318
	BUF/AMA	AAA	11	34	32	8	3	0	0	11	1	0	0	6	2	1	0	0	0	4	3	.250	.273	.344
87	TAC/PCL	AAA	79	261	215	54	13	0	5	82	35	3	1	34	8	8	2	6	3	30	32	.251	.356	.381
	OAK/AL		6	3	3	0	0	0	0	0	0	0	0	1	1	0	0	0	0	0	0	.000	.000	.000
88	TAC/PCL	AAA	77	275	234	54	8	1	2	70	37	0	2	41	6	2	0	2	2	28	23	.231	.341	.299
	OAK/AL		10	10	9	3	2	0	0	5	0	0	0	2	0	1	0	0	1	1	5	.333	.300	.556
89	TUC/PCL	AAA	34	115	96	22	5	0	0	27	13	0	1	16	2	4	1	1	1	11	8	.229	.324	.281
	DET/AL		13	27	25	3	0	0	0	3	1	0	1	3	1	0	0	0	0	2	1	.120	.185	.120
	CAL/PCL	AAA	12	36	32	11	1	0	0	12	3	0	0	5	0	1	0	0	0	2	4	.344	.400	.375
90	CAL/PCL	AAA	9	23	20	6	0	0	1	9	2	0	0	3	0	1	0	0	0	1	2	.300	.364	.450
	SEA/AL		30	57	50	15	1	0	0	16	4	0	0	10	3	3	0	1	0	2	1	.250	.333	.250
91	SEA/AL		5	9	8	2	0	0	0	2	1	0	0	1	0	0	0	0	0	1	1	.250	.333	.250
	CAL/PCL	AAA	40	153	131	34	8	0	3	51	16	0	1	20	5	3	2	1	1	13	19	.260	.340	.389
9 YR TOTALS			**122**	**248**	**224**	**45**	**6**	**1**	**1**	**56**	**17**	**1**	**1**	**30**	**10**	**5**	**1**	**2**	**1**	**20**	**21**	**.201**	**.259**	**.250**

Skinner, Joel Patrick — bats right — throws right — b.2/21/61 — 1991 positions: C 99

YR	TM/LG	CL	G	TPA	AB	H	2B	3B	HR	TB	BB	IBB	HB	SO	GDP	SH	SF	SB	CS	R	RBI	BA	OBA	SA
83	CHI/AL		6	11	11	3	0	0	0	3	0	0	0	1	2	0	0	0	0	2	1	.273	.273	.273
84	DEN/AMA	AAA	42	160	141	40	6	0	10	76	13	1	1	31	0	1	4	1	0	27	27	.284	.340	.539
	CHI/AL		43	88	80	17	2	0	0	19	7	0	0	19	2	0	1	1	0	4	3	.213	.273	.237
85	BUF/AMA	AAA	115	436	390	94	13	0	12	143	41	0	4	115	16	0	1	0	0	47	59	.241	.319	.367
	CHI/AL		22	50	44	15	4	1	1	24	5	0	0	13	2	1	0	0	0	9	5	.341	.408	.545
86	NY/AL		54	174	166	43	4	0	1	50	7	0	1	40	4	0	0	0	4	6	17	.259	.287	.301
	CHI/AL		60	162	149	30	5	1	4	49	9	0	1	43	2	2	1	1	0	17	20	.201	.250	.329
	YEAR		114	336	315	73	9	1	5	99	16	0	2	83	6	2	1	1	4	23	37	.232	.269	.314
87	COL/INT	AAA	49	192	178	43	10	2	6	75	10	0	1	44	1	1	2	0	1	19	27	.242	.283	.421
	NY/AL		64	154	139	19	4	0	3	32	8	0	1	46	9	4	2	0	0	9	14	.137	.187	.230
88	NY/AL		88	272	251	57	15	0	4	84	14	0	1	72	6	6	1	0	0	23	23	.227	.267	.335
89	CLE/AL		79	189	178	41	10	0	1	54	9	0	1	42	3	1	0	1	1	10	13	.230	.271	.303
90	CLE/AL		49	146	139	35	4	1	2	47	7	0	0	44	2	0	0	0	0	16	16	.252	.288	.338
91	CLE/AL		99	305	284	69	14	0	1	86	14	1	1	67	8	4	2	0	2	23	24	.243	.279	.303
9 YR TOTALS			**564**	**1551**	**1441**	**329**	**62**	**3**	**17**	**448**	**80**	**1**	**4**	**387**	**40**	**18**	**8**	**3**	**7**	**119**	**136**	**.228**	**.269**	**.311**

Slaught, Donald Martin "Don" — bats right — throws right — b.9/11/58 — 1991 positions: C 69, 3B 1

YR	TM/LG	CL	G	TPA	AB	H	2B	3B	HR	TB	BB	IBB	HB	SO	GDP	SH	SF	SB	CS	R	RBI	BA	OBA	SA
82	KC/AL		43	126	115	32	6	0	3	47	9	0	0	12	3	2	0	0	0	14	8	.278	.331	.409
83	KC/AL		83	290	276	86	13	4	0	107	11	0	0	27	8	1	2	3	1	21	28	.312	.336	.388
84	KC/AL		124	446	409	108	27	4	4	155	20	4	2	55	8	7	0	0	0	48	42	.264	.297	.379
85	TEX/AL		102	370	343	96	17	4	8	145	20	1	6	41	8	1	0	5	4	34	35	.280	.331	.423
86	OC/AMA	AAA	3	12	12	4	1	0	0	5	0	0	0	3	0	0	0	0	0	2	1	.333	.333	.417
	TEX/AL		95	341	314	83	17	1	13	141	16	0	5	59	8	3	3	0	2	39	46	.264	.308	.449
87	TEX/AL		95	266	237	53	15	2	8	96	24	3	1	51	7	4	0	0	3	25	16	.224	.298	.405
88	NY/AL		97	358	322	91	25	1	9	145	24	3	3	54	10	5	4	1	0	33	43	.283	.334	.450
89	NY/AL		117	392	350	88	21	3	5	130	30	3	3	57	9	2	5	1	1	34	38	.251	.315	.371
90	PIT/NL		84	267	230	69	18	3	4	105	27	2	3	27	2	3	4	0	1	27	29	.300	.375	.457
91	PIT/NL		77	250	220	65	17	1	1	87	21	1	2	32	6	5	1	1	0	19	29	.295	.363	.395
10 YR TOTALS			**917**	**3106**	**2816**	**771**	**176**	**23**	**55**	**1158**	**202**	**17**	**28**	**415**	**69**	**34**	**26**	**14**	**12**	**294**	**314**	**.274**	**.326**	**.411**

Smith, Gregory Allen "Greg" — bats both — throws right — b.4/5/67 — 1991 positions: 2B

YR	TM/LG	CL	G	TPA	AB	H	2B	3B	HR	TB	BB	IBB	HB	SO	GDP	SH	SF	SB	CS	R	RBI	BA	OBA	SA
85	WYT/APP	R+	51	205	179	42	6	2	0	52	20	1	2	27	1	3	1	8	1	28	15	.235	.317	.291
86	PEO/MID	A	53	192	170	43	6	3	2	61	19	1	1	45	2	2	0	9	2	24	26	.253	.332	.359
87	PEO/MID	A	124	522	444	120	23	5	6	171	62	5	4	90	11	7	5	26	9	69	56	.270	.361	.385
88	WIN/CAR	A+	95	418	361	101	12	2	4	129	46	2	2	50	5	6	3	52	12	62	29	.280	.362	.357
89	CHA/SOU	AA	126	528	467	138	23	6	5	188	42	1	6	52	8	9	4	38	13	59	64	.296	.358	.403
	CHI/NL		4	6	5	2	0	0	0	2	0	0	1	0	0	0	0	0	0	1	2	.400	.500	.400
90	IOW/AMA	AAA	105	442	398	116	19	1	5	152	37	0	1	57	8	4	1	26	14	54	44	.291	.354	.382
	CHI/NL		18	48	44	9	2	1	0	13	2	0	0	5	1	1	1	0	1	1	0	.205	.234	.295
91	LA/NL		5	4	3	0	0	0	0	0	0	0	0	1	0	1	0	0	0	1	0	.000	.000	.000
	ALB/PCL	AAA	48	173	161	35	3	2	0	42	10	1	1	30	7	1	0	11	1	25	17	.217	.262	.261
3 YR TOTALS			**27**	**58**	**52**	**11**	**2**	**1**	**0**	**15**	**2**	**0**	**1**	**7**	**1**	**2**	**1**	**1**	**0**	**6**	**7**	**.212**	**.250**	**.288**

Smith, John Dwight "Dwight" — bats left — throws right — b.11/8/63 — 1991 positions: OF 42

YR	TM/LG	CL	G	TPA	AB	H	2B	3B	HR	TB	BB	IBB	HB	SO	GDP	SH	SF	SB	CS	R	RBI	BA	OBA	SA
84	PIK/APP	R+	61	253	195	46	6	2	1	59	52	1	4	47	2	2	0	39	7	42	17	.236	.406	.303
85	GEN/NYP	A–	73	265	232	67	11	2	4	94	31	3	1	33	1	0	1	30	10	44	32	.289	.374	.405
86	PEO/MID	A	124	537	471	146	22	11	11	223	59	2	3	92	8	2	2	53	19	92	57	.310	.389	.473
87	PIT/EAS	AA	130	573	498	168	28	10	18	270	67	6	2	79	8	2	4	60	18	111	72	.337	.415	.542
88	IOW/AMA	AAA	129	569	505	148	26	3	9	207	54	1	5	90	9	5	0	25	20	76	48	.293	.367	.410
89	IOW/AMA	AAA	21	91	83	27	7	3	2	46	7	0	0	11	2	1	0	6	2	11	7	.325	.378	.554
	CHI/NL		109	381	343	111	19	6	9	169	31	0	2	51	4	4	1	9	4	52	52	.324	.382	.493
90	CHI/NL		117	322	290	76	15	0	6	109	28	2	2	46	7	0	2	11	6	34	27	.262	.329	.376
91	CHI/NL		90	180	167	38	7	2	3	58	11	2	1	32	2	1	0	2	3	16	21	.228	.279	.347
3 YR TOTALS			316	883	800	225	41	8	18	336	70	4	5	129	13	5	3	22	13	102	100	.281	.342	.420

Smith, Lonnie — bats right — throws right — b.12/22/55 — 1991 positions: OF 99

YR	TM/LG	CL	G	TPA	AB	H	2B	3B	HR	TB	BB	IBB	HB	SO	GDP	SH	SF	SB	CS	R	RBI	BA	OBA	SA
78	PHI/NL		17	8	4	0	0	0	0	0	4	0	0	3	0	0	0	4	0	6	0	.000	.500	.000
79	PHI/NL		17	31	30	5	2	0	0	7	1	0	0	7	0	0	0	2	1	4	3	.167	.194	.233
80	PHI/NL		100	331	298	101	14	4	3	132	26	2	4	48	5	1	0	33	13	69	20	.339	.397	.443
81	PHI/NL		62	202	176	57	14	3	2	83	18	1	5	14	1	3	0	21	10	40	11	.324	.402	.472
82	STL/NL		156	672	592	182	35	8	8	257	64	2	9	74	11	3	4	68	26	120	69	.307	.381	.434
83	STL/NL		130	547	492	158	31	5	8	223	41	2	9	55	11	1	4	43	18	83	45	.321	.381	.453
84	STL/NL		145	590	504	126	20	4	6	172	70	0	9	90	7	3	4	50	13	77	49	.250	.349	.341
85	STL/NL		28	115	96	25	2	2	0	31	15	0	3	20	2	1	0	12	6	15	7	.260	.377	.323
	KC/AL		120	498	448	115	23	4	6	164	41	0	4	69	2	0	5	40	7	77	41	.257	.321	.366
	YEAR		148	613	544	140	25	6	6	195	56	0	7	89	4	1	5	52	13	92	48	.257	.332	.358
86	KC/AL		134	568	508	146	25	7	3	209	46	0	10	78	10	2	2	26	9	80	44	.287	.357	.411
87	OMA/AMA	AAA	40	172	149	49	9	1	7	81	18	0	1	22	4	0	4	8	6	36	33	.329	.395	.544
	KC/AL		48	197	167	42	7	1	3	60	24	0	4	31	1	0	2	9	6	26	8	.251	.355	.359
88	RIC/INT	AAA	93	369	290	87	13	5	9	137	66	4	8	65	6	1	4	26	3	58	51	.300	.438	.472
	ATL/NL		43	125	114	27	3	0	3	39	10	0	0	25	0	0	1	4	2	14	9	.237	.296	.342
89	ATL/NL		134	577	482	152	34	4	21	257	76	3	11	95	7	1	7	25	12	89	79	.315	.415	.533
90	ATL/NL		135	537	466	142	27	9	9	214	58	3	6	69	2	1	6	10	10	72	42	.305	.384	.459
91	ATL/NL		122	416	353	97	19	1	7	139	50	3	9	64	4	2	2	9	5	58	44	.275	.377	.394
14 YR TOTALS			1391	5414	4730	1375	256	52	84	1987	544	16	83	742	63	18	39	356	136	830	471	.291	.371	.420

Smith, Osborne Earl "Ozzie" — bats both — throws right — b.12/26/54 — 1991 positions: SS 150

YR	TM/LG	CL	G	TPA	AB	H	2B	3B	HR	TB	BB	IBB	HB	SO	GDP	SH	SF	SB	CS	R	RBI	BA	OBA	SA
78	SD/NL		159	668	590	152	17	6	1	184	47	0	0	43	11	28	3	40	12	69	46	.258	.311	.312
79	SD/NL		156	649	587	124	18	6	0	154	37	5	2	37	11	22	1	28	7	77	27	.211	.260	.262
80	SD/NL		158	712	609	140	18	5	0	168	71	1	5	49	9	23	4	57	15	67	35	.230	.313	.276
81	SD/NL		110	507	450	100	11	2	0	115	41	1	5	37	8	10	1	22	12	53	21	.222	.294	.256
82	STL/NL		140	567	488	121	24	1	2	153	68	12	2	32	10	4	5	25	5	58	43	.248	.339	.314
83	STL/NL		159	626	552	134	30	6	3	185	64	9	1	36	10	7	2	34	7	69	50	.243	.321	.335
84	STL/NL		124	484	412	106	20	5	1	139	56	5	2	17	8	11	3	35	7	53	44	.257	.347	.337
85	STL/NL		158	615	537	148	22	3	6	194	65	11	2	27	13	9	2	31	8	70	54	.276	.355	.361
86	STL/NL		153	609	514	144	19	4	0	171	79	13	2	27	11	3	11	31	7	67	54	.280	.376	.333
87	STL/NL		158	706	600	182	40	4	0	230	89	3	1	36	9	12	4	43	9	104	75	.303	.392	.383
88	STL/NL		153	669	575	155	27	1	3	193	74	2	1	43	7	12	7	57	9	80	51	.270	.350	.336
89	STL/NL		155	664	593	162	30	8	2	214	55	3	2	37	10	11	3	29	9	82	50	.273	.335	.361
90	STL/NL		143	592	512	130	21	1	1	156	61	4	2	33	8	7	10	32	6	61	50	.254	.330	.305
91	STL/NL		150	641	550	157	30	3	3	202	83	2	1	36	6	8	1	35	9	96	50	.285	.380	.367
14 YR TOTALS			2076	8709	7569	1955	327	55	22	2458	890	71	28	490	131	173	49	499	120	1006	650	.258	.337	.325

Snyder, James Cory "Cory" — bats right — throws right — b.11/11/62 — 1991 positions: OF 43, 1B 4, 3B 3, DH 3

YR	TM/LG	CL	G	TPA	AB	H	2B	3B	HR	TB	BB	IBB	HB	SO	GDP	SH	SF	SB	CS	R	RBI	BA	OBA	SA
85	WAT/EAS	AA	139	575	512	144	25	1	28	255	44	2	4	123	12	3	12	5	9	77	94	.281	.336	.498
86	MAI/INT	AAA	49	214	192	58	19	0	9	104	17	1	1	39	5	1	3	2	3	25	32	.302	.357	.542
	CLE/AL		103	433	416	113	21	1	24	208	16	0	0	123	8	1	0	2	3	58	69	.272	.299	.500
87	CLE/AL		157	615	577	136	24	2	33	263	31	4	1	166	13	3	0	5	1	74	82	.236	.273	.456
88	CLE/AL		142	558	511	139	24	3	26	247	42	7	1	101	12	0	4	5	1	71	75	.272	.326	.483
89	CAN/EAS	AA	4	13	11	5	0	0	0	5	1	0	1	1	0	0	1	0	0	3	2	.455	.538	.455
	CLE/AL		132	518	489	105	17	0	18	176	23	1	2	134	11	0	4	6	5	49	59	.215	.251	.360
90	CLE/AL		123	468	438	102	27	0	14	177	21	3	2	118	11	1	6	1	4	46	55	.233	.268	.404
91	SYR/INT	AAA	17	74	67	18	3	0	6	39	4	0	1	16	0	0	2	0	0	11	17	.269	.311	.582
	CHI/AL		50	126	117	22	4	0	3	35	6	1	0	41	6	0	0	3	0	10	11	.188	.228	.299
	TOR/AL		21	54	49	7	0	0	3	9	3	0	0	19	1	1	1	0	0	4	6	.143	.189	.184
	YEAR		71	180	166	29	4	1	3	44	9	1	0	60	6	1	1	4	1	14	17	.175	.216	.265
6 YR TOTALS			728	2772	2597	624	117	10	118	1115	142	16	6	702	51	6	21	19	14	312	357	.240	.279	.429

Sojo, Luis Beltran (Sojo) — bats right — throws right — b.1/3/66 — 1991 positions: 2B 107, SS 2, 3B 1, OF 1, DH 1

YR	TM/LG	CL	G	TPA	AB	H	2B	3B	HR	TB	BB	IBB	HB	SO	GDP	SH	SF	SB	CS	R	RBI	BA	OBA	SA
87	MB/SAL	A	72	245	223	47	5	4	2	66	17	0	0	18	9	4	1	5	1	23	15	.211	.266	.296
88	MB/SAL	A	135	586	536	155	22	5	5	202	35	0	2	35	18	7	6	14	9	83	56	.289	.332	.377
89	SYR/INT	AAA	121	513	482	133	20	5	3	172	21	0	1	42	9	4	6	14	9	54	54	.276	.305	.357
90	SYR/INT	AAA	75	324	297	88	12	3	6	124	14	0	1	23	8	3	9	10	2	39	25	.296	.321	.418
	TOR/AL		33	85	80	18	3	0	1	24	5	0	0	5	1	0	0	1	1	14	9	.225	.271	.300

Sojo, Luis Beltran (Sojo) (continued)

YR	TM/LG	CL	G	TPA	AB	H	2B	3B	HR	TB	BB	IBB	HB	SO	GDP	SH	SF	SB	CS	R	RBI	BA	OBA	SA
91	CAL/AL		113	402	364	94	14	1	3	119	14	0	5	26	12	19	0	4	2	38	20	.258	.295	.327
2 YR TOTALS			**146**	**487**	**444**	**112**	**17**	**1**	**4**	**143**	**19**	**0**	**5**	**31**	**13**	**19**	**0**	**5**	**3**	**52**	**29**	**.252**	**.291**	**.322**

Sorrento, Paul Anthony — bats left — throws right — b.11/17/65 — 1991 positions: 1B 13, DH 2

YR	TM/LG	CL	G	TPA	AB	H	2B	3B	HR	TB	BB	IBB	HB	SO	GDP	SH	SF	SB	CS	R	RBI	BA	OBA	SA
86	QC/MID	A	53	204	177	63	11	2	6	96	24	0	2	40	4	0	1	0	0	33	34	.356	.436	.542
	PS/CAL	A+	16	66	62	15	3	0	1	21	4	1	0	15	3	0	0	0	0	5	7	.242	.288	.339
87	PS/CAL	A+	114	454	370	83	14	2	8	125	78	7	3	95	9	0	3	1	2	66	45	.224	.361	.338
88	PS/CAL	A+	133	582	465	133	30	6	14	217	110	5	2	101	10	0	5	3	4	91	99	.286	.421	.467
89	ORL/SOU	AA	140	604	509	130	35	2	27	250	84	7	7	119	7	0	4	1	1	81	112	.255	.366	.491
	MIN/AL		14	27	21	5	0	0	0	5	5	1	0	4	0	0	1	0	0	2	1	.238	.370	.238
90	POR/PCL	AAA	102	424	354	107	27	1	19	193	64	2	1	95	8	0	5	3	0	59	72	.302	.406	.545
	MIN/AL		41	135	121	25	4	1	5	46	12	0	1	31	3	0	1	1	1	11	13	.207	.281	.380
91	POR/PCL	AAA	113	485	409	126	30	2	13	199	62	5	8	65	15	0	6	1	0	59	79	.308	.404	.487
	MIN/AL		26	51	47	12	2	0	4	26	4	2	0	11	3	0	0	0	0	6	13	.255	.314	.553
3 YR TOTALS			**81**	**213**	**189**	**42**	**6**	**1**	**9**	**77**	**21**	**3**	**1**	**46**	**6**	**0**	**2**	**1**	**1**	**19**	**27**	**.222**	**.300**	**.407**

Sosa, Samuel Peralta "Sammy" — bats right — throws right — b.11/10/68 — 1991 positions: OF 111, DH 2

YR	TM/LG	CL	G	TPA	AB	H	2B	3B	HR	TB	BB	IBB	HB	SO	GDP	SH	SF	SB	CS	R	RBI	BA	OBA	SA
86	RAN/GCL		61	253	229	63	19	1	4	96	22	0	0	51	4	0	2	11	3	38	28	.275	.336	.419
87	GAS/SAL	A	129	548	519	145	27	4	11	213	21	0	5	123	7	0	3	22	8	73	59	.279	.312	.410
88	CHA/FSL	A+	131	549	507	116	13	12	9	180	35	0	3	106	14	0	3	42	24	70	51	.229	.282	.355
89	TUL/TEX	AA	66	295	273	81	15	4	7	125	15	0	3	52	4	0	2	16	11	45	31	.297	.338	.458
	TEX/AL		25	88	84	20	3	0	1	26	0	0	0	20	3	4	0	0	2	8	3	.238	.238	.310
	OC/AMA	AAA	10	41	39	4	2	0	0	6	2	0	0	8	0	0	0	4	2	3	3	.103	.146	.154
	VAN/PCL	AAA	13	56	49	18	3	0	1	24	7	0	0	6	1	0	0	3	1	7	5	.367	.446	.490
	CHI/AL		33	115	99	27	5	0	3	41	11	2	2	27	3	1	2	7	3	19	10	.273	.351	.414
	YEAR		58	203	183	47	8	0	4	67	11	2	2	47	6	5	2	7	5	27	13	.257	.303	.366
90	CHI/AL		153	579	532	124	26	10	15	215	33	4	6	150	10	0	8	32	16	72	70	.233	.282	.404
91	VAN/PCL	AAA	32	137	116	31	7	2	3	51	17	0	1	32	2	0	3	9	2	19	19	.267	.358	.440
	CHI/AL		116	338	316	64	10	1	10	106	14	2	2	98	5	5	1	13	6	39	33	.203	.240	.335
3 YR TOTALS			**327**	**1120**	**1031**	**235**	**44**	**11**	**29**	**388**	**58**	**8**	**10**	**295**	**21**	**12**	**9**	**52**	**27**	**138**	**116**	**.228**	**.273**	**.376**

Spehr, Timothy Joseph "Tim" — bats right — throws right — b.7/2/66 — 1991 positions: C 37

YR	TM/LG	CL	G	TPA	AB	H	2B	3B	HR	TB	BB	IBB	HB	SO	GDP	SH	SF	SB	CS	R	RBI	BA	OBA	SA
88	APP/MID	A	31	126	110	29	3	0	5	47	10	0	4	28	1	0	2	3	0	15	22	.264	.341	.427
89	BC/FSL	A+	18	71	64	16	5	0	1	24	5	0	0	17	1	2	0	1	0	8	7	.250	.304	.375
	MEM/SOU	AA	61	236	216	42	9	0	8	75	16	0	2	59	2	1	1	1	3	22	23	.194	.255	.347
90	OMA/AMA	AAA	102	366	307	69	10	2	6	101	41	0	10	88	4	6	2	5	5	42	34	.225	.333	.329
91	OMA/AMA	AAA	72	250	215	59	14	2	6	95	25	1	4	48	2	3	3	3	2	27	26	.274	.356	.442
	KC/AL		37	88	74	14	5	0	3	28	9	0	1	18	2	3	1	1	0	7	14	.189	.282	.378

Spiers, William James "Bill" — bats left — throws right — b.6/5/66 — 1991 positions: SS 128, OF 1

YR	TM/LG	CL	G	TPA	AB	H	2B	3B	HR	TB	BB	IBB	HB	SO	GDP	SH	SF	SB	CS	R	RBI	BA	OBA	SA
87	HEL/PIO	R+	6	25	22	9	1	0	0	10	3	0	0	3	0	0	0	2	0	4	3	.409	.480	.455
	BEL/MID	A	64	278	258	77	10	1	3	98	15	0	3	38	6	2	0	11	5	43	52	.298	.344	.380
88	STO/CAL	A+	84	409	353	95	17	3	5	133	42	1	5	41	5	7	2	27	7	68	52	.269	.353	.377
	EP/TEX	AA	47	186	168	47	5	2	3	65	15	0	0	20	7	0	1	4	4	22	21	.280	.344	.387
89	DEN/AMA	AAA	14	53	47	17	2	1	2	27	5	0	0	6	1	0	1	0	0	9	8	.362	.423	.574
	MIL/AL		114	373	345	88	9	3	4	115	21	1	1	63	2	4	2	10	2	44	33	.255	.298	.333
90	DEN/AMA	AAA	11	49	38	12	0	0	1	15	10	0	0	6	1	1	0	1	1	6	7	.316	.449	.395
	MIL/AL		112	389	363	88	15	3	2	115	16	0	1	46	12	6	3	10	4	44	36	.242	.274	.317
91	MIL/AL		133	464	414	117	13	6	8	166	34	0	2	55	9	10	4	15	10	71	54	.283	.337	.401
3 YR TOTALS			**359**	**1226**	**1122**	**293**	**37**	**12**	**14**	**396**	**71**	**1**	**4**	**164**	**23**	**20**	**9**	**35**	**16**	**159**	**123**	**.261**	**.305**	**.353**

Sprague, Edward Nelson Jr. "Ed" — bats right — throws right — b.7/25/67 — 1991 positions: 3B 35, 1B 22, C 2, DH 2

YR	TM/LG	CL	G	TPA	AB	H	2B	3B	HR	TB	BB	IBB	HB	SO	GDP	SH	SF	SB	CS	R	RBI	BA	OBA	SA
89	DUN/FSL	A+	52	217	192	42	9	2	7	76	16	2	7	40	1	0	2	1	1	21	23	.219	.300	.396
	SYR/INT	AAA	86	315	288	60	14	1	5	91	18	2	5	73	1	1	1	1	1	23	33	.208	.264	.316
90	SYR/INT	AAA	142	567	519	124	23	5	20	217	31	1	10	100	9	3	4	4	2	60	75	.239	.293	.418
91	SYR/INT	AAA	23	102	88	32	8	0	5	55	10	0	2	21	1	0	2	0	0	24	25	.364	.431	.625
	TOR/AL		61	183	160	44	7	0	4	63	19	2	3	43	2	0	1	0	3	17	20	.275	.361	.394

Stanley, Robert Michael "Mike" — bats right — throws right — b.6/25/63 — 1991 positions: C 58, 1B 12, 3B 6, DH 6, OF 1

YR	TM/LG	CL	G	TPA	AB	H	2B	3B	HR	TB	BB	IBB	HB	SO	GDP	SH	SF	SB	CS	R	RBI	BA	OBA	SA
85	SAL/CAR	A+	4	10	9	5	0	0	0	5	1	0	0	0	0	0	0	0	0	2	3	.556	.600	.556
	BUR/MID	A	13	49	42	13	0	0	1	18	6	0	0	5	1	0	0	1	1	8	6	.310	.388	.429
	TUL/TEX	AA	46	193	165	51	10	0	3	70	24	0	2	18	4	0	1	5	2	24	17	.309	.401	.424
86	TUL/TEX	AA	67	276	235	69	16	2	6	107	34	1	2	26	2	1	4	5	3	41	35	.294	.382	.455
	OC/AMA	AAA	56	249	202	74	13	3	5	108	44	0	0	42	4	1	0	1	0	37	49	.366	.480	.535
	TEX/AL		15	33	30	10	3	0	1	16	3	0	0	7	0	0	0	0	0	4	1	.333	.394	.533
87	OC/AMA	AAA	46	216	182	61	8	3	13	114	29	1	0	36	7	2	0	2	0	43	54	.335	.431	.626
	TEX/AL		78	253	216	59	8	1	6	87	31	1	0	48	6	1	4	0	2	34	37	.273	.361	.403
88	TEX/AL		94	292	249	57	8	0	3	74	37	1	0	62	6	1	4	1	1	21	27	.229	.323	.297
89	TEX/AL		67	137	122	30	3	1	1	38	12	1	0	29	5	1	0	1	0	9	11	.246	.324	.311

(continued)

Stanley, Robert Michael "Mike" (continued)

YR	TM/LG	CL	G	TPA	AB	H	2B	3B	HR	TB	BB	IBB	HB	SO	GDP	SH	SF	SB	CS	R	RBI	BA	OBA	SA
90	TEX/AL		103	226	189	47	8	1	2	63	30	2	0	25	4	6	1	1	0	21	19	.249	.350	.333
91	TEX/AL		95	223	181	45	13	1	3	69	34	0	2	44	2	5	1	0	0	25	25	.249	.372	.381
6 YR TOTALS			**452**	**1164**	**987**	**248**	**43**	**4**	**16**	**347**	**147**	**3**	**5**	**215**	**23**	**14**	**11**	**6**	**0**	**114**	**120**	**.251**	**.348**	**.352**

Staton, David Alan — bats right — throws right — b.4/12/68 — 1991 positions: 1B System SD/NL

YR	TM/LG	CL	G	TPA	AB	H	2B	3B	HR	TB	BB	IBB	HB	SO	GDP	SH	SF	SB	CS	R	RBI	BA	OBA	SA
89	SPO/NWL	A−	70	309	260	94	18	0	17	163	39	4	8	49	13	0	2	1	1	52	72	.362	.456	.627
90	RIV/CAL	A+	92	393	335	97	16	1	20	175	52	5	2	78	11	0	4	4	1	56	64	.290	.384	.522
	WIC/TEX	AA	45	188	164	50	11	0	6	79	22	0	1	37	6	0	1	0	0	26	31	.305	.388	.482
91	LV/PCL	AAA	107	425	375	100	19	1	22	187	44	4	3	89	12	0	3	1	0	61	74	.267	.346	.499

Steinbach, Terry Lee — bats right — throws right — b.3/2/62 — 1991 positions: C 117, 1B 9, DH 2

YR	TM/LG	CL	G	TPA	AB	H	2B	3B	HR	TB	BB	IBB	HB	SO	GDP	SH	SF	SB	CS	R	RBI	BA	OBA	SA
84	MAD/MID	A	135	535	474	140	24	6	11	209	49	1	7	59	12	4	5	7	5	6	57	79	.295	.358	.441
85	HUN/SOU	AA	128	515	456	124	31	3	9	188	45	2	3	36	9	4	7	4	1	64	72	.272	.337	.412
86	HUN/SOU	AA	138	611	505	164	33	2	24	273	94	1	5	74	12	0	7	10	9	113	132	.325	.430	.541
	OAK/AL		6	16	15	5	0	0	2	11	1	0	0	0	0	0	0	0	0	3	4	.333	.375	.733
87	OAK/AL		122	438	391	111	16	3	16	181	32	2	9	66	10	3	3	1	2	66	56	.284	.349	.463
88	OAK/AL		104	398	351	93	19	1	9	141	33	2	6	47	13	3	5	3	0	42	51	.265	.334	.402
89	OAK/AL		130	491	454	124	13	1	7	160	30	2	4	66	14	2	1	1	2	37	42	.273	.319	.352
90	OAK/AL		114	410	379	95	15	2	9	141	19	1	4	66	11	5	3	0	1	32	57	.251	.291	.372
91	OAK/AL		129	494	456	125	31	1	6	176	22	4	7	70	15	0	9	2	2	50	67	.274	.312	.386
6 YR TOTALS			**605**	**2247**	**2046**	**553**	**94**	**8**	**49**	**810**	**137**	**11**	**28**	**315**	**63**	**13**	**23**	**7**	**7**	**230**	**277**	**.270**	**.321**	**.396**

Stephens, Carl Ray "Ray" — bats right — throws right — b.9/22/62 — 1991 positions: C 6

YR	TM/LG	CL	G	TPA	AB	H	2B	3B	HR	TB	BB	IBB	HB	SO	GDP	SH	SF	SB	CS	R	RBI	BA	OBA	SA
85	ERI/NYP	A−	9	38	31	9	1	1	1	15	7	0	0	6	1	0	0	0	0	3	5	.290	.421	.484
	SAV/SAL	A	39	144	127	26	6	0	0	32	14	0	1	32	3	1	1	1	1	11	6	.205	.287	.252
86	SAV/SAL	A	95	388	325	71	10	0	13	120	57	1	3	76	6	1	2	2	4	52	56	.218	.339	.369
	LOU/AMA	AAA	12	34	31	6	1	0	1	10	1	0	1	13	0	0	1	0	0	2	2	.194	.235	.323
87	ARK/TEX	AA	100	351	307	77	20	0	8	121	37	4	3	68	10	2	2	6	2	35	42	.251	.335	.394
	LOU/AMA	AAA	9	36	30	4	0	0	0	4	5	1	0	9	3	0	1	0	1	1	2	.133	.250	.133
88	LOU/AMA	AAA	115	404	355	67	13	2	3	93	45	3	1	78	6	0	3	2	1	26	25	.189	.280	.262
89	ARK/TEX	AA	112	418	363	95	14	0	7	130	44	2	4	61	11	4	3	2	1	49	44	.262	.345	.358
90	LOU/AMA	AAA	98	335	294	65	8	1	3	84	27	3	4	74	9	1	0	1	0	20	27	.221	.294	.286
	STL/NL		5	15	15	2	1	0	1	6	0	0	0	3	2	0	0	0	0	2	1	.133	.133	.400
91	LOU/AMA	AAA	60	195	165	46	7	0	7	74	24	1	4	39	4	2	0	0	3	16	28	.279	.383	.448
	STL/NL		6	8	7	2	0	0	0	2	1	0	0	3	0	1	0	0	0	0	0	.286	.375	.286
2 YR TOTALS			**11**	**23**	**22**	**4**	**1**	**0**	**1**	**8**	**1**	**0**	**0**	**6**	**2**	**0**	**0**	**0**	**0**	**2**	**1**	**.182**	**.217**	**.364**

Stephenson, Phillip Raymond "Phil" — bats left — throws left — b.9/19/60 — 1991 positions: 1B

YR	TM/LG	CL	G	TPA	AB	H	2B	3B	HR	TB	BB	IBB	HB	SO	GDP	SH	SF	SB	CS	R	RBI	BA	OBA	SA
84	TAC/PCL	AAA	124	492	398	120	25	1	10	177	85	9	0	54	14	6	3	15	4	70	69	.302	.422	.445
85	TAC/PCL	AAA	56	220	171	36	11	0	5	62	46	1	0	32	1	1	2	5	1	30	24	.211	.374	.363
	MID/TEX	AA	50	212	176	52	14	0	7	87	35	3	1	27	4	0	0	5	2	39	41	.295	.415	.494
86	PIT/EAS	AA	140	565	423	115	29	2	12	184	129	8	2	67	9	3	8	30	18	72	68	.272	.438	.435
87	IOW/AMA	AAA	105	370	298	91	24	2	10	149	62	2	1	56	9	2	7	4	6	53	56	.305	.418	.500
88	IOW/AMA	AAA	118	484	426	125	28	11	22	241	50	9	1	76	9	2	5	9	5	69	81	.293	.365	.566
89	CHI/NL		17	23	21	3	0	0	0	3	2	0	0	3	0	0	0	1	0	0	0	.143	.217	.143
	IOW/AMA	AAA	84	353	290	87	17	3	13	149	58	9	0	41	4	0	4	28	3	52	62	.300	.414	.514
	SD/NL		10	22	17	6	0	0	2	12	3	0	1	2	0	0	0	0	0	4	2	.353	.450	.706
	YEAR		27	45	38	9	0	0	2	15	5	0	1	5	0	0	1	0	0	4	2	.237	.326	.395
90	SD/NL		103	213	182	38	9	1	4	61	30	1	0	43	0	0	1	2	1	26	19	.209	.319	.335
91	LV/PCL	AAA	7	20	18	4	0	0	0	6	1	0	0	1	0	1	1	1	1	1	5	.222	.250	.333
	WIC/TEX	AA	12	42	34	16	5	0	0	21	6	1	0	4	0	1	0	0	0	4	8	.471	.524	.618
	SD/NL		11	9	7	2	0	0	0	2	2	0	0	3	0	0	0	0	0	4	8	.286	.444	.286
3 YR TOTALS			**141**	**267**	**227**	**49**	**9**	**1**	**6**	**78**	**37**	**1**	**0**	**51**	**3**	**2**	**1**	**3**	**1**	**30**	**21**	**.216**	**.325**	**.344**

Stevens, De Wain Lee "Lee" — bats left — throws left — b.7/10/67 — 1991 positions: 1B 11, OF 9

YR	TM/LG	CL	G	TPA	AB	H	2B	3B	HR	TB	BB	IBB	HB	SO	GDP	SH	SF	SB	CS	R	RBI	BA	OBA	SA
86	SAL/NWL	A−	72	315	267	75	18	2	6	115	45	3	2	49	6	0	1	13	6	45	47	.281	.387	.431
87	PS/CAL	A+	140	601	532	130	29	2	19	220	61	5	4	117	18	0	4	1	9	82	97	.244	.324	.414
88	MID/TEX	AA	116	482	414	123	26	2	23	222	58	4	5	108	16	2	3	0	5	79	76	.297	.387	.536
89	EDM/PCL	AAA	127	513	446	110	29	9	14	199	61	3	4	115	14	0	2	5	3	72	74	.247	.341	.446
90	EDM/PCL	AAA	90	397	338	99	31	2	16	182	55	1	0	83	10	0	3	1	2	57	66	.293	.390	.538
	CAL/AL		67	275	248	53	10	0	7	84	22	3	0	75	8	0	2	1	0	28	32	.214	.275	.339
91	EDM/PCL	AAA	123	524	481	151	29	3	19	243	37	4	2	78	12	0	4	4	1	75	96	.314	.363	.505
	CAL/AL		18	66	58	17	7	0	0	24	6	2	0	12	0	1	1	1	2	8	9	.293	.354	.414
2 YR TOTALS			**85**	**341**	**306**	**70**	**17**	**0**	**7**	**108**	**28**	**5**	**0**	**87**	**8**	**3**	**4**	**2**	**3**	**36**	**41**	**.229**	**.290**	**.353**

Stillwell, Kurt Andrew — bats both — throws right — b.6/4/65 — 1991 positions: SS 118

YR	TM/LG	CL	G	TPA	AB	H	2B	3B	HR	TB	BB	IBB	HB	SO	GDP	SH	SF	SB	CS	R	RBI	BA	OBA	SA
84	CR/MID	A	112	461	382	96	15	1	4	125	70	1	1	53	3	3	5	24	9	63	33	.251	.365	.327
85	DEN/AMA	AAA	59	206	182	48	7	4	1	66	21	2	1	23	3	3	0	5	3	28	22	.264	.340	.363

Stillwell, Kurt Andrew (continued)

YR	TM/LG	CL	G	TPA	AB	H	2B	3B	HR	TB	BB	IBB	HB	SO	GDP	SH	SF	SB	CS	R	RBI	BA	OBA	SA
86	DEN/AMA	AAA	10	32	30	7	0	0	0	7	4	2	0	0	4	2	0	0	2	0	2	2	.233	.281	.233
	CIN/NL		104	315	279	64	6	1	0	72	30	1	2	47	5	4	0	6	2	31	26	.229	.309	.258
87	CIN/NL		131	433	395	102	20	7	4	148	32	2	2	50	5	2	2	4	6	54	33	.258	.316	.375
88	KC/AL		128	518	459	115	28	5	10	183	47	0	3	76	7	6	3	6	5	63	53	.251	.322	.399
89	KC/AL		130	516	463	121	20	7	7	176	42	2	3	64	3	5	3	9	6	52	54	.261	.325	.380
90	KC/AL		144	560	506	126	35	4	3	178	39	1	4	60	11	4	7	0	2	60	51	.249	.304	.352
91	KC/AL		122	428	385	102	17	1	6	139	33	5	1	56	8	5	4	3	4	44	51	.265	.322	.361
6 YR TOTALS			**759**	**2770**	**2487**	**630**	**126**	**25**	**30**	**896**	**223**	**11**	**15**	**353**	**39**	**26**	**19**	**28**	**25**	**304**	**268**	**.253**	**.316**	**.360**

Strange, Joseph Douglas "Doug" — bats both — throws right — b.4/13/64 — 1991 positions: 3B 3

YR	TM/LG	CL	G	TPA	AB	H	2B	3B	HR	TB	BB	IBB	HB	SO	GDP	SH	SF	SB	CS	R	RBI	BA	OBA	SA
85	BRI/APP	R+	65	258	226	69	16	1	6	105	22	1	3	30	6	4	3	6	0	43	45	.305	.370	.465
86	LAK/FSL	A+	126	546	466	119	29	4	2	162	65	5	2	59	18	7	6	18	6	59	63	.255	.345	.348
87	GF/EAS	AA	115	470	431	130	31	1	13	202	31	3	3	53	17	0	5	5	11	63	70	.302	.349	.469
	TOL/INT	AAA	16	51	45	11	2	0	1	16	4	0	0	7	1	1	1	3	2	7	5	.244	.300	.356
88	TOL/INT	AAA	82	292	278	56	8	2	6	86	8	0	2	38	8	2	2	9	7	23	19	.201	.228	.309
	GF/EAS	AA	57	243	218	61	11	1	1	77	16	2	0	28	5	1	8	11	1	32	36	.280	.318	.353
89	TOL/INT	AAA	83	344	304	75	15	2	8	118	34	2	2	49	11	2	2	8	3	38	42	.247	.325	.388
	DET/AL		64	217	196	42	4	1	1	51	17	0	1	36	6	3	0	3	3	16	14	.214	.280	.260
90	TUC/PCL	AAA	37	108	98	22	3	0	0	25	8	0	0	23	4	2	0	0	0	7	7	.224	.283	.255
	IOW/AMA	AAA	82	302	269	82	17	1	5	116	28	2	1	42	8	3	1	6	3	31	35	.305	.371	.431
91	IOW/AMA	AAA	131	573	509	149	35	5	8	218	49	9	1	75	12	7	1	10	5	76	56	.293	.352	.428
	CHI/NL		3	11	9	4	1	0	0	5	0	0	1	1	0	0	1	1	0	0	1	.444	.455	.556
2 YR TOTALS			**67**	**228**	**205**	**46**	**5**	**1**	**1**	**56**	**17**	**0**	**2**	**37**	**6**	**3**	**1**	**4**	**3**	**16**	**15**	**.224**	**.289**	**.273**

Strawberry, Darryl Eugene — bats left — throws left — b.3/12/62 — 1991 positions: OF 136

YR	TM/LG	CL	G	TPA	AB	H	2B	3B	HR	TB	BB	IBB	HB	SO	GDP	SH	SF	SB	CS	R	RBI	BA	OBA	SA
83	NY/NL		122	473	420	108	15	7	26	215	47	9	4	128	5	0	2	19	6	63	74	.257	.336	.512
84	NY/NL		147	602	522	131	27	4	26	244	75	15	0	131	8	1	4	27	8	75	97	.251	.343	.467
85	NY/NL		111	470	393	109	15	4	29	219	73	13	1	96	9	0	3	26	11	78	79	.277	.389	.557
86	NY/NL		136	562	475	123	27	5	27	241	72	9	6	141	4	0	9	28	12	76	93	.259	.358	.507
87	NY/NL		154	640	532	151	32	5	39	310	97	13	7	122	4	0	4	36	12	108	104	.284	.398	.583
88	NY/NL		153	640	543	146	27	3	39	296	85	21	3	127	6	0	9	29	14	101	101	.269	.366	.545
89	NY/NL		134	541	476	107	26	1	29	222	61	13	4	105	4	0	3	11	4	69	77	.225	.312	.466
90	NY/NL		152	621	542	150	18	1	37	281	70	15	4	110	5	0	5	15	8	92	108	.277	.361	.518
91	LA/NL		139	588	505	134	22	4	28	248	75	14	3	125	8	0	5	10	8	86	99	.265	.361	.491
9 YR TOTALS			**1248**	**5137**	**4408**	**1159**	**209**	**34**	**280**	**2276**	**655**	**112**	**29**	**1085**	**53**	**1**	**44**	**201**	**83**	**748**	**832**	**.263**	**.359**	**.516**

Stubbs, Franklin Lee — bats left — throws left — b.10/21/60 — 1991 positions: 1B 92, OF 4, DH 4

YR	TM/LG	CL	G	TPA	AB	H	2B	3B	HR	TB	BB	IBB	HB	SO	GDP	SH	SF	SB	CS	R	RBI	BA	OBA	SA
84	ALB/PCL	AAA	29	124	108	35	5	5	6	68	12	3	1	23	1	0	3	3	0	26	24	.324	.387	.630
	LA/NL		87	245	217	42	2	3	8	74	24	3	0	63	0	3	1	2	2	22	17	.194	.273	.341
85	ALB/PCL	AAA	132	509	421	118	23	5	32	247	83	10	1	105	8	1	3	23	3	86	93	.280	.398	.587
	LA/NL		10	9	9	2	0	0	0	2	0	0	0	3	0	0	0	0	0	0	0	.222	.222	.222
86	LA/NL		132	465	420	95	11	1	23	177	37	11	2	107	9	4	2	7	1	55	58	.226	.291	.421
87	LA/NL		129	423	386	90	16	3	16	160	31	9	1	85	7	3	2	8	1	48	52	.233	.290	.415
88	LA/NL		115	273	242	54	13	0	8	91	23	3	1	61	4	2	5	11	3	30	34	.223	.288	.376
89	LA/NL		69	120	103	30	6	0	4	48	16	2	0	27	3	1	0	3	2	11	15	.291	.387	.466
90	HOU/NL		146	501	448	117	23	2	23	213	48	3	2	114	4	1	2	19	6	59	71	.261	.334	.475
91	MIL/AL		103	404	362	77	16	2	11	130	35	3	2	71	4	0	5	13	3	48	38	.213	.282	.359
8 YR TOTALS			**791**	**2440**	**2187**	**507**	**87**	**11**	**93**	**895**	**214**	**34**	**8**	**531**	**31**	**14**	**17**	**63**	**19**	**273**	**287**	**.232**	**.300**	**.409**

Suero, William (Urban) — bats right — throws right — b.11/7/66 — 1991 positions: 2B System MIL/AL

YR	TM/LG	CL	G	TPA	AB	H	2B	3B	HR	TB	BB	IBB	HB	SO	GDP	SH	SF	SB	CS	R	RBI	BA	OBA	SA
86	MH/PIO	R+	64	297	273	76	7	5	2	99	15	0	3	36	7	4	2	13	4	39	28	.278	.321	.363
87	SC/NYP	A-	77	336	297	94	12	4	4	126	35	1	1	35	3	2	1	23	11	43	24	.316	.389	.424
88	MB/SAL	A	125	555	493	140	21	6	6	191	49	2	4	72	4	3	6	21	7	88	52	.284	.350	.387
89	DUN/FSL	A+	51	226	206	60	10	5	4	86	16	0	3	32	3	1	0	7	4	35	17	.291	.351	.417
	KNO/SOU	AA	87	363	324	84	17	5	4	123	34	0	3	50	2	2	0	7	4	42	29	.259	.335	.380
90	KNO/SOU	AA	133	576	483	127	29	7	16	218	78	5	6	78	5	6	2	40	21	80	60	.263	.372	.451
91	SYR/INT	AAA	98	445	393	78	18	1	1	101	38	0	7	51	9	4	3	17	13	49	28	.198	.279	.257
	DEN/AMA	AAA	20	83	70	27	3	2	0	34	10	0	0	8	3	2	1	3	0	20	15	.386	.457	.486

Surhoff, William James "B.J." — bats left — throws right — b.8/4/64 — 1991 positions: C 127, DH 6, 3B 5, OF 2, 2B 1

YR	TM/LG	CL	G	TPA	AB	H	2B	3B	HR	TB	BB	IBB	HB	SO	GDP	SH	SF	SB	CS	R	RBI	BA	OBA	SA
85	BEL/MID	A	76	318	289	96	13	4	7	138	22	0	0	35	3	2	5	10	9	39	58	.332	.373	.478
86	VAN/PCL	AAA	116	502	458	141	19	3	5	181	28	5	0	31	16	3	5	22	8	71	59	.308	.355	.395
87	MIL/AL		115	445	395	118	22	3	7	167	36	1	0	30	13	5	9	11	10	50	68	.299	.350	.423
88	MIL/AL		139	541	493	121	21	0	5	157	31	2	2	49	12	11	3	21	6	47	38	.245	.292	.318
89	MIL/AL		126	477	436	108	17	3	5	146	25	1	0	29	8	3	10	14	12	42	55	.248	.287	.339
90	MIL/AL		135	530	474	131	21	4	6	178	41	5	2	37	8	7	7	18	7	55	59	.276	.331	.376
91	MIL/AL		143	553	505	146	19	4	5	188	26	2	2	33	21	13	9	5	8	57	68	.289	.319	.372
5 YR TOTALS			**658**	**2546**	**2303**	**624**	**100**	**15**	**28**	**838**	**159**	**18**	**7**	**178**	**62**	**39**	**38**	**69**	**43**	**251**	**288**	**.271**	**.315**	**.364**

Sutko, Glenn Edward — bats right — throws right — b.5/9/68 — 1991 positions: C 9

YR	TM/LG	CL	G	TPA	AB	H	2B	3B	HR	TB	BB	IBB	HB	SO	GDP	SH	SF	SB	CS	R	RBI	BA	OBA	SA
88	BIL/PIO	R+	30	104	84	13	2	1	1	20	14	0	1	38	2	3	2	3	1	3	8	.155	.277	.238
89	GRE/SAL	A	109	387	333	78	21	0	7	120	47	1	4	105	5	0	3	1	3	44	41	.234	.333	.360
90	CR/MID	A	4	11	10	3	0	0	0	3	0	0	1	2	1	0	0	0	0	0	0	.300	.364	.300
	CHT/SOU	AA	53	183	174	29	7	1	2	44	8	1	1	66	2	0	0	1	1	12	11	.167	.208	.253
	CIN/NL		1	1	1	0	0	0	0	0	0	0	0	1	0	0	0	0	0	0	0	.000	.000	.000
91	CHT/SOU	AA	23	74	63	18	3	0	3	30	9	2	0	20	1	2	0	0	0	12	11	.286	.375	.476
	CIN/NL		10	12	10	1	0	0	0	1	2	0	0	6	0	0	0	0	1	0	1	.100	.250	.100
	NAS/AMA	AAA	45	156	134	28	2	1	3	41	22	3	0	67	3	0	0	1	0	9	15	.209	.321	.306
2 YR TOTALS			**11**	**13**	**11**	**1**	**0**	**0**	**0**	**1**	**2**	**0**	**0**	**7**	**0**	**0**	**0**	**0**	**0**	**0**	**1**	**.091**	**.231**	**.091**

Sveum, Dale Curtis — bats both — throws right — b.11/23/63 — 1991 positions: SS 51, 3B 38, DH 3, 2B 2

YR	TM/LG	CL	G	TPA	AB	H	2B	3B	HR	TB	BB	IBB	HB	SO	GDP	SH	SF	SB	CS	R	RBI	BA	OBA	SA
84	EP/TEX	AA	131	573	523	172	41	8	9	256	43	1	0	72	9	1	6	6	3	92	84	.329	.376	.489
85	VAN/PCL	AAA	122	468	415	98	17	3	6	139	48	6	2	79	17	1	2	4	5	42	48	.236	.317	.335
86	VAN/PCL	AAA	28	122	105	31	3	2	1	41	13	0	1	24	4	0	3	0	0	16	23	.295	.369	.390
	MIL/AL		91	356	317	78	13	2	7	116	32	0	1	63	7	5	1	4	3	35	35	.246	.316	.366
87	MIL/AL		153	586	535	135	27	3	25	243	40	4	1	133	11	5	5	2	6	86	95	.252	.303	.454
88	MIL/AL		129	495	467	113	14	4	9	162	21	0	1	122	6	3	3	1	0	41	51	.242	.274	.347
89	BEL/MID	A	6	20	15	2	1	0	0	3	5	2	0	6	0	0	1	0	0	0	2	.133	.350	.200
	STO/CAL	A+	11	50	43	8	0	0	1	11	6	1	0	14	2	0	1	0	0	5	5	.186	.280	.256
90	DEN/AMA	AAA	57	240	218	63	17	2	2	90	20	3	0	49	5	0	2	1	2	25	26	.289	.349	.413
	MIL/AL		48	133	117	23	7	0	1	33	12	0	2	30	2	2	0	1	1	15	12	.197	.278	.282
91	MIL/AL		90	308	266	64	19	1	4	97	32	0	4	78	8	5	4	2	4	33	43	.241	.320	.365
5 YR TOTALS			**511**	**1878**	**1702**	**413**	**80**	**10**	**46**	**651**	**137**	**4**	**6**	**426**	**34**	**18**	**15**	**9**	**14**	**210**	**236**	**.243**	**.299**	**.382**

Tabler, Patrick Sean "Pat" — bats right — throws right — b.2/2/58 — 1991 positions: DH 57, 1B 20, OF 1

YR	TM/LG	CL	G	TPA	AB	H	2B	3B	HR	TB	BB	IBB	HB	SO	GDP	SH	SF	SB	CS	R	RBI	BA	OBA	SA
81	CHI/NL		35	117	101	19	3	1	1	27	13	0	0	26	4	3	0	0	1	11	5	.188	.281	.267
82	CHI/NL		25	94	85	20	4	2	1	31	6	0	1	20	3	0	2	0	0	9	7	.235	.287	.365
83	CLE/AL		124	492	430	125	23	5	6	176	56	1	1	63	18	0	5	2	4	56	65	.291	.370	.409
84	CLE/AL		144	528	473	137	21	3	10	194	47	2	3	62	16	0	5	3	1	66	68	.290	.354	.410
85	CLE/AL		117	438	404	111	18	3	5	150	27	2	2	55	15	2	3	0	6	47	59	.275	.321	.371
86	MAI/INT	AAA	3	15	12	3	1	0	0	4	2	0	0	1	0	0	1	0	0	5	1	.250	.333	.333
	CLE/AL		130	508	473	154	29	2	6	205	29	3	3	75	11	2	1	3	1	61	48	.326	.368	.433
87	CLE/AL		151	618	553	170	34	3	11	243	51	6	6	84	6	3	5	5	2	66	86	.307	.369	.439
88	CLE/AL		41	168	143	32	5	1	1	42	23	1	1	27	3	0	1	0	0	16	17	.224	.333	.294
	KC/AL		89	330	301	93	17	2	1	117	23	0	2	41	6	0	4	2	3	37	49	.309	.358	.389
	YEAR		130	498	444	125	22	3	2	159	46	1	3	68	9	0	5	3	3	53	66	.282	.349	.358
89	KC/AL		123	434	390	101	11	1	2	120	37	0	2	42	14	3	2	0	0	36	42	.259	.325	.308
90	KC/AL		75	219	195	53	14	0	1	70	20	2	1	21	8	0	3	0	2	12	19	.272	.338	.359
	NY/NL		17	47	43	12	1	1	1	18	3	0	0	8	1	0	0	0	0	6	10	.279	.340	.419
	YEAR		92	266	238	65	15	1	2	88	23	2	2	29	8	0	3	0	2	18	29	.273	.338	.370
91	TOR/AL		82	222	185	40	5	1	1	50	29	5	1	21	3	2	5	0	0	20	21	.216	.318	.270
11 YR TOTALS			**1153**	**4215**	**3776**	**1067**	**185**	**25**	**47**	**1443**	**364**	**22**	**24**	**545**	**107**	**15**	**36**	**16**	**20**	**443**	**496**	**.283**	**.346**	**.382**

Tackett, Jeffery Wilson "Jeff" — bats right — throws right — b.12/1/65 — 1991 positions: C 6

YR	TM/LG	CL	G	TPA	AB	H	2B	3B	HR	TB	BB	IBB	HB	SO	GDP	SH	SF	SB	CS	R	RBI	BA	OBA	SA
84	BLU/APP	R+	34	123	98	16	2	0	0	18	23	0	0	28	1	0	2	1	1	9	12	.163	.317	.184
85	DB/FSL	A+	40	118	103	20	5	2	0	29	13	0	1	16	6	0	1	1	3	8	10	.194	.288	.282
	NEW/NYP	A-	62	215	187	39	6	0	0	45	22	0	2	33	4	3	1	2	2	21	22	.209	.297	.241
86	HAG/CAR	A+	83	288	246	70	15	1	0	87	36	0	5	36	2	1	1	2	2	53	21	.285	.385	.354
87	CHA/SOU	AA	61	221	205	46	6	1	0	54	12	0	2	34	2	1	1	5	5	18	13	.224	.273	.263
88	CHA/SOU	AA	81	317	272	56	9	0	0	65	42	0	2	46	7	0	1	6	4	24	18	.206	.315	.239
89	ROC/INT	AAA	67	223	199	36	3	1	2	47	19	0	1	45	3	2	2	3	1	13	17	.181	.253	.236
90	ROC/INT	AAA	108	363	306	73	8	3	4	99	47	0	7	50	3	3	0	4	8	37	33	.239	.353	.324
91	ROC/INT	AAA	126	496	433	102	18	2	6	142	54	0	2	60	15	4	3	3	3	64	50	.236	.321	.328
	BAL/AL		6	11	8	1	0	0	0	1	2	0	1	5	0	0	1	0	0	1	0	.125	.300	.125

Tartabull, Danilo (Mora) "Danny" — bats right — throws right — b.10/30/62 — 1991 positions: OF 124, DH 6

YR	TM/LG	CL	G	TPA	AB	H	2B	3B	HR	TB	BB	IBB	HB	SO	GDP	SH	SF	SB	CS	R	RBI	BA	OBA	SA
84	SLC/PCL	AAA	116	484	418	127	22	9	13	206	57	3	1	69	11	1	7	11	13	69	73	.304	.383	.493
	SEA/AL		10	24	20	6	1	0	2	13	2	0	1	3	0	0	1	0	0	3	7	.300	.375	.650
85	CAL/PCL	AAA	125	546	473	142	14	3	43	291	67	4	1	123	14	1	4	17	4	102	109	.300	.385	.615
	SEA/AL		19	69	61	20	7	1	1	32	8	0	0	14	1	0	0	1	0	8	7	.328	.406	.525
86	SEA/AL		137	578	511	138	25	6	25	250	61	2	1	157	10	2	3	4	8	76	96	.270	.347	.489
87	KC/AL		158	667	582	180	27	3	34	315	79	2	1	136	14	0	5	9	4	95	101	.309	.390	.541
88	KC/AL		146	593	507	139	38	3	26	261	76	4	4	119	10	0	6	8	5	80	102	.274	.369	.515
89	KC/AL		133	515	441	118	22	0	18	194	69	2	3	123	12	0	2	4	2	54	62	.268	.369	.440
90	KC/AL		88	352	313	84	19	0	15	148	36	0	3	93	9	0	3	1	1	41	60	.268	.341	.473
91	KC/AL		132	557	484	153	35	3	31	287	65	6	3	121	9	0	5	6	3	78	100	.316	.397	.593
8 YR TOTALS			**823**	**3355**	**2919**	**838**	**174**	**16**	**152**	**1500**	**396**	**16**	**13**	**766**	**65**	**2**	**25**	**33**	**23**	**435**	**535**	**.287**	**.372**	**.514**

Tatum, James Ray "Jimmy" — bats right — throws right — b.10/9/67 — 1991 positions: SS System MIL/AL

YR	TM/LG	CL	G	TPA	AB	H	2B	3B	HR	TB	BB	IBB	HB	SO	GDP	SH	SF	SB	CS	R	RBI	BA	OBA	SA
85	SPO/NWL	A–	74	311	281	64	9	1	1	78	20	0	5	60	7	4	1	0	1	21	32	.228	.290	.278
86	CHA/SAL	A	120	483	431	112	19	2	10	165	41	2	2	83	11	4	5	2	4	55	62	.260	.324	.383
87	CHS/SAL	A	128	535	468	131	22	2	9	184	46	2	8	65	16	4	9	8	5	52	72	.280	.348	.393
88	WIC/TEX	AA	118	446	402	105	26	1	8	157	30	2	5	73	5	6	3	2	3	38	54	.261	.318	.391
90	CAN/EAS	AA	30	115	106	19	6	0	2	31	6	1	1	19	2	0	2	1	0	6	11	.179	.226	.292
	STO/CAL	A+	70	285	260	68	16	0	12	120	13	0	8	49	7	0	4	4	5	41	59	.262	.312	.462
91	EP/TEX	AA	130	593	493	158	27	8	18	255	63	5	15	79	21	2	20	5	7	99	128	.320	.399	.517

Taubensee, Edward Kenneth "Eddie" — bats left — throws right — b.10/31/68 — 1991 positions: C 25

YR	TM/LG	CL	G	TPA	AB	H	2B	3B	HR	TB	BB	IBB	HB	SO	GDP	SH	SF	SB	CS	R	RBI	BA	OBA	SA
86	RED/GCL	R	35	118	107	21	3	0	1	27	11	0	0	33	2	0	0	0	1	8	11	.196	.271	.252
87	BIL/PIO	R+	55	190	162	43	7	0	5	65	25	5	1	47	2	0	2	2	2	24	28	.265	.363	.401
88	CHT/SOU	AA	5	15	12	2	0	0	1	5	3	0	0	4	0	0	0	0	0	2	1	.167	.333	.417
	GRE/SAL	A	103	380	330	85	16	1	10	133	44	5	4	93	2	1	1	8	4	36	41	.258	.351	.403
89	CR/MID	A	59	223	196	39	5	0	8	68	25	4	2	55	3	0	0	4	1	25	22	.199	.296	.347
	CHT/SOU	AA	45	142	127	24	2	0	3	35	11	2	0	28	3	1	3	0	0	11	13	.189	.248	.276
90	CR/MID	A	122	477	417	108	22	1	16	180	51	5	5	98	8	1	4	11	4	57	62	.259	.342	.432
91	CS/PCL	AAA	91	318	287	89	23	3	13	157	31	5	0	61	6	0	2	0	0	53	39	.310	.377	.547
	CLE/AL		26	73	66	16	2	1	0	20	5	1	0	16	1	0	2	0	0	5	8	.242	.288	.303

Templeton, Garry Lewis — bats both — throws right — b.3/24/56 — 1991 positions: SS 40, 1B 25, 3B 17, OF 2

YR	TM/LG	CL	G	TPA	AB	H	2B	3B	HR	TB	BB	IBB	HB	SO	GDP	SH	SF	SB	CS	R	RBI	BA	OBA	SA
76	STL/NL		53	225	213	62	8	2	1	77	7	0	1	33	1	2	2	11	7	32	17	.291	.314	.362
77	STL/NL		153	644	621	200	19	18	8	279	15	3	1	70	9	2	5	28	24	94	79	.322	.336	.449
78	STL/NL		155	675	647	181	31	13	2	244	22	3	1	87	7	3	3	34	11	82	47	.280	.303	.377
79	STL/NL		154	696	672	211	32	19	9	308	18	4	1	91	8	2	3	26	10	105	62	.314	.331	.458
80	STL/NL		118	524	504	161	19	9	4	210	18	6	1	43	13	1	1	31	15	83	43	.319	.342	.417
81	STL/NL		80	350	333	96	16	8	1	131	14	3	0	55	1	2	1	8	12	47	33	.288	.315	.393
82	SD/NL		141	601	563	139	25	8	6	198	26	7	0	57	16	7	5	16	6	39	40	.247	.294	.352
83	SD/NL		126	490	460	121	20	2	3	154	21	7	0	57	10	0	2	8	3	40	35	.263	.312	.335
84	SD/NL		148	535	493	127	19	3	2	158	39	23	1	81	10	0	2	8	3	63	55	.258	.332	.320
85	SD/NL		148	596	546	154	30	2	6	206	41	24	1	88	5	5	3	16	5	42	44	.282	.332	.377
86	SD/NL		147	549	510	126	21	2	2	157	35	21	1	86	12	1	2	10	5	42	48	.247	.296	.308
87	SD/NL		148	561	510	113	13	5	5	151	42	11	1	92	15	5	3	14	2	35	36	.222	.281	.296
88	SD/NL		110	392	362	90	15	7	3	128	20	10	0	50	6	7	3	8	2	43	40	.249	.286	.354
89	SD/NL		142	536	506	129	26	3	6	179	23	12	0	80	15	4	3	1	4	43	40	.255	.286	.354
90	SD/NL		144	541	505	125	25	3	9	183	24	7	0	59	17	8	4	1	4	45	59	.248	.280	.362
91	SD/NL		32	59	57	11	1	1	1	17	1	0	0	9	3	0	1	0	1	5	6	.193	.203	.298
	NY/NL		80	234	219	50	9	1	2	67	9	3	0	29	2	3	2	3	1	20	20	.228	.257	.306
	YEAR		112	293	276	61	10	2	3	84	10	3	0	38	10	4	3	3	2	25	26	.221	.246	.304
16 YR TOTALS			**2079**	**8208**	**7721**	**2096**	**329**	**106**	**70**	**2847**	**375**	**144**	**9**	**1092**	**167**	**57**	**46**	**242**	**129**	**893**	**728**	**.271**	**.304**	**.369**

Tettleton, Mickey Lee — bats both — throws right — b.9/16/60 — 1991 positions: C 125, DH 24, OF 3, 1B 1

YR	TM/LG	CL	G	TPA	AB	H	2B	3B	HR	TB	BB	IBB	HB	SO	GDP	SH	SF	SB	CS	R	RBI	BA	OBA	SA
84	ALB/EAS	AA	86	339	281	65	18	0	5	98	52	8	0	52	8	0	6	2	2	32	47	.231	.345	.349
	OAK/AL		33	88	76	20	2	1	1	27	11	0	0	21	3	0	1	0	0	10	5	.263	.352	.355
85	MOD/CAL	A+	4	14	14	3	3	0	0	6	0	0	0	4	0	0	0	0	0	1	0	.214	.214	.429
	OAK/AL		78	246	211	53	12	0	3	74	28	0	2	59	6	5	0	2	2	23	15	.251	.344	.351
86	MOD/CAL	A+	15	62	42	10	1	0	2	17	19	1	1	9	1	1	0	2	0	14	8	.238	.484	.405
	OAK/AL		90	262	211	43	9	0	10	82	39	0	1	51	3	7	4	7	1	26	35	.204	.325	.389
87	MOD/CAL	A+	3	12	11	4	1	0	2	11	1	0	0	4	0	0	0	0	0	4	2	.364	.417	1.000
	OAK/AL		82	248	211	41	3	0	8	68	30	0	0	65	3	5	2	1	1	19	26	.194	.292	.322
88	ROC/INT	AAA	19	50	41	10	3	1	1	18	7	0	0	15	0	0	2	0	1	9	4	.244	.380	.439
	BAL/AL		86	316	283	74	11	1	11	120	28	2	2	70	9	1	2	0	1	31	37	.261	.330	.424
89	BAL/AL		117	489	411	106	21	2	26	209	73	4	1	117	8	1	3	3	2	72	65	.258	.369	.509
90	BAL/AL		135	559	444	99	21	2	15	169	106	3	5	160	7	0	4	2	4	68	51	.223	.376	.381
91	DET/AL		154	608	501	132	17	2	31	246	101	9	2	131	12	0	4	3	3	85	89	.263	.387	.491
8 YR TOTALS			**775**	**2816**	**2348**	**568**	**96**	**8**	**105**	**995**	**416**	**18**	**13**	**674**	**51**	**19**	**20**	**18**	**14**	**334**	**323**	**.242**	**.356**	**.424**

Teufel, Timothy Shawn "Tim" — bats right — throws right — b.7/7/58 — 1991 positions: 2B 65, 3B 53, 1B 6

YR	TM/LG	CL	G	TPA	AB	H	2B	3B	HR	TB	BB	IBB	HB	SO	GDP	SH	SF	SB	CS	R	RBI	BA	OBA	SA
83	MIN/AL		21	82	78	24	7	1	3	42	2	0	0	8	1	2	0	0	0	11	6	.308	.325	.538
84	MIN/AL		157	652	568	149	30	3	14	227	76	8	2	73	18	2	4	1	3	76	61	.262	.349	.400
85	MIN/AL		138	496	434	113	24	3	10	173	48	2	3	70	14	7	4	4	2	58	50	.260	.324	.399
86	NY/NL		93	318	279	69	20	1	4	103	32	1	1	42	6	3	2	3	2	35	31	.247	.308	.369
87	NY/NL		97	350	299	92	29	0	14	163	44	2	1	53	7	3	2	3	2	55	61	.308	.398	.545
88	NY/NL		90	309	273	64	20	0	4	96	29	1	1	41	6	2	4	0	1	27	15	.234	.306	.352
89	NY/NL		83	254	219	56	7	2	2	73	32	1	1	50	4	0	1	0	3	28	24	.256	.350	.333
90	NY/NL		80	192	175	43	11	0	10	84	15	1	1	33	5	1	1	0	0	25	24	.246	.304	.480
91	NY/NL		20	36	34	4	0	0	1	7	2	0	0	9	0	0	0	0	0	2	2	.118	.167	.206
	SD/NL		97	363	307	70	16	0	11	119	49	4	1	77	8	4	2	2	9	39	42	.228	.319	.388
	YEAR		117	399	341	74	16	0	12	126	51	4	1	77	8	4	2	2	9	41	44	.217	.319	.370
9 YR TOTALS			**876**	**3052**	**2666**	**684**	**164**	**10**	**73**	**1087**	**329**	**20**	**11**	**447**	**69**	**24**	**22**	**19**	**16**	**366**	**323**	**.257**	**.338**	**.408**

Thomas, Frank Edward — bats right — throws right — b.5/27/68 — 1991 positions: DH 101, 1B 56

YR	TM/LG	CL	G	TPA	AB	H	2B	3B	HR	TB	BB	IBB	HB	SO	GDP	SH	SF	SB	CS	R	RBI	BA	OBA	SA
89	WS/GCL	R	17	66	52	19	5	0	1	27	11	0	1	3	0	0	2	1	0	8	11	.365	.470	.519
	SAR/FSL	A+	55	223	188	52	9	1	4	75	31	0	3	33	6	0	1	0	1	27	30	.277	.386	.399
90	BIR/SOU	AA	109	474	353	114	27	5	18	205	112	2	5	74	13	0	4	7	5	85	71	.323	.487	.581
	CHI/AL		60	240	191	63	11	3	7	101	44	0	2	54	5	0	3	0	1	39	31	.330	.454	.529
91	CHI/AL		158	700	559	178	31	2	32	309	138	13	1	112	20	0	2	1	2	104	109	.318	.453	.553
2 YR TOTALS			**218**	**940**	**750**	**241**	**42**	**5**	**39**	**410**	**182**	**13**	**3**	**166**	**25**	**0**	**5**	**1**	**3**	**143**	**140**	**.321**	**.453**	**.547**

Thome, James Howard "Jim" — bats left — throws right — b.8/27/70 — 1991 positions: 3B 27

YR	TM/LG	CL	G	TPA	AB	H	2B	3B	HR	TB	BB	IBB	HB	SO	GDP	SH	SF	SB	CS	R	RBI	BA	OBA	SA
89	IND/GCL	R	55	213	186	44	5	3	0	55	21	1	1	33	5	3	2	6	4	22	22	.237	.314	.296
90	BUR/APP	R+	34	149	118	44	7	1	12	89	27	3	4	18	2	0	0	6	3	31	34	.373	.503	.754
	KIN/CAR	A+	33	143	117	36	4	1	4	54	24	0	1	26	4	0	1	4	1	19	16	.308	.427	.462
91	CAN/EAS	AA	84	345	294	99	20	2	5	138	44	4	4	58	7	0	3	8	2	47	45	.337	.426	.469
	CS/PCL	AAA	41	166	151	43	7	3	2	62	12	0	0	29	4	0	3	0	0	20	28	.285	.331	.411
	CLE/AL		27	104	98	25	4	2	1	36	5	1	1	16	4	0	0	1	1	7	9	.255	.298	.367

Thompson, Milton Bernard "Milt" — bats left — throws right — b.1/5/59 — 1991 positions: OF 91

YR	TM/LG	CL	G	TPA	AB	H	2B	3B	HR	TB	BB	IBB	HB	SO	GDP	SH	SF	SB	CS	R	RBI	BA	OBA	SA
84	RIC/INT	AAA	134	593	503	145	11	3	4	174	83	3	3	86	9	2	2	47	17	91	40	.288	.391	.346
	ATL/NL		25	111	99	30	1	0	2	37	11	1	0	11	1	1	0	14	2	16	4	.303	.373	.374
85	RIC/INT	AAA	82	353	312	98	10	1	2	116	32	3	1	30	9	5	3	34	11	52	22	.314	.376	.372
	ATL/NL		73	193	182	55	7	2	0	66	7	1	0	36	1	1	0	9	4	17	6	.302	.339	.363
86	POR/PCL	AAA	41	179	161	56	10	2	1	73	15	1	1	20	3	1	1	20	3	26	16	.348	.404	.453
	PHI/NL		96	332	299	75	7	1	6	102	26	4	4	62	4	4	2	19	4	38	23	.251	.311	.341
87	PHI/NL		150	575	527	159	26	9	7	224	42	2	0	87	5	3	3	46	10	86	43	.302	.351	.425
88	PHI/NL		122	423	378	109	16	2	2	135	39	6	1	59	8	2	3	17	9	53	33	.288	.354	.357
89	STL/NL		155	591	545	158	28	8	4	214	39	5	4	91	12	0	3	27	8	60	68	.290	.340	.393
90	STL/NL		135	463	418	91	16	4	3	137	39	5	5	60	4	0	0	25	5	42	30	.218	.292	.328
91	STL/NL		115	361	326	100	16	5	6	144	32	7	0	53	4	2	1	16	9	55	34	.307	.368	.442
8 YR TOTALS			**871**	**3049**	**2774**	**777**	**115**	**34**	**33**	**1059**	**235**	**27**	**14**	**459**	**39**	**14**	**12**	**173**	**51**	**367**	**241**	**.280**	**.338**	**.382**

Thompson, Robert Randall "Robby" — bats right — throws right — b.5/10/62 — 1991 positions: 2B 144

YR	TM/LG	CL	G	TPA	AB	H	2B	3B	HR	TB	BB	IBB	HB	SO	GDP	SH	SF	SB	CS	R	RBI	BA	OBA	SA
84	FRE/CAL	A+	102	383	325	81	11	0	8	116	47	1	5	85	8	1	5	21	7	53	43	.249	.348	.357
85	SHR/TEX	AA	121	527	449	117	20	7	9	178	65	0	5	101	8	5	3	28	7	85	40	.261	.358	.396
86	SF/NL		149	615	549	149	27	3	7	203	42	0	5	112	11	18	1	12	15	73	47	.271	.328	.370
87	SF/NL		132	474	420	110	26	5	10	176	40	3	8	91	8	6	0	16	11	62	44	.262	.338	.419
88	SF/NL		138	540	477	126	24	6	7	183	40	0	4	111	14	5	5	14	5	66	48	.264	.323	.384
89	SF/NL		148	620	547	132	26	11	13	219	51	0	13	133	6	9	6	12	2	91	50	.241	.321	.400
90	SF/NL		144	549	498	122	22	3	15	195	34	1	6	96	9	8	3	14	4	67	56	.245	.299	.392
91	SF/NL		144	573	492	129	24	5	19	220	63	2	6	95	5	11	1	14	7	74	48	.262	.352	.447
6 YR TOTALS			**855**	**3371**	**2983**	**768**	**149**	**33**	**71**	**1196**	**270**	**6**	**42**	**638**	**46**	**66**	**10**	**82**	**44**	**433**	**293**	**.257**	**.327**	**.401**

Thon, Richard William "Dickie" — bats right — throws right — b.6/20/58 — 1991 positions: SS 146

YR	TM/LG	CL	G	TPA	AB	H	2B	3B	HR	TB	BB	IBB	HB	SO	GDP	SH	SF	SB	CS	R	RBI	BA	OBA	SA
79	CAL/AL		35	62	56	19	3	0	0	22	5	0	0	10	2	1	0	0	0	6	8	.339	.393	.393
80	CAL/AL		80	285	267	68	12	2	0	84	10	0	1	28	5	2	5	7	5	32	15	.255	.282	.315
81	HOU/NL		49	105	95	26	6	0	0	32	9	1	0	13	3	1	0	6	1	13	3	.274	.337	.337
82	HOU/NL		136	540	496	137	31	10	3	197	37	2	1	48	4	5	1	37	8	73	36	.276	.327	.397
83	HOU/NL		154	686	619	177	28	9	20	283	54	10	2	73	12	3	8	34	16	81	79	.286	.341	.457
84	HOU/NL		5	18	17	6	0	1	0	8	0	0	1	4	1	0	0	0	0	3	1	.353	.389	.471
85	HOU/NL		84	272	251	63	6	1	6	89	18	4	0	50	2	1	2	8	3	26	29	.251	.299	.355
86	HOU/NL		106	309	278	69	13	1	3	93	29	5	0	49	8	1	1	6	5	24	21	.248	.318	.335
87	TUC/PCL	AAA	14	56	48	13	4	0	0	17	6	0	1	12	1	1	0	1	1	10	6	.271	.364	.354
	HOU/NL		32	83	66	14	1	0	1	18	16	3	0	13	1	1	0	3	0	6	3	.212	.366	.273
88	SD/NL		95	296	258	68	12	2	1	87	33	0	1	49	4	2	2	19	4	36	18	.264	.347	.337
89	PHI/NL		136	472	435	118	18	1	15	189	33	0	6	81	6	1	3	6	3	45	60	.271	.321	.434
90	PHI/NL		149	595	552	141	20	4	8	193	37	10	1	77	14	1	2	12	5	54	48	.255	.305	.350
91	PHI/NL		146	570	539	136	18	4	9	189	25	6	0	84	9	2	4	11	5	44	44	.252	.283	.351
13 YR TOTALS			**1207**	**4293**	**3929**	**1042**	**168**	**38**	**66**	**1484**	**306**	**47**	**9**	**579**	**71**	**24**	**25**	**149**	**56**	**443**	**365**	**.265**	**.318**	**.378**

Thurman, Gary Montez — bats right — throws right — b.11/12/64 — 1991 positions: OF 72

YR	TM/LG	CL	G	TPA	AB	H	2B	3B	HR	TB	BB	IBB	HB	SO	GDP	SH	SF	SB	CS	R	RBI	BA	OBA	SA
84	CHA/SAL	A	129	571	478	109	6	8	6	149	81	1	8	127	6	1	3	44	17	71	51	.228	.347	.312
85	FM/FSL	A+	134	532	453	137	9	9	0	164	68	1	4	93	7	3	4	70	18	68	45	.302	.395	.362
86	MEM/SOU	AA	131	589	525	164	24	12	7	233	57	0	0	81	5	4	3	53	18	88	62	.312	.378	.444
	OMA/AMA	AAA	3	4	2	1	0	0	0	1	2	0	0	0	0	0	0	2	0	1	0	.500	.750	.500
87	OMA/AMA	AAA	115	509	450	132	14	9	8	188	48	0	3	84	4	5	3	58	7	88	39	.293	.363	.418
	KC/AL		27	90	81	24	2	0	0	26	6	0	1	20	1	1	0	7	2	12	5	.296	.360	.321
88	OMA/AMA	AAA	106	475	422	106	12	0	3	139	38	2	4	80		8	3	35	12	77	40	.251	.317	.329
	KC/AL		35	70	66	11	1	0	0	12	4	0	0	20	0	0	0	5	2	9	2	.167	.214	.182
89	OMA/AMA	AAA	17	71	64	14	3	2	0	21	7	0	0	18	0	0	0	5	1	6	2	.219	.296	.328
	KC/AL		72	105	87	17	2	1	0	21	15	0	0	26	0	2	1	16	0	24	3	.195	.311	.241

Thurman, Gary Montez (continued)

YR	TM/LG	CL	G	TPA	AB	H	2B	3B	HR	TB	BB	IBB	HB	SO	GDP	SH	SF	SB	CS	R	RBI	BA	OBA	SA
90	OMA/AMA	AAA	98	424	381	126	14	8	0	156	31	1	4	68	6	6	2	39	15	65	26	.331	.385	.409
	KC/AL		23	63	60	14	3	0	0	17	2	0	0	12	1	0	1	1	1	5	3	.233	.258	.283
91	KC/AL		80	200	184	51	9	0	2	66	11	0	1	42	4	3	1	15	5	24	13	.277	.320	.359
5 YR TOTALS			**237**	**528**	**478**	**117**	**17**	**1**	**2**	**142**	**40**	**0**	**1**	**120**	**7**	**7**	**2**	**44**	**9**	**71**	**28**	**.245**	**.303**	**.297**

Tingley, Ronald Irvin "Ron" — bats right — throws right — b.5/27/59 — 1991 positions: C 45

YR	TM/LG	CL	G	TPA	AB	H	2B	3B	HR	TB	BB	IBB	HB	SO	GDP	SH	SF	SB	CS	R	RBI	BA	OBA	SA
77	WW/NWL	A−	21	38	33	5	0	0	1	8	3	0	2	9	0	1	0	0	0	8	3	.152	.243	.242
78	WW/NWL	A−	43	168	140	29	2	0	2	37	21	1	5	38	2	1	1	2	0	22	21	.207	.329	.264
79	SC/CAL	A+	52	166	143	29	4	1	0	35	18	0	0	37	3	2	0	3		11	17	.203	.288	.245
	AMA/TEX	AA	30	105	90	23	4	1	1	32	14	0	0	17	2	1	0	2	1	16	6	.256	.356	.356
80	REN/CAL	A+	65	243	204	61	3	3	3	79	33	1	0	35	4	4	2	8	1	37	35	.299	.393	.387
81	AMA/TEX	AA	116	446	379	109	9	10	13	177	52	0	4	98	4	7	4	11	6	72	60	.288	.376	.467
82	HAW/PCL	AAA	115	427	362	95	13	8	6	142	56	0	2	103	4	5	2	11	6	45	42	.262	.363	.392
	SD/NL		8	21	20	2	0	0	0	2	0	0	0	7	0	1	0	0	0	0	0	.100	.100	.100
83	LV/PCL	AAA	92	338	294	83	15	6	10	140	39	2	1	85	2	1	3	9	4	44	48	.282	.365	.476
85	CAL/PCL	AAA	83	311	277	70	11	3	11	120	30	1	2	74	1	2	0	3	3	36	47	.253	.330	.433
86	RIC/INT	AAA	9	24	23	4	0	0	0	4	0	0	0	9	0	1	0	0	0	1	1	.174	.174	.174
	MAI/INT	AAA	49	166	151	31	2	1	3	44	12	0	0	27	7	2	1	1	0	12	12	.205	.262	.291
87	BUF/AMA	AAA	57	197	167	45	8	5	5	78	25	1	4	42	3	0	1	1	2	27	30	.269	.376	.467
88	CS/PCL	AAA	44	148	130	37	5	1	3	53	12	0	2	23	4	1	3	1	0	11	20	.285	.347	.408
	CLE/AL		9	26	24	4	0	0	1	7	2	0	0	8	1	0	0	0	0	1	2	.167	.231	.292
89	CS/PCL	AAA	66	234	207	54	8	2	6	84	19	1	1	49	6	1	6	2	1	28	39	.261	.318	.406
	CAL/AL		4	4	3	1	0	0	0	1	0	0	0	1	0	0	0	0	0	0	0	.333	.500	.333
90	EDM/PCL	AAA	54	198	172	46	9	2	5	74	21	0	2	39	6	1	2	1	1	27	23	.267	.350	.430
	CAL/AL		5	4	3	0	0	0	0	0	0	0	1	1	0	0	0	0	0	0	0	.000	.250	.000
91	EDM/PCL	AAA	17	65	55	16	5	0	3	30	8	0	1	14	0	1	1	1	0	11	15	.291	.391	.545
	CAL/AL		45	128	115	23	7	0	1	33	8	0	1	34	1	4	0	1	1	11	13	.200	.258	.287
5 YR TOTALS			**71**	**183**	**165**	**30**	**7**	**0**	**2**	**43**	**12**	**0**	**2**	**50**	**3**	**5**	**0**	**1**	**1**	**12**	**15**	**.182**	**.242**	**.261**

Tinsley, Lee Owen — bats right — throws right — b.3/4/69 — 1991 positions: OF System CLE/AL

YR	TM/LG	CL	G	TPA	AB	H	2B	3B	HR	TB	BB	IBB	HB	SO	GDP	SH	SF	SB	CS	R	RBI	BA	OBA	SA
87	MED/NWL	A−	45	174	132	23	3	2	0	30	35	0	2	57	1	1	4	9	3	22	13	.174	.347	.227
88	SO/NWL	A−	72	329	256	64	8	2	3	85	66	1	5	106	1	1	1	42	10	56	28	.250	.412	.332
89	MAD/MID	A	123	477	397	72	10	2	6	104	67	1	9	177	3	3	1	19	11	51	31	.181	.312	.262
90	MAD/MID	A	132	570	482	121	14	11	12	193	78	7	5	175	3	3	2	44	11	88	59	.251	.360	.400
91	HUN/SOU	AA	92	363	303	68	7	6	2	93	52	1	3	97	6	1	4	36	14	47	24	.224	.340	.307
	CAN/EAS	AA	38	163	139	41	7	2	3	61	18	2	4	37	2	2	0	18	5	26	8	.295	.391	.439

Tolentino, Jose Franco — bats left — throws left — b.6/3/61 — 1991 positions: 1B 10, OF 1

YR	TM/LG	CL	G	TPA	AB	H	2B	3B	HR	TB	BB	IBB	HB	SO	GDP	SH	SF	SB	CS	R	RBI	BA	OBA	SA
83	MED/NWL	A−	49	201	181	60	11	1	7	94	15	2	3	17	3	0	2	1	1	33	39	.331	.388	.519
84	MOD/CAL	A+	66	287	251	71	17	1	14	132	29	7	3	34	6	2	0	4	4	40	54	.283	.368	.526
	ALB/EAS	AA	71	278	257	73	13	1	5	103	16	0	0	35	5	2	3	2	1	38	41	.284	.322	.401
85	TAC/PCL	AAA	106	385	339	87	24	1	6	131	38	5	3	53	9	1	2	7	2	33	53	.257	.333	.386
86	HUN/SOU	AA	137	606	540	170	28	0	16	246	53	6	4	57	10	2	0	0	2	80	105	.315	.376	.456
87	TAC/PCL	AAA	59	225	202	46	6	0	6	63	21	0	0	28	4	1	1	1	0	20	25	.228	.300	.312
	HUN/SOU	AA	49	197	173	41	6	0	6	65	21	2	1	20	5	4	0	1	0	16	26	.237	.321	.376
88	OC/AMA	AAA	48	155	131	28	4	0	0	32	20	3	0	20	5	4	0	1	3	6	8	.214	.318	.244
	COL/SOU	AA	72	306	259	79	10	3	9	122	36	6	0	32	7	0	3	10	2	61	64	.305	.395	.471
89	TUC/PCL	AAA	128	486	408	111	27	0	9	167	62	2	5	44	12	3	10	2	3	69	78	.272	.364	.409
90	TUC/PCL	AAA	116	436	377	116	32	3	21	217	48	2	5	44	10	0	1	2	3	44	51	.308	.389	.576
91	TUC/PCL	AAA	90	350	303	88	24	5	6	140	44	8	2	44	10	2	0	1	0	6	6	.290	.383	.462
	HOU/NL		44	59	54	14	4	0	1	21	4	0	0	21	2	0	1	0	0	6	6	.259	.305	.389

Torve, Kelvin Curtis — bats left — throws right — b.1/10/60 — 1991 positions: 1B 1

YR	TM/LG	CL	G	TPA	AB	H	2B	3B	HR	TB	BB	IBB	HB	SO	GDP	SH	SF	SB	CS	R	RBI	BA	OBA	SA
81	CLI/MID	A	57	239	211	55	10	0	1	68	26	2	0	26	7	0	2	7	4	27	27	.261	.339	.322
82	SHR/TEX	AA	127	506	449	137	29	7	15	225	43	11	2	47	6	3	9	9	1	66	84	.305	.362	.501
83	PHO/PCL	AAA	115	438	392	102	21	5	4	145	34	2	1	33	7	4	2	6	4	58	54	.260	.316	.370
84	SHR/TEX	AA	114	367	316	94	21	5	16	173	43	3	2	42	8	0	6	2	0	59	62	.297	.379	.547
85	CHA/SOU	AA	134	570	482	140	34	1	15	221	75	9	2	53	16	4	7	5	2	85	77	.290	.383	.459
86	ROC/INT	AAA	109	397	356	86	16	0	4	116	37	0	0	43	8	0	5	2	2	39	41	.242	.310	.326
87	ROC/INT	AAA	86	296	252	66	10	0	9	103	38	6	0	36	3	5	0	0	0	27	32	.262	.357	.409
88	MIN/AL		12	17	16	3	0	0	1	6	1	0	0	2	0	0	0	0	0	1	2	.188	.235	.375
	POR/PCL	AAA	103	429	385	116	28	2	9	175	40	3	1	36	8	2	1	1	5	58	47	.301	.368	.455
89	POR/PCL	AAA	137	563	499	145	41	2	8	214	52	7	4	59	11	3	5	5	10	62	62	.291	.359	.429
90	TID/INT	AAA	115	469	402	122	25	2	11	182	56	6	6	43	13	0	5	9	2	62	76	.303	.392	.453
	NY/NL		20	44	38	11	4	0	0	15	4	0	0	2	9	1	0	0	0	0	2	.289	.360	.395
91	NY/NL		10	8	8	0	0	0	0	0	0	0	0	2	0	1	0	0	0	0	0	.000	.000	.000
	TID/INT	AAA	103	406	336	92	20	2	2	143	62	0	2	12	2	0	0	0	1	57	49	.274	.383	.426
3 YR TOTALS			**42**	**69**	**62**	**14**	**4**	**0**	**1**	**21**	**5**	**0**	**2**	**12**	**2**	**0**	**0**	**0**	**1**	**1**	**4**	**.226**	**.304**	**.339**

Trammell, Alan Stuart — bats right — throws right — b.2/21/58 — 1991 positions: SS 91, DH 6, 3B 1

YR	TM/LG	CL	G	TPA	AB	H	2B	3B	HR	TB	BB	IBB	HB	SO	GDP	SH	SF	SB	CS	R	RBI	BA	OBA	SA
77	DET/AL		19	48	43	8	0	0	0	8	4	0	0	12	1	1	0	0	0	6	0	.186	.255	.186
78	DET/AL		139	504	448	120	14	6	2	152	45	0	2	56	12	6	3	3	1	49	34	.268	.335	.339
79	DET/AL		142	520	460	127	11	4	6	164	43	0	0	55	6	12	5	17	14	68	50	.276	.335	.357
80	DET/AL		146	652	560	168	21	5	9	226	69	2	3	63	10	13	7	12	12	107	65	.300	.376	.404
81	DET/AL		105	463	392	101	15	3	2	128	49	2	3	31	10	16	3	10	3	52	31	.258	.342	.327
82	DET/AL		157	556	489	126	34	3	9	193	52	0	0	47	5	9	6	19	8	66	57	.258	.325	.395
83	DET/AL		142	581	505	161	31	2	14	238	57	2	0	64	7	15	4	30	10	83	66	.319	.385	.471
84	DET/AL		139	626	555	174	34	5	14	260	60	2	3	63	8	6	2	19	13	85	69	.314	.382	.468
85	DET/AL		149	677	605	156	21	7	13	230	50	4	2	71	6	11	9	14	5	79	57	.258	.312	.380
86	DET/AL		151	653	574	159	33	7	21	269	59	4	5	57	7	11	4	25	12	107	75	.277	.347	.469
87	DET/AL		151	668	597	205	34	3	28	329	60	8	3	47	11	2	6	21	2	109	105	.343	.402	.551
88	DET/AL		128	523	466	145	24	1	15	216	46	8	4	46	14	0	7	7	4	73	69	.311	.373	.464
89	DET/AL		121	506	449	109	20	3	5	150	45	1	4	45	9	3	5	10	2	54	43	.243	.314	.334
90	DET/AL		146	637	559	170	37	1	14	251	68	7	1	55	11	3	6	12	10	71	89	.304	.377	.449
91	DET/AL		101	421	375	93	20	0	9	140	37	1	3	39	7	5	1	11	2	57	55	.248	.320	.373
15 YR TOTALS			**1936**	**8035**	**7077**	**2022**	**349**	**50**	**161**	**2954**	**744**	**41**	**33**	**751**	**124**	**113**	**68**	**210**	**98**	**1066**	**865**	**.286**	**.353**	**.417**

Treadway, Hugh Jeffery "Jeff" — bats left — throws right — b.1/22/63 — 1991 positions: 2B 93

YR	TM/LG	CL	G	TPA	AB	H	2B	3B	HR	TB	BB	IBB	HB	SO	GDP	SH	SF	SB	CS	R	RBI	BA	OBA	SA
84	TAM/FSL	A+	119	441	372	115	16	0	0	131	54	8	5	40	10	7	3	13	7	44	44	.309	.401	.352
85	VER/EAS	AA	129	514	431	130	17	1	2	155	71	2	2	40	10	5	5	6	5	63	49	.302	.399	.360
86	VER/EAS	AA	33	148	122	41	8	1	1	54	23	2	1	12	2	0	2	3	1	18	16	.336	.439	.443
	DEN/AMA	AAA	72	227	204	67	11	4	3	95	19	2	1	12	4	1	2	3	1	20	23	.328	.385	.466
87	NAS/AMA	AAA	123	472	409	129	28	5	7	188	52	3	3	41	8	2	6	2	1	66	59	.315	.391	.460
	CIN/NL		23	90	84	28	4	0	2	38	2	0	1	6	1	3	0	1	0	9	4	.333	.356	.452
88	CIN/NL		103	341	301	76	19	4	2	109	27	7	3	30	4	4	6	2	0	30	23	.252	.315	.362
89	ATL/NL		134	514	473	131	18	3	8	179	30	3	0	38	9	6	5	3	2	58	40	.277	.317	.378
90	ATL/NL		128	511	474	134	20	2	11	191	25	1	3	42	10	5	4	3	4	56	59	.283	.320	.403
91	ATL/NL		106	336	306	98	17	2	3	128	23	1	2	19	8	2	3	2	2	41	32	.320	.368	.418
5 YR TOTALS			**494**	**1792**	**1638**	**467**	**78**	**11**	**26**	**645**	**107**	**12**	**9**	**135**	**32**	**20**	**18**	**11**	**8**	**194**	**158**	**.285**	**.329**	**.394**

Turner, Shane Lee — bats left — throws right — b.1/8/63 — 1991 positions: 2B 1

YR	TM/LG	CL	G	TPA	AB	H	2B	3B	HR	TB	BB	IBB	HB	SO	GDP	SH	SF	SB	CS	R	RBI	BA	OBA	SA
85	ONE/NYP	A—	64	269	228	56	7	3	0	69	35	2	3	44	2	1	2	12	0	35	26	.246	.351	.303
86	FL/FSL	A+	66	283	222	71	12	2	2	93	51	1	3	35	6	4	3	12	8	48	36	.320	.448	.419
87	COL/INT	AAA	25	82	76	17	0	2	0	21	5	0	0	16	2	1	0	2	1	10	7	.224	.272	.276
	ALB/EAS	AA	20	88	73	23	3	1	1	31	12	0	1	3	3	1	0	2	1	19	8	.315	.414	.425
	REA/EAS	AA	74	309	283	96	16	6	3	133	21	1	3	35	5	1	1	3	6	50	47	.339	.390	.470
88	MAI/INT	AAA	38	130	117	21	3	1	0	26	7	0	1	21	1	3	2	2	2	10	9	.179	.228	.222
	REA/EAS	AA	78	336	295	88	11	6	3	120	26	3	7	53	3	6	2	14	2	52	21	.298	.367	.407
	PHI/NL		18	40	35	6	0	0	0	6	5	0	0	9	1	0	0	0	0	1	1	.171	.275	.171
89	REA/EAS	AA	46	170	141	28	5	1	1	38	27	1	2	27	2	0		13	3	18	11	.199	.335	.270
	ROC/INT	AAA	59	219	194	43	6	1	2	57	19	1	1	33	5	4	1	6	4	31	19	.222	.293	.294
90	HAG/EAS	AA	10	38	38	9	1	0	0	10	0	0	0	10	1	0		1	0	5	1	.237	.237	.263
	ROC/INT	AAA	86	243	209	59	7	0	0	69	25	2	0	41	4	7	2	3	5	29	19	.282	.356	.330
91	BAL/AL		4	1	1	0	0	0	0	0	0	0	0	0	0	0	0	0	0	0	0	.000	.000	.000
	ROC/INT	AAA	110	457	404	114	13	2	1	134	47	1	3	75	13	1	2	6	7	49	57	.282	.360	.332
2 YR TOTALS			**22**	**41**	**36**	**6**	**0**	**0**	**0**	**6**	**5**	**0**	**0**	**9**	**1**	**0**	**0**	**0**	**0**	**1**	**1**	**.167**	**.268**	**.167**

Uribe, Jose Altagracia — bats both — throws right — b.1/21/59 — 1991 positions: SS 87

YR	TM/LG	CL	G	TPA	AB	H	2B	3B	HR	TB	BB	IBB	HB	SO	GDP	SH	SF	SB	CS	R	RBI	BA	OBA	SA
84	STL/NL		8	20	19	4	0	0	0	4	0	0	0	2	1	1	0	1	0	4	3	.211	.211	.211
85	SF/NL		147	513	476	113	20	4	3	150	30	8	2	57	5	5	0	8	2	46	26	.237	.285	.315
86	SF/NL		157	517	453	101	15	1	3	127	61	19	0	76	2	3	0	22	11	46	43	.223	.315	.280
87	SF/NL		95	340	309	90	16	5	5	131	24	9	1	35	1	5	1	12	2	44	30	.291	.343	.424
88	SF/NL		141	535	493	124	10	7	3	157	36	10	3	69	3	4	2	14	10	47	35	.252	.301	.318
89	SF/NL		151	497	453	100	12	1	1	127	34	12	6	74	7	6	4	6	6	34	30	.221	.273	.280
90	SF/NL		138	448	415	103	8	6	1	126	29	13	0	49	8	4	0	5	9	35	24	.248	.297	.304
91	SJ/CAL	A+	3	11	9	1	0	1	0	3	1	0	0	0	1	0	0	0	0	0	1	.111	.182	.333
	PHO/PCL	AAA	11	42	41	14	1	1	0	17	1	0	0	2	1	0	0	0	0	7	4	.341	.357	.415
	SF/NL		90	252	231	51	8	4	1	70	20	6	0	33	2	1	0	3	4	23	12	.221	.283	.303
8 YR TOTALS			**927**	**3122**	**2849**	**686**	**89**	**33**	**17**	**892**	**234**	**77**	**3**	**395**	**29**	**29**	**7**	**71**	**44**	**279**	**203**	**.241**	**.298**	**.313**

Valle, David "Dave" — bats right — throws right — b.10/30/60 — 1991 positions: C 129, 1B 2

YR	TM/LG	CL	G	TPA	AB	H	2B	3B	HR	TB	BB	IBB	HB	SO	GDP	SH	SF	SB	CS	R	RBI	BA	OBA	SA
84	SLC/PCL	AAA	86	335	284	79	13	1	12	130	45	1	3	36	6	0	3	0	1	54	54	.278	.379	.458
	SEA/AL		13	28	27	8	1	0	1	12	1	0	0	5	0	0	0	0	0	4	4	.296	.321	.444
85	CAL/PCL	AAA	42	151	131	45	8	0	6	71	20	1	0	19	6	0	0	0	0	17	26	.344	.430	.542
	SEA/AL		31	73	70	11	1	0	0	12	1	0	1	17	1	1	0	0	0	2	4	.157	.181	.171
86	CAL/PCL	AAA	105	404	353	110	21	2	21	198	41	0	7	43	13	1	2	5	1	71	72	.312	.392	.561
	SEA/AL		22	60	53	18	3	0	5	36	4	0	0	7	2	0	0	1	0	10	15	.340	.417	.679
87	SEA/AL		95	346	324	83	16	3	12	141	15	2	3	46	13	0	4	2	0	40	53	.256	.292	.435
88	SEA/AL		93	322	290	67	15	2	10	116	18	0	9	38	13	3	2	0	1	29	50	.231	.295	.400

Valle, David "Dave" (continued)

YR	TM/LG	CL	G	TPA	AB	H	2B	3B	HR	TB	BB	IBB	HB	SO	GDP	SH	SF	SB	CS	R	RBI	BA	OBA	SA
89	CAL/PCL	AAA	2	7	6	0	0	0	0	0	0	0	1	1	0	0	0	0	0	0	0	.000	.143	.000
	SEA/AL		94	355	316	75	10	3	7	112	29	2	6	32	13	1	3	0	0	32	34	.237	.311	.354
90	SEA/AL		107	364	308	66	15	0	7	102	45	0	7	48	11	4	0	1	2	37	33	.214	.328	.331
91	SEA/AL		132	376	324	63	8	1	8	97	34	0	9	49	19	6	3	0	2	38	32	.194	.286	.299
8 YR TOTALS			**587**	**1924**	**1712**	**391**	**69**	**9**	**50**	**628**	**150**	**4**	**35**	**242**	**72**	**15**	**12**	**3**	**5**	**192**	**225**	**.228**	**.302**	**.367**

Vanderwal, John Henry — bats left — throws left — b.4/29/66 — 1991 positions: OF 17

YR	TM/LG	CL	G	TPA	AB	H	2B	3B	HR	TB	BB	IBB	HB	SO	GDP	SH	SF	SB	CS	R	RBI	BA	OBA	SA
87	JAM/NYP	A—	18	73	69	33	12	3	3	60	3	0	0	14	2	0	1	3	2	24	15	.478	.493	.870
	WPB/FSL	A+	50	223	189	54	11	2	2	75	30	0	0	25	2	1	3	8	3	29	22	.286	.378	.397
88	WPB/FSL	A+	62	272	231	64	15	2	10	113	32	2	3	40	3	0	3	11	4	50	33	.277	.368	.489
	JAC/SOU	AA	58	227	208	54	14	0	3	77	17	1	1	49	3	0	1	3	4	22	14	.260	.317	.370
89	JAC/SOU	AA	71	242	217	55	9	2	6	86	22	1	1	51	5	0	2	2	3	30	24	.253	.322	.396
90	JAC/SOU	AA	77	321	277	84	25	3	8	139	39	2	3	46	7	0	2	6	3	45	40	.303	.393	.502
	IND/AMA	AAA	51	148	135	40	6	0	2	52	13	0	0	28	3	0	0	0	1	16	14	.296	.358	.385
91	IND/AMA	AAA	133	564	478	140	36	8	15	237	79	4	2	118	10	1	4	8	1	84	71	.293	.393	.496
	MON/NL		21	63	61	13	4	1	1	22	1	0	0	18	2	0	1	0	0			.213	.222	.361

Van Slyke, Andrew James "Andy" — bats left — throws right — b.12/21/60 — 1991 positions: OF 135

YR	TM/LG	CL	G	TPA	AB	H	2B	3B	HR	TB	BB	IBB	HB	SO	GDP	SH	SF	SB	CS	R	RBI	BA	OBA	SA
83	STL/NL		101	361	309	81	15	5	8	130	46	5	1	64	4	2	3	21	7	51	38	.262	.357	.421
84	STL/NL		137	426	361	88	16	4	7	133	63	9	0	71	5	0	2	28	5	45	50	.244	.354	.368
85	STL/NL		146	475	424	110	25	6	13	186	47	6	2	54	7	1	1	34	6	48	61	.259	.335	.439
86	STL/NL		137	470	418	113	23	7	13	189	47	5	1	85	2	1	3	21	8	48	61	.270	.343	.452
87	PIT/NL		157	630	564	165	36	11	21	286	56	4	4	122	6	3	3	34	8	93	82	.293	.359	.507
88	PIT/NL		154	659	587	169	23	15	25	297	57	2	1	126	8	1	13	30	9	101	100	.288	.345	.506
89	PIT/NL		130	531	476	113	18	9	9	176	47	3	3	100	13	1	4	16	4	64	53	.237	.308	.370
90	PIT/NL		136	567	493	140	26	6	17	229	66	2	1	89	5	0	11	14	4	67	77	.284	.367	.465
91	PIT/NL		138	577	491	130	24	7	17	219	71	1	4	85	5	0	11	10	3	87	83	.265	.355	.446
9 YR TOTALS			**1236**	**4696**	**4123**	**1109**	**206**	**70**	**130**	**1845**	**500**	**37**	**17**	**796**	**56**	**12**	**44**	**208**	**54**	**617**	**599**	**.269**	**.347**	**.447**

Varsho, Gary Andrew — bats left — throws right — b.6/20/61 — 1991 positions: OF 54, 1B 3

YR	TM/LG	CL	G	TPA	AB	H	2B	3B	HR	TB	BB	IBB	HB	SO	GDP	SH	SF	SB	CS	R	RBI	BA	OBA	SA
84	MID/TEX	AA	128	486	429	112	15	6	8	163	49	2	1	86	4	4	3	27	8	65	50	.261	.336	.380
85	PIT/EAS	AA	115	469	418	101	14	6	3	136	40	1	5	53	3	5	1	40	8	62	37	.242	.315	.325
86	PIT/EAS	AA	107	444	399	106	18	5	13	173	38	4	3	52	1	1	3	45	11	75	44	.266	.332	.434
87	IOW/AMA	AAA	132	555	504	152	23	9	9	220	41	2	3	65	6	3	4	37	17	87	48	.302	.355	.437
88	IOW/AMA	AAA	66	257	234	65	16	5	4	103	18	0	2	38	1	1	2	8	2	46	26	.278	.332	.440
	CHI/NL		46	75	73	20	3	0	0	23	1	0	0	20	2	0	0	5	0	6	5	.274	.280	.315
89	IOW/AMA	AAA	31	125	112	26	3	1	2	37	9	2	2	21	2	0	0	3	0	10	6	.232	.296	.330
	CHI/NL		61	91	87	16	4	2	0	24	4	1	0	13	0	0	0	3	0	10	6	.184	.220	.276
90	IOW/AMA	AAA	63	259	229	69	9	0	7	99	25	2	3	35	2	0	2	18	7	35	33	.301	.375	.432
	CHI/NL		46	49	48	12	4	0	0	16	1	0	0	6	1	0	0	2	0	10	1	.250	.265	.333
91	PIT/NL		99	210	187	51	11	2	4	78	19	2	2	34	2	1	1	9	2	23	23	.273	.344	.417
4 YR TOTALS			**252**	**425**	**395**	**99**	**22**	**4**	**4**	**141**	**25**	**4**	**2**	**59**	**3**	**1**	**2**	**19**	**2**	**49**	**35**	**.251**	**.297**	**.357**

Vatcher, James Ernest "Jim" — bats right — throws right — b.5/27/66 — 1991 positions: OF 11

YR	TM/LG	CL	G	TPA	AB	H	2B	3B	HR	TB	BB	IBB	HB	SO	GDP	SH	SF	SB	CS	R	RBI	BA	OBA	SA
87	UTI/NYP	A—	67	282	249	67	15	2	3	95	28	0	2	31	5	2	1	10	5	44	21	.269	.346	.382
88	SPA/SAL	A	137	605	496	150	32	2	12	222	89	1	8	73	10	9	3	26	13	90	72	.302	.414	.448
89	CLE/FSL	A+	92	394	349	105	30	5	4	157	41	0	2	49	11	0	2	7	3	27	32	.301	.376	.450
	REA/EAS	AA	48	202	171	56	11	3	4	85	26	1	1	29	8	0	0	4	0	5	4	.327	.411	.497
90	PHI/NL		36	50	46	12	1	0	0	16	4	0	0	6	1	0	0	0	0	3	3	.261	.320	.348
	SCR/INT	AAA	55	216	181	46	12	4	5	81	32	1	0	33	4	1	2	1	4	2	3	.254	.363	.448
	ATL/NL		21	28	27	7	1	1	0	10	1	0	0	15	1	0	0	0	0	7	7	.259	.286	.370
	YEAR		57	78	73	19	2	1	0	26	5	0	0	21	2	0	0	0	0	10	10	.260	.308	.356
91	LV/PCL	AAA	117	456	395	105	28	6	17	196	53	3	3	76	14	3	2	3	0			.266	.355	.496
	SD/NL		17	24	20	4	0	0	0	4	4	0	0	6	0	0	0	1	0			.200	.333	.200
2 YR TOTALS			**74**	**102**	**93**	**23**	**2**	**1**	**1**	**30**	**9**	**0**	**0**	**21**	**1**	**0**	**0**	**1**	**0**	**10**	**9**	**.247**	**.314**	**.323**

Vaughn, Gregory Lamont "Greg" — bats right — throws right — b.7/3/65 — 1991 positions: OF 135, DH 10

YR	TM/LG	CL	G	TPA	AB	H	2B	3B	HR	TB	BB	IBB	HB	SO	GDP	SH	SF	SB	CS	R	RBI	BA	OBA	SA
86	HEL/PIO	R+	66	300	258	75	13	2	16	140	30	1	2	69	1	5	5	23	5	64	54	.291	.363	.543
87	BEL/MID	A	139	608	492	150	31	6	33	292	102	2	5	115	3	8	6	36	9	120	105	.305	.425	.593
88	EP/TEX	AA	131	579	505	152	39	2	28	279	63	3	3	120	11	4	4	22	5	104	105	.301	.379	.552
89	DEN/AMA	AAA	110	452	387	107	17	5	26	212	62	4	0	94	10	2	1	20	3	74	92	.276	.376	.548
	MIL/AL		38	128	113	30	3	0	5	48	13	0	0	23	0	0	2	4	1	18	23	.265	.336	.425
90	MIL/AL		120	429	382	84	26	2	17	165	33	1	1	91	11	3	5	7	2	51	61	.220	.280	.432
91	MIL/AL		145	614	542	132	24	5	27	247	62	2	9	125	6	9	15	13	7	81	98	.244	.319	.456
3 YR TOTALS			**303**	**1171**	**1037**	**246**	**53**	**7**	**49**	**460**	**108**	**3**	**2**	**239**	**17**	**12**	**22**	**24**	**10**	**150**	**182**	**.237**	**.306**	**.444**

Vaughn, Maurice Samuel "Mo" — bats left — throws right — b.12/15/67 — 1991 positions: 1B 49, DH 16

YR	TM/LG	CL	G	TPA	AB	H	2B	3B	HR	TB	BB	IBB	HB	SO	GDP	SH	SF	SB	CS	R	RBI	BA	OBA	SA
89	NB/EAS	AA	73	275	245	68	15	0	8	107	25	3	3	47	7	1	1	1	3	28	38	.278	.350	.437
90	PAW/INT	AAA	108	438	386	114	26	1	22	208	44	2	6	87	10	0	2	3	2	62	72	.295	.374	.539

(continued)

Vaughn, Maurice Samuel "Mo" (continued)

YR	TM/LG	CL	G	TPA	AB	H	2B	3B	HR	TB	BB	IBB	HB	SO	GDP	SH	SF	SB	CS	R	RBI	BA	OBA	SA
91	PAW/INT	AAA	69	301	234	64	10	0	14	116	60	7	3	44	6	0	4	2	1	35	50	.274	.422	.496
	BOS/AL		74	251	219	57	12	0	4	81	26	2	2	43	7	0	4	2	1	21	32	.260	.339	.370

Velarde, Randy Lee — bats right — throws right — b.11/24/62 — 1991 positions: 3B 50, SS 31, OF 2

YR	TM/LG	CL	G	TPA	AB	H	2B	3B	HR	TB	BB	IBB	HB	SO	GDP	SH	SF	SB	CS	R	RBI	BA	OBA	SA
85	NF/NYP	A–	67	254	218	48	7	3	1	64	35	2	1	72	10	0	0	8	3	28	16	.220	.331	.294
86	BUF/AMA	AAA	9	23	20	4	1	0	0	5	2	0	1	4	1	0	0	1	0	2	2	.200	.304	.250
	APP/MID	A	124	487	417	105	31	4	11	177	58	1	7	96	10	1	4	13	6	55	50	.252	.350	.424
87	ALB/EAS	AA	71	294	263	83	20	2	7	128	25	0	3	47	9	2	1	8	6	40	32	.316	.380	.487
	COL/INT	AAA	49	204	185	59	10	6	5	96	14	0	4	36	2	0	1	8	2	21	33	.319	.377	.519
	NY/AL		8	22	22	4	0	0	0	4	0	0	0	6	1	0	0	0	0	1	1	.182	.182	.182
88	COL/INT	AAA	78	321	293	79	23	4	5	125	25	0	1	71	7	0	2	7	5	39	37	.270	.327	.427
	NY/AL		48	125	115	20	6	0	5	41	8	0	2	24	3	0	0	1	1	18	12	.174	.240	.357
89	COL/INT	AAA	103	431	387	103	26	3	11	168	38	0	5	105	8	1	0	3	5	59	53	.266	.340	.434
	NY/AL		33	111	100	34	4	2	2	48	7	0	1	14	0	3	0	0	3	12	11	.340	.389	.480
90	NY/AL		95	253	229	48	6	2	5	73	20	0	1	53	6	2	1	0	3	21	19	.210	.275	.319
91	NY/AL		80	210	184	45	11	1	1	61	18	0	3	43	6	3	0	3	3	19	15	.245	.322	.332
5 YR TOTALS			**264**	**721**	**650**	**151**	**27**	**5**	**13**	**227**	**53**	**0**	**7**	**140**	**16**	**10**	**1**	**4**	**8**	**71**	**58**	**.232**	**.297**	**.349**

Velasquez, Guillermo — bats left — throws right — b.4/23/68 — 1991 positions: 1B System SD/NL

YR	TM/LG	CL	G	TPA	AB	H	2B	3B	HR	TB	BB	IBB	HB	SO	GDP	SH	SF	SB	CS	R	RBI	BA	OBA	SA
87	CHS/SAL	A	102	312	295	65	12	0	3	86	16	0	0	65	13	1	0	2	0	32	30	.220	.260	.292
88	CHS/SAL	A	135	567	520	149	28	3	11	216	34	9	1	110	6	3	9	1	1	55	90	.287	.326	.415
89	RIV/CAL	A+	139	607	544	152	30	2	9	213	51	4	2	91	14	0	10	4	3	73	69	.279	.338	.392
90	WIC/TEX	AA	105	417	377	102	21	2	12	163	35	5	1	66	9	0	4	1	1	48	72	.271	.331	.432
91	WIC/TEX	AA	130	557	501	148	26	3	21	243	48	6	1	75	6	0	7	4	2	72	100	.295	.354	.485

Venable, William McKinley "Max" — bats left — throws right — b.6/6/57 — 1991 positions: OF 65, DH 3

YR	TM/LG	CL	G	TPA	AB	H	2B	3B	HR	TB	BB	IBB	HB	SO	GDP	SH	SF	SB	CS	R	RBI	BA	OBA	SA
79	SF/NL		55	97	85	14	1	1	0	17	10	1	1	18	0	1	0	3	3	12	3	.165	.260	.200
80	SF/NL		64	157	138	37	5	0	0	42	15	0	0	22	3	1	3	8	2	13	10	.268	.333	.304
81	SF/NL		18	36	32	6	0	2	0	10	4	0	0	3	0	0	0	3	1	2	1	.188	.278	.313
82	SF/NL		71	132	125	28	2	1	1	35	7	0	0	16	2	0	0	9	3	17	7	.224	.265	.280
83	SF/NL		94	256	228	50	7	4	6	83	22	1	3	34	2	1	2	15	2	28	27	.219	.295	.364
84	IND/AMA	AAA	99	381	330	82	13	3	9	128	41	4	1	42	6	4	5	22	4	57	47	.248	.329	.388
	MON/NL		38	76	71	17	2	0	2	25	3	1	1	7	0	0	1	1	0	7	7	.239	.276	.352
85	IND/AMA	AAA	14	57	53	19	4	2	1	30	4	1	0	3	1	0	0	2	2	10	9	.358	.404	.566
	DEN/AMA	AAA	32	128	119	23	3	3	0	41	8	1	0	16	2	1	0	8	1	17	10	.193	.244	.345
	CIN/NL		77	146	135	39	12	3	0	57	6	0	2	23	2	3	2	11	3	21	10	.289	.315	.422
86	CIN/NL		108	168	147	31	7	1	2	46	17	2	0	24	0	2	2	7	2	17	15	.211	.289	.313
87	CIN/NL		7	7	7	1	0	0	0	1	0	0	0	0	0	0	0	0	0	2	2	.143	.143	.143
	NAS/AMA	AAA	116	458	400	108	16	4	2	138	39	2	5	56	6	11	3	20	6	57	28	.270	.340	.345
89	EDM/PCL	AAA	95	387	329	89	14	4	1	114	46	2	1	59	1	7	4	13	3	52	45	.271	.358	.347
	CAL/AL		20	57	53	19	4	0	0	23	1	0	0	16	0	3	0	0	1	7	4	.358	.370	.434
90	CAL/AL		93	222	189	49	9	3	4	76	24	2	0	31	3	7	2	5	1	26	21	.259	.340	.402
91	CAL/AL		82	206	187	46	8	2	3	67	11	2	2	30	5	4	2	5	1	24	21	.246	.292	.358
12 YR TOTALS			**727**	**1560**	**1397**	**337**	**57**	**17**	**18**	**482**	**120**	**9**	**7**	**218**	**18**	**23**	**13**	**64**	**18**	**176**	**128**	**.241**	**.302**	**.345**

Ventura, Robin Mark — bats left — throws right — b.7/14/67 — 1991 positions: 3B 151, 1B 31

YR	TM/LG	CL	G	TPA	AB	H	2B	3B	HR	TB	BB	IBB	HB	SO	GDP	SH	SF	SB	CS	R	RBI	BA	OBA	SA
89	BIR/SOU	AA	129	563	454	126	25	2	3	164	93	12	6	51	9	4	6	9	7	75	67	.278	.403	.361
	CHI/AL		16	58	45	8	3	0	0	11	8	0	1	6	1	1	3	0	0	5	7	.178	.298	.244
90	CHI/AL		150	565	493	123	17	1	5	157	55	2	1	53	5	13	3	1	4	48	54	.249	.324	.318
91	CHI/AL		157	705	606	172	25	1	23	268	80	3	4	67	22	8	7	2	4	92	100	.284	.367	.442
3 YR TOTALS			**323**	**1328**	**1144**	**303**	**45**	**2**	**28**	**436**	**143**	**5**	**6**	**126**	**28**	**22**	**13**	**3**	**8**	**145**	**161**	**.265**	**.346**	**.381**

Villanueva, Hector (Balasquide) — bats right — throws right — b.10/2/64 — 1991 positions: C 55, 1B 6

YR	TM/LG	CL	G	TPA	AB	H	2B	3B	HR	TB	BB	IBB	HB	SO	GDP	SH	SF	SB	CS	R	RBI	BA	OBA	SA
85	PEO/MID	A	65	226	193	45	7	0	6	55	27	0	3	16	7	2	1	0	0	22	19	.233	.335	.285
86	WIN/CAR	A+	125	509	412	131	20	2	13	194	81	3	2	42	12	2	12	6	4	58	100	.318	.422	.471
87	PIT/EAS	AA	109	440	391	107	31	0	14	180	43	1	1	38	8	2	3	3	4	59	70	.274	.345	.460
88	PIT/EAS	AA	127	521	436	137	24	3	10	197	71	6	4	58	9	2	8	5	4	59	70	.314	.408	.452
89	IOW/AMA	AAA	120	480	444	112	25	1	12	175	32	2	1	95	6	1	2	1	1	50	75	.252	.303	.394
90	IOW/AMA	AAA	52	198	177	47	7	1	8	80	19	2	1	36	4	1	0	0	1	46	57	.266	.340	.452
	CHI/NL		52	120	114	31	4	0	7	58	4	2	1	30	4	0	0	0	0	20	34	.272	.308	.509
91	IOW/AMA	AAA	6	27	25	9	3	0	2	18	1	0	1	6	0	0	1	0	1	14	18	.360	.370	.720
	CHI/NL		71	214	192	53	10	1	13	104	21	3	0	30	3	0	1	0	0	23	32	.276	.346	.542
2 YR TOTALS			**123**	**334**	**306**	**84**	**14**	**2**	**20**	**162**	**25**	**3**	**2**	**57**	**6**	**0**	**1**	**1**	**0**	**37**	**50**	**.275**	**.332**	**.529**

Vizcaino, Jose Luis (Pimental) — bats both — throws right — b.3/26/68 — 1991 positions: 3B 57, SS 33, 2B 9

YR	TM/LG	CL	G	TPA	AB	H	2B	3B	HR	TB	BB	IBB	HB	SO	GDP	SH	SF	SB	CS	R	RBI	BA	OBA	SA
87	DOD/GCL	R	49	175	150	38	5	1	0	45	22	1	0	24	1	0	1	8	5	26	12	.253	.347	.300
88	BAK/CAL	A+	122	502	433	126	11	4	0	145	50	1	7	54	6	10	2	13	14	77	38	.291	.372	.335
89	ALB/PCL	AAA	129	483	434	123	10	4	1	144	33	2	1	41	10	12	3	16	14	60	44	.283	.333	.332
	LA/NL		7	11	10	2	0	0	0	2	0	0	0	1	0	0	0	0	0	2	0	.200	.200	.200

Vizcaino, Jose Luis (Pimental) (continued)

YR	TM/LG	CL	G	TPA	AB	H	2B	3B	HR	TB	BB	IBB	HB	SO	GDP	SH	SF	SB	CS	R	RBI	BA	OBA	SA
90	ALB/PCL	AAA	81	312	276	77	10	2	2	97	30	3	0	33	6	3	3	13	6	46	38	.279	.346	.351
	LA/NL		37	55	51	14	1	1	0	17	4	1	0	8	1	0	0	1	1	3	2	.275	.327	.333
91	CHI/NL		93	154	145	38	5	0	0	43	5	0	0	18	1	2	2	2	1	7	10	.262	.283	.297
3 YR TOTALS			**137**	**220**	**206**	**54**	**6**	**1**	**0**	**62**	**9**	**1**	**0**	**27**	**2**	**3**	**2**	**3**	**2**	**12**	**12**	**.262**	**.290**	**.301**

Vizquel, Omar Enrique (Gonzalez) — bats both — throws right — b.4/24/67 — 1991 positions: SS 138, 2B 1

YR	TM/LG	CL	G	TPA	AB	H	2B	3B	HR	TB	BB	IBB	HB	SO	GDP	SH	SF	SB	CS	R	RBI	BA	OBA	SA
84	BUT/PIO	R+	15	49	45	14	2	0	0	16	3	0	0	8	0	0	0	1	2	7	4	.311	.347	.356
85	BEL/NWL	A–	50	204	187	42	9	0	5	66	12	1	0	27	0	4	1	4	3	24	17	.225	.270	.353
86	WAU/MID	A	105	425	352	75	13	2	4	104	64	1	2	56	6	2	5	19	6	60	28	.213	.333	.295
87	SAL/CAL	A+	114	474	407	107	12	8	0	135	57	1	0	56	6	4	4	25	19	61	38	.263	.350	.332
88	VER/EAS	AA	103	430	374	95	18	2	2	123	42	1	0	44	6	3	8	30	11	54	35	.254	.328	.329
	CAL/PCL	AAA	33	113	107	24	7	0	1	35	5	1	0	14	1	1	0	2	4	10	12	.224	.259	.327
89	CAL/PCL	AAA	7	32	28	6	2	0	0	8	3	0	1	4	1	0	0	0	2	3	3	.214	.313	.286
	SEA/AL		143	431	387	85	7	3	1	101	28	0	0	40	6	13	2	1	4	45	20	.220	.273	.261
90	SB/CAL	A+	5	25	22	6	0	0	0	6	3	0	0	0	0	0	0	2	4	3	3	.273	.360	.273
	CAL/PCL	AAA	48	176	150	35	6	2	0	45	13	0	3	10	3	9	2	4	1	18	18	.233	.299	.300
	SEA/AL		81	285	255	63	3	2	1	76	18	0	0	22	7	10	2	4	1	19	18	.247	.295	.298
91	SEA/AL		142	482	426	98	16	4	1	125	45	0	1	37	8	8	3	7	2	42	41	.230	.302	.293
3 YR TOTALS			**366**	**1198**	**1068**	**246**	**26**	**9**	**4**	**302**	**91**	**0**	**1**	**99**	**21**	**31**	**7**	**12**	**7**	**106**	**79**	**.230**	**.290**	**.283**

Wakamatsu, Wilbur Donald "Don" — bats right — throws right — b.2/22/63 — 1991 positions: C 18

YR	TM/LG	CL	G	TPA	AB	H	2B	3B	HR	TB	BB	IBB	HB	SO	GDP	SH	SF	SB	CS	R	RBI	BA	OBA	SA
85	BIL/PIO	R+	58	228	196	49	7	0	0	56	25	2	0	36	7	5	2	1	0	20	24	.250	.332	.286
86	TAM/FSL	A+	112	427	361	100	18	2	1	125	53	2	5	66	11	0	8	6	1	41	66	.277	.370	.346
87	CR/MID	A	103	403	365	79	13	1	7	115	30	1	3	71	9	2	3	3	3	33	41	.216	.279	.315
88	CHA/SOU	AA	79	275	235	56	9	1	1	70	37	0	0	41	5	1	2	0	1	22	26	.238	.339	.298
89	BIR/SOU	AA	92	336	287	73	15	0	2	94	32	0	7	54	4	5	5	7	6	45	45	.254	.338	.328
90	VAN/PCL	AAA	62	209	187	49	10	0	0	59	13	1	7	35	2	1	1	2	2	20	13	.262	.332	.316
91	VAN/PCL	AAA	55	191	172	34	8	0	4	54	12	0	1	39	3	4	2	0	0	20	19	.198	.251	.314
	CHI/AL		18	32	31	7	0	0	0	7	1	0	0	6	0	3	0	0	0	2	0	.226	.250	.226

Walker, Cleotha "Chico" — bats both — throws right — b.11/25/57 — 1991 positions: 3B 57, OF 53, 2B 6

YR	TM/LG	CL	G	TPA	AB	H	2B	3B	HR	TB	BB	IBB	HB	SO	GDP	SH	SF	SB	CS	R	RBI	BA	OBA	SA
77	ELM/NYP	A–	64	263	227	50	4	3	1	63	29	3	0	39	2	6	1	10	1	26	14	.220	.307	.278
78	WH/FSL	A+	133	532	480	134	10	6	3	165	43	1	0	71	6	6	4	29	17	66	52	.279	.337	.344
79	BRI/EAS	AA	123	552	498	132	19	12	8	199	44	2	0	77	10	6	4	29	16	75	57	.265	.322	.400
80	PAW/INT	AAA	139	584	536	146	18	7	8	202	41	8	1	91	9	6	0	21	10	59	52	.272	.325	.377
	BOS/AL		19	66	57	12	0	0	1	15	6	1	1	10	1	1	1	3	2	3	5	.211	.292	.263
81	PAW/INT	AAA	138	596	535	148	21	5	17	230	49	8	0	110	13	9	3	24	12	50	68	.277	.336	.430
	BOS/AL		6	18	17	6	0	0	0	6	1	0	0	2	0	0	0	0	2	3	2	.353	.389	.353
82	PAW/INT	AAA	133	560	494	124	22	2	15	195	60	7	0	99	4	0	3	25	9	71	66	.251	.330	.395
83	PAW/INT	AAA	125	517	442	119	18	1	18	193	68	4	1	80	7	3	3	27	14	78	56	.269	.366	.437
	BOS/AL		4	5	5	2	0	2	0	6	0	0	0	0	0	0	0	0	0	2	1	.400	.400	1.200
84	BOS/AL		3	3	2	0	0	0	0	0	0	0	0	1	0	0	0	0	0	0	1	.000	.000	.000
	PAW/INT	AAA	130	587	499	131	26	5	18	221	80	9	0	88	8	4	4	42	17	91	51	.263	.362	.443
85	CHI/NL		21	12	12	1	0	0	0	1	0	0	0	1	0	0	0	0	0	0	0	.083	.083	.083
	IOW/AMA	AAA	89	388	331	94	17	8	5	142	50	1	2	60	9	4	1	42	11	47	46	.284	.380	.429
86	IOW/AMA	AAA	138	599	530	158	30	11	16	258	62	2	0	68	1	1	6	67	22	97	65	.298	.368	.487
	CHI/NL		28	112	101	28	3	2	1	38	10	0	0	20	1	0	2	15	4	21	7	.277	.339	.376
87	IOW/AMA	AAA	90	383	315	77	13	3	8	120	65	3	0	52	6	2	2	23	4	15	7	.244	.371	.381
	CHI/NL		47	121	105	21	4	0	0	25	12	1	0	23	1	2	2	11	4	8	7	.200	.277	.238
88	CAL/AL		33	86	78	12	1	0	0	13	6	0	0	15	2	1	0	4	0	15	7	.154	.214	.167
	EDM/PCL	AAA	79	337	304	88	17	4	7	134	29	2	0	47	9	4	0	25	4	58	39	.289	.347	.441
89	SYR/INT	AAA	123	495	431	103	11	5	12	160	58	8	1	61	7	1	6	37	10	61	63	.239	.328	.371
90	CHA/SOU	AA	88	359	310	82	16	1	12	136	44	1	0	70	1	1	4	9	3	30	19	.265	.351	.439
	IOW/AMA	AAA	32	141	114	41	7	1	6	68	25	5	1	17	1	1	0	9	3	51	34	.360	.479	.596
91	CHI/NL		124	411	374	96	10	1	6	126	33	2	0	57	10	3	5	13	5	54	29	.257	.315	.337
9 YR TOTALS			**285**	**834**	**751**	**178**	**18**	**5**	**8**	**230**	**68**	**4**	**1**	**133**	**10**	**6**	**8**	**45**	**18**	**106**	**59**	**.237**	**.298**	**.306**

Walker, Larry Kenneth Robert — bats left — throws right — b.12/1/66 — 1991 positions: OF 102, 1B 39

YR	TM/LG	CL	G	TPA	AB	H	2B	3B	HR	TB	BB	IBB	HB	SO	GDP	SH	SF	SB	CS	R	RBI	BA	OBA	SA
85	UTI/NYP	A–	62	241	215	48	8	2	2	66	18	4	5	57	1	0	2	12	1	24	26	.223	.297	.307
86	BUR/MID	A	95	390	332	96	12	6	29	207	46	1	9	112	4	0	3	16	8	67	74	.289	.387	.623
	WPB/FSL	A+	38	142	113	32	7	5	2	61	26	2	2	32	2	0	1	2	2	20	16	.283	.423	.540
87	JAC/SOU	AA	128	553	474	136	25	7	26	253	50	8	9	87	8	5	7	36	6	68	59	.287	.361	.534
89	IND/AMA	AAA	114	456	385	104	18	2	12	162	50	8	9	87	6	0	5	24	3	68	59	.270	.361	.421
	MON/NL		20	56	47	8	0	0	0	8	5	0	1	13	3	0	3	1	1	4	4	.170	.264	.170
90	MON/NL		133	478	419	101	18	3	19	182	49	5	5	112	8	0	3	21	7	59	51	.241	.326	.434
91	MON/NL		137	539	487	141	30	2	16	223	42	3	5	102	4	0	3	14	9	59	64	.290	.349	.458
3 YR TOTALS			**290**	**1073**	**953**	**250**	**48**	**5**	**35**	**413**	**96**	**8**	**11**	**227**	**15**	**0**	**6**	**36**	**17**	**122**	**119**	**.262**	**.335**	**.433**

Wallach, Timothy Charles "Tim" — bats right — throws right — b.9/14/57 — 1991 positions: 3B 149

YR	TM/LG	CL	G	TPA	AB	H	2B	3B	HR	TB	BB	IBB	HB	SO	GDP	SH	SF	SB	CS	R	RBI	BA	OBA	SA
80	MON/NL		5	12	11	2	0	0	1	5	1	0	0	5	0	0	0	0	0	1	2	.182	.250	.455

(continued)

Wallach, Timothy Charles "Tim" (continued)

YR	TM/LG	CL	G	TPA	AB	H	2B	3B	HR	TB	BB	IBB	HB	SO	GDP	SH	SF	SB	CS	R	RBI	BA	OBA	SA
81	MON/NL		71	231	212	50	9	1	4	73	15	2	4	37	3	0	0	0	1	19	13	.236	.299	.344
82	MON/NL		158	645	596	160	31	3	28	281	36	4	4	81	15	5	4	6	4	89	97	.268	.313	.471
83	MON/NL		156	647	581	156	33	3	19	252	55	8	6	97	9	0	5	0	3	54	70	.269	.335	.434
84	MON/NL		160	643	582	143	25	4	18	230	50	6	7	101	12	0	4	3	7	55	72	.246	.311	.395
85	MON/NL		155	617	569	148	36	3	22	256	38	8	5	79	17	0	5	9	9	70	81	.260	.310	.450
86	MON/NL		134	539	480	112	22	1	18	190	44	8	10	72	16	0	5	8	4	50	71	.233	.308	.396
87	MON/NL		153	644	593	177	42	4	26	305	37	5	7	98	6	0	7	9	5	89	123	.298	.343	.514
88	MON/NL		159	640	592	152	32	5	12	230	38	7	3	88	19	0	7	2	6	52	69	.257	.302	.389
89	MON/NL		154	639	573	159	42	0	13	240	58	10	1	81	21	0	7	3	6	76	77	.277	.341	.419
90	MON/NL		161	678	626	185	37	5	21	295	42	11	3	80	12	0	7	6	9	69	98	.296	.339	.471
91	MON/NL		151	637	577	130	22	1	13	193	50	8	6	100	12	0	4	2	4	60	73	.225	.292	.334
12 YR TOTALS			**1617**	**6572**	**5992**	**1574**	**331**	**30**	**195**	**2550**	**464**	**77**	**56**	**919**	**142**	**5**	**55**	**48**	**59**	**684**	**846**	**.263**	**.319**	**.426**

Walling, Dennis Martin "Denny" — bats left — throws right — b.4/17/54 — 1991 positions: 3B 14, OF 5

YR	TM/LG	CL	G	TPA	AB	H	2B	3B	HR	TB	BB	IBB	HB	SO	GDP	SH	SF	SB	CS	R	RBI	BA	OBA	SA
75	OAK/AL		6	8	8	1	1	0	0	2	0	0	0	4	0	0	0	0	0	0	2	.125	.125	.250
76	OAK/AL		3	11	11	3	0	0	0	3	0	0	0	3	0	0	0	0	0	1	0	.273	.273	.273
77	HOU/NL		6	23	21	6	0	1	0	8	2	0	0	4	0	0	0	1	1	1	6	.286	.348	.381
78	HOU/NL		120	280	247	62	11	3	3	88	30	3	1	24	0	0	2	9	2	30	36	.251	.332	.356
79	HOU/NL		82	165	147	48	8	4	3	73	17	2	0	21	2	0	1	3	2	21	31	.327	.394	.497
80	HOU/NL		100	321	284	85	6	5	1	110	35	4	0	26	2	0	2	4	3	30	29	.299	.374	.387
81	HOU/NL		65	189	158	37	6	0	1	58	28	1	0	17	3	1	2	2	1	23	23	.234	.346	.367
82	HOU/NL		85	170	146	30	4	1	1	39	23	3	0	19	6	0	1	4	2	22	14	.205	.312	.267
83	HOU/NL		100	152	135	40	5	3	3	60	15	1	0	16	1	1	1	2	1	24	19	.296	.364	.444
84	HOU/NL		87	268	249	70	11	5	3	100	16	2	1	28	6	0	2	7	1	37	31	.281	.325	.402
85	HOU/NL		119	374	345	93	20	1	7	136	25	2	0	26	8	0	4	5	2	44	45	.270	.316	.394
86	HOU/NL		130	422	382	119	23	1	13	183	36	8	0	31	8	0	4	1	1	54	58	.312	.367	.479
87	HOU/NL		110	370	325	92	21	4	5	136	39	9	2	37	9	2	4	5	1	45	33	.283	.356	.418
88	TUC/PCL	AAA	5	20	16	3	1	0	0	4	4	0	0	4	0	0	0	0	0	2	4	.188	.350	.250
	HOU/NL		65	192	176	43	10	2	1	60	15	3	0	18	2	1	0	1	0	19	20	.244	.304	.341
	STL/NL		19	60	58	13	3	0	0	16	2	0	0	7	1	0	0	0	1	3	1	.224	.250	.276
	YEAR		84	252	234	56	13	2	1	76	17	3	0	25	3	1	0	1	1	22	21	.239	.291	.325
89	STL/NL		69	93	79	24	7	0	1	34	14	2	0	12	1	0	0	0	0	9	11	.304	.409	.430
90	STL/NL		78	137	127	28	5	0	1	36	8	0	0	15	5	1	1	0	0	7	19	.220	.265	.283
91	OC/AMA	AAA	3	12	10	5	1	0	0	6	1	0	0	2	1	0	1	0	0	3	1	.500	.500	.600
	TEX/AL		24	49	44	4	1	0	0	5	3	0	2	8	3	0	0	0	0	1	2	.091	.184	.114
17 YR TOTALS			**1268**	**3284**	**2942**	**798**	**142**	**30**	**49**	**1147**	**308**	**29**	**4**	**316**	**57**	**6**	**24**	**44**	**18**	**371**	**380**	**.271**	**.339**	**.390**

Walton, Jerome O'Terrell — bats right — throws right — b.7/8/65 — 1991 positions: OF 101

YR	TM/LG	CL	G	TPA	AB	H	2B	3B	HR	TB	BB	IBB	HB	SO	GDP	SH	SF	SB	CS	R	RBI	BA	OBA	SA
86	WYT/APP	R+	62	269	229	66	7	4	5	96	28	0	6	40	3	3	3	21	3	48	34	.288	.376	.419
87	PEO/MID	A	128	580	472	158	24	11	6	222	91	2	11	91	9	5	1	49	25	102	38	.335	.452	.470
88	PIT/EAS	AA	120	470	414	137	26	2	3	176	41	1	8	69	6	4	3	42	13	64	49	.331	.399	.425
89	IOW/AMA	AAA	4	19	18	6	1	0	1	10	1	0	0	5	0	0	0	2	1	4	3	.333	.368	.556
	CHI/NL		116	515	475	139	23	3	5	183	27	1	6	77	6	2	5	24	7	64	46	.293	.335	.385
90	IOW/AMA	AAA	4	18	16	3	0	0	1	6	2	0	0	4	0	0	0	0	0	3	1	.188	.278	.375
	CHI/NL		101	449	392	103	16	2	2	129	50	1	4	70	4	1	2	14	7	63	21	.263	.350	.329
91	CHI/NL		123	298	270	59	13	1	5	89	19	0	3	55	7	3	3	7	3	42	17	.219	.275	.330
3 YR TOTALS			**340**	**1262**	**1137**	**301**	**52**	**6**	**12**	**401**	**96**	**2**	**13**	**202**	**17**	**6**	**10**	**45**	**17**	**169**	**84**	**.265**	**.326**	**.353**

Ward, Kevin Michael — bats right — throws right — b.9/28/61 — 1991 positions: OF 33

YR	TM/LG	CL	G	TPA	AB	H	2B	3B	HR	TB	BB	IBB	HB	SO	GDP	SH	SF	SB	CS	R	RBI	BA	OBA	SA
83	BEN/NWL	A−	55	234	199	61	12	2	2	83	31	2	4	35	2	0	0	18	8	33	29	.307	.410	.417
84	PEN/CAR	A+	130	526	456	119	18	5	13	186	53	3	6	90	11	4	7	21	3	84	69	.261	.341	.408
85	REA/EAS	AA	42	162	132	40	9	6	1	64	23	1	5	19	2	0	2	7	5	23	21	.303	.420	.485
86	REA/EAS	AA	119	478	398	109	27	6	7	169	66	1	6	66	9	1	7	28	14	79	59	.274	.379	.425
87	REA/EAS	AA	16	64	56	14	5	1	0	21	6	0	1	12	0	0	1	5	2	9	6	.250	.328	.375
	MAI/INT	AAA	106	364	326	68	13	3	13	126	30	0	1	68	9	1	2	14	8	48	37	.209	.284	.387
88	MAI/INT	AAA	134	537	456	105	22	8	11	176	62	1	7	118	9	9	3	17	11	60	63	.230	.330	.386
89	HUN/SOU	AA	27	117	84	26	4	4	3	47	29	0	1	18	1	0	3	15	0	20	18	.310	.479	.560
90	TAC/PCL	AAA	123	487	421	125	30	14	10	213	44	1	14	72	8	4	4	24	10	83	60	.297	.379	.506
91	LV/PCL	AAA	83	347	276	89	17	6	6	136	58	2	7	53	6	1	5	10	4	51	43	.322	.445	.493
	SD/NL		44	118	107	26	7	2	2	43	9	0	1	27	1	0	1	0	4	13	8	.243	.308	.402

Ward, Turner Max — bats both — throws right — b.4/11/65 — 1991 positions: OF 44

YR	TM/LG	CL	G	TPA	AB	H	2B	3B	HR	TB	BB	IBB	HB	SO	GDP	SH	SF	SB	CS	R	RBI	BA	OBA	SA
86	ONE/NYP	A−	63	259	221	62	4	1	1	71	31	1	2	39	4	2	3	6	6	42	19	.281	.370	.321
87	FL/FSL	A+	130	573	493	145	15	2	7	185	64	4	6	83	8	7	3	25	3	83	55	.294	.380	.375
88	COL/INT	AAA	134	551	490	123	24	1	7	170	48	5	3	100	7	8	2	28	5	55	50	.251	.320	.347
89	IND/GCL	R	4	17	15	3	0	0	0	3	2	0	0	1	0	0	0	1	0	2	1	.200	.294	.200
	CAN/EAS	AA	30	108	93	28	5	1	0	35	15	0	0	16	2	0	0	1	0	19	3	.301	.398	.376
90	CS/PCL	AAA	133	585	495	148	24	9	6	208	72	1	4	70	16	0	14	22	15	89	65	.299	.386	.420
	CLE/AL		14	49	46	16	2	1	1	23	3	0	0	8	1	0	0	3	0	10	10	.348	.388	.500

Ward, Turner Max (continued)

YR	TM/LG	CL	G	TPA	AB	H	2B	3B	HR	TB	BB	IBB	HB	SO	GDP	SH	SF	SB	CS	R	RBI	BA	OBA	SA
91	CLE/AL		40	114	100	23	7	0	0	30	10	0	0	16	1	4	0	0	0	11	5	.230	.300	.300
	CS/PCL	AAA	14	58	51	10	1	1	1	16	6	0	0	9	1	1	0	2	1	5	3	.196	.281	.314
	SYR/INT	AAA	59	266	218	72	11	3	7	110	47	1	0	22	5	1	0	9	6	40	32	.330	.449	.505
	TOR/AL		8	14	13	4	0	0	0	4	1	0	0	2	1	0	0	0	0	1	2	.308	.357	.308
	YEAR		48	128	113	27	7	0	0	34	11	0	0	18	2	4	0	0	0	12	7	.239	.306	.301
2 YR TOTALS			**62**	**177**	**159**	**43**	**9**	**1**	**1**	**57**	**14**	**0**	**0**	**26**	**3**	**4**	**0**	**3**	**0**	**22**	**17**	**.270**	**.329**	**.358**

Webster, Leonard Irell "Lenny" — bats right — throws right — b.2/10/65 — 1991 positions: C 17

YR	TM/LG	CL	G	TPA	AB	H	2B	3B	HR	TB	BB	IBB	HB	SO	GDP	SH	SF	SB	CS	R	RBI	BA	OBA	SA
86	KEN/MID	A	22	76	65	10	2	0	0	12	10	0	0	12	3	1	0	0	0	2	8	.154	.267	.185
	ELI/APP	R+	48	176	152	35	4	0	3	48	22	0	0	21	6	0	0	1	0	29	14	.230	.335	.316
87	KEN/MID	A	52	160	140	35	7	0	3	51	17	0	0	20	8	0	3	2	0	17	17	.250	.325	.364
88	KEN/MID	A	129	546	465	134	23	2	11	194	71	5	1	47	13	2	7	3	2	82	87	.288	.379	.417
89	VIS/CAL	A+	63	264	231	62	7	0	5	84	27	1	1	27	9	0	5	2	1	36	39	.268	.341	.364
	ORL/SOU	AA	59	242	191	45	7	0	2	58	44	1	3	20	3	2	2	2	0	29	17	.236	.383	.304
	MIN/AL		14	23	20	6	2	0	0	8	3	0	0	2	0	0	0	0	0	3	1	.300	.391	.400
90	ORL/SOU	AA	126	526	455	119	31	0	8	174	68	0	0	57	11	0	3	0	0	69	71	.262	.356	.382
	MIN/AL		2	7	6	2	1	0	0	3	1	0	0	1	0	0	0	0	0	1	0	.333	.429	.500
91	POR/PCL	AAA	87	353	325	82	18	0	7	121	24	2	1	32	14	0	3	1	4	43	34	.252	.303	.372
	MIN/AL		18	41	34	10	1	0	3	20	6	0	0	10	2	0	1	0	0	7	8	.294	.390	.588
3 YR TOTALS			**34**	**71**	**60**	**18**	**4**	**0**	**3**	**31**	**10**	**0**	**0**	**13**	**2**	**0**	**1**	**0**	**0**	**11**	**9**	**.300**	**.394**	**.517**

Webster, Mitchell Dean "Mitch" — bats both — throws left — b.5/16/59 — 1991 positions: OF 75, 1B 1

YR	TM/LG	CL	G	TPA	AB	H	2B	3B	HR	TB	BB	IBB	HB	SO	GDP	SH	SF	SB	CS	R	RBI	BA	OBA	SA
83	TOR/AL		11	12	11	2	0	0	0	2	1	0	0	1	0	0	0	0	0	2	0	.182	.250	.182
84	SYR/INT	AAA	95	420	360	108	22	5	3	149	51	4	0	36	4	9	0	16	4	60	25	.300	.387	.414
	TOR/AL		26	23	22	5	2	1	0	9	1	0	0	7	1	0	0	0	0	9	4	.227	.261	.409
85	TOR/AL		4	1	1	0	0	0	0	0	0	0	0	0	0	0	0	0	0	0	0	.000	.000	.000
	SYR/INT	AAA	47	215	189	52	5	3	3	72	20	1	0	24	3	1	1	5	4	32	23	.275	.346	.381
	MON/NL		74	234	212	58	8	2	11	103	20	3	0	33	3	1	1	15	9	32	30	.274	.335	.486
	YEAR		78	235	213	58	8	2	11	103	20	3	0	33	3	1	1	15	10	32	30	.272	.333	.484
86	MON/NL		151	645	576	167	31	13	8	248	57	4	4	78	9	3	5	36	15	89	49	.290	.355	.431
87	MON/NL		156	676	588	165	30	8	15	256	70	5	8	95	6	8	4	33	10	101	63	.281	.361	.435
88	CHI/NL		70	289	264	70	11	6	4	105	19	1	2	50	3	1	2	10	4	36	26	.265	.319	.398
	MON/NL		81	306	259	66	5	2	2	81	36	2	2	37	3	1	2	12	10	33	13	.255	.354	.313
	YEAR		151	595	523	136	16	8	6	186	55	3	4	87	6	5	4	22	14	69	39	.260	.337	.356
89	CHI/NL		98	308	272	70	12	4	3	99	30	5	1	55	3	3	2	14	2	40	19	.257	.331	.364
90	CLE/AL		128	477	437	110	20	6	12	178	20	1	3	61	6	11	6	22	6	58	55	.252	.285	.407
91	CLE/AL		13	36	32	4	0	0	0	4	3	0	0	9	1	0	1	2	2	2	0	.125	.200	.125
	PIT/NL		36	106	97	17	3	4	1	31	9	1	0	31	3	0	0	0	1	9	9	.175	.245	.320
	LA/NL		58	84	74	21	5	1	1	31	9	0	0	21	0	1	0	0	1	12	10	.284	.361	.419
	YEAR		107	226	203	42	8	5	2	66	21	1	0	61	3	2	0	2	3	23	19	.207	.281	.325
9 YR TOTALS			**906**	**3197**	**2845**	**755**	**127**	**47**	**57**	**1147**	**275**	**21**	**22**	**478**	**35**	**33**	**22**	**144**	**60**	**423**	**278**	**.265**	**.332**	**.403**

Wedge, Eric Michael — bats right — throws right — b.1/27/68 — 1991 positions: DH 1

YR	TM/LG	CL	G	TPA	AB	H	2B	3B	HR	TB	BB	IBB	HB	SO	GDP	SH	SF	SB	CS	R	RBI	BA	OBA	SA
89	ELM/NYP	A–	41	160	145	34	6	2	7	65	15	0	0	21	3	0	0	1	1	20	22	.234	.306	.448
	NB/EAS	AA	14	47	40	8	2	0	0	10	5	0	0	10	1	2	0	0	0	3	2	.200	.289	.250
90	NB/EAS	AA	103	396	339	77	13	1	5	107	51	2	1	54	14	0	5	1	3	36	48	.227	.326	.316
91	NB/EAS	AA	2	9	8	2	0	0	0	2	0	0	0	2	0	0	1	0	0	2	2	.250	.222	.250
	WH/FSL	A+	8	25	21	5	0	0	1	8	3	0	1	7	1	1	0	1	0	2	1	.238	.333	.381
	PAW/INT	AAA	53	196	163	38	14	1	5	69	25	0	5	26	3	2	5	1	2	24	18	.233	.330	.423
	BOS/AL		1	1	1	1	0	0	0	1	0	0	0	0	0	0	0	0	0	0	0	1.000	1.000	1.000

Wehner, John Paul — bats right — throws right — b.6/29/67 — 1991 positions: 3B 36

YR	TM/LG	CL	G	TPA	AB	H	2B	3B	HR	TB	BB	IBB	HB	SO	GDP	SH	SF	SB	CS	R	RBI	BA	OBA	SA
88	WAT/NYP	A–	70	293	265	73	6	0	3	88	21	0	2	39	4	1	4	18	6	41	31	.275	.329	.332
89	SAL/CAR	A+	137	559	515	155	32	6	14	241	42	4	1	81	14	0	1	21	10	69	73	.301	.354	.468
90	HAR/EAS	AA	138	565	511	147	27	1	4	188	40	4	4	51	12	4	6	24	11	72	62	.288	.340	.368
91	CAR/SOU	AA	61	268	234	62	5	1	3	78	24	1	2	32	7	3	5	17	5	30	21	.265	.332	.333
	BUF/AMA	AAA	31	128	112	34	9	2	1	50	14	1	0	12	5	0	2	6	4	18	15	.304	.375	.446
	PIT/NL		37	113	106	36	7	0	0	43	7	0	0	17	0	0	0	3	0	15	7	.340	.381	.406

Weiss, Walter William "Walt" — bats both — throws right — b.11/28/63 — 1991 positions: SS 40

YR	TM/LG	CL	G	TPA	AB	H	2B	3B	HR	TB	BB	IBB	HB	SO	GDP	SH	SF	SB	CS	R	RBI	BA	OBA	SA
85	POC/PIO	R+	40	175	158	49	9	3	0	64	12	0	1	18	5	0	4	6	0	19	21	.310	.354	.405
	MOD/CAL	A+	30	135	122	24	4	1	0	30	12	0	0	20	4	1	0	3	3	17	7	.197	.269	.246
86	MAD/MID	A	84	362	322	97	15	5	2	128	33	1	1	66	6	0	6	12	5	50	54	.301	.362	.398
	HUN/SOU	AA	46	175	160	40	2	1	0	44	11	0	2	39	4	1	1	5	1	19	13	.250	.305	.275
87	HUN/SOU	AA	91	394	337	96	16	2	1	119	47	2	2	67	5	6	2	23	3	35	17	.263	.364	.318
	TAC/PCL	AAA	46	211	179	47	4	3	0	57	28	0	1	31	5	1	2	1	1	3	1	.462	.500	.615
	OAK/AL		16	29	26	12	17	3	3	145	35	1	9	56	9	8	7	4	4	44	39	.250	.312	.321
88	OAK/AL		147	511	452	113																			

(continued)

Weiss, Walter William "Walt"(continued)

YR	TM/LG	CL	G	TPA	AB	H	2B	3B	HR	TB	BB	IBB	HB	SO	GDP	SH	SF	SB	CS	R	RBI	BA	OBA	SA
89	TAC/PCL	AAA	2	9	9	1	1	0	0	2	0	0	0	0	0	0	0	0	0	1	1	.111	.111	.222
	MOD/CAL	A+	5	14	8	3	0	0	0	3	4	0	1	1	1	0	1	0	0	1	1	.375	.571	.375
	OAK/AL		84	263	236	55	11	0	3	75	21	0	1	39	5	0	0	6	1	30	21	.233	.298	.318
90	OAK/AL		138	505	445	118	17	1	2	143	46	5	4	53	7	6	4	9	3	50	35	.265	.337	.321
91	OAK/AL		40	148	133	30	6	1	0	38	12	0	0	14	3	1	2	6	0	15	13	.226	.286	.286
5 YR TOTALS			**425**	**1456**	**1292**	**328**	**55**	**5**	**8**	**417**	**116**	**6**	**14**	**164**	**24**	**21**	**13**	**26**	**10**	**142**	**109**	**.254**	**.319**	**.323**

Whitaker, Louis Rodman "Lou" — bats left — throws right — b.5/12/57 — 1991 positions: 2B 135, DH 3

YR	TM/LG	CL	G	TPA	AB	H	2B	3B	HR	TB	BB	IBB	HB	SO	GDP	SH	SF	SB	CS	R	RBI	BA	OBA	SA
77	DET/AL		11	37	32	8	1	0	0	9	4	0	0	6	1	0	1	2	2	5	2	.250	.333	.281
78	DET/AL		139	567	484	138	12	7	3	173	61	0	1	65	9	13	8	7	7	71	58	.285	.361	.357
79	DET/AL		127	520	423	121	14	8	3	160	78	2	1	66	10	14	4	20	10	75	42	.286	.395	.378
80	DET/AL		145	568	477	111	19	1	1	135	73	0	0	79	9	12	6	8	4	68	45	.233	.331	.283
81	DET/AL		109	382	335	88	14	4	5	125	40	3	1	42	5	3	3	5	3	48	36	.263	.340	.373
82	DET/AL		152	619	560	160	22	8	15	243	48	4	1	58	8	6	4	11	3	76	65	.286	.341	.434
83	DET/AL		161	720	643	206	40	6	12	294	67	4	0	70	9	2	8	17	10	94	72	.320	.380	.457
84	DET/AL		143	629	558	161	25	1	13	227	62	0	0	63	9	4	5	6	5	90	56	.289	.357	.407
85	DET/AL		152	701	609	170	29	8	21	278	80	9	1	56	3	5	5	6	4	102	73	.279	.362	.456
86	DET/AL		144	651	584	157	26	6	20	255	63	5	0	70	20	0	4	13	5	95	73	.269	.338	.437
87	DET/AL		149	684	604	160	38	6	16	258	71	2	1	108	5	4	4	13	5	110	59	.265	.341	.427
88	DET/AL		115	477	403	111	18	2	12	169	66	5	0	61	8	6	2	2	0	54	55	.275	.376	.419
89	DET/AL		148	611	509	128	21	1	28	235	89	6	3	59	7	1	9	6	3	77	85	.251	.361	.462
90	DET/AL		132	552	472	112	22	2	18	192	74	7	0	71	10	1	5	8	2	75	60	.237	.338	.407
91	DET/AL		138	572	470	131	26	2	23	230	90	6	2	45	3	2	8	4	2	94	78	.279	.391	.489
15 YR TOTALS			**1965**	**8290**	**7163**	**1962**	**327**	**62**	**190**	**2983**	**966**	**62**	**12**	**919**	**115**	**74**	**75**	**128**	**68**	**1134**	**859**	**.274**	**.358**	**.416**

White, Devon Markes — bats both — throws right — b.12/29/62 — 1991 positions: OF 156

YR	TM/LG	CL	G	TPA	AB	H	2B	3B	HR	TB	BB	IBB	HB	SO	GDP	SH	SF	SB	CS	R	RBI	BA	OBA	SA
84	RED/CAL	A+	138	609	520	147	25	5	7	203	56	1	11	118	8	17	5	36	12	101	55	.283	.361	.390
85	MID/TEX	AA	70	310	260	77	10	4	4	107	35	2	6	46	2	3	6	38	8	52	35	.296	.384	.412
	EDM/PCL	AAA	66	309	277	70	16	5	4	108	24	0	4	77	5	1	3	21	9	53	39	.253	.318	.390
	CAL/AL		21	9	7	1	0	0	0	1	1	0	1	3	0	0	0	3	1	7	0	.143	.333	.143
86	EDM/PCL	AAA	112	497	461	134	25	10	14	221	31	8	3	90	2	1	1	42	12	84	60	.291	.339	.479
	CAL/AL		29	57	51	12	1	1	1	18	6	0	0	8	0	0	0	6	0	8	3	.235	.316	.353
87	CAL/AL		159	696	639	168	33	5	24	283	39	2	2	135	8	14	2	32	11	103	87	.263	.306	.443
88	CAL/AL		122	486	455	118	22	2	11	177	23	1	2	84	5	5	1	17	8	76	51	.259	.297	.389
89	CAL/AL		156	678	636	156	18	13	12	236	31	3	2	129	12	7	2	44	16	86	56	.245	.282	.371
90	EDM/PCL	AAA	14	62	55	20	4	4	0	32	7	2	0	12	1	0	0	4	2	9	6	.364	.435	.582
	CAL/AL		125	503	443	96	17	3	11	152	44	5	3	116	6	10	3	21	6	57	44	.217	.290	.343
91	TOR/AL		156	715	642	181	40	10	17	292	55	1	7	135	7	5	6	33	10	110	60	.282	.342	.455
7 YR TOTALS			**768**	**3144**	**2873**	**732**	**131**	**34**	**76**	**1159**	**199**	**12**	**17**	**610**	**38**	**41**	**14**	**156**	**52**	**447**	**301**	**.255**	**.306**	**.403**

Whiten, Mark Anthony — bats both — throws right — b.11/25/66 — 1991 positions: OF 109, DH 3

YR	TM/LG	CL	G	TPA	AB	H	2B	3B	HR	TB	BB	IBB	HB	SO	GDP	SH	SF	SB	CS	R	RBI	BA	OBA	SA
86	MH/PIO	R+	70	308	270	81	16	3	10	133	29	2	6	56	2	1	2	22	3	53	44	.300	.378	.493
87	MB/SAL	A	139	587	494	125	22	5	15	202	76	10	16	149	1	0	1	49	14	90	64	.253	.370	.409
88	DUN/FSL	A+	99	434	385	97	8	5	7	136	41	6	3	69	8	2	3	17	14	61	37	.252	.326	.353
	KNO/SOU	AA	28	121	108	28	3	1	2	39	12	1	1	20	5	0	0	6	0	20	9	.259	.339	.361
89	KNO/SOU	AA	129	496	423	109	13	6	12	170	60	1	11	114	7	0	2	11	10	75	47	.258	.363	.402
90	SYR/INT	AAA	104	434	390	113	19	4	14	182	37	5	3	72	8	0	4	14	5	65	48	.290	.353	.467
	TOR/AL		33	96	88	24	1	1	2	33	7	0	0	14	2	0	1	2	0	12	7	.273	.323	.375
91	TOR/AL		46	164	149	33	4	3	2	49	11	1	1	35	5	0	3	0	1	12	19	.221	.274	.329
	CLE/AL		70	281	258	66	14	4	7	109	19	1	2	50	8	0	2	4	2	34	26	.256	.310	.422
	YEAR		116	445	407	99	18	7	9	158	30	2	3	85	13	0	6	6	3	46	45	.243	.297	.388
2 YR TOTALS			**149**	**541**	**495**	**123**	**19**	**8**	**11**	**191**	**37**	**2**	**3**	**99**	**15**	**0**	**6**	**6**	**3**	**58**	**52**	**.248**	**.301**	**.386**

Whitt, Leo Ernest "Ernie" — bats left — throws right — b.6/13/52 — 1991 positions: C 20, DH 2

YR	TM/LG	CL	G	TPA	AB	H	2B	3B	HR	TB	BB	IBB	HB	SO	GDP	SH	SF	SB	CS	R	RBI	BA	OBA	SA
76	BOS/AL		8	20	18	4	2	0	1	9	2	0	0	2	0	0	0	0	0	4	3	.222	.300	.500
77	TOR/AL		23	45	41	7	3	0	0	10	2	0	0	12	1	0	0	2	0	4	6	.171	.200	.244
78	TOR/AL		2	5	4	0	0	0	0	0	0	0	0	1	0	0	0	0	0	0	0	.000	.200	.000
80	TOR/AL		106	325	295	70	12	2	6	104	22	0	0	30	11	5	3	1	3	23	34	.237	.287	.353
81	TOR/AL		74	222	195	46	9	0	1	58	20	3	0	30	2	7	0	1	3	16	16	.236	.307	.297
82	TOR/AL		105	316	284	74	14	2	11	125	26	5	0	34	5	1	5	3	1	28	42	.261	.317	.440
83	TOR/AL		123	400	344	88	15	2	17	158	50	5	0	55	5	1	1	1	1	53	56	.256	.346	.459
84	TOR/AL		124	364	315	75	12	1	15	134	43	7	1	49	2	4	1	1	1	35	46	.238	.327	.425
85	TOR/AL		139	465	412	101	21	1	19	183	47	7	1	59	7	3	2	3	6	55	64	.245	.323	.444
86	TOR/AL		131	433	395	106	19	2	16	177	35	3	0	39	11	2	1	3	3	48	56	.268	.323	.448
87	TOR/AL		135	494	446	120	24	1	19	203	44	4	1	50	17	0	3	0	1	57	75	.269	.334	.455
88	TOR/AL		127	468	398	100	11	2	16	163	61	4	1	38	9	6	4	2	2	63	70	.251	.348	.410
89	TOR/AL		129	440	385	101	24	1	11	160	52	2	0	53	9	1	2	5	4	42	53	.262	.349	.416
90	GRE/SOU	AA	4	14	12	4	1	0	0	5	2	0	0	2	0	0	0	0	0	1	0	.333	.429	.417
	ATL/NL		67	204	180	31	8	0	2	45	23	2	0	27	6	1	3	0	0	14	10	.172	.265	.250
91	BAL/AL		35	70	62	15	2	0	0	17	8	0	0	12	3	0	0	0	0	5	3	.242	.329	.274
15 YR TOTALS			**1328**	**4271**	**3774**	**938**	**176**	**15**	**134**	**1546**	**436**	**44**	**4**	**491**	**97**	**20**	**37**	**22**	**26**	**447**	**534**	**.249**	**.324**	**.410**

Wilkerson, Curtis Vernon — bats both — throws right — b.4/26/61 — 1991 positions: 2B 30, SS 15, 3B 14

YR	TM/LG	CL	G	TPA	AB	H	2B	3B	HR	TB	BB	IBB	HB	SO	GDP	SH	SF	SB	CS	R	RBI	BA	OBA	SA
83	TEX/AL		16	37	35	6	0	1	0	8	2	0	0	5	0	0	0	3	0	7	1	.171	.216	.229
84	TEX/AL		153	522	484	120	12	0	1	135	22	0	2	72	7	12	2	12	10	47	26	.248	.282	.279
85	TEX/AL		129	395	360	88	11	6	0	111	22	0	4	63	7	6	3	14	7	35	22	.244	.293	.308
86	TEX/AL		110	249	236	56	10	3	0	72	11	0	1	42	2	0	1	9	7	27	15	.237	.273	.305
87	TEX/AL		85	146	138	37	5	3	2	54	6	0	2	16	1	0	0	6	3	28	14	.268	.308	.391
88	TEX/AL		117	371	338	99	12	5	0	121	26	3	2	43	7	3	2	9	4	41	28	.293	.345	.358
89	CHI/NL		77	170	160	39	4	2	1	50	8	0	0	33	3	1	1	4	2	18	10	.244	.278	.313
90	CHI/NL		77	196	186	41	5	1	0	48	7	2	0	36	4	3	0	2	2	21	16	.220	.249	.258
91	PIT/NL		85	210	191	36	9	1	2	53	15	0	0	40	2	0	4	2	1	20	18	.188	.243	.277
9 YR TOTALS			**849**	**2296**	**2128**	**522**	**68**	**22**	**6**	**652**	**119**	**5**	**11**	**350**	**34**	**25**	**13**	**61**	**36**	**244**	**150**	**.245**	**.287**	**.306**

Wilkins, Richard David "Rick" — bats left — throws right — b.7/4/67 — 1991 positions: C 82

YR	TM/LG	CL	G	TPA	AB	H	2B	3B	HR	TB	BB	IBB	HB	SO	GDP	SH	SF	SB	CS	R	RBI	BA	OBA	SA
87	GEN/NYP	A−	75	302	243	61	8	2	8	97	58	8	1	40	3	0	0	7	2	35	43	.251	.397	.399
88	PEO/MID	A	137	575	490	119	30	1	8	175	67	6	7	110	12	2	9	4	6	54	63	.243	.337	.357
89	WIN/CAR	A+	132	512	445	111	24	1	12	173	50	6	8	87	11	2	7	6	3	61	54	.249	.331	.389
90	CHA/SOU	AA	127	501	449	102	17	1	17	172	43	5	5	97	9	1	3	4	5	48	71	.227	.300	.383
91	IOW/AMA	AAA	38	123	107	29	3	1	5	49	11	1	1	17	1	2	2	1	2	12	14	.271	.339	.458
	CHI/NL		86	235	203	45	9	0	6	72	19	2	5	56	3	7	0	3	3	21	22	.222	.307	.355

Willard, Gerald Duane "Jerry" — bats left — throws right — b.3/14/60 — 1991 positions: C 1

YR	TM/LG	CL	G	TPA	AB	H	2B	3B	HR	TB	BB	IBB	HB	SO	GDP	SH	SF	SB	CS	R	RBI	BA	OBA	SA
80	CO/NWL	A−	65	289	231	85	21	1	5	123	51	4	2	27	4	2	3	2	2	53	59	.368	.481	.532
81	PEN/CAR	A+	107	393	334	87	17	1	12	142	49	5	2	66	7	3	5	6	4	43	60	.260	.354	.425
82	REA/EAS	AA	81	325	281	82	10	1	12	130	38	3	4	48	7	0	2	1	3	43	51	.292	.382	.463
	OC/AMA	AAA	36	125	95	22	5	0	2	33	27	1	2	18	6	0	1	1	1	13	14	.232	.408	.347
83	CHA/INT	AAA	127	488	396	119	22	2	19	202	80	7	5	76	4	4	3	0	4	61	77	.301	.421	.510
84	CLE/AL		87	275	246	55	8	1	10	95	26	0	0	55	6	0	3	1	0	21	37	.224	.295	.386
85	MAI/INT	AAA	11	47	40	9	3	0	1	15	7	0	0	7	1	0	0	1	0	5	4	.225	.340	.375
	CLE/AL		104	334	300	81	13	0	7	115	28	1	1	59	3	4	1	0	0	39	36	.270	.333	.383
86	TAC/PCL	AAA	22	73	62	16	5	0	1	24	9	0	0	11	0	1	0	0	0	7	12	.258	.347	.387
	OAK/AL		75	193	161	43	7	0	4	62	22	0	2	28	4	4	4	4	0	17	26	.267	.354	.385
87	TAC/PCL	AAA	67	277	215	64	15	0	6	97	56	3	0	33	6	3	3	0	1	42	38	.298	.438	.451
	OAK/AL		7	8	6	1	0	0	0	1	2	0	0	1	0	0	0	0	0	1	0	.167	.375	.167
89	BIR/SOU	AA	5	17	10	3	1	0	0	4	7	1	0	2	0	0	0	0	0	5	1	.300	.588	.400
	VAN/PCL	AAA	90	331	283	78	18	1	7	119	43	5	4	56	6	0	1	0	2	32	38	.276	.378	.420
90	VAN/PCL	AAA	121	472	380	106	21	0	20	187	85	7	2	60	11	0	5	2	4	66	76	.279	.409	.492
	CHI/AL		3	3	3	0	0	0	0	0	0	0	0	2	0	0	0	0	0	0	0	.000	.000	.000
91	RIC/INT	AAA	91	330	277	83	24	0	8	131	45	4	5	46	2	2	1	1	3	42	39	.300	.405	.473
	ATL/NL		17	16	14	3	0	0	1	6	2	0	0	5	0	0	0	0	0	1	4	.214	.313	.429
6 YR TOTALS			**293**	**829**	**730**	**183**	**28**	**1**	**22**	**279**	**80**	**1**	**3**	**150**	**13**	**8**	**8**	**1**	**1**	**79**	**103**	**.251**	**.324**	**.382**

Williams, Bernabe (Figueroa) "Bernie" — bats both — throws right — b.9/13/68 — 1991 positions: OF 85

YR	TM/LG	CL	G	TPA	AB	H	2B	3B	HR	TB	BB	IBB	HB	SO	GDP	SH	SF	SB	CS	R	RBI	BA	OBA	SA
86	YAN/GCL	R	61	274	230	62	5	3	2	79	39	0	1	40	3	1	3	33	12	45	25	.270	.374	.343
87	FL/FSL	A+	25	94	71	11	3	0	0	14	18	1	3	22	1	2	0	9	1	11	4	.155	.348	.197
	ONE/NYP	A−	25	106	93	32	4	0	0	36	10	0	1	14	0	1	1	9	3	13	15	.344	.410	.387
88	PW/CAR	A+	92	408	337	113	16	7	7	164	66	6	4	66	5	0	1	29	11	72	45	.335	.449	.487
89	COL/INT	AAA	50	194	162	35	8	1	2	51	25	1	2	38	3	3	2	11	5	21	16	.216	.325	.315
	ALB/EAS	AA	91	384	314	79	11	8	11	139	60	4	6	72	9	3	1	26	13	63	42	.252	.381	.443
90	ALB/EAS	AA	134	571	466	131	28	5	8	193	98	6	4	97	12	1	2	39	18	91	54	.281	.409	.414
91	COL/INT	AAA	78	353	306	90	14	6	8	140	38	2	2	43	4	3	4	9	8	52	37	.294	.372	.458
	NY/AL		85	374	320	76	19	4	3	112	48	0	3	57	4	2	1	10	5	43	34	.237	.336	.350

Williams, Gerald Floyd — bats right — throws right — b.8/10/66 — 1991 positions: OF System NY/AL

YR	TM/LG	CL	G	TPA	AB	H	2B	3B	HR	TB	BB	IBB	HB	SO	GDP	SH	SF	SB	CS	R	RBI	BA	OBA	SA
87	ONE/NYP	A−	29	132	115	42	6	2	2	58	16	0	1	18	3	0	0	6	2	26	29	.365	.447	.504
88	PW/CAR	A+	54	176	159	29	3	0	2	38	15	0	0	47	4	1	1	6	1	20	18	.182	.251	.239
	FL/FSL	A+	63	232	212	40	7	2	2	57	16	0	3	56	4	1	0	4	3	21	17	.189	.255	.269
89	PW/CAR	A+	134	518	454	104	19	4	13	174	51	1	7	120	7	5	1	15	10	63	69	.229	.316	.383
90	FL/FSL	A+	50	224	204	59	4	5	7	94	16	1	2	52	1	0	2	19	5	25	43	.289	.344	.461
	ALB/EAS	AA	96	365	324	81	17	2	13	141	35	1	2	75	7	1	3	18	8	54	58	.250	.324	.435
91	ALB/EAS	AA	45	197	175	50	15	0	5	80	18	2	0	26	5	1	3	18	3	28	32	.286	.347	.457
	COL/INT	AAA	61	220	198	51	8	3	2	71	16	1	1	39	3	0	5	9	12	20	27	.258	.309	.359

Williams, Kenneth Royal "Kenny" — bats right — throws right — b.4/6/64 — 1991 positions: OF 33

YR	TM/LG	CL	G	TPA	AB	H	2B	3B	HR	TB	BB	IBB	HB	SO	GDP	SH	SF	SB	CS	R	RBI	BA	OBA	SA
84	APP/MID	A	38	167	147	42	11	2	5	72	15	0	2	48	0	1	2	13	5	23	26	.286	.355	.490
	GF/EAS	AA	97	339	309	76	7	5	8	117	21	1	4	70	7	1	4	16	7	35	47	.246	.299	.379
85	GF/EAS	AA	133	585	520	130	16	6	16	206	47	1	6	83	9	7	5	27	14	87	66	.250	.317	.396
86	BIR/SOU	AA	68	296	272	90	16	5	6	134	18	0	5	53	6	0	1	25	4	21	15	.212	.255	.317
	BUF/AMA	AAA	50	201	189	40	4	2	4	60	6	0	5	48	3	1	0	1	1	19	14	.129	.182	.226
	CHI/AL		15	33	31	4	0	0	0	4	1	0	0	11	1	0	1	1	1	2	1	.269	.310	.425
87	HAW/PCL	AAA	35	146	134	36	4	4	3	57	9	1	0	27	1	0	3	5	5	19	14	.281	.314	.422
	CHI/AL		116	414	391	110	18	2	11	165	10	0	9	83	5	3	1	21	10	48	50			

(continued)

Williams, Kenneth Royal "Kenny" (continued)

YR	TM/LG	CL	G	TPA	AB	H	2B	3B	HR	TB	BB	IBB	HB	SO	GDP	SH	SF	SB	CS	R	RBI	BA	OBA	SA
88	VAN/PCL	AAA	16	66	60	15	2	1	1	22	2	0	2	14	0	1	1	2	1	8	7	.250	.292	.367
	CHI/AL		73	243	220	35	4	2	8	67	10	0	8	64	2	3	2	6	5	18	28	.159	.221	.305
89	TOL/INT	AAA	14	57	51	13	2	0	3	24	5	0	1	9	1	0	0	2	0	8	8	.255	.333	.471
	DET/AL		94	285	258	53	5	1	6	78	18	0	5	63	6	2	2	9	4	29	23	.205	.269	.302
90	DET/AL		57	88	83	11	2	0	0	13	3	0	1	24	0	0	1	2	2	10	5	.133	.170	.157
	TOR/AL		49	81	72	14	6	1	0	22	7	0	1	18	1	0	1	7	2	13	8	.194	.272	.306
	YEAR		106	169	155	25	8	1	0	35	10	0	2	42	1	0	2	9	4	23	13	.161	.219	.226
91	SYR/INT	AAA	15	63	54	18	1	0	7	40	6	0	1	12	1	1	1	6	2	14	19	.333	.403	.741
	TOR/AL		13	35	29	6	2	0	1	11	4	0	1	5	1	0	1	1	0	5	3	.207	.314	.379
	IND/AMA	AAA	18	55	47	11	3	1	2	22	5	0	2	16	0	1	1	1	0	7	7	.234	.327	.468
	MON/NL		34	74	70	19	5	2	0	28	3	0	1	22	1	0	0	2	1	11	1	.271	.311	.400
	YEAR		47	109	99	25	7	2	1	39	7	0	2	27	2	0	1	3	1	16	4	.253	.312	.394
6 YR TOTALS			**451**	**1253**	**1154**	**252**	**42**	**8**	**27**	**391**	**56**	**0**	**27**	**290**	**17**	**8**	**8**	**49**	**25**	**136**	**119**	**.218**	**.269**	**.339**

Williams, Matthew Derrick "Matt" — bats right — throws right — b.11/28/65 — 1991 positions: 3B 155, SS 4

YR	TM/LG	CL	G	TPA	AB	H	2B	3B	HR	TB	BB	IBB	HB	SO	GDP	SH	SF	SB	CS	R	RBI	BA	OBA	SA
86	EVE/NWL	A—	4	19	17	4	0	1	1	9	1	0	0	4	0	0	1	0	0	3	10	.235	.263	.529
	CLI/MID	A	68	280	250	60	14	3	7	101	24	1	3	51	6	0	3	3	3	32	29	.240	.311	.404
87	PHO/PCL	AAA	56	235	211	61	15	2	6	98	19	3	0	53	2	3	2	6	2	36	37	.289	.345	.464
	SF/NL		84	266	245	46	9	2	8	83	16	4	0	68	5	3	1	4	1	28	21	.188	.240	.339
88	PHO/PCL	AAA	82	324	306	83	19	1	12	140	13	2	1	56	9	0	4	6	5	45	51	.271	.299	.458
	SF/NL		52	170	156	32	6	1	8	64	8	0	2	41	7	3	1	0	1	17	19	.205	.251	.410
89	PHO/PCL	AAA	76	320	284	91	20	2	26	193	32	4	3	51	8	0	1	9	3	61	61	.320	.394	.680
	SF/NL		84	311	292	59	18	1	18	133	14	1	2	72	5	1	2	1	2	31	50	.202	.242	.455
90	SF/NL		159	664	617	171	27	2	33	301	33	4	9	138	13	2	5	7	4	87	122	.277	.319	.488
91	SF/NL		157	635	589	158	24	5	34	294	33	6	6	128	11	0	7	5	5	72	98	.268	.310	.499
5 YR TOTALS			**536**	**2046**	**1899**	**466**	**84**	**11**	**101**	**875**	**104**	**20**	**18**	**447**	**41**	**9**	**16**	**17**	**15**	**235**	**310**	**.245**	**.289**	**.461**

Wilson, Craig — bats right — throws right — b.11/28/64 — 1991 positions: 3B 12, OF 5, 1B 4, 2B 3

YR	TM/LG	CL	G	TPA	AB	H	2B	3B	HR	TB	BB	IBB	HB	SO	GDP	SH	SF	SB	CS	R	RBI	BA	OBA	SA
84	ERI/NYP	A—	72	318	282	83	18	4	7	130	29	0	4	27	8	1	2	10	4	53	46	.294	.366	.461
85	SPR/MID	A	133	562	504	132	16	4	8	180	47	0	1	67	12	4	6	33	14	64	52	.262	.323	.357
86	SPR/MID	A	127	575	496	136	17	6	1	168	65	0	1	49	11	9	4	44	12	106	49	.274	.357	.339
87	SP/FSL	A+	38	176	162	58	6	4	0	72	14	0	0	5	3	0	0	12	8	35	28	.358	.409	.444
	LOU/AMA	AAA	21	76	70	15	2	0	1	20	3	0	0	5	2	1	0	2	2	10	8	.214	.243	.286
	ARK/TEX	AA	66	274	238	69	13	1	1	87	30	1	1	19	5	3	2	9	6	37	26	.290	.369	.366
88	LOU/AMA	AAA	133	561	497	127	27	2	1	161	54	1	0	46	13	6	4	6	4	59	46	.256	.326	.324
89	ARK/TEX	AA	55	250	224	71	12	1	1	88	21	1	1	14	4	3	1	8	5	41	40	.317	.377	.393
	LOU/AMA	AAA	75	298	278	81	18	3	1	108	14	0	2	25	5	3	1	1	3	37	30	.291	.329	.388
	STL/NL		6	5	4	1	0	0	0	1	1	0	0	2	0	0	0	0	0	1	1	.250	.400	.250
90	LOU/AMA	AAA	57	244	204	57	9	2	2	76	28	0	1	15	3	5	6	5	3	30	23	.279	.360	.373
	STL/NL		55	131	121	30	2	0	0	32	8	0	0	14	7	0	2	0	0	13	7	.248	.290	.264
91	STL/NL		60	90	82	14	2	0	0	16	6	2	0	10	2	0	2	0	0	5	13	.171	.222	.195
3 YR TOTALS			**121**	**226**	**207**	**45**	**4**	**0**	**0**	**49**	**15**	**2**	**0**	**26**	**9**	**0**	**4**	**0**	**2**	**19**	**21**	**.217**	**.265**	**.237**

Wilson, Daniel Allen "Dan" — bats right — throws right — b.3/25/69 — 1991 positions: C System CIN/NL

YR	TM/LG	CL	G	TPA	AB	H	2B	3B	HR	TB	BB	IBB	HB	SO	GDP	SH	SF	SB	CS	R	RBI	BA	OBA	SA
90	CHW/SAL	A	32	128	113	28	9	1	2	45	13	0	0	18	1	1	1	0	0	16	17	.248	.323	.398
91	CHW/SAL	A	52	225	197	62	11	1	3	84	25	0	2	21	6	0	1	1	1	25	25	.315	.396	.426
	CHT/SOU	AA	81	318	292	75	19	2	2	104	21	0	0	39	10	1	4	2	2	32	38	.257	.303	.356

Wilson, William Hayward "Mookie" — bats both — throws right — b.2/9/56 — 1991 positions: OF 41, DH 34

YR	TM/LG	CL	G	TPA	AB	H	2B	3B	HR	TB	BB	IBB	HB	SO	GDP	SH	SF	SB	CS	R	RBI	BA	OBA	SA
80	NY/NL		27	119	105	26	5	3	0	37	12	0	0	19	0	2	0	7	7	16	4	.248	.325	.352
81	NY/NL		92	350	328	89	8	8	3	122	20	3	2	59	3	0	0	24	12	49	14	.271	.317	.372
82	NY/NL		159	677	639	178	25	9	5	236	32	4	2	102	5	1	3	58	16	90	55	.279	.314	.369
83	NY/NL		152	663	638	176	25	6	7	234	18	3	4	103	6	2	1	54	16	91	51	.276	.300	.367
84	NY/NL		154	619	587	162	28	10	10	240	26	2	2	90	5	2	2	46	9	88	54	.276	.308	.409
85	NY/NL		93	367	337	93	16	8	6	143	28	6	0	52	9	1	1	24	9	56	26	.276	.331	.424
86	TID/INT	AAA	9	34	31	8	1	0	0	9	3	0	0	7	0	0	0	4	4	4	4	.258	.324	.290
	NY/NL		123	415	381	110	17	5	9	164	32	5	1	72	6	0	1	25	7	61	45	.289	.345	.430
87	NY/NL		124	425	385	115	19	7	9	175	35	8	2	85	2	2	1	21	6	58	34	.299	.359	.455
88	NY/NL		112	410	378	112	17	5	8	163	27	2	2	63	12	1	2	15	4	61	41	.296	.345	.431
89	NY/NL		80	262	249	51	10	1	3	72	10	0	1	47	0	1	2	7	4	22	18	.205	.237	.289
	TOR/AL		54	247	238	71	9	1	2	88	3	0	2	37	3	1	3	12	1	32	17	.298	.311	.370
	YEAR		134	509	487	122	19	2	5	160	13	0	3	84	3	2	5	19	5	54	35	.251	.273	.329
90	TOR/AL		147	629	588	156	36	4	3	209	31	0	6	102	10	6	4	23	4	81	51	.265	.300	.355
91	TOR/AL		86	258	241	58	12	4	2	84	8	0	5	35	4	2	2	11	3	26	28	.241	.277	.349
12 YR TOTALS			**1403**	**5441**	**5094**	**1397**	**227**	**71**	**67**	**1967**	**282**	**36**	**23**	**866**	**66**	**22**	**20**	**327**	**98**	**731**	**438**	**.274**	**.314**	**.386**

Wilson, Willie James — bats both — throws right — b.7/9/55 — 1991 positions: OF 87, DH 9

YR	TM/LG	CL	G	TPA	AB	H	2B	3B	HR	TB	BB	IBB	HB	SO	GDP	SH	SF	SB	CS	R	RBI	BA	OBA	SA
76	KC/AL		12	6	6	1	0	0	0	1	0	0	0	0	0	0	0	2	1	0	0	.167	.167	.167
77	KC/AL		13	37	34	11	2	0	0	13	1	0	0	8	1	2	0	6	3	10	1	.324	.343	.382
78	KC/AL		127	223	198	43	8	2	0	55	16	0	2	33	2	5	2	46	12	43	16	.217	.280	.278

Wilson, Willie James (continued)

YR	TM/LG	CL	G	TPA	AB	H	2B	3B	HR	TB	BB	IBB	HB	SO	GDP	SH	SF	SB	CS	R	RBI	BA	OBA	SA
79	KC/AL		154	640	588	185	18	13	6	247	28	3	7	92	1	13	4	83	12	113	49	.315	.351	.420
80	KC/AL		161	745	705	230	28	15	3	297	28	3	6	81	4	5	1	79	10	133	49	.326	.357	.421
81	KC/AL		102	465	439	133	10	7	1	160	18	3	4	42	5	3	1	34	8	54	32	.303	.335	.364
82	KC/AL		136	621	585	194	19	15	3	252	26	2	6	81	4	2	2	37	11	87	46	.332	.365	.431
83	KC/AL		137	611	576	159	22	8	2	203	33	2	1	75	4	1	0	59	8	90	33	.276	.316	.352
84	KC/AL		128	588	541	163	24	9	2	211	39	2	3	56	7	2	3	47	5	81	44	.301	.350	.390
85	KC/AL		141	642	605	168	25	21	4	247	29	3	5	94	6	2	1	43	11	87	43	.278	.316	.408
86	KC/AL		156	675	631	170	20	7	9	231	31	1	9	97	6	3	1	34	8	77	44	.269	.313	.366
87	KC/AL		146	653	610	170	18	15	4	230	32	2	6	88	9	4	1	59	11	97	30	.279	.320	.377
88	KC/AL		147	628	591	155	17	11	1	197	22	1	2	106	5	8	5	35	7	81	37	.262	.289	.333
89	KC/AL		112	423	383	97	17	7	3	137	27	0	1	78	8	6	6	24	6	58	43	.253	.300	.358
90	KC/AL		115	345	307	89	13	3	2	114	30	1	2	57	4	3	3	24	6	49	42	.290	.354	.371
91	OAK/AL		113	318	294	70	14	4	0	92	18	1	4	43	11	1	1	20	5	38	28	.238	.290	.313
16 YR TOTALS			**1900**	**7620**	**7093**	**2038**	**255**	**137**	**40**	**2687**	**378**	**24**	**58**	**1033**	**77**	**60**	**31**	**632**	**124**	**1098**	**537**	**.287**	**.327**	**.379**

Winfield, David Mark "Dave" — bats right — throws right — b.10/3/51 — 1991 positions: OF 115, DH 34

YR	TM/LG	CL	G	TPA	AB	H	2B	3B	HR	TB	BB	IBB	HB	SO	GDP	SH	SF	SB	CS	R	RBI	BA	OBA	SA
73	SD/NL		56	154	141	39	4	1	3	54	12	1	0	19	5	0	1	0	0	9	12	.277	.331	.383
74	SD/NL		145	544	498	132	18	4	20	218	40	2	1	96	14	0	5	9	7	57	75	.265	.318	.438
75	SD/NL		143	591	509	136	20	2	15	205	69	14	3	82	11	3	7	23	4	74	76	.267	.354	.403
76	SD/NL		137	567	492	139	26	4	13	212	65	8	3	78	14	2	5	26	7	81	69	.283	.366	.431
77	SD/NL		157	678	615	169	29	7	25	287	58	10	0	75	12	0	5	16	7	104	92	.275	.335	.467
78	SD/NL		158	649	587	181	30	5	24	293	55	20	2	81	13	0	5	21	9	88	97	.308	.367	.499
79	SD/NL		159	686	597	184	27	10	34	333	85	24	2	71	9	0	2	15	9	97	118	.308	.395	.558
80	SD/NL		162	643	558	154	25	6	20	251	79	14	2	83	13	0	4	23	7	89	87	.276	.365	.450
81	NY/AL		105	440	388	114	25	1	13	180	43	3	1	41	13	1	7	11	1	52	68	.294	.360	.464
82	NY/AL		140	597	539	151	24	8	37	302	45	7	0	64	20	5	8	5	3	84	106	.280	.331	.560
83	NY/AL		152	664	598	169	26	8	32	307	58	2	0	77	30	0	6	5	5	99	116	.283	.345	.513
84	NY/AL		141	626	567	193	34	4	19	292	53	9	0	71	14	0	6	6	4	106	100	.340	.393	.515
85	NY/AL		155	689	633	174	34	6	26	298	52	8	0	96	17	0	4	19	7	105	114	.275	.328	.471
86	NY/AL		154	652	565	148	31	5	24	261	77	9	2	106	20	0	2	6	5	90	104	.262	.349	.462
87	NY/AL		156	655	575	158	22	1	27	263	76	5	0	96	20	1	3	5	6	83	97	.275	.358	.457
88	NY/AL		149	631	559	180	37	2	25	296	69	10	0	88	19	0	1	9	4	96	107	.322	.398	.530
90	NY/AL		20	67	61	13	3	0	2	22	4	0	1	13	2	0	1	0	0	7	6	.213	.269	.361
	CAL/AL		112	470	414	114	18	2	19	193	48	3	1	68	15	1	6	0	1	63	72	.275	.348	.466
	YEAR		132	537	475	127	21	2	21	215	52	3	2	81	17	1	7	0	1	70	78	.267	.338	.453
91	CAL/AL		150	633	568	149	27	4	28	268	56	4	1	109	21	2	6	7	2	75	86	.262	.326	.472
18 YR TOTALS			**2551**	**10636**	**9464**	**2697**	**460**	**80**	**406**	**4535**	**1044**	**153**	**23**	**1414**	**282**	**17**	**88**	**216**	**89**	**1459**	**1602**	**.285**	**.354**	**.479**

Winningham, Herman Son "Herm" — bats left — throws right — b.12/1/61 — 1991 positions: OF 66

YR	TM/LG	CL	G	TPA	AB	H	2B	3B	HR	TB	BB	IBB	HB	SO	GDP	SH	SF	SB	CS	R	RBI	BA	OBA	SA
84	TID/INT	AAA	115	458	406	114	20	3	3	149	48	2	1	81	4	2	1	23	5	50	47	.281	.357	.367
	NY/NL		14	28	27	11	1	1	0	14	1	0	0	7	0	0	0	2	1	5	5	.407	.429	.519
85	IND/AMA	AAA	11	38	35	6	0	0	0	6	3	0	0	7	1	0	0	2	0	3	2	.171	.237	.171
	MON/NL		125	345	312	74	6	5	3	99	28	3	0	72	1	1	4	20	9	30	21	.237	.297	.317
86	IND/AMA	AAA	51	217	201	54	5	7	4	85	14	0	0	47	7	1	1	23	2	35	24	.269	.315	.423
	MON/NL		90	204	185	40	6	3	4	64	18	3	1	51	4	1	0	12	7	23	11	.216	.286	.346
87	MON/NL		137	386	347	83	20	3	4	121	34	7	0	68	10	1	4	29	10	34	41	.239	.304	.349
88	IND/AMA	AAA	3	10	10	2	0	1	0	4	0	0	0	3	1	0	0	1	0	2	1	.200	.200	.400
	MON/NL		47	103	90	21	2	1	0	25	12	1	0	18	2	0	1	4	5	10	6	.233	.320	.278
	CIN/NL		53	122	113	26	1	3	0	33	5	0	0	27	0	3	1	8	3	6	15	.230	.261	.292
	YEAR		100	225	203	47	3	4	0	58	17	1	0	45	2	3	2	12	8	16	21	.232	.288	.286
89	CIN/NL		115	278	251	63	11	3	3	89	24	1	0	50	5	3	0	14	5	40	13	.251	.316	.355
90	CIN/NL		84	177	160	41	8	5	3	68	14	1	0	31	0	2	1	6	4	20	17	.256	.314	.425
91	CIN/NL		98	182	169	38	6	1	1	49	11	1	0	40	1	2	0	4	4	17	4	.225	.272	.290
8 YR TOTALS			**763**	**1825**	**1654**	**397**	**61**	**25**	**18**	**562**	**147**	**17**	**0**	**364**	**24**	**13**	**11**	**99**	**48**	**185**	**133**	**.240**	**.300**	**.340**

Witmeyer, Ronald Herman "Ron" — bats left — throws left — b.6/28/67 — 1991 positions: 1B 8

YR	TM/LG	CL	G	TPA	AB	H	2B	3B	HR	TB	BB	IBB	HB	SO	GDP	SH	SF	SB	CS	R	RBI	BA	OBA	SA
89	MOD/CAL	A+	134	540	457	93	22	1	8	141	70	1	4	101	3	5	4	5	1	54	43	.204	.312	.309
90	TAC/PCL	AAA	10	32	31	9	2	0	1	14	1	0	0	3	1	0	0	0	0	5	7	.290	.313	.452
	MOD/CAL	A+	92	380	333	78	14	5	10	132	41	2	1	74	6	1	4	0	4	38	45	.234	.317	.396
	HUN/SOU	AA	27	108	91	29	4	0	5	48	15	0	2	16	2	0	0	0	0	18	18	.319	.426	.527
91	TAC/PCL	AAA	122	497	431	113	18	4	15	184	57	5	2	59	13	2	5	2	5	64	80	.262	.347	.427
	OAK/AL		11	19	19	1	0	0	0	1	0	0	0	3	1	0	0	0	0	0	0	.053	.053	.053

Wood, Edward Robert "Ted" — bats left — throws left — b.1/4/67 — 1991 positions: OF 8

YR	TM/LG	CL	G	TPA	AB	H	2B	3B	HR	TB	BB	IBB	HB	SO	GDP	SH	SF	SB	CS	R	RBI	BA	OBA	SA
89	SHR/TEX	AA	114	419	349	90	13	1	0	105	51	2	6	72	8	10	3	9	7	44	43	.258	.359	.301
90	SHR/TEX	AA	131	543	456	121	22	11	17	216	74	5	7	76	8	4	2	17	8	81	72	.265	.375	.474
91	PHO/PCL	AAA	137	612	512	159	38	6	11	242	86	4	4	96	13	0	10	12	7	90	109	.311	.407	.473
	SF/NL		10	28	25	3	0	0	0	3	2	0	0	11	0	1	0	0	0	0	1	.120	.185	.120

Worthington, Craig Richard — bats right — throws right — b.4/17/65 — 1991 positions: 3B 30

YR	TM/LG	CL	G	TPA	AB	H	2B	3B	HR	TB	BB	IBB	HB	SO	GDP	SH	SF	SB	CS	R	RBI	BA	OBA	SA
85	BLU/APP	R+	39	145	129	44	9	1	7	76	10	1	2	19	3	3	1	3	2	33	20	.341	.394	.589
86	HAG/CAR	A+	132	572	480	144	35	4	15	226	82	7	2	58	12	0	8	7	12	85	105	.300	.399	.471
87	ROC/INT	AAA	109	422	383	99	14	1	7	136	32	3	2	62	10	3	2	0	2	46	50	.258	.317	.355
88	ROC/INT	AAA	121	475	430	105	25	1	16	180	39	2	0	93	13	0	6	3	1	53	73	.244	.303	.419
	BAL/AL		26	90	81	15	2	0	2	23	9	0	0	24	2	0	0	1	0	5	4	.185	.267	.284
89	BAL/AL		145	566	497	123	23	0	15	191	61	4	4	114	10	3	1	1	2	57	70	.247	.334	.384
90	BAL/AL		133	501	425	96	17	0	8	137	63	2	3	96	13	7	3	1	2	46	44	.226	.328	.322
91	BAL/AL		31	116	102	23	3	0	4	38	12	0	1	14	3	1	0	1	2	11	12	.225	.313	.373
	ROC/INT	AAA	19	64	57	17	4	0	2	27	6	0	1	8	3	0	0	0	0	10	9	.298	.375	.474
4 YR TOTALS			**335**	**1273**	**1105**	**257**	**45**	**0**	**29**	**389**	**145**	**4**	**8**	**248**	**28**	**11**	**4**	**3**	**5**	**119**	**130**	**.233**	**.325**	**.352**

Yelding, Eric Girard — bats right — throws right — b.2/22/65 — 1991 positions: SS 72, OF 4

YR	TM/LG	CL	G	TPA	AB	H	2B	3B	HR	TB	BB	IBB	HB	SO	GDP	SH	SF	SB	CS	R	RBI	BA	OBA	SA
84	MH/PIO	R+	67	332	304	94	14	6	4	132	26	0	0	46	3	0	2	31	11	61	29	.309	.361	.434
85	KIN/CAR	A+	135	571	526	137	14	4	2	165	33	0	4	70	4	5	3	62	26	59	31	.260	.307	.314
86	VEN/CAL	A+	131	601	560	157	14	7	4	197	33	3	0	84	6	6	2	41	18	83	40	.280	.319	.352
87	KNO/SOU	AA	39	165	150	30	6	1	0	38	12	0	1	25	4	1	1	10	5	23	7	.200	.262	.253
	MB/SAL	A	88	384	357	109	12	1	1	128	18	0	4	30	5	1	4	73	13	53	31	.305	.342	.359
88	SYR/INT	AAA	138	594	556	139	15	2	1	161	36	3	0	102	4	2	0	59	23	69	38	.250	.296	.290
89	HOU/NL		70	102	90	21	2	0	0	23	7	0	1	19	2	2	1	11	5	19	9	.233	.290	.256
90	HOU/NL		142	559	511	130	9	5	1	152	39	1	0	87	11	4	5	64	25	69	28	.254	.305	.297
91	HOU/NL		78	293	276	67	11	1	1	83	13	1	3	46	4	3	1	11	9	19	20	.243	.276	.301
	TUC/PCL	AAA	11	49	43	17	3	0	0	20	4	0	2	4	0	0	0	4	2	6	3	.395	.469	.465
3 YR TOTALS			**290**	**954**	**877**	**218**	**22**	**6**	**2**	**258**	**59**	**4**	**1**	**152**	**17**	**9**	**8**	**86**	**39**	**107**	**57**	**.249**	**.294**	**.294**

Young, Eric Orlando — bats right — throws right — b.5/18/67 — 1991 positions: 2B System LA/NL

YR	TM/LG	CL	G	TPA	AB	H	2B	3B	HR	TB	BB	IBB	HB	SO	GDP	SH	SF	SB	CS	R	RBI	BA	OBA	SA
89	DOD/GCL	R	56	235	197	65	11	5	2	92	33	1	3	16	1	1	1	41	10	53	22	.330	.432	.467
90	VB/FSL	A+	127	544	460	132	23	7	2	175	69	1	6	35	4	5	4	76	16	101	50	.287	.384	.380
91	SA/TEX	AA	127	539	461	129	17	4	3	163	67	0	2	36	13	8	1	71	26	82	35	.280	.373	.354
	ALB/PCL	AAA	1	5	5	2	0	0	0	2	0	0	0	0	0	0	0	0	0	0	0	.400	.400	.400

Young, Gerald Anthony — bats both — throws right — b.10/22/64 — 1991 positions: OF 84

YR	TM/LG	CL	G	TPA	AB	H	2B	3B	HR	TB	BB	IBB	HB	SO	GDP	SH	SF	SB	CS	R	RBI	BA	OBA	SA
81	BIL/PIO	R+	47	151	135	44	7	0	1	54	13	1	0	19	3	2	1	3	1	22	23	.326	.383	.400
84	COL/SAL	A	124	491	396	84	14	3	1	107	84	1	2	69	7	6	3	43	7	69	52	.212	.351	.270
85	OSC/FSL	A+	133	576	474	121	20	9	3	168	86	5	5	48	17	2	9	31	13	88	48	.255	.369	.354
86	COL/SOU	AA	136	617	539	151	30	4	9	216	67	5	6	57	6	2	8	54	27	101	62	.280	.356	.401
87	TUC/PCL	AAA	86	394	340	99	15	5	2	130	47	0	3	32	6	2	2	43	12	59	31	.291	.380	.382
	HOU/NL		71	303	274	88	9	2	1	104	26	0	1	27	1	0	2	26	9	44	15	.321	.380	.380
88	HOU/NL		149	655	576	148	21	9	0	187	66	1	3	66	10	5	5	65	27	79	37	.257	.334	.325
89	HOU/NL		146	620	533	124	17	3	0	147	74	4	2	60	7	6	5	34	25	71	38	.233	.326	.276
90	TUC/PCL	AAA	49	227	183	61	7	4	0	76	40	1	0	18	5	2	2	14	11	37	24	.333	.449	.415
	HOU/NL		57	179	154	27	4	1	1	36	20	0	0	23	3	4	1	6	3	15	4	.175	.269	.234
91	TUC/PCL	AAA	24	95	79	24	2	3	0	32	14	1	0	8	2	1	1	3	1	14	17	.304	.404	.405
	HOU/NL		108	169	142	31	3	1	1	39	24	0	0	17	3	1	2	16	5	26	11	.218	.327	.275
5 YR TOTALS			**531**	**1926**	**1679**	**418**	**54**	**16**	**3**	**513**	**210**	**5**	**6**	**193**	**24**	**16**	**15**	**147**	**69**	**235**	**105**	**.249**	**.332**	**.306**

Yount, Robin R — bats right — throws right — b.9/16/55 — 1991 positions: OF 117, DH 13

YR	TM/LG	CL	G	TPA	AB	H	2B	3B	HR	TB	BB	IBB	HB	SO	GDP	SH	SF	SB	CS	R	RBI	BA	OBA	SA
74	MIL/AL		107	364	344	86	14	5	3	119	12	0	1	46	4	5	2	7	7	48	26	.250	.276	.346
75	MIL/AL		147	607	558	149	28	2	8	205	33	3	1	69	8	10	5	12	4	67	52	.267	.307	.367
76	MIL/AL		161	690	638	161	19	3	2	192	38	3	0	69	13	8	6	16	11	59	54	.252	.292	.301
77	MIL/AL		154	663	605	174	34	4	4	228	41	1	2	80	11	11	4	16	7	66	49	.288	.333	.377
78	MIL/AL		127	545	502	147	23	9	9	215	24	1	1	43	5	13	5	16	5	66	71	.293	.323	.428
79	MIL/AL		149	626	577	154	26	5	8	214	35	1	3	52	15	10	3	11	8	72	51	.267	.308	.371
80	MIL/AL		143	647	611	179	49	10	23	317	26	1	1	67	8	6	3	20	5	121	87	.293	.321	.519
81	MIL/AL		96	411	377	103	15	5	10	158	22	1	2	37	4	4	6	4	1	50	49	.273	.312	.419
82	MIL/AL		156	704	635	210	46	12	29	367	54	2	1	63	19	4	10	14	3	129	114	.331	.379	.578
83	MIL/AL		149	662	578	178	42	10	17	291	72	6	3	58	11	1	8	12	5	102	80	.308	.383	.503
84	MIL/AL		160	702	624	186	27	7	16	275	67	1	2	67	22	1	9	14	4	105	80	.298	.362	.441
85	MIL/AL		122	527	466	129	26	3	15	206	49	3	2	56	8	1	9	10	4	76	68	.277	.342	.442
86	MIL/AL		140	595	522	163	31	7	9	235	62	1	4	73	9	5	2	14	5	82	46	.312	.388	.450
87	MIL/AL		158	723	635	198	25	9	21	304	76	10	1	94	9	5	3	19	9	99	103	.312	.384	.479
88	MIL/AL		162	696	621	190	38	11	13	289	63	10	3	63	21	2	7	22	4	92	91	.306	.369	.465
89	MIL/AL		160	690	614	195	38	9	21	314	63	9	6	71	9	3	4	19	3	101	103	.318	.384	.511
90	MIL/AL		158	683	587	145	17	5	17	223	78	6	6	89	7	4	8	15	8	98	77	.247	.337	.380
91	MIL/AL		130	571	503	131	20	4	10	189	54	8	4	79	13	1	9	6	4	66	77	.260	.332	.376
18 YR TOTALS			**2579**	**11106**	**9997**	**2878**	**518**	**120**	**235**	**4341**	**869**	**81**	**40**	**1176**	**196**	**95**	**105**	**247**	**97**	**1499**	**1278**	**.288**	**.344**	**.434**

Zeile, Todd Edward — bats right — throws right — b.9/9/65 — 1991 positions: 3B 154

YR	TM/LG	CL	G	TPA	AB	H	2B	3B	HR	TB	BB	IBB	HB	SO	GDP	SH	SF	SB	CS	R	RBI	BA	OBA	SA
86	ERI/NYP	A-	70	294	248	64	14	1	14	122	37	1	2	52	3	1	6	5	1	40	63	.258	.352	.492
87	SPR/MID	A	130	561	487	142	24	4	25	249	70	7	1	85	10	1	0	3	1	94	106	.292	.380	.511

Zeile, Todd Edward (continued)

YR	TM/LG	CL	G	TPA	AB	H	2B	3B	HR	TB	BB	IBB	HB	SO	GDP	SH	SF	SB	CS	R	RBI	BA	OBA	SA
88	ARK/TEX	AA	129	518	430	117	33	2	19	211	83	8	1	64	11	0	4	6	5	95	75	.272	.388	.491
89	LOU/AMA	AAA	118	506	453	131	26	3	19	220	45	1	1	78	10	0	7	0	1	71	85	.289	.350	.486
	STL/NL		28	93	82	21	3	1	1	29	9	1	0	14	1	1	1	0	0	7	8	.256	.326	.354
90	STL/NL		144	570	495	121	25	3	15	197	67	3	2	77	11	0	6	2	4	62	57	.244	.333	.398
91	STL/NL		155	638	565	158	36	3	11	233	62	3	5	94	15	0	6	17	11	76	81	.280	.353	.412
3 YR TOTALS			**327**	**1301**	**1142**	**300**	**64**	**7**	**27**	**459**	**138**	**7**	**7**	**185**	**27**	**1**	**13**	**19**	**15**	**145**	**146**	**.263**	**.342**	**.402**

Zosky, Edward James "Eddie" — bats right — throws right — b.2/10/68 — 1991 positions: SS 18

YR	TM/LG	CL	G	TPA	AB	H	2B	3B	HR	TB	BB	IBB	HB	SO	GDP	SH	SF	SB	CS	R	RBI	BA	OBA	SA
89	KNO/SOU	AA	56	221	208	46	5	3	2	63	10	0	0	32	4	2	1	1	1	21	14	.221	.256	.303
90	KNO/SOU	AA	115	490	450	122	20	7	3	165	26	1	5	73	7	6	3	3	13	53	45	.271	.316	.367
91	SYR/INT	AAA	119	563	511	135	18	4	6	179	35	1	5	82	11	7	5	9	4	69	39	.264	.315	.350
	TOR/AL		18	28	27	4	1	1	0	7	0	0	0	8	1	1	0	0	0	2	2	.148	.148	.259

Zupcic, Robert "Bob" — bats right — throws right — b.8/18/66 — 1991 positions: OF 16

YR	TM/LG	CL	G	TPA	AB	H	2B	3B	HR	TB	BB	IBB	HB	SO	GDP	SH	SF	SB	CS	R	RBI	BA	OBA	SA
87	ELM/NYP	A−	66	262	238	72	12	2	7	109	17	0	2	35	5	3	2	5	4	39	37	.303	.351	.458
88	LYN/CAR	A+	135	565	482	143	33	5	13	225	60	4	8	64	6	7	8	10	6	69	97	.297	.378	.467
89	PAW/INT	AAA	27	99	94	24	7	1	1	36	3	0	0	15	2	0	2	1	3	8	11	.255	.273	.383
	NB/EAS	AA	94	375	346	75	12	2	2	97	19	0	1	55	7	7	2	15	1	37	28	.217	.258	.280
90	NB/EAS	AA	132	516	461	98	26	1	2	132	36	2	6	63	7	6	7	10	8	45	41	.213	.275	.286
91	PAW/INT	AAA	129	505	429	103	27	1	18	186	55	2	1	58	5	12	8	10	6	70	70	.240	.323	.434
	BOS/AL		18	27	25	4	0	0	1	7	1	0	0	6	0	1	0	0	0	3	3	.160	.192	.280

Zuvella, Paul — bats right — throws right — b.10/31/58 — 1991 positions: 3B 2

YR	TM/LG	CL	G	TPA	AB	H	2B	3B	HR	TB	BB	IBB	HB	SO	GDP	SH	SF	SB	CS	R	RBI	BA	OBA	SA
80	BRA/GCL	R	2	8	8	1	0	0	0	1	0	0	0	0	0	0	0	0	0	0	1	.125	.125	.125
	DUR/CAR	A+	48	177	149	47	7	0	2	60	23	0	2	12	1	1	2	3	4	21	19	.315	.409	.403
81	SAV/SOU	AA	138	545	485	145	17	2	11	199	31	2	10	42	12	14	5	10	8	61	68	.299	.350	.410
82	RIC/INT	AAA	133	510	455	128	15	2	9	174	39	2	4	41	10	9	3	8	7	63	54	.281	.341	.382
	ATL/NL		2	1	1	0	0	0	0	0	0	0	0	0	0	0	0	0	0	0	0	.000	.000	.000
83	RIC/INT	AAA	117	455	415	119	13	2	6	154	28	1	7	34	16	3	2	4	4	53	64	.287	.341	.371
	ATL/NL		3	8	5	0	0	0	0	0	2	0	1	1	0	0	0	0	0	0	0	.000	.375	.000
84	RIC/INT	AAA	127	535	462	140	18	6	6	188	58	3	8	39	22	4	3	14	6	77	55	.303	.388	.407
	ATL/NL		11	27	25	5	1	0	0	6	2	0	0	3	0	0	0	0	0	2	1	.200	.259	.240
85	RIC/INT	AAA	8	35	32	7	0	1	0	10	2	0	1	3	1	1	0	0	0	3	3	.219	.265	.313
	ATL/NL		81	210	190	48	8	1	0	58	16	1	0	14	3	4	0	2	0	16	4	.253	.311	.305
86	RIC/INT	AAA	66	293	252	80	10	1	1	95	33	0	1	11	7	6	1	8	2	44	24	.317	.397	.377
	NY/AL		21	57	48	4	1	0	0	5	5	0	0	4	1	4	0	0	0	2	2	.083	.170	.104
	COL/INT	AAA	23	90	82	21	3	0	1	27	8	0	0	8	2	0	0	3	0	12	7	.256	.322	.329
87	NY/AL		14	36	34	6	0	0	0	6	0	0	0	4	1	2	0	0	0	2	0	.176	.176	.176
	COL/INT	AAA	69	299	269	81	15	4	2	110	22	1	3	21	3	3	2	13	2	47	25	.301	.358	.409
88	CS/PCL	AAA	68	257	232	67	11	3	1	87	17	2	1	19	4	2	5	6	3	33	28	.289	.333	.375
	CLE/AL		51	146	130	30	5	1	0	37	8	0	0	13	3	8	0	0	0	9	7	.231	.275	.285
89	CS/PCL	AAA	96	414	387	128	23	3	10	187	24	0	1	27	12	1	1	8	6	61	66	.331	.370	.483
	CLE/AL		24	60	58	16	2	0	2	24	1	0	1	11	0	0	0	0	0	10	6	.276	.300	.414
90	OMA/AMA	AAA	111	456	407	115	16	1	5	148	38	1	3	39	15	6	2	11	10	47	41	.283	.347	.364
91	KC/AL		2	0	0	0	0	0	0	0	0	0	0	0	0	0	0	0	0	0	0	.000	.000	.000
	OMA/AMA	AAA	64	248	219	59	14	1	1	78	23	2	3	15	5	1	2	3	2	28	20	.269	.344	.356
9 YR TOTALS			**209**	**545**	**491**	**109**	**17**	**2**	**2**	**136**	**34**	**1**	**2**	**50**	**8**	**18**	**0**	**2**	**0**	**41**	**20**	**.222**	**.275**	**.277**

Abbott, James Anthony "Jim" — bats left — throws left — b.9/19/67

YR	TM/LG	CL	G	TBF	GS	CG	SHO	GF	IP	H	HR	BB	IBB	HB	SO	SH	SF	WP	BK	R	ER	W	L	PCT	SV	ERA
89	CAL/AL		29	788	29	4	2	0	181.1	190	13	74	3	4	115	11	5	8	2	95	79	12	12	.500	0	3.92
90	CAL/AL		33	925	33	4	1	0	211.2	246	16	72	6	5	105	9	6	4	3	116	106	10	14	.417	0	4.51
91	CAL/AL		34	1002	34	5	1	0	243.0	222	14	73	6	5	158	7	7	1	4	85	78	18	11	.621	0	2.89
3 YR TOTALS			**96**	**2715**	**96**	**13**	**4**	**0**	**636.0**	**658**	**43**	**219**	**15**	**14**	**378**	**27**	**18**	**13**	**9**	**296**	**263**	**40**	**37**	**.519**	**0**	**3.72**

Abbott, Lawrence Kyle "Kyle" — bats left — throws left — b.2/18/68

YR	TM/LG	CL	G	TBF	GS	CG	SHO	GF	IP	H	HR	BB	IBB	HB	SO	SH	SF	WP	BK	R	ER	W	L	PCT	SV	ERA
89	QC/MID	A	13	303	12	0	0	1	73.2	55	5	30	0	4	95	0	0	3	5	26	21	5	4	.556	0	2.57
90	MID/TEX	AA	24	565	24	2	0	0	128.1	124	8	73	0	8	91	4	4	6	3	75	59	6	9	.400	0	4.14
	EDM/PCL	AAA	3	61	3	0	0	0	10.1	26	4	4	0	0	14	0	1	4	0	18	17	1	0	1.000	0	14.81
91	EDM/PCL	AAA	27	732	27	4	2	0	180.1	173	22	46	1	1	120	7	6	7	0	84	80	14	10	.583	0	3.99
	CAL/AL		5	90	3	0	0	0	19.2	22	2	13	0	0	12	3	0	1	1	11	10	1	2	.333	0	4.58

Abbott, Paul David — bats right — throws right — b.9/15/67

YR	TM/LG	CL	G	TBF	GS	CG	SHO	GF	IP	H	HR	BB	IBB	HB	SO	SH	SF	WP	BK	R	ER	W	L	PCT	SV	ERA
85	ELI/APP	R+	10	172	10	1	0	0	35.0	33	3	32	0	0	34	1	0	7	1	32	27	1	5	.167	0	6.94
86	KEN/MID	A	25	462	15	1	0	7	98.0	102	13	73	3	2	73	3	2	7	0	62	49	6	10	.375	0	4.50
87	KEN/MID	A	26	620	25	1	0	0	145.1	102	11	103	0	3	138	5	6	11	2	76	59	13	6	.684	0	3.65
88	VIS/CAL	A+	28	799	28	4	2	0	172.1	141	9	143	5	4	205	8	6	12	9	95	80	11	9	.550	0	4.18
89	ORL/SOU		17	389	17	1	0	0	90.2	71	6	48	0	0	102	2	1	7	7	48	44	9	3	.750	0	4.37
90	POR/PCL	AAA	23	568	23	4	1	0	128.1	110	9	82	0	1	129	3	3	8	5	75	65	5	14	.263	0	4.56
	MIN/AL		7	162	7	0	0	0	34.2	37	0	28	0	1	25	1	1	1	0	24	23	0	5	.000	0	5.97
91	POR/PCL	AAA	8	193	8	1	1	0	44.0	36	2	28	0	3	40	0	1	1	0	19	19	2	3	.400	0	3.89
	MIN/AL		15	210	3	0	0	1	47.1	38	5	36	1	0	43	7	3	5	0	27	25	3	1	.750	0	4.75
2 YR TOTALS			**22**	**372**	**10**	**0**	**0**	**1**	**82.0**	**75**	**5**	**64**	**1**	**1**	**68**	**8**	**4**	**6**	**0**	**51**	**48**	**3**	**6**	**.333**	**0**	**5.27**

Acker, James Justin "Jim" — bats right — throws right — b.9/24/58

YR	TM/LG	CL	G	TBF	GS	CG	SHO	GF	IP	H	HR	BB	IBB	HB	SO	SH	SF	WP	BK	R	ER	W	L	PCT	SV	ERA
83	TOR/AL		38	426	5	0	0	8	97.2	103	7	38	1	8	44	1	2	1	0	52	47	5	1	.833	1	4.33
84	TOR/AL		32	312	3	0	0	9	72.0	79	3	25	3	6	33	4	1	5	0	39	35	3	5	.375	1	4.38
85	TOR/AL		61	370	0	0	0	26	86.1	86	7	43	1	3	42	1	2	2	0	35	31	7	2	.778	10	3.23
86	TOR/AL		23	259	5	0	0	6	60.0	63	6	22	3	2	32	6	5	3	1	34	29	2	4	.333	0	4.35
	ATL/NL		21	402	14	0	0	3	95.0	100	7	26	3	1	37	6	4	2	0	47	40	3	8	.273	0	3.79
	YEAR		44	661	19	0	0	9	155.0	163	13	48	6	3	69	12	9	5	1	81	69	5	12	.294	0	4.01
87	ATL/NL		68	491	0	0	0	41	114.2	109	11	51	4	4	68	3	3	1	0	57	53	4	9	.308	14	4.16
88	GRE/SOU	AA	8	54	4	0	0	0	15.2	7	1	3	0	0	5	0	0	0	0	3	3	0	0	.000	0	1.72
	ATL/NL		21	184	1	0	0	7	42.0	45	6	14	3	1	25	5	3	2	0	26	22	0	4	.000	0	4.71
89	ATL/NL		59	383	0	0	0	23	97.2	84	5	20	8	1	68	5	3	2	0	29	29	0	6	.000	2	2.67
	TOR/AL		14	116	0	0	0	3	28.1	24	1	12	3	1	24	1	0	1	0	7	5	2	1	.667	0	1.59
	YEAR		73	499	0	0	0	26	126.0	108	6	32	11	2	92	6	3	3	0	36	34	2	7	.222	2	2.43
90	TOR/AL		59	403	0	0	0	19	91.2	103	9	30	5	3	54	3	1	4	1	49	39	4	4	.500	1	3.83
91	TOR/AL		54	374	4	0	0	11	88.1	77	16	36	5	2	44	7	5	7	0	53	51	3	5	.375	1	5.20
9 YR TOTALS			**450**	**3720**	**32**	**0**	**0**	**156**	**873.2**	**873**	**78**	**317**	**39**	**32**	**471**	**42**	**29**	**30**	**2**	**428**	**381**	**33**	**49**	**.402**	**30**	**3.92**

Agosto, Juan Roberto (Gonzalez) — bats left — throws left — b.2/23/58

YR	TM/LG	CL	G	TBF	GS	CG	SHO	GF	IP	H	HR	BB	IBB	HB	SO	SH	SF	WP	BK	R	ER	W	L	PCT	SV	ERA
81	CHI/AL		2	22	0	0	0	1	5.2	5	1	0	0	1	3	0	0	0	0	3	3	0	0	.000	0	4.76
82	CHI/AL		1	13	0	0	0	1	2.0	7	0	0	0	1	0	0	0	0	0	4	4	0	0	.000	0	18.00
83	CHI/AL		39	166	0	0	0	13	41.2	41	2	11	1	1	29	5	4	2	0	20	19	2	2	.500	7	4.10
84	CHI/AL		49	243	0	0	0	18	55.1	54	2	34	7	4	26	5	1	1	0	20	19	2	1	.667	7	3.09
85	BUF/AMA	AAA	6	52	0	0	0	5	12.2	13	0	2	0	0	11	1	0	0	0	3	3	0	0	.000	2	2.13
	CHI/AL		54	246	0	0	0	21	60.1	45	3	23	1	3	39	3	3	0	0	27	24	4	3	.571	1	3.58
86	CHI/AL		9	24	0	0	0	1	4.2	6	0	4	0	0	3	0	0	0	0	5	4	0	2	.000	0	7.71
	MIN/AL		17	115	0	0	0	3	20.1	43	1	14	0	2	9	2	0	1	0	25	20	1	2	.333	1	8.85
	YEAR		26	139	0	0	0	4	25.0	49	1	18	0	2	12	2	0	1	0	30	24	1	4	.200	1	8.64
	TOL/INT	AAA	21	149	0	0	0	18	35.0	33	0	14	0	1	29	1	0	4	0	11	9	4	3	.571	6	2.31
87	TUC/PCL	AAA	44	214	0	0	0	24	50.0	48	1	19	2	2	31	4	0	4	1	16	11	4	2	.667	7	1.98
	HOU/NL		27	118	0	0	0	13	27.1	26	1	10	1	0	6	3	0	1	0	12	8	1	1	.500	2	2.63
88	HOU/NL		75	371	0	0	0	33	91.2	74	6	30	13	0	33	9	5	3	5	27	23	10	2	.833	4	2.26
89	HOU/NL		71	361	0	0	0	28	83.0	81	4	32	10	2	46	6	4	1	1	32	27	4	5	.444	1	2.93
90	HOU/NL		82	404	0	0	0	29	92.1	91	4	39	8	7	50	7	2	1	0	46	44	9	8	.529	4	4.29
91	STL/NL		72	377	0	0	0	22	86.0	92	4	39	4	8	34	11	3	6	0	52	46	5	3	.625	2	3.80
11 YR TOTALS			**498**	**2460**	**1**	**0**	**0**	**183**	**570.1**	**565**	**27**	**236**	**45**	**27**	**279**	**50**	**24**	**19**	**6**	**273**	**241**	**38**	**29**	**.567**	**29**	**3.80**

Aguilera, Richard Warren "Rick" — bats right — throws right — b.12/31/61

YR	TM/LG	CL	G	TBF	GS	CG	SHO	GF	IP	H	HR	BB	IBB	HB	SO	SH	SF	WP	BK	R	ER	W	L	PCT	SV	ERA
84	LYN/CAR	A+	13	364	13	6	3	0	88.1	72	3	28	1	6	101	3	2	6	2	29	23	8	3	.727	0	2.34
	JAC/TEX	AA	11	284	11	2	1	0	67.0	68	5	19	1	0	71	2	1	2	0	37	34	4	4	.500	0	4.57
85	TID/INT	AAA	11	314	11	2	1	0	79.0	64	5	17	0	1	55	1	1	2	2	24	22	6	4	.600	0	2.51
	NY/NL		21	507	19	2	0	1	122.1	118	8	37	2	3	74	4	5	5	0	49	44	10	7	.588	0	3.24
86	NY/NL		28	605	20	2	0	2	141.2	145	15	36	1	7	104	6	5	5	3	70	61	10	7	.588	0	3.88
87	TID/INT	AAA	3	47	2	0	0	0	13.0	8	0	4	0	0	10	0	0	0	0	2	1	1	1	.500	0	0.69
	NY/NL		18	494	17	1	0	0	115.0	124	12	33	2	3	77	7	2	9	0	53	46	11	3	.786	0	3.60

Aguilera, Richard Warren "Rick" (continued)

YR	TM/LG	CL	G	TBF	GS	CG	SHO	GF	IP	H	HR	BB	IBB	HB	SO	SH	SF	WP	BK	R	ER	W	L	PCT	SV	ERA
88	SL/FSL	A+	2	30	2	0	0	0	7.0	8	0	1	0	0	5	3	0	1	0	1	1	0	0	.000	0	1.29
	TID/INT	AAA	1	25	1	0	0	0	6.0	6	0	1	0	0	4	0	1	0	0	1	1	0	0	.000	0	1.50
	NY/NL		11	111	3	0	0	2	24.2	29	2	10	2	1	16	2	0	1	1	20	19	0	4	.000	0	6.93
89	NY/NL		36	284	0	0	0	19	69.1	59	3	21	3	2	80	5	1	3	3	19	18	6	6	.500	7	2.34
	MIN/AL		11	310	11	3	0	0	75.2	71	5	17	1	1	57	2	0	1	0	32	27	3	5	.375	0	3.21
	YEAR		47	594	11	3	0	19	145.0	130	8	38	4	3	137	7	1	4	3	51	45	9	11	.450	7	2.79
90	MIN/AL		56	268	0	0	0	54	65.1	55	5	19	6	4	61	0	0	3	0	27	20	5	3	.625	32	2.76
91	MIN/AL		63	275	0	0	0	60	69.0	44	3	30	6	1	61	1	3	3	0	20	18	4	5	.444	42	2.35
7 YR TOTALS			**244**	**2854**	**70**	**8**	**0**	**138**	**683.0**	**645**	**53**	**203**	**23**	**21**	**530**	**30**	**15**	**30**	**9**	**290**	**253**	**49**	**40**	**.551**	**81**	**3.33**

Akerfelds, Darrel Wayne — bats right — throws right — b.6/12/62

YR	TM/LG	CL	G	TBF	GS	CG	SHO	GF	IP	H	HR	BB	IBB	HB	SO	SH	SF	WP	BK	R	ER	W	L	PCT	SV	ERA
84	MAD/MID	A	24	665	24	6	1	0	151.0	156	7	74	2	5	137	4	2	19	1	86	74	11	6	.647	0	4.41
85	HUN/SOU	AA	17	418	17	1	1	0	96.1	75	12	64	0	1	56	2	3	4	0	42	37	9	6	.600	0	3.46
86	OAK/AL		2	26	0	0	0	2	5.1	7	2	3	1	0	5	0	0	2	0	5	4	0	0	.000	0	6.75
	TAC/PCL	AAA	25	656	24	2	0	0	150.0	158	12	62	3	6	91	3	7	10	2	91	79	8	12	.400	0	4.74
87	TAC/PCL	AAA	19	549	19	3	0	0	129.2	117	9	57	1	4	84	2	3	9	1	52	51	10	3	.769	0	3.54
	CLE/AL		16	347	13	1	0	0	74.2	84	18	38	1	7	42	2	2	7	0	60	56	2	6	.250	0	6.75
88	CS/PCL	AAA	49	270	0	0	0	41	58.0	70	9	26	3	2	50	6	2	6	2	43	28	3	7	.300	6	4.34
89	OC/AMA	AAA	33	458	11	1	0	15	108.0	89	5	59	4	5	75	3	1	5	1	45	40	5	5	.500	4	3.33
	TEX/AL		6	50	0	0	0	2	11.0	11	1	5	2	0	9	0	1	1	0	6	4	0	1	.000	0	3.27
90	PHI/NL		71	395	0	0	0	18	93.0	65	10	54	9	3	42	9	5	7	1	45	39	5	2	.714	3	3.77
91	PHI/NL		30	229	0	0	0	11	49.2	49	5	27	4	3	31	6	2	4	0	30	29	2	1	.667	0	5.26
	SCR/INT	AAA	11	239	11	0	0	0	52.2	52	9	39	0	0	36	3	1	5	1	37	37	3	3	.500	0	6.32
5 YR TOTALS			**125**	**1047**	**13**	**1**	**0**	**33**	**233.2**	**216**	**36**	**127**	**16**	**13**	**129**	**17**	**12**	**21**	**1**	**146**	**132**	**9**	**10**	**.474**	**3**	**5.08**

Aldred, Scott Phillip — bats left — throws left — b.6/12/68

YR	TM/LG	CL	G	TBF	GS	CG	SHO	GF	IP	H	HR	BB	IBB	HB	SO	SH	SF	WP	BK	R	ER	W	L	PCT	SV	ERA
87	FAY/SAL	A	21	485	20	0	0	0	111.0	101	5	69	0	3	91	2	7	8	1	56	44	4	9	.308	0	3.57
88	LAK/FSL	A+	25	583	25	1	1	0	131.1	122	6	72	1	8	102	3	3	5	4	61	52	8	7	.533	0	3.56
89	LON/EAS	AA	20	513	20	3	1	0	122.0	98	11	59	0	5	97	3	3	9	2	55	52	10	6	.625	0	3.84
90	TOL/INT	AAA	29	687	29	2	0	0	158.0	145	16	81	1	4	133	2	10	9	4	93	86	6	15	.286	0	4.90
	DET/AL		4	63	3	0	0	0	14.1	13	0	10	1	1	7	2	1	0	0	6	6	1	2	.333	0	3.77
91	DET/AL		11	253	11	1	0	0	57.1	58	9	30	2	0	35	3	2	3	1	37	33	2	4	.333	0	5.18
	TOL/INT	AAA	22	581	20	2	0	2	135.1	127	7	72	1	4	95	8	3	4	0	65	59	8	8	.500	1	3.92
2 YR TOTALS			**15**	**316**	**14**	**1**	**0**	**0**	**71.2**	**71**	**9**	**40**	**3**	**1**	**42**	**5**	**3**	**3**	**1**	**43**	**39**	**3**	**6**	**.333**	**0**	**4.90**

Alexander, Gerald Paul — bats right — throws right — b.3/26/68

YR	TM/LG	CL	G	TBF	GS	CG	SHO	GF	IP	H	HR	BB	IBB	HB	SO	SH	SF	WP	BK	R	ER	W	L	PCT	SV	ERA
89	RAN/GCL	R	6	19	0	0	0	5	6.1	3	0	0	0	0	9	0	0	0	0	0	0	0	0	.000	4	0.00
	CHA/FSL	A+	14	215	6	0	0	5	53.0	36	1	16	0	2	41	2	1	5	0	12	10	2	3	.400	2	1.70
90	CHA/FSL	A+	7	163	7	0	0	0	42.2	24	0	14	0	1	39	0	0	2	0	7	3	6	1	.857	0	0.63
	OC/AMA	AAA	20	510	20	2	1	0	118.2	126	6	45	0	3	94	2	4	6	1	58	54	13	2	.867	0	4.10
	TEX/AL		3	39	2	0	0	1	7.0	14	0	5	0	1	8	0	1	0	0	6	6	0	0	.000	0	7.71
91	OC/AMA	AAA	2	46	2	0	0	0	10.2	10	0	4	0	0	10	1	0	0	0	5	5	1	1	.500	0	4.22
	TEX/AL		30	402	9	0	0	4	89.1	93	11	48	7	3	50	6	3	3	1	56	52	5	3	.625	0	5.24
2 YR TOTALS			**33**	**441**	**11**	**0**	**0**	**5**	**96.1**	**107**	**11**	**53**	**7**	**4**	**58**	**6**	**4**	**3**	**1**	**62**	**58**	**5**	**3**	**.625**	**0**	**5.42**

Allison, Dana Eric — bats right — throws left — b.8/14/66

YR	TM/LG	CL	G	TBF	GS	CG	SHO	GF	IP	H	HR	BB	IBB	HB	SO	SH	SF	WP	BK	R	ER	W	L	PCT	SV	ERA
89	MAD/MID	A	13	100	0	0	0	11	24.0	24	0	3	2	0	16	3	0	1	0	6	3	2	3	.400	1	1.13
	SO/NWL	A–	11	108	2	0	0	6	29.1	17	0	4	0	1	27	0	1	2	1	8	6	0	0	.000	4	1.84
90	MOD/CAL	A+	10	76	0	0	0	8	19.1	13	0	3	0	0	19	0	1	0	1	9	5	0	0	.000	4	2.33
	HUN/SOU	AA	35	216	0	0	0	14	52.2	52	2	6	3	0	36	7	2	1	0	14	14	7	1	.875	2	2.39
	TAC/PCL	AAA	2	6	0	0	0	1	1.1	1	0	1	0	0	2	0	0	0	0	0	0	0	0	.000	0	0.00
91	OAK/AL		11	49	0	0	0	4	11.0	16	0	5	1	0	4	1	1	0	0	9	9	1	1	.500	0	7.36
	TAC/PCL	AAA	18	101	0	0	0	4	22.2	25	2	11	2	1	13	2	0	0	1	12	11	3	1	.750	0	4.37

Alvarez, Wilson Eduardo (Fuenmayor) — bats left — throws left — b.3/24/70

YR	TM/LG	CL	G	TBF	GS	CG	SHO	GF	IP	H	HR	BB	IBB	HB	SO	SH	SF	WP	BK	R	ER	W	L	PCT	SV	ERA
87	GAS/SAL	A	8	153	6	0	0	1	32.0	39	5	23	0	4	19	0	1	0	0	24	23	1	5	.167	0	6.47
	RAN/GCL	R	10	193	10	0	0	0	44.2	41	6	21	0	3	46	1	1	3	0	29	26	2	5	.286	0	5.24
88	GAS/SAL	A	23	552	23	1	0	0	127.0	113	5	49	1	7	134	4	6	5	10	63	42	4	11	.267	0	2.98
	OC/AMA	AAA	5	71	3	0	0	0	16.2	17	2	6	0	1	9	0	2	0	0	8	7	1	1	.500	0	3.78
89	CHA/FSL	A+	13	331	13	3	2	0	81.0	68	1	21	0	4	51	3	3	2	1	29	19	7	4	.636	0	2.11
	TUL/TEX	AA	7	196	7	1	1	0	48.0	40	1	16	3	0	29	2	2	1	4	14	11	2	2	.500	0	2.06
	TEX/AL		1	5	1	0	0	0	0.0	3	2	2	0	0	0	0	0	0	0	3	3	0	1	.000	0	0.00
	BIR/SOU	AA	6	149	6	0	0	0	35.2	32	2	16	0	1	18	2	0	1	0	12	12	2	1	.667	0	3.03
90	VAN/PCL	AAA	17	350	15	1	0	0	75.0	91	7	51	0	4	35	2	3	1	0	54	50	7	5	.500	0	6.00
	BIR/SOU	AA	7	204	7	1	0	0	46.1	44	5	25	0	0	36	0	0	2	0	24	22	5	1	.833	0	4.27
91	BIR/SOU	AA	23	634	23	3	2	0	152.1	109	4	74	0	3	165	3	9	9	3	46	31	10	6	.625	0	1.83
	CHI/AL		10	237	10	2	1	0	56.1	47	9	29	0	0	32	3	1	2	0	26	22	3	2	.600	0	3.51
2 YR TOTALS			**11**	**242**	**10**	**2**	**1**	**0**	**56.1**	**50**	**11**	**31**	**0**	**0**	**32**	**3**	**1**	**2**	**0**	**29**	**25**	**3**	**3**	**.500**	**0**	**3.99**

Andersen, Larry Eugene — bats right — throws right — b.5/6/53

YR	TM/LG	CL	G	TBF	GS	CG	SHO	GF	IP	H	HR	BB	IBB	HB	SO	SH	SF	WP	BK	R	ER	W	L	PCT	SV	ERA
75	CLE/AL		3	23	0	0	0	1	5.2	4	0	2	0	0	4	0	1	2	0	3	3	0	0	.000	0	4.76
77	CLE/AL		11	62	0	0	0	7	14.1	10	1	9	3	0	8	3	0	1	0	7	5	0	1	.000	0	3.14
79	CLE/AL		8	77	0	0	0	4	16.2	25	3	4	0	0	7	1	2	0	0	14	14	0	0	.000	0	7.56
81	SEA/AL		41	273	0	0	0	23	67.2	57	4	18	2	2	40	0	3	0	0	27	20	3	3	.500	5	2.66
82	SEA/AL		40	354	1	0	0	14	79.2	100	16	23	1	4	32	2	3	2	0	56	53	0	0	.000	1	5.99
83	PHI/NL		17	106	0	0	0	4	26.1	19	0	9	1	0	14	1	1	1	1	7	7	1	0	1.000	0	2.39
84	PHI/NL		64	376	0	0	0	25	90.2	85	5	25	6	0	54	4	4	2	1	32	24	3	7	.300	4	2.38
85	PHI/NL		57	318	0	0	0	19	73.0	78	5	26	4	3	50	3	1	1	1	41	35	3	3	.500	3	4.32
86	PHI/NL		10	55	0	0	0	1	12.2	19	0	3	0	0	9	2	1	0	0	8	6	0	0	.000	0	4.26
	HOU/NL		38	268	0	0	0	7	64.2	64	2	23	10	1	33	8	4	1	0	22	20	2	1	.667	1	2.78
	YEAR		48	323	0	0	0	8	77.1	83	2	26	10	1	42	10	5	1	0	30	26	2	1	.667	1	3.03
87	HOU/NL		67	440	0	0	0	31	101.2	95	7	41	10	2	94	7	4	1	0	46	39	9	5	.643	5	3.45
88	HOU/NL		53	350	0	0	0	25	82.2	82	3	20	8	1	66	3	3	1	2	29	27	2	4	.333	5	2.94
89	HOU/NL		60	351	0	0	0	21	87.2	63	2	24	4	0	85	4	5	2	1	19	15	4	4	.500	3	1.54
90	HOU/NL		50	301	0	0	0	20	73.2	61	2	24	5	1	68	6	5	2	0	19	16	5	2	.714	6	1.95
	BOS/AL		15	86	0	0	0	4	22.0	18	0	3	0	1	25	0	0	2	0	3	3	0	0	.000	1	1.23
	YEAR		65	387	0	0	0	24	95.2	79	2	27	5	2	93	5	5	4	0	22	19	5	2	.714	7	1.79
91	SD/NL		38	188	0	0	0	24	47.0	39	0	13	3	0	40	4	2	1	0	13	12	3	4	.429	13	2.30
14 YR TOTALS			572	3628	1	0	0	230	866.0	819	50	267	57	15	629	47	39	19	6	346	299	35	34	.507	47	3.11

Anderson, Allan Lee — bats left — throws left — b.1/7/64

YR	TM/LG	CL	G	TBF	GS	CG	SHO	GF	IP	H	HR	BB	IBB	HB	SO	SH	SF	WP	BK	R	ER	W	L	PCT	SV	ERA
84	VIS/CAL	A+	26	0	26	8	5	0	188.2	152	3	105	1	2	151	0	0	8	1	80	60	12	7	.632	0	2.86
85	TOL/INT	AAA	27	753	27	5	0	0	176.0	176	19	79	0	2	94	8	5	4	3	81	67	7	11	.389	0	3.43
86	TOL/INT	AAA	11	298	11	2	0	0	67.0	78	3	31	2	0	37	3	3	3	1	39	34	2	5	.286	0	4.57
	MIN/AL		21	371	10	1	0	3	84.1	106	11	30	3	1	51	2	3	2	2	54	52	3	6	.333	0	5.55
87	MIN/AL		4	61	2	0	0	0	12.1	20	3	10	2	0	10	0	0	0	0	15	15	1	0	1.000	0	10.95
	POR/PCL	AAA	19	456	15	3	0	0	98.0	127	9	49	4	1	45	5	4	5	1	77	61	4	8	.333	0	5.60
88	POR/PCL	AAA	3	58	3	1	0	0	14.1	11	0	5	0	1	9	0	1	0	0	4	2	1	1	.500	0	1.26
	MIN/AL		30	815	30	3	1	0	202.1	199	14	37	1	7	83	3	5	1	4	70	55	16	9	.640	0	2.45
89	MIN/AL		33	846	33	4	1	0	196.2	214	15	53	1	7	69	4	5	5	0	97	83	17	10	.630	0	3.80
90	MIN/AL		31	797	31	5	1	0	188.2	214	20	39	1	5	82	4	8	4	3	106	95	7	18	.280	0	4.53
91	POR/PCL	AAA	5	138	5	2	0	0	32.1	33	2	7	0	2	16	1	0	1	0	15	11	4	1	.800	0	3.06
	MIN/AL		29	584	22	2	0	4	134.1	148	24	42	4	5	51	4	6	3	0	82	74	5	11	.313	0	4.96
6 YR TOTALS			148	3474	128	15	3	7	818.2	901	87	211	12	25	339	17	27	15	9	424	374	49	54	.476	0	4.11

Appier, Robert Kevin "Kevin" — bats right — throws right — b.12/6/67

YR	TM/LG	CL	G	TBF	GS	CG	SHO	GF	IP	H	HR	BB	IBB	HB	SO	SH	SF	WP	BK	R	ER	W	L	PCT	SV	ERA
87	EUG/NWL	A–	15	340	15	0	0	0	77.0	81	2	29	0	2	72	0	1	7	1	43	26	5	2	.714	0	3.04
88	BC/FSL	A+	24	601	24	1	0	0	147.1	134	1	39	5	2	112	4	6	7	4	58	45	10	9	.526	0	2.75
	MEM/SOU	AA	3	75	3	0	0	0	19.2	11	0	7	0	0	18	0	1	1	0	5	4	2	0	1.000	0	1.83
89	KC/AL		6	106	5	0	0	0	21.2	34	0	12	1	0	10	0	3	0	0	22	22	1	4	.200	0	9.14
	OMA/AMA	AAA	22	594	22	3	2	0	139.0	141	6	42	1	2	109	2	4	5	1	70	61	8	8	.500	0	3.95
90	OMA/AMA	AAA	3	69	3	0	0	0	18.0	15	0	3	0	1	17	0	0	0	0	3	3	2	0	1.000	0	1.50
	KC/AL		32	784	24	3	3	1	185.2	179	13	54	2	6	127	5	9	6	1	67	57	12	8	.600	0	2.76
91	KC/AL		34	881	31	6	3	1	207.2	205	13	61	3	2	158	8	6	7	1	97	79	13	10	.565	0	3.42
3 YR TOTALS			72	1771	60	9	6	2	415.0	418	29	127	6	8	295	13	18	13	2	186	158	26	22	.542	0	3.43

Aquino, Luis Antonio (Colon) — bats right — throws right — b.5/19/64

YR	TM/LG	CL	G	TBF	GS	CG	SHO	GF	IP	H	HR	BB	IBB	HB	SO	SH	SF	WP	BK	R	ER	W	L	PCT	SV	ERA
84	KIN/CAR	A+	53	292	0	0	0	42	70.0	50	3	37	4	3	78	7	0	2	1	21	21	5	6	.455	20	2.70
	KNO/SOU	AA	3	19	0	0	0	2	4.0	3	1	3	1	1	7	0	1	0	1	4	4	0	0	.000	0	9.00
85	KNO/SOU	AA	50	336	0	0	0	42	83.0	58	4	32	0	0	82	5	3	1	0	29	24	5	7	.417	20	2.60
86	SYR/INT	AAA	43	351	6	0	0	27	84.1	70	7	34	2	1	60	1	2	5	0	30	27	3	7	.300	10	2.88
	TOR/AL		7	50	0	0	0	1	11.1	14	2	3	1	0	5	1	0	1	0	8	8	1	1	.500	0	6.35
87	SYR/INT	AAA	26	379	11	0	0	6	84.2	75	11	51	1	8	68	1	2	2	1	46	45	6	7	.462	0	4.78
	OMA/AMA	AAA	14	203	4	1	1	5	50.2	42	2	16	1	1	29	2	1	0	0	15	13	3	2	.600	1	2.31
88	OMA/AMA	AAA	25	525	16	1	1	3	129.1	106	3	50	3	3	93	3	3	1	2	43	41	8	3	.727	0	2.85
	KC/AL		7	136	5	1	0	0	29.0	33	1	17	0	1	11	0	1	1	1	15	9	1	0	1.000	0	2.79
89	KC/AL		34	591	16	2	1	7	141.1	148	6	35	4	4	68	2	4	4	0	62	55	6	8	.429	0	3.50
90	KC/AL		20	287	3	1	0	3	68.1	59	6	27	4	4	28	5	2	3	1	25	24	4	1	.800	0	3.16
91	KC/AL		38	661	18	1	1	9	157.0	152	10	47	5	4	80	2	7	1	0	67	60	8	4	.667	0	3.44
5 YR TOTALS			106	1725	42	5	3	22	407.0	406	25	129	16	13	192	9	15	10	2	177	156	20	14	.588	3	3.45

Ard, Broni John "Johnny" — bats right — throws right — b.6/1/67 — System SF/NL

YR	TM/LG	CL	G	TBF	GS	CG	SHO	GF	IP	H	HR	BB	IBB	HB	SO	SH	SF	WP	BK	R	ER	W	L	PCT	SV	ERA
88	ELI/APP	R+	9	242	8	1	1	0	59.1	40	2	26	0	3	71	0	0	1	6	17	13	4	1	.800	0	1.97
	KEN/MID	A	4	90	3	0	0	0	25.2	14	0	4	0	1	16	1	0	1	0	3	3	1	0	1.000	0	1.05
89	VIS/CAL	A+	28	776	28	4	0	0	186.0	155	13	84	0	10	153	2	5	4	4	87	68	13	7	.650	0	3.29
90	ORL/SOU	AA	29	787	29	4	2	0	180.1	167	11	85	0	7	101	5	4	8	2	90	76	12	9	.571	0	3.79
91	PHO/PCL	AAA	10	286	10	1	0	0	62.1	76	6	33	0	2	30	2	1	1	0	42	40	3	5	.375	0	5.78
	SHR/TEX	AA	13	367	13	4	3	0	88.2	77	4	36	0	2	58	2	2	4	1	31	27	9	3	.750	0	2.74

Armstrong, Jack William — bats right — throws right — b.3/7/65

YR	TM/LG	CL	G	TBF	GS	CG	SHO	GF	IP	H	HR	BB	IBB	HB	SO	SH	SF	WP	BK	R	ER	W	L	PCT	SV	ERA
87	BIL/PIO	R+	5	87	4	0	0	0	20.1	16	0	12	0	0	29	1	0	1	0	7	6	2	1	.667	0	2.66
	VER/EAS	AA	5	152	5	2	1	0	35.2	24	0	23	4	1	39	3	2	3	1	12	12	1	2	.333	0	3.03
88	NAS/AMA	AAA	17	476	17	4	1	0	120.0	84	6	38	1	2	116	5	6	3	7	44	40	5	5	.500	0	3.00
	CIN/NL		14	293	13	0	0	0	65.1	63	8	38	2	0	45	4	5	3	2	44	42	4	7	.364	0	5.79
89	NAS/AMA	AAA	25	738	24	12	6	0	182.2	144	10	58	2	6	152	10	2	5	4	63	59	13	9	.591	0	2.91
	CIN/NL		9	187	8	0	0	1	42.2	40	5	21	4	0	23	2	1	0	0	24	22	2	3	.400	0	4.64
90	CIN/NL		29	704	27	2	1	1	166.0	151	9	59	7	6	110	8	5	7	5	72	63	12	9	.571	0	3.42
91	NAS/AMA	AAA	6	143	6	2	0	0	37.1	31	4	5	0	1	28	1	3	0	0	14	11	2	0	1.000	0	2.65
	CIN/NL		27	611	24	1	0	1	139.2	158	25	54	2	2	93	6	9	2	1	90	85	7	13	.350	0	5.48
4 YR TOTALS			**79**	**1795**	**72**	**3**	**1**	**3**	**413.2**	**412**	**47**	**172**	**15**	**8**	**271**	**20**	**20**	**12**	**8**	**230**	**212**	**25**	**32**	**.439**	**0**	**4.61**

Arnsberg, Bradley James "Brad" — bats right — throws right — b.8/20/63

YR	TM/LG	CL	G	TBF	GS	CG	SHO	GF	IP	H	HR	BB	IBB	HB	SO	SH	SF	WP	BK	R	ER	W	L	PCT	SV	ERA
84	GRE/SAL	A	23	652	23	10	4	0	158.2	121	9	59	2	4	112	5	2	10	3	61	52	12	5	.706	0	2.95
85	ALB/EAS	AA	20	553	20	9	2	0	141.1	105	0	35	0	8	82	5	5	3	1	34	25	14	2	.875	0	1.59
86	COL/INT	AAA	28	743	28	6	2	0	177.1	168	15	53	1	1	96	5	7	4	5	106	83	8	12	.400	0	4.21
	NY/AL		2	39	1	0	0	1	8.0	13	1	1	0	0	3	0	0	0	0	3	3	0	0	.000	0	3.38
87	COL/INT	AAA	19	590	19	9	2	0	144.0	140	9	37	1	0	83	3	2	2	1	55	46	12	5	.706	0	2.88
	NY/AL		6	91	2	0	0	2	19.1	22	5	13	3	0	14	0	2	1	0	12	12	1	3	.250	0	5.59
89	OC/AMA	AAA	18	482	18	4	1	0	115.1	117	6	34	1	6	61	2	3	4	6	58	52	6	8	.429	0	4.06
	TEX/AL		16	209	1	0	0	3	48.0	45	6	22	0	3	26	1	1	6	2	27	22	2	1	.667	1	4.13
90	OC/AMA	AAA	14	130	3	0	0	7	29.2	35	4	10	0	1	17	1	1	4	1	19	17	0	4	.000	2	5.16
	TEX/AL		53	277	0	0	0	20	62.2	56	4	33	1	2	44	2	2	8	0	20	15	6	1	.857	5	2.15
91	OC/AMA	AAA	9	38	0	0	0	6	10.2	3	1	3	0	0	10	0	0	0	0	2	2	1	0	1.000	1	1.69
	TEX/AL		9	44	0	0	0	2	9.2	10	5	5	0	0	8	0	0	1	1	9	9	0	1	.000	0	8.38
5 YR TOTALS			**86**	**660**	**4**	**0**	**0**	**28**	**147.2**	**146**	**21**	**74**	**4**	**5**	**95**	**3**	**5**	**16**	**3**	**71**	**61**	**9**	**6**	**.600**	**6**	**3.72**

Ashby, Andrew Jason "Andy" — bats right — throws right — b.7/11/67

YR	TM/LG	CL	G	TBF	GS	CG	SHO	GF	IP	H	HR	BB	IBB	HB	SO	SH	SF	WP	BK	R	ER	W	L	PCT	SV	ERA
86	BEN/NWL	A—	16	0	6	0	0	4	60.0	56	3	34	1	2	45	0	0	3	1	40	33	1	2	.333	2	4.95
87	SPA/SAL	A—	13	301	13	1	0	0	64.1	73	8	38	2	2	52	3	1	9	1	45	40	4	6	.400	0	5.60
	UTI/NYP	A—	13	264	13	0	0	0	60.0	56	3	36	3	1	51	2	1	7	0	38	27	3	7	.300	0	4.05
88	BAT/NYP	A—	6	174	6	2	1	0	44.2	25	3	16	0	1	32	2	0	0	2	11	8	3	1	.750	0	1.61
	SPA/SAL	A	3	68	3	0	0	0	16.2	13	0	7	0	0	16	0	0	2	3	7	5	1	1	.500	0	2.70
89	SPA/SAL	A	17	463	17	3	1	0	106.2	95	8	49	0	5	100	3	0	8	0	48	34	5	9	.357	0	2.87
	CLE/FSL	A+	6	173	6	2	1	0	43.2	28	0	21	0	0	44	1	0	4	1	9	6	1	4	.200	0	1.24
90	REA/EAS	AA	23	591	23	4	1	0	139.2	134	3	48	0	4	94	5	4	10	2	65	53	10	7	.588	0	3.42
91	SCR/INT	AAA	26	691	26	6	3	0	161.1	144	12	60	2	9	113	3	4	6	0	78	62	11	11	.500	0	3.46
	PHI/NL		8	186	8	0	0	0	42.0	41	5	19	0	3	26	1	3	6	0	28	28	1	5	.167	0	6.00

Assenmacher, Paul Andre — bats left — throws left — b.12/10/60

YR	TM/LG	CL	G	TBF	GS	CG	SHO	GF	IP	H	HR	BB	IBB	HB	SO	SH	SF	WP	BK	R	ER	W	L	PCT	SV	ERA
84	DUR/CAR	A+	26	640	24	3	1	1	147.1	153	16	52	0	4	147	11	3	5	1	78	70	6	11	.353	0	4.28
85	DUR/CAR	A+	14	170	0	0	0	11	38.1	38	1	13	4	2	36	6	0	0	0	16	14	3	2	.600	1	3.29
	GRE/SOU	AA	29	212	0	0	0	21	52.2	47	0	11	3	1	59	3	1	1	0	16	15	6	0	1.000	4	2.56
86	ATL/NL		61	287	0	0	0	27	68.1	61	5	26	4	0	56	7	1	2	3	23	19	7	3	.700	7	2.50
87	RIC/INT	AAA	4	107	4	0	0	0	24.2	30	4	8	1	0	21	0	0	1	0	11	10	1	2	.333	0	3.65
	ATL/NL		52	251	0	0	0	10	54.2	58	8	24	4	1	39	2	1	0	0	41	31	1	1	.500	2	5.10
88	ATL/NL		64	329	0	0	0	32	79.1	72	4	32	11	1	71	8	1	7	0	28	27	8	7	.533	5	3.06
89	ATL/NL		49	247	0	0	0	14	57.2	55	2	16	7	1	64	7	2	3	1	26	23	1	3	.250	0	3.59
	CHI/NL		14	84	0	0	0	3	19.0	19	1	12	1	0	15	2	1	0	0	11	11	2	1	.667	0	5.21
	YEAR		63	331	0	0	0	17	76.2	74	3	28	8	1	79	9	3	3	1	37	34	3	4	.429	0	3.99
90	CHI/NL		74	426	0	0	0	21	103.0	90	10	36	8	1	95	10	3	2	0	33	32	7	2	.778	10	2.80
91	CHI/NL		75	427	0	0	0	31	102.2	85	10	31	6	3	117	8	4	4	0	41	37	7	8	.467	15	3.24
6 YR TOTALS			**389**	**2051**	**1**	**0**	**0**	**138**	**484.2**	**440**	**40**	**177**	**41**	**7**	**457**	**44**	**13**	**18**	**4**	**203**	**180**	**33**	**25**	**.569**	**39**	**3.34**

August, Donald Glenn "Don" — bats right — throws right — b.7/3/63

YR	TM/LG	CL	G	TBF	GS	CG	SHO	GF	IP	H	HR	BB	IBB	HB	SO	SH	SF	WP	BK	R	ER	W	L	PCT	SV	ERA
85	COL/SOU	AA	27	752	27	4	2	0	176.1	183	11	49	4	3	78	1	7	9	1	77	58	14	8	.636	0	2.96
86	TUC/PCL	AAA	24	659	24	3	0	0	154.2	166	7	44	4	1	60	3	10	7	1	78	58	8	9	.471	0	3.38
	VAN/PCL	AAA	3	102	3	1	0	0	24.1	26	0	7	1	0	10	0	3	0	0	10	9	2	1	.667	0	3.33
87	DEN/AMA	AAA	28	787	27	8	0	1	179.1	220	16	55	3	5	91	2	6	4	0	124	111	10	9	.526	0	5.57
88	DEN/AMA	AAA	10	302	10	3	0	0	71.2	79	6	14	0	1	58	0	1	2	3	37	28	4	1	.800	0	3.52
	MIL/AL		24	614	22	6	1	0	148.1	137	12	48	6	0	66	4	3	5	0	55	51	13	7	.650	0	3.09
89	DEN/AMA	AAA	4	108	4	0	0	0	23.2	35	3	5	0	1	12	1	0	1	0	18	13	1	1	.500	0	4.94
3:	MIL/AL		31	648	25	2	1	2	142.1	175	17	58	2	2	51	2	7	3	1	93	84	12	12	.500	0	5.31
90	DEN/AMA	AAA	22	553	22	3	1	0	124.0	164	17	27	1	5	67	0	2	1	1	98	93	7	7	.500	0	6.75
	MIL/AL		5	51	0	0	0	1	11.0	13	4	5	0	0	2	2	0	0	0	10	8	0	3	.000	0	6.55
91	DEN/AMA	AAA	1	18	1	0	0	0	5.0	3	0	0	0	0	1	0	0	0	0	0	0	1	0	1.000	0	0.00
	MIL/AL		28	613	23	1	1	3	138.1	166	18	47	2	2	62	9	3	5	0	87	84	9	8	.529	0	5.47
4 YR TOTALS			**88**	**1926**	**70**	**9**	**3**	**6**	**440.0**	**491**	**47**	**158**	**10**	**5**	**181**	**17**	**13**	**15**	**1**	**245**	**227**	**34**	**30**	**.531**	**0**	**4.64**

Austin, James Parker "Jim" — bats right — throws right — b.12/7/63

YR	TM/LG	CL	G	TBF	GS	CG	SHO	GF	IP	H	HR	BB	IBB	HB	SO	SH	SF	WP	BK	R	ER	W	L	PCT	SV	ERA
86	SPO/NWL	A−	28	0	0	0	0	19	59.2	53	1	22	2	1	74	0	0	7	0	24	15	5	4	.556	5	2.26
87	CHS/SAL	A	31	642	21	2	1	3	152.0	138	10	56	2	1	123	4	1	20	1	89	71	7	10	.412	0	4.20
88	RIV/CAL	A+	12	333	12	2	1	0	80.0	65	5	35	0	0	73	2	3	2	0	31	24	6	2	.750	0	2.70
	WIC/TEX	AA	12	313	12	4	1	0	73.0	76	9	23	0	0	52	2	3	10	1	46	39	5	6	.455	0	4.81
89	STO/CAL	A+	7	204	7	0	0	0	48.1	51	3	14	0	0	44	2	1	2	0	19	14	3	3	.500	0	2.61
	EP/TEX	AA	22	406	13	2	0	5	85.0	121	6	34	1	4	69	2	3	4	0	60	55	3	10	.231	1	5.82
90	EP/TEX	AA	38	384	3	0	0	24	92.1	91	5	26	4	1	77	2	3	8	0	36	25	11	3	.786	6	2.44
91	DEN/AMA	AAA	20	184	3	0	0	10	44.0	35	4	24	3	2	37	2	0	1	0	12	12	6	3	.667	3	2.45
	MIL/AL		5	46	0	0	0	1	8.2	8	1	11	1	3	3	2	1	1	0	8	8	0	0	.000	0	8.31

Avery, Steven Thomas "Steve" — bats left — throws left — b.4/14/70

YR	TM/LG	CL	G	TBF	GS	CG	SHO	GF	IP	H	HR	BB	IBB	HB	SO	SH	SF	WP	BK	R	ER	W	L	PCT	SV	ERA
88	PUL/APP	R+	10	249	10	3	2	0	66.0	38	2	19	0	1	80	1	1	5	1	16	11	7	1	.875	0	1.50
89	DUR/CAR	A+	13	337	13	3	1	0	86.2	59	5	20	1	1	90	5	0	4	1	22	14	6	4	.600	0	1.45
	GRE/SOU	AA	13	341	13	1	0	0	84.1	68	3	34	0	1	75	4	1	4	0	32	26	6	3	.667	0	2.77
90	RIC/INT	AAA	13	343	13	3	0	0	82.1	85	7	21	0	2	69	6	2	5	0	35	32	5	5	.500	0	3.50
	ATL/NL		21	466	20	1	1	1	99.0	121	7	45	2	2	75	14	4	5	1	79	62	3	11	.214	0	5.64
91	ATL/NL		35	868	35	3	1	0	210.1	189	21	65	0	3	137	8	4	4	1	89	79	18	8	.692	0	3.38
2 YR TOTALS			56	1334	55	4	2	1	309.1	310	28	110	2	5	212	22	8	9	2	168	141	21	19	.525	0	4.10

Bailes, Scott Alan — bats left — throws left — b.12/18/61

YR	TM/LG	CL	G	TBF	GS	CG	SHO	GF	IP	H	HR	BB	IBB	HB	SO	SH	SF	WP	BK	R	ER	W	L	PCT	SV	ERA
84	NAS/EAS	AA	54	380	1	0	0	34	87.0	80	4	46	10	2	61	6	5	8	0	43	33	6	8	.429	3	3.41
85	NAS/EAS	AA	29	205	0	0	0	20	47.1	45	2	20	2	0	40	1	1	4	0	22	15	3	3	.500	8	2.85
	WAT/EAS	AA	13	334	11	3	1	2	79.0	78	5	23	0	4	53	3	0	4	2	36	23	6	3	.667	1	2.62
86	CLE/AL		62	500	10	0	0	22	112.2	123	12	43	5	1	60	7	4	4	0	70	62	10	10	.500	7	4.95
87	CLE/AL		39	551	17	0	0	15	120.1	145	21	47	1	4	65	4	6	3	0	75	62	7	8	.467	6	4.64
88	CLE/AL		37	617	21	5	2	7	145.0	149	22	46	0	2	53	5	4	2	3	89	79	9	14	.391	0	4.90
89	CLE/AL		34	473	11	0	0	9	113.1	116	7	29	4	3	47	5	5	3	0	57	54	5	9	.357	0	4.28
90	CAL/AL		27	173	0	0	0	6	35.1	46	8	20	1	0	16	1	5	0	0	30	25	2	0	1.000	0	6.37
	EDM/PCL	AAA	9	79	3	0	0	1	18.0	21	3	8	0	0	12	1	2	0	1	13	12	0	1	.000	0	6.00
91	CAL/AL		42	219	0	0	0	14	51.2	41	5	22	5	4	41	3	2	2	0	26	24	1	2	.333	0	4.18
6 YR TOTALS			241	2533	59	5	2	73	578.2	620	75	207	15	15	282	25	26	14	5	347	306	34	43	.442	13	4.76

Ballard, Jeffrey Scott "Jeff" — bats left — throws left — b.8/13/63

YR	TM/LG	CL	G	TBF	GS	CG	SHO	GF	IP	H	HR	BB	IBB	HB	SO	SH	SF	WP	BK	R	ER	W	L	PCT	SV	ERA
85	NEW/NYP	A−	13	381	13	6	3	0	96.0	78	2	20	1	0	91	1	1	1	1	20	15	10	2	.833	0	1.41
86	HAG/CAR	A+	17	466	17	5	2	0	112.0	106	3	32	1	3	115	0	1	3	2	39	23	9	5	.643	0	1.85
	CHA/SOU	AA	10	261	10	0	0	0	59.2	70	7	20	0	1	35	0	0	0	1	29	22	5	2	.714	0	3.32
	ROC/INT	AAA	2	34	2	0	0	0	6.1	11	1	3	0	1	7	0	1	0	0	6	5	0	2	.000	0	7.11
87	ROC/INT	AAA	23	647	23	4	1	0	160.1	151	15	35	2	5	114	3	6	2	0	60	55	13	4	.765	0	3.09
	BAL/AL		14	327	14	0	0	0	69.2	100	15	35	1	0	27	0	1	0	1	60	51	2	8	.200	0	6.59
88	ROC/INT	AAA	9	247	8	3	1	0	60.2	56	4	11	0	1	32	1	1	3	1	26	20	4	3	.571	0	2.97
	BAL/AL		25	654	25	6	1	0	153.1	167	15	42	2	6	41	3	3	2	2	83	75	8	12	.400	0	4.40
89	BAL/AL		35	912	35	4	1	0	215.1	240	16	57	5	4	62	10	5	3	0	95	82	18	8	.692	0	3.43
90	BAL/AL		44	578	17	0	0	6	133.1	152	22	42	6	3	50	5	2	2	1	79	73	2	11	.154	0	4.93
91	ROC/INT	AAA	7	221	7	3	0	0	51.0	63	2	10	0	0	19	1	6	1	0	27	25	3	3	.500	0	4.41
	BAL/AL		26	540	22	0	0	1	123.2	153	16	28	2	3	37	1	3	3	1	91	77	6	12	.333	0	5.60
5 YR TOTALS			144	3011	113	10	2	7	695.1	812	84	204	16	15	217	19	14	10	5	408	358	36	51	.414	0	4.63

Bankhead, Michael Scott "Scott" — bats right — throws right — b.7/31/63

YR	TM/LG	CL	G	TBF	GS	CG	SHO	GF	IP	H	HR	BB	IBB	HB	SO	SH	SF	WP	BK	R	ER	W	L	PCT	SV	ERA
85	MEM/SOU	AA	24	592	24	2	1	0	140.1	117	16	56	0	3	128	0	3	3	0	63	56	8	6	.571	0	3.59
86	OMA/AMA	AAA	7	187	7	2	0	0	48.1	31	2	14	1	0	34	3	0	1	3	11	8	2	2	.500	0	1.49
	KC/AL		24	517	17	0	0	2	121.0	121	14	37	7	3	94	5	5	1	0	66	62	8	9	.471	0	4.61
87	SEA/AL		27	642	25	2	0	1	149.1	168	35	37	0	3	95	3	6	2	2	96	90	9	8	.529	0	5.42
88	SB/CAL	A+	2	43	2	0	0	0	11.0	6	0	4	0	1	6	1	0	0	0	3	2	0	0	.000	0	1.64
	CAL/PCL	AAA	2	51	2	0	0	0	11.0	15	2	5	0	0	5	0	0	0	0	9	9	1	1	.500	0	7.36
	SEA/AL		21	557	21	2	1	0	135.0	115	8	38	5	1	102	3	1	3	0	53	46	7	9	.438	0	3.07
89	SEA/AL		33	862	33	3	2	0	210.1	187	19	63	1	3	140	4	8	2	0	84	78	14	6	.700	0	3.34
90	CAL/PCL	AAA	2	32	2	0	0	0	7.0	9	1	3	0	0	6	0	0	0	0	6	5	0	1	.000	0	6.43
	SEA/AL		4	63	4	0	0	0	13.0	18	2	7	0	0	10	0	2	1	0	16	16	0	2	.000	0	11.08
91	SB/CAL	A+	2	24	2	0	0	0	5.1	4	2	2	0	1	4	0	0	0	0	4	3	0	1	.000	0	5.06
	BEL/NWL	A−	1	14	0	0	0	0	4.0	1	0	0	0	0	8	0	0	0	0	0	0	1	0	1.000	0	0.00
	CAL/PCL	AAA	5	33	0	0	0	0	8.2	7	0	1	0	0	10	0	0	0	0	1	1	0	0	.000	1	1.04
	SEA/AL		17	271	9	0	0	2	60.2	73	8	21	2	2	28	0	2	0	0	35	33	3	6	.333	0	4.90
6 YR TOTALS			126	2912	109	7	3	5	689.1	682	86	203	15	12	469	15	24	9	3	350	325	41	40	.506	0	4.24

Banks, Willie Anthony — bats right — throws right — b.2/27/69

YR	TM/LG	CL	G	TBF	GS	CG	SHO	GF	IP	H	HR	BB	IBB	HB	SO	SH	SF	WP	BK	R	ER	W	L	PCT	SV	ERA
87	ELI/APP	R+	13	332	13	0	0	0	65.2	73	3	62	0	3	71	3	4	28	3	71	51	1	8	.111	0	6.99
88	KEN/MID	A	24	580	24	0	0	0	125.2	109	3	107	2	4	113	2	5	14	2	73	52	10	10	.500	0	3.72
89	VIS/CAL	A+	27	723	27	7	4	0	174.0	122	5	85	0	10	173	2	7	22	1	70	50	12	9	.571	0	2.59

Banks, Willie Anthony (continued)

YR	TM/LG	CL	G	TBF	GS	CG	SHO	GF	IP	H	HR	BB	IBB	HB	SO	SH	SF	WP	BK	R	ER	W	L	PCT	SV	ERA
	ORL/SOU	AA	1	30	1	0	0	0	7.0	10	0	0	0	0	9	0	0	2	0	4	4	1	0	1.000	0	5.14
90	ORL/SOU	AA	28	737	28	1	0	0	162.2	161	15	98	0	7	114	1	8	6	1	93	71	7	9	.438	0	3.93
91	POR/PCL	AAA	25	653	24	1	1	1	146.1	156	6	76	1	6	63	2	4	14	1	81	74	9	8	.529	0	4.55
	MIN/AL		5	85	3	0	0	2	17.1	21	1	12	0	0	16	0	0	3	0	15	11	1	1	.500	0	5.71

Bannister, Floyd Franklin — bats left — throws left — b.6/10/55

YR	TM/LG	CL	G	TBF	GS	CG	SHO	GF	IP	H	HR	BB	IBB	HB	SO	SH	SF	WP	BK	R	ER	W	L	PCT	SV	ERA
77	HOU/NL		24	622	23	4	1	0	142.2	138	11	68	1	4	112	2	4	6	2	70	64	8	9	.471	0	4.04
78	HOU/NL		28	502	16	2	2	3	110.1	120	13	63	4	1	94	7	3	7	2	59	59	3	9	.250	0	4.81
79	SEA/AL		30	792	30	6	2	0	182.1	185	25	68	4	4	115	5	3	1	0	92	82	10	15	.400	0	4.05
80	SEA/AL		32	918	32	8	0	0	217.2	200	24	66	6	2	155	8	5	7	0	96	84	9	13	.409	0	3.47
81	SEA/AL		21	522	20	5	2	0	121.1	128	14	39	0	3	85	2	0	7	1	62	60	9	9	.500	0	4.45
82	SEA/AL		35	1022	35	5	3	0	247.0	225	32	77	0	3	209	10	5	6	0	112	94	12	13	.480	0	3.43
83	CHI/AL		34	902	34	5	2	0	217.1	191	19	71	3	2	193	4	4	8	1	88	81	16	10	.615	0	3.35
84	CHI/AL		34	936	33	4	0	0	218.0	211	30	80	2	6	152	3	10	10	0	127	117	14	11	.560	0	4.83
85	CHI/AL		34	928	34	4	1	0	210.2	211	30	100	5	4	198	9	8	11	0	121	114	10	14	.417	0	4.87
86	CHI/AL		28	688	27	6	1	0	165.1	162	17	48	0	2	92	7	5	5	0	81	65	10	14	.417	0	3.54
87	CHI/AL		34	939	34	11	2	0	228.2	216	38	49	0	0	124	9	1	5	0	100	91	16	11	.593	0	3.58
88	KC/AL		31	816	31	2	0	0	189.1	182	22	68	6	5	113	8	2	6	2	102	91	12	13	.480	0	4.33
89	KC/AL		14	323	14	0	0	0	75.1	87	8	18	1	1	35	2	2	1	0	40	39	4	1	.800	0	4.66
91	CAL/AL		16	104	0	0	0	2	25.0	25	5	10	1	0	16	0	0	1	0	12	11	0	0	.000	0	3.96
	PS/CAL	A+	7	128	5	0	0	1	28.2	32	1	9	1	2	27	1	2	1	0	24	21	0	3	.000	1	6.59
14 YR TOTALS			**395**	**10014**	**363**	**62**	**16**	**5**	**2351.0**	**2281**	**288**	**825**	**33**	**37**	**1693**	**76**	**54**	**81**	**9**	**1162**	**1052**	**133**	**142**	**.484**	**0**	**4.03**

Barfield, John David — bats left — throws left — b.10/15/64

YR	TM/LG	CL	G	TBF	GS	CG	SHO	GF	IP	H	HR	BB	IBB	HB	SO	SH	SF	WP	BK	R	ER	W	L	PCT	SV	ERA
86	DB/FSL	A+	3	69	3	0	0	0	17.1	14	0	1	0	1	13	0	0	0	0	9	8	1	1	.500	0	4.15
	SAL/CAR	A+	13	250	11	0	0	0	56.0	71	7	22	0	1	39	2	0	3	1	43	31	2	5	.286	0	4.98
87	CHA/FSL	A+	25	654	25	3	2	0	153.2	145	3	55	0	3	79	1	8	6	3	75	63	10	7	.588	0	3.69
88	TUL/TEX	AA	24	702	24	5	0	0	169.0	159	8	66	2	3	125	6	2	13	2	69	54	9	9	.500	0	2.88
89	OC/AMA	AAA	28	739	28	7	3	0	175.1	178	14	68	2	2	58	6	6	11	1	93	79	10	8	.556	0	4.06
	TEX/AL		4	52	2	0	0	1	11.2	15	0	4	0	0	9	1	0	1	0	10	8	0	1	.000	0	6.17
90	OC/AMA	AAA	19	182	3	0	0	2	43.1	44	3	21	3	1	25	6	0	0	2	21	17	1	6	.143	1	3.53
	TEX/AL		33	178	0	0	0	10	44.1	42	2	13	3	1	17	3	4	1	1	25	23	4	3	.571	1	4.67
91	TEX/AL		28	361	9	0	0	4	83.1	96	11	22	3	0	27	3	4	0	2	51	42	4	4	.500	1	4.54
3 YR TOTALS			**65**	**591**	**11**	**0**	**0**	**15**	**139.1**	**153**	**13**	**39**	**6**	**1**	**53**	**7**	**8**	**2**	**3**	**86**	**73**	**8**	**8**	**.500**	**2**	**4.72**

Barnes, Brian Keith — bats left — throws left — b.3/25/67

YR	TM/LG	CL	G	TBF	GS	CG	SHO	GF	IP	H	HR	BB	IBB	HB	SO	SH	SF	WP	BK	R	ER	W	L	PCT	SV	ERA
89	JAM/NYP	A−	2	33	2	0	0	0	9.0	4	0	3	0	0	15	0	0	1	1	1	1	1	0	1.000	0	1.00
	WPB/FSL	A+	7	187	7	4	3	0	50.0	25	0	16	0	0	67	3	1	4	0	9	4	4	3	.571	0	0.72
	IND/AMA	AAA	1	24	1	0	0	0	6.0	5	0	2	0	0	5	0	0	0	0	1	1	1	0	1.000	0	1.50
90	JAC/SOU	AA	29	828	28	3	1	0	201.1	144	12	87	2	9	213	7	5	8	1	78	62	13	7	.650	0	2.77
	MON/NL		4	115	4	1	0	0	28.0	25	2	7	0	0	23	2	0	2	0	10	9	1	1	.500	0	2.89
91	WPB/FSL	A+	2	27	2	0	0	0	7.0	3	0	4	0	0	6	0	0	3	0	0	0	0	0	.000	0	0.00
	IND/AMA	AAA	2	44	2	0	0	0	11.0	6	0	8	0	1	10	1	0	0	0	2	2	1	0	1.000	0	1.64
	MON/NL		28	684	27	1	0	0	160.0	135	16	84	2	6	117	9	5	5	1	82	75	5	8	.385	0	4.22
2 YR TOTALS			**32**	**799**	**31**	**2**	**0**	**0**	**188.0**	**160**	**18**	**91**	**2**	**6**	**140**	**11**	**5**	**7**	**1**	**92**	**84**	**6**	**9**	**.400**	**0**	**4.02**

Bautista, Jose Joaquin (Arias) — bats right — throws right — b.7/25/64

YR	TM/LG	CL	G	TBF	GS	CG	SHO	GF	IP	H	HR	BB	IBB	HB	SO	SH	SF	WP	BK	R	ER	W	L	PCT	SV	ERA
81	KIN/APP	R+	13	0	11	3	2	0	66.0	84	0	17	0	0	34	0	0	0	0	54	34	3	6	.333	0	4.64
82	KIN/APP	R+	14	0	4	0	0	0	38.0	61	3	19	0	0	13	0	0	3	1	44	38	0	4	.000	0	9.00
83	MET/GCL	R	13	0	13	2	0	0	81.0	66	2	32	0	0	44	0	0	5	0	31	21	4	3	.571	0	2.33
84	COL/SAL	A	19	544	18	5	3	0	135.0	121	10	35	3	0	96	7	2	3	1	52	47	13	4	.765	0	3.13
85	LYN/CAR	A+	27	674	25	7	3	1	169.0	145	8	33	0	3	109	2	3	3	1	49	44	15	8	.652	1	2.34
86	JAC/TEX	AA	7	109	4	0	0	0	21.2	36	3	8	0	1	13	0	0	1	0	22	20	0	1	.000	0	8.31
	LYN/CAR	A+	18	486	18	5	1	0	118.2	120	12	24	1	3	62	6	4	3	3	58	52	8	8	.500	0	3.94
87	JAC/TEX	AA	28	712	25	2	1	2	169.1	174	9	43	3	4	95	6	3	3	0	76	61	10	5	.667	0	3.24
88	BAL/AL		33	721	25	3	0	5	171.2	171	21	45	2	3	76	2	3	4	5	86	82	6	15	.286	0	4.30
89	ROC/INT	AAA	15	398	13	3	1	1	98.2	84	10	26	1	4	47	3	4	4	2	41	31	4	4	.500	0	2.83
	BAL/AL		15	325	10	0	0	4	78.0	84	17	15	0	1	30	1	1	0	0	46	46	3	4	.429	0	5.31
90	ROC/INT	AAA	27	442	13	3	0	4	108.2	115	10	15	0	4	50	3	5	3	5	51	49	7	8	.467	2	4.06
	BAL/AL		22	112	0	0	0	9	26.2	28	4	7	3	0	15	1	1	2	0	15	12	1	0	1.000	0	4.05
91	OC/AMA	AAA	11	139	12	3	1	0	32.1	38	4	6	0	1	22	1	0	0	0	23	19	2	4	.333	0	5.29
	MIA/FSL	A+	11	293	11	4	3	0	76.1	63	5	11	0	1	69	6	5	4	1	23	23	8	2	.800	0	2.71
	BAL/AL		5	34	0	0	0	3	5.1	13	1	5	0	1	3	0	0	1	0	10	10	0	1	.000	0	16.88
	ROC/INT	AAA	6	56	0	0	0	5	15.1	8	1	3	2	0	7	2	0	0	0	1	1	1	0	1.000	1	0.59
4 YR TOTALS			**75**	**1192**	**35**	**3**	**0**	**21**	**281.2**	**296**	**43**	**72**	**6**	**9**	**124**	**4**	**5**	**7**	**5**	**157**	**150**	**10**	**20**	**.333**	**0**	**4.79**

Beasley, Christopher Charles "Chris" — bats right — throws right — b.6/23/62

YR	TM/LG	CL	G	TBF	GS	CG	SHO	GF	IP	H	HR	BB	IBB	HB	SO	SH	SF	WP	BK	R	ER	W	L	PCT	SV	ERA
84	BAT/NYP	A−	14	399	13	4	1	0	89.2	97	11	33	2	1	70	1	3	8	1	54	40	6	5	.545	0	4.01
85	WAT/MID	A	17	511	17	6	1	0	120.0	110	6	47	2	2	87	3	2	7	1	55	44	6	7	.462	0	3.30

(continued)

Beasley, Christopher Charles "Chris" (continued)

YR	TM/LG	CL	G	TBF	GS	CG	SHO	GF	IP	H	HR	BB	IBB	HB	SO	SH	SF	WP	BK	R	ER	W	L	PCT	SV	ERA
	WAT/EAS	AA	9	238	9	4	0	0	56.0	44	4	35	1	3	27	4	0	1	0	28	26	2	6	.250	0	4.18
86	WAT/EAS	AA	27	675	25	5	2	0	155.2	152	10	67	2	7	105	3	4	10	2	83	66	8	9	.471	0	3.82
87	WIL/EAS	AA	11	316	11	1	0	0	66.1	93	8	30	1	3	37	2	3	5	0	63	49	2	6	.250	0	6.65
	CHT/SOU	AA	14	250	8	0	0	4	56.1	73	4	22	0	1	26	0	2	2	0	33	23	2	4	.333	0	3.67
89	PS/CAL	A+	10	294	10	3	0	0	71.0	60	1	18	0	8	44	1	2	5	1	31	21	4	3	.571	0	2.66
	MID/TEX	AA	16	442	15	4	1	1	104.1	101	2	33	0	4	48	3	4	6	1	53	45	8	4	.667	1	3.88
90	EDM/PCL	AAA	28	792	27	5	0	0	176.1	201	15	70	5	16	108	2	5	5	0	107	88	12	9	.571	0	4.49
91	EDM/PCL	AAA	23	377	10	1	1	3	89.0	99	10	26	3	5	51	1	4	3	0	55	52	3	5	.375	1	5.26
	CAL/AL		22	113	0	0	0	8	26.2	26	2	10	1	1	14	0	1	2	0	14	10	0	1	.000	0	3.38

Beatty, Gordon Blaine "Blaine" — bats left — throws left — b.4/25/64

YR	TM/LG	CL	G	TBF	GS	CG	SHO	GF	IP	H	HR	BB	IBB	HB	SO	SH	SF	WP	BK	R	ER	W	L	PCT	SV	ERA
86	NEW/NYP	A-	15	475	15	8	3	0	119.1	98	6	30	3	1	93	5	2	6	0	37	28	11	3	.786	0	2.11
87	HAG/CAR	A+	13	389	13	4	1	0	100.0	81	7	11	0	1	65	3	1	5	0	32	28	11	1	.917	0	2.52
	CHA/SOU	AA	15	438	15	3	1	0	105.2	110	2	20	2	1	57	1	4	4	0	38	36	6	5	.545	0	3.07
88	JAC/TEX	AA	30	824	28	12	5	1	208.2	191	13	34	3	0	103	12	6	3	7	64	57	16	8	.667	0	2.46
89	TID/INT	AAA	27	764	27	6	3	0	185.0	173	14	43	4	1	90	4	8	3	2	86	68	12	10	.545	0	3.31
	NY/NL		2	25	1	0	0	0	6.0	5	1	2	0	0	3	0	0	0	0	1	1	0	0	.000	0	1.50
91	TID/INT	AAA	28	750	28	3	1	0	175.1	192	18	43	6	5	74	7	4	0	1	86	80	12	9	.571	0	4.11
	NY/NL		5	42	0	0	0	1	9.2	9	0	4	1	0	7	1	1	1	0	3	3	0	0	.000	0	2.79
2 YR TOTALS			7	67	1	0	0	1	15.2	14	1	6	1	0	10	1	1	1	0	4	4	0	0	.000	0	2.30

Beck, Rodney Roy "Rod" — bats right — throws right — b.8/3/68

YR	TM/LG	CL	G	TBF	GS	CG	SHO	GF	IP	H	HR	BB	IBB	HB	SO	SH	SF	WP	BK	R	ER	W	L	PCT	SV	ERA
86	MED/NWL	A-	13	0	6	0	0	5	32.2	47	4	11	1	1	21	0	0	4	0	25	19	1	3	.250	1	5.23
87	MED/NWL	A-	17	431	12	2	0	1	92.0	106	5	26	0	4	69	4	4	12	1	74	53	5	8	.385	0	5.18
88	CLI/MID	A	28	706	23	5	1	1	177.0	177	11	27	2	0	123	4	1	3	5	68	59	12	7	.632	0	3.00
89	SJ/CAL	A+	13	402	13	4	0	0	97.1	91	5	26	0	1	88	1	3	2	1	29	26	11	2	.846	0	2.40
	SHR/TEX	AA	16	416	14	4	1	0	99.0	108	6	16	3	3	74	2	2	3	2	45	39	7	3	.700	0	3.55
90	PHO/PCL	AAA	12	345	12	2	0	0	76.2	100	8	18	1	1	43	2	4	6	0	51	42	4	7	.364	0	4.93
	SHR/TEX	AA	14	366	14	2	1	0	93.0	85	4	17	1	1	71	4	1	7	0	26	23	10	3	.769	0	2.23
91	PHO/PCL	AAA	23	280	5	3	0	14	71.1	56	3	13	2	2	35	2	4	2	0	18	16	4	3	.571	6	2.02
	SF/NL		31	214	0	0	0	10	52.1	53	4	13	2	1	38	4	2	0	0	22	22	1	1	.500	1	3.78

Bedrosian, Stephen Wayne "Steve" — bats right — throws right — b.12/6/57

YR	TM/LG	CL	G	TBF	GS	CG	SHO	GF	IP	H	HR	BB	IBB	HB	SO	SH	SF	WP	BK	R	ER	W	L	PCT	SV	ERA
81	ATL/NL		15	106	1	0	0	5	24.1	15	2	15	2	1	9	0	1	0	0	14	12	1	2	.333	0	4.44
82	ATL/NL		64	567	3	0	0	30	137.2	102	7	57	5	4	123	9	2	0	0	39	37	8	6	.571	11	2.42
83	ATL/NL		70	504	1	0	0	52	120.0	100	11	51	8	4	114	8	4	2	0	50	48	9	10	.474	19	3.60
84	ATL/NL		40	345	4	0	0	28	83.2	65	5	33	5	1	81	1	1	4	0	23	22	9	6	.600	11	2.37
85	ATL/NL		37	907	37	0	0	0	206.2	198	17	111	6	5	134	4	7	6	0	101	88	7	15	.318	0	3.83
86	PHI/NL		68	381	0	0	0	56	90.1	79	12	34	10	0	82	3	3	5	2	39	34	8	6	.571	29	3.39
87	PHI/NL		65	366	0	0	0	56	89.0	79	11	28	5	1	74	2	1	3	1	31	28	5	3	.625	40	2.83
88	MAI/INT	AAA	5	28	0	0	0	2	6.2	6	0	2	0	0	5	0	0	0	2	0	0	0	0	.000	0	0.00
	PHI/NL		57	322	0	0	0	49	74.1	75	6	27	5	0	61	0	3	0	0	34	31	6	6	.500	28	3.75
89	PHI/NL		28	135	0	0	0	27	33.2	21	7	17	1	1	24	0	1	2	0	13	12	2	3	.400	6	3.21
	SF/NL		40	207	0	0	0	33	51.0	35	5	22	4	0	34	1	2	0	0	18	15	1	4	.200	17	2.65
	YEAR		68	342	0	0	0	60	84.2	56	12	39	5	1	58	1	4	2	0	31	27	3	7	.300	23	2.87
90	SF/NL		68	349	0	0	0	53	79.1	72	6	44	9	2	43	3	1	3	0	40	37	9	9	.500	17	4.20
91	MIN/AL		56	332	0	0	0	22	77.1	70	11	35	6	3	44	2	4	2	0	42	38	5	3	.625	6	4.42
11 YR TOTALS			608	4521	46	0	0	411	1067.1	911	100	474	66	22	823	35	31	27	3	444	402	70	73	.490	184	3.39

Belcher, Timothy Wayne "Tim" — bats right — throws right — b.10/19/61

YR	TM/LG	CL	G	TBF	GS	CG	SHO	GF	IP	H	HR	BB	IBB	HB	SO	SH	SF	WP	BK	R	ER	W	L	PCT	SV	ERA
84	MAD/MID	A	16	427	16	3	1	0	98.1	80	6	48	1	8	111	2	5	6	0	45	39	9	4	.692	0	3.57
	ALB/EAS	AA	10	242	10	2	0	0	54.0	37	2	41	0	3	40	0	3	2	1	30	20	3	4	.429	0	3.33
85	HUN/SOU	AA	29	688	26	3	1	1	149.2	145	12	99	0	7	90	0	12	11	2	99	78	11	10	.524	0	4.69
86	HUN/SOU	AA	9	176	9	0	0	0	37.0	50	3	22	1	0	25	0	2	3	0	28	27	2	5	.286	0	6.57
87	TAC/PCL	AAA	29	743	28	2	1	0	163.0	143	8	133	2	1	136	2	6	8	2	89	80	9	11	.450	0	4.42
	LA/NL		6	135	5	0	0	1	34.0	30	2	7	0	0	23	2	1	0	1	11	9	4	2	.667	0	2.38
88	LA/NL		36	719	27	4	1	5	179.2	143	8	51	7	2	152	6	1	4	0	65	58	12	6	.667	4	2.91
89	LA/NL		39	937	30	10	8	6	230.0	182	20	80	5	7	200	6	6	7	2	81	72	15	12	.556	1	2.82
90	LA/NL		24	627	24	5	2	0	153.0	136	17	48	2	6	102	5	6	6	1	76	68	9	9	.500	0	4.00
91	LA/NL		33	880	33	2	1	0	209.1	189	10	75	3	2	156	11	3	7	0	76	61	10	9	.526	0	2.62
5 YR TOTALS			138	3298	119	21	12	12	806.0	680	57	261	15	13	633	30	17	24	4	309	268	50	38	.568	5	2.99

Belinda, Stanley Peter "Stan" — bats right — throws right — b.8/6/66

YR	TM/LG	CL	G	TBF	GS	CG	SHO	GF	IP	H	HR	BB	IBB	HB	SO	SH	SF	WP	BK	R	ER	W	L	PCT	SV	ERA
86	PIR/GCL	R	17	84	0	0	0	15	20.1	23	1	2	0	1	17	1	2	0	0	12	6	3	2	.600	7	2.66
	WAT/NYP	A-	5	29	0	0	0	5	8.0	5	1	2	0	0	5	0	0	0	0	3	3	0	0	.000	2	3.38
87	MAC/SAL	A	50	329	0	0	0	45	82.0	59	4	27	1	4	75	3	5	4	0	26	19	6	4	.600	16	2.09
88	SAL/CAR	A+	53	308	0	0	0	42	71.2	54	9	32	4	2	63	4	3	4	0	33	22	6	4	.600	14	2.76
89	HAR/EAS	AA	32	171	0	0	0	28	38.2	32	1	25	1	1	33	1	4	2	2	13	10	1	4	.200	13	2.33
	BUF/AMA	AAA	19	114	0	0	0	15	28.1	13	1	13	3	2	28	3	1	1	1	5	3	2	2	.500	9	0.95

Belinda, Stanley Peter "Stan" (continued)

YR	TM/LG	CL	G	TBF	GS	CG	SHO	GF	IP	H	HR	BB	IBB	HB	SO	SH	SF	WP	BK	R	ER	W	L	PCT	SV	ERA
	PIT/NL		8	46	0	0	0	2	10.1	13	0	2	0	1	10	0	0	1	0	8	7	0	1	.000	0	6.10
90	BUF/AMA	AAA	15	96	0	0	0	10	23.2	20	1	8	1	1	25	2	1	0	1	8	5	3	1	.750	5	1.90
	PIT/NL		55	245	0	0	0	17	58.1	48	4	29	3	1	55	2	2	1	0	23	23	3	4	.429	8	3.55
91	PIT/NL		60	318	0	0	0	37	78.1	50	10	35	4	4	71	4	3	2	0	30	30	7	5	.583	16	3.45
3 YR TOTALS			**123**	**609**	**0**	**0**	**0**	**56**	**147.0**	**111**	**14**	**66**	**7**	**5**	**136**	**6**	**5**	**4**	**0**	**61**	**60**	**10**	**10**	**.500**	**24**	**3.67**

Bell, Eric Alvin — bats left — throws left — b.10/27/63

YR	TM/LG	CL	G	TBF	GS	CG	SHO	GF	IP	H	HR	BB	IBB	HB	SO	SH	SF	WP	BK	R	ER	W	L	PCT	SV	ERA
82	BLU/APP	R+	11	0	9	0	0	0	51.0	42	2	36	0	2	30	0	0	2	0	19	12	4	1	.800	0	2.12
83	NEW/NYP	A–	18	0	5	2	0	0	60.0	71	5	30	0	1	56	0	0	4	0	44	33	3	2	.600	6	4.95
84	HAG/CAR	A+	3	23	1	0	0	0	3.2	6	0	5	0	1	6	0	1	0	0	4	4	0	0	.000	0	9.82
	NEW/NYP	A–	15	424	15	4	1	0	102.1	82	6	26	0	2	114	2	2	8	1	40	28	8	3	.727	0	2.46
85	HAG/CAR	A+	26	664	26	5	2	0	158.1	141	7	63	0	1	162	3	3	4	0	73	55	11	6	.647	0	3.13
	BAL/AL		4	24	0	0	0	3	5.2	4	1	4	0	0	4	0	0	0	0	3	3	0	0	.000	0	4.76
86	CHA/SOU	AA	18	539	18	6	1	0	129.2	109	7	66	0	1	104	3	1	5	0	49	44	9	6	.600	0	3.05
	ROC/INT	AAA	11	323	11	4	0	0	76.2	68	3	35	1	0	59	0	1	7	0	26	26	7	3	.700	0	3.05
	BAL/AL		4	105	4	0	0	0	23.1	23	4	14	0	0	18	1	1	0	0	14	13	1	2	.333	0	5.01
87	BAL/AL		33	729	29	2	0	1	165.0	174	32	78	0	2	111	4	2	11	1	113	100	10	13	.435	0	5.45
88	ROC/INT	AAA	7	148	7	0	0	0	36.1	28	0	13	0	0	33	3	1	1	2	10	8	3	1	.750	0	1.98
89	HAG/EAS	AA	9	170	7	0	0	1	43.0	32	3	11	1	1	35	1	0	0	1	11	9	4	2	.667	1	1.88
	ROC/INT	AAA	7	172	7	0	0	0	39.2	40	5	15	0	0	27	1	2	4	2	24	22	1	2	.333	0	4.99
90	ROC/INT	AAA	27	667	27	3	0	0	148.0	168	16	65	0	9	90	4	8	11	1	90	80	9	6	.600	0	4.86
91	CAN/EAS	AA	18	402	16	1	0	0	93.1	82	3	37	1	2	84	3	5	6	0	47	30	9	5	.643	0	2.89
	CS/PCL	AAA	4	108	4	1	1	0	25.1	23	1	11	1	0	16	1	0	1	0	6	6	2	1	.667	0	2.13
	CLE/AL		10	61	0	0	0	3	18.0	5	0	5	0	1	7	0	0	0	0	2	1	4	0	1.000	0	0.50
4 YR TOTALS			**51**	**919**	**33**	**2**	**0**	**7**	**212.0**	**206**	**37**	**101**	**0**	**3**	**140**	**5**	**3**	**11**	**1**	**132**	**117**	**15**	**15**	**.500**	**0**	**4.97**

Benes, Andrew Charles "Andy" — bats right — throws right — b.8/20/67

YR	TM/LG	CL	G	TBF	GS	CG	SHO	GF	IP	H	HR	BB	IBB	HB	SO	SH	SF	WP	BK	R	ER	W	L	PCT	SV	ERA
89	WIC/TEX	AA	16	437	16	5	3	0	108.1	79	6	39	1	2	115	5	2	1	2	32	26	8	4	.667	0	2.16
	LV/PCL	AAA	5	133	5	0	0	0	26.2	41	8	12	0	0	29	2	0	2	2	29	24	2	1	.667	0	8.10
	SD/NL		10	280	10	0	0	0	66.2	51	7	31	0	1	66	6	2	0	3	28	26	6	3	.667	0	3.51
90	SD/NL		32	811	31	2	0	1	192.1	177	18	69	5	1	140	5	6	2	5	87	77	10	11	.476	0	3.60
91	SD/NL		33	908	33	4	1	0	223.0	194	23	59	7	4	167	5	4	3	4	76	75	15	11	.577	0	3.03
3 YR TOTALS			**75**	**1999**	**74**	**6**	**1**	**1**	**482.0**	**422**	**48**	**159**	**12**	**6**	**373**	**16**	**12**	**5**	**12**	**191**	**178**	**31**	**25**	**.554**	**0**	**3.32**

Berenguer, Juan Bautista — bats right — throws right — b.11/30/54

YR	TM/LG	CL	G	TBF	GS	CG	SHO	GF	IP	H	HR	BB	IBB	HB	SO	SH	SF	WP	BK	R	ER	W	L	PCT	SV	ERA
78	NY/NL		5	65	3	0	0	1	13.0	17	1	11	0	1	8	0	1	0	0	12	12	0	2	.000	0	8.31
79	NY/NL		5	126	5	0	0	0	30.2	28	2	12	0	1	25	1	1	0	2	13	10	1	1	.500	0	2.93
80	NY/NL		6	46	0	0	0	4	9.1	9	1	10	2	0	7	0	0	0	0	9	6	0	1	.000	0	5.79
81	KC/AL		8	97	3	0	0	4	19.2	22	4	16	0	2	20	0	3	1	0	21	19	0	0	.000	0	8.69
	TOR/AL		12	308	11	1	0	0	71.0	62	7	35	1	3	29	2	4	1	0	41	34	2	9	.182	0	4.31
	YEAR		20	405	14	1	0	0	90.2	84	11	51	1	5	49	2	7	2	0	62	53	2	13	.133	0	5.26
82	DET/AL		2	34	1	0	0	0	6.2	5	0	9	1	0	6	0	0	0	0	5	5	0	0	.000	0	6.75
83	DET/AL		37	650	19	2	1	7	157.2	110	19	71	3	6	129	1	2	3	1	58	55	9	5	.643	1	3.14
84	DET/AL		31	720	27	2	1	0	168.1	146	14	79	2	5	118	2	6	7	2	75	65	11	10	.524	0	3.48
85	DET/AL		31	424	13	0	0	9	95.0	96	12	48	3	1	82	1	4	4	1	67	59	5	6	.455	0	5.59
86	SF/NL		46	314	4	0	0	17	73.1	64	4	44	3	2	72	5	2	4	0	23	22	2	3	.400	4	2.70
87	MIN/AL		47	473	6	0	0	13	112.0	100	10	47	7	0	110	2	4	6	0	51	49	8	1	.889	4	3.94
88	MIN/AL		57	428	1	0	0	27	100.0	74	7	61	7	1	99	5	4	3	5	44	44	8	4	.667	3	3.96
89	MIN/AL		56	452	0	0	0	17	106.0	96	11	47	0	2	93	7	5	5	3	44	41	9	3	.750	3	3.48
90	MIN/AL		51	434	0	0	0	13	100.1	85	9	58	4	2	77	5	2	5	0	43	38	8	5	.615	0	3.41
91	ATL/NL		49	255	0	0	0	35	64.1	43	5	20	2	3	53	2	2	0	0	18	16	0	3	.000	17	2.24
14 YR TOTALS			**443**	**4826**	**93**	**5**	**2**	**147**	**1127.1**	**957**	**106**	**568**	**35**	**29**	**930**	**30**	**39**	**39**	**16**	**524**	**475**	**63**	**57**	**.525**	**31**	**3.79**

Bielecki, Michael Joseph "Mike" — bats right — throws right — b.7/31/59

YR	TM/LG	CL	G	TBF	GS	CG	SHO	GF	IP	H	HR	BB	IBB	HB	SO	SH	SF	WP	BK	R	ER	W	L	PCT	SV	ERA
84	HAW/PCL	AAA	28	0	28	9	2	0	187.2	162	11	88	2	2	162	0	0	4	3	70	62	19	3	.864	0	2.97
	PIT/NL		4	17	0	0	0	1	4.1	4	0	0	0	0	1	1	0	0	1	0	0	0	0	.000	0	0.00
85	HAW/PCL	AAA	20	0	20	2	0	0	129.1	117	13	56	1	1	111	0	0	6	1	58	55	8	6	.571	0	3.83
	PIT/NL		12	211	7	0	0	1	45.2	45	5	31	1	1	22	4	0	1	1	26	23	2	3	.400	0	4.53
86	PIT/NL		31	667	27	0	0	0	148.2	149	16	83	3	8	83	7	6	11	5	87	77	6	11	.353	0	4.66
87	VAN/PCL	AAA	26	802	26	3	3	0	181.0	194	12	78	3	5	140	8	5	12	2	89	76	12	10	.545	0	3.78
	PIT/NL		8	192	8	2	0	0	45.2	43	6	12	0	1	25	5	2	3	0	25	24	2	3	.400	0	4.73
88	IOW/AMA	AAA	23	212	3	1	1	12	54.2	34	3	20	1	2	50	2	0	0	1	19	16	3	2	.600	5	2.63
	CHI/NL		19	215	5	0	0	7	48.1	55	4	16	1	0	33	1	4	3	3	22	18	2	2	.500	0	3.35
89	CHI/NL		33	882	33	4	3	0	212.1	187	16	81	8	0	147	9	3	9	4	82	74	18	7	.720	0	3.14
90	CHI/NL		36	749	29	0	0	6	168.0	188	13	70	11	5	103	16	4	11	0	101	92	8	11	.421	0	4.93
91	CHI/NL		39	718	25	0	0	8	172.0	169	18	54	6	2	72	10	6	6	0	91	86	13	11	.542	0	4.50
	ATL/NL		2	9	0	0	0	1	1.2	2	0	2	0	0	3	0	0	0	0	0	0	0	0	.000	0	0.00
	YEAR		41	727	25	0	0	9	173.2	171	18	56	6	2	75	10	6	6	0	91	86	13	11	.542	0	4.46
8 YR TOTALS			**184**	**3660**	**134**	**6**	**3**	**24**	**846.2**	**842**	**72**	**349**	**30**	**11**	**489**	**53**	**25**	**40**	**14**	**434**	**394**	**51**	**48**	**.515**	**1**	**4.19**

Bitker, Joseph Anthony "Joe" — bats right — throws right — b.2/12/64

YR	TM/LG	CL	G	TBF	GS	CG	SHO	GF	IP	H	HR	BB	IBB	HB	SO	SH	SF	WP	BK	R	ER	W	L	PCT	SV	ERA
84	SPO/NWL	A–	14	0	14	2	0	0	87.0	85	2	33	0	2	60	0	0	8	0	48	33	4	4	.500	0	3.41
85	CHA/SAL	A	13	380	13	6	4	0	90.1	74	3	31	0	2	85	4	3	3	3	35	26	9	3	.750	0	2.59
	BEA/TEX	AA	15	422	14	4	1	0	98.0	91	3	41	2	2	64	3	4	3	1	43	34	8	1	.889	0	3.12
86	BEA/TEX	AA	18	497	17	2	2	1	114.2	114	2	52	4	6	91	5	4	4	1	55	45	7	7	.500	0	3.53
	LV/PCL	AAA	5	112	4	0	0	0	27.1	24	3	9	0	2	19	2	0	4	0	10	10	2	0	1.000	0	3.29
87	LV/PCL	AAA	36	736	27	3	0	2	160.1	184	14	79	1	7	80	9	3	9	1	97	86	11	9	.550	1	4.83
88	LV/PCL	AAA	28	769	27	3	1	0	178.1	195	11	41	3	4	106	7	10	4	4	98	71	8	10	.444	0	3.58
89	LV/PCL	AAA	18	104	0	0	0	10	22.2	29	1	8	1	0	11	2	1	1	1	12	10	0	1	.000	2	3.97
	TAC/PCL	AAA	24	207	2	0	0	6	51.0	38	3	12	1	3	37	3	0	3	0	26	20	3	3	.500	1	3.53
90	OAK/AL		1	10	0	0	0	1	3.0	1	0	1	0	0	2	0	0	0	0	0	0	0	0	.000	0	0.00
	TAC/PCL	AAA	48	235	0	0	0	43	56.1	51	6	20	0	0	52	3	1	2	0	22	20	2	3	.400	26	3.20
	TEX/AL		5	38	0	0	0	4	9.0	7	0	3	0	1	6	0	1	0	0	3	3	0	0	.000	0	3.00
	YEAR		6	48	0	0	0	5	12.0	8	0	4	0	1	8	0	1	0	0	3	3	0	0	.000	0	2.25
91	TEX/AL		9	70	0	0	0	2	14.2	17	4	8	3	0	16	0	0	2	0	11	11	1	0	1.000	0	6.75
	OC/AMA	AAA	23	115	0	0	0	20	26.2	30	1	9	2	0	33	1	0	1	0	16	12	0	5	.000	7	4.05
2 YR TOTALS			**15**	**118**	**0**	**0**	**0**	**7**	**26.2**	**25**	**4**	**12**	**3**	**1**	**24**	**0**	**1**	**2**	**0**	**14**	**14**	**1**	**0**	**1.000**	**0**	**4.72**

Black, Harry Ralston "Bud" — bats left — throws left — b.6/30/57

YR	TM/LG	CL	G	TBF	GS	CG	SHO	GF	IP	H	HR	BB	IBB	HB	SO	SH	SF	WP	BK	R	ER	W	L	PCT	SV	ERA
81	SEA/AL		2	7	0	0	0	0	1.0	2	0	3	1	0	0	0	0	1	0	0	0	0	0	.000	0	0.00
82	KC/AL		22	386	14	0	0	2	88.1	92	10	34	6	3	40	4	3	4	7	48	45	4	6	.400	0	4.58
83	KC/AL		24	672	24	3	0	0	161.1	159	19	43	1	2	58	4	5	4	0	75	68	10	7	.588	0	3.79
84	KC/AL		35	1045	35	8	1	0	257.0	226	22	64	2	4	140	6	1	2	2	99	89	17	12	.586	0	3.12
85	KC/AL		33	885	33	5	2	0	205.2	216	17	59	4	8	122	8	4	9	1	111	99	10	15	.400	0	4.33
86	KC/AL		56	503	4	0	0	26	121.0	100	14	43	5	7	68	4	4	2	2	49	43	5	10	.333	9	3.20
87	KC/AL		29	520	18	0	0	4	122.1	126	16	35	2	5	61	1	3	6	0	63	49	8	6	.571	1	3.60
88	KC/AL		17	98	0	0	0	5	22.0	23	2	11	2	0	19	1	0	0	2	12	12	2	1	.667	0	4.91
	WIL/EAS	AA	1	15	1	0	0	0	5.0	0	0	0	0	0	0	0	0	0	0	0	0	1	0	1.000	0	0.00
	CLE/AL		16	260	7	0	0	4	59.0	59	6	23	1	4	44	5	3	5	0	35	33	2	3	.400	1	5.03
	YEAR		33	358	7	0	0	9	81.0	82	8	34	3	4	63	6	3	5	6	47	45	4	4	.500	1	5.00
89	CLE/AL		33	912	32	6	3	0	222.1	213	14	52	0	1	88	9	5	13	5	95	83	12	11	.522	0	3.36
90	CLE/AL		29	796	29	5	2	0	191.0	171	17	58	1	4	103	4	5	6	1	79	75	11	10	.524	0	3.53
	TOR/AL		3	61	2	0	0	1	15.2	10	2	3	0	1	3	2	2	0	0	7	7	2	1	.667	0	4.02
	YEAR		32	857	31	5	2	1	206.2	181	19	61	1	5	106	6	7	6	1	86	82	13	11	.542	0	3.57
91	SF/NL		34	893	34	3	3	0	214.1	201	25	71	8	4	104	11	7	6	6	104	95	12	16	.429	0	3.99
11 YR TOTALS			**333**	**7038**	**232**	**30**	**11**	**42**	**1681.0**	**1598**	**164**	**499**	**33**	**43**	**850**	**59**	**42**	**58**	**30**	**777**	**698**	**95**	**98**	**.492**	**11**	**3.74**

Blair, William Allen "Willie" — bats right — throws right — b.12/18/65

YR	TM/LG	CL	G	TBF	GS	CG	SHO	GF	IP	H	HR	BB	IBB	HB	SO	SH	SF	WP	BK	R	ER	W	L	PCT	SV	ERA
86	ST./NYP	A–	21	204	0	0	0	18	53.2	32	1	20	1	0	55	1	0	3	0	10	10	5	0	1.000	12	1.68
87	DUN/FSL	A+	50	375	0	0	0	45	85.1	99	5	29	0	1	72	5	6	9	0	51	42	2	9	.182	13	4.43
88	DUN/FSL	A+	4	26	0	0	0	1	6.2	5	0	4	1	0	5	1	0	2	0	2	2	2	0	1.000	0	2.70
	KNO/SOU	AA	34	429	9	0	0	14	102.0	94	7	35	2	4	76	1	5	4	2	49	41	5	5	.500	3	3.62
89	SYR/INT	AAA	19	451	17	3	1	2	106.2	94	10	38	1	2	76	2	2	1	2	55	47	5	6	.455	0	3.97
90	SYR/INT	AAA	3	83	3	0	0	0	19.0	20	1	8	1	0	6	1	1	0	0	13	10	0	2	.000	0	4.74
	TOR/AL		27	297	6	0	0	8	68.2	66	4	28	4	1	43	0	4	3	0	33	31	3	5	.375	0	4.06
91	CS/PCL	AAA	26	496	15	0	0	10	113.2	130	10	30	2	2	57	3	3	3	1	74	63	9	6	.600	4	4.99
	CLE/AL		11	168	5	0	0	1	36.0	58	7	10	0	1	13	1	2	1	0	27	27	2	3	.400	0	6.75
2 YR TOTALS			**38**	**465**	**11**	**0**	**0**	**9**	**104.2**	**124**	**11**	**38**	**4**	**2**	**56**	**1**	**6**	**4**	**0**	**60**	**58**	**5**	**8**	**.385**	**0**	**4.99**

Blyleven, Rik Aalbert "Bert" — bats right — throws right — b.4/6/51

YR	TM/LG	CL	G	TBF	GS	CG	SHO	GF	IP	H	HR	BB	IBB	HB	SO	SH	SF	WP	BK	R	ER	W	L	PCT	SV	ERA
70	MIN/AL		27	675	25	5	1	1	164.0	143	17	47	6	2	135	8	2	2	3	66	58	10	9	.526	0	3.18
71	MIN/AL		38	1126	38	17	5	0	278.1	267	21	59	1	5	224	12	3	5	1	95	87	16	15	.516	0	2.81
72	MIN/AL		39	1158	38	11	3	1	287.1	247	22	69	7	10	228	14	6	7	1	93	87	17	17	.500	0	2.73
73	MIN/AL		40	1321	40	25	9	0	325.0	296	16	67	4	9	258	11	13	7	2	109	91	20	17	.541	0	2.52
74	MIN/AL		37	1149	37	19	3	0	281.0	244	14	77	3	9	249	13	5	3	0	99	83	17	17	.500	0	2.66
75	MIN/AL		35	1104	35	20	3	0	275.2	219	24	84	2	4	233	10	8	7	0	104	92	15	10	.600	0	3.00
76	MIN/AL		12	406	12	4	0	0	95.1	101	3	35	5	4	75	7	3	0	2	39	33	4	5	.444	0	3.12
	TEX/AL		24	819	24	14	6	0	202.1	182	11	46	1	8	144	11	3	7	0	67	62	9	11	.450	0	2.76
	YEAR		36	1225	36	18	6	0	297.2	283	14	81	6	12	219	18	6	7	2	106	95	13	16	.448	0	2.87
77	TEX/AL		30	935	30	15	5	0	234.2	181	20	69	1	7	182	10	5	6	0	81	71	14	12	.538	0	2.72
78	PIT/NL		34	1011	34	11	4	0	243.2	217	17	66	5	6	182	13	2	6	2	94	82	14	10	.583	0	3.03
79	PIT/NL		37	1018	37	4	0	0	237.1	238	21	92	8	6	172	14	9	9	0	102	95	12	5	.706	0	3.60
80	PIT/NL		34	907	32	5	2	1	216.2	219	20	59	5	0	168	10	2	2	1	102	92	8	13	.381	0	3.82
81	CLE/AL		20	644	20	9	1	0	159.1	145	9	40	1	5	107	3	3	3	1	52	51	11	7	.611	0	2.88
82	CLE/AL		4	89	4	0	0	0	20.1	16	2	11	0	0	19	0	2	0	0	14	11	2	2	.500	0	4.87
83	CLE/AL		24	660	24	5	0	0	156.1	160	8	44	4	10	123	2	5	5	1	74	68	7	10	.412	0	3.91
84	CLE/AL		33	1004	32	12	4	0	245.0	204	19	74	4	6	170	6	8	6	0	86	78	19	7	.731	0	2.87
85	CLE/AL		23	743	23	15	4	0	179.2	163	14	49	1	7	129	4	4	1	0	76	65	9	11	.450	0	3.26
	MIN/AL		14	460	14	9	1	0	114.0	101	9	26	0	2	77	1	4	3	0	45	38	8	5	.615	0	3.00
	YEAR		37	1203	37	24	5	0	293.2	264	23	75	1	9	206	5	8	4	1	121	103	17	16	.515	0	3.16
86	MIN/AL		36	1126	36	16	3	0	271.2	262	50	58	4	10	215	5	4	4	0	134	121	17	14	.548	0	4.01
87	MIN/AL		37	1122	37	8	1	0	267.0	249	46	101	4	9	196	4	6	13	0	132	119	15	12	.556	0	4.01

Blyleven, Rik Aalbert "Bert" (continued)

YR	TM/LG	CL	G	TBF	GS	CG	SHO	GF	IP	H	HR	BB	IBB	HB	SO	SH	SF	WP	BK	R	ER	W	L	PCT	SV	ERA
88	MIN/AL		33	895	33	7	0	0	207.1	240	21	51	1	16	145	6	6	5	3	128	125	10	17	.370	0	5.43
89	CAL/AL		33	973	33	8	5	0	241.0	225	14	44	2	8	131	7	7	2	0	76	73	17	5	.773	0	2.73
90	CAL/AL		23	578	23	2	0	0	134.0	163	15	25	0	7	69	2	6	6	0	85	78	8	7	.533	0	5.24
21 YR TOTALS			667	19923	661	241	60	3	4837.0	4482	413	1293	69	150	3631	173	116	111	18	1953	1760	279	238	.540	0	3.27

Boddicker, Michael James "Mike" — bats right — throws right — b.8/23/57

YR	TM/LG	CL	G	TBF	GS	CG	SHO	GF	IP	H	HR	BB	IBB	HB	SO	SH	SF	WP	BK	R	ER	W	L	PCT	SV	ERA
80	BAL/AL		1	34	1	0	0	0	7.1	6	1	5	0	0	4	0	0	0	0	6	5	0	1	.000	0	6.14
81	BAL/AL		2	25	0	0	0	1	5.2	6	1	2	0	0	2	0	0	2	0	4	3	0	0	.000	0	4.76
82	BAL/AL		7	110	0	0	0	4	25.2	25	2	12	2	0	20	1	0	1	0	10	10	1	0	1.000	0	3.51
83	BAL/AL		27	711	26	10	5	1	179.0	141	13	52	1	0	120	4	3	5	0	65	55	16	8	.667	0	2.77
84	BAL/AL		34	1051	34	16	4	0	261.1	218	23	81	1	5	128	2	7	6	1	95	81	20	11	.645	0	2.79
85	BAL/AL		32	899	32	9	2	0	203.1	227	13	89	7	5	135	9	2	5	0	104	92	12	17	.414	0	4.07
86	BAL/AL		33	934	33	7	0	0	218.1	214	30	74	4	11	175	3	6	7	0	125	114	14	12	.538	0	4.70
87	BAL/AL		33	950	33	7	2	0	226.0	212	29	78	4	7	152	7	4	10	0	114	105	10	12	.455	0	4.18
88	BAL/AL		21	636	21	4	0	0	147.0	149	14	51	5	11	100	3	8	3	4	72	63	6	12	.333	0	3.86
	BOS/AL		15	365	14	1	1	0	89.0	85	3	26	1	3	56	1	4	3	0	30	26	7	3	.700	0	2.63
	YEAR		36	1001	35	5	1	0	236.0	234	17	77	6	14	156	4	12	6	4	102	89	13	15	.464	0	3.39
89	BOS/AL		34	912	34	3	2	0	211.2	217	19	71	4	10	145	8	10	4	1	101	94	15	11	.577	0	4.00
90	BOS/AL		34	956	34	4	0	0	228.0	225	16	69	6	10	143	3	1	10	0	92	85	17	8	.680	0	3.36
91	KC/AL		30	775	29	1	0	1	180.2	188	13	59	0	13	79	10	1	3	2	89	82	12	12	.500	0	4.08
12 YR TOTALS			303	8358	291	62	16	7	1983.0	1913	177	669	35	75	1259	51	46	58	8	907	815	130	107	.549	0	3.70

Boever, Joseph Martin "Joe" — bats right — throws right — b.10/4/60

YR	TM/LG	CL	G	TBF	GS	CG	SHO	GF	IP	H	HR	BB	IBB	HB	SO	SH	SF	WP	BK	R	ER	W	L	PCT	SV	ERA
84	ARK/TEX	AA	8	56	0	0	0	8	11.0	10	1	12	0	0	12	0	0	1	0	11	10	0	1	.000	3	8.18
	SP/FSL	A+	48	325	0	0	0	38	77.2	52	2	45	0	1	81	1	2	1	1	31	26	6	4	.600	14	3.01
85	ARK/TEX	AA	27	151	0	0	0	20	37.2	21	1	23	4	0	45	3	1	2	0	5	5	3	1	.750	9	1.19
	LOU/AMA	AAA	21	156	0	0	0	13	35.1	28	0	22	0	0	37	0	1	3	1	11	8	3	2	.600	1	2.04
	STL/NL		13	69	0	0	0	5	16.1	17	3	4	1	0	20	1	1	1	0	8	8	0	0	.000	0	4.41
86	LOU/AMA	AAA	51	375	0	0	0	26	88.0	71	1	48	6	2	75	7	5	10	1	25	22	4	5	.444	5	2.25
	STL/NL		11	93	0	0	0	4	21.2	19	2	11	0	0	8	0	0	1	0	5	4	0	1	.000	0	1.66
87	LOU/AMA	AAA	43	263	0	0	0	36	59.0	52	7	27	2	1	79	1	3	1	0	22	22	3	2	.600	21	3.36
	RIC/INT	AAA	6	38	0	0	0	4	9.0	8	0	1	1	0	8	0	1	0	0	1	1	1	0	1.000	1	1.00
	ATL/NL		14	93	0	0	0	10	18.1	29	4	12	1	0	18	1	1	1	0	15	15	1	0	1.000	0	7.36
88	RIC/INT	AAA	48	279	0	0	0	43	71.1	47	5	22	4	1	71	2	2	3	1	17	17	6	3	.667	22	2.14
	ATL/NL		16	70	0	0	0	13	20.1	12	1	1	0	1	7	2	0	0	0	4	4	0	2	.000	1	1.77
89	ATL/NL		66	349	0	0	0	53	82.1	78	6	34	5	1	68	5	0	5	0	37	36	4	11	.267	21	3.94
90	ATL/NL		33	198	0	0	0	21	42.1	40	6	35	10	0	35	2	2	2	0	23	22	1	3	.250	6	4.68
	PHI/NL		34	190	0	0	0	13	46.0	37	0	16	2	0	40	2	0	1	2	12	11	2	3	.400	6	2.15
	YEAR		67	388	0	0	0	34	88.1	77	6	51	12	0	75	4	2	3	2	35	33	3	6	.333	14	3.36
91	PHI/NL		68	431	0	0	0	27	98.1	90	10	54	11	0	89	3	6	6	1	45	42	3	5	.375	0	3.84
7 YR TOTALS			255	1493	0	0	0	146	345.2	322	32	167	30	2	285	16	10	17	3	149	142	11	25	.306	36	3.70

Bohanon, Brian Edward — bats left — throws left — b.8/1/68

YR	TM/LG	CL	G	TBF	GS	CG	SHO	GF	IP	H	HR	BB	IBB	HB	SO	SH	SF	WP	BK	R	ER	W	L	PCT	SV	ERA
87	RAN/GCL	R	5	84	4	0	0	0	21.0	15	1	5	0	0	21	0	0	2	0	13	11	0	2	.000	0	4.71
88	CHA/FSL	A+	2	31	2	0	0	0	6.2	6	0	5	0	0	9	0	0	0	1	4	4	0	0	.000	0	5.40
89	CHA/FSL	A+	11	213	7	0	0	3	54.2	40	1	20	0	2	33	1	1	1	0	16	11	0	3	.000	1	1.81
	TUL/TEX	AA	11	297	11	1	1	0	73.2	59	3	27	0	3	44	3	2	2	1	30	18	5	0	1.000	0	2.20
90	TEX/AL		11	158	6	0	0	0	34.0	40	6	18	0	2	15	0	1	2	1	30	25	0	3	.000	0	6.62
	OC/AMA	AAA	14	135	4	0	0	4	32.0	35	0	8	0	0	22	2	1	2	1	16	13	1	2	.333	1	3.66
91	CHA/FSL	A+	2	47	2	0	0	0	11.2	6	0	4	0	2	7	0	2	1	0	5	5	1	0	1.000	0	3.86
	TUL/TEX	AA	2	54	2	0	0	0	11.2	9	0	11	0	0	6	1	0	0	0	8	3	0	0	.000	0	2.31
	OC/AMA	AAA	7	197	7	0	0	0	46.1	49	2	15	1	0	37	2	2	2	0	19	15	0	4	.000	0	2.91
	TEX/AL		11	273	11	1	0	0	61.1	66	4	23	0	2	34	2	5	3	1	35	33	4	3	.571	0	4.84
2 YR TOTALS			22	431	17	1	0	1	95.1	106	10	41	0	4	49	2	8	4	1	65	58	4	6	.400	0	5.48

Bolton, Rodney Earl — bats right — throws right — b.9/23/68 — System CHI/AL

YR	TM/LG	CL	G	TBF	GS	CG	SHO	GF	IP	H	HR	BB	IBB	HB	SO	SH	SF	WP	BK	R	ER	W	L	PCT	SV	ERA
90	UTI/NYP	A–	6	168	6	1	1	0	44.0	27	0	11	0	3	45	1	0	0	0	4	2	5	1	.833	0	0.41
	SB/MID	A	7	196	7	3	1	0	51.0	34	0	12	1	1	50	1	1	1	1	14	11	5	1	.833	0	1.94
91	SAR/FSL	A+	15	412	15	5	2	0	103.2	81	2	23	0	2	77	5	1	3	1	29	22	7	6	.538	0	1.91
	BIR/SOU	AA	12	360	12	3	2	0	89.0	73	3	21	1	8	57	0	3	3	0	26	16	8	4	.667	0	1.62

Bolton, Thomas Edward "Tom" — bats left — throws left — b.5/6/62

YR	TM/LG	CL	G	TBF	GS	CG	SHO	GF	IP	H	HR	BB	IBB	HB	SO	SH	SF	WP	BK	R	ER	W	L	PCT	SV	ERA
80	ELM/NYP	A–	23	237	1	1	1	15	56.0	43	4	22	0	0	43	1	1	0	0	26	15	6	2	.750	5	2.41
81	WH/FSL	A+	24	420	0	0	0	3	92.0	125	5	41	0	3	47	2	3	1	0	62	46	2	3	.400	0	4.50
82	WH/FSL	A+	28	682	25	4	0	1	163.0	161	8	63	0	4	77	6	4	7	4	67	54	9	8	.529	0	2.98
83	NB/EAS	AA	16	416	16	2	1	0	99.2	93	7	41	0	1	62	1	0	5	0	36	32	7	3	.700	0	2.89
	PAW/INT	AAA	6	144	6	0	0	0	29.0	33	4	25	0	1	20	1	0	1	1	26	21	0	5	.000	0	6.52
84	NB/EAS	AA	33	380	9	0	0	11	87.0	87	5	34	3	4	66	2	3	6	2	54	40	4	4	.444	1	4.14
85	NB/EAS	AA	34	437	10	1	0	14	101.0	106	3	40	1	2	74	5	3	3	2	53	48	5	6	.455	1	4.28

(continued)

Bolton, Thomas Edward "Tom" (continued)

YR	TM/LG	CL	G	TBF	GS	CG	SHO	GF	IP	H	HR	BB	IBB	HB	SO	SH	SF	WP	BK	R	ER	W	L	PCT	SV	ERA
86	PAW/INT	AAA	29	356	7	1	0	11	86.0	80	6	25	2	0	58	9	2	1	1	30	26	3	4	.429	2	2.72
87	PAW/INT	AAA	5	93	4	0	0	1	21.2	25	0	12	1	0	8	0	1	1	0	14	13	2	1	.667	0	5.40
	BOS/AL		29	287	0	0	0	5	61.2	83	5	27	2	2	49	3	3	3	0	33	30	1	0	1.000	0	4.38
88	PAW/INT	AAA	18	81	1	0	0	8	19.1	17	0	10	0	0	15	0	0	2	0	7	6	3	0	1.000	0	2.79
	BOS/AL		28	140	0	0	0	8	30.1	35	1	14	1	0	21	2	1	2	1	17	16	1	3	.250	1	4.75
89	BOS/AL		4	83	4	0	0	0	17.1	21	1	10	1	0	9	0	1	1	0	18	16	0	4	.000	0	8.31
	PAW/INT	AAA	25	606	22	5	2	2	143.1	140	13	47	2	4	99	6	1	0	1	57	46	12	5	.706	1	2.89
90	PAW/INT	AAA	4	50	2	0	0	1	11.2	9	2	7	0	0	8	0	1	2	0	6	5	1	0	1.000	0	3.86
	BOS/AL		21	501	16	3	0	2	119.2	111	6	47	3	3	65	3	5	1	1	46	45	10	5	.667	0	3.38
91	BOS/AL		25	499	19	0	0	4	110.0	136	16	51	2	1	64	2	4	3	0	72	64	8	9	.471	0	5.24
5 YR TOTALS			**107**	**1510**	**39**	**3**	**0**	**19**	**339.0**	**386**	**29**	**149**	**9**	**6**	**208**	**10**	**14**	**10**	**2**	**186**	**171**	**20**	**21**	**.488**	**1**	**4.54**

Bones, Ricardo "Ricky" — bats right — throws right — b.4/7/69

YR	TM/LG	CL	G	TBF	GS	CG	SHO	GF	IP	H	HR	BB	IBB	HB	SO	SH	SF	WP	BK	R	ER	W	L	PCT	SV	ERA
86	SPO/NWL	A–	18	0	9	0	0	4	58.0	63	3	29	1	1	46	0	0	7	2	44	36	1	3	.250	0	5.59
87	CHS/SAL	A	26	729	26	4	1	0	170.1	183	9	45	4	6	130	4	1	5	2	81	69	12	5	.706	0	3.65
88	RIV/CAL	A+	25	742	25	5	2	0	175.1	162	11	64	3	4	129	2	2	14	5	80	71	15	6	.714	0	3.64
89	WIC/TEX	AA	24	611	24	2	0	0	136.1	162	22	47	5	2	88	4	3	7	3	103	87	10	9	.526	0	5.74
90	WIC/TEX	AA	21	591	21	2	1	0	137.0	138	15	45	0	5	96	7	5	6	4	66	53	9	6	.600	0	3.48
	LV/PCL	AAA	5	158	5	0	0	0	36.1	45	2	10	0	1	25	0	3	1	0	17	14	2	1	.667	0	3.47
91	LV/PCL	AAA	23	611	23	1	0	0	136.1	155	10	43	3	4	95	2	4	6	3	90	64	8	6	.571	0	4.22
	SD/NL		11	234	11	0	0	0	54.0	57	3	18	0	0	31	0	4	4	0	33	29	4	6	.400	0	4.83

Bosio, Christopher Louis "Chris" — bats right — throws right — b.4/3/63

YR	TM/LG	CL	G	TBF	GS	CG	SHO	GF	IP	H	HR	BB	IBB	HB	SO	SH	SF	WP	BK	R	ER	W	L	PCT	SV	ERA
84	BEL/MID	A	26	759	26	11	2	0	181.0	159	12	56	0	5	156	4	3	17	4	83	55	17	6	.739	0	2.73
85	EP/TEX	AA	28	780	25	6	1	3	181.1	186	14	49	4	4	155	9	6	4	5	108	77	11	6	.647	2	3.82
86	VAN/PCL	AAA	44	254	0	0	0	34	67.0	47	1	13	4	0	60	1	0	0	0	18	17	7	3	.700	16	2.28
	MIL/AL		10	154	4	0	0	0	34.2	41	9	13	0	0	29	1	0	2	1	27	27	0	4	.000	0	7.01
87	MIL/AL		46	734	19	2	1	8	170.0	187	18	50	3	1	150	3	3	14	2	102	99	11	8	.579	2	5.24
88	DEN/AMA	AAA	2	56	2	1	0	0	14.0	13	0	4	0	0	12	2	0	1	0	6	6	1	0	1.000	0	3.86
	MIL/AL		38	766	22	9	1	15	182.0	190	13	38	6	2	84	7	9	1	2	80	68	7	15	.318	6	3.36
89	MIL/AL		33	969	33	8	2	0	234.2	225	16	48	1	6	173	5	5	4	2	90	77	15	10	.600	0	2.95
90	BEL/MID	A	1	15	1	0	0	0	3.0	4	0	1	0	0	2	0	0	0	0	2	1	0	0	.000	0	3.00
	MIL/AL		20	557	20	4	1	0	132.2	131	15	38	1	3	76	4	4	7	0	67	59	4	9	.308	0	4.00
91	MIL/AL		32	840	32	5	1	0	204.2	187	15	58	0	8	117	2	6	5	0	80	74	14	10	.583	0	3.25
6 YR TOTALS			**179**	**4020**	**130**	**28**	**6**	**26**	**958.2**	**961**	**86**	**245**	**11**	**20**	**629**	**22**	**27**	**33**	**7**	**446**	**404**	**51**	**56**	**.477**	**8**	**3.79**

Boskie, Shawn Kealoha — bats right — throws right — b.3/28/67

YR	TM/LG	CL	G	TBF	GS	CG	SHO	GF	IP	H	HR	BB	IBB	HB	SO	SH	SF	WP	BK	R	ER	W	L	PCT	SV	ERA
86	WYT/APP	R+	14	268	12	1	0	0	54.0	42	4	57	0	1	40	0	1	15	0	41	32	4	4	.500	0	5.33
87	PEO/MID	A	26	657	25	1	0	0	149.0	149	12	56	2	17	100	4	5	7	5	91	72	9	11	.450	0	4.35
88	WIN/CAR	A+	27	825	27	4	2	0	186.0	176	9	89	1	17	164	4	7	14	4	83	70	12	7	.632	0	3.39
89	CHA/SOU	AA	28	813	28	5	0	0	181.0	196	10	84	3	19	164	3	8	11	1	105	88	11	8	.579	0	4.38
90	IOW/AMA	AAA	8	217	8	1	0	0	51.0	46	1	21	1	2	51	2	1	1	0	22	18	4	2	.667	0	3.18
	CHI/NL		15	415	15	1	0	0	97.2	99	8	31	3	1	49	8	2	3	2	42	40	5	6	.455	0	3.69
91	IOW/AMA	AAA	7	186	6	2	0	0	45.1	43	1	11	0	2	29	1	1	1	0	19	18	2	2	.500	0	3.57
	CHI/NL		28	582	20	0	0	2	129.0	150	14	52	4	5	62	8	6	1	1	78	75	4	9	.308	0	5.23
2 YR TOTALS			**43**	**997**	**35**	**1**	**0**	**2**	**226.2**	**249**	**22**	**83**	**7**	**6**	**111**	**16**	**8**	**4**	**3**	**120**	**115**	**9**	**15**	**.375**	**0**	**4.57**

Boucher, Denis — bats right — throws left — b.3/7/68

YR	TM/LG	CL	G	TBF	GS	CG	SHO	GF	IP	H	HR	BB	IBB	HB	SO	SH	SF	WP	BK	R	ER	W	L	PCT	SV	ERA
88	MB/SAL	A	33	809	32	1	0	0	196.2	161	11	63	1	8	169	7	6	15	21	81	62	13	12	.520	0	2.84
89	DUN/FSL	A+	33	675	28	1	1	1	164.2	142	6	58	2	6	117	3	8	13	8	80	56	10	10	.500	0	3.06
90	DUN/FSL	A+	9	226	9	2	2	0	60.0	45	1	8	0	2	62	0	0	4	0	8	5	7	0	1.000	0	0.75
	SYR/INT	AAA	17	449	17	2	1	0	107.2	100	7	37	2	2	80	4	5	6	0	51	46	8	5	.615	0	3.85
91	TOR/AL		7	162	7	0	0	0	35.1	39	6	16	1	2	16	3	1	0	0	20	18	0	3	.000	0	4.58
	SYR/INT	AAA	8	241	8	1	0	0	56.2	57	5	19	1	3	28	4	1	2	0	24	20	2	1	.667	0	3.18
	CLE/AL		5	108	5	0	0	0	22.2	35	6	8	0	0	13	0	1	0	0	21	21	1	0	.200	0	8.34
	CS/PCL	AAA	3	59	3	0	0	0	14.1	14	1	2	0	0	9	0	1	0	0	8	8	1	0	1.000	0	5.02
	YEAR		12	270	12	0	0	0	58.0	74	12	24	1	2	29	3	1	1	4	41	39	1	7	.125	0	6.05
1 YR TOTALS			**12**	**270**	**12**	**0**	**0**	**0**	**58.0**	**74**	**12**	**24**	**1**	**2**	**29**	**3**	**1**	**1**	**4**	**41**	**39**	**1**	**7**	**.125**	**0**	**6.05**

Bowen, Ryan Eugene — bats right — throws right — b.2/10/68

YR	TM/LG	CL	G	TBF	GS	CG	SHO	GF	IP	H	HR	BB	IBB	HB	SO	SH	SF	WP	BK	R	ER	W	L	PCT	SV	ERA
87	ASH/SAL	A	26	704	26	6	2	0	160.1	143	12	78	1	5	126	7	4	8	2	86	72	12	5	.706	0	4.04
88	OSC/FSL	A+	4	65	4	0	0	0	13.2	12	0	10	0	1	12	1	0	2	0	8	6	1	0	1.000	0	3.95
89	COL/SOU	AA	27	655	27	1	1	0	139.2	123	11	116	0	8	136	7	4	12	0	83	66	8	6	.571	0	4.25
90	TUC/PCL	AAA	10	177	7	0	0	0	34.2	41	5	38	1	0	29	2	0	0	0	36	36	1	3	.250	0	9.35
	COL/SOU	AA	18	491	18	2	2	0	113.0	103	7	49	0	0	109	4	6	5	1	59	47	8	6	.667	0	3.74
91	TUC/PCL	AAA	18	450	18	2	2	0	98.2	114	3	56	2	3	78	3	2	6	0	56	48	5	5	.500	0	4.38
	HOU/NL		14	319	13	0	0	0	71.2	73	4	36	1	4	28	2	6	8	1	43	41	6	4	.600	0	5.15

Boyd, Dennis Ray "Oil Can" — bats right — throws right — b.10/6/59

YR	TM/LG	CL	G	TBF	GS	CG	SHO	GF	IP	H	HR	BB	IBB	HB	SO	SH	SF	WP	BK	R	ER	W	L	PCT	SV	ERA
82	BOS/AL		3	37	1	0	0	0	8.1	11	2	2	0	0	2	0	0	0	0	5	5	0	1	.000	0	5.40
83	BOS/AL		15	413	13	5	0	2	98.2	103	9	23	0	1	43	1	5	3	1	46	36	4	8	.333	0	3.28
84	PAW/INT	AAA	5	149	3	2	0	1	37.1	30	2	12	0	1	45	0	0	0	0	12	12	3	1	.750	0	2.89
	BOS/AL		29	835	26	10	3	2	197.2	207	18	53	5	1	134	4	8	5	1	109	96	12	12	.500	0	4.37
85	BOS/AL		35	1132	35	13	3	0	272.1	273	26	67	3	4	154	9	7	1	1	117	112	15	13	.536	0	3.70
86	BOS/AL		30	893	30	10	0	0	214.1	222	32	45	1	2	129	3	6	3	0	99	90	16	10	.615	0	3.78
87	PAW/INT	AAA	3	51	3	0	0	0	12.0	12	2	4	0	0	8	1	0	0	0	6	6	1	1	.500	0	4.50
	BOS/AL		7	167	7	0	0	0	36.2	47	6	9	1	2	12	4	3	0	2	31	24	1	3	.250	0	5.89
88	BOS/AL		23	561	23	1	0	0	129.2	147	25	41	2	2	71	3	6	0	5	82	77	9	7	.563	0	5.34
89	PAW/INT	AAA	2	25	2	0	0	0	7.0	4	0	0	0	0	11	0	0	0	0	1	1	0	0	.000	0	0.00
	NB/EAS	AA	1	20	1	0	0	0	5.0	3	0	1	0	0	4	0	0	0	0	1	1	0	0	.000	0	1.80
	BOS/AL		10	246	10	0	0	0	59.0	57	8	19	0	0	26	0	1	2	0	31	29	3	2	.600	0	4.42
90	MON/NL		31	774	31	3	3	0	190.2	164	19	52	10	3	113	12	4	3	3	64	62	10	6	.625	0	2.93
91	MON/NL		19	496	19	1	1	0	120.1	115	9	40	2	0	82	2	4	2	3	49	47	6	8	.429	0	3.52
	TEX/AL		12	277	12	0	0	0	62.0	81	12	17	1	0	33	2	0	0	1	47	46	2	7	.222	0	6.68
	YEAR		31	773	31	1	1	0	182.1	196	21	57	3	0	115	4	4	2	4	96	93	8	15	.348	0	4.59
10 YR TOTALS			214	5831	207	43	10	4	1389.2	1427	166	368	25	15	799	40	45	20	17	680	624	78	77	.503	0	4.04

Brantley, Clifford "Cliff" — bats right — throws right — b.4/12/68

YR	TM/LG	CL	G	TBF	GS	CG	SHO	GF	IP	H	HR	BB	IBB	HB	SO	SH	SF	WP	BK	R	ER	W	L	PCT	SV	ERA
86	UTI/NYP	A–	11	280	11	0	0	0	60.2	68	5	25	1	4	42	2	4	5	1	37	29	3	5	.375	0	4.30
87	SPA/SAL	A	20	494	20	3	0	0	110.1	114	2	58	2	9	86	2	2	10	3	69	59	3	10	.231	0	4.81
88	CLE/FSL	A+	24	689	24	6	1	0	166.2	126	2	74	6	5	124	4	6	20	0	55	48	8	11	.421	0	2.59
	REA/EAS	AA	1	26	1	0	0	0	6.0	5	1	2	0	1	5	0	0	0	0	4	4	1	0	1.000	0	6.00
89	REA/EAS	AA	11	227	9	0	0	1	49.0	49	1	28	0	2	35	1	2	2	1	29	18	3	4	.429	1	3.31
	CLE/FSL	A+	8	228	8	1	0	0	49.2	60	3	19	1	0	33	1	3	6	2	31	24	0	5	.000	0	4.35
90	CLE/FSL	A+	8	201	8	2	0	0	49.0	44	3	17	1	0	37	4	0	5	0	20	16	1	4	.200	0	2.94
	REA/EAS	AA	17	386	17	0	0	0	87.0	93	4	39	0	3	69	3	3	4	1	51	44	4	9	.308	0	4.55
91	REA/EAS	AA	11	279	11	2	1	0	69.2	50	3	25	1	4	51	0	2	0	0	17	15	4	3	.571	0	1.94
	SCR/INT	AAA	8	206	8	0	0	0	47.1	44	2	25	0	2	28	1	0	0	2	26	20	2	4	.333	0	3.80
	PHI/NL		6	140	5	0	0	0	31.2	26	0	19	0	2	22	2	3	2	0	12	12	2	2	.500	0	3.41

Brantley, Jeffrey Hoke "Jeff" — bats right — throws right — b.9/5/63

YR	TM/LG	CL	G	TBF	GS	CG	SHO	GF	IP	H	HR	BB	IBB	HB	SO	SH	SF	WP	BK	R	ER	W	L	PCT	SV	ERA
85	FRE/CAL	A+	14	0	13	3	0	0	94.2	83	4	37	0	1	85	0	0	7	0	39	35	8	2	.800	0	3.33
86	SHR/TEX	AA	26	686	26	8	3	0	165.2	139	13	68	0	6	125	5	3	11	2	78	64	8	10	.444	0	3.48
87	SHR/TEX	AA	2	48	2	0	0	0	11.2	12	1	4	0	1	7	0	0	1	0	7	4	0	1	.000	0	3.09
	PHO/PCL	AAA	29	761	28	2	0	0	170.1	187	13	82	3	11	111	5	5	5	7	110	88	6	11	.353	0	4.65
88	PHO/PCL	AAA	27	533	19	1	0	1	122.2	130	6	39	2	5	83	2	7	2	8	65	59	9	5	.643	0	4.33
	SF/NL		9	88	1	0	0	2	20.2	22	2	6	1	1	11	1	0	0	0	13	13	0	1	.000	1	5.66
89	PHO/PCL	AAA	7	56	0	0	0	5	14.1	6	1	6	1	1	20	1	0	0	0	2	2	1	1	.500	3	1.26
	SF/NL		59	422	1	0	0	15	97.1	101	10	37	8	2	69	7	3	3	2	50	44	7	1	.875	0	4.07
90	SF/NL		55	361	0	0	0	32	86.2	77	3	33	6	3	61	2	2	0	3	18	15	5	3	.625	19	1.56
91	SF/NL		67	411	0	0	0	39	95.1	78	8	52	10	5	81	4	4	6	0	27	26	5	2	.714	15	2.45
4 YR TOTALS			190	1282	2	0	0	88	300.0	278	23	128	25	11	222	14	9	9	6	108	98	17	7	.708	35	2.94

Briscoe, John Eric — bats right — throws right — b.9/22/67

YR	TM/LG	CL	G	TBF	GS	CG	SHO	GF	IP	H	HR	BB	IBB	HB	SO	SH	SF	WP	BK	R	ER	W	L	PCT	SV	ERA
88	ATH/ARI	R	7	105	6	0	0	0	25.2	26	1	6	0	1	23	0	1	3	3	14	10	1	1	.500	0	3.51
89	MAD/MID	A	21	524	20	1	0	1	117.2	121	7	57	0	9	69	10	9	11	1	66	55	7	5	.583	0	4.21
90	MOD/CAL	A+	29	373	12	1	0	12	86.1	72	12	52	0	4	66	4	1	6	0	50	44	3	6	.333	4	4.59
	HUN/SOU	AA	3	30	0	0	0	0	4.2	9	1	7	0	0	7	0	0	0	0	7	7	0	0	.000	0	13.50
91	HUN/SOU	AA	2	19	0	0	0	0	4.1	1	0	6	0	0	6	0	0	0	0	1	1	0	0	.000	0	2.08
	OAK/AL		11	62	0	0	0	9	14.0	12	3	10	0	0	9	0	1	3	0	11	11	0	0	.000	0	7.07
	TAC/PCL	AAA	22	342	9	0	0	6	76.1	73	7	44	1	5	66	2	2	3	0	35	31	3	5	.375	1	3.66

Bross, Terrence Paul "Terry" — bats right — throws right — b.3/30/66

YR	TM/LG	CL	G	TBF	GS	CG	SHO	GF	IP	H	HR	BB	IBB	HB	SO	SH	SF	WP	BK	R	ER	W	L	PCT	SV	ERA
87	LF/NYP	A–	10	129	3	0	0	1	28.0	22	3	20	0	0	21	2	1	1	1	23	12	2	0	1.000	0	3.86
88	LF/NYP	A–	20	248	6	0	0	8	55.1	43	2	38	0	0	59	1	2	2	2	25	19	2	1	.667	1	3.09
89	SL/FSL	A+	35	234	0	0	0	26	58.0	39	1	26	3	1	47	0	4	3	1	21	18	8	2	.800	11	2.79
90	JAC/TEX	AA	58	289	0	0	0	48	71.2	46	4	40	5	2	51	5	3	4	4	21	21	3	4	.429	28	2.64
91	TID/INT	AAA	27	159	0	0	0	10	33.0	31	1	32	2	1	23	1	1	3	2	12	7	2	0	1.000	2	2.49
	WIL/EAS	AA	20	98	0	0	0	16	25.1	13	1	11	0	0	28	1	1	0	0	5	5	0	0	.000	2	1.80
	NY/NL		8	39	0	0	0	4	10.0	7	1	3	0	0	7	1	0	0	0	2	2	0	0	.000	0	1.80

Brown, James Kevin "Kevin" — bats right — throws right — b.3/14/65

YR	TM/LG	CL	G	TBF	GS	CG	SHO	GF	IP	H	HR	BB	IBB	HB	SO	SH	SF	WP	BK	R	ER	W	L	PCT	SV	ERA
86	RAN/GCL	R	3	26	0	0	0	0	6.0	7	0	2	0	0	3	1	0	0	1	4	4	0	0	.000	0	6.00
	TUL/TEX	AA	3	47	2	0	0	0	10.0	9	0	5	0	0	10	1	0	0	0	7	5	0	0	.000	0	4.50
	TEX/AL		1	19	1	0	0	0	5.0	6	0	0	0	0	4	0	0	0	0	2	2	1	0	1.000	0	3.60
87	TUL/TEX	AA	8	193	8	2	0	0	42.0	53	3	18	1	1	26	0	2	1	0	36	34	1	4	.200	0	7.29
	OC/AMA	AAA	5	124	5	0	0	0	24.1	32	2	17	0	4	9	0	0	1	0	32	29	0	5	.000	0	10.73
	CHA/FSL	A+	6	153	6	1	0	0	36.1	33	1	17	0	0	21	3	0	1	0	14	11	0	2	.000	0	2.72

(continued)

Brown, James Kevin "Kevin" (continued)

YR	TM/LG	CL	G	TBF	GS	CG	SHO	GF	IP	H	HR	BB	IBB	HB	SO	SH	SF	WP	BK	R	ER	W	L	PCT	SV	ERA
88	TUL/TEX	AA	26	741	26	5	0	0	174.1	174	5	61	1	10	118	3	0	13	8	94	68	12	10	.545	0	3.51
	TEX/AL		4	110	4	1	0	0	23.1	33	2	8	0	1	12	1	0	1	0	15	11	1	1	.500	0	4.24
89	TEX/AL		28	798	28	7	0	0	191.0	167	10	70	2	4	104	3	6	7	2	81	71	12	9	.571	0	3.35
90	TEX/AL		26	757	26	6	2	0	180.0	175	13	60	3	3	88	2	7	9	2	84	72	12	10	.545	0	3.60
91	TEX/AL		33	934	33	0	0	0	210.2	233	17	90	5	13	96	6	4	12	3	116	103	9	12	.429	0	4.40
5 YR TOTALS			**92**	**2618**	**92**	**14**	**2**	**0**	**610.0**	**614**	**42**	**228**	**10**	**21**	**304**	**12**	**17**	**29**	**7**	**298**	**259**	**35**	**32**	**.522**	**0**	**3.82**

Brown, Keith Edward — bats both — throws right — b.2/14/64

YR	TM/LG	CL	G	TBF	GS	CG	SHO	GF	IP	H	HR	BB	IBB	HB	SO	SH	SF	WP	BK	R	ER	W	L	PCT	SV	ERA
86	RED/GCL	R	7	179	7	1	0	0	47.1	29	0	5	1	2	26	2	1	3	0	15	5	4	1	.800	0	0.95
	BIL/PIO	R+	4	0	3	0	0	1	21.1	18	0	7	0	1	14	0	0	1	0	6	5	2	0	1.000	0	2.11
	VER/EAS	AA	4	58	2	1	0	0	14.0	12	2	8	0	0	11	1	1	1	0	10	8	1	1	.500	0	5.14
87	CR/MID	A	17	481	17	3	1	0	124.1	91	5	27	0	3	86	2	1	3	0	28	22	13	4	.765	0	1.59
88	CHT/SOU	AA	10	273	10	2	0	0	69.2	47	3	20	1	4	34	2	1	1	0	11	11	9	1	.900	0	1.42
	NAS/AMA	AAA	12	354	12	3	1	0	85.1	72	1	28	2	1	43	6	2	2	1	33	18	6	3	.667	0	1.90
	CIN/NL		4	63	3	0	0	1	16.1	14	1	4	0	0	6	0	0	1	0	5	5	2	1	.667	0	2.76
89	NAS/AMA	AAA	29	695	27	4	2	0	161.1	171	13	51	2	1	85	10	4	5	2	99	86	8	13	.381	0	4.80
90	NAS/AMA	AAA	39	379	9	1	0	26	94.1	83	6	24	2	4	50	8	2	4	1	37	25	7	8	.467	9	2.39
	CIN/NL		8	46	0	0	0	2	11.1	12	2	3	0	0	8	1	0	0	0	6	6	0	0	.000	0	4.76
91	CIN/NL		11	56	0	0	0	3	12.0	15	0	6	1	0	4	1	0	1	0	4	3	0	0	.000	0	2.25
	NAS/AMA	AAA	47	274	1	0	0	32	62.0	64	3	32	4	2	53	5	2	5	0	26	24	2	5	.286	16	3.48
3 YR TOTALS			**23**	**165**	**3**	**0**	**0**	**6**	**39.2**	**41**	**3**	**13**	**1**	**0**	**18**	**2**	**0**	**2**	**0**	**15**	**14**	**2**	**1**	**.667**	**0**	**3.18**

Brown, Kevin Dewayne — bats left — throws left — b.3/5/66

YR	TM/LG	CL	G	TBF	GS	CG	SHO	GF	IP	H	HR	BB	IBB	HB	SO	SH	SF	WP	BK	R	ER	W	L	PCT	SV	ERA
86	IF/PIO	R+	12	0	12	1	0	0	68.0	65	5	41	0	0	44	0	0	2	0	48	38	3	6	.333	0	5.03
87	SUM/SAL	A	9	232	9	0	0	0	56.0	53	2	19	0	1	45	2	1	5	0	14	12	7	1	.875	0	1.93
	DUR/CAR	A+	13	330	12	1	0	1	72.2	78	6	42	0	0	41	0	1	5	2	46	42	4	4	.500	0	5.20
88	JAC/TEX	AA	5	129	5	1	1	0	32.2	24	1	11	0	0	24	1	2	2	0	9	8	1	2	.333	0	2.20
	SL/FSL	A+	20	533	20	5	1	0	134.0	96	3	37	1	6	113	3	2	10	2	42	27	5	7	.417	0	1.81
89	JAC/TEX	AA	8	216	8	2	2	0	51.2	51	0	11	0	4	40	1	1	4	4	15	13	5	2	.714	0	2.26
	TID/INT	AAA	13	326	13	4	0	0	75.0	81	2	31	0	0	46	3	1	2	0	41	37	6	6	.500	0	4.44
90	NY/NL		2	9	0	0	0	1	2.0	2	0	1	0	0	0	0	0	0	0	0	0	0	0	.000	0	0.00
	TID/INT	AAA	26	592	24	3	0	0	134.1	138	4	60	0	2	109	7	0	3	2	71	53	10	6	.625	0	3.55
	MIL/AL		5	87	3	0	0	1	21.0	14	1	7	1	1	12	1	1	2	0	7	6	1	1	.500	0	2.57
	YEAR		7	96	3	0	0	2	23.0	16	1	8	1	1	12	1	1	2	0	7	6	1	1	.500	0	2.35
91	MIL/AL		15	285	10	0	0	0	63.2	66	6	34	2	1	30	5	1	6	0	39	39	2	4	.333	0	5.51
	DEN/AMA	AAA	12	277	11	1	0	0	61.2	71	4	34	0	2	31	3	0	2	2	36	32	4	3	.571	0	4.67
2 YR TOTALS			**22**	**381**	**13**	**0**	**0**	**2**	**86.2**	**82**	**7**	**42**	**3**	**2**	**42**	**6**	**2**	**8**	**0**	**46**	**45**	**3**	**5**	**.375**	**0**	**4.67**

Browning, Thomas Leo "Tom" — bats left — throws left — b.4/28/60

YR	TM/LG	CL	G	TBF	GS	CG	SHO	GF	IP	H	HR	BB	IBB	HB	SO	SH	SF	WP	BK	R	ER	W	L	PCT	SV	ERA
84	WIC/AMA	AAA	30	801	28	8	1	1	189.1	169	24	73	1	6	160	5	5	2	0	88	83	12	10	.545	0	3.95
	CIN/NL		3	95	3	0	0	0	23.1	27	0	5	0	0	14	1	0	1	0	4	4	1	0	1.000	0	1.54
85	CIN/NL		38	1083	38	6	4	0	261.1	242	29	73	8	3	155	13	7	2	0	111	103	20	9	.690	0	3.55
86	CIN/NL		39	1016	39	4	2	0	243.1	225	26	70	6	1	147	14	12	3	0	123	103	14	13	.519	0	3.81
87	NAS/AMA	AAA	5	138	5	1	1	0	29.2	37	5	12	0	0	28	1	2	1	0	22	20	2	3	.400	0	6.07
	CIN/NL		32	791	31	2	0	1	183.0	201	27	61	7	5	117	10	6	2	4	107	102	10	13	.435	0	5.02
88	CIN/NL		36	1001	36	5	2	0	250.2	205	36	64	3	7	124	6	8	2	4	98	95	18	5	.783	0	3.41
89	CIN/NL		37	1031	37	9	2	0	249.2	241	31	64	10	3	118	12	6	2	1	109	94	15	12	.556	0	3.39
90	CIN/NL		35	957	35	2	1	0	227.2	235	24	52	13	5	99	13	5	5	1	98	96	15	9	.625	0	3.80
91	CIN/NL		36	983	36	1	0	0	230.1	241	32	56	4	4	115	8	9	3	1	124	107	14	14	.500	0	4.18
8 YR TOTALS			**256**	**6957**	**255**	**29**	**11**	**1**	**1669.1**	**1617**	**205**	**445**	**51**	**28**	**889**	**77**	**54**	**20**	**11**	**774**	**704**	**107**	**75**	**.588**	**0**	**3.80**

Burba, David Allen "Dave" — bats right — throws right — b.7/7/66

YR	TM/LG	CL	G	TBF	GS	CG	SHO	GF	IP	H	HR	BB	IBB	HB	SO	SH	SF	WP	BK	R	ER	W	L	PCT	SV	ERA
87	BEL/NWL	A-	5	97	5	0	0	0	23.1	20	0	3	0	0	24	0	0	4	0	10	5	3	1	.750	0	1.93
	SAL/CAL	A+	9	246	9	0	0	0	54.2	53	3	29	0	2	46	3	2	3	0	31	28	1	6	.143	0	4.61
88	SB/CAL	A+	20	485	20	1	0	0	114.0	106	4	54	1	4	102	4	2	5	0	41	34	5	7	.417	0	2.68
89	WIL/EAS	AA	25	651	25	5	1	0	156.2	138	7	55	0	3	89	5	4	4	5	69	55	11	7	.611	0	3.16
90	CAL/PCL	AAA	31	493	18	1	0	8	113.2	124	11	45	0	2	47	4	3	5	3	64	59	10	6	.625	2	4.67
	SEA/AL		6	35	0	0	0	2	8.0	8	0	2	0	1	4	2	0	0	0	6	4	0	0	.000	0	4.50
91	CAL/PCL	AAA	23	315	9	0	0	2	71.1	82	4	27	0	4	42	4	1	3	2	35	28	6	4	.600	4	3.53
	SEA/AL		22	153	2	0	0	11	36.2	34	6	14	3	0	16	0	1	1	0	16	15	2	2	.500	1	3.68
2 YR TOTALS			**28**	**188**	**2**	**0**	**0**	**13**	**44.2**	**42**	**6**	**16**	**3**	**1**	**20**	**2**	**1**	**1**	**0**	**22**	**19**	**2**	**2**	**.500**	**1**	**3.83**

Burke, Timothy Philip "Tim" — bats right — throws right — b.2/19/59

YR	TM/LG	CL	G	TBF	GS	CG	SHO	GF	IP	H	HR	BB	IBB	HB	SO	SH	SF	WP	BK	R	ER	W	L	PCT	SV	ERA
84	IND/AMA	AAA	35	766	27	1	0	4	180.2	192	15	61	5	4	108	4	5	10	2	81	70	11	8	.579	2	3.49
85	MON/NL		78	483	0	0	0	31	120.1	86	9	44	14	7	87	6	3	7	0	32	32	9	4	.692	8	2.39
86	MON/NL		68	451	2	0	0	25	101.1	103	7	46	13	4	82	6	2	4	0	37	33	9	7	.563	4	2.93
87	MON/NL		55	354	0	0	0	30	91.0	64	3	17	6	0	58	8	2	2	0	18	12	7	0	1.000	18	1.19
88	MON/NL		61	350	0	0	0	39	82.0	84	7	25	13	3	42	5	3	1	0	36	31	3	5	.375	18	3.40
89	MON/NL		68	333	0	0	0	52	84.2	68	6	22	7	0	54	4	5	1	0	24	24	9	3	.750	28	2.55

Burke, Timothy Philip "Tim" (continued)

YR	TM/LG	CL	G	TBF	GS	CG	SHO	GF	IP	H	HR	BB	IBB	HB	SO	SH	SF	WP	BK	R	ER	W	L	PCT	SV	ERA
90	MON/NL		58	316	0	0	0	35	75.0	71	6	21	6	2	47	3	3	1	1	29	21	3	3	.500	20	2.52
91	MON/NL		37	190	0	0	0	16	46.0	41	3	14	6	4	25	2	1	1	0	24	21	3	4	.429	5	4.11
	NY/NL		35	231	0	0	0	15	55.2	55	5	12	2	0	34	1	2	2	0	22	17	3	3	.500	1	2.75
	YEAR		72	421	0	0	0	31	101.2	96	8	26	8	4	59	3	3	3	0	46	38	6	7	.462	6	3.36
7 YR TOTALS			**460**	**2708**	**2**	**0**	**0**	**243**	**656.0**	**572**	**46**	**201**	**67**	**20**	**429**	**40**	**23**	**21**	**2**	**222**	**191**	**46**	**29**	**.613**	**102**	**2.62**

Burkett, John David — bats right — throws right — b.11/28/64

YR	TM/LG	CL	G	TBF	GS	CG	SHO	GF	IP	H	HR	BB	IBB	HB	SO	SH	SF	WP	BK	R	ER	W	L	PCT	SV	ERA
84	CLI/MID	A	20	553	20	2	0	0	126.2	128	5	38	1	6	83	7	3	9	1	81	61	7	6	.538	0	4.33
85	FRE/CAL	A+	20	0	20	1	1	0	109.2	98	3	46	0	6	72	0	0	6	0	43	35	7	4	.636	0	2.87
86	FRE/CAL	A+	4	118	4	0	0	0	24.2	34	2	8	0	2	14	1	0	3	0	19	15	0	3	.000	0	5.47
	SHR/TEX	AA	22	513	21	4	2	0	128.2	99	7	42	0	4	73	4	0	3	3	46	38	10	6	.625	0	2.66
87	SHR/TEX	AA	27	759	27	6	1	0	177.2	181	11	53	2	7	126	6	6	3	1	75	66	14	6	.636	0	3.34
	SF/NL		3	28	0	0	0	1	6.0	7	2	3	0	1	5	1	0	0	0	4	3	0	0	.000	0	4.50
88	SHR/TEX	AA	7	199	7	2	1	0	50.2	33	3	18	1	2	34	3	2	1	1	15	12	5	1	.833	0	2.13
	PHO/PCL	AAA	21	524	21	0	0	0	114.0	142	7	49	3	5	74	5	7	1	2	79	66	5	11	.313	0	5.21
89	PHO/PCL	AAA	28	745	28	2	1	0	167.2	197	19	59	3	8	105	6	6	2	2	111	94	10	11	.476	0	5.05
90	PHO/PCL	AAA	3	86	3	2	1	0	23.0	18	2	3	0	0	14	2	1	0	0	8	7	2	1	.667	0	2.74
	SF/NL		33	857	32	2	0	1	204.0	201	18	61	7	4	118	6	5	3	3	92	86	14	7	.667	1	3.79
91	SF/NL		36	890	34	3	1	0	206.2	223	19	60	2	10	131	8	8	5	0	103	96	12	11	.522	0	4.18
3 YR TOTALS			**72**	**1775**	**66**	**5**	**1**	**2**	**416.2**	**431**	**39**	**124**	**9**	**15**	**254**	**15**	**13**	**8**	**3**	**199**	**185**	**26**	**18**	**.591**	**1**	**4.00**

Burns, Todd Edward — bats right — throws right — b.7/6/63

YR	TM/LG	CL	G	TBF	GS	CG	SHO	GF	IP	H	HR	BB	IBB	HB	SO	SH	SF	WP	BK	R	ER	W	L	PCT	SV	ERA
84	MED/NWL	A-	22	0	0	0	0	18	36.1	21	0	12	1	0	63	0	0	0	0	4	2	3	0	1.000	8	0.50
	MAD/MID	A	10	55	0	0	0	9	14.0	11	1	3	0	0	20	3	0	0	1	4	4	3	2	.600	1	2.57
85	MAD/MID	A	20	506	19	5	3	0	123.0	109	8	40	0	3	94	1	3	12	0	55	50	8	8	.500	0	3.66
	HUN/SOU	AA	4	94	4	1	1	0	22.2	16	0	13	0	0	8	0	2	0	0	6	3	3	1	.750	0	1.19
86	HUN/SOU	AA	20	525	18	5	3	0	124.2	122	16	39	1	3	77	1	6	6	3	59	52	7	7	.500	0	3.75
	TAC/PCL	AAA	11	66	0	0	0	9	16.2	11	1	12	1	0	14	0	1	0	0	4	4	0	2	.000	2	2.16
87	HUN/SOU	AA	34	257	0	0	0	27	63.2	49	4	17	4	1	54	3	1	3	0	24	21	3	4	.429	7	2.97
	TAC/PCL	AAA	21	122	0	0	0	10	27.2	27	3	16	1	0	30	1	2	0	2	16	15	2	2	.500	0	4.88
88	TAC/PCL	AAA	21	310	5	1	0	3	73.1	74	4	26	2	1	59	3	2	2	4	39	30	4	3	.571	1	3.68
	OAK/AL		17	425	14	2	0	0	102.2	93	8	34	1	2	57	2	2	3	6	38	36	8	2	.800	1	3.16
89	OAK/AL		50	374	2	0	0	22	96.1	66	3	28	5	1	49	7	1	4	0	27	24	6	5	.545	8	2.24
90	OAK/AL		43	337	2	0	0	9	78.2	78	8	32	4	0	43	5	3	5	0	28	26	3	3	.500	3	2.97
91	MOD/CAL	A+	2	31	1	0	0	0	6.0	9	1	3	0	1	8	0	1	3	0	7	7	1	0	1.000	0	10.50
	OAK/AL		9	57	0	0	0	5	13.1	10	2	8	1	0	12	0	0	3	0	5	5	1	0	1.000	0	3.38
	TAC/PCL	AAA	13	112	0	0	0	4	25.1	30	5	7	2	0	24	1	3	2	0	16	15	0	2	.000	2	5.33
4 YR TOTALS			**119**	**1193**	**18**	**2**	**0**	**39**	**291.0**	**247**	**21**	**102**	**11**	**2**	**152**	**15**	**8**	**13**	**6**	**98**	**91**	**18**	**10**	**.643**	**12**	**2.81**

Cadaret, Gregory James "Greg" — bats left — throws left — b.2/27/62

YR	TM/LG	CL	G	TBF	GS	CG	SHO	GF	IP	H	HR	BB	IBB	HB	SO	SH	SF	WP	BK	R	ER	W	L	PCT	SV	ERA
84	MOD/CAL	A+	26	0	26	6	2	0	171.1	162	7	82	0	1	138	0	0	14	2	79	58	13	8	.619	0	3.05
85	HUN/SOU	AA	17	387	17	0	0	0	82.1	96	9	57	0	0	60	2	4	9	0	61	56	3	7	.300	0	6.12
	MOD/CAL	A+	12	0	12	1	1	0	61.1	59	4	54	0	1	43	0	0	10	0	50	40	3	9	.250	0	5.87
86	HUN/SOU	AA	28	666	28	1	0	0	141.1	166	6	98	0	1	113	1	4	15	0	106	85	12	5	.706	0	5.41
87	HUN/SOU	AA	24	172	0	0	0	21	40.1	31	6	20	3	0	48	1	0	6	1	16	13	5	2	.714	9	2.90
	TAC/PCL	AAA	7	57	0	0	0	4	13.0	5	1	13	0	0	12	0	1	0	0	6	5	1	2	.333	1	3.46
	OAK/AL		29	176	0	0	0	7	39.2	37	6	24	1	1	30	2	1	2	0	22	20	6	2	.750	0	4.54
88	OAK/AL		58	311	0	0	0	16	71.2	60	2	36	1	1	64	5	3	5	3	26	23	5	2	.714	3	2.89
89	OAK/AL		26	119	0	0	0	1	27.2	21	0	19	3	0	14	0	2	1	0	9	7	0	0	.000	0	2.28
	NY/AL		20	412	13	1	0	1	92.1	109	7	38	1	2	66	3	3	6	2	53	47	5	5	.500	0	4.58
	YEAR		46	531	13	1	0	1	120.0	130	7	57	4	2	80	3	5	6	2	62	54	5	5	.500	0	4.05
90	NY/AL		54	525	6	0	0	9	121.1	120	8	64	5	1	80	9	4	14	0	62	56	5	4	.556	3	4.15
91	NY/AL		68	517	5	0	0	17	121.2	110	8	59	6	1	105	6	3	3	1	52	49	8	6	.571	3	3.62
5 YR TOTALS			**255**	**2060**	**24**	**3**	**1**	**56**	**474.1**	**457**	**31**	**240**	**17**	**7**	**359**	**25**	**17**	**29**	**6**	**224**	**202**	**29**	**19**	**.604**	**9**	**3.83**

Campbell, Kevin Wade — bats right — throws right — b.12/12/64

YR	TM/LG	CL	G	TBF	GS	CG	SHO	GF	IP	H	HR	BB	IBB	HB	SO	SH	SF	WP	BK	R	ER	W	L	PCT	SV	ERA
86	GF/PIO	R+	15	0	15	3	0	0	85.0	99	5	32	0	3	66	0	0	6	0	62	44	5	6	.455	0	4.66
87	VB/FSL	A+	28	807	28	5	1	0	184.0	200	11	64	4	9	112	6	6	11	4	100	80	7	14	.333	0	3.91
88	VB/FSL	A+	26	677	26	5	1	0	163.2	166	6	49	2	3	115	10	4	6	1	67	50	8	12	.400	0	2.75
89	BAK/CAL	A+	31	255	0	0	0	17	60.1	43	0	28	1	0	63	2	5	2	0	23	17	1	5	.167	2	2.54
	SA/TEX	AA	17	127	0	0	0	7	27.0	29	3	16	1	0	28	2	2	1	0	22	20	1	3	.250	8	6.67
90	SA/TEX	AA	49	329	0	0	0	29	81.0	67	1	25	6	3	84	3	3	5	1	29	21	9	2	.818	2	2.33
91	TAC/PCL	AAA	35	304	0	0	0	12	75.0	53	0	35	1	0	56	3	1	5	0	18	15	9	2	.818	2	1.80
	OAK/AL		14	94	0	0	0	2	23.0	13	0	14	0	1	16	1	0	0	0	7	7	1	0	1.000	2	2.74

Candelaria, John Robert "John" or "Candy Man" — bats left — throws left — b.11/6/53

YR	TM/LG	CL	G	TBF	GS	CG	SHO	GF	IP	H	HR	BB	IBB	HB	SO	SH	SF	WP	BK	R	ER	W	L	PCT	SV	ERA
75	PIT/NL		18	497	18	4	1	0	120.2	95	8	36	9	2	95	6	4	1	0	47	37	8	6	.571	0	2.76
76	PIT/NL		32	881	31	11	4	1	220.0	173	22	60	5	6	138	13	6	0	0	87	77	16	7	.696	1	3.15
77	PIT/NL		33	917	33	6	1	0	230.2	197	29	50	2	2	133	9	6	1	2	64	60	20	5	.800	0	2.34

(continued)

Candelaria, John Robert "John" or "Candy Man" (continued)

YR	TM/LG	CL	G	TBF	GS	CG	SHO	GF	IP	H	HR	BB	IBB	HB	SO	SH	SF	WP	BK	R	ER	W	L	PCT	SV	ERA
78	PIT/NL		30	796	29	3	1	1	189.0	191	15	49	6	5	94	8	2	3	3	73	68	12	11	.522	1	3.24
79	PIT/NL		33	850	30	8	0	2	207.0	201	25	41	6	3	101	4	7	2	0	83	74	14	9	.609	0	3.22
80	PIT/NL		35	969	34	7	0	1	233.1	246	14	50	4	3	97	14	12	0	2	114	104	11	14	.440	1	4.01
81	PIT/NL		6	168	6	0	0	0	40.2	42	3	11	1	0	14	1	1	0	0	17	16	2	2	.500	0	3.54
82	PIT/NL		31	704	30	1	1	1	174.2	166	13	37	3	4	133	5	6	1	0	62	57	12	7	.632	1	2.94
83	PIT/NL		33	797	32	2	0	0	197.2	191	15	45	3	2	157	4	4	3	2	73	71	15	8	.652	0	3.23
84	PIT/NL		33	751	28	3	1	4	185.1	179	19	34	3	1	133	10	6	1	1	69	56	12	11	.522	2	2.72
85	PIT/NL		37	229	0	0	0	26	54.1	57	7	14	2	1	47	3	4	0	0	23	22	2	4	.333	9	3.64
	CAL/AL		13	301	13	1	1	0	71.0	70	7	24	1	3	53	4	3	2	0	33	30	7	3	.700	0	3.80
	YEAR		50	530	13	1	1	26	125.1	127	14	38	3	4	100	7	7	2	0	56	52	9	7	.563	9	3.73
86	PS/CAL	A+	2	27	2	0	0	0	7.0	4	0	2	0	0	8	0	0	0	0	2	2	0	0	.000	0	2.57
	CAL/AL		16	365	16	0	0	0	91.2	68	4	26	2	3	81	3	3	2	1	30	26	10	2	.833	0	2.55
87	CAL/AL		20	487	20	0	0	0	116.2	127	17	20	0	1	74	6	5	0	0	70	61	8	6	.571	0	4.71
	NY/NL		3	57	3	0	0	0	12.1	17	1	3	0	0	10	2	1	0	1	8	8	2	0	1.000	0	5.84
	YEAR		23	544	23	0	0	0	129.0	144	18	23	0	1	84	8	6	0	1	78	69	10	6	.625	0	4.81
88	NY/AL		25	640	24	6	2	1	157.0	150	18	23	2	2	121	4	6	2	12	69	59	13	7	.650	1	3.38
89	YAN/GCL	R	2	31	2	0	0	0	8.0	6	0	1	0	0	12	0	0	0	1	0	0	1	0	1.000	0	0.00
	NY/AL		10	206	6	1	0	1	49.0	49	8	12	1	0	37	2	2	2	1	28	28	3	3	.500	0	5.14
	MON/NL		12	68	0	0	0	2	16.1	17	3	4	2	0	14	1	3	0	0	8	6	0	2	.000	0	3.31
	YEAR		22	274	6	1	0	3	65.1	66	11	16	3	0	51	3	5	2	1	36	34	3	5	.375	0	4.68
90	MIN/AL		34	239	1	0	0	10	58.1	55	9	9	2	0	44	2	3	3	0	23	22	7	3	.700	4	3.39
	TOR/AL		13	106	2	0	0	5	21.1	32	2	11	3	2	19	0	2	2	0	13	13	0	3	.000	1	5.48
	YEAR		47	345	3	0	0	15	79.2	87	11	20	5	2	63	2	5	5	0	36	35	7	6	.538	5	3.95
91	LA/NL		59	138	0	0	0	10	33.2	31	3	11	2	0	38	1	3	1	1	16	14	1	1	.500	2	3.74
17 YR TOTALS			**526**	**10166**	**356**	**54**	**13**	**65**	**2480.2**	**2354**	**242**	**570**	**59**	**36**	**1633**	**102**	**90**	**26**	**26**	**1010**	**909**	**175**	**114**	**.606**	**23**	**3.30**

Candiotti, Thomas Caesar "Tom" — bats right — throws right — b.8/31/57

YR	TM/LG	CL	G	TBF	GS	CG	SHO	GF	IP	H	HR	BB	IBB	HB	SO	SH	SF	WP	BK	R	ER	W	L	PCT	SV	ERA
83	MIL/AL		10	233	8	2	1	1	55.2	62	4	16	0	2	21	0	2	0	0	21	20	4	4	.500	0	3.23
84	VAN/PCL	AAA	15	0	15	4	0	0	96.2	96	4	22	0	2	53	0	3	3	1	36	31	8	4	.667	0	2.89
	BEL/MID	A	2	49	2	0	0	0	10.0	12	1	5	0	0	12	1	0	1	0	5	3	0	1	.000	0	2.70
	MIL/AL		8	147	6	0	0	0	32.1	38	5	10	0	0	23	0	0	1	0	21	19	2	2	.500	0	2.70
85	EP/TEX	AA	4	122	4	1	1	0	29.1	29	2	7	1	0	16	2	0	0	0	11	9	1	1	1.000	0	2.76
	VAN/PCL	AAA	24	0	24	5	1	0	150.2	178	14	36	2	4	97	0	0	0	5	83	66	9	13	.409	0	3.94
86	CLE/AL		36	1078	34	17	3	1	252.1	234	18	106	0	8	167	3	9	12	4	112	100	16	12	.571	0	3.57
87	CLE/AL		32	888	32	7	2	0	201.2	193	28	93	2	4	111	8	10	13	2	132	107	7	18	.280	0	4.78
88	CLE/AL		31	903	31	11	1	0	216.2	225	15	53	3	6	137	12	5	5	7	86	79	14	8	.636	0	3.28
89	CLE/AL		31	847	31	4	0	0	206.0	188	10	55	5	4	124	6	4	4	8	80	71	13	10	.565	0	3.10
90	CLE/AL		31	856	29	3	1	1	202.0	207	23	55	1	6	128	4	3	9	3	92	82	15	11	.577	0	3.65
91	CLE/AL		15	442	15	3	0	0	108.1	88	6	28	0	2	86	1	7	6	0	35	27	7	6	.538	0	2.24
	TOR/AL		19	539	19	3	0	0	129.2	114	6	45	1	4	81	3	4	5	0	47	43	6	7	.462	0	2.98
	YEAR		34	981	34	6	0	0	238.0	202	12	73	1	6	167	4	11	11	0	82	70	13	13	.500	0	2.65
8 YR TOTALS			**213**	**5933**	**205**	**50**	**8**	**3**	**1404.2**	**1349**	**115**	**461**	**12**	**36**	**878**	**37**	**44**	**55**	**24**	**626**	**548**	**84**	**78**	**.519**	**0**	**3.51**

Capel, Michael Lee "Mike" — bats right — throws right — b.10/13/61

YR	TM/LG	CL	G	TBF	GS	CG	SHO	GF	IP	H	HR	BB	IBB	HB	SO	SH	SF	WP	BK	R	ER	W	L	PCT	SV	ERA
83	MID/SOU	AA	3	0	3	0	0	0	14.0	22	3	8	0	0	8	0	0	0	0	12	11	1	1	.500	0	7.07
	QC/MID	A	8	0	6	1	0	0	44.0	32	6	14	0	6	35	0	0	5	0	15	12	3	2	.600	0	2.45
84	MID/TEX	AA	16	281	11	0	0	3	61.1	69	7	37	0	1	20	2	0	11	0	53	43	1	10	.091	0	6.31
	LOD/CAL	A+	20	0	6	1	0	3	69.0	54	4	35	2	1	46	0	0	6	1	38	28	0	7	.000	1	3.65
85	PIT/EAS	AA	33	339	4	0	0	16	73.1	74	4	47	2	1	53	4	3	6	1	44	40	3	6	.333	0	4.91
86	PIT/EAS	AA	38	258	0	0	0	27	62.2	51	2	22	4	0	50	5	2	1	0	20	13	4	4	.500	13	1.87
87	IOW/AMA	AAA	53	476	8	1	0	20	108.1	117	14	43	11	6	75	5	5	14	0	72	69	7	10	.412	4	5.73
88	IOW/AMA	AAA	32	248	2	0	0	13	57.2	60	2	23	1	1	49	5	2	4	3	24	22	3	2	.600	3	3.43
	CHI/NL		22	134	0	0	0	11	29.1	34	5	13	2	0	19	2	0	5	0	19	16	2	1	.667	0	4.91
89	IOW/AMA	AAA	64	414	0	0	0	28	97.0	87	9	41	4	3	62	9	1	7	2	43	35	4	7	.364	5	3.25
90	MIL/AL		2	9	0	0	0	0	0.1	6	0	1	0	1	1	0	0	1	0	6	5	0	0	.000	0	135.00
	DEN/AMA	AAA	41	432	3	0	0	11	101.1	98	6	39	0	5	60	6	6	3	2	55	48	4	3	.571	2	4.26
91	HOU/NL		25	143	0	0	0	13	32.2	33	3	15	1	0	23	3	1	2	0	14	11	1	3	.250	3	3.03
	TUC/PCL	AAA	30	227	0	0	0	9	56.1	49	1	17	2	5	44	1	0	4	0	16	15	4	2	.667	3	2.40
3 YR TOTALS			**49**	**286**	**0**	**0**	**0**	**24**	**62.1**	**73**	**8**	**29**	**3**	**4**	**43**	**5**	**1**	**5**	**0**	**39**	**32**	**3**	**4**	**.429**	**3**	**4.62**

Carman, Donald Wayne "Don" — bats left — throws left — b.8/14/59

YR	TM/LG	CL	G	TBF	GS	CG	SHO	GF	IP	H	HR	BB	IBB	HB	SO	SH	SF	WP	BK	R	ER	W	L	PCT	SV	ERA
83	PHI/NL		1	3	0	0	0	0	1.0	0	0	0	0	0	0	0	0	0	0	0	0	0	0	.000	1	0.00
84	POR/PCL	AAA	39	0	2	0	0	24	55.2	66	8	22	6	3	53	0	0	0	3	36	33	1	1	.500	3	5.34
	PHI/NL		11	61	0	0	0	9	13.1	14	2	6	4	0	16	0	0	3	0	9	8	0	1	.000	0	5.34
85	PHI/NL		71	342	0	0	0	33	86.1	52	6	38	3	2	87	5	5	1	0	25	20	9	4	.692	7	2.08
86	PHI/NL		50	545	14	2	1	13	134.1	113	11	52	11	3	98	5	3	6	2	50	48	10	5	.667	1	3.22
87	PHI/NL		35	886	35	3	2	0	211.0	194	34	69	7	5	125	11	4	3	1	110	99	13	11	.542	0	4.22
88	PHI/NL		36	873	32	2	0	0	201.1	211	20	70	6	4	116	9	8	3	0	101	96	10	14	.417	0	4.29
89	PHI/NL		49	683	20	0	0	5	149.1	152	21	86	6	3	81	5	5	7	3	98	87	5	15	.250	0	5.24
90	PHI/NL		59	368	1	0	0	11	86.2	69	13	38	7	4	58	6	4	6	1	43	40	6	2	.750	1	5.24
91	CIN/NL		28	164	0	0	0	10	36.0	40	8	19	1	1	15	3	1	2	0	23	21	0	2	.000	1	5.25

Carman, Donald Wayne "Don" (continued)

YR	TM/LG	CL	G	TBF	GS	CG	SHO	GF	IP	H	HR	BB	IBB	HB	SO	SH	SF	WP	BK	R	ER	W	L	PCT	SV	ERA
	OMA/AMA	AAA	14	112	2	0	0	1	25.0	29	0	13	1	0	14	2	0	2	0	12	11	3	3	.500	0	3.96
9 YR TOTALS			340	3925	102	7	3	82	919.1	845	115	378	45	22	596	44	31	36	10	459	419	53	54	.495	11	4.10

Carpenter, Cris Howell — bats right — throws right — b.4/5/65

YR	TM/LG	CL	G	TBF	GS	CG	SHO	GF	IP	H	HR	BB	IBB	HB	SO	SH	SF	WP	BK	R	ER	W	L	PCT	SV	ERA
88	STL/NL		8	203	8	1	0	0	47.2	56	3	9	2	1	24	1	4	1	0	27	25	2	3	.400	0	4.72
	LOU/AMA	AAA	13	359	13	1	1	0	87.2	81	7	26	0	0	45	2	1	1	0	28	28	6	2	.750	0	2.87
89	LOU/AMA	AAA	27	154	0	0	0	23	36.2	39	3	9	3	0	29	1	2	1	0	17	13	5	3	.625	11	3.19
	STL/NL		36	303	5	0	0	10	68.0	70	4	26	9	2	35	4	4	1	0	30	24	4	4	.500	0	3.18
90	STL/NL		4	32	0	0	0	1	8.0	5	2	2	1	0	6	0	0	0	0	4	4	0	0	.000	0	4.50
	LOU/AMA	AAA	22	591	22	2	1	0	143.1	146	16	21	2	6	100	6	5	1	1	61	59	10	8	.556	0	3.70
91	STL/NL		59	266	0	0	0	19	66.0	53	6	20	9	0	47	3	2	1	0	31	31	10	4	.714	0	4.23
4 YR TOTALS			107	804	13	1	0	30	189.2	184	15	57	21	3	112	8	10	3	0	92	84	16	11	.593	0	3.99

Carreno, Amalio Rafael (Adrian) — bats right — throws right — b.4/11/64

YR	TM/LG	CL	G	TBF	GS	CG	SHO	GF	IP	H	HR	BB	IBB	HB	SO	SH	SF	WP	BK	R	ER	W	L	PCT	SV	ERA
84	YAN/GCL	R	9	166	7	1	0	2	33.0	37	1	26	0	0	31	1	2	4	2	28	18	1	6	.143	0	4.91
85	YAN/GCL	R	1	9	0	0	0	0	2.0	1	0	1	0	0	1	0	0	1	0	1	1	0	0	.000	0	4.50
86	YAN/GCL	R	7	184	7	2	1	0	47.2	36	0	12	0	1	27	0	2	1	0	12	9	5	0	1.000	0	1.70
	FT./FSL	A+	3	70	3	1	0	0	15.2	16	0	7	1	0	8	0	0	3	0	11	7	1	1	.500	0	4.02
87	COL/INT	AAA	11	80	0	0	0	5	17.1	26	2	5	0	0	11	0	1	0	0	15	15	1	1	.500	1	7.79
	PW/CAR	A+	26	271	4	2	0	14	62.1	53	2	30	2	1	49	1	3	14	0	30	21	5	2	.714	2	3.03
	ALB/EAS	AA	9	116	3	0	0	4	24.0	32	6	15	1	0	18	1	0	1	0	23	21	0	3	.000	1	7.87
88	COL/INT	AAA	1	18	0	0	0	0	3.1	8	0	0	0	1	2	0	0	1	0	4	4	0	0	.000	0	10.80
	ALB/EAS	AA	9	175	7	1	0	2	38.1	38	3	21	2	3	24	1	1	1	1	20	15	2	4	.333	0	3.52
	REA/EAS	AA	5	93	4	0	0	1	21.1	22	1	11	0	1	7	0	1	1	0	12	12	1	0	1.000	0	5.06
89	REA/EAS	AA	31	443	11	2	1	11	101.2	99	9	41	2	4	56	3	6	9	0	57	49	5	7	.417	1	4.34
90	REA/EAS	AA	25	565	23	3	1	1	128.0	137	5	47	4	5	86	3	3	8	0	62	52	4	13	.235	1	3.66
91	PHI/NL		3	20	0	0	0	0	3.1	5	1	3	0	2	2	0	0	0	0	6	6	0	0	.000	0	16.20
	SCR/INT	AAA	33	358	8	0	0	12	81.0	88	7	26	3	1	52	4	4	1	1	51	48	4	8	.333	0	5.33

Carter, Jeffrey Allen "Jeff" — bats right — throws right — b.12/3/64

YR	TM/LG	CL	G	TBF	GS	CG	SHO	GF	IP	H	HR	BB	IBB	HB	SO	SH	SF	WP	BK	R	ER	W	L	PCT	SV	ERA
87	JAM/NYP	A–	31	178	0	0	0	20	42.1	39	1	17	0	0	42	1	3	5	0	15	11	2	3	.400	5	2.34
88	ROC/MID	A	39	447	11	1	0	11	107.1	100	8	35	3	1	91	0	0	7	3	38	33	11	5	.688	3	2.77
89	WPB/FSL	A+	7	148	7	0	0	0	35.0	36	0	8	0	1	29	1	2	1	0	14	10	4	1	.800	0	2.57
	JAC/SOU	AA	6	143	6	1	0	0	36.0	23	2	14	1	0	21	1	0	2	1	11	10	1	4	.200	0	2.50
90	JAC/SOU	AA	52	466	7	2	1	30	117.1	90	4	33	1	1	76	10	4	3	1	36	24	8	3	.727	15	1.84
91	VAN/PCL	AAA	41	344	4	0	0	26	79.2	78	3	35	5	1	40	7	3	3	0	33	27	3	7	.300	4	3.05
	CHI/AL		5	49	2	0	0	1	12.0	8	1	5	0	0	2	0	0	1	0	8	7	0	1	.000	0	5.25

Cary, Charles Douglas "Chuck" — bats left — throws left — b.3/3/60

YR	TM/LG	CL	G	TBF	GS	CG	SHO	GF	IP	H	HR	BB	IBB	HB	SO	SH	SF	WP	BK	R	ER	W	L	PCT	SV	ERA
84	BIR/SOU	AA	22	484	20	1	0	1	108.1	118	10	46	1	1	62	4	6	9	3	61	58	6	4	.600	0	4.82
85	NAS/AMA	AAA	48	269	0	0	0	16	66.0	55	6	27	1	3	54	2	3	4	0	27	22	2	1	.667	8	3.00
	DET/AL		16	95	0	0	0	6	23.2	16	2	8	1	2	22	0	1	0	0	9	9	0	1	.000	2	3.42
86	NAS/AMA	AAA	22	126	0	0	0	13	26.1	29	3	15	2	0	19	1	2	2	0	21	16	1	4	.200	0	5.47
	DET/AL		22	140.0	0	0	0	6	31.2	33	3	15	4	0	21	2	2	1	1	18	12	1	2	.333	0	3.41
87	RIC/INT	AAA	40	454	9	1	0	16	105.2	104	12	43	0	0	128	5	4	8	0	64	55	4	6	.400	3	4.68
	ATL/NL		13	70	0	0	0	6	16.2	17	3	4	3	1	15	1	0	1	0	7	7	1	1	.500	1	3.78
88	BRA/GCL	R	4	51	4	0	0	0	12.0	11	0	2	0	1	9	0	2	1	0	10	5	0	2	.000	0	3.75
	RIC/INT	AAA	5	26	0	0	0	2	6.1	4	0	2	0	1	3	0	0	0	0	6	1	0	0	.000	1	1.42
	ATL/NL		7	39	0	0	0	1	8.1	8	1	4	0	1	7	2	0	0	0	6	6	0	0	.000	0	6.48
89	COL/INT	AAA	11	97	2	0	0	6	23.1	17	1	13	1	0	27	0	1	1	2	9	8	1	1	.500	0	3.09
	NY/AL		22	404	11	2	0	4	99.1	78	13	29	6	0	79	1	1	6	1	42	36	4	4	.500	0	3.26
90	NY/AL		28	661	27	4	0	1	156.2	155	21	55	1	1	134	3	5	11	2	77	73	6	12	.333	0	4.19
91	COL/INT	AAA	8	207	8	0	0	0	45.2	44	9	26	0	0	28	2	0	6	2	31	29	5	3	.625	0	5.72
	NY/AL		10	247	9	0	0	0	53.1	61	6	32	2	0	34	1	0	2	1	35	35	1	5	.143	0	5.91
7 YR TOTALS			118	1656	47	4	0	24	389.2	368	49	147	17	5	312	10	9	22	5	194	178	13	26	.333	3	4.11

Casian, Lawrence Paul "Larry" — bats right — throws left — b.10/28/65

YR	TM/LG	CL	G	TBF	GS	CG	SHO	GF	IP	H	HR	BB	IBB	HB	SO	SH	SF	WP	BK	R	ER	W	L	PCT	SV	ERA
87	VIS/CAL	A+	18	400	15	2	1	3	97.0	89	3	49	0	7	96	1	2	7	0	35	27	10	3	.769	2	2.51
88	ORL/SOU	AA	27	723	26	4	1	0	174.0	165	14	62	1	7	104	6	4	12	8	72	57	9	9	.500	0	2.95
	POR/PCL	AAA	1	14	0	0	0	1	2.2	5	1	0	0	0	2	1	0	0	0	3	0	0	0	.000	0	0.00
89	POR/PCL	AAA	28	738	27	0	0	0	169.1	201	13	63	0	6	65	5	6	5	2	97	85	7	12	.368	0	4.52
90	POR/PCL	AAA	37	682	23	1	0	4	156.2	171	14	59	5	3	89	8	4	2	2	90	78	9	9	.500	0	4.48
	MIN/AL		5	90	3	0	0	1	22.1	26	2	4	0	0	11	0	1	0	0	9	8	2	1	.667	0	3.22
91	MIN/AL		15	87	0	0	0	4	18.1	28	4	7	2	1	6	0	0	0	0	16	15	0	0	.000	0	7.36
	POR/PCL	AAA	34	215	6	0	0	10	52.0	51	3	16	1	1	24	0	2	1	2	25	20	6	3	.667	0	3.46
2 YR TOTALS			20	177	3	0	0	5	40.2	54	6	11	2	1	17	0	1	2	0	25	23	2	1	.667	0	5.09

Castillo, Antonio Jose (Jimenez) "Tony" — bats left — throws left — b.3/1/63

YR	TM/LG	CL	G	TBF	GS	CG	SHO	GF	IP	H	HR	BB	IBB	HB	SO	SH	SF	WP	BK	R	ER	W	L	PCT	SV	ERA
83	BJ/GCL	R	1	0	0	0	0	0	3.0	3	0	0	0	0	0	0	0	0	0	1	1	0	0	.000	1	3.00
84	FLO/SAL	A	25	592	24	4	1	0	137.1	123	11	50	0	0	96	2	2	4	0	71	52	11	8	.579	0	3.41
85	KIN/CAR	A+	36	546	12	0	0	8	127.2	111	5	48	3	3	136	5	0	2	0	44	27	11	7	.611	3	1.90
87	DUN/FSL	A+	39	293	0	0	0	18	69.2	62	2	19	1	5	62	3	1	4	0	30	26	6	2	.750	6	3.36
88	DUN/FSL	A+	30	166	0	0	0	23	42.2	31	0	10	1	0	46	4	2	0	2	9	7	4	3	.571	12	1.48
	KNO/SOU	AA	5	27	0	0	0	2	8.0	2	0	1	0	0	11	0	0	0	0	0	0	1	0	1.000	2	0.00
	TOR/AL		14	54	0	0	0	6	15.0	10	0	2	0	0	14	0	2	0	0	5	5	1	0	1.000	3	3.00
89	SYR/INT	AAA	27	171	0	0	0	19	41.2	33	7	15	2	0	37	3	1	1	1	15	13	1	3	.250	5	2.81
	TOR/AL		17	86	0	0	0	8	17.2	23	0	10	5	1	10	2	4	3	0	14	12	1	1	.500	1	6.11
	ATL/NL		12	41	0	0	0	1	9.1	8	0	4	1	0	5	1	0	0	0	5	5	0	1	.000	0	4.82
	YEAR		29	127	0	0	0	9	27.0	31	0	14	6	1	15	3	4	3	0	19	17	1	2	.333	1	5.67
90	RIC/INT	AAA	5	93	4	1	1	1	25.0	14	5	6	0	0	27	1	1	1	0	7	7	3	1	.750	0	2.52
	ATL/NL		52	337	3	0	0	7	76.2	93	5	20	3	1	64	4	4	2	2	41	36	5	1	.833	1	4.23
91	RIC/INT	AAA	23	462	17	0	0	0	118.0	89	4	32	1	0	78	5	2	2	2	47	38	5	6	.455	0	2.90
	ATL/NL		7	44	0	0	0	5	8.2	13	3	5	0	0	8	1	0	0	0	9	7	1	1	.500	0	7.27
	NY/NL		10	104	3	0	0	5	23.2	27	1	6	1	0	18	1	1	1	0	7	5	1	0	1.000	0	1.90
	YEAR		17	148	3	0	0	5	32.1	40	4	11	1	0	18	2	1	1	0	16	12	2	1	.667	0	3.34
4 YR TOTALS			112	666	6	0	0	28	151.0	174	11	47	10	2	111	9	11	5	2	81	70	9	4	.692	2	4.17

Castillo, Frank Anthony — bats right — throws right — b.4/1/69

YR	TM/LG	CL	G	TBF	GS	CG	SHO	GF	IP	H	HR	BB	IBB	HB	SO	SH	SF	WP	BK	R	ER	W	L	PCT	SV	ERA
87	WYT/APP	R+	12	372	12	5	0	0	90.1	86	4	21	0	5	83	3	2	2	1	31	23	10	1	.909	0	2.29
	GEN/NYP	A-	1	23	1	0	0	0	6.0	3	0	1	0	0	6	0	0	0	0	1	0	1	0	1.000	0	0.00
88	PEO/MID	A	9	186	8	2	2	0	51.0	25	1	10	0	1	58	0	0	0	0	5	4	6	1	.857	0	0.71
89	WIN/CAR	A+	18	521	18	8	1	0	129.1	118	5	24	1	3	114	2	1	1	1	42	36	9	6	.600	0	2.51
	CHA/SOU	AA	10	283	10	4	0	0	68.0	73	7	12	3	1	43	4	2	1	0	35	29	3	4	.429	0	3.84
90	CHA/SOU	AA	18	471	18	4	1	0	111.1	113	8	27	4	8	112	6	3	5	1	54	48	6	6	.500	0	3.88
91	IOW/AMA	AAA	4	98	4	1	1	0	25.0	20	0	7	1	0	20	0	1	2	0	7	7	3	1	.750	0	2.52
	CHI/NL		18	467	18	4	0	0	111.2	107	5	33	2	0	73	6	3	5	1	56	54	6	7	.462	0	4.35

Cerutti, John Joseph — bats left — throws left — b.4/28/60

YR	TM/LG	CL	G	TBF	GS	CG	SHO	GF	IP	H	HR	BB	IBB	HB	SO	SH	SF	WP	BK	R	ER	W	L	PCT	SV	ERA
84	SYR/INT	AAA	29	639	22	6	0	3	148.0	152	20	52	3	2	114	7	8	5	4	89	73	7	13	.350	0	4.44
85	SYR/INT	AAA	28	757	27	7	2	1	182.0	165	10	60	2	2	110	10	8	6	1	84	60	11	9	.550	0	2.97
	TOR/AL		4	36	1	0	0	1	6.2	10	1	4	0	1	5	0	0	2	0	7	4	0	2	.000	0	5.40
86	SYR/INT	AAA	7	191	7	2	1	0	43.2	44	5	16	0	0	22	1	1	1	2	27	20	1	3	.250	0	4.12
	TOR/AL		34	616	20	2	1	3	145.1	150	25	47	2	1	89	4	5	8	0	73	67	9	4	.692	1	4.15
87	TOR/AL		44	638	21	2	0	6	151.1	144	30	59	5	1	92	3	2	5	1	75	74	11	4	.733	0	4.40
88	TOR/AL		46	524	12	0	0	11	123.2	120	12	42	4	3	65	8	3	7	3	56	43	6	7	.462	1	3.13
89	TOR/AL		33	856	31	3	1	1	205.1	214	19	53	2	4	69	7	5	4	2	90	70	11	11	.500	0	3.07
90	TOR/AL		30	609	23	0	0	1	140.0	162	23	49	3	4	49	5	5	2	0	77	74	9	9	.500	0	4.76
91	DET/AL		38	389	8	1	0	10	88.2	94	9	37	9	2	29	7	3	4	1	49	45	3	6	.333	2	4.57
7 YR TOTALS			229	3668	116	8	2	33	861.0	894	119	291	27	18	398	34	23	34	8	427	377	49	43	.533	4	3.94

Chapin, Darrin John — bats right — throws right — b.2/1/66

YR	TM/LG	CL	G	TBF	GS	CG	SHO	GF	IP	H	HR	BB	IBB	HB	SO	SH	SF	WP	BK	R	ER	W	L	PCT	SV	ERA
86	YAN/GCL	R	13	341	13	2	2	0	83.1	71	2	27	1	2	67	3	3	10	1	42	30	4	3	.571	0	3.24
87	ONE/NYP	A-	25	170	0	0	0	21	40.0	31	1	17	5	0	26	2	1	6	0	8	3	1	1	.500	12	0.68
88	ALB/EAS	AA	3	26	0	0	0	3	4.0	11	0	2	0	1	4	0	0	0	0	7	5	0	0	.000	0	11.25
	FT./FSL	A+	38	234	0	0	0	33	63.0	39	1	19	1	0	57	4	1	3	1	8	6	6	4	.600	15	0.86
89	ALB/EAS	AA	7	32	0	0	0	7	8.2	5	0	1	1	0	16	0	0	2	0	0	0	1	0	1.000	3	0.00
	COL/INT	AAA	27	167	0	0	0	21	40.0	33	3	15	4	1	38	3	1	3	1	15	13	2	4	.333	5	2.93
90	COL/INT	AAA	6	41	0	0	0	6	8.2	10	0	6	0	0	8	0	0	1	0	8	7	0	1	.000	2	7.27
	ALB/EAS	AA	43	223	0	0	0	40	52.2	43	2	21	1	4	61	1	4	4	0	20	16	3	2	.600	21	2.73
91	COL/INT	AAA	55	328	0	0	0	28	78.1	54	5	40	3	1	69	5	3	5	1	23	17	10	3	.769	12	1.95
	NY/AL		3	25	0	0	0	2	5.1	3	0	6	0	0	5	0	0	2	0	3	3	0	1	.000	0	5.06

Charlton, Norman Wood "Norm" — bats both — throws left — b.1/6/63

YR	TM/LG	CL	G	TBF	GS	CG	SHO	GF	IP	H	HR	BB	IBB	HB	SO	SH	SF	WP	BK	R	ER	W	L	PCT	SV	ERA
84	WPB/FSL	A+	8	187	8	0	0	0	39.1	51	2	22	0	1	27	2	3	1	1	27	20	1	4	.200	0	4.58
85	WPB/FSL	A+	24	571	23	5	2	0	128.0	135	7	79	1	4	71	4	4	9	0	79	65	7	10	.412	0	4.57
86	VER/EAS	AA	22	578	22	6	1	0	136.2	109	4	74	2	3	96	6	9	8	0	55	43	10	6	.625	0	2.83
87	NAS/AMA	AAA	18	426	17	3	1	0	98.1	97	8	44	1	1	74	6	2	7	2	57	47	2	8	.200	0	4.30
88	NAS/AMA	AAA	27	743	27	8	1	0	182.0	149	7	56	1	2	161	9	3	13	17	69	61	11	10	.524	0	3.02
	CIN/NL		10	259	10	0	0	0	61.1	60	6	20	2	2	39	1	2	3	2	27	27	4	5	.444	0	3.96
89	CIN/NL		69	393	0	0	0	27	95.1	67	5	40	7	2	98	9	2	2	3	31	31	8	3	.727	0	2.93
90	CIN/NL		56	650	16	1	1	13	154.1	131	10	70	4	2	117	7	2	9	2	53	47	12	9	.571	2	2.74
91	CIN/NL		39	438	11	0	0	10	108.1	92	6	34	4	6	77	1	1	11	0	37	35	3	5	.375	1	2.91
4 YR TOTALS			174	1740	37	1	1	50	419.1	350	27	164	17	14	331	24	7	25	7	155	140	27	22	.551	3	3.00

Chiamparino, Scott Michael — bats right — throws right — b.8/22/66

YR	TM/LG	CL	G	TBF	GS	CG	SHO	GF	IP	H	HR	BB	IBB	HB	SO	SH	SF	WP	BK	R	ER	W	L	PCT	SV	ERA
87	MED/NWL	A-	13	288	11	3	1	1	67.2	64	2	20	0	3	65	1	3	6	0	29	19	5	4	.556	0	2.53
88	MOD/CAL	A+	16	456	16	5	3	0	106.2	89	1	56	0	0	117	2	2	17	4	40	32	5	7	.417	0	2.70

Chiamparino, Scott Michael (continued)

YR	TM/LG	CL	G	TBF	GS	CG	SHO	GF	IP	H	HR	BB	IBB	HB	SO	SH	SF	WP	BK	R	ER	W	L	PCT	SV	ERA
	HUN/SOU	AA	13	365	13	4	0	0	84.0	88	3	26	2	1	49	1	7	5	1	36	30	4	5	.444	0	3.21
89	HUN/SOU	AA	17	440	17	2	1	0	101.2	109	8	29	0	4	87	4	3	8	0	60	52	8	6	.571	0	4.60
90	TAC/PCL	AAA	26	744	26	4	2	0	173.0	174	10	72	1	5	110	5	4	9	1	79	63	13	9	.591	0	3.28
	TEX/AL		6	160	6	0	0	0	37.2	36	1	12	0	2	19	1	1	5	0	14	11	1	2	.333	0	2.63
91	TEX/AL		5	101	5	0	0	0	22.1	26	1	12	0	0	8	1	0	0	0	11	10	1	0	1.000	0	4.03
2 YR TOTALS			**11**	**261**	**11**	**0**	**0**	**0**	**60.0**	**62**	**2**	**24**	**0**	**2**	**27**	**2**	**1**	**5**	**0**	**25**	**21**	**2**	**2**	**.500**	**0**	**3.15**

Chitren, Stephen Vincent "Steve" — bats right — throws right — b.6/8/67

YR	TM/LG	CL	G	TBF	GS	CG	SHO	GF	IP	H	HR	BB	IBB	HB	SO	SH	SF	WP	BK	R	ER	W	L	PCT	SV	ERA
89	SO/NWL	A-	2	20	0	0	0	1	5.0	3	0	2	0	0	3	0	1	0	0	2	1	0	0	.000	0	1.80
	MAD/MID	A	20	85	0	0	0	18	22.2	13	1	4	0	2	17	0	2	0	0	3	3	2	1	.667	7	1.19
90	HUN/SOU	AA	48	218	0	0	0	39	53.2	32	4	22	1	3	61	0	0	2	0	18	10	2	4	.333	27	1.68
	TAC/PCL	AAA	1	3	0	0	0	1	0.2	1	0	0	0	0	0	0	0	0	0	0	0	0	0	.000	0	0.00
	OAK/AL		8	64	0	0	0	4	17.2	7	0	4	0	0	19	0	0	2	0	2	2	1	0	1.000	0	1.02
91	OAK/AL		56	271	0	0	0	20	60.1	59	8	32	4	4	47	4	2	2	1	31	29	1	4	.200	4	4.33
2 YR TOTALS			**64**	**335**	**0**	**0**	**0**	**24**	**78.0**	**66**	**8**	**36**	**4**	**4**	**66**	**4**	**2**	**4**	**1**	**33**	**31**	**2**	**4**	**.333**	**4**	**3.58**

Christopher, Michael Wayne "Mike" — bats right — throws right — b.11/3/63

YR	TM/LG	CL	G	TBF	GS	CG	SHO	GF	IP	H	HR	BB	IBB	HB	SO	SH	SF	WP	BK	R	ER	W	L	PCT	SV	ERA
85	ONE/NYP	A-	15	317	9	2	2	3	80.1	58	1	22	0	3	84	1	2	3	0	21	13	8	1	.889	0	1.46
86	ALB/EAS	AA	11	273	11	2	0	0	60.2	75	6	12	1	3	34	2	4	3	0	48	34	3	5	.375	0	5.04
	FT./FSL	A+	15	421	14	3	1	0	102.2	92	2	36	0	1	56	4	2	1	1	37	30	7	3	.700	0	2.63
87	FT./FSL	A+	24	694	24	9	4	0	169.1	183	5	28	1	0	81	6	4	4	0	63	46	13	8	.619	0	2.44
88	ALB/EAS	AA	24	648	24	5	1	0	152.2	166	7	44	3	6	67	4	5	2	4	75	65	13	7	.650	0	3.83
89	COL/INT	AAA	13	331	11	1	0	0	73.0	95	6	21	3	3	42	6	5	1	0	45	39	5	6	.455	0	4.81
	ALB/EAS	AA	8	213	8	3	0	0	53.2	48	1	7	0	1	33	0	1	0	0	17	15	6	1	.857	0	2.52
90	ALB/PCL	AAA	54	287	0	0	0	25	68.2	62	3	23	3	2	47	5	4	0	0	20	15	6	1	.857	8	1.97
91	ALB/PCL	AAA	63	334	0	0	0	34	77.1	73	2	30	5	3	67	4	1	7	1	25	21	7	2	.778	16	2.44
	LA/NL		3	15	0	0	0	2	4.0	2	0	3	0	0	0	0	0	0	0	0	0	0	0	.000	0	0.00

Clancy, James "Jim" — bats right — throws right — b.12/18/55

YR	TM/LG	CL	G	TBF	GS	CG	SHO	GF	IP	H	HR	BB	IBB	HB	SO	SH	SF	WP	BK	R	ER	W	L	PCT	SV	ERA
77	TOR/AL		13	346	13	4	1	0	76.2	80	7	47	1	0	44	6	7	4	0	47	43	4	9	.308	0	5.05
78	TOR/AL		31	846	30	7	0	0	193.2	199	10	91	1	1	106	8	10	10	0	96	88	10	12	.455	0	4.09
79	TOR/AL		12	278	11	2	0	0	63.2	65	8	31	0	0	33	3	5	2	0	44	39	2	7	.222	0	5.51
80	TOR/AL		34	1075	34	15	2	0	250.2	217	19	128	4	2	152	9	4	10	0	108	92	13	16	.448	0	3.30
81	TOR/AL		22	556	22	2	0	0	125.0	126	12	64	0	5	56	2	4	12	0	77	68	6	12	.333	0	4.90
82	TOR/AL		40	1100	40	11	3	0	266.2	251	26	77	1	2	139	5	4	6	0	122	110	16	14	.533	0	3.71
83	TOR/AL		34	955	34	11	1	0	223.0	238	23	61	0	1	99	4	12	3	0	115	97	15	11	.577	0	3.91
84	TOR/AL		36	966	36	5	0	0	219.2	249	25	88	2	3	118	4	4	10	0	132	125	13	15	.464	0	5.12
85	KNO/SOU	AA	2	32	2	0	0	0	8.0	7	0	2	0	0	2	0	0	0	0	3	3	1	0	1.000	0	3.38
	TOR/AL		23	527	23	0	0	0	128.2	117	15	37	0	0	66	0	5	2	0	54	54	9	6	.600	0	3.78
86	TOR/AL		34	913	34	6	3	0	219.1	202	24	63	0	4	126	0	9	4	0	100	96	14	14	.500	0	3.94
87	TOR/AL		37	1008	37	5	1	0	241.1	234	24	80	5	1	180	5	4	12	1	103	95	15	11	.577	0	3.54
88	TOR/AL		36	827	31	4	0	5	196.1	207	26	47	3	9	118	4	4	4	0	106	98	11	13	.458	1	4.49
89	HOU/NL		33	655	26	1	0	3	147.0	155	13	66	15	3	91	9	4	6	3	71	63	7	14	.333	0	3.92
90	TUC/PCL	AAA	10	186	5	0	0	0	42.1	48	1	9	2	2	34	1	1	0	1	17	14	3	2	.600	0	2.98
	HOU/NL		33	352	10	0	0	8	76.0	100	4	33	9	3	44	1	4	3	0	58	55	2	8	.200	0	6.51
91	HOU/NL		30	215	0	0	0	13	55.0	37	5	20	3	0	33	1	2	5	0	19	17	0	3	.000	5	2.78
	ATL/NL		24	153	0	0	0	9	34.2	36	3	14	1	1	17	1	2	5	0	23	22	3	2	.600	3	5.71
	YEAR		54	368	0	0	0	22	89.2	73	8	34	4	1	50	2	4	10	0	42	39	3	5	.375	8	3.91
15 YR TOTALS			**472**	**10772**	**381**	**74**	**11**	**38**	**2517.1**	**2513**	**244**	**947**	**45**	**32**	**1422**	**70**	**84**	**101**	**4**	**1304**	**1182**	**140**	**167**	**.456**	**10**	**4.23**

Clark, Mark Willard — bats right — throws right — b.5/12/68

YR	TM/LG	CL	G	TBF	GS	CG	SHO	GF	IP	H	HR	BB	IBB	HB	SO	SH	SF	WP	BK	R	ER	W	L	PCT	SV	ERA
88	HAM/NYP	A-	15	385	15	2	0	0	94.1	88	10	32	2	0	60	4	3	2	1	39	32	6	7	.462	0	3.05
89	SAV/SAL	A	27	712	27	4	2	0	173.2	143	8	52	0	1	132	4	4	11	3	61	47	14	9	.609	0	2.44
90	SP/FSL	A+	10	254	10	1	1	0	62.0	63	3	14	0	1	58	2	2	3	1	33	21	3	2	.600	0	3.05
	ARK/TEX	AA	19	479	19	4	0	0	115.1	111	11	37	2	0	87	6	4	5	0	56	49	5	11	.313	0	3.82
91	ARK/TEX	AA	15	398	15	4	1	0	92.1	99	2	30	1	4	76	3	2	0	0	50	41	5	5	.500	0	4.00
	LOU/AMA	AAA	7	189	6	1	1	0	45.1	43	4	15	0	0	29	1	3	2	0	17	15	3	2	.600	0	2.98
	STL/NL		7	93	2	0	0	1	22.1	17	3	11	0	0	13	0	3	2	0	10	10	1	1	.500	0	4.03

Clemens, William Roger "Roger" — bats right — throws right — b.8/4/62

YR	TM/LG	CL	G	TBF	GS	CG	SHO	GF	IP	H	HR	BB	IBB	HB	SO	SH	SF	WP	BK	R	ER	W	L	PCT	SV	ERA
84	PAW/INT	AAA	7	189	6	3	1	1	46.2	39	3	14	0	0	50	3	1	0	0	12	10	2	3	.400	0	1.93
	BOS/AL		21	575	20	5	1	0	133.1	146	13	29	3	2	126	2	3	4	0	67	64	9	4	.692	0	4.32
85	BOS/AL		15	407	15	3	1	0	98.1	83	5	37	0	3	74	1	2	1	3	38	36	7	5	.583	0	3.29
86	BOS/AL		33	997	33	10	1	0	254.0	179	21	67	0	4	238	4	6	11	3	77	70	24	4	.857	0	2.48
87	BOS/AL		36	1157	36	18	7	0	281.2	248	19	83	4	9	256	6	4	4	3	100	93	20	9	.690	0	2.97
88	BOS/AL		35	1063	35	14	8	0	264.0	217	17	62	4	6	291	9	5	7	0	101	88	17	11	.607	0	3.13
89	BOS/AL		35	1044	35	8	3	0	253.1	215	20	93	5	3	230	7	5	8	0	59	49	21	6	.778	0	1.93
90	BOS/AL		31	920	31	7	4	0	228.1	193	7	54	1	6	209	5	5	5	0							

(continued)

Clemens, William Roger "Roger" (continued)

YR	TM/LG	CL	G	TBF	GS	CG	SHO	GF	IP	H	HR	BB	IBB	HB	SO	SH	SF	WP	BK	R	ER	W	L	PCT	SV	ERA
91	BOS/AL		35	1077	35	13	4	0	271.1	219	15	65	12	5	241	6	8	6	0	93	79	18	10	.643	0	2.62
8 YR TOTALS			241	7240	240	78	29	0	1784.1	1500	117	490	31	44	1665	41	36	45	16	628	565	134	61	.687	0	2.85

Clemens, Patrick Brian "Pat" — bats right — throws left — b.2/2/62

YR	TM/LG	CL	G	TBF	GS	CG	SHO	GF	IP	H	HR	BB	IBB	HB	SO	SH	SF	WP	BK	R	ER	W	L	PCT	SV	ERA
83	PEO/MID	A	15	0	14	4	0	0	92.0	113	5	24	0	3	67	0	0	8	0	56	46	4	7	.364	0	4.50
84	WAT/EAS	AA	43	286	2	1	0	28	67.0	59	2	29	4	3	44	5	6	6	0	28	20	4	2	.667	9	2.69
85	CAL/AL		41	247	0	0	0	12	62.0	47	4	25	2	2	19	4	0	1	0	23	23	5	0	1.000	3	3.34
	PIT/NL		27	153	0	0	0	7	34.1	39	2	15	3	0	17	2	1	2	0	14	14	0	2	.000	2	3.67
	YEAR		68	400	0	0	0	19	96.1	86	6	40	5	2	36	6	1	3	0	37	37	5	2	.714	3	3.46
86	PIT/NL		65	256	0	0	0	19	61.0	53	1	32	6	2	31	7	4	2	0	20	19	0	4	.000	2	2.80
87	COL/INT	AAA	4	75	2	0	0	1	19.0	19	3	2	0	0	7	0	0	0	0	8	8	1	0	1.000	0	3.79
	NY/AL		55	347	0	0	0	20	80.0	91	4	30	2	3	36	6	4	8	2	45	44	3	3	.500	7	4.95
88	COL/INT	AAA	32	585	16	0	0	9	144.0	136	5	34	5	5	69	6	3	2	0	55	44	6	7	.462	5	2.75
	NY/AL		6	41	1	0	0	1	8.1	12	1	4	0	0	3	0	2	1	0	8	6	0	0	.000	0	6.48
89	LV/PCL	AAA	18	241	6	0	0	4	55.0	57	5	24	5	1	34	1	3	3	0	31	25	3	1	.750	2	4.09
	SD/NL		23	167	1	0	0	8	39.0	39	4	15	5	0	18	5	1	1	0	17	17	4	1	.800	0	3.92
90	SD/NL		9	63	0	0	0	3	13.0	20	1	7	1	0	6	0	0	0	0	9	6	0	0	.000	0	4.15
	LV/PCL	AAA	26	394	13	0	0	5	86.1	106	7	34	3	0	57	2	1	0	2	68	58	4	3	.571	0	6.05
91	LV/PCL	AAA	11	54	0	0	0	4	12.0	15	3	5	1	0	4	0	0	1	1	11	11	0	0	.000	0	8.25
	SD/NL		12	63	0	0	0	4	14.1	13	0	9	4	0	8	0	3	0	0	8	6	1	0	1.000	0	3.77
7 YR TOTALS			238	1337	2	0	0	74	312.0	314	17	137	23	7	138	24	15	16	2	144	135	13	10	.565	12	3.89

Combs, Patrick Dennis "Pat" — bats left — throws left — b.10/29/66

YR	TM/LG	CL	G	TBF	GS	CG	SHO	GF	IP	H	HR	BB	IBB	HB	SO	SH	SF	WP	BK	R	ER	W	L	PCT	SV	ERA
89	CLE/FSL	A+	6	165	6	1	0	0	41.2	35	0	11	0	1	24	3	0	0	1	8	6	2	1	.667	0	1.30
	REA/EAS	AA	19	512	19	4	0	0	125.0	104	16	40	2	4	77	6	2	5	2	57	47	8	7	.533	0	3.38
	SW/INT	AAA	3	94	3	2	1	0	24.1	15	0	7	0	0	20	0	1	1	0	4	1	3	0	1.000	0	0.37
	PHI/NL		6	153	6	1	1	0	38.2	36	2	6	1	0	30	0	1	0	0	10	9	4	0	1.000	0	2.09
90	PHI/NL		32	800	31	3	2	0	183.1	179	12	86	7	4	108	7	7	9	1	90	83	10	10	.500	0	4.07
91	PHI/NL		14	300	13	1	0	0	64.1	64	7	43	1	2	41	1	2	7	0	41	35	2	6	.250	0	4.90
	SCR/INT	AAA	6	132	6	1	0	0	27.0	39	0	16	0	0	14	2	3	1	0	23	20	2	2	.500	0	6.67
3 YR TOTALS			52	1253	50	5	3	0	286.1	279	21	135	9	6	179	10	9	21	1	141	127	16	16	.500	0	3.99

Comstock, Keith Martin — bats left — throws left — b.12/23/55

YR	TM/LG	CL	G	TBF	GS	CG	SHO	GF	IP	H	HR	BB	IBB	HB	SO	SH	SF	WP	BK	R	ER	W	L	PCT	SV	ERA
76	IF/PIO	R+	15	0	2	0	0	0	37.0	33	1	32	0	0	45	0	0	2	2	18	16	1	4	.200	5	3.89
77	DAV/MID	A	18	0	0	0	0	0	32.0	22	5	18	0	1	39	0	0	0	2	18	18	1	0	1.000	5	5.06
	SAL/CAL	A+	23	0	0	0	0	0	33.0	35	3	18	0	1	41	0	0	2	0	26	17	1	1	.500	6	4.64
78	SAL/CAL	A+	27	0	6	5	1	0	82.0	70	8	46	0	0	71	0	0	3	3	31	26	6	4	.600	2	2.85
79	EP/TEX	AA	16	0	8	1	0	0	63.0	95	12	35	0	2	18	0	0	5	1	64	50	2	5	.286	0	7.14
80	WH/EAS	AA	29	0	3	2	0	0	73.0	64	8	37	0	0	52	0	0	10	0	40	34	4	4	.333	1	4.19
81	WH/EAS	AA	35	0	22	1	0	0	145.0	123	18	80	0	1	133	0	0	13	2	76	66	8	7	.533	0	4.10
82	TAC/PCL	AAA	5	0	5	0	0	0	27.0	34	4	12	0	1	22	0	0	0	0	24	22	1	2	.333	0	7.33
	WH/EAS	AA	24	0	18	4	2	0	125.0	99	11	69	0	3	132	0	0	8	0	48	42	9	5	.643	0	3.02
83	BIR/SOU	AA	37	0	14	4	3	0	145.0	130	14	63	0	2	136	0	0	5	0	58	52	12	3	.800	1	3.23
84	MIN/AL		4	28	0	0	0	2	6.1	6	4	4	0	0	2	1	0	0	0	6	6	0	0	.000	0	8.53
	TOL/INT	AAA	23	670	23	6	0	0	164.1	132	13	56	0	0	154	4	3	5	4	58	51	12	6	.667	0	2.79
87	PHO/PCL	AAA	17	158	1	0	0	7	39.0	24	0	23	0	0	35	0	1	1	1	12	12	4	2	.667	2	2.77
	SF/NL		15	87	0	0	0	3	20.2	19	1	10	2	0	21	1	1	3	1	8	7	2	0	1.000	1	3.05
	SD/NL		26	157	0	0	0	12	36.0	33	4	21	3	0	38	2	3	3	0	22	22	0	1	.000	0	5.50
	YEAR		41	244	0	0	0	15	56.2	52	5	31	5	0	59	3	4	6	1	30	29	2	1	.667	1	4.61
88	SD/NL		7	35	0	0	0	3	8.0	8	1	3	1	0	9	0	0	2	1	6	6	0	0	.000	0	6.75
	LV/PCL	AAA	50	312	0	0	0	39	71.2	67	5	31	1	0	78	2	2	5	2	32	25	5	4	.556	17	3.14
89	LV/PCL	AAA	28	206	0	0	0	23	48.1	40	3	20	3	0	60	9	2	3	0	17	17	7	1	.875	9	3.17
	CAL/PCL	AAA	5	30	0	0	0	4	7.0	5	0	1	0	2	4	2	0	1	0	2	1	2	1	.667	1	1.29
	SEA/AL		31	111	0	0	0	7	25.2	26	2	10	2	0	22	2	2	2	0	8	8	1	2	.333	0	2.81
90	SEA/AL		60	228	0	0	0	19	56.0	40	4	26	5	0	50	5	3	2	1	22	18	7	4	.636	2	2.89
91	CAL/PCL	AAA	15	148	0	0	0	4	35.2	25	4	16	0	0	38	2	1	2	2	16	13	3	1	.750	2	3.28
	SEA/AL		1	4	0	0	0	0	0.1	2	0	1	0	0	0	0	0	0	0	2	2	0	0	.000	0	54.00
6 YR TOTALS			144	650	0	0	0	46	153.0	134	14	75	13	0	142	11	9	12	3	74	69	10	7	.588	3	4.06

Cone, David Bryan — bats left — throws right — b.1/2/63

YR	TM/LG	CL	G	TBF	GS	CG	SHO	GF	IP	H	HR	BB	IBB	HB	SO	SH	SF	WP	BK	R	ER	W	L	PCT	SV	ERA
84	MEM/SOU	AA	29	804	29	9	1	0	178.2	162	9	114	1	5	110	6	9	27	4	103	85	8	12	.400	0	4.28
85	OMA/AMA	AAA	28	710	27	5	1	0	158.2	157	13	93	3	2	115	8	7	4	4	90	82	9	15	.375	0	4.65
86	OMA/AMA	AAA	39	296	2	2	0	33	71.0	60	3	25	4	3	63	2	6	6	1	23	22	8	4	.667	14	2.79
	KC/AL		11	108	0	0	0	5	22.2	29	2	13	1	1	21	0	0	3	0	14	14	0	0	.000	0	5.56
87	TID/INT	AAA	3	51	3	0	0	0	11.0	10	1	6	0	1	7	1	0	0	0	8	7	0	1	.000	0	5.73
	NY/NL		21	420	13	1	0	3	99.1	87	11	44	1	5	68	4	3	2	4	46	41	5	6	.455	1	3.71
88	NY/NL		35	936	28	8	4	0	231.1	178	10	80	7	4	213	11	5	10	10	67	57	20	3	.870	0	2.22
89	NY/NL		34	910	33	7	2	0	219.2	183	20	74	4	9	190	6	4	14	4	92	86	14	8	.636	0	3.52
90	NY/NL		31	860	30	6	2	1	211.2	177	21	65	4	10	233	6	4	10	4	84	76	14	10	.583	0	3.23
91	NY/NL		34	966	34	5	2	0	232.2	204	13	73	2	5	241	13	7	17	1	95	85	14	14	.500	0	3.29
6 YR TOTALS			166	4200	138	27	10	9	1017.1	858	77	349	18	20	966	38	25	56	23	398	359	67	41	.620	1	3.18

Cook, Dennis Bryan — bats left — throws left — b.10/4/62

YR	TM/LG	CL	G	TBF	GS	CG	SHO	GF	IP	H	HR	BB	IBB	HB	SO	SH	SF	WP	BK	R	ER	W	L	PCT	SV	ERA
85	CLI/MID	A	13	343	13	1	0	0	83.0	73	7	27	0	2	40	0	4	5	4	35	31	5	4	.556	0	3.36
86	FRE/CAL	A+	27	735	25	2	1	2	170.0	141	16	100	1	5	173	5	6	7	3	92	75	12	7	.632	0	3.97
87	SHR/TEX	AA	16	426	16	1	1	0	105.2	94	1	20	1	1	98	3	2	4	4	32	25	9	2	.818	0	2.13
	PHO/PCL	AAA	12	277	11	1	0	0	62.0	72	8	26	2	1	24	5	1	4	4	45	36	2	5	.286	0	5.23
88	PHO/PCL	AAA	26	600	25	5	1	0	141.1	138	14	51	1	3	110	3	6	5	4	73	61	11	9	.550	0	3.88
	SF/NL		4	86	4	1	1	0	22.0	9	1	11	1	0	13	0	3	1	0	8	7	2	1	.667	0	2.86
89	PHO/PCL	AAA	12	319	12	3	1	0	78.0	73	4	19	0	1	85	1	4	4	2	29	27	7	4	.636	0	3.12
	SF/NL		2	58	2	1	0	0	15.0	13	1	5	0	0	9	0	0	1	0	3	3	1	0	1.000	0	1.80
	PHI/NL		21	441	16	1	1	1	106.0	97	17	33	6	2	58	5	2	3	2	56	47	6	8	.429	0	3.99
	YEAR		23	499	18	2	1	1	121.0	110	18	38	6	2	67	5	2	4	2	59	50	7	8	.467	0	3.72
90	PHI/NL		42	594	13	2	1	4	141.2	132	13	54	9	2	58	5	5	6	3	61	56	8	3	.727	1	3.56
	LA/NL		5	69	3	0	0	0	14.1	23	7	2	0	0	6	2	2	0	0	13	12	1	1	.500	0	7.53
	YEAR		47	663	16	2	1	4	156.0	155	20	56	9	2	64	7	7	6	3	74	68	9	4	.692	1	3.92
91	ALB/PCL	AAA	14	373	14	1	0	0	91.2	73	9	32	0	2	84	5	3	5	5	46	37	7	3	.700	0	3.63
	SA/TEX	AA	7	202	7	1	0	0	50.2	43	2	10	1	1	45	3	3	0	4	20	14	1	3	.250	0	2.49
	LA/NL		20	69	1	0	0	5	17.2	12	0	7	1	0	8	1	2	0	0	3	1	1	0	1.000	0	0.51
4 YR TOTALS			**94**	**1317**	**39**	**5**	**3**	**10**	**316.2**	**286**	**39**	**112**	**17**	**4**	**152**	**13**	**14**	**11**	**5**	**144**	**126**	**19**	**13**	**.594**	**1**	**3.58**

Corbin, Archie Ray — bats right — throws right — b.12/30/67

YR	TM/LG	CL	G	TBF	GS	CG	SHO	GF	IP	H	HR	BB	IBB	HB	SO	SH	SF	WP	BK	R	ER	W	L	PCT	SV	ERA
86	KIN/APP	R+	18	149	1	0	0	9	30.1	31	3	28	0	0	30	0	1	8	1	23	16	1	1	.500	0	4.75
87	KIN/APP	R+	6	128	6	0	0	0	25.2	24	3	26	0	2	17	0	0	6	0	21	18	2	3	.400	0	6.31
88	KIN/APP	R+	11	277	10	4	1	0	69.1	47	5	17	0	3	47	2	0	1	1	23	12	7	2	.778	0	1.56
89	COL/SAL	A	27	664	23	4	2	3	153.2	149	16	72	0	5	130	4	4	2	0	86	77	9	9	.500	1	4.51
90	SL/FSL	A+	20	494	18	3	0	2	118.0	97	2	59	0	7	105	4	3	10	0	47	39	7	8	.467	0	2.97
91	MEM/SOU	AA	28	692	25	1	0	0	156.1	139	7	90	1	8	166	4	6	13	0	90	81	8	8	.500	0	4.66
	KC/AL		2	12	0	0	0	2	2.1	3	0	2	0	0	1	0	0	0	1	1	1	0	0	.000	0	3.86

Cormier, Rheal Paul — bats left — throws left — b.4/23/67

YR	TM/LG	CL	G	TBF	GS	CG	SHO	GF	IP	H	HR	BB	IBB	HB	SO	SH	SF	WP	BK	R	ER	W	L	PCT	SV	ERA
89	SP/FSL	A+	26	669	26	4	2	0	169.2	141	9	33	2	0	122	6	3	4	7	63	42	12	7	.632	0	2.23
90	ARK/TEX	AA	22	530	21	3	1	1	121.1	133	9	30	2	5	102	6	2	5	1	81	68	5	12	.294	0	5.04
	LOU/AMA	AAA	4	92	4	0	0	0	24.0	18	1	3	0	0	9	0	0	4	0	8	6	1	1	.500	0	2.25
91	LOU/AMA	AAA	21	543	21	3	3	0	127.2	140	5	31	1	6	74	10	6	6	1	64	60	7	9	.438	0	4.23
	STL/NL		11	281	10	2	0	1	67.2	74	5	8	1	2	38	1	3	2	1	35	31	4	5	.444	0	4.12

Corsi, James Bernard "Jim" — bats right — throws right — b.9/9/61

YR	TM/LG	CL	G	TBF	GS	CG	SHO	GF	IP	H	HR	BB	IBB	HB	SO	SH	SF	WP	BK	R	ER	W	L	PCT	SV	ERA
82	ONE/NYP	A−	1	4	0	0	0	0	3.0	5	0	2	0	0	6	0	0	0	0	0	0	0	0	.000	0	0.00
	PAI/APP	R+	8	0	4	0	0	0	31.0	32	0	13	0	0	20	0	0	2	1	11	10	0	2	.000	0	2.90
83	GRE/SAL	A	12	0	7	1	0	0	50.0	59	1	33	0	5	37	0	0	8	0	37	23	2	2	.500	1	4.14
	ONE/NYP	A−	11	0	10	0	0	0	59.0	76	1	21	0	1	47	0	0	2	0	38	28	3	6	.333	0	4.27
85	GRE/SAL	A	41	363	2	1	0	36	78.2	94	1	23	3	4	84	4	3	4	0	49	37	5	8	.385	9	4.23
86	NB/EAS	AA	29	220	0	0	0	19	51.1	52	2	20	5	1	38	6	0	2	0	13	13	2	3	.400	3	2.28
87	MOD/CAL	A+	19	121	0	0	0	10	30.0	23	1	10	1	0	45	1	0	4	0	16	12	3	1	.750	6	3.60
	HUN/SOU	AA	28	182	0	0	0	18	48.0	30	1	15	1	0	33	2	0	5	0	17	15	8	1	.889	2	2.81
88	TAC/PCL	AAA	50	247	0	0	0	45	59.0	60	2	23	10	1	48	4	1	5	2	25	18	2	5	.286	16	2.75
	OAK/AL		11	89	1	0	0	7	21.1	20	1	6	1	0	10	0	3	1	1	10	9	0	1	.000	0	3.80
89	TAC/PCL	AAA	23	131	0	0	0	18	28.1	40	1	9	4	1	23	2	0	4	0	17	13	2	3	.400	8	4.13
	OAK/AL		22	149	0	0	0	14	38.1	26	2	10	0	1	21	2	2	0	0	8	8	1	2	.333	0	1.88
90	TAC/PCL	AAA	5	26	0	0	0	2	6.0	9	0	1	0	0	6	0	0	2	0	2	1	0	0	.000	0	1.50
91	TUC/PCL	AAA	2	11	0	0	0	2	3.0	2	0	0	0	0	4	0	0	0	0	0	0	0	0	.000	0	0.00
	HOU/NL		47	322	0	0	0	15	77.2	76	6	23	6	1	53	3	2	1	1	37	32	0	5	.000	0	3.71
3 YR TOTALS			**80**	**560**	**1**	**0**	**0**	**36**	**137.1**	**122**	**9**	**39**	**6**	**1**	**84**	**8**	**7**	**2**	**2**	**55**	**49**	**1**	**8**	**.111**	**0**	**3.21**

Costello, John Reilly — bats right — throws right — b.12/24/60

YR	TM/LG	CL	G	TBF	GS	CG	SHO	GF	IP	H	HR	BB	IBB	HB	SO	SH	SF	WP	BK	R	ER	W	L	PCT	SV	ERA
84	SAV/SAL	A	26	711	26	2	0	0	166.0	142	9	86	1	5	114	5	8	5	1	80	62	13	9	.591	0	3.36
85	SPR/MID	A	28	805	28	7	0	0	188.0	188	17	60	1	4	127	7	2	9	2	105	87	8	13	.381	0	4.16
86	ARK/TEX	AA	10	66	0	0	0	5	15.0	17	1	10	1	2	11	0	0	1	0	11	9	0	0	.000	1	5.40
	SP/FSL	A+	15	293	12	2	1	2	71.2	65	1	24	1	2	32	3	1	0	0	21	19	8	2	.800	1	2.39
87	ARK/TEX	AA	44	303	0	0	0	25	74.0	64	5	22	5	3	67	4	3	2	0	27	19	5	2	.714	7	2.31
	LOU/AMA	AAA	6	53	1	0	0	0	10.1	14	0	7	1	1	5	0	0	1	0	6	5	2	0	1.000	0	4.35
88	LOU/AMA	AAA	20	112	0	0	0	17	29.1	17	3	7	1	0	34	0	0	0	0	7	6	2	0	1.000	11	1.84
	STL/NL		36	214	0	0	0	15	49.2	44	3	25	4	0	38	1	1	0	1	11	10	5	2	.714	1	1.81
89	LOU/AMA	AAA	4	21	0	0	0	2	5.0	5	0	1	0	0	4	0	0	0	0	1	1	0	0	.000	1	1.80
	STL/NL		48	252	0	0	0	11	62.1	48	5	20	7	2	40	0	5	0	0	24	23	5	4	.556	3	3.32
90	STL/NL		4	21	0	0	0	3	4.1	7	1	1	0	1	1	1	0	0	0	3	3	0	0	.000	0	6.23
	MON/NL		4	26	0	0	0	1	6.1	5	2	1	0	0	3	1	0	0	0	5	4	0	0	.000	0	5.68
	YEAR		8	47	0	0	0	4	10.2	12	3	2	0	1	4	2	0	0	0	26	24	0	3	.000	0	7.04
	IND/AMA	AAA	22	145	0	0	0	7	30.2	36	8	20	1	0	32	2	2	1	0	16	7	1	2	.333	3	2.15
91	LV/PCL	AAA	17	131	0	0	0	6	29.1	31	1	7	1	2	24	1	0	0	0	15	12	1	0	1.000	0	3.09
	SD/NL		27	157	0	0	0	6	35.0	37	2	17	3	0	24	4	0	2	1	15	12	1	0	1.000	0	3.09
4 YR TOTALS			**119**	**670**	**0**	**0**	**0**	**36**	**157.2**	**141**	**13**	**64**	**15**	**3**	**104**	**5**	**9**	**2**	**2**	**62**	**52**	**11**	**6**	**.647**	**4**	**2.97**

Cox, Danny Bradford — bats right — throws right — b.9/21/59

YR	TM/LG	CL	G	TBF	GS	CG	SHO	GF	IP	H	HR	BB	IBB	HB	SO	SH	SF	WP	BK	R	ER	W	L	PCT	SV	ERA
81	JC/APP	R+	13	0	13	10	4	0	109.0	80	3	36	0	1	87	0	0	3	0	27	25	9	4	.692	0	2.06
82	SPR/MID	A	15	0	13	2	0	0	84.0	82	7	29	0	4	68	0	0	8	1	46	24	5	3	.625	0	2.57
83	ARK/TEX	AA	11	0	11	7	1	0	86.0	60	4	24	0	1	73	0	0	0	0	31	22	8	3	.727	0	2.30
	SP/FSL	A+	5	0	5	2	0	0	32.0	26	0	14	0	0	22	0	0	1	0	10	9	2	2	.500	0	2.53
	LOU/AMA	AAA	2	0	2	0	0	0	11.0	10	1	0	0	0	8	0	0	1	0	3	3	0	0	.000	0	2.45
	STL/NL		12	352	12	0	0	0	83.0	92	6	23	2	0	36	6	1	2	0	38	30	3	6	.333	0	3.25
84	LOU/AMA	AAA	6	168	6	4	0	0	42.1	34	3	7	0	0	34	2	1	0	1	16	10	4	1	.800	0	2.13
	STL/NL		29	668	27	1	1	0	156.1	171	9	54	6	7	70	10	5	2	4	81	70	9	11	.450	0	4.03
85	STL/NL		35	989	35	10	4	0	241.0	226	19	64	5	3	131	12	9	3	1	91	77	18	9	.667	0	2.88
86	STL/NL		32	881	32	8	0	0	220.0	189	14	60	6	3	108	8	3	3	4	85	71	12	13	.480	0	2.90
87	STL/NL		31	864	31	2	0	0	199.1	224	17	71	6	3	101	14	4	5	1	99	86	11	9	.550	0	3.88
88	LOU/AMA	AAA	3	50	3	0	0	0	11.2	11	1	6	0	0	7	1	0	0	2	7	4	0	0	.000	0	3.09
	STL/NL		13	361	13	0	0	0	86.0	89	6	25	7	1	47	5	3	4	0	40	38	3	8	.273	0	3.98
90	SPR/MID	A	1	16	1	0	0	0	5.0	1	0	0	0	0	3	0	0	0	0	0	0	0	0	.000	0	0.00
	ARK/TEX	AA	1	25	1	1	0	0	7.0	3	0	1	0	0	3	0	0	0	0	1	1	1	0	1.000	0	1.29
	LOU/AMA	AAA	4	68	4	0	0	0	11.0	22	3	10	0	0	6	0	1	8	3	20	19	0	3	.000	0	15.55
91	CLE/FSL	A+	3	62	3	0	0	0	18.0	4	0	4	0	0	15	0	0	0	0	0	0	3	0	1.000	0	0.00
	SCR/INT	AAA	1	24	1	0	0	0	6.0	5	0	2	0	0	3	1	0	0	0	2	2	1	0	1.000	0	3.00
	PHI/NL		23	433	17	0	0	2	102.1	98	14	39	2	1	46	6	7	7	1	57	52	4	6	.400	0	4.57
7 YR TOTALS			**175**	**4548**	**167**	**21**	**5**	**2**	**1088.0**	**1089**	**85**	**336**	**34**	**17**	**539**	**61**	**32**	**26**	**14**	**491**	**424**	**60**	**62**	**.492**	**0**	**3.51**

Crawford, Steven Ray "Steve" — bats right — throws right — b.4/29/58

YR	TM/LG	CL	G	TBF	GS	CG	SHO	GF	IP	H	HR	BB	IBB	HB	SO	SH	SF	WP	BK	R	ER	W	L	PCT	SV	ERA
78	WIN/CAR	A+	19	0	14	5	1	0	110.0	109	5	42	0	4	60	0	0	3	0	53	42	9	5	.643	0	3.44
79	WIN/CAR	A+	29	0	28	15	3	0	211.0	208	4	67	0	2	127	0	0	13	0	88	69	11	11	.500	0	2.94
80	BRI/EAS	AA	24	0	23	10	2	0	177.0	170	6	64	0	5	97	0	0	8	1	68	52	9	7	.563	0	2.64
	BOS/AL		6	142	4	2	0	1	32.1	41	3	8	2	0	10	0	0	0	0	14	13	1	0	1.000	0	3.62
81	BOS/AL		14	257	11	0	0	2	57.2	69	10	18	0	3	29	3	4	2	0	38	32	0	5	.000	0	4.99
82	PAW/INT	AAA	10	0	10	0	0	0	46.0	55	4	15	0	0	20	0	0	0	0	25	21	1	4	.200	0	4.11
	BOS/AL		5	41	0	0	0	4	9.0	14	0	0	0	0	2	0	0	0	0	3	2	1	0	1.000	0	2.00
83	PAW/INT	AAA	27	0	27	4	1	0	154.0	181	17	80	0	3	104	0	0	7	0	98	89	8	11	.421	0	5.20
84	PAW/INT	AAA	7	74	0	0	0	5	18.1	11	2	9	3	0	8	4	0	0	0	10	4	2	1	.667	2	1.96
	BOS/AL		35	268	0	0	0	19	62.0	69	6	21	5	1	21	1	4	2	0	31	23	5	0	1.000	0	3.34
85	BOS/AL		44	394	1	0	0	26	91.0	103	5	28	8	0	58	6	3	5	0	47	38	6	5	.545	12	3.76
86	PAW/INT	AAA	5	28	0	0	0	4	6.0	10	1	1	0	0	1	0	0	0	0	4	4	1	1	.500	2	6.00
	BOS/AL		40	248	0	0	0	15	57.1	69	5	19	7	0	32	3	2	2	0	29	25	0	2	.000	4	3.92
87	BOS/AL		29	324	0	0	0	7	72.2	91	13	32	2	2	43	0	0	2	0	48	43	5	4	.556	0	5.33
88	SA/TEX	AA	3	20	0	0	0	1	6.0	2	0	0	0	0	4	0	0	0	1	0	0	1	0	1.000	1	0.00
	ALB/PCL	AAA	32	246	2	0	0	14	54.1	59	5	25	4	2	36	2	1	2	5	31	23	3	6	.333	3	3.81
89	OMA/AMA	AAA	22	179	0	0	0	6	43.0	41	6	9	1	2	32	1	3	1	0	18	14	3	1	.750	0	2.93
	KC/AL		25	224	0	0	0	5	54.0	48	2	19	3	3	33	3	1	0	0	19	17	3	1	.750	0	2.83
90	OMA/AMA	AAA	4	23	0	0	0	0	6.0	2	0	2	0	1	11	0	0	1	0	0	0	0	0	.000	0	0.00
	KC/AL		46	341	0	0	0	14	80.0	79	7	23	3	3	54	2	2	1	0	38	37	5	4	.556	1	4.16
91	KC/AL		33	216	0	0	0	17	46.2	60	3	18	5	1	38	1	3	5	0	31	31	3	2	.600	1	5.98
10 YR TOTALS			**277**	**2455**	**16**	**2**	**0**	**110**	**562.2**	**643**	**54**	**186**	**35**	**13**	**320**	**19**	**19**	**19**	**0**	**298**	**261**	**30**	**23**	**.566**	**19**	**4.17**

Crews, Stanley Timothy "Tim" — bats right — throws right — b.4/3/61

YR	TM/LG	CL	G	TBF	GS	CG	SHO	GF	IP	H	HR	BB	IBB	HB	SO	SH	SF	WP	BK	R	ER	W	L	PCT	SV	ERA
81	BUR/MID	A	21	0	20	8	1	0	144.0	148	16	27	0	1	98	0	0	4	0	82	67	10	4	.714	0	4.19
82	STO/CAL	A+	19	0	19	8	1	0	139.0	151	9	28	0	0	83	0	0	6	3	66	52	10	4	.714	0	3.37
83	EP/TEX	AA	27	0	26	2	0	0	163.0	207	25	53	0	4	99	0	0	6	0	129	119	9	8	.529	0	6.57
84	EP/TEX	AA	8	168	8	1	0	0	36.0	56	1	10	0	1	22	1	1	0	0	32	27	2	3	.400	0	6.75
85	STO/CAL	A+	16	0	14	0	0	1	90.0	101	4	17	0	2	56	0	1	1	0	46	33	8	1	.889	0	3.30
86	EP/TEX	AA	15	387	15	4	1	0	90.2	114	13	18	1	0	50	0	6	3	1	53	48	5	5	.500	0	4.76
	VAN/PCL	AAA	10	148	3	0	0	4	33.1	39	1	14	3	0	28	0	0	1	0	15	15	2	1	.667	1	4.05
87	ALB/PCL	AAA	42	311	0	0	0	31	72.0	73	5	25	4	0	60	3	1	6	0	34	29	7	2	.778	12	3.62
	LA/NL		20	124	0	0	0	7	29.0	30	2	8	1	2	20	1	1	0	0	9	8	1	1	.500	3	2.48
88	ALB/PCL	AAA	10	53	0	0	0	7	13.1	13	1	2	0	1	7	0	1	1	1	5	4	1	1	.500	3	2.70
	LA/NL		42	301	0	0	0	12	71.2	77	3	16	7	0	45	3	5	0	0	29	25	4	0	1.000	0	3.14
89	ALB/PCL	AAA	2	10	0	0	0	2	2.1	3	0	0	0	0	3	0	0	0	0	2	2	0	1	.000	0	7.71
	LA/NL		44	275	0	0	0	16	61.2	69	7	23	9	0	56	7	0	2	0	27	22	0	1	.000	1	3.21
90	LA/NL		66	440	2	0	0	18	107.1	98	9	24	6	1	76	1	3	2	0	40	33	4	5	.444	5	2.77
91	LA/NL		60	318	0	0	0	17	76.0	75	7	19	11	0	53	4	2	3	1	30	29	2	3	.400	6	3.43
5 YR TOTALS			**232**	**1458**	**2**	**0**	**0**	**70**	**345.2**	**349**	**28**	**90**	**34**	**5**	**250**	**16**	**11**	**7**	**1**	**135**	**117**	**11**	**10**	**.524**	**15**	**3.05**

Crim, Charles Robert "Chuck" — bats right — throws right — b.7/23/61

YR	TM/LG	CL	G	TBF	GS	CG	SHO	GF	IP	H	HR	BB	IBB	HB	SO	SH	SF	WP	BK	R	ER	W	L	PCT	SV	ERA
84	EP/TEX	AA	55	360	0	0	0	33	90.0	77	4	25	4	2	69	5	4	2	0	20	15	7	4	.636	17	1.50
85	VAN/PCL	AAA	48	0	5	0	0	23	106.2	110	8	38	3	4	68	0	0	3	4	58	54	3	6	.333	6	4.56
86	EP/TEX	AA	16	156	0	0	0	13	39.0	35	5	2	2	2	32	2	0	0	0	16	12	2	4	.333	6	2.77
	VAN/PCL	AAA	26	204	0	0	0	13	45.1	64	2	15	4	1	26	1	2	1	0	32	25	0	3	.000	1	4.96
87	MIL/AL		53	549	5	0	0	18	130.0	133	15	39	5	3	56	6	1	2	1	60	53	6	8	.429	12	3.67
88	MIL/AL		70	425	0	0	0	25	105.0	95	11	28	3	2	58	6	6	2	0	38	34	7	6	.538	9	2.91
89	MIL/AL		76	487	0	0	0	31	117.2	114	7	36	9	2	59	3	4	0	0	42	37	9	7	.563	7	2.83

Crim, Charles Robert "Chuck" (continued)

YR	TM/LG	CL	G	TBF	GS	CG	SHO	GF	IP	H	HR	BB	IBB	HB	SO	SH	SF	WP	BK	R	ER	W	L	PCT	SV	ERA
90	BEL/MID	A	1	10	1	0	0	0	2.0	3	0									2	2	0	0	.000	0	4.50
	MIL/AL		67	367	0	0	0	25	85.2	88	7	23	4	2	39	1	4	0	1	39	33	3	5	.375	11	3.47
91	MIL/AL		66	408	0	0	0	29	91.1	115	9	25	9	2	39	3	1	3	3	52	47	8	5	.615	3	4.63
5 YR TOTALS			**332**	**2236**	**5**	**0**	**0**	**128**	**529.2**	**545**	**49**	**151**	**30**	**11**	**251**	**18**	**18**	**19**	**7**	**231**	**204**	**33**	**31**	**.516**	**42**	**3.47**

Dalton, Michael Edward "Mike" — bats right — throws left — b.3/27/63

YR	TM/LG	CL	G	TBF	GS	CG	SHO	GF	IP	H	HR	BB	IBB	HB	SO	SH	SF	WP	BK	R	ER	W	L	PCT	SV	ERA
83	ELM/NYP	A-	21	0	1	0	0	0	51.0	48	0	15	0	0	49	0	0	0	0	19	15	3	1	.750	5	2.65
84	WH/FSL	A+	38	476	9	2	0	23	107.2	115	2	52	4	2	43	5	8	8	1	56	38	5	8	.385	6	3.18
85	WH/FSL	A+	49	281	0	0	0	42	72.0	45	0	27	2	0	41	5	3	1	0	14	9	2	3	.400	18	1.13
86	PAW/INT	AAA	37	324	6	0	0	22	71.2	84	4	34	3	4	49	1	3	7	0	43	40	6	2	.750	1	5.02
87	NB/EAS	AA	4	18	0	0	0	4	5.0	1	0	2	0	0	7	0	0	0	0	0	0	1	0	1.000	0	0.00
	PAW/INT	AAA	39	375	1	0	0	19	88.2	83	10	40	2	0	45	4	2	6	1	49	41	1	2	.333	2	4.16
88	NB/EAS	AA	52	356	1	1	0	38	84.1	65	2	39	10	1	61	6	2	3	0	32	21	6	5	.545	8	2.24
89	NB/EAS	AA	18	135	1	1	1	7	32.2	25	0	15	3	2	15	1	1	1	0	13	9	3	1	.750	3	2.48
	PAW/INT	AAA	26	206	3	1	1	10	45.2	55	2	16	2	0	20	6	1	1	0	26	26	1	3	.250	4	5.12
90	PAW/INT	AAA	49	412	2	1	0	21	99.0	94	6	22	2	3	49	9	5	2	0	42	28	7	4	.636	5	2.55
91	DET/AL		4	38	0	0	0	0	8.0	12	2	2	0	0	4	0	0	2	0	3	3	0	0	.000	0	3.38
	TOL/INT	AAA	39	294	0	0	0	18	65.1	72	7	24	4	2	28	5	1	6	0	33	30	3	3	.500	4	4.13

Darling, Ronald Maurice "Ron" — bats right — throws right — b.8/19/60

YR	TM/LG	CL	G	TBF	GS	CG	SHO	GF	IP	H	HR	BB	IBB	HB	SO	SH	SF	WP	BK	R	ER	W	L	PCT	SV	ERA
83	NY/NL		5	148	5	1	0	0	35.1	31	0	17	1	3	23	3	0	3	2	11	11	1	3	.250	0	2.80
84	NY/NL		33	884	33	2	2	0	205.2	179	17	104	3	5	136	7	6	7	1	97	87	12	9	.571	0	3.81
85	NY/NL		36	1043	35	4	2	1	248.0	214	21	114	1	3	167	13	4	7	1	93	80	16	6	.727	0	2.90
86	NY/NL		34	967	34	4	2	0	237.0	203	21	81	2	3	184	10	6	7	3	84	74	15	6	.714	0	2.81
87	NY/NL		32	891	32	2	0	0	207.2	183	24	96	3	3	167	5	3	6	3	111	99	12	8	.600	0	4.29
88	NY/NL		34	971	34	7	4	0	240.2	218	24	60	2	5	161	10	8	7	2	97	87	17	9	.654	0	3.25
89	NY/NL		33	922	33	4	0	0	217.1	214	19	70	7	3	153	7	13	12	4	100	85	14	14	.500	0	3.52
90	NY/NL		33	554	18	1	0	3	126.0	135	20	44	4	5	99	7	3	5	1	73	63	7	9	.438	0	4.50
91	NY/NL		17	427	17	0	0	0	102.1	96	9	28	1	6	58	7	4	9	4	50	44	5	6	.455	0	3.87
	MON/NL		3	81	3	0	0	0	17.0	25	6	5	0	1	11	0	0	4	0	16	14	0	2	.000	0	7.41
	OAK/AL		12	319	12	0	0	0	75.0	64	7	38	2	2	60	5	4	3	1	34	34	3	7	.300	0	4.08
	YEAR		32	827	32	0	0	0	194.1	185	22	71	3	9	129	12	8	16	5	100	92	8	15	.348	0	4.26
9 YR TOTALS			**272**	**7207**	**256**	**25**	**10**	**4**	**1712.0**	**1562**	**168**	**657**	**25**	**39**	**1219**	**74**	**51**	**70**	**22**	**766**	**678**	**102**	**79**	**.564**	**0**	**3.56**

Darwin, Daniel Wayne "Danny" — bats right — throws right — b.10/25/55

YR	TM/LG	CL	G	TBF	GS	CG	SHO	GF	IP	H	HR	BB	IBB	HB	SO	SH	SF	WP	BK	R	ER	W	L	PCT	SV	ERA
78	TEX/AL		3	36	1	0	0	2	8.2	11	0	1	0	0	8	0	1	0	0	4	4	1	0	1.000	0	4.15
79	TEX/AL		20	313	6	1	0	4	78.0	50	5	30	2	5	58	3	6	0	1	36	35	4	4	.500	0	4.04
80	TEX/AL		53	468	2	0	0	35	109.2	98	4	50	7	2	104	5	7	3	0	37	32	13	4	.765	8	2.63
81	TEX/AL		22	601	22	6	2	0	146.0	115	12	57	5	6	98	8	3	1	0	67	59	9	9	.500	0	3.64
82	TEX/AL		56	394	1	0	0	41	89.0	95	6	37	8	2	61	10	5	2	1	38	34	10	8	.556	7	3.44
83	TEX/AL		28	780	26	9	2	0	183.0	175	9	62	3	3	92	7	4	2	0	86	71	8	13	.381	0	3.49
84	TEX/AL		35	955	32	5	1	2	223.2	249	19	54	2	4	123	3	3	3	0	110	98	8	12	.400	0	3.94
85	MIL/AL		39	919	29	11	1	8	217.2	212	34	65	4	4	125	7	9	6	0	112	92	8	18	.308	3	3.80
86	MIL/AL		27	537	14	5	1	4	130.1	120	13	35	1	3	80	6	5	5	0	62	51	6	8	.429	0	3.52
	HOU/NL		12	222	8	0	0	2	54.1	50	3	9	0	0	40	1	3	2	1	19	14	5	2	.714	0	2.32
	YEAR		39	759	22	6	1	6	184.2	170	16	44	1	3	120	6	9	4	1	81	65	11	10	.524	0	3.17
87	HOU/NL		33	833	30	3	1	0	195.2	184	17	69	12	5	134	9	9	3	1	86	82	9	10	.474	0	3.59
88	HOU/NL		44	804	20	3	0	9	192.0	189	20	48	9	7	129	10	9	1	2	86	82	8	13	.381	3	3.84
89	HOU/NL		68	482	0	0	0	26	122.0	92	8	33	9	2	104	8	5	2	0	34	32	11	4	.733	2	2.36
90	HOU/NL		48	646	17	3	0	14	162.2	136	11	31	4	4	109	4	2	0	2	42	40	11	4	.733	2	2.21
91	BOS/AL		12	292	12	0	0	0	68.0	71	15	15	1	4	42	1	2	2	0	39	39	3	6	.333	0	5.16
14 YR TOTALS			**500**	**8282**	**220**	**47**	**8**	**147**	**1980.2**	**1847**	**176**	**596**	**67**	**51**	**1307**	**80**	**71**	**32**	**11**	**859**	**761**	**114**	**115**	**.498**	**29**	**3.46**

Davis, George Earl "Storm" — bats right — throws right — b.12/26/61

YR	TM/LG	CL	G	TBF	GS	CG	SHO	GF	IP	H	HR	BB	IBB	HB	SO	SH	SF	WP	BK	R	ER	W	L	PCT	SV	ERA
82	BAL/AL		29	412	8	1	0	9	100.2	96	8	28	4	0	67	4	6	2	1	40	39	8	4	.667	0	3.49
83	BAL/AL		34	831	29	6	1	0	200.1	180	14	64	4	2	125	5	4	7	2	90	80	13	7	.650	0	3.59
84	BAL/AL		35	923	31	10	2	3	225.0	205	7	71	6	5	105	7	9	6	1	86	78	14	9	.609	1	3.12
85	BAL/AL		31	750	28	8	1	0	175.0	172	11	70	5	1	93	3	3	2	1	92	88	10	8	.556	0	4.53
86	HAG/CAR	A+	1	18	1	0	0	0	4.0	3	0	3	0	0	6	0	0	0	0	0	0	0	0	.000	0	0.00
	BAL/AL		25	657	25	2	0	0	154.0	166	16	49	2	0	96	3	2	5	0	70	62	9	12	.429	0	3.62
87	WIC/TEX	AA	1	17	1	0	0	0	4.0	4	0	0	0	0	5	0	0	0	0	0	0	0	1	.000	0	0.00
	REN/CAL	A+	1	22	1	0	0	0	5.0	2	0	6	0	0	5	0	0	0	0	2	2	0	0	.000	0	3.60
	SD/NL		21	292	10	0	0	5	62.2	70	5	36	6	2	37	2	2	1	1	48	43	2	7	.222	0	6.18
	OAK/AL		5	128	5	0	0	0	30.1	28	3	11	0	0	28	0	1	2	0	13	11	1	1	.500	0	3.26
	YEAR		26	420	15	0	0	5	93.0	98	8	47	6	2	65	2	3	3	1	61	54	3	8	.273	0	5.23
88	OAK/AL		33	872	33	0	0	0	201.2	211	16	91	2	1	127	3	7	8	2	91	82	16	7	.696	0	3.70
89	OAK/AL		31	733	31	1	0	0	169.1	187	19	68	1	3	91	5	4	2	0	91	82	19	7	.731	0	4.36
90	KC/AL		21	498	20	0	1	0	112.0	129	9	35	1	0	62	1	3	1	0	66	59	7	10	.412	0	4.74
91	KC/AL		51	515	9	1	0	22	114.1	140	11	46	9	0	53	6	4	1	0	69	63	3	9	.250	2	4.96
10 YR TOTALS			**316**	**6611**	**229**	**30**	**5**	**39**	**1545.1**	**1584**	**119**	**569**	**40**	**15**	**884**	**39**	**49**	**64**	**10**	**751**	**688**	**102**	**81**	**.557**	**3**	**4.01**

Davis, Mark William — bats left — throws left — b.10/19/60

YR	TM/LG	CL	G	TBF	GS	CG	SHO	GF	IP	H	HR	BB	IBB	HB	SO	SH	SF	WP	BK	R	ER	W	L	PCT	SV	ERA
80	PHI/NL		2	30	1	0	0	0	7.0	4	0	5	0	0	5	0	0	0	0	2	2	0	0	.000	0	2.57
81	PHI/NL		9	194	9	0	0	0	43.0	49	7	24	0	0	29	2	4	1	1	37	37	1	4	.200	0	7.74
83	SF/NL		20	469	20	2	2	0	111.0	93	14	50	4	3	83	2	4	8	1	51	43	6	4	.600	0	3.49
84	SF/NL		46	766	27	1	0	6	174.2	201	25	54	12	5	124	10	10	8	4	113	104	5	17	.227	0	5.36
85	SF/NL		77	465	1	0	0	38	114.1	89	13	41	7	3	131	13	1	6	1	49	45	5	12	.294	7	3.54
86	SF/NL		67	342	2	0	0	20	84.1	63	6	34	7	1	90	5	5	3	0	33	28	5	7	.417	4	2.99
87	SF/NL		20	301	11	0	1	0	70.2	72	5	28	1	4	51	3	2	4	2	38	37	4	5	.444	0	4.71
	SD/NL		43	265	0	0	0	17	62.1	51	5	31	7	2	47	4	2	5	0	26	22	1	2	.625	2	3.18
	YEAR		63	566	11	1	0	18	133.0	123	14	59	8	6	98	7	2	6	2	64	59	9	8	.529	2	3.99
88	SD/NL		62	402	0	0	0	52	98.1	70	2	42	11	0	102	7	1	9	1	24	22	5	10	.333	28	2.01
89	SD/NL		70	370	0	0	0	65	92.2	66	6	31	1	2	92	3	4	8	0	21	19	4	3	.571	44	1.85
90	KC/AL		53	334	3	0	0	28	68.2	71	9	52	3	4	73	2	2	6	0	43	39	2	7	.222	6	5.11
91	OMA/AMA	AAA	6	142	6	0	0	0	35.2	27	1	9	0	1	36	0	2	1	0	11	8	4	1	.800	0	2.02
	KC/AL		29	276	5	0	0	8	62.2	55	6	39	0	1	47	2	5	1	0	36	31	6	3	.667	1	4.45
11 YR TOTALS			**498**	**4214**	**79**	**4**	**2**	**235**	**989.2**	**884**	**102**	**431**	**53**	**25**	**874**	**53**	**38**	**56**	**10**	**473**	**429**	**48**	**75**	**.390**	**92**	**3.90**

Dayley, Kenneth Grant "Ken" — bats left — throws left — b.2/25/59

YR	TM/LG	CL	G	TBF	GS	CG	SHO	GF	IP	H	HR	BB	IBB	HB	SO	SH	SF	WP	BK	R	ER	W	L	PCT	SV	ERA
82	ATL/NL		20	313	11	0	0	3	71.1	79	9	25	2	0	34	7	5	2	0	39	36	5	6	.455	0	4.54
83	ATL/NL		24	436	16	0	0	3	104.2	100	12	39	2	2	70	3	3	3	0	59	50	5	8	.385	0	4.30
84	ATL/NL		4	92	4	0	0	0	18.2	28	5	6	1	1	10	3	0	0	0	18	11	0	3	.000	0	5.30
	RIC/INT	AAA	9	275	9	2	1	0	62.1	66	6	24	0	0	45	1	0	4	1	31	28	5	1	.833	0	4.04
	STL/NL		3	32	0	0	0	1	5.0	16	1	5	0	0	1	0	0	0	0	10	10	0	2	.000	0	18.00
	YEAR		7	124	6	0	0	1	23.2	44	6	11	1	1	10	4	0	0	0	28	21	0	5	.000	0	7.99
	LOU/AMA	AAA	13	386	13	3	0	0	96.1	86	6	22	1	2	79	6	0	3	0	42	35	4	6	.400	0	3.27
85	STL/NL		57	271	0	0	0	27	65.1	65	2	18	9	0	62	4	2	4	0	24	20	4	4	.500	11	2.76
86	STL/NL		31	170	0	0	0	13	38.2	42	1	11	3	1	33	4	1	0	0	19	14	0	3	.000	5	3.26
87	LOU/AMA	AAA	1	9	1	0	0	0	2.0	1	0	1	0	0	1	0	0	1	0	1	1	0	0	.000	0	4.50
	SPR/MID	A	2	14	2	0	0	0	3.2	1	0	1	0	0	2	0	0	0	0	0	0	0	0	.000	0	0.00
	STL/NL		53	260	0	0	0	29	61.0	52	2	33	8	2	63	2	1	5	0	21	18	9	5	.643	4	2.66
88	STL/NL		54	226	0	0	0	21	55.1	48	2	19	7	1	38	4	1	2	0	20	17	2	7	.222	5	2.77
89	STL/NL		71	310	0	0	0	28	75.1	63	3	30	10	0	40	3	1	2	0	26	24	4	3	.571	12	2.87
90	STL/NL		58	307	0	0	0	17	73.1	63	5	30	7	0	51	2	5	6	0	32	29	4	4	.500	2	3.56
91	DUN/FSL	A+	3	21	2	0	0	0	6.0	1	0	2	0	0	2	0	0	0	0	0	0	0	0	.000	0	0.00
	SYR/INT	AAA	10	79	0	0	0	2	14.0	26	2	11	0	0	13	0	1	2	0	16	15	0	1	.000	1	9.64
	TOR/AL		8	26	0	0	0	3	4.1	7	0	5	1	1	3	0	1	2	0	3	3	0	0	.000	0	6.23
10 YR TOTALS			**383**	**2443**	**33**	**0**	**0**	**145**	**573.0**	**563**	**42**	**221**	**49**	**8**	**404**	**33**	**20**	**26**	**1**	**271**	**232**	**33**	**45**	**.423**	**39**	**3.64**

DeJesus, Jose Luis — bats right — throws right — b.1/6/65

YR	TM/LG	CL	G	TBF	GS	CG	SHO	GF	IP	H	HR	BB	IBB	HB	SO	SH	SF	WP	BK	R	ER	W	L	PCT	SV	ERA
85	FM/FSL	A+	27	563	26	3	1	0	129.2	119	9	59	0	7	94	1	4	4	3	70	62	8	10	.444	0	4.30
86	FM/FSL	A+	22	500	22	1	0	0	110.0	87	4	82	0	4	97	3	2	8	3	64	42	4	9	.308	0	3.44
87	MEM/SOU	AA	25	589	24	2	0	0	130.1	106	8	99	0	4	79	3	7	11	2	78	65	4	11	.267	0	4.49
88	MEM/SOU	AA	20	502	20	4	1	0	116.0	88	5	70	0	5	149	3	2	9	2	56	50	9	9	.500	0	3.88
	OMA/AMA	AAA	7	208	7	3	0	0	49.2	44	1	14	0	2	57	3	3	3	1	22	19	2	3	.400	0	3.44
	KC/AL		2	19	1	0	0	0	2.2	6	0	5	0	0	2	0	0	0	0	10	8	0	1	.000	0	27.00
89	OMA/AMA	AAA	31	638	21	2	0	7	145.1	112	9	98	1	6	158	4	6	11	2	78	61	8	11	.421	1	3.78
	KC/AL		3	37	1	0	0	1	8.0	7	1	8	0	0	2	0	0	0	0	4	4	0	0	.000	0	4.50
90	SW/INT	AAA	10	249	10	1	0	0	56.0	41	2	39	0	2	45	2	3	6	4	30	21	1	4	.200	0	3.38
	PHI/NL		22	544	22	3	1	0	130.0	97	10	73	3	2	87	8	0	4	0	63	54	7	8	.467	0	3.74
91	PHI/NL		31	801	29	3	0	1	181.2	147	7	128	4	4	118	11	3	10	0	74	69	10	9	.526	1	3.42
4 YR TOTALS			**58**	**1401**	**53**	**6**	**1**	**2**	**322.1**	**257**	**18**	**214**	**8**	**6**	**209**	**19**	**3**	**14**	**0**	**151**	**135**	**17**	**18**	**.486**	**1**	**3.77**

De la Rosa, Francisco — bats both — throws right — b.3/3/66

YR	TM/LG	CL	G	TBF	GS	CG	SHO	GF	IP	H	HR	BB	IBB	HB	SO	SH	SF	WP	BK	R	ER	W	L	PCT	SV	ERA
85	BJ/GCL	R	16	148	0	0	0	13	31.0	43	1	5	1	2	19	2	4	0	2	24	19	0	1	.000	1	5.52
88	HAG/CAR	A+	29	182	1	0	0	16	41.0	34	2	29	4	1	47	1	2	0	2	21	21	3	4	.429	2	4.61
89	FRE/CAR	A+	23	101	0	0	0	19	22.2	17	1	11	2	2	31	0	2	0	0	9	6	3	4	.429	5	2.38
	HAG/EAS	AA	18	133	0	0	0	15	29.2	27	1	20	1	1	34	3	1	0	0	15	15	1	1	.500	8	4.55
90	HAG/EAS	AA	23	531	20	2	0	2	131.0	97	5	51	0	4	105	3	4	1	1	42	30	9	5	.643	0	2.06
	ROC/INT	AAA	2	4	0	0	0	1	0.2	0	0	1	0	0	0	0	0	0	0	0	0	0	0	.000	1	0.00
91	ROC/INT	AAA	38	342	4	0	0	16	84.1	71	6	33	1	0	61	2	1	2	2	28	25	4	1	.800	3	2.67
	BAL/AL		2	20	0	0	0	1	4.0	6	0	2	0	0	1	0	1	0	0	3	2	0	0	.000	0	4.50

DeLeon, Jose (Chestaro) — bats right — throws right — b.12/20/60

YR	TM/LG	CL	G	TBF	GS	CG	SHO	GF	IP	H	HR	BB	IBB	HB	SO	SH	SF	WP	BK	R	ER	W	L	PCT	SV	ERA
83	PIT/NL		15	438	15	3	2	0	108.0	75	5	47	2	1	118	4	3	5	2	36	34	7	3	.700	0	2.83
84	PIT/NL		30	795	28	5	1	0	192.1	147	10	92	5	3	153	7	7	6	2	86	80	7	13	.350	0	3.74
85	HAW/PCL	AAA	5	0	5	4	2	0	41.0	15	3	10	0	1	45	0	0	0	0	4	4	4	0	1.000	0	0.88
	PIT/NL		31	700	25	1	0	5	162.2	138	15	89	3	3	149	7	4	7	1	93	85	2	19	.095	3	4.70
86	PIT/NL		9	83	1	0	0	0	16.1	17	2	17	3	1	11	1	0	1	0	16	15	1	3	.250	1	8.27
	HAW/PCL	AAA	15	431	14	7	1	1	106.0	87	5	44	3	1	83	5	4	3	0	32	29	5	8	.385	0	2.46
	CHI/AL		13	325	13	1	0	0	79.0	49	7	42	0	4	68	4	1	3	0	30	26	4	5	.444	0	2.96
	YEAR		22	408	14	1	0	5	95.1	66	9	59	3	5	79	5	1	7	0	46	41	5	8	.385	1	3.87

DeLeon, Jose (Chestaro) (continued)

YR	TM/LG	CL	G	TBF	GS	CG	SHO	GF	IP	H	HR	BB	IBB	HB	SO	SH	SF	WP	BK	R	ER	W	L	PCT	SV	ERA
87	CHI/AL		33	889	31	2	0	0	206.0	177	24	97	4	10	153	6	6	6	1	106	92	11	12	.478	0	4.02
88	STL/NL		34	940	34	3	1	0	225.1	198	13	86	7	2	208	10	7	10	0	95	92	13	10	.565	0	3.67
89	STL/NL		36	972	36	5	3	0	244.2	173	16	80	5	6	201	5	3	2	0	96	83	16	12	.571	0	3.05
90	STL/NL		32	793	32	0	0	0	182.2	168	15	86	9	5	164	11	8	5	0	96	90	7	19	.269	0	4.43
91	STL/NL		28	679	28	1	0	0	162.2	144	15	61	1	6	118	5	4	1	1	57	49	5	9	.357	0	2.71
9 YR TOTALS			**261**	**6614**	**243**	**21**	**7**	**10**	**1579.2**	**1286**	**122**	**697**	**39**	**41**	**1343**	**60**	**43**	**49**	**7**	**711**	**646**	**73**	**105**	**.410**	**4**	**3.68**

DeLucia, Richard Anthony "Rich" — bats right — throws right — b.10/7/64

YR	TM/LG	CL	G	TBF	GS	CG	SHO	GF	IP	H	HR	BB	IBB	HB	SO	SH	SF	WP	BK	R	ER	W	L	PCT	SV	ERA
86	BEL/NWL	A–	13	0	11	1	1	1	74.0	44	4	24	0	1	69	0	0	3	0	20	14	8	2	.800	0	1.70
88	SB/CAL	A+	22	541	22	0	0	0	127.2	110	4	59	3	7	118	2	6	6	2	57	44	7	8	.467	0	3.10
89	WIL/EAS	AA	10	234	10	0	0	0	54.2	59	5	13	0	1	41	3	2	5	0	28	23	3	4	.429	0	3.79
90	SB/CAL	A+	5	116	5	1	0	0	30.2	19	4	3	0	4	35	1	0	0	0	9	7	4	1	.800	0	2.05
	WIL/EAS	AA	18	447	18	2	1	0	115.0	92	7	30	2	2	76	3	3	1	0	30	27	6	6	.500	0	2.11
	CAL/PCL	AAA	5	139	5	1	0	0	32.1	30	2	12	0	2	23	0	3	3	0	17	13	2	2	.500	0	3.62
	SEA/AL		5	144	5	1	0	0	36.0	30	4	9	0	0	20	2	0	0	0	9	8	1	2	.333	0	2.00
91	SEA/AL		32	779	31	0	0	0	182.0	176	31	78	4	4	98	5	14	10	0	107	103	12	13	.480	0	5.09
2 YR TOTALS			**37**	**923**	**36**	**1**	**0**	**0**	**218.0**	**206**	**33**	**87**	**4**	**4**	**118**	**7**	**14**	**10**	**0**	**116**	**111**	**13**	**15**	**.464**	**0**	**4.58**

Deshaies, James Joseph "Jim" — bats left — throws left — b.6/23/60

YR	TM/LG	CL	G	TBF	GS	CG	SHO	GF	IP	H	HR	BB	IBB	HB	SO	SH	SF	WP	BK	R	ER	W	L	PCT	SV	ERA
84	NAS/SOU	AA	7	196	7	1	0	0	45.0	33	3	29	1	1	42	2	0	1	3	20	14	3	2	.600	0	2.80
	NY/AL		2	40	2	0	0	0	7.0	14	1	7	0	0	5	0	1	0	0	9	9	0	1	.000	0	11.57
	COL/INT	AAA	18	552	18	9	4	0	135.2	99	9	62	4	1	117	3	4	3	1	45	36	10	5	.667	0	2.39
85	COL/INT	AAA	21	564	21	3	0	0	131.2	124	16	59	1	1	106	4	7	3	4	67	63	8	6	.571	0	4.31
	HOU/NL		2	10	0	0	0	0	3.0	1	0	0	0	0	2	0	0	0	0	0	0	0	0	.000	0	0.00
86	HOU/NL		26	599	26	1	1	0	144.0	124	16	59	2	2	128	4	3	0	7	58	52	12	5	.706	0	3.25
87	HOU/NL		26	648	25	1	0	0	152.0	149	22	57	0	4	104	9	3	4	5	81	78	11	6	.647	0	4.62
88	HOU/NL		31	847	31	3	2	0	207.0	164	20	72	5	2	127	8	13	1	6	77	69	11	14	.440	0	3.00
89	HOU/NL		34	928	34	3	1	0	225.2	180	15	79	8	4	153	11	5	8	1	80	73	15	10	.600	0	2.91
90	HOU/NL		34	881	34	2	0	0	209.1	186	21	84	9	8	119	17	12	3	3	93	88	7	12	.368	0	3.78
91	HOU/NL		28	686	28	1	0	0	161.0	156	19	72	5	4	98	4	7	0	5	90	89	5	12	.294	0	4.98
8 YR TOTALS			**183**	**4639**	**180**	**14**	**6**	**0**	**1109.0**	**974**	**114**	**430**	**36**	**17**	**736**	**53**	**44**	**16**	**27**	**488**	**458**	**61**	**60**	**.504**	**0**	**3.72**

DeSilva, John Reed — bats right — throws right — b.9/30/67 — System DET/AL

YR	TM/LG	CL	G	TBF	GS	CG	SHO	GF	IP	H	HR	BB	IBB	HB	SO	SH	SF	WP	BK	R	ER	W	L	PCT	SV	ERA
89	NF/NYP	A–	4	95	4	0	0	0	24.0	15	0	8	0	2	24	1	0	3	1	5	5	3	0	1.000	0	1.88
	FAY/SAL	A	9	215	9	1	0	0	52.2	40	4	21	0	0	54	1	2	2	3	23	16	2	2	.500	0	2.73
90	LAK/FSL	A+	14	349	14	0	0	0	91.0	54	4	25	0	4	113	1	2	3	1	18	15	8	1	.889	0	1.48
	LON/EAS	AA	14	372	14	1	1	0	89.0	87	4	27	0	2	76	1	4	3	0	47	37	5	6	.455	0	3.74
91	LON/EAS	AA	11	294	11	2	0	0	73.2	51	4	24	0	1	80	2	2	1	0	24	23	5	4	.556	0	2.81
	TOL/INT	AAA	11	254	11	1	0	0	58.2	62	10	21	0	1	56	0	1	1	0	33	30	5	4	.556	0	4.60

Dibble, Robert Keith "Rob" — bats left — throws right — b.1/24/64

YR	TM/LG	CL	G	TBF	GS	CG	SHO	GF	IP	H	HR	BB	IBB	HB	SO	SH	SF	WP	BK	R	ER	W	L	PCT	SV	ERA
84	TAM/FSL	A+	15	279	11	2	0	1	64.2	59	2	29	4	1	39	4	3	3	0	31	21	5	2	.714	0	2.92
85	CR/MID	A	45	290	1	0	0	30	65.2	67	3	28	0	0	73	4	2	6	0	37	28	5	5	.500	12	3.84
86	VER/EAS	AA	31	246	1	1	0	20	55.1	53	0	28	3	0	37	1	1	5	1	29	19	3	2	.600	10	3.09
	DEN/AMA	AAA	5	27	0	0	0	3	6.2	9	0	2	0	0	4	0	0	0	0	4	4	1	0	1.000	0	5.40
87	NAS/AMA	AAA	44	276	0	0	0	19	61.0	72	5	27	4	1	51	4	2	5	1	34	32	2	4	.333	4	4.72
88	NAS/AMA	AAA	31	140	0	0	0	25	35.0	21	2	14	0	1	41	1	2	3	0	9	9	1	1	.500	13	2.31
	CIN/NL		37	235	0	0	0	6	59.1	43	3	21	5	1	59	2	3	3	2	12	12	1	1	.500	2	1.82
89	CIN/NL		74	401	0	0	0	18	99.0	62	4	39	3	3	141	3	4	7	0	23	23	10	5	.667	2	2.09
90	CIN/NL		68	384	0	0	0	29	98.0	62	3	34	3	1	136	4	6	3	1	22	19	8	3	.727	11	1.74
91	CIN/NL		67	334	0	0	0	57	82.1	67	5	25	2	0	124	5	3	5	0	32	29	3	5	.375	31	3.17
4 YR TOTALS			**246**	**1354**	**0**	**0**	**0**	**110**	**338.2**	**234**	**14**	**119**	**21**	**5**	**460**	**14**	**16**	**18**	**3**	**89**	**83**	**22**	**14**	**.611**	**44**	**2.21**

Dickson, Lance Michael — bats right — throws left — b.10/19/69 — System CHI/NL

YR	TM/LG	CL	G	TBF	GS	CG	SHO	GF	IP	H	HR	BB	IBB	HB	SO	SH	SF	WP	BK	R	ER	W	L	PCT	SV	ERA
90	GEN/NYP	A–	3	56	3	0	0	0	17.0	5	1	4	0	0	29	0	0	0	0	1	1	2	1	.667	0	0.53
	PEO/MID	A	5	138	5	1	0	0	35.2	22	1	11	0	0	54	1	0	2	4	9	6	3	1	.750	0	1.51
	CHA/SOU	AA	3	87	3	1	1	0	23.2	13	0	3	0	0	28	1	0	2	0	1	1	2	1	.667	0	0.38
	CHI/NL		3	61	3	0	0	0	13.2	20	2	4	1	0	9	0	0	1	0	12	11	0	3	.000	0	7.24
91	IOW/AMA	AAA	18	427	18	1	1	1	101.1	85	5	57	1	0	101	8	3	5	1	39	35	4	4	.500	0	3.11
1 YR TOTALS			**3**	**61**	**3**	**0**	**0**	**0**	**13.2**	**20**	**2**	**4**	**1**	**0**	**9**	**0**	**0**	**1**	**0**	**12**	**11**	**0**	**3**	**.000**	**0**	**7.24**

DiPino, Frank Michael bats left — throws left — b.10/22/56

YR	TM/LG	CL	G	TBF	GS	CG	SHO	GF	IP	H	HR	BB	IBB	HB	SO	SH	SF	WP	BK	R	ER	W	L	PCT	SV	ERA
81	MIL/AL		2	10	0	0	0	2	2.1	0	0	3	0	0	3	0	0	0	0	0	0	0	0	.000	0	0.00
82	HOU/NL		6	122	6	0	0	0	28.1	32	1	11	1	0	25	3	1	3	0	20	19	2	2	.500	0	6.04
83	HOU/NL		53	279	0	0	0	32	71.1	52	2	20	5	1	67	1	3	3	0	21	21	3	4	.429	20	2.65
84	HOU/NL		57	329	0	0	0	44	75.1	69	7	43	6	2	49	3	3	3	1	32	28	4	9	.308	14	3.35
85	HOU/NL		54	329	0	0	0	29	76.0	69	7	43	6	2	49	3	3	3	1	44	34	3	7	.300	6	4.03

(continued)

DiPino, Frank Michael bats left (continued)

YR	TM/LG	CL	G	TBF	GS	CG	SHO	GF	IP	H	HR	BB	IBB	HB	SO	SH	SF	WP	BK	R	ER	W	L	PCT	SV	ERA
86	HOU/NL		31	167	0	0	0	14	40.1	27	5	16	1	2	27	5	1	0	0	18	16	1	3	.250	3	3.57
	CHI/NL		30	178	0	0	0	12	40.0	47	6	14	5	0	43	4	2	3	0	27	23	2	4	.333	0	5.17
	YEAR		61	345	0	0	0	26	80.1	74	11	30	6	2	70	9	3	3	0	45	39	3	7	.300	3	4.37
87	CHI/NL		69	343	0	0	0	20	80.0	75	7	34	2	1	61	6	4	5	0	31	28	3	3	.500	4	3.15
88	CHI/NL		63	398	0	0	0	23	90.1	102	6	32	7	0	69	2	6	6	1	54	50	2	3	.400	6	4.98
89	ST./NL		67	347	0	0	0	8	88.1	73	6	20	7	0	44	1	5	2	0	26	24	9	0	1.000	0	2.45
90	STL/NL		62	360	0	0	0	24	81.0	92	8	31	12	1	49	8	7	2	1	45	41	5	2	.714	3	4.56
91	LOU/AMA	AAA	2	7	0	0	0	0	1.0	2	0	3	0	0	0	0	0	0	0	4	4	0	0	.000	0	36.00
10 YR TOTALS			**494**	**2862**	**6**	**0**	**0**	**208**	**673.1**	**643**	**51**	**260**	**57**	**8**	**502**	**38**	**35**	**28**	**4**	**318**	**284**	**34**	**37**	**.479**	**56**	**3.80**

Dopson, John Robert — bats left — throws right — b.7/14/63

YR	TM/LG	CL	G	TBF	GS	CG	SHO	GF	IP	H	HR	BB	IBB	HB	SO	SH	SF	WP	BK	R	ER	W	L	PCT	SV	ERA
84	JAC/SOU	AA	26	726	26	6	1	0	170.2	198	10	41	2	1	76	13	2	5	0	83	70	10	8	.556	0	3.69
85	JAC/SOU	AA	5	129	5	1	0	0	32.1	27	2	10	0	1	20	2	0	1	0	5	4	3	0	1.000	0	1.11
	IND/AMA	AAA	18	412	18	3	2	0	95.1	88	7	44	1	3	48	5	2	3	0	44	40	4	7	.364	0	3.78
	MON/NL		4	70	3	0	0	0	13.0	25	4	4	0	0	4	0	0	0	0	17	16	0	2	.000	0	11.08
86	WPB/FSL	A+	2	43	2	0	0	0	10.2	8	0	4	0	1	8	0	0	0	0	0	0	1	0	1.000	0	0.00
	IND/AMA	AAA	4	76	4	0	0	0	16.0	18	0	11	0	0	6	0	0	2	1	12	8	0	3	.000	0	4.50
87	JAC/SOU	AA	21	504	21	1	1	0	118.1	123	8	30	1	1	75	0	1	0	0	58	50	7	5	.583	0	3.80
88	IND/AMA	AAA	3	71	3	0	0	0	18.0	19	0	5	0	0	15	2	0	0	0	7	7	0	0	.000	0	3.50
	MON/NL		26	704	26	1	0	0	168.2	150	15	58	3	1	101	5	2	3	1	69	57	3	11	.214	0	3.04
89	PAW/INT	AAA	2	43	2	0	0	0	8.2	13	1	1	0	0	9	0	0	0	0	9	7	0	2	.000	0	7.27
	BOS/AL		29	727	28	2	0	0	169.1	166	14	69	0	2	95	5	4	7	15	84	75	12	8	.600	0	3.99
90	BOS/AL		4	75	4	0	0	0	17.2	13	2	9	0	0	9	0	1	0	0	7	4	0	0	.000	0	2.04
	PAW/INT	AAA	5	95	5	0	0	0	22.0	28	3	8	1	0	13	1	0	0	3	12	12	2	1	.667	0	4.91
91	WH/FSL	A+	6	116	6	0	0	0	26.2	26	0	8	0	1	26	0	1	2	5	14	10	2	2	.500	0	3.38
	BOS/AL		1	6	0	0	0	1	1.0	2	0	1	0	0	0	0	1	0	0	2	2	0	0	.000	0	18.00
5 YR TOTALS			**64**	**1582**	**61**	**3**	**0**	**1**	**369.2**	**356**	**35**	**141**	**3**	**3**	**209**	**10**	**8**	**12**	**16**	**179**	**154**	**15**	**21**	**.417**	**0**	**3.75**

Downs, Kelly Robert — bats right — throws right — b.10/25/60

YR	TM/LG	CL	G	TBF	GS	CG	SHO	GF	IP	H	HR	BB	IBB	HB	SO	SH	SF	WP	BK	R	ER	W	L	PCT	SV	ERA
84	POR/PCL	AAA	30	0	25	5	0	2	163.0	166	12	65	3	4	104	0	0	7	2	106	96	7	12	.368	0	5.30
85	PHO/PCL	AAA	37	0	19	2	1	6	137.0	138	9	56	4	1	109	0	0	7	4	69	61	9	10	.474	1	4.01
86	PHO/PCL	AAA	18	466	18	4	0	0	108.0	116	11	28	1	3	68	2	3	6	2	54	41	8	5	.615	0	3.42
	SF/NL		14	372	14	1	0	0	88.1	78	5	30	7	3	64	4	4	3	2	29	27	4	4	.500	0	2.75
87	SF/NL		41	797	28	4	3	4	186.0	185	14	67	11	4	137	7	1	12	4	83	75	12	9	.571	1	3.63
88	SF/NL		27	685	26	6	3	0	168.0	140	11	47	8	3	118	4	9	7	4	67	62	13	9	.591	0	3.32
89	PHO/PCL	AAA	3	42	3	0	0	0	9.1	11	1	5	0	0	9	0	0	0	2	9	9	1	1	.500	0	8.68
	SJ/CAL	A+	1	21	1	0	0	0	5.0	1	0	4	0	0	7	0	0	0	0	0	0	0	0	.000	0	0.00
	SF/NL		18	349	15	0	0	1	82.2	82	7	26	4	1	49	4	4	3	3	47	44	4	8	.333	0	4.79
90	SJ/CAL	A+	1	19	1	0	0	0	5.0	5	0	0	0	1	3	0	0	1	0	2	1	0	1	.000	0	1.80
	PHO/PCL	AAA	1	20	1	0	0	0	5.0	5	1	0	0	0	4	1	1	0	0	3	1	0	0	.000	0	1.80
	SF/NL		13	265	9	0	0	1	63.0	56	2	20	4	2	31	2	1	2	1	26	24	3	2	.600	0	3.43
91	SF/NL		45	479	11	0	0	4	111.2	99	12	53	9	3	62	4	4	4	1	59	52	10	4	.714	0	4.19
6 YR TOTALS			**158**	**2947**	**103**	**11**	**6**	**10**	**699.2**	**640**	**51**	**243**	**43**	**16**	**461**	**25**	**23**	**31**	**15**	**311**	**284**	**46**	**36**	**.561**	**1**	**3.65**

Drabek, Douglas Dean "Doug" — bats right — throws right — b.7/25/62

YR	TM/LG	CL	G	TBF	GS	CG	SHO	GF	IP	H	HR	BB	IBB	HB	SO	SH	SF	WP	BK	R	ER	W	L	PCT	SV	ERA
84	APP/MID	A	1	21	1	0	0	0	5.0	3	0	3	0	0	6	0	0	0	0	1	1	1	0	1.000	0	1.80
	GF/EAS	AA	19	497	17	7	3	2	124.2	90	6	44	2	2	75	4	8	6	0	34	31	12	5	.706	0	2.24
	NAS/SOU	AA	4	131	4	2	0	0	31.0	30	1	10	0	0	22	0	3	2	1	11	8	1	2	.333	0	2.32
85	ALB/EAS	AA	26	777	26	9	2	0	192.2	153	12	55	2	6	153	7	6	2	0	71	64	13	7	.650	0	2.99
86	COL/INT	AAA	8	198	8	0	0	0	42.0	50	9	25	0	0	23	0	1	0	0	36	34	1	4	.200	0	7.29
	NY/AL		27	561	21	0	0	2	131.2	126	13	50	1	3	76	5	2	2	0	64	60	7	8	.467	0	4.10
87	PIT/NL		29	721	28	1	1	0	176.1	165	22	46	2	0	120	3	4	5	1	86	76	11	12	.478	0	3.88
88	PIT/NL		33	880	32	3	1	0	219.1	194	21	50	4	6	127	7	5	4	1	83	75	15	7	.682	0	3.08
89	PIT/NL		35	994	34	8	5	1	244.1	215	21	69	3	3	123	13	7	3	0	83	76	14	12	.538	0	2.80
90	PIT/NL		33	918	33	9	3	0	231.1	190	15	56	2	3	131	10	3	5	0	78	71	22	6	.786	0	2.76
91	PIT/NL		35	977	35	5	2	0	234.2	245	16	62	6	3	142	12	6	5	0	92	80	15	14	.517	0	3.07
6 YR TOTALS			**192**	**5051**	**183**	**26**	**12**	**3**	**1237.2**	**1135**	**108**	**333**	**18**	**18**	**719**	**50**	**27**	**25**	**2**	**486**	**438**	**84**	**59**	**.587**	**0**	**3.19**

Drahman, Brian Stacy — bats right — throws right — b.11/7/66

YR	TM/LG	CL	G	TBF	GS	CG	SHO	GF	IP	H	HR	BB	IBB	HB	SO	SH	SF	WP	BK	R	ER	W	L	PCT	SV	ERA
86	HEL/PIO	R+	18	0	10	0	0	5	65.1	79	4	33	1	0	40	0	0	4	0	49	43	4	6	.400	2	5.92
87	BEL/MID	A	46	318	0	0	0	41	79.0	63	3	22	3	3	60	4	2	5	1	28	19	6	5	.545	18	2.16
88	STO/CAL	A+	44	266	0	0	0	40	62.1	57	2	27	3	1	50	1	0	3	0	17	14	4	5	.444	14	2.02
89	EP/TEX	AA	19	151	0	0	0	8	31.0	52	3	11	1	1	23	3	0	3	0	31	25	3	4	.429	1	7.26
	STO/CAL	A+	12	112	0	0	0	10	27.2	22	0	9	0	2	30	1	0	2	0	11	10	3	2	.600	4	3.25
	SAR/FSL	A+	7	73	2	0	0	3	16.2	18	1	5	1	1	9	1	0	1	0	9	6	0	1	.000	1	3.24
90	BIR/SOU	AA	50	383	1	0	0	31	90.1	90	6	24	2	3	72	9	4	12	1	50	41	6	4	.600	17	4.08
91	VAN/PCL	AAA	22	106	0	0	0	21	24.1	21	1	13	1	0	17	4	0	1	1	12	12	2	3	.400	12	4.44
	CHI/AL		28	125	0	0	0	8	30.2	21	4	18	2	1	0	8	1	0	0	12	11	3	2	.600	0	3.23

Drees, Thomas Kent "Tom" — bats both — throws left — b.6/17/63

YR	TM/LG	CL	G	TBF	GS	CG	SHO	GF	IP	H	HR	BB	IBB	HB	SO	SH	SF	WP	BK	R	ER	W	L	PCT	SV	ERA
85	WS/GCL	R	12	314	12	2	0	0	74.1	75	1	17	0	4	75	2	2	6	1	29	23	6	3	.667	0	2.78
86	PEN/CAR	A+	37	440	10	1	0	14	94.2	108	5	61	1	4	54	2	3	7	1	64	50	5	7	.417	2	4.75
87	DB/FSL	A+	27	747	26	8	3	1	168.2	195	10	58	4	6	76	5	7	9	1	87	70	10	14	.417	0	3.74
88	BIR/SOU	AA	22	664	21	6	2	0	158.0	149	5	52	0	4	94	5	3	3	10	63	49	9	7	.563	0	2.79
89	VAN/PCL	AAA	26	701	26	4	3	0	168.1	142	12	72	2	4	66	8	5	2	10	76	63	12	11	.522	0	3.37
90	VAN/PCL	AAA	17	430	16	4	1	0	97.1	94	3	51	0	4	63	0	2	1	0	49	43	8	5	.615	0	3.98
91	VAN/PCL	AAA	22	619	22	3	3	0	143.0	130	15	62	0	3	89	3	7	1	2	70	56	8	8	.500	0	3.52
	CHI/AL		4	37	0	0	0	1	7.1	10	4	6	0	0	2	1	1	2	0	10	10	0	0	.000	0	12.27

Dressendorfer, Kirk Richard — bats right — throws right — b.4/8/69

YR	TM/LG	CL	G	TBF	GS	CG	SHO	GF	IP	H	HR	BB	IBB	HB	SO	SH	SF	WP	BK	R	ER	W	L	PCT	SV	ERA
90	SO/NWL	A-	7	78	4	0	0	0	19.1	18	0	2	0	1	22	1	1	1	0	7	5	0	1	.000	0	2.33
91	OAK/AL		7	159	7	0	0	0	34.2	33	5	21	0	0	17	2	1	3	0	28	21	3	3	.500	0	5.45
	TAC/PCL	AAA	8	120	7	0	0	0	24.0	31	4	20	0	1	19	1	2	2	0	29	29	1	3	.250	0	10.88

DuBois, Brian Andrew bats left — throws left — b.4/18/67

YR	TM/LG	CL	G	TBF	GS	CG	SHO	GF	IP	H	HR	BB	IBB	HB	SO	SH	SF	WP	BK	R	ER	W	L	PCT	SV	ERA
85	BLU/APP	R+	10	231	9	2	1	1	57.2	42	1	20	0	2	67	3	1	5	0	23	16	5	4	.556	0	2.50
86	HAG/CAR	A+	5	95	5	0	0	0	20.1	29	1	11	0	1	17	1	1	2	1	19	16	1	2	.333	0	7.08
	BLU/APP	R+	3	37	1	0	0	0	9.1	8	0	2	0	0	8	0	0	1	1	2	1	1	1	.500	0	0.96
87	HAG/CAR	A+	27	662	25	3	0	0	155.0	162	13	73	2	5	96	7	5	5	0	81	67	8	9	.471	0	3.89
88	VIR/CAR	A+	9	228	9	0	0	0	48.2	66	2	20	0	0	35	0	1	2	1	42	30	2	5	.286	0	5.55
	HAG/CAR	A+	19	556	19	7	1	0	135.0	129	5	30	0	0	112	4	2	6	3	71	55	12	4	.750	0	3.67
89	HAG/EAS	AA	15	440	15	6	2	0	112.0	93	1	18	0	1	82	6	1	4	0	36	31	6	4	.600	0	2.49
	ROC/INT	AAA	4	121	4	0	0	0	30.0	24	3	12	0	0	16	0	0	0	0	8	6	3	1	.750	0	1.80
	TOL/INT	AAA	3	93	3	0	0	0	24.0	17	3	6	0	0	13	0	1	0	0	6	6	1	1	.500	0	2.25
	DET/AL		6	153	5	0	0	0	36.0	29	2	17	3	2	13	0	1	0	0	14	7	0	4	.000	1	1.75
90	DET/AL		12	255	11	0	0	0	58.1	70	9	22	1	4	34	2	4	5	1	37	33	3	5	.375	0	5.09
	TOL/INT	AAA	13	297	10	2	1	0	69.2	67	6	26	1	2	47	2	2	2	0	27	21	5	4	.556	0	2.71
91	ORI/GCL	R	1	0	1	0	0	0	0.0	0	0	0	0	0	0	0	0	0	0	0	0	0	0	.000	0	0.00
2 YR TOTALS			18	408	16	0	0	1	94.1	99	11	39	4	3	47	2	5	5	2	51	40	3	9	.250	1	3.82

Eckersley, Dennis Lee — bats right — throws right — b.10/3/54

YR	TM/LG	CL	G	TBF	GS	CG	SHO	GF	IP	H	HR	BB	IBB	HB	SO	SH	SF	WP	BK	R	ER	W	L	PCT	SV	ERA
75	CLE/AL		34	794	24	6	2	5	186.2	147	16	90	8	7	152	6	7	4	2	61	54	13	7	.650	2	2.60
76	CLE/AL		36	821	30	9	3	3	199.1	155	13	78	2	5	200	10	4	6	1	82	76	13	12	.520	1	3.43
77	CLE/AL		33	1006	33	12	3	0	247.1	214	31	54	11	7	191	11	6	3	0	100	97	14	13	.519	0	3.53
78	BOS/AL		35	1121	35	16	3	0	268.1	258	30	71	8	7	162	7	8	3	0	99	89	20	8	.714	0	2.99
79	BOS/AL		33	1018	33	17	2	0	246.2	234	29	59	4	6	150	10	6	1	1	89	82	17	10	.630	0	2.99
80	BOS/AL		30	818	30	8	0	0	197.2	188	25	44	7	2	121	7	8	0	0	101	94	12	14	.462	0	4.28
81	BOS/AL		23	649	23	8	2	0	154.0	160	9	35	2	3	79	6	5	0	0	82	73	9	8	.529	0	4.27
82	BOS/AL		33	926	33	11	3	0	224.1	228	31	43	3	6	127	4	4	1	0	101	93	13	13	.500	0	3.73
83	BOS/AL		28	787	28	2	0	0	176.1	223	27	39	4	6	77	1	5	1	0	119	110	9	13	.409	0	5.61
84	BOS/AL		9	270	9	2	0	0	64.2	71	10	13	2	1	33	3	3	2	0	38	36	4	4	.500	0	5.01
	CHI/NL		24	662	24	2	0	0	160.1	152	11	36	7	4	81	8	6	1	2	59	54	10	8	.556	0	3.03
	YEAR		33	932	33	4	0	0	225.0	223	21	49	9	5	114	11	9	3	2	97	90	14	12	.538	0	3.60
85	CHI/NL		25	664	25	6	2	0	169.1	145	15	19	4	3	117	6	2	0	3	61	58	11	7	.611	0	3.08
86	CHI/NL		33	862	32	1	0	0	201.0	226	21	43	3	3	137	13	10	2	5	109	102	6	11	.353	0	4.57
87	OAK/AL		54	460	2	0	0	33	115.2	99	11	17	3	3	113	3	5	1	0	41	39	6	8	.429	16	3.03
88	OAK/AL		60	279	0	0	0	53	72.2	52	5	11	2	1	70	1	3	0	2	20	19	4	2	.667	45	2.35
89	OAK/AL		51	206	0	0	0	46	57.2	32	5	3	0	1	55	0	4	0	0	10	10	4	0	1.000	33	1.56
90	OAK/AL		63	262	0	0	0	61	73.1	41	2	4	1	0	73	0	1	0	0	9	5	4	2	.667	48	0.61
91	OAK/AL		67	299	0	0	0	59	76.0	60	11	9	3	1	87	1	0	1	0	26	25	5	4	.556	43	2.96
17 YR TOTALS			671	11904	361	100	20	260	2891.1	2685	302	668	74	62	2025	97	85	26	16	1207	1116	174	144	.547	188	3.47

Edens, Thomas Patrick "Tom" — bats right — throws right — b.6/9/61

YR	TM/LG	CL	G	TBF	GS	CG	SHO	GF	IP	H	HR	BB	IBB	HB	SO	SH	SF	WP	BK	R	ER	W	L	PCT	SV	ERA
84	COL/SAL	A	16	409	15	4	1	1	95.1	65	1	58	1	1	60	2	4	10	1	44	33	7	4	.636	0	3.12
	LYN/CAR	A+	3	65	2	0	0	0	14.1	11	1	8	0	0	15	1	0	1	0	6	4	1	1	.500	0	2.51
85	LYN/CAR	A+	16	353	16	4	0	0	82.0	86	4	34	0	2	48	2	5	3	2	40	35	6	4	.600	0	3.84
86	JAC/TEX	AA	16	431	16	4	0	0	106.0	76	4	41	1	1	72	5	2	10	0	36	30	9	4	.692	0	2.55
	TID/INT	AAA	11	280	11	2	1	0	61.1	71	5	28	1	1	31	1	2	1	4	33	31	5	3	.625	0	4.55
87	NY/NL		2	42	2	0	0	0	8.0	15	2	4	0	0	2	0	0	0	0	6	6	0	0	.000	0	6.75
	TID/INT	AAA	25	605	22	2	0	1	138.0	140	10	55	0	2	61	6	6	2	1	69	55	9	7	.563	0	3.59
88	TID/INT	AAA	24	582	21	3	0	0	135.1	128	7	28	2	4	89	1	0	3	1	67	52	7	6	.538	0	3.46
89	TID/INT	AAA	18	295	8	0	0	3	65.0	76	4	28	2	4	31	0	2	2	0	43	38	1	5	.167	1	5.26
	SW/INT	AAA	7	177	6	0	0	0	42.1	45	2	11	2	1	16	1	2	2	0	16	15	1	1	.500	0	3.19
90	DEN/AMA	AAA	19	154	0	0	0	9	36.2	32	3	22	0	0	26	1	0	1	3	23	22	1	1	.500	4	5.40
	MIL/AL		35	387	6	0	0	9	89.0	89	8	33	3	4	40	6	4	1	0	52	44	4	5	.444	2	4.45
91	POR/PCL	AAA	25	668	24	3	1	0	161.1	145	6	62	3	7	100	5	5	4	0	67	54	10	7	.588	0	3.01
	MIN/AL		8	143	6	0	0	0	33.0	34	1	10	1	0	19	0	0	0	0	15	15	2	2	.500	0	4.09
3 YR TOTALS			45	572	14	0	0	9	130.0	138	12	47	4	4	63	8	4	4	0	73	65	6	7	.462	2	4.50

Edwards, Wayne Maurice — bats left — throws left — b.3/7/64

YR	TM/LG	CL	G	TBF	GS	CG	SHO	GF	IP	H	HR	BB	IBB	HB	SO	SH	SF	WP	BK	R	ER	W	L	PCT	SV	ERA
85	WS/GCL	R	11	274	11	3	0	0	68.2	52	0	18	0	3	61	1	1	2	0	26	19	7	3	.700	0	2.49
86	PEN/CAR	A+	24	574	21	0	0	2	128.1	149	10	68	1	2	86	6	2	8	2	80	60	8	8	.500	0	4.21
87	DB/FSL	A+	29	862	28	15	2	0	199.2	211	4	68	3	9	121	5	6	17	0	91	80	16	8	.667	0	3.61
88	BIR/SOU	AA	27	762	27	6	1	0	167.0	176	9	92	3	5	136	5	10	16	7	108	91	9	12	.429	0	4.90
	VAN/PCL	AAA	2	9	0	0	0	1	3.0	0	0	0	0	0	2	0	0	0	0	0	0	0	0	.000	0	0.00
89	BIR/SOU	AA	24	660	19	5	0	1	158.0	131	6	65	1	5	122	4	1	6	4	69	56	10	4	.714	1	3.19
	CHI/AL		7	30	0	0	0	2	7.1	7	1	3	0	0	9	0	1	0	0	3	3	0	0	.000	0	3.68
90	CHI/AL		42	396	5	0	0	8	95.0	81	6	41	2	3	63	4	2	1	0	39	34	5	3	.625	2	3.22
91	CHI/AL		13	106	0	0	0	3	23.1	22	2	17	3	0	12	2	2	2	0	14	10	0	2	.000	0	3.86
	VAN/PCL	AAA	14	304	12	0	0	1	64.2	73	4	37	0	5	35	3	2	4	0	50	45	3	9	.250	0	6.26
3 YR TOTALS			**62**	**532**	**5**	**0**	**0**	**13**	**125.2**	**110**	**9**	**61**	**5**	**3**	**84**	**6**	**5**	**3**	**0**	**56**	**47**	**5**	**5**	**.500**	**2**	**3.37**

Egloff, Bruce Edward — bats right — throws right — b.4/10/65

YR	TM/LG	CL	G	TBF	GS	CG	SHO	GF	IP	H	HR	BB	IBB	HB	SO	SH	SF	WP	BK	R	ER	W	L	PCT	SV	ERA
86	BAT/NYP	A–	12	302	12	1	0	0	70.0	79	8	17	0	3	62	0	1	7	0	42	31	1	2	.333	0	3.99
87	WAT/MID	A	7	106	7	0	0	0	22.2	30	1	10	0	4	14	2	1	1	1	14	13	1	2	.333	0	5.16
89	WAT/NYP	A–	22	207	0	0	0	17	48.2	33	2	24	1	1	63	3	1	9	2	19	14	1	1	.500	8	2.59
90	CAN/EAS	AA	34	226	0	0	0	24	54.2	44	5	15	1	3	53	0	4	6	1	16	12	3	2	.600	15	1.98
91	CLE/AL		6	28	0	0	0	2	5.2	8	0	4	1	0	8	0	0	2	0	3	3	0	0	.000	0	4.76
	CS/PCL	AAA	15	126	0	0	0	7	29.1	31	2	13	2	1	17	3	0	1	3	14	11	1	2	.333	2	3.38

Eichhorn, Mark Anthony — bats right — throws right — b.11/21/60

YR	TM/LG	CL	G	TBF	GS	CG	SHO	GF	IP	H	HR	BB	IBB	HB	SO	SH	SF	WP	BK	R	ER	W	L	PCT	SV	ERA
82	TOR/AL		7	171	7	0	0	0	38.0	40	4	14	1	0	16	1	2	3	0	28	23	0	3	.000	0	5.45
84	SYR/INT	AAA	36	541	18	3	1	7	117.2	147	13	51	0	4	54	3	3	8	0	92	78	5	9	.357	0	5.97
85	KNO/SOU	AA	26	473	10	2	1	2	116.1	101	11	34	2	4	76	5	4	2	1	49	39	5	1	.833	0	3.02
	SYR/INT	AAA	8	154	7	0	0	1	37.1	38	5	7	0	0	27	2	1	1	0	24	20	2	5	.286	0	4.82
86	TOR/AL		69	612	0	0	0	38	157.0	105	8	45	14	7	166	9	2	2	1	32	30	14	6	.700	10	1.72
87	TOR/AL		89	540	0	0	0	27	127.2	110	14	52	13	6	96	7	4	3	1	47	45	10	6	.625	4	3.17
88	SYR/INT	AAA	18	162	1	0	0	8	38.1	35	0	15	5	4	34	0	2	0	0	9	5	4	4	.500	2	1.17
	TOR/AL		37	302	0	0	0	17	66.2	79	3	27	4	6	28	8	1	3	6	32	31	0	3	.000	1	4.18
89	RIC/INT	AAA	25	152	0	0	0	24	41.0	29	1	6	0	2	33	2	2	0	0	6	6	1	0	1.000	19	1.32
	ATL/NL		45	286	0	0	0	13	68.1	70	6	19	8	1	49	7	4	0	1	36	33	5	5	.500	0	4.35
90	CAL/AL		60	374	0	0	0	40	84.2	98	2	23	0	6	69	2	4	2	0	36	29	2	5	.286	13	3.08
91	CAL/AL		70	311	0	0	0	23	81.2	63	2	13	1	2	49	5	3	0	0	21	18	3	3	.500	1	1.98
7 YR TOTALS			**377**	**2596**	**7**	**0**	**0**	**158**	**624.0**	**565**	**39**	**193**	**41**	**28**	**473**	**39**	**20**	**13**	**9**	**232**	**209**	**34**	**31**	**.523**	**29**	**3.01**

Eiland, David William "Dave" — bats right — throws right — b.7/5/66

YR	TM/LG	CL	G	TBF	GS	CG	SHO	GF	IP	H	HR	BB	IBB	HB	SO	SH	SF	WP	BK	R	ER	W	L	PCT	SV	ERA
87	ONE/NYP	A–	5	109	5	0	0	0	29.1	20	1	3	0	0	16	0	0	2	0	6	6	4	0	1.000	0	1.84
	FT./FSL	A+	8	248	8	4	1	0	62.1	57	0	8	0	0	28	2	0	1	1	17	13	5	3	.625	0	1.88
88	ALB/EAS	AA	18	472	18	7	2	0	119.1	95	8	22	3	1	66	4	5	2	0	39	34	9	5	.643	0	2.56
	NY/AL		3	57	3	0	0	0	12.2	15	6	4	0	2	7	0	0	0	0	9	9	0	0	.000	0	6.39
	COL/INT	AAA	4	106	4	0	0	0	24.1	25	4	6	0	1	13	0	1	0	0	8	7	1	1	.500	0	2.59
89	NY/AL		6	152	6	0	0	0	34.1	44	5	13	3	2	11	1	2	0	0	25	22	1	3	.250	0	5.77
	COL/INT	AAA	18	427	18	2	0	0	103.0	107	10	21	0	1	45	1	3	1	1	47	43	9	4	.692	0	3.76
90	COL/INT	AAA	27	707	26	11	3	0	175.1	155	8	32	0	1	96	3	1	2	2	63	56	16	5	.762	0	2.87
	NY/AL		5	127	5	0	0	0	30.1	31	2	5	0	0	16	0	0	0	0	14	12	2	1	.667	0	3.56
91	COL/INT	AAA	9	244	9	2	0	0	60.0	54	7	7	0	2	18	1	1	1	0	22	16	6	1	.857	0	2.40
	NY/AL		18	317	13	0	0	4	72.2	87	10	23	1	3	30	0	3	0	0	51	43	2	5	.286	0	5.33
4 YR TOTALS			**32**	**653**	**27**	**0**	**0**	**4**	**150.0**	**177**	**23**	**45**	**4**	**7**	**52**	**1**	**5**	**0**	**0**	**99**	**86**	**5**	**9**	**.357**	**0**	**5.16**

Eldred, Calvin John "Cal" — bats right — throws right — b.11/24/67

YR	TM/LG	CL	G	TBF	GS	CG	SHO	GF	IP	H	HR	BB	IBB	HB	SO	SH	SF	WP	BK	R	ER	W	L	PCT	SV	ERA
89	BEL/MID	A	5	127	5	0	0	0	31.1	23	0	11	1	1	32	1	1	0	0	10	8	2	1	.667	0	2.30
90	STO/CAL	A+	7	197	7	3	1	0	50.0	31	2	19	0	3	75	0	0	2	1	12	9	4	2	.667	0	1.62
	EP/TEX	AA	19	485	19	0	0	0	110.1	126	9	47	0	2	93	3	3	4	1	61	55	5	4	.556	0	4.49
91	DEN/AMA	AAA	29	784	29	3	1	0	185.0	161	13	84	2	12	168	4	8	8	2	82	77	13	9	.591	0	3.75
	MIL/AL		3	73	3	0	0	0	16.0	20	2	6	0	0	10	0	0	0	0	9	8	2	0	1.000	0	4.50

Erickson, Scott Gavin — bats right — throws right — b.2/2/68

YR	TM/LG	CL	G	TBF	GS	CG	SHO	GF	IP	H	HR	BB	IBB	HB	SO	SH	SF	WP	BK	R	ER	W	L	PCT	SV	ERA
89	VIS/CAL	A+	12	320	12	2	0	0	78.2	79	3	22	0	0	59	0	0	3	4	29	26	3	4	.429	0	2.97
90	ORL/SOU	AA	15	397	15	3	1	0	101.0	75	3	24	0	5	69	1	2	4	1	38	34	8	3	.727	0	3.03
	MIN/AL		19	485	17	1	0	1	113.0	108	9	51	4	5	53	5	2	3	0	49	36	8	4	.667	0	2.87
91	MIN/AL		32	851	32	5	3	0	204.0	189	13	71	3	6	108	5	7	4	0	80	72	20	8	.714	0	3.18
2 YR TOTALS			**51**	**1336**	**49**	**6**	**3**	**1**	**317.0**	**297**	**22**	**122**	**7**	**11**	**161**	**10**	**9**	**7**	**0**	**129**	**108**	**28**	**12**	**.700**	**0**	**3.07**

Fajardo, Hector (Navarette) — bats right — throws right — b.11/6/70

YR	TM/LG	CL	G	TBF	GS	CG	SHO	GF	IP	H	HR	BB	IBB	HB	SO	SH	SF	WP	BK	R	ER	W	L	PCT	SV	ERA
89	PIR/GCL	R	10	154	6	0	0	0	34.2	38	0	20	0	0	19	0	1	1	0	24	23	0	5	.000	0	5.97
90	PIR/GCL	R	5	92	4	0	0	0	21.0	23	0	8	0	3	17	1	1	0	0	10	9	1	1	.500	0	3.86
	AUG/SAL	A	7	173	7	0	0	0	39.2	41	1	15	0	2	28	1	0	0	1	18	17	2	2	.500	0	3.86

Fajardo, Hector (Navarette) (continued)

YR	TM/LG	CL	G	TBF	GS	CG	SHO	GF	IP	H	HR	BB	IBB	HB	SO	SH	SF	WP	BK	R	ER	W	L	PCT	SV	ERA
91	AUG/SAL	A	11	250	11	1	1	0	60.1	44	1	24	0	2	79	1	2	3	1	26	18	4	3	.571	0	2.69
	SAL/CAR	A+	1	30	1	1	0	0	7.2	4	1	1	1	0	7	1	0	0	0	3	2	0	1	.000	0	2.35
	CAR/SOU	AA	10	258	10	1	0	0	61.0	55	4	24	0	0	53	2	3	3	2	32	28	3	4	.429	0	4.13
	PIT/NL		2	35	2	0	0	0	6.1	10	0	7	0	0	8	0	0	3	0	7	7	0	0	.000	0	9.95
	BUF/AMA	AAA	8	36	0	0	0	4	9.1	6	0	3	0	0	12	0	0	0	0	1	1	1	0	1.000	1	0.96
	TEX/AL		4	84	3	0	0	1	19.0	25	2	4	0	1	15	0	3	0	0	13	12	0	2	.000	0	5.68
	YEAR		6	119	5	0	0	1	25.1	35	2	11	0	1	23	0	3	3	0	20	19	0	2	.000	0	6.75
1 YR TOTALS			**6**	**119**	**5**	**0**	**0**	**1**	**25.1**	**35**	**2**	**11**	**0**	**1**	**23**	**0**	**3**	**3**	**0**	**20**	**19**	**0**	**2**	**.000**	**0**	**6.75**

Farmer, Howard Earl — bats right — throws right — b.1/18/66 — System MON/NL

YR	TM/LG	CL	G	TBF	GS	CG	SHO	GF	IP	H	HR	BB	IBB	HB	SO	SH	SF	WP	BK	R	ER	W	L	PCT	SV	ERA
87	JAM/NYP	A–	15	404	15	3	1	0	96.1	93	4	30	0	3	63	1	2	4	2	42	35	9	6	.600	0	3.27
88	ROC/MID	A	27	774	25	8	2	0	193.2	153	10	58	2	8	145	3	5	10	9	70	54	15	7	.682	0	2.51
89	JAC/SOU	AA	26	724	26	5	2	0	184.0	122	5	50	0	4	151	7	4	6	10	59	45	12	9	.571	0	2.20
	IND/AMA	AAA	1	28	1	0	0	0	7.0	3	0	3	0	0	3	0	0	0	0	1	0	1	0	1.000	0	0.00
90	IND/AMA	AAA	26	640	26	4	2	0	148.0	150	12	48	2	6	99	4	4	5	2	84	64	7	9	.438	0	3.89
	MON/NL		6	99	4	0	0	0	23.0	26	9	10	1	0	14	2	1	1	0	18	18	0	3	.000	0	7.04
91	IND/AMA	AAA	20	444	19	0	0	0	105.0	93	5	37	0	6	67	7	4	5	2	55	45	6	4	.600	0	3.86
1 YR TOTALS			**6**	**99**	**4**	**0**	**0**	**0**	**23.0**	**26**	**9**	**10**	**1**	**0**	**14**	**2**	**1**	**1**	**0**	**18**	**18**	**0**	**3**	**.000**	**0**	**7.04**

Farr, Steven Michael "Steve" — bats right — throws right — b.12/12/56

YR	TM/LG	CL	G	TBF	GS	CG	SHO	GF	IP	H	HR	BB	IBB	HB	SO	SH	SF	WP	BK	R	ER	W	L	PCT	SV	ERA
84	MAI/INT	AAA	6	179	6	2	1	0	45.0	37	3	8	0	0	40	3	0	0	2	14	13	4	0	1.000	0	2.60
	CLE/AL		31	488	16	0	0	4	116.0	106	14	46	3	5	83	2	3	2	2	61	59	3	11	.214	1	4.58
85	OMA/AMA	AAA	17	532	16	7	3	0	133.2	105	6	41	0	4	98	3	2	1	1	36	30	10	4	.714	0	2.02
	KC/AL		16	164	3	0	0	5	37.2	34	2	20	4	2	36	1	2	2	0	15	13	2	1	.667	1	3.11
86	KC/AL		56	443	0	0	0	33	109.1	90	10	39	8	4	83	3	2	4	1	39	38	8	4	.667	8	3.13
87	OMA/AMA	AAA	8	50	0	0	0	8	12.2	6	0	6	1	0	15	0	0	0	0	3	2	0	0	.000	4	1.42
	KC/AL		47	408	1	0	0	19	91.0	97	9	44	4	2	88	3	1	3	4	47	42	4	3	.571	1	4.15
88	KC/AL		62	344	1	0	0	49	82.2	74	5	30	6	2	72	1	3	4	2	25	23	5	4	.556	20	2.50
89	KC/AL		51	279	2	0	0	40	63.1	75	5	22	5	1	56	0	1	2	0	35	29	2	5	.286	18	4.12
90	KC/AL		57	515	6	1	1	20	127.0	99	6	48	9	5	94	10	1	2	0	32	28	13	7	.650	1	1.98
91	NY/AL		60	285	0	0	0	48	70.0	57	4	20	3	5	60	0	0	2	0	19	17	5	5	.500	23	2.19
8 YR TOTALS			**380**	**2926**	**28**	**1**	**1**	**218**	**697.0**	**632**	**55**	**269**	**42**	**26**	**572**	**17**	**17**	**20**	**5**	**273**	**249**	**42**	**40**	**.512**	**73**	**3.22**

Farrell, John Edward — bats right — throws right — b.8/4/62

YR	TM/LG	CL	G	TBF	GS	CG	SHO	GF	IP	H	HR	BB	IBB	HB	SO	SH	SF	WP	BK	R	ER	W	L	PCT	SV	ERA
84	WAT/MID	A	9	213	9	2	0	0	43.1	59	4	33	0	1	29	3	0	4	2	34	31	0	5	.000	0	6.44
	MAI/INT	AAA	5	117	5	0	0	0	26.1	20	2	20	2	1	12	1	2	1	0	11	11	2	1	.667	0	3.76
85	WAT/EAS	AA	25	678	25	5	1	0	149.0	161	8	76	1	5	75	8	4	3	1	106	86	7	13	.350	0	5.19
86	WAT/EAS	AA	26	732	26	9	3	0	173.1	158	15	54	2	10	104	4	4	3	0	82	59	9	10	.474	0	3.06
87	BUF/AMA	AAA	25	681	24	2	0	1	156.0	155	26	64	2	8	91	3	5	9	1	109	101	6	12	.333	0	5.83
	CLE/AL		10	297	9	1	0	1	69.0	68	7	22	1	5	28	3	1	1	1	29	26	5	1	.833	0	3.39
88	CLE/AL		31	895	30	4	0	0	210.1	216	15	67	3	9	92	9	6	2	3	106	99	14	10	.583	0	4.24
89	CLE/AL		31	895	31	7	2	0	208.0	196	14	71	4	7	132	8	6	4	0	97	84	9	14	.391	0	3.63
90	CAN/EAS	AA	2	46	2	0	0	0	10.0	13	1	2	0	1	5	0	0	1	0	8	8	1	1	.500	0	7.20
	CLE/AL		17	418	17	1	0	0	96.2	108	10	33	1	1	44	5	2	1	0	49	46	4	5	.444	0	4.28
4 YR TOTALS			**89**	**2505**	**87**	**13**	**2**	**1**	**584.0**	**588**	**46**	**193**	**9**	**22**	**296**	**25**	**15**	**8**	**4**	**281**	**255**	**32**	**30**	**.516**	**0**	**3.93**

Fassero, Jeffrey Joseph "Jeff" — bats left — throws left — b.1/5/63

YR	TM/LG	CL	G	TBF	GS	CG	SHO	GF	IP	H	HR	BB	IBB	HB	SO	SH	SF	WP	BK	R	ER	W	L	PCT	SV	ERA
84	JC/APP	R+	13	292	11	2	0	2	66.2	65	2	39	0	0	59	0	4	1	1	42	34	4	7	.364	1	4.59
85	SPR/MID	A	29	533	15	1	0	2	119.0	125	11	45	3	3	65	4	3	4	3	78	53	4	8	.333	1	4.01
86	SP/FSL	A+	26	720	26	6	1	0	176.0	156	5	56	4	0	112	7	3	5	3	63	48	13	7	.650	0	2.45
87	ARK/TEX	AA	28	674	27	2	1	0	151.1	168	16	67	7	1	118	10	2	7	1	90	69	10	7	.588	0	4.10
88	ARK/TEX	AA	70	375	1	0	0	36	78.0	97	1	41	13	3	72	7	2	5	2	48	31	5	5	.500	17	3.58
89	ARK/TEX	AA	6	174	6	2	1	0	44.0	32	1	12	0	1	38	1	0	1	1	11	8	4	1	.800	0	1.64
	LOU/AMA	AAA	22	511	19	0	0	0	112.0	136	13	47	1	2	73	8	3	8	4	79	65	3	10	.231	0	5.22
90	CAN/EAS	AA	61	281	0	0	0	30	64.1	66	5	24	6	1	61	1	0	2	0	24	20	5	4	.556	6	2.80
91	IND/AMA	AAA	18	71	0	0	0	11	18.1	11	1	7	1	1	12	1	0	1	0	3	3	3	0	1.000	4	1.47
	MON/NL		51	223	0	0	0	30	55.1	39	1	17	1	1	42	6	0	4	0	17	15	2	5	.286	8	2.44

Fernandez, Alexander "Alex" — bats right — throws right — b.8/13/69

YR	TM/LG	CL	G	TBF	GS	CG	SHO	GF	IP	H	HR	BB	IBB	HB	SO	SH	SF	WP	BK	R	ER	W	L	PCT	SV	ERA
90	WS/GCL	R	2	43	2	0	0	0	10.0	11	0	1	0	2	16	0	1	1	0	4	4	1	0	1.000	0	3.60
	SAR/FSL	A+	2	59	2	0	0	0	14.2	9	0	3	0	0	23	0	1	0	1	4	3	1	1	.500	0	1.84
	BIR/SOU	AA	4	99	4	0	0	0	25.0	20	0	6	0	0	27	0	0	0	0	7	3	3	0	1.000	0	1.08
	CHI/AL		13	378	13	3	0	0	87.2	89	6	34	0	3	61	5	0	1	0	40	37	5	5	.500	0	3.80
91	CHI/AL		34	827	32	2	0	1	191.2	186	16	88	2	2	145	7	11	4	1	100	96	9	13	.409	0	4.51
2 YR TOTALS			**47**	**1205**	**45**	**5**	**0**	**1**	**279.1**	**275**	**22**	**122**	**2**	**5**	**206**	**12**	**11**	**5**	**1**	**140**	**133**	**14**	**18**	**.438**	**0**	**4.29**

Fernandez, Charles Sidney "Sid" — bats left — throws left — b.10/12/62

YR	TM/LG	CL	G	TBF	GS	CG	SHO	GF	IP	H	HR	BB	IBB	HB	SO	SH	SF	WP	BK	R	ER	W	L	PCT	SV	ERA
83	LA/NL		2	33	1	0	0	0	6.0	7	0	7	0	1	9	0	0	0	0	4	4	0	1	.000	0	6.00

(continued)

YR	TM/LG	CL	G	TBF	GS	CG	SHO	GF	IP	H	HR	BB	IBB	HB	SO	SH	SF	WP	BK	R	ER	W	L	PCT	SV	ERA
84	TID/INT	AAA	17	451	17	3	0	0	105.2	69	2	63	1	3	123	5	3	8	0	39	30	6	5	.545	0	2.56
	NY/NL		15	371	15	0	0	0	90.0	74	8	34	3	0	62	5	5	1	4	40	35	6	6	.500	0	3.50
85	TID/INT	AAA	5	142	5	1	0	0	35.1	17	2	21	0	0	42	0	1	1	0	8	8	4	1	.800	0	2.04
	NY/NL		26	685	26	3	0	0	170.1	108	14	80	3	2	180	4	3	3	2	56	53	9	9	.500	0	2.80
86	NY/NL		32	855	31	2	1	1	204.1	161	13	91	1	2	200	9	7	6	0	82	80	16	6	.727	1	3.52
87	NY/NL		28	665	27	3	1	0	156.0	130	16	67	8	2	134	3	6	2	0	75	66	12	8	.600	0	3.81
88	NY/NL		31	751	31	1	1	0	187.0	127	15	70	1	6	189	2	7	4	9	69	63	12	10	.545	0	3.03
89	NY/NL		35	883	32	6	2	0	219.1	157	21	75	3	6	198	4	4	1	3	73	69	14	5	.737	0	2.83
90	NY/NL		30	735	30	2	1	0	179.1	130	18	67	4	5	181	7	6	1	0	79	69	9	14	.391	0	3.46
91	SL/FSL	A+	1	11	1	0	0	0	3.0	1	0	1	0	0	4	0	0	0	0	0	0	0	0	.000	0	0.00
	WIL/EAS	AA	1	23	1	0	0	0	6.0	3	0	1	0	0	5	0	0	0	0	0	0	0	0	.000	0	0.00
	TID/INT	AAA	3	58	3	0	0	0	15.2	9	0	6	0	0	22	0	1	0	0	2	2	1	0	1.000	0	1.15
	NY/NL		8	177	8	0	0	0	44.0	36	4	9	0	0	31	5	1	0	0	18	14	1	3	.250	0	2.86
9 YR TOTALS			207	5155	201	17	6	1	1256.1	930	109	500	23	30	1184	39	39	18	18	496	453	79	62	.560	1	3.25

Fetters, Michael Lee "Mike" — bats right — throws right — b.12/19/64

YR	TM/LG	CL	G	TBF	GS	CG	SHO	GF	IP	H	HR	BB	IBB	HB	SO	SH	SF	WP	BK	R	ER	W	L	PCT	SV	ERA
86	SAL/NWL	A-	12	0	12	1	0	0	72.0	60	4	51	0	3	72	0	0	4	1	39	27	4	2	.667	0	3.38
87	PS/CAL	A+	19	518	19	2	0	1	116.0	106	2	73	0	6	105	4	5	22	1	62	46	9	7	.563	0	3.57
88	MID/TEX	AA	20	522	20	2	0	0	114.0	116	10	67	3	7	101	2	4	18	14	78	75	8	8	.500	0	5.92
	EDM/PCL	AAA	2	57	2	1	0	0	14.0	8	0	10	0	0	11	0	0	0	0	3	3	2	0	1.000	0	1.93
89	EDM/PCL	AAA	26	704	26	6	2	0	168.0	160	11	72	2	7	144	1	1	16	2	80	71	12	8	.600	0	3.80
	CAL/AL		1	16	1	0	0	0	3.1	5	1	1	0	0	4	0	0	0	0	4	3	0	0	.000	0	8.10
90	EDM/PCL	AAA	5	116	5	1	1	0	27.1	22	0	13	0	1	26	1	0	2	1	9	3	1	1	.500	0	0.99
	CAL/AL		26	291	2	0	0	10	67.2	77	9	20	0	2	35	1	0	3	0	33	31	1	1	.500	0	4.12
91	EDM/PCL	AAA	11	264	11	1	0	0	61.0	65	5	26	0	3	43	1	1	2	3	39	33	2	7	.222	0	4.87
	CAL/AL		19	206	4	0	0	8	44.2	53	4	28	2	3	24	1	0	4	0	29	24	2	5	.286	0	4.84
3 YR TOTALS			46	513	6	0	0	18	115.2	135	14	49	2	5	63	2	0	9	0	66	58	3	6	.333	1	4.51

Finley, Charles Edward "Chuck" — bats left — throws left — b.11/26/62

YR	TM/LG	CL	G	TBF	GS	CG	SHO	GF	IP	H	HR	BB	IBB	HB	SO	SH	SF	WP	BK	R	ER	W	L	PCT	SV	ERA
85	SAL/NWL	A-	18	0	0	0	0	12	29.0	34	1	10	0	0	32	0	0	4	0	21	15	3	1	.750	5	4.66
86	QC/MID	A	10	43	0	0	0	9	12.0	4	0	3	0	0	16	0	0	1	1	0	0	1	0	1.000	6	0.00
	CAL/AL		25	198	0	0	0	7	46.1	40	2	23	1	1	37	4	0	2	0	17	17	3	1	.750	0	3.30
87	CAL/AL		35	405	3	0	0	17	90.2	102	7	43	3	3	63	2	2	4	3	54	47	2	7	.222	0	4.67
88	CAL/AL		31	831	31	2	0	0	194.1	191	15	82	7	6	111	7	10	5	8	95	90	9	15	.375	0	4.17
89	CAL/AL		29	827	29	9	1	0	199.2	171	13	82	0	2	156	7	3	4	2	64	57	16	9	.640	0	2.57
90	CAL/AL		32	962	32	7	2	0	236.0	210	17	81	3	2	177	12	3	9	0	77	63	18	9	.667	0	2.40
91	CAL/AL		34	955	34	4	2	0	227.1	205	23	101	1	8	171	4	3	6	3	102	96	18	9	.667	0	3.80
6 YR TOTALS			186	4178	129	22	5	24	994.1	919	77	412	15	22	715	36	21	30	16	409	370	66	50	.569	0	3.35

Flanagan, Michael Kendall "Mike" — bats left — throws left — b.12/16/51

YR	TM/LG	CL	G	TBF	GS	CG	SHO	GF	IP	H	HR	BB	IBB	HB	SO	SH	SF	WP	BK	R	ER	W	L	PCT	SV	ERA
75	BAL/AL		2	42	1	0	0	0	9.2	9	0	6	1	0	7	0	0	0	0	4	3	0	1	.000	0	2.79
76	BAL/AL		20	358	10	4	0	7	85.0	83	7	33	0	0	56	2	4	2	1	41	39	3	5	.375	0	4.13
77	BAL/AL		36	974	33	15	2	2	235.0	235	17	70	5	2	149	10	7	5	0	100	95	15	10	.600	1	3.64
78	BAL/AL		40	1160	40	17	2	0	281.1	271	22	87	2	3	167	9	4	6	1	128	126	19	15	.559	0	4.03
79	BAL/AL		39	1085	38	16	5	0	265.2	245	23	70	1	3	190	9	4	6	0	107	91	23	9	.719	0	3.08
80	BAL/AL		37	1065	37	12	2	0	251.1	278	27	71	3	2	128	9	12	12	1	121	115	16	13	.552	0	4.12
81	BAL/AL		20	482	20	3	2	0	116.0	108	11	37	1	2	72	0	0	6	0	55	54	9	6	.600	0	4.19
82	BAL/AL		36	991	35	11	1	1	236.0	233	24	76	5	4	103	5	6	9	2	110	104	15	11	.577	0	3.97
83	BAL/AL		20	528	20	3	1	0	125.1	135	10	31	2	2	50	4	6	1	0	53	46	12	4	.750	0	3.30
84	BAL/AL		34	947	34	10	2	0	226.2	213	24	81	5	1	115	8	6	8	0	103	89	13	13	.500	0	3.53
85	HAG/CAR	A+	1	20	1	0	0	0	6.0	1	0	4	0	0	2	0	0	0	0	0	0	0	0	.000	0	0.00
	BAL/AL		15	379	15	1	0	0	86.0	101	14	28	0	2	42	7	2	3	0	49	49	4	5	.444	0	5.13
86	BAL/AL		29	747	28	2	0	0	172.0	179	15	66	4	1	96	10	6	8	1	95	81	7	11	.389	0	4.24
87	ROC/INT	AAA	3	51	3	0	0	0	12.0	12	0	3	0	0	11	1	1	0	0	5	4	0	0	.000	0	3.00
	BAL/AL		16	410	16	4	0	0	94.2	102	9	36	1	0	50	6	1	1	0	57	52	3	6	.333	0	4.94
	TOR/AL		7	209	7	0	0	0	49.1	46	3	15	3	0	43	0	0	1	0	15	13	3	2	.600	0	2.37
	YEAR		23	619	23	4	0	0	144.0	148	12	51	4	0	93	6	1	2	0	72	65	6	8	.429	0	4.06
88	TOR/AL		34	916	34	2	1	0	211.0	220	23	80	1	1	99	14	4	3	4	106	98	13	13	.500	0	4.18
89	TOR/AL		30	726	30	1	1	0	171.2	186	10	47	0	5	47	8	8	4	0	82	75	8	10	.444	0	3.93
90	TOR/AL		5	94	5	0	0	0	20.1	28	3	8	0	0	5	1	0	1	0	14	12	2	2	.500	0	5.31
91	BAL/AL		64	391	1	0	0	24	98.1	84	6	25	5	3	55	4	3	2	2	27	26	2	7	.222	3	2.38
17 YR TOTALS			484	11504	404	101	19	34	2735.1	2756	248	867	40	36	1474	108	74	80	12	1267	1168	167	143	.539	4	3.84

Fleming, David Anthony "Dave" — bats left — throws left — b.11/7/69

YR	TM/LG	CL	G	TBF	GS	CG	SHO	GF	IP	H	HR	BB	IBB	HB	SO	SH	SF	WP	BK	R	ER	W	L	PCT	SV	ERA
90	SB/CAL	A+	12	328	12	4	0	0	79.2	64	0	30	1	1	77	1	1	1	5	29	23	7	3	.700	0	2.60
91	JAC/SOU	AA	21	567	20	6	1	0	140.0	129	7	25	2	2	109	5	2	6	0	50	42	10	6	.625	0	2.70
	CAL/PCL	AAA	3	60	2	1	0	0	16.0	10	1	3	0	0	16	0	1	0	0	2	2	2	0	1.000	0	1.13
	SEA/AL		9	73	3	0	0	3	17.2	19	1	3	0	3	11	0	0	1	0	13	13	1	0	1.000	0	6.62

Fossas, Emilio Antonio (Morejon) "Tony" — bats left — throws left — b.9/23/57

YR	TM/LG	CL	G	TBF	GS	CG	SHO	GF	IP	H	HR	BB	IBB	HB	SO	SH	SF	WP	BK	R	ER	W	L	PCT	SV	ERA
79	RAN/GCL	R	10	0	9	1	0	0	60.0	54	2	26	0	3	49	0	0	2	0	28	20	2	1	.667	0	3.00
	TUL/TEX	AA	2	0	2	0	0	0	11.0	14	1	4	0	3	3	0	0	1	0	10	8	1	1	.500	0	6.55
80	ASH/SAL	A	30	0	27	8	2	0	197.0	187	11	69	0	5	140	0	0	14	7	64	69	12	8	.600	0	3.15
81	TUL/TEX	AA	38	0	12	1	1	0	106.0	113	4	44	0	3	57	0	0	4	2	65	49	5	6	.455	0	4.16
82	BUR/MID	A	25	0	18	10	1	0	146.0	121	9	33	0	7	115	0	0	4	0	63	50	8	9	.471	0	3.08
83	TUL/TEX	AA	24	0	16	6	1	0	133.0	123	11	46	0	3	103	0	0	3	0	77	62	8	7	.533	0	4.20
	OC/AMA	AAA	10	0	5	0	0	0	35.0	55	2	12	0	1	23	0	0	2	0	33	31	1	2	.333	0	7.97
84	TUL/TEX	AA	4	43	0	0	0	4	10.0	12	0	3	0	0	7	0	0	0	0	5	5	0	1	.000	0	4.50
	OC/AMA	AAA	29	529	15	3	0	5	121.0	143	12	34	1	2	74	8	2	3	0	65	58	5	9	.357	0	4.31
85	OC/AMA	AAA	30	465	13	2	0	8	110.0	121	6	36	1	1	49	7	4	3	2	65	58	7	6	.538	2	4.75
86	EDM/PCL	AAA	7	186	7	2	1	0	43.1	53	4	12	0	0	15	2	1	1	0	23	22	3	3	.500	0	4.57
87	EDM/PCL	AAA	40	520	15	1	0	9	117.1	152	8	29	7	8	54	6	5	8	2	76	65	6	8	.429	0	4.99
88	TEX/AL		5	28	0	0	0	1	5.2	11	0	2	0	0	0	0	0	1	0	3	3	0	0	.000	0	4.76
	OC/AMA	AAA	52	271	0	0	0	14	66.2	64	2	16	3	2	42	4	0	3	3	21	21	3	0	1.000	4	2.83
89	DEN/AMA	AAA	24	141	1	0	0	7	35.1	27	0	11	1	1	35	0	0	2	1	9	8	5	1	.833	6	2.04
	MIL/AL		51	256	0	0	0	16	61.0	57	3	22	7	1	42	7	3	1	3	27	24	2	2	.500	1	3.54
90	MIL/AL		32	146	0	0	0	9	29.1	44	5	10	2	0	24	2	1	0	0	23	21	2	3	.400	0	6.44
	DEN/AMA	AAA	25	141	0	0	0	14	35.2	29	1	10	3	1	45	3	0	4	0	8	6	5	2	.714	4	1.51
91	BOS/AL		64	244	0	0	0	18	57.0	49	3	28	9	3	29	5	0	2	0	27	22	3	2	.600	1	3.47
4 YR TOTALS			**152**	**674**	**0**	**0**	**0**	**44**	**153.0**	**161**	**11**	**62**	**18**	**4**	**95**	**14**	**4**	**4**	**3**	**80**	**70**	**7**	**7**	**.500**	**2**	**4.12**

Foster, Stephen Eugene "Steve" — bats right — throws right — b.8/16/66

YR	TM/LG	CL	G	TBF	GS	CG	SHO	GF	IP	H	HR	BB	IBB	HB	SO	SH	SF	WP	BK	R	ER	W	L	PCT	SV	ERA
88	BIL/PIO	R+	18	114	0	0	0	14	30.1	15	0	7	1	3	27	3	2	1	7	5	4	2	3	.400	7	1.19
89	CR/MID	A	51	245	0	0	0	47	59.0	46	2	19	6	5	55	2	1	5	5	16	14	0	3	.000	23	2.14
90	CHT/SOU	AA	50	277	0	0	0	42	59.1	69	6	33	4	4	51	3	8	2	2	38	35	5	10	.333	20	5.31
91	CHT/SOU	AA	17	64	0	0	0	16	15.2	10	0	4	0	3	18	1	0	2	1	4	2	0	2	.000	10	1.15
	NAS/AMA	AAA	41	237	0	0	0	25	54.2	46	4	29	5	1	52	2	3	0	0	17	13	2	3	.400	12	2.14
	CIN/NL		11	53	0	0	0	5	14.0	7	1	4	0	0	11	0	0	0	0	5	3	0	0	.000	0	1.93

Franco, John Anthony — bats left — throws left — b.9/17/60

YR	TM/LG	CL	G	TBF	GS	CG	SHO	GF	IP	H	HR	BB	IBB	HB	SO	SH	SF	WP	BK	R	ER	W	L	PCT	SV	ERA
84	WIC/AMA	AAA	6	39	0	0	0	3	9.1	8	1	4	0	0	11	1	0	0	0	6	6	1	0	1.000	0	5.79
	CIN/NL		54	335	0	0	0	30	79.1	74	3	36	4	2	55	4	4	2	0	28	23	6	2	.750	4	2.61
85	CIN/NL		67	407	0	0	0	33	99.0	83	5	40	8	1	61	11	1	4	0	27	24	12	3	.800	12	2.18
86	CIN/NL		74	429	0	0	0	52	101.0	90	7	44	12	2	84	8	3	4	2	40	33	6	6	.500	29	2.94
87	CIN/NL		68	344	0	0	0	60	82.0	76	6	27	0	0	61	5	2	1	0	26	23	8	5	.615	32	2.52
88	CIN/NL		70	336	0	0	0	61	86.0	60	3	27	3	0	46	5	1	1	2	18	15	6	6	.500	39	1.57
89	CIN/NL		60	345	0	0	0	50	80.2	77	3	36	8	0	60	7	3	3	2	35	28	4	8	.333	32	3.12
90	NY/NL		55	287	0	0	0	48	67.2	66	4	21	0	0	56	3	1	7	2	22	19	5	3	.625	33	2.53
91	NY/NL		52	247	0	0	0	48	55.1	61	2	18	4	1	45	3	0	6	0	27	18	5	9	.357	30	2.93
8 YR TOTALS			**500**	**2730**	**0**	**0**	**0**	**382**	**651.0**	**587**	**33**	**249**	**47**	**6**	**468**	**46**	**15**	**28**	**8**	**223**	**183**	**52**	**42**	**.553**	**211**	**2.53**

Fraser, William Patrick "Willie" — bats right — throws right — b.5/26/64

YR	TM/LG	CL	G	TBF	GS	CG	SHO	GF	IP	H	HR	BB	IBB	HB	SO	SH	SF	WP	BK	R	ER	W	L	PCT	SV	ERA
85	QC/MID	A	13	370	13	1	0	0	81.2	95	8	32	0	8	72	2	1	12	2	53	49	2	6	.250	0	5.40
86	PS/CAL	A+	19	516	19	2	0	0	124.1	115	8	29	0	7	99	2	3	4	0	60	49	9	2	.818	0	3.55
	EDM/PCL	AAA	6	151	6	2	2	0	40.0	25	5	8	0	0	24	1	0	0	0	15	14	4	1	.800	0	3.15
	CAL/AL		1	20	1	0	0	0	4.1	6	0	1	0	0	2	1	1	0	0	4	4	0	0	.000	0	8.31
87	CAL/AL		36	744	23	5	1	6	176.2	160	26	63	3	6	106	5	4	12	1	85	77	10	10	.500	1	3.92
88	CAL/AL		34	861	32	2	0	0	194.2	203	33	80	7	9	86	2	9	12	6	129	117	12	13	.480	0	5.41
89	CAL/AL		44	375	0	0	0	21	91.2	80	6	23	4	5	46	4	3	5	0	33	33	4	7	.364	2	3.24
90	EDM/PCL	AAA	3	62	3	0	0	0	14.1	11	1	6	1	0	12	0	1	2	0	8	5	1	0	1.000	0	3.14
	CAL/AL		45	315	0	0	0	20	76.0	69	4	24	3	0	37	2	3	1	0	29	26	5	4	.556	2	3.08
91	TOR/AL		13	123	1	0	0	5	26.1	33	4	11	2	3	12	0	0	0	2	20	18	0	0	.000	0	6.15
	SYR/INT	AAA	7	59	0	0	0	2	14.2	12	1	6	0	0	12	1	0	1	0	7	6	0	1	.000	1	3.68
	STL/NL		35	210	0	0	0	16	49.1	44	9	21	3	3	25	1	3	4	0	28	27	3	3	.500	0	4.93
	YEAR		48	333	1	0	0	22	75.2	77	13	32	5	6	37	1	3	6	0	48	45	3	5	.375	0	5.35
6 YR TOTALS			**208**	**2648**	**57**	**7**	**1**	**69**	**619.0**	**595**	**82**	**223**	**22**	**26**	**309**	**15**	**23**	**36**	**7**	**328**	**302**	**34**	**39**	**.466**	**5**	**4.39**

Freeman, Marvin — bats right — throws right — b.4/10/63

YR	TM/LG	CL	G	TBF	GS	CG	SHO	GF	IP	H	HR	BB	IBB	HB	SO	SH	SF	WP	BK	R	ER	W	L	PCT	SV	ERA
84	BEN/NWL	A−	15	0	15	2	1	0	89.2	64	1	52	0	1	79	0	0	7	0	41	26	8	5	.615	0	2.61
85	REA/EAS	AA	11	293	11	2	0	0	65.1	51	11	52	1	1	35	5	5	3	0	41	39	1	7	.125	0	5.37
	CLE/FSL	A+	14	366	13	3	3	1	88.1	72	0	36	1	1	55	1	4	7	1	32	30	6	5	.545	0	3.06
86	REA/EAS	AA	27	720	27	4	2	0	163.0	130	12	111	3	1	113	5	8	11	1	89	73	13	6	.684	0	4.03
	PHI/NL		3	61	3	0	0	0	16.0	6	0	10	0	0	8	0	1	0	0	4	4	2	0	1.000	0	2.25
87	MAI/INT	AAA	10	223	10	2	0	0	46.0	56	8	30	0	0	29	1	0	6	0	38	32	0	7	.000	0	6.26
	REA/EAS	AA	9	222	9	0	0	0	49.2	45	7	32	1	0	40	0	0	6	1	30	28	3	3	.500	0	5.07
88	MAI/INT	AAA	18	325	14	2	1	0	74.0	62	8	46	0	0	37	3	1	11	0	43	38	5	5	.500	0	4.62
	PHI/NL		11	249	11	0	0	0	51.2	55	2	43	2	1	37	5	1	3	1	36	35	2	3	.400	0	6.10
89	PHI/NL		1	16	1	0	0	0	3.0	2	0	5	0	0	1	0	0	0	0	2	2	0	0	.000	0	6.00
	SW/INT	AAA	5	57	5	0	0	0	14.0	11	0	5	0	0	8	0	1	0	0	8	7	1	1	.500	0	4.50

(continued)

Freeman, Marvin (continued)

YR	TM/LG	CL	G	TBF	GS	CG	SHO	GF	IP	H	HR	BB	IBB	HB	SO	SH	SF	WP	BK	R	ER	W	L	PCT	SV	ERA
90	SW/INT	AAA	7	163	7	0	0	0	35.1	39	5	19	0	1	33	3	0	3	1	23	20	2	4	.333	0	5.09
	PHI/NL		16	147	3	0	0	4	32.1	34	5	14	2	3	26	1	0	4	0	21	20	0	2	.000	1	5.57
	RIC/INT	AAA	7	159	7	1	1	0	39.0	33	3	22	0	0	23	0	1	1	1	20	20	2	3	.400	0	4.62
	ATL/NL		9	60	0	0	0	1	15.2	7	0	3	0	2	12	1	0	1	0	3	3	1	0	1.000	0	1.72
	YEAR		25	207	3	0	0	5	48.0	41	5	17	2	5	38	2	0	4	0	24	23	1	2	.333	1	4.31
91	ATL/NL		34	190	0	0	0	6	48.0	37	2	13	1	2	34	1	1	4	0	19	16	1	0	1.000	1	3.00
5 YR TOTALS			**74**	**723**	**18**	**0**	**0**	**11**	**166.2**	**141**	**9**	**88**	**5**	**8**	**117**	**8**	**3**	**12**	**2**	**85**	**80**	**6**	**5**	**.545**	**2**	**4.32**

Frey, Steven Francis "Steve" — bats right — throws left — b.7/29/63

YR	TM/LG	CL	G	TBF	GS	CG	SHO	GF	IP	H	HR	BB	IBB	HB	SO	SH	SF	WP	BK	R	ER	W	L	PCT	SV	ERA
84	FT./FSL	A+	47	281	0	0	0	25	64.2	46	2	34	2	0	66	1	3	4	0	26	15	4	2	.667	4	2.09
85	FT./FSL	A+	19	89	0	0	0	13	22.1	11	0	12	0	1	15	1	0	0	0	4	3	1	1	.500	7	1.21
	ALB/EAS	AA	40	261	0	0	0	14	61.1	53	4	25	5	3	54	2	1	0	0	30	26	4	7	.364	3	3.82
86	COL/INT	AAA	11	93	0	0	0	2	19.0	29	3	10	1	0	11	0	2	0	0	17	17	0	2	.000	0	8.05
	ALB/EAS	AA	40	287	0	0	0	26	73.0	50	5	18	1	2	62	2	4	2	0	25	17	3	4	.429	4	2.10
87	ALB/EAS	AA	14	111	0	0	0	10	28.0	20	0	7	1	0	19	1	0	1	0	6	6	0	2	.000	1	1.93
	COL/INT	AAA	23	196	0	0	0	11	47.1	45	2	10	0	0	35	0	3	4	0	19	16	2	1	.667	6	3.04
88	TID/INT	AAA	58	230	1	0	0	22	54.2	38	3	25	6	3	58	4	2	1	3	23	19	6	3	.667	6	3.13
89	MON/NL		20	103	0	0	0	11	21.1	29	4	11	1	1	15	0	2	1	0	15	13	3	2	.600	0	5.48
	IND/AMA	AAA	21	97	0	0	0	8	25.1	18	1	6	1	0	23	2	0	0	0	7	5	2	1	.667	3	1.78
90	IND/AMA	AAA	2	10	0	0	0	1	3.0	0	0	1	0	0	3	0	0	0	0	0	0	0	0	.000	1	0.00
	MON/NL		51	236	0	0	0	21	55.2	44	4	29	6	1	29	3	2	0	0	15	13	8	2	.800	9	2.10
91	IND/AMA	AAA	30	145	0	0	0	15	35.2	25	1	15	2	1	45	1	0	1	1	6	6	3	1	.750	3	1.51
	MON/NL		31	182	0	0	0	5	39.2	43	3	23	4	1	21	3	2	3	1	31	22	0	1	.000	1	4.99
3 YR TOTALS			**102**	**521**	**0**	**0**	**0**	**37**	**116.2**	**116**	**11**	**63**	**11**	**3**	**65**	**6**	**6**	**4**	**2**	**61**	**48**	**11**	**5**	**.688**	**10**	**3.70**

Frohwirth, Todd Gerard — bats right — throws right — b.9/28/62

YR	TM/LG	CL	G	TBF	GS	CG	SHO	GF	IP	H	HR	BB	IBB	HB	SO	SH	SF	WP	BK	R	ER	W	L	PCT	SV	ERA
84	BEN/NWL	A–	29	0	0	0	0	25	49.2	26	0	31	4	3	60	0	0	1	0	17	9	4	4	.500	11	1.63
85	PEN/CAR	A+	54	363	0	0	0	48	82.0	70	2	48	3	4	74	3	1	6	3	33	20	7	5	.583	18	2.20
86	CLE/FSL	A+	32	227	0	0	0	23	52.0	54	1	18	2	2	39	1	2	2	0	29	23	3	3	.500	10	3.98
	REA/EAS	AA	29	175	0	0	0	23	42.0	39	1	10	4	2	23	2	1	0	0	20	15	0	4	.000	12	3.21
87	MAI/INT	AAA	27	141	0	0	0	18	32.1	30	3	15	7	0	21	2	3	0	0	12	9	1	4	.200	3	2.51
	REA/EAS	AA	36	217	0	0	0	31	58.0	36	3	13	0	2	44	1	4	1	0	14	12	2	4	.333	19	1.86
	PHI/NL		10	43	0	0	0	2	11.0	12	0	2	0	0	9	0	0	0	0	0	0	1	0	1.000	0	0.00
88	PHI/NL		12	62	0	0	0	6	12.0	16	2	11	6	0	11	1	1	1	0	11	11	1	2	.333	0	8.25
	MAI/INT	AAA	49	258	0	0	0	38	62.2	52	3	19	3	5	39	5	0	3	1	21	17	7	3	.700	13	2.44
89	SW/INT	AAA	21	134	0	0	0	17	32.1	29	1	11	3	1	29	2	0	0	0	11	8	3	2	.600	7	2.23
	PHI/NL		45	258	0	0	0	11	62.2	56	4	18	0	3	39	1	1	1	1	26	25	1	0	1.000	0	3.59
90	PHI/NL		5	12	0	0	0	0	1.0	3	0	6	2	0	1	0	0	1	0	2	2	0	1	.000	0	18.00
	SW/INT	AAA	67	349	0	0	0	52	83.0	77	3	32	3	8	56	6	3	0	0	34	28	9	7	.563	21	3.04
91	ROC/INT	AAA	20	97	0	0	0	16	24.2	17	1	5	0	2	15	2	2	1	0	12	10	1	3	.250	8	3.65
	BAL/AL		51	372	0	0	0	10	96.1	64	2	29	3	1	77	4	1	3	0	24	20	7	3	.700	3	1.87
5 YR TOTALS			**123**	**747**	**0**	**0**	**0**	**29**	**183.0**	**151**	**8**	**66**	**11**	**4**	**137**	**8**	**3**	**3**	**1**	**63**	**58**	**10**	**6**	**.625**	**3**	**2.85**

Gakeler, Daniel Michael "Dan" — bats right — throws right — b.5/1/64

YR	TM/LG	CL	G	TBF	GS	CG	SHO	GF	IP	H	HR	BB	IBB	HB	SO	SH	SF	WP	BK	R	ER	W	L	PCT	SV	ERA
84	ELM/NYP	A–	14	341	13	0	0	1	76.2	67	9	41	3	7	54	5	2	2	2	47	35	4	6	.400	0	4.11
85	GRE/SAL	A	23	509	16	3	1	2	108.0	135	8	54	0	3	51	2	3	4	0	86	66	7	5	.583	0	5.50
86	GRE/SAL	A	24	679	23	5	1	1	154.1	158	6	69	1	4	154	4	4	11	2	73	57	7	6	.538	1	3.32
87	NB/EAS	AA	30	769	25	5	1	3	173.0	188	14	63	5	7	90	2	7	7	3	112	89	8	13	.381	0	4.63
88	NB/EAS	AA	26	660	25	5	2	0	153.2	157	4	54	1	5	110	3	1	9	3	74	63	6	13	.316	0	3.69
89	JAC/SOU	AA	14	365	14	2	1	0	86.2	70	1	39	1	3	76	4	1	6	1	31	23	5	4	.556	0	2.39
	IND/AMA	AAA	11	280	11	1	0	0	66.1	53	1	28	1	3	41	4	1	4	0	29	23	3	6	.333	0	3.12
90	IND/AMA	AAA	22	509	21	1	1	0	120.0	101	2	55	1	7	89	7	2	6	0	55	43	5	5	.500	0	3.22
91	TOL/INT	AAA	23	187	2	0	0	12	43.2	44	5	13	1	1	32	2	1	3	0	22	17	2	3	.400	4	3.50
	DET/AL		31	331	7	0	0	11	73.2	73	5	39	6	1	43	3	3	7	0	52	47	1	4	.200	2	5.74

Garcia, Ramon Antonio (Fortunata) — bats right — throws right — b.12/9/69

YR	TM/LG	CL	G	TBF	GS	CG	SHO	GF	IP	H	HR	BB	IBB	HB	SO	SH	SF	WP	BK	R	ER	W	L	PCT	SV	ERA
89	WS/GCL	R	14	209	7	2	1	2	53.0	34	1	17	0	2	52	0	1	1	4	21	18	6	4	.600	0	3.06
90	SAR/FSL	A+	26	665	26	1	0	0	157.1	155	10	45	1	12	130	5	4	4	13	84	69	9	14	.391	0	3.95
	VAN/PCL	AAA	1	5	0	0	0	1	1.0	2	0	0	0	0	1	0	0	0	0	0	0	0	0	.000	0	0.00
91	BIR/SOU	AA	6	152	6	2	1	0	38.2	27	0	11	0	3	38	1	0	1	2	5	4	4	0	1.000	0	0.93
	VAN/PCL	AAA	4	110	4	0	0	0	26.2	24	3	7	0	0	17	1	0	0	0	13	12	2	2	.500	0	4.05
	CHI/AL		16	332	15	0	0	0	78.1	79	13	31	2	4	40	3	2	0	2	50	47	4	4	.500	0	5.40

Garcia, Victoriano "Victor" — bats right — throws right — b.9/15/69 — System CIN/NL

YR	TM/LG	CL	G	TBF	GS	CG	SHO	GF	IP	H	HR	BB	IBB	HB	SO	SH	SF	WP	BK	R	ER	W	L	PCT	SV	ERA
88	RED/GCL	R	13	302	13	0	0	0	71.1	60	2	30	1	0	47	2	1	6	9	27	18	4	4	.500	0	2.27
89	GRE/SAL	A	43	355	0	0	0	20	85.0	54	5	39	0	5	108	6	4	2	2	36	26	10	1	.909	5	2.75
90	CR/MID	A	49	262	0	0	0	26	71.0	36	6	18	5	0	106	5	0	4	0	15	12	8	3	.727	15	1.52
91	CHT/SOU	AA	40	209	0	0	0	25	50.0	41	3	20	1	1	51	0	1	5	0	12	11	5	3	.625	5	1.98
	NAS/AMA	AAA	15	97	0	0	0	9	24.0	15	2	14	0	1	12	1	3	2	0	7	7	2	0	1.000	0	2.63

Gardella, Michael Jeremy "Mike" — bats left — throws left — b.1/18/67 — System NY/AL

YR	TM/LG	CL	G	TBF	GS	CG	SHO	GF	IP	H	HR	BB	IBB	HB	SO	SH	SF	WP	BK	R	ER	W	L	PCT	SV	ERA
89	ONE/NYP	A—	28	153	0	0	0	26	37.2	23	2	15	0	0	66	2	1	2	0	8	7	2	0	1.000	19	1.67
90	PW/CAR	A+	62	301	0	0	0	57	71.2	61	0	31	3	1	86	5	0	7	0	18	16	4	3	.571	30	2.01
91	ALB/EAS	AA	53	344	0	0	0	27	77.2	70	1	55	6	1	76	10	3	3	0	37	33	4	5	.444	11	3.82

Gardiner, Michael James "Mike" — bats both — throws right — b.10/19/65

YR	TM/LG	CL	G	TBF	GS	CG	SHO	GF	IP	H	HR	BB	IBB	HB	SO	SH	SF	WP	BK	R	ER	W	L	PCT	SV	ERA
87	BEL/NWL	A—	2	35	1	0	0	0	10.0	6	0	1	0	0	11	0	0	0	0	0	0	2	0	1.000	0	0.00
	WAU/MID	A	13	368	13	2	1	0	81.0	91	9	33	2	3	80	2	5	3	1	54	47	3	5	.375	0	5.22
88	WAU/MID	A	11	132	6	0	0	4	31.1	31	1	13	0	1	24	0	0	1	1	16	11	2	1	.667	1	3.16
89	WAU/MID	A	15	120	1	0	0	11	30.1	21	1	11	0	1	48	2	0	0	0	5	2	4	0	1.000	7	0.59
	WIL/EAS	AA	30	274	3	1	0	14	63.1	54	6	32	6	1	60	1	3	4	1	25	20	4	6	.400	2	2.84
90	WIL/EAS	AA	26	697	26	5	1	0	179.2	136	8	29	1	1	149	4	3	4	1	47	38	12	8	.600	0	1.90
	SEA/AL		5	66	3	0	0	0	12.2	22	1	5	0	2	6	0	1	0	0	17	15	0	0	.000	0	10.66
91	PAW/INT	AAA	8	220	8	2	1	0	57.2	39	2	11	0	1	42	3	2	0	0	16	15	7	1	.875	0	2.34
	BOS/AL		22	562	22	0	0	0	130.0	140	18	47	2	0	91	1	3	1	0	79	70	9	10	.474	0	4.85
2 YR TOTALS			**27**	**628**	**25**	**0**	**0**	**1**	**142.2**	**162**	**19**	**52**	**2**	**2**	**97**	**1**	**4**	**1**	**0**	**96**	**85**	**9**	**12**	**.429**	**0**	**5.36**

Gardner, Christopher John "Chris" — bats right — throws right — b.3/30/69

YR	TM/LG	CL	G	TBF	GS	CG	SHO	GF	IP	H	HR	BB	IBB	HB	SO	SH	SF	WP	BK	R	ER	W	L	PCT	SV	ERA
88	AST/GCL	R	12	226	9	0	0	0	55.1	37	0	23	0	4	41	3	1	4	4	18	9	4	3	.571	0	1.46
89	ASH/SAL	A	15	360	15	2	0	0	77.1	76	5	58	0	1	49	1	3	8	10	53	33	3	8	.273	0	3.84
90	ASH/SAL	A	23	560	23	3	1	0	134.0	102	6	69	2	7	81	1	2	8	3	57	39	5	10	.333	0	2.62
91	JAC/TEX	AA	22	559	22	1	1	0	131.1	116	6	75	1	8	72	5	4	9	1	57	46	13	5	.722	0	3.15
	HOU/NL		5	103	4	0	0	0	24.2	19	5	14	1	0	12	0	0	0	0	12	11	1	2	.333	0	4.01

Gardner, Mark Allan — bats right — throws right — b.3/1/62

YR	TM/LG	CL	G	TBF	GS	CG	SHO	GF	IP	H	HR	BB	IBB	HB	SO	SH	SF	WP	BK	R	ER	W	L	PCT	SV	ERA
85	JAM/NYP	A—	3	54	3	0	0	0	13.0	9	0	4	0	1	16	1	0	0	1	4	4	0	0	.000	0	2.77
	WPB/FSL	A+	10	257	9	4	0	1	60.2	54	4	18	1	2	44	3	2	6	1	24	16	5	4	.556	0	2.37
86	JAC/SOU	AA	29	726	28	3	1	1	168.2	144	8	90	1	8	140	5	5	15	1	88	72	10	11	.476	0	3.84
87	IND/AMA	AAA	9	207	9	0	0	0	46.0	48	8	28	1	1	41	0	1	2	1	32	29	3	3	.500	0	5.67
	JAC/SOU	AA	17	434	17	1	0	0	101.0	101	13	42	0	0	78	5	3	4	0	50	47	4	6	.400	0	4.19
88	JAC/SOU	AA	15	443	15	4	2	0	112.1	72	4	36	0	5	130	3	1	2	0	24	20	6	3	.667	0	1.60
	IND/AMA	AAA	13	351	13	3	1	0	84.1	65	5	32	0	5	71	6	1	3	1	30	26	4	2	.667	0	2.77
89	IND/AMA	AAA	24	660	23	4	2	1	163.1	122	8	59	1	5	175	9	6	7	1	51	43	12	4	.750	0	2.37
	MON/NL		7	117	4	0	0	1	26.1	26	2	11	1	2	21	0	0	0	0	16	15	0	3	.000	0	5.13
90	MON/NL		27	642	26	3	3	1	152.2	129	13	61	5	9	135	4	7	2	4	62	58	7	9	.438	0	3.42
91	IND/AMA	AAA	6	133	6	0	0	0	31.0	26	3	16	0	3	38	0	2	2	0	13	12	2	0	1.000	0	3.48
	MON/NL		27	692	27	0	0	0	168.1	139	17	75	1	4	107	7	2	2	1	78	72	9	11	.450	0	3.85
3 YR TOTALS			**61**	**1451**	**57**	**3**	**3**	**2**	**347.1**	**294**	**32**	**147**	**7**	**15**	**263**	**11**	**9**	**4**	**5**	**156**	**145**	**16**	**23**	**.410**	**0**	**3.76**

Gardner, Wesley Brian "Wes" — bats right — throws right — b.4/29/61

YR	TM/LG	CL	G	TBF	GS	CG	SHO	GF	IP	H	HR	BB	IBB	HB	SO	SH	SF	WP	BK	R	ER	W	L	PCT	SV	ERA
84	TID/INT	AAA	40	221	0	0	0	37	56.0	40	2	19	3	0	36	1	2	1	0	11	10	1	2	.333	20	1.61
	NY/NL		21	116	0	0	0	12	25.1	34	0	8	2	0	19	1	1	1	0	19	18	1	1	.500	1	6.39
85	TID/INT	AAA	53	314	0	0	0	42	76.2	57	6	34	3	1	75	3	3	5	0	31	24	7	6	.538	18	2.82
	NY/NL		9	61	0	0	0	8	12.0	18	1	6	0	1	11	4	1	1	0	14	7	0	2	.000	0	5.25
86	BOS/AL		1	4	0	0	0	0	1.0	1	0	0	0	0	0	0	0	0	0	1	1	0	0	.000	0	9.00
87	PAW/INT	AAA	5	36	0	0	0	4	8.2	8	0	3	1	0	9	0	0	0	0	3	3	1	0	1.000	2	3.12
	BOS/AL		49	401	1	0	0	29	89.2	98	17	42	7	2	70	4	2	4	0	55	54	3	6	.333	10	5.42
88	BOS/AL		36	620	18	1	0	12	149.0	119	17	64	2	3	106	5	6	5	0	61	58	8	6	.571	2	3.50
89	BOS/AL		22	393	16	0	0	2	86.0	97	10	47	0	1	81	3	4	3	0	64	57	3	7	.300	0	5.97
90	BOS/AL		34	340	9	0	0	9	77.1	77	6	35	0	2	58	4	2	1	1	43	42	3	7	.300	0	4.89
91	SD/NL		14	99	0	0	0	8	20.1	27	1	12	1	0	9	0	1	0	0	16	16	0	1	.000	1	7.08
	OMA/AMA	AAA	9	84	1	0	0	3	18.1	27	0	5	0	0	2	0	3	3	0	11	10	3	1	.750	0	4.91
	KC/AL		3	26	0	0	0	2	5.2	5	0	2	0	0	3	0	0	0	0	4	1	0	0	.000	0	1.59
	YEAR		17	125	0	0	0	4	26.0	32	1	14	1	0	12	0	1	0	0	20	17	0	1	.000	1	5.88
8 YR TOTALS			**189**	**2060**	**44**	**1**	**0**	**76**	**466.1**	**476**	**52**	**218**	**21**	**8**	**358**	**21**	**17**	**17**	**1**	**277**	**254**	**18**	**30**	**.375**	**14**	**4.90**

Garrelts, Scott William — bats right — throws right — b.10/30/61

YR	TM/LG	CL	G	TBF	GS	CG	SHO	GF	IP	H	HR	BB	IBB	HB	SO	SH	SF	WP	BK	R	ER	W	L	PCT	SV	ERA
82	SF/NL		1	11	0	0	0	1	2.0	3	0	2	0	0	4	0	0	0	0	3	3	0	0	.000	0	13.50
83	SF/NL		5	154	5	1	1	0	35.2	33	4	19	4	2	16	3	0	4	1	11	10	2	2	.500	0	2.52
84	PHO/PCL	AAA	21	0	19	2	1	0	97.2	97	8	82	2	2	69	0	0	9	0	75	64	5	7	.417	0	5.90
	SF/NL		21	206	3	0	0	0	43.0	45	4	34	1	1	32	5	2	3	0	33	27	2	3	.400	0	5.65
85	SF/NL		74	454	0	0	0	44	105.2	76	2	58	12	3	106	6	3	7	1	37	27	9	6	.600	13	2.30
86	SF/NL		53	717	18	2	0	27	173.2	144	17	74	11	2	125	10	7	9	1	65	60	13	9	.591	10	3.11
87	SF/NL		64	428	0	0	0	43	106.1	70	10	55	4	0	127	7	2	5	1	41	38	11	7	.611	12	3.22
88	SF/NL		65	413	0	0	0	40	98.0	80	3	46	10	2	86	9	2	6	4	42	39	5	9	.357	13	3.58
89	SF/NL		30	766	29	2	1	0	193.1	149	11	46	3	4	119	9	7	7	2	58	49	14	5	.737	0	2.28
90	SF/NL		31	786	31	4	2	0	182.0	190	16	70	8	3	80	10	5	4	0	91	84	12	11	.522	0	4.15
91	SF/NL		8	90	0	0	0	2	19.2	25	5	9	0	0	6	1	0	1	0	14	14	1	1	.500	0	6.41
10 YR TOTALS			**352**	**4025**	**89**	**9**	**4**	**162**	**959.1**	**815**	**74**	**413**	**53**	**13**	**703**	**59**	**29**	**48**	**10**	**395**	**351**	**69**	**53**	**.566**	**48**	**3.29**

George, Christopher Sean "Chris" — bats right — throws right — b.9/24/66

YR	TM/LG	CL	G	TBF	GS	CG	SHO	GF	IP	H	HR	BB	IBB	HB	SO	SH	SF	WP	BK	R	ER	W	L	PCT	SV	ERA
88	BEL/MID	A	22	243	4	0	0	10	58.0	52	1	14	4	5	58	1	1	4	1	27	19	7	4	.636	6	2.95
89	STO/CAL	A+	55	345	0	0	0	52	79.2	61	1	37	8	1	85	6	5	8	2	30	19	7	7	.500	22	2.15
90	DEN/AMA	AAA	7	36	0	0	0	1	5.1	17	1	4	0	0	4	0	0	1	0	11	11	1	1	.500	0	18.56
	EP/TEX	AA	39	226	0	0	0	30	55.2	41	1	20	7	3	38	7	1	7	1	16	11	8	3	.727	13	1.78
91	DEN/AMA	AAA	43	350	1	0	0	16	85.0	74	6	26	5	0	65	6	7	4	0	31	22	4	5	.444	4	2.33
	MIL/AL		2	25	1	0	0	1	6.0	8	0	0	0	0	2	0	1	0	0	2	2	0	0	.000	0	3.00

Gibson, Paul Marshall — bats left — throws right — b.1/4/60

YR	TM/LG	CL	G	TBF	GS	CG	SHO	GF	IP	H	HR	BB	IBB	HB	SO	SH	SF	WP	BK	R	ER	W	L	PCT	SV	ERA
84	ORL/SOU	AA	27	529	12	3	1	7	121.0	125	9	54	0	1	64	4	2	6	0	71	52	7	7	.500	1	3.87
85	BIR/SOU	AA	36	615	14	2	2	5	144.1	135	13	63	1	0	79	4	4	4	0	73	66	8	8	.500	1	4.12
86	GF/EAS	AA	9	81	1	0	0	3	19.2	16	0	7	0	0	21	0	0	0	0	3	3	3	1	.750	1	1.37
	NAS/AMA	AAA	30	489	14	2	0	9	113.1	121	12	40	5	2	91	3	3	8	0	58	50	5	6	.455	2	3.97
87	TOL/INT	AAA	27	753	27	7	2	0	179.0	173	14	57	6	3	118	2	5	6	1	83	69	14	7	.667	0	3.47
88	DET/AL		40	390	1	0	0	18	92.0	83	6	34	8	2	50	3	5	3	1	33	30	4	2	.667	0	2.93
89	DET/AL		45	573	13	0	0	16	132.0	129	11	57	12	6	77	7	5	4	1	71	68	4	8	.333	0	4.64
90	DET/AL		61	422	0	0	0	17	97.1	99	10	44	12	1	56	4	5	1	1	36	33	5	4	.556	3	3.05
91	DET/AL		68	432	0	0	0	28	96.0	112	10	48	8	3	52	2	2	4	0	51	49	5	7	.417	8	4.59
4 YR TOTALS			**214**	**1817**	**14**	**0**	**0**	**79**	**417.1**	**423**	**37**	**183**	**40**	**12**	**235**	**16**	**17**	**12**	**3**	**191**	**180**	**18**	**21**	**.462**	**11**	**3.88**

Glavine, Thomas Michael "Tom" — bats left — throws left — b.3/25/66

YR	TM/LG	CL	G	TBF	GS	CG	SHO	GF	IP	H	HR	BB	IBB	HB	SO	SH	SF	WP	BK	R	ER	W	L	PCT	SV	ERA
84	BRA/GCL	R	8	141	7	0	0	1	32.1	29	0	13	0	1	34	2	1	12	0	17	12	2	3	.400	0	3.34
85	SUM/SAL	A	26	680	26	2	1	0	168.2	114	6	73	0	9	174	5	2	19	0	58	44	9	6	.600	0	2.35
86	GRE/SOU	AA	22	629	22	2	1	0	145.1	129	14	70	3	2	114	7	4	8	0	62	55	11	6	.647	0	3.41
	RIC/INT	AAA	7	186	7	1	1	0	40.0	40	4	27	0	2	12	1	2	5	0	29	25	1	5	.167	0	5.63
87	RIC/INT	AAA	22	643	22	4	1	0	150.1	142	15	56	3	5	91	7	2	8	0	70	56	6	12	.333	0	3.35
	ATL/NL		9	238	9	0	0	0	50.1	55	5	33	4	3	20	2	3	1	1	34	31	2	4	.333	0	5.54
88	ATL/NL		34	844	34	1	0	0	195.1	201	12	63	7	8	84	17	11	2	2	111	99	7	17	.292	0	4.56
89	ATL/NL		29	766	29	6	4	0	186.0	172	20	40	3	2	90	11	4	2	0	88	76	14	8	.636	0	3.68
90	ATL/NL		33	929	33	1	0	0	214.1	232	18	78	10	1	129	21	2	8	1	111	102	10	12	.455	0	4.28
91	ATL/NL		34	989	34	9	1	0	246.2	201	17	69	6	2	192	7	6	10	2	83	70	20	11	.645	0	2.55
5 YR TOTALS			**139**	**3766**	**139**	**17**	**5**	**0**	**892.2**	**861**	**72**	**283**	**30**	**16**	**515**	**58**	**26**	**23**	**6**	**427**	**378**	**53**	**52**	**.505**	**0**	**3.81**

Gleaton, Jerry Don — bats left — throws left — b.9/14/57

YR	TM/LG	CL	G	TBF	GS	CG	SHO	GF	IP	H	HR	BB	IBB	HB	SO	SH	SF	WP	BK	R	ER	W	L	PCT	SV	ERA
79	TEX/AL		5	45	2	0	0	1	9.2	15	0	2	0	1	2	1	1	1	0	7	7	0	1	.000	0	6.52
80	TEX/AL		5	30	0	0	0	2	7.0	5	0	4	0	0	2	0	2	0	0	2	2	0	0	.000	0	2.57
81	SEA/AL		20	369	13	1	0	3	85.1	88	10	38	2	2	31	3	4	3	0	50	45	4	7	.364	0	4.75
82	SEA/AL		3	24	0	0	0	1	4.2	7	3	2	0	1	1	0	0	0	0	7	7	0	0	.000	0	13.50
84	SLC/PCL	AAA	29	0	2	0	0	13	49.2	62	6	17	0	2	39	0	0	1	1	39	32	4	1	.800	2	5.80
	CHI/AL		11	81	1	0	0	4	18.1	20	2	6	0	1	4	0	4	4	0	12	7	1	2	.333	2	3.44
	DEN/AMA	AAA	12	84	0	0	0	8	20.0	20	0	4	0	1	10	4	1	0	0	5	4	1	0	.500	3	1.80
85	BUF/AMA	AAA	38	240	0	0	0	26	55.1	62	2	21	3	0	37	3	1	0	0	17	15	8	2	.800	7	2.44
	CHI/AL		31	135	0	0	0	9	29.2	37	3	13	3	0	22	4	1	3	0	19	19	1	0	1.000	1	5.76
86	BUF/AMA	AAA	46	341	3	1	0	24	78.1	79	5	35	4	1	77	6	3	0	0	34	28	4	3	.571	7	3.22
87	OMA/AMA	AAA	6	64	0	0	0	1	15.0	14	2	6	2	0	9	1	0	2	0	6	5	2	0	1.000	0	3.00
	KC/AL		48	210	0	0	0	22	50.2	38	4	28	3	0	44	3	3	4	1	28	24	4	4	.500	5	4.26
88	OMA/AMA	AAA	15	149	0	0	0	11	37.1	30	0	14	0	0	40	0	2	2	0	7	6	4	2	.667	0	1.45
	KC/AL		42	164	0	0	0	20	38.0	33	2	17	1	3	29	2	0	2	0	17	15	0	4	.000	0	3.55
89	OMA/AMA	AAA	24	230	0	0	0	9	56.2	40	0	22	1	0	57	3	1	3	2	12	7	3	3	.500	4	1.11
	KC/AL		15	66	0	0	0	5	14.1	20	0	6	0	0	9	0	2	0	1	10	9	0	0	.000	0	5.65
90	DET/AL		57	325	0	0	0	34	82.2	62	5	25	2	3	56	2	4	2	1	27	27	1	3	.250	13	2.94
91	DET/AL		47	319	0	0	0	16	75.1	74	7	39	8	0	47	1	4	1	1	37	34	3	2	.600	2	4.06
11 YR TOTALS			**284**	**1768**	**16**	**1**	**0**	**117**	**415.2**	**399**	**36**	**180**	**19**	**11**	**247**	**16**	**25**	**20**	**4**	**216**	**196**	**14**	**23**	**.378**	**26**	**4.24**

Gohr, Gregory James "Greg" — bats right — throws right — b.10/29/67 — System DET/AL

YR	TM/LG	CL	G	TBF	GS	CG	SHO	GF	IP	H	HR	BB	IBB	HB	SO	SH	SF	WP	BK	R	ER	W	L	PCT	SV	ERA
89	FAY/SAL	A	4	50	4	0	0	0	11.1	11	3	6	0	0	10	0	1	0	0	9	9	0	2	.000	0	7.15
90	LAK/FSL	A+	25	577	25	0	0	0	137.2	125	0	50	0	5	90	2	1	11	6	52	40	13	5	.722	0	2.62
91	LON/EAS	AA	2	42	2	0	0	0	11.0	9	0	2	0	0	10	0	0	0	0	0	0	0	0	.000	0	0.00
	TOL/INT	AAA	26	627	26	2	1	0	148.1	125	11	66	0	4	96	9	5	14	3	86	76	10	8	.556	0	4.61

Gooden, Dwight Eugene "Dwight" or "Doc" — bats right — throws right — b.11/16/64

YR	TM/LG	CL	G	TBF	GS	CG	SHO	GF	IP	H	HR	BB	IBB	HB	SO	SH	SF	WP	BK	R	ER	W	L	PCT	SV	ERA
84	NY/NL		31	879	31	7	3	0	218.0	161	7	73	2	2	276	3	2	3	7	72	63	17	9	.654	0	2.60
85	NY/NL		35	1065	35	16	8	0	276.2	198	13	69	4	2	268	6	2	4	2	51	47	24	4	.857	0	1.53
86	NY/NL		33	1020	33	12	2	0	250.0	197	17	80	3	4	200	10	8	4	4	92	79	17	6	.739	0	2.84
87	LYN/CAR	A+	1	15	1	0	0	0	4.0	2	0	2	0	0	3	0	0	0	0	0	0	0	0	.000	0	0.00
	TID/INT	AAA	4	96	4	0	0	0	22.0	20	0	9	0	2	24	0	1	0	0	7	5	3	0	1.000	0	2.05
	NY/NL		25	730	25	7	3	0	179.2	162	11	53	2	2	148	5	5	1	1	68	64	15	7	.682	0	3.21
88	NY/NL		34	1024	34	10	3	0	248.1	242	8	57	4	6	175	10	6	5	5	98	88	18	9	.667	0	3.19
89	NY/NL		19	497	17	0	0	1	118.1	93	9	47	2	2	101	4	3	7	5	42	38	9	4	.692	1	2.89

Gooden, Dwight Eugene "Dwight" or "Doc" (continued)

YR	TM/LG	CL	G	TBF	GS	CG	SHO	GF	IP	H	HR	BB	IBB	HB	SO	SH	SF	WP	BK	R	ER	W	L	PCT	SV	ERA
90	NY/NL		34	983	34	2	1	0	232.2	229	10	70	3	7	223	10	7	6	3	106	99	19	7	.731	0	3.83
91	NY/NL		27	789	27	3	1	0	190.0	185	12	56	2	3	150	5	4	5	2	80	76	13	7	.650	0	3.60
8 YR TOTALS			**238**	**6987**	**236**	**57**	**21**	**1**	**1713.2**	**1467**	**87**	**505**	**22**	**28**	**1541**	**53**	**37**	**37**	**29**	**609**	**554**	**132**	**53**	**.714**	**1**	**2.91**

Gordon, Thomas "Tom" — bats right — throws right — b.11/18/67

YR	TM/LG	CL	G	TBF	GS	CG	SHO	GF	IP	H	HR	BB	IBB	HB	SO	SH	SF	WP	BK	R	ER	W	L	PCT	SV	ERA
86	ROY/GCL	R	9	184	7	2	1	1	44.0	31	0	23	1	0	47	0	1	7	1	12	5	3	1	.750	1	1.02
	OMA/AMA	AAA	1	12	0	0	0	0	1.1	6	0	2	0	0	3	0	0	0	0	7	7	0	0	.000	0	47.25
87	FM/FSL	A+	3	60	3	0	0	0	13.2	5	0	17	0	2	11	0	0	0	0	4	4	1	0	1.000	0	2.63
	EUG/NWL	A–	15	315	13	0	0	1	72.1	48	2	47	0	3	91	3	0	4	4	33	23	9	0	1.000	1	2.86
88	APP/MID	A	17	473	17	5	1	0	118.0	69	3	43	1	0	172	1	5	10	4	30	27	7	5	.583	0	2.06
	MEM/SOU	AA	6	174	6	2	2	0	47.1	16	1	17	0	1	62	0	0	1	0	3	2	6	0	1.000	0	0.38
	OMA/AMA	AAA	3	85	3	0	0	0	20.1	11	0	15	0	0	29	0	0	0	0	3	3	1	0	1.000	0	1.33
	KC/AL		5	67	2	0	0	0	15.2	16	1	7	0	0	18	0	0	0	0	9	9	0	2	.000	0	5.17
89	KC/AL		49	677	16	1	1	16	163.0	122	10	86	4	1	153	4	4	12	0	67	66	17	9	.654	1	3.64
90	KC/AL		32	858	32	6	1	0	195.1	192	17	99	1	3	175	8	2	11	0	99	81	12	11	.522	0	3.73
91	KC/AL		45	684	14	1	0	11	158.0	129	16	87	6	4	167	5	3	5	0	76	68	9	14	.391	1	3.87
4 YR TOTALS			**131**	**2286**	**64**	**8**	**2**	**27**	**532.0**	**459**	**44**	**279**	**11**	**8**	**513**	**17**	**9**	**28**	**0**	**251**	**224**	**38**	**36**	**.514**	**2**	**3.79**

Gossage, Richard Michael "Rich" or "Goose" — bats right — throws right — b.7/5/51

YR	TM/LG	CL	G	TBF	GS	CG	SHO	GF	IP	H	HR	BB	IBB	HB	SO	SH	SF	WP	BK	R	ER	W	L	PCT	SV	ERA
72	CHI/AL		36	352	1	0	0	7	80.0	72	2	44	3	4	57	10	2	7	0	44	38	7	1	.875	2	4.28
73	CHI/AL		20	232	4	1	0	4	49.2	57	9	37	2	3	33	5	4	6	0	44	41	0	4	.000	0	7.43
74	CHI/AL		39	397	3	0	0	19	89.1	92	4	47	7	2	64	6	4	2	1	45	41	4	6	.400	1	4.13
75	CHI/AL		62	583	0	0	0	49	141.2	99	3	70	15	5	130	15	0	3	0	32	29	9	8	.529	26	1.84
76	CHI/AL		31	956	29	15	0	1	224.0	214	16	90	3	9	135	8	7	6	0	104	98	9	17	.346	1	3.94
77	PIT/NL		72	523	0	0	0	55	133.0	78	9	49	6	2	151	7	6	2	0	27	24	11	9	.550	26	1.62
78	NY/AL		63	543	0	0	0	55	134.1	87	9	59	8	2	122	9	8	5	0	41	30	10	11	.476	27	2.01
79	NY/AL		36	234	0	0	0	33	58.1	48	5	19	4	0	41	4	0	3	0	18	17	5	3	.625	18	2.62
80	NY/AL		64	401	0	0	0	58	99.0	74	5	37	3	1	103	8	4	4	0	29	25	6	2	.750	33	2.27
81	NY/AL		32	173	0	0	0	30	46.2	22	2	14	1	1	48	1	1	1	0	6	4	3	2	.600	20	0.77
82	NY/AL		56	356	0	0	0	43	93.0	63	5	28	5	0	102	5	2	1	0	23	23	4	5	.444	30	2.23
83	NY/AL		57	367	0	0	0	47	87.1	82	5	25	5	1	90	5	6	0	0	27	22	13	5	.722	22	2.27
84	SD/NL		62	412	0	0	0	51	102.1	75	6	36	4	3	84	4	3	2	2	34	33	10	6	.625	25	2.90
85	SD/NL		50	308	0	0	0	38	79.0	64	1	17	1	1	52	3	4	0	0	21	16	5	3	.625	26	1.82
86	SD/NL		45	281	0	0	0	38	64.2	69	8	20	0	2	63	2	4	0	0	36	32	5	7	.417	21	4.45
87	SD/NL		40	217	0	0	0	30	52.0	47	4	19	6	0	44	2	3	2	0	18	18	5	4	.556	11	3.12
88	CHI/NL		46	194	0	0	0	33	43.2	50	3	15	5	3	30	1	3	2	2	23	21	4	4	.500	13	4.33
89	SF/NL		31	182	0	0	0	22	43.2	32	2	27	3	0	24	2	2	2	0	16	13	2	1	.667	4	2.68
	NY/NL		11	56	0	0	0	6	14.1	14	0	3	1	1	6	1	0	1	0	6	6	1	0	1.000	1	3.77
	YEAR		42	238	0	0	0	28	58.0	46	2	30	4	1	30	3	2	3	0	22	19	3	1	.750	5	2.95
91	OC/AMA	AAA	2	10	0	0	0	1	2.0	2	1	1	0	1	3	0	0	1	0	4	4	0	0	.000	0	18.00
	TEX/AL		44	167	0	0	0	16	40.1	33	4	16	1	3	28	3	0	3	0	16	16	4	2	.667	1	3.57
19 YR TOTALS			**897**	**6934**	**37**	**16**	**0**	**635**	**1676.1**	**1372**	**102**	**672**	**83**	**41**	**1407**	**103**	**61**	**57**	**5**	**610**	**547**	**117**	**100**	**.539**	**308**	**2.94**

Gott, James William "Jim" — bats right — throws right — b.8/3/59

YR	TM/LG	CL	G	TBF	GS	CG	SHO	GF	IP	H	HR	BB	IBB	HB	SO	SH	SF	WP	BK	R	ER	W	L	PCT	SV	ERA
82	TOR/AL		30	600	23	1	1	4	136.0	134	15	66	2	3	82	3	2	8	0	76	67	5	10	.333	0	4.43
83	TOR/AL		34	776	30	6	1	2	176.2	195	15	68	5	5	121	4	3	2	0	103	93	9	14	.391	0	4.74
84	TOR/AL		35	464	12	1	1	11	109.2	93	7	49	3	6	73	7	6	1	0	54	49	7	6	.538	2	4.02
85	SF/NL		26	629	26	2	0	0	148.1	144	10	51	3	1	78	6	4	3	2	73	64	7	10	.412	0	3.88
86	SF/NL		9	66	2	0	0	3	13.0	16	0	13	2	0	9	1	1	1	1	12	11	0	0	.000	1	7.62
	PHO/PCL	AAA	2	12	2	0	0	0	2.2	2	0	3	0	0	2	0	0	0	0	2	2	0	0	.000	0	6.75
87	SF/NL		30	253	3	0	0	8	56.0	53	4	32	5	2	63	1	1	3	0	32	28	1	0	1.000	0	4.50
	PIT/NL		25	129	0	0	0	22	31.0	28	0	8	2	0	27	1	0	2	0	11	5	0	2	.000	13	1.45
	YEAR		55	382	3	0	0	30	87.0	81	4	40	7	2	90	2	1	5	0	43	33	1	2	.333	13	3.41
88	PIT/NL		67	314	0	0	0	59	77.1	68	4	22	5	2	76	7	2	3	0	30	30	6	6	.500	34	3.49
89	PIT/NL		1	4	0	0	0	0	0.2	1	0	1	0	0	1	0	0	0	0	0	0	0	0	.000	0	0.00
90	BAK/CAL	A+	7	56	3	0	0	1	13.0	13	0	4	0	1	16	2	0	2	1	5	4	0	0	.000	0	2.77
	LA/NL		50	270	0	0	0	24	62.0	59	5	34	7	0	44	2	4	4	0	27	20	3	5	.375	3	2.90
91	LA/NL		55	322	0	0	0	26	76.0	63	5	32	7	1	73	6	1	6	3	28	25	4	3	.571	2	2.96
10 YR TOTALS			**362**	**3827**	**96**	**10**	**3**	**159**	**886.2**	**854**	**70**	**376**	**39**	**17**	**647**	**38**	**25**	**31**	**12**	**446**	**392**	**42**	**56**	**.429**	**55**	**3.98**

Gozzo, Mauro Paul — bats right — throws right — b.3/7/66

YR	TM/LG	CL	G	TBF	GS	CG	SHO	GF	IP	H	HR	BB	IBB	HB	SO	SH	SF	WP	BK	R	ER	W	L	PCT	SV	ERA
84	LF/NYP	A–	24	176	0	0	0	8	38.1	40	3	28	4	0	30	0	2	7	1	27	24	4	3	.571	2	5.63
85	COL/SAL	A	49	330	0	0	0	42	78.0	62	2	39	7	2	66	3	5	4	1	22	22	11	4	.733	14	2.54
86	LYN/CAR	A+	60	341	0	0	0	46	78.1	80	3	35	3	2	50	5	2	4	1	30	27	9	4	.692	9	3.10
87	MEM/SOU	AA	19	400	14	1	0	2	91.1	95	13	36	2	4	56	1	2	3	3	58	46	6	5	.545	0	4.53
88	MEM/SOU	AA	33	430	12	0	0	9	92.2	127	9	36	1	1	48	2	7	14	3	64	59	7	9	.308	3	5.73
89	KNO/SOU	AA	18	245	6	2	1	6	60.1	59	1	12	1	1	37	0	5	2	1	27	20	7	0	1.000	2	2.98
	SYR/INT	AAA	12	251	7	3	2	1	62.0	56	3	19	2	0	34	1	2	0	0	22	19	5	1	.833	2	2.76
	TOR/AL		9	133	3	0	0	2	31.2	35	1	9	1	1	10	0	2	0	0	19	17	4	1	.800	0	4.83

(continued)

Gozzo, Mauro Paul (continued)

YR	TM/LG	CL	G	TBF	GS	CG	SHO	GF	IP	H	HR	BB	IBB	HB	SO	SH	SF	WP	BK	R	ER	W	L	PCT	SV	ERA
	SYR/INT	AAA	34	409	10	0	0	19	98.0	87	5	44	3	3	62	3	1	2	1	46	39	3	8	.273	7	3.58
	CLE/AL		2	13	0	0	0	0	3.0	2	0	2	0	0	2	0	0	0	0	0	0	0	0	.000	0	0.00
91	CLE/AL		2	28	2	0	0	0	4.2	9	0	7	0	0	3	0	1	2	0	10	10	0	0	.000	0	19.29
	CS/PCL	AAA	25	588	20	3	0	4	130.1	143	9	68	3	6	81	3	7	7	4	86	76	10	6	.625	1	5.25
3 YR TOTALS			**13**	**174**	**5**	**0**	**0**	**3**	**39.1**	**46**	**1**	**18**	**1**	**1**	**15**	**0**	**3**	**2**	**0**	**29**	**27**	**4**	**1**	**.800**	**0**	**6.18**

Grahe, Joseph Milton "Joe" — bats right — throws right — b.8/14/67

YR	TM/LG	CL	G	TBF	GS	CG	SHO	GF	IP	H	HR	BB	IBB	HB	SO	SH	SF	WP	BK	R	ER	W	L	PCT	SV	ERA
90	MID/TEX	AA	18	519	18	1	0	0	119.0	145	10	34	1	4	58	2	2	10	1	75	68	7	5	.583	0	5.14
	EDM/PCL	AAA	5	159	5	2	0	0	40.0	35	4	11	0	0	21	0	0	0	0	10	6	3	0	1.000	0	1.35
	CAL/AL		8	200	8	0	0	0	43.1	51	3	23	1	3	25	0	0	1	0	30	24	3	4	.429	0	4.98
91	EDM/PCL	AAA	14	428	14	3	1	0	94.1	121	3	30	0	3	55	4	2	6	0	55	42	9	3	.750	0	4.01
	CAL/AL		18	330	10	1	0	2	73.0	84	2	33	0	3	40	1	1	2	0	43	39	3	7	.300	0	4.81
2 YR TOTALS			**26**	**530**	**18**	**1**	**0**	**2**	**116.1**	**135**	**5**	**56**	**1**	**6**	**65**	**1**	**1**	**3**	**0**	**73**	**63**	**6**	**11**	**.353**	**0**	**4.87**

Grant, Mark Andrew — bats right — throws right — b.10/24/63

YR	TM/LG	CL	G	TBF	GS	CG	SHO	GF	IP	H	HR	BB	IBB	HB	SO	SH	SF	WP	BK	R	ER	W	L	PCT	SV	ERA
84	PHO/PCL	AAA	17	0	17	4	1	0	111.1	102	7	61	2	1	78	0	0	8	0	64	49	5	7	.417	0	3.96
	SF/NL		11	231	10	0	0	1	53.2	56	6	19	0	1	32	2	3	3	3	40	38	1	4	.200	1	6.37
85	PHO/PCL	AAA	29	0	29	4	3	0	183.0	182	17	90	5	3	133	0	0	18	0	101	92	8	15	.348	0	4.52
86	PHO/PCL	AAA	28	785	27	10	3	0	181.2	204	13	46	4	3	93	2	9	8	0	105	99	14	7	.667	0	4.90
	SF/NL		4	39	1	0	0	3	10.0	6	0	5	0	0	5	0	0	0	1	4	4	0	1	.000	0	3.60
87	PHO/PCL	AAA	3	93	3	2	0	0	23.0	20	2	5	0	1	12	0	1	0	0	8	8	2	1	.667	0	3.13
	SF/NL		16	264	8	0	0	2	61.0	66	6	21	5	1	32	7	1	2	2	29	24	1	2	.333	1	3.54
	SD/NL		17	456	17	2	1	0	102.1	104	16	52	3	0	58	8	0	6	1	59	53	6	7	.462	0	4.66
	YEAR		33	720	25	2	1	2	163.1	170	22	73	8	1	90	15	1	8	3	88	77	7	9	.438	1	4.24
88	SD/NL		33	410	11	0	0	9	97.2	97	14	36	6	2	61	6	4	5	0	41	40	2	8	.200	0	3.69
89	SD/NL		50	466	0	0	0	19	116.1	105	11	32	6	3	69	5	2	2	0	45	43	8	2	.800	2	3.33
90	SD/NL		26	180	0	0	0	5	39.0	47	5	19	8	2	29	4	3	1	1	23	21	1	1	.500	0	4.85
	ATL/NL		33	231	1	0	0	16	52.1	61	4	18	3	1	40	2	2	1	0	30	27	1	2	.333	3	4.64
	YEAR		59	411	1	0	0	21	91.1	108	9	37	11	3	69	6	5	2	1	53	48	2	3	.400	3	4.73
91	RIC/INT	AAA	1	10	1	0	0	0	3.0	2	0	1	0	1	3	0	0	0	0	0	0	0	0	.000	0	0.00
6 YR TOTALS			**190**	**2277**	**48**	**2**	**1**	**55**	**532.1**	**542**	**62**	**202**	**31**	**8**	**326**	**34**	**15**	**20**	**5**	**271**	**250**	**20**	**27**	**.426**	**7**	**4.23**

Grater, Mark Anthony — bats right — throws right — b.1/19/64

YR	TM/LG	CL	G	TBF	GS	CG	SHO	GF	IP	H	HR	BB	IBB	HB	SO	SH	SF	WP	BK	R	ER	W	L	PCT	SV	ERA
86	JC/APP	R+	24	163	0	0	0	19	41.1	25	2	14	3	2	46	0	2	7	0	14	11	5	2	.714	8	2.40
87	SAV/SAL	A	50	319	0	0	0	28	74.0	54	4	48	9	6	59	5	1	11	1	35	25	6	10	.375	6	3.04
88	SPR/MID	A	53	318	0	0	0	28	81.0	60	1	27	7	4	66	4	1	5	3	23	16	7	2	.778	11	1.78
89	SP/FSL	A+	56	279	0	0	0	49	67.1	44	1	24	4	7	59	4	3	2	0	23	14	3	8	.273	32	1.87
90	LOU/AMA	AAA	24	124	0	0	0	15	28.1	24	1	15	4	0	18	3	2	0	0	13	10	0	2	.000	3	3.18
	ARK/TEX	AA	29	182	0	0	0	22	44.0	31	1	18	0	4	43	2	1	6	0	18	14	2	0	1.000	17	2.86
91	STL/NL		3	15	0	0	0	2	3.0	5	0	2	0	0	0	0	0	0	0	0	0	0	0	.000	0	0.00
	LOU/AMA	AAA	58	329	0	0	0	41	80.1	68	1	33	7	3	53	6	0	4	0	20	18	3	5	.375	12	2.02

Gray, Jeffrey Edward "Jeff" — bats right — throws right — b.4/10/63

YR	TM/LG	CL	G	TBF	GS	CG	SHO	GF	IP	H	HR	BB	IBB	HB	SO	SH	SF	WP	BK	R	ER	W	L	PCT	SV	ERA
84	PHI/GCL	R	26	170	0	0	0	24	41.1	35	0	10	5	1	26	2	0	0	0	9	6	6	4	.600	7	1.31
85	CLE/FSL	A+	55	381	0	0	0	47	87.2	80	4	33	9	1	80	9	3	6	1	38	31	5	9	.357	23	3.18
86	VER/EAS	AA	55	344	0	0	0	42	84.1	71	4	26	5	6	65	3	3	2	0	24	22	14	2	.875	15	2.35
87	NAS/AMA	AAA	53	374	0	0	0	29	83.1	97	9	26	9	0	70	7	2	6	1	52	45	4	10	.286	14	4.86
88	CIN/NL		5	45	0	0	0	1	9.1	12	0	4	2	0	5	3	2	0	0	4	4	0	0	.000	0	3.86
	NAS/AMA	AAA	42	287	0	0	0	18	73.0	59	4	18	2	1	73	3	2	2	0	17	16	8	5	.615	7	1.97
89	NAS/AMA	AAA	44	286	0	0	0	33	66.1	76	3	12	3	0	58	5	3	3	0	33	27	4	4	.500	7	3.66
90	PAW/INT	AAA	21	124	0	0	0	8	31.2	20	4	7	1	1	35	1	2	3	0	14	12	0	0	.000	1	3.41
	BOS/AL		41	217	0	0	0	28	50.2	53	3	15	3	1	50	2	1	2	0	27	25	2	4	.333	9	4.44
91	BOS/AL		50	231	0	0	0	20	61.2	39	3	10	4	1	41	3	1	2	0	17	16	2	3	.400	1	2.34
3 YR TOTALS			**96**	**493**	**0**	**0**	**0**	**49**	**121.2**	**104**	**10**	**29**	**9**	**2**	**96**	**8**	**4**	**4**	**0**	**48**	**45**	**4**	**7**	**.364**	**10**	**3.33**

Greene, Ira Thomas "Tommy" — bats right — throws right — b.4/6/67

YR	TM/LG	CL	G	TBF	GS	CG	SHO	GF	IP	H	HR	BB	IBB	HB	SO	SH	SF	WP	BK	R	ER	W	L	PCT	SV	ERA
85	PUL/APP	R+	12	226	12	1	1	0	50.2	49	7	27	0	2	32	1	1	4	0	45	43	2	5	.286	0	7.64
86	SUM/SAL	A	28	758	28	5	3	0	174.2	162	17	82	3	8	169	4	3	15	7	95	91	11	7	.611	0	4.69
87	GRE/SOU	AA	23	590	23	4	2	0	142.1	103	13	66	1	4	101	4	2	7	2	60	52	11	8	.579	0	3.29
88	RIC/INT	AAA	29	765	29	8	0	0	177.1	169	10	70	1	3	130	7	8	5	8	98	94	7	17	.292	0	4.77
89	RIC/INT	AAA	26	638	26	2	1	0	152.0	136	9	50	0	2	125	9	5	10	0	74	61	9	12	.429	0	3.61
	ATL/NL		4	103	4	1	1	0	26.1	22	5	6	1	0	17	1	2	1	0	12	12	1	2	.333	0	4.10
90	ATL/NL		5	61	2	0	0	0	12.1	14	3	9	0	1	4	2	0	0	0	11	11	1	0	1.000	0	8.03
	RIC/INT	AAA	19	459	18	0	0	0	109.0	88	5	65	3	0	65	5	3	8	3	49	45	5	8	.385	0	3.72
	SW/INT	AAA	1	27	1	0	0	0	7.0	5	0	2	0	0	4	0	0	0	0	0	0	0	0	.000	0	0.00
	PHI/NL		10	166	7	0	0	1	39.0	36	5	17	1	0	17	3	0	1	0	20	18	2	3	.400	0	4.15
	YEAR		15	227	9	0	0	1	51.1	50	8	26	1	1	21	5	0	1	0	31	29	3	3	.500	0	5.08
91	PHI/NL		36	857	27	3	2	3	207.2	177	19	66	4	3	154	9	11	9	1	85	78	13	7	.650	0	3.38
3 YR TOTALS			**55**	**1187**	**40**	**4**	**3**	**4**	**285.1**	**249**	**32**	**98**	**6**	**4**	**192**	**15**	**13**	**11**	**1**	**128**	**119**	**17**	**12**	**.586**	**0**	**3.75**

Grimsley, Jason Alan — bats right — throws right — b.8/7/67

YR	TM/LG	CL	G	TBF	GS	CG	SHO	GF	IP	H	HR	BB	IBB	HB	SO	SH	SF	WP	BK	R	ER	W	L	PCT	SV	ERA
85	BEN/NWL	A−	6	0	1	0	0	2	11.1	12	0	25	0	1	10	0	0	3	0	21	17	0	1	.000	0	13.50
86	UTI/NYP	A−	14	342	14	3	0	2	64.2	63	3	77	0	11	46	1	2	18	0	61	46	1	10	.091	0	6.40
87	SPA/SAL	A	23	380	9	3	0	7	88.1	59	4	54	2	6	98	2	5	12	0	48	31	7	4	.636	0	3.16
88	CLE/FSL	A+	16	422	15	2	0	1	101.1	80	2	37	1	9	90	4	4	12	2	48	42	4	7	.364	0	3.73
	REA/EAS	AA	5	98	4	0	0	1	21.1	20	1	13	1	1	14	1	1	1	0	19	17	1	3	.250	0	7.17
89	REA/EAS	AA	26	727	26	8	2	0	172.0	121	13	109	4	10	134	6	3	12	0	65	57	11	8	.579	0	2.98
	PHI/NL		4	91	4	0	0	0	18.1	19	2	19	1	0	7	1	0	2	0	13	12	1	3	.250	0	5.89
90	SW/INT	AAA	22	563	22	0	0	0	128.1	111	7	78	1	4	99	4	6	18	3	68	56	8	5	.615	0	3.93
	PHI/NL		11	255	11	0	0	0	57.1	47	1	43	0	2	41	2	1	6	1	21	21	3	2	.600	0	3.30
91	PHI/NL		12	272	12	0	0	0	61.0	54	4	41	3	2	42	3	2	14	0	34	33	1	7	.125	0	4.87
	SCR/INT	AAA	9	231	9	0	0	0	51.2	48	3	37	2	2	43	3	0	2	2	28	25	2	3	.400	0	4.35
3 YR TOTALS			**27**	**618**	**27**	**0**	**0**	**0**	**136.2**	**120**	**7**	**103**	**4**	**5**	**90**	**6**	**3**	**22**	**1**	**68**	**66**	**5**	**12**	**.294**	**0**	**4.35**

Gross, Kevin Frank — bats right — throws right — b.6/8/61

YR	TM/LG	CL	G	TBF	GS	CG	SHO	GF	IP	H	HR	BB	IBB	HB	SO	SH	SF	WP	BK	R	ER	W	L	PCT	SV	ERA
83	PHI/NL		17	418	17	1	1	0	96.0	100	13	35	3	3	66	2	1	4	1	46	38	4	6	.400	0	3.56
84	PHI/NL		44	566	14	1	0	9	129.0	140	8	44	4	5	84	9	3	4	4	66	59	8	5	.615	1	4.12
85	PHI/NL		38	873	31	6	2	0	205.2	194	11	81	6	7	151	7	5	2	0	86	78	15	13	.536	0	3.41
86	PHI/NL		37	1040	36	7	2	0	241.2	240	28	94	2	8	154	8	5	2	1	115	108	12	12	.500	0	4.02
87	PHI/NL		34	878	33	3	1	1	200.2	205	26	87	7	10	110	8	6	3	7	107	97	9	16	.360	0	4.35
88	PHI/NL		33	989	33	5	1	0	231.2	209	18	89	5	11	162	9	4	5	7	101	95	12	14	.462	0	3.69
89	MON/NL		31	867	31	4	3	0	201.1	188	20	88	6	6	158	10	3	5	5	105	98	11	12	.478	0	4.38
90	MON/NL		31	712	26	2	1	3	163.1	171	9	65	7	4	111	6	9	4	1	86	83	9	12	.429	0	4.57
91	LA/NL		46	509	10	0	0	16	115.2	123	10	50	6	2	95	6	4	3	0	55	46	10	11	.476	3	3.58
9 YR TOTALS			**311**	**6852**	**231**	**29**	**11**	**29**	**1585.0**	**1570**	**143**	**633**	**46**	**56**	**1091**	**65**	**40**	**32**	**26**	**767**	**702**	**90**	**101**	**.471**	**4**	**3.99**

Gross, Kip Lee — bats right — throws right — b.8/24/64

YR	TM/LG	CL	G	TBF	GS	CG	SHO	GF	IP	H	HR	BB	IBB	HB	SO	SH	SF	WP	BK	R	ER	W	L	PCT	SV	ERA
87	LYN/CAR	A+	16	379	15	2	0	0	89.1	92	1	22	1	6	39	2	3	1	1	37	27	7	4	.636	0	2.72
88	SL/FSL	A+	28	736	27	7	3	1	178.1	153	1	53	6	7	124	1	3	10	11	72	52	13	9	.591	0	2.62
89	JAC/TEX	AA	16	444	16	4	0	0	112.0	96	9	13	2	2	60	4	2	4	4	47	31	6	5	.545	0	2.49
	TID/INT	AAA	12	289	12	0	0	0	70.1	72	3	17	0	1	39	5	2	1	1	33	31	4	4	.500	0	3.97
90	NAS/AMA	AAA	40	521	11	2	1	11	127.0	113	6	47	3	7	62	6	2	6	3	54	47	12	7	.632	3	3.33
	CIN/NL		5	25	0	0	0	2	6.1	6	0	2	0	1	0	0	1	0	0	3	3	0	0	.000	0	4.26
91	NAS/AMA	AAA	14	195	6	1	1	3	47.2	39	3	16	0	4	39	2	1	3	1	13	11	5	3	.625	0	2.08
	CIN/NL		29	381	9	1	0	6	85.2	93	8	40	2	0	40	6	2	5	1	43	33	6	4	.600	0	3.47
2 YR TOTALS			**34**	**406**	**9**	**1**	**0**	**8**	**92.0**	**99**	**8**	**42**	**2**	**0**	**43**	**6**	**3**	**5**	**1**	**46**	**36**	**6**	**4**	**.600**	**0**	**3.52**

Gubicza, Mark Steven — bats right — throws right — b.8/14/62

YR	TM/LG	CL	G	TBF	GS	CG	SHO	GF	IP	H	HR	BB	IBB	HB	SO	SH	SF	WP	BK	R	ER	W	L	PCT	SV	ERA
84	KC/AL		29	800	29	4	2	0	189.0	172	13	75	0	5	111	4	9	3	1	90	85	10	14	.417	0	4.05
85	KC/AL		29	760	28	0	0	0	177.1	160	14	77	0	5	99	1	6	12	0	88	80	14	10	.583	0	4.06
86	KC/AL		35	765	24	3	2	2	180.2	155	8	84	2	5	118	4	8	15	0	77	73	12	6	.667	0	3.64
87	KC/AL		35	1036	35	10	2	0	241.2	231	18	120	3	6	166	6	11	14	1	114	107	13	18	.419	0	3.98
88	KC/AL		35	1111	35	8	4	0	269.2	237	11	83	3	6	183	3	6	12	4	94	81	20	8	.714	0	2.70
89	KC/AL		36	1060	36	8	2	0	255.0	252	10	63	5	8	173	11	8	9	0	100	86	15	11	.577	0	3.04
90	KC/AL		16	409	16	2	0	0	94.0	101	5	38	4	4	71	6	4	2	1	48	47	4	7	.364	0	4.50
91	OMA/AMA	AAA	3	71	3	0	0	0	16.1	20	0	4	0	1	12	0	0	4	0	7	6	2	1	.667	0	3.31
	KC/AL		26	601	26	0	0	0	133.0	168	10	42	1	6	89	3	5	5	0	90	84	9	12	.429	0	5.68
8 YR TOTALS			**241**	**6542**	**229**	**35**	**12**	**2**	**1540.1**	**1476**	**89**	**582**	**21**	**42**	**1010**	**38**	**57**	**72**	**7**	**701**	**643**	**97**	**86**	**.530**	**0**	**3.76**

Guetterman, Arthur Lee "Lee" — bats left — throws left — b.11/22/58

YR	TM/LG	CL	G	TBF	GS	CG	SHO	GF	IP	H	HR	BB	IBB	HB	SO	SH	SF	WP	BK	R	ER	W	L	PCT	SV	ERA
84	CHT/SOU	AA	24	652	24	5	2	0	157.0	174	7	38	2	4	47	6	2	5	1	68	59	11	7	.611	0	3.38
	SEA/AL		3	22	0	0	0	1	4.1	9	0	2	0	0	2	0	0	1	0	2	2	0	0	.000	0	4.15
85	CAL/PCL	AAA	20	0	18	2	0	1	110.1	138	7	44	0	1	48	0	0	6	0	86	71	5	8	.385	0	5.79
86	CAL/PCL	AAA	4	82	4	0	0	0	19.1	24	0	7	0	0	8	0	0	0	0	12	12	1	0	1.000	0	5.59
	SEA/AL		41	353	4	1	0	8	76.0	108	4	30	3	4	38	3	5	2	0	67	62	0	4	.000	0	7.34
87	CAL/PCL	AAA	16	186	2	1	0	5	44.0	41	1	17	1	1	29	1	2	3	0	14	14	5	1	.833	1	2.86
	SEA/AL		25	483	17	2	1	3	113.1	117	13	35	2	2	42	2	5	3	0	60	48	11	4	.733	0	3.81
88	COL/INT	AAA	18	493	18	6	0	0	120.2	109	2	26	2	3	49	5	5	4	0	46	37	9	6	.600	0	2.76
	NY/AL		20	177	2	0	0	7	40.2	49	2	14	1	0	15	1	1	2	0	21	21	1	2	.333	0	4.65
89	NY/AL		70	412	0	0	0	38	103.0	98	6	26	0	0	51	0	2	4	0	31	28	5	5	.500	13	2.45
90	NY/AL		64	376	0	0	0	21	93.0	80	6	26	7	0	48	0	3	1	0	37	35	11	7	.611	2	3.39
91	NY/AL		64	376	0	0	0	37	88.0	91	6	25	5	3	35	4	4	4	0	42	36	4	6	.429	6	3.68
7 YR TOTALS			**287**	**2199**	**23**	**3**	**1**	**115**	**518.1**	**552**	**40**	**158**	**26**	**10**	**231**	**22**	**20**	**17**	**1**	**260**	**232**	**31**	**26**	**.544**	**21**	**4.03**

Gullickson, William Lee "Bill" — bats right — throws right — b.2/20/59

YR	TM/LG	CL	G	TBF	GS	CG	SHO	GF	IP	H	HR	BB	IBB	HB	SO	SH	SF	WP	BK	R	ER	W	L	PCT	SV	ERA
79	MON/NL		1	4	0	0	0	1	1.0	2	0	0	0	0	0	0	0	0	0	0	0	0	0	.000	0	0.00
80	MON/NL		24	593	19	5	2	1	141.0	127	6	50	2	2	120	3	4	5	0	53	47	10	5	.667	0	3.00
81	MON/NL		22	640	22	3	2	0	157.1	142	3	34	4	4	115	5	2	4	0	54	49	7	9	.438	0	2.80
82	MON/NL		34	990	34	6	0	0	236.2	231	25	61	4	4	155	9	6	11	3	101	94	12	14	.462	0	3.57
83	MON/NL		34	990	34	10	1	0	242.1	230	19	59	4	4	120	4	7	4	1	108	101	17	12	.586	0	3.75

(continued)

Gullickson, William Lee "Bill" (continued)

YR	TM/LG	CL	G	TBF	GS	CG	SHO	GF	IP	H	HR	BB	IBB	HB	SO	SH	SF	WP	BK	R	ER	W	L	PCT	SV	ERA
84	MON/NL		32	919	32	3	0	0	226.2	230	27	37	7	1	100	8	4	5	0	100	91	12	9	.571	0	3.61
85	MON/NL		29	759	29	4	1	0	181.1	187	8	47	9	1	68	12	8	1	1	78	71	14	12	.538	0	3.52
86	CIN/NL		37	1014	37	6	2	0	244.2	245	24	60	10	2	121	12	13	3	0	103	92	15	12	.556	0	3.38
87	CIN/NL		27	698	27	3	1	0	165.0	172	33	39	6	2	89	6	6	4	1	99	89	10	11	.476	0	4.85
	NY/AL		8	198	8	1	0	0	48.0	46	7	11	1	1	28	2	2	0	0	29	26	4	2	.667	0	4.88
	YEAR		35	896	35	4	1	0	213.0	218	40	50	7	3	117	8	8	4	1	128	115	14	13	.519	0	4.86
90	HOU/NL		32	846	32	2	1	0	193.1	221	21	61	14	2	73	6	8	3	2	100	82	10	14	.417	0	3.82
91	DET/AL		35	954	35	4	0	0	226.1	256	22	44	13	4	91	8	8	4	0	109	98	20	9	.690	0	3.90
11 YR TOTALS			**315**	**8605**	**309**	**47**	**10**	**2**	**2063.2**	**2089**	**195**	**503**	**72**	**27**	**1080**	**75**	**68**	**44**	**8**	**934**	**840**	**131**	**109**	**.546**	**0**	**3.66**

Gunderson, Eric Andrew — bats right — throws left — b.3/29/66

YR	TM/LG	CL	G	TBF	GS	CG	SHO	GF	IP	H	HR	BB	IBB	HB	SO	SH	SF	WP	BK	R	ER	W	L	PCT	SV	ERA
87	EVE/NWL	A–	15	406	15	5	3	0	98.2	80	4	34	1	3	99	2	2	4	3	34	27	8	4	.667	0	2.46
88	SJ/CAL	A+	20	640	20	5	4	0	149.1	131	2	52	0	17	151	7	3	14	6	56	44	12	5	.706	0	2.65
	SHR/TEX	AA	7	166	6	0	0	1	36.2	45	1	13	0	1	28	1	1	0	1	25	21	1	2	.333	0	5.15
89	SHR/TEX	AA	11	298	11	2	1	0	72.2	68	1	23	0	1	61	1	3	1	1	24	22	8	2	.800	0	2.72
	PHO/PCL	AAA	14	375	14	0	0	0	85.2	93	7	36	2	2	56	5	6	7	1	51	48	2	4	.333	0	5.04
90	PHO/PCL	AAA	16	418	16	0	0	0	82.0	137	11	46	1	3	41	5	3	4	2	87	75	5	7	.417	0	8.23
	SHR/TEX	AA	8	225	8	1	1	0	52.2	51	7	17	1	2	44	1	1	3	0	24	19	2	2	.500	0	3.25
	SF/NL		7	94	4	0	0	1	19.2	24	2	11	1	0	14	1	0	0	0	14	12	1	2	.333	0	5.49
91	PHO/PCL	AAA	40	511	14	0	0	8	107.0	153	10	44	4	3	53	3	4	3	0	85	73	7	6	.538	3	6.14
	SF/NL		2	18	0	0	0	1	3.1	6	0	1	0	0	2	0	0	0	0	4	2	0	0	.000	1	5.40
2 YR TOTALS			**9**	**112**	**4**	**0**	**0**	**2**	**23.0**	**30**	**2**	**12**	**1**	**0**	**16**	**1**	**0**	**0**	**0**	**18**	**14**	**1**	**2**	**.333**	**1**	**5.48**

Guthrie, Mark Andrew — bats both — throws right — b.9/22/65

YR	TM/LG	CL	G	TBF	GS	CG	SHO	GF	IP	H	HR	BB	IBB	HB	SO	SH	SF	WP	BK	R	ER	W	L	PCT	SV	ERA
87	VIS/CAL	A+	4	48	1	0	0	1	12.0	10	0	5	1	0	9	2	0	2	0	7	6	2	1	.667	0	4.50
88	VIS/CAL	A+	25	742	25	4	1	0	171.1	169	6	86	1	3	182	5	3	14	7	81	63	12	9	.571	0	3.31
89	ORL/SOU	AA	14	382	14	0	0	0	96.0	75	4	38	0	2	103	4	0	3	6	32	21	8	3	.727	0	1.97
	POR/PCL	AAA	7	189	7	1	0	0	44.1	45	4	16	0	0	35	1	3	2	0	21	18	3	4	.429	0	3.65
	MIN/AL		13	254	8	0	0	2	57.1	66	7	21	1	1	38	1	5	1	0	32	29	2	4	.333	0	4.55
90	POR/PCL	AAA	9	178	8	1	0	1	42.1	47	1	12	0	2	39	1	1	0	1	19	14	1	3	.250	0	2.98
	MIN/AL		24	603	21	3	1	0	144.2	154	8	39	3	1	101	6	0	9	0	65	61	7	9	.438	0	3.79
91	MIN/AL		41	432	12	0	0	13	98.0	116	11	41	2	1	72	4	3	7	0	52	47	7	5	.583	2	4.32
3 YR TOTALS			**78**	**1289**	**41**	**3**	**1**	**15**	**300.0**	**336**	**26**	**101**	**6**	**3**	**211**	**11**	**8**	**17**	**0**	**149**	**137**	**16**	**18**	**.471**	**2**	**4.11**

Guzman, Jose Alberto (Mirabal) — bats right — throws right — b.4/9/63

YR	TM/LG	CL	G	TBF	GS	CG	SHO	GF	IP	H	HR	BB	IBB	HB	SO	SH	SF	WP	BK	R	ER	W	L	PCT	SV	ERA
84	TUL/TEX	AA	25	597	25	7	1	0	140.1	137	6	55	1	0	82	1	8	8	0	75	65	7	9	.438	0	4.17
85	OC/AMA	AAA	25	606	23	4	1	2	149.2	131	11	40	0	2	76	5	6	2	2	60	52	10	5	.667	1	3.13
	TEX/AL		5	140	5	0	0	0	32.2	27	3	14	1	0	24	0	1	0	0	13	10	3	2	.600	0	2.76
86	TEX/AL		29	757	29	2	0	0	172.1	199	23	60	2	6	87	7	4	3	0	101	87	9	15	.375	0	4.54
87	TEX/AL		37	880	30	6	0	1	208.1	196	30	82	0	3	143	6	8	6	5	115	108	14	14	.500	0	4.67
88	TEX/AL		30	876	30	6	2	0	206.2	180	20	82	3	5	157	4	6	10	12	99	85	11	13	.458	0	3.70
90	CHA/FSL	A+	2	37	2	0	0	0	8.1	10	0	4	0	1	7	1	1	0	0	3	2	0	1	.000	0	2.16
	TUL/TEX	AA	1	12	1	0	0	0	3.0	3	0	0	0	0	2	0	0	0	0	2	2	0	0	.000	0	6.00
	OC/AMA	AAA	7	126	7	0	0	0	28.2	35	2	9	0	2	26	2	3	1	1	20	18	0	3	.000	0	5.65
91	OC/AMA	AAA	3	84	3	0	0	0	20.2	18	1	4	0	0	18	1	0	2	1	9	9	1	1	.500	0	3.92
	TEX/AL		25	730	25	5	1	0	169.2	152	10	84	1	4	125	2	3	8	1	67	58	13	7	.650	0	3.08
5 YR TOTALS			**126**	**3383**	**119**	**19**	**3**	**1**	**789.2**	**754**	**86**	**322**	**7**	**18**	**536**	**19**	**21**	**28**	**18**	**395**	**348**	**50**	**51**	**.495**	**0**	**3.97**

Guzman, Juan Andres (Correa) — bats right — throws right — b.10/28/66

YR	TM/LG	CL	G	TBF	GS	CG	SHO	GF	IP	H	HR	BB	IBB	HB	SO	SH	SF	WP	BK	R	ER	W	L	PCT	SV	ERA
85	DOD/GCL	R	21	189	3	0	0	12	42.0	39	2	25	3	1	43	3	2	15	3	26	18	5	1	.833	4	3.86
86	VB/FSL	A+	26	594	24	3	0	0	131.1	114	3	90	4	4	96	4	3	16	2	69	51	10	9	.526	0	3.49
87	BAK/CAL	A+	22	508	21	0	0	0	110.0	106	4	84	0	1	113	0	1	19	1	71	58	5	6	.455	0	4.75
88	KNO/SOU	AA	46	363	2	0	0	23	84.0	52	1	61	5	1	90	4	4	6	6	29	22	4	5	.444	6	2.36
89	SYR/INT	AAA	14	99	0	0	0	4	20.1	13	0	30	0	1	28	0	1	5	0	9	9	1	1	.500	0	3.98
	KNO/SOU	AA	22	232	8	0	0	7	47.2	34	2	60	0	2	50	2	1	8	1	36	33	1	4	.200	0	6.23
90	KNO/SOU	AA	37	685	21	2	0	7	157.0	145	10	80	6	3	138	6	11	21	8	84	74	11	9	.550	1	4.24
91	SYR/INT	AAA	12	287	11	0	0	0	67.0	46	4	42	0	2	67	1	3	7	2	39	30	4	5	.444	0	4.03
	TOR/AL		23	574	23	1	1	0	138.2	98	6	66	0	4	123	2	5	10	0	53	46	10	3	.769	0	2.99

Guzman, Ramon Dionny (Estrella) "Johnny" — bats right — throws left — b.1/21/71

YR	TM/LG	CL	G	TBF	GS	CG	SHO	GF	IP	H	HR	BB	IBB	HB	SO	SH	SF	WP	BK	R	ER	W	L	PCT	SV	ERA
88	ATH/ARI	R	16	116	1	0	0	5	23.0	37	1	8	0	1	18	2	1	4	4	27	22	0	2	.000	1	8.61
89	MOD/CAL	A+	5	81	3	0	0	1	16.2	23	0	13	0	0	12	0	0	2	1	11	9	0	2	.000	0	4.86
	MAD/MID	A	9	201	9	1	0	0	45.2	41	3	21	0	2	36	0	1	1	4	26	19	3	3	.500	0	3.74
90	MOD/CAL	A+	13	337	13	1	1	0	84.2	67	3	23	2	4	58	4	2	2	1	25	18	7	4	.636	0	1.91
	HUN/SOU	AA	16	458	16	0	0	0	105.2	89	9	54	1	7	63	4	1	6	2	52	42	5	6	.455	0	3.58
91	OAK/AL		5	24	1	0	0	1	5.0	11	0	2	0	0	3	0	0	0	0	5	5	1	0	1.000	0	9.00
	TAC/PCL	AAA	17	394	13	0	0	2	79.2	113	8	51	0	2	40	3	4	4	6	74	60	2	5	.286	0	6.78
	HUN/SOU	AA	7	194	7	0	0	0	44.0	46	3	25	0	1	23	2	1	4	5	17	17	2	1	.667	0	3.48

Haas, Robert David "Dave" — bats right — throws right — b.10/19/65

YR	TM/LG	CL	G	TBF	GS	CG	SHO	GF	IP	H	HR	BB	IBB	HB	SO	SH	SF	WP	BK	R	ER	W	L	PCT	SV	ERA
88	FAY/SAL	A	11	243	11	0	0	0	54.2	59	0	19	1	6	46	1	1	2	4	20	11	4	3	.571	0	1.81
89	LAK/FSL	A+	10	247	10	1	1	0	62.0	50	1	16	0	6	46	0	1	1	1	16	14	4	1	.800	0	2.03
	LON/EAS	AA	18	460	18	2	1	0	103.2	107	13	51	1	11	75	5	2	5	1	69	65	3	11	.214	0	5.64
90	LON/EAS	AA	27	740	27	3	1	0	177.2	151	10	74	1	10	116	4	3	14	1	64	59	13	8	.619	0	2.99
91	TOL/INT	AAA	28	718	28	1	0	0	158.1	187	11	77	3	8	133	8	3	8	1	103	92	8	10	.444	0	5.23
	DET/AL		11	50	0	0	0	0	10.2	8	1	12	3	1	6	2	2	1	0	8	8	1	0	1.000	0	6.75

Habyan, John Gabriel — bats right — throws right — b.1/29/63

YR	TM/LG	CL	G	TBF	GS	CG	SHO	GF	IP	H	HR	BB	IBB	HB	SO	SH	SF	WP	BK	R	ER	W	L	PCT	SV	ERA
82	BLU/APP	R+	12	0	12	2	1	0	81.0	68	3	24	0	1	55	0	0	4	1	35	32	9	2	.818	0	3.56
	HAG/CAR	A+	1	0	1	0	0	0	0.0	0	0	5	2	0	1	0	0	0	0	5	5	0	0	.000	0	0.00
83	HAG/CAR	A+	11	0	11	1	0	0	48.0	54	3	29	0	1	42	0	0	5	0	41	31	2	3	.400	0	5.81
	NEW/NYP	A−	11	0	11	1	1	0	71.0	68	6	29	0	2	64	0	0	4	0	34	27	5	3	.625	0	3.42
84	HAG/CAR	A+	13	342	13	4	0	0	81.1	64	6	33	0	0	81	4	1	5	0	41	32	9	4	.692	0	3.54
	CHA/SOU	AA	13	340	13	1	0	0	77.0	84	8	34	1	0	55	2	6	6	1	46	38	4	7	.364	0	4.44
85	CHA/SOU	AA	28	799	28	8	2	0	189.2	157	11	90	0	2	123	5	10	13	0	73	69	13	5	.722	0	3.27
	BAL/AL		2	12	0	0	0	1	2.2	3	0	0	0	0	2	0	0	0	0	1	0	1	0	1.000	0	0.00
86	ROC/INT	AAA	26	686	25	5	1	0	157.1	168	13	69	2	1	93	5	3	10	1	82	75	12	7	.632	0	4.29
	BAL/AL		6	117	5	0	0	1	26.1	24	1	18	2	0	14	2	1	1	0	17	13	1	3	.250	0	4.44
87	ROC/INT	AAA	7	209	7	2	1	0	49.0	47	5	20	0	1	39	0	2	0	0	23	21	3	2	.600	0	3.86
	BAL/AL		27	493	13	0	0	4	116.1	110	20	40	1	2	64	4	4	3	0	67	62	6	7	.462	1	4.80
88	BAL/AL		7	68	0	0	0	1	14.2	22	2	4	0	0	4	0	2	1	1	10	7	1	0	1.000	0	4.30
	ROC/INT	AAA	23	635	23	8	1	0	147.1	161	13	46	2	0	91	8	6	7	9	78	73	9	9	.500	0	4.46
89	ROC/INT	AAA	7	154	5	0	0	2	37.1	38	2	5	0	0	22	2	0	1	0	15	9	1	2	.333	0	2.17
	COL/INT	AAA	8	207	8	2	0	0	46.1	65	2	9	0	1	30	2	3	2	0	29	28	2	3	.400	0	5.44
90	COL/INT	AAA	36	459	11	1	0	11	112.0	99	9	30	4	1	77	4	5	5	0	52	40	7	7	.500	6	3.21
	NY/AL		6	37	0	0	0	1	8.2	10	0	2	0	1	4	0	0	1	0	2	2	0	0	.000	0	2.08
91	NY/AL		66	349	0	0	0	16	90.0	73	2	20	2	2	70	2	1	1	2	28	23	4	2	.667	2	2.30
6 YR TOTALS			**114**	**1076**	**18**	**0**	**0**	**24**	**258.2**	**242**	**27**	**84**	**5**	**5**	**158**	**8**	**8**	**7**	**3**	**125**	**107**	**13**	**12**	**.520**	**3**	**3.72**

Hammaker, Charlton Atlee "Atlee" — bats both — throws left — b.1/24/58

YR	TM/LG	CL	G	TBF	GS	CG	SHO	GF	IP	H	HR	BB	IBB	HB	SO	SH	SF	WP	BK	R	ER	W	L	PCT	SV	ERA
81	KC/AL		10	169	6	0	0	2	39.0	44	2	12	1	0	11	2	1	0	1	24	24	1	3	.250	0	5.54
82	SF/NL		29	725	27	4	1	0	175.0	189	16	28	8	2	102	12	4	2	4	86	80	12	8	.600	0	4.11
83	SF/NL		23	695	23	8	3	0	172.1	147	9	32	12	3	127	10	4	6	2	57	43	10	9	.526	0	2.25
84	PHO/PCL	AAA	2	0	2	0	0	0	8.0	14	0	2	0	0	5	0	0	0	0	7	4	0	1	.000	0	4.50
	SF/NL		6	139	6	0	0	0	33.0	32	2	9	1	0	24	3	2	0	2	10	8	2	0	1.000	0	2.18
85	SF/NL		29	713	29	1	1	0	170.2	161	17	47	5	0	100	8	6	4	4	81	71	5	12	.294	0	3.74
87	SHR/TEX	AA	1	27	1	0	0	0	7.0	6	0	0	0	0	3	1	0	0	0	2	1	0	1	.000	0	1.29
	PHO/PCL	AAA	3	76	3	0	0	0	17.1	19	1	6	0	1	8	0	1	0	0	9	8	1	2	.333	0	4.15
	SF/NL		31	706	27	2	0	1	168.1	159	22	57	10	3	107	3	3	8	7	73	67	10	10	.500	0	3.58
88	SF/NL		43	607	17	3	1	11	144.2	136	11	41	9	3	65	10	4	1	2	68	60	9	9	.500	5	3.73
89	SF/NL		28	322	9	0	0	5	76.2	78	5	23	2	1	30	6	4	1	2	34	32	6	6	.500	0	3.76
90	SF/NL		25	282	6	0	0	5	67.1	69	7	21	4	0	28	4	3	1	1	33	32	4	5	.444	0	4.28
	SD/NL		9	81	1	0	0	3	19.1	16	1	6	1	0	16	0	0	1	1	11	10	0	4	.000	0	4.66
	YEAR		34	363	7	0	0	8	86.2	85	8	27	5	0	44	4	4	2	2	44	42	4	9	.308	0	4.36
91	HD/CAL	A+	2	34	2	0	0	0	8.0	9	1	3	0	0	3	0	0	2	0	3	2	0	0	.000	0	2.25
	LV/PCL	AAA	3	67	3	0	0	0	15.1	21	1	3	0	0	9	1	0	2	1	11	11	0	0	.000	0	6.46
	WIC/TEX	AA	5	32	0	0	0	1	7.2	10	0	3	0	0	9	1	0	0	0	3	3	0	0	.000	0	3.52
	SD/NL		1	27	0	0	0	0	4.2	8	0	3	0	1	2	0	1	0	0	7	3	0	0	.000	0	5.79
10 YR TOTALS			**234**	**4466**	**152**	**18**	**6**	**27**	**1071.0**	**1039**	**92**	**279**	**53**	**12**	**611**	**60**	**32**	**27**	**26**	**484**	**430**	**59**	**67**	**.468**	**5**	**3.61**

Hammond, Christopher Andrew "Chris" — bats left — throws left — b.1/21/66

YR	TM/LG	CL	G	TBF	GS	CG	SHO	GF	IP	H	HR	BB	IBB	HB	SO	SH	SF	WP	BK	R	ER	W	L	PCT	SV	ERA
86	RED/GCL	R	7	176	7	1	0	0	41.2	27	0	17	1	0	53	1	0	5	0	21	13	3	2	.600	0	2.81
	TAM/FSL	A+	5	100	5	0	0	0	21.2	25	0	13	1	1	5	0	0	1	0	8	8	0	2	.000	0	3.32
87	TAM/FSL	A+	25	745	24	6	0	1	170.0	174	10	60	1	3	126	4	4	6	3	81	67	11	11	.500	0	3.55
88	CHT/SOU	AA	26	743	26	4	2	0	182.2	127	2	77	3	3	127	1	3	5	4	48	35	16	5	.762	0	1.72
89	NAS/AMA	AAA	24	697	24	3	1	0	157.1	144	7	96	1	3	142	6	4	9	2	69	59	11	7	.611	0	3.38
90	CIN/NL		3	56	3	0	0	0	11.1	13	2	12	1	0	4	1	0	1	0	9	8	0	2	.000	0	6.35
	NAS/AMA	AAA	24	611	24	5	3	0	149.0	118	7	63	1	5	149	1	3	6	7	43	36	15	1	.938	0	2.17
91	CIN/NL		20	425	18	0	0	0	99.2	92	4	48	3	2	50	6	1	3	0	51	45	7	7	.500	0	4.06
2 YR TOTALS			**23**	**481**	**21**	**0**	**0**	**0**	**111.0**	**105**	**6**	**60**	**4**	**2**	**54**	**7**	**1**	**4**	**3**	**60**	**53**	**7**	**9**	**.438**	**0**	**4.30**

Haney, Christopher Deane "Chris" — bats left — throws left — b.11/16/68

YR	TM/LG	CL	G	TBF	GS	CG	SHO	GF	IP	H	HR	BB	IBB	HB	SO	SH	SF	WP	BK	R	ER	W	L	PCT	SV	ERA
90	JAM/NYP	A−	6	109	5	0	0	1	28.0	17	1	11	0	4	26	1	0	1	0	3	3	3	0	1.000	1	0.96
	ROC/MID	A	8	204	8	3	0	0	53.0	40	1	6	0	1	45	3	2	0	0	15	13	2	4	.333	0	2.21
	JAC/SOU	AA	1	25	1	0	0	0	6.0	6	0	3	0	0	6	0	0	0	0	1	0	1	0	1.000	0	0.00
91	HAR/EAS	AA	12	334	12	3	0	0	83.1	65	4	31	1	3	68	8	2	3	1	21	20	5	3	.625	0	2.16
	IND/AMA	AAA	2	50	2	0	0	0	10.1	14	2	6	0	1	8	0	0	2	0	10	5	1	1	.500	0	4.35
	MON/NL		16	387	16	0	0	0	84.2	94	6	43	1	1	51	6	1	9	0	49	38	3	7	.300	0	4.04

Hanson, Erik Brian — bats right — throws right — b.5/18/65

YR	TM/LG	CL	G	TBF	GS	CG	SHO	GF	IP	H	HR	BB	IBB	HB	SO	SH	SF	WP	BK	R	ER	W	L	PCT	SV	ERA
86	CHT/SOU	AA	3	43	2	0	0	0	9.1	10	1	4	1	2	11	0	0	1	1	4	4	0	0	.000	0	3.86
87	CHT/SOU	AA	21	538	21	1	0	0	131.1	102	10	43	0	3	131	1	2	11	1	56	38	8	10	.444	0	2.60
	CAL/PCL	AAA	8	201	7	0	0	0	47.1	38	4	21	0	2	43	2	2	2	0	23	19	1	3	.250	0	3.61
88	CAL/PCL	AAA	27	691	26	2	1	1	161.2	167	9	57	0	0	154	2	5	10	4	92	76	12	7	.632	0	4.23
	SEA/AL		6	168	6	0	0	0	41.2	35	4	12	1	1	36	3	0	2	2	17	15	2	3	.400	0	3.24
89	CAL/PCL	AAA	8	175	8	1	0	0	38.0	51	4	11	0	2	37	1	1	4	0	30	29	4	2	.667	0	6.87
	SEA/AL		17	465	17	1	0	0	113.1	103	7	32	1	5	75	4	1	3	0	44	40	9	5	.643	0	3.18
90	SEA/AL		33	964	33	5	1	0	236.0	205	15	68	6	2	211	5	6	10	1	88	85	18	9	.667	0	3.24
91	CAL/PCL	AAA	1	21	1	0	0	0	6.0	1	0	2	0	0	5	1	0	1	0	1	1	0	0	.000	0	1.50
	SEA/AL		27	744	27	2	1	0	174.2	182	16	56	2	5	143	2	8	14	1	82	74	8	8	.500	0	3.81
4 YR TOTALS			**83**	**2341**	**83**	**8**	**2**	**0**	**565.2**	**525**	**42**	**168**	**10**	**10**	**465**	**14**	**15**	**29**	**4**	**231**	**214**	**37**	**25**	**.597**	**0**	**3.40**

Harkey, Michael Anthony "Mike" — bats right — throws right — b.10/25/66

YR	TM/LG	CL	G	TBF	GS	CG	SHO	GF	IP	H	HR	BB	IBB	HB	SO	SH	SF	WP	BK	R	ER	W	L	PCT	SV	ERA
87	PEO/MID	A	12	343	12	3	0	0	76.0	81	3	28	2	6	48	6	2	2	3	45	30	2	3	.400	0	3.55
	PIT/EAS	AA	1	6	0	0	0	0	2.0	1	0	0	0	0	2	0	0	0	0	0	0	0	0	.000	0	0.00
88	PIT/EAS	AA	13	358	13	3	1	0	85.2	66	1	35	1	3	73	3	0	5	5	29	13	9	2	.818	0	1.37
	IOW/AMA	AAA	12	317	12	3	1	0	78.2	55	6	33	0	1	62	3	3	3	1	36	31	7	2	.778	0	3.55
	CHI/NL		5	155	5	0	0	0	34.2	33	0	15	3	2	18	5	0	2	1	14	10	0	3	.000	0	2.60
89	IOW/AMA	AAA	12	277	12	0	0	0	63.0	67	7	25	0	3	37	1	3	3	1	37	31	2	7	.222	0	4.43
90	CHI/NL		27	728	27	2	1	0	173.2	153	14	59	8	7	94	5	4	8	1	71	63	12	6	.667	0	3.26
91	CHI/NL		4	84	4	0	0	0	18.2	21	3	6	1	0	15	0	1	1	0	11	11	0	2	.000	0	5.30
3 YR TOTALS			**36**	**967**	**36**	**2**	**1**	**0**	**227.0**	**207**	**17**	**80**	**12**	**9**	**127**	**10**	**5**	**11**	**2**	**96**	**84**	**12**	**11**	**.522**	**0**	**3.33**

Harnisch, Peter Thomas "Pete" — bats both — throws right — b.9/23/66

YR	TM/LG	CL	G	TBF	GS	CG	SHO	GF	IP	H	HR	BB	IBB	HB	SO	SH	SF	WP	BK	R	ER	W	L	PCT	SV	ERA
87	BLU/APP	R+	9	216	9	0	0	0	52.2	38	0	26	1	1	64	1	1	4	1	19	15	3	1	.750	0	2.56
	HAG/CAR	A+	4	91	4	0	0	0	20.0	17	0	14	0	1	18	0	1	3	1	7	5	1	2	.333	0	2.25
88	CHA/SOU	AA	20	552	20	4	2	0	132.1	113	6	52	0	4	141	1	3	4	4	55	38	7	6	.538	0	2.58
	ROC/INT	AAA	7	230	7	3	2	0	58.1	44	2	14	1	1	43	3	2	1	1	16	14	4	1	.800	0	2.16
	BAL/AL		2	61	2	0	0	0	13.0	13	1	9	0	0	10	2	0	1	0	8	8	0	0	.000	0	5.54
89	ROC/INT	AAA	12	354	12	3	1	0	87.1	60	7	35	0	4	59	4	5	3	2	27	25	5	5	.500	0	2.58
	BAL/AL		18	468	17	2	0	1	103.1	97	10	64	3	5	70	4	5	5	1	55	53	5	9	.357	0	4.62
90	BAL/AL		31	821	31	3	0	0	188.2	189	17	86	5	1	122	6	5	2	2	96	91	11	11	.500	0	4.34
91	HOU/NL		33	900	33	4	2	0	216.2	169	14	83	3	5	172	9	7	5	2	71	65	12	9	.571	0	2.70
4 YR TOTALS			**84**	**2250**	**83**	**9**	**2**	**1**	**521.2**	**468**	**42**	**242**	**12**	**11**	**374**	**21**	**17**	**13**	**5**	**230**	**217**	**28**	**31**	**.475**	**0**	**3.74**

Harris, Greg Allen — bats both — throws right — b.11/2/55

YR	TM/LG	CL	G	TBF	GS	CG	SHO	GF	IP	H	HR	BB	IBB	HB	SO	SH	SF	WP	BK	R	ER	W	L	PCT	SV	ERA
81	NY/NL		16	300	14	0	0	2	68.2	65	8	28	2	2	54	4	1	3	2	36	34	3	5	.375	1	4.46
82	CIN/NL		34	398	10	1	0	9	91.1	96	12	37	1	2	67	5	3	2	2	56	49	2	6	.250	1	4.83
83	CIN/NL		1	9	0	0	0	0	1.0	2	0	3	1	1	1	0	0	0	0	3	3	0	0	.000	0	27.00
84	MON/NL		15	68	0	0	0	4	17.2	10	0	7	1	2	15	1	0	0	0	4	4	0	1	.000	2	2.04
	IND/AMA	AAA	14	199	6	0	0	4	44.2	44	7	29	0	3	45	1	2	3	0	27	22	4	4	.500	1	4.43
	SD/NL		19	158	1	0	0	10	36.2	28	3	18	0	2	30	1	3	3	0	14	11	2	1	.667	1	2.70
	YEAR		34	226	1	0	0	14	54.1	38	3	25	1	4	45	2	3	3	0	18	15	2	2	.500	3	2.48
85	TEX/AL		58	450	0	0	0	35	113.0	74	7	43	3	5	111	3	2	2	1	35	31	5	4	.556	11	2.47
86	TEX/AL		73	462	0	0	0	63	111.1	103	12	42	6	1	95	3	6	2	1	40	35	10	8	.556	20	2.83
87	TEX/AL		42	629	19	0	0	14	140.2	157	18	56	3	4	106	7	3	4	2	92	76	5	10	.333	0	4.86
88	MAI/INT	AAA	3	22	0	0	0	3	4.2	5	1	1	1	0	5	2	0	0	0	3	1	0	1	.000	1	1.93
	PHI/NL		66	446	1	0	0	19	107.0	80	7	52	14	4	71	6	2	8	2	34	28	4	6	.400	1	2.36
89	PHI/NL		44	324	0	0	0	17	75.1	64	7	43	7	2	51	3	2	10	0	34	30	2	2	.500	1	3.58
	BOS/AL		15	118	0	0	0	7	28.0	21	1	15	2	0	25	1	1	2	0	12	8	2	2	.500	0	2.57
	YEAR		59	442	0	0	0	24	103.1	85	8	58	9	2	76	4	3	12	0	46	38	4	4	.500	1	3.31
90	BOS/AL		34	803	30	1	0	3	184.1	186	13	77	7	6	117	8	9	8	1	90	82	13	9	.591	0	4.00
91	BOS/AL		53	731	21	0	0	15	173.0	157	13	69	5	5	127	4	8	6	1	79	74	11	12	.478	2	3.85
11 YR TOTALS			**470**	**4896**	**96**	**3**	**0**	**198**	**1148.0**	**1043**	**101**	**490**	**53**	**36**	**870**	**47**	**40**	**50**	**12**	**529**	**465**	**59**	**66**	**.472**	**40**	**3.65**

Harris, Gregory Wade "Greg" — bats right — throws right — b.12/1/63

YR	TM/LG	CL	G	TBF	GS	CG	SHO	GF	IP	H	HR	BB	IBB	HB	SO	SH	SF	WP	BK	R	ER	W	L	PCT	SV	ERA
85	SPO/NWL	A−	13	0	13	1	0	0	87.1	80	5	36	0	3	90	0	0	6	0	36	33	5	4	.556	0	3.40
86	CHA/SAL	A	27	803	27	8	2	0	191.1	176	13	54	2	3	176	10	5	6	0	69	56	13	7	.650	0	2.63
87	WIC/TEX	AA	27	780	27	7	2	0	174.1	205	32	49	3	3	170	4	2	7	6	103	83	12	11	.522	0	4.28
88	LV/PCL	AAA	26	692	25	5	2	0	159.2	160	15	65	2	1	147	4	4	8	5	84	73	9	5	.643	0	4.11
	SD/NL		3	68	1	1	0	2	18.0	13	0	3	0	0	15	0	0	0	0	3	3	2	0	1.000	0	1.50
89	SD/NL		56	554	8	0	0	25	135.0	106	8	52	9	2	106	5	2	3	3	43	39	8	9	.471	6	2.60
90	SD/NL		73	488	0	0	0	33	117.1	92	6	49	13	4	97	9	7	2	3	35	30	8	8	.500	9	2.30
91	LV/PCL	AAA	4	92	4	0	0	0	20.2	24	1	8	0	0	16	0	2	0	1	20	17	1	2	.333	0	7.40
	SD/NL		20	537	20	3	2	0	133.0	116	16	27	6	1	95	9	2	2	0	42	33	9	5	.643	0	2.23
4 YR TOTALS			**152**	**1647**	**29**	**4**	**2**	**60**	**403.1**	**327**	**30**	**131**	**28**	**7**	**313**	**23**	**11**	**7**	**6**	**123**	**105**	**27**	**22**	**.551**	**15**	**2.34**

Harris, Reginald Allen "Reggie" — bats right — throws right — b.8/12/68

YR	TM/LG	CL	G	TBF	GS	CG	SHO	GF	IP	H	HR	BB	IBB	HB	SO	SH	SF	WP	BK	R	ER	W	L	PCT	SV	ERA
87	ELM/NYP	A−	9	212	8	1	1	0	46.2	50	3	22	0	6	25	1	1	3	0	29	26	2	3	.400	0	5.01

Harris, Reginald Allen "Reggie" (continued)

YR	TM/LG	CL	G	TBF	GS	CG	SHO	GF	IP	H	HR	BB	IBB	HB	SO	SH	SF	WP	BK	R	ER	W	L	PCT	SV	ERA
88	LYN/CAR	A+	17	310	11	0	0	2	64.0	86	8	34	5	4	48	0	3	5	7	60	53	1	8	.111	0	7.45
	ELM/NYP	A–	10	237	10	0	0	0	54.1	56	5	28	0	2	46	1	3	1	2	37	32	3	6	.333	0	5.30
89	WH/FSL	A+	29	670	26	1	0	2	153.1	144	6	77	2	7	85	5	11	7	4	81	68	10	13	.435	0	3.99
90	HUN/SOU	AA	5	131	5	0	0	0	29.2	26	3	16	0	4	34	1	1	4	0	12	10	0	2	.000	0	3.03
	OAK/AL		16	168	1	0	0	9	41.1	25	5	21	1	2	31	1	2	2	0	16	16	1	0	1.000	0	3.48
91	OAK/AL		2	15	0	0	0	0	3.0	5	0	3	1	0	2	0	1	2	0	4	4	0	0	.000	0	12.00
	TAC/PCL	AAA	16	380	15	0	0	0	83.0	83	11	58	0	3	72	0	4	5	0	55	46	5	4	.556	0	4.99
2 YR TOTALS			**18**	**183**	**1**	**0**	**0**	**10**	**44.1**	**30**	**5**	**24**	**2**	**2**	**33**	**1**	**3**	**4**	**0**	**20**	**20**	**1**	**0**	**1.000**	**0**	**4.06**

Harris, Tyrone Eugene "Gene" — bats right — throws right — b.12/5/64

YR	TM/LG	CL	G	TBF	GS	CG	SHO	GF	IP	H	HR	BB	IBB	HB	SO	SH	SF	WP	BK	R	ER	W	L	PCT	SV	ERA
86	JAM/NYP	A–	4	86	4	0	0	0	20.1	15	0	11	0	0	16	0	2	0	1	8	5	0	2	.000	0	2.21
	BUR/MID	A	7	210	6	4	3	0	53.1	37	1	15	0	1	32	0	3	2	1	12	8	4	2	.667	0	1.35
	WPB/FSL	A+	2	52	2	0	0	0	11.0	14	0	7	0	0	5	2	1	0	0	7	5	0	0	.000	0	4.09
87	WPB/FSL	A+	26	773	26	7	1	0	179.0	178	7	77	1	2	121	5	4	11	3	101	87	9	7	.563	0	4.37
88	JAC/SOU	AA	18	500	18	7	0	0	126.2	95	4	45	0	2	103	2	2	7	4	43	37	9	5	.643	0	2.63
89	MON/NL		11	84	0	0	0	7	20.0	16	1	10	1	0	11	7	1	3	0	11	11	1	1	.500	0	4.95
	IND/AMA	AAA	6	46	0	0	0	4	11.0	4	0	10	1	0	9	4	0	0	0	0	0	2	0	1.000	2	0.00
	CAL/PCL	AAA	5	20	0	0	0	4	6.0	4	0	1	0	0	4	0	0	0	0	0	0	0	0	.000	2	0.00
	SEA/AL		10	152	6	0	0	2	33.1	47	3	15	1	1	14	0	3	0	0	27	24	1	4	.200	1	6.48
	YEAR		21	236	6	0	0	9	53.1	63	4	25	1	1	25	7	4	3	0	38	35	2	5	.286	1	5.91
90	CAL/PCL	AAA	6	30	0	0	0	6	7.2	7	0	4	0	0	9	0	0	2	0	2	2	3	0	1.000	2	2.35
	SEA/AL		25	176	0	0	0	12	38.0	31	5	30	5	1	43	0	2	2	0	25	20	1	2	.333	0	4.74
91	CAL/PCL	AAA	25	152	0	0	0	18	35.0	37	2	11	1	1	23	1	3	2	1	16	13	4	0	1.000	4	3.34
	SEA/AL		8	66	0	0	0	3	13.1	15	1	10	3	0	6	1	0	1	0	8	6	0	0	.000	1	4.05
3 YR TOTALS			**54**	**478**	**6**	**0**	**0**	**24**	**104.2**	**109**	**10**	**65**	**9**	**2**	**74**	**8**	**6**	**6**	**0**	**71**	**61**	**3**	**7**	**.300**	**2**	**5.25**

Hartley, Michael Edward "Mike" — bats right — throws right — b.8/31/61

YR	TM/LG	CL	G	TBF	GS	CG	SHO	GF	IP	H	HR	BB	IBB	HB	SO	SH	SF	WP	BK	R	ER	W	L	PCT	SV	ERA
84	SP/FSL	A+	31	622	23	4	1	1	139.1	142	3	84	10	4	88	7	2	16	2	81	65	8	14	.364	0	4.20
85	SPR/MID	A	33	516	12	0	0	10	114.1	119	9	62	2	8	100	7	6	9	0	77	65	2	7	.222	0	5.12
86	SPR/MID	A	8	82	0	0	0	5	15.0	22	4	14	1	1	10	0	1	2	0	17	16	0	0	.000	1	9.60
	SAV/SAL	A	39	248	0	0	0	25	56.0	38	0	37	1	1	55	0	1	9	0	31	18	5	7	.417	8	2.89
87	BAK/CAL	A+	33	236	0	0	0	27	56.0	44	3	24	5	4	72	4	2	7	0	19	16	5	4	.556	14	2.57
	SA/TEX	AA	25	161	0	0	0	19	41.0	21	2	18	5	2	37	4	1	6	0	8	6	3	4	.429	3	1.32
	ALB/PCL	AAA	2	14	0	0	0	0	2.2	5	0	3	1	0	3	0	0	0	0	3	2	0	1	.000	0	6.75
88	SA/TEX	AA	30	177	0	0	0	25	45.0	25	2	18	2	1	57	1	1	1	1	5	4	5	1	.833	9	0.80
	ALB/PCL	AAA	18	99	0	0	0	11	20.2	22	1	12	1	2	16	4	0	0	1	11	10	2	2	.500	3	4.35
89	ALB/PCL	AAA	58	315	0	0	0	50	77.1	53	4	34	2	2	76	3	3	4	1	31	24	7	4	.636	18	2.79
	LA/NL		5	20	0	0	0	3	6.0	2	0	0	0	0	6	0	0	0	0	1	1	0	0	.000	0	1.50
90	ALB/PCL	AAA	3	14	0	0	0	2	3.0	3	0	2	0	0	3	0	0	0	0	0	0	0	0	.000	2	0.00
	LA/NL		32	325	6	1	1	8	79.1	58	7	30	2	2	76	2	1	3	0	32	26	6	3	.667	1	2.95
91	LA/NL		40	258	0	0	0	11	57.0	53	7	37	1	1	44	1	1	8	1	29	28	2	1	1.000	1	4.42
	PHI/NL		18	110	0	0	0	5	26.1	21	4	10	1	3	19	1	0	2	1	11	11	2	1	.667	1	3.76
	YEAR		58	368	0	0	0	16	83.1	74	11	47	2	4	63	2	1	10	2	40	39	4	1	.800	2	4.21
3 YR TOTALS			**95**	**713**	**6**	**1**	**1**	**27**	**168.2**	**134**	**18**	**77**	**10**	**8**	**143**	**4**	**2**	**13**	**2**	**73**	**66**	**10**	**5**	**.667**	**3**	**3.52**

Harvey, Bryan Stanley — bats right — throws right — b.6/2/63

YR	TM/LG	CL	G	TBF	GS	CG	SHO	GF	IP	H	HR	BB	IBB	HB	SO	SH	SF	WP	BK	R	ER	W	L	PCT	SV	ERA
85	QC/MID	A	30	345	7	0	0	17	81.2	66	5	37	0	2	111	5	2	4	2	37	32	5	6	.455	4	3.53
86	PS/CAL	A+	43	244	0	0	0	29	57.0	38	1	38	6	3	68	4	5	2	0	24	17	3	4	.429	15	2.68
87	MID/TEX	AA	43	225	0	0	0	36	53.0	40	1	28	5	0	78	0	4	10	0	14	12	2	2	.500	20	2.04
	CAL/AL		3	22	0	0	0	2	5.0	6	0	2	0	0	3	0	0	3	0	0	0	0	0	.000	0	0.00
88	EDM/PCL	AAA	5	30	0	0	0	5	5.2	7	0	4	0	0	10	0	0	3	0	2	2	0	0	.000	2	3.18
	CAL/AL		50	303	0	0	0	38	76.0	59	4	20	6	1	67	3	3	4	1	22	18	7	5	.583	17	2.13
89	CAL/AL		51	245	0	0	0	42	55.0	36	6	41	1	0	78	5	2	5	0	21	21	3	3	.500	25	3.44
90	CAL/AL		54	267	0	0	0	47	64.1	45	6	35	6	0	82	4	4	7	1	24	23	4	4	.500	25	3.22
91	CAL/AL		67	309	0	0	0	63	78.2	51	6	17	3	1	101	3	2	2	2	20	14	2	4	.333	46	1.60
5 YR TOTALS			**225**	**1146**	**0**	**0**	**0**	**192**	**279.0**	**197**	**20**	**115**	**16**	**2**	**331**	**15**	**11**	**21**	**4**	**87**	**76**	**16**	**16**	**.500**	**113**	**2.45**

Hawblitzel, Ryan Wade — bats right — throws right — b.4/30/71 — System CHI/NL

YR	TM/LG	CL	G	TBF	GS	CG	SHO	GF	IP	H	HR	BB	IBB	HB	SO	SH	SF	WP	BK	R	ER	W	L	PCT	SV	ERA
90	HUN/APP	R+	14	322	14	2	1	0	75.2	72	8	25	0	6	71	0	0	2	0	38	33	6	5	.545	0	3.93
91	WIN/CAR	A+	20	552	20	5	2	0	134.0	110	7	47	0	7	103	5	7	8	1	40	34	15	2	.882	0	2.28
	CHA/SOU	AA	5	141	5	1	1	0	33.2	31	1	12	3	3	25	5	2	0	0	14	12	1	2	.333	0	3.21

Hawkins, Melton Andrew "Andy" — bats right — throws right — b.1/21/60

YR	TM/LG	CL	G	TBF	GS	CG	SHO	GF	IP	H	HR	BB	IBB	HB	SO	SH	SF	WP	BK	R	ER	W	L	PCT	SV	ERA
82	SD/NL		15	281	10	1	0	2	63.2	66	4	27	3	2	25	6	5	2	3	33	29	2	5	.286	0	4.10
83	SD/NL		21	501	19	4	1	1	119.2	106	8	48	4	5	59	10	4	4	1	50	39	5	7	.417	0	2.93
84	SD/NL		36	650	22	2	1	9	146.0	143	13	72	9	2	77	10	4	1	2	90	76	8	9	.471	0	4.68
85	SD/NL		33	953	33	5	2	0	228.2	229	18	65	8	4	69	13	12	3	3	88	80	18	8	.692	0	3.15
86	SD/NL		37	905	35	3	1	0	209.1	218	24	75	7	5	117	7	6	6	2	111	100	10	8	.556	0	4.30
87	SD/NL		24	516	20	0	0	2	117.2	131	16	49	2	2	51	5	3	2	3	71	66	3	10	.231	0	5.05

(continued)

YR	TM/LG	CL	G	TBF	GS	CG	SHO	GF	IP	H	HR	BB	IBB	HB	SO	SH	SF	WP	BK	R	ER	W	L	PCT	SV	ERA
88	SD/NL		33	906	33	4	2	0	217.2	196	16	76	4	6	91	14	6	1	3	88	81	14	11	.560	0	3.35
89	NY/AL		34	908	34	5	2	0	208.1	238	23	76	6	6	98	3	3	1	2	127	111	15	15	.500	0	4.80
90	NY/AL		28	692	26	2	1	1	157.2	156	20	82	3	2	74	4	5	2	1	101	94	5	12	.294	0	5.37
91	NY/AL		4	66	3	0	0	1	12.2	23	5	6	0	0	5	0	0	1	0	15	14	0	2	.000	0	9.95
	OAK/AL		15	333	14	1	0	1	77.0	68	5	36	0	5	40	0	4	3	0	41	41	4	4	.500	0	4.79
	YEAR		19	399	17	1	0	2	89.2	91	10	42	0	5	45	2	3	1	1	56	55	4	6	.400	0	5.52
10 YR TOTALS			**280**	**6711**	**249**	**27**	**10**	**17**	**1558.1**	**1574**	**152**	**612**	**39**	**39**	**706**	**74**	**51**	**23**	**21**	**815**	**731**	**84**	**91**	**.480**	**0**	**4.22**

Heaton, Neal — bats left — throws left — b.3/3/60

YR	TM/LG	CL	G	TBF	GS	CG	SHO	GF	IP	H	HR	BB	IBB	HB	SO	SH	SF	WP	BK	R	ER	W	L	PCT	SV	ERA
82	CLE/AL		8	142	4	0	0	0	31.0	32	1	16	0	0	14	1	2	4	0	21	18	0	2	.000	0	5.23
83	CLE/AL		39	637	16	4	3	19	149.1	157	11	44	10	1	75	3	5	1	0	79	69	11	7	.611	7	4.16
84	CLE/AL		38	880	34	4	1	2	198.2	231	21	75	5	0	75	6	10	3	1	128	115	12	15	.444	0	5.21
85	CLE/AL		36	921	33	5	1	2	207.2	244	19	80	2	7	82	7	8	2	2	119	113	9	17	.346	0	4.90
86	CLE/AL		12	324	12	2	0	0	74.1	73	8	34	4	1	24	2	0	2	0	42	35	3	6	.333	0	4.24
	MIN/AL		21	526	17	3	0	2	124.1	128	18	47	4	1	66	4	5	2	0	60	55	4	9	.308	1	3.98
	YEAR		33	850	29	5	0	2	198.2	201	26	81	8	2	90	6	5	4	0	102	90	7	15	.318	1	4.08
87	MON/NL		32	807	32	3	1	0	193.1	207	25	37	3	3	105	5	5	2	5	103	97	13	10	.565	0	4.52
88	MON/NL		32	415	11	0	0	7	97.1	98	14	43	5	3	43	5	3	1	5	54	54	3	10	.231	2	4.99
89	PIT/NL		42	620	18	1	0	5	147.1	127	12	55	12	6	67	12	3	4	5	55	50	6	7	.462	0	3.05
90	PIT/NL		30	599	24	0	0	2	146.0	143	17	38	1	2	68	10	6	4	1	66	56	12	9	.571	0	3.45
91	PIT/NL		42	293	1	0	0	5	68.2	72	6	21	2	4	34	3	3	0	1	37	33	3	3	.500	0	4.33
10 YR TOTALS			**332**	**6164**	**202**	**22**	**6**	**44**	**1438.0**	**1512**	**152**	**490**	**48**	**28**	**653**	**58**	**50**	**25**	**20**	**764**	**695**	**76**	**95**	**.444**	**10**	**4.35**

Henke, Thomas Anthony "Tom" — bats right — throws right — b.12/21/57

YR	TM/LG	CL	G	TBF	GS	CG	SHO	GF	IP	H	HR	BB	IBB	HB	SO	SH	SF	WP	BK	R	ER	W	L	PCT	SV	ERA
82	TEX/AL		8	67	0	0	0	6	15.2	14	0	8	2	1	9	1	0	0	0	2	2	1	0	1.000	0	1.15
83	TEX/AL		8	65	0	0	0	5	16.0	16	1	4	0	0	17	0	0	0	0	6	6	1	0	1.000	1	3.38
84	OC/AMA	AAA	39	270	0	0	0	34	64.2	59	1	25	6	1	65	1	1	5	1	21	19	6	2	.750	7	2.64
	TEX/AL		25	141	0	0	0	13	28.1	36	1	20	2	1	25	1	4	2	2	21	20	1	2	.500	2	6.35
85	SYR/INT	AAA	39	185	0	0	0	32	51.1	13	2	18	2	1	60	2	3	1	0	5	5	2	1	.667	18	0.88
	TOR/AL		28	153	0	0	0	22	40.0	29	4	8	2	0	42	2	2	0	0	12	9	3	3	.500	13	2.03
86	TOR/AL		63	370	0	0	0	51	91.1	63	6	32	4	1	118	2	6	3	1	39	34	9	5	.643	27	3.35
87	TOR/AL		72	363	0	0	0	62	94.0	62	10	25	3	0	128	3	5	5	0	27	26	0	6	.000	34	2.49
88	TOR/AL		52	285	0	0	0	44	68.0	60	6	24	3	2	66	4	2	0	0	23	22	4	4	.500	25	2.91
89	TOR/AL		64	356	0	0	0	56	89.0	66	5	25	4	2	116	4	3	2	0	20	19	8	3	.727	20	1.92
90	TOR/AL		61	297	0	0	0	58	74.2	58	8	19	2	1	75	4	1	6	0	18	18	2	4	.333	32	2.17
91	TOR/AL		49	190	0	0	0	43	50.1	33	4	11	2	0	53	0	0	1	0	13	13	0	2	.000	32	2.32
10 YR TOTALS			**430**	**2287**	**0**	**0**	**0**	**360**	**567.1**	**437**	**44**	**176**	**24**	**8**	**649**	**21**	**23**	**19**	**3**	**181**	**169**	**29**	**28**	**.509**	**186**	**2.68**

Henneman, Michael Alan "Mike" — bats right — throws right — b.12/11/61

YR	TM/LG	CL	G	TBF	GS	CG	SHO	GF	IP	H	HR	BB	IBB	HB	SO	SH	SF	WP	BK	R	ER	W	L	PCT	SV	ERA
84	BIR/SOU	AA	29	258	1	0	0	16	59.1	48	1	33	2	2	39	2	1	3	0	22	16	4	2	.667	6	2.43
85	BIR/SOU	AA	46	327	0	0	0	38	70.1	88	6	28	4	7	40	2	2	3	0	50	45	3	5	.375	9	5.76
86	NAS/AMA	AAA	31	254	0	0	0	18	58.0	57	5	23	1	4	39	3	6	5	1	27	19	2	5	.286	1	2.95
87	TOL/INT	AAA	11	62	0	0	0	9	18.1	5	0	3	0	0	19	0	0	1	0	3	3	1	1	.500	4	1.47
	DET/AL		55	399	0	0	0	28	96.2	86	8	30	5	3	75	2	2	7	0	36	32	11	3	.786	7	2.98
88	DET/AL		65	364	0	0	0	51	91.1	72	7	24	10	2	58	5	2	8	1	23	19	9	6	.600	22	1.87
89	DET/AL		60	401	0	0	0	35	90.0	84	4	51	15	5	69	7	3	0	1	46	37	11	4	.733	8	3.70
90	DET/AL		69	399	0	0	0	53	94.1	90	4	33	12	3	50	5	2	3	0	36	32	8	6	.571	22	3.05
91	DET/AL		60	358	0	0	0	50	84.1	81	2	34	8	0	61	5	5	5	0	29	27	10	2	.833	21	2.88
5 YR TOTALS			**309**	**1921**	**0**	**0**	**0**	**217**	**456.2**	**413**	**25**	**172**	**50**	**13**	**313**	**24**	**14**	**23**	**2**	**170**	**147**	**49**	**21**	**.700**	**80**	**2.90**

Henry, Dwayne Allen — bats right — throws right — b.2/16/62

YR	TM/LG	CL	G	TBF	GS	CG	SHO	GF	IP	H	HR	BB	IBB	HB	SO	SH	SF	WP	BK	R	ER	W	L	PCT	SV	ERA
80	RAN/GCL	R	11	0	11	1	1	0	54.0	36	2	28	0	1	47	0	0	6	0	23	16	5	1	.833	0	2.67
81	ASH/SAL	A	25	0	25	1	1	0	134.0	120	21	58	0	4	86	0	0	8	0	81	66	8	7	.533	0	4.43
82	BUR/MID	A	4	0	4	0	0	0	18.0	6	0	6	0	1	25	0	0	0	0	0	0	2	0	1.000	0	0.00
83	TUL/TEX	AA	9	0	2	0	0	0	14.0	16	2	19	0	0	14	0	0	0	1	14	9	0	0	.000	0	5.79
	RAN/GCL	R	3	0	2	0	0	0	9.0	10	0	1	0	1	11	0	0	0	0	6	4	0	0	.000	1	4.00
84	TUL/TEX	AA	33	373	12	1	1	15	85.0	65	1	60	2	1	79	1	4	6	1	42	32	5	8	.385	8	3.39
	TEX/AL		3	25	0	0	0	1	4.1	5	0	7	0	1	2	1	0	0	0	4	4	0	1	.000	0	8.31
85	TUL/TEX	AA	34	339	11	0	0	19	81.1	51	1	44	1	1	97	3	2	8	1	32	24	7	6	.538	3	2.66
	TEX/AL		16	86	0	0	0	10	21.0	16	1	7	0	0	20	2	1	1	0	7	6	2	2	.500	3	2.57
86	OC/AMA	AAA	28	204	1	0	0	16	44.1	51	3	27	0	0	41	2	3	7	1	30	29	2	1	.667	5	5.89
	TEX/AL		19	93	0	0	0	4	19.1	14	1	22	1	0	17	1	2	7	1	11	10	1	0	1.000	0	4.66
87	OC/AMA	AAA	30	317	8	0	0	15	69.0	66	11	50	0	0	55	1	3	3	0	39	38	4	5	.500	3	4.96
	TEX/AL		5	50	0	0	0	1	10.0	12	2	9	0	0	7	0	0	0	1	10	10	0	0	.000	0	9.00
88	OC/AMA	AAA	46	336	3	0	0	24	75.2	57	3	54	0	0	98	3	6	11	1	51	47	5	5	.500	7	5.59
	TEX/AL		11	59	0	0	0	5	10.1	15	1	9	0	0	14	0	0	1	0	10	10	0	1	.000	1	8.71
89	RIC/INT	AAA	41	359	6	0	0	20	84.2	43	4	61	3	3	101	3	3	7	0	28	23	11	5	.688	1	2.44
	ATL/NL		12	55	0	0	0	6	12.2	12	2	5	1	0	16	2	0	1	0	6	6	0	2	.000	0	4.26
90	RIC/INT	AAA	13	109	0	0	0	6	27.0	12	1	16	1	0	36	2	0	0	0	7	7	1	2	.500	2	2.33
	ATL/NL		34	176	0	0	0	14	38.1	41	3	25	0	0	34	0	0	1	1	26	24	2	2	.500	0	5.63

Henry, Dwayne Allen (continued)

YR	TM/LG	CL	G	TBF	GS	CG	SHO	GF	IP	H	HR	BB	IBB	HB	SO	SH	SF	WP	BK	R	ER	W	L	PCT	SV	ERA
91	HOU/NL		52	282	0	0	0	25	67.2	51	7	39	7	2	51	6	2	5	0	25	24	3	2	.600	2	3.19
8 YR TOTALS			**152**	**826**	**0**	**0**	**0**	**66**	**183.2**	**166**	**16**	**123**	**9**	**6**	**157**	**12**	**7**	**20**	**3**	**99**	**94**	**8**	**10**	**.444**	**7**	**4.61**

Henry, Richard Douglas "Doug" — bats right — throws right — b.12/10/63

YR	TM/LG	CL	G	TBF	GS	CG	SHO	GF	IP	H	HR	BB	IBB	HB	SO	SH	SF	WP	BK	R	ER	W	L	PCT	SV	ERA
86	BEL/MID	A	27	639	24	4	1	1	143.1	153	16	56	4	6	115	3	5	9	4	95	74	7	8	.467	1	4.65
87	BEL/MID	A	31	593	15	1	0	5	132.2	145	6	51	5	5	106	2	4	7	0	83	72	8	9	.471	2	4.88
88	STO/CAL	A+	23	280	1	1	0	14	70.2	46	1	31	1	1	71	1	1	5	4	19	14	7	1	.875	7	1.78
	EP/TEX	AA	14	182	3	3	1	1	45.2	33	4	19	0	1	50	0	0	0	0	16	16	4	0	1.000	0	3.15
89	EP/TEX	AA	1	11	1	0	0	0	2.0	3	1	3	0	0	2	0	0	0	0	3	3	0	0	.000	0	13.50
	STO/CAL	A+	4	43	3	0	0	0	11.0	9	0	3	0	0	9	0	0	0	0	4	0	0	0	.000	0	0.00
90	STO/CAL	A+	4	35	0	0	0	3	8.0	4	0	3	0	2	13	0	1	1	0	1	1	1	0	1.000	1	1.13
	EP/TEX	AA	15	131	0	0	0	12	30.2	31	1	11	0	0	25	0	1	0	2	13	10	1	0	1.000	9	2.93
	DEN/AMA	AAA	27	219	0	0	0	15	50.2	46	4	27	2	0	54	3	1	3	0	26	25	2	3	.400	8	4.44
91	DEN/AMA	AAA	32	234	0	0	0	27	57.2	47	4	20	3	0	47	4	2	4	2	16	14	3	2	.600	14	2.18
	MIL/AL		32	137	0	0	0	25	36.0	16	1	14	1	0	28	1	2	0	0	4	4	1	0	.667	15	1.00

Hentgen, Patrick George "Pat" — bats right — throws right — b.11/13/68

YR	TM/LG	CL	G	TBF	GS	CG	SHO	GF	IP	H	HR	BB	IBB	HB	SO	SH	SF	WP	BK	R	ER	W	L	PCT	SV	ERA
86	ST./NYP	A–	13	191	11	0	0	2	40.0	38	3	30	1	2	30	2	1	3	0	27	20	0	4	.000	1	4.50
87	MB/SAL	A	32	753	31	2	2	0	188.0	145	5	60	1	8	131	4	2	14	3	62	49	11	5	.688	0	2.35
88	DUN/FSL	A+	31	651	30	0	0	1	151.1	139	10	65	1	4	125	4	4	14	4	80	58	3	12	.200	0	3.45
89	DUN/FSL	A+	29	633	28	0	0	0	151.1	123	5	71	1	2	148	6	7	16	4	53	45	9	8	.529	0	2.68
90	KNO/SOU	AA	28	633	26	0	0	0	153.1	121	10	68	0	3	142	3	5	8	2	57	52	9	5	.643	0	3.05
91	SYR/INT	AAA	31	729	28	1	0	2	171.0	146	17	90	1	2	155	5	6	11	2	91	85	8	9	.471	0	4.47
	TOR/AL		3	30	1	0	0	1	7.1	5	1	3	0	2	3	1	0	1	0	2	2	0	0	.000	0	2.45

Heredia, Gilbert "Gil" — bats right — throws right — b.10/26/65

YR	TM/LG	CL	G	TBF	GS	CG	SHO	GF	IP	H	HR	BB	IBB	HB	SO	SH	SF	WP	BK	R	ER	W	L	PCT	SV	ERA
87	EVE/NWL	A–	3	80	3	1	0	0	20.0	24	2	1	0	0	14	0	0	1	0	8	8	2	0	1.000	0	3.60
	FRE/CAL	A+	11	321	11	5	2	0	80.2	62	8	23	1	0	60	2	5	2	2	28	26	5	3	.625	0	2.90
88	SJ/CAL	A+	27	863	27	9	0	0	206.1	216	9	46	0	4	121	9	7	9	0	107	80	13	12	.520	0	3.49
89	SHR/TEX	AA	7	104	2	1	0	1	24.2	28	1	4	0	1	17	0	1	0	2	10	7	1	0	1.000	0	2.55
90	PHO/PCL	AAA	29	626	19	0	0	2	147.0	159	7	37	0	3	75	6	6	4	1	81	67	9	7	.563	1	4.10
91	PHO/PCL	AAA	33	592	15	5	1	7	140.1	155	7	28	5	2	75	9	2	4	0	60	44	9	11	.450	1	2.82
	SF/NL		7	126	4	0	0	1	33.0	27	4	7	2	0	13	2	1	0	0	14	14	0	2	.000	0	3.82

Hernandez, Francis Xavier "Xavier" — bats left — throws right — b.8/16/65

YR	TM/LG	CL	G	TBF	GS	CG	SHO	GF	IP	H	HR	BB	IBB	HB	SO	SH	SF	WP	BK	R	ER	W	L	PCT	SV	ERA
86	ST./NYP	A–	13	284	10	1	1	3	70.2	55	6	16	0	6	69	1	0	5	2	27	21	5	5	.500	0	2.67
87	ST./NYP	A–	13	242	11	0	0	0	55.0	57	4	16	0	4	49	1	1	2	0	39	31	3	3	.500	0	5.07
88	MB/SAL	A	23	585	22	2	2	1	148.0	116	5	28	1	7	111	1	3	10	4	52	42	13	6	.684	0	2.55
	KNO/SOU	AA	11	290	11	2	0	0	68.1	73	3	15	0	3	33	2	1	2	1	32	22	2	4	.333	0	2.90
89	KNO/SOU	AA	4	112	4	1	1	0	24.0	25	1	11	0	1	17	0	1	1	0	11	11	1	1	.500	0	4.13
	TOR/AL		7	101	0	0	0	2	22.2	25	2	8	0	1	7	0	2	0	0	15	12	1	0	1.000	0	4.76
	SYR/INT	AAA	15	411	15	2	1	0	99.1	95	7	22	0	2	47	4	4	4	2	42	39	5	6	.455	0	3.53
90	HOU/NL		34	268	1	0	0	10	62.1	60	8	24	5	4	24	2	4	6	0	34	32	2	1	.667	0	4.62
91	TUC/PCL	AAA	16	151	3	0	0	8	36.0	35	1	9	0	2	34	1	3	4	2	16	11	2	0	1.000	4	2.75
	HOU/NL		32	285	6	0	0	8	63.0	66	6	32	7	0	55	1	1	0	0	34	33	2	7	.222	3	4.71
3 YR TOTALS			**73**	**654**	**7**	**0**	**0**	**20**	**148.0**	**151**	**16**	**64**	**12**	**5**	**86**	**3**	**7**	**7**	**0**	**83**	**77**	**5**	**8**	**.385**	**3**	**4.68**

Hernandez, Jeremy Stuart — bats right — throws right — b.7/6/66

YR	TM/LG	CL	G	TBF	GS	CG	SHO	GF	IP	H	HR	BB	IBB	HB	SO	SH	SF	WP	BK	R	ER	W	L	PCT	SV	ERA
87	ERI/NYP	A–	16	412	16	1	0	0	99.1	87	7	41	3	2	62	2	3	7	1	36	31	5	4	.556	0	2.81
88	SPR/MID	A	24	615	24	3	1	0	147.1	133	8	34	2	7	97	0	3	4	8	73	58	12	6	.667	0	3.54
89	SP/FSL	A+	3	63	3	0	0	0	14.0	17	0	5	0	0	5	2	1	2	0	14	12	0	2	.000	0	7.71
	CHS/SAL	A	10	260	10	2	1	0	58.2	65	2	16	1	3	39	2	0	1	3	37	23	3	5	.375	0	3.53
	RIV/CAL	A+	9	264	9	4	1	0	67.0	55	2	11	0	4	65	0	1	1	4	17	13	5	2	.714	0	1.75
	WIC/TEX	AA	4	91	3	0	1	0	19.0	30	6	8	0	0	9	1	1	4	0	18	18	2	1	.667	0	8.53
90	WIC/TEX	AA	26	675	26	1	0	0	155.0	163	18	50	0	7	101	1	7	6	1	92	78	7	6	.538	0	4.53
91	LV/PCL	AAA	56	309	0	0	0	45	68.1	76	1	25	10	4	67	5	2	2	1	36	36	4	8	.333	13	4.74
	SD/NL		9	56	0	0	0	7	14.1	8	0	5	0	0	11	1	0	0	0	0	0	0	0	.000	2	0.00

Hernandez, Roberto Manuel — bats right — throws right — b.11/11/64

YR	TM/LG	CL	G	TBF	GS	CG	SHO	GF	IP	H	HR	BB	IBB	HB	SO	SH	SF	WP	BK	R	ER	W	L	PCT	SV	ERA
86	SAL/NWL	A–	10	0	10	0	0	0	55.0	57	3	42	1	1	38	0	0	6	0	37	28	2	2	.500	0	4.58
87	QC/MID	A	7	102	6	0	0	1	21.0	24	2	12	0	2	21	0	0	5	0	21	16	2	3	.400	1	6.86
88	QC/MID	A	24	699	24	6	1	0	164.2	157	8	48	0	6	114	6	4	7	5	70	58	9	10	.474	0	3.17
	MID/TEX	AA	3	59	3	0	0	0	12.1	16	0	8	0	1	7	0	0	1	0	13	9	0	2	.000	0	6.57
89	MID/TEX	AA	12	305	12	0	0	0	64.0	94	6	30	0	2	42	1	5	4	1	57	49	2	7	.222	0	6.89
	PS/CAL	A+	7	188	7	0	0	0	42.2	49	1	16	0	2	33	1	1	4	0	27	22	1	4	.200	0	4.64
	SB/MID	A	4	95	4	1	0	0	24.1	19	0	7	0	0	17	2	0	0	0	9	9	1	1	.500	0	3.33
90	BIR/SOU	AA	17	469	17	3	1	0	108.0	103	6	43	2	6	62	5	5	3	1	57	44	8	5	.615	0	3.67
	VAN/PCL	AAA	11	329	11	3	1	0	79.1	73	4	26	0	2	49	3	3	3	0	33	25	3	5	.375	0	2.84

(continued)

Hernandez, Roberto Manuel (continued)

YR	TM/LG	CL	G	TBF	GS	CG	SHO	GF	IP	H	HR	BB	IBB	HB	SO	SH	SF	WP	BK	R	ER	W	L	PCT	SV	ERA
91	VAN/PCL	AAA	7	195	7	0	0	0	44.2	41	2	23	0	0	40	1	1	1	0	17	16	4	1	.800	0	3.22
	WS/GCL	R	1	18	1	0	0	0	6.0	2	0	0	0	0	7	0	0	0	0	0	0	0	0	.000	0	0.00
	BIR/SOU	AA	4	85	4	0	0	0	22.2	11	2	6	0	2	25	0	1	2	0	5	5	2	1	.667	0	1.99
	CHI/AL		9	69	3	0	0	1	15.0	18	0	7	0	0	6	0	0	1	0	15	13	1	0	1.000	0	7.80

Hershiser, Orel Leonard — bats right — throws right — b.9/16/58

YR	TM/LG	CL	G	TBF	GS	CG	SHO	GF	IP	H	HR	BB	IBB	HB	SO	SH	SF	WP	BK	R	ER	W	L	PCT	SV	ERA
83	LA/NL		8	37	0	0	0	4	8.0	7	1	6	0	0	5	1	0	1	0	6	3	0	0	.000	1	3.38
84	LA/NL		45	771	20	8	4	10	189.2	160	9	50	8	4	150	2	3	8	1	65	56	11	8	.579	2	2.66
85	LA/NL		36	953	34	9	5	1	239.2	179	8	68	5	6	157	5	4	5	0	72	54	19	3	.864	0	2.03
86	LA/NL		35	988	35	8	1	0	231.1	213	13	86	11	5	153	14	6	12	3	112	99	14	14	.500	0	3.85
87	LA/NL		37	1093	35	10	1	2	264.2	247	17	74	5	9	190	8	2	11	2	105	90	16	16	.500	1	3.06
88	LA/NL		35	1068	34	15	8	1	267.0	208	18	73	10	4	178	9	6	6	5	73	67	23	8	.742	1	2.26
89	LA/NL		35	1047	33	8	4	0	256.2	226	9	77	14	3	178	19	6	8	4	75	66	15	15	.500	0	2.31
90	LA/NL		4	106	4	0	0	0	25.1	26	1	4	0	1	16	1	0	0	1	12	12	1	1	.500	0	4.26
91	ALB/PCL	AAA	1	19	1	0	0	0	5.0	5	0	0	0	0	5	0	0	1	0	0	0	0	0	.000	0	0.00
	BAK/CAL	A+	2	40	2	0	0	0	11.0	5	0	1	0	0	6	1	0	0	0	2	1	2	0	1.000	0	0.82
	SA/TEX	AA	1	31	1	0	0	0	7.0	11	1	1	0	0	5	0	0	0	1	3	2	0	1	.000	0	2.57
	LA/NL		21	473	21	0	0	0	112.0	112	3	32	6	5	73	2	1	2	4	43	43	7	2	.778	0	3.46
9 YR TOTALS			**256**	**6536**	**216**	**58**	**23**	**18**	**1594.1**	**1378**	**79**	**470**	**59**	**37**	**1100**	**61**	**28**	**53**	**20**	**563**	**490**	**106**	**67**	**.613**	**5**	**2.77**

Hesketh, Joseph Thomas "Joe" — bats right — throws left — b.2/15/59

YR	TM/LG	CL	G	TBF	GS	CG	SHO	GF	IP	H	HR	BB	IBB	HB	SO	SH	SF	WP	BK	R	ER	W	L	PCT	SV	ERA
84	IND/AMA	AAA	22	595	22	5	1	0	147.2	120	8	54	2	3	135	6	6	10	3	60	50	12	3	.800	0	3.05
	MON/NL		11	182	5	1	1	2	45.0	38	2	15	3	0	32	2	2	1	3	12	9	2	2	.500	1	1.80
85	MON/NL		25	618	25	2	1	0	155.1	125	10	45	2	0	113	8	2	3	3	52	43	10	5	.667	0	2.49
86	MON/NL		15	362	15	0	0	0	82.2	92	11	31	4	2	67	2	4	4	3	46	46	6	5	.545	0	5.01
87	EXP/GCL	R	2	20	1	0	0	0	4.1	7	0	0	0	0	8	0	0	1	0	4	4	0	0	.000	0	8.31
	JAC/SOU	AA	6	78	3	0	0	1	19.2	18	1	4	1	0	22	0	0	1	0	6	5	1	0	1.000	1	2.29
	MON/NL		18	128	0	0	0	3	28.2	23	2	15	3	2	31	2	0	1	0	12	10	0	0	.000	1	3.14
88	IND/AMA	AAA	8	47	0	0	0	3	11.0	10	1	5	0	0	16	0	0	0	0	5	4	0	0	.000	2	3.27
	MON/NL		60	304	0	0	0	23	72.2	63	1	35	9	0	64	5	4	5	1	30	23	4	3	.571	9	2.85
89	IND/AMA	AAA	5	40	1	0	0	3	9.1	11	0	5	0	0	9	0	1	1	0	4	4	0	0	.000	1	3.86
	MON/NL		43	219	0	0	0	17	48.1	54	5	26	6	0	44	6	2	1	3	34	31	6	4	.600	3	5.77
90	MON/NL		2	12	0	0	0	0	3.0	3	0	2	1	0	3	0	0	0	0	0	0	1	0	1.000	0	0.00
	ATL/NL		31	135	0	0	0	15	31.0	30	5	12	0	1	21	0	1	5	0	23	20	0	2	.000	5	5.81
	BOS/AL		12	122	2	0	0	4	25.2	37	2	11	1	0	26	0	0	3	0	12	10	0	4	.000	0	3.51
	YEAR		45	269	2	0	0	19	59.2	69	7	25	1	1	50	0	1	8	0	35	30	1	6	.143	5	4.53
91	BOS/AL		39	631	17	0	0	5	153.1	142	19	53	3	0	104	7	3	8	0	59	56	12	4	.750	0	3.29
8 YR TOTALS			**256**	**2713**	**64**	**3**	**2**	**69**	**645.2**	**606**	**57**	**245**	**32**	**5**	**505**	**32**	**16**	**31**	**13**	**280**	**248**	**41**	**29**	**.586**	**19**	**3.46**

Hibbard, James Gregory "Greg" — bats left — throws left — b.9/13/64

YR	TM/LG	CL	G	TBF	GS	CG	SHO	GF	IP	H	HR	BB	IBB	HB	SO	SH	SF	WP	BK	R	ER	W	L	PCT	SV	ERA
86	EUG/NWL	A—	26	0	1	0	0	15	39.0	30	2	19	0	2	44	0	0	0	0	23	15	5	2	.714	5	3.46
87	APP/MID	A	9	265	9	2	1	0	64.2	53	3	18	3	2	61	1	0	2	0	17	8	7	2	.778	0	1.11
	FM/FSL	A+	3	92	3	3	1	0	24.0	20	0	3	0	1	20	2	0	0	0	5	5	2	1	.667	0	1.88
	MEM/SOU	AA	16	431	16	3	1	0	106.0	102	7	21	1	2	56	3	3	1	0	48	38	7	6	.538	0	3.23
88	VAN/PCL	AAA	25	617	24	4	1	0	144.1	155	7	44	4	4	65	7	5	6	2	74	66	11	11	.500	0	4.12
89	VAN/PCL	AAA	9	231	9	2	1	0	58.0	47	3	11	0	1	45	1	3	5	0	24	17	2	3	.400	0	2.64
	CHI/AL		23	581	23	2	0	0	137.1	142	5	41	0	0	55	5	4	4	0	58	49	6	7	.462	0	3.21
90	CHI/AL		33	871	33	3	1	0	211.0	202	11	55	2	6	92	8	10	2	1	80	74	14	9	.609	0	3.16
91	VAN/PCL	AAA	1	24	1	0	0	0	5.1	4	0	3	0	0	3	0	0	0	0	3	2	0	0	.000	0	3.38
	CHI/AL		32	806	29	5	0	1	194.0	196	23	57	1	2	71	8	2	1	0	107	93	11	11	.500	0	4.31
3 YR TOTALS			**88**	**2258**	**85**	**10**	**1**	**1**	**542.1**	**540**	**39**	**153**	**3**	**10**	**218**	**21**	**16**	**7**	**1**	**245**	**216**	**31**	**27**	**.534**	**0**	**3.58**

Hickerson, Bryan David — bats left — throws left — b.10/13/63

YR	TM/LG	CL	G	TBF	GS	CG	SHO	GF	IP	H	HR	BB	IBB	HB	SO	SH	SF	WP	BK	R	ER	W	L	PCT	SV	ERA
86	VIS/CAL	A+	11	302	11	3	0	0	72.1	72	3	25	1	1	69	9	3	5	0	37	34	4	3	.571	0	4.23
87	CLI/MID	A	17	371	10	2	1	3	94.0	60	1	37	0	1	103	3	1	5	0	17	13	11	0	1.000	1	1.24
	SHR/TEX	AA	4	70	3	0	0	0	16.0	20	0	4	0	0	23	1	1	1	0	7	7	1	2	.333	0	3.94
89	SJ/CAL	A+	21	561	21	1	1	0	134.0	111	1	57	0	1	110	6	5	3	2	52	38	11	6	.647	0	2.55
90	SHR/TEX	AA	27	294	6	0	0	7	66.0	71	2	26	2	1	63	4	2	2	2	37	31	3	6	.333	1	4.23
	PHO/PCL	AAA	12	162	4	0	0	3	34.1	48	3	16	2	0	26	2	2	0	1	25	21	0	0	.000	0	5.50
91	SHR/TEX	AA	23	165	0	0	0	6	39.0	36	1	14	1	0	41	6	0	1	0	15	13	3	4	.429	2	3.00
	PHO/PCL	AAA	12	97	0	0	0	7	21.1	29	1	5	1	0	21	1	1	1	0	10	9	1	1	.500	0	3.80
	SF/NL		17	212	6	0	0	4	50.0	53	3	17	3	0	43	2	0	2	0	20	20	2	2	.500	0	3.60

Hickey, Kevin John — bats left — throws left — b.2/25/57

YR	TM/LG	CL	G	TBF	GS	CG	SHO	GF	IP	H	HR	BB	IBB	HB	SO	SH	SF	WP	BK	R	ER	W	L	PCT	SV	ERA
81	CHI/AL		41	188	0	0	0	14	44.1	38	3	18	5	1	17	3	2	1	0	22	18	0	2	.000	3	3.65
82	CHI/AL		60	327	0	0	0	20	78.0	73	4	30	6	2	38	6	4	0	0	32	26	4	4	.500	0	3.00
83	CHI/AL		23	98	0	0	0	13	20.2	23	5	11	0	0	8	0	0	1	0	14	12	1	2	.333	5	5.23
84	GF/EAS	AA	3	10	0	0	0	1	1.2	5	1	0	0	0	1	0	0	0	0	1	1	0	2	.000	0	5.40
	APP/MID	A	10	200	8	1	0	2	49.2	45	5	11	0	0	40	0	2	1	0	18	13	4	3	.571	1	2.36

Hickey, Kevin John (continued)

YR	TM/LG	CL	G	TBF	GS	CG	SHO	GF	IP	H	HR	BB	IBB	HB	SO	SH	SF	WP	BK	R	ER	W	L	PCT	SV	ERA
	DEN/AMA	AAA	16	222	7	0	0	2	47.1	61	6	23	2	0	20	3	2	2	0	39	33	2	2	.500	1	6.27
	COL/INT	AAA	5	46	1	0	0	0	9.1	14	1	8	0	0	3	0	0	1	0	10	9	1	1	.500	0	8.68
85	ALB/EAS	AA	11	55	0	0	0	4	12.1	11	0	7	2	1	11	1	1	0	0	5	4	1	0	1.000	1	2.92
	REA/EAS	AA	33	199	0	0	0	27	48.0	42	3	15	1	2	33	4	3	1	0	17	14	4	5	.444	10	2.63
86	POR/PCL	AAA	33	298	5	0	0	11	65.0	76	7	29	0	0	44	0	4	2	0	54	47	1	3	.250	2	6.51
87	HAW/PCL	AAA	43	328	4	0	0	18	73.2	83	8	31	4	1	44	1	4	2	1	50	44	4	5	.444	8	5.38
	PHO/PCL	AAA	3	35	0	0	0	0	9.0	5	0	5	0	0	4	0	1	0	0	2	2	0	0	.000	0	2.00
88	CHA/SOU	AA	6	45	1	0	0	2	9.2	10	1	8	0	0	7	1	1	0	0	4	4	1	1	.500	0	3.72
	ROC/INT	AAA	27	149	0	0	0	11	37.0	31	1	9	2	1	24	3	0	0	3	7	6	2	0	1.000	2	1.46
89	BAL/AL		51	199	0	0	0	17	49.1	38	3	23	4	1	28	2	0	1	0	16	16	2	3	.400	2	2.92
90	ROC/INT	AAA	16	104	0	0	0	8	23.1	31	2	7	1	0	28	1	1	0	0	15	15	2	1	.667	3	5.79
	BAL/AL		37	113	0	0	0	9	26.1	26	3	13	2	0	17	1	1	1	0	16	15	1	3	.250	1	5.13
91	HAG/EAS	AA	15	78	0	0	0	11	19.2	15	1	6	0	0	20	0	0	0	0	6	4	0	1	.000	3	1.83
	BAL/AL		19	62	0	0	0	6	14.0	15	3	6	0	0	10	0	0	2	0	14	14	1	0	1.000	0	9.00
	PHO/PCL	AAA	5	36	0	0	0	1	5.2	18	3	1	0	0	5	0	0	2	1	13	13	0	0	.000	0	20.65
6 YR TOTALS			**231**	**987**	**0**	**0**	**0**	**79**	**232.2**	**213**	**21**	**101**	**19**	**4**	**118**	**12**	**9**	**6**	**2**	**114**	**101**	**9**	**14**	**.391**	**17**	**3.91**

Higuera, Teodoro Valenzuela (Valenzuela) "Teddy" — bats both — throws left — b.11/9/58

YR	TM/LG	CL	G	TBF	GS	CG	SHO	GF	IP	H	HR	BB	IBB	HB	SO	SH	SF	WP	BK	R	ER	W	L	PCT	SV	ERA
84	EP/TEX	AA	19	530	19	4	0	2	121.0	116	11	43	0	1	99	4	1	5	2	57	35	8	7	.533	0	2.60
	VAN/PCL	AAA	8	0	6	0	0	2	40.0	49	3	14	0	0	29	0	0	0	2	26	21	1	4	.200	0	4.72
85	MIL/AL		32	874	30	7	2	2	212.1	186	22	63	0	3	127	5	10	4	3	105	92	15	8	.652	0	3.90
86	MIL/AL		34	1031	34	15	4	0	248.1	226	26	74	5	3	207	7	11	3	0	84	77	20	11	.645	0	2.79
87	MIL/AL		35	1084	35	14	3	0	261.2	236	24	87	2	2	240	6	9	4	2	120	112	18	10	.643	0	3.85
88	MIL/AL		31	895	31	8	1	0	227.1	168	15	59	4	6	192	10	7	0	6	66	62	16	9	.640	0	2.45
89	EP/TEX	AA	1	21	1	0	0	0	5.0	5	0	1	0	0	4	0	0	0	0	2	1	0	1	.000	0	1.80
	MIL/AL		22	567	22	2	1	0	135.1	125	9	48	2	4	91	6	5	0	1	56	52	9	6	.600	0	3.46
90	MIL/AL		27	720	27	4	1	0	170.0	167	16	50	2	3	129	10	4	2	1	80	71	11	10	.524	0	3.76
91	DEN/AMA	AAA	2	38	2	0	0	0	8.2	6	1	6	0	0	6	0	0	0	0	3	2	1	0	1.000	0	2.08
	MIL/AL		7	153	6	0	0	1	36.1	37	2	10	0	1	33	0	1	0	0	18	18	3	2	.600	0	4.46
7 YR TOTALS			**188**	**5324**	**185**	**50**	**12**	**3**	**1291.1**	**1145**	**114**	**391**	**15**	**22**	**1019**	**44**	**47**	**13**	**13**	**529**	**484**	**92**	**56**	**.622**	**0**	**3.37**

Hill, Kenneth Wade "Ken" — bats right — throws right — b.12/14/65

YR	TM/LG	CL	G	TBF	GS	CG	SHO	GF	IP	H	HR	BB	IBB	HB	SO	SH	SF	WP	BK	R	ER	W	L	PCT	SV	ERA
85	GAS/SAL	A	15	318	12	0	0	0	69.0	60	5	57	1	1	48	2	2	15	0	51	38	3	6	.333	0	4.96
86	GAS/SAL	A	22	524	16	1	0	4	122.2	95	4	80	0	5	86	2	5	14	1	51	38	9	5	.643	0	2.79
	GF/EAS	AA	1	31	1	0	0	0	7.0	4	1	6	0	0	4	0	0	3	0	4	4	0	1	.000	0	5.14
	ARK/TEX	AA	3	75	3	0	0	0	18.0	18	0	7	0	0	9	1	0	3	1	10	9	1	2	.333	0	4.50
87	ARK/TEX	AA	18	244	8	0	0	5	53.2	60	1	30	3	0	48	0	1	8	0	33	31	3	5	.375	2	5.20
	SP/FSL	A+	18	172	4	0	0	10	41.0	38	2	17	1	1	33	2	2	1	0	19	19	1	3	.250	2	4.17
88	ARK/TEX	AA	22	511	22	3	1	0	115.1	129	7	50	1	1	107	2	3	8	5	76	63	9	9	.500	0	4.92
	STL/NL		4	62	1	0	0	0	14.0	16	0	6	0	0	6	0	0	1	0	9	8	0	1	.000	0	5.14
89	LOU/AMA	AAA	3	79	3	0	0	0	18.0	13	1	10	0	0	18	0	0	1	0	8	7	0	2	.000	0	3.50
	STL/NL		33	862	33	2	1	0	196.2	186	9	99	6	5	112	14	5	11	2	92	83	7	15	.318	0	3.80
90	LOU/AMA	AAA	12	326	12	2	1	0	85.1	47	6	27	1	1	104	4	1	2	0	20	17	6	1	.857	0	1.79
	STL/NL		17	343	14	1	0	1	78.2	79	7	33	1	0	58	5	5	5	0	49	48	5	6	.455	0	5.49
91	LOU/AMA	AAA	1	3	1	0	0	0	1.0	0	0	0	0	0	2	0	0	0	0	0	0	0	0	.000	0	0.00
	STL/NL		30	743	30	0	0	1	181.1	147	15	67	4	6	121	7	7	7	1	76	72	11	10	.524	0	3.57
4 YR TOTALS			**84**	**2010**	**78**	**3**	**1**	**1**	**470.2**	**428**	**31**	**205**	**11**	**12**	**297**	**26**	**17**	**24**	**3**	**226**	**211**	**23**	**32**	**.418**	**0**	**4.03**

Hill, Milton Giles "Milt" — bats right — throws right — b.8/22/65

YR	TM/LG	CL	G	TBF	GS	CG	SHO	GF	IP	H	HR	BB	IBB	HB	SO	SH	SF	WP	BK	R	ER	W	L	PCT	SV	ERA
87	BIL/PIO	R+	21	125	0	0	0	19	32.2	25	1	4	2	0	40	1	0	5	0	10	6	3	1	.750	7	1.65
88	CR/MID	A	44	300	0	0	0	38	78.1	52	3	17	7	1	69	3	1	4	8	21	18	9	4	.692	13	2.07
89	CHT/SOU	AA	51	281	0	0	0	42	70.0	49	4	28	6	0	63	1	5	1	4	19	16	6	5	.545	13	2.06
90	NAS/AMA	AAA	48	276	0	0	0	11	71.1	51	4	18	1	0	58	1	5	4	2	20	18	4	4	.500	3	2.27
91	NAS/AMA	AAA	37	269	0	0	0	16	67.1	59	3	15	1	0	62	3	3	3	1	26	22	3	3	.500	0	2.94
	CIN/NL		22	137	0	0	0	8	33.1	36	1	8	0	2	20	4	3	1	0	14	14	1	1	.500	0	3.78

Hillegas, Shawn Patrick — bats right — throws right — b.8/21/64

YR	TM/LG	CL	G	TBF	GS	CG	SHO	GF	IP	H	HR	BB	IBB	HB	SO	SH	SF	WP	BK	R	ER	W	L	PCT	SV	ERA
84	VB/FSL	A+	13	379	13	4	2	0	93.1	71	1	33	3	3	64	3	1	1	1	25	19	5	3	.625	0	1.83
85	SA/TEX	AA	23	606	23	3	0	0	139.1	134	6	67	1	3	56	9	5	5	3	72	49	4	10	.286	0	3.17
86	SA/TEX	AA	17	549	17	7	1	0	132.1	107	7	58	1	2	97	1	2	7	0	60	45	9	5	.643	0	3.06
	ALB/PCL	AAA	9	216	9	1	0	0	46.2	48	1	31	2	2	43	0	3	4	0	35	32	1	5	.167	0	6.17
87	ALB/PCL	AAA	24	709	24	4	1	0	165.2	172	4	64	1	0	105	6	6	7	1	79	62	13	5	.722	0	3.37
	LA/NL		12	252	10	0	0	0	58.0	52	5	31	0	0	51	4	1	4	0	27	23	4	3	.571	0	3.57
88	LA/NL		11	239	10	0	0	0	56.2	54	5	17	1	3	30	1	2	3	0	26	26	3	4	.429	0	4.13
	ALB/PCL	AAA	16	411	15	2	2	0	100.2	93	8	22	0	1	66	2	2	3	0	44	39	6	4	.600	0	3.49
	CHI/AL		6	166	6	0	0	0	40.0	30	4	18	0	1	26	0	0	0	0	16	14	3	2	.600	0	3.15
	YEAR		17	405	16	0	0	0	96.2	84	9	35	1	4	56	1	2	3	0	42	40	6	6	.500	0	3.72
89	CHI/AL		50	533	13	0	0	12	119.2	132	12	51	4	3	76	4	2	4	1	67	63	7	11	.389	3	4.74
90	VAN/PCL	AAA	36	261	0	0	0	23	67.1	49	4	15	0	1	52	4	3	2	1	22	13	5	3	.625	9	1.74
	CHI/AL		7	43	0	0	0	3	11.1	4	0	5	1	0	5	1	1	2	0	1	1	0	0	.000	0	0.79

(continued)

Hillegas, Shawn Patrick (continued)

YR	TM/LG	CL	G	TBF	GS	CG	SHO	GF	IP	H	HR	BB	IBB	HB	SO	SH	SF	WP	BK	R	ER	W	L	PCT	SV	ERA
91	CLE/AL		51	359	3	0	0	31	83.0	67	7	46	7	2	66	4	7	5	0	42	40	3	4	.429	7	4.34
5 YR TOTALS			**137**	**1592**	**42**	**0**	**0**	**47**	**368.2**	**339**	**33**	**168**	**13**	**9**	**254**	**14**	**15**	**18**	**1**	**179**	**167**	**20**	**24**	**.455**	**10**	**4.08**

Holman, Brian Scott — bats right — throws right — b.1/25/65

YR	TM/LG	CL	G	TBF	GS	CG	SHO	GF	IP	H	HR	BB	IBB	HB	SO	SH	SF	WP	BK	R	ER	W	L	PCT	SV	ERA
84	WPB/FSL	A+	4	62	4	0	0	0	8.0	14	0	21	0	0	14	0	1	2	1	19	16	0	3	.000	0	18.00
	GAS/SAL	A	20	443	20	1	0	0	90.2	76	5	98	0	1	94	1	5	14	1	58	48	5	8	.385	0	4.76
85	WPB/FSL	A+	25	633	24	6	2	0	143.1	124	6	90	1	2	103	6	3	10	1	79	63	9	9	.500	0	3.96
86	JAC/SOU	AA	27	736	27	3	0	0	157.2	146	16	122	1	0	118	8	7	10	2	111	90	11	9	.550	0	5.14
87	IND/AMA	AAA	6	161	6	0	0	0	34.2	41	5	23	2	1	27	0	2	2	2	28	24	0	4	.000	0	6.23
	JAC/SOU	AA	22	613	22	6	1	0	151.1	114	8	56	0	7	115	2	2	8	2	52	42	14	5	.737	0	2.50
88	IND/AMA	AAA	14	372	13	2	1	1	91.1	78	6	30	0	0	70	1	3	9	2	26	24	8	1	.889	0	2.36
	MON/NL		18	422	16	1	1	1	100.1	101	3	34	2	0	58	4	1	2	0	39	36	4	8	.333	0	3.23
89	MON/NL		10	145	3	0	0	0	31.2	34	2	15	0	1	23	2	1	3	1	18	17	1	2	.333	0	4.83
	SEA/AL		23	688	22	6	2	1	159.2	160	9	62	6	6	82	4	3	5	0	68	61	8	10	.444	0	3.44
	YEAR		33	833	25	6	2	1	191.1	194	11	77	6	7	105	6	4	8	1	86	78	9	12	.429	0	3.67
90	SEA/AL		28	804	28	3	0	0	189.2	188	17	66	4	6	121	4	3	8	2	92	85	11	11	.500	0	4.03
91	SEA/AL		30	839	30	5	3	0	195.1	199	16	77	0	10	108	6	3	8	1	86	80	13	14	.481	0	3.69
4 YR TOTALS			**109**	**2898**	**99**	**15**	**6**	**2**	**676.2**	**682**	**47**	**254**	**10**	**23**	**392**	**17**	**15**	**26**	**4**	**303**	**279**	**37**	**45**	**.451**	**0**	**3.71**

Holmes, Darren Lee — bats right — throws right — b.4/25/66

YR	TM/LG	CL	G	TBF	GS	CG	SHO	GF	IP	H	HR	BB	IBB	HB	SO	SH	SF	WP	BK	R	ER	W	L	PCT	SV	ERA
84	GF/PIO	R+	18	0	6	1	0	4	44.2	53	5	30	1	2	29	0	0	3	3	41	33	2	5	.286	0	6.65
85	VB/FSL	A+	33	277	0	0	0	20	63.2	57	0	35	2	0	46	4	5	6	1	31	22	4	3	.571	2	3.11
86	VB/FSL	A+	11	288	10	0	0	1	64.2	55	0	39	2	3	59	3	0	5	0	30	21	3	6	.333	0	2.92
87	VB/FSL	A+	19	455	19	1	1	0	99.2	111	4	53	0	1	46	4	6	5	1	60	50	6	4	.600	0	4.52
88	ALB/PCL	AAA	2	22	0	0	0	0	5.1	6	0	1	0	0	1	0	0	0	0	3	3	0	1	.000	0	5.06
89	SA/TEX	AA	17	471	16	3	2	1	110.1	102	5	44	2	3	81	2	4	8	6	59	47	5	8	.385	1	3.83
	ALB/PCL	AAA	9	177	8	0	0	1	38.2	50	8	18	1	0	31	0	2	2	0	32	32	1	4	.200	0	7.45
90	ALB/PCL	AAA	56	389	0	0	0	30	92.2	78	3	39	2	4	99	0	4	5	2	34	32	12	2	.857	13	3.11
	LA/NL		14	77	0	0	0	1	17.1	15	1	11	3	0	19	1	2	0	0	10	10	0	1	.000	0	5.19
91	DEN/AMA	AAA	1	6	0	0	0	1	1.0	1	0	2	0	0	2	0	0	0	0	1	1	0	0	.000	0	9.00
	BEL/MID	A	2	6	0	0	0	2	2.0	0	0	0	0	0	3	0	0	0	0	0	0	0	0	.000	2	0.00
	MIL/AL		40	344	0	0	0	9	76.1	90	6	27	1	1	59	8	3	6	0	43	40	1	4	.200	3	4.72
2 YR TOTALS			**54**	**421**	**0**	**0**	**0**	**10**	**93.2**	**105**	**7**	**38**	**4**	**1**	**78**	**9**	**5**	**7**	**0**	**53**	**50**	**1**	**5**	**.167**	**3**	**4.80**

Honeycutt, Frederick Wayne "Rick" — bats left — throws left — b.6/29/52

YR	TM/LG	CL	G	TBF	GS	CG	SHO	GF	IP	H	HR	BB	IBB	HB	SO	SH	SF	WP	BK	R	ER	W	L	PCT	SV	ERA
77	SEA/AL		10	125	3	0	0	3	29.0	26	7	11	2	3	17	0	2	2	1	16	14	0	1	.000	0	4.34
78	SEA/AL		26	594	24	4	1	0	134.1	150	12	49	5	3	50	9	7	3	0	81	73	5	11	.313	0	4.89
79	SEA/AL		33	839	28	8	1	2	194.0	201	22	67	7	6	83	11	6	5	1	103	87	11	12	.478	0	4.04
80	SEA/AL		30	871	30	9	1	0	203.1	221	22	60	7	3	79	11	7	4	0	99	89	10	17	.370	0	3.94
81	TEX/AL		20	509	20	8	2	0	127.2	120	12	17	1	0	40	5	0	1	0	49	47	11	6	.647	0	3.31
82	TEX/AL		30	728	26	4	1	3	164.0	201	20	54	4	3	64	4	8	3	1	103	96	5	17	.227	0	5.27
83	TEX/AL		25	693	25	5	2	0	174.2	168	9	37	2	6	56	3	6	1	2	59	47	14	8	.636	0	2.42
	LA/NL		9	172	7	1	0	0	39.0	46	6	13	4	2	18	2	0	0	1	26	25	2	3	.400	0	5.77
	YEAR		34	865	32	6	2	0	213.2	214	15	50	6	8	74	5	6	1	3	85	72	16	11	.593	0	3.03
84	LA/NL		29	762	28	6	2	0	183.2	180	11	51	11	2	75	6	5	1	2	72	58	10	9	.526	0	2.84
85	LA/NL		31	600	25	1	0	2	142.0	141	9	49	7	1	67	5	4	2	0	71	54	8	12	.400	0	3.42
86	LA/NL		32	713	28	0	0	2	171.0	164	9	45	4	3	100	6	1	4	1	71	63	11	9	.550	0	3.32
87	LA/NL		27	525	20	1	1	0	115.2	133	10	45	4	3	92	6	4	2	1	74	59	2	12	.143	0	4.59
	OAK/AL		7	106	4	0	0	1	23.2	25	3	9	0	1	10	1	3	1	1	17	14	1	4	.200	0	5.32
	YEAR		34	631	24	1	1	1	139.1	158	13	54	4	4	102	6	1	3	5	91	73	3	16	.158	0	4.72
88	OAK/AL		55	330	0	0	0	17	79.2	74	6	25	2	3	47	3	6	3	8	36	31	3	2	.600	7	3.50
89	OAK/AL		64	305	0	0	0	24	76.2	56	5	26	3	1	52	5	2	6	1	26	20	2	2	.500	12	2.35
90	OAK/AL		63	256	0	0	0	13	63.1	46	2	22	2	1	38	2	6	1	1	23	19	2	2	.500	7	2.70
91	MOD/CAL	A+	3	17	3	0	0	0	5.0	4	0	1	0	0	5	0	0	1	0	1	0	0	0	.000	0	0.00
	MAD/MID	A	1	7	1	0	0	0	1.0	4	0	0	0	0	2	0	0	1	0	2	2	0	1	.000	0	18.00
	OAK/AL		43	167	0	0	0	7	37.2	37	3	20	3	2	26	2	1	0	0	16	15	2	4	.333	0	3.58
15 YR TOTALS			**534**	**8295**	**268**	**47**	**11**	**74**	**1959.1**	**1989**	**168**	**600**	**68**	**43**	**914**	**75**	**64**	**41**	**20**	**942**	**811**	**99**	**131**	**.430**	**27**	**3.73**

Horsman, Vincent Stanley Joseph "Vince" — bats right — throws left — b.3/9/67

YR	TM/LG	CL	G	TBF	GS	CG	SHO	GF	IP	H	HR	BB	IBB	HB	SO	SH	SF	WP	BK	R	ER	W	L	PCT	SV	ERA
85	MH/PIO	R+	18	0	1	0	0	2	40.1	56	1	23	3	0	30	0	0	1	0	31	28	0	3	.000	1	6.25
86	FLO/SAL	A	29	419	9	1	1	10	90.2	93	8	49	0	1	64	1	6	5	4	56	41	4	3	.571	1	4.07
87	MB/SAL	A	30	621	28	0	0	1	149.0	144	20	37	2	2	109	6	5	5	4	74	55	7	7	.500	0	3.32
88	KNO/SOU	AA	20	260	6	1	0	6	58.1	57	5	28	3	3	40	4	4	4	1	34	30	3	2	.600	0	4.63
	DUN/FSL	A+	14	159	2	0	0	3	39.2	28	1	13	2	1	34	1	1	4	1	7	6	3	1	.750	1	1.36
89	DUN/FSL	A+	35	330	1	0	0	23	79.0	72	3	27	3	1	60	1	1	3	4	24	22	5	6	.455	8	2.51
	KNO/SOU	AA	4	19	0	0	0	1	5.0	3	0	2	1	0	4	0	0	0	0	1	1	0	0	.000	1	1.80
90	DUN/FSL	A+	28	209	0	0	0	14	50.0	53	0	15	2	1	41	2	2	2	0	21	18	4	7	.364	1	3.24
	KNO/SOU	AA	8	51	0	0	0	2	11.2	11	1	5	0	0	10	1	0	1	1	7	6	1	2	.667	1	4.63
91	KNO/SOU	AA	42	335	2	0	0	17	80.2	80	2	19	5	0	80	3	1	3	1	23	21	4	1	.800	3	2.34
	TOR/AL		4	16	0	0	0	2	4.0	2	0	3	1	0	2	1	0	0	0	0	0	0	0	.000	0	0.00

Hough, Charles Oliver "Charlie" — bats right — throws right — b.1/5/48

YR	TM/LG	CL	G	TBF	GS	CG	SHO	GF	IP	H	HR	BB	IBB	HB	SO	SH	SF	WP	BK	R	ER	W	L	PCT	SV	ERA
70	LA/NL		8	79	0	0	0	5	17.0	18	7	11	0	0	8	0	0	0	0	11	10	0	0	.000	2	5.29
71	LA/NL		4	19	0	0	0	3	4.1	3	1	3	0	0	4	1	0	0	0	3	2	0	0	.000	0	4.15
72	LA/NL		2	13	0	0	0	2	2.2	2	0	2	0	1	4	0	0	0	0	1	1	0	0	.000	0	3.38
73	LA/NL		37	309	0	0	0	18	71.2	52	3	45	2	6	70	4	3	2	0	24	22	4	2	.667	5	2.76
74	LA/NL		49	389	0	0	0.	16	96.0	65	12	40	2	4	63	6	8	4	0	45	40	9	4	.692	3	3.75
75	LA/NL		38	266	0	0	0	24	61.0	43	3	34	0	8	34	3	0	4	1	25	20	3	7	.300	4	2.95
76	LA/NL		77	600	0	0	0	55	142.2	102	6	77	3	8	81	4	1	9	0	43	35	12	8	.600	18	2.21
77	LA/NL		70	551	1	0	0	53	127.1	98	10	70	6	7	105	10	4	8	0	53	47	6	12	.333	22	3.32
78	LA/NL		55	390	0	0	0	31	93.1	69	6	48	4	5	66	0	0	6	0	38	34	5	5	.500	7	3.28
79	LA/NL		42	662	14	0	0	10	151.1	152	16	66	2	8	76	9	4	9	1	88	80	7	5	.583	0	4.76
80	LA/NL		19	156	1	0	0	5	32.1	37	4	21	0	2	25	3	3	3	0	21	20	1	3	.250	1	5.57
	TEX/AL		16	270	2	2	1	7	61.1	54	2	37	2	3	47	4	1	8	0	30	27	2	2	.500	0	3.96
	YEAR		35	426	3	2	1	12	93.2	91	6	58	2	5	72	7	4	11	0	51	47	3	5	.375	1	4.52
81	TEX/AL		21	330	5	2	0	9	82.0	61	4	31	1	3	69	1	1	4	0	30	27	4	1	.800	1	2.96
82	TEX/AL		34	954	34	12	2	0	228.0	217	21	72	5	7	128	7	4	9	0	111	100	16	13	.552	0	3.95
83	TEX/AL		34	1030	33	11	3	1	252.0	219	22	95	2	3	152	5	5	6	1	96	89	15	13	.536	0	3.18
84	TEX/AL		36	1133	36	17	1	0	266.0	260	26	94	3	9	164	5	7	12	2	127	111	16	14	.533	0	3.76
85	TEX/AL		34	1018	34	14	1	0	250.1	198	23	83	1	7	141	7	11	3	3	102	92	14	16	.467	0	3.31
86	OC/AMA	AAA	1	22	1	0	0	0	5.0	7	1	1	0	0	3	0	1	0	0	5	5	0	1	.000	0	9.00
	TEX/AL		33	958	33	7	2	0	230.1	188	32	89	2	9	146	9	1	16	0	115	97	17	10	.630	0	3.79
87	TEX/AL		40	1231	40	13	0	0	285.1	238	36	124	1	19	223	5	14	12	9	159	120	18	13	.581	0	3.79
88	TEX/AL		34	1067	34	10	0	0	252.0	202	20	126	1	12	174	8	8	10	10	111	93	15	16	.484	0	3.32
89	TEX/AL		30	795	30	5	1	0	182.0	168	28	95	2	6	94	3	6	7	5	97	88	10	13	.435	0	4.35
90	TEX/AL		32	950	32	5	0	0	218.2	190	24	119	2	11	114	2	11	4	0	108	99	12	12	.500	0	4.07
91	CHI/AL		31	858	29	4	1	1	199.1	167	21	94	0	11	107	8	16	5	1	98	89	9	10	.474	0	4.02
22 YR TOTALS			**776**	**14028**	**358**	**102**	**12**	**240**	**3307.0**	**2803**	**327**	**1476**	**39**	**149**	**2095**	**98**	**104**	**149**	**33**	**1536**	**1343**	**195**	**179**	**.521**	**61**	**3.65**

Howe, Steven Roy "Steve" — bats left — throws left — b.3/10/58

YR	TM/LG	CL	G	TBF	GS	CG	SHO	GF	IP	H	HR	BB	IBB	HB	SO	SH	SF	WP	BK	R	ER	W	L	PCT	SV	ERA
80	LA/NL		59	359	0	0	0	36	84.2	83	1	22	10	2	39	8	3	1	0	33	25	7	9	.438	17	2.66
81	LA/NL		41	227	0	0	0	25	54.0	51	2	18	7	0	32	4	4	0	0	17	15	5	3	.625	8	2.50
82	LA/NL		66	393	0	0	0	41	99.1	87	3	17	11	0	49	10	3	1	0	27	23	7	5	.583	13	2.08
83	LA/NL		46	274	0	0	0	33	68.2	55	2	12	7	1	52	5	3	3	0	15	11	4	7	.364	18	1.44
85	LA/NL		19	104	0	0	0	14	22.0	30	2	5	1	1	11	2	2	2	0	17	12	1	1	.500	4	4.91
	MIN/AL		13	94	0	0	0	5	19.0	28	1	7	2	0	10	0	3	1	0	16	13	2	3	.400	0	6.16
	YEAR		32	198	0	0	0	19	41.0	58	3	12	4	1	21	2	5	3	0	33	25	3	4	.429	3	5.49
86	SJ/CAL	A+	14	190	8	0	0	5	49.0	40	0	5	0	2	37	1	2	1	0	14	8	3	2	.600	2	1.47
87	OC/AMA	AAA	7	85	3	0	0	1	20.2	26	1	5	0	1	14	1	1	1	0	8	8	2	2	.500	0	3.48
	TEX/AL		24	131	0	0	0	15	31.1	33	2	8	1	3	19	2	1	1	1	15	15	3	3	.500	1	4.31
90	SAL/CAL	A+	10	78	6	0	0	2	17.0	19	0	5	0	1	14	2	0	2	2	8	4	0	1	.000	0	2.12
91	COL/INT	AAA	12	72	0	0	0	9	18.0	11	0	8	2	1	13	2	0	1	0	1	0	2	1	.667	5	0.00
	NY/AL		37	189	0	0	0	10	48.1	39	1	7	2	3	34	2	1	2	0	12	9	3	1	.750	3	1.68
7 YR TOTALS			**305**	**1771**	**0**	**0**	**0**	**179**	**427.1**	**406**	**14**	**96**	**42**	**10**	**246**	**33**	**19**	**12**	**1**	**152**	**123**	**32**	**32**	**.500**	**63**	**2.59**

Howell, Jay Canfield — bats right — throws right — b.11/26/55

YR	TM/LG	CL	G	TBF	GS	CG	SHO	GF	IP	H	HR	BB	IBB	HB	SO	SH	SF	WP	BK	R	ER	W	L	PCT	SV	ERA
80	CIN/NL		5	19	0	0	0	1	3.1	8	0	0	0	1	1	0	1	0	0	5	5	0	0	.000	0	13.50
81	CHI/AL		10	97	2	0	0	1	22.1	23	3	10	2	2	10	1	1	0	0	13	12	2	0	1.000	0	4.84
82	NY/AL		6	138	6	0	0	0	28.0	42	1	13	0	0	21	0	2	1	0	25	24	2	3	.400	0	7.71
83	NY/AL		19	368	12	2	0	3	82.0	89	7	35	0	3	61	1	5	2	1	53	49	1	5	.167	0	5.38
84	NY/AL		61	426	1	0	0	23	103.2	86	5	34	3	0	109	3	3	4	0	33	31	9	4	.692	7	2.69
85	OAK/AL		63	414	0	0	0	58	98.0	98	5	31	3	1	68	3	4	4	1	32	31	9	8	.529	29	2.85
86	MOD/CAL	A+	2	12	2	0	0	0	2.0	5	1	1	0	0	1	0	0	0	0	3	3	0	0	.000	0	13.50
	OAK/AL		38	230	0	0	0	33	53.1	53	3	23	4	1	42	3	1	4	0	23	20	3	6	.333	16	3.38
87	OAK/AL		36	200	0	0	0	27	44.1	48	6	21	1	1	35	3	2	4	0	30	29	3	4	.429	16	5.89
88	LA/NL		50	262	0	0	0	38	65.0	44	1	21	2	1	70	3	3	2	2	16	15	5	3	.625	21	2.08
89	LA/NL		56	312	0	0	0	41	79.2	60	5	22	6	0	55	4	2	1	0	15	14	5	3	.625	28	1.58
90	LA/NL		45	271	0	0	0	35	66.0	59	5	20	3	6	59	1	0	4	0	17	16	5	5	.500	16	2.18
91	LA/NL		44	202	0	0	0	35	51.0	39	3	11	3	1	40	5	2	0	0	19	18	6	5	.545	16	3.18
12 YR TOTALS			**433**	**2939**	**21**	**2**	**0**	**295**	**696.2**	**649**	**42**	**241**	**27**	**17**	**571**	**27**	**26**	**26**	**5**	**281**	**264**	**50**	**46**	**.521**	**149**	**3.41**

Howell, Kenneth "Ken" — bats right — throws right — b.11/28/60

YR	TM/LG	CL	G	TBF	GS	CG	SHO	GF	IP	H	HR	BB	IBB	HB	SO	SH	SF	WP	BK	R	ER	W	L	PCT	SV	ERA
84	ALB/PCL	AAA	18	0	9	3	0	7	72.1	79	10	37	1	0	58	0	0	7	1	48	37	8	2	.800	2	4.60
	LA/NL		32	207	1	0	0	19	51.1	51	1	9	4	1	54	2	4	0	0	21	19	5	5	.500	6	3.33
85	LA/NL		56	356	0	0	0	31	86.0	66	8	35	3	0	85	4	0	4	2	41	36	4	7	.364	12	3.77
86	LA/NL		62	437	0	0	0	36	97.2	86	7	63	9	3	104	8	3	4	0	48	42	6	12	.333	12	3.87
87	LA/NL		40	239	2	0	0	17	55.0	54	7	29	2	0	60	6	0	5	1	32	30	3	4	.429	1	4.91
	ALB/PCL	AAA	2	50	2	0	0	0	13.0	6	0	7	0	0	13	0	0	1	0	1	1	1	0	1.000	0	0.00
88	BAK/CAL	A+	3	56	3	0	0	0	13.2	8	1	9	0	0	13	0	1	1	0	5	2	0	1	.000	0	1.32
	ALB/PCL	AAA	18	435	16	0	0	2	107.1	92	6	42	0	0	95	3	3	3	0	43	39	10	1	.909	0	3.27
	LA/NL		4	55	1	0	0	0	12.2	16	0	4	1	0	12	1	0	0	0	10	9	0	1	.000	0	6.39
89	PHL/NL		33	827	32	1	1	0	204.0	155	11	86	6	2	164	8	9	21	1	84	78	12	12	.500	0	3.44
90	PHL/NL		18	467	18	2	0	0	106.2	106	12	49	6	3	70	6	1	8	0	60	55	8	7	.533	0	4.64

(continued)

Howell, Kenneth "Ken" (continued)

YR	TM/LG	CL	G	TBF	GS	CG	SHO	GF	IP	H	HR	BB	IBB	HB	SO	SH	SF	WP	BK	R	ER	W	L	PCT	SV	ERA
91	SCR/INT	AAA	6	113	6	0	0	0	24.2	30	3	16	0	2	20	2	0	4	1	15	14	2	0	1.000	0	5.11
	7 YR TOTALS		245	2588	54	3	1	105	613.1	534	46	275	31	9	549	35	17	42	4	296	269	38	48	.442	31	3.95

Huismann, Mark Lawrence — bats right — throws right — b.5/11/58

YR	TM/LG	CL	G	TBF	GS	CG	SHO	GF	IP	H	HR	BB	IBB	HB	SO	SH	SF	WP	BK	R	ER	W	L	PCT	SV	ERA
80	ROY/GCL	R	28	0	0	0	0	0	59.0	50	1	14	0	1	46	0	0	5	0	20	16	1	2	.333	0	2.44
81	FM/FSL	A+	14	0	0	0	0	0	21.0	15	1	16	0	2	19	0	0	1	0	9	8	3	1	.750	0	3.43
	CHS/SAL	A	28	0	0	0	0	0	44.0	36	0	17	0	1	42	0	0	4	0	16	8	3	2	.600	0	1.64
82	FM/FSL	A+	14	0	0	0	0	0	23.0	16	0	4	0	1	21	0	0	1	0	1	1	3	1	.750	0	0.39
	JAC/SOU	AA	36	0	0	0	0	0	54.0	52	5	15	0	3	60	0	0	3	1	18	13	4	4	.500	0	2.17
83	JAC/SOU	AA	37	0	0	0	0	0	61.0	60	1	25	0	3	46	0	0	6	0	25	22	6	3	.667	10	3.25
	OMA/AMA	AAA	17	0	0	0	0	0	24.0	21	2	9	0	1	25	0	0	1	0	7	5	0	2	.000	8	1.88
	KC/AL		13	135	0	0	0	5	30.2	29	1	17	3	0	20	1	1	4	1	20	19	2	1	.667	0	5.58
84	OMA/AMA	AAA	15	71	0	0	0	14	19.0	11	0	5	2	0	18	1	0	1	1	0	0	2	0	1.000	0	0.00
	KC/AL		38	324	0	0	0	23	75.0	84	7	21	3	1	54	3	5	3	0	38	35	3	3	.500	3	4.20
85	OMA/AMA	AAA	59	345	0	0	0	56	89.1	70	4	14	2	2	70	5	3	7	0	20	20	5	5	.500	33	2.01
	KC/AL		9	70	0	0	0	6	18.2	14	1	3	0	0	9	1	2	0	0	4	4	1	0	1.000	1	1.93
86	KC/AL		10	74	0	0	0	5	17.1	18	1	6	0	0	13	0	1	1	0	8	8	0	1	.000	1	4.15
	SEA/AL		36	334	1	0	0	14	80.0	80	18	19	0	1	59	0	2	4	0	39	33	3	3	.500	4	3.71
	YEAR		46	408	1	0	0	19	97.1	98	19	25	0	1	72	0	3	5	0	47	41	3	4	.429	5	3.79
87	SEA/AL		6	61	0	0	0	1	14.2	10	1	4	0	2	15	3	1	0	0	10	8	0	0	.000	0	4.91
	CLE/AL		20	151	0	0	0	10	35.1	38	6	8	0	0	23	1	2	3	0	22	20	2	3	.400	2	5.09
	YEAR		26	212	0	0	0	11	50.0	48	7	12	0	2	38	4	3	3	0	32	28	2	3	.400	2	5.04
	BUF/AMA	AAA	13	148	3	0	0	5	33.1	43	9	8	2	1	31	0	3	0	1	32	28	1	0	.500	0	7.56
88	TOL/INT	AAA	48	237	0	0	0	45	57.2	50	2	15	5	1	61	6	5	1	3	20	12	4	6	.400	21	1.87
	DET/AL		5	23	0	0	0	2	5.1	6	0	2	1	0	6	0	0	0	0	3	3	1	0	1.000	0	5.06
89	ROC/INT	AAA	16	75	0	0	0	13	21.0	9	1	3	1	1	20	1	0	0	0	4	4	2	1	.667	8	1.71
	BAL/AL		8	48	0	0	0	1	11.1	13	0	0	0	0	13	0	1	1	0	8	8	0	1	.000	1	6.35
90	PIT/NL		2	15	0	0	0	1	3.0	6	2	1	0	1	2	0	0	1	0	5	3	1	0	1.000	0	9.00
	BUF/AMA	AAA	49	313	0	0	0	24	76.0	69	3	15	6	1	32	7	2	3	1	23	22	6	2	.750	4	2.61
91	PIT/NL		5	25	0	0	0	1	5.0	7	1	2	1	0	5	0	0	0	0	6	4	0	0	.000	0	7.20
	BUF/AMA	AAA	13	118	1	0	0	6	26.1	32	4	6	1	0	16	0	1	2	0	15	14	1	1	.500	2	4.78
	OMA/AMA	AAA	32	168	0	0	0	31	42.0	38	3	12	2	1	34	1	2	0	0	13	10	5	4	.556	15	2.14
	9 YR TOTALS		152	1260	1	0	0	67	296.1	305	37	83	8	5	219	9	15	17	1	163	145	13	11	.542	11	4.40

Hunter, James Mac Gregor "Jim" — bats right — throws right — b.6/22/64

YR	TM/LG	CL	G	TBF	GS	CG	SHO	GF	IP	H	HR	BB	IBB	HB	SO	SH	SF	WP	BK	R	ER	W	L	PCT	SV	ERA
85	JAM/NYP	A–	14	310	13	1	0	1	70.2	65	1	34	1	1	41	2	1	3	0	30	22	3	3	.500	0	2.80
86	BUR/MID	A	9	210	9	1	0	0	45.0	52	1	25	0	2	28	0	1	2	1	28	23	2	3	.400	0	4.60
	BEL/MID	A	15	382	15	2	0	0	89.1	91	4	22	3	5	52	2	1	5	1	47	37	4	5	.444	0	3.73
87	STO/CAL	A+	8	214	8	0	0	0	51.1	39	1	20	0	5	44	1	2	2	0	16	14	6	1	.857	0	2.45
	EP/TEX	AA	16	421	15	1	0	1	95.2	117	14	33	1	2	62	1	2	4	0	60	49	5	5	.500	0	4.61
88	EP/TEX	AA	26	666	26	2	0	0	147.2	163	15	77	2	8	103	3	4	4	3	107	93	8	11	.421	0	5.67
89	EP/TEX	AA	19	547	19	4	0	0	124.2	149	9	45	1	4	68	3	4	5	0	70	58	7	10	.412	0	4.19
90	EP/TEX	AA	9	258	9	2	0	0	62.0	64	9	15	0	1	37	0	0	1	0	31	27	6	3	.667	0	3.92
	DEN/AMA	AAA	20	512	20	2	0	0	117.0	138	5	45	1	5	57	4	8	1	0	76	61	6	8	.429	0	4.69
91	MIL/AL		8	152	6	0	0	0	31.0	45	5	17	0	4	14	1	1	3	0	26	25	0	5	.000	0	7.26
	DEN/AMA	AAA	14	374	14	0	0	0	87.1	94	6	27	0	5	43	4	1	2	0	38	32	7	4	.636	0	3.30

Hurst, Bruce Vee — bats left — throws left — b.3/24/58

YR	TM/LG	CL	G	TBF	GS	CG	SHO	GF	IP	H	HR	BB	IBB	HB	SO	SH	SF	WP	BK	R	ER	W	L	PCT	SV	ERA
80	BOS/AL		12	147	7	0	0	2	30.2	39	4	16	0	2	16	0	2	4	2	33	31	2	2	.500	0	9.10
81	BOS/AL		5	104	5	0	0	0	23.0	23	1	12	2	1	11	0	2	2	0	11	11	2	0	1.000	0	4.30
82	BOS/AL		28	535	19	0	0	3	117.0	161	16	40	2	3	53	2	7	5	0	87	75	3	7	.300	0	5.77
83	BOS/AL		33	903	32	6	2	0	211.1	241	22	62	5	3	115	3	4	1	2	102	96	12	12	.500	0	4.09
84	BOS/AL		33	958	33	9	2	0	218.0	232	25	88	3	6	136	3	4	1	1	106	95	12	12	.500	0	3.92
85	BOS/AL		35	973	31	6	1	0	229.1	243	31	70	4	3	189	6	4	3	4	123	115	11	13	.458	0	4.51
86	BOS/AL		25	721	25	11	4	0	174.1	169	18	50	2	3	167	5	3	6	0	63	58	13	8	.619	0	2.99
87	BOS/AL		33	1001	33	15	3	0	238.2	239	35	76	5	1	190	5	3	6	0	124	117	15	13	.536	0	4.41
88	BOS/AL		33	922	32	7	1	0	216.2	222	21	65	1	2	166	5	5	5	1	98	88	18	6	.750	0	3.66
89	SD/NL		33	990	33	10	2	0	244.2	214	16	66	7	0	179	18	3	8	0	84	73	15	11	.577	0	2.69
90	SD/NL		33	903	33	9	4	0	223.2	188	21	63	5	1	162	15	1	7	1	85	78	11	9	.550	0	3.14
91	SD/NL		31	909	31	4	0	0	221.2	201	17	59	3	3	141	8	4	5	1	89	81	15	8	.652	0	3.29
	12 YR TOTALS		334	9066	314	77	19	5	2149.0	2172	227	667	39	28	1525	73	47	50	15	1005	918	129	101	.561	0	3.84

Ignasiak, Michael James "Mike" — bats both — throws right — b.3/12/66

YR	TM/LG	CL	G	TBF	GS	CG	SHO	GF	IP	H	HR	BB	IBB	HB	SO	SH	SF	WP	BK	R	ER	W	L	PCT	SV	ERA
88	HEL/PIO	R+	7	53	0	0	0	7	11.2	10	1	7	0	1	18	0	0	2	0	5	4	2	0	1.000	1	3.09
	BEL/MID	A	9	232	9	1	0	0	56.1	52	4	12	1	2	66	3	2	1	1	21	17	2	4	.333	0	2.72
89	STO/CAL	A+	28	763	28	4	4	0	179.0	140	4	97	0	5	142	4	5	12	1	67	54	11	6	.647	0	2.72
90	STO/CAL	A+	6	130	6	1	0	0	32.0	18	3	17	0	2	23	0	0	2	1	14	14	3	1	.750	0	3.94
	EP/TEX	AA	15	368	15	1	0	0	82.2	96	5	34	1	1	39	2	3	4	3	45	40	6	3	.667	0	4.35
91	DEN/AMA	AAA	24	587	22	1	0	1	137.2	119	14	57	2	6	103	1	1	4	3	68	65	9	5	.643	1	4.25
	MIL/AL		4	51	1	0	0	0	12.2	7	2	8	0	0	10	0	0	0	0	8	8	2	1	.667	0	5.68

Innis, Jeffrey David "Jeff" — bats right — throws right — b.7/5/62

YR	TM/LG	CL	G	TBF	GS	CG	SHO	GF	IP	H	HR	BB	IBB	HB	SO	SH	SF	WP	BK	R	ER	W	L	PCT	SV	ERA
83	LF/NYP	A–	28	0	0	0	0	0	46.0	29	0	28			68			4		8	7	8	0	1.000	8	1.37
84	JAC/TEX	AA	42	283	0	0	0	27	59.1	65	3	40	8	0	63	4	0	6	1	34	28	6	5	.545	8	4.25
85	LYN/CAR	A+	53	311	0	0	0	39	77.0	46	2	40	1	1	91	6	2	3	0	26	20	6	3	.667	14	2.34
86	JAC/TEX	AA	56	359	0	0	0	48	92.0	69	2	24	3	1	75	3	6	2	0	30	25	4	5	.444	25	2.45
87	TID/INT	AAA	29	171	0	0	0	18	44.1	26	3	16	4	0	28	2	0	1	0	10	10	6	1	.857	5	2.03
	NY/NL		17	109	1	0	0	8	25.2	29	5	4	1	1	28	0	1	1	0	9	9	0	0	.000	0	3.16
88	NY/NL		12	80	0	0	0	7	19.0	19	0	2	1	0	14	1	1	0	0	6	4	1	1	.500	0	1.89
	TID/INT	AAA	34	213	0	0	0	19	48.1	43	3	25	8	0	43	3	1	1	0	22	19	0	5	.000	4	3.54
89	TID/INT	AAA	25	127	0	0	0	18	29.2	28	0	8	2	1	14	3	1	1	0	9	7	3	1	.750	10	2.12
	NY/NL		29	160	0	0	0	12	39.2	38	2	8	1	1	16	1	1	0	0	16	14	0	1	.000	0	3.18
90	TID/INT	AAA	40	209	0	0	0	33	52.2	34	1	17	5	2	42	4	1	0	1	11	10	5	2	.714	19	1.71
	NY/NL		18	104	0	0	0	12	26.1	19	4	10	3	1	12	0	2	1	0	9	7	1	3	.250	0	2.39
91	NY/NL		69	336	0	0	0	29	84.2	66	2	23	6	0	47	6	5	4	0	30	25	0	2	.000	0	2.66
5 YR TOTALS			**145**	**789**	**1**	**0**	**0**	**68**	**195.1**	**171**	**13**	**47**	**11**	**3**	**117**	**8**	**9**	**6**	**2**	**70**	**59**	**2**	**8**	**.200**	**1**	**2.72**

Irvine, Daryl Keith — bats right — throws right — b.11/15/64

YR	TM/LG	CL	G	TBF	GS	CG	SHO	GF	IP	H	HR	BB	IBB	HB	SO	SH	SF	WP	BK	R	ER	W	L	PCT	SV	ERA
85	GRE/SAL	A	8	173	7	0	0	0	37.0	46	3	17	0	1	19	1	0	3	1	26	18	4	2	.667	0	4.38
86	WH/FSL	A+	26	702	24	3	0	0	161.0	162	3	67	3	7	73	9	3	13	1	73	57	9	8	.529	0	3.19
87	NB/EAS	AA	37	588	16	3	0	8	127.0	156	7	59	4	2	70	9	6	16	9	101	75	4	13	.235	0	5.31
88	NB/EAS	AA	39	536	14	4	1	13	125.1	113	4	57	4	5	82	5	2	8	7	62	43	5	11	.313	0	3.09
89	NB/EAS	AA	54	366	1	0	0	45	91.1	74	0	23	2	3	50	5	0	9	0	24	13	4	6	.400	16	1.28
90	PAW/INT	AAA	42	216	0	0	0	30	50.0	47	1	19	5	3	35	6	1	1	1	24	18	2	5	.286	12	3.24
	BOS/AL		11	75	0	0	0	6	17.1	15	0	10	3	0	9	1	3	1	1	10	9	1	1	.500	0	4.67
91	PAW/INT	AAA	27	132	0	0	0	25	33.0	27	2	13	1	0	19	1	0	9	0	11	11	1	1	.500	17	3.00
	BOS/AL		9	90	0	0	0	5	18.0	25	2	9	1	2	8	1	0	1	0	13	12	0	0	.000	0	6.00
2 YR TOTALS			**20**	**165**	**0**	**0**	**0**	**11**	**35.1**	**40**	**2**	**19**	**4**	**2**	**17**	**2**	**3**	**2**	**1**	**23**	**21**	**1**	**1**	**.500**	**0**	**5.35**

Jackson, Danny Lynn — bats right — throws left — b.1/5/62

YR	TM/LG	CL	G	TBF	GS	CG	SHO	GF	IP	H	HR	BB	IBB	HB	SO	SH	SF	WP	BK	R	ER	W	L	PCT	SV	ERA
83	KC/AL		4	87	3	0	0	0	19.0	26	1	6	0	0	9	1	0	0	0	12	11	1	1	.500	0	5.21
84	OMA/AMA	AAA	16	459	16	10	3	0	110.1	91	8	45	3	1	82	5	2	3	0	50	45	5	8	.385	0	3.67
	KC/AL		15	338	11	1	0	3	76.0	84	4	35	0	5	40	3	0	3	2	41	36	2	6	.250	0	4.26
85	KC/AL		32	893	32	4	3	0	208.0	209	7	76	2	6	114	5	4	4	2	94	79	14	12	.538	0	3.42
86	KC/AL		32	789	27	4	1	3	185.2	177	13	79	1	4	115	10	4	7	0	83	66	11	12	.478	1	3.20
87	KC/AL		36	981	34	11	2	1	224.0	219	11	109	1	7	152	8	7	5	0	115	100	9	18	.333	0	4.02
88	CIN/NL		35	1034	35	15	6	0	260.2	206	13	71	6	2	161	13	5	5	2	86	79	23	8	.742	0	2.73
89	CIN/NL		20	519	20	1	0	0	115.2	122	10	57	7	1	70	6	4	3	2	78	72	6	11	.353	0	5.60
90	CHW/SAL	A	1	12	1	0	0	0	3.0	2	0	1	0	0	2	0	0	0	0	2	2	0	0	.000	0	6.00
	NAS/AMA	AAA	2	45	2	0	0	0	11.0	9	0	4	0	0	3	1	0	0	0	1	0	1	0	1.000	0	0.00
	CIN/NL		22	499	21	0	0	1	117.1	119	11	40	4	2	76	4	5	3	1	54	47	6	6	.500	0	3.61
91	IOW/AMA	AAA	1	19	1	0	0	0	5.0	2	0	2	0	0	4	0	0	0	0	1	1	0	0	.000	0	1.80
	CHI/NL		17	347	14	0	0	0	70.2	89	8	48	4	1	31	8	2	1	1	59	53	1	5	.167	0	6.75
9 YR TOTALS			**213**	**5487**	**197**	**36**	**12**	**8**	**1277.0**	**1251**	**78**	**521**	**25**	**28**	**768**	**58**	**31**	**31**	**10**	**622**	**543**	**73**	**79**	**.480**	**1**	**3.83**

Jackson, Michael Ray "Mike" — bats right — throws right — b.12/22/64

YR	TM/LG	CL	G	TBF	GS	CG	SHO	GF	IP	H	HR	BB	IBB	HB	SO	SH	SF	WP	BK	R	ER	W	L	PCT	SV	ERA
84	SPA/SAL	A–	14	352	14	0	0	0	80.2	53	8	50	0	7	77	3	1	4	1	35	24	7	2	.778	0	2.68
85	PEN/CAR	A+	31	554	18	0	0	2	125.1	127	11	53	1	5	96	2	4	6	7	71	64	7	9	.438	1	4.60
86	REA/EAS	AA	30	174	0	0	0	23	43.1	25	1	22	2	1	42	0	2	4	1	9	8	2	3	.400	6	1.66
	POR/PCL	AAA	17	100	0	0	0	10	22.2	18	2	13	4	1	23	2	1	5	0	8	8	3	1	.750	3	3.18
	PHI/NL		9	54	0	0	0	4	13.1	12	2	5	1	0	13	1	0	0	0	5	5	0	0	.000	0	3.38
87	MAI/INT	AAA	2	46	2	0	0	0	11.0	9	0	5	1	0	13	1	0	2	1	5	1	1	0	1.000	0	0.82
	PHI/NL		55	468	7	0	0	8	109.1	88	16	56	6	3	93	3	4	6	8	55	51	3	10	.231	1	4.20
88	SEA/AL		62	412	0	0	0	29	99.1	74	10	43	10	2	76	3	10	6	6	37	29	6	5	.545	4	2.63
89	SEA/AL		65	431	0	0	0	27	99.1	81	8	54	6	6	94	6	2	1	2	43	35	4	6	.400	7	3.17
90	SEA/AL		63	338	0	0	0	28	77.1	64	9	44	12	2	69	8	5	9	2	42	39	5	7	.417	3	4.54
91	SEA/AL		72	363	0	0	0	35	88.2	64	5	34	11	6	74	4	0	3	0	35	32	7	7	.500	14	3.25
6 YR TOTALS			**326**	**2066**	**7**	**0**	**0**	**131**	**487.1**	**383**	**49**	**235**	**46**	**21**	**409**	**24**	**21**	**25**	**18**	**217**	**191**	**25**	**35**	**.417**	**29**	**3.53**

Jeffcoat, James Michael "Mike" — bats left — throws left — b.8/3/59

YR	TM/LG	CL	G	TBF	GS	CG	SHO	GF	IP	H	HR	BB	IBB	HB	SO	SH	SF	WP	BK	R	ER	W	L	PCT	SV	ERA
83	CLE/AL		11	140	2	0	0	1	32.2	32	1	13	1	1	9	1	0	1	1	13	12	1	3	.250	0	3.31
84	CLE/AL		63	327	1	0	0	12	75.1	82	7	24	7	1	41	3	7	8	1	28	25	5	2	.714	1	2.99
85	CLE/AL		9	44	0	0	0	3	9.2	8	1	6	1	0	4	2	2	0	0	5	3	0	0	.000	0	2.79
	PHO/PCL	AAA	10	0	10	2	0	0	59.2	64	11	9	2	2	28	0	0	2	1	26	24	4	5	.444	0	3.62
	SF/NL		19	99	1	0	0	7	22.0	27	4	6	3	2	10	2	1	1	0	18	16	0	2	.000	0	4.55
	YEAR		28	143	1	0	0	10	31.2	35	5	12	4	2	14	4	3	1	0	40	35	4	7	.778	0	4.20
86	PHO/PCL	AAA	54	340	0	0	0	18	75.0	81	7	31	7	2	57	3	6	1	1	13	13	1	0	.000	0	12.86
87	TEX/AL		2	35	2	0	0	0	7.0	11	4	4	0	0	4	0	0	0	0	99	85	11	8	.579	0	4.79
	OC/AMA	AAA	26	701	24	3	2	0	159.2	193	14	41	0	1	101	5	5	3	2	53	49	9	5	.643	0	2.80
88	OC/AMA	AAA	22	639	22	6	2	0	157.1	137	8	41	2	0	95	6	4	4	0	13	13	0	0	.000	0	11.70
	TEX/AL		5	52	2	0	0	0	10.0	19	1	5	0	0	5	1	2	0	0	31	26	4	4	.500	0	3.22
89	OC/AMA	AAA	11	313	11	0	0	0	72.2	81	1	21	1	1	50	3	3	1	0							

(continued)

Jeffcoat, James Michael "Mike" (continued)

YR	TM/LG	CL	G	TBF	GS	CG	SHO	GF	IP	H	HR	BB	IBB	HB	SO	SH	SF	WP	BK	R	ER	W	L	PCT	SV	ERA
89	TEX/AL		22	559	22	2	2	0	130.2	139	7	33	0	4	64	3	5	0	1	65	52	9	6	.600	0	3.58
90	TEX/AL		44	466	12	1	0	11	110.2	122	12	28	5	2	58	3	2	1	0	57	55	5	6	.455	5	4.47
91	TEX/AL		70	363	0	0	0	21	79.2	104	8	25	3	4	43	5	4	3	0	46	41	5	3	.625	5	4.63
8 YR TOTALS			245	2085	42	3	2	57	477.2	544	45	144	21	16	235	20	21	14	3	250	224	25	25	.500	7	4.22

Johnson, David Wayne "Dave" — bats right — throws right — b.10/24/59

YR	TM/LG	CL	G	TBF	GS	CG	SHO	GF	IP	H	HR	BB	IBB	HB	SO	SH	SF	WP	BK	R	ER	W	L	PCT	SV	ERA
84	PW/CAR	A+	13	348	13	3	1	0	88.1	60	2	35	0	1	48	3	1	3	0	22	13	7	5	.583	0	1.32
	NAS/EAS	AA	12	366	12	4	0	0	83.2	95	2	31	1	3	47	1	6	7	1	52	45	1	8	.111	0	4.84
85	NAS/EAS	AA	34	624	18	4	1	9	153.0	129	9	45	1	2	84	11	2	6	0	66	53	6	9	.400	2	3.12
86	HAW/PCL	AAA	22	624	22	6	1	0	150.1	150	6	35	0	3	71	8	7	0	0	68	53	8	7	.533	0	3.17
87	PIT/NL		5	31	0	0	0	3	6.1	13	1	2	0	0	4	0	0	0	0	7	7	0	0	.000	0	9.95
	VAN/PCL	AAA	23	650	22	9	2	1	153.2	133	9	68	0	10	76	7	4	8	3	74	60	8	10	.444	0	3.51
88	BUF/AMA	AAA	29	829	29	9	2	0	192.1	213	9	55	2	2	90	6	7	5	7	93	75	15	12	.556	0	3.51
89	ROC/INT	AAA	18	444	14	2	0	2	105.0	104	4	31	2	4	60	3	3	4	1	45	38	7	6	.538	1	3.26
	BAL/AL		14	378	14	4	0	0	89.1	90	11	28	1	4	26	3	3	0	2	44	42	4	7	.364	0	4.23
90	BAL/AL		30	758	29	3	0	0	180.0	196	30	43	2	3	68	5	7	1	2	83	82	13	9	.591	0	4.10
91	HAG/EAS	AA	3	68	3	0	0	0	18.0	13	0	3	0	0	9	1	0	0	0	3	3	1	1	1.000	0	1.00
	ROC/INT	AAA	2	56	2	1	0	0	13.0	18	1	5	0	0	8	1	2	1	0	7	6	0	1	.000	0	4.15
	BAL/AL		22	393	14	0	0	4	84.0	127	18	24	3	4	38	0	1	0	0	68	66	4	8	.333	0	7.07
4 YR TOTALS			71	1560	57	7	0	7	359.2	426	60	97	6	11	136	8	11	1	4	202	197	21	24	.467	0	4.93

Johnson, Randall David "Randy" — bats right — throws left — b.9/10/63

YR	TM/LG	CL	G	TBF	GS	CG	SHO	GF	IP	H	HR	BB	IBB	HB	SO	SH	SF	WP	BK	R	ER	W	L	PCT	SV	ERA
85	JAM/NYP	A–	8	130	8	0	0	0	27.1	29	1	24	0	0	21	1	4	3	1	22	18	0	3	.000	0	5.93
86	WPB/FSL	A+	26	535	26	2	1	0	119.2	89	3	94	0	6	133	10	4	13	4	49	42	8	7	.533	0	3.16
87	JAC/SOU	AA	25	629	24	0	0	1	140.0	100	10	128	0	9	163	1	1	12	2	63	58	11	8	.579	0	3.73
88	IND/AMA	AAA	20	489	19	0	0	0	113.1	85	6	72	0	3	111	4	3	8	20	52	41	8	7	.533	0	3.26
	MON/NL		4	109	4	1	0	0	26.0	23	3	7	0	0	25	0	0	3	0	8	7	3	0	1.000	0	2.42
89	MON/NL		7	143	6	0	0	1	29.2	29	2	26	1	0	26	3	4	2	0	25	22	0	4	.000	0	6.67
	IND/AMA	AAA	3	77	3	0	0	0	18.0	13	0	9	0	1	17	0	0	0	0	5	4	1	1	.500	0	2.00
	SEA/AL		22	572	22	2	0	0	131.0	118	11	70	1	3	104	7	9	5	5	75	64	7	9	.438	0	4.40
	YEAR		29	715	28	2	0	1	160.2	147	13	96	2	3	130	10	13	7	7	100	86	7	13	.350	0	4.82
90	SEA/AL		33	944	33	5	2	0	219.2	174	26	120	2	5	194	7	6	4	2	103	89	14	11	.560	0	3.65
91	SEA/AL		33	889	33	2	1	0	201.1	151	15	152	0	12	228	9	8	12	2	96	89	13	10	.565	0	3.98
4 YR TOTALS			99	2657	98	10	3	1	607.2	495	57	375	4	20	577	26	27	26	11	307	271	37	34	.521	0	4.01

Johnson, William Jeffrey "Jeff" — bats right — throws left — b.8/4/66

YR	TM/LG	CL	G	TBF	GS	CG	SHO	GF	IP	H	HR	BB	IBB	HB	SO	SH	SF	WP	BK	R	ER	W	L	PCT	SV	ERA
88	ONE/NYP	A–	14	371	14	0	0	0	87.2	67	2	39	0	2	91	3	3	3	2	35	29	6	1	.857	0	2.98
89	PW/CAR	A+	25	578	24	0	0	0	138.2	125	7	55	1	0	99	8	2	14	2	59	45	4	10	.286	0	2.92
90	FT./FSL	A+	17	439	17	1	0	0	103.2	101	4	25	0	3	84	5	2	5	2	55	42	6	8	.429	0	3.65
	ALB/EAS	AA	9	239	9	3	1	0	60.2	44	0	15	0	2	41	2	0	1	0	14	11	4	3	.571	0	1.63
91	COL/INT	AAA	10	261	10	0	0	0	62.0	58	1	25	0	1	40	4	1	1	3	27	18	4	0	1.000	0	2.61
	NY/AL		23	562	23	0	0	0	127.0	156	15	33	1	6	62	7	4	5	1	89	84	6	11	.353	0	5.95

Johnston, Joel Raymond — bats right — throws right — b.3/8/67

YR	TM/LG	CL	G	TBF	GS	CG	SHO	GF	IP	H	HR	BB	IBB	HB	SO	SH	SF	WP	BK	R	ER	W	L	PCT	SV	ERA
88	EUG/NWL	A–	14	295	14	0	0	0	64.0	64	1	34	0	7	64	4	3	7	6	49	37	4	7	.364	0	5.20
89	BC/FSL	A+	26	586	26	0	0	0	131.2	135	6	63	2	11	76	2	6	8	5	84	72	9	4	.692	0	4.92
90	MEM/SOU	AA	4	40	3	0	0	1	6.2	5	1	16	0	0	6	0	0	3	0	9	5	0	0	.000	0	6.75
	BC/FSL	A+	31	251	7	1	0	18	55.1	36	2	49	0	3	60	6	3	6	1	37	30	2	4	.333	7	4.88
	OMA/AMA	AAA	2	9	0	0	0	0	3.0	1	0	1	0	0	3	0	0	0	0	0	0	0	0	.000	0	0.00
91	OMA/AMA	AAA	47	318	0	0	0	27	74.1	60	12	42	2	1	63	4	0	6	0	43	43	4	7	.364	8	5.21
	KC/AL		13	85	0	0	0	1	22.1	9	0	9	3	0	21	1	0	0	0	1	1	1	0	1.000	0	0.40

Jones, Barry Louis — bats right — throws right — b.2/15/63

YR	TM/LG	CL	G	TBF	GS	CG	SHO	GF	IP	H	HR	BB	IBB	HB	SO	SH	SF	WP	BK	R	ER	W	L	PCT	SV	ERA
84	WAT/NYP	A–	14	376	14	2	1	0	86.2	75	4	49	0	4	61	1	2	8	1	41	33	6	3	.667	0	3.43
85	PW/CAR	A+	28	154	0	0	0	23	37.1	26	0	19	3	0	42	6	0	9	0	7	5	3	2	.600	10	1.21
	NAS/EAS	AA	23	111	0	0	0	20	29.0	19	1	10	0	0	24	1	1	4	0	6	5	3	2	.600	12	1.55
	HAW/PCL	AAA	1	0	0	0	0	1	3.0	5	0	1	0	0	2	0	0	0	0	5	3	0	0	.000	0	9.00
86	HAW/PCL	AAA	35	203	0	0	0	32	48.0	41	3	20	4	2	28	5	1	0	0	20	19	3	6	.333	7	3.56
	PIT/NL		26	159	0	0	0	10	37.1	29	3	21	0	0	29	1	2	0	0	16	12	3	4	.429	3	2.89
87	VAN/PCL	AAA	20	112	0	0	0	10	25.1	21	2	14	1	0	27	0	0	2	0	9	9	1	2	.333	11	3.20
	PIT/NL		32	203	0	0	0	10	43.1	55	6	23	6	0	28	3	2	3	0	34	27	2	4	.333	1	5.61
88	PIT/NL		42	241	0	0	0	15	56.1	57	3	21	6	1	31	5	4	7	1	21	19	1	1	.500	0	3.04
	CHI/AL		17	106	0	0	0	10	26.0	15	3	17	1	0	17	0	1	6	1	7	7	2	2	.500	2	2.42
	YEAR		59	347	0	0	0	25	82.1	72	6	38	7	1	48	5	5	13	2	28	26	3	3	.500	2	2.84
89	WS/GCL	R	7	70	4	0	0	2	18.1	12	0	5	0	0	14	0	0	0	0	7	3	0	1	.000	1	1.47
	SB/MID	A	3	17	0	0	0	0	3.2	6	0	0	0	0	2	0	0	0	0	3	2	0	0	.000	0	4.91
	CHI/AL		22	121	0	0	0	8	30.1	22	2	8	0	1	17	4	2	1	0	12	8	3	2	.600	0	2.37
90	CHI/AL		65	310	0	0	0	9	74.0	62	4	33	7	1	45	7	1	5	0	20	19	11	4	.733	1	2.31
91	MON/NL		77	353	0	0	0	46	88.2	76	5	33	8	1	46	7	3	1	1	35	33	4	9	.308	13	3.35
6 YR TOTALS			281	1493	0	0	0	108	356.0	316	27	156	30	4	213	28	18	20	4	145	125	26	26	.500	22	3.16

Jones, Calvin Douglas — bats right — throws right — b.9/26/63

YR	TM/LG	CL	G	TBF	GS	CG	SHO	GF	IP	H	HR	BB	IBB	HB	SO	SH	SF	WP	BK	R	ER	W	L	PCT	SV	ERA
84	BEL/NWL	A–	10	0	9	0	0	0	59.2	29	0	36	0	7	59	0	0	8	1	23	16	5	0	1.000	0	2.41
85	WAU/MID	A	20	473	19	1	0	0	106.0	96	10	65	1	5	71	0	0	9	2	59	46	4	11	.267	0	3.91
86	SAL/CAL	A+	26	680	25	2	0	0	157.1	141	9	90	2	4	137	4	4	15	2	76	63	11	8	.579	0	3.60
87	CHT/SOU	AA	26	372	10	0	0	12	81.1	90	5	38	0	2	77	5	1	4	0	58	45	2	9	.182	2	4.98
88	VER/EAS	AA	24	312	4	0	0	6	74.2	52	1	47	2	0	58	0	2	4	3	26	22	7	5	.583	0	2.65
89	SB/CAL	A+	5	49	0	0	0	4	12.1	8	0	7	0	0	15	0	1	0	2	1	1	2	0	1.000	1	0.73
	WIL/EAS		5	34	0	0	0	3	6.2	13	1	4	0	0	5	0	0	1	0	9	9	0	0	.000	0	12.15
90	SB/CAL	A+	53	298	0	0	0	27	67.0	43	4	54	2	4	94	1	3	6	0	32	22	5	3	.625	8	2.96
91	CAL/PCL	AAA	20	109	0	0	0	15	23.0	19	1	19	1	2	25	0	0	6	2	12	10	1	1	.500	7	3.91
	SEA/AL		27	194	0	0	0	6	46.1	33	0	29	5	1	42	6	0	6	0	14	13	2	2	.500	2	2.53

Jones, Douglas Reid "Doug" — bats right — throws right — b.6/24/57

YR	TM/LG	CL	G	TBF	GS	CG	SHO	GF	IP	H	HR	BB	IBB	HB	SO	SH	SF	WP	BK	R	ER	W	L	PCT	SV	ERA
82	MIL/AL		4	14	0	0	0	2	2.2	5	1	1	0	1	1	0	0	0	0	3	3	0	0	.000	0	10.13
84	VAN/PCL	AAA	3	0	0	0	0	0	8.0	9	3	3	0	1	2	0	0	2	0	9	9	1	0	1.000	0	10.13
	EP/TEX	AA	16	479	16	7	0	0	109.1	120	12	35	2	4	62	6	3	3	0	61	52	6	8	.429	0	4.28
85	WAT/EAS	AA	39	506	1	0	0	25	116.0	123	11	36	8	3	113	5	4	8	0	59	47	9	4	.692	3	3.65
86	MAI/INT	AAA	43	472	3	0	0	21	116.1	105	6	27	5	0	98	1	1	4	0	35	27	5	6	.455	9	2.09
	CLE/AL		11	79	0	0	0	5	18.0	18	0	6	1	1	12	1	1	0	0	5	5	1	0	1.000	1	2.50
87	BUF/AMA	AAA	23	240	0	0	0	18	61.2	49	3	12	2	0	61	3	1	4	0	18	14	5	2	.714	7	2.04
	CLE/AL		49	400	0	0	0	29	91.1	101	4	24	5	6	87	5	5	0	0	45	32	6	5	.545	8	3.15
88	CLE/AL		51	338	0	0	0	46	83.1	69	1	16	2	2	72	3	0	2	3	26	21	3	4	.429	37	2.27
89	CLE/AL		59	331	0	0	0	53	80.2	76	4	13	4	1	65	8	6	1	1	25	21	7	10	.412	32	2.34
90	CLE/AL		66	331	0	0	0	64	84.1	66	5	22	4	2	55	2	5	1	0	26	24	5	5	.500	43	2.56
91	CS/PCL	AAA	17	135	2	1	1	14	35.2	30	3	5	0	1	29	4	1	0	0	14	13	2	2	.500	7	3.28
	CLE/AL		36	293	4	0	0	29	63.1	87	7	17	5	0	48	2	2	1	0	42	39	4	8	.333	7	5.54
7 YR TOTALS			**276**	**1786**	**4**	**0**	**0**	**228**	**423.2**	**422**	**22**	**99**	**22**	**12**	**340**	**21**	**16**	**6**	**4**	**172**	**145**	**26**	**32**	**.448**	**128**	**3.08**

Jones, James Condia "Jimmy" — bats right — throws right — b.4/20/64

YR	TM/LG	CL	G	TBF	GS	CG	SHO	GF	IP	H	HR	BB	IBB	HB	SO	SH	SF	WP	BK	R	ER	W	L	PCT	SV	ERA
82	WW/NWL	A–	14	0	14	2	0	0	78.0	64	4	71	0	1	78	0	0	7	1	49	28	4	6	.400	0	3.23
83	REN/CAL	A+	17	0	17	6	1	0	116.0	96	5	49	0	3	79	0	0	3	0	50	35	7	5	.583	0	2.72
84	BEA/TEX	AA	13	354	13	0	0	0	85.2	63	5	39	0	0	49	7	3	4	0	28	20	7	2	.778	0	2.10
85	BEA/TEX	AA	16	389	16	1	0	0	85.0	84	3	66	3	0	57	3	5	5	5	51	44	7	5	.583	0	4.66
86	LV/PCL	AAA	28	696	27	4	2	0	157.2	168	10	72	0	1	114	6	5	9	5	84	77	9	10	.474	0	4.40
	SD/NL		3	65	3	1	1	0	18.0	10	1	3	0	0	11	0	0	3	0	6	5	2	0	1.000	0	2.50
87	LV/PCL	AAA	4	104	4	1	0	0	24.1	24	1	8	0	0	11	0	0	3	0	16	16	2	0	1.000	0	5.92
	SD/NL		30	639	22	2	1	4	145.2	154	14	54	2	5	51	5	5	3	2	85	67	9	7	.563	0	4.14
88	SD/NL		29	760	29	3	0	0	179.0	192	14	44	3	3	82	11	9	4	1	98	82	9	14	.391	0	4.12
89	COL/INT	AAA	20	509	20	4	1	0	124.0	110	9	31	1	2	94	1	1	2	0	54	52	8	6	.571	0	3.77
	NY/AL		11	211	6	0	0	3	48.0	56	7	16	1	2	25	1	1	1	0	29	28	2	2	.667	0	5.25
90	COL/INT	AAA	11	299	11	3	1	0	73.0	46	3	35	1	5	78	1	1	1	2	20	19	5	2	.714	0	2.34
	NY/AL		17	238	7	0	0	9	50.0	72	8	23	0	1	25	1	4	3	0	42	35	1	2	.333	0	6.30
91	HOU/NL		26	593	22	1	1	0	135.1	143	9	51	3	3	88	7	2	4	0	73	66	8	8	.429	0	4.39
6 YR TOTALS			**116**	**2506**	**89**	**7**	**3**	**16**	**576.0**	**627**	**53**	**191**	**9**	**14**	**286**	**26**	**21**	**15**	**3**	**333**	**283**	**29**	**32**	**.475**	**0**	**4.42**

Jones, Joseph Stacy "Stacy" — bats right — throws right — b.5/26/67

YR	TM/LG	CL	G	TBF	GS	CG	SHO	GF	IP	H	HR	BB	IBB	HB	SO	SH	SF	WP	BK	R	ER	W	L	PCT	SV	ERA
88	ERI/NYP	A–	7	218	7	3	2	0	54.1	51	1	15	2	0	40	1	0	2	0	12	8	3	3	.500	0	1.33
	HAG/CAR	A+	6	156	6	3	2	0	37.2	35	2	12	0	1	23	1	4	2	0	14	12	3	1	.750	0	2.87
89	FRE/CAR	A+	15	374	15	3	1	0	82.2	93	11	35	0	2	58	1	3	3	4	57	45	5	6	.455	0	4.90
90	FRE/CAR	A+	15	119	0	0	0	11	26.2	31	0	7	1	1	24	0	1	1	1	13	10	1	2	.333	2	3.38
	HAG/EAS	AA	19	176	0	0	0	11	40.1	46	1	11	1	1	41	4	1	2	0	27	23	1	6	.143	5	5.13
91	HAG/EAS	AA	12	130	0	0	0	4	30.1	24	1	15	1	1	26	2	0	1	0	6	6	0	1	.000	1	1.78
	BAL/AL		4	49	0	0	0	2	11.0	11	1	5	0	0	10	0	1	0	0	6	5	0	0	.000	0	4.09
	ROC/INT	AAA	33	221	1	0	0	21	50.2	53	4	20	2	0	47	7	2	2	1	22	19	4	4	.500	8	3.38

Juden, Jeffrey Daniel "Jeff" — bats right — throws right — b.1/19/71

YR	TM/LG	CL	G	TBF	GS	CG	SHO	GF	IP	H	HR	BB	IBB	HB	SO	SH	SF	WP	BK	R	ER	W	L	PCT	SV	ERA
89	AST/GCL	R	9	177	8	0	0	0	39.2	33	0	17	0	3	49	1	3	7	2	21	15	1	4	.200	0	3.40
90	OSC/FSL	A+	15	390	15	2	0	0	91.0	72	2	42	0	5	85	3	1	7	4	37	23	10	1	.909	0	2.27
	COL/SOU	AA	11	250	11	0	0	0	52.0	55	2	42	2	4	40	2	1	9	2	36	31	1	3	.250	0	5.37
91	JAC/TEX	AA	16	408	16	0	0	0	95.2	84	4	44	0	3	75	8	4	5	2	43	33	6	3	.667	0	3.10
	TUC/PCL	AAA	10	245	10	0	0	0	56.2	56	2	25	0	0	51	4	3	7	0	28	20	3	2	.600	0	3.18
	HOU/NL		4	81	3	0	0	0	18.0	19	2	10	0	1	11	2	2	1	0	14	14	1	1	.500	0	6.00

Kaiser, Jeffrey Patrick "Jeff" — bats right — throws left — b.7/24/60

YR	TM/LG	CL	G	TBF	GS	CG	SHO	GF	IP	H	HR	BB	IBB	HB	SO	SH	SF	WP	BK	R	ER	W	L	PCT	SV	ERA
82	MED/NWL	A–	15	0	15	1	0	0	78.0	91	5	57	0	2	69	0	0	12	1	56	46	8	1	.889	0	5.31
83	MOD/CAL	A+	25	0	25	4	0	0	164.0	160	4	80	0	5	102	0	1	9	0	84	70	12	9	.571	0	3.84
84	ALB/EAS	AA	7	187	7	1	1	0	47.2	36	0	15	0	1	20	3	1	1	1	11	10	5	1	.833	0	1.89
	TAC/PCL	AAA	14	0	12	0	0	1	74.2	81	4	28	1	1	38	0	0	1	1	52	38	4	7	.364	1	4.58
85	TAC/PCL	AAA	27	0	0	0	0	11	46.1	33	3	18	4	0	36	0	0	2	0	10	9	4	2	.667	5	1.75
	OAK/AL		15	97	0	0	0	4	16.2	25	6	20	2	1	10	1	2	0	0	32	27	0	0	.000	0	14.58

(continued)

Kaiser, Jeffrey Patrick "Jeff" (continued)

YR	TM/LG	CL	G	TBF	GS	CG	SHO	GF	IP	H	HR	BB	IBB	HB	SO	SH	SF	WP	BK	R	ER	W	L	PCT	SV	ERA
86	TAC/PCL	AAA	34	498	18	2	1	10	110.2	123	5	52	2	5	63	2	4	6	5	70	53	4	4	.500	2	4.31
87	BUF/AMA	AAA	22	333	8	0	0	5	71.1	87	9	32	1	3	53	2	5	2	2	52	41	5	3	.625	1	5.17
	CLE/AL		2	18	0	0	0	0	3.1	4	1	3	0	1	2	0	0	0	0	6	6	0	0	.000	0	16.20
88	CLE/AL		3	11	0	0	0	1	2.2	2	0	1	0	0	0	2	1	0	0	0	0	0	0	.000	0	0.00
	CS/PCL	AAA	36	229	0	0	0	21	53.0	56	5	19	2	1	47	4	3	1	0	23	22	3	2	.600	6	3.74
89	CS/PCL	AAA	31	213	1	0	0	12	45.1	64	1	18	1	1	46	4	0	3	1	29	22	3	6	.333	3	4.37
	CLE/AL		6	22	0	0	0	1	3.2	5	1	5	0	0	4	2	0	0	0	5	3	0	1	.000	0	7.36
90	CLE/AL		5	60	0	0	0	0	12.2	16	2	7	1	0	9	0	1	0	0	5	5	0	0	.000	0	3.55
	CS/PCL	AAA	25	182	0	0	0	11	43.0	36	3	22	2	2	46	0	3	5	1	16	14	2	2	.500	2	2.93
91	DEN/AMA	AAA	8	85	0	0	0	1	18.2	16	0	13	1	1	12	1	1	1	1	9	8	0	1	.000	0	3.86
	TOL/INT	AAA	16	145	3	0	0	6	34.2	35	3	11	0	1	28	1	0	4	2	9	8	3	0	1.000	1	2.08
	DET/AL		10	26	0	0	0	7	5.0	6	1	5	0	0	4	0	0	0	0	5	5	0	1	.000	2	9.00
6 YR TOTALS			**41**	**234**	**0**	**0**	**0**	**10**	**44.0**	**58**	**11**	**41**	**5**	**2**	**29**	**3**	**5**	**3**	**0**	**53**	**46**	**0**	**2**	**.000**	**2**	**9.41**

Kamieniecki, Scott Andrew — bats right — throws right — b.4/19/64

YR	TM/LG	CL	G	TBF	GS	CG	SHO	GF	IP	H	HR	BB	IBB	HB	SO	SH	SF	WP	BK	R	ER	W	L	PCT	SV	ERA
87	PW/CAR	A+	19	499	19	1	0	0	112.1	91	7	78	3	5	84	1	2	9	2	61	52	9	5	.643	0	4.17
	ALB/EAS	AA	10	176	7	0	0	1	37.0	41	0	33	3	1	19	5	0	3	1	25	22	1	3	.250	0	5.35
88	PW/CAR	A+	15	451	15	7	2	0	100.1	115	3	50	1	2	72	2	0	10	1	62	49	6	7	.462	0	4.40
	FT./FSL	A+	12	329	11	1	1	0	77.0	71	0	40	1	1	51	1	2	7	0	36	31	3	6	.333	0	3.62
89	ALB/EAS	AA	24	636	23	6	3	1	151.0	142	13	57	1	2	140	1	3	5	0	67	62	10	9	.526	0	3.70
90	ALB/EAS	AA	22	562	21	3	1	1	132.0	113	5	61	2	0	99	6	6	4	1	55	47	10	9	.526	0	3.20
91	COL/INT	AAA	11	308	11	3	1	0	76.1	61	2	20	0	3	58	3	2	2	3	25	20	6	3	.667	0	2.36
	NY/AL		9	239	9	0	0	0	55.1	54	8	22	1	3	34	2	1	1	0	24	24	4	4	.500	0	3.90

Key, James Edward "Jimmy" — bats right — throws left — b.4/22/61

YR	TM/LG	CL	G	TBF	GS	CG	SHO	GF	IP	H	HR	BB	IBB	HB	SO	SH	SF	WP	BK	R	ER	W	L	PCT	SV	ERA
84	TOR/AL		63	285	0	0	0	24	62.0	70	8	32	8	1	44	6	1	3	1	37	32	4	5	.444	10	4.65
85	TOR/AL		35	856	32	3	0	0	212.2	188	22	50	1	2	85	5	5	6	1	77	71	14	6	.700	0	3.00
86	TOR/AL		36	959	35	4	2	0	232.0	222	24	74	1	3	141	10	6	3	0	98	92	14	11	.560	0	3.57
87	TOR/AL		36	1033	36	8	1	0	261.0	210	24	66	6	2	161	11	3	8	5	93	80	17	8	.680	0	2.76
88	DUN/FSL	A+	4	83	4	0	0	0	21.1	15	0	1	0	0	11	1	0	0	1	2	0	1	0	1.000	0	0.00
	TOR/AL		21	551	21	2	2	0	131.1	127	13	30	2	5	65	4	3	1	0	55	48	12	5	.706	0	3.29
89	TOR/AL		33	886	33	5	1	0	216.0	226	18	27	2	3	118	9	9	4	1	99	93	13	14	.481	0	3.88
90	DUN/FSL	A+	3	77	3	0	0	0	18.0	21	0	3	0	1	14	0	1	1	0	7	5	2	0	1.000	0	2.50
	TOR/AL		27	636	27	0	0	0	154.2	169	20	22	2	1	88	5	6	0	1	79	73	13	7	.650	0	4.25
91	TOR/AL		33	877	33	2	2	0	209.1	207	12	44	3	3	125	10	5	1	1	84	71	16	12	.571	0	3.05
8 YR TOTALS			**284**	**6083**	**217**	**24**	**8**	**24**	**1479.0**	**1419**	**141**	**345**	**25**	**20**	**827**	**60**	**38**	**26**	**9**	**622**	**560**	**103**	**68**	**.602**	**10**	**3.41**

Kiecker, Dana Ervin — bats right — throws right — b.2/25/61

YR	TM/LG	CL	G	TBF	GS	CG	SHO	GF	IP	H	HR	BB	IBB	HB	SO	SH	SF	WP	BK	R	ER	W	L	PCT	SV	ERA
84	WIN/CAR	A+	29	615	19	5	1	8	137.2	142	12	55	2	1	82	2	3	12	2	86	67	6	11	.353	1	4.38
85	WH/FSL	A+	29	789	29	9	2	0	193.2	176	4	59	2	2	60	7	10	7	0	72	56	12	12	.500	0	2.60
86	NB/EAS	AA	24	675	24	7	0	0	156.1	171	8	48	3	4	71	5	8	10	5	88	72	7	12	.368	0	4.14
87	NB/EAS	AA	39	691	17	2	0	18	153.0	164	6	66	5	10	66	5	6	9	1	76	65	7	10	.412	6	3.82
88	NB/EAS	AA	1	22	1	0	0	0	6.0	3	0	0	0	1	1	0	0	0	0	0	0	1	0	1.000	0	0.00
	PAW/INT	AAA	23	556	22	4	1	1	132.1	120	7	46	2	6	74	2	4	5	0	65	54	7	7	.500	0	3.67
89	PAW/INT	AAA	28	644	19	3	0	3	147.1	163	12	36	2	4	87	4	6	6	0	83	60	8	8	.500	0	3.67
90	BOS/AL		32	641	25	0	0	4	152.0	145	9	54	2	9	93	1	5	5	1	74	67	8	9	.471	0	3.97
91	PAW/INT	AAA	8	175	7	0	0	0	38.0	42	4	19	2	3	23	3	0	2	0	24	16	2	3	.400	0	3.79
	BOS/AL		18	194	5	0	0	2	40.1	56	6	23	4	2	21	5	1	3	2	34	33	2	3	.400	0	7.36
2 YR TOTALS			**50**	**835**	**30**	**0**	**0**	**6**	**192.1**	**201**	**13**	**77**	**6**	**11**	**114**	**6**	**6**	**12**	**3**	**108**	**100**	**10**	**12**	**.455**	**0**	**4.68**

Kiely, John Francis — bats right — throws right — b.10/4/64

YR	TM/LG	CL	G	TBF	GS	CG	SHO	GF	IP	H	HR	BB	IBB	HB	SO	SH	SF	WP	BK	R	ER	W	L	PCT	SV	ERA
88	BRI/APP	R+	8	53	0	0	0	6	11.2	9	0	7	0	0	14	2	0	2	0	9	8	2	2	.500	1	6.17
89	LAK/FSL	A+	36	267	0	0	0	22	63.2	52	2	27	4	0	56	4	3	1	2	26	17	4	3	.571	8	2.40
90	LON/EAS	AA	46	321	0	0	0	25	76.2	63	2	42	6	2	52	2	4	2	0	17	15	3	0	1.000	12	1.76
91	DET/AL		7	42	0	0	0	3	6.2	13	0	9	2	1	2	1	1	1	0	11	11	0	1	.000	0	14.85
	TOL/INT	AAA	42	301	0	0	0	27	72.0	57	3	35	3	2	60	4	2	2	0	25	17	4	2	.667	6	2.13

Kile, Darryl Andrew — bats right — throws right — b.12/2/68

YR	TM/LG	CL	G	TBF	GS	CG	SHO	GF	IP	H	HR	BB	IBB	HB	SO	SH	SF	WP	BK	R	ER	W	L	PCT	SV	ERA
88	AST/GCL	R	12	263	12	0	0	0	59.2	48	1	33	0	3	54	3	1	9	8	34	21	5	3	.625	0	3.17
89	COL/SOU	AA	20	508	20	6	2	0	125.2	74	5	68	1	6	108	3	4	5	6	47	36	11	6	.647	0	2.58
	TUC/PCL	AAA	6	122	6	1	1	0	25.2	33	1	13	0	1	18	0	0	1	1	20	17	2	1	.667	0	5.96
90	TUC/PCL	AAA	26	575	23	1	0	1	123.1	147	16	68	1	5	77	2	5	13	4	97	91	5	10	.333	0	6.64
91	HOU/NL		37	689	22	0	0	5	153.2	144	16	84	6	3	100	9	5	5	4	81	63	7	11	.389	0	3.69

Kilgus, Paul Nelson — bats left — throws left — b.2/2/62

YR	TM/LG	CL	G	TBF	GS	CG	SHO	GF	IP	H	HR	BB	IBB	HB	SO	SH	SF	WP	BK	R	ER	W	L	PCT	SV	ERA
84	TRI/NWL	A−	14	0	14	0	0	0	78.1	87	1	31	0	3	60	0	0	4	0	38	25	7	5	.583	0	2.87
85	SAL/CAR	A+	38	346	0	0	0	19	84.1	69	5	24	6	4	67	0	4	1	0	28	19	3	1	.750	10	2.03
86	TUL/TEX	AA	41	447	7	2	0	24	103.2	102	7	36	5	4	59	3	4	5	1	56	43	3	7	.300	8	3.73

Kilgus, Paul Nelson (continued)

YR	TM/LG	CL	G	TBF	GS	CG	SHO	GF	IP	H	HR	BB	IBB	HB	SO	SH	SF	WP	BK	R	ER	W	L	PCT	SV	ERA
87	OC/AMA	AAA	21	104	0	0	0	17	24.2	23	2	10	3	2	14	1	1	1	1	12	11	2	0	1.000	7	4.01
	TEX/AL		25	385	12	0	0	2	89.1	95	14	31	2	2	42	2	0	0	0	45	41	2	7	.222	0	4.13
88	TEX/AL		32	871	32	5	3	0	203.1	190	18	71	2	10	88	4	4	6	4	105	94	12	15	.444	0	4.16
89	IOW/AMA	AAA	1	37	1	1	0	0	9.0	9	0	2	0	0	5	1	1	2	0	3	3	1	0	1.000	0	3.00
	CHI/NL		35	642	23	0	0	5	145.2	164	9	49	6	5	61	5	4	3	2	90	71	6	10	.375	2	4.39
90	TOR/AL		11	74	0	0	0	4	16.1	19	2	7	1	1	7	1	3	0	0	11	11	0	0	.000	0	6.06
	SYR/INT	AAA	20	516	17	1	0	8	125.2	116	10	39	4	5	75	5	1	4	3	47	41	6	8	.429	0	2.94
91	BAL/AL		38	267	0	0	0	14	62.0	60	8	24	2	3	32	2	4	2	0	38	35	0	2	.000	1	5.08
5 YR TOTALS			141	2239	67	5	3	25	516.2	528	51	182	13	21	230	14	15	11	6	289	252	20	34	.370	3	4.39

King, Eric Steven — bats right — throws right — b.4/10/64

YR	TM/LG	CL	G	TBF	GS	CG	SHO	GF	IP	H	HR	BB	IBB	HB	SO	SH	SF	WP	BK	R	ER	W	L	PCT	SV	ERA
84	CLI/MID	A	35	650	21	2	0	12	147.1	142	5	76	2	1	124	9	1	15	1	74	55	5	10	.333	3	3.36
85	SHR/TEX	AA	15	415	15	2	1	0	104.2	74	8	30	0	4	80	3	2	1	0	34	27	5	3	.625	0	2.32
86	NAS/AMA	AAA	6	158	6	1	0	0	38.1	29	1	16	2	1	38	1	1	2	0	16	15	3	2	.600	0	3.52
	DET/AL		33	579	16	3	1	9	138.1	108	11	63	3	8	79	6	1	4	3	54	54	11	4	.733	3	3.51
87	DET/AL		55	513	4	0	0	26	116.0	111	15	60	10	4	89	3	3	5	1	67	63	6	9	.400	9	4.89
88	TOL/INT	AAA	10	279	10	2	0	0	69.0	54	4	23	4	1	51	3	2	1	1	26	25	3	4	.429	0	3.26
	DET/AL		23	303	5	0	0	8	68.2	60	5	34	2	5	45	5	2	4	2	28	26	4	1	.800	3	3.41
89	WS/GCL	R	2	49	2	0	0	0	11.0	13	0	3	1	1	8	1	1	2	1	8	5	1	1	.500	0	4.09
	SAR/FSL	A+	1	33	1	1	0	0	9.0	9	0	0	0	0	7	0	0	0	0	1	1	1	0	1.000	0	1.00
	CHI/AL		25	666	25	1	1	0	159.1	144	13	64	1	4	72	3	4	5	4	69	60	9	10	.474	0	3.39
90	SAR/FSL	A+	2	33	2	0	0	0	8.0	8	0	2	0	0	5	0	0	0	1	4	2	1	0	1.000	0	2.25
	CHI/AL		25	623	25	2	2	0	151.0	135	10	40	0	6	70	4	1	4	3	59	55	12	4	.750	0	3.28
91	CS/PCL	AAA	3	56	3	0	0	0	11.1	18	1	5	0	0	3	0	0	1	1	12	12	1	0	1.000	0	9.53
	CLE/AL		25	656	24	2	1	0	150.2	166	7	44	3	3	59	7	8	2	2	83	77	6	11	.353	0	4.60
6 YR TOTALS			186	3340	99	8	5	43	784.0	724	61	305	20	30	414	30	19	22	15	360	335	48	39	.552	15	3.85

Kipper, Robert Wayne "Bob" — bats right — throws left — b.7/8/64

YR	TM/LG	CL	G	TBF	GS	CG	SHO	GF	IP	H	HR	BB	IBB	HB	SO	SH	SF	WP	BK	R	ER	W	L	PCT	SV	ERA
84	RED/CAL	A+	26	0	26	8	3	0	185.0	147	4	65	3	3	98	0	0	5	0	61	42	18	8	.692	0	2.04
85	CAL/AL		2	20	1	0	0	0	3.1	7	1	3	0	0	0	2	0	0	0	8	8	0	1	.000	0	21.60
	MID/TEX	AA	9	204	9	1	1	0	49.2	52	5	10	2	3	31	2	3	1	1	22	17	3	3	.500	0	3.08
	EDM/PCL	AAA	1	0	1	0	0	0	8.1	7	1	2	0	0	8	0	0	0	0	3	2	0	0	.000	0	2.16
	HAW/PCL	AAA	6	0	5	1	1	1	41.1	29	3	10	0	1	34	0	0	1	0	12	9	1	2	.333	0	1.96
	PIT/NL		5	104	4	0	0	1	24.2	21	4	7	0	0	13	1	1	0	0	16	14	1	2	.333	0	5.11
	YEAR		7	124					28.0	28	5	10	0	0	13	1	3	0	0	24	22	1	3	.250	0	7.07
86	NAS/EAS	AA	4	72	4	0	0	0	18.1	14	1	3	0	3	19	0	1	1	0	7	7	0	1	.000	0	3.44
	PIT/NL		20	496	19	0	0	1	114.0	123	17	34	3	2	81	3	3	3	3	60	51	6	8	.429	0	4.03
87	VAN/PCL	AAA	6	102	2	0	0	0	25.1	23	2	4	1	0	22	2	1	1	0	7	5	0	2	.000	0	1.78
	PIT/NL		24	493	20	1	1	0	110.2	117	25	52	4	2	83	4	3	5	0	74	73	5	9	.357	0	5.94
88	PIT/NL		50	267	0	0	0	15	65.0	54	7	26	4	2	39	5	3	1	1	33	27	2	6	.250	0	3.74
89	PIT/NL		52	334	0	0	0	15	83.0	55	5	33	6	0	58	5	3	5	2	29	27	3	4	.429	4	2.93
90	BUF/AMA	AAA	5	21	1	0	0	0	4.2	6	1	1	0	0	6	0	0	0	0	4	4	0	0	.000	0	7.71
	PIT/NL		41	260	1	0	0	7	62.2	44	7	26	1	3	35	2	3	1	5	24	21	5	2	.714	3	3.02
91	PIT/NL		52	264	0	0	0	18	60.0	66	7	22	3	0	38	1	2	2	2	34	31	2	2	.500	4	4.65
7 YR TOTALS			246	2238	45	1	1	57	523.1	487	73	203	21	9	347	21	20	15	12	278	252	24	34	.414	11	4.33

Kiser, Garland Routhard — bats left — throws left — b.7/8/68

YR	TM/LG	CL	G	TBF	GS	CG	SHO	GF	IP	H	HR	BB	IBB	HB	SO	SH	SF	WP	BK	R	ER	W	L	PCT	SV	ERA
86	BEN/NWL	A−	14	0	12	0	0	2	70.2	79	4	48	2	2	46	0	0	6	1	58	43	4	5	.444	0	5.48
87	SPA/SAL	A	21	204	5	0	0	6	43.0	49	2	24	2	4	27	4	1	6	0	37	31	0	5	.000	1	6.49
88	IND/GCL	R	7	221	7	2	0	1	56.0	31	0	17	0	2	45	0	0	0	2	12	8	5	1	.833	0	1.29
	BUR/APP	R+	7	123	5	1	0	0	31.0	22	0	9	0	0	29	0	0	1	2	11	7	2	2	.500	0	2.03
89	KIN/CAR	A+	6	60	0	0	0	1	12.2	14	1	7	0	2	7	1	1	0	0	10	10	0	0	.000	0	7.11
	WAT/NYP	A−	12	304	9	2	0	2	74.0	66	4	18	0	2	74	4	0	5	2	36	28	7	1	.875	0	3.41
90	KIN/CAR	A+	55	388	0	0	0	24	94.2	81	3	27	1	3	82	3	4	5	0	25	18	5	3	.625	9	1.71
91	KIN/CAR	A+	31	197	0	0	0	12	48.1	35	2	14	2	1	52	3	0	3	0	11	8	6	1	.857	5	1.49
	CAN/EAS	AA	17	170	4	0	0	6	44.1	35	1	11	2	1	34	1	0	1	0	5	5	0	0	.000	0	2.03
	CLE/AL		7	25	0	0	0	2	4.2	7	0	4	0	1	3	0	0	0	0	5	5	0	0	.000	0	9.64

Klink, Joseph Charles "Joe" — bats left — throws left — b.2/3/62

YR	TM/LG	CL	G	TBF	GS	CG	SHO	GF	IP	H	HR	BB	IBB	HB	SO	SH	SF	WP	BK	R	ER	W	L	PCT	SV	ERA
84	COL/SAL	A	31	172	0	0	0	27	38.2	30	1	28	0	1	49	4	3	5	1	19	15	5	4	.556	11	3.49
85	LYN/CAR	A+	44	221	0	0	0	17	51.2	41	1	26	2	0	59	4	2	1	2	16	13	3	3	.500	5	2.26
86	ORL/SOU	AA	45	297	0	0	0	41	68.0	59	5	37	1	2	63	5	1	1	0	24	19	4	5	.444	11	2.51
87	MIN/AL		12	116	0	0	0	5	23.0	37	4	11	0	0	17	1	1	0	0	18	17	0	1	.000	0	6.65
	POR/PCL	AAA	12	107	0	0	0	7	23.0	25	1	13	1	0	14	1	3	1	0	14	11	0	0	.000	0	4.30
88	HUN/SOU	AA	21	143	0	0	0	12	34.2	25	3	14	1	0	30	0	0	3	4	6	3	1	2	.333	3	0.78
	TAC/PCL	AAA	27	185	0	0	0	15	38.2	48	2	17	1	1	32	5	3	3	0	29	22	2	1	.667	1	5.12
89	TAC/PCL	AAA	6	23	0	0	0	5	6.2	2	0	2	0	1	6	0	0	0	0	0	0	0	0	.000	0	0.00
	HUN/SOU	AA	57	249	0	0	0	53	60.2	46	2	23	0	2	59	3	4	6	1	19	19	4	4	.500	26	2.82
90	OAK/AL		40	165	0	0	0	19	39.2	34	1	18	0	0	19	1	0	3	1	9	9	0	0	.000	1	2.04

(continued)

Klink, Joseph Charles "Joe" (continued)

YR	TM/LG	CL	G	TBF	GS	CG	SHO	GF	IP	H	HR	BB	IBB	HB	SO	SH	SF	WP	BK	R	ER	W	L	PCT	SV	ERA
91	MOD/CAL	A+	3	19	3	0	0	0	5.0	4	2	1	0	0	1	0	0	0	0	2	2	0	0	.000	0	3.60
	OAK/AL		62	266	0	0	0	10	62.0	60	4	21	5	5	34	8	0	4	0	30	30	10	3	.769	2	4.35
3 YR TOTALS			**114**	**547**	**0**	**0**	**0**	**34**	**124.2**	**131**	**9**	**50**	**5**	**5**	**70**	**10**	**1**	**8**	**1**	**57**	**56**	**10**	**4**	**.714**	**3**	**4.04**

Knudson, Mark Richard — bats right — throws right — b.10/28/60

YR	TM/LG	CL	G	TBF	GS	CG	SHO	GF	IP	H	HR	BB	IBB	HB	SO	SH	SF	WP	BK	R	ER	W	L	PCT	SV	ERA
84	COL/SOU	AA	14	414	14	3	0	0	101.0	100	2	27	4	0	54	7	2	2	0	32	25	4	5	.444	0	2.23
	TUC/PCL	AAA	13	0	13	1	0	0	84.0	93	6	20	3	1	42	0	0	1	0	41	34	4	6	.400	0	3.64
85	TUC/PCL	AAA	24	0	22	4	2	0	146.0	171	10	37	1	1	68	0	0	6	0	69	65	8	5	.615	0	4.01
	HOU/NL		2	53	2	0	0	0	11.0	21	0	3	0	0	4	1	0	0	0	11	11	0	2	.000	0	9.00
86	HOU/NL		9	191	7	0	0	1	42.2	48	5	15	5	0	20	3	0	1	0	23	20	1	5	.167	0	4.22
	TUC/PCL	AAA	15	401	14	3	1	0	94.0	111	4	21	0	0	55	2	2	3	2	46	41	5	5	.500	0	3.93
	VAN/AMA	AAA	2	54	2	0	0	0	12.2	13	2	5	1	0	8	0	0	0	0	8	8	1	1	.500	0	5.68
	MIL/AL		4	82	1	0	0	1	17.2	22	7	5	1	0	9	0	0	1	0	15	15	0	1	.000	0	7.64
	YEAR		13	273	8	0	0	2	60.1	70	12	20	6	1	29	3	0	2	0	38	35	1	6	.143	0	5.22
87	DEN/AMA	AAA	14	345	14	1	0	0	78.1	89	11	30	0	2	37	3	1	4	1	53	51	7	2	.778	0	5.86
	MIL/AL		15	288	8	1	0	3	62.0	88	7	14	1	0	26	3	5	1	0	46	37	4	4	.500	0	5.37
88	DEN/AMA	AAA	24	677	22	6	0	1	164.1	180	4	33	1	5	66	1	9	6	4	67	62	11	8	.579	0	3.40
	MIL/AL		5	63	1	0	0	3	16.0	17	1	2	0	0	7	0	0	1	0	3	2	0	0	.000	0	1.13
89	MIL/AL		40	499	7	1	0	16	123.2	110	15	29	2	3	47	1	2	2	0	50	46	8	5	.615	0	3.35
90	MIL/AL		30	719	27	4	2	0	168.1	187	14	40	1	3	56	3	9	6	0	84	77	10	9	.526	0	4.12
91	MIL/AL		12	174	7	0	0	0	35.0	54	8	15	0	1	23	3	3	1	0	33	31	1	3	.250	0	7.97
	DEN/AMA	AAA	13	234	10	2	0	0	51.2	73	5	13	1	2	28	6	1	1	0	34	31	4	4	.500	1	5.40
7 YR TOTALS			**117**	**2069**	**59**	**6**	**2**	**27**	**476.1**	**547**	**57**	**123**	**10**	**8**	**192**	**15**	**18**	**13**	**0**	**265**	**239**	**24**	**29**	**.453**	**0**	**4.52**

Kramer, Thomas Joseph "Tom" — bats both — throws right — b.1/9/68

YR	TM/LG	CL	G	TBF	GS	CG	SHO	GF	IP	H	HR	BB	IBB	HB	SO	SH	SF	WP	BK	R	ER	W	L	PCT	SV	ERA
87	BUR/APP	R+	12	292	11	2	1	1	71.2	57	2	26	0	1	71	0	1	0	0	31	24	7	3	.700	1	3.01
88	WAT/MID	A	27	814	27	10	2	0	198.2	173	9	60	3	3	152	10	3	5	3	70	56	14	7	.667	0	2.54
89	KIN/CAR	A+	18	527	17	5	1	1	131.2	97	7	42	3	4	89	5	3	4	1	44	38	9	5	.643	0	2.60
	CAN/EAS	AA	10	202	8	1	0	0	43.1	58	6	20	0	0	26	3	4	3	0	34	30	1	6	.143	0	6.23
90	KIN/CAR	A+	16	402	16	2	1	0	98.0	82	5	29	0	2	96	1	2	2	1	34	31	7	4	.636	0	2.85
	CAN/EAS	AA	12	287	10	2	0	0	72.0	67	3	14	1	0	46	2	1	1	0	25	24	6	3	.667	0	3.00
91	CAN/EAS	AA	35	320	5	0	0	13	79.1	61	5	34	3	1	61	6	1	3	0	23	21	7	3	.700	6	2.38
	CS/PCL	AAA	10	43	1	0	0	6	11.1	5	1	5	0	0	18	0	0	1	0	1	1	1	0	1.000	4	0.79
	CLE/AL		4	30	0	0	0	1	4.2	10	1	6	0	0	4	0	3	0	0	9	9	0	0	.000	0	17.36

Krueger, William Culp "Bill" — bats left — throws left — b.4/24/58

YR	TM/LG	CL	G	TBF	GS	CG	SHO	GF	IP	H	HR	BB	IBB	HB	SO	SH	SF	WP	BK	R	ER	W	L	PCT	SV	ERA
83	OAK/AL		17	473	16	2	0	0	109.2	104	7	53	1	2	58	0	5	1	1	54	44	7	6	.538	0	3.61
84	TAC/PCL	AAA	5	0	5	2	0	0	31.2	29	3	21	1	0	20	0	0	0	0	17	13	2	2	.500	0	3.69
	OAK/AL		26	647	24	1	0	0	142.0	156	9	85	2	2	61	4	8	5	1	95	75	10	10	.500	0	4.75
85	TAC/PCL	AAA	2	0	2	0	0	0	9.2	12	2	6	0	0	6	0	0	0	0	10	10	1	0	1.000	0	9.31
	OAK/AL		32	674	23	2	0	4	151.1	165	13	69	1	2	56	1	5	6	3	95	76	9	10	.474	0	4.52
86	MAD/MID	A	1	7	0	0	0	0	2.0	1	0	1	0	1	0	0	0	0	0	0	0	0	0	.000	0	0.00
	TAC/PCL	AAA	8	235	8	2	1	0	52.1	53	4	27	1	1	41	3	2	2	0	32	27	3	3	.500	0	4.64
	OAK/AL		11	149	3	0	0	0	34.1	40	4	13	0	0	10	1	2	3	1	25	23	1	2	.333	1	6.03
87	OAK/AL		9	33	0	0	0	0	5.2	9	0	8	3	0	2	0	1	0	0	7	6	0	3	.000	0	9.53
	TAC/PCL	AAA	10	273	10	1	1	0	62.1	64	2	27	2	4	37	3	0	8	2	26	24	3	3	.500	0	3.47
	ALB/PCL	AAA	14	376	14	5	1	0	84.0	94	3	39	0	0	60	3	0	3	4	48	42	6	4	.600	0	4.50
	LA/NL		2	13	0	0	0	0	2.1	3	0	1	0	0	2	0	0	0	0	2	0	0	0	.000	0	0.00
	YEAR		11	46	0	0	0	1	8.0	12	0	9	3	0	4	0	1	0	0	9	6	0	3	.000	0	6.75
88	LA/NL		1	14	1	0	0	0	2.1	4	0	2	1	1	1	0	0	0	0	3	3	0	0	.000	0	11.57
	ALB/PCL	AAA	27	747	26	7	4	0	173.1	167	14	69	1	0	114	4	6	8	1	74	58	15	5	.750	0	3.01
89	DEN/AMA	AAA	2	54	2	0	0	0	13.1	10	1	6	0	0	9	0	0	0	0	4	3	1	1	.500	0	2.03
	MIL/AL		34	403	5	0	0	4	93.2	96	9	33	3	0	72	5	1	10	1	43	40	3	2	.600	3	3.84
90	BEL/MID	A	1	20	1	0	0	0	6.0	4	0	2	0	0	4	0	1	0	0	1	1	1	0	1.000	0	1.50
	MIL/AL		30	566	17	0	0	4	129.0	137	10	54	1	3	64	3	10	8	0	70	57	6	8	.429	0	3.98
91	SEA/AL		35	751	25	1	0	2	175.0	194	15	60	4	4	91	4	6	9	1	82	70	11	8	.579	0	3.60
9 YR TOTALS			**197**	**3723**	**114**	**6**	**0**	**23**	**845.1**	**908**	**67**	**378**	**21**	**14**	**417**	**20**	**40**	**43**	**9**	**476**	**394**	**47**	**49**	**.490**	**4**	**4.19**

LaCoss, Michael James "Mike" — bats right — throws right — b.5/30/56

YR	TM/LG	CL	G	TBF	GS	CG	SHO	GF	IP	H	HR	BB	IBB	HB	SO	SH	SF	WP	BK	R	ER	W	L	PCT	SV	ERA
78	CIN/NL		16	420	15	2	1	0	96.0	104	5	46	9	1	31	6	6	2	1	56	48	4	8	.333	0	4.50
79	CIN/NL		35	868	32	6	1	0	205.2	202	13	79	8	2	73	12	6	3	3	92	80	14	8	.636	0	3.50
80	CIN/NL		34	762	29	4	2	1	169.1	207	9	68	4	1	49	7	3	3	2	101	87	10	12	.455	0	4.62
81	CIN/NL		20	354	13	1	1	3	78.0	102	7	30	4	1	22	4	5	1	0	55	53	4	7	.364	0	6.12
82	HOU/NL		41	488	8	0	0	11	115.0	107	3	54	6	4	51	5	0	5	1	41	37	6	6	.500	2	2.90
83	HOU/NL		38	590	17	2	0	6	138.0	142	10	56	11	2	53	6	6	9	1	81	68	5	7	.417	0	4.43
84	HOU/NL		39	565	18	2	1	6	132.0	132	3	55	5	0	86	3	2	9	1	64	59	7	5	.583	3	4.02
85	KC/AL		21	193	0	0	0	7	40.2	49	2	29	6	0	26	3	0	2	0	25	23	1	1	.500	1	5.09
	OMA/AMA	AAA	4	101	4	1	0	0	22.1	23	1	15	0	1	11	0	0	0	0	12	12	1	2	.333	0	3.22
86	SF/NL		37	842	31	4	2	1	204.1	179	14	70	8	2	86	16	3	5	5	99	81	10	13	.435	0	3.57
87	SF/NL		39	728	26	2	1	4	171.0	184	16	63	12	2	79	9	3	6	1	78	70	13	10	.565	0	3.68

LaCoss, Michael James "Mike" (continued)

YR	TM/LG	CL	G	TBF	GS	CG	SHO	GF	IP	H	HR	BB	IBB	HB	SO	SH	SF	WP	BK	R	ER	W	L	PCT	SV	ERA
88	SF/NL		19	477	19	1	1	0	114.1	99	5	47	3	1	70	5	1	6	2	55	46	7	7	.500	0	3.62
89	SF/NL		45	647	18	1	0	16	150.1	143	3	65	4	7	78	8	7	1	5	62	53	10	10	.500	6	3.17
90	SJ/CAL	A+	1	20	1	0	0	0	6.0	5	1	0	0	0	6	0	0	0	0	1	1	1	0	1.000	0	1.50
	SF/NL		13	337	12	1	0	0	77.2	75	5	39	2	0	39	4	4	1	1	37	34	6	4	.600	0	3.94
91	SF/NL		18	225	5	0	0	6	47.1	61	4	24	1	2	30	3	2	2	0	39	38	1	5	.167	0	7.23
14 YR TOTALS			**415**	**7496**	**243**	**26**	**9**	**61**	**1739.2**	**1786**	**99**	**725**	**86**	**29**	**783**	**91**	**48**	**55**	**23**	**885**	**777**	**98**	**103**	**.488**	**12**	**4.02**

Lamp, Dennis Patrick — bats right — throws right — b.9/23/52

YR	TM/LG	CL	G	TBF	GS	CG	SHO	GF	IP	H	HR	BB	IBB	HB	SO	SH	SF	WP	BK	R	ER	W	L	PCT	SV	ERA
77	CHI/NL		11	137	3	0	0	4	30.0	43	3	8	4	2	12	1	1	0	1	21	21	0	2	.000	0	6.30
78	CHI/NL		37	928	36	6	3	0	223.2	221	16	56	8	4	73	10	3	2	2	96	82	7	15	.318	0	3.30
79	CHI/NL		38	843	32	6	1	3	200.1	223	14	46	9	5	86	9	5	1	0	96	78	11	10	.524	0	3.50
80	CHI/NL		41	921	37	2	1	3	202.2	259	16	82	7	1	83	17	4	10	0	123	117	10	14	.417	0	5.20
81	CHI/AL		27	514	10	3	0	5	127.0	103	4	43	1	1	71	5	0	4	1	41	34	7	6	.538	0	2.41
82	CHI/AL		44	817	27	3	2	11	189.2	206	9	59	3	6	78	12	2	5	0	96	84	11	8	.579	5	3.99
83	CHI/AL		49	483	5	1	0	31	116.1	123	6	29	7	4	44	2	1	0	0	52	48	7	7	.500	15	3.71
84	TOR/AL		56	387	4	0	0	37	85.0	97	7	38	1	3	45	7	1	2	0	53	43	8	8	.500	9	4.55
85	TOR/AL		53	426	1	0	0	11	105.2	96	7	27	3	1	68	6	5	5	0	42	39	11	0	1.000	2	3.32
86	TOR/AL		40	329	2	0	0	11	73.0	93	5	23	6	0	30	4	1	2	0	50	41	2	6	.250	2	5.05
87	TAC/PCL	AAA	6	53	0	0	0	0	12.1	9	0	8	1	0	10	0	1	0	1	4	4	1	0	1.000	0	2.92
	OAK/AL		36	262	5	0	0	10	56.2	76	5	22	3	0	36	3	3	4	0	38	32	1	3	.250	0	5.08
88	BOS/AL		46	350	0	0	0	14	82.2	92	3	19	3	2	49	3	2	5	8	39	32	7	6	.538	0	3.48
89	BOS/AL		42	445	0	0	0	14	112.1	96	4	27	6	0	61	5	5	1	1	37	29	4	2	.667	0	2.32
90	BOS/AL		47	453	1	0	0	5	105.2	114	10	30	8	3	49	8	4	2	0	61	55	3	5	.375	0	4.68
91	BOS/AL		51	403	0	0	0	12	92.0	100	8	31	7	3	57	3	2	1	0	54	48	6	3	.667	0	4.70
15 YR TOTALS			**618**	**7698**	**163**	**21**	**7**	**171**	**1802.2**	**1942**	**119**	**540**	**82**	**33**	**842**	**94**	**40**	**44**	**13**	**899**	**783**	**95**	**95**	**.500**	**35**	**3.91**

Lancaster, Lester Wayne "Les" — bats right — throws right — b.4/21/62

YR	TM/LG	CL	G	TBF	GS	CG	SHO	GF	IP	H	HR	BB	IBB	HB	SO	SH	SF	WP	BK	R	ER	W	L	PCT	SV	ERA
85	WYT/APP	R+	20	433	10	7	1	8	102.0	98	6	24	5	1	81	4	3	4	0	49	41	7	4	.636	3	3.62
86	WIN/CAR	A+	13	396	13	3	0	0	97.0	88	6	30	2	2	52	3	4	1	1	37	30	8	3	.727	0	2.78
	PIT/EAS	AA	14	389	14	2	0	0	88.0	105	4	34	2	5	49	2	4	2	1	46	41	5	6	.455	0	4.19
87	IOW/AMA	AAA	15	268	6	0	0	6	67.0	59	9	17	3	1	62	3	1	0	1	24	24	5	3	.625	4	3.22
	CHI/NL		27	578	18	0	0	4	132.1	138	14	51	5	1	78	5	6	7	8	76	72	8	3	.727	0	4.90
88	CHI/NL		44	371	3	1	0	15	85.2	89	4	34	7	1	36	3	7	3	3	42	36	4	6	.400	5	3.78
89	IOW/AMA	AAA	17	389	14	3	2	0	91.1	76	6	43	0	3	56	4	4	2	4	38	27	5	7	.417	0	2.66
	CHI/NL		42	288	0	0	0	15	72.2	60	2	15	1	0	56	3	4	2	1	12	11	4	2	.667	8	1.36
90	IOW/AMA	AAA	6	74	0	0	0	2	17.2	20	0	5	0	0	15	0	1	1	0	10	8	0	1	.000	1	4.08
	CHI/NL		55	479	6	1	1	26	109.0	121	11	40	1	1	65	6	5	7	0	57	56	9	5	.643	3	4.62
91	CHI/NL		64	653	11	1	0	21	156.0	150	13	49	7	4	102	9	2	2	2	68	61	9	7	.563	3	3.52
5 YR TOTALS			**232**	**2369**	**38**	**3**	**1**	**81**	**555.2**	**558**	**44**	**189**	**28**	**7**	**337**	**26**	**26**	**21**	**14**	**255**	**236**	**34**	**23**	**.596**	**22**	**3.82**

Landrum, Thomas William "Bill" — bats right — throws right — b.8/17/57

YR	TM/LG	CL	G	TBF	GS	CG	SHO	GF	IP	H	HR	BB	IBB	HB	SO	SH	SF	WP	BK	R	ER	W	L	PCT	SV	ERA
84	WIC/AMA	AAA	47	545	9	2	0	16	130.1	120	8	52	1	1	120	6	7	4	2	58	50	7	4	.636	2	3.45
85	DEN/AMA	AAA	29	596	19	3	1	6	138.0	148	9	49	1	3	88	7	2	4	7	72	61	6	6	.500	2	3.98
86	DEN/AMA	AAA	24	166	2	0	0	19	36.1	36	1	25	2	0	36	1	0	3	1	20	14	1	3	.250	8	3.47
	CIN/NL		10	65	0	0	0	4	13.1	23	0	4	0	0	14	1	1	0	0	11	10	0	0	.000	0	6.75
87	NAS/AMA	AAA	19	164	2	0	0	5	38.2	30	0	19	3	0	47	0	3	2	2	9	9	4	0	1.000	1	2.09
	CIN/NL		44	276	2	0	0	14	65.0	68	3	34	6	0	42	7	2	4	1	35	34	3	2	.600	2	4.71
88	CHI/NL		7	55	0	0	0	5	12.1	19	1	3	0	0	6	0	0	1	1	7	7	1	0	1.000	3	2.95
	IOW/AMA	AAA	9	81	0	0	0	6	21.1	13	2	6	0	1	22	0	0	0	1	2	2	3	0	1.000	0	0.71
89	BUF/AMA	AAA	5	91	3	0	0	1	25.1	16	0	6	0	0	20	0	0	0	0			3	0	1.000	0	
	PIT/NL		56	325	0	0	0	40	81.0	60	2	28	8	0	51	3	2	0	0	18	15	2	3	.400	26	1.67
90	PIT/NL		54	292	0	0	0	41	71.2	69	4	21	5	0	39	5	3	1	1	22	17	3	3	.700	13	2.13
91	PIT/NL		61	322	0	0	0	43	76.1	76	4	19	5	0	45	1	1	3	2	32	27	4	4	.500	17	3.18
6 YR TOTALS			**232**	**1335**	**2**	**0**	**0**	**147**	**319.2**	**315**	**14**	**109**	**24**	**0**	**197**	**17**	**9**	**11**	**5**	**126**	**111**	**17**	**12**	**.586**	**58**	**3.13**

Langston, Mark Edward — bats right — throws left — b.8/20/60

YR	TM/LG	CL	G	TBF	GS	CG	SHO	GF	IP	H	HR	BB	IBB	HB	SO	SH	SF	WP	BK	R	ER	W	L	PCT	SV	ERA
84	SEA/AL		35	965	33	5	2	0	225.0	188	16	118	5	8	204	13	7	4	2	99	85	17	10	.630	0	3.40
85	SEA/AL		24	577	24	2	0	0	126.2	122	22	91	2	2	72	3	2	3	2	85	77	7	14	.333	0	5.47
86	SEA/AL		37	1057	36	9	0	1	239.1	234	30	123	1	4	245	5	8	10	3	142	129	12	14	.462	0	4.85
87	SEA/AL		35	1152	35	14	3	0	272.0	242	30	114	0	5	262	6	5	9	2	132	116	19	13	.594	0	3.84
88	SEA/AL		35	1078	35	9	3	0	261.1	222	32	110	2	3	235	6	5	7	4	108	97	15	11	.577	0	3.34
89	SEA/AL		10	297	10	2	1	0	73.1	60	3	19	0	4	60	0	3	1	2	30	29	4	5	.444	0	3.56
	MON/NL		24	740	24	6	4	0	176.2	138	13	93	6	0	175	9	4	5	2	57	47	12	9	.571	0	2.39
	YEAR		34	1037	34	8	5	0	250.0	198	16	112	6	4	235	9	7	6	4	87	76	16	14	.533	0	2.74
90	CAL/AL		33	950	33	5	1	0	223.0	215	13	104	1	5	195	6	6	6	0	120	109	10	17	.370	0	4.40
91	CAL/AL		34	992	34	7	0	0	246.1	190	30	96	3	2	183	4	5	6	3	89	82	19	8	.704	0	3.00
8 YR TOTALS			**267**	**7808**	**264**	**59**	**14**	**1**	**1843.2**	**1611**	**189**	**868**	**20**	**33**	**1631**	**58**	**47**	**53**	**18**	**862**	**771**	**115**	**101**	**.532**	**0**	**3.76**

LaPoint, David Jeffrey "Dave" — bats left — throws left — b.7/29/59

YR	TM/LG	CL	G	TBF	GS	CG	SHO	GF	IP	H	HR	BB	IBB	HB	SO	SH	SF	WP	BK	R	ER	W	L	PCT	SV	ERA
80	MIL/AL		5	75	3	0	0	1	15.0	17	2	13	1	0	5	2	2	0	1	14	10	1	0	1.000	1	6.00
81	STL/NL		3	45	2	0	0	0	10.2	12	1	2	0	1	4	1	0	0	0	5	5	1	0	1.000	0	4.22
82	STL/NL		42	656	21	0	0	6	152.2	170	8	52	8	3	81	9	5	4	2	63	58	9	3	.750	0	3.42
83	STL/NL		37	832	29	1	0	1	191.1	191	12	84	7	4	113	17	11	11	4	92	84	12	9	.571	0	3.95
84	STL/NL		33	827	33	2	1	0	193.0	205	9	77	8	1	130	8	3	15	3	94	85	12	10	.545	0	3.96
85	SF/NL		31	886	31	2	1	0	206.2	215	18	74	6	0	122	7	5	10	0	99	82	7	17	.292	0	3.57
86	DET/AL		16	314	8	0	0	2	67.2	85	11	32	3	0	36	4	1	2	1	49	43	3	6	.333	0	5.72
	SD/NL		24	274	4	0	0	4	61.1	67	8	24	4	1	41	5	1	1	4	37	29	1	4	.200	0	4.26
	YEAR		40	588	12	0	0	6	129.0	152	19	56	7	1	77	9	2	3	5	86	72	4	10	.286	0	5.02
87	LOU/AMA	AAA	14	386	13	4	0	0	91.2	93	8	27	0	0	70	0	2	4	0	45	41	5	5	.500	0	4.03
	STL/NL		6	79	2	0	0	3	16.0	26	4	5	0	0	8	0	0	1	0	12	12	1	1	.500	0	6.75
	CHI/AL		14	341	12	2	1	0	82.2	69	7	31	0	1	43	1	0	3	0	29	27	6	3	.667	0	2.94
	YEAR		20	420	14	2	1	3	98.2	95	11	36	0	1	51	1	0	4	0	41	39	7	4	.636	0	3.56
88	CHI/AL		25	677	25	1	1	0	161.1	151	10	47	1	2	79	8	3	1	5	69	61	10	11	.476	0	3.40
	PIT/NL		8	215	8	1	0	0	52.0	54	4	10	2	0	19	5	1	0	2	18	16	4	2	.667	0	2.77
	YEAR		33	892	33	2	1	0	213.1	205	14	57	3	2	98	13	4	1	7	87	77	14	13	.519	0	3.25
89	NY/AL		20	524	20	0	0	0	113.2	146	12	45	4	2	51	2	4	1	2	73	71	6	9	.400	0	5.62
90	NY/AL		28	694	27	2	0	0	157.2	180	11	57	3	1	67	8	11	4	0	84	72	7	10	.412	0	4.11
91	PHI/NL		2	32	2	0	0	0	5.0	10	1	6	0	1	3	1	1	0	0	10	9	0	1	.000	0	16.20
	DEN/AMA	AAA	7	164	7	0	0	0	35.0	48	3	12	0	2	25	2	1	1	2	30	29	0	2	.000	0	7.46
	IOW/AMA	AAA	26	144	1	0	0	11	30.1	37	3	13	1	3	17	2	1	0	1	26	18	3	0	1.000	1	5.34
12 YR TOTALS			294	6471	227	11	4	17	1486.2	1598	117	559	47	17	802	78	48	53	25	748	664	80	86	.482	1	4.02

Layana, Timothy Joseph "Tim" — bats right — throws right — b.3/2/64

YR	TM/LG	CL	G	TBF	GS	CG	SHO	GF	IP	H	HR	BB	IBB	HB	SO	SH	SF	WP	BK	R	ER	W	L	PCT	SV	ERA
86	ONE/NYP	A–	3	71	3	0	0	0	19.0	10	1	5	0	1	24	1	0	1	0	5	5	2	0	1.000	0	2.37
	FT./FSL	A+	11	276	10	3	1	1	68.1	59	1	19	1	4	52	2	0	5	1	19	17	5	4	.556	1	2.24
87	ALB/EAS	AA	8	195	7	1	0	1	46.1	51	4	18	0	2	19	2	1	1	1	28	26	2	4	.333	0	5.05
	PW/CAR	A+	7	111	3	0	0	2	22.2	29	3	11	0	1	17	1	2	5	2	22	16	2	1	.667	0	6.35
	COL/INT	AAA	13	310	13	0	0	0	70.0	77	6	37	2	1	36	3	1	3	0	37	37	4	5	.444	0	4.76
88	ALB/EAS	AA	14	378	14	1	0	0	87.0	90	4	30	2	6	42	3	3	2	8	52	42	5	7	.417	0	4.34
	COL/INT	AAA	11	216	9	0	0	0	47.2	54	2	25	0	6	25	0	1	2	4	34	32	1	7	.125	0	6.04
89	ALB/EAS	AA	40	261	1	0	0	37	67.2	53	2	15	3	3	48	5	1	2	4	17	13	7	4	.636	17	1.73
90	CIN/NL		55	344	0	0	0	17	80.0	71	7	44	6	2	53	4	3	5	4	33	31	5	3	.625	2	3.49
91	CIN/NL		22	95	0	0	0	9	20.2	23	1	11	0	0	14	1	0	3	0	18	16	0	2	.000	0	6.97
	NAS/AMA	AAA	26	210	2	0	0	4	47.1	41	3	28	0	2	43	3	1	0	1	17	17	3	1	.750	0	3.23
2 YR TOTALS			77	439	0	0	0	26	100.2	94	8	55	6	2	67	5	3	8	4	51	47	5	5	.500	2	4.20

Leach, Terry Hester — bats right — throws right — b.3/13/54

YR	TM/LG	CL	G	TBF	GS	CG	SHO	GF	IP	H	HR	BB	IBB	HB	SO	SH	SF	WP	BK	R	ER	W	L	PCT	SV	ERA
81	NY/NL		21	139	1	0	0	3	35.1	26	2	12	1	0	16	0	0	0	0	11	10	1	1	.500	0	2.55
82	NY/NL		21	194	1	1	1	12	45.1	46	2	18	5	0	30	5	1	0	0	22	21	2	1	.667	3	4.17
84	RIC/INT	AAA	12	78	0	0	0	10	14.2	28	3	3	1	1	6	1	1	0	0	16	15	1	2	.333	1	9.20
	TID/INT	AAA	31	329	0	0	0	16	80.1	70	3	27	4	0	53	2	1	0	0	26	17	10	2	.833	1	1.90
85	TID/INT	AAA	24	178	0	0	0	12	45.1	33	1	8	1	0	25	2	2	0	0	12	8	1	0	1.000	4	1.59
	NY/NL		22	226	4	1	1	4	55.2	48	3	14	3	1	30	5	2	0	0	19	18	3	4	.429	1	2.91
86	NY/NL		6	30	0	0	0	0	6.2	6	0	3	0	0	4	0	0	0	0	3	2	0	0	.000	0	2.70
	TID/INT	AAA	34	327	4	1	0	15	79.2	69	8	21	1	2	55	4	5	1	1	30	22	4	4	.500	7	2.49
87	NY/NL		44	542	12	1	1	7	131.1	132	14	29	5	1	61	8	1	0	1	54	47	11	1	.917	3	3.22
88	NY/NL		52	392	0	0	0	21	92.0	95	5	24	4	3	51	8	0	0	0	32	26	7	2	.778	3	2.54
89	NY/NL		10	85	0	0	0	4	21.1	19	1	4	0	1	12	2	0	2	0	11	10	0	0	.000	0	4.22
	KC/AL		30	328	3	0	0	6	73.2	78	4	36	9	1	34	6	4	1	1	46	34	5	6	.455	0	4.15
	YEAR		40	413	3	0	0	10	95.0	97	5	40	9	2	36	6	4	1	1	57	44	5	6	.455	0	4.17
90	MIN/AL		55	344	0	0	0	29	81.2	84	2	21	10	1	46	7	2	1	1	31	29	2	5	.286	2	3.20
91	MIN/AL		50	292	0	0	0	22	67.1	82	3	14	5	0	32	3	1	1	0	28	27	1	2	.333	0	3.61
9 YR TOTALS			311	2572	21	3	3	109	610.1	616	36	175	42	8	306	42	16	3	3	257	224	32	22	.593	9	3.30

Leary, Timothy James "Tim" — bats right — throws right — b.12/23/58

YR	TM/LG	CL	G	TBF	GS	CG	SHO	GF	IP	H	HR	BB	IBB	HB	SO	SH	SF	WP	BK	R	ER	W	L	PCT	SV	ERA
81	NY/NL		1	7	1	0	0	0	2.0	0	0	1	0	0	3	0	0	0	0	0	0	0	0	.000	0	0.00
83	NY/NL		2	53	2	1	0	0	10.2	15	0	4	0	0	9	1	1	0	0	10	4	1	1	.500	0	3.38
84	TID/INT	AAA	10	241	10	0	0	0	53.1	47	4	42	0	3	27	0	3	4	0	26	24	4	4	.500	0	4.05
	NY/NL		20	237	7	0	0	3	53.2	61	2	18	3	2	29	1	2	2	3	28	24	3	3	.500	0	4.02
85	VAN/PCL	AAA	27	0	27	3	1	0	177.2	174	9	57	1	5	136	0	0	6	1	85	79	10	7	.588	0	4.00
	MIL/AL		5	146	5	0	0	0	33.1	40	5	8	0	1	29	0	0	0	0	18	15	1	4	.200	0	4.05
86	MIL/AL		33	817	30	3	2	2	188.1	216	20	53	4	7	110	4	6	7	0	97	88	12	12	.500	0	4.21
87	LA/NL		39	469	12	0	0	11	107.2	121	15	36	5	2	61	6	1	3	1	62	57	3	11	.214	1	4.76
88	LA/NL		35	932	34	9	6	0	228.2	201	13	56	4	4	180	7	3	9	6	87	74	17	11	.607	0	2.91
89	LA/NL		19	481	17	2	0	0	117.1	107	9	37	7	2	59	4	4	4	0	45	44	6	7	.462	0	3.38
	CIN/NL		14	393	14	0	0	0	89.2	98	8	31	8	3	64	3	4	6	0	39	37	2	7	.222	0	3.71
	YEAR		33	874	31	2	0	0	207.0	205	17	68	15	5	123	7	8	10	0	84	81	8	14	.364	0	3.52
90	NY/AL		31	881	31	6	1	0	208.0	202	18	78	1	7	138	4	4	23	0	105	95	9	19	.321	0	4.11
91	NY/AL		28	551	18	1	0	4	120.2	150	20	57	1	4	83	2	2	10	0	89	87	4	10	.286	0	6.49
10 YR TOTALS			227	4967	171	22	9	20	1160.0	1211	110	379	33	34	765	42	27	66	11	580	525	58	85	.406	1	4.07

Lee, Mark Owen — bats left — throws left — b.7/20/64

YR	TM/LG	CL	G	TBF	GS	CG	SHO	GF	IP	H	HR	BB	IBB	HB	SO	SH	SF	WP	BK	R	ER	W	L	PCT	SV	ERA
85	BRI/APP	R+	15	127	1	0	0	11	33.0	18	1	12	0	0	40	1	0	2	0	5	4	3	0	1.000	5	1.09
86	LAK/FSL	A+	41	281	0	0	0	31	62.2	73	4	21	8	2	39	4	1	5	0	44	36	2	5	.286	10	5.17
87	GF/EAS	AA	7	38	0	0	0	4	8.1	13	1	1	0	0	3	1	1	0	0	9	8	0	0	.000	0	8.64
	LAK/FSL	A+	30	223	0	0	0	15	53.0	48	1	18	3	1	42	0	1	1	0	17	15	3	2	.600	4	2.55
88	LAK/FSL	A+	10	73	0	0	0	2	19.0	16	0	4	1	0	15	2	3	0	1	7	3	1	0	1.000	1	1.42
	GF/EAS	AA	14	106	0	0	0	6	26.0	27	0	4	2	0	25	2	1	0	0	10	7	3	0	1.000	1	2.42
	TOL/INT	AAA	22	79	0	0	0	6	19.1	18	0	7	2	0	13	0	0	2	0	7	6	0	1	.000	0	2.79
	KC/AL		4	21	0	0	0	4	5.0	6	0	1	0	0	0	0	0	0	0	2	2	0	0	.000	0	3.60
89	MEM/SOU	AA	25	558	24	0	0	1	122.2	149	13	44	2	3	79	4	4	6	8	84	71	5	11	.313	0	5.21
90	STO/CAL	A+	5	32	0	0	0	2	7.2	5	0	3	0	0	7	1	0	0	0	2	2	1	0	1.000	1	2.35
	DEN/AMA	AAA	20	110	0	0	0	6	28.0	25	2	4	0	0	35	1	0	1	1	7	7	3	1	.750	4	2.25
	MIL/AL		11	85	0	0	0	1	21.1	20	1	4	0	0	14	1	2	0	0	5	5	1	0	1.000	0	2.11
91	MIL/AL		62	291	0	0	0	9	67.2	72	10	31	7	1	43	4	1	0	0	33	29	2	5	.286	1	3.86
3 YR TOTALS			**77**	**397**	**0**	**0**	**0**	**14**	**94.0**	**98**	**11**	**36**	**7**	**1**	**57**	**5**	**3**	**0**	**0**	**40**	**36**	**3**	**5**	**.375**	**1**	**3.45**

Lefferts, Craig Lindsey — bats left — throws left — b.9/29/57

YR	TM/LG	CL	G	TBF	GS	CG	SHO	GF	IP	H	HR	BB	IBB	HB	SO	SH	SF	WP	BK	R	ER	W	L	PCT	SV	ERA
83	CHI/NL		56	367	5	0	0	10	89.0	80	13	29	3	2	60	7	0	2	0	35	31	3	4	.429	1	3.13
84	SD/NL		62	420	0	0	0	29	105.2	88	4	24	1	1	56	4	6	2	2	29	25	3	4	.429	10	2.13
85	SD/NL		60	345	0	0	0	24	83.1	75	7	30	4	0	48	7	1	2	0	34	31	7	6	.538	2	3.35
86	SD/NL		83	446	0	0	0	36	107.2	98	7	44	11	1	72	9	5	1	1	41	37	9	8	.529	4	3.09
87	SD/NL		33	225	0	0	0	8	51.1	56	9	15	5	2	39	2	0	5	2	29	25	2	2	.500	2	4.38
	SF/NL		44	191	0	0	0	14	47.1	36	4	18	6	0	18	4	2	1	1	18	17	3	3	.500	4	3.23
	YEAR		77	416	0	0	0	22	98.2	92	13	33	11	2	57	6	2	6	3	47	42	5	5	.500	6	3.83
88	SF/NL		64	362	0	0	0	30	92.1	74	7	23	5	1	58	6	3	4	0	33	30	3	8	.273	11	2.92
89	SF/NL		70	430	0	0	0	32	107.0	93	11	22	5	1	71	4	4	4	1	38	32	2	4	.333	20	2.69
90	SD/NL		56	327	0	0	0	44	78.2	68	10	22	4	1	60	5	1	1	0	26	22	7	5	.583	23	2.52
91	SD/NL		54	290	0	0	0	40	69.0	74	5	14	3	1	48	10	5	3	1	35	30	1	6	.143	23	3.91
9 YR TOTALS			**582**	**3403**	**5**	**0**	**0**	**267**	**831.1**	**742**	**77**	**241**	**47**	**10**	**530**	**58**	**27**	**25**	**8**	**318**	**280**	**40**	**50**	**.444**	**100**	**3.03**

Leibrandt, Charles Louis "Charlie" — bats right — throws left — b.10/4/56

YR	TM/LG	CL	G	TBF	GS	CG	SHO	GF	IP	H	HR	BB	IBB	HB	SO	SH	SF	WP	BK	R	ER	W	L	PCT	SV	ERA
79	CIN/NL		3	16	0	0	0	1	4.1	2	0	2	0	0	1	0	1	0	0	2	0	0	0	.000	0	0.00
80	CIN/NL		36	754	27	5	2	3	173.2	200	15	54	4	2	62	12	2	1	6	84	82	10	9	.526	0	4.25
81	CIN/NL		7	128	4	1	1	0	30.0	28	0	15	2	0	9	4	2	0	0	12	12	1	1	.500	0	3.60
82	CIN/NL		36	484	11	0	0	10	107.2	130	4	48	9	2	34	10	2	6	1	68	61	5	7	.417	2	5.10
84	OMA/AMA	AAA	9	278	9	4	3	0	72.2	51	4	16	2	3	38	1	0	0	0	14	10	7	1	.875	0	1.24
	KC/AL		23	621	23	0	0	0	143.2	158	11	38	2	3	53	3	7	5	1	65	58	11	7	.611	0	3.63
85	KC/AL		33	983	33	8	3	0	237.2	223	17	68	3	2	108	8	5	4	3	86	71	17	9	.654	0	2.69
86	KC/AL		35	975	34	8	1	0	231.1	238	18	63	0	4	108	14	5	2	1	112	105	14	11	.560	0	4.09
87	KC/AL		35	1015	35	8	3	0	240.1	235	23	74	2	1	151	5	5	9	3	104	91	16	11	.593	0	3.41
88	KC/AL		35	1002	35	7	2	0	243.0	244	20	62	3	4	125	5	7	10	4	98	86	13	12	.520	0	3.19
89	KC/AL		33	712	27	3	1	3	161.0	196	13	54	4	2	73	8	4	9	2	98	92	5	11	.313	0	5.14
90	GRE/SOU	AA	2	46	2	0	0	0	13.0	5	0	5	0	0	12	0	0	1	0	4	0	1	0	1.000	0	0.00
	ATL/NL		24	680	24	5	2	0	162.1	164	9	35	4	3	76	7	4	6	3	72	57	9	11	.450	0	3.16
91	ATL/NL		36	949	36	1	1	0	229.2	212	18	56	3	4	128	19	6	5	3	105	89	15	13	.536	0	3.49
12 YR TOTALS			**336**	**8319**	**289**	**46**	**16**	**17**	**1964.2**	**2030**	**148**	**569**	**35**	**28**	**928**	**95**	**52**	**55**	**27**	**906**	**804**	**116**	**102**	**.532**	**2**	**3.68**

Leiter, Alois Terry "Al" — bats left — throws left — b.10/23/65

YR	TM/LG	CL	G	TBF	GS	CG	SHO	GF	IP	H	HR	BB	IBB	HB	SO	SH	SF	WP	BK	R	ER	W	L	PCT	SV	ERA
84	ONE/NYP	A–	10	250	10	0	0	0	57.0	52	1	26	0	2	48	2	4	5	1	32	23	3	2	.600	0	3.63
85	FT./FSL	A+	17	386	17	1	0	0	82.0	87	3	57	1	0	44	4	1	5	1	70	59	1	6	.143	0	6.48
	ONE/NYP	A–	6	157	6	2	0	0	38.0	27	0	25	0	0	34	4	1	5	0	14	10	3	2	.600	0	2.37
86	FT./FSL	A+	22	526	21	1	1	0	117.2	96	2	90	1	5	101	4	2	7	1	64	53	4	8	.333	0	4.05
87	ALB/EAS	AA	15	327	14	2	0	0	78.0	64	4	37	0	2	71	4	4	3	2	34	29	3	3	.500	0	3.35
	COL/INT	AAA	5	101	5	0	0	0	23.1	21	1	15	0	0	23	1	1	3	0	18	16	1	4	.200	0	6.17
	NY/AL		4	104	4	0	0	0	22.2	24	2	15	0	0	28	1	0	2	0	16	16	2	2	.500	0	6.35
88	COL/INT	AAA	4	58	4	0	0	0	13.0	5	0	14	0	3	12	0	0	0	1	7	5	0	1	.000	0	3.46
	NY/AL		14	251	14	1	0	0	57.1	49	7	33	0	1	60	1	0	1	4	27	25	4	4	.500	0	3.92
89	NY/AL		4	123	4	0	0	0	26.2	23	1	21	0	2	22	1	1	1	1	20	18	1	2	.333	0	6.07
	TOR/AL		1	31	1	0	0	0	6.2	9	1	2	0	0	4	0	1	1	0	3	3	0	0	.000	0	4.05
	YEAR		5	154	5	0	0	0	33.1	32	2	23	0	2	26	1	1	2	1	23	21	1	2	.333	0	5.67
	DUN/FSL	A+	3	39	3	0	0	0	8.0	11	0	5	0	0	5	0	0	1	0	8	7	0	0	.000	0	2.63
90	DUN/FSL	A+	6	99	6	0	0	0	24.0	18	1	12	0	0	14	0	1	2	0	8	7	0	0	.000	0	2.63
	SYR/INT	AAA	15	353	14	1	1	0	78.0	59	4	68	0	1	69	1	5	5	6	43	40	3	8	.273	0	4.62
	TOR/AL		4	22	0	0	0	2	6.1	1	0	2	0	0	5	0	0	0	0	0	0	0	0	.000	0	0.00
91	TOR/AL		3	13	0	0	0	1	1.2	3	0	5	0	0	1	0	1	0	0	5	5	0	0	.000	0	27.00
	DUN/FSL	A+	4	40	3	0	0	0	9.2	5	0	5	0	0	14	1	0	1	0	2	2	0	0	.000	0	1.86
5 YR TOTALS			**30**	**544**	**23**	**0**	**0**	**3**	**121.1**	**109**	**11**	**78**	**0**	**7**	**120**	**4**	**1**	**7**	**5**	**71**	**67**	**7**	**8**	**.467**	**0**	**4.97**

Leiter, Mark Edward — bats right — throws right — b.4/13/63

YR	TM/LG	CL	G	TBF	GS	CG	SHO	GF	IP	H	HR	BB	IBB	HB	SO	SH	SF	WP	BK	R	ER	W	L	PCT	SV	ERA
83	BLU/APP	R+	6	0	6	2	0	0	36.0	33	0	13	0	3	35	0	0	2	0	17	11	2	1	.667	0	2.75
	HAG/CAR	A+	8	0	8	0	0	0	36.0	42	0	28	0	3	18	0	0	3	0	31	29	1	5	.167	0	7.25

(continued)

Leiter, Mark Edward (continued)

YR	TM/LG	CL	G	TBF	GS	CG	SHO	GF	IP	H	HR	BB	IBB	HB	SO	SH	SF	WP	BK	R	ER	W	L	PCT	SV	ERA
84	HAG/CAR	A+	27	643	24	5	1	2	139.1	132	13	108	2	8	105	6	4	13	1	96	87	8	13	.381	0	5.62
85	HAG/CAR	A+	34	351	6	1	0	22	83.1	77	2	29	3	7	82	4	4	3	0	44	32	2	8	.200	8	3.46
	CHA/SOU	AA	5	23	0	0	0	2	6.1	3	1	2	0	0	8	0	0	0	0	1	1	0	0	.000	0	1.42
89	FT./FSL	A+	6	143	4	1	0	1	35.1	27	1	5	0	2	22	0	1	0	1	9	6	2	2	.500	1	1.53
	COL/INT	AAA	22	404	12	0	0	2	90.0	102	5	34	2	5	70	2	3	3	5	50	50	9	6	.600	0	5.00
90	COL/INT	AAA	30	508	14	2	1	6	122.2	114	5	27	0	1	115	2	3	7	0	56	49	9	4	.692	1	3.60
	NY/AL		8	119	3	0	0	0	26.1	33	5	9	0	2	21	2	1	0	0	20	20	1	1	.500	0	6.84
91	TOL/INT	AAA	5	29	0	0	0	3	6.2	6	0	3	0	1	7	0	0	0	0	0	0	1	0	1.000	0	0.00
	DET/AL		38	578	15	1	0	7	134.2	125	16	50	4	6	103	5	6	2	0	66	63	9	7	.563	1	4.21
2 YR TOTALS			**46**	**697**	**18**	**1**	**0**	**9**	**161.0**	**158**	**21**	**59**	**4**	**8**	**124**	**7**	**7**	**2**	**0**	**86**	**83**	**10**	**8**	**.556**	**1**	**4.64**

Lewis, James Steven "Jim" — bats right — throws right — b.7/20/64

YR	TM/LG	CL	G	TBF	GS	CG	SHO	GF	IP	H	HR	BB	IBB	HB	SO	SH	SF	WP	BK	R	ER	W	L	PCT	SV	ERA
85	SPO/NWL	A−	20	0	6	1	0	0	67.1	60	4	21	0	2	54	0	0	6	0	34	29	4	4	.500	0	3.88
86	CHA/SAL	A	51	366	1	1	1	25	84.0	87	4	32	4	0	61	6	3	4	1	48	32	4	8	.333	4	3.43
87	REN/CAL	A+	13	135	2	1	1	3	29.1	34	3	21	0	1	28	0	1	2	0	26	20	2	2	.500	0	6.14
88	RIV/CAL	A+	44	444	1	0	0	18	98.1	99	7	54	4	1	80	9	1	9	0	57	39	7	7	.500	7	3.57
89	WIC/TEX	AA	63	359	0	0	0	50	83.1	83	3	33	5	3	53	5	2	2	0	28	25	8	4	.667	18	2.70
90	LV/PCL	AAA	59	424	0	0	0	18	93.0	109	6	46	3	2	54	3	7	7	0	60	47	5	6	.455	5	4.55
91	WIC/TEX	AA	2	15	0	0	0	1	2.2	4	0	4	0	1	4	0	0	0	0	2	0	0	0	.000	1	0.00
	LV/PCL	AAA	48	381	0	0	0	15	85.1	93	4	34	4	3	76	3	6	2	0	41	32	6	3	.667	3	3.38
	SD/NL		12	64	0	0	0	2	13.0	14	2	11	2	0	10	2	0	1	0	7	6	0	0	.000	0	4.15

Lewis, Scott Allen — bats right — throws right — b.12/5/65

YR	TM/LG	CL	G	TBF	GS	CG	SHO	GF	IP	H	HR	BB	IBB	HB	SO	SH	SF	WP	BK	R	ER	W	L	PCT	SV	ERA
88	BEN/NWL	A−	9	262	9	2	0	0	61.2	63	3	12	0	5	53	1	3	3	2	33	24	5	3	.625	0	3.50
	QC/MID	A	3	85	3	1	0	0	21.1	19	0	5	0	0	20	1	0	1	2	12	11	1	2	.333	0	4.64
	PS/CAL	A+	2	37	1	0	0	0	8.0	12	3	2	0	0	7	0	0	0	0	5	5	0	1	.000	0	5.63
89	MID/TEX	AA	25	729	25	4	1	0	162.1	195	15	55	9	8	104	2	3	12	9	121	89	11	12	.478	0	4.93
90	EDM/PCL	AAA	27	749	27	6	0	0	177.2	198	16	35	1	7	124	4	3	2	0	90	77	13	11	.542	0	3.90
	CAL/AL		2	60	2	0	0	0	16.1	10	2	9	0	0	9	0	0	0	0	4	4	1	1	.500	0	2.20
91	EDM/PCL	AAA	17	489	17	4	0	0	110.0	132	7	26	2	8	87	4	4	5	3	71	55	3	9	.250	0	4.50
	CAL/AL		16	281	11	0	0	0	60.1	81	9	21	0	2	37	2	0	3	0	43	42	3	5	.375	0	6.27
2 YR TOTALS			**18**	**341**	**13**	**1**	**0**	**0**	**76.2**	**91**	**11**	**23**	**0**	**2**	**46**	**2**	**0**	**3**	**0**	**47**	**46**	**4**	**6**	**.400**	**0**	**5.40**

Lilliquist, Derek Jansen — bats left — throws left — b.2/20/66

YR	TM/LG	CL	G	TBF	GS	CG	SHO	GF	IP	H	HR	BB	IBB	HB	SO	SH	SF	WP	BK	R	ER	W	L	PCT	SV	ERA
87	BRA/GCL	R	2	44	2	0	0	0	13.0	3	0	0	0	0	16	0	0	0	0	0	0	0	0	.000	0	0.00
	DUR/CAR	A+	3	94	3	2	0	0	25.0	13	1	6	0	1	29	0	1	0	0	9	8	2	1	.667	0	2.88
88	RIC/INT	AAA	28	716	28	2	0	0	170.2	179	11	36	1	1	80	6	7	5	6	70	64	10	12	.455	0	3.38
89	ATL/NL		32	718	30	0	0	0	165.2	202	16	34	5	2	79	8	3	4	3	87	73	8	10	.444	0	3.97
90	ATL/NL		12	279	11	0	0	1	61.2	75	10	19	4	1	34	6	4	0	2	45	43	2	8	.200	0	6.28
	RIC/INT	AAA	5	143	5	1	0	0	35.0	31	3	11	0	0	24	0	1	0	0	11	10	4	0	1.000	0	2.57
	SD/NL		16	258	7	1	1	2	60.1	61	6	23	1	2	29	3	1	2	1	29	29	3	3	.500	0	4.33
	YEAR		28	537	18	1	1	3	122.0	136	16	42	5	3	63	9	5	2	3	74	72	5	11	.313	0	5.31
91	LV/PCL	AAA	33	491	14	0	0	8	105.1	142	10	33	7	2	89	6	6	4	3	79	63	4	6	.400	2	5.38
	SD/NL		6	70	2	0	0	1	14.1	25	3	4	0	0	7	0	0	0	0	14	14	0	2	.000	0	8.79
3 YR TOTALS			**66**	**1325**	**50**	**1**	**1**	**4**	**302.0**	**363**	**35**	**80**	**11**	**5**	**149**	**17**	**8**	**6**	**6**	**175**	**159**	**13**	**23**	**.361**	**0**	**4.74**

Long, William Douglas "Bill" — bats right — throws right — b.2/29/60

YR	TM/LG	CL	G	TBF	GS	CG	SHO	GF	IP	H	HR	BB	IBB	HB	SO	SH	SF	WP	BK	R	ER	W	L	PCT	SV	ERA
84	BEA/TEX	AA	25	678	24	4	2	1	159.2	149	8	67	1	1	114	2	1	5	1	56	52	14	5	.737	0	2.93
85	CHI/AL		4	71	3	0	0	1	14.0	25	4	5	2	0	13	1	1	1	0	17	16	0	1	.000	0	10.29
	BUF/AMA	AAA	25	623	22	7	1	1	151.1	146	12	43	2	1	71	2	1	1	2	69	59	13	6	.684	0	3.51
86	BUF/AMA	AAA	22	629	22	5	0	0	146.0	159	15	44	2	1	86	6	7	4	0	73	63	9	9	.500	0	3.88
87	HAW/PCL	AAA	2	59	2	0	0	0	13.0	15	0	4	0	0	6	0	0	0	0	7	6	2	0	1.000	0	4.15
	CHI/AL		29	699	23	5	2	2	169.0	179	20	28	1	3	72	6	3	0	1	85	82	8	8	.500	1	4.37
88	CHI/AL		47	732	18	3	0	14	174.0	187	21	43	4	4	77	8	8	2	0	89	78	8	11	.421	2	4.03
89	VAN/PCL	AAA	3	95	3	2	1	0	26.0	17	2	7	0	0	14	0	1	0	1	8	8	1	2	.333	0	2.77
	CHI/AL		30	432	8	0	0	8	98.2	101	8	37	0	4	51	4	6	3	0	49	43	5	5	.500	1	3.92
90	CHI/AL		4	26	0	0	0	0	5.2	6	2	2	0	1	6	0	0	0	0	5	4	0	1	.000	0	6.35
	CHI/NL		42	244	0	0	0	21	55.2	66	8	21	4	1	32	3	0	1	0	29	27	6	1	.857	5	4.37
	YEAR		46	270	0	0	0	21	61.1	72	10	23	4	2	34	4	0	1	0	34	31	6	2	.750	5	4.55
91	MON/NL		3	12	0	0	0	0	1.2	4	0	4	0	0	0	0	0	0	0	2	2	0	0	.000	0	10.80
	IND/AMA	AAA	10	144	4	0	1	1	33.1	32	6	14	0	0	17	2	0	0	0	20	19	1	4	.200	0	5.13
6 YR TOTALS			**159**	**2216**	**52**	**8**	**2**	**42**	**518.2**	**568**	**63**	**140**	**11**	**12**	**247**	**23**	**18**	**7**	**1**	**276**	**252**	**27**	**27**	**.500**	**9**	**4.37**

MacDonald, Robert Joseph "Rob" — bats left — throws left — b.4/27/65

YR	TM/LG	CL	G	TBF	GS	CG	SHO	GF	IP	H	HR	BB	IBB	HB	SO	SH	SF	WP	BK	R	ER	W	L	PCT	SV	ERA
87	ST./NYP	A−	1	20	1	0	0	0	4.0	8	0	0	0	0	4	0	0	0	0	4	2	0	0	.000	0	4.50
	MH/PIO	R+	13	109	0	0	0	9	24.2	22	0	12	1	1	26	1	0	5	0	13	8	3	1	.750	2	2.92
	MB/SAL	A	10	94	0	0	0	4	20.2	24	1	7	0	0	24	0	0	2	0	18	13	2	1	.667	0	5.66
88	MB/SAL	A	52	222	0	0	0	48	53.1	42	2	18	3	0	43	3	1	2	0	13	10	3	4	.429	15	1.69
89	KNO/SOU	AA	43	264	0	0	0	27	63.0	52	0	23	2	0	58	5	0	0	0	27	23	3	5	.375	9	3.29

MacDonald, Robert Joseph "Rob" (continued)

YR	TM/LG	CL	G	TBF	GS	CG	SHO	GF	IP	H	HR	BB	IBB	HB	SO	SH	SF	WP	BK	R	ER	W	L	PCT	SV	ERA
	SYR/INT	AAA	12	75	0	0	0	4	16.0	16	0	6	0	1	12	3	1	0	0	10	10	1	0	1.000	0	5.63
90	KNO/SOU	AA	36	237	0	0	0	29	57.0	37	2	29	4	0	54	9	1	3	0	17	12	1	2	.333	15	1.89
	SYR/INT	AAA	9	35	0	0	0	5	8.1	4	1	9	0	0	6	0	0	0	0	5	5	0	2	.000	2	5.40
	TOR/AL		4	8	0	0	0	1	2.1	0	0	2	0	0	0	0	0	0	0	0	0	0	0	.000	0	0.00
91	SYR/INT	AAA	7	29	0	0	0	5	6.0	5	1	5	0	0	6	0	0	3	0	3	1	0	0	1.000	1	4.50
	TOR/AL		45	231	0	0	0	10	53.2	51	5	25	4	0	24	2	2	1	1	19	17	3	3	.500	0	2.85
2 YR TOTALS			**49**	**239**	**0**	**0**	**0**	**11**	**56.0**	**51**	**5**	**27**	**4**	**0**	**24**	**2**	**2**	**1**	**1**	**19**	**17**	**3**	**3**	**.500**	**0**	**2.73**

Machado, Julio Segundo (Rondon) — bats right — throws right — b.12/1/65

YR	TM/LG	CL	G	TBF	GS	CG	SHO	GF	IP	H	HR	BB	IBB	HB	SO	SH	SF	WP	BK	R	ER	W	L	PCT	SV	ERA
85	SPA/SAL	A	32	363	3	1	0	13	81.1	75	5	38	1	4	71	6	7	4	3	50	39	4	5	.444	0	4.32
86	SPA/SAL	A	43	366	5	2	1	28	79.2	68	1	52	3	3	81	5	6	5	1	39	33	2	5	.286	7	3.73
87	CLE/FSL	A+	7	153	5	0	0	1	34.2	31	2	19	2	2	32	1	2	0	2	11	10	2	0	1.000	0	2.60
	REA/EAS	AA	21	472	17	2	2	2	108.1	112	9	40	2	4	89	4	7	6	7	70	57	4	5	.444	0	4.74
88	CLE/FSL	A+	13	154	3	0	0	7	36.2	34	3	14	1	2	45	0	1	3	2	13	12	1	4	.200	5	2.95
	REA/EAS	AA	26	291	5	0	0	9	63.0	69	1	34	3	5	52	6	6	3	2	41	38	6	1	.857	3	5.43
89	PEN/CAR	A+	4	17	0	0	0	3	3.2	2	0	2	0	1	1	0	0	0	0	0	0	1	0	1.000	2	0.00
	SL/FSL	A+	4	39	0	0	0	2	10.2	5	0	3	0	0	14	1	0	0	0	1	0	1	0	1.000	2	0.00
	JAC/TEX	AA	32	239	0	0	0	16	57.0	42	0	27	4	2	67	5	2	1	1	23	18	3	5	.375	3	2.84
	TID/INT	AAA	14	116	1	0	0	9	29.0	16	0	17	2	0	37	2	0	2	0	2	2	1	2	.333	5	0.62
	NY/NL		10	45	0	0	0	9	11.0	9	0	3	0	0	14	0	0	1	0	4	4	0	0	.000	0	3.27
90	NY/NL		27	151	0	0	0	14	34.1	32	4	17	4	2	27	1	2	3	0	13	12	4	1	.800	0	3.15
	TID/INT	AAA	16	88	0	0	0	13	21.1	16	1	8	2	0	24	3	0	1	0	7	4	0	0	.000	8	1.69
	MIL/AL		10	56	0	0	0	7	13.0	9	0	8	2	0	12	0	1	0	0	1	1	0	0	.000	3	0.69
	YEAR		37	207	0	0	0	21	47.1	41	4	25	6	2	39	1	3	3	0	14	13	4	1	.800	3	2.47
91	MIL/AL		54	371	0	0	0	13	88.2	65	12	55	1	3	98	3	2	5	0	36	34	3	3	.500	3	3.45
3 YR TOTALS			**101**	**623**	**0**	**0**	**0**	**43**	**147.0**	**115**	**16**	**83**	**7**	**5**	**151**	**4**	**5**	**8**	**0**	**54**	**51**	**7**	**5**	**.583**	**6**	**3.12**

Maddux, Gregory Alan "Greg" — bats right — throws right — b.4/14/66

YR	TM/LG	CL	G	TBF	GS	CG	SHO	GF	IP	H	HR	BB	IBB	HB	SO	SH	SF	WP	BK	R	ER	W	L	PCT	SV	ERA
84	PIK/APP	R+	14	361	12	2	2	1	85.2	63	2	41	2	8	62	2	3	4	1	35	25	6	2	.750	0	2.63
85	PEO/MID	A	27	787	27	6	0	0	186.0	176	9	52	0	6	125	8	3	5	2	86	66	13	9	.591	0	3.19
86	PIT/EAS	AA	8	249	8	4	2	0	63.2	49	1	15	0	1	35	1	3	1	4	22	19	4	3	.571	0	2.69
	IOW/AMA	AAA	18	538	18	5	2	0	128.1	127	3	30	3	12	65	4	2	0	5	49	43	10	1	.909	0	3.02
	CHI/NL		6	144	5	1	0	1	31.0	44	3	11	2	1	20	1	0	2	0	20	19	2	4	.333	0	5.52
87	IOW/AMA	AAA	4	109	4	2	2	0	27.2	17	1	12	0	2	22	0	0	2	0	3	3	3	0	1.000	0	0.98
	CHI/NL		30	701	27	1	1	2	155.2	181	17	74	13	4	101	7	1	4	7	111	97	6	14	.300	0	5.61
88	CHI/NL		34	1047	34	9	3	0	249.0	230	13	81	16	2	140	11	2	3	6	97	88	18	8	.692	0	3.18
89	CHI/NL		35	1002	35	7	1	0	238.1	222	13	82	13	4	135	18	6	5	3	90	78	19	12	.613	0	2.95
90	CHI/NL		35	1011	35	8	2	0	237.0	242	11	71	10	4	144	18	3	6	3	116	91	15	15	.500	0	3.46
91	CHI/NL		37	1070	37	7	2	0	263.0	232	18	66	9	6	198	16	3	6	3	113	98	15	11	.577	0	3.35
6 YR TOTALS			**177**	**4975**	**173**	**33**	**9**	**3**	**1174.0**	**1151**	**75**	**385**	**63**	**30**	**738**	**71**	**17**	**23**	**22**	**547**	**471**	**75**	**64**	**.540**	**0**	**3.61**

Maddux, Michael Ausley "Mike" — bats left — throws right — b.8/27/61

YR	TM/LG	CL	G	TBF	GS	CG	SHO	GF	IP	H	HR	BB	IBB	HB	SO	SH	SF	WP	BK	R	ER	W	L	PCT	SV	ERA
84	REA/EAS	AA	20	527	19	4	0	2	116.0	143	10	49	2	2	77	9	4	12	0	82	65	3	12	.200	0	5.04
	POR/PCL	AAA	8	0	8	1	0	0	44.2	58	5	17	2	1	22	0	0	2	0	32	29	2	4	.333	0	5.84
85	POR/PCL	AAA	27	0	26	6	1	1	166.0	195	15	51	4	4	96	0	0	13	2	106	98	9	12	.429	0	5.31
86	POR/PCL	AAA	12	334	12	3	0	0	84.0	70	5	22	0	1	65	3	2	1	1	26	22	5	2	.714	0	2.36
	PHI/NL		16	351	16	0	0	0	78.0	88	6	34	4	3	44	3	3	4	2	56	47	3	7	.300	0	5.42
87	MAI/INT	AAA	18	446	16	3	1	1	103.1	116	9	26	3	2	71	2	2	5	1	58	50	6	6	.500	0	4.35
	PHI/NL		7	72	2	0	0	0	17.0	17	0	5	1	0	15	0	1	0	0	5	5	2	0	1.000	0	2.65
88	MAI/INT	AAA	5	109	3	1	0	0	23.2	25	3	10	0	2	18	1	0	1	3	18	11	2	0	.000	0	4.18
	PHI/NL		25	380	11	0	0	4	88.2	91	6	34	4	5	59	7	3	4	2	41	37	4	3	.571	0	3.76
89	SW/INT	AAA	19	515	17	3	1	1	123.0	119	7	26	2	7	100	5	5	8	1	55	50	7	7	.500	0	3.66
	PHI/NL		16	191	4	2	1	1	43.2	52	3	14	3	2	26	0	3	1	1	29	25	1	3	.250	1	5.15
90	LA/NL		11	88	2	0	0	2	20.2	24	4	4	1	1	11	0	1	2	0	15	15	0	1	.000	0	6.53
	ALB/PCL	AAA	20	473	19	4	2	0	108.0	122	8	32	2	4	85	3	2	7	0	59	51	8	5	.615	0	4.25
91	SD/NL		64	388	1	0	0	27	98.2	78	4	27	3	1	57	2	2	5	0	30	27	7	2	.778	5	2.46
6 YR TOTALS			**139**	**1470**	**36**	**2**	**1**	**35**	**346.2**	**350**	**22**	**118**	**14**	**12**	**212**	**18**	**10**	**19**	**5**	**176**	**156**	**17**	**16**	**.515**	**6**	**4.05**

Magnante, Michael Anthony "Mike" — bats left — throws left — b.6/17/65

YR	TM/LG	CL	G	TBF	GS	CG	SHO	GF	IP	H	HR	BB	IBB	HB	SO	SH	SF	WP	BK	R	ER	W	L	PCT	SV	ERA
88	EUG/NWL	A–	3	59	3	0	0	0	16.0	10	0	2	0	0	26	0	0	1	0	6	1	1	1	.500	0	0.56
	APP/MID	A	9	199	8	0	0	0	47.2	48	3	15	0	0	40	4	1	3	0	20	17	3	2	.600	0	3.21
	BC/FSL	A+	4	95	4	1	0	0	24.0	19	1	8	0	0	19	1	0	0	0	12	11	1	1	.500	0	4.13
89	MEM/SOU	AA	26	659	26	4	1	0	157.1	137	10	53	3	9	118	6	2	8	0	70	64	8	9	.471	0	3.66
90	OMA/AMA	AAA	13	320	13	2	0	0	76.2	72	6	25	0	2	56	3	0	3	1	39	35	2	5	.286	0	4.11
91	OMA/AMA	AAA	10	264	10	2	1	0	65.2	53	2	23	0	1	50	2	2	0	0	23	22	6	1	.857	0	3.02
	KC/AL		38	236	0	0	0	10	55.0	55	4	23	3	0	42	0	1	1	0	19	15	0	1	.000	0	2.45

Magrane, Joseph David "Joe" — bats right — throws left — b.7/2/64

YR	TM/LG	CL	G	TBF	GS	CG	SHO	GF	IP	H	HR	BB	IBB	HB	SO	SH	SF	WP	BK	R	ER	W	L	PCT	SV	ERA
85	JC/APP	R+	6	113	5	2	2	0	30.0	15	0	11	0	1	31	0	0	0	2	4	2	2	1	.667	0	0.60

(continued)

Magrane, Joseph David "Joe" (continued)

YR	TM/LG	CL	G	TBF	GS	CG	SHO	GF	IP	H	HR	BB	IBB	HB	SO	SH	SF	WP	BK	R	ER	W	L	PCT	SV	ERA
	SP/FSL	A+	5	137	5	1	1	0	34.2	21	0	14	0	1	17	0	0	2	1	8	4	3	1	.750	0	1.04
86	ARK/TEX	AA	13	353	13	5	2	0	89.1	66	3	31	0	2	66	4	1	8	0	29	24	8	4	.667	0	2.42
	LOU/AMA	AAA	15	457	15	8	2	0	113.1	93	4	33	1	5	72	2	5	7	4	34	26	9	6	.600	0	2.42
87	LOU/AMA	AAA	3	88	3	1	1	0	23.1	16	1	3	0	0	17	0	0	0	1	7	5	1	0	1.000	0	1.93
	STL/NL		27	722	26	4	2	0	170.1	157	9	60	6	10	101	9	3	9	7	75	67	9	7	.563	0	3.54
88	LOU/AMA	AAA	4	86	4	1	0	0	20.0	19	1	7	0	2	18	0	0	1	4	7	7	2	1	.667	0	3.15
	STL/NL		24	677	24	4	3	0	165.1	133	6	51	4	2	100	8	8	8	8	57	40	5	9	.357	0	2.18
89	ST./NL		34	971	33	9	3	1	234.2	219	5	72	7	6	127	14	8	14	8	81	76	18	9	.667	0	2.91
90	STL/NL		31	855	31	3	2	0	203.1	204	10	59	7	8	100	8	6	11	5	86	81	10	17	.370	0	3.59
4 YR TOTALS			**116**	**3225**	**114**	**20**	**10**	**1**	**773.2**	**713**	**30**	**242**	**24**	**26**	**428**	**39**	**21**	**42**	**21**	**299**	**264**	**42**	**42**	**.500**	**0**	**3.07**

Mahler, Richard Keith "Rick" — bats right — throws right — b.8/5/53

YR	TM/LG	CL	G	TBF	GS	CG	SHO	GF	IP	H	HR	BB	IBB	HB	SO	SH	SF	WP	BK	R	ER	W	L	PCT	SV	ERA
79	ATL/NL		15	101	0	0	0	5	22.0	28	4	11	0	0	12	0	0	1	1	16	15	0	0	.000	0	6.14
80	ATL/NL		2	13	0	0	0	0	3.2	2	0	0	0	0	1	0	0	0	0	1	1	0	0	.000	0	2.45
81	ATL/NL		34	478	14	1	0	10	112.1	109	5	43	5	1	54	8	3	3	1	41	35	8	6	.571	2	2.80
82	ATL/NL		39	857	33	5	2	0	205.1	213	18	62	5	1	105	6	6	8	2	105	96	9	10	.474	0	4.21
83	ATL/NL		10	66	2	0	0	1	14.1	16	0	9	1	0	7	1	2	0	0	8	8	0	0	.000	0	5.02
84	ATL/NL		38	918	29	9	1	1	222.0	209	13	62	7	3	106	13	6	3	1	86	77	13	10	.565	0	3.12
85	ATL/NL		39	1110	39	6	1	0	266.2	272	24	79	8	1	107	10	5	3	1	116	103	17	15	.531	0	3.48
86	ATL/NL		39	1056	39	9	1	0	237.2	283	25	95	10	3	137	10	8	5	1	139	129	14	18	.438	0	4.88
87	ATL/NL		39	849	28	3	1	1	197.0	212	24	85	8	2	95	9	3	2	2	118	109	8	13	.381	0	4.98
88	ATL/NL		39	1063	34	5	0	2	249.0	279	17	42	6	8	131	19	5	5	8	125	102	9	16	.360	0	3.69
89	CIN/NL		40	940	31	5	2	1	220.2	242	15	51	13	10	102	15	5	4	4	113	94	9	13	.409	0	3.83
90	NAS/AMA	AAA	1	29	1	0	0	0	7.1	6	1	3	0	0	5	0	0	2	0	2	2	0	1	.000	0	2.45
	CIN/NL		35	564	16	2	1	9	134.2	134	16	39	4	3	68	4	4	3	2	67	64	7	6	.538	4	4.28
91	MON/NL		10	158	6	0	0	1	37.1	37	2	15	0	2	17	4	1	0	0	17	15	1	3	.250	0	3.62
	ATL/NL		13	133	2	0	0	1	28.2	33	2	13	1	0	10	1	0	1	0	20	18	1	1	.500	0	5.65
	YEAR		23	291	8	0	0	2	66.0	70	4	28	1	2	27	5	1	1	0	37	33	2	4	.333	0	4.50
13 YR TOTALS			**392**	**8306**	**271**	**43**	**9**	**32**	**1951.1**	**2069**	**165**	**606**	**70**	**35**	**952**	**100**	**50**	**41**	**23**	**972**	**866**	**96**	**111**	**.464**	**6**	**3.99**

Mahomes, Patrick Lavon "Pat" — bats right — throws right — b.8/9/70 — System MIN/AL

YR	TM/LG	CL	G	TBF	GS	CG	SHO	GF	IP	H	HR	BB	IBB	HB	SO	SH	SF	WP	BK	R	ER	W	L	PCT	SV	ERA
88	ELI/APP	R+	13	344	13	3	0	0	78.0	66	4	51	0	0	93	3	1	9	2	45	32	6	3	.667	0	3.69
89	KEN/MID	A	25	668	25	3	1	0	156.1	120	4	100	3	2	167	0	9	9	3	66	57	13	7	.650	0	3.28
90	VIS/CAL	A+	28	784	28	5	1	0	185.1	136	14	118	1	4	178	3	4	19	1	77	68	11	11	.500	0	3.30
91	ORL/SOU	AA	18	463	17	2	0	0	116.0	77	5	57	0	3	136	0	2	3	0	30	23	8	5	.615	0	1.78
	POR/PCL	AAA	9	244	9	2	0	0	55.0	50	2	36	1	0	41	0	2	3	1	26	21	3	5	.375	0	3.44

Maldonado, Carlos Cesar (Delgado) — bats both — throws right — b.10/18/66

YR	TM/LG	CL	G	TBF	GS	CG	SHO	GF	IP	H	HR	BB	IBB	HB	SO	SH	SF	WP	BK	R	ER	W	L	PCT	SV	ERA
86	ROY/GCL	R	10	136	4	0	0	2	34.1	29	0	10	1	1	16	1	1	3	0	10	7	0	2	.000	1	1.83
87	APP/MID	A	2	13	0	0	0	1	2.1	4	0	3	0	0	4	0	1	0	0	3	3	0	0	.000	0	11.57
	ROY/GCL	R	20	223	0	0	0	8	58.0	32	2	19	2	2	56	2	0	2	1	18	16	5	1	.833	4	2.48
88	BC/FSL	A+	16	242	7	0	0	2	52.2	46	5	39	0	7	44	2	1	3	0	35	31	1	5	.167	0	5.30
89	BC/FSL	A+	28	300	5	0	0	19	76.2	47	3	24	1	1	66	3	1	2	0	14	10	11	3	.786	9	1.17
90	MEM/SOU	AA	55	325	0	0	0	48	77.1	61	5	39	0	1	77	3	4	1	0	29	25	4	5	.444	20	2.91
	KC/AL		4	31	0	0	0	1	6.0	9	0	3	0	0	6	0	0	4	0	6	6	0	0	.000	0	9.00
91	OMA/AMA	AAA	41	282	1	0	0	31	61.0	67	6	42	1	2	46	3	2	6	0	31	29	1	1	.500	9	4.28
	KC/AL		5	43	0	0	0	2	7.2	11	0	9	1	0	11	1	0	4	0	9	7	0	0	.000	0	8.22
2 YR TOTALS			**9**	**74**	**0**	**0**	**0**	**3**	**13.2**	**20**	**0**	**13**	**1**	**0**	**10**	**1**	**1**	**5**	**0**	**15**	**13**	**0**	**0**	**.000**	**0**	**8.56**

Mallicoat, Robbin Dale "Rob" — bats left — throws left — b.11/16/64

YR	TM/LG	CL	G	TBF	GS	CG	SHO	GF	IP	H	HR	BB	IBB	HB	SO	SH	SF	WP	BK	R	ER	W	L	PCT	SV	ERA
84	AUB/NYP	A-	1	25	1	0	0	0	5.0	8	1	3	0	0	6	0	0	1	0	3	3	0	0	.000	0	5.40
	ASH/SAL	A	11	276	11	2	0	0	64.1	49	5	36	0	4	57	1	1	7	2	30	28	3	4	.429	0	3.92
85	OSC/FSL	A+	26	717	25	5	2	0	178.2	119	2	74	3	3	158	6	5	14	2	41	27	16	6	.727	0	1.36
86	TUC/PCL	AAA	3	68	3	0	0	0	14.0	18	1	8	0	0	9	1	0	1	0	14	10	0	2	.000	0	6.43
	COL/SOU	AA	10	281	10	1	0	0	58.0	61	2	45	1	3	52	0	4	2	0	38	31	0	6	.000	0	4.81
87	COL/SOU	AA	24	656	24	3	0	0	152.1	132	13	78	3	5	141	8	4	8	0	68	49	10	7	.588	0	2.89
	TUC/PCL	AAA	2	45	2	0	0	0	9.2	9	0	7	0	0	4	1	0	1	0	5	4	0	0	.000	0	3.72
	HOU/NL		4	31	1	0	0	0	6.2	8	0	6	0	0	6	0	0	0	0	5	4	0	0	.000	0	5.40
90	AST/GCL	R	7	78	4	0	0	0	16.1	15	0	15	0	1	21	3	1	4	1	15	9	0	0	.000	0	6.75
	OSC/FSL	A+	3	51	3	0	0	0	12.0	8	0	9	0	0	10	0	0	1	0	9	7	0	0	.000	0	4.96
91	JAC/TEX	AA	18	121	0	0	0	9	31.0	20	1	11	1	2	34	0	3	2	1	15	13	0	0	.000	0	0.00
	TUC/PCL	AAA	19	221	6	0	0	4	47.2	43	3	38	4	3	32	4	0	3	2	15	13	4	1	.800	1	3.77
	HOU/NL		24	103	0	0	0	4	23.1	22	2	13	1	2	18	1	1	2	0	32	29	0	2	.000	1	5.48
2 YR TOTALS			**28**	**134**	**1**	**0**	**0**	**4**	**30.0**	**30**	**2**	**19**	**1**	**2**	**22**	**1**	**2**	**1**	**0**	**15**	**15**	**0**	**2**	**.000**	**1**	**4.50**

Manuel, Barry Paul — bats right — throws right — b.8/12/65

YR	TM/LG	CL	G	TBF	GS	CG	SHO	GF	IP	H	HR	BB	IBB	HB	SO	SH	SF	WP	BK	R	ER	W	L	PCT	SV	ERA
87	RAN/GCL	R	1	7	0	0	0	0	1.0	3	0	1	0	0	1	0	0	0	0	2	2	0	0	.000	0	18.00
	CHA/FSL	A+	13	138	5	0	0	3	30.0	33	2	18	0	3	19	1	2	1	0	24	22	1	0	.000	0	6.60
88	CHA/FSL	A+	37	259	0	0	0	22	60.1	47	4	32	0	4	55	1	1	8	3	24	17	4	3	.571	4	2.54

Manuel, Barry Paul (continued)

YR	TM/LG	CL	G	TBF	GS	CG	SHO	GF	IP	H	HR	BB	IBB	HB	SO	SH	SF	WP	BK	R	ER	W	L	PCT	SV	ERA
89	TUL/TEX	AA	11	237	11	0	0	0	49.1	49	5	39	0	9	40	3	6	3	3	44	41	3	4	.429	0	7.48
	CHA/FSL	A+	15	330	14	0	0	0	76.1	77	6	30	0	8	51	4	3	6	1	43	40	4	7	.364	0	4.72
90	CHA/FSL	A+	57	238	0	0	0	56	56.1	39	2	30	2	3	60	4	2	1	0	23	18	1	5	.167	36	2.88
91	TUL/TEX	AA	56	300	0	0	0	48	68.1	63	5	34	1	5	45	4	2	0	1	29	25	2	7	.222	25	3.29
	TEX/AL		8	58	0	0	0	5	16.0	7	0	6	0	0	5	0	3	2	0	2	2	1	0	1.000	0	1.13

Manzanillo, Josias (Adams) — bats right — throws right — b.10/16/67

YR	TM/LG	CL	G	TBF	GS	CG	SHO	GF	IP	H	HR	BB	IBB	HB	SO	SH	SF	WP	BK	R	ER	W	L	PCT	SV	ERA
83	ELM/NYP	A–	12	0	4	0	0	0	38.0	52	7	20	0	2	19	0	0	5	0	44	34	1	5	.167	0	8.05
84	ELM/NYP	A–	14	128	0	0	0	7	25.2	27	1	26	1	1	15	1	1	9	0	24	15	2	3	.400	1	5.26
85	GRE/SAL	A	7	62	0	0	0	2	12.0	12	1	18	0	0	10	0	0	2	0	13	13	1	1	.500	0	9.75
	ELM/NYP	A–	19	181	4	0	0	10	39.2	36	1	36	4	2	43	0	1	12	0	19	17	2	4	.333	1	3.86
86	WH/FSL	A+	23	601	21	3	2	2	142.2	110	3	81	0	3	102	6	4	9	0	51	36	13	5	.722	0	2.27
87	NB/EAS	AA	2	45	2	0	0	0	10.0	8	1	8	0	0	12	0	0	0	0	5	5	2	0	1.000	0	4.50
89	NB/EAS	AA	26	657	26	3	1	0	147.2	129	11	85	7	5	93	4	5	16	2	78	60	9	10	.474	0	3.66
90	NB/EAS	AA	12	317	12	2	1	0	74.0	66	3	37	1	2	51	1	0	7	3	34	28	4	4	.500	0	3.41
	PAW/INT	AAA	15	368	15	5	0	0	82.2	75	9	45	0	2	77	1	2	8	0	57	51	4	7	.364	0	5.55
91	NB/EAS	AA	7	212	7	0	0	0	49.2	37	0	28	1	1	35	5	0	2	1	25	16	2	2	.500	0	2.90
	PAW/INT	AAA	20	459	16	0	0	0	102.2	109	12	53	0	4	65	2	4	9	1	69	64	5	5	.500	0	5.61
	BOS/AL		1	8	0	0	0	1	1.0	2	0	2	0	0	1	0	0	0	0	2	2	0	0	.000	0	18.00

Marak, Paul Patrick — bats right — throws right — b.8/2/65

YR	TM/LG	CL	G	TBF	GS	CG	SHO	GF	IP	H	HR	BB	IBB	HB	SO	SH	SF	WP	BK	R	ER	W	L	PCT	SV	ERA
85	BRA/GCL	R	12	305	12	0	0	0	63.0	80	1	36	0	1	33	3	1	11	0	58	39	2	6	.250	0	5.57
86	IF/PIO	R+	12	0	12	1	0	0	61.0	82	6	25	1	4	52	0	0	12	1	57	34	2	5	.286	0	5.02
87	SUM/SAL	A	50	495	6	0	0	14	118.0	101	6	44	1	6	98	5	3	9	0	50	41	12	5	.706	2	3.13
88	GRE/SOU	AA	12	84	0	0	0	3	16.1	25	6	11	0	0	9	1	1	2	1	19	19	0	0	.000	0	10.47
	DUR/CAR	A+	32	419	7	3	1	7	100.2	90	5	33	4	5	84	4	5	6	3	40	30	7	4	.636	0	2.68
89	RIC/INT	AAA	2	23	1	0	0	0	4.0	8	1	4	1	0	2	0	0	1	0	4	4	0	1	.000	0	9.00
	GRE/SOU	AA	43	510	14	0	0	10	121.2	102	7	47	1	3	81	5	5	5	0	53	41	8	7	.533	5	3.03
90	RIC/INT	AAA	32	603	16	5	0	6	148.0	130	9	50	0	2	75	3	4	6	1	49	41	9	8	.529	0	2.49
	ATL/NL		7	172	7	1	1	0	39.0	39	2	19	3	3	15	3	1	2	0	16	16	1	2	.333	0	3.69
91	RIC/INT	AAA	29	787	26	2	1	1	172.1	220	18	80	1	7	57	5	10	8	1	123	112	10	13	.435	0	5.85
1 YR TOTALS			**7**	**172**	**7**	**1**	**1**	**0**	**39.0**	**39**	**2**	**19**	**3**	**3**	**15**	**3**	**1**	**2**	**0**	**16**	**16**	**1**	**2**	**.333**	**0**	**3.69**

Martinez, Jose Dennis (Emilia) "Dennis" — bats right — throws right — b.5/14/55

YR	TM/LG	CL	G	TBF	GS	CG	SHO	GF	IP	H	HR	BB	IBB	HB	SO	SH	SF	WP	BK	R	ER	W	L	PCT	SV	ERA
76	BAL/AL		4	106	2	1	0	1	27.2	23	1	8	0	0	18	1	0	1	0	8	8	1	2	.333	0	2.60
77	BAL/AL		42	709	13	5	0	19	166.2	157	10	64	5	8	107	8	8	5	0	86	76	14	7	.667	4	4.10
78	BAL/AL		40	1140	38	15	2	0	276.1	257	20	93	4	3	142	8	7	8	0	121	108	16	11	.593	0	3.52
79	BAL/AL		40	1206	39	18	3	0	292.1	279	28	78	1	1	132	12	12	9	2	129	119	15	16	.484	0	3.66
80	BAL/AL		25	428	12	2	0	8	99.2	103	12	44	2	2	42	1	3	0	1	44	44	6	4	.600	1	3.97
81	BAL/AL		25	753	24	9	2	0	179.0	173	10	62	1	2	88	2	5	6	1	84	66	14	5	.737	0	3.32
82	BAL/AL		40	1093	39	10	2	0	252.0	262	30	87	2	7	111	11	7	7	1	123	118	16	12	.571	0	4.21
83	BAL/AL		32	688	25	4	0	3	153.0	209	21	45	2	2	71	3	5	2	0	108	94	7	16	.304	0	5.53
84	BAL/AL		34	599	20	2	0	4	141.2	145	26	37	2	2	77	0	5	7	0	81	79	6	9	.400	0	5.02
85	BAL/AL		33	789	31	3	1	1	180.0	203	29	63	3	9	68	0	11	4	1	110	103	13	11	.542	0	5.15
86	BAL/AL		4	33	0	0	0	1	6.2	11	0	2	0	0	2	0	1	1	0	5	5	0	0	.000	0	6.75
	ROC/INT	AAA	4	83	4	0	0	0	19.1	18	5	9	0	0	14	0	1	0	0	14	13	2	1	.667	0	6.05
	MON/NL		19	416	15	1	1	1	98.0	103	11	28	4	3	63	8	1	2	2	52	50	3	6	.333	0	4.59
	YEAR		23	449	15	1	1	2	104.2	114	11	30	4	3	65	8	2	3	2	57	55	3	6	.333	0	4.73
87	MIA/FSL	A+	3	89	3	0	0	0	19.0	21	0	3	0	1	11	0	1	0	0	20	19	1	3	.600	0	4.46
	IND/AMA	AAA	7	161	7	1	1	0	38.1	32	5	13	1	1	30	3	1	0	0	59	53	11	4	.733	0	3.30
	MON/NL		22	599	22	2	1	0	144.2	133	9	40	2	6	84	4	3	4	2	59	53	11	4	.733	0	3.30
88	MON/NL		34	968	34	9	2	0	235.1	215	21	55	2	6	120	2	6	5	10	94	71	15	13	.536	0	2.72
89	MON/NL		34	950	33	5	2	1	232.0	227	21	49	4	7	142	2	2	5	2	88	82	16	7	.696	0	3.18
90	MON/NL		32	908	32	7	2	0	226.0	191	16	49	9	6	156	11	3	1	1	70	59	10	11	.476	0	2.95
91	MON/NL		31	905	31	9	5	0	222.0	187	9	62	3	4	123	4	4	1	0	70	59	14	11	.560	0	2.39
16 YR TOTALS			**491**	**12290**	**410**	**102**	**23**	**39**	**2933.0**	**2878**	**274**	**866**	**49**	**71**	**1546**	**86**	**82**	**70**	**23**	**1342**	**1209**	**177**	**145**	**.550**	**5**	**3.71**

Martinez, Pedro Jaime — bats right — throws right — b.7/25/71 — System LA/NL

YR	TM/LG	CL	G	TBF	GS	CG	SHO	GF	IP	H	HR	BB	IBB	HB	SO	SH	SF	WP	BK	R	ER	W	L	PCT	SV	ERA
90	GF/PIO	R+	14	346	14	0	0	0	77.0	74	5	40	1	8	82	2	2	6	1	39	31	8	3	.727	0	3.62
91	BAK/CAL	A+	10	243	10	0	0	0	61.1	41	3	19	0	5	83	0	2	1	1	17	14	8	0	1.000	0	2.05
	SA/TEX	AA	12	310	12	4	3	0	76.2	57	1	31	1	3	74	5	1	5	1	21	15	7	5	.583	0	1.76
	ALB/PCL	AAA	6	157	6	0	0	0	39.1	28	3	16	0	0	35	0	3	3	0	17	16	3	3	.500	0	3.66

Martinez, Ramon Jaime — bats right — throws right — b.3/22/68

YR	TM/LG	CL	G	TBF	GS	CG	SHO	GF	IP	H	HR	BB	IBB	HB	SO	SH	SF	WP	BK	R	ER	W	L	PCT	SV	ERA
85	DOD/GCL	R	23	254	6	0	0	6	59.0	57	1	23	0	1	42	5	2	5	0	30	17	4	1	.800	1	2.59
86	BAK/CAL	A+	20	494	20	2	1	0	106.0	119	3	63	2	2	78	6	5	4	2	73	56	4	8	.333	0	4.75
87	VB/FSL	A+	25	699	25	6	1	0	170.1	128	3	78	1	4	148	5	2	5	2	45	41	16	5	.762	0	2.17
88	SA/TEX	AA	14	392	14	2	1	0	95.0	79	3	34	2	1	89	1	2	4	8	29	26	8	4	.667	0	2.46
	ALB/PCL	AAA	10	249	10	2	1	0	58.2	43	3	32	0	0	49	1	2	1	0	24	18	5	2	.714	0	2.76

(continued)

Martinez, Ramon Jaime (continued)

YR	TM/LG	CL	G	TBF	GS	CG	SHO	GF	IP	H	HR	BB	IBB	HB	SO	SH	SF	WP	BK	R	ER	W	L	PCT	SV	ERA
	LA/NL		9	151	6	0	0	0	35.2	27	0	22	1	0	23	4	0	1	0	17	15	1	3	.250	0	3.79
89	ALB/PCL	AAA	18	476	18	2	1	0	113.0	92	6	50	0	1	127	4	2	5	0	40	35	10	2	.833	0	2.79
	LA/NL		15	410	15	2	2	0	98.2	79	11	41	1	5	89	4	2	5	4	39	35	6	4	.600	0	3.19
90	LA/NL		33	950	33	12	3	0	234.1	191	22	67	5	4	223	7	5	3	3	89	76	20	6	.769	0	2.92
91	LA/NL		33	916	33	6	4	0	220.1	190	18	69	4	7	150	8	4	6	0	89	80	17	13	.567	0	2.92
4 YR TOTALS			**90**	**2427**	**87**	**20**	**9**	**0**	**589.0**	**487**	**51**	**199**	**11**	**16**	**485**	**23**	**9**	**11**	**3**	**234**	**206**	**44**	**26**	**.629**	**0**	**3.15**

Mason, Roger LeRoy — bats right — throws right — b.9/18/58

YR	TM/LG	CL	G	TBF	GS	CG	SHO	GF	IP	H	HR	BB	IBB	HB	SO	SH	SF	WP	BK	R	ER	W	L	PCT	SV	ERA
81	MAC/SAL	A	26	0	26	4	1	0	148.0	153	10	50	0	7	105	0	0	4	0	77	64	10	10	.500	0	3.89
82	LAK/FSL	A+	22	0	22	5	0	0	132.0	124	9	52	0	6	72	0	0	3	0	60	51	7	7	.500	0	3.48
83	BIR/SOU	AA	17	0	17	4	1	0	126.0	116	10	43	0	7	83	0	0	3	0	45	29	7	4	.636	0	2.07
	EVA/AMA	AAA	11	0	11	2	0	0	78.0	84	6	21	0	0	43	0	0	4	0	39	37	5	5	.500	0	4.27
84	EVA/AMA	AAA	25	651	25	6	2	0	151.2	175	10	64	1	1	88	5	2	6	1	78	64	9	7	.563	0	3.80
	DET/AL		5	97	2	0	0	2	22.0	23	1	10	0	0	15	0	2	2	0	11	11	1	1	.500	1	4.50
85	PHO/PCL	AAA	24	0	24	5	2	0	167.1	145	12	72	6	4	120	0	0	6	0	67	62	12	1	.923	0	3.33
	SF/NL		5	128	5	1	1	0	29.2	28	5	11	0	0	26	0	0	0	0	13	7	1	3	.250	0	2.12
86	PHO/PCL	AAA	1	22	1	0	0	0	6.0	2	0	1	0	0	2	0	0	0	0	0	0	0	1	1.000	0	0.00
	SF/NL		11	262	11	1	0	0	60.0	56	5	30	3	3	43	2	3	1	0	35	32	3	4	.429	0	4.80
87	SF/NL		5	110	5	0	0	0	26.0	30	4	10	0	0	18	0	1	1	1	15	13	1	1	.500	0	4.50
	PHO/PCL	AAA	10	265	10	1	0	0	61.0	62	4	20	0	0	49	2	3	5	1	34	28	5	1	.833	0	4.13
88	PHO/PCL	AAA	19	397	17	1	0	2	90.2	90	7	38	2	4	62	3	1	0	2	62	49	2	9	.182	0	4.86
89	TUC/PCL	AAA	25	621	25	5	1	0	155.0	125	7	46	1	2	105	6	5	5	0	71	61	7	12	.368	0	3.54
	HOU/NL		2	8	0	0	0	1	1.1	2	0	2	0	0	3	0	0	0	0	3	3	0	0	.000	0	20.25
90	BUF/AMA	AAA	29	325	2	0	0	6	77.0	78	3	25	4	1	44	4	1	2	1	21	18	3	3	.375	3	2.10
91	BUF/AMA	AAA	34	521	15	2	1	6	122.2	115	11	44	1	6	80	6	4	2	0	47	42	7	5	.643	0	3.08
	PIT/NL		24	114	0	0	0	9	29.2	21	2	6	1	1	21	1	1	2	0	11	10	3	2	.600	3	3.03
6 YR TOTALS			**52**	**719**	**23**	**2**	**1**	**9**	**168.2**	**160**	**13**	**69**	**5**	**4**	**126**	**6**	**6**	**6**	**1**	**88**	**76**	**9**	**11**	**.450**	**4**	**4.06**

Mathews, Terry Alan — bats left — throws right — b.10/5/64

YR	TM/LG	CL	G	TBF	GS	CG	SHO	GF	IP	H	HR	BB	IBB	HB	SO	SH	SF	WP	BK	R	ER	W	L	PCT	SV	ERA
87	GAS/SAL	A	34	234	1	0	0	13	48.1	53	5	32	4	2	46	4	5	7	1	35	30	3	3	.500	0	5.59
88	CHA/FSL	A+	27	672	26	2	1	0	163.2	141	6	49	2	4	94	3	3	11	3	68	51	13	6	.684	0	2.80
89	TUL/TEX	AA	10	211	10	1	0	0	45.1	53	3	24	1	2	32	2	6	3	3	40	31	2	5	.286	0	6.15
	CHA/FSL	A+	10	241	10	0	0	0	59.1	55	2	17	0	2	30	1	3	2	0	28	24	4	2	.667	0	3.64
90	TUL/TEX	AA	14	375	14	4	2	0	86.1	88	4	36	2	3	48	1	6	9	0	50	41	5	7	.417	0	4.27
	OC/AMA	AAA	12	307	11	1	1	0	70.2	81	4	15	0	3	36	3	4	2	0	39	29	2	7	.222	0	3.69
91	OC/AMA	AAA	18	410	13	1	0	2	95.1	98	2	34	3	2	63	3	3	4	1	39	37	5	6	.455	1	3.49
	TEX/AL		34	236	2	0	0	8	57.1	54	5	18	3	1	51	2	0	5	0	24	23	4	0	1.000	1	3.61

Mauser, Timothy Edward "Tim" — bats right — throws right — b.10/4/66

YR	TM/LG	CL	G	TBF	GS	CG	SHO	GF	IP	H	HR	BB	IBB	HB	SO	SH	SF	WP	BK	R	ER	W	L	PCT	SV	ERA
88	SPA/SAL	A	4	88	3	0	0	0	23.0	15	0	5	0	1	18	2	1	0	0	6	5	2	1	.667	0	1.96
	REA/EAS	AA	5	120	5	0	0	0	28.1	27	4	6	0	2	17	2	0	0	1	14	11	2	3	.400	0	3.49
89	CLE/FSL	A+	16	457	16	5	0	0	107.0	105	4	40	0	5	73	2	0	2	1	40	32	6	7	.462	0	2.69
	REA/EAS	AA	11	302	11	4	2	0	72.0	62	5	33	0	1	54	0	2	3	1	36	29	7	4	.636	0	3.62
90	REA/EAS	AA	8	194	8	1	0	0	46.1	35	2	15	0	3	40	0	2	4	0	20	17	3	4	.429	0	3.30
	SW/INT	AAA	16	396	16	4	1	0	98.1	75	10	34	1	3	54	1	3	4	0	48	40	5	7	.417	0	3.66
91	PHI/NL		3	53	0	0	0	1	10.2	18	3	3	0	0	5	1	0	0	0	10	9	0	0	.000	0	7.59
	SCR/INT	AAA	26	544	18	1	0	3	128.1	119	11	55	3	2	75	4	3	3	0	66	53	6	11	.353	1	3.72

May, Scott Francis — bats right — throws right — b.11/11/61

YR	TM/LG	CL	G	TBF	GS	CG	SHO	GF	IP	H	HR	BB	IBB	HB	SO	SH	SF	WP	BK	R	ER	W	L	PCT	SV	ERA
83	LET/PIO	R+	13	0	6	1	1	0	46.0	46	3	30	0	2	36	0	0	2	0	29	26	2	1	.667	1	5.09
84	BAK/CAL	A+	25	0	23	7	1	2	152.2	128	7	81	1	2	107	0	0	6	0	78	65	8	10	.444	0	3.83
85	SA/TEX	AA	26	829	26	9	2	0	191.2	181	15	99	3	1	125	6	8	10	4	85	74	10	6	.625	0	3.47
86	ALB/PCL	AAA	27	320	8	0	0	12	65.0	97	6	39	2	2	57	4	2	4	1	59	50	0	7	.000	0	6.92
	SA/TEX	AA	4	106	4	2	1	0	24.0	31	3	7	0	1	12	1	1	1	0	15	14	2	0	1.000	0	5.25
87	SA/TEX	AA	30	516	16	2	1	4	111.1	136	19	52	1	4	108	2	3	11	1	83	74	8	8	.500	0	5.98
88	OC/AMA	AAA	36	628	17	4	1	6	151.2	132	11	57	0	5	103	1	1	5	6	56	50	8	7	.533	0	2.97
	TEX/AL		3	33	1	0	0	0	7.1	8	3	4	1	0	4	1	0	1	1	7	7	0	0	.000	0	8.59
89	OC/AMA	AAA	17	471	16	4	2	0	111.0	100	6	41	4	2	77	1	2	1	0	61	46	6	7	.462	0	3.73
	DEN/AMA	AAA	12	319	12	1	0	0	69.1	80	4	38	3	3	52	1	2	0	0	46	43	3	6	.333	0	5.58
90	DEN/AMA	AAA	7	143	5	2	1	0	28.0	45	3	13	0	2	20	1	4	0	0	26	25	1	1	.500	0	8.04
	EP/TEX	AA	22	437	13	2	0	3	99.2	113	3	38	1	4	75	3	4	4	0	48	42	6	4	.600	0	3.79
91	CHI/NL		2	12	0	0	0	1	2.0	6	0	1	0	0	1	0	0	0	0	4	4	0	0	.000	0	18.00
	IOW/AMA	AAA	57	404	2	0	0	26	94.0	75	7	54	3	2	93	5	0	2	1	38	31	4	4	.500	10	2.97
2 YR TOTALS			**5**	**45**	**1**	**0**	**0**	**1**	**9.1**	**14**	**3**	**5**	**1**	**0**	**5**	**2**	**1**	**0**	**0**	**11**	**11**	**0**	**0**	**.000**	**0**	**10.61**

McCarthy, Gregory O'Neil "Greg" — bats left — throws left — b.10/30/68

YR	TM/LG	CL	G	TBF	GS	CG	SHO	GF	IP	H	HR	BB	IBB	HB	SO	SH	SF	WP	BK	R	ER	W	L	PCT	SV	ERA
87	UTI/NYP	A–	20	130	0	0	0	13	29.2	14	0	23	1	0	40	2	1	1	2	9	3	4	1	.800	3	0.91
88	SPA/SAL	A	34	297	1	0	0	20	64.2	52	3	52	0	10	65	1	3	1	2	36	29	4	2	.667	2	4.04
89	SPA/SAL	A	24	499	15	2	1	4	112.0	90	3	80	0	9	115	3	5	8	6	58	52	5	8	.385	0	4.18
90	CLE/FSL	A+	42	265	0	0	0	19	59.2	47	4	38	1	1	67	2	4	5	5	32	22	1	3	.250	5	3.32

McCaskill, Kirk Edward — bats right — throws right — b.4/9/61

YR	TM/LG	CL	G	TBF	GS	CG	SHO	GF	IP	H	HR	BB	IBB	HB	SO	SH	SF	WP	BK	R	ER	W	L	PCT	SV	ERA
84	EDM/PCL	AAA	24	0	22	2	0	0	143.0	162	19	74	1	1	75	0	0	1	2	104	91	7	11	.389	0	5.73
85	EDM/PCL	AAA	3	0	3	0	0	0	17.2	17	1	6	0	0	18	0	0	0	0	7	4	1	1	.500	0	2.04
	CAL/AL		30	807	29	6	1	0	189.2	189	23	64	1	4	102	2	5	5	0	105	99	12	12	.500	0	4.70
86	CAL/AL		34	1013	33	10	2	1	246.1	207	19	92	1	5	202	6	5	10	2	98	92	17	10	.630	0	3.36
87	PS/CAL	A+	2	35	2	0	0	0	10.0	4	0	3	0	0	7	0	0	0	0	1	0	2	0	1.000	0	0.00
	EDM/PCL	AAA	1	24	1	0	0	0	6.0	3	0	4	0	0	4	0	0	0	0	2	2	1	0	1.000	0	3.00
	CAL/AL		14	334	13	1	1	0	74.2	84	14	34	0	2	56	3	1	1	0	52	47	4	6	.400	0	5.67
88	CAL/AL		23	635	23	4	2	0	146.1	155	9	61	3	1	98	1	6	13	2	78	70	8	6	.571	0	4.31
89	CAL/AL		32	864	32	6	4	0	212.0	202	16	59	1	3	107	3	4	7	2	73	69	15	10	.600	0	2.93
90	CAL/AL		29	738	29	2	1	0	174.1	161	9	72	1	2	78	3	1	6	1	77	63	12	11	.522	0	3.25
91	CAL/AL		30	762	30	1	0	0	177.2	193	19	66	1	3	71	6	6	6	0	93	84	10	19	.345	0	4.26
7 YR TOTALS			**192**	**5153**	**189**	**30**	**11**	**1**	**1221.0**	**1191**	**109**	**448**	**8**	**20**	**714**	**24**	**28**	**48**	**7**	**576**	**524**	**78**	**74**	**.513**	**0**	**3.86**

McClellan, Paul William — bats right — throws right — b.2/8/66

YR	TM/LG	CL	G	TBF	GS	CG	SHO	GF	IP	H	HR	BB	IBB	HB	SO	SH	SF	WP	BK	R	ER	W	L	PCT	SV	ERA
86	EVE/NWL	A–	13	0	13	2	0	0	86.1	71	2	46	0	0	74	0	0	8	0	39	32	5	4	.556	0	3.34
87	CLI/MID	A	28	756	27	5	2	0	177.1	141	18	100	2	6	209	1	1	10	2	86	64	12	10	.545	0	3.25
88	SHR/TEX	AA	27	701	27	4	1	0	167.0	146	11	62	4	4	128	7	5	3	22	89	75	10	12	.455	0	4.04
89	SHR/TEX	AA	12	339	12	2	0	0	84.1	56	4	35	0	1	56	3	3	5	3	26	21	8	3	.727	0	2.24
	PHO/PCL	AAA	9	248	9	0	0	0	56.2	56	6	29	1	4	25	0	4	4	2	34	31	3	4	.429	0	4.92
90	PHO/PCL	AAA	28	770	27	1	0	0	172.1	192	17	78	3	5	102	9	10	7	6	112	99	7	16	.304	0	5.17
	SF/NL		4	44	1	0	0	2	7.2	14	3	6	1	0	2	1	0	0	0	10	10	0	1	.000	0	11.74
91	SHR/TEX	AA	14	384	14	1	1	0	95.2	75	4	30	0	2	63	1	2	8	2	12	12	11	1	.917	0	2.82
	PHO/PCL	AAA	5	160	5	2	0	0	38.1	27	2	21	0	0	18	3	1	2	1	12	12	2	2	.500	0	2.82
	SF/NL		13	300	12	1	0	1	71.0	68	12	25	1	1	44	3	1	5	0	41	36	3	6	.333	0	4.56
2 YR TOTALS			**17**	**344**	**13**	**1**	**0**	**3**	**78.2**	**82**	**15**	**31**	**1**	**2**	**46**	**4**	**1**	**5**	**0**	**51**	**46**	**3**	**7**	**.300**	**0**	**5.26**

McClure, Robert Craig "Bob" — bats right — throws left — b.4/29/52

YR	TM/LG	CL	G	TBF	GS	CG	SHO	GF	IP	H	HR	BB	IBB	HB	SO	SH	SF	WP	BK	R	ER	W	L	PCT	SV	ERA
75	KC/AL		12	66	0	0	0	4	15.1	4	0	14	2	0	15	0	0	0	2	0	0	1	0	1.000	1	0.00
76	KC/AL		8	22	0	0	0	0	4.0	3	0	8	0	0	3	0	0	0	0	4	4	0	0	.000	0	9.00
77	MIL/AL		68	302	0	0	0	31	71.1	64	2	34	5	5	57	5	5	1	2	25	20	2	1	.667	6	2.52
78	MIL/AL		44	283	0	0	0	29	65.0	53	8	30	4	4	47	7	2	1	1	30	27	2	6	.250	9	3.74
79	MIL/AL		36	229	0	0	0	16	51.0	53	6	24	0	3	37	2	3	5	0	29	22	5	2	.714	5	3.88
80	MIL/AL		52	390	5	2	1	23	90.2	83	6	37	2	4	47	1	5	0	2	34	31	5	8	.385	10	3.52
81	MIL/AL		4	34	0	0	0	1	7.2	7	1	4	1	0	6	0	0	0	0	3	3	0	0	.000	0	3.52
82	MIL/AL		34	734	26	5	0	5	172.2	160	21	74	4	4	99	6	4	5	5	90	81	12	7	.632	0	4.22
83	MIL/AL		24	625	23	4	0	0	142.0	152	11	68	1	5	68	0	4	4	6	75	71	9	9	.500	0	4.50
84	MIL/AL		39	616	18	1	0	5	139.2	154	9	52	2	4	68	8	1	3	3	76	68	4	8	.333	1	4.38
85	MIL/AL		38	370	1	0	0	12	85.2	91	10	30	2	3	57	3	2	5	0	43	41	4	1	.800	3	4.31
86	MIL/AL		13	75	0	0	0	7	16.1	18	2	10	1	0	11	1	1	0	0	7	7	2	1	.667	0	3.86
	MON/NL		52	257	0	0	0	15	62.2	53	2	23	2	1	42	3	2	1	1	22	21	2	5	.286	6	3.02
	YEAR		65	332	0	0	0	22	79.0	71	4	33	3	1	53	4	3	1	1	29	28	4	6	.400	6	3.19
87	MON/NL		52	222	0	0	0	16	52.1	47	5	20	3	0	33	5	2	0	1	30	20	6	1	.857	5	3.44
88	MON/NL		19	87	0	0	0	8	19.0	23	4	6	0	1	12	3	2	0	3	13	13	1	3	.250	2	6.16
	NY/NL		14	46	0	0	0	5	11.0	12	1	2	0	1	7	0	1	0	0	5	5	1	0	1.000	1	4.09
	YEAR		33	133	0	0	0	13	30.0	35	4	8	0	2	19	3	2	1	3	18	18	2	3	.400	3	5.40
89	CAL/AL		48	205	0	0	0	27	52.1	39	2	15	1	4	36	1	4	2	1	14	9	6	1	.857	3	1.55
90	PS/CAL	A+	2	10	1	0	0	0	3.0	0	0	1	0	0	6	0	0	0	0	0	0	0	0	.000	0	0.00
	CAL/AL		11	30	0	0	0	1	7.0	7	0	3	0	0	6	1	0	0	0	6	5	1	0	1.000	0	6.43
91	CAL/AL		13	48	0	0	0	2	9.2	13	3	5	0	1	5	0	1	2	1	11	10	0	0	.000	0	9.31
	STL/NL		32	98	0	0	0	9	23.0	24	1	8	2	1	20	1	3	0	0	8	8	1	1	.500	0	3.13
	YEAR		45	146	0	0	0	11	32.2	37	4	13	2	2	20	1	4	2	1	19	18	1	1	.500	0	4.96
17 YR TOTALS			**613**	**4739**	**73**	**12**	**1**	**216**	**1098.1**	**1060**	**96**	**467**	**34**	**32**	**671**	**47**	**48**	**28**	**30**	**525**	**466**	**65**	**54**	**.546**	**52**	**3.82**

McDonald, Larry Benard "Ben" — bats right — throws right — b.11/14/67

YR	TM/LG	CL	G	TBF	GS	CG	SHO	GF	IP	H	HR	BB	IBB	HB	SO	SH	SF	WP	BK	R	ER	W	L	PCT	SV	ERA
89	FRE/CAR	A+	2	35	2	0	0	0	9.0	10	0	0	0	0	9	0	0	1	2	2	2	0	0	.000	0	2.00
	BAL/AL		6	33	0	0	0	2	7.1	8	2	4	0	0	3	0	1	1	1	7	7	1	0	1.000	0	8.59
90	HAG/EAS	AA	3	48	3	0	0	0	11.0	11	1	3	0	1	15	0	0	0	1	8	8	0	1	.000	0	6.55
	ROC/INT	AAA	7	183	7	0	0	0	44.0	33	4	21	1	2	37	2	0	4	0	18	14	3	3	.500	0	2.86
	BAL/AL		21	472	15	3	2	2	118.2	88	9	35	0	0	65	3	5	5	0	36	32	8	5	.615	0	2.43
91	ROC/INT	AAA	2	36	2	0	0	0	7.0	10	1	5	0	0	7	0	0	1	0	7	6	0	1	.000	0	7.71
	BAL/AL		21	532	21	1	0	0	126.1	126	16	43	2	1	85	2	3	3	0	71	68	6	8	.429	0	4.84
3 YR TOTALS			**48**	**1037**	**36**	**4**	**2**	**4**	**252.1**	**222**	**27**	**82**	**2**	**1**	**153**	**5**	**9**	**9**	**1**	**114**	**107**	**15**	**13**	**.536**	**0**	**3.82**

McDowell, Jack Burns — bats right — throws right — b.1/16/66

YR	TM/LG	CL	G	TBF	GS	CG	SHO	GF	IP	H	HR	BB	IBB	HB	SO	SH	SF	WP	BK	R	ER	W	L	PCT	SV	ERA
87	WS/GCL	R	2	28	1	0	0	1	7.0	4	0	1	0	1	12	0	1	0	0	3	2	0	1	.000	0	2.57
	BIR/SOU	AA	4	89	4	1	1	0	20.2	19	5	8	0	1	17	0	0	3	1	20	18	1	2	.333	0	7.84
	CHI/AL		4	103	4	0	0	0	28.0	16	1	6	0	2	15	0	0	0	0	6	6	3	0	1.000	0	1.93
88	CHI/AL		26	687	26	1	0	0	158.2	147	12	68	5	7	84	6	7	11	5	85	70	5	10	.333	0	3.97
89	WS/GCL	R	4	93	4	0	0	0	24.0	19	0	4	0	1	25	0	0	0	0	2	2	2	0	1.000	0	0.75
	VAN/PCL	AAA	16	397	16	1	0	0	86.2	97	6	50	0	3	65	3	4	2	1	60	59	5	5	.455	0	6.13

(continued)

McDowell, Jack Burns (continued)

YR	TM/LG	CL	G	TBF	GS	CG	SHO	GF	IP	H	HR	BB	IBB	HB	SO	SH	SF	WP	BK	R	ER	W	L	PCT	SV	ERA
90	CHI/AL		33	866	33	4	0	0	205.0	189	20	77	0	7	165	1	5	7	1	93	87	14	9	.609	0	3.82
91	CHI/AL		35	1028	35	15	3	0	253.2	212	19	82	2	4	191	8	4	10	1	97	96	17	10	.630	0	3.41
4 YR TOTALS			98	2684	98	20	3	0	645.1	564	52	233	7	20	455	15	16	28	3	281	259	39	29	.574	0	3.61

McDowell, Roger Alan — bats right — throws right — b.12/21/60

YR	TM/LG	CL	G	TBF	GS	CG	SHO	GF	IP	H	HR	BB	IBB	HB	SO	SH	SF	WP	BK	R	ER	W	L	PCT	SV	ERA
84	JAC/TEX	AA	3	32	0	0	0	0	7.1	9	0	1	0	0	8	0	0	0	0	3	3	0	0	.000	0	3.68
85	NY/NL		62	516	2	0	0	36	127.1	108	9	37	8	1	70	6	2	6	2	43	40	6	5	.545	17	2.83
86	NY/NL		75	524	0	0	0	52	128.0	107	4	42	5	3	65	7	3	3	3	48	43	14	9	.609	22	3.02
87	NY/NL		56	384	0	0	0	45	88.2	95	7	28	4	2	32	5	5	3	1	41	41	7	5	.583	25	4.16
88	NY/NL		62	378	0	0	0	41	89.0	80	1	31	7	3	46	3	5	6	1	31	26	5	5	.500	16	2.63
89	NY/NL		25	156	0	0	0	15	35.1	34	1	16	3	2	15	3	1	3	1	21	13	1	5	.167	4	3.31
	PHI/NL		44	231	0	0	0	41	56.2	45	2	22	5	1	32	3	0	0	0	15	7	3	3	.500	19	1.11
	YEAR		69	387	0	0	0	56	92.0	79	3	38	8	3	47	6	1	3	1	36	20	4	8	.333	23	1.96
90	PHI/NL		72	373	0	0	0	60	86.1	92	2	35	9	2	39	10	4	1	1	41	37	6	8	.429	22	3.86
91	PHI/NL		38	271	0	0	0	16	59.0	61	1	32	12	2	28	7	1	1	0	28	21	3	6	.333	3	3.20
	LA/NL		33	174	0	0	0	18	42.1	39	3	16	8	2	22	4	2	1	0	12	12	6	3	.667	7	2.55
	YEAR		71	445	0	0	0	34	101.1	100	4	48	20	2	50	11	3	2	0	40	33	9	9	.500	10	2.93
7 YR TOTALS			467	3007	2	0	0	324	712.2	661	30	259	61	16	349	48	23	24	9	280	240	51	49	.510	135	3.03

McElroy, Charles Dwayne "Chuck" — bats left — throws left — b.10/1/67

YR	TM/LG	CL	G	TBF	GS	CG	SHO	GF	IP	H	HR	BB	IBB	HB	SO	SH	SF	WP	BK	R	ER	W	L	PCT	SV	ERA
86	UTI/NYP	A–	14	386	14	5	1	0	94.2	85	4	28	0	2	91	8	2	2	0	40	31	4	6	.400	0	2.95
87	SPA/SAL	A	24	535	21	5	2	0	130.1	117	6	48	2	0	115	4	1	7	1	51	45	14	4	.778	0	3.11
	CLE/FSL	A+	2	27	2	0	0	0	7.1	1	0	4	0	0	7	0	1	0	0	1	0	1	0	1.000	0	0.00
88	REA/EAS	AA	28	698	26	4	2	0	160.0	173	9	70	2	2	92	2	6	4	1	89	80	9	12	.429	0	4.50
89	REA/EAS	AA	32	188	0	0	0	24	47.0	39	0	14	2	3	39	3	2	3	0	14	14	3	1	.750	12	2.68
	SW/INT	AAA	14	68	0	0	0	9	15.1	13	1	11	1	1	12	1	1	0	0	6	5	1	2	.333	3	2.93
	PHI/NL		11	46	0	0	0	4	10.1	12	1	4	1	0	8	0	0	0	0	2	2	0	0	.000	0	1.74
90	SW/INT	AAA	57	324	1	0	0	26	76.0	62	6	34	4	5	78	7	2	2	0	24	23	6	8	.429	7	2.72
	PHI/NL		16	76	0	0	0	8	14.0	24	0	10	2	0	16	0	1	0	0	13	12	0	1	.000	0	7.71
91	CHI/NL		71	419	0	0	0	12	101.1	73	7	57	7	0	92	9	6	1	0	33	22	6	2	.750	3	1.95
3 YR TOTALS			98	541	0	0	0	24	125.2	109	8	71	10	0	116	9	7	1	0	48	36	6	3	.667	3	2.58

McGaffigan, Andrew Joseph "Andy" — bats right — throws right — b.10/25/56

YR	TM/LG	CL	G	TBF	GS	CG	SHO	GF	IP	H	HR	BB	IBB	HB	SO	SH	SF	WP	BK	R	ER	W	L	PCT	SV	ERA
81	NY/AL		2	31	0	0	0	0	7.0	5	1	3	0	1	2	1	2	0	1	3	2	0	0	.000	0	2.57
82	SF/NL		4	30	0	0	0	2	8.0	5	0	1	0	1	4	0	0	0	0	1	0	1	0	1.000	0	0.00
83	SF/NL		43	560	16	0	0	11	134.1	131	17	39	5	1	93	5	2	8	7	67	64	3	9	.250	2	4.29
84	MON/NL		21	184	3	0	0	8	46.0	37	2	15	2	0	39	0	1	1	2	14	13	3	4	.429	1	2.54
	CIN/NL		9	98	3	0	0	2	23.0	23	2	8	0	0	18	2	0	0	0	14	14	0	2	.000	0	5.48
	YEAR		30	282	6	0	0	10	69.0	60	4	23	2	0	57	2	1	1	2	28	27	3	6	.333	1	3.52
85	DEN/AMA	AAA	26	454	13	4	2	8	106.2	105	3	37	1	2	91	5	2	4	4	43	35	11	5	.688	2	2.95
	CIN/NL		15	392	15	2	0	0	94.1	88	4	30	4	2	83	4	0	2	0	40	39	3	3	.500	0	3.72
86	MON/NL		48	583	14	1	1	8	142.2	114	9	55	8	2	104	10	5	5	4	49	42	10	5	.667	2	2.65
87	MON/NL		69	500	0	0	0	30	120.1	105	5	42	7	3	100	5	3	6	0	38	32	5	2	.714	12	2.39
88	MON/NL		63	392	0	0	0	24	91.1	81	4	37	7	2	71	4	2	2	2	31	28	6	0	1.000	4	2.76
89	MON/NL		57	333	0	0	0	23	75.0	85	3	30	4	3	40	6	4	3	1	40	39	3	5	.375	2	4.68
90	SF/NL		4	27	0	0	0	1	4.2	10	2	4	0	0	4	1	0	0	0	9	9	0	0	.000	0	17.36
	OMA/AMA	AAA	10	74	0	0	0	3	17.0	22	0	5	0	1	17	1	0	0	0	7	7	2	1	.667	0	3.71
	KC/AL		24	336	11	0	0	2	78.2	75	8	28	1	2	49	1	2	3	0	40	27	4	3	.571	1	3.09
	YEAR		28	363	11	0	0	3	83.1	85	8	32	1	2	53	2	2	3	0	49	36	4	3	.571	1	3.89
91†	OMA/AMA	AAA	23	227	4	0	6	11	50.1	56	3	22	1	1	31	1	3	6	0	27	23	0	0	.000	0	4.11
	KC/AL		4	39	0	0	0	1	8.0	14	0	2	0	0	3	0	0	0	0	5	4	0	0	.000	0	4.50
	DEN/PCL	AAA	10	64	0	0	1	2	15.0	16	2	4	1	0	14	1	1	0	0	6	3	0	0	.000	0	1.80
11 YR TOTALS			363	3505	62	3	1	112	833.1	773	55	294	38	16	610	39	22	30	16	351	313	38	33	.535	24	3.38

Meacham, Russell Loren "Rusty" — bats right — throws right — b.1/27/68

YR	TM/LG	CL	G	TBF	GS	CG	SHO	GF	IP	H	HR	BB	IBB	HB	SO	SH	SF	WP	BK	R	ER	W	L	PCT	SV	ERA
88	FAY/SAL	A	6	117	5	0	0	0	24.2	37	3	6	1	2	16	0	1	2	5	19	17	0	3	.000	0	6.20
	BRI/APP	R+	13	303	9	2	2	1	75.1	55	2	22	0	7	85	1	1	5	1	14	12	9	1	.900	0	1.43
89	FAY/SAL	A	16	413	15	2	0	1	102.0	103	4	23	0	1	74	1	4	2	3	33	26	10	3	.769	0	2.29
	LAK/FSL	A+	11	259	9	4	2	1	64.2	59	3	12	2	2	39	3	0	0	0	15	14	5	4	.556	0	1.95
90	LON/EAS	AA	26	722	26	9	3	0	178.0	160	11	36	4	4	123	3	7	5	1	70	62	15	9	.625	0	3.13
91	DET/AL		10	126	4	0	0	1	27.2	35	4	11	0	0	14	1	3	0	1	17	16	2	1	.667	0	5.20
	TOL/INT	AAA	26	517	17	3	1	4	125.1	117	8	40	3	1	70	2	5	6	0	53	43	9	7	.563	2	3.09

Melendez, Jose Luis (Garcia) — bats right — throws right — b.9/2/65

YR	TM/LG	CL	G	TBF	GS	CG	SHO	GF	IP	H	HR	BB	IBB	HB	SO	SH	SF	WP	BK	R	ER	W	L	PCT	SV	ERA
84	WAT/NYP	A–	15	372	15	3	1	0	91.0	61	6	40	0	6	68	1	2	4	2	37	28	5	7	.417	0	2.77
85	PW/CAR	A+	9	180	8	1	0	1	44.1	25	2	26	0	0	41	0	3	2	0	17	12	3	2	.600	1	2.44
86	PW/CAR	A+	28	768	27	6	1	0	186.1	141	9	81	1	2	146	7	5	4	5	75	54	13	10	.565	0	2.61
87	HAR/EAS	AA	6	91	6	0	0	0	18.1	28	4	11	0	0	13	1	0	1	0	24	22	1	3	.250	0	10.80
	SAL/CAR	A+	20	493	20	1	1	0	116.1	96	17	56	0	8	86	0	5	4	0	62	59	9	6	.600	0	4.56

Melendez, Jose Luis (Garcia) (continued)

YR	TM/LG	CL	G	TBF	GS	CG	SHO	GF	IP	H	HR	BB	IBB	HB	SO	SH	SF	WP	BK	R	ER	W	L	PCT	SV	ERA
88	SAL/CAR	A+	8	233	8	2	1	0	53.2	55	10	19	0	1	50	0	0	2	1	26	24	4	2	.667	1	4.02
	HAR/EAS	AA	22	274	4	2	2	6	71.1	46	2	19	1	1	38	2	3	3	4	20	18	5	3	.625	1	2.27
89	WIL/EAS	AA	11	295	11	0	0	0	73.1	54	7	22	1	2	56	1	2	0	6	23	20	3	4	.429	0	2.45
	CAL/PCL	AAA	17	184	2	0	0	4	40.2	42	6	19	2	3	24	2	3	1	0	27	26	1	2	.333	0	5.75
90	CAL/PCL	AAA	45	525	10	1	0	14	124.2	119	11	44	2	6	95	2	5	2	1	61	54	11	4	.733	2	3.90
	SEA/AL		3	28	0	0	0	1	5.1	8	2	3	0	1	7	0	0	1	0	8	7	0	0	.000	0	11.81
91	LV/PCL	AAA	9	238	8	1	0	1	58.2	54	8	11	0	3	45	1	4	0	0	27	26	7	0	1.000	0	3.99
	SD/NL		31	381	9	0	0	10	93.2	77	11	24	3	1	60	2	6	3	2	35	34	8	5	.615	3	3.27
2 YR TOTALS			**34**	**409**	**9**	**0**	**0**	**11**	**99.0**	**85**	**13**	**27**	**3**	**2**	**67**	**2**	**6**	**4**	**2**	**43**	**41**	**8**	**5**	**.615**	**3**	**3.73**

Mercker, Kent Franklin — bats left — throws left — b.2/1/68

YR	TM/LG	CL	G	TBF	GS	CG	SHO	GF	IP	H	HR	BB	IBB	HB	SO	SH	SF	WP	BK	R	ER	W	L	PCT	SV	ERA
86	BRA/GCL	R	9	203	8	0	0	1	47.1	37	1	16	1	0	42	2	0	0	1	21	13	4	3	.571	0	2.47
87	DUR/CAR	A+	3	49	3	0	0	1	11.2	11	1	6	0	0	14	0	0	1	0	8	7	0	1	.000	0	5.40
88	DUR/CAR	A+	19	527	19	5	0	0	127.2	102	5	47	0	2	159	0	1	7	1	44	39	11	4	.733	0	2.75
	GRE/SOU	AA	9	207	9	0	0	0	48.1	36	2	26	1	1	60	1	0	2	2	20	18	3	1	.750	0	3.35
89	RIC/INT	AAA	27	698	27	4	0	0	168.2	107	17	95	4	3	144	7	7	7	2	66	60	9	12	.429	0	3.20
	ATL/NL		2	26	1	0	0	1	4.1	8	1	6	0	0	4	0	0	0	0	6	6	0	0	.000	0	12.46
90	RIC/INT	AAA	12	260	10	0	0	1	58.1	60	1	27	1	0	69	0	1	5	1	30	23	5	4	.556	1	3.55
	ATL/NL		36	211	0	0	0	28	48.1	43	6	24	3	2	39	1	2	2	0	22	17	4	7	.364	7	3.17
91	ATL/NL		50	306	4	0	0	28	73.1	56	5	35	3	1	62	2	2	4	1	23	21	5	3	.625	6	2.58
3 YR TOTALS			**88**	**543**	**5**	**0**	**0**	**57**	**126.0**	**107**	**11**	**65**	**6**	**3**	**105**	**3**	**4**	**6**	**1**	**51**	**44**	**9**	**10**	**.474**	**13**	**3.14**

Mesa, Jose Ramon — bats right — throws right — b.5/22/66

YR	TM/LG	CL	G	TBF	GS	CG	SHO	GF	IP	H	HR	BB	IBB	HB	SO	SH	SF	WP	BK	R	ER	W	L	PCT	SV	ERA
84	FLO/SAL	A	7	177	7	0	0	0	38.1	38	3	25	0	0	35	1	2	2	1	24	16	4	3	.571	0	3.76
	KIN/CAR	A+	10	221	9	0	0	0	50.2	51	2	28	0	1	24	1	1	2	1	23	22	5	2	.714	0	3.91
85	KIN/CAR	A+	30	508	20	0	0	5	106.2	110	11	79	2	9	71	1	10	12	1	89	73	5	10	.333	1	6.16
86	VEN/CAL	A+	24	614	24	2	1	0	142.1	141	6	58	0	1	113	2	1	9	2	71	61	10	6	.625	0	3.86
	KNO/SOU	AA	9	190	8	2	1	1	41.1	40	6	23	0	2	30	0	0	5	0	32	20	2	2	.500	0	4.35
87	KNO/SOU	AA	35	881	35	4	2	0	193.1	206	19	104	0	3	115	8	9	13	3	131	112	10	13	.435	0	5.21
	BAL/AL		6	143	5	0	0	0	31.1	38	7	15	0	0	17	0	0	4	0	23	21	1	3	.250	0	6.03
88	ROC/INT	AAA	11	81	2	0	0	5	15.2	21	2	14	0	2	15	1	0	0	0	20	15	0	3	.000	0	8.62
89	HAG/EAS	AA	3	51	3	0	0	0	13.0	9	0	4	0	0	12	0	0	0	0	2	2	0	0	.000	0	1.38
	ROC/INT	AAA	7	45	1	0	0	4	10.0	10	2	6	0	1	3	0	0	1	0	6	6	0	2	.000	0	5.40
90	HAG/EAS	AA	15	333	15	3	1	0	79.0	77	4	30	0	1	72	3	1	2	0	35	30	5	5	.500	0	3.42
	ROC/INT	AAA	4	106	4	0	0	0	26.0	21	2	12	0	0	23	0	0	3	0	11	7	1	2	.333	0	2.42
	BAL/AL		7	202	7	0	0	0	46.2	37	2	27	2	1	24	2	2	1	1	20	20	3	2	.600	0	3.86
91	ROC/INT	AAA	8	216	8	1	1	0	51.1	37	4	30	0	2	48	1	1	3	1	25	22	3	3	.500	0	3.86
	BAL/AL		23	566	23	2	1	0	123.2	151	11	62	3	3	64	5	4	3	0	86	82	6	11	.353	0	5.97
3 YR TOTALS			**36**	**911**	**35**	**2**	**1**	**0**	**201.2**	**226**	**20**	**104**	**4**	**4**	**105**	**7**	**6**	**8**	**1**	**129**	**123**	**10**	**16**	**.385**	**0**	**5.49**

Milacki, Robert "Bob" — bats right — throws right — b.7/28/64

YR	TM/LG	CL	G	TBF	GS	CG	SHO	GF	IP	H	HR	BB	IBB	HB	SO	SH	SF	WP	BK	R	ER	W	L	PCT	SV	ERA
84	HAG/CAR	A+	15	339	13	1	0	1	77.2	69	2	48	0	0	62	1	2	6	0	35	29	4	5	.444	0	3.36
85	DB/FSL	A+	8	167	6	2	0	1	38.1	32	0	26	1	0	24	2	3	7	1	23	17	1	4	.200	0	3.99
	HAG/CAR	A+	7	174	7	1	0	0	40.2	32	1	22	0	2	37	0	0	0	0	16	12	3	2	.600	0	2.66
86	HAG/CAR	A+	13	292	12	1	1	0	60.2	69	4	37	2	1	46	1	4	6	1	59	32	4	5	.444	0	4.75
	MIA/FSL	A+	12	297	11	0	0	0	67.1	70	1	27	2	2	41	2	4	6	0	36	28	4	4	.500	0	3.74
	CHA/SOU	AA	1	28	1	0	0	0	5.1	7	0	4	0	0	6	1	0	2	0	4	4	0	1	.000	0	6.75
87	CHA/SOU	AA	29	662	24	2	0	2	148.0	168	10	66	0	3	101	2	3	10	0	86	75	11	9	.550	1	4.56
88	CHA/SOU	AA	5	150	5	1	0	0	37.2	26	1	12	1	3	29	1	1	1	1	11	10	3	1	.750	0	2.39
	ROC/INT	AAA	24	747	24	11	3	0	176.2	174	8	65	1	1	103	2	2	6	0	62	53	12	8	.600	0	2.70
	BAL/AL		3	101	3	1	1	0	25.0	9	1	9	0	0	18	0	0	0	0	2	2	2	0	1.000	0	0.72
89	BAL/AL		37	1022	36	3	2	1	243.0	233	21	88	4	2	113	7	6	1	1	105	101	14	12	.538	0	3.74
90	BAL/AL		27	594	24	1	1	0	135.1	143	18	61	2	0	60	5	5	2	1	73	67	5	8	.385	0	4.46
91	HAG/EAS	AA	3	67	3	0	0	0	17.0	14	1	3	0	0	18	0	0	0	0	3	2	3	0	1.000	0	1.06
	BAL/AL		31	758	26	3	0	1	184.0	175	17	53	3	1	108	7	5	1	2	86	82	10	9	.526	0	4.01
4 YR TOTALS			**98**	**2465**	**89**	**8**	**5**	**2**	**587.1**	**560**	**57**	**211**	**9**	**3**	**299**	**19**	**16**	**4**	**4**	**266**	**252**	**31**	**29**	**.517**	**0**	**3.86**

Militello, Sam Salvatore — bats right — throws right — b.11/26/69 — System NY/AL

YR	TM/LG	CL	G	TBF	GS	CG	SHO	GF	IP	H	HR	BB	IBB	HB	SO	SH	SF	WP	BK	R	ER	W	L	PCT	SV	ERA
90	ONE/NYP	A–	13	332	13	3	2	0	88.2	53	2	24	0	1	119	0	2	0	2	14	12	8	2	.800	0	1.22
91	PW/CAR	A+	16	397	16	1	0	0	103.1	65	1	27	1	4	113	1	4	1	1	19	14	12	2	.857	0	1.22
	ALB/EAS	AA	7	191	7	0	0	0	46.0	40	3	19	1	3	55	1	1	0	0	14	12	2	2	.500	0	2.35

Miller, Paul Robert — bats right — throws right — b.4/27/65

YR	TM/LG	CL	G	TBF	GS	CG	SHO	GF	IP	H	HR	BB	IBB	HB	SO	SH	SF	WP	BK	R	ER	W	L	PCT	SV	ERA
87	PIR/GCL	R	12	292	12	1	1	0	70.1	55	3	26	0	2	62	4	1	3	0	34	25	3	6	.333	0	3.20
88	AUG/SAL	A	15	374	15	2	2	0	90.1	80	3	28	1	4	51	3	5	8	5	34	29	6	5	.545	0	2.89
89	SAL/CAR	A+	26	599	20	2	1	0	133.2	138	17	64	0	8	82	2	4	8	1	86	62	6	12	.333	0	4.17
90	SAL/CAR	A+	22	628	22	5	1	0	150.2	145	6	33	1	7	83	3	6	5	0	58	41	8	6	.571	0	2.45
	HAR/EAS	AA	5	148	5	2	1	0	37.0	27	1	10	0	2	11	1	2	2	0	9	9	2	1	.667	0	2.19

(continued)

Miller, Paul Robert (continued)

YR	TM/LG	CL	G	TBF	GS	CG	SHO	GF	IP	H	HR	BB	IBB	HB	SO	SH	SF	WP	BK	R	ER	W	L	PCT	SV	ERA
91	CAR/SOU	AA	15	369	15	1	0	0	89.1	69	4	35	4	3	69	7	1	5	1	29	24	7	2	.778	0	2.42
	PIT/NL		1	21	1	0	0	0	5.0	4	0	3	0	0	2	0	0	0	0	3	3	0	0	.000	0	5.40
	BUF/AMA	AAA	10	272	10	2	0	0	67.0	41	2	29	0	5	30	4	0	1	1	17	11	5	2	.714	0	1.48

Mills, Alan Bernard — bats right — throws right — b.10/18/66

YR	TM/LG	CL	G	TBF	GS	CG	SHO	GF	IP	H	HR	BB	IBB	HB	SO	SH	SF	WP	BK	R	ER	W	L	PCT	SV	ERA
86	SAL/NWL	A-	14	0	14	1	0	0	83.2	77	1	60	0	5	50	0	0	5	0	58	43	6	6	.500	0	4.63
87	PW/CAR	A+	35	424	8	0	0	11	85.2	102	7	64	3	4	53	7	0	9	0	75	58	2	11	.154	1	6.09
88	PW/CAR	A+	42	416	5	0	0	19	93.2	93	4	43	2	5	59	5	5	6	1	56	43	3	8	.273	4	4.13
89	FT./FSL	A+	22	140	0	0	0	15	31.0	40	0	9	1	4	25	3	3	3	2	15	13	1	4	.200	6	3.77
	PW/CAR	A+	26	155	0	0	0	26	39.2	22	0	13	1	5	44	1	2	6	0	5	4	6	1	.857	7	0.91
90	COL/INT	AAA	17	123	0	0	0	13	29.1	22	0	14	2	2	30	1	1	2	0	11	11	3	3	.500	6	3.38
	NY/AL		36	200	0	0	0	18	41.2	48	4	33	6	1	24	4	1	3	0	21	19	1	5	.167	0	4.10
91	COL/INT	AAA	38	522	15	0	0	18	113.2	109	3	75	1	6	77	5	6	12	1	65	56	7	5	.583	8	4.43
	NY/AL		6	72	2	0	0	3	16.1	16	1	8	0	0	11	0	1	2	0	9	8	1	1	.500	0	4.41
2 YR TOTALS			42	272	2	0	0	21	58.0	64	5	41	6	1	35	4	2	5	0	30	27	2	6	.250	0	4.19

Minutelli, Gino Michael — bats left — throws left — b.5/23/64

YR	TM/LG	CL	G	TBF	GS	CG	SHO	GF	IP	H	HR	BB	IBB	HB	SO	SH	SF	WP	BK	R	ER	W	L	PCT	SV	ERA
85	TRI/NWL	A-	20	0	10	0	0	7	57.0	61	3	57	0	6	79	0	0	6	0	57	51	4	8	.333	0	8.05
86	CR/MID	A	27	671	27	3	2	0	152.2	133	14	76	1	5	149	4	6	16	2	73	62	15	5	.750	0	3.66
87	TAM/FSL	A+	17	461	15	5	1	1	104.1	98	4	48	4	5	70	10	3	13	1	51	44	7	6	.538	0	3.80
	VER/EAS	AA	6	168	6	0	0	0	39.2	34	1	16	0	2	39	0	0	2	1	15	14	4	1	.800	0	3.18
88	CHT/SOU	AA	2	27	2	0	0	0	5.2	6	0	4	0	1	3	0	0	0	2	2	1	0	0	.000	0	1.59
89	RED/GCL	R	1	4	1	0	0	0	1.0	0	0	1	0	0	0	0	0	0	1	0	0	0	0	.000	0	0.00
	CHT/SOU	AA	6	140	6	1	0	0	29.0	28	1	23	0	6	20	1	0	1	0	19	17	1	1	.500	0	5.28
90	CHT/SOU	AA	17	467	17	5	0	0	108.1	106	9	46	1	2	75	5	2	5	13	52	48	9	5	.643	0	3.99
	NAS/AMA	AAA	11	315	11	3	0	0	78.1	65	5	31	0	1	61	1	1	1	0	34	28	5	2	.714	0	3.22
	CIN/NL		2	6	0	0	0	0	1.0	0	0	2	0	1	0	0	0	1	0	1	1	0	0	.000	0	9.00
91	CHW/SAL	A	2	28	2	0	0	0	8.0	2	0	4	0	0	8	0	0	0	0	0	0	1	0	1.000	0	0.00
	NAS/AMA	AAA	13	325	13	1	1	0	80.1	57	3	35	2	1	64	6	2	6	1	25	17	4	7	.364	0	1.90
	CIN/NL		16	124	3	0	0	2	25.1	30	5	18	1	0	21	0	2	3	0	17	17	0	0	.000	0	6.04
2 YR TOTALS			18	130	3	0	0	2	26.1	30	5	20	1	1	21	0	2	4	0	18	18	0	2	.000	0	6.15

Miranda, Angel — bats left — throws left — b.11/9/69 — System MIL/AL

YR	TM/LG	CL	G	TBF	GS	CG	SHO	GF	IP	H	HR	BB	IBB	HB	SO	SH	SF	WP	BK	R	ER	W	L	PCT	SV	ERA
87	BUT/PIO	R+	12	91	0	0	0	5	21.2	15	3	10	0	1	28	1	0	1	1	13	9	1	1	.500	0	3.74
	HEL/PIO	R+	13	95	0	0	0	8	21.2	12	1	16	0	0	32	0	0	0	0	9	6	0	1	.000	3	2.49
88	STO/CAL	A+	16	139	0	0	0	5	26.1	20	1	37	0	2	36	2	0	7	0	30	21	0	1	.000	2	7.18
	HEL/PIO	R+	14	284	11	0	0	1	60.2	54	2	58	0	2	75	0	1	6	3	32	26	5	2	.714	0	3.86
89	BEL/MID	A	43	264	0	0	0	40	63.0	39	1	32	6	1	88	7	5	3	1	13	6	6	5	.545	16	0.86
90	STO/CAL	A+	52	443	9	2	1	40	108.1	75	7	49	1	2	138	6	4	2	1	37	32	9	4	.692	24	2.66
91	EP/TEX	AA	38	317	0	0	0	24	74.1	55	2	41	1	1	86	1	4	7	0	27	21	4	2	.667	11	2.54
	DEN/AMA	AAA	11	60	0	0	0	8	11.2	10	0	17	1	0	14	2	0	1	0	9	8	0	1	.000	2	6.17

Mmahat, Kevin Paul — bats left — throws left — b.11/9/64 — System NY/AL

YR	TM/LG	CL	G	TBF	GS	CG	SHO	GF	IP	H	HR	BB	IBB	HB	SO	SH	SF	WP	BK	R	ER	W	L	PCT	SV	ERA
87	RAN/GCL	R	12	222	9	1	0	1	53.1	37	1	30	1	2	60	1	2	6	2	22	19	3	3	.500	0	3.21
88	FT./FSL	A+	17	456	16	3	0	1	102.1	95	1	57	1	8	78	2	6	11	2	60	47	7	7	.500	0	4.13
	ALB/EAS	AA	6	166	6	0	0	0	38.1	30	1	24	0	1	32	1	4	3	3	19	17	2	3	.400	0	3.99
89	ALB/EAS	AA	8	201	8	1	1	0	51.1	35	0	19	0	2	48	0	1	3	0	11	9	5	1	.833	0	1.58
	COL/INT	AAA	15	357	15	0	0	0	82.0	70	2	49	0	3	50	2	3	2	1	44	35	3	4	.429	0	3.84
	NY/AL		4	44	2	0	0	1	7.2	13	2	8	0	3	3	0	3	0	0	12	11	0	2	.000	0	12.91
90	COL/INT	AAA	20	491	20	1	0	0	115.0	99	5	61	0	2	81	5	5	8	3	52	48	11	5	.688	0	3.76
91	COL/INT	AAA	12	279	11	2	2	0	65.1	54	0	34	0	2	59	2	2	0	0	26	26	3	3	.500	0	3.58
1 YR TOTALS			4	44	2	0	0	1	7.2	13	2	8	0	3	3	0	3	0	0	12	11	0	2	.000	0	12.91

Monteleone, Richard "Rich" — bats right — throws right — b.3/22/63

YR	TM/LG	CL	G	TBF	GS	CG	SHO	GF	IP	H	HR	BB	IBB	HB	SO	SH	SF	WP	BK	R	ER	W	L	PCT	SV	ERA
82	BRI/APP	R+	12	0	12	2	0	0	71.0	66	8	23	0	1	52	0	0	4	1	41	31	4	6	.400	0	3.93
83	LAK/FSL	A+	24	0	24	1	0	0	142.0	146	6	80	0	3	124	0	0	12	0	80	65	9	8	.529	0	4.12
	BIR/SOU	AA	3	0	3	0	0	0	15.0	25	4	6	0	0	9	0	0	0	0	12	12	1	1	.500	0	7.20
84	BIR/SOU	AA	19	537	19	4	0	0	123.2	116	9	67	1	4	74	2	5	11	2	69	64	7	8	.467	0	4.66
	EVA/AMA	AAA	11	279	11	2	0	0	64.0	64	7	36	0	0	42	1	2	0	1	33	32	5	3	.625	0	4.50
85	NAS/AMA	AAA	27	652	26	3	0	0	145.1	149	14	87	2	2	97	7	3	11	0	89	82	6	12	.333	0	5.08
86	CAL/PCL	AAA	39	728	21	0	0	14	158.2	177	16	89	5	5	101	7	8	8	3	108	93	8	12	.400	5	5.28
87	SEA/AL		3	34	0	0	0	1	7.0	10	2	4	0	1	2	0	0	0	0	5	5	0	0	.000	0	6.43
	CAL/PCL	AAA	51	309	0	0	0	33	65.1	59	5	63	8	2	38	7	3	4	0	45	40	6	13	.316	15	5.51
88	CAL/PCL	AAA	10	56	0	0	0	3	9.1	21	4	4	0	1	5	0	1	0	3	19	13	0	0	.000	0	12.54
	EDM/PCL	AAA	20	478	16	3	1	1	113.0	120	10	23	1	0	92	4	3	3	4	65	56	4	7	.364	0	4.46
	CAL/AL		3	20	0	0	0	2	4.1	4	0	1	1	1	3	0	0	0	0	0	0	0	0	.000	0	0.00
89	EDM/PCL	AAA	13	234	8	2	0	0	57.0	50	3	16	1	2	47	6	0	2	0	23	22	3	3	.333	0	3.47
	CAL/AL		24	170	0	0	0	8	39.2	39	3	13	1	1	27	1	2	2	0	15	14	2	2	.500	0	3.18
90	EDM/PCL	AAA	5	52	1	0	0	1	14.0	7	1	4	0	0	9	1	0	0	0	3	3	1	0	1.000	1	1.93

Monteleone, Richard "Rich" (continued)

YR	TM/LG	CL	G	TBF	GS	CG	SHO	GF	IP	H	HR	BB	IBB	HB	SO	SH	SF	WP	BK	R	ER	W	L	PCT	SV	ERA
	COL/INT	AAA	38	265	0	0	0	27	64.1	51	4	23	4	1	60	5	3	3	0	17	16	4	4	.500	9	2.24
	NY/AL		5	31	0	0	0	2	7.1	8	0	2	0	0	8	0	0	0	0	5	5	0	1	.000	0	6.14
91	COL/INT	AAA	32	182	0	0	0	25	46.2	36	1	7	0	0	51	3	1	3	0	15	11	1	3	.250	17	2.12
	NY/AL		26	201	0	0	0	10	47.0	42	5	19	3	0	34	2	2	1	1	27	19	3	1	.750	0	3.64
5 YR TOTALS			**61**	**456**	**0**	**0**	**0**	**23**	**105.1**	**103**	**10**	**39**	**5**	**3**	**74**	**3**	**4**	**3**	**2**	**52**	**43**	**5**	**4**	**.556**	**0**	**3.67**

Montgomery, Jeffrey Thomas "Jeff" — bats right — throws right — b.1/7/62

YR	TM/LG	CL	G	TBF	GS	CG	SHO	GF	IP	H	HR	BB	IBB	HB	SO	SH	SF	WP	BK	R	ER	W	L	PCT	SV	ERA
84	TAM/FSL	A+	31	190	0	0	0	28	44.1	29	1	30	6	0	56	2	2	1	0	15	12	5	3	.625	14	2.44
	VER/EAS	AA	22	112	0	0	0	11	25.1	14	0	24	2	0	20	3	0	1	1	7	6	2	0	1.000	4	2.13
85	VER/EAS	AA	53	405	1	0	0	33	101.0	63	6	48	4	1	89	6	1	2	0	25	23	5	3	.625	9	2.05
86	DEN/AMA	AAA	30	652	22	2	1	4	151.2	162	13	57	0	3	78	4	5	11	3	88	74	11	7	.611	0	4.39
87	NAS/AMA	AAA	24	594	21	1	0	0	139.0	132	17	51	3	3	121	3	4	3	4	76	64	8	5	.615	0	4.14
	CIN/NL		14	89	1	0	0	6	19.1	25	2	9	1	0	13	0	0	1	1	15	14	2	2	.500	0	6.52
88	OMA/AMA	AAA	20	106	0	0	0	18	28.1	15	1	11	0	0	36	1	0	0	0	6	6	1	2	.333	13	1.91
	KC/AL		45	271	0	0	0	13	62.2	54	6	30	4	2	47	3	2	3	6	25	24	7	2	.778	1	3.45
89	KC/AL		63	363	0	0	0	39	92.0	66	3	25	4	2	94	1	1	1	6	36	25	7	3	.700	18	1.37
90	KC/AL		73	400	0	0	0	59	94.1	81	6	34	8	5	94	2	2	3	0	36	25	6	5	.545	24	2.39
91	KC/AL		67	376	0	0	0	55	90.0	83	6	28	2	2	77	6	2	6	0	32	29	4	4	.500	33	2.90
5 YR TOTALS			**262**	**1499**	**1**	**0**	**0**	**172**	**358.1**	**309**	**23**	**126**	**16**	**11**	**325**	**12**	**7**	**19**	**8**	**124**	**106**	**26**	**16**	**.619**	**76**	**2.66**

Moore, Michael Wayne "Mike" — bats right — throws right — b.11/26/59

YR	TM/LG	CL	G	TBF	GS	CG	SHO	GF	IP	H	HR	BB	IBB	HB	SO	SH	SF	WP	BK	R	ER	W	L	PCT	SV	ERA
82	SEA/AL		28	651	27	1	1	0	144.1	159	21	79	0	2	73	8	4	6	0	91	86	7	14	.333	0	5.36
83	SEA/AL		22	556	21	3	2	1	128.0	130	10	60	4	3	108	1	6	7	0	75	67	6	8	.429	0	4.71
84	SEA/AL		34	937	33	6	0	0	212.0	236	16	85	10	5	158	5	6	7	2	127	117	7	17	.292	0	4.97
85	SEA/AL		35	1016	34	14	2	1	247.0	230	18	70	2	4	155	2	7	10	3	100	95	17	10	.630	0	3.46
86	SEA/AL		38	1145	37	11	1	1	266.0	279	28	94	6	12	146	10	6	4	1	141	127	11	13	.458	1	4.30
87	SEA/AL		33	1020	33	12	0	0	231.0	268	29	84	3	0	115	9	8	4	2	145	121	9	19	.321	0	4.71
88	SEA/AL		33	918	32	9	3	3	228.2	196	24	63	1	3	182	3	4	3	0	104	96	9	15	.375	1	3.78
89	OAK/AL		35	976	35	6	3	0	241.2	193	14	83	1	2	172	5	6	17	0	82	70	19	11	.633	0	2.61
90	OAK/AL		33	862	33	3	0	0	199.1	204	14	84	2	3	73	4	7	13	0	113	103	13	15	.464	0	4.65
91	OAK/AL		33	887	33	3	1	0	210.0	176	11	105	1	5	153	5	4	14	0	75	69	17	8	.680	0	2.96
10 YR TOTALS			**328**	**8968**	**318**	**68**	**13**	**6**	**2108.0**	**2071**	**185**	**807**	**35**	**39**	**1335**	**52**	**57**	**86**	**11**	**1053**	**951**	**115**	**130**	**.469**	**2**	**4.06**

Morgan, Michael Thomas "Mike" — bats right — throws right — b.10/8/59

YR	TM/LG	CL	G	TBF	GS	CG	SHO	GF	IP	H	HR	BB	IBB	HB	SO	SH	SF	WP	BK	R	ER	W	L	PCT	SV	ERA
78	OAK/AL		3	60	3	1	0	0	12.1	19	1	8	0	0	0	1	0	0	0	12	10	0	3	.000	0	7.30
79	OAK/AL		13	368	13	2	0	0	77.1	102	7	50	0	3	17	4	4	7	0	57	51	2	10	.167	0	5.94
82	NY/AL		30	661	23	2	0	2	150.1	167	15	67	5	2	71	2	4	6	0	77	73	7	11	.389	0	4.37
83	TOR/AL		16	198	4	0	0	2	45.1	48	6	21	0	1	22	0	1	3	0	26	26	0	3	.000	0	5.16
84	SYR/INT	AAA	34	803	28	10	4	4	185.2	167	11	100	3	2	105	6	5	11	0	101	84	13	11	.542	1	4.07
85	SEA/AL		2	33	2	0	0	0	6.0	11	2	5	0	0	2	0	0	1	0	8	8	1	1	.500	0	12.00
	CAL/PCL	AAA	1	0	1	0	0	0	2.0	3	0	0	0	0	0	0	0	0	0	1	1	0	0	.000	0	4.50
86	SEA/AL		37	951	33	9	1	2	216.1	243	24	86	3	4	116	7	3	8	1	122	109	11	17	.393	1	4.53
87	SEA/AL		34	898	31	8	2	2	207.0	245	25	53	3	5	85	8	5	11	0	117	107	12	17	.414	0	4.65
88	ROC/INT	AAA	3	74	3	1	0	0	17.0	19	1	6	0	0	7	0	1	1	0	10	9	0	0	.000	0	4.76
	BAL/AL		22	299	10	2	0	6	71.1	70	6	23	1	1	29	1	0	5	0	45	43	1	6	.143	1	5.43
89	LA/NL		40	604	19	0	0	7	152.2	130	6	33	8	2	72	8	6	6	0	51	43	8	11	.421	0	2.53
90	LA/NL		33	891	33	6	4	0	211.0	216	19	60	5	5	106	11	4	4	1	100	88	11	15	.423	0	3.75
91	LA/NL		34	949	33	5	1	1	236.1	197	12	61	10	3	140	10	4	6	0	85	73	14	10	.583	1	2.78
11 YR TOTALS			**264**	**5912**	**204**	**35**	**8**	**22**	**1386.0**	**1448**	**123**	**467**	**35**	**25**	**660**	**52**	**31**	**57**	**2**	**700**	**631**	**67**	**104**	**.392**	**3**	**4.10**

Morris, John Scott "Jack" — bats right — throws right — b.5/16/55

YR	TM/LG	CL	G	TBF	GS	CG	SHO	GF	IP	H	HR	BB	IBB	HB	SO	SH	SF	WP	BK	R	ER	W	L	PCT	SV	ERA
77	DET/AL		7	189	6	1	0	0	45.2	38	4	23	0	0	28	3	1	2	0	20	19	1	1	.500	0	3.74
78	DET/AL		28	469	7	0	0	10	106.0	107	8	49	5	3	48	8	9	4	0	57	51	3	5	.375	0	4.33
79	DET/AL		27	806	27	9	1	0	197.2	179	19	59	4	4	113	3	6	4	0	76	72	17	7	.708	0	3.28
80	DET/AL		36	1074	36	11	2	0	250.0	252	20	87	5	4	112	10	13	6	2	125	116	16	15	.516	0	4.18
81	DET/AL		25	798	25	15	1	0	198.0	153	14	78	11	2	97	8	9	2	2	69	67	14	7	.667	0	3.05
82	DET/AL		37	1107	37	17	3	0	266.1	247	37	96	7	0	135	4	5	10	0	131	120	17	16	.515	0	4.06
83	DET/AL		37	1204	37	20	1	0	293.2	257	30	83	5	3	232	8	9	18	0	117	109	20	13	.606	0	3.34
84	DET/AL		35	1015	35	9	1	0	240.1	221	20	87	7	2	148	5	3	14	0	108	96	19	11	.633	0	3.60
85	DET/AL		35	1077	35	13	4	0	257.0	212	21	110	7	5	191	11	7	15	0	102	95	16	11	.593	0	3.33
86	DET/AL		35	1092	35	15	6	0	267.0	229	40	82	5	7	223	7	3	12	0	105	97	21	8	.724	0	3.27
87	DET/AL		34	1101	34	13	0	0	266.0	227	39	93	7	1	208	6	5	24	1	111	100	18	11	.621	0	3.38
88	DET/AL		34	997	34	10	2	0	235.0	225	20	83	7	4	168	12	3	11	1	115	103	15	13	.536	0	3.94
89	LAK/FSL	A+	3	30	3	0	0	0	8.0	7	0	0	0	0	2	0	0	0	0	2	2	0	0	.000	0	2.25
	DET/AL		24	743	24	10	0	0	170.1	189	23	59	3	2	115	6	7	12	1	102	92	6	14	.300	0	4.86
90	DET/AL		36	1073	36	11	3	0	249.2	231	26	97	13	6	162	7	10	16	2	144	125	15	18	.455	0	4.51
91	MIN/AL		35	1032	35	10	2	0	246.2	226	18	92	5	5	163	5	8	15	1	107	94	18	12	.600	0	3.43
15 YR TOTALS			**465**	**13777**	**443**	**164**	**26**	**10**	**3289.1**	**2993**	**339**	**1178**	**93**	**41**	**2143**	**103**	**98**	**170**	**24**	**1489**	**1356**	**216**	**162**	**.571**	**0**	**3.71**

Morton, Kevin Joseph — bats right — throws left — b.8/3/68

YR	TM/LG	CL	G	TBF	GS	CG	SHO	GF	IP	H	HR	BB	IBB	HB	SO	SH	SF	WP	BK	R	ER	W	L	PCT	SV	ERA
89	RS/GCL	R	2	22	1	0	0	1	6.0	2	0	1	0	1	11	0	0	0	0	0	0	1	0	1.000	1	0.00
	ELM/NYP	A–	3	90	3	2	0	0	24.0	11	0	6	0	1	32	2	2	1	0	6	5	1	1	.500	0	1.88
	LYN/CAR	A+	9	253	9	4	2	0	65.0	42	2	17	0	2	68	0	2	3	0	20	17	4	5	.444	0	2.35
90	NB/EAS	AA	26	685	26	7	2	0	163.0	151	10	48	0	14	131	4	3	6	5	86	69	8	14	.364	0	3.81
91	PAW/INT	AAA	16	412	15	1	1	0	98.0	91	8	30	1	2	80	2	2	3	2	41	38	7	3	.700	0	3.49
	BOS/AL		16	379	15	1	0	0	86.1	93	9	40	2	1	45	3	7	1	1	49	44	6	5	.545	0	4.59

Moyer, Jamie — bats left — throws left — b.11/18/62

YR	TM/LG	CL	G	TBF	GS	CG	SHO	GF	IP	H	HR	BB	IBB	HB	SO	SH	SF	WP	BK	R	ER	W	L	PCT	SV	ERA
84	GEN/NYP	A–	14	407	14	5	2	0	104.2	59	5	31	0	5	120	1	1	7	1	27	22	9	3	.750	0	1.89
85	WIN/CAR	A+	12	391	12	6	2	1	94.0	82	1	22	3	5	94	7	3	0	3	36	24	8	2	.800	0	2.30
	PIT/EAS	AA	15	419	15	3	0	0	96.2	99	4	32	1	5	51	5	4	4	1	49	40	7	6	.538	0	3.72
86	PIT/EAS	AA	6	162	6	2	0	0	41.0	27	2	16	0	4	42	1	0	3	1	10	4	3	1	.750	0	0.88
	IOW/AMA	AAA	6	165	6	2	0	0	42.1	25	2	11	0	0	25	0	1	1	0	14	12	3	2	.600	0	2.55
	CHI/NL		16	395	16	1	1	0	87.1	107	10	42	1	3	45	3	3	3	3	52	49	7	4	.636	0	5.05
87	CHI/NL		35	899	33	1	0	1	201.0	210	28	97	9	5	147	14	7	11	2	127	114	12	15	.444	0	5.10
88	CHI/NL		34	855	30	3	1	0	202.0	212	20	55	7	4	121	14	4	4	0	84	78	9	15	.375	0	3.48
89	RAN/GCL	R	3	42	3	0	0	0	11.0	8	0	1	0	0	18	0	0	0	0	4	2	1	0	1.000	0	1.64
	TUL/TEX	AA	2	53	2	1	1	0	12.1	16	1	3	0	0	9	0	0	1	1	8	7	1	1	.500	0	5.11
	TEX/AL		15	337	15	1	1	0	76.0	84	10	33	0	2	44	1	4	1	0	51	41	4	9	.308	0	4.86
90	TEX/AL		33	447	10	1	0	6	102.1	115	6	39	4	4	58	1	7	1	0	59	53	2	6	.250	0	4.66
91	STL/NL		8	142	7	0	0	1	31.1	38	5	16	0	1	20	1	4	2	1	21	20	0	5	.000	0	5.74
	LOU/AMA	AAA	20	536	20	1	0	0	125.2	125	16	43	4	3	69	6	3	8	3	64	53	5	10	.333	0	3.80
6 YR TOTALS			**141**	**3075**	**111**	**7**	**2**	**9**	**700.0**	**766**	**79**	**282**	**21**	**19**	**435**	**37**	**27**	**22**	**6**	**394**	**355**	**34**	**54**	**.386**	**0**	**4.56**

Mulholland, Terence John "Terry" — bats right — throws left — b.3/9/63

YR	TM/LG	CL	G	TBF	GS	CG	SHO	GF	IP	H	HR	BB	IBB	HB	SO	SH	SF	WP	BK	R	ER	W	L	PCT	SV	ERA
84	EVE/NWL	A–	3	0	3	0	0	0	19.0	10	0	4	0	1	15	0	0	0	0	2	0	1	0	1.000	0	0.00
	FRE/CAL	A+	9	0	9	0	0	0	42.2	32	1	36	0	0	39	0	0	1	0	17	14	5	2	.714	0	2.95
85	SHR/TEX	AA	26	761	26	8	3	0	176.2	166	9	87	2	2	122	8	1	6	0	79	57	9	8	.529	0	2.90
86	PHO/PCL	AAA	17	482	17	3	0	0	111.0	112	6	56	4	1	77	7	2	4	4	60	55	8	5	.615	0	4.46
	SF/NL		15	245	10	0	0	1	54.2	51	3	35	2	1	27	5	1	6	0	33	30	1	7	.125	0	4.94
87	PHO/PCL	AAA	37	799	29	3	0	4	172.1	200	7	90	0	4	94	5	7	17	3	124	97	7	12	.368	1	5.07
88	PHO/PCL	AAA	19	447	14	3	2	1	100.2	116	3	44	0	0	57	3	2	5	4	45	40	7	3	.700	0	3.58
	SF/NL		9	191	6	2	1	1	46.0	50	3	15	1	0	18	5	0	1	0	20	19	2	1	.667	0	3.72
89	PHO/PCL	AAA	13	313	12	1	1	0	78.1	67	3	26	2	3	61	5	2	2	3	30	26	4	5	.444	0	2.99
	SF/NL		5	51	1	0	0	2	11.0	15	0	4	0	0	6	0	0	0	0	5	5	0	0	.000	0	4.09
	PHI/NL		20	462	17	2	1	2	104.1	122	8	32	3	4	60	7	1	3	0	61	58	4	7	.364	0	5.00
	YEAR		25	513	18	2	1	4	115.1	137	8	36	3	4	66	7	1	3	0	66	63	4	7	.364	0	4.92
90	SW/INT	AAA	1	27	1	0	0	0	6.0	9	0	2	0	0	2	0	0	0	0	4	2	0	1	.000	0	3.00
	PHI/NL		33	746	26	6	1	2	180.2	172	15	42	7	2	75	7	12	7	2	78	67	9	10	.474	0	3.34
91	PHI/NL		34	956	34	8	3	0	232.0	231	15	49	2	3	142	11	6	3	0	100	93	16	13	.552	0	3.61
5 YR TOTALS			**116**	**2651**	**94**	**18**	**6**	**8**	**628.2**	**641**	**44**	**169**	**14**	**11**	**328**	**35**	**20**	**20**	**2**	**297**	**272**	**32**	**38**	**.457**	**0**	**3.89**

Munoz, Michael Anthony "Mike" — bats left — throws left — b.7/12/65

YR	TM/LG	CL	G	TBF	GS	CG	SHO	GF	IP	H	HR	BB	IBB	HB	SO	SH	SF	WP	BK	R	ER	W	L	PCT	SV	ERA
86	GF/PIO	R+	14	0	14	2	2	0	81.1	85	4	38	0	1	49	0	0	3	0	44	29	4	4	.500	0	3.21
87	BAK/CAL	A+	52	524	12	0	0	23	118.0	125	5	43	3	0	80	11	2	6	1	68	49	8	7	.533	8	3.74
88	SA/TEX	AA	56	302	0	0	0	35	71.2	63	0	24	1	1	71	5	1	6	0	18	8	7	2	.778	14	1.00
89	ALB/PCL	AAA	60	345	0	0	0	27	79.0	72	2	40	8	0	81	6	3	6	0	32	27	6	4	.600	16	3.08
	LA/NL		3	14	0	0	0	1	2.2	5	1	2	0	0	3	0	0	0	0	5	5	0	0	.000	0	16.88
90	LA/NL		8	24	0	0	0	3	5.2	7	0	3	0	0	2	1	0	0	0	2	2	0	0	.000	0	3.18
	ALB/PCL	AAA	49	258	0	0	0	14	59.1	65	8	19	3	0	40	4	2	3	1	33	28	4	1	.800	6	4.25
91	DET/AL		6	46	0	0	0	4	9.1	14	0	5	0	0	3	0	1	0	0	10	10	0	0	.000	0	9.64
	TOL/INT	AAA	38	235	1	0	0	19	54.0	44	4	35	4	0	38	2	1	2	0	30	23	2	3	.400	8	3.83
3 YR TOTALS			**17**	**84**	**0**	**0**	**0**	**8**	**17.2**	**25**	**1**	**10**	**0**	**0**	**8**	**1**	**1**	**1**	**0**	**17**	**17**	**0**	**1**	**.000**	**0**	**8.66**

Murphy, Robert Albert "Rob" — bats left — throws left — b.5/26/60

YR	TM/LG	CL	G	TBF	GS	CG	SHO	GF	IP	H	HR	BB	IBB	HB	SO	SH	SF	WP	BK	R	ER	W	L	PCT	SV	ERA
84	VER/EAS	AA	45	313	1	0	0	25	69.2	57	0	35	3	1	69	9	4	7	0	23	21	2	3	.400	15	2.71
85	DEN/AMA	AAA	41	395	0	0	0	18	84.0	94	8	57	4	2	66	5	2	8	0	55	43	5	5	.500	5	4.61
	CIN/NL		2	12	0	0	0	2	3.0	2	1	2	0	0	1	0	0	0	0	2	2	0	0	.000	0	6.00
86	DEN/AMA	AAA	27	180	0	0	0	16	42.2	33	0	24	1	0	36	3	1	0	1	12	9	3	4	.429	7	1.90
	CIN/NL		34	195	0	0	0	12	50.1	26	0	21	2	0	36	3	3	5	0	4	4	6	0	1.000	1	0.72
87	CIN/NL		87	415	0	0	0	21	100.2	91	7	32	5	0	99	1	2	1	0	37	34	8	5	.615	3	3.04
88	CIN/NL		76	350	0	0	0	28	84.2	69	3	38	6	1	74	9	1	1	0	31	29	0	6	.000	3	3.08
89	BOS/AL		74	438	0	0	0	27	105.0	97	7	41	8	1	107	7	3	6	0	38	32	5	7	.417	9	2.74
90	BOS/AL		68	285	0	0	0	20	57.0	85	10	32	3	1	54	4	4	4	0	46	40	0	6	.000	7	6.32
91	SEA/AL		57	211	0	0	0	26	48.0	47	4	19	1	1	34	3	0	4	0	17	16	0	1	.000	4	3.00
7 YR TOTALS			**398**	**1906**	**0**	**0**	**0**	**136**	**448.2**	**417**	**32**	**185**	**28**	**4**	**405**	**27**	**13**	**25**	**1**	**175**	**157**	**19**	**25**	**.432**	**27**	**3.15**

Mussina, Michael Cole "Mike" — bats right — throws right — b.12/8/68

YR	TM/LG	CL	G	TBF	GS	CG	SHO	GF	IP	H	HR	BB	IBB	HB	SO	SH	SF	WP	BK	R	ER	W	L	PCT	SV	ERA
90	HAG/EAS	AA	7	168	7	2	1	0	42.1	34	1	7	0	0	40	1	1	3	1	10	7	3	0	1.000	0	1.49

Mussina, Michael Cole "Mike" (continued)

YR	TM/LG	CL	G	TBF	GS	CG	SHO	GF	IP	H	HR	BB	IBB	HB	SO	SH	SF	WP	BK	R	ER	W	L	PCT	SV	ERA
	ROC/INT	AAA	2	50	2	0	0	0	13.1	8	2	4	0	0	15	0	0	0	0	2	2	0	0	.000	0	1.35
91	ROC/INT	AAA	19	497	19	3	1	0	122.1	108	9	31	0	2	107	3	1	6	1	42	39	10	4	.714	0	2.87
	BAL/AL		12	349	12	2	0	0	87.2	77	7	21	0	1	52	3	2	3	1	31	28	4	5	.444	0	2.87

Mutis, Jeffrey Thomas "Jeff" — bats left — throws left — b.12/20/66

YR	TM/LG	CL	G	TBF	GS	CG	SHO	GF	IP	H	HR	BB	IBB	HB	SO	SH	SF	WP	BK	R	ER	W	L	PCT	SV	ERA
88	BUR/APP	R+	3	79	3	0	0	0	22.0	8	0	6	0	0	20	0	0	1	2	1	1	3	0	1.000	0	0.41
	KIN/CAR	A+	1	24	1	0	0	0	5.2	6	0	3	0	0	2	1	0	1	0	1	1	1	0	1.000	0	1.59
89	KIN/CAR	A+	16	406	15	5	2	1	99.2	87	6	20	0	2	68	1	4	3	2	42	29	7	3	.700	0	2.62
90	CAN/EAS	AA	26	702	26	7	3	0	165.0	178	6	44	2	3	94	3	2	5	1	73	58	11	10	.524	0	3.16
91	CLE/AL		3	68	3	0	0	0	12.1	23	1	7	1	0	6	2	1	1	0	16	16	0	3	.000	0	11.68
	CAN/EAS	AA	25	682	24	7	4	0	169.2	138	5	51	2	6	89	4	3		1	42	34	11	5	.688	0	1.80

Myers, Randall Kirk "Randy" — bats left — throws left — b.9/19/62

YR	TM/LG	CL	G	TBF	GS	CG	SHO	GF	IP	H	HR	BB	IBB	HB	SO	SH	SF	WP	BK	R	ER	W	L	PCT	SV	ERA
84	LYN/CAR	A+	23	641	22	7	1	1	157.0	123	7	61	0	3	171	5	1	11	0	46	36	13	5	.722	0	2.06
	JAC/TEX	AA	5	148	5	1	0	0	35.0	29	2	16	1	0	35	2	2	2	1	14	8	2	1	.667	0	2.06
85	JAC/TEX	AA	19	517	19	2	1	0	120.1	99	4	69	1	1	116	5	5	8	1	61	53	4	8	.333	0	3.96
	TID/INT	AAA	8	184	7	0	0	0	44.0	40	1	20	1	1	25	1	1	4	0	13	9	1	1	.500	0	1.84
	NY/NL		1	7	0	0	0	1	2.0	0	0	1	0	0	2	0	0	0	0	0	0	0	0	.000	0	0.00
86	TID/INT	AAA	45	278	0	0	0	35	65.0	44	2	44	3	2	79	3	0	0	0	19	17	6	7	.462	12	2.35
	NY/NL		10	53	0	0	0	5	10.2	11	1	9	1	0	13	0	0	0	0	5	5	0	0	.000	0	4.22
87	TID/INT	AAA	5	33	0	0	0	4	7.1	6	0	4	0	1	13	1	0	0	0	4	4	0	0	.000	3	4.91
	NY/NL		54	314	0	0	0	18	75.0	61	6	30	5	0	92	7	6	3	0	36	33	3	6	.333	6	3.96
88	NY/NL		55	261	0	0	0	44	68.0	45	5	17	2	2	69	3	2	2	0	15	13	7	3	.700	26	1.72
89	NY/NL		65	349	0	0	0	47	84.1	62	4	40	4	0	88	6	2	3	0	23	22	7	4	.636	24	2.35
90	CIN/NL		66	353	0	0	0	59	86.2	59	6	38	8	3	98	4	2	1	0	24	20	4	6	.400	31	2.08
91	CIN/NL		58	575	12	1	0	18	132.0	116	8	80	5	1	108	8	6	2	1	61	52	6	13	.316	6	3.55
7 YR TOTALS			**309**	**1912**	**12**	**1**	**0**	**192**	**458.2**	**354**	**30**	**215**	**25**	**7**	**470**	**28**	**18**	**12**	**2**	**164**	**145**	**27**	**32**	**.458**	**93**	**2.85**

Nabholz, Christopher William "Chris" — bats left — throws left — b.1/5/67

YR	TM/LG	CL	G	TBF	GS	CG	SHO	GF	IP	H	HR	BB	IBB	HB	SO	SH	SF	WP	BK	R	ER	W	L	PCT	SV	ERA
89	ROC/MID	A	24	654	23	3	3	0	161.1	132	6	41	0	0	149	5	4	11	2	54	39	13	5	.722	0	2.18
90	JAC/SOU	AA	11	304	11	0	0	0	74.1	62	6	27	0	0	77	1	1	6	1	28	25	7	2	.778	0	3.03
	IND/AMA	AAA	10	274	10	0	0	0	63.1	66	7	28	0	1	44	1	6	3	0	38	34	0	6	.000	0	4.83
	MON/NL		11	282	11	0	0	0	70.0	43	6	32	1	2	53	1	2	1	0	23	22	6	2	.750	0	2.83
91	IND/AMA	AAA	4	74	4	0	0	0	19.1	13	2	5	0	0	16	1	0	0	0	5	4	2	2	.500	0	1.86
	MON/NL		24	631	24	1	0	0	153.2	134	5	57	4	2	99	2	4	3	1	66	62	8	7	.533	0	3.63
2 YR TOTALS			**35**	**913**	**35**	**2**	**1**	**0**	**223.2**	**177**	**11**	**89**	**5**	**4**	**152**	**3**	**6**	**4**	**2**	**89**	**84**	**14**	**9**	**.609**	**0**	**3.38**

Nagy, Charles Harrison — bats left — throws right — b.5/5/67

YR	TM/LG	CL	G	TBF	GS	CG	SHO	GF	IP	H	HR	BB	IBB	HB	SO	SH	SF	WP	BK	R	ER	W	L	PCT	SV	ERA
89	KIN/CAR	A+	13	373	13	6	4	0	95.1	69	0	24	0	4	99	1	3	3	0	22	16	8	4	.667	0	1.51
	CAN/EAS	AA	15	400	14	2	0	0	94.0	102	4	32	0	2	65	3	2	7	0	44	35	4	5	.444	0	3.35
90	CAN/EAS	AA	23	694	23	9	2	0	175.0	132	9	39	0	6	99	4	4	3	3	62	49	13	8	.619	0	2.52
	CLE/AL		9	208	8	0	0	1	45.2	58	7	21	0	1	26	1	1	1	1	31	30	2	4	.333	0	5.91
91	CLE/AL		33	914	33	6	1	0	211.1	228	15	66	1	6	109	5	9	6	2	103	97	10	15	.400	0	4.13
2 YR TOTALS			**42**	**1122**	**41**	**6**	**1**	**1**	**257.0**	**286**	**22**	**87**	**7**	**7**	**135**	**6**	**10**	**7**	**3**	**134**	**127**	**12**	**19**	**.387**	**0**	**4.45**

Navarro, Jaime (Cintron) — bats right — throws right — b.3/27/67

YR	TM/LG	CL	G	TBF	GS	CG	SHO	GF	IP	H	HR	BB	IBB	HB	SO	SH	SF	WP	BK	R	ER	W	L	PCT	SV	ERA
87	HEL/PIO	R+	13	356	13	3	0	0	85.2	87	5	18	1	1	95	2	2	5	1	37	34	4	3	.571	0	3.57
88	STO/CAL	A+	26	727	26	4	1	0	174.2	148	6	74	1	6	151	4	1	22	2	70	60	15	5	.750	0	3.09
89	EP/TEX	AA	11	316	11	1	0	0	76.2	61	3	35	1	1	78	1	0	5	1	29	21	5	2	.714	0	2.47
	DEN/AMA	AAA	3	87	3	1	0	1	20.0	24	0	7	2	0	17	1	1	0	0	8	8	1	1	.500	0	3.60
	MIL/AL		19	470	17	1	0	1	109.2	119	6	32	3	1	56	5	2	3	0	47	38	7	8	.467	0	3.12
90	DEN/AMA	AAA	6	176	6	0	0	0	40.2	41	1	14	0	0	28	1	1	0	0	27	19	2	3	.400	0	4.20
	MIL/AL		32	654	22	3	0	2	149.1	176	11	41	3	4	75	4	5	6	5	83	74	8	7	.533	0	4.46
91	MIL/AL		34	1002	34	10	2	0	234.0	237	18	73	4	6	114	7	8	10	0	117	102	15	12	.556	0	3.92
3 YR TOTALS			**85**	**2126**	**73**	**14**	**2**	**3**	**493.0**	**532**	**35**	**146**	**9**	**11**	**245**	**16**	**15**	**19**	**5**	**247**	**214**	**30**	**27**	**.526**	**1**	**3.91**

Neagle, Dennis Edward "Denny" — bats left — throws left — b.9/13/68

YR	TM/LG	CL	G	TBF	GS	CG	SHO	GF	IP	H	HR	BB	IBB	HB	SO	SH	SF	WP	BK	R	ER	W	L	PCT	SV	ERA
89	ELI/APP	R+	6	91	3	0	0	3	22.0	20	1	8	0	1	32	1	1	1	1	11	11	1	2	.333	1	4.50
	KEN/MID	A	6	166	6	1	1	0	43.2	25	3	16	0	1	40	5	1	1	0	9	8	2	1	.667	0	1.65
90	VIS/CAL	A+	10	241	10	0	0	0	63.0	39	2	16	0	0	92	1	1	0	2	13	10	8	0	1.000	0	1.43
	ORL/SOU	AA	17	486	17	4	1	0	121.1	94	11	31	0	5	94	4	2	2	0	40	33	12	3	.800	0	2.45
91	POR/PCL	AAA	19	438	17	1	1	1	104.2	101	6	32	1	2	94	4	2	4	0	41	38	9	4	.692	0	3.27
	MIN/AL		7	92	3	0	0	2	20.0	28	3	7	2	0	14	0	0		0	9	9	0	0	.000	0	4.05

Nelson, Jeffrey Allan "Jeff" — bats right — throws right — b.11/17/66 — System SEA/AL

YR	TM/LG	CL	G	TBF	GS	CG	SHO	GF	IP	H	HR	BB	IBB	HB	SO	SH	SF	WP	BK	R	ER	W	L	PCT	SV	ERA
84	GF/PIO	R+	1	0	0	0	0	0	0.2	3	1	3	0	1	1	0	0	0	0	4	4	0	0	.000	0	54.00
	DOD/GCL	R	9	56	0	0	0	3	13.1	6	0	6	0	1	7	0	0	1	1	3	2	0	0	.000	0	1.35

(continued)

Nelson, Jeffrey Allan "Jeff" (continued)

YR	TM/LG	CL	G	TBF	GS	CG	SHO	GF	IP	H	HR	BB	IBB	HB	SO	SH	SF	WP	BK	R	ER	W	L	PCT	SV	ERA
85	DOD/GCL	R	14	242	7	0	0	3	47.1	72	1	32	0	0	31	0	1	8	1	50	29	0	5	.000	0	5.51
86	GF/PIO	R+	3	0	0	0	0	2	2.0	5	0	3	2	0	1	0	0	2	0	3	3	0	0	.000	0	13.50
	BAK/CAL	A+	24	412	11	0	0	6	71.1	79	9	84	1	4	37	1	9	10	0	83	53	0	7	.000	0	6.69
87	SAL/CAL	A+	17	389	16	1	0	0	80.0	80	2	71	0	4	43	4	3	17	0	61	51	3	7	.300	0	5.74
88	SB/CAL	A+	27	677	27	1	1	0	149.1	163	9	91	2	8	94	2	8	20	0	115	92	8	9	.471	0	5.54
89	WIL/EAS	AA	15	392	15	2	0	0	92.1	72	3	53	1	4	61	0	3	9	1	41	34	7	5	.583	0	3.31
90	WIL/EAS	AA	10	203	10	0	0	0	43.1	65	2	18	1	2	14	0	2	2	0	35	31	1	4	.200	0	6.44
	PEN/CAR	A+	18	247	7	1	1	8	60.0	47	5	25	1	1	49	1	0	2	0	21	21	2	2	.500	6	3.15
91	JAC/SOU	AA	21	113	0	0	0	20	28.1	23	0	9	0	0	34	2	0	2	0	5	4	4	0	1.000	12	1.27
	CAL/PCL	AAA	28	146	0	0	0	21	32.1	39	1	15	3	0	26	2	3	2	1	19	14	3	4	.429	7	3.90

Nelson, Wayland Eugene "Gene" — bats right — throws right — b.12/3/60

YR	TM/LG	CL	G	TBF	GS	CG	SHO	GF	IP	H	HR	BB	IBB	HB	SO	SH	SF	WP	BK	R	ER	W	L	PCT	SV	ERA
81	NY/AL		8	179	7	0	0	0	39.1	40	5	23	1	1	16	0	2	2	0	24	21	3	1	.750	0	4.81
82	SEA/AL		22	545	19	2	1	2	122.2	133	16	60	1	2	71	4	2	4	2	70	63	6	9	.400	0	4.62
83	SEA/AL		10	153	5	1	0	2	32.0	38	6	21	2	1	11	2	0	1	0	29	28	0	3	.000	0	7.87
84	SLC/PCL	AAA	17	0	17	6	1	0	112.0	138	15	54	3	5	89	0	0	11	1	75	70	6	8	.429	0	5.63
	CHI/AL		20	304	9	2	0	4	74.2	72	9	17	0	1	36	1	2	4	1	38	37	3	5	.375	1	4.46
85	CHI/AL		46	643	18	1	0	11	145.2	144	23	67	4	7	101	9	2	11	1	74	69	10	10	.500	2	3.85
86	CHI/AL		54	488	1	0	0	26	114.2	118	7	41	5	3	70	7	1	3	0	52	49	6	5	.500	6	3.85
87	OAK/AL		54	530	6	0	0	15	123.2	120	12	35	0	5	94	3	5	7	0	58	54	6	5	.545	3	3.93
88	OAK/AL		54	456	1	0	0	20	111.2	93	9	38	4	3	67	3	4	4	6	42	38	9	6	.600	3	3.06
89	OAK/AL		50	335	0	0	0	15	80.0	60	5	30	3	2	70	3	1	5	0	33	29	3	5	.375	3	3.26
90	OAK/AL		51	291	0	0	0	17	74.2	55	5	17	1	3	38	1	5	1	0	14	13	3	3	.500	5	1.57
91	OAK/AL		44	229	0	0	0	11	48.2	60	12	23	1	3	23	3	4	0	0	38	37	1	5	.167	0	6.84
11 YR TOTALS			413	4153	66	6	1	123	967.2	933	109	372	22	31	597	36	31	42	10	472	438	50	58	.463	23	4.07

Newman, Alan Spencer — bats left — throws left — b.10/2/69 — System MIN/AL

YR	TM/LG	CL	G	TBF	GS	CG	SHO	GF	IP	H	HR	BB	IBB	HB	SO	SH	SF	WP	BK	R	ER	W	L	PCT	SV	ERA
88	ELI/APP	R+	13	279	12	2	0	0	55.1	57	3	56	0	2	51	2	2	17	3	62	50	2	8	.200	0	8.13
89	KEN/MID	A	18	398	18	1	0	0	88.2	65	2	74	0	4	82	5	0	3	9	41	28	3	9	.250	0	2.84
90	KEN/MID	A	22	614	22	5	1	0	154.0	94	2	78	2	6	158	4	0	10	2	41	28	10	4	.714	0	1.64
	VIS/CAL	A+	5	155	5	0	0	0	36.1	29	0	22	0	1	42	3	2	1	0	15	9	3	1	.750	0	2.23
91	VIS/CAL	A+	15	411	15	0	0	0	92.1	86	2	49	2	6	79	4	0	11	0	49	36	6	5	.545	0	3.51
	ORL/SOU	AA	11	275	11	2	0	0	67.0	53	0	30	1	1	53	2	1	8	0	28	20	5	4	.556	0	2.69

Nichols, Rodney Lea "Rod" — bats right — throws right — b.12/29/64

YR	TM/LG	CL	G	TBF	GS	CG	SHO	GF	IP	H	HR	BB	IBB	HB	SO	SH	SF	WP	BK	R	ER	W	L	PCT	SV	ERA
85	BAT/NYP	A−	13	361	13	3	0	0	84.0	74	10	33	0	3	93	0	2	6	0	40	28	5	5	.500	0	3.00
86	WAT/MID	A	20	493	20	3	1	0	115.1	128	8	21	1	13	83	3	4	3	0	56	52	8	5	.615	0	4.06
87	KIN/CAR	A+	9	231	8	1	1	1	56.0	53	3	14	0	1	61	0	2	4	0	27	25	4	2	.667	0	4.02
	WIL/EAS	AA	16	441	16	1	0	0	100.0	107	9	33	0	9	60	2	3	5	1	53	41	4	3	.571	0	3.69
88	KIN/CAR	A+	4	109	4	0	0	0	24.0	26	1	15	0	0	19	0	2	2	0	13	12	3	1	.750	0	4.50
	CS/PCL	AAA	10	256	9	2	0	1	58.2	69	8	17	2	3	43	1	2	3	2	41	37	2	6	.250	0	5.68
	CLE/AL		11	297	10	3	0	1	69.1	73	5	23	1	2	31	2	2	2	3	41	39	1	7	.125	0	5.06
89	CS/PCL	AAA	10	274	10	2	0	0	65.1	57	2	30	0	1	41	1	3	1	2	28	26	8	1	.889	0	3.58
	CLE/AL		15	315	11	0	0	2	71.2	81	9	24	0	2	42	3	2	0	0	42	35	4	6	.400	0	4.40
90	CLE/AL		4	79	2	0	0	0	16.0	24	5	6	0	2	3	1	0	0	0	14	14	0	3	.000	0	7.87
	CS/PCL	AAA	22	602	22	4	2	0	133.1	160	12	48	3	11	74	0	4	3	2	84	76	12	9	.571	0	5.13
91	CLE/AL		31	578	16	3	1	4	137.1	145	6	30	3	6	76	6	4	3	0	63	54	2	11	.154	1	3.54
4 YR TOTALS			61	1269	39	6	1	7	294.1	323	25	83	4	12	152	12	8	5	3	160	142	7	27	.206	1	4.34

Nolte, Eric Carl — bats left — throws left — b.4/28/64

YR	TM/LG	CL	G	TBF	GS	CG	SHO	GF	IP	H	HR	BB	IBB	HB	SO	SH	SF	WP	BK	R	ER	W	L	PCT	SV	ERA
85	SPO/NWL	A−	14	0	14	0	0	0	76.2	79	6	46	0	3	52	0	0	11	2	50	34	3	8	.273	0	3.99
86	CHA/SAL	A	26	694	26	3	0	0	164.0	154	11	68	1	1	121	5	5	10	1	80	71	12	9	.571	0	3.90
87	REN/CAL	A+	11	282	11	1	0	0	64.0	76	4	24	0	1	47	4	4	2	1	38	31	3	4	.429	0	4.36
	WIC/TEX	AA	10	308	10	2	1	0	75.0	62	4	19	0	2	67	1	1	3	0	28	24	4	2	.667	0	2.88
	SD/NL		12	293	12	1	0	0	67.1	57	6	36	2	2	44	2	1	3	1	28	24	2	6	.250	0	3.21
88	SD/NL		2	14	0	0	0	1	3.0	3	1	2	0	0	1	0	0	0	1	2	2	0	0	.000	0	6.00
	LV/PCL	AAA	27	597	25	1	0	1	128.1	168	11	53	2	1	68	5	5	7	8	97	86	8	7	.533	0	6.03
89	LV/PCL	AAA	23	524	21	3	0	1	116.1	121	7	54	2	3	89	5	5	13	5	74	67	6	9	.400	0	5.18
	SD/NL		3	49	1	0	0	1	9.0	15	0	7	1	0	8	1	1	3	0	12	11	0	0	.000	0	11.00
90	LV/PCL	AAA	33	592	18	1	0	4	122.2	187	15	49	4	1	79	6	4	8	7	130	117	2	11	.154	0	8.58
91	SD/NL		6	111	6	0	0	0	22.0	37	6	10	0	1	15	0	1	1	1	27	27	3	2	.600	0	11.05
	TEX/AL		3	14	0	0	0	2	2.2	3	0	3	0	0	1	0	0	1	0	1	1	0	0	.000	0	3.38
	YEAR		9	125	6	0	0	2	24.2	40	6	13	0	1	16	0	3	1	1	28	28	3	2	.600	0	10.22
	OC/AMA	AAA	25	269	9	0	0	6	56.1	74	4	31	0	2	41	1	4	3	2	39	37	1	3	.250	1	5.91
4 YR TOTALS			26	481	19	1	0	4	104.0	115	14	58	3	2	69	4	5	7	3	70	65	5	8	.385	0	5.63

Novoa, Rafael Angel — bats left — throws left — b.10/26/67

YR	TM/LG	CL	G	TBF	GS	CG	SHO	GF	IP	H	HR	BB	IBB	HB	SO	SH	SF	WP	BK	R	ER	W	L	PCT	SV	ERA
89	EVE/NWL	A−	3	73	3	0	0	0	15.0	20	2	8	0	1	20	0	0	3	1	11	8	0	1	.000	0	4.80
	CLI/MID	A	13	267	10	0	0	0	63.2	58	1	18	1	4	61	9	1	1	6	20	18	5	4	.556	0	2.54

Novoa, Rafael Angel (continued)

YR	TM/LG	CL	G	TBF	GS	CG	SHO	GF	IP	H	HR	BB	IBB	HB	SO	SH	SF	WP	BK	R	ER	W	L	PCT	SV	ERA
90	CLI/MID	A	15	397	14	3	1	0	97.2	73	6	30	0	4	113	2	3	2	2	32	26	9	2	.818	0	2.40
	SHR/TEX	AA	11	297	10	2	1	1	71.2	60	3	25	0	3	66	1	2	1	0	21	21	5	4	.556	0	2.64
	SF/NL		7	88	2	0	0	2	18.2	21	3	13	1	0	14	0	1	0	0	14	14	0	1	.000	1	6.75
91	PHO/PCL	AAA	17	450	17	0	0	0	93.2	135	16	37	3	5	46	5	6	3	1	83	62	6	6	.500	0	5.96
1 YR TOTALS			**7**	**88**	**2**	**0**	**0**	**2**	**18.2**	**21**	**3**	**13**	**1**	**0**	**14**	**0**	**1**	**0**	**0**	**14**	**14**	**0**	**1**	**.000**	**1**	**6.75**

Nunez, Edwin (Martinez) — bats right — throws right — b.5/27/63

YR	TM/LG	CL	G	TBF	GS	CG	SHO	GF	IP	H	HR	BB	IBB	HB	SO	SH	SF	WP	BK	R	ER	W	L	PCT	SV	ERA
79	BEL/NWL	A–	6	0	6	2	0	0	39.0	39	0	5	0	0	30	0	0	0	0	14	9	4	1	.800	0	2.08
80	WAU/MID	A	22	0	19	8	2	0	138.0	145	0	58	0	0	91	0	0	0	0	71	57	9	7	.563	0	3.72
81	WAU/MID	A	25	0	25	13	0	0	186.0	143	0	58	0	0	205	0	0	0	0	61	51	16	3	.842	0	2.47
82	SEA/AL		8	153	5	0	0	0	35.1	36	7	16	0	0	27	3	0	0	2	18	18	1	2	.333	0	4.58
	SLC/PCL	AAA	11	0	8	1	0	0	55.0	40	0	23	0	0	42	0	0	0	0	26	21	4	3	.571	0	3.44
83	SEA/AL		14	170	5	0	0	4	37.0	40	3	22	1	3	35	1	0	0	2	21	18	0	4	.000	0	4.38
	SLC/PCL	AAA	14	0	12	3	0	0	77.0	99	0	36	0	0	52	0	0	0	0	70	61	3	2	.500	0	7.13
84	SLC/PCL	AAA	18	0	0	0	0	13	27.2	24	2	12	1	1	26	0	0	0	0	12	11	3	2	.600	3	3.58
	SEA/AL		37	280	0	0	0	23	67.2	55	8	21	2	3	57	1	3	1	0	26	24	2	2	.500	7	3.19
85	SEA/AL		70	378	0	0	0	53	90.1	79	13	34	5	0	58	4	3	2	1	36	31	7	3	.700	16	3.09
86	CAL/PCL	AAA	6	65	0	0	0	4	14.0	19	2	4	0	0	17	1	2	1	0	13	11	1	2	.333	0	7.07
	SEA/AL		14	93	1	0	0	6	21.2	25	5	5	1	0	17	0	0	0	0	15	14	1	2	.333	0	5.82
87	SEA/AL		48	198	0	0	0	40	47.1	45	7	18	3	1	34	3	4	2	0	20	20	3	4	.429	12	3.80
88	CAL/PCL	AAA	3	65	3	0	0	0	15.1	15	0	4	0	1	12	0	0	0	0	9	8	2	0	1.000	0	4.70
	SEA/AL		14	145	3	0	0	2	29.1	45	4	14	3	2	19	2	0	0	1	33	26	1	4	.200	0	7.98
	NY/NL		10	65	0	0	0	4	14.0	21	1	3	0	0	8	0	0	1	0	7	7	1	0	1.000	0	4.50
	YEAR		24	210	3	0	0	6	43.1	66	5	17	3	2	27	2	4	1	1	40	33	2	4	.333	0	6.85
89	TOL/INT	AAA	13	239	8	1	0	3	59.1	47	9	18	2	2	53	3	1	1	3	20	17	1	5	.167	1	2.58
	DET/AL		27	238	0	0	0	12	54.0	49	6	36	13	0	41	6	3	2	1	33	25	3	4	.429	0	4.17
90	DET/AL		42	343	0	0	0	15	80.1	65	4	37	6	2	66	5	1	4	0	26	20	3	1	.750	6	2.24
91	BEL/MID	A	5	37	1	0	0	3	9.0	9	1	0	0	0	9	0	0	1	0	5	4	0	1	.000	1	4.00
	MIL/AL		23	119	0	0	0	18	25.1	28	6	13	2	0	24	3	2	0	1	20	17	2	1	.667	8	6.04
10 YR TOTALS			**307**	**2182**	**14**	**0**	**0**	**177**	**502.1**	**488**	**64**	**219**	**36**	**11**	**386**	**28**	**20**	**12**	**8**	**255**	**220**	**24**	**27**	**.471**	**50**	**3.94**

Ojeda, Robert Michael "Bob" — bats left — throws left — b.12/17/57

YR	TM/LG	CL	G	TBF	GS	CG	SHO	GF	IP	H	HR	BB	IBB	HB	SO	SH	SF	WP	BK	R	ER	W	L	PCT	SV	ERA
80	BOS/AL		7	122	7	0	0	0	26.0	39	2	14	1	0	12	0	1	0	0	20	20	1	1	.500	0	6.92
81	BOS/AL		10	267	10	2	0	0	66.1	50	6	25	2	2	28	3	1	0	0	25	23	6	2	.750	0	3.12
82	BOS/AL		22	352	14	0	0	6	78.1	95	13	29	0	1	52	0	1	5	0	53	49	4	6	.400	0	5.63
83	BOS/AL		29	746	28	5	0	0	173.2	173	15	73	2	3	94	6	11	2	0	85	78	12	7	.632	0	4.04
84	BOS/AL		33	928	32	8	5	0	216.2	211	17	96	2	6	137	8	6	0	1	106	96	12	12	.500	0	3.99
85	BOS/AL		39	671	22	5	0	10	157.2	166	11	48	9	2	102	10	3	3	3	74	70	9	11	.450	0	4.00
86	NY/NL		32	871	30	7	2	1	217.1	185	15	52	3	2	148	10	3	2	0	72	62	18	5	.783	0	2.57
87	NY/NL		10	192	7	0	0	0	46.1	45	5	10	1	0	21	3	1	1	0	23	20	3	5	.375	0	3.88
88	NY/NL		29	752	29	5	5	0	190.1	158	6	33	2	4	133	6	6	4	7	74	61	10	13	.435	0	2.88
89	NY/NL		31	824	31	5	2	0	192.0	179	16	78	5	2	95	6	7	0	2	83	74	13	11	.542	0	3.47
90	NY/NL		38	500	12	0	0	9	118.0	123	10	40	4	2	62	3	3	2	3	53	48	7	6	.538	0	3.66
91	LA/NL		31	802	31	2	1	0	189.1	181	15	70	9	3	120	15	9	4	2	78	67	12	9	.571	0	3.18
12 YR TOTALS			**311**	**7027**	**253**	**39**	**15**	**26**	**1672.0**	**1605**	**131**	**568**	**40**	**23**	**1004**	**70**	**51**	**24**	**19**	**746**	**668**	**107**	**88**	**.549**	**1**	**3.60**

Olin, Steven Robert "Steve" — bats right — throws right — b.10/10/65

YR	TM/LG	CL	G	TBF	GS	CG	SHO	GF	IP	H	HR	BB	IBB	HB	SO	SH	SF	WP	BK	R	ER	W	L	PCT	SV	ERA
87	BUR/APP	R+	26	231	0	0	0	25	57.1	42	0	17	5	1	75	3	0	4	0	21	15	4	4	.500	7	2.35
88	WAT/MID	A	29	163	0	0	0	23	39.1	26	0	14	3	2	48	3	1	4	2	7	6	3	0	1.000	15	1.37
	KIN/CAR	A+	33	234	0	0	0	22	56.2	49	1	15	2	0	45	0	1	0	0	23	19	5	2	.714	8	3.02
89	CS/PCL	AAA	42	195	0	0	0	38	50.1	34	6	15	3	3	46	2	0	0	0	18	18	4	1	.800	24	3.22
	CLE/AL		25	152	0	0	0	8	36.0	35	1	14	2	0	24	1	0	2	0	16	15	1	4	.200	1	3.75
90	CS/PCL	AAA	14	117	0	0	0	8	27.1	18	0	15	1	1	30	1	0	0	0	9	2	3	1	.750	2	0.66
	CLE/AL		50	394	1	0	0	16	92.1	96	3	26	2	6	64	5	2	0	0	41	35	4	4	.500	1	3.41
91	CS/PCL	AAA	22	190	0	0	0	16	44.1	45	1	10	5	6	36	4	1	2	2	25	22	3	2	.600	6	4.47
	CLE/AL		48	249	0	0	0	32	56.1	61	2	23	7	1	38	2	0	0	0	26	21	3	6	.333	17	3.36
3 YR TOTALS			**123**	**795**	**1**	**0**	**0**	**56**	**184.2**	**192**	**6**	**63**	**11**	**7**	**126**	**8**	**2**	**2**	**0**	**83**	**71**	**8**	**14**	**.364**	**19**	**3.46**

Olivares, Omar (Palqu) — bats right — throws right — b.7/6/67

YR	TM/LG	CL	G	TBF	GS	CG	SHO	GF	IP	H	HR	BB	IBB	HB	SO	SH	SF	WP	BK	R	ER	W	L	PCT	SV	ERA
87	CHS/SAL	A	31	744	24	5	0	3	170.1	182	9	57	4	7	86	6	10	3	1	107	87	4	14	.222	0	4.60
88	CHS/SAL	A	24	746	24	10	3	0	185.1	166	3	43	2	3	94	5	7	9	7	63	46	13	6	.684	0	2.23
	RIV/CAL	A+	4	96	3	1	0	0	23.1	18	2	9	0	2	16	1	0	1	1	9	3	3	0	1.000	0	1.16
89	WIC/TEX	AA	26	771	26	6	1	0	185.2	175	10	61	6	10	79	3	8	10	1	87	70	12	11	.522	0	3.39
90	LOU/AMA	AAA	23	643	23	5	2	0	159.1	127	6	59	1	9	88	4	2	6	2	58	50	10	11	.476	0	2.82
	STL/NL		9	201	6	0	0	0	49.1	45	2	17	2	1	20	1	0	1	1	17	16	1	1	.500	0	2.92
91	LOU/AMA	AAA	6	158	6	0	0	0	36.1	39	1	16	1	1	27	1	1	2	1	15	14	1	2	.333	0	3.47
	STL/NL		28	688	24	0	0	2	167.1	148	13	61	1	5	91	11	2	3	1	72	69	11	7	.611	1	3.71
2 YR TOTALS			**37**	**889**	**30**	**0**	**0**	**2**	**216.2**	**193**	**15**	**78**	**1**	**7**	**111**	**12**	**2**	**4**	**2**	**89**	**85**	**12**	**8**	**.600**	**1**	**3.53**

Oliveras, Francisco Javier (Noa) — bats right — throws right — b.1/31/63

YR	TM/LG	CL	G	TBF	GS	CG	SHO	GF	IP	H	HR	BB	IBB	HB	SO	SH	SF	WP	BK	R	ER	W	L	PCT	SV	ERA
81	IF/PIO	R+	14	0	14	2	1	0	92.0	132	1	27	0	3	71	0	0	3	0	59	51	6	4	.600	0	4.99
	MIA/FSL	A+	19	0	18	4	0	0	108.0	103	5	48	0	6	80	0	0	3	1	55	46	6	5	.545	0	3.83
82	CHA/SOU	AA	24	0	24	10	2	0	162.0	132	17	64	0	6	97	0	0	10	1	71	64	10	9	.526	0	3.56
83	CHA/SOU	AA	25	0	25	5	2	0	151.0	173	23	73	0	3	89	0	0	5	0	94	78	8	14	.364	0	4.65
84	CHA/SOU	AA	19	329	6	0	0	4	75.0	68	8	39	2	4	52	4	4	9	0	45	35	3	7	.300	0	4.20
	ROC/INT	AAA	12	195	7	2	0	1	40.2	58	6	19	1	1	39	0	0	2	0	37	36	1	3	.250	0	7.97
85	DB/FSL	A+	3	89	3	2	0	0	23.2	13	0	9	0	1	25	0	3	1	0	6	5	3	0	1.000	0	1.90
	CHA/SOU	AA	12	201	7	0	0	2	40.2	57	3	25	0	1	20	2	6	5	0	40	30	2	1	.667	0	6.64
	BEA/TEX	AA	7	112	4	0	0	0	27.0	23	2	9	0	1	24	2	1	2	0	17	15	3	1	.750	0	5.00
86	CHA/SOU	AA	33	828	25	5	1	3	194.0	185	27	71	1	5	127	4	7	7	1	112	90	12	9	.571	0	4.18
87	CHA/SOU	AA	23	407	10	3	1	6	100.0	99	9	21	0	5	67	2	4	5	1	43	40	6	3	.667	0	3.60
	ROC/INT	AAA	6	115	4	0	0	1	27.0	31	3	7	0	0	18	0	0	2	0	14	13	3	0	1.000	0	4.33
88	ORL/SOU	AA	7	189	7	0	0	0	43.0	44	8	18	0	1	42	1	0	0	2	24	23	3	1	.750	0	4.81
	POR/PCL	AAA	21	566	21	4	0	0	133.2	134	10	43	0	2	95	0	7	0	6	69	64	11	10	.524	0	4.31
89	MIN/AL		12	239	8	1	0	1	55.0	64	8	15	0	1	24	0	1	0	2	28	28	3	4	.429	0	4.53
	POR/PCL	AAA	17	414	13	3	1	2	97.2	108	11	24	1	1	54	0	3	2	2	54	54	6	4	.600	0	4.98
90	POR/PCL	AAA	11	247	6	1	0	0	62.0	44	2	22	0	3	56	3	3	1	1	23	20	3	4	.429	0	2.90
	SJ/CAL	A+	1	15	1	0	0	0	3.2	4	0	1	0	0	3	0	0	0	0	2	1	0	0	.000	0	2.45
	SF/NL		33	231	2	0	0	9	55.1	47	5	21	6	2	41	1	3	2	1	22	17	2	2	.500	2	2.77
91	PHO/PCL	AAA	3	79	3	1	1	0	18.1	18	1	7	0	1	12	0	0	1	2	5	5	2	0	1.000	0	2.45
	SF/NL		55	316	1	0	0	17	79.1	69	12	22	4	1	48	5	3	2	2	36	34	6	6	.500	3	3.86
3 YR TOTALS			**100**	**786**	**11**	**1**	**0**	**27**	**190.1**	**180**	**25**	**58**	**10**	**4**	**113**	**6**	**7**	**4**	**5**	**86**	**79**	**11**	**12**	**.478**	**5**	**3.74**

Olson, Greggory William "Gregg" — bats right — throws right — b.10/11/66

YR	TM/LG	CL	G	TBF	GS	CG	SHO	GF	IP	H	HR	BB	IBB	HB	SO	SH	SF	WP	BK	R	ER	W	L	PCT	SV	ERA
88	HAG/CAR	A+	8	33	0	0	0	8	9.0	5	1	2	0	0	9	1	0	0	1	2	2	1	0	1.000	4	2.00
	CHA/SOU	AA	8	78	0	0	0	3	15.1	24	2	6	0	0	22	1	1	2	0	13	10	0	1	.000	1	5.87
	BAL/AL		10	51	0	0	0	4	11.0	10	1	10	1	0	9	0	0	0	1	4	4	1	1	.500	3	3.27
89	BAL/AL		64	356	0	0	0	52	85.0	57	1	46	10	1	90	1	1	9	3	17	16	5	2	.714	27	1.69
90	BAL/AL		64	305	0	0	0	58	74.1	57	3	31	3	3	74	1	2	5	0	20	20	6	5	.545	37	2.42
91	BAL/AL		72	319	0	0	0	62	73.2	74	1	29	5	1	72	5	1	8	1	28	26	4	6	.400	31	3.18
4 YR TOTALS			**210**	**1031**	**0**	**0**	**0**	**176**	**244.0**	**198**	**6**	**116**	**19**	**5**	**245**	**10**	**4**	**22**	**5**	**69**	**66**	**16**	**14**	**.533**	**95**	**2.43**

Ontiveros, Steven "Steve" — bats right — throws right — b.3/5/61

YR	TM/LG	CL	G	TBF	GS	CG	SHO	GF	IP	H	HR	BB	IBB	HB	SO	SH	SF	WP	BK	R	ER	W	L	PCT	SV	ERA
84	TAC/PCL	AAA	2	0	2	0	0	0	11.1	18	3	5	0	1	6	0	0	0	0	11	10	1	1	.500	0	7.94
	MAD/MID	A	5	122	5	2	0	0	30.2	23	0	6	0	1	26	1	1	1	0	10	7	3	1	.750	0	2.05
85	TAC/PCL	AAA	15	0	0	0	0	7	33.2	26	1	21	2	2	30	0	0	1	0	13	11	3	0	1.000	2	2.94
	OAK/AL		39	284	0	0	0	18	74.2	45	4	19	2	2	36	2	2	1	0	17	16	1	3	.250	8	1.93
86	OAK/AL		46	305	0	0	0	27	72.2	72	10	25	3	1	54	1	6	4	0	40	38	2	2	.500	10	4.71
87	TAC/PCL	AAA	1	12	1	0	0	0	3.0	1	0	2	0	0	1	0	0	1	0	1	1	0	0	.000	0	3.00
	OAK/AL		35	645	22	2	1	6	150.2	141	19	50	3	4	97	6	2	4	1	78	67	10	8	.556	1	4.00
88	OAK/AL		10	241	10	0	0	0	54.2	57	6	21	1	0	30	5	0	5	5	32	28	3	4	.429	0	4.61
89	SW/INT	AAA	1	15	1	0	0	0	3.1	3	0	3	0	0	0	0	0	0	0	0	0	0	0	.000	0	0.00
	PHL/NL		6	134	5	0	0	0	30.2	34	2	15	1	0	12	1	0	2	0	15	13	2	1	.667	0	3.82
90	CLE/FSL	A+	3	29	2	0	0	0	7.2	4	0	3	0	0	2	0	0	0	1	2	2	0	0	.000	0	2.35
	REA/EAS	AA	2	29	2	0	0	0	6.0	7	0	2	0	2	8	0	0	0	0	6	6	0	2	.000	0	9.00
	PHL/NL		5	43	0	0	0	1	10.0	9	1	0	0	0	6	0	0	0	0	3	3	0	0	.000	0	2.70
91	SCR/INT	AAA	7	127	7	0	0	0	31.0	29	1	10	0	0	21	0	1	2	0	11	10	2	1	.667	0	2.90
6 YR TOTALS			**141**	**1652**	**37**	**2**	**1**	**52**	**393.1**	**358**	**40**	**133**	**10**	**7**	**235**	**15**	**10**	**16**	**6**	**185**	**165**	**18**	**18**	**.500**	**19**	**3.78**

Orosco, Jesse Russell — bats right — throws left — b.4/21/57

YR	TM/LG	CL	G	TBF	GS	CG	SHO	GF	IP	H	HR	BB	IBB	HB	SO	SH	SF	WP	BK	R	ER	W	L	PCT	SV	ERA
79	NY/NL		18	154	2	0	0	6	35.0	33	4	22	0	2	22	3	0	0	0	20	19	1	2	.333	0	4.89
81	NY/NL		8	69	0	0	0	4	17.1	13	2	6	2	0	18	2	0	0	1	4	3	0	1	.000	1	1.56
82	NY/NL		54	451	2	0	0	22	109.1	92	7	40	2	2	89	5	4	3	2	37	33	4	10	.286	4	2.72
83	NY/NL		62	432	0	0	0	42	110.0	76	3	38	7	1	84	4	3	1	2	27	18	13	7	.650	17	1.47
84	NY/NL		60	355	0	0	0	52	87.0	58	7	34	6	2	85	3	3	1	1	29	25	10	6	.625	31	2.59
85	NY/NL		54	331	0	0	0	39	79.0	66	6	34	7	0	68	1	1	4	0	26	24	8	6	.571	17	2.73
86	NY/NL		58	338	0	0	0	40	81.0	64	6	35	3	3	62	4	3	2	0	23	21	8	6	.571	21	2.33
87	NY/NL		58	335	0	0	0	41	77.0	78	5	31	9	2	78	5	4	2	0	41	38	3	9	.250	16	4.44
88	LA/NL		55	229	0	0	0	21	53.0	41	4	30	3	2	43	3	3	1	0	18	16	3	2	.600	9	2.72
89	CLE/AL		69	312	0	0	0	29	78.0	54	7	26	4	2	79	8	3	0	0	20	18	3	4	.429	3	2.08
90	CLE/AL		55	289	0	0	0	28	64.2	58	9	38	7	0	55	5	1	1	0	35	28	5	4	.556	2	3.90
91	CLE/AL		47	202	0	0	0	20	45.2	52	4	15	8	1	36	5	3	1	1	20	19	2	0	1.000	2	3.74
12 YR TOTALS			**598**	**3497**	**4**	**0**	**0**	**344**	**837.0**	**685**	**64**	**349**	**58**	**17**	**719**	**42**	**30**	**16**	**7**	**300**	**262**	**60**	**57**	**.513**	**121**	**2.82**

Osborne, Donovan Alan — bats right — throws left — b.6/21/69 — System STL/NL

YR	TM/LG	CL	G	TBF	GS	CG	SHO	GF	IP	H	HR	BB	IBB	HB	SO	SH	SF	WP	BK	R	ER	W	L	PCT	SV	ERA
90	HAM/NYP	A—	4	86	4	0	0	0	20.0	21	0	5	1	0	14	1	1	1	2	8	8	0	2	.000	0	3.60
	SAV/SAL	A	6	169	6	1	0	0	41.1	40	2	7	0	3	28	1	1	2	3	20	12	2	2	.500	0	2.61
91	ARK/TEX	AA	26	696	26	3	0	0	166.0	177	6	43	3	4	130	9	4	4	4	82	67	8	12	.400	0	3.63

Osuna, Alfonso "Al" — bats right — throws left — b.8/10/65

YR	TM/LG	CL	G	TBF	GS	CG	SHO	GF	IP	H	HR	BB	IBB	HB	SO	SH	SF	WP	BK	R	ER	W	L	PCT	SV	ERA
87	AUB/NYP	A–	8	75	0	0	0	3	15.2	16	1	14	2	0	20	0	0	0	2	16	10	1	0	1.000	0	5.74
	ASH/SAL	A	14	81	0	0	0	7	19.2	20	1	6	0	0	20	0	0	0	3	6	6	2	0	1.000	2	2.75
88	OSC/FSL	A+	8	58	0	0	0	2	11.2	12	1	9	1	0	5	0	1	0	0	9	9	0	1	.000	0	6.94
	ASH/SAL	A	31	212	0	0	0	19	50.0	41	1	25	2	2	41	1	0	4	9	19	11	6	1	.857	3	1.98
89	OSC/FSL	A+	46	283	0	0	0	26	67.2	50	2	27	4	2	62	7	2	5	5	27	20	3	4	.429	7	2.66
90	COL/SOU	AA	60	289	0	0	0	26	69.1	57	4	33	2	3	82	3	1	4	1	30	26	7	5	.583	6	3.38
	HOU/NL		12	48	0	0	0	2	11.1	10	1	6	1	3	6	0	2	3	0	6	6	2	0	1.000	0	4.76
91	HOU/NL		71	353	0	0	0	32	81.2	59	5	46	5	3	68	6	5	3	1	39	31	7	6	.538	12	3.42
2 YR TOTALS			**83**	**401**	**0**	**0**	**0**	**34**	**93.0**	**69**	**6**	**52**	**6**	**6**	**74**	**6**	**7**	**6**	**1**	**45**	**37**	**9**	**6**	**.600**	**12**	**3.58**

Otto, David Alan "Dave" — bats left — throws left — b.11/12/64

YR	TM/LG	CL	G	TBF	GS	CG	SHO	GF	IP	H	HR	BB	IBB	HB	SO	SH	SF	WP	BK	R	ER	W	L	PCT	SV	ERA
85	MED/NWL	A–	11	0	11	0	0	0	42.1	42	1	22	0	2	27	0	0	5	0	27	19	2	2	.500	0	4.04
86	MAD/MID	A	26	724	26	6	1	0	169.0	154	9	71	0	2	125	10	5	6	1	72	50	13	7	.650	0	2.66
87	MAD/MID	A	1	11	1	0	0	0	3.0	2	0	0	0	0	2	0	0	0	0	0	0	0	0	.000	0	0.00
	HUN/SOU	AA	9	192	8	1	0	0	50.0	36	1	11	0	0	25	0	1	4	0	14	13	4	1	.800	0	2.34
	OAK/AL		3	24	0	0	0	3	6.0	7	1	1	0	0	3	0	0	0	0	6	6	0	0	.000	0	9.00
88	TAC/PCL	AAA	21	564	21	2	0	0	127.2	124	7	63	3	0	80	1	4	7	4	71	50	4	9	.308	0	3.52
	OAK/AL		3	43	2	0	0	1	10.0	9	0	6	0	0	7	0	0	0	0	2	2	0	0	.000	0	1.80
89	TAC/PCL	AAA	29	714	28	2	1	0	169.0	164	6	61	3	1	122	3	4	18	2	84	69	10	13	.435	0	3.67
	OAK/AL		1	26	1	0	0	0	6.2	6	0	2	0	0	4	0	0	0	0	2	2	0	0	.000	0	2.70
90	OAK/AL		2	13	0	0	0	2	2.1	3	0	3	0	0	2	0	0	0	0	3	2	0	0	.000	0	7.71
	TAC/PCL	AAA	2	10	0	0	0	0	2.0	3	0	1	0	0	2	0	0	1	0	1	1	0	0	.000	0	4.50
91	CS/PCL	AAA	17	418	15	1	0	1	94.2	110	7	43	2	1	62	3	3	7	3	56	50	5	6	.455	0	4.75
	CLE/AL		18	425	14	1	0	0	100.0	108	7	27	6	4	47	8	4	3	0	52	47	2	8	.200	0	4.23
5 YR TOTALS			**27**	**531**	**17**	**1**	**0**	**6**	**125.0**	**133**	**8**	**39**	**6**	**4**	**63**	**9**	**4**	**3**	**1**	**65**	**59**	**2**	**8**	**.200**	**0**	**4.25**

Palacios, Vicente (Diaz) — bats right — throws right — b.7/19/63

YR	TM/LG	CL	G	TBF	GS	CG	SHO	GF	IP	H	HR	BB	IBB	HB	SO	SH	SF	WP	BK	R	ER	W	L	PCT	SV	ERA
83	VER/MEX	AAA	22	0	22	10	3	0	165.0	121	6	60	0	4	125	0	0	6	0	53	48	12	6	.667	0	2.62
84	GF/EAS	AA	5	110	5	0	0	0	25.1	23	0	11	0	0	10	0	0	1	0	12	7	1	2	.333	0	2.49
85	GF/EAS	AA	8	185	4	0	0	1	39.2	44	1	29	1	2	20	0	3	5	4	25	21	1	1	.500	1	4.76
87	VAN/PCL	AAA	27	765	26	7	5	0	185.0	140	10	85	1	5	148	11	1	5	6	63	53	13	5	.722	0	2.58
	PIT/NL		6	120	4	0	0	0	29.1	27	1	9	1	1	13	2	0	0	2	14	14	2	1	.667	0	4.30
88	PIT/NL		7	113	3	0	0	0	24.1	28	3	15	1	0	15	2	1	2	3	18	18	1	2	.333	0	6.66
	BUF/AMA	AAA	5	126	5	1	0	0	31.2	26	0	5	0	1	23	0	1	2	1	7	7	3	0	1.000	0	1.99
89	BUF/AMA	AAA	2	45	2	0	0	0	10.0	9	2	8	0	1	8	0	2	1	1	8	8	0	2	.000	0	7.20
90	BUF/AMA	AAA	28	762	28	5	2	0	183.2	173	8	53	2	1	137	6	4	9	2	77	70	13	7	.650	0	3.43
	PIT/NL		7	50	0	0	0	4	15.0	4	0	2	0	0	8	0	0	2	0	0	0	0	0	.000	3	0.00
91	BUF/AMA	AAA	3	27	0	0	0	2	6.1	7	0	2	0	0	7	0	0	0	0	1	1	0	0	.000	0	1.42
	PIT/NL		36	347	7	1	1	8	81.2	69	12	38	2	1	64	4	1	6	2	34	34	6	3	.667	3	3.75
4 YR TOTALS			**56**	**630**	**14**	**1**	**1**	**12**	**150.1**	**128**	**16**	**64**	**4**	**2**	**100**	**8**	**2**	**10**	**7**	**66**	**66**	**9**	**6**	**.600**	**6**	**3.95**

Pall, Donn Steven — bats right — throws right — b.1/11/62

YR	TM/LG	CL	G	TBF	GS	CG	SHO	GF	IP	H	HR	BB	IBB	HB	SO	SH	SF	WP	BK	R	ER	W	L	PCT	SV	ERA
85	WS/GCL	R	13	342	13	4	2	0	86.0	68	2	10	0	2	63	3	5	3	3	34	16	7	5	.583	0	1.67
86	APP/MID	A	11	317	11	3	1	0	78.0	71	2	14	1	4	51	2	0	4	0	29	20	5	5	.500	0	2.31
	BIR/SOU	AA	21	313	9	0	0	6	73.0	77	9	27	3	2	41	3	2	5	2	38	36	3	4	.429	1	4.44
87	BIR/SOU	AA	30	718	23	3	0	3	158.0	173	18	63	4	8	139	3	8	9	2	100	75	8	11	.421	0	4.27
88	VAN/PCL	AAA	44	293	0	0	0	25	72.2	61	2	20	2	3	41	2	1	2	1	21	18	5	2	.714	10	2.23
	CHI/AL		17	130	0	0	0	6	28.2	39	1	8	1	0	16	2	1	1	0	11	11	0	2	.000	0	3.45
89	SB/MID	A	2	12	0	0	0	0	3.1	1	0	1	0	0	4	0	0	0	0	0	0	0	0	.000	0	0.00
	CHI/AL		53	370	0	0	0	27	87.0	90	9	19	3	8	58	8	2	4	1	35	32	4	5	.444	6	3.31
90	CHI/AL		56	306	0	0	0	11	76.0	63	7	24	8	4	39	4	2	2	0	33	28	3	5	.375	2	3.32
91	CHI/AL		51	282	0	0	0	7	71.0	59	7	20	3	2	40	4	0	2	0	22	19	7	2	.778	0	2.41
4 YR TOTALS			**177**	**1088**	**0**	**0**	**0**	**51**	**262.2**	**251**	**24**	**71**	**15**	**15**	**153**	**18**	**5**	**9**	**1**	**101**	**90**	**14**	**14**	**.500**	**8**	**3.08**

Parrett, Jeffrey Dale "Jeff" — bats right — throws right — b.8/26/61

YR	TM/LG	CL	G	TBF	GS	CG	SHO	GF	IP	H	HR	BB	IBB	HB	SO	SH	SF	WP	BK	R	ER	W	L	PCT	SV	ERA
84	BEL/MID	A	29	413	5	1	1	6	91.2	76	8	71	1	1	95	5	6	13	0	50	46	4	3	.571	2	4.52
85	STO/CAL	A+	45	0	2	0	0	21	127.2	97	5	75	2	1	120	0	0	7	2	50	39	7	4	.636	11	2.75
86	MON/NL		12	91	0	0	0	6	20.1	19	3	13	0	0	21	0	1	2	0	11	11	0	1	.000	0	4.87
	IND/AMA	AAA	25	297	8	0	0	7	69.0	54	6	35	2	0	76	3	3	7	0	44	38	2	5	.286	2	4.96
87	IND/AMA	AAA	20	91	0	0	0	19	22.1	15	0	13	0	0	17	1	0	3	0	5	5	2	1	.667	9	2.01
	MON/NL		45	267	0	0	0	26	62.0	53	8	30	4	0	56	5	1	6	1	33	29	7	6	.538	6	4.21
88	MON/NL		61	369	0	0	0	34	91.2	66	8	45	9	1	62	9	6	4	1	29	27	12	4	.750	6	2.65
89	PHI/NL		72	444	0	0	0	34	105.2	90	6	44	13	0	98	7	5	7	3	43	35	12	6	.667	6	2.98
90	PHI/NL		47	355	5	0	0	14	81.2	92	10	36	8	1	69	3	1	3	1	51	47	4	9	.308	1	5.18
	ATL/NL		20	124	0	0	0	5	27.0	27	1	19	2	1	17	4	4	2	0	11	9	1	1	.500	1	3.00
	YEAR		67	479	5	0	0	19	108.2	119	11	55	10	2	86	7	5	5	1	62	56	5	10	.333	2	4.64
91	ATL/NL		18	109	0	0	0	9	21.1	31	2	12	2	0	14	2	0	4	0	18	15	1	2	.333	1	6.33
	RIC/INT	AAA	19	352	14	0	0	2	79.2	72	2	46	1	1	88	2	3	5	0	45	40	2	7	.222	0	4.52
6 YR TOTALS			**275**	**1759**	**5**	**0**	**0**	**128**	**409.2**	**378**	**38**	**199**	**38**	**3**	**337**	**30**	**18**	**28**	**6**	**196**	**173**	**37**	**29**	**.561**	**21**	**3.80**

Patterson, Kenneth Brian "Ken" — bats left — throws left — b.7/8/64

YR	TM/LG	CL	G	TBF	GS	CG	SHO	GF	IP	H	HR	BB	IBB	HB	SO	SH	SF	WP	BK	R	ER	W	L	PCT	SV	ERA
85	ONE/NYP	A–	6	103	6	0	0	0	22.1	23	0	14	0	2	21	1	0	1	0	14	12	2	2	.500	0	4.84
86	FT./FSL	A+	5	100	5	0	0	0	18.2	30	2	16	0	3	13	0	0	2	0	20	16	0	2	.000	0	7.71
	ONE/NYP	A–	15	399	15	5	4	0	100.1	67	2	45	0	4	102	1	1	7	1	25	15	9	3	.750	0	1.35
87	FT./FSL	A+	9	202	9	0	0	0	42.2	46	0	31	0	2	36	1	2	5	1	34	30	1	3	.250	0	6.33
	ALB/EAS	AA	24	272	8	1	0	14	63.2	59	2	31	1	2	47	3	3	4	0	31	28	3	6	.333	5	3.96
	HAW/PCL	AAA	3	14	0	0	0	3	3.1	1	0	3	0	0	5	0	0	0	0	0	0	0	2	.000	0	0.00
88	VAN/PCL	AAA	55	349	4	1	0	23	86.1	64	4	36	7	2	89	5	4	7	2	37	31	6	5	.545	13	3.23
	CHI/AL		9	92	2	0	0	3	20.2	25	2	7	0	0	8	0	0	1	1	11	11	0	2	.000	1	4.79
89	VAN/PCL	AAA	2	35	2	0	0	0	9.0	6	0	1	0	1	17	1	1	2	0	2	1	0	1	.000	0	1.00
	CHI/AL		50	284	1	0	0	18	65.2	64	11	28	3	2	43	1	4	3	1	37	33	6	1	.857	0	4.52
90	CHI/AL		43	283	0	0	0	15	66.1	58	6	34	1	2	40	2	5	2	0	27	25	2	1	.667	2	3.39
91	CHI/AL		43	265	0	0	0	13	63.2	48	5	35	1	1	32	3	2	2	0	22	20	3	0	1.000	1	2.83
4 YR TOTALS			**145**	**924**	**3**	**0**	**0**	**49**	**216.1**	**195**	**24**	**104**	**5**	**5**	**123**	**6**	**11**	**8**	**2**	**97**	**89**	**11**	**4**	**.733**	**4**	**3.70**

Patterson, Robert Chandler "Bob" — bats right — throws right — b.5/16/59

YR	TM/LG	CL	G	TBF	GS	CG	SHO	GF	IP	H	HR	BB	IBB	HB	SO	SH	SF	WP	BK	R	ER	W	L	PCT	SV	ERA
84	LV/PCL	AAA	60	0	7	1	0	41	143.1	129	12	37	1	1	97	0	0	3	0	63	52	8	9	.471	13	3.27
85	LV/PCL	AAA	42	0	20	7	1	16	186.1	187	19	52	5	1	146	0	0	5	2	80	65	10	11	.476	6	3.14
	SD/NL		3	26	0	0	0	2	4.0	13	2	3	0	0	1	0	0	0	1	11	11	0	0	.000	0	24.75
86	HAW/PCL	AAA	25	653	21	6	1	2	156.0	146	9	44	0	1	137	6	4	3	0	68	59	9	6	.600	1	3.40
	PIT/NL		11	159	5	0	0	2	36.1	49	0	5	2	0	20	1	1	0	1	20	20	2	3	.400	0	4.95
87	VAN/PCL	AAA	14	348	12	5	1	1	89.0	62	5	30	0	0	92	2	0	2	1	21	21	5	2	.714	0	2.12
	PIT/NL		15	201	7	0	0	2	43.0	49	5	22	4	1	27	6	3	1	0	34	32	1	4	.200	0	6.70
88	BUF/AMA	AAA	4	120	4	1	0	0	31.0	26	0	4	0	0	20	2	0	0	1	12	8	2	0	1.000	0	2.32
89	BUF/AMA	AAA	31	725	25	4	1	3	177.1	177	13	35	2	2	103	8	5	3	0	69	66	12	6	.667	1	3.35
	PIT/NL		12	109	3	0	0	2	26.2	23	3	8	2	0	20	1	1	0	0	13	12	4	3	.571	0	4.05
90	PIT/NL		55	386	0	0	0	19	94.2	88	9	21	7	3	70	5	3	1	2	33	31	8	5	.615	5	2.95
91	PIT/NL		54	270	1	0	0	19	65.2	67	7	15	1	0	57	2	2	0	0	32	30	4	3	.571	2	4.11
6 YR TOTALS			**150**	**1151**	**21**	**0**	**0**	**46**	**270.1**	**289**	**26**	**74**	**16**	**4**	**195**	**15**	**10**	**2**	**4**	**143**	**136**	**19**	**18**	**.514**	**8**	**4.53**

Pavlas, David Lee "Dave" — bats right — throws right — b.8/12/62

YR	TM/LG	CL	G	TBF	GS	CG	SHO	GF	IP	H	HR	BB	IBB	HB	SO	SH	SF	WP	BK	R	ER	W	L	PCT	SV	ERA
85	PEO/MID	A	17	452	15	3	1	2	110.0	90	7	32	0	3	86	3	1	6	1	40	32	8	3	.727	1	2.62
86	WIN/CAR	A+	28	739	26	5	2	0	173.1	172	8	57	2	6	143	6	4	11	1	91	74	14	6	.700	0	3.84
87	PIT/EAS	AA	7	199	7	0	0	0	45.0	49	6	17	0	3	27	0	3	1	1	25	19	6	1	.857	0	3.80
	TUL/TEX	AA	13	280	12	0	0	1	59.2	79	9	27	0	3	46	1	0	7	0	51	51	1	6	.143	0	7.69
88	TUL/TEX	AA	26	299	5	1	0	9	77.1	52	3	18	1	5	69	6	2	4	6	26	17	5	2	.714	2	1.98
	OC/AMA	AAA	13	237	8	0	0	2	52.1	59	1	28	0	3	40	1	2	2	1	29	26	3	1	.750	0	4.47
89	OC/AMA	AAA	29	652	21	4	0	4	143.2	175	7	67	4	7	94	6	7	8	1	89	75	2	14	.125	0	4.70
90	IOW/AMA	AAA	53	421	3	0	0	22	99.1	84	4	48	6	10	96	4	3	8	1	38	36	8	3	.727	8	3.26
	CHI/NL		13	93	0	0	0	3	21.1	23	2	6	2	0	12	0	2	3	0	7	5	2	0	1.000	0	2.11
91	CHI/NL		1	5	0	0	0	1	1.0	3	1	0	0	0	0	1	0	0	0	2	2	0	0	.000	0	18.00
	IOW/AMA	AAA	61	418	0	0	0	29	97.1	92	5	43	9	5	54	10	5	13	0	49	43	5	6	.455	7	3.98
2 YR TOTALS			**14**	**98**	**0**	**0**	**0**	**4**	**22.1**	**26**	**3**	**6**	**2**	**0**	**12**	**1**	**2**	**3**	**0**	**9**	**7**	**2**	**0**	**1.000**	**0**	**2.82**

Pena, Alejandro (Vasquez) — bats right — throws right — b.6/25/59

YR	TM/LG	CL	G	TBF	GS	CG	SHO	GF	IP	H	HR	BB	IBB	HB	SO	SH	SF	WP	BK	R	ER	W	L	PCT	SV	ERA
81	LA/NL		14	104	0	0	0	7	25.1	18	2	11	1	0	14	0	0	0	0	8	8	1	1	.500	2	2.84
82	LA/NL		29	160	0	0	0	11	35.2	37	2	21	7	1	20	2	0	1	1	24	19	0	2	.000	0	4.79
83	LA/NL		34	730	26	4	3	4	177.0	152	7	51	7	1	120	8	5	2	1	67	54	12	9	.571	1	2.75
84	LA/NL		28	813	28	8	4	0	199.1	186	7	46	7	3	135	6	2	5	1	67	55	12	6	.667	0	2.48
85	LA/NL		2	23	1	0	0	0	4.1	7	1	3	1	0	2	0	0	0	0	5	4	0	1	.000	0	8.31
86	VB/FSL	A+	4	69	4	0	0	0	15.2	22	1	4	0	1	11	0	2	1	0	15	13	0	2	.000	0	7.47
	LA/NL		24	309	10	0	0	6	70.0	74	6	30	5	1	46	3	1	1	1	40	38	1	2	.333	1	4.89
87	LA/NL		37	377	7	0	0	17	87.1	82	9	37	5	2	76	5	6	0	1	41	34	2	7	.222	11	3.50
88	LA/NL		60	378	0	0	0	31	94.1	75	4	27	6	1	83	3	3	3	2	29	20	6	7	.462	12	1.91
89	LA/NL		53	306	0	0	0	28	76.0	62	6	18	4	2	75	3	1	1	1	20	18	4	3	.571	5	2.13
90	NY/NL		52	320	0	0	0	32	76.0	71	4	22	5	1	76	1	6	0	0	31	27	3	3	.500	5	3.20
91	NY/NL		44	261	0	0	0	24	63.0	63	5	19	4	0	49	2	4	1	2	20	19	6	1	.857	4	2.71
	ATL/NL		15	70	0	0	0	12	19.1	11	1	3	0	0	13	1	0	0	0	3	3	2	0	1.000	11	1.40
	YEAR		59	331	0	0	0	36	82.1	74	6	22	4	0	62	3	4	1	2	23	22	8	1	.889	15	2.40
11 YR TOTALS			**392**	**3851**	**72**	**12**	**7**	**172**	**927.2**	**838**	**54**	**288**	**52**	**12**	**709**	**34**	**28**	**14**	**10**	**355**	**299**	**49**	**42**	**.538**	**52**	**2.90**

Perez, Melido Turpen Gross — bats right — throws right — b.2/15/66

YR	TM/LG	CL	G	TBF	GS	CG	SHO	GF	IP	H	HR	BB	IBB	HB	SO	SH	SF	WP	BK	R	ER	W	L	PCT	SV	ERA
84	CHA/SAL	A	16	387	15	0	0	0	89.0	99	9	19	0	2	55	2	2	4	1	52	43	5	7	.417	0	4.35
85	EUG/NWL	A–	17	0	15	2	0	1	101.0	116	13	35	2	1	88	0	0	4	2	65	61	6	7	.462	0	5.44
86	BUR/MID	A	28	712	23	13	1	5	170.1	148	15	49	3	3	153	5	10	8	1	83	70	10	12	.455	0	3.70
87	FM/FSL	A+	8	247	8	5	1	0	64.1	51	3	7	0	0	51	3	1	3	0	20	17	4	3	.571	0	2.38
	MEM/SOU	AA	20	538	20	5	2	0	133.2	125	13	20	1	0	126	1	1	4	0	60	51	8	5	.615	0	3.43
	KC/AL		3	53	3	0	0	0	10.1	18	2	5	0	0	5	0	0	0	0	12	9	1	1	.500	0	7.84
88	CHI/AL		32	836	32	3	1	0	197.0	186	26	72	0	2	138	5	8	13	3	105	83	12	10	.545	0	3.79
89	CHI/AL		31	810	31	2	0	0	183.1	187	23	90	3	3	141	5	4	12	5	106	102	11	14	.440	0	5.01
90	CHI/AL		35	833	35	3	3	0	197.0	177	14	86	1	2	161	4	6	8	4	111	101	13	14	.481	0	4.61

Perez, Melido Turpen Gross (continued)

YR	TM/LG	CL	G	TBF	GS	CG	SHO	GF	IP	H	HR	BB	IBB	HB	SO	SH	SF	WP	BK	R	ER	W	L	PCT	SV	ERA
91	CHI/AL		49	553	8	0	0	16	135.2	111	15	52	0	1	128	4	1	11	1	49	47	8	7	.533	1	3.12
5 YR TOTALS			150	3085	109	8	4	16	723.1	679	80	305	4	8	573	18	19	44	13	383	342	45	46	.495	1	4.26

Perez, Michael Irvin (Ortega) "Mike" — bats right — throws right — b.10/19/64

YR	TM/LG	CL	G	TBF	GS	CG	SHO	GF	IP	H	HR	BB	IBB	HB	SO	SH	SF	WP	BK	R	ER	W	L	PCT	SV	ERA
86	JC/APP	R+	18	314	8	2	0	6	72.2	69	3	22	0	5	72	1	2	1	0	35	24	3	5	.375	3	2.97
87	SPR/MID	A	58	321	0	0	0	51	84.1	47	2	21	3	2	119	3	2	2	0	12	8	6	2	.750	41	0.85
88	ARK/TEX	AA	11	75	0	0	0	6	14.1	18	2	13	2	1	17	1	2	2	3	18	18	1	3	.250	0	11.30
	SP/FSL	A+	35	173	0	0	0	28	43.1	24	0	16	1	4	45	2	3	2	4	12	10	2	2	.500	17	2.08
89	ARK/TEX	AA	57	329	0	0	0	51	76.2	68	5	32	2	2	74	0	2	3	1	34	31	4	6	.400	33	3.64
90	LOU/AMA	AAA	57	298	0	0	0	50	67.1	64	9	33	4	2	69	4	1	3	0	34	32	7	7	.500	31	4.28
	STL/NL		13	55	0	0	0	7	13.2	12	0	3	0	0	5	0	2	0	0	6	6	1	0	1.000	0	3.95
91	STL/NL		14	75	0	0	0	2	17.0	19	1	7	2	1	7	1	0	0	1	11	11	0	2	.000	0	5.82
	LOU/AMA	AAA	37	225	0	0	0	23	47.0	54	5	25	6	2	38	5	2	5	0	38	32	3	5	.375	4	6.13
2 YR TOTALS			27	130	0	0	0	9	30.2	31	1	10	2	1	12	1	2	0	1	17	17	1	2	.333	1	4.99

Perez, Pascual Gross — bats right — throws right — b.5/17/57

YR	TM/LG	CL	G	TBF	GS	CG	SHO	GF	IP	H	HR	BB	IBB	HB	SO	SH	SF	WP	BK	R	ER	W	L	PCT	SV	ERA
80	PIT/NL		2	51	2	0	0	0	12.0	15	0	2	0	2	7	1	2	0	0	6	5	0	1	.000	0	3.75
81	PIT/NL		17	380	13	2	0	1	86.1	92	5	34	9	3	46	6	0	5	1	50	38	2	7	.222	0	3.96
82	ATL/NL		16	333	11	0	0	2	79.1	85	4	17	3	0	29	5	3	2	1	35	27	4	4	.500	0	3.06
83	ATL/NL		33	889	33	7	1	0	215.1	213	20	51	5	4	144	12	4	7	0	88	82	15	8	.652	0	3.43
84	ATL/NL		30	864	30	4	1	0	211.2	208	26	51	5	3	145	6	4	4	5	96	88	14	8	.636	0	3.74
85	ATL/NL		22	453	22	0	0	0	95.1	115	10	57	10	1	57	5	3	2	2	72	65	1	13	.071	0	6.14
87	IND/AMA	AAA	19	544	19	8	2	0	133.0	128	12	34	4	1	125	5	2	4	2	65	56	9	7	.563	0	3.79
	MON/NL		10	273	10	2	0	0	70.1	52	5	16	1	1	58	3	1	1	1	21	18	7	0	1.000	0	2.30
88	IND/AMA	AAA	2	30	2	0	0	0	7.2	4	0	4	0	1	7	0	0	0	0	1	1	0	0	.000	0	1.17
	MON/NL		27	741	27	4	2	0	188.0	133	15	44	6	7	131	10	3	5	10	59	51	12	8	.600	0	2.44
89	MON/NL		33	811	28	2	0	3	198.1	178	15	45	13	4	152	6	4	6	1	85	73	9	13	.409	0	3.31
90	NY/AL		3	52	3	0	0	0	14.0	8	0	3	0	1	12	0	1	0	0	3	2	1	2	.333	0	1.29
	FT./FSL	A+	1	12	1	0	0	0	3.0	3	1	1	0	0	1	0	0	0	0	2	2	0	0	.000	0	6.00
91	ALB/EAS	AA	2	22	2	0	0	0	5.1	5	0	1	0	0	6	0	0	0	0	1	1	0	0	.000	0	1.69
	NY/AL		14	299	14	0	0	0	73.2	68	7	24	1	0	41	3	0	3	2	26	26	2	4	.333	0	3.18
11 YR TOTALS			207	5146	193	21	4	6	1244.1	1167	107	344	53	25	822	57	24	36	23	541	475	67	68	.496	0	3.44

Perez, Yorkis Miguel — bats left — throws left — b.9/30/67

YR	TM/LG	CL	G	TBF	GS	CG	SHO	GF	IP	H	HR	BB	IBB	HB	SO	SH	SF	WP	BK	R	ER	W	L	PCT	SV	ERA
83	ELI/APP	R+	3	0	1	0	0	0	4.0	5	1	9	0	0	6	0	0	0	0	9	9	0	1	.000	0	20.25
84	ELI/APP	R+	1	6	0	0	0	0	1.1	1	0	1	0	0	1	0	0	0	0	0	0	0	0	.000	0	0.00
86	KEN/MID	A	31	591	18	3	0	9	131.0	120	9	88	1	3	144	4	4	13	1	81	75	4	11	.267	0	5.15
87	JAC/SOU	AA	12	263	10	1	1	1	60.0	61	4	30	0	1	60	0	5	4	0	34	27	2	7	.222	1	4.05
	WPB/FSL	A+	15	413	15	3	0	0	100.0	78	4	46	0	0	111	2	3	8	1	36	26	6	2	.750	0	2.34
88	JAC/SOU	AA	27	618	25	2	1	1	130.0	142	11	94	0	4	105	2	6	13	9	96	84	8	12	.400	0	5.82
89	WPB/FSL	A+	18	385	12	0	0	3	94.2	62	2	54	0	3	85	1	2	5	4	34	29	7	6	.538	1	2.76
	JAC/SOU	AA	20	164	0	0	0	3	35.0	25	0	34	1	0	50	1	0	1	2	16	14	4	3	.571	1	3.60
90	JAC/SOU	AA	28	200	2	0	0	8	42.0	36	1	34	2	1	39	2	1	4	0	34	28	2	2	.500	1	6.00
	IND/AMA	AAA	9	49	0	0	0	2	11.2	8	1	6	0	0	8	2	0	0	0	5	3	1	1	.500	0	2.31
91	RIC/INT	AAA	36	459	10	0	0	5	107.0	99	7	53	1	2	102	3	7	7	2	47	45	12	3	.800	1	3.79
	CHI/NL		3	16	0	0	0	0	4.1	2	0	2	0	0	3	0	2	2	0	1	1	1	0	1.000	0	2.08

Peterson, Adam Charles — bats right — throws right — b.12/11/65

YR	TM/LG	CL	G	TBF	GS	CG	SHO	GF	IP	H	HR	BB	IBB	HB	SO	SH	SF	WP	BK	R	ER	W	L	PCT	SV	ERA
84	WS/GCL	R	12	206	8	0	0	3	43.0	49	4	19	1	1	31	1	4	5	1	39	26	1	4	.200	0	5.44
85	NF/NYP	A–	14	384	14	5	0	0	92.1	74	9	34	1	0	79	4	1	5	1	39	31	7	6	.538	0	3.02
86	PEN/CAR	A+	24	632	23	1	0	1	147.0	150	16	58	4	3	84	1	7	9	2	92	75	9	8	.529	0	4.59
	BIR/SOU	AA	6	145	5	2	0	0	32.1	34	8	16	1	1	21	1	1	0	0	16	15	1	3	.250	0	4.18
87	BIR/SOU	AA	26	740	26	2	1	0	170.2	165	12	73	1	7	124	2	7	6	0	79	74	12	9	.571	0	3.90
	CHI/AL		1	22	1	0	0	0	4.0	8	1	3	0	0	1	0	1	0	0	6	6	0	0	.000	0	13.50
88	VAN/PCL	AAA	28	739	28	4	1	0	171.0	161	10	81	1	7	103	8	5	10	6	69	63	14	7	.667	0	3.32
	CHI/AL		2	31	2	0	0	0	6.0	6	0	6	1	0	5	0	0	0	0	9	9	0	1	.000	0	13.50
89	CHI/AL		3	31	2	0	0	0	5.1	13	1	2	0	0	3	1	0	0	0	9	9	0	1	.000	0	15.19
	VAN/PCL	AAA	25	721	24	6	1	0	172.0	141	12	71	0	5	116	6	6	2	0	60	52	14	5	.737	0	2.72
90	VAN/PCL	AAA	6	164	6	3	2	0	43.0	26	3	15	0	1	30	1	0	3	0	11	10	4	1	.800	0	2.09
	CHI/AL		20	357	11	2	0	4	85.0	90	12	29	2	2	29	2	3	3	0	46	43	2	5	.286	0	4.55
91	SD/NL		13	241	11	0	0	0	54.2	50	10	28	2	0	37	4	2	7	1	33	27	3	4	.429	0	4.45
	LV/PCL	AAA	8	187	8	0	0	0	42.0	41	3	20	2	2	37	4	2	3	1	25	21	2	2	.500	0	4.50
5 YR TOTALS			39	682	27	2	0	4	155.0	167	24	65	3	2	75	7	6	11	1	103	94	5	11	.313	0	5.46

Petkovsek, Mark Joseph — bats right — throws right — b.11/18/65

YR	TM/LG	CL	G	TBF	GS	CG	SHO	GF	IP	H	HR	BB	IBB	HB	SO	SH	SF	WP	BK	R	ER	W	L	PCT	SV	ERA
87	RAN/GCL	R	3	26	1	0	0	0	5.2	4	0	2	0	2	7	0	0	0	0	2	2	0	0	.000	0	3.18
	CHA/FSL	A+	11	249	10	0	0	1	56.0	67	2	17	0	0	23	3	3	5	1	36	25	3	4	.429	0	4.02
88	CHA/FSL	A+	28	708	28	7	5	0	175.2	156	5	42	2	3	95	6	7	11	4	71	58	10	11	.476	0	2.97
89	OC/AMA	AAA	6	147	6	0	0	0	30.2	39	3	18	1	3	8	1	1	2	0	27	25	0	4	.000	0	7.34

(continued)

Petkovsek, Mark Joseph (continued)

YR	TM/LG	CL	G	TBF	GS	CG	SHO	GF	IP	H	HR	BB	IBB	HB	SO	SH	SF	WP	BK	R	ER	W	L	PCT	SV	ERA
	TUL/TEX	AA	21	585	21	1	0	0	140.0	144	7	35	0	3	66	6	7	5	0	63	54	8	5	.615	0	3.47
90	OC/AMA	AAA	28	669	28	2	1	0	151.0	187	9	42	1	4	81	3	2	8	0	103	88	7	14	.333	0	5.25
91	TEX/AL		4	53	1	0	0	1	9.1	21	4	4	0	0	6	0	1	2	0	16	15	0	1	.000	0	14.46
	OC/AMA	AAA	25	646	24	3	1	0	149.2	162	9	38	2	7	67	5	9	10	1	89	82	9	8	.529	0	4.93

Petry, Daniel Joseph "Dan" — bats right — throws right — b.11/13/58

YR	TM/LG	CL	G	TBF	GS	CG	SHO	GF	IP	H	HR	BB	IBB	HB	SO	SH	SF	WP	BK	R	ER	W	L	PCT	SV	ERA
79	DET/AL		15	401	15	2	0	0	98.0	90	11	33	5	4	43	5	5	3	1	46	43	6	5	.545	0	3.95
80	DET/AL		27	716	25	4	3	1	164.2	156	9	83	14	1	88	10	5	5	2	82	72	10	9	.526	0	3.94
81	DET/AL		23	583	22	7	2	1	141.0	115	10	57	4	1	79	9	2	3	1	53	47	10	9	.526	0	3.00
82	DET/AL		35	1031	35	8	1	0	246.0	220	15	100	5	4	132	8	8	9	0	98	88	15	9	.625	0	3.22
83	DET/AL		38	1115	38	9	2	0	266.1	256	37	99	7	6	122	5	5	12	0	126	116	19	11	.633	0	3.92
84	DET/AL		35	968	35	7	2	0	233.1	231	21	66	4	3	144	5	2	7	0	94	84	18	8	.692	0	3.24
85	DET/AL		34	962	34	8	0	0	238.2	190	24	81	9	3	109	0	2	6	0	98	89	15	13	.536	0	3.36
86	LAK/FSL	A+	3	45	3	0	0	0	10.1	13	0	1	0	2	6	0	0	0	0	8	8	1	1	.500	0	6.97
	DET/AL		20	520	20	2	0	0	116.0	122	15	53	3	5	56	3	3	5	0	78	60	5	10	.333	0	4.66
87	DET/AL		30	628	21	0	0	3	134.2	148	22	76	5	10	93	4	7	8	1	101	84	9	7	.563	0	5.61
88	PS/CAL	A+	3	75	3	0	0	0	15.0	19	0	11	0	0	11	1	1	1	0	14	11	1	2	.333	0	6.60
	CAL/AL		22	604	22	4	1	0	139.2	139	18	59	5	6	64	5	6	5	2	70	68	3	9	.250	0	4.38
89	CAL/AL		19	223	4	0	0	3	51.0	53	8	23	0	1	21	1	5	2	0	32	31	3	2	.600	0	5.47
90	DET/AL		32	655	23	1	0	2	149.2	148	14	77	7	1	73	8	6	10	0	78	74	10	9	.526	0	4.45
91	DET/AL		17	240	6	0	0	1	54.2	66	9	19	3	0	18	1	0	0	0	35	30	2	3	.400	0	4.94
	ATL/NL		10	116	0	0	0	4	24.1	29	2	14	1	1	9	3	0	2	0	17	15	0	0	.000	0	5.55
	BOS/AL		13	98	0	0	0	7	22.1	21	3	12	2	1	12	0	1	0	0	17	11	0	0	.000	1	4.43
	YEAR		40	454	6	0	0	12	101.1	116	14	45	6	2	39	4	1	2	0	69	56	2	3	.400	1	4.97
13 YR TOTALS			**370**	**8860**	**300**	**52**	**11**	**22**	**2080.1**	**1984**	**218**	**852**	**74**	**47**	**1063**	**67**	**57**	**77**	**7**	**1025**	**912**	**125**	**104**	**.546**	**1**	**3.95**

Piatt, Douglas William "Doug" — bats left — throws right — b.9/26/65

YR	TM/LG	CL	G	TBF	GS	CG	SHO	GF	IP	H	HR	BB	IBB	HB	SO	SH	SF	WP	BK	R	ER	W	L	PCT	SV	ERA
88	BUR/APP	R+	2	9	0	0	0	1	1.1	4	0	1	0	0	1	0	0	0	0	2	2	0	0	.000	1	13.50
	WAT/MID	A	26	153	0	0	0	22	36.2	33	2	11	1	0	40	1	1	1	1	18	9	2	1	.667	12	2.21
89	KIN/CAR	A+	20	115	0	0	0	12	28.2	24	1	8	0	3	31	3	0	1	0	8	8	2	0	1.000	6	2.51
	WAT/NYP	A—	15	137	0	0	0	15	35.0	21	0	9	4	0	43	1	0	2	0	5	2	4	2	.667	6	0.51
	ROC/MID	A	11	86	0	0	0	6	19.2	19	1	11	1	1	24	1	0	2	0	7	7	2	2	.500	2	3.20
90	WPB/FSL	A+	21	111	0	0	0	13	27.1	12	0	16	1	1	41	2	0	2	0	6	3	4	1	.800	9	0.99
	JAC/SOU	AA	35	206	0	0	0	22	49.0	30	4	29	2	3	51	2	1	1	0	17	12	5	1	.833	6	2.20
91	IND/AMA	AAA	44	210	0	0	0	32	47.0	40	2	27	1	3	61	3	3	5	1	24	18	6	4	.600	13	3.45
	MON/NL		21	145	0	0	0	3	34.2	29	3	17	0	0	29	2	0	1	0	11	10	0	0	.000	2	2.60

Plesac, Daniel Thomas "Dan" — bats left — throws left — b.2/4/62

YR	TM/LG	CL	G	TBF	GS	CG	SHO	GF	IP	H	HR	BB	IBB	HB	SO	SH	SF	WP	BK	R	ER	W	L	PCT	SV	ERA
84	STO/CAL	A+	16	0	16	2	0	0	108.1	106	7	50	0	2	101	0	0	3	2	51	40	6	6	.500	0	3.32
	EP/TEX	AA	7	171	7	0	0	0	39.0	43	2	16	0	0	24	3	1	0	0	19	15	2	2	.500	0	3.46
85	EP/TEX	AA	25	662	24	2	0	0	150.1	171	12	68	1	0	128	5	9	13	1	91	83	12	5	.706	0	4.97
86	MIL/AL		51	377	0	0	0	33	91.0	81	5	29	1	0	75	6	5	4	0	34	30	10	7	.588	14	2.97
87	MIL/AL		57	325	0	0	0	47	79.1	63	8	23	1	3	89	1	2	6	0	30	23	5	6	.455	23	2.61
88	MIL/AL		50	211	0	0	0	48	52.1	46	2	12	2	0	52	2	0	4	6	14	14	1	2	.333	30	2.41
89	MIL/AL		52	242	0	0	0	51	61.1	47	6	17	1	0	52	0	4	0	0	16	16	3	4	.429	33	2.35
90	MIL/AL		66	299	0	0	0	52	69.0	67	5	31	6	3	65	2	2	2	0	36	34	3	7	.300	24	4.43
91	MIL/AL		45	402	10	0	0	25	92.1	92	12	39	1	3	61	3	7	2	1	49	44	2	7	.222	8	4.29
6 YR TOTALS			**321**	**1856**	**10**	**0**	**0**	**256**	**445.1**	**396**	**38**	**151**	**12**	**9**	**394**	**14**	**20**	**18**	**7**	**179**	**161**	**24**	**33**	**.421**	**132**	**3.25**

Plunk, Eric Vaughn — bats right — throws right — b.9/3/63

YR	TM/LG	CL	G	TBF	GS	CG	SHO	GF	IP	H	HR	BB	IBB	HB	SO	SH	SF	WP	BK	R	ER	W	L	PCT	SV	ERA
84	FT./FSL	A+	28	791	28	7	1	0	176.1	153	5	123	1	6	152	5	8	17	7	85	56	12	12	.500	0	2.86
85	HUN/SOU	AA	13	347	13	2	1	0	79.1	61	9	56	0	2	68	1	3	4	1	36	30	8	2	.800	0	3.40
	TAC/PCL	AAA	11	0	10	0	0	0	53.0	51	3	50	3	2	43	0	0	4	3	41	34	0	5	.000	0	5.77
86	TAC/PCL	AAA	6	147	6	0	0	0	32.2	25	4	33	0	0	31	2	3	3	2	18	17	2	3	.400	0	4.68
	OAK/AL		26	537	15	0	0	2	120.1	91	14	102	2	5	98	2	3	9	6	75	71	4	7	.364	0	5.31
87	TAC/PCL	AAA	24	140	0	0	0	19	34.2	21	1	17	2	0	56	1	0	6	0	8	6	1	1	.500	9	1.56
	OAK/AL		32	432	11	0	0	11	95.0	91	8	62	3	2	90	3	5	5	2	53	50	4	6	.400	2	4.74
88	OAK/AL		49	331	0	0	0	22	78.0	62	6	39	4	1	79	3	2	4	7	27	26	7	2	.778	5	3.00
89	OAK/AL		23	113	0	0	0	12	28.2	17	1	12	0	1	24	1	0	4	0	7	7	1	1	.500	1	2.20
	NY/AL		27	332	7	0	0	5	75.2	65	9	52	2	0	61	2	4	6	3	36	31	7	5	.583	0	3.69
	YEAR		50	445	7	0	0	17	104.1	82	10	64	2	1	85	3	4	10	3	43	38	6	6	.571	1	3.28
90	NY/AL		47	310	0	0	0	16	72.2	58	6	43	4	2	67	7	0	4	2	27	22	6	3	.667	0	2.72
91	NY/AL		43	521	8	0	0	6	111.2	128	18	62	1	1	103	6	4	6	2	69	59	2	5	.286	0	4.76
6 YR TOTALS			**247**	**2576**	**41**	**0**	**0**	**74**	**582.0**	**512**	**62**	**372**	**16**	**12**	**522**	**24**	**18**	**38**	**22**	**294**	**266**	**31**	**29**	**.517**	**8**	**4.11**

Plympton, Jeffrey Hunter "Jeff" — bats right — throws right — b.11/24/65

YR	TM/LG	CL	G	TBF	GS	CG	SHO	GF	IP	H	HR	BB	IBB	HB	SO	SH	SF	WP	BK	R	ER	W	L	PCT	SV	ERA
87	NB/EAS	AA	23	281	6	1	0	7	63.2	61	2	34	2	2	60	1	3	4	3	35	27	4	1	.800	1	3.82
88	LYN/CAR	A+	41	360	0	0	0	22	83.0	69	5	45	8	2	105	7	2	6	1	30	24	5	4	.556	12	2.60
89	NB/EAS	AA	38	332	6	0	0	17	72.2	72	3	39	5	5	63	2	6	4	0	36	30	4	4	.500	5	3.72

Plympton, Jeffrey Hunter "Jeff" (continued)

YR	TM/LG	CL	G	TBF	GS	CG	SHO	GF	IP	H	HR	BB	IBB	HB	SO	SH	SF	WP	BK	R	ER	W	L	PCT	SV	ERA
90	NB/EAS	AA	37	265	0	0	0	30	64.0	62	1	16	5	1	55	0	5	0	2	31	19	3	4	.429	13	2.67
	PAW/INT	AAA	11	71	0	0	0	8	17.1	10	0	11	4	1	11	1	1	0	0	0	0	1	0	1.000	3	0.00
91	PAW/INT	AAA	41	299	1	0	0	26	69.1	65	11	29	2	6	58	1	1	1	1	31	24	2	6	.250	7	3.12
	BOS/AL		4	24	0	0	0	3	5.1	5	0	4	0	0	2	0	1	1	0	0	0	0	0	.000	0	0.00

Poole, James Richard "Jim" — bats left — throws left — b.4/28/66

YR	TM/LG	CL	G	TBF	GS	CG	SHO	GF	IP	H	HR	BB	IBB	HB	SO	SH	SF	WP	BK	R	ER	W	L	PCT	SV	ERA
88	VB/FSL	A+	10	63	0	0	0	6	14.1	13	0	9	1	1	12	1	1	1	1	7	6	1	1	.500	0	3.77
89	VB/FSL	A+	60	306	0	0	0	50	78.1	57	0	24	7	2	93	5	0	3	0	16	14	11	4	.733	19	1.61
	BAK/CAL	A+	1	7	0	0	0	1	1.2	2	0	0	0	0	1	0	0	0	0	1	0	0	0	.000	0	0.00
90	SA/TEX	AA	54	278	0	0	0	35	63.2	55	3	27	5	2	77	8	0	6	0	31	17	6	7	.462	16	2.40
	LA/NL		16	46	0	0	0	4	10.2	7	1	8	4	0	6	0	0	1	0	5	5	0	0	.000	0	4.22
91	OC/AMA	AAA	10	41	0	0	0	7	12.1	4	0	1	0	0	14	0	2	0	0	0	0	0	0	.000	3	0.00
	TEX/AL		5	31	0	0	0	2	6.0	10	0	3	0	0	4	0	1	0	0	4	3	0	0	.000	1	4.50
	ROC/INT	AAA	27	123	0	0	0	19	29.0	29	1	9	0	0	25	0	1	3	0	11	9	3	2	.600	9	2.79
	BAL/AL		24	135	0	0	0	3	36.0	19	3	9	2	0	34	3	2	2	0	10	8	3	2	.600	1	2.00
	YEAR		29	166	0	0	0	5	42.0	29	3	12	2	0	38	3	3	2	0	14	11	3	2	.600	1	2.36
2 YR TOTALS			45	212	0	0	0	9	52.2	36	4	20	6	0	44	3	3	3	0	19	16	3	2	.600	1	2.73

Portugal, Mark Steven — bats right — throws right — b.10/30/62

YR	TM/LG	CL	G	TBF	GS	CG	SHO	GF	IP	H	HR	BB	IBB	HB	SO	SH	SF	WP	BK	R	ER	W	L	PCT	SV	ERA
84	ORL/SOU	AA	27	849	27	10	3	0	196.0	171	16	113	2	3	110	4	4	9	0	80	65	14	7	.667	0	2.98
85	TOL/INT	AAA	19	547	19	5	1	0	128.2	129	10	60	0	0	89	2	2	4	3	60	54	8	5	.615	0	3.78
	MIN/AL		6	105	4	0	0	0	24.1	24	3	14	0	0	12	0	2	1	1	16	15	1	3	.250	0	5.55
86	TOL/INT	AAA	6	191	6	3	1	0	45.0	34	2	23	0	2	30	0	2	1	0	15	13	5	1	.833	0	2.60
	MIN/AL		27	481	15	3	0	7	112.2	112	10	50	1	1	67	5	3	5	0	56	54	6	10	.375	1	4.31
87	MIN/AL		13	204	7	0	0	3	44.0	58	13	24	1	1	28	0	1	2	0	40	38	1	3	.250	0	7.77
	POR/PCL	AAA	17	451	16	2	0	1	102.0	108	9	50	1	0	69	1	3	5	2	75	68	1	10	.091	0	6.00
88	POR/PCL	AAA	3	80	3	1	1	0	19.2	15	0	8	0	0	9	2	2	1	0	3	3	2	0	1.000	0	1.37
	MIN/AL		26	242	0	0	0	9	57.2	60	11	17	1	1	31	2	3	2	2	30	29	3	3	.500	3	4.53
89	TUC/PCL	AAA	17	480	17	5	0	0	116.2	107	6	32	1	3	90	2	1	3	1	55	49	7	5	.583	0	3.78
	HOU/NL		20	440	15	2	1	1	108.0	91	7	37	0	2	86	8	3	3	0	34	33	7	1	.875	0	2.75
90	HOU/NL		32	831	32	1	0	0	196.2	187	21	67	4	4	136	7	6	6	0	90	79	11	10	.524	0	3.62
91	HOU/NL		32	710	27	1	0	3	168.1	163	19	59	5	2	120	6	6	4	1	91	84	10	12	.455	1	4.49
7 YR TOTALS			156	3013	100	7	1	23	711.2	695	84	268	12	11	480	28	22	23	4	357	332	39	42	.481	5	4.20

Power, Ted Henry — bats right — throws right — b.1/31/55

YR	TM/LG	CL	G	TBF	GS	CG	SHO	GF	IP	H	HR	BB	IBB	HB	SO	SH	SF	WP	BK	R	ER	W	L	PCT	SV	ERA
81	LA/NL		5	66	2	0	0	1	14.1	16	0	7	2	1	7	0	2	0	0	6	5	1	3	.250	0	3.14
82	LA/NL		12	160	4	0	0	4	33.2	38	4	23	1	0	15	4	1	3	3	27	25	1	1	.500	0	6.68
83	CIN/NL		49	480	6	1	0	14	111.0	120	10	49	4	1	57	4	6	1	0	62	56	5	6	.455	2	4.54
84	CIN/NL		78	456	0	0	0	42	108.2	93	4	46	8	0	81	9	8	3	0	37	34	9	7	.563	11	2.82
85	CIN/NL		64	342	0	0	0	50	80.0	65	2	45	6	1	42	6	4	1	0	27	24	8	6	.571	27	2.70
86	CIN/NL		56	537	10	0	0	30	129.0	115	13	52	10	1	95	9	6	5	1	59	53	10	6	.625	1	3.70
87	CIN/NL		34	887	34	2	1	0	204.0	213	28	71	7	3	133	8	7	3	2	115	102	10	13	.435	0	4.50
88	KC/AL		22	360	12	2	2	3	80.1	98	7	30	3	0	44	2	4	3	2	54	53	5	6	.455	0	5.94
	DET/AL		4	83	2	0	0	0	18.2	23	1	8	4	0	13	0	0	1	0	13	12	1	1	.500	0	5.79
	YEAR		26	443	14	2	2	3	99.0	121	8	38	7	0	57	2	4	4	2	67	65	6	7	.462	0	5.91
89	LOU/AMA	AAA	8	152	7	1	1	0	37.0	29	3	15	1	2	36	0	1	1	0	13	13	4	3	.571	0	3.16
	STL/NL		23	407	15	0	0	2	97.0	96	7	21	3	1	43	5	3	1	0	47	40	7	7	.500	0	3.71
90	PIT/NL		40	218	0	0	0	25	51.2	50	5	17	6	4	42	3	2	1	0	23	21	1	3	.250	7	3.66
91	CIN/NL		68	371	0	0	0	22	87.0	87	6	31	5	2	51	6	4	6	1	37	35	5	3	.625	3	3.62
11 YR TOTALS			455	4367	85	5	3	193	1015.1	1014	87	400	61	13	623	56	47	28	9	507	460	63	62	.504	51	4.08

Radinsky, Scott David — bats left — throws left — b.3/3/68

YR	TM/LG	CL	G	TBF	GS	CG	SHO	GF	IP	H	HR	BB	IBB	HB	SO	SH	SF	WP	BK	R	ER	W	L	PCT	SV	ERA
86	WS/GCL	R	7	122	7	0	0	0	26.2	24	0	17	0	0	18	1	3	2	1	20	10	1	0	1.000	0	3.38
87	PEN/CAR	A+	12	187	8	0	0	2	39.0	43	3	32	0	3	37	2	2	3	1	30	25	1	7	.125	0	5.77
	WS/GCL	R	11	249	10	0	0	0	58.1	43	1	39	0	4	41	0	2	5	1	23	15	3	3	.500	0	2.31
88	WS/GCL	R	5	17	0	0	0	2	3.1	2	0	4	0	0	7	0	0	1	2	2	2	0	0	.000	0	5.40
89	SB/MID	A	53	248	0	0	0	49	61.2	39	1	19	2	5	83	4	2	2	2	21	12	7	5	.583	31	1.75
90	CHI/AL		62	237	0	0	0	18	52.1	47	1	36	1	2	46	2	2	2	1	29	28	6	1	.857	4	4.82
91	CHI/AL		67	289	0	0	0	19	71.1	53	4	23	2	1	49	4	4	0	0	18	16	5	5	.500	8	2.02
2 YR TOTALS			129	526	0	0	0	37	123.2	100	5	59	3	3	95	6	6	2	1	47	44	11	6	.647	12	3.20

Rasmussen, Dennis Lee — bats left — throws left — b.4/18/59

YR	TM/LG	CL	G	TBF	GS	CG	SHO	GF	IP	H	HR	BB	IBB	HB	SO	SH	SF	WP	BK	R	ER	W	L	PCT	SV	ERA
83	SD/NL		4	58	1	0	0	1	13.2	10	1	8	0	0	13	0	0	1	0	5	3	0	0	.000	0	1.98
84	COL/INT	AAA	6	177	6	3	1	0	43.2	24	1	27	0	0	30	1	1	8	0	15	15	4	1	.800	0	3.09
	NY/AL		24	616	24	1	0	0	147.2	127	16	60	0	4	110	3	7	8	2	79	75	9	6	.600	0	4.57
85	COL/INT	AAA	7	196	7	1	0	0	45.0	41	1	25	0	1	43	3	3	3	1	24	19	0	3	.000	0	3.80
	NY/AL		22	429	16	2	0	0	101.2	97	10	42	1	1	63	1	5	5	0	56	45	3	5	.375	0	3.98
86	NY/AL		31	819	31	3	1	0	202.0	160	28	74	0	2	131	4	5	5	0	91	87	18	6	.750	0	3.88
87	COL/INT	AAA	1	26	1	0	0	0	7.0	5	0	0	0	0	4	0	1	0	0	1	1	1	0	1.000	0	1.29

(continued)

Rasmussen, Dennis Lee (continued)

YR	TM/LG	CL	G	TBF	GS	CG	SHO	GF	IP	H	HR	BB	IBB	HB	SO	SH	SF	WP	BK	R	ER	W	L	PCT	SV	ERA
	NY/AL		26	627	25	2	0	0	146.0	145	31	55	1	4	89	5	5	6	0	78	77	9	7	.563	0	4.75
	CIN/NL		7	187	7	0	0	0	45.1	39	5	12	0	1	39	3	1	1	2	22	20	4	1	.800	0	3.97
	YEAR		33	814	32	2	0	0	191.1	184	36	67	1	5	128	8	6	7	2	100	97	13	8	.619	0	4.56
88	CIN/NL		11	255	11	1	1	0	56.1	68	8	22	4	2	27	2	2	1	5	36	36	2	6	.250	0	5.75
	SD/NL		20	599	20	6	0	0	148.1	131	9	36	0	2	85	8	2	6	0	48	42	14	4	.778	0	2.55
	YEAR		31	854	31	7	1	0	204.2	199	17	58	4	4	112	10	4	7	5	84	78	16	10	.615	0	3.43
89	SD/NL		33	799	33	1	0	0	183.2	190	18	72	6	3	87	9	11	4	2	100	87	10	10	.500	0	4.26
90	SD/NL		32	825	32	3	1	0	187.2	217	28	62	4	3	86	14	4	9	1	110	94	11	15	.423	0	4.51
91	LV/PCL	AAA	5	114	5	1	0	0	26.1	23	2	15	0	2	12	1	1	1	1	18	16	1	3	.250	0	5.47
	SD/NL		24	633	24	1	1	0	146.2	155	12	49	3	2	75	4	6	1	1	74	61	6	13	.316	0	3.74
9 YR TOTALS			234	5847	224	20	4	2	1379.0	1339	166	492	19	24	805	50	48	45	14	699	627	86	73	.541	0	4.09

Reardon, Jeffrey James "Jeff" — bats right — throws right — b.10/1/55

YR	TM/LG	CL	G	TBF	GS	CG	SHO	GF	IP	H	HR	BB	IBB	HB	SO	SH	SF	WP	BK	R	ER	W	L	PCT	SV	ERA
79	NY/NL		18	81	0	0	0	10	20.2	12	2	9	3	0	10	2	1	2	0	7	4	1	2	.333	2	1.74
80	NY/NL		61	475	0	0	0	35	110.1	96	10	47	15	0	101	8	5	2	0	36	32	8	7	.533	6	2.61
81	NY/NL		18	124	0	0	0	14	28.2	27	2	12	4	1	28	0	1	0	0	11	11	1	0	1.000	2	3.45
	MON/NL		25	155	0	0	0	19	41.2	21	3	9	0	1	21	3	0	1	0	6	6	2	0	1.000	6	1.30
	YEAR		43	279	0	0	0	33	70.1	48	5	21	4	2	49	3	1	1	0	17	17	3	0	1.000	8	2.18
82	MON/NL		75	444	0	0	0	53	109.0	87	6	36	4	2	86	8	4	2	0	28	25	7	4	.636	26	2.06
83	MON/NL		66	403	0	0	0	53	92.0	87	7	44	9	1	78	8	2	2	0	34	31	7	9	.438	21	3.03
84	MON/NL		68	363	0	0	0	58	87.0	70	5	37	7	3	79	3	2	4	0	31	28	7	7	.500	23	2.90
85	MON/NL		63	356	0	0	0	50	87.2	68	7	26	4	1	67	3	1	2	0	31	31	2	8	.200	41	3.18
86	MON/NL		62	368	0	0	0	48	89.0	83	12	26	2	1	67	9	1	0	0	42	39	7	9	.438	35	3.94
87	MIN/AL		63	337	0	0	0	58	80.1	70	14	28	4	3	83	1	3	2	0	41	40	8	8	.500	31	4.48
88	MIN/AL		63	299	0	0	0	58	73.0	68	6	15	2	1	56	4	1	0	3	21	20	2	4	.333	42	2.47
89	MIN/AL		65	297	0	0	0	61	73.0	68	8	12	3	3	46	1	5	1	1	33	33	5	4	.556	31	4.07
90	BOS/AL		47	210	0	0	0	37	51.1	39	5	19	4	1	33	1	0	0	0	19	18	5	3	.625	21	3.16
91	BOS/AL		57	248	0	0	0	51	59.1	54	9	16	3	1	44	0	2	0	0	21	20	1	4	.200	40	3.03
13 YR TOTALS			751	4160	0	0	0	605	1003.0	850	96	336	64	20	799	51	28	18	4	361	338	63	69	.477	327	3.03

Reed, Richard Allen "Rick" — bats right — throws right — b.8/16/64

YR	TM/LG	CL	G	TBF	GS	CG	SHO	GF	IP	H	HR	BB	IBB	HB	SO	SH	SF	WP	BK	R	ER	W	L	PCT	SV	ERA
86	PIR/GCL	R	8	96	3	0	0	1	24.0	20	0	6	0	0	15	1	3	0	1	12	10	0	2	.000	0	3.75
	MAC/SAL	A	1	26	1	0	0	0	6.1	5	0	2	1	0	1	1	0	0	0	3	2	0	0	.000	0	2.84
87	MAC/SAL	A	46	388	0	0	0	20	93.2	80	6	29	3	9	92	3	4	4	0	38	26	8	4	.667	7	2.50
88	SAL/CAR	A+	15	294	8	4	1	2	72.1	56	6	17	1	5	73	0	1	3	1	28	22	6	2	.750	0	2.74
	HAR/EAS	AA	2	60	2	0	0	0	16.0	11	0	2	0	0	17	0	0	0	0	2	2	1	0	1.000	0	1.13
	PIT/NL		2	47	2	0	0	0	12.0	10	1	2	0	0	6	2	0	0	0	4	4	1	0	1.000	0	3.00
	BUF/AMA	AAA	10	301	9	3	2	0	77.0	62	0	12	2	1	50	6	1	1	1	15	14	5	2	.714	0	1.64
89	BUF/AMA	AAA	20	522	20	3	0	0	125.2	130	9	28	0	1	75	6	3	3	0	58	52	9	8	.529	0	3.72
	PIT/NL		15	232	7	0	0	2	54.2	62	5	11	3	2	34	2	3	0	3	35	34	1	4	.200	0	5.60
90	PIT/NL		13	238	8	1	1	2	53.2	62	6	12	6	1	27	2	1	0	0	32	26	2	3	.400	1	4.36
	BUF/AMA	AAA	15	369	15	2	2	0	91.0	82	4	21	0	6	63	6	0	1	0	37	35	7	4	.636	0	3.46
91	PIT/NL		1	21	1	0	0	0	4.1	8	1	1	0	0	2	0	0	0	0	6	5	0	0	.000	0	10.38
	BUF/AMA	AAA	25	660	25	5	2	0	167.2	151	3	26	3	2	102	9	6	2	1	45	40	14	4	.778	0	2.15
4 YR TOTALS			31	538	18	1	1	4	124.2	142	13	26	9	3	69	6	4	0	3	77	69	4	7	.364	1	4.98

Remlinger, Michael John "Mike" — bats left — throws left — b.3/23/66

YR	TM/LG	CL	G	TBF	GS	CG	SHO	GF	IP	H	HR	BB	IBB	HB	SO	SH	SF	WP	BK	R	ER	W	L	PCT	SV	ERA
87	EVE/NWL	A–	2	19	1	0	0	0	5.0	1	0	5	0	0	11	0	0	1	0	2	2	0	0	.000	0	3.60
	CLI/MID	A	6	124	5	0	0	0	30.0	21	2	14	0	1	43	1	1	3	1	12	11	2	1	.667	0	3.30
	SHR/TEX	AA	6	142	6	0	0	0	34.1	14	2	22	0	1	51	0	1	2	1	11	9	4	2	.667	0	2.36
88	SHR/TEX	AA	3	50	3	0	0	0	13.0	7	0	3	0	3	18	0	0	1	3	4	1	1	0	1.000	0	0.69
89	SHR/TEX	AA	16	399	16	0	0	0	90.2	68	2	73	0	3	92	1	1	16	2	43	30	4	6	.400	0	2.98
	PHO/PCL	AAA	11	233	10	0	0	0	43.0	51	8	52	0	2	28	1	2	5	0	47	44	1	6	.143	0	9.21
90	SHR/TEX	AA	25	644	25	2	1	0	147.2	149	9	72	1	8	75	8	4	16	0	82	64	9	11	.450	0	3.90
91	PHO/PCL	AAA	19	508	19	1	1	0	108.2	134	15	59	0	1	68	4	5	6	1	86	77	5	5	.500	0	6.38
	SF/NL		8	155	6	1	1	1	35.0	36	5	20	1	0	19	1	1	1	0	17	17	2	1	.667	0	4.37

Renfroe, Cohen Williams "Laddie" — bats both — throws right — b.5/9/62

YR	TM/LG	CL	G	TBF	GS	CG	SHO	GF	IP	H	HR	BB	IBB	HB	SO	SH	SF	WP	BK	R	ER	W	L	PCT	SV	ERA
84	GEN/NYP	A–	24	170	0	0	0	18	39.0	34	1	10	5	3	33	4	1	1	0	10	6	3	3	.500	10	1.38
85	PEO/MID	A	57	396	0	0	0	37	95.2	79	2	39	2	5	56	4	3	1	0	36	34	10	6	.625	8	3.20
86	WIN/CAR	A+	65	356	0	0	0	54	83.0	84	2	27	5	2	51	3	0	3	0	37	27	6	6	.500	21	2.93
87	PIT/EAS	AA	40	205	0	0	0	37	46.1	56	2	15	8	0	27	3	0	3	0	22	21	4	5	.444	16	4.08
	IOW/AMA	AAA	8	56	0	0	0	1	14.1	8	1	5	0	0	9	0	0	1	0	9	8	0	1	.000	0	5.02
88	IOW/AMA	AAA	16	109	0	0	0	5	24.0	28	2	11	1	0	12	1	0	0	2	13	13	1	3	.250	0	4.88
	PIT/EAS	AA	29	441	7	1	0	11	110.1	102	4	24	5	4	57	10	1	3	1	32	24	9	4	.692	1	1.96
89	CHA/SOU	AA	78	554	1	1	1	58	132.0	127	12	34	10	1	85	11	1	2	1	52	46	19	7	.731	15	3.14
90	IOW/AMA	AAA	44	517	14	1	0	22	118.0	146	12	30	7	1	56	4	1	0	1	68	65	7	3	.700	9	4.96
91	CHI/NL		4	27	0	0	0	2	4.2	11	1	2	1	0	4	0	0	1	0	7	7	0	0	.000	0	13.50
	IOW/AMA	AAA	63	422	1	1	0	40	98.1	101	10	32	5	3	52	5	6	2	0	52	46	8	5	.615	18	4.21

Reuschel, Rickey Eugene "Rick" — bats right — throws right — b.5/16/49

YR	TM/LG	CL	G	TBF	GS	CG	SHO	GF	IP	H	HR	BB	IBB	HB	SO	SH	SF	WP	BK	R	ER	W	L	PCT	SV	ERA
72	CHI/NL		21	527	18	5	4	1	129.0	127	3	29	6	2	87	4	2	1	2	46	42	10	8	.556	0	2.93
73	CHI/NL		36	1003	36	7	3	0	237.0	244	15	62	6	5	168	5	2	10	1	95	79	14	15	.483	0	3.00
74	CHI/NL		41	1061	38	8	2	2	240.2	262	18	83	12	6	160	14	8	7	1	130	115	13	12	.520	0	4.30
75	CHI/NL		38	1007	37	6	0	1	234.0	244	17	67	8	7	155	20	4	4	1	116	97	11	17	.393	1	3.73
76	CHI/NL		38	1078	37	9	2	1	260.0	260	17	64	5	8	146	11	13	7	1	117	100	14	12	.538	1	3.46
77	CHI/NL		39	1030	37	8	4	2	252.0	233	13	74	11	5	166	3	4	9	1	84	78	20	10	.667	1	2.79
78	CHI/NL		35	1007	35	9	1	0	242.2	235	16	54	8	5	115	16	8	13	1	98	92	14	15	.483	0	3.41
79	CHI/NL		36	1021	36	5	1	0	239.0	251	16	75	8	10	125	13	6	5	0	104	96	18	12	.600	0	3.62
80	CHI/NL		38	1094	38	6	0	0	257.0	281	13	76	10	4	140	19	14	3	1	111	97	11	13	.458	0	3.40
81	CHI/NL		13	358	13	1	0	0	85.2	87	4	23	4	4	53	5	0	5	0	40	33	4	7	.364	0	3.47
	NY/AL		12	282	11	3	0	1	70.2	75	4	10	0	1	22	1	2	0	0	24	21	4	4	.500	0	2.67
	YEAR		25	640	24	4	0	1	156.1	162	8	33	4	5	75	6	2	5	0	64	54	8	11	.421	0	3.11
83	CHI/NL		4	88	4	0	0	0	20.2	18	1	10	2	0	9	0	1	0	0	9	9	1	1	.500	0	3.92
84	CHI/NL		19	405	14	1	0	2	92.1	123	7	23	0	3	43	7	9	2	0	57	53	5	5	.500	0	5.17
85	HAW/PCL	AAA	8	0	8	2	0	0	54.0	52	2	12	1	0	46	0	0	5	1	18	15	6	2	.750	0	2.50
	PIT/NL		31	773	26	9	1	4	194.0	153	7	52	10	3	138	5	3	4	0	58	49	14	8	.636	1	2.27
86	PIT/NL		35	930	34	4	2	0	215.2	232	20	57	2	8	125	9	10	6	1	106	95	9	16	.360	0	3.96
87	PIT/NL		25	715	25	9	3	0	177.0	163	12	35	1	6	80	4	7	5	0	63	54	8	6	.571	0	2.75
	SF/NL		9	205	8	3	1	0	50.0	44	1	7	2	2	27	4	1	2	0	28	24	5	3	.625	0	4.32
	YEAR		34	920	33	12	4	0	227.0	207	13	42	3	8	107	8	8	7	0	91	78	13	9	.591	0	3.09
88	SF/NL		36	1000	36	7	2	0	245.0	242	11	42	8	6	92	9	14	4	0	88	85	19	11	.633	0	3.12
89	SF/NL		32	860	32	2	0	0	208.1	195	18	54	4	2	111	7	7	1	0	75	68	17	8	.680	0	2.94
90	SF/NL		15	390	13	0	0	1	87.0	102	8	31	9	1	49	10	5	1	0	40	38	3	6	.333	1	3.93
91	SF/NL		4	54	1	0	0	1	10.2	17	0	7	1	0	4	1	0	0	0	5	5	0	2	.000	0	4.22
19 YR TOTALS			**557**	**14888**	**529**	**102**	**26**	**16**	**3548.1**	**3588**	**221**	**935**	**117**	**88**	**2015**	**167**	**120**	**89**	**10**	**1494**	**1330**	**214**	**191**	**.528**	**5**	**3.37**

Reynoso, Armando Martin (Gutierrez) — bats right — throws right — b.5/1/66

YR	TM/LG	CL	G	TBF	GS	CG	SHO	GF	IP	H	HR	BB	IBB	HB	SO	SH	SF	WP	BK	R	ER	W	L	PCT	SV	ERA
90	RIC/INT	AAA	4	102	3	0	0	0	24.0	26	3	7	0	0	15	1	1	0	3	7	6	3	1	.750	0	2.25
91	RIC/INT	AAA	22	544	19	3	3	1	131.0	117	9	39	1	10	97	7	3	8	6	44	38	10	6	.625	0	2.61
	ATL/NL		6	103	5	0	0	1	23.1	26	4	10	1	3	10	3	0	2	0	18	16	2	1	.667	0	6.17

Rhodes, Arthur Lee "Arthur Lee" — bats left — throws left — b.10/24/69

YR	TM/LG	CL	G	TBF	GS	CG	SHO	GF	IP	H	HR	BB	IBB	HB	SO	SH	SF	WP	BK	R	ER	W	L	PCT	SV	ERA
88	BLU/APP	R+	11	155	7	0	0	3	35.1	29	1	15	0	1	44	0	1	9	2	17	13	3	4	.429	0	3.31
89	ERI/NYP	A—	5	115	5	1	0	0	31.0	13	1	10	0	0	45	0	0	2	1	7	4	2	0	1.000	0	1.16
	FRE/CAR	A+	7	109	6	0	0	0	24.1	19	2	19	0	1	28	0	1	4	1	16	14	2	2	.500	0	5.18
90	FRE/CAR	A+	13	322	13	4	0	0	80.2	62	6	21	0	1	103	0	1	3	1	25	19	4	6	.400	0	2.12
	HAG/EAS	AA	12	303	12	0	0	0	72.1	62	3	39	0	0	60	1	3	5	0	32	30	3	4	.429	0	3.73
91	HAG/EAS	AA	19	428	19	2	2	0	106.2	73	4	47	1	0	115	1	3	10	0	37	32	7	4	.636	0	2.70
	BAL/AL		8	174	8	0	0	0	36.0	47	4	23	0	0	23	1	3	2	0	35	32	0	3	.000	0	8.00

Rice, Patrick Edward "Pat" — bats right — throws right — b.11/2/63

YR	TM/LG	CL	G	TBF	GS	CG	SHO	GF	IP	H	HR	BB	IBB	HB	SO	SH	SF	WP	BK	R	ER	W	L	PCT	SV	ERA
86	SLC/PIO	R+	18	0	6	0	0	7	59.1	67	1	15	0	1	39	0	0	5	0	33	22	1	3	.250	0	3.34
87	WAU/MID	A	28	732	27	4	1	0	166.1	192	13	43	2	7	127	4	6	15	1	100	71	12	11	.522	0	3.84
88	SB/CAL	A+	33	518	12	3	1	8	121.0	120	10	32	1	8	114	4	3	5	3	56	46	7	7	.500	3	3.42
	VER/EAS	AA	6	111	3	0	0	1	26.0	22	2	7	1	1	16	1	0	1	3	7	3	3	0	1.000	0	1.04
89	WIL/EAS	AA	13	190	5	2	1	3	47.1	39	0	12	2	0	40	1	1	2	1	13	12	4	1	.800	0	2.28
	CAL/PCL	AAA	17	247	5	0	0	3	55.2	63	8	21	1	0	35	1	1	1	0	32	30	6	3	.667	1	4.85
90	CAL/PCL	AAA	15	129	2	0	0	2	28.1	34	2	13	2	1	27	1	1	4	0	21	20	1	1	.500	2	6.35
	WIL/EAS	AA	25	313	8	0	0	4	72.1	77	4	24	1	1	58	1	4	5	0	36	32	4	4	.500	4	3.98
91	SEA/AL		7	91	2	0	0	1	21.0	18	3	10	1	1	12	0	3	0	0	10	7	1	1	.500	0	3.00
	CAL/PCL	AAA	21	520	21	1	0	0	121.2	138	18	37	0	2	59	2	5	5	0	70	68	13	4	.765	0	5.03

Righetti, David Allan "Dave" — bats left — throws left — b.11/28/58

YR	TM/LG	CL	G	TBF	GS	CG	SHO	GF	IP	H	HR	BB	IBB	HB	SO	SH	SF	WP	BK	R	ER	W	L	PCT	SV	ERA
79	NY/AL		3	67	3	0	0	0	17.1	10	2	10	0	0	13	1	1	0	0	7	7	0	1	.000	0	3.63
81	NY/AL		15	422	15	2	0	0	105.1	75	1	38	0	0	89	0	1	2	1	25	24	8	4	.667	0	2.05
82	NY/AL		33	804	27	4	0	3	183.0	155	11	108	4	6	163	8	5	9	5	88	77	11	10	.524	1	3.79
83	NY/AL		31	900	31	7	2	0	217.0	194	12	67	2	2	169	10	4	10	1	96	83	14	8	.636	0	3.44
84	NY/AL		64	400	0	0	0	53	96.1	79	5	37	7	0	90	4	2	4	0	29	25	5	6	.455	31	2.34
85	NY/AL		74	452	0	0	0	60	107.0	96	5	45	7	0	92	8	5	4	1	36	33	12	7	.632	29	2.78
86	NY/AL		74	435	0	0	0	68	106.2	88	4	35	7	2	83	5	4	1	0	31	29	8	8	.500	46	2.45
87	NY/AL		60	419	0	0	0	54	95.0	95	9	44	4	4	77	6	5	1	3	45	37	8	6	.571	31	3.51
88	NY/AL		60	377	0	0	0	41	87.0	86	5	37	2	1	70	4	0	2	0	35	34	5	4	.556	25	3.52
89	NY/AL		55	300	0	0	0	53	69.0	73	3	26	6	1	51	1	1	2	0	32	23	2	6	.250	25	3.00
90	NY/AL		53	235	0	0	0	47	53.0	48	8	26	2	2	43	1	1	2	0	24	21	1	1	.500	36	3.57
91	SF/NL		61	304	0	0	0	49	71.2	64	4	28	4	1	51	4	2	1	0	29	27	2	7	.222	24	3.39
12 YR TOTALS			**583**	**5115**	**76**	**13**	**2**	**428**	**1208.1**	**1063**	**69**	**501**	**43**	**19**	**991**	**56**	**33**	**34**	**17**	**477**	**420**	**76**	**68**	**.528**	**248**	**3.13**

Rijo, Jose Antonio (Abreu) — bats right — throws right — b.5/13/65

YR	TM/LG	CL	G	TBF	GS	CG	SHO	GF	IP	H	HR	BB	IBB	HB	SO	SH	SF	WP	BK	R	ER	W	L	PCT	SV	ERA
84	NY/AL		24	289	5	0	0	8	62.1	74	5	33	1	1	47	6	1	2	1	40	33	2	8	.200	2	4.76

(continued)

Rijo, Jose Antonio (Abreu) (continued)

YR	TM/LG	CL	G	TBF	GS	CG	SHO	GF	IP	H	HR	BB	IBB	HB	SO	SH	SF	WP	BK	R	ER	W	L	PCT	SV	ERA
	COL/INT	AAA	11	294	11	0	0	0	65.1	67	7	40	0	1	47	0	1	4	1	35	32	3	3	.500	0	4.41
85	TAC/PCL	AAA	24	0	24	3	1	0	149.0	116	6	108	3	0	179	0	1	4	11	64	48	7	10	.412	0	2.90
	OAK/AL		12	272	9	0	0	1	63.2	57	6	28	2	1	65	5	0	0	0	26	25	6	4	.600	0	3.53
86	OAK/AL		39	856	26	4	0	9	193.2	172	24	108	7	4	176	10	9	6	4	116	100	9	11	.450	1	4.65
87	TAC/PCL	AAA	9	230	8	0	0	0	54.2	44	5	28	0	1	67	1	0	8	2	27	24	2	4	.333	0	3.95
	OAK/AL		21	394	14	1	0	3	82.1	106	10	41	1	2	67	0	3	5	2	67	54	2	7	.222	0	5.90
88	CIN/NL		49	653	19	0	0	12	162.0	120	10	63	7	3	160	8	5	1	4	47	43	13	8	.619	0	2.39
89	CIN/NL		19	464	19	1	1	0	111.0	101	6	48	3	2	86	3	6	4	3	39	35	7	6	.538	0	2.84
90	NAS/AMA	AAA	1	19	1	0	0	0	4.1	5	0	2	0	0	2	0	0	0	1	4	4	0	0	.000	0	8.31
	CIN/NL		29	801	29	7	1	0	197.0	151	10	78	1	2	152	8	1	2	5	65	59	14	8	.636	0	2.70
91	CIN/NL		30	825	30	3	1	0	204.1	165	8	55	4	3	172	4	8	2	4	69	57	15	6	.714	0	2.51
8 YR TOTALS			**223**	**4554**	**151**	**16**	**3**	**33**	**1076.1**	**946**	**76**	**454**	**26**	**18**	**925**	**44**	**33**	**22**	**23**	**469**	**406**	**68**	**58**	**.540**	**3**	**3.39**

Ritchie, Wallace Reid "Wally" — bats left — throws left — b.7/12/65

YR	TM/LG	CL	G	TBF	GS	CG	SHO	GF	IP	H	HR	BB	IBB	HB	SO	SH	SF	WP	BK	R	ER	W	L	PCT	SV	ERA
85	BEN/NWL	A—	2	0	1	0	0	0	10.0	10	0	5	0	1	3	0	0	0	0	11	5	1	0	1.000	0	4.50
	CLE/FSL	A+	14	196	6	0	0	3	46.2	49	5	12	0	0	24	1	2	0	0	30	18	3	1	.750	1	3.47
86	CLE/FSL	A+	32	206	0	0	0	22	52.2	40	0	16	2	0	39	4	3	2	0	15	13	4	1	.800	10	2.22
	REA/EAS	AA	28	129	0	0	0	15	30.0	29	4	9	0	1	13	3	5	0	0	13	9	4	1	.800	4	2.70
87	MAI/INT	AAA	13	91	0	0	0	9	22.0	17	1	8	0	1	16	1	0	1	0	6	5	3	1	.750	2	2.05
	PHI/NL		49	273	0	0	0	13	62.1	60	8	29	11	1	45	5	2	2	3	27	26	3	2	.600	3	3.75
88	PHI/NL		19	115	0	0	0	6	26.0	19	1	17	2	1	8	2	3	2	0	14	9	0	0	.000	0	3.12
	MAI/INT	AAA	16	340	14	0	0	0	78.2	88	4	29	2	0	49	3	4	6	1	49	41	4	5	.444	0	4.69
89	SW/INT	AAA	34	582	20	4	1	6	135.2	143	16	38	2	2	73	2	7	3	0	70	63	7	4	.636	0	4.18
90	SW/INT	AAA	20	350	13	1	1	1	82.1	75	7	28	1	2	47	5	1	2	0	46	38	4	3	.571	0	4.15
91	SCR/INT	AAA	7	99	2	0	0	3	26.0	17	2	7	0	0	25	0	0	0	0	8	7	1	0	1.000	2	2.42
	PHI/NL		39	213	0	0	0	13	50.1	44	4	17	5	2	26	2	4	1	0	17	14	1	2	.333	0	2.50
3 YR TOTALS			**107**	**601**	**0**	**0**	**0**	**34**	**138.2**	**123**	**13**	**63**	**18**	**4**	**79**	**9**	**9**	**5**	**3**	**58**	**49**	**4**	**4**	**.500**	**3**	**3.18**

Ritz, Kevin D — bats right — throws right — b.6/8/65

YR	TM/LG	CL	G	TBF	GS	CG	SHO	GF	IP	H	HR	BB	IBB	HB	SO	SH	SF	WP	BK	R	ER	W	L	PCT	SV	ERA
86	GAS/SAL	A	7	155	7	0	0	0	36.1	29	2	21	0	0	34	0	1	6	0	19	17	1	2	.333	0	4.21
	LAK/FSL	A+	18	393	15	0	0	2	85.2	114	3	45	1	2	39	2	2	6	0	60	53	3	9	.250	1	5.57
87	GF/EAS	AA	25	680	25	1	0	0	152.2	171	5	71	1	4	78	10	4	11	3	95	83	8	8	.500	0	4.89
88	GF/EAS	AA	26	583	24	4	2	0	136.2	115	3	70	0	4	75	2	4	6	4	68	58	8	10	.444	0	3.82
89	TOL/INT	AAA	16	447	16	1	0	0	102.2	95	3	60	1	8	74	3	1	4	2	48	36	7	8	.467	0	3.16
	DET/AL		12	334	12	1	0	0	74.0	75	2	44	1	6	56	1	5	6	0	41	36	4	6	.400	0	4.38
90	DET/AL		4	52	4	0	0	0	7.1	14	0	14	2	0	3	3	0	3	0	12	9	0	4	.000	0	11.05
	TOL/INT	AAA	20	418	18	0	0	1	89.2	93	5	59	0	9	57	5	4	6	3	68	52	3	6	.333	0	5.22
91	TOL/INT	AAA	20	535	19	3	0	1	126.1	116	9	60	2	3	105	3	2	6	1	50	46	8	7	.533	0	3.28
	DET/AL		11	86	5	0	0	3	15.1	17	1	22	1	2	9	1	2	0	0	22	20	0	3	.000	0	11.74
3 YR TOTALS			**27**	**472**	**21**	**1**	**0**	**3**	**96.2**	**106**	**3**	**80**	**8**	**3**	**68**	**5**	**7**	**9**	**0**	**75**	**65**	**4**	**13**	**.235**	**0**	**6.05**

Robinson, Don Allen — bats right — throws right — b.6/8/57

YR	TM/LG	CL	G	TBF	GS	CG	SHO	GF	IP	H	HR	BB	IBB	HB	SO	SH	SF	WP	BK	R	ER	W	L	PCT	SV	ERA
78	PIT/NL		35	937	32	9	1	1	228.1	203	20	57	4	3	135	8	8	9	4	98	88	14	6	.700	1	3.47
79	PIT/NL		29	684	25	4	0	1	160.2	171	12	52	5	4	96	6	5	6	1	74	69	8	8	.500	0	3.87
80	PIT/NL		29	671	24	3	2	1	160.1	157	14	45	5	5	103	8	3	7	2	74	71	7	10	.412	1	3.99
81	PIT/NL		16	182	2	0	0	4	38.1	47	4	23	4	0	17	7	2	3	0	27	25	0	3	.000	0	5.87
82	PIT/NL		38	977	30	6	0	3	227.0	213	26	103	11	3	165	12	8	17	1	123	108	15	13	.536	0	4.28
83	PIT/NL		9	168	6	0	0	2	36.1	43	5	21	3	0	28	2	0	2	0	21	18	2	2	.500	0	4.46
84	PIT/NL		51	500	1	0	0	28	122.0	99	6	49	4	0	110	4	9	5	0	45	41	5	6	.455	10	3.02
85	PIT/NL		44	418	6	0	0	22	95.1	95	6	42	11	2	65	2	2	2	0	49	41	5	11	.313	3	3.87
86	PW/CAR	A+	3	54	3	1	0	0	12.2	13	0	1	0	0	13	0	2	1	0	7	1	1	1	.500	0	0.71
	PIT/NL		50	295	0	0	0	41	69.1	61	5	27	2	2	53	5	4	4	1	27	26	3	4	.429	14	3.38
87	PIT/NL		42	276	0	0	0	37	65.1	66	6	22	3	0	53	6	1	6	1	29	28	6	6	.500	12	3.86
	SF/NL		25	184	0	0	0	17	42.2	39	1	18	3	2	26	1	2	1	0	13	13	5	1	.833	7	2.74
	YEAR		67	460	0	0	0	54	108.0	105	7	40	6	2	79	7	3	7	1	42	41	11	7	.611	19	3.42
88	SF/NL		51	725	19	3	2	19	176.2	152	11	49	12	3	122	7	8	4	2	63	48	10	5	.667	6	2.45
89	SF/NL		34	793	32	5	1	2	197.0	184	22	37	4	2	96	6	5	4	4	80	75	12	11	.522	0	3.43
90	SJ/CAL	A+	2	28	2	0	0	0	7.0	6	1	1	0	1	6	1	0	0	0	3	3	1	0	1.000	0	3.86
	SF/NL		26	667	25	4	0	0	157.2	173	18	41	8	1	78	4	3	2	0	84	80	10	7	.588	0	4.57
91	SF/NL		34	525	16	0	0	7	121.1	123	12	50	7	1	78	4	5	1	0	64	59	5	9	.357	1	4.38
14 YR TOTALS			**513**	**8002**	**218**	**34**	**6**	**185**	**1898.1**	**1826**	**168**	**636**	**89**	**26**	**1225**	**82**	**63**	**73**	**15**	**871**	**790**	**107**	**102**	**.512**	**57**	**3.75**

Robinson, Jeffrey Daniel "Jeff" — bats right — throws right — b.12/13/60

YR	TM/LG	CL	G	TBF	GS	CG	SHO	GF	IP	H	HR	BB	IBB	HB	SO	SH	SF	WP	BK	R	ER	W	L	PCT	SV	ERA
84	SF/NL		34	749	33	1	1	0	171.2	195	12	52	4	7	102	5	8	7	2	99	87	7	15	.318	0	4.56
85	PHO/PCL	AAA	29	0	29	5	1	0	161.0	192	14	60	7	4	80	0	0	11	0	107	92	9	9	.500	0	5.14
	SF/NL		8	59	0	0	0	0	12.1	16	2	10	1	0	8	0	1	1	0	11	7	0	0	.000	0	5.11
86	SF/NL		64	431	1	0	0	22	104.1	92	8	32	7	1	90	1	3	11	0	46	39	6	3	.667	8	3.36
87	SF/NL		63	395	0	0	0	33	96.2	69	10	48	10	1	82	9	4	2	0	34	30	6	8	.429	10	2.79
	PIT/NL		18	100	0	0	0	7	26.2	20	1	6	1	0	19	1	0	2	0	9	9	2	1	.667	4	3.04
	YEAR		81	495	0	0	0	40	123.1	89	11	54	11	1	101	10	4	4	0	43	39	8	9	.471	14	2.85

Robinson, Jeffrey Daniel "Jeff" (continued)

YR	TM/LG	CL	G	TBF	GS	CG	SHO	GF	IP	H	HR	BB	IBB	HB	SO	SH	SF	WP	BK	R	ER	W	L	PCT	SV	ERA
88	PIT/NL		75	513	0	0	0	35	124.2	113	6	39	5	3	87	2	6	11	0	44	42	11	5	.688	9	3.03
89	PIT/NL		50	643	19	0	0	18	141.1	161	14	59	11	1	95	7	7	14	2	92	72	7	13	.350	4	4.58
90	NY/AL		54	372	4	1	0	12	88.2	82	8	34	3	1	43	5	1	2	0	35	34	3	6	.333	0	3.45
91	CAL/AL		39	252	0	0	0	16	57.0	56	9	29	4	2	57	3	2	10	0	34	34	0	3	.000	3	5.37
8 YR TOTALS			**405**	**3514**	**57**	**2**	**1**	**143**	**823.1**	**804**	**70**	**309**	**46**	**16**	**583**	**33**	**32**	**61**	**6**	**404**	**354**	**42**	**54**	**.438**	**38**	**3.87**

Robinson, Jeffrey Mark "Jeff" — bats right — throws right — b.12/14/61

YR	TM/LG	CL	G	TBF	GS	CG	SHO	GF	IP	H	HR	BB	IBB	HB	SO	SH	SF	WP	BK	R	ER	W	L	PCT	SV	ERA
84	LAK/FSL	A+	10	262	10	2	1	0	61.2	62	3	26	0	1	33	2	4	1	2	30	23	2	3	.400	0	3.36
	BIR/SOU	AA	20	495	19	1	0	0	113.0	111	10	56	0	2	47	6	5	7	1	64	59	6	6	.500	0	4.70
85	BIR/SOU	AA	22	541	22	2	1	0	115.0	142	14	59	0	6	67	2	3	14	0	79	65	4	8	.333	0	5.09
86	NAS/AMA	AAA	25	664	24	3	0	0	150.0	162	12	72	6	2	72	1	2	9	3	86	73	9	6	.600	0	4.38
87	DET/AL		29	569	21	2	1	2	127.1	132	16	54	3	7	98	2	2	4	3	86	76	9	6	.600	0	5.37
88	DET/AL		24	698	23	6	2	0	172.0	121	19	72	5	3	114	2	6	8	1	61	57	13	6	.684	0	2.98
89	LAK/FSL	A+	4	49	4	0	0	0	11.0	12	1	4	0	0	5	0	0	0	0	8	8	0	0	.000	0	6.55
	DET/AL		16	347	16	1	1	0	78.0	76	10	46	1	1	40	1	3	5	0	47	41	4	5	.444	0	4.73
90	DET/AL		27	654	27	1	1	0	145.0	141	23	88	9	6	76	3	5	16	1	101	96	10	9	.526	0	5.96
91	BAL/AL		21	472	19	0	0	0	104.1	119	12	51	2	6	65	3	0	4	0	62	60	4	9	.308	0	5.18
	ROC/INT	AAA	8	98	1	0	0	3	21.0	23	3	15	0	1	13	2	1	2	0	18	15	1	2	.333	1	6.43
5 YR TOTALS			**117**	**2740**	**106**	**10**	**5**	**2**	**626.2**	**589**	**80**	**311**	**20**	**23**	**393**	**13**	**16**	**41**	**5**	**357**	**330**	**40**	**35**	**.533**	**0**	**4.74**

Robinson, Ronald Dean "Ron" — bats right — throws right — b.3/24/62

YR	TM/LG	CL	G	TBF	GS	CG	SHO	GF	IP	H	HR	BB	IBB	HB	SO	SH	SF	WP	BK	R	ER	W	L	PCT	SV	ERA
84	WIC/AMA	AAA	25	659	24	3	2	0	150.1	168	11	60	1	4	98	9	2	1	1	86	77	9	6	.600	0	4.61
	CIN/NL		12	166	5	1	0	2	39.2	35	3	13	3	0	24	1	1	0	2	18	12	1	2	.333	0	2.72
85	DEN/AMA	AAA	6	169	6	0	0	0	39.2	39	1	12	0	2	24	2	2	1	2	17	12	2	1	.667	0	2.72
	CIN/NL		33	453	12	0	0	9	108.1	107	11	32	3	1	76	3	4	3	0	53	48	7	7	.500	1	3.99
86	CIN/NL		70	487	0	0	0	32	116.2	110	10	43	8	2	117	4	3	3	0	44	42	10	3	.769	14	3.24
87	CIN/NL		48	638	18	0	0	14	154.0	148	14	43	8	1	99	8	7	2	0	71	63	7	5	.583	4	3.68
88	NAS/AMA	AAA	2	18	2	0	0	0	3.2	4	0	3	0	0	4	0	0	0	0	3	3	0	0	.000	0	7.36
	CIN/NL		17	347	16	0	0	0	78.2	88	5	26	4	2	38	5	5	3	0	47	36	3	7	.300	0	4.12
89	NAS/AMA	AAA	3	75	3	0	0	0	19.0	12	1	6	0	0	11	1	1	0	0	5	4	2	0	1.000	0	1.89
	CHT/SOU	AA	1	19	1	0	0	0	5.0	3	0	1	0	0	5	0	0	0	0	1	1	0	0	.000	0	1.80
	CIN/NL		15	353	15	0	0	0	83.1	80	8	28	2	2	36	5	1	2	0	36	31	5	3	.625	0	3.35
90	CIN/NL		6	137	5	0	0	0	31.1	36	2	14	0	0	14	1	0	1	0	18	17	2	2	.500	0	4.88
	MIL/AL		22	627	22	7	2	0	148.1	158	5	37	1	6	57	3	7	2	0	60	48	12	5	.706	0	2.91
	YEAR		28	764	27	7	2	0	179.2	194	7	51	1	6	71	4	7	3	0	78	65	14	7	.667	0	3.26
91	MIL/AL		1	21	1	0	0	0	4.1	6	0	3	1	1	0	0	0	0	0	3	3	0	1	.000	0	6.23
8 YR TOTALS			**224**	**3229**	**94**	**8**	**2**	**57**	**764.2**	**768**	**58**	**239**	**30**	**15**	**461**	**30**	**28**	**16**	**2**	**350**	**300**	**47**	**35**	**.573**	**19**	**3.53**

Rodriguez, Richard Anthony "Rich" — bats left — throws left — b.3/1/63

YR	TM/LG	CL	G	TBF	GS	CG	SHO	GF	IP	H	HR	BB	IBB	HB	SO	SH	SF	WP	BK	R	ER	W	L	PCT	SV	ERA
84	LF/NYP	A−	25	171	1	0	0	6	35.1	28	0	36	7	1	27	4	2	3	0	21	11	2	1	.667	0	2.80
85	COL/SAL	A	49	365	3	0	0	19	80.1	89	4	36	2	1	71	6	1	7	1	41	36	6	3	.667	6	4.03
86	JAC/TEX	AA	13	161	5	1	0	2	33.0	51	5	15	2	0	15	2	2	2	0	35	33	3	4	.429	0	9.00
	LYN/CAR	A+	36	184	0	0	0	16	45.1	37	2	19	0	1	38	1	1	4	1	20	18	2	1	.667	3	3.57
87	LYN/CAR	A+	69	291	0	0	0	30	68.0	69	3	26	6	0	59	1	2	7	8	23	21	3	1	.750	5	2.78
38	JAC/TEX	AA	47	335	1	0	0	25	78.1	66	3	42	6	1	68	9	4	6	5	35	25	2	7	.222	6	2.87
89	WIC/TEX	AA	54	319	0	0	0	38	74.1	74	3	37	11	2	40	3	1	4	1	30	30	8	3	.727	8	3.63
90	LV/PCL	AAA	27	243	2	0	0	13	59.0	50	5	22	1	1	46	1	3	3	1	24	23	3	4	.429	4	3.51
	SD/NL		32	201	0	0	0	15	47.2	52	4	16	4	1	22	2	1	1	1	17	15	1	1	.500	1	2.83
91	SD/NL		64	335	1	0	0	19	80.0	66	6	44	8	0	40	7	2	4	1	31	29	3	1	.750	0	3.26
2 YR TOTALS			**96**	**536**	**1**	**0**	**0**	**34**	**127.2**	**118**	**10**	**60**	**12**	**1**	**62**	**9**	**3**	**5**	**2**	**48**	**44**	**4**	**2**	**.667**	**1**	**3.10**

Rodriguez, Rosario Isabel (Echavarria) — bats right — throws left — b.7/8/69

YR	TM/LG	CL	G	TBF	GS	CG	SHO	GF	IP	H	HR	BB	IBB	HB	SO	SH	SF	WP	BK	R	ER	W	L	PCT	SV	ERA
87	RED/GCL	R	17	271	10	0	0	4	64.1	64	2	21	5	2	33	2	2	1	2	32	22	1	5	.167	1	3.08
88	GRE/SAL	A	23	267	3	1	1	13	65.1	49	2	24	3	3	53	5	1	4	8	15	11	6	4	.600	2	1.52
	CR/MID	A	13	314	11	0	0	0	70.0	73	6	25	2	5	47	2	4	3	11	41	31	3	4	.429	0	3.99
89	CHT/SOU	AA	28	195	0	0	0	11	44.1	48	6	18	2	4	36	3	2	6	3	24	22	3	0	1.000	2	4.47
	CIN/NL		7	19	0	0	0	4	4.1	3	0	3	1	0	0	0	0	1	0	2	2	1	1	.500	0	4.15
90	NAS/AMA	AAA	5	19	0	0	0	1	4.1	4	1	3	0	0	1	0	0	0	0	5	5	0	1	.000	0	10.38
	CHT/SOU	AA	36	256	0	1	0	22	53.2	52	5	48	5	6	39	11	0	7	3	29	26	2	2	.500	7	4.36
	CIN/NL		9	47	0	0	0	4	10.1	15	3	2	0	1	8	1	1	1	0	7	7	0	0	.000	0	6.10
91	BUF/AMA	AAA	48	218	0	0	0	21	51.0	38	1	31	1	2	43	7	1	3	1	22	17	4	3	.571	8	3.00
	PIT/NL		18	89	0	0	0	8	15.1	14	1	8	0	1	10	1	0	2	0	7	7	1	1	.500	6	4.11
3 YR TOTALS			**34**	**133**	**0**	**0**	**0**	**16**	**30.0**	**32**	**4**	**13**	**1**	**2**	**18**	**2**	**1**	**3**	**0**	**16**	**16**	**2**	**2**	**.500**	**6**	**4.80**

Rogers, Charles Kevin "Kevin" — bats right — throws left — b.8/20/68 — System SF/NL

YR	TM/LG	CL	G	TBF	GS	CG	SHO	GF	IP	H	HR	BB	IBB	HB	SO	SH	SF	WP	BK	R	ER	W	L	PCT	SV	ERA
88	POC/PIO	R+	13	314	13	1	0	0	69.2	73	4	35	0	2	71	0	3	5	4	51	48	2	8	.200	0	6.20
89	CLI/MID	A	29	722	28	4	0	0	169.1	128	4	78	1	6	168	2	6	5	7	74	48	13	8	.619	0	2.55
90	SJ/CAL	A+	28	731	26	1	1	1	172.0	143	9	68	1	11	186	5	5	19	3	86	69	14	5	.737	0	3.61
91	SHR/TEX	AA	22	528	22	2	0	0	118.0	124	8	54	4	2	108	5	5	11	2	63	44	4	6	.400	0	3.36

(continued)

Rogers, Kenneth Scott "Kenny" — bats left — throws left — b.11/10/64

YR	TM/LG	CL	G	TBF	GS	CG	SHO	GF	IP	H	HR	BB	IBB	HB	SO	SH	SF	WP	BK	R	ER	W	L	PCT	SV	ERA
84	BUR/MID	A	39	396	4	1	1	16	92.2	87	9	33	3	4	93	5	0	8	0	52	41	4	7	.364	3	3.98
85	DB/FSL	A+	6	54	0	0	0	1	10.0	12	0	11	1	1	9	1	1	3	0	9	8	0	1	.000	0	7.20
	BUR/MID	A	33	411	4	2	1	12	95.0	67	3	62	9	6	96	4	6	5	1	34	30	2	5	.286	4	2.84
86	SAL/CAR	A+	12	297	12	0	0	0	66.0	75	9	26	0	1	46	2	2	2	1	54	46	2	7	.222	0	6.27
	TUL/TEX	AA	10	135	4	0	0	2	26.1	39	4	18	1	0	23	0	0	3	1	30	29	0	3	.000	0	9.91
87	CHA/FSL	A+	5	76	3	0	0	1	17.0	17	1	8	1	0	14	1	0	2	0	13	9	0	3	.000	0	4.76
	TUL/TEX	AA	28	316	6	0	0	8	69.0	80	5	35	3	2	59	3	1	14	0	51	41	1	5	.167	2	5.35
88	CHA/FSL	A+	8	138	6	0	0	1	35.1	22	1	11	0	2	26	0	2	1	2	8	5	2	0	1.000	1	1.27
	TUL/TEX	AA	13	354	13	2	0	0	83.1	73	6	34	0	3	76	3	1	3	4	43	37	4	6	.400	0	4.00
89	TEX/AL		73	314	0	0	0	24	73.2	60	2	42	9	4	63	6	3	6	0	28	24	3	4	.429	2	2.93
90	TEX/AL		69	428	3	0	0	46	97.2	93	6	42	5	1	74	7	4	5	0	40	34	10	6	.625	15	3.13
91	TEX/AL		63	511	9	0	0	20	109.2	121	14	61	7	6	73	9	5	3	1	80	66	10	10	.500	5	5.42
3 YR TOTALS			**205**	**1253**	**12**	**0**	**0**	**90**	**281.0**	**274**	**22**	**145**	**21**	**11**	**210**	**22**	**12**	**14**	**1**	**148**	**124**	**23**	**20**	**.535**	**22**	**3.97**

Rojas, Melquiades (Medrano) "Mel" — bats right — throws right — b.12/10/66

YR	TM/LG	CL	G	TBF	GS	CG	SHO	GF	IP	H	HR	BB	IBB	HB	SO	SH	SF	WP	BK	R	ER	W	L	PCT	SV	ERA
86	EXP/GCL	R	13	261	12	1	0	1	55.1	63	0	37	0	0	34	3	3	4	0	39	30	4	5	.444	0	4.88
87	BUR/MID	A	25	686	25	4	1	0	158.2	146	10	67	1	3	100	4	6	8	0	84	67	8	9	.471	0	3.80
88	ROC/MID	A	12	302	12	3	0	0	73.1	52	3	29	0	2	72	3	1	3	2	30	20	6	4	.600	0	2.45
	WPB/FSL	A+	2	19	2	0	0	0	5.0	4	1	1	0	0	4	0	0	0	0	2	2	1	0	1.000	0	3.60
89	JAC/SOU	AA	34	447	12	1	1	17	112.0	62	1	57	0	5	104	7	4	8	1	39	31	10	7	.588	5	2.49
90	IND/AMA	AAA	17	412	17	0	0	0	97.2	84	9	47	3	1	64	5	2	3	1	42	34	2	4	.333	0	3.13
	MON/NL		23	173	0	0	0	5	40.0	34	5	24	4	2	26	2	0	2	0	17	16	3	1	.750	1	3.60
91	IND/AMA	AAA	14	221	10	0	0	2	52.2	50	4	14	1	1	55	5	1	2	1	29	24	4	2	.667	0	4.10
	MON/NL		37	200	0	0	0	13	48.0	42	4	13	1	1	37	0	2	3	0	21	20	3	3	.500	6	3.75
2 YR TOTALS			**60**	**373**	**0**	**0**	**0**	**18**	**88.0**	**76**	**9**	**37**	**5**	**3**	**63**	**2**	**2**	**5**	**0**	**38**	**36**	**6**	**4**	**.600**	**7**	**3.68**

Rosenberg, Steven Allen "Steve" — bats left — throws left — b.10/31/64

YR	TM/LG	CL	G	TBF	GS	CG	SHO	GF	IP	H	HR	BB	IBB	HB	SO	SH	SF	WP	BK	R	ER	W	L	PCT	SV	ERA
86	ONE/NYP	A–	4	31	0	0	0	0	9.0	4	0	2	0	0	10	0	0	1	0	1	1	0	0	.000	3	1.00
	FT./FSL	A+	25	130	0	0	0	15	29.2	24	1	18	1	0	26	0	1	1	1	7	7	6	1	.857	3	2.12
87	ALB/EAS	AA	32	157	0	0	0	31	40.0	33	1	12	1	0	24	2	3	0	2	11	10	4	4	.500	15	2.25
	COL/INT	AAA	21	157	0	0	0	14	35.1	43	3	18	2	2	27	2	1	1	2	17	16	4	1	.800	2	4.08
88	VAN/PCL	AAA	20	99	0	0	0	5	24.1	15	0	11	3	0	17	0	1	0	4	9	9	2	0	1.000	3	3.33
	CHI/AL		33	203	0	0	0	18	46.0	53	5	19	0	0	28	3	3	1	0	22	22	0	1	.000	1	4.30
89	CHI/AL		38	617	21	2	0	2	142.0	148	14	58	1	1	77	7	9	7	2	92	78	4	13	.235	0	4.94
90	VAN/PCL	AAA	40	366	7	0	0	21	88.1	66	5	44	3	4	74	6	5	2	0	43	35	6	5	.545	8	3.57
	CHI/AL		6	44	0	0	0	3	10.0	10	2	5	0	0	4	0	0	0	0	6	6	1	0	1.000	0	5.40
91	SD/NL		10	49	0	0	0	5	11.2	11	3	5	1	0	6	0	0	2	0	9	9	1	1	.500	0	6.94
	LV/PCL	AAA	36	319	8	0	0	9	68.0	95	6	26	5	2	61	4	3	2	1	62	57	2	4	.333	0	7.54
4 YR TOTALS			**87**	**913**	**21**	**2**	**0**	**28**	**209.2**	**222**	**24**	**87**	**2**	**1**	**115**	**10**	**12**	**10**	**2**	**129**	**115**	**6**	**15**	**.286**	**1**	**4.94**

Rosenthal, Wayne Scott — bats right — throws right — b.2/19/65

YR	TM/LG	CL	G	TBF	GS	CG	SHO	GF	IP	H	HR	BB	IBB	HB	SO	SH	SF	WP	BK	R	ER	W	L	PCT	SV	ERA
86	RAN/GCL	R	23	234	3	1	1	16	61.2	36	0	11	0	0	73	1	0	4	0	9	5	4	2	.667	9	0.73
87	GAS/SAL	A	56	273	0	0	0	55	68.2	44	6	25	5	0	101	5	3	10	0	19	13	1	5	.167	30	1.70
88	CHA/FSL	A+	23	98	0	0	0	19	26.1	20	1	4	0	0	21	1	0	1	1	6	6	1	2	.333	7	2.05
89	CHA/FSL	A+	20	95	0	0	0	16	24.1	13	1	8	1	0	26	4	1	1	1	8	6	2	1	.667	10	2.22
	TUL/TEX	AA	31	209	0	0	0	22	50.0	40	2	21	3	0	47	1	3	0	0	20	17	2	4	.333	10	3.06
90	TUL/TEX	AA	12	62	0	0	0	10	15.0	9	1	9	1	0	18	1	1	3	1	6	4	2	2	.500	4	2.40
	OC/AMA	AAA	42	200	0	0	0	33	48.0	40	1	18	3	2	39	2	1	5	1	24	16	3	4	.429	14	3.00
91	OC/AMA	AAA	32	226	0	0	0	16	51.2	52	2	22	2	3	59	3	3	3	1	24	23	3	2	.600	5	4.01
	TEX/AL		36	321	0	0	0	8	70.1	72	9	36	1	1	61	1	3	8	1	43	41	1	4	.200	1	5.25

Ross, Mark Joseph — bats right — throws right — b.8/8/57

YR	TM/LG	CL	G	TBF	GS	CG	SHO	GF	IP	H	HR	BB	IBB	HB	SO	SH	SF	WP	BK	R	ER	W	L	PCT	SV	ERA
79	AST/GCL	R	2	0	1	0	0	0	7.0	5	0	1	0	1	2	0	0	0	0	3	3	1	0	1.000	0	3.86
80	DB/FSL	A+	30	0	1	1	0	0	58.0	50	0	11	0	0	39	0	0	2	0	14	11	5	3	.625	0	1.71
	COL/SOU	AA	14	0	0	0	0	0	27.0	30	1	4	0	0	13	0	0	1	0	11	11	2	2	.500	0	3.67
81	COL/SOU	AA	64	0	0	0	0	0	116.0	103	3	32	1	5	70	0	0	3	0	35	29	8	10	.444	0	2.25
82	TUC/PCL	AAA	43	0	1	0	0	0	83.0	106	5	32	0	3	35	0	0	2	0	55	45	4	3	.571	0	4.88
83	COL/SOU	AA	13	0	0	0	0	0	27.0	27	0	16	0	0	12	0	0	2	0	8	8	1	1	.500	5	2.67
	TUC/PCL	AAA	6	0	0	0	0	0	6.0	14	1	4	0	0	3	0	0	2	0	10	7	0	2	.000	0	10.50
84	TUC/PCL	AAA	57	0	0	0	0	45	92.0	88	5	24	2	4	32	0	0	1	0	35	30	5	6	.455	20	2.93
	HOU/NL		2	8	0	0	0	0	2.1	1	0	0	0	0	1	0	0	0	0	0	0	1	0	1.000	0	0.00
85	TUC/PCL	AAA	46	0	0	0	0	38	77.0	109	3	21	0	4	31	0	0	2	0	38	31	8	5	.615	11	3.62
	HOU/NL		8	52	0	0	0	4	13.0	12	2	2	0	0	3	0	0	2	0	7	7	0	2	.000	1	4.85
86	TUC/PCL	AAA	48	331	0	0	0	37	73.1	99	4	20	1	2	26	5	2	1	1	37	34	5	5	.500	8	4.17
87	PIT/NL		1	4	0	0	0	1	1.0	1	1	0	0	0	0	0	0	0	0	1	1	0	0	.000	0	9.00
	VAN/PCL	AAA	32	372	1	0	0	15	89.1	87	5	21	4	2	48	6	2	1	0	40	30	5	6	.455	4	3.02
88	TOR/AL		3	32	0	0	0	2	7.1	7	0	4	0	0	4	0	1	0	0	6	4	0	0	.000	0	4.91
	SYR/INT	AAA	17	413	15	2	0	1	99.2	101	8	19	2	1	57	5	2	5	1	50	40	3	8	.273	0	3.61
89	SYR/INT	AAA	26	403	8	2	0	7	95.0	102	4	11	0	3	58	4	4	1	1	43	31	8	5	.615	0	2.94
90	PIT/NL		9	50	0	0	0	6	12.2	11	2	4	2	0	5	1	0	1	0	5	5	1	0	1.000	0	3.55

Ross, Mark Joseph (continued)

YR	TM/LG	CL	G	TBF	GS	CG	SHO	GF	IP	H	HR	BB	IBB	HB	SO	SH	SF	WP	BK	R	ER	W	L	PCT	SV	ERA
	BUF/AMA	AAA	47	298	0	0	0	36	71.1	73	1	12	6	2	35	14	5	0		23	16	6	8	.429	11	2.02
91	RIC/INT	AAA	39	338	1	0	0	22	82.1	84	2	13	7	1	50	8	5	1	0	35	32	3	6	.333	9	3.50
15 YR TOTALS			**23**	**146**	**0**	**0**	**0**	**13**	**36.1**	**30**	**5**	**10**	**3**	**0**	**13**	**1**	**1**	**3**	**0**	**19**	**17**	**2**	**2**	**.500**	**1**	**4.21**

Ruffin, Bruce Wayne — bats both — throws left — b.10/4/63

YR	TM/LG	CL	G	TBF	GS	CG	SHO	GF	IP	H	HR	BB	IBB	HB	SO	SH	SF	WP	BK	R	ER	W	L	PCT	SV	ERA
85	CLE/FSL	A+	14	399	14	3	1	0	97.0	87	2	34	1	2	74	2	1	3	1	33	31	5	5	.500	0	2.88
86	REA/EAS	AA	16	380	13	4	2	0	90.1	89	3	26	1	0	68	1	4	2	0	41	33	8	4	.667	0	3.29
	PHI/NL		21	600	21	6	0	0	146.1	138	6	44	6	1	70	2	4	0	1	53	40	9	4	.692	0	2.46
87	PHI/NL		35	884	35	3	1	0	204.2	236	17	73	4	2	93	8	10	6	0	118	99	11	14	.440	0	4.35
88	PHI/NL		55	646	15	3	0	14	144.1	151	7	80	6	3	82	10	3	12	0	86	71	6	10	.375	3	4.43
89	SW/INT	AAA	9	225	9	0	0	0	50.0	44	2	39	1	2	44	2	2	9	0	28	26	5	1	.833	0	4.68
	PHI/NL		24	576	23	1	0	0	125.2	152	10	62	6	0	70	8	1	8	0	69	62	6	10	.375	0	4.44
90	PHI/NL		32	678	25	2	1	1	149.0	178	14	62	7	1	79	10	6	3	2	99	89	6	13	.316	0	5.38
91	SCR/INT	AAA	13	337	13	1	0	0	75.1	82	4	41	1	0	50	5	3	3	0	43	39	4	5	.444	0	4.66
	PHI/NL		31	508	15	1	1	2	119.0	125	6	38	3	1	85	6	4	4	0	52	50	4	7	.364	0	3.78
6 YR TOTALS			**198**	**3892**	**134**	**16**	**3**	**17**	**889.0**	**980**	**60**	**359**	**32**	**8**	**479**	**44**	**28**	**33**	**3**	**477**	**411**	**42**	**58**	**.420**	**3**	**4.16**

Ruskin, Scott Drew — bats right — throws left — b.6/8/63

YR	TM/LG	CL	G	TBF	GS	CG	SHO	GF	IP	H	HR	BB	IBB	HB	SO	SH	SF	WP	BK	R	ER	W	L	PCT	SV	ERA
89	SAL/CAR	A+	14	359	13	3	0	0	84.2	71	5	33	0	4	92	1	1	6	4	35	21	4	5	.444	1	2.23
	HAR/EAS	AA	12	278	10	2	0	0	63.0	64	5	32	0	1	56	2	3	2	2	38	34	2	3	.400	0	4.86
90	PIT/NL		44	221	0	0	0	8	47.2	50	2	28	3	2	34	3	2	3	1	21	16	2	2	.500	2	3.02
	MON/NL		23	115	0	0	0	4	27.2	25	2	10	3	0	23	2	0	0	0	7	7	1	0	1.000	0	2.28
	YEAR		67	336	0	0	0	12	75.1	75	4	38	6	2	57	5	2	3	1	28	23	3	2	.600	2	2.75
91	MON/NL		64	275	0	0	0	24	63.2	57	4	30	2	3	46	5	0	5	0	31	30	4	4	.500	6	4.24
2 YR TOTALS			**131**	**611**	**0**	**0**	**0**	**36**	**139.0**	**132**	**8**	**68**	**8**	**5**	**103**	**10**	**2**	**8**	**1**	**59**	**53**	**7**	**6**	**.538**	**8**	**3.43**

Russell, Jeffrey Lee "Jeff" — bats right — throws right — b.9/2/61

YR	TM/LG	CL	G	TBF	GS	CG	SHO	GF	IP	H	HR	BB	IBB	HB	SO	SH	SF	WP	BK	R	ER	W	L	PCT	SV	ERA
83	CIN/NL		10	282	10	2	0	0	68.1	58	7	22	3	0	40	6	5	1	1	30	23	4	5	.444	0	3.03
84	CIN/NL		33	787	30	4	2	1	181.2	186	15	65	8	4	101	8	3	3	3	97	86	6	18	.250	0	4.26
85	DEN/AMA	AAA	16	440	16	1	1	0	102.1	94	5	46	1	1	81	6	4	5	3	51	48	6	4	.600	0	4.22
	OC/AMA	AAA	2	53	2	0	0	0	13.0	11	1	5	0	0	13	0	0	1	0	4	4	1	0	1.000	0	2.77
	TEX/AL		13	295	13	0	0	0	62.0	85	10	27	1	2	44	1	3	2	0	55	52	3	6	.333	0	7.55
86	OC/AMA	AAA	11	306	11	1	0	0	70.2	63	5	38	0	2	34	4	2	1	1	32	31	4	1	.800	0	3.95
	TEX/AL		37	338	0	0	0	9	82.0	74	11	31	2	1	54	1	2	5	0	40	31	5	2	.714	2	3.40
87	CHA/FSL	A+	2	44	2	0	0	0	11.0	8	1	5	0	0	3	0	1	0	0	3	3	0	0	.000	0	2.45
	OC/AMA	AAA	4	23	0	0	0	2	6.1	5	0	1	0	0	5	0	1	0	1	1	1	0	0	.000	0	1.42
	TEX/AL		52	442	2	0	0	12	97.1	109	9	52	5	2	56	0	5	4	0	56	48	5	4	.556	3	4.44
88	TEX/AL		34	793	24	5	0	1	188.2	183	15	66	3	7	88	4	3	5	7	86	80	10	9	.526	0	3.82
89	TEX/AL		71	278	0	0	0	66	72.2	45	4	24	5	3	77	1	3	6	0	21	16	6	4	.600	38	1.98
90	CHA/FSL	A+	1	1	0	0	0	0	0.0	1	0	0	0	0	0	0	0	0	0	1	1	0	0	.000	0	0.00
	TEX/AL		27	111	0	0	0	22	25.1	23	1	16	5	0	16	3	1	2	0	15	12	1	5	.167	10	4.26
91	TEX/AL		68	336	0	0	0	56	79.1	71	11	26	1	1	52	3	4	6	0	36	29	6	4	.600	30	3.29
9 YR TOTALS			**345**	**3662**	**79**	**11**	**2**	**167**	**857.1**	**834**	**83**	**329**	**33**	**20**	**528**	**27**	**29**	**36**	**12**	**436**	**377**	**46**	**57**	**.447**	**83**	**3.96**

Ryan, Lynn Nolan "Nolan" — bats right — throws right — b.1/31/47

YR	TM/LG	CL	G	TBF	GS	CG	SHO	GF	IP	H	HR	BB	IBB	HB	SO	SH	SF	WP	BK	R	ER	W	L	PCT	SV	ERA
66	NY/NL		2	17	1	0	0	0	3.0	5	1	3	1	0	6	0	0	1	0	5	5	0	1	.000	0	15.00
68	NY/NL		21	559	18	3	0	1	134.0	93	12	75	4	4	133	12	4	7	0	50	46	6	9	.400	0	3.09
69	NY/NL		25	375	10	2	0	4	89.1	60	3	53	3	1	92	2	2	1	3	38	35	6	3	.667	1	3.53
70	NY/NL		27	570	19	5	2	4	131.2	86	10	97	2	4	125	8	4	6	0	59	50	7	11	.389	1	3.42
71	NY/NL		30	705	26	3	0	1	152.0	125	8	116	4	15	137	3	0	6	1	78	67	10	14	.417	0	3.97
72	CAL/AL		39	1154	39	20	9	0	284.0	166	14	157	4	10	329	11	3	18	0	80	72	19	16	.543	0	2.28
73	CAL/AL		41	1355	39	26	4	2	326.0	238	18	162	2	7	383	7	7	15	0	113	104	21	16	.568	1	2.87
74	CAL/AL		42	1392	41	26	3	1	332.2	221	18	202	3	9	367	12	4	9	0	127	107	22	16	.579	0	2.89
75	CAL/AL		28	864	28	10	5	0	198.0	152	13	132	0	7	186	4	7	12	0	90	76	14	12	.538	0	3.45
76	CAL/AL		39	1196	39	21	7	0	284.1	193	13	183	2	9	327	13	4	5	2	117	106	17	18	.486	0	3.36
77	CAL/AL		37	1272	37	22	4	0	299.0	198	12	204	7	9	341	22	10	21	3	110	92	19	16	.543	0	2.77
78	CAL/AL		31	1008	31	14	3	0	234.2	183	12	148	7	3	260	11	14	13	2	106	97	10	13	.435	0	3.72
79	CAL/AL		34	937	34	17	5	0	222.2	169	15	114	3	6	223	8	10	9	0	104	89	16	14	.533	0	3.60
80	HOU/NL		35	982	35	4	2	0	233.2	205	10	98	3	3	200	7	7	10	1	100	87	11	10	.524	0	3.35
81	HOU/NL		21	605	21	5	3	0	149.0	99	2	68	1	2	140	5	3	16	2	34	28	11	5	.688	0	1.69
82	HOU/NL		35	1050	35	10	3	0	250.1	196	20	109	3	4	245	9	3	18	1	100	88	16	12	.571	0	3.16
83	HOU/NL		29	804	29	5	2	0	196.1	134	9	101	3	4	183	7	5	5	1	74	65	14	9	.609	0	2.98
84	HOU/NL		30	760	30	5	2	0	183.2	143	12	69	2	4	197	4	6	6	3	78	62	12	11	.522	0	3.04
85	HOU/NL		35	983	35	4	0	0	232.0	205	12	95	8	9	209	11	12	14	2	108	98	10	12	.455	0	3.80
86	HOU/NL		30	729	30	1	0	0	178.0	119	14	82	5	4	194	5	4	15	0	72	66	12	8	.600	0	3.34
87	HOU/NL		34	873	34	0	0	0	211.2	154	14	87	2	4	270	9	1	10	2	75	65	8	16	.333	0	2.76
88	HOU/NL		33	930	33	4	1	0	220.0	186	18	87	3	9	228	10	8	10	7	98	86	12	11	.522	0	3.52
89	TEX/AL		32	988	32	6	2	0	239.1	162	17	98	3	9	301	4	5	19	1	96	85	16	10	.615	0	3.20
90	TEX/AL		30	818	30	5	2	0	204.0	137	18	74	2	7	232	3	5	9	1	86	78	13	9	.591	0	3.44

(continued)

Ryan, Lynn Nolan "Nolan" (continued)

YR	TM/LG	CL	G	TBF	GS	CG	SHO	GF	IP	H	HR	BB	IBB	HB	SO	SH	SF	WP	BK	R	ER	W	L	PCT	SV	ERA
91	TEX/AL		27	683	27	2	2	0	173.0	102	12	72	0	5	203	3	9	8	0	58	56	12	6	.667	0	2.91
25 YR TOTALS			767	21609	733	220	61	13	5162.1	3731	307	2686	78	145	5511	197	137	265	33	2056	1810	314	278	.530	3	3.16

Saberhagen, Bret William — bats right — throws right — b.4/11/64

YR	TM/LG	CL	G	TBF	GS	CG	SHO	GF	IP	H	HR	BB	IBB	HB	SO	SH	SF	WP	BK	R	ER	W	L	PCT	SV	ERA
84	KC/AL		38	634	18	2	1	9	157.2	138	13	36	4	2	73	8	5	7	1	71	61	10	11	.476	1	3.48
85	KC/AL		32	931	32	10	1	0	235.1	211	19	38	1	1	158	9	7	1	3	79	75	20	6	.769	0	2.87
86	KC/AL		30	652	25	4	2	4	156.0	165	15	29	1	2	112	3	3	1	1	77	72	7	12	.368	0	4.15
87	KC/AL		33	1048	33	15	4	0	257.0	246	27	53	2	6	163	8	5	6	1	99	96	18	10	.643	0	3.36
88	KC/AL		35	1089	35	9	0	0	260.2	271	18	59	5	4	171	8	10	9	0	122	110	14	16	.467	0	3.80
89	KC/AL		36	1021	35	12	4	0	262.1	209	13	43	6	2	193	9	6	8	1	74	63	23	6	.793	0	2.16
90	KC/AL		20	561	20	5	0	0	135.0	146	9	28	1	1	87	4	4	1	0	52	49	5	9	.357	0	3.27
91	KC/AL		28	789	28	7	2	0	196.1	165	12	45	5	9	136	8	3	8	1	76	67	13	8	.619	0	3.07
8 YR TOTALS			252	6725	226	64	14	13	1660.1	1551	126	331	25	27	1093	57	43	41	8	650	593	110	78	.585	1	3.21

St.Claire, Randy Anthony — bats right — throws right — b.8/23/60

YR	TM/LG	CL	G	TBF	GS	CG	SHO	GF	IP	H	HR	BB	IBB	HB	SO	SH	SF	WP	BK	R	ER	W	L	PCT	SV	ERA
79	CAL/PIO	R+	6	0	6	0	0	0	33.0	30	0	15	0	0	17	0	0	0	0	22	16	1	2	.333	0	4.36
80	CAL/PIO	R+	21	0	4	0	0	0	57.0	65	0	23	0	0	51	0	0	0	0	36	27	5	7	.417	0	4.26
81	JAM/NYP	A–	13	0	3	1	1	0	51.0	53	0	17	0	0	36	0	0	0	0	22	11	4	1	.800	0	1.94
82	SJ/CAL	A+	9	0	8	2	0	0	61.0	58	0	20	0	0	44	0	0	0	0	32	28	2	5	.286	0	4.13
	WPB/FSL	A+	19	0	5	2	0	0	65.0	74	0	17	0	0	38	0	0	0	0	41	38	3	8	.273	2	5.26
83	WPB/FSL	A+	42	0	0	0	0	0	98.0	72	0	31	0	0	77	0	0	0	0	33	23	5	7	.417	11	2.11
84	JAC/SOU	AA	48	316	0	0	0	40	75.0	64	4	29	14	2	56	11	2	2	0	35	24	10	7	.588	15	2.88
	IND/AMA	AAA	13	73	0	0	0	13	17.2	15	0	6	1	0	17	0	1	1	0	2	2	1	1	.500	8	1.02
	MON/NL		4	38	0	0	0	4	8.0	11	0	2	1	1	4	1	2	0	0	5	4	0	0	.000	0	4.50
85	IND/AMA	AAA	11	80	0	0	0	10	19.2	21	1	3	1	0	11	1	1	1	0	5	4	0	1	.000	6	1.83
	MON/NL		42	294	0	0	0	14	68.2	69	3	26	7	1	25	6	1	1	0	32	30	5	3	.625	0	3.93
86	IND/AMA	AAA	57	423	0	0	0	35	99.1	105	10	29	4	4	72	4	3	4	1	49	44	5	7	.417	15	3.99
	MON/NL		11	76	0	0	0	2	19.0	13	2	6	1	0	21	0	0	1	0	5	5	2	0	1.000	1	2.37
87	IND/AMA	AAA	18	82	0	0	0	14	20.2	12	1	12	1	0	15	1	2	0	0	5	5	0	1	.000	7	2.18
	MON/NL		44	282	0	0	0	24	67.0	64	9	20	4	1	43	1	3	4	0	31	30	3	3	.500	1	4.03
88	MON/NL		6	38	0	0	0	3	7.1	11	2	5	1	0	6	0	1	0	1	5	5	0	0	.000	0	6.14
	IND/AMA	AAA	27	125	0	0	0	21	31.1	25	2	7	1	2	21	2	3	3	1	13	10	0	3	.000	8	2.87
	NAS/AMA	AAA	9	37	0	0	0	6	9.0	10	0	2	0	0	4	0	0	0	0	2	2	0	0	.000	5	2.00
	CIN/NL		10	60	0	0	0	6	13.2	13	3	8	3	0	8	0	1	0	0	8	4	1	0	1.000	0	2.63
	YEAR		16	98	0	0	0	9	21.0	24	5	13	3	0	14	0	2	0	0	13	9	1	0	1.000	0	3.86
89	MIN/AL		14	98	0	0	0	8	22.1	19	4	10	2	2	14	1	1	1	0	13	13	1	0	1.000	1	5.24
	POR/PCL	AAA	27	191	1	0	0	17	45.1	39	1	17	1	0	48	0	1	6	1	21	16	4	0	1.000	3	3.18
90	TUC/PCL	AAA	23	161	0	0	0	16	31.1	45	3	21	5	1	16	1	3	6	0	22	19	4	3	.571	0	5.46
	OC/AMA	AAA	29	221	0	0	0	13	53.2	45	3	12	1	3	68	2	0	5	0	15	12	1	2	.333	1	2.01
91	RIC/INT	AAA	29	245	0	0	0	14	68.0	39	1	11	2	4	60	3	1	7	0	10	9	6	2	.750	2	1.19
	ATL/NL		19	123	0	0	0	5	28.2	31	4	9	3	0	30	3	1	4	0	17	13	0	0	.000	0	4.08
7 YR TOTALS			150	1009	0	0	0	66	234.2	231	27	83	21	5	151	12	10	11	1	115	104	12	6	.667	9	3.99

Salkeld, Roger W. — bats right — throws right — b.3/6/71 — System SEA/AL

YR	TM/LG	CL	G	TBF	GS	CG	SHO	GF	IP	H	HR	BB	IBB	HB	SO	SH	SF	WP	BK	R	ER	W	L	PCT	SV	ERA
89	BEL/NWL	A–	8	168	6	0	0	1	42.0	27	0	10	0	4	55	0	1	3	3	17	6	2	2	.500	0	1.29
90	SB/CAL	A+	25	677	25	2	0	0	153.1	140	3	83	0	3	167	7	1	9	2	77	58	11	5	.688	0	3.40
91	JAC/SOU	AA	23	634	23	5	0	0	153.2	131	9	55	1	10	159	5	5	12	2	56	52	8	8	.500	0	3.05
	CAL/PCL	AAA	4	90	4	0	0	0	19.1	18	2	13	0	4	21	1	0	1	0	16	11	2	1	.667	0	5.12

Sampen, William Albert "Bill" — bats right — throws right — b.1/18/63

YR	TM/LG	CL	G	TBF	GS	CG	SHO	GF	IP	H	HR	BB	IBB	HB	SO	SH	SF	WP	BK	R	ER	W	L	PCT	SV	ERA
85	WAT/NYP	A–	5	48	0	0	0	2	10.0	9	0	7	0	1	11	1	1	2	0	3	2	0	0	.000	1	1.80
86	WAT/NYP	A–	9	130	5	0	0	3	29.2	27	0	13	0	1	29	1	2	3	0	18	14	0	3	.000	0	4.25
87	SAL/CAR	A+	26	650	26	2	1	0	152.1	126	16	72	1	7	137	5	5	3	2	77	65	9	8	.529	0	3.84
88	SAL/CAR	A+	8	217	8	1	0	0	51.1	47	4	14	0	0	59	1	1	1	2	22	19	3	3	.500	0	3.33
	HAR/EAS	AA	13	349	12	3	0	0	82.2	72	3	27	1	2	65	1	2	2	2	38	34	6	3	.667	0	3.70
89	HAR/EAS	AA	26	691	26	6	0	0	165.2	148	8	40	3	5	134	7	8	6	0	75	59	11	9	.550	0	3.21
90	MON/NL		59	394	4	0	0	26	90.1	94	7	33	6	2	69	5	3	4	0	34	30	12	7	.632	2	2.99
91	MON/NL		43	409	8	0	0	8	92.1	96	13	46	7	3	52	4	4	3	1	49	41	9	5	.643	0	4.00
	IND/AMA	AAA	7	170	7	0	0	0	39.2	33	1	19	0	1	41	1	1	2	0	13	9	4	0	1.000	0	2.04
2 YR TOTALS			102	803	12	0	0	34	182.2	190	20	79	13	5	121	9	7	7	1	83	71	21	12	.636	2	3.50

Sanderson, Scott Douglas — bats right — throws right — b.7/22/56

YR	TM/LG	CL	G	TBF	GS	CG	SHO	GF	IP	H	HR	BB	IBB	HB	SO	SH	SF	WP	BK	R	ER	W	L	PCT	SV	ERA
78	MON/NL		10	251	9	1	1	1	61.0	52	3	21	0	1	50	3	2	2	0	20	17	4	2	.667	0	2.51
79	MON/NL		34	696	24	5	3	3	168.0	148	16	54	4	3	138	5	7	2	3	69	64	9	8	.529	1	3.43
80	MON/NL		33	875	33	7	3	0	211.1	206	18	56	3	3	125	11	5	6	0	76	73	16	11	.593	0	3.11
81	MON/NL		22	560	22	4	1	0	137.1	122	10	31	2	1	77	7	4	2	0	50	45	9	7	.563	0	2.95
82	MON/NL		32	922	32	7	0	0	224.0	212	24	58	3	4	158	9	6	2	1	98	86	12	12	.500	0	3.46
83	MON/NL		18	346	16	0	0	0	81.1	98	12	20	0	0	55	2	2	1	0	50	42	6	7	.462	1	4.65
84	LOD/CAL	A+	1	0	1	0	0	0	5.0	7	1	0	0	0	5	0	0	0	0	2	2	0	1	.000	0	3.60

Sanderson, Scott Douglas (continued)

YR	TM/LG	CL	G	TBF	GS	CG	SHO	GF	IP	H	HR	BB	IBB	HB	SO	SH	SF	WP	BK	R	ER	W	L	PCT	SV	ERA
	CHI/NL		24	571	24	3	0	0	140.2	140	5	24	3	2	76	6	8	3	2	54	49	8	5	.615	0	3.14
85	CHI/NL		19	480	19	2	0	0	121.0	100	13	27	4	0	80	7	7	1	0	49	42	5	6	.455	0	3.12
86	CHI/NL		37	697	28	1	1	2	169.2	165	21	37	2	2	124	6	5	3	1	85	79	9	11	.450	1	4.19
87	CHI/NL		32	631	22	0	0	5	144.2	156	23	50	5	3	106	4	5	1	0	72	69	8	9	.471	2	4.29
88	PEO/MID	A	1	20	1	0	0	0	5.0	4	0	0	0	0	3	0	0	0	2	1	0	0	0	.000	0	0.00
	IOW/AMA	AAA	3	55	3	0	0	0	13.1	13	1	2	0	1	4	0	0	0	0	7	7	1	0	1.000	0	4.72
	CHI/NL		11	62	0	0	0	3	15.1	13	1	3	1	0	6	0	3	0	0	9	9	1	2	.333	0	5.28
89	CHI/NL		37	611	23	2	0	2	146.1	155	16	31	6	2	86	8	3	1	3	69	64	11	9	.550	0	3.94
90	OAK/AL		34	885	34	2	1	0	206.1	205	27	66	2	4	128	4	8	7	1	99	89	17	11	.607	0	3.88
91	NY/AL		34	837	34	2	2	0	208.0	200	22	29	0	3	130	5	5	4	1	95	88	16	10	.615	0	3.81
14 YR TOTALS			**377**	**8424**	**320**	**36**	**12**	**17**	**2035.0**	**1972**	**211**	**507**	**37**	**27**	**1339**	**77**	**69**	**34**	**12**	**895**	**816**	**131**	**110**	**.544**	**5**	**3.61**

Sanford, Meredith Leroy "Mo" — bats right — throws right — b.12/24/66

YR	TM/LG	CL	G	TBF	GS	CG	SHO	GF	IP	H	HR	BB	IBB	HB	SO	SH	SF	WP	BK	R	ER	W	L	PCT	SV	ERA
88	RED/GCL	R	14	217	11	0	0	1	53.0	34	6	25	1	0	64	0	1	3	4	24	19	3	4	.429	1	3.23
89	GRE/SAL	A	25	629	25	3	1	0	153.2	112	8	64	0	2	160	4	2	6	3	52	48	12	6	.667	0	2.81
90	CR/MID	A	25	628	25	2	1	0	157.2	112	15	55	1	4	180	3	2	8	1	50	48	13	4	.765	0	2.74
91	CHT/SOU	AA	16	395	16	1	1	0	95.1	69	7	55	2	1	124	4	3	1	0	37	29	7	4	.636	0	2.74
	NAS/AMA	AAA	5	140	5	2	2	0	33.2	19	0	22	0	1	38	0	0	3	0	7	6	3	0	1.000	0	1.60
	CIN/NL		5	118	5	0	0	0	28.0	19	3	15	1	1	31	0	0	4	0	14	12	1	2	.333	0	3.86

Sauveur, Richard Daniel "Rich" — bats left — throws left — b.11/23/63

YR	TM/LG	CL	G	TBF	GS	CG	SHO	GF	IP	H	HR	BB	IBB	HB	SO	SH	SF	WP	BK	R	ER	W	L	PCT	SV	ERA
83	WAT/NYP	A—	16	0	12	1	0	0	93.0	80	6	31	0	1	73	0	0	2	0	41	24	7	5	.583	0	2.32
84	PW/CAR	A+	10	240	10	0	0	0	54.2	43	5	31	0	1	54	2	1	3	0	22	19	3	3	.500	0	3.13
	NAS/EAS	AA	10	291	10	2	2	0	70.2	54	4	34	1	3	48	4	1	2	4	27	23	5	3	.625	0	2.93
85	NAS/EAS	AA	25	666	25	4	2	0	157.1	146	7	78	2	3	85	9	6	7	4	73	62	9	10	.474	0	3.55
86	NAS/EAS	AA	5	141	5	2	1	0	38.0	21	1	11	0	1	28	0	1	1	1	5	5	3	1	.750	0	1.18
	PIT/NL		3	57	3	0	0	0	12.0	17	3	6	2	0	6	2	1	0	0	8	8	0	0	.000	0	6.00
	HAW/PCL	AAA	14	391	14	6	1	0	92.0	73	3	45	1	6	68	2	4	0	8	40	31	7	6	.538	0	3.03
87	HAR/EAS	AA	30	825	27	7	1	0	195.0	174	9	96	3	9	160	7	9	9	7	71	62	13	6	.684	0	2.86
88	JAC/SOU	AA	8	32	0	0	0	4	6.2	7	0	5	0	0	8	0	0	0	0	5	3	0	2	.000	1	4.05
	IND/AMA	AAA	43	318	3	0	0	18	81.1	60	8	28	5	1	58	5	1	3	3	26	22	7	4	.636	10	2.43
	MON/NL		4	14	0	0	0	4	3.0	3	1	2	0	0	4	0	0	0	0	2	2	0	0	.000	0	6.00
89	IND/AMA	AAA	8	44	0	0	0	4	9.2	10	1	6	0	0	8	0	1	0	0	8	8	0	1	.000	0	7.45
90	MIA/FSL	A+	11	178	6	1	0	2	40.2	41	2	17	0	4	34	0	2	0	3	16	15	0	0	.000	0	3.32
	IND/AMA	AAA	14	232	7	0	0	0	56.0	45	1	25	0	3	24	2	2	1	3	14	12	2	2	.500	0	1.93
91	NY/NL		6	19	0	0	0	0	3.1	7	1	2	0	0	4	2	0	0	0	4	4	0	0	.000	0	10.80
	TID/INT	AAA	42	188	0	0	0	21	45.1	31	0	23	5	0	49	4	0	3	3	14	12	2	2	.500	6	2.38
3 YR TOTALS			**13**	**90**	**3**	**0**	**0**	**0**	**18.1**	**27**	**5**	**10**	**2**	**0**	**13**	**3**	**0**	**0**	**2**	**14**	**14**	**0**	**0**	**.000**	**0**	**6.87**

Scanlan, Robert Guy "Bob" — bats right — throws right — b.8/9/66

YR	TM/LG	CL	G	TBF	GS	CG	SHO	GF	IP	H	HR	BB	IBB	HB	SO	SH	SF	WP	BK	R	ER	W	L	PCT	SV	ERA
84	PHI/GCL	R	13	173	6	0	0	2	33.1	43	0	30	0	0	17	3	2	4	1	31	24	0	2	.000	0	6.48
85	SPA/SAL	A	26	669	25	4	1	0	152.1	160	7	53	3	6	108	3	6	8	0	95	70	8	12	.400	0	4.14
86	CLE/FSL	A+	24	559	22	5	0	0	125.2	146	1	45	4	5	51	6	4	4	1	73	58	8	12	.400	0	4.15
87	REA/EAS	AA	27	718	26	3	1	0	164.0	187	12	55	3	11	91	9	9	4	1	98	93	15	5	.750	0	5.10
88	MAI/INT	AA	28	713	27	4	1	0	161.0	181	10	50	7	8	79	13	7	17	8	110	100	5	18	.217	0	5.59
89	REA/EAS	AA	31	531	17	0	0	8	118.1	124	9	58	1	5	63	3	5	12	1	88	76	8	10	.375	0	5.78
90	SW/INT	AAA	23	565	23	1	0	0	130.0	128	11	59	3	7	74	3	4	3	0	79	70	8	11	.421	0	4.85
91	IOW/AMA	AAA	4	79	3	0	0	1	18.1	14	0	10	1	0	15	2	0	3	0	8	6	2	0	1.000	0	2.95
	CHI/NL		40	482	13	0	0	16	111.0	114	5	40	3	3	44	12	4	5	1	60	48	7	8	.467	1	3.89

Schatzeder, Daniel Ernest "Dan" — bats left — throws left — b.12/1/54

YR	TM/LG	CL	G	TBF	GS	CG	SHO	GF	IP	H	HR	BB	IBB	HB	SO	SH	SF	WP	BK	R	ER	W	L	PCT	SV	ERA
77	MON/NL		6	93	3	1	1	0	21.2	16	0	13	0	0	14	0	1	1	0	6	6	2	1	.667	0	2.49
78	MON/NL		29	586	18	2	0	1	143.2	108	10	68	5	2	69	5	4	4	3	54	49	7	7	.500	0	3.07
79	MON/NL		32	677	21	3	0	4	162.0	136	17	59	2	1	106	10	3	6	0	57	51	10	5	.667	0	2.83
80	DET/AL		32	794	26	9	2	2	192.2	178	23	58	9	3	94	6	3	8	0	88	86	11	13	.458	0	4.02
81	DET/AL		17	318	14	1	0	1	71.1	74	13	29	1	2	20	4	4	3	0	49	48	6	8	.429	0	6.06
82	SF/NL		13	155	3	0	0	1	33.1	47	3	12	4	0	18	1	1	2	0	30	27	1	4	.200	0	7.29
	MON/NL		26	152	1	0	0	10	36.0	37	1	12	5	2	15	2	2	2	0	16	14	0	2	.000	0	3.50
	YEAR		39	307	4	0	0	11	69.1	84	4	24	9	2	33	3	3	4	0	46	41	1	6	.143	0	5.32
83	MON/NL		58	369	2	0	0	23	87.0	88	3	25	6	5	48	5	2	5	0	44	41	7	7	.500	0	2.71
84	MON/NL		36	547	14	1	1	6	136.0	112	13	36	1	2	89	4	4	3	0	58	48	6	2	.750	0	5.31
85	IND/AMA	AAA	1	12	1	0	0	0	3.0	2	0	1	0	0	0	0	0	0	0	0	0	0	0	.000	0	0.00
	MON/NL		24	431	15	1	0	2	104.1	101	13	31	0	0	64	0	7	3	0	52	44	3	5	.375	0	3.80
86	MON/NL		30	244	1	0	0	9	59.0	53	6	19	2	0	33	2	2	1	0	29	21	3	3	.500	1	3.20
	PHI/NL		25	131	1	0	0	10	29.1	28	5	16	7	0	14	3	1	0	0	14	11	3	3	.500	2	3.38
	YEAR		55	375	1	0	0	19	88.1	81	9	35	2	4	28	2	4	1	0	43	32	6	5	.545	3	3.26
87	PHI/NL		26	164	0	0	0	8	37.2	40	4	14	7	0	28	2	4	0	0	21	17	3	0	.750	0	4.06
	MIN/AL		30	208	1	0	0	5	43.2	64	8	18	3	1	30	4	2	0	0	37	31	3	1	.750	0	6.39
	YEAR		56	372	1	0	0	13	81.1	104	12	32	10	1	58	6	6	0	0	58	48	6	2	.750	0	5.31
88	CLE/AL		15	77	0	0	0	8	16.0	26	6	2	0	1	10	0	0	2	0	19	17	0	2	.000	3	9.56

(continued)

Schatzeder, Daniel Ernest "Dan" (continued)

YR	TM/LG	CL	G	TBF	GS	CG	SHO	GF	IP	H	HR	BB	IBB	HB	SO	SH	SF	WP	BK	R	ER	W	L	PCT	SV	ERA
	POR/PCL	AAA	13	356	12	4	1	1	86.2	82	7	24	0	3	55	2	0	2	0	26	25	6	4	.600	0	2.60
	MIN/AL		10	44	0	0	0	2	10.1	8	1	5	1	1	7	1	0	0	0	2	2	0	1	.000	0	1.74
	YEAR		25	121	0	0	0	10	26.1	34	7	7	1	2	17	1	0	0	0	21	19	0	3	.000	0	6.49
89	TUC/PCL	AAA	11	74	1	0	0	5	16.0	15	1	10	1	1	15	0	0	0	0	8	7	0	2	.000	1	3.94
	HOU/NL		36	259	0	0	0	7	56.2	64	2	28	6	3	46	5	0	7	1	33	28	4	1	.800	1	4.45
90	HOU/NL		45	264	2	0	0	13	64.0	61	2	23	4	0	37	2	5	2	0	23	17	1	3	.250	0	2.39
	NY/NL		6	19	0	0	0	3	5.2	5	0	0	0	0	2	0	0	0	0	0	0	0	0	.000	0	0.00
	YEAR		51	283	2	0	0	16	69.2	66	2	23	4	0	39	2	5	2	0	23	17	1	3	.250	0	2.20
91	KC/AL		8	37	0	0	0	2	6.2	11	0	7	1	0	4	0	0	0	0	9	7	0	0	.000	0	9.45
	TID/INT	AAA	9	73	1	0	0	0	14.2	22	1	13	3	0	10	2	0	0	1	13	12	0	0	.000	0	7.36
15 YR TOTALS			**504**	**5569**	**121**	**18**	**4**	**117**	**1317.0**	**1257**	**128**	**475**	**64**	**23**	**748**	**59**	**41**	**56**	**5**	**617**	**548**	**69**	**68**	**.504**	**10**	**3.74**

Schilling, Curtis Montague "Curt" — bats right — throws right — b.11/14/66

YR	TM/LG	CL	G	TBF	GS	CG	SHO	GF	IP	H	HR	BB	IBB	HB	SO	SH	SF	WP	BK	R	ER	W	L	PCT	SV	ERA
86	ELM/NYP	A-	16	399	15	2	1	1	93.2	92	3	30	1	2	75	4	1	4	2	34	27	7	3	.700	0	2.59
87	GRE/SAL	A	29	777	28	7	3	1	184.0	179	10	65	8	2	189	5	3	10	2	96	78	8	15	.348	0	3.82
88	NB/EAS	AA	21	440	17	4	1	1	106.0	91	3	40	1	0	62	4	3	2	6	44	35	8	5	.615	0	2.97
	CHA/SOU	AA	7	189	7	2	1	0	45.1	36	3	23	0	0	32	6	0	3	2	19	16	5	2	.714	0	3.18
	BAL/AL		4	76	4	0	0	0	14.2	22	3	10	1	1	4	0	3	2	0	19	16	0	3	.000	0	9.82
89	ROC/INT	AAA	27	762	27	9	3	0	185.1	176	11	59	0	1	109	7	3	5	6	76	66	13	11	.542	0	3.21
	BAL/AL		5	38	1	0	0	0	8.2	10	2	3	0	0	6	0	0	1	0	6	6	0	1	.000	0	6.23
90	ROC/INT	AAA	15	374	14	1	0	0	87.1	95	10	25	1	2	83	4	0	0	2	46	38	4	4	.500	0	3.92
	BAL/AL		35	191	0	0	0	16	46.0	38	1	19	0	0	32	2	4	0	0	13	13	1	2	.333	3	2.54
91	TUC/PCL	AAA	13	99	0	0	0	5	23.2	16	0	12	1	0	21	1	0	0	0	9	9	0	3	.000	3	3.42
	HOU/NL		56	336	0	0	0	34	75.2	79	2	39	7	0	71	5	4	1	1	35	32	3	5	.375	8	3.81
4 YR TOTALS			**100**	**641**	**5**	**0**	**0**	**50**	**145.0**	**149**	**8**	**71**	**8**	**1**	**113**	**7**	**8**	**7**	**1**	**73**	**67**	**4**	**11**	**.267**	**11**	**4.16**

Schiraldi, Calvin Drew — bats right — throws right — b.6/16/62

YR	TM/LG	CL	G	TBF	GS	CG	SHO	GF	IP	H	HR	BB	IBB	HB	SO	SH	SF	WP	BK	R	ER	W	L	PCT	SV	ERA
84	NY/NL		5	80	3	0	0	0	17.1	20	3	10	0	0	16	0	0	0	0	13	11	0	2	.000	0	5.71
85	NY/NL		10	131	4	0	0	2	26.1	43	4	11	0	3	21	0	0	2	1	27	26	2	1	.667	0	8.89
86	BOS/AL		25	198	0	0	0	21	51.0	36	5	15	2	1	55	2	1	1	0	8	8	4	2	.667	9	1.41
87	BOS/AL		62	361	1	0	0	52	83.2	75	15	40	5	1	93	5	2	5	2	45	41	8	5	.615	6	4.41
88	CHI/NL		29	717	27	2	1	2	166.1	166	13	63	7	2	140	2	4	6	3	87	81	9	13	.409	0	4.38
89	CHI/NL		54	342	0	0	0	24	78.2	60	7	50	2	1	54	2	2	3	0	34	33	3	6	.333	4	3.78
	SD/NL		5	87	4	0	0	1	21.1	12	1	13	0	0	17	0	0	1	1	6	6	3	1	.750	0	2.53
	YEAR		59	429	4	0	0	25	100.0	72	8	63	2	1	71	2	2	4	1	40	39	6	7	.462	4	3.51
90	SD/NL		42	468	8	0	0	14	104.0	105	11	60	6	1	74	7	3	3	1	59	51	3	8	.273	1	4.41
91	TEX/AL		3	25	0	0	0	1	4.2	5	3	5	0	1	1	0	0	0	0	6	6	0	1	.000	0	11.57
	AST/GCL	R	15	272	7	1	0	2	59.1	56	2	37	0	4	64	3	0	7	5	36	23	4	3	.571	0	3.49
8 YR TOTALS			**235**	**2409**	**47**	**2**	**1**	**117**	**553.1**	**522**	**62**	**267**	**22**	**9**	**471**	**19**	**12**	**21**	**8**	**285**	**263**	**32**	**39**	**.451**	**21**	**4.28**

Schmidt, David Joseph "Dave" — bats right — throws right — b.4/22/57

YR	TM/LG	CL	G	TBF	GS	CG	SHO	GF	IP	H	HR	BB	IBB	HB	SO	SH	SF	WP	BK	R	ER	W	L	PCT	SV	ERA
81	TEX/AL		14	132	1	0	0	8	31.2	31	1	11	3	1	13	0	0	3	1	11	11	0	1	.000	1	3.13
82	TEX/AL		33	462	8	0	0	14	109.2	118	5	25	5	5	69	6	3	2	0	45	39	4	6	.400	6	3.20
83	TEX/AL		31	191	0	0	0	20	46.1	42	3	14	1	1	29	1	1	2	0	20	20	3	3	.500	2	3.88
84	TEX/AL		43	293	0	0	0	37	70.1	69	3	20	2	0	46	7	3	4	0	30	20	6	6	.500	2	2.56
85	TEX/AL		51	356	4	1	1	35	85.2	81	6	22	4	0	46	3	2	1	0	36	30	7	6	.538	5	3.15
86	CHI/AL		49	394	1	0	0	21	92.1	94	10	27	7	5	67	3	3	5	0	37	34	3	6	.333	8	3.31
87	BAL/AL		35	515	14	2	2	7	124.0	128	13	26	2	1	70	0	1	2	0	57	52	10	5	.667	1	3.77
88	BAL/AL		41	541	9	0	0	11	129.2	129	14	38	5	2	67	5	3	3	0	58	49	8	5	.615	2	3.40
89	BAL/AL		38	686	26	2	0	5	156.2	196	24	36	2	2	46	9	7	3	1	102	99	10	13	.435	0	5.69
90	JAC/SOU	AA	3	24	2	0	0	0	6.0	4	1	0	0	4	0	0	0	0	0	3	3	0	1	.000	0	4.50
	MON/NL		34	213	0	0	0	20	48.0	58	3	13	4	1	22	4	1	1	0	26	23	3	3	.500	13	4.31
91	WPB/FSL	A+	9	58	4	0	0	2	14.0	12	0	0	0	0	11	0	1	1	0	9	5	1	1	.500	1	3.21
	IND/AMA	AAA	13	87	4	0	0	1	20.2	19	2	8	1	0	9	0	1	0	2	13	9	0	1	.000	0	3.92
	MON/NL		4	24	0	0	0	2	4.1	9	2	2	1	0	3	1	0	0	0	5	5	0	1	.000	0	10.38
	OC/AMA	AAA	11	75	0	0	0	6	16.1	20	1	9	5	0	10	2	0	0	0	4	3	0	2	.000	1	1.65
11 YR TOTALS			**373**	**3807**	**63**	**5**	**3**	**179**	**898.2**	**955**	**84**	**234**	**47**	**18**	**478**	**39**	**24**	**27**	**3**	**427**	**382**	**54**	**55**	**.495**	**50**	**3.83**

Schooler, Michael Ralph "Mike" — bats right — throws right — b.8/10/62

YR	TM/LG	CL	G	TBF	GS	CG	SHO	GF	IP	H	HR	BB	IBB	HB	SO	SH	SF	WP	BK	R	ER	W	L	PCT	SV	ERA
85	BEL/NWL	A-	10	0	10	0	0	0	55.1	42	5	15	0	2	48	0	0	1	1	24	18	4	3	.571	0	2.93
86	WAU/MID	A	26	700	26	6	1	0	166.1	166	20	44	0	4	171	3	3	10	2	83	62	12	10	.545	0	3.35
87	CHT/SOU	AA	28	748	28	3	2	0	175.0	183	14	48	1	6	144	2	5	4	7	87	77	13	8	.619	0	3.96
88	CAL/PCL	AAA	26	139	0	0	0	21	33.2	33	2	6	1	0	47	5	1	3	0	19	12	4	4	.500	8	3.21
	SEA/AL		40	214	0	0	0	33	48.1	45	4	24	4	1	54	2	3	4	1	21	19	5	8	.385	15	3.54
89	SEA/AL		67	329	0	0	0	60	77.0	81	2	19	3	2	69	3	1	6	1	27	24	1	7	.125	33	2.81
90	SEA/AL		49	229	0	0	0	45	56.0	47	5	16	5	1	45	3	2	1	0	18	14	1	4	.200	30	2.25
91	JAC/SOU	AA	11	50	2	0	0	3	11.1	13	2	3	0	0	12	0	1	0	0	9	7	1	1	.500	1	5.56
	SEA/AL		34	138	0	0	0	23	34.1	25	2	10	0	0	31	1	1	2	1	14	14	3	3	.500	7	3.67
4 YR TOTALS			**190**	**910**	**0**	**0**	**0**	**161**	**215.2**	**198**	**13**	**69**	**12**	**4**	**199**	**9**	**7**	**13**	**3**	**80**	**71**	**10**	**22**	**.313**	**85**	**2.96**

Schourek, Peter Alan "Pete" — bats left — throws left — b.5/10/69

YR	TM/LG	CL	G	TBF	GS	CG	SHO	GF	IP	H	HR	BB	IBB	HB	SO	SH	SF	WP	BK	R	ER	W	L	PCT	SV	ERA
87	KIN/APP	R+	12	336	12	2	0	0	78.1	70	7	34	0	2	57	4	1	2	1	37	32	4	5	.444	0	3.68
89	COL/SAL	A	27	593	19	5	1	3	136.0	120	11	66	2	2	131	7	4	5	3	66	43	5	9	.357	1	2.85
	ST./FSL	A+	2	16	1	0	0	1	4.0	3	0	2	0	0	4	0	0	0	0	1	1	0	0	.000	0	2.25
90	TID/INT	AAA	2	54	2	1	1	0	14.0	9	0	5	0	1	14	2	0	0	0	4	4	1	0	1.000	0	2.57
	SL/FSL	A+	5	143	5	2	2	0	37.0	29	0	8	0	2	28	0	0	0	0	4	4	4	1	.800	0	0.97
	JAC/TEX	AA	19	518	19	4	0	0	124.1	109	8	39	2	8	94	5	7	5	1	53	42	11	4	.733	0	3.04
91	TID/INT	AAA	4	100	4	0	0	0	25.0	18	3	10	0	10	17	1	0	0	0	7	7	1	1	.500	0	2.52
	NY/NL		35	385	8	1	1	7	86.1	82	7	43	4	2	67	5	4	1	0	49	41	5	4	.556	2	4.27

Scott, Michael Warren "Mike" — bats right — throws right — b.4/26/55

YR	TM/LG	CL	G	TBF	GS	CG	SHO	GF	IP	H	HR	BB	IBB	HB	SO	SH	SF	WP	BK	R	ER	W	L	PCT	SV	ERA
79	NY/NL		18	229	9	0	0	0	52.1	59	4	20	3	0	21	4	1	1	1	35	31	1	3	.250	0	5.33
80	NY/NL		6	132	6	1	1	0	29.1	40	1	8	1	0	13	2	1	1	0	14	14	1	1	.500	0	4.30
81	NY/NL		23	551	23	1	0	0	136.0	130	11	34	1	1	54	12	5	1	2	65	59	5	10	.333	0	3.90
82	NY/NL		37	670	22	1	0	10	147.0	185	13	60	2	3	63	21	11	1	2	100	84	7	13	.350	3	5.14
83	HOU/NL		24	612	24	2	2	0	145.0	143	8	46	0	5	73	1	5	4	4	67	60	10	6	.625	0	3.72
84	HOU/NL		31	675	29	0	0	0	154.0	179	7	43	4	3	83	8	11	2	2	96	80	5	11	.313	0	4.68
85	HOU/NL		36	922	35	4	2	1	221.2	194	20	80	0	3	137	6	6	7	2	91	81	18	8	.692	0	3.29
86	HOU/NL		37	1065	37	7	5	0	275.1	182	17	72	6	2	306	8	6	3	0	73	68	18	10	.643	0	2.22
87	HOU/NL		36	1010	36	8	3	0	247.2	199	21	79	6	4	233	8	3	10	2	94	89	16	13	.552	0	3.23
88	HOU/NL		32	875	32	8	5	0	218.2	162	19	53	6	8	190	16	4	1	1	74	71	14	8	.636	0	2.92
89	HOU/NL		33	924	32	9	2	0	229.0	180	23	62	12	3	172	7	4	7	0	87	79	20	10	.667	0	3.10
90	HOU/NL		32	871	32	4	2	0	205.2	194	27	66	6	1	121	7	8	0	3	102	87	9	13	.409	0	3.81
91	HOU/NL		2	35	2	0	0	0	7.0	11	2	6	1	1	3	0	0	0	0	10	10	0	2	.000	0	12.86
13 YR TOTALS			**347**	**8571**	**319**	**45**	**22**	**13**	**2068.2**	**1858**	**173**	**627**	**53**	**33**	**1469**	**100**	**65**	**39**	**19**	**908**	**813**	**124**	**108**	**.534**	**3**	**3.54**

Scott, Timothy Dale "Tim" — bats right — throws right — b.11/16/66

YR	TM/LG	CL	G	TBF	GS	CG	SHO	GF	IP	H	HR	BB	IBB	HB	SO	SH	SF	WP	BK	R	ER	W	L	PCT	SV	ERA
84	GF/PIO	R+	13	0	13	3	2	0	78.0	90	4	38	1	2	44	0	0	5	2	58	38	5	4	.556	0	4.38
85	BAK/CAL	A+	12	0	10	2	0	1	63.2	84	4	28	0	1	31	0	2	4	4	46	41	3	4	.429	0	5.80
86	VB/FSL	A+	20	418	13	3	1	2	95.1	113	2	34	2	2	37	4	9	5	5	44	36	5	4	.556	0	3.40
87	SA/TEX	AA	2	33	2	0	0	0	5.1	14	2	2	0	1	6	0	0	1	0	10	10	0	1	.000	0	16.88
	BAK/CAL	A+	7	137	5	1	0	1	32.1	33	2	10	1	2	29	0	1	2	0	19	16	2	3	.400	0	4.45
88	BAK/CAL	A+	36	272	2	0	0	25	64.1	52	3	26	5	2	59	4	4	2	0	34	26	4	7	.364	4	3.64
89	SA/TEX	AA	48	308	0	0	0	28	68.0	71	3	36	5	0	64	5	3	1	4	30	28	4	2	.667	4	3.71
90	ALB/PCL	AAA	17	73	0	0	0	8	15.0	14	1	14	2	0	15	0	0	0	0	9	7	2	1	.667	3	4.20
	SA/TEX	AA	30	186	0	0	0	20	47.1	35	5	14	0	1	52	0	1	0	0	17	15	3	3	.500	7	2.85
91	SD/NL		2	5	0	0	0	0	1.0	2	0	0	0	0	1	0	0	0	0	2	1	0	0	.000	0	9.00
	LV/PCL	AAA	41	497	11	0	0	9	111.0	133	8	39	1	4	74	5	2	1	0	78	64	8	8	.500	0	5.19

Scudder, William Scott "Scott" — bats right — throws right — b.2/14/68

YR	TM/LG	CL	G	TBF	GS	CG	SHO	GF	IP	H	HR	BB	IBB	HB	SO	SH	SF	WP	BK	R	ER	W	L	PCT	SV	ERA
86	BIL/PIO	R+	12	0	8	0	0	1	52.2	42	1	36	0	3	38	0	0	8	0	34	28	1	3	.250	0	4.78
87	CR/MID	A	26	660	26	0	0	0	153.2	129	16	76	0	7	128	8	2	15	3	86	70	7	12	.368	0	4.10
88	CR/MID	A	16	405	15	1	1	0	102.1	61	3	41	0	2	126	2	1	5	0	30	23	7	3	.700	0	2.02
	CHA/SOU	AA	11	290	11	0	0	0	70.0	53	7	30	0	1	52	1	3	5	1	27	24	6	2	.750	0	2.68
89	NAS/AMA	AAA	12	339	12	3	3	0	80.2	54	1	48	0	3	64	2	3	1	1	27	21	7	1	.875	0	2.34
	CIN/NL		23	451	17	0	0	3	100.1	91	14	61	11	1	66	7	2	0	1	54	50	4	9	.308	0	4.49
90	NAS/AMA	AAA	11	315	11	1	0	0	80.2	53	1	32	0	0	60	0	1	0	3	27	21	7	1	.875	0	2.34
	CIN/NL		21	316	10	0	0	3	71.2	74	12	30	4	3	42	3	1	2	2	41	39	5	5	.500	0	4.90
91	CIN/NL		27	443	14	0	0	4	101.1	91	6	56	4	6	51	8	3	7	0	52	49	6	9	.400	0	4.35
3 YR TOTALS			**71**	**1210**	**41**	**0**	**0**	**10**	**273.1**	**256**	**32**	**147**	**19**	**10**	**159**	**18**	**6**	**9**	**3**	**147**	**138**	**15**	**23**	**.395**	**1**	**4.54**

Seanez, Rudy Caballero — bats right — throws right — b.10/20/68

YR	TM/LG	CL	G	TBF	GS	CG	SHO	GF	IP	H	HR	BB	IBB	HB	SO	SH	SF	WP	BK	R	ER	W	L	PCT	SV	ERA
86	BUR/APP	R+	13	318	12	1	1	1	76.0	59	5	32	0	3	56	1	3	6	0	37	27	5	2	.714	0	3.20
87	WAT/MID	A	10	159	10	0	0	0	34.2	35	6	23	0	1	23	0	2	2	2	29	26	0	4	.000	0	6.75
88	WAT/MID	A	22	505	22	1	1	0	113.1	98	10	68	0	6	93	2	2	14	2	69	59	6	6	.500	0	4.69
89	KIN/CAR	A+	25	539	25	1	0	0	113.0	94	0	111	1	5	149	1	1*	13	1	66	52	8	10	.444	0	4.14
	CS/PCL	AAA	1	4	0	0	0	0	1.0	1	0	0	0	0	0	0	0	0	0	2	2	0	0	.000	0	0.00
	CLE/AL		5	20	0	0	0	2	5.0	1	0	4	1	0	7	0	2	1	1	2	2	0	0	.000	0	3.60
90	CAN/EAS	AA	15	68	0	0	0	11	16.2	9	0	12	0	1	27	2	0	0	0	4	4	1	0	1.000	5	2.16
	CLE/AL		24	127	0	0	0	12	27.1	22	2	25	1	1	24	0	1	5	0	17	17	2	1	.667	1	5.60
	CS/PCL	AAA	12	59	0	0	0	10	12.0	15	2	10	0	0	7	0	1	3	0	10	9	1	4	.200	1	6.75
91	CAN/EAS	AA	25	161	0	0	0	18	38.1	17	2	30	1	1	73	0	1	5	0	12	11	4	2	.667	7	2.58
	CLE/AL		5	33	0	0	0	0	5.0	10	1	7	0	0	7	0	1	1	1	14	9	0	0	.000	0	16.20
	CS/PCL	AAA	16	86	0	0	0	11	17.1	17	2	22	0	1	19	0	1	5	0	14	13	0	0	.000	0	7.27
3 YR TOTALS			**34**	**180**	**0**	**0**	**0**	**14**	**37.1**	**33**	**4**	**36**	**2**	**1**	**38**	**0**	**3**	**8**	**1**	**31**	**28**	**2**	**1**	**.667**	**0**	**6.75**

Searcy, William Steven "Steve" — bats left — throws left — b.6/4/64

YR	TM/LG	CL	G	TBF	GS	CG	SHO	GF	IP	H	HR	BB	IBB	HB	SO	SH	SF	WP	BK	R	ER	W	L	PCT	SV	ERA
85	BRI/APP	R+	4	83	4	2	1	0	22.0	15	0	2	0	0	24	0	1	1	1	6	5	1	1	.500	0	2.05
	BIR/SOU	AA	7	172	7	0	0	0	36.2	39	1	23	1	2	19	0	2	2	0	17	13	2	2	.500	0	3.19
86	GF/EAS	AA	27	733	27	3	0	0	172.0	166	6	74	1	3	139	5	2	12	2	79	63	11	6	.647	0	3.30

(continued)

Searcy, William Steven "Steve" (continued)

YR	TM/LG	CL	G	TBF	GS	CG	SHO	GF	IP	H	HR	BB	IBB	HB	SO	SH	SF	WP	BK	R	ER	W	L	PCT	SV	ERA
87	TOL/INT	AAA	10	233	10	0	0	0	53.1	49	4	32	0	1	54	3	4	7	2	26	25	3	4	.429	0	4.22
88	TOL/INT	AAA	27	717	27	3	0	0	170.0	131	8	79	2	12	176	3	6	7	13	61	49	13	7	.650	0	2.59
	DET/AL		2	37	2	0	0	0	8.0	8	3	4	0	0	5	0	0	0	0	6	5	0	2	.000	0	5.63
89	LAK/FSL	A+	9	230	9	0	0	0	52.2	40	0	33	0	0	44	1	2	4	4	21	15	2	3	.400	0	2.56
	TOL/INT	AAA	9	182	9	0	0	0	37.0	41	2	37	2	1	26	1	0	2	3	36	31	2	3	.400	0	7.54
	DET/AL		8	100	2	0	0	3	22.1	27	3	12	1	0	11	0	0	0	0	16	15	1	1	.500	0	6.04
90	TOL/INT	AAA	17	429	17	2	2	0	104.2	71	5	52	1	0	105	1	3	3	5	40	34	10	5	.667	0	2.92
	DET/AL		16	341	12	1	0	2	75.1	76	9	51	3	0	66	2	6	3	0	44	39	2	7	.222	0	4.66
91	DET/AL		16	201	5	0	0	4	40.2	52	8	30	0	0	32	2	3	4	0	40	38	1	2	.333	0	8.41
	PHI/NL		18	134	5	0	0	4	30.1	29	2	14	1	0	21	3	2	1	1	16	14	2	1	.667	0	4.15
	YEAR		34	335	10	0	0	8	71.0	81	10	44	1	0	53	5	5	5	1	56	52	3	3	.500	0	6.59
4 YR TOTALS			**60**	**813**	**21**	**1**	**0**	**13**	**176.2**	**192**	**25**	**111**	**5**	**0**	**135**	**7**	**11**	**8**	**1**	**122**	**111**	**6**	**13**	**.316**	**0**	**5.65**

Segura, Jose Altagracia (Mota) — bats right — throws right — b.1/26/63

YR	TM/LG	CL	G	TBF	GS	CG	SHO	GF	IP	H	HR	BB	IBB	HB	SO	SH	SF	WP	BK	R	ER	W	L	PCT	SV	ERA
81	HEL/PIO	R+	25	0	0	0	0	0	35.0	42	1	15	0	0	27	0	0	1	0	26	17	2	3	.400	0	4.37
82	SPA/SAL	A	20	0	2	0	0	0	29.0	32	2	18	0	4	17	0	0	6	0	28	25	2	2	.500	0	7.76
	BEN/NWL	A-	24	0	0	0	0	0	36.0	27	1	28	0	0	43	0	0	9	0	16	7	4	4	.500	0	1.75
83	SPA/SAL	A	40	0	1	0	0	0	65.0	77	4	42	0	2	54	0	0	15	0	59	47	1	6	.143	5	6.51
84	KIN/CAR	A+	16	402	14	2	1	1	97.1	88	7	35	1	1	55	2	3	7	0	48	43	7	4	.636	0	3.98
	KNO/SOU	AA	12	322	12	1	0	0	69.0	75	4	47	1	1	26	2	1	8	1	47	34	4	6	.400	0	4.43
85	KIN/CAR	A+	34	499	15	1	1	10	110.1	109	7	69	4	7	73	1	3	7	0	62	51	4	6	.400	0	4.16
86	KNO/SOU	AA	24	491	17	1	0	3	106.2	101	7	72	1	6	55	0	7	11	1	72	50	4	13	.235	1	4.22
87	SYR/INT	AAA	43	499	12	0	0	12	107.0	136	13	59	2	10	54	2	10	14	1	90	78	5	8	.385	4	6.56
88	CHI/AL		4	52	0	0	0	1	8.2	19	1	8	0	0	9	0	0	0	3	17	13	0	0	.000	0	13.50
	VAN/PCL	AAA	20	507	19	0	0	0	111.0	127	4	60	0	3	39	5	7	3	6	69	56	6	6	.500	0	4.54
89	VAN/PCL	AAA	44	263	0	0	0	32	66.2	50	0	19	0	2	52	1	3	1	3	21	17	1	2	.333	17	2.30
	CHI/AL		7	34	0	0	0	3	6.0	13	2	3	1	0	4	2	1	0	1	11	10	0	1	.000	0	15.00
90	VAN/PCL	AAA	40	246	0	0	0	27	54.2	49	0	35	1	2	47	2	5	6	0	34	31	1	3	.250	8	5.10
91	PHO/PCL	AAA	32	177	0	0	0	27	39.1	46	4	17	2	1	21	3	2	6	2	15	15	1	3	.250	8	3.43
	SF/NL		11	72	0	0	0	2	16.1	20	1	5	0	0	10	1	3	0	2	11	8	0	0	.000	0	4.41
3 YR TOTALS			**22**	**158**	**0**	**0**	**0**	**5**	**31.0**	**52**	**4**	**16**	**1**	**0**	**16**	**3**	**1**	**4**	**3**	**39**	**31**	**0**	**2**	**.000**	**0**	**9.00**

Seminara, Frank Peter — bats right — throws right — b.5/16/67 — System SD/NL

YR	TM/LG	CL	G	TBF	GS	CG	SHO	GF	IP	H	HR	BB	IBB	HB	SO	SH	SF	WP	BK	R	ER	W	L	PCT	SV	ERA
88	ONE/NYP	A-	16	350	13	0	0	2	78.1	86	2	32	2	5	60	3	2	11	6	49	38	4	7	.364	1	4.37
89	PW/CAR	A+	21	158	0	0	0	12	36.2	26	0	22	3	5	23	1	3	5	6	23	15	2	4	.333	2	3.68
	ONE/NYP	A-	11	280	10	3	1	0	70.0	51	0	18	0	0	70	3	0	1	3	25	16	7	2	.778	0	2.06
90	PW/CAR	A+	25	692	25	4	2	0	170.1	136	5	52	1	10	132	1	2	12	2	51	36	16	8	.667	0	1.90
91	WIC/TEX	AA	27	761	27	6	1	0	176.0	173	10	68	0	9	107	4	5	12	3	86	66	15	10	.600	0	3.38

Shaw, Jeffrey Lee "Jeff" — bats right — throws right — b.7/7/66

YR	TM/LG	CL	G	TBF	GS	CG	SHO	GF	IP	H	HR	BB	IBB	HB	SO	SH	SF	WP	BK	R	ER	W	L	PCT	SV	ERA
86	BAT/NYP	A-	14	367	12	3	1	1	88.2	79	5	35	0	5	71	3	4	10	0	32	24	8	4	.667	0	2.44
87	WAT/MID	A	28	788	28	6	4	0	184.1	192	15	56	0	6	117	4	6	8	5	89	72	11	11	.500	0	3.52
88	WIL/EAS	AA	27	718	27	6	1	0	163.2	173	11	75	1	10	61	10	10	12	4	94	66	5	19	.208	0	3.63
89	CAN/EAS	AA	30	661	22	6	3	3	154.1	134	9	67	3	14	95	5	7	7	0	84	62	7	10	.412	0	3.62
90	CS/PCL	AAA	17	438	16	4	0	0	98.2	98	7	52	0	3	55	4	5	7	0	54	47	10	3	.769	0	4.29
	CLE/AL		12	229	9	0	0	0	48.2	73	11	20	0	0	25	1	3	3	0	38	36	3	4	.429	0	6.66
91	CS/PCL	AAA	12	329	12	1	0	0	75.2	77	9	25	0	4	55	0	2	1	1	47	39	6	3	.667	0	4.64
	CLE/AL		29	311	1	0	0	9	72.1	72	6	27	5	4	31	2	1	6	0	34	27	0	5	.000	1	3.36
2 YR TOTALS			**41**	**540**	**10**	**0**	**0**	**9**	**121.0**	**145**	**17**	**47**	**5**	**4**	**56**	**2**	**7**	**9**	**0**	**72**	**63**	**3**	**9**	**.250**	**1**	**4.69**

Sherrill, Timothy Shawn "Tim" — bats left — throws left — b.9/10/65

YR	TM/LG	CL	G	TBF	GS	CG	SHO	GF	IP	H	HR	BB	IBB	HB	SO	SH	SF	WP	BK	R	ER	W	L	PCT	SV	ERA
87	JC/APP	R+	25	172	0	0	0	18	42.0	25	1	18	2	2	62	1	0	0	0	18	14	3	4	.429	8	3.00
88	SAV/SAL	A	31	173	0	0	0	29	45.1	26	2	13	2	1	62	5	2	0	1	12	9	3	2	.600	16	1.79
	SP/FSL	A+	16	87	0	0	0	11	23.1	14	0	8	1	1	25	0	3	0	2	4	4	2	0	1.000	6	1.54
89	SAV/SAL	A	3	16	0	0	0	3	3.2	3	0	1	0	0	6	0	1	0	0	0	0	0	0	.000	2	0.00
	SP/FSL	A+	52	269	0	0	0	21	68.0	52	3	23	3	0	48	7	2	4	0	19	16	4	0	1.000	6	2.12
90	LOU/AMA	AAA	52	253	0	0	0	20	61.1	49	4	21	2	1	57	4	1	4	0	17	17	4	3	.571	6	2.49
	STL/NL		8	25	0	0	0	2	4.1	10	2	3	0	0	3	0	0	0	0	5	3	0	0	.000	0	6.23
91	STL/NL		10	67	0	0	0	3	14.1	20	2	6	1	0	11	2	0	1	0	13	13	0	0	.000	0	8.16
	LOU/AMA	AAA	42	257	0	0	0	29	60.1	56	3	26	3	0	38	3	0	2	0	21	21	5	5	.500	10	3.13
2 YR TOTALS			**18**	**92**	**0**	**0**	**0**	**5**	**18.2**	**30**	**2**	**6**	**1**	**2**	**7**	**2**	**2**	**2**	**0**	**18**	**16**	**0**	**0**	**.000**	**0**	**7.71**

Show, Eric Vaughn — bats right — throws right — b.5/19/56

YR	TM/LG	CL	G	TBF	GS	CG	SHO	GF	IP	H	HR	BB	IBB	HB	SO	SH	SF	WP	BK	R	ER	W	L	PCT	SV	ERA
81	SD/NL		15	92	0	0	0	4	23.0	17	2	9	3	1	22	2	0	0	0	9	8	1	3	.250	3	3.13
82	SD/NL		47	611	14	2	2	12	150.0	117	10	48	3	5	88	13	6	2	0	49	44	10	6	.625	3	2.64
83	SD/NL		35	857	33	4	2	0	200.2	201	25	74	2	5	120	9	4	2	0	97	93	15	12	.556	0	4.17
84	SD/NL		32	862	32	3	1	0	206.2	175	18	88	4	4	104	17	4	6	2	88	78	15	9	.625	0	3.40
85	SD/NL		35	977	35	5	2	0	233.0	212	27	87	5	5	141	9	4	4	0	95	80	12	11	.522	0	3.09
86	SD/NL		24	569	22	2	0	1	136.1	109	11	69	4	4	94	10	1	3	2	47	45	9	5	.643	0	2.97

Show, Eric Vaughn (continued)

YR	TM/LG	CL	G	TBF	GS	CG	SHO	GF	IP	H	HR	BB	IBB	HB	SO	SH	SF	WP	BK	R	ER	W	L	PCT	SV	ERA
87	SD/NL		34	887	34	5	3	0	206.1	188	26	85	7	9	117	9	5	6	5	99	88	8	16	.333	0	3.84
88	SD/NL		32	936	32	13	1	0	234.2	201	22	53	5	6	144	3	5	4	5	86	85	16	11	.593	0	3.26
89	SD/NL		16	464	16	1	0	0	106.1	113	9	39	3	2	66	6	5	2	2	59	50	8	6	.571	0	4.23
90	SD/NL		39	482	12	0	0	14	106.1	131	16	41	9	4	55	5	4	3	3	74	68	6	8	.429	1	5.76
91	MOD/CAL	A+	1	15	1	0	0	0	2.2	6	1	1	0	0	1	0	0	0	0	6	5	0	1	.000	0	16.88
	TAC/PCL	AAA	8	161	8	1	1	0	40.1	36	4	9	0	0	27	0	0	1	3	15	12	3	2	.600	0	2.68
	OAK/AL		23	231	5	0	0	6	51.2	62	5	17	1	0	20	2	4	2	1	36	34	1	2	.333	0	5.92
11 YR TOTALS			**332**	**6968**	**235**	**35**	**11**	**37**	**1655.0**	**1526**	**171**	**610**	**49**	**46**	**971**	**85**	**43**	**36**	**22**	**739**	**673**	**101**	**89**	**.532**	**7**	**3.66**

Simons, Douglas Eugene "Doug" — bats left — throws left — b.9/15/66

YR	TM/LG	CL	G	TBF	GS	CG	SHO	GF	IP	H	HR	BB	IBB	HB	SO	SH	SF	WP	BK	R	ER	W	L	PCT	SV	ERA
88	VIS/CAL	A+	17	467	16	5	2	1	107.1	100	10	46	0	5	123	4	3	6	1	59	47	6	5	.545	0	3.94
89	VIS/CAL	A+	14	372	14	1	0	0	90.2	77	4	33	1	5	79	1	4	4	1	33	15	6	2	.750	0	1.49
	ORL/SOU	AA	14	374	14	3	0	0	87.1	83	7	37	0	2	58	2	2	1	2	39	37	7	3	.700	0	3.81
90	ORL/SOU	AA	29	765	28	5	0	0	188.0	160	13	43	2	6	109	9	4	7	1	76	53	15	12	.556	0	2.54
91	NY/NL		42	258	1	0	0	11	60.2	55	5	19	2	0	38	9	4	3	0	40	35	2	3	.400	1	5.19

Sisk, Douglas Randall "Doug" — bats right — throws right — b.9/26/57

YR	TM/LG	CL	G	TBF	GS	CG	SHO	GF	IP	H	HR	BB	IBB	HB	SO	SH	SF	WP	BK	R	ER	W	L	PCT	SV	ERA
82	NY/NL		8	34	0	0	0	4	8.2	5	1	4	2	1	4	0	0	0	0	1	1	0	1	.000	1	1.04
83	NY/NL		67	447	0	0	0	39	104.1	88	1	59	7	4	33	6	4	5	1	38	26	5	4	.556	11	2.24
84	NY/NL		50	329	0	0	0	31	77.2	57	1	54	5	3	32	7	0	1	0	24	18	1	3	.250	15	2.09
85	TID/INT	AAA	4	71	3	0	0	0	15.0	15	0	13	0	0	4	1	0	2	0	12	12	0	2	.000	0	7.20
	NY/NL		42	341	0	0	0	22	73.0	86	3	40	2	2	26	3	0	1	1	48	43	4	5	.444	2	5.30
86	TID/INT	AAA	9	128	4	0	0	3	30.0	34	2	9	0	1	19	0	1	2	0	16	14	2	3	.400	2	4.20
	NY/NL		41	312	0	0	0	15	70.2	77	0	31	5	5	31	3	0	2	1	31	24	4	2	.667	1	3.06
87	NY/NL		55	339	0	0	0	17	78.0	83	5	22	4	3	37	5	2	2	0	38	30	3	1	.750	1	3.46
88	ROC/INT	AAA	6	48	1	0	0	5	10.2	15	1	3	1	0	5	1	0	0	0	7	7	0	2	.000	3	5.91
	BAL/AL		52	410	0	0	0	29	94.1	109	3	45	6	2	26	5	2	3	0	43	39	3	3	.500	0	3.72
90	CS/PCL	AAA	8	37	0	0	0	2	7.2	8	0	5	0	0	7	1	0	0	0	8	6	1	0	1.000	0	7.04
	TID/INT	AAA	8	169	6	0	0	1	41.2	39	1	10	0	1	20	0	0	1	0	16	13	5	1	.833	0	2.81
	ATL/NL		3	13	0	0	0	2	2.1	1	0	4	0	0	1	0	1	0	0	1	1	0	0	.000	0	3.86
91	ATL/NL		14	73	0	0	0	5	14.1	21	0	8	2	0	9	1	1	0	0	14	8	2	1	.667	0	5.02
	RIC/INT	AAA	9	45	0	0	0	4	11.1	14	0	4	0	0	2	0	0	1	0	3	2	0	0	.000	2	1.59
9 YR TOTALS			**332**	**2298**	**0**	**0**	**0**	**161**	**523.1**	**527**	**15**	**267**	**33**	**20**	**195**	**30**	**11**	**15**	**3**	**238**	**190**	**22**	**20**	**.524**	**33**	**3.27**

Slocumb, Heathcliff — bats right — throws right — b.6/7/66

YR	TM/LG	CL	G	TBF	GS	CG	SHO	GF	IP	H	HR	BB	IBB	HB	SO	SH	SF	WP	BK	R	ER	W	L	PCT	SV	ERA
84	KIN/APP	R+	1	3	0	0	0	0	0.1	0	0	1	0	0	1	0	0	0	0	1	.0	0	0	.000	0	0.00
	LF/NYP	A—	4	51	1	0	0	0	9.0	8	0	16	0	1	10	0	0	4	0	11	11	0	0	.000	0	11.00
85	KIN/APP	R+	11	232	9	1	0	0	52.1	47	0	31	0	1	29	2	1	15	0	32	22	3	2	.600	0	3.78
86	LF/NYP	A—	25	186	0	0	0	13	43.2	24	3	36	1	0	41	1	0	8	0	17	8	3	1	.750	1	1.65
87	WIN/CAR	A+	9	135	4	0	0	1	27.1	26	1	26	0	0	27	2	3	0	1	25	19	1	2	.333	0	6.26
	PEO/MID	A	16	455	16	3	1	0	103.2	97	2	42	3	3	81	0	1	15	0	44	30	10	4	.714	0	2.60
88	WIN/CAR	A+	25	567	19	2	1	3	119.2	122	5	90	1	3	78	2	5	19	2	75	66	6	6	.500	0	4.96
89	PEO/MID	A	49	233	0	0	0	43	55.2	31	0	33	4	1	52	5	3	6	0	16	11	3	3	.500	22	1.78
90	CHA/SOU	AA	43	232	0	0	0	37	50.1	50	0	32	5	3	37	6	2	4	0	20	12	3	1	.750	12	2.15
	IOW/AMA	AAA	20	115	0	0	0	10	27.0	16	1	18	2	2	21	2	1	3	0	10	6	1	0	1.000	1	2.00
91	IOW/AMA	AAA	12	59	0	0	0	6	13.1	10	0	6	0	1	9	1	0	1	0	8	6	1	0	1.000	1	4.05
	CHI/NL		52	274	0	0	0	21	62.2	53	3	30	6	3	34	6	6	9	0	29	24	2	1	.667	1	3.45

Slusarski, Joseph Andrew "Joe" — bats right — throws right — b.12/19/66

YR	TM/LG	CL	G	TBF	GS	CG	SHO	GF	IP	H	HR	BB	IBB	HB	SO	SH	SF	WP	BK	R	ER	W	L	PCT	SV	ERA
89	MOD/CAL	A+	27	753	27	4	1	0	184.0	155	15	50	0	8	160	5	3	13	1	78	65	13	10	.565	0	3.18
90	HUN/SOU	AA	17	471	17	2	0	0	108.2	114	9	35	0	3	75	2	9	5	0	65	54	6	8	.429	0	4.47
	TAC/PCL	AAA	9	241	9	0	0	0	55.2	54	3	22	0	2	37	1	3	1	1	24	21	4	2	.667	0	3.40
91	TAC/PCL	AAA	7	182	7	0	0	0	46.1	42	4	10	0	0	25	0	0	0	2	20	14	4	2	.667	0	2.72
	OAK/AL		20	486	19	1	0	0	109.1	121	14	52	1	4	60	1	1	0	0	69	64	5	7	.417	0	5.27

Smiley, John Patrick — bats left — throws left — b.3/17/65

YR	TM/LG	CL	G	TBF	GS	CG	SHO	GF	IP	H	HR	BB	IBB	HB	SO	SH	SF	WP	BK	R	ER	W	L	PCT	SV	ERA
84	MAC/SAL	A	21	553	19	2	0	2	130.0	119	12	41	1	2	73	4	4	4	1	73	57	5	11	.313	1	3.95
85	PW/CAR	A+	10	259	10	0	0	0	56.0	64	3	27	0	4	45	4	3	3	2	36	32	2	2	.500	0	5.14
	MAC/SAL	A	16	384	16	1	1	0	88.2	84	12	37	0	2	70	5	2	4	1	55	46	3	8	.273	0	4.67
86	PW/CAR	A+	48	371	2	0	0	36	90.0	64	2	40	1	1	93	5	3	2	2	35	31	3	6	.333	14	3.10
	PIT/NL		12	42	0	0	0	2	11.2	4	0	4	0	0	9	0	0	3	0	6	5	1	0	1.000	0	3.86
87	PIT/NL		63	336	0	0	0	19	75.0	69	7	50	8	0	58	0	3	5	1	49	48	5	5	.500	4	5.76
88	PIT/NL		34	835	32	5	1	0	205.0	185	15	46	4	3	129	11	8	6	1	81	74	13	11	.542	0	3.25
89	PIT/NL		28	835	28	8	1	0	205.1	174	22	49	5	4	123	6	7	5	2	83	64	12	8	.600	0	2.81
90	PIT/NL		26	632	25	2	0	0	149.1	161	15	36	1	2	86	5	4	2	0	78	77	9	10	.474	0	4.64
91	PIT/NL		33	836	32	2	1	0	207.2	194	17	44	0	3	129	11	4	3	1	78	71	20	8	.714	0	3.08
6 YR TOTALS			**196**	**3516**	**117**	**17**	**3**	**21**	**854.0**	**787**	**78**	**229**	**18**	**12**	**534**	**32**	**26**	**21**	**12**	**375**	**339**	**60**	**42**	**.588**	**4**	**3.57**

Smith, Bryn Nelson — bats right — throws right — b.8/11/55

YR	TM/LG	CL	G	TBF	GS	CG	SHO	GF	IP	H	HR	BB	IBB	HB	SO	SH	SF	WP	BK	R	ER	W	L	PCT	SV	ERA
81	MON/NL		7	53	0	0	0	1	13.0	14	1	3	0	0	9	0	0	2	0	4	4	1	0	1.000	0	2.77
82	MON/NL		47	335	1	0	0	16	79.1	81	5	23	5	0	50	1	4	5	1	43	37	2	4	.333	3	4.20
83	MON/NL		49	636	12	5	3	17	155.1	142	13	43	6	5	101	14	2	5	3	51	43	6	11	.353	2	2.49
84	MON/NL		28	751	28	4	2	0	179.0	178	15	51	7	3	101	7	2	2	2	72	66	12	13	.480	0	3.32
85	MON/NL		32	890	32	4	2	0	222.1	193	12	41	3	1	127	13	4	1	1	85	72	18	5	.783	0	2.91
86	MON/NL		30	807	30	1	0	0	187.1	182	15	63	6	6	105	10	3	4	2	101	82	10	8	.556	0	3.94
87	WPB/FSL	A+	4	76	4	0	0	0	17.2	19	2	1	0	3	16	1	0	1	0	10	8	0	2	.000	0	4.08
	MON/NL		26	643	26	2	0	0	150.1	164	16	31	4	2	94	7	5	2	0	81	73	10	9	.526	0	4.37
88	MON/NL		32	791	32	1	0	0	198.0	179	15	32	2	10	122	7	6	2	5	79	66	12	10	.545	0	3.00
89	MON/NL		33	864	32	3	1	0	215.2	177	16	54	4	4	129	7	5	3	1	76	68	10	11	.476	0	2.84
90	STL/NL		26	605	25	0	0	0	141.1	160	11	30	1	4	78	7	5	2	0	81	67	9	8	.529	0	4.27
91	STL/NL		31	818	31	3	0	0	198.2	188	16	45	3	7	94	10	7	3	1	95	85	12	9	.571	0	3.85
11 YR TOTALS			**341**	**7193**	**249**	**23**	**8**	**34**	**1740.1**	**1658**	**135**	**416**	**41**	**42**	**1010**	**83**	**43**	**31**	**16**	**768**	**663**	**102**	**88**	**.537**	**6**	**3.43**

Smith, Daryl Clinton — bats right — throws right — b.7/29/60 — System KC/AL

YR	TM/LG	CL	G	TBF	GS	CG	SHO	GF	IP	H	HR	BB	IBB	HB	SO	SH	SF	WP	BK	R	ER	W	L	PCT	SV	ERA
80	ASH/SAL	A	22	0	7	0	0	0	66.0	72	4	41	0	1	30	0	0	7	1	40	35	5	3	.625	0	4.77
	RAN/GCL	R	4	0	0	0	0	0	12.0	13	0	4	0	0	4	0	0	2	0	9	6	1	1	.500	0	4.50
81	ASH/SAL	A	29	0	22	7	0	0	160.0	136	7	57	0	4	64	0	0	9	0	65	49	16	5	.762	0	2.76
82	TUL/TEX	AA	9	0	7	0	0	0	37.0	51	4	24	0	5	18	0	0	5	0	35	30	2	5	.286	0	7.30
	BUR/MID	A	19	0	10	0	0	0	80.0	78	5	40	0	7	32	0	0	7	4	40	30	3	5	.375	0	3.38
83	SAL/CAR	A+	13	0	3	1	1	0	55.0	53	3	32	0	1	35	0	0	5	0	30	26	1	2	.333	1	4.25
	TUL/TEX	AA	6	0	1	0	0	0	14.0	14	1	6	0	0	5	0	0	0	0	3	3	0	0	.000	0	1.93
84	TUL/TEX	AA	7	57	0	0	0	1	10.2	18	0	9	0	1	6	1	1	3	0	17	17	0	1	.000	0	14.34
	SAL/CAR	A+	16	297	12	0	0	1	67.0	67	6	44	1	2	38	0	0	5	0	40	32	6	3	.667	0	4.30
85	WAT/MID	A	1	18	0	0	0	0	4.2	4	1	2	0	0	5	0	0	1	0	1	1	0	0	.000	0	1.93
	WAT/EAS	AA	16	231	6	1	0	8	53.2	42	5	37	1	1	38	1	2	5	0	25	21	2	2	.500	1	3.52
86	WAT/EAS	AA	21	368	11	4	1	4	89.0	71	8	48	0	3	55	0	2	11	0	37	35	4	3	.571	0	3.54
87	WIL/EAS	AA	2	37	2	0	0	0	8.0	11	1	3	0	0	5	0	1	1	0	8	7	1	1	.500	0	7.87
	REA/EAS	AA	19	349	12	1	0	2	79.1	75	5	43	2	4	53	3	3	5	1	38	31	6	2	.750	1	3.52
	MAI/INT	AAA	4	103	4	0	0	0	22.2	21	4	13	0	2	16	1	2	0	0	18	17	1	3	.250	0	6.75
88	BIR/SOU	AA	40	226	0	0	0	33	53.0	42	0	27	3	0	44	2	4	6	6	25	19	1	4	.200	7	3.23
90	MEM/SOU	AA	21	211	0	0	0	5	48.1	46	1	23	0	0	48	3	6	10	0	27	17	2	1	.667	1	3.17
	OMA/AMA	AAA	11	268	10	0	0	1	64.0	59	5	32	0	2	56	2	0	3	4	25	22	6	2	.750	0	3.09
	KC/AL		2	27	1	0	0	1	6.2	5	0	4	0	0	6	0	2	0	0	3	3	0	1	.000	0	4.05
91	OMA/AMA	AAA	23	389	14	0	0	4	93.0	82	10	33	1	0	94	4	2	4	2	38	35	4	5	.444	0	3.39
1 YR TOTALS			**2**	**27**	**1**	**0**	**0**	**1**	**6.2**	**5**	**0**	**4**	**0**	**0**	**6**	**0**	**2**	**0**	**0**	**3**	**3**	**0**	**1**	**.000**	**0**	**4.05**

Smith, David Stanley "Dave" — bats right — throws right — b.1/21/55

YR	TM/LG	CL	G	TBF	GS	CG	SHO	GF	IP	H	HR	BB	IBB	HB	SO	SH	SF	WP	BK	R	ER	W	L	PCT	SV	ERA
80	HOU/NL		57	422	0	0	0	35	102.2	90	1	32	7	4	85	6	1	3	1	24	22	7	5	.583	10	1.93
81	HOU/NL		42	305	0	0	0	22	75.0	54	2	23	4	2	52	6	1	4	0	26	23	5	3	.625	8	2.76
82	HOU/NL		49	286	1	0	0	29	63.1	69	4	31	4	0	28	9	4	2	4	30	27	5	4	.556	11	3.84
83	HOU/NL		42	323	0	0	0	24	72.2	72	2	36	4	0	41	3	5	1	1	32	25	3	1	.750	6	3.10
84	HOU/NL		53	304	0	0	0	24	77.1	60	5	20	3	1	45	2	1	1	1	22	19	5	4	.556	5	2.21
85	HOU/NL		64	315	0	0	0	46	79.1	69	3	17	5	1	40	3	1	4	1	26	20	9	5	.643	27	2.27
86	HOU/NL		54	223	0	0	0	51	56.0	39	5	22	3	1	46	4	1	2	0	17	17	4	7	.364	33	2.73
87	HOU/NL		50	240	0	0	0	44	60.0	39	0	21	8	1	73	4	1	3	2	13	11	2	3	.400	24	1.65
88	HOU/NL		51	249	0	0	0	39	57.1	60	1	19	8	1	38	4	1	1	3	26	17	4	5	.444	27	2.67
89	HOU/NL		52	239	0	0	0	44	58.0	49	1	19	7	1	31	8	1	2	2	20	17	3	4	.429	25	2.64
90	HOU/NL		49	239	0	0	0	42	60.1	45	4	20	4	0	50	4	1	5	5	18	16	6	6	.500	23	2.39
91	CHI/NL		35	151	0	0	0	28	33.0	39	6	19	5	1	16	2	0	1	1	22	22	0	6	.000	17	6.00
12 YR TOTALS			**598**	**3296**	**1**	**0**	**0**	**428**	**795.0**	**685**	**34**	**279**	**62**	**13**	**545**	**54**	**18**	**28**	**21**	**276**	**236**	**53**	**53**	**.500**	**216**	**2.67**

Smith, Lee Arthur — bats right — throws right — b.12/4/57

YR	TM/LG	CL	G	TBF	GS	CG	SHO	GF	IP	H	HR	BB	IBB	HB	SO	SH	SF	WP	BK	R	ER	W	L	PCT	SV	ERA
80	CHI/NL		18	97	0	0	0	6	21.2	21	0	14	5	0	17	1	1	0	0	9	7	2	0	1.000	0	2.91
81	CHI/NL		40	280	1	0	0	12	66.2	57	2	31	8	1	50	8	2	7	1	31	26	3	6	.333	1	3.51
82	CHI/NL		72	480	5	0	0	38	117.0	105	5	37	5	3	99	6	5	6	1	38	35	2	5	.286	17	2.69
83	CHI/NL		66	413	0	0	0	56	103.1	70	5	41	14	1	91	9	2	5	2	23	19	4	10	.286	29	1.65
84	CHI/NL		69	428	0	0	0	59	101.0	98	6	35	7	0	86	4	5	6	0	42	41	9	7	.563	33	3.65
85	CHI/NL		65	397	0	0	0	57	97.2	87	9	32	6	1	112	3	1	4	0	35	33	7	4	.636	33	3.04
86	CHI/NL		66	372	0	0	0	59	90.1	69	7	42	11	0	93	6	3	2	0	32	31	9	9	.500	31	3.09
87	CHI/NL		62	360	0	0	0	52	83.2	84	4	32	5	0	96	4	4	0	0	30	29	4	10	.286	36	3.12
88	BOS/AL		64	363	0	0	0	57	83.2	72	7	37	6	1	96	3	2	0	0	34	26	4	5	.444	29	2.80
89	BOS/AL		64	290	0	0	0	50	70.2	53	6	33	6	0	96	3	2	2	0	30	28	6	1	.857	25	3.57
90	BOS/AL		11	64	0	0	0	8	14.1	13	0	9	2	0	17	0	0	1	0	4	3	2	1	.667	4	1.88
	STL/NL		53	280	0	0	0	45	68.2	58	3	20	5	0	70	2	3	1	0	20	16	3	4	.429	27	2.10
	YEAR		64	344	0	0	0	53	83.0	71	3	29	7	0	87	2	3	2	0	24	19	5	5	.500	31	2.06
91	STL/NL		67	300	0	0	0	61	73.0	70	5	13	5	0	67	1	1	0	0	19	19	6	3	.667	47	2.34
12 YR TOTALS			**717**	**4124**	**6**	**0**	**0**	**563**	**991.2**	**857**	**59**	**376**	**85**	**7**	**990**	**53**	**27**	**40**	**4**	**347**	**313**	**61**	**65**	**.484**	**312**	**2.84**

Smith, LeRoy Purdy "Roy" — bats right — throws right — b.9/6/61

YR	TM/LG	CL	G	TBF	GS	CG	SHO	GF	IP	H	HR	BB	IBB	HB	SO	SH	SF	WP	BK	R	ER	W	L	PCT	SV	ERA
79	HEL/PIO	R+	5	0	5	2	0	0	36.0	21	2	16	0	0	42	0	0	4	0	16	10	5	0	1.000	0	2.50
80	PEN/CAR	A+	27	0	27	5	3	0	163.0	101	7	63	0	5	134	0	0	6	1	54	47	17	6	.739	0	2.60
81	REA/EAS	AA	27	0	27	4	2	0	161.0	123	13	97	0	10	117	0	0	14	1	92	79	11	8	.579	0	4.42
82	REA/EAS	AA	26	0	26	4	0	0	166.0	141	15	82	0	4	122	0	0	12	1	81	71	10	8	.556	0	3.85
83	CHA/INT	AAA	27	0	27	4	2	0	155.0	166	21	75	0	2	95	0	0	4	0	101	89	6	8	.429	0	5.17
84	MAI/INT	AAA	12	343	12	2	0	0	80.2	77	9	29	0	2	48	5	2	6	0	47	39	5	4	.556	0	4.35
	CLE/AL		22	382	14	0	0	0	86.1	91	14	40	0	1	55	1	3	3	2	49	44	5	5	.500	0	4.59
85	MAI/INT	AAA	15	430	15	6	0	0	109.1	84	10	29	0	0	65	2	2	2	0	33	29	10	4	.714	0	2.39
	CLE/AL		12	285	11	1	0	0	62.1	84	8	17	0	1	28	1	4	1	0	40	37	1	4	.200	0	5.34
86	MIN/AL		5	50	0	0	0	2	10.1	13	1	5	1	1	8	0	0	0	0	8	8	0	2	.000	0	6.97
	TOL/INT	AAA	9	216	9	1	0	0	53.2	42	4	16	0	0	39	1	1	4	0	12	9	2	1	.667	0	1.51
87	POR/PCL	AAA	24	712	24	6	0	0	166.1	176	12	41	0	5	106	1	9	3	3	84	70	9	12	.429	0	3.79
	MIN/AL		7	78	1	0	0	1	16.1	20	3	6	0	2	8	0	1	0	0	10	9	1	0	1.000	0	4.96
88	POR/PCL	AAA	22	627	22	7	2	0	150.0	152	10	31	1	2	110	2	6	3	9	82	72	12	9	.571	0	4.32
	MIN/AL		9	152	4	0	0	1	37.0	29	3	12	1	1	17	0	1	1	4	12	11	3	0	1.000	0	2.68
89	MIN/AL		32	733	26	2	0	1	172.1	180	22	51	5	5	92	5	3	5	1	82	75	10	6	.625	0	3.92
90	MIN/AL		32	671	23	1	1	1	153.1	191	20	47	4	0	87	2	11	10	0	91	82	5	10	.333	0	4.81
91	BAL/AL		17	348	14	0	0	0	80.1	99	9	24	0	1	25	2	3	3	1	52	50	5	4	.556	0	5.60
	ROC/INT	AAA	11	303	11	2	0	0	74.2	65	3	17	0	3	40	1	5	2	0	31	29	6	2	.750	0	3.50
8 YR TOTALS			**136**	**2699**	**93**	**4**	**1**	**7**	**618.1**	**707**	**80**	**202**	**16**	**12**	**320**	**11**	**26**	**23**	**8**	**344**	**316**	**30**	**31**	**.492**	**1**	**4.60**

Smith, Peter John "Pete" — bats right — throws right — b.2/27/66

YR	TM/LG	CL	G	TBF	GS	CG	SHO	GF	IP	H	HR	BB	IBB	HB	SO	SH	SF	WP	BK	R	ER	W	L	PCT	SV	ERA
84	PHI/GCL	R	8	155	8	0	0	0	37.0	28	0	16	0	0	35	3	1	2	0	11	6	1	2	.333	0	1.46
85	CLE/FSL	A+	26	663	25	4	1	0	153.0	135	2	80	1	2	86	1	7	3	6	68	56	12	10	.545	0	3.29
86	GRE/SOU	AA	24	499	19	0	0	1	104.2	117	11	78	0	4	64	7	8	4	2	88	68	1	8	.111	0	5.85
87	GRE/SOU	AA	29	744	25	5	1	2	177.1	162	10	67	0	3	119	1	4	11	3	76	66	9	9	.500	1	3.35
	ATL/NL		6	143	6	0	0	0	31.2	39	3	14	0	0	11	0	2	3	1	21	17	1	2	.333	0	4.83
88	ATL/NL		32	837	32	5	3	0	195.1	183	15	88	3	1	124	12	4	5	7	89	80	7	15	.318	0	3.69
89	ATL/NL		28	613	27	1	0	0	142.0	144	13	57	0	2	115	4	4	5	7	83	75	5	14	.263	0	4.75
90	ATL/NL		13	327	13	3	0	0	77.0	77	11	24	0	0	56	4	3	2	1	45	41	5	6	.455	0	4.79
	GRE/SOU	AA	2	12	2	0	0	0	3.1	1	0	0	0	0	2	0	0	0	0	0	0	0	0	.000	0	0.00
91	MAC/SAL	A	3	45	3	0	0	0	9.2	15	1	2	0	0	14	0	0	2	0	11	9	0	0	.000	0	8.38
	RIC/INT	AAA	10	239	10	1	0	0	51.0	66	10	24	0	0	41	1	5	2	1	44	41	3	3	.500	0	7.24
	ATL/NL		14	211	10	0	0	2	48.0	48	5	22	3	0	29	2	4	1	4	33	27	1	3	.250	0	5.06
5 YR TOTALS			**93**	**2131**	**88**	**9**	**3**	**2**	**494.0**	**491**	**47**	**205**	**10**	**1**	**335**	**22**	**18**	**14**	**20**	**271**	**240**	**19**	**40**	**.322**	**0**	**4.37**

Smith, Zane William — bats left — throws left — b.12/28/60

YR	TM/LG	CL	G	TBF	GS	CG	SHO	GF	IP	H	HR	BB	IBB	HB	SO	SH	SF	WP	BK	R	ER	W	L	PCT	SV	ERA
84	GRE/SOU	AA	9	239	9	3	1	0	60.0	47	0	23	0	1	35	2	1	1	0	13	11	7	0	1.000	0	1.65
	RIC/INT	AAA	19	534	19	3	0	0	123.2	113	11	65	1	3	68	4	3	7	1	62	57	7	4	.636	0	4.15
	ATL/NL		3	87	3	0	0	0	20.0	16	1	13	2	0	16	1	0	0	0	7	5	1	0	1.000	0	2.25
85	ATL/NL		42	631	18	2	2	3	147.0	135	4	80	5	3	85	16	1	1	2	70	62	9	10	.474	1	3.80
86	ATL/NL		38	889	32	3	1	2	204.2	209	8	105	6	5	139	13	6	6	8	109	92	8	16	.333	0	4.05
87	ATL/NL		36	1035	36	9	3	0	242.0	245	19	91	6	5	130	12	5	5	5	130	110	15	10	.600	0	4.09
88	ATL/NL		23	609	22	3	0	0	140.1	159	8	44	4	3	59	15	2	2	2	72	67	5	10	.333	0	4.30
89	ATL/NL		17	432	17	0	0	0	99.0	102	5	33	3	2	58	10	5	3	0	65	49	1	12	.077	0	4.45
	MON/NL		31	202	0	0	0	10	48.0	39	2	19	4	1	35	5	0	1	0	11	8	0	1	.000	2	1.50
	YEAR		48	634	17	0	0	10	147.0	141	7	52	7	3	93	15	5	4	0	76	57	1	13	.071	2	3.49
90	MON/NL		22	578	21	1	0	0	139.1	141	11	41	3	3	80	2	2	1	0	57	50	6	7	.462	0	3.23
	PIT/NL		11	282	10	3	2	1	76.0	55	4	9	1	0	50	1	1	1	0	20	11	6	2	.750	0	1.30
	YEAR		33	860	31	4	2	1	215.1	196	15	50	4	3	130	3	3	2	0	77	61	12	9	.571	0	2.55
91	PIT/NL		35	916	35	6	3	0	228.0	234	15	29	3	2	120	7	5	1	0	95	81	16	10	.615	0	3.20
8 YR TOTALS			**258**	**5661**	**194**	**27**	**11**	**16**	**1344.1**	**1335**	**77**	**464**	**37**	**24**	**772**	**82**	**27**	**24**	**3**	**636**	**535**	**67**	**78**	**.462**	**3**	**3.58**

Smoltz, John Andrew — bats right — throws right — b.5/15/67

YR	TM/LG	CL	G	TBF	GS	CG	SHO	GF	IP	H	HR	BB	IBB	HB	SO	SH	SF	WP	BK	R	ER	W	L	PCT	SV	ERA
86	LAK/FSL	A+	17	395	14	2	1	0	96.0	86	7	31	0	5	47	0	4	2	6	44	38	7	8	.467	0	3.56
87	GF/EAS	AA	21	582	21	0	0	0	130.0	131	17	81	2	7	86	3	2	6	8	89	82	4	10	.286	0	5.68
	RIC/INT	AAA	3	76	3	0	0	0	16.0	17	2	11	0	1	5	0	0	1	1	11	11	0	1	.000	0	6.19
88	RIC/INT	AAA	20	552	20	3	0	0	135.1	118	5	37	1	2	115	4	3	6	2	49	42	10	5	.667	0	2.79
	ATL/NL		12	297	12	0	0	0	64.0	74	10	33	4	2	37	2	0	2	1	40	39	2	7	.222	0	5.48
89	ATL/NL		29	847	29	5	0	0	208.0	160	15	72	2	2	168	10	7	8	3	79	68	12	11	.522	0	2.94
90	ATL/NL		34	966	34	6	2	0	231.1	206	20	90	3	1	170	9	8	14	2	109	99	14	11	.560	0	3.85
91	ATL/NL		36	947	36	5	0	0	229.2	206	16	77	4	1	148	9	9	20	2	101	97	14	13	.519	0	3.80
4 YR TOTALS			**111**	**3057**	**111**	**16**	**2**	**0**	**733.0**	**646**	**61**	**272**	**10**	**8**	**523**	**30**	**24**	**44**	**9**	**329**	**303**	**42**	**42**	**.500**	**0**	**3.72**

Stanton, William Michael "Mike" — bats left — throws left — b.6/2/67

YR	TM/LG	CL	G	TBF	GS	CG	SHO	GF	IP	H	HR	BB	IBB	HB	SO	SH	SF	WP	BK	R	ER	W	L	PCT	SV	ERA
87	PUL/APP	R+	15	354	13	3	2	1	83.1	64	7	42	0	3	82	3	4	2	1	37	30	4	8	.333	0	3.24
88	BUR/MID	A	30	675	23	1	1	3	154.0	154	7	69	2	1	160	4	3	16	1	86	62	11	5	.688	0	3.62
	DUR/CAR	A+	2	55	2	1	1	0	12.1	14	0	5	0	0	14	0	0	1	1	3	2	1	0	1.000	0	1.46
89	GRE/SOU	AA	47	207	0	0	0	36	51.1	32	1	31	3	0	58	5	2	4	0	10	9	4	1	.800	19	1.58
	RIC/INT	AAA	13	77	0	0	0	11	20.0	6	0	13	2	1	20	1	0	1	0	0	0	2	0	1.000	8	0.00

(continued)

Stanton, William Michael "Mike" (continued)

YR	TM/LG	CL	G	TBF	GS	CG	SHO	GF	IP	H	HR	BB	IBB	HB	SO	SH	SF	WP	BK	R	ER	W	L	PCT	SV	ERA
	ATL/NL		20	94	0	0	0	10	24.0	17	0	8	1	0	27	4	0	1	0	4	4	0	1	.000	7	1.50
90	ATL/NL		7	42	0	0	0	4	7.0	16	1	4	2	1	7	1	0	1	0	16	14	0	3	.000	2	18.00
	GRE/SOU	AA	4	27	4	0	0	0	5.2	7	1	3	0	0	4	0	0	0	0	1	1	0	1	.000	0	1.59
91	ATL/NL		74	314	0	0	0	20	78.0	62	6	21	6	1	54	6	0	0	0	27	25	5	5	.500	7	2.88
3 YR TOTALS			**101**	**450**	**0**	**0**	**0**	**34**	**109.0**	**95**	**7**	**33**	**9**	**2**	**88**	**11**	**0**	**2**	**0**	**47**	**43**	**5**	**9**	**.357**	**16**	**3.55**

Stewart, David Keith "Dave" — bats right — throws right — b.2/19/57

YR	TM/LG	CL	G	TBF	GS	CG	SHO	GF	IP	H	HR	BB	IBB	HB	SO	SH	SF	WP	BK	R	ER	W	L	PCT	SV	ERA
78	LA/NL		1	6	0	0	0	1	2.0	1	0	0	0	0	1	0	0	0	0	0	0	0	0	.000	0	0.00
81	LA/NL		32	184	0	0	0	14	43.1	40	3	14	5	0	29	7	3	4	0	13	12	4	3	.571	6	2.49
82	LA/NL		45	616	14	0	0	9	146.1	137	14	49	11	2	80	10	5	3	0	72	62	9	8	.529	1	3.81
83	LA/NL		46	328	1	0	0	25	76.0	67	4	33	7	2	54	7	3	2	0	28	25	5	2	.714	8	2.96
	TEX/AL		8	237	8	2	0	0	59.0	50	2	17	0	2	24	2	1	1	0	15	14	5	2	.714	0	2.14
	YEAR		54	565	9	2	0	25	135.0	117	6	50	7	4	78	9	4	3	0	43	39	10	4	.714	8	2.60
84	TEX/AL		32	847	27	3	0	2	192.1	193	26	87	3	4	119	4	5	12	0	106	101	7	14	.333	0	4.73
85	TEX/AL		42	361	5	0	0	29	81.1	86	13	37	5	2	64	5	2	5	1	53	49	0	6	.000	4	5.42
	PHI/NL		4	22	0	0	0	3	4.1	5	0	4	0	0	2	0	0	2	0	4	3	0	0	.000	0	6.23
	YEAR		46	383	5	0	0	32	85.2	91	13	41	5	2	66	5	2	7	1	57	52	0	6	.000	4	5.46
86	PHI/NL		8	56	0	0	0	2	12.1	15	1	4	0	0	9	0	0	3	1	9	9	0	0	.000	0	6.57
	TAC/PCL	AAA	1	13	0	0	0	0	3.0	4	0	1	0	0	3	0	0	0	0	1	0	0	0	.000	0	0.00
	OAK/AL		29	644	17	4	1	2	149.1	137	15	65	0	3	102	4	4	9	0	67	62	9	5	.643	0	3.74
	YEAR		37	700	17	4	1	4	161.2	152	16	69	0	3	111	4	4	7	10	3	76	71	9	5	.643	0	3.95
87	OAK/AL		37	1103	37	8	1	0	261.1	224	24	105	2	6	205	7	5	11	0	121	107	20	13	.606	0	3.68
88	OAK/AL		37	1156	37	14	2	0	275.2	240	14	110	5	3	192	7	9	14	16	111	99	21	12	.636	0	3.23
89	OAK/AL		36	1081	36	8	0	0	257.2	260	23	69	0	6	155	9	10	13	0	105	95	21	9	.700	0	3.32
90	OAK/AL		36	1088	36	11	4	0	267.0	226	16	83	1	5	166	10	10	8	0	84	76	22	11	.667	0	2.56
91	OAK/AL		35	1014	35	2	1	0	226.0	245	24	105	1	9	144	5	15	13	0	135	130	11	11	.500	0	5.18
12 YR TOTALS			**428**	**8743**	**253**	**52**	**9**	**87**	**2054.0**	**1926**	**179**	**782**	**40**	**44**	**1346**	**77**	**75**	**98**	**20**	**923**	**844**	**134**	**96**	**.583**	**19**	**3.70**

Stieb, David Andrew "Dave" — bats right — throws right — b.7/22/57

YR	TM/LG	CL	G	TBF	GS	CG	SHO	GF	IP	H	HR	BB	IBB	HB	SO	SH	SF	WP	BK	R	ER	W	L	PCT	SV	ERA
79	TOR/AL		18	563	18	7	1	0	129.1	139	11	48	3	4	52	4	4	3	1	70	62	8	8	.500	0	4.31
80	TOR/AL		34	1004	32	14	4	0	242.2	232	12	83	6	6	108	12	9	6	2	108	100	12	15	.444	0	3.71
81	TOR/AL		25	748	25	11	2	0	183.2	148	10	61	2	11	89	5	7	1	2	70	65	11	10	.524	0	3.19
82	TOR/AL		38	1187	38	19	5	0	288.1	271	27	75	4	5	141	10	3	3	1	116	104	17	14	.548	0	3.25
83	TOR/AL		36	1141	36	14	4	0	278.0	223	21	93	6	14	187	6	6	9	0	105	94	17	12	.586	0	3.04
84	TOR/AL		35	1085	35	11	2	0	267.0	215	19	88	1	11	198	8	6	2	0	87	84	16	8	.667	0	2.83
85	TOR/AL		36	1087	36	8	2	0	265.0	206	22	96	3	9	167	14	2	4	1	89	73	14	13	.519	0	2.48
86	TOR/AL		37	919	34	1	1	2	205.0	239	29	87	1	15	127	6	6	7	0	128	108	7	12	.368	1	4.74
87	TOR/AL		33	789	31	3	1	1	185.0	164	16	87	4	7	115	5	5	4	0	92	84	13	9	.591	0	4.09
88	TOR/AL		32	844	31	8	4	1	207.1	157	15	79	0	13	147	0	4	4	5	76	70	16	8	.667	0	3.04
89	TOR/AL		33	850	33	3	2	0	206.2	164	12	76	2	13	101	10	3	6	0	83	77	17	8	.680	0	3.35
90	TOR/AL		33	861	33	2	2	0	208.2	179	11	64	0	10	125	6	3	5	0	73	68	18	6	.750	0	2.93
91	TOR/AL		9	244	9	1	0	0	59.2	52	4	23	0	2	29	4	1	0	0	22	21	4	3	.571	0	3.17
13 YR TOTALS			**399**	**11322**	**391**	**102**	**30**	**4**	**2726.1**	**2389**	**209**	**960**	**32**	**120**	**1586**	**90**	**62**	**47**	**14**	**1119**	**1010**	**170**	**126**	**.574**	**1**	**3.33**

Stottlemyre, Todd Vernon — bats left — throws right — b.5/20/65

YR	TM/LG	CL	G	TBF	GS	CG	SHO	GF	IP	H	HR	BB	IBB	HB	SO	SH	SF	WP	BK	R	ER	W	L	PCT	SV	ERA
86	VEN/CAL	A+	17	428	17	2	0	0	103.2	76	4	36	0	2	104	4	1	7	2	39	28	9	4	.692	0	2.43
	KNO/SOU	AA	18	432	18	1	0	0	99.0	93	5	49	1	1	81	2	5	4	2	56	46	8	7	.533	0	4.18
87	SYR/INT	AAA	34	827	34	1	0	0	186.2	189	14	87	3	6	143	2	10	10	1	103	92	11	13	.458	0	4.44
88	SYR/INT	AAA	7	187	7	1	0	0	48.1	36	1	8	0	0	51	1	1	2	2	12	11	5	0	1.000	0	2.05
	TOR/AL		28	443	16	0	0	2	98.0	109	15	46	5	4	67	5	3	2	3	70	62	4	8	.333	0	5.69
89	SYR/INT	AAA	10	233	9	2	0	1	55.2	46	4	15	0	2	45	1	3	0	1	23	20	3	2	.600	0	3.23
	TOR/AL		27	545	18	0	0	4	127.2	137	11	44	4	5	63	3	7	4	1	56	55	7	7	.500	0	3.88
90	TOR/AL		33	866	33	4	0	0	203.0	214	18	69	4	8	115	3	5	6	1	101	98	13	17	.433	0	4.34
91	TOR/AL		34	921	34	1	0	0	219.0	194	21	75	3	12	116	0	8	4	0	97	92	15	8	.652	0	3.78
4 YR TOTALS			**122**	**2775**	**101**	**5**	**0**	**6**	**647.2**	**654**	**65**	**234**	**16**	**29**	**361**	**11**	**23**	**16**	**5**	**324**	**307**	**39**	**40**	**.494**	**0**	**4.27**

Sutcliffe, Richard Lee "Rick" — bats left — throws right — b.6/21/56

YR	TM/LG	CL	G	TBF	GS	CG	SHO	GF	IP	H	HR	BB	IBB	HB	SO	SH	SF	WP	BK	R	ER	W	L	PCT	SV	ERA
76	LA/NL		1	17	1	0	0	0	5.0	2	0	1	0	0	3	0	0	0	0	0	0	0	0	.000	0	0.00
78	LA/NL		2	9	0	0	0	0	1.2	2	0	1	0	1	0	0	0	0	0	0	0	0	0	.000	0	0.00
79	LA/NL		39	1016	30	5	1	2	242.0	217	16	97	6	2	117	16	9	8	6	104	93	17	10	.630	0	3.46
80	LA/NL		42	491	10	1	1	19	110.0	122	10	55	2	1	59	4	3	6	4	73	68	3	9	.250	5	5.56
81	LA/NL		14	197	6	0	0	5	47.0	41	5	20	2	1	16	1	2	0	0	24	21	2	2	.500	0	4.02
82	CLE/AL		34	887	27	6	1	3	216.0	174	16	98	2	4	142	7	8	6	1	81	71	14	8	.636	1	2.96
83	CLE/AL		36	1061	35	10	2	0	243.1	251	23	102	5	6	160	8	9	7	3	131	116	17	11	.607	0	4.29
84	CLE/AL		15	428	15	2	0	0	94.1	111	7	46	3	2	58	4	3	3	1	60	54	4	5	.444	0	5.15
	CHI/NL		20	602	20	7	3	0	150.1	123	9	39	0	1	155	1	1	3	2	53	45	16	1	.941	0	2.69
	YEAR		35	1030	35	9	3	0	244.2	234	16	85	3	3	213	5	4	6	3	113	99	20	6	.769	0	3.64
85	CHI/NL		20	549	20	6	3	0	130.0	119	12	44	3	3	102	3	3	4	0	51	46	8	8	.500	0	3.18
86	CHI/NL		28	764	27	4	1	0	176.2	166	18	96	6	2	122	6	2	13	1	92	91	5	14	.263	0	4.64
87	CHI/NL		34	1012	34	6	1	0	237.1	223	24	106	14	4	174	9	8	9	4	106	97	18	10	.643	0	3.68

Sutcliffe, Richard Lee "Rick" (continued)

YR	TM/LG	CL	G	TBF	GS	CG	SHO	GF	IP	H	HR	BB	IBB	HB	SO	SH	SF	WP	BK	R	ER	W	L	PCT	SV	ERA
88	CHI/NL		32	958	32	12	2	0	226.0	232	18	70	9	2	144	17	5	11	4	97	97	13	14	.481	0	3.86
89	CHI/NL		35	938	34	5	1	0	229.0	202	18	69	8	2	153	15	10	12	6	98	93	16	11	.593	0	3.66
90	IOW/AMA	AAA	2	62	2	0	0	0	12.2	18	2	7	0	0	12	0	1	0	1	13	11	0	2	.000	0	7.82
	CHI/NL		5	97	5	0	0	0	21.1	25	2	12	0	0	7	1	2	4	0	14	14	0	2	.000	0	5.91
91	PEO/MID	A	1	40	1	0	0	0	9.0	12	0	2	0	1	6	1	1	0	0	6	6	0	0	.000	0	6.00
	IOW/AMA	AAA	3	65	2	0	0	1	13.0	23	2	6	0	0	8	0	1	2	1	14	14	1	2	.333	0	9.69
	CHI/NL		19	422	18	0	0	0	96.2	96	4	45	2	0	52	5	8	2	2	52	44	6	5	.545	0	4.10
15 YR TOTALS			**376**	**9448**	**314**	**64**	**16**	**29**	**2226.2**	**2106**	**182**	**901**	**64**	**31**	**1464**	**97**	**74**	**88**	**35**	**1036**	**950**	**139**	**110**	**.558**	**6**	**3.84**

Swan, Russell Howard "Russ" — bats left — throws left — b.1/3/64

YR	TM/LG	CL	G	TBF	GS	CG	SHO	GF	IP	H	HR	BB	IBB	HB	SO	SH	SF	WP	BK	R	ER	W	L	PCT	SV	ERA
86	EVE/NWL	A–	7	0	7	2	0	0	46.0	30	2	22	0	1	45	0	0	1	1	17	11	5	0	1.000	0	2.15
	CLI/MID	A	7	179	7	2	1	0	43.2	36	2	8	0	1	37	0	2	1	1	18	15	3	3	.500	0	3.09
87	FRE/CAL	A+	12	274	12	0	0	0	64.0	54	5	29	0	1	59	4	0	4	0	40	27	6	3	.667	0	3.80
88	SJ/CAL	A+	11	301	11	2	1	0	76.2	53	2	26	0	1	62	7	0	2	0	28	19	7	0	1.000	0	2.23
89	SHR/TEX	AA	11	304	11	0	0	0	75.1	62	2	22	1	1	56	1	1	3	2	25	22	2	3	.400	0	2.63
	SF/NL		2	34	2	0	0	0	6.2	11	4	4	0	0	2	2	0	0	0	10	8	0	2	.000	0	10.80
	PHO/PCL	AAA	14	348	13	1	0	0	83.0	75	8	29	0	3	49	5	2	0	3	37	31	4	3	.571	0	3.36
90	SF/NL		2	18	1	0	0	0	2.1	6	0	4	0	0	1	0	0	1	0	4	1	0	1	.000	0	3.86
	PHO/PCL	AAA	6	153	6	0	0	0	33.2	41	1	15	0	2	21	1	1	1	1	17	13	2	4	.333	0	3.48
	CAL/PCL	AAA	5	105	5	0	0	0	23.0	28	0	12	0	0	14	1	0	3	0	18	15	1	2	.333	0	5.87
	SEA/AL		11	195	8	0	0	0	47.0	42	3	18	2	0	15	2	3	0	1	22	19	2	3	.400	0	3.64
	YEAR		13	213	9	0	0	0	49.1	48	3	22	2	0	16	2	3	1	1	26	20	2	4	.333	0	3.65
91	SEA/AL		63	336	1	0	0	11	78.2	81	8	28	7	0	33	6	1	8	0	35	30	6	2	.750	2	3.43
3 YR TOTALS			**78**	**583**	**11**	**0**	**0**	**11**	**134.2**	**140**	**15**	**54**	**9**	**0**	**51**	**10**	**4**	**9**	**1**	**71**	**58**	**8**	**8**	**.500**	**2**	**3.88**

Swift, William Charles "Bill" — bats right — throws right — b.10/27/61

YR	TM/LG	CL	G	TBF	GS	CG	SHO	GF	IP	H	HR	BB	IBB	HB	SO	SH	SF	WP	BK	R	ER	W	L	PCT	SV	ERA
85	CHT/SOU	AA	7	166	7	0	0	0	39.0	34	2	21	0	2	21	2	2	3	0	16	16	2	1	.667	0	3.69
	SEA/AL		23	532	21	0	0	0	120.2	131	8	48	5	5	55	6	3	5	3	71	64	6	10	.375	0	4.77
86	CAL/PCL	AAA	10	240	8	3	1	2	57.0	57	5	22	2	2	29	1	1	2	0	33	25	4	4	.500	1	3.95
	SEA/AL		29	534	17	1	0	3	115.1	148	5	55	2	7	55	5	3	2	1	85	70	2	9	.182	0	5.46
87	CAL/PCL	AAA	5	95	5	0	0	0	18.1	32	2	13	1	0	5	0	2	2	1	22	18	0	0	.000	0	8.84
88	SEA/AL		38	757	24	6	1	4	174.2	199	10	65	3	8	47	5	3	6	2	99	89	8	12	.400	0	4.59
89	SB/CAL	A+	2	36	2	0	0	0	10.0	8	0	2	0	0	4	0	0	0	0	0	0	1	0	1.000	0	0.00
	SEA/AL		37	551	16	0	0	7	130.0	140	7	38	4	2	45	4	3	4	1	72	64	7	3	.700	1	4.43
90	SEA/AL		55	533	8	0	0	18	128.0	135	4	21	6	7	42	5	4	8	3	46	34	6	4	.600	6	2.39
91	SEA/AL		71	359	0	0	0	30	90.1	74	3	26	4	1	48	2	0	2	1	22	20	1	2	.333	17	1.99
6 YR TOTALS			**253**	**3266**	**86**	**7**	**1**	**62**	**759.0**	**827**	**37**	**253**	**24**	**30**	**292**	**27**	**16**	**27**	**11**	**395**	**341**	**30**	**40**	**.429**	**24**	**4.04**

Swindell, Forrest Gregory "Greg" — bats right — throws left — b.1/2/65

YR	TM/LG	CL	G	TBF	GS	CG	SHO	GF	IP	H	HR	BB	IBB	HB	SO	SH	SF	WP	BK	R	ER	W	L	PCT	SV	ERA
86	WAT/MID	A	3	68	3	0	0	0	18.0	12	1	3	0	0	25	0	0	0	0	2	2	2	1	.667	0	1.00
	CLE/AL		9	255	9	1	0	0	61.2	57	9	15	0	1	46	3	1	3	2	35	29	5	2	.714	0	4.23
87	CLE/AL		16	441	15	4	1	0	102.1	112	18	37	1	1	97	4	3	0	1	62	58	3	8	.273	0	5.10
88	CLE/AL		33	988	33	12	4	0	242.0	234	18	45	3	1	180	9	5	5	0	97	86	18	14	.563	0	3.20
89	CLE/AL		28	749	28	5	2	0	184.1	170	16	51	1	0	129	4	4	3	1	71	69	13	6	.684	0	3.37
90	CLE/AL		34	912	34	3	0	0	214.2	245	27	47	2	1	135	4	6	3	2	110	105	12	9	.571	0	4.40
91	CLE/AL		33	971	33	7	0	0	238.0	241	21	31	1	3	169	13	8	3	1	112	92	9	16	.360	0	3.48
6 YR TOTALS			**153**	**4316**	**152**	**32**	**7**	**0**	**1043.0**	**1059**	**109**	**226**	**8**	**7**	**756**	**41**	**27**	**17**	**7**	**487**	**439**	**60**	**55**	**.522**	**0**	**3.79**

Tanana, Frank Daryl — bats left — throws left — b.7/3/53

YR	TM/LG	CL	G	TBF	GS	CG	SHO	GF	IP	H	HR	BB	IBB	HB	SO	SH	SF	WP	BK	R	ER	W	L	PCT	SV	ERA
73	CAL/AL		4	108	4	2	1	0	26.1	20	2	8	0	0	22	0	0	2	0	11	9	2	2	.500	0	3.08
74	CAL/AL		39	1127	35	12	4	2	268.2	262	27	77	4	8	180	10	4	4	2	104	93	14	19	.424	0	3.12
75	CAL/AL		34	1029	33	16	5	1	257.1	211	21	73	6	7	269	13	4	8	1	80	75	16	9	.640	0	2.62
76	CAL/AL		34	1142	34	23	2	0	288.1	212	24	73	5	9	261	14	3	5	0	88	78	19	10	.655	0	2.43
77	CAL/AL		31	973	31	20	7	0	241.1	201	19	61	2	12	205	~8	7	8	·1	72	68	15	9	.625	0	2.54
78	CAL/AL		33	1014	33	10	4	0	239.0	239	26	60	7	9	137	8	10	5	8	108	97	18	12	.600	0	3.65
79	CAL/AL		18	382	17	2	1	0	90.1	93	9	25	0	2	46	1	2	6	1	44	39	7	5	.583	0	3.89
80	CAL/AL		32	870	31	7	0	1	204.0	223	18	45	0	8	113	8	4	3	1	107	94	11	12	.478	0	4.15
81	BOS/AL		24	596	23	5	2	0	141.1	142	17	43	4	4	78	9	4	2	0	70	63	4	10	.286	0	4.01
82	TEX/AL		30	832	30	7	0	0	194.1	199	16	55	10	2	87	13	4	0	1	102	91	7	18	.280	0	4.21
83	TEX/AL		29	667	22	3	0	1	159.1	144	14	49	5	7	108	7	3	6	1	70	56	7	9	.438	0	3.16
84	TEX/AL		35	1054	35	9	1	0	246.1	234	30	81	3	6	141	6	5	12	4	117	89	15	15	.500	0	3.25
85	TEX/AL		13	340	13	0	0	0	77.2	89	15	23	2	1	52	4	3	0	0	53	51	2	7	.222	0	5.91
	DET/AL		20	567	20	4	0	0	137.1	131	13	34	6	2	107	4	2	1	1	59	51	10	7	.588	0	3.34
	YEAR		33	907	33	4	0	0	215.0	220	28	57	8	3	159	8	5	1	1	112	102	12	14	.462	0	4.27
86	DET/AL		32	812	31	3	1	1	188.1	196	23	65	9	3	119	8	5	7	1	95	87	12	9	.571	0	4.16
87	DET/AL		34	924	34	5	3	0	218.2	216	27	56	5	5	146	8	11	6	0	106	95	15	10	.600	0	3.91
88	DET/AL		32	876	32	5	0	0	203.0	213	25	64	7	4	127	6	3	6	0	105	95	14	11	.560	0	4.21
89	DET/AL		33	955	33	6	1	0	223.2	227	21	74	8	9	147	7	10	8	0	105	89	10	14	.417	0	3.58
90	DET/AL		34	763	29	1	0	4	176.1	190	25	66	7	9	114	3	7	5	1	104	104	9	8	.529	1	5.31

(continued)

Tanana, Frank Daryl (continued)

YR	TM/LG	CL	G	TBF	GS	CG	SHO	GF	IP	H	HR	BB	IBB	HB	SO	SH	SF	WP	BK	R	ER	W	L	PCT	SV	ERA
91	DET/AL		33	920	33	3	2	0	217.1	217	26	78	9	2	107	12	9	3	1	98	91	13	12	.520	0	3.77
19 YR TOTALS			**574**	**15951**	**553**	**140**	**34**	**10**	**3799.0**	**3659**	**398**	**1110**	**99**	**113**	**2566**	**146**	**103**	**101**	**24**	**1698**	**1515**	**220**	**208**	**.514**	**1**	**3.59**

Tapani, Kevin Ray — bats right — throws right — b.2/18/64

YR	TM/LG	CL	G	TBF	GS	CG	SHO	GF	IP	H	HR	BB	IBB	HB	SO	SH	SF	WP	BK	R	ER	W	L	PCT	SV	ERA
86	MED/NWL	A−	2	0	2	0	0	0	8.1	6	0	3	0	0	9	0	0	0	0	3	0	1	0	1.000	0	0.00
	TAC/PCL	AAA	1	14	1	0	0	0	2.1	5	1	1	0	0	1	0	0	1	0	6	4	0	1	.000	0	15.43
	MOD/CAL	A+	11	293	11	1	0	0	69.0	74	2	22	1	1	44	2	0	1	0	26	19	6	1	.857	0	2.48
	HUN/SOU	AA	1	26	1	0	0	0	6.0	8	0	1	0	0	2	0	1	0	0	4	4	1	0	1.000	0	6.00
87	MOD/CAL	A+	24	627	24	6	1	0	148.1	122	14	60	2	5	121	6	1	21	0	74	62	10	7	.588	0	3.76
88	SL/FSL	A+	3	76	3	0	0	0	19.0	17	1	4	0	0	11	0	0	2	0	5	3	1	0	1.000	0	1.42
	JAC/TEX	AA	24	248	5	0	0	9	62.1	46	3	19	2	0	35	5	2	1	3	23	19	5	1	.833	0	2.74
89	NY/NL		3	31	0	0	0	1	7.1	5	1	4	0	0	2	0	1	0	1	3	3	0	0	.000	0	3.68
	TID/INT	AAA	17	459	17	2	1	0	109.0	113	6	25	2	1	63	1	0	3	1	49	42	7	5	.583	0	3.47
	POR/PCL	AAA	6	170	6	1	0	0	41.0	38	4	12	1	0	30	1	0	0	1	15	10	4	2	.667	0	2.20
	MIN/AL		5	138	5	0	0	0	32.2	34	2	8	1	0	21	1	1	0	0	15	14	2	2	.500	0	3.86
	YEAR		8	169	5	0	0	1	40.0	39	3	12	1	0	23	1	2	0	1	18	17	2	2	.500	0	3.83
90	MIN/AL		28	659	28	1	1	0	159.1	164	12	29	2	2	101	3	4	1	0	75	72	12	8	.600	0	4.07
91	MIN/AL		34	974	34	4	1	0	244.0	225	23	40	0	2	135	9	6	3	3	84	81	16	9	.640	0	2.99
3 YR TOTALS			**70**	**1802**	**67**	**5**	**2**	**1**	**443.1**	**428**	**38**	**81**	**3**	**4**	**259**	**13**	**12**	**4**	**4**	**177**	**170**	**30**	**19**	**.612**	**0**	**3.45**

Taylor, Wade Eric — bats right — throws right — b.10/19/65

YR	TM/LG	CL	G	TBF	GS	CG	SHO	GF	IP	H	HR	BB	IBB	HB	SO	SH	SF	WP	BK	R	ER	W	L	PCT	SV	ERA
87	BEL/NWL	A−	12	259	10	0	0	2	58.1	58	4	22	0	13	53	1	2	4	1	31	29	3	5	.375	1	4.47
88	FT./FSL	A+	24	532	17	7	1	4	122.2	109	3	57	6	7	90	6	3	7	3	53	47	4	11	.267	0	3.45
89	PW/CAR	A+	25	603	25	4	1	0	142.2	131	9	56	2	5	104	4	3	9	5	63	53	9	8	.529	0	3.34
90	ALB/EAS	AA	12	332	12	1	0	0	84.1	71	3	18	0	2	44	3	4	2	2	30	27	6	4	.600	0	2.88
	COL/INT	AAA	14	402	14	4	3	0	98.2	91	3	30	1	3	57	3	3	0	3	25	24	6	4	.600	0	2.19
91	COL/INT	AAA	9	259	9	3	1	0	61.0	59	4	22	1	3	36	3	3	0	1	27	24	4	1	.800	0	3.54
	NY/AL		23	528	22	0	0	0	116.1	144	13	53	0	7	72	2	7	3	3	85	81	7	12	.368	0	6.27

Telford, Anthony Charles — bats right — throws right — b.3/6/66

YR	TM/LG	CL	G	TBF	GS	CG	SHO	GF	IP	H	HR	BB	IBB	HB	SO	SH	SF	WP	BK	R	ER	W	L	PCT	SV	ERA
87	NEW/NYP	A−	6	72	2	0	0	3	17.2	16	0	3	0	0	27	0	0	0	0	2	2	1	0	1.000	0	1.02
	HAG/CAR	A+	2	46	2	0	0	0	11.1	9	0	5	0	1	10	0	0	0	0	2	2	1	0	1.000	0	1.59
	ROC/INT	AAA	1	9	0	0	0	0	2.0	0	0	3	0	0	3	0	0	0	1	0	0	0	0	.000	0	0.00
88	HAG/CAR	A+	1	24	1	0	0	0	7.0	3	0	0	0	0	10	0	0	1	0	0	0	1	0	1.000	0	0.00
89	FRE/CAR	A+	9	116	5	0	0	2	25.2	25	1	12	0	2	19	1	2	2	0	15	12	2	1	.667	1	4.21
90	FRE/CAR	A+	8	207	8	1	0	0	53.2	35	1	11	1	4	49	0	0	4	0	15	10	4	2	.667	0	1.68
	HAG/EAS	AA	14	384	13	3	1	1	96.0	80	3	25	1	3	73	5	3	4	0	26	21	10	2	.833	0	1.97
	BAL/AL		8	168	8	0	0	0	36.1	43	4	19	0	1	20	0	2	1	0	22	20	3	3	.500	0	4.95
91	ROC/INT	AAA	27	666	25	3	0	0	157.1	166	18	48	2	4	115	5	3	7	1	82	69	12	9	.571	0	3.95
	BAL/AL		9	109	1	0	0	4	26.2	27	3	6	1	0	24	0	1	1	0	12	12	0	0	.000	0	4.05
2 YR TOTALS			**17**	**277**	**9**	**0**	**0**	**4**	**63.0**	**70**	**7**	**25**	**1**	**1**	**44**	**0**	**3**	**2**	**0**	**34**	**32**	**3**	**3**	**.500**	**0**	**4.57**

Terrell, Charles Walter "Walt" — bats left — throws right — b.5/11/58

YR	TM/LG	CL	G	TBF	GS	CG	SHO	GF	IP	H	HR	BB	IBB	HB	SO	SH	SF	WP	BK	R	ER	W	L	PCT	SV	ERA
82	NY/NL		3	97	3	0	0	0	21.0	22	2	14	2	0	8	1	0	1	1	12	8	0	3	.000	0	3.43
83	NY/NL		21	561	20	4	2	1	133.2	123	7	55	7	2	59	9	5	5	0	57	53	8	8	.500	0	3.57
84	NY/NL		33	926	33	3	1	0	215.0	232	16	80	1	4	114	11	8	6	0	99	84	11	12	.478	0	3.52
85	DET/AL		34	983	34	5	3	0	229.0	221	9	95	5	4	130	11	7	5	0	107	98	15	10	.600	0	3.85
86	DET/AL		34	918	33	9	2	1	217.1	199	30	98	5	3	93	2	3	5	0	116	110	15	10	.600	0	3.85
87	DET/AL		35	1057	35	10	1	0	244.2	254	30	94	7	3	143	3	10	8	0	123	110	17	10	.630	0	4.05
88	LAK/FSL	A+	2	42	2	0	0	0	9.2	13	1	1	0	0	6	0	0	0	0	7	7	1	1	.500	0	6.52
	DET/AL		29	870	29	11	1	0	206.1	199	20	78	8	2	84	13	6	7	2	101	91	7	16	.304	0	3.97
89	SD/NL		19	520	19	4	1	0	123.1	134	14	26	1	0	63	8	2	4	0	65	55	5	13	.278	0	4.01
	NY/AL		13	362	13	1	1	0	83.0	102	9	24	2	2	30	2	2	2	2	52	48	6	5	.545	0	5.20
	YEAR		32	882	32	5	2	0	206.1	236	23	50	3	2	93	10	4	6	2	117	103	11	18	.379	0	4.49
90	PIT/NL		16	377	16	0	0	0	82.2	98	13	33	1	4	34	6	2	7	0	59	54	2	7	.222	0	5.88
	DET/AL		13	333	12	0	0	0	75.1	86	7	24	3	8	30	1	0	0	0	39	38	6	4	.600	0	4.54
	YEAR		29	710	28	0	0	0	158.0	184	20	57	4	12	64	9	3	7	2	98	92	8	11	.421	0	5.24
91	DET/AL		35	954	33	8	2	1	218.2	257	16	79	10	2	80	10	9	8	0	115	103	12	14	.462	0	4.24
10 YR TOTALS			**285**	**7958**	**280**	**55**	**14**	**3**	**1850.0**	**1927**	**173**	**700**	**50**	**34**	**868**	**79**	**55**	**58**	**5**	**945**	**852**	**104**	**114**	**.477**	**0**	**4.14**

Terry, Scott Ray — bats right — throws right — b.11/21/59

YR	TM/LG	CL	G	TBF	GS	CG	SHO	GF	IP	H	HR	BB	IBB	HB	SO	SH	SF	WP	BK	R	ER	W	L	PCT	SV	ERA
84	VER/EAS	AA	20	555	20	9	6	0	144.0	110	1	43	0	1	100	3	3	5	1	31	24	14	3	.824	0	1.50
	WIC/AMA	AAA	2	43	2	0	0	0	9.1	13	1	7	1	0	6	1	0	1	0	6	6	0	0	.000	0	5.79
85	DEN/AMA	AAA	28	788	28	4	1	0	178.2	203	11	76	2	3	101	3	8	14	2	105	88	11	12	.478	0	4.43
86	CIN/NL		28	258	3	0	0	7	55.2	66	8	32	3	0	32	1	2	2	0	40	38	1	2	.333	0	6.14
	DEN/AMA	AAA	10	90	1	0	0	4	19.1	22	0	6	0	0	13	1	0	2	0	13	5	1	2	.333	0	2.33
87	NAS/AMA	AAA	27	775	27	10	0	0	181.2	199	13	48	1	3	91	3	4	2	0	94	80	11	10	.524	2	3.96
	STL/NL		11	59	0	0	0	2	13.1	13	0	4	2	0	9	1	0	0	0	5	5	0	0	.000	0	3.38
88	LOU/AMA	AAA	3	18	3	0	0	0	5.0	2	0	1	0	0	1	0	0	0	0	0	0	0	0	.000	0	0.00

Terry, Scott Ray (continued)

YR	TM/LG	CL	G	TBF	GS	CG	SHO	GF	IP	H	HR	BB	IBB	HB	SO	SH	SF	WP	BK	R	ER	W	L	PCT	SV	ERA
	STL/NL		51	524	11	1	0	14	129.1	119	5	34	6	0	65	6	3	1	2	48	42	9	6	.600	3	2.92
89	STL/NL		31	619	24	1	0	5	148.2	142	14	43	6	3	69	8	4	2	2	65	59	8	10	.444	2	3.57
90	STL/NL		50	323	2	0	0	26	72.0	75	7	27	5	4	35	3	5	2	0	45	38	2	6	.250	2	4.75
91	STL/NL		65	339	0	0	0	13	80.1	76	1	32	14	0	52	2	0	0	0	31	25	4	4	.500	1	2.80
6 YR TOTALS			**236**	**2122**	**40**	**2**	**0**	**67**	**499.1**	**491**	**35**	**176**	**36**	**7**	**262**	**25**	**13**	**7**	**4**	**234**	**207**	**24**	**28**	**.462**	**8**	**3.73**

Tewksbury, Robert Alan "Bob" — bats right — throws right — b.11/30/60

YR	TM/LG	CL	G	TBF	GS	CG	SHO	GF	IP	H	HR	BB	IBB	HB	SO	SH	SF	WP	BK	R	ER	W	L	PCT	SV	ERA
81	ONE/NYP	A—	14	0	14	6	1	0	90.0	85	8	37	0	2	62	0	0	5	1	43	34	7	3	.700	0	3.40
82	FT./FSL	A+	24	0	23	13	5	0	182.0	146	6	47	0	5	92	0	0	11	1	46	38	15	4	.789	0	1.88
83	FT./FSL	A+	2	0	2	1	0	0	16.0	6	0	1	0	0	5	0	0	0	0	0	0	2	0	1.000	0	0.00
	NAS/SOU	AA	7	0	7	3	0	0	51.0	49	6	10	1	1	15	0	0	0	0	20	16	5	1	.833	0	2.82
84	NAS/SOU	AA	26	724	26	6	0	0	172.0	185	8	42	3	4	78	3	4	4	1	69	54	11	9	.550	0	2.83
85	ALB/EAS	AA	17	434	17	4	2	0	106.2	101	9	19	0	2	63	3	3	2	1	48	42	6	5	.545	0	3.54
	COL/INT	AAA	6	160	6	1	1	0	44.0	27	2	5	0	0	21	0	0	0	1	5	5	3	0	1.000	0	1.02
86	COL/INT	AAA	2	37	2	0	0	0	10.0	6	0	2	0	0	4	0	0	0	1	3	3	1	0	1.000	0	2.70
	NY/AL		23	558	20	2	0	0	130.1	144	8	31	0	3	49	4	7	3	2	58	48	9	5	.643	0	3.31
87	COL/INT	AAA	11	300	11	3	0	0	74.2	68	5	11	0	1	32	2	1	0	2	23	21	6	1	.857	0	2.53
	NY/AL		8	149	6	0	0	1	33.1	47	5	7	1	1	12	2	0	0	0	26	25	1	4	.200	0	6.75
	CHI/NL		7	93	3	0	0	3	18.0	32	1	13	3	0	10	3	1	1	2	15	13	0	4	.000	0	6.50
	YEAR		15	242	9	0	0	4	51.1	79	6	20	3	1	22	5	1	1	2	41	38	1	8	.111	0	6.66
88	CHI/NL		1	18	1	0	0	0	3.1	6	1	2	0	0	1	0	0	0	0	5	3	0	0	.000	0	8.10
	IOW/AMA	AAA	10	277	10	2	2	0	67.0	73	8	10	0	2	43	1	2	1	6	28	28	4	2	.667	0	3.76
89	LOU/AMA	AAA	28	767	28	2	1	1	189.0	170	9	34	1	2	72	1	1	0	1	63	51	13	5	.722	0	2.43
	STL/NL		7	125	4	1	1	2	30.0	25	2	10	3	2	17	1	1	0	0	12	11	1	0	1.000	0	3.30
90	LOU/AMA	AAA	6	159	6	2	0	0	40.2	41	2	3	0	2	22	1	0	0	1	15	11	3	2	.600	0	2.43
	STL/NL		28	595	20	3	2	1	145.1	151	7	15	3	3	50	5	7	2	0	67	56	10	9	.526	1	3.47
91	STL/NL		30	798	30	3	0	0	191.0	206	13	38	2	5	75	12	10	0	0	86	69	11	12	.478	0	3.25
6 YR TOTALS			**104**	**2336**	**84**	**9**	**3**	**7**	**551.1**	**611**	**37**	**116**	**11**	**16**	**214**	**27**	**27**	**6**	**4**	**269**	**225**	**32**	**34**	**.485**	**1**	**3.67**

Thigpen, Robert Thomas "Bobby" — bats right — throws right — b.7/17/63

YR	TM/LG	CL	G	TBF	GS	CG	SHO	GF	IP	H	HR	BB	IBB	HB	SO	SH	SF	WP	BK	R	ER	W	L	PCT	SV	ERA
85	NF/NYP	A—	28	211	1	0	0	25	52.1	30	0	19	2	1	74	1	1	2	0	12	10	2	3	.400	9	1.72
	APP/MID	A	1	11	0	0	0	0	2.2	1	0	1	1	0	4	0	0	0	0	0	0	1	0	1.000	0	0.00
86	BIR/SOU	AA	25	707	25	5	0	0	159.2	182	12	54	1	11	90	3	7	4	2	97	83	8	11	.421	0	4.68
	CHI/AL		20	142	0	0	0	14	35.2	26	1	12	0	1	20	1	1	0	0	7	7	2	0	1.000	7	1.77
87	HAW/PCL	AAA	9	234	9	2	1	0	52.2	72	5	14	1	1	17	1	1	0	1	38	36	2	3	.400	0	6.15
	CHI/AL		51	369	0	0	0	37	89.0	86	10	24	5	3	52	6	0	0	0	30	27	7	5	.583	16	2.73
88	CHI/AL		68	398	0	0	0	59	90.0	96	6	33	3	4	62	4	5	6	2	38	33	5	8	.385	34	3.30
89	CHI/AL		61	336	0	0	0	56	79.0	62	10	40	1	1	47	5	5	2	1	34	33	2	6	.250	34	3.76
90	CHI/AL		77	347	0	0	0	73	88.2	60	5	32	3	1	70	4	3	2	0	20	18	4	6	.400	57	1.83
91	CHI/AL		67	309	0	0	0	58	69.2	63	10	38	8	4	47	7	3	2	0	32	27	7	5	.583	30	3.49
6 YR TOTALS			**344**	**1901**	**0**	**0**	**0**	**297**	**452.0**	**393**	**42**	**179**	**22**	**14**	**298**	**27**	**17**	**12**	**3**	**161**	**145**	**27**	**30**	**.474**	**178**	**2.89**

Timlin, Michael August "Mike" — bats right — throws right — b.3/10/66

YR	TM/LG	CL	G	TBF	GS	CG	SHO	GF	IP	H	HR	BB	IBB	HB	SO	SH	SF	WP	BK	R	ER	W	L	PCT	SV	ERA
87	MH/PIO	R+	13	326	12	2	0	0	75.1	79	4	26	0	5	66	1	2	9	5	50	43	4	8	.333	0	5.14
88	MB/SAL	A	35	653	22	0	0	1	151.0	119	4	77	2	19	106	2	2	8	4	68	48	10	6	.625	0	2.86
89	DUN/FSL	A+	33	397	7	1	0	16	88.2	90	2	36	2	5	64	9	3	10	3	44	32	5	8	.385	7	3.25
90	DUN/FSL	A+	42	203	0	0	0	40	50.1	36	0	16	2	1	46	3	0	3	0	11	8	7	2	.778	22	1.43
	KNO/SOU	AA	17	105	0	0	0	15	26.0	20	0	7	1	1	21	0	0	0	0	6	5	1	2	.333	8	1.73
91	TOR/AL		63	463	3	0	0	17	108.1	94	6	50	11	1	85	6	2	5	0	43	38	11	6	.647	3	3.16

Tomlin, Randy Leon — bats left — throws left — b.6/14/66

YR	TM/LG	CL	G	TBF	GS	CG	SHO	GF	IP	H	HR	BB	IBB	HB	SO	SH	SF	WP	BK	R	ER	W	L	PCT	SV	ERA
88	WAT/NYP	A—	15	407	15	5	2	0	103.1	75	4	25	1	6	87	3	3	4	2	31	25	7	5	.583	0	2.18
89	SAL/CAR	A+	21	582	21	3	2	0	138.2	131	11	43	0	3	99	2	2	7	0	60	50	12	6	.667	0	3.25
	HAR/EAS	AA	5	119	5	1	0	0	32.0	18	0	6	0	1	31	1	3	0	0	6	3	2	2	.500	0	0.84
90	BUF/AMA	AAA	3	33	1	0	0	1	8.0	12	1	1	0	0	3	0	1	0	0	3	3	0	0	.000	0	3.38
	HAR/EAS	AA	19	521	18	4	3	0	126.1	101	3	34	4	2	92	2	4	2	1	43	32	9	6	.600	0	2.28
	PIT/NL		12	297	12	2	0	0	77.2	62	5	12	1	1	42	2	2	1	3	24	22	4	4	.500	0	2.55
91	PIT/NL		31	736	27	4	2	0	175.0	170	9	54	4	6	104	5	2	2	3	75	58	8	7	.533	0	2.98
2 YR TOTALS			**43**	**1033**	**39**	**6**	**2**	**0**	**252.2**	**232**	**14**	**66**	**5**	**7**	**146**	**7**	**4**	**3**	**6**	**99**	**80**	**12**	**11**	**.522**	**0**	**2.85**

Trombley, Michael Scott "Mike" — bats right — throws right — b.4/14/67 — System MIN/AL

YR	TM/LG	CL	G	TBF	GS	CG	SHO	GF	IP	H	HR	BB	IBB	HB	SO	SH	SF	WP	BK	R	ER	W	L	PCT	SV	ERA
89	KEN/MID	A	12	202	3	0	0	6	49.0	45	1	13	0	3	41	1	0	4	3	23	17	5	1	.833	2	3.12
	VIS/CAL	A+	6	165	6	2	1	0	42.0	31	2	11	0	3	36	2	0	2	0	12	10	2	2	.500	0	2.14
90	VIS/CAL	A+	27	739	25	3	1	1	176.0	163	12	50	0	11	164	3	3	8	1	79	67	14	6	.700	0	3.43
91	ORL/SOU	AA	27	773	27	7	2	0	191.0	153	12	57	3	7	175	7	6	2	1	65	54	12	7	.632	0	2.54

Tsamis, George Alex — bats right — throws left — b.6/14/67 — System MIN/AL

YR	TM/LG	CL	G	TBF	GS	CG	SHO	GF	IP	H	HR	BB	IBB	HB	SO	SH	SF	WP	BK	R	ER	W	L	PCT	SV	ERA
89	VIS/CAL	A+	15	387	13	3	0	1	94.1	85	10	34	0	2	87	3	0	9	3	36	32	6	3	.667	0	3.05

(continued)

Tsamis, George Alex (continued)

YR	TM/LG	CL	G	TBF	GS	CG	SHO	GF	IP	H	HR	BB	IBB	HB	SO	SH	SF	WP	BK	R	ER	W	L	PCT	SV	ERA
90	VIS/CAL	A+	26	731	26	4	3	0	183.2	168	4	61	0	4	145	3	2	7	1	62	45	17	4	.810	0	2.21
91	ORL/SOU	AA	1	28	1	0	0	0	7.0	3	0	4	0	0	5	0	0	0	0	2	0	0	0	.000	0	0.00
	POR/PCL	AAA	29	716	27	2	1	0	167.2	183	11	66	0	5	75	8	6	7	1	75	61	10	8	.556	0	3.27

Valdez, Efrain Antonio — bats left — throws left — b.7/11/66

YR	TM/LG	CL	G	TBF	GS	CG	SHO	GF	IP	H	HR	BB	IBB	HB	SO	SH	SF	WP	BK	R	ER	W	L	PCT	SV	ERA
83	SPO/NWL	A–	13	0	1	0	0	0	29.0	40	3	17	0	2	27	0	0	3	0	32	23	0	0	.000	0	7.14
84	SPO/NWL	A–	13	0	1	0	0	6	16.2	26	1	8	0	0	15	0	0	0	0	18	14	1	2	.333	0	7.56
86	TUL/TEX	AA	4	52	2	0	0	1	12.1	12	1	6	0	1	4	1	0	0	1	8	8	0	1	.000	0	5.84
87	TUL/TEX	AA	11	235	8	1	1	1	49.1	62	9	24	3	2	38	1	3	3	0	44	39	1	4	.200	0	7.11
	CHA/FSL	A+	17	301	8	0	0	2	70.1	67	6	28	2	1	45	2	3	3	2	32	29	3	6	.333	0	3.71
88	TUL/TEX	AA	43	276	3	0	0	21	63.1	63	6	24	2	4	52	3	2	3	1	37	32	6	5	.545	6	4.55
89	CAN/EAS	AA	44	318	0	0	0	18	75.1	60	1	33	3	4	55	6	3	4	0	26	18	2	4	.333	1	2.15
90	CS/PCL	AAA	46	330	1	0	0	17	75.2	72	6	30	8	4	52	6	4	5	4	38	32	4	2	.667	6	3.81
	CLE/AL		13	104	0	0	0	4	23.2	20	2	14	3	0	13	1	3	1	0	10	8	1	1	.500	0	3.04
91	CLE/AL		7	27	0	0	0	0	6.0	5	0	3	1	1	1	1	1	0	0	1	1	0	0	.000	0	1.50
	CS/PCL	AAA	14	133	0	0	0	5	30.2	26	1	13	0	0	25	3	1	1	2	15	13	3	1	.750	1	3.82
	SYR/INT	AAA	21	201	1	0	0	4	43.2	50	7	25	0	0	30	2	2	3	0	27	26	3	2	.600	0	5.36
2 YR TOTALS			**20**	**131**	**0**	**0**	**0**	**4**	**29.2**	**25**	**2**	**17**	**4**	**1**	**14**	**2**	**4**	**1**	**0**	**11**	**9**	**1**	**1**	**.500**	**0**	**2.73**

Valdez, Rafael Emilio (Diaz) — bats right — throws right — b.12/17/68 — System SD/NL

YR	TM/LG	CL	G	TBF	GS	CG	SHO	GF	IP	H	HR	BB	IBB	HB	SO	SH	SF	WP	BK	R	ER	W	L	PCT	SV	ERA
88	CHS/SAL	A	28	603	17	4	1	6	152.1	117	6	46	4	1	100	3	3	9	6	42	38	11	4	.733	0	2.25
89	RIV/CAL	A+	21	567	21	5	3	0	143.1	89	6	58	1	4	137	2	1	6	0	40	36	10	5	.667	0	2.26
	WIC/TEX	AA	6	172	6	2	0	0	41.2	28	1	24	2	1	26	0	1	1	1	10	9	5	0	1.000	0	1.94
90	SD/NL		3	30	0	0	0	2	5.2	11	4	2	0	0	3	0	0	0	0	7	7	0	1	.000	0	11.12
	LV/PCL	AAA	17	401	17	0	0	0	86.0	82	6	65	0	2	79	5	3	4	3	58	47	4	7	.364	0	4.92
91	LV/PCL	AAA	5	86	5	0	0	0	16.2	22	2	16	2	0	9	1	2	0	0	13	11	0	2	.000	0	5.94
1 YR TOTALS			**3**	**30**	**0**	**0**	**0**	**2**	**5.2**	**11**	**4**	**2**	**0**	**0**	**3**	**0**	**0**	**0**	**0**	**7**	**7**	**0**	**1**	**.000**	**0**	**11.12**

Valdez, Sergio Sanchez — bats right — throws right — b.9/7/64

YR	TM/LG	CL	G	TBF	GS	CG	SHO	GF	IP	H	HR	BB	IBB	HB	SO	SH	SF	WP	BK	R	ER	W	L	PCT	SV	ERA
83	CAL/PIO	R+	13	0	13	1	0	0	72.0	88	7	31	0	2	41	0	0	3	0	55	45	6	3	.667	0	5.63
84	WPB/FSL	A+	5	54	0	0	0	2	11.1	15	2	8	0	1	6	0	0	1	1	11	11	0	0	.000	0	8.74
	JAM/NYP	A–	13	340	12	5	1	1	76.0	78	3	33	0	1	46	5	3	4	1	47	34	2	7	.222	0	4.03
85	UTI/NYP	A–	15	454	15	5	0	0	105.2	98	6	36	1	1	86	2	4	8	3	53	36	6	5	.545	0	3.07
86	WPB/FSL	A+	24	589	24	6	4	0	145.2	119	9	46	0	4	108	1	1	3	5	48	40	16	6	.727	0	2.47
	MON/NL		5	120	5	0	0	0	25.0	39	2	11	0	1	20	0	0	2	0	20	19	0	0	.000	0	6.84
87	IND/AMA	AAA	27	714	27	2	2	0	158.1	191	14	64	4	7	128	5	6	8	2	108	90	10	7	.588	0	5.12
88	IND/AMA	AAA	14	351	14	0	0	0	84.0	80	8	28	0	2	61	2	2	1	4	38	32	5	4	.556	0	3.43
89	IND/AMA	AAA	19	374	12	0	0	4	90.2	78	4	26	2	5	81	4	2	5	4	38	33	6	3	.667	1	3.28
	ATL/NL		19	145	1	0	0	8	32.2	31	5	17	3	0	26	2	0	2	0	24	22	1	2	.333	0	6.06
90	ATL/NL		6	26	0	0	0	3	5.1	6	0	3	0	0	3	1	0	1	0	4	4	0	0	.000	0	6.75
	CS/PCL	AAA	7	195	7	2	1	0	43.1	55	7	13	0	1	33	0	0	4	1	29	25	4	3	.571	0	5.19
	CLE/AL		24	440	13	0	0	4	102.1	109	17	35	2	5	63	4	5	3	0	62	54	6	6	.500	0	4.75
	YEAR		30	466	13	0	0	7	107.2	115	17	38	2	5	66	5	5	4	0	66	58	6	6	.500	0	4.85
91	CLE/AL		6	70	0	0	0	1	16.1	15	3	5	1	0	11	1	1	1	0	11	10	1	0	1.000	0	5.51
	CS/PCL	AAA	26	542	15	4	0	6	131.1	139	12	27	6	7	71	3	4	9	2	67	60	4	12	.250	0	4.11
4 YR TOTALS			**60**	**801**	**19**	**0**	**0**	**16**	**181.2**	**200**	**27**	**71**	**6**	**2**	**123**	**8**	**6**	**9**	**0**	**121**	**109**	**8**	**12**	**.400**	**0**	**5.40**

Valenzuela, Fernando (Anguamea) — bats left — throws left — b.11/1/60

YR	TM/LG	CL	G	TBF	GS	CG	SHO	GF	IP	H	HR	BB	IBB	HB	SO	SH	SF	WP	BK	R	ER	W	L	PCT	SV	ERA
80	LA/NL		10	66	0	0	0	4	17.2	8	0	5	0	0	16	1	1	0	1	2	0	2	0	1.000	1	0.00
81	LA/NL		25	758	25	11	8	0	192.1	140	11	61	4	1	180	9	3	4	0	55	53	13	7	.650	0	2.48
82	LA/NL		37	1156	37	18	4	0	285.0	247	13	83	12	2	199	19	6	4	0	105	91	19	13	.594	0	2.87
83	LA/NL		35	1094	35	9	4	0	257.0	245	16	99	10	3	189	27	5	12	1	122	107	15	10	.600	0	3.75
84	LA/NL		34	1078	34	12	2	0	261.0	218	14	106	4	2	240	11	7	11	1	109	88	12	17	.414	0	3.03
85	LA/NL		35	1109	35	14	5	0	272.1	211	14	101	5	1	208	13	8	10	1	92	74	17	10	.630	0	2.45
86	LA/NL		34	1102	34	20	3	0	269.1	226	18	85	5	1	242	15	3	13	0	104	94	21	11	.656	0	3.14
87	LA/NL		34	1116	34	12	1	0	251.0	254	25	124	4	4	190	18	2	14	1	120	111	14	14	.500	0	3.98
88	LA/NL		23	626	22	3	0	1	142.1	142	11	76	4	0	64	15	5	7	1	71	67	5	8	.385	1	4.24
89	LA/NL		31	852	31	3	0	0	196.2	185	11	98	6	2	116	7	7	6	4	89	75	10	13	.435	0	3.43
90	LA/NL		33	900	33	5	2	0	204.0	223	19	77	4	0	115	11	4	13	1	112	104	13	13	.500	0	4.59
91	PS/CAL	A+	1	19	1	0	0	0	4.0	4	0	3	0	0	2	0	0	0	0	1	0	0	0	.000	0	0.00
	CAL/AL		2	36	2	0	0	0	6.2	14	3	3	0	0	5	1	1	1	0	10	9	0	2	.000	0	12.15
	MID/TEX	AA	4	93	4	1	0	0	23.0	18	1	6	0	1	17	2	0	5	0	5	5	3	1	.750	0	1.96
	EDM/PCL	AAA	7	170	7	0	0	0	36.2	48	9	17	1	1	36	0	2	0	0	34	29	3	3	.500	0	7.12
12 YR TOTALS			**333**	**9893**	**322**	**107**	**29**	**5**	**2355.1**	**2113**	**155**	**918**	**58**	**16**	**1764**	**147**	**52**	**95**	**11**	**991**	**873**	**141**	**118**	**.544**	**2**	**3.34**

Valera, Julio Enrique (Torres) — bats right — throws right — b.10/13/68

YR	TM/LG	CL	G	TBF	GS	CG	SHO	GF	IP	H	HR	BB	IBB	HB	SO	SH	SF	WP	BK	R	ER	W	L	PCT	SV	ERA
86	KIN/APP	R+	13	356	13	2	1	0	76.1	91	5	29	2	0	64	4	0	4	1	58	44	3	10	.231	0	5.19
87	COL/SAL	A	22	522	22	2	2	0	125.1	114	7	31	0	4	97	2	1	6	0	53	39	8	7	.533	0	2.80
88	COL/SAL	A	30	775	27	8	0	3	191.0	171	8	51	3	4	144	5	7	9	6	77	68	15	11	.577	1	3.20

Valera, Julio Enrique (Torres) (continued)

YR	TM/LG	CL	G	TBF	GS	CG	SHO	GF	IP	H	HR	BB	IBB	HB	SO	SH	SF	WP	BK	R	ER	W	L	PCT	SV	ERA
89	SL/FSL	A+	6	173	6	3	2	0	45.0	34	1	6	1	0	45	2	0	0	0	5	5	4	2	.667	0	1.00
	JAC/TEX	AA	19	566	19	6	2	0	137.1	123	4	36	2	8	107	7	3	10	0	47	38	10	6	.625	0	2.49
	TID/INT	AAA	2	52	2	0	0	0	13.0	8	1	5	0	1	10	0	0	1	0	3	3	1	1	.500	0	2.08
90	TID/INT	AAA	24	648	24	9	2	0	158.0	146	12	39	3	5	133	6	5	7	5	66	53	10	10	.500	0	3.02
	NY/NL		3	64	3	0	0	0	13.0	20	1	7	0	0	4	0	0	0	0	11	10	1	1	.500	0	6.92
91	NY/NL		2	11	0	0	0	1	2.0	1	0	4	1	0	3	0	0	0	0	0	0	0	0	.000	0	0.00
	TID/INT	AAA	26	739	26	3	1	0	176.1	152	12	70	4	6	117	8	6	8	3	79	75	10	10	.500	0	3.83
2 YR TOTALS			**5**	**75**	**3**	**0**	**0**	**1**	**15.0**	**21**	**1**	**11**	**1**	**0**	**7**	**0**	**0**	**0**	**0**	**11**	**10**	**1**	**1**	**.500**	**0**	**6.00**

Van Poppel, Todd Matthew — bats right — throws right — b.12/9/71

YR	TM/LG	CL	G	TBF	GS	CG	SHO	GF	IP	H	HR	BB	IBB	HB	SO	SH	SF	WP	BK	R	ER	W	L	PCT	SV	ERA
90	SO/NWL	A–	5	92	5	0	0	0	24.0	10	1	9	0	2	32	0	1	0	0	5	3	1	1	.500	0	1.13
	MAD/MID	A	3	61	3	0	0	0	13.2	8	0	10	0	1	17	0	1	0	0	11	6	2	1	.667	0	3.95
91	HUN/SOU	AA	24	607	24	1	1	0	132.1	118	2	90	0	6	115	4	6	12	1	69	51	6	13	.316	0	3.47
	OAK/AL		1	21	1	0	0	0	4.2	7	1	2	0	0	6	0	0	0	0	5	5	0	0	.000	0	9.64

Viola, Frank John — bats left — throws left — b.4/19/60

YR	TM/LG	CL	G	TBF	GS	CG	SHO	GF	IP	H	HR	BB	IBB	HB	SO	SH	SF	WP	BK	R	ER	W	L	PCT	SV	ERA
82	MIN/AL		22	543	22	3	1	0	126.0	152	22	38	2	0	84	2	0	4	1	77	73	4	10	.286	0	5.21
83	MIN/AL		35	949	34	4	0	0	210.0	242	34	92	7	8	127	5	2	6	2	141	128	7	15	.318	0	5.49
84	MIN/AL		35	1047	35	10	4	0	257.2	225	28	73	1	4	149	1	5	6	1	101	92	18	12	.600	0	3.21
85	MIN/AL		36	1059	36	9	0	0	250.2	262	26	68	3	2	135	5	5	6	2	136	114	18	14	.563	0	4.09
86	MIN/AL		37	1053	37	7	0	0	245.2	257	37	83	0	3	191	4	5	12	0	136	123	16	13	.552	0	4.51
87	MIN/AL		36	1037	36	7	1	0	251.2	230	29	66	1	6	197	7	3	1	1	91	81	17	10	.630	0	2.90
88	MIN/AL		35	1031	35	7	2	0	255.1	236	20	54	2	3	193	6	6	5	1	80	75	24	7	.774	0	2.64
89	MIN/AL		24	731	24	7	1	0	175.2	171	17	47	1	3	138	9	4	5	1	80	74	8	12	.400	0	3.79
	NY/NL		12	351	12	2	1	0	85.1	75	5	27	3	1	73	3	2	3	0	35	32	5	5	.500	0	3.38
	YEAR		36	1082	36	9	2	0	261.0	246	22	74	4	4	211	12	6	8	1	115	106	13	17	.433	0	3.66
90	NY/NL		35	1016	35	7	3	0	249.2	227	15	60	2	2	182	13	3	11	0	83	74	20	12	.625	0	2.67
91	NY/NL		35	980	35	3	0	0	231.1	259	25	54	1	4	132	15	5	6	1	112	102	13	15	.464	0	3.97
10 YR TOTALS			**342**	**9797**	**341**	**66**	**14**	**0**	**2339.0**	**2336**	**258**	**662**	**26**	**33**	**1601**	**70**	**40**	**65**	**10**	**1072**	**968**	**150**	**125**	**.545**	**0**	**3.72**

Wagner, Hector Raul Guerrero — bats right — throws right — b.11/26/68

YR	TM/LG	CL	G	TBF	GS	CG	SHO	GF	IP	H	HR	BB	IBB	HB	SO	SH	SF	WP	BK	R	ER	W	L	PCT	SV	ERA
87	ROY/GCL	R	13	226	12	0	0	0	53.0	63	0	12	0	2	28	2	2	0	0	26	18	1	3	.250	0	3.06
88	EUG/NWL	A–	15	365	15	0	0	0	85.2	76	3	28	0	4	67	0	1	3	1	46	35	4	9	.308	0	3.68
89	APP/MID	A	24	557	23	3	0	1	130.1	149	9	29	1	6	71	1	1	6	1	79	66	6	11	.353	0	4.56
90	MEM/SOU	AA	40	538	11	1	1	8	133.1	114	7	41	0	2	63	5	1	3	0	37	30	12	4	.750	1	2.03
	KC/AL		5	112	5	0	0	0	23.1	32	4	11	1	0	14	0	2	3	0	24	21	0	2	.000	0	8.10
91	KC/AL		2	49	2	0	0	0	10.0	16	2	3	0	0	5	0	0	0	0	10	8	1	1	.500	0	7.20
	OMA/AMA	AAA	17	380	14	1	0	0	86.1	88	4	38	0	5	36	4	0	0	0	45	33	5	6	.455	0	3.44
2 YR TOTALS			**7**	**161**	**7**	**0**	**0**	**0**	**33.1**	**48**	**6**	**14**	**1**	**0**	**19**	**0**	**2**	**3**	**0**	**34**	**29**	**1**	**3**	**.250**	**0**	**7.83**

Wainhouse, David Paul "Dave" — bats left — throws right — b.11/7/67

YR	TM/LG	CL	G	TBF	GS	CG	SHO	GF	IP	H	HR	BB	IBB	HB	SO	SH	SF	WP	BK	R	ER	W	L	PCT	SV	ERA
89	WPB/FSL	A+	13	286	13	0	0	0	66.1	75	4	19	0	8	26	3	2	6	3	35	30	1	5	.167	0	4.07
90	WPB/FSL	A+	12	327	12	2	1	0	76.2	68	1	34	0	5	58	0	3	2	3	28	18	6	3	.667	0	2.11
	JAC/SOU	AA	17	428	16	2	0	0	95.2	97	8	47	2	7	59	2	3	3	0	59	46	7	7	.500	0	4.33
91	HAR/EAS	AA	33	224	0	0	0	27	52.0	49	1	17	2	4	46	2	0	3	0	17	15	2	2	.500	11	2.60
	IND/AMA	AAA	14	127	0	0	0	8	28.2	28	1	15	1	3	13	2	1	0	0	14	13	2	0	1.000	1	4.08
	MON/NL		2	14	0	0	0	1	2.2	2	0	4	0	0	1	0	1	2	0	2	2	0	1	.000	0	6.75

Walk, Robert Vernon "Bob" — bats right — throws right — b.11/26/56

YR	TM/LG	CL	G	TBF	GS	CG	SHO	GF	IP	H	HR	BB	IBB	HB	SO	SH	SF	WP	BK	R	ER	W	L	PCT	SV	ERA
80	PHI/NL		27	673	27	2	0	0	151.2	163	8	71	2	2	94	5	5	6	3	82	77	11	7	.611	0	4.57
81	ATL/NL		12	189	8	0	0	1	43.1	41	6	23	0	0	16	2	0	1	0	25	22	1	4	.200	0	4.57
82	ATL/NL		32	717	27	3	1	1	164.1	179	19	59	2	6	84	8	5	7	0	101	89	11	9	.550	0	4.87
83	ATL/NL		1	20	1	0	0	0	3.2	7	0	2	0	0	4	1	0	0	0	3	3	0	0	.000	0	7.36
84	HAW/PCL	AAA	18	0	18	5	3	0	127.1	100	3	42	0	0	23	0	0	2	0	39	32	9	5	.643	0	2.26
	PIT/NL		2	44	2	0	0	0	10.1	8	1	4	1	0	10	0	0	0	0	5	3	1	1	.500	0	2.61
85	HAW/PCL	AAA	24	0	24	12	1	0	173.0	143	10	61	1	4	124	0	0	12	4	57	51	16	5	.762	0	2.65
	PIT/NL		9	248	9	1	1	0	58.2	60	3	18	2	0	40	3	1	2	3	27	24	2	3	.400	0	3.68
86	PIT/NL		44	592	15	1	1	7	141.2	129	14	64	7	3	78	6	5	12	1	66	59	7	8	.467	2	3.75
87	PIT/NL		39	498	12	1	1	6	117.0	107	11	51	3	3	78	6	2	7	3	52	43	8	2	.800	0	3.31
88	PIT/NL		32	881	32	1	1	0	212.2	183	6	65	5	2	81	14	5	13	9	75	64	12	10	.545	0	2.71
89	PIT/NL		33	843	31	2	0	1	196.0	208	15	65	4	4	83	4	2	7	4	106	96	13	10	.565	0	4.41
90	PIT/NL		26	549	24	1	1	0	129.2	136	17	36	2	4	73	3	3	5	3	59	54	7	5	.583	1	3.75
91	CAR/SOU	AA	1	19	1	0	0	0	5.0	5	0	2	0	0	3	0	1	0	0	1	1	0	1	.000	0	1.80
	PIT/NL		25	484	20	0	0	0	115.0	104	10	35	2	5	67	7	4	11	2	53	46	9	2	.818	0	3.60
12 YR TOTALS			**282**	**5738**	**208**	**12**	**6**	**17**	**1344.0**	**1325**	**110**	**493**	**26**	**29**	**708**	**59**	**32**	**71**	**28**	**654**	**580**	**82**	**61**	**.573**	**3**	**3.88**

Walker, Michael Charles "Mike" — bats right — throws right — b.10/4/66

YR	TM/LG	CL	G	TBF	GS	CG	SHO	GF	IP	H	HR	BB	IBB	HB	SO	SH	SF	WP	BK	R	ER	W	L	PCT	SV	ERA
86	BUR/APP	R+	14	339	13	1	0	0	70.1	75	9	45	0	4	42	2	5	1	0	65	46	4	6	.400	0	5.89

(continued)

Walker, Michael Charles "Mike" (continued)

YR	TM/LG	CL	G	TBF	GS	CG	SHO	GF	IP	H	HR	BB	IBB	HB	SO	SH	SF	WP	BK	R	ER	W	L	PCT	SV	ERA
87	WAT/MID	A	23	637	23	8	1	0	145.1	133	11	68	1	13	144	4	3	14	0	74	58	11	7	.611	0	3.59
	KIN/CAR	A+	3	91	3	0	0	0	20.2	17	0	14	0	0	19	0	2	2	0	7	6	3	0	1.000	0	2.61
88	WIL/EAS	AA	28	717	27	3	0	1	164.1	162	11	74	1	9	144	5	3	17	2	82	68	15	7	.682	0	3.72
	CLE/AL		3	42	1	0	0	0	8.2	8	0	10	0	0	7	1	0	0	0	7	7	0	1	.000	0	7.27
89	CS/PCL	AAA	28	772	28	4	0	0	168.0	193	21	93	0	14	97	8	7	12	0	124	108	6	15	.286	0	5.79
90	CS/PCL	AAA	18	374	12	0	0	2	79.0	96	6	36	5	7	50	3	9	6	0	62	49	2	7	.222	1	5.58
	CAN/EAS	AA	1	29	1	0	0	0	7.0	4	0	4	0	0	3	0	0	0	0	0	0	1	0	1.000	0	0.00
	CLE/AL		18	350	11	0	0	2	75.2	82	6	42	4	6	34	4	2	3	1	49	41	2	6	.250	0	4.88
91	CLE/AL		5	22	0	0	0	3	4.1	6	0	2	1	1	2	0	0	0	0	1	1	0	1	.000	0	2.08
	CAN/EAS	AA	45	347	1	0	0	34	77.1	68	2	45	6	1	42	5	1	13	0	36	24	9	4	.692	11	2.79
3 YR TOTALS			**26**	**414**	**12**	**0**	**0**	**5**	**88.2**	**96**	**6**	**54**	**5**	**7**	**43**	**5**	**2**	**3**	**1**	**57**	**49**	**2**	**8**	**.200**	**0**	**4.97**

Walton, Bruce Kenneth — bats right — throws right — b.12/25/62

YR	TM/LG	CL	G	TBF	GS	CG	SHO	GF	IP	H	HR	BB	IBB	HB	SO	SH	SF	WP	BK	R	ER	W	L	PCT	SV	ERA
85	POC/PIO	R+	18	0	9	2	0	6	76.2	89	2	27	3	1	69	0	0	2	0	46	35	3	7	.300	3	4.11
86	MOD/CAL	A+	27	778	27	4	0	0	176.0	204	16	41	1	9	107	10	5	7	1	96	80	13	7	.650	0	4.09
	MAD/MID	A	1	21	1	0	0	0	5.0	5	0	1	0	0	1	0	0	0	0	3	3	0	0	.000	0	5.40
87	MOD/CAL	A+	16	437	16	3	1	0	106.1	97	6	27	0	4	84	1	3	2	0	44	34	8	6	.571	0	2.88
	HUN/SOU	AA	18	248	2	0	0	6	58.0	61	4	13	1	1	40	2	3	4	2	24	20	2	2	.500	2	3.10
88	HUN/SOU	AA	42	502	3	0	0	17	116.1	126	10	23	7	5	82	5	3	2	6	64	59	4	5	.444	3	4.56
89	TAC/PCL	AAA	32	461	14	1	1	7	107.2	118	7	27	1	1	76	4	4	3	2	59	45	8	6	.571	0	3.76
90	TAC/PCL	AAA	46	403	5	0	0	21	98.1	103	12	23	5	2	67	4	7	1	5	42	34	5	5	.500	7	3.11
91	TAC/PCL	AAA	38	184	0	0	0	38	46.2	39	0	5	1	0	49	2	0	2	0	11	7	1	1	.500	20	1.35
	OAK/AL		12	56	0	0	0	5	13.0	11	3	6	1	0	10	0	1	3	0	9	9	1	0	1.000	0	6.23

Wapnick, Steven Lee "Steve" — bats right — throws right — b.9/25/65

YR	TM/LG	CL	G	TBF	GS	CG	SHO	GF	IP	H	HR	BB	IBB	HB	SO	SH	SF	WP	BK	R	ER	W	L	PCT	SV	ERA
87	ST./NYP	A−	20	272	6	0	0	4	65.2	53	5	21	0	2	63	1	1	3	1	28	22	3	4	.429	1	3.02
88	MB/SAL	A	54	252	0	0	0	27	60.1	44	2	31	5	0	69	2	2	3	3	18	15	4	3	.571	12	2.24
89	DUN/FSL	A+	24	262	1	0	0	11	66.0	48	2	22	1	3	59	0	1	9	1	19	15	4	0	1.000	7	2.05
	KNO/SOU	AA	12	73	0	0	0	9	18.1	12	1	7	0	0	20	1	0	0	1	1	1	1	0	1.000	2	0.49
	SYR/INT	AAA	6	51	1	0	0	4	13.0	9	0	5	0	1	10	1	0	0	0	1	1	1	0	1.000	0	0.69
90	DET/AL		4	37	0	0	0	1	7.0	8	0	10	0	0	6	0	0	0	0	5	5	0	0	.000	0	6.43
	SYR/INT	AAA	11	70	1	0	0	6	16.0	16	2	6	0	1	19	1	1	1	0	9	9	0	1	.000	2	5.06
91	SYR/INT	AAA	53	302	0	0	0	42	71.2	68	4	25	4	2	58	7	2	4	1	23	22	6	3	.667	20	2.76
	CHI/AL		6	22	0	0	0	4	5.0	2	0	4	0	0	1	0	0	0	0	1	1	0	1	.000	0	1.80
2 YR TOTALS			**10**	**59**	**0**	**0**	**0**	**5**	**12.0**	**10**	**0**	**14**	**0**	**0**	**7**	**0**	**0**	**0**	**0**	**6**	**6**	**0**	**1**	**.000**	**0**	**4.50**

Ward, Roy Duane "Duane" — bats right — throws right — b.5/28/64

YR	TM/LG	CL	G	TBF	GS	CG	SHO	GF	IP	H	HR	BB	IBB	HB	SO	SH	SF	WP	BK	R	ER	W	L	PCT	SV	ERA
84	GRE/SOU	AA	21	471	20	4	0	0	104.2	108	9	57	0	2	54	4	6	8	1	71	58	4	9	.308	0	4.99
85	GRE/SOU	AA	28	671	24	3	0	1	150.0	141	4	105	1	4	100	3	5	9	0	83	70	11	10	.524	0	4.20
	RIC/INT	AAA	5	30	1	0	0	3	5.1	8	1	8	0	1	3	0	0	0	0	9	7	0	1	.000	0	11.81
86	ATL/NL		10	73	0	0	0	6	16.0	22	2	8	0	0	8	2	0	0	1	13	13	0	1	.000	0	7.31
	RIC/INT	AAA	6	158	6	0	0	0	34.2	34	0	23	0	1	17	3	0	0	1	13	13	1	1	.500	0	3.38
	SYR/INT	AAA	14	359	14	3	0	0	83.0	91	9	29	0	2	50	2	1	4	1	43	39	6	4	.600	0	4.23
	TOR/AL		2	15	1	0	0	1	2.0	3	0	4	0	1	1	0	0	1	0	4	3	0	0	.000	0	13.50
	YEAR		12	88	1	0	0	7	18.0	25	2	12	0	1	9	2	0	1	1	17	16	0	1	.000	0	8.00
87	SYR/INT	AAA	46	319	3	0	0	29	76.1	59	7	42	1	2	67	2	2	7	1	35	33	2	2	.500	14	3.89
	TOR/AL		12	57	1	0	0	4	11.2	14	0	12	2	0	10	1	1	0	0	9	9	1	0	1.000	0	6.94
88	TOR/AL		64	487	0	0	0	32	111.2	101	5	60	8	5	91	4	5	10	3	46	41	9	3	.750	15	3.30
89	TOR/AL		66	494	0	0	0	39	114.2	94	4	58	11	5	122	12	11	13	0	55	48	4	10	.286	15	3.77
90	TOR/AL		73	508	0	0	0	39	127.2	101	9	42	10	1	112	6	2	5	0	51	49	2	8	.200	11	3.45
91	TOR/AL		81	428	0	0	0	46	107.1	80	3	33	3	2	132	3	4	6	0	36	33	7	6	.538	23	2.77
6 YR TOTALS			**308**	**2062**	**2**	**0**	**0**	**167**	**491.0**	**415**	**23**	**217**	**34**	**14**	**476**	**28**	**23**	**35**	**4**	**214**	**196**	**23**	**29**	**.442**	**64**	**3.59**

Wayne, Gary Anthony — bats left — throws left — b.11/30/62

YR	TM/LG	CL	G	TBF	GS	CG	SHO	GF	IP	H	HR	BB	IBB	HB	SO	SH	SF	WP	BK	R	ER	W	L	PCT	SV	ERA
84	WPB/FSL	A+	13	342	12	2	0	0	74.1	70	1	49	0	3	46	3	2	9	2	38	32	3	5	.375	0	3.87
85	JAC/SOU	AA	21	471	20	2	0	0	102.0	108	3	70	3	1	62	2	4	11	1	67	60	3	12	.200	0	5.29
	WPB/FSL	A+	8	147	4	0	0	1	30.2	37	1	22	0	0	18	5	1	5	0	23	19	2	2	.500	0	5.58
86	WPB/FSL	A+	47	255	0	0	0	41	61.1	48	1	25	2	1	55	2	2	3	1	16	11	2	5	.286	25	1.61
87	JAC/SOU	AA	56	324	0	0	0	28	80.1	56	0	35	0	2	78	2	2	2	1	23	21	5	1	.833	10	2.35
88	IND/AMA	AAA	8	33	0	0	0	0	7.1	9	0	3	0	0	6	1	0	0	0	5	5	0	0	.000	1	6.14
89	MIN/AL		60	302	0	0	0	21	71.0	55	4	36	4	0	41	4	2	7	0	28	26	3	4	.429	1	3.30
90	POR/PCL	AAA	22	134	0	0	0	13	31.2	29	1	13	1	0	30	0	1	3	1	14	12	2	4	.333	5	3.41
	MIN/AL		38	166	0	0	0	12	38.2	38	5	13	1	2	28	1	2	4	0	19	18	1	1	.500	1	4.19
91	POR/PCL	AAA	51	296	0	0	0	32	67.2	63	4	31	4	2	66	4	4	4	2	27	21	4	5	.444	8	2.79
	MIN/AL		8	52	0	0	0	2	12.1	11	1	4	0	1	7	1	0	0	0	7	7	1	0	1.000	1	5.11
3 YR TOTALS			**106**	**520**	**0**	**0**	**0**	**35**	**122.0**	**104**	**10**	**53**	**4**	**3**	**76**	**6**	**5**	**11**	**0**	**54**	**51**	**5**	**5**	**.500**	**3**	**3.76**

Weathers, John David "Dave" — bats right — throws right — b.9/25/69

YR	TM/LG	CL	G	TBF	GS	CG	SHO	GF	IP	H	HR	BB	IBB	HB	SO	SH	SF	WP	BK	R	ER	W	L	PCT	SV	ERA
88	ST./NYP	A−	15	267	12	0	0	2	62.2	58	3	26	0	2	36	2	0	5	4	30	21	4	4	.500	0	3.02

Weathers, John David "Dave" (continued)

YR	TM/LG	CL	G	TBF	GS	CG	SHO	GF	IP	H	HR	BB	IBB	HB	SO	SH	SF	WP	BK	R	ER	W	L	PCT	SV	ERA
89	MB/SAL	A	31	759	31	2	0	0	172.2	163	3	86	2	7	111	5	2	12	1	99	74	11	13	.458	0	3.86
90	DUN/FSL	A+	27	675	27	2	0	0	158.0	158	2	59	0	9	96	4	7	10	9	82	65	10	7	.588	0	3.70
91	KNO/SOU	AA	24	575	22	5	2	0	139.1	121	3	49	1	8	114	1	3	7	2	51	38	10	7	.588	0	2.45
	TOR/AL		15	79	0	0	0	4	14.2	15	1	17	3	2	13	2	1	0	0	9	8	1	0	1.000	0	4.91

Wegman, William Edward "Bill" — bats right — throws right — b.12/19/62

YR	TM/LG	CL	G	TBF	GS	CG	SHO	GF	IP	H	HR	BB	IBB	HB	SO	SH	SF	WP	BK	R	ER	W	L	PCT	SV	ERA
84	EP/TEX	AA	10	265	10	4	0	0	64.0	62	5	15	0	3	42	1	0	1	0	25	19	4	5	.444	0	2.67
	VAN/PCL	AAA	6	0	3	0	0	2	27.2	30	0	8	0	1	16	0	0	0	1	11	6	0	3	.000	1	1.95
85	VAN/PCL	AAA	28	0	28	8	2	0	188.0	187	21	52	5	5	113	0	0	2	0	93	84	10	11	.476	0	4.02
	MIL/AL		3	73	3	0	0	0	17.2	17	3	3	0	0	6	0	1	0	1	8	7	2	0	1.000	0	3.57
86	MIL/AL		35	836	32	2	0	1	198.1	217	32	43	2	7	82	4	5	5	2	120	113	5	12	.294	0	5.13
87	MIL/AL		34	934	33	7	0	0	225.0	229	31	53	2	6	102	4	6	0	2	113	106	12	11	.522	0	4.24
88	MIL/AL		32	847	31	4	1	0	199.0	207	24	50	5	4	84	3	10	1	1	104	91	13	13	.500	0	4.12
89	MIL/AL		11	240	8	0	0	1	51.0	69	6	21	2	0	27	0	4	2	0	44	38	2	6	.250	0	6.71
90	DEN/AMA	AAA	3	54	3	0	0	0	13.2	10	0	7	0	1	14	1	1	0	0	5	5	1	0	1.000	0	3.29
	MIL/AL		8	132	5	1	1	0	29.2	37	6	6	1	0	20	1	1	0	0	21	16	2	2	.500	0	4.85
	BEL/MID	A	1	7	1	0	0	0	2.0	1	0	1	0	0	0	0	0	0	0	0	0	0	0	.000	0	0.00
91	BEL/MID	A	3	45	3	0	0	0	11.0	11	0	1	0	1	12	0	0	0	0	5	2	0	0	.000	0	1.64
	DEN/AMA	AAA	1	26	1	0	0	0	7.0	6	0	1	0	1	1	0	0	0	0	2	2	0	0	.000	0	2.57
	MIL/AL		28	785	28	7	2	0	193.1	176	16	40	1	4	89	6	4	6	0	76	61	15	7	.682	0	2.84
7 YR TOTALS			151	3847	140	21	4	2	914.0	952	118	216	12	24	410	18	31	14	6	486	432	51	51	.500	0	4.25

Welch, Robert Lynn "Bob" — bats right — throws right — b.11/3/56

YR	TM/LG	CL	G	TBF	GS	CG	SHO	GF	IP	H	HR	BB	IBB	HB	SO	SH	SF	WP	BK	R	ER	W	L	PCT	SV	ERA
78	LA/NL		23	439	13	4	3	6	111.1	92	6	26	2	1	66	4	6	2	2	28	25	7	4	.636	3	2.02
79	LA/NL		25	349	12	1	0	10	81.1	82	7	32	4	3	64	4	1	0	0	42	36	5	6	.455	5	3.98
80	LA/NL		32	889	32	3	2	0	213.2	190	15	79	6	3	141	12	10	7	5	85	78	14	9	.609	0	3.29
81	LA/NL		23	601	23	2	1	0	141.1	141	11	41	0	3	88	9	4	2	0	56	54	9	5	.643	0	3.44
82	LA/NL		36	965	36	9	3	0	235.2	199	19	81	5	5	176	7	4	5	1	94	88	16	11	.593	0	3.36
83	LA/NL		31	828	31	4	3	0	204.0	164	13	72	4	3	156	8	7	4	6	73	60	15	12	.556	0	2.65
84	LA/NL		31	771	29	3	1	0	178.2	191	11	58	7	2	126	10	2	4	2	86	75	13	13	.500	0	3.78
85	VB/FSL	A+	3	65	3	0	0	0	17.0	15	0	1	0	0	9	1	0	0	0	4	4	0	0	.000	0	2.12
	LA/NL		23	675	23	8	3	0	167.1	141	16	35	2	6	96	6	2	7	4	49	43	14	4	.778	0	2.31
86	LA/NL		33	981	33	7	3	0	235.2	227	14	55	6	7	183	7	8	2	1	95	86	7	13	.350	0	3.28
87	LA/NL		35	1027	35	6	4	0	251.2	204	21	86	6	4	196	10	6	4	4	94	90	15	9	.625	0	3.22
88	OAK/AL		36	1034	36	4	2	0	244.2	237	22	81	1	10	158	12	8	3	13	107	99	17	9	.654	0	3.64
89	OAK/AL		33	884	33	1	0	0	209.2	191	13	78	3	6	137	3	4	5	0	82	70	17	8	.680	0	3.00
90	OAK/AL		35	979	35	2	2	0	238.0	214	26	77	4	5	127	6	5	2	2	90	78	27	6	.818	0	2.95
91	OAK/AL		35	950	35	7	1	0	220.0	220	25	91	3	11	101	6	5	2	2	124	112	12	13	.480	0	4.58
14 YR TOTALS			431	11372	406	61	28	16	2733.0	2493	219	892	53	69	1815	104	73	50	42	1105	994	188	122	.606	8	3.27

Wells, David Lee — bats left — throws left — b.5/20/63

YR	TM/LG	CL	G	TBF	GS	CG	SHO	GF	IP	H	HR	BB	IBB	HB	SO	SH	SF	WP	BK	R	ER	W	L	PCT	SV	ERA
84	KIN/CAR	A+	7	192	7	0	0	0	42.0	51	1	19	1	1	44	1	2	4	1	29	22	1	6	.143	0	4.71
	KNO/SOU	AA	8	239	8	3	1	0	59.0	58	3	17	0	0	34	0	1	1	0	22	17	3	2	.600	0	2.59
86	FLO/SAL	A	4	54	1	0	0	0	12.2	7	1	9	0	0	14	0	1	0	0	6	5	0	0	.000	0	3.55
	VEN/CAL	A+	5	72	2	0	0	0	19.0	13	0	4	0	0	26	2	1	0	0	5	4	2	1	.667	0	1.89
	KNO/SOU	AA	10	174	7	1	0	2	40.0	42	1	18	0	1	32	2	3	4	0	24	18	1	3	.250	0	4.05
	SYR/INT	AAA	3	17	0	0	0	1	3.2	6	0	1	0	0	2	1	0	0	0	4	4	0	1	.000	0	9.82
87	SYR/INT	AAA	43	453	12	0	0	17	109.1	102	9	32	0	0	106	7	3	9	1	49	47	4	6	.400	6	3.87
	TOR/AL		18	132	2	0	0	6	29.1	37	7	12	0	0	32	1	0	4	0	14	13	4	3	.571	1	3.99
88	SYR/INT	AAA	6	28	0	0	0	3	5.2	7	0	2	1	0	8	0	0	2	1	1	0	0	0	.000	3	0.00
	TOR/AL		41	279	0	0	0	15	64.1	65	12	31	9	2	56	2	2	6	2	36	33	3	5	.375	4	4.62
89	TOR/AL		54	352	0	0	0	19	86.1	66	5	28	7	0	78	3	2	6	3	25	23	7	4	.636	2	2.40
90	TOR/AL		43	759	25	0	0	8	189.0	165	14	45	3	2	115	9	2	7	1	72	66	11	6	.647	3	3.14
91	TOR/AL		40	811	28	2	0	3	198.1	188	24	49	1	2	106	6	6	10	3	88	82	15	10	.600	1	3.72
5 YR TOTALS			196	2333	55	2	0	51	567.1	521	55	165	20	6	387	21	12	33	9	235	217	40	28	.588	11	3.44

Wendell, Steven John "Turk" — bats left — throws right — b.5/19/67 — System CHI/NL

YR	TM/LG	CL	G	TBF	GS	CG	SHO	GF	IP	H	HR	BB	IBB	HB	SO	SH	SF	WP	BK	R	ER	W	L	PCT	SV	ERA
88	PUL/APP	R+	14	418	14	6	1	0	101.0	85	3	30	0	6	87	5	2	7	6	50	43	3	8	.273	0	3.83
89	BUR/MID	A	22	643	22	9	5	0	159.0	127	7	41	1	3	153	2	0	1	6	63	39	9	11	.450	0	2.21
	GRE/SOU	AA	1	19	1	0	0	0	3.2	7	3	1	0	0	3	0	0	0	0	5	4	0	0	.000	0	9.82
	DUR/CAR	A+	3	89	3	1	0	0	24.0	13	0	6	0	0	27	0	0	0	0	4	3	2	0	1.000	0	1.13
90	GRE/SOU	AA	36	434	13	1	1	13	91.0	105	5	48	2	11	85	5	6	8	2	70	58	4	9	.308	2	5.74
	DUR/CAR	A+	6	154	5	1	0	0	38.2	24	3	15	1	2	26	0	0	2	0	10	8	1	3	.250	0	1.86
91	GRE/SOU	AA	25	613	20	1	1	3	147.2	130	4	51	5	6	122	2	2	11	0	47	42	11	3	.786	0	2.56
	RIC/INT	AAA	3	97	3	1	0	0	21.0	20	3	16	0	3	18	1	0	2	0	9	8	0	2	.000	0	3.43

West, David Lee — bats left — throws left — b.9/1/64

YR	TM/LG	CL	G	TBF	GS	CG	SHO	GF	IP	H	HR	BB	IBB	HB	SO	SH	SF	WP	BK	R	ER	W	L	PCT	SV	ERA
84	COL/SAL	A	12	288	12	0	0	0	60.2	41	2	68	1	2	60	4	2	14	1	47	42	3	5	.375	0	6.23
	LF/NYP	A-	13	290	11	0	0	1	62.0	43	1	62	0	1	79	3	4	16	2	35	23	6	4	.600	0	3.34

(continued)

West, David Lee (continued)

YR	TM/LG	CL	G	TBF	GS	CG	SHO	GF	IP	H	HR	BB	IBB	HB	SO	SH	SF	WP	BK	R	ER	W	L	PCT	SV	ERA
85	COL/SAL	A	26	677	25	5	2	0	150.0	105	6	111	1	9	194	3	4	23	3	97	76	10	9	.526	0	4.56
86	LYN/CAR	A+	13	343	13	1	0	0	75.0	76	3	53	0	3	70	5	3	4	1	50	43	1	6	.143	0	5.16
	COL/SAL	A	13	403	13	3	1	0	92.2	74	4	56	1	3	101	3	3	14	2	41	30	10	3	.769	0	2.91
87	JAC/TEX	AA	25	730	25	4	2	0	166.2	152	5	81	1	4	186	4	4	5	3	67	52	10	7	.588	0	2.81
88	TID/INT	AAA	23	675	23	7	1	0	160.1	106	5	97	1	9	143	11	3	5	3	42	32	12	4	.750	0	1.80
	NY/NL		2	25	1	0	0	0	6.0	6	0	3	0	0	3	0	0	0	2	2	2	1	0	1.000	0	3.00
89	TID/INT	AAA	12	343	12	5	1	0	87.1	60	9	29	0	0	69	6	4	3	1	31	23	7	4	.636	0	2.37
	NY/NL		11	112	2	0	0	0	24.1	25	4	14	2	1	19	0	1	1	0	20	20	0	2	.000	0	7.40
	MIN/AL		10	182	5	0	0	4	39.1	48	5	19	1	2	31	2	2	1	0	29	28	3	2	.600	0	6.41
	YEAR		21	294	7	0	0	4	63.2	73	9	33	3	3	50	2	3	2	0	49	48	3	4	.429	0	6.79
90	MIN/AL		29	646	27	2	0	0	146.1	142	21	78	1	4	92	6	4	4	1	88	83	7	9	.438	0	5.10
91	ORL/SOU	AA	1	1	1	0	0	0	0.1	0	0	0	0	0	0	0	0	0	0	0	0	0	0	.000	0	0.00
	POR/PCL	AAA	4	68	4	0	0	0	15.2	12	3	12	0	0	15	1	1	0	0	11	11	1	1	.500	0	6.32
	MIN/AL		15	305	12	0	0	0	71.1	66	13	28	0	1	52	2	3	3	0	37	36	4	4	.500	0	4.54
4 YR TOTALS			**67**	**1270**	**47**	**2**	**0**	**4**	**287.1**	**287**	**43**	**142**	**4**	**8**	**197**	**10**	**10**	**9**	**3**	**176**	**169**	**15**	**17**	**.469**	**0**	**5.29**

Weston, Michael Lee "Mickey" — bats right — throws right — b.3/26/61

YR	TM/LG	CL	G	TBF	GS	CG	SHO	GF	IP	H	HR	BB	IBB	HB	SO	SH	SF	WP	BK	R	ER	W	L	PCT	SV	ERA
82	LF/NYP	A–	17	0	13	2	0	0	92.0	105	16	22	0	4	67	0	0	9	0	63	52	7	6	.538	0	5.09
83	COL/SAL	A	37	0	1	0	0	0	74.0	87	5	22	0	1	46	0	0	8	0	48	36	2	2	.500	6	4.38
84	COL/SAL	A	32	272	2	0	0	20	63.2	58	2	27	6	2	40	6	1	5	0	27	13	6	5	.545	2	1.84
85	LYN/CAR	A+	49	407	3	1	1	24	100.1	81	4	22	2	0	62	3	2	4	1	29	24	6	5	.545	10	2.15
86	JAC/TEX	AA	34	308	4	0	0	7	70.2	73	9	27	3	4	36	3	2	3	0	40	34	4	4	.500	2	4.33
87	JAC/TEX	AA	58	346	1	0	0	21	82.0	96	4	18	5	1	50	0	1	6	1	39	31	8	4	.667	3	3.40
88	JAC/TEX	AA	30	507	14	1	0	4	125.1	127	3	20	4	0	61	8	5	4	0	50	31	8	5	.615	0	2.23
	TID/INT	AAA	4	115	4	2	1	0	29.2	21	0	5	1	1	16	3	0	1	0	6	5	2	1	.667	0	1.52
89	ROC/INT	AAA	23	445	14	2	1	7	112.0	103	6	19	0	1	51	2	2	1	0	30	26	8	3	.727	4	2.09
	BAL/AL		7	55	0	0	0	2	13.0	18	1	2	0	1	7	0	0	0	0	8	8	1	0	1.000	1	5.54
90	ROC/INT	AAA	29	432	12	2	0	13	109.1	93	3	22	0	0	58	1	1	2	0	36	24	11	4	.917	6	1.98
	BAL/AL		9	94	2	0	0	4	21.0	28	4	6	1	0	9	1	0	1	0	20	18	0	1	.000	0	7.71
91	TOR/AL		2	8	0	0	0	2	2.0	1	0	1	1	0	1	0	0	0	0	0	0	0	1	.000	0	0.00
	SYR/INT	AAA	27	710	25	3	0	1	166.0	193	7	36	1	3	60	4	5	10	0	85	69	12	6	.667	0	3.74
3 YR TOTALS			**18**	**157**	**2**	**0**	**0**	**8**	**36.0**	**47**	**7**	**9**	**2**	**1**	**17**	**1**	**0**	**1**	**0**	**28**	**26**	**1**	**1**	**.500**	**1**	**6.50**

Wetteland, John Karl — bats right — throws right — b.8/21/66

YR	TM/LG	CL	G	TBF	GS	CG	SHO	GF	IP	H	HR	BB	IBB	HB	SO	SH	SF	WP	BK	R	ER	W	L	PCT	SV	ERA
85	GF/PIO	R+	11	0	2	0	0	3	20.2	17	0	15	1	0	23	0	0	0	0	10	9	1	1	.500	0	3.92
86	BAK/CAL	A+	15	313	12	4	0	1	67.0	71	6	46	1	1	38	2	4	10	1	50	43	0	7	.000	0	5.78
	GF/PIO	R+	12	0	12	1	0	0	69.1	70	8	40	0	3	59	0	0	7	1	51	42	4	3	.571	0	5.45
87	VB/FSL	A+	27	759	27	7	2	0	175.2	150	11	92	0	2	144	3	4	17	0	81	61	12	7	.632	0	3.13
88	SA/TEX	AA	25	684	25	3	1	0	162.1	141	10	77	1	1	140	7	5	22	2	74	70	10	8	.556	0	3.88
89	ALB/PCL	AAA	10	286	10	1	0	0	69.0	61	11	20	0	0	73	2	0	0	0	28	28	5	3	.625	0	3.65
	LA/NL		31	411	12	0	0	7	102.2	81	8	34	4	0	96	4	2	16	1	46	43	5	8	.385	1	3.77
90	ALB/PCL	AAA	8	120	5	1	0	2	29.0	27	5	13	0	0	26	1	1	0	0	19	18	2	2	.500	0	5.59
	LA/NL		22	190	5	0	0	7	43.0	44	6	17	3	4	36	1	1	8	0	28	23	2	4	.333	0	4.81
91	ALB/PCL	AAA	41	245	0	0	0	34	61.1	48	5	26	1	1	55	4	3	5	1	22	19	4	3	.571	20	2.79
	LA/NL		6	36	0	0	0	3	9.0	5	0	3	0	1	9	0	1	1	0	2	0	1	0	1.000	0	0.00
3 YR TOTALS			**59**	**637**	**17**	**0**	**0**	**17**	**154.2**	**130**	**14**	**54**	**7**	**5**	**141**	**5**	**4**	**25**	**1**	**76**	**66**	**8**	**12**	**.400**	**1**	**3.84**

Whitehurst, Walter Richard "Wally" — bats right — throws right — b.4/11/64

YR	TM/LG	CL	G	TBF	GS	CG	SHO	GF	IP	H	HR	BB	IBB	HB	SO	SH	SF	WP	BK	R	ER	W	L	PCT	SV	ERA
85	MED/NWL	A–	14	0	14	2	0	0	88.0	92	6	29	1	7	91	0	0	11	2	51	35	7	5	.583	0	3.58
	MOD/CAL	A+	2	0	2	0	0	0	10.0	10	1	5	0	1	5	0	0	0	0	3	2	1	0	1.000	0	1.80
86	MAD/MID	A	8	234	8	5	4	0	61.0	42	1	16	0	1	57	1	0	4	0	8	4	6	1	.857	0	0.59
	HUN/SOU	AA	19	468	19	2	0	0	104.2	114	4	46	3	7	54	5	2	12	3	66	54	9	5	.643	0	4.64
87	HUN/SOU	AA	28	766	28	5	3	0	183.1	192	12	42	3	2	106	6	6	9	0	104	81	11	10	.524	0	3.98
88	TID/INT	AAA	26	664	26	3	1	0	165.0	145	7	32	3	8	113	8	4	10	9	65	56	10	11	.476	0	3.05
89	TID/INT	AAA	21	551	20	3	1	1	133.0	123	8	32	2	1	95	3	2	3	2	54	48	8	7	.533	0	3.25
	NY/NL		9	64	1	0	0	4	14.0	17	2	5	0	0	9	0	0	0	0	7	7	1	0	1.000	0	4.50
90	TID/INT	AAA	2	34	2	0	0	0	9.0	7	0	1	0	1	10	0	0	0	0	2	2	1	0	1.000	0	2.00
	NY/NL		38	263	0	0	0	16	65.2	63	5	9	2	0	46	3	0	2	0	27	24	1	0	1.000	2	3.29
91	NY/NL		36	556	20	0	0	6	133.1	142	12	25	3	4	87	6	3	3	4	67	62	7	12	.368	1	4.18
3 YR TOTALS			**83**	**883**	**21**	**0**	**0**	**26**	**213.0**	**222**	**19**	**39**	**5**	**4**	**142**	**9**	**4**	**6**	**4**	**101**	**93**	**8**	**13**	**.381**	**3**	**3.93**

Whitson, Eddie Lee "Ed" — bats right — throws right — b.5/19/55

YR	TM/LG	CL	G	TBF	GS	CG	SHO	GF	IP	H	HR	BB	IBB	HB	SO	SH	SF	WP	BK	R	ER	W	L	PCT	SV	ERA
77	PIT/NL		5	66	2	0	0	1	15.2	11	0	9	1	0	10	1	2	0	0	6	6	1	0	1.000	0	3.45
78	PIT/NL		43	318	0	0	0	14	74.1	66	5	37	5	2	64	3	4	1	0	31	27	5	6	.455	4	3.27
79	PIT/NL		19	263	7	0	0	4	57.2	53	6	36	3	0	31	3	0	2	1	36	28	2	3	.400	1	4.37
	SF/NL		18	439	17	2	0	1	100.1	98	5	39	6	4	62	7	3	3	1	47	44	3	5	.385	0	3.95
	YEAR		37	702	24	2	0	5	158.0	151	11	75	9	4	93	10	3	5	2	83	72	5	8	.385	1	4.10
80	SF/NL		34	898	34	6	2	0	211.2	222	7	56	7	4	90	10	5	9	1	88	73	11	13	.458	0	3.10
81	SF/NL		22	534	22	2	1	0	123.0	130	10	47	5	2	65	6	3	2	2	61	55	6	9	.400	0	4.02
82	CLE/AL		40	467	9	1	1	18	107.2	91	6	58	3	0	61	7	8	4	1	43	39	4	2	.667	2	3.26

Whitson, Eddie Lee "Ed" (continued)

YR	TM/LG	CL	G	TBF	GS	CG	SHO	GF	IP	H	HR	BB	IBB	HB	SO	SH	SF	WP	BK	R	ER	W	L	PCT	SV	ERA
83	SD/NL		31	617	21	2	0	4	144.1	143	23	50	1	1	81	3	4	2	0	73	69	5	7	.417	1	4.30
84	SD/NL		31	773	31	1	0	0	189.0	181	16	42	1	3	103	10	7	3	1	72	68	14	8	.636	0	3.24
85	NY/AL		30	705	30	2	2	0	158.2	201	19	43	0	2	89	3	7	1	0	100	86	10	8	.556	0	4.88
86	NY/AL		14	189	4	0	0	6	37.0	54	5	23	1	0	27	2	3	2	0	37	31	5	2	.714	0	7.54
	SD/NL		17	337	12	0	0	0	75.2	85	8	37	0	0	46	2	2	1	0	48	47	1	7	.125	0	5.59
	YEAR		31	526	16	0	0	6	112.2	139	13	60	1	0	73	4	5	3	0	85	78	6	9	.400	0	6.23
87	SD/NL		36	858	34	3	1	0	205.2	197	36	64	3	3	135	4	2	2	1	113	108	10	13	.435	0	4.73
88	SD/NL		34	846	33	3	1	0	205.1	202	17	45	1	1	118	13	8	2	2	93	86	13	11	.542	0	3.77
89	SD/NL		33	914	33	5	1	0	227.0	198	22	48	6	5	117	12	8	2	3	77	67	16	11	.593	0	2.66
90	SD/NL		32	918	32	6	3	0	228.2	215	13	47	8	1	127	9	6	2	0	73	66	14	9	.609	0	2.60
91	SD/NL		13	337	12	2	0	0	78.2	93	13	17	3	0	40	6	3	1	1	47	44	4	6	.400	0	5.03
15 YR TOTALS			**452**	**9479**	**333**	**35**	**12**	**48**	**2240.1**	**2240**	**211**	**698**	**54**	**29**	**1266**	**101**	**78**	**32**	**14**	**1045**	**944**	**126**	**123**	**.506**	**8**	**3.79**

Wilkins, Dean Allan — bats right — throws right — b.8/24/66

YR	TM/LG	CL	G	TBF	GS	CG	SHO	GF	IP	H	HR	BB	IBB	HB	SO	SH	SF	WP	BK	R	ER	W	L	PCT	SV	ERA
86	ONE/NYP	A–	15	337	12	1	0	3	83.1	64	5	24	0	8	80	5	1	4	1	32	29	9	0	1.000	1	3.13
87	ALB/EAS	AA	2	55	2	0	0	0	12.0	18	3	1	0	1	8	0	1	0	0	11	9	0	0	.000	0	6.75
	FT./FSL	A+	15	435	14	5	2	1	105.2	95	2	39	1	1	76	1	1	7	4	41	32	8	5	.615	0	2.73
	WIN/CAR	A+	13	224	6	3	0	1	50.1	49	3	24	0	1	29	2	3	1	0	31	23	4	4	.500	1	4.11
88	PIT/EAS	AA	59	295	0	0	0	49	71.2	53	0	30	5	2	59	6	1	9	0	25	13	5	7	.417	26	1.63
89	IOW/AMA	AAA	38	604	16	0	0	17	138.0	149	5	58	5	4	82	3	4	15	1	74	65	8	11	.421	3	4.24
	CHI/NL		11	67	0	0	0	1	15.2	13	2	9	2	0	14	1	0	0	0	9	8	1	0	1.000	0	4.60
90	CHI/NL		7	41	0	0	0	3	7.1	11	1	7	0	1	3	0	0	3	0	8	8	0	0	.000	0	9.82
	IOW/AMA	AAA	52	325	2	0	0	33	73.0	75	4	38	5	6	61	2	3	10	2	37	30	6	2	.750	11	3.70
91	TUC/PCL	AAA	65	375	0	0	0	47	83.2	84	2	43	5	5	65	6	4	5	0	47	39	8	7	.533	20	4.20
	HOU/NL		7	51	0	0	0	3	8.0	16	0	10	2	0	4	2	0	1	0	14	10	2	1	.667	1	11.25
3 YR TOTALS			**25**	**159**	**0**	**0**	**0**	**7**	**31.0**	**40**	**3**	**26**	**4**	**1**	**21**	**3**	**0**	**4**	**0**	**31**	**26**	**3**	**1**	**.750**	**2**	**7.55**

Williams, Brian O'Neal — bats right — throws right — b.2/15/69

YR	TM/LG	CL	G	TBF	GS	CG	SHO	GF	IP	H	HR	BB	IBB	HB	SO	SH	SF	WP	BK	R	ER	W	L	PCT	SV	ERA
90	AUB/NYP	A–	3	34	3	0	0	0	6.2	6	0	6	0	1	7	1	0	1	1	5	3	0	0	.000	0	4.05
91	OSC/FSL	A+	15	378	15	0	0	0	89.2	72	0	40	1	2	67	3	6	3	5	41	29	6	4	.600	0	2.91
	JAC/TEX	AA	3	66	3	0	0	0	15.0	17	1	7	0	0	15	0	0	3	0	8	7	2	1	.667	0	4.20
	TUC/PCL	AAA	7	177	7	0	0	0	38.1	39	3	22	0	2	29	4	0	3	4	25	21	0	1	.000	0	4.93
	HOU/NL		2	49	2	0	0	0	12.0	11	2	4	0	1	4	0	0	0	0	5	5	0	1	.000	0	3.75

Williams, Mitchell Steven "Mitch" — bats left — throws left — b.11/17/64

YR	TM/LG	CL	G	TBF	GS	CG	SHO	GF	IP	H	HR	BB	IBB	HB	SO	SH	SF	WP	BK	R	ER	W	L	PCT	SV	ERA
84	REN/CAL	A+	26	0	26	3	1	0	164.0	163	11	127	1	9	165	0	0	19	3	113	91	9	8	.529	0	4.99
85	SAL/CAR	A+	22	471	21	1	0	1	99.0	57	6	117	0	6	138	2	2	12	1	64	60	6	9	.400	0	5.45
	TUL/TEX	AA	6	165	6	0	0	0	33.0	17	1	48	0	2	37	2	1	3	1	24	17	2	2	.500	0	4.64
86	TEX/AL		80	435	0	0	0	38	98.0	69	8	79	8	11	90	1	3	5	5	39	39	8	6	.571	8	3.58
87	TEX/AL		85	469	1	0	0	32	108.2	63	9	94	7	7	129	4	3	4	2	47	39	8	6	.571	6	3.23
88	TEX/AL		67	296	0	0	0	51	68.0	48	4	47	3	4	61	3	4	5	6	38	35	2	7	.222	18	4.63
89	CHI/NL		76	365	0	0	0	61	81.2	71	6	52	4	8	67	2	5	6	4	27	25	4	4	.500	36	2.76
90	CHI/NL		59	310	2	0	0	39	66.1	60	4	50	6	1	55	5	3	4	2	38	29	1	8	.111	16	3.93
91	PHI/NL		69	386	0	0	0	60	88.1	56	4	62	6	8	84	4	4	4	1	24	23	12	5	.706	30	2.34
6 YR TOTALS			**436**	**2261**	**3**	**0**	**0**	**281**	**511.0**	**367**	**35**	**384**	**33**	**41**	**486**	**19**	**22**	**28**	**20**	**213**	**190**	**35**	**36**	**.493**	**114**	**3.35**

Williamson, Mark Alan — bats right — throws right — b.7/21/59

YR	TM/LG	CL	G	TBF	GS	CG	SHO	GF	IP	H	HR	BB	IBB	HB	SO	SH	SF	WP	BK	R	ER	W	L	PCT	SV	ERA
84	REN/CAL	A+	56	0	1	0	0	46	93.0	105	2	23	10	2	69	0	0	4	0	41	30	10	12	.455	15	2.90
85	BEA/TEX	AA	42	333	0	0	0	32	78.2	72	1	23	7	2	64	6	2	3	0	27	25	10	9	.526	8	2.86
86	LV/PCL	AAA	65	445	0	0	0	36	104.1	103	10	36	10	0	81	3	5	2	1	47	39	10	3	.769	16	3.36
87	ROC/INT	AAA	1	18	0	0	0	1	4.0	6	0	1	0	1	1	0	1	0	0	3	3	0	1	.000	0	6.75
	BAL/AL		61	520	2	0	0	36	125.0	122	12	41	15	3	73	5	3	0	0	59	56	8	9	.471	3	4.03
88	ROC/INT	AAA	12	131	3	1	0	8	29.2	38	2	5	2	0	25	0	0	3	0	11	11	2	3	.400	2	3.34
	BAL/AL		37	507	10	2	0	11	117.2	125	14	40	8	2	69	4	2	5	3	70	64	5	8	.385	2	4.90
89	BAL/AL		65	445	0	0	0	38	107.1	105	4	30	9	2	55	7	3	0	0	35	35	10	5	.667	9	2.93
90	BAL/AL		49	343	0	0	0	15	85.1	65	8	28	4	6	60	6	7	1	0	25	21	8	2	.800	1	2.21
91	BAL/AL		65	357	0	0	0	21	80.1	87	9	35	7	2	53	1	5	7	0	42	40	5	5	.500	4	4.48
5 YR TOTALS			**277**	**2172**	**12**	**2**	**0**	**121**	**515.2**	**504**	**47**	**174**	**41**	**7**	**310**	**23**	**20**	**16**	**3**	**231**	**216**	**36**	**29**	**.554**	**19**	**3.77**

Willis, Carl Blake — bats left — throws right — b.12/28/60

YR	TM/LG	CL	G	TBF	GS	CG	SHO	GF	IP	H	HR	BB	IBB	HB	SO	SH	SF	WP	BK	R	ER	W	L	PCT	SV	ERA
83	BRI/APP	R+	2	0	0	0	0	0	2.0	0	0	4	0	0	3	0	0	0	0	1	1	0	1	.000	0	4.50
	LAK/FSL	A+	4	0	0	0	0	0	9.0	6	0	5	0	0	7	0	0	0	0	0	0	3	0	1.000	0	0.00
	BIR/SOU	AA	14	0	0	0	0	0	20.0	16	0	7	0	0	13	0	0	2	0	9	9	3	1	.750	2	4.05
84	DET/AL		10	74	2	0	0	4	16.0	25	1	5	2	0	4	0	0	0	0	13	13	0	0	.000	0	7.31
	EVA/AMA	AAA	40	242	1	0	0	32	60.1	59	8	20	2	0	27	3	2	3	3	26	25	5	3	.625	16	3.73
	CIN/NL		7	39	0	0	0	2	9.2	8	1	2	0	0	3	1	0	0	0	4	4	0	1	.000	1	3.72
	YEAR		17	113	2	0	0	5	25.2	33	2	7	2	0	7	1	0	0	0	17	17	0	1	.000	1	5.96
85	DEN/AMA	AAA	37	338	1	0	0	24	78.0	82	7	30	2	1	27	1	6	8	1	39	36	4	5	.500	8	4.15
	CIN/NL		11	69	0	0	0	6	13.2	21	3	5	0	0	6	1	2	1	0	18	14	1	0	1.000	0	9.22

(continued)

Willis, Carl Blake (continued)

YR	TM/LG	CL	G	TBF	GS	CG	SHO	GF	IP	H	HR	BB	IBB	HB	SO	SH	SF	WP	BK	R	ER	W	L	PCT	SV	ERA
86	DEN/AMA	AAA	20	139	1	0	0	16	32.2	29	3	16	1	1	16	2	0	2	1	22	17	1	3	.250	8	4.68
	CIN/NL		29	233	0	0	0	7	52.1	54	4	32	9	1	24	5	1	3	1	29	26	1	3	.250	0	4.47
87	NAS/AMA	AAA	53	369	0	0	0	25	83.2	97	5	30	5	2	54	4	3	7	1	39	31	6	4	.600	5	3.33
88	CHI/AL		6	55	0	0	0	0	12.0	17	3	7	1	0	6	0	1	2	0	12	11	0	0	.000	0	8.25
	VAN/PCL	AAA	40	285	1	0	0	21	64.0	77	3	16	0	1	44	3	1	1	0	36	30	4	4	.500	4	4.22
89	EDM/PCL	AAA	36	493	10	0	0	12	112.1	137	9	36	3	1	47	3	1	4	3	54	46	5	7	.417	5	3.69
90	CS/PCL	AAA	41	457	6	0	0	5	98.2	136	9	32	3	1	42	4	6	3	0	80	70	5	3	.625	2	6.39
91	POR/PCL	AAA	3	41	1	0	0	1	11.0	5	0	0	0	1	0	1	1	0	0	4	2	1	1	.500	0	1.64
	MIN/AL		40	355	0	0	0	9	89.0	76	4	19	1	1	53	3	4	4	1	31	26	8	3	.727	2	2.63
5 YR TOTALS			**103**	**825**	**2**	**0**	**0**	**27**	**192.2**	**201**	**16**	**70**	**13**	**2**	**96**	**10**	**8**	**10**	**2**	**107**	**94**	**10**	**9**	**.526**	**4**	**4.39**

Wills, Frank Lee — bats right — throws right — b.10/26/58

YR	TM/LG	CL	G	TBF	GS	CG	SHO	GF	IP	H	HR	BB	IBB	HB	SO	SH	SF	WP	BK	R	ER	W	L	PCT	SV	ERA
83	KC/AL		6	152	4	0	0	1	34.2	35	2	15	0	0	23	0	2	3	0	17	16	2	1	.667	0	4.15
84	OMA/AMA	AAA	15	381	15	2	1	0	89.2	75	9	49	0	0	69	2	5	2	0	32	28	7	4	.636	0	2.81
	KC/AL		10	161	5	0	0	2	37.0	39	3	13	0	0	21	0	4	2	0	21	21	2	3	.400	0	5.11
85	CAL/PCL	AAA	9	0	9	3	2	0	46.1	44	5	25	0	0	31	0	3	3	0	27	25	4	3	.571	0	4.86
	SEA/AL		24	541	18	1	0	2	123.0	122	18	68	3	0	67	4	3	8	1	85	82	5	11	.313	1	6.00
86	MAI/INT	AAA	22	137	1	0	0	17	31.1	37	4	10	1	1	21	2	0	1	0	10	10	4	3	.571	6	2.87
	CLE/AL		26	182	0	0	0	16	40.1	43	6	16	4	0	32	6	2	2	0	23	22	4	4	.500	4	4.91
87	CLE/AL		6	26	0	0	0	4	5.1	3	0	7	0	0	4	1	1	0	0	3	3	0	1	.000	1	5.06
	BUF/AMA	AAA	36	243	0	0	0	30	56.2	53	5	22	2	0	45	1	4	1	3	28	21	3	2	.600	6	3.34
88	SYR/INT	AAA	25	343	10	0	0	4	80.2	70	4	25	2	4	53	2	5	7	4	40	29	6	4	.600	3	3.24
	TOR/AL		10	89	0	0	0	4	20.2	22	2	6	2	0	19	1	1	1	0	12	12	0	0	.000	0	5.23
89	SYR/INT	AAA	14	70	0	0	0	11	17.0	8	1	8	0	0	13	0	1	1	0	7	3	1	0	1.000	5	1.59
	TOR/AL		24	302	4	0	0	6	71.1	65	4	30	2	1	41	1	1	4	0	31	29	3	1	.750	0	3.66
90	TOR/AL		44	422	4	0	0	6	99.0	101	13	38	7	1	72	2	1	1	0	54	52	6	4	.600	0	4.73
91	TOR/AL		4	27	0	0	0	3	4.1	8	2	5	0	1	2	2	0	0	0	8	8	0	1	.000	0	16.62
	SYR/INT	AAA	22	270	0	0	0	12	61.1	71	4	21	0	3	38	3	1	2	4	35	33	3	5	.375	1	4.84
9 YR TOTALS			**154**	**1902**	**35**	**1**	**0**	**44**	**435.2**	**438**	**50**	**198**	**18**	**6**	**281**	**17**	**20**	**22**	**1**	**254**	**245**	**22**	**26**	**.458**	**6**	**5.06**

Wilson, Stephen Douglas "Steve" — bats left — throws left — b.12/13/64

YR	TM/LG	CL	G	TBF	GS	CG	SHO	GF	IP	H	HR	BB	IBB	HB	SO	SH	SF	WP	BK	R	ER	W	L	PCT	SV	ERA
85	BUR/MID	A	21	317	10	0	0	4	72.2	71	11	27	1	2	76	1	4	1	3	44	37	3	5	.375	0	4.58
86	TUL/TEX	AA	24	617	24	2	0	0	136.2	117	10	103	0	7	95	5	8	12	6	83	74	7	13	.350	0	4.87
87	CHA/FSL	A+	20	442	17	1	1	1	107.0	81	5	44	0	3	80	0	2	5	2	41	29	9	5	.643	0	2.44
88	TUL/TEX	AA	25	698	25	5	3	0	165.1	147	14	53	1	8	132	6	4	3	1	72	58	15	7	.682	0	3.16
	TEX/AL		3	31	0	0	0	1	7.2	7	1	4	1	0	1	0	0	0	0	5	5	0	0	.000	0	5.87
89	CHI/NL		53	364	8	0	0	9	85.2	83	6	31	5	1	65	5	4	0	1	43	40	6	4	.600	2	4.20
90	CHI/NL		45	597	15	1	0	6	139.0	140	17	43	6	2	95	9	3	2	1	77	74	4	9	.308	1	4.79
91	IOW/AMA	AAA	25	482	16	1	0	4	114.0	102	11	45	2	7	83	0	1	7	0	55	49	3	8	.273	0	3.87
	CHI/NL		8	53	0	0	0	2	12.1	13	1	5	1	0	9	0	1	0	0	7	6	0	0	.000	0	4.38
	LA/NL		11	28	0	0	0	3	8.1	1	0	4	0	0	5	0	0	0	0	0	0	0	0	.000	2	0.00
	YEAR		19	81	0	0	0	5	20.2	14	1	9	1	0	14	0	1	0	0	7	6	0	0	.000	2	2.61
4 YR TOTALS			**120**	**1073**	**23**	**1**	**0**	**20**	**253.0**	**244**	**25**	**87**	**13**	**3**	**175**	**14**	**8**	**2**	**2**	**132**	**125**	**10**	**13**	**.435**	**5**	**4.45**

Wilson, Trevor Kirk — bats left — throws left — b.6/7/66

YR	TM/LG	CL	G	TBF	GS	CG	SHO	GF	IP	H	HR	BB	IBB	HB	SO	SH	SF	WP	BK	R	ER	W	L	PCT	SV	ERA
85	EVE/NWL	A–	17	0	7	0	0	8	55.1	67	2	26	0	1	50	0	0	6	2	36	26	2	4	.333	3	4.23
86	CLI/MID	A	34	569	21	0	0	7	130.2	126	6	64	1	6	84	3	3	5	2	70	62	6	11	.353	2	4.27
87	CLI/MID	A	26	668	26	3	2	0	161.1	130	3	77	0	6	146	2	6	9	2	60	36	10	6	.625	0	2.01
88	SHR/TEX	AA	12	291	11	0	0	0	72.2	55	0	23	1	0	53	2	3	1	13	19	15	5	4	.556	0	1.86
	PHO/PCL	AAA	11	233	9	0	0	0	51.2	49	3	33	2	0	49	3	1	1	4	35	29	2	3	.400	0	5.05
	SF/NL		4	96	4	0	0	0	22.0	25	1	8	0	0	15	3	1	0	1	14	10	0	2	.000	0	4.09
89	PHO/PCL	AAA	23	504	20	2	0	2	115.1	109	5	76	1	2	77	5	4	5	7	49	40	7	7	.500	0	3.12
	SF/NL		14	167	4	0	0	2	39.1	28	2	24	0	4	22	3	1	0	1	20	19	2	3	.400	0	4.35
90	PHO/PCL	AAA	11	290	10	2	1	0	66.0	63	2	44	2	0	44	4	3	1	3	31	28	5	5	.500	0	3.82
	SF/NL		27	457	17	3	2	3	110.1	87	11	49	3	1	66	6	2	5	2	52	49	8	7	.533	0	4.00
91	SF/NL		44	841	29	2	1	6	202.0	173	13	77	14	5	139	14	5	5	3	87	80	13	11	.542	0	3.56
4 YR TOTALS			**89**	**1561**	**54**	**5**	**3**	**11**	**373.2**	**313**	**27**	**158**	**7**	**10**	**242**	**26**	**9**	**10**	**7**	**173**	**158**	**23**	**23**	**.500**	**0**	**3.81**

Witt, Michael Atwater "Mike" — bats right — throws right — b.7/20/60

YR	TM/LG	CL	G	TBF	GS	CG	SHO	GF	IP	H	HR	BB	IBB	HB	SO	SH	SF	WP	BK	R	ER	W	L	PCT	SV	ERA
81	CAL/AL		22	555	21	7	1	1	129.0	123	9	47	4	11	75	3	4	2	0	60	47	8	9	.471	0	3.28
82	CAL/AL		33	748	26	5	1	2	179.2	177	8	47	2	7	85	8	5	8	1	77	70	8	6	.571	0	3.51
83	CAL/AL		43	683	19	2	0	15	154.0	173	14	75	7	6	77	5	7	8	1	90	84	7	14	.333	5	4.91
84	CAL/AL		34	1032	34	9	2	0	246.2	227	17	84	3	5	196	7	7	7	1	103	95	15	11	.577	0	3.47
85	CAL/AL		35	1049	35	6	1	0	250.0	228	22	98	6	4	180	4	5	11	1	115	99	15	9	.625	0	3.56
86	CAL/AL		34	1071	34	14	3	0	269.0	218	22	73	2	3	208	3	5	6	0	95	85	18	10	.643	0	2.84
87	CAL/AL		36	1065	36	10	0	0	247.0	252	34	84	4	4	192	6	4	5	0	128	110	16	14	.533	0	4.01
88	CAL/AL		34	1080	34	12	2	0	249.2	263	14	87	7	5	133	11	10	9	2	130	115	13	16	.448	0	4.15
89	CAL/AL		33	937	33	5	0	0	220.0	252	26	48	1	2	123	10	13	7	0	119	111	9	15	.375	0	4.54
90	CAL/AL		10	92	0	0	0	4	20.1	19	1	13	2	1	14	1	1	1	0	9	4	0	3	.000	1	1.77
	NY/AL		16	406	16	2	1	0	96.2	87	8	34	2	4	60	0	5	6	0	53	48	5	6	.455	0	4.47

Witt, Michael Atwater "Mike" (continued)

YR	TM/LG	CL	G	TBF	GS	CG	SHO	GF	IP	H	HR	BB	IBB	HB	SO	SH	SF	WP	BK	R	ER	W	L	PCT	SV	ERA
	YEAR		26	498	16	2	1	4	117.0	106	9	47	4	5	74	1	6	7	0	62	52	5	9	.357	1	4.00
91	NY/AL		2	26	2	0	0	0	5.1	8	1	1	0	0	0	0	0	1	0	7	6	0	1	.000	0	10.13
	COL/INT	AAA	1	22	1	0	0	0	4.0	7	0	3	0	1	5	0	0	1	0	4	4	0	0	.000	0	9.00
	ALB/EAS	AA	1	10	1	0	0	0	2.0	2	0	2	0	0	2	0	0	1	0	2	2	0	0	.000	0	9.00
11 YR TOTALS			332	8744	290	72	11	22	2067.1	2027	176	691	40	52	1343	58	68	72	5	986	874	114	114	.500	6	3.80

Witt, Robert Andrew "Bobby" — bats right — throws right — b.5/11/64

YR	TM/LG	CL	G	TBF	GS	CG	SHO	GF	IP	H	HR	BB	IBB	HB	SO	SH	SF	WP	BK	R	ER	W	L	PCT	SV	ERA
85	TUL/TEX	AA	11	167	8	0	0	1	35.0	26	1	44	0	1	39	0	1	7	1	26	25	0	6	.000	0	6.43
86	TEX/AL		31	741	31	0	0	0	157.2	130	18	143	2	3	174	3	9	22	3	104	96	11	9	.550	0	5.48
87	OC/AMA	AAA	1	23	1	0	0	0	5.0	5	1	3	0	0	2	0	1	0	0	5	5	1	0	1.000	0	9.00
	TUL/TEX	AA	1	28	1	0	0	0	5.0	5	1	6	0	0	2	0	0	0	0	9	3	0	1	.000	0	5.40
	TEX/AL		26	673	25	1	0	0	143.0	114	10	140	1	3	160	5	5	7	2	82	78	8	10	.444	0	4.91
88	OC/AMA	AAA	11	341	11	3	0	0	76.2	69	1	47	0	2	70	3	2	6	4	42	37	4	6	.400	0	4.34
	TEX/AL		22	736	22	13	2	0	174.1	134	13	101	1	1	148	7	6	16	8	83	76	8	10	.444	0	3.92
89	TEX/AL		31	869	31	5	1	0	194.1	182	14	114	3	2	166	11	8	7	4	123	112	12	13	.480	0	5.14
90	TEX/AL		33	954	32	7	1	1	222.0	197	12	110	3	4	221	5	6	11	2	98	83	17	10	.630	0	3.36
91	OC/AMA	AAA	2	35	2	0	0	0	8.0	3	0	8	0	0	12	0	0	0	0	1	1	1	1	.500	0	1.13
	TEX/AL		17	413	16	1	1	0	88.2	84	4	74	1	1	82	3	4	8	0	66	60	3	7	.300	0	6.09
6 YR TOTALS			160	4386	157	27	5	1	980.0	841	71	682	12	14	951	34	38	71	19	556	504	59	59	.500	0	4.63

Wohlers, Mark Edward — bats right — throws right — b.1/23/70

YR	TM/LG	CL	G	TBF	GS	CG	SHO	GF	IP	H	HR	BB	IBB	HB	SO	SH	SF	WP	BK	R	ER	W	L	PCT	SV	ERA
88	PUL/APP	R+	13	275	9	1	0	4	59.2	47	0	50	0	0	49	1	3	6	2	37	22	5	3	.625	0	3.32
89	SUM/SAL	A	14	326	14	0	0	0	68.0	74	3	59	0	4	51	3	3	10	1	55	49	2	7	.222	0	6.49
	PUL/APP	R+	14	219	8	0	0	2	46.0	48	5	28	0	2	50	1	0	2	0	36	28	1	1	.500	0	5.48
90	SUM/SAL	A	37	208	2	0	0	16	52.2	27	1	20	0	4	85	1	2	0	0	13	11	5	4	.556	5	1.88
	GRE/SOU	AA	14	72	0	0	0	11	15.2	14	0	14	0	1	21	0	1	1	0	7	7	0	1	.000	6	4.02
91	GRE/SOU	AA	28	116	0	0	0	27	31.1	9	0	13	0	0	44	3	2	3	0	4	2	0	0	.000	21	0.57
	RIC/INT	AAA	23	111	0	0	0	21	26.1	23	1	12	1	1	22	4	0	1	1	4	3	1	0	1.000	11	1.03
	ATL/NL		17	89	0	0	0	4	19.2	17	1	13	3	2	13	2	1	0	0	7	7	3	1	.750	2	3.20

Worrell, Todd Roland — bats right — throws right — b.9/28/59

YR	TM/LG	CL	G	TBF	GS	CG	SHO	GF	IP	H	HR	BB	IBB	HB	SO	SH	SF	WP	BK	R	ER	W	L	PCT	SV	ERA
84	ARK/TEX	AA	18	474	18	5	0	0	100.1	109	8	67	4	0	88	7	4	8	1	72	50	3	10	.231	0	4.49
	SP/FSL	A+	8	209	7	2	0	0	47.1	41	0	24	2	0	33	2	0	4	0	22	11	3	2	.600	0	2.09
85	LOU/AMA	AAA	34	532	17	2	1	15	127.2	114	8	47	1	4	126	2	6	5	1	59	51	8	6	.571	11	3.60
86	STL/NL		74	430	0	0	0	60	103.2	86	9	41	16	1	73	7	6	1	0	29	24	9	10	.474	36	2.08
87	STL/NL		75	395	0	0	0	54	94.2	86	8	34	11	0	92	4	2	1	0	29	28	8	6	.571	33	2.66
88	STL/NL		68	366	0	0	0	54	90.0	69	7	34	14	1	78	3	5	6	2	32	30	5	9	.357	32	3.00
89	LOU/AMA	AAA	1	3	1	0	0	0	1.0	0	0	0	0	0	1	0	0	0	0	0	0	0	0	.000	0	0.00
	ST./NL		47	219	0	0	0	39	51.2	42	4	26	13	0	41	3	1	3	3	21	17	3	5	.375	20	2.96
91	LOU/AMA	AAA	3	16	0	0	0	0	3.0	4	1	3	0	0	4	0	0	1	0	6	6	0	0	.000	0	18.00
4 YR TOTALS			264	1410	0	0	0	207	340.0	283	28	135	54	2	284	17	14	11	5	111	99	25	30	.455	121	2.62

York, Michael David "Mike" — bats right — throws right — b.9/6/64

YR	TM/LG	CL	G	TBF	GS	CG	SHO	GF	IP	H	HR	BB	IBB	HB	SO	SH	SF	WP	BK	R	ER	W	L	PCT	SV	ERA
83	ONE/NYP	A—	9	0	0	0	0	0	11.0	19	0	8	0	2	3	0	0	3	0	13	10	0	0	.000	0	8.18
84	WS/GCL	R	5	70	1	0	0	0	14.2	18	1	9	0	0	19	1	0	0	0	9	6	1	0	1.000	0	3.68
85	BRI/APP	R+	21	168	0	0	0	18	38.0	24	1	34	2	2	31	5	2	6	1	12	10	9	2	.818	2	2.37
86	LAK/FSL	A+	16	214	0	0	0	13	40.2	49	2	43	0	3	29	1	3	9	0	42	29	1	3	.250	0	6.42
	GAS/SAL	A	22	153	0	0	0	20	34.0	26	0	27	0	6	27	3	6	5	0	15	13	2	2	.500	9	3.44
87	MAC/SAL	A	28	700	28	3	2	0	165.2	129	11	88	1	2	169	5	3	9	3	71	56	17	6	.739	0	3.04
88	SAL/CAR	A+	13	360	13	2	1	0	84.0	65	3	52	0	2	77	2	2	5	4	31	25	9	2	.818	0	2.68
	HAR/EAS	AA	13	381	13	2	0	0	82.1	92	5	45	2	1	61	5	5	3	2	43	34	0	5	.000	0	3.72
89	HAR/EAS	AA	18	492	18	3	2	0	121.0	105	6	40	2	2	106	1	5	8	0	37	31	11	5	.688	0	2.31
	BUF/AMA	AAA	8	193	8	0	0	0	41.0	48	3	25	0	1	28	2	0	1	0	29	27	1	3	.250	0	5.93
90	BUF/AMA	AAA	27	707	26	3	1	0	158.2	165	0	78	2	5	130	7	2	7	5	87	74	8	7	.533	0	4.20
	PIT/NL		4	56	1	0	0	0	12.2	13	0	5	0	1	4	2	1	0	1	5	4	1	1	.500	0	2.84
91	BUF/AMA	AAA	7	181	7	1	0	0	43.1	36	0	23	0	0	22	1	2	2	0	17	14	5	1	.833	0	2.91
	CS/PCL	AAA	5	130	5	0	0	0	26.0	40	2	16	0	1	13	0	1	1	0	19	17	0	1	.000	0	5.88
	CLE/AL		14	163	4	0	0	3	34.2	45	2	19	2	2	19	3	4	2	1	29	26	1	4	.200	0	6.75
2 YR TOTALS			18	219	5	0	0	3	47.1	58	2	24	2	3	23	5	5	2	1	34	30	2	5	.286	0	5.70

Young, Anthony Wayne — bats right — throws right — b.1/19/66

YR	TM/LG	CL	G	TBF	GS	CG	SHO	GF	IP	H	HR	BB	IBB	HB	SO	SH	SF	WP	BK	R	ER	W	L	PCT	SV	ERA
87	LF/NYP	A—	14	247	9	0	0	0	53.2	58	6	25	1	1	48	2	2	4	0	37	27	3	4	.429	0	4.53
88	LF/NYP	.A—	15	304	10	4	0	2	73.2	51	1	34	0	0	75	1	3	9	1	33	18	3	5	.375	0	2.20
89	COL/SAL	A	21	548	17	8	1	2	129.0	115	5	55	1	4	127	1	3	7	3	60	50	15	3	.833	0	1.65
90	JAC/TEX	AA	23	633	23	3	1	0	158.0	116	8	52	5	3	95	6	1	7	1	38	29	7	9	.438	0	1.65
91	TID/INT	AAA	25	702	25	3	1	0	164.0	172	13	67	2	1	93	9	5	6	1	74	68	7	9	.438	0	3.73
	NY/NL		10	202	8	0	0	2	49.1	48	4	12	1	1	20	1	1	1	0	20	17	2	5	.286	0	3.10

Young, Clifford Raphael "Cliff" — bats left — throws left — b.8/2/64

YR	TM/LG	CL	G	TBF	GS	CG	SHO	GF	IP	H	HR	BB	IBB	HB	SO	SH	SF	WP	BK	R	ER	W	L	PCT	SV	ERA
83	CAL/PIO	R+	13		13	4	0	0	79.1	98	8	32	0	0	72			2	1	55	45	7	1	.875	0	5.11
84	GAS/SAL	A	24	614	24	7	2	0	144.1	117	10	68	2	1	121	7	7	9	0	77	67	8	10	.444	0	4.18
85	WPB/FSL	A+	25	664	25	7	0	0	153.2	149	13	57	0	6	112	3	6	6	4	77	68	15	5	.750	0	3.98
86	KNO/SOU	AA	31	880	31	1	0	0	203.2	232	25	71	1	2	121	3	4	3	5	111	88	12	14	.462	0	3.89
87	KNO/SOU	AA	42	541	12	0	0	10	119.1	148	15	43	5	3	81	5	4	12	2	76	59	8	9	.471	1	4.45
88	SYR/INT	AAA	33	608	18	4	1	7	147.1	133	13	32	0	3	75	2	5	3	4	68	56	9	6	.600	1	3.42
89	EDM/PCL	AAA	31	591	21	2	1	3	139.0	158	16	32	1	5	89	6	4	3	4	80	74	8	9	.471	0	4.79
90	EDM/PCL	AAA	30	208	0	0	0	14	52.0	45	1	10	1	1	30	6	1	0	2	15	14	7	4	.636	4	2.42
	CAL/AL		17	137	0	0	0	5	30.2	40	2	7	1	1	19	2	4	1	0	14	12	1	1	.500	0	3.52
91	EDM/PCL	AAA	34	328	8	0	0	15	71.2	88	2	25	1	4	39	4	3	8	0	53	39	4	8	.333	5	4.90
	CAL/AL		11	49	0	0	0	6	12.2	12	3	3	1	0	6	0	0	0	0	6	6	1	0	1.000	0	4.26
2 YR TOTALS			**28**	**186**	**0**	**0**	**0**	**11**	**43.1**	**52**	**5**	**10**	**2**	**1**	**25**	**2**	**4**	**1**	**0**	**20**	**18**	**2**	**1**	**.667**	**0**	**3.74**

Young, Curtis Allen "Curt" — bats right — throws left — b.4/16/60

YR	TM/LG	CL	G	TBF	GS	CG	SHO	GF	IP	H	HR	BB	IBB	HB	SO	SH	SF	WP	BK	R	ER	W	L	PCT	SV	ERA
83	OAK/AL		8	50	2	0	0	0	9.0	17	1	5	0	1	5	0	0	1	0	17	16	0	1	.000	0	16.00
84	TAC/PCL	AAA	14	0	14	5	1	0	95.1	88	8	28	1	1	61	0	0	5	0	45	40	6	4	.600	0	3.78
	OAK/AL		20	475	17	2	1	0	108.2	118	9	31	0	8	41	1	4	3	0	53	49	9	4	.692	0	4.06
85	MOD/CAL	A+	2	0	2	0	0	0	5.2	7	0	6	0	0	3	0	0	0	0	4	3	0	0	.000	0	4.76
	TAC/PCL	AAA	3	0	3	0	0	0	15.0	10	1	7	0	0	8	0	0	0	0	7	6	2	0	1.000	0	3.60
	OAK/AL		19	214	7	0	0	5	46.0	57	15	22	0	1	19	0	1	1	0	38	37	0	4	.000	0	7.24
86	TAC/PCL	AAA	4	99	4	1	0	0	27.0	16	1	6	0	0	28	0	0	0	0	7	6	4	0	1.000	0	2.00
	OAK/AL		29	826	27	5	2	0	198.0	176	19	57	1	7	116	8	9	7	2	88	76	13	9	.591	0	3.45
87	OAK/AL		31	828	31	6	0	0	203.0	194	38	44	0	3	124	6	4	2	1	102	92	13	7	.650	0	4.08
88	OAK/AL		26	651	26	1	0	0	156.1	162	23	50	3	4	69	3	5	3	6	77	72	11	8	.579	0	4.14
89	OAK/AL		25	495	20	1	0	2	111.0	117	10	47	2	3	55	1	0	4	4	56	46	5	9	.357	0	3.73
90	OAK/AL		26	527	21	0	0	0	124.1	124	17	53	1	2	56	4	2	3	0	70	67	9	6	.600	0	4.85
91	OAK/AL		41	306	1	0	0	6	68.1	74	8	34	2	2	27	3	1	2	1	38	38	4	2	.667	0	5.00
9 YR TOTALS			**225**	**4372**	**152**	**15**	**3**	**13**	**1024.2**	**1039**	**140**	**343**	**9**	**31**	**512**	**26**	**26**	**26**	**14**	**539**	**493**	**64**	**50**	**.561**	**0**	**4.33**

Young, Matthew John "Matt" — bats left — throws left — b.8/9/58

YR	TM/LG	CL	G	TBF	GS	CG	SHO	GF	IP	H	HR	BB	IBB	HB	SO	SH	SF	WP	BK	R	ER	W	L	PCT	SV	ERA
83	SEA/AL		33	851	32	5	2	0	203.2	178	17	79	2	7	130	4	8	4	2	86	74	11	15	.423	0	3.27
84	SLC/PCL	AAA	6	0	6	0	0	0	41.2	32	0	20	0	2	37	0	0	4	0	9	7	6	0	1.000	0	1.51
	SEA/AL		22	524	22	1	0	0	113.1	141	11	57	3	1	73	1	5	3	1	81	72	6	8	.429	0	5.72
85	SEA/AL		37	951	35	5	2	2	218.1	242	23	76	3	7	136	7	3	6	2	135	119	12	19	.387	1	4.91
86	SEA/AL		65	458	5	1	0	32	103.2	108	9	46	2	8	82	4	3	7	1	50	44	8	6	.571	13	3.82
87	LA/NL		47	234	0	0	0	31	54.1	62	3	17	5	0	42	1	1	3	0	30	27	5	8	.385	11	4.47
89	MOD/CAL	A+	3	50	3	0	0	0	12.0	9	0	6	0	0	13	0	0	1	0	1	1	0	0	.000	0	0.75
	TAC/PCL	AAA	2	45	2	0	0	0	11.0	8	0	5	0	0	6	0	1	0	0	4	3	1	1	.500	0	2.45
	OAK/AL		26	183	4	0	0	1	37.1	42	2	31	2	0	27	4	1	5	0	31	28	1	4	.200	0	6.75
90	SEA/AL		34	963	33	7	1	0	225.1	198	15	107	7	6	176	7	7	16	0	106	88	8	18	.308	0	3.51
91	PAW/INT	AAA	2	38	2	0	0	0	8.0	8	0	6	0	0	7	0	0	0	0	4	4	1	0	1.000	0	4.50
	BOS/AL		19	404	16	0	0	1	88.2	92	4	53	2	2	69	1	2	5	0	55	51	3	7	.300	0	5.18
8 YR TOTALS			**283**	**4568**	**147**	**19**	**5**	**67**	**1044.2**	**1063**	**84**	**466**	**26**	**31**	**735**	**29**	**30**	**49**	**6**	**574**	**503**	**54**	**85**	**.388**	**25**	**4.33**

Zancanaro, David Michael "Dave" — bats right — throws left — b.1/8/69 — System OAK/AL

YR	TM/LG	CL	G	TBF	GS	CG	SHO	GF	IP	H	HR	BB	IBB	HB	SO	SH	SF	WP	BK	R	ER	W	L	PCT	SV	ERA
90	SO/NWL	A-	10	188	8	0	0	0	44.1	44	2	13	0	1	42	1	0	3	4	22	19	3	0	1.000	0	3.86
	MOD/CAL	A+	4	64	2	0	0	0	13.0	13	1	14	0	0	7	0	0	0	0	9	9	1	2	.333	0	6.23
91	HUN/SOU	AA	29	727	28	0	0	1	165.0	151	7	92	0	6	104	3	4	8	4	87	62	5	10	.333	0	3.38